WEBSTER'S
New Explorer
Spanish-English
Dictionary

WEBSTER'S New Explorer Spanish-English Dictionary

Created in Cooperation with
the Editors of
MERRIAM-WEBSTER

FEDERAL STREET PRESS

A Division of Merriam-Webster, Incorporated
Springfield, Massachusetts

This edition published by
Federal Street Press,
A Division of Merriam-Webster, Incorporated
P.O. Box 281
Springfield, MA 01102

Federal Street Press books are available for bulk purchase for sales promotion and premium use.
For details write the manager of special sales,
Federal Street Press, P.O. Box 281, Springfield, MA 01102

Library of Congress Catalog Card Number: 99-62653

ISBN 1-892859-08-4

Printed in the United States of America

04 05 06 20 19 18 17 16 15 14

Contents		Índice
Preface	7a	
Explanatory Notes	9a	
Abbreviations in this Work	24a	
Pronunciation Symbols	25a	
Spanish Grammar	26a	
Spanish Numbers	42a	
Conjugation of Spanish Verbs	44a	
Spanish-English Dictionary	**1**	
English-Spanish Dictionary	**289**	
Common Spanish Abbreviations	727	Abreviaturas comunes en español
Common English Abbreviations	732	Abreviaturas comunes en inglés
Metric System: Conversions	739	Sistema métrica: conversiones

Preface

WEBSTER'S NEW EXPLORER SPANISH-ENGLISH DICTIONARY is a completely new dictionary designed to meet the needs of English and Spanish speakers in a time of ever-expanding communication among the countries of the Western Hemisphere. It is intended for language learners, teachers, office workers, tourists, business travelers—anyone who needs to communicate effectively in the Spanish and English languages as they are spoken and written in the Americas. This new dictionary provides accurate and up-to-date coverage of current vocabulary in both languages, as well as abundant examples of words used in context to illustrate idiomatic usage. The selection of Spanish words and idioms was based on evidence drawn from a wide variety of modern Latin-American sources and interpreted by trained Merriam-Webster bilingual lexicographers. The English entries were chosen by Merriam-Webster editors from the most recent Merriam-Webster dictionaries, and they represent the current basic vocabulary of American English.

All of this material is presented in a format which is based firmly upon and, in many important ways, is similar to the traditional styling found in the Merriam-Webster monolingual dictionaries. The reader who is familiar with Merriam-Webster dictionaries will immediately recognize this style, with its emphasis on convenience and ease of use, clarity and conciseness of the information presented, precise discrimination of senses, and frequent inclusion of example phrases showing words in actual use. Also included are pronunciations (in the International Phonetic Alphabet) for all English words, full coverage of irregular verbs in both languages, a section on basic Spanish grammar, a table of the most common Spanish abbreviations, and a detailed Explanatory Notes section which answers any questions the reader might have concerning the use of this book.

Webster's New Explorer Spanish-English Dictionary represents the combined efforts of many members of the Merriam-Webster Editorial Department, along with advice and assistance from consultants outside the company. The primary defining work was done by Charlene M. Chateauneuf, Seán O'Mannion-Espejo, Karen L. Wilkinson, and Jocelyn Woods; early contributions to the text were also submitted by Cèsar Alegre, Hilton Alers, Marién Díaz, Anne Gatschet, and María D. Guijarro, with Victoria E. Neufeldt, Ph.D. and James L.

Rader providing helpful suggestions regarding style. Proofreading was done by Susan L. Brady, Daniel B. Brandon, Charlene M. Chateauneuf, Deanna Chiasson, Seán O'Mannion-Espejo, James L. Rader, Donna L. Rickerby, Adrienne M. Scholz, Amy West, Karen L. Wilkinson, and Linda Picard Wood. Brian M. Sietsema, Ph.D. provided the pronunciations. Cross-reference services were provided by Donna L. Rickerby. Karen L. Levister assisted in inputting revisions. Carol Fugiel contributed many hours of clerical assistance and other valuable support. The editorial work relating to typesetting and production was begun by Jennifer S. Goss and continued by Susan L. Brady, who also offered helpful suggestions regarding format. Madeline L. Novak provided guidance on typographic matters. John M. Morse was responsible for the conception of this book as well as for numerous ideas and continued support along the way.

Eileen M. Haraty
Editor

Explanatory Notes

Entries

1. Main Entries

A boldface letter, word, or phrase appearing flush with the left-hand margin of each column of type is a main entry or entry word. The main entry may consist of letters set solid, of letters joined by a hyphen, or of letters separated by a space:

cafetalero[1], **-ra** *adj*. . .
eye–opener. . . *n*. . .
walk out *vi* . . .

The main entry, together with the material that follows it on the same line and succeeding indented lines, constitutes a dictionary entry.

2. Order of Main Entries

Alphabetical order throughout the book follows the order of the English alphabet, with one exception: words beginning with the Spanish letter *ñ* follow all entries for the letter *n*. The main entries follow one another alphabetically letter by letter without regard to intervening spaces or hyphens; for example, *shake-up* follows *shaker.*

Homographs (words with the same spelling) having different parts of speech are usually given separate dictionary entries. These entries are distinguished by superscript numerals following the entry word:

hail[1]. . . *vt*. . .

hail[2] *n*. . .

hail[3] *interj*. . .

madrileño[1], **-ña** *adj*. . .

madrileño[2], **-ña** *n*. . .

Numbered homograph entries are listed in the following order: verb, adverb, adjective, noun, conjunction, preposition, pronoun, interjection, article.

Homographs having the same part of speech are normally included at the same dictionary entry, without regard to their different semantic origins. On the English-to-Spanish side, however, separate entries are made if the homographs have distinct inflected forms or if they have distinct pronunciations.

3. Guide Words

A pair of guide words is printed at the top of each page, indicating the first and last main entries that appear on that page:

fregar • fuego

4. Variants

When a main entry is followed by the word *or* and another spelling, the two spellings are variants. Both are standard, and either one may be used according to personal inclination:

jailer *or* **jailor**. . . *n*. . .
quizá *or* **quizás** *adv*. . .

Occasionally, a variant spelling is used only for a particular sense of a word. In these cases, the variant spelling is listed after the sense number of the sense to which it pertains:

electric. . . *adj* **1** *or* **electrical**. . .

Sometimes the entry word is used interchangeably with a longer phrase containing the entry word. For the purposes of this dictionary, such phrases are considered variants of the headword:

bunk^2 *n* **1** *or* **bunk bed**. . .

angina *nf* **1** *or* **angina de pecho** : angina . . .

Variant wordings of boldface phrases may also be shown:

> **madera** *nf.* . . **3 madera dura** *or* **madera noble**. . .
>
> **atención**[1] *nf.* . . **2 poner atención** *or* **prestar atención**. . .

5. Run-On Entries

A main entry may be followed by one or more derivatives or by a homograph with a different functional label. These are run-on entries. Each is introduced by a boldface dash and each has a functional label. They are not defined, however, since their equivalents can be readily derived by adding the corresponding foreign-language suffix to the terms used to define the entry word or, in the case of homographs, simply substituting the appropriate part of speech:

> **illegal**. . . *adj* **:** ilegal — **illegally** *adv*
>
> (the Spanish adverb is *ilegalmente*)
>
> **transferir**. . . *vt* TRASLADAR **:** to transfer — **transferible** *adj*
>
> (the English adjective is **transferable**)
>
> **Bosnian** *n* **:** bosnio *m,* -nia *f* — **Bosnian** *adj*
>
> (the Spanish adjective is *bosnio, -nia*)

On the Spanish side of the book, reflexive verbs are sometimes run on undefined:

> **enrollar** *vt* **:** to roll up, to coil — **enrollarse** *vr*

The absence of a definition means that *enrollarse* has the simple reflexive meaning "to become rolled up or coiled," "to roll itself up."

6. Bold Notes

A main entry may be followed by one or more phrases containing the entry word or an inflected form of the entry word. These are bold notes. Each bold note is defined at its own numbered sense:

> **álamo** *nm* **1 :** poplar **2 álamo temblón :** aspen
>
> **hold**[1]. . . *vi*. . . **4 to hold to :**. . . **5 to hold with :**. . .

If the bold note consists only of the entry word and a single preposition, the entry word is represented by a boldface swung dash **~**.

> **pegar** . . . *vi* . . . **3 ~ con :** to match, to go with . . .

The same bold note phrase may appear at two or more senses if it has more than one distinct meaning:

> **wear**[1]. . . *vt*. . . **3 to wear out :** gastar <he wore out his shoes. . . > **4 to wear out** EXHAUST **:** agotar, fatigar <to wear oneself out . . .> . . .
>
> **estar** . . . *vi* . . . **15 ~ por :** to be in favor of **16 ~ por :** to be about to <está por cerrar . . .> . . .

If the use of the entry word is commonly restricted to one particular phrase, then a bold note may be given as the entry word's only sense:

> **ward**[1]. . . *vt* **to ward off :**. . .

Pronunciation

1. Pronunciation of English Entry Words

The matter between a pair of brackets [ ] following the entry word of an English-to-Spanish entry indicates the pronunciation. The symbols used are explained in the International Phonetic Alphabet chart on page 25a.

The presence of variant pronunciations indicates that not all educated speakers pronounce words the same way. A second-place variant is not to be regarded as less acceptable than the pronunciation that is given first. It may, in fact, be used by as many educated speakers as the first variant, but the requirements of the printed page are such that one must precede the other:

tomato [tə'meɪt̬o, -'mɑ-] . . .

When a compound word has less than a full pronunciation, the missing part is to be supplied from the pronunciation at the entry for the unpronounced element of the compound:

gamma ray ['gæmə]. . .

ray ['reɪ]. . .

smoke[1] ['smo:k]. . .

smoke detector [dɪ'tɛktər]. . .

In general, no pronunciation is given for open compounds consisting of two or more English words that are main entries at their own alphabetical place:

water lily *n* **:** nenúfar *m*

Only the first entry in a series of numbered homographs is given a pronunciation if their pronunciations are the same:

dab[1] ['dæb] *vt*. . .

dab[2] *n*. . .

No pronunciation is shown for principal parts of verbs that are formed by regular suffixation, nor for other derivative words formed by common suffixes.

2. Pronunciation of Spanish Entry Words

Spanish pronunciation is highly regular, so no pronunciations are given for most Spanish-to-English entries. Exceptions have been made for certain words (such as foreign borrowings) whose Spanish pronunciations are not evident from their spellings:

pizza ['pitsa, 'pisa] . . .

footing ['fu,tɪŋ]. . .

Functional Labels

An italic label indicating a part of speech or some other functional classification follows the pronunciation or, if no pronunciation is given, the main entry. The eight traditional parts of speech, adjective, adverb, conjunction, interjection, noun, preposition, pronoun, and verb, are indicated as follows:

daily[2] *adj*. . .

vagamente *adv*. . .

and. . . *conj*. . .

huy *interj*. . .

jackal. . . *n*. . .

para *prep*. . .

neither[3] *pron*. . .

leer. . . *v*. . .

Verbs that are intransitive are labeled *vi,* and verbs that are transitive are labeled *vt.* Entries for verbs that are both transitive and intransitive are labeled *v;* if such an entry includes irregular verb inflections, it is labeled *v* immediately after the main entry, with the labels *vi* and *vt* serving to introduce transitive and intransitive subdivisions when both are present:

deliberar *vi* **:** to deliberate

necessitate. . . *vt* **-tated; -tating :** necesitar, requerir

satisfy. . . *v* **-fied; -fying** *vt*. . . — *vi*. . .

Two other labels are used to indicate functional classifications of verbs: *v aux* (auxiliary verb) and *v impers* (impersonal verb).

may. . . *v aux, past* **might**. . .

haber[1]. . . *v aux* **1 :** have. . . — *v impers* **1 hay :** there is, there are. . .

Gender Labels

In Spanish-to-English noun entries, the gender of the entry word is indicated by an italic *m* (masculine), *f* (feminine), or *mf* (masculine or feminine), immediately following the functional label:

magnesio *nm*. . .

galaxia *nf*. . .

turista *nmf*. . .

If both the masculine and feminine forms are shown for a noun referring to a person, the label is simply *n:*

director, -tora *n*. . .

Spanish noun equivalents of English entry words are also labeled for gender:

amnesia. . . *n* **:** amnesia *f*

earache. . . *n* **:** dolor *m* de oído

gamekeeper. . . *n* **:** guardabosque *mf*

Inflected Forms

1. Nouns

The plurals of nouns are shown in this dictionary when they are irregular, when plural suffixation brings about a change in accentuation or in the spelling of the root word, when an English noun ends in a consonant plus *-o* or in *-ey,* when an English noun ends in *-oo,* when an English noun is a compound that pluralizes any element but the last, when a noun has variant plurals, or whenever the dictionary user might have reasonable doubts regarding the spelling of a plural:

> **tooth**. . . *n, pl* **teeth**. . .
>
> **garrafón** *nm, pl* **-fones**. . .
>
> **potato**. . . *n, pl* **-toes**. . .
>
> **abbey**. . . *n, pl* **-beys**. . .
>
> **cuckoo**[2] *n, pl* **-oos**. . .
>
> **brother–in–law**. . . *n, pl* **brothers–in–law** . . .
>
> **quail**[2] *n, pl* **quail** *or* **quails**. . .
>
> **hábitat** *nm, pl* **-tats**. . .
>
> **tahúr** *nm, pl* **tahúres**. . .

Cutback inflected forms are used for most nouns on the English-to-Spanish side, regardless of the number of syllables. On the Spanish-to-English side, cutback inflections are given for nouns that have three or more syllables; plurals for shorter words are written out in full:

> **shampoo**[2] *n, pl* **-poos**. . .
>
> **calamity** . . . *n, pl* **-ties**. . .
>
> **mouse** . . . *n, pl* **mice**. . .
>
> **sartén** *nmf, pl* **sartenes**. . .
>
> **hámster** *nm, pl* **hámsters**. . .
>
> **federación** *nf, pl* **-ciones**. . .

If only one gender form has a plural which is irregular, that plural form will be given with the appropriate label:

> **campeón, -ona** *n, mpl* **-ones :** champion

The plurals of nouns are usually not shown when the base word is unchanged by the addition of the regular plural suffix or when the noun is unlikely to occur in the plural:

apple. . . *n* **:** manzana *f*

inglés[3] *nm* **:** English (language)

Nouns that are plural in form and that regularly occur in plural constructions are labeled as *npl* (for English nouns), *nmpl* (for Spanish masculine nouns), or *nfpl* (for Spanish feminine nouns):

knickers. . . *npl*. . .

enseres *nmpl*. . .

mancuernas *nfpl*. . .

Entry words that are unchanged in the plural are labeled *ns & pl* (for English nouns), *nms & pl* (for Spanish masculine nouns), *nfs & pl* (for Spanish feminine nouns), and *nmfs & pl* (for Spanish gender-variable nouns):

deer. . . *ns & pl* . . .

lavaplatos *nms & pl*. . .

tesis *nfs & pl* . . .

rompehuelgas *nmfs & pl* . . .

2. Verbs

ENGLISH VERBS

The principal parts of verbs are shown in English-to-Spanish entries when they are irregular, when suffixation brings about a change in spelling of the root word, when the verb ends in *-ey,* when there are variant inflected forms, or whenever it is believed that the dictionary user might have reasonable doubts about the spelling of an inflected form:

break[1]. . . *v* **broke**. . .; **broken**. . .; **breaking**. . .

drag[1]. . . *v* **dragged; dragging**. . .

monkey[1]. . . *vi* **-keyed; -keying**. . .

label[1]. . . *vt* **-beled** *or* **-belled; -beling** *or* **-belling**. . .

imagine. . . *vt* **-ined; -ining**. . .

Cutback inflected forms are usually used when the verb has two or more syllables:

multiply. . . *v* **-plied; -plying**. . .

bevel[1]. . . *v* **-eled** *or* **-elled; -eling** *or* **-elling**. . .

forgo *or* **forego**. . . *vt* **-went; -gone; -going**. . .

commit . . . *vt* **-mitted; -mitting** . . .

The principal parts of an English verb are not shown when the base word is unchanged by suffixation:

delay[1]. . . *vt*

pitch[1]. . . *vt*

SPANISH VERBS

Entries for irregular Spanish verbs are cross-referenced by number to the model conjugations appearing in the Conjugation of Spanish Verbs section:

abnegarse {49} *vr*. . .

volver {89} *vi*. . .

Entries for Spanish verbs with regular conjugations are not cross-referenced; however, model conjugations for regular Spanish verbs are included in the Conjugation of Spanish Verbs section beginning on page 44a.

Adverbs and Adjectives

The comparative and superlative forms of English adjective and adverb main entries are shown when suffixation brings about a change in spelling of the root word, when the inflection is irregular, and when there are variant inflected forms:

wet[2] *adj* **wetter; wettest**. . .

good[2] *adj* **better**. . . ; **best**. . .

evil[1]. . . *adj* **eviler** *or* **eviller; evilest** *or* **evillest**. . .

The superlative forms of adjectives and adverbs of two or more syllables are usually cut back; the superlative is shown in full, however, when it is desirable to indicate the pronunciation of the inflected form:

early[1]. . . *adv* **earlier; -est**. . .

gaudy. . . *adj* **gaudier; -est**. . .

secure[2] *adj* **-curer; -est**. . .

but

young[1]. . . *adj* **younger** [ˈjʌŋgər]; **youngest** [-gəst]. . .

At a few entries only the superlative form is shown:

mere *adj, superlative* **merest**. . .

The absence of the comparative form indicates that there is no evidence of its use.

The comparative and superlative forms of adjectives and adverbs are usually not shown when the base word is unchanged by suffixation:

quiet[3] *adj* **1**. . .

Usage

1. Usage Labels

Two types of usage labels are used in this dictionary—regional and stylistic. Spanish words that are limited in use to a specific area or areas of Latin America, or to Spain, are given labels indicating the countries in which they are most commonly used:

> **guarachear** *vi Cuba, PRi fam. . .*
>
> **bucket**. . . *n* **:**. . . cubeta *f Mex*

The following regional labels are used in this book: *Arg* (Argentina), *Bol* (Bolivia), *CA* (Central America), *Car* (Caribbean), *Chile* (Chile), *Col* (Colombia), *CoRi* (Costa Rica), *Cuba* (Cuba), *DomRep* (Dominican Republic), *Ecua* (Ecuador), *Sal* (El Salvador), *Guat* (Guatemala), *Hond* (Honduras), *Mex* (Mexico), *Nic* (Nicaragua), *Pan* (Panama), *Par* (Paraguay), *Peru* (Peru), *PRi* (Puerto Rico), *Spain* (Spain), *Uru* (Uruguay), *Ven* (Venezuela).

Since this book focuses on the Spanish spoken in Latin America, only the most common regionalisms from Spain have been included in order to allow for more thorough coverage of Latin-American forms.

A number of Spanish words are given a *fam* (familiar) label as well, indicating that these words are suitable for informal contexts but would not normally be used in formal writing or speaking. The stylistic label *usu considered vulgar* is added for a word which is usually considered vulgar or offensive but whose widespread use justifies its inclusion in this book. The label is intended to warn the reader that the word in question may be inappropriate in polite conversation.

2. Usage Notes

Definitions are sometimes preceded by parenthetical usage notes that give supplementary semantic information:

> **not**. . . *adv* **1** (*used to form a negative*) **:** no. . .
>
> **within**[2] *prep* . . . **2** (*in expressions of distance*) **:**. . . **3** (*in expressions of time*) **:** . . .

> **e**[2] *conj* (*used instead of* **y** *before words beginning with i or hi*) **:**. . .
>
> **poder**[1]. . . *v aux*. . . **2** (*expressing possibility*) **:**. . . **3** (*expressing permission*) **:**. . .

Additional semantic orientation is also sometimes given in the form of parenthetical notes appearing within the definition:

> **calibrate**. . . *vt*. . . **:** calibrar (armas), graduar (termómetros)
>
> **palco** *nm* **:** box (in a theater or stadium)

Occasionally a usage note is used in place of a definition. This is usually done when the entry word has no single foreign-language equivalent. This type of usage note will be accompanied by examples of common use:

> **shall**. . . *v aux*. . . **1** (*used to express a command*) <you shall do as I say **:** harás lo que te digo> . . .

3. Illustrations of Usage

Definitions are sometimes followed by verbal illustrations that show a typical use of the word in context or a common idiomatic usage. These verbal illustrations include a translation and are enclosed in angle brackets:

> **lejos** *adv* **1 :** far away, distant <a lo lejos **:** in the distance, far off> . . .
>
> **make**[1]. . . **9** . . .**:** ganar <to make a living **:** ganarse la vida> . . .

Sense Division

A boldface colon is used to introduce a definition:

> **fable**. . . *n* **:** fábula *f*

Boldface Arabic numerals separate the senses of a word that has more than one sense:

laguna *nf* **1 :** lagoon **2 :** lacuna, gap

Whenever some information (such as a synonym, a boldface word or phrase, a usage note, a cross-reference, or a label) follows a sense number, it applies only to that specific numbered sense and not to any other boldface numbered senses:

abanico *nm*. . . **2** GAMA **:**. . .

tonic² *n*. . . **2** *or* **tonic water :**. . .

grillo *nm*. . . **2 grillos** *nmpl* **:**. . .

fairy. . . *n, pl* **fairies**. . . **2 fairy tale :**. . .

myself. . . *pron* **1** (*used reflexively*) **:**. . .

pike. . . *n*. . . **3 → turnpike**

atado² *nm*. . . **2** *Arg* **:**. . .

Cross-References

Three different kinds of cross-references are used in this dictionary: synonymous, cognate, and inflectional. In each instance the cross-reference is readily recognized by the boldface arrow following the entry word.

Synonymous and cognate cross-references indicate that a definition at the entry cross-referred to can be substituted for the entry word:

scapula. . . **→ shoulder blade**

amuck. . . **→ amok**

An inflectional cross-reference is used to identify the entry word as an inflected form of another word (as a noun or verb):

fue, etc. → ir, ser

mice → mouse

Synonyms

At many entries or senses in this book, a synonym in small capital letters is provided before the boldface colon and the following defining text. These synonyms are all main entries or bold notes elsewhere in the book. They serve as a helpful guide to the meaning of the entry or sense and also give the reader an additional term that might be substituted in a similar context. On the English-to-Spanish side synonyms are particularly abundant, since special care has been taken to guide the English speaker—by means of synonyms, verbal illustrations, or usage notes—to the meaning of the Spanish terms at each sense of a multisense entry.

Abbreviations in this Work

adj	adjective
adv	adverb
Arg	Argentina
Bol	Bolivia
Brit	British
CA	Central America
Car	Caribbean region
Col	Colombia
conj	conjuction
CoRi	Costa Rica
DomRep	Dominican Republic
Ecua	Ecuador
esp	especially
f	feminine
fam	familiar or colloquial
fpl	feminine plural
Guat	Guatemala
Hond	Honduras
interj	interjection
m	masculine
Mex	Mexico
mf	masculine or feminine
mpl	masculine plural
n	noun
nf	feminine noun
nfpl	feminine plural noun
nfs & pl	invariable singular or plural feminine noun
Nic	Nicaragua
nm	masculine noun
nmf	masculine or feminine noun
nmfpl	plural noun invariable for gender
nmfs & pl	noun invariable for both gender and number
nmpl	masculine plural noun
nms & pl	invariable singular or plural masculine noun
npl	plural noun
ns & pl	noun invariable for plural
Pan	Panama
Par	Paraguay
pl	plural
pp	past participle
prep	preposition
PRi	Puerto Rico
pron	pronoun
s	singular
Sal	El Salvador
Uru	Uruguay
usu	usually
v	verb (transitive and intransitive)
v aux	auxiliary verb
Ven	Venezuela
vi	intransitive verb
v impers	impersonal verb
vr	reflexive verb
vt	transitive verb

Pronunciation Symbols

VOWELS

æ	**a**sk, b**a**t, gl**a**d
ɑ	c**o**t, b**o**mb
a	*New England* **au**nt, *British* **a**sk, gl**a**ss, *Spanish* c**a**s**a**
e	*Spanish* p**e**so, j**e**fe
ɛ	**e**gg, b**e**t, f**e**d
ə	**a**bout, jav**e**lin, **A**l**a**bam**a**
ə	when italicized as in *ə*l, *ə*m, *ə*n, indicates a syllabic pronunciation of the consonant as in bott**le**, pris**m**, butt**on**
i	ver**y**, an**y**, thirt**y**, *Spanish* p**i**ña
iː	**ea**t, b**ea**d, b**ee**
ɪ	**i**d, b**i**d, p**i**t
o	**O**hi**o**, yell**o**wer, potat**o**, *Spanish* **ó**valo
oː	**oa**ts, **ow**n, z**o**ne, bl**ow**
ɔ	**aw**l, m**au**l, c**au**ght, p**aw**
ʊ	s**u**re, sh**ou**ld, c**ou**ld
u	*Spanish* **u**va, c**u**lpa
uː	b**oo**t, f**ew**, c**oo**
ʌ	**u**nder, p**u**tt, b**u**d
eɪ	**ei**ght, w**a**de, b**ay**
aɪ	**i**ce, b**i**te, t**ie**
aʊ	**ou**t, g**ow**n, pl**ow**
ɔɪ	**oy**ster, c**oi**l, b**oy**
ɒ	*British* b**o**nd, g**o**d
ø	*French* d**eu**x, *German* H**öh**le
œ	*French* b**œu**f, *German* H**ö**lle
y	*French* l**u**ne, *German* f**üh**len
ʏ	*German* f**ü**llt
~	(tilde as in ã, ɔ̃, ɛ̃) *French* v**in**, b**on**, bi**en**
ː	indicates that the preceding vowel is long. Long vowels are almost always diphthongs in English, but not in Spanish.

STRESS MARKS

ˈ	high stress	**pen**manship
ˌ	low stress	penman**ship**

CONSONANTS

b	**b**a**b**y, la**b**or, ca**b**
β	*Spanish* ca**b**o, ó**v**alo
d	**d**ay, rea**d**y, ki**d**
dʒ	**j**ust, ba**dg**er, fu**dge**
ð	**th**en, ei**th**er, ba**the**
f	**f**oe, tou**gh**, bu**ff**
g	**g**o, bi**gg**er, ba**g**
ɣ	*Spanish* tra**g**ar, da**g**a
h	**h**ot, a**h**a
j	**y**es, vine**y**ard
ʲ	marks palatalization as in *French* digne [dinʲ]
k	**c**at, **k**eep, la**cqu**er, flo**ck**
l	**l**aw, ho**ll**ow, boi**l**
m	**m**at, he**m**p, ha**mm**er, ri**m**
n	**n**ew, te**n**t, te**n**or, ru**n**
ŋ	ru**ng**, ha**ng**, swi**ng**er
ɲ	*Spanish* caba**ñ**a, pi**ñ**a
p	**p**ay, la**p**se, to**p**
r	**r**ope, bu**r**n, ta**r**
s	**s**ad, mi**s**t, ki**ss**
ʃ	**sh**oe, mi**ss**ion, slu**sh**
t	**t**oe, bu**tt**on, ma**t**
t̬	indicates that some speakers of English pronounce this as a voiced alveolar flap [ɾ], as in later, catty, battle
tʃ	**ch**oose, ba**tch**
θ	**th**in, e**th**er, ba**th**
v	**v**at, ne**v**er, ca**v**e
w	**w**et, soft**w**are
x	*German* Ba**ch**, *Scots* lo**ch**, *Spanish* **g**ente, **j**efe
z	**z**oo, ea**s**y, bu**zz**
ʒ	**j**aborandi, a**z**ure, bei**ge**
ʔ	indicates a glottal stop, the sound beginning the syllables in **uh-oh**
h, k, p, t	when italicized indicate sounds which are present in the pronunciation of some speakers of English but absent in that of others, so that *whence* [ˈ*h*wɛn*t*s] can be pronounced as [ˈwɛns], [ˈhwɛns], [ˈwɛnts], or [ˈhwɛnts]

Spanish Grammar

Accentuation

Spanish word stress is generally determined according to the following rules:

- Words ending in a vowel, or in *-n* or *-s,* are stressed on the penultimate syllable (*za**pa**to, **lla**man*).
- Words ending in a consonant other than *-n* or *-s* are stressed on the last syllable (*per**diz**, curiosi**dad***).

Exceptions to these rules have a written accent mark over the stressed vowel (***fá**cil, habla**rá**, **úl**timo*). There are also a few words which take accent marks in order to distinguish them from homonyms (*si, sí; que, qué; el, él;* etc.).

Adverbs ending in *-mente* have two stressed syllables since they retain both the stress of the root word and of the *-mente* suffix (***len**ta**men**te, di**fí**cil**men**te*). Many compounds also have two stressed syllables (***lim**piapara**bri**sas*).

Punctuation and Capitalization

Questions and exclamations in Spanish are preceded by an inverted question mark ¿ and an inverted exclamation mark ¡, respectively:

¿Cuándo llamó Ana?
Y tú, ¿qué piensas?

¡No hagas eso!
Pero, ¡qué lástima!

In Spanish, unlike English, the following words are not capitalized:

- Names of days, months, and languages (*jueves, octubre, español*).
- Spanish adjectives or nouns derived from proper nouns (*los nicaragüenses, una teoría marxista*).

Articles

1. Definite Article

Spanish has five forms of the definite article: *el* (masculine singular), *la* (feminine singular), *los* (masculine plural), *las* (feminine plural), and *lo* (neuter). The first four agree in gender and number with the nouns they limit (*el carro,* the car; *las tijeras,* the scissors), although the form *el* is used with feminine singular nouns beginning with a stressed *a-* or *ha-* (*el águila, el hambre*).

The neuter article *lo* is used with the masculine singular form of an adjective to express an abstract concept (*lo mejor de este método,* the best thing about this method; *lo meticuloso de su trabajo,* the meticulousness of her work; *lo mismo para mí,* the same for me).

Whenever the masculine article *el* immediately follows the words *de* or *a,* it combines with them to form the contractions *del* and *al,* respectively (*viene* ***del*** *campo, vi* ***al*** *hermano de Roberto*).

The use of *el, la, los,* and *las* in Spanish corresponds largely to the use of *the* in English; some exceptions are noted below.

The definite article is used:

- When referring to something as a class (*los gatos son ágiles,* cats are agile; *me gusta el café,* I like coffee).
- In references to meals and in most expressions of time (*¿comiste el almuerzo?,* did you eat lunch?; *vino el año pasado,* he came last year; *son las dos,* it's two o'clock; *prefiero el verano,* I prefer summer; *la reunión es el lunes,*

the meeting is on Monday; but: *hoy es lunes,* today is Monday).

- Before titles (except *don, doña, san, santo, santa, fray,* and *sor*) in third-person references to people (*la señora Rivera llamó,* Mrs. Rivera called; but: *hola, señora Rivera,* hello, Mrs. Rivera).
- In references to body parts and personal possessions (*me duele la cabeza,* my head hurts; *dejó el sombrero,* he left his hat).
- To mean "the one" or "the ones" when the subject is already understood (*la de madera,* the wooden one; *los que vi ayer,* the ones I saw yesterday).

The definite article is omitted:

- Before a noun in apposition, if the noun is not modified (*Caracas, capital de Venezuela;* but: *Pico Bolívar, la montaña más alta de Venezuela*).
- Before a number in a royal title (*Carlos Quinto,* Charles the Fifth).

2. Indefinite Article

The forms of the indefinite article in Spanish are *un* (masculine singular), *una* (feminine singular), *unos* (masculine plural), and *unas* (feminine plural). They agree in number and gender with the nouns they limit (*una mesa,* a table; *unos platos,* some plates), although the form *un* is used with feminine singular nouns beginning with a stressed *a-* or *ha-* (*un ala, un hacha*).

The use of *un, una, unos,* and *unas* in Spanish corresponds largely to the use of *a, an,* and *some* in English, with some exceptions:

- Indefinite articles are generally omitted before nouns identifying someone or something as a member of a class or category (*Paco es profesor/católico,* Paco is a professor/Catholic; *se llama páncreas,* it's called a pancreas).

- They are also often omitted in instances where quantity is understood from context (*vine sin chaqueta,* I came without a jacket; *no tengo carro,* I don't have a car).

Nouns

1. Gender

Nouns in Spanish are either masculine or feminine. A noun's gender can often be determined according to the following guidelines:

- Nouns ending in *-aje, -o,* or *-or* are usually masculine (*el traje, el libro, el sabor*), with some exceptions (*la mano, la foto, la labor,* etc.).
- Nouns ending in *-a, -dad, -ión, -tud,* or *-umbre* are usually feminine (*la alfombra, la capacidad, la excepción, la juventud, la certidumbre*). Exceptions include: *el día, el mapa,* and many learned borrowings ending in *-ma* (*el idioma, el tema*).

Most nouns referring to people or animals agree in gender with the subject (*el hombre, la mujer; el hermano, la hermana; el perro, la perra*). However, some nouns referring to people, including those ending in *-ista,* use the same form for both sexes (*el artista, la artista; el modelo, la modelo;* etc.).

A few names of animals exist in only one gender form (*la jirafa, el sapo,* etc.). In these instances, the adjectives *macho* and *hembra* are sometimes used to distinguish males and females (*una jirafa macho,* a male giraffe).

2. Pluralization

Plurals of Spanish nouns are formed as follows:

- Nouns ending in an unstressed vowel or an accented *-é* are pluralized by adding *-s* (*la vaca, las vacas; el café, los cafés*).

- Nouns ending in a consonant other than *-s,* or in a stressed vowel other than *-é,* are generally pluralized by adding *-es* (*el papel, los papeles; el rubí, los rubíes*). Exceptions include *papá* (*papás*) and *mamá* (*mamás*).

- Nouns with an unstressed final syllable ending in *-s* usually have a zero plural (*la crisis, las crisis; el jueves, los jueves*). Other nouns ending in *-s* add *-es* to form the plural (*el mes, los meses; el país, los países*).

- Nouns ending in *-z* are pluralized by changing the *-z* to *-c* and adding *-es* (*el lápiz, los lápices; la vez, las veces*).

- Many compound nouns have a zero plural (*el paraguas, los paraguas; el aguafiestas, los aguafiestas*).

- The plurals of *cualquiera* and *quienquiera* are *cualesquiera* and *quienesquiera,* respectively.

Adjectives

1. Gender and Number

Most adjectives agree in gender and number with the nouns they modify (un chico *alto,* una chica *alta,* unos chicos *altos,* unas chicas *altas*). Some adjectives, including those ending in *-e* and *-ista* (*fuerte, altruista*) and comparative adjectives ending in *-or* (*mayor, mejor*), vary only for number.

Adjectives whose masculine singular forms end in *-o* generally change the *-o* to *-a* to form the feminine (*pequeño* → *pequeña*). Masculine adjectives ending in *-án, -ón,* or *-dor,* and masculine adjectives of nationality which end in a consonant, usually add *-a* to form the feminine (*holgazán* → *holgazana*; *llorón* → *llorona*; *trabajador* → *trabajadora*; *irlandés* → *irlandesa*).

Adjectives are pluralized in much the same manner as nouns:

- The plurals of adjectives ending in an unstressed vowel or an accented *-é* are formed by adding an *-s* (un postre *rico,* unos postres *ricos;* una camisa *café,* unas camisas *cafés*).

- Adjectives ending in a consonant, or in a stressed vowel other than *-é,* are generally pluralized by adding *-es* (un niño *cortés,* unos niños *corteses;* una persona *iraní,* unas personas *iraníes*).

- Adjectives ending in *-z* are pluralized by changing the *-z* to *-c* and adding *-es* (una respuesta *sagaz,* unas respuestas *sagaces*).

2. Shortening

- The following masculine singular adjectives drop their final *-o* when they occur before a masculine singular noun: *bueno* (*buen*), *malo* (*mal*), *uno* (*un*), *alguno* (*algún*), *ninguno* (*ningún*), *primero* (*primer*), *tercero* (*tercer*).

- *Grande* shortens to *gran* before any singular noun.

- *Ciento* shortens to *cien* before any noun.

- The title *Santo* shortens to *San* before all masculine names except those beginning with *To-* or *Do-* (*San Juan, Santo Tomás*).

3. Position

Descriptive adjectives generally follow the nouns they modify (*una cosa útil, un actor famoso*). However, adjectives that express an inherent quality often precede the noun (*la blanca nieve*).

Some adjectives change meaning depending on whether they occur before or after the noun: *un pobre niño,* a poor (pitiable) child; *un niño pobre,* a poor (not rich) child; *un gran hombre,* a great man; *un hombre grande,* a big man; *el único libro,* the only book; *el libro único,* the unique book, etc.

4. Comparative and Superlative Forms

The comparative of Spanish adjectives is generally rendered as *más . . . que* (more . . . than) or *menos . . . que* (less . . . than): *soy más alta que él,* I'm taller than he; *son menos inteligentes que tú,* they're less intelligent than you.

The superlative of Spanish adjectives usually follows the formula *definite article* + (*noun* +) *más/menos* + *adjective: ella es la estudiante más trabajadora,* she is the hardest-working student; *él es el menos conocido,* he's the least known.

A few Spanish adjectives have irregular comparative and superlative forms:

Adjective	Comparative/Superlative
bueno (good)	**mejor** (better, best)
malo (bad)	**peor** (worse, worst)
grande[1] (big, great), **viejo** (old)	**mayor** (greater, older; greatest, oldest)
pequeño[1] (little), **joven** (young)	**menor** (lesser, younger; least, youngest)
mucho (much), **muchos** (many)	**más** (more, most)
poco (little), **pocos** (few)	**menos** (less, least)

[1]These words have regular comparative and superlative forms when used in reference to physical size: *él es más grande que yo; nuestra casa es la más pequeña.*

ABSOLUTE SUPERLATIVE

The absolute superlative is formed by placing *muy* before the adjective, or by adding the suffix *-ísimo* (*ella es muy simpática* or *ella es simpatiquísima,* she is very nice). The absolute superlative using *-ísimo* is formed according to the following rules:

- Adjectives ending in a consonant other than *-z* simply add the *-ísimo* ending (*fácil* → *facilísimo*).
- Adjectives ending in *-z* change this consonant to *-c* and add *-ísimo* (*feliz* → *felicísimo*).
- Adjectives ending in a vowel or diphthong drop the vowel or diphthong and add *-ísimo* (*claro* → *clarísimo; amplio* → *amplísimo*).

- Adjectives ending in *-co* or *-go* change these endings to *qu* and *gu*, respectively, and add *-ísimo* (*rico* → *riquísimo; largo* → *larguísimo*).
- Adjectives ending in *-ble* change this ending to *-bil* and add *-ísimo* (*notable* → *notabilísimo*).
- Adjectives containing the stressed diphthong *ie* or *ue* will sometimes change these to *e* and *o*, respectively (*ferviente* → *fervientísimo* or *ferventísimo; bueno* → *buenísimo* or *bonísimo*).

Adverbs

Adverbs can be formed by adding the adverbial suffix *-mente* to virtually any adjective (*fácil* → *fácilmente*). If the adjective varies for gender, the feminine form is used as the basis for forming the adverb (*rápido* → *rápidamente*).

Pronouns

1. Personal Pronouns

The personal pronouns in Spanish are:

Person		Singular	Plural	
FIRST	**yo**	I	**nosotros, nosotras**	we
SECOND	**tú**	you (familiar)	**vosotros**[2], **vosotras**[2]	you, all of you
	vos[1]	you		
	usted	you (formal)	**ustedes**[3]	you, all of you
THIRD	**él**	he	**ellos, ellas**	they
	ella	she		
	ello	it (neuter)		

[1] Familiar form used in addition to *tú* in South and Central America.
[2] Familiar form used in Spain.
[3] Formal form used in Spain; familiar and formal form used in Latin America.

FAMILIAR VS. FORMAL

The second person personal pronouns exist in both familiar and formal forms. The familiar forms are generally used when addressing relatives, friends, and children, although usage varies considerably from region to region; the formal forms are used in other contexts to show courtesy, respect, or emotional distance.

In Spain and in the Caribbean, *tú* is used exclusively as the familiar singular "you." In South and Central America, however, *vos* either competes with *tú* to varying degrees or replaces it entirely. (For a more detailed explanation of *vos* and its corresponding verb forms, refer to the Conjugation of Spanish Verbs section.)

The plural familiar form *vosotros, -as* is used only in Spain, where *ustedes* is reserved for formal contexts. In Latin America, *vosotros, -as* is not used, and *ustedes* serves as the all-purpose plural "you."

It should be noted that while *usted* and *ustedes* are regarded as second person pronouns, they take the third person form of the verb.

USAGE

In Spanish, personal pronouns are generally omitted (*voy al cine,* I'm going to the movies; *¿llamaron?,* did they call?), although they are sometimes used for purposes of emphasis or clarity (*se lo diré yo,* I will tell them; *vino ella, pero él se quedó,* she came, but he stayed behind). The forms *usted* and *ustedes* are usually included out of courtesy (*¿cómo está usted?,* how are you?).

Personal pronouns are not generally used in reference to inanimate objects or living creatures other than humans; in these instances, the pronoun is most often omitted (*¿es nuevo? no, es viejo,* is it new? no, it's old).

The neuter third person pronoun *ello* is reserved for indefinite subjects (as abstract concepts): *todo ello implica . . . ,* all of this implies . . . ; *por si ello fuera poco . . . ,* as if that weren't enough . . . . It most commonly appears in formal writing and speech. In less formal contexts, *ello* is often either omitted or replaced with *esto, eso,* or *aquello.*

2. Prepositional Pronouns

Prepositional pronouns are used as the objects of prepositions (*¿es para mí?,* is it for me?; *se lo dio a ellos,* he gave it to them).

The prepositional pronouns in Spanish are:

Singular		Plural	
mí	me	**nosotros, nosotras**	us
ti	you	**vosotros[1], vosotras[1]**	you
usted	you (formal)	**ustedes**	you
él	him	**ellos, ellas**	them
ella	her		
ello	it (neuter)		
sí	yourself, himself, herself, itself, oneself	**sí**	yourselves, themselves

[1]Used primarily in Spain.

When the preposition *con* is followed by *mí, ti,* or *sí,* both words are replaced by *conmigo, contigo,* and *consigo,* respectively (*¿vienes conmigo?,* are you coming with me?; *habló contigo,* he spoke with you; *no lo trajo consigo,* she didn't bring it with her).

3. Object Pronouns

DIRECT OBJECT PRONOUNS

Direct object pronouns represent the primary goal or result of the action of a verb. The direct object pronouns in Spanish are:

Singular		Plural	
me	me	**nos**	us
te	you	**os[1]**	you
le[2]	you, him	**les[2]**	you, them
lo	you, him, it	**los**	you, them
la	you, her, it	**las**	you, them

[1]Used only in Spain.
[2]Used mainly in Spain.

Agreement

The third person forms agree in both gender and number with the nouns they replace or the people they refer to (*pintó las paredes,* she painted the walls → *las pintó,* she painted them; *visitaron al señor Juárez,* they visited Mr. Juárez → *lo visitaron*, they visited him). The remaining forms vary only for number.

Position

Direct object pronouns are normally affixed to the end of an affirmative command, a simple infinitive, or a present participle (*¡hazlo!,* do it!; *es difícil hacerlo,* it's difficult to do it; *haciéndolo, aprenderás,* you'll learn by doing it). With constructions involving an auxiliary verb and an infinitive or present participle, the pronoun may occur either immediately before the construction or suffixed to it (*lo voy a hacer* or *voy a hacerlo,* I'm going to do it; *estoy haciéndolo* or *lo estoy haciendo,* I'm doing it). In all other cases, the pronoun immediately precedes the conjugated verb (*no lo haré,* I won't do it).

Regional Variation

In Spain and in a few areas of Latin America, *le* and *les* are used in place of *lo* and *los* when referring to or addressing people (*le vieron,* they saw him; *les vistió,* she dressed them). In most parts of Latin America, however, *los* and *las* are used for the second person plural in both formal and familiar contexts.

The second person plural familiar form *os* is restricted to Spain.

INDIRECT OBJECT PRONOUNS

Indirect object pronouns represent the secondary goal of the action of a verb (*me dio el regalo,* he gave me the gift; *les dije que no,* I told them no). The indirect object pronouns in Spanish are:

Singular		Plural	
me	(to, for, from) me	**nos**	(to, for, from) us
te	(to, for, from) you	**os**[1]	(to, for, from) you
le	(to, for, from) you, him, her, it	**les**	(to, for, from) you, them
se[2]		**se**[2]	

[1]Used only in Spain.
[2]See explanation below.

Position

Indirect object pronouns follow the same rules as direct object pronouns with regard to their position in relation to verbs. When they occur with direct object pronouns, the indirect object pronoun always precedes (*nos lo dio,* she gave it to us; *estoy trayéndotela,* I'm bringing it to you).

Use of *Se*

When the indirect object pronouns *le* or *les* occur before any direct object pronoun beginning with an *l-*, the indirect object pronouns *le* and *les* convert to *se* (*les mandé la carta,* I sent them the letter → *se la mandé,* I sent it to them; *vamos a comprarle los aretes,* let's buy her the earrings → *vamos a comprárselos,* let's buy them for her).

4. Reflexive Pronouns

Reflexive pronouns are used to refer back to the subject of the verb (*me hice daño,* I hurt myself; *se vistieron,* they got dressed, they dressed themselves; *nos lo compramos,* we bought it for ourselves).

The reflexive pronouns in Spanish are:

Singular		Plural	
me	myself	**nos**	ourselves
te	yourself	**os**[1]	yourselves
se	yourself, himself, herself, itself	**se**	yourselves, themselves

[1]Used only in Spain.

Reflexive pronouns are also used:

- When the verb describes an action performed to one's own body, clothing, etc. (*me quité los zapatos,* I took off my shoes; *se arregló el pelo,* he fixed his hair).

- In the plural, to indicate reciprocal action (*se hablan con frecuencia,* they speak with each other frequently).
- In the third person singular and plural, as an indefinite subject reference (*se dice que es verdad,* they say it's true; *nunca se sabe,* one never knows; *se escribieron miles de páginas,* thousands of pages were written).

It should be noted that many verbs which take reflexive pronouns in Spanish have intransitive equivalents in English (*ducharse,* to shower; *quejarse,* to complain; etc.).

5. Relative Pronouns

Relative pronouns introduce subordinate clauses acting as nouns or modifiers (*el libro que escribió . . . ,* the book that he wrote . . . ; *las chicas a quienes conociste . . . ,* the girls whom you met . . .). In Spanish, the relative pronouns are:

que (that, which, who, whom)

quien, quienes (who, whom, that, whoever, whomever)

el cual, la cual, los cuales, las cuales (which, who)

el que, la que, los que, las que (which, who, whoever)

lo cual (which)

lo que (what, which, whatever)

cuanto, cuanta, cuantos, cuantas (all those that, all that, whatever, whoever, as much as, as many as)

Relative pronouns are not omitted in Spanish as they often are in English: *el carro que vi ayer,* the car (that) I saw yesterday. When relative pronouns are used with prepositions, the preposition precedes the clause (*la película sobre la cual le hablé,* the film I spoke to you about).

The relative pronoun *que* can be used in reference to both people and things. Unlike other relative pronouns, *que* does not take the personal *a* when used as a direct object referring to a person (*el hombre que llamé,* the man that I called; but: *el hombre a quien llamé,* the man whom I called).

Quien is used only in reference to people. It varies in number with the explicit or implied antecedent (*las mujeres con quienes charlamos . . .,* the women we chatted with; *quien lo hizo pagará,* whoever did it will pay).

El cual and *el que* vary for both number and gender, and are therefore often used in situations where *que* or *quien(es)* might create ambiguity: *nos contó algunas cosas sobre los libros, las cuales eran interesantes,* he told us some things about the books which (the things) were interesting.

Lo cual and *lo que* are used to refer back to a whole clause, or to something indefinite (*dijo que iría, lo cual me alegró,* he said he would go, which made me happy; *pide lo que quieras,* ask for whatever you want).

Cuanto varies for both number and gender with the implied antecedent: *conté a cuantas (personas) pude,* I counted as many (people) as I could. If an indefinite mass quantity is referred to, the masculine singular form is used (*anoté cuanto decía,* I jotted down whatever he said).

Possessives

1. Possessive Adjectives

UNSTRESSED FORMS

Singular		Plural	
mi(s)	my	**nuestro(s), nuestra(s)**	our
tu(s)	your	**vuestro(s)**[1], **vuestra(s)**[1]	your
su(s)	your, his, her, its	**su(s)**	your, their

[1]Used only in Spain.

STRESSED FORMS

Singular		Plural	
mío(s), mía(s)	my, mine, of mine	**nuestro(s), nuestra(s)**	our, ours, of ours
tuyo(s), tuya(s)	your, yours, of yours	**vuestro(s)**[1], **vuestra(s)**[1]	your, yours, of yours
suyo(s), suya(s)	your, yours, of yours; his, of his; her, hers, of hers; its, of its	**suyo(s), suya(s)**	your, yours, of yours; their, theirs, of theirs

[1]Used only in Spain.

The unstressed forms of possessive adjectives precede the nouns they modify (*mis zapatos,* my shoes; *nuestra escuela,* our school).

The stressed forms occur after the noun and are often used for purposes of emphasis (*el carro tuyo,* your car; *la pluma es mía,* the pen is mine; *unos amigos nuestros,* some friends of ours).

All possessive adjectives agree with the noun in number. The stressed forms, as well as the unstressed forms *nuestro* and *vuestro,* also vary for gender.

2. Possessive Pronouns

The possessive pronouns have the same forms as the stressed possessive adjectives (see table above). They are always preceded by the definite article, and they agree in number and gender with the nouns they replace (*las llaves mías,* my keys → *las mías,* mine; *los guantes nuestros,* our gloves → *los nuestros,* ours).

Demonstratives

1. Demonstrative Adjectives

The demonstrative adjectives in Spanish are:

Singular		Plural	
este, esta	this	**estos, estas**	these
ese, esa	that	**esos, esas**	those
aquel, aquella	that	**aquellos, aquellas**	those

Demonstrative adjectives agree with the nouns they modify in gender and number (*esta chica, aquellos árboles*). They normally precede the noun, but may occasionally occur after for purposes of emphasis or to express contempt: *en la época aquella de cambio,* in that era of change; *el perro ese ha ladrado toda la noche,* that (awful, annoying, etc.) dog barked all night long.

The forms *aquel, aquella, aquellos,* and *aquellas* are generally used in reference to people and things that are relatively distant from the speaker in space or time: *ese libro,* that book (a few feet away); *aquel libro,* that book (way over there).

2. Demonstrative Pronouns

The demonstrative pronouns in Spanish are orthographically identical to the demonstrative adjectives except that they take an accent mark over the stressed vowel (*éste, ése, aquél,* etc.). In addition, there are three neuter forms—*esto, eso,* and *aquello*—which are used when referring to abstract ideas or unidentified things (*¿te dijo eso?,* he said that to you?; *¿qué es esto?,* what is this?; *tráeme todo aquello,* bring me all that stuff).

Except for the neuter forms, demonstrative pronouns agree in gender and number with the nouns they replace (*esta silla,* this chair → *ésta,* this one; *aquellos vasos,* those glasses → *aquéllos,* those ones).

Spanish Numbers

Cardinal Numbers

1	uno	33	treinta y tres
2	dos	34	treinta y cuatro
3	tres	35	treinta y cinco
4	cuatro	36	treinta y seis
5	cinco	37	treinta y siete
6	seis	38	treinta y ocho
7	siete	39	treinta y nueve
8	ocho	40	cuarenta
9	nueve	41	cuarenta y uno
10	diez	50	cincuenta
11	once	60	sesenta
12	doce	70	setenta
13	trece	80	ochenta
14	catorce	90	noventa
15	quince	100	cien
16	dieciséis	101	ciento uno
17	diecisiete	102	ciento dos
18	dieciocho	200	doscientos
19	diecinueve	300	trescientos
20	veinte	400	cuatrocientos
21	veintiuno	500	quinientos
22	veintidós	600	seiscientos
23	veintitrés	700	setecientos
24	veinticuatro	800	ochocientos
25	veinticinco	900	novecientos
26	veintiséis	1,000	mil
27	veintisiete	1,001	mil uno
28	veintiocho	2,000	dos mil
29	veintinueve	100,000	cien mil
30	treinta	1,000,000	un millón
31	treinta y uno	1,000,000,000	mil millones
32	treinta y dos		

Ordinal Numbers

1st	primero, -ra	18th	decimoctavo, -va
2nd	segundo, -da	19th	decimonoveno, -na; *or* decimonono, -na
3rd	tercero, -ra	20th	vigésimo, -ma
4th	cuarto, -ta	21st	vigésimoprimero, vigésimaprimera
5th	quinto, -ta	22nd	vigésimosegundo, vigésimasegunda
6th	sexto, -ta	30th	trigésimo, -ma
7th	séptimo, -ma	40th	cuadragésimo, -ma
8th	octavo, -va	50th	quincuagésimo, -ma
9th	noveno, -na	60th	sexagésimo, -ma
10th	décimo, -ma	70th	septuagésimo, -ma
11th	undécimo, -ma	80th	octogésimo, -ma
12th	duodécimo, -ma	90th	nonagésimo, -ma
13th	decimotercero, -ra	100th	centésimo, -ma
14th	decimocuarto, -ta		
15th	decimoquinto, -ta		
16th	decimosexto, -ta		
17th	decimoséptimo, -ma		

Conjugation of Spanish Verbs

Simple Tenses

TENSE	REGULAR VERBS ENDING IN -AR hablar	
PRESENT INDICATIVE	hablo	hablamos
	hablas	habláis
	habla	hablan
PRESENT SUBJUNCTIVE	hable	hablemos
	hables	habléis
	hable	hablen
PRETERIT INDICATIVE	hablé	hablamos
	hablaste	hablasteis
	habló	hablaron
IMPERFECT INDICATIVE	hablaba	hablábamos
	hablabas	hablabais
	hablaba	hablaban
IMPERFECT SUBJUNCTIVE	hablara	habláramos
	hablaras	hablarais
	hablara	hablaran
	or	
	hablase	hablásemos
	hablases	hablaseis
	hablase	hablasen
FUTURE INDICATIVE	hablaré	hablaremos
	hablarás	hablaréis
	hablará	hablarán
FUTURE SUBJUNCTIVE	hablare	habláremos
	hablares	hablareis
	hablare	hablaren
CONDITIONAL	hablaría	hablaríamos
	hablarías	hablaríais
	hablaría	hablarían
IMPERATIVE		hablemos
	habla	hablad
	hable	hablen
PRESENT PARTICIPLE (GERUND)	hablando	
PAST PARTICIPLE	hablado	

REGULAR VERBS ENDING IN -ER		REGULAR VERBS ENDING IN -IR	
comer		vivir	
como	comemos	vivo	vivimos
comes	coméis	vives	vivís
come	comen	vive	viven
coma	comamos	viva	vivamos
comas	comáis	vivas	viváis
coma	coman	viva	vivan
comí	comimos	viví	vivimos
comiste	comisteis	viviste	vivisteis
comió	comieron	vivió	vivieron
comía	comíamos	vivía	vivíamos
comías	comíais	vivías	vivíais
comía	comían	vivía	vivían
comiera	comiéramos	viviera	viviéramos
comieras	comierais	vivieras	vivierais
comiera	comieran	viviera	vivieran
or		*or*	
comiese	comiésemos	viviese	viviésemos
comieses	comieseis	vivieses	vivieseis
comiese	comiesen	viviese	viviesen
comeré	comeremos	viviré	viviremos
comerás	comeréis	vivirás	viviréis
comerá	comerán	vivirá	vivirán
comiere	comiéremos	viviere	viviéremos
comieres	comiereis	vivieres	viviereis
comiere	comieren	viviere	vivieren
comería	comeríamos	viviría	viviríamos
comerías	comeríais	vivirías	viviríais
comería	comerían	viviría	vivirían
	comamos		vivamos
come	comed	vive	vivid
coma	coman	viva	vivan
comiendo		viviendo	
comido		vivido	

Compound Tenses

1. Perfect Tenses

The perfect tenses are formed with *haber* and the past participle:

PRESENT PERFECT

he hablado, etc. (*indicative*);
haya hablado, etc. (*subjunctive*)

PAST PERFECT

había hablado, etc. (*indicative*);
hubiera hablado, etc. (*subjuntive*)
or
hubiese hablado, etc. (*subjunctive*)

PRETERIT PERFECT

hube hablado, etc. (*indicative*)

FUTURE PERFECT

habré hablado, etc. (*indicative*)

CONDITIONAL PERFECT

habría hablado, etc. (*indicative*)

2. Progressive Tenses

The progressive tenses are formed with *estar* and the present participle:

PRESENT PROGRESSIVE

estoy llamando, etc. (*indicative*);
esté llamando, etc. (*subjunctive*)

IMPERFECT PROGRESSIVE

estaba llamando, etc. (*indicative*);
estuviera llamando, etc. (*subjunctive*)
or
estuviese llamando, etc. (*subjunctive*)

PRETERIT PROGRESSIVE

estuve llamando, etc. (*indicative*)

FUTURE PROGRESSIVE

estaré llamando, etc. (*indicative*)

CONDITIONAL PROGRESSIVE

estaría llamando, etc. (*indicative*)

PRESENT PERFECT PROGRESSIVE

he estado llamando, etc. (*indicative*);
haya estado llamando, etc. (*subjunctive*)

PAST PERFECT PROGRESSIVE

había estado llamando, etc. (*indicative*);
hubiera estado llamando, etc. (*subjunctive*)
or
hubiese estado llamando, etc. (*subjunctive*)

Use of *Vos*

In parts of South and Central America, *vos* often replaces or competes with *tú* as the second person familiar personal pronoun. It is particularly well established in the Río de la Plata region and much of Central America.

The pronoun *vos* often takes a distinct set of verb forms, usually in the present tense and the imperative. These vary widely from region to region; examples of the most common forms are shown below.

INFINITIVE FORM	hablar	comer	vivir
PRESENT INDICATIVE	vos hablás	vos comés	vos vivís
PRESENT SUBJUNCTIVE	vos hablés	vos comás	vos vivás
IMPERATIVE	hablá	comé	viví

In some areas, *vos* may take the *tú* or *vosotros* forms of the verb, while in others (as Uruguay), *tú* is combined with the *vos* verb forms.

Irregular Verbs

The *imperfect subjunctive,* the *future subjunctive,* the *conditional,* and the remaining forms of the *imperative* are not included in the model conjugations list, but can be derived as follows:

The *imperfect subjunctive* and the *future subjunctive* are formed from the third person plural form of the preterit tense by removing the last syllable (*-ron*) and adding the appropriate suffix:

PRETERIT INDICATIVE, THIRD PERSON PLURAL (querer)	quisieron
IMPERFECT SUBJUNCTIVE (querer)	quisiera, quisieras, etc. *or* quisiese, quisieses, etc.
FUTURE SUBJUNCTIVE (querer)	quisiere, quisieres, etc.

The conditional uses the same stem as the future indicative:

FUTURE INDICATIVE (poner)	pondré, pondrás, etc.
CONDITIONAL (poner)	pondría, pondrías, etc.

The third person singular, first person plural, and third person plural forms of the *imperative* are the same as the corresponding forms of the present subjunctive.

The second person plural *(vosotros)* form of the *imperative* is formed by removing the final *-r* of the infinitive form and adding a *-d* (ex.: *oír* → *oíd).*

Model Conjugations of Irregular Verbs

The model conjugations below include the following simple tenses: the *present indicative* (*IND*), the *present subjunctive* (*SUBJ*), the *preterit indicative* (*PRET*), the *imperfect indicative* (*IMPF*), the *future indicative* (*FUT*), the second person singular form of the *imperative* (*IMPER*), the *present participle* or *gerund* (*PRP*), and the *past participle* (*PP*). Each set of conjugations is preceded by the corresponding infinitive form of the verb, shown in bold type. Only tenses containing irregularities are listed, and the irregular verb forms within each tense are displayed in bold type.

Conjugation of Spanish Verbs

Each irregular verb entry in the Spanish-English section of this dictionary is cross-referred by number to one of the following model conjugations. These cross-reference numbers are shown in curly braces { } immediately following the entry's functional label.

1 **abolir** *(defective verb)* **:** *IND* abolimos, abolís *(other forms not used);* *SUBJ (not used);* *IMPER (only second person plural is used)*

2 **abrir :** *PP* abierto

3 **actuar :** *IND* **actúo**, **actúas**, **actúa**, actuamos, actuáis, **actúan;** *SUBJ* **actúe, actúes, actúe,** actuemos, actuéis, **actúen;** *IMPER* **actúa**

4 **adquirir :** *IND* **adquiero, adquieres, adquiere,** adquirimos, adquirís, **adquieren;** *SUBJ* **adquiera, adquieras, adquiera,** adquiramos, adquiráis, **adquieran;** *IMPER* **adquiere**

5 **airar :** *IND* **aíro, aíras, aíra,** airamos, airáis, **aíran;** *SUBJ* **aíre, aíres, aíre,** airemos, airéis, **aíren;** *IMPER* **aíra**

6 **andar :** *PRET* **anduve, anduviste, anduvo, anduvimos, anduvisteis, anduvieron**

7 **asir :** *IND* **asgo,** ases, ase, asimos, asís, asen; *SUBJ* **asga, asgas, asga, asgamos, asgáis, asgan**

8 **aunar :** *IND* **aúno, aúnas, aúna,** aunamos, aunáis, **aúnan;** *SUBJ* **aúne, aúnes, aúne,** aunemos, aunéis, **aúnen;** *IMPER* **aúna**

9 **avergonzar :** IND **avergüenzo, avergüenzas, avergüenza,** avergonzamos, avergonzáis, **avergüenzan;** *SUBJ* **avergüence, avergüences, avergüence, avergoncemos, avergoncéis, avergüencen;** *PRET* **avergoncé;** *IMPER* **avergüenza**

10 **averiguar :** *SUBJ* **averigüe, averigües, averigüe, averigüemos, averigüéis, averigüen;** *PRET* **averigüé,** averiguaste, averiguó, averiguamos, averiguasteis, averiguaron

11 **bendecir :** *IND* **bendigo, bendices, bendice,** bendecimos, bendecís, **bendicen;** *SUBJ* **bendiga, bendigas, bendiga, bendigamos, bendigáis, bendigan;** *PRET* **bendije, bendijiste, bendijo, bendijimos, bendijisteis, bendijeron;** *IMPER* **bendice**

12 **caber :** *IND* **quepo,** cabes, cabe, cabemos, cabéis, caben; *SUBJ* **quepa, quepas, quepa, quepamos, quepáis, quepan;** *PRET* **cupe, cupiste, cupo, cupimos, cupisteis, cupieron;** *FUT* **cabré, cabrás, cabrá, cabremos, cabréis, cabrán**

13 **caer :** *IND* **caigo,** caes, cae, caemos, caéis, caen; *SUBJ* **caiga, caigas, caiga, caigamos, caigáis, caigan;** *PRET* caí, **caíste, cayó, caímos, caísteis, cayeron;** *PRP* **cayendo;** *PP* **caído**

14 **cocer :** *IND* **cuezo, cueces, cuece,** cocemos, cocéis, **cuecen;** *SUBJ* **cueza, cuezas, cueza, cozamos, cozáis, cuezan;** *IMPER* **cuece**

15 **coger :** *IND* **cojo,** coges, coge, cogemos, cogéis, cogen; *SUBJ* **coja, cojas, coja, cojamos, cojáis, cojan**

16 **colgar :** *IND* **cuelgo, cuelgas, cuelga,** colgamos, colgáis, **cuelgan;** *SUBJ* **cuelgue, cuelgues, cuelgue, colguemos, colguéis, cuelguen;** *PRET* **colgué,** colgaste, colgó, colgamos, colgasteis, colgaron; *IMPER* **cuelga**

17 **concernir** *(defective verb; used only in the third person singular and plural of the present indicative, present subjunctive, and imperfect subjunctive) see* 25 **discernir**

18 **conocer :** *IND* **conozco,** conoces, conoce, conocemos, conocéis, conocen; *SUBJ* **conozca, conozcas, conozca, conozcamos, conozcáis, conozcan**

19 **contar :** *IND* **cuento, cuentas, cuenta,** contamos, contáis, **cuentan;** *SUBJ* **cuente, cuentes, cuente,** contemos, contéis, **cuenten;** *IMPER* **cuenta**

20 **creer :** *PRET* creí, **creíste, creyó, creímos, creísteis, creyeron;** *PRP* **creyendo;** *PP* **creído**

21 **cruzar :** *SUBJ* **cruce, cruces, cruce, crucemos, crucéis, crucen;** *PRET* **crucé,** cruzaste, cruzó, cruzamos, cruzasteis, cruzaron

22 **dar :** *IND* **doy,** das, da, damos, **dais,** dan; *SUBJ* **dé,** des, **dé,** demos, **deis,** den; *PRET* **di, diste, dio, dimos, disteis, dieron**

23 **decir :** *IND* **digo, dices, dice,** decimos, decís, **dicen;** *SUBJ* **diga, digas, diga, digamos, digáis, digan;** *PRET* **dije, dijiste, dijo,**

dijimos, dijisteis, dijeron; *FUT* **diré, dirás, dirá, diremos, diréis, dirán;** *IMPER* **di;** *PRP* **diciendo;** *PP* **dicho**

24 **delinquir :** *IND* **delinco,** delinques, delinque, delinquimos, delinquís, delinquen; *SUBJ* **delinca, delincas, delinca, delincamos, delincáis, delincan**

25 **discernir :** *IND* **discierno, disciernes, discierne,** discernimos, discernís, **disciernen;** *SUBJ* **discierna, disciernas, discierna,** discernamos, discernáis, **disciernan;** *IMPER* **discierne**

26 **distinguir :** *IND* **distingo,** distingues, distingue, distinguimos, distinguís, distinguen; *SUBJ* **distinga, distingas, distinga, distingamos, distingáis, distingan**

27 **dormir :** *IND* **duermo, duermes, duerme,** dormimos, dormís, **duermen;** *SUBJ* **duerma, duermas, duerma, durmamos, durmáis, duerman;** *PRET* dormí, dormiste, **durmió,** dormimos, dormisteis, **durmieron;** *IMPER* **duerme;** *PRP* **durmiendo**

28 **elegir :** *IND* **elijo, eliges, elige,** elegimos, elegís, **eligen;** *SUBJ* **elija, elijas, elija, elijamos, elijáis, elijan;** *PRET* elegí, elegiste, **eligió,** elegimos, elegisteis, **eligieron;** *IMPER* **elige;** *PRP* **eligiendo**

29 **empezar :** *IND* **empiezo, empiezas, empieza,** empezamos, empezáis, **empiezan;** *SUBJ* **empiece, empieces, empiece, empecemos, empecéis, empiecen;** *PRET* **empecé,** empezaste, empezó, empezamos, empezasteis, empezaron; *IMPER* **empieza**

30 **enraizar :** *IND* **enraízo, enraízas, enraíza,** enraizamos, enraizáis, **enraízan;** *SUBJ* **enraíce, enraíces, enraíce, enraicemos, enraicéis, enraícen;** *PRET* **enraicé,** enraizaste, enraizó, enraizamos, enraizasteis, enraizaron; *IMPER* **enraíza**

31 **erguir :** *IND* **irgo** *or* **yergo, irgues** *or* **yergues, irgue** *or* **yergue,** erguimos, erguís, **irguen** *or* **yerguen;** *SUBJ* **irga** *or* **yerga, irgas** *or* **yergas, irga** *or* **yerga, irgamos, irgáis, irgan** *or* **yergan;** *PRET* erguí, erguiste, **irguió,** erguimos, erguisteis, **irguieron;** *IMPER* **irgue** *or* **yergue;** *PRP* **irguiendo**

32 **errar :** *IND* **yerro, yerras, yerra,** erramos, erráis, **yerran;** *SUBJ* **yerre, yerres, yerre,** erremos, erréis, **yerren;** *IMPER* **yerra**

33 **escribir :** *PP* **escrito**

34 **estar :** *IND* **estoy, estás, está,** estamos, estáis, **están;** *SUBJ* **esté, estés, esté,** estemos, estéis, **estén;** *PRET* **estuve, estuviste, estuvo, estuvimos, estuvisteis, estuvieron;** *IMPER* **está**

35 **exigir :** *IND* **exijo,** exiges, exige, exigimos, exigís, exigen; *SUBJ* **exija, exijas, exija, exijamos, exijáis, exijan**

36 **forzar :** *IND* **fuerzo, fuerzas, fuerza,** forzamos, forzáis, **fuerzan;** *SUBJ* **fuerce, fuerces, fuerce, forcemos, forcéis, fuercen;** *PRET* **forcé,** forzaste, forzó, forzamos, forzasteis, forzaron; *IMPER* **fuerza**

37 **freír :** *IND* **frío, fríes, fríe, freímos,** freís, **fríen;** *SUBJ* **fría, frías, fría, friamos, friáis, frían;** *PRET* freí, **freíste, frió, freímos, freísteis, frieron;** *IMPER* **fríe;** *PRP* **friendo;** *PP* **frito**

38 **gruñir :** *PRET* gruñí, gruñiste, **gruñó,** gruñimos, gruñisteis, **gruñeron;** *PRP* **gruñendo**

39 **haber :** *IND* **he, has, ha, hemos,** habéis, **han;** *SUBJ* **haya, hayas, haya, hayamos, hayáis, hayan;** *PRET* **hube, hubiste, hubo, hubimos, hubisteis, hubieron;** *FUT* **habré, habrás, habrá, habremos, habréis, habrán;** *IMPER* **he**

40 **hacer :** *IND* **hago,** haces, hace, hacemos, hacéis, hacen; *SUBJ* **haga, hagas, haga, hagamos, hagáis, hagan;** *PRET* **hice, hiciste, hizo, hicimos, hicisteis, hicieron;** *FUT* **haré, harás, hará, haremos, haréis, harán;** *IMPER* **haz;** *PP* **hecho**

41 **huir :** *IND* **huyo, huyes, huye,** huimos, huís, **huyen;** *SUBJ* **huya, huyas, huya, huyamos, huyáis, huyan;** *PRET* huí, huiste, **huyó,** huimos, huisteis, **huyeron;** *IMPER* **huye;** *PRP* **huyendo**

42 **imprimir :** *PP* **impreso**

43 **ir :** *IND* **voy, vas, va, vamos, vais, van;** *SUBJ* **vaya, vayas, vaya, vayamos, vayáis, vayan;** *PRET* **fui, fuiste, fue, fuimos, fuisteis, fueron;** *IMPF* **iba, ibas, iba, íbamos, ibais, iban;** *IMPER* **ve;** *PRP* **yendo;** *PP* **ido**

44 **jugar :** *IND* **juego, juegas, juega,** jugamos, jugáis, **juegan;** *SUBJ* **juegue, juegues, juegue, juguemos, juguéis, jueguen;** *PRET* **jugué,** jugaste, jugó, jugamos, jugasteis, jugaron; *IMPER* **juega**

45 **lucir :** *IND* **luzco,** luces, luce, lucimos, lucís, lucen; *SUBJ* **luzca, luzcas, luzca, luzcamos, luzcáis, luzcan**

46 **morir :** *IND* **muero, mueres, muere,** morimos, morís, **mueren;** *SUBJ* **muera, mueras, muera, muramos, muráis, mueran;** *PRET* morí, moriste, **murió,** morimos, moristeis, **murieron;** *IMPER* **muere;** *PRP* **muriendo;** *PP* **muerto**

47 **mover :** *IND* **muevo, mueves, mueve,** movemos, movéis, **mueven;** *SUBJ* **mueva, muevas, mueva,** movamos, mováis, **muevan;** *IMPER* **mueve**

48 **nacer :** *IND* **nazco,** naces, nace, nacemos, nacéis, nacen; *SUBJ* **nazca, nazcas, nazca, nazcamos, nazcáis, nazcan**

49 **negar :** *IND* **niego, niegas, niega,** negamos, negáis, **niegan;** *SUBJ* **niegue, niegues, niegue, neguemos, neguéis, nieguen;** *PRET* **negué,** negaste, negó, negamos, negasteis, negaron; *IMPER* **niega**

50 **oír :** *IND* **oigo, oyes, oye, oímos,** oís, **oyen;** *SUBJ* **oiga, oigas, oiga, oigamos, oigáis, oigan;** *PRET* oí, **oíste, oyó, oímos, oísteis, oyeron;** *IMPER* **oye;** *PRP* **oyendo;** *PP* **oído**

51 **oler :** *IND* **huelo, hueles, huele,** olemos, oléis, **huelen;** *SUBJ* **huela, huelas, huela,** olamos, oláis, **huelan;** *IMPER* **huele**

52 **pagar :** *SUBJ* **pague, pagues, pague, paguemos, paguéis, paguen;** *PRET* **pagué,** pagaste, pagó, pagamos, pagasteis, pagaron

53 **parecer :** *IND* **parezco,** pareces, parece, parecemos, parecéis, parecen; *SUBJ* **parezca, parezcas, parezca, parezcamos, parezcáis, parezcan**

54 **pedir :** *IND* **pido, pides, pide,** pedimos, pedís, **piden;** *SUBJ* **pida, pidas, pida, pidamos, pidáis, pidan;** *PRET* pedí, pediste, **pidió,** pedimos, pedisteis, **pidieron;** *IMPER* **pide;** *PRP* **pidiendo**

55 **pensar :** *IND* **pienso, piensas, piensa,** pensamos, pensáis, **piensan;** *SUBJ* **piense, pienses, piense,** pensemos, penséis, **piensen;** *IMPER* **piensa**

56 **perder :** *IND* **pierdo, pierdes, pierde,** perdemos, perdéis, **pierden;** *SUBJ* **pierda, pierdas, pierda,** perdamos, perdáis, **pierdan;** *IMPER* **pierde**

57 **placer** : *IND* **plazco,** places, place, placemos, placéis, placen; *SUBJ* **plazca, plazcas, plazca, plazcamos, plazcáis, plazcan;** *PRET* plací, placiste, plació *or* **plugo,** placimos, placisteis, placieron *or* **pluguieron**

58 **poder** : *IND* **puedo, puedes, puede,** podemos, podéis, **pueden;** *SUBJ* **pueda, puedas, pueda,** podamos, podáis, **puedan;** *PRET* **pude, pudiste, pudo, pudimos, pudisteis, pudieron;** *FUT* **podré, podrás, podrá, podremos, podréis, podrán;** *IMPER* **puede;** *PRP* **pudiendo**

59 **podrir** *or* **pudrir** : *PP* **podrido** *(all other forms based on* pudrir*)*

60 **poner** : *IND* **pongo,** pones, pone, ponemos, ponéis, ponen; *SUBJ* **ponga, pongas, ponga, pongamos, pongáis, pongan;** *PRET* **puse, pusiste, puso, pusimos, pusisteis, pusieron;** *FUT* **pondré, pondrás, pondrá, pondremos, pondréis, pondrán;** *IMPER* **pon;** *PP* **puesto**

61 **producir** : *IND* **produzco,** produces, produce, producimos, producís, producen; *SUBJ* **produzca, produzcas, produzca, produzcamos, produzcáis, produzcan;** *PRET* **produje, produjiste, produjo, produjimos, produjisteis, produjeron**

62 **prohibir** : *IND* **prohíbo, prohíbes, prohíbe,** prohibimos, prohibís, **prohíben;** *SUBJ* **prohíba, prohíbas, prohíba,** prohibamos, prohibáis, **prohíban;** *IMPER* **prohíbe**

63 **proveer** : *PRET* proveí, **proveíste, proveyó, proveímos, proveísteis, proveyeron;** *PRP* **proveyendo;** *PP* **provisto**

64 **querer** : *IND* **quiero, quieres, quiere,** queremos, queréis, **quieren;** *SUBJ* **quiera, quieras, quiera,** queramos, queráis, **quieran;** *PRET* **quise, quisiste, quiso, quisimos, quisisteis, quisieron;** *FUT* **querré, querrás, querrá, querremos, querréis, querrán;** *IMPER* **quiere**

65 **raer** : *IND* rao *or* **raigo** *or* **rayo,** raes, rae, raemos, raéis, raen; *SUBJ* **raiga** *or* **raya, raigas** *or* **rayas, raiga** *or* **raya, raigamos** *or* **rayamos, raigáis** *or* **rayáis, raigan** *or* **rayan;** *PRET* **raí, raíste, rayó, raímos, raísteis, rayeron;** *PRP* **rayendo;** *PP* **raído**

66 **reír** : *IND* **río, ríes, ríe, reímos,** reís, **ríen;** *SUBJ* **ría, rías, ría, riamos, riáis, rían;** *PRET* reí, **reíste, rió, reímos, reísteis, rieron;** *IMPER* **ríe;** *PRP* **riendo;** *PP* **reído**

67 **reñir :** *IND* **riño, riñes, riñe,** reñimos, reñís, **riñen;** *SUBJ* **riña, riñas, riña, riñamos, riñáis, riñan;** *PRET* reñí, reñiste, **riñó,** reñimos, reñisteis, **riñeron;** *PRP* **riñendo**

68 **reunir :** *IND* **reúno, reúnes, reúne,** reunimos, reunís, **reúnen;** *SUBJ* **reúna, reúnas, reúna,** reunamos, reunáis, **reúnan;** *IMPER* **reúne**

69 **roer :** *IND* roo *or* **roigo** *or* **royo,** roes, roe, roemos, roéis, roen; *SUBJ* roa *or* **roiga** *or* **roya,** roas *or* **roigas** *or* **royas,** roa *or* **roiga** *or* **roya,** roamos *or* **roigamos** *or* **royamos,** roáis *or* **roigáis** *or* **royáis,** roan *or* **roigan** *or* **royan;** *PRET* roí, **roíste, royó, roímos, roísteis, royeron;** *PRP* **royendo;** *PP* **roído**

70 **romper :** *PP* **roto**

71 **saber :** *IND* **sé,** sabes, sabe, sabemos, sabéis, saben; *SUBJ* **sepa, sepas, sepa, sepamos, sepáis, sepan;** *PRET* **supe, supiste, supo, supimos, supisteis, supieron;** *FUT* **sabré, sabrás, sabrá, sabremos, sabréis, sabrán**

72 **sacar :** *SUBJ* **saque, saques, saque, saquemos, saquéis, saquen;** *PRET* **saqué,** sacaste, sacó, sacamos, sacasteis, sacaron

73 **salir :** *IND* **salgo,** sales, sale, salimos, salís, salen; *SUBJ* **salga, salgas, salga, salgamos, salgáis, salgan;** *FUT* **saldré, saldrás, saldrá, saldremos, saldréis, saldrán;** *IMPER* **sal**

74 **satisfacer :** *IND* **satisfago,** satisfaces, satisface, satisfacemos, satisfacéis, satisfacen; *SUBJ* **satisfaga, satisfagas, satisfaga, satisfagamos, satisfagáis, satisfagan;** *PRET* **satisfice, satisficiste, satisfizo, satisficimos, satificisteis, satisficieron;** *FUT* **satisfaré, satisfarás, satisfará, satisfaremos, satisfaréis, satisfarán;** *IMPER* **satisfaz** *or* **satisface;** *PP* **satisfecho**

75 **seguir :** *IND* **sigo, sigues, sigue,** seguimos, seguís, **siguen;** *SUBJ* **siga, sigas, siga, sigamos, sigáis, sigan;** *PRET* seguí, seguiste, **siguió,** seguimos, seguisteis, **siguieron;** *IMPER* **sigue;** *PRP* **siguiendo**

76 **sentir :** *IND* **siento, sientes, siente,** sentimos, sentís, **sienten;** *SUBJ* **sienta, sientas, sienta, sintamos, sintáis, sientan;** *PRET* sentí, sentiste, **sintió,** sentimos, sentisteis, **sintieron;** *IMPER* **siente;** *PRP* **sintiendo**

77 **ser** : *IND* **soy, eres, es, somos, sois, son;** *SUBJ* **sea, seas, sea, seamos, seáis, sean;** *PRET* **fui, fuiste, fue, fuimos, fuisteis, fueron;** *IMPF* **era, eras, era, éramos, erais, eran;** *IMPER* **sé;** *PRP* **siendo;** *PP* **sido**

78 **soler** *(defective verb; used only in the present, preterit, and imperfect indicative, and the present and imperfect subjunctive) see* 47 **mover**

79 **tañer** : *PRET* tañí, tañiste, **tañó,** tañimos, tañisteis, **tañeron;** *PRP* **tañendo**

80 **tener** : *IND* **tengo, tienes, tiene,** tenemos, tenéis, **tienen;** *SUBJ* **tenga, tengas, tenga, tengamos, tengáis, tengan;** *PRET* **tuve, tuviste, tuvo, tuvimos, tuvisteis, tuvieron;** *FUT* **tendré, tendrás, tendrá, tendremos, tendréis, tendrán;** *IMPER* **ten**

81 **traer** : *IND* **traigo,** traes, trae, traemos, traéis, traen; *SUBJ* **traiga, traigas, traiga, traigamos, traigáis, traigan;** *PRET* **traje, trajiste, trajo, trajimos, trajisteis, trajeron;** *PRP* **trayendo;** *PP* **traído**

82 **trocar** : *IND* **trueco, truecas, trueca,** trocamos, trocáis, **truecan;** *SUBJ* **trueque, trueques, trueque, troquemos, troquéis, truequen;** *PRET* **troqué,** trocaste, trocó, trocamos, trocasteis, trocaron; *IMPER* **trueca**

83 **uncir** : *IND* **unzo,** unces, unce, uncimos, uncís, uncen; *SUBJ* **unza, unzas, unza, unzamos, unzáis, unzan**

84 **valer** : *IND* **valgo,** vales, vale, valemos, valéis, valen; *SUBJ* **valga, valgas, valga, valgamos, valgáis, valgan;** *FUT* **valdré, valdrás, valdrá, valdremos, valdréis, valdrán**

85 **variar** : *IND* **varío, varías, varía,** variamos, variáis, **varían;** *SUBJ* **varíe, varíes, varíe,** variemos, variéis, **varíen;** *IMPER* **varía**

86 **vencer** : *IND* **venzo,** vences, vence, vencemos, vencéis, vencen; *SUBJ* **venza, venzas, venza, venzamos, venzáis, venzan**

87 **venir** : *IND* **vengo, vienes, viene,** venimos, venís, **vienen;** *SUBJ* **venga, vengas, venga, vengamos, vengáis, vengan;** *PRET* **vine, viniste, vino, vinimos, vinisteis, vinieron;** *FUT* **vendré, vendrás, vendrá, vendremos, vendréis, vendrán;** *IMPER* **ven;** *PRP* **viniendo**

88 **ver :** *IND* veo, **ves, ve, vemos, veis, ven;** *PRET* **vi, viste, vio, vimos, visteis, vieron;** *IMPER* **ve;** *PRP* **viendo;** *PP* **visto**

89 **volver :** *IND* **vuelvo, vuelves, vuelve,** volvemos, volvéis, **vuelven;** *SUBJ* **vuelva, vuelvas, vuelva,** volvamos, volváis, **vuelvan;** *IMPER* **vuelve;** *PP* **vuelto**

90 **yacer :** *IND* **yazco** *or* **yazgo** *or* **yago,** yaces, yace, yacemos, yacéis, yacen; *SUBJ* **yazca** *or* **yazga** *or* **yaga, yazcas** *or* **yazgas** *or* **yagas, yazca** *or* **yazga** *or* **yaga, yazcamos** *or* **yazgamos** *or* **yagamos, yazcáis** *or* **yazgáis** *or* **yagáis, yazcan** *or* **yazgan** *or* **yagan;** *IMPER* yace *or* **yaz**

Spanish–English Dictionary

A

a[1] *nf* : first letter of the Spanish alphabet

a[2] *prep* **1** : to <nos vamos a México : we're going to Mexico> **2** (*used before direct or indirect objects referring to persons*) <¿llamaste a tu papá? : did you call your dad?> <como a usted le guste : as you wish> **3** : in the manner of <papas a la francesa : french fries> **4** : on, by means of <a pie : on foot> **5** : per, each <tres pastillas al día : three pills per day> **6** (*with infinitive*) <enséñales a leer : teach them to read> <problemas a resolver : problems to be solved>

ábaco *nm* : abacus

abad *nm* : abbot

abadesa *nf* : abbess

abadía *nf* : abbey

abajo *adv* **1** : down <póngalo más abajo : put it further down> <arriba y abajo : up and down> **2** : downstairs **3** : under, beneath <el abajo firmante : the undersigned> **4** : down with <¡abajo la inflación! : down with inflation!> **5 ~ de** : under, beneath **6 de ~** : bottom <el cajón de abajo : the bottom drawer> **7 hacia ~** *or* **para ~** : downwards **8 cuesta abajo** : downhill **9 río abajo** : downstream

abalanzarse {21} *vr* : to hurl oneself, to rush

abanderado, -da *n* : standard-bearer

abandonado, -da *adj* **1** : abandoned, deserted **2** : neglected **3** : slovenly, unkempt

abandonar *vt* **1** DEJAR : to abandon, to leave **2** : to give up, to quit <abandonaron la búsqueda : they gave up the search> — **abandonarse** *vr* **1** : to neglect oneself **2 ~ a** : to succumb to, to give oneself over to

abandono *nm* **1** : abandonment **2** : neglect **3** : withdrawal <ganar por abandono : to win by default>

abanicar {72} *vt* : to fan — **abanicarse** *vr*

abanico *nm* **1** : fan **2** GAMA : range, gamut

abaratamiento *nm* : price reduction

abaratar *vt* : to lower the price of — **abaratarse** *vr* : to go down in price

abarcar {72} *vt* **1** : to cover, to include, to embrace **2** : to undertake **3** : to monopolize

abaritonado, -da *adj* : baritone

abarrotado, -da *adj* : packed, crammed

abarrotar *vt* : to fill up, to pack

abarrotería *nf CA, Mex* : grocery store

abarrotero, -ra *n Col, Mex* : grocer

abarrotes *nmpl* **1** : groceries, supplies **2 tienda de abarrotes** : general store, grocery store

abastecedor, -dora *n* : supplier

abastecer {53} *vt* : to supply, to stock — **abastecerse** *vr* : to stock up

abastecimiento → **abasto**

abasto *nm* : supply, supplying <no da abasto : there isn't enough for all>

abatido, -da *adj* : dejected, depressed

abatimiento *nm* **1** : drop, reduction **2** : dejection, depression

abatir *vt* **1** DERRIBAR : to demolish, to knock down **2** : to shoot down **3** DEPRIMIR : to depress, to bring low — **abatirse** *vr* **1** DEPRIMIRSE : to get depressed **2 ~ sobre** : to swoop down on

abdicación *nf, pl* **-ciones** : abdication

abdicar {72} *vt* : to relinquish, to abdicate

abdomen *nm, pl* **-dómenes** : abdomen

abdominal *adj* : abdominal

abecé *nm* : ABC

abecedario *nm* ALFABETO : alphabet

abedul *nm* : birch (tree)

abeja *nf* : bee

abejorro *nm* : bumblebee

aberración *nf, pl* **-ciones** : aberration

aberrante *adj* : aberrant, perverse

abertura *nf* **1** : aperture, opening **2** AGUJERO : hole **3** : slit (in a skirt, etc.) **4** GRIETA : crack

abeto *nm* : fir (tree)

abierto[1] *pp* → **abrir**

abierto[2], **-ta** *adj* **1** : open **2** : candid, frank **3** : generous — **abiertamente** *adv*

abigarrado, -da *adj* : multicolored, variegated

abigeato *nm* : rustling (of livestock)

abismal *adj* : abysmal, vast

abismo *nm* : abyss, chasm <al borde del abismo : on the brink of ruin>

abjurar *vi* **~ de** : to abjure — **abjuración** *nf*

ablandamiento *nm* : softening, moderation

ablandar *vt* **1** SUAVIZAR : to soften **2** CALMAR : to soothe, to appease — *vi* : to moderate, to get milder — **ablandarse** *vr* **1** : to become soft, to soften **2** CEDER : to yield, to relent

ablución *nf, pl* **-ciones** : ablution

abnegación *nf, pl* **-ciones** : abnegation, self-denial

abnegado, -da *adj* : self-sacrificing, selfless

abnegarse {49} *vr* : to deny oneself

abobado, -da *adj* **1** : silly, stupid **2** : bewildered

abocarse {72} *vr* **1** DIRIGIRSE : to head, to direct oneself **2** DEDICARSE : to dedicate oneself

abochornar *vt* AVERGONZAR : to embarrass, to shame — **abochornarse** *vr*

abofetear *vt* : to slap

abogacía *nf* : law, legal profession

abogado, -da *n* : lawyer, attorney

abogar {52} *vi* **~ por** : to plead for, to defend, to advocate
abolengo *nm* LINAJE : lineage, ancestry
abolición *nf, pl* **-ciones** : abolition
abolir {1} *vt* DEROGAR : to abolish, to repeal
abolladura *nf* : dent
abollar *vt* : to dent
abombar *vt* : to warp, to cause to bulge — **abombarse** *vr* : to decompose, to go bad
abominable *adj* ABORRECIBLE : abominable
abominación *nf, pl* **-ciones** : abomination
abominar *vt* ABORRECER : to abominate, to abhor
abonado, -da *n* : subscriber
abonar *vt* **1** : to pay **2** FERTILIZAR : to fertilize — **abonarse** *vr* : to subscribe
abono *nm* **1** : payment, installment **2** FERTILIZANTE : fertilizer **3** : season ticket
abordaje *nm* : boarding
abordar *vt* **1** : to address, to broach **2** : to accost, to waylay **3** : to come on board
aborigen[1] *adj, pl* **-rígenes** : aboriginal, native
aborigen[2] *nmf, pl* **-rígenes** : aborigine, indigenous inhabitant
aborrecer {53} *vt* ABOMINAR, ODIAR : to abhor, to detest, to hate
aborrecible *adj* ABOMINABLE, ODIOSO : abominable, detestable
aborrecimiento *nm* : abhorrence, loathing
abortar *vi* : to have an abortion — *vt* **1** : to abort **2** : to quash, to suppress
abortista *nmf* : abortionist
abortivo, -va *adj* : abortive
aborto *nm* **1** : abortion **2** : miscarriage
abotonar *vt* : to button — **abotonarse** *vr* : to button up
abovedado, -da *adj* : vaulted
abrasador, -dora *adj* : burning, scorching
abrasar *vt* QUEMAR : to burn, to sear, to scorch
abrasivo[1], **-va** *adj* : abrasive
abrasivo[2] *nm* : abrasive
abrazadera *nf* : clamp, brace
abrazar {21} *vt* : to hug, to embrace — **abrazarse** *vr*
abrazo *nm* : hug, embrace
abrebotellas *nms & pl* : bottle opener
abrelatas *nms & pl* : can opener
abrevadero *nm* BEBEDERO : watering trough
abreviación *nf, pl* **-ciones** : abbreviation
abreviar *vt* **1** : to abbreviate **2** : to shorten, to cut short
abreviatura *nf* → **abreviación**
abridor *nm* : bottle opener, can opener
abrigadero *nm* : shelter, windbreak
abrigado, -da *adj* **1** : sheltered **2** : warm, wrapped up (with clothing)
abrigar {52} *vt* **1** : to shelter, to protect **2** : to keep warm, to dress warmly **3** : to cherish, to harbor <abrigar esperanzas : to cherish hopes> — **abrigarse** *vr* : to dress warmly
abrigo *nm* **1** : coat, overcoat **2** : shelter, refuge
abril *nm* : April
abrillantador *nm* : polish
abrillantar *vt* : to polish, to shine
abrir {2} *vt* **1** : to open **2** : to unlock, to undo **3** : to turn on (a tap or faucet) — *vi* : to open, to open up — **abrirse** *vr* **1** : to open up **2** : to clear (of the skies)
abrochar *vt* : to button, to fasten — **abrocharse** *vr* : to fasten, to hook up
abrogación *nf, pl* **-ciones** : abrogation, annulment, repeal
abrogar {52} *vt* : to abrogate, to annul, to repeal
abrojo *nm* : bur (of a plant)
abrumador, -dora *adj* : crushing, overwhelming
abrumar *vt* **1** AGOBIAR : to overwhelm **2** OPRIMIR : to oppress, to burden
abrupto, -ta *adj* **1** : abrupt **2** ESCARPADO : steep — **abruptamente** *adv*
absceso *nm* : abscess
absolución *nf, pl* **-ciones** **1** : absolution **2** : acquittal
absolutismo *nm* : absolutism
absoluto, -ta *adj* **1** : absolute, unconditional **2 en ~** : not at all <no me gustó en absoluto : I did not like it at all> — **absolutamente** *adv*
absolver {89} *vt* **1** : to absolve **2** : to acquit
absorbente *adj* **1** : absorbent **2** : absorbing, engrossing
absorber *vt* **1** : to absorb, to soak up **2** : to occupy, to take up, to engross
absorción *nf, pl* **-ciones** : absorption
absorto, -ta *adj* : absorbed, engrossed
abstemio[1], **-mia** *adj* : abstemious, teetotal
abstemio[2], **-mia** *n* : teetotaler
abstención *nf, pl* **-ciones** : abstention
abstenerse {80} *vr* : to abstain, to refrain
abstinencia *nf* : abstinence
abstracción *nf, pl* **-ciones** : abstraction
abstracto, -ta *adj* : abstract
abstraer {81} *vt* : to abstract — **abstraerse** *vr* : to lose oneself in thought
abstraído, -da *adj* : preoccupied, withdrawn
abstruso, -sa *adj* : abstruse
abstuvo, etc. → **abstenerse**
absuelto *pp* → **absolver**
absurdo[1], **-da** *adj* DISPARATADO, RIDÍCULO : absurd, ridiculous — **absurdamente** *adv*
absurdo[2] *nm* : absurdity
abuchear *vt* : to boo, to jeer
abucheo *nm* : booing, jeering
abuela *nf* **1** : grandmother **2** : old woman **3 ¡tu abuela!** *fam* : no way!, forget about it!

abuelo *nm* **1 :** grandfather **2 :** old man **3 abuelos** *nmpl* **:** grandparents, ancestors

abulia *nf* **:** apathy, lethargy

abúlico, -ca *adj* **:** lethargic, apathetic

abultado, -da *adj* **:** bulging, bulky

abultar *vi* **:** to bulge — *vt* **:** to enlarge, to expand

abundancia *nf* **:** abundance

abundante *adj* **:** abundant, plentiful — **abundantemente** *adv*

abundar *vi* **1 :** to abound, to be plentiful **2 ~ en :** to be in agreement with

aburrido, -da *adj* **1 :** bored, tired, fed up **2** TEDIOSO **:** boring, tedious

aburrimiento *nm* **:** boredom, weariness

aburrir *vt* **:** to bore, to tire — **aburrirse** *vr* **:** to get bored

abusado, -da *adj Mex fam* **:** sharp, on the ball

abusador, -dora *n* **:** abuser

abusar *vi* **1 :** to go too far, to do something to excess **2 ~ de :** to abuse (as drugs) **3 ~ de :** to take unfair advantage of

abusivo, -va *adj* **1 :** abusive **2 :** outrageous, excessive

abuso *nm* **1 :** abuse **2 :** injustice, outrage

abyecto, -ta *adj* **:** despicable, contemptible

acá *adv* AQUÍ **:** here, over here <¡ven acá! : come here!>

acabado[1], -da *adj* **1 :** finished, done, completed **2 :** old, worn-out

acabado[2] *nm* **:** finish <un acabado brillante : a glossy finish>

acabar *vi* **1** TERMINAR **:** to finish, to end **2 ~ de :** to have just (done something) <acabo de ver a tu hermano : I just saw your brother> **3 ~ con :** to put an end to, to stamp out — *vt* TERMINAR **:** to finish — **acabarse** *vr* TERMINARSE **:** to come to an end, to run out <se me acabó el dinero : I ran out of money>

academia *nf* **:** academy

académico[1], -ca *adj* **:** academic, scholastic — **académicamente** *adv*

académico[2], -ca *n* **:** academic, academician

acaecer {53} *vi* (*3rd person only*) **:** to happen, to take place

acalambrarse *vr* **:** to cramp up, to get a cramp

acallar *vt* **:** to quiet, to silence

acalorado, -da *adj* **:** emotional, heated

acaloramiento *nm* **1 :** heat **2 :** ardor, passion

acalorar *vt* **:** to heat up, to inflame — **acalorarse** *vr* **:** to get upset, to get worked up

acampada *nf* **:** camp, camping <ir de acampada : to go camping>

acampar *vi* **:** to camp

acanalar *vt* **1 :** to groove, to furrow **2 :** to corrugate

acantilado *nm* **:** cliff

acanto *nm* **:** acanthus

acantonar *vt* **:** to station, to quarter

acaparador, -dora *adj* **:** greedy, selfish

acaparar *vt* **1 :** to stockpile, to hoard **2 :** to monopolize

acápite *nm* **:** paragraph

acariciar *vt* **:** to caress, to stroke, to pet

ácaro *nm* **:** mite

acarrear *vt* **1 :** to haul, to carry **2 :** to bring, to give rise to <los problemas que acarrea : the problems that come along with it>

acarreo *nm* **:** transport, haulage

acartonarse *vr* **1 :** to stiffen **2 :** to become wizened

acaso *adv* **1 :** perhaps, by any chance **2 por si acaso :** just in case

acatamiento *nm* **:** compliance, observance

acatar *vt* **:** to comply with, to respect

acaudalado, -da *adj* RICO **:** wealthy, rich

acaudillar *vt* **:** to lead, to command

acceder *vi* **~ a 1 :** to accede to, to agree to **2 :** to assume (a position) **3 :** to gain access to

accesar *vt* **:** to access (on a computer)

accesibilidad *nf* **:** accessibility

accesible *adj* ASEQUIBLE **:** accessible, attainable

acceso *nm* **1 :** access **2 :** admittance, entrance

accesorio[1], -ria *adj* **1 :** accessory **2 :** incidental

accesorio[2] *nm* **1 :** accessory **2 :** prop (in the theater)

accidentado[1], -da *adj* **1 :** eventful, turbulent **2 :** rough, uneven **3 :** injured

accidentado[2], -da *n* **:** accident victim

accidental *adj* **:** accidental, unintentional — **accidentalmente** *adv*

accidentarse *vr* **:** to have an accident

accidente *nm* **1 :** accident **2 :** unevenness **3 accidente geográfico :** geographical feature

acción *nf, pl* **acciones 1 :** action **2** ACTO **:** act, deed **3 :** share, stock

accionamiento *nm* **:** activation

accionar *vt* **:** to put into motion, to activate — *vi* **:** to gesticulate

accionario, -ria *adj* **:** stock <mercado accionario : stock market>

accionista *nmf* **:** stockholder, shareholder

acebo *nm* **:** holly

acechar *vt* **1 :** to watch, to spy on **2 :** to stalk, to lie in wait for

acecho *nm* **al acecho :** lying in wait

acedera *nf* **:** sorrel (herb)

acéfalo, -la *adj* **:** leaderless

aceitar *vt* **:** to oil

aceite *nm* **1 :** oil **2 aceite de ricino :** castor oil **3 aceite de oliva :** olive oil

aceitera *nf* **1 :** cruet (for oil) **2 :** oilcan **3** *Mex* **:** oil refinery

aceitoso, -sa *adj* **:** oily

aceituna *nf* OLIVA **:** olive

aceituno *nm* OLIVO **:** olive tree

aceleración *nf, pl* **-ciones** : acceleration, speeding up
acelerado, -da *adj* : accelerated, speedy
acelerador *nm* : accelerator
aceleramiento *nm* → **aceleración**
acelerar *vt* **1** : to accelerate, to speed up **2** AGILIZAR : to expedite — *vi* : to accelerate (of an automobile) — **acelerarse** *vr* : to hasten, to hurry up
acelga *nf* : chard, Swiss chard
acendrado, -da *adj* : pure, unblemished
acendrar *vt* : to purify, to refine
acento *nm* **1** : accent **2** : stress, emphasis
acentuación *nf, pl* **-ciones** : accentuation
acentuado, -da *adj* : marked, pronounced
acentuar {3} *vt* **1** : to accent **2** : to emphasize, to stress — **acentuarse** *vr* : to become more pronounced
acepción *nf, pl* **-ciones** SIGNIFICADO : sense, meaning
aceptabilidad *nf* : acceptability
aceptable *adj* : acceptable
aceptación *nf, pl* **-ciones 1** : acceptance **2** APROBACIÓN : approval
aceptar *vt* **1** : to accept **2** : to approve
acequia *nf* **1** : irrigation ditch **2** *Mex* : sewer
acera *nf* : sidewalk
acerado, -da *adj* **1** : made of steel **2** : steely, tough
acerbo, -ba *adj* **1** : harsh, cutting <comentarios acerbos : cutting remarks> **2** : bitter — **acerbamente** *adv*
acerca *prep* **~ de** : about, concerning
acercamiento *nm* : rapprochement, reconciliation
acercar {72} *vt* APROXIMAR, ARRIMAR : to bring near, to bring closer — **acercarse** *vr* APROXIMARSE, ARRIMARSE : to approach, to draw near
acería *nf* : steel mill
acerico *nm* : pincushion
acero *nm* : steel <acero inoxidable : stainless steel>
acérrimo, -ma *adj* **1** : staunch, steadfast **2** : bitter <un acérrimo enemigo : a bitter enemy>
acertado, -da *adj* CORRECTO : accurate, correct, on target — **acertadamente** *adv*
acertante[1] *adj* : winning
acertante[2] *nmf* : winner
acertar {55} *vt* : to guess correctly — *vi* ATINAR : to be accurate, to be on target
acertijo *nm* ADIVINANZA : riddle
acervo *nm* **1** : pile, heap **2** : wealth, heritage <el acervo artístico del instituto : the artistic treasures of the institute>
acetato *nm* : acetate
acético, -ca *adj* : acetic <ácido acético : acetic acid>
acetileno *nm* : acetylene
acetona *nf* **1** : acetone **2** : nail-polish remover
achacar {72} *vt* : to attribute, to impute <te achaca todos sus problemas : he blames all his problems on you>
achacoso, -sa *adj* : frail, sickly
achaparrado, -da *adj* : stunted, scrubby <árboles achaparrados : scrubby trees>
achaque *nm* DOLENCIA : ailment, malady, discomfort
achatar *vt* : to flatten
achicar {72} *vt* **1** REDUCIR : to make smaller, to reduce **2** : to intimidate **3** : to bail out (water) — **achicarse** *vr* : to become intimidated
achicharrar *vt* : to scorch, to burn to a crisp
achicoria *nf* : chicory
achispado, -da *adj fam* : tipsy
achote *or* **achiote** *nm* : annatto seed
achuchón *nm, pl* **-chones 1** : push, shove **2** *fam* : squeeze, hug **3** *fam* : mild illness
aciago, -ga *adj* : fateful, unlucky
acicalar *vt* **1** PULIR : to polish **2** : to dress up, to adorn — **acicalarse** *vr* : to get dressed up
acicate *nm* **1** : spur **2** INCENTIVO : incentive, stimulus
acidez *nf, pl* **-deces 1** : acidity **2** : sourness **3 acidez estomacal** : heartburn
acidificar {72} *vt* : to acidify
ácido[1], -da *adj* AGRIO : acid, sour
ácido[2] *nm* : acid
acierto *nm* **1** : correct answer, right choice **2** : accuracy, skill, deftness
acimut *nm* : azimuth
acitronar *vt Mex* : to fry until crisp
aclamación *nf, pl* **-ciones** : acclaim, acclamation
aclamar *vt* : to acclaim, to cheer, to applaud
aclaración *nf, pl* **-ciones** CLARIFICACIÓN : clarification, explanation
aclarar *vt* **1** CLARIFICAR : to clarify, to explain, to resolve **2** : to lighten **3 aclarar la voz** : to clear one's throat — *vi* **1** : to get light, to dawn **2** : to clear up — **aclararse** *vr* : to become clear
aclaratorio, -ria *adj* : explanatory
aclimatar *vt* : to acclimatize — **aclimatarse** *vr* **~ a** : to get used to — **aclimatación** *nf*
acné *nm* : acne
acobardar *vt* INTIMIDAR : to frighten, to intimidate — **acobardarse** *vr* : to be frightened, to cower
acodarse *vr* **~ en** : to lean (one's elbows) on
acogedor, -dora *adj* : cozy, warm, friendly
acoger {15} *vt* **1** REFUGIAR : to take in, to shelter **2** : to receive, to welcome — **acogerse** *vr* **1** REFUGIARSE : to take refuge **2 ~ a** : to resort to, to avail oneself of

acogida *nf* **1** AMPARO, REFUGIO **:** refuge, protection **2** RECIBIMIENTO **:** reception, welcome

acolchar *vt* **1 :** to pad (a wall, etc.) **2 :** to quilt

acólito *nm* **1** MONAGUILLO **:** altar boy **2 :** follower, helper, acolyte

acomedido, -da *adj* **:** helpful, obliging

acometer *vt* **1** ATACAR **:** to attack, to assail **2** EMPRENDER **:** to undertake, to begin — *vi* **~ contra :** to rush against

acometida *nf* ATAQUE **:** attack, assault

acomodado, -da *adj* **1 :** suitable, appropriate **2 :** well-to-do, prosperous

acomodador, -dora *n* **:** usher, usherette *f*

acomodar *vt* **1 :** to accommodate, to make room for **2 :** to adjust, to adapt — **acomodarse** *vr* **1 :** to settle in **2 ~ a :** to adapt to

acomodaticio, -cia *adj* **:** accommodating, obliging

acomodo *nm* **1 :** job, position **2 :** arrangement, placement **3 :** accommodation, lodging

acompañamiento *nm* **:** accompaniment

acompañante *nmf* **1** COMPAÑERO **:** companion **2 :** accompanist

acompañar *vt* **:** to accompany, to go with

acompasado, -da *adj* **:** rhythmic, regular, measured

acomplejado, -da *adj* **:** full of complexes, neurotic

acondicionado, -da *adj* **1 :** equipped, fitted-out **2 bien acondicionado :** in good shape, in a fit state

acondicionador *nm* **1 :** conditioner **2 acondicionador de aire :** air conditioner

acondicionar *vt* **1 :** to condition **2 :** to fit out, to furnish

acongojado, -da *adj* **:** distressed, upset

acongojarse *vr* **:** to grieve, to become distressed

aconsejable *adj* **:** advisable

aconsejar *vt* **:** to advise, to counsel

acontecer {53} *vi* (*3rd person only*) **:** to occur, to happen

acontecimiento *nm* SUCESO **:** event

acopiar *vt* **:** to gather, to collect, to stockpile

acopio *nm* **:** collection, stock

acoplamiento *nm* **:** connection, coupling

acoplar *vt* **:** to couple, to connect — **acoplarse** *vr* **:** to fit together

acoquinar *vt* **:** to intimidate

acorazado[1], -da *adj* BLINDADO **:** armored

acorazado[2] *nm* **:** battleship

acordado, -da *adj* **:** agreed upon

acordar {19} *vt* **1 :** to agree on **2** OTORGAR **:** to award, to bestow — **acordarse** *vr* RECORDAR **:** to remember, to recall

acorde[1] *adj* **1 :** in agreement, in accordance **2 ~ con :** in keeping with

acorde[2] *nm* **:** chord

acordeón *nm, pl* **-deones :** accordion — **acordeonista** *nmf*

acordonar *vt* **1 :** to cordon off **2 :** to lace up **3 :** to mill (coins)

acorralar *vt* ARRINCONAR **:** to corner, to hem in, to corral

acortar *vt* **:** to shorten, to cut short — **acortarse** *vr* **1 :** to become shorter **2 :** to end early

acosar *vt* PERSEGUIR **:** to pursue, to hound, to harass

acoso *nm* ASEDIO **:** harassment <acoso sexual **:** sexual harassment>

acostar {19} *vt* **1 :** to lay (something) down **2 :** to put to bed — **acostarse** *vr* **1 :** to lie down **2 :** to go to bed

acostumbrado, -da *adj* **1** HABITUADO **:** accustomed **2** HABITUAL **:** usual, customary

acostumbrar *vt* **:** to accustom — *vi* **:** to be accustomed, to be in the habit — **acostumbrarse** *vr*

acotación *nf, pl* **-ciones 1 :** marginal note **2 :** stage direction

acotado, -da *adj* **:** enclosed

acotamiento *nm Mex* **:** shoulder (of a road)

acotar *vt* **1** ANOTAR **:** to note, to annotate **2** DELIMITAR **:** to mark off (land), to demarcate

acre[1] *adj* **1 :** acrid, pungent **2** MORDAZ **:** caustic, biting

acre[2] *nm* **:** acre

acrecentamiento *nm* **:** growth, increase

acrecentar {55} *vt* AUMENTAR **:** to increase, to augment

acreditación *nf, pl* **-ciones :** accreditation

acreditado, -da *adj* **1 :** accredited, authorized **2 :** reputable

acreditar *vt* **1 :** to accredit, to authorize **2 :** to credit **3 :** to prove, to verify — **acreditarse** *vr* **:** to gain a reputation

acreedor[1], -dora *adj* **:** deserving, worthy

acreedor[2], -dora *n* **:** creditor

acribillar *vt* **1 :** to riddle, to pepper (with bullets, etc.) **2 :** to hound, to harass

acrílico *nm* **:** acrylic

acrimonia *nf* **1 :** pungency **2 :** acrimony

acrimonioso, -sa *adj* **:** acrimonious

acriollarse *vr* **:** to adopt local customs, to go native

acritud *nf* **1 :** pungency, bitterness **2 :** intensity, sharpness **3 :** harshness, asperity

acrobacia *nf* **:** acrobatics

acróbata *nmf* **:** acrobat

acrónimo *nm* **:** acronym

acta *nf* **1 :** document, certificate <acta de nacimiento **:** birth certificate> **2 actas** *nfpl* **:** minutes (of a meeting)

actitud *nf* **1 :** attitude **2 :** posture, position

activación *nf, pl* **-ciones 1 :** activation, stimulation **2** ACELERACIÓN **:** acceleration, speeding up

activar *vt* **1 :** to activate **2 :** to stimulate, to energize **3 :** to speed up

actividad *nf* **:** activity

activista *nmf* **:** activist

activo[1], **-va** *adj* **:** active — **activamente** *adv*

activo[2] *nm* **:** assets *pl* <activo y pasivo : assets and liabilities>

acto *nm* **1** ACCIÓN **:** act, deed **2 :** act (in a play) **3 el acto sexual :** sexual intercourse **4 en el acto :** right away, on the spot **5 acto seguido :** immediately after

actor *nm* ARTISTA **:** actor

actriz *nf, pl* **actrices** ARTISTA **:** actress

actuación *nf, pl* **-ciones 1 :** performance **2 actuaciones** *nfpl* DILIGENCIAS **:** proceedings

actual *adj* PRESENTE **:** present, current

actualidad *nf* **1 :** present time <en la actualidad : at present> **2 actualidades** *nfpl* **:** current affairs

actualización *nf, pl* **-ciones :** updating, modernization

actualizar {21} *vt* **:** to modernize, to bring up to date

actualmente *adv* **:** at present, nowadays

actuar {3} *vi* **:** to act, to perform

actuarial *adj* **:** actuarial

actuario, -ria *n* **:** actuary

acuarela *nf* **:** watercolor

acuario *nm* **:** aquarium

Acuario *nmf* **:** Aquarius, Aquarian

acuartelar *vt* **:** to quarter (troops)

acuático, -ca *adj* **:** aquatic, water

acuchillar *vt* APUÑALAR **:** to knife, to stab

acuciante *adj* **:** pressing, urgent

acucioso, -sa → **acuciante**

acudir *vi* **1 :** to go, to come (someplace for a specific purpose) <acudió a la puerta : he went to the door> <acudimos en su ayuda : we came to her aid> **2 :** to be present, to show up <acudí a la cita : I showed up for the appointment> **3 ~ a :** to turn to, to have recourse to <hay que acudir al médico : you must consult the doctor>

acueducto *nm* **:** aqueduct

acuerdo *nm* **1 :** agreement **2 estar de acuerdo :** to agree **3 de acuerdo con :** in accordance with **4 de ~ :** OK, all right

acuicultura *nf* **:** aquaculture

acullá *adv* **:** yonder, over there

acumulación *nf, pl* **-ciones :** accumulation

acumulador *nm* **:** storage battery

acumular *vt* **:** to accumulate, to amass — **acumularse** *vr* **:** to build up, to pile up

acumulativo, -va *adj* **:** cumulative — **acumulativamente** *adv*

acunar *vt* **:** to rock, to cradle

acuñar *vt* **:** to coin, to mint

acuoso, -sa *adj* **:** aqueous, watery

acupuntura *nf* **:** acupuncture

acurrucarse {72} *vr* **:** to cuddle, to nestle, to curl up

acusación *nf, pl* **-ciones 1 :** accusation, charge **2 la acusación :** the prosecution

acusado[1], **-da** *adj* **:** prominent, marked

acusado[2], **-da** *n* **:** defendant

acusador, -dora *n* **1 :** accuser **2** FISCAL **:** prosecutor

acusar *vt* **1 :** to accuse, to charge **2 :** to reveal, to betray <sus ojos acusaban la desconfianza : his eyes revealed distrust> — **acusarse** *vr* **:** to confess

acusatorio, -ria *adj* **:** accusatory

acuse *nm* **acuse de recibo :** acknowledgment of receipt

acústica *nf* **:** acoustics

acústico, -ca *adj* **:** acoustic

adagio *nm* **1** REFRÁN **:** adage, proverb **2 :** adagio

adalid *nm* **:** leader, champion

adaptable *adj* **:** adaptable — **adaptabilidad** *nf*

adaptación *nf, pl* **-ciones :** adaptation, adjustment

adaptado, -da *adj* **:** suited, adapted

adaptador *nm* **:** adapter (in electricity)

adaptar *vt* **1** MODIFICAR **:** to adapt **2 :** to adjust, to fit — **adaptarse** *vr* **:** to adapt oneself, to conform

adecentar *vt* **:** to tidy up

adecuación *nf, pl* **-ciones** ADAPTACIÓN **:** adaptation

adecuadamente *adv* **:** adequately

adecuado, -da *adj* **1** IDÓNEO **:** suitable, appropriate **2 :** adequate

adecuar {8} *vt* **:** to adapt, to make suitable — **adecuarse** *vr* **~ a :** to be appropriate for, to fit in with

adefesio *nm* **:** eyesore, monstrosity

adelantado, -da *adj* **1 :** advanced, ahead **2 :** fast (of a clock or watch) **3 por ~ :** in advance

adelantamiento *nm* **1 :** advancement **2 :** speeding up

adelantar *vt* **1 :** to advance, to move forward **2 :** to overtake, to pass **3 :** to reveal (information) in advance **4 :** to advance, to lend (money) — **adelantarse** *vr* **1 :** to advance, to get in front **2 ~ a :** to forestall, to preempt

adelante *adv* **1 :** ahead, in front, forward **2 más adelante :** further on, later on **3 ¡adelante! :** come in!

adelanto *nm* **1 :** advance, progress **2 :** advance payment **3 :** earliness <llevamos una hora de adelanto : we're running an hour ahead of time>

adelfa *nf* **:** oleander

adelgazar {21} *vt* **:** to thin, to reduce — *vi* **:** to lose weight

ademán *nm, pl* **-manes 1** GESTO **:** gesture **2 ademanes** *nmpl* **:** manners

además *adv* **1 :** besides, furthermore **2 ~ de :** in addition to, as well as

adenoides *nfpl* : adenoids

adentrarse *vr* **~ en** : to go into, to penetrate

adentro *adv* : inside, within

adentros *nmpl* **decirse para sus adentros** : to say to oneself <me dije para mis adentros que nunca regresaría : I told myself that I'd never go back>

adepto[1], -ta *adj* : supportive <ser adepto a : to be a follower of>

adepto[2], -ta *n* PARTIDARIO : follower, supporter

aderezar {21} *vt* **1** SAZONAR : to season, to dress (salad) **2** : to embellish, to adorn

aderezo *nm* **1** : dressing, seasoning **2** : adornment, embellishment

adeudar *vt* **1** : to debit **2** DEBER : to owe

adeudo *nm* **1** DÉBITO : debit **2** *Mex* : debt, indebtedness

adherencia *nf* **1** : adherence, adhesiveness **2** : appendage, accretion

adherente *adj* : adhesive, sticky

adherirse {76} *vr* : to adhere, to stick

adhesión *nf, pl* **-siones 1** : adhesion **2** : attachment, commitment (to a cause, etc.)

adhesivo[1], -va *adj* : adhesive

adhesivo[2] *nm* : adhesive

adicción *nf, pl* **-ciones** : addiction

adición *nf, pl* **-ciones** : addition

adicional *adj* : additional — **adicionalmente** *adv*

adicionar *vt* : to add

adicto[1], -ta *adj* **1** : addicted **2** : devoted, dedicated

adicto[2], -ta *n* **1** : addict **2** PARTIDARIO : supporter, advocate

adiestrador, -dora *n* : trainer

adiestramiento *nm* : training

adiestrar *vt* : to train

adinerado, -da *adj* : moneyed, wealthy

adiós *nm, pl* **adioses 1** DESPEDIDA : farewell, good-bye **2 ¡adiós!** : good-bye!

aditamento *nm* : attachment, accessory

aditivo *nm* : additive

adivinación *nf, pl* **-ciones 1** : guess **2** : divination, prediction

adivinanza *nf* ACERTIJO : riddle

adivinar *vt* **1** : to guess **2** : to foretell, to predict

adivino, -na *n* : fortune-teller

adjetivo[1], -va *adj* : adjectival

adjetivo[2] *nm* : adjective

adjudicación *nf, pl* **-ciones 1** : adjudication **2** : allocation, awarding, granting

adjudicar {72} *vt* **1** : to adjudge, to adjudicate **2** : to assign, to allocate <adjudicar la culpa : to assign the blame> **3** : to award, to grant

adjuntar *vt* : to enclose, to attach

adjunto[1], -ta *adj* : enclosed, attached

adjunto[2], -ta *n* : deputy, assistant

adjunto[3] *nm* : adjunct

administración *nf, pl* **-ciones 1** : administration, management **2 administración de empresas** : business administration

administrador, -dora *n* : administrator, manager

administrar *vt* : to administer, to manage, to run

administrativo, -va *adj* : administrative

admirable *adj* : admirable, impressive — **admirablemente** *adv*

admiración *nf, pl* **-ciones** : admiration

admirador, -dora *n* : admirer

admirar *vt* **1** : to admire **2** : to amaze, to astonish — **admirarse** *vr* : to be amazed

admirativo, -va *adj* : admiring

admisibilidad *nf* : admissibility

admisible *adj* : admissible, allowable

admisión *nf, pl* **-siones** : admission, admittance

admitir *vt* **1** : to admit, to let in **2** : to acknowledge, to concede **3** : to allow, to make room for <la ley no admite cambios : the law doesn't allow for changes>

admonición *nf, pl* **-ciones** : admonition, warning

admonitorio, -ria *adj* : admonitory

ADN *nm* : DNA

adobar *vt* : to marinate

adobe *nm* : adobe

adobo *nm* **1** : marinade, seasoning **2** *Mex* : spicy marinade used for cooking pork

adoctrinamiento *nm* : indoctrination

adoctrinar *vt* : to indoctrinate

adolecer {53} *vi* PADECER : to suffer <adolece de timidez : he suffers from shyness>

adolescencia *nf* : adolescence

adolescente[1] *adj* : adolescent, teenage

adolescente[2] *nmf* : adolescent, teenager

adonde *conj* : where <el lugar adonde vamos es bello : the place where we're going is beautiful>

adónde *adv* : where <¿adónde vamos? : where are we going?>

adondequiera *adv* : wherever, anywhere <adondequiera que vayas : anywhere you go>

adopción *nf, pl* **-ciones** : adoption

adoptar *vt* **1** : to adopt (a measure), to take (a decision) **2** : to adopt (children)

adoptivo, -va *adj* **1** : adopted (children, country) **2** : adoptive (parents)

adoquín *nm, pl* **-quines** : paving stone, cobblestone

adorable *adj* : adorable, lovable

adoración *nf, pl* **-ciones** : adoration, worship

adorador[1], -dora *adj* : adoring, worshipping

adorador[2], -dora *n* : worshipper

adorar *vt* : to adore, to worship

adormecer {53} *vt* **1** : to make sleepy, to lull to sleep **2** : to numb — **ador-**

mecerse *vr* **1 :** to doze off **2 :** to go numb
adormecimiento *nm* **1** SUEÑO **:** drowsiness, sleepiness **2** INSENSIBILIDAD **:** numbness
adormilarse *vr* **:** to doze, to drowse
adornar *vt* DECORAR **:** to decorate, to adorn
adorno *nm* **:** ornament, decoration
adquirido, -da *adj* **1 :** acquired **2 mal adquirido :** ill-gotten
adquirir {4} *vt* **1 :** to acquire, to gain **2** COMPRAR **:** to purchase
adquisición *nf, pl* **-ciones 1 :** acquisition **2** COMPRA **:** purchase
adquisitivo, -va *adj* **poder adquisitivo :** purchasing power
adrede *adv* **:** intentionally, on purpose
adrenalina *nf* **:** adrenaline
adscribir {33} *vt* **:** to assign, to appoint — **adscribirse** *vr* **~ a :** to become a member of
adscripción *nf, pl* **-ciones :** assignment, appointment
adscrito *pp* → **adscribir**
aduana *nf* **:** customs, customs office
aduanero[1], **-ra** *adj* **:** customs
aduanero[2], **-ra** *n* **:** customs officer
aducir {61} *vt* **:** to adduce, to offer as proof
adueñarse *vr* **~ de :** to take possession of, to take over
adulación *nf, pl* **-ciones :** adulation, flattery
adulador[1], **-dora** *adj* **:** flattering
adulador[2], **-dora** *n* **:** flatterer, toady
adular *vt* LISONJEAR **:** to flatter
adulteración *nf, pl* **-ciones :** adulteration
adulterar *vt* **:** to adulterate
adulterio *nm* **:** adultery
adúltero[1], **-ra** *adj* **:** adulterous
adúltero[2], **-ra** *n* **:** adulterer
adultez *nf* **:** adulthood
adulto, -ta *adj & n* **:** adult
adusto, -ta *adj* **:** harsh, severe
advenedizo, -za *n* **1 :** upstart, parvenu **2 :** newcomer
advenimiento *nm* **:** advent
adventicio, -cia *adj* **:** adventitious
adverbio *nm* **:** adverb — **adverbial** *adj*
adversario[1], **-ria** *adj* **:** opposing, contrary
adversario[2], **-ria** *n* OPOSITOR **:** adversary, opponent
adversidad *nf* **:** adversity
adverso, -sa *adj* DESFAVORABLE **:** adverse, unfavorable — **adversamente** *adv*
advertencia *nf* AVISO **:** warning
advertir {76} *vt* **1** AVISAR **:** to warn **2 :** to notice, to tell <no advertí que estuviera enojada : I couldn't tell she was angry>
adviento *nm* **:** Advent
adyacente *adj* **:** adjacent
aéreo, -rea *adj* **1 :** aerial, air **2 correo aéreo :** airmail
aeróbic *nm* **:** aerobics
aeróbico, -ca *adj* **:** aerobic
aerobio, -bia *adj* **:** aerobic
aerodinámica *nf* **:** aerodynamics
aerodinámico, -ca *adj* **:** aerodynamic, streamlined
aeródromo *nm* **:** airfield
aeroespacial *adj* **:** aerospace
aerolínea *nf* **:** airline
aeromozo, -za *n* **:** flight attendant, steward *m,* stewardess *f*
aeronáutica *nf* **:** aeronautics
aeronáutico, -ca *adj* **:** aeronautical
aeronave *nf* **:** aircraft
aeropostal *adj* **:** airmail
aeropuerto *nm* **:** airport
aerosol *nm* **:** aerosol, aerosol spray
aeróstata *nmf* **:** baloonist
aerotransportado, -da *adj* **:** airborne
aerotransportar *vt* **:** to airlift
afabilidad *nf* **:** affability
afable *adj* **:** affable — **afablemente** *adv*
afamado, -da *adj* **:** well-known, famous
afán *nm, pl* **afanes 1** ANHELO **:** eagerness, desire **2** EMPEÑO **:** effort, determination
afanador, -dora *n Mex* **:** cleaning person, cleaner
afanarse *vr* **:** to toil, to strive
afanosamente *adv* **:** zealously, industriously, busily
afanoso, -sa *adj* **1 :** eager, industrious **2 :** arduous, hard
afear *vt* **:** to make ugly, to disfigure
afección *nf, pl* **-ciones 1 :** fondness, affection **2 :** illness, complaint
afectación *nf, pl* **-ciones :** affectation
afectado, -da *adj* **1 :** affected, mannered **2 :** influenced **3 :** afflicted **4 :** feigned
afectar *vt* **1 :** to affect **2 :** to upset **3 :** to feign, to pretend
afectísimo, -ma *adj* **suyo afectísimo :** yours truly
afectivo, -va *adj* **:** emotional
afecto[1], **-ta** *adj* **1 :** affected, afflicted **2 :** fond, affectionate
afecto[2] *nm* CARIÑO **:** affection
afectuoso, -sa *adj* CARIÑOSO **:** affectionate, caring
afeitar *vt* RASURAR **:** to shave — **afeitarse** *vr*
afelpado, -da *adj* **:** plush
afeminado, -da *adj* **:** effeminate
aferrado, -da *adj* **:** obstinate, stubborn
aferrarse {55} *vr* **:** to cling, to hold on
AFI *nm* (*Alfabeto Fonético Internacional*) **:** IPA
affidávit *nm, pl* **-dávits :** affidavit
afgano, -na *adj & n* **:** Afghan
afianzar {21} *vt* **1 :** to secure, to strengthen **2 :** to guarantee, to vouch for — **afianzarse** *vr* ESTABLECERSE **:** to establish oneself
afiche *nm* **:** poster
afición *nf, pl* **-ciones 1 :** enthusiasm, penchant, fondness <afición al de-

porte : love of sports> **2** PASATIEMPO : hobby

aficionado[1], -da *adj* ENTUSIASTA : enthusiastic, keen

aficionado[2], -da *n* **1** ENTUSIASTA : enthusiast, fan **2** : amateur

áfido *nm* : aphid

afiebrado, -da *adj* : feverish

afilado, -da *adj* **1** : sharp **2** : long, pointed <una nariz afilada : a sharp nose>

afilador *nm* : sharpener

afilalápices *nms & pl* : pencil sharpener

afilar *vt* : to sharpen

afiliación *nf, pl* **-ciones** : affiliation

afiliado[1], -da *adj* : affiliated

afiliado[2], -da *n* : member

afiliarse *vr* : to become a member, to join, to affiliate

afín *adj, pl* **afines 1** PARECIDO : related, similar <la biología y disciplinas afines : biology and related disciplines> **2** PRÓXIMO : adjacent, nearby

afinación *nf, pl* **-ciones 1** : tune-up **2** : tuning (of an instrument)

afinador, -dora *n* : tuner (of musical instruments)

afinar *vt* **1** : to perfect, to refine **2** : to tune (an instrument) — *vi* : to sing or play in tune

afincarse {72} *vr* : to establish oneself, to settle in

afinidad *nf* : affinity, similarity

afirmación *nf, pl* **-ciones 1** : statement **2** : affirmation

afirmar *vt* **1** : to state, to affirm **2** REFORZAR : to make firm, to strengthen

afirmativo, -va *adj* : affirmative — **afirmativamente** *adj*

aflicción *nf, pl* **-ciones** DESCONSUELO, PESAR : grief, sorrow

afligido, -da *adj* : grief-stricken, sorrowful

afligir {35} *vt* **1** : to distress, to upset **2** : to afflict — **afligirse** *vr* : to grieve

aflojar *vt* **1** : to loosen, to slacken **2** *fam* : to pay up, to fork over — *vi* : to slacken, to ease up — **aflojarse** *vr* : to become loose, to slacken

afloramiento *nm* : outcropping, emergence

aflorar *vi* : to come to the surface, to emerge

afluencia *nf* **1** : flow, influx **2** : abundance, plenty

afluente *nm* : tributary

afluir {41} *vi* **1** : to flock <la gente afluía a la frontera : people were flocking to the border> **2** : to flow

aforismo *nm* : aphorism

aforo *nm* **1** : appraisal, assessment **2** : maximum capacity (of a theater, highway, etc.)

afortunado, -da *adj* : fortunate, lucky — **afortunadamente** *adv*

afrecho *nm* : bran, mash

afrenta *nf* : affront, insult

afrentar *vt* : to affront, to dishonor, to insult

africano, -na *adj & n* : African

afroamericano, -na *adj & n* : Afro-American

afrodisiaco *or* **afrodisíaco** *nm* : aphrodisiac

afrontamiento *nm* : confrontation

afrontar *vt* : to confront, to face up to

afrutado, -da *adj* : fruity

afuera *adv* **1** : out <¡afuera! : get out!> **2** : outside, outdoors

afueras *nfpl* ALEDAÑOS : outskirts

agachadiza *nf* : snipe (bird)

agachar *vt* : to lower (a part of the body) <agachar la cabeza : to bow one's head> — **agacharse** *vr* : to crouch, to stoop, to bend down

agalla *nf* **1** BRANQUIA : gill **2 tener agallas** *fam* : to have guts, to have courage

agarradera *nf* ASA, ASIDERO : handle, grip

agarrado, -da *adj fam* : cheap, stingy

agarrar *vt* **1** : to grab, to grasp **2** : to catch, to take — *vi* **agarrar y** *fam* : to do (something) abruptly <el día siguiente agarró y se fue : the next day he up and left> — **agarrarse** *vr* **1** : to hold on, to cling **2** *fam* : to get into a fight <se agarraron a golpes : they came to blows>

agarre *nm* : grip, grasp

agasajar *vt* : to fête, to wine and dine

agasajo *nm* : lavish attention

ágata *nf* : agate

agave *nm* : agave

agazaparse *vr* **1** AGACHARSE : to crouch **2** : to hide

agencia *nf* : agency, office

agenciar *vt* : to obtain, to procure — **agenciarse** *vr* : to manage, to get by

agenda *nf* **1** : agenda **2** : appointment book

agente *nmf* **1** : agent **2 agente de viajes** : travel agent **3 agente de bolsa** : stockbroker **4 agente de tráfico** : traffic officer

agigantado, -da *adj* GIGANTESCO : gigantic

agigantar *vt* **1** : to increase greatly, to enlarge **2** : to exaggerate

ágil *adj* **1** : agile, nimble **2** : sharp, lively (of a response, etc.) — **ágilmente** *adv*

agilidad *nf* : agility, nimbleness

agilizar {21} *vt* ACELERAR : to expedite, to speed up

agitación *nf, pl* **-ciones 1** : agitation **2** NERVIOSISMO : nervousness

agitado, -da *adj* **1** : agitated, excited **2** : choppy, rough, turbulent

agitador, -dora *n* PROVOCADOR : agitator

agitar *vt* **1** : to agitate, to shake **2** : to wave, to flap **3** : to stir up — **agitarse** *vr* **1** : to toss about, to flap around **2** : to get upset

aglomeración *nf, pl* **-ciones 1 :** conglomeration, mass **2** GENTÍO **:** crowd

aglomerar *vt* **:** to cluster, to amass — **aglomerarse** *vr* **:** to crowd together

aglutinar *vt* **:** to bring together, to bind

agnóstico, -ca *adj & n* **:** agnostic

agobiado, -da *adj* **:** weary, worn-out, weighted-down

agobiante *adj* **1 :** exhausting, overwhelming **2 :** stifling, oppressive

agobiar *vt* **1** OPRIMIR **:** to oppress, to burden **2** ABRUMAR **:** to overwhelm **3 :** to wear out, to exhaust

agonía *nf* **:** agony, death throes

agonizante *adj* **:** dying

agonizar {21} *vi* **1 :** to be dying **2 :** to be in agony **3 :** to dim, to fade

agorero, -ra *adj* **:** ominous

agostar *vt* **1 :** to parch **2 :** to wither — **agostarse** *vr*

agosto *nm* **1 :** August **2 hacer uno su agosto :** to make a fortune, to make a killing

agotado, -da *adj* **1 :** exhausted, used up **2 :** sold out **3** FATIGADO **:** worn-out, tired

agotador, -dora *adj* **:** exhausting

agotamiento *nm* FATIGA **:** exhaustion

agotar *vt* **1 :** to exhaust, to use up **2 :** to weary, to wear out — **agotarse** *vr*

agraciado[1], -da *adj* **1 :** attractive **2 :** fortunate

agraciado[2], -da *n* **:** winner

agradable *adj* GRATO, PLACENTERO **:** pleasant, agreeable — **agradablemente** *adv*

agradar *vi* **:** to be pleasing <nos agradó mucho el resultado : we were very pleased with the result>

agradecer {53} *vt* **1 :** to be grateful for **2 :** to thank

agradecido, -da *adj* **:** grateful, thankful

agradecimiento *nm* **:** gratitude, thankfulness

agrado *nm* **1** GUSTO **:** taste, liking <no es de su agrado : it's not to his liking> **2 :** graciousness, agreeableness **3 con ~ :** with pleasure, willingly <lo haré con agrado : I will be happy to do it>

agrandar *vt* **1 :** to exaggerate **2 :** to enlarge — **agrandarse** *vr*

agrario, -ria *adj* **:** agrarian, agricultural

agravación *nf, pl* **-ciones :** aggravation, worsening

agravante *adj* **:** aggravating

agravar *vt* **1 :** to increase (weight), to make heavier **2** EMPEORAR **:** to aggravate, to worsen — **agravarse** *vr*

agraviar *vt* INJURIAR, OFENDER **:** to offend, to insult

agravio *nm* INJURIA **:** affront, offense, insult

agredir {1} *vt* **:** to assail, to attack

agregado[1], -da *n* **1 :** attaché **2 :** assistant professor

agregado[2] *nm* **1 :** aggregate **2** AÑADIDURA **:** addition, something added

agregar {52} *vt* **1** AÑADIR **:** to add, to attach **2 :** to appoint — **agregarse** *vr* **:** to join

agresión *nf, pl* **-siones 1 :** aggression **2** ATAQUE **:** attack

agresividad *nf* **:** aggressiveness, aggression

agresivo, -va *adj* **:** aggressive — **agresivamente** *adv*

agresor[1], -sora *adj* **:** hostile, attacking

agresor[2], -sora *n* **1 :** aggressor **2 :** assailant, attacker

agreste *adj* **1** CAMPESTRE **:** rural **2 :** wild, untamed

agriar *vt* **1 :** to sour, to make sour **2 :** to embitter — **agriarse** *vr* **:** to turn sour

agrícola *adj* **:** agricultural

agricultor, -tora *n* **:** farmer, grower

agricultura *nf* **:** agriculture, farming

agridulce *adj* **1 :** bittersweet **2 :** sweet-and-sour

agrietar *vt* **:** to crack — **agrietarse** *vr* **1 :** to crack **2 :** to chap

agrimensor, -sora *n* **:** surveyor

agrimensura *nf* **:** surveying

agrio, agria *adj* **1** ÁCIDO **:** sour **2 :** caustic, acrimonious

agriparse *vr* **:** to catch the flu

agroindustria *nf* **:** agribusiness

agronomía *nf* **:** agronomy

agropecuario, -ria *adj* **:** pertaining to livestock and agriculture

agrupación *nf, pl* **-ciones** GRUPO **:** group, association

agrupamiento *nm* **:** grouping, concentration

agrupar *vt* **:** to group together

agua *nf* **1 :** water **2 agua oxigenada :** hydrogen peroxide **3 aguas negras** *or* **aguas residuales :** sewage **4 como agua para chocolate** *Mex fam* **:** furious **5 echar aguas** *Mex fam* **:** to keep an eye out, to be on the lookout

aguacate *nm* **:** avocado

aguacero *nm* **:** shower, downpour

aguado, -da *adj* **1** DILUIDO **:** watered-down, diluted **2** *CA, Col, Mex fam* **:** soft, flabby **3** *Mex, Peru fam* **:** dull, boring

aguafiestas *nmfs & pl* **:** killjoy, stick-in-the-mud, spoilsport

aguafuerte *nm* **:** etching

aguamanil *nm* **:** ewer, pitcher

aguanieve *nf* **:** sleet <caer aguanieve : to be sleeting>

aguantar *vt* **1** SOPORTAR **:** to bear, to tolerate, to withstand **2 :** to hold **3 aguantar las ganas :** to resist an urge <no pude aguantar las ganas de reír : I couldn't keep myself from laughing> — *vi* **:** to hold out, to last — **aguantarse** *vr* **1 :** to resign oneself **2 :** to restrain oneself

aguante *nm* **1** TOLERANCIA **:** tolerance, patience **2** RESISTENCIA **:** endurance, strength

aguar {10} *vt* **1 :** to water down, to dilute **2 aguar la fiesta** *fam* **:** to spoil the party

aguardar *vt* ESPERAR **:** to wait for, to await — *vi* **:** to be in store

aguardiente *nm* **:** clear brandy

aguarrás *nm* **:** turpentine

agudeza *nf* **1 :** keenness, sharpness **2 :** shrillness **3 :** witticism

agudizar {21} *vt* **:** to intensify, to heighten

agudo, -da *adj* **1 :** acute, sharp **2 :** shrill, high-pitched **3** PERSPICAZ **:** clever, shrewd

agüero *nm* AUGURIO, PRESAGIO **:** augury, omen

aguijón *nm, pl* **-jones 1 :** stinger (of a bee, etc.) **2 :** goad

aguijonear *vt* **:** to goad

águila *nf* **1 :** eagle **2 águila o sol** *Mex* **:** heads or tails

aguileño, -ña *adj* **:** aquiline

aguilera *nf* **:** aerie, eagle's nest

aguilón *nm, pl* **-lones :** gable

aguinaldo *nm* **1 :** Christmas bonus, year-end bonus **2** *PRi, Ven* **:** Christmas carol

agüitarse *vr Mex fam* **:** to have the blues, to feel discouraged

aguja *nf* **1 :** needle **2 :** steeple, spire

agujerear *vt* **:** to make a hole in, to pierce

agujero *nm* **1 :** hole **2 agujero negro :** black hole (in astronomy)

agujeta *nf* **1** *Mex* **:** shoelace **2 agujetas** *nfpl* **:** muscular soreness or stiffness

agusanado, -da *adj* **:** worm-eaten

aguzar {21} *vt* **1 :** to sharpen <aguzar el ingenio : to sharpen one's wits> **2 aguzar el oído :** to prick up one's ears

ahí *adv* **1 :** there <ahí está : there it is> **2 por ~ :** somewhere, thereabouts **3 de ahí que :** with the result that, so that

ahijado, -da *n* **:** godchild, godson *m*, goddaughter *f*

ahijar {5} *vt* **:** to adopt (a child)

ahínco *nm* **:** eagerness, zeal

ahogar {52} *vt* **1 :** to drown **2 :** to smother **3 :** to choke back, to stifle — **ahogarse** *vr*

ahogo *nm* **:** breathlessness, suffocation

ahondar *vt* **:** to deepen — *vi* **:** to elaborate, to go into detail

ahora *adv* **1 :** now **2 ahora mismo :** right now **3 hasta ~ :** so far **4 por ~ :** for the time being

ahorcar {72} *vt* **:** to hang, to kill by hanging — **ahorcarse** *vr*

ahorita *adv fam* **:** right now, right away

ahorquillado, -da *adj* **:** forked

ahorrador, -dora *adj* **:** thrifty

ahorrar *vt* **1 :** to save (money) **2 :** to spare, to conserve — *vi* **:** to save up — **ahorrarse** *vr* **:** to spare oneself

ahorrativo, -va *adj* **:** thrifty, frugal

ahorro *nm* **:** saving <cuenta de ahorros : savings account>

ahuecar {72} *vt* **1 :** to hollow out **2 :** to cup (one's hands) **3 :** to plump up, to fluff up

ahuizote *nm Mex fam* **:** annoying person, pain in the neck

ahumar {8} *vt* **:** to smoke, to cure

ahuyentar *vt* **1 :** to scare away, to chase away **2 :** to banish, to dispel <ahuyentar las dudas : to dispel doubts>

airado, -da *adj* FURIOSO **:** angry, irate

airar {5} *vt* **:** to make angry, to anger

aire *nm* **1 :** air **2 aire acondicionado :** air-conditioning **3 darse aires :** to give oneself airs

airear *vt* **:** to air, to air out — **airearse** *vr* **:** to get some fresh air

airoso, -sa *adj* **1 :** elegant, graceful **2 salir airoso :** to come out winning

aislacionismo *nm* **:** isolationism

aislacionista *adj & nmf* **:** isolationist

aislado, -da *adj* **:** isolated, alone

aislamiento *nm* **1 :** isolation **2 :** insulation

aislante *nm* **:** insulator, nonconductor

aislar {5} *vt* **1 :** to isolate **2 :** to insulate

ajado, -da *adj* **1 :** worn, shabby **2 :** wrinkled, crumpled

ajar *vt* **:** to wear out, to spoil

ajardinado, -da *adj* **:** landscaped

ajedrecista *nmf* **:** chess player

ajedrez *nm, pl* **-dreces 1 :** chess **2 :** chess set

ajeno, -na *adj* **1 :** alien **2 :** of another, of others <propiedad ajena : somebody else's property> **3 ~ a :** foreign to **4 ~ de :** devoid of, free from

ajetreado, -da *adj* **:** hectic, busy

ajetrearse *vr* **:** to bustle about, to rush around

ajetreo *nm* **:** hustle and bustle, fuss

ají *nm, pl* **ajíes :** chili pepper

ajo *nm* **:** garlic

ajonjolí *nm, pl* **-líes :** sesame

ajuar *nm* **:** trousseau

ajustable *adj* **:** adjustable

ajustado, -da *adj* **1** CEÑIDO **:** tight, tight-fitting **2 :** reasonable, fitting

ajustar *vt* **1 :** to adjust, to adapt **2 :** to take in (clothing) **3 :** to settle, to resolve — **ajustarse** *vr* **:** to fit, to conform

ajuste *nm* **1 :** adjustment **2 :** tightening

ajusticiar *vt* EJECUTAR **:** to execute, to put to death

al (*contraction of* **a** *and* **el**) → **a**[2]

ala *nf* **1 :** wing **2 :** brim (of a hat)

Alá *nm* **:** Allah

alabanza *nf* ELOGIO **:** praise

alabar *vt* **:** to praise — **alabarse** *vr* **:** to boast

alabastro *nm* **:** alabaster

alabear *vt* **:** to warp — **alabearse** *vr*

alabeo *nm* **:** warp, warping

alacena *nf* **:** cupboard, larder

alacrán *nm, pl* **-cranes** ESCORPIÓN **:** scorpion

alado, -da *adj* **:** winged

alambique *nm* **:** still (to distill alcohol)

alambre *nm* **1 :** wire **2 alambre de púas :** barbed wire

alameda *nf* **1 :** poplar grove **2 :** tree-lined avenue

álamo *nm* **1 :** poplar **2 álamo temblón :** aspen

alar *nm* **:** eaves *pl*

alarde *nm* **1 :** show, display **2 hacer alarde de :** to make show of, to boast about

alardear *vi* PRESUMIR **:** to boast, to brag

alargado, -da *adj* **:** elongated, slender

alargamiento *nm* **:** lengthening, extension, elongation

alargar {52} *vt* **1 :** to extend, to lengthen **2** PROLONGAR **:** to prolong — **alargarse** *vr*

alarido *nm* **:** howl, shriek

alarma *nf* **:** alarm

alarmante *adj* **:** alarming — **alarmantemente** *adv*

alarmar *vt* **:** to alarm

alazán *nm, pl* **-zanes :** sorrel (color or animal)

alba *nf* AMANECER **:** dawn, daybreak

albacea *nmf* TESTAMENTARIO **:** executor, executrix *f*

albahaca *nf* **:** basil

albanés, -nesa *adj & n, mpl* **-neses :** Albanian

albañil *nmf* **:** bricklayer, mason

albañilería *nf* **:** bricklaying, masonry

albaricoque *nm* **:** apricot

albatros *nm* **:** albatross

albedrío *nm* **:** will <libre albedrío : free will>

alberca *nf* **1 :** reservoir, tank **2** *Mex* **:** swimming pool

albergar {52} *vt* ALOJAR **:** to house, to lodge, to shelter

albergue *nm* **1 :** shelter, refuge **2 :** hostel

albino, -na *adj & n* **:** albino — **albinismo** *nm*

albóndiga *nf* **:** meatball

albor *nm* **1 :** dawning, beginning **2** BLANCURA **:** whiteness

alborada *nf* **:** dawn

alborear *v impers* **:** to dawn

alborotado, -da *adj* **1 :** excited, agitated **2 :** rowdy, unruly

alborotador[1], -dora *adj* **1 :** noisy, boisterous **2 :** rowdy, unruly

alborotador[2], -dora *n* **:** agitator, troublemaker, rioter

alborotar *vt* **1 :** to excite, to agitate **2 :** to incite, to stir up — **alborotarse** *vr* **:** to riot

alboroto *nm* **1 :** disturbance, ruckus **2** MOTÍN **:** riot

alborozado, -da *adj* **:** jubilant

alborozar {21} *vt* **:** to gladden, to cheer

alborozo *nm* **:** joy, elation

álbum *nm* **:** album <álbum de recortes : scrapbook>

albúmina *nf* **:** albumin

albur *nm* **1 :** chance, risk **2** *Mex* **:** pun

alca *nf* **:** auk

alcachofa *nf* **:** artichoke

alcahuete, -ta *n* CHISMOSO **:** gossip

alcaide *nm* **:** warden (in a prison)

alcalde, -desa *n* **:** mayor

alcaldía *nf* **1 :** mayoralty **2** AYUNTAMIENTO **:** city hall

álcali *nm* **:** alkali

alcalino, -na *adj* **:** alkaline — **alcalinidad** *nf*

alcance *nm* **1 :** reach **2 :** range, scope

alcancía *nf* **1 :** piggy bank, money box **2 :** collection box (for alms, etc.)

alcanfor *nm* **:** camphor

alcantarilla *nf* CLOACA **:** sewer, drain

alcanzar {21} *vt* **1 :** to reach **2 :** to catch up with **3** LOGRAR **:** to achieve, to attain — *vi* **1** DAR **:** to suffice, to be enough **2 ~ a :** to manage to

alcaparra *nf* **:** caper

alcapurria *nf PRi* **:** stuffed fritter made with taro and green banana

alcaravea *nf* **:** caraway

alcatraz *nm, pl* **-traces :** gannet

alcázar *nm* **:** fortress, castle

alce[1], etc. → **alzar**

alce[2] *nm* **:** moose, European elk

alcoba *nf* **:** bedroom

alcohol *nm* **:** alcohol

alcohólico, -ca *adj & n* **:** alcoholic

alcoholismo *nm* **:** alcoholism

alcoholizarse {21} *vr* **:** to become an alcoholic

alcornoque *nm* **1 :** cork oak **2** *fam* **:** idiot, fool

alcurnia *nf* **:** ancestry, lineage

aldaba *nf* **:** door knocker

aldea *nf* **:** village

aldeano[1], -na *adj* **:** village, rustic

aldeano[2], -na *n* **:** villager

aleación *nf, pl* **-ciones :** alloy

alear *vt* **:** to alloy

aleatorio, -ria *adj* **:** random, fortuitous — **aleatoriamente** *adv*

alebrestar *vt* **:** to excite, to make nervous — **alebrestarse** *vr*

aledaño, -ña *adj* **:** bordering, neighboring

aledaños *nmpl* AFUERAS **:** outskirts, surrounding area

alegar {52} *vt* **:** to assert, to allege — *vi* DISCUTIR **:** to argue

alegato *nm* **1 :** allegation, claim **2** *Mex* **:** argument, summation (in law) **3 :** argument, dispute

alegoría *nf* **:** allegory

alegórico, -ca *adj* **:** allegorical

alegrar *vt* **:** to make happy, to cheer up — **alegrarse** *vr* **:** to be glad, to rejoice

alegre *adj* **1 :** glad, cheerful **2 :** colorful, bright **3** *fam* **:** tipsy

alegremente *adv* **:** happily, cheerfully

alegría *nf* **:** joy, cheer, happiness

alejado, -da *adj* **:** remote

alejamiento *nm* **1 :** removal, separation **2 :** estrangement

alejar *vt* **1 :** to remove, to move away **2 :** to estrange, to alienate — **alejarse** *vr* **1 :** to move away, to stray **2 :** to drift apart

alelado, -da *adj* **1 :** bewildered, stupefied **2 :** foolish, stupid

aleluya *interj* **:** hallelujah!, alleluia!

alemán[1], **-mana** *adj & n, mpl* **-manes** : German

alemán[2] *nm* : German (language)

alentador, -dora *adj* : encouraging

alentar {55} *vt* : to encourage, to inspire — *vi* : to breathe

alerce *nm* : larch

alérgeno *nm* : allergen

alergia *nf* : allergy

alérgico, -ca *adj* : allergic

alergista *nmf* : allergist

alero *nm* **1** : eaves *pl* **2** : forward (in basketball)

alerón *nm, pl* **-rones** : aileron

alerta[1] *adv* : on the alert

alerta[2] *nf* : alert, alarm

alertar *vt* : to alert

alerto, -ta *adj* : alert, watchful

aleta *nf* **1** : fin **2** : flipper **3** : small wing

aletargado, -da *adj* : lethargic, sluggish, torpid

aletargarse {52} *vr* : to feel drowsy, to become lethargic

aleteo *nm* : flapping, flutter

alevosía *nf* **1** : treachery **2** : premeditation

alevoso, -sa *adj* : treacherous

alfabético, -ca *adj* : alphabetical — **alfabéticamente** *adv*

alfabetismo *nm* : literacy

alfabetizado, -da *adj* : literate

alfabetizar {21} *vt* : to alphabetize

alfabeto *nm* : alphabet

alfalfa *nf* : alfalfa

alfanje *nm* : cutlass, scimitar

alfarería *nf* : pottery

alfarero, -ra *n* : potter

alféizar *nm* : sill, windowsill

alfeñique *nm fam* : wimp, weakling

alférez *nmf, pl* **-reces 1** : second lieutenant **2** : ensign

alfiler *nm* **1** : pin **2** BROCHE : brooch

alfiletero *nm* : pincushion

alfombra *nf* : carpet, rug

alfombrado *nm* : carpeting

alfombrar *vt* : to carpet

alfombrilla *nf* : small rug, mat

alforfón *nm, pl* **-fones** : buckwheat

alforja *nf* : saddlebag

alforza *nf* : pleat, tuck

alga *nf* **1** : aquatic plant, alga **2** : seaweed

algáceo, -cea *adj* : algal

algarabía *nf* **1** : gibberish, babble **2** : hubbub, uproar

álgebra *nf* : algebra

algebraico, -ca *adj* : algebraic

álgido, -da *adj* **1** : critical, decisive **2** : icy cold

algo[1] *adv* : somewhat, rather <es simpático, pero algo tacaño : he's nice but rather stingy>

algo[2] *pron* **1** : something **2 ~ de** : some, a little <tengo algo de dinero : I've got some money>

algodón *nm, pl* **-dones** : cotton

algoritmo *nm* : algorithm

alguacil *nm* : constable

alguien *pron* : somebody, someone

alguno[1], **-na** *adj* (**algún** *before masculine singular nouns*) **1** : some, any <algún día : someday, one day> **2** (*in negative constructions*) : not any, not at all <no tengo noticia alguna : I have no news at all> **3 algunas veces** : sometimes

alguno[2], **-na** *pron* **1** : one, someone, somebody <alguno de ellos : one of them> **2 algunos, -nas** *pron pl* : some, a few <algunos quieren trabajar : some want to work>

alhaja *nf* : jewel, gem

alhajar *vt* : to adorn with jewels

alharaca *nf* : fuss

alhelí *nm* : wallflower

aliado[1], **-da** *adj* : allied

aliado[2], **-da** *n* : ally

alianza *nf* : alliance

aliarse {85} *vr* : to form an alliance, to ally oneself

alias *adv & nm* : alias

alicaído, -da *adj* : depressed, discouraged

alicates *nmpl* PINZAS : pliers

aliciente *nm* **1** INCENTIVO : incentive **2** ATRACCIÓN : attraction

alienación *nf, pl* **-ciones** : alienation, derangement

alienar *vt* ENAJENAR : to alienate

aliento *nm* **1** : breath **2** : courage, strength **3 dar aliento a** : to encourage

aligerar *vt* **1** : to lighten **2** ACELERAR : to hasten, to quicken

alijo *nm* : cache, consignment (of contraband)

alimaña *nf* : pest, vermin

alimentación *nf, pl* **-ciones** NUTRICIÓN : nutrition, nourishment

alimentar *vt* **1** NUTRIR : to feed, to nourish **2** MANTENER : to support (a family) **3** FOMENTAR : to nurture, to foster — **alimentarse** *vr* **~ con** : to live on

alimentario, -ria → **alimenticio**

alimenticio, -cia *adj* **1** : nutritional, food, dietary **2** : nutritious, nourishing

alimento *nm* : food, nourishment

alineación *nf, pl* **-ciones 1** : alignment **2** : lineup (in sports)

alineamiento *nm* : alignment

alinear *vt* **1** : to align **2** : to line up — **alinearse** *vr* **1** : to fall in, to line up **2 ~ con** : to align oneself with

aliño *nm* : seasoning, dressing

alipús *nm, pl* **-puses** *Mex fam* : booze, drink

alisar *vt* : to smooth

aliso *nm* : alder

alistamiento *nm* : enlistment, recruitment

alistar *vt* **1** : to recruit **2** : to make ready — **alistarse** *vr* : to join up, to enlist

aliteración *nf, pl* **-ciones** : alliteration

aliterado, -da *adj* : alliterative

aliviar *vt* MITIGAR : to relieve, to alleviate, to soothe — **aliviarse** *vr* : to recover, to get better

alivio *nm* : relief

aljaba *nf* : quiver (for arrows)

aljibe *nm* : cistern, well

allá *adv* **1** : there, over there **2 más allá** : farther away **3 más allá de** : beyond **4 allá tú** : that's up to you

allanamiento *nm* **1** : (police) raid **2 allanamiento de morada** : breaking and entering

allanar *vt* **1** : to raid, to search **2** : to resolve, to solve **3** : to smooth, to level out

allegado[1], **-da** *adj* : close, intimate

allegado[2], **-da** *n* : close friend, relation <parientes y allegados : friends and relations>

allegar {52} *vt* : to gather, to collect

allende[1] *adv* : beyond, on the other side

allende[2] *prep* : beyond <allende las montañas : beyond the mountains>

allí *adv* : there, over there <allí mismo : right there> <hasta allí : up to that point>

alma *nf* **1** : soul **2** : person, human being **3 no tener alma** : to be pitiless **4 tener el alma en un hilo** : to have one's heart in one's mouth

almacén *nm, pl* **-cenes 1** BODEGA : warehouse, storehouse **2** TIENDA : shop, store **3 gran almacén** *Spain* : department store

almacenaje → **almacenamiento**

almacenamiento *nm* : storage <almacenamiento de datos : data storage>

almacenar *vt* : to store, to put in storage

almacenero, -ra *n* : shopkeeper

almacenista *nm* MAYORISTA : wholesaler

almádena *nf* : sledgehammer

almanaque *nm* : almanac

almeja *nf* : clam

almendra *nf* **1** : almond **2** : kernel

almendro *nm* : almond tree

almiar *nm* : haystack

almíbar *nm* : syrup

almidón *nm, pl* **-dones** : starch

almidonar *vt* : to starch

alminar *nm* MINARETE : minaret

almirante *nm* : admiral

almizcle *nm* : musk

almohada *nf* : pillow

almohadilla *nf* **1** : small pillow, cushion **2** : bag, base (in baseball)

almohadón *nm, pl* **-dones** : bolster, cushion

almohazar {21} *vt* : to curry (a horse)

almoneda *nf* SUBASTA : auction

almorranas *nfpl* HEMORROIDES : hemorrhoids, piles

almorzar {36} *vi* : to have lunch — *vt* : to have for lunch

almuerzo *nm* : lunch

alocado, -da *adj* **1** : crazy **2** : wild, reckless **3** : silly, scatterbrained

alocución *nf, pl* **-ciones** : speech, address

áloe *or* **aloe** *nm* : aloe

alojamiento *nm* : lodging, accommodations *pl*

alojar *vt* ALBERGAR : to house, to lodge — **alojarse** *vr* : to lodge, to room

alondra *nf* : lark, skylark

alpaca *nf* : alpaca

alpinismo *nm* : mountain climbing, mountaineering

alpinista *nmf* : mountain climber

alpino, -na *adj* : Alpine, alpine

alpiste *nm* : birdseed

alquilar *vt* ARRENDAR : to rent, to lease

alquiler *nm* ARRENDAMIENTO : rent, rental

alquimia *nf* : alchemy

alquimista *nmf* : alchemist

alquitrán *nm, pl* **-tranes** BREA : tar

alquitranar *vt* : to tar, to cover with tar

alrededor[1] *adv* **1** : around, about <todo temblaba alrededor : all around things were shaking> **2 ~ de** : around, approximately <alrededor de quince personas : around fifteen people>

alrededor[2] *prep* **~ de** : around, about <corrió alrededor de la casa : she ran around the house> <llegaré alrededor de diciembre : I will get there around December>

alrededores *nmpl* ALEDAÑOS : surroundings, outskirts

alta *nf* **1** : admission, entry, enrollment **2 dar de alta** : to release, to discharge (a patient)

altanería *nf* ALTIVEZ, ARROGANCIA : arrogance, haughtiness

altanero, -ra *adj* ALTIVO, ARROGANTE : arrogant, haughty — **altaneramente** *adv*

altar *nm* : altar

altavoz *nm, pl* **-voces** ALTOPARLANTE : loudspeaker

alteración *nf, pl* **-ciones 1** MODIFICACIÓN : alteration, modification **2** PERTURBACIÓN : disturbance, disruption

alterado, -da *adj* : upset

alterar *vt* **1** MODIFICAR : to alter, to modify **2** PERTURBAR : to disturb, to disrupt — **alterarse** *vr* : to get upset, to get worked up

altercado *nm* DISCUSIÓN, DISPUTA : altercation, argument, dispute

alternador *nm* : alternator

alternancia *nf* : alternation, rotation

alternar *vi* **1** : to alternate **2** : to mix, to socialize — *vt* : to alternate — **alternarse** *vr* : to take turns

alternativa *nf* OPCIÓN : alternative, option

alternativo, -va *adj* **1** : alternating **2** : alternative — **alternativamente** *adv*

alterno, -na *adj* : alternate <corriente alterna : alternating current>

alteza *nf* **1** : loftiness, lofty height **2 Alteza** : Highness

altibajos *nmpl* **1 :** unevenness (of terrain) **2 :** ups and downs
altímetro *nm* **:** altimeter
altiplano *nm* **:** high plateau
altisonante *adj* **1 :** pompous, affected (of language) **2** *Mex* **:** rude, obscene (of language)
altitud *nf* **:** altitude
altivez *nf, pl* **-veces** ALTANERÍA, ARROGANCIA **:** arrogance, haughtiness
altivo, -va *adj* ALTANERO, ARROGANTE **:** arrogant, haughty
alto[1] *adv* **1 :** high **2 :** loud, loudly
alto[2]**, -ta** *adj* **1 :** tall, high **2 :** loud <en voz alta : aloud, out loud>
alto[3] *nm* **1** ALTURA **:** height, elevation **2 :** stop, halt **3 altos** *nmpl* **:** upper floors
alto[4] *interj* **:** halt!, stop!
altoparlante *nm* ALTAVOZ **:** loudspeaker
altozano *nm* **:** hillock
altruismo *nm* **:** altruism
altruista[1] *adj* **:** altruistic
altruista[2] *nmf* **:** altruist
altura *nf* **1 :** height **2 :** altitude **3 :** loftiness, nobleness **4 a la altura de :** near, up by <en la avenida San Antonio a la altura de la Calle Tres : on San Antonio Avenue up near Third Street> **5 a estas alturas :** at this point, at this stage of the game
alubia *nf* **:** kidney bean
alucinación *nf, pl* **-ciones :** hallucination
alucinante *adj* **:** hallucinatory
alucinar *vi* **:** to hallucinate
alucinógeno[1]**, -na** *adj* **:** hallucinogenic
alucinógeno[2] *nm* **:** hallucinogen
alud *nm* AVALANCHA **:** avalanche, landslide
aludido, -da *n* **1 :** person in question <el aludido : the aforesaid> **2 darse por aludido :** to take personally
aludir *vi* **:** to allude, to refer
alumbrado *nm* ILUMINACIÓN **:** lighting
alumbramiento *nm* **1 :** lighting **2 :** childbirth
alumbrar *vt* **1** ILUMINAR **:** to light, to illuminate **2 :** to give birth to
alumbre *nm* **:** alum
aluminio *nm* **:** aluminum
alumnado *nm* **:** student body
alumno, -na *n* **1 :** pupil, student **2 ex–alumno, -na :** alumnus, alumna *f* **3 ex–alumnos, -nas** *npl* **:** alumni, alumnae *f*
alusión *nf, pl* **-siones :** allusion, reference
alusivo, -va *adj* **1 :** allusive **2 ~ a :** in reference to, regarding
aluvión *nm, pl* **-viones :** flood, barrage
alza *nf* SUBIDA **:** rise <precios en alza : rising prices>
alzamiento *nm* LEVANTAMIENTO **:** uprising, insurrection
alzar {21} *vt* **1** ELEVAR, LEVANTAR **:** to lift, to raise **2 :** to erect — **alzarse** *vr* LEVANTARSE **:** to rise up
ama *nf* → **amo**
amabilidad *nf* **:** kindness
amable *adj* **:** kind, nice — **amablemente** *adv*
amado[1]**, -da** *adj* **:** beloved, darling
amado[2]**, -da** *n* **:** sweetheart, loved one
amaestrar *vt* **:** to train (animals)
amafiarse *vr Mex fam* **:** to conspire, to be in cahoots
amagar {52} *vt* **1 :** to show signs of (an illness, etc.) **2 :** to threaten — *vi* **1 :** to be imminent, to threaten **2 :** to feint, to dissemble
amago *nm* **1** AMENAZA **:** threat **2 :** sign, hint
amainar *vi* **:** to abate, to ease up, to die down
amalgama *nf* **:** amalgam
amalgamar *vt* **:** to amalgamate, to unite
amamantar *v* **:** to breast-feed, to nurse, to suckle
amanecer[1] {53} *v impers* **1 :** to dawn **2 :** to begin to show, to appear **3 :** to wake up (in the morning)
amanecer[2] *nm* ALBA **:** dawn, daybreak
amanerado, -da *adj* **:** affected, mannered
amansar *vt* **1 :** to tame **2 :** to soothe, to calm down — **amansarse** *vr*
amante[1] *adj* **:** loving, fond
amante[2] *nmf* **:** lover
amañar *vt* **:** to rig, to fix, to tamper with — **amañarse** *vr* **amañárselas :** to manage
amaño *nm* **1 :** skill, dexterity **2 :** trick, ruse
amapola *nf* **:** poppy
amar *vt* **:** to love — **amarse** *vr*
amargado, -da *adj* **:** embittered, bitter
amargar {52} *vt* **:** to make bitter, to embitter — *vi* **:** to taste bitter
amargo[1]**, -ga** *adj* **:** bitter — **amargamente** *adv*
amargo[2] *nm* **:** bitterness, tartness
amargura *nf* **1 :** bitterness **2 :** grief, sorrow
amarilis *nf* **:** amaryllis
amarillear *vi* **:** to yellow, to turn yellow
amarillento, -ta *adj* **:** yellowish
amarillismo *nm* **:** yellow journalism, sensationalism
amarillo[1]**, -lla** *adj* **:** yellow
amarillo[2] *nm* **:** yellow
amarra *nf* **1 :** mooring, mooring line **2 soltar las amarras de :** to loosen one's grip on
amarrar *vt* **1 :** to moor (a boat) **2** ATAR **:** to fasten, to tie up, to tie down
amartillar *vt* **:** to cock (a gun)
amasar *vt* **1 :** to amass **2 :** to knead **3 :** to mix, to prepare
amasijo *nm* **:** jumble, hodgepodge
amasio, -sia *n* **:** lover, paramour
amateur *adj & nmf* **:** amateur — **amateurismo** *nm*
amatista *nf* **:** amethyst
amatorio, -ria *adj* **:** amatory, love

amazona *nf* **1 :** Amazon (in mythology) **2 :** horsewoman

amazónico, -ca *adj* **:** amazonian

ambages *mpl* **sin ~ :** without hesitation, straight to the point

ámbar *nm* **1 :** amber **2 ámbar gris :** ambergris

ambición *nf, pl* **-ciones :** ambition

ambicionar *vt* **:** to aspire to, to seek

ambicioso, -sa *adj* **:** ambitious — **ambiciosamente** *adv*

ambidextro, -tra *adj* **:** ambidextrous

ambientación *nf, pl* **-ciones :** setting, atmosphere

ambiental *adj* **:** environmental — **ambientalmente** *adv*

ambientalista *nmf* **:** environmentalist

ambientar *vt* **:** to give atmosphere to, to set (in literature and drama) — **ambientarse** *vr* **:** to adjust, to get one's bearings

ambiente *nm* **1 :** atmosphere **2 :** environment **3 :** surroundings *pl*

ambigüedad *nf* **:** ambiguity

ambiguo, -gua *adj* **:** ambiguous

ámbito *nm* **:** domain, field, area

ambivalencia *nf* **:** ambivalence

ambivalente *adj* **:** ambivalent

ambos, -bas *adj & pron* **:** both

ambulancia *nf* **:** ambulance

ambulante *adj* **1 :** traveling, itinerant **2 vendedor ambulante :** street vendor

ameba *nf* **:** amoeba

amedrentar *vt* **:** to frighten, to intimidate — **amedrentarse** *vr*

amén *nm* **1 :** amen **2 ~ de :** in addition to, besides **3 en un decir amén :** in an instant

amenaza *nf* **:** threat, menace

amenazador, -dora *adj* **:** threatening, menacing

amenazante → **amenazador**

amenazar {21} *v* **:** to threaten

amenguar {10} *vt* **1 :** to diminish **2 :** to belittle, to dishonor

amenidad *nf* **:** pleasantness, amenity

amenizar {21} *vt* **1 :** to make pleasant **2 :** to brighten up, to add life to

ameno, -na *adj* **:** agreeable, pleasant

amento *nm* **:** catkin

americano, -na *adj & n* **:** American

amerindio, -dia *adj & n* **:** Amerindian

ameritar *vt* MERECER **:** to deserve

ametralladora *nf* **:** machine gun

amianto *nm* **:** asbestos

amiba *nf* → **ameba**

amigable *adj* **:** friendly, amicable — **amigablemente** *adv*

amígdala *nf* **:** tonsil

amigdalitis *nf* **:** tonsilitis

amigo[1]**, -ga** *adj* **:** friendly, close

amigo[2]**, -ga** *n* **:** friend

amigote *nm* **:** crony, pal

amilanar *vt* **1 :** to frighten **2 :** to daunt, to discourage — **amilanarse** *vr* **:** to lose heart

aminoácido *nm* **:** amino acid

aminorar *vt* **:** to reduce, to lessen — *vi* **:** to diminish

amistad *nf* **:** friendship

amistoso, -sa *adj* **:** friendly — **amistosamente** *adv*

amnesia *nf* **:** amnesia

amnésico, -ca *adj & n* **:** amnesiac, amnesic

amnistía *nf* **:** amnesty

amnistiar {85} *vt* **:** to grant amnesty to

amo, ama *n* **1 :** master *m*, mistress *f* **2 :** owner, keeper (of an animal) **3 ama de casa :** housewife **4 ama de llaves :** housekeeper

amodorrado, -da *adj* **:** drowsy

amolar {19} *vt* **1 :** to grind, to sharpen **2 :** to pester, to annoy

amoldable *adj* **:** adaptable

amoldar *vt* **1 :** to mold **2 :** to adapt, to adjust — **amoldarse** *vr*

amonestación *nf, pl* **-ciones 1** APERCIBIMIENTO **:** admonition, warning **2** AMONESTACIONES *nfpl* **:** banns

amonestar *vt* APERCIBIR **:** to admonish, to warn

amoníaco *or* **amoniaco** *nm* **:** ammonia

amontonamiento *nm* **:** accumulation, piling up

amontonar *vt* **1** APILAR **:** to pile up, to heap up **2 :** to collect, to gather **3 :** to hoard — **amontonarse** *vr*

amor *nm* **1 :** love **2 :** loved one, beloved **3 amor propio :** self-esteem **4 hacer el amor :** to make love

amoral *adj* **:** amoral

amoratado, -da *adj* **:** black-and-blue, bruised, livid

amordazar {21} *vt* **1 :** to gag, to muzzle **2 :** to silence

amorfo, -fa *adj* **:** shapeless, amorphous

amorío *nm* **:** love affair, fling

amoroso, -sa *adj* **1 :** loving, affectionate **2 :** amorous <una mirada amorosa : an amorous glance> **3 :** charming, cute — **amorosamente** *adv*

amortiguación *nf* **:** cushioning, absorption

amortiguador *nm* **:** shock absorber

amortiguar {10} *vt* **:** to soften (an impact)

amortizar {21} *vt* **:** to amortize, to pay off — **amortización** *nf*

amotinado[1]**, -da** *adj* **:** rebellious, insurgent, mutinous

amotinado[2]**, -da** *n* **:** rebel, insurgent, mutineer

amotinamiento *nm* **:** uprising, rebellion

amotinar *vt* **:** to incite (to riot), to agitate — **amotinarse** *vr* **1 :** to riot, to rebel **2 :** to mutiny

amparar *vt* **:** to safeguard, to protect — **ampararse** *vr* **1 ~ de :** to take shelter from **2 ~ en :** to have recourse to

amparo *nm* ACOGIDA, REFUGIO **:** protection, refuge

amperímetro *nm* **:** ammeter

amperio *nm* : ampere
ampliable *adj* : expandable, enlargeable, extendible
ampliación *nf, pl* **-ciones** : expansion, extension
ampliar {85} *vt* **1** : to expand, to extend **2** : to widen **3** : to enlarge (photographs) **4** : to elaborate on, to develop (ideas)
amplificador *nm* : amplifier
amplificar {72} *vt* : to amplify — **amplificación** *nf*
amplio, -plia *adj* : broad, wide, ample — **ampliamente** *adj*
amplitud *nf* **1** : breadth, extent **2** : spaciousness
ampolla *nf* **1** : blister **2** : vial, ampoule
ampollar *vt* : to blister — **ampollarse** *vr*
ampolleta *nf* **1** : small vial **2** : hourglass **3** *Chile* : light bulb
ampulosidad *nf* : pompousness, bombast
ampuloso, -sa *adj* GRANDILOCUENTE : pompous, bombastic — **ampulosamente** *adv*
amputar *vt* : to amputate — **amputación** *nf*
amueblar *vt* : to furnish
amuleto *nm* TALISMÁN : amulet, charm
amurallar *vt* : to wall in, to fortify
anacardo *nm* : cashew nut
anaconda *nf* : anaconda
anacrónico, -ca *adj* : anachronistic
anacronismo *nm* : anachronism
ánade *nmf* **1** : duck **2 ánade real** : mallard
anagrama *nm* : anagram
anal *adj* : anal
anales *nmpl* : annals
analfabetismo *nm* : illiteracy
analfabeto, -ta *adj & n* : illiterate
analgésico[1], -ca *adj* : analgesic, painkilling
analgésico[2] *nm* : painkiller, analgesic
análisis *nm* : analysis
analista *nmf* **1** : analyst **2** : annalist
analítico, -ca *adj* : analytical, analytic — **analíticamente** *adv*
analizar {21} *vt* : to analyze
analogía *nf* : analogy
analógico, -ca *adj* **1** : analogical **2** : analog <computadora analógica : analog computer>
análogo, -ga *adj* : analogous, similar
ananá *or* **ananás** *nm, pl* **-nás** : pineapple
anaquel *nm* REPISA : shelf
anaranjado[1], -da *adj* NARANJA : orange-colored
anaranjado[2] *nm* NARANJA : orange (color)
anarquía *nf* : anarchy
anárquico, -ca *adj* : anarchic
anarquismo *nm* : anarchism
anarquista *adj & nmf* : anarchist
anatema *nm* : anathema
anatomía *nf* : anatomy — **anatomista** *nmf*
anatómico, -ca *adj* : anatomical — **anatómicamente** *adv*
anca *nm* **1** : haunch, hindquarter **2 ancas de rana** : frogs' legs
ancestral *adj* **1** : ancient, traditional **2** : ancestral
ancestro *nm* ASCENDIENTE : ancestor, forefather *m*
ancho[1], -cha *adj* **1** : wide, broad **2** : ample, loose-fitting
ancho[2] *nm* : width, breadth
anchoa *nf* : anchovy
anchura *nf* : width, breadth
ancianidad *nf* SENECTUD : old age
anciano[1], -na *adj* : aged, old, elderly
anciano[2], -na *n* : elderly person
ancla *nf* : anchor
ancladero *nm* → **anclaje**
anclaje *nm* : anchorage
anclar *v* FONDEAR : to anchor
andadas *nfpl* **1** : tracks **2 volver a las andadas** : to go back to one's old ways, to backslide
andador[1] *nm* **1** : walker, baby walker **2** *Mex* : walkway
andador[2], -dora *n* : walker, one who walks
andadura *nf* : course, journey <su agotadora andadura al campeonato : his exhausting journey to the championship>
andaluz, -luza *adj & n, mpl* **-luces** : Andalusian
andamiaje *nm* **1** : scaffolding **2** ESTRUCTURA : structure, framework
andamio *nm* : scaffold
andanada *nf* **1** : volley, broadside **2 soltar una andanada a** : to reprimand
andanzas *nfpl* : adventures
andar[1] {6} *vi* **1** CAMINAR : to walk **2** IR : to go, to travel **3** FUNCIONAR : to run, to function <el auto anda bien : the car runs well> **4** : to ride <andar a caballo : to ride on horseback> **5** : to be <anda sin dinero : he's broke> — *vt* : to walk, to travel
andar[2] *nm* : walk, gait
andas *nfpl* : stand (for a coffin), bier
andén *nm, pl* **andenes 1** : (train) platform **2** *CA, Col* : sidewalk
andino, -na *adj* : Andean
andorrano, -na *adj & n* : Andorran
andrajos *nmpl* : rags, tatters
andrajoso, -sa *adj* : ragged, tattered
andrógino, -na *adj* : androgynous
andurriales *nmpl* : remote place
anea *nf* : cattail
anduvo, etc. → **andar**
anécdota *nf* : anecdote
anecdótico, -ca *adj* : anecdotal
anegar {52} *vt* **1** INUNDAR : to flood **2** AHOGAR : to drown **3** : to overwhelm — **anegarse** *vr* : to be flooded
anejo *nm* → **anexo[2]**
anemia *nf* : anemia
anémico, -ca *adj* : anemic
anémona *nf* : anemone
anestesia *nf* : anesthesia

anestesiar *vt* : to anesthetize
anestésico[1], **-ca** *adj* : anesthetic
anestésico[2] *nm* : anesthetic
anestesista *nmf* : anesthetist
aneurisma *nmf* : aneurism
anexar *vt* : to annex, to attach
anexión *nf, pl* **-xiones** : annexation
anexo[1], **-xa** *adj* : attached, joined, annexed
anexo[2] *nm* **1** : annex **2** : supplement (to a book), appendix
anfetamina *nf* : amphetamine
anfibio[1], **-bia** *adj* : amphibious
anfibio[2] *nm* : amphibian
anfiteatro *nm* **1** : amphitheater **2** : lecture hall
anfitrión, -triona *n, mpl* **-triones** : host, hostess *f*
ánfora *nf* **1** : amphora **2** *Mex, Peru* : ballot box
ángel *nm* : angel
angelical *adj* : angelic, angelical
angina *nf* **1** *or* **angina de pecho** : angina **2** *Mex* : tonsil
anglicano, -na *adj & n* : Anglican
angloparlante[1] *adj* : English-speaking
angloparlante[2] *nmf* : English speaker
anglosajón, -jona *adj & n, mpl* **-jones** : Anglo-Saxon
angoleño, -ña *adj & n* : Angolan
angora *nf* : angora
angostar *vt* : to narrow — **angostarse** *vr*
angosto, -ta *adj* : narrow
angostura *nf* : narrowness
anguila *nf* : eel
angular *adj* : angular — **angularidad** *nf*
ángulo *nm* **1** : angle **2** : corner **3 ángulo muerto** : blind spot
anguloso, -sa *adj* : angular, sharp <una cara angulosa : an angular face> — **angulosidad** *nf*
angustia *nf* **1** CONGOJA : anguish, distress **2** : anxiety, worry
angustiar *vt* **1** : to anguish, to distress **2** : to worry — **angustiarse** *vr*
angustioso, -sa *adj* **1** : anguished, distressed **2** : distressing, worrisome
anhelante *adj* : yearning, longing
anhelar *vt* : to yearn for, to crave
anhelo *nm* : longing, yearning
anidar *vi* **1** : to nest **2** : to make one's home, to dwell — *vt* : to shelter
anillo *nm* SORTIJA : ring
ánima *n* ALMA : soul
animación *nf, pl* **-ciones 1** : animation **2** VIVEZA : liveliness
animado, -da *adj* **1** : animated, lively **2** : cheerful — **animadamente** *adv*
animador, -dora *n* **1** : (television) host **2** : cheerleader
animadversión *nf, pl* **-siones** ANIMOSIDAD : animosity, antagonism
animal[1] *adj* **1** : animal **2** ESTÚPIDO : stupid, idiotic **3** : rough, brutish
animal[2] *nm* : animal
animal[3] *nmf* **1** IDIOTA : idiot, fool **2** : brute, beastly person
animar *vt* **1** ALENTAR : to encourage, to inspire **2** : to animate, to enliven **3** : to brighten up, to cheer up — **animarse** *vr*
anímico, -ca *adj* : mental <estado anímico : state of mind>
ánimo *nm* **1** ALMA : spirit, soul **2** : mood, spirits *pl* **3** : encouragement **4** PROPÓSITO : intention, purpose <sociedad sin ánimo de lucro : nonprofit organization> **5** : energy, vitality
animosidad *nf* ANIMADVERSIÓN : animosity, ill will
animoso, -sa *adj* : brave, spirited
aniñado, -da *adj* : childlike
aniquilación *nf* → **aniquilamiento**
aniquilamiento *nm* : annihilation, extermination
aniquilar *vt* **1** : to annihilate, to wipe out **2** : to overwhelm, to bring to one's knees — **aniquilarse** *vr*
anís *nm* **1** : anise **2 semilla de anís** : aniseed
aniversario *nm* : anniversary
ano *nm* : anus
anoche *adv* : last night
anochecer[1] {53} *v impers* : to get dark
anochecer[2] *nm* : dusk, nightfall
anodino, -na *adj* : insipid, dull
ánodo *nm* : anode
anomalía *nf* : anomaly
anómalo, -la *adj* : anomalous
anonadado, -da *adj* : dumbfounded, speechless
anonadar *vt* : to dumbfound, to stun
anonimato *nm* : anonymity
anónimo, -ma *adj* : anonymous — **anónimamente** *adv*
anorexia *nf* : anorexia
anoréxico, -ca *adj* : anorexic
anormal *adj* : abnormal — **anormalmente** *adv*
anormalidad *nf* : abnormality
anotación *nf, pl* **-ciones 1** : annotation, note **2** : scoring (in sports) <lograron una anotación : they managed to score a goal>
anotar *vt* **1** : to annotate **2** APUNTAR, ESCRIBIR : to write down, to jot down **3** : to score (in sports) — *vi* : to score
anquilosado, -da *adj* **1** : stiff-jointed **2** : stagnated, stale
anquilosamiento *nm* **1** : stiffness (of joints) **2** : stagnation, paralysis
anquilosarse *vr* **1** : to stagnate **2** : to become stiff or paralyzed
anquilostoma *nm* : hookworm
ánsar *nm* : goose
ansarino *nm* : gosling
ansia *nf* **1** INQUIETUD : apprehensiveness, uneasiness **2** ANGUSTIA : anguish, distress **3** ANHELO : longing, yearning
ansiar {85} *vt* : to long for, to yearn for
ansiedad *nf* : anxiety
ansioso, -sa *adj* **1** : anxious, worried **2** : eager — **ansiosamente** *adv*
antagónico, -ca *adj* : conflicting, opposing
antagonismo *nm* : antagonism

antagonista[1] *adj* : antagonistic
antagonista[2] *nmf* : antagonist, opponent
antaño *adv* : yesteryear, long ago
antártico, -ca *adj* **1** : antarctic **2 círculo antártico** : antarctic circle
ante[1] *nm* **1** : elk, moose **2** : suede
ante[2] *prep* **1** : before, in front of **2** : considering, in view of **3 ante todo** : first and foremost, above all
anteanoche *adv* : the night before last
anteayer *adv* : the day before yesterday
antebrazo *nm* : forearm
antecedente[1] *adj* : previous, prior
antecedente[2] *nm* **1** : precedent **2 antecedentes** *nmpl* : record, background
anteceder *v* : to precede
antecesor, -sora *n* **1** ANTEPASADO : ancestor **2** PREDECESOR : predecessor
antedicho, -cha *adj* : aforesaid, above
antelación *nf, pl* **-ciones 1** : advance notice **2 con ∼** : in advance, beforehand
antemano *adv* **de ∼** : in advance <se lo agradezco de antemano : I thank you in advance>
antena *nf* : antenna
antenoche → **anteanoche**
anteojera *nf* **1** : eyeglass case **2 anteojeras** *nfpl* : blinders
anteojos *nmpl* GAFAS : glasses, eyeglasses
antepasado[1], **-da** *adj* : before last <el domingo antepasado : the Sunday before last>
antepasado[2], **-da** *n* ANTECESOR : ancestor
antepecho *nm* **1** : guardrail **2** : ledge, sill
antepenúltimo, -ma *adj* : third from last
anteponer {60} *vt* **1** : to place before <anteponer al interés de la nación el interés de la comunidad : to place the interests of the community before national interest> **2** : to prefer
anteproyecto *nm* **1** : draft, proposal **2 anteproyecto de ley** : bill
antera *nf* : anther
anterior *adj* **1** : previous **2** : earlier <tiempos anteriores : earlier times> **3** : anterior, forward, front
anterioridad *nf* **1** : priority **2 con ∼** : beforehand, in advance
anteriormente *adv* : previously, beforehand
antes *adv* **1** : before, earlier **2** : formerly, previously **3** : rather, sooner <antes prefiero morir : I'd rather die> **4 ∼ de** : before, previous to <antes de hoy : before today> **5 antes que** : before <antes que llegue Luis : before Luis arrives> **6 cuanto antes** : as soon as possible **7 antes bien** : on the contrary
antesala *nf* **1** : anteroom, waiting room, lobby **2** : prelude, prologue
antiaborto, -ta *adj* : antiabortion
antiácido *nm* : antacid
antiadherente *adj* : nonstick
antiaéreo, -rea *adj* : antiaircraft
antiamericano, -na *adj* : anti-American
antibalas *adj* : bulletproof
antibiótico[1], **-ca** *adj* : antibiotic
antibiótico[2] *nm* : antibiotic
antichoque *adj* : shockproof
anticipación *nf, pl* **-ciones 1** : expectation, anticipation **2 con ∼** : in advance
anticipado, -da *adj* **1** : advance, early **2 por ∼** : in advance
anticipar *vt* **1** : to anticipate, to forestall, to deal with in advance **2** : to pay in advance — **anticiparse** *vr* **1** : to be early **2** ADELANTARSE : to get ahead
anticipo *nm* **1** : advance (payment) **2** : foretaste, preview
anticlerical *adj* : anticlerical
anticlimático, -ca : anticlimatic
anticlímax *nm* : anticlimax
anticomunismo *nm* : anticommunism
anticomunista *adj & nmf* : anticommunist
anticoncepción *nf, pl* **-ciones** : birth control, contraception
anticonceptivo *nm* : contraceptive
anticongelante *nm* : antifreeze
anticuado, -da *adj* : antiquated, outdated
anticuario[1], **-ria** *adj* : antique, antiquarian
anticuario[2], **-ria** *n* : antiquarian, antiquary
anticuario[3] *nm* : antique shop
anticuerpo *nm* : antibody
antidemocrático, -ca *adj* : antidemocratic
antideportivo, -va *adj* : unsportsmanlike
antidepresivo *nm* : antidepressant
antídoto *nm* : antidote
antidrogas *adj* : antidrug
antier → **anteayer**
antiestético, -ca *adj* : unsightly, unattractive
antifascista *adj & nmf* : antifascist
antifaz *nm, pl* **-faces** : mask
antifeminista *adj & nmf* : antifeminist
antífona *nf* : anthem
antígeno *nm* : antigen
antigualla *nf* **1** : antique **2** : relic, old thing
antiguamente *adv* **1** : formerly, once **2** : long ago
antigüedad *nf* **1** : antiquity **2** : seniority **3** : age <con siglos de antigüedad : centuries-old> **4 antigüedades** *nfpl* : antiques
antiguo, -gua *adj* **1** : ancient, old **2** : former **3** : old-fashioned <a la antigua : in the old-fashioned way>
antihigiénico, -ca *adj* INSALUBRE : unhygienic, unsanitary
antihistamínico *nm* : antihistamine
antiimperialismo *nm* : anti-imperialism

antiimperialista *adj & nmf* : anti-imperialist

antiinflacionario, -ria *adj* : anti-inflationary

antiinflamatorio, -ria *adj* : anti-inflammatory

antillano[1], -na *adj* CARIBEÑO : Caribbean, West Indian

antillano[2], -na *n* : West Indian

antílope *nm* : antelope

antimilitarismo *nm* : antimilitarism

antimilitarista *adj & nmf* : antimilitarist

antimonio *nm* : antimony

antimonopolista *adj* : antimonopoly, antitrust

antinatural *adj* : unnatural, perverse

antipatía *nf* : aversion, dislike

antipático, -ca *adj* : obnoxious, unpleasant

antipatriótico, -ca *adj* : unpatriotic

antirrábico, -ca *adj* : antirabies <vacuna antirrábica : rabies vaccine>

antirreglamentario, -ria *adj* **1** : unlawful, illegal **2** : foul (in sports)

antirrevolucionario, -ria *adj & n* : antirevolutionary

antirrobo, -ba *adj* : antitheft

antisemita *adj* : anti-Semitic

antisemitismo *nm* : anti-Semitism

antiséptico[1], -ca *adj* : antiseptic

antiséptico[2] *nm* : antiseptic

antisocial *adj* : antisocial

antitabaco *adj* : antismoking

antiterrorista *adj* : antiterrorist

antítesis *nf* : antithesis

antitoxina *nf* : antitoxin

antitranspirante *nm* : antiperspirant

antojadizo, -za *adj* CAPRICHOSO : capricious

antojarse *vr* **1** APETECER : to be appealing, to be desirable <se me antoja un helado : I feel like having ice cream> **2** : to seem, to appear <los árboles se antojaban fantasmas : the trees seemed like ghosts>

antojitos *nmpl Mex* : traditional Mexican snack foods

antojo *nm* **1** CAPRICHO : whim **2** : craving

antología *nf* **1** : anthology **2 de ~** *fam* : fantastic, incredible

antónimo *nm* : antonym

antonomasia *nf* **por ~** : par excellence

antorcha *nf* : torch

antracita *nf* : anthracite

antro *nm* **1** : cave, den **2** : dive, seedy nightclub

antropofagia *nf* CANIBALISMO : cannibalism

antropófago[1], -ga *adj* : cannibalistic

antropófago[2], -ga *n* CANÍBAL : cannibal

antropoide *adj & nmf* : anthropoid

antropología *nf* : anthropology

antropológico, -ca *adj* : anthropological

antropólogo, -ga *n* : anthropologist

anual *adj* : annual, yearly — **anualmente** *adv*

anualidad *nf* : annuity

anuario *nm* : yearbook, annual

anudar *vt* : to knot, to tie in a knot — **anudarse** *vr*

anuencia *nf* : consent

anulación *nf, pl* **-ciones** : annulment, nullification

anular *vt* : to annul, to cancel

anunciador, -dora *n* → **anunciante**

anunciante *nmf* : advertiser

anunciar *vt* **1** : to announce **2** : to advertise

anuncio *nm* **1** : announcement **2** : advertisement, commercial

anzuelo *nm* **1** : fishhook **2 morder el anzuelo** : to take the bait

añadido *nm* : addition

añadidura *nf* **1** : additive, addition **2 por ~** : in addition, furthermore

añadir *vt* **1** AGREGAR : to add **2** AUMENTAR : to increase

añejar *vt* : to age, to ripen

añejo, -ja *adj* **1** : aged, vintage **2** : age-old, musty, stale

añicos *nmpl* : smithereens, bits <hacer(se) añicos : to shatter>

añil *nm* **1** : indigo **2** : bluing

año *nm* **1** : year <en el año 1990 : in (the year) 1990> <tiene diez años : she is ten years old> **2** : grade <cuarto año : fourth grade> **3 año bisiesto** : leap year **4 año luz** : light-year **5 Año Nuevo** : New Year

añoranza *nf* : longing, yearning

añorar *vt* **1** DESEAR : to long for **2** : to grieve for, to miss — *vi* : to mourn, to grieve

añoso, -sa *adj* : aged, old

aorta *nf* : aorta

apabullante *adj* : overwhelming, crushing

apabullar *vt* : to overwhelm

apacentar {55} *vt* : to pasture, to put to pasture

apache *adj & nmf* : Apache

apachurrado, -da *adj fam* : depressed, down

apachurrar *vt* : to crush, to squash

apacible *adj* : gentle, mild, calm — **apaciblemente** *adv*

apaciguador, -dora *adj* : calming

apaciguamiento *nm* : appeasement

apaciguar {10} *vt* APLACAR : to appease, to pacify — **apaciguarse** *vr* : to calm down

apadrinar *vt* **1** : to be a godparent to **2** : to sponsor, to support

apagado, -da *adj* **1** : off, out <la luz está apagada : the light is off> **2** : dull, subdued

apagador *nm Mex* : switch

apagar {52} *vt* **1** : to turn off, to shut off **2** : to extinguish, to put out — **apagarse** *vr* **1** : to go out, to fade **2** : to wane, to die down

apagón *nm, pl* **-gones** : blackout (of power)

apalancamiento *nm* **:** leverage

apalancar {72} *vt* **1 :** to jack up **2 :** to pry open

apalear *vt* **:** to beat up, to thrash

apantallar *vt Mex* **:** to dazzle, to impress

apañar *vt* **1 :** to seize, to grasp **2 :** to repair, to mend — **apañarse** *vr* **:** to manage, to get along

apaño *nm fam* **1 :** patch **2** HABILIDAD **:** skill, knack

apapachar *vt Mex fam* **:** to cuddle, to caress — **apapacharse** *vr*

aparador *nm* **1 :** sideboard, cupboard **2** ESCAPARATE, VITRINA **:** shop window

aparato *nm* **1 :** machine, appliance, apparatus <aparato auditivo : hearing aid> <aparato de televisión : television set> **2 :** system <aparato digestivo : digestive system> **3 :** display, ostentation <sin aparato : without ceremony> **4 aparatos** *nmpl* **:** braces (for the teeth)

aparatoso, -sa *adj* **1 :** ostentatious **2 :** spectacular

aparcamiento *nm Spain* **1 :** parking **2 :** parking lot

aparcar {72} *v Spain* **:** to park

aparcero, -ra *n* **:** sharecropper

aparear *vt* **1 :** to mate (animals) **2 :** to match up — **aparearse** *vr* **:** to mate

aparecer {53} *vi* **1 :** to appear **2** PRESENTARSE **:** to show up **3 :** to turn up, to be found — **aparecerse** *vr* **:** to appear

aparejado, -da *adj* **1 ir aparejado con :** to go hand in hand with **2 llevar aparejado :** to entail

aparejar *vt* **1** PREPARAR **:** to prepare, to make ready **2 :** to harness (a horse) **3 :** to fit out (a ship)

aparejo *nm* **1 :** equipment, gear **2 :** harness, saddle **3 :** rig, rigging (of a ship)

aparentar *vt* **1 :** to seem, to appear <no aparentas tu edad : you don't look your age> **2** FINGIR **:** to feign, to pretend

aparente *adj* **1 :** apparent **2 :** showy, striking — **aparentemente** *adv*

aparición *nf, pl* **-ciones 1 :** appearance **2** PUBLICACIÓN **:** publication, release **3** FANTASMA **:** apparition, vision

apariencia *nf* **1** ASPECTO **:** appearance, look **2 en ~ :** seemingly, apparently

apartado *nm* **1 :** section, paragraph **2 apartado postal :** post office box

apartamento *nm* DEPARTAMENTO **:** apartment

apartar *vt* **1** ALEJAR **:** to move away, to put at a distance **2 :** to put aside, to set aside, to separate — **apartarse** *vr* **1 :** to step aside, to move away **2** DESVIARSE **:** to stray

aparte¹ *adv* **1 :** apart, aside <modestia aparte : if I say so myself> **2 :** separately **3 ~ de :** apart from, besides

aparte² *adj* **:** separate, special

aparte³ *nm* **:** aside (in theater)

apartheid *nm* **:** apartheid

apasionado, -da *adj* **:** passionate, enthusiastic — **apasionadamente** *adv*

apasionante *adj* **:** fascinating, exciting

apasionar *vt* **:** to enthuse, to excite — **apasionarse** *vr*

apatía *nf* **:** apathy

apático, -ca *adj* **:** apathetic

apearse *vr* **1** DESMONTAR **:** to dismount **2 :** to get out of or off (a vehicle)

apedrear *vt* **:** to stone, to throw stones at

apegado, -da *adj* **:** attached, close, devoted <es muy apegado a su familia : he is very devoted to his family>

apegarse {52} *vr* **~ a :** to become attached to, to grow fond of

apego *nm* AFICIÓN **:** attachment, fondness, inclination

apelación *nf, pl* **-ciones :** appeal (in court)

apelar *vi* **1 :** to appeal **2 ~ a :** to resort to

apelativo *nm* APELLIDO **:** last name, surname

apellidarse *vr* **:** to have for a last name <¿cómo se apellida? : what is your last name?>

apellido *nm* **:** last name, surname

apelotonar *vt* **:** to roll into a ball, to bundle up

apenar *vt* **:** to aggrieve, to sadden — **apenarse** *vr* **1 :** to be saddened **2 :** to become embarrassed

apenas¹ *adv* **:** hardly, scarcely

apenas² *conj* **:** as soon as

apéndice *nm* **1 :** appendix **2 :** appendage

apendicectomía *nf* **:** appendectomy

apendicitis *nf* **:** appendicitis

apercibimiento *nm* **1 :** preparation **2** AMONESTACIÓN **:** warning

apercibir *vt* **1** DISPONER **:** to prepare, to make ready **2** AMONESTAR **:** to warn **3** OBSERVAR **:** to observe, to perceive — **apercibirse** *vr* **1 :** to get ready **2 ~ de :** to notice

aperitivo *nm* **1 :** appetizer **2 :** aperitif

apero *nm* **:** tool, implement

apertura *nf* **1 :** opening, aperture **2 :** commencement, beginning **3 :** openness

apesadumbrar *vt* **:** to distress, to sadden — **apesadumbrarse** *vr* **:** to be weighed down

apestar *vt* **1 :** to infect with the plague **2 :** to corrupt — *vi* **:** to stink

apestoso, -sa *adj* **:** stinking, foul

apetecer {53} *vt* **1 :** to crave, to long for <apeteció la fama : he longed for fame> **2 :** to appeal to <me apetece un bistec : I feel like having a steak> <¿cuándo te apetece ir? : when do you want to go?> — *vi* **:** to be appealing

apetecible *adj* **:** appetizing, appealing

apetito *nm* **:** appetite

apetitoso, -sa *adj* **:** appetizing

apiario *nm* **:** apiary

ápice *nm* **1 :** apex, summit **2** PIZCA **:** bit, smidgen

apicultor, -tora *n* : beekeeper

apicultura *nf* : beekeeping

apilar *vt* AMONTONAR : to heap up, to pile up — **apilarse** *vr*

apiñado, -da *adj* : jammed, crowded

apiñar *vt* : to pack, to cram — **apiñarse** *vr* : to crowd together, to huddle

apio *nm* : celery

apisonadora *nf* : steamroller

apisonar *vt* : to pack down, to tamp

aplacamiento *nm* : appeasement

aplacar {72} *vt* APACIGUAR : to appease, to placate — **aplacarse** *vr* : to calm down

aplanadora *nf* : steamroller

aplanar *vt* : to flatten, to level

aplastante *adj* : crushing, overwhelming

aplastar *vt* : to crush, to squash

aplaudir *v* : to applaud

aplauso *nm* **1** : applause, clapping **2** : praise, acclaim

aplazamiento *nm* : postponement

aplazar {21} *vt* : to postpone, to defer

aplicable *adj* : applicable — **aplicabilidad** *nf*

aplicación *nf, pl* **-ciones** **1** : application **2** : diligence, dedication

aplicado, -da *adj* : diligent, industrious

aplicador *nm* : applicator

aplicar {72} *vt* : to apply — **aplicarse** *vr* : to apply oneself

aplique *or* **apliqué** *nm* : appliqué

aplomar *vt* : to plumb, to make vertical

aplomo *nm* : aplomb, composure

apocado, -da *adj* : timid

apocalipsis *nms & pl* : apocalypse <el Libro del Apocalipsis : the Book of Revelation>

apocalíptico, -ca *adj* : apocalyptic

apocamiento *nm* : timidity

apocarse {72} *vr* **1** : to shy away, to be intimidated **2** : to humble oneself, to sell oneself short

apócrifo, -fa *adj* : apocryphal

apodar *vt* : to nickname, to call — **apodarse** *vr*

apoderado, -da *n* : proxy, agent

apoderar *vt* : to authorize, to empower — **apoderarse** *vr* **~ de** : to seize, to take over

apodo *nm* SOBRENOMBRE : nickname

apogeo *nm* : acme, peak, zenith

apología *nf* : defense, apology

apoplejía *nf* : apoplexy, stroke

apoplético, -ca *adj* : apoplectic

aporrear *vt* : to bang on, to beat, to bludgeon

aportación *nf, pl* **-ciones** : contribution

aportar *vt* CONTRIBUIR : to contribute, to provide

aporte *nm* → **aportación**

apostador, -dora *n* : bettor, better

apostar {19} *v* : to bet, to wager <I bet he's not coming : apuesto que no viene>

apostasía *nf* : apostasy

apóstata *nmf* : apostate

apostilla *nf* : note

apostillar *vt* : to annotate

apóstol *nm* : apostle

apostólico, -ca *adj* : apostolic

apóstrofe *nmf* : apostrophe

apostura *nf* : elegance, gracefulness

apoyacabezas *nms & pl* : headrest

apoyapiés *nms & pl* : footrest

apoyar *vt* **1** : to support, to back **2** : to lean, to rest — **apoyarse** *vr* **1 ~ en** : to lean on **2 ~ en** : to be based on, to rest on

apoyo *nm* : support, backing

apreciable *adj* : appreciable, substantial, considerable

apreciación *nf, pl* **-ciones** **1** : appreciation **2** : appraisal, evaluation

apreciar *vt* **1** ESTIMAR : to appreciate, to value **2** EVALUAR : to appraise, to assess — **apreciarse** *vr* : to appreciate, to increase in value

aprecio *nm* **1** ESTIMO : esteem, appreciation **2** EVALUACIÓN : appraisal, assessment

aprehender *vt* **1** : to apprehend, to capture **2** : to conceive of, to grasp

aprehensión *nf, pl* **-siones** : apprehension, capture, arrest

apremiante *adj* : pressing, urgent

apremiar *vt* INSTAR : to pressure, to urge — *vi* URGIR : to be urgent <el tiempo apremia : time is of the essence>

apremio *nm* : pressure, urgency

aprender *v* : to learn — **aprenderse** *vr*

aprendiz, -diza *n, mpl* **-dices** : apprentice, trainee

aprendizaje *nm* : apprenticeship

aprensión *nf, pl* **-siones** : apprehension, dread

aprensivo, -va *adj* : apprehensive, worried

apresamiento *nm* : seizure, capture

apresar *vt* : to capture, to seize

aprestar *vt* : to make ready, to prepare — **aprestarse** *vr* : to get ready

apresuradamente *adv* **1** : hurriedly **2** : hastily, too fast

apresurado, -da *adj* : hurried, in a rush

apresuramiento *nm* : hurry, haste

apresurar *vt* : to quicken, to speed up — **apresurarse** *vr* : to hurry up, to make haste

apretado, -da *adj* **1** : tight **2** *fam* : cheap, tightfisted — **apretadamente** *adv*

apretar {55} *vt* **1** : to press, to push (a button) **2** : to tighten **3** : to squeeze — *vi* **1** : to press, to push **2** : to fit tightly, to be too tight <los zapatos me aprietan : my shoes are tight>

apretón *nm, pl* **-tones** **1** : squeeze **2** **apretón de manos** : handshake

apretujar *vt* : to squash, to squeeze — **apretujarse** *vr*

aprieto *nm* APURO : predicament, difficulty <estar en un aprieto : to be in a fix>

aprisa *adv* : quickly, hurriedly

aprisionar *vt* **1** : to imprison **2** : to trap, to box in

aprobación *nf, pl* **-ciones** : approval, endorsement

aprobar {19} *vt* **1** : to approve of **2** : to pass (a law, an exam) — *vi* : to pass (in school)

aprobatorio, -ria *adj* : approving

apropiación *nf, pl* **-ciones** : appropriation

apropiado, -da *adj* : appropriate, proper, suitable — **apropiadamente** *adv*

apropiarse *vr* **~ de** : to take possession of, to appropriate

aprovechable *adj* : usable

aprovechado[1], -da *adj* **1** : diligent, hardworking **2** : pushy, opportunistic

aprovechado[2], -da *n* : pushy person, opportunist

aprovechamiento *nm* : use, exploitation

aprovechar *vt* : to take advantage of, to make good use of — *vi* **1** : to be of use **2** : to progress, to improve — **aprovecharse** *vr* **~ de** : to take advantage of, to exploit

aprovisionamiento *nm* : provisions *pl*, supplies *pl*

aprovisionar *vt* : to provide, to supply (with provisions)

aproximación *nf, pl* **-ciones 1** : approximation, estimate **2** : rapprochement

aproximado, -da *adj* : approximate, estimated — **aproximadamente** *adv*

aproximar *vt* ACERCAR, ARRIMAR : to approximate, to bring closer — **aproximarse** *vr* ACERCARSE, ARRIMARSE : to approach, to move closer

aptitud *nf* : aptitude, capability

apto, -ta *adj* **1** : suitable, suited, fit **2** HÁBIL : capable, competent

apuesta *nf* : bet, wager

apuesto, -ta *adj* : elegant, good-looking

apuntador, -dora *n* : prompter

apuntalar *vt* : to prop up, to shore up

apuntar *vt* **1** : to aim, to point **2** ANOTAR : to write down, to jot down **3** INDICAR, SEÑALAR : to point to, to point out **4** : to prompt (in the theater) — *vi* **1** : to take aim **2** : to become evident — **apuntarse** *vr* **1** : to sign up, to enroll **2** : to score, to chalk up

apunte *nm* : note

apuñalar *vt* : to stab

apuradamente *adv* **1** : with difficulty **2** : hurriedly, hastily

apurado, -da *adj* **1** APRESURADO : rushed, pressured **2** : poor, needy **3** : difficult, awkward **4** : embarrassed

apurar *vt* **1** APRESURAR : to hurry, to rush **2** : to use up, to exhaust **3** : to trouble — **apurarse** *vr* **1** APRESURARSE : to hurry up **2** PREOCUPARSE : to worry

apuro *nm* **1** APRIETO : predicament, jam **2** : rush, hurry **3** : embarrassment

aquejar *vt* : to afflict

aquel, aquella *adj, mpl* **aquellos** : that, those

aquél, aquélla *pron, mpl* **aquéllos 1** : that (one), those (ones) **2** : the former

aquello *pron* (*neuter*) : that, that matter, that business <aquello fue algo serio : that was something serious>

aquí *adv* **1** : here **2** : now <de aquí en adelante : from now on> **3 por ~** : around here, hereabouts

aquiescencia *nf* : acquiescence, approval

aquietar *vt* : to allay, to calm — **aquietarse** *vr* : to calm down

aquilatar *vt* **1** : to assay **2** : to assess, to size up

ara *nf* **1** : altar **2 en aras de** : in the interests of, for the sake of

árabe[1] *adj & nmf* : Arab, Arabian

árabe[2] *nm* : Arabic (language)

arabesco *nm* : arabesque — **arabesco, -ca** *adj*

arábigo, -ga *adj* **1** : Arabic, Arabian **2 número arábigo** : Arabic numeral

arable *adj* : arable

arado *nm* : plow

aragonés, -nesa *adj & n, mpl* **-neses** : Aragonese

arancel *nm* : tariff, duty

arándano *nm* : blueberry

arandela *nf* : washer (for a faucet, etc.)

araña *nf* **1** : spider **2** : chandelier

arañar *v* : to scratch, to claw

arañazo *nm* : scratch

arar *v* : to plow

arbitraje *nm* **1** : arbitration **2** : refereeing (in sports)

arbitrar *v* **1** : to arbitrate **2** : to referee, to umpire

arbitrariedad *nf* **1** : arbitrariness **2** INJUSTICIA : injustice, wrong

arbitrario, -ria *adj* **1** : arbitrary **2** : unfair, unjust — **arbitrariamente** *adv*

arbitrio *nm* **1** ALBEDRÍO : will **2** JUICIO : judgment

árbitro, -tra *n* **1** : arbitrator, arbiter **2** : referee, umpire

árbol *nm* **1** : tree **2 árbol genealógico** : family tree

arbolado[1], -da *adj* : wooded

arbolado[2] *nm* : woodland

arboleda *nf* : grove, wood

arbóreo, -rea *adj* : arboreal

arbusto *nm* : shrub, bush, hedge

arca *nf* **1** : ark **2** : coffer, chest

arcada *nf* **1** : arcade, series of arches **2 arcadas** *nfpl* : retching <hacer arcadas : to retch>

arcaico, -ca *adj* : archaic

arcángel *nm* : archangel

arcano, -na *adj* : arcane

arce *nm* **:** maple tree

arcén *nm, pl* **arcenes :** hard shoulder, berm

archidiócesis *nfs & pl* **:** archdiocese

archipiélago *nm* **:** archipelago

archivador *nm* **:** filing cabinet

archivar *vt* **1 :** to file **2 :** to archive

archivista *nmf* **:** archivist

archivo *nm* **1 :** file **2 :** archive, archives *pl*

arcilla *nf* **:** clay

arco *nm* **1 :** arch, archway **2 :** bow (in archery) **3 :** arc **4 :** wicket (in croquet) **5** PORTERÍA **:** goal, goalposts *pl* **6 arco iris :** rainbow

arder *vi* **1 :** to burn <el bosque está ardiendo : the forest is in flames> <arder de ira : to burn with anger, to be seething> **2 :** to smart, to sting, to burn <le ardía el estómago : he had heartburn>

ardid *nm* **:** scheme, ruse

ardiente *adj* **1 :** burning **2 :** ardent, passionate — **ardientemente** *adv*

ardilla *nf* **1 :** squirrel **2** *or* **ardilla listada :** chipmunk

ardor *nm* **1 :** heat **2 :** passion, ardor

ardoroso, -sa *adj* **:** heated, impassioned

arduo, -dua *adj* **:** arduous, grueling — **arduamente** *adv*

área *nf* **:** area

arena *nf* **1 :** sand <arena movediza : quicksand> **2 :** arena

arenga *nf* **:** harangue, lecture

arengar {52} *vt* **:** to harangue, to lecture

arenilla *nf* **1 :** fine sand **2 arenillas** *nfpl* **:** kidney stones

arenisca *nf* **:** sandstone

arenoso, -sa *adj* **:** sandy, gritty

arenque *nm* **:** herring

arepa *nf* **:** cornmeal bread

arete *nm* **:** earring

argamasa *nf* **:** mortar (cement)

argelino, -na *adj & n* **:** Algerian

argentino, -na *adj & n* **:** Argentinian, Argentine

argolla *nf* **:** hoop, ring

argón *nm* **:** argon

argot *nm* **:** slang

argucia *nf* **:** sophistry, subtlety

argüir {41} *vi* **:** to argue — *vt* **1** ARGUMENTAR **:** to contend, to argue **2** INFERIR **:** to deduce **3** PROBAR **:** to prove

argumentación *nf, pl* **-ciones :** line of reasoning, argument

argumentar *vt* **:** to argue, to contend

argumento *nm* **1 :** argument, reasoning **2 :** plot, story line

aria *nf* **:** aria

aridez *nf, pl* **-deces :** aridity, dryness

árido, -da *adj* **:** arid, dry

Aries *nmf* **:** Aries

ariete *nm* **:** battering ram

arisco, -ca *adj* **:** surly, sullen, unsociable

arista *nf* **1 :** ridge, edge **2 :** beard (of a plant) **3 aristas** *nfpl* **:** rough edges, complications, problems

aristocracia *nf* **:** aristocracy

aristócrata *nmf* **:** aristocrat

aristocrático, -ca *adj* **:** aristocratic

aritmética *nf* **:** arithmetic

aritmético, -ca *adj* **:** arithmetic, arithmetical — **aritméticamente** *adv*

arlequín *nm, pl* **-quines :** harlequin

arma *nf* **1 :** weapon **2 armas** *nfpl* **:** armed forces **3 arma de fuego :** firearm

armada *nf* **:** navy, fleet

armadillo *nm* **:** armadillo

armado, -da *adj* **1 :** armed **2 :** assembled, put together **3** *PRi* **:** obstinate, stubborn

armador, -dora *n* **:** shipowner

armadura *nf* **1 :** armor **2** ARMAZÓN **:** skeleton, framework

armamento *nm* **:** armament, arms *pl*, weaponry

armar *vt* **1 :** to assemble, to put together **2 :** to create, to cause <armar un escándalo : to cause a scene> **3 :** to arm — **armarse** *vr* **armarse de valor :** to steel oneself

armario *nm* **1** CLÓSET, ROPERO **:** closet **2** ALACENA **:** cupboard

armatoste *nm fam* **:** monstrosity, contraption

armazón *nmf, pl* **-zones 1** ESQUELETO **:** framework, skeleton <armazón de acero : steel framework> **2 :** frames *pl* (of eyeglasses)

armenio, -nia *adj & n* **:** Armenian

armería *nf* **1 :** armory **2 :** arms museum **3 :** gunsmith's shop **4 :** gunsmith's craft

armiño *nm* **:** ermine

armisticio *nm* **:** armistice

armonía *nf* **:** harmony

armónica *nf* **:** harmonica

armónico, -ca *adj* **1 :** harmonic **2 :** harmonious — **armónicamente** *adv*

armonioso, -sa *adj* **:** harmonious — **armoniosamente** *adv*

armonizar {21} *vt* **1 :** to harmonize **2 :** to reconcile — *vi* **:** to harmonize, to blend together

arnés *nm, pl* **arneses :** harness

aro *nm* **1 :** hoop **2 :** napkin ring **3** *Arg, Chile, Uru* **:** earring

aroma *nm* **:** aroma, scent

aromático, -ca *adj* **:** aromatic

arpa *nf* **:** harp

arpegio *nm* **:** arpeggio

arpía *nf* **:** shrew, harpy

arpista *nmf* **:** harpist

arpón *nm, pl* **arpones :** harpoon — **arponear** *vt*

arquear *vt* **:** to arch, to bend — **arquearse** *vr* **:** to bend, to bow

arqueología *nf* **:** archaeology

arqueológico, -ca *adj* **:** archaeological

arqueólogo, -ga *n* **:** archaeologist

arquero, -ra *n* **1 :** archer **2** PORTERO **:** goalkeeper, goalie

arquetípico, -ca *adj* **:** archetypal
arquetipo *nm* **:** archetype
arquitecto, -ta *n* **:** architect
arquitectónico, -ca *adj* **:** architectural — **aquitectónicamente** *adv*
arquitectura *nf* **:** architecture
arrabal *nm* **1 :** slum **2 arrabales** *nmpl* **:** outskirts, outlying area
arracada *nf* **:** hoop earring
arracimarse *vr* **:** to cluster together
arraigado, -da *adj* **:** deep-seated, ingrained
arraigar {52} *vi* **:** to take root, to become established — **arraigarse** *vr*
arraigo *nm* **:** roots *pl* <con mucho arraigo : deep-rooted>
arrancar {72} *vt* **1 :** to pull out, to tear out **2 :** to pick, to pluck (a flower) **3 :** to start (an engine) **4 :** to boot (a computer) — *vi* **1 :** to start an engine **2 :** to get going — **arrancarse** *vr* **:** to pull out, to pull off
arrancón *nm, pl* **-cones** *Mex* **1 :** sudden loud start (of a car) **2 carrera de arrancones :** drag race
arranque *nm* **1 :** starter (of a car) **2** ARREBATO **:** outburst, fit **3 punto de arranque :** beginning, starting point
arrasar *vt* **1 :** to level, to smooth **2 :** to devastate, to destroy **3 :** to fill to the brim
arrastrar *vt* **1 :** to drag, to tow **2 :** to draw, to attract — *vi* **:** to hang down, to trail — **arrastrarse** *vr* **1 :** to crawl **2 :** to grovel
arrastre *nm* **1 :** dragging **2 :** pull, attraction **3 red de arrastre :** dragnet, trawling net
arrayán *nm, pl* **-yanes 1** MIRTO **:** myrtle **2 arrayán brabántico :** bayberry, wax myrtle
arrear *vt* **:** to urge on, to drive — *vi* **:** to hurry along
arrebatado, -da *adj* **1** PRECIPITADO **:** impetuous, hotheaded, rash **2 :** flushed, blushing
arrebatar *vt* **1 :** to snatch, to seize **2** CAUTIVAR **:** to captivate — **arrebatarse** *vr* **:** to get carried away (with anger, etc.)
arrebato *nm* ARRANQUE **:** fit, outburst
arreciar *vi* **:** to intensify, to worsen
arrecife *nm* **:** reef
arreglado, -da *adj* **1 :** fixed, repaired **2 :** settled, sorted out **3 :** neat, tidy **4 :** smart, dressed-up
arreglar *vt* **1** COMPONER **:** to repair, to fix **2 :** to tidy up <arregla tu cuarto : pick up your room> **3 :** to solve, to work out <quiero arreglar este asunto : I want to settle this matter> — **arreglarse** *vr* **1 :** to get dressed (up) <arreglarse el pelo : to get one's hair done> **2 arreglárselas** *fam* **:** to get by, to manage
arreglo *nm* **1 :** repair **2 :** arrangement **3 :** agreement, understanding
arrellanarse *vr* **:** to settle (in a chair)
arremangarse {52} *vr* **:** to roll up one's sleeves
arremeter *vi* EMBESTIR **:** to attack, to charge
arremetida *nf* EMBESTIDA **:** attack, onslaught
arremolinarse *vr* **1 :** to crowd around, to mill about **2 :** to swirl (about)
arrendador, -dora *n* **1 :** landlord, landlady *f* **2 :** tenant, lessee
arrendajo *nm* **:** jay
arrendamiento *nm* **1** ALQUILER **:** rental, leasing **2 contrato de arrendamiento :** lease
arrendar {55} *vt* ALQUILAR **:** to rent, to lease
arrendatario, -ria *n* **:** tenant, lessee, renter
arreos *nmpl* GUARNICIONES **:** tack, harness, trappings
arrepentido, -da *adj* **:** repentant, remorseful
arrepentimiento *nm* **:** regret, remorse, repentance
arrepentirse {76} *vr* **1 :** to regret, to be sorry **2 :** to repent
arrestar *vt* DETENER **:** to arrest, to detain
arresto *nm* **1** DETENCIÓN **:** arrest **2 arrestos** *nmpl* **:** boldness, daring
arriate *nm Mex, Spain* **:** bed (for plants), border
arriba *adv* **1 :** up, upwards **2 :** above, overhead **3 :** upstairs **4 ~ de :** more than **5 de arriba abajo :** from top to bottom, from head to foot
arribar *vi* **1 :** to arrive **2 :** to dock, to put into port
arribista *nmf* **:** parvenu, upstart
arribo *nm* **:** arrival
arriendo *nm* ARRENDAMIENTO **:** rent, rental
arriero, -ra *n* **:** mule driver, muleteer
arriesgado, -da *adj* **1 :** risky **2 :** bold, daring
arriesgar {52} *vt* **:** to risk, to venture — **arriesgarse** *vr* **:** to take a chance
arrimado, -da *n Mex fam* **:** sponger, freeloader
arrimar *vt* ACERCAR, APROXIMAR **:** to bring closer, to draw near — **arrimarse** *vr* ACERCARSE, APROXIMARSE **:** to approach, to get close
arrinconar *vt* **1** ACORRALAR **:** to corner, to box in **2 :** to push aside, to abandon
arroba *nf* **:** arroba (Spanish unit of measurement)
arrobamiento *nm* **:** rapture, ecstasy
arrobar *vt* **:** to enrapture, to enchant — **arrobarse** *vr*
arrocero¹, -ra *adj* **:** rice
arrocero², -ra *n* **:** rice grower
arrodillarse *vr* **:** to kneel (down)
arrogancia *nf* ALTANERÍA, ALTIVEZ **:** arrogance, haughtiness
arrogante *adj* ALTANERO, ALTIVO **:** arrogant, haughty
arrogarse {52} *vr* **:** to usurp, to arrogate

arrojado, -da *adj* : daring, fearless
arrojar *vt* **1** : to hurl, to cast, to throw **2** : to give off, to spew out **3** : to yield, to produce **4** *fam* : to vomit — **arrojarse** *vr* PRECIPITARSE : to throw oneself, to leap
arrojo *nm* : boldness, fearlessness
arrollador, -dora *adj* : sweeping, overwhelming
arrollar *vt* **1** : to sweep away, to carry away **2** : to crush, to overwhelm **3** : to run over (with a vehicle)
arropar *vt* : to clothe, to cover (up) — **arroparse** *vr*
arrostrar *vt* : to confront, to face (up to)
arroyo *nm* **1** RIACHUELO : brook, creek, stream **2** : gutter
arroz *nm, pl* **arroces** : rice
arrozal *nm* : rice field, rice paddy
arruga *nf* : wrinkle, fold, crease
arrugado, -da *adj* : wrinkled, creased, lined
arrugar {52} *vt* : to wrinkle, to crease, to pucker — **arrugarse** *vr*
arruinar *vt* : to ruin, to wreck — **arruinarse** *vr* **1** : to be ruined **2** : to fall into ruin, to go bankrupt
arrullar *vt* : to lull to sleep — *vi* : to coo
arrullo *nm* **1** : lullaby **2** : coo (of a dove)
arrumaco *nm fam* : kissing, cuddling
arrumbar *vt* **1** : to lay aside, to put away **2** : to floor, to leave speechless
arsenal *nm* : arsenal
arsénico *nm* : arsenic
arte *nmf* (*usually m in singular, f in plural*) **1** : art <artes y oficios : arts and crafts> <bellas artes : fine arts> **2** HABILIDAD : skill **3** : cunning, cleverness
artefacto *nm* **1** : artifact **2** DISPOSITIVO : device
artemisa *nf* : sagebrush
arteria *nf* : artery — **arterial** *adj*
arteriosclerosis *nf* : arteriosclerosis, hardening of the arteries
artero, -ra *adj* : wily, crafty
artesanal *adj* : pertaining to crafts or craftsmanship, handmade
artesanía *nm* **1** : craftsmanship **2** : handicrafts *pl*
artesano, -na *n* : artisan, craftsman *m,* craftsperson
artesiano, -na *adj* : artesian <pozo artesiano : artesian well>
ártico, -ca *adj* : arctic
articulación *nf, pl* **-ciones** **1** : articulation, pronunciation **2** COYUNTURA : joint
articular *vt* **1** : to articulate, to utter **2** : to connect with a joint **3** : to coordinate, to orchestrate
articulista *nmf* : columnist
artículo *nm* **1** : article, thing **2** : item, feature, report **3 artículo de comercio** : commodity **4 artículos de primera necesidad** : essentials **5 artículos de tocador** : toiletries
artífice *nmf* **1** ARTESANO : artisan **2** : mastermind, architect
artificial *adj* **1** : artificial, man-made **2** : feigned, false — **artificialmente** *adv*
artificio *nm* **1** HABILIDAD : skill **2** APARATO : device, appliance **3** ARDID : artifice, ruse
artificioso, -sa *adj* **1** : skillful **2** : cunning, deceptive
artillería *nf* : artillery
artillero, -ra *n* : artilleryman *m,* gunner
artilugio *nm* : gadget, contraption
artimaña *nf* : ruse, trick
artista *nmf* **1** : artist **2** ACTOR, ACTRIZ : actor, actress *f*
artístico, -ca *adj* : artistic — **artísticamente** *adv*
artrítico, -ca *adj* : arthritic
artritis *nms & pl* : arthritis
artrópodo *nm* : arthropod
arveja *nf* GUISANTE : pea
arzobispado *nm* : archbishopric
arzobispo *nm* : archbishop
as *nm* : ace
asa *nf* AGARRADERA, ASIDERO : handle, grip
asado[1]**, -da** *adj* : roasted, grilled, broiled
asado[2] *nm* **1** : roast **2** : barbecued meat **3** : barbecue, cookout
asador *nm* : spit, rotisserie
asaduras *nfpl* : entrails, offal
asalariado[1]**, -da** *adj* : wage-earning, salaried
asalariado[2]**, -da** *n* : wage earner
asaltante *nmf* **1** : mugger, robber **2** : assailant
asaltar *vt* **1** : to assault **2** : to mug, to rob **3 asaltar al poder** : to seize power
asalto *nm* **1** : assault **2** : mugging, robbery **3** : round (in boxing) **4 asalto al poder** : coup d'etat
asamblea *nf* : assembly, meeting
asambleísta *nmf* : assemblyman *m,* assemblywoman *f*
asar *vt* : to roast, to grill — **asarse** *vr fam* : to roast, to be dying from heat
asbesto *nm* : asbestos
ascendencia *nf* **1** : ancestry, descent **2** **~ sobre** : influence over
ascendente *adj* : ascending, upward <un curso ascendente : an upward trend>
ascender {56} *vi* **1** : to ascend, to rise up **2** : to be promoted <ascendió a gerente : she was promoted to manager> **3** **~ a** : to amount to, to reach <las deudas ascienden a 20 millones de pesos : the debt amounts to 20 million pesos> — *vt* : to promote
ascendiente[1] *nmf* ANCESTRO : ancestor
ascendiente[2] *nm* INFLUENCIA : influence, ascendancy

ascensión *nf, pl* **-siones 1 :** ascent, rise **2 Fiesta de la Ascensión :** Ascension Day

ascenso *nm* **1 :** ascent, rise **2 :** promotion

ascensor *nm* ELEVADOR **:** elevator

asceta *nmf* **:** ascetic

ascético, -ca *adj* **:** ascetic

ascetismo *nm* **:** asceticism

asco *nm* **1 :** disgust <¡qué asco! : that's disgusting!, how revolting!> **2 darle asco (a alguien) :** to sicken, to revolt **3 estar hecho un asco :** to be filthy **4 hacerle ascos a :** to turn up one's nose at

ascua *nf* **1** BRASA **:** ember **2 estar en ascuas** *fam* **:** to be on edge

asear *vt* **1 :** to wash, to clean **2 :** to tidy up — **asearse** *vr*

asechanza *nf* **:** snare, trap

asechar *vt* **:** to set a trap for

asediar *vt* **1** SITIAR **:** to besiege **2** ACOSAR **:** to harass

asedio *nm* **1 :** siege **2** ACOSO **:** harassment

asegurador[1], -dora *adj* **1 :** insuring, assuring **2 :** pertaining to insurance

asegurador[2], -dora *n* **:** insurer, underwriter

aseguradora *nf* **:** insurance company

asegurar *vt* **1 :** to assure **2 :** to secure **3 :** to insure — **asegurarse** *vr* **1** CERCIORARSE **:** to make sure **2 :** to take out insurance, to insure oneself

asemejar *vt* **1 :** to make similar <ese bigote te asemeja a tu abuelo : that mustache makes you look like your grandfather> **2** *Mex* **:** to be similar to, to resemble — **asemejarse** *vr* **~ a :** to be look like, to resemble

asentaderas *nfpl fam* **:** bottom, buttocks *pl*

asentado, -da *adj* **:** settled, established

asentamiento *nm* **:** settlement

asentar {55} *vt* **1 :** to lay down, to set down, to place **2 :** to settle, to establish **3** *Mex* **:** to state, to affirm — **asentarse** *vr* **1 :** to settle **2** ESTABLECERSE **:** to settle down, to establish oneself

asentimiento *nm* **:** assent, consent

asentir {76} *vi* **:** to consent, to agree

aseo *nm* **:** cleanliness

aséptico, -ca *adj* **:** aseptic, germ-free

asequible *adj* ACCESIBLE **:** accessible, attainable

aserción *nf* → **aserto**

aserradero *nm* **:** sawmill

aserrar {55} *vt* **:** to saw

aserrín *nm, pl* **-rrines :** sawdust

aserto *nm* **:** assertion, affirmation

asesinar *vt* **1 :** to murder **2 :** to assassinate

asesinato *nm* **1 :** murder **2 :** assassination

asesino[1], -na *adj* **:** murderous, homicidal

asesino[2], -na *n* **1 :** murderer, killer **2 :** assassin

asesor, -sora *n* **:** advisor, consultant

asesoramiento *nm* **:** advice, counsel

asesorar *vt* **:** to advise, to counsel — **asesorarse** *vr* **~ de :** to consult

asesoría *nf* **1 :** consulting, advising **2 :** consultant's office

asestar {55} *vt* **1 :** to aim, to point (a weapon) **2 :** to deliver, to deal (a blow)

aseveración *nf, pl* **-ciones :** assertion, statement

aseverar *vt* **:** to assert, to state

asexual *adj* **:** asexual — **asexualmente** *adv*

asfaltado[1], -da *adj* **:** asphalted, paved

asfaltado[2] *nm* PAVIMENTO **:** pavement, asphalt

asfaltar *vt* **:** to pave, to blacktop

asfalto *nm* **:** asphalt

asfixia *nf* **:** asphyxia, asphyxiation, suffocation

asfixiar *vt* **:** to asphyxiate, to suffocate, to smother — **asfixiarse** *vr*

asga, etc. → **asir**

así[1] *adv* **1 :** like this, like that **2 :** so, thus <así sea : so be it> **3 ~ de :** so, about so <una caja así de grande : a box about so big> **4 así que :** so, therefore **5 ~ como :** as well as **6 así así :** so-so, fair

así[2] *adj* **:** such, such a <un talento así es inestimable : a talent like that is priceless>

así[3] *conj* AUNQUE **:** even if, even though <no irá, así le paguen : he won't go, even if they pay him>

asiático[1], -ca *adj* **:** Asian, Asiatic

asiático[2], -ca *n* **:** Asian

asidero *nm* **1** AGARRADA, ASA **:** grip, handle **2** AGARRE **:** grip, hold

asiduamente *adv* **:** regularly, frequently

asiduidad *nf* **1 :** assiduousness **2 :** regularity, frequency

asiduo, -dua *adj* **1 :** assiduous **2 :** frequent, regular

asiento *nm* **1 :** seat, chair <asiento trasero : back seat> **2 :** location, site

asignación *nf, pl* **-ciones 1 :** allocation **2 :** appointment, designation **3 :** allowance, pay **4** *PRi* **:** homework, assignment

asignar *vt* **1 :** to assign, to allocate **2 :** to appoint

asignatura *nf* MATERIA **:** subject, course

asilado, -da *n* **:** exile, refugee

asilo *nm* **:** asylum, refuge, shelter

asimetría *nf* **:** asymmetry

asimétrico, -ca *adj* **:** asymmetrical, asymmetric

asimilación *nf, pl* **-ciones :** assimilation

asimilar *vt* **:** to assimilate — **asimilarse** *vr* **~ a :** to be similar to, to resemble

asimismo *adv* **1** IGUALMENTE **:** similarly, likewise **2** TAMBIÉN **:** as well, also

asir {7} *vt* : to seize, to grasp — **asirse** *vr* ~ **a** : to cling to

asistencia *nf* **1** : attendance **2** : assistance **3** : assist (in sports)

asistente[1] *adj* : attending, in attendance

asistente[2] *nmf* **1** : assistant **2 los asistentes** : those present, those in attendance

asistir *vi* : to attend, to be present <asistir a clase : to attend class> — *vt* : to aid, to assist

asma *nf* : asthma

asmático, -ca *adj* : asthmatic

asno *nm* BURRO : ass, donkey

asociación *nf, pl* **-ciones 1** : association, relationship **2** : society, group, association

asociado[1], **-da** *adj* : associate, associated

asociado[2], **-da** *n* : associate, partner

asociar *vt* **1** : to associate, to connect **2** : to pool (resources) **3** : to take into partnership — **asociarse** *vr* **1** : to become partners **2** ~ **a** : to join, to become a member of

asolar {19} *vt* : to devastate, to destroy

asoleado, -da *adj* : sunny

asolear *vt* : to put in the sun — **asolearse** *vr* : to sunbathe

asomar *vt* : to show, to stick out — *vi* : to appear, to become visible — **asomarse** *vr* **1** : to show, to appear **2** : to lean out, to look out <se asomó por la ventana : he leaned out the window>

asombrar *vt* MARAVILLAR : to amaze, to astonish — **asombrarse** *vr* : to marvel, to be amazed

asombro *nm* : amazement, astonishment

asombroso, -sa *adj* : amazing, astonishing — **asombrosamente** *adv*

asomo *nm* **1** : hint, trace **2 ni por asomo** : by no means

aspa *nf* : blade (of a fan or propeller)

aspaviento *nm* : exaggerated movement, fuss, flounce

aspecto *nm* **1** : aspect **2** APARIENCIA : appearance, look

aspereza *nf* RUDEZA : roughness, coarseness

áspero, -ra *adj* : rough, coarse, abrasive — **ásperamente** *adv*

aspersión *nf, pl* **-siones** : sprinkling

aspersor *nm* : sprinkler

aspiración *nf, pl* **-ciones 1** : inhalation, breathing in **2** ANHELO : aspiration, desire

aspiradora *nf* : vacuum cleaner

aspirante *nmf* : applicant, candidate

aspirar *vi* ~ **a** : to aspire to — *vt* : to inhale, to breathe in

aspirina *nf* : aspirin

asquear *vt* : to sicken, to disgust

asquerosidad *nf* : filth, foulness

asqueroso, -sa *adj* : disgusting, sickening, repulsive — **asquerosamente** *adv*

asta *nf* **1** : flagpole <a media asta : at half-mast> **2** : horn, antler **3** : shaft (of a weapon)

ástaco *nm* : crayfish

astado, -da *adj* : horned

áster *nm* : aster

asterisco *nm* : asterisk

asteroide *nm* : asteroid

astigmatismo *nm* : astigmatism

astil *nm* : shaft (of an arrow or feather)

astilla *nf* **1** : splinter, chip **2 de tal palo, tal astilla** : like father, like son

astillar *vt* : to splinter — **astillarse** *vr*

astillero *nm* : dry dock, shipyard

astral *adj* : astral

astringente *adj & nm* : astringent — **astringencia** *nf*

astro *nm* **1** : heavenly body **2** : star

astrología *nf* : astrology

astrológico, -ca *adj* : astrological

astrólogo, -ga *n* : astrologer

astronauta *nmf* : astronaut

astronáutica *nf* : astronautics

astronautico, -ca *adj* : astronautic, astronautical

astronave *nf* : spaceship

astronomía *nf* : astronomy

astronómico, -ca *adj* : astronomical — **astronómicamente** *adv*

astrónomo, -ma *n* : astronomer

astroso, -sa *adj* DESALIÑADO : slovenly, untidy

astucia *nf* **1** : astuteness, shrewdness **2** : cunning, guile

astuto, -ta *adj* **1** : astute, shrewd **2** : crafty, tricky — **astutamente** *adv*

asueto *nm* : time off, break

asumir *vt* **1** : to assume, to take on <asumir el cargo : to take office> **2** SUPONER : to assume, to suppose

asunción *nf, pl* **-ciones** : assumption

asunto *nm* **1** CUESTIÓN, TEMA : affair, matter, subject **2 asuntos** *nmpl* : affairs, business

asustadizo, -za *adj* : nervous, jumpy, skittish

asustado, -da *adj* : frightened, afraid

asustar *vt* ESPANTAR : to scare, to frighten — **asustarse** *vr*

atacante *nmf* : assailant, attacker

atacar {72} *v* : to attack

atado[1], **-da** *adj* : shy, inhibited

atado[2] *nm* **1** : bundle, bunch **2** *Arg* : pack (of cigarettes)

atadura *nf* LIGADURA : tie, bond

atajar *vt* **1** IMPEDIR : to block, to stop **2** INTERRUMPIR : to interrupt, to cut off **3** CONTENER : to hold back, to restrain — *vi* ~ **por** : to take a shortcut through

atajo *nm* : shortcut

atalaya *nf* **1** : watchtower **2** : vantage point

atañer {79} *vi* (*3rd person only*) : to concern, to have to do with <eso no me atañe : that does not concern me>

ataque *nm* **1** : attack, assault **2** : fit <ataque de risa : fit of laughter> **3 ataque de nervios** : nervous breakdown **4 ataque cardíaco** *or* **ataque al corazón :** heart attack

atar *vt* AMARRAR **:** to tie, to tie up, to tie down — **atarse** *vr*

atarantado, -da *adj fam* **1 :** restless **2 :** dazed, stunned

atarantar *vt fam* **:** to daze, to stun

atarazana *nf* **:** shipyard

atardecer[1] {53} *v impers* **:** to get dark

atardecer[2] *v impers* **:** late afternoon, dusk

atareado, -da *adj* **:** busy, overworked

atascar {72} *vt* **1** ATORAR **:** to block, to clog, to stop up **2 :** to hinder — **atascarse** *vr* **1 :** to become obstructed **2 :** to get bogged down **3** PARARSE **:** to stall

atasco *nm* **1 :** blockage **2** EMBOTELLAMIENTO **:** traffic jam

ataúd *nm* **:** coffin, casket

ataviar {85} *vt* **:** to dress, to clothe — **ataviarse** *vr* **:** to dress up

atavío *nm* ATUENDO **:** dress, attire

ateísmo *nm* **:** atheism

atemorizar {21} *vt* **:** to frighten, to intimidate — **atemorizarse** *vr*

atemperar *vt* **:** to temper, to moderate

atención[1] *nf, pl* **-ciones 1 :** attention **2 poner atención** *or* **prestar atención :** to pay attention **3 llamar la atención :** to attract attention **4 en atención a :** in view of

atención[2] *interj* **1 :** attention! **2 :** watch out!

atender {56 } *vt* **1 :** to help, to wait on **2 :** to look after, to take care of **3 :** to heed, to listen to — *vi* **:** to pay attention

atenerse {80} *vr* **:** to abide <tendrás que atenerte a las reglas : you will have to abide by the rules>

atentado *nm* **:** attack, assault

atentamente *adv* **1 :** attentively, carefully **2** (*used in correspondence*) **:** sincerely, sincerely yours

atentar {55} *vi* **~ contra :** to make an attempt on, to threaten <atentaron contra su vida : they made an attempt on his life>

atento, -ta *adj* **1 :** attentive, mindful **2** CORTÉS **:** courteous

atenuación *nf, pl* **-ciones 1 :** lessening **2 :** understatement

atenuante[1] *adj* **:** extenuating, mitigating

atenuante[2] *nmf* **:** extenuating circumstance, excuse

atenuar {3} *vt* **1** MITIGAR **:** to extenuate, to mitigate **2 :** to dim (light), to tone down (colors) **3 :** to minimize, to lessen

ateo[1], **atea** *adj* **:** atheistic

ateo[2], **atea** *n* **:** atheist

aterciopelado, -da *adj* **:** velvety, downy

aterido, -da *adj* **:** freezing, frozen

aterrador, -dora *adj* **:** terrifying

aterrar {55} *vt* **:** to terrify, to frighten

aterrizaje *nm* **:** landing (of a plane)

aterrizar {21} *vi* **:** to land, to touch down

aterrorizar {21} *vt* **1 :** to terrify **2 :** to terrorize — **aterrorizarse** *vr* **:** to be terrified

atesorar *vt* **:** to hoard, to amass

atestado, -da *adj* **:** crowded, packed

atestar {55} *vt* **1** ATIBORRAR **:** to crowd, to pack **2 :** to witness, to testify to — *vi* **:** to testify

atestiguar {10} *vt* **:** to testify to, to bear witness to — *vi* DECLARAR **:** to testify

atiborrar *vt* **:** to pack, to crowd — **atiborrarse** *vr* **:** to stuff oneself

ático *nm* **1 :** penthouse **2** BUHARDILLA, DESVÁN **:** attic

atigrado, -da *adj* **:** tabby (of cats), striped (of fur)

atildado, -da *adj* **:** smart, neat, dapper

atildar *vt* **1 :** to put a tilde over **2 :** to clean up, to smarten up — **atildarse** *vr* **:** to get spruced up

atinar *vi* ACERTAR **:** to be accurate, to be on target

atingencia *nf* **:** bearing, relevance

atípico, -ca *adj* **:** atypical

atiplado, -da *adj* **:** shrill, high-pitched

atirantar *vt* **:** to make taut, to tighten

atisbar *vt* **1 :** to spy on, to watch **2 :** to catch a glimpse of, to make out

atisbo *nm* **:** glimpse, sign, hint

atizador *nm* **:** poker (for a fire)

atizar {21} *vt* **1 :** to poke, to stir, to stoke (a fire) **2 :** to stir up, to rouse **3** *fam* **:** to give, to land (a blow)

atlántico, -ca *adj* **:** Atlantic

atlas *nm* **:** atlas

atleta *nmf* **:** athlete

atlético, -ca *adj* **:** athletic

atletismo *nm* **:** athletics

atmósfera *nf* **:** atmosphere

atmosférico, -ca *adj* **:** atmospheric

atole *nm Mex* **1 :** thick hot beverage prepared with corn flour **2 darle atole con el dedo (a alguien) :** to string (someone) along

atollarse *vr* **:** to get stuck, to get bogged down

atolón *nm, pl* **-lones :** atoll

atolondrado, -da *adj* **1** ATURDIDO **:** bewildered, dazed **2** DESPISTADO **:** scatterbrained, absentminded

atómico, -ca *adj* **:** atomic

atomizador *nm* **:** atomizer

atomizar {21} *vt* FRAGMENTAR **:** to fragment, to break into bits

átomo *nm* **:** atom

atónito, -ta *adj* **:** astonished, amazed

atontar *vt* **1 :** to stupefy **2 :** to bewilder, to confuse

atorar *vt* ATASCAR **:** to block, to clog — **atorarse** *vr* **1** ATASCARSE **:** to get stuck **2** ATRAGANTARSE **:** to choke

atormentador, -dora *n* **:** tormenter

atormentar *vt* **:** to torment, to torture — **atormentarse** *vr* **:** to torment oneself, to agonize

atornillar *vt* **:** to screw (in, on, down)

atorrante *nmf Arg* : bum, loafer
atosigar {52} *vt* : to harass, to annoy
atracadero *nm* : dock, pier
atracador, -dora *n* : robber, mugger
atracar {72} *vi* : to dock, to land — *vt* : to hold up, to rob, to mug — **atracarse** *vr fam* **~ de** : to gorge oneself with
atracción *nf, pl* **-ciones** : attraction
atraco *nm* : holdup, robbery
atractivo[1], **-va** *adj* : attractive
atractivo[2] *nm* : attraction, appeal, charm
atraer {81} *vt* : to attract — **atraerse** *vr* **1** : to attract (each other) **2** GANARSE : to gain, to win
atragantarse *vr* : to choke (on food)
atrancar {72} *vt* : to block, to bar — **atrancarse** *vr*
atrapada *nf* : catch
atrapar *vt* : to trap, to capture
atrás *adv* **1** DETRÁS : back, behind <se quedó atrás : he stayed behind> **2** ANTES : ago <mucho tiempo atrás : long ago> **3 para ~** *or* **hacia ~** : backwards, toward the rear **4 ~ de** : in back of, behind
atrasado, -da *adj* **1** : late, overdue **2** : backwards **3** : old-fashioned **4** : slow (of a clock or watch)
atrasar *vt* : to delay, to put off — *vi* : to lose time — **atrasarse** *vr* : to fall behind
atraso *nm* **1** RETRASO : lateness, delay <llegó con 20 minutos de atraso : he was 20 minutes late> **2** : backwardness **3 atrasos** *nmpl* : arrears
atravesar {55} *vt* **1** CRUZAR : to cross, to go across **2** : to pierce **3** : to lay across **4** : to go through (a situation or crisis) — **atravesarse** *vr* **1** : to be in the way <se me atravesó : it blocked my path> **2** : to interfere, to meddle
atrayente *adj* : attractive
atreverse *vr* **1** : to dare **2** : to be insolent
atrevido, -da *adj* **1** : bold, daring **2** : insolent
atrevimiento *nm* **1** : daring, boldness **2** : insolence
atribución *nf, pl* **-ciones** : attribution
atribuible *adj* IMPUTABLE : attributable, ascribable
atribuir {41} *vt* **1** : to attribute, to ascribe **2** : to grant, to confer — **atribuirse** *vr* : to take credit for
atribular *vt* : to afflict, to trouble — **atribularse** *vr*
atributo *nm* : attribute
atril *nm* : lectern, stand
atrincherar *vt* : to entrench — **atrincherarse** *vr* **1** : to dig in, to entrench oneself **2 ~ en** : to hide behind
atrio *nm* **1** : atrium **2** : portico
atrocidad *nf* : atrocity
atrofia *nf* : atrophy
atrofiar *v* : to atrophy
atronador, -dora *adj* : thunderous, deafening
atropellado, -da *adj* **1** : rash, hasty **2** : brusque, abrupt
atropellamiento *nm* → **atropello**
atropellar *vt* **1** : to knock down, to run over **2** : to violate, to abuse — **atropellarse** *vr* : to rush through (a task), to trip over one's words
atropello *nm* : abuse, violation, outrage
atroz *adj, pl* **atroces** : atrocious, appalling — **atrozamente** *adv*
atuendo *nm* ATAVÍO : attire, costume
atufar *vt* : to vex, to irritate — **atufarse** *vr* **1** : to get angry **2** : to smell bad, to stink
atún *nm, pl* **atunes** : tuna fish, tuna
aturdimiento *nm* : bewilderment, confusion
aturdir *vt* **1** : to stun, to shock **2** : to bewilder, to confuse, to stupefy
atuvo, etc. → **atenerse**
audacia *nf* OSADÍA : boldness, audacity
audaz *adj, pl* **audaces** : bold, audacious, daring — **audazmente** *adv*
audible *adj* : audible
audición *nf, pl* **-ciones** **1** : hearing **2** : audition
audiencia *nf* : audience
audífono *nm* **1** : hearing aid **2 audífonos** *nmpl* : headphones, earphones
audio *nm* : audio
audiovisual *adj* : audiovisual
auditar *vt* : to audit
auditivo, -va *adj* : auditory, hearing, aural <aparato auditivo : hearing aid>
auditor, -tora *n* : auditor
auditoría *nf* : audit
auditorio *nm* **1** : auditorium **2** : audience
auge *nm* **1** : peak, height **2** : boom, upturn
augurar *vt* : to predict, to foretell
augurio *nm* AGÜERO, PRESAGIO : augury, omen
augusto, -ta *adj* : august
aula *nf* : classroom
aullar {8} *vi* : to howl, to wail
aullido *nm* : howl, wail
aumentar *vt* ACRECENTAR : to increase, to raise — *vi* : to rise, to increase, to grow
aumento *nm* INCREMENTO : increase, rise
aun *adv* **1** : even <ni aun en coche llegaría a tiempo : I wouldn't arrive on time even if I drove> **2 aun así** : even so **3 aun más** : even more
aún *adv* **1** TODAVÍA : still, yet <¿aún no ha llegado el correo? : the mail still hasn't come?> **2 más aún** : furthermore
aunar {8} *vt* : to join, to combine — **aunarse** *vr* : to unite
aunque *conj* **1** : though, although, even if, even though **2 aunque sea** : at least
aura *nf* **1** : aura **2** : turkey buzzard
áureo, -rea *adj* : golden

aureola *nf* **1 :** halo **2 :** aura (of power, fame, etc.)

aurícula *nf* **:** auricle

auricular *nm* **:** telephone receiver

aurora *nf* **1 :** dawn **2 aurora boreal :** aurora borealis

ausencia *nf* **:** absence

ausentarse *vr* **1 :** to leave, to go away **2 ~ de :** to stay away from

ausente[1] *adj* **:** absent, missing

ausente[2] *nmf* **1 :** absentee **2 :** missing person

auspiciar *vt* **1** PATROCINAR **:** to sponsor **2** FOMENTAR **:** to foster, to promote

auspicios *nmpl* **:** sponsorship, auspices

austeridad *nf* **:** austerity

austero, -ra *adj* **:** austere

austral[1] *adj* **:** southern

austral[2] *nm* **:** former monetary unit of Argentina

australiano, -na *adj & n* **:** Australian

austriaco *or* **austríaco, -ca** *adj & n* **:** Austrian

autenticar {72} *vt* **:** to authenticate — **autenticación** *nf*

autenticidad *nf* **:** authenticity

auténtico, -ca *adj* **:** authentic — **auténticamente** *adv*

autentificar {72} *vt* **:** to authenticate — **autentificación** *nf*

autismo *nm* **:** autism

autista *adj* **:** autistic

auto *nm* **:** auto, car

autoayuda *nf* **:** self-help

autobiografía *nf* **:** autobiography

autobiográfico, -ca *adj* **:** autobiographical

autobús *nm, pl* **-buses :** bus

autocompasión *nf* **:** self-pity

autocontrol *nm* **:** self-control

autocracia *nf* **:** autocracy

autócrata *nmf* **:** autocrat

autocrático, -ca *adj* **:** autocratic

autóctono, -na *adj* **:** indigenous, native <arte autóctono : indigenous art>

autodefensa *nf* **:** self-defense

autodestrucción *nf* **:** self-destruction — **autodestructivo, -va** *adj*

autodeterminación *nf* **:** self-determination

autodidacta *adj* **:** self-taught

autodisciplina *nf* **:** self-discipline

autoestima *nf* **:** self-esteem

autogobierno *nm* **:** self-government

autografiar *vt* **:** to autograph

autógrafo *nm* **:** autograph

autoinfligido, -da *adj* **:** self-inflicted

automación *nf* → **automatización**

autómata *nm* **:** automaton

automático, -ca *adj* **:** automatic — **automáticamente** *adv*

automatización *nf* **:** automation

automatizar {21} *vt* **:** to automate

automotor, -tora *adj* **1 :** self-propelled **2 :** automotive, car

automotriz[1] *adj, pl* **-trices :** automotive, car

automotriz[2] *nf, pl* **-trices :** car dealership

automóvil *nm* **:** automobile

automovilista *nmf* **:** motorist

automovilístico, -ca *adj* **:** automobile, car <accidente automovilístico : automobile accident>

autonombrado, -da *adj* **:** self-appointed

autonomía *nf* **:** autonomy

autónomo, -ma *adj* **:** autonomous — **autónomamente** *adv*

autopista *nf* **:** expressway, highway

autopropulsado, -da *adj* **:** self-propelled

autopsia *nf* **:** autopsy

autor, -tora *n* **1 :** author **2 :** perpetrator

autoría *nf* **:** authorship

autoridad *nf* **:** authority

autoritario, -ria *adj* **:** authoritarian

autorización *nf, pl* **-ciones :** authorization

autorizado, -da *adj* **1 :** authorized **2 :** authoritative

autorizar {21} *vt* **:** to authorize, to approve

autorretrato *nm* **:** self-portrait

autoservicio *nm* **1 :** self-service restaurant **2** SUPERMERCADO **:** supermarket

autostop *nm* **1 :** hitchhiking **2 hacer autostop :** to hitchhike

autostopista *nmf* **:** hitchhiker

autosuficiencia *nf* **:** self-sufficiency — **autosuficiente** *adj*

auxiliar[1] *vt* **:** to aid, to assist

auxiliar[2] *adj* **:** assistant, auxiliary

auxiliar[3] *nmf* **1 :** assistant, helper **2 auxiliar de vuelo :** flight attendant

auxilio *nm* **1 :** aid, assistance **2 primeros auxilios :** first aid

aval *nm* **:** guarantee, endorsement

avalancha *nf* ALUD **:** avalanche

avalar *vt* **:** to guarantee, to endorse

avaluar {3} *vt* **:** to evaluate, to appraise

avalúo *nm* **:** appraisal, evaluation

avance *nm* ADELANTO **:** advance

avanzado, -da *adj* **1 :** advanced **2 :** progressive

avanzar {21} *v* **:** to advance, to move forward

avaricia *nf* CODICIA **:** greed, avarice

avaricioso, -sa *adj* **:** avaricious, greedy

avaro[1]**, -ra** *adj* **:** miserly, greedy

avaro[2]**, -ra** *n* **:** miser

avasallador, -dora *adj* **:** overwhelming

avasallamiento *nm* **:** subjugation, domination

avasallar *vt* **:** to overpower, to subjugate

ave *nf* **1 :** bird **2 aves de corral :** poultry **3 ave rapaz** *or* **ave de presa :** bird of prey

avecinarse *vr* **:** to approach, to come near

avecindarse *vr* **:** to settle, to take up residence

avellana *nf* **:** hazelnut, filbert

avena *nf* **1 :** oat, oats *pl* **2 :** oatmeal

avenencia *nf* **:** agreement, pact
avenida *nf* **:** avenue
avenir {87} *vt* **:** to reconcile, to harmonize — **avenirse** *vr* **1 :** to agree, to come to terms **2 :** to get along
aventajado, -da *adj* **:** outstanding
aventajar *vt* **1 :** to be ahead of, to lead **2 :** to surpass, to outdo
aventar {55} *vt* **1 :** to fan **2 :** to winnow **3** *Col, Mex* **:** to throw, to toss — **aventarse** *vr* **1** *Col, Mex* **:** to hurl oneself **2** *Mex fam* **:** to dare, to take a chance
aventón *nm, pl* **-tones** *Col, Mex fam* **:** ride, lift
aventura *nf* **1 :** adventure **2** RIESGO **:** venture, risk **3 :** love affair
aventurado, -da *adj* **:** hazardous, risky
aventurar *vt* **:** to venture, to risk — **aventurarse** *vr* **:** to take a risk
aventurero[1], -ra *adj* **:** adventurous
aventurero[2], -ra *n* **:** adventurer
avergonzado, -da *adj* **1 :** ashamed **2 :** embarrassed
avergonzar {9} *vt* APENAR **:** to shame, to embarrass — **avergonzarse** *vr* APENARSE **:** to be ashamed, to be embarrassed
avería *nf* **1 :** damage **2 :** breakdown, malfunction
averiado, -da *adj* **1 :** damaged, faulty **2 :** broken down
averiar {85} *vt* **:** to damage — **averiarse** *vr* **:** to break down
averiguación *nf, pl* **-ciones :** investigation, inquiry
averiguar {10} *vt* **1 :** to find out, to ascertain **2 :** to investigate
aversión *nf, pl* **-siones :** aversion, dislike
avestruz *nm, pl* **-truces :** ostrich
avezado, -da *adj* **:** seasoned, experienced
aviación *nf, pl* **-ciones :** aviation
aviador, -dora *n* **:** aviator, flyer
aviar {85} *vt* **1 :** to prepare, to make ready **2 :** to tidy up **3 :** to equip, to supply
avicultor, -tora *n* **:** poultry farmer
avicultura *nf* **:** poultry farming
avidez *nf, pl* **-deces :** eagerness
ávido, -da *adj* **:** eager, avid — **ávidamente** *adv*
avieso, -sa *adj* **1 :** twisted, distorted **2 :** wicked, depraved
avinagrado, -da *adj* **:** vinegary, sour
avío *nm* **1 :** preparation, provision **2 :** loan (for agriculture or mining) **3 avíos** *nmpl* **:** gear, equipment
avión *nm, pl* **aviones :** airplane
avioneta *nf* **:** light airplane
avisar *vt* **1 :** to notify, to inform **2 :** to advise, to warn
aviso *nm* **1 :** notice **2 :** advertisement, ad **3** ADVERTENCIA **:** warning **4 estar sobre aviso :** to be on the alert
avispa *nf* **:** wasp
avispado, -da *adj fam* **:** clever, sharp
avispero *nm* **:** wasps' nest
avispón *nm, pl* **-pones :** hornet
avistar *vt* **:** to sight, to catch sight of
avituallar *vt* **:** to suppy with food, to provision
avivar *vt* **1 :** to enliven, to brighten **2 :** to strengthen, to intensify
avizorar *vt* **1** ACECHAR **:** to spy on, to watch **2 :** to observe, to perceive <se avizoran dificultades : difficulties are expected>
axila *nf* **:** underarm, armpit
axioma *nm* **:** axiom
axiomático, -ca *adj* **:** axiomatic
ay *interj* **1 :** oh! **2 :** ouch!, ow!
ayer[1] *adv* **:** yesterday
ayer[2] *nm* ANTAÑO **:** yesteryear, days gone by
ayote *nm CA, Mex* **:** squash, pumpkin
ayuda *nf* **1 :** help, assistance **2 ayuda de cámara :** valet
ayudante *nmf* **:** helper, assistant
ayudar *vt* **:** to help, to assist — **ayudarse** *vr* **~ de :** to make use of
ayunar *vi* **:** to fast
ayunas *nfpl* **en ~ :** fasting <este medicamento ha de tomarse en ayunas : this medication should be taken on an empty stomach>
ayuno *nm* **:** fast
ayuntamiento *nm* **1 :** town hall, city hall **2 :** town or city council
azabache *nm* **:** jet <negro azabache : jet black>
azada *nf* **:** hoe
azafata *nf* **1 :** stewardess *f* **2 :** hostess *f* (on a TV show)
azafrán *nm, pl* **-franes 1 :** saffron **2 :** crocus
azahar *nm* **:** orange blossom
azalea *nf* **:** azalea
azar *nm* **1 :** chance <juegos de azar : games of chance> **2 :** accident, misfortune **3 al azar :** at random, randomly
azaroso, -sa *adj* **1 :** perilous, hazardous **2 :** turbulent, eventful
azimut *nm* **:** azimuth
azogue *nm* **:** mercury, quicksilver
azorar *vt* **1 :** to alarm, to startle **2 :** to fluster, to embarrass — **azorarse** *vr* **:** to get embarrassed
azotar *vt* **1 :** to whip, to flog **2 :** to lash, to batter **3 :** to devastate, to afflict
azote *nm* **1** LÁTIGO **:** whip, lash **2** *fam* **:** spanking, licking **3 :** calamity, scourge
azotea *nf* **:** flat roof, terraced roof
azteca *adj & nmf* **:** Aztec
azúcar *nmf* **:** sugar — **azucarar** *vt*
azucarado, -da *adj* **:** sweetened, sugary
azucarera *nf* **:** sugar bowl
azucarero, -ra *adj* **:** sugar <industria azucarera : sugar industry>
azucena *nf* **:** white lily
azuela *nf* **:** adz
azufre *nm* **:** sulphur — **azufroso, -sa** *adj*

azul *adj & nm* **:** blue
azulado, -da *adj* **:** bluish
azulejo *nm* **:** ceramic tile, floor tile
azulete *nm* **:** bluing
azuloso, -sa *adj* **:** bluish
azur[1] *adj* CELESTE **:** azure
azur[2] *n* CELESTE **:** azure, sky blue
azuzar {21} *vt* **:** to incite, to egg on

B

b *nf* **:** second letter of the Spanish alphabet
baba *nf* **1 :** spittle, saliva **2 :** dribble, drool (of a baby) **3 :** slime, ooze
babear *vi* **1 :** to drool, to slobber **2 :** to ooze
babel *nf* **:** babel, chaos, bedlam
babero *nm* **:** bib
babor *nm* **:** port, port side
babosa *nf* **:** slug (mollusk)
babosada *nf CA, Mex* **:** silly act or remark
baboso, -sa *adj* **1 :** drooling, slobbering **2 :** slimy **3** *CA, Mex fam* **:** silly, dumb
babucha *nf* **:** slipper
babuino *nm* **:** baboon
bacalao *nm* **:** cod (fish)
bache *nm* **1 :** pothole **2** *PRi* **:** deep puddle **3 :** bad period, rough time <bache económico : economic slump>
bachiller *nmf* **:** high school graduate
bachillerato *nm* **:** high school diploma
bacilo *nm* **:** bacillus
backgammon *nm* **:** backgammon
bacon *nm Spain* **:** bacon
bacteria *nf* **:** bacterium
bacteriano, -na *adj* **:** bacterial
bacteriología *nf* **:** bacteriology
bacteriológico, -ca *adj* **:** bacteriologic, bacteriological
bacteriólogo, -ga *n* **:** bacteriologist
báculo *nm* **1 :** staff, stick **2 :** comfort, support
badajo *nm* **:** clapper (of a bell)
badén *nm, pl* **badenes 1 :** (paved) ford, channel **2 :** dip, ditch (in a road)
bádminton *nm* **:** badminton
bafle *or* **baffle** *nm* **1 :** baffle **2 :** speaker, loudspeaker
bagaje *nm* **1** EQUIPAJE **:** baggage, luggage **2 :** background <bagaje cultural : cultural baggage>
bagatela *nf* **:** trifle, trinket
bagre *nm* **:** catfish
bahía *nf* **:** bay
bailar *vt* **:** to dance — *vi* **1 :** to dance **2 :** to spin **3 :** to be loose, to be too big
bailarín[1], **-rina** *adj, mpl* **-rines 1 :** dancing **2 :** fond of dancing
bailarín[2], **-rina** *n, mpl* **-rines 1 :** dancer **2 :** ballet dancer, ballerina *f*
baile *nm* **1 :** dance **2 :** dance party, ball **3 llevarse al baile a** *Mex fam* **:** to take for a ride, to take advantage of
baja *nf* **1** DESCENSO **:** fall, drop **2 :** slump, recession **3 :** loss, casualty **4 dar de baja :** to discharge, to dismiss **5 darse de baja :** to withdraw, to drop out
bajada *nf* **1 :** descent **2 :** dip, slope **3 :** decrease, drop
bajar *vt* **1** DESCENDER **:** to lower, to let down, to take down **2** REDUCIR **:** to reduce (prices) 3 INCLINAR **:** to lower, to bow (the head) **4 :** to go down, to descend **5 bajar de categoría :** to downgrade — *vi* **1 :** to drop, to fall **2 :** to come down, to go down **3 :** to ebb (of tides) — **bajarse** *vr* **~ de :** to get off, to get out of (a vehicle)
bajeza *nf* **1 :** low or despicable act **2 :** baseness
bajío *nm* **1 :** lowland **2 :** shoal, sandbank, shallows
bajista *nmf* **:** bass player, bassist
bajo[1] *adv* **1 :** down, low **2 :** softly, quietly <habla más bajo : speak more softly>
bajo[2], **-ja** *adj* **1 :** low **2 :** short (of stature) **3 :** soft, faint, deep (of sounds) **4 :** lower <el bajo Amazonas : the lower Amazon> **5 :** lowered <con la mirada baja : with lowered eyes> **6 :** base, vile **7 los bajos fondos :** the underworld
bajo[3] *nm* **1 :** bass (musical instrument) **2 :** first floor, ground floor **3 :** hemline
bajo[4] *prep* **:** under, beneath, below
bajón *nm, pl* **bajones :** sharp drop, slump
bajorrelieve *m* **:** bas-relief
bala *nf* **1 :** bullet **2 :** bale
balacera *nf* TIROTEO **:** shoot-out, gunfight
balada *nf* **:** ballad
balance *nm* **1 :** balance **2 :** balance sheet
balancear *vt* **1 :** to balance **2 :** to swing (one's arms, etc.) **3 :** to rock (a boat) — **balancearse** *vr* **1** OSCILAR **:** to swing, to sway, to rock **2** VACILAR **:** to hesitate, to vacillate
balanceo *nm* **1 :** swaying, rocking **2 :** vacillation
balancín *nm, pl* **-cines 1 :** rocking chair **2** SUBIBAJA **:** seesaw
balandra *nf* **:** sloop
balanza *nf* BÁSCULA **:** scales *pl,* balance
balar *vi* **:** to bleat
balaustrada *nf* **:** balustrade
balaustre *nm* **:** baluster
balazo *nm* **1** TIRO **:** shot, gunshot **2 :** bullet wound
balboa *nf* **:** balboa (monetary unit of Panama)

balbucear *vi* **1 :** to mutter, to stammer **2 :** to prattle, to babble <los niños están balbuceando : the children are prattling away>

balbuceo *nm* **:** mumbling, stammering

balbucir → **balbucear**

balcánico, -ca *adj* **:** Balkan

balcón *nm, pl* **balcones :** balcony

balde *nm* **1** CUBO **:** bucket, pail **2 en ~ :** in vain, to no avail

baldío[1], **-día** *adj* **1 :** fallow, uncultivated **2 :** useless, vain

baldío[2] *nm* **1 :** wasteland **2** *Mex* **:** vacant lot

baldosa *nf* LOSETA **:** floor tile

balear *vt* **:** to shoot, to shoot at

balero *nm* **1** *Mex* **:** ball bearing **2** *Mex, PRi* **:** cup-and-ball toy

balido *nm* **:** bleat

balín *nm, pl* **balines :** pellet

balística *nf* **:** ballistics

balístico, -ca *adj* **:** ballistic

baliza *nf* **1 :** buoy **2 :** beacon (for aircraft)

ballena *nf* **:** whale

ballenero[1], **-ra** *adj* **:** whaling

ballenero[2], **-ra** *n* **:** whaler

ballenero[3] *nm* **:** whaleboat, whaler

ballesta *nf* **1 :** crossbow **2 :** spring (of an automobile)

ballet *nm* **:** ballet

balneario *nm* **:** spa, bathing resort

balompié *nm* FUTBOL **:** soccer

balón *nm, pl* **balones :** ball

baloncesto *nm* BASQUETBOL **:** basketball

balsa *nf* **1 :** raft **2 :** balsa

balsámico, -ca *adj* **:** soothing

bálsamo *nm* **:** balsam, balm

báltico, -ca *adj* **:** Baltic

baluarte *nm* BASTIÓN **:** bulwark, bastion

bambolear *vi* **1 :** to sway, to swing **2 :** to wobble — **bambolearse** *vr*

bamboleo *nm* **1 :** swaying, swinging **2 :** wobbling

bambú *nm, pl* **bambúes** *or* **bambús :** bamboo

banal *adj* **:** banal, trivial

banalidad *nf* **:** banality

banana *nf* **:** banana

bananero[1], **-ra** *adj* **:** banana

bananero[2] *nm* **:** banana tree

banano *nm* **1 :** banana tree **2** *CA,Col* **:** banana

banca *nf* **1 :** banking **2** BANCO **:** bench

bancada *nf* **1 :** group, faction **2 :** workbench

bancal *nm* **1 :** terrace (in agriculture) **2 :** plot (of land)

bancario, -ria *adj* **:** bank, banking

bancarrota *nf* QUIEBRA **:** bankruptcy

banco *nm* **1 :** bank <banco central : central bank> <banco de datos : data bank> <banco de arena : sandbank> <banco de sangre : blood bank> **2** BANCA **:** stool, bench **3 :** pew **4 :** school (of fish)

banda *nf* **1 :** band, strip **2** *Mex* **:** belt <banda transportadora : conveyor belt> **3 :** band (of musicians) **4 :** gang (of persons), flock (of birds) **5 banda de rodadura :** tread (of a tire, etc.) **6 banda sonora** *or* **banda de sonido :** sound track

bandada *nf* **:** flock (of birds), school (of fish)

bandazo *nm* **:** swerving, lurch

bandearse *vr* **:** to look after oneself, to cope

bandeja *nf* **:** tray, platter

bandera *nf* **:** flag, banner

banderazo *nm* **:** starting signal (in sports)

banderilla *nf* **:** banderilla, dart (in bullfighting)

banderín *nm, pl* **-rines :** pennant, small flag

bandidaje *nm* **:** banditry

bandido, -da *n* BANDOLERO **:** bandit, outlaw

bando *nm* **1** FACCIÓN **:** faction, side **2** EDICTO **:** proclamation

bandolerismo *nm* **:** banditry

bandolero, -ra *n* BANDIDO **:** bandit, outlaw

banjo *nm* **:** banjo

banquero, -ra *n* **:** banker

banqueta *nf* **1 :** footstool, stool, bench **2** *Mex* **:** sidewalk

banquete *nm* **:** banquet

banquetear *v* **:** to feast

banquillo *nm* **1 :** bench (in sports) **2 :** dock, defendant's seat

bañadera *nf* → **bañera**

bañar *vt* **1 :** to bathe, to wash **2 :** to immerse, to dip **3 :** to coat, to cover <bañado en lágrimas : bathed in tears> — **bañarse** *vr* **1 :** to take a bath, to bathe **2 :** to go for a swim

bañera *nf* TINA **:** bathtub

bañista *nmf* **:** bather

baño *nm* **1 :** bath **2 :** swim, dip **3 :** bathroom **4 baño María :** double-boiler

baqueta *nf* **1 :** ramrod **2 baquetas** *nfpl* **:** drumsticks

bar *nm* **:** bar, tavern

baraja *nf* **:** deck of cards

barajar *vt* **1 :** to shuffle (cards) **2 :** to consider, to toy with

baranda *nf* **:** rail, railing

barandal *nm* **1 :** rail, railing **2 :** bannister, handrail

barandilla *nf Spain* **:** bannister, handrail, railing

barata *nf* **1** *Mex* **:** sale, bargain **2** *Chile* **:** cockroach

baratija *nf* **:** bauble, trinket

baratillo *nm* **:** rummage sale, flea market

barato[1] *adv* **:** cheap, cheaply <te lo vendo barato : I'll sell it to you cheap>

barato[2], **-ta** *adj* **:** cheap, inexpensive

baratura *nf* **1 :** cheapness **2 :** cheap thing

barba *nf* **1 :** beard, stubble **2 :** chin

barbacoa *nf* **:** barbecue

bárbaramente *adv* : barbarously

barbaridad *nf* **1** : barbarity, atrocity **2 ¡qué barbaridad!** : that's outrageous!

barbarie *nf* : barbarism, savagery

bárbaro[1] *adv fam* : wildly <anoche lo pasamos bárbaro : we had a wild time last night>

bárbaro[2], **-ra** *adj* **1** : barbarous, wild, uncivilized **2** *fam* : great, fantastic

bárbaro[3], **-ra** *n* : barbarian

barbecho *nm* : fallow land <dejar en barbecho : to leave fallow>

barbero, -ra *n* : barber

barbilla *nf* MENTÓN : chin

barbitúrico *nm* : barbiturate

barbudo[1], **-da** *adj* : bearded

barbudo[2] *nm* : bearded man

barca *nf* **1** : boat **2 barca de pasaje** : ferryboat

barcaza *nf* : barge

barcia *nf* : chaff

barco *nm* **1** BARCA : boat **2** BUQUE, NAVE : ship

bardo *nm* : bard

bario *nm* : barium

barítono *nm* : baritone

barlovento *nm* : windward

barman *nm* : bartender

barniz *nm, pl* **barnices 1** LACA : varnish, lacquer **2** : glaze (on ceramics, etc.)

barnizar {21} *vt* **1** : to varnish **2** : to glaze

barométrico, -ca *adj* : barometric

barómetro *nm* : barometer

barón *nm, pl* **barones** : baron

baronesa *nf* : baroness

baronet *nm* : baronet

barquero, -ra : boatman *m,* boatwoman *f*

barquillo *nm* : wafer, thin cookie or cracker

barra *nf* : bar

barraca *nf* **1** CABAÑA, CHOZA : hut, cabin **2** : booth, stall

barracuda *nf* : barracuda

barranca *nf* **1** : hillside, slope **2** → **barranco**

barranco *nm* : ravine, gorge

barredora *nf* : street sweeper (machine)

barrena *nf* **1** TALADRO : drill, auger, gimlet **2** : tailspin

barrenar *vt* **1** : to drill **2** : to undermine

barrendero, -ra *n* : sweeper, street cleaner

barrer *v* : to sweep — **barrerse** *vr* : to slide (in sports)

barrera *nf* OBSTÁCULO : barrier, obstacle <barrera de sonido : sound barrier>

barreta *nf* : crowbar

barriada *nf* **1** : district, quarter **2** : slums *pl*

barrica *nf* BARRIL, TONEL : barrel, cask, keg

barricada *nf* : barricade

barrida *nf* **1** : sweep **2** : slide (in sports)

barrido *nm* : sweeping

barriga *nf* PANZA : belly, paunch

barrigón, -gona *adj, mpl* **-gones** *fam* : potbellied, paunchy

barril *nm* **1** BARRICA : barrel, keg **2 cerveza de barril** : draft beer

barrio *nm* **1** : neighborhood, district **2 barrios bajos** : slums *pl*

barro *nm* **1** LODO : mud **2** ARCILLA : clay **3** ESPINILLA, GRANO : pimple, blackhead

barroco, -ca *adj* : baroque

barroso, -sa *adj* ENLODADO : muddy

barrote *nm* : bar (on a window)

barrunto *nm* **1** SOSPECHA : suspicion **2** INDICIO : sign, indication, hint

bártulos *nmpl* : things, belongings <liar los bártulos : to pack one's things>

barullo *nm* BULLA : racket, ruckus

basa *nf* : base, pedestal

basalto *nm* : basalt

basar *vt* FUNDAR : to base — **basarse** *vr* FUNDARSE **~ en** : to be based on

báscula *nf* BALANZA : balance, scales *pl*

base *nf* **1** : base, bottom **2** : base (in baseball) **3** FUNDAMENTO : basis, foundation **4 base de datos** : database **5 a base de** : based on, by means of **6 en base a** : based on, on the basis of

básico, -ca *adj* FUNDAMENTAL : basic — **básicamente** *adv*

basílica *nf* : basilica

basquetbol *or* **básquetbol** *nm* BALONCESTO : basketball

basset *nm* : basset hound

bastante[1] *adv* **1** : enough, sufficiently <he trabajado bastante : I have worked enough> **2** : fairly, rather, quite <llegaron bastante temprano : they arrived quite early>

bastante[2] *adj* : enough, sufficient

bastante[3] *pron* : enough <hemos visto bastante : we have seen enough>

bastar *vi* : to be enough, to suffice

bastardilla *nf* CURSIVA : italic type, italics *pl*

bastardo, -da *adj & n* : bastard

bastidor *nm* **1** : framework, frame **2** : wing (in theater) <entre bastidores : backstage, behind the scenes>

bastilla *nf* : hem

bastión *nf, pl* **bastiones** BALUARTE : bastion, bulwark

basto, -ta *adj* : coarse, rough

bastón *nm, pl* **bastones 1** : cane, walking stick **2** : baton **3 bastón de mando** : staff (of authority)

basura *nf* DESECHOS : garbage, waste, refuse

basurero[1], **-ra** *n* : garbage collector

basurero[2] *nm Mex* : garbage can

bata *nf* **1** : bathrobe, housecoat **2** : smock, coverall, lab coat

batalla *nf* **1** : battle **2** : fight, struggle **3 de ~** : ordinary, everyday <mis

zapatos de batalla : my everyday shoes>
batallar *vi* LIDIAR, LUCHAR : to battle, to fight
batallón *nm, pl* **-llones** : battalion
batata *nf* : yam, sweet potato
batazo *nm* HIT : hit (in baseball)
bate *nm* : baseball bat
batea *nf* **1** : tray, pan **2** : flat-bottomed boat, punt
bateador, -dora *n* : batter, hitter
batear *vi* : to bat — *vt* : to hit
batería *nf* **1** PILA : battery **2** : drum kit, drums *pl* **3** : artillery **4 batería de cocina** : kitchen utensils *pl*
baterista *nmf* : drummer
batido *nm* LICUADO : milk shake
batidor *nm* : eggbeater, whisk, mixer
batidora *nf* : (electric) mixer
batir *vt* **1** GOLPEAR : to beat, to hit **2** VENCER : to defeat **3** REVOLVER : to mix, to beat **4** : to break (a record) — **batirse** *vr* : to fight
batista *nf* : batiste, cambric
batuta *nf* **1** : baton **2 llevar la batuta** : to be the leader, to call the tune
baúl *nm* : trunk, chest
bautismal *adj* : baptismal
bautismo *nm* : baptism, christening
bautista *adj & nmf* : Baptist
bautizar {21} *vt* : to baptize, to christen
bautizo *nm* → **bautismo**
bávaro, -ra *adj & n* : Bavarian
baya *nf* **1** : berry **2 baya de saúco** : elderberry
bayeta *nf* : cleaning cloth
bayoneta *nf* : bayonet
baza *nf* **1** : trick (in card games) **2 meter baza en** : to butt in on
bazar *nm* : bazaar
bazo *nm* : spleen
bazofia *nf* **1** : table scraps *pl* **2** : slop, swill **3** : hogwash, rubbish
bazuca *nf* : bazooka
beagle *nm* : beagle
beatificar {72} *vt* : to beatify — **beatificación** *nf*
beatífico, -ca *adj* : beatific
beatitud *nf* : beatitude
beato, -ta *adj* **1** : blessed **2** : pious, devout **3** : sanctimonious, overly devout
bebé *nm* : baby
bebedero *nm* **1** ABREVADERO : watering trough **2** *Mex* : drinking fountain
bebedor, -dora *n* : drinker
beber *v* TOMAR : to drink
bebida *nf* : drink, beverage
beca *nf* : grant, scholarship
becado, -da *n* : scholar, scholarship holder
becerro, -rra *n* : calf
begonia *nf* : begonia
beige *adj & nm* : beige
beisbol *or* **béisbol** *nm* : baseball
beisbolista *nmf* : baseball player
beldad *nf* BELLEZA, HERMOSURA : beauty
belén *nf, pl* **belenes** NACIMIENTO : Nativity scene
belga *adj & nmf* : Belgian
beliceño, -ña *adj & n* : Belizean
belicista[1] *adj* : militaristic
belicista[2] *nmf* : warmonger
bélico, -ca *adj* GUERRERO : war, fighting <esfuerzos bélicos : war efforts>
belicosidad *nf* : bellicosity
belicoso, -sa *adj* **1** : warlike, martial **2** : aggressive, belligerent
beligerancia *nf* : belligerence
beligerante *adj & nmf* : belligerent
bellaco[1], **-ca** *adj* : sly, cunning
bellaco[2], **-ca** *n* : rogue, scoundrel
belleza *nf* BELDAD, HERMOSURA : beauty
bello, -lla *adj* **1** HERMOSO : beautiful **2 bellas artes** : fine arts
bellota *nf* : acorn
bemol *nm* : flat (in music) — **bemol** *adj*
benceno *nm* : benzene
bendecir {11} *vt* **1** CONSAGRAR : to bless, to consecrate **2** ALABAR : to praise, to extol **3 bendecir la mesa** : to say grace
bendición *nf, pl* **-ciones** : benediction, blessing
bendiga, bendijo, etc. → **bendecir**
bendito, -ta *adj* **1** : blessed, holy **2** : fortunate **3** : silly, simple-minded
benedictino, -na *adj & n* : Benedictine
benefactor[1], **-tora** *adj* : beneficent
benefactor[2], **-tora** *n* : benefactor, benefactress *f*
beneficencia *nf* : beneficence, charity
beneficiar *vt* : to benefit, to be of assistance to — **beneficiarse** *vr* : to benefit, to profit
beneficiario, -ria *n* : beneficiary
beneficio *nm* **1** GANANCIA, PROVECHO : gain, profit **2** : benefit
beneficioso, -sa *adj* PROVECHOSO : beneficial
benéfico, -ca *adj* : charitable, beneficent
benemérito, -ta *adj* : meritorious, worthy
beneplácito *nm* : approval, consent
benevolencia *nf* BONDAD : benevolence, kindness
benévolo, -la *adj* BONDADOSO : benevolent, kind, good
bengala *nf* **luz de bengala 1** : flare (signal) **2** : sparkler
bengalí[1] *adj & nmf* : Bengali
bengalí[2] *nm* : Bengali (language)
benignidad *nf* : mildness, kindness
benigno, -na *adj* : benign, mild
beninés, -nesa *adj & n* : Beninese
benjamín, -mina *n, mpl* **-mines** : youngest child
beodo[1], **-da** *adj* : drunk, inebriated
beodo[2], **-da** *n* : drunkard
berberecho *nm* : cockle
berbiquí *nm* : brace (in carpentry)
berenjena *nf* : eggplant
bergantín *nm, pl* **-tines** : brig (ship)
berilo *nm* : beryl

bermudas *nfpl* : Bermuda shorts

berrear *vi* **1 :** to bellow, to low **2 :** to bawl, to howl

berrido *nm* **1 :** bellowing **2 :** howl, scream

berrinche *nm fam* **:** tantrum, conniption

berro *nm* : watercress

berza *nf* : cabbage

besar *vt* : to kiss

beso *nm* : kiss

bestia[1] *adj* **1 :** ignorant, stupid **2 :** boorish, rude

bestia[2] *nf* : beast, animal

bestia[3] *nmf* **1** IGNORANTE **:** ignoramus **2 :** brute

bestial *adj* **1 :** bestial, beastly **2** *fam* **:** huge, enormous <hace un frío bestial : it's terribly cold> **3** *fam* **:** great, fantastic

besuquear *vt fam* **:** to cover with kisses — **besuquearse** *vr fam* **:** to neck, to smooch

betabel *nm Mex* **:** beet

betún *nm, pl* **betunes 1 :** shoe polish **2** *Mex* **:** icing

bianual *adj* **:** biannual

biatlón *nm, pl* **-lones :** biathlon

biberón *nm, pl* **-rones :** baby's bottle

biblia *nf* **1 :** bible **2 la Biblia :** the Bible

bíblico, -ca *adj* **:** biblical

bibliografía *nf* **:** bibliography

bibliográfico, -ca *adj* **:** bibliographic, bibliographical

bibliógrafo, -fa *n* **:** bibliographer

biblioteca *nf* **:** library

bibliotecario, -ria *n* **:** librarian

bicameral *adj* **:** bicameral

bicarbonato *nm* **1 :** bicarbonate **2 bicarbonato de soda :** sodium bicarbonate, baking soda

bicentenario *nm* **:** bicentennial

bíceps *nms & pl* **:** biceps

bicho *nm* **:** small animal, bug, insect

bici *nf fam* **:** bike

bicicleta *nf* **:** bicycle

bicolor *adj* **:** two-tone

bicúspide *adj* **:** bicuspid

bidón *nm, pl* **bidones :** large can, (oil) drum

bien[1] *adv* **1 :** well <¿dormiste bien? : did you sleep well?> **2** CORRECTAMENTE **:** correctly, properly, right <hay que hacerlo bien : it must be done correctly> **3 :** very, quite <el libro era bien divertido : the book was very amusing> **4 :** easily <bien puede acabarlo en un día : he can easily finish it in a day> **5 :** willingly, readily <bien lo aceptaré : I'll gladly accept it> **6 bien que :** although **7 más bien :** rather

bien[2] *adj* **1 :** well, OK, all right <¿te sientes bien? : are you feeling all right?> **2 :** pleasant, agreeable <las flores huelen bien : the flowers smell very nice> **3 :** satisfactory **4 :** correct, right

bien[3] *nm* **1 :** good <el bien y el mal : good and evil> **2 bienes** *nmpl* **:** property, goods, possessions

bienal *adj & nf* **:** biennial — **bienalmente** *adv*

bienaventurado, -da *adj* **1 :** blessed **2 :** fortunate, happy

bienaventuranzas *nfpl* **:** Beatitudes

bienestar *nm* **1 :** welfare, well-being **2** CONFORT **:** comfort

bienhechor[1], **-chora** *adj* **:** beneficent, benevolent

bienhechor[2], **-chora** *n* **:** benefactor, benefactress *f*

bienintencionado, -da *adj* **:** well-meaning

bienvenida *nf* **1 :** welcome **2 dar la bienvenida a :** to welcome

bienvenido, -da *adj* **:** welcome

bies *nm* **:** bias (in sewing)

bife *nm Arg, Chile, Uru* **:** steak

bífido, -da *adj* **:** forked

bifocal *adj* **:** bifocal

bifocales *nmpl* **:** bifocals

bifurcación *nf, pl* **-ciones :** fork (in a river or road)

bifurcarse {72} *vr* **:** to fork

bigamia *nf* **:** bigamy

bígamo, -ma *n* **:** bigamist

bigote *nm* **1 :** mustache **2 :** whisker (of an animal)

bigotudo, -da *adj* **:** mustached, having a big mustache

bikini *nm* **:** bikini

bilateral *adj* **:** bilateral — **bilateralmente** *adv*

bilingüe *adj* **:** bilingual

bilioso, -sa *adj* **1 :** bilious **2 :** irritable

bilis *nf* **:** bile

billar *nm* **:** pool, billiards

billete *nm* **1 :** bill <un billete de cinco dólares : a five-dollar bill> **2** BOLETO **:** ticket <billete de ida y vuelta : round-trip ticket>

billetera *nf* **:** billfold, wallet

billón *nm, pl* **billones 1 :** billion (Great Britain) **2 :** trillion (U.S.A.)

bimestral *adj* **:** bimonthly — **bimestralmente** *adv*

bimotor *adj* **:** twin-engined

binacional *adj* **:** binational

binario, -ria *adj* **:** binary

binocular *adj* **:** binocular

binoculares *nmpl* **:** binoculars

binomio *nm* **:** binomial

biodegradable *adj* **:** biodegradable

biodegradarse *vr* **:** to biodegrade

biodiversidad *nf* **:** biodiversity

biofísica *nf* **:** biophysics

biofísico[1], **-ca** *adj* **:** biophysical

biofísico[2], **-ca** *n* **:** biophysicist

biografía *nf* **:** biography

biográfico, -ca *adj* **:** biographical

biógrafo, -fa *n* **:** biographer

biología *nf* **:** biology

biológico, -ca *adj* **:** biological, biologic — **biológicamente** *adv*

biólogo, -ga *n* **:** biologist

biombo *nm* MAMPARA **:** folding screen, room divider
biomecánica *nf* **:** biomechanics
biopsia *nf* **:** biopsy
bioquímica *nf* **:** biochemistry
bioquímico[1], -ca *adj* **:** biochemical
bioquímico[2], -ca *n* **:** biochemist
biosfera *or* **biósfera** *nf* **:** biosphere
biotecnología *nf* **:** biotechnology
biótico, -ca *adj* **:** biotic
bipartidismo *nm* **:** two-party system
bipartidista *adj* **:** bipartisan
bípedo *nm* **:** biped
birlar *vt fam* **:** to swipe, to pinch
birmano, -na *adj & n* **:** Burmese
bis[1] *adv* **1 :** twice, again (in music) **2 :** a, A <artículo 47 bis : Article 47A> <calle Bolívar, número 70 bis : Bolívar Street, number 70A>
bis[2] *nm* **:** encore
bisabuelo, -la *n* **:** great-grandfather *m,* great-grandmother *f,* great-grandparent
bisagra *nf* **:** hinge
bisbisar *vt fam* **:** to mutter, to mumble
bisecar {72} *vt* **:** bisect — **bisección** *nf*
bisel *nm* **:** bevel
biselar *vt* **:** to bevel
bisexual *adj* **:** bisexual
bisiesto *adj* **año bisiesto :** leap year
bismuto *nm* **:** bismuth
bisnieto, -ta *n* **:** great-grandson *m,* great-granddaughter *f,* great-grandchild
bisonte *nm* **:** bison, buffalo
bisoñé *nm* **:** hairpiece, toupee
bisoño[1], -ña *adj* **:** inexperienced, green
bisoño[2], -ña *n* **:** rookie, greenhorn
bistec *nm* **:** steak, beefsteak
bisturí *nm* ESCALPELO **:** scalpel
bisutería *nf* **:** costume jewelry
bit *nm* **:** bit (unit of information)
bituminoso, -sa *adj* **:** bituminous
bivalvo *nm* **:** bivalve
bizarría *nf* **1 :** courage, gallantry **2 :** generosity
bizarro, -rra *adj* **1** VALIENTE **:** courageous, valiant **2** GENEROSO **:** generous
bizco, -ca *adj* **:** cross-eyed
bizcocho *nm* **1 :** sponge cake **2 :** biscuit **3** *Mex* **:** breadstick
bizquera *nf* **:** crossed eyes, squint
blanco[1], -ca *adj* **:** white
blanco[2], -ca *n* **:** white person
blanco[3] *nm* **1 :** white **2 :** target, bull's-eye <dar en el blanco : to hit the target, to hit the nail on the head> **3 :** blank space, blank <un cheque en blanco : a blank check>
blancura *nf* **:** whiteness
blancuzco, -ca *adj* **1 :** whitish, off-white **2** PÁLIDO **:** pale
blandir {1} *vt* **:** to wave, to brandish
blando, -da *adj* **1** SUAVE **:** soft, tender **2 :** weak (in character) **3 :** lenient
blandura *nf* **1 :** softness, tenderness **2 :** leniency
blanqueador *nm* **:** bleach, whitener
blanquear *vt* **1 :** to whiten, to bleach **2 :** to shut out (in sports) **3 :** to launder (money) — *vi* **:** to turn white
blanquillo *nm CA, Mex* **:** egg
blasfemar *vi* **:** to blaspheme
blasfemia *nf* **:** blasphemy
blasfemo, -ma *adj* **:** blasphemous
blazer *nm* **:** blazer
bledo *nm* **no me importa un bledo** *fam* **:** I couldn't care less, I don't give a damn
blindado, -da *adj* ACORAZADO **:** armored
blindaje *nm* **1 :** armor, armor plating **2 :** shield (for cables, machinery, etc.)
bloc *nm, pl* **blocs :** writing pad, pad of paper
blof *nm Col, Mex* **:** bluff
blofear *vi Col, Mex* **:** to bluff
blondo, -da *adj* **:** blond, flaxen
bloque *nm* **1 :** block **2** GRUPO **:** bloc <el bloque comunista : the Communist bloc>
bloquear *vt* **1** OBSTRUIR **:** to block, to obstruct **2 :** to blockade
bloqueo *nm* **1** OBSTRUCCIÓN **:** blockage, obstruction **2 :** blockade
blusa *nf* **:** blouse
blusón *nm, pl* **blusones :** loose shirt, smock
boa *nf* **:** boa
boato *nm* **:** ostentation, show
bobada *nf* **:** folly, nonsense
bobalicón, -cona *adj, mpl* **-cones** *fam* **:** silly, stupid
bobina *nf* CARRETE **:** bobbin, reel
bobo[1], -ba *adj* **:** silly, stupid
bobo[2], -ba *n* **:** fool, simpleton
boca *nf* **1 :** mouth **2 boca arriba :** face up, on one's back **3 boca abajo :** face down, prone **4 boca de riego :** hydrant **5 en boca de :** according to
bocacalle *nf* **:** entrance to a street <gire a la última bocacalle : take the last turning>
bocadillo *nm Spain* **:** sandwich
bocado *nm* **1 :** bite, mouthful **2** FRENO **:** bit (of a bridle)
bocajarro *nm* **a ~ :** point-blank, directly
bocallave *nf* **:** keyhole
bocanada *nf* **1 :** swig, swallow **2 :** puff, mouthful (of smoke) **3 :** gust (of air) **4 :** stream (of people)
boceto *nm* **:** sketch, outline
bochinche *nm fam* **:** ruckus, uproar
bochorno *nm* **1** VERGÜENZA **:** embarrassment **2 :** hot and humid weather **3 :** hot flash
bochornoso, -sa *adj* **1** EMBARAZOSO **:** embarrassing **2 :** hot and muggy
bocina *nf* **1 :** horn, trumpet **2 :** automobile horn **3 :** mouthpiece (of a telephone) **4** *Mex* **:** loudspeaker
bocinazo *nm* **:** honk (of a horn)
bocio *nm* **:** goiter
bocón, -cona *n, mpl* **bocones** *fam* **:** blabbermouth, loudmouth
boda *nf* **:** wedding

bodega *nf* **1** : wine cellar **2** *Chile, Col, Mex* : storeroom, warehouse **3** (*in various countries*) : grocery store

bofetada *nf* CACHETADA : slap on the face

bofetear *vt* CACHETEAR : to slap

bofetón *nm* → **bofetada**

bofo, -fa *adj* : flabby

boga *nf* : fashion, vogue <estar en boga : to be in style>

bogotano[1], -na *adj* : of or from Bogotá

bogotano[2], -na *n* : person from Bogotá

bohemio, -mia *adj & n* : bohemian, Bohemian

boicot *nm, pl* **boicots** : boycott

boicotear *vt* : to boycott

boina *nf* : beret

boiserie *nf* : wood paneling, wainscoting

boj *nm, pl* **bojes** : box (plant), boxwood

bola *nf* **1** : ball <bola de nieve : snowball> **2** *fam* : lie, fib **3** *Mex fam* : bunch, group <una bola de rateros : a bunch of thieves> **4** *Mex* : uproar, tumult

bolear *vt Mex* : to polish (shoes)

bolera *nf* : bowling alley

bolero *nm* : bolero

boleta *nf* **1** : ballot **2** : ticket **3** : receipt

boletería *nf* TAQUILLA : box office, ticket office

boletín *nm, pl* **-tines 1** : bulletin **2** : journal, review **3 boletín de prensa** : press release

boleto *nm* BILLETE : ticket

boliche *nm* **1** BOLOS : bowling **2** *Arg* : bar, tavern

bolígrafo *nm* : ballpoint pen

bolillo *nm* **1** : bobbin **2** *Mex* : roll, bun

bolívar *nm* : bolivar (monetary unit of Venezuela)

boliviano[1], -na *adj & n* : Bolivian

boliviano[2] *nm* : boliviano (monetary unit of Bolivia)

bollo *nm* : bun, sweet roll

bolo *nm* : bowling pin, tenpin

bolos *nmpl* BOLICHE : bowling

bolsa *nf* **1** : bag, sack **2** *Mex* : pocketbook, purse **3** *Mex* : pocket **4 la Bolsa** : the stock market, the stock exchange **5 bolsa de trabajo** : employment agency

bolsear *vi Mex* : to pick pockets

bolsillo *nm* **1** : pocket **2 dinero de bolsillo** : pocket change, loose change

bolso *nm* : pocketbook, handbag

bomba *nf* **1** : bomb **2** : bubble **3** : pump <bomba de gasolina : gas pump>

bombachos *nmpl* : baggy pants, bloomers

bombardear *vt* **1** : to bomb **2** : to bombard

bombardeo *nm* **1** : bombing, shelling **2** : bombardment

bombardero *nm* : bomber (airplane)

bombástico, -ca *adj* : bombastic

bombear *vt* : to pump

bombero, -ra *n* : firefighter, fireman *m*

bombilla *nf* : lightbulb

bombillo *nm CA, Col, Ven* : lightbulb

bombo *nm* **1** : bass drum **2** *fam* : exaggerated praise, hype <con bombos y platillos : with great fanfare>

bombón *nm, pl* **bombones 1** : bonbon, chocolate **2** *Mex* : marshmallow

bonachón[1], -chona *adj, mpl* **-chones** *fam* : good-natured, kindhearted

bonachón[2], -chona *n, mpl* **-chones** *fam* BUENAZO : kindhearted person

bonaerense[1] *adj* : of or from Buenos Aires

bonaerense[2] *nmf* : person from Buenos Aires

bonanza *nf* **1** PROSPERIDAD : prosperity <bonanza económica : economic boom> **2** : calm weather **3** : rich ore deposit, bonanza

bondad *nf* BENEVOLENCIA : goodness, kindness <tener la bondad de hacer algo : to be kind enough to do something>

bondadoso, -sa *adj* BENÉVOLO : kind, kindly, good — **bondadosamente** *adv*

bonete *nm* : cap, mortarboard

boniato *nm* : sweet potato

bonificación *nf, pl* **-ciones 1** : discount **2** : bonus, extra

bonito[1] *adv* : nicely, well <¡qué bonito canta tu hermana! : your sister sings wonderfully!>

bonito[2], -ta *adj* LINDO : pretty, lovely <tiene un apartamento bonito : she has a nice apartment>

bonito[3] *nm* : bonito (tuna)

bono *nm* **1** : bond <bono bancario : bank bond> **2** : voucher

boqueada *nf* : gasp <to give one's last gasp : dar la última boqueada>

boquear *vi* **1** : to gasp **2** : to be dying

boquete *nm* : gap, opening, breach

boquiabierto, -ta *adj* : open-mouthed, speechless, agape

boquilla *nf* : mouthpiece (of a musical instrument)

borbollar *vi* : to bubble

borbotar *or* **borbotear** *vi* : to boil, to bubble, to gurgle

borboteo *nm* : bubbling, gurgling

borda *nf* : gunwale

bordado *nm* : embroidery, needlework

bordar *v* : to embroider

borde *nm* **1** : border, edge **2 al borde de** : on the verge of <estoy al borde de la locura : I'm about to go crazy>

bordear *vt* **1** : to border, to skirt <el Río Este bordea Manhattan : the East River borders Manhattan> **2** : to border on <bordea la irrealidad : it borders on unreality> **3** : to line <una calle bordeada de árboles : a street lined with trees>

bordillo *nm* : curb

bordo *nm* **a ~** : aboard, on board

boreal *adj* : northern

borgoña *nf* : burgundy

bórico, -ca *adj* : boric <ácido bórico : boric acid>

boricua *adj & nmf fam* : Puerto Rican

borinqueño, -ña → **boricua**

borla *nf* **1** : pom-pom, tassel **2** : powder puff

boro *nm* : boron

borrachera *nf* : drunkenness <agarró una borrachera : he got drunk>

borrachín, -china *n, mpl* **-chines** *fam* : lush, drunk

borracho[1], **-cha** *adj* EBRIO : drunk, intoxicated

borracho[2], **-cha** *n* : drunk, drunkard

borrador *nm* **1** : rough copy, first draft <en borrador : in the rough> **2** : eraser

borrar *vt* : to erase, to blot out — **borrarse** *vr* **1** : to fade, to fade away **2** : to resign, to drop out **3** *Mex fam* : to split, to leave <me borro : I'm out of here>

borrascoso, -sa *adj* : gusty, blustery

borrego, -ga *n* **1** : lamb, sheep **2** : simpleton, fool

borrico *nm* → **burro**

borrón *nm, pl* **borrones** : smudge, blot <borrón y cuenta nueva : let's start on a clean slate, let's start over again>

borronear *vt* : to smudge, to blot

borroso, -sa *adj* **1** : blurry, smudgy **2** CONFUSO : unclear, confused

boscoso, -sa *adj* : wooded

bosnio, -nia *adj & n* : Bosnian

bosque *nm* : woods, forest

bosquecillo *nm* : grove, copse, thicket

bosquejar *vt* ESBOZAR : to outline, to sketch

bosquejo *nm* **1** TRAZADO : outline, sketch **2** : draft

bostezar {21} *vi* : to yawn

bostezo *nm* : yawn

bota *nf* **1** : boot **2** : wineskin

botana *nf Mex* : snack, appetizer

botanear *vi Mex* : to have a snack

botánica *nf* : botany

botánico[1], **-ca** *adj* : botanical

botánico[2], **-ca** *n* : botanist

botar *vt* **1** ARROJAR : to throw, to fling, to hurl **2** TIRAR : to throw out, to throw away **3** : to launch (a ship)

bote *nm* **1** : small boat <bote de remos : rowboat> **2** : can, jar **3** : jump, bounce **4** *Mex fam* : jail

botella *nf* : bottle

botica *nf* FARMACIA : drugstore, pharmacy

boticario, -ria *n* FARMACÉUTICO : pharmacist, druggist

botín *nm, pl* **botines 1** : baby's bootee **2** : ankle boot **3** : booty, plunder

botiquín *nm, pl* **-quines 1** : medicine cabinet **2** : first-aid kit

botón *nm, pl* **botones 1** : button **2** : bud **3** INSIGNIA : badge

botones *nmfs & pl* : bellhop

botulismo *nm* : botulism

boulevard [ˌbuleˈvar] *nm* → **bulevar**

bouquet *nm* **1** : fragrance, bouquet (of wine) **2** RAMILLETE : bouquet (of flowers)

boutique *nf* : boutique

bóveda *nf* **1** : vault, dome **2** CRIPTA : crypt

bovino, -na *adj* : bovine

box *nm, pl* **boxes 1** : pit (in auto racing) **2** *Mex* : boxing

boxeador, -dora *n* : boxer

boxear *vi* : to box

boxeo *nm* : boxing

boya *nf* : buoy

boyante *adj* **1** : buoyant **2** : prosperous, thriving

bozal *nm* **1** : muzzle **2** : halter (for a horse)

bracear *vi* **1** : to wave one's arms **2** : to make strokes (in swimming)

bracero, -ra *n* : migrant worker, day laborer

braguero *nm* : truss (in medicine)

bragueta *nf* : fly, pants zipper

braille *adj & nm* : braille

bramante *nm* : twine, string

bramar *vi* **1** RUGIR : to roar, to bellow **2** : to howl (of the wind)

bramido *nm* : bellowing, roar

brandy *nm* : brandy

branquia *nf* AGALLA : gill

brasa *nf* ASCUA : ember, live coal

brasero *nm* : brazier

brasier *nm Col, Mex* : brassiere, bra

brasileño, -ña *adj & n* : Brazilian

bravata *nf* **1** JACTANCIA : boast, bravado **2** AMENAZA : threat

bravo, -va *adj* **1** FEROZ : ferocious, fierce <un perro bravo : a ferocious dog> **2** EXCELENTE : excellent, great <¡bravo! : bravo!, well done!> **3** : rough, rugged, wild **4** : annoyed, angry

bravucón, -cona *n, mpl* **-cones** : bully

bravuconadas *nfpl* : bravado

bravura *nf* **1** FEROCIDAD : fierceness, ferocity **2** VALENTÍA : bravery

braza *nf* **1** : breaststroke **2** : fathom (unit of length)

brazada *nf* : stroke (in swimming)

brazalete *nm* PULSERA : bracelet, bangle

brazo *nm* **1** : arm **2 brazo derecho** : right-hand man **3 brazos** *nmpl* : hands, laborers

brea *nf* ALQUITRÁN : tar, pitch

brebaje *nm* : potion, brew

brecha *nf* **1** : gap, breach <estar siempre en la brecha : to be always there when needed, to stay in the thick of things> **2** : gash

brécol *nm* : broccoli

brega *nf* **1** LUCHA : struggle, fight **2** : hard work

bregar {52} *vi* **1** LUCHAR : to struggle **2** : to toil, to work hard **3 ~ con** : to deal with

brete *nm* : jam, tight spot

breve *adj* **1** CORTO : brief, short **2 en ~** : shortly, in short — **brevemente** *adv*

brevedad *nf* : brevity, shortness

breviario *nm* : breviary

brezal *nm* : heath, moor
brezo *nm* : heather
bribón, -bona *n, mpl* **bribones** : rascal, scamp
bricolaje *or* **bricolage** *nm* : do-it-yourself
brida *nf* : bridle
brigada *nf* **1** : brigade **2** : gang, team, squad
brigadier *nm* : brigadier
brillante[1] *adj* : brilliant, bright — **brillantemente** *adv*
brillante[2] *nm* DIAMANTE : diamond
brillantez *nf* : brilliance, brightness
brillar *vi* : to shine, to sparkle
brillo *nm* **1** LUSTRE : luster, shine **2** : brilliance
brilloso, -sa *adj* LUSTROSO : lustrous, shiny
brincar {72} *vi* **1** SALTAR : to jump around, to leap about **2** : to frolic, to gambol
brinco *nm* **1** SALTO : jump, leap, skip **2** **pegar un brinco** : to give a start, to jump
brindar *vi* : to drink a toast <brindó por los vencedores : he toasted the victors> — *vt* OFRECER, PROPORCIONAR : to offer, to provide — **brindarse** *vr* : to offer one's assistance, to volunteer
brindis *nm* : toast, drink <hacer un brindis : to drink a toast>
brinque, etc. → **brincar**
brío *nm* **1** : force, determination **2** : spirit, verve
brioso, -sa *adj* : spirited, lively
briqueta *nf* : briquette
brisa *nf* : breeze
británico[1], **-ca** *adj* : British
británico[2], **-ca** *n* **1** : British person **2** **los británicos** : the British
brizna *nf* **1** : strand, thread **2** : blade (of grass)
brocado *nm* : brocade
brocha *nf* : paintbrush
broche *nm* **1** ALFILER : brooch **2** : fastener, clasp **3** **broche de oro** : finishing touch
brocheta *nf* : skewer
brócoli *nm* : broccoli
broma *nf* **1** CHISTE : joke, prank **2** : fun, merriment **3** **en ~** : in jest, jokingly
bromear *vi* : to joke, to fool around <sólo estaba bromeando : I was only kidding>
bromista[1] *adj* : fun-loving, joking
bromista[2] *nmf* : joker, prankster
bromo *nm* : bromine
bronca *nf fam* : fight, quarrel, fuss
bronce *nm* : bronze
bronceado[1], **-da** *adj* **1** : tanned, suntanned **2** : bronze
bronceado[2] *nm* **1** : suntan, tan **2** : bronzing
broncearse *vr* : to get a suntan
bronco, -ca *adj* **1** : harsh, rough **2** : untamed, wild
bronquial *adj* : bronchial
bronquio *nm* : bronchial tube, bronchus
bronquitis *nf* : bronchitis
broqueta *nf* : skewer
brotar *vi* **1** : to bud, to sprout **2** : to spring up, to stream, to gush forth **3** : to break out, to appear
brote *nm* **1** : outbreak **2** : sprout, bud, shoot
broza *nf* **1** : brushwood **2** MALEZA : scrub, undergrowth
brujería *nf* HECHICERÍA : witchcraft, sorcery
brujo[1], **-ja** *adj* : bewitching
brujo[2], **-ja** *n* : warlock *m,* witch *f,* sorcerer
brújula *nf* : compass
bruma *nf* : haze, mist
brumoso, -sa *adj* : hazy, misty
bruñir {38} *vt* : to burnish, to polish (metals)
brusco, -ca *adj* **1** SÚBITO : sudden, abrupt **2** : curt, brusque — **bruscamente** *adv*
brusquedad *nf* **1** : abruptness, suddenness **2** : brusqueness
brutal *adj* **1** : brutal **2** *fam* : incredible, terrific — **brutalmente** *adv*
brutalidad *nf* CRUELDAD : brutality
brutalizar {21} *vt* : to brutalize, to maltreat
bruto[1], **-ta** *adj* **1** : gross <peso bruto : gross weight> <ingresos brutos : gross income> **2** : unrefined <petróleo bruto : crude oil> **3** : brutish, stupid
bruto[2], **-ta** *n* **1** : brute **2** : dunce, blockhead
bucal *adj* : oral
bucanero *nm* : buccaneer, pirate
buccino *nm* : whelk
buceador, -dora *n* : diver, scuba diver
bucear *vi* **1** : to dive, to swim underwater **2** : to explore, to delve
buceo *nm* **1** : diving, scuba diving **2** : exploration, searching
buche *nm* **1** : crop (of a bird) **2** *fam* : belly, gut **3** : mouthful <hacer buches : to rinse one's mouth>
bucle *nm* **1** : curl, ringlet **2** : loop
bucólico, -ca *adj* : bucolic
budín *nm, pl* **budines** : pudding
budismo *nm* : Buddhism
budista *adj & nmf* : Buddhist
buen → **bueno**[1]
buenamente *adv* **1** : easily **2** : willingly
buenaventura *nf* **1** : good luck **2** : fortune, future <le dijo la buenaventura : she told his fortune>
buenazo, -za *n fam* BONACHÓN : kind-hearted person
bueno[1], **-na** *adj* (**buen** *before masculine singular nouns*) **1** : good <una buena idea : a good idea> **2** BONDADOSO : nice, kind **3** APROPIADO : proper, appropriate **4** SANO : well, healthy **5** : considerable, goodly <una buena cantidad : a lot> **6** **buenos días**

: hello, good day **7 buenas tardes** : good afternoon **8 buenas noches** : good evening, good night

bueno[2] *interj* **1** : OK!, all right! **2** *Mex* : hello! (on the telephone)

buey *nm* : ox, steer

búfalo *nm* **1** : buffalo **2 búfalo de agua** : water buffalo

bufanda *nf* : scarf, muffler

bufar *vi* : to snort

bufet *or* **bufé** *nm* : buffet-style meal

bufete *nm* **1** : law firm, law office **2** : writing desk

bufido *nm* : snort

bufo, -fa *adj* : comic

bufón, -fona *n, mpl* **bufones** : clown, buffoon, jester

bufonada *nf* **1** : jest, buffoonery **2** : sarcasm

buhardilla *nf* **1** ÁTICO, DESVÁN : attic **2** : dormer window

búho *nm* **1** : owl **2** *fam* : hermit, recluse

buhonero, -ra *n* MERCACHIFLE : peddler

buitre *nm* : vulture

bujía *nf* : spark plug

bulbo *nm* : bulb

bulboso, -sa *adj* : bulbous

bulevar *nm* : boulevard

búlgaro, -ra *adj & n* : Bulgarian

bulla *nf* BARULLO : racket, rowdiness

bullicio *nm* **1** : ruckus, uproar **2** : hustle and bustle

bullicioso, -sa *adj* : noisy, busy, turbulent

bullir {38} *vi* **1** HERVIR : to boil **2** MOVERSE : to stir, to bustle about

bulto *nm* **1** : package, bundle **2** : piece of luggage, bag **3** : size, bulk, volume **4** : form, shape **5** : lump (on the body), swelling, bulge

bumerán *nm, pl* **-ranes** : boomerang

búnker *nm, pl* **búnkers** : bunker

búnquer *nm* → **búnker**

buñuelo *nm* : fried pastry

buque *nm* BARCO : ship, vessel

burbuja *nf* : bubble, blister (on a surface)

burbujear *vi* **1** : to bubble **2** : to fizz

burbujeo *nm* : bubbling

burdel *nm* : brothel, whorehouse

burdo, -da *adj* **1** : coarse, rough **2** : crude, clumsy <una burda mentira : a clumsy lie> — **burdamente** *adj*

burgués, -guesa *adj & n, mpl* **burgueses** : bourgeois

burguesía *nf* : bourgeoisie, middle class

burla *nf* **1** : mockery, ridicule **2** : joke, trick **3 hacer burla de** : to make fun of, to mock

burlar *vt* ENGAÑAR : to trick, to deceive — **burlarse** *vr* **~ de** : to make fun of, to ridicule

burlesco, -ca *adj* : burlesque, comic

burlón[1], **-lona** *adj, mpl* **burlones** : joking, mocking

burlón[2], **-lona** *n, mpl* **burlones** : joker

burocracia *nf* : bureaucracy

burócrata *nmf* : bureaucrat

burocrático, -ca *adj* : bureaucratic

burrada *nf fam* : stupid act, nonsense

burrito *nm* : burrito

burro[1], **-rra** *adj fam* : dumb, stupid

burro[2], **-rra** *n* **1** ASNO : donkey, ass **2** *fam* : dunce, poor student

burro[3] *nm* **1** : sawhorse **2** *Mex* : ironing board **3** *Mex* : stepladder

bursátil *adj* : stock-market

burundés, -desa *adj & n* : Burundian

bus *nm* : bus

busca *nf* : search

buscador, -dora *n* : hunter (for treasure, etc.), prospector

buscapleitos *nmfs & pl* : troublemaker

buscar {72} *vt* **1** : to look for, to seek **2** : to pick up, to collect **3** : to provoke — *vi* : to look, to search <buscó en los bolsillos : he searched through his pockets>

buscavidas *nmfs & pl* **1** : busybody **2** : go-getter

busque, etc. → **buscar**

búsqueda *nf* : search

busto *nm* : bust

butaca *nf* **1** SILLÓN : armchair **2** : seat (in a theatre) **3** *Mex* : pupil's desk

butano *nm* : butane

buzo[1], **-za** *adj Mex fam* : smart, astute <¡ponte buzo! : get with it!, get on the ball!>

buzo[2] *nm* : diver, scuba diver

buzón *nm, pl* **buzones** : mailbox

byte *nm* : byte

C

c *nf* : third letter of the Spanish alphabet

cabal *adj* **1** : exact, correct **2** : complete **3** : upright, honest

cabales *nmpl* **no estar en sus cabales** : not to be in one's right mind

cabalgar {52} *vi* : to ride (on horseback)

cabalgata *nf* : cavalcade, procession

cabalidad *nf* **a ~** : thoroughly, conscientiously

caballa *nf* : mackerel

caballada *nf* **1** : herd of horses **2** *fam* : nonsense, stupidity, outrageousness

caballar *adj* EQUINO : horse, equine

caballeresco, -ca *adj* : gallant, chivalrous

caballería *nf* **1** : cavalry **2** : horse, mount **3** : knighthood, chivalry

caballeriza *nf* : stable

caballero[1] → **caballeroso**

caballero[2] *nm* **1** : gentleman **2** : knight

caballerosidad *nf* **:** chivalry, gallantry
caballeroso, -sa *adj* **:** gentlemanly, chivalrous
caballete *nm* **1 :** ridge **2 :** easel **3 :** trestle (for a table, etc.) **4 :** bridge (of the nose) **5 :** sawhorse
caballista *nmf* **:** horseman *m,* horsewoman *f*
caballito *nm* **1 :** rocking horse **2 caballito de mar :** seahorse **3 caballitos** *nmpl* **:** merry-go-round
caballo *nm* **1 :** horse **2 :** knight (in chess) **3 caballo de fuerza** *or* **caballo de vapor :** horsepower
cabalmente *adv* **:** fully, exactly
cabaña *nf* CHOZA **:** cabin, hut
cabaret *nm, pl* **-rets :** nightclub, cabaret
cabecear *vt* **:** to head (in soccer) — *vi* **1 :** to nod one's head **2 :** to lurch, to pitch
cabecera *nf* **1 :** headboard **2 :** head <cabecera de la mesa : head of the table> **3 :** heading, headline **4 :** headwaters *pl* **5 médico de cabecera :** family doctor **6 cabecera municipal** *CA, Mex* **:** downtown area
cabecilla *nmf* **:** ringleader, kingpin
cabellera *nf* **:** head of hair, mane
cabello *nm* **:** hair
cabelludo, -da *adj* **1 :** hairy **2 cuero cabelludo :** scalp
caber {12} *vi* **1 :** to fit, to go <no sé si cabremos todos en el coche : I don't know if we'll all fit in the car> **2 :** to be possible <no cabe duda alguna : there's no doubt about it> <cabe que llegue mañana : he may come tomorrow>
cabestro *nm* **:** halter (for an animal)
cabeza *nf* **1 :** head **2 cabeza hueca :** scatterbrain **3 de ~ :** head first **4 dolor de cabeza :** headache
cabezada *nf* **1 :** butt, blow with the head **2 :** nod <echar una cabezada : to take a nap, to doze off>
cabezal *nm* **:** bolster
cabezazo *nm* **:** butt, blow with the head
cabezón, -zona *adj, mpl* **-zones** *fam* **1 :** having a big head **2 :** pigheaded, stubborn
cabida *nf* **1 :** room, space, capacity **2 dar cabida a :** to accomodate, to hold
cabildear *vi* **:** to lobby
cabildeo *nm* **:** lobbying
cabildero, -ra *n* **:** lobbyist
cabildo *nm* AYUNTAMIENTO **1 :** town or city hall **2 :** town or city council
cabina *nf* **1 :** cabin **2 :** booth **3 :** cab (of a truck), cockpit (of an airplane)
cabizbajo, -ja *adj* **:** dejected, downcast
cable *nm* **:** cable
cableado *nm* **:** wiring
cabo *nm* **1 :** end <al cabo de dos semanas : at the end of two weeks> **2 :** stub, end piece **3 :** corporal **4 :** cape, headland <el Cabo Cañaveral : Cape Canaveral> **5 al fin y al cabo :** after all, in the end **6 llevar a cabo :** to carry out, to do
caboverdiano, -na *adj & n* **:** Cape Verdean
cabrá, etc. → **caber**
cabra *nf* **:** goat
cabrestante *nm* **:** windlass
cabrío, -ría *adj* **:** goat, caprine
cabriola *nf* **1 :** skip, jump **2 hacer cabriolas :** to prance
cabriolar *vi* **:** to prance
cabrito *nm* **:** kid, baby goat
cabús *nm, pl* **cabuses** *Mex* **:** caboose
cacahuate *or* **cacahuete** *nm* **:** peanut
cacalote *nm Mex* **:** crow
cacao *nm* **:** cacao, cocoa bean
cacarear *vi* **:** to crow, to cackle, to cluck — *vt fam* **:** to boast about, to crow about <cacarear un huevo : to brag about an accomplishment>
cacatúa *nf* **:** cockatoo
cace, etc. → **cazar**
cacería *nf* **1** CAZA **:** hunt, hunting **2 :** hunting party
cacerola *nf* **:** pan, saucepan
cacha *nf* **:** butt (of a gun)
cachar *vt fam* **:** to catch
cacharro *nm* **1** *fam* **:** thing, piece of junk **2** *fam* **:** jalopy **3 cacharros** *nmpl* **:** pots and pans
cache *nm* **:** cache, cache memory
cachear *vt* **:** to search, to frisk
cachemir *nm* **:** cashmere
cachetada *nf* BOFETADA **:** slap on the face
cachete *nm* **:** cheek
cachetear *vt* BOFETEAR **:** to slap
cachiporra *nf* **:** bludgeon, club, blackjack
cachirul *nm Mex fam* **:** cheating <hacer cachirul : to cheat>
cachivache *nm fam* **:** thing <mete tus cachivaches en el maletero : put your stuff in the trunk>
cacho *nm fam* **:** piece, bit
cachorro, -rra *n* **1 :** cub **2** PERRITO **:** puppy
cachucha *nf Mex* **:** cap, baseball cap
cacique *nm* **1 :** chief (of a tribe) **2 :** boss (in politics)
cacofonía *nf* **:** cacophony
cacofónico, -ca *adj* **:** cacophonous
cacto *nm* **:** cactus
cactus *nm* → **cacto**
cada *adj* **1 :** each <cuestan diez pesos cada una : they cost ten pesos each> **2 :** every <cada vez : every time> **3 :** such, some <sales con cada historia : you come up with such crazy stories> **4 cada vez más :** more and more, increasingly **5 cada vez menos :** less and less
cadalso *nm* **:** scaffold, gallows
cadáver *nm* **:** corpse, cadaver
cadavérico, -ca *adj* **1 :** cadaverous **2** PÁLIDO **:** deathly pale
caddie *or* **caddy** *nmf, pl* **caddies :** caddy

cadena *nf* **1** : chain **2** : network, channel **3 cadena de montaje** : assembly line **4 cadena perpetua** : life sentence

cadencia *nf* : cadence, rhythm

cadencioso, -sa *adj* : rhythmic, rhythmical

cadera *nf* : hip

cadete *nmf* : cadet

cadmio *nm* : cadmium

caducar {72} *vi* : to expire

caducidad *nf* : expiration

caduco, -ca *adj* **1** : outdated, obsolete **2** : deciduous

caer {13} *vi* **1** : to fall, to drop **2** : to collapse **3** : to hang (down) **4 caer bien** *fam* : to be pleasant, to be likeable <me caes bien : I like you> **5 caer mal** *or* **caer gordo** *fam* : to be unpleasant, to be unlikeable — **caerse** *vr* : to fall down

café[1] *adj* : brown <ojos cafés : brown eyes>

café[2] *nm* **1** : coffee **2** : café

cafeína *nf* : caffeine

cafetal *nm* : coffee plantation

cafetalero[1], **-ra** *adj* : coffee <cosecha cafetalera : coffee harvest>

cafetalero[2], **-ra** *n* : coffee grower

cafetera *nf* : coffeepot, coffeemaker

cafetería *nf* **1** : coffee shop, café **2** : lunchroom, cafeteria

cafetero[1], **-ra** *adj* : coffee-producing

cafetero[2], **-ra** *n* : coffee grower

cafeticultura *nf Mex* : coffee industry

caguama *nf* **1** : large Caribbean turtle **2** *Mex* : large bottle of beer

caída *nf* **1** BAJA, DESCENSO : fall, drop **2** : collapse, downfall

caiga, etc. → **caer**

caimán *nm, pl* **caimanes** : alligator, caiman

caimito *nm* : star apple

caja *nf* **1** : box, case **2** : cash register, checkout counter **3** : bed (of a truck) **4** *fam* : coffin **5 caja fuerte** *or* **caja de caudales** : safe **6 caja de seguridad** : safe-deposit box **7 caja torácica** : rib cage

cajero, -ra *n* **1** : cashier **2** : teller **3 cajero automático** : automated teller machine, ATM

cajeta *nf Mex* : a sweet carmel-flavored spread

cajetilla *nf* : pack (of cigarettes)

cajón *nm, pl* **cajones 1** : drawer, till **2** : crate, case **3 cajón de estacionamiento** *Mex* : parking space

cajuela *nf Mex* : trunk (of a car)

cal *nf* : lime, quicklime

cala *nf* : cove, inlet

calabacín *nm, pl* **-cines** : zucchini

calabacita *nf Mex* : zucchini

calabaza *nf* **1** : pumpkin, squash **2** : gourd **3 dar calabazas a** : to give the brush-off to, to jilt

calabozo *nm* **1** : prison **2** : jail cell

calado[1], **-da** *adj* **1** : drenched **2** : openworked

calado[2] *nm* **1** : draft (of a ship) **2** : openwork

calafatear *vt* : to caulk

calamar *nm* **1** : squid **2 calamares** *nmpl* : calamari

calambre *nm* **1** ESPASMO : cramp **2** : electric shock, jolt

calamidad *nf* DESASTRE : calamity, disaster

calamina *nf* : calamine

calamitoso, -sa *adj* : calamitous, disastrous

calaña *nf* : ilk, kind, sort <una persona de mala calaña : a bad sort>

calar *vt* **1** : to soak through **2** : to pierce, to penetrate — *vi* : to catch on — **calarse** *vr* : to get drenched

calavera[1] *nf* **1** : skull **2** *Mex* : taillight

calavera[2] *nm* : rake, rogue

calcar {72} *vt* **1** : to trace **2** : to copy, to imitate

calce, etc. → **calzar**

calceta *nf* : knee-high stocking

calcetería *nf* : hosiery

calcetín *nm, pl* **-tines** : sock

calcificar {72} *v* : to calcify — **calcificarse** *vr*

calcinar *vt* : to char, to burn

calcio *nm* : calcium

calco *nm* **1** : transfer, tracing **2** : copy, image

calcomanía *nf* : decal, transfer

calculador, -dora *adj* : calculating

calculadora *nf* : calculator

calcular *vt* **1** : to calculate, to estimate **2** : to plan, to scheme

cálculo *nm* **1** : calculation, estimation **2** : calculus **3** : plan, scheme **4 cálculo biliar** : gallstone **5 hoja de cálculo** : spreadsheet

caldas *nfpl* : hot springs

caldear *vt* : to heat, to warm — **caldearse** *vr* **1** : to heat up **2** : to become heated, to get tense

caldera *nf* **1** : cauldron **2** : boiler

caldo *nm* **1** CONSOMÉ : broth, stock **2 caldo de cultivo** : culture medium, breeding ground

caldoso, -sa *adj* : watery

calefacción *nf, pl* **-ciones** : heating, heat

calefactor *nm* : heater

caleidoscopio *nm* → **calidoscopio**

calendario *nm* **1** : calendar **2** : timetable, schedule

caléndula *nf* : marigold

calentador *nm* : heater

calentamiento *nm* **1** : heating, warming **2** : warm-up (in sports)

calentar {55} *vt* **1** : to heat, to warm **2** *fam* : to annoy, to anger **3** *fam* : to excite, to turn on — **calentarse** *vr* **1** : to get warm, to heat up **2** : to warm up (in sports) **3** *fam* : to become sexually aroused **4** *fam* : to get mad

calentura *nf* **1** FIEBRE : temperature, fever **2** : cold sore

calibrador *nm* : gauge, calipers *pl*

calibrar *vt* : to calibrate — **calibración** *nf*
calibre *nm* **1** : caliber, gauge **2** : importance, excellence **3** : kind, sort <un problema de grueso calibre : a serious problem>
calidad *nf* **1** : quality, grade **2** : position, status **3 en calidad de** : as, in the capacity of
cálido, -da *adj* **1** : hot <un clima cálido : a hot climate> **2** : warm <una cálida bienvenida : a warm welcome>
calidoscopio *nm* : kaleidoscope
caliente *adj* **1** : hot, warm <mantenerse caliente : to stay warm> **2** : heated, fiery <una disputa caliente : a heated argument> **3** *fam* : sexually excited, horny
califa *nm* : caliph
calificación *nf, pl* **-ciones 1** NOTA : grade (for a course) **2** : rating, score **3** CLASIFICACIÓN : qualification, qualifying <ronda de calificación : qualifying round>
calificar {72} *vt* **1** : to grade **2** : to describe, to rate <la calificaron de buena alumna : they described her as a good student> **3** : to qualify, to modify (in grammar)
calificativo[1], **-va** *adj* : qualifying
calificativo[2] *nm* : qualifier, epithet
caligrafía *nf* **1** ESCRITURA : handwriting **2** : calligraphy
calistenia *nf* : calisthenics
cáliz *nm, pl* **cálices 1** : chalice, goblet **2** : calyx
caliza *nf* : limestone
callado, -da *adj* : quiet, silent — **calladamente** *adv*
callar *vi* : to keep quiet, to be silent — *vt* **1** : to silence, to hush <¡calla a los niños! : keep the children quiet!> **2** : to keep secret — **callarse** *vr* : to remain silent <¡cállate! : be quiet!, shut up!>
calle *nf* : street, road
callejear *vi* : to wander about the streets, to hang out
callejero, -ra *adj* : street <perro callejero : stray dog>
callejón *nm, pl* **-jones 1** : alley **2 callejón sin salida** : dead-end street
callo *nm* : callus, corn
calloso, -sa *adj* : callous
calma *nf* : calm, quiet
calmante[1] *adj* : calming, soothing
calmante[2] *nm* : tranquilizer, sedative
calmar *vt* TRANQUILIZAR : to calm, to soothe — **calmarse** *vr* : to calm down
calmo, -ma *adj* TRANQUILO : calm, tranquil
calmoso, -sa *adj* **1** TRANQUILO : calm, quiet **2** LENTO : slow, sluggish
calor *nm* **1** : heat <hace calor : it's hot outside> <tener calor : to feel hot> **2** : warmth, affection **3** : ardor, passion
caloría *nf* : calorie
calórico, -ca *adj* : caloric
calque, etc. → **calcar**
calumnia *nf* : slander, libel — **calumnioso, -sa** *adj*
calumniar *vt* : to slander, to libel
caluroso, -sa *adj* **1** : hot **2** : warm, enthusiastic
calva *nf* : bald spot, bald head
calvario *nm* **1** : Calvary **2** : Stations of the Cross *pl* **3 vivir un calvario** : to suffer great adversity
calvicie *nf* : baldness
calvo[1], **-va** *adj* : bald
calvo[2], **-va** *n* : bald person
calza *nf* : block, wedge
calzada *nf* : roadway, avenue
calzado *nm* : footwear
calzador *nm* : shoehorn
calzar {21} *vt* **1** : to wear (shoes) <¿de cuál calza? : what is your shoe size?> <siempre calzaban tenis : they always wore sneakers> **2** : to provide with shoes
calzo *nm* : chock, wedge
calzoncillos *nmpl* : underpants, briefs
calzones *nmpl* : underpants, panties
cama *nf* **1** : bed **2 cama elástica** : trampoline
camada *nf* : litter, brood
camafeo *nm* : cameo
camaleón *nm, pl* **-leones** : chameleon
cámara *nf* **1** : camera **2** : chamber, room **3** : house (in government) **4** : inner tube
camarada *nmf* **1** : comrade, companion **2** : colleague
camaradería *nf* : camaraderie
camarero, -ra *n* **1** MESERO : waiter, waitress *f* **2** : bellboy *m*, chambermaid *f* (in a hotel) **3** : steward *m*, stewardess *f* (on a ship, etc.)
camarilla *nf* : political clique
camarógrafo, -fa *n* : cameraman *m*, camerawoman *f*
camarón *nm, pl* **-rones 1** : shrimp **2** : prawn
camarote *nm* : cabin, stateroom
camastro *nm* : small hard bed, pallet
cambalache *nm fam* : swap
cambiante *adj* **1** : changing **2** VARIABLE : changeable, variable
cambiar *vt* **1** ALTERAR, MODIFICAR : to change **2** : to exchange, to trade — *vi* **1** : to change **2 cambiar de velocidad** : to shift gears — **cambiarse** *vr* **1** : to change (clothing) **2** MUDARSE : to move (to a new address)
cambio *nm* **1** : change, alteration **2** : exchange **3** : change (money) **4 en cambio** : instead **5 en cambio** : however, on the other hand
cambista *nmf* : exchange broker
camboyano, -na *adj & n* : Cambodian
cambur *nm Ven* : banana
camelia *nf* : camellia
camello *nm* : camel
camellón *nm, pl* **-llones** *Mex* : traffic island
camerino *nm* : dressing room
camerunés, -nesa *adj, mpl* **-neses** : Cameroonian

camilla *nf* : stretcher

camillero, -ra *n* : orderly (in a hospital)

caminante *nmf* : wayfarer, walker

caminar *vi* ANDAR : to walk, to move — *vt* : to walk, to cover (a distance)

caminata *nf* : hike, long walk

camino *nm* **1** : path, road **2** : journey <ponerse en camino : to set off> **3** : way <a medio camino : halfway there>

camión *nm, pl* **camiones 1** : truck **2** *Mex* : bus

camionero, -ra *n* **1** : truck driver **2** *Mex* : bus driver

camioneta *nm* : light truck, van

camisa *nf* **1** : shirt **2 camisa de fuerza** : straitjacket

camiseta *nf* **1** : T-shirt **2** : undershirt

camisón *nm, pl* **-sones** : nightshirt, nightgown

camorra *nf fam* : fight, trouble <buscar camorra : to pick a fight>

camote *nm* **1** : root vegetable similar to the sweet potato **2 hacerse camote** *Mex fam* : to get mixed up

campal *adj* : pitched, fierce <batalla campal : pitched battle>

campamento *nm* : camp

campana *nf* : bell

campanada *nf* TAÑIDO : stroke (of a bell), peal

campanario *nm* : bell tower, belfry

campanilla *nf* **1** : small bell, handbell **2** : uvula

campante *adj* : nonchalant, smug <seguir tan campante : to go on as if nothing had happened>

campaña *nf* **1** CAMPO : countryside, country **2** : campaign **3 tienda de campaña** : tent

campañol *nm* : vole

campechana *nf Mex* : puff pastry

campechanía *nf* : geniality

campechano, -na *adj* : open, cordial, friendly

campeón, -peona *n, mpl* **-peones** : champion

campeonato *nm* : championship

cámper *nm* : camper (vehicle)

campero, -ra *adj* : country, rural

campesino, -na *n* : peasant, farm laborer

campestre *adj* : rural, rustic

camping *nm* **1** : camping **2** : campsite

campiña *nf* CAMPO : countryside, country

campista *nmf* : camper

campo *nm* **1** CAMPAÑA : countryside, country **2** : field <campo de aviación : airfield> <su campo de responsabilidad : her field of responsibility>

camposanto *nm* : graveyard, cemetery

campus *nms & pl* : campus

camuflaje *nm* : camouflage

camuflajear *vt* : to camouflage

camuflar → **camuflajear**

can *nm* : hound, dog

cana *nf* **1** : gray hair **2 salirle canas** : to go gray, to get gray hair **3 echar una cana al aire** : to let one's hair down

canadiense *adj & nmf* : Canadian

canal[1] *nm* **1** : canal **2** : channel

canal[2] *nmf* : gutter, groove

canalé *nm* : rib, ribbing (in fabric)

canaleta *nf* : gutter

canalete *nm* : paddle

canalizar {21} *vt* : to channel

canalla[1] *adj fam* : low, rotten

canalla[2] *nmf fam* : bastard, swine

canapé *nm* **1** : hors d'oeuvre, canapé **2** SOFÁ : couch, sofa

canario[1], **-ria** *adj* : of or from the Canary Islands

canario[2], **-ria** *n* : Canarian, Canary Islander

canario[3] *nm* : canary

canasta *nf* **1** : basket **2** : canasta (card game)

cancel *nm* **1** : sliding door **2** : partition

cancelación *nf, pl* **-ciones 1** : cancellation **2** : payment in full

cancelar *vt* **1** : to cancel **2** : to pay off, to settle

cáncer *nm* : cancer

Cáncer *nmf* : Cancer

cancerígeno[1], **-na** *adj* : carcinogenic

cancerígeno[2] *nm* : carcinogen

canceroso, -sa *adj* : cancerous

cancha *nf* : court, field (for sports)

canciller *nm* : chancellor

cancillería *nf* : chancellery, ministry

canción *nf, pl* **canciones 1** : song **2 canción de cuna** : lullaby

cancionero[1] *nm* : songbook

cancionero[2], **-ra** *n Mex* : songster, songstress *f*

candado *nm* : padlock

candela *nf* **1** : flame, fire **2** : candle

candelabro *nm* : candelabra

candelero *nm* **1** : candlestick **2 estar en el candelero** : to be the center of attention

candente *adj* : red-hot

candidato, -ta *n* : candidate, applicant

candidatura *nf* : candidacy

candidez *nf* **1** : simplicity **2** INGENUIDAD : naïveté, ingenuousness

cándido, -da *adj* **1** : simple, unassuming **2** INGENUO : naive, ingenuous

candil *nm* : oil lamp

candilejas *nfpl* : footlights

candor *nm* : naïveté, innocence

candoroso, -sa *adj* : naive, innocent

canela *nf* : cinnamon

canesú *nm* : yoke (of clothing)

cangrejo *nm* JAIBA : crab

canguro *nm* **1** : kangaroo **2 hacer de canguro** *Spain* : to baby-sit

caníbal[1] *adj* : cannibalistic

caníbal[2] *nmf* ANTROPÓFAGO : cannibal

canibalismo *nm* ANTROPOFAGIA : cannibalism

canibalizar {21} *vt* : to cannibalize

canica *nf* **1** : marble **2 canicas** *nfpl* : marbles (toys)

caniche *nm* : poodle

canijo, -ja *adj* **1** *fam* : puny, weak **2** *Mex fam* : tough, hard <un examen muy canijo : a very tough exam>

canilla *nf* **1** : shin, shinbone **2** *Arg, Uru* : faucet

canino[1], -na *adj* : canine

canino[2] *nm* **1** COLMILLO : canine (tooth) **2** : dog, canine

canje *nm* INTERCAMBIO : exchange, trade

canjear *vt* INTERCAMBIAR : to exchange, to trade

cannabis *nm* : cannabis

cano, -na *adj* : gray <un hombre de pelo cano : a gray-haired man>

canoa *nf* : canoe

canon *nm, pl* **cánones** : canon

canónico, -ca *adj* **1** : canonical **2 derecho canónico** : canon law

canonizar {21} *vt* : to canonize — **canonización** *nf*

canoso, -sa → **cano**

cansado, -da *adj* **1** : tired <estar cansado : to be tired> **2** : tiresome, wearying <ser cansado : to be tiring>

cansancio *nm* FATIGA : fatigue, weariness

cansar *vt* FATIGAR : to wear out, to tire — *vi* : to be tiresome — **cansarse** *vr* **1** : to wear oneself out **2** : to get bored

cansino, -na *adj* : slow, weary, lethargic

cantaleta *nf fam* : nagging <la misma cantaleta : the same old story>

cantalupo *nm* : cantaloupe

cantante *nmf* : singer

cantar[1] *v* : to sing

cantar[2] *nm* : song, ballad

cántaro *nm* **1** : pitcher, jug **2 llover a cántaros** *fam* : to rain cats and dogs

cantata *nf* : cantata

cantera *nf* : quarry <cantera de piedra : stone quarry>

cántico *nm* : canticle, chant

cantidad[1] *adv fam* : really <ese carro me costó cantidad : that car cost me plenty>

cantidad[2] *nf* **1** : quantity **2** : sum, amount (of money) **3** *fam* : a lot, a great many <había cantidad de niños en el parque : there were tons of kids in the park>

cantimplora *nf* : canteen, water bottle

cantina *nf* **1** : tavern, bar **2** : canteen, mess, dining quarters *pl*

cantinero, -ra *n* : bartender

canto *nm* **1** : singing **2** : chant <canto gregoriano : Gregorian chant> **3** : song (of a bird) **4** : edge, end <de canto : on end, sideways> **5 canto rodado** : boulder

cantón *nm, pl* **cantones 1** : canton **2** *Mex fam* : place, home

cantor[1], -tora *adj* **1** : singing **2 pájaro cantor** : songbird

cantor[2], -tora *n* **1** : singer **2** : cantor

caña *nf* **1** : cane <caña de azúcar : sugarcane> **2** : reed **3 caña de pescar** : fishing rod **4 caña del timón** : tiller (of a boat)

cañada *nf* : ravine, gully

cáñamo *nm* : hemp

cañaveral *nm* : sugarcane field

cañería *nf* TUBERÍA : pipes *pl*, piping

caño *nm* **1** : pipe **2** : spout **3** : channel (for navigation)

cañón *nm, pl* **cañones 1** : cannon **2** : barrel (of a gun) **3** : canyon

cañonear *vt* : to shell, to bombard

cañoneo *nm* : shelling, bombardment

cañonero *nm* : gunboat

caoba *nf* : mahogany

caos *nm* : chaos

caótico, -ca *adj* : chaotic

capa *nf* **1** : cape, cloak **2** : coating **3** : layer, stratum **4** : (social) class, stratum

capacidad *nf* **1** : capacity **2** : capability, ability

capacitación *nf, pl* **-ciones** : training

capacitar *vt* : to train, to qualify

caparazón *nm, pl* **-zones** : shell, carapace

capataz *nmf, pl* **-taces** : foreman *m*, forewoman *f*

capaz *adj, pl* **capaces 1** APTO : capable, able **2** COMPETENTE : competent **3** : spacious <capaz para : with room for>

capcioso, -sa *adj* : cunning, deceptive <pregunta capciosa : trick question>

capea *nf* : amateur bullfight

capear *vt* **1** : to make a pass with the cape (in bullfighting) **2** : to dodge, to weather <capear el temporal : to ride out the storm>

capellán *nm, pl* **-llanes** : chaplain

capilar *nm* : capillary — **capilar** *adj*

capilla *nf* : chapel

capirotada *nf Mex* : traditional bread pudding

capirotazo *nm* : flip, flick

capital[1] *adj* **1** : capital **2** : chief, principal

capital[2] *nm* : capital <capital de riesgo : venture capital>

capital[3] *nf* : capital, capital city

capitalino[1], -na *adj* : of or from a capital city

capitalino[2], -na *n* : inhabitant of a capital city

capitalismo *nm* : capitalism

capitalista *adj & nmf* : capitalist

capitalizar {21} *vt* : to capitalize — **capitalización** *nf*

capitán, -tana *n, mpl* **-tanes** : captain

capitanear *vt* : to captain, to command

capitanía *nf* : captaincy

capitel *nm* : capital (of a column)

capitolio *nm* : capitol

capitulación *nf, pl* **-ciones** : capitulation

capitular *vi* : to capitulate, to surrender

capítulo *nm* **1** : chapter, section **2** : matter, subject

capó *nm* : hood (of a car)

capón *nm, pl* **capones** : capon

caporal *nm* **1 :** chief, leader **2 :** foreman (on a ranch)
capota *nf* **:** top (of a convertible)
capote *nm* **1 :** cloak, overcoat **2 :** bullfighter's cape **3** *Mex* COFRE **:** hood (of a car)
capricho *nm* ANTOJO **:** whim, caprice
caprichoso, -sa *adj* ANTOJADIZO **:** capricious, fickle
Capricornio *nmf* **:** Capricorn
cápsula *nf* **:** capsule
captar *vt* **1 :** to catch, to grasp **2 :** to gain, to attract **3 :** to harness, to collect (waters)
captor, -tora *n* **:** captor
captura *nf* **:** capture, seizure
capturar *vt* **:** to capture, to seize
capucha *nf* **:** hood, cowl
capuchina *nf* **:** nasturtium
capuchino *nm* **1 :** Capuchin (monk) **2 :** capuchin (monkey) **3 :** cappuccino
capullo *nm* **1 :** cocoon **2 :** bud (of a flower)
caqui *adj & nm* **:** khaki
cara *nf* **1 :** face **2** ASPECTO **:** look, appearance <¡qué buena cara tiene ese pastel! : that cake looks delicious!> **3** *fam* **:** nerve, gall **4 ~ a** *or* **de cara a :** facing **5 de cara a :** in view of, in the light of
carabina *nf* **:** carbine
caracol *nm* **1 :** snail **2** CONCHA **:** conch, seashell **3 :** cochlea **4 :** ringlet
caracola *nf* **:** conch
carácter *nm, pl* **caracteres 1** ÍNDOLE **:** character, kind, nature **2** TEMPERAMENTO **:** disposition, temperament **3 :** letter, symbol <caracteres chinos : Chinese characters>
característica *nf* RASGO **:** trait, feature, characteristic
característico, -ca *adj* **:** characteristic — **característicamente** *adv*
caracterizar {21} *vt* **:** to characterize — **caracterización** *nf*
caramba *interj* **:** darn!, heck!
carámbano *nm* **:** icicle
carambola *nf* **1 :** carom **2 :** ruse, trick <por carambola : by a lucky chance>
caramelo *nm* **1 :** caramel **2** DULCE **:** candy
caramillo *nm* **1 :** pipe, small flute **2 :** heap, pile
caraqueño[1], -ña *adj* **:** of or from Caracas
caraqueño[2], -ña *n* **:** person from Caracas
carátula *nf* **1 :** title page **2 :** cover, dust jacket **3** CARETA **:** mask **4** *Mex* **:** face, dial (of a clock or watch)
caravana *nf* **1 :** caravan **2 :** convoy, motorcade **3** REMOLQUE **:** trailer
caray → **caramba**
carbohidrato *nm* **:** carbohydrate
carbón *nm, pl* **carbones 1 :** coal **2 :** charcoal
carbonatado, -da *adj* **:** carbonated
carbonato *nm* **:** carbonate
carboncillo *nm* **:** charcoal
carbonera *nf* **:** coal cellar, coal bunker (on a ship)
carbonero, -ra *adj* **:** coal
carbonizar {21} *vt* **:** to carbonize, to char
carbono *nm* **:** carbon
carbunco *or* **carbunclo** *nm* **:** carbuncle
carburador *nm* **:** carburetor
carca *nmf fam* **:** old fogy
carcacha *nf fam* **:** jalopy, wreck
carcaj *nm* **:** quiver (for arrows)
carcajada *nf* **:** loud laugh, guffaw <reírse a carcajadas : to roar with laughter>
carcajearse *vr* **:** to roar with laughter, to be in stitches
cárcel *nf* PRISIÓN **:** jail, prison
carcelero, -ra *n* **:** jailer
carcinogénico, -ca *adj* **:** carcinogenic
carcinógeno *nm* CANCERÍGENO **:** carcinogen
carcinoma *nm* **:** carcinoma
carcomer *vt* **:** to eat away at, to consume
carcomido, -da *adj* **1 :** worm-eaten **2 :** decayed, rotten
cardán *nm, pl* **cardanes :** universal joint
cardar *vt* **:** to card, to comb
cardenal *nm* **1 :** cardinal (in religion) **2 :** bruise
cardíaco *or* **cardiaco, -ca** *adj* **:** cardiac, heart
cárdigan *nm, pl* **-gans :** cardigan
cardinal *adj* **:** cardinal
cardiología *nf* **:** cardiology
cardiólogo, -ga *n* **:** cardiologist
cardiovascular *adj* **:** cardiovascular
cardo *nm* **:** thistle
cardumen *nm* **:** school of fish
carear *vt* **:** to bring face-to-face
carecer {53} *vi* **~ de :** to lack <el cheque carecía de fondos : the check lacked funds>
carencia *nf* **1** FALTA **:** lack **2** ESCASEZ **:** shortage **3** DEFICIENCIA **:** deficiency
carente *adj* **~ de :** lacking (in)
carero, -ra *adj fam* **:** pricey
carestía *nf* **1 :** rise in cost <la carestía de la vida : the high cost of living> **2 :** dearth, scarcity
careta *nf* MÁSCARA **:** mask
carey *nm* **1 :** hawksbill turtle, sea turtle **2 :** tortoiseshell
carga *nf* **1 :** loading **2 :** freight, load, cargo **3 :** burden, responsibility **4 :** charge <carga eléctrica : electrical charge> **5 :** attack, charge
cargado, -da *adj* **1 :** loaded **2 :** bogged down, weighted down **3 :** close, stuffy **4 :** charged <cargado de tensión : charged with tension> **5** FUERTE **:** strong <café cargado : strong coffee> **6 cargado de hombros :** stoop-shouldered
cargador[1], -dora *n* **:** longshoreman *m*, longshorewoman *f*

cargador[2] *nm* **1 :** magazine (for a firearm) **2 :** charger (for batteries)
cargamento *nm* **:** cargo, load
cargar {52} *vt* **1 :** to carry **2 :** to load, to fill **3 :** to charge — *vi* **1 :** to load **2 :** to rest (in architecture) **3 ~ sobre :** to fall upon
cargo *nm* **1 :** burden, load **2 :** charge <a cargo de : in charge of> **3 :** position, office
cargue, etc. → **cargar**
carguero[1], **-ra** *adj* **:** freight, cargo <tren carguero : freight train>
carguero[2] *nm* **:** freighter, cargo ship
cariarse *vr* **:** to decay (of teeth)
caribe *adj* **:** Caribbean <el mar caribe : the Caribbean Sea>
caribeño, -ña *adj* **:** Caribbean
caribú *nm* **:** caribou
caricatura *nf* **1 :** caricature **2 :** cartoon
caricaturista *nmf* **:** caricaturist, cartoonist
caricaturizar {21} *vt* **:** to caricature
caricia *nf* **1 :** caress **2 hacer caricias :** to pet, to stroke
caridad *nf* **1 :** charity **2** LIMOSNA **:** alms *pl*
caries *nfs & pl* **:** cavity (in a tooth)
carillón *nm, pl* **-llones 1 :** carillon **2 :** glockenspiel
cariño *nm* AFECTO **:** affection, love
cariñoso, -sa *adj* AFECTUOSO **:** affectionate, loving — **cariñosamente** *adv*
carioca[1] *adj* **:** of or from Rio de Janeiro
carioca[2] *nmf* **:** person from Rio de Janeiro
carisma *nf* **:** charisma
carismático, -ca *adj* **:** charismatic
carita *adj Mex fam* **:** cute (said of a man) <tu primo se cree muy carita : your cousin thinks he's gorgeous>
caritativo, -va *adj* **:** charitable
cariz *nm, pl* **carices :** appearance, aspect
carmesí *adj & nm* **:** crimson
carmín *nm, pl* **carmines 1 :** carmine **2 carmín de labios :** lipstick
carnada *nf* CEBO **:** bait
carnal *adj* **1 :** carnal **2 primo carnal :** first cousin
carnaval *nm* **:** carnival
carnaza *nf* **:** bait
carne *nf* **1 :** meat <carne molida : ground beef> **2 :** flesh <carne de gallina : goose bumps>
carné *nm* → **carnet**
carnero *nm* **1 :** ram, sheep **2 :** mutton
carnet *nm* **1 :** identification card, ID **2 :** membership card **3 carnet de conducir** *Spain* **:** driver's license
carnicería *nf* **1 :** butcher shop **2** MATANZA **:** slaughter, carnage
carnicero, -ra *n* **:** butcher
carnívoro[1], **-ra** *adj* **:** carnivorous
carnívoro[2] *nm* **:** carnivore
carnoso, -sa *adj* **:** fleshy, meaty
caro[1] *adv* **:** dearly, a lot <pagué caro : I paid a high price>
caro[2], **-ra** *adj* **1 :** expensive, dear **2** QUERIDO **:** dear, beloved
carpa *nf* **1 :** carp **2 :** big top (of a circus) **3 :** tent
carpelo *nm* **:** carpel
carpeta *nf* **:** folder, binder, portfolio (of drawings, etc.)
carpetazo *nm* **dar carpetazo a :** to shelve, to defer
carpintería *nf* **1 :** carpentry **2 :** carpenter's workshop
carpintero, -ra *n* **:** carpenter
carraspear *vi* **:** to clear one's throat
carraspera *nf* **:** hoarseness <tener carraspera : to have a frog in one's throat>
carrera *nf* **1 :** run, running <a la carrera : at full speed> <de carrera : hastily> **2 :** race **3 :** course of study **4 :** career, profession **5 :** run (in baseball)
carreta *nf* **:** cart, wagon
carrete *nm* **1** BOBINA **:** reel, spool **2 :** roll of film
carretel *nm* → **carrete**
carretera *nf* **:** highway, road <carretera de peaje : turnpike>
carretero, -ra *adj* **:** highway <el sistema carretero nacional : the national highway system>
carretilla *nf* **1 :** wheelbarrow **2 carretilla elevadora :** forklift
carril *nm* **1 :** lane <carretera de doble carril : two-lane highway> **2 :** rail (on a railroad track)
carrillo *nm* **:** cheek, jowl
carrito *nm* **:** cart <carrito de compras : shopping cart>
carrizo *nm* JUNCO **:** reed
carro *nm* **1** COCHE **:** car **2 :** cart **3** *Chile, Mex* **:** coach (of a train) **4 carro alegórico :** float (in a parade)
carrocería *nf* **:** bodywork
carroña *nf* **:** carrion
carroñero, -ra *n* **:** scavenger (animal)
carroza *nf* **1 :** carriage **2 :** float (in a parade)
carruaje *nm* **:** carriage
carrusel *nm* **1 :** merry-go-round **2 :** carousel <carrusel de equipaje : luggage carousel>
carta *nf* **1 :** letter **2** NAIPE **:** playing card **3 :** charter, constitution **4** MENÚ **:** menu **5 :** map, chart **6 tomar cartas en :** to intervene in
cártamo *nm* **:** safflower
cartearse *vr* ESCRIBIRSE **:** to write to one another, to correspond
cartel *nm* **:** sign, poster
cártel *or* **cartel** *nm* **:** cartel
cartelera *nf* **1 :** billboard **2 :** marquee
cartera *nf* **1** BILLETERA **:** wallet, billfold **2** BOLSO **:** pocketbook, purse **3 :** portfolio <cartera de acciones : stock portfolio>
carterista *nmf* **:** pickpocket
cartero, -ra *n* **:** letter carrier, mailman *m*

cartilaginoso, -sa *adj* : cartilaginous, gristly
cartílago *nm* : cartilage
cartilla *nf* **1** : primer, reader **2** : booklet <cartilla de ahorros : bankbook>
cartografía *nf* : cartography
cartógrafo, -fa *n* : cartographer
cartón *nm, pl* **cartones 1** : cardboard <cartón madera : fiberboard> **2** : carton
cartucho *nm* : cartridge
cartulina *nf* : poster board, cardboard
carúncula *nf* : wattle (of a bird)
casa *nf* **1** : house, building **2** HOGAR : home **3** : household, family **4** : company, firm **5 echar la casa por la ventana** : to spare no expense
casaca *nf* : jacket
casado[1], -da *adj* : married
casado[2], -da *n* : married person
casamentero, -ra *n* : matchmaker
casamiento *nm* **1** : marriage **2** BODA : wedding
casar *vt* : to marry — *vi* : to go together, to match up — **casarse** *vr* **1** : to get married **2 ~ con** : to marry
casateniente *nmf Mex* : landlord, landlady *f*
cascabel[1] *nm* : small bell
cascabel[2] *nf* : rattlesnake
cascada *nf* CATARATA, SALTO : waterfall, cascade
cascajo *nm* **1** : pebble, rock fragment **2** *fam* : piece of junk
cascanueces *nms & pl* : nutcracker
cascar {72} *vt* : to crack (a shell) — **cascarse** *vr* : to crack, to chip
cáscara *nf* **1** : skin, peel, rind, husk **2** : shell (of a nut or egg)
cascarón *nm, pl* **-rones 1** : eggshell **2** *Mex* : shell filled with confetti
cascarrabias *nmfs & pl fam* : grouch, crab
casco *nm* **1** : helmet **2** : hull **3** : hoof **4** : fragment, shard **5** : center (of a town) **6** *Mex* : empty bottle **7 cascos** *nmpl* : headphones
caserío *nm* **1** : country house **2** : hamlet
casero[1], -ra *adj* **1** : domestic, household **2** : homemade
casero[2], -ra *n* DUEÑO : landlord *m,* landlady *f*
caseta *nf* : booth, stand, stall <caseta telefónica : telephone booth>
casete *nmf* → **cassette**
casi *adv* **1** : almost, nearly, virtually **2** (*in negative phrases*) : hardly <casi nunca : hardly ever>
casilla *nf* **1** : booth **2** : pigeonhole **3** : box (on a form)
casino *nm* **1** : casino **2** : (social) club
caso *nm* **1** : case **2 en caso de** : in case of, in the event of **3 hacer caso de** : to pay attention to, to notice **4 hacer caso omiso de** : to ignore, to take no notice of **5 no venir al caso** : to be beside the point
caspa *nf* : dandruff
casque, etc. → **cascar**
casquete *nm* **1** : skullcap **2 casquete glaciar** : ice cap **3 casquete corto** *Mex* : crew cut
cassette *nmf* : cassette
casta *nf* **1** : caste **2** : lineage, stock <de casta : thoroughbred, purebred> **3 sacar la casta** *Mex* : to come out ahead
castaña *nf* : chestnut
castañetear *vi* : to chatter (of teeth)
castaño[1], -ña *adj* : chestnut, brown
castaño[2], -ña *nm* **1** : chestnut tree **2** : chestnut, brown
castañuela *nf* : castanet
castellano[1], -na *adj & n* : Castilian
castellano[2] *nm* ESPAÑOL : Spanish, Castilian (language)
castidad *nf* : chastity
castigar {52} *vt* : to punish
castigo *nm* : punishment
castillo *nm* **1** : castle **2 castillo de proa** : forecastle
casto, -ta *adj* : chaste, pure — **castamente** *adv*
castor *nm* : beaver
castración *nf, pl* **-ciones** : castration
castrar *vt* **1** : to castrate, to spay, to neuter, to geld **2** DEBILITAR : to weaken, to debilitate
castrense *adj* : military
casual *adj* **1** FORTUITO : fortuitous, accidental **2** *Mex* : casual (of clothing)
casualidad *nf* **1** : chance **2 por ~** *or* **de ~** : by chance, by any chance
casualmente *adv* : accidentally, by chance
casucha *or* **casuca** *nf* : shanty, hovel
cataclismo *nm* : cataclysm
catacumbas *nfpl* : catacombs
catador, -dora *n* : wine taster
catalán[1], -lana *adj & n, mpl* **-lanes** : Catalan
catalán[2] *nm* : Catalan (language)
catálisis *nm* : catalysis
catalítico, -ca *adj* : catalytic
catalizador *nm* **1** : catalyst **2** : catalytic converter
catalogar {52} *vt* : to catalog, to classify
catálogo *nm* : catalog
catamarán *nm, pl* **-ranes** : catamaran
cataplasma *nf* : poultice
catapulta *nf* : catapult
catapultar *vt* : to catapult
catar *vt* **1** : to taste, to sample **2** : to look at, to examine
catarata *nf* **1** CASCADA, SALTO : waterfall **2** : cataract
catarro *nm* RESFRIADO : cold, catarrh
catarsis *nf* : catharsis
catártico, -ca *adj* : cathartic
catástrofe *nf* DESASTRE : catastrophe, disaster
catastrófico, -ca *adj* DESASTROSO : catastrophic, disastrous
catcher *nmf* : catcher (in baseball)
catecismo *nm* : catechism

cátedra *nf* **1** : chair, professorship **2** : subject, class **3 libertad de cátedra** : academic freedom
catedral *nf* : cathedral
catedrático, -ca *n* PROFESOR : professor
categoría *nf* **1** CLASE : category **2** RANGO : rank, standing **3 categoría gramatical** : part of speech **4 de ~** : first-rate, outstanding
categórico, -ca *adj* : categorical, unequivocal — **categóricamente** *adv*
catéter *nm* : catheter
cátodo *nm* : cathode
catolicismo *nm* : Catholicism
católico, -ca *adj & n* : Catholic
catorce *adj & nm* : fourteen
catorceavo *nm* : fourteenth
catre *nm* : cot
catsup *nm* : ketchup
caucásico, -ca *adj & n* : Caucasian
cauce *nm* **1** LECHO : riverbed **2** : means *pl,* channel
caucho *nm* **1** GOMA : rubber **2** : rubber tree **3** *Ven* : tire
caución *nf, pl* **cauciones** FIANZA : bail, security
caudal *nm* **1** : volume of water **2** RIQUEZA : capital, wealth **3** ABUNDANCIA : abundance
caudillaje *nm* : leadership
caudillo *nm* : leader, commander
causa *nf* **1** MOTIVO : cause, reason, motive <a causa de : because of> **2** IDEAL : cause <morir por una causa : to die for a cause> **3** : lawsuit
causal[1] *adj* : causal
causal[2] *nm* : cause, grounds *pl*
causalidad *nf* : causality
causante[1] *adj* **~ de** : causing, responsible for
causante[2] *nmf Mex* : taxpayer
causar *vt* **1** : to cause **2** : to provoke, to arouse <eso me causa gracia : that strikes me as being funny>
cáustico, -ca *adj* : caustic
cautela *nf* : caution, prudence
cautelar *adj* : precautionary, preventive
cauteloso, -sa *adj* : cautious, prudent — **cautelosamente** *adv*
cauterizar {21} *vt* : to cauterize
cautivador, -dora *adj* : captivating
cautivar *vt* HECHIZAR : to captivate, to charm
cautiverio *nm* : captivity
cautivo, -va *adj & n* : captive
cauto, -ta *adj* : cautious, careful
cavar *vt* : to dig — *vi* **~ en** : to delve into, to probe
caverna *nf* : cavern, cave
cavernoso, -sa *adj* **1** : cavernous **2** : deep, resounding
caviar *nm* : caviar
cavidad *nf* : cavity
cavilar *vi* : to ponder, to deliberate
cayado *nm* : crook, staff, crosier
cayena *nf* : cayenne pepper
cayó, etc. → **caer**
caza[1] *nf* **1** CACERÍA : hunt, hunting **2** : game
caza[2] *nm* : fighter plane
cazador, -dora *n* **1** : hunter **2 cazador furtivo** : poacher
cazar {21} *vt* **1** : to hunt **2** : to catch, to bag **3** *fam* : to land (a job, a spouse) — *vi* : to go hunting
cazatalentos *nmfs & pl* : talent scout
cazo *nm* **1** : saucepan, pot **2** CUCHARÓN : ladle
cazuela *nf* **1** : pan, saucepan **2** : casserole
cazurro, -ra *adj* : sullen, surly
CD *nm* : CD, compact disk
cebada *nf* : barley
cebar *vt* **1** : to bait **2** : to feed, to fatten **3** : to prime (a pump, etc.) — **cebarse** *vr* **~ en** : to take it out on
cebo *nm* **1** CARNADA : bait **2** : feed **3** : primer (for firearms)
cebolla *nf* : onion
cebolleta *nf* : scallion, green onion
cebollino *nm* **1** : chive **2** : scallion
cebra *nf* : zebra
cebú *nm, pl* **cebús** *or* **cebúes** : zebu (cattle)
cecear *vi* : to lisp
ceceo *nm* : lisp
cecina *nf* : dried beef, beef jerky
cedazo *nm* : sieve
ceder *vi* **1** : to yield, to give way **2** : to diminish, to abate **3** : to give in, to relent — *vt* : to cede, to hand over
cedro *nm* : cedar
cédula *nf* : document, certificate
céfiro *nm* : zephyr
cegador, -dora *adj* : blinding
cegar {49} *vt* **1** : to blind **2** : to block, to stop up — *vi* : to be blinded, to go blind
cegatón, -tona *adj, mpl* **-tones** *fam* : blind as a bat
ceguera *nf* : blindness
ceiba *nf* : ceiba, silk-cotton tree
ceja *nf* **1** : eyebrow <fruncir las cejas : to knit one's brows> **2** : flange, rim
cejar *vi* : to give in, to back down
celada *nf* : trap, ambush
celador, -dora *n* GUARDIA : guard, warden
celda *nf* : cell (of a jail)
celebración *nf, pl* **-ciones** : celebration
celebrado, -da *adj* CÉLEBRE, FAMOSO : famous, celebrated
celebrante *nmf* OFICIANTE : celebrant
celebrar *vt* **1** FESTEJAR : to celebrate **2** : to hold (a meeting) **3** : to say (Mass) **4** : to welcome, to be happy about — *vi* : to be glad — **celebrarse** *vr* **1** : to be celebrated, to fall **2** : to be held, to take place
célebre *adj* CELEBRADO, FAMOSO : celebrated, famous
celebridad *nf* **1** : celebrity **2** FAMA : fame, renown
celeridad *nf* : celerity, swiftness
celeste[1] *adj* **1** : celestial **2** : sky blue, azure

celeste[2] *nm* : sky blue

celestial *adj* : heavenly, celestial

celibato *nm* : celibacy

célibe *adj & nmf* : celibate

cello *nm* : cello

celo *nm* **1** : zeal, fervor **2** : heat (of females), rut (of males) **3 celos** *nmpl* : jealousy <tenerle celos a alguien : to be jealous of someone>

celofán *nm, pl* **-fanes** : cellophane

celosía *nf* **1** : lattice window **2** : latticework, trellis

celoso, -sa *adj* **1** : jealous **2** : zealous — **celosamente** *adv*

celta[1] *adj* : Celtic

celta[2] *nmf* : Celt

célula *nf* : cell

celular *adj* : cellular

celuloide *nm* **1** : celluloid **2** : film, cinema

celulosa *nf* : cellulose

cementar *vt* : to cement

cementerio *nm* : cemetery

cemento *nm* : cement

cena *nf* : supper, dinner

cenador *nm* : arbor

cenagal *nm* : bog, quagmire

cenagoso, -sa *adj* : swampy

cenar *vi* : to have dinner, to have supper — *vt* : to have for dinner or supper <anoche cenamos tamales : we had tamales for supper last night>

cencerro *nm* : cowbell

cenicero *nm* : ashtray

ceniciento, -ta *adj* : ashen

cenit *nm* : zenith, peak

ceniza *nf* **1** : ash **2 cenizas** *nfpl* : ashes (of a deceased person)

cenizo, -za *n* : jinx

cenote *nm Mex* : natural deposit of spring water

censar *vt* : to take a census of

censo *nm* : census

censor, -sora *n* : censor, critic

censura *nf* **1** : censorship **2** : censure, criticism

censurable *adj* : reprehensible, blameworthy

censurar *vt* **1** : to censor **2** : to censure, to criticize

centauro *nm* : centaur

centavo *nm* **1** : cent (in English-speaking countries) **2** : unit of currency in various Latin-American countries

centella *nf* **1** : lightning flash **2** : spark

centellear *vi* **1** : to twinkle **2** : to gleam, to sparkle

centelleo *nm* : twinkling, sparkle

centenar *nm* **1** : hundred **2 a centenares** : by the hundreds

centenario[1], **-ria** *adj & n* : centenarian

centenario[2] *nm* : centennial

centeno *nm* : rye

centésimo[1], **-ma** *adj* : hundredth

centésimo[2] *nm* : hundredth

centígrado *adj* : centigrade, Celsius

centigramo *nm* : centigram

centímetro *nm* : centimeter

centinela *nmf* : sentinel, sentry

central[1] *adj* **1** : central **2** PRINCIPAL : main, principal

central[2] *nf* **1** : main office, headquarters **2 central camionera** *Mex* : bus terminal

centralita *nf* : switchboard

centralizar {21} *vt* : to centralize — **centralización** *nf*

centrar *vt* **1** : to center **2** : to focus — **centrarse** *vr* **~ en** : to focus on, to concentrate on

céntrico, -ca *adj* : central

centrífugo, -ga *adj* : centrifugal

centrípeto, -ta *adj* : centripetal

centro[1] *nmf* : center (in sports)

centro[2] *nm* **1** MEDIO : center <centro de atención : center of attention> <centro de gravedad : center of gravity> **2** : downtown **3 centro de mesa** : centerpiece

centroamericano, -na *adj & n* : Central American

ceñido, -da *adj* AJUSTADO : tight, tight-fitting

ceñir {67} *vt* **1** : to encircle, to surround **2** : to hug, to cling to <me ciñe demasiado : it's too tight on me> — **ceñirse** *vr* **~ a** : to restrict oneself to, to stick to

ceño *nm* **1** : frown, scowl **2 fruncir el ceño** : to frown, to knit one's brows

cepa *nf* **1** : stump (of a tree) **2** : stock (of a vine) **3** LINAJE : ancestry, stock

cepillar *vt* **1** : to brush **2** : to plane (wood) — **cepillarse** *vr*

cepillo *nm* **1** : brush <cepillo de dientes : toothbrush> **2** : plane (for woodworking)

cepo *nm* : trap (for animals)

cera *nf* **1** : wax <cera de abejas : beeswax> **2** : polish

cerámica *nf* **1** : ceramics *pl* **2** : pottery

cerámico, -ca *adj* : ceramic

ceramista *nmf* ALFARERO : potter

cerca[1] *adv* **1** : close, near, nearby **2 ~ de** : nearly, almost

cerca[2] *nf* **1** : fence **2** : (stone) wall

cercado *nm* : enclosure

cercanía *nf* **1** PROXIMIDAD : proximity, closeness **2 cercanías** *nfpl* : outskirts, suburbs

cercano, -na *adj* : near, close

cercar {72} *vt* **1** : to fence in, to enclose **2** : to surround

cercenar *vt* **1** : to cut off, to amputate **2** : to diminish, to curtail

cerceta *nf* : teal (duck)

cerciorarse *vr* ASEGURARSE **~ de** : to make sure of, to verify

cerco *nm* **1** : siege **2** : cordon, circle **3** : fence

cerda *nf* **1** : bristle **2** : sow

cerdo *nm* **1** : pig, hog **2 carne de cerdo** : pork

cereal *nm* : cereal — **cereal** *adj*

cerebelo *nm* : cerebellum

cerebral *adj* : cerebral

cerebro *nm* : brain

ceremonia *nf* : ceremony — **ceremonial** *adj*
ceremonioso, -sa *adj* : ceremonious
cereza *nf* : cherry
cerezo *nm* : cherry tree
cerilla *nf* **1** : match **2** : earwax
cerillo *nm* (*in various countries*) : match
cerner {56} *vt* : to sift — **cernerse** *vr* **1** : to hover **2 ~ sobre** : to loom over, to threaten
cernidor *nm* : sieve
cernir → **cerner**
cero *nm* : zero
ceroso, -sa *adj* : waxy
cerque, etc. → **cercar**
cerquita *adv fam* : very close, very near
cerrado, -da *adj* **1** : closed, shut **2** : thick, broad <tiene un acento cerrado : she has a thick accent> **3** : cloudy, overcast **4** : quiet, reserved **5** : dense, stupid
cerradura *nf* : lock
cerrajería *nf* : locksmith's shop
cerrajero, -ra *n* : locksmith
cerrar {55} *vt* **1** : to close, to shut **2** : to turn off **3** : to bring to an end — *vi* **1** : to close up, to lock up **2** : to close down — **cerrarse** *vr* **1** : to close **2** : to fasten, to button up **3** : to conclude, to end
cerrazón *nf, pl* **-zones** : obstinacy, stubbornness
cerro *nm* COLINA, LOMA : hill
cerrojo *nm* PESTILLO : bolt, latch
certamen *nm, pl* **-támenes** : competition, contest
certero, -ra *adj* : accurate, precise — **certeramente** *adv*
certeza *nf* : certainty
certidumbre *nf* : certainty
certificable *adj* : certifiable
certificación *nf, pl* **-ciones** : certification
certificado[1], -da *adj* **1** : certified **2** : registered (of mail)
certificado[2] *nm* **1** : certificate **2** : registered letter
certificar {72} *vt* **1** : to certify **2** : to register (mail)
cervato *nm* : fawn
cervecería *nf* **1** : brewery **2** : beer hall, bar
cerveza *nf* : beer <cerveza de barril : draft beer>
cervical *adj* : cervical
cerviz *nf, pl* **cervices** : nape of the neck, cervix
cesación *nf, pl* **-ciones** : cessation, suspension
cesante *adj* : laid off, unemployed
cesantía *nf* : unemployment
cesar *vi* : to cease, to stop — *vt* : to dismiss, to lay off
cesárea *nf* : cesarean, C-section
cese *nm* **1** : cessation, stop <cese del fuego : cease-fire> **2** : dismissal
cesio *nm* : cesium
cesión *nf, pl* **cesiones** : transfer, assignment <cesión de bienes : transfer of property>
césped *nm* : lawn, grass
cesta *nf* **1** : basket **2** : jai alai racket
cesto *nm* **1** : hamper **2** : basket (in basketball) **3 cesto de (la) basura** : wastebasket
cetrería *nf* : falconry
cetrino, -na *adj* : sallow
cetro *nm* : scepter
chabacano[1], -na *adj* : tacky, tasteless
chabacano[2] *nm Mex* : apricot
chacal *nm* : jackal
cháchara *nf fam* **1** : small talk, chatter **2 cháchara**s *nfpl* : trinkets, junk
chacharear *vi fam* : to chatter, to gab
chacra *nf Arg, Chile, Peru* : small farm
chadiano, -na *adj & n* : Chadian
chal *nm* MANTÓN : shawl
chalado[1], -da *adj fam* : crazy, nuts
chalado[2], -da *n* : nut, crazy person
chalán *nm, pl* **chalanes** *Mex* : barge
chalé *nm* → **chalet**
chaleco *nm* : vest
chalet *nm Spain* : house
chalupa *nf* **1** : small boat **2** *Mex* : small stuffed tortilla
chamaco, -ca *n Mex fam* : kid, boy *m*, girl *f*
chamarra *nf* **1** : sheepskin jacket **2** : poncho, blanket
chamba *nf Mex, Peru fam* : job, work
chambear *vi Mex, Peru fam* : to work
chamo -ma *n Ven fam* **1** : kid, boy *m*, girl *f* **2** : buddy, pal
champaña *or* **champán** *nm* : champagne
champiñón *nm, pl* **-ñones** : mushroom
champú *nm, pl* **-pus** *or* **-púes** : shampoo
champurrado *nm Mex* : hot chocolate thickened with cornstarch
chamuco *nm Mex fam* : devil
chamuscar {72} *vt* : to singe, to scorch — **chamuscarse** *vr*
chamusquina *nf* : scorch
chance *nm* OPORTUNIDAD : chance, opportunity
chancho[1], -cha *adj fam* : dirty, filthy, gross
chancho[2], -cha *n* **1** : pig, hog **2** *fam* : slob
chanchullero, -ra *adj fam* : shady, crooked
chanchullo *nm fam* : shady deal, scam
chancla *nf* **1** : thong sandal, slipper **2** : old shoe
chancleta *nf* → **chancla**
chanclo *nm* **1** : clog **2 chanclos** *nmpl* : overshoes, galoshes, rubbers
chancro *nm* : chancre
changarro *nm Mex* : small shop, stall
chango, -ga *n Mex* : monkey
chantaje *nm* : blackmail
chantajear *vt* : to blackmail
chantajista *nmf* : blackmailer
chanza *nf* **1** : joke, jest **2** *Mex fam* : chance, opportunity

chapa *nf* **1** : sheet, panel, veneer **2** : lock **3** : badge

chapado, -da *adj* **1** : plated **2 chapado a la antigua** : old-fashioned

chapar *vt* **1** : to veneer **2** : to plate (metals)

chaparrón *nm, pl* **-rrones 1** : downpour **2** : great quantity, torrent

chapeado, -da *adj Col, Mex* : flushed

chapopote *nm Mex* : tar, blacktop

chapotear *vi* : to splash about

chapucero[1], -ra *adj* **1** : crude, shoddy **2** *Mex fam* : dishonest

chapucero[2], -ra *n* **1** : sloppy worker, bungler **2** *Mex fam* : cheat, swindler

chapulín *nm, pl* **-lines** *CA, Mex* : grasshopper, locust

chapuza *nf* **1** : botched job **2** *Mex fam* : fraud, trick <hacer chapuzas : to cheat>

chapuzón *nm, pl* **-zones** : dip, swim <darse un chapuzón : to go for a quick dip>

chaqueta *nf* : jacket

charada *nf* : charades (game)

charango *nm* : traditional Andean stringed instrument

charca *nf* : pond, pool

charco *nm* : puddle, pool

charcutería *nf* : delicatessen

charla *nf* : chat, talk

charlar *vi* : to chat, to talk

charlatán[1], -tana *adj* : talkative, chatty

charlatán[2], -tana *n, mpl* **-tanes 1** : chatterbox **2** FARSANTE : charlatan, phony

charlatanear *vi* : to chatter away

charol *nm* **1** : lacquer, varnish **2** : patent leather **3** : tray

charola *nf Bol, Mex, Peru* : tray

charreada *nf Mex* : charro show, rodeo

charretera *nf* : epaulet

charro[1], -rra *adj* **1** : gaudy, tacky **2** *Mex* : pertaining to charros

charro[2], -rra *n Mex* : charro (Mexican cowboy or cowgirl)

chascarrillo *nm fam* : joke, funny story

chasco *nm* **1** BROMA : trick, joke **2** DECEPCIÓN, DESILUSIÓN : disillusionment, disappointment

chasis *or* **chasís** *nm* : chassis

chasquear *vt* **1** : to click (the tongue, fingers, etc.) **2** : to snap (a whip)

chasquido *nm* **1** : click (of the tongue or fingers) **2** : snap, crack

chatarra *nf* : scrap metal

chato, -ta *adj* **1** : pug-nosed **2** : flat

chauvinismo *nm* : chauvinism

chauvinista[1] *adj* : chauvinistic

chauvinista[2] *nmf* : chauvinist

chaval, -vala *n fam* : kid, boy *m*, girl *f*

chavo[1], -va *adj Mex fam* : young

chavo[2], -va *n Mex fam* : kid, boy *m*, girl *f*

chavo[3] *nm fam* : cent, buck <no tengo un chavo : I'm broke>

chayote *nm* : chayote (plant, fruit)

checar {72} *vt Mex* : to check, to verify

checo[1], -ca *adj & n* : Czech

checo[2] *nm* : Czech (language)

checoslovaco, -ca *adj & n* : Czechoslovakian

chef *nm* : chef

chelín *nm, pl* **chelines** : shilling

cheque[1], etc. → **checar**

cheque[2] *nm* **1** : check **2 cheque de viajero** : traveler's check

chequear *vt* **1** : to check, to verify **2** : to check in (baggage)

chequeo *nm* **1** INSPECCIÓN : check, inspection **2** : checkup, examination

chequera *nf* : checkbook

chévere *adj fam* : great, fantastic

chic *adj & nm* : chic

chica → **chico**

chicano, -na *adj & n* : Chicano, Chicana *f*

chicha *nf* : fermented alcoholic beverage made from corn

chícharo *nm* : pea

chicharra *nf* **1** CIGARRA : cicada **2** : buzzer

chicharrón *nm, pl* **-rrones 1** : pork rind **2 darle chicharrón a** *Mex fam* : to get rid of

chichón *nm, pl* **chichones** : bump, swelling

chicle *nm* : chewing gum

chicloso *nm Mex* : taffy

chico[1], -ca *adj* **1** : little, small **2** : young

chico[2], -ca *n* **1** : child, boy *m*, girl *f* **2** : young man *m*, young woman *f*

chicote *nm* LÁTIGO : whip, lash

chiffon *nm* → **chifón**

chiflado[1], -da *adj fam* : nuts, crazy

chiflado[2], -da *n fam* : crazy person, lunatic

chiflar *vi* : to whistle — *vt* : to whistle at, to boo — **chiflarse** *vr fam* **~ por** : to be crazy about

chiflido *nm* : whistle, whistling

chiflón *nm, pl* **chiflones** : draft (of air)

chifón *nm, pl* **chifones** : chiffon

chilango[1], -ga *adj Mex fam* : of or from Mexico City

chilango[2], -ga *n Mex fam* : person from Mexico City

chilaquiles *nmpl Mex* : shredded tortillas in sauce

chile *nm* : chili pepper

chileno, -na *adj & n* : Chilean

chillar *vi* **1** : to squeal, to screech **2** : to scream, to yell **3** : to be gaudy, to clash

chillido *nm* **1** : scream, shout **2** : squeal, screech, cry (of an animal)

chillo *nm PRi* : red snapper

chillón, -llona *adj, mpl* **chillones 1** : piercing, shrill **2** : loud, gaudy

chilpayate *nmf Mex fam* : child, little kid

chimenea *nf* **1** : chimney **2** : fireplace

chimichurri *nm Arg* : traditional hot sauce

chimpancé *nm* **:** chimpanzee
china *nf* **1 :** pebble, small stone **2** *PRi* **:** orange
chinchar *vt fam* **:** to annoy, to pester — **chincharse** *vr fam* **:** to put up with something, to grin and bear it
chinchayote *nm Mex* **:** chayote root
chinche[1] *nf* **1 :** bedbug **2** *Ven* **:** ladybug **3 :** thumbtack
chinche[2] *nmf fam* **:** nuisance, pain in the neck
chinchilla *nf* **:** chinchilla
chino[1], **-na** *adj* **1 :** Chinese **2** *Mex* **:** curly, kinky
chino[2], **-na** *n* **:** Chinese person
chino[3] *nm* **:** Chinese (language)
chip *nm, pl* **chips :** chip <chip de memoria : memory chip>
chipote *nm Mex fam* **:** bump (on the head)
chipotle *nm Mex* **:** type of chili pepper
chipriota *adj & nmf* **:** Cypriot
chiquear *vt Mex* **:** to spoil, to indulge
chiquero *nm* POCILGA **:** pigpen, pigsty
chiquillada *nf* **:** childish prank
chiquillo[1], **-lla** *adj* **:** very young, little
chiquillo[2], **-lla** *n* **:** kid, youngster
chiquito[1], **-ta** *adj* **:** tiny
chiquito[2], **-ta** *n* **:** little one, baby
chiribita *nf* **1 :** spark **2 chiribitas** *nfpl* **:** spots before the eyes
chiribitil *nm* **1** DESVÁN **:** attic, garret **2 :** cubbyhole
chirigota *nf fam* **:** joke
chirimía *nf* **:** traditional reed pipe
chirimoya *nf* **:** cherimoya, custard apple
chiripa *nf* **1 :** fluke **2 de ~ :** by sheer luck
chirivía *nf* **:** parsnip
chirona *nf fam* **:** slammer, jail
chirriar {85} *vi* **1 :** to squeak, to creak **2 :** to screech — **chirriante** *adj*
chirrido *nm* **1 :** squeak, squeaking **2 :** screech, screeching
chirrión *nm, pl* **chirriones** *Mex* **:** whip, lash
chisme *nm* **1 :** gossip, tale **2** *Spain fam* **:** gadget, thingamajig
chismear *vi* **:** to gossip
chismoso[1], **-sa** *adj* **:** gossipy, gossiping
chismoso[2], **-sa** *n* **1 :** gossiper, gossip **2** *Mex fam* **:** tattletale
chispa[1] *adj* **1** *Mex fam* **:** lively, vivacious <un perrito chispa : a frisky puppy> **2** *Spain fam* **:** tipsy
chispa[2] *nf* **1 :** spark **2 echar chispas :** to be furious
chispeante *adj* **:** sparkling, scintillating
chispear *vi* **1 :** to give off sparks **2 :** to sparkle
chisporrotear *vi* **:** to crackle, to sizzle
chiste *nm* **1 :** joke, funny story **2 tener chiste :** to be funny **3 tener su chiste** *Mex* **:** to be tricky
chistoso[1], **-sa** *adj* **1 :** funny, humorous **2 :** witty
chistoso[2], **-sa** *n* **:** wit, joker
chivas *nfpl Mex fam* **:** stuff, odds and ends
chivo[1], **-va** *n* **1 :** kid, young goat **2 chivo expiatorio :** scapegoat
chivo[2] *nm* **1 :** billy goat **2 :** fit of anger
chocante *adj* **1 :** shocking **2 :** unpleasant, rude
chocar {72} *vi* **1 :** to crash, to collide **2 :** to clash, to conflict **3 :** to be shocking <le chocó : he was shocked> **4** *Mex, Ven fam* **:** to be unpleasant or obnoxious <me choca tu jefe : I can't stand your boss> — *vt* **1 :** to shake (hands) **2 :** to clink glasses
chochear *vi* **1 :** to be senile **2 ~ por :** to dote on, to be soft on
chochín *nm, pl* **-chines :** wren
chocho, -cha *adj* **1 :** senile **2 :** doting
choclo *nm* **1 :** ear of corn, corncob **2 :** corn **3 meter el choclo** *Mex fam* **:** to make a mistake
chocolate *nm* **1 :** chocolate **2 :** hot chocolate, cocoa
chofer *or* **chófer** *nm* **1 :** chauffeur **2 :** driver
choke *nm* **:** choke (of an automobile)
chole *interj Mex fam* **¡ya chole! :** enough!, cut it out!
cholo, -la *adj & n* **:** mestizo
cholla *nf fam* **:** head
chollo *nm Spain fam* **:** bargain
chongo *nm Mex* **1 :** bun (chignon) **2 chongos** *nmpl Mex* **:** dessert made with fried bread
choque[1], **etc.** → **chocar**
choque[2] *nm* **1 :** crash, collision **2 :** clash, conflict **3 :** shock
chorizo *nm* **:** chorizo, sausage
chorrear *vi* **1 :** to drip **2 :** to pour out, to gush out
chorrito *nm* **:** squirt, splash
chorro *nm* **1 :** flow, stream, jet **2** *Mex fam* **:** heap, ton
choteado, -da *adj Mex fam* **:** worn-out, stale <esa canción está bien choteada : that song's been played to death>
chotear *vt* **:** to make fun of
choteo *nm* **:** joking around, kidding
chovinismo, chovinista → **chauvinismo, chauvinista**
choza *nf* BARRACA, CABAÑA **:** hut, shack
chubasco *nm* **:** downpour, storm
chuchería *nf* **:** knickknack, trinket
chueco, -ca *adj* **1 :** crooked, bent **2** *Chile, Mex fam* **:** dishonest, shady
chulada *nf Mex, Spain fam* **:** cute or pretty thing <¡qué chulada de vestido! : what a lovely dress!>
chulear *vt Mex fam* **:** to compliment
chuleta *nf* **:** cutlet, chop
chulo[1], **-la** *adj* **1** *fam* **:** cute, pretty **2** *Spain fam* **:** cocky, arrogant
chulo[2] *nm Spain* **:** pimp
chupada *nf* **1 :** suck, sucking **2 :** puff, drag (on a cigarette)
chupado, -da *adj fam* **1 :** gaunt, skinny **2 :** plastered, drunk
chupaflor *nm* COLIBRÍ **:** hummingbird
chupamirto *nm Mex* **:** hummingbird

chupar *vt* **1 :** to suck **2 :** to absorb **3 :** to puff on **4** *fam* **:** to drink, to guzzle — *vi* **:** to suckle — **chuparse** *vr* **1 :** to waste away **2** *fam* **:** to put up with **3 ¡chúpate esa!** *fam* **:** take that!

chupete *nm* **1 :** pacifier **2** *Chile, Peru* **:** lollipop

chupetear *vt* **:** to suck (at)

chupón *nm, pl* **chupones 1 :** sucker (of a plant) **2 :** baby bottle, pacifier

churrasco *nm* **1 :** steak **2 :** barbecued meat

churro *nm* **1 :** fried dough **2** *fam* **:** botch, mess **3** *fam* **:** attractive person, looker

chusco, -ca *adj* **:** funny, amusing

chusma *nf* GENTUZA **:** riffraff, rabble

chutar *vi* **:** to shoot (in soccer)

chute *nm* **:** shot (in soccer)

cianuro *nm* **:** cyanide

cibernética *nf* **:** cybernetics

cicatriz *nf, pl* **-trices :** scar

cicatrizarse {21} *vr* **:** to form a scar, to heal

cíclico, -ca *adj* **:** cyclical

ciclismo *nm* **:** bicycling

ciclista *nmf* **:** bicyclist

ciclo *nm* **:** cycle

ciclomotor *nm* **:** moped

ciclón *nm, pl* **ciclones :** cyclone

cicuta *nf* **:** hemlock

cidra *nf* **:** citron (fruit)

ciega, ciegue, etc. → **cegar**

ciego[1], -ga *adj* **1** INVIDENTE **:** blind **2 a ciegas :** blindly **3 quedarse ciego :** to go blind — **ciegamente** *adv*

ciego[2], -ga *n* INVIDENTE **:** blind person

cielo *nm* **1 :** sky **2 :** heaven **3 :** ceiling

ciempiés *nms & pl* **:** centipede

cien[1] *adj* **1 :** a hundred, hundred <las primeras cien páginas : the first hundred pages> **2 cien por cien** *or* **cien por ciento :** a hundred percent, through and through, wholeheartedly

cien[2] *nm* **:** one hundred

ciénaga *nf* **:** swamp, bog

ciencia *nf* **1 :** science **2 :** learning, knowledge **3 a ciencia cierta :** for a fact, for certain

cieno *nm* **:** mire, mud, silt

científico[1], -ca *adj* **:** scientific — **científicamente** *adv*

científico[2], -ca *n* **:** scientist

ciento[1] *adj* (*used in compound numbers*) **:** one hundred <ciento uno : one hundred and one>

ciento[2] *nm* **1 :** hundred, group of a hundred **2 por ~ :** percent

cierne, etc. → **cerner**

cierra, etc. → **cerrar**

cierre *nm* **1 :** closing, closure **2 :** fastener, clasp, zipper

cierto, -ta *adj* **1 :** true, certain, definite <lo cierto es que... : the fact is that...> **2 :** certain, one <cierto día de verano : one summer day> <bajo ciertas circunstancias : under certain circumstances> **3 por ~ :** in fact, as a matter of fact — **ciertamente** *adv*

ciervo, -va *n* **:** deer, stag *m,* hind *f*

cifra *nf* **1 :** figure, number **2 :** quantity, amount **3** CLAVE **:** code, cipher

cifrar *vt* **1 :** to write in code **2 :** to place, to pin <cifró su esperanza en la lotería : he pinned his hopes on the lottery> — **cifrarse** *vr* **:** to amount <la multa se cifra en millares : the fine amounts to thousands>

cigarra *nf* CHICHARRA **:** cicada

cigarrera *nf* **:** cigarette case

cigarrillo *nm* **:** cigarrette

cigarro *nm* **1 :** cigarette **2** PURO **:** cigar

cigoto *nm* **:** zygote

cigüeña *nf* **:** stork

cilantro *nm* **:** cilantro, coriander

cilíndrico, -ca *adj* **:** cylindrical

cilindro *nm* **:** cylinder

cima *nf* CUMBRE **:** peak, summit, top

cimarrón, -rrona *adj, mpl* **-rrones :** untamed, wild

címbalo *nm* **:** cymbal

cimbel *nm* **:** decoy

cimbrar *vt* **:** to shake, to rock — **cimbrarse** *vr* **:** to sway, to swing

cimentar {55} *vt* **1 :** to lay the foundation of, to establish **2 :** to strengthen, to cement

cimientos *nmpl* **:** base, foundation(s)

cinc *nm* **:** zinc

cincel *nm* **:** chisel

cincelar *vt* **1 :** to chisel **2 :** to engrave

cincha *nf* **:** cinch, girth

cinchar *vt* **:** to cinch (a horse)

cinco *adj & nm* **:** five

cincuenta *adj & nm* **:** fifty

cincuentavo[1], -va *adj* **:** fiftieth

cincuentavo[2] *nm* **:** fiftieth (fraction)

cine *nm* **1 :** cinema, movies *pl* **2 :** movie theater

cineasta *nmf* **:** filmmaker

cinematográfico, -ca *adj* **:** movie, film, cinematic <la industria cinematográfica : the film industry>

cingalés[1], -lesa *adj & n* **:** Sinhalese

cingalés[2] *nm* **:** Sinhalese (language)

cínico[1], -ca *adj* **1 :** cynical **2 :** shameless, brazen — **cínicamente** *adv*

cínico[2], -ca *n* **:** cynic

cinismo *nm* **:** cynicism

cinta *nf* **1 :** ribbon **2 :** tape <cinta métrica : tape measure> **3 :** strap, belt <cinta transportadora : conveyor belt>

cinto *nm* **:** strap, belt

cintura *nf* **1 :** waist, waistline **2 meter en cintura** *fam* **:** to bring into line, to discipline

cinturón *nm, pl* **-rones 1 :** belt **2 cinturón de seguridad :** seat belt

ciñe, etc. → **ceñir**

ciprés *nm, pl* **cipreses :** cypress

circo *nm* **:** circus

circón *nm, pl* **circones :** zircon

circonio *nm* **:** zirconium

circuitería *nf* **:** circuitry

circuito *nm* **:** circuit

circulación *nf, pl* **-ciones 1 :** circulation **2 :** movement **3 :** traffic

circular[1] *vi* **1 :** to circulate **2 :** to move along **3 :** to drive
circular[2] *adj* **:** circular
circular[3] *nf* **:** circular, flier
circulatorio, -ria *adj* **:** circulatory
círculo *nm* **1 :** circle **2 :** club, group
circuncidar *vt* **:** to circumcise
circuncisión *nf, pl* **-siones :** circumcision
circundar *vt* **:** to surround — **circundante** *adj*
circunferencia *nf* **:** circumference
circunflejo, -ja *adj* **acento circunflejo :** circumflex
circunlocución *nf, pl* **-ciones :** circumlocution
circunloquio *nm* → **circunlocución**
circunnavegar {52} *vt* **:** to circumnavigate — **circunnavegación** *nf*
circunscribir {33} *vt* **:** to circumscribe, to constrict, to limit — **circunscribirse** *vr*
circunscripción *nf, pl* **-ciones 1 :** limitation, restriction **2 :** constituency
circunscrito *pp* → **circunscribir**
circunspección *nf, pl* **-ciones :** circumspection, prudence
circunspecto, -ta *adj* **:** circumspect, prudent
circunstancia *nf* **:** circumstance
circunstancial *adj* **:** circumstantial, incidental
circunstante *nmf* **1 :** onlooker, bystander **2 los circunstantes :** those present
circunvalación *nf, pl* **-ciones :** surrounding, encircling <carretera de circunvalación : bypass, beltway>
circunvecino, -na *adj* **:** surrounding, neighboring
cirio *nm* **:** large candle
cirro *nm* **:** cirrus (cloud)
cirrosis *nf* **:** cirrhosis
ciruela *nf* **1 :** plum **2 ciruela pasa :** prune
cirugía *nf* **:** surgery
cirujano, -na *n* **:** surgeon
cisma *nm* **:** schism, rift
cisne *nm* **:** swan
cisterna *nf* **:** cistern, tank
cita *nf* **1 :** quote, quotation **2 :** appointment, date
citable *adj* **:** quotable
citación *nf, pl* **-ciones** EMPLAZAMIENTO **:** summons, subpoena
citadino[1], **-na** *adj* **:** of the city, urban
citadino[2], **-na** *n* **:** city dweller
citado, -da *adj* **:** said, aforementioned
citar *vt* **1 :** to quote, to cite **2 :** to make an appointment with **3 :** to summon (to court), to subpoena — **citarse** *vr* **~ con :** to arrange to meet (someone)
cítara *nf* **:** zither
citatorio *nm* **:** subpoena
citoplasma *nm* **:** cytoplasm
cítrico[1], **-ca** *adj* **:** citric
cítrico[2] *nm* **:** citrus fruit
ciudad *nf* **1 :** city, town **2 ciudad universitaria :** college or university campus **3 ciudad perdida** *Mex* **:** shantytown
ciudadanía *nf* **1 :** citizenship **2 :** citizenry, citizens *pl*
ciudadano[1], **-na** *adj* **:** civic, city
ciudadano[2], **-na** *n* **1** NACIONAL **:** citizen **2** HABITANTE **:** resident, city dweller
ciudadela *nf* **:** citadel, fortress
cívico, -ca *adj* **1 :** civic **2 :** public-spirited
civil[1] *adj* **1 :** civil **2 :** civilian
civil[2] *nmf* **:** civilian
civilidad *nf* **:** civility, courtesy
civilización *nf, pl* **-ciones :** civilization
civilizar {21} *vt* **:** to civilize
civismo *nm* **:** community spirit, civic-mindedness, civics
cizaña *nf* **:** discord, rift
clamar *vi* **:** to clamor, to raise a protest — *vt* **:** to cry out for
clamor *nm* **:** clamor, outcry
clamoroso, -sa *adj* **:** clamorous, resounding, thunderous
clan *nm* **:** clan
clandestinidad *nf* **:** secrecy <en la clandestinidad : underground>
clandestino, -na *adj* **:** clandestine, secret
clara *nf* **:** egg white
claraboya *nf* **:** skylight
claramente *adv* **:** clearly
clarear *v impers* **1 :** to clear, to clear up **2 :** to get light, to dawn — *vi* **:** to go gray, to turn white
claridad *nf* **1** NITIDEZ **:** clarity, clearness **2 :** brightness, light
clarificación *nf, pl* **-ciones** ACLARACIÓN **:** clarification, explanation
clarificar {72} *vt* ACLARAR **:** to clarify, to explain
clarín *nm, pl* **clarines :** bugle
clarinete *nm* **:** clarinet
clarividencia *nf* **1 :** clairvoyance **2 :** perspicacity, discernment
clarividente[1] *adj* **1 :** clairvoyant **2 :** perspicacious, discerning
clarividente[2] *nmf* **:** clairvoyant
claro[1] *adv* **1 :** clearly <habla más claro : speak more clearly> **2 :** of course, surely <¡claro!, ¡claro que sí! : absolutely!, of course!> <claro que entendió : of course she understood>
claro[2], **-ra** *adj* **1 :** bright, clear **2 :** pale, fair, light **3 :** clear, evident
claro[3] *nm* **1 :** clearing **2 claro de luna :** moonlight
clase *nf* **1 :** class **2** ÍNDOLE, TIPO **:** sort, kind, type
clasicismo *nm* **:** classicism
clásico[1], **-ca** *adj* **1 :** classic **2 :** classical
clásico[2] *nm* **:** classic
clasificación *nf, pl* **-ciones 1 :** classification, sorting out **2 :** rating **3** CALIFICACIÓN **:** qualification (in competitions)
clasificado, -da *adj* **:** classified <aviso clasificado : classified ad>
clasificar {72} *vt* **1 :** to classify, to sort out **2 :** to rate, to rank — *vi* CALIFICAR

: to qualify (in competitions) — **clasificarse** *vr*

claudicación *nf, pl* **-ciones** : surrender, abandonment of one's principles

claudicar {72} *vi* : to back down, to abandon one's principles

claustro *nm* : cloister

claustrofobia *nf* : claustrophobia

claustrofóbico, -ca *adj* : claustrophobic

cláusula *nf* : clause

clausura *nf* **1** : closure, closing **2** : closing ceremony **3** : cloister

clausurar *vt* **1** : to close, to bring to a close **2** : to close down

clavadista *nmf* : diver

clavado[1], -da *adj* **1** : nailed, fixed, stuck **2** *fam* : punctual, on the dot **3** *fam* : identical <es clavado a su padre : he's the image of his father>

clavado[2] *nm* : dive

clavar *vt* **1** : to nail, to hammer **2** HINCAR : to plunge, to stick **3** : to fix (one's eyes) on — **clavarse** *vr* : to stick oneself (with a sharp object)

clave[1] *adj* : key, essential

clave[2] *nf* **1** CIFRA : code **2** : key <la clave del misterio : the key to the mystery> **3** : clef **4** : keystone

clavel *nm* : carnation

clavelito *nm* : pink (flower)

clavicémbalo *nm* : harpsichord

clavícula *nf* : collarbone

clavija *nf* **1** : plug **2** : peg, pin

clavo *nm* **1** : nail <clavo grande : spike> **2** : clove **3 dar en el clavo** : to hit the nail on the head

claxon *nm, pl* **cláxones** : horn (of an automobile)

clemencia *nf* : clemency, mercy

clemente *adj* : merciful

cleptomanía *nf* : kleptomania

cleptómano, -na *n* : kleptomaniac

clerecía *nf* : ministry, ministers *pl*

clerical *adj* : clerical

clérigo, -ga *n* : cleric, member of the clergy

clero *nm* : clergy

cliché *nm* **1** : cliché **2** : stencil **3** : negative (of a photograph)

cliente, -ta *n* : customer, client

clientela *nf* : clientele, customers *pl*

clima *nm* **1** : climate **2** AMBIENTE : atmosphere, ambience

climático, -ca *adj* : climatic

climatización *nf, pl* **-ciones** : air-conditioning

climatizar {21} *vt* : to air-condition — **climatizado, -da** *adj*

clímax *nm* : climax

clínica *nf* : clinic

clínico, -ca *adj* : clinical — **clínicamente** *adv*

clip *nm* **1** : clip **2** : paper clip

clítoris *nms & pl* : clitoris

cloaca *nf* ALCANTARILLA : sewer

clocar {82} *vi* : to cluck

cloche *nm CA, Car, Col, Ven* : clutch (of an automobile)

clon *nm* : clone

cloqué, etc. → **clocar**

cloquear *vi* : to cluck

clorar *vt* : to chlorinate — **cloración** *nf*

cloro *nm* : chlorine

clorofila *nf* : chlorophyll

cloroformo *nm* : chloroform

cloruro *nm* : chloride

clóset *nm, pl* **clósets 1** : closet **2** : cupboard

club *nm* : club

clueca, clueque, etc. → **clocar**

coa *nf Mex* : hoe

coacción *nf, pl* **-ciones** : coercion, duress

coaccionar *vt* : to coerce

coactivo, -va *adj* : coercive

coagular *v* : to clot, to coagulate — **coagulación** *nf*

coágulo *nm* : clot

coalición *nf, pl* **-ciones** : coalition

coartada *nf* : alibi

coartar *vt* : to restrict, to limit

cobalto *nm* : cobalt

cobarde[1] *adj* : cowardly

cobarde[2] *nmf* : coward

cobardía *nf* : cowardice

cobaya *nf* : guinea pig

cobertizo *nm* : shed, shelter

cobertor *nm* COLCHA : bedspread, quilt

cobertura *nf* **1** : coverage **2** : cover, collateral

cobija *nf* FRAZADA, MANTA : blanket

cobijar *vt* : to shelter — **cobijarse** *vr* : to take shelter

cobra *nf* : cobra

cobrador, -dora *n* **1** : collector **2** : conductor (of a bus or train)

cobrar *vt* **1** : to charge **2** : to collect, to draw, to earn **3** : to acquire, to gain **4** : to recover, to retrieve **5** : to cash (a check) **6** : to claim, to take (a life) **7** : to shoot (game), to bag — *vi* **1** : to be paid **2 llamar por cobrar** *Mex* : to call collect

cobre *nm* : copper

cobro *nm* : collection (of money), cashing (of a check)

coca *nf* **1** : coca **2** *fam* : coke, cocaine

cocaína *nf* : cocaine

cocal *nm* : coca plantation

cocción *nf, pl* **cocciones** : cooking

cocear *vi* : to kick (of an animal)

cocer {14} *vt* **1** COCINAR : to cook **2** HERVIR : to boil

cochambre *nmf fam* : filth, grime

cochambroso, -sa *adj* : filthy, grimy

coche *nm* **1** : car, automobile **2** : coach, carriage **3 coche cama** : sleeping car **4 coche fúnebre** : hearse

cochecito *nm* : baby carriage, stroller

cochera *nf* : garage, carport

cochinada *nf fam* **1** : filthy language **2** : disgusting behavior **3** : dirty trick

cochinillo *nm* : suckling pig, piglet

cochino[1], -na *adj* **1** : dirty, filthy, disgusting **2** *fam* : rotten, lousy

cochino[2], -na *n* : pig, hog

cocido[1], **-da** *adj* **1 :** boiled, cooked **2 bien cocido :** well-done

cocido[2] *nm* ESTOFADO, GUISADO **:** stew

cociente *nm* **:** quotient

cocimiento *nm* **:** cooking, baking

cocina *nf* **1 :** kitchen **2 :** stove **3 :** cuisine, cooking

cocinar *v* **:** to cook

cocinero, -ra *n* **:** cook, chef

cocineta *nf Mex* **:** kitchenette

coco *nm* **1 :** coconut **2** *fam* **:** head **3** *fam* **:** bogeyman

cocoa *nf* **:** cocoa, hot chocolate

cocodrilo *nm* **:** crocodile

cocotero *nm* **:** coconut palm

coctel *or* **cóctel** *nm* **1 :** cocktail **2 :** cocktail party

coctelera *nf* **:** cocktail shaker

codazo *nm* **1 darle un codazo a :** to elbow, to nudge **2 abrirse paso a codazos :** to elbow one's way through

codearse *vr* **:** to rub elbows, to hobnob

códice *nm* **:** codex, manuscript

codicia *nf* AVARICIA **:** avarice, covetousness

codiciar *vt* **:** to covet

codicilo *nm* **:** codicil

codicioso, -sa *adj* **:** avaricious, covetous

codificación *nf, pl* **-ciones 1 :** codification **2 :** coding, encoding

codificar {72} *vt* **1 :** to codify **2 :** to code, to encode

código *nm* **1 :** code **2 código postal :** zip code **3 código morse :** Morse code

codo[1], **-da** *adj Mex* **:** cheap, stingy

codo[2], **-da** *n Mex* **:** tightwad, cheapskate

codo[3] *nm* **:** elbow

codorniz *nf, pl* **-nices :** quail

coeficiente *nm* **1 :** coefficient **2 coeficiente intelectual :** IQ, intelligence quotient

coexistir *vi* **:** to coexist — **coexistencia** *nf*

cofa *nm* **:** crow's nest

cofre *nm* **1** BAÚL **:** trunk, chest **2** *Mex* CAPOTE **:** hood (of a car)

coger {15} *vt* **1 :** to seize, to take hold of **2 :** to catch **3 :** to pick up **4 :** to gather, to pick **5 :** to gore — **cogerse** *vr* AGARRARSE **:** to hold on

cogida *nf* **1 :** gathering, harvest **2 :** goring

cognición *nf, pl* **-ciones :** cognition

cognitivo, -va *adj* **:** cognitive

cogollo *nm* **1 :** heart (of a vegetable) **2 :** bud, bulb **3 :** core, crux <el cogollo de la cuestión : the heart of the matter>

cogote *nm* **:** scruff, nape

cohabitar *vi* **:** to cohabit — **cohabitación** *nf*

cohechar *vt* SOBORNAR **:** to bribe

cohecho *nm* SOBORNO **:** bribe, bribery

coherencia *nf* **:** coherence — **coherente** *adj*

cohesión *nf, pl* **-siones :** cohesion

cohesivo, -va *adj* **:** cohesive

cohete *nm* **:** rocket

cohibición *nf, pl* **-ciones 1 :** (legal) restraint **2** INHIBICIÓN **:** inhibition

cohibido, -da *adj* **:** inhibited, shy

cohibir {62} *vt* **:** to inhibit, to make self-conscious — **cohibirse** *vr* **:** to feel shy or embarrassed

cohorte *nf* **:** cohort

coima *nf Arg, Chile, Peru* **:** bribe

coimear *vt Arg, Chile, Peru* **:** to bribe

coincidencia *nf* **:** coincidence

coincidir *vi* **1 :** to coincide **2 :** to agree

coito *nm* **:** sexual intercourse, coitus

coja, etc. → **coger**

cojear *vi* **1 :** to limp **2 :** to wobble, to rock **3 cojear del mismo pie :** to be two of a kind

cojera *nf* **:** limp

cojín *nm, pl* **cojines :** cushion, throw pillow

cojinete *nm* **1 :** bearing, bushing **2 cojinete de bola :** ball bearing

cojo[1], **-ja** *adj* **1 :** limping, lame **2 :** wobbly **3 :** weak, ineffectual

cojo[2], **-ja** *n* **:** lame person

cojones *nmpl usu considered vulgar* **1 :** testicles *pl* **2 :** guts *pl,* courage

col *nf* **1** REPOLLO **:** cabbage **2 col de Bruselas :** Brussels sprout **3 col rizada :** kale

cola *nf* **1** RABO **:** tail <cola de caballo : ponytail> **2** FILA **:** line (of people) <hacer cola : to wait in line> **3 :** cola, drink **4 :** train (of a dress) **5 :** tails *pl* (of a tuxedo) **6** PEGAMENTO **:** glue **7** *fam* **:** buttocks *pl,* rear end

colaboracionista *nmf* **:** collaborator, traitor

colaborador, -dora *n* **1 :** contributor (to a periodical) **2 :** collaborator

colaborar *vi* **:** to collaborate — **colaboración** *nf*

colación *nf, pl* **-ciones 1 :** light meal **2 :** comparison, collation <sacar a colación : to bring up, to broach> **3 :** conferral (of a degree)

colador *nm* **1 :** colander, strainer **2** *PRi* **:** small coffeepot

colapso *nm* **1 :** collapse **2 :** standstill

colar {19} *vt* **:** to strain, to filter — **colarse** *vr* **1 :** to sneak in, to cut in line, to gate-crash **2 :** to slip up, to make a mistake

colateral[1] *adj* **:** collateral — **colateralmente** *adv*

colateral[2] *nm* **:** collateral

colcha *nf* COBERTOR **:** bedspread, quilt

colchón *nm, pl* **colchones 1 :** mattress **2 :** cushion, padding, buffer

colchoneta *nf* **:** mat (for gymnastic sports)

colear *vi* **1 :** to wag its tail **2 vivito y coleando** *fam* **:** alive and kicking

colección *nf, pl* **-ciones :** collection

coleccionar *vt* **:** to collect, to keep a collection of

coleccionista *nmf* **:** collector

colecta *nf* **:** collection (of donations)

colectar *vt* : to collect
colectividad *nf* : community, group
colectivo[1], **-va** *adj* : collective — **colectivamente** *adv*
colectivo[2] *nm* **1** : collective **2** *Arg, Bol, Peru* : city bus
colector[1], **-tora** *n* : collector <colector de impuestos : tax collector>
colector[2] *nm* **1** : sewer **2** : manifold (of an engine)
colega *nmf* **1** : colleague **2** HOMÓLOGO : counterpart **3** *fam* : buddy
colegiado[1], **-da** *adj* : collegiate
colegiado[2], **-da** *n* **1** ÁRBITRO : referee **2** : member (of a professional association)
colegial[1], **-giala** *adj* **1** : school, collegiate **2** *Mex fam* : green, inexperienced
colegial[2], **-giala** *n* : schoolboy *m*, schoolgirl *f*
colegiatura *nf Mex* : tuition
colegio *nm* **1** : school **2** : college <colegio electoral : electoral college> **3** : professional association
colegir {28} *vt* **1** JUNTAR : to collect, to gather **2** INFERIR : to infer, to deduce
cólera[1] *nm* : cholera
cólera[2] *nf* FURIA, IRA : anger, rage
colérico, -ca *adj* **1** FURIOSO : angry **2** IRRITABLE : irritable
colesterol *nm* : cholesterol
coleta *nf* **1** : ponytail **2** : pigtail
coletazo *nm* : lash, flick (of a tail)
colgado, -da *adj* **1** : hanging, hanged **2** : pending **3 dejar colgado a** : to disappoint, to let down
colgante[1] *adj* : hanging, dangling
colgante[2] *nm* : pendant, charm (on a bracelet)
colgar {16} *vt* **1** : to hang (up), to put up **2** AHORCAR : to hang (someone) **3** : to hang up (a telephone) **4** *fam* : to fail (an exam) — **colgarse** *vr* **1** : to hang, to be suspended **2** AHORCARSE : to hang oneself **3** : to hang up a telephone
colibrí *nm* CHUPAFLOR : hummingbird
cólico *nm* : colic
coliflor *nf* : cauliflower
colilla *nf* : butt (of a cigarette)
colina *nf* CERRO, LOMA : hill
colindante *adj* CONTIGUO : adjacent, neighboring
colindar *vi* : to adjoin, to be adjacent
coliseo *nm* : coliseum
colisión *nf, pl* **-siones** : collision
colisionar *vi* : to collide
collage *nm* : collage
collar *nm* **1** : collar (for an animal) **2** : necklace <collar de perlas : string of pearls>
colmado, -da *adj* : heaping
colmar *vt* **1** : to fill to the brim **2** : to fulfill, to satisfy **3** : to heap, to shower <me colmaron de regalos : they showered me with gifts>
colmena *nf* : beehive
colmenar *nm* APIARIO : apiary
colmillo *nm* **1** CANINO : canine (tooth), fang **2** : tusk
colmilludo, -da *adj Mex, PRi* : astute, shrewd, crafty
colmo *nm* : height, extreme, limit <el colmo de la locura : the height of folly> <¡eso es el colmo! : that's the last straw!>
colocación *nf, pl* **-ciones 1** : placement, placing **2** : position, job **3** : investment
colocar {72} *vt* **1** PONER : to place, to put **2** : to find a job for **3** : to invest — **colocarse** *vr* **1** SITUARSE : to position oneself **2** : to get a job
colofón *nm, pl* **-fones 1** : ending, finale **2** : colophon
colofonia *nf* : rosin
colombiano, -na *adj & n* : Colombian
colon *nm* : (intestinal) colon
colón *nm, pl* **colones** : Costa Rican and Salvadoran unit of currency
colonia *nf* **1** : colony **2** : cologne **3** *Mex* : residential area, neighborhood
colonial *adj* : colonial
colonización *nf, pl* **-ciones** : colonization
colonizador[1], **-dora** *adj* : colonizing
colonizador[2], **-dora** *n* : colonizer, colonist
colonizar {21} *vt* : to colonize, to settle
colono, -na *n* **1** : settler, colonist **2** : tenant farmer
coloquial *adj* : colloquial
coloquio *nm* **1** : discussion, talk **2** : conference, symposium
color *nm* **1** : color **2** : paint, dye **3 colores** *nmpl* : colored pencils
coloración *nf, pl* **-ciones** : coloring, coloration
colorado[1], **-da** *adj* **1** ROJO : red **2 ponerse colorado** : to blush **3 chiste colorado** *Mex* : off-color joke
colorado[2] *nm* ROJO : red
colorante *nm* : coloring <colorante de alimentos : food coloring>
colorear *vt* : to color — *vi* **1** : to redden **2** : to ripen
colorete *nm* : rouge, blusher
colorido *nm* : color, coloring
colorín *nm, pl* **-rines 1** : bright color **2** : goldfinch
colosal *adj* : colossal
coloso *nm* : colossus
coludir *vi* : to be in collusion, to conspire
columna *nf* **1** : column **2 columna vertebral** : spine, backbone
columnata *nf* : colonnade
columnista *nmf* : columnist
columpiar *vt* : to push (on a swing) — **columpiarse** *vr* : to swing
columpio *nm* : swing
colusión *nf, pl* **-siones** : collusion
colza *nf* : rape (plant)
coma[1] *nm* : coma
coma[2] *nf* : comma
comadre *nf* **1** : godmother of one's child **2** : mother of one's godchild **3**

fam : neighbor, female friend **4** *fam* : gossip

comadrear *vi fam* : to gossip

comadreja *nf* : weasel

comadrona *nf* : midwife

comanche *nmf* : Comanche

comandancia *nf* **1** : command headquarters **2** : command

comandante *nmf* **1** : commander, commanding officer **2** : major

comandar *vt* : to command, to lead

comando *nm* **1** : commando **2** : command (for computers)

comarca *nf* REGIÓN : region

comarcal *adj* REGIONAL : regional, local

combar *vt* : to bend, to curve — **combarse** *vr* **1** : to bend, to buckle **2** : to warp, to bulge, to sag

combate *nm* **1** : combat **2** : fight, boxing match

combatiente *nmf* : combatant, fighter

combatir *vt* : to combat, to fight against — *vi* : to fight

combatividad *nf* : fighting spirit

combativo, -va *adj* : combative, spirited

combinación *nf, pl* **-ciones 1** : combination **2** : connection (in travel)

combinar *vt* **1** UNIR : to combine, to mix together **2** : to match, to put together — **combinarse** *vr* : to get together, to conspire

combo *nm* **1** : (musical) band **2** *Chile, Peru* : sledgehammer **3** *Chile, Peru* : punch

combustible[1] *adj* : combustible

combustible[2] *nm* : fuel

combustión *nf, pl* **-tiones** : combustion

comedero *nm* : trough, feeder

comedia *nf* : comedy

comediante *nmf* : actor, actress *f*

comedido, -da *adj* MESURADO : moderate, restrained

comediógrafo, -fa *n* : playwright

comedor *nm* : dining room

comején *nm, pl* **-jenes** : termite

comelón[1], **-lona** *adj, mpl* **-lones** *fam* : gluttonous

comelón[2] **-lona** *n, pl* **-lones** *fam* : big eater, glutton

comensal *nmf* : dinner guest

comentador, -dora *n* → **comentarista**

comentar *vt* **1** : to comment on, to discuss **2** : to mention, to remark

comentario *nm* **1** : comment, remark <sin comentarios : no comment> **2** : commentary

comentarista *nmf* : commentator

comenzar {29} *v* EMPEZAR : to begin, to start

comer[1] *vt* **1** : to eat **2** : to consume, to eat up, to eat into — *vi* **1** : to eat **2** CENAR : to have a meal **3 dar de comer** : to feed — **comerse** *vr* : to eat up

comer[2] *nm* : eating, dining

comercial *adj & nm* : commercial — **comercialmente** *adv*

comercializar {21} *vt* **1** : to commercialize **2** : to market

comerciante *nmf* : merchant, dealer

comerciar *vi* : to do business, to trade

comercio *nm* **1** : commerce, trade **2** NEGOCIO : business, place of business

comestible *adj* : edible

comestibles *nmpl* VÍVERES : groceries, food

cometa[1] *nm* : comet

cometa[2] *nf* : kite

cometer *vt* **1** : to commit **2 cometer un error** : to make a mistake

cometido *nm* : assignment, task

comezón *nf, pl* **-zones** PICAZÓN : itchiness, itching

comible *adj fam* : eatable, edible

comic *or* **cómic** *nm* : comic strip, comic book

comicastro, -tra *n* : second-rate actor, ham

comicidad *nf* HUMOR : humor, wit

comicios *nmpl* : elections, voting

cómico[1], **-ca** *adj* : comic, comical

cómico[2], **-ca** *n* HUMORISTA : comic, comedian, comedienne *f*

comida *nf* **1** : food **2** : meal **3** : dinner **4 comida basura** : junk food **5 comida rápida** : fast food

comidilla *nf* : talk, gossip

comienzo *nm* **1** : start, beginning **2 al comienzo** : at first **3 dar comienzo** : to begin

comillas *nfpl* : quotation marks <entre comillas : in quotes>

comilón, -lona → **comelón, -lona**

comilona *nf fam* : feast

comino *nm* **1** : cumin **2 me vale un comino** *fam* : not to matter to someone <no me importa un comino : I couldn't care less>

comisaría *nf* : police station

comisario, -ria *n* : commissioner

comisión *nf, pl* **-siones 1** : commission, committing **2** : committee **3** : percentage, commission <comisión sobre las ventas : sales commission>

comisionado[1], **-da** *adj* : commissioned, entrusted

comisionado[2], **-da** *n* → **comisario**

comisionar *vt* : to commission

comité *nm* : committee

comitiva *nf* : retinue, entourage

como[1] *adv* **1** : around, about <cuesta como 500 pesos : it costs around 500 pesos> **2** : kind of, like <tengo como mareos : I'm kind of dizzy>

como[2] *conj* **1** : how, as <hazlo como dijiste que lo harías : do it the way you said you would> **2** : since, given that <como estaba lloviendo, no salí : since it was raining, I didn't go out> **3** : if <como lo vuelva a hacer lo arrestarán : if he does that again he'll be arrested> **4 como quiera** : in any way

como[3] *prep* **1 :** like, as <ligero como una pluma : light as a feather> **2 así como :** as well as
cómo *adv* **:** how <¿cómo estás? : how are you?> <¿a cómo están las manzanas? : how much are the apples?> <¿cómo? : excuse me?, what was that?> <¿se puede? ¡cómo no! : may I? please do!>
cómoda *nf* **:** bureau, chest of drawers
comodidad *nf* **1 :** comfort **2 :** convenience
comodín *nm, pl* **-dines 1 :** joker, wild card **2 :** all-purpose word or thing **3 :** pretext, excuse
cómodo, -da *adj* **1** CONFORTABLE **:** comfortable **2 :** convenient — **cómodamente** *adv*
comodoro *nm* **:** commodore
comoquiera *adv* **1 :** in any way **2 comoquiera que :** in whatever way, however <comoquiera que sea eso : however that may be>
compa *nm fam* **:** buddy, pal
compactar *vt* **:** to compact, to compress
compacto, -ta *adj* **:** compact
compadecer {53} *vt* **:** to sympathize with, to feel sorry for — **compadecerse** *vr* **1 ~ de :** to take pity on, to commiserate with **2 ~ con :** to fit, to accord (with)
compadre *nm* **1 :** godfather of one's child **2 :** father of one's godchild **3** *fam* **:** buddy, pal
compaginar *vt* **1** COORDINAR **:** to combine, to coordinate **2 :** to collate
compañerismo *nm* **:** comradeship, camaraderie
compañero, -ñera *n* **:** companion, mate, partner
compañía *nf* **1 :** company <llegó en compañía de su madre : he arrived with his mother> **2** EMPRESA, FIRMA **:** firm, company
comparable *adj* **:** comparable
comparación *nf, pl* **-ciones :** comparison
comparado, -da *adj* **:** comparative <literatura comparada : comparative literature>
comparar *vt* **:** to compare
comparativo[1]**, -va** *adj* **:** comparative, relative — **comparativamente** *adv*
comparativo[2] *nm* **:** comparative degree or form
comparecencia *nf* **1 :** appearance (in court) **2 orden de comparecencia :** subpoena, summons
comparecer {53} *vi* **:** to appear (in court)
compartimiento *or* **compartimento** *nm* **:** compartment
compartir *vt* **:** to share
compás *nm, pl* **-pases 1 :** beat, rhythm, time **2 :** compass
compasión *nf, pl* **-siones :** compassion, pity
compasivo, -va *adj* **:** compassionate, sympathetic
compatibilidad *nf* **:** compatibility
compatible *adj* **:** compatible
compatriota *nmf* PAISANO **:** compatriot, fellow countryman
compeler *vt* **:** to compel
compendiar *vt* **:** to summarize, to condense
compendio *nm* **:** summary
compenetración *nf, pl* **-ciones :** rapport, mutual understanding
compenetrarse *vr* **1 :** to understand each other **2 ~ con :** to identify oneself with
compensación *nf, pl* **-ciones :** compensation
compensar *vt* **:** to compensate for, to make up for — *vi* **:** to be worth one's while
compensatorio, -ria *adj* **:** compensatory
competencia *nf* **1 :** competition, rivalry **2 :** competence
competente *adj* **:** competent, able — **competentemente** *adv*
competición *nf, pl* **-ciones :** competition
competidor[1]**, -dora** *adj* RIVAL **:** competing, rival
competidor[2]**, -dora** *n* RIVAL **:** competitor, rival
competir {54} *vi* **:** to compete
competitividad *nf* **:** competitiveness
competitivo, -va *adj* **:** competitive — **competitivamente** *adv*
compilar *vt* **:** to compile — **compilación** *nf*
compinche *nmf fam* **1 :** buddy, pal **2 :** partner in crime, accomplice
complacencia *nf* **:** pleasure, satisfaction
complacer {57} *vt* **:** to please — **complacerse** *vr* **~ en :** to take pleasure in
complaciente *adj* **:** obliging, eager to please
complejidad *nf* **:** complexity
complejo[1]**, -ja** *adj* **:** complex
complejo[2] *nm* **:** complex
complementar *vt* **:** to complement, to supplement — **complementarse** *vr*
complementario, -ria *adj* **:** complementary
complemento *nm* **1 :** complement, supplement **2 :** supplementary pay, allowance
completamente *adv* **:** completely, totally
completar *vt* TERMINAR **:** to complete, to finish
completo, -ta *adj* **1 :** complete **2 :** perfect, absolute **3 :** full, detailed — **completamente** *adv*
complexión *nf, pl* **-xiones :** (physical) constitution
complicación *nf, pl* **-ciones :** complication
complicado, -da *adj* **:** complicated

complicar {72} *vt* **1 :** to complicate **2 :** to involve — **complicarse** *vr*
cómplice *nmf* **:** accomplice
complicidad *nf* **:** complicity
complot *nm, pl* **complots** CONFABULACIÓN, CONSPIRACIÓN **:** conspiracy, plot
componenda *nf* **:** shady deal, scam
componente *adj & nm* **:** component, constituent
componer {60} *vt* **1** ARREGLAR **:** to fix, to repair **2** CONSTITUIR **:** to make up, to compose **3 :** to compose, to write **4 :** to set (a bone) — **componerse** *vr* **1 :** to improve, to get better **2 ~ de :** to consist of
comportamiento *nm* CONDUCTA **:** behavior, conduct
comportarse *vr* **:** to behave, to conduct oneself
composición *nf, pl* **-ciones 1** OBRA **:** composition, work **2 :** makeup, arrangement
compositor, -tora *n* **:** composer, songwriter
compostura *nf* **1 :** composure **2 :** mending, repair
compra *nf* **1 :** purchase **2 ir de compras :** to go shopping **3 orden de compra :** purchase order
comprador, -dora *n* **:** buyer, shopper
comprar *vt* **:** to buy, to purchase
compraventa *nf* **:** buying and selling
comprender *vt* **1** ENTENDER **:** to comprehend, to understand **2** ABARCAR **:** to cover, to include — *vi* **:** to understand <¡ya comprendo! : now I understand!>
comprensible *adj* **:** understandable — **comprensiblemente** *adv*
comprensión *nf, pl* **-siones 1 :** comprehension, understanding, grasp **2 :** understanding, sympathy
comprensivo, -va *adj* **:** understanding
compresa *nf* **1 :** compress **2** *or* **compresa higiénica :** sanitary napkin
compresión *nf, pl* **-siones :** compression
compresor *nm* **:** compressor
comprimido *nm* PÍLDORA, TABLETA **:** pill, tablet
comprimir *vt* **:** to compress
comprobable *adj* **:** verifiable, provable
comprobación *nf, pl* **-ciones :** verification, confirmation
comprobante *nm* **1 :** proof <comprobante de identidad : proof of identity> **2 :** voucher, receipt <comprobante de ventas : sales slip>
comprobar {19} *vt* **1 :** to verify, to check **2 :** to prove
comprometedor, -dora *adj* **:** compromising
comprometer *vt* **1 :** to compromise **2 :** to jeopardize **3 :** to commit, to put under obligation — **comprometerse** *vr* **1 :** to commit oneself **2 ~ con :** to get engaged to
comprometido, -da *adj* **1 :** compromising, awkward **2 :** committed, obliged **3 :** engaged (to be married)
compromiso *nm* **1 :** obligation, commitment **2 :** engagement <anillo de compromiso : engagement ring> **3 :** agreement **4 :** awkward situation, fix
compuerta *nf* **:** floodgate
compuesto[1] *pp* → **componer**
compuesto[2], **-ta** *adj* **1 :** fixed, repaired **2 :** compound, composite **3 :** decked out, spruced up **4 ~ de :** made up of, consisting of
compuesto[3] *nm* **:** compound
compulsión *nf, pl* **-siones :** compulsion
compulsivo, -va *adj* **1 :** compelling, urgent **2 :** compulsive — **compulsivamente** *adv*
compungido, -da *adj* **:** contrite, remorseful
compungirse {35} *vr* **:** to feel remorse
compuso, etc. → **componer**
computación *nf, pl* **-ciones :** computing, computers *pl*
computador *nm* → **computadora**
computadora *nf* **1 :** computer **2 computadora portátil :** laptop computer
computar *vt* **:** to compute, to calculate
computarizar {21} *vt* **:** to computerize
cómputo *nm* **:** computation, calculation
comulgar {52} *vi* **:** to receive Communion
común *adj, pl* **comunes 1 :** common **2 común y corriente :** ordinary, regular **3 por lo común :** generally, as a rule
comuna *nf* **:** commune
comunal *adj* **:** communal
comunicación *nf, pl* **-ciones 1 :** communication **2 :** access, link **3 :** message, report
comunicado *nm* **1 :** communiqué **2 comunicado de prensa :** press release
comunicar {72} *vt* **1 :** to communicate, to convey **2 :** to notify — **comunicarse** *vr* **~ con 1 :** to contact, to get in touch with **2 :** to be connected to
comunicativo, -va *adj* **:** communicative, talkative
comunidad *nf* **:** community
comunión *nf, pl* **-niones 1 :** communion, sharing **2 :** Communion
comunismo *nm* **:** communism, Communism
comúnmente *adv* **:** commonly
con *prep* **1 :** with <vengo con mi padre : I'm going with my father> <¿con quién hablas? : who are you speaking to?> **2 :** in spite of <con todo : in spite of it all> **3 :** to, towards <ella es amable con los niños : she is kind to the children> **4 :** by <con llegar temprano : by arriving early> **5 con (tal) que :** as long as, so long as
conato *nm* **:** attempt, effort <conato de robo : attempted robbery>

cóncavo, -va *adj* **:** concave

concebible *adj* **:** conceivable

concebir {54} *vt* **1 :** to conceive **2 :** to conceive of, to imagine — *vi* **:** to conceive, to become pregnant

conceder *vt* **1 :** to grant, to bestow **2 :** to concede, to admit

concejal, -jala *n* **:** councilman *m,* councilwoman *f,* alderman *m,* alderwoman *f*

concejo *nm* **:** council <concejo municipal : town council>

concentración *nf, pl* **-ciones :** concentration

concentrado *nm* **:** concentrate

concentrar *vt* **:** to concentrate — **concentrarse** *vr*

concéntrico, -ca *adj* **:** concentric

concepción *nf, pl* **-ciones :** conception

concepto *nm* NOCIÓN **:** concept, idea, opinion

conceptuar {3} *vt* **:** to regard, to judge

concernir {17} *vi* **:** to be of concern

concertar {55} *vt* **1 :** to arrange, to set up **2 :** to agree on, to settle **3 :** to harmonize — *vi* **:** to be in harmony

concesión *nf, pl* **-siones 1 :** concession **2 :** awarding, granting

concha *nf* **:** conch, seashell

conciencia *nf* **1 :** conscience **2 :** consciousness, awareness

concientizar {21} *vt* **:** to make aware — **concientizarse** *vr* **~ de :** to realize, to become aware of

concienzudo, -da *adj* **:** conscientious

concierto *nm* **1 :** concert **2 :** agreement **3 :** concerto

conciliador[1]**, -dora** *adj* **:** conciliatory

conciliador[2]**, -dora** *n* **:** arbitrator, peacemaker

conciliar *vt* **:** to conciliate, to reconcile — **conciliación** *nf*

concilio *nm* **:** (church) council

conciso, -sa *adj* **:** concise — **concisión** *nf*

conciudadano, -na *n* **:** fellow citizen

cónclave *nm* **:** conclave, private meeting

concluir {41} *vt* **1** TERMINAR **:** to conclude, to finish **2** DEDUCIR **:** to deduce, to infer — *vi* **:** to end, to conclude

conclusión *nf, pl* **-siones :** conclusion

concluyente *adj* **:** conclusive

concomitante *adj* **:** concomitant

concordancia *nf* **:** agreement, accordance

concordar {19} *vi* **:** to agree, to coincide — *vt* **:** to reconcile

concordia *nf* **:** concord, harmony

concretar *vt* **1 :** to pinpoint, to specify **2 :** to fulfill, to realize — **concretarse** *vr* **:** to become real, to take shape

concretizar → **concretar**

concreto[1]**, -ta** *adj* **1 :** concrete, actual **2 :** definite, specific <en concreto : specifically> — **concretamente** *adv*

concreto[2] *nm* HORMIGÓN **:** concrete

concubina *nf* **:** concubine

concurrencia *nf* **1 :** audience, turnout **2 :** concurrence

concurrente *adj* **:** concurrent — **concurrentemente** *adv*

concurrido, -da *adj* **:** busy, crowded

concurrir *vi* **1 :** to converge, to come together **2 :** to concur, to agree **3 :** to take part, to participate **4 :** to attend, to be present <concurrir a una reunión : to attend a meeting> **5 ~ a :** to contribute to

concursante *nmf* **:** contestant, competitor

concursar *vt* **:** to compete in — *vi* **:** to compete, to participate

concurso *nm* **1 :** contest, competition **2 :** concurrance, coincidence **3 :** crowd, gathering **4 :** cooperation, assistance

condado *nm* **1 :** county **2 :** earldom

conde, -desa *n* **:** count *m,* earl *m,* countess *f*

condecoración *nf, pl* **-ciones :** decoration, medal

condecorar *vt* **:** to decorate, to award (a medal)

condena *nf* **1** REPROBACIÓN **:** disapproval, condemnation **2** SENTENCIA **:** sentence, conviction

condenación *nf, pl* **-ciones 1 :** condemnation **2 :** damnation

condenado[1]**, -da** *adj* **1 :** fated, doomed **2 :** convicted, sentenced **3** *fam* **:** darn, damned

condenado[2]**, -da** *n* **:** convict

condenar *vt* **1 :** to condemn **2 :** to sentence **3 :** to board up, to wall up — **condenarse** *vr* **:** to be damned

condensación *nf, pl* **-ciones :** condensation

condensar *vt* **:** to condense

condesa *nf* → **conde**

condescendencia *nf* **:** condescension

condescender {56} *vi* **1 :** to condescend **2 :** to agree, to acquiesce

condición *nf, pl* **-ciones 1 :** condition, state **2 :** capacity, position **3 condiciones** *nfpl* **:** conditions, circumstances <condiciones de vida : living conditions>

condicional *adj* **:** conditional — **condicionalmente** *adv*

condicionamiento *nm* **:** conditioning

condicionar *vt* **1 :** to condition, to determine **2 ~ a :** to be contingent on, to depend on

condimentar *vt* SAZONAR **:** to season, to spice

condimento *nm* **:** condiment, seasoning, spice

condolencia *nf* **:** condolence, sympathy

condolerse {47} *vr* **:** to sympathize

condominio *nm* **:** condominium, condo

condón *nm, pl* **condones :** condom

cóndor *nm* **:** condor

conducción *nf, pl* **-ciones 1 :** conduction (of electricity, etc.) **2** DIRECCIÓN **:** management, direction

conducir {61} *vt* **1** DIRIGIR, GUIAR **:** to direct, to lead **2** MANEJAR **:** to drive (a vehicle) — *vi* **1 :** to drive a vehicle **2 ~ a :** to lead to — **conducirse** *vr* PORTARSE **:** to behave, to conduct oneself
conducta *nf* COMPORTAMIENTO **:** conduct, behavior
conducto *nm* **:** conduit, channel, duct
conductor[1], **-tora** *adj* **:** conducting, leading
conductor[2], **-tora** *n* **:** driver
conductor[3] *nm* **:** conductor (of electricity, etc.)
conectar *vt* **:** to connect — *vi* **~ con :** to link up with, to communicate with
conector *nm* **:** connector
conejera *nf* **:** rabbit hutch
conejillo *nm* **conejillo de Indias :** guinea pig
conejo, -ja *n* **:** rabbit
conexión *nf, pl* **-xiones :** connection
confabulación *nf, pl* **-ciones** COMPLOT, CONSPIRACIÓN **:** plot, conspiracy
confabularse *vr* **:** to plot, to conspire
confección *nf, pl* **-ciones 1 :** preparation **2 :** tailoring, dressmaking
confeccionar *vt* **:** to make, to produce, to prepare
confederación *nf, pl* **-ciones :** confederation
confederarse *vr* **:** to confederate, to form a confederation
conferencia *nf* **1** REUNIÓN **:** conference, meeting **2 :** lecture
conferenciante *nmf* **:** lecturer
conferencista *nmf* → **conferenciante**
conferir {76} *vt* **:** to confer, to bestow
confesar {55} *v* **:** to confess — **confesarse** *vr* **:** to go to confession
confesión *nf, pl* **-siones 1 :** confession **2 :** creed, denomination
confesionario *nm* **:** confessional
confesor *nm* **:** confessor
confeti *nm* **:** confetti
confiable *adj* **:** trustworthy, reliable
confiado, -da *adj* **1 :** confident, self-confident **2 :** trusting — **confiadamente** *adv*
confianza *nf* **1 :** trust <de poca confiaza : untrustworthy> **2 :** confidence, self-confidence
confianzudo, -da *adj* **:** forward, presumptuous
confiar {85} *vi* **:** to have trust, to be trusting — *vt* **1 :** to confide **2 :** to entrust — **confiarse** *vr* **1 :** to be overconfident **2 ~ a :** to confide in
confidencia *nf* **:** confidence, secret
confidencial *adj* **:** confidential — **confidencialmente** *adv*
confidencialidad *nf* **:** confidentiality
confidente *nmf* **1 :** confidant, confidante *f* **2 :** informer
configuración *nf, pl* **-ciones :** configuration, shape
configurar *vt* **:** to shape, to form
confín *nm, pl* **confines :** boundary, limit
confinamiento *nm* **:** confinement
confinar *vt* **1 :** to confine, to limit **2 :** to exile — *vi* **~ con :** to border on
confirmación *nf, pl* **-ciones :** confirmation
confirmar *vt* **:** to confirm, to substantiate
confiscar {72} *vt* DECOMISAR **:** to confiscate, to seize
confitado, -da *adj* **:** candied
confite *nm* **:** comfit, candy
confitería *nm* **1** DULCERÍA **:** candy store, confectionery **2 :** tearoom, café
confitero, -ra *n* **:** confectioner
confitura *nf* **:** preserves, jam
conflagración *nf, pl* **-ciones 1 :** conflagration, fire **2 :** war
conflictivo, -va *adj* **1 :** troubled **2 :** controversial
conflicto *nm* **:** conflict
confluencia *nf* **:** junction, confluence
confluir {41} *vi* **1 :** to converge, to join **2 :** to gather, to assemble
conformar *vt* **1 :** to form, to create **2 :** to constitute, to make up — **conformarse** *vr* **1** RESIGNARSE **:** to resign oneself **2 :** to comply, to conform **3 ~ con :** to content oneself with, to be satisfied with
conforme[1] *adj* **1 :** content, satisfied **2 ~ a :** in accordance with
conforme[2] *conj* **:** as <entreguen sus tareas conforme vayan saliendo : hand in your homework as you leave>
conformidad *nf* **1 :** agreement, consent **2 :** resignation
confort *nm* **:** comfort
confortable *adj* CÓMODO **:** comfortable
confortar *vt* CONSOLAR **:** to comfort, to console
confraternidad *nf* **:** brotherhood, fraternity
confrontación *nf, pl* **-ciones :** confrontation
confrontar *vt* **1** ENCARAR **:** to confront **2 :** to compare **3 :** to bring face-to-face — *vi* **:** to border — **confrontarse** *vr* **~ con :** to face up to
confundir *vt* **:** to confuse, to mix up — **confundirse** *vr* **:** to make a mistake, to be confused <confundirse de número : to get the wrong number>
confusión *nf, pl* **-siones :** confusion
confuso, -sa *adj* **1 :** confused, mixed-up **2 :** obscure, indistinct
congelación *nf, pl* **-ciones 1 :** freezing **2 :** frostbite
congelado, -da *adj* HELADO **:** frozen
congelador *nm* HELADORA **:** freezer
congelamiento *nm* → **congelación**
congelar *vt* **:** to freeze — **congelarse** *vr*
congeniar *vi* **:** to get along (with someone)
congénito, -ta *adj* **:** congenital
congestión *nf, pl* **-tiones :** congestion
congestionado, -da *adj* **:** congested
congestionamiento *nm* → **congestión**

congestionarse *vr* **1 :** to become flushed **2 :** to become congested
conglomerado[1], -da *adj* **:** conglomerate, mixed
conglomerado[2] *nm* **:** conglomerate, conglomeration
congoja *nf* ANGUSTIA **:** anguish, grief
congoleño, -ña *adj & n* **:** Congolese
congraciarse *vr* **:** to ingratiate oneself
congratular *vt* FELICITAR **:** to congratulate
congregación *nf, pl* **-ciones :** congregation, gathering
congregar {52} *vt* **:** to bring together — **congregarse** *vr* **:** to congregate, to assemble
congresista *nmf* **:** congressman *m*, congresswoman *f*
congreso *nm* **:** congress, conference
congruencia *nf* **1 :** congruence **2** COHERENCIA **:** coherence — **congruente** *adj*
cónico, -ca *adj* **:** conical, conic
conífera *nf* **:** conifer
conífero, -ra *adj* **:** coniferous
conjetura *nf* **:** conjecture, guess
conjeturar *vt* **:** to guess, to conjecture
conjugación *nf, pl* **-ciones :** conjugation
conjugar {52} *vt* **1 :** to conjugate **2 :** to combine
conjunción *nf, pl* **-ciones :** conjunction
conjuntivo, -va *adj* **:** connective <tejido conjuntivo : connective tissue>
conjunto[1], -ta *adj* **:** joint
conjunto[2] *nm* **1 :** collection, group **2 :** ensemble, outfit <conjunto musical : musical ensemble> **3 :** whole, entirety <en conjunto : as a whole, altogether>
conjurar *vt* **1 :** to exorcise **2 :** to avert, to ward off — *vi* CONSPIRAR **:** to conspire, to plot
conjuro *nm* **1 :** exorcism **2 :** spell
conllevar *vt* **1 :** to bear, to suffer **2** IMPLICAR **:** to entail, to involve
conmemorar *vt* **:** to commemorate — **conmemoración** *nf*
conmemorativo, -va *adj* **:** commemorative, memorial
conmigo *pron* **:** with me <habló conmigo : he talked with me>
conminar *vt* AMENAZAR **:** to threaten, to warn
conmiseración *nf, pl* **-ciones :** pity, conmiseration
conmoción *nf, pl* **-ciones 1 :** shock, upheaval **2** *or* **conmoción cerebral :** concussion
conmocionar *vt* **:** to shake, to shock
conmovedor, -dora *adj* EMOCIONANTE **:** moving, touching
conmover {47} *vt* **1** EMOCIONAR **:** to move, to touch **2 :** to shake up — **conmoverse** *vr*
conmutador *nm* **1 :** switch **2 :** switchboard
connivencia *nf* **:** connivance
connotación *nf, pl* **-ciones :** connotation
connotar *vt* **:** to connote, to imply
cono *nm* **:** cone
conocedor[1], -dora *adj* **:** knowledgeable
conocedor[2], -dora *n* **:** connoisseur, expert
conocer {18} *vt* **1 :** to know, to be acquainted with <ya la conocí : I've already met him> **2 :** to meet **3** RECONOCER **:** to recognize — **conocerse** *vr* **1 :** to know each other **2 :** to meet **3 :** to know oneself
conocido[1], -da *adj* **1 :** familiar **2 :** well-known, famous
conocido[2], -da *n* **:** acquaintance
conocimiento *nm* **1 :** knowledge **2** SENTIDO **:** consciousness
conque *conj* **:** so, so then, and so <¡ah, conque esas tenemos! : oh, so that's what's going on!>
conquista *nf* **:** conquest
conquistador[1], -dora *adj* **:** conquering
conquistador[2], -dora *n* **:** conqueror
conquistar *vt* **:** to conquer
consabido, -da *adj* **:** usual, typical
consagración *nf, pl* **-ciones :** consecration
consagrar *vt* **1 :** to consecrate **2** DEDICAR **:** to dedicate, to devote
consciencia *nf* → **conciencia**
consciente *adj* **:** conscious, aware — **conscientemente** *adv*
conscripción *nf, pl* **-ciones :** conscription, draft
conscripto, -ta *n* **:** conscript, inductee
consecución *nf, pl* **-ciones :** attainment
consecuencia *nf* **1 :** consequence, result <a consecuencia de : as a result of> **2 en ~ :** accordingly
consecuente *adj* **:** consistent — **consecuentemente** *adv*
consecutivo, -va *adj* **:** consecutive, successive — **consecutivamente** *adv*
conseguir {75} *vt* **1 :** to get, to obtain **2 :** to achieve, to attain **3 :** to manage to <consiguió acabar el trabajo : she managed to finish the job>
consejero, -ra *n* **:** adviser, counselor
consejo *nm* **1 :** advice, counsel **2 :** council <consejo de guerra : court-martial>
consenso *nm* **:** consensus
consentido, -da *adj* **:** spoiled, pampered
consentimiento *nm* **:** consent, permission
consentir {76} *vt* **1** PERMITIR **:** to consent to, to allow **2** MIMAR **:** to pamper, to spoil — *vi* **~ en :** to agree to, to approve of
conserje *nmf* **:** custodian, janitor, caretaker
conserva *nf* **1 :** preserve(s), jam **2 conservas** *nfpl* **:** canned goods
conservación *nf, pl* **-ciones :** conservation, preservation

conservacionista *nmf* **:** conservationist

conservador[1], **-dora** *adj & n* **:** conservative

conservador[2] *nm* **:** preservative

conservadurismo *nf* **:** conservatism

conservante *nm* **:** preservative

conservar *vt* **1 :** to preserve **2** GUARDAR **:** to keep, to conserve

conservatorio *nm* **:** conservatory

considerable *adj* **:** considerable — **considerablemente** *adv*

consideración *nf, pl* **-ciones 1 :** consideration **2 :** respect **3 de ~ :** considerable, important

considerado, -da *adj* **1 :** considerate, thoughtful **2 :** respected

considerar *vt* **1 :** to consider, to think over **2 :** to judge, to deem **3 :** to treat with respect

consigna *nf* **1** ESLOGAN **:** slogan **2 :** assignment, orders *pl* **3 :** checkroom

consignar *vt* **1 :** to consign **2 :** to record, to write down **3 :** to assign, to allocate

consigo *pron* **:** with her, with him, with you, with oneself <se llevó las llaves consigo : she took the keys with her>

consiguiente *adj* **1 :** resulting, consequent **2 por ~ :** consequently, as a result

consistencia *nf* **:** consistency

consistente *adj* **1 :** firm, strong, sound **2 :** consistent — **consistentemente** *adv*

consistir *vi* **1 ~ en :** to consist of **2 ~ en :** to lie in, to consist in

consola *nf* **:** console

consolación *nf, pl* **-ciones :** consolation <premio de consolación : consolation prize>

consolar {19} *vt* CONFORTAR **:** to console, to comfort

consolidar *vt* **:** to consolidate — **consolidación** *nf*

consomé *nm* CALDO **:** consommé, clear soup

consonancia *nf* **1 :** consonance, harmony **2 en consonancia con :** in accordance with

consonante[1] *adj* **:** consonant, harmonious

consonante[2] *nf* **:** consonant

consorcio *nm* **:** consortium

consorte *nmf* **:** consort, spouse

conspicuo, -cua *adj* **:** eminent, famous

conspiración *nf, pl* **-ciones** COMPLOT, CONFABULACIÓN **:** conspiracy, plot

conspirador, -dora *n* **:** conspirator

conspirar *vi* CONJURAR **:** to conspire, to plot

constancia *nf* **1** PRUEBA **:** proof, certainty **2 :** record, evidence <que quede constancia : for the record> **3 :** perseverance, constancy

constante[1] *adj* **:** constant — **constantemente** *adv*

constante[2] *nm* **:** constant

constar *vi* **1 :** to be evident, to be on record <que conste : believe me, have no doubt> **2 ~ de :** to consist of

constatación *nf, pl* **-ciones :** confirmation, proof

constatar *vt* **1 :** to verify **2 :** to state

constelación *nf, pl* **-ciones :** constellation

consternación *nf, pl* **-ciones :** consternation, dismay

consternar *vt* **:** to dismay, to appall

constipación *nf, pl* **-ciones :** constipation

constipado[1], **-da** *adj* **estar constipado :** to have a cold

constipado[2] *nm* RESFRIADO **:** cold

constiparse *vr* **:** to catch a cold

constitución *nf, pl* **-ciones :** constitution — **constitucional** *adj* — **constitucionalmente** *adv*

constitucionalidad *nf* **:** constitutionality

constituir {41} *vt* **1** FORMAR **:** to constitute, to make up, to form **2** FUNDAR **:** to establish, to set up — **constituirse** *vr* **~ en :** to set oneself up as, to become

constitutivo, -va *adj* **:** constituent, component

constituyente *adj & nmf* **:** constituent

constreñir {67} *vt* **1** FORZAR, OBLIGAR **:** to constrain, to oblige **2** LIMITAR **:** to restrict, to limit

construcción *nf, pl* **-ciones :** construction, building

constructivo, -va *adj* **:** constructive — **constructivamente** *adv*

constructor, -tora *n* **:** builder

constructora *nf* **:** construction company

construir {41} *vt* **:** to build, to construct

consuelo *nm* **:** consolation, comfort

consuetudinario, -ria *adj* **1 :** customary, habitual **2 derecho consuetudinario :** common law

cónsul *nmf* **:** consul — **consular** *adj*

consulado *nm* **:** consulate

consulta *nf* **1 :** consultation **2 :** inquiry

consultar *vt* **:** to consult

consultor[1], **-tora** *adj* **:** consulting <firma consultora : consulting firm>

consultor[2], **-tora** *n* **:** consultant

consultorio *nm* **:** office (of a doctor or dentist)

consumación *nf, pl* **-ciones :** consummation

consumado, -da *adj* **:** consummate, perfect

consumar *vt* **1 :** to consummate, to complete **2 :** to commit, to carry out

consumible *adj* **:** consumable

consumición *nf, pl* **-ciones 1 :** consumption **2 :** drink (in a restaurant)

consumido, -da *adj* **:** thin, emaciated

consumidor, -dora *n* **:** consumer

consumir *vt* **:** to consume — **consumirse** *vr* **:** to waste away

consumo *nm* **:** consumption

contabilidad *nf* **1 :** accounting, bookkeeping **2 :** accountancy
contabilizar {21} *vt* **:** to enter, to record (in accounting)
contable[1] *adj* **:** countable
contable[2] *nmf Spain* **:** accountant, bookkeeper
contactar *vt* **:** to contact — *vi* **~ con :** to get in touch with, to contact
contacto *nm* **:** contact
contado[1], **-da** *adj* **1 :** counted <tenía los días contados : his days were numbered> **2 :** rare, scarce <en contadas ocasiones : on rare occasions>
contado[2] *nm* **al contado :** cash <pagar al contado : to pay in cash>
contador[1], **-dora** *n* **:** accountant
contador[2] *nm* **:** meter <contador de agua : water meter>
contaduría *nf* **1 :** accounting office **2** CONTABILIDAD **:** accountancy
contagiar *vt* **1 :** to infect **2 :** to transmit (a disease) — **contagiarse** *vr* **1 :** to be contagious **2 :** to become infected
contagio *nm* **:** contagion, infection
contagioso, -sa *adj* **:** contagious, catching
contaminación *nf, pl* **-ciones :** contamination, pollution
contaminante *nm* **:** pollutant, contaminant
contaminar *vt* **:** to contaminate, to pollute
contar {19} *vt* **1 :** to count **2 :** to tell **3 :** to include — *vi* **1 :** to count (up) **2 :** to matter, to be of concern <eso no cuenta : that doesn't matter> **3 ~ con :** to rely on, to count on — **contarse** *vr* **~ entre :** to be numbered among
contemplación *nf, pl* **-ciones :** contemplation — **contemplativo, -va** *adj*
contemplar *vt* **1 :** to contemplate, to ponder **2 :** to gaze at, to look at
contemporáneo, -nea *adj & n* **:** contemporary
contención *nf, pl* **-ciones :** containment, holding
contencioso, -sa *adj* **:** contentious
contender {56} *vi* **1 :** to contend, to compete **2 :** to fight
contendiente *nmf* **:** contender
contenedor *nm* **1 :** container, receptacle **2 :** Dumpster™
contener {80} *vt* **1 :** to contain, to hold **2** ATAJAR **:** to restrain, to hold back — **contenerse** *vr* **:** to restrain oneself
contenido[1], **-da** *adj* **:** restrained, reserved
contenido[2] *nm* **:** contents *pl,* content
contentar *vt* **:** to please, to make happy — **contentarse** *vr* **:** to be satisfied, to be pleased
contento[1], **-ta** *adj* **:** contented, glad, happy
contento[2] *nm* **:** joy, happiness
contestación *nf, pl* **-ciones 1 :** answer, reply **2 :** protest
contestar *vt* RESPONDER **:** to answer — *vi* **1** RESPONDER **:** to answer, to reply **2** REPLICAR **:** to answer back
contexto *nm* **:** context
contienda *nf* **1 :** dispute, conflict **2 :** contest, competition
contigo *pron* **:** with you <voy contigo : I'm going with you>
contiguo, -gua *adj* COLINDANTE **:** contiguous, adjacent
continencia *nf* **:** continence
continente *nm* **:** continent — **continental** *adj*
contingencia *nf* **:** contingency, eventuality
contingente *adj & nm* **:** contingent
continuación *nf, pl* **-ciones 1 :** continuation **2 a ~ :** next <lo demás sigue a continuación : the rest follows> **3 a continuación de :** after, following
continuar {3} *v* **:** to continue
continuidad *nf* **:** continuity
continuo, -nua *adj* **:** continuous, steady, constant — **continuamente** *adv*
contonearse *vr* **:** to sway one's hips
contoneo *nm* **:** swaying, wiggling (of the hips)
contorno *nm* **1 :** outline **2 contornos** *nmpl* **:** outskirts
contorsión *nf, pl* **-siones :** contortion
contra[1] *nf* **1** *fam* **:** difficulty, snag **2 llevar la contra a :** to oppose, to contradict
contra[2] *nm* **:** con <los pros y los contras : the pros and cons>
contra[3] *prep* **:** against
contraalmirante *nm* **:** rear admiral
contraatacar {72} *v* **:** to counterattack — **contraataque** *nm*
contrabajo *nm* **:** double bass
contrabalancear *vt* **:** to counterbalance — **contrabalanza** *nf*
contrabandear *v* **:** to smuggle
contrabandista *nmf* **:** smuggler, black marketeer
contrabando *nm* **1 :** smuggling **2 :** contraband
contracción *nf, pl* **-ciones :** contraction
contracepción *nf, pl* **-ciones :** contraception
contrachapado *nm* **:** plywood
contraconceptivo *nm* ANTICONCEPTIVO **:** contraceptive — **contracepción** *nf*
contracorriente *nf* **1 :** crosscurrent **2 ir a contracorriente :** to go against the tide
contractual *adj* **:** contractual
contradecir {11} *vt* DESMENTIR **:** to contradict — **contradecirse** *vr* DESDECIRSE **:** to contradict oneself
contradicción *nf, pl* **-ciones :** contradiction
contradictorio, -ria *adj* **:** contradictory
contraer {81} *vt* **1 :** to contract (a disease) **2 :** to establish by contract

<contraer matrimonio : to get married> **3 :** to tighten, to contract — **contraerse** *vr* **:** to contract, to tighten up

contrafuerte *nm* **:** buttress

contragolpe *nm* **1 :** counterblow **2 :** backlash

contrahecho, -cha *adj* **:** deformed, hunchbacked

contraindicado, -da *adj* **:** contraindicated — **contraindicación** *nf*

contralor, -lora *n* **:** comptroller

contralto *nmf* **:** contralto

contramaestre *nm* **1 :** boatswain **2 :** foreman

contramandar *vt* **:** to countermand

contramano *nm* **a ~ :** the wrong way (on a street)

contramedida *nf* **:** countermeasure

contraorden *nf* **:** countermand

contraparte *nf* **1 :** counterpart **2 en ~ :** on the other hand

contrapartida *nf* **:** compensation

contrapelo *nm* **a ~ :** in the wrong direction, against the grain

contrapeso *nm* **:** counterbalance

contraponer {60} *vt* **1 :** to counter, to oppose **2 :** to contrast, to compare

contraposición *nf, pl* **-ciones :** comparison

contraproducente *adj* **:** counterproductive

contrapunto *nm* **:** counterpoint

contrariar {85} *vt* **1 :** to contradict, to oppose **2 :** to vex, to annoy

contrariedad *nf* **1 :** setback, obstacle **2 :** vexation, annoyance

contrario, -ria *adj* **1 :** contrary, opposite <al contrario : on the contrary> **2 :** conflicting, opposed

contrarrestar *vt* **:** to counteract

contrarrevolución *nf, pl* **-ciones** **:** counterrevolution — **contrarrevolucionario, -ria** *adj & n*

contrasentido *nm* **:** contradiction

contraseña *nf* **:** password

contrastante *adj* **:** contrasting

contrastar *vt* **1 :** to resist **2 :** to check, to confirm — *vi* **:** to contrast

contraste *nm* **:** contrast

contratar *vt* **1 :** to contract for **2 :** to hire, to engage

contratiempo *nm* **1** PERCANCE **:** mishap, accident **2** DIFICULTAD **:** setback, difficulty

contratista *nmf* **:** contractor

contrato *nm* **:** contract

contravenir {87} *vt* **:** to contravene, to infringe

contraventana *nf* **:** shutter

contribución *nf, pl* **-ciones :** contribution

contribuidor, -dora *n* **:** contributor

contribuir {41} *vt* **1** APORTAR **:** to contribute **2 :** to pay (in taxes) — *vi* **1 :** contribute, to help out **2 :** to pay taxes

contribuyente[1] *adj* **:** contributing

contribuyente[2] *nmf* **:** taxpayer

contrición *nf, pl* **-ciones :** contrition

contrincante *nmf* **:** rival, opponent

contrito, -ta *adj* **:** contrite, repentant

control *nm* **1 :** control **2 :** inspection, check **3 :** checkpoint, roadblock

controlador, -dora *n* **:** controller <controlador aéreo : air traffic controller>

controlar *vt* **1 :** to control **2 :** to monitor, to check

controversia *nf* **:** controversy

controversial → **controvertido**

controvertido, -da *adj* **:** controversial

controvertir {76} *vt* **:** to dispute, to argue about — *vi* **:** to argue, to debate

contubernio *nm* **:** conspiracy

contumacia *nf* **:** obstinacy, stubbornness

contumaz *adj, pl* **-maces :** obstinate, stubbornly disobedient

contundencia *nf* **1 :** forcefulness, weight **2 :** severity

contundente *adj* **1 :** blunt <un objeto contundente : a blunt instrument> **2 :** forceful, convincing — **contundentemente** *adv*

contusión *nf, pl* **-siones :** bruise, contusion

contuvo, etc. → **contener**

convalecencia *nf* **:** convalescence

convalecer {53} *vi* **:** to convalesce, to recover

convaleciente *adj & nmf* **:** convalescent

convección *nf, pl* **-ciones :** convection

convencer {86} *vt* **:** to convince, to persuade — **convencerse** *vr*

convencimiento *nm* **:** belief, conviction

convención *nf, pl* **-ciones 1 :** convention, conference **2 :** pact, agreement **3 :** convention, custom

convencional *adj* **:** conventional — **convencionalmente** *adv*

convencionalismo *nm* **:** conventionality

conveniencia *nf* **1 :** convenience **2 :** fitness, suitability, advisability

conveniente *adj* **1 :** convenient **2 :** suitable, advisable

convenio *nm* PACTO **:** agreement, pact

convenir {87} *vi* **1 :** to be suitable, to be advisable **2 :** to agree

convento *nm* **1 :** convent **2 :** monastery

convergencia *nf* **:** convergence

convergente *adj* **:** convergent, converging

converger {15} *vi* **1 :** to converge **2 ~ en :** to concur on

conversación *nf, pl* **-ciones :** conversation

conversador, -dora *n* **:** conversationalist, talker

conversar *vi* **:** to converse, to talk

conversión *nf, pl* **-siones :** conversion

converso, -sa *n* **:** convert

convertible *adj & nm* **:** convertible

convertidor *nm* **:** converter

convertir {76} *vt* **1 :** to convert **2 :** to transform, to change **3 :** to exchange (money) — **convertirse** *vr* **~ en :** to turn into
convexo, -xa *adj* **:** convex
convicción *nf, pl* **-ciones :** conviction
convicto[1], -ta *adj* **:** convicted
convicto[2], -ta *n* **:** convict, prisoner
convidado, -da *n* **:** guest
convidar *vt* **1** INVITAR **:** to invite **2 :** to offer
convincente *adj* **:** convincing — **convincentemente** *adv*
convivencia *nf* **1 :** coexistence **2 :** cohabitation
convivir *vi* **1 :** to coexist **2 :** to live together
convocación *nf, pl* **-ciones :** convocation
convocar {72} *vt* **:** to convoke, to call together
convocatoria *nf* **:** summons, call
convoy *nm* **:** convoy
convulsión *nf, pl* **-siones 1 :** convulsion **2 :** agitation, upheaval
convulsivo, -va *adj* **:** convulsive
conyugal *adj* **:** conjugal
cónyuge *nmf* **:** spouse, partner
coñac *nm* **:** cognac, brandy
cooperación *nf, pl* **-ciones :** cooperation
cooperador, -dora *adj* **:** cooperative
cooperar *vi* **:** to cooperate
cooperativa *nf* **:** cooperative, co-op
cooperativo, -va *adj* **:** cooperative
cooptar *vt* **:** to co-opt
coordenada *nf* **:** coordinate
coordinación *nf, pl* **-ciones :** coordination
coordinador, -dora *n* **:** coordinator
coordinar *vt* COMPAGINAR **:** to coordinate, to combine
copa *nf* **1 :** wineglass, goblet **2 :** drink <irse de copas : to go out drinking> **3 :** cup, trophy
copar *vt* **1 :** to take <ya está copado el puesto : the job is already taken> **2 :** to fill, to crowd
copartícipe *nmf* **:** joint partner
copete *nm* **1 :** tuft (of hair) **2 estar hasta el copete :** to be completely fed up
copia *nf* **1 :** copy **2 :** imitation, replica
copiadora *nf* **:** photocopier
copiar *vt* **:** to copy
copiloto *nmf* **:** copilot
copioso, -sa *adj* **:** copious, abundant
copla *nf* **1 :** popular song or ballad **2 :** couplet, stanza
copo *nm* **1 :** snowflake **2 copos de avena :** rolled oats **3 copos de maíz :** cornflakes
copra *nf* **:** copra
cópula *nf* **:** copulation
copular *vi* **:** to copulate
coque *nm* **:** coke (fuel)
coqueta *nf* **:** dressing table
coquetear *vi* **:** to flirt
coqueteo *nm* **:** flirting, coquetry
coqueto[1], -ta *adj* **:** flirtatious, coquettish
coqueto[2], -ta *n* **:** flirt
coraje *nm* **1** VALOR **:** valor, courage **2** IRA **:** anger <darle coraje a alguien : to make someone angry>
coral[1] *nm* **1 :** coral **2 :** chorale
coral[2] *nf* **:** choir
Corán *nm* **el Corán :** the Koran
coraza *nf* **1 :** armor, armor plating **2 :** shell (of an animal)
corazón *nm, pl* **-zones 1 :** heart <de todo corazón : wholeheartedly> <de buen corazón : kindhearted> **2 :** core **3 :** darling, sweetheart
corazonada *nf* **:** hunch, impulse
corbata *nf* **:** tie, necktie
corcel *nm* **:** steed, charger
corchete *nm* **1 :** hook and eye, clasp **2 :** square bracket
corcho *nm* **:** cork
corcholata *nf Mex* **:** cap, bottle top
corcovear *vi* **:** to buck
cordel *nm* **:** cord, string
cordero *nm* **:** lamb
cordial[1] *adj* **:** cordial, affable — **cordialmente** *adv*
cordial[2] *nm* **:** cordial (liqueur)
cordialidad *nf* **:** cordiality, warmth
cordillera *nf* **:** mountain range
córdoba *nf* **:** Nicaraguan unit of currency
cordón *nm, pl* **cordones 1 :** cord <cordón umbilical : umbilical cord> **2 :** cordon
cordura *nf* **1 :** sanity **2 :** prudence, good judgment
coreano[1], -na *adj & n* **:** Korean
coreano[2] *nm* **:** Korean (language)
corear *vt* **:** to chant, to chorus
coreografía *nf* **:** choreography
coreografiar {85} *vt* **:** to choreograph
coreográfico, -ca *adj* **:** choreographic
coreógrafo, -fa *n* **:** choreographer
cormorán *nm, pl* **-ranes :** cormorant
cornada *nf* **:** goring, butt (with the horns)
córnea *nf* **:** cornea
cornear *vt* **:** to gore
cornejo *nm* **:** dogwood (tree)
corneta *nf* **:** bugle, horn, cornet
cornisa *nf* **:** cornice
cornudo, -da *adj* **:** horned
coro *nm* **1 :** choir **2 :** chorus
corola *nf* **:** corolla
corolario *nm* **:** corollary
corona *nf* **1 :** crown **2 :** wreath, garland **3 :** corona (in astronomy)
coronación *nf, pl* **-ciones :** coronation
coronar *vt* **1 :** to crown **2 :** to reach the top of, to culminate
coronel, -nela *n* **:** colonel
coronilla *nf* **1 :** crown (of the head) **2 estar hasta la coronilla :** to be completely fed up
corpiño *nm* **1 :** bodice **2** *Arg* **:** brassiere, bra
corporación *nf, pl* **-ciones :** corporation

corporal *adj* **:** corporal, bodily
corporativo, -va *adj* **:** corporate
corpóreo, -rea *adj* **:** corporeal, physical
corpulencia *nf* **:** corpulence, stoutness, sturdiness
corpulento, -ta *adj* ROBUSTO **:** robust, stout, sturdy
corpúsculo *nm* **:** corpuscle
corral *nm* **1 :** farmyard **2 :** corral, pen, stockyard **3** *or* **corralito :** playpen
correa *nf* **:** strap, belt
correcaminos *nms & pl* **:** roadrunner
corrección *nf, pl* **-ciones 1 :** correction **2 :** correctness, propriety **3 :** rebuke, reprimand **4 corrección de pruebas :** proofreading
correccional *nm* REFORMATORIO **:** reformatory
correctivo, -va *adj* **:** corrective <lentes correctivos : corrective lenses>
correcto, -ta *adj* **1 :** correct, right **2 :** courteous, polite — **correctamente** *adv*
corrector, -tora *n* **:** proofreader
corredizo, -za *adj* **:** sliding <puerta corrediza : sliding door>
corredor[1], -dora *n* **1 :** runner, racer **2 :** agent, broker <corredor de bolsa : stockbroker>
corredor[2] *nm* PASILLO **:** corridor, hallway
correduría *nf* → **corretaje**
corregir {28} *vt* **1** ENMENDAR **:** to correct, to emend **2 :** to reprimand **3 corregir pruebas :** to proofread — **corregirse** *vr* **:** to reform, to mend one's ways
correlación *nf, pl* **-ciones :** correlation
correo *nm* **1 :** mail <correo aéreo : airmail> **2 :** post office
correoso, -sa *adj* **:** leathery, rough
correr *vi* **1 :** to run, to race **2 :** to rush **3 :** to flow — *vt* **1 :** to travel over, to cover **2 :** to move, to slide, to roll, to draw (curtains) **3 correr un riesgo :** to run a risk — **correrse** *vr* **1 :** to move along **2 :** to run, to spill over
correspondencia *nf* **1 :** correspondence, mail **2 :** equivalence **3 :** connection, interchange
corresponder *vi* **1 :** to correspond **2 :** to pertain, to belong **3 :** to be appropriate, to fit **4 :** to reciprocate — **corresponderse** *vr* **:** to write to each other
correspondiente *adj* **:** corresponding, respective
corresponsal *nmf* **:** correspondent
corretaje *nm* **:** brokerage
corretear *vi* **1** VAGAR **:** to loiter, to wander about **2 :** to run around, to scamper about — *vt* **:** to pursue, to chase
corrida *nf* **1 :** run, dash **2 :** bullfight
corrido[1], -da *adj* **1 :** straight, continuous **2 :** wordly, experienced
corrido[2] *nm* **:** Mexican narrative folk song
corriente[1] *adj* **1 :** common, everyday **2 :** current, present **3** *Mex* **:** cheap, trashy **4 perro corriente** *Mex* **:** mutt
corriente[2] *nf* **1 :** current <corriente alterna : alternating current> <direct current : corriente continua> **2 :** draft **3** TENDENCIA **:** tendency, trend
corrillo *nm* **:** small group, clique
corro *nm* **:** ring, circle (of people)
corroborar *vt* **:** to corroborate
corroer {69} *vt* **1 :** to corrode **2 :** to erode, to wear away
corromper *vt* **1 :** to corrupt **2 :** to rot — **corromperse** *vr*
corrompido, -da *adj* CORRUPTO **:** corrupt, rotten
corrosión *nf, pl* **-siones :** corrosion
corrosivo, -va *adj* **:** corrosive
corrugar {52} *vt* **:** to corrugate — **corrugación** *nf*
corrupción *nf, pl* **-ciones 1 :** decay **2 :** corruption
corruptela *nf* **:** corruption, abuse of power
corrupto, -ta *adj* CORROMPIDO **:** corrupt
corsario *nm* **:** privateer
corsé *nm* **:** corset
cortada *nf* **:** cut, gash
cortador, -dora *n* **:** cutter
cortadora *nf* **:** cutter, slicer
cortadura *nm* **:** cut, slash
cortafuego *nm* **:** firebreak
cortante *adj* **:** cutting, sharp
cortar *vt* **1 :** to cut, to slice, to trim **2 :** to cut out, to omit **3 :** to cut off, to interrupt **4 :** to block, to close off **5 :** to curdle (milk) — *vi* **1 :** to cut **2 :** to break up **3 :** to hang up (the telephone) — **cortarse** *vr* **1 :** to cut oneself <cortarse el pelo : to cut one's hair> **2 :** to be cut off **3 :** to sour (of milk)
cortauñas *nms & pl* **:** nail clippers
corte[1] *nm* **1 :** cut, cutting <corte de pelo : haircut> **2 :** style, fit
corte[2] *nf* **1 :** court <corte suprema : supreme court> **2 hacer la corte a :** to court, to woo
cortejar *vt* GALANTEAR **:** to court, to woo
cortejo *nm* **1** GALANTEO **:** courtship **2 :** retinue, entourage
cortés *adj* **:** courteous, polite — **cortésmente** *adv*
cortesano[1], -na *adj* **:** courtly
cortesano[2], -na *n* **:** courtier
cortesía *nf* **1 :** courtesy, politeness **2 de ∼ :** complimentary, free
corteza *nf* **1 :** bark **2 :** crust **3 :** peel, rind **4 :** cortex <corteza cerebral : cerebral cortex>
cortijo *nm* **:** farmhouse
cortina *nm* **:** curtain
cortisona *nf* **:** cortisone
corto, -ta *adj* **1 :** short (in length or duration) **2 :** scarce **3 :** timid, shy **4 corto de vista :** nearsighted
cortocircuito *nm* **:** short circuit
corvo, -va *adj* **:** curved, bent

cosa *nf* **1** : thing, object **2** : matter, affair **3 otra cosa** : anything else, something else

cosecha *nf* : harvest, crop

cosechador, -dora *n* : harvester, reaper

cosechadora *nf* : harvester (machine)

cosechar *vt* **1** : to harvest, to reap **2** : to win, to earn, to garner — *vi* : to harvest

coser *vt* **1** : to sew **2** : to stitch up — *vi* : to sew

cosmético[1], -ca *adj* : cosmetic

cosmético[2] *nm* : cosmetic

cósmico, -ca *adj* : cosmic

cosmonauta *nmf* : cosmonaut

cosmopolita *adj & nmf* : cosmopolitan

cosmos *nm* : cosmos

cosquillas *nfpl* **1** : tickling **2 hacer cosquillas** : to tickle

cosquilleo *nm* : tickling sensation, tingle

cosquilloso, -sa *adj* : ticklish

costa *nf* **1** : coast, shore **2** : cost <a toda costa : at all costs>

costado *nm* **1** : side **2 al costado** : alongside

costar {19} *v* : to cost <¿cuánto cuesta? : how much does it cost?>

costarricense *adj & nmf* : Costa Rican

costarriqueño, -ña → **costarricense**

coste *nm* → **costo**

costear *vt* : to pay for, to finance

costero, -ra *adj* : coastal, coast

costilla *nf* **1** : rib **2** : chop, cutlet **3** *fam* : better half, wife

costo *nm* **1** : cost, price **2 costo de vida** : cost of living

costoso, -sa *adj* : costly, expensive

costra *nf* **1** : crust **2** POSTILLA : scab

costumbre *nf* **1** : custom **2** HÁBITO : habit

costura *nf* **1** : seam **2** : sewing, dressmaking **3 alta costura** : haute couture

costurera *nf* : seamstress *f*

cotejar *vt* : to compare, to collate

cotejo *nm* : comparison, collation

cotidiano, -na *adj* : daily, everyday <la vida cotidiana : daily life>

cotización *nf, pl* **-ciones** **1** : market price **2** : quote, estimate

cotizado, -da *adj* : in demand, sought after

cotizar {21} *vt* : to quote, to value — **cotizarse** *vr* : to be worth

coto *nm* **1** : enclosure, reserve **2 poner coto a** : to put a stop to

cotorra *nf* **1** : small parrot **2** *fam* : chatterbox, windbag

cotorrear *vi fam* : to chatter, to gab, to blab

cotorreo *nm fam* : chatter, prattle

coyote *nm* **1** : coyote **2** *Mex fam* : smuggler (of illegal immigrants)

coyuntura *nf* **1** ARTICULACIÓN : joint **2** : occasion, moment

coz *nm, pl* **coces** : kick (of an animal)

crac *nm, pl* **cracs** : crash (of the stock market)

cozamos, etc. → **cocer**

craneal *adj* : cranial

cráneo *nf* : cranium, skull — **craneano, -na** *adj*

cráter *nm* : crater

creación *nf, pl* **-ciones** : creation

creador[1], -dora *adj* : creative, creating

creador[2], -dora *n* : creator

crear *vt* **1** : to create, to cause **2** : to originate

creatividad *nf* : creativity

creativo, -va *adj* : creative

crecer {53} *vi* **1** : to grow **2** : to increase

crecida *nf* : flooding, floodwater

crecido, -da *adj* **1** : grown, grown-up **2** : large (of numbers)

creciente *adj* **1** : growing, increasing **2 luna creciente** : waxing moon

crecientemente *adv* : increasingly

crecimiento *nm* **1** : growth **2** : increase

credencial *adj* **cartas credenciales** : credentials

credenciales *nfpl* : documents, documentation, credentials

credibilidad *nf* : credibility

crédito *nm* : credit

credo *nm* : creed, credo

credulidad *nf* : credulity

crédulo, -la *adj* : credulous, gullible

creencia *nf* : belief

creer {20} *v* **1** : to believe **2** : to suppose, to think <creo que sí : I think so> — **creerse** *vr* **1** : to believe, to think **2** : to regard oneself as <se cree guapísimo : he thinks he's so handsome>

creíble *adj* : believable, credible

creído, -da *adj* **1** *fam* : conceited **2** : confident, sure

crema *nf* **1** : cream **2 la crema y nata** : the pick of the crop

cremación *nf, pl* **-ciones** : cremation

cremallera *nf* : zipper

cremar *vt* : to cremate

cremoso, -sa *adj* : creamy

crepa *nf Mex* : crepe (pancake)

crepe *or* **crep** *nmf* : crepe (pancake)

crepé *nm* **1** → **crespón** **2 papel crepé** : crepe paper

crepitar *vi* : to crackle

crepúsculo *nm* : twilight

crescendo *nm* : crescendo

crespo, -pa *adj* : curly, frizzy

crespón *nm, pl* **crespones** : crepe (fabric)

cresta *nf* **1** : crest **2** : comb (of a rooster)

creta *nf* : chalk (mineral)

cretino, -na *n* : cretin

creyente *nmf* : believer

creyó, etc. → **creer**

crezca, etc. → **crecer**

cría *nf* **1** : breeding, rearing **2** : young **3** : litter

criadero *nm* : hatchery

criado[1], -da *adj* **1** : raised, brought up **2 bien criado** : well-bred

criado[2], -da *n* : servant, maid *f*

criador, -dora *n* : breeder

crianza *nf* : upbringing, rearing
criar {85} *vt* **1** : to breed **2** : to bring up, to raise
criatura *nf* **1** : baby, child **2** : creature
criba *nf* : sieve, screen
cribar *vt* : to sift
cric *nm, pl* **crics** : jack
crimen *nm, pl* **crímenes** : crime
criminal *adj & nmf* : criminal
crin *nf* **1** : mane **2** : horsehair
criollo[1], **-lla** *adj* **1** : Creole **2** : native, national <comida criolla : native cuisine>
criollo[2], **-lla** *n* : Creole
criollo[3] *nm* : Creole (language)
cripta *nf* : crypt
críptico, -ca *adj* **1** : cryptic, coded **2** : enigmatic, cryptic
criptón *nm* : krypton
críquet *nm* : cricket (game)
crisálida *nf* : chrysalis, pupa
crisantemo *nm* : chrysanthemum
crisis *nf* **1** : crisis **2 crisis nerviosa** : nervous breakdown
crisma *nf fam* : head <romperle la crisma a alguien : to knock someone's block off>
crisol *nm* **1** : crucible **2** : melting pot
crispar *vt* **1** : to cause to contract **2** : to irritate, to set on edge <eso me crispa : that gets on my nerves> — **crisparse** *vr* : to tense up
cristal *nm* **1** VIDRIO : glass, piece of glass **2** : crystal
cristalería *nf* **1** : glassware shop <como chivo en cristalería : like a bull in a china shop> **2** : glassware, crystal
cristalino[1], **-na** *adj* : crystalline, clear
cristalino[2] *nm* : lens (of the eye)
cristalizar {21} *vi* : to crystallize — **cristalización** *nf*
cristianismo *nm* : Christianity
cristiano, -na *adj & n* : Christian
criterio *nm* **1** : criterion **2** : judgment, sense
crítica *nf* **1** : criticism **2** : review, critique
criticar {72} *vt* : to criticize
crítico[1], **-ca** *adj* : critical — **críticamente** *adv*
crítico[2], **-ca** *n* : critic
criticón[1], **-cona** *adj, mpl* **-cones** *fam* : hypercritical, captious
criticón[2], **-cona** *n, mpl* **-cones** *fam* : faultfinder, critic
croar *vi* : to croak
croata *adj & nmf* : Croatian
crocante *adj* : crunchy
croché *or* **crochet** *nm* : crochet
cromático, -ca *adj* : chromatic
cromo *nm* **1** : chromium, chrome **2** : picture card, sports card
cromosoma *nm* : chromosome
crónica *nf* **1** : news report **2** : chronicle, history
crónico, -ca *adj* : chronic
cronista *nmf* **1** : reporter, newscaster **2** HISTORIADOR : chronicler, historian
cronología *nf* : chronology
cronológico, -ca *adj* : chronological — **cronológicamente** *adv*
cronometrador, -dora *n* : timekeeper
cronometrar *vt* : to time, to clock
cronómetro *nm* : chronometer
croquet *nm* : croquet
croqueta *nf* : croquette
croquis *nm* : rough sketch
cruce[1], **etc.** → **cruzar**
cruce[2] *nm* **1** : crossing, cross **2** : crossroads, intersection <cruce peatonal : crosswalk>
crucero *nm* **1** : cruise **2** : cruiser, warship **3** *Mex* : intersection
crucial *adj* : crucial — **crucialmente** *adv*
crucificar {72} *vt* : to crucify
crucifijo *nm* : crucifix
crucifixión *nf, pl* **-xiones** : crucifixion
crucigrama *nm* : crossword puzzle
crudo[1], **-da** *adj* **1** : raw **2** : crude, harsh
crudo[2] *nm* : crude oil
cruel *adj* : cruel — **cruelmente** *adv*
crueldad *nf* : cruelty
cruento, -ta *adj* : bloody
crujido *nm* **1** : rustling **2** : creaking **3** : crackling (of a fire) **4** : crunching
crujiente *adj* : crunchy, crisp
crujir *vi* **1** : to rustle **2** : to creak, to crack **3** : to crunch
crup *nm* : croup
crustáceo *nm* : crustacean
crutón *nm, pl* **crutones** : crouton
cruz *nf, pl* **cruces** : cross
cruza *nf* : cross (hybrid)
cruzada *nf* : crusade
cruzado[1], **-da** *adj* : crossed <espadas cruzadas : crossed swords>
cruzado[2] *nm* **1** : crusader **2** : Brazilian unit of currency
cruzar {21} *vt* **1** : to cross **2** : to exchange (words, greetings) **3** : to cross, to interbreed — **cruzarse** *vr* **1** : to intersect **2** : to meet, to pass each other
cuaderno *nm* LIBRETA : notebook
cuadra *nf* **1** : city block **2** : stable
cuadrado[1], **-da** *adj* : square
cuadrado[2] *nm* : square <elevar al cuadrado : to square (a number)>
cuadragésimo[1] *adj* : fortieth, forty-
cuadragésimo[2], **-ma** *n* : fortieth, forty- (in a series)
cuadrante *nm* **1** : quadrant **2** : dial
cuadrar *vi* : to conform, to agree — *vt* : to square — **cuadrarse** *vr* : to stand at attention
cuadriculado *nm* : grid (on a map, etc.)
cuadrilátero *nm* **1** : quadrilateral **2** : ring (in sports)
cuadrilla *nf* : gang, team, group
cuadro *nm* **1** : square <una blusa a cuadros : a checkered blouse> **2** : painting, picture **3** : baseball diamond, infield **4** : panel, board, cadre
cuadrúpedo *nm* : quadruped
cuadruple *adj* : quadruple

cuadruplicar {72} *vt* : to quadruple — **cuadruplicarse** *vr*

cuajada *nf* : curd

cuajar *vi* **1** : to curdle **2** COAGULAR : to clot, to coagulate **3** : to set, to jell **4** : to be accepted <su idea no cuajó : his idea didn't catch on> — *vt* **1** : to curdle **2** : to adorn

cual[1] *prep* : like, as

cual[2] *pron* **1 el cual, la cual, los cuales, las cuales** : who, whom, which <la razón por la cual lo dije : the reason I said it> **2 lo cual** : which <se rió, lo cual me dio rabia : he laughed, which made me mad> **3 cada cual** : everyone, everybody

cuál[1] *adj* : which, what <¿cuáles libros? : which books?>

cuál[2] *pron* **1** (*in questions*) : which (one), what (one) <¿cuál es el mejor? : which one is the best?> <¿cuál es tu apellido? : what is your last name?> **2 cuál más, cuál menos** : some more, some less

cualidad *nf* : quality, trait

cualitativo, -va *adj* : qualitative — **cualitativamente** *adv*

cualquier → **cualquiera**[1]

cualquiera[1] (**cualquier** *before nouns*) *adj, pl* **cualesquiera 1** : any, whichever <cualquier persona : any person> **2** : everyday, ordinary <un hombre cualquiera : an ordinary man>

cualquiera[2] *pron, pl* **cualesquiera 1** : anyone, anybody, whoever **2** : whatever, whichever

cuán *adv* : how <¡cuán risible fue todo eso! : how funny it all was!>

cuando[1] *conj* **1** : when <cuando llegó : when he arrived> **2** : since, if <cuando lo dices : if you say so> **3 cuando más** : at the most **4 de vez en cuando** : from time to time

cuando[2] *prep* : during, at the time of <cuando la guerra : during the war>

cuándo *adv & conj* **1** : when <¿cuándo llegará? : when will she arrive?> <no sabemos cuándo será : we don't know when it will be> **2 ¿de cuándo acá?** : since when?, how come?

cuantía *nf* **1** : quantity, extent **2** : significance, import

cuántico, -ca *adj* : quantum <teoría cuántica : quantum theory>

cuantioso, -sa *adj* **1** : abundant, considerable **2** : heavy, grave <cuantiosos daños : heavy damage>

cuantitativo, -va *adj* : quantitative — **cuantitativamente** *adv*

cuanto[1] *adv* **1** : as much as <come cuanto puedas : eat as much as you can> **2 cuanto antes** : as soon as possible **3 en ~** : as soon as **4 en cuanto a** : as for, as regards

cuanto[2], **-ta** *adj* : as many, whatever <llévate cuantas flores quieras : take as many flowers as you wish>

cuanto[3], **-ta** *pron* **1** : as much as, all that, everything <tengo cuanto deseo : I have all that I want> **2 unos cuantos, unas cuantas** : a few

cuánto[1] *adv* : how much, how many <¿a cuánto están las manzanas? : how much are the apples?> <no sé cuánto desean : I don't know how much they want>

cuánto[2], **-ta** *adj* : how much, how many <¿cuántos niños tiene? : how many children do you have?>

cuánto[3] *pron* : how much, how many <¿cuántos quieren participar? : how many want to take part?> <¿cuánto cuesta? : how much does it cost?>

cuarenta *adj & nm* : forty

cuarentavo[1] *adj* : fortieth

cuarentavo[2] *nm* : fortieth (fraction)

cuarentena *nf* **1** : group of forty **2** : quarantine

Cuaresma *nf* : Lent

cuartear *vt* **1** : to quarter **2** : to divide up — **cuartearse** *vr* AGRIETARSE : to crack, to split

cuartel *nm* **1** : barracks, headquarters **2** : mercy <una guerra sin cuartel : a merciless war>

cuartelazo *nm* : coup d'état

cuarteto *nm* : quartet

cuartilla *nf* : sheet (of paper)

cuarto[1], **-ta** *adj* : fourth

cuarto[2], **-ta** *n* : fourth (in a series)

cuarto[3] *nm* **1** : quarter, fourth <cuarto de galón : quart> **2** HABITACIÓN : room

cuarzo *nm* : quartz

cuate, -ta *n Mex* **1** : twin **2** *fam* : buddy, pal

cuatrero, -ra *n* : rustler

cuatrillizo, -za *n* : quadruplet

cuatro *adj & nm* : four

cuatrocientos[1], **-tas** *adj* : four hundred

cuatrocientos[2] *nms & pl* : four hundred

cuba *nf* BARRÍL : cask, barrel

cubano, -na *adj & n* : Cuban

cubertería *nf* : flatware, silverware

cubeta *nf* **1** : keg, cask **2** : bulb (of a thermometer) **3** *Mex* : bucket, pail

cúbico, -ca *adj* : cubic, cubed

cubículo *nm* : cubicle

cubierta *nf* **1** : covering **2** FORRO : cover, jacket (of a book) **3** : deck

cubierto[1] *pp* → **cubrir**

cubierto[2] *nm* **1** : cover, shelter <bajo cubierto : under cover> **2** : table setting **3** : utensil, piece of silverware

cubil *nm* : den, lair

cúbito *nm* : ulna

cubo *nm* **1** : cube **2** BALDE : pail, bucket, can <cubo de basura : garbage can> **3** : hub (of a wheel)

cubrecama *nm* COLCHA : bedspread

cubrir {2} *vt* : to cover — **cubrirse** *vr*

cucaracha *nf* : cockroach, roach

cuchara *nf* : spoon

cucharada *nf* : spoonful

cucharilla *or* **cucharita** *nf* : teaspoon

cucharón *nf, pl* **-rones** : ladle

cuchichear *vi* : to whisper

cuchicheo *nm* : whisper

cuchilla *nf* **1 :** kitchen knife, cleaver **2 :** blade <cuchilla de afeitar : razor blade> **3 :** crest, ridge

cuchillada *nf* **:** stab, knife wound

cuchillo *nm* **:** knife

cuclillas *nfpl* **en ~ :** squatting, crouching

cuco[1], -ca *adj fam* **:** pretty, cute

cuco[2] *nm* **:** cuckoo

cuece, cueza, etc. → cocer

cuela, etc. → colar

cuelga, cuelgue, etc. → colgar

cuello *nm* **1 :** neck **2 :** collar (of a shirt) **3 cuello del útero :** cervix

cuenca *nf* **1 :** river basin **2 :** eye socket

cuenco *nm* **:** bowl, basin

cuenta[1], etc. → contar

cuenta[2] *nf* **1 :** calculation, count **2 :** account **3 :** check, bill **4 darse cuenta :** to realize **5 tener en cuenta :** to bear in mind

cuentagotas *nfs & pl* **1 :** dropper **2 con ~ :** little by little

cuentista *nmf* **1 :** short story writer **2** *fam* **:** liar, fibber

cuento *nm* **1 :** story, tale **2 cuento de hadas :** fairy tale **3 sin ~ :** countless

cuerda *nf* **1 :** cord, rope, string **2 cuerdas vocales :** vocal cords **3 darle cuerda a :** to wind up (a clock, a toy, etc.)

cuerdo, -da *adj* **:** sane, sensible

cuerno *nm* **1 :** horn, antler **2 :** cusp (of the moon) **3 :** horn (musical instrument)

cuero *nm* **1 :** leather, hide **2 cuero cabelludo :** scalp

cuerpo *nm* **1 :** body **2 :** corps

cuervo *nm* **:** crow, raven

cuesta[1], etc. → costar

cuesta[2] *nf* **1 :** slope <cuesta arriba : uphill> **2 a cuestas :** on one's back

cuestión *nf, pl* **-tiones** ASUNTO, TEMA **:** matter, affair

cuestionable *adj* **:** questionable, dubious

cuestionar *vt* **:** to question

cuestionario *nm* **1 :** questionnaire **2 :** quiz

cueva *nf* **:** cave

cuidado *nm* **1 :** care **2 :** worry, concern **3 tener cuidado :** to be careful **4 ¡cuidado! :** watch out!, be careful!

cuidadoso, -sa *adj* **:** careful, attentive — **cuidadosamente** *adv*

cuidar *vt* **1 :** to take care of, to look after **2 :** to pay attention to — *vi* **1 ~ de :** to look after **2 cuidar de que :** to make sure that — **cuidarse** *vr* **:** to take care of oneself

culata *nf* **:** butt (of a gun)

culatazo *nf* **:** kick, recoil

culebra *nf* SERPIENTE **:** snake

culi *nmf* **:** coolie

culinario, -ria *adj* **:** culinary

culminante *adj* **punto culminante :** peak, high point, climax

culminar *vi* **:** to culminate — **culminación** *nf*

culo *nm* **1** *fam* **:** backside, behind **2 :** bottom (of a glass)

culpa *nf* **1 :** fault, blame <echarle la culpa a alguien : to blame someone> **2 :** sin

culpabilidad *nf* **:** guilt

culpable[1] *adj* **:** guilty

culpable[2] *nmf* **:** culprit, guilty party

culpar *vt* **:** to blame

cultivado, -da *adj* **1 :** cultivated, farmed **2 :** cultured

cultivador, -dora *n* **:** cultivator

cultivar *vt* **1 :** to cultivate **2 :** to foster

cultivo *nm* **1 :** cultivation, farming **2 :** crop

culto[1], -ta *adj* **:** cultured, educated

culto[2] *nm* **1 :** worship **2 :** cult

cultura *nf* **:** culture

cultural *adj* **:** cultural — **culturalmente** *adv*

cumbre *nf* CIMA **:** top, peak, summit

cumpleaños *nms & pl* **:** birthday

cumplido[1], -da *adj* **1 :** complete, full **2 :** courteous, correct

cumplido[2] *nm* **:** compliment, courtesy <por cumplido : out of courtesy> <andarse con cumplidos : to stand on ceremony, to be formal>

cumplimentar *vt* **1 :** to congratulate **2 :** to carry out, to perform

cumplimiento *nm* **1 :** completion, fulfillment **2 :** performance

cumplir *vt* **1 :** to accomplish, to carry out **2 :** to comply with, to fulfill **3 :** to attain, to reach <su hermana cumple los 21 el viernes : her sister will be 21 on Friday> — *vi* **1 :** to expire, to fall due **2 :** to fulfill one's obligations <cumplir con el deber : to do one's duty> <cumplir con la palabra : to keep one's word> — **cumplirse** *vr* **1 :** to come true, to be fulfilled <se cumplieron sus sueños : her dreams came true> **2 :** to run out, to expire

cúmulo *nm* **1** MONTÓN **:** heap, pile **2 :** cumulus

cuna *nf* **1 :** cradle **2 :** birthplace <Puerto Rico es la cuna de la música salsa : Puerto Rico is the birthplace of salsa music>

cundir *vi* **1 :** to propagate, to spread <cundió el pánico en el vecindario : panic spread throughout the neighborhood> **2 :** to progress, to make headway

cuneta *nf* **:** ditch (in a road), gutter

cuña *nf* **:** wedge

cuñado, -da *n* **:** brother-in-law *m*, sister-in-law *f*

cuño *nm* **:** die (for stamping)

cuota *nf* **1 :** fee, dues **2 :** quota, share **3 :** installment, payment

cupé *nm* **:** coupe

cupo[1], etc. → caber

cupo[2] *nm* **1 :** quota, share **2 :** capacity, room

cupón *nm, pl* **cupones 1 :** coupon, voucher **2 cupón federal :** food stamp

cúpula *nf* **:** dome, cupola

cura[1] *nm* : priest

cura[2] *nf* **1** CURACIÓN, TRATAMIENTO : cure, treatment **2** : dressing, bandage

curación *nf, pl* **-ciones** CURA, TRATAMIENTO : cure, treatment

curandero, -ra *nm* **1** : witch doctor **2** : quack, charlatan

curar *vt* **1** : to cure, to heal **2** : to treat, to dress **3** CURTIR : to tan **4** : to cure (meat) — *vi* : to get well, to recover — **curarse** *vr*

curativo, -va *adj* : curative, healing

curiosear *vi* **1** : to snoop, to pry **2** : to browse — *vt* : to look over, to check

curiosidad *nf* **1** : curiosity **2** : curio

curioso, -sa *adj* **1** : curious, inquisitive **2** : strange, unusual, odd — **curiosamente** *adv*

currículo *nm* → **currículum**

currículum *nm, pl* **-lums 1** : résumé, curriculum vitae **2** : curriculum, course of study

curry ['kurri] *nm, pl* **-rries 1** : curry powder **2** : curry (dish)

cursar *vt* **1** : to attend (school), to take (a course) **2** : to dispatch, to pass on

cursi *adj fam* : affected, pretentious

cursilería *nf* **1** : vulgarity, poor taste **2** : pretentiousness

cursiva *nf* BASTARDILLA : italic type, italics *pl*

curso *nm* **1** : course, direction **2** : school year **3** : course, subject (in school)

cursor *nm* : cursor

curtido, -da *adj* : weather-beaten, leathery (of skin)

curtidor, -dora *n* : tanner

curtiduría *nf* : tannery

curtir *vt* **1** : to tan **2** : to harden, to weather — **curtirse** *vr*

curva *nf* : curve, bend

curvar *vt* : to bend

curvatura *nf* : curvature

curvilíneo, -nea *adj* : curvaceous, shapely

curvo, -va *adj* : curved, bent

cúspide *nf* : zenith, apex, peak

custodia *nf* : custody

custodiar *vt* : to guard, to look after

custodio, -dia *n* : keeper, guardian

cúter *nm* : cutter (boat)

cutícula *nf* : cuticle

cutis *nms & pl* : skin, complexion

cuyo, -ya *adj* **1** : whose, of whom, of which **2 en cuyo caso** : in which case

D

d *nf* : fourth letter of the Spanish alphabet

dable *adj* : feasible, possible

dactilar *adj* **huellas dactilares** : fingerprints

dádiva *nf* : gift, handout

dadivoso, -sa *adj* : generous

dado, -da *adj* **1** : given **2 dado que** : given that, since

dador, -dora *n* : giver, donor

dados *nmpl* : dice

daga *nf* : dagger

dalia *nf* : dahlia

dálmata *nm* : dalmatian

daltónico, -ca *adj* : color-blind

daltonismo *nm* : color blindness

dama *nf* **1** : lady **2 damas** *nfpl* : checkers

damasco *nm* : damask

damisela *nf* : damsel

damnificado, -da *n* : victim (of a disaster)

damnificar {72} *vt* : to damage, to injure

dance, etc. → **danzar**

dandi *nm* : dandy, fop

danés[1], **-nesa** *adj* : Danish

danés[2], **-nesa** *n, mpl* **daneses** : Dane, Danish person

danza *nf* : dance, dancing <danza folklórica : folk dance>

danzante, -ta *n* BAILARÍN : dancer

danzar {21} *v* BAILAR : to dance

dañar *vt* **1** : to damage, to spoil **2** : to harm, to hurt — **dañarse** *vr*

dañino, -na *adj* : harmful

daño *nm* **1** : damage **2** : harm, injury **3 hacer daño a** : to harm, to damage **4 daños y perjuicios** : damages

dar {22} *vt* **1** : to give **2** ENTREGAR : to deliver, to hand over **3** : to hit, to strike **4** : to yield, to produce **5** : to perform **6** : to give off, to emit **7 ~ como** *or* **~ por** : to regard as, to consider — *vi* **1** ALCANZAR : to suffice, to be enough <no me da para dos pasajes : I don't have enough for two fares> **2 ~ a** *or* **~ sobre** : to overlook, to look out on **3 ~ con** : to run into **4 ~ con** : to hit upon (an idea) **5 dar de sí** : to give, to stretch — **darse** *vr* **1** : to give in, to surrender **2** : to occur, to arise **3** : to grow, to come up **4 ~ con** *or* **~ contra** : to hit oneself against **5 dárselas de** : to boast about <se las da de muy listo : he thinks he's very smart>

dardo *nm* : dart

datar *vt* : to date — *vi* **~ de** : to date from, to date back to

dátil *nm* : date (fruit)

dato *nm* **1** : fact, piece of information **2 datos** *nmpl* : data, information

dé → **dar**

de *prep* **1** : of <la casa de Pepe : Pepe's house> <un niño de tres años : a three-year-old boy> **2** : from <es de Managua : she's from Managua> <salió del edificio : he left the building> **3** : in, at <a las tres de la mañana

: at three in the morning> <salen de noche : they go out at night> **4** : than <más de tres : more than three>

deambular *vi* : to wander, to roam

debajo *adv* **1** : underneath, below, on the bottom **2 ~ de** : under, underneath **3 por ~** : below, beneath

debate *nm* : debate

debatir *vt* : to debate, to discuss — **debatirse** *vr* : to struggle

debe *nm* : debit column, debit

deber[1] *vt* : to owe — *v aux* **1** : must, have to <debo ir a la oficina : I must go to the office> **2** : should, ought to <deberías buscar trabajo : you ought to look for work> **3** (*expressing probability*) : must <debe ser mexicano : he must be Mexican> — **deberse** *vr* **~ a** : to be due to

deber[2] *nm* **1** OBLIGACIÓN : duty, obligation **2 deberes** *nmpl Spain* : homework

debidamente *adv* : properly, duly

debido, -da *adj* **1** : right, proper, due **2 ~ a** : due to, owing to

débil *adj* : weak, feeble — **débilmente** *adv*

debilidad *nf* : weakness, debility, feebleness

debilitamiento *nm* : debilitation, weakening

debilitar *vt* : to debilitate, to weaken — **debilitarse** *vr*

debilucho[1], **-cha** *adj* : weak, frail

debilucho[2], **-cha** *n* : weakling

debitar *vt* : to debit

débito *nm* **1** DEUDA : debt **2** : debit

debut [de'but] *nm, pl* **debuts** : debut

debutante[1] *nmf* : beginner, newcomer

debutante[2] *nf* : debutante *f*

debutar *vi* : to debut, to make a debut

década *nf* DECENIO : decade

decadencia *nf* **1** : decadence **2** : decline

decadente *adj* **1** : decadent **2** : declining

decaer {13} *vi* **1** : to decline, to decay, to deteriorate **2** FLAQUEAR : to weaken, to flag

decaiga, etc. → **decaer**

decano, -na *n* **1** : dean **2** : senior member

decantar *vt* : to decant

decapitar *vt* : to decapitate, to behead

decayó, etc. → **decaer**

decena *nf* : group of ten

decencia *nf* : decency

decenio *nm* DÉCADA : decade

decente *adj* : decent — **decentemente** *adv*

decepción *nf, pl* **-ciones** : disappointment, letdown

decepcionante *adj* : disappointing

decepcionar *vt* : to disappoint, to let down — **decepcionarse** *vr*

deceso *nm* DEFUNCIÓN : death, passing

dechado *nm* **1** : sampler (of embroidery) **2** : model, paragon

decibelio *or* **decibel** *nm* : decibel

decidido, -da *adj* : decisive, determined, resolute — **decididamente** *adv*

decidir *vt* **1** : to decide, to determine <no he decidido nada : I haven't made a decision> **2** : to persuade, to decide <su padre lo decidió a estudiar : his father persuaded him to study> — *vi* : to decide — **decidirse** *vr* : to make up one's mind

decimal *adj* : decimal

décimo, -ma *adj* : tenth — **décimo, -ma** *n*

decimoctavo[1], **-va** *adj* : eighteenth

decimoctavo[2], **-va** *nm* : eighteenth (in a series)

decimocuarto[1], **-ta** *adj* : fourteenth

decimocuarto[2], **-ta** *nm* : fourteenth (in a series)

decimonoveno[1], **-na** *or* **decimonono, -na** *adj* : nineteenth

decimonoveno[2], **-na** *or* **decimonono, -na** *nm* : nineteenth (in a series)

decimoquinto[1], **-ta** *adj* : fifteenth

decimoquinto[2], **-ta** *nm* : fifteenth (in a series)

decimoséptimo[1], **-ma** *adj* : seventeenth

decimoséptimo[2], **-ma** *nm* : seventeenth (in a series)

decimosexto[1], **-ta** *adj* : sixteenth

decimosexto[2], **-ta** *nm* : sixteenth (in a series)

decimotercero[1], **-ra** *adj* : thirteenth

decimotercero[2], **-ra** *nm* : thirteenth (in a series)

decir[1] {23} *vt* **1** : to say <dice que no quiere ir : she says she doesn't want to go> **2** : to tell <dime lo que estás pensando : tell me what you're thinking> **3** : to speak, to talk <no digas tonterías : don't talk nonsense> **4** : to call <me dicen Rosy : they call me Rosy> **5 es decir** : that is to say **6 querer decir** : to mean — **decirse** *vr* **1** : to say to oneself **2** : to be said <¿cómo se dice "lápiz" en francés? : how do you say "pencil" in French?>

decir[2] *nm* DICHO : saying, expression

decisión *nf, pl* **-siones** : decision, choice

decisivo, -va *adj* : decisive, conclusive — **decisivamente** *adv*

declamar *vi* : to declaim — *vt* : to recite

declaración *nf, pl* **-ciones 1** : declaration, statement **2** TESTIMONIO : deposition, testimony **3 declaración de derechos** : bill of rights **4 declaración jurada** : affidavit

declarado, -da *adj* : professed, open — **declaradamente** *adv*

declarar *vt* : to declare, to state — *vi* ATESTIGUAR : to testify — **declararse** *vr* **1** : to declare oneself, to make a statement **2** : to confess one's love **3**

: to plead (in court) <declararse inocente : to plead not guilty>
declinación *nf, pl* **-ciones 1 :** drop, downward trend **2 :** declination **3 :** declension (in grammar)
declinar *vt* **:** to decline, to turn down — *vi* **1 :** to draw to a close **2 :** to diminish, to decline
declive *nm* **1** DECADENCIA **:** decline **2 :** slope, incline
decodificador *nm* **:** decoder
decolar *vi Chile, Col, Ecua* **:** to take off (of an airplane)
decolorar *vt* **:** to bleach — **decolorarse** *vr* **:** to fade
decomisar *vt* CONFISCAR **:** to seize, to confiscate
decomiso *nm* **:** seizure, confiscation
decoración *nf, pl* **-ciones 1 :** decoration **2 :** decor **3 :** stage set, scenery
decorado *nm* **:** stage set, scenery
decorador, -dora *n* **:** decorator
decorar *vt* ADORNAR **:** to decorate, to adorn
decorativo, -va *adj* **:** decorative, ornamental
decoro *nm* **:** decorum, propriety
decoroso, -sa *adj* **:** decent, proper, respectable
decrecer {53} *vi* **:** to decrease, to wane, to diminish — **decreciente** *adj*
decrecimiento *nm* **:** decrease, decline
decrépito, -ta *adj* **:** decrepit
decretar *vt* **:** to decree, to order
decreto *nm* **:** decree
decúbito *nm* **:** horizontal position <en decúbito prono : prone> <en decúbito supino : supine>
dedal *nm* **:** thimble
dedalera *nf* DIGITAL **:** foxglove
dedicación *nf, pl* **-ciones :** dedication, devotion
dedicar {72} *vt* CONSAGRAR **:** to dedicate, to devote — **dedicarse** *vr* **~ a :** to devote oneself to, to engage in
dedicatoria *nf* **:** dedication (of a book, song, etc.)
dedo *nm* **1 :** finger <dedo meñique : little finger> **2 dedo del pie :** toe
deducción *nf, pl* **-ciones :** deduction
deducible *adj* **1 :** deducible, inferable **2 :** deductible
deducir {61} *vt* **1** INFERIR **:** to deduce **2** DESCONTAR **:** to deduct
defecar {72} *vi* **:** to defecate — **defecación** *nf*
defecto *nm* **1 :** defect, flaw, shortcoming **2 en su defecto :** lacking that, in the absence of that
defectuoso, -sa *adj* **:** defective, faulty
defender {56} *vt* **:** to defend, to protect — **defenderse** *vr* **1 :** to defend oneself **2 :** to get by, to know the basics <su inglés no es perfecto pero se defiende : his English isn't perfect but he gets by>
defendible *adj* **:** defensible, tenable
defensa[1] *nf* **:** defense
defensa[2] *nmf* **:** defender, back (in sports)
defensiva *nf* **:** defensive, defense
defensivo, -va *adj* **:** defensive — **defensivamente** *adv*
defensor[1], **-sora** *adj* **:** defending, defense
defensor[2], **-sora** *n* **1 :** defender, advocate **2 :** defense counsel
defeño, -ña *n* **:** person from the Federal District (Mexico City)
deficiencia *nf* **:** deficiency, flaw
deficiente *adj* **:** deficient
déficit *nm, pl* **-cits 1 :** deficit **2 :** shortage, lack
definición *nf, pl* **-ciones :** definition
definido, -da *adj* **:** definite, well-defined
definir *vt* **1 :** to define **2 :** to determine
definitivamente *adv* **1 :** finally **2 :** permanently, for good **3 :** definitely, absolutely
definitivo, -va *adj* **1 :** definitive, conclusive **2 en definitiva :** all in all, on the whole **3 en definitiva** *Mex* **:** permanently, for good
deflación *nf, pl* **-ciones :** deflation
deforestación *nf, pl* **-ciones :** deforestation
deformación *nf, pl* **-ciones 1 :** deformation **2 :** distortion
deformar *vt* **1 :** to deform, to disfigure **2 :** to distort — **deformarse** *vr*
deforme *adj* **:** deformed, misshapen
deformidad *nf* **:** deformity
defraudación *nf, pl* **-ciones :** fraud
defraudar *vt* **1** ESTAFAR **:** to defraud, to cheat **2 :** to disappoint
defunción *nf, pl* **-ciones** DECESO **:** death, passing
degeneración *nf, pl* **-ciones 1 :** degeneration **2 :** degeneracy, depravity
degenerado, -da *adj* DEPRAVADO **:** degenerate
degenerar *vi* **:** to degenerate
degenerativo, -va *adj* **:** degenerative
degollar {19} *vt* **1 :** to slit the throat of, to slaughter **2** DECAPITAR **:** to behead **3 :** to ruin, to destroy
degradación *nf, pl* **-ciones 1 :** degradation **2 :** demotion
degradar *vt* **1 :** to degrade, to debase **2 :** to demote
degustación *nf, pl* **-ciones :** tasting, sampling
degustar *vt* **:** to taste
deidad *nf* **:** deity
deificar {72} *vt* **:** to idolize, to deify
dejado, -da *adj* **1 :** slovenly **2 :** careless, lazy
dejar *vt* **1 :** to leave **2** ABANDONAR **:** to abandon, to forsake **3 :** to let be, to let go **4** PERMITIR **:** to allow, to permit — *vi* **~ de :** to stop, to quit <dejar de fumar : to quit smoking> — **dejarse** *vr* **1 :** to let oneself be <se deja insultar : he lets himself be insulted> **2 :** to forget, to leave <me dejé las llaves en el carro : I left the keys in

the car> **3 :** to neglect oneself, to let oneself go **4 :** to grow <nos estamos dejando el pelo largo **:** we're growing our hair long>

dejo *nm* **1 :** aftertaste **2 :** touch, hint **3 :** (regional) accent

delación *nf, pl* **-ciones :** denunciation, betrayal

delantal *nm* **1 :** apron **2 :** pinafore

delante *adv* **1** ENFRENTE **:** ahead, in front **2 ~ de :** before, in front of

delantera *nf* **1 :** front, front part, front row <tomar la delantera **:** to take the lead> **2 :** forward line (in sports)

delantero[1], -ra *adj* **1 :** front, forward **2 tracción delantera :** front-wheel drive

delantero[2], -ra *n* **:** forward (in sports)

delatar *vt* **1 :** to betray, to reveal **2 :** to denounce, to inform against

delegación *nf, pl* **-ciones :** delegation

delegado, -da *n* **:** delegate, representative

delegar {52} *vt* **:** to delegate

deleitar *vt* **:** to delight, to please — **deleitarse** *vr*

deleite *nm* **:** delight, pleasure

deletrear *vi* **:** to spell <¿como se deletrea? **:** how do you spell it?>

deleznable *adj* **1 :** brittle, crumbly **2 :** slippery **3 :** weak, fragile <una excusa deleznable **:** a weak excuse>

delfín *nm, pl* **delfines 1 :** dolphin **2 :** dauphin, heir apparent

delgadez *nf* **:** thinness, skinniness

delgado, -da *adj* **1** FLACO **:** thin, skinny **2** ESBELTO **:** slender, slim **3** DELICADO **:** delicate, fine **4** AGUDO **:** sharp, clever

deliberación *nf, pl* **-ciones :** deliberation

deliberado, -da *adj* **:** deliberate, intentional — **deliberadamente** *adv*

deliberar *vi* **:** to deliberate

deliberativo, -va *adj* **:** deliberative

delicadeza *nf* **1 :** delicacy, fineness **2 :** gentleness, softness **3 :** tact, discretion, consideration

delicado, -da *adj* **1 :** delicate, fine **2 :** sensitive, frail **3 :** difficult, tricky **4 :** fussy, hard to please **5 :** tactful, considerate

delicia *nf* **:** delight

delicioso, -sa *adj* **1** RICO **:** delicious **2 :** delightful

delictivo, -va *adj* **:** criminal

delictuoso, -sa → **delictivo**

delimitación *nf, pl* **-ciones 1 :** demarcation **2 :** defining, specifying

delimitar *vt* **1 :** to demarcate **2 :** to define, to specify

delincuencia *nf* **:** delinquency, crime

delincuente[1] *adj* **:** delinquent

delincuente[2] *nmf* CRIMINAL **:** delinquent, criminal

delinear *vt* **1 :** to delineate, to outline **2 :** to draft, to draw up

delinquir {24} *vi* **:** to break the law

delirante *adj* **:** delirious

delirar *vi* DESVARIAR **1 :** to be delirious **2 :** to rave, to talk nonsense

delirio *nm* **1** DESVARÍO **:** delirium **2** DISPARATE **:** nonsense, ravings *pl* <delirios de grandeza **:** delusions of grandeur> **3** FRENESÍ **:** mania, frenzy <¡fue el delirio! **:** it was wild!>

delito *nm* **:** crime, offense

delta *nm* **:** delta

demacrado, -da *adj* **:** emaciated, gaunt

demagogia *nf* **:** demagogy

demagógico, -ca *adj* **:** demagogic, demagogical

demagogo, -ga *n* **:** demagogue

demanda *nf* **1 :** demand <la oferta y la demanda **:** supply and demand> **2 :** petition, request **3 :** lawsuit

demandado, -da *n* **:** defendant

demandante *nmf* **:** plaintiff

demandar *vt* **1 :** to demand **2** REQUERIR **:** to call for, to require **3 :** to sue, to file a lawsuit against

demarcar {72} *vt* **:** to demarcate — **demarcación** *nf*

demás[1] *adj* **:** remaining <acabó las demás tareas **:** she finished the rest of the chores>

demás[2] *pron* **1 lo (la, los, las) demás :** the rest, everyone else, everything else <Pepe, Rosa, y los demás **:** Pepe, Rosa, and everybody else> **2 estar por demás :** to be of no use, to be pointless <no estaría por demás **:** it couldn't hurt, it's worth a try> **3 por demás :** extremely **4 por lo demás :** otherwise **5 y demás :** and so on, et cetera

demasía *nf* **en ~ :** excessively, in excess

demasiado[1] *adv* **1 :** too <vas demasiado aprisa **:** you're going too fast> **2 :** too much <estoy comiendo demasiado **:** I'm eating too much>

demasiado[2], -da *adj* **:** too much, too many, excessive

demencia *nf* **1 :** dementia **2** LOCURA **:** madness, insanity

demente[1] *adj* **:** insane, mad

demente[2] *nmf* **:** insane person

demeritar *vt* **1 :** to detract from **2 :** to discredit

demérito *nm* **1 :** fault **2 :** discredit, disrepute

democracia *nf* **:** democracy

demócrata[1] *adj* **:** democratic

demócrata[2] *nmf* **:** democrat

democrático, -ca *adj* **:** democratic — **democráticamente** *adv*

democratizar {21} *vt* **:** to democratize, to make democratic

demografía *nf* **:** demography

demográfico, -ca *adj* **:** demographic

demoledor, -dora *adj* **:** devastating

demoler {47} *vt* DERRIBAR, DERRUMBAR **:** to demolish, to destroy

demolición *nf, pl* **-ciones :** demolition

demonio *nm* DIABLO **:** devil, demon

demora *nf* **:** delay

demorar *vt* **1** RETRASAR **:** to delay **2** TARDAR **:** to take, to last <la reparación demorará varios días : the repair will take several days> — *vi* **:** to delay, to linger — **demorarse** *vr* **1 :** to be slow, to take a long time **2 :** to take too long

demostración *nf, pl* **-ciones :** demonstration

demostrar {19} *vt* **:** to demonstrate, to show

demostrativo, -va *adj* **:** demonstrative

demudar *vt* **:** to change, to alter — **demudarse** *vr* **:** to change one's expression

denegación *nf, pl* **-ciones :** denial, refusal

denegar {49} *vt* **:** to deny, to turn down

denigrante *adj* **:** degrading, humiliating

denigrar *vt* **1** DIFAMAR **:** to denigrate, to disparage **2 :** to degrade, to humiliate

denodado, -da *adj* **:** bold, dauntless

denominación *nf, pl* **-ciones 1 :** name, designation **2 :** denomination (of money)

denominador *nm* **:** denominator

denominar *vt* **:** to designate, to name

denostar {19} *vt* **:** to revile

denotar *vt* **:** to denote, to show

densidad *nf* **:** density, thickness

denso, -sa *adj* **:** dense, thick — **densamente** *adv*

dentado, -da *adj* SERRADO **:** serrated, jagged

dentadura *nf* **1 :** teeth *pl* **2 dentadura postiza :** dentures *pl*

dental *adj* **:** dental

dentellada *nf* **1 :** bite **2 :** tooth mark

dentera *nf* **1 :** envy, jealousy **2 dar dentera :** to set one's teeth on edge

dentición *nf, pl* **-ciones 1 :** teething **2 :** dentition, set of teeth

dentífrico *nm* **:** toothpaste

dentista *nmf* **:** dentist

dentro *adv* **1 :** in, inside **2 :** indoors **3 ~ de :** within, inside, in **4 dentro de poco :** soon, shortly **5 dentro de todo :** all in all, all things considered **6 por ~ :** inwardly, inside

denuedo *nm* **:** valor, courage

denuesto *nm* **:** insult

denuncia *nf* **1 :** denunciation, condemnation **2 :** police report

denunciante *nmf* **:** accuser (of a crime)

denunciar *vt* **1 :** to denounce, to condemn **2 :** to report (to the authorities)

deparar *vt* **:** to have in store for, to provide with <no sabemos lo que nos depara el destino : we don't know what fate has in store for us>

departamental *adj* **1 :** departmental **2 tienda departamental** *Mex* **:** department store

departamento *nm* **1 :** department **2** APARTAMENTO **:** apartment

departir *vi* **:** to converse

dependencia *nf* **1 :** dependence, dependency <dependencia emocional : emotional dependence> <dependencia del alcohol : dependence on alcohol> **2 :** agency, branch office

depender *vi* **1 :** to depend **2 ~ de :** to depend on **3 ~ de :** to be subordinate to

dependiente[1] *adj* **:** dependent

dependiente[2], -ta *n* **:** clerk, salesperson

deplorable *adj* **:** deplorable

deplorar *vt* **1 :** to deplore **2** LAMENTAR **:** to regret

deponer {60} *vt* **1 :** to depose, to overthrow **2 :** to abandon (an attitude or stance) **3 deponer las armas :** to lay down one's arms — *vi* **1** TESTIFICAR **:** to testify, to make a statement **2** EVACUAR **:** to defecate

deportación *nf, pl* **-ciones :** deportation

deportar *vt* **:** to deport

deporte *nm* **:** sport, sports *pl* <hacer deporte : to engage in sports>

deportista[1] *adj* **1 :** fond of sports **2 :** sporty

deportista[2] *nmf* **1 :** sports fan **2 :** athlete, sportsman *m,* sportswoman *f*

deportividad *nf Spain* **:** sportsmanship

deportivo, -va *adj* **1 :** sports, sporting <artículos deportivos : sporting goods> **2 :** sporty

deposición *nf, pl* **-ciones 1 :** statement, testimony **2 :** removal from office

depositante *nmf* **:** depositor

depositar *vt* **1 :** to deposit, to place **2 :** to store — **depositarse** *vr* **:** to settle

depósito *nm* **1 :** deposit **2 :** warehouse, storehouse

depravado, -da *adj* DEGENERADO **:** depraved, degenerate

depravar *vt* **:** to deprave, to corrupt

depreciación *nf, pl* **-ciones :** depreciation

depreciar *vt* **:** to depreciate, to reduce the value of — **depreciarse** *vr* **:** to lose value

depredación *nf* SAQUEO **:** depredation, plunder

depredador[1], -dora *adj* **:** predatory

depredador[2] *nm* **1 :** predator **2** SAQUEADOR **:** plunderer

depresión *nf, pl* **-siones 1 :** depression **2 :** hollow, recess **3 :** drop, fall **4 :** slump, recession

depresivo[1], -va *adj* **1 :** depressive **2 :** depressant

depresivo[2] *nm* **:** depressant

deprimente *adj* **:** depressing

deprimir *vt* **1 :** to depress **2 :** to lower — **deprimirse** *vr* ABATIRSE **:** to get depressed

depuesto *pp* → **deponer**

depuración *nf, pl* **-ciones 1** PURIFICACIÓN **:** purification **2** PURGA **:** purge **3 :** refinement, polish

depurar *vt* **1** PURIFICAR **:** to purify **2** PURGAR **:** to purge

depuso, etc. → **deponer**

derecha *nf* **1 :** right **2 :** right hand, right side **3 :** right wing, right (in politics)

derechazo *nm* **1 :** pass with the cape on the right hand (in bullfighting) **2 :** right (in boxing) **3 :** forehand (in tennis)
derechista[1] *adj* **:** rightist, right-wing
derechista[2] *nmf* **:** right-winger
derecho[1] *adv* **1 :** straight **2 :** upright **3 :** directly
derecho[2], **-cha** *adj* **1 :** right **2 :** right-hand **3 :** RECTO **:** straight, upright, erect
derecho[3] *nm* **1 :** right <derechos humanos : human rights> **2 :** law <derecho civil : civil law> **3 :** right side (of cloth or clothing)
deriva *nf* **1 :** drift **2 a la deriva :** adrift
derivación *nf, pl* **-ciones :** derivation
derivar *vi* **1 :** to drift **2 ~ de :** to come from, to derive from **3 ~ en :** to result in — *vt* **:** to steer, to direct <derivó la discusión hacia la política : he steered the discussion over to politics> — **derivarse** *vr* **:** to be derived from, to arise from
dermatología *nf* **:** dermatology
dermatológico, -ca *adj* **:** dermatological
dermatólogo, -ga *n* **:** dermatologist
derogación *nf, pl* **-ciones :** abolition, repeal
derogar {52} *vt* ABOLIR **:** to abolish, to repeal
derramamiento *nm* **1 :** spilling, overflowing **2 derramamiento de sangre :** bloodshed
derramar *vt* **1 :** to spill **2 :** to shed (tears, blood) — **derramarse** *vr* **1 :** to spill over **2 :** to scatter
derrame *nm* **1 :** spilling, shedding **2 :** leakage, overflow **3 :** discharge, hemorrhage
derrapar *vi* **:** to skid
derrape *nm* **:** skid
derredor *nm* **al derredor** *or* **en derredor :** around, round about
derrengado, -da *adj* **1 :** bent, twisted **2 :** exhausted
derretir {54} *vt* **:** to melt, to thaw — **derretirse** *vr* **1 :** to melt, to thaw **2 ~ por** *fam* **:** to be crazy about
derribar *vt* **1** DEMOLER, DERRUMBAR **:** to demolish, to knock down **2 :** to shoot down, to bring down (an airplane) **3** DERROCAR **:** to overthrow
derribo *nm* **1 :** demolition, razing **2 :** shooting down **3 :** overthrow
derrocamiento *nm* **:** overthrow
derrocar {72} *vt* DERRIBAR **:** to overthrow, to topple
derrochador[1], **-dora** *adj* **:** extravagant, wasteful
derrochador[2], **-dora** *n* **:** spendthrift
derrochar *vt* **:** to waste, to squander
derroche *nm* **:** extravagance, waste
derrota *nf* **1 :** defeat, rout **2 :** course (at sea)
derrotar *vt* **:** to defeat
derrotero *nm* RUTA **:** course
derrotista *adj & nmf* **:** defeatist
derruir {41} *vt* **:** to demolish, to tear down
derrumbamiento *nm* **:** collapse
derrumbar *vt* **1** DEMOLER, DERRIBAR **:** to demolish, to knock down **2** DESPEÑAR **:** to cast down, to topple — **derrumbarse** *vr* DESPLOMARSE **:** to collapse, to break down
derrumbe *nm* **1** DESPLOME **:** collapse, fall <el derrumbe del comunismo : the fall of Communism> **2 :** landslide
desabastecimiento *nm* **:** shortage, scarcity
desabasto *nm Mex* **:** shortage, scarcity
desabrido, -da *adj* **:** tasteless, bland
desabrigar {52} *vt* **1 :** to undress **2 :** to uncover **3 :** to deprive of shelter
desabrochar *vt* **:** to unbutton, to undo — **desabrocharse** *vr* **:** to come undone
desacato *nm* **1 :** disrespect **2 :** contempt (of court)
desacelerar *vi* **:** to decelerate, to slow down
desacertado, -da *adj* **1 :** mistaken **2 :** unwise
desacertar {55} *vi* ERRAR **:** to err, to be mistaken
desacierto *nm* ERROR **:** error, mistake
desaconsejado, -da *adj* **:** ill-advised, unwise
desacorde *adj* **1 :** conflicting **2 :** discordant
desacostumbrado, -da *adj* **:** unaccustomed, unusual
desacreditar *vt* DESPRESTIGIAR **:** to discredit, to disgrace
desactivar *vt* **:** to deactivate, to defuse
desacuerdo *nm* **:** disagreement
desafiante *adj* **:** defiant
desafiar {85} *vt* RETAR **:** to defy, to challenge
desafilado, -da *adj* **:** blunt
desafinado, -da *adj* **:** out-of-tune, off-key
desafinarse *vr* **:** to go out of tune
desafío *nm* **1** RETO **:** challenge **2** RESISTENCIA **:** defiance
desafortunado, -da *adj* **:** unfortunate, unlucky — **desafortunadamente** *adv*
desafuero *nm* ABUSO **:** injustice, outrage
desagradable *adj* **:** unpleasant, disagreeable — **desagradablemente** *adv*
desagradar *vi* **:** to be unpleasant, to be disagreeable
desagradecido, -da *adj* **:** ungrateful
desagrado *nm* **1 :** displeasure **2 con ~ :** reluctantly
desagravio *nm* **1 :** apology **2 :** amends, reparation
desagregarse {52} *vr* **:** to break up, to disintegrate
desaguar {10} *vi* **:** to drain, to empty
desagüe *nm* **1 :** drain **2 :** drainage
desahogado, -da *adj* **1 :** well-off, comfortable **2 :** spacious, roomy

desahogar {52} *vt* **1 :** to relieve, to ease **2 :** to give vent to — **desahogarse** *vr* **1 :** to recover, to feel better **2 :** to unburden oneself, to let off steam
desahogo *nm* **1 :** relief, outlet **2 con ~ :** comfortably
desahuciar *vt* **1 :** to deprive of hope **2 :** to evict — **desahuciarse** *vr* **:** to lose all hope
desahucio *nm* **:** eviction
desairar {5} *vt* **:** to snub, to rebuff
desaire *nm* **:** rebuff, snub, slight
desajustar *vt* **1 :** to disarrange, to put out of order **2 :** to upset (plans)
desajuste *nm* **1 :** maladjustment **2 :** imbalance **3 :** upset, disruption
desalentar {55} *vt* DESANIMAR **:** to discourage, to dishearten — **desalentarse** *vr*
desaliento *nm* **:** discouragement
desaliñado, -da *adj* **:** slovenly, untidy
desalmado, -da *adj* **:** heartless, callous
desalojar *vt* **1 :** to remove, to clear **2** EVACUAR **:** to evacuate, to vacate **3 :** to evict
desalojo *nm* **1 :** removal, expulsion **2 :** evacuation **3 :** eviction
desamor *nm* **1** FRIALDAD **:** indifference **2** ENEMISTAD **:** dislike, enmity
desamparado, -da *adj* DESVALIDO **:** helpless, destitute
desamparar *vt* **:** to abandon, to forsake
desamparo *nm* **1 :** abandonment, neglect **2 :** helplessness
desamueblado, -da *adj* **:** unfurnished
desandar {6} *vt* **:** to go back, to return to the starting point
desangelado, -da *adj* **:** dull, lifeless
desangrar *vt* **:** to bleed, to bleed dry — **desangrarse** *vr* **1 :** to be bleeding **2 :** to bleed to death
desanimar *vt* DESALENTAR **:** to discourage, to dishearten — **desanimarse** *vr*
desánimo *nm* DESALIENTO **:** discouragement, dejection
desanudar *vt* **:** to untie, to disentangle
desapacible *adj* **:** unpleasant, disagreeable
desaparecer {53} *vt* **:** to cause to disappear — *vi* **:** to disappear, to vanish
desaparecido¹, -da *adj* **1 :** late, deceased **2 :** missing
desaparecido², -da *n* **:** missing person
desaparición *nf, pl* **-ciones :** disappearance
desapasionado, -da *adj* **:** dispassionate, impartial — **desapasionadamente** *adv*
desapego *nm* **:** coolness, indifference
desapercibido, -da *adj* **1 :** unnoticed **2** DESPREVENIDO **:** unprepared, off guard
desaprobación *nf, pl* **-ciones :** disapproval
desaprobar {19} *vt* REPROBAR **:** to disapprove of
desaprovechar *vt* MALGASTAR **:** to waste, to misuse — *vi* **:** to lose ground, to slip back
desarmador *nm Mex* **:** screwdriver
desarmar *vt* **1 :** to disarm **2** DESMONTAR **:** to disassemble, to take apart
desarme *nm* **:** disarmament
desarraigado, -da *adj* **:** rootless
desarraigar {52} *vt* **:** to uproot, to root out
desarreglado, -da *adj* **:** untidy, disorganized
desarreglar *vt* **1 :** to mess up **2 :** to upset, to disrupt
desarreglo *nm* **1 :** untidiness **2 :** disorder, confusion
desarrollar *vt* **:** to develop — **desarrollarse** *vr* **:** to take place
desarrollo *nm* **:** development
desarticulación *nf, pl* **-ciones 1 :** dislocation **2 :** breaking up, dismantling
desarticular *vt* **1** DISLOCAR **:** to dislocate **2 :** to break up, to dismantle
desaseado, -da *adj* **1 :** dirty **2 :** messy, untidy
desastre *nm* CATÁSTROFE **:** disaster
desastroso, -sa *adj* **:** disastrous, catastrophic
desatar *vt* **1 :** to undo, to untie **2 :** to unleash **3 :** to trigger, to precipitate — **desatarse** *vr* **:** to break out, to erupt
desatascar {72} *vt* **:** to unblock, to clear
desatención *nf, pl* **-ciones 1 :** absent-mindedness, distraction **2 :** discourtesy
desatender {56} *vt* **1 :** to disregard **2 :** to neglect
desatento, -ta *adj* **1** DISTRAÍDO **:** absent-minded **2** GROSERO **:** discourteous, rude
desatinado, -da *adj* **:** foolish, silly
desatino *nm* **:** folly, mistake
desautorizar {21} *vt* **:** to deprive of authority, to discredit
desavenencia *nf* DISCORDANCIA **:** disagreement, dispute
desayunar *vi* **:** to have breakfast — *vt* **:** to have for breakfast
desayuno *nm* **:** breakfast
desazón *nf, pl* **-zones** INQUIETUD **:** uneasiness, anxiety
desbalance *nm* **:** imbalance
desbancar {72} *vt* **:** to displace, to oust
desbandada *nf* **:** scattering, dispersal
desbarajuste *nm* DESORDEN **:** disarray, disorder, mess
desbaratar *vt* **1** ARRUINAR **:** to destroy, to ruin **2** DESCOMPONER **:** to break, to break down — **desbaratarse** *vr* **:** to fall apart
desbloquear *vt* **1 :** to open up, to clear, to break through **2 :** to free, to release
desbocado, -da *adj* **:** unbridled, rampant
desbocarse {72} *vr* **:** to run away, to bolt
desbordamiento *nm* **:** overflowing
desbordante *adj* **:** overflowing, bursting <desbordante de energía : bursting with energy>
desbordar *vt* **1 :** to overflow, to spill over **2 :** to surpass, to exceed **3 :** to

burst with, to brim with — **desbordarse** *vr*

descabellado, -da *adj* **:** outlandish, ridiculous

descafeinado, -da *adj* **:** decaffeinated

descalabrar *vt* **:** to hit on the head — **descalabrarse** *vr*

descalabro *nm* **:** setback, misfortune, loss

descalificar {72} *vt* **:** to disqualify — **descalificarse** *vr*

descalzarse {21} *vr* **:** take off one's shoes

descalzo, -za *adj* **:** barefoot

descansado, -da *adj* **1 :** rested, refreshed **2 :** restful, peaceful

descansar *vi* **:** to rest, to relax — *vt* **:** to rest <descansar la vista **:** to rest one's eyes>

descansillo *nm* **:** landing (of a staircase)

descanso *nm* **1 :** rest, relaxation **2 :** break **3 :** landing (of a staircase) **4 :** intermission

descapotable *adj & nm* **:** convertible

descarado, -da *adj* **:** brazen, impudent — **descaradamente** *adv*

descarga *nf* **1 :** discharge **2 :** unloading

descargar {52} *vt* **1 :** to discharge **2 :** to unload **3 :** to release, to free **4 :** to take out, to vent (anger, etc.) — **descargarse** *vr* **1 :** to unburden oneself **2 :** to quit **3 :** to lose power

descargo *nm* **1 :** unloading **2 :** defense <testigo de descargo **:** witness for the defense>

descarnado, -da *adj* **:** scrawny, gaunt

descaro *nm* **:** audacity, nerve

descarriado, -da *adj* **:** lost, gone astray

descarrilar *vi* **:** to derail — **descarrilarse** *vr*

descartar *vt* **:** to rule out, to reject — **descartarse** *vr* **:** to discard

descascarar *vt* **:** to peel, to shell, to husk — **descascararse** *vr* **:** to peel off, to chip

descendencia *nf* **1 :** descendants *pl* **2** LINAJE **:** descent, lineage

descendente *adj* **:** downward, descending

descender {56} *vt* **1 :** to descend, to go down **2** BAJAR **:** to lower, to take down, to let down — *vi* **1 :** to descend, to come down **2 :** to drop, to fall **3 ~ de :** to be a descendant of

descendiente *adj & nm* **:** descendant

descenso *nm* **1 :** descent **2** BAJA, CAÍDA **:** drop, fall

descentralizar {21} *vt* **:** to decentralize — **descentralizarse** *vr* — **descentralización** *nf*

descifrable *adj* **:** decipherable

descifrar *vt* **:** to decipher, to decode

descolgar {16} *vt* **1 :** to take down, to let down **2 :** to pick up, to answer (the telephone)

descollar {19} *vi* SOBRESALIR **:** to stand out, to be outstanding, to excel

descolorarse *vr* **:** to fade

descolorido, -da *adj* **:** discolored, faded

descomponer {60} *vt* **1 :** to rot, to decompose **2** DESBARATAR **:** to break, to break down — **descomponerse** *vr* **1 :** to break down **2 :** to decompose

descomposición *nf, pl* **-ciones 1 :** breakdown, decomposition **2 :** decay

descompresión *nf* **:** decompression

descompuesto[1] *pp* → **descomponer**

descompuesto[2], -ta *adj* **1 :** broken down, out of order **2 :** rotten, decomposed

descomunal *adj* **1** ENORME **:** enormous, huge **2** EXTRAORDINARIO **:** extraordinary

desconcertante *adj* **:** disconcerting

desconcertar {55} *vt* **:** to disconcert — **desconcertarse** *vr*

desconchar *vt* **:** to chip — **desconcharse** *vr* **:** to chip off, to peel

desconcierto *nm* **:** uncertainty, confusion

desconectar *vt* **1 :** to disconnect, to switch off **2 :** to unplug

desconfiado, -da *adj* **:** distrustful, suspicious

desconfianza *nf* RECELO **:** distrust, suspicion

desconfiar {85} *vi* **~ de :** to distrust, to be suspicious of

descongelar *vt* **1 :** to thaw **2 :** to defrost **3 :** to unfreeze (assets) — **descongelarse** *vr*

descongestionante *adj & nm* **:** decongestant

desconocer {18} *vt* **1** IGNORAR **:** to be unaware of **2 :** to fail to recognize

desconocido[1], -da *adj* **:** unknown, unfamiliar

desconocido[2], -da *n* EXTRAÑO **:** stranger

desconocimiento *nm* **:** ignorance

desconsiderado, -da *adj* **:** inconsiderate, thoughtless — **desconsideradamente** *adv*

desconsolado, -da *adj* **:** disconsolate, heartbroken

desconsuelo *nm* AFLICCIÓN **:** grief, distress, despair

descontaminar *vt* **:** to decontaminate — **descontaminación** *nf*

descontar {19} *vt* **1 :** to discount, to deduct **2** EXCEPTUAR **:** to except, to exclude

descontento[1], -ta *adj* **:** discontented, dissatisfied

descontento[2] *nm* **:** discontent, dissatisfaction

descontrol *nm* **:** lack of control, disorder, chaos

descontrolarse *vr* **:** to get out of control, to be out of hand

descorazonado, -da *adj* **:** disheartened, discouraged

descorrer *vt* **:** to draw back

descortés *adj, pl* **-teses :** discourteous, rude

descortesía *nf* **:** discourtesy, rudeness

descrédito *nm* DESPRESTIGIO **:** discredit

descremado, -da *adj* **:** nonfat, skim

describir {33} *vt* **:** to describe

descripción *nf, pl* **-ciones :** description

descriptivo, -va *adj* **:** descriptive

descrito *pp* → **describir**

descuartizar {21} *vt* **1 :** to cut up, to quarter **2 :** to tear to pieces

descubierto[1] *pp* → **descubrir**

descubierto[2], **-ta** *adj* **1 :** exposed, revealed **2 al descubierto :** out in the open

descubridor, -dora *n* **:** discoverer, explorer

descubrimiento *nm* **:** discovery

descubrir {2} *vt* **1** HALLAR **:** to discover, to find out **2** REVELAR **:** to uncover, to reveal — **descubrirse** *vr*

descuento *nm* REBAJA **:** discount

descuidado, -da *adj* **1 :** neglectful, careless **2 :** neglected, unkempt

descuidar *vt* **:** to neglect, to overlook — *vi* **:** to be careless — **descuidarse** *vr* **1 :** to be careless, to drop one's guard **2 :** to let oneself go

descuido *nm* **1 :** carelessness, negligence **2 :** slip, oversight

desde *prep* **1 :** from **2 :** since **3 desde ahora :** from now on **4 desde entonces :** since then **5 desde hace :** for, since (a time) <ha estado nevando desde hace dos días : it's been snowing for two days> **6 desde luego :** of course **7 desde que :** since, ever since **8 desde ya :** right now, immediately

desdecir {11} *vi* **~ de 1 :** to be unworthy of **2 :** to clash with — **desdecirse** *vr* **1** CONTRADECIRSE **:** to contradict oneself **2** RETRACTARSE **:** to go back on one's word

desdén *nm, pl* **desdenes** DESPRECIO **:** disdain, scorn

desdentado, -da *adj* **:** toothless

desdeñar *vt* DESPRECIAR **:** to disdain, to scorn, to despise

desdeñoso, -sa *adj* **:** disdainful, scornful — **desdeñosamente** *adv*

desdibujar *vt* **:** to blur — **desdibujarse** *vr*

desdicha *nf* **1 :** misery **2 :** misfortune

desdichado[1], **-da** *adj* **1 :** unfortunate **2 :** miserable, unhappy

desdichado[2], **-da** *n* **:** wretch

desdicho *pp* → **desdecir**

desdiga, desdijo, etc. → **desdecir**

desdoblar *vt* DESPLEGAR **:** to unfold

deseable *adj* **:** desirable

desear *vt* **1 :** to wish <te deseo buena suerte : I wish you good luck> **2** QUERER **:** to want, to desire

desechable *adj* **:** disposable

desechar *vt* **1 :** to discard, to throw away **2** RECHAZAR **:** to reject

desecho *nm* **1 :** reject **2 desechos** *nmpl* RESIDUOS **:** rubbish, waste

desembarazarse {21} *vr* **~ de :** to get rid of

desembarcadero *nm* **:** jetty, landing pier

desembarcar {72} *vi* **:** to disembark — *vt* **:** to unload

desembarco *nm* **1 :** landing, arrival **2 :** unloading

desembarque *nm* → **desembarco**

desembocadura *nf* **1 :** mouth (of a river) **2 :** opening, end (of a street)

desembocar {72} *vi* **~ en** *or* **~ a 1 :** to flow into, to join **2 :** to lead to, to result in

desembolsar *vt* PAGAR **:** to disburse, to pay out

desembolso *nm* PAGO **:** disbursement, payment

desempacar {72} *v* **:** to unpack

desempate *nm* **:** tiebreaker, play-off

desempeñar *vt* **1 :** to play (a role) **2 :** to fulfill, to carry out **3 :** to redeem (from a pawnshop) — **desempeñarse** *vr* **:** to function, to act

desempeño *nm* **1 :** fulfillment, carrying out **2 :** performance

desempleado[1], **-da** *adj* **:** unemployed

desempleado[2], **-da** *n* **:** unemployed person

desempleo *nm* **:** unemployment

desempolvar *vt* **1 :** to dust off **2 :** to resurrect, to revive

desencadenar *vt* **1 :** to unchain **2 :** to trigger, to unleash — **desencadenarse** *vr*

desencajar *vt* **1 :** to dislocate **2 :** to disconnect, to disengage

desencantar *vt* **:** to disenchant, to disillusion — **desencantarse** *vr*

desencanto *nm* **:** disenchantment, disillusionment

desenchufar *vt* **:** to disconnect, to unplug

desenfadado, -da *adj* **1 :** uninhibited, carefree **2 :** confident, self-assured

desenfado *nm* **1** DESENVOLTURA **:** self-assurance, confidence **2 :** naturalness, ease

desenfrenadamente *adv* **:** wildly, with abandon

desenfrenado, -da *adj* **:** unbridled, unrestrained

desenfreno *nm* **:** abandon, unrestraint

desenganchar *vt* **:** to unhitch, to uncouple

desengañar *vt* **:** to disillusion, to disenchant — **desengañarse** *vr*

desengaño *nm* **:** disenchantment, disillusionment

desenlace *nm* **:** ending, outcome

desenlazar {21} *vt* **1 :** to untie **2 :** to clear up, to resolve

desenmarañar *vt* **:** to disentangle, to unravel

desenmascarar *vt* **:** to unmask, to expose

desenredar *vt* **:** to untangle, to disentangle

desenrollar *vt* **:** to unroll, to unwind

desentenderse {56} *vr* **~ de 1 :** to want nothing to do with, to be uninterested in **2 :** to pretend ignorance of

desenterrar {55} *vt* **1** EXHUMAR **:** to exhume **2 :** to unearth, to dig up
desentonar *vi* **1 :** to clash, to conflict **2 :** to be out of tune, to sing off-key
desentrañar *vt* **:** to get to the bottom of, to unravel
desenvainar *vt* **:** to draw, to unsheathe (a sword)
desenvoltura *nf* **1** DESENFADO **:** confidence, self-assurance **2** ELOCUENCIA **:** eloquence, fluency
desenvolver {89} *vt* **:** to unwrap, to open — **desenvolverse** *vr* **1 :** to unfold, to develop **2 :** to manage, to cope
desenvuelto[1] *pp* → **desenvolver**
desenvuelto[2], **-ta** *adj* **:** confident, relaxed, self-assured
deseo *nm* **:** wish, desire
deseoso, -sa *adj* **:** eager, anxious
desequilibrar *vt* **:** to unbalance, to throw off balance — **desequilibrarse** *vr*
desequilibrio *nm* **:** imbalance
deserción *nf, pl* **-ciones :** desertion, defection
desertar *vi* **1 :** to desert, to defect **2 ~ de :** to abandon, to neglect
desertor, -tora *n* **:** deserter, defector
desesperación *nf, pl* **-ciones :** desperation, despair
desesperado, -da *adj* **:** desperate, despairing, hopeless — **desesperadamente** *adv*
desesperanza *nf* **:** despair, hopelessness
desesperar *vt* **:** to exasperate — *vi* **:** to despair, to lose hope — **desesperarse** *vr* **:** to become exasperated
desestimar *vt* **1 :** to reject, to disallow **2 :** to have a low opinion of
desfachatez *nf, pl* **-teces :** audacity, nerve, cheek
desfalcador, -dora *n* **:** embezzler
desfalcar {72} *vt* **:** to embezzle
desfalco *nm* **:** embezzlement
desfallecer {53} *vi* **1 :** to weaken **2 :** to faint
desfallecimiento *nm* **1 :** weakness **2 :** fainting
desfasado, -da *adj* **1 :** out of sync **2 :** out of step, behind the times
desfase *nm* **:** gap, lag <desfase horario : jet lag>
desfavorable *adj* **:** unfavorable, adverse — **desfavorablemente** *adv*
desfavorecido, -da *adj* **:** underprivileged
desfigurar *vt* **1 :** to disfigure, to mar **2 :** to distort, to misrepresent
desfiladero *nm* **:** narrow gorge, defile
desfilar *vi* **:** to parade, to march
desfile *nm* **:** parade, procession
desfogar {52} *vt* **1 :** to vent **2** *Mex* **:** to unclog, to unblock — **desfogarse** *vr* **:** to vent one's feelings, to let off steam
desforestación *nf, pl* **-ciones :** deforestation
desgajar *vt* **1 :** to tear off **2 :** to break apart — **desgajarse** *vr* **:** to come apart
desgana *nf* **1** INAPETENCIA **:** lack of appetite **2** APATÍA **:** apathy, unwillingness, reluctance
desgano *nm* → **desgana**
desgarbado, -da *adj* **:** ungainly
desgarrador, -dora *adj* **:** heartrending, heartbreaking
desgarradura *nf* **:** tear, rip
desgarrar *vt* **1 :** to tear, to rip **2 :** to break (one's heart) — **desgarrarse** *vr*
desgarre *nm* → **desgarro**
desgarro *nm* **:** tear
desgarrón *nm, pl* **-rrones :** rip, tear
desgastar *vt* **1 :** to use up **2 :** to wear away, to wear down
desgaste *nm* **:** deterioration, wear and tear
desglosar *vt* **:** to break down, to itemize
desglose *nm* **:** breakdown, itemization
desgobierno *nm* **:** anarchy, disorder
desgracia *nf* **1 :** misfortune **2 :** disgrace **3 por ~ :** unfortunately
desgraciadamente *adv* **:** unfortunately
desgraciado[1], **-da** *adj* **1 :** unfortunate, unlucky **2 :** vile, wretched
desgraciado[2], **-da** *n* **:** unfortunate person, wretch
desgranar *vt* **:** to shuck, to shell
deshabitado, -da *adj* **:** unoccupied, uninhabited
deshacer {40} *vt* **1 :** to destroy, to ruin **2** DESATAR **:** to undo, to untie **3 :** to break apart, to crumble **4 :** to dissolve, to melt **5 :** to break, to cancel — **deshacerse** *vr* **1 :** to fall apart, to come undone **2 ~ de :** to get rid of
deshecho[1] *pp* → **deshacer**
deshecho[2], **-cha** *adj* **1 :** destroyed, ruined **2 :** devastated, shattered **3 :** undone, untied
desherbar {55} *vt* **:** to weed
desheredado, -da *adj* MARGINADO **:** dispossessed, destitute
desheredar *vt* **:** to disinherit
deshicieron, etc. → **deshacer**
deshidratar *vt* **:** to dehydrate — **deshidratación** *nf*
deshielo *nm* **:** thaw, thawing
deshilachar *vt* **:** to fray — **deshilacharse** *vr*
deshizo → **deshacer**
deshonestidad *nf* **:** dishonesty
deshonesto, -ta *adj* **:** dishonest
deshonra *nf* **:** dishonor, disgrace
deshonrar *vt* **:** to dishonor, to disgrace
deshonroso, -sa *adj* **:** dishonorable, disgraceful
deshuesar *vt* **1 :** to pit (a fruit, etc.) **2 :** to bone, to debone
deshumanizar {21} *vt* **:** to dehumanize — **deshumanización** *nf*
desidia *nf* **1** APATÍA **:** apathy, indolence **2** NEGLIGENCIA **:** negligence, sloppiness
desierto[1], **-ta** *adj* **:** deserted, uninhabited

desierto[2] *nm* : desert
designación *nf, pl* **-ciones** NOMBRAMIENTO : appointment, naming (to an office, etc.)
designar *vt* NOMBRAR : to designate, to appoint, to name
designio *nm* : plan
desigual *adj* **1** : unequal **2** DISPAREJO : uneven
desigualdad *nf* **1** : inequality **2** : unevenness
desilusión *nf, pl* **-siones** DESENCANTO, DESENGAÑO : disillusionment, disenchantment
desilusionar *vt* DESENCANTAR, DESENGAÑAR : to disillusion, to disenchant — **desilusionarse** *vr*
desinfectante *adj & nm* : disinfectant
desinfectar *vt* : to disinfect — **desinfección** *nf*
desinflar *vt* : to deflate — **desinflarse** *vr*
desinhibido, -da *adj* : unihibited, unrestrained
desintegración *nf, pl* **-ciones** : disintegration
desintegrar *vt* : to disintegrate, to break up — **desintegrarse** *vr*
desinterés *nm* **1** : lack of interest, indifference **2** : unselfishness
desinteresado, -da *adj* GENEROSO : unselfish
desintoxicar {72} *vt* : to detoxify, to detox
desistir *vi* **1** : to desist, to stop **2 ~ de** : to give up, to relinquish
deslave *nm Mex* : landslide
desleal *adj* INFIEL : disloyal — **deslealmente** *adv*
deslealtad *nf* : disloyalty
desleír {66} *vt* : to dilute, to dissolve
desligar {52} *vt* **1** : to separate, to undo **2** : to free (from an obligation) — **desligarse** *vr* **~ de** : to extricate oneself from
deslindar *vt* **1** : to mark the limits of, to demarcate **2** : to define, to clarify
deslinde *nm* : demarcation
desliz *nm, pl* **deslices** : error, mistake, slip <desliz de la lengua : slip of the tongue>
deslizar {21} *vt* **1** : to slide, to slip **2** : to slip in — **deslizarse** *vr* **1** : to slide, to glide **2** : to slip away
deslucido, -da *adj* **1** : unimpressive, dull **2** : faded, dingy, tarnished
deslucir {45} *vt* **1** : to spoil **2** : to fade, to dull, to tarnish **3** : to discredit
deslumbrar *vt* : to dazzle — **deslumbrante** *adj*
deslustrado, -da *adj* : dull, lusterless
deslustrar *vt* : to tarnish, to dull
deslustre *nm* : tarnish
desmán *nm, pl* **desmanes 1** : outrage, abuse **2** : misfortune
desmandarse *vr* : to behave badly, to get out of hand
desmantelar *vt* DESMONTAR : to dismantle
desmañado, -da *adj* : clumsy, awkward
desmayado, -da *adj* **1** : fainting, weak **2** : dull, pale
desmayar *vi* : to lose heart, to falter — **desmayarse** *vr* DESVANECERSE : to faint, to swoon
desmayo *nm* **1** : faint, fainting **2 sufrir un desmayo** : to faint
desmedido, -da *adj* DESMESURADO : excessive, undue
desmejorar *vt* : to weaken, to make worse — *vi* : to decline (in health), to get worse
desmembramiento *nm* : dismemberment
desmembrar {55} *vt* **1** : to dismember **2** : to break up
desmemoriado, -da *adj* : absent-minded, forgetful
desmentido *nm* : denial
desmentir {76} *vt* **1** NEGAR : to deny, to refute **2** CONTRADECIR : to contradict
desmenuzar {21} *vt* **1** : to break down, to scrutinize **2** : to crumble, to shred — **desmenuzarse** *vr*
desmerecer {53} *vt* : to be unworthy of — *vi* **1** : to decline in value **2 ~ de** : to compare unfavorably with
desmesurado, -da *adj* DESMEDIDO : excessive, inordinate — **desmesuradamente** *adv*
desmigajar *vt* : to crumble — **desmigajarse** *vr*
desmilitarizado, -da *adj* : demilitarized
desmontar *vt* **1** : to clear, to level off **2** DESMANTELAR : to dismantle, to take apart — *vi* : to dismount
desmonte *nm* : clearing, leveling
desmoralizador, -dora *adj* : demoralizing
desmoralizar {21} *vt* DESALENTAR : to demoralize, to discourage
desmoronamiento *nm* : crumbling, falling apart
desmoronar *vt* : to wear away, to erode — **desmoronarse** *vr* : to crumble, to deteriorate, to fall apart
desmotadora *nf* : gin, cotton gin
desmovilizar {21} *vt* : to demobilize — **desmovilización** *nf*
desnaturalizar {21} *vt* **1** : to denature **2** : to distort, to alter
desnivel *nm* **1** : disparity, difference **2** : unevenness (of a surface) **3 paso a desnivel** *Mex* : underpass
desnivelado, -da *adj* **1** : uneven **2** : unbalanced
desnudar *vt* **1** : to undress **2** : to strip, to lay bare — **desnudarse** *vr* : to undress, to strip off one's clothing
desnudez *nf, pl* **-deces** : nudity, nakedness
desnudismo *nm* → **nudismo**
desnudista → **nudista**
desnudo[1]**, -da** *adj* : nude, naked, bare
desnudo[2] *nm* : nude

desnutrición *nf, pl* **-ciones** : MALNUTRICIÓN : malnutrition, undernourishment

desnutrido, -da *adj* MALNUTRIDO : malnourished, undernourished

desobedecer {53} *v* : to disobey

desobediencia *nf* : disobedience — **desobediente** *adj*

desocupación *nf, pl* **-ciones** : unemployment

desocupado, -da *adj* **1** : vacant, empty **2** : free, unoccupied **3** : unemployed

desocupar *vt* **1** : to empty **2** : to vacate, to move out of — **desocuparse** *vr* : to leave, to quit (a job)

desodorante *adj & nm* : deodorant

desolación *nf, pl* **-ciones** : desolation

desolado, -da *adj* **1** : desolate **2** : devastated, distressed

desolador, -dora *adj* **1** : devastating **2** : bleak, desolate

desollar *vt* : to skin, to flay

desorbitado, -da *adj* **1** : excessive, exorbitant **2 con los ojos desorbitados** : with eyes popping out of one's head

desorden *nm, pl* **desórdenes 1** DESBARAJUSTE : disorder, mess **2** : disorder, disturbance, upset

desordenado, -da *adj* **1** : untidy, messy **2** : disorderly, unruly

desorganización *nf, pl* **-ciones** : disorganization

desorganizar {21} *vt* : to disrupt, to disorganize

desorientación *nf, pl* **-ciones** : disorientation, confusion

desorientar *vt* : to disorient, to mislead, to confuse — **desorientarse** *vr* : to become disoriented, to lose one's way

desovar *vi* : to spawn

despachar *vt* **1** : to complete, to conclude **2** : to deal with, to take care of, to handle **3** : to dispatch, to send off **4** *fam* : to finish off, to kill — **despacharse** *vr fam* : to gulp down, to polish off

despacho *nm* **1** : dispatch, shipment **2** OFICINA : office, study

despacio *adv* LENTAMENTE, LENTO : slowly, slow <¡despacio! : take it easy!, easy does it!>

desparasitar *vt* : to worm (an animal), to delouse

desparpajo *nm* **1** *fam* : self-confidence, nerve **2** *CA fam* : confusion, muddle

desparramar *vt* **1** : to spill, to splatter **2** : to spread, to scatter

despatarrarse *vr* : to sprawl (out)

despavorido, -da *adj* : terrified, horrified

despecho *nm* **1** : spite **2 a despecho de** : despite, in spite of

despectivo, -va *adj* **1** : contemptuous, disparaging **2** : derogatory, pejorative

despedazar {21} *vt* : to cut to pieces, to tear apart

despedida *nf* **1** : farewell, good-bye **2 despedida de soltera** : bridal shower

despedir {54} *vt* **1** : to see off, to show out **2** : to dismiss, to fire **3** EMITIR : to give off, to emit <despedir un olor : to give off an odor> — **despedirse** *vr* : to take one's leave, to say good-bye

despegado, -da *adj* **1** : separated, detached **2** : cold, distant

despegar {52} *vt* : to remove, to detach — *vi* : to take off, to lift off, to blast off

despegue *nm* : takeoff, liftoff

despeinado, -da *adj* : disheveled, tousled <estoy despeinada : my hair's a mess>

despejado, -da *adj* **1** : clear, fair **2** : alert, clear-headed **3** : uncluttered, unobstructed

despejar *vt* **1** : to clear, to free **2** : to clarify — *vi* **1** : to clear up **2** : to punt (in sports)

despeje *nm* **1** : clearing **2** : punt (in sports)

despellejar *vt* : to skin (an animal)

despenalizar {21} *vt* : to legalize — **despenalización** *nf*

despensa *nf* **1** : pantry, larder **2** PROVISIONES : provisions *pl,* supplies *pl*

despeñar *vt* : to hurl down

despepitar *vt* : to seed, to remove the seeds from

desperdiciar *vt* **1** DESAPROVECHAR, MALGASTAR : to waste **2** : to miss, to miss out on

desperdicio *nm* **1** : waste **2 desperdicios** *nmpl* RESIDUOS : refuse, scraps, rubbish

desperdigar {52} *vt* DISPERSAR : to disperse, to scatter

desperfecto *nm* **1** DEFECTO : flaw, defect **2** : damage

despertador *nm* : alarm clock

despertar {55} *vi* : to awaken, to wake up — *vt* **1** : to arouse, to wake **2** EVOCAR : to elicit, to evoke — **despertarse** *vr* : to wake (oneself) up

despiadado, -da *adj* CRUEL : cruel, merciless, pitiless — **despiadadamente** *adv*

despido *nm* : dismissal, layoff

despierto, -ta *adj* **1** : awake, alert **2** LISTO : clever, sharp <con la mente despierta : with a sharp mind>

despilfarrador[1], -dora *adj* : extravagant, wasteful

despilfarrador[2], -dora *n* : spendthrift, prodigal

despilfarrar *vt* MALGASTAR : to squander, to waste

despilfarro *nm* : extravagance, wastefulness

despintar *vt* : to strip the paint from — **despintarse** *vr* : to fade, to wash off, to peel off

despistado[1], -da *adj* **1** DISTRAÍDO : absentminded, forgetful **2** CONFUSO : confused, bewildered

despistado[2], **-da** *n* : scatterbrain, absentminded person
despistar *vt* : to throw off the track, to confuse — **despistarse** *vr*
despiste *nm* **1** : absentmindedness **2** : mistake, slip
desplantador *nm* : garden trowel
desplante *nm* : insolence, rudeness
desplazamiento *nm* **1** : movement, displacement **2** : journey
desplazar {21} *vt* **1** : to replace, to displace **2** TRASLADAR : to move, to shift
desplegar {49} *vt* **1** : to display, to show, to manifest **2** DESDOBLAR : to unfold, to unfurl **3** : to spread (out) **4** : to deploy
despliegue *nm* **1** : display **2** : deployment
desplomarse *vr* **1** : to plummet, to fall **2** DERRUMBARSE : to collapse, to break down
desplome *nm* **1** : fall, drop **2** : collapse
desplumar *vt* : to pluck (a chicken, etc.)
despoblado[1], **-da** *adj* : uninhabited, deserted
despoblado[2] *nm* : open country, deserted area
despoblar {19} *vt* : to depopulate
despojar *vt* **1** : to strip, to clear **2** : to divest, to deprive — **despojarse** *vr* **1** ~ **de** : to remove (clothing) **2** ~ **de** : to relinquish, to renounce
despojos *nmpl* **1** : remains, scraps **2** : plunder, spoils
desportilladura *nf* : chip, nick
desportillar *vt* : to chip — **desportillarse** *vr*
desposeer {20} *vt* : to dispossess
déspota *nmf* : despot, tyrant
despotismo *nm* : despotism — **despótico, -ca** *adj*
despotricar {72} *vi* : to rant and rave, to complain excessively
despreciable *adj* **1** : despicable, contemptible **2** : negligible <nada despreciable : not inconsiderable, significant>
despreciar *vt* DESDEÑAR, MENOSPRECIAR : to despise, to scorn, to disdain
despreciativo, -va *adj* : scornful, disdainful
desprecio *nm* DESDÉN, MENOSPRECIO : disdain, contempt, scorn
desprender *vt* **1** SOLTAR : to detach, to loosen, to unfasten **2** EMITIR : to emit, to give off — **desprenderse** *vr* **1** : to come off, to come undone **2** : to be inferred, to follow **3** ~ **de** : to part with, to get rid of
desprendido, -da *adj* : generous, unselfish, disinterested
desprendimiento *nm* **1** : detachment **2** GENEROSIDAD : generosity **3 desprendimiento de tierras** : landslide
despreocupación *nf, pl* **-ciones** : indifference, lack of concern
despreocupado, -da *adj* : carefree, easygoing, unconcerned
desprestigiar *vt* DESACREDITAR : to discredit, to disgrace — **desprestigiarse** *vr* : to lose prestige
desprestigio *nm* DESCRÉDITO : discredit, disrepute
desprevenido, -da *adj* DESAPERCIBIDO : unprepared, off guard, unsuspecting
desproporción *nf, pl* **-ciones** : disproportion, disparity
desproporcionado, -da : out of proportion
despropósito *nm* : piece of nonsense, absurdity
desprotegido, -da *adj* : unprotected, vulnerable
desprovisto, -ta *adj* ~ **de** : devoid of, lacking in
después *adv* **1** : afterward, later **2** : then, next **3** ~ **de** : after, next after <después de comer : after eating> **4 después (de) que** : after <después que lo acabé : after I finished it> **5 después de todo** : after all **6 poco después** : shortly after, soon thereafter
despuntado, -da *adj* : blunt, dull
despuntar *vt* : to blunt — *vi* **1** : to dawn **2** : to sprout **3** : to excel, to stand out
desquiciar *vt* **1** : to unhinge (a door) **2** : to drive crazy — **desquiciarse** *vr* : to go crazy
desquitarse *vr* **1** : to get even, to retaliate **2** ~ **con** : to take it out on
desquite *nm* : revenge
desregulación *nf, pl* **-ciones** : deregulation
desregular *vt* : to deregulate
destacadamente *adv* : outstandingly, prominently
destacado, -da *adj* **1** : outstanding, prominent **2** : stationed, posted
destacar {72} *vt* **1** ENFATIZAR, SUBRAYAR : to emphasize, to highlight, to stress **2** : to station, to post — *vi* : to stand out
destajo *nm* **1** : piecework **2 a** ~ : by the item, by the job
destapador *nm* : bottle opener
destapar *vt* **1** : to open, to take the top off **2** DESCUBRIR : to reveal, to uncover **3** : to unblock, to unclog
destape *nm* : uncovering, revealing
destartalado, -da *adj* : dilapidated, tumbledown
destellar *vi* **1** : to sparkle, to flash, to glint **2** : to twinkle
destello *nm* **1** : flash, sparkle, twinkle **2** : glimmer, hint
destemplado, -da *adj* **1** : out of tune **2** : irritable, out of sorts **3** : unpleasant (of weather)
desteñir {67} *vi* : to run, to fade — **desteñirse** DESCOLORARSE : to fade
desterrado[1], **-da** *adj* : banished, exiled
desterrado[2], **-da** *n* : exile

desterrar {55} *vt* **1** EXILIAR : to banish, to exile **2** ERRADICAR : to eradicate, to do away with
destetar *vt* : to wean
destiempo *adv* **a ~** : at the wrong time
destierro *nm* EXILIO : exile
destilación *nf, pl* **-ciones** : distillation
destilador, -dora *n* : distiller
destilar *vt* **1** : to exude **2** : to distill
destilería *nf* : distillery
destinación *nf, pl* **-ciones** DESTINO : destination
destinado, -da *adj* : destined, bound
destinar *vt* **1** : to appoint, to assign **2** ASIGNAR : to earmark, to allot
destinatario, -ria *n* **1** : addressee **2** : payee
destino *nm* **1** : destiny, fate **2** DESTINACIÓN : destination **3** : use **4** : assignment, post
destitución *nf, pl* **-ciones** : dismissal, removal from office
destituir {41} *vt* : to dismiss, to remove from office
destorcer {14} *vt* : to untwist
destornillador *nm* : screwdriver
destornillar *vt* : to unscrew
destrabar *vt* **1** : to untie, to undo, to ease up **2** : to separate
destreza *nf* HABILIDAD : dexterity, skill
destronar *vt* : to depose, to dethrone
destrozado, -da *adj* **1** : ruined, destroyed **2** : devastated, brokenhearted
destrozar {21} *vt* **1** : to smash, to shatter **2** : to destroy, to wreck — **destrozarse** *vr*
destrozo *nm* **1** DAÑO : damage **2** : havoc, destruction
destrucción *nf, pl* **-ciones** : destruction
destructivo, -va *adj* : destructive
destructor[1]**, -tora** *adj* : destructive
destructor[2] *nm* : destroyer (ship)
destruir {41} *vt* : to destroy — **destruirse** *vr*
desubicado, -da *adj* **1** : out of place **2** : confused, disoriented
desunión *nf, pl* **-niones** : disunity
desunir *vt* : to split, to divide
desusado, -da *adj* **1** INSÓLITO : unusual **2** OBSOLETO : obsolete, disused, antiquated
desuso *nm* : disuse, obsolescence <caer en desuso : to fall into disuse>
desvaído, -da *adj* **1** : pale, washed-out **2** : vague, blurred
desvainar *vt* : to shell
desvalido, -da *adj* DESAMPARADO : destitute, helpless
desvalijar *vt* **1** : to ransack **2** : to rob
desvalorización *nf, pl* **-ciones** **1** DEVALUACIÓN : devaluation **2** : depreciation
desvalorizar {21} *vt* : to devalue
desván *nm, pl* **desvanes** ÁTICO, BUHARDILLA : attic
desvanecer {53} *vt* **1** DISIPAR : to make disappear, to dispel **2** : to fade, to blur — **desvanecerse** *vr* **1** : to vanish, to disappear **2** : to fade **3** DESMAYARSE : to faint, to swoon
desvanecimiento *nm* **1** : disappearance **2** DESMAYO : faint **3** : fading
desvariar {85} *vi* **1** DELIRAR : to be delirious **2** : to rave, to talk nonsense
desvarío *nm* DELIRIO : delirium
desvelado, -da *adj* : sleepless
desvelar *vt* **1** : to keep awake **2** REVELAR : to reveal, to disclose — **desvelarse** *vr* **1** : to stay awake **2** : to do one's utmost
desvelo *nm* **1** : sleeplessness **2** **desvelos** *nmpl* : efforts, pains
desvencijado, -da *adj* : dilapidated, rickety
desventaja *nf* : disadvantage, drawback
desventajoso, -sa *adj* : disadvantageous, unfavorable
desventura *nf* INFORTUNIO : misfortune
desventurado, -da *adj* : unfortunate, ill-fated
desvergonzado, -da *adj* : shameless, impudent
desvergüenza *nf* : shamelessness, impudence
desvestir {54} *vt* : to undress — **desvestirse** *vr* : to get undressed
desviación *nf, pl* **-ciones** **1** : deviation, departure **2** : detour, diversion
desviar {85} *vt* **1** : to change the course of, to divert **2** : to turn away, to deflect — **desviarse** *vr* **1** : to branch off **2** APARTARSE : to stray
desvinculación *nf, pl* **-ciones** : dissociation
desvincular *vt* **~ de** : to separate from, to dissociate from — **desvincularse** *vr*
desvío *nm* **1** : diversion, detour **2** : deviation
desvirtuar {3} *vt* **1** : to impair, to spoil **2** : to detract from **3** : to distort, to misrepresent
detalladamente *adv* : in detail, at great length
detallar *vt* : to detail
detalle *nm* **1** : detail **2** **al detalle** : retail
detallista[1] *adj* **1** : meticulous **2** : retail
detallista[2] *nmf* **1** : perfectionist **2** : retailer
detección *nf, pl* **-ciones** : detection
detectar *vt* : to detect — **detectable** *adj*
detective *nmf* : detective
detector *nm* : detector <detector de mentiras : lie detector>
detención *nf, pl* **-ciones** **1** ARRESTO : detention, arrest **2** : stop, halt **3** : delay, holdup
detener {80} *vt* **1** ARRESTAR : to arrest, to detain **2** PARAR : to stop, to halt **3** : to keep, to hold back — **detenerse** *vr* **1** : to stop **2** : to delay, to linger
detenidamente *adv* : thoroughly, at length
detenimiento *nm* **con ~** : carefully, in detail

detentar *vt* : to hold, to retain
detergente *nm* : detergent
deteriorado, -da *adj* : damaged, worn
deteriorar *vt* ESTROPEAR : to damage, to spoil — **deteriorarse** *vr* **1** : to get damaged, to wear out **2** : to deteriorate, to worsen
deterioro *nm* **1** : deterioration, wear **2** : worsening, decline
determinación *nf, pl* **-ciones 1** : determination, resolve **2 tomar una determinación** : to make a decision
determinado, -da *adj* **1** : certain, particular **2** : determined, resolute
determinante[1] *adj* : determining, deciding
determinante[2] *nm* : determinant
determinar *vt* **1** : to determine **2** : to cause, to bring about — **determinarse** *vr* : to make up one's mind, to decide
detestar *vt* : to detest — **detestable** *adj*
detonación *nf, pl* **-ciones** : detonation
detonador *nm* : detonator
detonante[1] *adj* : detonating, explosive
detonante[2] *nm* **1** → **detonador 2** : catalyst, cause
detonar *vi* : to detonate, to explode
detractor, -tora *n* : detractor, critic
detrás *adv* **1** : behind **2 ~ de** : in back of **3 por ~** : from behind
detuvo, etc. → **detener**
deuda *nf* **1** DÉBITO : debt **2 en deuda con** : indebted to
deudo, -da *n* : relative
deudor[1]**, -dora** *adj* : indebted
deudor[2]**, -dora** *n* : debtor
devaluación *nf, pl* **-ciones** DESVALORIZACIÓN : devaluation
devaluar {3} *vt* : to devalue — **devaluarse** *vr* : to depreciate
devanarse *vr* **devanarse los sesos** : to rack one's brains
devaneo *nm* **1** : flirtation, fling **2** : idle pursuit
devastador, -dora *adj* : devastating
devastar *vt* : to devastate — **devastación** *nf*
devenir {87} *vi* **1** : to come about **2 ~ en** : to become, to turn into
devoción *nf, pl* **-ciones** : devotion
devolución *nf, pl* **-ciones** REEMBOLSO : return, refund
devolver {89} *vt* **1** : to return, to give back **2** REEMBOLSAR : to refund, to pay back **3** : to vomit, to bring up — *vi* : to vomit, to throw up — **devolverse** *vr* : to return, to come back, to go back
devorar *vt* **1** : to devour **2** : to consume
devoto[1]**, -ta** *adj* : devout — **devotamente** *adv*
devoto[2]**, -ta** *n* : devotee, admirer
di → **dar, decir**
día *nm* **1** : day <todos los días : every day> **2** : daytime, daylight <de día : by day, in the daytime> <en pleno día : in broad daylight> **3 al día** : up-to-date **4 en su día** : in due time
diabetes *nf* : diabetes
diabético, -ca *adj & n* : diabetic
diablillo *nm* : little devil, imp
diablo *nm* DEMONIO : devil
diablura *nf* **1** : prank **2 diabluras** *nfpl* : mischief
diabólico, -ca *adj* : diabolical, diabolic, devilish
diaconisa *nf* : deaconess
diácono *nm* : deacon
diadema *nf* : diadem, crown
diáfano, -na *adj* : diaphanous
diafragma *nm* : diaphragm
diagnosticar {72} *vt* : to diagnose
diagnóstico[1]**, -ca** *adj* : diagnostic
diagnóstico[2] *nm* : diagnosis
diagonal *adj & nf* : diagonal — **diagonalmente** *adv*
diagrama *nm* **1** : diagram **2 diagrama de flujo** ORGANIGRAMA : flowchart
dialecto *nm* : dialect
dialogar {52} *vi* : to have a talk, to converse
diálogo *nm* : dialogue
diamante *nm* : diamond
diametral *adj* : diametric, diametrical — **diametralmente** *adv*
diámetro *nm* : diameter
diana *nf* **1** : target, bull's-eye **2** *or* **toque de diana** : reveille
diapositiva *nf* : slide, transparency
diario[1] *adv Mex* : every day, daily
diario[2]**, -ria** *adj* : daily, everyday — **diariamente** *adv*
diario[3] *nm* **1** : diary **2** PERIÓDICO : newspaper
diarrea *nf* : diarrhea
diatriba *nf* : diatribe, tirade
dibujante *nmf* **1** : draftsman *m*, draftswoman *f* **2** CARICATURISTA : cartoonist
dibujar *vt* **1** : to draw, to sketch **2** : to portray, to depict
dibujo *nm* **1** : drawing **2** : design, pattern **3 dibujos animados** : (animated) cartoons
dicción *nf, pl* **-ciones** : diction
diccionario *nm* : dictionary
dícese → **decir**
dicha *nf* **1** SUERTE : good luck **2** FELICIDAD : happiness, joy
dicho[1] *pp* → **decir**
dicho[2]**, -cha** *adj* : said, aforementioned
dicho[3] *nm* DECIR : saying, proverb
dichoso, -sa *adj* **1** : blessed **2** FELIZ : happy **3** AFORTUNADO : fortunate, lucky
diciembre *nm* : December
diciendo → **decir**
dictado *nm* : dictation
dictador, -dora *n* : dictator
dictadura *nf* : dictatorship
dictamen *nm, pl* **dictámenes 1** : report **2** : judgment, opinion
dictaminar *vt* : to report — *vi* : to give an opinion, to pass judgment
dictar *vt* **1** : to dictate **2** : to pronounce (a judgment) **3** : to give, to deliver <dictar una conferencia : to give a lecture>
dictatorial *adj* : dictatorial

didáctico, -ca *adj* : didactic

diecinueve *adj & nm* : nineteen

diecinueveavo[1], **-va** *adj* : nineteenth

diecinueveavo[2] *nm* : nineteenth (fraction)

dieciocho *adj & nm* : eighteen

dieciochoavo[1], **-va** *or* **dieciochavo, -va** *adj* : eighteenth

dieciochoavo[2] *or* **dieciochavo** *nm* : eighteenth (fraction)

dieciséis *adj & nm* : sixteen

dieciseisavo[1], **-va** *adj* : sixteenth

dieciseisavo[2] *nm* : sixteenth (fraction)

diecisietaeavo[1], **-va** *adj* : seventeenth

diecisietaeavo[2] *nm* : seventeenth (fraction)

diecisiete *adj & nm* : seventeen

diecisieteavo[1], **-va** *adj* : seventeenth

diecisieteavo[2] *nm* : seventeenth

diente *nm* **1** : tooth <diente canino : eyetooth, canine tooth> **2** : tusk, fang **3** : prong, tine **4 diente de león** : dandelion

dieron, etc. → **dar**

diesel [ˈdisɛl] *nm* : diesel

diestra *nf* : right hand

diestramente *adv* : skillfully, adroitly

diestro[1], **-tra** *adj* **1** : right **2** : skillful, accomplished

diestro[2] *nm* : bullfighter, matador

dieta *nf* : diet

dietética *nf* : dietetics

dietético, -ca *adj* : dietetic

dietista *nmf* : dietitian

diez *adj & nm, pl* **dieces** : ten

difamación *nf, pl* **-ciones** : defamation, slander

difamar *vt* : to defame, to slander

difamatorio, -ria *adj* : slanderous, defamatory, libelous

diferencia *nf* **1** : difference **2 a diferencia de** : unlike, in contrast to

diferenciación *nf, pl* **-ciones** : differentiation

diferenciar *vt* : to differentiate between, to distinguish — **diferenciarse** *vr* : to differ

diferendo *nm* : dispute, conflict

diferente *adj* DISTINTO : different — **diferentemente** *adv*

diferir {76} *vt* DILATAR, POSPONER : to postpone, to put off — *vi* : to differ

difícil *adj* : difficult, hard

difícilmente *adv* **1** : with difficulty **2** : hardly

dificultad *nf* : difficulty

dificultar *vt* : to make difficult, to obstruct

dificultoso, -sa *adj* : difficult, hard

difteria *nf* : diphtheria

difundir *vt* **1** : to diffuse, to spread out **2** : to broadcast, to spread

difunto, -ta *adj & n* FALLECIDO : deceased

difusión *nf, pl* **-siones 1** : spreading **2** : diffusion (of heat, etc.) **3** : broadcast, broadcasting <los medios de difusión : the media>

difuso, -sa *adj* : diffuse, widespread

diga, etc. → **decir**

digerir {76} *vt* : to digest — **digerible** *adj*

digestión *nf, pl* **-tiones** : digestion

digestivo, -va *adj* : digestive

digital[1] *adj* : digital — **digitalmente** *adv*

digital[2] *nm* **1** DEDALERA : foxglove **2** : digitalis

dígito *nm* : digit

dignarse *vr* : to deign, to condescend <no se dignó contestar : he didn't deign to answer>

dignatario, -ria *n* : dignitary

dignidad *nf* **1** : dignity **2** : dignitary

dignificar {72} *vt* : to dignify

digno, -na *adj* **1** HONORABLE : honorable **2** : worthy — **dignamente** *adv*

digresión *nf, pl* **-ciones** : digression

dije *nm* : charm (on a bracelet)

dijo, etc. → **decir**

dilación *nf, pl* **-ciones** : delay

dilapidar *vt* : to waste, to squander

dilatar *vt* **1** : to dilate, to widen, to expand **2** DIFERIR, POSPONER : to put off, to postpone — **dilatarse** *vr* **1** : to expand (of gases, metals, etc.) **2** *Mex* : to take long, to be long

dilatorio, -ria *adj* : dilatory, delaying

dilema *nm* : dilemma

diligencia *nf* **1** : diligence, care **2** : promptness, speed **3** : action, step **4** : task, errand **5** : stagecoach **6 diligencias** *nfpl* : judicial procedures, formalities

diligente *adj* : diligent — **diligentemente** *adv*

dilucidar *vt* : to elucidate, to clarify

diluir {41} *vt* : to dilute

diluviar *v impers* : to pour (with rain), to pour down

diluvio *nm* **1** : flood **2** : downpour

dimensión *nf, pl* **-siones** : dimension — **dimensional** *adj*

dimensionar *vt* : to measure, to gauge

diminuto, -ta *adj* : minute, tiny

dimisión *nf, pl* **-siones** : resignation

dimitir *vi* : to resign, to step down

dimos → **dar**

dinámica *nf* : dynamics

dinámico, -ca *adj* : dynamic — **dinámicamente** *adv*

dinamita *nf* : dynamite

dinamitar *vt* : to dynamite

dínamo *or* **dinamo** *nm* : dynamo

dinastía *nf* : dynasty

dineral *nm* : fortune, large sum of money

dinero *nm* : money

dinosaurio *nm* : dinosaur

dintel *nm* : lintel

dio, etc. → **dar**

diocesano, -na *adj* : diocesan

diócesis *nfs & pl* : diocese

dios, diosa *n* : god, goddess *f*

Dios *nm* : God

diploma *nm* : diploma

diplomacia *nf* : diplomacy

diplomado[1], -da *adj* : qualified, trained
diplomado[2] *nm Mex* : seminar
diplomático[1], -ca *adj* : diplomatic — **diplomáticamente** *adv*
diplomático[2], -ca *n* : diplomat
diputación *nf, pl* **-ciones** : deputation, delegation
diputado, -da *n* : delegate, representative
dique *nm* : dike
dirá, etc. → **decir**
dirección *nf, pl* **-ciones 1** : address **2** : direction **3** : management, leadership **4** : steering (of an automobile)
direccional[1] *adj* : directional
direccional[2] *nf* : directional, turn signal
directa *nf* : high gear
directamente *adv* : straight, directly
directiva *nf* **1** ORDEN : directive **2** DIRECTORIO, JUNTA : board of directors
directivo[1], -va *adj* : executive, managerial
directivo[2], -va *n* : executive, director
directo, -ta *adj* **1** : direct, straight, immediate **2 en ~** : live (in broadcasting)
director, -tora *n* **1** : director, manager, head **2** : conductor (of an orchestra)
directorial *adj* : managing, executive
directorio *nm* **1** : directory **2** DIRECTIVA, JUNTA : board of directors
directriz *nf, pl* **-trices** : guideline
dirigencia *nf* : leaders *pl*, leadership
dirigente[1] *adj* : directing, leading
dirigente[2] *nmf* : director, leader
dirigible *nm* : dirigible, blimp
dirigir {35} *vt* **1** : to direct, to lead **2** : to address **3** : to aim, to point **4** : to conduct (music) — **dirigirse** *vr* **~ a 1** : to go towards **2** : to speak to, to address
dirimir *vt* **1** : to resolve, to settle **2** : to annul, to dissolve (a marriage)
discapacidad *nf* MINUSVALÍA : disability, handicap
discapacitado[1], -da *adj* : disabled, handicapped
discapacitado[2], -da *n* : disabled person, handicapped person
discernimiento *nm* : discernment
discernir {25} *v* : to discern, to distinguish
disciplina *nf* : discipline
disciplinar *vt* : to discipline — **disciplinario, -ria** *adj*
discípulo, -la *n* : disciple, follower
disc jockey [ˌdiskˈjoke, -ˈdʒo-] *nmf* : disc jockey
disco *nm* **1** : phonograph record **2** : disc, disk <disco compacto : compact disc> **3** : discus
díscolo, -la *adj* : unruly, disobedient
disconforme *adj* : in disagreement
discontinuidad *nf* : discontinuity
discontinuo, -nua *adj* : discontinuous
discordancia *nf* DESAVENENCIA : conflict, disagreement
discordante *adj* **1** : discordant **2** : conflicting
discordia *nf* : discord
discoteca *nf* **1** : disco, discotheque **2** *CA, Mex* : record store
discreción *nf, pl* **-ciones** : discretion
discrecional *adj* : discretionary
discrepancia *nf* : discrepancy
discrepar *vi* **1** : to disagree **2** : to differ
discreto, -ta *adj* : discreet — **discretamente** *adv*
discriminación *nf, pl* **-ciones** : discrimination
discriminar *vt* **1** : to discriminate against **2** : to distinguish, to differentiate
discriminatorio, -ria *adj* : discriminatory
disculpa *nf* **1** : apology **2** : excuse
disculpable *adj* : excusable
disculpar *vt* : to excuse, to pardon — **disculparse** *vr* : to apologize
discurrir *vi* **1** : to flow **2** : to pass, to go by **3** : to ponder, to reflect
discurso *nm* **1** ORACIÓN : speech, address **2** : discourse, treatise
discusión *nf, pl* **-siones 1** : discussion **2** ALTERCADO, DISPUTA : argument
discutible *adj* : arguable, debatable
discutidor, -dora *adj* : argumentative
discutir *vt* **1** : to discuss **2** : to dispute — *vi* ALTERCAR : to argue, to quarrel
disecar {72} *vt* **1** : to dissect **2** : to stuff (for preservation)
disección *nf, pl* **-ciones** : dissection
diseminación *nf, pl* **-ciones** : dissemination, spreading
diseminar *vt* : to disseminate, to spread
disensión *nf, pl* **-siones** : dissension, disagreement
disentería *nf* : dysentery
disentir {76} *vi* : to dissent, to disagree
diseñador, -dora *n* : designer
diseñar *vt* **1** : to design, to plan **2** : to lay out, to outline
diseño *nm* : design
disertación *nf, pl* **-ciones 1** : lecture, talk **2** : dissertation
disertar *vi* : to lecture, to give a talk
disfraz *nm, pl* **disfraces 1** : disguise **2** : costume **3** : front, pretense
disfrazar {21} *vt* **1** : to disguise **2** : to mask, to conceal — **disfrazarse** *vr* : to wear a costume, to be in disguise
disfrutar *vt* : to enjoy — *vi* : to enjoy oneself, to have a good time
disfrute *nm* : enjoyment
disfunción *nf, pl* **-ciones** : dysfunction — **disfuncional** *adj*
disgresión *nf* → **digresión**
disgustar *vt* : to upset, to displease, to make angry — **disgustarse** *vr*
disgusto *nm* **1** : annoyance, displeasure **2** : argument, quarrel **3** : trouble, misfortune
disidencia *nf* : dissidence, dissent
disidente *adj & nmf* : dissident
disímbolo, -la *adj Mex* : dissimilar

disímil *adj* **:** dissimilar
disimulado, -da *adj* **1 :** concealed, disguised **2 :** furtive, sly
disimular *vi* **:** to dissemble, to pretend — *vt* **:** to conceal, to hide
disimulo *nm* **1 :** dissembling, pretense **2 :** slyness, furtiveness **3 :** tolerance
disipar *vt* **1 :** to dissipate **2 :** to dispel — **disiparse** *vr*
diskette [di'skɛt] *nm* **:** floppy disk, diskette
dislocar {72} *vt* **:** to dislocate — **dislocación** *nf*
disminución *nf, pl* **-ciones :** decrease, drop, fall
disminuir {41} *vt* REDUCIR **:** to reduce, to decrease, to lower — *vi* **1 :** to lower **2 :** to drop, to fall
disociación *nf, pl* **-ciones :** dissociation
disociar *vt* **:** to dissociate, to separate
disolución *nf, pl* **-ciones 1 :** dissolution, dissolving **2 :** breaking up **3 :** dissipation
disoluto, -ta *adj* **:** dissolute, dissipated
disolver {89} *vt* **1 :** to dissolve **2 :** to break up — **disolverse** *vr*
disonancia *nf* **:** dissonance — **disonante** *adj*
disparado, -da *adj* **salir disparado** *fam* **:** to take off in a hurry, to rush away
disparar *vi* **1 :** to fire (a gun) **2** *Mex fam* **:** to pay — *vt* **1 :** to shoot **2 :** to rush off **3** *Mex fam* **:** to treat to, to buy — **dispararse** *vr* **:** to shoot up, to skyrocket
disparatado, -da *adj* ABSURDO, RIDÍCULO **:** absurd, ridiculous, crazy
disparate *nm* **:** silliness, stupidity <decir disparates **:** to talk nonsense>
disparejo, -ja *adj* DESIGUAL **:** uneven
disparidad *nf* **:** disparity
disparo *nm* TIRO **:** shot
dispendio *nm* **:** wastefulness, extravagance
dispendioso, -sa *adj* **:** wasteful, extravagant
dispensa *nf* **:** dispensation
dispensable *adj* **1 :** dispensable **2 :** excusable
dispensar *vt* **1 :** to dispense, to give, to grant **2** EXCUSAR **:** to excuse, to forgive **3** EXIMIR **:** to exempt
dispensario *nm* **1 :** dispensary, clinic **2** *Mex* **:** dispenser
dispersar *vt* DESPERDIGAR **:** to disperse, to scatter
dispersión *nf, pl* **-siones :** dispersion
disperso, -sa *adj* **:** dispersed, scattered
displicencia *nf* **:** indifference, coldness, disdain
displicente *adj* **:** indifferent, cold, disdainful
disponer {60} *vt* **1 :** to arrange, to lay out **2 :** to stipulate, to order **3 :** to prepare — *vi* **~ de :** to have at one's disposal — **disponerse** *vr* **~ a :** to prepare to, to be about to
disponibilidad *nf* **:** availability
disponible *adj* **:** available
disposición *nf, pl* **-ciones 1 :** disposition **2 :** aptitude, talent **3 :** order, arrangement **4 :** willingness, readiness **5 última disposición :** last will and testament
dispositivo *nm* **1** APARATO, MECANISMO **:** device, mechanism **2 :** force, detachment
dispuesto[1] *pp* → **disponer**
dispuesto[2]**, -ta** *adj* PREPARADO **:** ready, prepared, disposed
dispuso, etc. → **disponer**
disputa *nf* ALTERCADO, DISCUSIÓN **:** dispute, argument
disputar *vi* **:** to argue, to contend, to vie — *vt* **:** to dispute, to question — **disputarse** *vr* **:** to be in competition for <se disputan la corona **:** they're fighting for the crown>
disquera *nf* **:** record label, recording company
disquete *nm* → **diskette**
disquisición *nf, pl* **-ciones 1 :** formal discourse **2 disquisiciones** *nfpl* **:** digressions
distancia *nf* **:** distance
distanciamiento *nm* **1 :** distancing **2 :** rift, estrangement
distanciar *vt* **1 :** to space out **2 :** to draw apart — **distanciarse** *vr* **:** to grow apart, to become estranged
distante *adj* **1 :** distant, far-off **2 :** aloof
distar *vi* **~ de :** to be far from <dista de ser perfecto **:** he is far from perfect>
diste → **dar**
distender {56} *vt* **:** to distend, to stretch
distensión *nf, pl* **-siones :** distension
distinción *nf, pl* **-ciones :** distinction
distinguido, -da *adj* **:** distinguished, refined
distinguir {26} *vt* **1 :** to distinguish **2 :** to honor — **distinguirse** *vr*
distintivo, -va *adj* **:** distinctive, distinguishing
distinto, -ta *adj* **1** DIFERENTE **:** different **2** CLARO **:** distinct, clear, evident
distorsión *nf, pl* **-siones :** distortion
distorsionar *vt* **:** to distort
distracción *nf, pl* **-ciones 1 :** distraction, amusement **2 :** forgetfulness **3 :** oversight
distraer {81} *vt* **1 :** to distract **2** ENTRETENER **:** to entertain, to amuse — **distraerse** *vr* **1 :** to get distracted **2 :** to amuse oneself
distraídamente *adv* **:** absentmindedly
distraído[1] *pp* → **distraer**
distraído[2]**, -da** *adj* **1 :** distracted, preoccupied **2** DESPISTADO **:** absentminded
distribución *nf, pl* **-ciones :** distribution
distribuidor, -dora *n* **:** distributor
distribuir {41} *vt* **:** to distribute
distrital *adj* **:** district, of the district

distrito *nm* : district
distrofia *nf* : dystrophy <distrofia muscular : muscular dystrophy>
disturbio *nm* : disturbance
disuadir *vt* : to dissuade, to discourage
disuasión *nf, pl* **-siones** : dissuasion
disuasorio, -ria *adj* : discouraging
disuelto *pp* → **disolver**
disyuntiva *nf* : dilemma
diurético[1], **-ca** *adj* : diuretic
diurético[2] *nm* : diuretic
diurno, -na *adj* : day, daytime
diva *nf* → **divo**
divagar {52} *vi* : to digress
diván *nm, pl* **divanes** : divan
divergencia *nf* : divergence, difference
divergente *adj* : divergent, differing
divergir {35} *vi* **1** : to diverge **2** : to differ, to disagree
diversidad *nf* : diversity, variety
diversificación *nf, pl* **-ciones** : diversification
diversificar {72} *vt* : to diversify
diversión *nf, pl* **-siones** ENTRETENIMIENTO : fun, amusement, diversion
diverso, -sa *adj* : diverse, various
divertido, -da *adj* **1** : amusing, funny **2** : entertaining, enjoyable
divertir {76} *vt* ENTRETENER : to amuse, to entertain — **divertirse** *vr* : to have fun, to have a good time
dividendo *nm* : dividend
dividir *vt* **1** : to divide, to split **2** : to distribute, to share out — **dividirse** *vr*
divieso *nm* : boil
divinidad *nf* : divinity
divino, -na *adj* : divine
divisa *nf* **1** : currency **2** LEMA : motto **3** : emblem, insignia
divisar *vt* : to discern, to make out
divisible *adj* : divisible
división *nf, pl* **-siones** : division
divisionismo *nm* : factionalism
divisivo, -va *adj* : divisive
divisor *nm* : denominator
divisorio, -ria *adj* : dividing
divo, -va *n* **1** : prima donna **2** : celebrity, star
divorciado[1], **-da** *adj* **1** : divorced **2** : split, divided
divorciado[2], **-da** *n* : divorcé *m*, divorcée *f*
divorciar *vt* : to divorce — **divorciarse** *vr* : to get a divorce
divorcio *nm* : divorce
divulgación *nf, pl* **-ciones 1** : spreading, dissemination **2** : popularization
divulgar {52} *vt* **1** : to spread, to circulate **2** REVELAR : to divulge, to reveal **3** : to popularize — **divulgarse** *vr*
dizque *adv* : supposedly, apparently
dobladillar *vt* : to hem
dobladillo *nm* : hem
doblar *vt* **1** : to double **2** PLEGAR : to fold, to bend **3** : to turn <doblar la esquina : to turn the corner> **4** : to dub — *vi* **1** : to turn **2** : to toll, to ring — **doblarse** *vr* **1** : to fold up, to double over **2** : to give in, to yield
doble[1] *adj* : double — **doblemente** *adv*
doble[2] *nm* **1** : double **2** : toll (of a bell), knell
doble[3] *nmf* : stand-in, double
doblegar {52} *vt* **1** : to fold, to crease **2** : to force to yield — **doblegarse** *vr* : to yield, to bow
doblez[1] *nm, pl* **dobleces** : fold, crease
doblez[2] *nmf* : duplicity, deceitfulness
doce *adj & nm* : twelve
doceavo[1], **-va** *adj* : twelfth
doceavo[2] *nm* : twelfth (fraction)
docena *nf* **1** : dozen **2 docena de fraile** : baker's dozen
docencia *nf* : teaching
docente[1] *adj* : educational, teaching
docente[2] *n* : teacher, lecturer
dócil *adj* : docile — **dócilmente** *adv*
docilidad *nf* : docility
docto, -ta *adj* : learned, erudite
doctor, -tora *n* : doctor
doctorado *nm* : doctorate
doctrina *nf* : doctrine — **doctrinal** *adj*
documentación *nf, pl* **-ciones** : documentation
documental *adj & nm* : documentary
documentar *vt* : to document
documento *nm* : document
dogma *nm* : dogma
dogmático, -ca *adj* : dogmatic
dogmatismo *nm* : dogmatism
dólar *nm* : dollar
dolencia *nf* : ailment, malaise
doler {47} *vi* **1** : to hurt, to ache **2** : to grieve — **dolerse** *vr* **1** : to be distressed **2** : to complain
doliente *nmf* : mourner, bereaved
dolor *nm* **1** : pain, ache <dolor de cabeza : headache> **2** PENA, TRISTEZA : grief, sorrow
dolorido, -da *adj* **1** : sore, aching **2** : hurt, upset
doloroso, -sa *adj* **1** : painful **2** : distressing — **dolorosamente** *adv*
doloso, -sa *adj* : fraudulent — **dolosamente** *adv*
domador, -dora *n* : tamer
domar *vt* : to tame, to break in
domesticado, -da *adj* : domesticated, tame
domesticar {72} *vt* : to domesticate, to tame
doméstico, -ca *adj* : domestic, household
domiciliado, -da *adj* : residing
domiciliario, -ria *adj* **1** : home **2 arresto domiciliario** : house arrest
domiciliarse *vr* RESIDIR : to reside
domicilio *nm* : home, residence <cambio de domicilio : change of address>
dominación *nf, pl* **-ciones** : domination
dominancia *nf* : dominance
dominante *adj* **1** : dominant **2** : domineering

dominar *vt* **1** : to dominate **2** : to master, to be proficient at — *vi* : to predominate, to prevail — **dominarse** *vr* : to control oneself
domingo *nm* : Sunday
dominical *adj* : Sunday <periódico dominical : Sunday newspaper>
dominicano, -na *adj & n* : Dominican
dominio *nm* **1** : dominion, power **2** : mastery **3** : domain, field
dominó *nm, pl* **-nós 1** : domino (tile) **2** : dominoes *pl* (game)
domo *nm* : dome
don[1] *nm* **1** : gift, present **2** : talent
don[2] *nm* **1** : title of courtesy preceding a man's first name **2 don nadie** : nobody, insignificant person
dona *nf Mex* : doughnut, donut
donación *nf, pl* **-ciones** : donation
donador, -dora *n* : donor
donaire *nm* **1** GARBO : grace, poise **2** : witticism
donante *nf* → **donador**
donar *vt* : to donate
donativo *nm* : donation
doncella *nf* : maiden, damsel
doncellez *nf* : maidenhood
donde[1] *conj* : where, in which <el pueblo donde vivo : the town where I live>
donde[2] *prep* : over by <lo encontré donde la silla : I found it over by the chair>
dónde *adv* : where <¿dónde está su casa? : where is your house?>
dondequiera *adv* **1** : anywhere, no matter where **2 dondequiera que** : wherever, everywhere
doña *nf* : title of courtesy preceding a woman's first name
doquier *adv* **por ~** : everywhere, all over
dorado[1], **-da** *adj* : gold, golden
dorado[2], **-da** *nm* : gilt
dorar *vt* **1** : to gild **2** : to brown
dormido, -da *adj* **1** : asleep **2** : numb <tiene el pie dormido : her foot's numb, her foot's gone to sleep>
dormilón, -lona *n* : sleepyhead, late riser
dormir {27} *vt* : to put to sleep — *vi* : to sleep — **dormirse** *vr* : to fall asleep
dormitar *vi* : to snooze, to doze
dormitorio *nm* **1** : bedroom **2** : dormitory
dorsal[1] *adj* : dorsal
dorsal[2] *nm* : number (worn in sports)
dorso *nm* **1** : back <el dorso de la mano : the back of the hand> **2** *Mex* : backstroke
dos *adj & nm* : two
doscientos[1], **-tas** *adj* : two hundred
doscientos[2] *nms & pl* : two hundred
dosel *nm* : canopy
dosificación *nf, pl* **-ciones** : dosage
dosis *nfs & pl* **1** : dose **2** : amount, quantity
dotación *nf, pl* **-ciones 1** : endowment, funding **2** : staff, personnel
dotado, -da *adj* **1** : gifted **2 ~ de** : endowed with, equipped with
dotar *vt* **1** : to provide, to equip **2** : to endow
dote *nf* **1** : dowry **2 dotes** *nfpl* : talent, gift
doy → **dar**
draga *nf* : dredge
dragado *nm* : dredging
dragar {52} *vt* : to dredge
dragón *nm, pl* **dragones 1** : dragon **2** : snapdragon
drague, etc. → **dragar**
drama *nm* : drama
dramático, -ca *adj* : dramatic — **dramáticamente** *adv*
dramatizar {21} *vt* : to dramatize — **dramatización** *nf*
dramaturgo, -ga *n* : dramatist, playwright
drástico, -ca *adj* : drastic — **drásticamente** *adv*
drenaje *nm* : drainage
drenar *vt* : to drain
drene *nm Mex* : drain
driblar *vi* : to dribble (in basketball)
drible *nm* : dribble (in basketball)
droga *nf* : drug
drogadicción *nf, pl* **-ciones** : drug addiction
drogadicto, -ta *n* : drug addict
drogar {52} *vt* : to drug — **drogarse** *vr* : to take drugs
drogue, etc. → **drogar**
droguería *nf* FARMACIA : drugstore
dual *adj* : dual
dualidad *nf* : duality
dualismo *nm* : dualism
ducha *nf* : shower <darse una ducha : to take a shower>
ducharse *vr* : to take a shower
ducho, -cha *adj* : experienced, skilled, expert
ducto *nm* **1** : duct, shaft **2** : pipeline
duda *nf* : doubt <no cabe duda : there's no doubt about it>
dudar *vt* : to doubt — *vi* **~ en** : to hesitate to <no dudes en pedirme ayuda : don't hesitate to ask me for help>
dudoso, -sa *adj* **1** : doubtful **2** : dubious, questionable — **dudosamente** *adv*
duele, etc. → **doler**
duelo *nm* **1** : duel **2** LUTO : mourning
duende *nm* **1** : elf, goblin **2** ENCANTO : magic, charm <una bailarina que tiene duende : a dancer with a certain magic>
dueño, -na *nmf* **1** : owner, proprietor, proprietress *f* **2** : landlord, landlady *f*
duerme, etc. → **dormir**
dueto *nm* : duet
dulce[1] *adv* : sweetly, softly
dulce[2] *adj* **1** : sweet **2** : mild, gentle, mellow — **dulcemente** *adv*
dulce[3] *nm* : candy, sweet

dulcería *nf* **:** candy store
dulcificante *nm* **:** sweetener
dulzura *nf* **1 :** sweetness **2 :** gentleness, mellowness
duna *nf* **:** dune
dúo *nm* **:** duo, duet
duodécimo[1], -ma *adj* **:** twelfth
duodécimo[2], -ma *nm* **:** twelfth (in a series)
dúplex *nms & pl* **:** duplex apartment
duplicación *nf, pl* **-ciones :** duplication, copying
duplicado *nm* **:** duplicate, copy
duplicar {72} *vt* **1 :** to double **2 :** to duplicate, to copy
duplicidad *nf* **:** duplicity
duque *nm* **:** duke
duquesa *nf* **:** duchess
durabilidad *nf* **:** durability
durable → duradero
duración *nf, pl* **-ciones :** duration, length
duradero, -ra *adj* **:** durable, lasting
duramente *adv* **1 :** harshly, severely **2 :** hard
durante *prep* **:** during <durante todo el día : all day long> <trabajó durante tres horas : he worked for three hours>
durar *vi* **:** to last, to endure
durazno *nm* **1 :** peach **2 :** peach tree
dureza *nf* **1 :** hardness, toughness **2 :** severity, harshness
durmiente[1] *adj* **:** sleeping
durmiente[2] *nmf* **:** sleeper
durmió, etc. → dormir
duro[1] *adv* **:** hard <trabajé tan duro : I worked so hard>
duro[2], -ra *adj* **1 :** hard, tough **2 :** harsh, severe

E

e[1] *nf* **:** fifth letter of the Spanish alphabet
e[2] *conj* (*used instead of* **y** *before words beginning with i or hi*) **:** and
ebanista *nmf* **:** cabinetmaker
ebanistería *nf* **:** cabinetmaking
ébano *nm* **:** ebony
ebriedad *nf* EMBRIAGUEZ **:** inebriation, drunkenness
ebrio, -bria *adj* EMBRIAGADO **:** inebriated, drunk
ebullición *nf, pl* **-ciones :** boiling
eccéntrico → excéntrico
echar *vt* **1** LANZAR **:** to throw, to cast, to hurl **2** EXPULSAR **:** to throw out, to expel **3** EMITIR **:** to emit, give off **4** BROTAR **:** to sprout, to put forth **5** DESPEDIR **:** to fire, to dismiss **6 :** to put in, to add **7 echar a perder :** to spoil, to ruin **8 echar de menos :** to miss <echan de menos a su madre : they miss their mother> — *vi* **1 :** to start off **2 ~ a :** to begin to — **echarse** *vr* **1 :** to throw oneself **2 :** to lie down **3 :** to put on **4 ~ a :** to start to **5 echarse a perder :** to go bad, to spoil **6 echárselas de :** to pose as
ecléctico, -ca *adj* **:** eclectic
eclesiástico[1], -ca *adj* **:** ecclesiastical, ecclesiastic
eclesiástico[2] *nm* CLÉRIGO **:** cleric, clergyman
eclipsar *vt* **1 :** to eclipse **2 :** to outshine, to surpass
eclipse *nm* **:** eclipse
eco *nm* **:** echo
ecografía *nf* **:** ultrasound scanning
ecología *nf* **:** ecology
ecológico, -ca *adj* **:** ecological — **ecológicamente** *adv*
ecologista *nmf* **:** ecologist, environmentalist
ecólogo, -ga *n* **:** ecologist
economía *nf* **1 :** economy **2 :** economics
económicamente *adv* **:** financially
económico, -ca *adj* **:** economic, economical
economista *nmf* **:** economist
economizar {21} *vt* **:** to save, to economize on — *vi* **:** to save up, to be frugal
ecosistema *nm* **:** ecosystem
ecuación *nf, pl* **-ciones :** equation
ecuador *nm* **:** equator
ecuánime *adj* **1 :** even-tempered **2 :** impartial
ecuanimidad *nf* **1 :** equanimity **2 :** impartiality
ecuatorial *adj* **:** equatorial
ecuatoriano, -na *adj & n* **:** Ecuadorian
ecuestre *adj* **:** equestrian
ecuménico, -ca *adj* **:** ecumenical
eczema *nm* **:** eczema
edad *nf* **1 :** age <¿qué edad tiene? : how old is she?> **2** ÉPOCA, ERA **:** epoch, era
edema *nm* **:** edema
Edén *nm, pl* **Edenes :** Eden, paradise
edición *nf, pl* **-ciones 1 :** edition **2 :** publication, publishing
edicto *nm* **:** edict, proclamation
edificación *nf, pl* **-ciones 1 :** edification **2 :** construction, building
edificante *adj* **:** edifying
edificar {72} *vt* **1 :** to edify **2** CONSTRUIR **:** to build, to construct
edificio *nm* **:** building, edifice
editar *vt* **1 :** to edit **2** PUBLICAR **:** to publish
editor[1], -tora *adj* **:** publishing <casa editora : publishing house>
editor[2], -tora *n* **1 :** editor **2 :** publisher
editora *nf* **:** publisher, publishing company
editorial[1] *adj* **1 :** publishing **2 :** editorial
editorial[2] *nm* **:** editorial
editorial[3] *nf* **:** publishing house

editorializar {21} *vi* **:** to editorialize

edredón *nm, pl* **-dones** COBERTOR, COLCHA **:** comforter, eiderdown, quilt

educable *adj* **:** educable, teachable

educación *nf, pl* **-ciones 1** ENSEÑANZA **:** education **2 :** manners *pl* — **educacional** *adj*

educado, -da *adj* **:** polite, well-mannered

educador, -dora *n* **:** educator

educando, -da *n* ALUMNO, PUPILO **:** pupil, student

educar {72} *vt* **1 :** to educate **2** CRIAR **:** to bring up, to raise **3 :** to train — **educarse** *vr* **:** to be educated

educativo, -va *adj* **:** educational

efectista *adj* **:** dramatic, sensational

efectivamente *adv* **:** really, actually

efectividad *nf* **:** effectiveness

efectivo[1], -va *adj* **1 :** effective **2 :** real, actual **3 :** permanent, regular (of employment)

efectivo[2] *nm* **:** cash

efecto *nm* **1 :** effect **2 en ~ :** actually, in fact **3 efectos** *nmpl* **:** goods, property <efectos personales : personal effects>

efectuar {3} *vt* **:** to carry out, to bring about

efervescencia *nf* **1 :** effervescence **2 :** vivacity, high spirits *pl*

efervescente *adj* **1 :** effervescent **2 :** vivacious

eficacia *nf* **1 :** effectiveness, efficacy **2 :** efficiency

eficaz *adj, pl* **-caces 1 :** effective **2** EFICIENTE **:** efficient — **eficazmente** *adv*

eficiencia *nf* **:** efficiency

eficiente *adj* EFICAZ **:** efficient — **eficientemente** *adv*

eficientizar {21} *vt Mex* **:** to streamline, to make more efficient

efigie *nf* **:** effigy

efímera *nf* **:** mayfly

efímero, -ra *adj* **:** ephemeral

efusión *nf, pl* **-siones 1 :** effusion **2 :** warmth, effusiveness **3 con ~ :** effusively

efusivo, -va *adj* **:** effusive — **efusivamente** *adv*

egipcio, -cia *adj & n* **:** Egyptian

eglefino *nm* **:** haddock

ego *nm* **:** ego

egocéntrico, -ca *adj* **:** egocentric, self-centered

egoísmo *nm* **:** selfishness, egoism

egoísta[1] *adj* **:** selfish, egoistic

egoísta[2] *nmf* **:** egoist, selfish person

egotismo *nm* **:** egotism, conceit

egotista[1] *adj* **:** egotistic, egotistical, conceited

egotista[2] *nmf* **:** egotist, conceited person

egresado, -da *n* **:** graduate

egresar *vi* **:** to graduate

egreso *nm* **1 :** graduation **2 ingresos y egresos :** income and expenditure

eje *nm* **1 :** axle **2 :** axis

ejecución *nf, pl* **-ciones :** execution

ejecutante *nmf* **:** performer

ejecutar *vt* **1 :** to execute, to put to death **2 :** to carry out, to perform

ejecutivo, -va *adj & n* **:** executive

ejecutor, -tora *n* **:** executor

ejemplar[1] *adj* **:** exemplary, model

ejemplar[2] *nm* **1 :** copy (of a book, magazine, etc.) **2 :** specimen, example

ejemplificar {72} *vt* **:** to exemplify, to illustrate

ejemplo *nm* **1 :** example **2 por ~ :** for example **3 dar ejemplo :** to set an example

ejercer {86} *vi* **~ de :** to practice as, to work as — *vt* **1 :** to practice **2 :** exercise (a right) **3 :** to exert

ejercicio *nm* **1 :** exercise **2 :** practice

ejercitar *vt* **1 :** to exercise **2** ADIESTRAR **:** to drill, to train

ejército *nm* **:** army

ejidal *adj Mex* **:** cooperative

ejido *nm* **1 :** common land **2** *Mex* **:** cooperative

ejote *nm Mex* **:** green bean

el[1] *pron* (*referring to masculine nouns*) **1 :** the one <tengo mi libro y el tuyo : I have my book and yours> <de los cantantes me gusta el de México : I prefer the singer from México> **2 el que :** he who, whoever, the one that <el que vino ayer : the one who came yesterday> <el que trabaja duro estará contento : he who works hard will be happy>

el[2], la *art, pl* **los, las :** the <los niños están en la casa : the boys are in the house> <me duele el pie : my foot hurts>

él *pron* **:** he, him <él es mi amigo : he's my friend> <hablaremos con él : we will speak with him>

elaboración *nf, pl* **-ciones 1** PRODUCCIÓN **:** production, making **2 :** preparation, devising

elaborado, -da *adj* **:** elaborate

elaborar *vt* **1 :** to make, to produce **2 :** to devise, to draw up

elasticidad *nf* **:** elasticity

elástico[1], -ca *adj* **1** FLEXIBLE **:** flexible **2 :** elastic

elástico[2] *nm* **1 :** elastic (material) **2 :** rubber band

elección *nf, pl* **-ciones 1** SELECCIÓN **:** choice, selection **2 :** election

electivo, -va *adj* **:** elective

electo, -ta *adj* **:** elect <el presidente electo : the president-elect>

elector, -tora *n* **:** elector, voter

electorado *nm* **:** electorate

electoral *adj* **:** electoral, election

electricidad *nf* **:** electricity

electricista *nmf* **:** electrician

eléctrico, -ca *adj* **:** electric, electrical

electrificar {72} *vt* **:** to electrify — **electrificación** *nf*

electrizar {21} *vt* **:** to electrify, to thrill — **electrizante** *adj*

electrocardiógrafo *nm* : electrocardiograph
electrocardiograma *nm* : electrocardiogram
electrocutar *vt* : to electrocute — **electrocución** *nf*
electrodo *nm* : electrode
electrodoméstico *nm* : electric appliance
electroimán *nm, pl* **-manes** : electromagnet
electrólisis *nfs & pl* : electrolysis
electrolito *nm* : electrolyte
electromagnético, -ca *adj* : electromagnetic
electromagnetismo *nm* : electromagnetism
electrón *nm, pl* **-trones** : electron
electrónica *nf* : electronics
electrónico, -ca *adj* : electronic — **electrónicamente** *adv*
elefante, -ta *n* : elephant
elegancia *nf* : elegance
elegante *adj* : elegant, smart — **elegantemente** *adv*
elegía *nf* : elegy
elegíaco, -ca *adj* : elegiac
elegibilidad *nf* : eligibility
elegible *adj* : eligible
elegido, -da *adj* **1** : chosen, selected **2** : elected
elegir {28} *vt* **1** ESCOGER, SELECCIONAR : to choose, to select **2** : to elect
elemental *adj* **1** : elementary, basic **2** : fundamental, essential
elemento *nm* : element
elenco *nm* : cast (of actors)
elepé *nm* : long-playing record
elevación *nf, pl* **-ciones** : elevation, height
elevado, -da *adj* **1** : elevated, lofty **2** : high
elevador *nm* ASCENSOR : elevator
elevar *vt* **1** ALZAR : to raise, to lift **2** AUMENTAR : to raise, to increase **3** : to elevate (in a hierarchy), to promote **4** : to present, to submit — **elevarse** *vr* : to rise
elfo *nm* : elf
eliminación *nf, pl* **-ciones** : elimination, removal
eliminar *vt* **1** : to eliminate, to remove **2** : to do in, to kill
elipse *nf* : ellipse
elipsis *nf* : ellipsis
elíptico, -ca *adj* : elliptical, elliptic
elite *or* **élite** *nf* : elite
elixir *or* **elíxir** *nm* : elixir
ella *pron* : she, her <ella es mi amiga : she is my friend> <nos fuimos con ella : we left with her>
ello *pron* : it <es por ello que me voy : that's why I'm going>
ellos, ellas *pron pl* **1** : they, them **2 de ellos, de ellas** : theirs
elocución *nf, pl* **-ciones** : elocution
elocuencia *nf* : eloquence
elocuente *adj* : eloquent — **elocuentemente** *adv*
elogiar *vt* ENCOMIAR : to praise
elogio *nm* : praise
elote *nm* **1** *Mex* : corn, maize **2** *CA, Mex* : corncob
elucidación *nf, pl* **-ciones** ESCLARECIMIENTO : elucidation
elucidar *vt* ESCLARECER : to elucidate
eludir *vt* EVADIR : to evade, to avoid, to elude
emanación *nf, pl* **-ciones** : emanation
emanar *vi* **~ de** : to emanate from — *vt* : to exude
emancipar *vt* : to emancipate — **emancipación** *nf*
embadurnar *vt* EMBARRAR : to smear, to daub
embajada *nf* : embassy
embajador, -dora *n* : ambassador
embalaje *nm* : packing, packaging
embalar *vt* EMPAQUETAR : to pack
embaldosar *vt* : to tile, to pave with tiles
embalsamar *vt* : to embalm
embalsar *vt* : to dam, to dam up
embalse *nm* : dam, reservoir
embarazada *adj* ENCINTA, PREÑADA : pregnant, expecting
embarazar {21} *vt* **1** : to obstruct, to hamper **2** PREÑAR : to make pregnant
embarazo *nm* : pregnancy
embarazoso, -sa *adj* : embarrassing, awkward
embarcación *nf, pl* **-ciones** : boat, craft
embarcadero *nm* : wharf, pier, jetty
embarcar {72} *vi* : to embark, to board — *vt* : to load
embarco *nm* : embarkation
embargar {52} *vt* **1** : to seize, to impound **2** : to overwhelm
embargo *nm* **1** : seizure **2** : embargo **3 sin ~** : however, nevertheless
embarque *nm* **1** : embarkation **2** : shipment
embarrancar {72} *vi* **1** : to run aground **2** : to get bogged down
embarrar *vt* **1** : to cover with mud **2** EMBADURNAR : to smear
embarullar *vt fam* : to muddle, to confuse — **embarullarse** *vr fam* : to get mixed up
embate *nm* **1** : onslaught **2** : battering (of waves or wind)
embaucador, -dora *n* : swindler, deceiver
embaucar {72} *vt* : to trick, to swindle
embeber *vt* : to absorb, to soak up — *vi* : to shrink
embelesado, -da *adj* : spellbound
embelesar *vt* : to enchant, to captivate
embellecer {53} *vt* : to embellish, to beautify
embellecimiento *nm* : beautification, embellishment
embestida *nf* **1** : charge (of a bull) **2** ARREMETIDA : attack, onslaught
embestir {54} *vt* : to hit, to run into, to charge at — *vi* ARREMETER : to charge, to attack

emblanquecer {53} *vt* BLANQUEAR **:** to bleach, to whiten **— emblanquecerse** *vr* **:** to turn white

emblema *nm* **:** emblem

emblemático, -ca *adj* **:** emblematic

embolia *nf* **:** embolism

émbolo *nm* **:** piston

embolsarse *vr* **1 :** to pocket (money) **2 :** to collect (payment)

emborracharse *vr* EMBRIAGARSE **:** to get drunk

emborronar *vt* **1 :** to blot, to smudge **2** GARABATEAR **:** to scribble

emboscada *nf* **:** ambush

emboscar {72} *vt* **:** to ambush **— emboscarse** *vr* **:** to lie in ambush

embotadura *nf* **:** bluntness, dullness

embotar *vt* **1 :** to dull, to blunt **2 :** to weaken, to enervate

embotellamiento *nm* ATASCO **:** traffic jam

embotellar *vt* ENVASAR **:** to bottle

embragar {52} *vi* **:** to engage the clutch

embrague *nm* **:** clutch

embravecerse {53} *vr* **1 :** to get furious **2 :** to get rough <el mar se embraveció : the sea became tempestuous>

embriagado, -da *adj* **:** inebriated, drunk

embriagador, -dora *adj* **:** intoxicating

embriagarse {52} *vr* EMBORRACHARSE **:** to get drunk

embriaguez *nf* EBRIEDAD **:** drunkenness, inebriation

embrión *nm, pl* **embriones :** embryo

embrionario, -ria *adj* **:** embryonic

embrollo *nm* ENREDO **:** imbroglio, confusion

embrujar *vt* HECHIZAR **:** to bewitch

embrujo *nm* **:** spell, curse

embudo *nm* **:** funnel

embuste *nm* **1** MENTIRA **:** lie, fib **2** ENGAÑO **:** trick, hoax

embustero[1], -ra *adj* **:** lying, deceitful

embustero[2], -ra *n* **:** liar, cheat

embutido *nm* **1 :** sausage **2 :** inlaid work

embutir *vt* **1 :** to cram, to stuff, to jam **2 :** to inlay

emergencia *nf* **1 :** emergency **2 :** emergence

emergente *adj* **1 :** emergent **2 :** consequent, resultant

emerger {15} *vi* **:** to emerge, to surface

emético[1], -ca *adj* **:** emetic

emético[2] *nm* **:** emetic

emigración *nf, pl* **-ciones 1 :** emigration **2 :** migration

emigrante *adj & nmf* **:** emigrant

emigrar *vi* **1 :** to emigrate **2 :** to migrate

eminencia *nf* **:** eminence

eminente *adj* **:** eminent, distinguished

eminentemente *adv* **:** basically, essentially

emisario[1], -ria *n* **:** emissary

emisario[2] *nm* **:** outlet (of a body of water)

emisión *nf, pl* **-siones 1 :** emission **2 :** broadcast **3 :** issue <emisión de acciones : stock issue>

emisor *nm* TRANSMISOR **:** television or radio transmitter

emisora *nf* **:** radio station

emitir *vt* **1 :** to emit, to give off **2 :** to broadcast **3 :** to issue **4 :** to cast (a vote)

emoción *nf, pl* **-ciones :** emotion **— emocional** *adj* **— emocionalmente** *adv*

emocionado, -da *adj* **1 :** moved, affected by emotion **2** ENTUSIASMADO **:** excited

emocionante *adj* **1** CONMOVEDOR **:** moving, touching **2** EXCITANTE **:** exciting, thrilling

emocionar *vt* **1** CONMOVER **:** to move, to touch **2 :** to excite, to thrill **— emocionarse** *vr*

emotivo, -va *adj* **:** emotional, moving

empacador, -dora *n* **:** packer

empacar {72} *vt* **1** EMPAQUETAR **:** to pack **2 :** to bale **—** *vi* **:** to pack **— empacarse** *vr* **1 :** to balk, to refuse to budge **2** *Col, Mex fam* **:** to eat ravenously, to devour

empachar *vt* **1** ESTORBAR **:** to obstruct **2 :** to give indigestion to **3** DISFRAZAR **:** to disguise, to mask **— empacharse** *vr* **1** INDIGESTARSE **:** to get indigestion **2** AVERGONZARSE **:** to be embarrassed

empacho *nm* **1** INDIGESTIÓN **:** indigestion **2** VERGÜENZA **:** embarrassment **3 no tener empacho en :** to have no qualms about

empadronarse *vr* **:** to register to vote

empalagar {52} *vt* **1 :** to cloy, to surfeit **2** FASTIDIAR **:** to annoy, to bother

empalagoso, -sa *adj* MELOSO **:** cloying, excessively sweet

empalar *vt* **:** to impale

empalizada *nf* **:** palisade (fence)

empalmar *vt* **1 :** to splice, to link **2 :** to combine **—** *vi* **:** to meet, to converge

empalme *nm* **1** CONEXIÓN **:** connection, link **2 :** junction

empanada *nf* **:** pie, turnover

empanadilla *nf* **:** meat or seafood pie

empanar *vt* **:** to bread

empantanado, -da *adj* **:** bogged down, delayed

empañar *vt* **1 :** to steam up **2 :** to tarnish, to sully

empapado, -da *adj* **:** soggy, sodden

empapar *vt* MOJAR **:** to soak, to drench **— empaparse** *vr* **1 :** to get soaking wet **2 ~ de :** to absorb, to be imbued with

empapelar *vt* **:** to wallpaper

empaque *nm fam* **1 :** presence, bearing **2 :** pomposity **3** DESCARO **:** impudence, nerve

empaquetar *vt* EMBALAR **:** to pack, to package **— empaquetarse** *vr fam* **:** to dress up

emparedado *nm* **:** sandwich

emparedar *vt* **:** to wall in, to confine

emparejar *vt* **1 :** to pair, to match up **2 :** to make even — *vi* **:** to catch up — **emparejarse** *vr* **:** to pair up

emparentado, -da *adj* **:** related

emparentar {55} *vi* **:** to become related by marriage

emparrillado *nm Mex* **:** gridiron (in football)

empastar *vt* **1 :** to fill (a tooth) **2 :** to bind (a book)

empaste *nm* **:** filling (of a tooth)

empatar *vt* **:** to tie, to connect — *vi* **:** to result in a draw, to be tied — **empatarse** *vr Ven* **:** to hook up, to link together

empate *nm* **:** draw, tie

empatía *nf* **:** empathy

empecinado, -da *adj* TERCO **:** stubborn

empecinarse *vr* OBSTINARSE **:** to be stubborn, to persist

empedernido, -da *adj* INCORREGIBLE **:** hardened, inveterate

empedrado *nm* **:** paving, pavement

empedrar {55} *vt* **:** to pave (with stones)

empeine *nm* **:** instep

empellón *nm, pl* **-llones :** shove, push

empelotado, -da *adj* **1** *Mex fam* **:** madly in love **2** *fam* **:** stark naked

empeñado, -da *adj* **:** determined, committed

empeñar *vt* **1 :** to pawn **2 :** to pledge, to give (one's word) — **empeñarse** *vr* **1 :** to insist stubbornly **2 :** to make an effort

empeño *nm* **1 :** pledge, commitment **2 :** insistence **3** ESFUERZO **:** effort, determination **4 :** pawning <casa de empeños : pawnshop>

empeoramiento *nm* **:** worsening, deterioration

empeorar *vi* **:** to deteriorate, to get worse — *vt* **:** to make worse

empequeñecer {53} *vi* **:** to diminish, to become smaller — *vt* **:** to minimize, to make smaller

emperador *nm* **:** emperor

emperatriz *nf, pl* **-trices :** empress

empero *conj* **:** however, nevertheless

empezar {29} *v* COMENZAR **:** to start, to begin

empinado, -da *adj* **:** steep

empinar *vt* ELEVAR **:** to lift, to raise — **empinarse** *vr* **:** to stand on tiptoe

empírico, -ca *adj* **:** empirical — **empíricamente** *adv*

emplasto *nm* **:** poultice, dressing

emplazamiento *nm* **1 :** location, site **2** CITACIÓN **:** summons, subpoena

emplazar {21} *vt* **1** CONVOCAR **:** to convene, to summon **2 :** to subpoena **3** UBICAR **:** to place, to position

empleado, -da *n* **:** employee

empleador, -dora *n* PATRÓN **:** employer

emplear *vt* **1 :** to employ **2** USAR **:** to use — **emplearse** *vr* **1 :** to get a job **2 :** to occupy oneself

empleo *nm* **1** OCUPACIÓN **:** employment, occupation, job **2 :** use, usage

empobrecer {53} *vt* **:** to impoverish — *vi* **:** to become poor — **empobrecerse** *vr*

empobrecimiento *nm* **:** impoverishment

empollar *vi* **:** to brood eggs — *vt* **:** to incubate

empolvado, -da *adj* **1 :** dusty **2 :** powdered, powdery

empolvar *vt* **1 :** to cover with dust **2 :** to powder — **empolvarse** *vr* **1 :** to gather dust **2 :** to powder one's face

emporio *nm* **1 :** center, capital, empire <un emporio cultural : a cultural center> <un emporio financiero : a financial empire> **2 :** department store

empotrado, -da *adj* **:** built-in <armarios empotrados : built-in cabinets>

empotrar *vt* **:** to build into, to embed

emprendedor, -dora *adj* **:** enterprising

emprender *vt* **:** to undertake, to begin

empresa *nf* **1** COMPAÑÍA, FIRMA **:** company, corporation, firm **2 :** undertaking, venture

empresariado *nm* **1 :** business world **2 :** management, managers *pl*

empresarial *adj* **:** business, managerial, corporate

empresario, -ria *n* **1 :** manager **2 :** businessman *m*, businesswoman *f* **3 :** impresario

empujar *vi* **:** to push, to shove — *vt* **1 :** to push **2** PRESIONAR **:** to spur on, to press

empuje *nm* **:** impetus, drive

empujón *nm, pl* **-jones :** push, shove

empuñadura *nf* MANGO **:** hilt, handle

empuñar *vt* **1** ASIR **:** to grasp **2 empuñar las armas :** to take up arms

emú *nm* **:** emu

emular *vt* IMITAR **:** to emulate — **emulación** *nf*

emulsión *nf, pl* **-siones :** emulsion

emulsionante *nm* **:** emulsifier

emulsionar *vt* **:** to emulsify

en *prep* **1 :** in <en el bolsillo : in one's pocket> <en una semana : in a week> **2 :** on <en la mesa : on the table> **3 :** at <en casa : at home> <en el trabajo : at work> <en ese momento : at that moment>

enagua *nf* **:** petticoat, slip

enajenación *nf, pl* **-ciones 1 :** transfer (of property) **2 :** alienation **3 :** absentmindedness

enajenado, -da *adj* **:** out of one's mind

enajenar *vt* **1 :** to transfer (property) **2 :** to alienate **3 :** to enrapture — **enajenarse** *vr* **1 :** to become estranged **2 :** to go mad

enaltecer {53} *vt* **:** to praise, to extol

enamorado[1], -da *adj* **:** in love

enamorado[2], -da *n* **:** lover, sweetheart

enamoramiento *nm* **:** infatuation, crush

enamorar *vt* **:** to enamor, to win the love of — **enamorarse** *vr* **:** to fall in love
enamoriscarse {72} *vr fam* **:** to have a crush, to be infatuated
enamorizado, -da *adj* **:** amorous, passionate
enano[1], -na *adj* **:** tiny, minute
enano[2], -na *n* **:** dwarf, midget
enarbolar *vt* **1 :** to hoist, to raise **2 :** to brandish
enarcar {72} *vt* **:** to arch, to raise
enardecer {53} *vt* **1 :** to arouse (anger, passions) **2 :** to stir up, to excite — **enardecerse** *vr*
encabezado *nm Mex* **:** headline
encabezamiento *nm* **1 :** heading **2 :** salutation, opening
encabezar {21} *vt* **1 :** to head, to lead **2 :** to put a heading on
encabritarse *vr* **1 :** to rear up **2** *fam* **:** to get angry
encadenar *vt* **1 :** to chain **2 :** to connect, to link **3** INMOVILIZAR **:** to immobilize
encajar *vi* **:** to fit, to fit together, to fit in — *vt* **1 :** to insert, to stick **2 :** to take, to cope with <encajó el golpe : he withstood the blow>
encaje *nm* **1 :** lace **2 :** financial reserve
encajonar *vt* **1 :** to box, to crate **2 :** to cram in
encalar *vt* **:** to whitewash
encallar *vi* **1 :** to run aground **2 :** to get stuck
encallecido, -da *adj* **:** callused
encamar *vt* **:** to confine to a bed
encaminado, -da *adj* **1 :** on the right track **2 ~ a :** aimed at, designed to
encaminar *vt* **1 :** to direct, to channel **2 :** to head in the right direction — **encaminarse** *vr* **~ a :** to head for, to aim at
encandilar *vt* **:** to dazzle
encanecer {53} *vi* **:** to gray, to go gray
encantado, -da *adj* **1 :** charmed, bewitched **2 :** delighted
encantador[1], -dora *adj* **:** charming, delightful
encantador[2], -dora *n* **:** magician
encantamiento *nm* **:** enchantment, spell
encantar *vt* **1 :** to enchant, to bewitch **2 :** to charm, to delight <me encanta esta canción : I love this song>
encanto *nm* **1 :** charm, fascination **2** HECHIZO **:** spell **3 :** delightful person or thing
encañonar *vt* **:** to point (a gun) at, to hold up
encapotado, -da *adj* **:** cloudy, overcast
encapotarse *vr* **:** to cloud over, to become overcast
encaprichado, -da *adj* **:** infatuated
encaprichamiento *nm* **:** infatuation
encapuchado, -da *adj* **:** hooded
encarado, -da *adj* **estar mal encarado** *fam* **:** to be ugly-looking, to look mean
encaramar *vt* **:** to raise, to lift up — **encaramarse** *vr* **:** to perch
encarar *vt* CONFRONTAR **:** to face, to confront
encarcelación *nf* → **encarcelamiento**
encarcelamiento *nm* **:** incarceration, imprisonment
encarcelar *vt* **:** to incarcerate, to imprison
encarecer {53} *vt* **1 :** to increase, to raise (price, value) **2 :** to beseech, to entreat — **encarecerse** *vr* **:** to become more expensive
encarecidamente *adv* **:** insistently, urgently
encarecimiento *nm* **:** increase, rise (in price)
encargado[1], -da *adj* **:** in charge
encargado[2], -da *n* **:** manager, person in charge
encargar {52} *vt* **1 :** to put in charge of **2 :** to recommend, to advise **3 :** to order, to request — **encargarse** *vr* **~ de :** to take charge of
encargo *nm* **1 :** errand **2 :** job assignment **3 :** order <hecho de encargo : custom-made, made to order>
encariñarse *vr* **~ con :** to become fond of, to grow attached to
encarnación *nf, pl* **-ciones :** incarnation, embodiment
encarnado[1], -da *adj* **1 :** incarnate **2 :** flesh-colored **3 :** red **4 :** ingrown
encarnado[2] *nm* **:** red
encarnar *vt* **:** to incarnate, to embody — **encarnarse** *vr* **encarnarse una uña :** to have an ingrown nail
encarnizado, -da *adj* **1 :** bloodshot, inflamed **2 :** fierce, bloody
encarnizar {21} *vt* **:** to enrage, to infuriate — **encarnizarse** *vr* **:** to be brutal, to attack viciously
encarrilar *vt* **:** to guide, to put on the right track
encasillar *vt* CLASIFICAR **:** to classify, to pigeonhole, to categorize
encausar *vt* **:** to prosecute, to charge
encauzar {21} *vt* **:** to channel, to guide — **encauzarse** *vr*
encebollado, -da *adj* **:** cooked with onions
encefalitis *nms & pl* **:** encephalitis
encendedor *nm* **:** lighter
encender {56} *vi* **:** to light — *vt* **1 :** to light, to set fire to **2** PRENDER **:** to switch on **3 :** to start (a motor) **4 :** to arouse, to kindle — **encenderse** *vr* **1 :** to get excited **2 :** to blush
encendido[1], -da *adj* **1 :** burning **2 :** flushed **3 :** fiery, passionate
encendido[2] *nm* **:** ignition
encerado *nm* **1 :** waxing, polishing **2 :** blackboard
encerar *vt* **:** to wax, to polish
encerrar {55} *vt* **1 :** to lock up, to shut away **2 :** to contain, to include **3 :** to involve, to entail
encerrona *nf* **1** TRAMPA **:** trap, setup **2** **prepararle una encerrona a alguien**

: to set a trap for someone, to set someone up

encestar *vi* **:** to make a basket (in basketball)

enchapado *nm* **:** plating, coating (of metal)

encharcamiento *nm* **:** flood, flooding

encharcar {72} *vt* **:** to flood, to swamp — **encharcarse** *vr*

enchilada *nf* **:** enchilada

enchilar *vt Mex* **:** to season with chili

enchuecar {72} *vt Chile, Mex fam* **:** to make crooked, to twist

enchufar *vt* **1 :** to plug in **2 :** to connect, to fit together

enchufe *nm* **1 :** connection **2 :** plug, socket

encía *nf* **:** gum (tissue)

encíclica *nf* **:** encyclical

enciclopedia *nf* **:** encyclopedia

enciclopédico, -ca *adj* **:** encyclopedic

encierro *nm* **1 :** confinement **2 :** enclosure

encima *adv* **1 :** on top, above **2** ADEMÁS **:** as well, besides **3 ~ de :** on, on top of, over **4 por encima de :** above, beyond <por encima de la ley : above the law> **5 echarse encima :** to take upon oneself **6 estar encima de** *fam* **:** to nag, to criticize **7 quitarse de encima :** to get rid of

encina *nf* **:** evergreen oak

encinta *adj* EMBARAZADA, PREÑADA **:** pregnant, expecting

enclaustrado, -da *adj* **:** cloistered, shut away

enclavado, -da *adj* **:** buried

enclenque *adj* **:** weak, sickly

encoger {15} *vt* **1 :** to shrink, to make smaller **2 :** to intimidate — *vi* **:** to shrink, to contract — **encogerse** *vr* **1 :** to shrink **2 :** to be intimidated, to cower, to cringe **3 encogerse de hombros :** to shrug <one's shoulders>

encogido, -da *adj* **1 :** shriveled, shrunken **2** TÍMIDO **:** shy, inhibited

encogimiento *nm* **1 :** shrinking, shrinkage **2 :** shrug **3** TIMIDEZ **:** shyness

encolar *vt* **:** to paste, to glue

encolerizar {21} *vt* ENFURECER **:** to enrage, to infuriate — **encolerizarse** *vr*

encomendar {55} *vt* CONFIAR **:** to entrust, to commend — **encomendarse** *vr*

encomiable *adj* **:** commendable, praiseworthy

encomiar *vt* ELOGIAR **:** to praise, to pay tribute to

encomienda *nf* **1 :** charge, mission **2 :** royal land grant **3 :** parcel

encomio *nm* **:** praise, eulogy

encomioso, -sa *adj* **:** eulogistic, laudatory

enconar *vt* **1 :** to irritate, to anger **2 :** to inflame — **enconarse** *vr* **1 :** to become heated **2 :** to fester

encono *nm* **1** RENCOR **:** animosity, rancor **2 :** inflamation, infection

encontrado, -da *adj* **:** contrary, opposing

encontrar {19} *vt* **1** HALLAR **:** to find **2 :** to encounter, to meet — **encontrarse** *vr* **1** REUNIRSE **:** to meet **2 :** to clash, to conflict **3 :** to be <su abuelo se encuentra mejor : her grandfather is doing better>

encorvar *vt* **:** to bend, to curve — **encorvarse** *vr* **:** to hunch over, to stoop

encrespar *vt* **1 :** to curl, to ruffle, to ripple **2 :** to annoy, to irritate — **encresparse** *vr* **1 :** to curl one's hair **2 :** to become choppy **3 :** to get annoyed

encrucijada *nf* **:** crossroads

encuadernación *nf, pl* **-ciones :** bookbinding

encuadernar *vt* EMPASTAR **:** to bind (a book)

encuadrar *vt* **1** ENMARCAR **:** to frame **2** ENCAJAR **:** to fit, to insert **3** COMPRENDER **:** to contain, to include

encubierto *pp* → **encubrir**

encubrimiento *nm* **:** cover-up

encubrir {2} *vt* **:** to cover up, to conceal

encuentro *nm* **1 :** meeting, encounter **2 :** conference, congress

encuerado, -da *adj fam* **:** naked

encuerar *vt fam* **:** to undress

encuesta *nf* **1** INVESTIGACIÓN, PESQUISA **:** inquiry, investigation **2** SONDEO **:** survey

encuestador, -dora *n* **:** pollster

encuestar *vt* **:** to poll, to take a survey of

encumbrado, -da *adj* **1 :** lofty, high **2 :** eminent, distinguished

encumbrar *vt* **1 :** to exalt, to elevate **2 :** to extol — **encumbrarse** *vr* **:** to reach the top

encurtir *vt* ESCABECHAR **:** to pickle

ende *adv* **por ~ :** therefore, consequently

endeble *adj* **:** feeble, weak

endeblez *nf* **:** weakness, frailty

endémico, -ca *adj* **:** endemic

endemoniado, -da *adj* **:** fiendish, diabolical

endentecer {53} *vi* **:** to teethe

enderezar {21} *vt* **1 :** to straighten (out) **2 :** to stand on end, to put upright

endeudado, -da *adj* **:** in debt, indebted

endeudamiento *nm* **:** indebtedness

endeudarse *vr* **1 :** to go into debt **2 :** to feel obliged

endiabladamente *adv* **:** extremely, diabolically

endiablado, -da *adj* **1 :** devilish, diabolical **2 :** complicated, difficult

endibia *or* **endivia** *nm* **:** endive

endilgar {52} *vt fam* **:** to spring, to foist <me endilgó la responsabilidad : he saddled me with the responsibility>

endocrino, -na *adj* **:** endocrine

endogamia *nf* **:** inbreeding

endosar *vt* **:** to endorse

endoso *nm* **:** endorsement

endulzante *nm* **:** sweetener

endulzar {21} *vt* **1 :** to sweeten **2 :** to soften, to mellow — **endulzarse** *vr*

endurecer {53} *vt* **:** to harden, to toughen — **endurecerse** *vr*

enebro *nm* **:** juniper

eneldo *nm* **:** dill

enema *nm* **:** enema

enemigo, -ga *adj & n* **:** enemy

enemistad *nf* **:** enmity, hostility

enemistar *vt* **:** to make enemies of — **enemistarse** *vr* **~ con :** to fall out with

energía *nf* **:** energy

enérgico, -ca *adj* **1 :** energetic, vigorous **2 :** forceful, emphatic — **enérgicamente** *adv*

energúmeno, -na *n fam* **:** lunatic, crazy person

enero *nm* **:** January

enervar *vt* **1 :** to enervate **2** *fam* **:** to annoy, to get on one's nerves — **enervante** *adj*

enésimo, -ma *adj* **:** umpteenth, nth

enfadar *vt* **1 :** to annoy, to make angry **2** *Mex fam* **:** to bore — **enfadarse** *vr* **:** to get angry, to get annoyed

enfado *nm* **:** anger, annoyance

enfadoso, -sa *adj* **:** irritating, annoying

enfardar *vt* **:** to bale

énfasis *nms & pl* **:** emphasis

enfático, -ca *adj* **:** emphatic — **enfáticamente** *adv*

enfatizar {21} *vt* DESTACAR, SUBRAYAR **:** to emphasize

enfermar *vt* **:** to make sick — *vi* **:** to fall ill, to get sick — **enfermarse** *vr*

enfermedad *nf* **1** INDISPOSICIÓN **:** sickness, illness **2 :** disease

enfermería *nf* **:** infirmary

enfermero, -ra *n* **:** nurse

enfermizo, -za *adj* **:** sickly

enfermo[1], -ma *adj* **:** sick, ill

enfermo[2], -ma *n* **1 :** sick person, invalid **2** PACIENTE **:** patient

enfilar *vt* **1 :** to take, to go along <enfiló la carretera de Montevideo : she went up the road to Montevideo> **2 :** to line up, to put in a row **3 :** to string, to thread **4 :** to aim, to direct — *vi* **:** to make one's way

enflaquecer {53} *vi* **:** to lose weight, to become thin — *vt* **:** to emaciate

enfocar {72} *vt* **1 :** to focus (on) **2 :** to consider, to look at

enfoque *nm* **:** focus

enfrascamiento *nm* **:** immersion, absorption

enfrascarse {72} *vr* **~ en :** to immerse oneself in, to get caught up in

enfrentamiento *nm* **:** clash, confrontation

enfrentar *vt* **:** to confront, to face — **enfrentarse** *vr* **1 ~ con :** to clash with **2 ~ a :** to face up to

enfrente *adv* **1** DELANTE **:** in front **2 :** opposite

enfriamiento *nm* **1** CATARRO **:** chill, cold **2 :** cooling off, damper

enfriar {85} *vt* **1 :** to chill, to cool **2 :** to cool down, to dampen — *vi* **:** to get cold — **enfriarse** *vr* **:** to get chilled, to catch a cold

enfundar *vt* **:** to sheathe, to encase

enfurecer {53} *vt* ENCOLERIZAR **:** to infuriate — **enfurecerse** *vr* **:** to fly into a rage

enfurecido, -da *adj* **:** furious, raging

enfurruñarse *vr fam* **:** to sulk

engalanar *vt* **:** to decorate, to deck out — **engalanarse** *vr* **:** to dress up

enganchar *vt* **1 :** to hook, to snag **2 :** to attach, to hitch up — **engancharse** *vr* **1 :** to get snagged, to get hooked **2 :** to enlist

enganche *nm* **1 :** hook **2 :** coupling, hitch **3** *Mex* **:** down payment

engañar *vt* **1** EMBAUCAR **:** to trick, to deceive, to mislead **2 :** to cheat on, to be unfaithful to — **engañarse** *vr* **1 :** to be mistaken **2 :** to deceive oneself

engaño *nm* **1 :** deception, trick **2 :** fake, feint (in sports)

engañoso, -sa *adj* **1 :** deceitful **2 :** misleading, deceptive

engarrotarse *vr* **:** to stiffen up, to go numb

engatusamiento *nm* **:** cajolery

engatusar *vt* **:** to coax, to cajole

engendrar *vt* **1 :** to beget, to father **2 :** to give rise to, to engender

engentarse *vr Mex* **:** to be in a daze

englobar *vt* **:** to include, to embrace

engomar *vt* **:** to glue

engordar *vt* **:** to fatten, to fatten up — *vi* **:** to gain weight

engorro *nm* **:** nuisance, bother

engorroso, -sa *adj* **:** bothersome

engranaje *nm* **:** gears *pl,* cogs *pl*

engranar *vt* **:** to mesh, to engage — *vi* **:** to mesh gears

engrandecer {53} *vt* **1 :** to enlarge **2 :** to exaggerate **3 :** to exalt

engrandecimiento *nm* **1 :** enlargement **2 :** exaggeration **3 :** exaltation

engrane *nm Mex* **:** cogwheel

engrapadora *nf* **:** stapler

engrapar *vt* **:** to staple

engrasar *vt* **:** to grease, to lubricate

engrase *nm* **:** greasing, lubrication

engreído, -da *adj* PRESUMIDO, VANIDOSO **:** vain, conceited, stuck-up

engreimiento *nm* ARROGANCIA **:** arrogance, conceit

engreír {66} *vt* ENVANECER **:** to make vain — **engreírse** *vr* **:** to become conceited

engrosar {19} *vt* **:** to enlarge, to increase, to swell — *vi* ENGORDAR **:** to gain weight

engrudo *nm* **:** paste

engullir {38} *vt* **:** to gulp down, to gobble up — **engullirse** *vr*

enharinar *vt* **:** to flour

enhebrar *vt* ENSARTAR **:** to string, to thread

enhiesto, -ta *adj* **1 :** erect, upright **2 :** lofty, towering
enhilar *vt* **:** to thread (a needle, etc.)
enhorabuena *nf* FELICIDADES **:** congratulations *pl*
enigma *nm* **:** enigma, mystery
enigmático, -ca *adj* **:** enigmatic — **enigmáticamente** *adv*
enjabonar *vt* **:** to soap up, to lather — **enjabonarse** *vr*
enjaezar {21} *vt* **:** to harness
enjalbegar {52} *vt* **:** to whitewash
enjambrar *vi* **:** to swarm
enjambre *nm* **1 :** swarm **2** MUCHEDUMBRE **:** crowd, mob
enjaular *vt* **1 :** to cage **2** *fam* **:** to jail, to lock up
enjuagar {52} *vt* **:** to rinse — **enjuagarse** *vr* **:** to rinse out
enjuague *nm* **1 :** rinse **2 enjuague bucal :** mouthwash
enjugar {52} *vt* **:** to wipe away (tears)
enjuiciar *vt* **1 :** to indict, to prosecute **2** JUZGAR **:** to try
enjundioso, -sa *adj* **:** substantial, weighty
enjuto, -ta *adj* **:** lean, gaunt
enlace *nm* **1 :** bond, link, connection **2 :** liaison
enladrillado *nm* **:** brick paving
enladrillar *vt* **:** to pave with bricks
enlatar *vt* ENVASAR **:** to can
enlazar {21} *v* **:** to join, to link, to fit together
enlistar *vt* **:** to list — **enlistarse** *vr* **:** to enlist
enlodado, -da *adj* BARROSO **:** muddy
enlodar *vt* **1 :** to cover with mud **2 :** to stain, to sully — **enlodarse** *vr*
enlodazar → **enlodar**
enloquecedor, -dora *adj* **:** maddening
enloquecer {53} *vt* ALOCAR **:** to drive crazy — **enloquecerse** *vr* **:** to go crazy
enlosado *nm* **:** flagstone pavement
enlosar *vt* **:** to pave with flagstone
enlutarse *vr* **:** to go into mourning
enmaderado *nm* **1 :** wood paneling **2 :** hardwood floor
enmarañar *vt* **1 :** to tangle **2 :** to complicate **3 :** to confuse, to mix up — **enmarañarse** *vr*
enmarcar {72} *vt* **1** ENCUADRAR **:** to frame **2 :** to provide the setting for
enmascarar *vt* **:** to mask, to disguise
enmasillar *vt* **:** to putty, to caulk
enmendar {55} *vt* **1 :** to amend **2** CORREGIR **:** to emend, to correct **3** COMPENSAR **:** to compensate for — **enmendarse** *vr* **:** to mend one's ways
enmienda *nf* **1 :** amendment **2 :** correction, emendation
enmohecerse {53} *vr* **1 :** to become moldy **2** OXIDARSE **:** to rust, to become rusty
enmudecer {53} *vt* **:** to mute, to silence — *vi* **:** to fall silent
enmugrar *vt* **:** to soil, to make dirty — **enmugrarse** *vr* **:** to get dirty
ennegrecer {53} *vt* **:** to blacken, to darken — **ennegrecerse** *vr*
ennoblecer {53} *vt* **1 :** to ennoble **2 :** to embellish
enojadizo, -za *adj* IRRITABLE **:** irritable, cranky
enojado, -da *adj* **1 :** annoyed **2 :** angry, mad
enojar *vt* **1 :** to anger **2 :** to annoy, to upset — **enojarse** *vr*
enojo *nm* **1** CÓLERA **:** anger **2 :** annoyance
enojón, -jona *adj, pl* **-jones** *Chile, Mex fam* **:** irritable, cranky
enojoso, -sa *adj* FASTIDIOSO, MOLESTOSO **:** annoying, irritating
enorgullecer {53} *vt* **:** to make proud — **enorgullecerse** *vr* **:** to pride oneself
enorme *adj* INMENSO **:** enormous, huge — **enormemente** *adv*
enormidad *nf* **1 :** enormity, seriousness **2 :** immensity, hugeness
enraizado, -da *adj* **:** deep-seated, deeply rooted
enraizar {30} *vi* **:** to take root
enramada *nf* **:** arbor, bower
enramar *vt* **:** to cover with branches
enrarecer {53} *vt* **:** to rarefy — **enrarecerse** *vr*
enredadera *nf* **:** climbing plant, vine
enredar *vt* **1 :** to tangle up, to entangle **2 :** to confuse, to complicate **3 :** to involve, to implicate — **enredarse** *vr*
enredo *nm* **1** EMBROLLO **:** muddle, confusion **2** MARAÑA **:** tangle
enredoso, -sa *adj* **:** complicated, tricky
enrejado *nm* **1 :** railing **2 :** grating, grille **3 :** trellis, lattice
enrevesado, -da *adj* **:** complicated, involved
enriquecer {53} *vt* **:** to enrich — **enriquecerse** *vr* **:** to get rich
enriquecido, -da *adj* **:** enriched
enriquecimiento *nm* **:** enrichment
enrojecer {53} *vt* **:** to make red, to redden — **enrojecerse** *vr* **:** to blush
enrolar *vt* RECLUTAR **:** to recruit — **enrolarse** *vr* INSCRIBIRSE **:** to enlist, to sign up
enrollar *vt* **:** to roll up, to coil — **enrollarse** *vr*
enronquecerse {53} *vr* **:** to become hoarse
enroscar {72} *vt* TORCER **:** to twist — **enroscarse** *vr* **:** to coil, to twine
ensacar {72} *vt* **:** to bag (up)
ensalada *nf* **:** salad
ensaladera *nf* **:** salad bowl
ensalmo *nm* **:** incantation, spell
ensalzar {21} *vt* **1 :** to praise, to extol **2** EXALTAR **:** to exalt
ensamblaje *nm* **:** assembly
ensamblar *vt* **1 :** to assemble **2 :** to join, to fit together
ensanchar *vt* **1 :** to widen **2 :** to expand, to extend — **ensancharse** *vr*
ensanche *nm* **1 :** widening **2 :** expansion, development

ensangrentado, -da *adj* **:** bloody, bloodstained

ensañarse *vr* **:** to act cruelly, to be merciless

ensartar *vt* **1** ENHEBRAR **:** to string, to thread **2 :** to skewer, to pierce

ensayar *vi* **:** to rehearse — *vt* **1 :** to try out, to test **2 :** to assay

ensayista *nmf* **:** essayist

ensayo *nm* **1 :** essay **2 :** trial, test **3 :** rehearsal **4 :** assay (of metals)

enseguida *adv* INMEDIATAMENTE **:** right away, immediately, at once

ensenada *nf* **:** cove, inlet

enseña *nf* **1** INSIGNIA **:** emblem, insignia **2 :** standard, banner

enseñanza *nf* **1** EDUCACIÓN **:** education **2 :** teaching

enseñar *vt* **1 :** to teach **2** MOSTRAR **:** to show, to display — **enseñarse** *vr* **~ a :** to learn to, to get used to

enseres *nmpl* **:** equipment, furnishings *pl* <enseres domésticos : household goods>

ensillar *vt* **:** to saddle (up)

ensimismado, -da *adj* **:** absorbed, engrossed

ensimismarse *vr* **:** to lose oneself in thought

ensoberbecerse {53} *vr* **:** to become haughty

ensombrecer {53} *vt* **:** to cast a shadow over, to darken — **ensombrecerse** *vr*

ensoñación *nf, pl* **-ciones :** fantasy

ensopar *vt* **1 :** to drench **2 :** to dunk, to dip

ensordecedor, -dora *adj* **:** deafening, thunderous

ensordecer {53} *vt* **:** to deafen — *vi* **:** to go deaf

ensuciar *vt* **:** to soil, to dirty — **ensuciarse** *vr*

ensueño *nm* **1 :** daydream, revery **2** FANTASÍA **:** illusion, fantasy

entablar *vt* **1 :** to cover with boards **2 :** to initiate, to enter into, to start

entallar *vt* AJUSTAR **:** to tailor, to fit, to take in — *vi* QUEDAR **:** to fit

ente *nm* **1 :** being, entity **2 :** body, organization <ente rector : ruling body> **3** *fam* **:** eccentric, crackpot

enteco, -ca *adj* **:** gaunt, frail

entenado, -da *n Mex* **:** stepchild, stepson *m,* stepdaughter *f*

entender[1] {56} *vt* **1** COMPRENDER **:** to understand **2** OPINAR **:** to think, to believe **3** QUERER **:** to mean, to intend **4** DEDUCIR **:** to infer, to deduce — *vi* **1 :** to understand <¡ya entiendo! : now I understand!> **2 ~ de :** to know about, to be good at **3 ~ en :** to be in charge of — **entenderse** *vr* **1 :** to be understood **2 :** to get along well, to understand each other **3 ~ con :** to deal with

entender[2] *nm* **a mi entender :** in my opinion

entendible *adj* **:** understandable

entendido[1], -da *adj* **1 :** skilled, expert **2 tener entendido :** to understand, to be under the impression <teníamos entendido que vendrías : we were under the impression you would come> **3 darse por entendido :** to go without saying

entendido[2] *nm* **:** expert, authority, connoisseur

entendimiento *nm* **1 :** intellect, mind **2 :** understanding, agreement

enterado, -da *adj* **:** aware, well-informed <estar enterado de : to be privy to>

enteramente *adv* **:** entirely, completely

enterar *vt* INFORMAR **:** to inform — **enterarse** *vr* INFORMARSE **:** to find out, to learn

entereza *nf* **1** INTEGRIDAD **:** integrity **2** FORTALEZA **:** fortitude **3** FIRMEZA **:** resolve

enternecedor, -dora *adj* CONMOVEDOR **:** touching, moving

enternecer {53} *vt* CONMOVER **:** to move, to touch

entero[1], -ra *adj* **1 :** entire, whole **2 :** complete, absolute **3 :** intact — **enteramente** *adv*

entero[2] *nm* **1 :** integer, whole number **2 :** point (in finance)

enterramiento *nm* **:** burial

enterrar {55} *vt* **:** to bury

entibiar *vt* **:** to cool (down) — **entibiarse** *vr* **:** to become lukewarm

entidad *nf* **1** ENTE **:** entity **2 :** body, organization **3 :** firm, company **4 :** importance, significance

entierro *nm* **1 :** burial **2 :** funeral

entintar *vt* **:** to ink

entoldado *nm* **:** awning

entomología *nf* **:** entomology

entomólogo, -ga *n* **:** entomologist

entonación *nf, pl* **-ciones :** intonation

entonar *vi* **:** to be in tune — *vt* **1 :** to intone **2 :** to tone up

entonces *adv* **1 :** then **2 desde ~ :** since then **3 en aquel entonces :** in those days

entornado, -da *adj* ENTREABIERTO **:** half-closed, ajar

entornar *vt* ENTREABRIR **:** to leave ajar

entorno *nm* **:** surroundings *pl,* environment

entorpecer {53} *vt* **1 :** to hinder, to obstruct **2 :** to dull — **entorpecerse** *vr* **:** to dull the senses

entrada *nf* **1 :** entrance, entry **2 :** ticket, admission **3 :** beginning, onset **4 :** entrée **5 :** cue (in music) **6 entradas** *nfpl* **:** income <entradas y salidas : income and expenditures> **7 tener entradas :** to have a receding hairline

entrado, -da *adj* **entrado en años :** elderly

entramado *nm* **:** framework

entrampar *vt* **1** ATRAPAR **:** to entrap, to ensnare **2** ENGAÑAR **:** to deceive, to trick

entrante *adj* **1 :** next, upcoming <el año entrante : next year> **2 :** incoming, new <el presidente entrante : the president elect>
entraña *nf* **1** MEOLLO **:** core, heart, crux **2 entrañas** *nfpl* VÍSCERAS **:** entrails
entrañable *adj* **:** close, intimate
entrañar *vt* **:** to entail, to involve
entrar *vi* **1 :** to enter, to go in, to come in **2 :** to begin — *vt* **1 :** to bring in, to introduce **2 :** to access
entre *prep* **1 :** between **2 :** among
entreabierto[1] *pp* → **entreabrir**
entreabierto[2], **-ta** *adj* ENTORNADO **:** half-open, ajar
entreabrir {2} *vt* ENTORNAR **:** to leave ajar
entreacto *nm* **:** intermission, interval
entrecano, -na *adj* **:** grayish, graying
entrecejo *nm* **fruncir el entrecejo :** to knit one's brows
entrecomillar *vt* **:** to place in quotation marks
entrecortado, -da *adj* **1 :** labored, difficult <respiración entrecortada : shortness of breath> **2 :** faltering, hesitant <con la voz entrecortada : with a catch in his voice>
entrecruzar {21} *vt* ENTRELAZAR **:** to interweave, to intertwine — **entrecruzarse** *vr*
entredicho *nm* **1** DUDA **:** doubt, question **2 :** prohibition
entrega *nf* **1 :** delivery **2 :** handing over, surrender **3 :** installment <entrega inicial : down payment>
entregar {52} *vt* **1 :** to deliver **2** DAR **:** to give, to present **3 :** to hand in, to hand over — **entregarse** *vr* **1 :** to surrender, to give in **2 :** to devote oneself
entrelazar {21} *vt* ENTRECRUZAR **:** to interweave, to intertwine
entremedias *adv* **1 :** in between, halfway **2 :** in the meantime
entremés *nm, pl* **-meses 1** APERITIVO **:** appetizer, hors d'oeuvre **2 :** interlude, short play
entremeterse → **entrometerse**
entremetido *nm* → **entrometido**
entremezclar *vt* **:** to intermingle
entrenador, -dora *n* **:** trainer, coach
entrenamiento *nm* **:** training, drill, practice
entrenar *vt* **:** to train, to drill, to practice — **entrenarse** *vr* **:** to train, to spar (in boxing)
entreoír {50} *vt* **:** to hear indistinctly
entrepierna *nf* **1 :** inner thigh **2 :** crotch **3 :** inseam
entrepiso *nm* ENTRESUELO **:** mezzanine
entresacar {72} *vt* **1** SELECCIONAR **:** to pick out, to select **2 :** to thin out
entresuelo *nm* ENTREPISO **:** mezzanine
entretanto[1] *adv* **:** meanwhile
entretanto[2] *nm* **en el entretanto :** in the meantime
entretejer *vt* **:** to interweave
entretela *nf* **:** facing (of a garment)
entretener {80} *vt* **1** DIVERTIR **:** to entertain, to amuse **2** DISTRAER **:** to distract **3** DEMORAR **:** to delay, to hold up — **entretenerse** *vr* **1 :** to amuse oneself **2 :** to dally
entretenido, -da *adj* DIVERTIDO **:** entertaining, amusing
entretenimiento *nm* **1 :** entertainment, pastime **2** DIVERSIÓN **:** fun, amusement
entrever {88} *vt* **1 :** to catch a glimpse of **2 :** to make out, to see indistinctly
entreverar *vt* **:** to mix, to intermingle
entrevero *nm* **:** confusion, disorder
entrevista *nf* **:** interview
entrevistador, -dora *n* **:** interviewer
entrevistar *vt* **:** to interview — **entrevistarse** *vr* REUNIRSE **~ con :** to meet with
entristecer {53} *vt* **:** to sadden
entrometerse *vr* **:** to interfere, to meddle
entrometido, -da *n* **:** meddler, busybody
entroncar {72} *vt* RELACIONAR **:** to establish a relationship between, to connect — *vi* **1 :** to be related **2 :** to link up, to be connected
entronque *nm* **1 :** kinship **2** VÍNCULO **:** link, connection
entuerto *nm* **:** wrong, injustice
entumecer {53} *vt* **:** to make numb, to be numb — **entumecerse** *vr* **:** to go numb, to fall asleep
entumecido, -da *adj* **1 :** numb **2 :** stiff (of muscles, joints, etc.)
entumecimiento *nm* **:** numbness
enturbiar *vt* **1 :** to cloud **2 :** to confuse — **enturbiarse** *vr*
entusiasmar *vt* **:** to excite, to fill with enthusiasm — **entusiasmarse** *vr* **:** to get excited
entusiasmo *nm* **:** enthusiasm
entusiasta[1] *adj* **:** enthusiastic
entusiasta[2] *nmf* AFICIONADO **:** enthusiast
enumerar *vt* **:** to enumerate — **enumeración** *nf*
enunciación *nf, pl* **-ciones :** enunciation, statement
enunciar *vt* **:** to enunciate, to state
envainar *vt* **:** to sheathe
envalentonar *vt* **:** to make bold, to encourage — **envalentonarse** *vr*
envanecer {53} *vt* ENGREÍR **:** to make vain — **envanecerse** *vr*
envasar *vt* **1** EMBOTELLAR **:** to bottle **2** ENLATAR **:** to can **3 :** to pack in a container
envase *nm* **1 :** packaging, packing **2 :** container **3** LATA **:** can **4 :** empty bottle
envejecer {53} *vt* **:** to age, to make look old — *vi* **:** to age, to grow old
envejecido, -da *adj* **:** aged, old-looking
envejecimiento *nm* **:** aging
envenenamiento *nm* **:** poisoning
envenenar *vt* **1 :** to poison **2 :** to embitter

envergadura *nf* **1 :** span, breadth, spread **2 :** importance, scope

envés *nm, pl* **enveses :** reverse, opposite side

enviado, -da *n* **:** envoy, correspondent

enviar {85} *vt* **1 :** to send **2 :** to ship

envidia *nf* **:** envy, jealousy

envidiar *vt* **:** to envy — **envidiable** *adj*

envidioso, -sa *adj* **:** envious, jealous

envilecer {53} *vt* **:** to degrade, to debase

envilecimiento *nm* **:** degradation, debasement

envío *nm* **1 :** shipment **2 :** remittance

enviudar *vi* **:** to be widowed, to become a widower

envoltorio *nm* **1 :** bundle, package **2 :** wrapping, wrapper

envoltura *nf* **:** wrapper, wrapping

envolver {89} *vt* **1 :** to wrap **2 :** to envelop, to surround **3 :** to entangle, to involve — **envolverse** *vr* **1 :** to become involved **2 :** to wrap oneself (up)

envuelto *pp* → **envolver**

enyerbar *vt Mex* **:** to bewitch

enyesar *vt* **1 :** to plaster **2** ESCAYOLAR **:** to put in a plaster cast

enzima *nf* **:** enzyme

éon *nm, pl* **eones :** aeon

eperlano *nm* **:** smelt (fish)

épico, -ca *adj* **:** epic

epicúreo[1]**, -rea** *adj* **:** epicurean

epicúreo[2]**, -rea** *n* **:** epicure

epidemia *nf* **:** epidemic

epidémico, -ca *adj* **:** epidemic

epidermis *nf* **:** epidermis

epifanía *nf* **:** feast of the Epiphany (January 6th)

epigrama *nm* **:** epigram

epilepsia *nf* **:** epilepsy

epiléptico, -ca *adj & n* **:** epileptic

epílogo *nm* **:** epilogue

episcopal *adj* **:** episcopal

episcopalista *adj & nmf* **:** Episcopalian

episódico, -ca *adj* **:** episodic

episodio *nm* **:** episode

epístola *nf* **:** epistle

epitafio *nm* **:** epitaph

epíteto *nm* **:** epithet, name

epítome *nm* **:** summary, abstract

época *nf* **1** EDAD, ERA, PERÍODO **:** epoch, age, period **2 :** time of year, season **3 de ~ :** vintage, antique

epopeya *nf* **:** epic poem

equidad *nf* JUSTICIA **:** equity, justice, fairness

equilátero, -ra *adj* **:** equilateral

equilibrado, -da *adj* **:** well-balanced

equilibrar *vt* **:** to balance — **equilibrarse** *vr*

equilibrio *nm* **1 :** balance, equilibrium <perder el equilibrio : to lose one's balance> <equilibrio político : balance of power> **2 :** poise, aplomb

equilibrista *nmf* ACRÓBATA, FUNÁMBULO **:** acrobat, tightrope walker

equino, -na *adj* **:** equine

equinoccio *nm* **:** equinox

equipaje *nm* BAGAJE **:** baggage, luggage

equipamiento *nm* **:** equipping, equipment

equipar *vt* **:** to equip — **equiparse** *vr*

equiparable *adj* **:** comparable

equiparar *vt* **1** IGUALAR **:** to put on a same level, to make equal **2** COMPARAR **:** to compare

equipo *nm* **1 :** team, crew **2 :** gear, equipment

equitación *nf, pl* **-ciones :** horseback riding, horsemanship

equitativo, -va *adj* JUSTO **:** equitable, fair, just — **equitativamente** *adv*

equivalencia *nf* **:** equivalence

equivalente *adj & nm* **:** equivalent

equivaler {84} *vi* **:** to be equivalent

equivocación *nf, pl* **-ciones** ERROR **:** error, mistake

equivocado, -da *adj* **:** mistaken, wrong — **equivocadamente** *adv*

equivocar {72} *vt* **:** to mistake, to confuse — **equivocarse** *vr* **:** to make a mistake, to be wrong

equívoco[1]**, -ca** *adj* AMBIGUO **:** ambiguous, equivocal

equívoco[2] *nm* **:** misunderstanding

era[1]**, etc.** → **ser**

era[2] *nf* EDAD, ÉPOCA **:** era, age

erario *nm* **:** public treasury

erección *nf, pl* **-ciones :** erection, raising

eremita *nmf* ERMITAÑO **:** hermit

ergonomía *nf* **:** ergonomic

erguido, -da *adj* **:** erect, upright

erguir {31} *vt* **:** to raise, to lift up — **erguirse** *vr* **:** to straighten up

erial *nm* **:** uncultivated land

erigir {35} *vt* **:** to build, to erect — **erigirse** *vr* **~ en :** to set oneself up as

erizado, -da : bristly

erizarse {21} *vr* **:** to bristle, to stand on end

erizo *nm* **1 :** hedgehog **2 erizo de mar :** sea urchin

ermitaño[1]**, -ña** *n* EREMITA **:** hermit, recluse

ermitaño[2] *nm* **:** hermit crab

erogación *nf, pl* **-ciones :** expenditure

erogar {52} *vt* **1 :** to pay out **2 :** to distribute

erosión *nf, pl* **-siones :** erosion

erosionar *vt* **:** to erode

erótico, -ca *adj* **:** erotic

erotismo *nm* **:** eroticism

errabundo, -da *adj* ERRANTE, VAGABUNDO **:** wandering

erradicar {72} *vt* **:** to eradicate — **erradicación** *nf*

errado, -da *adj* **:** wrong, mistaken

errante *adj* ERRABUNDO, VAGABUNDO **:** errant, wandering

errar {32} *vt* FALLAR **:** to miss — *vi* **1** DESACERTAR **:** to be wrong, to be mistaken **2** VAGAR **:** to wander

errata *nf* **:** misprint, error

errático, -ca *adj* : erratic — **erráticamente** *adv*
erróneo, -nea *adj* EQUIVOCADO : erroneous, wrong — **erróneamente** *adv*
error *nm* EQUIVOCACIÓN : error, mistake
eructar *vi* : to belch, to burp
eructo *nm* : belch, burp
erudición *nf, pl* **-ciones** : erudition, learning
erudito[1], **-ta** *adj* LETRADO : erudite, learned
erudito[2], **-ta** *n* : scholar
erupción *nf, pl* **-ciones 1** : eruption **2** SARPULLIDO : rash
eruptivo, -va *adj* : eruptive
es → **ser**
esbelto, -ta *adj* DELGADO : slender, slim
esbirro *nm* : henchman
esbozar {21} *vt* BOSQUEJAR : to sketch, to outline
esbozo *nm* **1** : sketch **2** : rough draft
escabechar *vt* **1** ENCURTIR : to pickle **2** *fam* : to kill, to rub out
escabeche *nm* : brine (for pickling)
escabechina *nf* MASACRE : massacre, bloodbath
escabel *nm* : footstool
escabroso, -sa *adj* **1** : rugged, rough **2** : difficult, tough **3** : risqué
escabullirse {38} *vr* : to slip away, to escape
escala *nf* **1** : scale **2** ESCALERA : ladder **3** : stopover
escalada *nf* : ascent, climb
escalador, -dora *n* ALPINISTA : mountain climber
escalafón *nm, pl* **-fones 1** : list of personnel **2** : salary scale, rank
escalar *vt* : to climb, to scale — *vi* **1** : to go climbing **2** : to escalate
escaldar *vt* : to scald
escalera *nf* **1** : ladder <escalera de tijera : stepladder> **2** : stairs *pl*, staircase **3 escalera mecánica** : escalator
escalfador *nm* : chafing dish
escalfar *vt* : to poach (eggs)
escalinata *nf* : flight of stairs
escalofriante *adj* : horrifying, bloodcurdling
escalofrío *nm* : shiver, chill, shudder
escalón *nm, pl* **-lones 1** : echelon **2** : step, rung
escalonado, -da *adj* GRADUAL : gradual, staggered
escalonar *vt* **1** : to terrace **2** : to stagger, to alternate
escalpelo *nm* BISTURÍ : scalpel
escama *nf* **1** : scale (of fish or reptiles) **2** : flake (of skin)
escamar *vt* **1** : to scale (fish) **2** : to make suspicious
escamocha *nf Mex* : fruit salad
escamoso, -sa *adj* : scaly
escamotear *vt* **1** : to palm, to conceal **2** *fam* : to lift, to swipe **3** : to hide, to cover up
escandalizar {21} *vt* : to shock, to scandalize — *vi* : to make a fuss — **escandalizarse** *vr* : to be shocked
escándalo *nm* **1** : scandal **2** : scene, commotion
escandaloso, -sa *adj* **1** : shocking, scandalous **2** RUIDOSO : noisy, rowdy **3** : flagrant, outrageous — **escandalosamente** *adv*
escandinavo, -va *adj & n* : Scandinavian
escandir *vt* : to scan (poetry)
escáner *nm* : scanner, scan
escaño *nm* **1** : seat (in a legislative body) **2** BANCO : bench
escapada *nf* HUIDA : flight, escape
escapar *vi* HUIR : to escape, to flee, to run away — **escaparse** *vr* : to escape notice, to leak out
escaparate *nm* **1** : shop window **2** : showcase
escapatoria *nf* **1** : loophole, excuse, pretext <no tener escapatoria : to have no way out> **2** ESCAPADA : escape, flight
escape *nm* **1** FUGA : escape **2** : exhaust (from a vehicle)
escapismo *nm* : escapism
escápula *nm* OMÓPLATO : scapula, shoulder blade
escapulario *nm* : scapular
escarabajo *nm* : beetle
escaramuza *nf* **1** : skirmish **2** : scrimmage
escaramuzar {21} *vi* : to skirmish
escarapela *nf* : rosette (ornament)
escarbar *vt* **1** : to dig, to scratch up **2** : to poke, to pick **3** ~ **en** : to investigate, to pry into
escarcha *nf* **1** : frost **2** *Mex, PRi* : glitter
escarchar *vt* **1** : to frost (a cake) **2** : to candy (fruit)
escardar *vt* **1** : to weed, to hoe **2** : to weed out
escariar *vt* : to ream
escarlata *adj & nf* : scarlet
escarlatina *nf* : scarlet fever
escarmentar {55} *vt* : to punish, to teach a lesson to — *vi* : to learn one's lesson
escarmiento *nm* **1** : lesson, warning **2** CASTIGO : punishment
escarnecer {53} *vt* RIDICULIZAR : to ridicule, to mock
escarnio *nm* : ridicule, mockery
escarola *nf* : escarole
escarpa *nf* : escarpment, steep slope
escarpado, -da *adj* : steep, sheer
escarpia *nf* : hook, spike
escasamente *adv* : scarcely, barely
escasear *vi* : to be scarce, to run short
escasez *nf, pl* **-seces** : shortage, scarcity
escaso, -sa *adj* **1** : scarce, scant **2** ~ **de** : short of
escatimar *vt* : to skimp on, to be sparing with <no escatimar esfuerzos : to spare no effort>
escayola *nf* **1** : plaster (for casts) **2** : plaster cast
escayolar *vt* : to put in a plaster cast

escena *nf* **1 :** scene **2 :** stage
escenario *nm* **1** ESCENA **:** stage **2 :** setting, scene <el escenario del crimen : the scene of the crime>
escénico, -ca *adj* **1 :** scenic **2 :** stage
escenificar {72} *vt* **:** to stage, to dramatize
escepticismo *nm* **:** skepticism
escéptico[1]**, -ca** *adj* **:** skeptical
escéptico[2]**, -ca** *n* **:** skeptic
escindirse *vr* **1 :** to split **2 :** to break away
escisión *nf, pl* **-siones 1 :** split, division **2 :** excision
esclarecer {53} *vt* **1** ELUCIDAR **:** to elucidate, to clarify **2** ILUMINAR **:** to illuminate, to light up
esclarecimiento *nm* ELUCIDACIÓN **:** elucidation, clarification
esclavitud *nf* **:** slavery
esclavización *nf, pl* **-ciones :** enslavement
esclavizar {21} *vt* **:** to enslave
esclavo, -va *n* **:** slave
esclerosis *nf* **esclerosis múltiple :** multiple sclerosis
esclusa *nf* **:** floodgate, lock (of a canal)
escoba *nf* **:** broom
escobilla *nf* **:** small broom, brush, whisk broom
escobillón *nm, pl* **-llones :** swab
escocer {14} *vi* ARDER **:** to smart, to sting — **escocerse** *vr* **:** to be sore
escocés[1]**, -cesa** *adj, mpl* **-ceses 1 :** Scottish **2 :** tartan, plaid
escocés[2]**, -cesa** *n, mpl* **-ceses :** Scottish person, Scot
escocés[3] *nm* **1 :** Scots (language) **2** *pl* **-ceses :** Scotch (whiskey)
escofina *nf* **:** file, rasp
escoger {15} *vt* ELEGIR, SELECCIONAR **:** to choose, to select
escogido, -da *adj* **:** choice, select
escolar[1] *adj* **:** school
escolar[2] *nmf* **:** student, pupil
escolaridad *nf* **:** schooling <escolaridad obligatoria : compulsory education>
escolarización *nf, pl* **-ciones :** education, schooling
escollo *nm* **1 :** reef **2** OBSTÁCULO **:** obstacle
escolta *nmf* **:** escort
escoltar *vt* **:** to escort, to accompany
escombro *nm* **1 :** debris, rubbish **2 escombros** *nmpl* **:** ruins, rubble
esconder *vt* OCULTAR **:** to hide, to conceal
escondidas *nfpl* **1 :** hide-and-seek **2 a ~ :** secretly, in secret
escondimiento *nm* **:** concealment
escondite *nm* **1** ENCONDRIJO **:** hiding place **2** ESCONDIDAS **:** hide-and-seek
escondrijo *nm* ESCONDITE **:** hiding place
escopeta *nf* **:** shotgun
escoplear *vt* **:** to chisel (out)
escoplo *nm* **:** chisel
escora *nf* **:** list, heeling
escorar *vi* **:** to list, to heel (of a boat)
escorbuto *nm* **:** scurvy
escoria *nf* **1 :** slag, dross **2** HEZ **:** dregs *pl,* scum <la escoria de la sociedad : the dregs of society>
Escorpio *or* **Escorpión** *nmf* **:** Scorpio
escorpión *nm, pl* **-piones** ALACRÁN **:** scorpion
escote *nm* **1 :** low neckline **2 pagar a escote :** to go dutch
escotilla *nf* **:** hatch, hatchway
escotillón *nf, pl* **-llones :** trapdoor
escozor *nm* **:** smarting, stinging
escriba *nm* **:** scribe
escribano, -na *n* **1 :** court clerk **2** NOTARIO **:** notary public
escribir {33} *v* **1 :** to write **2 :** to spell — **escribirse** *vr* CARTEARSE **:** to write to one another, to correspond
escrito[1] *pp* → **escribir**
escrito[2]**, -ta** *adj* **:** written
escrito[3] *nm* **1 :** written document **2 escritos** *nmpl* **:** writings, works
escritor, -tora *n* **:** writer
escritorio *nm* **:** desk
escritorzuelo, -la *n* **:** hack (writer)
escritura *nf* **1 :** writing, handwriting **2 :** deed
escroto *nm* **:** scrotum
escrúpulo *nm* **:** scruple
escrupuloso, -sa *adj* **1 :** scrupulous **2** METICULOSO **:** exact, meticulous — **escrupulosamente** *adv*
escrutador, -dora *adj* **:** penetrating, searching
escrutar *vt* ESCUDRIÑAR **:** to scrutinize, to examine closely
escrutinio *nm* **:** scrutiny
escuadra *nf* **1 :** square (instrument) **2 :** fleet, squadron
escuadrilla *nf* **:** squadron, formation, flight
escuadrón *nm, pl* **-drones :** squadron
escuálido, -da *adj* **1 :** skinny, scrawny **2** INMUNDO **:** filthy, squalid
escuchar *vt* **1 :** to listen to **2 :** to hear — *vi* **:** to listen — **escucharse** *vr*
escudar *vt* **:** to shield — **escudarse** *vr* **~ en :** to hide behind
escudero *nm* **:** squire
escudo *nm* **1 :** shield **2 escudo de armas :** coat of arms
escudriñar *vt* **1** ESCRUTAR **:** to scrutinize **2 :** to inquire into, to investigate
escuela *nf* **:** school
escueto, -ta *adj* **1 :** plain, simple **2 :** succinct, concise — **escuetamente** *adv*
escuincle, -cla *n Mex fam* **:** child, kid
esculcar {72} *vt* **:** to search
esculpir *vt* **1 :** to sculpt **2 :** to carve, to engrave — *vi* **:** to sculpt
escultor, -tora *n* **:** sculptor
escultórico, -ca *adj* **:** sculptural
escultura *nf* **:** sculpture
escultural *adj* **:** statuesque
escupidera *nf* **:** spittoon, cuspidor
escupir *v* **:** to spit
escupitajo *nm* **:** spit
escurridizo, -za *adj* **:** slippery, elusive

escurridor *nm* **1 :** dish rack **2 :** colander

escurrir *vt* **1 :** to wring out **2 :** to drain — *vi* **1 :** to drain **2 :** to drip, to drip-dry — **escurrirse** *vr* **:** to slip away

ese, esa *adj, mpl* **esos :** that, those

ése, ésa *pron, mpl* **ésos :** that one, those ones *pl*

esencia *nf* **:** essence

esencial *adj* **:** essential — **esencialmente** *adv*

esfera *nf* **1 :** sphere **2 :** face, dial (of a watch)

esférico[1], -ca *adj* **:** spherical

esférico[2] *nm* **:** ball (in sports)

esfinge *nf* **:** sphinx

esforzado, -da *adj* **1 :** energetic, vigorous **2** VALIENTE **:** courageous, brave

esforzar {36} *vt* **:** to strain — **esforzarse** *vr* **:** to make an effort

esfuerzo *nm* **1 :** effort **2** ÁNIMO, VIGOR **:** spirit, vigor **3 sin ~ :** effortlessly

esfumar *vt* **:** to tone down, to soften — **esfumarse** *vr* **1 :** to fade away, to vanish **2** *fam* **:** to take off, to leave

esgrima *nf* **:** fencing (sport)

esgrimidor, -dora *n* **:** fencer

esgrimir *vt* **1 :** to brandish, to wield **2 :** to use, to resort to — *vi* **:** to fence

esguince *nm* **:** sprain, strain (of a muscle)

eslabón *nm, pl* **-bones :** link

eslabonar *vt* **:** to link, to connect, to join

eslavo[1], -va *adj* **:** Slavic

eslavo[2], -va *n* **:** Slav

eslogan *nm, pl* **-lóganes :** slogan

eslovaco, -ca *adj & n* **:** Slovakian, Slovak

esloveno, -na *adj & nm* **:** Slovene, Slovenian

esmaltar *vt* **:** to enamel

esmalte *nm* **1 :** enamel **2 esmalte de uñas :** nail polish

esmerado, -da *adj* **:** careful, painstaking

esmeralda *nf* **:** emerald

esmerarse *vr* **:** to take great pains, to do one's utmost

esmeril *nm* **:** emery

esmero *nm* **:** meticulousness, great care

esmoquin *nm, pl* **-quins :** tuxedo

esnob[1] *adj, pl* **esnobs :** snobbish

esnob[2] *nmf, pl* **esnobs :** snob

esnobismo *nm* **:** snobbery, snobbishness

eso *pron* (*neuter*) **1 :** that <eso no me gusta : I don't like that> **2 ¡eso es! :** that's it!, that's right! **3 a eso de :** around <a eso de las tres : around three o'clock> **4 en ~ :** at that point, just then

esófago *nm* **:** esophagus

esos → **ese**

ésos → **ése**

esotérico, -ca *adj* **:** esoteric — **esotéricamente** *adv*

espabilado, -da *adj* **:** bright, smart

espabilarse *vr* **1 :** to awaken **2 :** to get a move on **3 :** to get smart, to wise up

espacial *adj* **1 :** space **2 :** spatial

espaciar *vt* DISTANCIAR **:** to space out, to spread out

espacio *nm* **1 :** space, room **2 :** period, length (of time) **3 espacio exterior :** outer space

espacioso, -sa *adj* **:** spacious, roomy

espada[1] *nf* **1 :** sword **2 espadas** *nfpl* **:** spades (in playing cards)

espada[2] *nm* MATADOR, TORERO **:** bullfighter, matador

espadaña *nf* **1 :** belfry **2 :** cattail

espadilla *nf* **:** scull, oar

espagueti *nm or* **espaguetis** *nmpl* **:** spaghetti

espalda *nf* **1 :** back **2 espaldas** *nfpl* **:** shoulders, back **3 por la espalda :** from behind

espaldarazo *nm* **1 :** recognition, support **2 :** slap on the back

espaldera *nf* **:** trellis

espantajo *nm* **:** scarecrow

espantapájaros *nms & pl* **:** scarecrow

espantar *vt* ASUSTAR **:** to scare, to frighten — **espantarse** *vr*

espanto *nm* **:** fright, fear, horror

espantoso, -sa *adj* **1 :** frightening, terrifying **2 :** frightful, dreadful

español[1], -ñola *adj* **:** Spanish

español[2], -ñola *n* **:** Spaniard

español[3] *nm* CASTELLANO **:** Spanish (language)

esparadrapo *nm* **:** adhesive bandage, Band-Aid™

esparcimiento *nm* **1** DIVERSIÓN, RECREO **:** entertainment, recreation **2** DESCANSO **:** relaxation **3** DISEMINACIÓN **:** dissemination, spreading

esparcir {83} *vt* DISPERSAR **:** to scatter, to spread — **esparcirse** *vr* **1 :** to spread out **2** DESCANSARSE **:** to take it easy **3** DIVERTIRSE **:** to amuse oneself

espárrago *nm* **:** asparagus

espartano, -na *adj* **:** severe, austere

espasmo *nm* **:** spasm

espasmódico, -ca *adj* **:** spasmodic

espástico, -ca *adj* **:** spastic

espátula *nf* **:** spatula

especia *nf* **:** spice

especial *adj & nm* **:** special

especialidad *nf* **:** specialty

especialista *nmf* **:** specialist, expert

especializarse {21} *vr* **:** to specialize

especialmente *adv* **:** especially, particularly

especie *nf* **1 :** species **2** CLASE, TIPO **:** type, kind, sort

especificación *nf, pl* **-ciones :** specification

especificar {72} *vt* **:** to specify

específico, -ca *adj* **:** specific — **específicamente** *adv*

espécimen *nm, pl* **especímenes :** specimen

especioso, -sa *adj* **:** specious

espectacular *adj* **:** spectacular — **espectacularmente** *adv*

espectáculo *nm* **1 :** spectacle, sight **2 :** show, performance
espectador, -dora *n* **:** spectator, onlooker
espectro *nm* **1 :** ghost, specter **2 :** spectrum
especulación *nf, pl* **-ciones :** speculation
especulador, -dora *n* **:** speculator
especular *vi* **:** to speculate
especulativo, -va *adj* **:** speculative
espejismo *nm* **1 :** mirage **2 :** illusion
espejo *nm* **:** mirror
espejuelos *nmpl* ANTEOJOS **:** spectacles, glasses
espeluznante *adj* **:** hair-raising, terrifying
espera *nf* **:** wait
esperanza *nf* **:** hope, expectation
esperanzado, -da *adj* **:** hopeful
esperanzador, -dora *adj* **:** encouraging, promising
esperanzar {21} *vt* **:** to give hope to
esperar *vt* **1** AGUARDAR **:** to wait for, to await **2 :** to expect **3 :** to hope <espero poder trabajar : I hope to be able to work> <espero que sí : I hope so> — *vi* **:** to wait — **esperarse** *vr* **1 :** to expect, to be hoped <como podría esperarse : as would be expected> **2 :** to hold on, to hang on <espérate un momento : hold on a minute>
esperma *nmf* **:** sperm
esperpéntico, -ca *adj* GROTESCO **:** grotesque
esperpento *nm fam* MAMARRACHO **:** sight, fright <voy hecha un esperpento : I really look a sight>
espesante *nm* **:** thickener
espesar *vt* **:** to thicken — **espesarse** *vr*
espeso, -sa *adj* **:** thick, heavy, dense
espesor *nm* **:** thickness, density
espesura *nf* **1 :** thickness **2 :** thicket
espetar *vt* **1 :** to blurt out **2 :** to skewer
espía *nmf* **:** spy
espiar {85} *vt* **:** to spy on, to observe — *vi* **:** to spy
espiga *nf* **1 :** ear (of wheat) **2 :** spike (of flowers)
espigado, -da *adj* **:** willowy, slender
espigar {52} *vt* **:** to glean, to gather — **espigarse** *vr* **:** to grow quickly, to shoot up
espigón *nm, pl* **-gones :** breakwater
espina *nf* **1 :** thorn **2 :** spine <espina dorsal : spinal column> **3 :** fish bone
espinaca *nf* **1 :** spinach (plant) **2 espinacas** *nfpl* **:** spinach (food)
espinal *adj* **:** spinal
espinazo *nm* **:** backbone
espineta *nf* **:** spinet
espinilla *nf* **1** BARRO, GRANO **:** pimple **2 :** shin
espino *nm* **:** hawthorn
espinoso, -sa *adj* **1 :** thorny, prickly **2 :** bony (of fish) **3 :** knotty, difficult
espionaje *nm* **:** espionage
espiración *nf, pl* **-ciones :** exhalation
espiral *adj & nf* **:** spiral
espirar *vt* EXHALAR **:** to breathe out, to give off — *vi* **:** to exhale
espiritismo *nm* **:** spiritualism
espiritista *nmf* **:** spiritualist
espíritu *nm* **1 :** spirit **2** ÁNIMO **:** state of mind, spirits *pl* **3 el Espíritu Santo :** the Holy Ghost
espiritual *adj* **:** spiritual — **espiritualmente** *adv*
espiritualidad *nf* **:** spirituality
espita *nf* **:** spigot, tap
esplendidez *nf, pl* **-deces** ESPLENDOR **:** magnificence, splendor
espléndido, -da *adj* **1 :** splendid, magnificent **2 :** generous, lavish — **espléndidamente** *adv*
esplendor *nm* ESPLENDIDEZ **:** splendor
esplendoroso, -sa *adj* MAGNÍFICO **:** magnificent, grand
espliego *nm* LAVANDA **:** lavender
espolear *vt* **:** to spur on
espoleta *nf* **1** DETONADOR **:** detonator, fuse **2 :** wishbone
espolón *nm, pl* **-lones :** spur (of poultry), fetlock (of a horse)
espolvorear *vt* **:** to sprinkle, to dust
esponja *nf* **1 :** sponge **2 tirar la esponja :** to throw in the towel
esponjado, -da *adj* **:** spongy
esponjoso, -sa *adj* **1 :** spongy **2 :** soft, fluffy
esponsales *nmpl* **:** betrothal, engagement
espontaneidad *nf* **:** spontaneity
espontáneo, -nea *adj* **:** spontaneous — **espontáneamente** *adv*
espora *nf* **:** spore
esporádico, -ca *adj* **:** sporadic — **esporádicamente** *adv*
esposar *vt* **:** to handcuff
esposas *nfpl* **:** handcuffs
esposo, -sa *n* **:** spouse, wife *f,* husband *m*
esprint *nm* **:** sprint
esprintar *vi* **:** to sprint
esprinter *nmf* **:** sprinter
espuela *nf* **:** spur
espuerta *nf* **:** two-handled basket
espulgar {52} *vt* **1 :** to delouse **2 :** to scrutinize
espuma *nf* **1 :** foam **2 :** lather **3 :** froth, head (on beer)
espumar *vi* **:** to foam, to froth — *vt* **:** to skim off
espumoso, -sa *adj* **:** foamy, frothy
espurio, -ria *adj* **:** spurious
esputar *v* **:** to expectorate, to spit
esputo *nm* **:** spit, sputum
esqueje *nm* **:** cutting (from a plant)
esquela *nf* **1 :** note **2 :** notice, announcement
esquelético, -ca *adj* **:** emaciated, skeletal
esqueleto *nm* **1 :** skeleton **2** ARMAZÓN **:** framework
esquema *nf* BOSQUEJO **:** outline, sketch, plan
esquemático, -ca *adj* **:** schematic

esquí *nm* **1 :** ski **2 esquí acuático :** water ski, waterskiing
esquiador, -dora *n* **:** skier
esquiar {85} *vi* **:** to ski
esquife *nm* **:** skiff
esquila *nf* **1** CENCERRO **:** cowbell **2 :** shearing
esquilar *vt* TRASQUILAR **:** to shear
esquimal *adj & nmf* **:** Eskimo
esquina *nf* **:** corner
esquinazo *nm* **1 :** corner **2 dar esquinazo a** *fam* **:** to stand up, to give the slip to
esquirla *nf* **:** splinter (of bone, glass, etc.)
esquirol *nm* ROMPEHUELGAS **:** strikebreaker, scab
esquisto *nm* **:** shale
esquivar *vt* **1** EVADIR **:** to dodge, to evade **2** EVITAR **:** to avoid
esquivez *nf, pl* **-veces 1 :** aloofness **2** TIMIDEZ **:** shyness
esquivo, -va *adj* **1** HURAÑO **:** aloof, unsociable **2 :** shy **3 :** elusive, evasive
esquizofrenia *nf* **:** schizophrenia
esquizofrénico, -ca *adj & n* **:** schizophrenic
esta → **este**[1]
ésta → **éste**
estabilidad *nf* **:** stability
estabilización *nf, pl* **-ciones :** stabilization
estabilizador *nm* **:** stabilizer
estabilizar {21} *vt* **:** to stabilize — **estabilizarse** *vr*
estable *adj* **:** stable, steady
establecer {53} *vt* FUNDAR, INSTITUIR **:** to establish, to found, to set up — **establecerse** *vr* INSTALARSE **:** to settle, to establish oneself
establecimiento *nm* **1 :** establishing **2 :** establishment, institution, office
establo *nm* **:** stable
estaca *nf* **:** stake, picket, post
estacada *nf* **1 :** picket fence **2 :** stockade
estacar {72} *vt* **1 :** to stake out **2 :** to fasten down with stakes — **estacarse** *vr* **:** to remain rigid
estación *nf, pl* **-ciones 1 :** station <estación de servicio : service station, gas station> **2 :** season
estacional *adj* **:** seasonal
estacionamiento *nm* **1 :** parking **2 :** parking lot
estacionar *vt* **1 :** to place, to station **2 :** to park — **estacionarse** *vr* **1 :** to park **2 :** to remain stationary
estacionario, -ria *adj* **1 :** stationary **2 :** stable
estada *nf* **:** stay
estadía *nf* ESTANCIA **:** stay, sojourn
estadio *nm* **1 :** stadium **2 :** phase, stage
estadista *nmf* **:** statesman
estadística *nf* **1 :** statistic, figure **2 :** statistics
estadístico[1], **-ca** *adj* **:** statistical — **estadísticamente** *adv*
estadístico[2], **-ca** *n* **:** statistician
estado *nm* **1 :** state **2 :** status <estado civil : marital status> **3** CONDICIÓN **:** condition
estadounidense *adj & nmf* AMERICANO, NORTEAMERICANO **:** American
estafa *nf* **:** swindle, fraud
estafador, -dora *n* **:** cheat, swindler
estafar *vt* DEFRAUDAR **:** to swindle, to defraud
estalactita *nf* **:** stalactite
estalagmita *nf* **:** stalagmite
estallar *vi* **1** REVENTAR **:** to burst, to explode, to erupt **2 :** to break out
estallido *nm* **1** EXPLOSIÓN **:** explosion **2 :** report (of a gun) **3 :** outbreak, outburst
estambre *nm* **1 :** worsted (fabric) **2 :** stamen
estampa *nf* **1** ILUSTRACIÓN, IMAGEN **:** printed image, illustration **2** ASPECTO **:** appearance, demeanor
estampado[1], **-da** *adj* **:** patterned, printed
estampado[2] *nm* **:** print, pattern
estampar *vt* **:** to stamp, to print, to engrave
estampida *nf* **:** stampede
estampilla *nf* **1 :** rubber stamp **2** SELLO, TIMBRE **:** postage stamp
estancado, -da *adj* **:** stagnant
estancamiento *nm* **:** stagnation
estancar {72} *vt* **1 :** to dam up, to hold back **2 :** to bring to a halt, to deadlock — **estancarse** *vr* **1 :** to stagnate **2 :** to be brought to a standstill, to be deadlocked
estancia *nf* **1** ESTADÍA **:** stay, sojourn **2 :** ranch, farm
estanciero, -ra *n* **:** rancher, farmer
estanco, -ca *adj* **:** watertight
estándar *adj & nm* **:** standard
estandarización *nf, pl* **-ciones :** standardization
estandarizar {21} *vt* **:** to standardize
estandarte *nm* **:** standard, banner
estanque *nm* **1 :** pool, pond **2 :** tank, reservoir
estante *nm* REPISA **:** shelf
estantería *nf* **:** shelves *pl*, bookcase
estaño *nm* **:** tin
estaquilla *nf* **1 :** peg **2** ESPIGA **:** spike
estar {34} *v aux* **:** to be <estoy aprendiendo inglés : I'm learning English> <está terminado : it's finished> — *vi* **1** (*indicating a state or condition*) **:** to be <está muy alto : he's so tall, he's gotten very tall><¿ya estás mejor? : are you feeling better now?> <estoy casado : I'm married> **2** (*indicating location*) **:** to be <están en la mesa : they're on the table> <estamos en la página 2 : we're on page 2> **3 :** to be at home <¿está María? : is Maria in?> **4 :** to remain <estaré aquí 5 días : I'll be here for 5 days> **5 :** to be ready, to be done <estará para las diez : it will be ready by ten o'clock> **6 :** to agree <¿estamos? : are we in agreement?> <estoy contigo : I'm with you> **7**

¿cómo estás? : how are you? **8 ¡está bien! :** all right!, that's fine! **9 ~ a :** to cost **10 ~ a :** to be <¿a qué dia estamos? : what's today's date?> **11 ~ con** to have <está con fiebre : she has a fever> **12 ~ de :** to be <estoy de vacaciones : I'm on vacation> <está de director hoy : he's acting as director today> **13 estar bien (mal) :** to be well (sick) **14 ~ para :** to be in the mood for **15 ~ por :** to be in favor of **16 ~ por :** to be about to <está por cerrar : it's on the verge of closing> **17 estar de más :** to be unnecessary **18 estar que :** to be (in a state or condition) <está que echa chispas : he's hopping mad> — **estarse** *vr* QUEDARSE **:** to stay, to remain <¡estáte quieto! : be still!>

estarcir {83} *vt* **:** to stencil

estatal *adj* **:** state, national

estática *nf* **:** static

estático, -ca *adj* **:** static

estatizar {21} *vt* **:** to nationalize — **estatización** *nf*

estatua *nf* **:** statue

estatuilla *nf* **:** statuette, figurine

estatura *nf* **:** height, stature <de mediana estatura : of medium height>

estatus *nm* **:** status, prestige

estatutario, -ria *adj* **:** statutory

estatuto *nm* **:** statute

este[1], **esta** *adj, mpl* **estos :** this, these

este[2] *adj* **:** eastern, east

este[3] *nm* **1** ORIENTE **:** east **2 :** east wind **3 el Este :** the East, the Orient

éste, ésta *pron, mpl* **éstos 1 :** this one, these ones *pl* **2 :** the latter

estela *nf* **1 :** wake (of a ship) **2** RASTRO **:** trail (of dust, smoke, etc.)

estelar *adj* **:** stellar

estelarizar {21} *vt Mex* **:** to star in, to be the star of

esténcil *nm* **:** stencil

estentóreo, -rea *adj* **:** loud, thundering

estepa *nf* **:** steppe

éster *nf* **:** ester

estera *nf* **:** mat

estercolero *nm* **:** dunghill

estéreo *adj & nm* **:** stereo

estereofónico, -ca *adj* **:** stereophonic

estereotipado, -da *adj* **:** stereotyped

estereotipar *vt* **:** to stereotype

estereotipo *nm* **:** stereotype

estéril *adj* **1 :** sterile, germ-free **2 :** infertile, barren **3 :** futile, vain

esterilidad *nf* **1 :** sterility **2 :** infertility

esterilizar {21} *vt* **1 :** to sterilize, to disinfect **2 :** to sterilize (a person), to spay (an animal) — **esterilización** *nf*

esterlina *adj* **:** sterling

esternón *nm, pl* **-nones :** sternum

estero *nm* **:** estuary

estertor *nm* **:** death rattle

estética *nf* **:** aesthetics

estético, -ca *adj* **:** aesthetic — **estéticamente** *adv*

estetoscopio *nm* **:** stethoscope

estibador, -dora *n* **:** longshoreman, stevedore

estibar *vt* **:** to load (freight)

estiércol *nm* **:** dung, manure

estigma *nm* **:** stigma

estigmatizar {21} *vt* **:** to stigmatize, to brand

estilarse *vr* **:** to be in fashion

estilete *nm* **:** stiletto

estilista *nmf* **:** stylist

estilizar {21} *vt* **:** to stylize

estilo *nm* **1 :** style **2 :** fashion, manner **3 :** stylus

estima *nf* ESTIMACIÓN **:** esteem, regard

estimable *adj* **1 :** considerable **2 :** estimable, esteemed

estimación *nf, pl* **-ciones 1** ESTIMA **:** esteem, regard **2 :** estimate

estimado, -da *adj* **:** esteemed, dear <Estimado señor Ortiz : Dear Mr. Ortiz>

estimar *vt* **1** APRECIAR **:** to esteem, to respect **2** EVALUAR **:** to estimate, to appraise **3** OPINAR **:** to consider, to deem

estimulación *nf, pl* **-ciones :** stimulation

estimulante[1] *adj* **:** stimulating

estimulante[2] *nm* **:** stimulant

estimular *vt* **1 :** to stimulate **2 :** to encourage

estímulo *nm* **1 :** stimulus **2** INCENTIVO **:** incentive, encouragement

estío *nm* **:** summertime

estipendio *nm* **1 :** salary **2 :** stipend, remuneration

estipular *vt* **:** to stipulate — **estipulación** *nf*

estirado, -da *adj* **1 :** stretched, extended **2** PRESUMIDO **:** stuck-up, conceited

estiramiento *nm* **1 :** stretching **2 estiramiento facial :** face-lift

estirar *vt* **:** to stretch (out), to extend — **estirarse** *vr*

estirón *nm, pl* **-rones 1 :** pull, tug **2 dar un estirón :** to grow quickly, to shoot up

estirpe *nf* LINAJE **:** lineage, stock

estival *adj* VERANIEGO **:** summer

esto *pron* (*neuter*) **1 :** this <¿qué es esto? : what is this?> **2 en ~ :** at this point **3 por ~ :** for this reason

estocada *nf* **1 :** final thrust (in bullfighting) **2 :** thrust, lunge (in fencing)

estofa *nf* CLASE **:** class, quality <de baja estofa : low-class, poor-quality>

estofado *nm* COCIDO, GUISADO **:** stew

estofar *vt* GUISAR **:** to stew

estoicismo *nm* **:** stoicism

estoico[1], **-ca** *adj* **:** stoic, stoical

estoico[2], **-ca** *n* **:** stoic

estola *nf* **:** stole

estomacal *adj* GÁSTRICO **:** stomach, gastric

estómago *nm* **:** stomach

estoniano, -na *adj & n* **:** Estonian

estopa *nf* **1 :** tow (yarn or cloth) **2 :** burlap

estopilla *nf* : cheesecloth
estoque *nm* : rapier, sword
estorbar *vt* OBSTRUIR : to obstruct, to hinder — *vi* : to get in the way
estorbo *nm* **1** : obstacle, hindrance **2** : nuisance
estornino *nm* : starling
estornudar *vi* : to sneeze
estornudo *nm* : sneeze
estos → **este**[1]
éstos → **éste**
estoy → **estar**
estrabismo *nm* : squint
estrado *nm* **1** : dais, platform, bench (of a judge) **2** ESTRADOS *nmpl* : courts of law
estrafalario, -ria *adj* ESTRAMBÓTICO, EXCÉNTRICO : eccentric, bizarre
estragar {52} *vt* DEVASTAR : to ruin, to devastate
estragón *nm* : tarragon
estragos *nmpl* **1** : ravages, destruction, devastation <los estragos de la guerra : the ravages of war> **2 hacer estragos en** *or* **causar estragos entre** : to play havoc with
estrambótico, -ca *adj* ESTRAFALARIO, EXCÉNTRICO : eccentric, bizarre
estrangulamiento *nm* : strangling, strangulation
estrangular *vt* AHOGAR : to strangle — **estrangulación** *nf*
estratagema *nf* ARTIMAÑA : stratagem, ruse
estratega *nmf* : strategist
estrategia *nf* : strategy
estratégico, -ca *adj* : strategic, tactical — **estratégicamente** *adv*
estratificación *nf, pl* **-ciones** : stratification
estratificado, -da *adj* : stratified
estrato *nm* : stratum, layer
estratosfera *nf* : stratosphere
estratosférico, -ca *adj* **1** : stratospheric **2** : astronomical, exorbitant
estrechamiento *nm* **1** : narrowing **2** : narrow point **3** : tightening, strengthening (of relations)
estrechar *vt* **1** : to narrow **2** : to tighten, to strengthen (a bond) **3** : to hug, to embrace **4 estrechar la mano de** : to shake hands with — **estrecharse** *vr*
estrechez *nf, pl* **-checes** **1** : tightness, narrowness **2 estrecheces** *nfpl* : financial problems
estrecho[1], **-cha** *adj* **1** : tight, narrow **2** ÍNTIMO : close — **estrechamente** *adv*
estrecho[2] *nm* : strait, narrows
estrella *nf* **1** ASTRO : star <estrella fugaz : shooting star> **2** : destiny <tener buena estrella : to be born lucky> **3** : movie star **4 estrella de mar** : starfish
estrellado, -da *adj* **1** : starry **2** : star-shaped **3 huevos estrellados** : fried eggs
estrellamiento *nm* : crash, collision
estrellar *vt* : to smash, to crash — **estrellarse** *vr* : to crash, to collide
estrellato *nm* : stardom
estremecedor, -dora *adj* : horrifying
estremecer {53} *vt* : to cause to shake — *vi* : to tremble, to shake — **estremecerse** *vr* : to shudder, to shiver (with emotion)
estremecimiento *nm* : trembling, shaking, shivering
estrenar *vt* **1** : to use for the first time **2** : to premiere, to open — **estrenarse** *vr* : to make one's debut
estreno *nm* DEBUT : debut, premiere
estreñimiento *nm* : constipation
estreñirse {67} *vr* : to be constipated
estrépito *nm* ESTRUENDO : clamor, din
estrepitoso, -sa *adj* : clamorous, noisy — **estrepitosamente** *adv*
estrés *nm, pl* **estreses** : stress
estresante *adj* : stressful
estresar *vt* : to stress, to stress out
estría *nf* : fluting, groove
estribación *nf, pl* **-ciones** **1** : spur, ridge **2 estribaciones** *nfpl* : foothills
estribar *vi* FUNDARSE **~ en** : to be due to, to stem from
estribillo *nm* : refrain, chorus
estribo *nm* **1** : stirrup **2** : abutment, buttress **3 perder los estribos** : to lose one's temper
estribor *nm* : starboard
estricnina *nf* : strychnine
estricto, -ta *adj* SEVERO : strict, severe — **estrictamente** *adv*
estridente *adj* : strident, shrill, loud — **estridentemente** *adv*
estrofa *nf* : stanza, verse
estrógeno *nm* : estrogen
estropajo *nm* : scouring pad
estropear *vt* **1** ARRUINAR : to ruin, to spoil **2** : to break, to damage — **estropearse** *vr* **1** : to spoil, to go bad **2** : to break down
estropicio *nm* DAÑO : damage, breakage
estructura *nf* : structure, framework
estructuración *nf, pl* **-ciones** : structuring, structure
estructural *adj* : structural — **estructuralmente** *adv*
estructurar *vt* : to structure, to organize
estruendo *nm* ESTRÉPITO : racket, din, roar
estruendoso, -sa *adj* : resounding, thunderous
estrujar *vt* APRETAR : to press, to squeeze
estuario *nm* : estuary
estuche *nm* : kit, case
estuco *nm* : stucco
estudiado, -da *adj* : affected, mannered
estudiantado *nm* : student body, students *pl*
estudiante *nmf* : student
estudiantil *adj* : student <la vida estudiantil : student life>

estudiar *v* : to study
estudio *nm* **1** : study **2** : studio **3 estudios** *nmpl* : studies, education
estudioso, -sa *adj* : studious
estufa *nf* **1** : stove, heater **2** *Col, Mex* : cooking stove, range
estupefacción *nf, pl* **-ciones** : stupefaction, astonishment
estupefaciente[1] *adj* : narcotic
estupefaciente[2] *nm* DROGA, NARCÓTICO : drug, narcotic
estupefacto, -ta *adj* : astonished, stunned
estupendo, -da *adj* MARAVILLOSO : stupendous, marvelous — **estupendamente** *adv*
estupidez *nf, pl* **-deces 1** : stupidity **2** : nonsense
estúpido[1], -da *adj* : stupid — **estúpidamente** *adj*
estúpido[2], -da *n* IDIOTA : idiot, fool
estupor *nm* **1** : stupor **2** : amazement
esturión *nm, pl* **-riones** : sturgeon
estuvo, etc. → **estar**
etano *nm* : ethane
etanol *nm* : ethanol
etapa *nf* FASE : stage, phase
etcétera[1] : et cetera, and so on
etcétera[2] *nmf* : etcetera
éter *nm* : ether
etéreo, -rea *adj* : ethereal, heavenly
eternidad *nf* : eternity
eternizar {21} *vt* PERPETUAR : to make eternal, to perpetuate — **eternizarse** *vr fam* : to take forever
eterno, -na *adj* : eternal, endless — **eternamente** *adv*
ética *nf* : ethics
ético, -ca *adj* : ethical — **éticamente** *adv*
etimología *nf* : etymology
etimológico, -ca *adj* : etymological
etimólogo, -ga *n* : etymologist
etíope *adj & nmf* : Ethiopian
etiqueta *nf* **1** : etiquette **2** : tag, label **3 de ~** : formal, dressy
etiquetar *vt* : to label
étnico, -ca *adj* : ethnic
etnología *nf* : ethnology
etnólogo, -ga *n* : ethnologist
eucalipto *nm* : eucalyptus
Eucaristía *nf* : Eucharist, communion
eucarístico, -ca *adj* : eucharistic
eufemismo *nm* : euphemism
eufemístico, -ca *adj* : euphemistic
eufonía *nf* : euphony
eufónico, -ca *adj* : euphonious
euforia *nf* : euphoria, joyousness
eufórico, -ca *adj* : euphoric, exuberant, joyous — **eufóricamente** *adv*
eunuco *nm* : eunuch
europeo, -pea *adj & n* : European
euskera *nm* : Basque (language)
eutanasia *nf* : euthanasia
evacuación *nf, pl* **-ciones** : evacuation
evacuar *vt* **1** : to evacuate, to vacate **2** : to carry out — *vi* : to have a bowel movement
evadir *vt* ELUDIR : to evade, to avoid — **evadirse** *vr* : to escape, to slip away
evaluación *nf, pl* **-ciones** : assessment, evaluation
evaluar {3} *vt* : to evaluate, to assess, to appraise
evangélico, -ca *adj* : evangelical — **evangélicamente** *adv*
evangelio *nm* : gospel
evangelismo *nm* : evangelism
evangelista *nm* : evangelist
evangelizador, -dora *n* : evangelist, missionary
evaporación *nf, pl* **-ciones** : evaporation
evaporar *vt* : to evaporate — **evaporarse** *vr* ESFUMARSE : to disappear, to vanish
evasión *nf, pl* **-siones 1** : escape, flight **2** : evasion, dodge
evasiva *nf* : excuse, pretext
evasivo, -va *adj* : evasive
evento *nm* : event
eventual *adj* **1** : possible **2** : temporary <trabajadores eventuales : temporary workers> — **eventualmente** *adv*
eventualidad *nf* : possibility, eventuality
evidencia *nf* **1** : evidence, proof **2 poner en evidencia** : to demonstrate, to make clear
evidenciar *vt* : to demonstrate, to show — **evidenciarse** *vr* : to be evident
evidente *adj* : evident, obvious, clear — **evidentemente** *adv*
eviscerar *vt* : to eviscerate
evitable *adj* : avoidable, preventable
evitar *vt* **1** : to avoid **2** PREVENIR : to prevent **3** ELUDIR : to escape, to elude
evocación *nf, pl* **-ciones** : evocation
evocador, -dora *adj* : evocative
evocar {72} *vt* **1** : to evoke **2** RECORDAR : to recall
evolución *nf, pl* **-ciones 1** : evolution **2** : development, progress
evolucionar *vi* **1** : to evolve **2** : to change, to develop
evolutivo, -va *adj* : evolutionary
exabrupto *nm* : pointed remark
exacción *nf, pl* **-ciones** : levying, exaction
exacerbar *vt* **1** : to exacerbate, to aggravate **2** : to irritate, to exasperate
exactamente *adv* : exactly
exactitud *nf* PRECISIÓN : accuracy, precision, exactitude
exacto, -ta *adj* PRECISO : accurate, precise, exact
exageración *nf, pl* **-ciones** : exaggeration
exagerado, -da *adj* **1** : exaggerated **2** : excessive — **exageradamente** *adv*
exagerar *v* : to exaggerate
exaltación *nf, pl* **-ciones 1** : exaltation **2** : excitement, agitation
exaltado[1], -da *adj* : excitable, hotheaded
exaltado[2], -da *n* : hothead

exaltar *vt* **1** ENSALZAR **:** to exalt, to extol **2 :** to excite, to agitate — **exaltarse** *vr* ACALORARSE **:** to get overexcited
ex–alumno → **alumno**
examen *nm, pl* **exámenes 1 :** examination, test **2 :** consideration, investigation
examinar *vt* **1 :** to examine **2** INSPECCIONAR **:** to inspect — **examinarse** *vr* **:** to take an exam
exánime *adj* **1 :** lifeless **2 :** exhausted
exasperar *vt* IRRITAR **:** to exasperate, to irritate — **exasperación** *nf*
excavación *nf, pl* **-ciones :** excavation
excavadora *nf* **:** excavator
excavar *v* **:** to excavate, to dig
excedente[1] *adj* **1 :** excessive **2 :** excess, surplus
excedente[2] *nm* **:** surplus, excess
exceder *vt* **:** to exceed, to surpass — **excederse** *vr* **:** to go too far
excelencia *nf* **1 :** excellence **2 :** excellency <Su Excelencia : His Excellency>
excelente *adj* **:** excellent — **excelentemente** *adv*
excelso, -sa *adj* **:** lofty, sublime
excentricidad *nf* **:** eccentricity
excéntrico, -ca *adj & n* **:** eccentric
excepción *nf, pl* **-ciones :** exception
excepcional *adj* EXTRAORDINARIO **:** exceptional, extraordinary, rare
excepto *prep* SALVO **:** except
exceptuar {3} *vt* EXCLUIR **:** to except, to exclude
excesivo, -va *adj* **:** excessive — **excesivamente** *adv*
exceso *nm* **1 :** excess **2 excesos** *nmpl* **:** excesses, abuses **3 exceso de velocidad :** speeding
excitabilidad *nf* **:** excitability
excitación *nf, pl* **-ciones :** excitement
excitante *adj* **:** exciting
excitar *vt* **:** to excite, to arouse — **excitarse** *vr*
exclamación *nf, pl* **-ciones :** exclamation
exclamar *v* **:** to exclaim
excluir {41} *vt* EXCEPTUAR **:** to exclude, to leave out
exclusión *nf, pl* **-siones :** exclusion
exclusividad *nf* **1 :** exclusiveness **2 :** exclusive rights *pl*
exclusivo, -va *adj* **:** exclusive — **exclusivamente** *adv*
excomulgar {52} *vt* **:** to excommunicate
excomunión *nf, pl* **-niones :** excommunication
excreción *nf, pl* **-ciones :** excretion
excremento *nm* **:** excrement
excretar *vt* **:** to excrete
exculpar *vt* **:** to exonerate, to exculpate — **exculpación** *nf*
excursión *nf, pl* **-siones :** excursion, outing
excursionista *nmf* **1 :** sightseer, tourist **2 :** hiker
excusa *nf* **1** PRETEXTO **:** excuse **2** DISCULPA **:** apology
excusar *vt* **1 :** to excuse **2 :** to exempt — **excusarse** *vr* **:** to apologize, to send one's regrets
execrable *adj* **:** detestable, abominable
exención *nf, pl* **-ciones :** exemption
exento, -ta *adj* **1 :** exempt, free **2 exento de impuestos :** tax-exempt
exequias *nfpl* FUNERALES **:** funeral rites
exhalar *vt* ESPIRAR **:** to exhale, to give off
exhaustivo, -va *adj* **:** exhaustive — **exhaustivamente** *adv*
exhausto, -ta *adj* AGOTADO **:** exhausted, worn-out
exhibición *nf, pl* **-ciones 1 :** exhibition, show **2 :** showing
exhibir *vt* **:** to exhibit, to show, to display — **exhibirse** *vr*
exhortación *nf, pl* **-ciones :** exhortation
exhortar *vt* **:** to exhort
exhumar *vt* DESENTERRAR **:** to exhume — **exhumación** *nf*
exigencia *nf* **:** demand, requirement
exigente *adj* **:** demanding, exacting
exigir {35} *vt* **1 :** to demand, to require **2 :** to exact, to levy
exiguo, -gua *adj* **:** meager
exiliado[1], **-da** *adj* **:** exiled, in exile
exiliado[2], **-da** *n* **:** exile
exiliar *vt* DESTERRAR **:** to exile, to banish — **exiliarse** *vr* **:** to go into exile
exilio *nm* DESTIERRO **:** exile
eximio, -mia *adj* **:** distinguished, eminent
eximir *vt* EXONERAR **:** to exempt
existencia *nf* **1 :** existence **2 existencias** *nfpl* MERCANCÍA **:** goods, stock
existente *adj* **1 :** existing, in existence **2 :** in stock
existir *vi* **:** to exist
éxito *nm* **1** TRIUNFO **:** success, hit **2 tener éxito :** to be successful
exitoso, -sa *adj* **:** successful — **exitosamente** *adv*
éxodo *nm* **:** exodus
exoneración *nf, pl* **-ciones** EXENCIÓN **:** exoneration, exemption
exonerar *vt* **1** EXIMIR **:** to exempt, to exonerate **2** DESPEDIR **:** to dismiss
exorbitante *adj* **:** exorbitant
exorcismo *nm* **:** exorcism — **exorcista** *nmf*
exorcizar {21} *vt* **:** to exorcize
exótico, -ca *adj* **:** exotic
expandir *vt* EXPANSIONAR **:** to expand — **expandirse** *vr* **:** to spread
expansión *nf, pl* **-siones 1 :** expansion, spread **2** DIVERSIÓN **:** recreation, relaxation
expansionar *vt* EXPANDIR **:** to expand — **expansionarse** *vr* **1 :** to expand **2** DIVERTIRSE **:** to amuse oneself, to relax
expansivo, -va *adj* **:** expansive
expatriado, -da *adj & n* **:** expatriate
expatriarse {85} *vr* **1** EMIGRAR **:** to emigrate **2 :** to go into exile

expectación *nf, pl* **-ciones :** expectation, anticipation
expectante *adj* **:** expectant
expectativa *nf* **1 :** expectation, hope **2 expectativas** *nfpl* **:** prospects
expedición *nf, pl* **-ciones :** expedition
expediente *nm* **1 :** expedient, means **2** ARCHIVO **:** file, dossier, record
expedir {54} *vt* **1** EMITIR **:** to issue **2** DESPACHAR **:** to dispatch, to send
expedito, -ta *adj* **1 :** free, clear **2 :** quick, easy
expeler *vt* **:** to expel, to eject
expendedor, -dora *n* **:** dealer, seller
expendio *nm* TIENDA **:** store, shop
expensas *nfpl* **1 :** expenses, costs **2 a expensas de :** at the expense of
experiencia *nf* **1 :** experience **2** EXPERIMENTO **:** experiment
experimentación *nf, pl* **-ciones :** experimentation
experimental *adj* **:** experimental
experimentar *vi* **:** to experiment — *vt* **1 :** to experiment with, to test out **2 :** to experience
experimento *nm* EXPERIENCIA **:** experiment
experto, -ta *adj & n* **:** expert
expiación *nf, pl* **-ciones :** expiation, atonement
expiar {85} *vt* **:** to expiate, to atone for
expiración *nf, pl* **-ciones** VENCIMIENTO **:** expiration
expirar *vi* **1** FALLECER, MORIR **:** to pass away, to die **2 :** to expire
explanada *nf* **:** esplanade, promenade
explayar *vt* **:** to extend — **explayarse** *vr* **:** to expound, to speak at length
explicable *adj* **:** explicable, explainable
explicación *nf, pl* **-ciones :** explanation
explicar {72} *vt* **:** to explain — **explicarse** *vr* **:** to understand
explicativo, -va *adj* **:** explanatory
explicitar *vt* **:** to state explicitly, to specify
explícito, -ta *adj* **:** explicit — **explícitamente** *adv*
exploración *nf, pl* **-ciones :** exploration
explorador, -dora *n* **:** explorer, scout
explorar *vt* **:** to explore — **exploratorio, -ria** *adj*
explosión *nf, pl* **-siones 1** ESTALLIDO **:** explosion **2 :** outburst <una explosión de ira **:** an outburst of anger>
explosivo, -va *adj* **:** explosive
explotación *nf, pl* **-ciones 1 :** exploitation **2 :** operation, running
explotar *vt* **1 :** to exploit **2 :** to operate, to run — *vi* ESTALLAR, REVENTAR **:** to explode
exponente *nm* **:** exponent
exponential *adj* **:** exponential — **exponentialmente** *adv*
exponer {60} *vt* **1 :** to exhibit, to show, to display **2 :** to explain, to present, to set forth **3 :** to expose, to risk — *vi* **:** to exhibit
exportación *nf, pl* **-ciones 1 :** exportation **2 exportaciones** *nfpl* **:** exports
exportador, -dora *n* **:** exporter
exportar *vt* **:** to export — **exportable** *adj*
exposición *nf, pl* **-ciones 1** EXHIBICIÓN **:** exposition, exhibition **2 :** exposure **3 :** presentation, statement
expositor, -tora *n* **1 :** exhibitor **2 :** exponent
exprés *nms & pl* **1 :** express, express train **2 :** espresso
expresamente *adv* **:** expressly, on purpose
expresar *vt* **:** to express — **expresarse** *vr*
expresión *nf, pl* **-siones :** expression
expresivo, -va *adj* **1 :** expressive **2** CARIÑOSO **:** affectionate — **expresivamente** *adv*
expreso[1], **-sa** *adj* **:** express, specific
expreso[2] *nm* **:** express train, express
exprimidor *nm* **:** squeezer, juicer
exprimir *vt* **1 :** to squeeze **2 :** to exploit
expropiar *vt* **:** to expropriate, to commandeer — **expropiación** *nf*
expuesto[1] *pp* → **exponer**
expuesto[2], **-ta** *adj* **1 :** exposed **2 :** hazardous, risky
expulsar *vt* **:** to expel, to eject
expulsión *nf, pl* **-siones :** expulsion
expurgar {52} *vt* **:** to expurgate
expuso, etc. → **exponer**
exquisitez *nf, pl* **-teces 1 :** exquisiteness, refinement **2 :** delicacy, special dish
exquisito, -ta *adj* **1 :** exquisite **2 :** delicious
extasiarse {85} *vr* **:** to be in ecstasy, to be enraptured
éxtasis *nms & pl* **:** ecstasy, rapture
extático, -ta *adj* **:** ecstatic
extemporáneo, -nea *adj* **1 :** unseasonable **2 :** untimely
extender {56} *vt* **1 :** to spread out, to stretch out **2 :** to broaden, to expand <extender la influencia **:** to broaden one's influence> **3 :** to draw up (a document), to write out (a check) — **extenderse** *vr* **1 :** to spread **2 :** to last
extendido, -da *adj* **1 :** outstretched **2 :** widespread
extensamente *adv* **:** extensively, at length
extensible *adj* **:** extensible, extendable
extensión *nf, pl* **-siones 1 :** extension, stretching **2 :** expanse, spread **3 :** extent, range **4 :** length, duration
extenso, -sa *adj* **1 :** extensive, detailed **2 :** spacious, vast
extenuar {3} *vt* **:** to exhaust, to tire out — **extenuarse** *vr* — **extenuante** *adj*
exterior[1] *adj* **1 :** exterior, external **2 :** foreign <asuntos exteriores **:** foreign affairs>
exterior[2] *nm* **1 :** outside **2 :** abroad
exteriorizar {21} *vt* **:** to express, to reveal
exteriormente *adv* **:** outwardly

exterminar *vt* : to exterminate — **exterminación** *nf*
exterminio *nm* : extermination
externar *vt Mex* : to express, to display
externo, -na *adj* : external, outward
extinción *nf, pl* **-ciones** : extinction
extinguidor *nm* : fire extinguisher
extinguir {26} *vt* **1** APAGAR : to extinguish, to put out **2** : to wipe out — **extinguirse** *vr* **1** APAGARSE : to go out, to fade out **2** : to die out, to become extinct
extinto, -ta *adj* : extinct
extintor *nm* : extinguisher
extirpación *n, pl* **-ciones** : removal, excision
extirpar *vt* : to eradicate, to remove, to excise — **extirparse** *vr*
extorsión *nf, pl* **-siones 1** : extortion **2** : harm, trouble
extorsionar *vt* : to extort
extra[1] *adv* : extra
extra[2] *adj* **1** : additional, extra **2** : superior, top-quality
extra[3] *nmf* : extra (in movies)
extra[4] *nm* : extra expense <paga extra : bonus>
extracción *nf, pl* **-ciones** : extraction
extracto *nm* **1** : extract <extracto de vainilla : vanilla extract> **2** : abstract, summary
extradición *nf, pl* **-ciones** : extradition
extraditar *vt* : to extradite
extraer {81} *vt* : to extract
extraído *pp* → **extraer**
extrajudicial *adj* : out-of-court
extramatrimonial *adj* : extramarital
extranjerizante *adj* : foreign-sounding, foreign-looking
extranjero[1], **-ra** *adj* : foreign
extranjero[2], **-ra** *n* : foreigner
extranjero[3] *nm* : foreign countries *pl* <viajó al extranjero : he traveled abroad> <trabajan en el extranjero : they work overseas>
extrañamente *adv* : strangely, oddly
extrañamiento *nm* ASOMBRO : amazement, surprise, wonder
extrañar *vt* : to miss (someone) — **extrañarse** *vr* : to be surprised
extrañeza *nf* **1** : strangeness, oddness **2** : surprise
extraño[1], **-ña** *adj* **1** RARO : strange, odd **2** EXTRANJERO : foreign
extraño[2], **-ña** *n* DESCONOCIDO : stranger
extraoficial *adj* OFICIOSO : unofficial — **extraoficialmente** *adv*
extraordinario, -ria *adj* EXCEPCIONAL : extraordinary — **extraordinariamente** *adv*
extrasensorial *adj* : extrasensory <percepción extrasensorial : extrasensory perception>
extraterrestre *adj & nmf* : extraterrestrial, alien
extravagancia *nf* : extravagance, outlandishness, flamboyance
extravagante *adj* : extravagant, outrageous, flamboyant
extraviar {85} *vt* **1** : to mislead, to lead astray **2** : to misplace, to lose — **extraviarse** *vr* : to get lost, to go astray
extravío *nm* **1** PÉRDIDA : loss, misplacement **2** : misconduct
extremado, -da *adj* : extreme — **extremadamente** *adv*
extremar *vt* : to carry to extremes — **extremarse** *vr* : to do one's utmost
extremidad *nf* **1** : extremity, tip, edge **2 extremidades** *nfpl* : extremities
extremista *adj & nmf* : extremist
extremo[1], **-ma** *adj* **1** : extreme, utmost **2** EXCESIVO : excessive **3 en caso extremo** : as a last resort
extremo[2] *nm* **1** : extreme, end **2 al extremo de** : to the point of **3 en ~** : in the extreme
extrovertido[1] **-da** *adj* : extroverted, outgoing
extrovertido[2], **-da** *n* : extrovert
extrudir *vt* : to extrude
exuberancia *nf* **1** : exuberance **2** : luxuriance, lushness
exuberante *adj* : exuberant, luxuriant — **exuberantemente** *adv*
exudar *vt* : to exude
exultación *nf, pl* **-ciones** : exultation, elation
exultante *adj* : exultant, elated — **exultantemente** *adv*
exultar *vi* : to exult, to rejoice
eyacular *vi* : to ejaculate — **eyaculación** *nf*
eyección *nf, pl* **-ciones** : ejection, expulsion
eyectar *vt* : to eject, to expel — **eyectarse** *vr*

F

f *nf* : sixth letter of the Spanish alphabet
fábrica *nf* FACTORÍA : factory
fabricación *nf, pl* **-ciones** : manufacture
fabricante *nmf* : manufacturer
fabricar {72} *vt* MANUFACTURAR : to manufacture, to make
fabril *adj* INDUSTRIAL : industrial, manufacturing
fábula *nf* **1** : fable **2** : fabrication, fib
fabuloso, -sa *adj* **1** : fabulous, fantastic **2** : mythical, fabled
facción *nf, pl* **facciones 1** : faction **2 facciones** *nfpl* RASGOS : features
faccioso, -sa *adj* : factious
faceta *nf* : facet
facha *nf* : appearance, look <estar hecho una facha : to look a sight>
fachada *nf* : facade

facial *adj* **:** facial

fácil *adj* **1 :** easy **2 :** likely, probable <es fácil que no pase : it probably won't happen>

facilidad *nf* **1 :** facility, ease **2 facilidades** *nfpl* **:** facilities, services **3 facilidades** *nfpl* **:** opportunities

facilitar *vt* **1 :** to facilitate **2 :** to provide, to supply

fácilmente *adv* **:** easily, readily

facsímil *or* **facsímile** *nm* **1 :** facsimile, copy **2 :** fax

facsimilar *adj* **:** facsimile

factibilidad *nf* **:** feasibility

factible *adj* **:** feasible, practicable

facticio, -cia *adj* **:** artificial, factitious

factor[1], -tora *n* **1 :** agent, factor **2 :** baggage clerk

factor[2] *nm* ELEMENTO **:** factor, element

factoría *nf* FÁBRICA **:** factory

factótum *nm* **:** factotum

factura *nf* **1 :** making, manufacturing **2 :** bill, invoice

facturación *nf, pl* **-ciones 1 :** invoicing, billing **2 :** check-in

facturar *vt* **1 :** to bill, to invoice **2 :** to register, to check in

facultad *nf* **1 :** faculty, ability <facultades mentales : mental faculties> **2 :** authority, power **3 :** school (of a university) <facultad de derecho : law school>

facultar *vt* **:** to authorize, to empower

facultativo, -va *adj* **1** OPTATIVO **:** voluntary, optional **2 :** medical <informe facultativo : medical report>

faena *nf* **:** task, job, work <faenas domésticas : housework>

faenar *vi* **1 :** to work, to labor **2** PESCAR **:** to fish

fagot *nm* **:** bassoon

faisán *nm, pl* **faisanes :** pheasant

faja *nf* **1 :** sash, belt **2 :** girdle **3 :** strip (of land)

fajar *vt* **1 :** to wrap (a sash or girdle) around **2 :** to hit, to thrash — **fajarse** *vr* **1 :** to put on a sash or girdle **2 :** to come to blows

fajo *nm* **:** bundle, sheaf <un fajo de billetes : a wad of cash>

falacia *nf* **:** fallacy

falaz, -laza *adj, mpl* **falaces** FALSO **:** fallacious, false

falda *nf* **1 :** skirt <falda escocesa : kilt> **2** REGAZO **:** lap (of the body) **3** VERTIENTE **:** side, slope

falible *adj* **:** fallible

fálico, -ca *adj* **:** phallic

falla *nf* **1 :** flaw, defect **2 :** (geological) fault **3 :** fault, failing

fallar *vi* **1** FRACASAR **:** to fail, to go wrong **2 :** to rule (in a court of law) — *vt* **1** ERRAR **:** to miss (a target) **2 :** to pronounce judgment on

fallecer {53} *vi* MORIR **:** to pass away, to die

fallecido, -da *adj & n* DIFUNTO **:** deceased

fallecimiento *nm* **:** demise, death

fallido, -da *adj* **:** failed, unsuccessful

fallo *nm* **1** SENTENCIA **:** sentence, judgment, verdict **2 :** error, fault

falo *nm* **:** phallus, penis

falsamente *adv* **:** falsely

falsear *vt* **1 :** to falsify, to fake **2 :** to distort — *vi* **1** CEDER **:** to give way **2 :** to be out of tune

falsedad *nf* **1 :** falseness, hypocrisy **2** MENTIRA **:** falsehood, lie

falsete *nm* **:** falsetto

falsificación *nf, pl* **-ciones 1 :** counterfeit, forgery **2 :** falsification

falsificador, -dora *n* **:** counterfeiter, forger

falsificar {72} *vt* **1 :** to counterfeit, to forge **2 :** to falsify

falso, -sa *adj* **1** FALAZ **:** false, untrue **2 :** counterfeit, forged

falta *nf* **1** CARENCIA **:** lack <hacer falta : to be lacking, to be needed> **2** DEFECTO **:** defect, fault, error **3 :** offense, misdemeanor **4 :** foul (in basketball), fault (in tennis)

faltar *vi* **1 :** to be lacking, to be needed <me falta ayuda : I need help> **2 :** to be absent, to be missing **3** QUEDAR **:** to remain, to be left <faltan pocos días para la fiesta : the party is just a few days away> **4 ¡no faltaba más! :** don't mention it!, you're welcome!

falto, -ta *adj* **~ de :** lacking (in), short of

fama *nf* **1 :** fame **2** REPUTACIÓN **:** reputation **3 de mala fama :** disreputable

famélico, -ca *adj* HAMBRIENTO **:** starving, famished

familia *nf* **1 :** family **2 familia política :** in-laws

familiar[1] *adj* **1** CONOCIDO **:** familiar **2 :** familial, family **3** INFORMAL **:** informal

familiar[2] *nmf* PARIENTE **:** relation, relative

familiaridad *nf* **1 :** familiarity **2 :** informality

familiarizarse {21} *vr* **~ con :** to familiarize oneself with

famoso[1], -sa *adj* CÉLEBRE **:** famous

famoso[2], -sa *n* **:** celebrity

fanal *nm* **1 :** beacon, signal light **2** *Mex* **:** headlight

fanático, -ca *adj & n* **:** fanatic

fanatismo *nm* **:** fanaticism

fandango *nm* **:** fandango

fanfarria *nf* **1 :** (musical) fanfare **2 :** pomp, ceremony

fanfarrón[1], -rrona *adj, mpl* **-rrones** *fam* **:** bragging, boastful

fanfarrón[2], -rrona *n, mpl* **-rrones** *fam* **:** braggart

fanfarronada *nf* **:** boast, bluster

fanfarronear *vi* **:** to brag, to boast

fango *nm* LODO **:** mud, mire

fangosidad *nf* **:** muddiness

fangoso, -sa *adj* LODOSO **:** muddy

fantasear *vi* **:** to fantasize, to daydream

fantasía *nf* **1 :** fantasy **2 :** imagination

fantasma *nm* : ghost, phantom
fantasmal *adj* : ghostly
fantástico, -ca *adj* **1** : fantastic, imaginary, unreal **2** *fam* : great, fantastic
faquir *nm* : fakir
farándula *nf* : show business, theater
faraón *nm, pl* **faraones** : pharaoh
fardo *nm* **1** : bale **2** : bundle
farfulla *nf* : jabbering
farfullar *v* : to jabber, to gabble
faringe *nf* : pharynx
faríngeo, -gea *adj* : pharyngeal
fariña *nf* : coarse manioc flour
farmacéutico[1], **-ca** *adj* : pharmaceutical
farmacéutico[2], **-ca** *n* : pharmacist
farmacia *nf* : drugstore, pharmacy
fármaco *nm* : medicine, drug
farmacodependencia *nf* : drug addiction
farmacología *nf* : pharmacology
faro *nm* **1** : lighthouse **2** : headlight
farol *nm* **1** : streetlight **2** : lantern, lamp **3** *fam* : bluff **4** *Mex* : headlight
farola *nf* **1** : lamppost **2** : streetlight
farolero, -ra *n fam* : bluffer
farra *nf* : spree, revelry
fárrago *nm* REVOLTIJO : hodgepodge, jumble
farsa *nf* **1** : farce **2** : fake, sham
farsante *nmf* CHARLATÁN : charlatan, fraud, phony
fascículo *nm* : fascicle, part (of a publication)
fascinación *nf, pl* **-ciones** : fascination
fascinante *adj* : fascinating
fascinar *vt* **1** : to fascinate **2** : to charm, to captivate
fascismo *nm* : fascism
fascista *adj & nmf* : fascist
fase *nf* : phase, stage
fastidiar *vt* **1** MOLESTAR : to annoy, to bother, to hassle **2** ABURRIR : to bore — *vi* : to be annoying or bothersome
fastidio *nm* **1** MOLESTIA : annoyance, nuisance, hassle **2** ABURRIMIENTO : boredom
fastidioso, -sa *adj* **1** MOLESTO : annoying, bothersome **2** ABURRIDO : boring
fatal *adj* **1** MORTAL : fatal **2** *fam* : awful, terrible **3** : fateful, unavoidable
fatalidad *nf* **1** : fatality **2** DESGRACIA : misfortune, bad luck
fatalismo *nm* : fatalism
fatalista[1] *adj* : fatalistic
fatalista[2] *nmf* : fatalist
fatalmente *adv* **1** : unavoidably **2** : unfortunately
fatídico, -ca *adj* : fateful, momentous
fatiga *nf* CANSANCIO : fatigue
fatigado, -da *adj* AGOTADO : weary, tired
fatigar {52} *vt* CANSAR : to fatigue, to tire — **fatigarse** *vr* : to wear oneself out
fatigoso, -sa *adj* : fatiguing, tiring
fatuidad *nf* **1** : fatuousness **2** VANIDAD : vanity, conceit
fatuo, -tua *adj* **1** : fatuous **2** PRESUMIDO : vain
fauces *nfpl* : jaws *pl,* maw
faul *nm, pl* **fauls** : foul, foul ball
fauna *nf* : fauna
fausto *nm* : splendor, magnificence
favor *nm* **1** : favor **2 a favor de** : in favor of **3 por ~** : please
favorable *adj* : favorable — **favorablemente** *adv*
favorecedor, -dora *adj* : becoming, flattering
favorecer {53} *vt* **1** : to favor **2** : to look well on, to suit
favorecido, -da *adj* **1** : flattering **2** : fortunate
favoritismo *nm* : favoritism
favorito, -ta *adj & n* : favorite
fax *nm* : fax, facsimile
fayuca *nf Mex* **1** : contraband **2** : black market
fayuquero *nm Mex* : smuggler, black marketeer
faz *nf* **1** : face, countenance <la faz de la tierra : the face of the earth> **2** : side (of coins, fabric, etc.)
fe *nf* **1** : faith **2** : assurance, testimony <dar fe de : to bear witness to> **3** : intention, will <de buena fe : bona fide, in good faith>
fealdad *nf* : ugliness
febrero *nm* : February
febril *adj* : feverish — **febrilmente** *adv*
fecal *adj* : fecal
fecha *nf* **1** : date **2 fecha de caducidad** *or* **fecha de vencimiento** : expiration date **3 fecha límite** : deadline
fechar *vt* : to date, to put a date on
fechoría *nf* : misdeed
fécula *nf* : starch
fecundar *vt* : to fertilize (an egg) — **fecundación** *nf*
fecundidad *nf* **1** : fecundity, fertility **2** : productiveness
fecundo, -da *adj* FÉRTIL : fertile, fecund
federación *nf, pl* **-ciones** : federation
federal *adj* : federal
federalismo *nm* : federalism
federalista *adj & nmf* : federalist
federar *vt* : to federate
fehaciente *adj* : reliable, irrefutable — **fehacientemente** *adv*
feldespato *nm* : feldspar
felicidad *nf* **1** : happiness **2 ¡felicidades!** : best wishes!, congratulations!, happy birthday!
felicitación *nf, pl* **-ciones** **1** : congratulation <¡felicitaciones! : congratulations!> **2** : greeting card
felicitar *vt* CONGRATULAR : to congratulate — **felicitarse** *vr* : to be glad about
feligrés, -gresa *n, mpl* **-greses** : parishioner
feligresía *nf* : parish
felino, -na *adj & n* : feline
feliz *adj, pl* **felices** **1** : happy **2 Feliz Navidad** : Merry Christmas

felizmente *adv* **1** : happily **2** : fortunately, luckily
felonía *nf* : felony
felpa *nf* **1** : terry cloth **2** : plush
felpudo *nm* : doormat
femenil *adj* : women's, girls' <futbol femenil : women's soccer>
femenino, -na *adj* **1** : feminine **2** : women's <derechos femeninos : women's rights> **3** : female
femineidad *nf* : femininity
feminidad *nf* : femininity
feminismo *nm* : feminism
feminista *adj & nmf* : feminist
femoral *adj* : femoral
fémur *nm* : femur, thighbone
fenecer {53} *vi* **1** : to die, to pass away **2** : to come to an end, to cease
fénix *nm* : phoenix
fenomenal *adj* **1** : phenomenal **2** *fam* : fantastic, terrific — **fenomenalmente** *adv*
fenómeno *nm* **1** : phenomenon **2** : prodigy, genius
feo[1] *adv* : badly, bad
feo[2], **fea** *adj* **1** : ugly **2** : unpleasant, nasty
féretro *nm* ATAÚD : coffin, casket
feria *nf* **1** : fair, market **2** : festival, holiday **3** *Mex* : change (money)
feriado, -da *adj* **día feriado** : public holiday
ferial *nm* : fairground
fermentar *v* : to ferment — **fermentación** *nf*
fermento *nm* : ferment
ferocidad *nf* : ferocity, fierceness
feroz *adj, pl* **feroces** FIERO : ferocious, fierce — **ferozmente** *adv*
férreo, -rrea *adj* **1** : iron **2** : strong, steely <una voluntad férrea : an iron will> **3** : strict, severe **4** **vía férrea** : railroad track
ferretería *nf* **1** : hardware store **2** : hardware **3** : foundry, ironworks
férrico, -ca *adj* : ferric
ferrocarril *nm* : railroad, railway
ferrocarrilero → **ferroviario**
ferroso, -sa *adj* : ferrous
ferroviario, -ria *adj* : rail, railroad
ferry *nm, pl* **ferrys** : ferry
fértil *adj* FECUNDO : fertile, fruitful
fertilidad *nf* : fertility
fertilizante[1] *adj* : fertilizing <droga fertilizante : fertility drug>
fertilizante[2] *nm* ABONO : fertilizer
fertilizar *vt* ABONAR : to fertilize — **fertilización** *nf*
ferviente *adj* FERVOROSO : fervent
fervor *nm* : fervor, zeal
fervoroso, -sa *adj* FERVIENTE : fervent, zealous
festejar *vt* **1** CELEBRAR : to celebrate **2** AGASAJAR : to entertain, to wine and dine **3** *Mex fam* : to thrash, to beat
festejo *nm* : celebration, festivity
festín *nm, pl* **festines** : banquet, feast
festinar *vt* : to hasten, to hurry up
festival *nm* : festival
festividad *nf* **1** : festivity **2** : (religious) feast, holiday
festivo, -va *adj* **1** : festive **2** **día festivo** : holiday — **festivamente** *adv*
fetal *adj* : fetal
fetiche *nm* : fetish
fétido, -da *adj* : fetid, foul
feto *nm* : fetus
feudal *adj* : feudal — **feudalismo** *nm*
feudo *nm* **1** : fief **2** : domain, territory
fiabilidad *nf* : reliability, trustworthiness
fiable *adj* : trustworthy, reliable
fiado, -da *adj* : on credit
fiador, -dora *n* : bondsman, guarantor
fiambrería *nf* : delicatessen
fiambres *nfpl* : cold cuts
fianza *nf* **1** CAUCIÓN : bail, bond **2** : surety, deposit
fiar {85} *vt* **1** : to sell on credit **2** : to guarantee — **fiarse** *vr* **~ de** : to place trust in
fiasco *nm* FRACASO : fiasco, failure
fibra *nf* **1** : fiber **2** **fibra de vidrio** : fiberglass
fibrilar *vi* : to fibrillate — **fibrilación** *nf*
fibroso, -sa *adj* : fibrous
ficción *nf, pl* **ficciones** **1** : fiction **2** : fabrication, lie
ficha *nf* **1** : index card **2** : file, record **3** : token **4** : domino, checker, counter, poker chip
fichar *vt* **1** : to open a file on **2** : to sign up — *vi* : to punch in, to punch out
fichero *nm* **1** : card file **2** : filing cabinet
ficticio, -cia *adj* : fictitious
fidedigno, -na *adj* FIABLE : reliable, trustworthy
fideicomisario, -ria *n* : trustee
fideicomiso *nm* : trusteeship, trust <guardar en fideicomiso : to hold in trust>
fidelidad *nf* : fidelity, faithfulness
fideo *nm* : noodle
fiduciario[1], **-ria** *adj* : fiduciary
fiduciario[2], **-ria** *n* : trustee
fiebre *nf* **1** CALENTURA : fever, temperature <fiebre amarilla : yellow fever> <fiebre palúdica : malaria> **2** : fever, excitement
fiel[1] *adj* **1** : faithful, loyal **2** : accurate — **fielmente** *adv*
fiel[2] *nm* **1** : pointer (of a scale) **2** **los fieles** : the faithful
fieltro *nm* : felt
fiera *nf* **1** : wild animal, beast **2** : fiend, demon <una fiera para el trabajo : a demon for work>
fiero, -ra *adj* FEROZ : fierce, ferocious
fierro *nm* HIERRO : iron
fiesta *nf* **1** : party, fiesta **2** : holiday, feast day
figura *nf* **1** : figure **2** : shape, form **3** **figura retórica** : figure of speech
figurado, -da *adj* : figurative — **figuradamente** *adv*

figurar *vi* **1 :** to figure, to be included <Rivera figura entre los más grandes pintores de México : Rivera is among Mexico's greatest painters> **2 :** to be prominent, to stand out — *vt* **:** to represent <esta línea figura el horizonte : this line represents the horizon> — **figurarse** *vr* **:** to imagine, to think <¡figúrate el lío en que se metió! : imagine the mess she got into!>

fijación *nf, pl* **-ciones 1 :** fixation, obsession **2 :** fixing, establishing **3 :** fastening, securing

fijador *nm* **1 :** fixative **2 :** hair spray

fijamente *adv* **:** fixedly

fijar *vt* **1 :** to fasten, to affix **2** ESTABLECER **:** to establish, to set up **3** CONCRETAR **:** to set, to fix <fijar la fecha : to set the date> — **fijarse** *vr* **1 :** to settle, to become fixed **2 ~ en :** to notice, to pay attention to

fijeza *nf* **1 :** firmness (of convictions) **2 :** persistence, constancy <mirar con fijeza a : to stare at>

fijiano, -na *adj & n* **:** Fijian

fijo, -ja *adj* **1 :** fixed, firm, steady **2** PERMANENTE **:** permanent

fila *nf* **1** HILERA **:** line, file <ponerse en fila : to get in line> **2 :** rank, row **3 filas** *nfpl* **:** ranks <cerrar filas : to close ranks>

filamento *nm* **:** filament

filantropía *nf* **:** philanthropy

filantrópico, -ca *adj* **:** philanthropic

filántropo, -pa *n* **:** philanthropist

filatelia *nf* **:** philately, stamp collecting

filatelista *nmf* **:** stamp collector, philatelist

filete *nm* **1 :** fillet **2** SOLOMILLO **:** sirloin **3 :** thread (of a screw)

filiación *nf, pl* **-ciones 1 :** affiliation, connection **2 :** particulars *pl,* (police) description

filial[1] *adj* **:** filial

filial[2] *nf* **:** affiliate, subsidiary

filibustero *nm* **:** freebooter, pirate

filigrana *nf* **1 :** filigree **2 :** watermark (on paper)

filipino, -na *adj & n* **:** Filipino

filmación *nf, pl* **-ciones :** filming, shooting

filmar *vt* **:** to film, to shoot

filme *or* **film** *nm* PELÍCULA **:** film, movie

filmina *nf* **:** slide, transparency

filo *nm* **1 :** cutting edge, blade **2 :** edge <al filo del escritorio : at the edge of the desk> <al filo de la medianoche : at the stroke of midnight>

filología *nf* **:** philology

filólogo, -ga *n* **:** philologist

filón *nm, pl* **filones 1 :** seam, vein (of minerals) **2** *fam* **:** successful business, gold mine

filoso, -sa *adj* **:** sharp

filosofar *vi* **:** to philosophize

filosofía *nf* **:** philosophy

filosófico, -ca *adj* **:** philosophic, philosophical — **filosóficamente** *adv*

filósofo, -fa *n* **:** philosopher

filtración *nf* **:** seepage, leaking

filtrar *v* **:** to filter — **filtrarse** *vr* **:** to seep through, to leak

filtro *nm* **:** filter

filudo, -da *adj* **:** sharp

fin *nm* **1 :** end **2 :** purpose, aim, objective **3 en ~ :** in short **4 fin de semana :** weekend **5 por ~ :** finally, at last

finado, -da *adj & n* DIFUNTO **:** deceased

final[1] *adj* **:** final, ultimate — **finalmente** *adv*

final[2] *nm* **1 :** end, conclusion, finale **2 finales** *nmpl* **:** play-offs

finalidad *nf* **1 :** purpose, aim **2 :** finality

finalista *nmf* **:** finalist

finalización *nf* **:** completion, end

finalizar {21} *v* **:** to finish, to end

financiación *nf, pl* **-ciones :** financing, funding

financiamiento *nm* → **financiación**

financiar *vt* **:** to finance, to fund

financiero[1], **-ra** *adj* **:** financial

financiero[2], **-ra** *n* **:** financier

financista *nmf* **:** financier

finanzas *nfpl* **:** finances, finance <altas finanzas : high finance>

finca *nf* **1 :** farm, ranch **2 :** country house

fineza *nf* FINURA, REFINAMIENTO **:** refinement

fingido, -da *adj* **:** false, feigned

fingimiento *nm* **:** pretense

fingir {35} *v* **:** to feign, to pretend

finiquitar *vt* **1 :** to settle (an account) **2 :** to conclude, to bring to an end

finiquito *nm* **:** settlement (of an account)

finito, -ta *adj* **:** finite

finja, etc. → **fingir**

finlandés, -desa *adj & n* **:** Finnish

fino, -na *adj* **1 :** fine, excellent **2 :** delicate, slender **3** REFINADO **:** refined **4 :** sharp, acute <olfato fino : keen sense of smell> **5 :** subtle

finta *nf* **:** feint

fintar *or* **fintear** *vi* **:** to feint

finura *nf* **1 :** fineness, high quality **2** FINEZA, REFINAMIENTO **:** refinement

fiordo *nm* **:** fjord

fique *nm* **:** sisal

firma *nf* **1 :** signature **2 :** signing **3** EMPRESA **:** firm, company

firmamento *nm* **:** firmament, sky

firmante *nmf* **:** signer, signatory

firmar *v* **:** to sign

firme *adj* **1 :** firm, resolute **2 :** steady, stable

firmemente *adv* **:** firmly

firmeza *nf* **1 :** firmness, stability **2 :** strength, resolve

firuletes *nmpl* **:** frills, adornments

fiscal[1] *adj* **:** fiscal — **fiscalmente** *adv*

fiscal[2] *nmf* **:** district attorney, prosecutor

fiscalizar {21} *vt* **1 :** to audit, to inspect **2 :** to oversee **3 :** to criticize

fisco *nm* **:** national treasury, exchequer

fisgar {52} *vt* HUSMEAR **:** to pry into, to snoop on
fisgón, -gona *n, mpl* **fisgones :** snoop, busybody
fisgonear *vi* **:** to snoop, to pry
fisgue, etc. → **fisgar**
física *nf* **:** physics
físico[1], -ca *adj* **:** physical — **físicamente** *adv*
físico[2], -ca *n* **:** physicist
físico[3] *nm* **:** physique, figure
fisiología *nf* **:** physiology
fisiológico, -ca *adj* **:** physiological, physiologic
fisiólogo, -ga *n* **:** physiologist
fisión *nf, pl* **fisiones :** fission — **fisionable** *adj*
fisionomía *nf* → **fisonomía**
fisioterapeuta *nmf* **:** physical therapist
fisioterapia *nf* **:** physical therapy
fisonomía *nf* **:** physiognomy, features *pl*
fistol *nm Mex* **:** tie clip
fisura *nf* **:** fissure, crevasse
fláccido, -da *or* **flácido, -da** *adj* **:** flaccid, flabby
flaco, -ca *adj* **1** DELGADO **:** thin, skinny **2 :** feeble, weak <una excusa flaca : a feeble excuse>
flagelar *vt* **:** to flagellate — **flagelación** *nf*
flagelo *nm* **1 :** scourge, whip **2 :** calamity
flagrante *adj* **:** flagrant, glaring, blatant — **flagrantemente** *adv*
flama *nf* LLAMA **:** flame
flamante *adj* **1 :** bright, brilliant **2 :** brand-new
flamear *vi* **1** LLAMEAR **:** to flame, to blaze **2** ONDEAR **:** to flap, to flutter
flamenco[1], -ca *adj* **1 :** flamenco **2 :** Flemish
flamenco[2], -ca *n* **:** Fleming, Flemish person
flamenco[3] *nm* **1 :** Flemish (language) **2 :** flamingo **3 :** flamenco (music or dance)
flanco *nm* **:** flank, side
flanquear *vt* **:** to flank
flaquear *vi* DECAER **:** to flag, to weaken
flaqueza *nf* **1** DEBILIDAD **:** frailty, feebleness **2 :** thinness **3 :** weakness, failing
flato *nm* **:** gloom, melancholy
flatulento, -ta *adj* **:** flatulent — **flatulencia** *nf*
flauta *nf* **1 :** flute **2 flauta dulce :** recorder
flautín *nm, pl* **flautines :** piccolo
flautista *nmf* **:** flute player, flutist
flebitis *nf* **:** phlebitis
flecha *nf* **:** arrow
fleco *nm* **1 :** bangs *pl* **2 :** fringe
flema *nf* **:** phlegm
flemático, -ca *adj* **:** phlegmatic, stolid, impassive
flequillo *nm* **:** bangs *pl*
fletar *vt* **1 :** to charter, to hire **2 :** to load (freight)
flete *nm* **1 :** charter fee **2 :** shipping cost **3 :** freight, cargo
fletero *nm* **:** shipper, carrier
flexibilidad *nf* **:** flexibility
flexibilizar {21} *vt* **:** to make more flexible
flexible[1] *adj* **:** flexible
flexible[2] *nm* **1 :** flexible electrical cord **2 :** soft hat
flirtear *vi* **:** to flirt
flojear *vi* **1** DEBILITARSE **:** to weaken, to flag **2 :** to idle, to loaf around
flojedad *nf* **:** weakness
flojera *nf fam* **1 :** lethargy, feeling of weakness **2 :** laziness
flojo, -ja *adj* **1** SUELTO **:** loose, slack **2 :** weak, poor <está flojo en las ciencias : he's weak in science> **3** PEREZOSO **:** lazy
flor *nf* **1 :** flower **2 flor de Pascua :** poinsettia
flora *nf* **:** flora
floración *nf* **:** flowering <en plena floración : in full bloom>
floral *adj* **:** floral
floreado, -da *adj* **:** flowered, flowery
florear *vi* FLORECER **:** to flower, to bloom — *vt* **1 :** to adorn with flowers **2** *Mex* **:** to flatter, to compliment
florecer {53} *vi* **1 :** to bloom, to blossom **2 :** to flourish, to thrive
floreciente *adj* **1 :** flowering **2** PROSPERO **:** flourishing, thriving
florecimiento *nm* **:** flowering
floreo *nm* **:** flourish
florería *nf* **:** flower shop, florist's
florero[1], -ra *n* **:** florist
florero[2] *nm* JARRÓN **:** vase
floresta *nf* **1 :** glade, grove **2** BOSQUE **:** woods
florido, -da *adj* **1 :** full of flowers **2 :** florid, flowery <escritos floridos : flowery prose>
florista *nmf* **:** florist
floritura *nf* **:** frill, embellishment
flota *nf* **:** fleet
flotabilidad *nf* **:** buoyancy
flotación *nf, pl* **-ciones :** flotation
flotador *nm* **1 :** float **2 :** life preserver
flotante *adj* **:** floating, buoyant
flotar *vi* **:** to float
flote *nm* **a ~ :** afloat
flotilla *nf* **:** flotilla, fleet
fluctuar {3} *vi* **1 :** to fluctuate **2** VACILAR **:** to vacillate — **fluctuación** *nf* — **fluctuante** *adj*
fluidez *nf* **1 :** fluency **2 :** fluidity
fluido[1], -da *adj* **1 :** flowing **2 :** fluent **3 :** fluid
fluido[2] *nm* **:** fluid
fluir {41} *vi* **:** to flow
flujo *nm* **1 :** flow **2 :** discharge
flúor *nm* **:** fluorine
fluoración *nf, pl* **-ciones :** fluoridation
fluorescencia *nf* **:** fluorescence — **fluorescente** *adj*
fluorizar {21} *vt* **:** to fluoridate
fluoruro *nm* **:** fluoride
fluvial *adj* **:** fluvial, river

fluye, etc. → **fluir**
fobia *nf* : phobia
foca *nf* : seal (animal)
focal *adj* : focal
focha *nf* : coot
foco *nm* **1** : focus **2** : center, pocket **3** : lightbulb **4** : spotlight **5** : headlight
fofo, -fa *adj* **1** ESPONJOSO : soft, spongy **2** : flabby
fogaje *nm* **1** FUEGO : skin eruption, cold sore **2** BOCHORNO : hot and humid weather
fogata *nf* : bonfire
fogón *nm, pl* **fogones** : bonfire
fogonazo *nm* : flash, explosion
fogonero, -ra *n* : stoker (of a furnace), fireman
fogoso, -sa *adj* ARDIENTE : ardent
foguear *vt* : to inure, to accustom
foja *nf* : sheet (of paper)
folículo *nm* : follicle
folio *nm* : folio, leaf
folklore *nm* : folklore
folklórico, -ca *adj* : folk, traditional
follaje *nm* : foliage
folleto *nm* : pamphlet, leaflet, circular
fomentar *vt* **1** : to foment, to stir up **2** PROMOVER : to promote, to foster
fomento *nm* : promotion, encouragement
fonda *nf* **1** POSADA : inn **2** : small restaurant
fondeado, -da *adj fam* : rich, in the money
fondear *vt* **1** : to sound **2** : to sound out, to examine **3** *Mex* : to fund, to finance — *vi* ANCLAR : to anchor — **fondearse** *vr fam* : to get rich
fondeo *nm* **1** : anchoring **2** *Mex* : funding, financing
fondillos *mpl* : seat, bottom (of clothing)
fondo *nm* **1** : bottom **2** : rear, back, end **3** : depth **4** : background **5** : sea bed **6** : fund <fondo de inversiones : investment fund> **7** *Mex* : slip, petticoat **8 fondos** *nmpl* : funds, resources <cheque sin fondos : bounced check> **9 a ~** : thoroughly, in depth **10 en ~** : abreast
fonema *nm* : phoneme
fonética *nf* : phonetics
fonético, -ca *adj* : phonetic
fontanería *nf* PLOMERÍA : plumbing
fontanero, -ra *n* PLOMERO : plumber
footing [ˈfuˌtɪŋ] *nm* : jogging <hacer footing : to jog>
foque *nm* : jib
forajido, -da *n* : bandit, fugitive, outlaw
foráneo, -nea *adj* : foreign, strange
forastero, -ra *n* : stranger, outsider
forcejear *vi* : to struggle
forcejeo *nm* : struggle
fórceps *nms & pl* : forceps *pl*
forense *adj* : forensic, legal
forestal *adj* : forest
forja *nf* FRAGUA : forge
forjar *vt* **1** : to forge **2** : to shape, to create <forjar un compromiso : to hammer out a compromise> **3** : to invent, to concoct
forma *nf* **1** : form, shape **2** MANERA, MODO : manner, way **3** : fitness <estar en forma : to be fit, to be in shape> **4 formas** *nfpl* : appearances, conventions
formación *nf, pl* **-ciones 1** : formation **2** : training <formación profesional : vocational training>
formal *adj* **1** : formal **2** : serious, dignified **3** : dependable, reliable
formaldehído *nm* : formaldehyde
formalidad *nf* **1** : formality **2** : seriousness, dignity **3** : dependability, reliability
formalizar {21} *vt* : to formalize, to make official
formalmente *adv* : formally
formar *vt* **1** : to form, to make **2** CONSTITUIR : to constitute, to make up **3** : to train, to educate — **formarse** *vr* **1** DESARROLLARSE : to develop, to take shape **2** EDUCARSE : to be educated
formatear *vt* : to format
formativo, -va *adj* : formative
formato *nm* : format
formidable *adj* **1** : formidable, tremendous **2** *fam* : fantastic, terrific
formón *nm, pl* **formones** : chisel
fórmula *nf* : formula
formulación *nf, pl* **-ciones** : formulation
formular *vt* **1** : to formulate, to draw up **2** : to make, to lodge (a protest or complaint)
formulario *nm* : form <rellenar un formulario : to fill out a form>
fornicar {72} *vi* : to fornicate — **fornicación** *nf*
fornido, -da *adj* : well-built, burly, hefty
foro *nm* **1** : forum **2** : public assembly, open discussion
forraje *nm* **1** : forage, fodder **2** : foraging **3** *fam* : hodgepodge
forrajear *vi* : to forage
forrar *vt* **1** : to line (a garment) **2** : to cover (a book)
forro *nm* **1** : lining **2** CUBIERTA : book cover
forsitia *nf* : forsythia
fortachón, -chona *adj, pl* **-chones** *fam* : brawny, strong, tough
fortalecer {53} *vt* : to strengthen, to fortify — **fortalecerse** *vr*
fortalecimiento *nm* **1** : strengthening, fortifying **2** : fortifications
fortaleza *nf* **1** : fortress **2** FUERZA : strength **3** : resolution, fortitude
fortificación *nf, pl* **-ciones** : fortification
fortificar {72} *vt* **1** : to fortify **2** : to strengthen
fortín *nm, pl* **fortines** : small fort
fortuito, -ta *adj* : fortuitous

fortuna *nf* **1** SUERTE **:** fortune, luck **2** RIQUEZA **:** wealth, fortune
forzar {36} *vt* **1** OBLIGAR **:** to force, to compel **2 :** to force open **3 :** to strain <forzar los ojos : to strain one's eyes>
forzosamente *adv* **1 :** forcibly, by force **2 :** necessarily, inevitably <forzosamente tendrán que pagar : they'll have no choice but to pay>
forzoso, -sa *adj* **1 :** forced, compulsory **2 :** necessary, inevitable
fosa *nf* **1 :** ditch, pit <fosa séptica : septic tank> **2** TUMBA **:** grave **3 :** cavity <fosas nasales : nasal cavities, nostrils>
fosfato *nm* **:** phosphate
fosforescencia *nf* **:** phosphorescence — **fosforescente** *adj*
fósforo *nm* **1** CERILLA **:** match **2 :** phosphorus
fósil[1] *adj* **:** fossilized, fossil
fósil[2] *nm* **:** fossil
fosilizarse {21} *vr* **:** to fossilize, to become fossilized
foso *nm* **1** FOSA, ZANJA **:** ditch **2 :** pit (of a theater) **3 :** moat
foto *nf* **:** photo, picture
fotocopia *nf* **:** photocopy — **fotocopiar** *vt*
fotocopiadora *nf* COPIADORA **:** photocopier
fotoeléctrico, -ca *adj* **:** photoelectric
fotogénico, -ca *adj* **:** photogenic
fotografía *nf* **1 :** photograph **2 :** photography
fotografiar {85} *vt* **:** to photograph
fotográfico, -ca *adj* **:** photographic — **fotográficamente** *adv*
fotógrafo, -fa *n* **:** photographer
fotosíntesis *nf* **:** photosynthesis
fotosintético, -ca *adj* **:** photosynthetic
fracasado[1]**, -da** *adj* **:** unsuccessful, failed
fracasado[2]**, -da** *n* **:** failure
fracasar *vi* **1** FALLAR **:** to fail **2 :** to fall through
fracaso *nm* FIASCO **:** failure
fracción *nf, pl* **fracciones 1 :** fraction **2 :** part, fragment **3 :** faction, splinter group
fraccionamiento *nm* **1 :** division, breaking up **2** *Mex* **:** residential area, housing development
fraccionar *vt* **:** to divide, to break up
fractura *nf* **1 :** fracture **2 fractura complicada :** compound fracture
fracturarse *vr* QUEBRARSE, ROMPERSE **:** to fracture, to break <fracturarse el brazo : to break one's arm>
fragancia *nf* **:** fragrance, scent
fragante *adj* **:** fragrant
fragata *nf* **:** frigate
frágil *adj* **1 :** fragile **2 :** frail, delicate
fragilidad *nf* **1 :** fragility **2 :** frailty, delicacy
fragmentar *vt* **:** to fragment — **fragmentación** *nf*
fragmentario, -ria *adj* **:** fragmentary, sketchy
fragmento *nm* **1 :** fragment, shard **2 :** bit, snippet **3 :** excerpt, passage
fragor *nm* **:** clamor, din, roar
fragoroso, -sa *adj* **:** thunderous, deafening
fragoso, -sa *adj* **1 :** rough, uneven **2 :** thick, dense
fragua *nf* FORJA **:** forge
fraguar {10} *vt* **1 :** to forge **2 :** to conceive, to concoct, to hatch — *vi* **:** to set, to solidify
fraile *nm* **:** friar, monk
frambuesa *nf* **:** raspberry
francamente *adv* **1 :** frankly, candidly **2** REALMENTE **:** really <es francamente admirable : it's really impressive>
francés[1]**, -cesa** *adj, mpl* **franceses :** French
francés[2]**, -cesa** *n, mpl* **franceses :** French person, Frenchman *m,* Frenchwoman *f*
francés[3] *nm* **:** French (language)
franciscano, -na *adj & n* **:** Franciscan
francmasón, -sona *n, mpl* **-sones :** Freemason — **francmasonería** *nf*
franco[1]**, -ca** *adj* **1** CÁNDIDO **:** frank, candid **2** PATENTE **:** clear, obvious **3 :** free <franco a bordo : free on board>
franco[2] *nm* **:** franc
francotirador, -dora *n* **:** sniper
franela *nf* **:** flannel
franja *nf* **1 :** stripe, band **2 :** border, fringe
franquear *vt* **1 :** to clear **2** ATRAVESAR **:** to cross, to go through **3 :** to pay the postage on
franqueo *nm* **:** postage
franqueza *nf* **:** frankness
franquicia *nf* **1** EXENCIÓN **:** exemption **2 :** franchise
frasco *nm* **:** small bottle, flask, vial
frase *nf* **1 :** phrase **2** ORACIÓN **:** sentence
frasear *vt* **:** to phrase
fraternal *adj* **:** fraternal, brotherly
fraternidad *nf* **1 :** brotherhood **2 :** fraternity
fraternizar {21} *vi* **:** to fraternize — **fraternización** *nf*
fraterno, -na *adj* **:** fraternal, brotherly
fratricida *adj* **:** fratricidal
fratricidio *nm* **:** fratricide
fraude *nm* **:** fraud
fraudulento, -ta *adj* **:** fraudulent — **fraudulentamente** *adv*
fray *nm* **:** brother (title of a friar) <Fray Bartolomé : Brother Bartholomew>
frazada *nf* COBIJA, MANTA **:** blanket
frecuencia *nf* **:** frequency
frecuentar *vt* **:** to frequent, to haunt
frecuente *adj* **:** frequent — **frecuentemente** *adv*
fregadera *nf fam* **:** hassle, pain in the neck
fregadero *nm* **:** kitchen sink
fregado[1]**, -da** *adj fam* **:** annoying, bothersome
fregado[2] *nm* **1 :** scrubbing, scouring **2** *fam* **:** mess, muddle

fregar {49} *vt* **1 :** to scrub, to scour, to wash <fregar los trastes : to do the dishes> <fregar el suelo : to scrub the floor> **2** *fam* **:** to annoy — *vi* **1 :** to wash the dishes **2 :** to clean, to scrub **3** *fam* **:** to be annoying

freidera *nf Mex* **:** frying pan

freír {37} *vt* **:** to fry — **freírse** *vr*

frenar *vt* **1 :** to brake **2** DETENER **:** to curb, to check — *vi* **:** to apply the brakes — **frenarse** *vr* **:** to restrain oneself

frenesí *nm* **:** frenzy

frenético, -ca *adj* **:** frantic, frenzied — **frenéticamente** *adv*

freno *nm* **1 :** brake **2 :** bit (of a bridle) **3 :** check, restraint **4 frenos** *nmpl Mex* **:** braces (for teeth)

frente[1] *nm* **1 :** front <al frente de : at the head of> <en frente : in front, opposite> **2 :** facade **3 :** front line, sphere of activity **4 :** front (in meteorology) <frente frío : cold front> **5 hacer frente a :** to face up to, to brave

frente[2] *nf* **1 :** forehead, brow **2 frente a frente :** face to face

fresa *nf* **1 :** strawberry **2 :** drill (in dentistry)

fresco[1], **-ca** *adj* **1 :** fresh **2 :** cool **3** *fam* **:** insolent, nervy

fresco[2] *nm* **1 :** coolness **2 :** fresh air <al fresco : in the open air, outdoors> **3 :** fresco

frescor *nm* **:** cool air <el frescor de la noche : the cool of the evening>

frescura *nf* **1 :** freshness **2 :** coolness **3 :** calmness **4** DESCARO **:** nerve, audacity

fresno *nm* **:** ash (tree)

freza *nf* **:** spawn, roe

frezar {21} *vi* DESOVAR **:** to spawn

friable *adj* **:** friable

frialdad *nf* **1 :** coldness **2** INDIFERENCIA **:** indifference, unconcern

fríamente *adv* **:** coldly, indifferently

fricasé *nm* **:** fricassee

fricción *nf, pl* **fricciones 1 :** friction **2 :** rubbing, massage **3 :** discord, disagreement <fricción entre los hermanos : friction between the brothers>

friccionar *vt* **1** FROTAR **:** to rub **2 :** to massage

friega[1], **friegue, etc.** → **fregar**

friega[2] *nf* **1** FRICCIÓN **:** rubdown, massage **2 :** annoyance, bother

frigidez *nf* **:** (sexual) frigidity

frigorífico *nm Spain* **:** refrigerator

frijol *nm* **:** bean <frijoles refritos : refried beans>

frío[1], **fría** *adj* **1 :** cold **2** INDIFERENTE **:** cool, indifferent

frío[2] *nm* **1 :** cold <hace mucho frío esta noche : it's very cold tonight> **2** INDIFERENCIA **:** coldness, indifference **3 tener frío :** to feel cold <tengo frío : I'm cold> **4 tomar frío** RESFRIARSE **:** to catch a cold

friolento, -ta *adj* **:** sensitive to cold

friolera *nf* (*used ironically or humorously*) **:** trifling amount <una friolera de mil dólares : a mere thousand dollars>

friso *nm* **:** frieze

fritar *vt* **:** to fry

frito[1] *pp* → **freír**

frito[2], **-ta** *adj* **1 :** fried **2** *fam* **:** worn-out, fed up <tener frito a alguien : to get on someone's nerves> **3** *fam* **:** fast asleep <se quedó frito en el sofá : she fell asleep on the couch>

fritura *nf* **1 :** frying **2 :** fried food

frivolidad *nf* **:** frivolity

frívolo, -la *adj* **:** frivolous — **frívolamente** *adv*

fronda *nf* **1 :** frond **2 frondas** *nfpl* **:** foliage

frondoso, -sa *adj* **:** leafy, luxuriant

frontal *adj* **:** frontal, head-on <un choque frontal : a head-on collision>

frontalmente *adv* **:** head-on

frontera *nf* **:** border, frontier

fronterizo, -za *adj* **:** border, on the border <estados fronterizos : neighboring states>

frotar *vt* **1 :** to rub **2 :** to strike (a match) — **frotarse** *vr* **:** to rub (together)

frote *nm* **:** rubbing, rub

fructífero, -ra *adj* **:** fruitful, productive

fructificar {72} *vi* **1 :** to bear or produce fruit **2 :** to be productive

fructuoso, -sa *adj* **:** fruitful

frugal *adj* **:** frugal, thrifty — **frugalmente** *adv*

frugalidad *adj* **:** frugality

frunce *nm* **:** gather (in cloth), pucker

fruncido *nm* **:** gathering, shirring

fruncir {83} *vt* **1 :** to gather, to shirr **2 fruncir el ceño :** to knit one's brow, to frown **3 fruncir la boca :** to pucker up, to purse one's lips

frunza, etc. → **fruncir**

frustración *nf, pl* **-ciones :** frustration

frustrado, -da *adj* **1 :** frustrated **2 :** failed, unsuccessful

frustrante *adj* **:** frustrating

frustrar *vt* **:** to frustrate, to thwart — **frustrarse** *vr* FRACASAR **:** to fail, to come to nothing <se frustraron sus esperanzas : his hopes were dashed>

fruta *nf* **:** fruit

frutal[1] *adj* **:** fruit, fruit-bearing

frutal[2] *nm* **:** fruit tree

frutilla *nf* **:** South American strawberry

fruto *nm* **1 :** fruit, agricultural product <los frutos de la tierra : the fruits of the earth> **2 :** result, consequence <los frutos de su trabajo : the fruits of his labor>

fucsia *adj & nm* **:** fuchsia

fue, etc. → **ir, ser**

fuego *nm* **1 :** fire **2 :** light <¿tienes fuego? : have you got a light?> **3 :** flame, burner (on a stove) **4 :** ardor, passion **5** FOGAJE **:** skin eruption, cold sore 6 **fuegos artificiales** *nmpl* : fireworks

fuelle *nm* : bellows

fuente *nf* **1** MANANTIAL : spring **2** : fountain **3** ORIGEN : source <fuentes informativas : sources of information> **4** : platter, serving dish

fuera *adv* **1** : outside, out **2** : abroad, away **3 ~ de** : outside of, out of, beyond **4 ~ de** : besides, in addition to <fuera de eso : aside from that> **5 fuera de lugar** : out of place, amiss

fuerce, fuerza, etc. → **forzar**

fuero *nm* **1** JURISDICCIÓN : jurisdiction **2** : privilege, exemption **3 fuero interno** : conscience, heart of hearts

fuerte[1] *adv* **1** : strongly, tightly, hard **2** : loudly **3** : abundantly

fuerte[2] *adj* **1** : strong **2** : intense <un fuerte dolor : an intense pain> **3** : loud **4** : extreme, excessive

fuerte[3] *nm* **1** : fort, stronghold **2** : forte, strong point

fuerza *nf* **1** : strength, vigor <fuerza de voluntad : willpower> **2** : force <fuerza bruta : brute force> **3** : power, might <fuerza de brazos : manpower> **4 fuerzas** *nfpl* : forces <fuerzas armadas : armed forces> **5 a fuerza de** : by, by dint of

fuetazo *nm* : lash

fuga *nf* **1** HUIDA : flight, escape **2** : fugue **3** : leak <fuga de gas : gas leak>

fugarse {52} *vr* **1** : to escape **2** HUIR : to flee, to run away **3** : to elope

fugaz *adj, pl* **fugaces** : brief, fleeting

fugitivo, -va *adj & n* : fugitive

fulana *nf* : hooker, slut

fulano, -na *n* : so-and-so, what's-his-name, what's-her-name <fulano, mengano, y zutano : Tom, Dick, and Harry> <señora fulana de tal : Mrs. so-and-so>

fulcro *nm* : fulcrum

fulgor *nm* : brilliance, splendor

fulgurar *vi* : to shine brightly, to gleam, to glow

fulminante *adj* **1** : fulminating, explosive **2** : devastating, terrible <una mirada fulminante : a withering look>

fulminar *vt* **1** : to strike with lightning **2** : to strike down <fulminar a alguien con la mirada : to look daggers at someone>

fumador, -dora *n* : smoker

fumar *v* : to smoke

fumble *nm* : fumble (in football)

fumblear *vt* : to fumble (in football)

fumigante *nm* : fumigant

fumigar {52} *vt* : to fumigate — **fumigación** *nf*

funámbulo, -la *n* EQUILIBRISTA : tightrope walker

función *nf, pl* **funciones 1** : function **2** : duty **3** : performance, show

funcional *adj* : functional — **funcionalmente** *adv*

funcionamiento *nm* **1** : functioning **2 en ~** : in operation

funcionar *vi* **1** : to function **2** : to run, to work

funcionario, -ria *n* : civil servant, official

funda *nf* **1** : case, cover, sheath **2** : pillowcase

fundación *nf, pl* **-ciones** : foundation, establishment

fundado, -da *adj* : well-founded, justified

fundador, -dora *n* : founder

fundamental *adj* BÁSICO : fundamental, basic — **fundamentalmente** *adv*

fundamentar *vt* **1** : to lay the foundations for **2** : to support, to back up **3** : to base, to found

fundamento *nm* : basis, foundation, groundwork

fundar *vt* **1** ESTABLECER, INSTITUIR : to found, to establish **2** BASAR : to base — **fundarse** *vr* **~ en** : to be based on, to stem from

fundición *nf, pl* **-ciones 1** : founding, smelting **2** : foundry

fundir *vt* **1** : to melt down, to smelt **2** : to fuse, to merge **3** : to burn out (a lightbulb) — **fundirse** *vr* **1** : to fuse together, to blend, to merge **2** : to melt, to thaw **3** : to fade (in television or movies)

fúnebre *adj* **1** : funeral, funereal **2** LÚGUBRE : gloomy, mournful

funeral[1] *adj* : funeral, funerary

funeral[2] *nm* **1** : funeral **2 funerales** *nmpl* EXEQUIAS : funeral rites

funeraria *nf* **1** : funeral home, funeral parlor **2 director de funeraria** : funeral director, undertaker

funerario, -ria *adj* : funeral

funesto, -ta *adj* : terrible, disastrous <consecuencias funestas : disastrous consequences>

fungicida[1] *adj* : fungicidal

fungicida[2] *nm* : fungicide

fungir {35} *vi* : to act, to function <fungir de asesor : to act as a consultant>

fungoso, -sa *adj* : fungous

funja, etc. → **fungir**

furgón *nm, pl* **furgones 1** : van, truck **2** : freight car, boxcar **3 furgón de cola** : caboose

furgoneta *nf* : van

furia *nf* **1** CÓLERA, IRA : fury, rage **2** : violence, fury <la furia de la tormenta : the fury of the storm>

furibundo, -da *adj* : furious

furiosamente *adv* : furiously, frantically

furioso, -sa *adj* **1** AIRADO : furious, irate **2** : intense, violent

furor *nm* **1** : fury, rage **2** : violence (of the elements) **3** : passion, frenzy **4** : enthusiasm <hacer furor : to be all the rage>

furtivo, -va *adj* : furtive — **furtivamente** *adv*

furúnculo *nm* DIVIESO **:** boil

fuselaje *nm* **:** fuselage

fusible *nm* **:** (electrical) fuse

fusil *nm* **:** rifle

fusilar *vt* **1 :** to shoot, to execute (by firing squad) **2** *fam* **:** to plagiarize, to pirate

fusilería *nf* **1 :** rifles *pl,* rifle fire **2 descarga de fusilería :** fusillade

fusión *nf, pl* **fusiones 1 :** fusion **2 :** union, merger

fusionar *vt* **1 :** to fuse **2 :** to merge, to amalgamate — **fusionarse** *vr*

fusta *nf* **:** riding crop

fustigar {52} *vt* **1** AZOTAR **:** to whip, to lash **2 :** to upbraid, to berate

futbol *or* **fútbol** *nm* **1 :** soccer **2 futbol americano :** football

futbolista *nmf* **:** soccer player

futesa *nf* **1 :** small thing, trifle **2 futesas** *nfpl* **:** small talk

fútil *adj* **:** trifling, trivial

futurista *adj* **:** futuristic

futuro[1], -ra *adj* **:** future

futuro[2] *nm* PORVENIR **:** future

G

g *nf* **:** seventh letter of the Spanish alphabet

gabán *nm, pl* **gabanes :** topcoat, overcoat

gabardina *nf* **1 :** gabardine **2 :** trench coat, raincoat

gabarra *nf* **:** barge

gabinete *nm* **1 :** cabinet (in government) **2 :** study, office (in the home) **3 :** (professional) office

gablete *nm* **:** gable

gabonés, -nesa *adj & n, mpl* **-neses :** Gabonese

gacela *nf* **:** gazelle

gaceta *nf* **:** gazette, newspaper

gachas *nfpl* **:** porridge

gacho, -cha *adj* **1 :** drooping, turned downward **2** *Mex fam* **:** nasty, awful **3 ir a gachas** *fam* **:** to go on all fours

gaélico[1], -ca *adj* **:** Gaelic

gaélico[2] *nm* **:** Gaelic (language)

gafas *nfpl* ANTEOJOS **:** eyeglasses, glasses

gaita *nf* **:** bagpipes *pl*

gajes *nmpl* **gajes del oficio :** occupational hazards

gajo *nm* **1 :** broken branch (of a tree) **2 :** cluster, bunch (of fruit) **3 :** segment (of citrus fruit)

gala *nf* **1 :** gala <vestido de gala : formal dress> <tener algo a gala : to be proud of something> **2 galas** *nfpl* **:** finery, attire

galáctico, -ca *adj* **:** galactic

galán *nm, pl* **galanes 1 :** ladies' man, gallant **2 :** leading man, hero **3 :** boyfriend, suitor

galano, -na *adj* **1 :** elegant **2** *Mex* **:** mottled

galante *adj* **:** gallant, attentive — **galantemente** *adv*

galantear *vt* **1** CORTEJAR **:** to court, to woo **2 :** to flirt with

galanteo *nm* **1** CORTEJO **:** courtship **2 :** flirtation, flirting

galantería *nf* **1 :** gallantry, attentiveness **2 :** compliment

galápago *nm* **:** aquatic turtle

galardón *nm, pl* **-dones :** award, prize

galardonado, -da *adj* **:** prize-winning

galardonar *vt* **:** to give an award to

galaxia *nf* **:** galaxy

galeno *nm fam* **:** physician, doctor

galeón *nm, pl* **galeones :** galleon

galera *nf* **:** galley

galería *nf* **1 :** gallery, balcony (in a theater) <galería comercial : shopping mall> **2 :** corridor, passage

galerón *nm, pl* **-rones** *Mex* **:** large hall

galés[1], -lesa *adj* **:** Welsh

galés[2], -lesa *n, mpl* **galeses 1 :** Welshman *m,* Welshwoman *f* **2 los galeses :** the Welsh

galés[3] *nm* **:** Welsh (language)

galgo *nm* **:** greyhound

galimatías *nms & pl* **:** gibberish, nonsense

galio *nm* **:** gallium

gallardete *nm* **:** pennant, streamer

gallardía *nf* **1** VALENTÍA **:** bravery **2** APOSTURA **:** elegance, gracefulness

gallardo, -da *adj* **1** VALIENTE **:** brave **2** APUESTO **:** elegant, graceful

gallear *vi* **:** to show off, to strut around

gallego[1], -ga *adj* **1 :** Galician **2** *fam* **:** Spanish

gallego[2], -ga *n* **1 :** Galician **2** *fam* **:** Spaniard

galleta *nf* **1 :** cookie **2 :** cracker

gallina *nf* **1 :** hen **2 gallina de Guinea :** guinea fowl

gallinazo *nm* **:** vulture, buzzard

gallinero *nm* **:** chicken coop, henhouse

gallito, -ta *adj fam* **:** cocky, belligerent

gallo *nm* **1 :** rooster, cock **2** *fam* **:** squeak or crack in the voice **3** *Mex* **:** serenade **4 gallo de pelea :** gamecock

galo[1], -la *adj* **1 :** Gaulish **2 :** French

galo[2], -la *n* **:** Frenchman *m,* Frenchwoman *f*

galocha *nf* **:** galosh

galón *nm, pl* **galones 1 :** gallon **2 :** stripe (military insignia)

galopada *nf* **:** gallop

galopante *adj* **:** galloping <inflación galopante : galloping inflation>

galopar *vi* **:** to gallop

galope *nm* **:** gallop

galpón *nm, pl* **galpones** : shed, storehouse
galvanizar {21} *vt* : to galvanize — **galvanización** *nf*
gama *nf* **1** : range, spectrum, gamut **2** → **gamo**
gamba *nf* : large shrimp, prawn
gameto *nm* : gamete
gamo, -ma *n* : fallow deer
gamuza *nf* **1** : suede **2** : chamois
gana *nf* **1** : desire, inclination **2 de buena gana** : willingly, readily, gladly **3 de mala gana** : reluctantly, half-heartedly **4 tener ganas de** : to feel like, to be in the mood for <tengo ganas de bailar : I feel like dancing> **5 ponerle ganas a algo** : to put effort into something
ganadería *nf* **1** : cattle raising, stockbreeding **2** : cattle ranch **3** GANADO : cattle *pl,* livestock
ganadero[1], -ra *adj* : cattle, ranching
ganadero[2], -ra *n* : rancher, stockbreeder
ganado *nm* **1** : cattle *pl,* livestock **2 ganado ovino** : sheep *pl* **3 ganado porcino** : swine *pl*
ganador[1], -dora *adj* : winning
ganador[2], -dora *n* : winner
ganancia *nf* **1** : profit **2 ganancias** *nfpl* : winnings, gains
ganancioso, -sa *adj* : profitable
ganar *vt* **1** : to win **2** : to gain <ganar tiempo : to buy time> **3** : to earn <ganar dinero : to make money> **4** : to acquire, to obtain — *vi* **1** : to win **2** : to profit <salir ganando : to come out ahead> — **ganarse** *vr* **1** : to gain, to win <ganarse a alguien : to win someone over> **2** : to earn <ganarse la vida : to make a living> **3** : to deserve
gancho *nm* **1** : hook **2** : clothes hanger **3** : hairpin, bobby pin **4** *Col* : safety pin
gandul[1] *nm CA, Car, Col* : pigeon pea
gandul[2], -dula *n fam* : idler, lazybones
gandulear *vi* : to idle, to loaf, to lounge about
ganga *nf* : bargain
ganglio *nm* **1** : ganglion **2** : gland
gangrena *nf* : gangrene — **gangrenoso, -sa** *adj*
gángster *nmf, pl* **gángsters** : gangster
gansada *nf* : silly thing, nonsense
ganso, -sa *n* **1** : goose, gander *m* **2** : idiot, fool
gañido *nm* : yelp (of a dog)
gañir {38} *vi* : to yelp
garabatear *v* : to scribble, to scrawl, to doodle
garabato *nm* **1** : doodle **2 garabatos** *nmpl* : scribble, scrawl
garaje *nm* : garage
garante *nmf* : guarantor
garantía *nf* **1** : guarantee, warranty **2** : security <garantía de trabajo : job security>
garantizar {21} *vt* : to guarantee
garapiña *nf* : pineapple drink
garapiñar *vt* : to candy
garbanzo *nm* : chickpea, garbanzo
garbo *nm* **1** DONAIRE : grace, poise **2** : jauntiness
garboso, -sa *adj* **1** : graceful **2** : elegant, stylish
garceta *nf* : egret
gardenia *nf* : gardenia
garfio *nm* : hook, gaff, grapnel
gargajo *nm* : phlegm
garganta *nf* **1** : throat **2** : neck (of a person or a bottle) **3** : ravine, narrow pass
gargantilla *nf* : choker, necklace
gárgara *nf* **1** : gargle, gargling **2 hacer gárgaras** : to gargle
gargarizar *vi* : to gargle
gárgola *nf* : gargoyle
garita *nf* **1** : cabin, hut **2** : sentry box, lookout post
garoso, -sa *adj Col, Ven* : gluttonous, greedy
garra *nf* **1** : claw **2** : hand, paw **3 garras** *nfpl* : claws, clutches <caer en las garras de alguien : to fall into someone's clutches>
garrafa *nf* : decanter, carafe
garrafal *adj* : terrible, monstrous
garrafón *nm, pl* **-fones** : large decanter, large bottle
garrapata *nf* : tick
garrobo *nm CA* : large lizard, iguana
garrocha *nf* **1** PICA : lance, pike **2** : pole <salto con garrocha : pole vault>
garrotazo *nm* : blow (with a club)
garrote *nm* **1** : club, stick **2** *Mex* : brake
garúa *nf* : drizzle
garuar {3} *v impers* LLOVIZNAR : to drizzle
garza *nf* : heron
gas *nm* : gas, vapor, fumes *pl* <gas lacrimógeno : tear gas>
gasa *nf* : gauze
gasear *vt* **1** : to gas **2** : to aerate (a liquid)
gaseosa *nf* REFRESCO : soda, soft drink
gaseoso, -sa *adj* **1** : gaseous **2** : carbonated, fizzy
gasoducto *nm* : gas pipeline
gasolina *nf* : gasoline, gas
gasolinera *nf* : gas station, service station
gastado, -da *adj* **1** : spent **2** : worn, worn-out
gastador[1], -dora *adj* : extravagant, spendthrift
gastador[2], -dora *n* : spendthrift
gastar *vt* **1** : to spend **2** CONSUMIR : to consume, to use up **3** : to squander, to waste **4** : to wear <gasta un bigote : he sports a mustache> — **gastarse** *vr* **1** : to spend, to expend **2** : to run down, to wear out
gasto *nm* **1** : expense, expenditure **2** DETERIORO : wear **3 gastos generales** *or* **gastos indirectos** : overhead
gástrico, -ca *adj* : gastric
gastritis *nf* : gastritis

gastronomía *nf* : gastronomy

gastronómico, -ca *adj* : gastronomic

gastrónomo, -ma *n* : gourmet

gatas *adv* **andar a gatas** : to crawl, to go on all fours

gatear *vi* **1** : to crawl **2** : to climb, to clamber (up)

gatillero *nm Mex* : gunman

gatillo *nm* : trigger

gatito, -ta *n* : kitten

gato[1]**, -ta** *n* : cat

gato[2] *nm* : jack (for an automobile)

gauchada *nf Arg, Uru* : favor, kindness

gaucho *nm* : gaucho

gaveta *nf* **1** CAJÓN : drawer **2** : till

gavilla *nf* **1** : gang, band **2** : sheaf

gaviota *nf* : gull, seagull

gay [ˈge, ˈgai] *adj* : gay (homosexual)

gaza *nf* : loop

gazapo *nm* **1** : young rabbit **2** : misprint, error

gazmoñería *nf* MOJIGATERÍA : prudery, primness

gazmoño[1]**, -ña** *adj* : prudish, prim

gazmoño[2]**, -ña** *n* MOJIGATO : prude, prig

gaznate *nm* : throat, gullet

gazpacho *nm* : gazpacho

géiser *or* **géyser** *nm* : geyser

gel *nm* : gel

gelatina *nf* : gelatin

gélido, -da *adj* : icy, freezing cold

gelificarse *vr* : to jell

gema *nf* : gem

gemelo[1]**, -la** *adj & n* MELLIZO : twin

gemelo[2] *nm* **1** : cuff link **2 gemelos** *nmpl* BINOCULARES : binoculars

gemido *nm* : moan, groan, wail

Géminis *nmf* : Gemini

gemir {54} *vi* : to moan, to groan, to wail

gen *or* **gene** *nm* : gene

gendarme *nmf* POLICÍA : police officer, policeman *m*, policewoman *f*

gendarmería *nf* : police

genealogía *nf* : genealogy

genealógico, -ca *adj* : genealogical

generación *nf, pl* **-ciones 1** : generation <tercera generación : third generation> **2** : generating, creating **3** : class <la generación del '97 : the class of '97>

generacional *adj* : generation, generational

generador *nm* : generator

general[1] *adj* **1** : general **2 en ~** *or* **por lo general** : in general, generally

general[2] *nmf* **1** : general **2 general de división** : major general

generalidad *nf* **1** : generality, generalization **2** : majority

generalización *nf, pl* **-ciones 1** : generalization **2** : escalation, spread

generalizado, -da *adj* : generalized, widespread

generalizar {21} *vi* : to generalize — *vt* : to spread, to spread out — **generalizarse** *vr* : to become widespread

generalmente *adv* : usually, generally

generar *vt* : to generate — **generarse** *vr*

genérico, -ca *adj* : generic

género *nm* **1** : genre, class, kind <el género humano : the human race, mankind> **2** : gender (in grammar) **3 géneros** *nmpl* : goods, commodities

generosidad *nf* : generosity

generoso, -sa *adj* **1** : generous, unselfish **2** : ample — **generosamente** *adv*

genética *nf* : genetics

genético, -ca *adj* : genetic — **genéticamente** *adv*

genetista *nmf* : geneticist

genial *adj* **1** AGRADABLE : genial, pleasant **2** : brilliant <una obra genial : a work of genius> **3** *fam* FORMIDABLE : fantastic, terrific

genialidad *nf* **1** : genius **2** : stroke of genius **3** : eccentricity

genio *nm* **1** : genius **2** : temper, disposition <de mal genio : bad-tempered> **3** : genie

genital *adj* : genital

genitales *nmpl* : genitals, genitalia

genocidio *nm* : genocide

genotipo *nm* : genotype

gente *nf* **1** : people **2** : relatives *pl*, folks *pl* **3 gente menuda** *fam* : children, kids *pl* **4 ser buena gente** : to be nice, to be kind

gentil[1] *adj* **1** AMABLE : kind **2** : gentile

gentil[2] *nmf* : gentile

gentileza *nf* **1** AMABILIDAD : kindness **2** CORTESÍA : courtesy

gentilicio, -cia *adj* **1** : national, tribal **2** : family

gentío *nm* MUCHEDUMBRE, MULTITUD : crowd, mob

gentuza *nf* CHUSMA : riffraff, rabble

genuflexión *nf, pl* **-xiones 1** : genuflection **2 hacer una genuflexión** : to genuflect

genuino, -na *adj* : genuine — **genuinamente** *adv*

geofísica *nf* : geophysics

geofísico, -ca *adj* : geophysical

geografía *nf* : geography

geográfico, -ca *adj* : geographic, geographical — **geográficamente** *adv*

geógrafo, -fa *n* : geographer

geología *nf* : geology

geológico, -ca *adj* : geologic, geological — **geológicamente** *adv*

geólogo, -ga *n* : geologist

geometría *nf* : geometry

geométrico, -ca *adj* : geometric, geometrical — **geométricamente** *adv*

geopolítica *nf* : geopolitics

geopolítico, -ca *adj* : geopolitical

georgiano, -na *adj & n* : Georgian

geranio *nm* : geranium

gerbo *nm* : gerbil

gerencia *nf* : management, administration

gerencial *adj* : managerial

gerente *nmf* : manager, director

geriatría *nf* : geriatrics

geriátrico, -ca *adj* : geriatric
germanio *nm* : germanium
germano, -na *adj* : Germanic, German
germen *nm, pl* **gérmenes** : germ
germicida *nf* : germicide
germinación *nf, pl* **-ciones** : germination
germinar *vi* : to germinate, to sprout
gerontología *nf* : gerontology
gerundio *nm* : gerund
gesta *nf* : deed, exploit
gestación *nf, pl* **-ciones** : gestation
gesticulación *nf, pl* **-ciones** : gesturing, gesticulation
gesticular *vi* : to gesticulate, to gesture
gestión *nf, pl* **gestiones** **1** TRÁMITE : procedure, step **2** ADMINISTRACIÓN : management **3** **gestiones** *nfpl* : negotiations
gestionar *vt* **1** : to negotiate, to work towards **2** ADMINISTRAR : to manage, to handle
gesto *nm* **1** ADEMÁN : gesture **2** : facial expression **3** MUECA : grimace
gestor[1]**, -tora** *adj* : facilitating, negotiating, managing
gestor[2]**, -tora** *n* : facilitator, manager
géyser *nm* → **géiser**
ghanés, -nesa *adj & n, mpl* **ghaneses** : Ghanaian
ghetto → **gueto**
giba *nf* **1** : hump (of an animal) **2** : hunchback (of a person)
gibón *nm, pl* **gibones** : gibbon
giboso[1]**, -sa** *adj* : hunchbacked, humpbacked
giboso[2]**, -sa** *n* : hunchback, humpback
gigante[1] *adj* : giant, gigantic
gigante[2]**, -ta** *n* : giant
gigantesco, -ca *adj* : gigantic, huge
gime, etc. → **gemir**
gimnasia *nf* : gymnastics
gimnasio *nm* : gymnasium, gym
gimnasta *nmf* : gymnast
gimnástico, -ca *adj* : gymnastic
gimotear *vi* LLORIQUEAR : to whine, to whimper
gimoteo *nm* : whimpering
ginebra *nf* : gin
ginecología *nf* : gynecology
ginecológico, -ca *adj* : gynecologic, gynecological
ginecólogo, -ga *n* : gynecologist
gira *nf* : tour
giralda *nf* : weather vane
girar *vi* **1** : to turn around, to revolve **2** : to swing around, to swivel — *vt* **1** : to turn, to twist, to rotate **2** : to draft (checks) **3** : to transfer (funds)
girasol *nm* MIRASOL : sunflower
giratorio, -ria *adj* : revolving
giro *nm* **1** VUELTA : turn, rotation **2** : change of direction <giro de 180 grados : U-turn, about-face> **3** **giro bancario** : bank draft **4** **giro postal** : money order
giroscopio *or* **giróscopo** *nm* : gyroscope
gis *nm Mex* : chalk
gitano, -na *adj & n* : Gypsy
glacial *adj* : glacial, icy — **glacialmente** *adv*
glaciar *nm* : glacier
gladiador *nm* : gladiator
gladiolo *or* **gladíolo** *nm* : gladiolus
glándula *nf* : gland — **glandular** *adj*
glaseado *nm* : glaze, icing
glasear *vt* : to glaze
glaucoma *nm* : glaucoma
glicerina *nf* : glycerin, glycerol
glicinia *nf* : wisteria
global *adj* **1** : global, worldwide **2** : full, comprehensive **3** : total, overall
globalizar {21} *vt* **1** ABARCAR : to include, to encompass **2** : to extend worldwide
globalmente *adv* : globally, as a whole
globo *nm* **1** : globe, sphere **2** : balloon **3** **globo ocular** : eyeball
glóbulo *nm* **1** : globule **2** : blood cell, corpuscle
gloria *nf* **1** : glory **2** : fame, renown **3** : delight, enjoyment **4** : star, legend <las glorias del cine : the great names in motion pictures>
glorieta *nf* **1** : rotary, traffic circle **2** : bower, arbor
glorificar {72} *vt* ALABAR : to glorify — **glorificación** *nf*
glorioso, -sa *adj* : glorious — **gloriosamente** *adv*
glosa *nf* **1** : gloss **2** : annotation, commentary
glosar *vt* **1** : to gloss **2** : to annotate, to comment on (a text)
glosario *nm* : glossary
glotis *nf* : glottis
glotón[1]**, -tona** *adj, mpl* **glotones** : gluttonous
glotón[2]**, -tona** *n, mpl* **glotones** : glutton
glotón[3] *nm, pl* **glotones** : wolverine
glotonería *nf* GULA : gluttony
glucosa *nf* : glucose
glutinoso, -sa *adj* : glutinous
gnomo *nm* : gnome
gobernación *nf, pl* **-ciones** : governing, government
gobernador, -dora *n* : governor
gobernante[1] *adj* : ruling, governing
gobernante[2] *nmf* : ruler, leader, governor
gobernar {55} *vt* **1** : to govern, to rule **2** : to steer, to sail (a ship) — *vi* **1** : to govern **2** : to steer
gobierno *nm* : government
goce[1]**, etc.** → **gozar**
goce[2] *nm* **1** PLACER : enjoyment, pleasure **2** : use, possession
gol *nm* : goal (in soccer)
golear *vt* : to rout, to score many goals against (in soccer)
goleta *nf* : schooner
golf *nm* : golf
golfista *nmf* : golfer
golfo *nm* : gulf, bay
golondrina *nf* **1** : swallow (bird) **2** **golondrina de mar** : tern

golosina *nf* : sweet, snack

goloso, -sa *adj* : fond of sweets <ser goloso : to have a sweet tooth>

golpazo *nm* : heavy blow, bang, thump

golpe *nm* **1** : blow <caerle a golpes a alguien : to give someone a beating> **2** : knock **3 de ~** : suddenly **4 de un golpe** : all at once, in one fell swoop **5 golpe de estado** : coup, coup d'etat **6 golpe de suerte** : stroke of luck

golpeado, -da *adj* **1** : beaten, hit **2** : bruised (of fruit) **3** : dented

golpear *vt* **1** : to beat (up), to hit **2** : to slam, to bang, to strike — *vi* **1** : to knock (at a door) **2** : to beat <la lluvia golpeaba contra el tejado : the rain beat against the roof> — **golpearse** *vr*

golpetear *v* : to knock, to rattle, to tap

golpeteo *nm* : banging, knocking, tapping

goma *nf* **1** : gum <goma de mascar : chewing gum> **2** CAUCHO : rubber <goma espuma : foam rubber> **3** PEGAMENTO : glue **4** : rubber band **5** *Arg* : tire **6** *or* **goma de borrar** : eraser

gomita *nf* : rubber band

gomoso, -sa *adj* : gummy, sticky

góndola *nf* : gondola

gong *nm* : gong

gonorrea *nf* : gonorrhea

gorda *nf Mex* : thick corn tortilla

gordinflón[1], -flona *adj, mpl* **-flones** *fam* : chubby, pudgy

gordinflón[2], -flona *n, mpl* **-flones** *fam* : chubby person

gordo[1], -da *adj* **1** : fat **2** : thick **3** : fatty, greasy, oily **4** : unpleasant <me cae gorda tu tía : I can't stand your aunt>

gordo[2], -da *n* : fat person

gordo[3] *nm* **1** GRASA : fat **2** : jackpot

gordura *nf* : fatness, flab

gorgojo *nm* : weevil

gorgotear *vi* : to gurgle, to bubble

gorgoteo *nm* : gurgle

gorila *nm* : gorilla

gorjear *vi* **1** : to chirp, to tweet, to warble **2** : to gurgle

gorjeo *nm* **1** : chirping, warbling **2** : gurgling

gorra *nf* **1** : bonnet **2** : cap **3 de ~** *fam* : for free, at someone else's expense <vivir de gorra : to sponge, to freeload>

gorrear *vt fam* : to bum, to scrounge — *vi fam* : to freeload

gorrero, -ra *n fam* : freeloader, sponger

gorrión *nm, pl* **gorriones** : sparrow

gorro *nm* **1** : cap **2 estar hasta el gorro** : to be fed up

gorrón, -rrona *n fam, mpl* **gorrones** : freeloader, scrounger

gorronear *vt fam* : to bum, to scrounge — *vi fam* : to freeload

gota *nf* **1** : drop <una gota de sudor : a bead of sweat> <como dos gotas de agua : like two peas in a pod> <sudar la gota gorda : to sweat buckets, to work very hard> **2** : gout

gotear *v* **1** : to drip **2** : to leak — *v impers* LLOVIZNAR : to drizzle

goteo *nm* : drip, dripping

gotera *nf* **1** : leak **2** : stain (from dripping water)

gotero *nm* : (medicine) dropper

gótico, -ca *adj* : Gothic

gourmet *nmf* : gourmet

gozar {21} *vi* **1** : to enjoy oneself, to have a good time **2 ~ de** : to enjoy, to have, to possess <gozar de buena salud : to enjoy good health> **3 ~ con** : to take delight in

gozne *nm* BISAGRA : hinge

gozo *nm* **1** : joy **2** PLACER : enjoyment, pleasure

gozoso, -sa *adj* : joyful

grabación *nf, pl* **-ciones** : recording

grabado *nm* **1** : engraving **2 grabado al aguafuerte** : etching

grabador, -dora *n* : engraver

grabadora *nf* : tape recorder

grabar *vt* **1** : to engrave **2** : to record, to tape — *vi* **grabar al aguafuerte** : to etch — **grabarse** *vr* **grabársele a alguien en la memoria** : to become engraved on someone's mind

gracia *nf* **1** : grace **2** : favor, kindness **3** : humor, wit <su comentario no me hizo gracia : I wasn't amused by his remark> **4 gracias** *nfpl* : thanks <¡gracias! : thank you!> <dar gracias : to give thanks>

grácil *adj* **1** : graceful **2** : delicate, slender, fine

gracilidad *nm* : gracefulness

gracioso, -sa *adj* **1** CHISTOSO : funny, amusing **2** : cute, attractive

grada *nf* **1** : harrow **2** PELDAÑO : step, stair **3 gradas** *nfpl* : bleachers, grandstand

gradación *nf, pl* **-ciones** : gradation, scale

gradar *vt* : to harrow, to hoe

gradería *nf* : tiers *pl,* stands *pl,* rows *pl* (in a theater)

gradiente *nf* : gradient, slope

grado *nm* **1** : degree (in meteorology and mathematics) <grado centígrado : degree centigrade> **2** : extent, level, degree <en grado sumo : greatly, to the highest degree> **3** RANGO : rank **4** : year, class (in education) **5 de buen grado** : willingly, readily

graduable *adj* : adjustable

graduación *nf, pl* **-ciones 1** : graduation (from a school) **2** GRADO : rank **3** : alcohol content, proof

graduado[1], -da *adj* **1** : graduated **2 lentes graduados** : prescription lenses

graduado[2], -da *n* : graduate

gradual *adj* : gradual — **gradualmente** *adv*

graduar {3} *v* **1** : to regulate, to adjust **2** CALIBRAR : to calibrate, to gauge —

graduarse *vr* : to graduate (from a school)
gráfica *nf* → **gráfico**[2]
gráfico[1], **-ca** *adj* : graphic — **gráficamente** *adv*
gráfico[2] *nm* **1** : graph, chart **2** : graphic (for a computer, etc.) **3 gráfico de barras** : bar graph
grafismo *nm* : graphics *pl*
grafito *nm* : graphite
gragea *nf* **1** : coated pill or tablet **2 grageas** *nfpl* : sprinkles, jimmies
grajo *nm* : rook (bird)
grama *nf* : grass
gramática *nf* : grammar
gramatical *adj* : grammatical — **gramaticalmente** *adv*
gramo *nm* : gram
gran → **grande**
grana *nf* : scarlet, deep red
granada *nf* **1** : pomegranate **2** : grenade <granada de mano : hand grenade>
granadero *nm* **1** : grenadier **2 granaderos** *nmpl Mex* : riot squad
granadino, -na *adj & n* : Grenadian
granado, -da *adj* **1** DISTINGUIDO : distinguished **2** : choice, select
granate *nm* **1** : garnet **2** : deep red, maroon
grande *adj* (**gran** *before singular nouns*) **1** : large, big <un libro grande : a big book> **2** ALTO : tall **3** NOTABLE : great <un gran autor : a great writer> **4** (*indicating intensity*) : great <con gran placer : with great pleasure> **5** : old, grown-up <hijos grandes : grown children>
grandeza *nf* **1** MAGNITUD : greatness, size **2** : nobility **3** : generosity, graciousness **4** : grandeur, magnificence
grandilocuencia *nf* : grandiloquence — **grandilocuente** *adj*
grandiosidad *nf* : grandeur
grandioso, -sa *adj* **1** MAGNÍFICO : grand, magnificent **2** : grandiose
granel *adv* **1 a ~** : galore, in great quantities **2 a ~** : in bulk <vender a granel : to sell in bulk>
granero *nm* : barn, granary
granito *nm* : granite
granizada *nf* : hailstorm
granizar {21} *v impers* : to hail
granizo *nm* : hail
granja *nf* : farm
granjear *vt* : to earn, to win — **granjearse** *vr* : to gain, to earn
granjero, -ra *n* : farmer
grano *nm* **1** PARTÍCULA : grain, particle <un grano de arena : a grain of sand> **2** : grain (of rice, etc.), bean (of coffee), seed **3** : grain (of wood or rock) **4** BARRO, ESPINILLA : pimple **5 ir al grano** : to get to the point
granuja *nmf* PILLUELO : rascal, urchin
granular[1] *vt* : to granulate — **granularse** *vr* : to break out in spots
granular[2] *adj* : granular, grainy
granza *nf* : chaff
grapa *nf* **1** : staple **2** : clamp
grapadora *nf* ENGRAPADORA : stapler
grapar *vt* ENGRAPAR : to staple
grasa *nf* **1** : grease **2** : fat **3** *Mex* : shoe polish
grasiento, -ta *adj* : greasy, oily
graso, -sa *adj* **1** : fatty **2** : greasy, oily
grasoso, -sa *adj* GRASIENTO : greasy, oily
gratificación *nf, pl* **-ciones 1** SATISFACCIÓN : gratification **2** : bonus **3** RECOMPENSA : recompense, reward
gratificar {72} *vt* **1** SATISFACER : to satisfy, to gratify **2** RECOMPENSAR : to reward **3** : to give a bonus to
gratinado, -da *adj* : au gratin
gratis[1] *adv* GRATUITAMENTE : free, for free, gratis
gratis[2] *adj* GRATUITO : free, gratis
gratitud *nf* : gratitude
grato, -ta *adj* AGRADABLE, PLACENTERO : pleasant, agreeable — **gratamente** *adv*
gratuitamente *adv* **1** : gratuitously **2** GRATIS : free, for free, gratis
gratuito, -ta *adj* **1** : gratuitous, unwarranted **2** GRATIS : free, gratis
grava *nf* : gravel
gravamen *nm, pl* **-vámenes 1** : burden, obligation **2** : (property) tax
gravar *vt* **1** : to burden, to encumber **2** : to levy (a tax)
grave *adj* **1** : grave, important **2** : serious, somber **3** : serious (of an illness)
gravedad *nf* **1** : gravity <centro de gravedad : center of gravity> **2** : seriousness, severity
gravemente *adv* : gravely, seriously
gravilla *nf* : (fine) gravel
gravitación *nf, pl* **-ciones** : gravitation
gravitar *vi* **1** : to gravitate **2 ~ sobre** : to rest on **3 ~ sobre** : to loom over
gravoso, -sa *adj* **1** ONEROSO : burdensome, onerous **2** : costly
graznar *vi* : to caw, to honk, to quack, to squawk
graznido *nm* : cawing, honking, quacking, squawking
gregario, -ria *adj* : gregarious
gregoriano, -na *adj* : Gregorian
gremial *adj* SINDICAL : union, labor
gremio *nm* SINDICATO : union, guild
greña *nf* **1** : mat, tangle **2 greñas** *nfpl* MELENAS : shaggy hair, mop
greñudo, -da *n* HIPPIE, MELENUDO : longhair, hippie
grey *nf* : congregation, flock
griego[1], **-ga** *adj & n* : Greek
griego[2] *nm* : Greek (language)
grieta *nf* : crack, crevice
grifo *nm* **1** : faucet <agua del grifo : tap water> **2** : griffin
grillete *nm* : shackle
grillo *nm* **1** : cricket **2 grillos** *nmpl* : fetters, shackles
grima *nf* **1** : disgust, uneasiness **2 darle grima a alguien** : to get on someone's nerves

gringo, -ga *adj & n* YANQUI **:** Yankee, gringo
gripa *nf Col, Mex* **:** flu
gripe *nf* **:** flu
gris *adj* **1 :** gray **2 :** overcast, cloudy
grisáceo, -cea *adj* **:** grayish
gritar *v* **:** to shout, to scream, to cry
gritería *nf* **:** shouting, clamor
grito *nm* **:** shout, scream, cry <a grito pelado : at the top of one's voice>
groenlandés, -desa *adj & n* **:** Greenlander
grogui *adj fam* **:** dazed, groggy
grosella *nf* **1 :** currant **2 grosella espinosa :** gooseberry
grosería *nf* **1 :** insult, coarse language **2 :** rudeness, discourtesy
grosero[1], -ra *adj* **1 :** rude, fresh **2 :** coarse, vulgar
grosero[2], -ra *n* **:** rude person
grosor *nm* **:** thickness
grosso *adj* **a grosso modo :** roughly, broadly, approximately
grotesco, -ca *adj* **:** grotesque, hideous
grúa *nf* **1 :** crane (machine) **2 :** tow truck
gruesa *nf* **:** gross
grueso[1], -sa *adj* **1 :** thick, bulky **2 :** heavy, big **3 :** heavyset, stout
grueso[2] *nm* **1 :** thickness **2 :** main body, mass **3 en ~ :** in bulk
grulla *nf* **:** crane (bird)
grumo *nm* **:** lump, glob
gruñido *nm* **:** growl, grunt
gruñir {38} *vi* **1 :** to growl, to grunt **2 :** to grumble
gruñón[1], -ñona *adj, mpl* **gruñones** *fam* **:** grumpy, crabby
gruñón[2], -ñona *n, mpl* **gruñones** *fam* **:** grumpy person, nag
grupa *nf* **:** rump, hindquarters *pl*
grupo *nm* **:** group
gruta *nf* **:** grotto, cave
guacal *nm Col, Mex, Ven* **:** crate
guacamayo *nm* **:** macaw
guacamole *or* **guacamol** *nm* **:** guacamole
guacamote *nm Mex* **:** yuca, cassava
guachinango → huachinango
guacho, -cha *adj* **1** *Arg, Col, Chile, Peru* **:** orphaned **2** *Chile, Peru* **:** odd, unmatched
guadaña *nf* **:** scythe
guagua *nf* **1** *Arg, Col, Chile, Peru* **:** baby **2** *Cuba, PRi* **:** bus
guaira *nf* **1** *CA* **:** traditional flute **2** *Peru* **:** smelting furnace
guajiro, -ra *n Cuba* **:** peasant
guajolote *nm Mex* **:** turkey
guanábana *nf* **:** guanabana, soursop (fruit)
guanaco *nm* **:** guanaco
guandú *nm CA, Car, Col* **:** pigeon pea
guango, -ga *adj Mex* **1 :** loose-fitting, baggy **2 :** slack, loose
guano *nm* **:** guano
guante *nm* **1 :** glove <guante de boxeo : boxing glove> **2 arrojarle el guante (a alguien) :** to throw down the gauntlet (to someone)
guantelete *nm* **:** gauntlet
guapo, -pa *adj* **1 :** handsome, good-looking, attractive **2 :** elegant, smart **3** *fam* **:** bold, dashing
guapura *nf fam* **:** handsomeness, attractiveness, good looks *pl* <¡qué guapura! : what a vision!>
guarache → huarache
guarachear *vi Cuba, PRi fam* **:** to go on a spree, to go out on the town
guaraní[1] *adj & nmf* **:** Guarani
guaraní[2] *nm* **:** Guarani (language of Paraguay)
guarda *nmf* **1** GUARDIÁN **:** security guard **2 :** keeper, custodian
guardabarros *nms & pl* **:** fender, mudguard
guardabosque *nmfs & pl* **:** forest ranger, gamekeeper
guardacostas[1] *nmfs & pl* **:** coastguardsman
guardacostas[2] *nms & pl* **:** coast guard vessel
guardaespaldas *nmfs & pl* **:** bodyguard
guardafangos *nms & pl* **:** fender, mudguard
guardameta *nmf* ARQUERO, PORTERO **:** goalkeeper, goalie
guardapelo *nm* **:** locket
guardapolvo *nm* **1 :** dustcover **2 :** duster, housecoat
guardar *vt* **1 :** to guard **2 :** to maintain, to preserve **3** CONSERVAR **:** to put away **4** RESERVAR **:** to save **5 :** to keep (a secret or promise) — **guardarse** *vr* **1 ~ de :** to refrain from **2 ~ de :** to guard against, to be careful not to
guardarropa *nm* **1 :** cloakroom, checkroom **2** ARMARIO **:** closet, wardrobe
guardería *nf* **:** nursery, day-care center
guardia[1] *nf* **1 :** guard, defense **2 :** guard duty, watch **3 en ~ :** on guard
guardia[2] *nmf* **1 :** sentry, guardsman, guard **2 :** police officer, policeman *m*, policewoman *f*
guardián, -diana *n, mpl* **guardianes 1** GUARDA **:** security guard, watchman **2 :** guardian, keeper **3 perro guardián :** watchdog
guarecer {53} *vt* **:** to shelter, to protect — **guarecerse** *vr* **:** to take shelter
guarida *nf* **1 :** den, lair **2 :** hideout
guarismo *nm* **:** figure, numeral
guarnecer {53} *vt* **1 :** to adorn **2 :** to garnish **3 :** to garrison
guarnición *nf, pl* **-ciones 1 :** garnish **2 :** garrison **3 :** decoration, trimming, setting (of a jewel)
guaro *nm CA* **:** liquor distilled from sugarcane
guasa *nf fam* **1 :** joking, fooling around **2 de ~ :** in jest, as a joke
guasón[1], -sona *adj, mpl* **guasones** *fam* **:** funny, witty

guasón[2], -sona *n, mpl* **guasones** *fam* : joker, clown

guatemalteco, -ca *adj & n* : Guatemalan

guau *interj* : wow!

guayaba *nf* : guava (fruit)

gubernamental *adj* : governmental

gubernativo, -va → **gubernamental**

gubernatura *nf Mex* : governing body

guepardo *nm* : cheetah

güero, -ra *adj Mex* : blond, fair

guerra *nf* **1** : war <declarar la guerra : to declare war> <guerra sin cuartel : all-out war> **2** : warfare **3** LUCHA : conflict, struggle

guerrear *vi* : to wage war

guerrero[1], -ra *adj* **1** : war, fighting **2** : warlike

guerrero[2], -ra *n* : warrior

guerrilla *nf* : guerrilla warfare

guerrillero, -ra *adj & n* : guerrilla

gueto *nm* : ghetto

guía[1] *nf* **1** : directory, guidebook **2** ORIENTACIÓN : guidance, direction <la conciencia me sirve como guía : conscience is my guide>

guía[2] *nmf* : guide, leader <guía de turismo : tour guide>

guiar {85} *vt* **1** : to guide, to lead **2** CONDUCIR : to manage — **guiarse** *vr* : to be guided by, to go by

guija *nf* : pebble

guijarro *nm* : pebble

guillotina *nf* : guillotine — **guillotinar** *vt*

guinda[1] *adj & nm Mex* : burgundy (color)

guinda[2] *nf* : morello (cherry)

guineo *nm Car* : banana

guinga *nf* : gingham

guiñada → **guiño**

guiñar *vi* : to wink

guiño *nm* : wink

guión *nm, pl* **guiones** **1** : script, screenplay **2** : hyphen, dash **3** ESTANDARTE : standard, banner

guirnalda *nf* : garland

guisa *nf* **1** : manner, fashion **2 a guisa de** : like, by way of **3 de tal guisa** : in such a way

guisado ESTOFADO *nm* : stew

guisante *nm* : pea

guisar *vt* **1** ESTOFAR : to stew **2** *Spain* : to cook

guiso *nm* **1** : stew **2** : casserole

güisqui → **whisky**

guita *nf* : string, twine

guitarra *nf* : guitar

guitarrista *nmf* : guitarist

gula *nf* GLOTONERÍA : gluttony, greed

gusano *nm* **1** LOMBRIZ : worm, earthworm <gusano de seda : silkworm> **2** : caterpillar, maggot, grub

gustar *vt* **1** : to taste **2** : to like <¿gustan pasar? : would you like to come in?> — *vi* **1** : to be pleasing <me gustan los dulces : I like sweets> <a María le gusta Carlos : Maria is attracted to Carlos> <no me gusta que me griten : I don't like to be yelled at> **2 ~ de** : to like, to enjoy <no gusta de chismes : she doesn't like gossip> **3 como guste** : as you wish, as you like

gustativo, -va *adj* : taste <papilas gustativas : taste buds>

gusto *nm* **1** : flavor, taste **2** : taste, style **3** : pleasure, liking **4** : whim, fancy <a gusto : at will> **5 a ~** : comfortable, at ease **6 al gusto** : to taste, as one likes **7 mucho gusto** : pleased to meet you

gustosamente *adv* : gladly

gustoso, -sa *adj* **1** : willing, glad <nuestra empresa participará gustosa : our company will be pleased to participate> **2** : zesty, tasty

gutural *adj* : guttural

H

h *nf* : eighth letter of the Spanish alphabet

ha → **haber**

haba *nf* : broad bean

habanero[1], -ra *adj* : of or from Havana

habanero[2], -ra *n* : native or resident of Havana

haber[1] {39} *v aux* **1** : have, has <no ha llegado el envío : the shipment hasn't arrived> **2 ~ de** : must <ha de ser tarde : it must be late> — *v impers* **1 hay** : there is, there are <hay dos mensajes : there are two messages> <¿qué hay de nuevo? : what's new?> **2 hay que** : it is necessary <hay que trabajar más rápido : you have to work faster>

haber[2] *nm* **1** : assets *pl* **2** : credit, credit side **3 haberes** *nmpl* : salary, income, remuneration

habichuela *nf* **1** : bean, kidney bean **2** : green bean

hábil *adj* **1** : able, skillful **2** : working <días hábiles : working days>

habilidad *nf* CAPACIDAD : ability, skill

habilidoso, -sa *adj* : skillful, clever

habilitación *nf, pl* **-ciones** **1** : authorization **2** : furnishing, equipping

habilitar *vt* **1** : to enable, to authorize, to empower **2** : to equip, to furnish

hábilmente *adv* : skillfully, expertly

habitable *adj* : habitable, inhabitable

habitación *nf, pl* **-ciones** **1** CUARTO : room **2** DORMITORIO : bedroom **3** : habitation, occupancy

habitante *nmf* : inhabitant, resident
habitar *vt* : to inhabit — *vi* : to reside, to dwell
hábitat *nm, pl* **-tats** : habitat
hábito *nm* **1** : habit, custom **2** : habit (of a monk or nun)
habitual *adj* : habitual, customary — **habitualmente** *adv*
habituar {3} *vt* : to accustom, to habituate — **habituarse** *vr* **~ a** : to get used to, to grow accustomed to
habla *nf* **1** : speech **2** : language, dialect **3 de ~** : speaking <de habla inglesa : English-speaking>
hablado, -da *adj* **1** : spoken **2 mal hablado** : foulmouthed
hablador[1], -dora *adj* : talkative
hablador[2], -dora *n* : chatterbox
habladuría *nf* **1** : rumor **2 habladurías** *nfpl* : gossip, scandal
hablante *nmf* : speaker
hablar *vi* **1** : to speak, to talk <hablar en broma : to be joking> **2 ~ de** : to mention, to talk about **3 dar que hablar** : to make people talk — *vt* **1** : to speak (a language) **2** : to talk about, to discuss <háblalo con tu jefe : discuss it with your boss> — **hablarse** *vr* **1** : to speak to each other, to be on speaking terms **2 se habla inglés (etc.)** : English (etc.) spoken
habrá, etc. → **haber**
hacedor, -dora *n* : creator, maker, doer
hacendado, -da *n* : landowner
hacer {40} *vt* **1** : to make **2** : to do, to perform **3** : to force, to oblige <los hice esperar : I made them wait> — *vi* : to act <haces bien : you're doing the right thing> — *v impers* **1** (*referring to weather*) <hacer frío : to be cold> <hace viento : it's windy> **2 hace** : ago <hace mucho tiempo : a long time ago, for a long time> **3 no le hace** : it doesn't matter, it makes no difference **4 hacer falta** : to be necessary, to be needed — **hacerse** *vr* **1** : to become **2** : to pretend, to act, to play <hacerse el tonto : to play dumb> **3** : to seem <el examen se me hizo difícil : the exam seemed difficult to me> **4** : to get, to grow <se hace tarde : it's growing late>
hacha *nf* : hatchet, ax
hachazo *nm* : blow, chop (with an ax)
hachís *nm* : hashish
hacia *prep* **1** : toward, towards <hacia abajo : downward> <hacia adelante : forward> **2** : near, around, about <hacia las seis : about six o'clock>
hacienda *nf* **1** : estate, ranch, farm **2** : property **3** : livestock **4 la Hacienda** : department of revenue, tax office
hacinar *vt* **1** : to pile up, to stack **2** : to overcrowd — **hacinarse** *vr* : to crowd together
hada *nf* : fairy
hado *nm* : destiny, fate
haga, etc. → **hacer**
haitiano, -na *adj & n* : Haitian
halagador[1], -dora *adj* : flattering
halagador[2], -dora *n* : flatterer
halagar {52} *vt* : to flatter, to compliment
halago *nm* : flattery, praise
halagüeño, -ña *adj* **1** : flattering **2** : encouraging, promising
halcón *nm, pl* **halcones** : hawk, falcon
halibut *nm, pl* **-buts** : halibut
hálito *nm* **1** : breath **2** : gentle breeze
hallar *vt* **1** ENCONTRAR : to find **2** DESCUBRIR : to discover, to find out — **hallarse** *vr* **1** : to be situated, to find oneself **2** : to feel <no se halla bien : he doesn't feel comfortable, he feels out of place>
hallazgo *nm* **1** : discovery **2** : find <¡es un verdadero hallazgo! : it's a real find!>
halo *nm* **1** : halo **2** : aura
halógeno *nm* : halogen
hamaca *nf* : hammock
hambre *nf* **1** : hunger **2** : starvation **3 tener hambre** : to be hungry **4 dar hambre** : to make hungry
hambriento, -ta *adj* : hungry, starving
hambruna *nf* : famine
hamburguesa *nf* : hamburger
hampa *nf* : criminal underworld
hampón, -pona *n, mpl* **hampones** : criminal, thug
hámster *nm, pl* **hámsters** : hamster
han → **haber**
handicap *or* **hándicap** [ˈhandiˌkap] *nm, pl* **-caps** : handicap (in sports)
hangar *nm* : hangar
hará, etc. → **hacer**
haragán[1], -gana *adj, mpl* **-ganes** : lazy, idle
haragán[2], -gana *n, mpl* **-ganes** HOLGAZÁN : slacker, good-for-nothing
haraganear *vi* : to be lazy, to waste one's time
haraganería *nf* : laziness
harapiento, -ta *adj* : ragged, tattered
harapos *nmpl* ANDRAJOS : rags, tatters
hardware [ˈhardˌwɛr] *nm* : computer hardware
harén *nm, pl* **harenes** : harem
harina *nf* **1** : flour **2 harina de maíz** : cornmeal
hartar *vt* **1** : to glut, to satiate **2** FASTIDIAR : to tire, to irritate, to annoy — **hartarse** *vr* : to be weary, to get fed up
harto[1] *adv* : most, extremely, very
harto[2], -ta *adj* **1** : full, satiated **2** : fed up
hartura *nf* **1** : surfeit **2** : abundance, plenty
has → **haber**
hasta[1] *adv* : even
hasta[2] *prep* **1** : until, up until <hasta entonces : until then> <¡hasta luego! : see you later!> **2** : as far as <nos fuimos hasta Managua : we went all the way to Managua> **3** : up to <hasta cierto punto : up to a certain point> **4 hasta que** : until

hastiar {85} *vt* **1 :** to make weary, to bore **2 :** to disgust, to sicken — **hastiarse** *vr* **~ de :** to get tired of

hastío *nm* **1** TEDIO **:** tedium **2** REPUGNANCIA **:** disgust

hato *nm* **1 :** flock, herd **2 :** bundle (of possessions)

hawaiano, -na *adj & n* **:** Hawaiian

hay → **haber**

haya[1], **etc.** → **haber**

haya[2] *nf* **:** beech (tree and wood)

hayuco *nm* **:** beechnut

haz[1] → **hacer**

haz[2] *nm, pl* **haces 1** FARDO **:** bundle **2 :** beam (of light)

haz[3] *nf, pl* **haces 1 :** face **2 haz de la tierra :** surface of the earth

hazaña *nf* PROEZA **:** feat, exploit

hazmerreír *nm fam* **:** laughingstock

he[1] {39} → **haber**

he[2] *v impers* **he aquí :** here is, here are, behold

hebilla *nf* **:** buckle, clasp

hebra *nf* **:** strand, thread

hebreo[1], **-brea** *adj & n* **:** Hebrew

hebreo[2] *nm* **:** Hebrew (language)

hecatombe *nm* **1** MATANZA **:** massacre **2 :** disaster

heces → **hez**

hechicería *nf* **1** BRUJERÍA **:** sorcery, witchcraft **2 :** curse, spell

hechicero[1], **-ra** *adj* **:** bewitching, enchanting

hechicero[2], **-ra** *n* **:** sorcerer, sorceress *f*

hechizar {21} *vt* **1** EMBRUJAR **:** to bewitch **2** CAUTIVAR **:** to charm

hechizo *nm* **1** SORTILEGIO **:** spell, enchantment **2** ENCANTO **:** charm, fascination

hecho[1] *pp* → **hacer**

hecho[2], **-cha** *adj* **1 :** made, done **2 :** ready-to-wear **3 :** complete, finished <hecho y derecho : full-fledged>

hecho[3] *nm* **1 :** fact **2 :** event <hechos históricos : historic events> **3 :** act, action **4 de ~ :** in fact, in reality

hechura *nf* **1 :** style **2 :** craftsmanship, workmanship **3 :** product, creation

hectárea *nf* **:** hectare

heder {56} *vi* **:** to stink, to reek

hediondez *nf* **:** stink, stench

hediondo, -da *adj* MALOLIENTE **:** foul-smelling, stinking

hedor *nm* **:** stench, stink

hegemonía *nf* **1 :** dominance **2 :** hegemony (in politics)

helada *nf* **:** frost (in meteorology)

heladería *nf* **:** ice-cream parlor, ice-cream stand

helado[1], **-da** *adj* **1** GÉLIDO **:** icy, freezing cold **2** CONGELADO **:** frozen

helado[2] *nm* **:** ice cream

heladora *nf* CONGELADOR **:** freezer

helar {55} *v* CONGELAR **:** to freeze — *v impers* **:** to produce frost <anoche heló : there was frost last night> — **helarse** *vr*

helecho *nm* **:** fern, bracken

hélice *nf* **1 :** spiral, helix **2 :** propeller

helicóptero *nm* **:** helicopter

helio *nm* **:** helium

helipuerto *nm* **:** heliport

hembra *adj & nf* **:** female

hemisférico, -ca *adj* **:** hemispheric, hemispherical

hemisferio *nm* **:** hemisphere

hemofilia *nf* **:** hemophilia

hemofílico, -ca *adj & n* **:** hemophiliac

hemoglobina *nf* **:** hemoglobin

hemorragia *nf* **1 :** hemorrhage **2 hemorragia nasal :** nosebleed

hemorroides *nfpl* ALMORRANAS **:** hemorrhoids, piles

hemos → **haber**

henchido, -da *adj* **:** swollen, bloated

henchir {54} *vt* **1 :** to stuff, to fill **2 :** to swell, to swell up — **henchirse** *vr* **:** to stuff oneself **2** LLENARSE **:** to fill up, to be full

hender {56} *vt* **:** to cleave, to split

hendidura *nf* **:** crack, crevice, fissure

henequén *nm, pl* **-quenes :** sisal hemp

heno *nm* **:** hay

hepatitis *nf* **:** hepatitis

heráldica *nf* **:** heraldry

heráldico, -ca *adj* **:** heraldic

heraldo *nm* **:** herald

herbario, -ria *adj* **:** herbal

herbicida *nm* **:** herbicide, weed killer

herbívoro[1], **-ra** *adj* **:** herbivorous

herbívoro[2] *nm* **:** herbivore

herbolario, -ria *n* **:** herbalist

hercúleo, -lea *adj* **:** herculean

heredar *vt* **:** to inherit

heredero, -ra *n* **:** heir, heiress *f*

hereditario, -ria *adj* **:** hereditary

hereje *nmf* **:** heretic

herejía *nf* **:** heresy

herencia *nf* **1 :** inheritance **2 :** heritage **3 :** heredity

herético, -ca *adj* **:** heretical

herida *nf* **:** injury, wound

herido[1], **-da** *adj* **1 :** injured, wounded **2 :** hurt, offended

herido[2], **-da** *n* **:** injured person, casualty

herir {76} *vt* **1 :** to injure, to wound **2 :** to hurt, to offend

hermafrodita *nmf* **:** hermaphrodite

hermanar *vt* **1 :** to unite, to bring together **2 :** to match up, to twin (cities)

hermanastro, -tra *n* **:** half brother *m*, half sister *f*

hermandad *nf* **1** FRATERNIDAD **:** brotherhood <hermandad de mujeres : sisterhood, sorority> **2 :** association

hermano, -na *n* **:** sibling, brother *m*, sister *f*

hermético, -ca *adj* **:** hermetic, watertight — **herméticamente** *adv*

hermoso, -sa *adj* BELLO **:** beautiful, lovely — **hermosamente** *adv*

hermosura *nf* BELLEZA **:** beauty, loveliness

hernia *nf* **:** hernia

héroe *nm* **:** hero

heroicidad *nf* **:** heroism, heroic deed

heroico, -ca *adj* : heroic — **heroicamente** *adv*
heroína *nf* **1** : heroine **2** : heroin
heroísmo *nm* : heroism
herpes *nms & pl* **1** : herpes **2** : shingles
herradura *nf* : horseshoe
herraje *nm* : ironwork
herramienta *nf* : tool
herrar {55} *vt* : to shoe (a horse)
herrería *nf* : blacksmith's shop
herrero, -ra *n* : blacksmith
herrumbre *nf* ORÍN : rust
herrumbroso, -sa *adj* OXIDADO : rusty
hertzio *nm* : hertz
hervidero *nm* **1** : mass, swarm **2** : hotbed (of crime, etc.)
hervidor *nm* : kettle
hervir {76} *vi* **1** BULLIR : to boil, to bubble **2 ~ de** : to teem with, to be swarming with — *vt* : to boil
hervor *nm* **1** : boiling **2** : fervor, ardor
heterogeneidad *nf* : heterogeneity
heterogéneo, -nea *adj* : heterogeneous
heterosexual *adj & nmf* : heterosexual
heterosexualidad *nf* : heterosexuality
hexágono *nm* : hexagon — **hexagonal** *adj*
hez *nf, pl* **heces 1** ESCORIA : scum, dregs *pl* **2** : sediment, lees *pl* **3 heces** *nfpl* : feces, excrement
hiato *nm* : hiatus
hibernar *vi* : to hibernate — **hibernación** *nf*
híbrido[1]**, -da** *adj* : hybrid
híbrido[2] *nm* : hybrid
hicieron, etc. → **hacer**
hidalgo, -ga *n* : nobleman *m,* noblewoman *f*
hidrante *nm CA, Col* : hydrant
hidratar *vt* : to moisturize — **hidratante** *adj*
hidrato *nm* **1** : hydrate **2 hidrato de carbono** : carbohydrate
hidráulico, -ca *adj* : hydraulic
hidroavión *nm, pl* **-viones** : seaplane
hidrocarburo *nm* : hydrocarbon
hidroeléctrico, -ca *adj* : hydroelectric
hidrofobia *nf* RABIA : hydrophobia, rabies
hidrófugo, -ga *adj* : water-repellent
hidrógeno *nm* : hydrogen
hidroplano *nm* : hydroplane
hiede, etc. → **heder**
hiedra *nf* **1** : ivy **2 hiedra venenosa** : poison ivy
hiel *nf* **1** BILIS : bile **2** : bitterness
hiela, etc. → **helar**
hielo *nm* **1** : ice **2** : coldness, reserve <romper el hielo : to break the ice>
hiena *nf* : hyena
hiende, etc. → **hender**
hierba *nf* **1** : herb **2** : grass **3 mala hierba** : weed
hierbabuena *nf* : mint, spearmint
hiere, etc. → **herir**
hierra, etc. → **herrar**
hierro *nm* **1** : iron <hierro fundido : cast iron> **2** : branding iron
hierve, etc. → **hervir**
hígado *nm* : liver
higiene *nf* : hygiene
higiénico, -ca *adj* : hygienic — **higiénicamente** *adv*
higienista *nmf* : hygienist
higo *nm* **1** : fig **2 higo chumbo** : prickly pear (fruit)
higrómetro *nm* : hygrometer
higuera *nf* : fig tree
hijastro, -tra *n* : stepson *m,* stepdaughter *f*
hijo, -ja *n* **1** : son *m,* daughter *f* **2 hijos** *nmpl* : children, offspring
híjole *interj Mex* : wow!, good grief!
hilacha *nf* **1** : ravel, loose thread **2 mostrar la hilacha** : to show one's true colors
hilado *nm* **1** : spinning **2** HILO : yarn, thread
hilar *vt* **1** : to spin (thread) **2** : to consider, to string together (ideas) — *vi* **1** : to spin **2 hilar delgado** : to split hairs
hilarante *adj* **1** : humorous, hilarious **2 gas hilarante** : laughing gas
hilaridad *nf* : hilarity
hilera *nf* FILA : file, row, line
hilo *nm* **1** : thread <colgar de un hilo : to hang by a thread> <hilo dental : dental floss> **2** LINO : linen **3** : (electric) wire **4** : theme, thread (of a discourse) **5** : trickle (of water, etc.)
hilvanar *vt* **1** : to baste, to tack **2** : to piece together
himnario *nm* : hymnal
himno *nm* **1** : hymn **2 himno nacional** : national anthem
hincapié *nm* **hacer hincapié en** : to emphasize, to stress
hincar {72} *vt* CLAVAR : to stick, to plunge — **hincarse** *vr* **hincarse de rodillas** : to kneel down, to fall to one's knees
hinchado, -da *adj* **1** : swollen, inflated **2** : pompous, overblown
hinchar *vt* **1** INFLAR : to inflate **2** : to exaggerate — **hincharse** *vr* **1** : to swell up **2** : to become conceited, to swell with pride
hinchazón *nf, pl* **-zones** : swelling
hinche, etc. → **henchir**
hindú *adj & nmf* : Hindu
hinduismo *nm* : Hinduism
hiniesta *nf* : broom (plant)
hinojo *nm* **1** : fennel **2 de hinojos** : on bended knee
hinque, etc. → **hincar**
hipar *vi* : to hiccup
hiperactividad *nf* : hyperactivity
hiperactivo, -va *adj* : hyperactive, overactive
hipérbole *nf* : hyperbole
hiperbólico, -ca *adj* : hyperbolic, exaggerated
hipercrítico, -ca *adj* : hypercritical
hipermetropía *nf* : farsightedness
hipersensibilidad *nf* : hypersensitivity
hipersensible *adj* : hypersensitive

hipertensión *nf, pl* **-siones** : hypertension, high blood pressure

hípico, -ca *adj* : equestrian <concurso hípico : horse show>

hipil *nm* → **huipil**

hipnosis *nfs & pl* : hypnosis

hipnótico, -ca *adj* : hypnotic

hipnotismo *nm* : hypnotism

hipnotizador[1], -dora *adj* **1** : hypnotic **2** : spellbinding, mesmerizing

hipnotizador[2], -dora *n* : hypnotist

hipnotizar {21} *vt* : to hypnotize

hipo *nm* : hiccup, hiccups *pl*

hipocampo *nm* : sea horse

hipocondría *nf* : hypochondria

hipocondríaco, -ca *adj & n* : hypochondriac

hipocresía *nf* : hypocrisy

hipócrita[1] *adj* : hypocritical — **hipócritamente** *adv*

hipócrita[2] *nmf* : hypocrite

hipodérmico, -ca *adj* **aguja hipodérmica** : hypodermic needle

hipódromo *nm* : racetrack

hipopótamo *nm* : hippopotamus

hipoteca *nf* : mortgage

hipotecar {72} *vt* **1** : to mortgage **2** : to compromise, to jeopardize

hipotecario, -ria *adj* : mortgage

hipotensión *nf* : low blood pressure

hipotenusa *nf* : hypotenuse

hipótesis *nfs & pl* : hypothesis

hipotético, -ca *adj* : hypothetical — **hipotéticamente** *adv*

hippie *or* **hippy** ['hipi] *nmf, pl* **hippies** [-pis] : hippie

hiriente *adj* : hurtful, offensive

hirió, etc. → **herir**

hirsuto, -ta *adj* **1** : hirsute, hairy **2** : bristly, wiry

hirviente *adj* : boiling

hirvió, etc. → **hervir**

hisopo *nm* **1** : hyssop **2** : cotton swab

hispánico, -ca *adj & n* : Hispanic

hispano[1], -na *adj* : Hispanic <de habla hispana : Spanish-speaking>

hispano[2], -na *n* : Hispanic (person)

hispanoamericano[1], -na *adj* LATINOAMERICANO : Latin-American

hispanoamericano[2], -na *n* LATINOAMERICANO : Latin American

hispanohablante[1] *adj* : Spanish-speaking

hispanohablante[2] *nmf* : Spanish speaker

histerectomía *nf* : hysterectomy

histeria *nf* **1** : hysteria **2** : hysterics

histérico, -ca *adj* : hysterical — **histéricamente** *adv*

histerismo *nm* **1** : hysteria **2** : hysterics

historia *nf* **1** : history **2** NARRACIÓN, RELATO : story

historiador, -dora *n* : historian

historial *nm* **1** : record, document **2** CURRÍCULUM : résumé, curriculum vitae

histórico, -ca *adj* **1** : historical **2** : historic, important — **históricamente** *adv*

historieta *nf* : comic strip

histrionismo *nm* : histrionics, acting

hit ['hit] *nm, pl* **hits 1** ÉXITO : hit, popular song **2** : hit (in baseball)

hito *nm* : milestone, landmark

hizo → **hacer**

hobby ['hɔbi] *nm, pl* **hobbies** [-bis] : hobby

hocico *nm* : snout, muzzle

hockey ['hɔke, -ki] *nm* : hockey

hogar *nm* **1** : home **2** : hearth, fireplace

hogareño, -ña *adj* **1** : home-loving **2** : domestic, homelike

hogaza *nf* : large loaf (of bread)

hoguera *nf* **1** FOGATA : bonfire **2 morir en la hoguera** : to burn at the stake

hoja *nf* **1** : leaf, petal, blade (of grass) **2** : sheet (of paper), page (of a book) <hoja de cálculo : spreadsheet> **3** FORMULARIO : form <hoja de pedido : order form> **4** : blade (of a knife) <hoja de afeitar : razor blade>

hojalata *nf* : tinplate

hojaldra *or* **hojaldre** *nm* : puff pastry

hojarasca *nf* : fallen leaves *pl*

hojear *vt* : to leaf through (a book or magazine)

hojuela *nf* **1** : leaflet, young leaf **2** : flake

hola *interj* : hello!, hi!

holandés[1], -desa *adj, mpl* **-deses** : Dutch

holandés[2], -desa *n, mpl* **-deses** : Dutch person, Dutchman *m*, Dutchwoman *f* <los holandeses : the Dutch>

holandés[3] *nm* : Dutch (language)

holgadamente *adv* : comfortably, easily <vivir holgadamente : to be well-off>

holgado, -da *adj* **1** : loose, baggy **2** : at ease, comfortable

holganza *nf* : leisure, idleness

holgazán[1], -zana *adj, mpl* **-zanes** : lazy

holgazán[2], -zana *n, mpl* **-zanes** HARAGÁN : slacker, idler

holgazanear *vi* HARAGANEAR : to laze around, to loaf

holgazanería *nf* PEREZA : idleness, laziness

holgura *nf* **1** : looseness **2** COMODIDAD : comfort, ease

holístico, -ca *adj* : holistic

hollar {19} *vt* : to tread on, to trample

hollín *nm, pl* **hollines** TIZNE : soot

holocausto *nm* : holocaust

holograma *nm* : hologram

hombre *nm* **1** : man <el hombre : man, mankind> **2 hombre de estado** : statesman **3 hombre de negocios** : businessman **4 hombre lobo** : werewolf

hombrera *nf* **1** : shoulder pad **2** : epaulet

hombría *nf* : manliness

hombro *nm* : shoulder <encogerse de hombros : to shrug one's shoulders>

hombruno, -na *adj* : mannish

homenaje *nm* **:** homage, tribute <rendir homenaje a **:** to pay tribute to>

homenajear *vt* **:** to pay homage to, to honor

homeopatía *nf* **:** homeopathy

homicida[1] *adj* **:** homicidal, murderous

homicida[2] *nmf* ASESINO **:** murderer

homicidio *nm* ASESINATO **:** homicide, murder

homilía *nf* **:** homily, sermon

homófono *nm* **:** homophone

homogeneidad *nf* **:** homogeneity

homogeneización *nf* **:** homogenization

homogeneizar {21} *vt* **:** to homogenize

homogéneo, -nea *adj* **:** homogeneous

homógrafo *nm* **:** homograph

homologación *nf, pl* **-ciones 1 :** sanctioning, approval **2 :** parity

homologar {52} *vt* **1 :** to sanction **2 :** to bring into line

homólogo[1]**, -ga** *adj* **:** homologous, equivalent

homólogo[2]**, -ga** *n* **:** counterpart

homónimo[1]**, -ma** *n* TOCAYO **:** namesake

homónimo[2] *nm* **:** homonym

homosexual *adj & nmf* **:** homosexual

homosexualidad *nf* **:** homosexuality

honda *nf* **:** sling

hondo[1] *adv* **:** deeply

hondo[2]**, -da** *adj* PROFUNDO **:** deep <en lo más hondo de **:** in the depths of> — **hondamente** *adv*

hondonada *nf* **1 :** hollow, depression **2 :** ravine, gorge

hondura *nf* **:** depth

hondureño, -ña *adj & n* **:** Honduran

honestidad *nf* **1 :** decency, modesty **2 :** honesty, uprightness

honesto, -ta *adj* **1 :** decent, virtuous **2 :** honest, honorable — **honestamente** *adv*

hongo *nm* **1 :** fungus **2 :** mushroom

honor *nm* **1 :** honor <en honor a la verdad **:** to be quite honest> **2 honores** *nmpl* **:** honors <hacer los honores **:** to do the honors>

honorable *adj* HONROSO **:** honorable — **honorablemente** *adv*

honorario, -ria *adj* **:** honorary

honorarios *nmpl* **:** payment, fees (for professional services)

honorífico, -ca *adj* **:** honorary <mención honorífica **:** honorable mention>

honra *nf* **1 :** dignity, self-respect <tener a mucha honra **:** to take great pride in> **2 :** good name, reputation

honradamente *adv* **:** honestly, decently

honradez *nf, pl* **-deces :** honesty, integrity, probity

honrado, -da *adj* **1** HONESTO **:** honest, upright **2 :** honored

honrar *vt* **1 :** to honor **2 :** to be a credit to <su generosidad lo honra **:** his generosity does him credit>

honroso, -sa *adj* HONORABLE **:** honorable — **honrosamente** *adv*

hora *nf* **1 :** hour <media hora **:** half an hour> <a la última hora **:** at the last minute> <a la hora en punto **:** on the dot> <horas de oficina **:** office hours> **2 :** time <¿qué hora es? **:** what time is it?> **3** CITA **:** appointment

horario *nm* **:** schedule, timetable, hours *pl* <horario de visita **:** visiting hours>

horca *nf* **1 :** gallows *pl* **2 :** pitchfork

horcajadas *nfpl* **a ~ :** astride, astraddle

horcón *nm, pl* **horcones :** wooden post, prop

horda *nf* **:** horde

horizontal *adj* **:** horizontal — **horizontalmente** *adv*

horizonte *nm* **:** horizon, skyline

horma *nf* **1 :** shoe tree **2 :** shoemaker's last

hormiga *nf* **:** ant

hormigón *nm, pl* **-gones** CONCRETO **:** concrete

hormigonera *nf* **:** cement mixer

hormigueo *nm* **1 :** tingling, pins and needles *pl* **2 :** uneasiness

hormiguero *nm* **1 :** anthill **2 :** swarm (of people)

hormona *nf* **:** hormone — **hormonal** *adj*

hornacina *nf* **:** niche, recess

hornada *nf* **:** batch

hornear *vt* **:** to bake

hornilla *nf* **:** burner (of a stove)

horno *nm* **1 :** oven <horno crematorio **:** crematorium> <horno de microondas **:** microwave oven> **2 :** kiln

horóscopo *nm* **:** horoscope

horqueta *nf* **1 :** fork (in a river or road) **2 :** crotch (in a tree) **3 :** small pitchfork

horquilla *nf* **1 :** hairpin, bobby pin **2 :** pitchfork

horrendo, -da *adj* **:** horrendous, horrible

horrible *adj* **:** horrible, dreadful — **horriblemente** *adv*

horripilante *adj* **:** horrifying, hair-raising

horripilar *vt* **:** to horrify, to terrify

horror *nm* **:** horror, dread

horrorizado, -da *adj* **:** terrified

horrorizar {21} *vt* **:** to horrify, to terrify — **horrorizarse** *vr*

horroroso, -sa *adj* **1 :** horrifying, terrifying **2 :** dreadful, bad

hortaliza *nf* **1 :** vegetable **2 hortalizas** *nfpl* **:** garden produce

hortera *adj Spain fam* **:** tacky, gaudy

hortícola *adj* **:** horticultural

horticultor, -ra *n* **:** horticulturist

horticultura *nf* **:** horticulture

hosco, -ca *adj* **:** sullen, gloomy

hospedaje *nm* **:** lodging, accomodations *pl*

hospedar *vt* **:** to provide with lodging, to put up — **hospedarse** *vr* **:** to stay, to lodge

hospicio *nm* : orphanage
hospital *nm* : hospital
hospitalario, -ria *adj* : hospitable
hospitalidad *nf* : hospitality
hospitalización *nf, pl* **-ciones** : hospitalization
hospitalizar {21} *vt* : to hospitalize — **hospitalizarse** *vr*
hostería *nf* POSADA : inn
hostia *nf* : host, Eucharist
hostigamiento *nm* : harassment
hostigar {52} *vt* ACOSAR, ASEDIAR : to harass, to pester
hostil *adj* : hostile
hostilidad *nf* **1** : hostility, antagonism **2 hostilidades** *nfpl* : (military) hostilities
hostilizar {21} *vt* : to harass
hotel *nm* : hotel
hotelero[1], **-ra** *adj* : hotel <la industria hotelera : the hotel business>
hotelero[2], **-ra** *n* : hotel manager, hotelier
hoy *adv* **1** : today <hoy mismo : right now, this very day> **2** : now, nowadays <de hoy en adelante : from now on>
hoyo *nm* AGUJERO : hole
hoyuelo *nm* : dimple
hoz *nf, pl* **hoces** : sickle
hozar {21} *vi* : to root (of a pig)
huachinango *nm Mex* : red snapper
huarache *nm* : huarache sandal
hubo, etc. → **haber**
hueco[1], **-ca** *adj* **1** : hollow, empty **2** : soft, spongy **3** : hollow-sounding, resonant **4** : proud, conceited **5** : superficial
hueco[2] *nm* **1** : hole, hollow, cavity **2** : gap, space **3** : recess, alcove
huele, etc. → **oler**
huelga *nf* **1** PARO : strike **2 hacer huelga** : to strike, to go on strike
huelguista *nmf* : striker
huella[1], **etc.** → **hollar**
huella[2] *nf* **1** : footprint <seguir las huellas de alguien : to follow in someone's footsteps> **2** : mark, impact <dejar huella : to leave one's mark> <sin dejar huella : without a trace> **3 huella digital** *or* **huella dactilar** : fingerprint
huérfano[1], **-na** *adj* **1** : orphan, orphaned **2** : defenseless **3 ~ de** : lacking, devoid of
huérfano[2], **-na** *n* : orphan
huerta *nf* **1** : large vegetable garden, truck farm **2** : orchard **3** : irrigated land
huerto *nm* **1** : vegetable garden **2** : orchard
hueso *nm* **1** : bone **2** : pit, stone (of a fruit)
huésped[1], **-peda** *n* INVITADO : guest
huésped[2] *nm* : host <organismo huésped : host organism>
huestes *nfpl* **1** : followers **2** : troops, army
huesudo, -da *adj* : bony
hueva *nf* : roe, spawn
huevo *nm* : egg <huevos revueltos : scrambled eggs>
huida *nf* : flight, escape
huidizo, -za *adj* **1** ESCURRIDIZO : elusive, slippery **2** : shy, evasive
huipil *nm CA, Mex* : traditional sleeveless blouse or dress
huir {41} *vi* **1** ESCAPAR : to escape, to flee **2 ~ de** : to avoid
huiro *nm Chile, Peru* : seaweed
huizache *nm* : huisache, acacia
hule *nm* **1** : oilcloth, oilskin **2** *Mex* : rubber **3 hule espuma** *Mex* : foam rubber
humanidad *nf* **1** : humanity, mankind **2** : humaneness **3 humanidades** *nfpl* : humanities *pl*
humanismo *nm* : humanism
humanista *nmf* : humanist
humanístico, -ca *adj* : humanistic
humanitario, -ria *adj & n* : humanitarian
humano[1], **-na** *adj* **1** : human **2** BENÉVOLO : humane , benevolent — **humanamente** *adv*
humano[2] *nm* : human being, human
humareda *nf* : cloud of smoke
humeante *adj* **1** : smoky **2** : smoking, steaming
humear *vi* **1** : to smoke **2** : to steam
humectante[1] *adj* : moisturizing
humectante[2] *nm* : moisturizer
humedad *nf* **1** : humidity **2** : dampness, moistness
humedecer {53} *vt* **1** : to humidify **2** : to moisten, to dampen
húmedo, -da *adj* **1** : humid **2** : moist, damp
humidificador *nm* : humidifier
humidificar {72} *vt* : to humidify
humildad *nf* **1** : humility **2** : lowliness
humilde *adj* **1** : humble **2** : lowly <gente humilde : poor people>
humildemente *adv* : meekly, humbly
humillación *nf, pl* **-ciones** : humiliation
humillante *adj* : humiliating
humillar *vt* : to humiliate — **humillarse** *vr* : to humble oneself <humillarse a hacer algo : to stoop to doing something>
humo *nm* **1** : smoke, steam, fumes **2 humos** *nmpl* : airs *pl*, conceit
humor *nm* **1** : humor **2** : mood, temper <está de buen humor : she's in a good mood>
humorada *nf* **1** BROMA : joke, witticism **2** : whim, caprice
humorismo *nm* : humor, wit
humorista *nmf* : humorist, comedian, comedienne *f*
humorístico, -ca *adj* : humorous — **humorísticamente** *adv*
humoso, -sa *adj* : smoky, steamy
humus *nm* : humus
hundido, -da *adj* **1** : sunken **2** : depressed

hundimiento *nm* **1 :** sinking **2 :** collapse, ruin

hundir *vt* **1 :** to sink **2 :** to destroy, to ruin — **hundirse** *vr* **1 :** to sink down **2 :** to cave in **3 :** to break down, to go to pieces

húngaro[1], **-ra** *adj & n* **:** Hungarian

húngaro[2] *nm* **:** Hungarian (language)

huracán *nm, pl* **-canes :** hurricane

huraño, -ña *adj* **1 :** unsociable, aloof **2 :** timid, skittish (of an animal)

hurgar {52} *vt* **:** to poke, to jab, to rake (a fire) — *vi* **~ en :** to rummage in, to poke through

hurgue, etc. → **hurgar**

hurón *nm, pl* **hurones :** ferret

huronear *vi* **:** to pry, to snoop

hurra *interj* **:** hurrah!, hooray!

hurtadillas *nfpl* **a ~ :** stealthily, on the sly

hurtar *vt* ROBAR **:** to steal

hurto *nm* **1 :** theft, robbery **2 :** stolen property, loot

husmear *vt* **1 :** to follow the scent of, to track **2 :** to sniff out, to pry into — *vi* **1 :** to pry, to snoop **2 :** to sniff around (of an animal)

huso *nm* **1 :** spindle **2 huso horario :** time zone

huy *interj* **:** ow!, ouch!

huye, etc. → **huir**

I

i *nf* **:** ninth letter of the Spanish alphabet

iba, etc. → **ir**

ibérico, -ca *adj* **:** Iberian

ibero, -ra *or* **íbero, -ra** *adj & n* **:** Iberian

iberoamericano, -na *adj* HISPANOAMERICANO, LATINOAMERICANO **:** Latin-American

ibis *nfs & pl* **:** ibis

ice, etc. → **izar**

iceberg *nm, pl* **icebergs :** iceberg

icono *nm* **:** icon

iconoclasia *nf* **:** iconoclasm

iconoclasta *nmf* **:** iconoclast

ictericia *nf* **:** jaundice

ida *nf* **1 :** going, departure **2 ida y vuelta :** round-trip **3 idas y venidas :** comings and goings

idea *nf* **1 :** idea, notion **2 :** opinion, belief **3** PROPÓSITO **:** intention

ideal *adj & nm* **:** ideal — **idealmente** *adv*

idealismo *nm* **:** idealism

idealista[1] *adj* **:** idealistic

idealista[2] *nmf* **:** idealist

idealizar {21} *vt* **:** to idealize — **idealización** *nf*

idear *vt* **:** to devise, to think up

ideario *nm* **:** ideology

ídem *nm* **:** idem, the same, ditto

idéntico, -ca *adj* **:** identical, alike — **idénticamente** *adv*

identidad *nf* **:** identity

identificable *adj* **:** identifiable

identificación *nf, pl* **-ciones 1 :** identification, identifying **2 :** identification document, ID

identificar {72} *vt* **:** to identify — **identificarse** *vr* **1 :** to identify oneself **2 ~ con :** to identify with

ideología *nf* **:** ideology — **ideológicamente** *adv*

ideológico, -ca *adj* **:** ideological

idílico, -ca *adj* **:** idyllic

idilio *nm* **:** idyll

idioma *nm* **:** language <el idioma inglés : the English language>

idiomático, -ca *adj* **:** idiomatic — **idiomáticamente** *adv*

idiosincrasia *nf* **:** idiosyncrasy

idiosincrásico, -ca *adj* **:** idiosyncratic

idiota[1] *adj* **:** idiotic, stupid, foolish

idiota[2] *nmf* **:** idiot, foolish person

idiotez *nf, pl* **-teces 1 :** idiocy **2 :** idiotic act or remark <¡no digas idioteces! : don't talk nonsense!>

ido *pp* → **ir**

idólatra[1] *adj* **:** idolatrous

idólatra[2] *nmf* **:** idolater

idolatrar *vt* **:** to idolize

idolatría *nf* **:** idolatry

ídolo *nm* **:** idol

idoneidad *nf* **:** suitability

idóneo, -nea *adj* ADECUADO **:** suitable, fitting

iglesia *nf* **:** church

iglú *nm* **:** igloo

ignición *nf, pl* **-ciones :** ignition

ignífugo, -ga *adj* **:** fire-resistant, fireproof

ignominia *nf* **:** ignominy, disgrace

ignominioso, -sa *adj* **:** ignominious, shameful

ignorancia *nf* **:** ignorance

ignorante[1] *adj* **:** ignorant

ignorante[2] *nmf* **:** ignorant person, ignoramus

ignorar *vt* **1 :** to ignore **2** DESCONOCER **:** to be unaware of <lo ignoramos por absoluto : we have no idea>

ignoto, -ta *adj* **:** unknown

igual[1] *adv* **1 :** in the same way **2 por ~ :** equally

igual[2] *adj* **1 :** equal **2** IDÉNTICO **:** the same, alike **3 :** even, smooth **4** SEMEJANTE **:** similar **5** CONSTANTE **:** constant

igual[3] *nmf* **:** equal, peer

igualación *nf* **1 :** equalization **2 :** leveling, smoothing **3 :** equating (in mathematics)

igualado, -da *adj* **1 :** even (of a score) **2 :** level **3** *Mex* **:** disrespectful

igualar *vt* **1 :** to equalize **2 :** to tie <igualar el marcador : to even the score>

igualdad *nf* **1 :** equality **2** UNIFORMIDAD **:** evenness, uniformity

igualmente *adv* **1 :** equally **2** ASIMISMO **:** likewise

iguana *nf* **:** iguana

ijada *nf* **:** flank, loin, side

ijar *nm* → **ijada**

ilegal[1] *adj* **:** illegal, unlawful — **ilegalmente** *adv*

ilegal[2] *nmf CA, Mex* **:** illegal alien

ilegalidad *nf* **:** illegality, unlawfulness

ilegibilidad *nf* **:** illegibility

ilegible *adj* **:** illegible — **ilegiblemente** *adv*

ilegitimidad *nf* **:** illegitimacy

ilegítimo, -ma *adj* **:** illegitimate, unlawful

ileso, -sa *adj* **:** uninjured, unharmed

ilícito, -ta *adj* **:** illicit — **ilícitamente** *adv*

ilimitado, -da *adj* **:** unlimited

ilógico, -ca *adj* **:** illogical — **ilógicamente** *adv*

iluminación *nf, pl* **-ciones 1 :** illumination **2** ALUMBRADO **:** lighting

iluminado, -da *adj* **:** illuminated, lighted

iluminar *vt* **1 :** to illuminate, to light (up) **2 :** to enlighten

ilusión *nf, pl* **-siones 1 :** illusion, delusion **2** ESPERANZA **:** hope <hacerse ilusiones : to get one's hopes up>

ilusionado, -da *adj* ESPERANZADO **:** hopeful, eager

ilusionar *vt* **:** to build up hope, to excite — **ilusionarse** *vr* **:** to get one's hopes up

iluso[1]**, -sa** *adj* **:** naive, gullible

iluso[2]**, -sa** *n* SOÑADOR **:** dreamer, visionary

ilusorio, -ria *adj* ENGAÑOSO **:** illusory, misleading

ilustración *nf, pl* **-ciones 1 :** illustration **2 :** erudition, learning <la Ilustración : the Enlightenment>

ilustrado, -da *adj* **1 :** illustrated **2** DOCTO **:** learned, erudite

ilustrador, -dora *n* **:** illustrator

ilustrar *vt* **1 :** to illustrate **2** ACLARAR, CLARIFICAR **:** to explain

ilustrativo, -va *adj* **:** illustrative

ilustre *adj* **:** illustrious, eminent

imagen *nf, pl* **imágenes :** image, picture

imaginable *adj* **:** imaginable, conceivable

imaginación *nf, pl* **-ciones :** imagination

imaginar *vt* **:** to imagine — **imaginarse** *vr* **1 :** to suppose, to imagine **2 :** to picture

imaginario, -ria *adj* **:** imaginary

imaginativo, -va *adj* **:** imaginative — **imaginativamente** *adv*

imán *nm, pl* **imanes :** magnet

imantar *vt* **:** to magnetize

imbatible *adj* **:** unbeatable

imbécil[1] *adj* **:** stupid, idiotic

imbécil[2] *nmf* **1 :** imbecile **2** *fam* **:** idiot, dope

imborrable *adj* **:** indelible

imbuir {41} *vt* **:** to imbue — **imbuirse** *vr*

imitación *nf, pl* **-ciones 1 :** imitation **2 :** mimicry, impersonation

imitador[1]**, -dora** *adj* **:** imitative

imitador[2]**, -dora** *n* **1 :** imitator **2 :** mimic

imitar *vt* **1 :** to imitate, to copy **2 :** to mimic, to impersonate

impaciencia *nf* **:** impatience

impacientar *vt* **:** to make impatient, to exasperate — **impacientarse** *vr*

impaciente *adj* **:** impatient — **impacientemente** *adv*

impactado, -da *adj* **:** shocked, stunned

impactante *adj* **1 :** shocking **2 :** impressive, powerful

impactar *vt* **1** GOLPEAR **:** to hit **2** IMPRESIONAR **:** to impact, to affect — **impactarse** *vr*

impacto *nm* **1 :** impact, effect **2 :** shock, collision

impagable *adj* **1 :** unpayable **2 :** priceless

impago *nm* **:** nonpayment

impalpable *adj* INTANGIBLE **:** impalpable, intangible

impar[1] *adj* **:** odd <números impares : odd numbers>

impar[2] *nm* **:** odd number

imparable *adj* **:** unstoppable

imparcial *adj* **:** impartial — **imparcialmente** *adv*

imparcialidad *nf* **:** impartiality

impartir *vt* **:** to impart, to give

impasible *adj* **:** impassive, unmoved — **impasiblemente** *adv*

impasse *nm* **:** impasse

impávido, -da *adj* **:** undaunted, unperturbed

impecable *adj* INTACHABLE **:** impeccable, faultless — **impecablemente** *adv*

impedido, -da *adj* **:** disabled, crippled

impedimento *nm* **1 :** impediment, obstacle **2 :** disability

impedir {54} *vt* **1 :** to prevent, to block **2 :** to impede, to hinder

impeler *vt* **1 :** to drive, to propel **2 :** to impel

impenetrable *adj* **:** impenetrable — **impenetrabilidad** *nf*

impenitente *adj* **:** unrepentant, impenitent

impensable *adj* **:** unthinkable

impensado, -da *adj* **:** unforeseen, unexpected

imperante *adj* **:** prevailing

imperar *vi* **1 :** to reign, to rule **2** PREDOMINAR **:** to prevail

imperativo[1]**, -va** *adj* **:** imperative

imperativo[2] *nm* **:** imperative

imperceptible *adj* **:** imperceptible — **imperceptiblemente** *adv*

imperdible *Spain nm* **:** safety pin

imperdonable *adj* : unpardonable, unforgivable
imperecedero, -ra *adj* **1** : imperishable **2** INMORTAL : immortal, everlasting
imperfección *nf, pl* **-ciones 1** : imperfection **2** DEFECTO : defect, flaw
imperfecto[1]**, -ta** *adj* : imperfect, flawed
imperfecto[2] *nm* : imperfect tense
imperial *adj* : imperial
imperialismo *nm* : imperialism
imperialista *adj & nmf* : imperialist
impericia *nf* : lack of skill, incompetence
imperio *nm* : empire
imperioso, -sa *adj* **1** : imperious **2** : pressing, urgent — **imperiosamente** *adv*
impermeabilizante *adj* : water-repellent
impermeabilizar {21} *vt* : to waterproof
impermeable[1] *adj* **1** : impervious **2** : impermeable, waterproof
impermeable[2] *nm* : raincoat
impersonal *adj* : impersonal — **impersonalmente** *adv*
impertinencia *nf* INSOLENCIA : impertinence, insolence
impertinente *adj* **1** INSOLENTE : impertinent, insolent **2** INOPORTUNO : inappropriate, uncalled-for **3** IRRELEVANTE : irrelevant
imperturbable *adj* : imperturbable, impassive, stolid
ímpetu *nm* **1** : impetus, momentum **2** : vigor, energy **3** : force, violence
impetuoso, -sa *adj* : impetuous, impulsive — **impetuosamente** *adv*
impiedad *nf* : impiety
impío, -pía *adj* : impious, ungodly
implacable *adj* : implacable, relentless — **implacablemente** *adv*
implantación *nf, pl* **-ciones 1** : implantation **2** ESTABLECIMIENTO : establishment, introduction
implantado, -da *adj* : well-established
implantar *vt* **1** : to implant **2** ESTABLECER : to establish, to introduce — **implantarse** *vr*
implante *nm* : implant
implementar *vt* : to implement — **implementarse** *vr* — **implementación** *nf*
implemento *nm* : implement, tool
implicación *nf, pl* **-ciones** : implication
implicar {72} *vt* **1** ENREDAR, ENVOLVER : to involve, to implicate **2** : to imply
implícito, -ta *adj* : implied, implicit — **implícitamente** *adv*
implorar *vt* : to implore
implosión *nf, pl* **-siones** : implosion — **implosivo, -va** *adj*
implosionar *vi* : to implode
imponderable *adj & nm* : imponderable
imponente *adj* : imposing, impressive
imponer {60} *vt* **1** : to impose **2** : to confer — *vi* : to be impressive, to command respect — **imponerse** *vr* **1** : to take on (a duty) **2** : to assert oneself **3** : to prevail
imponible *adj* : taxable
impopular *adj* : unpopular — **impopularidad** *nf*
importación *nf, pl* **-ciones 1** : importation **2 importaciones** *nfpl* : imports
importado, -da *adj* : imported
importador[1]**, -dora** *adj* : importing
importador[2]**, -dora** *n* : importer
importancia *nf* : importance
importante *adj* : important — **importantemente** *adv*
importar *vi* : to matter, to be important <no le importa lo que piensen : she doesn't care what they think> — *vt* : to import
importe *nm* **1** : price, cost **2** : sum, amount
importunar *vt* : to bother, to inconvenience — *vi* : to be inconvenient
importuno, -na *adj* **1** : inopportune, inconvenient **2** : bothersome, annoying
imposibilidad *nf* : impossibility
imposibilitado, -da *adj* **1** : disabled, crippled **2 verse imposibilitado** : to be unable (to do something)
imposibilitar *vt* **1** : to make impossible **2** : to disable, to incapacitate — **imposibilitarse** *vr* : to become disabled
imposible *adj* : impossible
imposición *nf, pl* **-ciones 1** : imposition **2** EXIGENCIA : demand, requirement **3** : tax **4** : deposit
impositivo, -va *adj* : tax <tasa impositiva : tax rate>
impostor, -tora *n* : impostor
impotencia *nf* **1** : impotence, powerlessness **2** : impotence (in medicine)
impotente *adj* **1** : powerless **2** : impotent
impracticable *adj* : impracticable
imprecisión *nf, pl* **-siones 1** : imprecision, vagueness **2** : inaccuracy
impreciso, -sa *adj* **1** : imprecise, vague **2** : inaccurate
impredecible *adj* : unpredictable
impregnar *vt* : to impregnate
imprenta *nf* **1** : printing **2** : printing shop, press
imprescindible *adj* : essential, indispensable
impresentable *adj* : unpresentable, unfit
impresión *nf, pl* **-siones 1** : print, printing **2** : impression, feeling
impresionable *adj* : impressionable
impresionante *adj* : impressive, incredible, amazing — **impresionantemente** *adv*
impresionar *vt* **1** : to impress, to strike **2** : to affect, to move — *vi* : to make an impression — **impresionarse** *vr* : to be affected, to be removed
impresionismo *nm* : impressionism

impresionista[1] *adj* **:** impressionist, impressionistic

impresionista[2] *nmf* **:** impressionist

impreso[1] *pp* → **imprimir**

impreso[2], **-sa** *adj* **:** printed

impreso[3] *nm* PUBLICACIÓN **:** printed matter, publication

impresor, -sora *n* **:** printer

impresora *nf* **:** (computer) printer

imprevisible *adj* **:** unforeseeable

imprevisión *nf, pl* **-siones :** lack of foresight, thoughtlessness

imprevisto[1], **-ta** *adj* **:** unexpected, unforeseen

imprevisto[2] *nm* **:** unexpected occurrence, contingency

imprimir {42} *vt* **1 :** to print **2 :** to imprint, to stamp, to impress

improbabilidad *nf* **:** improbability

improbable *adj* **:** improbable, unlikely

improcedente *adj* **1 :** inadmissible **2 :** inappropriate, improper

improductivo, -va *adj* **:** unproductive

improperio *nm* **:** affront, insult

impropio, -pia *adj* **1 :** improper, incorrect **2** INADECUADO **:** unsuitable, inappropriate

improvisación *nf, pl* **-ciones :** improvisation, ad-lib

improvisado, -da *adj* **:** improvised, ad-lib

improvisar *v* **:** to improvise, to ad-lib

improviso *adj* **de ~ :** all of a sudden, unexpectedly

imprudencia *nf* INDISCRECIÓN **:** imprudence, indiscretion

imprudente *adj* INDISCRETO **:** imprudent, indiscreet — **imprudentemente** *adv*

impúdico, -ca *adj* **:** shameless, indecent

impuesto[1] *pp* → **imponer**

impuesto[2] *nm* **:** tax

impugnar *vt* **:** to challenge, to contest

impulsar *vt* **:** to propel, to drive

impulsividad *nf* **:** impulsiveness

impulsivo, -va *adj* **:** impulsive — **impulsivamente** *adv*

impulso *nm* **1 :** drive, thrust **2 :** impulse, urge

impune *adj* **:** unpunished

impunemente *adv* **:** with impunity

impunidad *nf* **:** impunity

impureza *nf* **:** impurity

impuro, -ra *adj* **:** impure

impuso, etc. → **imponer**

imputable *adj* ATRIBUIBLE **:** attributable

imputación *nf, pl* **-ciones 1 :** attribution, imputation **2 :** accusation

imputar *vt* ATRIBUIR **:** to impute, to attribute

inacabable *adj* **:** endless

inacabado, -da *adj* INCONCLUSO **:** unfinished

inaccesibilidad *nf* **:** inaccessibility

inaccesible *adj* **1 :** inaccessible **2 :** unattainable

inacción *nf, pl* **-ciones :** inactivity, inaction

inaceptable *adj* **:** unacceptable

inactividad *nf* **:** inactivity, idleness

inactivo, -va *adj* **:** inactive, idle

inadaptado[1], **-da** *adj* **:** maladjusted

inadaptado[2], **-da** *n* **:** misfit

inadecuación *nf, pl* **-ciones :** inadequacy

inadecuado, -da *adj* **1 :** inadequate **2** IMPROPIO **:** inappropriate — **inadecuadamente** *adv*

inadmisible *adj* **1 :** inadmissible **2 :** unacceptable

inadvertencia *nf* **:** oversight

inadvertidamente *adv* **:** inadvertently

inadvertido, -da *adj* **1 :** unnoticed <pasar inadvertido : to go unnoticed> **2** DESPISTADO, DISTRAÍDO **:** inattentive, distracted

inagotable *adj* **:** inexhaustible

inaguantable *adj* INSOPORTABLE **:** insufferable, unbearable

inalámbrico, -ca *adj* **:** wireless, cordless

inalcanzable *adj* **:** unreachable, unattainable

inalienable *adj* **:** inalienable

inalterable *adj* **1 :** unalterable, unchangeable **2 :** impassive **3 :** colorfast

inamovible *adj* **:** immovable, fixed

inanición *nf, pl* **-ciones :** starvation

inanimado, -da *adj* **:** inanimate

inapelable *adj* **:** indisputable

inapetencia *nf* **:** lack of appetite

inaplicable *adj* **:** inapplicable

inapreciable *adj* **1 :** imperceptible, negligible **2 :** invaluable

inapropiado, -da *adj* **:** inappropriate, unsuitable

inarticulado, -da *adj* **:** inarticulate, unintelligible — **inarticuladamente** *adv*

inasequible *adj* **:** unattainable, inaccessible

inasistencia *nf* AUSENCIA **:** absence

inatacable *adj* **:** unassailable, indisputable

inaudible *adj* **:** inaudible

inaudito, -ta *adj* **:** unheard-of, unprecedented

inauguración *nf, pl* **-ciones :** inauguration

inaugural *adj* **:** inaugural, opening

inaugurar *vt* **1 :** to inaugurate **2 :** to open

inca *adj & nmf* **:** Inca

incalculable *adj* **:** incalculable

incalificable *adj* **:** indescribable

incandescencia *nf* **:** incandescence — **incandescente** *adj*

incansable *adj* INFATIGABLE **:** tireless — **incansablemente** *adv*

incapacidad *nf* **1 :** inability, incapacity **2 :** disability, handicap

incapacitado, -da *adj* **1 :** disqualified **2 :** disabled, handicapped

incapacitar *vt* **1 :** to incapacitate, to disable **2 :** to disqualify

incapaz *adj, pl* **-paces 1 :** incapable, unable **2 :** incompetent, inept

incautación *nf, pl* **-ciones** : seizure, confiscation

incautar *vt* CONFISCAR : to confiscate, to seize — **incautarse** *vr*

incauto, -ta *adj* : unwary, unsuspecting

incendiar *vt* : to set fire to, to burn (down) — **incendiarse** *vr* : to catch fire

incendiario[1], **-ria** *adj* : incendiary, inflammatory

incendiario[2], **-ria** *n* : arsonist

incendio *nm* **1** : fire **2 incendio premeditado** : arson

incentivar *vt* : to encourage, to stimulate

incentivo *nm* : incentive

incertidumbre *nf* : uncertainty, suspense

incesante *adj* : incessant — **incesantemente** *adv*

incesto *nm* : incest

incidencia *nf* **1** : incident **2** : effect, impact **3 por ~** : by chance, accidentally

incidental *adj* : incidental

incidentalmente *adv* : by chance

incidente *nm* : incident, occurrence

incidir *vi* **1 ~ en** : to fall into, to enter into <incidimos en el mismo error : we fell into the same mistake> **2 ~ en** : to affect, to influence, to have a bearing on

incienso *nm* : incense

incierto, -ta *adj* **1** : uncertain **2** : untrue **3** : unsteady, insecure

incineración *nf, pl* **-ciones 1** : incineration **2** : cremation

incinerador *nm* : incinerator

incinerar *vt* **1** : to incinerate **2** : to cremate

incipiente *adj* : incipient

incisión *nf, pl* **-siones** : incision

incisivo[1], **-va** *adj* : incisive

incisivo[2] *nm* : incisor

inciso *nm* : digression, aside

incitación *nf, pl* **-ciones** : incitement

incitante *adj* : provocative

incitar *vt* : to incite, to rouse

incivilizado, -da *adj* : uncivilized

inclemencia *nf* : inclemency, severity

inclemente *adj* : inclement

inclinación *nf, pl* **-ciones 1** PROPENSIÓN : inclination, tendency **2** : incline, slope

inclinado, -da *adj* **1** : sloping **2** : inclined, apt

inclinar *vt* : to tilt, to lean, to incline <inclinar la cabeza : to bow one's head> — **inclinarse** *vr* **1** : to lean, to lean over **2 ~ a** : to be inclined to

incluir {41} *vt* : to include

inclusión *nf, pl* **-siones** : inclusion

inclusive *adv* : inclusively, up to and including

inclusivo, -va *adj* : inclusive

incluso *adv* **1** AUN : even, in fact <es importante e incluso crucial : it is important and even crucial> **2** : inclusively

incógnita *nf* **1** : unknown quantity (in mathematics) **2** : mystery

incógnito, -ta *adj* **1** : unknown **2 de incógnito** : incognito

incoherencia *nf* : incoherence

incoherente *adj* : incoherent — **incoherentemente** *adv*

incoloro, -ra *adj* : colorless

incombustible *adj* : fireproof

incomible *adj* : inedible

incomodar *vt* **1** : to make uncomfortable **2** : to inconvenience — **incomodarse** *vr* : to put oneself out, to take the trouble

incomodidad *nf* **1** : discomfort, awkwardness **2** MOLESTIA : inconvenience, bother

incómodo, -da *adj* **1** : uncomfortable, awkward **2** INCONVENIENTE : inconvenient

incomparable *adj* : incomparable

incompatibilidad *nf* : incompatibility

incompatible *adj* : incompatible, uncongenial

incompetencia *nf* : incompetence

incompetente *adj & nmf* : incompetent

incompleto, -ta *adj* : incomplete

incomprendido, -da *adj* : misunderstood

incomprensible *adj* : incomprehensible

incomprensión *nf, pl* **-siones** : lack of understanding, incomprehension

incomunicación *nf, pl* **-ciones** : lack of communication

incomunicado, -da *adj* **1** : cut off, isolated **2** : in solitary confinement

inconcebible *adj* : inconceivable, unthinkable — **inconcebiblemente** *adv*

inconcluso, -sa *adj* INACABADO : unfinished

incondicional *adj* : unconditional — **incondicionalmente** *adv*

inconexo, -xa *adj* : unconnected, disconnected

inconfesable *adj* : unspeakable, shameful

inconforme *adj & nmf* : nonconformist

inconformidad *nf* : nonconformity

inconformista *adj & nmf* : nonconformist

inconfundible *adj* : unmistakable, obvious — **inconfundiblemente** *adv*

incongruencia *nf* : incongruity

incongruente *adj* : incongruous

inconmensurable *adj* : vast, immeasurable

inconquistable *adj* : unyielding

inconsciencia *nf* **1** : unconsciousness, unawareness **2** : irresponsibility

inconsciente[1] *adj* **1** : unconscious, unaware **2** : reckless, needless — **inconscientemente** *adv*

inconsciente[2] *n* **el inconsciente** : the unconscious

inconsecuente *adj* **:** inconsistent — **inconsecuencia** *nf*

inconsiderado, -da *adj* **:** inconsiderate, thoughtless

inconsistencia *nf* **:** inconsistency

inconsistente *adj* **1 :** weak, flimsy **2 :** watery, runny (of a sauce, etc.) **3 :** inconsistent, weak (of an argument)

inconsolable *adj* **:** inconsolable — **inconsolablemente** *adv*

inconstancia *nf* **:** inconstancy

inconstante *adj* **:** inconstant, fickle, changeable

inconstitucional *adj* **:** unconstitutional

inconstitucionalidad *nf* **:** unconstitutionality

incontable *adj* INNUMERABLE **:** countless, innumerable

incontenible *adj* **:** uncontrollable, unstoppable

incontestable *adj* INCUESTIONABLE, INDISCUTIBLE **:** irrefutable, indisputable

incontinencia *nf* **:** incontinence — **incontinente** *adj*

incontrolable *adj* **:** uncontrollable

incontrolado, -da *adj* **:** uncontrolled, out of control

incontrovertible *adj* **:** indisputable

inconveniencia *nf* **1 :** inconvenience, trouble **2 :** unsuitability, inappropriateness **3 :** tactless remark

inconveniente[1] *adj* **1** INCÓMODO **:** inconvenient **2** INAPROPIADO **:** improper, unsuitable

inconveniente[2] *nm* **:** obstacle, problem, snag <no tengo inconveniente en hacerlo : I don't mind doing it>

incorporación *nf, pl* **-ciones :** incorporation

incorporar *vt* **1 :** to incorporate **2 :** to add, to include — **incorporarse** *vr* **1 :** to sit up **2 ~ a :** to join

incorpóreo, -rea *adj* **:** incorporeal, bodiless

incorrección *n, pl* **-ciones :** impropriety, improper word or action

incorrecto, -ta *adj* **:** incorrect — **incorrectamente** *adv*

incorregible *adj* **:** incorrigible — **incorregibilidad** *nf*

incorruptible *adj* **:** incorruptible

incredulidad *nf* **:** incredulity, skepticism

incrédulo[1]**, -la** *adj* **:** incredulous, skeptical

incrédulo[2]**, -la** *n* **:** skeptic

increíble *adj* **:** incredible, unbelievable — **increíblemente** *adv*

incrementar *vt* **:** to increase — **incrementarse** *vr*

incremento *nm* AUMENTO **:** increase

incriminar *vt* **:** to incriminate — **incriminación** *nf*

incruento, -ta *adj* **:** bloodless

incrustación *nf, pl* **-ciones :** inlay

incrustar *vt* **1 :** to embed **2 :** to inlay — **incrustarse** *vr* **:** to become embedded

incubación *nf, pl* **-ciones :** incubation

incubadora *nf* **:** incubator

incubar *v* **:** to incubate

incuestionable *adj* INCONTESTABLE, INDISCUTIBLE **:** unquestionable, indisputable — **incuestionablemente** *adv*

inculcar {72} *vt* **:** to inculcate, to instill

inculpar *vt* ACUSAR **:** to accuse, to charge

inculto, -ta *adj* **1 :** uncultured, ignorant **2 :** uncultivated, fallow

incumbencia *nf* **:** obligation, responsibility

incumbir *vi* (*3rd person only*) **~ a :** to be incumbent upon, to be of concern to <a mí no me incumbe : it's not my concern>

incumplido, -da *adj* **:** irresponsible, unreliable

incumplimiento *nm* **1 :** nonfulfillment, neglect **2 incumplimiento de contrato :** breach of contract

incumplir *vt* **:** to fail to carry out, to break (a promise, a contract)

incurable *adj* **:** incurable

incurrir *vi* **1 ~ en :** to incur <incurrir en gastos : to incur expenses> **2 ~ en :** to fall into, to commit <incurrió en un error : he made a mistake>

incursión *nf, pl* **-siones :** incursion, raid

incursionar *vi* **1 :** to raid **2 ~ en :** to go into, to enter <el actor incursionó en el baile : the actor worked in dance for a while>

indagación *nf, pl* **-ciones :** investigation, inquiry

indagar {52} *vt* **:** to inquire into, to investigate

indebido, -da *adj* **:** improper, undue — **indebidamente** *adv*

indecencia *nf* **:** indecency, obscenity

indecente *adj* **:** indecent, obscene

indecible *adj* **:** indescribable, inexpressible

indecisión *nf, pl* **-siones :** indecision

indeciso, -sa *adj* **1** IRRESOLUTO **:** indecisive **2 :** undecided

indeclinable *adj* **:** unavoidable

indecoro *nm* **:** impropriety, indecorousness

indecoroso, -sa *adj* **:** indecorous, unseemly

indefectible *adj* **:** unfailing, sure

indefendible *adj* **:** indefensible

indefenso, -sa *adj* **:** defenseless, helpless

indefinido, -da *adj* **1 :** undefined, vague **2** INDETERMINADO **:** indefinite — **indefinidamente** *adv*

indeleble *adj* **:** indelible — **indeleblemente** *adv*

indelicado, -da *adj* **:** indelicate, tactless

indemnización *nf, pl* **-ciones 1 :** indemnity **2 indemnización por despido :** severance pay

indemnizar {21} *vt* **:** to indemnify, to compensate

independencia *nf* **:** independence

independiente *adj* : independent — **independientemente** *adv*
independizarse {21} *vr* : to become independent, to gain independence
indescifrable *adj* : indecipherable
indescriptible *adj* : indescribable — **indescriptiblemente** *adv*
indeseable *adj & nmf* : undesirable
indestructible *adj* : indestructible
indeterminación *nf, pl* **-ciones** : indeterminacy
indeterminado, -da *adj* **1** INDEFINIDO : indefinite **2** : indeterminate
indexar *vt* INDICIAR : to index (wages, prices, etc.)
indicación *nf, pl* **-ciones 1** : sign, signal **2** : direction, instruction **3** : suggestion, hint
indicado, -da *adj* **1** APROPIADO : appropriate, suitable **2** : specified, indicated <al día indicado : on the specified day>
indicador *nm* **1** : gauge, dial, meter **2** : indicator <indicadores económicos : economic indicators>
indicar {72} *vt* **1** SEÑALAR : to indicate **2** ENSEÑAR, MOSTRAR : to show
indicativo[1], **-va** *adj* : indicative
indicativo[2] *nm* : indicative (mood)
índice *nm* **1** : index **2** : index finger, forefinger **3** INDICIO : indication
indiciar *vt* : to index (prices, wages, etc.)
indicio *nm* : indication, sign
indiferencia *nf* : indifference
indiferente *adj* **1** : indifferent, unconcerned **2 ser indiferente** : to be of no concern <me es indiferente : it doesn't matter to me>
indígena[1] *adj* : indigenous, native
indígena[2] *nmf* : native
indigencia *nf* MISERIA : poverty, destitution
indigente *adj & nmf* : indigent
indigestarse *vr* **1** EMPACHARSE : to have indigestion **2** *fam* : to nauseate, to disgust <ese tipo se me indigesta : that guy makes me sick>
indigestión *nf, pl* **-tiones** EMPACHO : indigestion
indigesto, -ta *adj* : indigestible, difficult to digest
indignación *nf, pl* **-ciones** : indignation
indignado, -da *adj* : indignant
indignante *adj* : outrageous, infuriating
indignar *vt* : to outrage, to infuriate — **indignarse** *vr*
indignidad *nf* : indignity
indigno, -na *adj* : unworthy
indio[1], **-dia** *adj* **1** : American Indian, Indian, Amerindian **2** : Indian (from India)
indio[2], **-dia** *n* **1** : American Indian **2** : Indian (from India)
indirecta *nf* **1** : hint, innuendo **2 echar indirectas** *or* **lanzar indirectas** : to drop a hint, to insinuate
indirecto, -ta *adj* : indirect — **indirectamente** *adv*
indisciplina *nf* : indiscipline, unruliness
indisciplinado, -da *adj* : undisciplined, unruly
indiscreción *nf, pl* **-ciones 1** IMPRUDENCIA : indiscretion **2** : tactless remark
indiscreto, -ta *adj* IMPRUDENTE : indiscreet, imprudent — **indiscretamente** *adv*
indiscriminado, -da *adj* : indiscriminate — **indiscriminadamente** *adv*
indiscutible *adj* INCONTESTABLE, INCUESTIONABLE : indisputable, unquestionable — **indiscutiblemente** *adv*
indispensable *adj* : indispensable — **indispensablemente** *adv*
indisponer {60} *vt* **1** : to spoil, to upset **2** : to make ill — **indisponerse** *vr* **1** : to become ill **2 ~ con** : to fall out with
indisposición *nf, pl* **-ciones** : indisposition, illness
indispuesto, -ta *adj* : unwell, indisposed
indistinguible *adj* : indistinguishable
indistintamente *adv* **1** : indistinctly **2** : indiscriminately
indistinto, -ta *adj* : indistinct, vague, faint
individual *adj* : individual — **individualmente** *adv*
individualidad *nf* : individuality
individualismo *nm* : individualism
individualista[1] *adj* : individualistic
individualista[2] *nmf* : individualist
individualizar {21} *vt* : to individualize
individuo *nm* : individual, person
indivisible *adj* : indivisible — **indivisibilidad** *nf*
indocumentado, -da *n* : illegal immigrant
índole *nf* **1** : nature, character **2** CLASE, TIPO : sort, kind
indolencia *nf* : indolence, laziness
indolente *adj* : indolent, lazy
indoloro, -ra *adj* : painless
indomable *adj* **1** : indomitable **2** : unruly, unmanageable
indómito, -ta *adj* : indomitable
indonesio, -sia *adj & n* : Indonesian
inducción *nf, pl* **-ciones** : induction
inducir {61} *vt* **1** : to induce, to cause **2** : to infer, to deduce
inductivo, -va *adj* : inductive
indudable *adj* : unquestionable, beyond doubt
indudablemente *adv* : undoubtedly, unquestionably
indulgencia *nf* **1** : indulgence, leniency **2** : indulgence (in religion)
indulgente *adj* : indulgent, lenient
indultar *vt* : to pardon, to reprieve
indulto *nm* : pardon, reprieve
indumentaria *nf* : clothing, attire
industria *nf* : industry
industrial[1] *adj* : industrial

industrial[2] *nmf* : industrialist, manufacturer
industrialización *nf, pl* **-ciones** : industrialization
industrializar {21} *vt* : to industrialize
industrioso, -sa *adj* : industrious
inédito, -ta *adj* **1** : unpublished **2** : unprecedented
inefable *adj* : ineffable
ineficacia *nf* **1** : inefficiency **2** : ineffectiveness
ineficaz *adj, pl* **-caces 1** : inefficient **2** : ineffective — **ineficazmente** *adv*
ineficiencia *nf* : inefficiency
ineficiente *adj* : inefficient — **ineficientemente** *adv*
inelegancia *nf* : inelegance — **inelegante** *adj*
inelegible *adj* : ineligible — **inelegibilidad** *nf*
ineludible *adj* : inescapable, unavoidable — **ineludiblemente** *adv*
ineptitud *nf* : ineptitude, incompetence
inepto, -ta *adj* : inept, incompetent
inequidad *nf* : inequity
inequitativo, -va *adj* : inequitable
inequívoco, -ca *adj* : unequivocal, unmistakable — **inequívocamente** *adv*
inercia *nf* **1** : inertia **2** : apathy, passivity **3 por ~** : out of habit
inerme *adj* : unarmed, defenseless
inerte *adj* : inert
inescrupuloso, -sa *adj* : unscrupulous
inescrutable *adj* : inscrutable
inesperado, -da *adj* : unexpected — **inesperadamente** *adv*
inestabilidad *nf* : instability, unsteadiness
inestable *adj* : unstable, unsteady
inestimable *adj* : inestimable, invaluable
inevitabilidad *nf* : inevitability
inevitable *adj* : inevitable, unavoidable — **inevitablemente** *adv*
inexactitud *nf* : inaccuracy
inexacto, -ta *adj* : inexact, inaccurate
inexcusable *adj* : inexcusable, unforgivable
inexistencia *nf* : lack, nonexistence
inexistente *adj* : nonexistent
inexorable *adj* : inexorable — **inexorablemente** *adv*
inexperiencia *nf* : inexperience
inexperto, -ta *adj* : inexperienced, unskilled
inexplicable *adj* : inexplicable — **inexplicablemente** *adv*
inexplorado, -da *adj* : unexplored
inexpresable *adj* : inexpressible
inexpresivo, -va *adj* : inexpressive, expressionless
inextinguible *adj* **1** : inextinguishable **2** : unquenchable
inextricable *adj* : inextricable — **inextricablemente** *adv*
infalible *adj* : infallible — **infaliblemente** *adv*
infame *adj* **1** : infamous **2** : loathsome, vile <tiempo infame : terrible weather>
infamia *nf* : infamy, disgrace
infancia *nf* **1** NIÑEZ : infancy, childhood **2** : children *pl* **3** : beginnings *pl*
infante *nm* **1** : infante, prince **2** : infantryman
infantería *nf* : infantry
infantil *adj* **1** : childish, infantile **2** : child's, children's
infarto *nm* : heart attack
infatigable *adj* : indefatigable, tireless — **infatigablemente** *adv*
infección *nf, pl* **-ciones** : infection
infeccioso, -sa *adj* : infectious
infectar *vt* : to infect — **infectarse** *vr*
infecto, -ta *adj* **1** : infected **2** : repulsive, sickening
infecundidad *nf* : infertility
infecundo, -da *adj* : infertile, barren
infelicidad *nf* : unhappiness
infeliz[1] *adj, pl* **-lices 1** : unhappy **2** : hapless, unfortunate, wretched
infeliz[2] *nmf, pl* **-lices** : wretch
inferior[1] *adj* : inferior, lower
inferior[2] *nmf* : inferior, underling
inferioridad *nf* : inferiority
inferir {76} *vt* **1** DEDUCIR : to infer, to deduce **2** : to cause (harm or injury), to inflict
infernal *adj* : infernal, hellish
infestación *n, pl* **-ciones** : infestation
infestar *vt* **1** : to infest **2** : to overrun, to invade
infición *nf, pl* **-ciones** *Mex* : pollution
infidelidad *nf* : unfaithfulness, infidelity
infiel[1] *adj* : unfaithful, disloyal
infiel[2] *nmf* : infidel, heathen
infierno *nm* **1** : hell **2 el quinto infierno** : the middle of nowhere
infiltrar *vt* : to infiltrate — **infiltrarse** *vr* — **infiltración** *nf*
infinidad *nf* **1** : infinity **2** SINFÍN : great number, huge quantity <una infinidad de veces : countless times>
infinitesimal *adj* : infinitesimal
infinitivo *nm* : infinitive
infinito[1] *adv* : infinitely, vastly
infinito[2], **-ta** *adj* **1** : infinite **2** : limitless, endless **3 hasta lo infinito** : ad infinitum — **infinitamente** *adv*
infinito[3] *nm* : infinity
inflable *adj* : inflatable
inflación *nf, pl* **-ciones** : inflation
inflacionario, -ria *adj* : inflationary
inflamable *adj* : flammable
inflamación *nf, pl* **-ciones** : inflammation
inflamar *vt* : to inflame
inflamatorio, -ria *adj* : inflammatory
inflar *vt* HINCHAR : to inflate — **inflarse** *vr* **1** : to swell **2** : to become conceited
inflexibilidad *nf* : inflexibility
inflexible *adj* : inflexible, unyielding
inflexión *nf, pl* **-xiones** : inflection
infligir {35} *vt* : to inflict
influencia *nf* INFLUJO : influence

influenciable *adj* : easily influenced, suggestible

influenciar *vt* : to influence

influenza *nf* : influenza

influir {41} *vt* : to influence — *vi* **~ en** *or* **~ sobre** : to have an influence on, to affect

influjo *nm* INFLUENCIA : influence

influyente *adj* : influential

información *nf, pl* **-ciones 1** : information **2** INFORME : report, inquiry **3** NOTICIAS : news

informado, -da *adj* : informed <bien informado : well-informed>

informador, -dora *n* : informer, informant

informal *adj* **1** : unreliable (of persons) **2** : informal, casual — **informalmente** *adv*

informalidad *nf* : informality

informante *nmf* : informant

informar *vt* ENTERAR : to inform — *vi* : to report — **informarse** *vr* ENTERARSE : to get information, to find out

informática *nf* : computer science, computing

informativo[1], -va *adj* : informative

informativo[2] *nm* : news program, news

informatización *nf, pl* **-ciones** : computerization

informatizar {21} *vt* : to computerize

informe[1] *adj* AMORFO : shapeless, formless

informe[2] *nm* **1** : report **2** : reference (for employment) **3** INFORMES *nmpl* : information, data

infortunado, -da *adj* : unfortunate, unlucky

infortunio *nm* **1** DESGRACIA : misfortune **2** CONTRATIEMPO : mishap

infracción *nf, pl* **-ciones** : violation, offense, infraction

infractor, -tora *n* : offender

infraestructura *nf* : infrastructure

infrahumano, -na *adj* : subhuman

infranqueable *adj* **1** : impassable **2** : insurmountable

infrarrojo, -ja *adj* : infrared

infrecuente *adj* : infrequent

infringir {35} *vt* : to infringe, to breach

infructuoso, -sa *adj* : fruitless — **infructuosamente** *adv*

ínfulas *nfpl* **1** : conceit **2 darse ínfulas** : to put on airs

infundado, -da *adj* : unfounded, baseless

infundio *nm* : false story, lie, tall tale <todo eso son infundios : that's a pack of lies>

infundir *vt* **1** : to instill **2 infundir ánimo a** : to encourage **3 infundir miedo a** : to intimidate

infusión *nf, pl* **-siones** : infusion

ingeniar *vt* : to devise, to think up — **ingeniarse** *vr* : to manage, to find a way

ingeniería *nf* : engineering

ingeniero, -ra *n* : engineer

ingenio *nm* **1** : ingenuity **2** CHISPA : wit, wits **3** : device, apparatus **4 ingenio azucarero** : sugar refinery

ingenioso, -sa *adj* **1** : ingenious **2** : clever, witty — **ingeniosamente** *adv*

ingente *adj* : huge, enormous

ingenuidad *nf* : naïveté, ingenuousness

ingenuo[1], -nua *adj* CÁNDIDO : naive — **ingenuamente** *adv*

ingenuo[2], -nua *n* : naive person

ingerencia → **injerencia**

ingerir {76} *vt* : to ingest, to consume

ingestión *nf, pl* **-tiones** : ingestion

ingle *nf* : groin

inglés[1], -glesa *adj, mpl* **ingleses** : English

inglés[2], -glesa *n, mpl* **ingleses** : Englishman *m,* Englishwoman *f*

inglés[3] *nm* : English (language)

inglete *nm* : miter joint

ingobernable *adj* : ungovernable, lawless

ingratitud *nf* : ingratitude

ingrato[1], -ta *adj* **1** : ungrateful **2** : thankless

ingrato[2], -ta *n* : ingrate

ingrediente *nm* : ingredient

ingresar *vt* **1** : to admit <ingresaron a Luis al hospital : Luis was admitted into the hospital> **2** : to deposit — *vi* **1** : to enter, to go in **2 ~ en** : to join, to enroll in

ingreso *nm* **1** : entrance, entry **2** : admission **3 ingresos** *nmpl* : income, earnings *pl*

íngrimo, -ma *adj* : all alone, all by oneself

inhábil *adj* : unskillful, clumsy

inhabilidad *nf* **1** : unskillfulness **2** : unfitness

inhabilitar *vt* **1** : to disqualify, to bar **2** : to disable

inhabitable *adj* : uninhabitable

inhabituado, -da *adj* **~ a** : unaccustomed to

inhalante *nm* : inhalant

inhalar *vt* : to inhale — **inhalación** *nf*

inherente *adj* : inherent

inhibición *nf, pl* **-ciones** COHIBICIÓN : inhibition

inhibir *vt* : to inhibit — **inhibirse** *vr*

inhóspito, -ta *adj* : inhospitable

inhumación *nf, pl* **-ciones** : interment, burial

inhumanidad *nf* : inhumanity

inhumano, -na *adj* : inhuman, cruel, inhumane

inhumar *vt* : to inter, to bury

iniciación *nf, pl* **-ciones 1** : initiation **2** : introduction

iniciado, -da *n* : initiate

iniciador[1], -dora *adj* : initiatory

iniciador[2], -dora *n* : initiator, originator

inicial[1] *adj* : initial, original — **inicialmente** *adv*

inicial[2] *nf* : initial (letter)

iniciar *vt* COMENZAR : to initiate, to begin — **iniciarse** *vr*
iniciativa *nf* : initiative
inicio *nm* COMIENZO : beginning
inicuo, -cua *adj* : iniquitous, wicked
inigualado, -da *adj* : unequaled
inimaginable *adj* : unimaginable
inimitable *adj* : inimitable
ininteligible *adj* : unintelligible
ininterrumpido, -da *adj* : uninterrupted, continuous — **ininterrumpidamente** *adv*
iniquidad *nf* : iniquity, wickedness
injerencia *nf* : interference
injerirse {76} *vr* ENTROMETERSE, INMISCUIRSE : to meddle, to interfere
injertar *vt* : to graft
injerto *nm* : graft <injerto de piel : skin graft>
injuria *nf* AGRAVIO : affront, insult
injuriar *vt* INSULTAR : to insult, to revile
injurioso, -sa *adj* : insulting, abusive
injusticia *nf* : injustice, unfairness
injustificable *adj* : unjustifiable
injustificadamente *adv* : unjustifiably, unfairly
injustificado, -da *adj* : unjustified, unwarranted
injusto, -ta *adj* : unfair, unjust — **injustamente** *adv*
inmaculado, -da *adj* : immaculate, spotless
inmadurez *nf, pl* **-reces** : immaturity
inmaduro, -ra *adj* **1** : immature **2** : unripe
inmediaciones *nfpl* : environs, surrounding area
inmediatamente *adv* ENSEGUIDA : immediately
inmediatez *nf, pl* **-teces** : immediacy
inmediato, -ta *adj* **1** : immediate **2** CONTIGUO : adjoining **3 de ~** : immediately, right away **4 ~ a** : next to, close to
inmejorable *adj* : excellent, unbeatable
inmensidad *nf* : immensity, vastness
inmenso, -sa *adj* ENORME : immense, huge, vast — **inmensamente** *adv*
inmensurable *adj* : boundless, immeasurable
inmerecido, -da *adj* : undeserved — **inmerecidamente** *adv*
inmersión *nf, pl* **-siones** : immersion
inmerso, -sa *adj* **1** : immersed **2** : involved, absorbed
inmigración *nf, pl* **-ciones** : immigration
inmigrado, -da *adj & n* : immigrant
inmigrante *adj & nmf* : immigrant
inmigrar *vi* : to immigrate
inminencia *nf* : imminence
inminente *adj* : imminent — **inminentemente** *adv*
inmiscuirse {41} *vr* ENTROMETERSE, INJERIRSE : to meddle, to interfere
inmobiliario, -ria *adj* : real estate, property
inmoderación *n, pl* **-ciones** : immoderation, intemperance
inmoderado, -da *adj* : immoderate, excessive — **inmoderamente** *adv*
inmodestia *nf* : immodesty — **inmodesto, -ta** *adj*
inmolar *vt* : to immolate — **inmolación** *nf*
inmoral *adj* : immoral
inmoralidad *nf* : immorality
inmortal *adj & nmf* : immortal
inmortalidad *nf* : immortality
inmortalizar {21} *vt* : to immortalize
inmotivado, -da *adj* **1** : unmotivated **2** : groundless
inmovible *adj* : immovable, fixed
inmóvil *adj* **1** : still, motionless **2** : steadfast
inmovilidad *nf* : immobility
inmovilizar {21} *vt* : to immobilize
inmueble *nm* : building, property
inmundicia *nf* : dirt, filth, trash
inmundo, -da *adj* : dirty, filthy, nasty
inmune *adj* : immune
inmunidad *nf* : immunity
inmunizar {21} *vt* : to immunize — **inmunización** *nf*
inmunología *nf* : immunology
inmunológico, -ca *adj* : immune <sistema inmunológico : immune system>
inmutabilidad *nf* : immutability
inmutable *adj* : immutable, unchangeable
innato, -ta *adj* : innate, inborn
innecesario, -ria *adj* : unnecessary — **innecesariamente** *adv*
innegable *adj* : undeniable
innoble *adj* : ignoble — **innoblemente** *adv*
innovación *nf, pl* **-ciones** : innovation
innovador, -dora *adj* : innovative
innovar *vt* : to introduce — *vi* : to innovate
innumerable *adj* INCONTABLE : innumerable, countless
inobjetable *adj* : indisputable, unobjectionable
inocencia *nf* : innocence
inocente[1] *adj* **1** : innocent **2** INGENUO : naive — **inocentemente** *adv*
inocente[2] *nmf* : innocent person
inocentón[1], **-tona** *adj, mpl* **-tones** : naive, gullible
inocentón[2], **-tona** *n, mpl* **-tones** : simpleton, dupe
inocuidad *nf* : harmlessness
inocular *vt* : to inoculate, to vaccinate — **inoculación** *nf*
inocuo, -cua *adj* : innocuous, harmless
inodoro[1], **-ra** *adj* : odorless
inodoro[2] *nm* : toilet
inofensivo, -va *adj* : inoffensive, harmless
inolvidable *adj* : unforgettable
inoperable *adj* : inoperable
inoperante *adj* : ineffective, inoperative

inopinado, -da *adj* : unexpected — **inopinadamente** *adv*
inoportuno, -na *adj* : untimely, inopportune, inappropriate
inorgánico, -ca *adj* : inorganic
inoxidable *adj* **1** : rustproof **2 acero inoxidable** : stainless steel
inquebrantable *adj* : unshakable, unwavering
inquietante *adj* : disturbing, worrisome
inquietar *vt* PREOCUPAR : to disturb, to upset, to worry — **inquietarse** *vr*
inquieto, -ta *adj* **1** : anxious, uneasy, worried **2** : restless
inquietud *nf* **1** : anxiety, uneasiness, worry **2** AGITACIÓN : restlessness
inquilinato *nm* : tenancy
inquilino, -na *n* : tenant, occupant
inquina *nf* **1** : aversion, dislike **2** : ill will <tener inquina a alguien : to have a grudge against someone>
inquirir {4} *vi* : to make inquiries — *vt* : to investigate
inquisición *nf, pl* **-ciones** : investigation, inquiry
inquisidor, -dora *adj* : inquisitive
inquisitivo, -va *adj* : inquisitive, curious — **inquisitivamente** *adv*
insaciable *adj* : insatiable
insalubre *adj* **1** : unhealthy **2** ANTIHIGIÉNICO : unsanitary
insalubridad *nf* : unhealthiness
insalvable *adj* : insuperable, insurmountable
insano, -na *adj* **1** LOCO : insane, mad **2** INSALUBRE : unhealthy
insatisfacción *nf, pl* **-ciones** : dissatisfaction
insatisfactorio *nm* : unsatisfactory
insatisfecho, -cha *adj* **1** : dissatisfied **2** : unsatisfied
inscribir {33} *vt* **1** MATRICULAR : to enroll, to register **2** GRABAR : to engrave — **inscribirse** *vr* : to register, to sign up
inscripción *nf, pl* **-ciones 1** MATRÍCULA : enrollment, registration **2** : inscription
inscrito *pp* → **inscribir**
insecticida[1] *adj* : insecticidal
insecticida[2] *nm* : insecticide
insecto *nm* : insect
inseguridad *nf* **1** : insecurity **2** : lack of safety **3** : uncertainty
inseguro, -ra *adj* **1** : insecure **2** : unsafe **3** : uncertain
inseminar *vt* : to inseminate — **inseminación** *nf*
insensatez *nf, pl* **-teces** : foolishness, stupidity
insensato[1], **-ta** *adj* : foolish, senseless
insensato[2], **-ta** *n* : fool
insensibilidad *nf* : insensitivity
insensible *adj* : insensitive, unfeeling
inseparable *adj* : inseparable — **inseparablemente** *adv*
inserción *nf, pl* **-ciones** : insertion
insertar *vt* : to insert
inservible *adj* INÚTIL : useless, unusable
insidia *nf* **1** : snare, trap **2** : malice
insidioso, -sa *adj* : insidious
insigne *adj* : noted, famous
insignia *nf* ENSEÑA : insignia, emblem, badge
insignificancia *nf* **1** : insignificance **2** NIMIEDAD : trifle, triviality
insignificante *adj* : insignificant
insincero, -ra *adj* : insincere — **insinceridad** *nf*
insinuación *nf, pl* **-ciones** : insinuation, hint
insinuante *adj* : suggestive
insinuar {3} *vt* : to insinuate, to hint at — **insinuarse** *vr* **1 ~ a** : to make advances to **2 ~ en** : to worm one's way into
insipidez *nf, pl* **-deces** : insipidness, blandness
insípido, -da *adj* : insipid, bland
insistencia *nf* : insistence
insistente *adj* : insistent — **insistentemente** *adv*
insistir *v* : to insist
insociable *adj* : unsociable
insolación *nf, pl* **-ciones** : sunstroke
insolencia *nf* IMPERTINENCIA : insolence
insolente *adj* IMPERTINENTE : insolent
insólito, -ta *adj* : rare, unusual
insoluble *adj* : insoluble — **insolubilidad** *nf*
insolvencia *nf* : insolvency, bankruptcy
insolvente *adj* : insolvent, bankrupt
insomne *adj & nmf* : insomniac
insomnio *nm* : insomnia
insondable *adj* : fathomless, deep
insonorizado, -da *adj* : soundproof
insoportable *adj* INAGUANTABLE : unbearable, intolerable
insoslayable *adj* : unavoidable, inescapable
insospechado, -da *adj* : unexpected, unforeseen
insostenible *adj* : untenable
inspección *nf, pl* **-ciones** : inspection
inspeccionar *vt* : to inspect
inspector, -tora *n* : inspector
inspiración *nf, pl* **-ciones 1** : inspiration **2** INHALACIÓN : inhalation
inspirador, -dora *adj* : inspiring
inspirar *vt* : to inspire — *vi* INHALAR : to inhale
instalación *nf, pl* **-ciones** : installation
instalar *vt* **1** : to install **2** : to instate — **instalarse** *vr* ESTABLECERSE : to settle, to establish oneself
instancia *nf* **1** : petition, request **2 en última instancia** : as a last resort
instantánea *nf* : snapshot
instantáneo, -nea *adj* : instantaneous — **instantáneamente** *adv*
instante *nm* **1** : instant, moment **2 al instante** : immediately **3 a cada instante** : frequently, all the time **4 por instantes** : constantly, incessantly

instar *vt* APREMIAR **:** to urge, to press — *vi* URGIR **:** to be urgent or pressing <insta que vayamos pronto : it is imperative that we leave soon>
instauración *nf, pl* **-ciones :** establishment
instaurar *vt* **:** to establish
instigador, -dora *n* **:** instigator
instigar {52} *vt* **:** to instigate, to incite
instintivo, -va *adj* **:** instinctive — **instintivamente** *adv*
instinto *nm* **:** instinct
institución *nf, pl* **-ciones :** institution
institucional *adj* **:** institutional — **institucionalmente** *adv*
institucionalización *nf, pl* **-ciones :** institutionalization
institucionalizar {21} *vt* **:** to institutionalize
instituir {41} *vt* ESTABLECER, FUNDAR **:** to institute, to establish, to found
instituto *nm* **:** institute
institutriz *nf, pl* **-trices :** governess *f*
instrucción *nf, pl* **-ciones 1** EDUCACIÓN **:** education **2 instrucciones** *nfpl* **:** instructions, directions
instructivo, -va *adj* **:** instructive, educational
instructor, -tora *n* **:** instructor
instruir {41} *vt* **1** ADIESTRAR **:** to instruct, to train **2** ENSEÑAR **:** to educate, to teach
instrumentación *nf, pl* **-ciones :** orchestration
instrumental *adj* **:** instrumental
instrumentar *vt* **:** to orchestrate
instrumentista *nmf* **:** instrumentalist
instrumento *nm* **:** instrument
insubordinado, -da *adj* **:** insubordinate — **insubordinación** *nf*
insubordinarse *vr* **:** to rebel
insuficiencia *nf* **1 :** insufficiency, inadequacy **2 insuficiencia cardíaca :** heart failure
insuficiente *adj* **:** insufficient, inadequate — **insuficientemente** *adv*
insufrible *adj* **:** insufferable
insular *adj* **:** insular
insulina *nf* **:** insulin
insulso, -sa *adj* **1** INSÍPIDO **:** insipid, bland **2 :** dull
insultante *adj* **:** insulting
insultar *vt* **:** to insult
insulto *nm* **:** insult
insumos *nmpl* **:** supplies <insumos agrícolas : agricultural supplies>
insuperable *adj* **:** insuperable, insurmountable
insurgente *adj & nmf* **:** insurgent — **insurgencia** *nf*
insurrección *nf, pl* **-ciones :** insurrection, uprising
insustancial *adj* **:** insubstantial, flimsy
insustituible *adj* **:** irreplaceable
intachable *adj* **:** irreproachable, faultless
intacto, -ta *adj* **:** intact
intangible *adj* IMPALPABLE **:** intangible, impalpable
integración *nf, pl* **-ciones :** integration
integral *adj* **1 :** integral, essential **2 pan integral :** whole grain bread
integrante[1] *adj* **:** integrating, integral
integrante[2] *nmf* **:** member
integrar *vt* **:** to make up, to compose — **integrarse** *vr* **:** to integrate, to fit in
integridad *nf* **1** RECTITUD **:** integrity, honesty **2 :** wholeness, completeness
integrismo *nm* **:** fundamentalism
integrista *adj & nmf* **:** fundamentalist
íntegro, -gra *adj* **1 :** honest, upright **2** ENTERO **:** whole, complete **3 :** unabridged
intelecto *nm* **:** intellect
intelectual *adj & nmf* **:** intellectual — **intelectualmente** *adv*
intelectualidad *nf* **:** intelligentsia
inteligencia *nf* **:** intelligence
inteligente *adj* **:** intelligent — **inteligentemente** *adv*
inteligible *adj* **:** intelligible — **inteligibilidad** *nf*
intemperancia *adj* **:** intemperance, excess
intemperie *nf* **1 :** bad weather, elements *pl* **2 a la intemperie :** in the open air, outside
intempestivo, -va *adj* **:** inopportune, untimely — **intempestivamente** *adv*
intención *nf, pl* **-ciones :** intention, plan
intencional *adj* **:** intentional — **intencionalmente** *adv*
intendencia *nf* **:** management, administration
intendente *nmf* **:** quartermaster
intensidad *nf* **:** intensity
intensificar {72} *vt* **:** to intensify — **intensificarse** *vr*
intensivo, -va *adj* **:** intensive — **intensivamente** *adv*
intenso, -sa *adj* **:** intense — **intensamente** *adv*
intentar *vt* **:** to attempt, to try
intento *nm* **1** PROPÓSITO **:** intent, intention **2** TENTATIVA **:** attempt, try
interacción *nf, pl* **-ciones :** interaction
interactivo, -va *adj* **:** interactive
interactuar {3} *vi* **:** to interact
intercalar *vt* **:** to intersperse, to insert
intercambiable *adj* **:** interchangeable
intercambiar *vt* CANJEAR **:** to exchange, to trade
intercambio *nm* CANJE **:** exchange, trade
interceder *vi* **:** to intercede
intercepción *nf, pl* **-ciones :** interception
interceptar *vt* **1 :** to intercept, to block **2 interceptar las líneas :** to wiretap
intercesión *nf, pl* **-siones :** intercession
intercomunicación *nf, pl* **-ciones :** intercommunication
interconexión *nf, pl* **-xiones :** interconnection
interconfesional *adj* **:** interdenominational

interdependencia *nf* : interdependence — **interdependiente** *adj*

interdicción *nf, pl* **-ciones** : interdiction, prohibition

interés *nm, pl* **-reses** : interest

interesado, -da *adj* **1** : interested **2** : selfish, self-seeking

interesante *adj* : interesting

interesar *vt* : to interest — *vi* : to be of interest, to be interesting — **interesarse** *vr*

interestatal *adj* : interstate <autopista interestatal : interstate highway>

interestelar *adj* : interstellar

interfaz *nf, pl* **-faces** : interface

interferencia *nf* : interference, static

interferir {76} *vi* : to interfere, to meddle — *vt* : to interfere with, to obstruct

interín[1] *or* **ínterin** *adv* : meanwhile

interín[2] *or* **ínterin** *nm, pl* **-rines** : meantime, interim <en el interín : in the meantime>

interinamente *adv* : temporarily

interino, -na *adj* : acting, temporary, interim

interior[1] *adj* : interior, inner

interior[2] *nm* **1** : interior, inside **2** : inland region

interiormente *adv* : inwardly

interjección *nf, pl* **-ciones** : interjection

interlocutor, -tora *n* : interlocutor, speaker

intermediario, -ria *adj & n* : intermediary, go-between

intermedio[1], **-dia** *adj* : intermediate

intermedio[2] *nm* **1** : intermission **2 por intermedio de** : by means of

interminable *adj* : interminable, endless — **interminablemente** *adv*

intermisión *nf, pl* **-siones** : intermission, pause

intermitente[1] *adj* **1** : intermittent **2 luz intermitente** : strobe light — **intermitentemente** *adv*

intermitente[2] *nm* : blinker, turn signal

internacional *adj* : international — **internacionalmente** *adv*

internacionalismo *nm* : internationalism

internacionalizar {21} *vt* : to internationalize

internado *nm* : boarding school

internar *vt* : to commit, to confine — **internarse** *vr* **1** : to penetrate, to advance into **2 ~ en** : to go into, to enter

internista *nmf* : internist

interno[1], **-na** *adj* : internal — **internamente** *adv*

interno[2], **-na** *n* **1** : intern **2** : inmate, internee

interpelación *nf, pl* **-ciones** : appeal, plea

interpelar *vt* : to question (formally)

interpolar *vt* : to insert, to interpolate

interponer {60} *vt* : to interpose — **interponerse** *vr* : to intervene

interpretación *nf, pl* **-ciones** : interpretation

interpretar *vt* **1** : to interpret **2** : to play, to perform

interpretativo, -va *adj* : interpretive

intérprete *nmf* **1** TRADUCTOR : interpreter **2** : performer

interpuesto *pp* → **interponer**

interracial *adj* : interracial

interrelación *nf, pl* **-ciones** : interrelationship

interrelacionar *vi* : to interrelate

interrogación *nf, pl* **-ciones 1** : interrogation, questioning **2 signo de interrogación** : question mark

interrogador, -dora *n* : interrogator, questioner

interrogante[1] *adj* : questioning

interrogante[2] *nm* **1** : question mark **2** : query

interrogar {52} *vt* : to interrogate, to question

interrogativo, -va *adj* : interrogative

interrogatorio *nm* : interrogation, questioning

interrumpir *v* : to interrupt

interrupción *nf, pl* **-ciones** : interruption

interruptor *nm* **1** : (electrical) switch **2** : circuit breaker

intersección *nf, pl* **-ciones** : intersection

intersticio *nm* : interstice — **intersticial** *adj*

intervalo *nm* : interval

intervención *nf, pl* **-ciones 1** : intervention **2** : audit **3 intervención quirúrgica** : operation

intervencionista *adj & nmf* : interventionist

intervenir {87} *vi* **1** : to take part **2** INTERCEDER : to intervene, to intercede — *vt* **1** : to control, to supervise **2** : to audit **3** : to operate on **4** : to tap (a telephone)

interventor, -tora *n* **1** : inspector **2** : auditor, comptroller

intestado, -da *adj* : intestate

intestinal *adj* : intestinal

intestino *nm* : intestine

intimar *vi* **~ con** : to become friendly with — *vt* : to require, to call on

intimidación *nf, pl* **-ciones** : intimidation

intimidad *nf* **1** : intimacy **2** : privacy, private life

intimidar *vt* ACOBARDAR : to intimidate

íntimo, -ma *adj* **1** : intimate, close **2** PRIVADO : private — **íntimamente** *adv*

intitular *vt* : to entitle, to title

intocable *adj* : untouchable

intolerable *adj* : intolerable, unbearable

intolerancia *nf* : intolerance

intolerante[1] *adj* : intolerant

intolerante[2] *nmf* : intolerant person, bigot

intoxicación *nf, pl* **-ciones** : poisoning

intoxicante *nm* : poison

intoxicar {72} *vt* : to poison
intranquilidad *nf* PREOCUPACIÓN : worry, anxiety
intranquilizar {21} *vt* : to upset, to make uneasy — **intranquilizarse** *vr* : to get worried, to be anxious
intranquilo, -la *adj* PREOCUPADO : uneasy, worried
intransigencia *nf* : intransigence
intransigente *adj* : intransigent, unyielding
intransitable *adj* : impassable
intransitivo, -va *adj* : intransitive
intrascendente *adj* : unimportant, insignificant
intratable *adj* **1** : intractable **2** : awkward **3** : unsociable
intravenoso, -sa *adj* : intravenous
intrepidez *nf* : fearlessness
intrépido, -da *adj* : intrepid, fearless
intriga *nf* : intrigue
intrigante *nmf* : schemer
intrigar {52} *v* : to intrigue — **intrigante** *adj*
intrincado, -da *adj* : intricate, involved
intrínseco, -ca *adj* : intrinsic — **intrínsecamente** *adv*
introducción *nf, pl* **-ciones** : introduction
introducir {61} *vt* **1** : to introduce **2** : to bring in **3** : to insert **4** : to input, to enter — **introducirse** *vr* : to penetrate, to get into
introductorio, -ria *adj* : introductory
intromisión *nf, pl* **-siones** : interference, meddling
introspección *nf, pl* **-ciones** : introspection
introspectivo, -va *adj* : introspective
introvertido[1], -da *adj* : introverted
introvertido[2], -da *n* : introvert
intrusión *nf, pl* **-siones** : intrusion
intruso[1], -sa *adj* : intrusive
intruso[2], -sa *n* : intruder
intuición *nf, pl* **-ciones** : intuition
intuir {41} *vt* : to intuit, to sense
intuitivo, -va *adj* : intuitive — **intuitivamente** *adv*
inundación *nf, pl* **-ciones** : flood, inundation
inundar *vt* : to flood, to inundate
inusitado, -da *adj* : unusual, uncommon — **inusitadamente** *adv*
inusual *adj* : unusual, uncommon — **inusualmente** *adv*
inútil[1] *adj* INSERVIBLE : useless — **inútilmente** *adv*
inútil[2] *nmf* : good-for-nothing
inutilidad *nf* : uselessness
inutilizar {21} *vt* **1** : to make useless **2** INCAPACITAR : to disable, to put out of commission
invadir *vt* : to invade
invalidar *vt* : to nullify, to invalidate
invalidez *nf, pl* **-deces 1** : invalidity **2** : disablement
inválido, -da *adj & n* : invalid
invariable *adj* : invariable — **invariablemente** *adv*
invasión *nf, pl* **-siones** : invasion
invasivo, -va *adj* : invasive
invasor[1], -sora *adj* : invading
invasor[2], -sora *n* : invader
invectiva *nf* : invective, abuse
invencible *adj* **1** : invincible **2** : insurmountable
invención *nf, pl* **-ciones 1** INVENTO : invention **2** MENTIRA : fabrication, lie
inventar *vt* **1** : to invent **2** : to fabricate, to make up
inventariar {85} *vt* : to inventory
inventario *nm* : inventory
inventiva *nf* : ingenuity, inventiveness
inventivo, -va *adj* : inventive
invento *nm* INVENCIÓN : invention
inventor, -tora *n* : inventor
invernadero *nm* : greenhouse, hothouse
invernal *adj* : winter, wintry
invernar {55} *vi* **1** : to spend the winter **2** HIBERNAR : to hibernate
inverosímil *adj* : unlikely, farfetched
inversión *nf, pl* **-siones 1** : inversion **2** : investment
inversionista *nmf* : investor
inverso[1], -sa *adj* **1** : inverse, inverted **2** CONTRARIO : opposite **3 a la inversa** : on the contrary, vice versa **4 en orden inverso** : in reverse order — **inversamente** *adv*
inverso[2] *n* : inverse
inversor, -sora *n* : investor
invertebrado[1], -da *adj* : invertebrate
invertebrado[2] *nm* : invertebrate
invertir {76} *vt* **1** : to invert, to reverse **2** : to invest — *vi* : to make an investment — **invertirse** *vr* : to be reversed
investidura *nf* : investiture, inauguration
investigación *nf, pl* **-ciones 1** ENCUESTA, INDAGACIÓN : investigation, inquiry **2** : research
investigador[1], -dora *adj* : investigative
investigador[2], -dora *n* **1** : investigator **2** : researcher
investigar {52} *vt* **1** INDAGAR : to investigate **2** : to research — *vi* **~ sobre** : to do research into
investir {54} *vt* **1** : to empower **2** : to swear in, to inaugurate
inveterado, -da *adj* : inveterate, deep-seated
invicto, -ta *adj* : undefeated
invidente[1] *adj* CIEGO : blind, sightless
invidente[2] *nmf* CIEGO : blind person
invierno *nm* : winter, wintertime
inviolable *adj* : inviolable — **inviolabilidad** *nf*
inviolado, -da *adj* : inviolate, pure
invisibilidad *nf* : invisibility
invisible *adj* : invisible — **invisiblemente** *adv*
invitación *nf, pl* **-ciones** : invitation
invitado, -da *n* : guest

invitar *vt* : to invite
invocación *nf, pl* **-ciones** : invocation
invocar {72} *vt* : to invoke, to call on
involucramiento *nm* : involvement
involucrar *vt* : to implicate, to involve — **involucrarse** *vr* : to get involved
involuntario, -ria *adj* : involuntary — **involuntariamente** *adv*
invulnerable *adj* : invulnerable
inyección *nf, pl* **-ciones** : injection, shot
inyectado, -da *adj* **ojos inyectados** : bloodshot eyes
inyectar *vt* : to inject
ion *nm* : ion
ionizar {21} *vt* : to ionize — **ionización** *nf*
ionosfera *nf* : ionosphere
ir {43} *vi* **1** : to go <ir a pie : to go on foot, to walk> <ir a caballo : to ride horseback> <ir a casa : to go home> **2** : to lead, to extend, to stretch <el camino va de Cali a Bogotá : the road goes from Cali to Bogotá> **3** FUNCIONAR : to work, to function <esta computadora ya no va : this computer doesn't work anymore> **4** : to get on, to get along <¿cómo te va? : how are you?, how's it going?> <el negocio no va bien : the business isn't doing well> **5** : to suit <ese vestido te va bien : that dress really suits you> **6 ~ con** : to be <ir con prisa : to be in a hurry> **7 ~ por** : to follow, to go along <fueron por la costa : they followed the shoreline> **8 dejarse ir** : to let oneself go **9 ir a parar** : to end up **10 vamos a ver** : let's see — *v aux* **1** (*with present participle*) <ir caminando : to walk> <¡voy corriendo! : I'll be right there!> **2 ~ a** : to be going to <voy a hacerlo : I'm going to do it> <el avión va a despegar : the plane is about to take off> — **irse** *vr* **1** : to leave, to go <¡vámonos! : let's go!> <todo el mundo se fue : everyone left> **2** ESCAPARSE : to leak **3** GASTARSE : to be used up, to be gone
ira *nf* CÓLERA, FURIA : wrath, anger
iracundo, -da *adj* : irate, angry
iraní *adj & nmf* : Iranian
iraquí *adj & nmf* : Iraqi
irascible *adj* : irascible, irritable — **irascibilidad** *nf*
irga, irgue, etc. → **erguir**
iridio *nm* : iridium
iridiscencia *nf* : iridescence — **iridiscente** *adj*
iris *nms & pl* **1** : iris **2 arco iris** : rainbow
irlandés[1], **-desa** *adj, mpl* **-deses** : Irish
irlandés[2], **-desa** *n, pl* **-deses** : Irish person, Irishman *m,* Irishwoman *f*
irlandés[3] *nm* : Irish (language)
ironía *nf* : irony
irónico, -ca *adj* : ironic, ironical — **irónicamente** *adv*
irracional *adj* : irrational — **irracionalmente** *adv*
irracionalidad *nf* : irrationality
irradiar *vt* : to radiate, to irradiate
irrazonable *adj* : unreasonable
irreal *adj* : unreal
irrebatible *adj* : unanswerable, irrefutable
irreconciliable *adj* : irreconcilable
irreconocible *adj* : unrecognizable
irrecuperable *adj* : irrecoverable, irretrievable
irredimible *adj* : irredeemable
irreductible *adj* : unyielding
irreemplazable *adj* : irreplaceable
irreflexión *nf, pl* **-xiones** : thoughtlessness, impetuosity
irreflexivo, -va *adj* : rash, unthinking — **irreflexivamente** *adv*
irrefrenable *adj* : uncontrollable, unstoppable <un impulso irrefrenable : an irresistable urge>
irrefutable *adj* : irrefutable
irregular *adj* : irregular — **irregularmente** *adv*
irregularidad *nf* : irregularity
irrelevante *adj* : irrelevant — **irrelevancia** *nf*
irreligioso, -sa *adj* : irreligious
irremediable *adj* : incurable — **irremediablemente** *adv*
irreparable *adj* : irreparable
irreprimible *adj* : irrepressible
irreprochable *adj* : irreproachable
irresistible adj : irresistible — **irresistiblemente** adv
irresolución *nf, pl* **-ciones** : indecision, hesitation
irresoluto, -ta *adj* INDECISO : undecided
irrespeto *nm* : disrespect
irrespetuoso, -sa *adj* : disrespectful — **irrespetuosamente** *adv*
irresponsabilidad *nf* : irresponsibility
irresponsable *adj* : irresponsible — **irresponsablemente** *adv*
irrestricto, -ta *adj* : unrestricted, unconditional <apoyo irrestricto : unconditional support>
irreverencia *nf* : disrespect
irreverente *adj* : disrespectful
irreversible *adj* : irreversible
irrevocable *adj* : irrevocable — **irrevocablemente** *adv*
irrigar {52} *vt* : to irrigate — **irrigación** *nf*
irrisible *adj* : laughable
irrisión *nf, pl* **-siones** : derision, ridicule
irrisorio, -ria *adj* RISIBLE : ridiculous, ludicrous
irritabilidad *nf* : irritability
irritable *adj* : irritable
irritación *nf, pl* **-ciones** : irritation
irritante *adj* : irritating
irritar *vt* : to irritate — **irritación** *nf*
irrompible *adj* : unbreakable
irrumpir *vi* **~ en** : to burst into
irrupción *nf, pl* **-ciones 1** : irruption **2** : invasion
isla *nf* : island

islámico, -ca *adj* : Islamic, Muslim
islandés[1], **-desa** *adj, mpl* **-deses** : Icelandic
islandés[2], **-desa** *n, mpl* **-deses** : Icelander
islandés[3] *nm* : Icelandic (language)
isleño, -ña *n* : islander
islote *nm* : islet
isometría *nfs & pl* : isometrics
isométrico, -ca *adj* : isometric
isósceles *adj* : isosceles <triángulo isósceles : isosceles triangle>
isótopo *nm* : isotope
israelí *adj & nmf* : Israeli
istmo *nm* : isthmus
itacate *nm Mex* : pack, provisions *pl*
italiano[1], **-na** *adj & n* : Italian
italiano[2] *nm* : Italian (language)
iterbio *nm* : ytterbium
itinerante *adj* AMBULANTE : traveling, itinerant
itinerario *nm* : itinerary, route
itrio *nm* : yttrium
izar {21} *vt* : to hoist, to raise <izar la bandera : to raise the flag>
izquierda *nf* : left
izquierdista *adj & nmf* : leftist
izquierdo, -da *adj* : left

J

j *nf* : tenth letter of the Spanish alphabet
jabalí *nm* : wild boar
jabalina *nf* : javelin
jabón *nm, pl* **jabones** : soap
jabonar *vt* ENJABONAR : to soap up, to lather — **jabonarse** *vr*
jabonera *nf* : soap dish
jabonoso, -sa *adj* : soapy
jaca *nf* **1** : pony **2** YEGUA : mare
jacal *nm Mex* : shack, hut
jacinto *nm* : hyacinth
jactancia *nf* **1** : boastfulness **2** : boasting, bragging
jactancioso[1], **-sa** *adj* : boastful
jactancioso[2], **-sa** *n* : boaster, braggart
jactarse *vr* : to boast, to brag
jade *nm* : jade
jadear *vi* : to pant, to gasp, to puff — **jadeante** *adj*
jadeo *nm* : panting, gasping, puffing
jaez *nm, pl* **jaeces 1** : harness **2** : kind, sort, ilk **3 jaeces** *nmpl* : trappings
jaguar *nm* : jaguar
jai alai *nm* : jai alai
jaiba *nf* CANGREJO : crab
jalapeño *nm Mex* : jalapeño pepper
jalar *vt* **1** : to pull, to tug **2** *fam* : to attract, to draw in <las ideas nuevas lo jalan : new ideas appeal to him> — *vi* **1** : to pull, to pull together **2** *fam* : to hurry up, to get going **3** *Mex fam* : to be in working order <esta máquina no jala : this machine doesn't work>
jalbegue *nm* : whitewash
jalea *nf* : jelly
jalear *vt* : to encourage, to urge on
jaleo *nm fam* **1** : uproar, ruckus, racket **2** *fam* : confusion, hassle **3** : cheering and clapping (for a dance)
jalón *nm, pl* **jalones 1** : milestone, landmark **2** TIRÓN : pull, tug
jalonar *vt* : to mark, to stake out
jalonear *vt Mex, Peru fam* : to tug at — *vi* **1** *fam* : to pull, to tug **2** *CA fam* : to haggle
jamaica *nf* : hibiscus
jamaicano, -na → **jamaiquino**
jamaiquino, -na *adj & n* : Jamaican
jamás *adv* **1** NUNCA : never **2 nunca jamás** *or* **jamás de los jamases** : never ever **3 para siempre jamás** : for ever and ever
jamba *nf* : jamb
jamelgo *nm* : nag (horse)
jamón *nm, pl* **jamones** : ham
Janucá *nmf* : Hanukkah
japonés, -nesa *adj & n, mpl* **-neses** : Japanese
jaque *nm* **1** : check (in chess) <jaque mate : checkmate> **2 tener en jaque** : to intimidate, to bully
jaqueca *nf* : headache, migraine
jarabe *nm* **1** : syrup **2** : Mexican folk dance
jarana *nf* **1** *fam* : revelry, partying, spree **2** *fam* : joking, fooling around **3** : small guitar
jaranear *vi fam* : to go on a spree, to party
jarcia *nf* **1** : rigging **2** : fishing tackle
jardín *nm, pl* **jardines 1** : garden **2 jardín de niños** : kindergarten **3 los jardines** *nmpl* : the outfield
jardinería *nf* : gardening
jardinero, -ra *n* **1** : gardener **2** : outfielder (in baseball)
jarra *nf* **1** : pitcher, jug **2** : stein, mug **3 de jarras** *or* **en jarras** : akimbo
jarrete *nm* **1** : back of the knee **2** : hock (of an animal)
jarro *nm* **1** : pitcher, jug **2** : mug
jarrón *nm, pl* **jarrones** FLORERO : vase
jaspe *nm* : jasper
jaspeado, -da *adj* **1** VETEADO : streaked, veined **2** : speckled, mottled
jaula *nf* : cage
jauría *nf* : pack of hounds
javanés, -nesa *adj & n* : Javanese
jazmín *nm, pl* **jazmines** : jasmine
jazz ['jas, 'dʒas] *nm* : jazz
jeans ['jins, 'dʒins] *nmpl* : jeans
jeep ['jip, 'dʒip] *nm, pl* **jeeps** : jeep
jefatura *nf* **1** : leadership **2** : headquarters <jefatura de policía : police headquarters>
jefe, -fa *n* **1** : chief, head, leader <jefe de bomberos : fire chief> **2** : boss
Jehová *nm* : Jehovah

jején *nm, pl* **jejenes :** gnat, small mosquito

jengibre *nm* **:** ginger

jeque *nm* **:** sheikh, sheik

jerarca *nmf* **:** leader, chief

jerarquía *nf* **1 :** hierarchy **2** RANGO **:** rank

jerárquico, -ca *adj* **:** hierarchical

jerbo *nm* **:** gerbil

jerez *nm, pl* **jereces :** sherry

jerga *nf* **1 :** jargon, slang **2 :** coarse cloth

jerigonza *nf* GALIMATÍAS **:** mumbo jumbo, gibberish

jeringa *nf* **:** syringe

jeringar {52} *vt* **1 :** to inject **2** *fam* JOROBAR **:** to annoy, to pester — *vi fam* JOROBAR **:** to be annoying, to be a nuisance

jeringuear → **jeringar**

jeringuilla *nf* → **jeringa**

jeroglífico *nm* **:** hieroglyphic

jersey *nm, pl* **jerseys 1 :** jersey (fabric) **2** *Spain* **:** sweater

jesuita *adj & nm* **:** Jesuit

Jesús *nm* **:** Jesus

jeta *nf* **1 :** snout **2** *fam* **:** face, mug

jíbaro, -ra *adj* **1 :** Jivaro **2 :** rustic, rural

jibia *nf* **:** cuttlefish

jícama *nf* **:** jicama

jícara *nf Mex* **:** calabash

jilguero *nm* **:** European goldfinch

jinete *nmf* **:** horseman, horsewoman *f,* rider

jinetear *vt* **1 :** to ride, to perform (on horseback) **2** DOMAR **:** to break in (a horse) — *vi* CABALGAR **:** to ride horseback

jingoísmo [ˌjɪŋgoˈizmo, ˌdʒɪŋ-] *nm* **:** jingoism

jingoísta *adj* **:** jingoist, jingoistic

jiote *nm Mex* **:** rash

jira *nf* **:** outing, picnic

jirafa *nf* **1 :** giraffe **2 :** boom microphone

jirón *nm, pl* **jirones :** shred, rag <hecho jirones : in tatters>

jitomate *nm Mex* **:** tomato

jockey [ˈjɔki, ˈdʒɔ-] *nmf, pl* **jockeys** [-kis] **:** jockey

jocosidad *nf* **:** humor, jocularity

jocoso, -sa *adj* **:** playful, jocular — **jocosamente** *adv*

jofaina *nf* **:** washbowl

jogging [ˈjɔgɪŋ, ˈdʒɔ-] *nm* **:** jogging

jolgorio *nm* **:** merrymaking, fun

jonrón *nm, pl* **jonrones :** home run

jordano, -na *adj & n* **:** Jordanian

jornada *nf* **1 :** expedition, day's journey **2 jornada de trabajo :** working day **3 jornadas** *nfpl* **:** conference, congress

jornal *nm* **1 :** day's pay **2 a ~ :** by the day

jornalero, -ra *n* **:** day laborer

joroba *nf* **1** GIBA **:** hump **2** *fam* **:** nuisance, pain in the neck

jorobado[1], -da *adj* GIBOSO **:** hunchbacked, humpbacked

jorobado[2], -da *n* GIBOSO **:** hunchback, humpback

jorobar *vt fam* JERINGAR **:** to bother, to annoy — *vi fam* JERINGAR **:** to be annoying, to be a nuisance

jorongo *nm Mex* **:** full-length poncho

jota *nf* **1 :** jot, bit <no entiendo ni jota : I don't understand a word of it> <no se ve ni jota : you can't see a thing> **2 :** jack (in playing cards)

joven[1] *adj, pl* **jóvenes 1 :** young **2 :** youthful

joven[2] *nmf, pl* **jóvenes :** young man *m,* young woman *f,* young person

jovial *adj* **:** jovial, cheerful — **jovialmente** *adv*

jovialidad *nf* **:** joviality, cheerfulness

joya *nf* **1 :** jewel, piece of jewelry **2 :** treasure, gem <la nueva empleada es una joya : the new employee is a real gem>

joyería *nf* **1 :** jewelry store **2 :** jewelry **3 joyería de fantasía :** costume jewelry

joyero, -ra *n* **:** jeweler

juanete *nm* **:** bunion

jubilación *nf, pl* **-ciones 1 :** retirement **2** PENSIÓN **:** pension

jubilado[1], -da *adj* **:** retired, in retirement

jubilado[2], -da *nmf* **:** retired person, retiree

jubilar *vt* **1 :** to retire, to pension off **2** *fam* **:** to get rid of, to discard — **jubilarse** *vr* **:** to retire

jubileo *nm* **:** jubilee

júbilo *nm* **:** jubilation, joy

jubiloso, -sa *adj* **:** jubilant, joyous

judaico, -ca *adj* **:** Judaic, Jewish

judaísmo *nm* **:** Judaism

judía *nf* **1 :** bean **2** *or* **judía verde :** green bean, string bean

judicatura *nf* **1 :** judiciary, judges *pl* **2 :** office of judge

judicial *adj* **:** judicial — **judicialmente** *adv*

judío[1], -día *adj* **:** Jewish

judío[2], -día *n* **:** Jewish person, Jew

judo [ˈjuðo, ˈdʒu-] *nm* **:** judo

juega, juegue, etc. → **jugar**

juego *nm* **1 :** play, playing <poner en juego : to bring into play> **2 :** game, sport <juego de cartas : card game> <Juegos Olímpicos : Olympic Games> **3 :** gaming, gambling <estar en juego : to be at stake> **4 :** set <un juego de llaves : a set of keys> **5 hacer juego :** to go together, to match **6 juego de manos :** conjuring trick, sleight of hand

juerga *nf* **:** partying, binge <irse de juerga : to go on a spree>

juerguista *nmf* **:** reveler, carouser

jueves *nms & pl* **:** Thursday

juez *nmf, pl* **jueces 1 :** judge **2** ÁRBITRO **:** umpire, referee

jugada *nf* **1 :** play, move **2 :** trick <hacer una mala jugada : to play a dirty trick>
jugador, -dora *n* **1 :** player **2 :** gambler
jugar {44} *vi* **1 :** to play <jugar a la pelota : to play ball> **2** APOSTAR **:** to gamble, to bet **3 :** to joke, to kid — *vt* **1 :** to play <jugar un papel : to play a role> <jugar una carta : to play a card> **2 :** to bet — **jugarse** *vr* **1 :** to risk, to gamble away <jugarse la vida : to risk one's life> **2 jugarse el todo por el todo :** to risk everything
jugarreta *nf fam* **:** prank, dirty trick
juglar *nm* **:** minstrel
jugo *nm* **1 :** juice **2 :** substance, essence <sacarle el jugo a algo : to get the most out of something>
jugosidad *nf* **:** juiciness, succulence
jugoso, -sa *adj* **:** juicy
juguete *nm* **:** toy
juguetear *vi* **1 :** to play, to cavort, to frolic **2 :** to toy, to fiddle
juguetería *nf* **:** toy store
juguetón, -tona *adj, mpl* **-tones :** playful — **juguetonamente** *adv*
juicio *nm* **1 :** good judgment, reason, sense **2 :** opinion <a mi juicio : in my opinion> **3 :** trial <llevar a juicio : to take to court>
juicioso, -sa *adj* **:** judicious, wise — **juiciosamente** *adv*
julio *nm* **:** July
juncia *nf* **:** sedge
junco *nm* **1 :** reed, rush **2 :** junk (boat)
jungla *nf* **:** jungle
junio *nm* **:** June
junquillo *nm* **:** jonquil
junta *nf* **1 :** board, committee <junta directiva : board of directors> **2** REUNIÓN **:** meeting, session **3 :** junta **4 :** joint, gasket
juntamente *adv* **1 :** jointly, together <juntamente con : together with> **2 :** at the same time
juntar *vt* **1** UNIR **:** to unite, to combine, to put together **2** REUNIR **:** to collect, to gather together, to assemble **3 :** to close partway <juntar la puerta : to leave the door ajar> — **juntarse** *vr* **1 :** to join together **2 :** to socialize, to get together
junto, -ta *adj* **1** UNIDO **:** joined, united **2 :** close, adjacent <colgaron los dos retratos juntos : they hung the two paintings side by side> **3** (*used adverbially*) **:** together <llegamos juntos : we arrived together> **4 ~ a :** next to, alongside of **5 ~ con :** together with, along with
juntura *nf* **:** joint, coupling
Júpiter *nm* **:** Jupiter
jura *nf* **:** oath, pledge <jura de bandera : pledge of allegiance>
jurado[1] *nm* **:** jury
jurado[2]**, -da** *n* **:** juror
juramento *nm* **1 :** oath <juramento hipocrático : Hippocratic oath> **2 :** swearword, oath
jurar *vt* **1 :** to swear <jurar lealtad : to swear loyalty> **2 :** to take an oath <el alcalde juró su cargo : the mayor took the oath of office> — *vi* **:** to curse, to swear
jurídico, -ca *adj* **:** legal
jurisdicción *nf, pl* **-ciones :** jurisdiction
jurisdiccional *adj* **:** jurisdictional, territorial
jurisprudencia *nf* **:** jurisprudence, law
justa *nf* **1 :** joust **2** TORNEO **:** tournament, competition
justamente *adv* **1** PRECISAMENTE **:** precisely, exactly **2 :** justly, fairly
justar *vi* **:** to joust
justicia *nf* **1 :** justice, fairness <hacerle justicia a : to do justice to> <ser de justicia : to be only fair> **2 la justicia :** the law <tomarse la justicia por su mano : to take the law into one's own hands>
justiciero, -ra *adj* **:** righteous, avenging
justificable *adj* **:** justifiable
justificación *nf, pl* **-ciones :** justification
justificante *nm* **1 :** justification **2 :** proof, voucher
justificar {72} *vt* **1 :** to justify **2 :** to excuse, to vindicate
justo[1] *adv* **1 :** justly **2 :** right, exactly <justo a tiempo : just in time> **3 :** tightly
justo[2]**, -ta** *adj* **1 :** just, fair **2 :** right, exact **3 :** tight <estos zapatos me quedan muy justos : these shoes are too tight>
justo[3]**, -ta** *n* **:** just person <los justos : the just>
juvenil *adj* **1 :** juvenile, young, youthful **2** ADOLESCENTE **:** teenage
juventud *nf* **1 :** youth **2 :** young people
juzgado *nm* TRIBUNAL **:** court, tribunal
juzgar {52} *vt* **1 :** to try, to judge (a case in court) **2 :** to pass judgment on **3** CONSIDERAR **:** to consider, to deem
juzgue, etc. → **juzgar**

K

k *nf* **:** eleventh letter of the Spanish alphabet
kaki *adj & nm* → **caqui**
kaleidoscopio *nm* → **caleidoscopio**
kamikaze *adj & nm* **:** kamikaze
kampucheano, -na *adj & n* **:** Kampuchean
kan *nm* **:** khan
karaoke *nm* **:** karaoke
karate *or* **kárate** *nm* **:** karate

kayac *or* **kayak** *nm, pl* **kayacs** *or* **kayaks** : kayak
keniano, -na *adj & n* : Kenyan
kepí *nm* : kepi
kermesse *or* **kermés** [kɛrˈmɛs] *nf, pl* **kermesses** *or* **kermeses** [-ˈmɛsɛs] : charity fair, bazaar
kerosene *or* **kerosén** *or* **keroseno** *nm* : kerosene, paraffin
kilo *nm* **1 :** kilo, kilogram **2** *fam* **:** large amount
kilobyte [ˌkiloˈbait] *nm* : kilobyte
kilociclo *nm* : kilocycle
kilogramo *nm* : kilogram
kilohertzio *nm* : kilohertz
kilometraje *nm* : distance in kilometers, mileage
kilométrico, -ca *adj fam* : endless, very long
kilómetro *nm* : kilometer
kilovatio *nm* : kilowatt
kimono *nm* : kimono
kinder [ˈkɪndɛr] *nm* → **kindergarten**
kindergarten [ˌkɪndɛrˈgartɛn] *nm, pl* **kindergartens** [-tɛns] **:** kindergarten, nursery school
kinesiología *nf* **:** physical therapy
kinesiólogo, -ga *n* **:** physical therapist
kiosco *nm* → **quiosco**
kit *nm, pl* **kits** : kit
kiwi [ˈkiwi] *nm* **1** : kiwi (bird) **2** : kiwifruit
klaxon *nm* → **claxon**
knockout [nɔˈkaut] *nm* → **nocaut**
koala *nm* : koala bear
kriptón *nm* : krypton
kurdo[1], -da *adj* : Kurdish
kurdo[2], -da *n* : Kurd
kuwaití [kuˌwaiˈti] *adj & nmf* : Kuwaiti

L

l *nf* **:** twelfth letter of the Spanish alphabet
la[1] *pron* **1 :** her, it <llámala hoy : call her today> <sacó la botella y la abrió : he took out the bottle and opened it> **2** (*formal*) : you <no la vi a usted, Señora Díaz : I didn't see you, Mrs. Díaz> **3 :** the one <mi casa y la de la puerta roja : my house and the one with the red door> **4 la que :** the one who
la[2] *art* → **el[2]**
laberíntico, -ca *adj* : labyrinthine
laberinto *nm* : labyrinth, maze
labia *nf fam* : gift of gab <tu amigo tiene labia : your friend has a way with words>
labial *adj* : labial, lip <lápiz labial : lipstick>
labio *nm* **1 :** lip **2 labio leporino :** harelip
labor *nf* **:** work, labor
laborable *adj* **1 :** arable **2 día laborable :** workday, business day
laboral *adj* **1 :** work, labor <costos laborales : labor costs> **2 estancia laboral :** workstation
laborar *vi* : to work
laboratorio *nm* : laboratory, lab
laboriosidad *nf* **:** industriousness, diligence
laborioso, -sa *adj* **1 :** laborious, hard **2** : industrious, hard-working
labrado[1], -da *adj* **1 :** cultivated, tilled **2 :** carved, wrought
labrado[2] *nm* : cultivated field
labrador, -dora *n* : farmer
labranza *nf* **:** farming
labrar *vt* **1 :** to carve, to work (metal) **2 :** to cultivate, to till **3 :** to cause, to bring about
laca *nf* **1** : lacquer, shellac **2 :** hair spray **3 laca de uñas** : nail polish
lacayo *nm* : lackey
lace, etc. → **lazar**
lacear *vt* : to lasso
laceración *nf, pl* **-ciones :** laceration
lacerante *adj* : hurtful, wounding
lacerar *vt* **1 :** to lacerate, to cut **2 :** to hurt, to wound (one's feelings)
lacio, -cia *adj* **1** : limp, lank **2 pelo lacio** : straight hair
lacónico, -ca *adj* : laconic — **lacónicamente** *adv*
lacra *nf* **1 :** scar, mark (on the skin) **2** : stigma, blemish
lacrar *vt* : to seal (with wax)
lacrimógeno, -na *adj* **gas lacrimógeno :** tear gas
lacrimoso, -sa *adj* : tearful, moving
lactancia *nf* **1** : lactation **2** : breastfeeding
lactante *nmf* **:** nursing infant, suckling
lactar *v* : to breast-feed
lácteo, -tea *adj* **1 :** dairy **2 Vía Láctea** : Milky Way
láctico, -ca *adj* : lactic
lactosa *nf* **:** lactose
ladeado, -da *adj* **:** crooked, tilted, lopsided
ladear *vt* **:** to tilt, to tip — **ladearse** *vr* : to bend (over)
ladera *nf* **:** slope, hillside
ladino[1], -na *adj* **1 :** cunning, shrewd **2** *CA, Mex* : mestizo
ladino[2], -na *n* **1 :** trickster **2** *CA, Mex* : Spanish-speaking Indian **3** *CA, Mex* : mestizo
lado *nm* **1 :** side **2** PARTE **:** place <miró por todos lados : he looked everywhere> **3 al lado de :** next to, beside **4 de ~** : tilted, sideways <está de lado : it's lying on its side> **5 hacerse a un lado :** to step aside **6 lado a lado** : side by side **7 por otro lado :** on the other hand
ladrar *vi* : to bark
ladrido *nm* : bark (of a dog), barking

ladrillo *nm* **:** brick
ladrón, -drona *n, mpl* **ladrones :** robber, thief, burglar
lagartija *nf* **:** small lizard
lagarto *nm* **1 :** lizard **2 lagarto de Indias :** alligator
lago *nm* **:** lake
lágrima *nf* **:** tear, teardrop
lagrimear *vi* **1 :** to water (of eyes) **2 :** to weep easily
laguna *nf* **1 :** lagoon **2 :** lacuna, gap
laicado *nm* **:** laity
laico[1]**, -ca** *adj* **:** lay, secular
laico[2]**, -ca** *n* **:** layman *m,* laywoman *f*
laja *nf* **:** slab
lama[1] *nf* **:** slime, ooze
lama[2] *nm* **:** lama
lamber *vt* **:** to lick
lamentable *adj* **1 :** unfortunate, lamentable **2 :** pitiful, sad
lamentablemente *adv* **:** unfortunately, regrettably
lamentación *nf, pl* **-ciones :** lamentation, groaning, moaning
lamentar *vt* **1 :** to lament **2 :** to regret <lo lamento : I'm sorry> — **lamentarse** *vr* **:** to grumble, to complain
lamento *nm* **:** lament, groan, cry
lamer *vt* **1 :** to lick **2 :** to lap against
lamida *nf* **:** lick
lámina *nf* **1** PLANCHA **:** sheet, plate **2 :** plate, illustration
laminado[1]**, -da** *adj* **:** laminated
laminado[2] *nm* **:** laminate
laminar *vt* **:** to laminate — **laminación** *nf*
lámpara *nf* **:** lamp
lampiño, -ña *adj* **:** hairless
lamprea *nf* **:** lamprey
lana *nf* **1 :** wool <lana de acero : steel wool> **2** *Mex fam* **:** money, dough
lance[1]**, etc. → lanzar**
lance[2] *nm* **1** INCIDENTE **:** event, incident **2** RIÑA **:** quarrel **3 :** throw, cast (of a net, etc.) **4 :** move, play (in a game), throw (of dice)
lancear *vt* **:** to spear
lanceta *nf* **:** lancet
lancha *nf* **1 :** small boat, launch **2 lancha motora :** motorboat, speedboat
langosta *nf* **1 :** lobster **2 :** locust
langostino *nm* **:** prawn, crayfish
languidecer {53} *vi* **:** to languish
languidez *nf, pl* **-deces :** languor, listlessness
lánguido, -da *adj* **:** languid, listless — **lánguidamente** *adv*
lanolina *nf* **:** lanolin
lanudo, -da *adj* **:** woolly
lanza *nf* **:** spear, lance
lanzadera *nf* **1 :** shuttle (for weaving) **2 lanzadera espacial :** space shuttle
lanzado, -da *adj* **1 :** impulsive, brazen **2 :** forward, determined <ir lanzado : to hurtle along>
lanzador, -dora *n* **:** thrower, pitcher
lanzallamas *nms & pl* **:** flamethrower
lanzamiento *nm* **1 :** throw **2 :** pitch (in baseball) **3 :** launching, launch
lanzar {21} *vt* **1 :** to throw, to hurl **2 :** to pitch **3 :** to launch — **lanzarse** *vr* **1 :** to throw oneself (at, into) **2 ~ a :** to embark upon, to undertake
laosiano, -na *adj & n* **:** Laotian
lapicero *nm* **1 :** mechanical pencil **2** *CA, Peru* **:** ballpoint pen
lápida *nf* **:** marker, tombstone
lapidar *vt* APEDREAR **:** to stone
lapidario, -ria *adj & n* **:** lapidary
lápiz *nm, pl* **lápices 1 :** pencil **2 lápiz de labios** *or* **lápiz labial :** lipstick
lapón, -pona *adj & n, mpl* **lapones :** Lapp
lapso *nm* **:** lapse, space (of time)
lapsus *nms & pl* **:** error, slip
laquear *vt* **:** to lacquer, to varnish, to shellac
largamente *adv* **1 :** at length, extensively **2 :** easily, comfortably **3 :** generously
largar {52} *vt* **1** SOLTAR **:** to let loose, to release **2** AFLOJAR **:** to loosen, to slacken **3** *fam* **:** to give, to hand over **4** *fam* **:** to hurl, to let fly (insults, etc.) — **largarse** *vr fam* **:** to scram, to beat it
largo[1]**, -ga** *adj* **1 :** long **2 a lo largo :** lengthwise **3 a lo largo de :** along **4 a la larga :** in the long run
largo[2] *nm* **:** length <tres metros de largo : three meters long>
largometraje *nm* **:** feature film
largue, etc. → largar
larguero *nm* **:** crossbeam
largueza *nf* **:** generosity, largesse
larguirucho, -cha *adj fam* **:** lanky
largura *nf* **:** length
laringe *nf* **:** larynx
laringitis *nfs & pl* **:** laryngitis
larva *nf* **:** larva — **larval** *adj*
las → el[2]**, los**[1]
lasaña *nf* **:** lasagna
lasca *nf* **:** chip, chipping
lascivia *nf* **:** lasciviousness, lewdness
lascivo, -va *adj* **:** lascivious, lewd — **lascivamente** *adv*
láser *nm* **:** laser
lasitud *nf* **:** lassitude, weariness
laso, -sa *adj* **:** languid, weary
lástima *nf* **1 :** compassion, pity **2** PENA **:** shame, pity <¡qué lástima! : what a shame!>
lastimadura *nf* **:** injury, wound
lastimar *vt* **1** DAÑAR, HERIR **:** to hurt, to injure **2** AGRAVIAR **:** to offend — **lastimarse** *vr* **:** to hurt oneself
lastimero, -ra *adj* **:** pitiful, wretched
lastimoso, -sa *adj* **1 :** shameful **2 :** pitiful, terrible
lastrar *vt* **1 :** to ballast **2 :** to burden, to encumber
lastre *nm* **1 :** burden **2 :** ballast
lata *nf* **1 :** tinplate **2 :** tin can **3** *fam* **:** pest, bother, nuisance **4 dar lata** *fam* **:** to bother, to annoy
latencia *nf* **:** latency
latente *adj* **:** latent

lateral[1] *adj* **1 :** lateral, side **2 :** indirect — **lateralmente** *adv*
lateral[2] *nm* **:** end piece, side
látex *nms & pl* **:** latex
latido *nm* **:** beat, throb <latido del corazón : heartbeat>
latifundio *nm* **:** large estate
latigazo *nm* **:** lash (with a whip)
látigo *nm* AZOTE **:** whip
latín *nm* **:** Latin (language)
latino[1], **-na** *adj* **1 :** Latin **2** *fam* **:** Latin-American
latino[2], **-na** *n fam* **:** Latin American
latinoamericano[1], **-na** *adj* HISPANOAMERICANO **:** Latin American
latinoamericano, -na *n* **:** Latin American
latir *vi* **1 :** to beat, to throb **2 latirle a uno** *Mex fam* **:** to have a hunch <me late que no va a venir : I have a feeling he's not going to come>
latitud *nf* **1 :** latitude **2 :** breadth
lato, -ta *adj* **1 :** extended, lengthy **2 :** broad (in meaning)
latón *nm, pl* **latones :** brass
latoso[1], **-sa** *adj fam* **:** annoying, bothersome
latoso[2], **-sa** *n fam* **:** pest, nuisance
latrocinio *nm* **:** larceny
laúd *nm* **:** lute
laudable *adj* **:** laudable, praiseworthy
laudo *nm* **:** findings, decision
laureado, -da *adj & n* **:** laureate
laurear *vt* **:** to award, to honor
laurel *nm* **1 :** laurel **2 :** bay leaf **3 dormirse en sus laureles :** to rest on one's laurels
lava *nf* **:** lava
lavable *adj* **:** washable
lavabo *nm* **1** LAVAMANOS **:** sink, washbowl **2 :** lavatory, toilet
lavadero *nm* **:** laundry room
lavado *nm* **1 :** laundry, wash **2 :** laundering <lavado de dinero : money laundering>
lavadora *nf* **:** washing machine
lavamanos *nms & pl* LAVABO **:** sink, washbowl
lavanda *nf* ESPLIEGO **:** lavender
lavandería *nf* **:** laundry (service)
lavandero, -ra *n* **:** launderer, laundress *f*
lavaplatos *nms & pl* **1 :** dishwasher **2** *Chile, Col, Mex* **:** kitchen sink
lavar *vt* **1 :** to wash, to clean **2 :** to launder (money) **3 lavar en seco :** to dry-clean — **lavarse** *vr* **1 :** to wash oneself **2 lavarse las manos de :** to wash one's hands of
lavativa *nf* **:** enema
lavatorio *nm* **:** lavatory, washroom
lavavajillas *nms & pl* **:** dishwasher
laxante *adj & nm* **:** laxative
laxitud *nf* **:** laxity, slackness
laxo, -xa *adj* **:** lax, slack
lazada *nf* **:** bow, loop
lazar {21} *vt* **:** to rope, to lasso
lazo *nm* **1** VÍNCULO **:** link, bond **2 :** bow, ribbon **3 :** lasso, lariat

le *pron* **1 :** to her, to him, to it <¿qué le dijiste? : what did you tell him?> **2 :** from her, from him, from it <el ladrón le robó la cartera : the thief stole his wallet> **3 :** for her, for him, for it <cómprale flores a tu mamá : buy your mom some flowers> **4** (*formal*) **:** to you, for you <le traje un regalo : I brought you a gift>
leal *adj* **:** loyal, faithful — **lealmente** *adv*
lealtad *nf* **:** loyalty, allegiance
lebrel *nm* **:** hound
lección *nf, pl* **lecciones :** lesson
lechada *nf* **1 :** whitewash **2 :** grout
lechal *adj* **:** suckling, unweaned <cordero lechal : suckling lamb>
leche *nf* **1 :** milk <leche en polvo : powdered milk> <leche de magnesia : milk of magnesia> **2 :** milky sap
lechera *nf* **1 :** milk jug **2 :** dairymaid *f*
lechería *nf* **:** dairy store
lechero[1], **-ra** *adj* **:** dairy
lechero[2], **-ra** *n* **:** milkman *m,* milk dealer
lecho *nm* **1 :** bed <un lecho de rosas : a bed of roses> <lecho de muerte : deathbed> **2 :** riverbed **3 :** layer, stratum (in geology)
lechón, -chona *n, mpl* **lechones :** suckling pig
lechoso, -sa *adj* **:** milky
lechuga *nf* **:** lettuce
lechuza *nf* BÚHO **:** owl, barn owl
lectivo, -va *adj* **:** school <año lectivo : school year>
lector[1], **-tora** *adj* **:** reading <nivel lector : reading level>
lector[2], **-tora** *n* **:** reader
lector[3] *nm* **:** scanner, reader <lector óptico : optical scanner>
lectura *nf* **1 :** reading **2 :** reading matter
leer {20} *v* **:** to read
legación *nf, pl* **-ciones :** legation
legado *nm* **1 :** legacy, bequest **2 :** legate, emissary
legajo *nm* **:** dossier, file
legal *adj* **:** legal, lawful — **legalmente** *adv*
legalidad *nf* **:** legality, lawfulness
legalizar {21} *vt* **:** to legalize — **legalización** *nf*
legar {52} *vt* **1 :** to bequeath, to hand down **2** DELEGAR **:** to delegate
legendario, -ria *adj* **:** legendary
legible *adj* **:** legible
legión *nf, pl* **legiones :** legion
legionario, -ria *n* **:** legionnaire
legislación *nf* **1 :** legislation, lawmaking **2 :** laws *pl,* legislation
legislador[1], **-dora** *adj* **:** legislative
legislador[2], **-dora** *n* **:** legislator
legislar *vi* **:** to legislate
legislativo, -va *adj* **:** legislative
legislatura *nf* **1 :** legislature **2 :** term of office
legitimar *vt* **1 :** to legitimize **2 :** to authenticate — **legitimación** *nf*

legitimidad *nf* : legitimacy
legítimo, -ma *adj* **1** : legitimate **2** : genuine, authentic — **legítimamente** *adv*
lego[1], **-ga** *adj* **1** : secular, lay **2** : uniformed, ignorant
lego[2], **-ga** *n* : layperson, layman *m*, laywoman *f*
legua *nf* **1** : league **2 notarse a leguas** : to be very obvious <se notaba a leguas : you could tell from a mile away>
legue, etc. → **legar**
legumbre *nf* **1** HORTALIZA : vegetable **2** : legume
leíble *adj* : readable
leída *nf* : reading, read <de una leída : in one reading, at one go>
leído[1] *pp* → **leer**
leído[2], **-da** *adj* : well-read
lejanía *nf* : remoteness, distance
lejano, -na *adj* : remote, distant, far away
lejía *nf* **1** : lye **2** : bleach
lejos *adv* **1** : far away, distant <a lo lejos : in the distance, far off> <desde lejos : from a distance> **2** : long ago, a long way off <está lejos de los 50 años : he's a long way from 50 years old> **3 de ~** : by far <esta decisión fue de lejos la más fácil : this decision was by far the easiest> **4 ~ de** : far from <lejos de ser reprobado, recibió una nota de B : far from failing, he got a B>
lelo, -la *adj* : silly, stupid
lema *nm* : motto, slogan
lencería *nf* : lingerie
lengua *nf* **1** : tongue <morderse la lengua : to bite one's tongue> **2** IDIOMA : language <lengua materna : mother tongue, native language> <lengua muerta : dead language>
lenguado *nm* : sole, flounder
lenguaje *nm* **1** : language, speech **2 lenguaje gestual** *or* **lenguaje de gestos** : sign language **3 lenguaje de programación** : programming language
lengüeta *nf* **1** : tongue (of a shoe), tab, flap **2** : reed (of a musical instrument) **3** : barb, point
lengüetada *nf* **beber a lengüetadas** : to lap (up)
lenidad *nf* : leniency
lenitivo, -va *adj* : soothing
lente *nmf* **1** : lens <lentes de contacto : contact lenses> **2 lentes** *nmpl* ANTEOJOS : eyeglasses <lentes de sol : sunglasses>
lenteja *nf* : lentil
lentejuela *nf* : sequin, spangle
lentitud *nf* : slowness
lento[1] *adv* DESPACIO : slowly
lento[2], **-ta** *adj* **1** : slow **2** : slow-witted, dull — **lentamente** *adv*
leña *nf* : wood, firewood
leñador, -dora *n* : lumberjack, woodcutter
leñera *nf* : woodshed
leño *nm* : log
leñoso, -sa *adj* : woody
Leo *nmf* : Leo
león, -ona *n, mpl* **leones 1** : lion, lioness *f* **2** (*in various countries*) : puma, cougar
leonado, -da *adj* : tawny
leonino, -na *adj* **1** : leonine **2** : one-sided, unfair
leopardo *nm* : leopard
leotardo *nm* MALLA : leotard, tights *pl*
leperada *nf Mex* : obscenity
lépero, -ra *adj Mex* : vulgar, coarse
lepra *nf* : leprosy
leproso[1], **-sa** *adj* : leprous
leproso[2], **-sa** *n* : leper
lerdo, -da *adj* **1** : clumsy **2** : dull, oafish, slow-witted
les *pron* **1** : to them <dales una propina : give them a tip> **2** : from them <se les privó de su herencia : they were deprived of their inheritance> **3** : for them <les hice sus tareas : I did their homework for them> **4** : to you *pl*, for you *pl* <les compré un regalo : I bought you all a present>
lesbiana *nf* : lesbian — **lesbiano, -na** *adj*
lesbianismo *nm* : lesbianism
lesión *nf, pl* **lesiones** HERIDA : lesion, wound, injury <una lesión grave : a serious injury>
lesionado, -da *adj* HERIDO : injured, wounded
lesionar *vt* : to injure, to wound — **lesionarse** *vr* : to hurt oneself
lesivo, -va *adj* : harmful, damaging
letal *adj* MORTÍFERO : deadly, lethal — **letalmente** *adv*
letanía *nf* **1** : litany **2** *fam* : spiel, song and dance
letárgico, -ca *adj* : lethargic
letargo *nm* : lethargy, torpor
letón[1], **-tona** *adj & n, mpl* **letones** : Latvian
letón[2] *nm* : Latvian (language)
letra *nf* **1** : letter **2** CALIGRAFÍA : handwriting, lettering **3** : lyrics *pl* **4 al pie de la letra** : word for word, by the book **5 letras** *nfpl* : arts (in education)
letrado[1], **-da** *adj* ERUDITO : learned, erudite
letrado[2], **-da** *n* : attorney-at-law, lawyer
letrero *nm* RÓTULO : sign, notice
letrina *nf* : latrine
letrista *nmf* : lyricist, songwriter
leucemia *nf* : leukemia
levadizo, -za *adj* **1** : liftable **2 puente levadizo** : drawbridge
levadura *nf* **1** : yeast, leavening **2 levadura en polvo** : baking powder
levantamiento *nm* **1** ALZAMIENTO : uprising **2** : raising, lifting <levantamiento de pesas : weight lifting>
levantar *vt* **1** ALZAR : to lift, to raise **2** : to put up, to erect **3** : to call off, to adjourn **4** : to give rise to, to arouse

<levantar sospechas : to arouse suspicion> — **levantarse** *vr* **1 :** to rise, to stand up **2 :** to get out of bed
levar *vt* **levar anclas :** to weigh anchor
leve *adj* **1 :** light, slight **2 :** trivial, unimportant — **levemente** *adv*
levedad *nf* **:** lightness
levemente *adv* LIGERAMENTE **:** lightly, softly
léxico[1], **-ca** *adj* **:** lexical
léxico[2] *nm* **:** lexicon, glossary
lexicografía *nf* **:** lexicography
lexicográfico, -ca *adj* **:** lexicographical, lexicographic
lexicógrafo, -fa *n* **:** lexicographer
ley *nf* **1 :** law <fuera de la ley : outside the law> <la ley de gravedad : the law of gravity> **2 :** purity (of metals) <oro de ley : pure gold>
leyenda *nf* **1 :** legend **2 :** caption, inscription
leyó, etc. → **leer**
liar {85} *vt* **1** ATAR **:** to bind, to tie (up) **2 :** to roll (a cigarette) **3 :** to confuse — **liarse** *vr* **:** to get mixed up
libanés, -nesa *adj & n, mpl* **-neses** **:** Lebanese
libar *vt* **1 :** to suck (nectar) **2 :** to sip, to swig (liquor, etc.)
libelo *nm* **1 :** libel, lampoon **2 :** petition (in court)
libélula *nf* **:** dragonfly
liberación *nf, pl* **-ciones :** liberation, deliverance <liberación de la mujer : women's liberation>
liberado, -da *adj* **1 :** liberated <una mujer liberada : a liberated woman> **2 :** freed, delivered
liberal *adj & nmf* **:** liberal
liberalidad *nf* **:** generosity, liberality
liberalismo *nm* **:** liberalism
liberalizar {21} *vt* **:** to liberalize — **liberalización** *nf*
liberar *vt* **:** to liberate, to free — **liberarse** *vr* **:** to get free of
liberiano, -na *adj & n* **:** Liberian
libertad *nf* **1 :** freedom, liberty <tomarse la libertad de : to take the liberty of> **2 libertad bajo fianza :** bail **3 libertad condicional :** parole
libertador[1], **-dora** *adj* **:** liberating
libertador[2], **-dora** *n* **:** liberator
libertar *vt* LIBRAR **:** to set free
libertario, -ria *adj & n* **:** libertarian
libertinaje *nm* **:** licentiousness, dissipation
libertino[1], **-na** *adj* **:** licentious, dissolute
libertino[2], **-na** *n* **:** libertine
libidinoso, -sa *adj* **:** lustful, lewd
libido *nf* **:** libido
libio, -bia *adj & n* **:** Libyan
libra *nf* **1 :** pound **2 libra esterlina :** pound sterling
Libra *nmf* **:** Libra
libramiento *nm* **1 :** liberating, freeing **2** LIBRANZA **:** order of payment **3** *Mex* **:** beltway
libranza *nf* **:** order of payment
librar *vt* **1** LIBERTAR **:** to deliver, to set free **2 :** to wage <librar batalla : to do battle> **3 :** to issue <librar una orden : to issue an order> — **librarse** *vr* **~ de :** to free oneself from, to get out of
libre *adj* **1 :** free <un país libre : a free country> <libre de : free from, exempt from> <libre albedrío : free will> **2** DESOCUPADO **:** vacant **3 día libre :** day off
librea *nf* **:** livery
librecambio *nm* **:** free trade
libremente *adv* **:** freely
librería *nf* **:** bookstore
librero[1], **-ra** *n* **:** bookseller
librero[2] *nm Mex* **:** bookcase
libresco, -ca *adj* **:** bookish
libreta *nf* CUADERNO **:** notebook
libreto *nm* **:** libretto, script
libro *nm* **1 :** book <libro de texto : textbook> **2 libros** *nmpl* **:** books (in bookkeeping), accounts <llevar los libros : to keep the books>
licencia *nf* **1 :** permission **2 :** leave, leave of absence **3 :** permit, license <licencia de conducir : driver's license>
licenciado, -da *n* **1 :** university graduate **2** ABOGADO **:** lawyer
licenciar *vt* **1 :** to license, to permit, to allow **2 :** to discharge **3 :** to grant a university degree to — **licenciarse** *vr* **:** to graduate
licenciatura *nf* **1 :** college degree **2 :** course of study (at a college or university)
licencioso, -sa *adj* **:** licentious, lewd
liceo *nm* **:** secondary school, high school
licitación *nf, pl* **-ciones :** bid, bidding
licitar *vt* **:** to bid on
lícito, -ta *adj* **1 :** lawful, licit **2** JUSTO **:** just, fair
licor *nm* **1 :** liquor **2 :** liqueur
licorera *nf* **:** decanter
licuado *nm* BATIDO **:** milk shake
licuadora *nf* **:** blender
licuar {3} *vt* **:** to liquefy — **licuarse** *vr*
lid *nf* **1 :** fight, combat **2 :** argument, dispute **3 lides** *nfpl* **:** matters, affairs **4 en buena lid :** fair and square
líder[1] *adj* **:** leading, foremost
líder[2] *nmf* **:** leader
liderar *vt* DIRIGIR **:** to lead, to head
liderato *nm* **:** leadership, leading
liderazgo *nm* → **liderato**
lidiar *vt* **:** to fight — *vi* BATALLAR, LUCHAR **:** to struggle, to battle, to wrestle
liebre *nf* **:** hare
liendre *nf* **:** nit
lienzo *nm* **1 :** linen **2 :** canvas, painting **3 :** stretch of wall or fencing
liga *nf* **1** ASOCIACIÓN **:** league **2** GOMITA **:** rubber band **3 :** garter
ligado, -da *adj* **:** linked, connected
ligadura *nf* **1** ATADURA **:** tie, bond **2 :** ligature
ligamento *nm* **:** ligament
ligar {52} *vt* **:** to bind, to tie (up)

ligeramente *adv* 1 : slightly 2 LEVEMENTE : lightly, gently 3 : casually, flippantly

ligereza *nf* 1 : lightness 2 : flippancy 3 : agility

ligero, -ra *adj* 1 : light, lightweight 2 : slight, minor 3 : agile, quick 4 : lighthearted, superficial

ligue, etc. → **ligar**

lija *nf or* **papel de lija** : sandpaper

lijar *vt* : to sand

lila[1] *adj* : lilac, light purple

lila[2] *nf* : lilac

lima *nf* 1 : lime (fruit) 2 : file <lima de uñas : nail file>

limadora *nf* : polisher

limar *vt* 1 : to file 2 : to polish, to put the final touch on 3 : to smooth over <limar las diferencias : to iron out differences>

limbo *nm* 1 : limbo 2 : limb (in botany and astronomy)

limeño[1], -ña *adj* : of or from Lima, Peru

limeño[2], -ña *n* : person from Lima, Peru

limero *nm* : lime tree

limitación *nf, pl* **-ciones** 1 : limitation 2 : limit, restriction <sin limitación : unlimited>

limitado, -da *adj* 1 RESTRINGIDO : limited 2 : dull, slow-witted

limitar *vt* RESTRINGIR : to limit, to restrict — *vi* ~ **con** : to border on — **limitarse** *vr* ~ **a** : to limit oneself to

límite *nm* 1 : boundary, border 2 : limit <el límite de mi paciencia : the limit of my patience> <límite de velocidad : speed limit> 3 **fecha límite** : deadline

limítrofe *adj* LINDANTE, LINDERO : bordering, adjoining

limo *nm* : slime, mud

limón *nm, pl* **limones** 1 : lemon 2 : lemon tree 3 **limón verde** *Mex* : lime

limonada *nf* : lemonade

limosna *nf* : alms, charity

limosnear *vi* : to beg (for alms)

limosnero, -ra *n* MENDIGO : beggar

limoso, -sa *adj* : slimy

limpiabotas *nmfs & pl* : bootblack

limpiador[1], -dora *adj* : cleaning

limpiador[2], -dora *n* : cleaning person, cleaner

limpiamente *adv* : cleanly, honestly, fairly

limpiaparabrisas *nms & pl* : windshield wiper

limpiar *vt* 1 : to clean, to cleanse 2 : to clean up, to remove defects 3 *fam* : to clean out (in a game) 4 *fam* : to swipe, to pinch — *vi* : to clean — **limpiarse** *vr*

limpiavidrios *nmfs & pl Mex* : windshield wiper

límpido, -da *adj* : limpid

limpieza *nf* 1 : cleanliness, tidiness 2 : cleaning 3 HONRADEZ : integrity, honesty 4 DESTREZA : skill, dexterity

limpio[1] *adv* : fairly

limpio[2], -pia *adj* 1 : clean, neat 2 : honest <un juego limpio : a fair game> 3 : free <limpio de impurezas : pure, free from impurities> 4 : clear, net <ganancia limpia : clear profit>

limusina *nf* : limousine

linaje *nm* ABOLENGO : lineage, ancestry

linaza *nf* : linseed

lince *nm* : lynx

linchamiento *nm* : lynching

linchar *vt* : to lynch

lindante *adj* LIMÍTROFE, LINDERO : bordering, adjoining

lindar *vi* 1 ~ **con** : to border, to skirt 2 ~ **con** BORDEAR : to border on, to verge on

linde *nmf* : boundary, limit

lindero[1], -ra *adj* LIMÍTROFE, LINDANTE : bordering, adjoining

lindero[2] *nm* : boundary, limit

lindeza *nf* 1 : prettiness 2 : clever remark 3 **lindezas** *nfpl* (*used ironically*) : insults

lindo[1] *adv* 1 : beautifully, wonderfully <canta lindo tu mujer : your wife sings beautifully> 2 **de lo lindo** : a lot, a great deal <los zancudos nos picaban de lo lindo : the mosquitoes were biting away at us>

lindo[2], -da *adj* 1 BONITO : pretty, lovely 2 MONO : cute

línea *nf* 1 : line <línea divisoria : dividing line> <línea de banda : sideline> 2 : line, course, position <línea de conducta : course of action> <en líneas generales : in general terms, along general lines> 3 : line, service <línea aérea : airline> <línea telefónica : telephone line>

lineal *adj* : linear

linfa *nf* : lymph

linfático, -ca *adj* : lymphatic

lingote *nm* : ingot

lingüista *nmf* : linguist

lingüística *nf* : linguistics

lingüístico, -ca *adj* : linguistic

linimento *nm* : liniment

lino *nm* 1 : linen 2 : flax

linóleo *nm* : linoleum

linterna *nf* 1 : lantern 2 : flashlight

lío *nm fam* 1 : confusion, mess 2 : hassle, trouble, jam <meterse en un lío : to get into a jam> 3 : affair, liason

liofilizar {21} *vt* : to freeze-dry

lioso, -sa *adj fam* 1 : confusing, muddled 2 : troublemaking

liquen *nm* : lichen

liquidación *nf, pl* **-ciones** 1 : liquidation 2 : clearance sale 3 : settlement, payment

liquidar *vt* 1 : to liquefy 2 : to liquidate 3 : to settle, to pay off 4 *fam* : to rub out, to kill

liquidez *nf, pl* **-deces** : liquidity

líquido[1], **-da** *adj* **1 :** liquid, fluid **2 :** net <ingresos líquidos : net income>
líquido[2] *nm* **1 :** liquid, fluid <líquido de frenos : brake fluid> **2 :** ready cash, liquid assets
lira *nf* **:** lyre
lírica *nf* **:** lyric poetry
lírico, -ca *adj* **:** lyric, lyrical
lirio *nm* **1 :** iris **2 lirio de los valles** MUGUETE **:** lily of the valley
lirismo *nm* **:** lyricism
lirón *nm, pl* **lirones :** dormouse
lisiado[1], **-da** *adj* **:** disabled, crippled
lisiado[2], **-da** *n* **:** disabled person, cripple
lisiar *vt* **:** to cripple, to disable — **lisiarse** *vr*
liso, -sa *adj* **1 :** smooth **2 :** flat **3 :** straight <pelo liso : straight hair> **4 :** plain, unadorned <liso y llano : plain and simple>
lisonja *nf* **:** flattery
lisonjear *vt* ADULAR **:** to flatter
lista *nf* **1 :** list **2 :** roster, roll <pasar lista : to take attendance> **3 :** stripe, strip **4 :** menu
listado[1], **-da** *adj* **:** striped
listado[2] *nm* **:** listing
listar *vt* **:** to list
listeza *nf* **:** smartness, alertness
listo, -ta *adj* **1** DISPUESTO, PREPARADO **:** ready <¿estás listo? : are you ready?> **2 :** clever, smart
listón *nm, pl* **listones 1 :** ribbon **2 :** strip (of wood), lath **3 :** high bar (in sports)
lisura *nf* **:** smoothness
litera *nf* **:** bunk bed, berth
literal *adj* **:** literal — **literalmente** *adv*
literario, -ria *adj* **:** literary
literato, -ta *n* **:** writer, author
literatura *nf* **:** literature
litigante *adj & nmf* **:** litigant
litigar {52} *vi* **:** to litigate, to be in litigation
litigio *nm* **1 :** litigation, lawsuit **2 en ~ :** in dispute
litigioso, -sa *adj* **:** litigious
litio *nm* **:** lithium
litografía *nf* **1 :** lithography **2 :** lithograph
litógrafo, -fa *n* **:** lithographer
litoral[1] *adj* **:** coastal
litoral[2] *nm* **:** shore, seaboard
litosfera *nf* **:** lithosphere
litro *nm* **:** liter
lituano[1], **-na** *adj & n* **:** Lithuanian
lituano[2] *nm* **:** Lithuanian (language)
liturgia *nf* **:** liturgy
litúrgico, -ca *adj* **:** liturgical — **litúrgicamente** *adv*
liviandad *nf* LIGEREZA **:** lightness
liviano, -na *adj* **1 :** light, slight **2** INCONSTANTE **:** fickle
lividez *nf* PALIDEZ **:** pallor
lívido, -da *adj* **1** AMORATADO **:** livid **2** PÁLIDO **:** pallid, extremely pale
living *nm* **:** living room
llaga *nf* **:** sore, wound
llama *nf* **1 :** flame **2 :** llama
llamada *nf* **:** call <llamada a larga distancia : long-distance call> <llamada al orden : call to order>
llamado[1], **-da** *adj* **:** named, called <una mujer llamada Rosa : a woman called Rosa>
llamado[2] → **llamamiento**
llamador *nm* **:** door knocker
llamamiento *nm* **:** call, appeal
llamar *vt* **1 :** to name, to call **2 :** to call, to summon **3 :** to phone, to call up — **llamarse** *vr* **:** to be called, to be named <¿cómo te llamas? : what's your name?>
llamarada *nf* **1 :** flare-up, sudden blaze **2 :** flushing (of the face)
llamativo, -va *adj* **:** flashy, showy, striking
llameante *adj* **:** flaming, blazing
llamear *vi* **:** to flame, to blaze
llana *nf* **1 :** trowel **2** → **llano**[2]
llanamente *adv* **:** simply, plainly, straightforwardly
llaneza *nf* **:** simplicity, naturalness
llano[1], **-na** *adj* **1 :** even, flat **2 :** frank, open **3** LISO **:** plain, simple
llano[2] *nm* **:** plain
llanta *nf* **1** NEUMÁTICO **:** tire **2 :** rim
llantén *nm, pl* **llantenes :** plantain (weed)
llanto *nm* **:** crying, weeping
llanura *nf* **:** plain, prairie
llave *nf* **1 :** key **2 :** faucet **3** INTERRUPTOR **:** switch **4 :** brace (punctuation mark) **5 llave inglesa :** monkey wrench
llavero *nm* **:** key chain, key ring
llegada *nf* **:** arrival
llegar {52} *vi* **1 :** to arrive, to come **2 ~ a :** to arrive at, to reach, to amount to **3 ~ a :** to manage to <llegó a terminar la novela : she managed to finish the novel> **4 llegar a ser :** to become <llegó a ser un miembro permanente : he became a permanent member>
llegue, etc. → **llegar**
llenar *vt* **1 :** to fill, to fill up, to fill in **2 :** to meet, to fulfill <los regalos no llenaron sus expectativas : the gifts did not meet her expectations> — **llenarse** *vr* **:** to fill up, to become full
llenito, -ta *adj fam* REGORDETE **:** chubby, plump
lleno[1], **-na** *adj* **1 :** full, filled **2 de ~ :** completely, fully **3 estar lleno de sí mismo :** to be full of oneself
lleno[2] *nm* **1** *fam* **:** plenty, abundance **2 :** full house, sellout
llevadero, -ra *adj* **:** bearable
llevar *vt* **1 :** to take away, to carry <me gusta, me lo llevo : I like it, I'll take it> **2 :** to wear **3 :** to take, to lead <llevamos a Pedro al cine : we took Pedro to the movies> **4 llevar a cabo :** to carry out **5 llevar adelante :** to carry on, to keep going — *vi* **:** to lead <un problema lleva al otro : one problem leads to another> — *v aux* **:** to

have <llevo mucho tiempo buscándolo : I've been looking for it for a long time> <lleva leído medio libro : he's halfway through the book> — **llevarse** *vr* **1** : to take away, to carry off **2** : to get along <siempre nos llevábamos bien : we always got along well>

llorar *vi* : to cry, to weep — *vt* : to mourn, to bewail

lloriquear *vi* : to whimper, to whine

lloriqueo *nm* : whimpering, whining

llorón, -rona *n, mpl* **llorones** : crybaby, whiner

lloroso, -sa *adj* : tearful, sad

llovedizo, -za *adj* : rain <agua llovediza : rainwater>

llover {47} *v impers* : to rain <está lloviendo : it's raining> <llover a cántaros : to rain cats and dogs> — *vi* : to rain down, to shower <le llovieron regalos : he was showered with gifts>

llovizna *nf* : drizzle, sprinkle

lloviznar *v impers* : to drizzle, to sprinkle

llueve, etc. → **llover**

lluvia *nf* **1** : rain, rainfall **2** : barrage, shower

lluvioso, -sa *adj* : rainy

lo[1] *pron* **1** : him, it <lo vi ayer : I saw him yesterday> <lo entiendo : I understand it> <no lo creo : I don't believe so> **2** (*formal, masculine*) : you <disculpe, señor, no lo oí : excuse me sir, I didn't hear you> **3 lo que** : what, that which <eso es lo que más le gusta : that's what he likes the most>

lo[2] *art* **1** : the <lo mejor : the best, the best thing> **2** : how <sé lo bueno que eres : I know how good you are>

loa *nf* : praise

loable *adj* : laudable, praiseworthy — **loablemente** *adv*

loar *vt* : to praise, to laud

lobato, -ta *n* : wolf cub

lobby *nm* : lobby, pressure group

lobo, -ba *n* : wolf

lóbrego, -ga *adj* SOMBRÍO : gloomy, dark

lobulado, -da *adj* : lobed

lóbulo *nm* : lobe <lóbulo de la oreja : earlobe>

locación *nf, pl* **-ciones 1** : location (in moviemaking) **2** *Mex* : place

local[1] *adj* : local — **localmente** *adv*

local[2] *nm* : premises *pl*

localidad *nf* : town, locality

localización *nf, pl* **-ciones 1** : locating, localization **2** : location

localizar {21} *vt* **1** UBICAR : to locate, to find **2** : to localize — **localizarse** *vr* UBICARSE : to be located <se localiza en el séptimo piso : it is located on the seventh floor>

locatario, -ria *n* : tenant

loción *nf, pl* **lociones** : lotion

lócker *nm, pl* **lóckers** : locker

loco[1]**, -ca** *adj* **1** DEMENTE : crazy, insane, mad **2 a lo loco** : wildly, recklessly **3 volverse loco** : to go mad

loco[2]**, -ca** *n* **1** : crazy person, lunatic **2 hacerse el loco** : to act the fool

locomoción *nf, pl* **-ciones** : locomotion

locomotor, -tora *adj* : locomotive

locomotora *nf* **1** : locomotive **2** : driving force

locuacidad *nf* : loquacity, talkativeness

locuaz *adj, pl* **locuaces** : loquacious, talkative

locución *nf, pl* **-ciones** : locution, phrase <locución adverbial : adverbial phrase>

locura *nf* **1** : insanity, madness **2** : crazy thing, folly

locutor, -tora *n* : announcer

lodazal *nm* : bog, quagmire

lodo *nm* BARRO : mud, mire

lodoso, -sa *adj* : muddy

logaritmo *nm* : logarithm

logia *nf* : lodge <logia masónica : Masonic lodge>

lógica *nf* : logic

lógico, -ca *adj* : logical — **lógicamente** *adv*

logística *nf* : logistics *pl*

logístico, -ca *adj* : logistic, logistical

logo *nm* → **logotipo**

logotipo *nm* : logo

logrado, -da *adj* : successful, well done

lograr *vt* **1** : to get, to obtain **2** : to achieve, to attain — **lograrse** *vr* : to be successful

logro *nm* : achievement, attainment

loma *nf* : hill, hillock

lombriz *nf, pl* **lombrices** : worm <lombriz de tierra : earthworm, night crawler> <lombriz solitaria : tapeworm> <tener lombrices : to have worms>

lomo *nm* **1** : back (of an animal) **2** : loin <lomo de cerdo : pork loin> **3** : spine (of a book) **4** : blunt edge (of a knife)

lona *nf* : canvas

loncha *nf* LONJA, REBANADA : slice

lonche *nm* **1** ALMUERZO : lunch **2** *Mex* : submarine sandwich

lonchería *nf Mex* : luncheonette

londinense[1] *adj* : of or from London

londinense[2] *nmf* : Londoner

longaniza *nf* : spicy pork sausage

longevidad *nf* : longevity

longevo, -va *adj* : long-lived

longitud *nf* **1** LARGO : length <longitud de onda : wavelength> **2** : longitude

longitudinal *adj* : longitudinal

lonja *nf* LONCHA, REBANADA : slice

lontananza *nf* : background <en lontananza : in the distance, far away>

lord *nm, pl* **lores** (*title in England*) : lord

loro *nm* : parrot

los[1]**, las** *pron* **1** : them <hice galletas y se las di a los nuevos vecinos : I made cookies and gave them to the

new neighbors> **2 :** you <voy a llevarlos a los dos **:** I am going to take both of you> **3 los que, las que :** those, who, the ones <los que van a cantar deben venir temprano **:** those who are singing must come early> **4** (*used with* **haber**) <los hay en varios colores **:** they come in various colors>
los[2] → **el**[2]
losa *nf* **:** flagstone, paving stone
loseta *nf* BALDOSA **:** floor tile
lote *nm* **1 :** part, share **2 :** batch, lot **3 :** plot of land, lot
lotería *nf* **:** lottery
loto *nm* **:** lotus
loza *nf* **1 :** crockery, earthenware **2 :** china
lozanía *nf* **1 :** healthiness, robustness **2 :** luxuriance, lushness
lozano, -na *adj* **1 :** robust, healthy-looking <un rostro lozano **:** a smooth, fresh face> **2 :** lush, luxuriant
lubricante[1] *adj* **:** lubricating
lubricante[2] *nm* **:** lubricant
lubricar {72} *vt* **:** to lubricate, to oil — **lubricación** *nf*
lucero *nm* **:** bright star <lucero del alba **:** morning star>
lucha *nf* **1 :** struggle, fight **2 :** wrestling
luchador, -dora *n* **1 :** fighter **2 :** wrestler
luchar *vi* **1 :** to fight, to struggle **2 :** to wrestle
luchón, -chona *adj, mpl* **luchones** *Mex* **:** industrious, hardworking
lucidez *nf, pl* **-deces :** lucidity, clarity
lucido, -da *adj* MAGNÍFICO **:** magnificent, splendid
lúcido, -da *adj* **:** lucid
luciérnaga *nf* **:** firefly, glowworm
lucimiento *nm* **1 :** brilliance, splendor, sparkle **2 :** triumph, success <salir con lucimiento **:** to succeed with flying colors>
lucio *nm* **:** pike (fish)
lucir {45} *vi* **1 :** to shine **2 :** to look good, to stand out **3 :** to seem, to appear <ahora luce contento **:** he looks happy now> — *vt* **1 :** to wear, to sport **2 :** to flaunt, to show off — **lucirse** *vr* **1 :** to distinguish oneself, to excel **2 :** to show off
lucrarse *vr* **:** to make a profit
lucrativo, -va *adj* **:** lucrative, profitable — **lucrativamente** *adv*
lucro *nm* GANANCIA **:** profit, gain
luctuoso, -sa *adj* **:** mournful, tragic
luego[1] *adv* **1** DESPUÉS **:** then, afterwards **2 :** later (on) **3 desde ~ :** of course **4 ¡hasta luego! :** see you later! **5 luego que :** as soon as **6 luego luego** *Mex fam* **:** right away, immediately
luego[2] *conj* **:** therefore <pienso, luego existo **:** I think, therefore I am>
lugar *nm* **1 :** place, position <se llevó el primer lugar en su división **:** she took first place in her division> **2** ESPACIO **:** space, room **3 dar lugar a :** to give rise to, to lead to **4 en lugar de :** instead of **5 lugar común :** cliché, platitude **6 tener lugar :** to take place
lugareño[1], **-ña** *adj* **:** village, rural
lugareño[2], **-ña** *n* **:** villager
lugarteniente *nmf* **:** lieutenant, deputy
lúgubre *adj* **:** gloomy, lugubrious
lujo *nm* **1 :** luxury **2 de ~ :** deluxe
lujoso, -sa *adj* **:** luxurious
lujuria *nf* **:** lust, lechery
lujurioso, -sa *adj* **:** lustful, lecherous
lumbar *adj* **:** lumbar
lumbre *nf* **1** FUEGO **:** fire **2 :** brilliance, splendor **3 poner en la lumbre :** to put on the stove, to warm up
lumbrera *nf* **1 :** skylight **2 :** vent, port **3 :** brilliant person, luminary
luminaria *nf* **1 :** altar lamp **2** LUMBRERA **:** luminary, celebrity
luminiscencia *nf* **:** luminescence — **luminiscente** *adj*
luminosidad *nf* **:** luminosity, brightness
luminoso, -sa *adj* **:** shining, luminous
luna *nf* **1 :** moon **2 luna de miel :** honeymoon
lunar[1] *adj* **:** lunar
lunar[2] *nm* **1 :** mole, beauty spot **2 :** defect, blemish **3 :** polka dot
lunático, -ca *adj & n* **:** lunatic
lunes *nms & pl* **:** Monday
luneta *nf* **1 :** lens (of eyeglasses) **2 :** windshield (of an automobile) **3 :** crescent
lupa *nf* **:** magnifying glass
lúpulo *nm* **:** hops (plant)
lustrar *vt* **:** to shine, to polish
lustre *nm* **1** BRILLO **:** luster, shine **2 :** glory, distinction
lustroso, -sa *adj* BRILLOSO **:** lustrous, shiny
luto *nm* **:** mourning <estar de luto **:** to be in mourning>
luz *nf, pl* **luces 1 :** light **2 :** lighting **3** *fam* **:** electricity **4 :** window, opening **5 :** light, lamp **6 :** span, spread (between supports) **7 a la luz de :** in light of **8 dar a luz :** to give birth **9 traje de luces :** matador's costume
luzca, etc. → **lucir**

M

m *nf* **:** thirteenth letter of the Spanish alphabet
macabro, -bra *adj* **:** macabre
macaco[1], **-ca** *adj* **:** ugly, misshapen
macaco[2], **-ca** *n* **:** macaque
macadán *nm, pl* **-danes :** macadam
macana *nf* **1 :** club, cudgel **2** *fam* **:** nonsense, silliness **3** *fam* **:** lie, fib
macanudo, -da *adj fam* **:** great, fantastic

macarrón *nm, pl* **-rrones 1 :** macaroon **2 macarrones** *nmpl* **:** macaroni

maceta *nf* **1 :** flowerpot **2 :** mallet **3** *Mex fam* **:** head

machacar {72} *vt* **1 :** to crush, to grind **2 :** to beat, to pound — *vi* **:** to insist, to go on (about)

machacón, -cona *adj, mpl* **-cones :** insistent, tiresome

machete *nm* **:** machete

machetear *vt* **:** to hack with a machete — *vi Mex fam* **:** to plod, to work tirelessly

machismo *nm* **1 :** machismo **2 :** male chauvinism

machista *nm* **:** male chauvinist

macho[1] *adj* **1 :** male **2 :** macho, virile, tough

macho[2] *nm* **1 :** male **2 :** he-man

machote *nm* **1** *fam* **:** tough guy, he-man **2** *CA, Mex* **:** rough draft, model **3** *Mex* **:** blank form

machucar {72} *vt* **1 :** to pound, to beat, to crush **2 :** to bruise

machucón *nm, pl* **-cones 1** MORETÓN **:** bruise **2 :** smashing, pounding

macilento, -ta *adj* **:** gaunt, wan

macis *nm* **:** mace (spice)

macizo, -za *adj* **1 :** solid <oro macizo : solid gold> **2 :** strong, strapping **3 :** massive

macrocosmo *nm* **:** macrocosm

mácula *nf* **:** blemish, stain

madeja *nf* **1 :** skein, hank **2 :** tangle (of hair)

madera *nf* **1 :** wood **2 :** lumber, timber **3 madera dura** *or* **madera noble :** hardwood

maderero, -ra *adj* **:** timber, lumber

madero *nm* **:** piece of lumber, plank

madrastra *nf* **:** stepmother

madrazo *nm Mex fam* **:** punch, blow <se agarraron a madrazos : they beat each other up>

madre *nf* **1 :** mother **2 madre política :** mother-in-law **3 la Madre Patria :** the mother country (said of Spain)

madrear *vt Mex fam* **:** to beat up

madreperla *nf* NÁCAR **:** mother-of-pearl

madreselva *nf* **:** honeysuckle

madriguera *nf* **:** burrow, den, lair

madrileño[1], **-ña** *adj* **:** of or from Madrid

madrileño[2], **-ña** *n* **:** person from Madrid

madrina *nf* **1 :** godmother **2 :** bridesmaid **3 :** sponsor

madrugada *nf* **1 :** early morning, wee hours **2** ALBA **:** dawn, daybreak

madrugador, -dora *n* **:** early riser

madrugar {52} *vi* **1 :** to get up early **2 :** to get a head start

madurar *v* **1 :** to ripen **2 :** to mature

madurez *nf, pl* **-reces 1 :** maturity **2 :** ripeness

maduro, -ra *adj* **1 :** mature **2 :** ripe

maestría *nf* **1 :** mastery, skill **2 :** master's degree

maestro[1], **-tra** *adj* **1 :** masterly, skilled **2 :** chief, main **3 :** trained <un elefante maestro : a trained elephant>

maestro[2], **-tra** *n* **1 :** teacher (in grammar school) **2 :** expert, master **3 :** maestro

Mafia *nf* **:** Mafia

mafioso, -sa *n* **:** mafioso, gangster

magdalena *nf* **:** bun, muffin

magenta *adj & n* **:** magenta

magia *nf* **:** magic

mágico, -ca *adj* **:** magic, magical — **mágicamente** *adv*

magisterio *nm* **1 :** teaching **2 :** teachers *pl,* teaching profession

magistrado, -da *n* **:** magistrate, judge

magistral *adj* **1 :** masterful, skillful **2 :** magisterial

magistralmente *adv* **:** masterfully, brilliantly

magistratura *nf* **:** judgeship, magistracy

magma *nm* **:** magma

magnanimidad *nf* **:** magnanimity

magnánimo, -ma *adj* GENEROSO **:** magnanimous — **magnánimamente** *adv*

magnate *nmf* **:** magnate, tycoon

magnesia *nf* **:** magnesia

magnesio *nm* **:** magnesium

magnético, -ca *adj* **:** magnetic

magnetismo *nm* **:** magnetism

magnetizar {21} *vt* **:** to magnetize

magnetófono *nm* **:** tape recorder

magnetofónico, -ca *adj* **cinta magnetofónica :** magnetic tape

magnificar {72} *vt* **1 :** to magnify **2** EXAGERAR **:** to exaggerate **3** ENSALZAR **:** to exalt, to extol, to praise highly

magnificencia *nf* **:** magnificence, splendor

magnífico, -ca *adj* ESPLENDOROSO **:** magnificent, splendid — **magníficamente** *adv*

magnitud *nf* **:** magnitude

magnolia *nf* **:** magnolia (flower)

magnolio *nm* **:** magnolia (tree)

mago, -ga *n* **1 :** magician **2 :** wizard (in folk tales, etc.) **3 los Reyes Magos :** the Magi

magro, -gra *adj* **1 :** lean (of meat) **2 :** meager

maguey *nm* **:** maguey

magulladura *nf* MORETÓN **:** bruise

magullar *vt* **:** to bruise — **magullarse** *vr*

mahometano[1], **-na** *adj* ISLÁMICO **:** Islamic, Muslim

mahometano[2], **-na** *n* **:** Muslim

mahonesa *nf* → **mayonesa**

maicena *nf* **:** cornstarch

maíz *nm* **:** corn, maize

maizal *nm* **:** cornfield

maja *nf* **:** pestle

majadería *nf* **1** TONTERÍA **:** stupidity, foolishness **2** *Mex* LEPERADA **:** insult, obscenity

majadero[1], **-ra** *adj* **1 :** foolish, silly **2** *Mex* LÉPERO **:** crude, vulgar

majadero[2], **-ra** *n* **1** TONTO : fool **2** *Mex* : rude person, boor
majar *vt* : to crush, to mash
majestad *nf* : majesty <Su Majestad : Your Majesty>
majestuosamente *adv* : majestically
majestuosidad *nf* : majesty, grandeur
majestuoso, -sa *adj* : majestic, stately
majo, -ja *adj Spain* **1** : nice, likeable **2** GUAPO : attractive, good-looking
mal[1] *adv* **1** : badly, poorly <baila muy mal : he dances very badly> **2** : wrong, incorrectly <me entendió mal : she misunderstood me> **3** : with difficulty, hardly <mal puedo oírte : I can hardly hear you> **4 de mal en peor** : from bad to worse **5 menos mal** : it could have been worse
mal[2] *adj* → **malo**
mal[3] *nm* **1** : evil, wrong **2** DAÑO : harm, damage **3** DESGRACIA : misfortune **4** ENFERMEDAD : illness, sickness
malabar *adj* **juegos malabares** : juggling
malabarista *nmf* : juggler
malaconsejado, -da *adj* : ill-advised
malacostumbrado, -da *adj* CONSENTIDO : spoiled, pampered
malacostumbrar *vt* : to spoil
malagradecido, -da *adj* INGRATO : ungrateful
malaisio → **malasio**
malaquita *nf* : malachite
malaria *nf* PALUDISMO : malaria
malasio, -sia *adj & n* : Malaysian
malaventura *nf* : misadventure, misfortune
malaventurado, -da *adj* MALHADADO : ill-fated, unfortunate
malayo, -ya *adj & n* : Malay, Malayan
malbaratar *vt* **1** MALGASTAR : to squander **2** : to undersell
malcriado[1], **-da** *adj* **1** : ill-bred, bad-mannered **2** : spoiled, pampered
malcriado[2], **-da** *n* : spoiled brat
maldad *nf* **1** : evil, wickedness **2** : evil deed
maldecir {11} *vt* : to curse, to damn — *vi* **1** : to curse, to swear **2 ~ de** : to speak ill of, to slander, to defame
maldición *nf, pl* **-ciones** : curse
maldiga, maldijo, etc. → **maldecir**
maldito, -ta *adj* **1** : cursed, damned <¡maldita sea! : damn it all!> **2** : wicked
maldoso, -sa *adj Mex* : mischievous
maleable *adj* : malleable
maleante *nmf* : crook, thug
malecón *nm, pl* **-cones** : jetty, breakwater
maleducado, -da *adj* : ill-mannered, rude
maleficio *nm* : curse, hex
maléfico, -ca *adj* : evil, harmful
malentender {56} *vt* : to misunderstand
malentendido *nm* : misunderstanding
malestar *nm* **1** : discomfort **2** IRRITACIÓN : annoyance **3** INQUIETUD : uneasiness, unrest
maleta *nf* : suitcase, bag <haz tus maletas : pack your bags>
maletero[1], **-ra** *n* : porter
maletero[2] *nm* : trunk (of an automobile)
maletín *nm, pl* **-tines 1** PORTAFOLIO : briefcase **2** : overnight bag, satchel
malevolencia *nf* : malevolence, wickedness
malévolo, -la *adj* : malevolent, wicked
maleza *nf* **1** : thicket, underbrush **2** : weeds *pl*
malformación *nf, pl* **-ciones** : malformation
malgache *adj & nmf* : Madagascan
malgastar *vt* : to squander (resources), to waste (time, effort)
malhablado, -da *adj* : foul-mouthed
malhadado, -da *adj* MALAVENTURADO : ill-fated
malhechor, -chora *n* : criminal, delinquent, wrongdoer
malherir {76} *vt* : to injure seriously
malhumor *nm* : bad mood, sullenness
malhumorado, -da *adj* : bad-tempered, cross
malicia *nf* **1** : wickedness, malice **2** : mischief, naughtiness **3** : cunning, craftiness
malicioso, -sa *adj* **1** : malicious **2** PÍCARO : mischievous
malignidad *nf* **1** : malignancy **2** MALDAD : evil
maligno, -na *adj* **1** : malignant <un tumor maligno : a malignant tumor> **2** : evil, harmful, malign
malinchismo *nm Mex* : preference for foreign goods or people — **malinchista** *adj*
malintencionado, -da *adj* : malicious, spiteful
malinterpretar *vt* : to misinterpret
malla *nf* **1** : mesh **2** LEOTARDO : leotard, tights *pl* **3 malla de baño** : bathing suit
mallorquín, -quina *adj & n* : Majorcan
malnutrición *nf, pl* **-ciones** DESNUTRICIÓN : malnutrition
malnutrido, -da *adj* DESNUTRIDO : malnourished, undernourished
malo[1], **-la** *adj* (**mal** *before masculine singular nouns*) **1** : bad <mala suerte : bad luck> **2** : wicked, naughty **3** : cheap, poor (quality) **4** : harmful <malo para la salud : bad for one's health> **5** (*using the form* **mal**) : unwell <estar mal del corazón : to have heart trouble> **6 estar de malas** : to be in a bad mood
malo[2], **-la** *n* : villain, bad guy (in novels, movies, etc.)
malogrado, -da *adj* : failed, unsuccessful
malograr *vt* **1** : to spoil, to ruin **2** : to waste (an opportunity, time) — **mal-**

ograrse *vr* **1** FRACASAR **:** to fail **2 :** to die young

malogro *nm* **1 :** untimely death **2** FRACASO **:** failure

maloliente *adj* HEDIONDO **:** foul-smelling, smelly

malparado, -da *adj* **salir malparado** *or* **quedar malparado :** to come out of (something) badly, to end up in a bad state

malpensado, -da *adj* **:** distrustful, suspicious, nasty-minded

malquerencia *nf* AVERSIÓN **:** ill will, dislike

malquerer {64} *vt* **:** to dislike

malquiso, etc. → **malquerer**

malsano, -na *adj* **:** unhealthy

malsonante *adj* **:** rude, offensive <palabras malsonantes : foul language>

malta *nf* **:** malt

malteada *nf* **:** malted milk <malteada de chocolate : chocolate malt>

maltés, -tesa *adj & n, mpl* **malteses** **:** Maltese

maltratar *vt* **1 :** to mistreat, to abuse **2 :** to damage, to spoil

maltrato *nm* **:** mistreatment, abuse

maltrecho, -cha *adj* **:** battered, damaged

malucho, -cha *adj fam* **:** sick, under the weather

malva *adj & nm* **:** mauve

malvado[1], -da *adj* **:** evil, wicked

malvado[2], -da *n* **:** evildoer, wicked person

malvavisco *nm* **:** marshmallow

malvender *vt* **:** to sell at a loss

malversación *nf, pl* **-ciones :** misappropriation (of funds), embezzlement

malversador, -dora *n* **:** embezzler

malversar *vt* **:** to embezzle

malvivir *vi* **:** to live badly, to just scrape by

mamá *nf fam* **:** mom, mama

mamar *vi* **1 :** to suckle **2 darle de mamar a :** to breast-feed — *vt* **1 :** to suckle, to nurse **2 :** to learn from childhood, to grow up with — **mamarse** *vr fam* **:** to get drunk

mamario, -ria *adj* **:** mammary

mamarracho *nm fam* **1** ESPERPENTO **:** mess, sight **2 :** laughingstock, fool **3 :** rubbish, junk

mambo *nm* **:** mambo

mami *nf fam* **:** mommy

mamífero[1], -ra *adj* **:** mammalian

mamífero[2] *nm* **:** mammal

mamila *nf* **1 :** nipple **2** *Mex* **:** baby bottle, pacifier

mamografía *nf* **:** mammogram

mamola *nf* **:** pat, chuck under the chin

mamotreto *nm fam* **1 :** huge book, tome **2** ARMATOSTE **:** hulk, monstrosity

mampara *nf* BIOMBO **:** screen, room divider

mamparo *nm* **:** bulkhead

mampostería *nf* **:** masonry, stonemasonery

mampostero *nm* **:** mason, stonemason

mamut *nm, pl* **mamuts :** mammoth

maná *nm* **:** manna

manada *nf* **1 :** flock, herd, pack **2** *fam* **:** horde, mob <llegaron en manada : they came in droves>

manantial *nm* **1** FUENTE **:** spring **2 :** source

manar *vi* **1 :** to flow **2 :** to abound

manatí *nm* **:** manatee

mancha *nf* **1 :** stain, spot, mark <mancha de sangre : bloodstain> **2 :** blemish, blot <una mancha en su reputación : a blemish on his reputation> **3 :** patch

manchado, -da *adj* **:** stained

manchar *vt* **1** ENSUCIAR **:** to stain, to soil **2** DESHONRAR **:** to sully, to tarnish — **mancharse** *vr* **:** to get dirty

mancillar vt **:** to sully, to besmirch

manco, -ca *adj* **:** one-armed, one-handed

mancomunar *vt* **:** to combine, to pool — **mancomunarse** *vr* **:** to unite, to join together

mancomunidad *nf* **1 :** commonwealth **2 :** association, confederation

mancuernas *nfpl* **:** cuff links

mancuernillas *nf Mex* **:** cuff links

mandadero, -ra *n* **:** errand boy *m,* errand girl *f,* messenger

mandado *nm* **1 :** order, command **2 :** errand <hacer los mandados : to run errands, to go shopping>

mandamás *nmf, pl* **-mases** *fam* **:** boss, bigwig, honcho

mandamiento *nm* **1 :** commandment **2 :** command, order, warrant <mandamiento judicial : warrant, court order>

mandar *vt* **1** ORDENAR **:** to command, to order **2** ENVIAR **:** to send <te manda saludos : he sends you his regards> **3** ECHAR **:** to hurl, to throw **4 ¿mande?** *Mex* **:** yes?, pardon? — *vi* **:** to be the boss, to be in charge — **mandarse** *vr Mex* **:** to take liberties, to take advantage

mandarina *nf* **:** mandarin orange, tangerine

mandatario, -ria *n* **1 :** leader (in politics) <primer mandatario : head of state> **2 :** agent (in law)

mandato *nm* **1 :** term of office **2 :** mandate

mandíbula *nf* **1 :** jaw **2 :** mandible

mandil *nm* **1** DELANTAL **:** apron **2 :** horse blanket

mandilón *nm, pl* **-lones** *fam* **:** wimp, coward

mandioca *nf* **1 :** manioc, cassava **2 :** tapioca

mando *nm* **1 :** command, leadership **2 :** control (for a device) <mando a distancia : remote control> **3 al mando de :** in charge of **4 al mando de :** under the command of

mandolina *nf* **:** mandolin

mandón, -dona *adj, mpl* **mandones :** bossy, domineering

mandonear *vt fam* MANGONEAR **:** to boss around
mandrágora *nf* **:** mandrake
manecilla *nf* **:** hand (of a clock), pointer
manejable *adj* **1 :** manageable **2 :** docile, easily led
manejar *vt* **1** CONDUCIR **:** to drive (a car) **2** OPERAR **:** to handle, to operate **3 :** to manage **4 :** to manipulate (a person) — *vi* **:** to drive — **manejarse** *vr* **1** COMPORTARSE **:** to behave **2 :** to get along, to manage
manejo *nm* **1 :** handling, operation **2 :** management
manera *nf* **1** MODO **:** way, manner, fashion **2 de cualquier manera** *or* **de todas maneras :** anyway, anyhow **3 de manera que :** so, in order that **4 de ninguna manera :** by no means, absolutely not **5 manera de ser :** personality, demeanor
manga *nf* **1 :** sleeve **2** MANGUERA **:** hose
manganeso *nm* **:** manganese
mangle *nm* **:** mangrove
mango *nm* **1 :** hilt, handle **2 :** mango
mangonear *vt fam* **:** to boss around, to bully — *vi* **1 :** to be bossy **2 :** to loaf, to fool around
mangosta *nf* **:** mongoose
manguera *nf* **:** hose
maní *nm, pl* **maníes :** peanut
manía *nf* **1** OBSESIÓN **:** mania, obsession **2 :** craze, fad **3 :** odd habit, peculiarity **4 :** dislike, aversion
maníaco[1], -ca *adj* **:** maniacal
maníaco[2], -ca *n* **:** maniac
maniatar *vt* **:** to tie the hands of, to manacle
maniático[1], -ca *adj* **1** MANÍACO **:** maniacal **2 :** obsessive **3 :** fussy, finicky
maniático[2], -ca *n* **1** MANÍACO **:** maniac, lunatic **2 :** obsessive person, fanatic **3 :** eccentric, crank
manicomio *nm* **:** insane asylum, madhouse
manicura *nf* **:** manicure
manicuro, -ra *n* **:** manicurist
manido, -da *adj* **:** hackneyed, stale, trite
manifestación *nf, pl* **-ciones 1 :** manifestation, sign **2 :** demonstration, rally
manifestante *nmf* **:** demonstrator
manifestar {55} *vt* **1 :** to demonstrate, to show **2 :** to declare — **manifestarse** *vr* **1 :** to be or become evident **2 :** to state one's position <se han manifestado a favor del acuerdo : they have declared their support for the agreement> **3 :** to demonstrate, to rally
manifiesto[1], -ta *adj* **:** manifest, evident, clear — **manifiestamente** *adv*
manifiesto[2] *nm* **:** manifesto
manija *nf* MANGO **:** handle
manilla *nf* → **manecilla**
manillar *nm* **:** handlebars *pl*
maniobra *nf* **:** maneuver, stratagem
maniobrar *v* **:** to maneuver
manipulación *nf, pl* **-ciones :** manipulation
manipulador[1], -dora *adj* **:** manipulating, manipulative
manipulador[2], -dora *n* **:** manipulator
manipular *vt* **1 :** to manipulate **2** MANEJAR **:** to handle
maniquí[1] *nmf, pl* **-quíes :** mannequin, model
maniquí[2] *nm, pl* **-quíes :** mannequin, dummy
manirroto[1], -ta *adj* **:** extravagant
manirroto[2], -ta *n* **:** spendthrift
manivela *nf* **:** crank
manjar *nm* **:** delicacy, special dish
mano[1] *nf* **1 :** hand **2 :** coat (of paint or varnish) **3 a ~ :** by hand **4 a ~** *or* **a la mano :** handy, at hand, nearby **5 darse la mano :** to shake hands **6 de la mano :** hand in hand <la política y la economía van de la mano : politics and economics go hand in hand> **7 de primera mano :** firsthand, at firsthand **8 de segunda mano :** secondhand <ropa de segunda mano : secondhand clothing> **9 mano a mano :** one-on-one **10 mano de obra :** labor, manpower **11 mano de mortero :** pestle **12 echar una mano :** to lend a hand **13** *Mex fam* **mano negra :** shady dealings *pl*
mano[2], -na *n Mex fam* **:** buddy, pal <¡oye, mano! : hey man!>
manojo *nm* PUÑADO **:** handful, bunch
manopla *nf* **1 :** mitten, mitt **2 :** brass knuckles *pl*
manosear *vt* **1 :** to handle or touch excessively **2** ACARICIAR **:** to fondle, to caress
manotazo *nm* **:** slap, smack, swipe
manotear *vi* **:** to wave one's hands, to gesticulate
mansalva *adv* **a ~ :** at close range
mansarda *nf* BUHARDILLA **:** attic
mansedumbre *nf* **1 :** gentleness, meekness **2 :** tameness
mansión *nf, pl* **-siones :** mansion
manso, -sa *adj* **1 :** gentle, meek **2 :** tame — **mansamente** *adv*
manta *nf* **1** COBIJA, FRAZADA **:** blanket **2 :** poncho **3** *Mex* **:** coarse cotton fabric
manteca *nf* **1** GRASA **:** lard, fat **2 :** butter
mantecoso, -sa *adj* **:** buttery
mantel *nm* **1 :** tablecloth **2 :** altar cloth
mantelería *nf* **:** table linen
mantener {80} *vt* **1** SUSTENTAR **:** to support, to feed <mantener uno su familia : to support one's family> **2** CONSERVAR **:** to keep, to preserve **3** CONTINUAR **:** to keep up, to sustain <mantener una correspondencia : to keep up a correspondence> **4** AFIRMAR **:** to maintain, to affirm — **mantenerse** *vr* **1 :** to support oneself, to subsist **2 mantenerse firme :** to hold one's ground
mantenimiento *nm* **1 :** maintenance, upkeep **2 :** sustenance, food **3 :** preservation

mantequera *nf* **1 :** churn **2 :** butter dish

mantequería *nf* **1 :** creamery, dairy **2 :** grocery store

mantequilla *nf* **:** butter

mantilla *nf* **:** mantilla

manto *nm* **1 :** cloak **2 :** mantle (in geology)

mantón *nm, pl* **-tones** CHAL **:** shawl

mantuvo, etc. → **mantener**

manual[1] *adj* **1 :** manual <trabajo manual : manual labor> **2 :** handy, manageable — **manualmente** *adv*

manual[2] *nm* **:** manual, handbook

manualidades *nfpl* **:** handicrafts (in schools)

manubrio *nm* **1 :** handle, crank **2 :** handlebars *pl*

manufactura *nf* **1** FABRICACIÓN **:** manufacture **2 :** manufactured item, product **3** FÁBRICA **:** factory

manufacturar *vt* FABRICAR **:** to manufacture

manufacturero[1], -ra *adj* **:** manufacturing

manufacturero[2], -ra *n* FABRICANTE **:** manufacturer

manuscrito[1], -ta *adj* **:** handwritten

manuscrito[2] *nm* **:** manuscript

manutención *nf, pl* **-ciones :** maintenance, support

manzana *nf* **1 :** apple **2** CUADRA **:** block (enclosed by streets or buildings) **3** *or* **manzana de Adán :** Adam's apple

manzanal *nm* **1 :** apple orchard **2** MANZANO **:** apple tree

manzanar *nm* **:** apple orchard

manzanilla *nf* **1 :** chamomile **2 :** chamomile tea

manzano *nm* **:** apple tree

maña *nf* **1 :** dexterity, skill **2 :** cunning, guile **3 mañas** *or* **malas mañas** *nfpl* **:** bad habits, vices

mañana *nf* **1 :** morning **2 :** tomorrow

mañanero, -ra *adj* MATUTINO **:** morning <rocío mañanero : morning dew>

mañanitas *nfpl Mex* **:** birthday serenade

mañoso, -sa *adj* **1** HÁBIL **:** skillful **2** ASTUTO **:** cunning, crafty **3 :** fussy, finicky

mapa *nm* CARTA **:** map

mapache *nm* **:** raccoon

mapamundi *nm* **:** map of the world

maqueta *nf* **:** model, mock-up

maquillador, -dora *n* **:** makeup artist

maquillaje *nm* **:** makeup

maquillarse *vr* **:** to put on makeup, to make oneself up

máquina *nf* **1 :** machine <máquina de coser : sewing machine> <máquina de escribir : typewriter> **2** LOCOMOTORA **:** engine, locomotive **3 :** machine (in politics) **4 a toda máquina :** at full speed

maquinación *nf, pl* **-ciones :** machination, scheme, plot

maquinal *adj* **:** mechanical, automatic — **maquinalmente** *adv*

maquinar *vt* **:** to plot, to scheme

maquinaria *nf* **1 :** machinery **2 :** mechanism, works *pl*

maquinilla *nf* **1 :** small machine or device **2** *CA, Car* **:** typewriter

maquinista *nmf* **1 :** machinist **2 :** railroad engineer

mar *nmf* **1 :** sea <un mar agitado : a rough sea> <hacerse a la mar : to set sail> **2 alta mar :** high seas

maraca *nf* **:** maraca

maraña *nf* **1 :** thicket **2** ENREDO **:** tangle, mess

marasmo *nm* **:** paralysis, stagnation

maratón *nm, pl* **-tones :** marathon

maravilla *nf* **1 :** wonder, marvel <a las mil maravillas : wonderfully, marvelously> <hacer maravillas : to work wonders> **2 :** marigold

maravillar *vt* ASOMBRAR **:** to astonish, to amaze — **maravillarse** *vr* **:** to be amazed, to marvel

maravilloso, -sa *adj* ESTUPENDO **:** wonderful, marvelous — **maravillosamente** *adv*

marbete *nm* **1** ETIQUETA **:** label, tag **2** *PRi* **:** registration sticker (of a car)

marca *nf* **1 :** mark **2 :** brand, make **3 :** trademark <marca registrada : registered trademark> **4 :** record (in sports) <batir la marca : to beat the record>

marcado, -da *adj* **:** marked <un marcado contraste : a marked contrast>

marcador *nm* **1** TANTEADOR **:** scoreboard **2 :** marker, felt-tipped pen **3 marcador de libros :** bookmark

marcaje *nm* **1 :** scoring (in sports) **2 :** guarding (in sports)

marcapasos *nms & pl* **:** pacemaker

marcar {72} *vt* **1 :** to mark **2 :** to brand (livestock) **3 :** to indicate, to show **4** RESALTAR **:** to emphasize **5 :** to dial (a telephone) **6 :** to guard (an opponent) **7** ANOTAR **:** to score (a goal, a point) — *vi* **1** ANOTAR **:** to score **2 :** to dial

marcha *nf* **1 :** march **2 :** hike, walk <ir de marcha : to go hiking> **3 :** pace, speed <a toda marcha : at top speed> **4 :** gear (of an automobile) <marcha atrás : reverse, reverse gear> **5 en ~ :** in motion, in gear, under way

marchar *vi* **1** IR **:** to go, to travel **2** ANDAR **:** to walk **3** FUNCIONAR **:** to work, to go **4 :** to march — **marcharse** *vr* **:** to leave

marchitar *vi* **:** to make wither, to wilt — **marchitarse** *vr* **1 :** to wither, to shrivel up, to wilt **2 :** to languish, to fade away

marchito, -ta *adj* **:** withered, faded

marcial *adj* **:** martial, military

marco *nm* **1 :** frame, framework **2 :** goalposts *pl* **3** AMBIENTE **:** setting, atmosphere **4 :** mark (unit of currency)

marea *nf* **:** tide

mareado, -da *adj* **1 :** dizzy, lightheaded **2 :** queasy, nauseous **3 :** seasick

marear *vt* **1 :** to make sick <los gases me marearon : the fumes made me sick> **2 :** to bother, to annoy — **marearse** *vr* **1 :** to get sick, to become nauseated **2 :** to feel dizzy **3 :** to get tipsy
marejada *nf* **1 :** surge, swell (of the sea) **2 :** undercurrent, ferment, unrest
maremoto *nm* **:** tidal wave
mareo *nm* **1 :** dizzy spell **2 :** nausea **3 :** seasickness, motion sickness **4 :** annoyance, vexation
marfil *nm* **:** ivory
margarina *nf* **:** margarine
margarita *nf* **1 :** daisy **2 :** margarita (cocktail)
margen[1] *nf, pl* **márgenes :** bank (of a river), side (of a street)
margen[2] *nm, pl* **márgenes 1 :** edge, border **2 :** margin <margen de ganancia : profit margin>
marginación *nf, pl* **-ciones :** marginalization, exclusion
marginado[1], **-da** *adj* **1** DESHEREDADO **:** outcast, alienated, dispossessed **2 clases marginadas :** underclass
marginado[2], **-da** *n* **:** outcast, misfit
marginal *adj* **:** marginal, fringe
marginalidad *nf* **:** marginality
marginar *vt* **:** to ostracize, to exclude
mariachi *nm* **:** mariachi musician or band
maridaje *nm* **:** marriage, union
maridar *vt* UNIR **:** to marry, to unite
marido *nm* ESPOSO **:** husband
marihuana *or* **mariguana** *or* **marijuana** *nf* **:** marihuana
marimacho *nmf fam* **1 :** mannish woman **2 :** tomboy
marimba *nf* **:** marimba
marina *nf* **1 :** coast, coastal area **2 :** navy, fleet <marina mercante : merchant marine>
marinada *nf* **:** marinade
marinar *vt* **:** to marinate
marinero[1], **-ra** *adj* **1 :** seaworthy **2 :** sea, marine
marinero[2] *nm* **:** sailor
marino[1], **-na** *adj* **:** marine, sea
marino[2] *nm* **:** sailor, seaman
marioneta *nf* TÍTERE **:** puppet, marionette
mariposa *nf* **1 :** butterfly **2 mariposa nocturna :** moth
mariquita[1] *nf* **:** ladybug
mariquita[2] *nm fam* **:** sissy, wimp
mariscal *nm* **1 :** marshal **2 mariscal de campo :** field marshal (in the military), quarterback (in football)
marisco *nm* **1 :** shellfish **2 mariscos** *nmpl* **:** seafood
marisma *nf* **:** marsh, salt marsh
marital *adj* **:** marital, married <la vida marital : married life>
marítimo, -ma *adj* **:** maritime, shipping <la industria marítima : the shipping industry>
marmita *nf* **:** (cooking) pot
mármol *nm* **:** marble
marmóreo, -rea *adj* **:** marble, marmoreal
marmota *nf* **1 :** marmot **2 marmota de América :** woodchuck, groundhog
maroma *nf* **1 :** rope **2 :** acrobatic stunt **3** *Mex* **:** somersault
marque, etc. → **marcar**
marqués, -quesa *n, mpl* **marqueses :** marquis *m,* marquess *m,* marquise *f,* marchioness *f*
marquesina *nf* **:** marquee, canopy
marqueta *nf Mex* **:** block (of chocolate), lump (of sugar or salt)
marranada *nf* **1 :** disgusting thing **2 :** dirty trick
marrano[1], **-na** *adj* **:** filthy, disgusting
marrano[2], **-na** *n* **1** CERDO **:** pig, hog **2 :** dirty pig, slob
marrar *vt* **:** to miss (a target) — *vi* **:** to fail, to go wrong
marras *adv* **1 :** long ago **2 de ~ :** said, aforementioned <el individuo de marras : the individual in question>
marrasquino *nm* **:** maraschino
marrón *adj & nm, pl* **marrones** CASTAÑO **:** brown
marroquí *adj & nmf, pl* **-quíes :** Moroccan
marsopa *nf* **:** porpoise
marsupial *nm* **:** marsupial
marta *nf* **1 :** marten **2 marta cebellina :** sable (animal)
Marte *nm* **:** Mars
martes *nms & pl* **:** Tuesday
martillar *v* **:** to hammer
martillazo *nm* **:** blow with a hammer
martillo *nm* **1 :** hammer **2 martillo neumático :** jackhammer
martinete *nm* **1 :** heron **2 :** pile driver
mártir *nmf* **:** martyr
martirio *nm* **1 :** martyrdom **2 :** ordeal, torment
martirizar {21} *vt* **1 :** to martyr **2** ATORMENTAR **:** to torment
marxismo *nm* **:** Marxism
marxista *adj & nmf* **:** Marxist
marzo *nm* **:** March
mas *conj* PERO **:** but
más[1] *adv* **1 :** more <¿hay algo más grande? : is there anything bigger?> **2 :** most <Luis es el más alto : Luis is the tallest> **3 :** longer <el sabor dura más : the flavor lasts longer> **4 :** rather <más querría andar : I would rather walk> **5 a ~ :** besides, in addition **6 más allá :** further **7 qué . . . más . . . :** what . . ., what a . . . <¡qué día más bonito! : what a beautiful day!>
más[2] *adj* **1 :** more <dáme dos kilos más : give me two more kilos> **2 :** most <la que ganó más dinero : the one who earned the most money> **3 :** else <¿quién más quiere vino? : who else wants wine?>
más[3] *n* **:** plus sign
más[4] *prep* **:** plus <tres más dos es igual a cinco : three plus two equals five>

más[5] *pron* **1 :** more <¿tienes más? : do you have more?> **2 a lo más :** at most **3 de ~ :** extra, excess **4 más o menos :** more or less, approximately **5 por más que :** no matter how much <por más que corras no llegarás a tiempo : no matter how fast you run you won't arrive on time>

masa *nf* **1 :** mass, volume <masa atómica : atomic mass> <producción en masa : mass production> **2 :** dough, batter **3 masas** *nfpl* **:** people, masses <las masas populares : the common people> **4 masa harina** *Mex* **:** corn flour (for tortillas, etc.)

masacrar *vt* **:** to massacre

masacre *nf* **:** massacre

masaje *nm* **:** massage

masajear *vt* **:** to massage

masajista *nmf* **:** masseur *m,* masseuse *f*

mascar {72} *v* MASTICAR **:** to chew

máscara *nf* **1** CARETA **:** mask **2 :** appearance, pretense

mascarada *nf* **:** masquerade

mascarilla *nf* **1 :** mask (in medicine) <mascarilla de oxígeno : oxygen mask> **2 :** facial mask (in cosmetology)

mascota *nf* **:** mascot

masculinidad *nf* **:** masculinity

masculino, -na *adj* **1 :** masculine, male **2 :** manly **3 :** masculine (in grammar)

mascullar *v* **:** to mumble, to mutter

masificado, -da *adj* **:** overcrowded

masilla *nf* **:** putty

masivamente *adv* **:** en masse

masivo, -va *adj* **:** mass <comunicación masiva : mass communication>

masón *nm, pl* **masones** FRANCMASÓN **:** Mason, Freemason

masonería *nf* FRANCMASONERÍA **:** Masonry, Freemasonry

masónico, -ca *adj* **:** Masonic

masoquismo *nm* **:** masochism

masoquista[1] *adj* **:** masochistic

masoquista[2] *nmf* **:** masochist

masque, etc. → **mascar**

masticar {72} *v* MASCAR **:** to chew, to masticate

mástil *nm* **1 :** mast **2** ASTA **:** flagpole **3 :** neck (of a stringed instrument)

mastín *nm, pl* **mastines :** mastiff

mástique *nm* **:** putty, filler

mastodonte *nm* **:** mastodon

masturbación *nf, pl* **-ciones :** masturbation

masturbarse *vr* **:** to masturbate

mata *nf* **1** ARBUSTO **:** bush, shrub **2 :** plant <mata de tomate : tomato plant> **3 :** sprig, tuft **4 mata de pelo :** mop of hair

matadero *nm* **:** slaughterhouse, abattoir

matado, -da *adj Mex* **:** strenuous, exhausting

matador *nm* TORERO **:** matador, bullfighter

matamoscas *nms & pl* **:** flyswatter

matanza *nf* MASACRE **:** slaughter, butchering

matar *vt* **1 :** to kill **2 :** to slaughter, to butcher **3** APAGAR **:** to extinguish, to put out (fire, light) **4 :** to tone down (colors) **5 :** to pass, to waste (time) **6 :** to trump (in card games) — *vi* **:** to kill — **matarse** *vr* **1 :** to be killed **2** SUICIDARSE **:** to commit suicide **3** *fam* **:** to exhaust oneself <se mató tratando de terminarlo : he knocked himself out trying to finish it>

matasanos *nms & pl fam* **:** quack

matasellar *vt* **:** to cancel (a stamp), to postmark

matasellos *nms & pl* **:** postmark

matatena *nf Mex* **:** jacks

mate[1] *adj* **:** matte, dull

mate[2] *nm* **1 :** maté **2 jaque mate :** checkmate <darle mate a *or* darle jaque mate a : to checkmate>

matemática → **matemáticas**

matemáticas *nfpl* **:** mathematics, math

matemático[1]**, -ca** *adj* **:** mathematical — **matemáticamente** *adv*

matemático[2]**, -ca** *n* **:** mathematician

materia *nf* **1 :** matter <materia gris : gray matter> **2 :** material <materia prima : raw material> **3 :** (academic) subject **4 en materia de :** on the subject of, concerning

material[1] *adj* **1 :** material, physical, real **2 daños materiales :** property damage

material[2] *nm* **1 :** material <material de construcción : building material> **2** EQUIPO **:** equipment, gear

materialismo *nm* **:** materialism

materialista[1] *adj* **:** materialistic

materialista[2] *nmf* **1 :** materialist **2** *Mex* **:** truck driver

materializar {21} *vt* **:** to bring to fruition, to realize — **materializarse** *vr* **:** to materialize, to come into being

materialmente *adv* **1 :** materially, physically <materialmente imposible : physically impossible> **2 :** really, absolutely

maternal *adj* **:** maternal, motherly

maternidad *nf* **1 :** maternity, motherhood **2 :** maternity hospital, maternity ward

materno, -na *adj* **:** maternal

matinal *adj* MATUTINO **:** morning <la pálida luz matinal : the pale morning light>

matinée *or* **matiné** *nf* **:** matinee

matiz *nm, pl* **matices 1 :** hue, shade **2 :** nuance

matización *nf, pl* **-ciones 1 :** tinting, toning, shading **2 :** clarification (of a statement)

matizar {21} *vt* **1 :** to tinge, to tint (colors) **2 :** to vary, to modulate (sounds) **3 :** to qualify (statements)

matón *nm, pl* **matones :** thug, bully

matorral *nm* **1 :** thicket **2 :** scrub, scrubland

matraca *nf* **1** : rattle, noisemaker **2 dar la matraca a** : to pester, to nag

matriarca *nf* : matriarch

matriarcado *nm* : matriarchy

matrícula *nf* **1** : list, roll, register **2** INSCRIPCIÓN : registration, enrollment **3** : license plate, registration number

matriculación *nf, pl* **-ciones** : matriculation, registration

matricular *vt* **1** INSCRIBIR : to enroll, to register (a person) **2** : to register (a vehicle) — **matricularse** *vr* : to matriculate

matrimonial *adj* : marital, matrimonial <la vida matrimonial : married life>

matrimonio *nm* **1** : marriage, matrimony **2** : married couple

matríz *nf, pl* **matrices 1** : uterus, womb **2** : original, master copy **3** : main office, headquarters **4** : stub (of a check) **5** : matrix <matriz de puntos : dot matrix>

matrona *nf* : matron

matronal *adj* : matronly

matutino[1], -na *adj* : morning <la edición matutina : the morning edition>

matutino[2] *nm* : morning paper

maullar {8} *vi* : to meow

maullido *nm* : meow

mauritano, -na *adj & n* : Mauritanian

mausoleo *nm* : mausoleum

maxilar *nm* : jaw, jawbone

máxima *nf* : maxim

máxime *adv* ESPECIALMENTE : especially, principally

maximizar {21} *vt* : to maximize

máximo[1], -ma *adj* : maximum, greatest, highest

máximo[2] *nm* **1** : maximum **2 al máximo** : to the utmost **3 como ~** : at the most, at the latest

maya[1] *adj & nmf* : Mayan

maya[2] *nmf* : Maya, Mayan

mayo *nm* : May

mayonesa *nf* : mayonnaise

mayor[1] *adj* **1** (*comparative of* **grande**) : bigger, larger, greater, elder, older **2** (*superlative of* **grande**) : biggest, largest, greatest, eldest, oldest **3** : grown-up, mature **4** : main, major **5 mayor de edad** : of (legal) age **6 al por mayor** *or* **por ~** : wholesale

mayor[2] *nmf* **1** : major (in the military) **2** : adult

mayoral *nm* CAPATAZ : foreman, overseer

mayordomo *nm* : butler, majordomo

mayoreo *nm* : wholesale

mayores *nmpl* : grown-ups, elders

mayoría *nf* **1** : majority **2 en su mayoría** : on the whole

mayorista[1] *adj* ALMACENISTA : wholesale

mayorista[2] *nmf* : wholesaler

mayoritariamente *adv* : primarily, chiefly

mayoritario, -ria *adj & n* : majority <un consenso mayoritario : a majority consensus>

mayormente *adv* : primarily, chiefly

mayúscula *nf* : capital letter

mayúsculo, -la *adj* **1** : capital, uppercase **2** : huge, terrible <un problema mayúsculo : a huge problem>

maza *nf* **1** : mace (weapon) **2** : drumstick **3** *fam* : bore, pest

mazacote *nm* **1** : concrete **2** : lumpy mess (of food) **3** : eyesore, crude work of art

mazapán *nm, pl* **-panes** : marzipan

mazmorra *nf* CALABOZO : dungeon

mazo *nm* **1** : mallet **2** : pestle **3** MANOJO : handful, bunch

mazorca *nf* **1** CHOCLO : cob, ear of corn **2 pelar la mazorca** *Mex fam* : to smile from ear to ear

me *pron* **1** : me <me vieron : they saw me> **2** : to me, for me, from me <dame el libro : give me the book> <me lo compró : he bought it for me> <me robaron la cartera : they stole my pocketbook> **3** : myself, to myself, for myself, from myself <me preparé una buena comida : I cooked myself a good dinner> <me equivoqué : I made a mistake>

mecánica *nf* : mechanics

mecánico[1], -ca *adj* : mechanical — **mecánicamente** *adv*

mecánico[2], -ca *n* **1** : mechanic **2** : technician <mecánico dental : dental technician>

mecanismo *nm* : mechanism

mecanización *nf, pl* **-ciones** : mechanization

mecanizar {21} *vt* : to mechanize

mecanografía *nf* : typing

mecanografiar {85} *vt* : to type

mecanógrafo, -fa *n* : typist

mecate *nm CA, Mex, Ven* : rope, twine, cord

mecedor *nm* : glider (seat)

mecedora *nf* : rocking chair

mecenas *nmfs & pl* : patron (of the arts), sponsor

mecenazgo *nm* PATROCINIO : sponsorship, patronage

mecer {86} *vt* **1** : to rock **2** COLUMPIAR : to push (on a swing) — **mecerse** *vr* : to rock, to swing, to sway

mecha *nf* **1** : fuse **2** : wick **3 mechas** *nfpl* : highlights (in hair)

mechero *nm* **1** : burner **2** *Spain* : lighter

mechón *nm, pl* **mechones** : lock (of hair)

medalla *nf* : medal, medallion

medallista *nmf* : medalist

medallón *nm, pl* **-llones 1** : medallion **2** : locket

media *nf* **1** CALCETÍN : sock **2** : average, mean **3 medias** *nfpl* : stockings, hose, tights **4 a medias** : by halves, half and half, halfway <ir a medias : to go

halves> <verdad a medias : half-truth>

mediación *nf, pl* **-ciones** : mediation

mediado, -da *adj* **1** : half full, half empty, half over **2** : halfway through <mediada la tarea : halfway through the job>

mediador, -dora *n* : mediator

mediados *nmpl* **a mediados de** : halfway through, in the middle of <a mediados del mes : towards the middle of the month, mid-month>

medialuna *nf* **1** : crescent **2** : croissant, crescent roll

medianamente *adv* : fairly, moderately

medianero, -ra *adj* **1** : dividing **2** : mediating

medianía *nf* **1** : middle position **2** : mediocre person, mediocrity

mediano, -na *adj* **1** : medium, average <la mediana edad : middle age> **2** : mediocre

medianoche *nf* : midnight

mediante *prep* : through, by means of <Dios mediante : God willing>

mediar *vi* **1** : to mediate **2** : to be in the middle, to be halfway through **3** : to elapse, to pass <mediaron cinco años entre el inicio de la guerra y el armisticio : five years passed between the start of the war and the armistice> **4** : to be a consideration <media el hecho de que cuesta mucho : one must take into account that it is costly> **5** : to come up, to happen <medió algo urgente : something pressing came up>

mediatizar {21} *vt* : to influence, to interfere with

medicación *nf, pl* **-ciones** : medication, treatment

medicamento *nm* : medication, medicine, drug

medicar {72} *vt* : to medicate — **medicarse** *vr* : to take medicine

medicina *nf* : medicine

medicinal *adj* **1** : medicinal **2** : medicated

medicinar *vt* : to give medication to, to dose

medición *nf, pl* **-ciones** : measuring, measurement

médico[1], -ca *adj* : medical <una receta médica : a doctor's prescription>

médico[2], -ca *n* DOCTOR : doctor, physician

medida *nf* **1** : measurement, measure <hecho a medida : custom-made> **2** : measure, step <tomar medidas : to take steps> **3** : moderation, prudence <sin medida : immoderately> **4** : extent, degree <en gran medida : to a great extent>

medidor *nm* : meter, gauge

medieval *adj* : medieval — **medievalista** *nmf*

medievo *nm* → **medioevo**

medio[1] *adv* **1** : half <está medio dormida : she's half asleep> **2** : rather, kind of <está medio aburrida esta fiesta : this party is rather boring>

medio[2], -dia *adj* **1** : half <una media hora : half an hour> <medio hermano : half brother> <a media luz : in the half-light> <son las tres y media : it's half past three, it's three-thirty> **2** : midway, halfway <a medio camino : halfway there> **3** : middle <la clase media : the middle class> **4** : average <la temperatura media : the average temperature>

medio[3] *nm* **1** CENTRO : middle, center <en medio de : in the middle of, amid> **2** AMBIENTE : milieu, environment **3** : medium, spiritualist **4** : means *pl,* way <por medio de : by means of> <los medios de comunicación : the media> **5 medios** *nmpl* : means, resources

mediocre *adj* : mediocre, average

mediocridad *nf* : mediocrity

mediodía *nm* : noon, midday

medioevo *nm* : Middle Ages

medir {54} *vt* **1** : to measure **2** : to weigh, to consider <medir los riesgos : to weigh the risks> — *vi* : to measure — **medirse** *vr* : to be moderate, to exercise restraint

meditabundo, -da *adj* PENSATIVO : pensive, thoughtful

meditación *nf, pl* **-ciones** : meditation, thought

meditar *vi* : to meditate, to think <meditar sobre la vida : to contemplate life> — *vt* **1** : to think over, to consider **2** : to plan, to work out

meditativo, -va *adj* : pensive

mediterráneo, -nea *adj* : Mediterranean

medrar *vi* **1** PROSPERAR : to prosper, to thrive **2** AUMENTAR : to increase, to grow

medro *nm* PROSPERIDAD : prosperity, growth

medroso, -sa *adj* : fainthearted, fearful

médula *nf* **1** : marrow, pith **2 médula espinal** : spinal cord

medular *adj* : fundamental, core <el punto medular : the crux of the matter>

medusa *nf* : jellyfish, medusa

megabyte *nm* : megabyte

megáfono *nm* : megaphone

megahertzio *nm* : megahertz

megatón *nm, pl* **-tones** : megaton

megavatio *nm* : megawatt

mejicano → **mexicano**

mejilla *nf* : cheek

mejillón *nm, pl* **-llones** : mussel

mejor[1] *adv* **1** : better <Carla cocina mejor que Ana : Carla cooks better than Ana> **2** : best <ella es la que lo hace mejor : she's the one who does it best> **3** : rather <mejor morir que rendirme : I'd rather die than give up> **4** : it's better that . . . <mejor te

vas : you'd better go> **5 a lo mejor** : maybe, perhaps

mejor² *adj* **1** (*comparative of* **bueno**) : better <a falta de algo mejor : for lack of something better> **2** (*comparative of* **bien**) : better <está mucho mejor : he's much better> **3** (*superlative of* **bueno**) : best, the better <mi mejor amigo : my best friend> **4** (*superlative of* **bien**) : best, the better <duermo mejor en un clima seco : I sleep best in a dry climate> **5** PREFERIBLE : preferable, better **6 lo mejor** : the best thing, the best part

mejor³ *nmf* (*with definite article*) : the better (one), the best (one)

mejora *nf* : improvement

mejoramiento *nm* : improvement

mejorana *nf* : marjoram

mejorar *vt* : to improve, to make better — *vi* : to improve, to get better — **mejorarse** *vr*

mejoría *nf* : improvement, betterment

mejunje *nm* : concoction, brew

melancolía *nf* : melancholy, sadness

melancólico, -ca *adj* : melancholy, sad

melanoma *nm* : melanoma

melaza *nf* : molasses

maleficio *nm* : curse, spell

melena *nf* **1** : mane **2** : long hair **3 melenas** *nfpl* GREÑAS : shaggy hair, mop

melenudo¹, -da *adj fam* : longhaired

melenudo², -da *n* GREÑUDO : longhair, hippie

melindres *nmpl* **1** : affectation, airs *pl* **2** : finickiness

melindroso¹, -sa *adj* **1** : affected **2** : fussy, finicky

melindroso², -sa *n* : finicky person, fussbudget

melisa *nf* : lemon balm

mella *nf* **1** : dent, nick **2 hacer mella en** : to have an effect on, to make an impression on

mellado, -da *adj* **1** : chipped, dented **2** : gap-toothed

mellar *vt* : to dent, to nick

mellizo, -za *adj & n* GEMELO : twin

melocotón *nm, pl* **-tones** : peach

melodía *nf* : melody, tune

melódico, -ca *adj* : melodic

melodioso, -sa *adj* : melodious

melodrama *nm* : melodrama

melodramático, -ca *adj* : melodramatic

melón *nm, pl* **melones** : melon, cantaloupe

meloso, -sa *adj* **1** : honeyed, sweet **2** EMPALAGOSO : cloying, saccharine

membrana *nf* **1** : membrane **2 membrana interdigital** : web, webbing (of a bird's foot) — **membranoso, -sa** *adj*

membresía *nf* : membership, members *pl*

membrete *nm* : letterhead, heading

membrillo *nm* : quince

membrudo, -da *adj* FORNIDO : muscular, well-built

memez *nf, pl* **memeces** : stupid thing

memo, -ma *adj* : silly, stupid

memorabilia *nf* : memorabilia

memorable *adj* : memorable

memorándum *or* **memorando** *nm, pl* **-dums** *or* **-dos 1** : memorandum, memo **2** : memo book, appointment book

memoria *nf* **1** : memory <de memoria : by heart> <hacer memoria : to try to remember> <traer a la memoria : to call to mind> **2** RECUERDO : remembrance, memory <su memoria perdurará para siempre : his memory will live forever> **3** : report <memoria annual : annual report> **4 memorias** *nfpl* : memoirs

memorizar {21} *vt* : to memorize — **memorización** *nf*

mena *nf* : ore

menaje *nm* : household goods *pl,* furnishings *pl*

mención *nf, pl* **-ciones** : mention

mencionar *vt* : to mention, to refer to

mendaz *adj, pl* **mendaces** : mendacious, lying

mendicidad *nf* : begging

mendigar {52} *vi* : to beg — *vt* : to beg for

mendigo, -ga *n* LIMOSNERO : beggar

mendrugo *nm* : crust (of bread)

menear *vt* **1** : to shake (one's head) **2** : to sway, to wiggle (one's hips) **3** : to wag (a tail) **4** : to stir (a liquid) — **menearse** *vr* **1** : to wiggle one's hips **2** : to fidget

meneo *nm* **1** : movement **2** : shake, toss **3** : swaying, wagging, wiggling **4** : stir, stirring

menester *nm* **1** : activity, occupation, duties *pl* **2 ser menester** : to be necessary <es menester que vengas : you must come>

mengano, -na *n* → **fulano**

mengua *nf* **1** : decrease, decline **2** : lack, want **3** : discredit, dishonor

menguar *vt* : to diminish, to lessen — *vi* **1** : to decline, to decrease **2** : to wane — **menguante** *adj*

meningitis *nf* : meningitis

menisco *nm* : meniscus, cartilage

menjurje *nm* → **mejunje**

menopausia *nf* : menopause

menor¹ *adj* **1** (*comparative of* **pequeño**) : smaller, lesser, younger **2** (*superlative of* **pequeño**) : smallest, least, youngest **3** : minor **4 al por menor** : retail **5 ser menor de edad** : to be a minor, to be underage

menor² *nmf* : minor, juvenile

menos¹ *adv* **1** : less <llueve menos en agosto : it rains less in August> **2** : least <el coche menos caro : the least expensive car> **3 ~ de** : less than, fewer than

menos² *adj* **1** : less, fewer <tengo más trabajo y menos tiempo : I have more

work and less time> 2 : least, fewest <la clase que tiene menos estudiantes : the class that has the fewest students>

menos[3] *prep* **1** SALVO, EXCEPTO : except **2** : minus <quince menos cuatro son once : fifteen minus four is eleven>

menos[4] *pron* **1** : less, fewer <no deberías aceptar menos : you shouldn't accept less> **2 al menos** *or* **por lo menos** : at least **3 a menos que** : unless

menoscabar *vt* **1** : to lessen, to diminish **2** : to disgrace, to discredit **3** PERJUDICAR : to harm, to damage

menoscabo *nm* **1** : lessening, diminishing **2** : disgrace, discredit **3** : harm, damage

menospreciar *vt* **1** DESPRECIAR : to scorn, to look down on **2** : to underestimate, to undervalue

menosprecio *nm* DESPRECIO : contempt, scorn

mensaje *nm* : message

mensajero, -ra *n* : messenger

menso, -sa *adj Mex fam* : foolish, stupid

menstrual *adj* : menstrual

menstruar {3} *vi* : to menstruate — **menstruación** *nf*

mensual *adj* : monthly

mensualidad *nf* **1** : monthly payment, installment **2** : monthly salary

mensualmente *adv* : every month, monthly

mensurable *adj* : measurable

menta *nf* **1** : mint, peppermint **2 menta verde** : spearmint

mentado, -da *adj* **1** : aforementioned **2** FAMOSO : renowned, famous

mental *adj* : mental, intellectual — **mentalmente** *adv*

mentalidad *nf* : mentality

mentar {55} *vt* **1** : to mention, to name **2 mentar la madre a** *fam* : to insult, to swear at

mente *nf* : mind <tener en mente : to have in mind>

mentecato[1], **-ta** *adj* : foolish, simple

mentecato[2], **-ta** *n* : fool, idiot

mentir {76} *vi* : to lie

mentira *nf* : lie

mentiroso[1], **-sa** *adj* EMBUSTERO : lying, untruthful

mentiroso[2], **-sa** *n* EMBUSTERO : liar

mentís *nm, pl* **mentises** : denial, repudiation <dar el mentís a : to deny, to refute>

mentol *nm* : menthol

mentón *nm, pl* **mentones** BARBILLA : chin

mentor *nm* : mentor, counselor

menú *nm, pl* **menús** : menu

menudear *vi* : to occur frequently — *vt* : to do repeatedly

menudencia *nf* **1** : trifle **2 menudencias** *nfpl* : giblets

menudeo *nm* : retail, retailing

menudillos *nmpl* : giblets

menudo[1], **-da** *adj* **1** : minute, small **2 a ~** FRECUENTEMENTE : often, frequently

menudo[2] *nm* **1** *Mex* : tripe stew **2 menudos** *nmpl* : giblets

meñique *nm or* **dedo meñique** : little finger, pinkie

meollo *nm* **1** MÉDULA : marrow **2** SESO : brains *pl* **3** ENTRAÑA : essence, core <el meollo del asunto : the heart of the matter>

mequetrefe *nm fam* : good-for-nothing

mercachifle *nm* : peddler, hawker

mercadeo *nm* : marketing

mercadería *nf* : merchandise, goods *pl*

mercado *nm* : market <mercado de trabajo *or* mercado laboral : labor market> <mercado de valores *or* mercado bursátil : stock market>

mercadotecnia *nf* : marketing

mercancía *nf* : merchandise, goods *pl*

mercante *nmf* : merchant, dealer

mercantil *adj* COMERCIAL : commercial, mercantile

merced *nf* **1** : favor **2 ~ a** : thanks to, due to **3 a merced de** : at the mercy of

mercenario, -ria *adj & n* : mercenary

mercería *nf* : notions store

mercurio *nm* : mercury

Mercurio *nm* : Mercury (planet)

merecedor, -dora *adj* : deserving, worthy

merecer {53} *vt* : to deserve, to merit — *vi* : to be worthy

merecidamente *adv* : rightfully, deservedly

merecido *nm* : something merited, due <recibieron su merecido : they got their just deserts>

merecimiento *nm* : merit, worth

merendar {55} *vi* : to have an afternoon snack — *vt* : to have as an afternoon snack

merendero *nm* **1** : lunchroom, snack bar **2** : picnic area

merengue *nm* **1** : meringue **2** : merengue (dance)

meridiano[1], **-na** *adj* **1** : midday **2** : crystal clear

meridiano[2] *nm* : meridian

meridional *adj* SUREÑO : southern

merienda *nf* : afternoon snack, tea

mérito *nm* : merit

meritorio[1], **-ria** *adj* : deserving, meritorious

meritorio[2], **-ria** *n* : intern, trainee

merluza *nf* : hake

merma *nf* **1** : decrease, cut **2** : waste, loss

mermar *vi* : to decrease, to diminish — *vt* : to reduce, to cut down

mermelada *nf* : marmalade, jam

mero[1], **-ra** *adv Mex fam* **1** : nearly, almost <ya mero me caí : I almost fell> **2** : just, exactly <aquí mero : right here>

mero[2], -ra *adj* **1 :** mere, simple **2** *Mex fam* (*used as an intensifier*) **:** very <en el mero centro : in the very center of town>

mero[3] *nm* **:** grouper

merodeador, -dora *n* **1 :** marauder **2 :** prowler

merodear *vi* **1 :** to maraud, to pillage **2 :** to prowl around, to skulk

mes *nm* **:** month

mesa *nf* **1 :** table **2 :** committee, board

mesada *nf* **:** allowance, pocket money

mesarse *vr* **:** to pull at <mesarse los cabellos : to tear one's hair>

mesero, -ra *n* CAMARERO **:** waiter, waitress *f*

meseta *nf* **:** plateau, tableland

Mesías *nm* **:** Messiah

mesón *nm, pl* **mesones :** inn

mesonero, -ra *nm* **:** innkeeper

mestizo[1], -za *adj* **1 :** of mixed ancestry **2** HÍBRIDO **:** hybrid

mestizo[2], -za *n* **:** person of mixed ancestry

mesura *nf* **1** MODERACIÓN **:** moderation, discretion **2** CORTESÍA **:** courtesy **3** GRAVEDAD **:** seriousness, dignity

mesurado, -da *adj* COMEDIDO **:** moderate, restrained

mesurar *vt* **:** to moderate, to restrain, to temper — **mesurarse** *vr* **:** to restrain oneself

meta *nf* **:** goal, objective

metabólico, -ca *adj* **:** metabolic

metabolismo *nm* **:** metabolism

metabolizar {21} *vt* **:** to metabolize

metafísica *nf* **:** metaphysics

metafísico, -ca *adj* **:** metaphysical

metáfora *nf* **:** metaphor

metafórico, -ca *adj* **:** metaphoric, metaphorical

metal *nm* **1 :** metal **2 :** brass section (in an orchestra)

metálico, -ca *adj* **:** metallic, metal

metalistería *nf* **:** metalworking

metalurgia *nf* **:** metallurgy

metalúrgico[1], -ca *adj* **:** metallurgical

metalúrgico[2], -ca *n* **:** metallurgist

metamorfosis *nfs & pl* **:** metamorphosis

metano *nm* **:** methane

meteórico, -ca *adj* **:** meteoric

meteorito *nm* **:** meteorite

meteoro *nm* **:** meteor

meteorología *nf* **:** meteorology

meteorológico, -ca *adj* **:** meteorologic, meteorological

meteorólogo, -ga *n* **:** meteorologist

meter *vt* **1 :** to put (in) <metieron su dinero en el banco : they put their money in the bank> **2 :** to fit, to squeeze <puedes meter dos líneas más en esa página : you can fit two more lines on that page> **3 :** to place (in a job) <lo metieron de barrendero : they got him a job as a street sweeper> **4 :** to involve <lo metió en un buen lío : she got him in an awful mess> **5 :** to make, to cause <meten demasiado ruido : they make too much noise> **6 :** to spread (a rumor) **7 :** to strike (a blow) **8 :** to take up, to take in (clothing) **9 a todo meter :** at top speed — **meterse** *vr* **1 :** to get into, to enter **2** *fam* **:** to meddle <no te metas en lo que no te importa : mind your own business> **3 ~ con** *fam* **:** to pick a fight with, to provoke <no te metas conmigo : don't mess with me>

metiche[1] *adj Mex fam* **:** nosy

metiche[2] *nmf Mex fam* **:** busybody

meticulosidad *nf* **:** thoroughness, meticulousness

meticuloso, -sa *adj* **:** meticulous, thorough — **meticulosamente** *adv*

metida *nf* **metida de pata** *fam* **:** blunder, gaffe, blooper

metódico, -ca *adj* **:** methodical — **metódicamente** *adv*

metodista *adj & nmf* **:** Methodist

método *nm* **:** method

metodología *nf* **:** methodology

metomentodo *nmf fam* **:** busybody

metralla *nf* **:** shrapnel

metralleta *nf* **:** submachine gun

métrico, -ca *adj* **1 :** metric **2 cinta métrica :** tape measure

metro *nm* **1 :** meter **2 :** subway

metrónomo *nm* **:** metronome

metrópoli *nf or* **metrópolis** *nfs & pl* **:** metropolis

metropolitano, -na *adj* **:** metropolitan

mexicanismo *nm* **:** Mexican word or expression

mexicano, -na *adj & n* **:** Mexican

mexicoamericano, -na *adj & n* **:** Mexican-American

meza, etc. → **mecer**

mezcla *nf* **1 :** mixing **2 :** mixture, blend **3 :** mortar (masonry material)

mezclar *vt* **1 :** to mix, to blend **2 :** to mix up, to muddle **3** INVOLUCRAR **:** to involve — **mezclarse** *vr* **1 :** to get mixed up (in) **2 :** to mix, to mingle (socially)

mezclilla *nf Chile, Mex* **:** denim <pantalones de mezclilla : jeans>

mezcolanza *nf* **:** jumble, hodgepodge

mezquindad *nf* **1 :** meanness, stinginess **2 :** petty deed, mean action

mezquino[1], -na *adj* **1 :** mean, petty **2 :** stingy **3 :** paltry

mezquino[2] *nm Mex* **:** wart

mezquita *nf* **:** mosque

mezquite *nm* **:** mesquite

mi *adj* **:** my

mí *pron* **1 :** me <es para mí : it's for me> <a mí no me importa : it doesn't matter to me> **2 mí mismo, mí misma :** myself

miasma *nm* **:** miasma

miau *nm* **:** meow

mica *nf* **:** mica

mico *nm* **:** monkey, long-tailed monkey

micra *nf* **:** micron

microbio *nm* **:** microbe, germ

microbiología *nf* **:** microbiology

microbiólogico, -ca *adj* : microbiological
microbús *nm, pl* **-buses** : minibus
microcomputadora *nf* : microcomputer
microcosmos *nms & pl* : microcosm
microficha *nf* : microfiche
microfilm *nm, pl* **-films** : microfilm
micrófono *nm* : microphone
micrómetro *nm* : micrometer
microonda *nf* : microwave
microondas *nms & pl* : microwave, microwave oven
microordenador *nm Spain* : microcomputer
microorganismo *nm* : microorganism
microprocesador *nm* : microprocessor
microscópico, -ca *adj* : microscopic
microscopio *nm* : microscope
mide, etc. → **medir**
miedo *nm* **1** TEMOR : fear <le tiene miedo al perro : he's scared of the dog> <tenían miedo de hablar : they were afraid to speak> **2 dar miedo** : to frighten
miedoso, -sa *adj* TEMEROSO : fearful
miel *nf* : honey
miembro *nm* **1** : member **2** EXTREMIDAD : limb, extremity
mienta, etc. → **mentar**
miente, etc. → **mentir**
mientras[1] *adv* **1** *or* **mientras tanto** : meanwhile, in the meantime **2 mientras más** : the more <mientras más como, más quiero : the more I eat, the more I want>
mientras[2] *conj* **1** : while, as <roncaba mientras dormía : he snored while he was sleeping> **2** : as long as <luchará mientras pueda : he will fight as long as he is able> **3 mientras que** : while, whereas <él es alto mientras que ella es muy baja : he is tall, whereas she is very short>
miércoles *nms & pl* : Wednesday
miga *nf* **1** : crumb **2 hacer buenas (malas) migas con** : to get along well (poorly) with
migaja *nf* **1** : crumb **2 migajas** *nfpl* SOBRAS : leftovers, scraps
migración *nf, pl* **-ciones** : migration
migrante *nmf* : migrant
migraña *nf* : migraine
migratorio, -ria *adj* : migratory
mijo *nm* : millet
mil[1] *adj* : thousand
mil[2] *nm* : one thousand, a thousand
milagro *nm* : miracle <de milagro : miraculously>
milagroso, -sa *adj* : miraculous, marvelous — **milagrosamente** *adv*
milenio *nm* : millennium
milésimo, -ma *adj* : thousandth — **milésimo** *n*
milicia *nf* **1** : militia **2** : military service
miligramo *nm* : milligram
mililitro *nm* : milliliter
milímetro *nm* : millimeter
militancia *nf* : militancy
militante[1] *adj* : militant
militante[2] *nmf* : militant, activist
militar[1] *vi* **1** : to serve (in the military) **2** : to be active (in politics)
militar[2] *adj* : military
militar[3] *nmf* SOLDADO : soldier
militarizar {21} *vt* : to militarize
milla *nf* : mile
millar *nm* : thousand
millón *nm, pl* **millones** : million
millonario, -ria *n* : millionaire
millonésimo[1], **-ma** *adj* : millionth
millonésimo[2] *nm* : millionth
mil millones *nms & pl* : billion
milpa *nf CA, Mex* : cornfield
milpiés *nms & pl* : millipede
mimar *vt* CONSENTIR : to pamper, to spoil
mimbre *nm* : wicker
mimeógrafo *nm* : mimeograph
mímica *nf* **1** : mime, sign language **2** IMITACIÓN : mimicry
mimo *nm* **1** : pampering, indulgence <hacerle mimos a alguien : to pamper someone> **2** : mime
mimoso, -sa *adj* **1** : fussy, finicky **2** : affectionate, clinging
mina *nf* **1** : mine **2** : lead (for pencils)
minar *vt* **1** : to mine **2** DEBILITAR : to undermine
minarete *nm* ALMINAR : minaret
mineral *adj & nm* : mineral
minería *nf* : mining
minero[1], **-ra** *adj* : mining
minero[2], **-ra** *n* : miner, mine worker
miniatura *nf* : miniature
minicomputadora *nf* : minicomputer
minifalda *nf* : miniskirt
minifundio *nm* : small farm
minimizar {21} *vt* : to minimize
mínimo[1], **-ma** *adj* **1** : minimum <salario mínimo : minimum wage> **2** : least, smallest **3** : very small, minute
mínimo[2] *nm* **1** : minimum, least amount **2** : modicum, small amount **3 como ~** : at least
minino, -na *n fam* : pussy, pussycat
miniserie *nf* : miniseries
ministerial *adj* : ministerial
ministerio *nm* : ministry, department
ministro, -tra *n* : minister, secretary <primer ministro : prime minister> <Ministro de Defensa : Secretary of Defense>
minivan [ˌminiˈban, -ˈvan] *nf, pl* **-vanes** : minivan
minoría *nf* : minority
minorista[1] *adj* : retail
minorista[2] *nmf* : retailer
minoritario, -ria *adj* : minority
mintió, etc. → **mentir**
minuciosamente *adv* **1** : minutely **2** : in great detail **3** : thoroughly, meticulously
minucioso, -sa *adj* **1** : minute **2** DETALLADO : detailed **3** : thorough, meticulous
minué *nm* : minuet

minúsculo, -la *adj* DIMINUTO : tiny, miniscule

minusvalía *nf* : disability, handicap

minusválido[1], -da *adj* : handicapped, disabled

minusválido[2], -da *n* : handicapped person

minuta *nf* **1** BORRADOR : rough draft **2** : bill, fee

minutero *nm* : minute hand

minuto *nm* : minute

mío[1], mía *adj* **1** : my, of mine <¡Dios mío! : my God!, good heavens!> <una amiga mía : a friend of mine> **2** : mine <es mío : it's mine>

mío[2], mía *pron* (*with definite article*) : mine, my own <tus zapatos son iguales a los míos : your shoes are just like mine>

miope *adj* : nearsighted, myopic

miopía *nf* : myopia, nearsightedness

mira *nf* **1** : sight (of a firearm or instrument) **2** : aim, objective <con miras a : with the intention of, with a view to> <de amplias miras : broad-minded> <poner la mira en : to aim at, to aspire to>

mirada *nf* **1** : look, glance, gaze **2** EXPRESIÓN : look, expression <una mirada de sorpresa : a look of surprise>

mirado, -da *adj* **1** : cautious, careful **2** : considerate **3 bien mirado** : well thought of **4 mal mirado** : disliked, disapproved of

mirador *nm* : balcony, lookout, vantage point

miramiento *nm* **1** CONSIDERACIÓN : consideration, respect **2 sin miramientos** : without due consideration, carelessly

mirar *vt* **1** : to look at **2** OBSERVAR : to watch **3** REFLEXIONAR : to consider, to think over — *vi* **1** : to look **2** : to face, to overlook **3 ~ por** : to look after, to look out for — **mirarse** *vr* **1** : to look at oneself **2** : to look at each other

mirasol *nm* GIRASOL : sunflower

miríada *nf* : myriad

mirlo *nm* : blackbird

mirra *nf* : myrrh

mirto *nm* ARRAYÁN : myrtle

misa *nf* : Mass

misantropía *nf* : misanthropy

misantrópico, -ca *adj* : misanthropic

misántropo, -pa *n* : misanthrope

miscelánea *nf* : miscellany

misceláneo, -nea *adj* : miscellaneous

miserable *adj* **1** LASTIMOSO : miserable, wretched **2** : paltry, meager **3** MEZQUINO : stingy, miserly **4** : despicable, vile

miseria *nf* **1** POBREZA : poverty **2** : misery, suffering **3** : pittance, meager amount

misericordia *nf* COMPASIÓN : mercy, compassion

misericordioso, -sa *adj* : merciful

mísero, -ra *adj* **1** : wretched, miserable **2** : stingy **3** : paltry, meager

misil *nm* : missile

misión *nf, pl* **misiones** : mission

misionero, -ra *adj & n* : missionary

misiva *nf* : missive, letter

mismísimo, -ma *adj* (*used as an intensifier*) : very, selfsame <el mismísimo día : that very same day>

mismo[1] *adv* (*used as an intensifier*) : right, exactly <hazlo ahora mismo : do it right now> <te llamará hoy mismo : he'll definitely call you today>

mismo[2], -ma *adj* **1** : same **2** (*used as an intensifier*) : very <en ese mismo momento : at that very moment> **3** : oneself <lo hizo ella misma : she made it herself> **4 por lo mismo** : for that reason

misoginia *nf* : misogyny

misógino *nm* : misogynist

misterio *nm* : mystery

misterioso, -sa *adj* : mysterious — **misteriosamente** *adv*

misticismo *nm* : mysticism

místico[1], -ca *adj* : mystic, mystical

místico[2], -ca *n* : mystic

mitad *nf* **1** : half <mitad y mitad : half and half> **2** MEDIO : middle <a mitad de : halfway through> <por la mitad : in half>

mítico, -ca *adj* : mythical, mythic

mitigar {52} *vt* ALIVIAR : to mitigate, to alleviate — **mitigación** *nf*

mitin *nm, pl* **mítines** : (political) meeting, rally

mito *nm* LEYENDA : myth, legend

mitología *nm* : mythology

mitológico, -ca *adj* : mythological

mitosis *nfs & pl* : mitosis

mitra *nf* : miter (bishop's hat)

mixto, -ta *adj* **1** : mixed, joint **2** : coeducational

mixtura *nf* : mixture, blend

mnemónico, -ca *adj* : mnemonic

mobiliario *nm* : furniture

mocasín *nm, pl* **-sines** : moccasin

mocedad *nf* **1** JUVENTUD : youth **2** : youthful prank

mochila *nf* MORRAL : backpack, knapsack

moción *nf, pl* **-ciones 1** MOVIMIENTO : motion, movement **2** : motion (to a court or assembly)

moco *nm* **1** : mucus **2** *fam* : snot <limpiarse los mocos : to wipe one's (runny) nose>

mocoso, -sa *n* : kid, brat

moda *nf* **1** : fashion, style **2 a la moda** *or* **de ~** : in style, fashionable **3 moda pasajera** : fad

modales *nmpl* : manners

modalidad *nf* **1** CLASE : kind, type **2** MANERA : way, manner

modelar *vt* : to model, to mold — **modelarse** *vr* : to model oneself after, to emulate

modelo[1] *adj* : model <una casa modelo : a model home>
modelo[2] *nm* : model, example, pattern
modelo[3] *nmf* : model, mannequin
módem *or* **modem** [ˈmoðɛm] *nm* : modem
moderación *nf, pl* **-ciones** MESURA : moderation
moderado, -da *adj & n* : moderate — **moderadamente** *adv*
moderador, -dora *n* : moderator, chair
moderar *vt* **1** TEMPERAR : to temper, to moderate **2** : to curb, to reduce <moderar gastos : to curb spending> **3** PRESIDIR : to chair (a meeting) — **moderarse** *vr* **1** : to restrain oneself **2** : to diminish, to calm down
modernidad *nf* **1** : modernity, modernness **2** : modern age
modernismo *nm* : modernism
modernista[1] *adj* : modernist, modernistic
modernista[2] *nmf* : modernist
modernizar {21} *vt* : to modernize — **modernización** *nf*
moderno, -na *adj* : modern, up-to-date
modestia *nf* : modesty
modesto, -ta *adj* : modest — **modestamente** *adv*
modificación *nf, pl* **-ciones** : alteration
modificante *nm* : modifier
modificar {72} *vt* ALTERAR : to modify, to alter, to adapt
modismo *nm* : idiom
modista *nmf* **1** : dressmaker **2** : fashion designer
modo *nm* **1** MANERA : way, manner, mode <de un modo u otro : one way or another> <a mi modo de ver : to my way of thinking> **2** : mood (in grammar) **3** : mode (in music) **4 a modo de** : by way of, in the manner of, like <a modo de ejemplo : by way of example> **5 de cualquier modo** : in any case, anyway **6 de modo que** : so, in such a way that **7 de todos modos** : in any case, anyway **8 en cierto modo** : in a way, to a certain extent
modorra *nf* : drowsiness, lethargy
modular[1] *v* : to modulate — **modulación** *nf*
modular[2] *adj* : modular
módulo *nm* : module, unit
mofa *nf* **1** : mockery, ridicule **2 hacer mofa de** : to make fun of, to ridicule
mofarse *vr* **~ de** : to scoff at, to make fun of
mofeta *nf* ZORRILLO : skunk
mofle *nm CA, Mex* : muffler (of a car)
moflete *nm fam* : fat cheek
mofletudo, -da *adj fam* : fat-cheeked, chubby
mohín *nm, pl* **mohines** : grimace, face
mohino, -na *adj* : gloomy, melancholy
moho *nm* **1** : mold, mildew **2** : rust
mohoso, -sa *adj* **1** : moldy **2** : rusty
moisés *nm, pl* **moiseses** : bassinet, cradle
mojado[1], **-da** *adj* : wet
mojado[2], **-da** *n Mex fam* : illegal immigrant
mojar *vt* **1** : to wet, to moisten **2** : to dunk — **mojarse** *vr* : to get wet
mojigatería *nf* **1** : hypocrisy **2** GAZMOÑERÍA : primness, prudery
mojigato[1], **-ta** *adj* : prudish, prim — **mojigatamente** *adv*
mojigato[2], **-ta** *n* : prude, prig
mojón *nm, pl* **mojones** : boundary stone, marker
molar *nm* MUELA : molar
molcajete *nm Mex* : mortar
molde *nm* **1** : mold, form **2 letras de molde** : printing, block lettering
moldear *vt* **1** FORMAR : to mold, to shape **2** : to cast
moldura *nf* : molding
mole[1] *nm Mex* **1** : spicy sauce made with chilies and usually chocolate **2** : meat served with mole sauce
mole[2] *nf* : mass, bulk
molécula *nf* : molecule — **molecular** *adj*
moler {47} *vt* **1** : to grind, to crush **2** CANSAR : to exhaust, to wear out
molestar *vt* **1** FASTIDIAR : to annoy, to bother **2** : to disturb, to disrupt — *vi* : to be a nuisance — **molestarse** *vr* **~ en** : to take the trouble to
molestia *nf* **1** FASTIDIO : annoyance, bother, nuisance **2** : trouble <se tomó la molestia de investigar : she took the trouble to investigate> **3** MALESTAR : discomfort
molesto, -ta *adj* **1** ENOJADO : bothered, annoyed **2** FASTIDIOSO : bothersome, annoying
molestoso, -sa *adj* : bothersome, annoying
molido, -da *adj* **1** MACHACADO : ground, crushed **2 estar molido** : to be exhausted
molinero, -ra *n* : miller
molinillo *nm* : grinder, mill <molinillo de café : coffee grinder>
molino *nm* **1** : mill **2 molino de viento** : windmill
molla *nf* : soft fleshy part, flesh (of fruit), lean part (of meat)
molleja *nf* : gizzard
molusco *nm* : mollusk
momentáneamente *adv* : momentarily
momentáneo, -nea *adj* **1** : momentary **2** TEMPORARIO : temporary
momento *nm* **1** : moment, instant <espera un momentito : wait just a moment> **2** : time, period of time <momentos difíciles : hard times> **3** : present, moment <los atletas del momento : the athletes of the moment, today's popular athletes> **4** : momentum **5 al momento** : right away, at once **6 de ~** : at the moment, for the moment **7 de un momento a otro** : any time now **8 por momentos** : at times

momia *nf* : mummy
monaguillo *nm* ACÓLITO : altar boy
monarca *nmf* : monarch
monarquía *nf* : monarchy
monárquico, -ca *n* : monarchist
monasterio *nm* : monastery
monástico, -ca *adj* : monastic
mondadientes *nms & pl* PALILLO : toothpick
mondar *vt* : to peel
mondongo *nm* ENTRAÑAS : innards *pl,* insides *pl,* guts *pl*
moneda *nf* **1** : coin **2** : money, currency
monedero *nm* : change purse
monetario, -ria *adj* : monetary, financial
mongol, -gola *adj & n* : Mongol, Mongolian
monitor[1]**, -tora** *n* : instructor (in sports)
monitor[2] *nm* : monitor <monitor de televisión : television monitor>
monitorear *vt* : to monitor
monja *nf* : nun
monje *nm* : monk
mono[1]**, -na** *adj fam* : lovely, pretty, cute, darling
mono[2]**, -na** *n* : monkey
monóculo *nm* : monocle
monogamia *nf* : monogamy
monógamo -ma *adj* : monogamous
monografía *nf* : monograph
monograma *nm* : monogram
monolingüe *adj* : monolingual
monolítico, -ca *adj* : monolithic
monolito *nm* : monolith
monólogo *nm* : monologue
monomanía *nf* : obsession
monopatín *nm, pl* **-tines** : scooter
monopolio *nm* : monopoly
monopolizar {21} *vt* : to monopolize — **monopolización** *nf*
monosilábico, -ca *adj* : monosyllabic
monosílabo *nm* : monosyllable
monoteísmo *nm* : monotheism
monoteísta[1] *adj* : monotheistic
monoteísta[2] *nmf* : monotheist
monotonía *nf* **1** : monotony **2** : monotone
monótono, -na *adj* : monotonous — **monótonamente** *adv*
monóxido *nm* : monoxide <monóxido de carbono : carbon monoxide>
monserga *nf* : gibberish, drivel
monstruo *nm* : monster
monstruosidad *nf* : monstrosity
monstruoso, -sa *adj* : monstrous — **monstruosamente** *adv*
monta *nf* **1** : sum, total **2** : importance, value <de poca monta : unimportant, insignificant>
montaje *nm* **1** : assembling, assembly **2** : montage
montante *nm* : transom, fanlight
montaña *nf* **1** MONTE : mountain **2 montaña rusa** : roller coaster
montañero, -ra *n* : mountaineer, mountain climber
montañoso, -sa *adj* : mountainous
montar *vt* **1** : to mount **2** ESTABLECER : to set up, to establish **3** ARMAR : to assemble, to put together **4** : to edit (a film) **5** : to stage, to put on (a show) **6** : to cock (a gun) **7 montar en bicicleta** : to get on a bicycle **8 montar a caballo** CABALGAR : to ride horseback
monte *nm* **1** MONTAÑA : mountain, mount **2** : woodland, scrubland <monte bajo : underbrush> **3** : outskirts (of a town), surrounding country **4 monte de piedad** : pawnshop
montés *adj, pl* **monteses** : wild (of animals or plants)
montículo *nm* **1** : mound, heap **2** : hillock, knoll
monto *nm* : amount, total
montón *nm, pl* **-tones 1** : heap, pile **2** *fam* : ton, load <un montón de preguntas : a ton of questions> <montones de gente : loads of people>
montura *nf* **1** : mount (horse) **2** : saddle, tack **3** : setting, mounting (of jewelry) **4** : frame (of glasses)
monumental *adj fam* **1** : tremendous, terrific **2** : massive, huge
monumento *nm* : monument
monzón *nm, pl* **monzones** : monsoon
moño *nm* **1** : bun (chignon) **2** LAZO : bow, knot <corbata de moño : bow tie>
moquear *vi* : to snivel
moquillo *nm* : distemper
mora *nf* **1** : blackberry **2** : mulberry
morada *nf* RESIDENCIA : dwelling, abode
morado[1]**, -da** *adj* : purple
morado[2] *nm* : purple
morador, -dora *n* : dweller, inhabitant
moral[1] *adj* : moral — **moralmente** *adv*
moral[2] *nf* **1** MORALIDAD : ethics, morality, morals *pl* **2** ÁNIMO : morale, spirits *pl*
moraleja *nf* : moral (of a story)
moralidad *nf* : morality
moralista[1] *adj* : moralistic
moralista[2] *nmf* : moralist
morar *vi* : to dwell, to reside
moratoria *nf* : moratorium
morboso, -sa *adj* : morbid — **morbosidad** *nf*
morcilla *nf* : blood sausage, blood pudding
mordacidad *nf* : bite, sharpness
mordaz *adj* : caustic, scathing
mordaza *nf* **1** : gag **2** : clamp
mordedura *nf* : bite (of an animal)
morder {47} *v* : to bite
mordida *nf* **1** : bite **2** *CA, Mex* : bribe, payoff
mordisco *nm* : bite, nibble
mordisquear *vt* : to nibble (on), to bite
morena *nf* **1** : moraine **2** : moray (eel)
moreno[1]**, -na** *adj* **1** : brunette **2** : dark, dark-skinned
moreno[2]**, -na** *n* **1** : brunette **2** : dark-skinned person

moretón *nm, pl* **-tones :** bruise

morfina *nf* **:** morphine

morfología *nf* **:** morphology

morgue *nf* **:** morgue

moribundo[1], -da *adj* **:** dying, moribund

moribundo[2], -da *n* **:** dying person

morillo *nm* **:** andiron

morir {46} *vi* **1** FALLECER **:** to die **2** APAGARSE **:** to die out, to go out

mormón, -mona *adj & n, pl* **mormones :** Mormon

moro[1], -ra *adj* **:** Moorish

moro[2], -ra *n* **1 :** Moor **2 :** Muslim

morosidad *nf* **1 :** delinquency (in payment) **2 :** slowness

moroso, -sa *adj* **1 :** delinquent, in arrears <cuentas morosas **:** delinquent accounts> **2 :** slow, sluggish

morral *nm* MOCHILA **:** backpack, knapsack

morralla *nf* **1 :** small fish **2 :** trash, riffraff **3** *Mex* **:** small change

morriña *nf* **:** homesickness

morro *nm* HOCICO **:** snout

morsa *nf* **:** walrus

morse *nm* **:** Morse code

mortaja *nf* SUDARIO **:** shroud

mortal[1] *adj* **1 :** mortal **2** FATAL **:** fatal, deadly — **mortalmente** *adv*

mortal[2] *nmf* **:** mortal

mortalidad *nf* **:** mortality

mortandad *nf* **1 :** loss of life, death toll **2 :** carnage, slaughter

mortero *nm* **:** mortar (bowl, cannon, or building material)

mortífero, -ra *adj* LETAL **:** deadly, fatal

mortificación *nf, pl* **-ciones 1 :** mortification **2** TORMENTO **:** anguish, torment

mortificar {72} *vt* **1 :** to mortify **2** TORTURAR **:** to trouble, to torment — **mortificarse** *vr* **:** to be mortified, to feel embarrassed

mosaico *nm* **:** mosaic

mosca *nf* **1 :** fly **2 mosca común :** housefly

moscada *adj* **nuez moscada :** nutmeg

moscovita *adj & nmf* **:** Muscovite

mosquearse *vr* **1 :** to become suspicious **2 :** to take offense

mosquete *nm* **:** musket

mosquetero *nm* **:** musketeer

mosquitero *nm* **:** mosquito net

mosquito *nm* ZANCUDO **:** mosquito

mostachón *nm, pl* **-chones :** macaroon

mostaza *nf* **:** mustard

mostrador *nm* **:** counter (in a store)

mostrar {19} *vt* **1 :** to show **2** EXHIBIR **:** to exhibit, to display — **mostrarse** *vr* **:** to show oneself, to appear

mota *nf* **1 :** fleck, speck **2 :** defect, blemish

mote *nm* SOBRENOMBRE **:** nickname

moteado, -da *adj* **:** dotted, spotted, dappled

motel *nm* **:** motel

motín *nm, pl* **motines 1 :** riot **2 :** rebellion, mutiny

motivación *nf, pl* **-ciones :** motivation — **motivacional** *adj*

motivar *vt* **1** CAUSAR **:** to cause **2** IMPULSAR **:** to motivate

motivo *nm* **1** MÓVIL **:** motive **2** CAUSA **:** cause, reason **3** TEMA **:** theme, motif

moto *nf* **:** motorcycle, motorbike

motocicleta *nf* **:** motorcycle

motociclismo *nm* **:** motorcycling

motociclista *nmf* **:** motorcyclist

motor[1], -ra *adj* MOTRIZ **:** motor

motor[2] *nm* **1 :** motor, engine **2 :** driving force, cause

motorista *nmf* **:** motorist

motriz *adj, pl* **motrices :** driving

motu proprio *adv* **de motu proprio** [de'motu'proprio] **:** voluntarily, of one's own accord

mousse ['mus] *nm* **:** mousse

mover {47} *vt* **1** TRASLADAR **:** to move, to shift **2** AGITAR **:** to shake, to nod (the head) **3** ACCIONAR **:** to power, to drive **4** INDUCIR **:** to provoke, to cause **5 :** to excite, to stir — **moverse** *vr* **1 :** to move, to move over **2 :** to hurry, to get a move on **3 :** to get moving, to make an effort

movible *adj* **:** movable

movida *nf* **:** move (in a game)

móvil[1] *adj* **:** mobile

móvil[2] *nm* **1** MOTIVO **:** motive **2 :** mobile

movilidad *nf* **:** mobility

movilizar {21} *vt* **:** to mobilize — **movilización** *nf*

movimiento *nm* **:** movement, motion <movimiento del cuerpo **:** bodily movement> <movimiento sindicalista **:** labor movement>

mozo[1], -za *adj* **:** young, youthful

mozo[2], -za *n* **1** JOVEN **:** young man *m,* young woman *f,* youth **2 :** helper, servant

mucamo, -ma *n* **:** servant, maid *f*

muchacha *nf* **:** maid

muchacho, -cha *n* **1 :** kid, boy *m,* girl *f* **2** JOVEN **:** young man *m,* young woman *f*

muchedumbre *nf* MULTITUD **:** crowd, multitude

mucho[1] *adv* **1 :** much, a lot <mucho más **:** much more> <le gusta mucho **:** he likes it a lot> **2 :** long, a long time <tardó mucho en venir **:** he was a long time getting here> **3 por mucho que :** no matter how much

mucho[2], -cha *adj* **1 :** a lot of, many, much <mucha gente **:** a lot of people> <hace mucho tiempo que no lo veo **:** I haven't seen him in ages> **2 muchas veces :** often

mucho[3], -cha *pron* **1 :** a lot, many, much <hay mucho que hacer **:** there is a lot to do> <muchas no vinieron **:** many didn't come> **2 cuando ~** *or* **como ~ :** at most **3 con ~ :** by far **4 ni mucho menos :** not at all, far from it

mucílago *nm* **:** mucilage

mucosidad *nf* **:** mucus

mucoso, -sa *adj* : mucous, slimy
muda *nf* **1 :** change <muda de ropa : change of clothes> **2 :** molt, molting
mudanza *nf* **1** CAMBIO **:** change **2** TRASLADO **:** move, moving
mudar *v* **1** CAMBIAR **:** to change **2 :** to molt, to shed — **mudarse** *vr* **1** TRASLADARSE **:** to move (one's residence) **2 :** to change (clothes)
mudo[1], -da *adj* **1** SILENCIOSO **:** silent <el cine mudo : silent films> **2 :** mute, dumb
mudo[2], -da *n* **:** mute
mueble *nm* **1 :** piece of furniture **2 muebles** *nmpl* **:** furniture, furnishings
mueblería *nf* **:** furniture store
mueca *nf* **:** grimace, face
muela *nf* **1 :** tooth, molar <dolor de muelas : toothache> <muela de juicio : wisdom tooth> **2 :** millstone **3 :** whetstone
muele, etc. → **moler**
muelle[1] *adj* **:** soft, comfortable, easy
muelle[2] *nm* **1 :** wharf, dock **2** RESORTE **:** spring
muérdago *nm* **:** mistletoe
muerde, etc. → **morder**
muere, etc. → **morir**
muerte *nf* **:** death
muerto[1] *pp* → **morir**
muerto[2], -ta *adj* **1 :** dead **2 :** lifeless, flat, dull **3 ~ de :** dying of <estoy muerto de hambre : I'm dying of hunger>
muerto[3], -ta *nm* DIFUNTO **:** dead person, deceased
muesca *nf* **:** nick, notch
muestra[1], etc. → **mostrar**
muestra[2] *nf* **1 :** sample **2** SEÑAL **:** sign, show <una muestra de respeto : a show of respect> **3** EXPOSICIÓN **:** exhibition, exposition **4 :** pattern, model
mueve, etc. → **mover**
mugido *nm* **:** moo, lowing, bellow
mugir {35} *vi* **:** to moo, to low, to bellow
mugre *nf* SUCIEDAD **:** grime, filth
mugriento, -ta *adj* **:** filthy
muguete *nm* **:** lily of the valley
muja, etc. → **mugir**
mujer *nf* **1 :** woman **2** ESPOSA **:** wife
mulato, -ta *adj & n* **:** mulatto
muleta *nf* **:** crutch
mullido, -da *adj* **1 :** soft, fluffy **2 :** spongy, springy
mulo, -la *n* **:** mule
multa *nf* **:** fine
multicolor *adj* **:** multicolored
multicultural *adj* **:** multicultural
multidisciplinario, -ria *adj* **:** multidisciplinary
multifacético, -ca *adj* **:** multifaceted
multifamiliar *adj* **:** multifamily
multilateral *adj* **:** multilateral
multimedia *nf* **:** multimedia
multimillonario, -ria *n* **:** multimillionaire
multinacional *adj* **:** multinational
múltiple *adj* **:** multiple
multiplicación *nf, pl* **-ciones :** multiplication
multiplicar {72} *v* **1 :** to multiply **2 :** to increase — **multiplicarse** *vr* **:** to multiply, to reproduce
multiplicidad *nf* **:** multiplicity
múltiplo *nm* **:** multiple
multitud *nf* MUCHEDUMBRE **:** crowd, multitude
multiuso, -sa *adj* **:** multipurpose
multivitamínico, -ca *adj* **:** multivitamin
mundano, -na *adj* **:** worldly, earthly
mundial *adj* **:** world, worldwide
mundialmente *adv* **:** worldwide, all over the world
mundo *nm* **1 :** world **2 todo el mundo :** everyone, everybody
municiones *nfpl* **:** ammunition, munitions
municipal *adj* **:** municipal
municipio *nm* **1 :** municipality **2** AYUNTAMIENTO **:** town council
muñeca *nf* **1 :** doll **2** MANIQUÍ **:** mannequin **3 :** wrist
muñeco *nm* **1 :** doll, boy doll **2** MARIONETA **:** puppet
muñon *nm, pl* **muñones :** stump (of an arm or leg)
mural *adj & nm* **:** mural
muralista *nmf* **:** muralist
muralla *nf* **:** rampart, wall
murciélago *nm* **:** bat (animal)
murga *nf* **:** band of street musicians
murió, etc. → **morir**
murmullo *nm* **1 :** murmur, murmuring **2 :** rustling, rustle <el murmullo de las hojas : the rustling of the leaves>
murmurar *vt* **1 :** to murmur, to mutter **2 :** to whisper (gossip) — *vi* **1 :** to murmur **2** CHISMEAR **:** to gossip
muro *nm* **:** wall
musa *nf* **:** muse
musaraña *nf* **:** shrew
muscular *adj* **:** muscular
musculatura *nf* **:** muscles *pl,* musculature
músculo *nm* **:** muscle
musculoso, -sa *adj* **:** muscular, brawny
muselina *nf* **:** muslin
museo *nm* **:** museum
musgo *nm* **:** moss
musgoso, -sa *adj* **:** mossy
música *nf* **:** music
musical *adj* **:** musical — **musicalmente** *adv*
músico[1], -ca *adj* **:** musical
músico[2], -ca *n* **:** musician
musitar *vt* **:** to mumble, to murmur
muslo *nm* **:** thigh
musulmán, -mana *adj & n, mpl* **-manes :** Muslim
mutación *nf, pl* **-ciones :** mutation
mutante *adj & nm* **:** mutant
mutar *v* **:** to mutate
mutilar *vt* **:** to mutilate — **mutilación** *nf*
mutis *nm* **1 :** exit (in theater) **2 :** silence
mutual *adj* **:** mutual

mutuo, -tua *adj* **:** mutual, reciprocal — **mutuamente** *adv*

muy *adv* **1 :** very, quite <es muy inteligente : she's very intelligent> <muy bien : very well, fine> <eso es muy americano : that's typically American> **2 :** too <es muy grande para él : it's too big for him>

N

n *nf* **:** fourteenth letter of the Spanish alphabet

nabo *nm* **:** turnip

nácar *nm* MADREPERLA **:** nacre, mother-of-pearl

nacarado, -da *adj* **:** pearly

nacer {48} *vi* **1 :** to be born <nací en Guatemala : I was born in Guatemala> <no nació ayer : he wasn't born yesterday> **2 :** to hatch **3 :** to bud, to sprout **4 :** to rise, to originate **5 nacer para algo :** to be born to be something **6 volver a nacer :** to have a lucky escape

nacido[1], -da *adj* **1 :** born **2 recién nacido :** newborn

nacido[2], -da *n* **1 los nacidos :** those born (at a particular time) **2 recién nacido :** newborn baby

naciente *adj* **1 :** newfound, growing **2 :** rising <el sol naciente : the rising sun>

nacimiento *nm* **1 :** birth **2 :** source (of a river) **3 :** beginning, origin **4** BELÉN **:** Nativity scene, crèche

nación *nf, pl* **naciones :** nation, country, people (of a country)

nacional[1] *adj* **:** national

nacional[2] *nmf* CIUDADANO **:** national, citizen

nacionalidad *nf* **:** nationality

nacionalismo *nm* **:** nationalism

nacionalista[1] *adj* **:** nationalist, nationalistic

nacionalista[2] *nmf* **:** nationalist

nacionalización *nf, pl* **-ciones 1 :** nationalization **2 :** naturalization

nacionalizar {21} *vt* **1 :** to nationalize **2 :** to naturalize (as a citizen) — **nacionalizarse** *vr*

naco, -ca *adj Mex* **:** trashy, vulgar, common

nada[1] *adv* **:** not at all, not in the least <no estamos nada cansados : we are not at all tired>

nada[2] *nf* **1 :** nothingness **2 :** smidgen, bit <una nada le disgusta : the slightest thing upsets him>

nada[3] *pron* **1 :** nothing <no estoy haciendo nada : I'm not doing anything> **2 casi nada :** next to nothing **3 de ~ :** you're welcome **4 dentro de nada :** very soon, in no time **5 nada más :** nothing else, nothing more

nadador, -dora *n* **:** swimmer

nadar *vi* **1 :** to swim **2 ~ en :** to be swimming in, to be rolling in — *vt* **:** to swim

nadería *nf* **:** small thing, trifle

nadie *pron* **:** nobody, no one <no vi a nadie : I didn't see anyone>

nadir *nm* **:** nadir

nado *nm* **1** *Mex* **:** swimming **2 a ~ :** swimming <cruzó el río a nado : he swam across the river>

nafta *nf* **1 :** naphtha **2** (*in various countries*) **:** gasoline

naftalina *nf* **:** naphthalene, mothballs *pl*

náhuatl[1] *adj & nmf, pl* **nahuas :** Nahuatl

náhuatl[2] *nm* **:** Nahuatl (language)

nailon → **nilón**

naipe *nm* **:** playing card

nalga *nf* **1 :** buttock **2 nalgas** *nfpl* **:** buttocks, bottom

nalgada *nf* **:** smack on the bottom, spanking

namibio, -bia *adj & n* **:** Namibian

nana *nf* **1 :** lullaby **2** *fam* **:** grandma **3** *CA, Col, Mex, Ven* **:** nanny

nanay *interj fam* **:** no way!, not likely!

naranja[1] *adj & nm* **:** orange (color)

naranja[2] *nf* **:** orange (fruit)

naranjal *nm* **:** orange grove

naranjo *nm* **:** orange tree

narcisismo *nm* **:** narcissism

narcisista[1] *adj* **:** narcissistic

narcisista[2] *nmf* **:** narcissist

narciso *nm* **:** narcissus, daffodil

narcótico[1], -ca *adj* **:** narcotic

narcótico[2] *nm* **:** narcotic

narcotizar {21} *vt* **:** to drug, to dope

narcotraficante *nmf* **:** drug trafficker

narcotráfico *nm* **:** drug trafficking

narigón, -gona *adj, mpl* **-gones :** big-nosed

narigudo → **narigón**

nariz *nf, pl* **narices 1 :** nose <sonar(se) la nariz : to blow one's nose> **2 :** sense of smell

narración *nf, pl* **-ciones :** narration, account

narrador, -dora *n* **:** narrator

narrar *vt* **:** to narrate, to tell

narrativa *nf* **:** narrative, story

narrativo, -va *adj* **:** narrative

narval *nm* **:** narwhal

nasa *nf* **:** creel

nasal *adj* **:** nasal

nata *nf* **1 :** cream <nata batida : whipped cream> **2 :** skin (on boiled milk)

natación *nf, pl* **-ciones :** swimming

natal *adj* **:** native, natal

natalicio *nm* **:** birthday <el natalicio de George Washington : George Washington's birthday>

natalidad *nf* **:** birthrate

natillas *nfpl* : custard

natividad *nf* : birth, nativity

nativo, -va *adj & n* : native

natural[1] *adj* **1** : natural **2** : normal <como es natural : naturally, as expected> **3 ~ de** : native of, from **4 de tamaño natural** : life-size

natural[2] *nm* **1** CARÁCTER : disposition, temperament **2** : native <un natural de Venezuela : a native of Venezuela>

naturaleza *nf* **1** : nature <la madre naturaleza : mother nature> **2** ÍNDOLE : nature, disposition, constitution <la naturaleza humana : human nature> **3 naturaleza muerta** : still life

naturalidad *nf* : simplicity, naturalness

naturalismo *nm* : naturalism

naturalista[1] *adj* : naturalistic

naturalista[2] *nmf* : naturalist

naturalización *nf, pl* **-ciones** : naturalization

naturalizar {21} *vt* : to naturalize — **naturalizarse** *vr* NACIONALIZARSE : to become naturalized

naturalmente *adv* **1** : naturally, inherently **2** : of course

naufragar {52} *vi* **1** : to be shipwrecked **2** FRACASAR : to fail, to collapse

naufragio *nm* **1** : shipwreck **2** FRACASO : failure, collapse

náufrago[1], **-ga** *adj* : shipwrecked, castaway

náufrago[2], **-ga** *n* : shipwrecked person, castaway

náusea *nf* **1** : nausea **2 dar náuseas** : to nauseate, to disgust **3 náuseas matutinas** : morning sickness

nauseabundo, -da *adj* : nauseating, sickening

náutica *nf* : navigation

náutico, -ca *adj* : nautical

nautilo *nm* : nautilus

navaja *nf* **1** : pocketknife, penknife <navaja de muelle : switchblade> **2 navaja de afeitar** : straight razor, razor blade

navajo, -ja *adj & n* : Navajo

naval *adj* : naval

nave *nf* **1** : ship <nave capitana : flagship> <nave espacial : spaceship> **2** : nave <nave lateral : aisle> **3 quemar uno sus naves** : to burn one's bridges

navegabilidad *nf* : navigability

navegable *adj* : navigable

navegación *nf, pl* **-ciones** : navigation

navegante[1] *adj* : sailing, seafaring

navegante[2] *nmf* : navigator

navegar {52} *v* : to navigate, to sail

Navidad *nf* : Christmas, Christmastime <Feliz Navidad : Merry Christmas>

navideño, -ña *adj* : Christmas

naviero, -ra *adj* : shipping

náyade *nf* : naiad

nazca, etc. → **nacer**

nazi *adj & nmf* : Nazi

nazismo *nm* : Nazism

nébeda *nf* : catnip

neblina *nf* : light fog, mist

neblinoso, -sa *adj* : misty, foggy

nebulosa *nf* : nebula

nebulosidad *nf* : mistiness, haziness

nebuloso, -sa *adj* **1** : hazy, misty **2** : nebulous, vague

necedad *nf* : stupidity, foolishness <decir necedades : to talk nonsense>

necesariamente *adv* : necessarily

necesario, -ria *adj* **1** : necessary **2 si es necesario** : if need be **3 hacerse necesario** : to be required

neceser *nm* : toilet kit, vanity case

necesidad *nf* **1** : need, necessity **2** : poverty, want **3 necesidades** *nfpl* : hardships **4 hacer sus necesidades** : to relieve oneself

necesitado, -da *adj* : needy

necesitar *vt* **1** : to need **2** : to necessitate, to require — *vi* **~ de** : to have need of

necio[1], **-cia** *adj* **1** : foolish, silly, dumb **2** *fam* : naughty

necio[2], **-cia** *n* ESTÚPIDO : fool, idiot

necrología *nf* : obituary

necrópolis *nfs & pl* : cemetery

néctar *nm* : nectar

nectarina *nf* : nectarine

neerlandés[1], **-desa** *adj, mpl* **-deses** HOLANDÉS : Dutch

neerlandés[2], **-desa** *n, mpl* **-deses** HOLANDÉS : Dutch person, Dutchman *m*

nefando, -da *adj* : unspeakable, heinous

nefario, -ria *adj* : nefarious

nefasto, -ta *adj* **1** : ill-fated, unlucky **2** : disastrous, terrible

negación *nf, pl* **-ciones 1** : negation, denial **2** : negative (in grammar)

negar {49} *vt* **1** : to deny **2** REHUSAR : to refuse **3** : to disown — **negarse** *vr* **1** : to refuse **2** : to deny oneself

negativa *nf* **1** : denial **2** : refusal

negativo[1], **-va** *adj* : negative

negativo[2] *nm* : negative (of a photograph)

negligé *nm* : negligee

negligencia *nf* : negligence

negligente *adj* : neglectful, negligent — **negligentemente** *adv*

negociable *adj* : negotiable

negociación *nf, pl* **-ciones 1** : negotiation **2 negociación colectiva** : collective bargaining

negociador, -dora *n* : negotiator

negociante *nmf* : businessman *m*, businesswoman *f*

negociar *vt* : to negotiate — *vi* : to deal, to do business

negocio *nm* **1** : business, place of business **2** : deal, transaction **3 negocios** *nmpl* : commerce, trade, business

negrero, -ra *n* **1** : slave trader **2** *fam* : slave driver, brutal boss

negrita *nf* : boldface (type)

negro[1], **-gra** *adj* **1** : black, dark **2** BRONCEADO : suntanned **3** : gloomy, awful, desperate <la cosa se está poniendo negra : things are looking bad> **4 mercado negro** : black market

negro[2], **-gra** *n* **1** : dark-skinned person, black person **2** *fam* : darling, dear

negro[3] *nm* : black (color)

negrura *nf* : blackness

negruzco, -ca *adj* : blackish

nene, -na *n* : baby, small child

nenúfar *nm* : water lily

neocelandés → **neozelandés**

neoclasicismo *nm* : neoclassicism

neoclásico, -ca *adj* : neoclassical

neófito, -ta *n* : neophyte, novice

neologismo *nm* : neologism

neón *nm, pl* **neones** : neon

neoyorquino[1], **-na** *adj* : of or from New York

neoyorquino[2], **-na** *n* : New Yorker

neozelandés[1], **-desa** *adj, mpl* **-deses** : of or from New Zealand

neozelandés[2], **-desa** *n, mpl* **-deses** : New Zealander

nepalés, -lesa *adj & n, mpl* **-leses** : Nepali

nepotismo *nm* : nepotism

neptunio *nm* : neptunium

Neptuno *nm* : Neptune

nervio *nm* **1** : nerve **2** : tendon, sinew, gristle (in meat) **3** : energy, drive **4** : rib (of a vault) **5 nervios** *nmpl* : nerves <estar mal de los nervios : to be a bundle of nerves> <ataque de nervios : nervous breakdown>

nerviosamente *adv* : nervously

nerviosidad *nf* → **nerviosismo**

nerviosismo *nf* : nervousness, anxiety

nervioso, -sa *adj* **1** : nervous, nerve <sistema nervioso : nervous system> **2** : high-strung, restless, anxious <ponerse nervioso : to get nervous> **3** : vigorous, energetic

nervudo, -da *adj* : sinewy, wiry

neta *nf Mex fam* : truth <la neta es que me cae mal : the truth is, I don't like her>

netamente *adv* : clearly, obviously

neto, -ta *adj* **1** : net <peso neto : net weight> **2** : clear, distinct

neumático[1], **-ca** *adj* : pneumatic

neumático[2] *nm* LLANTA : tire

neumonía *nf* PULMONÍA : pneumonia

neural *adj* : neural

neuralgia *nf* : neuralgia

neuritis *nf* : neuritis

neurología *nf* : neurology

neurológico, -ca *adj* : neurological, neurologic

neurólogo, -ga *n* : neurologist

neurosis *nfs & pl* : neurosis

neurótico, -ca *adj & n* : neurotic

neutral *adj* : neutral

neutralidad *nf* : neutrality

neutralizar {21} *vt* : to neutralize — **neutralización** *nf*

neutro, -tra *adj* **1** : neutral **2** : neuter

neutrón *nm, pl* **neutrones** : neutron

nevada *nf* : snowfall

nevado, -da *adj* **1** : snowcapped **2** : snow-white

nevar {55} *v impers* : to snow

nevasca *nf* : snowstorm, blizzard

nevera *nf* REFRIGERADOR : refrigerator

nevería *nf Mex* : ice cream parlor

nevisca *nf* : light snowfall, flurry

nevoso, -sa *adj* : snowy

nexo *nm* VÍNCULO : link, connection, nexus

ni *conj* **1** : neither, nor <afuera no hace ni frío ni calor : it's neither cold nor hot outside> **2 ni que** : not even if, not as if <ni que me pagaran : not even if they paid me> <ni que fuera (yo) su madre : it's not as if I were his mother> **3 ni siquiera** : not even <ni siquiera nos llamaron : they didn't even call us>

nicaragüense *adj & nmf* : Nicaraguan

nicho *nm* : niche

nicotina *nf* : nicotine

nido *nm* **1** : nest **2** : hiding place, den

niebla *nf* : fog, mist

niega, niegue, etc. → **negar**

nieto, -ta *n* **1** : grandson *m,* granddaughter *f* **2 nietos** *nmpl* : grandchildren

nieva, etc. → **nevar**

nieve *nf* **1** : snow **2** *Cuba, Mex, PRi* : sherbet

nigeriano, -na *adj & n* : Nigerian

nigua *nf* : sand flea, chigger

nihilismo *nm* : nihilism

nilón *or* **nilon** *nm, pl* **nilones** : nylon

nimbo *nm* **1** : halo **2** : nimbus

nimiedad *nf* INSIGNIFICANCIA : trifle, triviality

nimio, -mia *adj* INSIGNIFICANTE : insignificant, trivial

ninfa *nf* : nymph

ningunear *vt Mex fam* : to disrespect

ninguno[1], **-na** (**ningún** *before masculine singular nouns*) *adj, mpl* **ningunos** : no, none <no es ninguna tonta : she's no fool> <no debe hacerse en ningún momento : that should never be done>

ninguno[2], **-na** *pron* **1** : neither, none <ninguno de los dos ha vuelto aún : neither one has returned yet> **2** : no one, no other <te quiero más que a ninguna : I love you more than any other>

niña *nf* **1** PUPILA : pupil (of the eye) **2 la niña de los ojos** : the apple of one's eye

niñada *nf* **1** : childishness **2** : trifle, silly thing

niñería *nf* → **niñada**

niñero, -ra *n* : baby-sitter, nanny

niñez *nf, pl* **niñeces** INFANCIA : childhood

niño, -ña *n* : child, boy *m,* girl *f*

niobio *nm* : niobium

nipón, -pona *adj & n, mpl* **nipones** JAPONÉS : Japanese

níquel *nm* : nickel

nitidez *nf, pl* **-deces** CLARIDAD : clarity, vividness, sharpness
nítido, -da *adj* CLARO : clear, vivid, sharp
nitrato *nm* : nitrate
nítrico, -ca *adj* **ácido nítrico** : nitric acid
nitrito *nm* : nitrite
nitrógeno *nm* : nitrogen
nitroglicerina *nf* : nitroglycerin
nivel *nm* **1** : level, height <nivel del mar : sea level> **2** : level, standard <nivel de vida : standard of living>
nivelar *vt* : to level (out)
nixtamal *nm Mex* : limed corn used for tortillas
no *adv* **1** : no <¿quieres ir al mercado? no, voy más tarde : do you want to go shopping? no, I'm going later> **2** : not <¡no hagas eso! : don't do that!> <creo que no : I don't think so> **3** : non- <no fumador : non-smoker> **4** **¡como no!** : of course! **5** **no bien** : as soon as, no sooner
nobelio *nm* : nobelium
noble[1] *adj* : noble — **noblemente** *adv*
noble[2] *nmf* : nobleman *m*, noblewoman *f*
nobleza *nf* **1** : nobility **2** HONRADEZ : honesty, integrity
nocaut *nm* : knockout, KO
noche *nf* **1** : night, nighttime, evening **2** **buenas noches** : good evening, good night **3** **de noche** *or* **por la noche** : at night **4** **hacerse de noche** : to get dark
Nochebuena *nf* : Christmas Eve
nochecita *nf* : dusk
Nochevieja *nf* : New Year's Eve
noción *nf, pl* **nociones** **1** CONCEPTO : notion, concept **2** **nociones** *nfpl* : smattering, rudiments *pl*
nocivo, -va *adj* DAÑINO : harmful, noxious
noctámbulo, -la *n* **1** : sleepwalker **2** : night owl
nocturno[1], -na *adj* : night, nocturnal
nocturno[2] *nm* : nocturne
nodriza *nf* : wet nurse
nódulo *nm* : nodule
nogal *nm* **1** : walnut tree **2** *Mex* : pecan tree **3** **nogal americano** : hickory
nómada[1] *adj* : nomadic
nómada[2] *nmf* : nomad
nomás *adv* : only, just <lo hice nomás porque sí : I did it just because> <nomás de recordarlo me enojo : I get angry just remembering it> <nomás faltan dos semanas para Navidad : there are only two weeks left till Christmas>
nombradía *nf* RENOMBRE : fame, renown
nombrado, -da *adj* : famous, well-known
nombramiento *nm* : appointment, nomination
nombrar *vt* **1** : to appoint **2** : to mention, to name
nombre *nm* **1** : name <nombre de pluma : pseudonym, pen name> <en nombre : on behalf of> <sin nombre : nameless> **2** : noun <nombre propio : proper noun> **3** : fame, renown
nomenclatura *nf* : nomenclature
nomeolvides *nmfs & pl* : forget-me-not
nómina *nf* : payroll
nominación *nf, pl* **-ciones** : nomination
nominal *adj* : nominal — **nominalmente** *adv*
nominar *vt* : to nominate
nominativo[1], -va *adj* : nominative
nominativo[2] *nm* : nominative (case)
nomo *nm* : gnome
non[1] *adj* IMPAR : odd, not even
non[2] *nm* : odd number
nonagésimo[1], -ma *adj* : ninetieth, ninety-
nonagésimo[2], -ma *n* : ninetieth, ninety- (in a series)
nono, -na *adj* : ninth — **nono** *nm*
nopal *nm* : nopal, cactus
nopalitos *nmpl Mex* : pickled cactus leaves
noquear *vt* : to knock out, to KO
norcoreano, -na *adj & n* : North Korean
nordeste[1] *or* **noreste** *adj* **1** : northeastern **2** : northeasterly
nordeste[2] *or* **noreste** *nm* : northeast
nórdico, -ca *adj & n* ESCANDINAVO : Scandinavian
noreste → **nordeste**
noria *nf* **1** : waterwheel **2** : Ferris wheel
norirlandés[1], -desa *adj, mpl* **-deses** : Northern Irish
norirlandés[2], -desa *n, mpl* **-deses** : person from Northern Ireland
norma *nf* **1** : rule, regulation **2** : norm, standard
normal *adj* **1** : normal, usual **2** : standard **3** **escuela normal** : teacher-training college
normalidad *nf* : normality, normalcy
normalización *nf, pl* **-ciones** *nf* **1** REGULARIZACIÓN : normalization **2** ESTANDARIZACIÓN : standardization
normalizar {21} *vt* **1** REGULARIZAR : to normalize **2** ESTANDARIZAR : to standardize — **normalizarse** *vr* : to return to normal
normalmente *adv* GENERALMENTE : ordinarily, generally
noroeste[1] *adj* **1** : northwestern **2** : northwesterly
noroeste[2] *nm* : northwest
norte[1] *adj* : north, northern
norte[2] *nm* **1** : north **2** : north wind **3** META : aim, objective
norteamericano, -na *adj & n* **1** : North American **2** AMERICANO, ESTADOUNIDENSE : American, native or inhabitant of the United States
norteño[1], -ña *adj* : northern
norteño[2], -ña *n* : Northerner

noruego[1], **-ga** *adj & n* : Norwegian

noruego[2] *nm* : Norwegian (language)

nos *pron* **1** : us <nos enviaron a la frontera : they sent us to the border> **2** : ourselves <nos divertimos muchísimo : we enjoyed ourselves a great deal> **3** : each other, one another <nos vimos desde lejos : we saw each other from far away> **4** : to us, for us, from us <nos lo dio : he gave it to us> <nos lo compraron : they bought it from us>

nosotros, -tras *pron* **1** : we <nosotros llegamos ayer : we arrived yesterday> **2** : us <ven con nosotros : come with us> **3 nosotros mismos** : ourselves <lo arreglamos nosotros mismos : we fixed it ourselves>

nostalgia *nf* **1** : nostalgia, longing **2** : homesickness

nostálgico, -ca *adj* **1** : nostalgic **2** : homesick

nota *nf* **1** : note, message **2** : announcement <nota de prensa : press release> **3** : grade, mark (in school) **4** : characteristic, feature, touch **5** : note (in music) **6** : bill, check (in a restaraunt)

notable *adj* **1** : notable, noteworthy **2** : outstanding

notar *vt* **1** : to notice <hacer notar algo : to point out something> **2** : to tell <la diferencia se nota inmediatamente : you can tell the difference right away> — **notarse** *vr* **1** : to be evident, to show **2** : to feel, to seem

notario, -ria *n* : notary, notary public

noticia *nf* **1** : news item, piece of news **2 noticias** *nfpl* : news

noticiero *nm* : news program, newscast

noticioso, -sa *adj* : news <agencia noticiosa : news agency>

notificación *nf, pl* **-ciones** : notification

notificar {72} *vt* : to notify, to inform

notoriedad *nf* **1** : knowledge, obviousness **2** : fame, notoriety

notorio, -ria *adj* **1** OBVIO : obvious, evident **2** CONOCIDO : well-known

novato[1], **-ta** *adj* : inexperienced, new

novato[2], **-ta** *n* : beginner, novice

novecientos[1], **-tas** *adj* : nine hundred

novecientos[2] *nms & pl* : nine hundred

novedad *nf* **1** : newness, novelty **2** : innovation

novedoso, -sa *adj* : original, novel

novel *adj* NOVATO : inexperienced, new

novela *nf* **1** : novel **2** : soap opera

novelar *vt* : to fictionalize, to make a novel out of

novelesco, -ca *adj* **1** : fictional **2** : fantastic, fabulous

novelista *nmf* : novelist

novena *nf* : novena

noveno, -na *adj* : ninth — **noveno, -na** *n*

noventa *adj & nm* : ninety

noventavo[1], **-va** *adj* : ninetieth

noventavo[2] *nm* : ninetieth (fraction)

noviazgo *nm* **1** : courtship, relationship **2** : engagement, betrothal

novicio, -cia *n* **1** : novice (in religion) **2** PRINCIPIANTE : novice, beginner

noviembre *nm* : November

novilla *nf* : heifer

novillada *nf* : bullfight featuring young bulls

novillero, -ra *n* : apprentice bullfighter

novillo *nm* : young bull

novio, -via *n* **1** : boyfriend *m,* girlfriend *f* **2** PROMETIDO : fiancé *m,* fiancée *f* **3** : bridegroom *m,* bride *f*

novocaína *nf* : novocaine

nubarrón *nm, pl* **-rrones** : storm cloud

nube *nf* **1** : cloud <andar en las nubes : to have one's head in the clouds> <por las nubes : sky-high> **2** : cloud (of dust), swarm (of insects, etc.)

nublado[1], **-da** *adj* **1** NUBOSO : cloudy, overcast **2** : clouded, dim

nublado[2] *nm* **1** : storm cloud **2** AMENAZA : menace, threat

nublar *vt* **1** : to cloud **2** OSCURECER : to obscure — **nublarse** *vr* : to get cloudy

nubosidad *nf* : cloudiness

nuboso, -sa *adj* NUBLADO : cloudy

nuca *nf* : nape, back of the neck

nuclear *adj* : nuclear

núcleo *nm* **1** : nucleus **2** : center, heart, core

nudillo *nm* : knuckle

nudismo *nm* : nudism

nudista *adj & nmf* : nudist

nudo *nm* **1** : knot <square knot : nudo de rizo> <un nudo en la garganta : a lump in one's throat> **2** : node **3** : junction, hub <nudo de comunicaciones : communication center> **4** : crux, heart (of a problem, etc.)

nudoso, -sa *adj* : knotty, gnarled

nuera *nf* : daughter-in-law

nuestro[1], **-tra** *adj* : our

nuestro[2], **-tra** *pron* (*with definite article*) : ours, our own <el nuestro es más grande : ours is bigger> <es de los nuestros : it's one of ours>

nuevamente *adv* : again, anew

nuevas *nfpl* : tidings *pl*

nueve *adj & nm* : nine

nuevecito, -ta *adj* : brand-new

nuevo, -va *adj* **1** : new <una casa nueva : a new house> <¿qué hay de nuevo? : what's new?> **2 de ~** : again, once more

nuez *nf, pl* **nueces 1** : nut **2** : walnut **3** *Mex* : pecan **4 nuez de Adán** : Adam's apple **5 nuez moscada** : nutmeg

nulidad *nf* **1** : nullity **2** : incompetent person <¡es una nulidad! : he's hopeless!>

nulo, -la *adj* **1** : null, null and void **2** INEPTO : useless, inept <es nula para la cocina : she's hopeless at cooking>

numen *nm* : poetic muse, inspiration

numerable *adj* : countable

numeración *nf, pl* **-ciones 1 :** numbering **2 :** numbers *pl,* numerals *pl* <numeración romana : Roman numerals>
numerador *nm* **:** numerator
numeral *adj* **:** numeral
numerar *vt* **:** to number
numerario, -ria *adj* **:** long-standing, permanent <profesor numerario : tenured professor>
numérico, -ca *adj* **:** numerical — **numéricamente** *adv*
número *nm* **1 :** number <número impar : odd number> <número ordinal : ordinal number> <número arábico : Arabic numeral> <número quebrado : fraction> **2 :** issue (of a publication) **3 sin ~ :** countless
numeroso, -sa *adj* **:** numerous
numismática *nf* **:** numismatics
nunca *adv* **1 :** never, ever <nunca es tarde : it's never too late> <no trabaja casi nunca : he hardly ever works> **2 nunca más :** never again **3 nunca jamás :** never ever
nuncio *nm* **:** harbinger, herald
nupcial *adj* **:** nuptial, wedding
nupcias *nfpl* **:** nuptials *pl,* wedding
nutria *nf* **1 :** otter **2 :** nutria
nutrición *nf, pl* **-ciones :** nutrition, nourishment
nutrido, -da *adj* **1 :** nourished <mal nutrido : undernourished, malnourished> **2 :** considerable, abundant <de nutrido : full of, abounding in>
nutriente *nm* **:** nutrient
nutrimento *nm* **:** nutriment
nutrir *vt* **1** ALIMENTAR **:** to feed, to nourish **2 :** to foster, to provide
nutritivo, -va *adj* **:** nourishing, nutritious
nylon *nm* → **nilón**

Ñ

ñ *nf* **:** fifteenth letter of the Spanish alphabet
ñame *nm* **:** yam
ñandú *nm* **:** rhea
ñapa *nf* **:** extra amount <de ñapa : for good measure>
ñoñear *vi fam* **:** to whine
ñoño, -ña *adj fam* **:** whiny, fussy <no seas tan ñoño : don't be such a wimp>
ñoquis *nmpl* **:** gnocchi *pl*
ñu *nm* **:** gnu, wildebeest

O

o[1] *nf* **:** sixteenth letter of the Spanish alphabet
o[2] *conj* (**u** *before words beginning with o- or ho-*) **1 :** or <¿vienes con nosotros o te quedas? : are you coming with us or staying?> **2 :** either <o vienes con nosotros o te quedas : either you come with us or you stay> **3 o sea :** that is to say, in other words
oasis *nms & pl* **:** oasis
obcecado, -da *adj* **1 :** blinded <obcecado por la ira : blinded by rage> **2 :** stubborn, obstinate
obcecar {72} *vt* **:** to blind (by emotions) — **obcecarse** *vr* **:** to become stubborn
obedecer {53} *vt* **:** to obey <obedecer órdenes : to obey orders> <obedece a tus padres : obey your parents> — *vi* **1 :** to obey **2 ~ a :** to respond to **3 ~ a :** to be due to, to result from
obediencia *nf* **:** obedience
obediente *adj* **:** obedient — **obedientemente** *adv*
obelisco *nm* **:** obelisk
obertura *nf* **:** overture
obesidad *nf* **:** obesity
obeso, -sa *adj* **:** obese
óbice *nm* **:** obstacle, impediment
obispado *nm* DIÓCESIS **:** bishopric, diocese
obispo *nm* **:** bishop
obituario *nm* **:** obituary
objeción *nf, pl* **-ciones :** objection <ponerle objeciones a algo : to object to something>
objetar *v* **:** to object <no tengo nada que objetar : I have no objections>
objetividad *nf* **:** objectivity
objetivo[1], **-va** *adj* **:** objective — **objetivamente** *adv*
objetivo[2] *nm* **1** META **:** objective, goal, target **2 :** lens
objeto *nm* **1** COSA **:** object, thing **2** OBJETIVO **:** objective, purpose <con objeto de : in order to, with the aim of> **3 objeto volador no identificado :** unidentified flying object
objetor, -tora *n* **:** objector <objetor de conciencia : conscientious objector>
oblea *nf* **1 :** wafer **2 hecho una oblea** *fam* **:** skinny as a rail
oblicuo, -cua *adj* **:** oblique — **oblicuamente** *adv*
obligación *nf, pl* **-ciones 1** DEBER **:** obligation, duty **2 :** bond, debenture
obligado, -da *adj* **1 :** obliged **2 :** obligatory, compulsory **3 :** customary
obligar {52} *vt* **:** to force, to require, to oblige — **obligarse** *vr* **:** to commit

oneself, to undertake (to do something)

obligatorio, -ria *adj* : mandatory, required, compulsory

obliterar *vt* : to obliterate, to destroy — **obliteración** *nf*

oblongo, -ga *adj* : oblong

obnubilación *nf, pl* **-ciones** : bewilderment, confusion

obnubilar *vt* : to daze, to bewilder

oboe[1] *nm* : oboe

oboe[2] *nmf* : oboist

obra *nf* **1** : work <obra de arte : work of art> <obra de teatro : play> <obra de consulta : reference work> **2** : deed <una buena obra : a good deed> **3** : construction work **4 obra maestra** : masterpiece **5 obras públicas** : public works **6 por obra de** : thanks to, because of

obrar *vt* : to work, to produce <obrar milagros : to work miracles> — *vi* **1** : to act, to behave <obrar con cautela : to act with caution> **2 obrar en poder de** : to be in possession of

obrero[1], **-ra** *adj* : working <la clase obrera : the working class>

obrero[2], **-ra** *n* : worker, laborer

obscenidad *nf* : obscenity

obsceno, -na *adj* : obscene

obscurecer, obscuridad, obscuro → **oscurecer, oscuridad, oscuro**

obsequiar *vt* REGALAR : to give, to present <lo obsequiaron con una placa : they presented him with a plaque>

obsequio *nm* REGALO : gift, present

obsequiosidad *nf* : attentiveness, deference

obsequioso, -sa *adj* : obliging, attentive

observación *nf, pl* **-ciones 1** : observation, watching **2** : remark, comment

observador[1], **-dora** *adj* : observant

observador[2], **-dora** *n* : observer, watcher

observancia *nf* : observance

observar *vt* **1** : to observe, to watch <estábamos observando a los niños : we were watching the children> **2** NOTAR : to notice **3** ACATAR : to obey, to abide by **4** COMENTAR : to remark, to comment

observatorio *nm* : observatory

obsesión *nf, pl* **-siones** : obsession

obsesionar *vt* : to obsess, to preoccupy excessively — **obsesionarse** *vr*

obsesivo, -va *adj* : obsessive

obseso, -sa *adj* : obsessed

obsolescencia *nf* DESUSO : obsolescence — **obsolescente** *adj*

obsoleto, -ta *adj* DESUSADO : obsolete

obstaculizar {21} *vt* IMPEDIR : to obstruct, to hinder

obstáculo *nm* IMPEDIMENTO : obstacle

obstante[1] *conj* **no obstante** : nevertheless, however

obstante[2] *prep* **no obstante** : in spite of, despite <mantuvo su inocencia no obstante la evidencia : he maintained his innocence in spite of the evidence>

obstar *v impers* **~ a** *or* **~ para** : to hinder, to prevent <eso no obsta para que me vaya : that doesn't prevent me from leaving>

obstetra *nmf* TOCÓLOGO : obstetrician

obstetricia *nf* : obstetrics

obstétrico, -ca *adj* : obstetric, obstetrical

obstinación *nf, pl* **-ciones 1** TERQUEDAD : obstinacy, stubbornness **2** : perseverance, tenacity

obstinado, -da *adj* **1** TERCO : obstinate, stubborn **2** : persistent — **obstinadamente** *adv*

obstinarse *vr* EMPECINARSE : to be obstinate, to be stubborn

obstrucción *nf, pl* **-ciones** : obstruction, blockage

obstruccionismo *nm* : obstructionism, filibustering

obstructor, -tora *adj* : obstructive

obstruir {41} *vt* BLOQUEAR : to obstruct, to block, to clog — **obstruirse** *vr*

obtención *nf* : obtaining, procurement

obtener {80} *vt* : to obtain, to secure, to get — **obtenible** *adj*

obturador *nm* : shutter (of a camera)

obtuso, -sa *adj* : obtuse

obtuvo, etc. → **obtener**

obviar *vt* : to get around (a difficulty), to avoid

obvio, -via *adj* : obvious — **obviamente** *adv*

oca *nf* : goose

ocasión *nf, pl* **-siones 1** : occasion, time **2** : opportunity, chance **3** : bargain **4 de ~** : secondhand **5 aviso de ocasión** *Mex* : classified ad

ocasional *adj* **1** : occasional **2** : chance, fortuitous

ocasionalmente *adv* **1** : occasionally **2** : by chance

ocasionar *vt* CAUSAR : to cause, to occasion

ocaso *nm* **1** ANOCHECER : sunset, sundown **2** DECADENCIA : decline, fall

occidental *adj* : western, occidental

occidente *nm* **1** OESTE, PONIENTE : west **2 el Occidente** : the West

oceánico, -ca *adj* : oceanic

océano *nm* : ocean

oceanografía *nf* : oceanography

oceanográfico, -ca *adj* : oceanographic

ocelote *nm* : ocelot

ochenta *adj & nm* : eighty

ochentavo[1], **-va** *adj* : eightieth

ochentavo[2] *nm* : eightieth (fraction)

ocho *adj & nm* : eight

ochocientos[1], **-tas** *adj* : eight hundred

ochocientos[2] *nms & pl* : eight hundred

ocio *nm* **1** : free time, leisure **2** : idleness

ociosidad *nf* : idleness, inactivity

ocioso, -sa *adj* **1** INACTIVO **:** idle, inactive **2** INÚTIL **:** pointless, useless

ocre *nm* **:** ocher

octágono *nm* **:** octagon — **octagonal** *adj*

octava *nf* **:** octave

octavo, -va *adj* **:** eighth — **octavo, -va** *n*

octeto *nm* **1 :** octet **2 :** byte

octogésimo[1], **-ma** *adj* **:** eightieth, eighty-

octogésimo[2], **-ma** *n* **:** eightieth, eighty- (in a series)

octubre *nm* **:** October

ocular *adj* **1 :** ocular, eye <músculos oculares : eye muscles> **2 testigo ocular :** eyewitness

oculista *nmf* **:** oculist, opthalmologist

ocultación *nf, pl* **-ciones :** concealment

ocultar *vt* ESCONDER **:** to conceal, to hide — **ocultarse** *vr*

oculto, -ta *adj* **1** ESCONDIDO **:** hidden, concealed **2 :** occult

ocupación *nf, pl* **-ciones 1 :** occupation, activity **2 :** occupancy **3** EMPLEO **:** employment, job

ocupacional *adj* **:** occupational, job-related

ocupado, -da *adj* **1 :** busy **2 :** taken <este asiento está ocupado : this seat is taken> **3 :** occupied <territorios ocupados : occupied territories> **4 señal de ocupado :** busy signal

ocupante *nmf* **:** occupant

ocupar *vt* **1 :** to occupy, to take possession of **2 :** to hold (a position) **3 :** to employ, to keep busy **4 :** to fill (space, time) **5 :** to inhabit (a dwelling) **6 :** to bother, to concern — **ocuparse** *vr* **~ de 1 :** to be concerned with **2 :** to take care of

ocurrencia *nf* **1 :** occurrence, event **2 :** witticism **3 :** bright idea

ocurrente *adj* **1 :** witty **2 :** clever, sharp

ocurrir *vi* **:** to occur, to happen — **ocurrirse** *vr* **~ a :** to occur to, to strike <se me ocurrió una mejor idea : a better idea occurred to me>

oda *nf* **:** ode

odiar *vt* ABOMINAR, ABORRECER **:** to hate

odio *nm* **:** hate, hatred

odioso, -sa *adj* ABOMINABLE, ABORRECIBLE **:** hateful, detestable

odisea *nf* **:** odyssey

odontología *nf* **:** dentistry, dental surgery

odontólogo, -ga *n* **:** dentist, dental surgeon

oeste[1] *adj* **1 :** west, western <la región oeste : the western region> **2 :** westerly

oeste[2] *nm* **1 :** west, West **2 :** west wind

ofender *vt* AGRAVIAR **:** to offend, to insult — *vi* **:** to offend, to be insulting — **ofenderse** *vr* **:** to take offense

ofensa *nf* **:** offense, insult

ofensiva *nf* **:** offensive <pasar a la ofensiva : to go on the offensive>

ofensivo, -va *adj* **:** offensive, insulting

ofensor, -sora *n* **:** offender

oferente *nmf* **1 :** supplier **2** FUENTE **:** source <un oferente no identificado : an unidentified source>

oferta *nf* **1 :** offer **2 :** sale, bargain <las camisas están en oferta : the shirts are on sale> **3 oferta y demanda :** supply and demand

ofertar *vt* OFRECER **:** to offer

oficial[1] *adj* **:** official — **oficialmente** *adv*

oficial[2] *nmf* **1 :** officer, police officer, commissioned officer (in the military) **2 :** skilled worker

oficializar {21} *vt* **:** to make official

oficiante *nmf* **:** celebrant

oficiar *vt* **1 :** to inform officially **2 :** to officiate at, to celebrate (Mass) — *vi* **~ de :** to act as

oficina *nf* **:** office

oficinista *nmf* **:** office worker

oficio *nm* **1 :** trade, profession <es electricista de oficio : he's an electrician by trade> **2 :** function, role **3 :** official communication **4 :** experience <tener oficio : to be experienced> **5 :** religious ceremony

oficioso, -sa *adj* **1** EXTRAOFICIAL **:** unofficial **2 :** officious — **oficiosamente** *adv*

ofrecer {53} *vt* **1 :** to offer **2 :** to provide, to give **3 :** to present (an appearance, etc.) — **ofrecerse** *vr* **1 :** to offer oneself, to volunteer **2 :** to open up, to present itself

ofrecimiento *nm* **:** offer, offering

ofrenda *nf* **:** offering

oftalmología *nf* **:** ophthalmology

oftalmólogo, -ga *n* **:** ophthalmologist

ofuscación *nf, pl* **-ciones :** blindness, confusion

ofuscar {72} *vt* **1 :** to blind, to dazzle **2** CONFUNDIR **:** to bewilder, to confuse — **ofuscarse** *vr* **~ con :** to be blinded by

ogro *nm* **:** ogre

ohm *nm, pl* **ohms :** ohm

ohmio *nm* → **ohm**

oídas *nfpl* **de ~ :** by hearsay

oído *nm* **1 :** ear <oído interno : inner ear> **2 :** hearing <duro de oído : hard of hearing> **3 tocar de oído :** to play by ear

oiga, etc. → **oír**

oír {50} *vi* **:** to hear — *vt* **1 :** to hear **2** ESCUCHAR **:** to listen to **3 :** to pay attention to, to heed **4 ¡oye!** *or* **¡oiga! :** listen!, excuse me!, look here!

ojal *nm* **:** buttonhole

ojalá *interj* **1 :** I hope so!, if only!, God willing! **2 :** I hope, I wish, hopefully <¡ojalá que le vaya bien! : I hope things go well for her!> <¡ojalá no llueva! : hopefully it won't rain!>

ojeada *nf* **:** glimpse, glance <echar una ojeada : to have a quick look>

ojear *vt* **:** to eye, to have a look at

ojete *nm* **:** eyelet

ojiva *nf* **:** warhead

ojo *nm* **1 :** eye **2 :** judgment, sharpness <tener buen ojo para : to be a good judge of, to have a good eye for> **3 :** hole (in cheese), eye (in a needle), center (of a storm) **4 :** span (of a bridge) **5 a ojos vistas :** openly, publicly **6 andar con ojo :** to be careful **7 ojo de agua** *Mex* **:** spring, source **8 ¡ojo! :** look out!, pay attention!

ola *nf* **1 :** wave **2 ola de calor :** heat wave

oleada *nf* **:** swell, wave <una oleada de protestas : a wave of protests>

oleaje *nm* **:** waves *pl*, surf

óleo *nm* **1 :** oil **2 :** oil painting

oleoducto *nm* **:** oil pipeline

oleoso, -sa *adj* **:** oily

oler {51} *vt* **1 :** to smell **2** INQUIRIR **:** to pry into, to investigate **3** AVERIGUAR **:** to smell out, to uncover — *vi* **1 :** to smell <huele mal : it smells bad> **2 ~ a :** to smell like, to smell of <huele a pino : it smells like pine> — **olerse** *vr* **:** to have a hunch, to suspect

olfatear *vt* **1 :** to sniff **2 :** to sense, to sniff out

olfativo, -va *adj* **:** olfactory

olfato *nm* **1 :** sense of smell **2 :** nose, instinct

oligarquía *nf* **:** oligarchy

olimpiada *or* **olimpíada** *nf* **:** Olympics *pl*, Olympic Games *pl*

olímpico, -ca *adj* **:** Olympic

olisquear *vt* **:** to sniff at

oliva *nf* ACEITUNA **:** olive <aceite de oliva : olive oil>

olivo *nm* **:** olive tree

olla *nf* **1 :** pot <olla de presión : pressure cooker> **2 olla podrida :** Spanish stew

olmeca *adj & nmf* **:** Olmec

olmo *nm* **:** elm

olor *nm* **:** smell, odor

oloroso, -sa *adj* **:** scented, fragrant

olote *nm Mex* **:** cob, corncob

olvidadizo, -za *adj* **:** forgetful, absent-minded

olvidar *vt* **1 :** to forget, to forget about <olvida lo que pasó : forget about what happened> **2 :** to leave behind <olvidé mi chequera en la casa : I left my checkbook at home> — **olvidarse** *vr* **:** to forget <se me olvidó mi cuaderno : I forgot my notebook> <se le olvidó llamarme : he forgot to call me>

olvido *nm* **1 :** forgetfulness **2 :** oblivion **3** DESCUIDO **:** oversight

omaní *adj & nmf* **:** Omani

ombligo *nm* **:** navel, belly button

ombudsman *nmfs & pl* **:** ombudsman

omelette *nmf* **:** omelet

ominoso, -sa *adj* **:** ominous — **ominosamente** *adv*

omisión *nf, pl* **-siones :** omission, neglect

omiso, -sa *adj* **1** NEGLIGENTE **:** neglectful **2 hacer caso omiso de :** to ignore

omitir *vt* **1 :** to omit, to leave out **2 :** to fail to <omitió dar su nombre : he failed to give his name>

ómnibus *n, pl* **-bus** *or* **-buses :** bus, coach

omnipotencia *nf* **:** omnipotence

omnipotente *adj* TODOPODEROSO **:** omnipotent, almighty

omnipresencia *nf* **:** ubiquity, omnipresence

omnipresente *adj* **:** ubiquitous, omnipresent

omnisciente *adj* **:** omniscient — **omnisciencia** *nf*

omnívoro, -ra *adj* **:** omnivorous

omóplato *or* **omoplato** *nm* **:** shoulder blade

once *adj & nm* **:** eleven

onceavo[1], -va *adj* **:** eleventh

onceavo[2] *nm* **:** eleventh (fraction)

onda *nf* **1 :** wave, ripple, undulation <onda sonora : sound wave> **2 :** wave (in hair) **3 :** scallop (on clothing) **4** *fam* **:** wavelength, understanding <agarrar la onda : to get the point> <en la onda : on the ball, with it> **5 ¿qué onda?** *fam* **:** what's happening?, what's up?

ondear *vi* **:** to ripple, to undulate, to flutter

ondulación *nf, pl* **-ciones :** undulation

ondulado, -da *adj* **1 :** wavy <pelo ondulado : wavy hair> **2 :** undulating

ondular *vt* **:** to wave (hair) — *vi* **:** to undulate, to ripple

oneroso, -sa *adj* GRAVOSO **:** onerous, burdensome

ónix *nm* **:** onyx

onza *nf* **:** ounce

opacar {72} *vt* **1 :** to make opaque or dull **2 :** to outshine, to overshadow

opacidad *nf* **1 :** opacity **2 :** dullness

opaco, -ca *adj* **1 :** opaque **2 :** dull

ópalo *nm* **:** opal

opción *nf, pl* **opciones 1** ALTERNATIVA **:** option, choice **2 :** right, chance <tener opción a : to be eligible for>

opcional *adj* **:** optional — **opcionalmente** *adv*

ópera *nf* **:** opera

operación *nf, pl* **-ciones 1 :** operation **2 :** transaction, deal

operacional *adj* **:** operational

operador, -dora *n* **1 :** operator **2 :** cameraman, projectionist

operante *adj* **:** operating, working

operar *vt* **1 :** to produce, to bring about **2** INTERVENIR **:** to operate on **3** *Mex* **:** to operate, to run (a machine) — *vi* **1 :** to operate, to function **2 :** to deal, to do business — **operarse** *vr* **1 :** to come about, to take place **2 :** to have an operation

operario, -ria *n* **:** laborer, worker

operático, -ca → **operístico**

operativo[1], -va *adj* **1 :** operating <capacidad operativa : operating capacity> **2 :** operative

operativo[2] *nm* : operation <operativo militar : military operation>
opereta *nf* : operetta
operístico, -ca *adj* : operatic
opiato *nm* : opiate
opinable *adj* : arguable
opinar *vi* **1** : to think, to have an opinion **2** : to express an opinion **3 opinar bien de** : to think highly of — *vt* : to think <opinamos lo mismo : we're of the same opinion, we're in agreement>
opinión *nf, pl* **-niones** : opinion, belief
opio *nm* : opium
oponente *nmf* : opponent
oponer {60} *vt* **1** CONTRAPONER : to oppose, to place against **2 oponer resistencia** : to resist, to put up a fight — **oponerse** *vr* **~ a** : to object to, to be against
oporto *nm* : port (wine)
oportunamente *adv* **1** : at the right time, opportunely **2** : appropriately
oportunidad *nf* : opportunity, chance
oportunismo *nm* : opportunism
oportunista[1] *adj* : opportunistic
oportunista[2] *nmf* : opportunist
oportuno, -na *adj* **1** : opportune, timely **2** : suitable, appropriate
oposición *nf, pl* **-ciones** : opposition
opositor, -tora *n* ADVERSARIO : opponent
oposum *nm* ZARIGÜEYA : opossum
opresión *nf, pl* **-siones 1** : oppression **2 opresión de pecho** : tightness in the chest
opresivo, -va *adj* : oppressive
opresor[1]**, -sora** *adj* : oppressive
opresor[2]**, -sora** *n* : oppressor
oprimir *vt* **1** : to oppress **2** : to press, to squeeze <oprima el botón : push the button>
oprobio *nm* : opprobrium, shame
optar *vi* **1 ~ por** : to opt for, to choose **2 ~ a** : to aspire to, to apply for <dos candidatos optan a la presidencia : two candidates are running for president>
optativo, -va *adj* FACULTATIVO : optional
óptica *nf* **1** : optics **2** : optician's shop **3** : viewpoint
óptico[1]**, -ca** *adj* : optical, optic
óptico[2]**, -ca** *n* : optician
optimismo *nm* : optimism
optimista[1] *adj* : optimistic
optimista[2] *nmf* : optimist
óptimo, -ma *adj* : optimum, optimal
optometría *nf* : optometry — **optometrista** *nmf*
opuesto[1] *pp* → **oponer**
opuesto[2] *adj* **1** : opposite, contrary **2** : opposed
opulencia *nf* : opulence — **opulento, -ta** *adj*
opus *nm* : opus
opuso, etc. → **oponer**
ora *conj* : now <los matices eran variados, ora verdes, ora ocres : the hues were varied, now green, now ocher>
oración *nf, pl* **-ciones 1** DISCURSO : oration, speech **2** PLEGARIA : prayer **3** FRASE : sentence, clause
oráculo *nm* : oracle
orador, -dora *n* : speaker, orator
oral *adj* : oral — **oralmente** *adv*
órale *interj Mex fam* **1** : sure!, OK! <¿los dos por cinco pesos? ¡órale! : both for five pesos? you've got a deal!> **2** : come on! <¡órale, vámonos! : come on, let's go!>
orangután *nm, pl* **-tanes** : orangutan
orar *vi* REZAR : to pray
oratoria *nf* : oratory
oratorio *nm* **1** CAPILLA : oratory, chapel **2** : oratorio
orbe *nm* **1** : orb, sphere **2** GLOBO : globe, world
órbita *nf* **1** : orbit **2** : eye socket **3** ÁMBITO : sphere, field
orbitador *nm* : space shuttle, orbiter
orbital *adj* : orbital
orden[1] *nm, pl* **órdenes 1** : order <todo está en orden : everything's in order> <por orden cronológico : in chronological order> **2 orden del día** : agenda (at a meeting) **3 orden público** : law and order
orden[2] *nf, pl* **órdenes 1** : order <una orden religiosa : a religious order> <una orden de tacos : an order of tacos> **2 orden de compra** : purchase order **3 estar a la orden del día** : to be the order of the day, to be prevalent
ordenación *nf, pl* **-ciones 1** : ordination **2** : ordering, organizing
ordenadamente *adv* : in an orderly fashion, neatly
ordenado, -da *adj* : orderly, neat
ordenador *nm Spain* : computer
ordenamiento *nm* **1** : ordering, organizing **2** : code (of laws)
ordenanza[1] *nf* REGLAMENTO : ordinance, regulation
ordenanza[2] *nm* : orderly (in the armed forces)
ordenar *vt* **1** MANDAR : to order, to command **2** ARREGLAR : to put in order, to arrange **3** : to ordain (a priest)
ordeñar *vt* : to milk
ordeño *nm* : milking
ordinal *nm* : ordinal (number)
ordinariamente *adv* **1** : usually **2** : coarsely
ordinariez *nf* : coarseness, vulgarity
ordinario, -ria *adj* **1** : ordinary **2** : coarse, common, vulgar **3 de ~** : usually
orear *vt* : to air
orégano *nm* : oregano
oreja *nf* : ear
orfanato *nm* : orphanage
orfanatorio *nm Mex* : orphanage
orfebre *nmf* : goldsmith, silversmith
orfebrería *nf* : articles of gold or silver

orfelinato *nm* : orphanage
orgánico, -ca *adj* : organic — **orgánicamente** *adv*
organigrama *nm* : organization chart, flowchart
organismo *nm* **1** : organism **2** : agency, organization
organista *nmf* : organist
organización *nf, pl* **-ciones** : organization
organizador¹, -dora *adj* : organizing
organizador², -dora *n* : organizer
organizar {21} *vt* : to organize, to arrange — **organizarse** *vr* : to get organized
organizativo, -va *adj* : organizational
órgano *nm* : organ
orgasmo *nm* : orgasm
orgía *nf* : orgy
orgullo *nm* : pride
orgulloso, -sa *adj* : proud — **orgullosamente** *adv*
orientación *nf, pl* **-ciones 1** : orientation **2** DIRECCIÓN : direction, course **3** GUÍA : guidance, direction
oriental¹ *adj* **1** : eastern **2** : oriental **3** *Arg, Uru* : Uruguayan
oriental² *nmf* **1** : Easterner **2** : Oriental **3** *Arg, Uru* : Uruguayan
orientar *vt* **1** : to orient, to position **2** : to guide, to direct — **orientarse** *vr* **1** : to orient oneself, to get one's bearings **2 ~ hacia** : to turn towards, to lean towards
oriente *nm* **1** : east, East **2 el Oriente** : the Orient
orífice *nmf* : goldsmith
orificio *nm* : orifice, opening
origen *nm, pl* **orígenes 1** : origin **2** : lineage, birth **3 dar origen a** : to give rise to **4 en su origen** : originally
original *adj & nm* : original — **originalmente** *adv*
originalidad *nf* : originality
originar *vt* : to originate, to give rise to — **originarse** *vr* : to originate, to begin
originario, -ria *adj* **~ de** : native of
originariamente *adv* : originally
orilla *nf* **1** BORDE : border, edge **2** : bank (of a river) **3** : shore
orillar *vt* **1** : to skirt, to go around **2** : to trim, to edge (cloth) **3** : to settle, to wind up **4** *Mex* : to pull over (a vehicle)
orín *nm* **1** HERRUMBRE : rust **2 orines** *nmpl* : urine
orina *nf* : urine
orinación *nf* : urination
orinal *nm* : urinal (vessel)
orinar *vi* : to urinate — **orinarse** *vr* : to wet oneself
oriol *nm* OROPÉNDOLA : oriole
oriundo, -da *adj* **~ de** : native of
orla *nf* : border, edging
orlar *vt* : to edge, to trim
ornamentación *nf, pl* **-ciones** : ornamentation
ornamental *adj* : ornamental
ornamentar *vt* ADORNAR : to ornament, to adorn
ornamento *nm* : ornament, adornment
ornar *vt* : to adorn, to decorate
ornitología *nf* : ornithology
ornitólogo, -ga *n* : ornithologist
ornitorrinco *nm* : platypus
oro *nm* : gold
orondo, -da *adj* **1** : rounded, potbellied (of a container) **2** *fam* : smug, self-satisfied
oropel *nm* : glitz, glitter, tinsel
oropéndola *nf* : oriole
orquesta *nf* : orchestra — **orquestal** *adj*
orquestar *vt* : to orchestrate — **orquestación** *nf*
orquídea *nf* : orchid
ortiga *nf* : nettle
ortodoncia *nf* : orthodontics
ortodoncista *nmf* : orthodontist
ortodoxia *nf* : orthodoxy
ortodoxo, -xa *adj* : orthodox
ortografía *nf* : orthography, spelling
ortográfico, -ca *adj* : orthographic, spelling
ortopedia *nf* : orthopedics
ortopedista *nmf* : orthopedist
oruga *nf* **1** : caterpillar **2** : track (of a tank, etc.)
orzuelo *nm* : sty, stye (in the eye)
os *pron pl* (*objective form of* **vosotros**) *Spain* **1** : you, to you **2** : yourselves, to yourselves **3** : each other, to each other
osa *nf* → **oso**
osadía *nf* **1** VALOR : boldness, daring **2** AUDACIA : audacity, nerve
osado, -da *adj* **1** : bold, daring **2** : audacious, impudent — **osadamente** *adv*
osamenta *nf* : skeletal remains *pl*, bones *pl*
osar *vi* : to dare
oscilación *nf, pl* **-ciones 1** : oscillation **2** : fluctuation **3** : vacillation, wavering
oscilar *vi* **1** BALANCEARSE : to swing, to sway, to oscillate **2** FLUCTUAR : to fluctuate **3** : to vacillate, to waver
oscuramente *adv* : obscurely
oscurecer {53} *vt* **1** : to darken **2** : to obscure, to confuse, to cloud **3 al oscurecer** : at dusk, at nightfall — *v impers* : to grow dark, to get dark — **oscurecerse** *vr* : to darken, to dim
oscuridad *nf* **1** : darkness **2** : obscurity
oscuro, -ra *adj* **1** : dark **2** : obscure **3 a oscuras** : in the dark, in darkness
óseo, ósea *adj* : skeletal, bony
ósmosis *or* **osmosis** *nf* : osmosis
oso, osa *n* **1** : bear **2 Osa Mayor** : Big Dipper **3 Osa Menor** : Little Dipper **4 oso blanco** : polar bear **5 oso hormiguero** : anteater **6 oso de peluche** : teddy bear
ostensible *adj* : ostensible, apparent — **ostensiblemente** *adv*
ostentación *nf, pl* **-ciones** : ostentation, display

ostentar *vt* **1 :** to display, to flaunt **2** POSEER **:** to have, to hold <ostenta el récord mundial : he holds the world record>

ostentoso, -sa *adj* **:** ostentatious, showy — **ostentosamente** *adv*

osteópata *nmf* **:** osteopath

osteopatía *n* **:** osteopathy

osteoporosis *nf* **:** osteoporosis

ostión *nm, pl* **ostiones 1** *Mex* **:** oyster **2** *Chile* **:** scallop

ostra *nf* **:** oyster

ostracismo *nm* **:** ostracism

otear *vt* **:** to scan, to survey, to look over

otero *nm* **:** knoll, hillock

otomana *nf* **:** ottoman

otoñal *adj* **:** autumn, autumnal

otoño *nm* **:** autumn, fall

otorgamiento *nm* **:** granting, awarding

otorgar {52} *vt* **1 :** to grant, to award **2 :** to draw up, to frame (a legal document)

otro[1]**, otra** *adj* **1 :** other **2 :** another <en otro juego, ellos ganaron : in another game, they won> **3 otra vez :** again **4 de otra manera :** otherwise **5 otra parte :** elsewhere **6 en otro tiempo :** once, formerly

otro[2]**, otra** *pron* **1 :** another one <dame otro : give me another> **2 :** other one <el uno o el otro : one or the other> **3 los otros, las otras :** the others, the rest <me dio una y se quedó con las otras : he gave me one and kept the rest>

ovación *nf, pl* **-ciones :** ovation

ovacionar *vt* **:** to cheer, to applaud

oval → **ovalado**

ovalado, -da *adj* **:** oval

óvalo *nm* **:** oval

ovárico, -ca *adj* **:** ovarian

ovario *nm* **:** ovary

oveja *nf* **1 :** sheep, ewe **2 oveja negra :** black sheep

overol *nm* **:** overalls *pl*

ovillar *vt* **:** to roll into a ball

ovillo *nm* **1 :** ball (of yarn) **2 :** tangle

ovni *or* **OVNI** *nm* (*objeto volador no identificado*) **:** UFO

ovoide *adj* **:** ovoid, ovoidal

ovulación *nf, pl* **-ciones :** ovulation

ovular *vi* **:** to ovulate

óvulo *nm* **:** ovum

oxidación *nf, pl* **-ciones 1 :** oxidation **2 :** rusting

oxidado, -da *adj* **:** rusty

oxidar *vt* **1 :** to cause to rust **2 :** to oxidize — **oxidarse** *vr* **:** to rust, to become rusty

óxido *nm* **1** HERRUMBRE, ORÍN **:** rust **2 :** oxide

oxigenar *vt* **1 :** to oxygenate **2 :** to bleach (hair)

oxígeno *nm* **:** oxygen

oxiuro *nm* **:** pinworm

oye, etc. → **oír**

oyente *nmf* **1 :** listener **2 :** auditor, auditing student

ozono *nm* **:** ozone

P

p *nf* **:** seventeenth letter of the Spanish alphabet

pabellón *nm, pl* **-llones 1 :** pavilion **2 :** summerhouse, lodge **3 :** flag (of a vessel)

pabilo *nm* MECHA **:** wick

paca *nf* FARDO **:** bale

pacana *nf* **:** pecan

pacer {48} *v* **:** to graze, to pasture

paces → **paz**

pachanga *nf fam* **:** party, bash

paciencia *nf* **:** patience

paciente *adj & nmf* **:** patient — **pacientemente** *adv*

pacificación *nf, pl* **-ciones :** pacification

pacíficamente *adv* **:** peacefully, peaceably

pacificar {72} *vt* **:** to pacify, to calm — **pacificarse** *vr* **:** to calm down, to abate

pacífico, -ca *adj* **:** peaceful, pacific

pacifismo *nm* **:** pacifism

pacifista *adj & nmf* **:** pacifist

pacotilla *nf* **de ~ :** shoddy, trashy

pactar *vt* **:** to agree on — *vi* **:** to come to an agreement

pacto *nm* CONVENIO **:** pact, agreement

padecer {53} *vt* **:** to suffer, to endure — *vi* ADOLECER **~ de :** to suffer from

padecimiento *nm* **1 :** suffering **2 :** ailment, condition

padrastro *nm* **1 :** stepfather **2 :** hangnail

padre[1] *adj Mex fam* **:** fantastic, great

padre[2] *nm* **1 :** father **2 padres** *nmpl* **:** parents

padrenuestro *nm* **:** Lord's Prayer, paternoster

padrino *nm* **1 :** godfather **2 :** best man **3 :** sponsor, patron

padrón *nm, pl* **padrones :** register, roll <padrón municipal : city register>

paella *nf* **:** paella

paga *nf* **1 :** payment **2 :** pay, wages *pl*

pagadero, -ra *adj* **:** payable

pagado, -da *adj* **1 :** paid **2 pagado de sí mismo :** self-satisfied, smug

pagador, -dora *n* **:** payer

paganismo *nm* **:** paganism

pagano, -na *adj & n* **:** pagan

pagar {52} *vt* **:** to pay, to pay for, to repay — *vi* **:** to pay

pagaré *nm* VALE **:** promissory note, IOU

página *nf* **:** page

pago *nm* **1 :** payment **2 en pago de :** in return for
pagoda *nf* **:** pagoda
pague, etc. → **pagar**
país *nm* **1** NACIÓN **:** country, nation **2** REGIÓN **:** region, territory
paisaje *nm* **:** scenery, landscape
paisano, -na *n* COMPATRIOTA **:** compatriot, fellow countryman
paja *nf* **1 :** straw **2** *fam* **:** trash, tripe
pajar *nm* **:** hayloft, haystack
pajarera *nf* **:** aviary
pájaro *nm* **:** bird <pájaro cantor : songbird> <pájaro bobo : penguin> <pájaro carpintero : woodpecker>
pajita *nf* **:** (drinking) straw
pajote *nm* **:** straw, mulch
pala *nf* **1 :** shovel, spade **2 :** blade (of an oar or a rotor) **3 :** paddle, racket
palabra *nf* **1** VOCABLO **:** word **2** PROMESA **:** word, promise <un hombre de palabra : a man of his word> **3** HABLA **:** speech **4 :** right to speak <tener la palabra : to have the floor>
palabrería *nf* **:** empty talk
palabrota *nf* **:** swearword
palacio *nm* **1 :** palace, mansion **2 palacio de justicia :** courthouse
paladar *nm* **1 :** palate **2** GUSTO **:** taste
paladear *vt* SABOREAR **:** to savor
paladín *nm, pl* **-dines :** champion, defender
palanca *nf* **1 :** lever, crowbar **2** *fam* **:** leverage, influence **3 palanca de cambio** *or* **palanca de velocidad :** gearshift
palangana *nf* **:** washbowl
palanqueta *nf* **:** jimmy, small crowbar
palco *nm* **:** box (in a theater or stadium)
palear *vt* **1 :** to shovel **2 :** to paddle
palenque *nm* **1** ESTACADA **:** stockade, palisade **2 :** arena, ring
paleontología *nf* **:** paleontology
paleontólogo, -ga *n* **:** paleontologist
palestino, -na *adj & n* **:** Palestinian
palestra *nf* **:** arena <salir a la palestra : to join the fray>
paleta *nf* **1 :** palette **2 :** trowel **3 :** spatula **4 :** blade, vane **5 :** paddle **6** *CA, Mex* **:** lollipop, Popsicle—
paletilla *nf* **:** shoulder blade
paliar *vt* MITIGAR **:** to alleviate, to palliate
paliativo[1], -va *adj* **:** palliative
paliativo[2] *nm* **:** palliative
palidecer {53} *vi* **:** to turn pale
palidez *nf, pl* **-deces :** paleness, pallor
pálido, -da *adj* **:** pale
palillo *nm* **1** MONDADIENTES **:** toothpick **2 palillos** *nmpl* **:** chopsticks **3 palillo de tambor :** drumstick
paliza *nf* **:** beating, pummeling <darle una paliza a : to beat, to thrash>
palma *nf* **1 :** palm (of the hand) **2 :** palm (tree or leaf) **3 batir palmas :** to clap, to applaud **4 llevarse la palma** *fam* **:** to take the cake
palmada *nf* **1 :** pat **2 :** slap **3 :** clap
palmarés *nm* **:** record (of achievements)
palmario, -ria *adj* MANIFIESTO **:** clear, manifest
palmeado, -da *adj* **:** webbed
palmear *vt* **:** to slap on the back — *vi* **:** to clap, to applaud
palmera *nf* **:** palm tree
palmo *nm* **1 :** span, small amount **2 palmo a palmo :** bit by bit, inch by inch **3 dejar con un palmo de narices :** to disappoint
palmotear *vi* **:** to applaud
palmoteo *nm* **:** clapping, applause
palo *nm* **1 :** stick, pole, post **2 :** shaft, handle <palo de escoba : broomstick> **3 :** mast, spar **4 :** wood **5 :** blow (with a stick) **6 :** suit (of cards)
paloma *nf* **1 :** pigeon, dove **2 paloma mensajera :** carrier pigeon
palomilla *nf* **:** moth
palomitas *nfpl* **:** popcorn
palpable *adj* **:** palpable, tangible
palpar *vt* **:** to feel, to touch
palpitación *nf, pl* **-ciones :** palpitation
palpitar *vi* **:** to palpitate, to throb — **palpitante** *adj*
palta *nf* **:** avocado
paludismo *nm* MALARIA **:** malaria
palurdo, -da *n* **:** boor, yokel, bumpkin
pampa *nf* **:** pampa
pampeano, -na *adj* **:** pampean, pampas
pampero → **pampeano**
pan *nm* **1 :** bread **2 :** loaf of bread **3 :** cake, bar <pan de jabón : bar of soap> **4 pan dulce** *CA, Mex* **:** traditional pastry **5 pan tostado :** toast **6 ser pan comido** *fam* **:** to be a piece of cake, to be a cinch
pana *nf* **:** corduroy
panacea *nf* **:** panacea
panadería *nf* **:** bakery, bread shop
panadero, -ra *n* **:** baker
panal *nm* **:** honeycomb
panameño, -ña *adj & n* **:** Panamanian
pancarta *nf* **:** placard, sign
pancita *nf Mex* **:** tripe
páncreas *nms & pl* **:** pancreas
panda *nmf* **:** panda
pandeado, -da *adj* **:** warped
pandearse *vr* **1 :** to warp **2 :** to bulge, to sag
pandemonio *or* **pandemónium** *nm* **:** pandemonium
pandereta *nf* **:** tambourine
pandero *nm* **:** tambourine
pandilla *nf* **1 :** group, clique **2 :** gang
panecito *nm* **:** roll, bread roll
panegírico[1], -ca *adj* **:** eulogistic, panegyrical
panegírico[2] *nm* **:** eulogy, panegyric
panel *nm* **:** panel — **panelista** *nmf*
panera *nf* **:** bread box
panfleto *nm* **:** pamphlet
pánico *nm* **:** panic
panorama *nm* **1** VISTA **:** panorama, view **2 :** scene, situation <el pa-

norama nacional : the national scene> 3 PERSPECTIVA : outlook

panorámico, -ca *adj* : panoramic

panqueque *nm* : pancake

pantaletas *nfpl* : panties

pantalla *nf* **1** : screen, monitor **2** : lampshade **3** : fan

pantalón *nm, pl* **-lones 1** : pants *pl,* trousers *pl* **2 pantalones vaqueros** : jeans **3 pantalones de mezclilla** *Chile, Mex* : jeans **4 pantalones de montar** : jodhpurs

pantano *nm* **1** : swamp, marsh, bayou **2** : reservoir **3** : obstacle, difficulty

pantanoso, -sa *adj* **1** : marshy, swampy **2** : difficult, thorny

panteón *nm, pl* **-teones 1** CEMENTERIO : cemetery **2** : pantheon, mausoleum

pantera *nf* : panther

pantimedias *nfpl Mex* : panty hose

pantomima *nf* : pantomime

pantorrilla *nf* : calf (of the leg)

pantufla *nf* ZAPATILLA : slipper

panza *nf* BARRIGA : belly, paunch

panzón, -zona *adj, mpl* **panzones** : potbellied, paunchy

pañal *nm* : diaper

pañería *nf* **1** : cloth, material **2** : fabric store

pañito *nm* : doily

paño *nm* **1** : cloth **2** : rag, dust cloth **3 paño de cocina** : dishcloth **4 paño higiénico** : sanitary napkin

pañuelo *nm* **1** : handkerchief **2** : scarf

papa¹ *nm* : pope

papa² *nf* **1** : potato **2 papa dulce** : sweet potato **3 papas fritas** : potato chips, french fries **4 papas a la francesa** *Mex* : french fries

papá *nm fam* **1** : dad, pop **2 papás** *nmpl* : parents, folks

papada *nf* **1** : double chin, jowl **2** : dewlap

papagayo *nm* LORO : parrot

papal *adj* : papal

papalote *nm Mex* : kite

papaya *nf* : papaya

papel *nm* **1** : paper, piece of paper **2** : role, part **3 papel de estaño** : tinfoil **4 papel de empapelar** *or* **papel pintado** : wallpaper **5 papel higiénico** : toilet paper **6 papel de lija** : sandpaper

papeleo *nm* : paperwork, red tape

papelera *nf* : wastebasket

papelería *nf* : stationery store

papelero, -ra *adj* : paper

papeleta *nf* **1** : ballot **2** : ticket, slip

paperas *nfpl* : mumps

papi *nm fam* : daddy, papa

papilla *nf* **1** : pap, mash **2 hacer papilla** : to beat to a pulp

papiro *nm* : papyrus

paquete *nm* BULTO : package, parcel

paquistaní *adj & nmf* : Pakistani

par¹ *adj* : even (in number)

par² *nm* **1** : pair, couple **2** : equal, peer <sin par : matchless, peerless> **3** : par (in golf) **4** : rafter **5 de par en par** : wide open

par³ *nf* **1** : par <por encima de la par : above par> **2 a la par que** : at the same time as, as well as <interesante a la par que instructivo : both interesting and informative>

para *prep* **1** : for <para ti : for you> <alta para su edad : tall for her age> <una cita para el lunes : an appointment for Monday> **2** : to, towards <para la derecha : to the right> <van para el río : they're heading towards the river> **3** : to, in order to <lo hace para molestarte : he does it to annoy you> **4** : around, by (a time) <para mañana estarán listos : they'll be ready by tomorrow> **5 para adelante** : forwards **6 para atrás** : backwards **7 para que** : so, so that, in order that <te lo digo para que sepas : I'm telling you so you'll know>

parabién *nm, pl* **-bienes** : congratulations *pl*

parábola *nf* **1** : parable **2** : parabola

parabrisas *nms & pl* : windshield

paracaídas *nms & pl* : parachute

paracaidista *nmf* **1** : parachutist **2** : paratrooper

parachoques *nms & pl* : bumper

parada *nf* **1** : stop <parada de autobús : bus stop> **2** : catch, save, parry (in sports) **3** DESFILE : parade

paradero *nm* : whereabouts

paradigma *nm* : paradigm

parado, -da *adj* **1** : motionless, idle, stopped **2** : standing (up) **3** : confused, bewildered **4 bien (mal) parado** : in good (bad) shape <salió bien parado : it turned out well for him>

paradoja *nf* : paradox

paradójico, -ca *adj* : paradoxical

parafernalia *nf* : paraphernalia

parafina *nf* : paraffin

parafrasear *vt* : to paraphrase

paráfrasis *nfs & pl* : paraphrase

paraguas *nms & pl* : umbrella

paraguayo, -ya *adj & n* : Paraguayan

paraíso *nm* **1** : paradise, heaven **2 paraíso fiscal** : tax shelter

paraje *nm* : spot, place

paralelismo *nm* : parallelism, similarity

paralelo¹, -la *adj* : parallel

paralelo² *nm* : parallel

paralelogramo *nm* : parallelogram

parálisis *nfs & pl* **1** : paralysis **2** : standstill **3 parálisis cerebral** : cerebral palsy

paralítico, -ca *adj & n* : paralytic

paralizar {21} *vt* **1** : to paralyze **2** : to bring to a standstill — **paralizarse** *vr*

parámetro *nm* : parameter

páramo *nm* : barren plateau, moor

parangón *nm, pl* **-gones 1** : comparison **2 sin ~** : incomparable

paraninfo *nm* : auditorium, assembly hall

paranoia *nf* **:** paranoia
paranoico, -ca *adj & n* **:** paranoid
parapeto *nm* **:** parapet, rampart
parapléjico, -ca *adj & n* **:** paraplegic
parar *vt* **1** DETENER **:** to stop **2 :** to stand, to prop — *vi* **1** CESAR **:** to stop **2 :** to stay, to put up **3 ir a parar :** to end up, to wind up — **pararse** *vr* **1 :** to stop **2** ATASCARSE **:** to stall (out) **3 :** to stand up, to get up
pararrayos *nms & pl* **:** lightning rod
parasitario, -ria *adj* **:** parasitic
parasitismo *nm* **:** parasitism
parásito *nm* **:** parasite
parasol *nm* SOMBRILLA **:** parasol
parcela *nf* **:** parcel, tract of land
parcelar *vt* **:** to parcel (land)
parchar *vt* **:** to patch, to patch up
parche *nm* **:** patch
parcial *adj* **:** partial — **parcialmente** *adv*
parcialidad *nf* **:** partiality, bias
parco, -ca *adj* **1 :** sparing, frugal **2 :** moderate, temperate
pardo, -da *adj* **:** brownish grey
pardusco → **pardo**
parecer[1] {53} *vi* **1 :** to seem, to look, to appear to be <parece bien fácil : it looks very easy> <así parece : so it seems> <pareces una princesa : you look like a princess> **2 :** to think, to have an opinion <me parece que sí : I think so> **3 :** to like, to be in agreement <si te parece : if you like, if it's all right with you> — **parecerse** *vr* **~ a :** to resemble
parecer[2] *nm* **1** OPINIÓN **:** opinion **2** ASPECTO **:** appearance <al parecer : apparently>
parecido[1], **-da** *adj* **1 :** similar, alike **2 bien parecido :** good-looking
parecido[2] *nm* **:** resemblance, similarity
pared *nf* **:** wall
pareja *nf* **1 :** couple, pair **2 :** partner, mate
parejo, -ja *adj* **1 :** even, smooth, level **2 :** equal, similar
parentela *nf* **:** relations *pl*, kinfolk
parentesco *nm* **:** relationship, kinship
paréntesis *nms & pl* **1 :** parenthesis **2 :** digression
parentético, -ca *adj* **:** parenthetic, parenthetical
paria *nmf* **:** pariah, outcast
paridad *nf* **:** parity, equality
pariente *nmf* **:** relative, relation
parir *vi* **:** to give birth — *vt* **:** to give birth to, to bear
parking *nm* **:** parking lot
parlamentar *vi* **:** to talk, to parley
parlamentario[1], **-ria** *adj* **:** parliamentary
parlamentario[2], **-ria** *n* **:** member of parliament
parlamento *nm* **1 :** parliament **2 :** negotiations *pl*, talks *pl*
parlanchín[1], **-china** *adj, mpl* **-chines :** chatty, talkative
parlanchín[2], **-china** *n, mpl* **-chines :** chatterbox
parlante *nm* ALTOPARLANTE **:** loudspeaker
parlotear *vi fam* **:** to gab, to chat, to prattle
parloteo *nm fam* **:** prattle, chatter
paro *nm* **1** HUELGA **:** strike **2 :** stoppage, stopping **3 paro forzoso :** layoff
parodia *nf* **:** parody
parodiar *vt* **:** to parody
parpadear *vi* **1 :** to blink **2 :** to flicker
parpadeo *nm* **1 :** blink, blinking **2 :** flickering
párpado *nm* **:** eyelid
parque *nm* **1 :** park **2 parque de atracciones :** amusement park
parquear *vt* **:** to park — **parquearse** *vr*
parqueo *nm* **:** parking
parquet *or* **parqué** *nm* **:** parquet
parquímetro *nm* **:** parking meter
parra *nf* **:** vine, grapevine
párrafo *nm* **:** paragraph
parranda *nf fam* **:** party, spree
parrilla *nf* **1 :** broiler, grill **2 :** grate
parrillada *nf* BARBACOA **:** barbecue
párroco *nm* **:** parish priest
parroquia *nf* **1 :** parish **2 :** parish church **3 :** customers *pl*, clientele
parroquial *adj* **:** parochial
parroquiano, -na *nm* **1 :** parishioner **2 :** customer, patron
parsimonia *nf* **1 :** calm **2 :** parsimony, thrift
parsimonioso, -sa *adj* **1 :** calm, unhurried **2 :** parsimonious, thrifty
parte[1] *nm* **:** report, dispatch
parte[2] *nf* **1 :** part, share **2 :** part, place <en alguna parte : somewhere> <por todas partes : everywhere> **3 :** party (in negotiations, etc.) **4 de parte de :** on behalf of **5 ¿de parte de quién? :** may I ask who's calling? **6 tomar parte :** to take part
partero, -ra *n* **:** midwife
partición *nf, pl* **-ciones :** division, sharing
participación *nf, pl* **-ciones 1 :** participation **2 :** share, interest **3 :** announcement, notice
participante *nmf* **1 :** participant **2 :** competitor, entrant
participar *vi* **1 :** to participate, to take part **2 ~ en :** to have a share in — *vt* **:** to announce, to notify
partícipe *nmf* **:** participant
participio *nm* **:** participle
partícula *nf* **:** particle
particular[1] *adj* **1 :** particular, specific **2 :** private, personal **3 :** special, unique
particular[2] *nm* **1 :** matter, detail **2 :** individual
particularidad *nf* **:** characteristic, peculiarity
particularizar {21} *vt* **1 :** to distinguish, to characterize **2 :** to specify

partida *nf* **1 :** departure **2 :** item, entry **3 :** certificate <partida de nacimiento : birth certificate> **4 :** game, match, hand **5 :** party, group

partidario, -ria *n* **:** follower, supporter

partido *nm* **1 :** (political) party **2 :** game, match <partido de futbol : soccer game> **3** APOYO **:** support, following **4** PROVECHO **:** profit, advantage <sacar partido de : to profit from>

partir *vt* **1 :** to cut, to split **2 :** to break, to crack **3 :** to share (out), to divide — *vi* **1 :** to leave, to depart **2 ~ de :** to start from **3 a partir de :** as of, from <a partir de hoy : as of today> — **partirse** *vr* **1 :** to smash, to split open **2 :** to chap

partisano, -na *adj & n* **:** partisan

partitura *nf* **:** (musical) score

parto *nm* **1 :** childbirth, delivery, labor <estar de parto : to be in labor> **2 :** product, creation, brainchild

parvulario *nm* **:** nursery school

párvulo, -la *n* **:** toddler, preschooler

pasa *nf* **1 :** raisin **2 pasa de Corinto :** currant

pasable *adj* **:** passable, tolerable — **pasablemente** *adv*

pasada *nf* **1 :** passage, passing **2 :** pass, wipe, coat (of paint) **3 de ~ :** in passing **4 mala pasada :** dirty trick

pasadizo *nm* **:** passageway, corridor

pasado^{1}, -da *adj* **1 :** past <el año pasado : last year> <pasado mañana : the day after tomorrow> <pasadas las siete : after seven o'clock> **2 :** stale, bad, overripe **3 :** old-fashioned, out-of-date **4 :** overripe, slightly spoiled

pasado^{2} *nm* **:** past

pasador *nm* **1 :** bolt, latch **2 :** barrette **3** *Mex* **:** bobby pin

pasaje *nm* **1 :** ticket (for travel) **2** TARIFA **:** fare **3 :** passageway **4 :** passengers *pl*

pasajero^{1}, -ra *adj* **:** passing, fleeting

pasajero^{2}, -ra *n* **:** passenger

pasamanos *nms & pl* **1 :** handrail **2 :** banister

pasante *nmf* **:** assistant

pasaporte *nm* **:** passport

pasar *vi* **1 :** to pass, to go by, to come by **2 :** to come in, to enter <¿se puede pasar? : may we come in?> **3 :** to happen <¿qué pasa? : what's happening?, what's going on?> **4 :** to manage, to get by **5 :** to be over, to end **6 ~ de :** to exceed, to go beyond **7 ~ por :** to pretend to be — *vt* **1 :** to pass, to give <¿me pasas la sal? : would you pass me the salt?> **2 :** to pass (a test) **3 :** to go over, to cross **4 :** to spend (time) **5 :** to tolerate **6 :** to go through, to suffer **7 :** to show (a movie, etc.) **8 :** to overtake, to pass, to surpass **9 :** to pass over, to wipe up **10 pasarlo bien** *or* **pasarla bien :** to have a good time **11 pasarlo mal** *or* **pasarla mal :** to have a bad time, to have a hard time **12 pasar por alto :** to overlook, to omit — **pasarse** *vr* **1 :** to move, to pass, to go away **2 :** to slip one's mind, to forget **3 :** to go too far

pasarela *nf* **1 :** gangplank **2 :** footbridge **3 :** runway, catwalk

pasatiempo *nm* **:** pastime, hobby

Pascua *nf* **1 :** Easter **2 :** Passover **3 :** Christmas **4 Pascuas** *nfpl* **:** Christmas season

pase *nm* **1** PERMISO **:** pass, permit **2 pase de abordar** *Mex* **:** boarding pass

pasear *vi* **:** to take a walk, to go for a ride — *vt* **1 :** to take for a walk **2 :** to parade around, to show off — **pasearse** *vr* **:** to walk around

paseo *nm* **1 :** walk, stroll **2 :** ride **3** EXCURSIÓN **:** outing, trip

pasiflora *nf* **:** passionflower

pasillo *nm* CORREDOR **:** hallway, corridor, aisle

pasión *nf, pl* **pasiones :** passion

pasional *adj* **:** passionate <crimen pasional : crime of passion>

pasionaria *nf* → **pasiflora**

pasivo^{1}, -va *adj* **:** passive — **pasivamente** *adv*

pasivo^{2} *nm* **1 :** liability <activos y pasivos : assets and liabilities> **2 :** debit side (of an account)

pasmado, -da *adj* **:** stunned, flabbergasted

pasmar *vt* **:** to amaze, to stun — **pasmarse** *vr*

pasmo *nm* **1 :** shock, astonishment **2 :** wonder, marvel

pasmoso, -sa *adj* **:** incredible, amazing — **pasmosamente** *adv*

paso^{1}, -sa *adj* **:** dried <ciruela pasa : prune>

paso^{2} *nm* **1 :** passage, passing <de paso : in passing, on the way> **2 :** way, path <abrirse paso : to make one's way> **3 :** crossing <paso de peatones : crosswalk> <paso a desnivel : underpass> <paso elevado : overpass> **4 :** step <paso a paso : step by step> **5 :** pace, gait <a buen paso : quickly, at a good rate>

pasta *nf* **1 :** paste <pasta de dientes *or* pasta dental : toothpaste> **2 :** pasta **3 :** pastry dough **4 libro en pasta dura :** hardcover book **5 tener pasta de :** to have the makings of

pastar *vi* **:** to graze — *vt* **:** to put to pasture

pastel^{1} *adj* **:** pastel

pastel^{2} *nm* **1 :** cake <pastel de cumpleaños : birthday cake> **2 :** pie, turnover **3 :** pastel

pastelería *nf* **:** pastry shop

pasteurización *nf, pl* **-ciones :** pasteurization

pasteurizar {21} *vt* **:** to pasteurize

pastilla *nf* **1** COMPRIMIDO, PÍLDORA **:** pill, tablet **2 :** lozenge <pastilla para la tos

: cough drop> **3** : cake (of soap), bar (of chocolate)
pastizal *nm* : pasture, grazing land
pasto *nm* **1** : pasture **2** HIERBA : grass, lawn
pastor, -tora *n* **1** : shepherd, shepherdess *f* **2** : minister, pastor
pastoral *adj & nf* : pastoral
pastorear *vt* : to shepherd, to tend
pastorela *nf* **1** : pastoral, pastourelle **2** *Mex* : a traditional Christmas play
pastoso, -sa *adj* **1** : pasty, doughy **2** : smooth, mellow (of sounds)
pata *nf* **1** : paw, leg (of an animal) **2** : foot, leg (of furniture) **3 patas de gallo** : crow's-feet **4 meter la pata** *fam* : to put one's foot in it, to make a blunder
patada *nf* **1** PUNTAPIÉ : kick **2** : stamp (of the foot)
patalear *vi* **1** : to kick **2** : to stamp one's feet
pataleta *nf fam* : tantrum
patán[1] *adj, pl* **patanes** : boorish, crude
patán[2] *nm, pl* **patanes** : boor, lout
patata *nf Spain* : potato
patear *vt* : to kick — *vi* : to stamp one's foot
patentar *vt* : to patent
patente[1] *adj* EVIDENTE : obvious, patent — **patentemente** *adv*
patente[2] *nf* : patent
paternal *adj* : fatherly, paternal
paternidad *nf* **1** : fatherhood, paternity **2** : parenthood **3** : authorship
paterno, -na *adj* : paternal <abuela paterna : paternal grandmother>
patético, -ca *adj* : pathetic, moving
patetismo *nm* : pathos
patíbulo *nm* : gallows, scaffold
patillas *nfpl* : sideburns
patín *nm, pl* **patines** : skate <patín de ruedas : roller skate>
patinador, -dora *n* : skater
patinaje *nm* : skating
patinar *vi* **1** : to skate **2** : to skid, to slip **3** *fam* : to slip up, to blunder
patinazo *nm* **1** : skid **2** *fam* : blunder, slipup
patineta *nf* **1** : scooter **2** : skateboard
patinete *nm* : scooter
patio *nm* **1** : courtyard, patio **2 patio de recreo** : playground
patito, -ta *n* : duckling
pato, -ta *n* **1** : duck **2 pato real** : mallard **3 pagar el pato** *fam* : to take the blame
patología *nf* : pathology
patológico, -ca *adj* : pathological
patólogo, -ga *n* : pathologist
patraña *nf* : tall tale, humbug, nonsense
patria *nf* : native land
patriarca *nm* : patriarch — **patriarcal** *adj*
patriarcado *nm* : patriarchy
patrimonio *nm* : patrimony, legacy
patrio, -tria *adj* **1** : native, home <suelo patrio : native soil> **2** : paternal
patriota[1] *adj* : patriotic
patriota[2] *nmf* : patriot
patriotería *nf* : jingoism, chauvinism
patriotero[1], -ra *adj* : jingoistic, chauvinistic
patriotero[2], -ra *n* : jingoist, chauvinist
patriótico, -ca *adj* : patriotic
patriotismo *nm* : patriotism
patrocinador, -dora *n* : sponsor, patron
patrocinar *vt* : to sponsor
patrocinio *nm* : sponsorship, patronage
patrón[1], -trona *n, mpl* **patrones 1** JEFE : boss **2** : patron saint
patrón[2] *nm, pl* **patrones 1** : standard **2** : pattern (in sewing)
patronal *adj* **1** : management, employers' <sindicato patronal : employers' association> **2** : pertaining to a patron saint <fiesta patronal : patron saint's day>
patronato *nm* **1** : board, council **2** : foundation, trust
patrono, -na *n* **1** : employer **2** : patron saint
patrulla *nf* **1** : patrol **2** : police car, cruiser
patrullar *v* : to patrol
patrullero *nm* **1** : police car **2** : patrol boat
paulatino, -na *adj* : gradual
paupérrimo, -ma *adj* : destitute, poverty-stricken
pausa *nf* : pause, break
pausado[1] *adv* : slowly, deliberately <habla más pausado : speak more slowly>
pausado[2], -da *adj* : slow, deliberate — **pausadamente** *adv*
pauta *nf* **1** : rule, guideline **2** : lines *pl* (on paper)
pava *nf Arg, Bol, Chile* : kettle
pavimentar *vt* : pave
pavimento *nm* : pavement
pavo, -va *n* **1** : turkey **2 pavo real** : peacock **3 comer pavo** : to be a wallflower
pavón *nm, pl* **pavones** : peacock
pavonearse *vr* : to strut, to swagger
pavoneo *nm* : strut, swagger
pavor *nm* TERROR : dread, terror
pavoroso, -sa *adj* ATERRADOR : dreadful, terrifying
payasada *nf* BUFONADA : antic, buffoonery
payasear *vi* : to clown around
payaso, -sa *n* : clown
paz *nf, pl* **paces 1** : peace **2 dejar en paz** : to leave alone **3 hacer las paces** : to make up, to reconcile
pazca, etc. → **pacer**
PC *nmf* : PC, personal computer
peaje *nm* : toll
peatón *nm, pl* **-tones** : pedestrian
peca *nf* : freckle

pecado *nm* **:** sin
pecador[1], **-dora** *adj* **:** sinful, sinning
pecador[2], **-dora** *n* **:** sinner
pecaminoso, -sa *adj* **:** sinful
pecar {72} *vi* **1 :** to sin **2 ~ de :** to be too much (something) <no pecan de amabilidad : they're not overly friendly>
pécari *or* **pecarí** *nm* **:** peccary
pececillo *nm* **:** small fish
pecera *nf* **:** fishbowl, fish tank
pecho *nm* **1 :** chest **2** SENO **:** breast, bosom **3 :** heart, courage **4 dar el pecho :** to breast-feed **5 tomar a pecho :** to take to heart
pechuga *nf* **:** breast (of fowl)
pecoso, -sa *adj* **:** freckled
pectoral *adj* **:** pectoral
peculado *nm* **:** embezzlement
peculiar *adj* **1** CARACTERÍSTICO **:** particular, characteristic **2** RARO **:** peculiar, uncommon
peculiaridad *nf* **:** peculiarity
pecuniario, -ria *adj* **:** pecuniary
pedagogía *nf* **:** pedagogy
pedagógico, -ca *adj* **:** pedagogic, pedagogical
pedagogo, -ga *n* **:** educator, pedagogue
pedal *nm* **:** pedal
pedalear *vi* **:** to pedal
pedante[1] *adj* **:** pedantic
pedante[2] *nmf* **:** pedant
pedantería *nf* **:** pedantry
pedazo *nm* TROZO **:** piece, bit, chunk <caerse a pedazos : to fall to pieces> <hacer pedazos : to tear into shreds, to smash to pieces>
pedernal *nm* **:** flint
pedestal *nm* **:** pedestal
pedestre *adj* **:** commonplace, pedestrian
pediatra *nmf* **:** pediatrician
pediatría *nf* **:** pediatrics
pediátrico, -ca *adj* **:** pediatric
pedido *nm* **1 :** order (of merchandise) **2 :** request
pedigrí *nm* **:** pedigree
pedir {54} *vt* **1 :** to ask for, to request <le pedí un préstamo a Claudia : I asked Claudia for a loan> **2 :** to order (food, merchandise) **3 pedir disculpas** *or* **pedir perdón :** to apologize — *vi* **1 :** to order **2 :** to beg
pedrada *nf* **1 :** blow (with a rock or stone) <la ventana se quebró de una pedrada : the window was broken by a rock> **2** *fam* **:** cutting remark, dig
pedregal *nm* **:** rocky ground
pedregoso, -sa *adj* **:** rocky, stony
pedrera *nf* CANTERA **:** quarry
pedrería *nf* **:** precious stones *pl*, gems *pl*
pegado, -da *adj* **1 :** glued, stuck, stuck together **2 ~ a :** right next to
pegajoso, -sa *adj* **1 :** sticky, gluey **2 :** catchy <una tonada pegajosa : a catchy tune>
pegamento *nm* **:** adhesive, glue
pegar {52} *vt* **1 :** to glue, to stick, to paste **2 :** to attach, to sew on **3 :** to infect with, to give <me pegó el resfriado : he gave me his cold> **4** GOLPEAR **:** to hit, to deal, to strike <me pegaron un puntapié : they gave me a kick> **5 :** to give (out with) <pegó un grito : she let out a yell> — *vi* **1 :** to adhere, to stick **2 ~ en :** to hit, to strike (against) **3 ~ con :** to match, to go with — **pegarse** *vr* **1** GOLPEARSE **:** to hit oneself, to hit each other **2 :** to stick, to take hold **3 :** to be contagious **4** *fam* **:** to tag along, to stick around
pegote *nm* **1 :** sticky mess **2** *Mex* **:** sticker, adhesive label
pegue, etc. → **pegar**
peinado *nm* **:** hairstyle, hairdo
peinador, -dora *n* **:** hairdresser
peinar *vt* **:** to comb — **peinarse** *vr*
peine *nm* **:** comb
peineta *nf* **:** ornamental comb
peladez *nf, pl* **-deces** *Mex fam* **:** obscenity, bad language
pelado, -da *adj* **1 :** bald, hairless **2 :** peeled **3 :** bare, barren **4 :** broke, penniless **5** *Mex fam* **:** coarse, crude
pelador *nm* **:** peeler
pelagra *nf* **:** pellagra
pelaje *nm* **:** coat (of an animal), fur
pelar *vt* **1 :** to peel, to shell **2 :** to skin **3 :** to pluck **4 :** to remove hair from **5** *fam* **:** to clean out (of money) — **pelarse** *vr* **1 :** to peel **2** *fam* **:** to get a haircut **3** *Mex fam* **:** to split, to leave
peldaño *nm* **1 :** step, stair **2 :** rung
pelea *nf* **1** LUCHA **:** fight **2 :** quarrel
pelear *vi* **1** LUCHAR **:** to fight **2** DISPUTAR **:** to quarrel — **pelearse** *vr*
peleón, -ona *adj, mpl* **-ones** *Spain* **:** quarrelsome, argumentative
peleonero, -ra *adj Mex* **:** quarrelsome
peletería *nf* **1 :** fur shop **2 :** fur trade
peletero, -ra *n* **:** furrier
peliagudo, -da *adj* **:** tricky, difficult, ticklish
pelícano *nm* **:** pelican
película *nf* **1 :** movie, film **2 :** (photographic) film **3 :** thin covering, layer
peligrar *vi* **:** to be in danger
peligro *nm* **1 :** danger, peril **2 :** risk <correr peligro de : to run the risk of>
peligroso, -sa *adj* **:** dangerous, hazardous
pelirrojo[1], **-ja** *adj* **:** red-haired, redheaded
pelirrojo[2], **-ja** *n* **:** redhead
pellejo *nm* **1 :** hide, skin **2 salvar el pellejo :** to save one's neck
pellizcar {72} *vt* **1 :** to pinch **2 :** to nibble on
pellizco *nm* **:** pinch
pelo *nm* **1 :** hair **2 :** fur **3 :** pile, nap **4 a pelo :** bareback **5 con pelos y señales :** in great detail **6 no tener pelos en la lengua :** to not mince words, to be blunt **7 tomarle el pelo a alguien :** to tease someone, to pull someone's leg

pelón, -lona *adj, mpl* **pelones 1 :** bald **2** *fam* **:** broke **3** *Mex fam* **:** tough, difficult

pelota *nf* **1 :** ball **2** *fam* **:** head **3 en pelotas** *fam* **:** naked **4 pelota vasca :** jai alai **5 pasar la pelota** *fam* **:** to pass the buck

pelotón *nm, pl* **-tones :** squad, detachment

peltre *nm* **:** pewter

peluca *nf* **:** wig

peluche *nm* **:** plush (fabric)

peludo, -da *adj* **:** hairy, shaggy, bushy

peluquería *nf* **1 :** hairdresser's, barber shop **2 :** hairdressing

peluquero, -ra *n* **:** barber, hairdresser

peluquín *nm, pl* **-quines** TUPÉ **:** hairpiece, toupee

pelusa *nf* **:** lint, fuzz

pélvico, -ca *adj* **:** pelvic

pelvis *nfs & pl* **:** pelvis

pena *nf* **1** CASTIGO **:** punishment, penalty <pena de muerte : death penalty> **2** AFLICCIÓN **:** sorrow, grief <morir de pena : to die of a broken heart> <¡que pena! : what a shame!, how sad!> **3** DOLOR **:** pain, suffering **4** DIFICULTAD **:** difficulty, trouble <a duras penas : with great difficulty> **5** VERGÜENZA **:** shame, embarrassment **6 valer la pena :** to be worthwhile

penacho *nm* **1 :** crest, tuft **2 :** plume (of feathers)

penal[1] *adj* **:** penal

penal[2] *nm* CÁRCEL **:** prison, penitentiary

penalidad *nf* **1 :** hardship **2 :** penalty, punishment

penalizar {21} *vt* **:** to penalize

penalty *nm* **:** penalty (in sports)

penar *vt* **:** to punish, to penalize — *vi* **:** to suffer, to grieve

pendenciero, -ra *adj* **:** argumentative, quarrelsome

pender *vi* **1 :** to hang **2 :** to be pending

pendiente[1] *adj* **1 :** pending **2 estar pendiente de :** to be watchful of, to be on the lookout for

pendiente[2] *nm Spain* **:** earring

pendiente[3] *nf* **:** slope, incline

pendón *nm, pl* **pendones :** banner

péndulo *nm* **:** pendulum

pene *nm* **:** penis

penetración *nf, pl* **-ciones 1 :** penetration **2 :** insight

penetrante *adj* **1 :** penetrating, piercing **2 :** sharp, acute **3 :** deep (of a wound)

penetrar *vi* **1 :** to penetrate, to sink in **2 ~ por** *or* **~ en :** to pierce, to go in, to enter into <el frío penetra por la ventana : the cold comes right in through the window> — *vt* **1 :** to penetrate, to permeate **2 :** to pierce <el dolor penetró su corazón : sorrow pierced her heart> **3 :** to fathom, to understand

penicilina *nf* **:** penicillin

península *nf* **:** peninsula — **peninsular** *adj*

penitencia *nf* **:** penance, penitence

penitenciaría *nf* **:** penitentiary

penitente *adj & nmf* **:** penitent

penol *nm* **:** yardarm

penoso, -sa *adj* **1 :** painful, distressing **2 :** difficult, arduous **3 :** shy, bashful

pensado, -da *adj* **1 bien pensado :** well thought-out **2 en el momento menos pensado :** when least expected **3 poco pensado :** badly thought-out **4 mal pensado :** evil-minded

pensador, -dora *n* **:** thinker

pensamiento *nm* **1 :** thought **2 :** thinking **3 :** pansy

pensar {55} *vi* **1 :** to think **2 ~ en :** to think about — *vt* **1 :** to think **2 :** to think about **3 :** to intend, to plan on — **pensarse** *vr* **:** to think over

pensativo, -va *adj* **:** pensive, thoughtful

pensión *nf, pl* **pensiones 1** JUBILACIÓN **:** pension **2 :** boarding house **3 pensión alimenticia :** alimony

pensionado, -da *n* → **pensionista**

pensionista *nmf* **1** JUBILADO **:** pensioner, retiree **2 :** boarder, lodger

pentágono *nm* **:** pentagon — **pentagonal** *adj*

pentagrama *nm* **:** staff (in music)

penúltimo, -ma *adj* **:** next to last, penultimate

penumbra *nf* **:** semidarkness

penuria *nf* **1** ESCASEZ **:** shortage, scarcity **2 :** poverty

peña *nf* **:** rock, crag

peñasco *nm* **:** crag, large rock

peñón *nm* → **peñasco**

peón *nm, pl* **peones 1 :** laborer, peon **2 :** pawn (in chess)

peonía *nf* **:** peony

peor[1] *adv* **1** (*comparative of* **mal**) **:** worse <se llevan peor que antes : they get along worse than before> **2** (*superlative of* **mal**) **:** worst <me fue peor que a nadie : I did the worst of all>

peor[2] *adj* **1** (*comparative of* **malo**) **:** worse <es peor que el original : it's worse than the original> **2** (*superlative of* **malo**) **:** worst <el peor de todos : the worst of all>

pepa *nf* **:** seed, pit (of a fruit)

pepenador, -dora *n CA, Mex* **:** scavenger

pepenar *vt CA, Mex* **:** to scavenge, to scrounge

pepinillo *nm* **:** pickle, gherkin

pepino *nm* **:** cucumber

pepita *nf* **1 :** seed, pip **2 :** nugget **3** *Mex* **:** dried pumpkin seed

peque, etc. → **pecar**

pequeñez *nf, pl* **-ñeces 1 :** smallness **2 :** trifle, triviality **3 pequeñez de espíritu :** pettiness

pequeño[1]**, -ña** *adj* **1 :** small, little <un libro pequeño : a small book> **2 :** young **3** BAJO **:** short

pequeño[2]**, -ña** *n* **:** child, little one

pera *nf* : pear

peraltar *vt* : to bank (a road)

perca *nf* : perch (fish)

percal *nm* : percale

percance *nm* : mishap, misfortune

percatarse *vr* **~ de** : to notice, to become aware of

percebe *nm* : barnacle

percepción *nf, pl* **-ciones 1** : perception **2** : idea, notion **3** COBRO : receipt (of payment), collection

perceptible *adj* : perceptible, noticeable — **perceptiblemente** *adv*

percha *nf* **1** : perch **2** : coat hanger **3** : coatrack, coat hook

perchero *nm* : coatrack

percibir *vt* **1** : to perceive, to notice, to sense **2** : to earn, to draw (a salary)

percudido, -da *adj* : grimy

percudir *vt* : to make grimy — **percudirse** *vr*

percusión *nf, pl* **-siones** : percussion

percusor *or* **percutor** *nm* : hammer (of a firearm)

perdedor[1], **-dora** *adj* : losing

perdedor[2], **-dora** *n* : loser

perder {56} *vt* **1** : to lose **2** : to miss <perdimos la oportunidad : we missed the opportunity> **3** : to waste (time) — *vi* : to lose — **perderse** *vr* EXTRAVIARSE : to get lost, to stray

perdición *nf, pl* **-ciones** : perdition, damnation

pérdida *nf* **1** : loss **2 pérdida de tiempo** : waste of time

perdidamente *adv* : hopelessly

perdido, -da *adj* **1** : lost **2** : inveterate, incorrigible <es un caso perdido : he's a hopeless case> **3** : in trouble, done for **4 de ~** *Mex fam* : at least

perdigón *nm, pl* **-gones** : shot, pellet

perdiz *nf, pl* **perdices** : partridge

perdón[1] *nm, pl* **perdones** : forgiveness, pardon

perdón[2] *interj* : excuse me!, sorry!

perdonable *adj* : forgivable

perdonar *vt* **1** DISCULPAR : to forgive, to pardon **2** : to exempt, to excuse

perdurable *adj* : lasting

perdurar *vi* : to last, to endure, to survive

perecedero, -ra *adj* : perishable

perecer {53} *vi* : to perish, to die

peregrinación *nf, pl* **-ciones** : pilgrimage

peregrinaje *nm* → **peregrinación**

peregrino[1], **-na** *adj* **1** : unusual, odd **2** MIGRATORIO : migratory

peregrino[2], **-na** *n* : pilgrim

perejil *nm* : parsley

perenne *adj* : perennial

pereza *nf* FLOJERA, HOLGAZANERÍA : laziness, idleness

perezoso[1], **-sa** *adj* FLOJO, HOLGAZÁN : lazy

perezoso[2] *nm* : sloth (animal)

perfección *nf, pl* **-ciones** : perfection

perfeccionamiento *nm* : perfecting, refinement

perfeccionar *vt* : to perfect, to refine

perfeccionismo *nm* : perfectionism

perfeccionista *nmf* : perfectionist

perfecto, -ta *adj* : perfect — **perfectamente** *adv*

perfidia *nf* : perfidy, treachery

pérfido, -da *adj* : perfidious

perfil *nm* **1** : profile **2 de ~** : sideways, from the side **3 perfiles** *nmpl* RASGOS : features, characteristics

perfilar *vt* : to outline, to define — **perfilarse** *vr* **1** : to be outlined, to be silhouetted **2** : to take shape

perforación *nf, pl* **-ciones 1** : perforation **2** : drilling

perforar *vt* **1** : to perforate, to pierce **2** : to drill, to bore

perfumar *vt* : to perfume, to scent — **perfumarse** *vr*

perfume *nm* : perfume, scent

pergamino *nm* : parchment

pérgola *nf* : pergola, arbor

pericia *nf* : skill, expertise

pericial *adj* : expert <testigo pericial : expert witness>

perico *nm* COTORRA : small parrot

periferia *nf* : periphery

periférico[1], **-ca** *adj* : peripheral

periférico[2] *nm* **1** *CA, Mex* : beltway **2** : peripheral

perilla *nf* **1** : goatee **2** : pommel (on a saddle) **3** *Col, Mex* : knob, handle **4 perilla de la oreja** : earlobe **5 de perillas** *fam* : handy, just right

perímetro *nm* : perimeter

periódico[1], **-ca** *adj* : periodic — **periódicamente** *adv*

periódico[2] *nm* DIARIO : newspaper

periodismo *nm* : journalism

periodista *nmf* : journalist

periodístico, -ca *adj* : journalistic, news

período *or* **periodo** *nm* : period

peripecia *nf* VICISITUD : vicissitude, reversal <las peripecias de su carrera : the ups and downs of her career>

periquito *nm* **1** : parakeet **2 periquito australiano** : budgerigar

periscopio *nm* : periscope

perito, -ta *adj & n* : expert

perjudicar {72} *vt* : to harm, to be detrimental to

perjudicial *adj* : harmful, detrimental

perjuicio *nm* **1** : harm, damage **2 en perjuicio de** : to the detriment of

perjurar *vi* : to perjure oneself

perjurio *nm* : perjury

perjuro, -ra *n* : perjurer

perla *nf* **1** : pearl **2 de perlas** *fam* : wonderfully <me viene de perlas : it suits me just fine>

permanecer {53} *vi* **1** QUEDARSE : to remain, to stay **2** SEGUIR : to remain, to continue to be

permanencia *nf* **1** : permanence, continuance **2** ESTANCIA : stay

permanente[1] *adj* **1** : permanent **2** : constant — **permanentemente** *adv*

permanente[2] *nf* : permanent (wave)

permeabilidad *nf* : permeability

permeable *adj* : permeable

permisible *adj* : permissible, allowable

permisividad *nf* : permissiveness

permisivo, -va *adv* : permissive

permiso *nm* **1** : permission **2** : permit, license **3** : leave, furlough **4 con ~** : excuse me, pardon me

permitir *vt* : to permit, to allow — **permitirse** *vr*

permuta *nf* : exchange

permutar *vt* INTERCAMBIAR : to exchange

pernicioso, -sa *adj* : pernicious, destructive

pernil *nm* **1** : haunch (of an animal) **2** : leg (of meat), ham **3** : trouser leg

perno *nm* : bolt, pin

pernoctar *vi* : to stay overnight, to spend the night

pero[1] *nm* **1** : fault, defect <ponerle peros a : to find fault with> **2** : objection

pero[2] *conj* : but

perogrullada *nf* : truism, platitude, cliché

peroné *nm* : fibula

perorar *vi* : to deliver a speech

perorata *nf* : oration, long-winded speech

peróxido *nm* : peroxide

perpendicular *adj & nf* : perpendicular

perpetrar *vt* : to perpetrate

perpetuar {3} *vt* ETERNIZAR : to perpetuate

perpetuidad *nf* : perpetuity

perpetuo, -tua *adj* : perpetual — **perpetuamente** *adv*

perplejidad *nf* : perplexity

perplejo, -ja *adj* : perplexed, puzzled

perrada *nf fam* : dirty trick

perrera *nf* : kennel, dog pound

perrero, -ra *n* : dogcatcher

perrito, -ta *n* CACHORRO : puppy, small dog

perro, -rra *n* **1** : dog, bitch *f* **2 perro caliente** : hot dog **3 perro salchicha** : dachsund **4 perro faldero** : lapdog **5 perro cobrador** : retriever

persa *adj & nmf* : Persian

persecución *nf, pl* **-ciones 1** : pursuit, chase **2** : persecution

perseguidor, -dora *n* **1** : pursuer **2** : persecutor

perseguir {75} *vt* **1** : to pursue, to chase **2** : to persecute **3** : to pester, to annoy

perseverancia *nf* : perseverance

perseverar *vi* : to persevere

persiana *nf* : blind, venetian blind

persignarse *vr* SANTIGUARSE : to cross oneself, to make the sign of the cross

persistir *vi* : to persist — **persistencia** *nf* — **persistente** *adj*

persona *nf* : person

personaje *nm* **1** : character (in drama or literature) **2** : personage, celebrity

personal[1] *adj* : personal — **personalmente** *adv*

personal[2] *nm* : personnel, staff

personalidad *nf* : personality

personalizar {21} *vt* : to personalize

personificar {72} *vi* : to personify — **personificación** *nf*

perspectiva *nf* **1** : perspective, view **2** : prospect, outlook

perspicacia *nf* : shrewdness, perspicacity, insight

perspicaz *adj, pl* **-caces** : shrewd, perspicacious

persuadir *vt* : to persuade — **persuadirse** *vr* : to become convinced

persuasión *nf, pl* **-siones** : persuasion

persuasivo, -va *adj* : persuasive

pertenecer {53} *vi* : to belong

perteneciente *adj* **~ a** : belonging to

pertenencia *nf* **1** : membership **2** : ownership **3 pertenencias** *nfpl* : belongings, possessions

pértiga *nf* GARROCHA : pole <salto de pértiga : pole vault>

pertinaz *adj, pl* **-naces 1** OBSTINADO : obstinate **2** PERSISTENTE : persistent

pertinencia *nf* : pertinence, relevance — **pertinente** *adj*

pertrechos *nmpl* : equipment, gear

perturbación *nf, pl* **-ciones** : disturbance, disruption

perturbador, -dora *adj* **1** INQUIETANTE : disturbing, troubling **2** : disruptive

perturbar *vt* **1** : to disturb, to trouble **2** : to disrupt

peruano, -na *adj & n* : Peruvian

perversidad *nf* : perversity, depravity

perversión *nf, pl* **-siones** : perversion

perverso, -sa *adj* : wicked, depraved

pervertido[1]**, -da** *adj* DEPRAVADO : perverted, depraved

pervertido[2]**, -da** *n* : pervert

pervertir {76} *vt* : to pervert, to corrupt

pesa *nf* **1** : weight **2 levantamiento de pesas** : weightlifting

pesadamente *adv* **1** : heavily **2** : slowly, clumsily

pesadez *nf, pl* **-deces 1** : heaviness **2** : slowness **3** : tediousness

pesadilla *nf* : nightmare

pesado[1]**, -da** *adj* **1** : heavy **2** : slow **3** : irritating, annoying **4** : tedious, boring **5** : tough, difficult

pesado[2]**, -da** *n fam* : bore, pest

pesadumbre *nf* AFLICCIÓN : grief, sorrow, sadness

pésame *nm* : condolences *pl* <mi más sentido pésame : my heartfelt condolences>

pesar[1] *vt* **1** : to weigh **2** EXAMINAR : to consider, to think over — *vi* **1** : to weigh <¿cuánto pesa? : how much does it weigh?> **2** : to be heavy **3** : to weigh heavily, to be a burden <no le pesa : it's not a burden on him> <pesa sobre mi corazón : it weighs upon my heart> **4** INFLUIR : to carry weight, to have bearing **5** (*with personal pro-*

nouns) : to grieve, to sadden <me pesa mucho : I'm very sorry> **6 pese a :** in spite of, despite

pesar² *nm* **1** AFLICCIÓN, PENA **:** sorrow, grief **2** REMORDIMIENTO **:** remorse **3 a pesar de :** in spite of, despite

pesaroso, -sa *adj* **1 :** sad, mournful **2** ARREPENTIDO **:** sorry, regretful

pesca *nf* **:** fishing

pescadería *nf* **:** fish market

pescado *nm* **:** fish (as food)

pescador, -dora *n* **:** fisherman *m*, fisherwoman *f*

pescar {72} *vt* **1 :** to fish for **2 :** to catch **3** *fam* **:** to get a hold of, to land — *vi* **:** to fish, to go fishing

pescuezo *nm* **:** neck

pesebre *nm* **:** manger

pesera *nf Mex* **:** minibus

peseta *nf* **:** peseta (Spanish unit of currency)

pesimismo *nm* **:** pessimism

pesimista¹ *adj* **:** pessimistic

pesimista² *nmf* **:** pessimist

pésimo, -ma *adj* **:** dreadful, abominable

peso *nm* **1 :** weight, heaviness **2 :** burden, responsibility **3 :** weight (in sports) **4** BÁSCULA **:** scales *pl* **5 :** peso

pesque, etc. → **pescar**

pesquería *nf* **:** fishery

pesquero¹, -ra *adj* **:** fishing <pueblo pesquero : fishing village>

pesquero² *nm* **:** fishing boat

pesquisa *nf* INVESTIGACIÓN **:** inquiry, investigation

pestaña *nf* **1 :** eyelash **2 :** flange, rim

pestañear *vi* **:** to blink

pestañeo *nm* **:** blink

peste *nf* **1 :** plague, pestilence **2 :** stench, stink **3 :** nuisance, pest

pesticida *nm* **:** pesticide

pestilencia *nf* **1 :** stench, foul odor **2 :** pestilence

pestilente *adj* **1 :** foul, smelly **2 :** pestilent

pestillo *nm* CERROJO **:** bolt, latch

petaca *nf* **1** *Mex* **:** suitcase **2 petacas** *nfpl Mex fam* **:** bottom, behind

pétalo *nm* **:** petal

petardear *vi* **:** to backfire

petardeo *nm* **:** backfiring

petardo *nm* **:** firecracker

petate *nm Mex* **:** mat

petición *nf, pl* **-ciones :** petition, request

peticionar *vt* **:** to petition

peticionario, -ria *n* **:** petitioner

petirrojo *nm* **:** robin

peto *nm* **:** bib (of clothing)

pétreo, -trea *adj* **:** stone, stony

petrificar {72} *vt* **:** to petrify

petróleo *nm* **:** oil, petroleum

petrolero¹, -ra *adj* **:** oil <industria petrolera : oil industry>

petrolero² *nm* **:** oil tanker

petulancia *nf* INSOLENCIA **:** insolence, petulance

petulante *adj* INSOLENTE **:** insolent, petulant — **petulantemente** *adv*

petunia *nf* **:** petunia

peyorativo, -va *adj* **:** pejorative

pez¹ *nm, pl* **peces 1 :** fish **2 pez de colores :** goldfish **3 pez espada :** swordfish **4 pez gordo :** big shot

pez² *nf, pl* **peces :** pitch, tar

pezón *nm, pl* **pezones :** nipple

pezuña *nf* **:** hoof <pezuña hendida : cloven hoof>

pi *nf* **:** pi

piadoso, -sa *adj* **1 :** compassionate, merciful **2** DEVOTO **:** pious, devout

pianista *nmf* **:** pianist, piano player

piano *nm* **:** piano

piar {85} *vi* **:** to chirp, to cheep, to tweet

pibe, -ba *n Arg, Uru fam* **:** kid, child

pica *nf* **1 :** pike, lance **2 :** goad (in bullfighting) **3 :** spade (in playing cards)

picada *nf* **1 :** bite, sting (of an insect) **2 :** sharp descent

picadillo *nm* **1 :** minced meat, hash **2 hacer picadillo a :** to beat to a pulp

picado, -da *adj* **1 :** perforated **2 :** minced, chopped **3 :** decayed (of teeth) **4 :** choppy, rough **5** *fam* **:** annoyed, miffed

picador *nm* **:** picador

picadura *nf* **1 :** sting, bite **2 :** prick, puncture **3 :** decay, cavity

picaflor *nm* COLIBRÍ **:** hummingbird

picana *nf* **:** goad, prod

picante¹ *adj* **1 :** hot, spicy **2 :** sharp, cutting **3 :** racy, risqué

picante² *nm* **1 :** spiciness **2 :** hot spices *pl*, hot sauce

picaporte *nm* **1 :** latch **2 :** door handle **3** ALDABA **:** door knocker

picar {72} *vt* **1 :** to sting, to bite **2 :** to peck at **3 :** to nibble on **4 :** to prick, to puncture, to punch (a ticket) **5 :** to grind, to chop **6 :** to goad, to incite **7 :** to pique, to provoke — *vi* **1 :** to itch **2 :** to sting **3 :** to be spicy **4 :** to nibble **5 :** to take the bait **6 ~ en :** to dabble in **7 picar muy alto :** to aim too high — **picarse** *vr* **1 :** to get a cavity, to decay **2 :** to get annoyed, to take offense

picardía *nf* **1 :** cunning, craftiness **2 :** prank, dirty trick

picaresco, -ca *adj* **1 :** picaresque **2 :** rascally, roguish

pícaro¹, -ra *adj* **1 :** mischievous **2 :** cunning, sly **3 :** off-color, risqué

pícaro², -ra *n* **1 :** rogue, scoundrel **2 :** rascal

picazón *nf, pl* **-zones** COMEZÓN **:** itch

picea *nf* **:** spruce (tree)

pichel *nm* **:** pitcher, jug

pichón, -chona *n, mpl* **pichones 1 :** young pigeon, squab **2** *Mex fam* **:** novice, greenhorn

picnic *nm* **:** picnic

pico *nm* **1 :** peak **2 :** point, spike **3 :** beak, bill **4 :** pick, pickax **5 y pico**

: and a little, and a bit <las siete y pico : a little after seven> <dos metros y pico : a bit over two meters>

picor *nm* : itch, irritation

picoso, -sa *adj Mex* : very hot, spicy

picota *nf* **1** : pillory, stock **2 poner a alguien en la picota** : to put someone on the spot

picotada *nf* → **picotazo**

picotazo *nm* : peck (of a bird)

picotear *vt* : to peck — *vi* : to nibble, to pick

pictórico, -ca *adj* : pictorial

picudo, -da *adj* **1** : pointy, sharp **2 ~ para** *Mex fam* : clever at, good at

pide, etc. → **pedir**

pie *nm* **1** : foot <a pie : on foot> <de pie : on one's feet, standing> **2** : base, bottom, stem, foot <pie de la cama : foot of the bed> <pie de una lámpera : base of a lamp> <pie de la escalera : bottom of the stairs> <pie de una copa : stem of a glass> **3** : foot (in measurement) <pie cuadrado : square foot> **4** : cue (in theater) **5 dar pie a** : to give cause for, to give rise to **6 en pie de igualidad** : on equal footing

piedad *nf* **1** COMPASIÓN : mercy, pity **2** DEVOCIÓN : piety, devotion

piedra *nf* **1** : stone **2** : flint (of a lighter) **3** : hailstone **4 piedra de afilar** : whetstone, grindstone **5 piedra angular** : cornerstone **6 piedra arenisca** : sandstone **7 piedra caliza** : limestone **8 piedra imán** : lodestone **9 piedra de molino** : millstone **10 piedra de toque** : touchstone

piel *nf* **1** : skin **2** CUERO : leather, hide <piel de venado : deerskin> **3** : fur, pelt **4** CÁSCARA : peel, skin **5 piel de gallina** : goose bumps *pl* <me pone la piel de gallina : it gives me goose bumps>

piélago *nm* **el piélago** : the deep, the ocean

piensa, etc. → **pensar**

pienso *nm* : feed, fodder

pierde, etc. → **perder**

pierna *nf* : leg

pieza *nf* **1** ELEMENTO : piece, part, component <vestido de dos piezas : two-piece dress> <pieza de recambio : spare part> <pieza clave : key element> **2** : piece (in chess) **3** OBRA : piece, work <pieza de teatro : play> **4** : room, bedroom

pifia *nf fam* : goof, blunder

pigargo *nm* : osprey

pigmentación *nf, pl* **-ciones** : pigmentation

pigmento *nm* : pigment

pigmeo, -mea *adj & n* : pygmy, Pygmy

pijama *nm* : pajamas *pl*

pila *nf* **1** BATERÍA : battery <pila de linterna : flashlight battery> **2** MONTÓN : pile, heap **3** : sink, basin, font <pila bautismal : baptismal font> <pila para pájaros : birdbath>

pilar *nm* **1** : pillar, column **2** : support, mainstay

píldora *nf* PASTILLA : pill

pillaje *nm* : pillage, plunder

pillar *vt fam* **1** : to catch <¡cuidado! ¡nos pillarán! : watch out! they'll catch us!> **2** : to grasp, to catch on <¿no lo pillas? : don't you get it?>

pillo¹, -lla *adj* : cunning, crafty

pillo², -lla *n* **1** : rascal, brat **2** : rogue, scoundrel

pilluelo, -la *n* : urchin

pilotar *vt* : to pilot, to drive

pilote *nm* : pile (stake)

pilotear → **pilotar**

piloto *nm* **1** : pilot, driver **2** : pilot light

piltrafa *nf* **1** : poor quality meat **2** : wretch **3 piltrafas** *nfpl* : food scraps

pimentero *nm* : pepper shaker

pimentón *nm, pl* **-tones 1** : paprika **2** : cayenne pepper

pimienta *nf* **1** : pepper (condiment) **2 pimienta de Jamaica** : allspice

pimiento *nm* : pepper (fruit) <pimiento verde : green pepper>

pináculo *nm* **1** : pinnacle (of a building) **2** : peak, acme

pincel *nm* : paintbrush

pincelada *nf* **1** : brushstroke **2 últimas pinceladas** : final touches

pinchar *vt* **1** PICAR : to puncture (a tire) **2** : to prick, to stick **3** : to goad, to tease, to needle — *vi* **1** : to be prickly **2** : to get a flat tire **3** *fam* : to get beaten, to lose out — **pincharse** *vr* : to give oneself an injection

pinchazo *nm* **1** : prick, jab **2** : puncture, flat tire

pingüe *adj* **1** : rich, huge (of profits) **2** : lucrative

pingüino *nm* : penguin

pininos *or* **pinitos** *nmpl* : first steps <hacer pininos : to take one's first steps, to toddle>

pino *nm* : pine, pine tree

pinta *nf* **1** : dot, spot **2** : pint **3** *fam* : aspect, appearance <las peras tienen buena pinta : the pears look good> **4 pintas** *nfpl Mex* : graffiti

pintadas *nfpl* : graffiti

pintar *vt* **1** : to paint **2** : to draw, to mark **3** : to describe, to depict — *vi* **1** : to paint, to draw **2** : to look <no pinta bien : it doesn't look good> **3** *fam* : to count <aquí no pinta nada : he has no say here> — **pintarse** *vr* **1** MAQUILLARSE : to put on makeup **2 pintárselas solo** *fam* : to manage by oneself, to know it all

pintarrajear *vt* : to daub (with paint)

pinto, -ta *adj* : speckled, spotted

pintor, -tora *n* **1** : painter **2 pintor de brocha gorda** : housepainter, dauber

pintoresco, -ca *adj* : picturesque, quaint

pintura *nf* **1** : paint **2** : painting (art, work of art)

pinza *nf* **1 :** clothespin **2 :** claw, pincer **3 :** pleat, dart **4 pinzas** *nfpl* **:** tweezers **5 pinzas** *nfpl* ALICATES **:** pliers, pincers

pinzón *nm, pl* **pinzones :** finch

piña *nf* **1 :** pineapple **2 :** pine cone

piñata *nf* **:** piñata

piñón *nm, pl* **piñones 1 :** pine nut **2 :** pinion

pío[1], pía *adj* **1** DEVOTO **:** pious, devout **2 :** piebald, pied, dappled

pío[2] *nm* **:** peep, tweet, cheep

piocha *nf* **1 :** pickax **2** *Mex* **:** goatee

piojo *nm* **:** louse

piojoso, -sa *adj* **1 :** lousy **2 :** filthy

pionero[1], -ra *adj* **:** pioneering

pionero[2], -ra *n* **:** pioneer

pipa *nf* **:** pipe (for smoking)

pipián *nm, pl* **pipianes** *Mex* **:** a spicy sauce or stew

pipiolo, -la *n fam* **1 :** greenhorn, novice **2 :** kid, youngster

pique[1], etc. → **picar**

pique[2] *nm* **1 :** pique, resentment **2 :** rivalry, competition **3 a pique de :** about to, on the verge of **4 irse a pique :** to sink, to founder

piqueta *nf* **:** pickax

piquete *nm* **1 :** picketers *pl*, picket line **2 :** squad, detachment **3** *Mex* **:** prick, jab

piquetear *vt* **1 :** to picket **2** *Mex* **:** to prick, to jab

pira *nf* **:** pyre

piragua *nf* **:** canoe — **piragüista** *nmf*

pirámide *nf* **:** pyramid

piraña *nf* **:** piranha

pirata[1] *adj* **:** bootleg, pirated

pirata[2] *nmf* **1 :** pirate **2 :** bootlegger **3 pirata aéreo :** hijacker

piratear *vt* **1 :** to hijack, to commandeer **2 :** to bootleg, to pirate

piratería *nf* **:** piracy, bootlegging

piromanía *nf* **:** pyromania

pirómano, -na *n* **:** pyromaniac

piropo *nm* **:** flirtatious compliment

pirotecnia *nf* **:** fireworks *pl*, pyrotechnics *pl*

pirotécnico, -ca *adj* **:** fireworks, pyrotechnic

pírrico, -ca *adj* **:** Pyrrhic

pirueta *nf* **:** pirouette

pirulí *nm* **:** cone-shaped lollipop

pisada *nf* **1 :** footstep **2** HUELLA **:** footprint

pisapapeles *nms & pl* **:** paperweight

pisar *vt* **1 :** to step on, to set foot in **2 :** to walk all over, to mistreat — *vi* **:** to step, to walk, to tread

piscina *nf* **1 :** swimming pool **2 :** fish pond

Piscis *nmf* **:** Pisces

piso *nm* **1** PLANTA **:** floor, story **2** SUELO **:** floor **3** *Spain* **:** apartment

pisotear *vt* **1 :** to stamp on, to trample **2** PISAR **:** to walk all over **3 :** to flout, to disregard

pisotón *nm, pl* **-tones :** stamp, step <sufrieron empujones y pisotones : they were pushed and stepped on>

pista *nf* **1** RASTRO **:** trail, track <siguen la pista de los sospechosos : they're on the trail of the suspects> **2 :** clue **3** CAMINO **:** road, trail **4 :** track, racetrack **5 :** ring, arena, rink **6 pista de aterrizaje :** runway, airstrip **7 pista de baile :** dance floor

pistacho *nm* **:** pistachio

pistilo *nm* **:** pistil

pistola *nf* **1 :** pistol, handgun **2 :** spray gun

pistolera *nf* **:** holster

pistolero *nm* **:** gunman

pistón *nm, pl* **pistones :** piston

pita *nf* **1 :** agave **2 :** pita fiber **3 :** twine

pitar *vi* **1 :** to blow a whistle **2 :** to whistle, to boo **3 :** to beep, to honk, to toot — *vt* **:** to whistle at, to boo

pitido *nm* **1 :** whistle, whistling **2 :** beep, honk, toot

pito *nm* **1** SILBATO **:** whistle **2 no me importa un pito** *fam* **:** I don't give a damn

pitón *nm, pl* **pitones** *nm* **1 :** python **2 :** point of a bull's horn

pituitario, -ria *adj* **:** pituitary

pívot *nmf, pl* **pívots :** center (in basketball)

pivote *nm* **:** pivot

piyama *nmf* **:** pajamas *pl*

pizarra *nf* **1 :** slate **2 :** blackboard **3 :** scoreboard

pizarrón *nm, pl* **-rrones :** blackboard, chalkboard

pizca *nf* **1 :** pinch <una pizca de canela : a pinch of cinnamon> **2 :** speck, trace <ni pizca : not a bit> **3** *Mex* **:** harvest

pizcar {72} *vt Mex* **:** to harvest

pizque, etc. → **pizcar**

pizza ['pitsa, 'pisa] *nf* **:** pizza

pizzería *nf* **:** pizzeria, pizza parlor

placa *nf* **1 :** sheet, plate **2 :** plaque, nameplate **3 :** plate (in photography) **4 :** badge, insignia **5 placa de matrícula :** license plate, tag **6 placa dental :** plaque, tartar

placebo *nm* **:** placebo

placenta *nf* **:** placenta, afterbirth

placentero, -ra *adj* AGRADABLE, GRATO **:** pleasant, agreeable

placer[1] {57} *vi* GUSTAR **:** to be pleasing <hazlo como te plazca : do it however you please>

placer[2] *nm* **1 :** pleasure, enjoyment **2 a ~ :** as much as one wants

plácido, -da *adj* TRANQUILO **:** placid, calm

plaga *nf* **1 :** plague, infestation, blight **2** CALAMIDAD **:** disaster, scourge

plagado, -da *adj* **~ de :** filled with, covered with

plagar {52} *vt* **:** to plague

plagiar *vt* **1 :** to plagiarize **2** SECUESTRAR **:** to kidnap, to abduct

plagiario, -ria *n* **1 :** plagiarist **2** SECUESTRADOR **:** kidnapper, abductor

plagio *nm* **1 :** plagiarism **2** SECUESTRO **:** kidnapping, abduction

plague, etc. → **plagar**

plan *nm* **1 :** plan, strategy, program <plan de inversiones : investment plan> <plan de estudios : curriculum> **2** PLANO **:** plan, diagram **3 :** attitude, intent, purpose <ponte en plan serio : be serious> <estamos en plan de divertirnos : we're looking to have some fun>

plana *nf* **1 :** page <noticias en primera plana : front-page news> **2 plana mayor :** staff (in the military)

plancha *nf* **1 :** iron, ironing **2 :** grill, griddle <a la plancha : grilled> **3 :** sheet, plate <plancha para hornear : baking sheet> **4** *fam* **:** blunder, blooper

planchada *nf* **:** ironing, pressing

planchado *nm* → **planchada**

planchar *v* **:** to iron

planchazo *nm fam* **:** goof, blunder

plancton *nm* **:** plankton

planeación *nf* → **planeamiento**

planeador *nm* **:** glider (aircraft)

planeamiento *nm* **:** plan, planning

planear *vt* **:** to plan — *vi* **:** to glide (in the air)

planeo *nm* **:** gliding, soaring

planeta *nm* **:** planet

planetario[1], -ria *adj* **1 :** planetary **2 :** global, worldwide

planetario[2] *nm* **:** planetarium

planicie *nf* **:** plain

planificación *nf* **:** planning <planificación familiar : family planning>

planificar {72} *vt* **:** to plan

planilla *nf* **1** LISTA **:** list **2** NÓMINA **:** payroll **3** TABLA **:** chart, table **4** *Mex* **:** slate, ticket (of candidates) **5 planilla de cálculo** *Arg, Chile* **:** spreadsheet

plano[1], -na *adj* **:** flat, level, plane

plano[2] *nm* **1** PLAN **:** map, plan **2 :** plane (surface) **3** NIVEL **:** level <en un plano personal : on a personal level> **4 :** shot (in photography) **5 de ~ :** flatly, outright, directly <se negó de plano : he flatly refused>

planta *nf* **1 :** plant <planta de interior : houseplant> **2** FÁBRICA **:** plant, factory **3** PISO **:** floor, story **4 :** staff, employees *pl* **5 :** sole (of the foot)

plantación *nf, pl* **-ciones 1 :** plantation **2 :** planting

plantar *vt* **1 :** to plant, to sow **2 :** to put in, to place **3** *fam* **:** to plant, to land <plantar un beso : to plant a kiss> **4** *fam* **:** to leave, to jilt — **plantarse** *vr* **1 :** to stand firm **2** *fam* **:** to arrive, to show up **3** *fam* **:** to balk

planteamiento *nm* **1 :** approach, position <el planteamiento feminista : the feminist viewpoint> **2 :** explanation, exposition **3 :** proposal, suggestion, plan

plantear *vt* **1 :** to set forth, to bring up, to suggest **2 :** to establish, to set up **3 :** to create, to pose (a problem) — **plantearse** *vr* **1 :** to think about **2 :** to arise

plantel *nm* **1 :** educational institution **2 :** staff, team

planteo *nm* → **planteamiento**

plantilla *nf* **1 :** insole **2 :** pattern, template, stencil **3** *Mex, Spain* **:** staff, roster of employees

plantío *nm* **:** field (planted with a crop)

plantón *nm, pl* **plantones 1 :** seedling **2 :** long wait <darle a alguien un plantón : to stand someone up>

plañidero[1], -ra *adj* **:** mournful

plañidero[2], -ra *nf* **:** hired mourner

plañir {38} *v* **:** to mourn, to lament

plasma *nm* **:** plasma

plasmar *vt* **:** to express, to give form to — **plasmarse** *vr*

plasta *nf* **:** soft mass, lump

plástica *nf* **:** modeling, sculpture

plasticidad *nf* **:** plasticity

plástico[1], -ca *adj* **:** plastic

plástico[2] *nm* **:** plastic

plastificar {72} *vt* **:** to laminate

plata *nf* **1 :** silver **2 :** money

plataforma *nf* **1** ESTRADO, TARIMA **:** platform, dais **2 :** platform (in politics) **3 :** springboard, stepping stone **4 plataforma continental :** continental shelf **5 plataforma de lanzamiento :** launchpad **6 plataforma petrolífera :** oil rig (at sea)

platal *nm* **:** large sum of money, fortune

platanal *nm* **:** banana plantation

platanero[1], -ra *adj* **:** banana, banana-producing

platanero[2], -ra *n* **:** banana grower

plátano *nm* **1 :** banana **2 :** plantain **3 plátano macho** *Mex* **:** plantain

platea *nf* **:** orchestra, pit (in a theater)

plateado, -da *adj* **1 :** silver, silvery **2 :** silver-plated

plática *nf* **1 :** talk, lecture **2 :** chat, conversation

platicar {72} *vi* **:** to talk, to chat — *vt Mex* **:** to tell, to say

platija *nf* **:** flatfish, flounder

platillo *nm* **1 :** saucer <platillo volador : flying saucer> **2 :** cymbal **3** *Mex* **:** dish <platillos típicos : local dishes>

platino *nm* **:** platinum

plato *nm* **1 :** plate, dish <lavar los platos : to do the dishes> **2 :** serving, helping **3 :** course (of a meal) **4 :** dish <plato típico : typical dish> **5 :** home plate (in baseball) **6 plato hondo :** soup bowl

plató *nm* **:** set (in the movies)

platónico, -ca *adj* **:** platonic

playa *nf* **:** beach, seashore

playera *nf* **1 :** canvas sneaker **2** *CA, Mex* **:** T-shirt

plaza *nf* **1 :** square, plaza **2 :** marketplace **3 :** room, space, seat (in a vehicle) **4 :** post, position **5 plaza fuerte**

: stronghold, fortified city **6 plaza de toros** : bullring
plazca, etc. → **placer**
plazo *nm* **1** : period, term <un plazo de cinco días : a period of five days> <a largo plazo : long-term> **2** ABONO : installment <pagar a plazos : to pay in installments>
pleamar *nf* : high tide
plebe *nf* : common people, masses *pl*
plebeyo[1], -ya *adj* : plebeian
plebeyo[2], -ya *n* : plebeian, commoner
plegable *adj* : folding, collapsible
plegadizo → **plegable**
plegar {49} *vt* DOBLAR : to fold, to bend — **plegarse** *vr* : to give in, to yield
plegaria *nf* ORACIÓN : prayer
pleito *nm* **1** : lawsuit **2** : fight, argument, dispute
plenamente *adv* COMPLETAMENTE : fully, completely
plenario, -ria *adj* : plenary, full
plenilunio *nm* : full moon
plenipotenciario, -ria *n* : plenipotentiary
plenitud *nf* : fullness, abundance
pleno, -na *adj* COMPLETO (*often used as an intensifier*) : full, complete <en pleno uso de sus facultades : in full command of his faculties> <en plena noche : in the middle of the night> <en pleno corazón de la ciudad : right in the heart of the city>
plétora *nf* : plethora
pleuresía *nf* : pleurisy
pliega, pliegue, etc. → **plegar**
pliego *nm* **1** HOJA : sheet of paper **2** : sealed document
pliegue *nm* **1** DOBLEZ : crease, fold **2** : pleat
plisar *vt* : to pleat
plomada *nf* **1** : plumb line **2** : sinker
plomería *nf* FONTANERÍA : plumbing
plomero, -ra *n* FONTANERO : plumber
plomizo, -za *adj* : leaden
plomo *nm* **1** : lead **2** : plumb line **3** : fuse **4** *fam* : bore, drag **5 a ~** : plumb, straight
plugo, etc. → **placer**
pluma *nf* **1** : feather **2** : pen **3 pluma fuente** : fountain pen
plumaje *nm* : plumage
plumero *nm* : feather duster
plumilla *nf* : nib
plumón *nm, pl* **plumones** : down
plumoso, -sa *adj* : feathery, downy
plural *adj & nm* : plural
pluralidad *nf* : plurality
pluralizar {21} *vt* : to pluralize
pluriempleado, -da *adj* : holding more than one job
pluriempleo *nm* : moonlighting
plus *nm* : bonus
plusvalía *nf* : appreciation, capital gain
Plutón *nm* : Pluto
plutocracia *nf* : plutocracy
plutonio *nm* : plutonium
población *nf, pl* **-ciones 1** : population **2** : city, town, village
poblado[1], -da *adj* **1** : inhabited, populated **2** : full, thick <cejas pobladas : bushy eyebrows>
poblado[2] *nm* : village, settlement
poblador, -dora *n* : settler
poblar {19} *vt* **1** : to populate, to inhabit **2** : to settle, to colonize **3 ~ de** : to stock with, to plant with — **poblarse** *vr* : to fill up, to become crowded
pobre[1] *adj* **1** : poor, impoverished **2** : unfortunate <¡pobre de mí! : poor me!> **3** : weak, deficient <una dieta pobre : a poor diet>
pobre[2] *nmf* : poor person <los pobres : the poor> <¡pobre! : poor thing!>
pobremente *adv* : poorly
pobreza *nf* : poverty
pocilga *nf* CHIQUERO : pigsty, pigpen
pocillo *nm* : small coffee cup, demitasse
poción *nf, pl* **pociones** : potion
poco[1] *adv* **1** : little, not much <poco probable : not very likely> <come poco : he doesn't eat much> **2** : a short time, a while <tardaremos poco : we won't be very long> **3 poco antes** : shortly before **4 poco después** : shortly after
poco[2], -ca *adj* **1** : little, not much, (a) few <tengo poco dinero : I don't have much money> <en no pocas ocasiones : on more than a few occasions> <poca gente : few people> **2 pocas veces** : rarely
poco[3], -ca *pron* **1** : little, few <le falta poco para terminar : he's almost finished> <uno de los pocos que quedan : one of the remaining few> **2 un poco** : a little, a bit <un poco de vino : a little wine> <un poco extraño : a bit strange> **3 a ~** *Mex* (*used to express disbelief*) <¿a poco no se te hizo difícil? : you mean you didn't find it difficult?> **4 de a poco** : little by little **5 hace poco** : not long ago **6 poco a poco** : little by little **7 dentro de poco** : shortly, in a little while **8 por ~** : nearly, almost
podar *vt* : to prune, to trim
poder[1] {58} *v aux* **1** : to be able to, can <no puede hablar : he can't speak> **2** (*expressing possibility*) : might, may <puede llover : it may rain at any moment> <¿cómo puede ser? : how can that be?> **3** (*expressing permission*) : can, may <¿puedo ir a la fiesta? : can I go to the party?> <¿se puede? : may I come in?> — *vi* **1** : to beat, to defeat <cree que le puede a cualquiera : he thinks he can beat anyone> **2** : to be possible <¿crees que vendrán? — puede (que sí) : do you think they'll come? — maybe> **3 ~ con** : to cope with, to manage <¡no puedo con estos niños! : I can't handle these children!> **4 no poder más** : to have had enough <no puede más : she can't take anymore> **5 no poder menos**

que : to not be able to help <no pudo menos que asombrarse : she couldn't help but be amazed>

poder[2] *nm* **1** : control, power <poder adquisitivo : purchasing power> **2** : authority <el poder legislativo : the legislature> **3** : possession <está en mi poder : it's in my hands> **4** : strength, force <poder militar : military might>

poderío *nm* **1** : power **2** : wealth, influence

poderoso, -sa *adj* **1** : powerful **2** : wealthy, influential **3** : effective

podiatría *nf* : podiatry

podio *nm* : podium

pódium *nm* → **podio**

podología *nf* : podiatry, chiropody

podólogo, -ga *n* : podiatrist, chiropodist

podrá, etc. → **poder**

podredumbre *nf* **1** : decay, rottenness **2** : corruption

podrido, -da *adj* **1** : rotten, decayed **2** : corrupt

podrir → **pudrir**

poema *nm* : poem

poesía *nf* **1** : poetry **2** POEMA : poem

poeta *nmf* : poet

poético, -ca *adj* : poetic, poetical

pogrom *nm* : pogrom

póker *or* **poker** *nm* : poker (card game)

polaco[1], **-ca** *adj* : Polish

polaco[2], **-ca** *n* : Pole, Polish person

polaco[3] *nm* : Polish (language)

polar *adj* : polar

polarizar {21} *vt* : to polarize — **polarizarse** *vr* — **polarización** *nf*

polea *nf* : pulley

polémica *nf* CONTROVERSIA : controversy, polemics

polémico, -ca *adj* CONTROVERTIDO : controversial, polemical

polen *nm, pl* **pólenes** : pollen

policía[1] *nf* : police

policía[2] *nmf* : police officer, policeman *m*, policewoman *f*

policíaco, -ca *or* **policiaco, -ca** *adj* : police <novela policíaca : detective story>

policial *adj* : police

poliéster *nm* : polyester

poligamia *nf* : polygamy

polígamo[1], **-ma** *adj* : polygamous

polígamo[2], **-ma** *n* : polygamist

polígono *nm* : polygon — **poligonal** *adj*

poliinsaturado, -da *adj* : polyunsaturated

polilla *nf* : moth

polimerizar {21} *vt* : to polymerize

polímero *nm* : polymer

polinesio, -sia *adj & n* : Polynesian

polinizar {21} *vt* : to pollinate — **polinización** *nf*

polio *nf* : polio

poliomielitis *nf* : poliomyelitis, polio

polisón *nm, pl* **-sones** : bustle (on clothing)

politécnico, -ca *adj* : polytechnic

politeísmo *nm* : polytheism — **politeísta** *adj & nmf*

política *nf* **1** : politics **2** : policy

políticamente *adv* : politically

político[1], **-ca** *adj* **1** : political **2** : tactful, politic **3** : by marriage <padre político : father-in-law>

político[2], **-ca** *n* : politician

póliza *nf* : policy <póliza de seguros : insurance policy>

polizón *nm, pl* **-zones** : stowaway <viajar de polizón : to stow away>

polla *nf* APUESTA : bet

pollera *nf* **1** : chicken coop **2** : skirt

pollero, -ra *n* **1** : poulterer **2** : poultry farm **3** *Mex fam* COYOTE : smuggler of illegal immigrants

pollito, -ta *n* : chick, young bird, fledgling

pollo, -lla *n* **1** : chicken **2** POLLITO : chick **3** JOVEN : young man *m*, young lady *f*

polluelo *nm* → **pollito**

polo *nm* **1** : pole <el Polo Norte : the North Pole> <polo negativo : negative pole> **2** : polo (sport) **3** : polo shirt **4** : focal point, center **5 polo opuesto** : exact opposite

polución *nf, pl* **-ciones** CONTAMINACIÓN : pollution

polvareda *nf* **1** : cloud of dust **2** : uproar, fuss

polvera *nf* : compact (for face powder)

polvo *nm* **1** : dust **2** : powder **3 polvos** *nmpl* : face powder **4 polvos de hornear** : baking powder **5 hacer polvo** *fam* : to crush, to shatter <vas a hacer polvo el reloj : you're going to destroy your watch>

pólvora *nf* **1** : gunpowder **2** : fireworks *pl*

polvoriento, -ta *adj* : dusty, powdery

polvorín *nm, pl* **-rines** : magazine, storehouse (for explosives)

pomada *nf* : ointment, cream

pomelo *nm* : grapefruit

pómez *nm or* **piedra pómez** : pumice

pomo *nm* **1** : pommel (on a sword) **2** : knob, handle **3** : perfume bottle

pompa *nf* **1** : bubble **2** : pomp, splendor **3 pompas fúnebres** : funeral

pompón *nm, pl* **pompones** BORLA : pom-pom

pomposidad *nf* **1** : pomp, splendor **2** : pomposity, ostentation

pomposo, -sa *adj* : pompous — **pomposamente** *adv*

pómulo *nm* : cheekbone

pon → **poner**

ponchadura *nf Mex* : puncture, flat (tire)

ponchar *vt* **1** : to strike out (in baseball) **2** *Mex* : to puncture — **poncharse** *vr* **1** *Col, Ven* : to strike out (in baseball) **2** *Mex* : to blow out (of a tire)

ponche *nm* **1 :** punch (drink) **2 ponche de huevo :** eggnog

poncho *nm* **:** poncho

ponderación *nf, pl* **-ciones 1 :** consideration, deliberation **2 :** high praise

ponderar *vt* **1 :** to weigh, to consider **2 :** to speak highly of

pondrá, etc. → **poner**

ponencia *nf* **1** DISCURSO **:** paper, presentation, address **2** INFORME **:** report

ponente *nmf* **:** speaker, presenter

poner {60} *vt* **1** COLOCAR **:** to put, to place <pon el libro en la mesa : put the book on the table> **2** AGREGAR, AÑADIR **:** to put in, to add **3 :** to put on (clothes) **4** CONTRIBUIR **:** to contribute **5** ESCRIBIR **:** to put in writing <no le puso su nombre : he didn't put his name on it> **6** IMPONER **:** to set, to impose **7** EXPONER **:** to put, to expose <lo puso en peligro : she put him in danger> **8 :** to prepare, to arrange <poner la mesa : to set the table> **9 :** to name <le pusimos Ana : we called her Ana> **10** ESTABLECER **:** to set up, to establish <puso un restaurante : he opened up a restaurant> **11** INSTALAR **:** to install, to put in **12** (*with an adjective or adverb*) **:** to make <siempre lo pones de mal humor : you always put him in a bad mood> **13 :** to turn on, to switch on **14** SUPONER **:** to suppose <pongamos que no viene : supposing he doesn't come> **15 :** to lay (eggs) **16 ~ a :** to start (someone doing something) <lo puse a trabajar : I put him to work> **17 ~ de :** to place as <la pusieron de directora : they made her director> **18 ~ en :** to put in (a state or condition) <poner en duda : to call into question — *vi* **1 :** to contribute **2 :** to lay eggs — **ponerse** *vr* **1 :** to move (into a position) <ponerse de pie : to stand up> **2 :** to put on, to wear **3 :** to become, to turn <se puso colorado : he turned red> **4 :** to set (of the sun or moon)

poni *or* **poney** *nm* **:** pony

ponga, etc. → **poner**

poniente *nm* **1** OCCIDENTE **:** west **2 :** west wind

ponqué *nm Col, Ven* **:** cake

pontifical *adj* **:** pontifical

pontificar {72} *vi* **:** to pontificate

pontífice *nm* **:** pontiff, pope

pontón *nm, pl* **pontones :** pontoon

ponzoña *nf* VENENO **:** poison — **ponzoñoso, -sa** *adj*

popa *nf* **1 :** stern **2 a ~ :** astern, abaft, aft

popelín *nm, pl* **-lines :** poplin

popelina *nf* **:** poplin

popote *nm Mex* **:** (drinking) straw

populachero, -ra *adj* **:** common, popular, vulgar

populacho *nm* **:** rabble, masses *pl*

popular *adj* **1 :** popular **2 :** traditional **3 :** colloquial

popularidad *nf* **:** popularity

popularizar {21} *vt* **:** to popularize — **popularizarse** *vr*

populista *adj & nmf* **:** populist — **populismo** *nm*

populoso, -sa *adj* **:** populous

popurrí *nm* **:** potpourri

por *prep* **1 :** for, during <se quedaron allí por la semana : they stayed there during the week> <por el momento : for now, at the moment> **2 :** around, during <por noviembre empieza a nevar : around November it starts to snow> <por la mañana : in the morning> **3 :** around (a place) <debe estar por allí : it must be over there> <por todas partes : everywhere> **4 :** by, through, along <por la puerta : through the door> <pasé por tu casa : I stopped by your house> <por la costa : along the coast> **5 :** for, for the sake of <lo hizo por su madre : he did it for his mother> <¡por Dios! : for heaven's sake!> **6 :** because of, on account of <llegué tarde por el tráfico : I arrived late because of the traffic> <dejar por imposible : to give up as impossible> **7 :** per <60 millas por hora : 60 miles per hour> <por docena : by the dozen> **8 :** for, in exchange for, instead of <su hermana habló por él : his sister spoke on his behalf> **9 :** by means of <hablar por teléfono : to talk on the phone> <por escrito : in writing> **10 :** as for <por mí : as far as I'm concerned> **11 :** times <tres por dos son seis : three times two is six> **12** SEGÚN **:** from, according to <por lo que dices : judging from what you're telling me> **13 :** as, for <por ejemplo : for example> **14 :** by <hecho por mi abuela : made by my grandmother> <por correo : by mail> **15 :** for, in order to <lucha por ganar su respeto : he struggles to win her respect> **16 estar por :** to be about to **17 por ciento :** percent **18 por favor :** please **19 por lo tanto :** therefore, consequently **20 ¿por qué? :** why? **21 por que** → **porque 22 por . . . que :** no matter how <por mucho que intente : no matter how hard I try> **23 por si** *or* **por si acaso :** just in case

porcelana *nf* **:** china, porcelain

porcentaje *nm* **:** percentage

porche *nm* **:** porch

porción *nf, pl* **porciones 1 :** portion **2** PARTE **:** part, share **3** RACIÓN **:** serving, helping

pordiosear *vi* MENDIGAR **:** beg

pordiosero, -ra *n* MENDIGO **:** beggar

porfiado, -da *adj* OBSTINADO, TERCO **:** obstinate, stubborn — **: porfiadamente** *adv*

porfiar {85} *vi* **:** to insist, to persist

pormenor *nm* DETALLE **:** detail

pormenorizar {21} *vi* **:** to go into detail — *vt* **:** to tell in detail

pornografía *nf* **:** pornography

pornográfico, -ca *adj* : pornographic
poro *nm* : pore
poroso, -sa *adj* : porous — **porosidad** *nf*
poroto *nm Arg, Chile, Uru* : bean
porque *conj* **1** : because **2** *or* **por que** : in order that
porqué *nm* : reason, cause
porquería *nf* **1** SUCIEDAD : dirt, filth **2** : nastiness, vulgarity **3** : worthless thing, trifle **4** : junk food
porra *nf* **1** : nightstick, club **2** *Mex* : cheer, yell <los aficionados le echaban porras : the fans cheered him on>
porrazo *nm* **1** : blow, whack **2 de golpe y porrazo** : suddenly
porrista *nmf* **1** : cheerleader **2** : fan, supporter
portaaviones *nms & pl* : aircraft carrier
portada *nf* **1** : title page **2** : cover **3** : facade, front
portador, -dora *n* : carrier, bearer
portafolio *or* **portafolios** *nm, pl* **-lios 1** MALETÍN : briefcase **2** : portfolio (of investments)
portal *nm* **1** : portal, doorway **2** VESTÍBULO : vestibule, hall
portar *vt* **1** : to carry, to bear **2** : to wear — **portarse** *vr* CONDUCIRSE : to behave <pórtate bien : behave yourself>
portátil *adj* : portable
portaviandas *nms & pl* : lunch box
portaviones *nm* → **portaaviones**
portavoz *nmf, pl* **-voces** : spokesperson, spokesman *m*, spokeswoman *f*
portazo *nm* : slam (of a door)
porte *nm* **1** ASPECTO : bearing, demeanor **2** TRANSPORTE : transport, carrying <porte pagado : postage paid>
portento *nm* MARAVILLA : marvel, wonder
portentoso, -sa *adj* MARAVILLOSO : marvelous, wonderful
porteño, -ña *adj* : of or from Buenos Aires
portería *nf* **1** ARCO : goal, goalposts *pl* **2** : superintendent's office
portero, -ra *n* **1** ARQUERO : goalkeeper, goalie **2** : doorman *m* **3** : janitor, superintendent
pórtico *nm* : portico
portilla *nf* : porthole
portón *nm, pl* **portones 1** : main door **2** : gate
portugués¹, -guesa *adj & n, mpl* **-gueses** : Portuguese
portugués² *nm* : Portuguese (language)
porvenir *nm* FUTURO : future
pos *adv* **en pos de** : in pursuit of
posada *nf* **1** : inn **2** *Mex* : Advent celebration
posadero, -ra *n* : innkeeper
posar *vi* : to pose — *vt* : to place, to lay — **posarse** *vr* **1** : to land, to light, to perch **2** : to settle, to rest
posavasos *nms & pl* : coaster (for drinks)
posdata *nf* → **postdata**
pose *nf* : pose
poseedor, -dora *n* : possessor, holder
poseer {20} *vt* : to possess, to hold, to have
poseído, -da *adj* : possessed
posesión *nf, pl* **-siones** : possession
posesionarse *vr* **~ de** : to take possession of, to take over
posesivo¹, -va *adj* : possessive
posesivo² *nm* : possessive case
posguerra *nf* : postwar period
posibilidad *nf* **1** : possibility **2 posibilidades** *nfpl* : means, income
posibilitar *vt* : to make possible, to permit
posible *adj* : possible — **posiblemente** *adv*
posición *nf, pl* **-ciones 1** : position, place **2** : status, standing **3** : attitude, stance
posicionar *vt* **1** : to position, to place **2** : to establish — **posicionarse** *vr*
positivo¹, -va *adj* : positive
positivo² *nm* : print (in photography)
poso *nm* **1** : sediment, dregs *pl* **2** : grounds *pl* (of coffee)
posoperatorio, -ria *adj* : postoperative
posponer {60} *vt* **1** : to postpone **2** : to put behind, to subordinate
pospuso, etc. → **posponer**
posta *nf* : relay race
postal¹ *adj* : postal
postal² *nm* : postcard
postdata *nf* : postscript
poste *nm* : post, pole <poste de teléfonos : telephone pole>
póster *or* **poster** *nm, pl* **pósters** *or* **posters** : poster, placard
postergación *nf, pl* **-ciones** : postponement, deferring
postergar {52} *vt* **1** : to delay, to postpone **2** : to pass over (an employee)
posteridad *nf* : posterity
posterior *adj* **1** ULTERIOR : later, subsequent **2** TRASERO : back, rear
postgrado *nm* : graduate course
postgraduado, -da *n* : graduate student, postgraduate
postigo *nm* **1** CONTRAVENTANA : shutter **2** : small door, wicket gate
postilla *nf* : scab
postizo, -za *adj* : artificial, false <dentadura postiza : dentures>
postnatal *adj* : postnatal
postor, -tora *n* : bidder <mejor postor : highest bidder>
postración *nf, pl* **-ciones 1** : prostration **2** ABATIMIENTO : depression
postrado, -da *adj* **1** : prostrate **2 postrado en cama** : bedridden
postrar *vt* DEBILITAR : to debilitate, to weaken — **postrarse** *vr* : to prostrate oneself
postre *nm* : dessert

postrero, -ra *adj* (**postrer** *before masculine singular nouns*) ÚLTIMO : last

postulación *nf, pl* **-ciones 1 :** collection **2 :** nomination (of a candidate)

postulado *nm* **:** postulate, assumption

postulante, -ta *n* **1 :** postulant **2 :** candidate, applicant

postular *vt* **1 :** to postulate **2 :** to nominate **3 :** to propose — **postularse** *vr* **:** to run, to be a candidate

póstumo, -ma *adj* **:** posthumous — **póstumamente** *adv*

postura *nf* **1 :** posture, position (of the body) **2** ACTITUD, POSICIÓN **:** position, stance

potable *adj* **:** drinkable, potable

potaje *nm* **:** thick vegetable soup, pottage

potasa *nf* **:** potash

potasio *nm* **:** potassium

pote *nm* **1** OLLA **:** pot **2 :** jar, container

potencia *nf* **1 :** power <potencias extranjeras : foreign powers> <elevado a la tercera potencia : raised to the third power> **2 :** capacity, potency

potencial *adj & nm* **:** potential

potenciar *vt* **:** to promote, to foster

potenciómetro *nm* **:** dimmer, dimmer switch

potentado, -da *n* **1** SOBERANO **:** potentate, sovereign **2** MAGNATE **:** tycoon, magnate

potente *adj* **1 :** powerful, strong **2 :** potent, virile

potestad *nf* **1** AUTORIDAD **:** authority, jurisdiction **2 patria potestad :** custody, guardianship

potrero *nm* **1 :** field, pasture **2 :** cattle ranch

potro[1], -tra *n* **:** colt *m,* filly *f*

potro[2] *nm* **1 :** rack (for torture) **2 :** horse (in gymnastics)

pozo *nm* **1 :** well <pozo de petróleo : oil well> **2 :** deep pool (in a river) **3 :** mine shaft **4** *Arg, Par, Uru* **:** pothole **5 pozo séptico :** cesspool

pozole *nm Mex* **:** spicy stew made with pork and hominy

práctica *nf* **1 :** practice, experience **2** EJERCICIO **:** exercising <la práctica de la medicina : the practice of medicine> **3** APLICACIÓN **:** application, practice <poner en práctica : to put into practice> **4 prácticas** *nfpl* **:** training

practicable *adj* **:** practicable, feasible

prácticamente *adv* **:** practically

practicante[1] *adj* **:** practicing <católicos practicantes : practicing Catholics>

practicante[2] *nmf* **:** practicer, practitioner

practicar {72} *vt* **1 :** to practice **2 :** to perform, to carry out **3 :** to exercise (a profession) — *vi* **:** to practice

práctico, -ca *adj* **:** practical, useful

pradera *nf* **:** grassland, prairie

prado *nm* **1** CAMPO **:** field, meadow **2 :** park

pragmático, -ca *adj* **:** pragmatic — **pragmáticamente** *adv*

pragmatismo *nm* **:** pragmatism

preámbulo *nm* **1** INTRODUCCIÓN **:** preamble, introduction **2** RODEO **:** evasion <gastar preámbulos : to beat around the bush>

prebélico, -ca *adj* **:** antebellum

prebenda *nf* **:** privilege, perquisite

precalentar {55} *vt* **:** to preheat

precariedad *nf* **:** precariousness

precario, -ria *adj* **:** precarious — **precariamente** *adv*

precaución *nf, pl* **-ciones 1 :** precaution <medidas de precaución : precautionary measures> **2** PRUDENCIA **:** caution, care <con precaución : cautiously>

precautorio, -ria *adj* **:** precautionary

precaver *vt* PREVENIR **:** to prevent, to guard against — **precaverse** *vr* PREVENIRSE **:** to take precautions, to be on guard

precavido, -da *adj* CAUTELOSO **:** cautious, prudent

precedencia *nf* **:** precedence, priority

precedente[1] *adj* **:** preceding, previous

precedente[2] *nm* **:** precedent

preceder *v* **:** to precede

precepto *nm* **:** rule, precept

preciado, -da *adj* **:** esteemed, prized, valuable

preciarse *vr* **1** JACTARSE **:** to boast, to brag **2 ~ de :** to pride oneself on

precinto *nm* **:** seal

precio *nm* **1 :** price **2 :** cost, sacrifice <a cualquier precio : whatever the cost>

preciosidad *nf* **:** beautiful thing <este vestido es una preciosidad : this dress is lovely>

precioso, -sa *adj* **1** HERMOSO **:** beautiful, exquisite **2** VALIOSO **:** precious, valuable

precipicio *nm* **1 :** precipice **2** RUINA **:** ruin

precipitación *nf, pl* **-ciones 1** PRISA **:** haste, hurry, rush **2 :** precipitation, rain, snow

precipitado, -da *adj* **1 :** hasty, sudden **2 :** rash — **precipitadamente** *adv*

precipitar *vt* **1** APRESURAR **:** to hasten, to speed up **2** ARROJAR **:** to hurl, to throw — **precipitarse** *vr* **1** APRESURARSE **:** to rush **2 :** to act rashly **3** ARROJARSE **:** to throw oneself

precisamente *adv* JUSTAMENTE **:** precisely, exactly

precisar *vt* **1 :** to specify, to determine exactly **2** NECESITAR **:** to need, to require — *vi* **:** to be necessary

precisión *nf, pl* **-siones 1** EXACTITUD **:** precision, accuracy **2** CLARIDAD **:** clarity (of style, etc.) **3** NECESIDAD **:** necessity <tener precisión de : to have need of>

preciso, -sa *adj* **1** EXACTO **:** precise **2 :** very, exact <en ese preciso instante : at that very instant> **3** NECESARIO **:** necessary

precocidad *nf* **:** precocity
precocinar *vt* **:** to precook
preconcebir {54} *vt* **:** to preconceive
precondición *nf, pl* **-ciones :** precondition
preconizar {21} *vt* **1 :** to recommend, to advocate **2 :** to extol
precoz *adj, pl* **precoces 1 :** precocious **2 :** early, premature — **precozmente** *adv*
precursor, -sora *n* **:** forerunner, precursor
predecesor, -sora *n* ANTECESOR **:** predecessor
predecir {11} *vt* **:** to foretell, to predict
predestinado, -da *adj* **:** predestined, fated
predestinar *vt* **:** to predestine — **predestinación** *nf*
predeterminar *vt* **:** to predetermine
prédica *nf* SERMÓN **:** sermon
predicado *nm* **:** predicate
predicador, -dora *n* **:** preacher
predicar {72} *v* **:** to preach
predicción *nf, pl* **-ciones 1 :** prediction **2** PRONÓSTICO **:** forecast <predicción del tiempo : weather forecast>
prediga, predijo, etc. → **predecir**
predilección *nf, pl* **-ciones :** predilection, preference
predilecto, -ta *adj* **:** favorite
predio *nm* **:** property, piece of land
predisponer {60} *vt* **1 :** to predispose, to incline **2 :** to prejudice, to bias
predisposición *nf, pl* **-ciones 1 :** predisposition, tendency **2 :** prejudice, bias
predominante *adj* **:** predominant — **predominantemente** *adv*
predominar *vi* PREVALECER **:** to predominate, to prevail
predominio *nm* **:** predominance, prevalence
preeminente *adj* **:** preeminent — **preeminencia** *nf*
preescolar *adj & nm* **:** preschool
preestreno *nm* **:** preview
prefabricado, -da *adj* **:** prefabricated
prefacio *nm* **:** preface
prefecto *nm* **:** prefect
preferencia *nf* **1 :** preference **2** PRIORIDAD **:** priority **3 de ~ :** preferably
preferencial *adj* **:** preferential
preferente *adj* **:** preferential, special <trato preferente : special treatment>
preferentemente *adv* **:** preferably
preferible *adj* **:** preferable
preferido, -da *adj & n* **:** favorite
preferir {76} *vt* **:** to prefer
prefijo *nm* **:** prefix
pregonar *vt* **1 :** to proclaim, to announce **2 :** to hawk (merchandise) **3 :** to extol **4 :** to reveal, to disclose
pregunta *nf* **1 :** question **2 hacer una pregunta :** to ask a question
preguntar *vt* **:** to ask, to question — *vi* **:** to ask, to inquire — **preguntarse** *vr* **:** to wonder
preguntón, -tona *adj, mpl* **-tones :** inquisitive
prehistórico, -ca *adj* **:** prehistoric
prejuicio *nm* **:** prejudice
prejuzgar {52} *vt* **:** to prejudge
prelado *nm* **:** prelate
preliminar *adj & nm* **:** preliminary
preludio *nm* **:** prelude
prematrimonial *adj* **:** premarital
prematuro, -ra *adj* **:** premature
premeditación *nf, pl* **-ciones :** premeditation
premeditar *vt* **:** to premeditate, to plan
premenstrual *adj* **:** premenstrual
premiado, -da *adj* **:** winning, prizewinning
premiar *vt* **1 :** to award a prize to **2 :** to reward
premier *nmf* **:** premier, prime minister
premio *nm* **1 :** prize <premio gordo : grand prize, jackpot> **2 :** reward **3 :** premium
premisa *nf* **:** premise, basis
premolar *nm* **:** bicuspid (tooth)
premonición *nf, pl* **-ciones :** premonition
premura *nf* **:** haste, urgency
prenatal *adj* **:** prenatal
prenda *nf* **1 :** piece of clothing **2 :** security, pledge
prendar *vt* **1 :** to charm, to captivate **2 :** to pawn, to pledge — **prendarse** *vr* **~ de :** to fall in love with
prendedor *nm* **:** brooch, pin
prender *vt* **1** SUJETAR **:** to pin, to fasten **2** APRESAR **:** to catch, to apprehend **3 :** to light (a cigarette, a match) **4 :** to turn on <prende la luz : turn on the light> **5 prender fuego a :** to set fire to — *vi* **1 :** to take root **2 :** to catch fire **3 :** to catch on
prensa *nf* **1 :** printing press **2 :** press <conferencia de prensa : press conference>
prensar *vt* **:** to press
prensil *adj* **:** prehensile
preñado, -da *adj* **1 :** pregnant **2 ~ de :** filled with
preñar *vt* EMBARAZAR **:** to make pregnant
preñez *nf, pl* **preñeces :** pregnancy
preocupación *nf, pl* **-ciones** INQUIETUD **:** worry, concern
preocupante *adj* **:** worrisome
preocupar *vt* INQUIETAR **:** to worry, to concern — **preocuparse** *vr* APURARSE **:** to worry, to be concerned
preparación *nf, pl* **-ciones 1 :** preparation, readiness **2 :** education, training **3 :** (medicinal) preparation
preparado[1]**, -da** *adj* **1 :** ready, prepared **2 :** trained
preparado[2] *nm* **:** preparation, mixture
preparar *vt* **1 :** to prepare, to make ready **2 :** to teach, to train, to coach — **prepararse** *vr*
preparativos *nmpl* **:** preparations
preparatoria *nf Mex* **:** high school
preparatorio, -ria *adj* **:** preparatory

preponderante *adj* : preponderant, predominant — **preponderancia** *nf* — **preponderantemente** *adv*

preposición *nf, pl* **-ciones** : preposition — **preposicional** *adj*

prepotente *adj* : arrogant, domineering, overbearing — **prepotencia** *nf*

prerrogativa *nf* : prerogative, privilege

presa *nf* **1** : capture, seizure <hacer presa de : to seize> **2** : catch, prey <presa de : prey to, seized with> **3** : claw, fang **4** DIQUE : dam **5** : morsel, piece (of food)

presagiar *vt* : to presage, to portend

presagio *nm* : omen, portent

presbiterio *nm* : presbytery, sanctuary (of a church)

presbítero *nm* : presbyter

presciencia *nf* : prescience

prescindir *vi* **~ de 1** : to do without, to dispense with **2** DESATENDER : to ignore, to disregard **3** OMITIR : to omit, to skip

prescribir {33} *vt* : to prescribe

prescripción *nf, pl* **-ciones** : prescription

prescrito *pp* → **prescribir**

presencia *nf* **1** : presence **2** ASPECTO : appearance

presenciar *vt* : to be present at, to witness

presentación *nf, pl* **-ciones 1** : presentation **2** : introduction **3** : appearance

presentador, -dora *n* : newscaster, anchorman *m,* anchorwoman *f*

presentar *vt* **1** : to present, to show **2** : to offer, to give **3** : to submit (a document), to launch (a product) **4** : to introduce (a person) — **presentarse** *vr* **1** : to show up, to appear **2** : to arise, to come up **3** : to introduce oneself

presente[1] *adj* **1** : present, in attendance **2** : present, current **3 tener presente** : to keep in mind

presente[2] *nm* **1** : present (time, tense) **2** : one present <entre los presentes se encontraban . . . : those present included . . .>

presentimiento *nm* : premonition, hunch, feeling

presentir {76} *vt* : to sense, to intuit <presentía lo que iba a pasar : he sensed what was going to happen>

preservación *nf, pl* **-ciones** : preservation

preservar *vt* **1** : to preserve **2** : to protect

preservativo *nm* CONDÓN : condom

presidencia *nf* **1** : presidency **2** : chairmanship

presidencial *adj* : presidential

presidente, -ta *n* **1** : president **2** : chair, chairperson **3** : presiding judge

presidiario, -ria *n* : convict, prisoner

presidio *nm* : prison, penitentiary

presidir *vt* **1** MODERAR : to preside over, to chair **2** : to dominate, to rule over

presilla *nf* : eye, loop, fastener

presión *nf, pl* **presiones 1** : pressure **2 presión arterial** : blood pressure

presionar *vt* **1** : to pressure **2** : to press, to push — *vi* : to put on the pressure

preso[1]**, -sa** *adj* : imprisoned

preso[2]**, -sa** *n* : prisoner

prestado, -da *adj* **1** : borrowed, on loan **2 pedir prestado** : to borrow

prestamista *nmf* : moneylender, pawnbroker

préstamo *nm* : loan

prestar *vt* **1** : to lend, to loan **2** : to render (a service), to give (aid) **3 prestar atención** : to pay attention **4 prestar juramento** : to take an oath — **prestarse** *vr* : to lend oneself <se presta a confusiones : it lends itself to confusion>

prestatario, -ria *n* : borrower

presteza *nf* : promptness, speed

prestidigitación *nf, pl* **-ciones** : sleight of hand, prestidigitation

prestidigitador, -dora *n* : conjurer, magician

prestigio *nm* : prestige — **prestigioso, -sa** *adj*

presto[1] *adv* : promptly, at once

presto[2]**, -ta** *adj* **1** : quick, prompt **2** DISPUESTO, PREPARADO : ready

presumido, -da *adj* VANIDOSO : conceited, vain

presumir *vt* SUPONER : to presume, to suppose — *vi* **1** ALARDEAR : to boast, to show off **2 ~ de** : to consider oneself <presume de inteligente : he thinks he's intelligent>

presunción *nf, pl* **-ciones 1** SUPOSICIÓN : presumption, supposition **2** VANIDAD : conceit, vanity

presunto, -ta *adj* : presumed, supposed, alleged — **presuntamente** *adv*

presuntuoso, -sa *adj* : conceited

presuponer {60} *vt* : to presuppose

presupuestal *adj* : budget, budgetary

presupuestar *vi* : to budget — *vt* : to budget for

presupuestario, -ria *adj* : budget, budgetary

presupuesto *nm* **1** : budget, estimate **2** : assumption, supposition

presurizar {21} *vt* : to pressurize

presuroso, -sa *adj* : hasty, quick

pretencioso, -sa *adj* : pretentious

pretender *vt* **1** INTENTAR : to attempt, to try <pretendo estudiar : I'm trying to study> **2** AFIRMAR : to claim <pretende ser pobre : he claims he's poor> **3** : to seek, to aspire to <¿qué pretendes tú? : what are you after?> **4** CORTEJAR : to court **5 pretender que** : to expect <¿pretendes que lo crea? : do you expect me to believe you?>

pretendiente[1] *nmf* **1** : candidate, applicant **2** : pretender, claimant (to a throne, etc.)

pretendiente[2] *nm* : suitor

pretensión *nf, pl* **-siones 1 :** intention, hope, plan **2 :** pretension <sin pretensiones : unpretentious>

pretexto *nm* EXCUSA **:** pretext, excuse

pretil *nm* **:** parapet, railing

prevalecer {53} *vi* **:** to prevail, to triumph

prevaleciente *adj* **:** prevailing, prevalent

prevalerse {84} *vr* **~ de :** to avail oneself of, to take advantage of

prevención *nf, pl* **-ciones 1 :** prevention **2 :** preparation, readiness **3 :** precautionary measure **4 :** prejudice, bias

prevenido, -da *adj* **1** PREPARADO **:** prepared, ready **2** ADVERTIDO **:** forewarned **3** CAUTELOSO **:** cautious

prevenir {87} *vt* **1 :** to prevent **2 :** to warn — **prevenirse** *vr* **~ contra** *or* **~ de :** to take precautions against

preventivo, -va *adj* **:** preventive, precautionary

prever {88} *vt* ANTICIPAR **:** to foresee, to anticipate

previo, -via *adj* **1 :** previous, prior **2 :** after, upon <previo pago : after paying, upon payment>

previsible *adj* **:** foreseeable

previsión *nf, pl* **-siones 1 :** foresight **2 :** prediction, forecast **3 :** precaution

previsor, -sora *adj* **:** farsighted, prudent

prieto, -ta *adj* **1 :** blackish, dark **2 :** dark-skinned, swarthy **3 :** tight, compressed

prima *nf* **1 :** premium **2 :** bonus **3** → **primo**

primacía *nf* **1 :** precedence, priority **2 :** superiority, supremacy

primado *nm* **:** primate (bishop)

primario, -ria *adj* **:** primary

primate *nm* **:** primate

primavera *nf* **1 :** spring (season) **2** PRÍMULA **:** primrose

primaveral *adj* **:** spring, springlike

primero[1] *adv* **1 :** first **2 :** rather, sooner

primero[2], -ra *adj* (**primer** *before masculine singular nouns*) **1 :** first **2 :** top, leading **3 :** fundamental, basic **4 de primera :** first-rate

primero[3], -ra *n* **:** first

primicia *nf* **1 :** first fruits **2 :** scoop, exclusive

primigenio, -nia *adj* **:** original, primary

primitivo, -va *adj* **1 :** primitive **2** ORIGINAL **:** original

primo, -ma *n* **:** cousin

primogénito, -ta *adj* & *n* **:** firstborn

primor *nm* **1 :** skill, care **2 :** beauty, elegance

primordial *adj* **1 :** primordial **2 :** basic, fundamental

primoroso, -sa *adj* **1 :** exquisite, fine, delicate **2 :** skillful

prímula *nf* **:** primrose

princesa *nf* **:** princess

principado *nm* **:** principality

principal[1] *adj* **1 :** main, principal **2 :** foremost, leading

principal[2] *nm* **:** capital, principal

príncipe *nm* **:** prince

prinipesco, -ca *adj* **:** princely

principiante[1] *adj* **:** beginning

principiante[2] *nmf* **:** beginner, novice

principiar *vt* EMPEZAR **:** to begin

principio *nm* **1** COMIENZO **:** beginning **2 :** principle **3 al principio :** at first **4 a principios de :** at the beginning of <a principios de agosto : at the beginning of August> **5 en ~ :** in principle

pringar {52} *vt* **1 :** to dip (in grease) **2 :** to soil, to spatter (with grease) — **pringarse** *vr*

pringoso, -sa *adj* **:** greasy

pringue[1], etc. → **pringar**

pringue[2] *nm* **:** grease, drippings *pl*

prior, priora *n* **:** prior *m,* prioress *f*

priorato *nm* **:** priory

prioridad *nf* **:** priority, precedence

prisa *nf* **1 :** hurry, rush **2 a ~** *or* **de ~ :** quickly, fast **3 a toda prisa :** as fast as possible **4 darse prisa :** to hurry **5 tener prisa :** to be in a hurry

prisión *nf, pl* **prisiones 1** CÁRCEL **:** prison, jail **2** ENCARCELAMIENTO **:** imprisonment

prisionero, -ra *n* **:** prisoner

prisma *nf* **:** prism

prismáticos *nmpl* **:** binoculars

prístino, -na *adj* **:** pristine

privacidad *nf* **:** privacy

privación *nf, pl* **-ciones 1 :** deprivation **2 :** privation, want

privado, -da *adj* **:** private — **privadamente** *adv*

privar *vt* **1** DESPOJAR **:** to deprive **2 :** to stun, to knock out — **privarse** *vr* **:** to deprive oneself

privativo, -va *adj* **:** exclusive, particular

privilegiado, -da *adj* **:** privileged

privilegiar *vt* **:** to grant a privilege to, to favor

privilegio *nm* **:** privilege

pro[1] *nm* **1 :** pro, advantage <los pros y contras : the pros and cons> **2 en pro de :** for, in favor of

pro[2] *prep* **:** for, in favor of <grupos pro derechos humanos : groups supporting human rights>

proa *nf* **:** bow, prow

probabilidad *nf* **:** probability

probable *adj* **:** probable, likely

probablemente *adv* **:** probably

probar {19} *vt* **1 :** to demonstrate, to prove **2 :** to test, to try out **3 :** to try on (clothing) **4 :** to taste, to sample — *vi* **:** to try — **probarse** *vr* **:** to try on (clothing)

probeta *nf* **:** test tube

probidad *nf* **:** probity

problema *nm* **:** problem

problemática *nf* **:** set of problems <la problemática que debemos enfrentar : the problems we must face>

probóscide *nf* **:** proboscis

problemático, -ca *adj* : problematic

procaz *adj, pl* **procaces 1** : insolent, impudent **2** : indecent

procedencia *nf* : origin, source

procedente *adj* **1** : proper, fitting **2 ~ de** : coming from

proceder *vi* **1** AVANZAR : to proceed **2** : to act, to behave **3** : to be appropriate, to be fitting **4 ~ de** : to originate from, to come from

procedimiento *nm* : procedure, process

prócer *nmf* : eminent person, leader

procesado, -da *n* : accused, defendant

procesador *nm* : processor <procesador de textos : word processor>

procesamiento *nm* : processing <procesamiento de datos : data processing>

procesar *vt* **1** : to prosecute, to try **2** : to process

procesión *nf, pl* **-siones** : procession

proceso *nm* **1** : process **2** : trial, proceedings *pl*

proclama *nf* : proclamation

proclamación *nf, pl* **-ciones** : proclamation

proclamar *vt* : to proclaim — **proclamarse** *vr*

proclive *adj* **~ a** : inclined to, prone to

proclividad *nf* : proclivity, inclination

procrear *vi* : to procreate — **procreación** *nf*

procurador, -dora *n* ABOGADO : attorney

procurar *vt* **1** INTENTAR : to try, to endeavor **2** CONSEGUIR : to obtain, to procure **3 procurar hacer** : to manage to do

prodigar {52} *vt* : to lavish, to be generous with

prodigio *nm* : wonder, marvel

prodigioso, -sa *adj* : prodigious, marvelous

pródigo[1], **-ga** *adj* **1** : generous, lavish **2** : wasteful, prodigal

pródigo[2], **-ga** *n* : spendthrift, prodigal

producción *nf, pl* **-ciones 1** : production **2 producción en serie** : mass production

producir {61} *vt* **1** : to produce, to make, to manufacture **2** : to cause, to bring about **3** : to bear (interest) — **producirse** *vr* : to take place, to occur

productividad *nf* : productivity

productivo, -va *adj* **1** : productive **2** LUCRATIVO : profitable

producto *nm* **1** : product **2** : proceeds *pl*, yield

productor, -tora *n* : producer

proeza *nf* HAZAÑA : feat, exploit

profanar *vt* : to profane, to desecrate — **profanación** *nf*

profano[1], **-na** *adj* **1** : profane **2** : worldly, secular

profano[2], **-na** *n* : nonspecialist

profecía *nf* : prophecy

proferir {76} *vt* **1** : to utter **2** : to hurl (insults)

profesar *vt* **1** : to profess, to declare **2** : to practice, to exercise

profesión *nf, pl* **-siones** : profession

profesional *adj & nmf* : professional — **profesionalmente** *adv*

profesionalismo *nm* : professionalism

profesionalizar {21} *vt* : to professionalize

profesionista *nmf Mex* : professional

profesor, -sora *n* **1** MAESTRO : teacher **2** : professor

profesorado *nm* **1** : faculty **2** : teaching profession

profeta *nm* : prophet

profético, -ca *adj* : prophetic

profetisa *nf* : prophetess, prophet

profetizar {21} *vt* : to prophesy

prófugo, -ga *adj & n* : fugitive

profundidad *nf* : depth, profundity

profundizar {21} *vt* **1** : to deepen **2** : to study in depth — *vi* **~ en** : to go deeply into, to study in depth

profundo, -da *adj* **1** HONDO : deep **2** : profound — **profundamente** *adv*

profusión *nf, pl* **-siones** : abundance, profusion

profuso, -sa *adj* : profuse, abundant, extensive

progenie *nf* : progeny, offspring

progenitor, -tora *n* ANTEPASADO : ancestor, progenitor

prognóstico *nm* : prognosis

programa *nm* **1** : program **2** : plan **3 programa de estudios** : curriculum

programable *adj* : programmable

programación *nf, pl* **-ciones 1** : programming **2** : planning

programador, -dora *n* : programmer

programar *vt* **1** : to schedule, to plan **2** : to program (a computer, etc.)

progresar *vi* : to progress, to make progress

progresista *adj & nmf* : progressive

progresivo, -va *adj* : progressive, gradual

progreso *nm* : progress

prohibición *nf, pl* **-ciones** : ban, prohibition

prohibir {62} *vt* : to prohibit, to ban, to forbid

prohibitivo, -va *adj* : prohibitive

prohijar {5} *vt* ADOPTAR : to adopt

prójimo *nm* : neighbor, fellow man

prole *nf* : offspring, progeny

proletariado *nm* : proletariat, working class

proletario, -ria *adj & n* : proletarian

proliferar *vi* : to proliferate — **proliferación** *nf*

prolífico, -ca *adj* : prolific

prolijo, -ja *adj* : wordy, long-winded

prólogo *nm* : prologue, preface, foreword

prolongación *nf, pl* **-ciones** : extension, lengthening

prolongar {52} *vt* **1 :** to prolong **2 :** to extend, to lengthen — **prolongarse** *vr* CONTINUAR **:** to last, to continue

promediar *vt* **1 :** to average **2 :** to divide in half — *vi* **:** to be half over

promedio *nm* **1 :** average **2 :** middle, mid-point

promesa *nf* **:** promise

prometedor, -dora *adj* **:** promising, hopeful

prometer *vt* **:** to promise — *vi* **:** to show promise — **prometerse** *vr* COMPROMETERSE **:** to get engaged

prometido[1], **-da** *adj* **:** engaged

prometido[2], **-da** *n* NOVIO **:** fiancé *m*, fiancée *f*

prominente *adj* **:** prominent — **prominencia** *nf*

promiscuo, -cua *adj* **:** promiscuous — **promiscuidad** *nf*

promisorio, -ria *adj* **1 :** promising **2 :** promissory

promoción *nf, pl* **-ciones 1 :** promotion **2 :** class, year **3 :** play-off (in soccer)

promocionar *vt* **:** to promote — **promocional** *adj*

promontorio *nm* **:** promontory, headland

promotor, -tora *n* **:** promoter

promover {47} *vt* **1 :** to promote, to advance **2** FOMENTAR **:** to foster, to encourage **3** PROVOCAR **:** to provoke, to cause

promulgación *nf, pl* **-ciones 1 :** enactment **2 :** proclamation, enactment

promulgar {52} *vt* **1 :** to promulgate, to proclaim **2 :** to enact (a law or decree)

prono, -na *adj* **:** prone

pronombre *nm* **:** pronoun

pronosticar {72} *vt* **:** to predict, to forecast

pronóstico *nm* **1** PREDICCIÓN **:** forecast, prediction **2 :** prognosis

prontitud *nf* **1** PRESTEZA **:** promptness, speed **2 con ~ :** promptly, quickly

pronto[1] *adv* **1 :** quickly, promptly **2 :** soon **3 de ~ :** suddenly **4 lo más pronto posible :** as soon as possible **5 tan pronto como :** as soon as

pronto[2], **-ta** *adj* **1** RÁPIDO **:** quick, speedy, prompt **2** PREPARADO **:** ready

pronunciación *nf, pl* **-ciones :** pronunciation

pronunciado, -da *adj* **1 :** pronounced, sharp, steep **2 :** marked, noticeable

pronunciar *vt* **1 :** to pronounce, to say **2 :** to give, to deliver (a speech) **3 pronunciar un fallo :** to pronounce sentence — **pronunciarse** *vr* **:** to declare oneself

propagación *nf, pl* **-ciones :** propagation, spreading

propaganda *nf* **1 :** propaganda **2** PUBLICIDAD **:** advertising

propagar {52} *vt* **1 :** to propagate **2 :** to spread, to disseminate — **propagarse** *vr*

propalar *vt* **1 :** to divulge **2 :** to spread

propano *nm* **:** propane

propasarse *vr* **:** to go too far, to overstep one's bounds

propensión *nf, pl* **-siones** INCLINACIÓN **:** inclination, propensity

propenso, -sa *adj* **:** prone, susceptible

propiamente *adv* **1 :** properly, correctly **2 :** exactly, precisely <propiamente dicho **:** strictly speaking>

propiciar *vt* **1 :** to propitiate **2 :** to favor, to foster

propicio, -cia *adj* **:** favorable, propitious

propiedad *nf* **1 :** property <propiedad privada **:** private property> **2 :** ownership **3** CUALIDAD **:** property, quality **4 :** suitability, appropriateness

propietario[1], **-ria** *adj* **:** proprietary

propietario[2], **-ria** *n* DUEÑO **:** owner, proprietor

propina *nf* **:** tip, gratuity

propinar *vt* **:** to give, to strike <propinar una paliza **:** to give a beating>

propio, -pia *adj* **1 :** own <su propia casa **:** his own house> <sus recursos propios **:** their own resources> **2** APROPIADO **:** appropriate, suitable **3** CARACTERÍSTICO **:** characteristic, typical **4** MISMO **:** oneself <el propio director **:** the director himself>

proponer {60} *vt* **1 :** to propose, to suggest **2 :** to nominate — **proponerse** *vr* **:** to intend, to plan, to set out <lo que se propone lo cumple **:** he does what he sets out to do>

proporción *nf, pl* **-ciones 1 :** proportion **2 :** ratio (in mathematics) **3 proporciones** *nfpl* **:** proportions, size <de grandes proporciones **:** very large>

proporcionado, -da *adj* **1 :** proportionate **2 :** proportioned <bien proporcionado **:** well-proportioned> — **proporcionadamente** *adv*

proporcional *adj* **:** proportional — **proporcionalmente** *adv*

proporcionar *vt* **1 :** to provide, to give **2 :** to proportion, to adapt

proposición *nf, pl* **-ciones :** proposal, proposition

propósito *nm* **1** INTENCIÓN **:** purpose, intention **2 a ~ :** by the way **3 a ~ :** on purpose, intentionally

propuesta *nf* PROPOSICIÓN **:** proposal

propulsar *vt* **1** IMPULSAR **:** to propel, to drive **2** PROMOVER **:** to promote, to encourage

propulsión *nf, pl* **-siones :** propulsion

propulsor *nm* **:** propellant

propuso, etc. → **proponer**

prorrata *nf* **1 :** share, quota **2 a ~ :** pro rata, proportionately

prórroga *nf* **1 :** extension, deferment **2 :** overtime (in sports)

prorrogar {52} *vt* **1 :** to extend (a deadline) **2 :** to postpone

prorrumpir *vi* **:** to burst forth, to break out <prorrumpí en lágrimas **:** I burst into tears>

prosa *nf* **:** prose

prosaico, -ca *adj* **:** prosaic, mundane

proscribir {33} *v* **1** PROHIBIR **:** to prohibit, to ban, to proscribe **2** DESTERRAR **:** to banish, to exile

proscripción *nf, pl* **-ciones 1** PROHIBICIÓN **:** ban, proscription **2** DESTIERRO **:** banishment

proscrito[1] *pp* → **proscribir**

proscrito[2], -ta *n* **1** DESTERRADO **:** exile **2 :** outlaw

prosecución *nf, pl* **-ciones 1 :** continuation **2 :** pursuit

proseguir {75} *vt* **1** CONTINUAR **:** to continue **2 :** to pursue (studies, goals) — *vi* **:** to continue, to go on

prosélito, -ta *n* **:** proselyte

prospección *nf, pl* **-ciones :** prospecting, exploration

prospectar *vi* **:** to prospect

prospecto *nm* **:** prospectus, leaflet, brochure

prosperar *vi* **:** to prosper, to thrive

prosperidad *nf* **:** prosperity

próspero, -ra *adj* **:** prosperous, flourishing

próstata *nf* **:** prostate

prostitución *nf, pl* **-ciones :** prostitution

prostituir {41} *vt* **:** to prostitute — **prostituirse** *vr* **:** to prostitute oneself

prostituto, -ta *n* **:** prostitute

protagonista *nmf* **1 :** protagonist, main character **2 :** leader

protagonizar {21} *vt* **:** to star in

protección *nf, pl* **-ciones :** protection

protector[1], -tora *adj* **:** protective

protector[2], -tora *n* **1 :** protector, guardian **2 :** patron

protector[3] *nm* **:** protector, guard <chaleco protector : chest protector>

protectorado *nm* **:** protectorate

proteger {15} *vt* **:** to protect, to defend — **protegerse** *vr*

protegido, -da *n* **:** protégé

proteína *nf* **:** protein

prótesis *nfs & pl* **:** prosthesis

protesta *nf* **1 :** protest **2** *Mex* **:** promise, oath

protestante *adj & nmf* **:** Protestant

protestantismo *nm* **:** Protestantism

protestar *vi* **:** to protest, to object — *vt* **1 :** to protest, to object to **2 :** to declare, to profess

protocolo *nm* **:** protocol

protón *nm, pl* **protones :** proton

protoplasma *nm* **:** protoplasm

prototipo *nm* **:** prototype

protozoario *or* **protozoo** *nm* **:** protozoan

protuberancia *nf* **:** protuberance — **protuberante** *adj*

provecho *nm* **:** benefit, advantage

provechoso, -sa *adj* BENEFICIOSO **:** beneficial, profitable, useful — **provechosamente** *adv*

proveedor, -dora *n* **:** provider, supplier

proveer {63} *vt* **:** to provide, to supply — **proveerse** *vr* **~ de :** to obtain, to supply oneself with

provenir {87} *vi* **~ de :** to come from

provenzal[1] *adj* **:** Provençal

provenzal[2] *nmf* **:** Provençal

provenzal[3] *nm* **:** Provençal (language)

proverbio *nm* REFRÁN **:** proverb — **proverbial** *adj*

providencia *nf* **1 :** providence, foresight **2 :** Providence, God **3 providencias** *nfpl* **:** steps, measures

providencial *adj* **:** providential

provincia *nf* **:** province — **provincial** *adj*

provinciano, -na *adj* **:** provincial, unsophisticated

provisión *nf, pl* **-siones :** provision

provisional *adj* **:** provisional, temporary

provisionalmente *adv* **:** provisionally, tentatively

provisorio, -ria *adj* **:** provisional, temporary

provisto *pp* → **proveer**

provocación *nf, pl* **-ciones :** provocation

provocador[1], -dora *adj* **:** provocative, provoking

provocador[2], -dora *n* AGITADOR **:** agitator

provocar {72} *vt* **1** CAUSAR **:** to provoke, to cause **2** IRRITAR **:** to provoke, to pique

provocativo, -va *adj* **:** provocative

proxeneta *nmf* **:** pimp *m*

próximamente *adv* **:** shortly, soon

proximidad *nf* **1 :** nearness, proximity **2 proximidades** *nfpl* **:** vicinity

próximo, -ma *adj* **1 :** near, close <la Navidad está próxima : Christmas is almost here> **2** SIGUIENTE **:** next, following <la próxima semana : the following week>

proyección *nf, pl* **-ciones 1 :** projection **2 :** showing, screening (of a film) **3 :** range, influence, diffusion

proyectar *vt* **1 :** to plan **2** LANZAR **:** to throw, to hurl **3 :** to project, to cast (light or shadow) **4 :** to show, to screen (a film)

proyectil *nm* **:** projectile, missile

proyecto *nm* **1 :** plan, project **2 proyecto de ley :** bill

proyector *nm* **1 :** projector **2 :** spotlight

prudencia *nf* **:** prudence, care, discretion

prudente *adj* **:** prudent, sensible, reasonable

prueba[1], etc. → **probar**

prueba[2] *nf* **1 :** proof, evidence **2 :** trial, test **3 :** proof (in printing or photography) **4 :** event, qualifying round (in sports) **5 a prueba de agua :** waterproof **6 prueba de fuego :** acid test **7 poner a prueba :** to put to the test

prurito *nm* **1 :** itching **2 :** desire, urge

psicoanálisis *nm* **:** psychoanalysis — **psicoanalista** *nmf*

psicoanalítico, -ca *adj* : psychoanalytic

psicoanalizar {21} *vt* : to psychoanalyze

psicología *nf* : psychology

psicológico, -ca *adj* : psychological — **psicológicamente** *adv*

psicólogo, -ga *n* : psychologist

psicópata *nmf* : psychopath

psicopático, -ca *adj* : psycopathic

psicosis *nfs & pl* : psychosis

psicosomático, -ca *adj* : psychosomatic

psicoterapeuta *nmf* : psychotherapist

psicoterapia *nf* : psychotherapy

psicótico, -ca *adj & n* : psychotic

psique *nf* : psyche

psiquiatra *nmf* : psychiatrist

psiquiatría *nf* : psychiatry

psiquiátrico¹, -ca *adj* : psychiatric

psiquiátrico² *nm* : mental hospital

psíquico, -ca *adj* : psychic

psiquis *nfs & pl* : psyche

psoriasis *nf* : psoriasis

ptomaína *nf* : ptomaine

púa *nf* **1** : barb <alambre de púas : barbed wire> **2** : tooth (of a comb) **3** : quill, spine

pubertad *nf* : puberty

pubiano → **púbico**

púbico, -ca *adj* : pubic

publicación *nf, pl* **-ciones** : publication

publicar {72} *vt* **1** : to publish **2** DIVULGAR : to divulge, to disclose

publicidad *nf* **1** : publicity **2** : advertising

publicista *nmf* : publicist

publicitar *vt* **1** : to publicize **2** : to advertise

publicitario, -ria *adj* : advertising, publicity <agencia publicitaria : advertising agency>

público¹, -ca *adj* : public — **públicamente** *adv*

público² *nm* **1** : public **2** : audience, spectators *pl*

puchero *nm* **1** : pot **2** : stew **3** : pout <hacer pucheros : to pout>

pucho *nm* **1** : waste, residue **2** : cigarette butt **3 a puchos** : little by little, bit by bit

púdico, -ca *adj* : chaste, modest

pudiente *adj* **1** : powerful **2** : rich, wealthy

pudín *nm, pl* **pudines** BUDÍN : pudding

pudo, etc. → **poder**

pudor *nm* : modesty, reserve

pudoroso, -sa *adj* : modest, reserved, shy

pudrir {59} *vt* **1** : to rot **2** *fam* : to annoy, to upset — **pudrirse** *vr* **1** : to rot **2** : to languish

pueblerino, -na *adj* : provincial, countrified

puebla, etc. → **poblar**

pueblo *nm* **1** NACIÓN : people **2** : common people **3** ALDEA, POBLADO : town, village

puede, etc. → **poder**

puente *nm* **1** : bridge <puente levadizo : drawbridge> **2** : denture, bridge **3 puente aéreo** : airlift

puerco¹, -ca *adj* : dirty, filthy

puerco², -ca *n* **1** CERDO, MARRANO : pig, hog **2** : pig, dirty or greedy person **3 puerco espín** : porcupine

pueril *adj* : childish, puerile

puerro *nm* : leek

puerta *nf* **1** : door, entrance, gate **2 a puerta cerrada** : behind closed doors

puerto *nm* **1** : port, harbor **2** : mountain pass **3 puerto marítimo** : seaport

puertorriqueño, -ña *adj & n* : Puerto Rican

pues *conj* **1** : since, because, for <no puedo ir, pues no tengo plata : I can't go, since I don't have any money> <lo hace, pues a él le gusta : he does it because he likes to> **2** (*used interjectionally*) : well, then <¡pues claro que sí! : well, of course!> <¡pues no voy! : well then, I'm not going!>

puesta *nf* **1** : setting <puesta del sol : sunset> **2** : laying (of eggs) **3 puesta a punto** : tune-up **4 puesta en marcha** : start, starting up

puestero, -ra *n* : seller, vendor

puesto¹ *pp* → **poner**

puesto², -ta *adj* : dressed <bien puesto : well-dressed>

puesto³ *nm* **1** LUGAR, SITIO : place, position **2** : position, job **3** : kiosk, stand, stall **4 puesto que** : since, given that

pugilato *nm* BOXEO : boxing, pugilism

pugilista *nm* BOXEADOR : boxer, pugilist

pugna *nf* **1** CONFLICTO, LUCHA : conflict, struggle **2 en ~** : at odds, in conflict

pugnar *vi* LUCHAR : to fight, to strive, to struggle

pugnaz *adj* : pugnacious

pujante *adj* : mighty, powerful

pujanza *nf* : strength, vigor <pujanza económica : economic strength>

pulcritud *nf* **1** : neatness, tidiness **2** ESMERO : meticulousness

pulcro, -cra *adj* **1** : clean, neat **2** : exquisite, delicate, refined

pulga *nf* **1** : flea **2 tener malas pulgas** : to be bad-tempered

pulgada *nf* : inch

pulgar *nm* **1** : thumb **2** : big toe

pulir *vt* **1** : to polish, to shine **2** REFINAR : to refine, to perfect

pulla *nf* **1** : cutting remark, dig, gibe **2** : obscenity

pulmón *nm, pl* **pulmones** : lung

pulmonar *adj* : pulmonary

pulmonía *nf* NEUMONÍA : pneumonia

pulpa *nf* : pulp, flesh

pulpería *nf* : small grocery store

púlpito *nm* : pulpit

pulpo *nm* : octopus

pulsación *nf, pl* **-ciones** **1** : beat, pulsation, throb **2** : keystroke

pulsar *vt* **1** APRETAR : to press, to push **2** : to strike (a key) **3** : to assess — *vi* : to beat, to throb

pulsera *nf* **:** bracelet

pulso *nm* **1 :** pulse <tomarle el pulso a alguien : to take someone's pulse> <tomarle el pulso a la opinión : to sound out opinion> **2 :** steadiness (of hand) <dibujo a pulso : freehand sketch>

pulular *vi* ABUNDAR **:** to abound, to swarm <en el río pululan los peces : the river is teeming with fish>

pulverizador *nm* **1 :** atomizer, spray **2 :** spray gun

pulverizar {21} *vt* **1 :** to pulverize, to crush **2 :** to spray

puma *nf* **:** cougar, puma

puna *nf* **:** bleak Andean tableland

punción *nf, pl* **punciones :** puncture

punible *adj* **:** punishable

punitivo, -va *adj* **:** punitive

punce, etc. → **punzar**

punta *nf* **1 :** tip, end <punta del dedo : fingertip> <en la punta de la lengua : at the tip of one's tongue> **2 :** point (of a weapon or pencil) <punta de lanza : spearhead> **3 :** point, headland **4 :** bunch, lot <una punta de ladrones : a bunch of thieves> **5 a punta de :** by, by dint of

puntada *nf* **1 :** stitch (in sewing) **2** PUNZADA **:** sharp pain, stitch, twinge **3** *Mex* **:** witticism, quip

puntal *nm* **1 :** prop, support **2 :** stanchion

puntapié *nm* PATADA **:** kick

puntazo *nm* CORNADA **:** wound (from a goring)

puntear *vt* **1 :** to pluck (a guitar) **2 :** to lead (in sports)

puntería *nf* **:** aim, marksmanship

puntero *nm* **1 :** pointer **2 :** leader

puntiagudo, -da *adj* **:** sharp, pointed

puntilla *nf* **1 :** lace edging **2 :** dagger (in bullfighting) **3 de puntillas :** on tiptoe

puntilloso, -sa *adj* **:** punctilious

punto *nm* **1 :** dot, point **2 :** period (in punctuation) **3 :** item, question **4 :** spot, place **5 :** moment, stage, degree **6 :** point (in a score) **7 :** stitch **8 en ~ :** on the dot, sharp <a las dos en punto : at two o'clock sharp> **9 al punto :** at once **10 a punto fijo :** exactly, certainly **11 dos puntos :** colon **12 hasta cierto punto :** up to a point **13 punto decimal :** decimal point **14 punto de vista :** point of view **15 punto y coma :** semicolon **16 y punto :** period <es el mejor que hay y punto : it's the best there is, period> **17 puntos cardinales :** points of the compass

puntuación *nf, pl* **-ciones 1 :** punctuation **2 :** scoring, score, grade

puntual *adj* **1 :** prompt, punctual **2 :** exact, accurate — **puntualmente** *adv*

puntualidad *nf* **1 :** promptness, punctuality **2 :** exactness, accuracy

puntualizar {21} *vt* **1 :** to specify, to state **2 :** to point out

puntuar {3} *vt* **:** to punctuate — *vi* **:** to score points

punzada *nf* **:** sharp pain, twinge, stitch

punzante *adj* **1 :** sharp **2** CÁUSTICO **:** biting, caustic

punzar {21} *vt* **:** to pierce, to puncture

punzón *nm, pl* **punzones 1 :** awl **2 :** hole punch

puñado *nm* **1 :** handful **2 a puñados :** lots of, by the handful

puñal *nm* DAGA **:** dagger

puñalada *nf* **:** stab, stab wound

puñetazo *nm* **:** punch (with the fist)

puño *nm* **1 :** fist **2 :** handful, fistful **3 :** cuff (of a shirt) **4 :** handle, hilt

pupila *nf* **:** pupil (of the eye)

pupilo, -la *n* **1 :** pupil, student **2 :** ward, charge

pupitre *nm* **:** writing desk

puré *nm* **:** purée <puré de papas : mashed potatoes>

pureza *nf* **:** purity

purga *nf* **1 :** laxative **2 :** purge

purgante *adj & nm* **:** laxative, purgative

purgar {52} *vt* **1 :** to purge, to cleanse **2 :** to liquidate (in politics) **3 :** to give a laxative to — **purgarse** *vr* **1 :** to take a laxative **2 ~ de :** to purge oneself of

purgatorio *nm* **:** purgatory

purgue, etc. → **purgar**

purificador *nm* **:** purifier

purificar {72} *vt* **:** to purify — **purificación** *nf*

puritano[1], -na *adj* **:** puritanical, puritan

puritano[2], -na *n* **1 :** Puritan **2 :** puritan

puro[1] *adv* **:** sheer, much <de puro terco : out of sheer stubbornness>

puro[2], -ra *adj* **1 :** pure <aire puro : fresh air> **2 :** plain, simple, sheer <por pura curiosidad : from sheer curiosity> **3 :** only, just <emplean puras mujeres : they only employ women> **4 pura sangre :** Thoroughbred horse

puro[3] *nm* **:** cigar

púrpura *nf* **:** purple

purpúreo, -rea *adj* **:** purple

purpurina *nf* **:** glitter (for decoration)

pus *nm* **:** pus

pusilánime *adj* COBARDE **:** pusillanimous, cowardly

puso, etc. → **poner**

pústula *nf* **:** pustule, pimple

puta *nf* **:** whore, slut

putrefacción *nf, pl* **-ciones :** putrefaction

putrefacto, -ta *adj* **1** PODRIDO **:** putrid, rotten **2 :** decayed

pútrido, -da *adj* **:** putrid, rotten

puya *nf* **1 :** point (of a lance) **2 lanzar una puya :** to gibe, to taunt

Q

q *nf* : eighteenth letter of the Spanish alphabet

que[1] *conj* **1 :** that <dice que está listo : he says that he's ready> <espero que lo haga : I hope that he does it> **2 :** than <más que nada : more than anything> **3** (*implying permission or desire*) <¡que entre! : send him in!> <¡que te vaya bien! : I wish you well!> **4** (*indicating a reason or cause*) <¡cuidado, que te caes! : be careful, you're about to fall!> <no provoques al perro, que te va a morder : don't provoke the dog or (else) he'll bite> **5 es que :** the thing is that, I'm afraid that **6 yo que tú :** if I were you

que[2] *pron* **1 :** who, that <la niña que viene : the girl who is coming> **2 :** whom, that <los alumnos que enseñé : the students that I taught> **3 :** that, which <el carro que me gusta : the car that I like> **4 el (la, lo, las, los) que** → **el**[1], **la**[1], **lo**[1], **los**[1]

qué[1] *adv* : how, what <¡qué bonito! : how pretty!>

qué[2] *adj* : what, which <¿qué hora es? : what time is it?>

qué[3] *pron* : what <¿qué quieres? : what do you want?>

quebracho *nm* : quebracho (tree)

quebrada *nf* DESFILADERO : ravine, gorge

quebradizo, -za *adj* FRÁGIL : breakable, delicate, fragile

quebrado[1], **-da** *adj* **1 :** bankrupt **2 :** rough, uneven **3** ROTO : broken

quebrado[2] *nm* : fraction

quebrantamiento *nm* **1 :** breaking **2 :** deterioration, weakening

quebrantar *vt* **1 :** to break, to split, to crack **2 :** to weaken **3 :** to violate (a law or contract)

quebranto *nm* **1 :** break, breaking **2** AFLICCIÓN : affliction, grief **3** PÉRDIDA : loss

quebrar {55} *vt* **1** ROMPER : to break **2** DOBLAR : to bend, to twist — *vi* **1 :** to go bankrupt **2 :** to fall out, to break up — **quebrarse** *vr*

queda *nf* : curfew

quedar *vi* **1** PERMANECER : to remain, to stay **2 :** to be <quedamos contentos con las mejoras : we were pleased with the improvements> **3 :** to be situated <queda muy lejos : it's very far, it's too far away> **4 :** to be left <quedan sólo dos alternativas : there are only two options left> **5 :** to fit, to suit <estos zapatos no me quedan : these shoes don't fit> **6 quedar bien (mal) :** to turn out well (badly) **7 ~ en :** to agree, to arrange <¿en qué quedamos? : what's the arrangement, then?> — **quedarse** *vr* **1 :** to stay <se quedó en casa : she stayed at home> **2 :** to keep on <se quedó esperando : he kept on waiting> **3 quedarse atrás :** to stay behind <no quedarse atrás : to be no slouch> **4 ~ con :** to remain <me quedé con hambre después de comer : I was still hungry after I ate>

quedo[1] *adv* : softly, quietly

quedo[2], **-da** *adj* : quiet, still

quehacer *nm* **1 :** work **2 quehaceres** *nmpl* : chores

queja *nf* : complaint

quejarse *vr* **1 :** to complain **2 :** to groan, to moan

quejido *nm* **1 :** groan, moan **2 :** whine, whimper

quejoso, -sa *adj* : complaining, whining

quejumbroso, -sa *adj* : querulous, whining

quema *nf* **1** FUEGO : fire **2 :** burning

quemado, -da *adj* **1 :** burned, burnt **2 :** annoyed **3 :** burned-out

quemador *nm* : burner

quemadura *nf* : burn

quemar *vt* : to burn, to set fire to — *vi* : to be burning hot — **quemarse** *vr*

quemarropa *nf* **a ~ :** point-blank

quemazón *nf, pl* **-zones 1 :** burning **2 :** intense heat **3 :** itch **4 :** cutting remark

quena *nf* : Peruvian reed flute

quepa, etc. → **caber**

querella *nf* **1 :** complaint **2 :** lawsuit

querellante *nmf* : plaintiff

querellarse *vr* **~ contra :** to bring suit against, to sue

querer[1] {64} *vt* **1** DESEAR : to want, to desire <quiere ser profesor : he wants to be a teacher> <¿cuánto quieres por esta computadora? : how much do you want for this computer?> **2 :** to love, to like, to be fond of <te quiero : I love you> **3** (*indicating a request*) <¿quieres pasarme la leche? : please pass the milk> **4 querer decir :** to mean **5 sin ~ :** unintentionally — *vi* : like, want <si quieras : if you like>

querer[2] *nm* : love, affection

querido[1], **-da** *adj* : dear, beloved

querido[2], **-da** *n* : dear, sweetheart

queroseno *nm* : kerosene

querúbico, -ca *adj* : cherubic

querrá, etc. → **querer**

querubín *nm, pl* **-bines :** cherub

quesadilla *nf* : quesadilla

quesería *nf* : cheese shop

queso *nm* : cheese

quetzal *nm* **1 :** quetzal (bird) **2 :** monetary unit of Guatemala

quicio *nm* **1 estar fuera de quicio :** to be beside oneself **2 sacar de quicio :** to exasperate, to drive crazy

quid *nm* : crux, gist <el quid de la cuestión : the crux of the matter>

quiebra[1], **etc.** → **quebrar**

quiebra[2] *nf* **1 :** break, crack **2** BANCARROTA **:** failure, bankruptcy

quien *pron, pl* **quienes 1 :** who, whom <no sé quien ganará : I don't know who will win> <las personas con quienes trabajo : the people with whom I work> **2 :** whoever, whomever <quien quiere salir que salga : whoever wants to can leave> **3 :** anyone, some people <hay quienes no están de acuerdo : some people don't agree>

quién *pron, pl* **quiénes 1 :** who, whom <¿quién sabe? : who knows?> <¿con quién hablo? : with whom am I speaking?> **2 de ~ :** whose <¿de quién es este libro? : whose book is this?>

quienquiera *pron, pl* **quienesquiera :** whoever, whomever

quiere, etc. → **querer**

quieto, -ta *adj* **1 :** calm, quiet **2** INMÓVIL **:** still

quietud *nf* **1 :** calm, tranquility **2** INMOVILIDAD **:** stillness

quijada *nf* **:** jaw, jawbone

quijotesco, -ca *adj* **:** quixotic

quilate *nm* **:** karat

quilla *nf* **:** keel

quimera *nf* **:** chimera, illusion

quimérico, -ca *adj* **:** chimeric, fanciful

química *nf* **:** chemistry

químico[1]**, -ca** *adj* **:** chemical

químico[2]**, -ca** *n* **:** chemist

quimioterapia *nf* **:** chemotherapy

quimono *nm* **:** kimono

quince *adj & nm* **:** fifteen

quinceañero, -ra *n* **:** fifteen-year-old, teenager

quinceavo[1]**, -va** *adj* **:** fifteenth

quinceavo[2] *nm* **:** fifteenth (fraction)

quincena *nf* **:** two week period, fortnight

quincenal *adj* **:** bimonthly, twice a month

quingombó *nm* **:** okra

quincuagésimo[1]**, -ma** *adj* **:** fiftieth, fifty-

quincuagésimo[2]**, -ma** *n* **:** fiftieth, fifty- (in a series)

quiniela *nf* **:** sports lottery

quinientos[1]**, -tas** *adj* **:** five hundred

quinientos[2] *nms & pl* **:** five hundred

quinina *nf* **:** quinine

quino *nm* **:** cinchona

quinqué *nm* **:** oil lamp

quinquenal *adj* **:** five-year <un plan quinquenal : a five-year plan>

quinta *nf* **:** country house, villa

quintaesencia *nf* **:** quintessence — **quintaesencial** *adj*

quintal *nm* **:** hundredweight

quinteto *nm* **:** quintet

quintillizo, -za *n* **:** quintuplet

quinto, -ta *adj* **:** fifth — **quinto, -ta** *n*

quíntuplo, -la *adj* **:** quintuple, fivefold

quiosco *nm* **1 :** kiosk **2 :** newsstand **3 quiosco de música :** bandstand

quirófano *nm* **:** operating room

quiromancia *nf* **:** palmistry

quiropráctica *nf* **:** chiropractic

quiropráctico, -ca *n* **:** chiropractor

quirúrgico, -ca *adj* **:** surgical — **quirúrgicamente** *adv*

quiso, etc. → **querer**

quisquilloso[1]**, -sa** *adj* **:** fastidious, fussy

quisquilloso[2]**, -sa** *n* **:** fussy person, fussbudget

quiste *nm* **:** cyst

quitaesmalte *nm* **:** nail polish remover

quitamanchas *nms & pl* **:** stain remover

quitanieves *nms & pl* **:** snowplow

quitar *vt* **1 :** to remove, to take away **2 :** to take off (clothes) **3 :** to get rid of, to relieve — **quitarse** *vr* **1 :** to withdraw, to leave **2 :** to take off (one's clothes) **3 ~ de :** to give up (a habit) **4 quitar de encima :** to get rid of

quitasol *nm* **:** parasol

quiteño[1]**, -ña** *adj* **:** of or from Quito

quiteño[2]**, -ña** *n* **:** person from Quito

quizá *or* **quizás** *adv* **:** maybe, perhaps

quórum *nm, pl* **quórums :** quorum

R

r *nf* **:** nineteenth letter of the Spanish alphabet

rábano *nm* **1 :** radish **2 rábano picante :** horseradish

rabí *nmf, pl* **rabíes :** rabbi

rabia *nf* **1** HIDROFOBIA **:** rabies, hydrophobia **2 :** rage, anger

rabiar *vi* **1 :** to rage, to be furious **2 :** to be in great pain **3 a ~** *fam* **:** like crazy, like mad

rabieta *nf* BERRINCHE **:** tantrum

rabino, -na *n* **:** rabbi

rabioso, -sa *adj* **1 :** enraged, furious **2 :** rabid

rabo *nm* **1** COLA **:** tail **2 el rabo del ojo :** the corner of one's eye

racha *nf* **1 :** gust of wind **2 :** run, series, string <racha perdedora : losing streak>

racheado, -da *adj* **:** gusty, windy

racial *adj* **:** racial

racimo *nm* **:** bunch, cluster <un racimo de uvas : a bunch of grapes>

raciocinio *nm* **:** reason, reasoning

ración *nf, pl* **raciones 1 :** share, ration **2** PORCIÓN **:** portion, helping

racional *adj* **:** rational, reasonable — **racionalmente** *adv*

racionalidad *nf* **:** rationality

racionalización *nf, pl* **-ciones** : rationalization
racionalizar {21} *vt* **1** : to rationalize **2** : to streamline
racionamiento *nm* : rationing
racionar *vt* : to ration
racismo *nm* : racism
racista *adj & nmf* : racist
radar *nm* : radar
radiación *nf, pl* **-ciones** : radiation, irradiation
radiactividad *nf* : radioactivity
radiactivo, -va *adj* : radioactive
radiador *nm* : radiator
radial *adj* **1** : radial **2** : radio, broadcasting <emisora radial : radio transmitter>
radiante *adj* : radiant
radiar *vt* **1** : to radiate **2** : to irradiate **3** : to broadcast (on the radio)
radical[1] *adj* : radical, extreme — **radicalmente** *adv*
radical[2] *nmf* : radical
radicalismo *nm* : radicalism
radicar {72} *vi* **1** : to be found, to lie **2** ARRAIGAR : to take root — **radicarse** *vr* : to settle, to establish oneself
radio[1] *nm* **1** : radius **2** : radium
radio[2] *nmf* : radio
radioactividad *nf* : radioactivity
radioactivo, -va *adj* : radioactive
radioaficionado, -da *n* : ham radio operator
radiodifusión *nf, pl* **-siones** : radio broadcasting
radiodifusora *nf* : radio station
radioemisora *nf* : radio station
radiofaro *nm* : radio beacon
radiofónico, -ca *adj* : radio <estación radiofónica pública : public radio station>
radiofrecuencia *nf* : radio frequency
radiografía *nf* : X ray (photograph)
radiografiar {85} *vt* : to x-ray
radiología *nf* : radiology
radiólogo, -ga *n* : radiologist
radón *nm* : radon
raer {65} *vt* RASPAR : to scrape, to scrape off
ráfaga *nf* **1** : gust (of wind) **2** : flash, burst <una ráfaga de luz : a flash of light>
raid *nm CA, Mex fam* : lift, ride
raído, -da *adj* : worn, shabby
raiga, etc. → **raer**
raíz *nf, pl* **raíces** **1** : root **2** : origin, source **3** **a raíz de** : following, as a result of **4** **echar raíces** : to take root
raja *nf* **1** : crack, slit **2** : slice, wedge
rajá *nm* : raja
rajadura *nf* : crack, split
rajar *vt* HENDER : to crack, to split — *vi* **1** *fam* : to chatter **2** *fam* : to boast, to brag — **rajarse** *vr* **1** : to crack, to split open **2** *fam* : to back out
rajatabla *adv* **a ~** : strictly, to the letter
ralea *nf* : kind, sort, ilk <son de la misma valea : they're two of a kind>
ralentí *nm* **dejar al ralentí** : to leave (a motor) idling
rallado, -da *adj* **1** : grated **2** **pan rallado** : bread crumbs *pl*
rallador *nm* : grater
rallar *vt* : to grate
ralo, -la *adj* : sparse, thin
rama *nf* : branch
ramaje *nm* : branches *pl*
ramal *nm* **1** : branchline **2** : halter, strap
ramera *nf* : harlot, prostitute
ramificación *nf, pl* **-ciones** : ramification
ramificarse {72} *vr* : to branch out, to divide into branches
ramillete *nm* **1** RAMO : bouquet **2** : select group, cluster
ramo *nm* **1** : branch **2** RAMILLETE : bouquet **3** : division (of science or industry) **4** **Domingo de Ramos** : Palm Sunday
rampa *nf* : ramp, incline
rana *nf* **1** : frog **2** **rana toro** : bullfrog
ranchera *nf Mex* : traditional folk song
ranchería *nf* : settlement
ranchero, -ra *n* : rancher, farmer
rancho *nm* **1** : ranch, farm **2** : hut **3** : settlement, camp **4** : food, mess (for soldiers, etc.)
rancio, -cia *adj* **1** : aged, mellow (of wine) **2** : ancient, old **3** : rancid
rango *nm* **1** : rank, status **2** : high social standing **3** : pomp, splendor
ranúnculo *nm* : buttercup
ranura *nf* : groove, slot
rapacidad *nf* : rapacity
rapar *vt* **1** : to crop **2** : to shave
rapaz[1] *adj, pl* **rapaces** : rapacious, predatory
rapaz[2], **-paza** *n, mpl* **rapaces** : youngster, child
rape *nm* : close haircut
rapé *nm* : snuff
rapidez *nf* : rapidity, speed
rápido[1] *adv* : quickly, fast <¡manejas tan rápido! : you drive so fast!>
rápido[2], **-da** *adj* : rapid, quick — **rápidamente** *adv*
rápido[3] *nm* **1** : express train **2** **rápidos** *nmpl* : rapids
rapiña *nf* **1** : plunder, pillage **2** **ave de rapiña** : bird of prey
raposa *nf* : vixen (fox)
rapsodia *nf* : rhapsody
raptar *vt* SEQUESTRAR : to abduct, to kidnap
rapto *nm* **1** SECUESTRO : kidnapping, abduction **2** ARREBATO : fit, outburst
raptor, -tora *n* SECUESTRADOR : kidnapper
raque *nm* : beachcombing
raquero, -ra *n* : beachcomber
raqueta *nf* **1** : racket (in sports) **2** : snowshoe
raquítico, -ca *adj* **1** : scrawny, weak **2** : measly, skimpy
raquitismo *nm* : rickets
raramente *adv* : seldom, rarely

rareza *nf* **1** : rarity **2** : peculiarity, oddity

raro, -ra *adj* **1** EXTRAÑO : odd, strange, peculiar **2** : unusual, rare **3** : exceptional **4** **rara vez** : seldom, rarely

ras *nm* **a ras de** : level with

rasar *vt* **1** : to skim, to graze **2** : to level

rascacielos *nms & pl* : skyscraper

rascar {72} *vt* **1** : to scratch **2** : to scrape — **rascarse** *vr* : to scratch an itch

rasgadura *nf* : tear, rip

rasgar {52} *vt* : to rip, to tear — **rasgarse** *vr*

rasgo *nm* **1** : stroke (of a pen) <a grandes rasgos : in broad outlines> **2** CARACTERÍSTICA : trait, characteristic **3** : gesture, deed **4** **rasgos** *nmpl* FACCIONES : features

rasgón *nm, pl* **rasgones** : rip, tear

rasgue, etc. → **rasgar**

rasguear *vt* : to strum

rasguñar *vt* **1** : to scratch **2** : to sketch, to outline

rasguño *nm* **1** : scratch **2** : sketch

raso[1], -sa *adj* **1** : level, flat **2** **soldado raso** : private (in the army) <los soldados rasos : the ranks>

raso[2] *nm* : satin

raspadura *nf* **1** : scratching, scraping **2** **raspaduras** *nfpl* : scrapings

raspar *vt* **1** : to scrape **2** : to file down, to smooth — *vi* : to be rough

rasque, etc. → **rascar**

rastra *nf* **1** : harrow **2** **a rastras** : by dragging, unwillingly

rastrear *vt* **1** : to track, to trace **2** : to comb, to search **3** : to trawl

rastrero, -ra *adj* **1** : creeping, crawling **2** : vile, despicable

rastrillar *vt* : to rake, to harrow

rastrillo *nm* **1** : rake **2** *Mex* : razor

rastro *nm* **1** PISTA : trail, track **2** VESTIGIO : trace, sign

rastrojo *nm* : stubble (of plants)

rasurar *vt* AFEITAR : to shave — **rasurarse** *vr*

rata[1] *nm fam* : pickpocket, thief

rata[2] *nf* **1** : rat **2** *Col, Pan, Peru* : rate, percentage

ratear *vt* : to pilfer, to steal

ratero, -ra *n* : petty thief

ratificación *nf, pl* **-ciones** : ratification

ratificar {72} *vt* **1** : to ratify **2** : to confirm

rato *nm* **1** : while **2** **pasar el rato** : to pass the time **3** **a cada rato** : all the time, constantly <les sacaba dinero a cada rato : he was always taking money from them> **4** **al poco rato** : later, shortly after

ratón[1], -tona *n, mpl* **ratones 1** : mouse **2** **ratón de biblioteca** *fam* : bookworm

ratón[2] *nm, pl* **ratones 1** : (computer) mouse **2** *CoRi* : biceps

ratonera *nf* : mousetrap

raudal *nm* **1** : torrent **2** **a raudales** : in abundance

raya[1], etc. → **raer**

raya[2] *nf* **1** : line **2** : stripe **3** : skate, ray **4** : part (in the hair) **5** : crease (in clothing)

rayar *vt* **1** ARAÑAR : to scratch **2** : to scrawl on, to mark up <rayaron las paredes : they covered the walls with graffiti> — *vi* **1** : to scratch **2** AMANECER : to dawn, to break <al rayar el alba : at break of day> **3** **~ con** : to be adjacent to, to be next to **4** **~ en** : to border on, to verge on <su respuesta raya en lo ridículo : his answer borders on the ridiculous> — **rayarse** *vr*

rayo *nm* **1** : ray, beam <rayo láser : laser beam> <rayo de gamma : gamma ray> <rayo de sol : sunbeam> **2** RELÁMPAGO : lightning bolt **3** **rayo X** : X ray

rayón *nm, pl* **rayones** : rayon

raza *nf* **1** : race <raza humana : human race> **2** : breed, strain **3** **de ~** : thoroughbred, pedigreed

razón *nf, pl* **razones 1** MOTIVO : reason, motive <en razón de : by reason of, because of> **2** JUSTICIA : rightness, justice <tener razón : to be right> **3** : reasoning, sense <perder la razón : to lose one's mind> **4** : ratio, proportion

razonable *adj* : reasonable — **razonablemente** *adv*

razonado, -da *adj* : itemized, detailed

razonamiento *nm* : reasoning

razonar *v* : to reason, to think

reabastecimiento *nm* : replenishment

reabierto *pp* → **reabrir**

reabrir {2} *vt* : to reopen — **reabrirse** *vr*

reacción *nf, pl* **-ciones 1** : reaction **2** **motor a reacción** : jet engine

reaccionar *vi* : to react, to respond

reaccionario, -ria *adj & n* : reactionary

reacio, -cia *adj* : resistant, opposed

reacondicionar *vt* : to recondition

reactor *nm* **1** : reactor <reactor nuclear : nuclear reactor> **2** : jet engine **3** : jet airplane, jet

reafirmar *vt* : to reaffirm, to assert, to strengthen

reajustar *vt* : to readjust, to adjust

reajuste *nm* : readjustment <reajuste de precios : price increase>

real *adj* **1** : real, true **2** : royal

realce *nm* **1** : embossing, relief **2** **dar realce** : to highlight, to bring out

realeza *nf* : royalty

realidad *nf* **1** : reality **2** **en ~** : in truth, actually

realinear *vt* : to realign

realismo *nm* **1** : realism **2** : royalism

realista[1] *adj* **1** : realistic **2** : realist **3** : royalist

realista[2] *nmf* **1** : realist **2** : royalist

realización *nf, pl* **-ciones** : execution, realization

realizar {21} *vt* **1** : to carry out, to execute **2** : to produce, to direct (a film or play) **3 :** to fulfill, to achieve **4 :** to realize (a profit) — **realizarse** *vr* **1 :** to come true **2 :** to fulfill oneself

realmente *adv* **:** really, in reality

realzar {21} *vt* **1 :** to heighten, to raise **2 :** to highlight, to enhance

reanimación *nf, pl* **-ciones :** revival, resuscitation

reanimar *vt* **1 :** to revive, to restore **2 :** to resuscitate — **reanimarse** *vr* **:** to come around, to recover

reanudar *vt* **:** to resume, to renew — **reanadarse** *vr* **:** to resume, to continue

reaparecer {53} *vi* **1 :** to reappear **2 :** to make a comeback

reaparición *nf, pl* **-ciones :** reappearance

reapertura *nf* **:** reopening

reata *nf* **1 :** rope **2** *Mex* **:** lasso, lariat **3 de ~ :** single file

reavivar *vt* **:** to revive, to reawaken

rebaja *nf* **1 :** reduction **2** DESCUENTO **:** discount **3 rebajas** *nfpl* **:** sale

rebajar *vt* **1 :** to reduce, to lower **2 :** to lessen, to diminish **3 :** to humiliate — **rebajarse** *vr* **: 1 :** to humble oneself **2 rebajarse a :** to stoop to

rebanada *nf* **:** slice

rebañar *vt* **:** to mop up, to sop up

rebaño *nm* **1 :** flock **2 :** herd

rebasar *vt* **1 :** to surpass, to exceed **2** *Mex* **:** to pass, to overtake

rebatiña *nf* **:** scramble, fight (over something)

rebatir *vt* REFUTAR **:** to refute

rebato *nm* **1 :** surprise attack **2 tocar a rebato :** to sound the alarm

rebelarse *vr* **:** to rebel

rebelde[1] *adj* **:** rebellious, unruly

rebelde[2] *nmf* **1 :** rebel **2 :** defaulter

rebeldía *nf* **1 :** rebelliousness **2 en ~ :** in default

rebelión *nf, pl* **-liones :** rebellion

rebobinar *vt* **:** to rewind

reborde *nm* **:** border, flange, rim

rebosante *adj* **:** brimming, overflowing <rebosante de salud : brimming with health>

rebosar *vi* **1 :** to overflow **2 ~ de :** to abound in, to be bursting with — *vt* **:** to radiate

rebotar *vi* **1 :** to bounce **2 :** to ricochet, to rebound

rebote *nm* **1 :** bounce **2 :** rebound, ricochet

rebozar {21} *vt* **:** to coat in batter

rebozo *nm* **1 :** shawl, wrap **2 sin ~ :** frankly, openly

rebullir {38} *v* **:** to move, to stir — **rebullirse** *vr*

rebuscado, -da *adj* **:** affected, pretentious

rebuscar {72} *vi* **:** to search thoroughly

rebuznar *vi* **:** to bray

rebuzno *nm* **:** bray, braying

recabar *vt* **1 :** to gather, to obtain, to collect **2 recabar fondos :** to raise money

recado *nm* **1 :** message <mandar recado : to send word> **2** *Spain* **:** errand

recaer {13} *vi* **1 :** to relapse **2 ~ en** *or* **~ sobre :** to fall on, to fall to

recaída *nf* **:** relapse

recaiga, etc. → **recaer**

recalar *vi* **:** to arrive

recalcar {72} *vt* **:** to emphasize, to stress

recalcitrante *adj* **:** recalcitrant

recalentar {55} *vt* **1 :** to reheat, to warm up **2 :** to overheat

recámara *nf* **1** *Col, Mex, Pan* **:** bedroom **2 :** chamber (of a firearm)

recamarera *nf Mex* **:** chambermaid

recambio *nm* **1 :** spare part **2 :** refill (for a pen, etc.)

recapacitar *vi* **1 :** to reconsider **2 ~ en :** to reflect on, to weigh

recapitular *v* **:** to recapitulate — **recapitulación** *nf*

recargable *adj* **:** rechargeable

recargado, -da *adj* **:** overly elaborate or ornate

recargar {52} *vt* **1 :** to recharge **2 :** to overload

recargo *nm* **:** surcharge

recatado, -da *adj* MODESTO **:** modest, demure

recato *nm* PUDOR **:** modesty

recaudación *nf, pl* **-ciones 1 :** collection **2 :** earnings *pl*, takings *pl*

recaudador, -dora *n* **recaudador de impuestos :** tax collector

recaudar *vt* **:** to collect

recaudo *nm* **:** safe place <a (buen) recaudo : in safe keeping>

recayó, etc. → **recaer**

rece, etc. → **rezar**

recelo *nm* **:** distrust, suspicion

receloso, -sa *adj* **:** distrustful, suspicious

recepción *nf, pl* **-ciones :** reception

recepcionista *nmf* **:** receptionist

receptáculo *nm* **:** receptacle

receptividad *nf* **:** receptivity, receptiveness

receptivo, -va *adj* **:** receptive

receptor[1]**, -tora** *adj* **:** receiving

receptor[2]**, -tora** *n* **1 :** recipient **2 :** catcher (in baseball), receiver (in football)

receptor[3] *nm* **:** receiver <receptor de televisión : television set>

recesión *nf, pl* **-siones :** recession

recesivo, -va *adj* **:** recessive

receso *nm* **:** recess, adjournment

receta *nf* **1 :** recipe **2 :** prescription

recetar *vt* **:** to prescribe (medications)

rechazar {21} *vt* **1 :** to reject **2 :** to turn down, to refuse

rechazo *nm* **:** rejection, refusal

rechifla *nf* **:** booing, jeering

rechinar *vi* **1 :** to squeak **2 :** to grind, to gnash <hacer rechinar los dientes : to grind one's teeth>

rechoncho, -cha *adj fam* **:** chubby, squat

recibidor *nm* **:** vestibule, entrance hall

recibimiento *nm* **:** reception, welcome

recibir *vt* **1 :** to receive, to get **2 :** to welcome — *vi* **:** to receive visitors — **recibirse** *vr* **~ de :** to qualify as

recibo *nm* **:** receipt

reciclable *adj* **:** recyclable

reciclado *nm* → **reciclaje**

reciclaje *nm* **1 :** recycling **2 :** retraining

reciclar *vt* **1 :** to recycle **2 :** to retrain

recién *adv* **1 :** newly, recently <recién nacido : newborn> <recién casados : newlyweds> <recién llegado : newcomer> **2 :** just, only just <recién ahora me acordé : I just now remembered>

reciente *adj* **:** recent — **recientemente** *adv*

recinto *nm* **1 :** enclosure **2 :** site, premises *pl*

recio[1] *adv* **1 :** strongly, hard **2 :** loudly, loud

recio[2]**, -cia** *adj* **1 :** severe, harsh **2 :** tough, strong

recipiente[1] *nm* **:** container, receptacle

recipiente[2] *nmf* **:** recipient

reciprocar {72} *vi* **:** to reciprocate

reciprocidad *nf* **:** reciprocity

recíproco, -ca *adj* **:** reciprocal, mutual

recitación *nf, pl* **-ciones :** recitation, recital

recital *nm* **:** recital

recitar *vt* **:** to recite

reclamación *nf, pl* **-ciones 1 :** claim, demand **2** QUEJA **:** complaint

reclamar *vt* **1** EXIGIR **:** to demand, to require **2 :** to claim — *vi* **:** to complain

reclamo *nm* **1 :** bird call, lure **2 :** lure, decoy **3 :** inducement, attraction **4 :** advertisement **5 :** complaint

reclinar *vt* **:** to rest, to lean — **reclinarse** *vr* **:** to recline, to lean back

recluir {41} *vt* **:** to confine, to lock up — **recluirse** *vr* **:** to shut oneself up, to withdraw

reclusión *nf, pl* **-siones :** imprisonment

recluso, -sa *n* **1 :** inmate, prisoner **2** SOLITARIO **:** recluse

recluta *nmf* **:** recruit, draftee

reclutamiento *nm* **:** recruitment, recruiting

reclutar *vt* ENROLAR **:** to recruit, to enlist

recobrar *vt* **:** to recover, to regain — **recobrarse** *vr* **:** to recover, to recuperate

recocer {14} *vt* **:** to overcook, to cook again

recodo *nm* **:** bend

recogedor *nm* **:** dustpan

recoger {15} *vt* **1 :** to collect, to gather **2 :** to get, to retrieve, to pick up **3 :** to clean up, to tidy (up)

recogido, -da *adj* **:** quiet, secluded

recogimiento *nm* **1 :** collecting, gathering **2 :** withdrawal **3 :** absorption, concentration

recolección *nf, pl* **-ciones 1 :** collection <recolección de basura : trash pickup> **2 :** harvest

recolectar *vt* **1 :** to gather, to collect **2 :** to harvest, to pick

recomendable *adj* **:** advisable, recommended

recomendación *nf, pl* **-ciones :** recommendation

recomendar {55} *vt* **1 :** to recommend **2** ACONSEJAR **:** to advise

recompensa *nf* **:** reward, recompense

recompensar *vt* **1** PREMIAR **:** to reward **2 :** to compensate

reconciliación *nf, pl* **-ciones :** reconciliation

reconciliar *vt* **:** to reconcile — **reconciliarse** *vr*

recóndito, -ta *adj* **1 :** remote, isolated **2 :** hidden, recondite **3 en lo más recóndito de :** in the depths of

reconfortar *vt* **:** to comfort — **reconfortante** *adj*

reconocer {18} *vt* **1 :** to recognize **2 :** to admit **3 :** to examine

reconocible *adj* **:** recognizable

reconocido, -da *adj* **1 :** recognized, accepted **2 :** grateful

reconocimiento *nm* **1 :** acknowledgment, recognition, avowal **2 :** (medical) examination **3 :** reconnaissance

reconsiderar *vt* **:** to reconsider — **reconsideración** *nf*

reconstrucción *nf, pl* **-ciones :** reconstruction

reconstruir {41} *vt* **:** to rebuild, to reconstruct

reconversión *nf, pl* **-siones :** restructuring

reconvertir {76} *vt* **1 :** to restructure **2 :** to retrain

recopilación *nf, pl* **-ciones 1 :** summary **2 :** collection, compilation

recopilar *vt* **:** to compile, to collect

récord *or* **record** [ˈrɛkɔr] *nm, pl* **récords** *or* **records** [-kɔrs] **:** record <record mundial : world record> — **récord** *or* **record** *adj*

recordar {19} *vt* **1 :** to recall, to remember **2 :** to remind — *vi* **1** ACORDARSE **:** to remember **2** DESPERTAR **:** to wake up

recordatorio[1]**, -ria** *adj* **:** commemorative

recordatorio[2] *nm* **:** reminder

recorrer *vt* **1 :** to travel through, to tour **2 :** to cover (a distance) **3 :** to go over, to look over

recorrido *nm* **1 :** journey, trip **2 :** path, route, course **3 :** round (in golf)

recortar *vt* **1 :** to cut, to reduce **2 :** to cut out **3 :** to trim, to cut off **4 :** to outline — **recortarse** *vr* **:** to stand out <los árboles se recortaban en el horizonte : the trees were silhouetted against the horizon>

recorte *nm* **1 :** cut, reduction **2 :** clipping <recortes de periódicos : newspaper clippings>

recostar {19} *vt* **:** to lean, to rest — **recostarse** *vr* **:** to lie down, recline

recoveco *nm* **1** VUELTA **:** bend, turn **2 :** nook, corner **3 recovecos** *nmpl* **:** intricacies, ins and outs

recreación *nf, pl* **-ciones 1 :** re-creation **2** DIVERSIÓN **:** recreation, entertainment

recrear *vt* **1 :** to re-create **2 :** to entertain, to amuse — **recrearse** *vr* **:** to enjoy oneself

recreativo, -va *adj* **:** recreational

recreo *nm* **1** DIVERSIÓN **:** entertainment, amusement **2 :** recess, break

recriminación *nf, pl* **-ciones :** reproach, recrimination

recriminar *vt* **:** to reproach — *vi* **:** to recriminate — **recriminarse** *vr*

recrudecer {53} *v* **:** to intensify, to worsen — **recrudecerse** *vr*

rectal *adj* **:** rectal

rectangular *adj* **:** rectangular

rectángulo *nm* **:** rectangle

rectificación *nf, pl* **-ciones :** rectification, correction

rectificar {72} *vt* **1 :** to rectify, to correct **2 :** to straighten (out)

rectitud *nf* **1 :** straightness **2 :** honesty, rectitude

recto[1] *adv* **:** straight

recto[2]**, -ta** *adj* **1 :** straight **2 :** upright, honorable **3 :** sound

recto[3] *nm* **:** rectum

rector[1]**, -tora** *adj* **:** governing, managing

rector[2]**, -tora** *n* **:** rector

rectoría *nf* **:** rectory

recubierto *pp* → **recubrir**

recubrir {2} *vt* **:** to cover, to coat

recuento *nm* **:** recount, count <un recuento de los votos : a recount of the votes>

recuerdo *nm* **1 :** memory **2 :** souvenir, memento **3 recuerdos** *nmpl* **:** regards

recuperación *nf, pl* **-ciones 1 :** recovery, recuperation **2 recuperación de datos :** data retrieval

recuperar *vt* **1 :** to recover, to get back, to retrieve **2 :** to recuperate **3 :** to make up for <recuperar el tiempo perdido : to make up for lost time> — **recuperarse** *vr* **~ de :** to recover from, to get over

recurrente *adj* **:** recurrent, recurring

recurrir *vi* **1 ~ a :** to turn to, to appeal to **2 ~ a :** to resort to **3 :** to appeal (in law)

recurso *nm* **1 :** recourse <el último recurso : the last resort> **2 :** appeal (in law) **3 recursos** *nmpl* **:** resources, means <recursos naturales : natural resources>

red *nf* **1 :** net, mesh **2 :** network, system, chain **3 :** trap, snare

redacción *nf, pl* **-ciones 1 :** writing, composition **2 :** editing

redactar *vt* **1 :** to write, to draft **2 :** to edit

redactor, -tora *n* **:** editor

redada *nf* **1 :** raid **2 :** catch, haul

redefinir *vt* **:** to redefine — **redefinición** *nf*

redención *nf, pl* **-ciones :** redemption

redentor[1]**, -tora** *adj* **:** redeeming

redentor[2]**, -tora** *n* **:** redeemer

redescubierto *pp* → **redescubrir**

redescubrir {2} *vt* **:** to rediscover

redicho, -cha *adj fam* **:** affected, pretentious

redil *nm* **1 :** sheepfold **2 volver al redil :** to return to the fold

redimir *vt* **:** to redeem, to deliver (from sin)

rediseñar *vt* **:** to redesign

redistribuir {41} *vt* **:** to redistribute — **redistribución** *nf*

rédito *nm* **:** return, yield

redituar {3} *vt* **:** to produce, to yield

redoblar *vt* **:** to redouble, to strengthen — **redoblado, -da** *adj*

redomado, -da *adj* **1 :** sly, crafty **2 :** utter, out-and-out

redonda *nf* **1 :** region, surrounding area **2 a la redonda** ALREDEDOR **:** around <de diez millas a la redonda : for ten miles around>

redondear *vt* **:** to round off, to round out

redondel *nm* **1 :** ring, circle **2 :** bullring, arena

redondez *nf* **:** roundness

redondo, -da *adj* **1 :** round <mesa redonda : round table> **2 :** great, perfect <un negocio redondo : an excellent deal> **3 :** straightforward, flat <un rechazo redondo : a flat refusal> **4** *Mex* **:** round-trip **5 en ~ :** around

reducción *nf, pl* **-ciones :** reduction, decrease

reducido, -da *adj* **1 :** reduced, limited **2 :** small

reducir {61} *vt* **1** DISMINUIR **:** to reduce, to decrease, to cut **2 :** to subdue **3 :** to boil down — **reducirse** *vr* **~ a :** to come down to, to be nothing more than

redundancia *nf* **:** reduncancy

redundante *adj* **:** redundant

reedición *nf, pl* **-ciones :** reprint

reelegir {28} *vt* **:** to reelect — **reelección** *nf*

reembolsable *adj* **:** refundable

reembolsar *vt* **1 :** to refund, to reimburse **2 :** to repay

reembolso *nm* **:** refund, reimbursement

reemplazable *adj* **:** replaceable

reemplazar {21} *vt* **:** to replace, to substitute

reemplazo *nm* **:** replacement, substitution

reencarnación *nf, pl* **-ciones :** reincarnation

reencuentro *nm* **:** reunion

reestablecer {53} *vt* **:** to reestablish

reestructurar *vt* : to restructure
reexaminar *vt* : to reexamine
refaccionar *vt* : to repair, to renovate
refacciones *nfpl* : repairs, renovations
referencia *nf* **1** : reference **2 hacer referencia a** : to refer to
referendo *nm* → **referéndum**
referéndum *nm, pl* **-dums** : referendum
referente *adj* **~ a** : concerning
réferi *or* **referi** ['rɛfɛri] *nmf* : referee
referir {76} *vt* **1** : to relate, to tell **2** : to refer <nos refirió al diccionario : she referred us to the dictionary> — **referirse** *vr* **1 ~ a** : to refer to **2 ~ a** : to be concerned, to be in reference to <en lo que se refiere a la educación : as far as education is concerned>
refinado[1], -da *adj* : refined
refinado[2] *nm* : refining
refinamiento *nm* **1** : refining **2** FINURA : refinement
refinanciar *vt* : to refinance
refinar *vt* : to refine
refinería *nf* : refinery
reflectante *adj* : reflective, reflecting
reflector[1], -tora *adj* : reflecting
reflector[2] *nm* **1** : spotlight, searchlight **2** : reflector
reflejar *vt* : to reflect — **reflejarse** *vr* : to be reflected <la decepción se refleja en su rostro : the disappointment shows on her face>
reflejo *nm* **1** : reflection **2** : reflex **3 reflejos** *nmpl* : highlights, streaks (in hair)
reflexión *nf, pl* **-xiones** : reflection, thought
reflexionar *vi* : to reflect, to think
reflexivo, -va *adj* **1** : reflective, thoughtful **2** : reflexive
reflujo *nm* : ebb, ebb tide
reforma *nf* **1** : reform **2** : alteration, renovation
reformador, -dora *n* : reformer
reformar *vt* **1** : to reform **2** : to change, to alter **3** : to renovate, to repair — **reformarse** *vr* : to mend one's ways
reformatorio *nm* : reformatory
reformular *vt* : to reformulate — **reformulación** *nf*
reforzar {36} *vt* **1** : to reinforce, to strengthen **2** : to encourage, to support
refracción *nf, pl* **-ciones** : refraction
refractar *vt* : to refract — **refractarse** *vr*
refractario, -ria *adj* : refractory, obstinate
refrán *nm, pl* **refranes** ADAGIO : proverb, saying
refregar {49} *vt* : to scrub
refrenar *vt* **1** : to rein in (a horse) **2** : to restrain, to check — **refrenarse** *vr* : to restrain oneself
refrendar *vt* **1** : to countersign, to endorse **2** : to stamp (a passport)
refrescante *adj* : refreshing
refrescar {72} *vt* **1** : to refresh, to cool **2** : to brush up (on) **3 refrescar la memoria** : to refresh one's memory — *vi* : to turn cooler
refresco *nm* : refreshment, soft drink
refriega *nf* : skirmish, scuffle
refrigeración *nf, pl* **-ciones 1** : refrigeration **2** : air-conditioning
refrigerador *nmf* NEVERA : refrigerator
refrigeradora *nf Col, Peru* : refrigerator
refrigerante *nm* : coolant
refrigerar *vt* **1** : to refrigerate **2** : to air-condition
refrigerio *nm* : snack, refreshments *pl*
refrito[1], -ta *adj* : refried
refrito[2] *nm* : rehash
refuerzo *nm* : reinforcement, support
refugiado, -da *n* : refugee
refugiar *vt* : to shelter — **refugiarse** *vr* ACOGERSE : to take refuge
refugio *nm* : refuge, shelter
refulgencia *nf* : brilliance, splendor
refulgir {35} *vi* : to shine brightly
refundir *vt* **1** : to recast (metals) **2** : to revise, to rewrite
refunfuñar *vi* : to grumble, to groan
refutar *vt* : to refute — **refutación** *nf*
regadera *nf* **1** : watering can **2** : shower head, shower **3** : sprinkler
regaderazo *nm Mex* : shower
regalar *vt* **1** OBSEQUIAR : to present (as a gift), to give away **2** : to regale, to entertain **3** : to flatter, to make a fuss over — **regalarse** *vr* : to pamper oneself
regalía *nf* : royalty, payment
regaliz *nm, pl* **-lices** : licorice
regalo *nm* **1** OBSEQUIO : gift, present **2** : pleasure, comfort **3** : treat
regañadientes *mpl* **a ~** : reluctantly, unwillingly
regañar *vt* : to scold, to give a talking to — *vi* **1** QUEJARSE : to grumble, to complain **2** REÑIR : to quarrel, to argue
regaño *nm fam* : scolding
regañon, -ñona *adj, mpl* **-ñones** *fam* : grumpy, irritable
regar {49} *vt* **1** : to irrigate **2** : to water **3** : to wash, to hose down **4** : to spill, to scatter
regata *nf* : regatta, yacht race
regate *nm* : dodge, feint
regatear *vt* **1** : to haggle over **2** ESCATIMAR : to skimp on, to be sparing with — *vi* : to bargain, to haggle
regateo *nm* : bargaining, haggling
regatón *nm, pl* **-tones** : ferrule, tip
regazo *nm* : lap (of a person)
regencia *nf* : regency
regenerar *vt* : to regenerate — **regenerarse** *vr* — **regeneración** *nf*
regentar *vt* : to run, to manage
regente *nmf* : regent
regidor, -dora *n* : town councillor
régimen *nm, pl* **regímenes 1** : regime **2** : diet **3** : regimen, rules *pl* <régimen de vida : lifestyle>
regimiento *nm* : regiment

regio, -gia *adj* **1 :** great, magnificent **2 :** regal, royal

región *nf, pl* **regiones :** region, area

regional *adj* **:** regional — **regionalmente** *adv*

regir {28} *vt* **1 :** to rule **2 :** to manage, to run **3 :** to control, to govern <las costumbres que rigen la conducta : the customs which govern behavior> — *vi* **:** to apply, to be in force <las leyes rigen en los tres países : the laws apply in all three countries> — **regirse** *vr* **~ por :** to go by, to be guided by

registrador[1], -dora *adj* **caja registradora :** cash register

registrador[2], -dora *n* **:** registrar, recorder

registrar *vt* **1 :** to register, to record **2** GRABAR **:** to record, to tape **3 :** to search, to examine — **registrarse** *vr* **1** INSCRIBIRSE **:** to register **2** OCURRIR **:** to happen, to occur

registro *nm* **1 :** register **2 :** registration **3 :** registry, record office **4 :** range (of a voice or musical instrument) **5 :** search

regla *nf* **1** NORMA **:** rule, regulation **2 :** ruler <regla de cálculo : slide rule> **3** MENSTRUACIÓN **:** period, menstruation

reglamentación *nf, pl* **-ciones 1 :** regulation **2 :** rules *pl*

reglamentar *vt* **:** to regulate, to set rules for

reglamentario, -ria *adj* **:** regulation, official <equipo reglamentario : standard equipment>

reglamento *nm* **:** regulations *pl*, rules *pl* <reglamento de tráfico : traffic regulations>

regocijar *vt* **:** to gladden, to delight — **regocijarse** *vr* **:** to rejoice

regocijo *nm* **:** delight, rejoicing

regordete *adj fam* LLENITO **:** chubby

regresar *vt* DEVOLVER **:** to give back — *vi* **:** to return, to come back, to go back

regresión *nf, pl* **-siones :** regression, return

regresivo, -va *adj* **:** regressive

regreso *nm* **1 :** return **2 estar de regreso :** to be back, to be home

reguero *nm* **1 :** irrigation ditch **2 :** trail, trace **3 propagarse como reguero de pólvora :** to spread like wildfire

regulable *adj* **:** adjustable

regulación *nf, pl* **-ciones :** regulation, control

regulador[1], -dora *adj* **:** regulating, regulatory

regulador[2] *nm* **1 :** regulator, governor **2 regulador de tiro :** damper (in a chimney)

regular[1] *vt* **:** to regulate, to control

regular[2] *adj* **1 :** regular **2 :** fair, OK, so-so **3 :** medium, average **4 por lo regular :** in general, generally

regularidad *nf* **:** regularity

regularización *nf, pl* **-ciones** NORMALIZACIÓN **:** normalization

regularizar {21} *vt* NORMALIZAR **:** to normalize, to make regular

regularmente *adv* **:** regularly

rehabilitar *vt* **1 :** to rehabilitate **2 :** to reinstate **3 :** renovate, to restore — **rehabilitación** *nf*

rehacer {40} *vt* **1 :** to redo **2 :** to remake, to repair, to renew — **rehacerse** *vr* **1 :** to recover **2 ~ de :** to get over

rehecho *pp* → **rehacer**

rehén *nm, pl* **rehenes :** hostage

rehicieron, etc. → **rehacer**

rehizo → **rehacer**

rehuir {41} *vt* **:** to avoid, to shun

rehusar {8} *v* **:** to refuse

reimprimir *vt* **:** to reprint

reina *nf* **:** queen

reinado *nm* **:** reign

reinante *adj* **1 :** reigning **2 :** prevailing, current

reinar *vi* **1 :** to reign **2 :** to prevail

reincidencia *nf* **:** recidivism, relapse

reincidente *nmf* **:** backslider, recidivist

reincidir *vi* **:** to backslide, to retrogress

reincorporar *vt* **:** to reinstate — **reincorporarse** *vr* **~ a :** to return to, to rejoin

reino *nm* **:** kingdom, realm <reino animal : animal kingdom>

reinstalar *vt* **1 :** to reinstall **2 :** to reinstate

reintegrar *vt* **1 :** to reintegrate, reinstate **2 :** to refund, to reimburse — **reintegrarse** *vr* **~ a :** to return to, to rejoin

reír {66} *vi* **:** to laugh — *vt* **:** to laugh at — **reírse** *vr*

reiteración *nf, pl* **-ciones :** reiteration, repetition

reiterado, -da *adj* **:** repeated <lo explicó en reiteradas ocasiones : he explained it repeatedly> — **reiteradamente** *adv*

reiterar *vt* **:** to reiterate, to repeat

reiterativo, -va *adj* **:** repetitive, repetitious

reivindicación *nf, pl* **-ciones 1 :** demand, claim **2 :** vindication

reivindicar {72} *vt* **1 :** to vindicate **2 :** to demand, to claim **3 :** to restore

reja *nf* **1 :** grill, grating <entre rejas : behind bars> **2 :** plowshare

rejilla *nf* **:** grille, grate, screen

rejuvenecer {53} *vt* **:** to rejuvenate — *vi* **:** to be rejuvenated — **rejuvenecerse** *vr*

rejuvencimiento *m* **:** rejuvenation

relación *nf, pl* **-ciones 1 :** relation, connection, relevance **2 :** relationship **3** RELATO **:** account **4** LISTA **:** list **5 con relación a** *or* **en relación con :** in relation to, concerning **6 relaciones públicas :** public relations

relacionar *vt* **:** to relate, to connect — **relacionarse** *vr* **~ con :** to be connected to, to be linked with

relajación *nf, pl* **-ciones** : relaxation

relajado, -da *adj* **1** : relaxed, loose **2** : dissolute, depraved

relajar *vt* : to relax, to slacken — *vi* : to be relaxing — **relajarse** *vr*

relajo *nm* **1** : commotion, ruckus **2** : joke, laugh <lo hizo de relajo : he did it for a laugh>

relamerse *vr* : to smack one's lips, to lick one's chops

relámpago *nm* : flash of lightning

relampaguear *vi* : to flash

relanzar {21} *vt* : to relaunch

relatar *vt* : to relate, to tell

relativo, -va *adj* **1** : relative **2 en lo relativo a** : with regard to, concerning — **relativamente** *adv*

relato *nm* **1** : story, tale **2** : account

releer {20} *vt* : to reread

relegar {52} *vt* **1** : to relegate **2 relegar al olvido** : to consign to oblivion

relevante *adj* : outstanding, important

relevar *vt* **1** : to relieve, to take over from **2 ~ de** : to exempt from — **relevarse** *vr* : to take turns

relevo *nm* **1** : relief, replacement **2** : relay <carrera de relevos : relay race>

relicario *nm* **1** : reliquary **2** : locket

relieve *nm* **1** : relief, projection <mapa en relieve : relief map> <letras en relieve : embossed letters> **2** : prominence, importance **3 poner en relieve** : to highlight, to emphasize

religión *nf, pl* **-giones** : religion

religiosamente *adv* : religiously, faithfully

religioso[1], -sa *adj* : religious

religioso[2], -sa *n* : monk *m*, nun *f*

relinchar *vi* : to neigh, to whinny

relincho *nm* : neigh, whinny

reliquia *nf* **1** : relic **2 reliquia de familia** : family heirloom

rellenar *vt* **1** : to refill **2** : to stuff, to fill **3** : to fill out

relleno[1], -na *adj* : stuffed, filled

relleno[2] *nm* : stuffing, filling

reloj *nm* **1** : clock **2** : watch **3 reloj de arena** : hourglass **4 reloj de pulsera** : wristwatch **5 como un reloj** : like clockwork

relojería *nf* **1** : watchmaker's shop **2** : watchmaking, clockmaking

reluciente *adj* : brilliant, shining

relucir {45} *vi* **1** : to glitter, to shine **2 salir a relucir** : to come to the surface **3 sacar a relucir** : to bring up, to mention

relumbrante *adj* : dazzling

relumbrar *vi* : to shine brightly

relumbrón *nm, pl* **-brones 1** : flash, glare **2 de ~** : flashy, showy

remachar *vt* **1** : to rivet **2** : to clinch (a nail) **3** : to stress, to drive home — *vi* : to smash, to spike (a ball)

remache *nm* **1** : rivet **2** : smash, spike (in sports)

remanente *nm* **1** : remainder, balance **2** : surplus

remanso *nm* : pool

remar *vi* **1** : to row, to paddle **2** : to struggle, to toil

remarcar {72} *vt* : to emphasize, to stress

rematado, -da *adj* : utter, complete

rematador, -dora *n* : auctioneer

rematar *vt* **1** : to finish off **2** : to auction — *vi* **1** : to shoot **2** : to end

remate *nm* **1** : shot (in sports) **2** : auction **3** : end, conclusion **4 como ~** : to top it off **5 de ~** : completely, utterly

remecer {86} *vt* : to sway, to swing

remedar *vt* **1** IMITAR : to imitate, to copy **2** : to mimic, to ape

remediar *vt* **1** : to remedy, to repair **2** : to help out, to assist **3** EVITAR : to prevent, to avoid

remedio *nm* **1** : remedy, cure **2** : solution **3** : option <no me quedó más remedio : I had no other choice> <no hay remedio : it can't be helped> **4 poner remedio a** : to put a stop to **5 sin ~** : unavoidable, inevitable

remedo *nm* : imitation

rememorar *vi* : to recall <rememorar los viejos tiempos : to reminisce>

remendar {55} *vt* **1** : to mend, to patch, to darn **2** : to correct

remero, -ra *n* : rower

remesa *nf* **1** : remittance **2** : shipment

remezón *nm, pl* **-zones** : mild earthquake, tremor

remiendo *nm* **1** : patch **2** : correction

remilgado, -da *adj* **1** : prim, prudish **2** : affected

remilgo *nm* : primness, affectation

reminiscencia *nf* : reminiscence

remisión *nf, pl* **-siones 1** ENVÍO : sending, delivery **2** : remission **3** : reference, cross-reference

remiso, -sa *adj* **1** : lax, remiss **2** : reluctant

remitente[1] *nm* : return address

remitente[2] *nmf* : sender (of a letter, etc.)

remitir *vt* **1** : to send, to remit **2 ~ a** : to refer to, to direct to <nos remitió al diccionario : he referred us to the dictionary> — *vi* : to subside, to let up

remo *nm* **1** : paddle, oar **2** : rowing (sport)

remoción *nf, pl* **-ciones 1** : removal **2** : dismissal

remodelación *nf, pl* **-ciones 1** : remodeling **2** : reorganization, restructuring

remodelar *vt* **1** : to remodel **2** : to restructure

remojar *vt* **1** : to soak, to steep **2** : to dip, to dunk **3** : to celebrate with a drink

remojo *nm* **1** : soaking, steeping **2 poner en remojo** : to soak, to leave soaking

remolacha *nf* : beet

remolcador *nm* : tugboat

remolcar {72} *vt* : to tow, to haul

remolino *nm* **1** : whirlwind **2** : eddy, whirlpool **3** : crowd, throng **4** : cowlick

remolque *nm* **1** : towing, tow **2** : trailer **3 a ~** : in tow

remontar *vt* **1** : to overcome **2** SUBIR : to go up — **remontarse** *vr* **1** : to soar **2 ~ a** : to date from, to go back to

rémora *nf* : obstacle, hindrance

remorder {47} *vt* INQUIETAR : to trouble, to distress

remordimiento *nm* : remorse

remotamente *adv* : remotely, vaguely

remoto, -ta *adj* **1** : remote, unlikely <hay una posibilidad remota : there is a slim possibility> **2** : distant, far-off

remover {47} *vt* **1** : to stir **2** : to move around, to turn over **3** : to stir up **4** : to remove **5** : to dismiss

remozamiento *nm* : renovation

remozar {21} *vt* **1** : to renew, to brighten up **2** : to redo, to renovate

remuneración *nf, pl* **-ciones** : remuneration, pay

remunerar *vt* : to pay, to remunerate

remunerativo, -va *adj* : remunerative

renacer {48} *vi* : to be reborn, to revive

renacimiento *nm* **1** : rebirth, revival **2 el Renacimiento** : the Renaissance

renacuajo *nm* : tadpole, pollywog

renal *adj* : renal, kidney

rencilla *nf* : quarrel

renco, -ca *adj* : lame

rencor *nm* **1** : rancor, enmity, hostility **2 guardar rencor** : to hold a grudge

rencoroso, -sa *adj* : resentful, rancorous

rendición *nf, pl* **-ciones** **1** : surrender, submission **2** : yield, return

rendido, -da *adj* **1** : submissive **2** : worn-out, exhausted **3** : devoted

rendija *nf* GRIETA : crack, split

rendimiento *nm* **1** : performance **2** : yield

rendir {54} *vt* **1** : to render, to give <rendir las gracias : to give thanks> <rendir homenaje a : to pay homage to> **2** : to yield **3** CANSAR : to exhaust — *vi* **1** CUNDIR : to progress, to make headway **2** : to last, to go a long way — **rendirse** *vr* : to surrender, to give up

renegado, -da *n* : renegade

renegar {49} *vi* **1 ~ de** : to renounce, to disown, to give up **2 ~ de** : to complain about — *vt* **1** : to deny vigorously **2** : to abhor, to hate

renegociar *vt* : to renegotiate — **renegociación** *nf*

renglón *nm, pl* **renglones** **1** : line (of writing) **2** : merchandise, line (of products)

rengo, -ga *adj* : lame

renguear *vi* : to limp

reno *nm* : reindeer

renombrado, -da *adj* : renowned, famous

renombre *nm* NOMBRADÍA : renown, fame

renovable *adj* : renewable

renovación *nf, pl* **-ciones** **1** : renewal <renovación de un contrato : renewal of a contract> **2** : change, renovation

renovar {19} *vt* **1** : to renew, to restore **2** : to renovate

renquear *vi* : to limp, to hobble

renquera *nf* COJERA : limp, lameness

renta *nf* **1** : income **2** : rent **3 impuesto sobre la renta** : income tax

rentable *adj* : profitable

rentar *vt* **1** : to produce, to yield **2** ALQUILAR : to rent

renuencia *nf* : reluctance, unwillingness

renuente *adj* : reluctant, unwilling

renuncia *nf* **1** : resignation **2** : renunciation **3** : waiver

renunciar *vi* **1** : to resign **2 ~ a** : to renounce, to relinquish <renunció al título : he relinquished the title>

reñido, -da *adj* **1** : tough, hard-fought **2** : at odds, on bad terms

reñir {67} *vi* **1** : to argue **2 ~ con** : to fall out with, to go up against — *vt* : to scold, to reprimand

reo, rea *n* **1** : accused, defendant **2** : offender, culprit

reojo *nm* **de ~** : out of the corner of one's eye <una mirada de reojo : a sidelong glance>

reorganizar {21} *vt* : to reorganize — **reorganización** *nf*

repantigarse {52} *vr* : to slouch, to loll about

reparación *nf, pl* **-ciones** **1** : reparation, amends **2** : repair

reparar *vt* **1** : to repair, to fix, to mend **2** : to make amends for **3** : to correct **4** : to restore, to refresh — *vi* **1 ~ en** : to observe, to take notice of **2 ~ en** : to consider, to think about

reparo *nm* **1** : repair, restoration **2** : reservation, qualm <no tuvieron reparos en decírmelo : they didn't hesitate to tell me> **3 poner reparos a** : to find fault with, to object to

repartición *nf, pl* **-ciones** **1** : distribution **2** : department, division

repartidor[1], -dora *adj* : delivery <camión repartidor : delivery truck>

repartidor[2], -dora *n* : delivery person, distributor

repartimiento *nm* → **repartición**

repartir *vt* **1** : to allocate **2** DISTRIBUIR : to distribute, to hand out **3** : to spread

reparto *nm* **1** : allocation **2** : distribution **3** : cast (of characters)

repasar *vt* **1** : to pass by again **2** : to review, to go over **3** : to mend

repaso *nm* **1** : review **2** : mending **3** : checkup, overhaul

repatriar {85} *vt* : to repatriate — **repatriación** *nf*

repavimentar *vt* : to resurface

repelente[1] *adj* : repellent, repulsive

repelente[2] *nm* **:** repellent <repelente de insectos : insect repellent>

repeler *vt* **1 :** to repel, to resist, to repulse **2 :** to reject **3 :** to disgust <el sabor me repele : I find the taste repulsive>

repensar {55} *v* **:** to rethink, to reconsider

repente *nm* **1 :** sudden movement, start <de repente : suddenly> **2 :** fit, outburst <un repente de ira : a fit of anger>

repentino, -na *adj* **:** sudden — **repentinamente** *adv*

repercusión *nf, pl* **-siones :** repercussion

repercutir *vi* **1 :** to reverberate, to echo **2 ~ en :** to have effects on, to have repercussions on

repertorio *nm* **:** repertoire

repetición *nf, pl* **-ciones 1 :** repetition **2 :** rerun, repeat

repetidamente *adv* **:** repeatedly

repetido, -da *adj* **1 :** repeated, numerous **2 repetidas veces :** repeatedly, time and again

repetir {54} *vt* **1 :** to repeat **2 :** to have a second helping of — **repetirse** *vr* **1 :** to repeat oneself **2 :** to recur

repetitivo, -va *adj* **:** repetitive, repetitious

repicar {72} *vt* **:** to ring — *vi* **:** to ring out, to peal

repique *nm* **:** ringing, pealing

repisa *nf* **:** shelf, ledge <repisa de chimenea : mantelpiece> <repisa de ventana : windowsill>

replantear *vt* **:** to redefine, to restate — **replantearse** *vr* **:** to reconsider

replegar {49} *vt* **:** to fold — **replegarse** *vr* RETIRARSE **:** to retreat, to withdraw

repleto, -ta *adj* **1 :** replete, full **2 ~ de :** packed with, crammed with

réplica *nf* **1 :** reply **2 :** replica, reproduction **3** *Chile, Mex* **:** aftershock

replicación *nf, pl* **-ciones :** replication

replicar {72} *vi* **1 :** to reply, to retort **2 :** to argue, to answer back

repliegue *nm* **1 :** fold **2 :** retreat, withdrawal

repollo *nm* COL **:** cabbage

reponer {60} *vt* **1 :** to replace, to put back **2 :** to reinstate **3 :** to reply — **reponerse** *vr* **:** to recover

reportaje *nm* **:** article, story, report

reportar *vt* **1 :** to check, to restrain **2 :** to bring, to carry, to yield <me reportó numerosos beneficios : it brought me many benefits> **3 :** to report — **reportarse** *vr* **1** CONTENERSE **:** to control oneself **2** PRESENTARSE **:** to report, to show up

reporte *nm* **:** report

reportear *vt* **:** to report on, to cover

reportero, -ra *n* **1 :** reporter **2 reportero gráfico :** photojournalist

reposado, -da *adj* **:** calm

reposar *vi* **1 :** to rest, to repose **2 :** to stand, to settle <deje reposar la masa media hora : let the dough stand for half an hour> **3 :** to lie, to be buried — **reposarse** *vr* **:** to settle

reposición *nf, pl* **-ciones 1 :** replacement **2 :** reinstatement **3 :** revival

repositorio *nm* **:** repository

reposo *nm* **:** repose, rest

repostar *vi* **1 :** to stock up **2 :** to refuel

repostería *nf* **1 :** confectioner's shop **2 :** pastry-making

repostero, -ra *n* **:** confectioner

repreguntar *vt* **:** to cross-examine

repreguntas *nfpl* **:** cross-examination

reprender *vt* **:** to reprimand, to scold

reprensible *adj* **:** reprehensible

represa *nf* **:** dam

represalia *nf* **1 :** reprisal, retaliation **2 tomar represalias :** to retaliate

represar *vt* **:** to dam

representación *nf, pl* **-ciones 1 :** representation **2 :** performance **3 en representación de :** on behalf of

representante *nmf* **1 :** representative **2 :** performer

representar *vt* **1 :** to represent, to act for **2 :** to perform **3 :** to look, to appear as **4 :** to symbolize, to stand for **5 :** to signify, to mean — **representarse** *vr* **:** to imagine, to picture

representativo, -va *adj* **:** representative

represión *nf, pl* **-siones :** repression

represivo, -va *adj* **:** repressive

reprimenda *nf* **:** reprimand

reprimir *vt* **1 :** to repress **2 :** to suppress, to stifle

reprobable *adj* **:** reprehensible, culpable

reprobación *nf* **:** disapproval

reprobar {19} *vt* **1** DESAPROBAR **:** to condemn, to disapprove of **2 :** to fail (a course)

reprobatorio, -ria *adj* **:** disapproving, admonitory

reprochar *vt* **:** to reproach — **reprocharse** *vr*

reproche *nm* **:** reproach

reproducción *nf, pl* **-ciones :** reproduction

reproducir {61} *vt* **:** to reproduce — **reproducirse** *vr* **1 :** to breed, to reproduce **2 :** to recur

reproductor, -tora *adj* **:** reproductive

reptar *vi* **:** to crawl, to slither

reptil[1] *adj* **:** reptilian

reptil[2] *nm* **:** reptile

república *nf* **:** republic

republicanismo *nm* **:** republicanism

republicano, -na *adj & n* **:** republican

repudiar *vt* **:** to repudiate — **repudiación** *nf*

repudio *nm* **:** repudiation

repuesto[1] *pp* → **reponer**

repuesto[2] *nm* **1 :** spare part **2 de ~ :** spare <rueda de repuesto : spare wheel>

repugnancia *nf* **:** repugnance

repugnante *adj* **:** repulsive, repugnant, revolting

repugnar *vt* **:** to cause repugnance, to disgust — **repugnarse** *vr*

repujar *vt* **:** to emboss

repulsivo, -va *adj* **:** repulsive

repuntar *vt Arg, Chile* **:** to round up (cattle) — *vi* **:** to begin to appear — **repuntarse** *vr* **:** to fall out, to quarrel

repuso, etc. → **reponer**

reputación *nf, pl* **-ciones :** reputation

reputar *vt* **:** to consider, to deem

requerir {76} *vt* **1 :** to require, to call for **2 :** to summon, to send for

requesón *nm, pl* **-sones :** curd cheese, cottage cheese

réquiem *nm* **:** requiem

requisa *nf* **1 :** requisition **2 :** seizure **3 :** inspection

requisar *vt* **1 :** to requisition **2 :** to seize **3** INSPECCIONAR **:** to inspect

requisito *nm* **1 :** requirement **2 requisito previo :** prerequisite

res *nf* **1 :** beast, animal **2** *CA, Mex* **:** beef **3 reses** *nfpl* **:** cattle <60 reses : 60 head of cattle>

resabio *nm* **1** VICIO **:** bad habit, vice **2** DEJO **:** aftertaste

resaca *nf* **1 :** undertow **2 :** hangover

resaltar *vi* **1** SOBRESALIR **:** to stand out **2 hacer resaltar :** to bring out, to highlight — *vt* **:** to stress, to emphasize

resarcimiento *nm* **1 :** compensation **2 :** reimbursement

resarcir {83} *vt* **:** to compensate, to indemnify — **resarcirse** *vr* **~ de :** to make up for

resbaladizo, -za *adj* **1** RESBALOSO **:** slippery **2 :** tricky, ticklish, delicate

resbalar *vi* **1 :** to slip, to slide **2 :** to slip up, to make a mistake **3 :** to skid — **resbalarse** *vr*

resbalón *nm, pl* **-lones :** slip

resbaloso, -sa *adj* **:** slippery

rescatar *vt* **1 :** to rescue, to save **2 :** to recover, to get back

rescate *nm* **1 :** rescue **2 :** recovery **3 :** ransom

rescindir *vt* **:** to rescind, to annul, to cancel

rescisión *nf, pl* **-siones :** annulment, cancelation

rescoldo *nm* **:** embers *pl*

resecar {72} *vt* **:** to make dry, to dry up — **resecarse** *vr* **:** to dry up

reseco, -ca *adj* **:** dry, dried-up

resentido, -da *adj* **:** resentful

resentimiento *nm* **:** resentment

resentirse {76} *vr* **1 :** to suffer, to be weakened **2** OFENDERSE **:** to be upset <se resintió porque la insultaron : she got upset when they insulted her, she resented being insulted> **3 ~ de :** to feel the effects of

reseña *nf* **1 :** report, summary, review **2 :** description

reseñar *vt* **1 :** to review **2** DESCRIBIR **:** to describe

reserva *nf* **1 :** reservation **2 :** reserve **3 :** confidence, privacy <con la mayor reserva : in strictest confidence> **4 de ~ :** spare, in reserve **5 reservas** *nfpl* **:** reservations, doubts

reservación *nf, pl* **-ciones :** reservation

reservado, -da *adj* **1 :** reserved, reticent **2 :** confidential

reservar *vt* **:** to reserve — **reservarse** *vr* **1 :** to save oneself **2 :** to conceal, to keep to oneself

reservorio *nm* **:** reservoir, reserve

resfriado *nm* CATARRO **:** cold

resfriar {85} *vt* **:** to cool — **resfriarse** *vr* **1 :** to cool off **2 :** to catch a cold

resfrío *nm* **:** cold

resguardar *vt* **:** to safeguard, to protect — **resguardarse** *vr*

resguardo *nm* **1 :** safeguard, protection **2 :** receipt, voucher **3 :** border guard, coast guard

residencia *nf* **1 :** residence **2 :** boarding house

residencial *adj* **:** residential

residente *adj & nmf* **:** resident

residir *vi* **1** VIVIR **:** to reside, to dwell **2 ~ en :** to lie in, to consist of

residual *adj* **:** residual

residuo *nm* **1 :** residue **2 :** remainder **3 residuos** *nmpl* **:** waste <residuos nucleares : nuclear waste>

resignación *nf, pl* **-ciones :** resignation

resignar *vt* **:** to resign — **resignarse** *vr* **~ a :** to resign oneself to

resina *nf* **1 :** resin **2 resina epoxídica :** epoxy

resistencia *nf* **1 :** resistance **2** AGUANTE **:** endurance, strength, stamina

resistente *adj* **1 :** resistant **2 :** strong, tough

resistir *vt* **1 :** to stand, to bear, to tolerate **2 :** to withstand — *vi* **:** to resist <resistió hasta el último minuto : he held out until the last minute> — **resistirse** *vr* **~ a :** to be resistent to, to be reluctant

resollar {19} *vi* **:** to breathe heavily, to wheeze

resolución *nf, pl* **-ciones 1 :** resolution, settlement **2 :** decision **3 :** determination, resolve

resolver {89} *vt* **1 :** to resolve, to settle **2 :** to decide — **resolverse** *vr* **:** to make up one's mind

resonancia *nf* **1 :** resonance **2 :** impact, repercussions *pl*

resonante *adj* **1 :** resonant **2 :** tremendous, resounding <un éxito resonante : a resounding success>

resonar {19} *vi* **:** to resound, to ring

resoplar *vi* **1 :** to puff, to pant **2 :** to snort

resoplo *nm* **1 :** puffing, panting **2 :** snort

resorte *nm* **1** MUELLE **:** spring **2 :** elasticity **3 :** influence, means *pl* <tocar resortes : to pull strings>

resortera *nf Mex* **:** slingshot

respaldar *vt* **:** to back, to support, to endorse — **respaldarse** *vr* **:** to lean back

respaldo *nm* **1 :** back (of an object) **2 :** support, backing

respectar *vt* **:** to concern, to relate to <por lo que a mí respecta **:** as far as I'm concerned>

respectivo, -va *adj* **:** respective — **respectivamente** *adv*

respecto *nm* **1 ~ a :** in regard to, concerning **2 al respecto :** on this matter, in this respect

respetable *adj* **:** respectable — **respetabilidad** *nf*

respetar *vt* **:** to respect

respeto *nm* **1 :** respect, consideration **2 respetos** *nmpl* **:** respects <presentar sus respetos **:** to pay one's respects>

respetuosidad *nf* **:** respectfulness

respetuoso, -sa *adj* **:** respectful — **respetuosamente** *adv*

respingo *nm* **:** start, jump

respiración *nf, pl* **-ciones :** respiration, breathing

respiradero *nm* **:** vent, ventilation shaft

respirador *nm* **:** respirator

respirar *v* **:** to breathe

respiratorio, -ria *adj* **:** respiratory

respiro *nm* **1 :** breath **2 :** respite, break

resplandecer {53} *vi* **1 :** to shine **2 :** to stand out

resplandeciente *adj* **1 :** resplendent, shining **2 :** radiant

resplandor *nm* **1 :** brightness, brilliance, radiance **2 :** flash

responder *vt* **:** to answer — *vi* **1 :** to answer, to reply, to respond **2 ~ a :** to respond to <responder al tratamiento **:** to respond to treatment> **3 ~ de :** to answer for, to vouch for (something) **4 ~ por :** to vouch for (someone)

responsabilidad *nf* **:** responsibility

responsable *adj* **:** responsible — **responsablemente** *adv*

respuesta *nf* **:** answer, response

resquebrajar *vt* **:** to split, to crack — **resquebrajarse** *vr*

resquemor *nm* **:** resentment, bitterness

resquicio *nm* **1 :** crack **2 :** opportunity, chance **3 :** trace <sin un resquicio de remordimiento **:** without a trace of remorse> **4 resquicio legal :** loophole

resta *nf* SUSTRACCIÓN **:** subtraction

restablecer {53} *vt* **:** to reestablish, to restore — **restablecerse** *vr* **:** to recover

restablecimiento *nm* **1 :** reestablishment, restoration **2 :** recovery

restallar *vi* **:** to crack, to crackle, to click

restallido *nm* **:** crack, crackle

restante *adj* **1 :** remaining **2 lo restante, los restantes :** the rest

restañar *vt* **:** to stanch

restar *vt* **1 :** to deduct, to subtract <restar un punto **:** to deduct a point> **2 :** to minimize, to play down — *vi* **:** to remain, to be left

restauración *nf, pl* **-ciones 1 :** restoration **2 :** catering, food service

restaurante *nm* **:** restaurant

restaurar *vt* **:** to restore

restitución *nf, pl* **-ciones :** restitution, return

restituir {41} *vt* **:** to return, to restore, to reinstate

resto *nm* **1 :** rest, remainder **2 restos** *nmpl* **:** remains <restos de comida **:** leftovers> <restos arqueológicos **:** archeological ruins> **3 restos mortales :** mortal remains

restorán *nm, pl* **-ranes :** restaurant

restregadura *nf* **:** scrub, scrubbing

restregar {49} *vt* **1 :** to rub **2 :** to scrub — **restregarse** *vr*

restricción *nf, pl* **-ciones :** restriction, limitation

restrictivo, -va *adj* **:** restrictive

restringido, -da *adj* LIMITADO **:** limited, restricted

restringir {35} *vt* LIMITAR **:** to restrict, to limit

restructuración *nf* **:** restructuring

restructurar *vt* **:** to restructure

resucitación *nf* **:** resuscitation <resucitación cardiopulmonar **:** CPR, cardiopulmonary resuscitation>

resucitar *vt* **1 :** to resuscitate, to revive, to resurrect **2 :** to revitalize

resuello *nm* **1 :** puffing, heavy breathing, wheezing **2 :** break, breather

resuelto[1] *pp* → **resolver**

resuelto[2]**, -ta** *adj* **:** determined, resolved, resolute

resulta *nf* **1 :** consequence, result **2 a resultas de** *or* **de resultas de :** as a result of

resultado *nm* **:** result, outcome

resultante *adj & nf* **:** resultant

resultar *vi* **1 :** to work, to work out <mi idea no resultó **:** my idea didn't work out> **2 :** to prove, to turn out to be <resultó bien simpático **:** he turned out to be very nice> **3 ~ en :** to lead to, to result in **4 ~ de :** to be the result of

resumen *nm, pl* **-súmenes 1 :** summary, summation **2 en ~ :** in summary, in short

resumidero *nm* **:** drain

resumir *v* **:** to summarize, to sum up

resurgimiento *nm* **:** resurgence

resurgir {35} *vi* **:** to reappear, to revive

resurrección *nf, pl* **-ciones :** resurrection

retablo *nm* **1 :** tableau **2 :** altarpiece

retador, -dora *n* **:** challenger (in sports)

retaguardia *nf* **:** rear guard

retahíla *nf* **:** string, series <una retahíla de insultos **:** a volley of insults>

retaliación *nf, pl* **-ciones :** retaliation

retama *nf* **:** broom (plant)

retar *vt* DESAFIAR **:** to challenge, to defy

retardante *adj* **:** retardant

retardar *vt* **1** RETRASAR **:** to delay, to retard **2 :** to postpone
retazo *nm* **1 :** remnant, scrap **2 :** fragment, piece <retazos de su obra : bits and pieces from his writings>
retención *nf, pl* **-ciones 1 :** retention **2 :** deduction, withholding
retener {80} *vt* **1 :** to retain, to keep **2 :** to withhold **3 :** to detain
retentivo, -va *adj* **:** retentive
reticencia *nf* **1 :** reluctance, reticence **2 :** insinuation
reticente *adj* **1 :** reluctant, reticent **2 :** insinuating, misleading
retina *nf* **:** retina
retintín *nm, pl* **-tines 1 :** jingle, jangle **2 con ~ :** sarcastically
retirada *nf* **1 :** retreat <batirse en retirada : to withdraw, to beat a retreat> **2 :** withdrawl (of funds) **3 :** retirement **4 :** refuge, haven
retirado, -da *adj* **1 :** remote, distant, far off **2 :** secluded, quiet
retirar *vt* **1 :** to remove, to take away, to recall **2 :** to withdraw, to take out — **retirarse** *vr* **1** REPLEGARSE **:** to retreat, to withdraw **2** JUBILARSE **:** to retire
retiro *nm* **1** JUBILACIÓN **:** retirement **2 :** withdrawal, retreat **3 :** seclusion
reto *nm* DESAFÍO **:** challenge, dare
retocar {72} *vt* **:** to touch up
retoñar *vi* **:** to sprout
retoño *nm* **:** sprout, shoot
retoque *nm* **:** retouching
retorcer {14} *vt* **1 :** to twist **2 :** to wring — **retorcerse** *vr* **1 :** to get twisted, to get tangled up **2 :** to squirm, to writhe, to wiggle about
retorcijón *nm, pl* **-jones :** cramp, sharp pain
retorcimiento *nm* **1 :** twisting, wringing **2 :** deviousness
retórica *nf* **:** rhetoric
retórico, -ca *adj* **:** rhetorical — **retóricamente** *adv*
retornar *v* **:** to return
retorno *nm* **:** return
retozar {21} *vi* **:** to frolic, to romp
retozo *nm* **:** frolicking
retozón, -zona *adj, mpl* **-zones :** playful
retracción *nf, pl* **-ciones :** retraction, withdrawal
retractable *adj* **:** retractable
retractación *nf, pl* **-ciones :** retraction (of a statement, etc.)
retractarse *vr* **1 :** to withdraw, to back down **2 ~ de :** to take back, to retract
retraer {81} *vt* **1 :** to bring back **2 :** to dissuade — **retraerse** *vr* **1** RETIRARSE **:** to withdraw, to retire **2** REFUGIARSE **:** to take refuge
retraído, -da *adj* **:** withdrawn, retiring, shy
retraimiento *nm* **1 :** shyness, timidity **2 :** withdrawal
retrasado, -da *adj* **1 :** retarded, mentally slow **2 :** behind, in arrears **3 :** backward (of a country) **4 :** slow (of a watch)
retrasar *vt* **1** DEMORAR, RETARDAR **:** to delay, to hold up **2 :** to put off, to postpone — **retrasarse** *vr* **1 :** to be late **2 :** to fall behind
retraso *nm* **1** ATRASO **:** delay, lateness **2 retraso mental :** mental retardation
retratar *vt* **1 :** to portray, to depict **2 :** to photograph **3 :** to paint a portrait of
retrato *nm* **1 :** depiction, portrayal **2 :** portrait, photograph
retrete *nm* **:** restroom, toilet
retribución *nf, pl* **-ciones 1 :** pay, payment **2 :** reward
retribuir {41} *vt* **1 :** to pay **2 :** to reward
retroactivo, -va *adj* **:** retroactive — **retroactivamente** *adv*
retroalimentación *nf, pl* **-ciones :** feedback
retroceder *vi* **1 :** to move back, to turn back **2 :** to back off, to back down **3 :** to recoil (of a firearm)
retroceso *nm* **1 :** backward movement **2 :** backing down **3 :** setback, relapse **4 :** recoil
retrógrado, -da *adj* **1 :** reactionary **2 :** retrograde
retropropulsión *nf* **:** jet propulsion
retrospectiva *nf* **:** retrospective, hindsight
retrospectivo, -va *adj* **1 :** retrospective **2 mirada retrospectiva :** backward glance
retrovisor *nm* **:** rearview mirror
retruécano *nm* **:** pun, play on words
retumbar *vi* **1 :** to boom, to thunder **2 :** to resound, to reverberate
retumbo *nm* **:** booming, thundering, roll
retuvo, etc. → **retener**
reubicar {72} *vt* **:** to relocate — **reubicación** *nf*
reuma *or* **reúma** *nmf* → **reumatismo**
reumático, -ca *adj* **:** rheumatic
reumatismo *nm* **:** rheumatism
reunión *nf, pl* **-niones 1 :** meeting **2 :** gathering, reunion
reunir {68} *vt* **1 :** to unite, to join, to bring together **2 :** to have, to possess <reunieron los requisitos necesarios : they fulfilled the necessary requirements> **3 :** to gather, to collect, to raise (funds) — **reunirse** *vr* **:** to meet
reutilizable *adj* **:** reusable
reutilizar {21} *vt* **:** to recycle, to reuse
revalidar *vt* **1 :** to confirm, to ratify **2 :** to defend (a title)
revaluar {3} *vt* **:** to reevaluate — **revaluación** *n*
revancha *nf* **1** DESQUITE **:** revenge, requital **2 :** rematch
revelación *nf, pl* **-ciones :** revelation
revelado *nm* **:** developing (of film)
revelador¹, -dora *adj* **:** revealing
revelador² *nm* **:** developer

revelar *vt* **1 :** to reveal, to disclose **2 :** to develop (film)

revendedor, -dora *n* **1 :** scalper **2** DETALLISTA **:** retailer

revender *vt* **1 :** to resell **2 :** to scalp

reventa *nf* **1 :** resale **2 :** scalping

reventar {55} *vi* **1** ESTALLAR, EXPLOTAR **:** to burst, to blow up **2 ~ de :** to be bursting with — *vt* **1 :** to burst **2** *fam* **:** to annoy, to rile

reventón *nm, pl* **-tones 1 :** burst, bursting **2 :** blowout, flat tire **3** *Mex fam* **:** bash, party

reverberar *vi* **:** to reverberate — **reverberación** *nf*

reverdecer {53} *vi* **1 :** to grow green again **2 :** to revive

reverencia *nf* **1 :** reverence **2 :** bow, curtsy

reverenciar *vt* **:** to revere, to venerate

reverendo[1], -da *adj* **1 :** reverend **2** *fam* **:** total, absolute <es un reverendo imbécil : he is a complete idiot>

reverendo[2], -da *n* **:** reverend

reverente *adj* **:** reverent

reversa *nf Col, Mex* **:** reverse (gear)

reversible *adj* **:** reversible

reversión *nf, pl* **-siones :** reversion

reverso *nm* **1 :** back, other side **2 el reverso de la medalla :** the complete opposite

revertir {76} *vi* **1 :** to revert, to go back **2 ~ en :** to result in, to end up as

revés *nm, pl* **reveses 1 :** back, wrong side **2 :** setback, reversal **3 :** backhand (in sports) **4 al revés :** the other way around, upside down, inside out **5 al revés de :** contrary to

revestimiento *nm* **:** covering, facing (of a building)

revestir {54} *vt* **1 :** to coat, to cover, to surface **2 :** to conceal, to disguise **3 :** to take on, to assume <la reunión revistió gravedad : the meeting took on a serious note>

revisar *vt* **1 :** to examine, to inspect, to check **2 :** to check over, to overhaul (machinery) **3 :** to revise

revisión *nf, pl* **-siones 1 :** revision **2 :** inspection, check

revisor, -sora *n* **1 :** inspector **2 :** conductor (on a train)

revista *nf* **1 :** magazine, journal **2 :** revue **3 pasar revista :** to review, to inspect

revistar *vt* **:** to review, to inspect

revitalizar {21} *vt* **:** to revitalize — **revitalización** *nf*

revivir *vi* **:** to revive, to come alive again — *vt* **:** to relive

revocación *nf, pl* **-ciones :** revocation, repeal

revocar {72} *vt* **1 :** to revoke, to repeal **2 :** to plaster (a wall)

revolcar {82} *vt* **:** to knock over, to knock down — **revolcarse** *vr* **:** to roll around, to wallow

revolcón *nm, pl* **-cones** *fam* **:** tumble, fall

revolotear *vi* **:** to flutter around, to flit

revoloteo *nm* **:** fluttering, flitting

revoltijo *nm* **1** FÁRRAGO **:** mess, jumble **2** *Mex* **:** traditional seafood dish

revoltoso, -sa *adj* **:** unruly, rebellious

revolución *nf, pl* **-ciones :** revolution

revolucionar *vt* **:** to revolutionize

revolucionario, -ria *adj & n* **:** revolutionary

revolver {89} *vt* **1 :** to move about, to mix, to shake, to stir **2 :** to upset (one's stomach) **3 :** to mess up, to rummage through <revolver la casa : to turn the house upside down> — **revolverse** *vr* **1 :** to toss and turn **2** VOLVERSE **:** to turn around

revólver *nm* **:** revolver

revoque *nm* **:** plaster

revuelo *nm* **1 :** fluttering **2 :** commotion, stir

revuelta *nf* **:** uprising, revolt

revuelto[1] *pp* → **revolver**

revuelto[2], -ta *adj* **1 :** choppy, rough <mar revuelto : rough sea> **2 :** untidy **3 huevos revueltos :** scrambled eggs

rey *nm* **:** king

reyerta *nf* **:** brawl, fight

rezagado, -da *n* **:** straggler, latecomer

rezagar {52} *vt* **1 :** to leave behind **2 :** to postpone — **rezagarse** *vr* **:** to fall behind, to lag

rezar {21} *vi* **1 :** to pray **2 :** to say <como reza el refrán : as the saying goes> **3 ~ con :** to concern, to have to do with — *vt* **:** to say, to recite <rezar un Ave María : to say a Hail Mary>

rezo *nm* **:** prayer, praying

rezongar {52} *vi* **:** to gripe, to grumble

rezumar *v* **:** to ooze, to leak

ría[1], etc. → **reír**

ría[2] *nf* **:** estuary

riachuelo *nm* ARROYO **:** brook, stream

riada *nf* **:** flood

ribera *nf* **:** bank, shore

ribete *nm* **1 :** border, trim **2 :** frill, adornment **3 ribetes** *nmpl* **:** hint, touch <tiene sus ribetes de genio : there's a touch of genius in him>

ribetear *vt* **:** to border, to edge, to trim

ricamente *adv* **:** richly, splendidly

rice, etc. → **rizar**

rico[1], -ca *adj* **1 :** rich, wealthy **2 :** fertile **3 :** luxurious, valuable **4 :** delicious **5 :** adorable, lovely **6 :** great, wonderful

rico[2], -ca *n* **:** rich person

ridiculez *nf, pl* **-leces :** ridiculousness, absurdity

ridiculizar {21} *vt* **:** to ridicule

ridículo[1], -la *adj* ABSURDO, DISPARATADO **:** ridiculous, ludicrous — **ridículamente** *adv*

ridículo[2], -la *n* **1 hacer el ridículo :** to make a fool of oneself **2 poner en ridículo :** to ridicule

ríe, etc. → **reír**

riega, riegue, etc. → **regar**

riego *nm* **:** irrigation

riel *nm* **:** rail, track
rienda *nf* **1 :** rein **2 dar rienda suelta a :** to give free rein to **3 llevar las riendas :** to be in charge **4 tomar las riendas :** to take control
riesgo *nm* **:** risk
riesgoso, -sa *adj* **:** risky
rifa *nf* **:** raffle
rifar *vt* **:** to raffle — *vi* **:** to quarrel, to fight
rifle *nm* **:** rifle
rige, rija, etc. → **regir**
rigidez *nf, pl* **-deces 1 :** rigidity, stiffness <rigidez cadavérica : rigor mortis> **2 :** inflexibility
rígido, -da *adj* **1 :** rigid, stiff **2 :** strict — **rígidamente** *adv*
rigor *nm* **1 :** rigor, harshness **2 :** precision, meticulousness **3 de ~ :** usual <la respuesta de rigor : the standard reply> **4 de ~ :** essential, obligatory **5 en ~ :** strictly speaking, in reality
riguroso, -sa *adj* **:** rigorous — **rigurosamente** *adv*
rima *nf* **1 :** rhyme **2 rimas** *nfpl* **:** verse, poetry
rimar *vi* **:** to rhyme
rimbombante *adj* **1 :** grandiose, showy **2 :** bombastic, pompous
rímel *or* **rimel** *nm* **:** mascara
rin *nm Col, Mex* **:** wheel, rim (of a tire)
rincón *nm, pl* **rincones :** corner, nook
rinde, etc. → **rendir**
rinoceronte *nm* **:** rhinoceros
riña *nf* **1 :** fight, brawl **2 :** dispute, quarrel
riñe, etc. → **reñir**
riñón *nm, pl* **riñones :** kidney
río[1] → **reír**
río[2] *nm* **1 :** river **2 :** torrent, stream <un río de lágrimas : a flood of tears>
ripio *nm* **1 :** debris, rubble **2 :** gravel
riqueza *nf* **1 :** wealth, riches *pl* **2 :** richness **3 riquezas naturales :** natural resources
risa *nf* **1 :** laughter, laugh **2 dar risa :** to make laugh <me dio mucha risa : I found it very funny> **3** *fam* **morirse de la risa :** to die laughing, to crack up
risco *nm* **:** crag, cliff
risible *adj* IRRISORIO **:** ludicrous, laughable
risita *nf* **:** giggle, titter, snicker
risotada *nf* **:** guffaw
ristra *nf* **:** string, series *pl*
risueño, -ña *adj* **1 :** cheerful, pleasant **2 :** promising
rítmico, -ca *adj* **:** rhythmical, rhythmic — **rítmicamente** *adv*
ritmo *nm* **1 :** rhythm **2 :** pace, tempo <trabajó a ritmo lento : she worked at a slow pace>
rito *nm* **:** rite, ritual
ritual *adj & nm* **:** ritual — **ritualmente** *adv*
rival *adj & nmf* COMPETIDOR **:** rival
rivalidad *nf* **:** rivalry, competition
rivalizar {21} *vi* **~ con :** to rival, to compete with
rizado, -da *adj* **1 :** curly **2 :** ridged **3 :** ripply, undulating
rizar {21} *vt* **1 :** to curl **2 :** to ripple, to ruffle (a surface) **3 :** to crumple, to fold — **rizarse** *vr* **1 :** to frizz **2 :** to ripple
rizo *nm* **1 :** curl **2 :** loop (in aviation)
robalo *or* **róbalo** *nm* **:** sea bass
robar *vt* **1 :** to steal **2 :** to rob, to burglarize **3** SECUESTRAR **:** to abduct, to kidnap **4 :** to captivate — *vi* **~ en :** to break into
roble *nm* **:** oak
robo *nm* **:** robbery, theft
robot *nm, pl* **robots :** robot
robótica *nf* **:** robotics
robustecer {53} *vt* **:** to grow stronger, to strengthen
robustez *nf* **:** sturdiness, robustness
robusto, -ta *adj* **:** robust, sturdy
roca *nf* **:** rock, boulder
roce[1], **etc.** → **rozar**
roce[2] *nm* **1 :** rubbing, chafing **2 :** brush, graze, touch **3 :** close contact, familiarity **4 :** friction, disagreement
rociador *nm* **:** sprinkler
rociar {85} *vt* **:** to spray, to sprinkle
rocío *nm* **1 :** dew **2 :** shower, light rain
rocola *nf* **:** jukebox
rocoso, -sa *adj* **:** rocky
rodada *nf* **:** track (of a tire), rut
rodado, -da *adj* **1 :** wheeled **2 :** dappled (of a horse)
rodaja *nf* **:** round, slice
rodaje *nm* **1 :** filming, shooting **2 :** breaking in (of a vehicle)
rodamiento *nm* **1 :** bearing <rodamiento de bolas : ball bearings> **2 :** rolling
rodar {19} *vi* **1 :** to roll, to roll down, to roll along <rodé por la escalera : I tumbled down the stairs> <todo rodaba bien : everthing was going along well> **2** GIRAR **:** to turn, to go around **3 :** to move about, to travel <andábamos rodando por todas partes : we drifted along from place to place> — *vt* **1 :** to film, to shoot **2 :** to break in (a new vehicle)
rodear *vt* **1 :** to surround **2 :** to round up (cattle) — *vi* **1 :** to go around **2 :** to beat around the bush — **rodearse** *vr* **~ de :** to surround oneself with
rodeo *nm* **1 :** rodeo, roundup **2** DESVÍO **:** detour **3 :** evasion <andar con rodeos : to beat around the bush> <sin rodeos : without reservations>
rodilla *nf* **:** knee
rodillo *nm* **1 :** roller **2 :** rolling pin
rododendro *nm* **:** rhododendron
roedor[1], **-dora** *adj* **:** gnawing
roedor[2] *nm* **:** rodent
roer {69} *vt* **1 :** to gnaw **2 :** to eat away at, to torment
rogar {16} *vt* **:** to beg, to request — *vi* **1 :** to beg, to plead **2 :** to pray
rojez *nf* **:** redness

roiga, etc. → **roer**

rojizo, -za *adj* : reddish

rojo[1], **-ja** *adj* **1** : red **2 ponerse rojo** : to blush

rojo[2] *nm* : red

rol *nm* **1** : role **2** : list, roll

rollo *nm* **1** : roll, coil <un rollo de cinta : a roll of tape> <en rollo : rolled up> **2** *fam* : roll of fat **3** *fam* : boring speech, lecture

romance *nm* **1** : Romance language **2** : ballad **3** : romance **4 en buen romance** : simply stated, simply put

romano, -na *adj & n* : Roman

romanticismo *nm* : romanticism

romántico, -ca *adj* : romantic — **románticamente** *adv*

rombo *nm* : rhombus

romería *nf* **1** : pilgrimage, procession **2** : crowd, gathering

romero[1], **-ra** *n* PEREGRINO : pilgrim

romero[2] *nm* : rosemary

romo, -ma *adj* : blunt, dull

rompecabezas *nms & pl* : puzzle, riddle

rompehielos *nms & pl* : icebreaker (ship)

rompehuelgas *nmfs & pl* ESQUIROL : strikebreaker, scab

rompenueces *nms & pl* : nutcracker

rompeolas *ns & pl* : breakwater, jetty

romper {70} *vt* **1** : to break, to smash **2** : to rip, to tear **3** : to break off (relations), to break (a contract) **4** : to break through, to break down **5** GASTAR : to wear out — *vi* **1** : to break <al romper del día : at the break of day> **2 ~ a** : to begin to, to burst out with <romper a llorar : to burst into tears> **3 ~ con** : to break off with

rompope *nm CA, Mex* : drink similar to eggnog

ron *nm* : rum

roncar {72} *vi* **1** : to snore **2** : to roar

ronco, -ca *adj* **1** : hoarse **2** : husky (of the voice) — **roncamente** *adv*

ronda *nf* **1** : beat, patrol **2** : round (of drinks, of negotiations, of a game)

rondar *vt* **1** : to patrol **2** : to hang around <siempre está rondando la calle : he's always hanging around the street> **3** : to be approximately <debe rondar los cincuenta : he must be about 50> — *vi* **1** : to be on patrol **2** : to prowl around, to roam about

ronque, etc. → **roncar**

ronquera *nf* : hoarseness

ronquido *nm* **1** : snore **2** : roar

ronronear *vi* : to purr

ronroneo *nm* : purr, purring

ronzal *nm* : halter (for an animal)

ronzar {21} *v* : to munch, to crunch

roña *nf* **1** : mange **2** : dirt, filth **3** *fam* : stinginess

roñoso, -sa *adj* **1** : mangy **2** : dirty **3** *fam* : stingy

ropa *nf* **1** : clothes *pl,* clothing **2 ropa interior** : underwear

ropaje *nm* : apparel, garments *pl,* regalia

ropero *nm* ARMARIO, CLÓSET : wardrobe, closet

rosa[1] *adj* : rose-colored, pink

rosa[2] *nm* : rose, pink (color)

rosa[3] *nf* : rose (flower)

rosáceo, -cea *adj* : pinkish

rosado[1], **-da** *adj* **1** : pink **2 vino rosado** : rosé

rosado[2] *nm* : pink (color)

rosal *nm* : rosebush

rosario *nm* **1** : rosary **2** : series <un rosario de islas : a string of islands>

rosbif *nm* : roast beef

rosca *nf* **1** : thread (of a screw) <una tapa a rosca : a screw top> **2** : ring, coil

roseta *nf* : rosette

rosquilla *nf* : ring-shaped pastry, doughnut

rostro *nm* : face, countenance

rotación *nf, pl* **-ciones** : rotation

rotar *vt* : to rotate, to turn — *vi* : to turn, to spin

rotativo[1], **-va** *adj* : rotary

rotativo[2] *nm* : newspaper

rotatorio, -ria → **rotativo**[1]

roto[1] *pp* → **romper**

roto[2], **-ta** *adj* **1** : broken **2** : ripped, torn

rotonda *nf* **1** : traffic circle, rotary **2** : rotunda

rotor *nm* : rotor

rótula *nf* : kneecap

rotular *vt* **1** : to head, to entitle **2** : to label

rótulo *nm* **1** : heading, title **2** : label, sign

rotundo, -da *adj* **1** REDONDO : round **2** : categorical, absolute <un éxito rotundo : a resounding success> — **rotundamente** *adv*

rotura *nf* : break, tear, fracture

roya *nf* : plant rust

roya, etc. → **roer**

rozado, -da *adj* GASTADO : worn

rozadura *nf* **1** : scratch, abrasion **2** : rubbed spot, sore

rozar {21} *vt* **1** : to chafe, to rub against **2** : to border on, to touch on **3** : to graze, to touch lightly — **rozarse** *vr* **~ con** *fam* : to rub shoulders with

ruandés, -desa *adj & n* : Rwandan

ruano, -na *adj* : roan

rubí *nm, pl* **rubíes** : ruby

rubio, -bia *adj & n* : blond

rublo *nm* : ruble

rubor *nm* **1** : flush, blush **2** : rouge, blusher

ruborizarse {21} *vr* : to blush

rubrica *nf* : title, heading

rubricar {72} *vt* **1** : sign with a flourish <firmado y rubricado : signed and sealed> **2** : to endorse, to sanction

rubro *nm* **1** : heading, title **2** : line, area (in business)

rudeza *nf* ASPEREZA : roughness, coarseness

rudimentario, -ria *adj* **:** rudimentary **— rudimentariamente** *adv*
rudimento *nm* **:** rudiment, basics *pl*
rudo, -da *adj* **1 :** rough, harsh **2 :** coarse, unpolished **— rudamente** *adv*
rueda[1], etc. → rodar
rueda[2] *nf* **1 :** wheel **2** RODAJA **:** round slice **3 :** circle, ring **4 rueda de andar :** treadmill **5 rueda de prensa :** press conference **6 ir sobre ruedas :** to go smoothly
ruedita *nf* **:** caster (on furniture)
ruedo *nm* **1 :** bullring, arena **2 :** rotation, turn **3 :** hem
ruega, ruegue, etc. → rogar
ruego *nm* **:** request, appeal, plea
rugido *nm* **:** roar
rugir {35} *vi* **:** to roar
ruibarbo *nm* **:** rhubarb
ruido *nm* **:** noise, sound
ruidoso, -sa *adj* **:** loud, noisy **— ruidosamente** *adv*
ruin *adj* **1 :** base, despicable **2 :** mean, stingy
ruina *nf* **1 :** ruin, destruction **2 :** downfall, collapse **3 ruinas** *nfpl* **:** ruins, remains
ruinoso, -sa *adj* **1 :** run-down, dilapidated **2 :** ruinous, disasterous
ruiseñor *nm* **:** nightingale
ruja, etc. → rugir
ruleta *nf* **:** roulette
rulo *nm* **:** curler, roller
rumano, -na *n* **:** Romanian, Rumanian
rumbo *nm* **1 :** direction, course <con rumbo a : bound for, heading for> <perder el rumbo : to go off course, to lose one's bearings> <sin rumbo : aimless, aimlessly> **2 :** ostentation, pomp **3 :** lavishness, generosity
rumiante *adj & nm* **:** ruminant
rumiar *vt* **:** to ponder, to mull over — *vi* **1 :** to chew the cud **2 :** to ruminate, to ponder
rumor *nm* **1 :** rumor **2 :** murmur
rumorearse *or* **rumorarse** *vr* **:** to be rumored <se rumorea que se va : rumor has it that she's leaving>
rumoroso, -sa *adj* **:** murmuring, babbling <un arroyo rumoroso : a babbling brook>
rupia *nf* **:** rupee
ruptura *nf* **1 :** break **2 :** breaking, breach (of a contract) **3 :** breaking off, breakup
rural *adj* **:** rural
ruso[1], -sa *adj & n* **:** Russian
ruso[2] *nm* **:** Russian (language)
rústico[1], -ca *adj* **:** rural, rustic
rústico[2], -ca *n* **:** rustic, country dweller
ruta *nf* **:** route
rutina *nf* **:** routine, habit
rutinario, -ria *adj* **:** routine, ordinary <visita rutinaria : routine visit> **— rutinariamente** *adv*

S

s *nf* **:** twentieth letter of the Spanish alphabet
sábado *nm* **1 :** Saturday **2 :** Sabbath
sábalo *nm* **:** shad
sabana *nf* **:** savanna
sábana *nf* **:** sheet, bedsheet
sabandija *nf* BICHO **:** bug, small reptile, pesky creature
sabático, -ca *adj* **:** sabbatical
sabedor, -dora *adj* **:** aware, informed
sabelotodo *nmf fam* **:** know-it-all
saber[1] {71} *vt* **1 :** to know **2 :** to know how to, to be able to <sabe tocar el violín : she can play the violin> **3 :** to learn, to find out **4 a ~ :** to wit, namely — *vi* **1 :** to know, to suppose **2 :** to be informed <supimos del desastre : we heard about the disaster> **3 :** to taste <esto no sabe bien : this doesn't taste right> **4 ~ a :** to taste like <sabe a naranja : it tastes like orange> **— saberse** *vr* **:** to know <ese chiste no me lo sé : I don't know that joke>
saber[2] *nm* **:** knowledge, learning
sabiamente *adv* **:** wisely
sabido, -da *adj* **:** well-known
sabiduría *nf* **1 :** wisdom **2 :** learning, knowledge
sabiendas *adv* **1 a ~ :** knowingly **2 a sabiendas de que :** knowing full well that
sabio[1], -bia *adj* **1** PRUDENTE **:** wise, sensible **2** DOCTO **:** learned
sabio[2], -bia *n* **1 :** wise person **2 :** savant, learned person
sable *nm* **:** saber, cutlass
sablear *vt fam* **:** to scrounge, to cadge
sabor *nm* **1 :** flavor, taste **2 sin ~ :** flavorless
saborear *vt* **1 :** to taste, to savor **2 :** to enjoy, to relish
sabotaje *nm* **:** sabotage
saboteador, -dora *n* **:** saboteur
sabotear *vt* **:** to sabotage
sabrá, etc. → saber
sabroso, -sa *adj* **1** RICO **:** delicious, tasty **2** AGRADABLE **:** pleasant, nice, lovely
sabueso *nm* **1 :** bloodhound **2** *fam* **:** detective, sleuth
sacacorchos *nms & pl* **:** corkscrew
sacapuntas *nms & pl* **:** pencil sharpener
sacar {72} *vt* **1 :** to pull out, to take out <saca el pollo del congelador : take the chicken out of the freezer> **2 :** to get, to obtain <saqué un 100 en el examen : I got 100 on the exam> **3 :** to get out, to extract <le saqué la infor-

mación : I got the information from him> **4 :** to stick out <sacar la lengua : to stick out one's tongue> **5 :** to bring out, to introduce <sacar un libro : to publish a book> <sacaron una moda nueva : they introduced a new style> **6 :** to take (photos) **7 :** to make (copies) — *vi* **1 :** to kick off (in soccer or football) **2 :** to serve (in sports)

sacarina *nf* **:** saccharin

sacarosa *nf* **:** sucrose

sacerdocio *nm* **:** priesthood

sacerdotal *adj* **:** priestly

sacerdote, -tisa *n* **:** priest *m*, priestess *f*

saciar *vt* **1** HARTAR **:** to sate, to satiate **2** SATISFACER **:** to satisfy

saciedad *nf* **:** satiety

saco *nm* **1 :** bag, sack **2 :** sac **3 :** jacket, sport coat

sacramento *nm* **:** sacrament — **sacramental** *adj*

sacrificar {72} *vt* **:** to sacrifice — **sacrificarse** *vr* **:** to sacrifice oneself, to make sacrifices

sacrificio *nm* **:** sacrifice

sacrilegio *nm* **:** sacrilege

sacrílego, -ga *adj* **:** sacrilegious

sacristán *nm, pl* **-tanes :** sexton, sacristan

sacristía *nf* **:** sacristy, vestry

sacro, -cra *adj* SAGRADO **:** sacred <arte sacro : sacred art>

sacrosanto, -ta *adj* **:** sacrosanct

sacudida *nf* **1 :** shaking **2 :** jerk, jolt, shock **3 :** shake-up, upheaval

sacudir *vt* **1 :** to shake, to beat **2 :** to jerk, to jolt **3 :** to dust off **4** CONMOVER **:** to shake up, to shock — **sacudirse** *vr* **:** to shake off

sacudón *nm, pl* **-dones :** intense jolt or shake-up

sádico[1], -ca *adj* **:** sadistic

sádico[2], -ca *n* **:** sadist

sadismo *nm* **:** sadism

safari *nm* **:** safari

saga *nf* **:** saga

sagacidad *nf* **:** sagacity, shrewdness

sagaz *adj, pl* **sagaces** PERSPICAZ **:** shrewd, discerning, sagacious

Sagitario *nmf* **:** Sagittarius, Sagittarian

sagrado, -da *adj* **:** sacred, holy

sainete *nm* **:** comedy sketch, one-act farce <este proceso es un sainete : these proceedings are a farce>

sajar *vt* **:** to lance, to cut open

sal[1] → **salir**

sal[2] *nf* **1 :** salt **2** *CA, Mex* **:** misfortune, bad luck

sala *nf* **1 :** living room **2 :** room, hall <sala de conferencias : lecture hall> <sala de urgencias : emergency room> <sala de baile : ballroom>

salado, -da *adj* **1 :** salty **2 agua salada :** salt water

salamandra *nf* **:** salamander

salami *nm* **:** salami

salar *vt* **1 :** to salt **2 :** to spoil, to ruin **3** *CoRi, Mex* **:** to jinx, to bring bad luck

salarial *adj* **:** salary, salary-related

salario *nm* **1 :** salary **2 salario mínimo :** minimum wage

salaz *adj, pl* **salaces :** salacious, lecherous

salchicha *nf* **1 :** sausage **2 :** frankfurter, wiener

salchichón *nf, pl* **-chones :** a type of deli meat

salchichonería *nf Mex* **1 :** delicatessen **2 :** cold cuts *pl*

saldar *vt* **:** to settle, to pay off <saldar una cuenta : to settle an account>

saldo *nm* **1 :** settlement, payment **2 :** balance <saldo de cuenta : account balance> **3 :** remainder, leftover merchandise

saldrá, etc. → **salir**

salero *nm* **1 :** saltshaker **2 :** wit, charm

salga, etc. → **salir**

salida *nf* **1 :** exit <salida de emergencia : emergency exit> **2 :** leaving, departure **3** SOLUCIÓN **:** way out, solution **4 :** start (of a race) **5** OCURRENCIA **:** wisecrack, joke **6 salida del sol :** sunrise

saliente[1] *adj* **1 :** departing, outgoing **2 :** projecting **3** DESTACADO **:** salient, prominent

saliente[2] *nm* **1 :** projection, protrusion **2 ventana en saliente :** bay window

salinidad *nf* **:** salinity, saltiness

salino, -na *adj* **:** saline <solución salina : saline solution>

salir {73} *vi* **1 :** to go out, to come out, to get out <salimos todas las noches : we go out every night> <su libro acaba de salir : her book just came out> **2** PARTIR **:** to leave, to depart **3** APARECER **:** to appear <salió en todos los diarios : it came out in all the papers> **4 :** to project, to stick out **5 :** to cost, to come to **6** RESULTAR **:** to turn out, to prove **7 :** to come up, to occur <salga lo que salga : whatever happens> <salió una oportunidad : an opportunity came up> **8 ~ a :** to take after, to look like, to resemble **9 ~ con :** to go out with, to date — **salirse** *vr* **1 :** to escape, to get out, to leak out **2 :** to come loose, to come off **3 salirse con la suya :** to get one's own way

saliva *nf* **:** saliva

salivar *vi* **:** to salivate

salmo *nm* **:** psalm

salmón[1] *adj* **:** salmon-colored

salmón[2] *nm, pl* **salmones :** salmon

salmuera *nf* **:** brine

salobre *adj* **:** brackish, briny

salón *nm, pl* **salones 1 :** hall, large room <salón de clase : classroom> <salón de baile : ballroom> **2 :** salon <salón de belleza : beauty salon> **3 :** parlor, sitting room

salpicadera *nf Mex* **:** fender

salpicadura *nf* **:** spatter, splash

salpicar {72} *vt* **1 :** to spatter, to splash **2 :** to sprinkle, to scatter about

salpimentar {55} *vt* **1 :** to season (with salt and pepper) **2 :** to spice up

salsa *nf* **1 :** sauce <salsa picante : hot sauce> <salsa inglesa : Worcestershire sauce> <salsa tártara : tartar sauce> **2 :** gravy **3 :** salsa (music) **4 salsa mexicana :** salsa (sauce)

salsero, -ra *n* **:** salsa musician

saltador, -dora *n* **:** jumper

saltamontes *nms & pl* **:** grasshopper

saltar *vi* **1** BRINCAR **:** to jump, to leap **2 :** to bounce **3 :** to come off, to pop out **4 :** to shatter, to break **5 :** to explode, to blow up — *vt* **1 :** to jump, to jump over **2 :** to skip, to miss — **saltarse** *vr* OMITIR **:** to skip, to omit <me salté ese capítulo : I skipped that chapter>

saltarín, -rina *adj, mpl* **-rines :** leaping, hopping <frijol saltarín : jumping bean>

salteado, -da *adj* **1 :** sautéed **2 :** jumbled up <los episodios se transmitieron salteados : the episodes were broadcast in random order>

salteador *nm* **:** highwayman

saltear *vt* **1** SOFREÍR **:** to sauté **2 :** to skip around, to skip over

saltimbanqui *nmf* **:** acrobat

salto *nm* **1** BRINCO **:** jump, leap, skip **2 :** jump, dive (in sports) **3 :** gap, omission **4 dar saltos :** to jump up and down **5** *or* **salto de agua** CATARATA **:** waterfall

saltón, -tona *adj, mpl* **saltones :** bulging, protruding

salubre *adj* **:** healthful, salubrious

salubridad *nf* **:** healthfulness, health

salud *nf* **1 :** health <buena salud : good health> **2 ¡salud! :** bless you! (when someone sneezes) **3 ¡salud! :** cheers!, to your health!

saludable *adj* **1** SALUBRE **:** healthful **2** SANO **:** healthy, well

saludar *vt* **1 :** to greet, to say hello to **2 :** to salute — **saludarse** *vr*

saludo *nm* **1 :** greeting, regards *pl* **2 :** salute

salutación *nf, pl* **-ciones :** salutation

salva *nf* **1 :** salvo, volley **2 salva de aplausos :** round of applause

salvación *nf, pl* **-ciones 1 :** salvation **2** RESCATE **:** rescue

salvado *nm* **:** bran

salvador, -dora *n* **1 :** savior, rescuer **2 el Salvador :** the Savior

salvadoreño, -ña *adj & n* **:** Salvadoran, El Salvadoran

salvaguardar *vt* **:** to safeguard

salvaguardia *or* **salvaguarda** *nf* **:** safeguard, defense

salvajada *nf* ATROCIDAD **:** atrocity, act of savagery

salvaje[1] *adj* **1 :** wild <animales salvajes : wild animals> **2 :** savage, cruel **3 :** primitive, uncivilized

salvaje[2] *nmf* **:** savage

salvajismo *nm* **:** savagery

salvamento *nm* **1 :** rescuing, lifesaving **2 :** salvation **3 :** refuge

salvar *vt* **1 :** to save, to rescue **2 :** to cover (a distance) **3 :** to get around (an obstacle), to overcome (a difficulty) **4 :** to cross, to jump across **5 salvando :** except for, excluding — **salvarse** *vr* **1 :** to survive, to escape **2 :** to save one's soul

salvavidas[1] *nms & pl* **1 :** life preserver **2 bote salvavidas :** lifeboat

salvavidas[2] *nmf* **:** lifeguard

salvedad *nf* **1** EXCEPCIÓN **:** exception **2 :** proviso, stipulation

salvia *nf* **:** sage (plant)

salvo[1], **-va** *adj* **1 :** unharmed, sound <sano y salvo : safe and sound> **2 a ~ :** safe from danger

salvo[2] *prep* **1** EXCEPTO **:** except (for), save <todos asistirán salvo Jaime : all will attend except for Jaime> **2 salvo que :** unless <salvo que llueva : unless it rains>

salvoconducto *nm* **:** safe-conduct

samba *nf* **:** samba

San → **santo**[1]

sanar *vt* **:** to heal, to cure — *vi* **:** to get well, to recover

sanatorio *nm* **1 :** sanatorium **2 :** clinic, private hospital

sanción *nf, pl* **sanciones :** sanction

sancionar *vt* **1 :** to penalize, to impose a sanction on **2 :** to sanction, to approve

sancochar *vt* **:** to parboil

sandalia *nf* **:** sandal

sándalo *nm* **:** sandalwood

sandez *nf, pl* **sandeces** ESTUPIDEZ **:** nonsense, silly thing to say

sandía *nf* **:** watermelon

sandwich [ˈsandwitʃ, ˈsaŋgwitʃ] *nm, pl* **sandwiches** [-dwitʃɛs, -gwi-] EMPAREDADO **:** sandwich

saneamiento *nm* **1 :** cleaning up, sanitation **2 :** reorganizing, streamlining

sanear *vt* **1 :** to clean up, to sanitize **2 :** to reorganize, to streamline

sangrante *adj* **1 :** bleeding **2 :** flagrant, blatant

sangrar *vi* **:** to bleed — *vt* **:** to indent (a paragraph, etc.)

sangre *nf* **1 :** blood **2 a sangre fría :** in cold blood **3 a sangre y fuego :** by violent force **4 pura sangre :** thoroughbred

sangría *nf* **1 :** bloodletting **2 :** sangria (wine punch) **3 :** drain, draining <una sangría fiscal : a financial drain> **4 :** indentation, indenting

sangriento, -ta *adj* **1 :** bloody **2 :** cruel

sanguijuela *nf* **1 :** leech, bloodsucker **2 :** sponger, leech

sanguinario, -ria *adj* **:** bloodthirsty

sanguíneo, -nea *adj* **1 :** blood <vaso sanguíneo : blood vessel> **2 :** sanguine, ruddy

sanidad *nf* **1 :** health **2 :** public health, sanitation

sanitario[1], -ria *adj* **1** : sanitary **2** : health <centro sanitario : health center>
sanitario[2], -ria *n* : sanitation worker
sanitario[3] *nm Col, Mex, Ven* : toilet <los sanitarios : the toilets, the restroom>
sano, -na *adj* **1** SALUDABLE : healthy **2** : wholesome **3** : whole, intact
santiaguino, -na *adj* : of or from Santiago, Chile
santiamén *nm* **en un santiamén** : in no time at all
santidad *nf* : holiness, sanctity
santificar {72} *vt* : to sanctify, to consecrate, to hallow
santiguarse {10} *vr* PERSIGNARSE : to cross oneself
santo[1], -ta *adj* **1** : holy, saintly <el Santo Padre : the Holy Father> <una vida santa : a saintly life> **2 Santo, Santa** (**San** *before names of masculine saints except those beginning with D or T*) : Saint <Santa Clara : Saint Claire> <Santo Tomás : Saint Thomas> <San Francisco : Saint Francis>
santo[2], -ta *n* : saint
santo[3] *nm* **1** : saint's day **2** CUMPLEAÑOS : birthday
santuario *nm* : sanctuary
santurrón, -rrona *adj, mpl* **-rrones** : overly pious, sanctimonious — **santurronamente** *adv*
saña *nf* **1** : fury, rage **2** : viciousness <con saña : viciously>
sapo *nm* : toad
saque[1], etc. → **sacar**
saque[2] *nm* **1** : kick-off (in soccer or football) **2** : serve, service (in sports)
saqueador, -dora *n* DEPREDADOR : plunderer, looter
saquear *vt* : to sack, to plunder, to loot
saqueo *nm* DEPREDACIÓN : sacking, plunder, looting
sarampión *nm* : measles *pl*
sarape *nm CA, Mex* : serape, blanket
sarcasmo *nm* : sarcasm
sarcástico, -ca *adj* : sarcastic
sarcófago *nm* : sarcophagus
sardina *nf* : sardine
sardónico, -ca *adj* : sardonic
sarga *nf* : serge
sargento *nmf* : sergeant
sarna *nf* : mange
sarnoso, -sa *adj* : mangy
sarpullido *nm* ERUPCIÓN : rash
sarro *nm* **1** : deposit, coating **2** : tartar, plaque
sartén *nmf, pl* **sartenes 1** : frying pan **2 tener la sartén por el mango** : to call the shots, to be in control
sasafrás *nm* : sassafras
sastre, -tra *n* : tailor
sastrería *nf* **1** : tailoring **2** : tailor's shop
Satanás *or* **Satán** *nm* : Satan, the devil
satánico, -ca *adj* : satanic
satélite *nm* : satellite
satín *or* **satén** *nm, pl* **satines** *or* **satenes** : satin
satinado, -da *adj* : satiny, glossy
sátira *nf* : satire
satírico, -ca *adj* : satirical, satiric
satirizar {21} *vt* : to satirize
sátiro *nm* : satyr
satisfacción *nf, pl* **-ciones** : satisfaction
satisfacer {74} *vt* **1** : to satisfy **2** : to fulfill, to meet **3** : to pay, to settle — **satisfacerse** *vr* **1** : to be satisfied **2** : to take revenge
satisfactorio, -ria *adj* : satisfactory — **satisfactoriamente** *adv*
satisfecho, -cha *adj* : satisfied, content, pleased
saturación *nf, pl* **-ciones** : saturation
saturar *vt* **1** : to saturate, to fill up **2** : to satiate, to surfeit
saturnismo *nm* : lead poisoning
Saturno *nm* : Saturn
sauce *nm* : willow
saúco *nm* : elder (tree)
saudí *or* **saudita** *adj & nmf* : Saudi, Saudi Arabian
sauna *nmf* : sauna
savia *nf* : sap
saxofón *nm, pl* **-fones** : saxophone
sazón[1] *nf, pl* **sazones 1** : flavor, seasoning **2** : ripeness, maturity <en sazón : in season, ripe> **3 a la sazón** : at that time, then
sazón[2] *nmf, pl* **sazones** *Mex* : flavor, seasoning
sazonar *vt* CONDIMENTAR : to season, to spice
sé → **saber, ser**
se *pron* **1** : to him, to her, to you, to them <se los daré a ella : I'll give them to her> **2** : each other, one another <se abrazaron : they hugged each other> **3** : himself, herself, itself, yourself, yourselves, themselves <se afeitó antes de salir : he shaved before leaving> **4** (*used in passive constructions*) <se dice que es hermosa : they say she's beautiful> <se habla inglés : English spoken>
sea, etc. → **ser**
sebo *nm* **1** : grease, fat **2** : tallow **3** : suet
secado *nm* : drying
secador *nm* : hair dryer
secadora *nf* **1** : dryer, clothes dryer **2** *Mex* : hair dryer
secante *nm* : blotting paper, blotter
secar {72} *v* : to dry — **secarse** *vr* **1** : to get dry **2** : to dry up
sección *nf, pl* **secciones 1** : section <sección transversal : cross section> **2** : department, division
seco, -ca *adj* **1** : dry **2** DISECADO : dried <fruta seca : dried fruit> **3** : thin, lean **4** : curt, brusque **5** : sharp <un golpe seco : a sharp blow> **6 a secas** : simply, just <se llama Chico, a secas : he's just called Chico> **7 en ~**

: abruptly, suddenly <frenar en seco : to make a sudden stop>

secoya *nf* : sequoia, redwood

secreción *nf, pl* **-ciones** : secretion

secretar *vt* : to secrete

secretaría *nf* **1** : secretariat, administrative department **2** *Mex* : ministry, cabinet office

secretariado *nm* **1** : secretariat **2** : secretarial profession

secretario, -ria *n* : secretary — **secretarial** *adj*

secreto[1], -ta *adj* **1** : secret **2** : secretive — **secretamente** *adv*

secreto[2] *nm* **1** : secret **2** : secrecy

secta *nf* : sect

sectario, -ria *adj & n* : sectarian

sector *nm* : sector

secuaz *nmf, pl* **secuaces** : follower, henchman, underling

secuela *nf* : consequence, sequel <las secuelas de la guerra : the aftermath of the war>

secuencia *nf* : sequence

secuestrador, -dora *n* **1** : kidnapper, abductor **2** : hijacker

secuestrar *vt* **1** RAPTAR : to kidnap, to abduct **2** : to hijack, to commandeer **3** CONFISCAR : to confiscate, to seize

secuestro *nm* **1** RAPTO : kidnapping, abduction **2** : hijacking **3** : seizure, confiscation

secular *adj* : secular — **secularismo** *nm* — **secularización** *nf*

secundar *vt* : to support, to second

secundaria *nf* **1** : secondary education, high school **2** *Mex* : junior high school, middle school

secundario, -ria *adj* : secondary

secuoya *nf* : sequoia

sed *nf* **1** : thirst <tener sed : to be thirsty> **2 tener sed de** : to hunger for, to thirst for

seda *nf* : silk

sedación *nf, pl* **-ciones** : sedation

sedal *nm* : fishing line

sedán *nm, pl* **sedanes** : sedan

sedante *adj & nm* CALMANTE : sedative

sedar *vt* : to sedate

sede *nf* **1** : seat, headquarters **2** : venue, site **3 la Santa Sede** : the Holy See

sedentario, -ria *adj* : sedentary

sedición *nf, pl* **-ciones** : sedition — **sedicioso, -sa** *adj*

sediento, -ta *adj* : thirsty, thirsting

sedimentación *nf, pl* **-ciones** : sedimentation

sedimentario, -ria *adj* : sedimentary

sedimento *nm* : sediment

sedoso, -sa *adj* : silky, silken

seducción *nf, pl* **-ciones** : seduction

seducir {61} *vt* **1** : to seduce **2** : to captivate, to charm

seductivo, -va *adj* : seductive

seductor[1], -tora *adj* **1** SEDUCTIVO : seductive **2** ENCANTADOR : charming, alluring

seductor[2], -tora *n* : seducer

segar {49} *vt* **1** : to reap, to harvest, to cut **2** : to sever abruptly <una vida segada por la enfermedad : a life cut short by illness>

seglar[1] *adj* LAICO : lay, secular

seglar[2] *nm* LAICO : layperson, layman *m,* laywoman *f*

segmentación *nm, pl* **-ciones** : segmentation

segmentado, -da *adj* : segmented

segmento *nm* : segment

segregar {52} *vt* **1** : to segregate **2** SECRETAR : to secrete

seguida *nf* **en ~** : right away, immediately <vuelvo en seguida : I'll be right back>

seguidamente *adv* **1** : next, immediately after **2** : without a break, continuously

seguido[1] *adv* **1** RECTO : straight, straight ahead **2** : often, frequently

seguido[2], -da *adj* **1** CONSECUTIVO : consecutive, successive <tres días seguidos : three days in a row> **2** : straight, unbroken **3 ~ por** *or* **~ de** : followed by

seguidor, -dora *n* : follower, supporter

seguimiento *nm* **1** : following, pursuit **2** : continuation **3** : tracking, monitoring

seguir {75} *vt* **1** : to follow <el sol sigue la lluvia : sunshine follows the rain> <seguiré tu consejo : I'll follow your advice> <me siguieron con la mirada : they followed me with their eyes> **2** : to go along, to keep on <seguimos toda la carretera panamericana : we continued along the Pan-American Highway> <siguió hablando : he kept on talking> <seguir el curso : to stay on course> **3** : to take (a course, a treatment) — *vi* **1** : to go on, to keep going <sigue adelante : keep going, carry on> **2** : to remain, to continue to be <¿todavía sigues aquí? : you're still here?> <sigue con vida : she's still alive> **3** : to follow, to come after <la frase que sigue : the following sentence>

según[1] *adv* : it depends <según y como : it all depends on>

según[2] *conj* **1** COMO, CONFORME : as, just as <según lo dejé : just as I left it> **2** : depending on how <según se vea : depending on how one sees it>

según[3] *prep* **1** : according to <según los rumores : according to the rumors> **2** : depending on <según los resultados : depending on the results>

segundo[1], -da *adj* : second <el segundo lugar : second place>

segundo[2], -da *n* **1** : second (in a series) **2** : second (person), second-in-command

segundo[3] *nm* : second <sesenta segundos : sixty seconds>

seguramente *adv* **1** : for sure, surely **2** : probably

seguridad *nf* **1** : safety, security **2** : (financial) security <seguridad social : Social Security> **3** CERTEZA : certainty, assurance <con toda seguridad : with complete certainty> **4** : confidence, self-confidence

seguro[1] *adv* : certainly, definitely <va a llover, seguro : it's going to rain for sure> <¡seguro que sí! : of course!>

seguro[2], **-ra** *adj* **1** : safe, secure **2** : sure, certain <estoy segura que es él : I'm sure that's him> **3** : reliable, trustworthy **4** : self-assured

seguro[3] *nm* **1** : insurance <seguro de vida : life insurance> **2** : fastener, clasp **3** *Mex* : safety pin

seis *adj & nm* : six

seiscientos[1], **-tas** *adj* : six hundred

seiscientos[2] *nms & pl* : six hundred

selección *nf, pl* **-ciones 1** ELECCIÓN : selection, choice **2 selección natural** : natural selection

seleccionar *vt* ELEGIR : to select, to choose

selectivo, -va *adj* : selective — **selectivamente** *adv*

selecto, -ta *adj* **1** : choice, select **2** EXCLUSIVO : exclusive

selenio *nm* : selenium

sellar *vt* **1** : to seal **2** : to stamp

sello *nm* **1** : seal **2** ESTAMPILLA, TIMBRE : postage stamp **3** : hallmark, characteristic

selva *nf* **1** BOSQUE : woods *pl,* forest <selva húmeda : rain forest> **2** JUNGLA : jungle

selvático, -ca *adj* **1** : forest, jungle <sendero selvático : jungle path> **2** : wild

semáforo *nm* **1** : traffic light **2** : stop signal

semana *nf* : week

semanal *adj* : weekly — **semanalmente** *adv*

semanario *nm* : weekly (publication)

semántica *nf* : semantics

semántico, -ca *adj* : semantic

semblante *nm* **1** : countenance, face **2** : appearance, look

semblanza *nf* : biographical sketch, profile

sembrado *nm* : cultivated field

sembrador, -dora *n* : planter, sower

sembradora *nf* : seeder (machine)

sembrar {55} *vt* **1** : to plant, to sow **2** : to scatter, to strew <sembrar el pánico : to spread panic>

semejante[1] *adj* **1** PARECIDO : similar, alike **2** TAL : such <nunca he visto cosa semejante : I have never seen such a thing>

semejante[2] *nm* PRÓJIMO : fellowman

semejanza *nf* PARECIDO : similarity, resemblance

semejar *vi* : to resemble, to look like — **semejarse** *vr* : to be similar, to look alike

semen *nm* : semen

semental *nm* : stud (animal) <caballo semental : stallion>

semestre *nm* : semester

semicírculo *nm* : semicircle, half circle

semiconductor *nm* : semiconductor

semidiós *nm, pl* **-dioses** : demigod *m*

semifinal *nf* : semifinal

semifinalista[1] *adj* : semifinal

semifinalista[2] *nmf* : semifinalist

semiformal *adj* : semiformal

semilla *nf* : seed

semillero *nm* **1** : seedbed **2** : hotbed, breeding ground

seminario *nm* **1** : seminary **2** : seminar, graduate course

seminarista *nm* : seminarian

semiprecioso, -sa *adj* : semiprecious

semita[1] *adj* : Semitic

semita[2] *nmf* : Semite

sémola *nf* : semolina

sempiterno, -na *adj* ETERNO : eternal, everlasting

senado *nm* : senate

senador, -dora *n* : senator

sencillamente *adv* : simply, plainly

sencillez *nf* : simplicity

sencillo[1], **-lla** *adj* **1** : simple, easy **2** : plain, unaffected **3** : single

sencillo[2] *nm* **1** : single (recording) **2** : small change (coins) **3** : one-way ticket

senda *nf* CAMINO, SENDERO : path, way

sendero *nm* CAMINO, SENDA : path, way

sendos, -das *adj pl* : each, both <llevaban sendos vestidos nuevos : they were each wearing a new dress>

senectud *nf* ANCIANIDAD : old age

senegalés, -lesa *adj & n, mpl* **-leses** : Senegalese

senil *adj* : senile — **senilidad** *nf*

seno *nm* **1** : breast, bosom <los senos : the breasts> <el seno de la familia : the bosom of the family> **2** : sinus **3 seno materno** : womb

sensación *nf, pl* **-ciones 1** IMPRESIÓN : feeling <tener la sensación : to have a feeling> **2** : sensation <causar sensación : to cause a sensation>

sensacional *adj* : sensational

sensacionalista *adj* : sensationalistic, lurid

sensatez *nf* **1** : good sense **2 con ~** : sensibly

sensato, -ta *n* : sensible, sound — **sensatamente** *adv*

sensibilidad *nf* **1** : sensitivity, sensibility **2** SENSACIÓN : feeling

sensibilizar {21} *vt* : to sensitize

sensible *adj* **1** : sensitive **2** APRECIABLE : considerable, significant

sensiblemente *adv* : considerably, significantly

sensiblería *nf* : sentimentality, mush

sensiblero, -ra *adj* : mawkish, sentimental, mushy

sensitivo, -va *adj* **1** : sense <órganos sensitivos : sense organs> **2** : sentient, capable of feeling

sensor *nm* : sensor

sensorial *adj* : sensory
sensual *adj* : sensual, sensuous — **sensualmente** *adv*
sensualidad *nf* : sensuality
sentado, -da *adj* **1 :** sitting, seated **2 :** established, settled <dar por sentado : to take for granted> <dejar sentado : to make clear> **3 :** sensible, steady, judicious
sentar {55} *vt* **1 :** to seat, to sit **2 :** to establish, to set — *vi* **1 :** to suit <ese color te sienta : that color suits you> **2 :** to agree with (of food or drink) <las cebollas no me sientan : onions don't agree with me> **3 :** to please <le sentó mal el paseo : she didn't enjoy the trip> — **sentarse** *vr* : to sit, to sit down <siéntese, por favor : please have a seat>
sentencia *nf* **1 :** sentence, judgment **2 :** maxim, saying
sentenciar *vt* : to sentence
sentido[1], -da *adj* **1 :** heartfelt, sincere <mi más sentido pésame : my sincerest condolences> **2 :** touchy, sensitive **3 :** offended, hurt
sentido[2] *nm* **1 :** sense <sentido común : common sense> <los cinco sentidos : the five senses> <sin sentido : senseless> **2** CONOCIMIENTO : consciousness **3** SIGNIFICADO : meaning, sense <doble sentido : double entendre> **4 :** direction <calle de sentido único : one-way street>
sentimental[1] *adj* **1 :** sentimental **2 :** love, romantic <vida sentimental : love life>
sentimental[2] *nmf* : sentimentalist
sentimentalismo *nm* : sentimentality, sentimentalism
sentimiento *nm* **1 :** feeling, emotion **2** PESAR : regret, sorrow
sentir {76} *vt* **1 :** to feel, to experience <no siento nada de dolor : I don't feel any pain> <sentía sed : he was feeling thirsty> <sentir amor : to feel love> **2** PERCIBIR : to perceive, to sense <sentir un ruido : to hear a noise> **3** LAMENTAR : to regret, to feel sorry for <lo siento mucho : I'm very sorry> — *vi* **1 :** to have feeling, to feel **2 sin ~ :** without noticing, inadvertently — **sentirse** *vr* **1 :** to feel <¿te sientes mejor? : are you feeling better?> **2** *Chile, Mex* : to take offense
seña *nf* **1 :** sign, signal **2 dar señas de :** to show signs of
señal *nf* **1 :** signal **2 :** sign <señal de tráfico : traffic sign> **3** INDICIO : indication <en señal de : as a token of> **4** VESTIGIO : trace, vestige **5 :** scar, mark **6 :** deposit, down payment
señalado, -da *adj* : distinguished, notable
señalador *nm* : marker <señalador de libros : bookmark>
señalar *vt* **1** INDICAR : to indicate, to show **2 :** to mark **3 :** to point out, to stress **4 :** to fix, to set — **señalarse** *vr* : to distinguish oneself
señor, -ñora *n* **1 :** gentleman *m,* man *m,* lady *f,* woman *f,* wife *f* **2 :** Sir *m,* Madam *f* <estimados señores : Dear Sirs> **3 :** Mr. *m,* Mrs. *f* **4 :** lord *m,* lady *f* <el Señor : the Lord>
señoría *nf* **1 :** lordship **2 Su Señoría :** Your Honor
señorial *adj* : stately, regal
señorío *nm* **1 :** manor, estate **2 :** dominion, power **3 :** elegance, class
señorita *nf* **1 :** young lady, young woman **2 :** Miss
señuelo *nm* **1 :** decoy **2 :** bait
sépalo *nm* : sepal
sepa, etc. → **saber**
separación *nf, pl* **-ciones 1 :** separation, division **2 :** gap, space
separadamente *adv* : separately, apart
separado, -da *adj* **1 :** separated **2 :** separate <vidas separadas : separate lives> **3 por ~ :** separately
separar *vt* **1 :** to separate, to divide **2 :** to split up, to pull apart — **separarse** *vr*
sepelio *nm* : interment, burial
sepia[1] *adj & nm* : sepia
sepia[2] *nf* : cuttlefish
septentrional *adj* : northern
séptico, -ca *adj* : septic
septiembre *nm* : September
séptimo[1], -ma *adj* : seventh
séptimo[2] *nm* : seventh
septuagésimo[1], -ma *adj* : seventieth
septuagésimo[2] *nm* : seventieth
sepulcral *adj* **1 :** sepulcral **2 :** dismal, gloomy
sepulcro *nm* TUMBA : tomb, sepulchre
sepultar *vt* ENTERRAR : to bury
sepultura *nf* **1 :** burial **2** TUMBA : grave, tomb
seque, etc. → **secar**
sequedad *nf* **1 :** dryness **2 :** brusqueness, curtness
sequía *nf* : drought
séquito *nm* : retinue, entourage
ser[1] {77} *vi* **1 :** to be <él es mi hermano : he is my brother> <Camila es linda : Camila is pretty> **2 :** to exist, to live <ser, o no ser : to be or not to be> **3 :** to take place, to occur <el concierto es el domingo : the concert is on Sunday> **4** (*used with expressions of time, date, season*) <son las diez : it's ten o'clock> <hoy es el 9 : today's the 9th> **5 :** to cost, to come to <¿cuánto es? : how much is it?> **6** (*with the future tense*) : to be able to be <¿será posible? : can it be possible?> **7 ~ de :** to come from <somos de Managua : we're from Managua> **8 ~ de :** to belong to <ese lápiz es de Juan : that's Juan's pencil> **9 es que :** the thing is that <es que no lo conozco : it's just that I don't know him> **10 ¡sea! :** agreed!, all right! **11 sea . . . sea :** either . . . or — *v aux* (*used in passive constructions*) : to be <la cuenta

ha sido pagada : the bill has been paid> <él fue asesinado : he was murdered>
ser[2] *nm* : being <ser humano : human being>
seráfico, -ca *adj* : angelic, seraphic
serbio[1], **-bia** *adj & n* : Serb, Serbian
serbio[2] *nm* : Serbian (language)
serbocroata[1] *adj* : Serbo-Croatian
serbocroata[2] *nm* : Serbo-Croatian (language)
serenar *vt* : to calm, to soothe — **serenarse** *vr* CALMARSE : to calm down
serenata *nf* : serenade
serendipia *nf* : serendipity
serenidad *nf* : serenity, calmness
sereno[1], **-na** *adj* **1** SOSEGADO : serene, calm, composed **2** : fair, clear (of weather) **3** : calm, still (of the sea) — **serenamente** *adv*
sereno[2] *nm* : night watchman
seriado, -da *adj* : serial
serial *nm* : serial (on radio or television)
seriamente *adv* : seriously
serie *nf* **1** : series **2** SERIAL : serial **3 fabricación en serie** : mass production **4 fuera de serie** : extraordinary, amazing
seriedad *nf* **1** : seriousness, earnestness **2** : gravity, importance
serio, -ria *adj* **1** : serious, earnest **2** : reliable, responsible **3** : important **4 en ~** : seriously, in earnest — **seriamente** *adv*
sermón *nm, pl* **sermones 1** : sermon **2** *fam* : harangue, lecture
sermonear *vt fam* : to harangue, to lecture
serpentear *vi* : to twist, to wind — **serpenteante** *adj*
serpentina *nf* : paper streamer
serpiente *nf* : serpent, snake
serrado, -da *adj* DENTADO : serrated
serranía *nf* : mountainous area
serrano, -na *adj* : from the mountains
serrar {55} *vt* : to saw
serrín *nm, pl* **serrines** : sawdust
serruchar *vt* : to saw up
serrucho *nm* : saw, handsaw
servicentro *nm Peru* : gas station
servicial *adj* : obliging, helpful
servicio *nm* **1** : service **2** SAQUE : serve (in sports) **3 servicios** *nmpl* : restroom
servidor, -dora *n* **1** : servant **2 su seguro servidor** : yours truly (in correspondence)
servidumbre *nf* **1** : servitude **2** : help, servants *pl*
servil *adj* **1** : servile, subservient **2** : menial
servilismo *nm* : servility, subservience
servilleta *nf* : napkin
servir {54} *vt* **1** : to serve, to be of use to **2** : to serve, to wait **3** SURTIR : to fill (an order) — *vi* **1** : to work <mi radio no sirve : my radio isn't working> **2** : to be of use, to be helpful <esa computadora no sirve para nada : that computer's perfectly useless> — **servirse** *vr* **1** : to help oneself to **2** : to be kind enough <sírvase enviarnos un catálogo : please send us a catalog>
sésamo *nm* AJONJOLÍ : sesame, sesame seeds *pl*
sesenta *adj & nm* : sixty
sesentavo[1], **-va** *adj* : sixtieth
sesentavo[2] *n* : sixtieth (fraction)
sesgado, -da *adj* **1** : inclined, tilted **2** : slanted, biased
sesgar {52} *vt* **1** : to cut on the bias **2** : to tilt **3** : to bias, to slant
sesgo *nm* : bias
sesgue, etc. → **sesgar**
sesión *nf, pl* **sesiones 1** : session **2** : showing, performance
sesionar *vi* REUNIRSE : to meet, to be in session
seso *nm* **1** : brains, intelligence **2 sesos** *nmpl* : brains (as food)
sesudo, -da *adj* **1** : prudent, sensible **2** : brainy
set *nm, pl* **sets** : set (in tennis)
seta *nf* : mushroom
setecientos[1], **-tas** *adj* : seven hundred
setecientos[2] *nms & pl* : seven hundred
setenta *adj & nm* : seventy
setentavo[1], **-va** *adj* : seventieth
setentavo[2] *nm* : seventieth
setiembre *nm* → **septiembre**
seto *nm* **1** : fence, enclosure **2 seto vivo** : hedge
seudónimo *nm* : pseudonym
severidad *nf* **1** : harshness, severity **2** : strictness
severo, -ra *adj* **1** : harsh, severe **2** ESTRICTO : strict — **severamente** *adv*
sexagésimo[1], **-ma** *adj* : sixtieth, sixty-
sexagésimo[2], **-ma** *n* : sixtieth, sixty- (in a series)
sexismo *nm* : sexism — **sexista** *adj & nmf*
sexo *nm* : sex
sextante *nm* : sextant
sexteto *nm* : sextet
sexto, -ta *adj* : sixth — **sexto, -ta** *n*
sexual *adj* : sexual, sex <educación sexual : sex education> — **sexualmente** *adv*
sexualidad *nf* : sexuality
sexy *adj, pl* **sexy** *or* **sexys** : sexy
shock [ˈʃɔk, ˈtʃɔk] *nm* : shock <estado de shock : state of shock>
short *nm, pl* **shorts** : shorts *pl*
show *nm, pl* **shows** : show
si *conj* **1** : if <lo haré si me pagan : I'll do it if they pay me> <si lo supiera te lo diría : if I knew it I would tell you> **2** : whether, if <no importa si funciona o no : it doesn't matter whether it works (or not)> **3** (*expressing desire, protest, or surprise*) <si supiera la verdad : if only I knew the truth> <¡si no quiero! : but I don't want to!> **4 si bien** : although <si bien se ha progresado : although progress has been made> **5 si no** : otherwise, or

else <si no, no voy : otherwise I won't go>

sí[1] *adv* **1 :** yes <sí, gracias : yes, please> <creo que sí : I think so> **2 sí que :** indeed, absolutely <esta vez sí que ganaré : this time I'm sure to win> **3 porque sí** *fam* **:** because, just because <lo hizo porque sí : she did it just because>

sí[2] *nm* **:** yes <dar el sí : to say yes, to express consent>

sí[3] *pron* **1 de por sí** *or* **en sí :** by itself, in itself, per se **2 fuera de sí :** beside oneself **3 para sí (mismo) :** to himself, to herself, for himself, for herself **4 entre ~ :** among themselves

siamés, -mesa *adj & n, mpl* **siameses :** Siamese

sibilante *adj & nf* **:** sibilant

siciliano, -na *adj & n* **:** Sicilian

sico- → **psico-**

sicomoro *or* **sicómoro** *nm* **:** sycamore

SIDA *or* **sida** *nm* **:** AIDS

siderurgia *nf* **:** iron and steel industry

siderúrgico, -ca *adj* **:** steel, iron <the steel industry : la industria siderúrgica>

sidra *nf* **:** hard cider

siega[1], **siegue, etc.** → **segar**

siega[2] *nf* **1 :** harvesting **2 :** harvest time **3 :** harvested crop

siembra[1], **etc.** → **sembrar**

siembra[2] *nf* **1 :** sowing **2 :** sowing season **3** SEMBRADO **:** cultivated field

siempre *adv* **1 :** always <siempre tienes hambre : you're always hungry> **2 :** still <¿siempre te vas? : are you still going?> **3** *Mex* **:** after all <siempre no fui : I didn't go after all> **4 siempre que :** whenever, every time <siempre que pasa : every time he walks by> **5 para ~ :** forever, for good **6 siempre y cuando :** provided that

sien *nf* **:** temple (on the forehead)

sienta, etc. → **sentar**

siente, etc. → **sentir**

sierpe *nf* **:** serpent, snake

sierra[1], **etc.** → **serrar**

sierra[2] *nf* **1 :** saw <sierra de vaivén : jigsaw> **2** CORDILLERA **:** mountain range **3 :** mountains *pl* <viven en la sierra : they live in the mountains>

siervo, -va *n* **1 :** slave **2 :** serf

siesta *nf* **:** nap, siesta

siete *adj & nm* **:** seven

sífilis *nf* **:** syphilis

sifón *nm, pl* **sifones :** siphon

siga, sigue, etc. → **seguir**

sigilo *nm* **:** secrecy, stealth

sigiloso, -sa *adj* FURTIVO **:** furtive, stealthy — **sigilosamente** *adv*

sigla *nf* **:** acronym, abbreviation

siglo *nm* **1 :** century **2 :** age <el Siglo de Oro : the Golden Age> <hace siglos que no te veo : I haven't seen you in ages> **3 :** world, secular life

signar *vt* **:** to sign (a treaty or agreement)

signatario, -ria *n* **:** signatory

significación *nf, pl* **-ciones 1 :** significance, importance **2 :** signification, meaning

significado *nm* **1 :** sense, meaning **2 :** significance

significante *adj* **:** significant

significar {72} *vt* **1 :** to mean, to signify **2 :** to express, to make known — **significarse** *vr* **1 :** to draw attention, to become known **2 :** to take a stance

significativo, -va *adj* **1 :** significant, important **2 :** meaningful — **significativamente** *adv*

signo *nm* **1 :** sign <signo de igual : equal sign> <un signo de alegría : a sign of happiness> **2 :** (punctuation) mark <signo de interrogación : question mark> <signo de admiración : exclamation point> <signo de intercalación : caret>

siguiente *adj* **:** next, following

sílaba *nf* **:** syllable

silábico, -ca *adj* **:** syllabic

silbar *v* **:** to whistle

silbato *nm* PITO **:** whistle

silbido *nm* **:** whistle, whistling

silenciador *nm* **1 :** muffler (of an automobile) **2 :** silencer

silenciar *vt* **1 :** to silence **2 :** to muffle

silencio *nm* **1 :** silence, quiet <¡silencio! : be quiet!> **2 :** rest (in music)

silencioso, -sa *adj* **:** silent, quiet — **silenciosamente** *adv*

sílice *nf* **:** silica

silicio *nm* **:** silicon

silla *nf* **1 :** chair **2 silla de ruedas :** wheelchair

sillón *nm, pl* **sillones :** armchair, easy chair

silo *nm* **:** silo

silueta *nf* **1 :** silhouette **2 :** figure, shape

silvestre *adj* **:** wild <flor silvestre : wildflower>

silvicultor, -tora *n* **:** forester

silvicultura *nf* **:** forestry

sima *nf* ABISMO **:** chasm, abyss

simbólico, -ca *adj* **:** symbolic — **simbólicamente** *adj*

simbolismo *nm* **:** symbolism

simbolizar {21} *vt* **:** to symbolize

símbolo *nm* **:** symbol

simetría *nf* **:** symmetry

simétrico, -ca *adj* **:** symmetrical, symmetric

simiente *nf* **:** seed

símil *nm* **1 :** simile **2 :** analogy, comparison

similar *adj* SEMEJANTE **:** similar, alike

similitud *nf* **:** similarity, resemblance

simio *nm* **:** ape

simpatía *nf* **1 :** liking, affection <tomarle simpatía a : to take a liking to> **2 :** warmth, friendliness **3 :** support, solidarity

simpático, -ca *adj* **:** nice, friendly, likeable

simpatizante *nf* **:** sympathizer, supporter

simpatizar {21} *vi* **1 :** to get along, to hit it off <simpaticé mucho con él : I really liked him> **2 ~ con :** to sympathize with, to support
simple[1] *adj* **1** SENCILLO **:** plain, simple, easy **2 :** pure, mere <por simple vanidad : out of pure vanity> **3 :** simpleminded, foolish
simple[2] *n* **:** fool, simpleton
simplemente *adv* **:** simply, merely, just
simpleza *nf* **1 :** foolishness, simpleness **2** NECEDAD **:** nonsense
simplicidad *nf* **:** simplicity
simplificar {72} *vt* **:** to simplify — **simplificación** *nf*
simposio *or* **simposium** *nm* **:** symposium
simulación *nf, pl* **-ciones :** simulation
simulacro *nm* **:** imitation, sham <simulacro de juicio : mock trial>
simular *vt* **1 :** to simulate **2 :** to feign, to pretend
simultáneo, -nea *adj* **:** simultaneous — **simultáneamente** *adv*
sin *prep* **1 :** without <sin querer : unintentionally> <sin refinar : unrefined> **2 sin que :** without <lo hicimos sin que él se diera cuenta : we did it without him noticing>
sinagoga *nf* **:** synagogue
sinceridad *nf* **:** sincerity
sincero, -ra *adj* **:** sincere, honest, true — **sinceramente** *adv*
síncopa *nf* **:** syncopation
sincopar *vt* **:** to syncopate
sincronizar {21} *vt* **:** to synchronize — **sincronización** *nf*
sindical *adj* GREMIAL **:** union, labor <representante sindical : union representative>
sindicalización *nf, pl* **-ciones :** unionizing, unionization
sindicalizar {21} *vt* **:** to unionize — **sindicalizarse** *vr* **1 :** to form a union **2 :** to join a union
sindicar → **sindicalizar**
sindicato *nm* GREMIO **:** union, guild
síndrome *nm* **:** syndrome
sinecura *nf* **:** sinecure
sinfín *nm* **:** endless number <un sinfín de problemas : no end of problems>
sinfonía *nf* **:** symphony
sinfónica *nf* **:** symphony orchestra
sinfónico, -ca *adj* **:** symphonic, symphony
singular[1] *adj* **1 :** singular, unique **2** PARTICULAR **:** peculiar, odd **3 :** singular (in grammar) — **singularmente** *adv*
singular[2] *nm* **:** singular
singularidad *nf* **:** uniqueness, singularity
singularizar {21} *vt* **:** to make unique or distinct — **singularizarse** *vr* **:** to stand out, to distinguish oneself
siniestrado, -da *adj* **:** damaged, wrecked <zona siniestrada : disaster zone>
siniestro[1], **-tra** *adj* **1** IZQUIERDO **:** left, left-hand **2** MALVADO **:** sinister, evil
siniestro[2] *nm* **:** accident, disaster
sinnúmero → **sinfín**
sino *conj* **1 :** but, rather <no será hoy, sino mañana : it won't be today, but tomorrow> **2** EXCEPTO **:** but, except <no hace sino despertar suspicacias : it does nothing but arouse suspicion>
sinónimo[1], **-ma** *adj* **:** synonymous
sinónimo[2] *nm* **:** synonym
sinopsis *nfs & pl* RESUMEN **:** synopsis, summary
sinrazón *nf, pl* **-zones :** wrong, injustice
sinsabores *nmpl* **:** woes, troubles
sinsonte *nm* **:** mockingbird
sintáctico, -ca *adj* **:** syntactic, syntactical
sintaxis *nfs & pl* **:** syntax
síntesis *nfs & pl* **1 :** synthesis, fusion **2** SINOPSIS **:** synopsis, summary
sintético, -ca *adj* **:** synthetic — **sintéticamente** *adv*
sintetizar {21} *vt* **1 :** to synthesize **2** RESUMIR **:** to summarize
sintió, etc. → **sentir**
síntoma *nm* **:** symptom
sintomático, -ca *adj* **:** symptomatic
sintonía *nf* **1 :** tuning in (of a radio) **2 en sintonía con :** in tune with, attuned to
sintonizador *nm* **:** tuner, knob for tuning (of a radio, etc.)
sintonizar {21} *vt* **:** to tune (in) to — *vi* **1 :** to tune in **2 ~ con :** to be in tune with, to empathize with
sinuosidad *nf* **:** sinuosity
sinuoso, -sa *adj* **1 :** winding, sinuous **2 :** devious
sinvergüenza[1] *adj* **1** DESCARADO **:** shameless, brazen, impudent **2** TRAVIESO **:** naughty
sinvergüenza[2] *nmf* **1 :** rogue, scoundrel **2 :** brat, rascal
sionista *adj & nmf* **:** Zionist — **sionismo** *nm*
siqui- → **psiqui-**
siquiera *adv* **1 :** at least <dame siquiera un poquito : at least give me a little bit> **2** (*in negative constructions*) **:** not even <ni siquiera nos saludaron : they didn't even say hello to us>
sirena *nf* **1 :** mermaid **2 :** siren <sirena de niebla : foghorn>
sirio, -ria *adj & n* **:** Syrian
sirope *nm* **:** syrup
sirve, etc. → **servir**
sirviente, -ta *n* **:** servant, maid *f*
sisal *nm* **:** sisal
sisear *vi* **:** to hiss
siseo *nm* **:** hiss
sísmico, -ca *adj* **:** seismic
sismo *nm* **1** TERREMOTO **:** earthquake **2** TEMBLOR **:** tremor
sismógrafo *nm* **:** seismograph
sistema *nm* **:** system

sistemático, -ca *adj* : systematic — **sistemáticamente** *adv*
sistematizar {21} *vt* : to systematize
sistémico, -ca *adj* : systemic
sitiar *vt* ASEDIAR : to besiege
sitio *nm* **1** LUGAR : place, site <vámonos a otro sitio : let's go somewhere else> **2** ESPACIO : room, space <hacer sitio a : to make room for> **3** : siege <estado de sitio : state of siege> **4** *Mex* : taxi stand
situación *nf, pl* **-ciones** : situation
situado, -da *adj* : situated, placed
situar {3} *vt* UBICAR : to situate, to place, to locate — **situarse** *vr* **1** : to be placed, to be located **2** : to make a place for oneself, to do well
sketch *nm* : sketch, skit
slip *nm* : briefs *pl*, underpants *pl*
smog *nm* : smog
smoking *nm* ESMOQUIN : tuxedo
snob → **esnob**
so *prep* : under <so pena de : under penalty of>
sobaco *nm* : armpit
sobado, -da *adj* **1** : worn, shabby **2** : well-worn, hackneyed
sobar *vt* **1** : to finger, to handle **2** : to knead **3** : to rub, to massage **4** *fam* : to beat, to pummel
soberanía *nf* : sovereignty
soberano, -na *adj & n* : sovereign
soberbia *nf* **1** ORGULLO : pride, arrogance **2** MAGNIFICENCIA : magnificence
soberbio, -bia *adj* **1** : proud, arrogant **2** : grand, magnificent
sobornable *adv* : venal, bribable
sobornar *vt* : to bribe
soborno *nm* **1** : bribery **2** : bribe
sobra *nf* **1** : excess, surplus **2 de ~** : extra, to spare **3 sobras** *nfpl* : leftovers, scraps
sobrado, -da *adj* : abundant, excessive, more than enough
sobrante[1] *adj* : remaining, superfluous
sobrante[2] *nm* : remainder, surplus
sobrar *vi* : to be in excess, to be superfluous <más vale que sobre a que falte : it's better to have too much than not enough>
sobre[1] *nm* **1** : envelope **2** : packet <un sobre de sazón : a packet of seasoning>
sobre[2] *prep* **1** : on, on top of <sobre la mesa : on the table> **2** : over, above **3** : about <¿tiene libros sobre Bolivia? : do you have books on Bolivia?> **4 sobre todo** : especially, above all
sobrealimentar *vt* : to overfeed
sobrecalentar {55} *vt* : to overheat — **sobrecalentarse** *vr*
sobrecama *nmf* : bedspread
sobrecargar {52} *vt* : to overload, to overburden, to weigh down
sobrecoger {15} *vt* **1** : to surprise, to startle **2** : to scare — **sobrecogerse** *vr*
sobrecubierta *nf* : dust jacket
sobredosis *nfs & pl* : overdose
sobreentender {56} *vt* : to infer, to understand
sobreestimar *vt* : to overestimate, to overrate
sobreexitado, -da *adj* : overexcited
sobreexponer {60} *vt* : to overexpose
sobregirar *vt* : to overdraw
sobregiro *nm* : overdraft
sobrehumano, -na *adj* : superhuman
sobrellevar *vt* : to endure, to bear
sobremanera *adv* : exceedingly
sobremesa *nf* : after-dinner conversation
sobrenatural *adj* : supernatural
sobrenombre *nm* APODO : nickname
sobrentender → **sobreentender**
sobrepasar *vt* : to exceed, to surpass — **sobrepasarse** *vr* PASARSE : to go too far
sobrepelliz *nf, pl* **-pellices** : surplice
sobrepeso *nm* **1** : excess weight **2** : overweight, obesity
sobrepoblación, sobrepoblado → **superpoblación, superpoblado**
sobreponer {60} *vt* **1** SUPERPONER : to superimpose **2** ANTEPONER : to put first, to give priority to — **sobreponerse** *vr* **1** : to pull oneself together **2 ~ a** : to overcome
sobreprecio *nm* : surcharge
sobreproducción *nf, pl* **-ciones** : overproduction
sobreproducir {61} *vt* : to overproduce
sobreprotector, -tora *adj* : overprotective
sobreproteger {15} *vt* : to overprotect
sobresaliente[1] *adj* **1** : protruding, projecting **2** : outstanding, noteworthy **3** : significant, salient
sobresaliente[2] *nmf* : understudy
sobresalir {73} *vi* **1** : to protrude, to jut out, to project **2** : to stand out, to excel
sobresaltar *vt* : to startle, to frighten — **sobresaltarse** *vr*
sobresalto *nm* : start, fright
sobresueldo *nm* : bonus, additional pay
sobretasa *nf* : surcharge <sobretasa a la gasolina : gas tax>
sobretodo *nm* : overcoat
sobrevalorar *or* **sobrevaluar** {3} *vt* : to overvalue, to overrate
sobrevender *vt* : to oversell
sobrevenir {87} *vi* ACAECER : to take place, to come about <podrían sobrevenir complicaciones : complications could occur>
sobrevivencia *nf* → **supervivencia**
sobreviviente → **superviviente**
sobrevivir *vi* : to survive — *vt* : to outlive, to outlast
sobrevolar {19} *vt* : to fly over, to overfly
sobriedad *nf* : sobriety, moderation
sobrino, -na *n* : nephew *m*, niece *f*
sobrio, -bria *adj* : sober — **sobriamente** *adv*

socarrón, -rrona *adj, mpl* **-rrones 1** : sly, cunning **2** : sarcastic
socavar *vt* : to undermine
sociabilidad *nf* : sociability
sociable *adj* : sociable
social *adj* : social — **socialmente** *adv*
socialista *adj & nmf* : socialist — **socialismo** *nm*
sociedad *nf* **1** : society **2** : company, enterprise **3 sociedad anónima** : incorporated company
socio, -cia *n* **1** : member **2** : partner
socioeconómico, -ca *adj* : socioeconomic
sociología *nf* : sociology
sociológico, -ca *adj* : sociological — **sociológicamente** *adv*
sociólogo, -ga *n* : sociologist
socorrer *vt* : to assist, to come to the aid of
socorrido, -da *adj* ÚTIL : handy, practical
socorrista *nmf* **1** : rescue worker **2** : lifeguard
socorro *nm* AUXILIO **1** : aid, help <equipo de socorro : rescue team> **2 ¡socorro!** : help!
soda *nf* : soda, soda water
sodio *nf* : sodium
soez *adj, pl* **soeces** GROSERO : rude, vulgar — **soezmente** *adv*
sofá *nm* : couch, sofa
sofistería *nf* : sophistry — **sofista** *nmf*
sofisticación *nf, pl* **-ciones** : sophistication
sofisticado, -da *adj* : sophisticated
sofocante *adj* : suffocating, stifling
sofocar {72} *vt* **1** AHOGAR : to suffocate, to smother **2** EXTINGUIR : to extinguish, to put out (a fire) **3** APLASTAR : to crush, to put down <sofocar una rebelión : to crush a rebellion> — **sofocarse** *vr* **1** : to suffocate **2** *fam* : to get upset, to get mad
sofreír {66} *vt* : to sauté
sofrito[1], **-ta** *adj* : sautéed
sofrito[2] *nm* : seasoning sauce
softbol *nm* : softball
software *nm* : software
soga *nf* : rope
soja *nf* → **soya**
sojuzgar *vt* : to subdue, to conquer, to subjugate
sol *nm* **1** : sun **2** : Peruvian unit of currency
solamente *adv* SÓLO : only, just
solapa *nf* **1** : lapel (of a jacket) **2** : flap (of an envelope)
solapado, -da *adj* : secret, underhanded
solapar *vt* : to cover up, to keep secret — **solaparse** *vr* : to overlap
solar[1] {19} *vt* : to floor, to tile
solar[2] *adj* : solar, sun
solar[3] *nm* **1** TERRENO : lot, piece of land, site **2** *Cuba, Peru* : tenement building
solariego, -ga *adj* : ancestral
solaz *nm, pl* **solaces 1** CONSUELO : solace, comfort **2** DESCANSO : relaxation, recreation
solazarse {21} *vr* : to relax, to enjoy oneself
soldado *nm* **1** : soldier **2 soldado raso** : private, enlisted man
soldador[1], **-dora** *n* : welder
soldador[2] *nm* : soldering iron
soldadura *nf* **1** : welding **2** : soldering, solder
soldar {19} *vt* **1** : to weld **2** : to solder
soleado, -da *adj* : sunny
soledad *nf* : loneliness, solitude
solemne *adj* : solemn — **solemnemente** *adv*
solemnidad *nf* : solemnity
soler {78} *vi* : to be in the habit of, to tend to <solía tomar café por la tarde : she usually drank coffee in the afternoon> <eso suele ocurrir : that frequently happens>
solera *nf* **1** : prop, support **2** : tradition
solicitante *nmf* : applicant
solicitar *vt* **1** : to request, to solicit **2** : to apply for <solicitar empleo : to apply for employment>
solícito, -ta *adj* : solicitous, attentive, obliging
solicitud *nf* **1** : solicitude, concern **2** : request **3** : application
solidaridad *nf* : solidarity
solidario, -ria *adj* : supportive, united in support <se declararon solidarios con la nueva ley : they declared their support for the new law> <espíritu solidario : spirit of solidarity>
solidarizar {21} *vi* : to be in solidarity <solidarizamos con la huelga : we support the strike>
solidez *nf* **1** : solidity, firmness **2** : soundness (of an argument, etc.)
solidificar {72} *vt* : to solidify, to make solid — **solidificarse** *vr* — **solidificación** *nf*
sólido[1], **-da** *adj* **1** : solid, firm **2** : sturdy, well-made **3** : sound, well-founded — **sólidamente** *adv*
sólido[2] *nm* : solid
soliloquio *nm* : soliloquy
solista *nmf* : soloist
solitaria *nf* TENIA : tapeworm
solitario[1], **-ria** *adj* **1** : lonely **2** : lone, solitary **3** DESIERTO : deserted, lonely <una calle solitaria : a deserted street>
solitario[2], **-ria** *n* : recluse, loner
solitario[3] *nm* : solitaire
sollozar {21} *vi* : to sob
sollozo *nm* : sob
solo[1], **-la** *adj* **1** : alone, by oneself **2** : lonely **3** ÚNICO : only, sole, unique <hay un solo problema : there's only one problem> **4 a solas** : alone
solo[2] *nm* : solo
sólo *adv* SOLAMENTE : just, only <sólo quieren comer : they just want to eat>
solomillo *nm* : sirloin, loin
solsticio *nm* : solstice

soltar {19} *vt* **1 :** to let go of, to drop **2 :** to release, to set free **3** AFLOJAR **:** to loosen, to slacken

soltería *nf* **:** bachelorhood, spinsterhood

soltero[1], **-ra** *adj* **:** single, unmarried

soltero[2], **-ra** *n* **1 :** bachelor *m,* single man *m,* single woman *f* **2 apellido de soltera :** maiden name

soltura *nf* **1 :** looseness, slackness **2 :** fluency (of language) **3 :** agility, ease of movement

soluble *adj* **:** soluble — **solubilidad** *nf*

solución *nf, pl* **-ciones 1 :** solution (in a liquid) **2 :** answer, solution

solucionar *vt* RESOLVER **:** to solve, to resolve — **solucionarse** *vr*

solvencia *nf* **1 :** solvency **2 :** settling, payment (of debts) **3 :** reliability <solvencia moral : trustworthiness>

solvente[1] *adj* **1 :** solvent **2 :** reliable, trustworthy

solvente[2] *nm* **:** solvent

somalí *adj & nmf* **:** Somalian

sombra *nf* **1 :** shadow **2 :** shade **3 sombras** *nfpl* **:** darkness, shadows *pl* **4 sin sombra de duda :** without a shadow of a doubt

sombreado, -da *adj* **1 :** shady **2 :** shaded, darkened

sombrear *vt* **:** to shade

sombrerero, -ra *n* **:** milliner, hatter

sombrero *nm* **1 :** hat **2 sin ~ :** bareheaded **3 sombrero hongo :** derby

sombrilla *nf* **:** parasol, umbrella

sombrío, -bría *adj* LÓBREGO **:** dark, somber, gloomy — **sombríamente** *adv*

someramente *adv* **:** cursorily, summarily

somero, -ra *adj* **:** superficial, cursory, shallow

someter *vt* **1 :** to subjugate, to conquer **2 :** to subordinate **3 :** to subject (to treatment or testing) **4 :** to submit, to present — **someterse** *vr* **1 :** to submit, to yield **2 :** to undergo

sometimiento *nm* **1 :** submission, subjection **2 :** presentation

somnífero[1], **-ra** *adj* **:** soporific

somnífero[2] *nm* **:** sleeping pill

somnolencia *nf* **:** drowsiness, sleepiness

somnoliento, -ta *adj* **:** drowsy, sleepy

somorgujo *or* **somormujo** *nm* **:** loon, grebe

somos → **ser**

son[1] → **ser**

son[2] *nm* **1 :** sound <al son de la trompeta : at the sound of the trumpet> **2 :** news, rumor **3 en son de :** as, in the manner of, by way of <en son de broma : as a joke> <en son de paz : in peace>

sonado, -da *adj* **:** celebrated, famous, much-discussed

sonaja *nf* **:** rattle

sonajero *nm* **:** rattle (toy)

sonámbulo, -la *n* **:** sleepwalker

sonar[1] {19} *vi* **1 :** to sound <suena bien : it sounds good> **2 :** to ring (bells) **3 :** to look or sound familiar <me suena ese nombre : that name rings a bell> **4 ~ a :** to sound like — *vt* **1 :** to ring **2 :** to blow (a trumpet, a nose) — **sonarse** *vr* **:** to blow one's nose

sonar[2] *nm* **:** sonar

sonata *nf* **:** sonata

sonda *nf* **1 :** sounding line **2 :** probe **3** CATÉTER **:** catheter

sondar *vt* **1 :** to sound, to probe (in medicine, drilling, etc.) **2 :** to probe, to explore (outer space)

sondear *vt* **1 :** to sound **2 :** to probe **3 :** to sound out, to test (opinions, markets)

sondeo *nm* **1 :** sounding, probing **2 :** drilling **3** ENCUESTA **:** survey, poll

soneto *nm* **:** sonnet

sónico, -ca *adj* **:** sonic

sonido *nm* **:** sound

sonoridad *nf* **:** sonority, resonance

sonoro, -ra *adj* **1 :** resonant, sonorous, voiced (in linguistics) **2 :** resounding, loud **3 banda sonora :** soundtrack

sonreír {66} *vi* **:** to smile

sonriente *adj* **:** smiling

sonrisa *nf* **:** smile

sonrojar *vt* **:** to cause to blush — **sonrojarse** *vr* **:** to blush

sonrojo *nm* RUBOR **:** blush

sonrosado, -da *adj* **:** rosy, pink

sonsacar {72} *vt* **:** to wheedle, to extract

sonsonete *nm* **1 :** tapping **2 :** drone **3 :** mocking tone

soñador[1], **-dora** *adj* **:** dreamy

soñador[2], **-dora** *n* **:** dreamer

soñar {19} *v* **1 :** to dream **2 ~ con :** to dream about **3 soñar despierto :** to daydream

soñoliento, -ta *adj* **:** sleepy, drowsy

sopa *nf* **1 :** soup **2 estar hecho una sopa :** to be soaked to the bone

sopera *nf* **:** soup tureen

sopesar *vt* **:** to weigh, to evaluate

soplar *vi* **:** to blow — *vt* **:** to blow on, to blow out, to blow off

soplete *nm* **:** blowtorch

soplido *nm* **:** puff

soplo *nm* **:** puff, gust

soplón, -plona *n, mpl* **soplones** *fam* **:** tattletale, sneak

sopor *nm* SOMNOLENCIA **:** drowsiness, sleepiness

soporífero, -ra *adj* **:** soporific

soportable *adj* **:** bearable, tolerable

soportar *vt* **1** SOSTENER **:** to support, to hold up **2** RESISTIR **:** to withstand, to resist **3** AGUANTAR **:** to bear, to tolerate

soporte *nm* **:** base, stand, support

soprano *nmf* **:** soprano

sor *nf* **:** Sister (religious title)

sorber *vt* **1 :** to sip, to suck in **2 :** to absorb, to soak up

sorbete *nm* **:** sherbet

sorbo *nm* **1 :** sip, gulp, swallow **2 beber a sorbos :** to sip

sordera *nf* : deafness

sordidez *nf, pl* **-deces** : sordidness, squalor

sórdido, -da *adj* : sordid, dirty, squalid

sordina *nf* : mute (for a musical instrument)

sordo, -da *adj* **1** : deaf **2** : muted, muffled

sordomudo, -da *n* : deaf-mute

sorgo *nm* : sorghum

soriasis *nfs & pl* : psoriasis

sorna *nf* : sarcasm, mocking tone

sorprendente *adj* : surprising — **sorprendentemente** *adv*

sorprender *vt* : to surprise — **sorprenderse** *vr*

sorpresa *nf* : surprise

sorpresivo, -va *adj* **1** : surprising, surprise **2** IMPREVISTO : sudden, unexpected

sortear *vt* **1** RIFAR : to raffle, to draw lots for **2** : to dodge, to avoid

sorteo *nm* : drawing, raffle

sortija *nf* **1** ANILLO : ring **2** : curl, ringlet

sortilegio *nm* **1** HECHIZO : spell, charm **2** HECHICERÍA : sorcery

SOS *nm* : SOS

sosegado, -da *adj* SERENO : calm, tranquil, serene

sosegar {49} *vt* : to calm, to pacify — **sosegarse** *vr*

sosiego *nm* : tranquillity, serenity, calm

soslayar *vt* ESQUIVAR : to dodge, to evade

soslayo *nm* **de ~** : obliquely, sideways <mirar de soslayo : to look askance>

soso, -sa *adj* **1** INSÍPIDO : bland, flavorless **2** ABURRIDO : dull, boring

sospecha *nf* : suspicion

sospechar *vt* : to suspect — *vi* : to be suspicious

sospechosamente *adv* : suspiciously

sospechoso[1], -sa *adj* : suspicious, suspect

sospechoso[2], -sa *n* : suspect

sostén *nm, pl* **sostenes 1** APOYO : support **2** : sustenance **3** : brassiere, bra

sostener {80} *vt* **1** : to support, to hold up **2** : to hold <sostenme la puerta : hold the door for me> <sostener una conversación : to hold a conversation> **3** : to sustain, to maintain — **sostenerse** *vr* **1** : to stand, to hold oneself up **2** : to continue, to remain

sostenible *adj* : sustainable, tenable

sostenido[1], -da *adj* **1** : sustained, prolonged **2** : sharp (in music)

sostenido[2] *nm* : sharp (in music)

sostuvo, etc. → **sostener**

sotana *nf* : cassock

sótano *nm* : basement

sotavento *nm* : lee <a sotavento : leeward>

soterrar {55} *vt* **1** : to bury **2** : to conceal, to hide away

soto *nm* : grove, copse

souvenir *nm, pl* **-nirs** RECUERDO : souvenir, memento

soviético, -ca *adj* : Soviet

soy → **ser**

soya *nf* : soy, soybean

spaghetti *nm* → **espagueti**

sport [ɛ'spor] *adj* : sport, casual

sprint [ɛ'sprin, -'sprint] *nm* : sprint — **sprinter** *nmf*

squash [ɛ'skwaʃ, -'skwatʃ] *nm* : squash (sport)

Sr. *nm* : Mr.

Sra. *nf* : Mrs., Ms.

Srta. *or* **Srita.** *nf* : Miss, Ms.

standard → **estándar**

stress *nm* → **estrés**

su *adj* **1** : his, her, its, their, one's <su libro : her book> <sus consecuencias : its consequences> **2** (*formal*) : your <tómese su medicina, señor : take your medicine, sir>

suave *adj* **1** BLANDO : soft **2** LISO : smooth **3** : gentle, mild **4** *Mex fam* : great, fantastic

suavemente *adj* : smoothly, gently, softly

suavidad *nf* : softness, smoothness, mellowness

suavizante *nm* : softener, fabric softener

suavizar {21} *vt* **1** : to soften, to smooth out **2** : to tone down — **suavizarse** *vr*

subacuático, -ca *adj* : underwater

subalterno[1], -na *adj* **1** SUBORDINADO : subordinate **2** SECUNDARIO : secondary

subalterno[2], -na *n* SUBORDINADO : subordinate

subarrendar {55} *vt* : to sublet

subasta *nf* : auction

subastador, -dora *n* : auctioneer

subastar *vt* : to auction, to auction off

subcampeón, -peona *n, mpl* **-peones** : runner-up

subcomité *nm* : subcommittee

subconsciente *adj & nm* : subconscious — **subconscientemente** *adv*

subcontratar *vt* : to subcontract

subcontratista *nmf* : subcontractor

subcultura *nf* : subculture

subdesarrollado, -da *adj* : underdeveloped

subdirector, -tora *n* : assistant manager

súbdito, -ta *n* : subject (of a monarch)

subdividir *vt* : to subdivide

subdivisión *nf, pl* **-siones** : subdivision

subestimar *vt* : to underestimate, to undervalue

subexponer {60} *vt* : to underexpose

subexposición *nf, pl* **-ciones** : underexposure

subgrupo *nm* : subgroup

subibaja *nm* : seesaw

subida *nf* **1** : ascent, climb **2** : rise, increase **3** : slope, hill <ir de subida : to go uphill>

subido, -da *adj* **1 :** intense, strong <amarillo subido : bright yellow> **2 subido de tono :** risqué

subir *vt* **1 :** to bring up, to take up **2 :** to climb, to go up **3 :** to raise — *vi* **1 :** to go up, to come up **2 :** to rise, to increase **3 :** to be promoted **4 ~ a :** to get on, to mount <subir a un tren : to get on a train> — **subirse** *vr* **1 :** to climb (up) **2 :** to pull up (clothing) **3 subirse a la cabeza :** to go to one's head

súbito, -ta *adj* **1** REPENTINO **:** sudden **2 de ~ :** all of a sudden, suddenly — **súbitamente** *adv*

subjetivo, -va *adj* **:** subjective — **subjetivamente** *adv* — **subjetividad** *nf*

subjuntivo[1], **-va** *adj* **:** subjunctive

subjuntivo[2] *nm* **:** subjunctive

sublevación *nf, pl* **-ciones** ALZAMIENTO **:** uprising, rebellion

sublevar *vt* **:** to incite to rebellion — **sublevarse** *vr* **:** to rebel, to rise up

sublimar *vt* **:** to sublimate — **sublimación** *nf*

sublime *adj* **:** sublime

submarinismo *nm* **:** scuba diving

submarinista *nmf* **:** scuba diver

submarino[1], **-na** *adj* **:** submarine, undersea

submarino[2] *nm* **:** submarine

suboficial *nmf* **:** noncommissioned officer, petty officer

subordinado, -da *adj & n* **:** subordinate

subordinar *vt* **:** to subordinate — **subordinarse** *vr* — **subordinación** *nf*

subproducto *nm* **:** by-product

subrayar *vt* **1 :** to underline, to underscore **2** ENFATIZAR **:** to highlight, to emphasize

subrepticio, -cia *adj* **:** surreptitious — **subrepticiamente** *adv*

subsahariano, -na *adj* **:** sub-Saharan

subsanar *vt* **1** RECTIFICAR **:** to rectify, to correct **2 :** to overlook, to excuse **3 :** to make up for

subscribir → **suscribir**

subsecretario, -ria *n* **:** undersecretary

subsecuente *adj* **:** subsequent — **subsecuentemente** *adv*

subsidiar *vt* **:** to subsidize

subsidiaria *nf* **:** subsidiary

subsidio *nm* **:** subsidy

subsiguiente *adj* **:** subsequent

subsistencia *nf* **1 :** subsistence **2 :** sustenance

subsistir *vi* **1 :** to subsist, to live **2 :** to endure, to survive

substancia *nf* → **sustancia**

subteniente *nmf* **:** second lieutenant

subterfugio *nm* **:** subterfuge

subterráneo[1], **-nea** *adj* **:** underground, subterranean

subterráneo[2] *nm* **1 :** underground passage, tunnel **2** *Arg, Uru* **:** subway

subtítulo *nm* **:** subtitle, subheading

subtotal *nm* **:** subtotal

suburbano, -na *adj* **:** suburban

suburbio *nm* **1 :** suburb **2 :** slum (outside a city)

subvención *nf, pl* **-ciones :** subsidy, grant

subvencionar *vt* **:** to subsidize

subversivo, -va *adj & n* **:** subversive — **subversión** *nf*

subvertir {76} *vt* **:** to subvert

subyacente *adj* **:** underlying

subyugar {52} *vt* **:** to subjugate — **subyugación** *nf*

succión *nf, pl* **succiones :** suction

succionar *vt* **:** to suck up, to draw in

sucedáneo *nm* **:** substitute <sucedáneo de azucar : sugar substitute>

suceder *vi* **1** OCURRIR **:** to happen, to occur <¿qué sucede? : what's going on?> <suceda lo que suceda : come what may> **2 ~ a :** to follow, to succeed <suceder al trono : to succeed to the throne> <a la primavera sucede el verano : summer follows sping>

sucesión *nf, pl* **-siones 1 :** succession **2 :** sequence, series **3 :** issue, heirs *pl*

sucesivamente *adv* **:** successively, consecutively <y así sucesivamente : and so on>

sucesivo, -va *adj* **:** successive <en los días sucesivos : in the days that followed>

suceso *nm* **1 :** event, happening, occurrence **2 :** incident, crime

sucesor, -sora *n* **:** successor

suciedad *nf* **1 :** dirtiness, filthiness **2** MUGRE **:** dirt, filth

sucinto, -ta *adj* CONCISO **:** succinct, concise — **sucintamente** *adv*

sucio, -cia *adj* **:** dirty, filthy

sucre *nm* **:** Ecuadoran unit of currency

suculento, -ta *adj* **:** succulent

sucumbir *vi* **:** to succumb

sucursal *nf* **:** branch (of a business)

sudadera *nf* **:** sweatshirt

sudado, -da → **sudoroso**

sudafricano, -na *adj & n* **:** South African

sudamericano, -na *adj & n* **:** South American

sudanés, -nesa *adj & n, mpl* **-neses :** Sudanese

sudar *vi* TRANSPIRAR **:** to sweat, to perspire

sudario *nm* **:** shroud

sudeste → **sureste**

sudoeste → **suroeste**

sudor *nm* TRANSPIRACIÓN **:** sweat, perspiration

sudoroso, -sa *adj* **:** sweaty

sueco[1], **-ca** *adj* **:** Swedish

sueco[2], **-ca** *n* **:** Swede

sueco[3] *nm* **:** Swedish (language)

suegro, -gra *n* **1 :** father-in-law *m*, mother-in-law *f* **2 suegros** *nmpl* **:** in-laws

suela *nf* **:** sole (of a shoe)

suelda, etc. → **soldar**

sueldo *nm* **:** salary, wage

suele, etc. → **soler**

suelo *nm* **1 :** ground <caerse al suelo : to fall down, to hit the ground> **2 :** floor, flooring **3** TIERRA **:** soil, land

suelta, etc. → **soltar**

suelto[1], -ta *adj* **:** loose, free, unattached

suelto[2] *nm* **:** loose change

suena, etc. → **sonar**

sueña, etc. → **soñar**

sueño *nm* **1 :** dream **2 :** sleep <perder el sueño : to lose sleep> **3 :** sleepiness <tener sueño : to be sleepy>

suero *nm* **1 :** serum **2 :** whey

suerte *nf* **1** FORTUNA **:** luck, fortune <tener suerte : to be lucky> <por suerte : luckily> **2** DESTINO **:** fate, destiny, lot **3** CLASE, GÉNERO **:** sort, kind <toda suerte de cosas : all kinds of things>

suertudo, -da *adj fam* **:** lucky

suéter *nm* **:** sweater

suficiencia *nf* **1 :** adequacy, sufficiency **2 :** competence, fitness **3 :** smugness, self-satisfaction

suficiente *adj* **1** BASTANTE **:** enough, sufficient <tener suficiente : to have enough> **2 :** suitable, fit **3 :** smug, complacent

suficientemente *adv* **:** sufficiently, enough

sufijo *nm* **:** suffix

suflé *nm* **:** soufflé

sufragar {52} *vt* **1** AYUDAR **:** to help out, to support **2 :** to defray (costs) — *vi* **:** to vote

sufragio *nm* **:** suffrage, vote

sufrido, -da *adj* **1 :** long-suffering, patient **2 :** sturdy, serviceable (of clothing)

sufrimiento *nm* **:** suffering

sufrir *vt* **1 :** to suffer <sufrir una pérdida : to suffer a loss> **2 :** to tolerate, to put up with <ella no lo puede sufrir : she can't stand him> — *vi* **:** to suffer

sugerencia *nf* **:** suggestion

sugerir {76} *vt* **1** PROPONER, RECOMENDAR **:** to suggest, to recommend, to propose **2 :** to suggest, to bring to mind

sugestión *nf, pl* **-tiones :** suggestion, prompting <poder de sugestión : power of suggestion>

sugestionable *adj* **:** suggestible, impressionable

sugestionar *vt* **:** to influence, to sway — **sugestionarse** *vr* **~ con :** to talk oneself into, to become convinced of

sugestivo, -va *adj* **1 :** suggestive **2 :** interesting, stimulating

suicida[1] *adj* **:** suicidal

suicida[2] *nmf* **:** suicide victim, suicide

suicidarse *vr* **:** to commit suicide

suicidio *nm* **:** suicide

suite *nf* **:** suite

suizo, -za *adj & n* **:** Swiss

sujeción *nf, pl* **-ciones 1 :** holding, fastening **2 :** subjection

sujetador *nm* **1 :** fastener **2 :** holder <sujetador de tazas : cup holder>

sujetalibros *nms & pl* **:** bookend

sujetapapeles *nms & pl* CLIP **:** paper clip

sujetar *vt* **1 :** to hold on to, to steady, to hold down **2** FIJAR **:** to fasten, to attach **3** DOMINAR **:** to subdue, to conquer — **sujetarse** *vr* **1 :** to hold on, to hang on **2 ~ a :** to abide by

sujeto[1], -ta *adj* **1 :** secure, fastened **2 ~ a :** subject to

sujeto[2] *nm* **1** INDIVIDUO **:** individual, character **2 :** subject (in grammar)

sulfúrico, -ca *adj* **:** sulfuric

sulfuro *nm* **:** sulfur

sultán *nm, pl* **sultanes :** sultan

suma *nf* **1** CANTIDAD **:** sum, quantity **2 :** addition

sumamente *adv* **:** extremely, exceedingly

sumar *vt* **1 :** to add, to add up **2 :** to add up to, to total — *vi* **:** to add up — **sumarse** *vr* **~ a :** to join

sumario[1], -ria *adj* SUCINTO **:** succinct, summary — **sumariamente** *adv*

sumario[2] *nm* **:** summary

sumergir {35} *vt* **:** to submerge, to immerse, to plunge — **sumergirse** *vr*

sumersión *nf, pl* **-siones :** submersion, immersion

sumidero *nm* **:** drain, sewer

suministrar *vt* **:** to supply, to provide

suministro *nm* **:** supply, provision

sumir *vt* SUMERGIR **:** to plunge, to immerse, to sink — **sumirse** *vr*

sumisión *nf, pl* **-siones 1 :** submission **2 :** submissiveness

sumiso, -sa *adj* **:** submissive, acquiescent, docile

sumo, -ma *adj* **1 :** extreme, great, high <la suma autoridad : the highest authority> **2 a lo sumo :** at the most — **sumamente** *adv*

suntuoso, -sa *adj* **:** sumptuous, lavish — **suntuosamente** *adv*

supeditar *vt* SUBORDINAR **:** to subordinate — **supeditación** *nf*

super[1] *or* **súper** *adj fam* **:** super, great

super[2] *nm* SUPERMERCADO **:** market, supermarket

superable *adj* **:** surmountable

superabundancia *nf* **:** overabundance, superabundance — **superabundante** *adj*

superar *vt* **1 :** to surpass, to exceed **2 :** to overcome, to surmount — **superarse** *vr* **:** to improve oneself

superávit *nm, pl* **-vit** *or* **-vits :** surplus

supercherĩa *nf* **:** trickery, fraud

superestructura *nf* **:** superstructure

superficial *adj* **:** superficial — **superficialmente** *adv*

superficialidad *nf* **:** superficiality

superficie *nf* **1 :** surface **2 :** area <el superficie de un triángulo : the area of a triangle>

superfluidad *nf* **:** superfluity

superfluo, -flua *adj* **:** superfluous

superintendente *nmf* **:** supervisor, superintendent

superior[1] *adj* **1 :** superior **2 :** upper <nivel superior : upper level> **3 :** higher <educación superior : higher education> **4 ~ a :** above, higher than, in excess of

superior[2] *nm* **:** superior

superioridad *nf* **:** superiority

superlativo[1]**, -va** *adj* **:** superlative

superlativo[2] *nm* **:** superlative

supermercado *nm* **:** supermarket

superpoblación *nf, pl* **-ciones :** overpopulation

superpoblado, -da *adj* **:** overpopulated

superponer {60} *vt* **:** to superimpose

superpotencia *nf* **:** superpower

superproducción *nf* → **sobreproducción**

supersónico, -ca *adj* **:** supersonic

superstición *nf, pl* **-ciones :** superstition

supersticioso, -sa *adj* **:** superstitious

supervisar *vt* **:** to supervise, to oversee

supervisión *nf, pl* **-siones :** supervision

supervisor, -sora *n* **:** supervisor, overseer

supervivencia *nf* **:** survival

superviviente *nmf* **:** survivor

supino, -na *adj* **:** supine

suplantar *vt* **:** to supplant, to replace

suplemental → **suplementario**

suplementario, -ria *adj* **:** supplementary, additional, extra

suplemento *nm* **:** supplement

suplencia *nf* **:** substitution, replacement

suplente *adj & nmf* **:** substitute <equipo suplente : replacement team>

supletorio, -ria *adj* **:** extra, additional <teléfono supletorio : extension phone> <cama supletoria : spare bed>

súplica *nf* **:** plea, entreaty

suplicar {72} *vt* IMPLORAR, ROGAR **:** to entreat, to implore, to supplicate

suplicio *nm* TORMENTO **:** ordeal, torture

suplir *vt* **1** COMPENSAR **:** to make up for, to compensate for **2** REEMPLAZAR **:** to replace, to substitute

supo, etc. → **saber**

suponer {60} *vt* **1** PRESUMIR **:** to suppose, to assume <supongo que sí : I guess so, I suppose so> <se supone que van a llegar mañana : they're supposed to arrive tomorrow> **2 :** to imply, to suggest **3 :** to involve, to entail <el éxito supone mucho trabajo : success involves a lot of work>

suposición *nf, pl* **-ciones** PRESUNCIÓN **:** supposition, assumption

supositorio *nm* **:** suppository

supremacía *nf* **:** supremacy

supremo, -ma *adj* **:** supreme

supresión *nf, pl* **-siones 1 :** suppression, elimination **2 :** deletion

suprimir *vt* **1 :** to suppress, to eliminate **2 :** to delete

supuestamente *adv* **:** supposedly, allegedly

supuesto, -ta *adj* **1 :** supposed, alleged **2 por ~ :** of course, absolutely

supurar *vi* **:** to ooze, to discharge

supuso, etc. → **suponer**

sur[1] *adj* **:** southern, southerly, south

sur[2] *nm* **1 :** south, South **2 :** south wind

surafricano, -na → **sudafricano**

suramericano, -na → **sudamericano**

surcar {72} *vt* **1 :** to plow (through) **2 :** to groove, to score, to furrow

surco *nm* **:** groove, furrow, rut

sureño[1]**, -ña** *adj* **:** southern, Southern

sureño[2]**, -ña** *n* **:** Southerner

sureste[1] *adj* **1 :** southeast, southeastern **2 :** southeasterly

sureste[2] *nm* **:** southeast, Southeast

surf *nm* **:** surfing

surfear *vi* **:** to surf

surfing *nm* → **surf**

surfista *nmf* **:** surfer

surgimiento *nm* **:** rise, emergence

surgir {35} *vi* **:** to rise, to arise, to emerge

suroeste[1] *adj* **1 :** southwest, southwestern **2 :** southwesterly

suroeste[2] *nm* **:** southwest, Southwest

surtido[1]**, -da** *adj* **1 :** assorted, varied **2 :** stocked, provisioned

surtido[2] *nm* **:** assortment, selection

surtidor *nm* **1 :** jet, spout **2** *Arg, Chile, Spain* **:** gas pump

surtir *vt* **1 :** to supply, to provide <surtir un pedido : to fill an order> **2 surtir efecto :** to have an effect — *vi* **:** to spout, to spurt up — **surtirse** vr **:** to stock up

susceptible *adj* **:** susceptible, sensitive — **susceptibilidad** *nf*

suscitar *vt* **:** to provoke, to give rise to

suscribir {33} *vt* **1 :** to sign (a formal document) **2 :** to endorse, to sanction — **suscribirse** *vr* **~ a :** to subscribe to

suscripción *nf, pl* **-ciones 1 :** subscription **2 :** endorsement, sanction **3 :** signing

suscriptor, -tora *n* **:** subscriber

susodicho, -cha *adj* **:** aforementioned, aforesaid

suspender *vt* **1** COLGAR **:** to suspend, to hang **2 :** to suspend, to discontinue **3 :** to suspend, to dismiss

suspensión *nf, pl* **-siones :** suspension

suspenso *nm* **:** suspense

suspicacia *nf* **:** suspicion, mistrust

suspicaz *adj, pl* **-caces** DESCONFIADO **:** suspicious, wary

suspirar *vi* **:** to sigh

suspiro *nm* **:** sigh

surque, etc. → **surcar**

suscrito *pp* → **suscribir**

sustancia *nf* **1 :** substance **2 sin ~ :** shallow, lacking substance

sustancial *adj* **1 :** substantial **2** ESENCIAL, FUNDAMENTAL **:** essential, fundamental — **sustancialmente** *adv*

sustancioso, -sa *adj* **1** NUTRITIVO **:** hearty, nutritious **2 :** substantial, solid
sustantivo *nm* **:** noun
sustentación *nf, pl* **-ciones** SOSTÉN **:** support
sustentar *vt* **1 :** to support, to hold up **2 :** to sustain, to nourish **3 :** to maintain, to hold (an opinion) — **sustentarse** *vr* **:** to support oneself
sustento *nm* **1 :** means of support, livelihood **2 :** sustenance, food
sustitución *nf, pl* **-ciones :** replacement, substitution
sustituir {41} *vt* **1 :** to replace, to substitute for **2 :** to stand in for
sustituto, -ta *n* **:** substitute, stand-in
susto *nm* **:** fright, scare
sustracción *nf, pl* **-ciones 1** RESTA **:** subtraction **2 :** theft
sustraer {81} *vt* **1 :** to remove, to take away **2** RESTAR **:** to subtract **3 :** to steal — **sustraerse** *vr* **~ a :** to avoid, to evade
susurrar *vi* **1 :** to whisper **2 :** to murmur **3 :** to rustle (leaves, etc.) — *vt* **:** to whisper
susurro *nm* **1 :** whisper **2 :** murmur **3 :** rustle, rustling
sutil *adj* **1 :** delicate, thin, fine **2 :** subtle
sutileza *nf* **1 :** delicacy **2 :** subtlety
sutura *nf* **:** suture
suturar *vt* **:** to suture
suyo[1], -ya *adj* **1 :** his, her, its, theirs <los libros suyos : his books> <un amigo suyo : a friend of hers> <esta casa es suya : this house is theirs> **2** (*formal*) **:** yours <¿este abrigo es suyo, señor? : is this your coat, sir?>
suyo[2], -ya *pron* **1 :** his, hers, theirs <mi guitarra y la suya : my guitar and hers> <ellos trajeron las suyas : they brought theirs, they brought their own> **2** (*formal*) **:** yours <usted olvidó la suya : you forgot yours>
switch *nm* **:** switch

T

t *nf* **:** twenty-first letter of the Spanish alphabet
taba *nf* **:** anklebone
tabacalero[1], -ra *adj* **:** tobacco <industria tabacalera : tobacco industry>
tabacalero[2], -ra *n* **:** tobacco grower
tabaco *nm* **:** tobacco
tábano *nm* **:** horsefly
taberna *nf* **:** tavern, bar
tabernáculo *nm* **:** tabernacle
tabicar {72} *vt* **:** to wall up
tabique *nm* **:** thin wall, partition
tabla *nf* **1 :** table, list <tabla de multiplicar : multiplication table> **2 :** board, plank, slab <tabla de planchar : ironing board> **3 :** plot, strip (of land) **4 tablas** *nfpl* **:** stage, boards *pl*
tablado *nm* **1 :** flooring, floorboards **2 :** platform, scaffold **3 :** stage
tablero *nm* **1 :** bulletin board **2 :** board (in games) <tablero de ajedrez : chessboard> <tablero de damas : checkerboard> **3** PIZARRA **:** blackboard **4 :** switchboard **5 tablero de instrumentos :** dashboard, instrument panel
tableta *nf* **1** COMPRIMIDO, PÍLDORA **:** tablet, pill **2 :** bar (of chocolate)
tabletear *vi* **:** to rattle, to clack
tableteo *nm* **:** clack, rattling
tablilla *nf* **1 :** small board or tablet **2 :** bulletin board **3 :** splint
tabloide *nm* **:** tabloid
tablón *nm, pl* **tablones 1 :** plank, beam **2 tablón de anuncios :** bulletin board
tabú[1] *adj* **:** taboo
tabú[2] *nm, pl* **tabúes** or **tabús :** taboo
tabulador *nm* **:** tabulator
tabular[1] *vt* **:** to tabulate
tabular[2] *adj* **:** tabular
taburete *nm* **:** footstool, stool
tacañería *nf* **:** miserliness, stinginess
tacaño[1], -ña *adj* MEZQUINO **:** stingy, miserly
tacaño[2], -ña *n* **:** miser, tightwad
tacha *nf* **1 :** flaw, blemish, defect **2 poner tacha a :** to find fault with **3 sin ~ :** flawless
tachadura *nf* **:** erasure, correction
tachar *vt* **1 :** to cross out, to delete **2 ~ de :** to accuse of, to label as <lo tacharon de mentiroso : they accused him of being a liar>
tachón *nm, pl* **tachones :** stud, hobnail
tachonar *vt* **:** to stud
tachuela *nf* **:** tack, hobnail, stud
tácito, -ta *adj* **:** tacit, implicit — **tácitamente** *adv*
taciturno, -na *adj* **1 :** taciturn **2 :** sullen, gloomy
tacle *nm* **:** tackle
taclear *vt* **:** to tackle (in football)
taco *nm* **1 :** wad, stopper, plug **2 :** pad (of paper) **3 :** cleat **4 :** heel (of a shoe) **5 :** cue (in billiards) **6 :** light snack, bite **7 :** taco
tacón *nm, pl* **tacones :** heel (of a shoe) <de tacón alto : high-heeled>
táctica *nf* **:** tactic, tactics *pl*
táctico[1], -ca *adj* **:** tactical
táctico[2], -ca *n* **:** tactician
táctil *adj* **:** tactile
tacto *nm* **1 :** touch, touching, feel **2** DELICADEZA **:** tact
tafetán *nm, pl* **-tanes :** taffeta
tahúr *nm, pl* **tahúres :** gambler
tailandés[1], -desa *adj & n, pl* **-deses :** Thai
tailandés[2] *nm* **:** Thai (language)

taimado, -da *adj* **1 :** crafty, sly **2** *Chile* **:** sullen, sulky

tajada *nf* **1 :** slice **2 sacar tajada** *fam* **:** to get one's share

tajante *adj* **1 :** cutting, sharp **2 :** decisive, categorical

tajantemente *adj* **:** emphatically, categorically

tajar *vt* **:** to cut, to slice

tajo *nm* **1 :** cut, slash, gash **2** ESCARPA **:** steep cliff

tal[1] *adv* **1 :** so, in such a way **2 tal como :** just as <tal como lo hice : just the way I did it> **3 con tal que :** provided that, as long as **4 ¿qué tal? :** how are you?, how's it going?

tal[2] *adj* **1 :** such, such a **2 tal vez :** maybe, perhaps

tal[3] *pron* **1 :** such a one, someone **2 :** such a thing, something **3 tal para cual :** two of a kind

tala *nf* **:** felling (of trees)

taladrar *vt* **:** to drill

taladro *nm* **:** drill, auger <taladro eléctrico : power drill>

talante *nm* **1** HUMOR **:** mood, disposition **2** VOLUNTAD **:** will, willingness

talar *vt* **1 :** to cut down, to fell **2** DEVASTAR **:** to devastate, to destroy

talco *nm* **1 :** talc **2 :** talcum powder

talego *nm* **:** sack

talento *nm* **:** talent, ability

talentoso, -sa *adj* **:** talented, gifted

talismán *nm, pl* **-manes** AMULETO **:** talisman, charm

talla *nf* **1** ESTATURA **:** height **2 :** size (in clothing) **3 :** stature, status **4 :** sculpture, carving

tallar *vt* **1 :** to sculpt, to carve **2 :** to measure (someone's height) **3 :** to deal (cards)

tallarín *nf, pl* **-rines :** noodle

talle *nm* **1 :** size **2 :** waist, waistline **3 :** figure, shape

taller *nm* **1 :** shop, workshop **2 :** studio (of an artist)

tallo *nm* **:** stalk, stem <tallo de maíz : cornstalk>

talón *nm, pl* **talones 1 :** heel (of the foot) **2 :** stub (of a check) **3 talón de Aquiles :** Achilles' heel

talud *nm* **:** slope, incline

tamal *nm* **:** tamale

tamaño[1], **-ña** *adj* **:** such a big <¿crees tamaña mentira? : do you believe such a lie?>

tamaño[2] *nm* **1 :** size **2 de tamaño natural :** life-size

tamarindo *nm* **:** tamarind

tambalearse *vr* **1 :** to teeter **2 :** to totter, to stagger, to sway — **tambaleante** *adj*

tambaleo *nm* **:** staggering, lurching, swaying

también *adv* **:** too, as well, also

tambor *nm* **:** drum

tamborilear *vi* **:** to drum, to tap

tamborileo *nm* **:** tapping, drumming

tamiz *nm* **:** sieve

tamizar {21} *vt* **:** to sift

tampoco *adv* **:** neither, not either <ni yo tampoco : me neither>

tampón *nm, pl* **tampones 1 :** ink pad **2 :** tampon

tam–tam *nm* **:** tom-tom

tan *adv* **1 :** so, so very <no es tan difícil : it is not that difficult> **2 :** as <tan pronto como : as soon as> **3 tan siquiera :** at least, at the least **4 tan sólo :** only, merely

tanda *nf* **1 :** turn, shift **2 :** batch, lot, series

tándem *nm* **1 :** tandem (bicycle) **2 :** duo, pair

tangente *adj & nf* **:** tangent — **tangencial** *adj*

tangible *adj* **:** tangible

tango *nm* **:** tango

tanino *nm* **:** tannin

tanque *nm* **1 :** tank, reservoir **2 :** tanker, tank (vehicle)

tanteador *nm* MARCADOR **:** scoreboard

tantear *vt* **1 :** to feel, to grope **2 :** to size up, to weigh — *vi* **1 :** to keep score **2 :** to feel one's way

tanteo *nm* **1 :** estimate, rough calculation **2 :** testing, sizing up **3 :** scoring

tanto[1] *adv* **1 :** so much <tanto mejor : so much the better> **2 :** so long <¿por qué te tardaste tanto? : why did you take so long?>

tanto[2], **-ta** *adj* **1 :** so much, so many, such <no hagas tantas preguntas : don't ask so many questions> <tiene tanto encanto : he has such charm, he's so charming> **2 :** as much, as many <come tantos dulces como yo : she eats as many sweets as I do> **3 :** odd, however many <cuarenta y tantos años : forty-odd years>

tanto[3] *nm* **1 :** certain amount **2 :** goal, point (in sports) **3 al tanto :** abreast, in the picture **4 un tanto :** somewhat, rather <un tanto cansado : rather tired>

tanto[4], **-ta** *pron* **1 :** so much, so many <tiene tanto que hacer : she has so much to do> <¡no me des tantos! : don't give me so many!> **2 entre ~ :** meanwhile **3 por lo tanto :** therefore

tañer {79} *vt* **1 :** to ring (a bell) **2 :** to play (a musical instrument)

tañido *nm* **1** CAMPANADA **:** ring, peal, toll **2 :** sound (of an instrument)

tapa *nf* **1 :** cover, top, lid **2** *Spain* **:** bar snack

tapacubos *nms & pl* **:** hubcap

tapadera *nf* **1 :** cover, lid **2 :** front, cover (for an organization or person)

tapar *vt* **1** CUBRIR **:** to cover, to cover up **2** OBSTRUIR **:** to block, to obstruct — **taparse** *vr*

tapete *nm* **1 :** small rug, mat **2 :** table cover **3 poner sobre el tapete :** to bring up for discussion

tapia *nf* **:** (adobe) wall, garden wall

tapiar *vt* **1 :** to wall in **2 :** to enclose, to block off

tapicería *nf* **1** : upholstery **2** TAPIZ : tapestry

tapicero, -ra *n* : upholsterer

tapioca *nf* : tapioca

tapir *nm* : tapir

tapiz *nm, pl* **tapices** : tapestry

tapizar {21} *vt* **1** : to upholster **2** : to cover, to carpet

tapón *nm, pl* **tapones 1** : cork **2** : bottle cap **3** : plug, stopper

tapujo *nm* **1** : deceit, pretension **2 sin tapujos** : openly, frankly

taquigrafía *nf* : stenography, shorthand

taquigráfico, -ca *adj* : stenographic

taquígrafo, -fa *n* : stenographer

taquilla *nf* **1** : box office, ticket office **2** : earnings *pl*, take

taquillero, -ra *adj* : box-office, popular <un éxito taquillero : a box-office success>

tarántula *nf* : tarantula

tararear *vt* : to hum

tardanza *nf* : lateness, delay

tardar *vi* **1** : to delay, to take a long time **2** : to be late **3 a más tardar** : at the latest — *vt* DEMORAR : to take (time) <tarda una hora : it takes an hour>

tarde[1] *adv* **1** : late **2 tarde o temprano** : sooner or later

tarde[2] *nf* **1** : afternoon, evening **2 ¡buenas tardes!** : good afternoon!, good evening! **3 en la tarde** *or* **por la tarde** : in the afternoon, in the evening

tardío, -día *adj* : late, tardy

tardo, -da *adj* : slow

tarea *nf* **1** : task, job **2** : homework

tarifa *nf* **1** : rate <tarifas postales : postal rates> **2** : fare (for transportation) **3** : price list **4** ARANCEL : duty

tarima *nf* PLATAFORMA : dais, platform, stage

tarjeta *nf* : card <tarjeta de crédito : credit card> <tarjeta postal : postcard>

tarro *nm* **1** : jar, pot **2** *Arg, Chile* : can, tin

tarta *nf* **1** : tart **2** : cake

tartaleta *nf* : tart

tartamudear *vi* : to stammer, to stutter

tartamudeo *nm* : stutter, stammer

tartán *nm, pl* **tartanes** : tartan, plaid

tártaro *nm* : tartar <cream of tartar : crémor, tártaro>

tasa *nf* **1** : rate <tasa de desempleo : unemployment rate> **2** : tax, fee **3** : appraisal, valuation

tasación *nf, pl* **-ciones** : appraisal, assessment

tasador, -dora *n* : assessor, appraiser

tasar *vt* **1** VALORAR : to appraise, to value **2** : to set the price of **3** : to ration, to limit

tasca *nf* : cheap bar, dive

tatuaje *nm* : tattoo, tattooing

tatuar {3} *vt* : to tattoo

taurino, -na *adj* : bull, bullfighting

Tauro *nmf* : Taurus

tauromaquia *nf* : (art of) bullfighting

taxi *nm, pl* **taxis** : taxi, taxicab

taxidermia *nf* : taxidermy

taxidermista *nmf* : taxidermist

taxímetro *nm* : taximeter

taxista *nmf* : taxi driver

taza *nf* **1** : cup **2** : cupful **3** : (toilet) bowl **4** : basin (of a fountain)

tazón *nm, pl* **tazones 1** : bowl **2** : large cup, mug

te *pron* **1** : you <te quiero : I love you> **2** : for you, to you, from you <me gustaría dártelo : I would like to give it to you> **3** : yourself, for yourself, to yourself, from yourself <¡cálmate! : calm yourself!> <¿te guardaste uno? : did you keep one for yourself?> **4** : thee

té *nm* **1** : tea **2** : tea party

tea *nf* : torch

teatral *adj* : theatrical — **teatralmente** *adv*

teatro *nm* **1** : theater **2 hacer teatro** : to put on an act, to exaggerate

teca *nf* : teak

techado *nm* **1** : roof **2 bajo techado** : under cover, indoors

techar *vt* : to roof, to shingle

techo *nm* **1** TEJADO : roof **2** : ceiling **3** : upper limit, ceiling

techumbre *nf* : roofing

tecla *nf* **1** : key (of a musical instrument or a machine) **2 dar en la tecla** : to hit the nail on the head

teclado *nm* : keyboard

teclear *vt* : to type in, to enter

técnica *nf* **1** : technique, skill **2** : technology

técnico[1]**, -ca** *adj* : technical — **técnicamente** *adv*

técnico[2]**, -ca** *n* : technician, expert, engineer

tecnología *nf* : technology

tecnológico, -ca *adj* : technological — **tecnológicamente** *adv*

tecolote *nm Mex* : owl

tedio *nm* : tedium, boredom

tedioso, -sa *adj* : tedious, boring — **tediosamente** *adv*

teja *nf* : tile

tejado *nm* TECHO : roof

tejedor, -dora *n* : weaver

tejer *vt* **1** : to knit, to crochet **2** : to weave **3** FABRICAR : to concoct, to make up, to fabricate

tejido *nm* **1** TELA : fabric, cloth **2** : weave, texture **3** : tissue <tejido muscular : muscle tissue>

tejo *nm* : yew

tejón *nm, pl* **tejones** : badger

tela *nf* **1** : fabric, cloth, material **2 tela de araña** : spiderweb **3 poner en tela de juicio** : to call into question, to doubt

telar *nm* : loom

telaraña *nf* : spiderweb, cobweb

tele *nf fam* : TV, television

telecomunicación *nf, pl* **-ciones** : telecommunication

teleconferencia *nf* **:** teleconference

teledifusión *nf, pl* **-siones :** television broadcasting

teledirigido, -da *adj* **:** remote-controlled

telefonear *v* **:** to telephone, to call

telefónico, -ca *adj* **:** phone, telephone <llamada telefónica : phone call>

telefonista *nmf* **:** telephone operator

teléfono *nm* **1 :** telephone **2 llamar por teléfono :** to telephone, to make a phone call

telegrafiar {85} *v* **:** to telegraph

telegráfico, -ca *adj* **:** telegraphic

telégrafo *nm* **:** telegaph

telegrama *nm* **:** telegram

telenovela *nf* **:** soap opera

telepatía *nf* **:** telepathy

telepático, -ca *adj* **:** telepathic — **telepáticamente** *adv*

telescópico, -ca *adj* **:** telescopic

telescopio *nm* **:** telescope

telespectador, -dora *n* **:** television viewer

telesquí *nm, pl* **-squís :** ski lift

televidente *nmf* **:** television viewer

televisar *vt* **:** to televise

televisión *nf, pl* **-siones :** television, TV

televisivo, -va *adj* **:** television <serie televisiva : television series>

televisor *nm* **:** television set

telón *nm, pl* **telones 1 :** curtain (in theater) **2 telón de fondo :** backdrop, background

tema *nm* **1** ASUNTO **:** theme, topic, subject **2** MOTIVO **:** motif, central theme

temario *nm* **1 :** set of topics (for study) **2 :** agenda

temática *nf* **:** subject matter

temático, -ca *adj* **:** thematic

temblar {55} *vi* **1 :** to tremble, to shake, to shiver <le temblaban las rodillas : his knees were shaking> **2 :** to shudder, to be afraid <tiemblo con sólo pensarlo : I shudder to think of it>

temblor *nm* **1 :** shaking, trembling **2 :** tremor, earthquake

tembloroso, -sa *adj* **:** tremulous, trembling, shaking <con la voz temblorosa : with a shaky voice>

temer *vt* **:** to fear, to dread — *vi* **:** to be afraid

temerario, -ria *adj* **:** reckless, rash — **temerariamente** *adv*

temeridad *nf* **1 :** temerity, recklessness, rashness **2 :** rash act

temeroso, -sa *adj* MIEDOSO **:** fearful, frightened

temible *adj* **:** fearsome, dreadful

temor *nm* MIEDO **:** fear, dread

témpano *nm* **:** ice floe

temperamento *nm* **:** temperament — **temperamental** *adj*

temperancia *nf* **:** temperance

temperar *vt* MODERAR **:** to temper, to moderate — *vi* **:** to have a change of air

temperatura *nf* **:** temperature

tempestad *nf* **1 :** storm, tempest **2 tempestad de arena :** sandstorm

tempestuoso, -sa *adj* **:** tempestuous, stormy

templado, -da *adj* **1 :** temperate, mild **2 :** moderate, restrained **3 :** warm, lukewarm **4** VALIENTE **:** courageous, bold

templanza *nf* **1 :** temperance, moderation **2 :** mildness (of weather)

templar *vt* **1 :** to temper (steel) **2 :** to restrain, to moderate **3 :** to tune (a musical instrument) **4 :** to warm up, to cool down — **templarse** *vr* **1 :** to be moderate **2 :** to warm up, to cool down

temple *nm* **1 :** temper (of steel, etc.) **2** HUMOR **:** mood <de buen temple : in a good mood> **3 :** tuning **4** VALOR **:** courage

templo *nm* **1 :** temple **2 :** church, chapel

tempo *nm* **:** tempo (in music)

temporada *nf* **1 :** season, time <temporada de béisbol : baseball season> **2 :** period, spell <por temporadas : on and off>

temporal[1] *adj* **1 :** temporal **2 :** temporary

temporal[2] *nm* **1 :** storm **2 capear el temporal :** to weather the storm

temporalmente *adv* **:** temporarily

temporario, -ria *adj* **:** temporary — **temporariamente** *adv*

temporero[1], **-ra** *adj* **:** temporary, seasonal

temporero[2], **-ra** *n* **:** temporary or seasonal worker

temporizador *nm* **:** timer

tempranero, -ra *adj* **1 :** early **2 :** early-rising

temprano[1] *adv* **:** early <lo más temprano posible : as soon as possible>

temprano[2], **-na** *adj* **:** early <la parte temprana del siglo : the early part of the century>

ten → **tener**

tenacidad *nf* **:** tenacity, perseverance

tenaz *adj, pl* **tenaces 1 :** tenacious, persistent **2 :** strong, tough

tenaza *nf or* **tenazas** *nfpl* **1 :** pliers, pincers **2 :** tongs **3 :** claw (of a crustacean)

tenazmente *adv* **:** tenaciously

tendedero *nm* **:** clothesline

tendencia *nf* **1** PROPENSIÓN **:** tendency, inclination **2 :** trend

tendencioso, -sa *adj* **:** tendencious, biased

tendente → **tendiente**

tender {56} *vt* **1** EXTENDER **:** to spread out, to lay out **2 :** to hang out (clothes) **3 :** to lay (cables, etc.) **4 :** to set (a trap) — *vi* **~ a :** to tend to, to have a tendency towards — **tenderse** *vr* **:** to stretch out, to lie down

tendero, -ra *n* **:** shopkeeper, storekeeper

tendido *nm* **1 :** laying (of cables, etc.) **2 :** seats *pl,* section (at a bullfight)
tendiente *adj* **~ a :** aimed at, designed to
tendón *nm, pl* **tendones :** tendon
tenebrosidad *nf* **:** darkness, gloom
tendrá, etc. → **tener**
tenebroso, -sa *adj* **1** OSCURO **:** gloomy, dark **2** SINIESTRO **:** sinister
tenedor[1]**, -dora** *n* **1 :** holder **2 tenedor de libros, tenedora de libros :** bookkeeper
tenedor[2] *nm* **:** table fork
tenencia *nf* **1 :** possession, holding **2 :** tenancy **3 :** tenure
tener {80} *vt* **1 :** to have <tiene ojos verdes : she has green eyes> <tengo mucho que hacer : I have a lot to do> <tiene veinte años : he's twenty years old> <tiene un metro de largo : it's one meter long> **2 :** to hold <ten esto un momento : hold this for a moment> **3 :** to feel, to make <tengo frío : I'm cold> <eso nos tiene contentos : that makes us happy> **4 ~ por :** to think, to consider <me tienes por loco : you think I'm crazy> — *v aux* **1 tener que :** to have to <tengo que salir : I have to leave> <tiene que estar aquí : it has to be here, it must be here> **2** (*with past participle*) <tenía pensado escribirte : I've been thinking of writing to you> — **tenerse** *vr* **1 :** to stand up **2 ~ por :** to consider oneself <me tengo por afortunado : I consider myself lucky>
tenería *nf* CURTIDURÍA **:** tannery
tenga, etc. → **tener**
tenia *nf* SOLITARIA **:** tapeworm
teniente *nmf* **1 :** lieutenant **2 teniente coronel :** lieutenant colonel
tenis *nms & pl* **1 :** tennis **2 tenis** *nmpl* **:** sneakers *pl*
tenista *nmf* **:** tennis player
tenor *nm* **1 :** tenor **2 :** tone, sense
tensar *vt* **1 :** to tense, to make taut **2 :** to draw (a bow) — **tensarse** *vr* **:** to become tense
tensión *nf, pl* **tensiones 1 :** tension, tautness **2 :** stress, strain **3 tensión arterial :** blood pressure
tenso, -sa *adj* **:** tense
tentación *nf, pl* **-ciones :** temptation
tentáculo *nm* **:** tentacle, feeler
tentador[1]**, -dora** *adj* **:** tempting
tentador[2]**, -dora** *n* **:** tempter, temptress *f*
tentar {55} *vt* **1** TOCAR **:** to feel, to touch **2** PROBAR **:** to test, to try **3** ATRAER **:** to tempt, to entice
tentativa *nf* **:** attempt, try
tentempié *nm fam* **:** snack, bite
tenue *adj* **1 :** tenuous **2 :** faint, weak, dim **3 :** light, fine **4 :** thin, slender
teñir {67} *vt* **1 :** to dye **2 :** to stain
teodolito *nm* **:** theodolite, transit (for surveying)
teología *nf* **:** theology
teológico, -ca *adj* **:** theological
teólogo, -ga *n* **:** theologian
teorema *nm* **:** theorem
teoría *nf* **:** theory
teórico[1]**, -ca** *adj* **:** theoretical — **teóricamente** *adv*
teórico[2]**, -ca** *n* **:** theorist
teorizar {21} *vi* **:** to theorize
tepe *nm* **:** sod, turf
teponaztle *nm Mex* **:** traditional drum
tequila *nm* **:** tequila
terapeuta *nmf* **:** therapist
terapéutica *nf* **:** therapeutics
terapéutico, -ca *adj* **:** therapeutic
terapia *nf* **1 :** therapy **2 terapia intensiva :** intensive care
tercer → **tercero**
tercermundista *adj* **:** third-world
tercero[1]**, -ra** *adj* (**tercer** *before masculine singular nouns*) **1 :** third **2 el Tercer Mundo :** the Third World
tercero[2]**, -ra** *n* **:** third (in a series)
terciar *vt* **1 :** to place diagonally **2 :** to divide into three parts — *vi* **1 :** to mediate **2 ~ en :** to take part in
terciario, -ria *adj* **:** tertiary
tercio[1]**, -cia** → **tercero**
tercio[2] *nm* **:** third <dos tercios : two thirds>
terciopelo *nm* **:** velvet
terco, -ca *adj* OBSTINADO **:** obstinate, stubborn
tergiversación *nf, pl* **-ciones :** distortion
tergiversar *vt* **:** to distort, to twist
termal *adj* **:** thermal, hot
termas *nfpl* **:** hot springs
térmico, -ca *adj* **:** thermal, heat <energía térmica : thermal energy>
terminación *nf, pl* **-ciones :** termination, conclusion
terminal[1] *adj* **:** terminal — **terminalmente** *adv*
terminal[2] *nm* (*in some regions f*) **:** (electric or electronic) terminal
terminal[3] *nf* (*in some regions m*) **:** terminal, station
terminante *adj* **:** final, definitive, categorical — **terminantemente** *adv*
terminar *vt* **1** CONCLUIR **:** to end, to conclude **2** ACABAR **:** to complete, to finish off — *vi* **1 :** to finish **2 :** to stop, to end — **terminarse** *vr* **1 :** to run out **2 :** to come to an end
término *nm* **1** CONCLUSIÓN **:** end, conclusion **2 :** term, expression **3 :** period, term of office **4 término medio :** happy medium **5 términos** *nmpl* **:** terms, specifications <los términos del acuerdo : the terms of the agreement>
terminología *nf* **:** terminology
termita *nf* **:** termite
termo *nm* **:** thermos
termodinámica *nf* **:** thermodynamics
termómetro *nm* **:** thermometer
termóstato *nm* **:** thermostat
ternera *nf* **:** veal
ternero, -ra *n* **:** calf

terno *nm* **1 :** set of three **2 :** three-piece suit

ternura *nf* **:** tenderness

terquedad *nf* OBSTINACIÓN **:** obstinacy, stubbornness

terracota *nf* **:** terra-cotta

terraplén *nm, pl* **-plenes :** terrace, embankment

terráqueo, -quea *adj* **1 :** earth **2 globo terráqueo :** the earth, globe (of the earth)

terrateniente *nmf* **:** landowner

terraza *nf* **1 :** terrace, veranda **2 :** balcony (in a theater) **3 :** terrace (in agriculture)

terremoto *nm* **:** earthquake

terrenal *adj* **:** worldly, earthly

terreno *nm* **1 :** terrain **2** SUELO **:** earth, ground **3 :** plot, tract of land **4 perder terreno :** to lose ground **5 preparar el terreno :** to pave the way

terrestre *adj* **:** terrestrial

terrible *adj* **:** terrible, horrible — **terriblemente** *adv*

terrier *nmf* **:** terrier

territorial *adj* **:** territorial

territorio *nm* **:** territory

terrón *nm, pl* **terrones 1 :** clod (of earth) **2 terrón de azúcar :** lump of sugar

terror *nm* **:** terror

terrorífico, -ca *adj* **:** horrific, terrifying

terrorismo *nm* **:** terrorism

terrorista *adj & nmf* **:** terrorist

terroso, -sa *adj* **:** earthy <colores terrosos : earthy colors>

terruño *nm* **:** native land, homeland

terso, -sa *adj* **1 :** smooth **2 :** glossy, shiny **3 :** polished, flowing (of a style)

tersura *nf* **1 :** smoothness **2 :** shine

tertulia *nf* **:** gathering, group <tertulia literaria : literary circle>

tesauro *nm* **:** thesaurus

tesis *nfs & pl* **:** thesis

tesón *nm* **:** persistence, tenacity

tesonero, -ra *adj* **:** persistent, tenacious

tesorería *nf* **:** treasurer's office

tesorero, -ra *n* **:** treasurer

tesoro *nm* **1 :** treasure **2 :** thesaurus

testaferro *nm* **:** figurehead

testamentario[1], -ria *adj* **:** testamentary

testamentario[2], -ria *n* ALBACEA **:** executor, executrix *f*

testamento *nm* **:** testament, will

testar *vi* **:** to draw up a will

testarudo, -da *adj* **:** stubborn, pigheaded

testículo *nm* **:** testicle

testificar {72} *v* **:** to testify

testigo *nmf* **:** witness

testimonial *adj* **1 :** testimonial **2 :** token

testimoniar *vi* **:** to testify

testimonio *nm* **:** testimony, statement

teta *nf* **:** teat

tétano *or* **tétanos** *nm* **:** tetanus, lockjaw

tetera *nf* **1 :** teapot **2 :** teakettle

tetilla *nf* **1 :** teat **2 :** nipple

tetina *nf* **:** nipple (on a bottle)

tétrico, -ca *adj* **:** somber, gloomy

textil *adj & nm* **:** textile

texto *nm* **:** text

textual *adj* **:** literal, exact — **textualmente** *adv*

textura *nf* **:** texture

tez *nf, pl* **teces :** complexion, coloring

ti *pron* **1 :** you <es para ti : it's for you> **2 ti mismo, ti misma :** yourself **3 :** thee

tía → **tío**

tiamina *nf* **:** thiamine

tianguis *nm Mex* **:** open-air market

tibetano, -na *adj & n* **:** Tibetan

tibia *nf* **:** tibia

tibieza *nf* **1 :** tepidness **2 :** halfheartedness

tibio, -bia *adj* **1 :** lukewarm, tepid **2 :** cool, unenthusiastic

tiburón *nm, pl* **-rones 1 :** shark **2 :** raider (in finance)

tic *nm* **1 :** click, tick **2 tic nervioso :** tic

tico, -ca *adj & n fam* **:** Costa Rican

tiembla, etc. → **temblar**

tiempo *nm* **1 :** time <justo a tiempo : just in time> <perder tiempo : to waste time> <tiempo libre : spare time> **2 :** period, age <en los tiempos que corren : nowadays> **3 :** season, moment <antes de tiempo : prematurely> **4 :** weather <hace buen tiempo : the weather is fine, it's nice outside> **5 :** tempo (in music) **6 :** half (in sports) **7 :** tense (in grammar)

tienda *nf* **1 :** store, shop **2** *or* **tienda de campaña :** tent

tiende, etc. → **tender**

tiene, etc. → **tener**

tienta[1], etc. → **tentar**

tienta[2] *nf* **andar a tientas :** to feel one's way, to grope around

tiernamente *adv* **:** tenderly

tierno, -na *adj* **1 :** affectionate, tender **2 :** tender, young

tierra *nf* **1 :** land **2** SUELO **:** ground, earth **3 :** country, homeland, soil **4 tierra natal :** native land **5 la Tierra :** the Earth

tieso, -sa *adj* **1 :** stiff, rigid **2 :** upright, erect

tiesto *nm* **1 :** potsherd **2** MACETA **:** flowerpot

tiesura *nf* **:** stiffness, rigidity

tifoidea *nf* **:** typhoid

tifoideo, -dea *adj* **:** typhoid <fiebre tifoidea : typhoid fever>

tifón *nm, pl* **tifones :** typhoon

tifus *nm* **:** typhus

tigre, -gresa *n* **1 :** tiger, tigress *f* **2 :** jaguar

tijera *nf* **1** *or* **tijeras** *nfpl* **:** scissors **2 de ~ :** folding <escalera de tijera : stepladder>

tijereta *nf* **:** earwig

tijeretada *nf or* **tijeretazo** *nm* **:** cut, snip

tildar *vt* **~ de :** to brand as, to call <lo tildaron de traidor : they branded him as a traitor>

tilde *nf* **1 :** accent mark **2 :** tilde (accent over *ñ*)

tilo *nm* **:** linden (tree)

timador, -dora *n* **:** swindler

timar *vt* **:** to swindle, to cheat

timbal *nm* **1 :** kettledrum **2 timbales** *nmpl* **:** timpani

timbre *nm* **1 :** bell <tocar el timbre : to ring the doorbell> **2 :** tone, timbre **3** SELLO **:** seal, stamp **4** *CA, Mex* **:** postage stamp

timidez *nf* **:** timidity, shyness

tímido, -da *adj* **:** timid, shy — **tímidamente** *adv*

timo *nm fam* **:** swindle, trick, hoax

timón *nm, pl* **timones :** rudder <estar al timón : to beat the helm>

timonel *nm* **:** helmsman, coxwain

timorato, -ta *adj* **1 :** timorous **2 :** sanctimonious

tímpano *nm* **1 :** eardrum **2 tímpanos** *nmpl* **:** timpani, kettledrums

tina *nf* **1** BAÑERA **:** tub, bathtub **2 :** vat

tinaco *nm Mex* **:** water tank

tinieblas *nfpl* **1** OSCURIDAD **:** darkness **2 :** ignorance

tino *nm* **1 :** good judgment, sense **2 :** tact, sensitivity, insight

tinta *nf* **:** ink

tinte *nm* **1 :** dye, coloring **2 :** overtone <tintes raciales : racial overtones>

tintero *nm* **1 :** inkwell **2 quedarse en el tintero :** to remain unsaid

tintinear *vt* **:** to jingle, to clink, to tinkle

tintineo *nm* **:** clink, jingle, tinkle

tinto, -ta *adj* **1 :** dyed, stained <tinto en sangre : bloodstained> **2 :** red (of wine)

tintorería *nf* **:** dry cleaner (service)

tintura *nf* **1 :** dye, tint **2 :** tincture <tintura de yodo : tincture of iodine>

tiña *nf* **:** ringworm

tiñe, etc. → **teñir**

tío, tía *n* **:** uncle *m,* aunt *f*

tiovivo *nm* **:** merry-go-round

tipi *nm* **:** tepee

típico, -ca *adj* **:** typical — **típicamente** *adv*

tipificar {72} *vt* **1 :** to classify, to categorize **2 :** to typify

tiple *nm* **:** soprano

tipo[1] *nm* **1** CLASE **:** type, kind, sort **2 :** figure, build, appearance **3 :** rate <tipo de interés : interest rate> **4 :** (printing) type, typeface **5 :** style, model <un vestido tipo 60's : a 60's-style dress>

tipo[2], **-pa** *n fam* **:** guy *m,* gal *f,* character

tipografía *nf* **:** typography, printing

tipográfico, -ca *adj* **:** typographic, typographical

tipográfo, -fa *n* **:** printer, typographer

tique *or* **tiquet** *nm* **1 :** ticket **2 :** receipt

tira *nf* **1 :** strip, strap **2 tira cómica :** comic, comic strip

tirabuzón *nf, pl* **-zones :** corkscrew

tirada *nf* **1 :** throw **2 :** distance, stretch **3** IMPRESIÓN **:** printing, issue

tiradero *nm Mex* **1 :** dump **2 :** mess, clutter

tirador[1] *nm* **:** handle, knob

tirador[2], **-dora** *n* **:** marksman *m,* markswoman *f*

tiragomas *nms & pl* **:** slingshot

tiranía *nf* **:** tyranny

tiránico, -ca *adj* **:** tyrannical

tiranizar {21} *vt* **:** to tyrannize

tirano[1], **-na** *adj* **:** tyrannical, despotic

tirano[2], **-na** *n* **:** tyrant

tirante[1] *adj* **1 :** tense, strained **2 :** taut

tirante[2] *nm* **1 :** shoulder strap **2 tirantes** *nmpl* **:** suspenders

tirantez *nf* **1 :** tautness **2 :** tension, friction, strain

tirar *vt* **1 :** to throw, to hurl, to toss **2** BOTAR **:** to throw away, to throw out, to waste **3** DERRIBAR **:** to knock down **4 :** to shoot, to fire, to launch **5 :** to take (a photo) **6 :** to print, to run off — *vi* **1 :** to pull, to draw **2 :** to shoot **3 :** to attract **4 :** to get by, to manage <va tirando : he's getting along, he's managing> **5 ~ a :** to tend towards, to be rather <tira a picante : it's a bit spicy> — **tirarse** *vr* **1 :** to throw oneself **2** *fam* **:** to spend (time)

tiritar *vi* **:** to shiver, to tremble

tiro *nm* **1** BALAZO, DISPARO **:** shot, gunshot **2 :** shot, kick (in sports) **3 :** flue **4 :** team (of horses, etc.) **5 a ~ :** within range **6 al tiro :** right away **7 tiro de gracia :** coup de grace, death blow

tiroideo, -dea *adj* **:** thyroid

tiroides *nmf* **:** thyroid, thyroid gland — **tiroides** *adj*

tirolés, -lesa *adj* **:** Tyrolean

tirón *nm, pl* **tirones 1 :** pull, tug, yank **2 de un tirón :** all at once, in one go

tiroteo *nm* **1 :** shooting **2 :** gunfight, shoot-out

tirria *nf fam* **tener tirria a :** to have a grudge against

titánico, -ca *adj* **:** titanic, huge

titanio *nm* **:** titanium

títere *nm* **:** puppet

tití *nm* **:** marmoset

titilar *vi* **:** to twinkle, to flicker

titileo *nm* **:** twinkle, flickering

titiritero, -ra *n* **1 :** puppeteer **2 :** acrobat

titubear *vi* **1 :** to hesitate **2 :** to stutter, to stammer — **titubeante** *adj*

titubeo *nm* **1 :** hesitation **2 :** stammering

titulado, -da *adj* **1 :** titled, entitled **2 :** qualified

titular[1] *vt* **:** to title, to entitle — **titularse** *vr* **1 :** to be called, to be entitled **2 :** to receive a degree

titular[2] *adj* **:** titular, official

titular[3] *nm* **:** headline

titular[4] *nmf* **1 :** owner, holder **2 :** officeholder, incumbent

título *nm* **1 :** title **2 :** degree, qualification **3 :** security, bond **4 a título de :** by way of, in the capacity of

tiza *nf* **:** chalk

tiznar *vt* **:** to blacken (with soot, etc.)

tizne *nm* HOLLÍN **:** soot

tiznón *nm, pl* **tiznones :** stain, smudge

tlapalería *nf Mex* **:** hardware store

TNT *nm* **:** TNT

toalla *nf* **:** towel

toallita *nf* **:** washcloth

tobillo *nm* **:** ankle

tobogán *nm, pl* **-ganes 1 :** toboggan, sled **2 :** slide, chute

tocadiscos *nms & pl* **:** record player, phonograph

tocado[1], **-da** *adj* **1 :** bad, bruised (of fruit) **2** *fam* **:** touched, not all there

tocado[2] *nm* **:** headdress

tocador[1] *nm* **1 :** dressing table, vanity table **2 artículos de tocador :** toiletries

tocador[2], **-dora** *n* **:** player (of music)

tocante *adj* **~ a :** with regard to, regarding

tocar {72} *vt* **1 :** to touch, to feel, to handle **2 :** to touch on, to refer to **3 :** to concern, to affect **4 :** to play (a musical instrument) — *vi* **1 :** to knock, to ring <tocar a la puerta : to rap on the door> **2 ~ en :** to touch on, to border on <eso toca en lo ridículo : that's almost ludicrous> **3 tocarle a :** to fall to, to be up to, to be one's turn <¿a quién le toca manejar? : whose turn is it to drive?>

tocayo, -ya *n* **:** namesake

tocineta *nf Col, Ven* **:** bacon

tocino *nm* **1 :** bacon **2 :** salt pork

tocología *nf* OBSTETRICIA **:** obstetrics

tocólogo, -ga *n* OBSTETRA **:** obstetrician

tocón *nm, pl* **tocones** CEPA **:** stump (of a tree)

todavía *adv* **1** AÚN **:** still, yet <todavía puedes verlo : you can still see it> **2 :** even <todavía más rápido : even faster> **3 todavía no :** not yet

todo[1], **-da** *adj* **1 :** all, whole, entire <con toda sinceridad : with all sincerity> <toda la comunidad : the whole community> **2 :** every, each <a todo nivel : at every level> **3 :** maximum <a toda velocidad : at top speed> **4 todo el mundo :** everyone, everybody

todo[2] *nm* **:** whole

todo[3], **-da** *pron* **1 :** everything, all, every bit <lo sabe todo : he knows it all> <es todo un soldado : he's every inch a soldier> **2 todos, -das** *pl* **:** everybody, everyone, all

todopoderoso, -sa *adj* OMNIPOTENTE **:** almighty, all-powerful

toga *nf* **1 :** toga **2 :** gown, robe (for magistrates, etc.)

toldo *nm* **:** awning, canopy

tolerable *adj* **:** tolerable — **tolerablemente** *adv*

tolerancia *nf* **:** tolerance, toleration

tolerante *adj* **:** tolerant — **tolerantemente** *adv*

tolerar *vt* **:** to tolerate

tolete *nm* **:** oarlock

tolva *nf* **:** hopper (container)

toma *nf* **1 :** taking, seizure, capture **2** DOSIS **:** dose **3 :** take, shot **4 toma de corriente :** wall socket, outlet **5 toma y daca :** give-and-take

tomar *vt* **1 :** to take <tomé el libro : I took the book> <tomar un taxi : to take a taxi> <tomar una foto : to take a photo> <toma dos años : it takes two years> <tomaron medidas drásticas : they took drastic measures> **2** BEBER **:** to drink **3** CAPTURAR **:** to capture, to seize **4 tomar el sol :** to sunbathe **5 tomar tierra :** to land — *vi* **:** to drink (alcohol) — **tomarse** *vr* **1 :** to take <tomarse la molestia de : to take the trouble to> **2 :** to drink, to eat, to have

tomate *nm* **:** tomato

tomillo *nm* **:** thyme

tomo *nm* **:** volume, tome

ton *nm* **sin ton ni son :** without rhyme or reason

tonada *nf* **1 :** tune, song **2 :** accent

tonalidad *nf* **:** tonality

tonel *nm* BARRICA **:** barrel, cask

tonelada *nf* **:** ton

tonelaje *nm* **:** tonnage

tónica *nf* **1 :** tonic (water) **2 :** tonic (in music) **3 :** trend, tone <dar la tónica : to set the tone>

tónico[1], **-ca** *adj* **:** tonic

tónico[2] *nm* **:** tonic <tónico capilar : hair tonic>

tono *nm* **1 :** tone <tono muscular : muscle tone> **2 :** shade (of colors) **3 :** key (in music)

tontamente *adv* **:** foolishly, stupidly

tontear *vi* **1 :** to fool around, to play the fool **2 :** to flirt

tontería *nf* **1 :** foolishness **2 :** stupid remark or action **3 decir tonterías :** to talk nonsense

tonto[1], **-ta** *adj* **1 :** dumb, stupid **2 :** silly **3 a tontas y a locas :** without thinking, haphazardly

tonto[2], **-ta** *n* **:** fool, idiot

topacio *nm* **:** topaz

toparse *vr* **~ con :** to bump into, to run into, to come across <me topé con algunas dificultades : I ran into some problems>

tope *nm* **1 :** limit, end <hasta el tope : to the limit, to the brim> **2 :** stop, check, buffer <tope de puerta : doorstop> **3 :** bump, collision **4** *Mex* **:** speed bump

tópico[1], **-ca** *adj* **1 :** topical, external **2 :** trite, commonplace

tópico[2] *nm* **1 :** topic, subject **2 :** cliché, trite expression

topo *nm* **1 :** mole (animal) **2** *fam* **:** clumsy person, blunderer

topografía *nf* **:** topography

topográfico, -ca *adj* **:** topographic, topographical

topógrafo, -fa *n* **:** topographer

toque[1], etc. → **tocar**

toque[2] *nm* **1 :** touch <el último toque : the finishing touch> <un toque de color : a touch of color> **2 :** ringing, peal, chime **3** *Mex* **:** shock, jolt **4 toque de queda :** curfew **5 toque de diana :** reveille

toquetear *vt* **:** to touch, to handle, to finger

tórax *nm* **:** thorax

torbellino *nm* **:** whirlwind

torcedura *nf* **1 :** twisting, buckling **2 :** sprain

torcer {14} *vt* **1 :** to bend, to twist **2 :** to sprain **3 :** to turn (a corner) **4 :** to wring, to wring out **5 :** to distort — *vi* **:** to turn — **torcerse** *vr*

torcido, -da *adj* **1 :** twisted, crooked **2 :** devious

tordo *nm* ZORZAL **:** thrush

torear *vt* **1 :** to fight (bulls) **2 :** to dodge, to sidestep

toreo *nm* **:** bullfighting

torero, -ra *n* MATADOR **:** bullfighter, matador

tormenta *nf* **1 :** storm <tormenta de nieve : snowstorm> **2 :** turmoil, frenzy

tormento *nm* **1 :** torment, anguish **2 :** torture

tormentoso, -sa *adj* **:** stormy, turbulent

tornado *nm* **:** tornado

tornamesa *nmf* **:** turntable

tornar *vt* **1 :** to return, to give back **2 :** to make, to render — *vi* **:** to go back — **tornarse** *vr* **:** to become, to turn into

tornasol *nm* **1 :** reflected light **2 :** sunflower **3 :** litmus

tornear *vt* **:** to turn (in carpentry)

torneo *nm* **:** tournament

tornillo *nm* **1 :** screw **2 tornillo de banco :** vise

torniquete *nm* **1 :** tourniquet **2 :** turnstile

torno *nm* **1 :** lathe **2 :** winch **3 torno de banco :** vise **4 en torno a :** around, about <en torno a este asunto : about this issue> <en torno suyo : around him>

toro *nm* **:** bull

toronja *nf* **:** grapefruit

toronjil *nm* **:** balm, lemon balm

torpe *adj* **1** DESMAÑADO **:** clumsy, awkward **2 :** stupid, dull — **torpemente** *adv*

torpedear *vt* **:** to torpedo

torpedo *nm* **:** torpedo

torpeza *nf* **1 :** clumsiness, awkwardness **2 :** stupidity **3 :** blunder

torre *nf* **1 :** tower <torre de perforación : oil rig> **2 :** turret **3 :** rook, castle (in chess)

torrencial *adj* **:** torrential — **torrencialmente** *adv*

torrente *nm* **1 :** torrent **2 torrente sanguíneo :** bloodstream

torreón *nm, pl* **-rreones :** tower (of a castle)

torreta *nf* **:** turret (of a tank, ship, etc.)

tórrido, -da *adj* **:** torrid

torsión *nf, pl* **torsiones :** torsion — **torsional** *adj*

torso *nm* **:** torso, trunk

torta *nf* **1 :** torte, cake **2** *Mex* **:** sandwich

tortazo *nm fam* **:** blow, wallop

tortilla *nf* **1 :** tortilla **2** *or* **tortilla de huevo :** omelet

tórtola *nf* **:** turtledove

tortuga *nf* **1 :** turtle, tortoise **2 tortuga de agua dulce :** terrapin **3 tortuga boba :** loggerhead

tortuoso, -sa *adj* **:** tortuous, winding

tortura *nf* **:** torture

torturador, -dora *n* **:** torturer

torturar *vt* **:** to torture, to torment

torvo, -va *adj* **:** grim, stern, baleful

torzamos, etc. → **torcer**

tos *nf* **1 :** cough **2 tos ferina :** whooping cough

tosco, -ca *adj* **:** rough, coarse

toser *vi* **:** to cough

tosquedad *nf* **:** crudeness, coarseness, roughness

tostada *nf* **1 :** piece of toast **2 :** tostada

tostador *nm* **1 :** toaster **2 :** roaster (for coffee)

tostar {19} *vt* **1 :** to toast **2 :** to roast (coffee) **3 :** to tan — **tostarse** *vr* **:** to get a tan

tostón *nm, pl* **tostones** *Car* **:** fried plantain chip

total[1] *adv* **:** in the end, so <total, que no fui : in short, I didn't go>

total[2] *adj & nm* **:** total — **totalmente** *adv*

totalidad *nf* **:** totality, whole

totalitario, -ria *adj & n* **:** totalitarian

totalitarismo *nm* **:** totalitarianism

totalizar {21} *vt* **:** total, to add up to

tótem *nm, pl* **tótems :** totem

totopo *nm CA, Mex* **:** tortilla chip

totuma *nf* **:** calabash

tour ['tur] *nm, pl* **tours :** tour, excursion

toxicidad *nf* **:** toxicity

tóxico[1], -ca *adj* **:** toxic, poisonous

tóxico[2] *nm* **:** poison

toxicomanía *nf* **:** drug addiction

toxicómano, -na *n* **:** drug addict

toxina *nf* **:** toxin

tozudez *nf* **:** stubbornness, obstinancy

tozudo, -da *adj* **:** stubborn, obstinate — **tozudamente** *adv*

traba *nf* **1 :** tie, bond **2 :** obstacle, hinderance

trabajador[1], -dora *adj* **:** hard-working

trabajador[2], -dora *n* **:** worker

trabajar *vi* **1 :** to work <trabaja mucho : he works hard> <trabajo de secretaria : I work as a secretary> **2 :** to strive <trabajan por mejores oportunidades : they're striving for better opportunities> **3 :** to act, to perform <trabajar en una película : to be in a movie> — *vt* **1 :** to work (metal) **2 :** to knead **3 :** to till **4 :** to work on <tienes que trabajar el español : you need to work on your Spanish>

trabajo *nm* **1 :** work, job **2** LABOR **:** labor, work <tengo mucho trabajo : I have a lot of work to do> **3** TAREA **:** task **4** ESFUERZA **:** effort **5 costar trabajo :** to be difficult **6 tomarse el trabajo :** to take the trouble **7 trabajo en equipo :** teamwork **8 trabajos** *nmpl* **:** hardships, difficulties

trabajoso, -sa *adj* LABORIOSO **:** laborious — **trabajosamente** *adv*

trabalenguas *nms & pl* **:** tongue twister

trabar *vt* **1 :** to join, to connect **2 :** to impede, to hold back **3 :** to strike up (a conversation), to form (a friendship) **4 :** to thicken (sauces) — **trabarse** *vr* **1 :** to jam **2 :** to become entangled **3 :** to be tongue-tied, to stammer

trabucar {72} *vt* **:** to confuse, to mix up

trabuco *nm* **:** blunderbuss

tracalero, -ra *adj Mex* **:** dishonest, tricky

tracción *nf* **:** traction

trace, etc. → **trazar**

tracto *nm* **:** tract

tractor *nm* **:** tractor

tradición *nf, pl* **-ciones :** tradition

tradicional *adj* **:** traditional — **tradicionalmente** *adv*

traducción *nf, pl* **-ciones :** translation

traducible *adj* **:** translatable

traducir {61} *vt* **1 :** to translate **2 :** to convey, to express — **traducirse** *vr* **~ en :** to result in

traductor, -dora *n* **:** translator

traer {81} *vt* **1 :** to bring <trae una ensalada : bring a salad> **2** CAUSAR **:** to cause, to bring about <el problema puede traer graves consecuencias : the problem could have serious consequences> **3 :** to carry, to have <todos los periódicos traían las mismas noticias : all of the newspapers carried the same news> **4** LLEVAR **:** to wear — **traerse** *vr* **1 :** to bring along **2 traérselas :** to be difficult

traficante *nmf* **:** dealer, trafficker

traficar {72} *vi* **1 :** to trade, to deal **2 ~ en :** to traffic in

tráfico *nm* **1 :** trade **2 :** traffic

tragaluz *nf, pl* **-luces :** skylight, fanlight

tragar {52} *v* **:** to swallow — **tragarse**

tragedia *nf* **:** tragedy

trágico, -ca *adj* **:** tragic — **trágicamente** *adv*

trago *nm* **1 :** swallow, swig **2 :** drink, liquor **3 trago amargo :** hard time

trague, etc. → **tragar**

traición *nf, pl* **traiciones 1 :** treason **2 :** betrayal, treachery

traicionar *vt* **:** to betray

traicionero, -ra → **traidor**

traidor[1]**, -dora** *adj* **:** traitorous, treasonous

traidor[2]**, -dora** *n* **:** traitor

traiga, etc. → **traer**

tráiler *or* **trailer** *nm* **:** trailer

traílla *nf* **1 :** leash **2 :** harrow

traje *nm* **1 :** suit **2 :** dress **3 :** costume **4 traje de baño :** bathing suit

trajín *nm, pl* **trajines 1 :** transport 2 *fam* **:** hustle and bustle

trajinar *vt* **:** to transport, to carry — *vi* **:** to rush around

trajo, etc. → **traer**

trama *nf* **1 :** plot **2 :** weave, weft (fabric)

tramar *vt* **1 :** to plot, to plan **2 :** to weave

tramitar *vt* **:** to transact, to negotiate, to handle

trámite *nm* **:** procedure, step

tramo *nm* **1 :** stretch, section **2 :** flight (of stairs)

trampa *nf* **1 :** trap **2 hacer trampas :** to cheat

trampear *vt* **:** to cheat

trampero, -ra *n* **:** trapper

trampilla *nf* **:** trapdoor

trampolín *nm, pl* **-lines 1 :** diving board **2 :** trampoline **3 :** springboard <un trampolín al éxito : a springboard to success>

tramposo[1]**, -sa** *adj* **:** crooked, cheating

tramposo[2]**, -sa** *n* **:** cheat, swindler

tranca *nf* **1 :** stick, club **2 :** bar, crossbar

trancar {72} *vt* **:** to bar (a door or window)

trancazo *nm* GOLPE **:** blow, hit

trance *nm* **1 :** critical juncture, tough time **2 :** trance **3 en trance de :** in the process of <en trance de extinción : on the verge of extinction>

tranco *nm* **1 :** stride **2** UMBRAL **:** threshold

tranque, etc. → **trancar**

tranquilidad *nf* **:** tranquility, peace

tranquilizador, -dora *adj* **1 :** soothing **2 :** reassuring

tranquilizante[1] *adj* **1 :** reassuring **2 :** tranquilizing

tranquilizante[2] *nm* **:** tranquilizer

tranquilizar {21} *vt* CALMAR **:** to calm down, to soothe <tranquilizar la conciencia : to ease the conscience> — **tranquilizarse** *vr*

tranquilo, -la *adj* CALMO **:** calm, tranquil <una vida tranquila : a quiet life> — **tranquilamente** *adv*

transacción *nf, pl* **-ciones :** transaction

transar *vi* TRANSIGIR **:** to give way, to compromise — *vt* **:** to buy and sell

transatlántico[1]**, -ca** *adj* **:** transatlantic

transatlántico[2] *nm* : ocean liner

transbordador *nm* **1** : ferry **2 transbordador espacial** : space shuttle

transbordar *v* : to transfer

transbordo *nm* : transfer

transcendencia *nf* → **trascendencia**

transcender → **trascender**

transcribir {33} *vt* : to transcribe

transcrito *pp* → **transcribir**

transcripción *nf, pl* **-ciones** : transcription

transcurrir *vi* : to elapse, to pass

transcurso *nm* : course, progression <en el transcurso de cien años : over the course of a hundred years>

transeúnte *nmf* **1** : passerby **2** : transient

transferencia *nf* : transfer, transference

transferir {76} *vt* TRASLADAR : to transfer — **transferible** *adj*

transfigurar *vt* : to transfigure, to transform — **transfiguración** *nf*

transformación *nf, pl* **-ciones** : transformation, conversion

transformador *nm* : transformer

transformar *vt* **1** CONVERTIR : to convert **2** : to transform, to change, to alter — **transformarse** *vr*

transfusión *nf, pl* **-siones** : transfusion

transgredir {1} *vt* : to transgress — **transgresión** *nf*

transgresor, -sora *n* : transgressor

transición *nf, pl* **-ciones** : transition <período de transición : transition period>

transido, -da *adj* : overcome, beset <transido de dolor : racked with pain>

transigir {35} *vi* **1** : to give in, to compromise **2 ~ con** : to tolerate, to put up with

transistor *nm* : transistor

transitable *adj* : passable

transitar *vi* : to go, to pass, to travel <transitar por la ciudad : to travel through the city>

transitivo, -va *adj* : transitive

tránsito *nm* **1** TRÁFICO : traffic <hora de máximo tránsito : rush hour> **2** : transit, passage, movement **3** : death, passing

transitorio, -ria *adj* **1** : transitory **2** : provisional, temporary — **transitoriamente** *adv*

translúcido, -da *adj* : translucent

translucir → **traslucir**

transmisión *nf, pl* **-siones 1** : transmission, broadcast **2** : transfer **3** : transmission (of an automobile)

transmisor *nm* : transmitter

transmitir *vt* **1** : to transmit, to broadcast **2** : to pass on, to transfer — *vi* : to transmit, to broadcast

transparencia *nf* : transparency

transparentar *vt* : to reveal, to betray — **transparentarse** *vr* **1** : to be transparent **2** : to show through

transparente[1] *adj* : transparent — **transparentemente** *adv*

transparente[2] *nm* : shade, blind

transpiración *nf, pl* **-ciones** SUDOR : perspiration, sweat

transpirado, -da *adj* : sweaty

transpirar *vi* **1** SUDAR : to perspire, to sweat **2** : to transpire

transplantar, transplante → **trasplantar, trasplante**

transponer {60} *vt* **1** : to transpose, to move about **2** TRASPLANTAR : to transplant — **transponerse** *vr* **1** OCULTARSE : to hide **2** PONERSE : to set, to go down (of the sun or moon) **3** DORMITAR : to doze off

transportación *nf, pl* **-ciones** : transportation

transportador *nm* **1** : protractor **2** : conveyor

transportar *vt* **1** : to transport, to carry **2** : to transmit **3** : to transpose (music) — **transportarse** *vr* : to get carried away

transporte *nm* : transport, transportation

transportista *nmf* : hauler, carrier, trucker

transpuso, etc. → **transponer**

transversal *adj* : transverse, cross <corte transversal : cross section>

transversalmente *adv* : obliquely

transverso, -sa *adj* : transverse

tranvía *nm* : streetcar, trolley

trapeador *nm* : mop

trapear *vt* : to mop

trapecio *nm* **1** : trapezoid **2** : trapeze

trapezoide *nm* : trapezoid

trapo *nm* **1** : cloth, rag <trapo de polvo : dust cloth> **2 soltar el trapo** : to burst into tears **3 trapos** *nmpl fam* : clothes

tráquea *nf* : trachea, windpipe

traquetear *vi* : to clatter, to jolt

traqueteo *nm* **1** : jolting **2** : clattering, clatter

tras *prep* **1** : after <día tras día : day after day> <uno tras otro : one after another> **2** : behind <tras la puerta : behind the door>

trasbordar, trasbordo → **transbordar, transbordo**

trascendencia *nf* **1** : importance, significance **2** : transcendence

trascendental *adj* **1** : transcendental **2** : important, momentous

trascendente *adj* **1** : important, significant **2** : transcendent

trascender {56} *vi* **1** : to leak out, to become known **2** : to spread, to have a wide effect **3 ~ a** : to smell of <la casa trascendía a flores : the house smelled of flowers> **4 ~ de** : to transcend, to go beyond — *vt* : to transcend

trasero[1], **-sa** *adj* POSTERIOR : rear, back

trasero[2] *nm* : buttocks

trasfondo *nm* **1** : background, backdrop **2** : undertone, undercurrent

trasformación *nf* → **transformación**

trasgo *nm* : goblin, imp

trasgredir → **transgredir**

trasladar *vt* **1** TRANSFERIR : to transfer, to move **2** POSPONER : to postpone **3** TRADUCIR : to translate **4** COPIAR : to copy, to transcribe — **trasladarse** *vr* MUDARSE : to move, to relocate

traslado *nm* **1** : transfer, move **2** : copy

traslapar *vt* : to overlap — **traslaparse** *vr*

traslapo *nm* : overlap

traslúcido, -da → **translúcido**

traslucir {45} *vi* : to reveal, to show — **traslucirse** *vr* : to show through

trasmano *nm* **a ~** : out of the way, out of reach

trasmisión, trasmitir → **transmisión, transmitir**

trasnochar *vi* : to stay up all night

trasparencia *nf,* **trasparente** → **transparencia, transparente**

traspasar *vt* **1** PERFORAR : to pierce, to go through **2** : to go beyond <traspasar los límites : to overstep the limits> **3** ATRAVESAR : to cross, to go across **4** : to sell, to transfer

traspaso *nm* : transfer, sale

traspié *nm* **1** : stumble **2** : blunder

traspiración *nf* → **transpiración**

trasplantar *vt* : to transplant

trasplante *nm* : transplant

trasponer → **transponer**

trasportar → **transportar**

trasquilar *vt* ESQUILAR : to shear

traste *nm* **1** : fret (on a guitar) **2** *CA, Mex, PRi* : kitchen utensil <lavar los trastes : to do the dishes> **3 dar al traste con** : to ruin, to destroy **4 irse al traste** : to fall through

trastornar *vt* : to disturb, to upset, to disrupt — **trastornarse** *vr*

trastorno *nm* **1** : disorder <trastorno mental : mental disorder> **2** : disturbance, upset

trastos *nmpl* **1** : implements, utensils **2** *fam* : pieces of junk, stuff

trasunto *nm* : image, likeness

tratable *adj* **1** : friendly, sociable **2** : treatable

tratado *nm* **1** : treatise **2** : treaty

tratamiento *nm* : treatment

tratante *nmf* : dealer, trader

tratar *vi* **1 ~ con** : to deal with, to have contact with <no trato mucho con los clientes : I don't have much contact with customers> **2 ~ de** : to try to <estoy tratando de comer : I am trying to eat> **3 ~ de** *or* **~ sobre** : to be about, to concern <el libro trata de las plantas : the book is about plants> **4 ~ en** : to deal in <trata en herramientas : he deals in tools> — *vt* **1** : to treat <tratan bien a sus empleados : they treat their employees well> **2** : to handle <trató el tema con delicadeza : he handled the subject tactfully> — **tratarse** *vr* **~ de** : to be about, to concern

trato *nm* **1** : deal, agreement **2** : relationship, dealings *pl* **3** : treatment <malos tratos : ill-treatment>

trauma *nm* : trauma

traumático, -ca *adj* : traumatic — **traumáticamente** *adv*

traumatismo *nm* : injury <traumatismo cervical : whiplash>

través *nm* **1 a través de** : across, through **2 al través** : crosswise, across **3 de través** : sideways

travesaño *nm* **1** : crossbar **2** : crossbeam, crosspiece, transom (of a window)

travesía *nf* : voyage, crossing (of the sea)

travesura *nf* **1** : prank, mischievous act **2 travesuras** *nfpl* : mischief

travieso, -sa *adj* : mischievous, naughty — **traviesamente** *adv*

trayecto *nm* **1** : journey **2** : route **3** : trajectory, path

trayectoria *nf* : course, path, trajectory

trayendo → **traer**

traza *nf* **1** DISEÑO : design, plan **2** : appearance

trazado *nm* **1** BOSQUEJO : outline, sketch **2** PLAN : plan, layout

trazar {21} *vt* **1** : to trace **2** : to draw up, to devise **3** : to outline, to sketch

trazo *nm* **1** : stroke, line **2** : sketch, outline

trébol *nm* **1** : clover, shamrock **2** : club (playing card)

trece *adj & nm* : thirteen

treceavo[1], -va *adj* : thirteenth

treceavo[2] *nm* : thirteenth (fraction)

trecho *nm* **1** : stretch, period <de trecho en trecho : at intervals> **2** : distance, space

tregua *nf* **1** : truce **2** : lull, respite **3 sin ~** : relentless, unrelenting

treinta *adj & nm* : thirty

treintavo[1], -va *adj* : thirtieth

treintavo[2] *nm* : thirtieth (fraction)

tremendo, -da *adj* **1** : tremendous, enormous **2** : terrible, dreadful **3** *fam* : great, super

trementina *nf* AGUARRÁS : turpentine

trémulo, -la *adj* **1** : trembling, shaky **2** : flickering

tren *nm* **1** : train **2** : set, assembly <tren de aterrizaje : landing gear> **3** : speed, pace <a todo tren : at top speed>

trence, etc. → **trenzar**

trenza *nf* : braid, pigtail

trenzar {21} *vt* : to braid — **trenzarse** *vr* : to get involved

trepador, -dora *adj* : climbing <rosal trepador : rambling rose>

trepadora *nf* **1** : climbing plant, climber **2** : nuthatch

trepar *vi* **1** : to climb <trepar a un árbol : to climb up a tree> **2** : to creep, to spread (of a plant)

trepidación *nf, pl* **-ciones** : vibration

trepidante *adj* **1** : vibrating **2** : fast, frantic

trepidar *vi* **1 :** to shake, to vibrate **2 :** to hesitate, to waver
tres *adj & nm* **:** three
trescientos[1], -tas *adj* **:** two hundred
trescientos[2] *nms & pl* **:** three hundred
treta *nf* **:** trick, ruse
tríada *nf* **:** triad
triángulo *nm* **:** triangle — **triangular** *adj*
tribal *adj* **:** tribal
tribu *nf* **:** tribe
tribulación *nf, pl* **-ciones :** tribulation
tribuna *nf* **1 :** dais, platform **2 :** stands *pl,* bleachers *pl,* grandstand
tribunal *nm* **:** court, tribunal
tributar *vt* **:** to pay, to render — *vi* **:** to pay taxes
tributario[1], -ria *adj* **:** tax <evasión tributaria : tax evasion>
tributario[2] *nm* **:** tributary
tributo *nm* **1 :** tax **2 :** tribute
triciclo *nm* **:** tricycle
tricolor *adj* **:** tricolor, tricolored
tridente *nm* **:** trident
tridimensional *adj* **:** three-dimensional, 3-D
trienal *adj* **:** triennial
trifulca *nf fam* **:** row, ruckus
trigésimo[1], -ma *adj* **:** thirtieth, thirty-
trigésimo[2], -ma *n* **:** thirtieth, thirty- (in a series)
trigo *nm* **1 :** wheat **2 trigo rubión :** buckwheat
trigonometría *nf* **:** trigonometry
trigueño, -ña *adj* **1 :** light brown (of hair) **2** MORENO **:** dark, olive-skinned
trillado, -da *adj* **:** trite, hackneyed
trilladora *nf* **:** thresher, threshing machine
trillar *vt* **:** to thresh
trillizo, -za *n* **:** triplet
trilogía *nf* **:** trilogy
trimestral *adj* **:** quarterly — **trimestralmente** *adv*
trinar *vi* **1 :** to thrill **2 :** to warble
trinchar *vt* **:** to carve, to cut up
trinchera *nf* **1 :** trench, ditch **2 :** trench coat
tridente *nm* **:** trident
trineo *nm* **:** sled, sleigh
trinidad *nf* **la Trinidad :** the Trinity
trino *nm* **:** trill, warble
trinquete *nm* **:** ratchet
trío *nm* **:** trio
tripa *nf* **1** INTESTINO **:** gut, intestine **2 tripas** *nfpl fam* **:** belly, tummy, insides *pl* <dolerle a uno las tripas : to have a stomach ache>
tripartito, -ta *adj* **:** tripartite
triple *adj & nm* **:** triple
triplicado *nm* **:** triplicate
triplicar {72} *vt* **:** to triple, to treble
trípode *nm* **:** tripod
tripulación *nf, pl* **-ciones :** crew
tripulante *nmf* **:** crew member
tripular *vt* **:** to man
tris *nm* **estar en un tris de :** to be within an inch of, to be very close to
triste *adj* **1 :** sad, gloomy <ponerse triste : to become sad> **2 :** desolate, dismal <una perspectiva triste : a dismal outlook> **3 :** sorry, sorry-looking <la triste verdad : the sorry truth>
tristeza *nf* DOLOR **:** sadness, grief
tristón, -tona *adj, mpl* **-tones :** melancholy, downhearted
tritón *nm, pl* **tritones :** newt
triturar *vt* **:** to crush, to grind
triunfal *adj* **:** triumphal, triumphant — **triunfalmente** *adv*
triunfante *adj* **:** triumphant, victorious
triunfar *vi* **:** to triumph, to win
triunfo *nm* **1 :** triumph, victory **2** ÉXITO **:** success **3 :** trump (in card games)
triunvirato *nm* **:** triumvirate
trivial *adj* **1 :** trivial **2 :** trite, commonplace
trivialidad *nf* **:** triviality
triza *nf* **1 :** shred, bit **2 hacer trizas :** to tear into shreds, to smash to pieces
trocar {82} *vt* **1** CAMBIAR **:** to exchange, to trade **2** CAMBIAR **:** to change, to alter, to transform **3** CONFUNDIR **:** to confuse, to mix up
trocha *nf* **:** path, trail
troce, etc. → **trozar**
trofeo *nm* **:** trophy
tromba *nf* **1 :** whirlwind **2 tromba de agua :** downpour, cloudburst
trombón *nm, pl* **trombones 1 :** trombone **2 :** trombonist — **trombonista** *nmf*
trombosis *nf* **:** thrombosis
trompa *nf* **1 :** trunk (of an elephant), proboscis (of an insect) **2 :** horn <trompa de caza : hunting horn> **3 :** tube, duct (in the body)
trompada *nf fam* **1 :** punch, blow **2 :** bump, collision (of persons)
trompeta *nf* **:** trumpet
trompetista *nmf* **:** trumpet player, trumpeter
trompo *nm* **:** spinning top
tronada *nf* **:** thunderstorm
tronar {19} *vi* **1 :** to thunder, to roar **2 :** to be furious, to rage **3** *CA, Mex fam* **:** to shoot — *v impers* **:** to thunder <está tronando : it's thundering>
tronchar *vt* **1 :** to snap, to break off **2 :** to cut off (relations)
tronco *nm* **1 :** trunk (of a tree) **2 :** log **3 :** torso
trono *nm* **1 :** throne **2** *fam* **:** toilet
tropa *nf* **1 :** troop, soldiers *pl* **2 :** crowd, mob **3 :** herd (of livestock)
tropel *nm* **:** mob, swarm
tropezar {29} *vi* **1 :** to trip, to stumble **2 :** to slip up, to blunder **3 ~ con :** to run into, to bump into **4 ~ con :** to come up against (a problem)
tropezón *nm, pl* **-zones 1 :** stumble **2 :** mistake, slip
tropical *adj* **:** tropical
trópico *nm* **1 :** tropic <trópico de Cáncer : tropic of Cancer> **2 el trópico :** the tropics

tropiezo *nm* **1** CONTRATIEMPO **:** snag, setback **2** EQUIVOCACIÓN **:** mistake, slip
troqué, etc. → **trocar**
troquel *nm* **:** die (for stamping)
trotamundos *nmf* **:** globe-trotter
trotar *vi* **1 :** to trot **2 :** to jog **3** *fam* **:** to rush about
trote *nm* **1 :** trot **2** *fam* **:** rush, bustle **3 de ~ :** durable, for everyday use
trovador, -dora *n* **:** troubadour
trozar {21} *vt* **:** to cut up, to dice
trozo *nm* **1** PEDAZO **:** piece, bit, chunk **2 :** passage, extract
trucha *nf* **:** trout
truco *nm* **1 :** trick **2 :** knack
truculento, -ta *adj* **:** horrifying, gruesome
trueca, trueque, etc. → **trocar**
truena, etc. → **tronar**
trueno *nm* **:** thunder
trueque *nm* **:** barter, exchange
trufa *nf* **:** truffle
truncar {72} *vt* **1 :** to truncate, to cut short **2 :** to thwart, to frustrate <truncó sus esperanzas : she shattered their hopes>
trunco, -ca *adj* **1 :** truncated **2 :** unfinished, incomplete
trunque, etc. → **truncar**
tu *adj* **1 :** your <tu vestido : your dress> <toma tus vitaminas : take your vitamins> **2 :** thy
tú *pron* **1 :** you <tú eres mi hijo : you are my son> **2 :** thou
tuba *nf* **:** tuba
tubérculo *nm* **:** tuber
tuberculosis *nf* **:** tuberculosis
tuberculoso, -sa *adj* **:** tuberculous, tubercular
tubería *nf* **:** pipes *pl*, tubing
tuberoso, -sa *adj* **:** tuberous
tubo *nm* **1 :** tube <tubo de ensayo : test tube> **2 :** pipe <tubo de desagüe : drainpipe> **3 tubo digestivo :** alimentary canal
tubular *adj* **:** tubular
tuerca *nf* **:** nut <tuercas y tornillos : nuts and bolts>
tuerce, etc. → **torcer**
tuerto, -ta *adj* **:** one-eyed, blind in one eye
tuerza, etc. → **torcer**
tuesta, etc. → **tostar**
tuétano *nm* **:** marrow
tufo *nm* **1 :** fume, vapor **2** *fam* **:** stench, stink
tugurio *nm* **:** hovel
tulipán *nm, pl* **-panes :** tulip
tumba *nf* **1** SEPULCRO **:** tomb **2** FOSA **:** grave **3 :** felling of trees
tumbar *vt* **1 :** to knock down **2 :** to fell, to cut down — *vi* **:** to fall down — **tumbarse** *vr* ACOSTARSE **:** to lie down
tumbo *nm* **1 :** tumble, fall **2 dar tumbos :** to jolt, to bump around
tumor *nm* **:** tumor
túmulo *nm* **:** burial mound
tumulto *nm* **1** ALBOROTO **:** commotion, tumult **2** MOTÍN **:** riot **3** MULTITUD **:** crowd
tumultuoso, -sa *adj* **:** tumultuous
tuna *nf* **:** prickly pear (fruit)
tundra *nf* **:** tundra
tunecino, -na *adj & n* **:** Tunisian
túnel *nm* **:** tunnel
tungsteno *nm* **:** tungsten
túnica *nf* **:** tunic
tupé *nm* PELUQUÍN **:** toupee
tupido, -da *adj* **1** DENSO **:** dense, thick **2** OBSTRUIDO **:** obstructed, blocked up
turba *nf* **1 :** peat **2 :** mob, throng
turbación *nf, pl* **-ciones 1 :** disturbance **2 :** alarm, concern **3 :** confusion
turbante *nm* **:** turban
turbar *vt* **1 :** to disturb, to disrupt **2 :** to worry, to upset **3 :** to confuse
turbina *nf* **:** turbine
turbio, -bia *adj* **1 :** cloudy, murky, turbid **2 :** dim, blurred **3 :** shady, crooked
turbopropulsor *nm* **:** turboprop
turborreactor *nm* **:** turbojet
turbulencia *nf* **:** turbulence
turbulento, -ta *adj* **:** turbulent
turco[1], -ca *adj* **:** Turkish
turco[2], -ca *n* **:** Turk
turgente *adj* **:** turgid, swollen
turismo *nm* **:** tourism, tourist industry
turista *nmf* **:** tourist, vacationer
turístico, -ca *adj* **:** tourist, travel
turnar *vi* **:** to take turns, to alternate
turno *nm* **1 :** turn <ya te tocará tu turno : you'll get your turn> **2 :** shift, duty <turno de noche : night shift> **3 por turno :** alternately
turón *nm, pl* **turones :** polecat
turquesa *nf* **:** turquoise
turrón *nm, pl* **turrones :** nougat
tusa *nf* **:** corn husk
tutear *vt* **:** to address as *tú*
tutela *nf* **1 :** guardianship **2 :** tutelage, protection
tuteo *nm* **:** addressing as *tú*
tutor, -tora *n* **1 :** tutor **2 :** guardian
tuvo, etc. → **tener**
tuyo[1], -ya *adj* **:** yours, of yours <un amigo tuyo : a friend of yours> <¿es tuya esta casa? : is this house yours?>
tuyo[2], -ya *pron* **1 :** yours <ése es el tuyo : that one is yours> <trae la tuya : bring your own> **2 los tuyos :** your relations, your friends <¿vendrán los tuyos? : are your folks coming?>
tweed [ˈtwið] *nm* **:** tweed

U

u[1] *nf* : twenty-second letter of the Spanish alphabet
u[2] *conj* (*used instead of* **o** *before words beginning with o- or ho-*) : or
ualabí *nm* : wallaby
uapití *nm* : American elk, wapiti
ubicación *nf, pl* **-ciones** : location, position
ubicar {72} *vt* **1** SITUAR : to place, to put, to position **2** LOCALIZAR : to locate, to find — **ubicarse** *vr* **1** LOCALIZARSE : to be placed, to be located **2** SITUARSE : to position oneself
ubicuidad *nf* OMNIPRESENCIA : ubiquity
ubicuo, -cua *adj* OMNIPRESENTE : ubiquitous
ubre *nf* : udder
ucraniano, -na *adj & n* : Ukranian
Ud., Uds. → **usted**
ufanarse *vr* **~ de** : to boast about, to pride oneself on
ufano, -na *adj* **1** ORGULLOSO : proud **2** : self-satisfied, smug
ugandés, -desa *adj & n, mpl* **-deses** : Ugandan
ukelele *nm* : ukulele
úlcera *nf* : ulcer — **ulceroso, -sa** *adj*
ulcerar *vt* : to ulcerate — **ulcerarse** *vr* — **ulceración** *nf*
ulceroso, -sa *adj* : ulcerous
ulterior *adj* : later, subsequent — **ulteriormente** *adv*
últimamente *adv* : lately, recently
ultimar *vt* **1** CONCLUIR : to complete, to finish, to finalize **2** MATAR : to kill
ultimátum *nm, pl* **-tums** : ultimatum
último, -ma *adj* **1** : last, final <la última galleta : the last cookie> <en último caso : as a last resort> **2** : last, latest, most recent <su último viaje a España : her last trip to Spain> <en los últimos años : in recent years> **3 por ~** : finally
ultrajar *vt* INSULTAR : to offend, to outrage, to insult
ultraje *nm* INSULTO : outrage, insult
ultramar *nm* **de ~** *or* **en ~** : overseas, abroad
ultranza *nf* **a ~ 1** : to the extreme <lo defendió a ultranza : she defended him fiercely> **2** : extreme, out-and-out <perfeccionismo a ultranza : rabid perfectionism>
ultrarrojo, -ja *adj* : infrared
ultravioleta *adj* : ultraviolet
ulular *vi* **1** : to hoot **2** : to howl, to wail
ululato *nm* : hoot (of an owl), wail (of a person)
umbilical *adj* : umbilical <cordón umbilical : umbilical cord>
umbral *nm* : threshold, doorstep
un[1] → **uno**[1]
un[2], **una** *art, mpl* **unos 1** : a, an **2 unos** *or* **unas** *pl* : some, a few <hace unas semanas : a few weeks ago> **3 unos** *or* **unas** *pl* : about, approximately <unos veinte años antes : about twenty years before>
unánime *adj* : unanimous — **unánimemente** *adv*
unanimidad *nf* **1** : unanimity **2 por ~** : unanimously
unción *nf, pl* **-ciones** : unction
uncir {83} *vt* : to yoke
undécimo[1], **-ma** *adj* : eleventh
undécimo[2], **-ma** *n* : eleventh (in a series)
ungir {35} *vt* : to anoint
ungüento *nm* : ointment, salve
únicamente *adv* : only, solely
unicelular *adj* : unicellular
único[1], **-ca** *adj* **1** : only, sole **2** : unique, extraordinary
único[2], **-ca** *n* : only one <los únicos que vinieron : the only ones who showed up>
unicornio *nm* : unicorn
unidad *nf* **1** : unity **2** : unit
unidireccional *adj* : unidirectional
unido, -da *adj* **1** : joined, united **2** : close <unos amigos muy unidos : very close friends>
unificar {72} *vt* : to unify — **unificación** *nf*
uniformado, -da *adj* : uniformed
uniformar *vt* ESTANDARIZAR : to standardize, to make uniform
uniforme[1] *adj* : uniform — **uniformemente** *adv*
uniforme[2] *nm* : uniform
uniformidad *nf* : uniformity
unilateral *adj* : unilateral — **unilateralmente** *adv*
unión *nf, pl* **uniones 1** : union **2** JUNTURA : joint, coupling
unir *vt* **1** JUNTAR : to unite, to join, to link **2** COMBINAR : to combine, to blend — **unirse** *vr* **1** : to join together **2** : to combine, to mix together **3 ~ a** : to join <se unieron al grupo : they joined the group>
unísono *nm* : unison <al unísono : in unison>
unitario, -ria *adj* : unitary, unit <precio unitario : unit price>
universal *adj* : universal — **universalmente** *adv*
universidad *nf* : university
universitario[1], **-ria** *adj* : university, college
universitario[2], **-ria** *n* : university student, college student
universo *nm* : universe
unja, etc. → **ungir**
uno[1], **una** *adj* (**un** *before masculine singular nouns*) : one <una silla : one chair> <tiene treinta y un años : he's thirty-one years old> <el tomo uno : volume one>
uno[2] *nm* : one, number one
uno[3], **una** *pron* **1** : one (number) <uno por uno : one by one> <es la una : it's

one o'clock> **2 :** one (person or thing) <una es mejor que las otras : one (of them) is better than the others> <hacerlo uno mismo : to do it oneself> **3 unos, unas** *pl* **:** some (ones), some people **4 uno y otro :** both **5 unos y otros :** all of them **6 el uno al otro :** one another, each other <se enseñaron los unos a los otros : they taught each other>

untar *vt* **1 :** to anoint **2 :** to smear, to grease **3 :** to bribe

unza, etc. → **uncir**

uña *nf* **1 :** fingernail, toenail **2 :** claw, hoof, stinger

uranio *nm* **:** uranium

Urano *nm* **:** Uranus

urbanidad *nf* **:** urbanity, courtesy

urbanización *nf, pl* **-ciones :** housing development, residential area

urbano, -na *adj* **1 :** urban **2** CORTÉS **:** urbane, polite

urbe *nf* **:** large city, metropolis

urdimbre *nf* **:** warp (in a loom)

uretra *nf* **:** urethra

urgencia *nf* **1 :** urgency **2** EMERGENCIA **:** emergency

urgente *adj* **:** urgent — **urgentemente** *adv*

urgir {35} *v impers* **:** to be urgent, to be pressing <me urge localizarlo : I urgently need to find him> <el tiempo urge : time is running out>

urinario[1], -ria *adj* **:** urinary

urinario[2] *nm* **:** urinal (place)

urja, etc. → **urgir**

urna *nf* **1 :** urn **2 :** ballot box <acudir a las urnas : to go to the polls>

urogallo *nm* **:** grouse (bird)

urraca *nf* **1 :** magpie **2 urraca de América :** blue jay

urticaria *nf* **:** hives

uruguayo, -ya *adj & n* **:** Uruguayan

usado, -da *adj* **1 :** used, secondhand **2 :** worn, worn-out

usanza *nf* **:** custom, usage

usar *vt* **1** EMPLEAR, UTILIZAR **:** to use, to make use of **2** CONSUMIR **:** to consume, to use (up) **3** LLEVAR **:** to wear **4 de usar y tirar :** disposable — **usarse 1 :** to be used **2 :** to be in fashion

uso *nm* **1** EMPLEO, UTILIZACIÓN **:** use <de uso personal : for personal use> <hacer uso de : to make use of> **2 :** wear <uso y desgaste : wear and tear> **3** USANZA **:** custom, usage, habit <al uso de : in the manner of, in the style of>

usted *pron* **1** (*formal form of address in most countries; often written as* **Ud.** *or* **Vd.**) **:** you **2 ustedes** *pl* (*often written as* **Uds.** *or* **Vds.**) **:** you, all of you

usual *adj* **:** usual, common, normal <poco usual : not very common> — **usualmente** *adv*

usuario, -ria *n* **:** user

usura *nf* **:** usury — **usurario, -ria** *adj*

usurero, -ra *n* **:** usurer

usurpador, -dora *n* **:** usurper

usurpar *vt* **:** to usurp — **usurpación** *nf*

utensilio *nm* **:** utensil, tool

uterino, -na *adj* **:** uterine

útero *nm* **:** uterus, womb

útil *adj* **:** useful, handy, helpful

útiles *nmpl* **:** implements, tools

utilidad *nf* **1 :** utility, usefulness **2 utilidades** *nfpl* **:** profits

utilitario, -ria *adj* **:** utilitarian

utilizable *adj* **:** usable, fit for use

utilización *nf, pl* **-ciones :** utilization, use

utilizar {21} *vt* **:** to use, to utilize

útilmente *adv* **:** usefully

utopía *nf* **:** utopia

utópico, -ca *adj* **:** utopian

uva *nf* **:** grape

uvular *adj* **:** uvular

V

v *nf* **:** twenty-third letter of the Spanish alphabet

va → **ir**

vaca *nf* **:** cow

vacación *nf, pl* **-ciones 1 :** vacation <dos semanas de vacaciones : two weeks of vacation> **2 estar de vacaciones :** to be on vacation **3 irse de vacaciones :** to go on vacation

vacacionar *vi Mex* **:** to vacation

vacacionista *nmf CA, Mex* **:** vacationer

vacante[1] *adj* **:** vacant, empty

vacante[2] *nf* **:** vacancy (for a job)

vaciado *nm* **:** cast, casting <vaciado de yeso : plaster cast>

vaciar {85} *vt* **1 :** to empty, to empty out, to drain **2** AHUECAR **:** to hollow out **3 :** to cast (in a mold) — *vi* **~ en :** to flow into, to empty into

vacilación *nf, pl* **-ciones :** hesitation, vacillation

vacilante *adj* **1 :** hesitant, unsure **2 :** shaky, unsteady **3 :** flickering

vacilar *vi* **1 :** to hesitate, to vacillate, to waver **2 :** to be unsteady, to wobble **3 :** to flicker **4** *fam* **:** to joke, to fool around

vacío[1], -cía *adj* **1 :** vacant **2 :** empty **3 :** meaningless

vacío[2] *nm* **1 :** emptiness, void **2 :** space, gap **3 :** vacuum **4 hacerle el vacío a alguien :** to ostracize someone, to give someone the cold shoulder

vacuidad *nf* **:** vacuity, vacuousness

vacuna *nf* **:** vaccine

vacunación *nf, pl* **-ciones** INOCULACIÓN **:** vaccination, inoculation

vacunar *vt* INOCULAR **:** to vaccinate, to inoculate

vacuno[1], -na *adj* **:** bovine <ganado vacuno **:** beef cattle>

vacuno[2] *nm* **:** bovine

vacuo, -cua *adj* **:** empty, shallow, inane

vadear *vt* **:** to ford, to wade across

vado *nm* **:** ford

vagabundear *vi* **:** to wander, to roam about

vagabundo[1], -da *adj* **1** ERRANTE **:** wandering **2 :** stray

vagabundo[2], -da *n* **:** vagrant, bum, vagabond

vagamente *adv* **:** vaguely

vagancia *nf* **1 :** vagrancy **2** PEREZA **:** laziness, idleness

vagar {52} *vi* ERRAR **:** to roam, to wander

vagina *nf* **:** vagina — **vaginal** *adj*

vago[1], -ga *adj* **1 :** vague **2** PEREZOSO **:** lazy, idle

vago[2], -ga *n* **1 :** idler, loafer **2** VAGABUNDO **:** vagrant, bum

vagón *nm, pl* **vagones :** car (of a train)

vague, etc. → **vagar**

vaguear *vi* **1 :** to loaf, to lounge around **2** VAGAR **:** to wander

vaguedad *nf* **:** vagueness

vahído *nm* **:** dizzy spell

vaho *nm* **1 :** breath **2 :** vapor, steam (on glass, etc.)

vaina *nf* **1 :** sheath, scabbard **2 :** pod (of a pea or bean) **3** *fam* **:** nuisance, bother

vainilla *nf* **:** vanilla

vaivén *nm, pl* **vaivenes 1 :** swinging, swaying, rocking **2 :** change, fluctuation <los vaivenes de la vida **:** life's ups and downs>

vajilla *nf* **:** dishes *pl*, set of dishes

valdrá, etc. → **valer**

vale *nm* **1 :** voucher **2** PAGARÉ **:** promissary note, IOU

valedero, -ra *adj* **:** valid

valentía *nf* **:** courage, valor

valer {84} *vt* **1 :** to be worth <valen una fortuna **:** they're worth a fortune> <no vale protestar **:** there's no point in protesting> <valer la pena **:** to be worth the trouble> **2 :** to cost <¿cuánto vale? **:** how much does it cost?> **3 :** to earn, to gain <le valió una reprimenda **:** it earned him a reprimand> **4 :** to protect, to aid <¡válgame Dios! **:** God help me!> **5 :** to be equal to — *vi* **1 :** to have value <sus consejos no valen para nada **:** his advice is worthless> **2 :** to be valid, to count <¡eso no vale! **:** that doesn't count!> **3 hacerse valer :** to assert oneself **4 más vale :** it's better <más vale que te vayas **:** you'd better go> — **valerse** *vr* **1 ~ de :** to take advantage of **2 valerse solo** *or* **valerse por sí mismo :** to look after oneself **3** *Mex* **:** to be fair <no se vale **:** it's not fair>

valeroso, -sa *adj* **:** brave, valiant

valet [ˈbalɛt, -ˈle] *nm* **:** jack (in playing cards)

valga, etc. → **valer**

valía *nf* **:** value, worth

validar *vt* **:** to validate — **validación** *nf*

validez *nf* **:** validity

válido, -da *adj* **:** valid

valiente *adj* **1 :** brave, valiant **2** (*used ironically*) **:** fine, great <¡valiente amiga! **:** what a fine friend!> — **valientemente** *adv*

valija *nf* **:** suitcase, valise

valioso, -sa *adj* PRECIOSO **:** valuable, precious

valla *nf* **1 :** fence, barricade **2 :** hurdle (in sports) **3 :** obstacle, hindrance

vallar *vt* **:** to fence, to put a fence around

valle *nm* **:** valley, vale

valor *nm* **1 :** value, worth, importance **2** CORAJE **:** courage, valor **3 valores** *nmpl* **:** values, principles **4 valores** *nmpl* **:** securities, bonds **5 sin ~ :** worthless

valoración *nf, pl* **-ciones 1** EVALUACIÓN **:** valuation, appraisal, assessment **2** APRECIACIÓN **:** appreciation

valorar *vt* **1** EVALUAR **:** to evaluate, to appraise, to assess **2** APRECIAR **:** to value, to appreciate

valorizarse {21} *vr* **:** to appreciate, to increase in value — **valorización** *nf*

vals *nm* **:** waltz

valsar *vi* **:** to waltz

valuación *nf, pl* **-ciones :** valuation, appraisal

valuar {3} *vt* **:** to value, to appraise, to assess

válvula *nf* **1 :** valve **2 válvula reguladora :** throttle

vamos → **ir**

vampiro *nm* **:** vampire

van → **ir**

vanadio *nm* **:** vanadium

vanagloriarse *vr* **:** to boast, to brag

vanamente *adv* **:** vainly, in vain

vandalismo : vandalism

vándalo *nm* **:** vandal — **vandalismo** *nm*

vanguardia *nf* **1 :** vanguard **2 :** avante-garde **3 a la vanguardia :** at the forefront

vanidad *nf* **:** vanity

vanidoso, -sa *adj* PRESUMIDO **:** vain, conceited

vano, -na *adj* **1** INÚTIL **:** vain, useless **2 :** vain, worthless <vanas promesas **:** empty promises> **3 en ~ :** in vain, of no avail

vapor *nm* **1 :** vapor, steam **2 :** steamer, steamship **3 al vapor :** steamed

vaporizador *nm* **:** vaporizer

vaporizar {21} *vt* **:** to vaporize — **vaporizarse** *vr* — **vaporización** *nf*

vaporoso, -sa *adj* **1 :** vaporous **2 :** sheer, airy

vapulear *vt* **:** to beat, to thrash

vaquero[1], **-ra** *adj* : cowboy <pantalón vaquero : jeans>

vaquero[2], **-ra** *n* : cowboy *m,* cowgirl *f*

vaqueros *nmpl* JEANS : jeans

vaquilla *nf* : heifer

vara *nf* **1** : pole, stick, rod **2** : staff (of office) **3** : lance, pike (in bullfighting) **4** : yardstick **5 vara de oro** : goldenrod

varado, -da *adj* **1** : beached, aground **2** : stranded

varar *vt* : to beach (a ship), to strand — *vi* : to run aground

variable *adj & nf* : variable — **variabilidad** *nf*

variación *nf, pl* **-ciones** : variation

variado, -da *adj* : varied, diverse

variante *adj & nf* : variant

varianza *nf* : variance

variar {85} *vt* **1** : to change, to alter **2** : to diversify — *vi* **1** : to vary, to change **2 variar de opinión** : to change one's mind

varicela *nf* : chicken pox

varices *or* **várices** *nfpl* : varicose veins

varicoso, -sa *adj* : varicose

variedad *nf* DIVERSIDAD : variety, diversity

varilla *nf* **1** : rod, bar **2** : spoke (of a wheel) **3** : rib (of an umbrella)

vario, -ria *adj* **1** : varied, diverse **2** : variegated, motley **3** : changeable **4 varios, varias** *pl* : various, several

variopinto, -ta *adj* : diverse, assorted, motley

varita *nf* : wand <varita mágica : magic wand>

varón *nm, pl* **varones 1** HOMBRE : man, male **2** NIÑO : boy

varonil *adj* **1** : masculine, manly **2** : mannish

vas → **ir**

vasallo *nm* : vassal — **vasallaje** *nm*

vasco[1], **-ca** *adj & n* : Basque

vasco[2] *nm* : Basque (language)

vascular *adj* : vascular

vasija *nf* : container, vessel

vaso *nm* **1** : glass, tumbler **2** : glassful **3** : vessel <vaso sanguíneo : blood vessel>

vástago *nm* **1** : offspring, descendent **2** : shoot (of a plant)

vastedad *nf* : vastness, immensity

vasto, -ta *adj* : vast, immense

vataje *nm* : wattage

vaticinar *vt* : to predict, to foretell

vaticinio *nm* : prediction, prophecy

vatio *nm* : watt

vaya, etc. → **ir**

Vd., Vds. → **usted**

ve, etc. → **ir, ver**

vea, etc. → **ver**

vecinal *adj* : local

vecindad *nf* **1** : neighborhood, vicinity **2 casa de vecindad** : tenement

vecindario *nm* **1** : neighborhood, area **2** : residents *pl*

vecino, -na *n* **1** : neighbor **2** : resident, inhabitant

veda *nf* **1** PROHIBICIÓN : prohibition **2** : closed season (for hunting or fishing)

vedar *vt* **1** : to prohibit, to ban **2** IMPEDIR : to impede, to prevent

vega *nf* : fertile lowland

vegetación *nf, pl* **-ciones 1** : vegetation **2 vegetaciones** *nfpl* : adenoids

vegetal *adj & nm* : vegetable, plant

vegetar *vi* : to vegetate

vegetarianismo *nm* : vegetarianism

vegetariano, -na *adj & n* : vegetarian

vegetativo, -va *adj* : vegetative

vehemente *adj* : vehement — **vehemencia** *nf*

vehículo *nm* : vehicle — **vehicular** *adj*

veía, etc. → **ver**

veinte *adj & nm* : twenty

veinteavo[1], **-va** *adj* : twentieth

veinteavo[2] *nm* : twentieth (fraction)

veintena *nf* : group of twenty, score <una veintena de participantes : about twenty participants>

vejación *nf, pl* **-ciones** : ill-treatment, humiliation

vejar *vt* : to mistreat, to ridicule, to harass

vejete *nm* : old fellow, codger

vejez *nf* : old age

vejiga *nf* **1** : bladder **2** AMPOLLA : blister

vela *nf* **1** VIGILIA : wakefulness <pasé la noche en vela : I stayed awake all night> **2** : watch, vigil, wake **3** : candle **4** : sail

velada *nf* : evening party, soirée

velado, -da *adj* **1** : veiled, hidden **2** : blurred **3** : muffled

velador[1], **-dora** *n* : guard, night watchman

velador[2] *nm* **1** : candlestick **2** : night table

velar *vt* **1** : to hold a wake over **2** : to watch over, to sit up with **3** : to blur, to expose (a photo) **4** : to veil, to conceal — *vi* **1** : to stay awake **2 ~ por** : to watch over, to look after

velatorio *nm* VELORIO : wake (for the dead)

veleidad *nf* **1** : fickleness **2** : whim, caprice

veleidoso, -sa : fickle, capricious

velero *nm* **1** : sailing ship **2** : sailboat

veleta *nf* : weather vane

vello *nm* **1** : body hair **2** : down, fuzz

vellocino *nm* : fleece

vellón *nm, pl* **vellones 1** : fleece, sheepskin **2** *PRi* : nickel (coin)

vellosidad *nf* : downiness, hairiness

velloso, -sa *adj* : downy, fluffy, hairy

velo *nm* : veil

velocidad *nf* **1** : speed, velocity <velocidad máxima : speed limit> **2** MARCHA : gear (of an automobile)

velocímetro *nm* : speedometer

velocista *nmf* : sprinter

velorio *nm* VELATORIO : wake (for the dead)

velour *nm* : velour, velours

veloz *adj, pl* **veloces** : fast, quick, swift — **velozmente** *adv*

ven → **venir**

vena *nf* **1** : vein <vena yugular : jugular vein> **2** : vein, seam, lode **3** : grain (of wood) **4** : style <en vena lírica : in a lyrical vein> **5** : strain, touch <una vena de humor : a touch of humor> **6** : mood

venado *nm* **1** : deer **2** : venison

venal *adj* : venal — **venalidad** *nf*

vencedor, -dora *n* : winner, victor

vencejo *nm* : swift (bird)

vencer {86} *vt* **1** DERROTAR : to vanquish, to defeat **2** SUPERAR : to overcome, to surmount — *vi* **1** GANAR : to win, to triumph **2** CADUCAR : to expire <el plazo vence el jueves : the deadline is Thursday> **3** : to fall due, to mature — **vencerse** *vr* **1** DOMINARSE : to control oneself **2** : to break, to collapse

vencido, -da *adj* **1** : defeated **2** : expired **3** : due, payable **4 darse por vencido** : to give up

vencimiento *nm* **1** : defeat **2** : expiration **3** : maturity (of a loan)

venda *nf* : bandage

vendaje *nm* : bandage, dressing

vendar *vt* **1** : to bandage **2 vendar los ojos** : to blindfold

vendaval *nm* : gale, strong wind

vendedor, -dora *n* : salesperson, salesman *m*, saleswoman *f*

vender *vt* **1** : to sell **2** : to sell out, to betray — **venderse 1** : to be sold <se vende : for sale> **2** : to sell out

vendetta *nf* : vendetta

vendible *adj* : salable, marketable

vendimia *nf* : grape harvest

vendrá, etc. → **venir**

veneno *nm* **1** : poison **2** : venom

venenoso, -sa *adj* : poisonous, venomous

venerable *adj* : venerable

veneración *nf, pl* **-ciones** : veneration, reverence

venerar *vt* : to venerate, to revere

venéreo, -rea *adj* : venereal

venero *nm* **1** VENA : seam, lode, vein **2** MANANTIAL : spring **3** FUENTE : origin, source

venezolano, -na *adj & n* : Venezuelan

venga, etc. → **venir**

vengador, -dora *n* : avenger

venganza *nf* : vengeance, revenge

vengar {52} *vt* : to avenge — **vengarse** *vr* : to get even, to revenge oneself

vengativo, -va *adj* : vindictive, vengeful

vengue, etc. → **vengar**

venia *nf* **1** PERMISO : permission, leave **2** PERDÓN : pardon **3** : bow (of the head)

venial *adj* : venial

venida *nf* **1** LLEGADA : arrival, coming **2** REGRESO : return **3 idas y venidas** : comings and goings

venidero, -ra *adj* : coming, future

venir {87} *vi* **1** : to come <lo vi venir : I saw him coming> <¡venga! : come on!> **2** : to arrive <vinieron en coche : they came by car> **3** : to come, to originate <sus zapatos vienen de Italia : her shoes are from Italy> **4** : to come, to be available <viene envuelto en plástico : it comes wrapped in plastic> **5** : to come back, to return **6** : to affect, to overcome <me vino un vahído : a dizzy spell came over me> **7** : to fit <te viene un poco grande : it's a little big for you> **8** (*with the present participle*) : to have been <viene entrenando diariamente : he's been training daily> **9 ~ a** (*with the infinitive*) : to end up, to turn out <viene a ser lo mismo : it comes out the same> **10 que viene** : coming, next <el año que viene : next year> **11 venir bien** : to be suitable, to be just right — **venirse** *vr* **1** : to come, to arrive **2** : to come back **3 venirse abajo** : to fall apart, to collapse

venta *nf* **1** : sale **2 venta al por menor** *or* **venta al detalle** : retail sales

ventaja *nf* **1** : advantage **2** : lead, head start **3 ventajas** *nfpl* : perks, extras

ventajoso, -sa *adj* **1** : advantageous **2** : profitable — **ventajosamente** *adv*

ventana *nf* **1** : window (of a building) **2 ventana de la nariz** : nostril

ventanal *nm* : large window

ventanilla *nf* **1** : window (of a vehicle or airplane) **2** : ticket window, box office

ventero, -ra *n* : innkeeper

ventilación *nf, pl* **-ciones** : ventilation

ventilador *nm* **1** : ventilator **2** : fan

ventilar *vt* **1** : to ventilate, to air out **2** : to air, to discuss **3** : to make public, to reveal — **ventilarse** *vr* : to get some air

ventisca *nf* : snowstorm, blizzard

ventisquero *nm* : snowdrift

ventosear *vi* : to break wind

ventosidad *nf* : wind, flatulence

ventoso, -sa *adj* : windy

ventrículo *nm* : ventricle

ventrílocuo, -cua *n* : ventriloquist

ventriloquia *nf* : ventriloquism

ventura *nf* **1** : fortune, luck, chance **2** : happiness **3 a la ventura** : at random, as it comes

venturoso, -sa *adj* **1** AFORTUNADO : fortunate, lucky **2** : successful

Venus *nm* : Venus

venza, etc. → **vencer**

ver[1] {88} *vt* **1** : to see <vimos la película : we saw the movie> **2** ENTENDER : to understand <ya lo veo : now I get it> **3** EXAMINAR : to examine, to look into <lo veré : I'll take a look at it> **4** JUZGAR : to see, to judge <a mi manera de ver : to my way of thinking> **5** VISITAR : to meet with, to visit **6** AVERIGUAR : to find out **7 a ver** *or* **vamos a ver** : let's see — *vi* **1** : to see **2** ENTERARSE : to learn, to find out **3**

ENTENDER : to understand — **verse** *vr* **1** HALLARSE : to find oneself **2** PARECER : to look, to appear **3** ENCONTRARSE : to see each other, to meet

ver[2] *nm* **1** : looks *pl*, appearance **2** : opinion <a mi ver : in my view>

vera *nf* : side <a la vera del camino : alongside the road>

veracidad *nf* : truthfulness, veracity

veranda *nf* : veranda

veraneante *nmf* : summer vacationer

veranear *vi* : to spend the summer

veraniego, -ga *adj* **1** ESTIVAL : summer <el sol veraniego : the summer sun> **2** : summery

verano *nm* : summer

veras *nfpl* **de ~** : really, truly

veraz *adj, pl* **veraces** : truthful, veracious

verbal *adj* : verbal — **verbalmente** *adv*

verbalizar {21} *vt* : to verbalize, to express

verbena *nf* **1** FIESTA : festival, fair **2** : verbena, vervain

verbigracia *adv* : for example

verbo *nm* : verb

verborrea *nf* : verbiage

verbosidad *nf* : verbosity, wordiness

verboso, -sa *adj* : verbose, wordy

verdad *nf* **1** : truth **2 de ~** : really, truly **3 ¿verdad?** : right?, isn't that so?

verdaderamente *adv* : really, truly

verdadero, -dera *adj* **1** REAL, VERÍDICO : true, real **2** AUTÉNTICO : genuine

verde[1] *adj* **1** : green (in color) **2** : green, unripe **3** : inexperienced, green **4** : dirty, risqué

verde[2] *nm* : green

verdear *vi* : to turn green, to become verdant

verdín *nm, pl* **verdines** : slime, scum

verdor *nm* **1** : greenness **2** : verdure

verdoso, -sa *adj* : greenish

verdugo *nm* **1** : executioner, hangman **2** : tyrant

verdugón *nm, pl* **-gones** : welt, wheal

verdura *nf* : vegetable(s), green(s)

vereda *nf* **1** SENDA : path, trail **2** : sidewalk, pavement

veredicto *nm* : verdict

verga *nf* : spar, yard (of a ship)

vergonzoso, -sa *adj* **1** : disgraceful, shameful **2** : bashful, shy — **vergonzosamente** *adv*

vergüenza *nf* **1** : disgrace, shame **2** : embarrassment **3** : bashfulness, shyness

vericueto *nm* : rough terrain

verídico, -ca *adj* **1** REAL, VERDADERO : true, real **2** VERAZ : truthful

verificación *nf, pl* **-ciones** **1** : verification **2** : testing, checking

verificador, -dora *n* : inspector, tester

verificar {72} *vt* **1** : to verify, to confirm **2** : to test, to check **3** : to carry out, to conduct — **verificarse** *vr* **1** : to take place, to occur **2** : to come true

verja *nf* **1** : rails *pl* (of a fence) **2** : grating, grille **3** : gate

vermut *nm, pl* **vermuts** : vermouth

vernáculo, -la *adj* : vernacular

vernal *adj* : vernal, spring

verosímil *adj* **1** : probable, likely **2** : credible, realistic

verosimilitud *nf* **1** : probability, likeliness **2** : verisimilitude

verraco *nm* : boar

verruga *nf* : wart

versado, -da *adj* **~ en** : versed in, knowledgeable about

versar *vi* **~ sobre** : to deal with, to be about

versátil *adj* **1** : versatile **2** : fickle

versatilidad *nf* **1** : versatility **2** : fickleness

versículo *nm* : verse (in the Bible)

versión *nf, pl* **versiones** **1** : version **2** : translation

verso *nm* : verse

versus *prep* : versus, against

vértebra *nf* : vertebra — **vertebral** *adj*

vertebrado[1], -da *adj* : vertebrate

vertebrado[2] *nm* : vertebrate

vertedero *nm* **1** : garbage dump **2** DESAGÜE : drain, outlet

verter {56} *vt* **1** : to pour **2** : to spill, to shed **3** : to empty out **4** : to express, to voice **5** : to translate, to render — *vi* : to flow

vertical *adj & nf* : vertical — **verticalmente** *adv*

vértice *nm* : vertex, apex

vertido *nm* : spilling, spill

vertiente *nf* **1** : slope **2** : aspect, side, element

vertiginoso, -sa *adj* : vertiginous — **vertiginosamente** *adv*

vértigo *nm* : vertigo, dizziness

vesícula *nf* **1** : vesicle **2 vesícula biliar** : gallbladder

vesicular *adj* : vesicular

vestíbulo *nm* : vestibule, hall, lobby, foyer

vestido *nm* **1** : dress, costume, clothes *pl* **2** : dress (garment)

vestidor *nm* : dressing room

vestiduras *nfpl* **1** : clothing, raiment, regalia **2** *or* **vestiduras sacerdotales** : vestments

vestigio *nm* : vestige, sign, trace

vestimenta *nf* ROPA : clothing, clothes *pl*

vestir {54} *vt* **1** : to dress, to clothe **2** LLEVAR : to wear **3** ADORNAR : to decorate, to dress up — *vi* **1** : to dress <vestir bien : to dress well> **2** : to look good, to suit the occasion — **vestirse** *vr* **1** : to get dressed **2 ~ de** : to dress up as <se vistieron de soldados : they dressed up as soldiers> **3 ~ de** : to wear, to dress in

vestuario *nm* **1** : wardrobe **2** : dressing room, locker room

veta *nf* **1** : grain (in wood) **2** : vein, seam, lode **3** : trace, streak <una veta de terco : a stubborn streak>

vetar *vt* : to veto
veteado, -da *adj* : streaked, veined
veterano, -na *adj & n* : veteran
veterinaria *nf* : veterinary medicine
veterinario[1], **-ria** *adj* : veterinary
veterinario[2], **-ria** *n* : veterinarian
veto *nm* : veto
vetusto, -ta *adj* ANTIGUO : ancient, very old
vez *nf, pl* **veces 1** : time, occasion <a la vez : at the same time> <a veces : at times, occasionally> <de vez en cuando : from time to time> **2** (*with numbers*) : time <una vez : once> <de una vez : all at once> <de una vez para siempre : once and for all> <dos veces : twice> **3** : turn <a su vez : in turn> <en vez de : instead of> <hacer las veces de : to act as, to stand in for>
vía[1] *nf* **1** RUTA, CAMINO : road, route, way <Vía Láctea : Milky Way> **2** MEDIO : means, way <por vía oficial : through official channels> **3** : track, line (of a railroad) **4** : tract, passage <por vía oral : orally> **5 en vías de** : in the process of <en vías de solución : on the road to a solution> **6 por ~** : by (in transportation) <por vía aérea : by air, airmail>
vía[2] *prep* : via
viable *adj* : viable, feasible — **viabilidad** *nf*
viaducto *nm* : viaduct
viajante *mf* : traveling salesman, traveling saleswoman
viajar *vi* : to travel, to journey
viaje *nm* : trip, journey <viaje de negocios : business trip>
viajero[1], **-ra** *adj* : traveling
viajero[2], **-ra** *n* **1** : traveler **2** PASAJERO : passenger
vial *adj* : road, traffic
viático *nm* : travel allowance, travel expenses *pl*
víbora *nf* : viper
vibración *nf, pl* **-ciones** : vibration
vibrador *nm* : vibrator
vibrante *adj* **1** : vibrant **2** : vibrating
vibrar *vi* : to vibrate
vibratorio, -ria *adj* : vibratory
vicario, -ria *n* : vicar
vicealmirante *nmf* : vice admiral
vicepresidente, -ta *n* : vice president — **vicepresidencia** *nf*
viceversa *adv* : vice versa, conversely
viciado, -da *adj* : stuffy, close
viciar *vt* **1** : to corrupt **2** : to invalidate **3** FALSEAR : to distort **4** : to pollute, to adulterate
vicio *nm* **1** : vice, depravity **2** : bad habit **3** : defect, blemish
vicioso, -sa *adj* : depraved, corrupt
vicisitud *nf* : vicissitude
víctima *nf* : victim
victimario, -ria *n* ASESINO : killer, murderer
victimizar {21} *vt Arg, Mex* : to victimize
victoria *nf* : victory — **victorioso, -sa** *adj* — **victoriosamente** *adv*
victoriano, -na *adj* : Victorian
vid *nf* : vine, grapevine
vida *nf* **1** : life <la vida cotidiana : everyday life> **2** : life span, lifetime **3** BIOGRAFÍA : biography, life **4** : way of life, lifestyle **5** : livelihood <ganarse la vida : to earn one's living> **6** VIVEZA : liveliness **7 media vida** : half-life
vidente *nmf* **1** : psychic, clairvoyant **2** : sighted person
video *or* **vídeo** *nm* : video
videocasete *or* **videocasette** *nm* : videocassette
videocasetera *or* **videocasettera** *nf* : videocassette recorder, VCR
videocinta *nf* : videotape
videograbar *vt* : to videotape
vidriado *nm* : glaze
vidriar *vt* : to glaze (pottery, tile, etc.)
vidriera *nf* **1** : stained-glass window **2** : glass door or window **3** : store window
vidriero, -ra *n* : glazier
vidrio *nm* **1** : glass, piece of glass **2** : windowpane
vidrioso, -sa *adj* **1** : brittle, fragile **2** : slippery **3** : glassy, glazed (of eyes) **4** : touchy, delicate
vieira *nf* **1** : scallop **2** : scallop shell
viejo[1], **-ja** *adj* **1** ANCIANO : old, elderly **2** ANTIGUO : former, longstanding <viejas tradiciones : old traditions> <viejos amigos : old friends> **3** GASTADO : old, worn, worn-out
viejo[2], **-ja** *n* ANCIANO : old man *m*, old woman *f*
viene, etc. → **venir**
viento *nm* **1** : wind **2 hacer viento** : to be windy **3 contra viento y marea** : against all odds **4 viento en popa** : splendidly, successfully
vientre *nm* **1** : abdomen, belly **2** : womb **3** : bowels *pl*
viernes *nms & pl* : Friday
vierte, etc. → **verter**
vietnamita *adj & nmf* : Vietnamese
viga *nf* **1** : beam, rafter, girder **2 viga voladiza** : cantilever
vigencia *nf* **1** : validity **2** : force, effect <entrar en vigencia : to go into effect>
vigente *adj* : valid, in force
vigésimo[1], **-ma** *adj* : twentieth, twenty- <la vigésima segunda edición : the twenty-second edition>
vigésimo[2], **-ma** *n* : twentieth, twenty- (in a series)
vigía *nmf* : lookout
vigilancia *nf* : vigilance, watchfulness <bajo vigilancia : under surveillance>
vigilante[1] *adj* : vigilant, watchful
vigilante[2] *nmf* : watchman, guard
vigilar *vt* **1** CUIDAR : to look after, to keep an eye on **2** GUARDAR : to watch over, to guard — *vi* **1** : to be watchful **2** : to keep watch

vigilia *nf* **1** VELA : wakefulness **2** : night work **3** : vigil (in religion)
vigor *nm* **1** : vigor, energy, strength **2** VIGENCIA : force, effect
vigorizante *adj* : envigorating
vigorizar {21} *vt* : to strengthen, to invigorate
vigoroso, -sa *adj* : vigorous — **vigorosamente** *adv*
VIH *nm* : HIV
vil *adj* : vile, dispicable
vileza *nf* **1** : vileness **2** : despicable action, villainy
vilipendiar *vt* : to vilify, to revile
villa *nf* **1** : town, village **2** : villa
villancico *nm* : carol, Christmas carol
villano, -na *n* **1** : villain **2** : peasant
vilo *nm* **en ~ 1** : in the air **2** : uncertain, in suspense
vinagre *nm* : vinegar
vinagrera *nf* : cruet (for vinegar)
vinatería *nf* : wine shop
vinculación *nf, pl* **-ciones 1** : linking **2** RELACIÓN : bond, link, connection
vincular *vt* CONECTAR, RELACIONAR : to tie, to link, to connect
vínculo *nm* LAZO : tie, link, bond
vindicación *nf, pl* **-ciones** : vindication
vindicar *vt* **1** : to vindicate **2** : to avenge
vinilo *nm* : vinyl
vino[1], etc. → **venir**
vino[2] *nm* : wine
viña *nf* : vineyard
viñedo *nm* : vineyard
vio, etc. → **ver**
viola *nf* : viola
violación *nf, pl* **-ciones 1** : violation, offense **2** : rape
violador[1], -dora *n* : violator, offender
violador[2] *nm* : rapist
violar *vt* **1** : to rape **2** : to violate (a law or right) **3** PROFANAR : to desecrate
violencia *nf* : violence
violentamente *adv* : by force, violently
violentar *vt* **1** FORZAR : to break open, to force **2** : to distort (words or ideas) — **violentarse** *vr* : to force oneself
violento, -ta *adj* **1** : violent **2** EMBARAZOSO, INCÓMODO : awkward, embarassing
violeta[1] *adj & nm* : violet (color)
violeta[2] *nf* : violet (flower)
violín *nm, pl* **-lines** : violin
violinista *nmf* : violinist
violonchelista *nmf* : cellist
violonchelo *nm* : cello, violoncello
VIP *nmf, pl* **VIPs** : VIP
vira *nf* : welt (of a shoe)
virago *nf* : virago, shrew
viraje *nm* **1** : turn, swerve **2** : change
viral *adj* : viral
virar *vi* : to tack, to turn, to veer
virgen[1] *adj* : virgin <lana virgen : virgin wool>
virgen[2] *nmf, pl* **vírgenes** : virgin <la Santísima Virgen : the Blessed Virgin>
virginal *adj* : virginal, chaste
virginidad *nf* : virginity
Virgo *nmf* : Virgo
vírico, -ca *adj* : viral
viril *adj* : virile — **virilidad** *nf*
virrey, -rreina *n* : viceroy *m,* vicereine *f*
virtual *adj* : virtual — **virtualmente** *adv*
virtud *nf* **1** : virtue **2 en virtud de** : by virtue of
virtuosismo *nm* : virtuosity
virtuoso[1], -sa *adj* : virtuous — **virtuosamente** *adv*
virtuoso[2], -sa *n* : virtuoso
viruela *nf* **1** : smallpox **2** : pockmark
virulencia *nf* : virulence
virulento, -ta *adj* : virulent
virus *nm* : virus
viruta *nf* : shaving
visa *nf* : visa
visado *nm Spain* : visa
visaje *nm* : face, grimace <hacer visajes : to make faces>
visceral *adj* : visceral
visceras *nfpl* : viscera, entrails
visconde, -desa *n* : viscount *m,* viscountess *f*
viscosidad *nf* : viscosity
viscoso, -sa *adj* : viscous
visera *nf* : visor
visibilidad *nf* : visibility
visible *adj* : visible — **visiblemente** *adv*
visión *nf, pl* **visiones 1** : vision, eyesight **2** : view, perspective **3** : vision, illusion <ver visiones : to be seeing things>
visionario, -ria *adj & n* : visionary
visita *nf* **1** : visit, call **2** : visitor **3 ir de visita** : to go visiting
visitador, -dora *n* : visitor, frequent caller
visitante[1] *adj* : visiting
visitante[2] *nmf* : visitor
visitar *vt* : to visit
vislumbrar *vt* **1** : to discern, to make out **2** : to begin to see, to have an inkling of
vislumbre *nf* : glimmer, gleam
viso *nm* **1** APARIENCIA : appearance <tener visos de : to seem, to show signs of> **2** DESTELLO : glint, gleam **3** : sheen, iridescence
visón *nm, pl* **visones** : mink
víspera *nf* **1** : eve, day before **2 vísperas** *nfpl* : vespers
vista *nf* **1** VISIÓN : vision, eyesight **2** MIRADA : look, gaze, glance **3** PANORAMA : view, vista, panorama **4** : hearing (in court) **5 a primera vista** : at first sight **6 en vista de** : in view of **7 hacer la vista gorda** : to turn a blind eye **8 ¡hasta la vista!** : so long!, see you! **9 perder de vista** : to lose sight of **10 punto de vista** : point of view
vistazo *nm* : glance, look
viste, etc. → **ver, vestir**

visto[1] *pp* → **ver**
visto[2], **-ta** *adj* **1** : obvious, clear **2** : in view of, considering **3 estar bien visto** : to be approved of **4 estar mal visto** : to be frowned upon **5 por lo visto** : apparently **6 nunca visto** : unheard-of **7 visto que** : since, given that
visto[3] *nm* **visto bueno** : approval
vistoso, -sa *adj* : colorful, bright
visual *adj* : visual — **visualmente** *adv*
visualización *nf, pl* **-ciones** : visualization
visualizar {21} *vt* **1** : to visualize **2** : to display (on a screen)
vital *adj* **1** : vital **2** : lively, dynamic
vitalicio, -cia *adj* : life, lifetime
vitalidad *nf* : vitality
vitamina *nf* : vitamin
vitamínico, -ca *adj* : vitamin <complejos vitamínicos : vitamin compounds>
vitorear *vt* : to cheer, to acclaim
vitral *nm* : stained-glass window
vítreo, -rea *adj* : vitreous, glassy
vitrina *nf* **1** : showcase, display case **2** : store window
vitriolo *nm* : vitriol
vituperar *vt* : to condemn, to vituperate against
vituperio *nm* : vituperation, censure
viudez *nf* : widowerhood, widowhood
viudo, -da *n* : widower *m*, widow *f*
vivacidad *nf* VIVEZA : vivacity, liveliness
vivamente *adv* **1** : in a lively manner **2** : vividly **3** : strongly, acutely <lo recomendamos vivamente : we strongly recommend it>
vivaque *nm* : bivouac
vivaquear *vi* : to bivouac
vivar *vi* : to cheer
vivaz *adj, pl* **vivaces 1** : lively, vivacious **2** : clever, sharp **3** : perennial
víveres *nmpl* : provisions, supplies, food
vivero *nm* **1** : nursery (for plants) **2** : hatchery, fish farm
viveza *nf* **1** VIVACIDAD : liveliness **2** BRILLO : vividness, brightness **3** ASTUCIA : cleverness, sharpness
vívido, -da *adj* : vivid, lively
vividor, -dora *n* : sponger, parasite
vivienda *nf* **1** : housing **2** MORADA : dwelling, home
viviente *adj* : living
vivificar {72} *vt* : to vivify, to give life to
vivir[1] *vi* **1** : to live, to be alive **2** SUBSISTIR : to subsist, to make a living **3** RESIDIR : to reside **4** : to spend one's life <vive para trabajar : she lives to work> **5 ~ de** : to live on — *vt* **1** : to live <vivir su vida : to live one's life> **2** EXPERIMENTAR : to go through, to experience
vivir[2] *nm* **1** : life, lifestyle **2 de mal vivir** : disreputable
vivisección *nf, pl* **-ciones** : vivisection
vivo, -va *adj* **1** : alive **2** INTENSO : vivid, bright, intense **3** ANIMADO : lively, vivacious **4** ASTUTO : sharp, clever **5 en ~** : live <transmisión en vivo : live broadcast> **6 al rojo vivo** : red-hot
vizconde, -desa *n* : viscount *m*, viscountess *f*
vocablo *nm* PALABRA : word
vocabulario *nm* : vocabulary
vocación *nf, pl* **-ciones** : vocation
vocacional *adj* : vocational
vocal[1] *adj* : vocal
vocal[2] *nmf* : member (of a committee, board, etc.)
vocal[3] *nf* : vowel
vocalista *nmf* CANTANTE : singer, vocalist
vocalizar {21} *vi* : to vocalize
vocear *v* : to shout
vocerío *nm* : clamor, shouting
vocero, -ra *n* PORTAVOZ : spokesperson, spokesman *m*, spokeswoman *f*
vociferante *adj* : vociferous
vociferar *vi* GRITAR : to shout, to yell
vodevil *nm* : vaudeville
vodka *nm* : vodka
voladizo[1], **-za** *adj* : projecting
voladizo[2] *nm* : projection
volador, -dora *adj* : flying
volando *adv* : quickly, in a hurry
volante[1] *adj* : flying
volante[2] *nm* **1** : steering wheel **2** FOLLETO : flier, circular **3** : shuttlecock **4** : flywheel **5** : balance wheel (of a watch) **6** : ruffle, flounce
volar {19} *vi* **1** : to fly **2** CORRER : to hurry, to rush <el tiempo vuela : time flies> <pasar volando : to fly past> **3** DIVULGARSE : to spread <unos rumores volaban : rumors were spreading around> **4** DESAPARECER : to disappear <el dinero ya voló : the money's already gone> — *vt* **1** : to blow up, to demolish **2** : to irritate
volátil *adj* : volatile — **volatilidad** *nf*
volatilizar {21} *vt* : to volatize — **volatilizarse** *vr*
volcán *nm, pl* **volcanes** : volcano
volcánico, -ca *adj* : volcanic
volcar {82} *vt, pl* **volcanes 1** : to upset, to knock over, to turn over **2** : to empty out **3** : to make dizzy **4** : to cause a change of mind in **5** : to irritate — *vi* **1** : to overturn, to tip over **2** : to capsize — **volcarse** *vr* **1** : to overturn **2** : to do one's utmost
volea *nf* : volley (in sports)
volear *vi* : to volley (in sports)
voleibol *nm* : volleyball
voleo *nm* **al voleo** : haphazardly, at random
volframio *nm* : wolfram, tungsten
volición *nf, pl* **-ciones** : volition
volqué, etc. → **volcar**
voltaje *nm* : voltage
voltear *vt* **1** : to turn over, to turn upside down **2** : to reverse, to turn inside out **3** : to turn <voltear la cara : to turn one's head> **4** : to knock

down — *vi* **1** : to roll over, to do somersaults **2** : to turn <volteó a la izquierda : he turned left> — **voltearse** *vr* **1** : to turn around **2** : to change one's allegiance

voltereta *nf* : somersault, tumble

voltio *nm* : volt

volubilidad *nf* : fickleness, changeableness

voluble *adj* : fickle, changeable

volumen *nm, pl* **-lúmenes 1** TOMO : volume, book **2** : capacity, size, bulk **3** CANTIDAD : amount <el volumen de ventas : the volume of sales> **4** : volume, loudness

voluminoso, -sa *adj* : voluminous, massive, bulky

voluntad *nf* **1** : will, volition **2** DESEO : desire, wish **3** INTENCIÓN : intention **4 a voluntad** : at will **5 buena voluntad** : good will **6 mala voluntad** : ill will **7 fuerza de voluntad** : willpower

voluntario[1], -ria *adj* : voluntary — **voluntariamente** *adv*

voluntario[2], -ria *n* : volunteer

voluntarioso, -sa *adj* **1** : stubborn **2** : willing, eager

voluptuosidad *nf* : voluptuousness

voluptuoso, -sa *adj* : voluptuous — **voluptuosamente** *adv*

voluta *nf* : spiral, column (of smoke)

volver {89} *vi* **1** : to return, to come or go back <volver a casa : to return home> **2** : to revert <volver al tema : to get back to the subject> **3 ~ a** : to do again <volvieron a llamar : they called again> **4 volver en sí** : to come to, to regain consciousness — *vt* **1** : to turn, to turn over, to turn inside out **2** : to return, to repay, to restore **3** : to cause, to make <la volvía loca : it was driving her crazy> — **volverse** *vr* **1** : to become <se volvió deprimido : he became depressed> **2** : to turn around

vomitar *vi* : to vomit — *vt* **1** : to vomit **2** : to spew out (lava, etc.)

vómito *nm* **1** : vomiting **2** : vomit

voracidad *nf* : voracity

vorágine *nf* : whirlpool, maelstrom

voraz *adj, pl* **voraces** : voracious — **vorazmente** *adv*

vórtice *nm* **1** : whirlpool, vortex **2** TORBELLINO : whirlwind

vos *pron* (*in some regions of Latin America*) : you

vosear *vt* : to address as *vos*

vosotros, -tras *pron pl Spain* **1** : you, yourselves **2** : ye

votación *nf, pl* **-ciones** : vote, voting

votante *nmf* : voter

votar *vi* : to vote — *vt* : to vote for

votivo, -va *adj* : votive

voto *nm* **1** : vote **2** : vow (in religion) **3 votos** *nmpl* : good wishes

voy → **ir**

voz *nf, pl* **voces 1** : voice **2** : opinion, say **3** GRITO : shout, yell **4** : sound **5** VOCABLO : word, term **6** : rumor **7 a voz en cuello** : at the top of one's lungs **8 dar voces** : to shout **9 en voz alta** : aloud, in a loud voice **10 en voz baja** : softly, in a low voice

vudú *nm* : voodoo

vuelco *nm* : upset, overturning <me dio un vuelco el corazón : my heart skipped a beat>

vuela, etc. → **volar**

vuelca, vuelque, etc. → **volcar**

vuelo *nm* **1** : flight, flying <alzar el vuelo : to take flight> **2** : flight (of an aircraft) <vuelo espacial : space flight> **3** : flare, fullness (of clothing) **4 al vuelo** : on the wing

vuelta *nf* **1** GIRO : turn <se dio la vuelta : he turned around> **2** REVOLUCIÓN : circle, revolution <dio la vuelta al mundo : she went around the world> <las ruedas daban vueltas : the wheels were spinning> **3** : flip, turn <le dio la vuelta : she flipped it over> **4** : bend, curve <a la vuelta de la esquina : around the corner> **5** REGRESO : return <de ida y vuelta : round trip> <a vuelta de correo : return mail> **6** : round, lap (in sports or games) **7** PASEO : walk, drive, ride <dio una vuelta : he went for a walk> **8** DORSO, REVÉS : back, other side <a la vuelta : on the back> **9** : cuff (of pants) **10 darle vueltas** : to think over **11 estar de vuelta** : to be back

vuelto *pp* → **volver**

vuelve, etc. → **volver**

vuestro[1], -stra *adj Spain* : your, of yours <vuestros coches : your cars> <una amiga vuestra : a friend of yours>

vuestro[2], -stra *pron Spain* (*with definite article*) : yours <la vuestra es más grande : yours is bigger> <esos son los vuestros : those are yours>

vulcanizar {21} *vt* : to vulcanize

vulgar *adj* **1** : common **2** : vulgar

vulgaridad *nf* : vulgarity

vulgarismo *nm* : vulgarism

vulgarizar {21} *vt* : to vulgarize, to popularize

vulgarmente *adv* : vulgarly, popularly

vulgo *nm* **el vulgo** : the masses, common people

vulnerable *adj* : vulnerable — **vulnerabilidad** *nf*

vulnerar *vt* **1** : to injure, to damage (one's reputation or honor) **2** : to violate, to break (a law or contract)

W

w *nf* **:** twenty-fourth letter of the Spanish alphabet
wafle *nm* **:** waffle
waflera *nf* **:** waffle iron
wapití *nm* **:** wapiti, elk
whisky *nm, pl* **whiskys** *or* **whiskies** **:** whiskey
wigwam *nm* **:** wigwam

X

x *nf* **:** twenty-fifth letter of the Spanish alphabet
xenofobia *nf* **:** xenophobia
xenófobo[1]**, -ba** *adj* **:** xenophobic
xenófobo[2]**, -ba** *n* **:** xenophobe
xenón *nm* **:** xenon
xerocopiar *vt* **:** to photocopy, to xerox
xilófono *nm* **:** xylophone

Y

y[1] *nf* **:** twenty-sixth letter of the Spanish alphabet
y[2] *conj* **1 :** and <mi hermano y yo : my brother and I> <¿y los demás? : and (what about) the others?> **2** (*used in numbers*) <cincuenta y cinco : fifty-five> **3** *fam* **:** well <y por supuesto : well, of course>
ya[1] *adv* **1 :** already <ya terminó : she's finished already> **2 :** now, right now <¡hazlo ya! : do it now!> <ya mismo : right away> **3 :** later, soon <ya iremos : we'll go later on> **4 :** no longer, anymore <ya no fuma : he no longer smokes> **5** (*used for emphasis*) **:** <¡ya lo sé! : I know!> <ya lo creo : of course> **6 no ya :** not only <no ya lloran sino gritan : they're not only crying but screaming> **7 ya que :** now that, since <ya que sabe la verdad : now that she knows the truth>
ya[2] *conj* **ya . . . ya :** whether . . . or, first . . . then <ya le gusta, ya no : first he likes it, then he doesn't>
yac *nm* **:** yak
yacer {90} *vi* **:** to lie <en esta tumba yacen sus abuelos : his grandparents lie in this grave>
yacimiento *nm* **:** bed, deposit <yacimiento petrolífero : oil field>
yaga, etc. → **yacer**
yanqui *adj & nmf* **:** Yankee
yarda *nf* **:** yard
yate *nm* **:** yacht
yaz, yazca, yazga, etc. → **yacer**
yedra *nf* **:** ivy
yegua *nf* **:** mare
yelmo *nm* **:** helmet
yema *nf* **1 :** bud, shoot **2 :** yolk (of an egg) **3 yema del dedo :** fingertip
yemenita *adj & nmf* **:** Yemenite
yendo → **ir**
yerba *nf* **1** *or* **yerba mate :** maté **2** → **hierba**
yerga, yergue, etc. → **erguir**
yermo[1]**, -ma** *adj* **:** barren, deserted
yermo[2] *nm* **:** wasteland
yerno *nm* **:** son-in-law
yerra, etc. → **errar**
yerro *nm* **:** blunder, mistake
yerto, -ta *adj* **:** rigid, stiff
yesca *nf* **:** tinder
yeso *nm* **1 :** plaster **2 :** gypsum
yo[1] *nm* **:** ego, self
yo[2] *pron* **1 :** I **2 :** me <todos menos yo : everyone except me> <tan bajo como yo : as short as me> **3 soy yo :** it is I, it's me
yodado, -da *adj* **:** iodized
yodo *nm* **:** iodine
yoduro *nm* **:** iodide
yoga *nm* **:** yoga
yogui *nm* **:** yogi
yogurt *or* **yogur** *nm* **:** yogurt
yola *nf* **:** yawl
yoyo *or* **yoyó** *nm* **:** yo-yo
yuca *nf* **1 :** yucca (plant) **2 :** cassava, manioc
yucateco[1]**, -ca** *adj* **:** of or from the Yucatán
yucateco[2]**, -ca** *n* **:** person from the Yucatán
yudo → **judo**
yugo *nm* **:** yoke
yugoslavo, -va *adj & n* **:** Yugoslavian
yugular *adj* **:** jugular <vena yugular : jugular vein>
yungas *nfpl Bol, Chile, Peru* **:** warm tropical valleys
yunque *nm* **:** anvil
yunta *nf* **:** yoke, team (of oxen)
yute *nm* **:** jute
yuxtaponer {60} *vt* **:** to juxtapose — **yuxtaposición** *nf*

Z

z *nf* **:** twenty-seventh letter of the Spanish alphabet
zacate *nm CA, Mex* **1 :** grass, forage **2 :** hay
zafacón *nm, pl* **-cones :** wastebasket
zafar *vt* **:** to loosen, to untie — **zafarse** *vr* **1 :** to loosen up, to come undone **2 :** to get free of
zafio, -fia *adj* **:** coarse, crude
zafiro *nm* **:** sapphire
zaga *nf* **1 :** defense (in sports) **2 a la zaga** *or* **en ~ :** behind, in the rear
zagual *nm* **:** paddle (of a canoe)
zaguán *nm, pl* **zaguanes :** front hall, vestibule
zaherir {76} *vt* **1 :** to criticize sharply **2 :** to wound, to mortify
zahones *nmpl* **:** chaps
zaino, -na *adj* **:** chestnut (color)
zalamería *nf* **:** flattery, sweet talk
zalamero[1]**, -ra** *adj* **:** flattering, fawning
zalamero[2]**, -ra** *n* **:** flatterer
zambiano, -na *adj & nmf* **:** Zambian
zambullida *nf* **:** dive, plunge
zambullirse {38} *vr* **:** to dive, to plunge
zanahoria *nf* **:** carrot
zancada *nf* **:** stride, step
zancadilla *nf* **1 :** trip, stumble **2** *fam* **:** trick, ruse
zancos *nmpl* **:** stilts
zancuda *nf* **:** wading bird
zancudo *nm* MOSQUITO **:** mosquito
zángano *nm* **:** drone, male bee
zanja *nf* **:** ditch, trench
zanjar *vt* ACLARAR **:** to settle, to clear up, to resolve
zapallo *nm Arg, Chile, Peru, Uru* **:** pumpkin
zapapico *nm* **:** pickax
zapata *nf* **:** brake shoe
zapatería *nf* **1 :** shoemaker's, shoe factory **2 :** shoe store
zapatero[1]**, -ra** *adj* **:** dry, tough, poorly cooked
zapatero[2]**, -ra** *n* **:** shoemaker, cobbler
zapatilla *nf* **1** PANTUFLA **:** slipper **2** *or* **zapatilla de deporte :** sneaker
zapato *nm* **:** shoe
zar, zarina *n* **:** czar *m,* czarina *f*
zarandear *vt* **1 :** to sift, to sieve **2 :** to shake, to jostle, to jiggle
zarapito *nm* **:** curlew
zarcillo *nm* **1 :** earring **2 :** tendril (of a plant)
zarigüeya *nf* **:** opossum
zarista *adj & nmf* **:** czarist
zarpa *nf* **:** paw
zarpar *vi* **:** to set sail, to raise anchor
zarza *nf* **:** bramble, blackberry bush
zarzamora *nf* **1 :** blackberry **2 :** bramble, blackberry bush
zarzaparrilla *nf* **:** sarsaparilla
zepelín *nm, pl* **-lines :** zeppelin
zigoto *nm* **:** zygote
zigzag *nm, pl* **zigzags** *or* **zigzagues :** zigzag
zigzaguear *vi* **:** to zigzag
zimbabuense *adj & nmf* **:** Zimbabwean
zinc *nm* **:** zinc
zinnia *nf* **:** zinnia
zíper *nm CA, Mex* **:** zipper
zircón *nm, pl* **zircones :** zircon
zócalo *nm Mex* **:** main square
zodíaco *nm* **:** zodiac — **zodíacal** *adj*
zombi *or* **zombie** *nmf* **:** zombie
zona *nf* **:** zone, district, area
zonzo[1]**, -za** *adj* **:** stupid, silly
zonzo[2]**, -za** *n* **:** idiot, nitwit
zoo *nm* **:** zoo
zoología *nf* **:** zoology
zoológico[1]**, -ca** *adj* **:** zoological
zoológico[2] *nm* **:** zoo
zoólogo, -ga *n* **:** zoologist
zoom *nm* **:** zoom lens
zopilote *nm CA, Mex* **:** buzzard
zoquete *nmf fam* **:** oaf, blockhead
zorrillo *nm* MOFETA **:** skunk
zorro[1]**, -rra** *adj* **:** sly, crafty
zorro[2]**, -rra** *n* **1 :** fox, vixen **2 :** sly crafty person
zorzal *nm* **:** thrush
zozobra *nf* **:** anxiety, worry
zozobrar *vi* **:** to capsize
zueco *nm* **:** clog (shoe)
zulú[1] *adj & nmf* **:** Zulu
zulú[2] *nm* **:** Zulu (language)
zumaque *nm* **:** sumac
zumbar *vi* **:** to buzz, to hum — *vt fam* **1 :** to hit, to thrash **2 :** to make fun of
zumbido *nm* **:** buzzing, humming
zumo *nf* JUGO **:** juice
zurcir {83} *vt* **:** to darn, to mend
zurdo[1]**, -da** *adj* **:** left-handed
zurdo[2]**, -da** *n* **:** left-handed person
zurza, etc. → **zurcir**
zutano, -na → **fulano**

English–Spanish Dictionary

A

a[1] [ˈeɪ] *n, pl* **a's** *or* **as** [ˈeɪz] **:** primera letra del alfabeto inglés

a[2] [ə, ˈeɪ] *art* (**an** [ən, ˈæn] *before vowel or silent h*) **1 :** un *m,* una *f* <a house : una casa> <half an hour : media hora> <what a surprise! : ¡qué sorpresa!> **2** PER **:** por, a la, al <30 kilometers an hour : 30 kilómetros por hora> <twice a month : dos veces al mes>

aardvark [ˈɑrd͵vɑrk] *n* **:** oso *m* hormiguero

aback [əˈbæk] *adv* **1 :** por sorpresa **2 to be taken aback :** quedarse desconcertado

abacus [ˈæbəkəs] *n, pl* **abaci** [ˈæbə͵saɪ, -͵kiː] *or* **abacuses :** ábaco *m*

abaft [əˈbæft] *adv* **:** a popa

abalone [͵æbəˈloːni] *n* **:** abulón *m,* oreja *f* marina

abandon[1] [əˈbændən] *vt* **1** DESERT, FORSAKE **:** abandonar, desamparar (a alguien), desertar de (algo) **2** GIVE UP, SUSPEND **:** renunciar a, suspender <he abandoned the search : suspendió la búsqueda> **3** EVACUATE, LEAVE **:** abandonar, evacuar, dejar <to abandon ship : abandonar el buque> **4 to abandon oneself :** entregarse, abandonarse

abandon[2] *n* **:** desenfreno *m* <with wild abandon : desenfrenadamente>

abandoned [əˈbændənd] *adj* **1** DESERTED **:** abandonado **2** UNRESTRAINED **:** desenfrenado, desinhibido

abandonment [əˈbændənmənt] *n* **:** abandono *m,* desamparo *m*

abase [əˈbeɪs] *vt* **abased; abasing :** degradar, humillar, rebajar

abash [əˈbæʃ] *vt* **:** avergonzar, abochornar

abashed [əˈbæʃt] *adj* **:** avergonzado

abate [əˈbeɪt] *vi* **abated; abating :** amainar, menguar, disminuir

abattoir [ˈæbə͵twɑr] *n* **:** matadero *m*

abbess [ˈæbɪs, -͵bɛs, -bəs] *n* **:** abadesa *f*

abbey [ˈæbi] *n, pl* **-beys :** abadía *f*

abbot [ˈæbət] *n* **:** abad *m*

abbreviate [əˈbriːvi͵eɪt] *vt* **-ated; -ating :** abreviar

abbreviation [ə͵briːviˈeɪʃən] *n* **:** abreviación *f,* abreviatura *f*

abdicate [ˈæbdɪ͵keɪt] *v* **-cated; -cating :** abdicar

abdication [͵æbdɪˈkeɪʃən] *n* **:** abdicación *f*

abdomen [ˈæbdəmən, æbˈdoːmən] *n* **:** abdomen *m,* vientre *m*

abdominal [æbˈdɑmənəl] *adj* **:** abdominal — **abdominally** *adv*

abduct [æbˈdʌkt] *vt* **:** raptar, secuestrar

abduction [æbˈdʌkʃən] *n* **:** rapto *m,* secuestro *m*

abductor [æbˈdʌktər] *n* **:** raptor *m,* -tora *f;* secuestrador *m,* -dora *f*

abed [əˈbɛd] *adv & adj* **:** en cama

aberrant [æˈbɛrənt, ˈæbərənt] *adj* **1** ABNORMAL **:** anormal, aberrante **2** ATYPICAL **:** anómalo, atípico

aberration [͵æbəˈreɪʃən] *n* **1 :** aberración *f* **2** DERANGEMENT **:** perturbación *f* mental

abet [əˈbɛt] *vt* **abetted; abetting** ASSIST **:** ayudar <to aid and abet : ser cómplice de>

abeyance [əˈbeɪənts] *n* **:** desuso *m,* suspensión *f*

abhor [əbˈhɔr, æb-] *vt* **-horred; -horring :** abominar, aborrecer

abhorrence [əbˈhɔrənts, æb-] *n* **:** aborrecimiento *m,* odio *m*

abhorrent [əbˈhɔrənt, æb-] *adj* **:** abominable, aborrecible, odioso

abide [əˈbaɪd] *v* **abode** [əˈboːd] *or* **abided; abiding** *vt* STAND **:** soportar, tolerar <I can't abide them : no los puedo ver> — *vi* **1** ENDURE **:** quedar, permanecer **2** DWELL **:** morar, residir **3 to abide by :** atenerse a

ability [əˈbɪləti] *n, pl* **-ties 1** CAPABILITY **:** aptitud *f,* capacidad *f,* facultad *f* **2** COMPETENCE **:** competencia *f* **3** TALENT **:** talento *m,* don *m,* habilidad *f*

abject [ˈæb͵dʒɛkt, æbˈ-] *adj* **1** WRETCHED **:** miserable, desdichado **2** HOPELESS **:** abatido, desesperado **3** SERVILE **:** servil <abject flattery : halagos serviles> — **abjectly** *adv*

ablaze [əˈbleɪz] *adj* **1** BURNING **:** ardiendo, en llamas **2** RADIANT **:** resplandeciente, radiante

able [ˈeɪbəl] *adj* **abler; ablest 1** CAPABLE **:** capaz, hábil **2** COMPETENT **:** competente

ablution [əˈbluːʃən] *n* **:** ablución *f* <to perform one's ablutions : lavarse>

ably [ˈeɪbəli] *adv* **:** hábilmente, eficientemente

abnormal [æbˈnɔrməl] *adj* **:** anormal — **abnormally** *adv*

abnormality [͵æbnərˈmæləti, -nɔr-] *n, pl* **-ties :** anormalidad *f*

aboard[1] [əˈbord] *adv* **:** a bordo

aboard[2] *prep* **:** a bordo de

abode[1] → **abide**

abode[2] [əˈboːd] *n* **:** morada *f,* residencia *f,* vivienda *f*

abolish [əˈbɑlɪʃ] *vt* **:** abolir, suprimir

abolition [͵æbəˈlɪʃən] *n* **:** abolición *f,* supresión *f*

abominable [əˈbɑmənəbəl] *adj* DETESTABLE **:** abominable, aborrecible, espantoso

abominate [əˈbɑmə͵neɪt] *vt* **-nated; -nating :** abominar, aborrecer

abomination [ə͵bɑməˈneɪʃən] *n* **:** abominación *f*

aboriginal [͵æbəˈrɪdʒənəl] *adj* **:** aborigen, indígena

aborigine [ˌæbəˈrɪdʒəni] *n* NATIVE : aborigen *mf,* indígena *mf*
abort [əˈbɔrt] *vt* **1** : abortar (en medicina) **2** CALL OFF : suspender, abandonar — *vi* : abortar, hacerse un aborto
abortion [əˈbɔrʃən] *n* : aborto *m*
abortive [əˈbɔrtɪv] *adj* UNSUCCESSFUL : fracasado, frustrado, malogrado
abound [əˈbaʊnd] *vi* **to abound in** : abundar en, estar lleno de
about[1] [əˈbaʊt] *adv* **1** APPROXIMATELY : aproximadamente, casi, más o menos **2** AROUND : por todas partes, alrededor <the children are running about : los niños están corriendo por todas partes> **3 to be about to** : estar a punto de **4 to be up and about** : estar levantado
about[2] *prep* **1** AROUND : alrededor de **2** CONCERNING : de, acerca de, sobre <he always talks about politics : siempre habla de política>
above[1] [əˈbʌv] *adv* **1** OVERHEAD : por encima, arriba **2** : más arriba <as stated above : como se indica más arriba>
above[2] *adj* : anterior, antedicho <for the above reasons : por las razones antedichas>
above[3] *prep* **1** OVER : encima de, arriba de, sobre **2** : superior a, por encima de <he's above those things : él está por encima de esas cosas> **3** : más de, superior a <he earns above $50,000 : gana más de $50,000> <a number above 10 : un número superior a 10> **4 above all** : sobre todo
aboveboard[1] [əˈbʌvˈbord, -ˌbord] *adv* **open and aboveboard** : sin tapujos
aboveboard[2] *adj* : legítimo, sincero
abrade [əˈbreɪd] *vt* **abraded; abrading** **1** ERODE : erosionar, corroer **2** SCRAPE : escoriar, raspar
abrasion [əˈbreɪʒən] *n* **1** SCRAPE, SCRATCH : raspadura *f,* rasguño *m* **2** EROSION : erosión *f*
abrasive[1] [əˈbreɪsɪv] *adj* **1** ROUGH : abrasivo, áspero **2** BRUSQUE, IRRITATING : brusco, irritante
abrasive[2] *n* : abrasivo *m*
abreast [əˈbrɛst] *adv* **1** : en fondo, al lado <to march three abreast : marchar de tres en fondo> **2 to keep abreast** : mantenerse al día
abridge [əˈbrɪdʒ] *vt* **abridged; abridging** : compendiar, resumir
abridgment *or* **abridgement** [əˈbrɪdʒmənt] *n* : compendio *m,* resumen *m*
abroad [əˈbrɔd] *adv* **1** ABOUT, WIDELY : por todas partes, en todas direcciones <the news spread abroad : la noticia corrió por todas partes> **2** OVERSEAS : en el extranjero, en el exterior
abrupt [əˈbrʌpt] *adj* **1** SUDDEN : abrupto, repentino, súbito **2** BRUSQUE, CURT : brusco, cortante — **abruptly** *adv*
abscess [ˈæbˌsɛs] *n* : absceso *m*
abscond [æbˈskɑnd] *vi* : huir, fugarse
absence [ˈæbsənts] *n* **1** : ausencia *f* (de una persona) **2** LACK : falta *f,* carencia *f*
absent[1] [æbˈsɛnt] *vt* **to absent oneself** : ausentarse
absent[2] [ˈæbsənt] *adj* : ausente
absentee [ˌæbsənˈtiː] *n* : ausente *mf*
absentminded [ˌæbsəntˈmaɪndəd] *adj* : distraído, despistado
absentmindedly [ˌæbsəntˈmaɪndədli] *adv* : distraídamente
absentmindedness [ˌæbsəntˈmaɪndədnəs] *n* : distracción *f,* despiste *m*
absolute [ˈæbsəˌluːt, ˌæbsəˈluːt] *adj* **1** COMPLETE, PERFECT : completo, pleno, perfecto **2** UNCONDITIONAL : absoluto, incondicional **3** DEFINITE : categórico, definitivo
absolutely [ˈæbsəˌluːtli, ˌæbsəˈluːtli] *adv* **1** COMPLETELY : completamente, absolutamente **2** CERTAINLY : desde luego <do you agree? absolutely! : ¿estás de acuerdo? ¡desde luego!>
absolution [ˌæbsəˈluːʃən] *n* : absolución *f*
absolve [əbˈzɑlv, æb-, -ˈsɑlv] *vt* **-solved; -solving** : absolver, perdonar
absorb [əbˈzɔrb, æb-, -ˈsɔrb] *vt* **1** : absorber, embeber (un líquido), amortiguar (un golpe, la luz) **2** ENGROSS : absorber **3** ASSIMILATE : asimilar
absorbed [əbˈzɔrbd, æb-, -ˈsɔrbd] *adj* ENGROSSED : absorto, ensimismado
absorbency [əbˈzɔrbəntsi, æb-, -ˈsɔr-] *n* : absorbencia *f*
absorbent [əbˈzɔrbənt, æb-, -ˈsɔr-] *adj* : absorbente
absorbing [əbˈzɔrbɪŋ, æb-, -ˈsɔr-] *adj* : absorbente, fascinante
absorption [əbˈzɔrpʃən, æb-, -ˈsɔrp-] *n* **1** : absorción *f* **2** CONCENTRATION : concentración *f*
abstain [əbˈsteɪn, æb-] *vi* : abstenerse
abstainer [əbˈsteɪnər, æb-] *n* : abstemio *m,* -mia *f*
abstemious [æbˈstiːmiəs] *adj* : abstemio, sobrio — **abstemiously** *adv*
abstention [əbˈstɛntʃən, æb-] *n* : abstención *f*
abstinence [ˈæbstənənts] *n* : abstinencia *f*
abstract[1] [æbˈstrækt, ˈæbˌ-] *vt* **1** EXTRACT : abstraer, extraer **2** SUMMARIZE : compendiar, resumir
abstract[2] *adj* : abstracto — **abstractly** [æbˈstræktli, ˈæbˌ-] *adv*
abstract[3] [ˈæbˌstrækt] *n* : resumen *m,* compendio *m,* sumario *m*
abstraction [æbˈstrækʃən] *n* **1** : abstracción *f,* idea *f* abstracta **2** ABSENTMINDEDNESS : distracción *f*
abstruse [əbˈstruːs, æb-] *adj* : abstruso, recóndito — **abstrusely** *adv*
absurd [əbˈsərd, -ˈzərd] *adj* : absurdo, ridículo, disparatado — **absurdly** *adv*
absurdity [əbˈsərdəti, -ˈzər-] *n, pl* **-ties** **1** : absurdo *m* **2** NONSENSE : disparate *m,* despropósito *m*

abundance [əˈbʌndənts] *n* : abundancia *f*

abundant [əˈbʌndənt] *adj* : abundante, cuantioso, copioso

abundantly [əˈbʌndəntli] *adv* : abundantemente, en abundancia

abuse[1] [əˈbju:z] *vt* **abused; abusing 1** MISUSE : abusar de **2** MISTREAT : maltratar **3** REVILE : insultar, injuriar, denostar

abuse[2] [əˈbju:s] *n* **1** MISUSE : abuso *m* **2** MISTREATMENT : abuso *m,* maltrato *m* **3** INSULTS : insultos *mpl,* improperios *mpl* <a string of abuse : una serie de improperios>

abuser [əˈbju:zər] *n* : abusador *m,* -dora *f*

abusive [əˈbju:sɪv] *adj* **1** ABUSING : abusivo **2** INSULTING : ofensivo, injurioso, insultante — **abusively** *adv*

abut [əˈbʌt] *v* **abutted; abutting** *vt* : bordear — *vi* **to abut on** : colindar con

abutment [əˈbʌtmənt] *n* **1** BUTTRESS : contrafuerte *m,* estribo *m* **2** CLOSENESS : contigüidad *f*

abysmal [əˈbɪzməl] *adj* **1** DEEP : abismal, insondable **2** TERRIBLE : atroz, desastroso

abysmally [əˈbɪzməli] *adv* : desastrosamente, terriblemente

abyss [əˈbɪs, ˈæbɪs] *n* : abismo *m,* sima *f*

acacia [əˈkeɪʃə] *n* : acacia *f*

academic[1] [ˌækəˈdɛmɪk] *adj* **1** : académico **2** THEORETICAL : teórico — **academically** [-mɪkli] *adv*

academic[2] *n* : académico *m,* -ca *f*

academy [əˈkædəmi] *n, pl* **-mies** : academia *f*

accede [ækˈsi:d] *vi* **-ceded; -ceding 1** AGREE : acceder, consentir **2** ASCEND : subir, acceder <he acceded to the throne : subió al trono>

accelerate [ɪkˈsɛləˌreɪt, æk-] *v* **-ated; -ating** *vt* : acelerar, apresurar — *vi* : acelerar (dícese de un carro)

acceleration [ɪkˌsɛləˈreɪʃən, æk-] *n* : aceleración *f*

accelerator [ɪkˈsɛləˌreɪt̬ər, æk-] *n* : acelerador *m*

accent[1] [ˈækˌsɛnt, ækˈsɛnt] *vt* : acentuar

accent[2] [ˈækˌsɛnt, -sənt] *n* **1** : acento *m* **2** EMPHASIS, STRESS : énfasis *m,* acento *m*

accentuate [ɪkˈsɛntʃʊˌeɪt, æk-] *vt* **-ated; -ating** : acentuar, poner énfasis en

accept [ɪkˈsɛpt, æk-] *vt* **1** : aceptar **2** ACKNOWLEDGE : admitir, reconocer

acceptability [ɪkˌsɛptəˈbɪlət̬i, æk-] *n* : aceptabilidad *f*

acceptable [ɪkˈsɛptəbəl, æk-] *adj* : aceptable, admisible — **acceptably** [-bli] *adv*

acceptance [ɪkˈsɛptənts, æk-] *n* : aceptación *f,* aprobación *f*

access[1] [ˈækˌsɛs] *vt* : obtener acceso a, entrar a

access[2] *n* : acceso *m*

accessible [ɪkˈsɛsəbəl, æk-] *adj* : accesible, asequible

accession [ɪkˈsɛʃən, æk-] *n* **1** : ascenso *f,* subida *f* (al trono, etc.) **2** ACQUISITION : adquisición *f*

accessory[1] [ɪkˈsɛsəri, æk-] *adj* : auxiliar

accessory[2] *n, pl* **-ries 1** : accesorio *m,* complemento *m* **2** ACCOMPLICE : cómplice *mf*

accident [ˈæksədənt] *n* **1** MISHAP : accidente *m* **2** CHANCE : casualidad *f*

accidental [ˌæksəˈdɛntəl] *adj* : accidental, casual, imprevisto, fortuito

accidentally [ˌæksəˈdɛntəli, -ˈdɛntli] *adv* **1** BY CHANCE : por casualidad **2** UNINTENTIONALLY : sin querer, involuntariamente

acclaim[1] [əˈkleɪm] *vt* : aclamar, elogiar

acclaim[2] *n* : aclamación *f,* elogio *m*

acclamation [ˌækləˈmeɪʃən] *n* : aclamación *f*

acclimate [ˈækləˌmeɪt, əˈklaɪmət] → **acclimatize**

acclimatize [əˈklaɪməˌtaɪz] *v* **-tized; -tizing** *vt* **1** : aclimatar **2 to acclimatize oneself** : aclimatarse

accolade [ˈækəˌleɪd, -ˌlɑd] *n* **1** PRAISE : elogio *m* **2** AWARD : galardón *m*

accommodate [əˈkɑməˌdeɪt] *vt* **-dated; -dating 1** ADAPT : acomodar, adaptar **2** SATISFY : tener en cuenta, satisfacer **3** HOLD : dar cabida a, tener cabida para

accommodation [əˌkɑməˈdeɪʃən] *n* **1** : adaptación *f,* adecuación *f* **2 accommodations** *npl* LODGING : alojamiento *m,* hospedaje *m*

accompaniment [əˈkʌmpənəmənt, -ˈkɑm-] *n* : acompañamiento *m*

accompanist [əˈkʌmpənɪst, -ˈkɑm-] *n* : acompañante *mf*

accompany [əˈkʌmpəni, -ˈkɑm-] *vt* **-nied; -nying** : acompañar

accomplice [əˈkɑmpləs, -ˈkʌm-] *n* : cómplice *mf*

accomplish [əˈkɑmplɪʃ, -ˈkʌm-] *vt* : efectuar, realizar, lograr, llevar a cabo

accomplished [əˈkɑmplɪʃt, -ˈkʌm-] *adj* : consumado, logrado

accomplishment [əˈkɑmplɪʃmənt, -ˈkʌm-] *n* **1** ACHIEVEMENT : logro *m,* éxito *m* **2** SKILL : destreza *f,* habilidad *f*

accord[1] [əˈkɔrd] *vt* GRANT : conceder, otorgar — *vi* **to accord with** : concordar con, conformarse con

accord[2] *n* **1** AGREEMENT : acuerdo *m,* convenio *m* **2** VOLITION : voluntad *f* <on one's own accord : voluntariamente, de motu proprio>

accordance [əˈkɔrdənts] *n* **1** ACCORD : acuerdo *m,* conformidad *f* **2 in ac-**

cordance with : conforme a, según, de acuerdo con

accordingly [ə'kɔrdɪŋli] *adv* **1** CORRESPONDINGLY : en consecuencia **2** CONSEQUENTLY : por consiguiente, por lo tanto

according to [ə'kɔrdɪŋ] *prep* : según, de acuerdo con, conforme a

accordion [ə'kɔrdiən] *n* : acordeón *m*

accordionist [ə'kɔrdiənɪst] *n* : acordeonista *mf*

accost [ə'kɔst] *vt* : abordar, dirigirse a

account[1] [ə'kaʊnt] *vt* : considerar, estimar <he accounts himself lucky : se considera afortunado> — *vi* **to account for** : dar cuenta de, explicar

account[2] *n* **1** : cuenta *f* <savings account : cuenta de ahorros> **2** EXPLANATION : versión *f*, explicación *f* **3** REPORT : relato *m*, informe *m* **4** IMPORTANCE : importancia *f* <to be of no account : no tener importancia> **5 on account of** BECAUSE OF : a causa de, debido a, por **6 on no account** : de ninguna manera

accountability [əˌkaʊntə'bɪlət̬i] *n* : responsabilidad *f*

accountable [ə'kaʊntəbəl] *adj* : responsable

accountant [ə'kaʊntənt] *n* : contador *m*, -dora *f*; contable *mf Spain*

accounting [ə'kaʊntɪŋ] *n* : contabilidad *f*

accoutrements *or* **accouterments** [ə'kuːtrəmənts, -'kuːt̬ər-] *npl* **1** EQUIPMENT : equipo *m*, avíos *mpl* **2** ACCESSORIES : accesorios *mpl* **3** TRAPPINGS : símbolos *mpl* <the accoutrements of power : los símbolos del poder>

accredit [ə'krɛdət] *vt* : acreditar, autorizar

accreditation [əˌkrɛdə'teɪʃən] *n* : acreditación *f*, homologación *f*

accrual [ə'kruːəl] *n* : incremento *m*, acumulación *f*

accrue [ə'kruː] *vi* **-crued; -cruing** : acumularse, aumentarse

accumulate [ə'kjuːmjəˌleɪt] *v* **-lated; -lating** *vt* : acumular, amontonar — *vi* : acumularse, amontonarse

accumulation [əˌkjuːmjə'leɪʃən] *n* : acumulación *f*, amontonamiento *m*

accuracy ['ækjərəsi] *n* : exactitud *f*, precisión *f*

accurate ['ækjərət] *adj* : exacto, correcto, fiel, preciso — **accurately** *adv*

accusation [ˌækjə'zeɪʃən] *n* : acusación *f*

accuse [ə'kjuːz] *vt* **-cused; -cusing** : acusar, delatar, denunciar

accused [ə'kjuːzd] *ns & pl* DEFENDANT : acusado *m*, -da *f*

accuser [ə'kjuːzər] *n* : acusador *m*, -dora *f*

accustom [ə'kʌstəm] *vt* : acostumbrar, habituar

ace ['eɪs] *n* : as *m*

acerbic [ə'sərbɪk, æ-] *adj* : acerbo, mordaz

acetate ['æsəˌteɪt] *n* : acetato *m*

acetylene [ə'sɛt̬ələn, -t̬əˌliːn] *n* : acetileno *m*

ache[1] ['eɪk] *vi* **ached; aching 1** : doler **2 to ache for** : anhelar, ansiar

ache[2] *n* : dolor *m*

achieve [ə'tʃiːv] *vt* **achieved; achieving** : lograr, alcanzar, conseguir, realizar

achievement [ə'tʃiːvmənt] *n* : logro *m*, éxito *m*, realización *f*

acid[1] ['æsəd] *adj* **1** SOUR : ácido, agrio **2** CAUSTIC, SHARP : acerbo, mordaz — **acidly** *adv*

acid[2] *n* : ácido *m*

acidic [ə'sɪdɪk, æ-] *adj* : ácido

acidity [ə'sɪdət̬i, æ-] *n, pl* **-ties** : acidez *f*

acknowledge [ɪk'nɑlɪdʒ, æk-] *vt* **-edged; -edging 1** ADMIT : reconocer, admitir **2** RECOGNIZE : reconocer **3 to acknowledge receipt of** : acusar recibo de

acknowledgment [ɪk'nɑlɪdʒmənt, æk-] *n* **1** RECOGNITION : reconocimiento *m* **2** THANKS : agradecimiento *m*

acme ['ækmi] *n* : colmo *m*, apogeo *m*, cúspide *f*

acne ['ækni] *n* : acné *m*

acorn ['eɪˌkɔrn, -kərn] *n* : bellota *f*

acoustic [ə'kuːstɪk] *or* **acoustical** [-stɪkəl] *adj* : acústico — **acoustically** *adv*

acoustics [ə'kuːstɪks] *ns & pl* : acústica *f*

acquaint [ə'kweɪnt] *vt* **1** INFORM : enterar, informar **2** FAMILIARIZE : familiarizar **3 to be acquainted with** : conocer a (una persona), estar al tanto de (un hecho)

acquaintance [ə'kweɪntənts] *n* **1** KNOWLEDGE : conocimiento *m* **2** : conocido *m*, -da *f* <friends and acquaintances : amigos y conocidos>

acquiesce [ˌækwi'ɛs] *vi* **-esced; -escing** : consentir, conformarse

acquiescence [ˌækwi'ɛsənts] *n* : consentimiento *m*, aquiescencia *f*

acquire [ə'kwaɪr] *vt* **-quired; -quiring** : adquirir, obtener

acquisition [ˌækwə'zɪʃən] *n* : adquisición *f*

acquisitive [ə'kwɪzət̬ɪv] *adj* : adquisitivo, codicioso

acquit [ə'kwɪt] *vt* **-quitted; -quitting 1** : absolver, exculpar **2 to acquit oneself** : comportarse, defenderse

acquittal [ə'kwɪt̬əl] *n* : absolución *f*, exculpación *f*

acre ['eɪkər] *n* : acre *m*

acreage ['eɪkərɪdʒ] *n* : superficie *f* en acres

acrid ['ækrəd] *adj* **1** BITTER : acre **2** CAUSTIC : acre, mordaz — **acridly** *adv*

acrimonious [ˌækrə'moːniəs] *adj* : áspero, cáustico, sarcástico

acrimony ['ækrəˌmoːni] *n, pl* **-nies** : acrimonia *f*

acrobat ['ækrə,bæt] *n* : acróbata *mf,* satimbanqui *mf*

acrobatic [,ækrə'bæṭɪk] *adj* : acrobático

acronym ['ækrə,nɪm] *n* : acrónimo *m*

across[1] [ə'krɔs] *adv* **1** CROSSWISE : al través **2** : a través, del otro lado <he's already across : ya está del otro lado> **3** : de ancho <40 feet across : 40 pies de ancho>

across[2] *prep* **1** : al otro lado de <across the street : al otro lado de la calle> **2** : a través de <a log across the road : un tronco a través del camino>

acrylic [ə'krɪlɪk] *n* : acrílico *m*

act[1] ['ækt] *vi* **1** PERFORM : actuar, interpretar **2** FEIGN, PRETEND : fingir, simular **3** BEHAVE : comportarse **4** FUNCTION : actuar, servir, funcionar **5** : tomar medidas <he acted to save the business : tomó medidas para salvar el negocio> **6 to act as** : servir de, hacer de

act[2] *n* **1** DEED : acto *m,* hecho *m,* acción *f* **2** DECREE : ley *f,* decreto *m* **3** : acto *m* (en una obra de teatro), número *m* (en un espectáculo) **4** PRETENSE : fingimiento *m*

action ['ækʃən] *n* **1** DEED : acción *f,* acto *m,* hecho *m* **2** BEHAVIOR : actuación *f,* comportamiento *m* **3** LAWSUIT : demanda *f* **4** MOVEMENT : movimiento *m* **5** COMBAT : combate *m* **6** PLOT : acción *f,* trama *f* **7** MECHANISM : mecanismo *m*

activate ['æktə,veɪt] *vt* **-vated; -vating** : activar

active ['æktɪv] *adj* **1** MOVING : activo, en movimiento **2** LIVELY : vigoroso, enérgico **3** : en actividad <an active volcano : un volcán en actividad> **4** OPERATIVE : vigente

actively ['æktɪvli] *adv* : activamente, enérgicamente

activity [æk'tɪvəṭi] *n, pl* **-ties 1** MOVEMENT : actividad *f,* movimiento *m* **2** VIGOR : vigor *m,* energía *f* **3** OCCUPATION : actividad *f,* ocupación *f*

actor ['æktər] *n* : actor *m,* artista *mf*

actress ['æktrəs] *n* : actriz *f*

actual ['æktʃʊəl] *adj* : real, verdadero

actuality [,æktʃʊ'æləṭi] *n, pl* **-ties** : realidad *f*

actually ['æktʃʊəli, -ʃəli] *adv* : realmente, en realidad

actuary ['æktʃʊ,ɛri] *n, pl* **-aries** : actuario *m,* -ria *f* de seguros

acumen [ə'kju:mən] *n* : perspicacia *f*

acupuncture ['ækjʊ,pʌŋktʃər] *n* : acupuntura *f*

acute [ə'kju:t] *adj* **acuter; acutest 1** SHARP : agudo **2** PERCEPTIVE : perspicaz, sagaz **3** KEEN : fino, muy desarrollado, agudo <an acute sense of smell : un fino olfato> **4** SEVERE : grave **5 acute angle** : ángulo *m* agudo

acutely [ə'kju:tli] *adv* : intensamente <to be acutely aware : estar perfectamente consciente>

acuteness [ə'kju:tnəs] *n* : agudeza *f*

ad ['æd] → **advertisement**

adage ['ædɪdʒ] *n* : adagio *m,* refrán *m,* dicho *m*

adamant ['ædəmənt, -,mænt] *adj* : firme, categórico, inflexible — **adamantly** *adv*

Adam's apple ['ædəmz] *n* : nuez *f* de Adán

adapt [ə'dæpt] *vt* : adaptar, ajustar — *vi* : adaptarse

adaptability [ə,dæptə'bɪləṭi] *n* : adaptabilidad *f,* flexibilidad *f*

adaptable [ə'dæptəbəl] *adj* : adaptable, amoldable

adaptation [,æ,dæp'teɪʃən, -dəp-] *n* **1** : adaptación *f,* modificación *f* **2** VERSION : versión *f*

adapter [ə'dæptər] *n* : adaptador *m*

add ['æd] *vt* **1** : añadir, agregar <to add a comment : añadir una observación> **2** : sumar <add these numbers : suma estos números> — *vi* : sumar (en total)

adder ['ædər] *n* : víbora *f*

addict[1] [ə'dɪkt] *vt* : causar adicción en

addict[2] ['ædɪkt] *n* **1** : adicto *m,* -ta *f* **2 drug addict** : drogadicto *m,* -ta *f;* toxicómano *m,* -na *f*

addiction [ə'dɪkʃən] *n* **1** : adicción *f,* dependencia *f* **2 drug addiction** : drogadicción *f*

addictive [ə'dɪktɪv] *adj* : adictivo

addition [ə'dɪʃən] *n* **1** : adición *f,* añadidura *f* **2 in ~** : además, también

additional [ə'dɪʃənəl] *adj* : extra, adicional, de más

additionally [ə'dɪʃənəli] *adv* : además, adicionalmente

additive ['ædəṭɪv] *n* : aditivo *m*

addle ['ædəl] *vt* **-dled; -dling** : confundir, enturbiar

address[1] [ə'drɛs] *vt* **1** : dirigirse a, pronunciar un discurso ante <to address a jury : dirigirse a un jurado> **2** : dirigir, ponerle la dirección a <to address a letter : dirigir una carta>

address[2] [ə'drɛs, 'æ,drɛs] *n* **1** SPEECH : discurso *m,* alocución *f* **2** : dirección *f* (de una residencia, etc.)

adenoids ['æd,nɔɪd, -dən,ɔɪd] *npl* : adenoides *fpl*

adept [ə'dɛpt] *adj* : experto, hábil — **adeptly** *adv*

adequacy ['ædɪkwəsi] *n, pl* **-cies** : cantidad *f* suficiente

adequate ['ædɪkwət] *adj* **1** SUFFICIENT : adecuado, suficiente **2** ACCEPTABLE, PASSABLE : adecuado, aceptable

adequately ['ædɪkwətli] *adv* : suficientemente, apropiadamente

adhere [æd'hɪr, əd-] *vi* **-hered; -hering 1** STICK : pegarse, adherirse **2 to adhere to** : adherirse a (una política, etc.), cumplir con (una promesa)

adherence [æd'hɪrənts, əd-] *n* : adhesión *f,* adherencia *f,* observancia *f* (de una ley, etc.)

adherent[1] [æd'hɪrənt, əd-] *adj* : adherente, adhesivo, pegajoso

adherent[2] *n* : adepto *m,* -ta *f;* partidario *m,* -ria *f*

adhesive[1] [æd'hiːsɪv, əd-, -zɪv] *adj* : adhesivo

adhesive[2] *n* : adhesivo *m,* pegamento *m*

adjacent [ə'dʒeɪsənt] *adj* : adyacente, colindante, contiguo

adjective ['ædʒɪktɪv] *n* : adjetivo *m* — **adjectival** [ˌædʒɪk'taɪvəl] *adj*

adjoin [ə'dʒɔɪn] *vt* : lindar con, colindar con

adjoining [ə'dʒɔɪnɪŋ] *adj* : contiguo, colindante

adjourn [ə'dʒərn] *vt* : levantar, suspender <the meeting is adjourned : se levanta la sesión> — *vi* : aplazarse

adjournment [ə'dʒərnmənt] *n* : suspensión *f,* aplazamiento *m*

adjudicate [ə'dʒuːdɪˌkeɪt] *vt* **-cated; -cating** : juzgar, arbitrar

adjunct ['æˌdʒʌŋkt] *n* : adjunto *m,* complemento *m*

adjust [ə'dʒʌst] *vt* : ajustar, arreglar, regular — *vi* **to adjust to** : adaptarse a

adjustable [ə'dʒʌstəbəl] *adj* : ajustable, regulable, graduable

adjustment [ə'dʒʌstmənt] *n* : ajuste *m,* modificación *f*

ad–lib[1] ['æd'lɪb] *v* **-libbed; -libbing** : improvisar

ad–lib[2] *adj* : improvisado

administer [æd'mɪnəstər, əd-] *vt* : administrar

administration [ædˌmɪnə'streɪʃən, əd-] *n* **1** MANAGING : administración *f,* dirección *f* **2** GOVERNMENT, MANAGEMENT : administración *f,* gobierno *m*

administrative [æd'mɪnəˌstreɪṭɪv, əd-] *adj* : administrativo — **administratively** *adv*

administrator [æd'mɪnəˌstreɪṭər, əd-] *n* : administrador *m,* -dora *f*

admirable ['ædmərəbəl] *adj* : admirable, loable — **admirably** *adv*

admiral ['ædmərəl] *n* : almirante *mf*

admiration [ˌædmə'reɪʃən] *n* : admiración *f*

admire [æd'maɪr] *vt* **-mired; -miring** : admirar

admirer [æd'maɪrər] *n* : admirador *m,* -dora *f*

admiring [æd'maɪrɪŋ] *adj* : admirativo, de admiración

admiringly [æd'maɪrɪŋli] *adv* : con admiración

admissible [æd'mɪsəbəl] *adj* : admisible, aceptable

admission [æd'mɪʃən] *n* **1** ADMITTANCE : entrada *f,* admisión *f* **2** ACKNOWLEDGMENT : reconocimiento *m,* admisión *f*

admit [æd'mɪt, əd-] *vt* **-mitted; -mitting 1** : admitir, dejar entrar <the museum admits children : el museo deja entrar a los niños> **2** ACKNOWLEDGE : reconocer, admitir

admittance [æd'mɪtənts, əd-] *n* : admisión *f,* entrada *f,* acceso *m*

admittedly [æd'mɪṭədli, əd-] *adv* : la verdad es que, lo cierto es que <admittedly we went too fast : la verdad es que fuimos demasiado de prisa>

admonish [æd'mɑnɪʃ, əd-] *vt* : amonestar, reprender

admonition [ˌædmə'nɪʃən] *n* : admonición *f*

ado [ə'duː] *n* **1** FUSS : ruido *m,* alboroto *m* **2** TROUBLE : dificultad *f,* lío *m* **3** **without further ado** : sin más preámbulos

adobe [ə'doːbi] *n* : adobe *m*

adolescence [ˌædəl'ɛsənts] *n* : adolescencia *f*

adolescent[1] [ˌædəl'ɛsənt] *adj* : adolescente, de adolescencia

adolescent[2] *n* : adolescente *mf*

adopt [ə'dɑpt] *vt* : adoptar

adoption [ə'dɑpʃən] *n* : adopción *f*

adorable [ə'dorəbəl] *adj* : adorable, encantador

adorably [ə'dorəbli] *adv* : de manera adorable

adoration [ˌædə'reɪʃən] *n* : adoración *f*

adore [ə'dor] *vt* **adored; adoring 1** WORSHIP : adorar **2** LOVE : querer, adorar **3** LIKE : encantarle (algo a uno), gustarle mucho (algo a uno) <I adore your new dress : me encanta tu vestido nuevo>

adorn [ə'dɔrn] *vt* : adornar, ornar, engalanar

adornment [ə'dɔrnmənt] *n* : adorno *m,* decoración *f*

adrift [ə'drɪft] *adj & adv* : a la deriva

adroit [ə'drɔɪt] *adj* : diestro, hábil — **adroitly** *adv*

adroitness [ə'drɔɪtnəs] *n* : destreza *f,* habilidad *f*

adult[1] [ə'dʌlt, 'æˌdʌlt] *adj* : adulto

adult[2] *n* : adulto *m,* -ta *f*

adulterate [ə'dʌltəˌreɪt] *vt* **-ated; -ating** : adulterar

adulterous [ə'dʌltərəs] *adj* : adúltero

adultery [ə'dʌltəri] *n, pl* **-teries** : adulterio *m*

adulthood [ə'dʌltˌhʊd] *n* : adultez *f,* edad *f* adulta

advance[1] [æd'vænts, əd-] *v* **-vanced; -vancing** *vt* **1** : avanzar, adelantar <to advance troops : avanzar las tropas> **2** PROMOTE : ascender, promover **3** PROPOSE : proponer, presentar **4** : adelantar, anticipar <they advanced me next month's salary : me adelantaron el sueldo del próximo mes> — *vi* **1** PROCEED : avanzar, adelantarse **2** PROGRESS : progresar

advance[2] *adj* : anticipado <advance notice : previo aviso>

advance[3] *n* **1** PROGRESSION : avance *m* **2** PROGRESS : adelanto *m,* mejora *f,* pro-

greso *m* 3 RISE : aumento *m,* alza *f* 4 LOAN : anticipo *m,* préstamo *m* **5 in ~** : por adelantado
advanced [æd'væntst, əd-] *adj* **1** DEVELOPED : avanzado, desarrollado **2** PRECOCIOUS : adelantado, precoz **3** HIGHER : superior
advancement [æd'væntsmənt, əd-] *n* **1** FURTHERANCE : fomento *m,* adelantamiento *m,* progreso *m* **2** PROMOTION : ascenso *m*
advantage [əd'væntɪdʒ, æd-] *n* **1** SUPERIORITY : ventaja *f,* superioridad *f* **2** GAIN : provecho *m,* partido *m* **3 to take advantage of** : aprovecharse de
advantageous [ˌædˌvæn'teɪdʒəs, -vən-] *adj* : ventajoso, provechoso — **advantageously** *adv*
advent ['ædˌvɛnt] *n* **1 Advent** : Adviento *m* **2** ARRIVAL : advenimiento *m,* venida *f*
adventure [æd'vɛntʃər, əd-] *n* : aventura *f*
adventurer [æd'vɛntʃərər, əd-] *n* : aventurero *m,* -ra *f*
adventurous [æd'vɛntʃərəs, əd-] *adj* **1** : intrépido, aventurero <an adventurous traveler : un viajero intrépido> **2** RISKY : arriesgado, aventurado
adverb ['ædˌvərb] *n* : adverbio *m* — **adverbial** [æd'vərbiəl] *adj*
adversary ['ædvərˌsɛri] *n, pl* **-saries** : adversario *m,* -ria *f*
adverse [æd'vərs, 'æd-ˌ] *adj* **1** OPPOSING : opuesto, contrario **2** UNFAVORABLE : adverso, desfavorable — **adversely** *adv*
adversity [æd'vərsəṭi, əd-] *n, pl* **-ties** : adversidad *f*
advertise ['ædvərˌtaɪz] *v* **-tised; -tising** *vt* : anunciar, hacerle publicidad a — *vi* : hacer publicidad, hacer propaganda
advertisement ['ædvərˌtaɪzmənt; æd'vərṭəzmənt] *n* : anuncio *m*
advertiser ['ædvərˌtaɪzər] *n* : anunciante *mf*
advertising ['ædvərˌtaɪzɪŋ] *n* : publicidad *f,* propaganda *f*
advice [æd'vaɪs] *n* : consejo *m,* recomendación *f* <take my advice : sigue mis consejos>
advisability [ædˌvaɪzə'bɪləṭi, əd-] *n* : conveniencia *f*
advisable [æd'vaɪzəbəl, əd-] *adj* : aconsejable, recomendable, conveniente
advise [æd'vaɪz, əd-] *v* **-vised; -vising** *vt* **1** COUNSEL : aconsejar, asesorar **2** RECOMMEND : recomendar **3** INFORM : informar, notificar — *vi* : dar consejo
adviser *or* **advisor** [æd'vaɪzər, əd-] *n* : consejero *m,* -ra *f;* asesor *m,* -sora *f*
advisory [æd'vaɪzəri, əd-] *adj* **1** : consultivo **2 in an advisory capacity** : como asesor
advocacy ['ædvəkəsi] *n* : promoción *f,* apoyo *m*
advocate[1] ['ædvəˌkeɪt] *vt* **-cated; -cating** : recomendar, abogar por, ser partidario de
advocate[2] ['ædvəkət] *n* : defensor *m,* -sora *f;* partidario *m,* -ria *f*
adze ['ædz] *n* : azuela *f*
aeon ['iːən, 'iːˌɑn] *n* : eón *m,* siglo *m,* eternidad *f*
aerate ['ærˌeɪt] *vt* **-ated; -ating** : gasear (un líquido), oxigenar (la sangre)
aerial[1] ['æriəl] *adj* : aéreo
aerial[2] *n* : antena *f*
aerie ['æri, 'ɪri, 'eɪəri] *n* : aguilera *f*
aerobic [ˌær'oːbɪk] *adj* : aerobio, aeróbico <aerobic exercises : ejercicios aeróbicos>
aerobics [ˌær'oːbɪks] *ns & pl* : aeróbic *m*
aerodynamic [ˌæroːdaɪ'næmɪk] *adj* : aerodinámico — **aerodynamically** [-mikli] *adv*
aerodynamics [ˌæroːdaɪ'næmɪks] *n* : aerodinámica *f*
aeronautical [ˌærə'nɔṭɪkəl] *adj* : aeronáutico
aeronautics [ˌærə'nɔṭɪks] *n* : aeronáutica *f*
aerosol ['ærəˌsɔl] *n* : aerosol *m*
aerospace[1] ['æroˌspeɪs] *adj* : aeroespacial
aerospace[2] *n* : espacio *m*
aesthetic [ɛs'θɛṭɪk] *adj* : estético — **aesthetically** [-ṭɪkli] *adv*
aesthetics [ɛs'θɛṭɪks] *n* : estética *f*
afar [ə'fɑr] *adv* : lejos, a lo lejos
affability [ˌæfə'bɪləṭi] *n* : afabilidad *f*
affable ['æfəbəl] *adj* : afable — **affably** *adv*
affair [ə'fær] *n* **1** MATTER : asunto *m,* cuestión *f,* caso *m* **2** EVENT : ocasión *f,* acontecimiento *m* **3** LIAISON : amorío *m,* aventura *f* **4 business affairs** : negocios *mpl* **5 current affairs** : actualidades *fpl*
affect [ə'fɛkt, æ-] *vt* **1** INFLUENCE, TOUCH : afectar, tocar **2** FEIGN : fingir
affectation [ˌæˌfɛk'teɪʃən] *n* : afectación *f*
affected [ə'fɛktəd, æ-] *adj* **1** FEIGNED : afectado, fingido **2** MOVED : conmovido
affecting [ə'fɛktɪŋ, æ-] *adj* : conmovedor
affection [ə'fɛkʃən] *n* : afecto *m,* cariño *m*
affectionate [ə'fɛkʃənət] *adj* : afectuoso, cariñoso — **affectionately** *adv*
affidavit [ˌæfə'deɪvət, 'æfəˌ-] *n* : declaración *f* jurada, affidávit *m*
affiliate[1] [ə'fɪliˌeɪt] *v* **-ated; -ating** *vt* : afiliar, asociar <to be affiliated with : estar afiliado a>
affiliate[2] [ə'fɪliət] *n* : afiliado *m,* -da *f* (persona), filial *f* (organización)
affiliation [əˌfɪli'eɪʃən] *n* : afiliación *f,* filiación *f*
affinity [ə'fɪnəṭi] *n, pl* **-ties** : afinidad *f*

affirm [ə'fərm] *vt* : afirmar, aseverar, declarar

affirmation [ˌæfər'meɪʃən] *n* : afirmación *f,* aserto *m,* declaración *f*

affirmative[1] [ə'fərmətɪv] *adj* : afirmativo <affirmative action : acción afirmativa>

affirmative[2] *n* **1** : afirmativa *f* **2 to answer in the affirmative** : responder afirmativamente, dar una respuesta afirmativa

affix [ə'fɪks] *vt* : fijar, poner, pegar

afflict [ə'flɪkt] *vt* **1** : afligir, aquejar **2 to be afflicted with** : padecer de, sufrir de

affliction [ə'flɪkʃən] *n* **1** TRIBULATION : aflicción *f,* tribulación *f* **2** AILMENT : enfermedad *f,* padecimiento *m*

affluence ['æˌflu:ən*t*s; æ'flu:-, ə-] *n* : afluencia *f,* abundancia *f,* prosperidad *f*

affluent ['æˌflu:ənt; æ'flu:-, ə-] *adj* : próspero, adinerado

afford [ə'ford] *vt* **1** : tener los recursos para, permitirse el lujo de <I can afford it : puedo permitírmelo, tengo con que comprarlo> **2** PROVIDE : ofrecer, proporcionar, dar

affront[1] [ə'frʌnt] *vt* : afrentar, insultar, ofender

affront[2] *n* : afrenta *f,* insulto *m,* ofensa *f*

Afghan ['æfˌgæn, -gən] *n* : afgano *m,* -na *f* — **Afghan** *adj*

afire [ə'faɪr] *adj* : ardiendo, en llamas

aflame [ə'fleɪm] *adj* : llameante, en llamas

afloat [ə'flo:t] *adv & adj* : a flote

afoot [ə'fʊt] *adj* **1** WALKING : a pie, andando **2** UNDER WAY : en marcha <something suspicious is afoot : algo sospechoso se está tramando>

aforesaid [ə'forˌsɛd] *adj* : antes mencionado, antedicho

afraid [ə'freɪd] *adj* **1 to be afraid** : tener miedo **2 to be afraid that** : temerse que <I'm afraid not : me temo que no>

afresh [ə'frɛʃ] *adv* **1** : de nuevo, otra vez **2 to start afresh** : volver a empezar

African ['æfrɪkən] *n* : africano *m,* -na *f* — **African** *adj*

Afro–American[1] [ˌæfroə'mɛrɪkən] *adj* : afroamericano *m,* -na *f*

Afro–American[2] *n* : afroamericano

aft ['æft] *adv* : a popa

after[1] ['æftər] *adv* **1** AFTERWARD : después **2** BEHIND : detrás, atrás

after[2] *adj* : posterior, siguiente <in after years : en los años posteriores>

after[3] *conj* : después de, después de que <after we ate : después de que comimos, después de comer>

after[4] *prep* **1** FOLLOWING : después de, tras <after Saturday : después del sábado> <day after day : día tras día> **2** BEHIND : tras de, después de <I ran after the dog : corrí tras del perro> **3** CONCERNING : por <they asked after you : preguntaron por ti> **4 after all** : después de todo

aftereffect ['æftərɪˌfɛkt] *n* : efecto *m* secundario

afterlife ['æftərˌlaɪf] *n* : vida *f* venidera, vida *f* después de la muerte

aftermath ['æftərˌmæθ] *n* : consecuencias *fpl,* resultados *mpl*

afternoon [ˌæftər'nu:n] *n* : tarde *f*

afterthought ['æftərˌθɔt] *n* : ocurrencia *f* tardía, idea *f* tardía

afterward ['æftərwərd] *or* **afterwards** [-wərdz] *adv* : después, luego <soon afterward : poco después>

again [ə'gɛn, -'gɪn] *adv* **1** ANEW, OVER : de nuevo, otra vez **2** BESIDES : además **3 then again** : por otra parte <I may stay, then again I may not : puede ser que me quede, por otra parte, puede que no>

against [ə'gɛn*t*st, -'gɪn*t*st] *prep* **1** TOUCHING : contra <against the wall : contra la pared> **2** OPPOSING : contra, en contra de <I will vote against the proposal : votaré en contra de la propuesta> <against the grain : a contrapelo>

agape [ə'geɪp] *adj* : boquiabierto

agate ['ægət] *n* : ágata *f*

age[1] ['eɪdʒ] *vi* **aged; aging** : envejecer, madurar

age[2] *n* **1** : edad *f* <ten years of age : diez años de edad> <to be of age : ser mayor de edad> **2** PERIOD : era *f,* siglo *m,* época *f* **3 old age** : vejez *f* **4 ages** *npl* : siglos *mpl,* eternidad *f*

aged *adj* **1** ['eɪdʒəd, 'eɪdʒd] OLD : anciano, viejo, vetusto **2** ['eɪdʒd] (*indicating a specified age*) <a girl aged 10 : una niña de 10 años de edad>

ageless ['eɪdʒləs] *adj* **1** YOUTHFUL : eternamente joven **2** TIMELESS : eterno, perenne

agency ['eɪdʒən*t*si] *n, pl* **-cies 1** : agencia *f,* oficina *f* <travel agency : agencia de viajes> **2 through the agency of** : a través de, por medio de

agenda [ə'dʒɛndə] *n* : agenda *f,* orden *m* del día

agent ['eɪdʒənt] *n* **1** MEANS : agente *m,* medio *m,* instrumento *m* **2** REPRESENTATIVE : agente *mf,* representante *mf*

aggravate ['ægrəˌveɪt] *vt* **-vated; -vating 1** WORSEN : agravar, empeorar **2** ANNOY : irritar, exasperar

aggravation [ˌægrə'veɪʃən] *n* **1** WORSENING : empeoramiento *m* **2** ANNOYANCE : molestia *f,* irritación *f,* exasperación *f*

aggregate[1] ['ægrɪˌgeɪt] *vt* **-gated; -gating** : juntar, sumar

aggregate[2] ['ægrɪgət] *adj* : total, global, conjunto

aggregate[3] ['ægrɪgət] *n* **1** CONGLOMERATE : agregado *m,* conglomerado *m* **2** WHOLE : total *m,* conjunto *m*

aggression [ə'grɛʃən] *n* **1** ATTACK : agresión *f* **2** AGGRESSIVENESS : agresividad *f*

aggressive [ə'grɛsɪv] *adj* : agresivo — **aggressively** *adv*

aggressiveness [ə'grɛsɪvnəs] *n* : agresividad *f*

aggressor [ə'grɛsər] *n* : agresor *m*, -sora *f*

aggrieved [ə'gri:vd] *adj* : ofendido, herido

aghast [ə'gæst] *adj* : espantado, aterrado, horrorizado

agile ['ædʒəl] *adj* : ágil

agility [ə'dʒɪləṭi] *n, pl* **-ties** : agilidad *f*

agitate ['ædʒə,teɪt] *v* **-tated; -tating** *vt* **1** SHAKE : agitar **2** UPSET : inquietar, perturbar — *vi* **to agitate against** : hacer campaña en contra de

agitation [,ædʒə'teɪʃən] *n* : agitación *f*, inquietud *f*

agitator ['ædʒə,teɪṭər] *n* : agitador *m*, -dora *f*

agnostic [æg'nɑstɪk] *n* : agnóstico *m*, -ca *f*

ago [ə'go:] *adv* : hace <two years ago : hace dos años> <long ago : hace tiempo, hace mucho tiempo>

agog [ə'gɑg] *adj* : ansioso, curioso

agonize ['ægə,naɪz] *vi* **-nized; -nizing** : tormentarse, angustiarse

agonizing ['ægə,naɪzɪŋ] *adj* : angustioso, terrible — **agonizingly** [-zɪŋli] *adv*

agony ['ægəni] *n, pl* **-nies** **1** PAIN : dolor *m* **2** ANGUISH : angustia *f*

agrarian [ə'grɛriən] *adj* : agrario

agree [ə'gri:] *v* **agreed; agreeing** *vt* ACKNOWLEDGE : estar de acuerdo <he agreed that I was right : estuvo de acuerdo en que tenía razón> — *vi* **1** CONCUR : estar de acuerdo **2** CONSENT : ponerse de acuerdo **3** TALLY : concordar **4 to agree with** : sentarle bien (a alguien) <this climate agrees with me : este clima me sienta bien>

agreeable [ə'gri:əbəl] *adj* **1** PLEASING : agradable, simpático **2** WILLING : dispuesto **3** AGREEING : de acuerdo, conforme

agreeably [ə'gri:əbli] *adv* : agradablemente

agreement [ə'gri:mənt] *n* **1** : acuerdo *m*, conformidad *f* <in agreement with : de acuerdo con> **2** CONTRACT, PACT : acuerdo *m*, pacto *m*, convenio *m* **3** CONCORD, HARMONY : concordia *f*

agriculture ['ægrɪ,kʌltʃər] *n* : agricultura *f* — **agricultural** [,ægrɪ'kʌltʃərəl] *adj*

aground [ə'graʊnd] *adj* : encallado, varado

ahead [ə'hɛd] *adv* **1** : al frente, delante, adelante <he walked ahead : caminó delante> **2** BEFOREHAND : por adelantado, con antelación **3** LEADING : a la delantera **4 to get ahead** : adelantar, progresar

ahead of *prep* **1** : al frente de, delante de, antes de **2 to get ahead of** : adelantarse a

ahoy [ə'hɔɪ] *interj* **ship ahoy!** : ¡barco a la vista!

aid[1] ['eɪd] *vt* : ayudar, auxiliar

aid[2] *n* **1** HELP : ayuda *f*, asistencia *f* **2** ASSISTANT : asistente *mf*

aide ['eɪd] *n* : ayudante *mf*

AIDS ['eɪdz] *n* : SIDA *m*, sida *m*

ail ['eɪl] *vt* : molestar, afligir — *vi* : sufrir, estar enfermo

aileron ['eɪlə,rɑn] *n* : alerón *m*

ailment ['eɪlmənt] *n* : enfermedad *f*, dolencia *f*, achaque *m*

aim[1] ['eɪm] *vt* **1** : apuntar (un arma), dirigir (una observación) **2** INTEND : proponerse, querer <he aims to do it tonight : se propone hacerlo esta noche> — *vi* **1** POINT : apuntar **2 to aim at** : aspirar a

aim[2] *n* **1** MARKSMANSHIP : puntería *f* **2** GOAL : propósito *m*, objetivo *m*, fin *m*

aimless ['eɪmləs] *adj* : sin rumbo, sin objeto

aimlessly ['eɪmləsli] *adv* : sin rumbo, sin objeto

air[1] ['ær] *vt* **1** : airear, ventilar <to air out a mattress : airear un colchón> **2** EXPRESS : airear, manifestar, comunicar **3** BROADCAST : transmitir, emitir

air[2] *n* **1** : aire *m* **2** MELODY : aire *m* **3** APPEARANCE : aire *m*, aspecto *m* **4 airs** *npl* : aires *mpl*, afectación *f* **5 by ~** : por avión (dícese de una carta), en avión (dícese de una persona) **6 to be on the air** : estar en el aire, estar emitiendo

airborne ['ær,born] *adj* **1** : aerotransportado <airborne troops : tropas aerotransportadas> **2** FLYING : volando, en el aire

air–condition [,ærkən'dɪʃən] *vt* : climatizar, condicionar con el aire

air conditioner [,ærkən'dɪʃənər] *n* : acondicionador *m* de aire

air–conditioning [,ærkən'dɪʃənɪŋ] *n* : aire *m* acondicionado

aircraft ['ær,kræft] *ns & pl* **1** : avión *m*, aeronave *f* **2 aircraft carrier** : portaaviones *m*

airfield ['ær,fi:ld] *n* : aeródromo *m*, campo *m* de aviación

air force *n* : fuerza *f* aérea

airlift ['ær,lɪft] *n* : puente *m* aéreo, transporte *m* aéreo

airline ['ær,laɪn] *n* : aerolínea *f*, línea *f* aérea

airliner ['ær,laɪnər] *n* : avión *m* de pasajeros

airmail[1] ['ær,meɪl] *vt* : enviar por vía aérea

airmail[2] *n* : correo *m* aéreo

airman ['ærmən] *n, pl* **-men** [-mən, -,mɛn] **1** AVIATOR : aviador *m*, -dora *f* **2** : soldado *m* de la fuerza aérea

airplane ['ær,pleɪn] *n* : avión *m*

airport ['ær,port] *n* : aeropuerto *m*

airship [ˈær,ʃɪp] *n* : dirigible *m,* zepelín *m*

airstrip [ˈær,strɪp] *n* : pista *f* de aterrizaje

airtight [ˈærˈtaɪt] *adj* : hermético, herméticamente cerrado

airwaves [ˈær,weɪvz] *npl* : radio *m,* televisión *f*

airy [ˈæri] *adj* **airier** [-iər]; **-est 1** DELICATE, LIGHT : delicado, ligero **2** BREEZY : aireado, bien ventilado

aisle [ˈaɪl] *n* : pasillo *m,* nave *f* lateral (de una iglesia)

ajar [əˈdʒɑr] *adj* : entreabierto, entornado

akimbo [əˈkɪmbo] *adj & adv* : en jarras

akin [əˈkɪn] *adj* **1** RELATED : emparentado **2** SIMILAR : semejante, parecido

alabaster [ˈælə,bæstər] *n* : alabastro *m*

alacrity [əˈlækrəti] *n* : presteza *f,* prontitud *f*

alarm¹ [əˈlɑrm] *vt* **1** WARN : alarmar, alertar **2** FRIGHTEN : asustar

alarm² *n* **1** WARNING : alarma *f,* alerta *f* **2** APPREHENSION, FEAR : aprensión *f,* inquietud *f,* temor *m* **3 alarm clock** : despertador *m*

alas [əˈlæs] *interj* : ¡ay!

Albanian [ælˈbeɪniən] *n* : albanés *m,* -nesa *f* — **Albanian** *adj*

albatross [ˈælbə,trɔs] *n, pl* **-tross** *or* **-trosses** : albatros *m*

albeit [ɔlˈbiːət, æl-] *conj* : aunque

albino [ælˈbaɪno] *n, pl* **-nos** : albino *m,* -na *f*

album [ˈælbəm] *n* : álbum *m*

albumen [ælˈbjuːmən] *n* **1** : clara *f* de huevo **2** → **albumin**

albumin [ælˈbjuːmən] *n* : albúmina *f*

alcohol [ˈælkə,hɔl] *n* **1** ETHANOL : alcohol *m,* etanol *m* **2** LIQUOR : alcohol *m,* bebidas *fpl* alcohólicas

alcoholic¹ [,ælkəˈhɔlɪk] *adj* : alcohólico

alcoholic² *n* : alcohólico *m,* -ca *f*

alcoholism [ˈælkəhɔ,lɪzəm] *n* : alcoholismo *m*

alcove [ˈæl,koːv] *n* : nicho *m,* hueco *m*

alderman [ˈɔldərmən] *n, pl* **-men** [-mən, -,mɛn] : concejal *mf*

ale [ˈeɪl] *n* : cerveza *f*

alert¹ [əˈlərt] *vt* : alertar, poner sobre aviso

alert² *adj* **1** WATCHFUL : alerta, vigilante **2** QUICK : listo, vivo

alert³ *n* : alerta *f,* alarma *f*

alertly [əˈlərtli] *adv* : con listeza

alertness [əˈlərtnəs] *n* **1** WATCHFULNESS : vigilancia *f* **2** ASTUTENESS : listeza *f,* viveza *f*

alfalfa [ælˈfælfə] *n* : alfalfa *f*

alga [ˈælgə] *n, pl* **-gae** [ˈæl,dʒiː] : alga *f*

algebra [ˈældʒəbrə] *n* : álgebra *m*

algebraic [,ældʒəˈbreɪɪk] *adj* : algebraico — **algebraically** [-ɪkli] *adv*

Algerian [ælˈdʒɪriən] *n* : argelino *m,* -na *f* — **Algerian** *adj*

alias¹ [ˈeɪliəs] *adv* : alias

alias² *n* : alias *m*

alibi¹ [ˈælə,baɪ] *vi* : ofrecer una coartada

alibi² *n* **1** : coartada *f* **2** EXCUSE : pretexto *m,* excusa *f*

alien¹ [ˈeɪliən] *adj* **1** STRANGE : ajeno, extraño **2** FOREIGN : extranjero, foráneo **3** EXTRATERRESTRIAL : extraterrestre

alien² *n* **1** FOREIGNER : extranjero *m,* -ra *f;* forastero *m,* -ra *f* **2** EXTRATERRESTRIAL : extraterrestre *mf*

alienate [ˈeɪliə,neɪt] *vt* **-ated; -ating 1** ESTRANGE : alienar, enajenar **2 to alienate oneself** : alejarse, distanciarse

alienation [,eɪliəˈneɪʃən] *n* : alienación *f,* enajenación *f*

alight [əˈlaɪt] *vi* **1** DISMOUNT : bajarse, apearse **2** LAND : posarse, aterrizar

align [əˈlaɪn] *vt* : alinear

alignment [əˈlaɪnmənt] *n* : alineación *f,* alineamiento *m*

alike¹ [əˈlaɪk] *adv* : igual, del mismo modo

alike² *adj* : igual, semejante, parecido

alimentary [,æləˈmɛntəri] *adj* **1** : alimenticio **2 alimentary canal** : tubo *m* digestivo

alimony [ˈælə,moːni] *n, pl* **-nies** : pensión *f* alimenticia

alive [əˈlaɪv] *adj* **1** LIVING : vivo, viviente **2** LIVELY : animado, activo **3** ACTIVE : vigente, en uso **4** AWARE : consciente <alive to the danger : consciente del peligro>

alkali [ˈælkə,laɪ] *n, pl* **-lies** [-,laɪz] *or* **-lis** [-,laɪz] : álcali *m*

alkaline [ˈælkələn, -,laɪn] *adj* : alcalino

all¹ [ˈɔl] *adv* **1** COMPLETELY : todo, completamente **2** : igual <the score is 14 all : es 14 iguales, están empatados a 14> **3 all the better** : tanto mejor **4 all the more** : aún más, todavía más

all² *adj* : todo <all the children : todos los niños> <in all likelihood : con toda probabilidad, con la mayor probabilidad>

all³ *pron* **1** : todo, -da <they ate it all : lo comieron todo> <that's all : eso es todo> <enough for all : suficiente para todos> **2 all in all** : en general **3 not at all** (*in negative constructions*) : en absoluto, para nada

Allah [ˈɑlɑ, ɑˈlɑ] *n* : Alá *m*

all–around [,ɔləˈraʊnd] *adj* : completo, amplio

allay [əˈleɪ] *vt* **1** ALLEVIATE : aliviar, mitigar **2** CALM : aquietar, calmar

allegation [,ælɪˈgeɪʃən] *n* : alegato *m,* acusación *f*

allege [əˈlɛdʒ] *vt* **-leged; -leging 1** : alegar, afirmar **2 to be alleged** : decirse, pretenderse <she is alleged

to be wealthy : se dice que es adinerada>

alleged [ə'lɛdʒd, ə'lɛdʒəd] *adj* : presunto, supuesto

allegedly [ə'lɛdʒədli] : *adv* : supuestamente, según se alega

allegiance [ə'li:dʒən*t*s] *n* : lealtad *f,* fidelidad *f*

allegorical [ˌælə'gɔrɪkəl] *adj* : alegórico

allegory ['æləˌgori] *n, pl* **-ries** : alegoría *f*

alleluia [ˌɑlə'lu:jə, ˌæ-] → **hallelujah**

allergic [ə'lərdʒɪk] *adj* : alérgico

allergy ['ælərdʒi] *n, pl* **-gies** : alergia *f*

alleviate [ə'li:viˌeɪt] *vt* **-ated; -ating** : aliviar, mitigar, paliar

alleviation [əˌli:vi'eɪʃən] *n* : alivio *m*

alley ['æli] *n, pl* **-leys 1** : callejón *m* **2 bowling alley** : bolera *f*

alliance [ə'laɪən*t*s] *n* : alianza *f,* coalición *f*

alligator ['æləˌgeɪt̬ər] *n* : caimán *m*

alliteration [əˌlɪt̬ə'reɪʃən] *n* : aliteración *f*

allocate ['æləˌkeɪt] *vt* **-cated; -cating** : asignar, adjudicar

allocation [ˌælə'keɪʃən] *n* : asignación *f,* reparto *m,* distribución *f*

allot [ə'lɑt] *vt* **-lotted; -lotting** : repartir, distribuir, asignar

allotment [ə'lɑtmənt] *n* : reparto *m,* asignación *f,* distribución *f*

allow [ə'laʊ] *vt* **1** PERMIT : permitir, dejar **2** ALLOT : conceder, dar **3** ADMIT, CONCEDE : admitir, conceder — *vi* **to allow for** : tener en cuenta

allowable [ə'laʊəbəl] *adj* **1** PERMISSIBLE : permisible, lícito **2** : deducible <allowable expenditure : gasto deducible>

allowance [ə'laʊən*t*s] *n* **1** : complemento *m* (para gastos, etc.), mesada *f* (para niños) **2 to make allowance(s)** : tener en cuenta, disculpar

alloy ['æˌlɔɪ] *n* : aleación *f*

all right[1] *adv* **1** YES : sí, por supuesto **2** WELL : bien <I did all right : me fue bien> **3** DEFINITELY : bien, ciertamente, sin duda <he's sick all right : está bien enfermo>

all right[2] *adj* **1** OK : bien <are you all right? : ¿estás bien?> **2** SATISFACTORY : bien, bueno <your work is all right : tu trabajo es bueno>

all–round [ˌɔl'raʊnd] → **all–around**

allspice ['ɔlspaɪs] *n* : pimienta *f* de Jamaica

allude [ə'lu:d] *vi* **-luded; -luding** : aludir, referirse

allure[1] [ə'lʊr] *vt* **-lured; -luring** : cautivar, atraer

allure[2] *n* : atractivo *m,* encanto *m*

allusion [ə'lu:ʒən] *n* : alusión *f*

ally[1] [ə'laɪ, 'æˌlaɪ] *vi* **-lied; -lying** : aliarse

ally[2] ['æˌlaɪ, ə'laɪ] *n* : aliado *m,* -da *f*

almanac ['ɔlməˌnæk, 'æl-] *n* : almanaque *m*

almighty [ɔl'maɪt̬i] *adj* : omnipotente, todopoderoso

almond ['ɑmənd, 'ɑl-, 'æ-, 'æl-] *n* : almendra *f*

almost ['ɔlˌmo:st, ɔl'mo:st] *adv* : casi, prácticamente

alms ['ɑmz, 'ɑlmz, 'ælmz] *ns & pl* : limosna *f,* caridad *f*

aloft [ə'lɔft] *adv* : en alto, en el aire

alone[1] [ə'lo:n] *adv* : sólo, solamente, únicamente

alone[2] *adj* : solo <they're alone in the house : están solos en la casa>

along[1] [ə'lɔŋ] *adv* **1** FORWARD : adelante <farther along : más adelante> <move along! : ¡circulen, por favor!> **2 to bring along** : traer **3 ~ with** : con, junto con **4 all along** : desde el principio

along[2] *prep* **1** : por, a lo largo de <along the coast : a lo largo de la costa> **2** : en, en el curso de, por <along the way : en el curso del viaje>

alongside[1] [əˌlɔŋ'saɪd] *adv* : al costado, al lado

alongside[2] *or* **alongside of** *prep* : junto a, al lado de

aloof [ə'lu:f] *adj* : distante, reservado

aloofness [ə'lu:fnəs] *n* : reserva *f,* actitud *f* distante

aloud [ə'laʊd] *adv* : en voz alta

alpaca [æl'pækə] *n* : alpaca *f*

alphabet ['ælfəˌbɛt] *n* : alfabeto *m*

alphabetical [ˌælfə'bɛt̬ɪkəl] *or* **alphabetic** [-'bɛtɪk] *adj* : alfabético — **alphabetically** [-tɪkli] *adv*

alphabetize ['ælfəbəˌtaɪz] *vt* **-ized; -izing** : alfabetizar, poner en orden alfabético

already [ɔl'rɛdi] *adv* : ya

also ['ɔlˌso:] *adv* : también, además

altar ['ɔltər] *n* : altar *m*

alter ['ɔltər] *vt* : alterar, cambiar, modificar

alteration [ˌɔltə'reɪʃən] *n* : alteración *f,* cambio *m,* modificación *f*

altercation [ˌɔltər'keɪʃən] *n* : altercado *m,* disputa *f*

alternate[1] ['ɔltərˌneɪt] *v* **-nated; -nating** : alternar

alternate[2] ['ɔltərnət] *adj* **1** : alterno <alternate cycles of inflation and depression : ciclos alternos de inflación y depresión> **2** : uno sí y uno no <he cooks on alternate days : cocina un día sí y otro no>

alternate[3] ['ɔltərnət] *n* : suplente *mf;* sustituto *m,* -ta *f*

alternately ['ɔltərnətli] *adv* : alternativamente, por turno

alternating current ['ɔltərˌneɪt̬ɪŋ] *n* : corriente *f* alterna

alternation [ˌɔltər'neɪʃən] *n* : alternancia *f,* rotación *f*

alternative[1] [ɔl'tərnət̬ɪv] *adj* : alternativo

alternative[2] *n* : alternativa *f*

alternator [ˈɔltərˌneɪt̬ər] *n* : alternador *m*

although [ɔlˈðoː] *conj* : aunque, a pesar de que

altitude [ˈæltəˌtuːd, -ˌtjuːd] *n* : altitud *f*, altura *f*

alto [ˈælˌtoː] *n, pl* **-tos** : alto *mf*, contralto *mf*

altogether [ˌɔltəˈgɛðər] *adv* **1** COMPLETELY : completamente, totalmente, del todo **2** ON THE WHOLE : en suma, en general

altruism [ˈæltrʊˌɪzəm] *n* : altruismo *m*

altruistic [ˌæltrʊˈɪstɪk] *adj* : altruista — **altruistically** [-tɪkli] *adv*

alum [ˈæləm] *n* : alumbre *m*

aluminum [əˈluːmənəm] *n* : aluminio *m*

alumna [əˈlʌmnə] *n, pl* **-nae** [-ˌniː] : ex-alumna *f*

alumnus [əˈlʌmnəs] *n, pl* **-ni** [-ˌnaɪ] : ex-alumno *m*

always [ˈɔlwiz, -ˌweɪz] *adv* **1** INVARIABLY : siempre, invariablemente **2** FOREVER : para siempre

am → **be**

amalgam [əˈmælgəm] *n* : amalgama *f*

amalgamate [əˈmælgəˌmeɪt] *vt* **-ated; -ating** : amalgamar, unir, fusionar

amalgamation [əˌmælgəˈmeɪʃən] *n* : fusión *f*, unión *f*

amaryllis [ˌæməˈrɪləs] *n* : amarilis *f*

amass [əˈmæs] *vt* : amasar, acumular

amateur [ˈæmətʃər, -tər, -ˌtʊr, -ˌtjʊr] *n* **1** : amateur *mf* **2** BEGINNER : principiante *mf*; aficionado *m*, -da *f*

amateurish [ˈæməˌtʃərɪʃ, -ˌtər-, -ˌtʊr-, -ˌtjʊr-] *adj* : amateur, inexperto

amaze [əˈmeɪz] *vt* **amazed; amazing** : asombrar, maravillar, pasmar

amazement [əˈmeɪzmənt] *n* : asombro *m*, sorpresa *f*

amazing [əˈmeɪzɪŋ] *adj* : asombroso, sorprendente — **amazingly** [-zɪŋli] *adv*

ambassador [æmˈbæsədər] *n* : embajador *m*, -dora *f*

amber [ˈæmbər] *n* : ámbar *m*

ambergris [ˈæmbərˌgrɪs, -ˌgriːs] *n* : ámbar *m* gris

ambidextrous [ˌæmbɪˈdɛkstrəs] *adj* : ambidextro — **ambidextrously** *adv*

ambience *or* **ambiance** [ˈæmbiən*t*s, ˈɑmbiˌɑn*t*s] *n* : ambiente *m*, atmósfera *f*

ambiguity [ˌæmbəˈgjuːət̬i] *n, pl* **-ties** : ambigüedad *f*

ambiguous [æmˈbɪgjʊəs] *adj* : ambiguo

ambition [æmˈbɪʃən] *n* : ambición *f*

ambitious [æmˈbɪʃəs] *adj* : ambicioso — **ambitiously** *adv*

ambivalence [æmˈbɪvələn*t*s] *n* : ambivalencia *f*

ambivalent [æmˈbɪvələnt] *adj* : ambivalente

amble[1] [ˈæmbəl] *vi* **-bled; -bling** : ir tranquilamente, pasearse despreocupadamente

amble[2] *n* : paseo *m* tranquilo

ambulance [ˈæmbjələn*t*s] *n* : ambulancia *f*

ambush[1] [ˈæmˌbʊʃ] *vt* : emboscar

ambush[2] *n* : emboscada *f*, celada *f*

ameliorate [əˈmiːljəˌreɪt] *v* **-rated; -rating** IMPROVE : mejorar

amelioration [əˌmiːljəˈreɪʃən] *n* : mejora *f*

amen [ˈeɪˈmɛn, ˈɑ-] *interj* : amén

amenable [əˈmiːnəbəl, -ˈmɛ-] *adj* RESPONSIVE : susceptible, receptivo, sensible

amend [əˈmɛnd] *vt* **1** IMPROVE : mejorar, enmendar **2** CORRECT : enmendar, corregir

amendment [əˈmɛndmənt] *n* : enmienda *f*

amends [əˈmɛndz] *ns & pl* : compensación *f*, reparación *f*, desagravio *m*

amenity [əˈmɛnət̬i, -ˈmiː-] *n, pl* **-ties 1** PLEASANTNESS : lo agradable, amenidad *f* **2 amenities** *npl* : servicios *mpl*, comodidades *fpl*

American [əˈmɛrɪkən] *n* : americano *m*, -na *f* — **American** *adj*

American Indian *n* : indio *m* (americano), india *f* (americana)

amethyst [ˈæməθəst] *n* : amatista *f*

amiability [ˌeɪmiːəˈbɪlət̬i] *n* : amabilidad *f*, afabilidad *f*

amiable [ˈeɪmiːəbəl] *adj* : amable, afable — **amiably** [-bli] *adv*

amicable [ˈæmɪkəbəl] *adj* : amigable, amistoso, cordial — **amicably** [-bli] *adv*

amid [əˈmɪd] *or* **amidst** [əˈmɪdst] *prep* : en medio de, entre

amino acid [əˈmiːno] *n* : aminoácido *m*

amiss[1] [əˈmɪs] *adv* : mal, fuera de lugar <to take amiss : tomar a mal, llevar a mal>

amiss[2] *adj* **1** WRONG : malo, inoportuno **2 there's something amiss** : pasa algo, algo anda mal

ammeter [ˈæˌmiːt̬ər] *n* : amperímetro *m*

ammonia [əˈmoːnjə] *n* : amoníaco *m*

ammunition [ˌæmjəˈnɪʃən] *n* **1** : municiones *fpl* **2** ARGUMENTS : argumentos *mpl*

amnesia [æmˈniːʒə] *n* : amnesia *f*

amnesty [ˈæmnəsti] *n, pl* **-ties** : amnistía *f*

amoeba [əˈmiːbə] *n, pl* **-bas** *or* **-bae** [-ˌbiː] : ameba *f*

amoebic [əˈmiːbɪk] *adj* : amébico

amok [əˈmʌk, -ˈmɑk] *adv* **to run amok** : correr a ciegas, enloquecerse, desbocarse (dícese de la economía, etc.)

among [əˈmʌŋ] *prep* : entre

amorous [ˈæmərəs] *adj* **1** PASSIONATE : enamoradizo, apasionado **2** ENAM-

ORED : enamorado 3 LOVING : amoroso, cariñoso
amorously [ˈæmərəsli] *adv* : con cariño
amorphous [əˈmɔrfəs] *adj* : amorfo, informe
amortize [ˈæmərˌtaɪz, əˈmɔr-] *vt* **-tized; -tizing** : amortizar
amount[1] [əˈmaʊnt] *vi* **to amount to 1** : equivaler a, significar <that amounts to treason : eso equivale a la traición> 2 : ascender (a) <my debts amount to $2000 : mis deudas ascienden a $2000>
amount[2] *n* : cantidad *f,* suma *f*
ampere [ˈæmˌpɪr] *n* : amperio *m*
ampersand [ˈæmpərˌsænd] *n* : el signo &
amphibian [æmˈfɪbiən] *n* : anfibio *m*
amphibious [æmˈfɪbiəs] *adj* : anfibio
amphitheater [ˈæmfəˌθiːət̬ər] *n* : anfiteatro *m*
ample [ˈæmpəl] *adj* **-pler; -plest 1** LARGE, SPACIOUS : amplio, extenso, grande **2** ABUNDANT : abundante, generoso
amplifier [ˈæmpləˌfaɪər] *n* : amplificador *m*
amplify [ˈæmpləˌfaɪ] *vt* **-fied; -fying** : amplificar
amply [ˈæmpli] *adv* : ampliamente, abundantemente, suficientemente
amputate [ˈæmpjəˌteɪt] *vt* **-tated; -tating** : amputar
amputation [ˌæmpjəˈteɪʃən] *n* : amputación *f*
amuck [əˈmʌk] → **amok**
amulet [ˈæmjələt] *n* : amuleto *m,* talismán *m*
amuse [əˈmjuːz] *vt* **amused; amusing 1** ENTERTAIN : entretener, distraer **2** : hacer reír, divertir <the joke amused us : la broma nos hizo reír>
amusement [əˈmjuːzmənt] *n* **1** ENTERTAINMENT : diversión *f,* entretenimiento *m,* pasatiempo *m* **2** LAUGHTER : risa *f*
an → **a**[2]
anachronism [əˈnækrəˌnɪzəm] *n* : anacronismo *m*
anachronistic [əˌnækrəˈnɪstɪk] *adj* : anacrónico
anaconda [ˌænəˈkɑndə] *n* : anaconda *f*
anagram [ˈænəˌgræm] *n* : anagrama *m*
anal [ˈeɪnəl] *adj* : anal
analgesic [ˌænəlˈdʒiːzɪk, -sɪk] *n* : analgésico *m*
analogical [ˌænəˈlɑdʒɪkəl] *adj* : analógico — **analogically** [-kli] *adv*
analogous [əˈnæləgəs] *adj* : análogo
analogy [əˈnælədʒi] *n, pl* **-gies** : analogía *f*
analysis [əˈnæləsəs] *n, pl* **-yses** [-ˌsiːz] **1** : análisis *m* **2** PSYCHOANALYSIS : psicoanálisis *m*
analyst [ˈænəlɪst] *n* **1** : analista *mf* **2** PSYCHOANALYST : psicoanalista *mf*
analytic [ˌænəˈlɪt̬ɪk] *or* **analytical** [-tɪkəl] *adj* : analítico — **analytically** [-t̬ɪkli] *adv*
analyze [ˈænəˌlaɪz] *vt* **-lyzed; -lyzing** : analizar
anarchic [æˈnɑrkɪk] *adj* : anárquico — **anarchically** [-kɪkli] *adv*
anarchism [ˈænərˌkɪzəm, -nɑr-] *n* : anarquismo *m*
anarchist [ˈænərkɪst, -nɑr-] *n* : anarquista *mf*
anarchy [ˈænərki, -nɑr-] *n* : anarquía *f*
anathema [əˈnæθəmə] *n* : anatema *m*
anatomic [ˌænəˈtɑmɪk] *or* **anatomical** [-mɪkəl] *adj* : anatómico — **anatomically** [-mɪkli] *adv*
anatomy [əˈnæt̬əmi] *n, pl* **-mies** : anatomía *f*
ancestor [ˈænˌsɛstər] *n* : antepasado *m,* -da *f;* antecesor *m,* -sora *f*
ancestral [ænˈsɛstrəl] *adj* : ancestral, de los antepasados
ancestry [ˈænˌsɛstri] *n* **1** DESCENT : ascendencia *f,* linaje *m,* abolengo *m* **2** ANCESTORS : antepasados *mpl,* -das *fpl*
anchor[1] [ˈæŋkər] *vt* **1** MOOR : anclar, fondear **2** FASTEN : sujetar, asegurar, fijar
anchor[2] *n* **1** : ancla *f* **2** : presentador *m,* -dora *f* (en televisión)
anchorage [ˈæŋkərɪdʒ] *n* : anclaje *m*
anchovy [ˈænˌtʃoːvi, ænˈtʃoː-] *n, pl* **-vies** *or* **-vy** : anchoa *f*
ancient [ˈeɪntʃənt] *adj* **1** : antiguo <ancient history : historia antigua> **2** OLD : viejo
ancients [ˈeɪntʃənts] *npl* : los antiguos *mpl*
and [ˈænd] *conj* **1** : y (e *before words beginning with i- or hi-*) **2** : con <ham and eggs : huevos con jamón> **3** : a <go and see : ve a ver> **4** : de <try and finish it soon : trata de terminarlo pronto>
andiron [ˈænˌdaɪərn] *n* : morillo *m*
Andorran [ænˈdɔrən] *n* : andorrano *m,* -na *f* — **Andorran** *adj*
androgynous [ænˈdrɑdʒənəs] *adj* : andrógino
anecdotal [ˌænɪkˈdoːt̬əl] *adj* : anecdótico
anecdote [ˈænɪkˌdoːt] *n* : anécdota *f*
anemia [əˈniːmiə] *n* : anemia *f*
anemic [əˈniːmɪk] *adj* : anémico
anemone [əˈnɛməni] *n* : anémona *f*
anesthesia [ˌænəsˈθiːʒə] *n* : anestesia *f*
anesthetic[1] [ˌænəsˈθɛt̬ɪk] *adj* : anestésico
anesthetic[2] *n* : anestésico *m*
anesthetist [əˈnɛsθətɪst] *n* : anestesista *mf*
anesthetize [əˈnɛsθəˌtaɪz] *vt* **-tize; -tized** : anestesiar
anew [əˈnuː, -ˈnjuː] *adv* : de nuevo, otra vez, nuevamente
angel [ˈeɪndʒəl] *n* : ángel *m*

angelic [æn'dʒɛlɪk] *or* **angelical** [-lɪkəl] *adj* **:** angélico — **angelically** [-lɪkli] *adv*

anger[1] ['æŋgər] *vt* **:** enojar, enfadar

anger[2] *n* **:** enojo *m,* enfado *m,* ira *f,* cólera *f,* rabia *f*

angina [æn'dʒaɪnə] *n* **:** angina *f*

angle[1] ['æŋgəl] *v* **angled; angling** *vt* DIRECT, SLANT **:** orientar, dirigir — *vi* FISH **:** pescar (con caña)

angle[2] *n* **1 :** ángulo *m* **2** POINT OF VIEW **:** perspectiva *f,* punto *m* de vista

angler ['æŋglər] *n* **:** pescador *m,* -dora *f*

Anglo–Saxon[1] [ˌæŋglo'sæksən] *adj* **:** anglosajón

Anglo–Saxon[2] *n* **:** anglosajón *m,* -jona *f*

Angolan [æŋ'goːlən, æn-] *n* **:** angoleño *m,* -ña *f* — **Angolan** *adj*

angora [æŋ'gorə, æn-] *n* **:** angora *f*

angrily ['æŋgrəli] *adv* **:** furiosamente, con ira

angry ['æŋgri] *adj* **-grier; -est :** enojado, enfadado, furioso

anguish ['æŋgwɪʃ] *n* **:** angustia *f,* congoja *f*

anguished ['æŋgwɪʃt] *adj* **:** angustiado, acongojado

angular ['æŋgjələr] *adj* **:** angular (dícese de las formas), anguloso (dícese de las caras)

animal ['ænəməl] *n* **1 :** animal *m* **2** BRUTE **:** bruto *m,* -ta *f*

animate[1] ['ænəˌmeɪt] *vt* **-mated; -mating :** animar

animate[2] ['ænəmət] *adj* **:** animado

animated ['ænəˌmeɪt̬əd] *adj* **1** LIVELY **:** animado, vivo, vivaz **2 animated cartoon :** dibujos *mpl* animados

animation [ˌænə'meɪʃən] *n* **:** animación *f*

animosity [ˌænə'mɑsət̬i] *n, pl* **-ties :** animosidad *f,* animadversión *f*

anise ['ænəs] *n* **:** anís *m*

aniseed ['ænəsˌsiːd] *n* **:** anís *m,* semilla *f* de anís

ankle ['æŋkəl] *n* **:** tobillo *m*

anklebone ['æŋkəlˌboːn] *n* **:** taba *f*

annals ['ænəlz] *npl* **:** anales *mpl,* crónica *f*

anneal [ə'niːl] *vt* **1** TEMPER **:** templar **2** STRENGTHEN **:** fortalecer

annex[1] [ə'nɛks, 'æˌnɛks] *vt* **:** anexar

annex[2] ['æˌnɛks, -nɪks] *n* **:** anexo *m,* anejo *m*

annexation [ˌæˌnɛk'seɪʃən] *n* **:** anexión *f*

annihilate [ə'naɪəˌleɪt] *vt* **-lated; -lating :** aniquilar

annihilation [əˌnaɪə'leɪʃən] *n* **:** aniquilación *f,* aniquilamiento *m*

anniversary [ˌænə'vərsəri] *n, pl* **-ries :** aniversario *m*

annotate ['ænəˌteɪt] *vt* **-tated; -tating :** anotar

annotation [ˌænə'teɪʃən] *n* **:** anotación *f*

announce [ə'naʊnts] *vt* **-nounced; -nouncing :** anunciar

announcement [ə'naʊntsmənt] *n* **:** anuncio *m*

announcer [ə'naʊntsər] *n* **:** anunciador *m,* -dora *f;* comentarista *mf;* locutor *m,* -tora *f*

annoy [ə'nɔɪ] *vt* **:** molestar, fastidiar, irritar

annoyance [ə'nɔɪənts] *n* **1** IRRITATION **:** irritación *f,* fastidio *m* **2** NUISANCE **:** molestia *f,* fastidio *m*

annoying [ə'nɔɪɪŋ] *adj* **:** molesto, fastidioso, engorroso — **annoyingly** [-ɪŋli] *adv*

annual[1] ['ænjʊəl] *adj* **:** anual — **annually** *adv*

annual[2] *n* **1 :** planta *f* anual **2** YEARBOOK **:** anuario *m*

annuity [ə'nuːət̬i] *n, pl* **-ties :** anualidad *f*

annul [ə'nʌl] *vt* **anulled; anulling :** anular, invalidar

annulment [ə'nʌlmənt] *n* **:** anulación *f*

anode ['æˌnoːd] *n* **:** ánodo

anoint [ə'nɔɪnt] *vt* **:** ungir

anomalous [ə'nɑmələs] *adj* **:** anómalo

anomaly [ə'nɑməli] *n, pl* **-lies :** anomalía *f*

anonymity [ˌænə'nɪmət̬i] *n* **:** anonimato *m*

anonymous [ə'nɑnəməs] *adj* **:** anónimo — **anonymously** *adv*

another[1] [ə'nʌðər] *adj* **:** otro

another[2] *pron* **:** otro, otra

answer[1] ['æntsər] *vt* **1 :** contestar (a), responder (a) <to answer the telephone **:** contestar el teléfono> **2** FULFILL **:** satisfacer **3 to answer for :** ser responsable de, pagar por <she'll answer for that mistake **:** pagará por ese error> — *vi* **:** contestar, responder

answer[2] *n* **1** REPLY **:** respuesta *f,* contestación *f* **2** SOLUTION **:** solución *f*

answerable ['æntsərəbəl] *adj* **:** responsable

ant ['ænt] *n* **:** hormiga *f*

antagonism [æn'tægəˌnɪzəm] *n* **:** antagonismo *m,* hostilidad *f*

antagonist [æn'tægənɪst] *n* **:** antagonista *mf*

antagonistic [ænˌtægə'nɪstɪk] *adj* **:** antagonista, hostil

antagonize [æn'tægəˌnaɪz] *vt* **-nized; -nizing :** antagonizar

antarctic [ænt'ɑrktɪk, -'ɑrt̬ɪk] *adj* **:** antártico

antarctic circle *n* **:** círculo *m* antártico

antebellum [ˌæntɪ'bɛləm] *adj* **:** prebélico

antecedent[1] [ˌæntə'siːdənt] *adj* **:** antecedente, precedente

antecedent[2] *n* **:** antecedente *mf;* precursor *m,* -sora *f*

antelope ['æntəlˌoːp] *n, pl* **-lope** *or* **-lopes :** antílope *m*

antenna [æn'tɛnə] *n, pl* **-nae** [-ˌniː, -ˌnaɪ] *or* **-nas :** antena *f*

anterior [æn'tɪriər] *adj* **:** anterior

anthem ['ænθəm] *n* **:** himno *m* <national anthem **:** himno nacional>

anther [ˈænθər] *n* : antera *f*
anthill [ˈæntˌhɪl] *n* : hormiguero *m*
anthology [ænˈθɑlədʒi] *n, pl* **-gies** : antología *f*
anthracite [ˈænθrəˌsaɪt] *n* : antracita *f*
anthropoid[1] [ˈænθrəˌpɔɪd] *adj* : antropoide
anthropoid[2] *n* : antropoide *mf*
anthropological [ˌænθrəpəˈlɑdʒɪkəl] *adj* : antropológico
anthropologist [ˌænθrəˈpɑlədʒɪst] *n* : antropólogo *m*, -ga *f*
anthropology [ˌænθrəˈpɑlədʒi] *n* : antropología *f*
antiabortion [ˌæntiəˈbɔrʃən, ˌæntaɪ-] *adj* : antiaborto
antiaircraft [ˌæntiˈærˌkræft, ˌæntaɪ-] *adj* : antiaéreo
anti–American [ˌæntiəˈmɛrɪkən, ˌæntaɪ-] *adj* : antiamericano
antibiotic[1] [ˌæntibaɪˈɑt̬ɪk, ˌæntaɪ-, -bi-] *adj* : antibiótico
antibiotic[2] *n* : antibiótico *m*
antibody [ˈæntiˌbɑdi] *n, pl* **-bodies** : anticuerpo *m*
antic[1] [ˈæntɪk] *adj* : extravagante, juguetón
antic[2] *n* : payasada *f*, travesura *f*
anticipate [ænˈtɪsəˌpeɪt] *vt* **-pated; -pating 1** FORESEE : anticipar, prever **2** EXPECT : esperar, contar con
anticipation [ænˌtɪsəˈpeɪʃən] *n* **1** FORESIGHT : previsión *f* **2** EXPECTATION : anticipación *f*, expectación *f*, esperanza *f*
anticipatory [ænˈtɪsəpəˌtori] *adj* : en anticipación, en previsión
anticlimactic [ˌæntiklaɪˈmæktɪk] *adj* : anticlimático, decepcionante
anticlimax [ˌæntiˈklaɪˌmæks] *n* : anticlímax *m*
anticommunism [ˌæntiˈkɑmjəˌnɪzəm, ˌæntaɪ-] *n* : anticomunismo *m*
anticommunist[1] [ˌæntiˈkɑmjənɪst, ˌæntaɪ-] *adj* : anticomunista
anticommunist[2] *n* : anticomunista *mf*
antidemocratic [ˌæntiˌdɛməˈkræt̬ɪk, ˌæntaɪ-] *adj* : antidemocrático
antidote [ˈæntɪˌdoːt] *n* : antídoto *m*
antidrug [ˌæntiˈdrʌg, ˌæntaɪ-; ˈæntiˌdrʌg, ˈæntaɪ-] *adj* : antidrogas
antifascist [ˌæntiˈfæʃɪst, ˌæntaɪ-] *adj* : antifascista
antifeminist [ˌæntiˈfɛmənɪst, ˌæntaɪ-] *adj* : antifeminista
antifreeze [ˈæntiˌfriːz] *n* : anticongelante *m*
anti–imperialism [ˌæntiɪmˈpɪriəˌlɪzəm, ˌæntaɪ-] *n* : antiimperialismo *m*
anti–imperialist [ˌæntiɪmˈpɪriəlɪst, ˌæntaɪ-] *adj* : antiimperialista
anti–inflationary [ˌæntiɪnˈfleɪʃəˌnɛri, ˌæntaɪ-] *adj* : antiinflacionario
antimony [ˈæntəˌmoːni] *n* : antimonio *m*
antipathy [ænˈtɪpəθi] *n, pl* **-thies** : antipatía *f*, aversión *f*
antiperspirant [ˌæntiˈpərspərənt, ˌæntaɪ-] *n* : antitranspirante *m*
antiquarian[1] [ˌæntəˈkwɛriən] *adj* : antiguo, anticuario <an antiquarian book : un libro antiguo>
antiquarian[2] *n* : anticuario *m*, -ria *f*
antiquary [ˈæntəˌkwɛri] → **antiquarian**[2]
antiquated [ˈæntəˌkweɪt̬əd] *adj* : anticuado, pasado de moda
antique[1] [ænˈtiːk] *adj* **1** OLD : antiguo, de época <an antique mirror : un espejo antiguo> **2** OLD-FASHIONED : anticuado, pasado de moda
antique[2] *n* : antigüedad *f*
antiquity [ænˈtɪkwət̬i] *n, pl* **-ties** : antigüedad
antirevolutionary [ˌæntiˌrɛvəˈluːʃəˌnɛri, ˌæntaɪ-] *adj* : antirrevolucionario
anti–Semitic [ˌæntisəˈmɪt̬ɪk, ˌæntaɪ-] *adj* : antisemita
anti–Semitism [ˌæntiˈsɛməˌtɪzəm, ˌæntaɪ-] *n* : antisemitismo *m*
antiseptic[1] [ˌæntəˈsɛptɪk] *adj* : antiséptico — **antiseptically** [-tɪkli] *adv*
antiseptic[2] *n* : antiséptico *m*
antismoking [ˌæntiˈsmoːkɪŋ, ˌæntaɪ-] *adj* : antitabaco
antisocial [ˌæntiˈsoːʃəl, ˌæntaɪ-] *adj* **1** : antisocial **2** UNSOCIABLE : poco sociable
antitheft [ˌæntiˈθɛft, ˌæntaɪ-] *adj* : antirrobo
antithesis [ænˈtɪθəsɪs] *n, pl* **-eses** [-ˌsiːz] : antítesis *f*
antitoxin [ˌæntiˈtɑksən, ˌæntaɪ-] *n* : antitoxina *f*
antitrust [ˌæntiˈtrʌst, ˌæntaɪ-] *adj* : antimonopolista
antler [ˈæntlər] *n* : asta *f*, cuerno *m*
antonym [ˈæntəˌnɪm] *n* : antónimo *m*
anus [ˈeɪnəs] *n* : ano *m*
anvil [ˈænvəl, -vɪl] *n* : yunque *m*
anxiety [æŋkˈzaɪət̬i] *n, pl* **-eties 1** UNEASINESS : inquietud *f*, preocupación *f*, ansiedad *f* **2** APPREHENSION : ansiedad *f*, angustia *f*
anxious [ˈæŋkʃəs] *adj* **1** WORRIED : inquieto, preocupado, ansioso **2** WORRISOME : preocupante, inquietante **3** EAGER : ansioso, deseoso
anxiously [ˈæŋkʃəsli] *adv* : con inquietud, con ansiedad
any[1] [ˈɛni] *adv* **1** : algo <is it any better? : ¿está (algo) mejor?> **2** : para nada <it is not any good : no sirve para nada>
any[2] *adj* **1** : alguno <is there any doubt? : ¿hay alguna duda?> <call me if you have any questions : llámeme si tiene alguna pregunta> **2** : cualquier <I can answer any question : puedo responder a cualquier pregunta> **3** : todo <in any case : en todo caso> **4** : ningún <he would not accept it under any circumstances : no lo aceptaría bajo ninguna circunstancia>
any[3] *pron* **1** : alguno *m*, -na *f* <are there any left? : ¿queda alguno?> **2** : nin-

guno *m,* -na *f* <I don't want any : no quiero ninguno>

anybody ['ɛni͵bʌdi, -͵bɑ-] → **anyone**

anyhow ['ɛni͵haʊ] *adv* **1** HAPHAZARDLY : de cualquier manera **2** IN ANY CASE : de todos modos, en todo caso

anymore [͵ɛni'mor] *adv* **1** : ya, ya más <he doesn't dance anymore : ya no baila más> **2** : todavía <do they sing anymore? : ¿cantan todavía?>

anyone ['ɛni͵wʌn] *pron* **1** : alguien <is anyone here? : ¿hay alguien aquí?> <if anyone wants to come : si alguno quiere venir> **2** : cualquiera <anyone can play : cualquiera puede jugar> **3** : nadie <I don't want anyone here : no quiero a nadie aquí>

anyplace ['ɛni͵pleɪs] → **anywhere**

anything ['ɛni͵θɪŋ] *pron* **1** : algo, alguna cosa <do you want anything? : ¿quieres algo?, ¿quieres alguna cosa?> **2** : nada <hardly anything : casi nada> **3** : cualquier cosa <I eat anything : como de todo>

anytime ['ɛni͵taɪm] *adv* : en cualquier momento, a cualquier hora, cuando sea

anyway ['ɛni͵weɪ] → **anyhow**

anywhere ['ɛni͵*h*wɛr] *adv* **1** : en algún sitio, en alguna parte <do you see it anywhere? : ¿lo ves en alguna parte?> **2** : en ningún sitio, por ninguna parte <I can't find it anywhere : no puedo encontrarlo por ninguna parte> **3** : en cualquier parte, dondequiera, donde sea <put it anywhere : ponlo dondequiera>

aorta [eɪ'ɔrt̬ə] *n, pl* **-tas** *or* **-tae** [-t̬i, -taɪ] : aorta *f*

apart [ə'pɑrt] *adv* **1** SEPARATELY : aparte, separadamente **2** ASIDE : aparte, a un lado **3 to fall apart** : deshacerse, hacerse pedazos **4 to take apart** : desmontar, desmantelar

apartheid [ə'pɑr͵teɪt, -͵taɪt] *n* : apartheid *m*

apartment [ə'pɑrtmənt] *n* : apartamento *m,* departamento *m,* piso *m Spain*

apathetic [͵æpə'θɛt̬ɪk] *adj* : apático, indiferente — **apathetically** [-t̬ɪkli] *adv*

apathy ['æpəθi] *n* : apatía *f,* indiferencia *f*

ape[1] ['eɪp] *vt* **aped; aping** : imitar, remedar

ape[2] *n* : simio *m;* mono *m,* -na *f*

aperture ['æpərtʃər, -͵tʃʊr] *n* : abertura *f,* rendija *f,* apertura *f* (en fotografía)

apex ['eɪ͵pɛks] *n, pl* **apexes** *or* **apices** ['eɪpə͵si:z, 'æ-] : ápice *m,* cúspide *f,* cima *f*

aphid ['eɪfɪd, 'æ-] *n* : áfido *m*

aphorism ['æfə͵rɪzəm] *n* : aforismo *m*

aphoristic [͵æfə'rɪstɪk] *adj* : aforístico

aphrodisiac [͵æfrə'di:zi͵æk, -'dɪ-] *n* : afrodisíaco *m*

apiary ['eɪpi͵ɛri] *n, pl* **-aries** : apiario *m,* colmenar *m*

apiece [ə'pi:s] *adv* : cada uno

aplenty [ə'plɛnti] *adj* : en abundancia

aplomb [ə'plɑm, -'plʌm] *n* : aplomo *m*

apocalypse [ə'pɑkə͵lɪps] *n* : apocalipsis *m*

apocalyptic [ə͵pɑkə'lɪptɪk] *adj* : apocalíptico

apocrypha [ə'pɑkrəfə] *n* : textos *mpl* apócrifos

apocryphal [ə'pɑkrəfəl] *adj* : apócrifo

apologetic [ə͵pɑlə'dʒɛt̬ɪk] *adj* : lleno de disculpas

apologetically [ə͵pɑlə'dʒɛt̬ɪkli] *adv* : disculpándose, con aire de disculpas

apologize [ə'pɑlə͵dʒaɪz] *vi* **-gized; -gizing** : disculparse, pedir perdón

apology [ə'pɑlədʒi] *n, pl* **-gies** : disculpa *f,* excusa *f*

apoplectic [͵æpə'plɛktɪk] *adj* : apoplético

apoplexy ['æpə͵plɛksi] *n* : apoplejía *f*

apostasy [ə'pɑstəsi] *n, pl* **-sies** : apostasía *f*

apostate [ə'pɑs͵teɪt] *n* : apóstata *mf*

apostle [ə'pɑsəl] *n* : apóstol *m*

apostleship [ə'pɑsəl͵ʃɪp] *n* : apostolado *m*

apostolic [͵æpə'stɑlɪk] *adj* : apostólico

apostrophe [ə'pɑstrə͵fi:] *n* : apóstrofo *m*

apothecary [ə'pɑθə͵kɛri] *n, pl* **-caries** : boticario *m,* -ria *f*

appall [ə'pɔl] *vt* : consternar, horrorizar

apparatus [͵æpə'ræt̬əs, -'reɪ-] *n, pl* **-tuses** *or* **-tus** : aparato *m,* equipo *m*

apparel [ə'pærəl] *n* : atavío *m,* ropa *f*

apparent [ə'pærənt] *adj* **1** VISIBLE : visible **2** OBVIOUS : claro, evidente, manifiesto **3** SEEMING : aparente, ostensible

apparently [ə'pærəntli] *adv* : aparentemente, al parecer

apparition [͵æpə'rɪʃən] *n* : aparición *f,* visión *f*

appeal[1] [ə'pi:l] *vt* **1** : apelar <to appeal a decision : apelar contra una decisión> — *vi* **1 to appeal for** : pedir, solicitar **2 to appeal to** : atraer a <that doesn't appeal to me : eso no me atrae>

appeal[2] *n* **1** : apelación *f* (en derecho) **2** PLEA : ruego *m,* súplica *f* **3** ATTRACTION : atracción *f,* atractivo *m,* interés *m*

appear [ə'pɪr] *vi* **1** : aparecer, aparecerse, presentarse <he suddenly appeared : apareció de repente> **2** COME OUT : aparecer, salir, publicarse **3** : comparecer (ante el tribunal), actuar (en el teatro) **4** SEEM : parecer

appearance [ə'pɪrənts] *n* **1** APPEARING : aparición *f,* presentación *f,* comparecencia *f* (ante un tribunal), publicación *f* (de un libro) **2** LOOK : apariencia *f,* aspecto *m*

appease [əˈpiːz] *vt* **-peased; -peasing** **1** CALM, PACIFY : aplacar, apaciguar, sosegar **2** SATISFY : satisfacer, mitigar

appeasement [əˈpiːzmənt] *n* : aplacamiento *m,* apaciguamiento *m*

append [əˈpɛnd] *vt* : agregar, añadir, adjuntar

appendage [əˈpɛndɪdʒ] *n* **1** ADDITION : apéndice *m,* añadidura *f* **2** LIMB : miembro *m,* extremidad *f*

appendectomy [ˌæpənˈdɛktəmi] *n, pl* **-mies** : apendicectomía *f*

appendicitis [əˌpɛndəˈsaɪt̬əs] *n* : apendicitis *f*

appendix [əˈpɛndɪks] *n, pl* **-dixes** *or* **-dices** [-dəˌsiːz] : apéndice *m*

appetite [ˈæpəˌtaɪt] *n* **1** CRAVING : apetito *m,* deseo *m,* ganas *fpl* **2** PREFERENCE : gusto *m,* preferencia *f* <the cultural appetites of today : los gustos culturales de hoy>

appetizer [ˈæpəˌtaɪzər] *n* : aperitivo *m,* entremés *m,* botana *f Mex,* tapa *f Spain*

appetizing [ˈæpəˌtaɪzɪŋ] *adj* : apetecible, apetitoso — **appetizingly** [-zɪŋli] *adv*

applaud [əˈplɔd] *v* : aplaudir

applause [əˈplɔz] *n* : aplauso *m*

apple [ˈæpəl] *n* : manzana *f*

appliance [əˈplaɪən*t*s] *n* **1** : aparato *m* **2 household appliance** : electrodoméstico *m,* aparato *m* electrodoméstico

applicability [ˌæplɪkəˈbɪlət̬i, əˌplɪkə-] *n* : aplicabilidad *f*

applicable [ˈæplɪkəbəl, əˈplɪkə-] *adj* : aplicable, pertinente

applicant [ˈæplɪkənt] *n* : solicitante *mf,* aspirante *mf,* postulante *mf;* candidato *m,* -ta *f*

application [ˌæpləˈkeɪʃən] *n* **1** USE : aplicación *f,* empleo *m,* uso *m* **2** DILIGENCE : aplicación *f,* diligencia *f,* dedicación *f* **3** REQUEST : solicitud *f,* petición *f,* demanda *f*

applicator [ˈæpləˌkeɪt̬ər] *n* : aplicador *m*

appliqué[1] [ˌæpləˈkeɪ] *vt* : decorar con apliques

appliqué[2] *n* : aplique *m*

apply [əˈplaɪ] *v* **-plied; -plying** *vt* **1** : aplicar (una sustancia, los frenos, el conocimiento) **2 to apply oneself** : dedicarse, aplicarse — *vi* **1** : aplicarse, referirse <the rules apply to everyone : las reglas se aplican a todos> **2 to apply for** : solicitar, pedir

appoint [əˈpɔɪnt] *vt* **1** NAME : nombrar, designar **2** FIX, SET : fijar, señalar, designar <to appoint a date : fijar una fecha> **3** EQUIP : equipar <a well-appointed office : una oficina bien equipada>

appointee [əˌpɔɪnˈtiː, ˌæ-] *n* : persona *f* designada

appointment [əˈpɔɪntmənt] *n* **1** APPOINTING : nombramiento *m,* designación *f* **2** ENGAGEMENT : cita *f,* hora *f* **3** POST : puesto *m*

apportion [əˈporʃən] *vt* : distribuir, repartir

apportionment [əˈporʃənmənt] *n* : distribución *f,* repartición *f,* reparto *m*

apposite [ˈæpəzət] *adj* : apropiado, oportuno, pertinente — **appositely** *adv*

appraisal [əˈpreɪzəl] *n* : evaluación *f,* valoración *f,* tasación *f,* apreciación *f*

appraise [əˈpreɪz] *vt* **-praised; -praising** : evaluar, valorar, tasar, apreciar

appraiser [əˈpreɪzər] *n* : tasador *m,* -dora *f*

appreciable [əˈpriːʃəbəl, -ˈprɪʃiə-] *adj* : apreciable, sensible, considerable — **appreciably** [-bli] *adv*

appreciate [əˈpriːʃiˌeɪt, -ˈprɪ-] *v* **-ated; -ating** *vt* **1** VALUE : apreciar, valorar **2** : agradecer <we appreciate his frankness : agradecemos su franqueza> **3** UNDERSTAND : darse cuenta de, entender — *vi* : apreciarse, valorizarse

appreciation [əˌpriːʃiˈeɪʃən, -ˌprɪ-] *n* **1** GRATITUDE : agradecimiento *m,* reconocimiento *m* **2** VALUING : apreciación *f,* valoración *f,* estimación *f* <art appreciation : apreciación artística> **3** UNDERSTANDING : comprensión *f,* entendimiento *m*

appreciative [əˈpriːʃət̬ɪv, -ˈprɪ-; əˈpriːʃiˌeɪ-] *adj* **1** : apreciativo <an appreciative audience : un público apreciativo> **2** GRATEFUL : agradecido **3** ADMIRING : de admiración

apprehend [ˌæprɪˈhɛnd] *vt* **1** ARREST : aprehender, detener, arrestar **2** DREAD : temer **3** COMPREHEND : comprender, entender

apprehension [ˌæprɪˈhɛntʃən] *n* **1** ARREST : arresto *m,* detención *f,* aprehensión *f* **2** ANXIETY : aprensión *f,* ansiedad *f,* temor *m* **3** UNDERSTANDING : comprensión *f,* percepción *f*

apprehensive [ˌæprɪˈhɛn*t*sɪv] *adj* : aprensivo, inquieto — **apprehensively** *adv*

apprentice[1] [əˈprɛntɪs] *vt* **-ticed; -ticing** : colocar de aprendiz

apprentice[2] *n* : aprendiz *m,* -diza *f*

apprenticeship [əˈprɛntɪsˌʃɪp] *n* : aprendizaje *f*

apprise [əˈpraɪz] *vt* **-prised; -prising** : informar, avisar

approach[1] [əˈproːtʃ] *vt* **1** NEAR : acercarse a **2** APPROXIMATE : aproximarse a **3** : abordar, dirigirse a <I approached my boss with the proposal : me dirigí a mi jefe con la propuesta> **4** TACKLE : abordar, enfocar, considerar — *vi* : acercarse, aproximarse

approach[2] *n* **1** NEARING : acercamiento *m,* aproximación *f* **2** POSITION : enfoque *m,* planteamiento *m* **3** OFFER : propuesta *f,* oferta *f* **4** ACCESS : acceso *m,* vía *f* de acceso

approachable [əˈproːtʃəbəl] *adj* : accesible, asequible

approbation [ˌæprəˈbeɪʃən] *n* : aprobación *f*
appropriate¹ [əˈproːpriˌeɪt] *vt* **-ated; -ating 1** SEIZE : apropiarse de **2** ALLOCATE : destinar, asignar
appropriate² [əˈproːpriət] *adj* : apropiado, adecuado, idóneo — **appropriately** *adv*
appropriateness [əˈproːpriətnəs] *n* : idoneidad *f*, propiedad *f*
appropriation [əˌproːpriˈeɪʃən] *n* **1** SEIZURE : apropiación *f* **2** ALLOCATION : asignación *f*
approval [əˈpruːvəl] *n* **1** : aprobación *f*, visto *m* bueno **2 on approval** : a prueba
approve [əˈpruːv] *vt* **-proved; -proving 1** : aprobar, sancionar, darle el visto bueno a **2 to approve of** : consentir en, aprobar <he doesn't approve of smoking : está en contra del tabaco>
approximate¹ [əˈprɑksəˌmeɪt] *vt* **-mated; -mating** : aproximarse a, acercarse a
approximate² [əˈprɑksəmət] *adj* : aproximado
approximately [əˈprɑksəmətli] *adv* : aproximadamente, más o menos
approximation [əˌprɑksəˈmeɪʃən] *n* : aproximación *f*
appurtenance [əˈpərtənənts] *n* : accesorio *m*
apricot [ˈæprəˌkɑt, ˈeɪ-] *n* : albaricoque *m*, chabacano *m Mex*
April [ˈeɪprəl] *n* : abril *m*
apron [ˈeɪprən] *n* : delantal *m*, mandil *m*
apropos¹ [ˌæprəˈpoː, ˈæprəˌpoː] *adv* : a propósito
apropos² *adj* : pertinente, oportuno, acertado
apropos of *prep* : a propósito de
apt [ˈæpt] *adj* **1** FITTING : apto, apropiado, acertado, oportuno **2** LIABLE : propenso, inclinado **3** CLEVER, QUICK : listo, despierto
aptitude [ˈæptəˌtuːd, -ˌtjuːd] *n* **1** : aptitud *f*, capacidad *f* <aptitude test : prueba de aptitud> **2** TALENT : talento *m*, facilidad *f*
aptly [ˈæptli] *adv* : acertadamente
aqua [ˈækwə, ˈɑ-] *n* : color *m* aguamarina
aquarium [əˈkwæriəm] *n*, *pl* **-iums** *or* **-ia** [-iə] : acuario *m*
Aquarius [əˈkwæriəs] *n* : Acuario *mf*
aquatic [əˈkwɑtɪk, -ˈkwæ-] *adj* : acuático
aqueduct [ˈækwəˌdʌkt] *n* : acueducto *m*
aquiline [ˈækwəˌlaɪn, -lən] *adj* : aguileño
Arab¹ [ˈærəb] *adj* : árabe
Arab² *n* : árabe *mf*
arabesque [ˌærəˈbɛsk] *n* : arabesco *m*
Arabian¹ [əˈreɪbiən] *adj* : árabe
Arabian² *n* → **Arab²**
Arabic¹ [ˈærəbɪk] *adj* : árabe
Arabic² *n* : árabe *m* (idioma)
arable [ˈærəbəl] *adj* : arable, cultivable
arbiter [ˈɑrbətər] *n* : árbitro *m*, -tra *f*
arbitrary [ˈɑrbəˌtrɛri] *adj* : arbitrario — **arbitrarily** [ˌɑrbəˈtrɛrəli] *adv*
arbitrate [ˈɑrbəˌtreɪt] *v* **-trated; -trating** : arbitrar
arbitration [ˌɑrbəˈtreɪʃən] *n* : arbitraje *m*
arbitrator [ˈɑrbəˌtreɪtər] *n* : árbitro *m*, -tra *f*
arbor [ˈɑrbər] *n* : cenador *m*, pérgola *f*
arboreal [ɑrˈboriəl] *adj* : arbóreo
arc¹ [ˈɑrk] *vi* **arced; arcing** : formar un arco
arc² *n* : arco *m*
arcade [ɑrˈkeɪd] *n* **1** ARCHES : arcada *f* **2** MALL : galería *f* comercial
arcane [ɑrˈkeɪn] *adj* : arcano, secreto, misterioso
arch¹ [ˈɑrtʃ] *vt* : arquear, enarcar — *vi* : formar un arco, arquearse
arch² *adj* **1** CHIEF : principal **2** MISCHIEVOUS : malicioso, pícaro
arch³ *n* : arco *m*
archaeological [ˌɑrkiəˈlɑdʒɪkəl] *adj* : arqueológico
archaeologist [ˌɑrkiˈɑlədʒɪst] *n* : arqueólogo *m*, -ga *f*
archaeology *or* **archeology** [ˌɑrkiˈɑlədʒi] *n* : arqueología *f*
archaic [ɑrˈkeɪɪk] *adj* : arcaico — **archaically** [-ɪkli] *adv*
archangel [ˈɑrkˌeɪndʒəl] *n* : arcángel *m*
archbishop [ɑrtʃˈbɪʃəp] *n* : arzobispo *m*
archdiocese [ɑrtʃˈdaɪəsəs, -ˌsiːz, -ˌsiːs] *n* : archidiócesis *f*
archer [ˈɑrtʃər] *n* : arquero *m*, -ra *f*
archery [ˈɑrtʃəri] *n* : tiro *m* al arco
archetype [ˈɑrkɪˌtaɪp] *n* : arquetipo *m*
archipelago [ˌɑrkəˈpɛləˌgoː, ˌɑrtʃə-] *n*, *pl* **-goes** *or* **-gos** [-goːz] : archipiélago *m*
architect [ˈɑrkəˌtɛkt] *n* : arquitecto *m*, -ta *f*
architectural [ˌɑrkəˈtɛktʃərəl] *adj* : arquitectónico — **architecturally** *adv*
architecture [ˈɑrkəˌtɛktʃər] *n* : arquitectura *f*
archives [ˈɑrˌkaɪvz] *npl* : archivo *m*
archivist [ˈɑrkəvɪst, -ˌkaɪ-] *n* : archivero *m*, -ra *f*; archivista *mf*
archway [ˈɑrtʃˌweɪ] *n* : arco *m*, pasadizo *m* abovedado
arctic [ˈɑrktɪk, ˈɑrt-] *adj* **1** : ártico <arctic regions : zonas árticas> **2** FRIGID : glacial
arctic circle *n* : círculo *m* ártico
ardent [ˈɑrdənt] *adj* **1** PASSIONATE : ardiente, fogoso, apasionado **2** FERVENT : ferviente, fervoroso — **ardently** *adv*
ardor [ˈɑrdər] *n* : ardor *m*, pasión *f*, fervor *m*
arduous [ˈɑrdʒʊəs] *adj* : arduo, duro, riguroso — **arduously** *adv*

arduousness [ˈɑrdʒʊəsnəs] *n* **:** dureza *f,* rigor *m*
are → **be**
area [ˈæriə] *n* **1** SURFACE **:** área *f,* superficie *f* **2** REGION **:** área *f,* región *f,* zona *f* **3** FIELD **:** área *f,* terreno *m,* campo *m* (de conocimiento)
area code *n* **:** código *m* de la zona, prefijo *m Spain*
arena [əˈriːnə] *n* **1 :** arena *f,* estadio *m* <sports arena : estadio deportivo> **2 :** arena *f,* ruedo *m* <the political arena : el ruedo político>
Argentine [ˈɑrdʒənˌtaɪn, -ˌtiːn] *or* **Argentinean** *or* **Argentinian** [ˌɑrdʒənˈtɪniən] *n* **:** argentino *m,* -na *f* — **Argentine** *or* **Argentinean** *or* **Argentinian** *adj*
argon [ˈɑrˌgɑn] *n* **:** argón *m*
argot [ˈɑrgət, -ˌgoː] *n* **:** argot *m*
arguable [ˈɑrgjʊəbəl] *adj* **:** discutible
argue [ˈɑrˌgjuː] *v* **-gued; -guing** *vi* **1** REASON **:** argüir, argumentar, razonar **2** DISPUTE **:** discutir, pelear(se), alegar — *vt* **1** SUGGEST **:** sugerir **2** MAINTAIN **:** alegar, argüir, sostener **3** DISCUSS **:** discutir, debatir
argument [ˈɑrgjəmənt] *n* **1** REASONING **:** argumento *m,* razonamiento *m* **2** DISCUSSION **:** discusión *f,* debate *m* **3** QUARREL **:** pelea *f,* riña *f,* disputa *f*
argumentative [ˌɑrgjəˈmɛntət̬ɪv] *adj* **:** discutidor
argyle [ˈɑrˌgaɪl] *n* **:** diseño *m* de rombos
aria [ˈɑriə] *n* **:** aria *f*
arid [ˈærəd] *adj* **:** árido
aridity [əˈrɪdət̬i, æ-] *n* **:** aridez *f*
Aries [ˈɛriːz, -iˌiːz] *n* **:** Aries *mf*
arise [əˈraɪz] *vi* **arose** [əˈroːz]; **arisen** [əˈrɪzən]; **arising 1** ASCEND **:** ascender, subir, elevarse **2** ORIGINATE **:** originarse, surgir, presentarse **3** GET UP **:** levantarse
aristocracy [ˌærəˈstɑkrəsi] *n, pl* **-cies :** aristocracia *f*
aristocrat [əˈrɪstəˌkræt] *n* **:** aristócrata *mf*
aristocratic [əˌrɪstəˈkræt̬ɪk] *adj* **:** aristocrático, noble
arithmetic¹ [ˌærɪθˈmɛt̬ɪk] *or* **arithmetical** [-t̬ɪkəl] *adj* **:** aritmético
arithmetic² [əˈrɪθməˌtɪk] *n* **:** aritmética
ark [ˈɑrk] *n* **:** arca *f*
arm¹ [ˈɑrm] *vt* **:** armar — *vi* **:** armarse
arm² *n* **1 :** brazo *m* (del cuerpo o de un sillón), manga *f* (de una prenda) **2** BRANCH **:** rama *f,* sección *f* **3** WEAPON **:** arma *f* <to take up arms : tomar las armas> **4 coat of arms :** escudo *m* de armas
armada [ɑrˈmɑdə, -ˈmeɪ-] *n* **:** armada *f,* flota *f*
armadillo [ˌɑrməˈdɪlo] *n, pl* **-los :** armadillo *m*
armament [ˈɑrməmənt] *n* **:** armamento *m*
armed [ˈɑrmd] *adj* **1 :** armado <armed robbery : robo a mano armada> **2 armed forces :** fuerzas *fpl* armadas
Armenian [ɑrˈmiːniən] *n* **:** armenio *m,* -nia *f* — **Armenian** *adj*
armistice [ˈɑrməstɪs] *n* **:** armisticio *m*
armor [ˈɑrmər] *n* **:** armadura *f,* coraza *f*
armored [ˈɑrmərd] *adj* **:** blindado, acorazado
armory [ˈɑrməri] *n, pl* **-mories :** arsenal *m* (almacén), armería *f* (museo), fábrica *f* de armas
armpit [ˈɑrmˌpɪt] *n* **:** axila *f,* sobaco *m*
army [ˈɑrmi] *n, pl* **-mies 1 :** ejército *m* (militar) **2** MULTITUDE **:** legión *f,* multitud *f,* ejército *m*
aroma [əˈroːmə] *n* **:** aroma *f*
aromatic [ˌærəˈmæt̬ɪk] *adj* **:** aromático
around¹ [əˈraʊnd] *adv* **1 :** de circunferencia <a tree three feet around : un árbol de tres pies de circunferencia> **2 :** alrededor, a la redonda <for miles around : por millas a la redonda> <all around : por todos lados, todo alrededor> **3 :** por ahí <they're somewhere around : deben estar por ahí> **4** APPROXIMATELY **:** más o menos, aproximadamente <around 5 o'clock : a eso de las 5> **5 to turn around :** darse la vuelta, voltearse
around² *prep* **1** SURROUNDING **:** alrededor de, en torno a **2** THROUGH **:** por, en <he traveled around Mexico : viajó por México> <around the house : en casa> **3 :** a la vuelta de <around the corner : a la vuelta de la esquina> **4** NEAR **:** alrededor de, cerca de
arousal [əˈraʊzəl] *n* **:** excitación *f*
arouse [əˈraʊz] *vt* **aroused; arousing 1** AWAKE **:** despertar **2** EXCITE **:** despertar, suscitar, excitar
arraign [əˈreɪn] *vt* **:** hacer comparecer (ante un tribunal)
arraignment [əˈreɪnmənt] *n* **:** orden *m* de comparecencia, acusación *f*
arrange [əˈreɪndʒ] *vt* **-ranged; -ranging 1** ORDER **:** arreglar, poner en orden, disponer **2** SETTLE **:** arreglar, fijar, concertar **3** ADAPT **:** arreglar, adaptar
arrangement [əˈreɪndʒmənt] *n* **1** ORDER **:** arreglo *m,* orden *m* **2** ARRANGING **:** disposición *f* <floral arrangement : arreglo floral> **3** AGREEMENT **:** arreglo *m,* acuerdo *m,* convenio *m* **4 arrangements** *npl* **:** preparativos *mpl,* planes *mpl*
array¹ [əˈreɪ] *vt* **1** ORDER **:** poner en orden, presentar, formar **2** GARB **:** vestir, ataviar, engalanar
array² *n* **1** ORDER **:** orden *m,* formación *f* **2** ATTIRE **:** atavío *m,* galas *mpl* **3** RANGE, SELECTION **:** selección *f,* serie *f,* gama *f* <an array of problems : una serie de problemas>
arrears [əˈrɪrz] *npl* **:** atrasos *mpl* <to be in arrears : estar atrasado en los pagos>

arrest[1] [ə'rɛst] *vt* **1** APPREHEND : arrestar, detener **2** CHECK, STOP : detener, parar

arrest[2] *n* **1** APPREHENSION : arresto *m,* detención *f* <under arrest : detenido> **2** STOPPING : paro *m*

arrival [ə'raɪvəl] *n* : llegada *f,* venida *f,* arribo *m*

arrive [ə'raɪv] *vi* **-rived; -riving 1** COME : llegar, arribar **2** SUCCEED : triunfar, tener éxito

arrogance ['ærəgənts] *n* : arrogancia *f,* soberbia *f,* altanería *f,* altivez *f*

arrogant ['ærəgənt] *adj* : arrogante, soberbio, altanero, altivo — **arrogantly** *adv*

arrogate ['ærə,geɪt] *vt* **-gated; -gating to arrogate to oneself** : arrogarse

arrow ['æro] *n* : flecha *f*

arrowhead ['æro,hɛd] *n* : punta *f* de flecha

arroyo [ə'rɔɪo] *n* : arroyo *m*

arsenal ['ɑrsənəl] *n* : arsenal *m*

arsenic ['ɑrsənɪk] *n* : arsénico *m*

arson ['ɑrsən] *n* : incendio *m* premeditado

arsonist *n* ['ɑrsənɪst] : incendiario *m,* -ria *f;* pirómano *m,* -na *f*

art ['ɑrt] *n* **1** : arte *m* **2** SKILL : destreza *f,* habilidad *f,* maña *f* **3 arts** *npl* : letras *fpl* (en la educación) **4 fine arts** : bellas artes *fpl*

arterial [ɑr'tɪriəl] *adj* : arterial

arteriosclerosis [ɑr,tɪriosklə'roːsɪs] *n* : arteriosclerosis *f*

artery ['ɑrtəri] *n, pl* **-teries 1** : arteria *f* **2** THOROUGHFARE : carretera *f* principal, arteria *f*

artesian well [ɑr'tiːʒən] *n* : pozo *m* artesiano

artful ['ɑrtfəl] *adj* **1** INGENIOUS : ingenioso, diestro **2** CRAFTY : astuto, taimado, ladino, artero — **artfully** *adv*

arthritic [ɑr'θrɪtɪk] *adj* : artrítico

arthritis [ɑr'θraɪtəs] *n, pl* **-tides** [ɑr'θrɪtə,diːz] : artritis *f*

arthropod ['ɑrθrə,pɑd] *n* : artrópodo *m*

artichoke ['ɑrtə,tʃoːk] *n* : alcachofa *f*

article ['ɑrtɪkəl] *n* **1** ITEM : artículo *m,* objeto *m* **2** ESSAY : artículo *m* **3** CLAUSE : artículo *m,* cláusula *f* **4** : artículo *m* <definite article : artículo determinado>

articulate[1] [ɑr'tɪkjə,leɪt] *vt* **-lated; -lating 1** UTTER : articular, enunciar, expresar **2** CONNECT : articular (en anatomía)

articulate[2] [ɑr'tɪkjələt] *adj* **to be articulate** : poder articular palabras, expresarse bien

articulately [ɑr'tɪkjələtli] *adv* : elocuentemente, con fluidez

articulateness [ɑr'tɪkjələtnəs] *n* : elocuencia *f,* fluidez *f*

articulation [ɑr,tɪkjə'leɪʃən] *n* **1** JOINT : articulación *f* **2** UTTERANCE : articulación *f,* declaración *f* **3** ENUNCIATION : articulación *f,* pronunciación *f*

artifact ['ɑrtə,fækt] *n* : artefacto *m*

artifice ['ɑrtəfəs] *n* : artificio *m*

artificial [,ɑrtə'fɪʃəl] *adj* **1** SYNTHETIC : artificial, sintético **2** FEIGNED : artificial, falso, afectado

artificially [,ɑrtə'fɪʃəli] *adv* : artificialmente, con afectación

artillery [ɑr'tɪləri] *n, pl* **-leries** : artillería *f*

artisan ['ɑrtəzən, -sən] *n* : artesano *m,* -na *f*

artist ['ɑrtɪst] *n* : artista *mf*

artistic [ɑr'tɪstɪk] *adj* : artístico — **artistically** [-tɪkli] *adv*

artistry ['ɑrtəstri] *n* : maestría *f,* arte *m*

artless ['ɑrtləs] *adj* : sencillo, natural, ingenuo, cándido — **artlessly** *adv*

artlessness ['ɑrtləsnəs] *n* : ingenuidad *f,* candidez *f*

arty ['ɑrti] *adj* **artier; -est** : pretenciosamente artístico

as[1] ['æz] *adv* **1** : tan, tanto <this one's not as difficult : éste no es tan difícil> **2** : como <some trees, as oak and pine : algunos árboles, como el roble y el pino>

as[2] *conj* **1** LIKE : como, igual que **2** WHEN, WHILE : cuando, mientras, a la vez que **3** BECAUSE : porque **4** THOUGH : aunque, por más que <strange as it may appear : por extraño que parezca> **5 as is** : tal como está

as[3] *prep* **1** : de <I met her as a child : la conocí de pequeña> **2** LIKE : como <behave as a man : compórtate como un hombre>

as[4] *pron* : que <in the same building as my brother : en el mismo edificio que mi hermano>

asbestos [æz'bɛstəs, æs-] *n* : asbesto *m,* amianto *m*

ascend [ə'sɛnd] *vi* : ascender, subir — *vt* : subir, subir a, escalar

ascendancy [ə'sɛndəntsi] *n* : ascendiente *m,* predominio *m*

ascendant[1] [ə'sɛndənt] *adj* **1** RISING : ascendente **2** DOMINANT : superior, dominante

ascendant[2] *n* **to be in the ascendant** : estar en alza, ir ganando predominio

ascension [ə'sɛntʃən] *n* : ascensión *f*

ascent [ə'sɛnt] *n* **1** RISE : ascensión *f,* subida *f,* ascenso *m* **2** SLOPE : cuesta *f,* pendiente *f*

ascertain [,æsər'teɪn] *vt* : determinar, establecer, averiguar

ascertainable [,æsər'teɪnəbəl] *adj* : determinable, averiguable

ascetic[1] [ə'sɛtɪk] *adj* : ascético

ascetic[2] *n* : asceta *mf*

asceticism [ə'sɛtə,sɪzəm] *n* : ascetismo *m*

ascribable [ə'skraɪbəbəl] *adj* : atribuible, imputable

ascribe [ə'skraɪb] *vt* **-cribed; -cribing** : atribuir, imputar

aseptic [eɪ'sɛptɪk] *adj* : aséptico

as for *prep* CONCERNING : en cuanto a, respecto a, para

ash ['æʃ] *n* **1 :** ceniza *f* <to reduce to ashes : reducir a cenizas> **2 :** fresno *m* (árbol)

ashamed [ə'ʃeɪmd] *adj* **:** avergonzado, abochornado, apenado — **ashamedly** [ə'ʃeɪmədli] *adv*

ashen ['æʃən] *adj* **:** lívido, ceniciento, pálido

ashore [ə'ʃor] *adv* **1 :** en tierra **2 to go ashore :** desembarcar

ashtray ['æʃ,treɪ] *n* **:** cenicero *m*

Asian[1] ['eɪʒən, -ʃən] *adj* **:** asiático

Asian[2] *n* **:** asiático *m*, -ca *f*

aside [ə'saɪd] *adv* **1 :** a un lado <to step aside : hacerse a un lado> **2 :** de lado, aparte <jesting aside : bromas aparte> **3 to set aside :** guardar, apartar, reservar

aside from *prep* **1** BESIDES **:** además de **2** EXCEPT **:** aparte de, menos

as if *conj* **:** como si

asinine ['æsən,aɪn] *adj* **:** necio, estúpido

ask ['æsk] *vt* **1 :** preguntar <ask him if he's coming : pregúntale si viene> **2** REQUEST **:** pedir, solicitar <to ask a favor : pedir un favor> **3** INVITE **:** invitar — *vi* **1** INQUIRE **:** preguntar <I asked about her children : pregunté por sus niños> **2** REQUEST **:** pedir <we asked for help : pedimos ayuda>

askance [ə'skænts] *adv* **1** SIDELONG **:** de reojo, de soslayo **2** SUSPICIOUSLY **:** con recelo, con desconfianza

askew [ə'skjuː] *adj* **:** torcido, ladeado

asleep [ə'sliːp] *adj* **1 :** dormido, durmiendo **2 to fall asleep :** quedarse dormido

as of *prep* **:** desde, a partir de

asparagus [ə'spærəgəs] *n* **:** espárrago *m*

aspect ['æ,spɛkt] *n* **:** aspecto *m*

aspen ['æspən] *n* **:** álamo *m* temblón

asperity [æ'spɛrəṭi, ə-] *n, pl* **-ties :** aspereza *f*

aspersion [ə'spərʒən] *n* **:** difamación *f*, calumnia *f*

asphalt ['æs,fɔlt] *n* **:** asfalto *m*

asphyxia [æ'sfɪksiə, ə-] *n* **:** asfixia *f*

asphyxiate [æ'sfɪksi,eɪt] *v* **-ated; -ating** *vt* **:** asfixiar — *vi* **:** asfixiarse

asphyxiation [æ,sfɪksi'eɪʃən] *n* **:** asfixia *f*

aspirant ['æspərənt, ə'spaɪrənt] *n* **:** aspirante *mf*, pretendiente *mf*

aspiration [,æspə'reɪʃən] *n* **1** DESIRE **:** aspiración *f*, anhelo *m*, ambición *f* **2** BREATHING **:** aspiración *f*

aspire [ə'spaɪr] *vi* **-pired; -piring :** aspirar

aspirin ['æsprən, 'æspə-] *n, pl* **aspirin** *or* **aspirins :** aspirina *f*

ass ['æs] *n* **1 :** asno *m* **2** IDIOT **:** imbécil *mf*, idiota *mf*

assail [ə'seɪl] *vt* **:** atacar, asaltar

assailant [ə'seɪlənt] *n* **:** asaltante *mf*, atacante *mf*

assassin [ə'sæsən] *n* **:** asesino *m*, -na *f*

assassinate [ə'sæsən,eɪt] *vt* **-nated; -nating :** asesinar

assassination [ə,sæsən'eɪʃən] *n* **:** asesinato *m*

assault[1] [ə'sɔlt] *vt* **:** atacar, asaltar, agredir

assault[2] *n* **:** ataque *m*, asalto *m*, agresión *f*

assay[1] [æ'seɪ, 'æ,seɪ] *vt* **:** ensayar

assay[2] ['æ,seɪ, æ'seɪ] *n* **:** ensayo *m*

assemble [ə'sɛmbəl] *v* **-bled; -bling** *vt* **1** GATHER **:** reunir, recoger, juntar **2** CONSTRUCT **:** ensamblar, montar, construir — *vi* **:** reunirse, congregarse

assembly [ə'sɛmbli] *n, pl* **-blies 1** MEETING **:** reunión *f* **2** CONSTRUCTING **:** ensamblaje *m*, montaje *m*

assemblyman [ə'sɛmblimən] *n, pl* **-men** [-mən, -,mɛn] **:** asambleísta *m*

assemblywoman [ə'sɛmbli,wʊmən] *n, pl* **-women** [-,wɪmən] **:** asambleísta *f*

assent[1] [ə'sɛnt] *vi* **:** asentir, consentir

assent[2] *n* **:** asentimiento *m*, aprobación *f*

assert [ə'sərt] *vt* **1** AFFIRM **:** afirmar, aseverar, mantener **2 to assert oneself :** imponerse, hacerse valer

assertion [ə'sərʃən] *n* **:** afirmación *f*, aseveración *f*, aserto *m*

assertive [ə'sərṭɪv] *adj* **:** firme, enérgico

assertiveness [ə'sərṭɪvnəs] *n* **:** seguridad *f* en sí mismo

assess [ə'sɛs] *vt* **1** IMPOSE **:** gravar (un impuesto), imponer **2** EVALUATE **:** evaluar, valorar, aquilatar

assessment [ə'sɛsmənt] *n* **:** evaluación *f*, valoración *f*

assessor [ə'sɛsər] *n* **:** evaluador *m*, -dora *f*; tasador *m*, -dora *f*

asset ['æ,sɛt] *n* **1 :** ventaja *f*, recurso *m* **2 assets** *npl* **:** bienes *mpl*, activo *m* <assets and liabilities : activo y pasivo>

assiduous [ə'sɪdʒʊəs] *adj* **:** diligente, aplicado, asiduo — **assiduously** *adv*

assign [ə'saɪn] *vt* **1** APPOINT **:** designar, nombrar **2** ALLOT **:** asignar, señalar **3** ATTRIBUTE **:** atribuir, dar, conceder

assignment [ə'saɪnmənt] *n* **1** TASK **:** función *f*, tarea *f*, misión *f* **2** HOMEWORK **:** tarea *f*, asignación *f PRi*, deberes *mpl Spain* **3** APPOINTMENT **:** nombramiento *m* **4** ALLOCATION **:** asignación *f*

assimilate [ə'sɪmə,leɪt] *v* **-lated; -lating** *vt* **:** asimilar — *vi* **:** adaptarse, integrarse

assimilation [ə,sɪmə'leɪʃən] *n* **:** asimilación *f*

assist[1] [ə'sɪst] *vt* **:** asistir, ayudar

assist[2] *n* **:** asistencia *f*, contribución *f*

assistance [ə'sɪstənts] *n* **:** asistencia *f*, ayuda *f*, auxilio *m*

assistant [ə'sɪstənt] *n* **:** ayudante *mf*, asistente *mf*

associate[1] [ə'soːʃi,eɪt, -si-] *v* **-ated; -ating** *vt* **1** CONNECT, RELATE **:** asociar, relacionar **2 to be associated with**

: estar relacionado con, estar vinculado a — *vi* **to associate with** : relacionarse con, frecuentar

associate² [ə'soːʃiət, -siət] *n* : asociado *m*, -da *f*; colega *mf*; socio *m*, -cia *f*

association [əˌsoːʃi'eɪʃən, -si-] *n* **1** ORGANIZATION : asociación *f*, sociedad *f* **2** RELATIONSHIP : asociación *f*, relación *f*

as soon as *conj* : en cuanto, tan pronto como

assorted [ə'sɔrt̬əd] *adj* : surtido

assortment [ə'sɔrtmənt] *n* : surtido *m*, variedad *f*, colección *f*

assuage [ə'sweɪdʒ] *vt* **-suaged; -suaging 1** EASE : aliviar, mitigar **2** CALM : calmar, aplacar **3** SATISFY : saciar, satisfacer

assume [ə'suːm] *vt* **-sumed; -suming 1** SUPPOSE : suponer, asumir **2** UNDERTAKE : asumir, encargarse de **3** TAKE ON : adquirir, adoptar, tomar <to assume importance : tomar importancia> **4** FEIGN : adoptar, afectar, simular

assumption [ə'sʌmpʃən] *n* : asunción *f*, presunción *f*

assurance [ə'ʃʊrənts] *n* **1** CERTAINTY : certidumbre *f*, certeza *f* **2** CONFIDENCE : confianza *f*, aplomo *m*, seguridad *f*

assure [ə'ʃʊr] *vt* **-sured; -suring** : asegurar, garantizar <I assure you that I'll do it : te aseguro que lo haré>

assured [ə'ʃʊrd] *adj* **1** CERTAIN : seguro, asegurado **2** CONFIDENT : confiado, seguro de sí mismo

aster ['æstər] *n* : áster *m*

asterisk ['æstəˌrɪsk] *n* : asterisco *m*

astern [ə'stərn] *adv* **1** BEHIND : detrás, a popa **2** BACKWARDS : hacia atrás

asteroid ['æstəˌrɔɪd] *n* : asteroide *m*

asthma ['æzmə] *n* : asma *m*

asthmatic [æz'mæt̬ɪk] *adj* : asmático

as though → **as if**

astigmatism [ə'stɪgməˌtɪzəm] *n* : astigmatismo *m*

as to *prep* **1** ABOUT : sobre, acerca de **2** → **according to**

astonish [ə'stɑnɪʃ] *vt* : asombrar, sorprender, pasmar

astonishing [ə'stɑnɪʃɪŋ] *adj* : asombroso, sorprendente, increíble — **astonishingly** *adv*

astonishment [ə'stɑnɪʃmənt] *n* : asombro *m*, estupefacción *f*, sorpresa *f*

astound [ə'staʊnd] *vt* : asombrar, pasmar, dejar estupefacto

astounding [ə'staʊndɪŋ] *adj* : asombroso, pasmoso — **astoundingly** *adv*

astraddle [ə'strædəl] *adv* : a horcajadas

astral ['æstrəl] *adj* : astral

astray [ə'streɪ] *adv & adj* : perdido, extraviado, descarriado

astride [ə'straɪd] *adv* : a horcajadas

astringency [ə'strɪndʒəntsi] *n* : astringencia *f*

astringent¹ [ə'strɪndʒənt] *adj* : astringente

astringent² *n* : astringente *m*

astrologer [ə'strɑlədʒər] *n* : astrólogo *m*, -ga *f*

astrological [ˌæstrə'lɑdʒɪkəl] *adj* : astrológico

astrology [ə'strɑlədʒi] *n* : astrología *f*

astronaut ['æstrəˌnɔt] *n* : astronauta *mf*

astronautic [ˌæstrə'nɔt̬ɪk] *or* **astronautical** [-t̬ɪkəl] *adj* : astronáutico

astronautics [ˌæstrə'nɔt̬ɪks] *ns & pl* : astronáutica *f*

astronomer [ə'strɑnəmər] *n* : astrónomo *m*, -ma *f*

astronomical [ˌæstrə'nɑmɪkəl] *adj* **1** : astronómico **2** ENORMOUS : astronómico, enorme, gigantesco

astronomy [ə'strɑnəmi] *n, pl* **-mies** : astronomía *f*

astute [ə'stuːt, -'stjuːt] *adj* : astuto, sagaz, perspicaz — **astutely** *adv*

astuteness [ə'stuːtnəs, -'stjuːt-] *n* : astucia *f*, sagacidad *f*, perspicacia *f*

asunder [ə'sʌndər] *adv* : en dos, en pedazos <to tear asunder : hacer pedazos>

as well as¹ *conj* : tanto como

as well as² *prep* BESIDES : además de, aparte de

as yet *adv* : aún, todavía

asylum [ə'saɪləm] *n* **1** REFUGE : refugio *m*, santuario *m*, asilo *m* **2 insane asylum** : manicomio *m*

asymmetrical [ˌeɪsə'mɛtrɪkəl] *or* **asymmetric** [-'mɛtrɪk] *adj* : asimétrico

asymmetry [ˌeɪ'sɪmətri] *n* : asimetría *f*

at ['æt] *prep* **1** : en <at the top : en lo alto> <at peace : en paz> <at Ana's house : en casa de Ana> **2** : a <at the rear : al fondo> <at 10 o'clock : a las diez> **3** : por <at last : por fin> <to be surprised at something : sorprenderse por algo> **4** : de <he's laughing at you : está riéndose de ti> **5** : para <you're good at this : eres bueno para esto>

at all *adv* : en absoluto, para nada

ate → **eat**

atheism *n* ['eɪθiˌɪzəm] : ateísmo *m*

atheist ['eɪθiɪst] *n* : ateo *m*, atea *f*

atheistic [ˌeɪθi'ɪstɪk] *adj* : ateo

athlete ['æθˌliːt] *n* : atleta *mf*

athletic [æθ'lɛt̬ɪk] *adj* : atlético

athletics [æθ'lɛt̬ɪks] *ns & pl* : atletismo *m*

atlas ['ætləs] *n* : atlas *m*

atmosphere ['ætməˌsfɪr] *n* **1** AIR : atmósfera *f*, aire *m* **2** AMBIENCE : ambiente *m*, atmósfera *f*, clima *m*

atmospheric [ˌætmə'sfɪrɪk, -'sfɛr-] *adj* : atmosférico — **atmospherically** [-ɪkli] *adv*

atoll ['æˌtɔl, 'eɪ-, -ˌtɑl] *n* : atolón *m*

atom ['æt̬əm] *n* **1** : átomo *m* **2** SPECK : ápice *m*, pizca *f*

atomic [ə'tɑmɪk] *adj* : atómico

atomic bomb *n* **:** bomba *f* atómica
atomizer [ˈæt̬əˌmaɪzər] *n* **:** atomizador *m,* pulverizador *m*
atone [əˈtoːn] *vt* **atoned; atoning to atone for :** expiar
atonement [əˈtoːnmənt] *n* **:** expiación *f,* desagravio *m*
atop[1] [əˈtɑp] *adj* **:** encima
atop[2] *prep* **:** encima de, sobre
atrium [ˈeɪtriəm] *n, pl* **atria** [-triə] *or* **atriums 1 :** atrio *m* **2 :** aurícula *f* (del corazón)
atrocious [əˈtroːʃəs] *adj* **:** atroz — **atrociously** *adv*
atrocity [əˈtrɑsət̬i] *n, pl* **-ties :** atrocidad *f*
atrophy[1] [ˈætrəfi] *vt* **-phied; -phying :** atrofiar
atrophy[2] *n, pl* **-phies :** atrofia *f*
atropine [ˈætrəˌpiːn] *n* **:** atropina *f*
attach [əˈtætʃ] *vt* **1** FASTEN **:** sujetar, atar, amarrar, pegar **2** JOIN **:** juntar, adjuntar **3** ATTRIBUTE **:** dar, atribuir <I attached little importance to it : le di poca importancia> **4** SEIZE **:** embargar **5 to become attached to someone :** encariñarse con alguien
attaché [ˌæt̬əˈʃeɪ, ˌæˌtæ-, əˌtæ-] *n* **:** agregado *m,* -da *f*
attachment [əˈtætʃmənt] *n* **1** ACCESSORY **:** accesorio *m* **2** CONNECTION **:** conexión *f,* acoplamiento *m* **3** FONDNESS **:** apego *m,* cariño *m,* afición *f*
attack[1] [əˈtæk] *vt* **1** ASSAULT **:** atacar, asaltar, agredir **2** TACKLE **:** acometer, combatir, enfrentarse con
attack[2] *n* **1 :** ataque *m,* asalto *m,* acometida *f* <to launch an attack : lanzar un ataque> **2 :** ataque *m,* crisis *f* <heart attack : ataque cardíaco, infarto> <attack of nerves : crisis nerviosa>
attacker [əˈtækər] *n* **:** asaltante *mf*
attain [əˈteɪn] *vt* **1** ACHIEVE **:** lograr, conseguir, alcanzar, realizar **2** REACH **:** alcanzar, llegar a
attainable [əˈteɪnəbəl] *adj* **:** alcanzable, realizable, asequible
attainment [əˈteɪnmənt] *n* **:** logro *m,* consecución *f,* realización *f*
attempt[1] [əˈtɛmpt] *vt* **:** intentar, tratar de
attempt[2] *n* **:** intento *m,* tentativa *f*
attend [əˈtɛnd] *vt* **1 :** asistir a <to attend a meeting : asistir a una reunión> **2 :** atender, ocuparse de, cuidar <to attend a patient : atender a un paciente> **3** HEED **:** atender a, hacer caso de **4** ACCOMPANY **:** acompañar
attendance [əˈtɛndənts] *n* **1** ATTENDING **:** asistencia *f* **2** TURNOUT **:** concurrencia *f*
attendant[1] [əˈtɛndənt] *adj* **:** concomitante, inherente
attendant[2] *n* **:** asistente *mf,* acompañante *mf,* guarda *mf*
attention [əˈtɛntʃən] *n* **1 :** atención *f* **2 to pay attention :** prestar atención, hacer caso **3 to stand at attention :** estar firme
attentive [əˈtɛntɪv] *adj* **:** atento — **attentively** *adv*
attentiveness [əˈtɛntɪvnəs] *n* **1** THOUGHTFULNESS **:** cortesía *f,* consideración *f* **2** CONCENTRATION **:** atención *f,* concentración *f*
attest [əˈtɛst] *vt* **:** atestiguar, dar fe de
attestation [ˌæˌtɛsˈteɪʃən] *n* **:** testimonio *m*
attic [ˈætɪk] *n* **:** ático *m,* desván *m,* buhardilla *f*
attire[1] [əˈtaɪr] *vt* **-tired; -tiring :** ataviar
attire[2] *n* **:** atuendo *m,* atavío *m*
attitude [ˈæt̬əˌtuːd, -ˌtjuːd] *n* **1** FEELING **:** actitud *f* **2** POSTURE **:** postura *f*
attorney [əˈtərni] *n, pl* **-neys :** abogado *m,* -da *f*
attract [əˈtrækt] *vt* **1 :** atraer **2 to attract attention :** llamar la atención
attraction [əˈtrækʃən] *n* **:** atracción *f,* atractivo *m*
attractive [əˈtræktɪv] *adj* **:** atractivo, atrayente
attractively [əˈtræktɪvli] *adv* **:** de manera atractiva, de buen gusto, hermosamente
attractiveness [əˈtræktɪvnəs] *n* **:** atractivo *m*
attributable [əˈtrɪbjʊt̬əbəl] *adj* **:** atribuible, imputable
attribute[1] [əˈtrɪˌbjuːt] *vt* **-tributed; -tributing :** atribuir
attribute[2] [ˈætrəˌbjuːt] *n* **:** atributo *m,* cualidad *f*
attribution [ˌætrəˈbjuːʃən] *n* **:** atribución *f*
attune [əˈtuːn, -ˈtjuːn] *vt* **-tuned; -tuning 1** ADAPT **:** adaptar, adecuar **2 to be attuned to :** estar en armonía con
auburn [ˈɔbərn] *adj* **:** castaño rojizo
auction[1] [ˈɔkʃən] *vt* **:** subastar, rematar
auction[2] *n* **:** subasta *f,* remate *m*
auctioneer [ˌɔkʃəˈnɪr] *n* **:** subastador *m,* -dora *f;* rematador *m,* -dora *f*
audacious [ɔˈdeɪʃəs] *adj* **:** audaz, atrevido
audacity [ɔˈdæsət̬i] *n, pl* **-ties :** audacia *f,* atrevimiento *m,* descaro *m*
audible [ˈɔdəbəl] *adj* **:** audible — **audibly** [-bli] *adv*
audience [ˈɔdiənts] *n* **1** INTERVIEW **:** audiencia *f* **2** PUBLIC **:** audiencia *f,* público *m,* auditorio *m,* espectadores *mpl*
audio[1] [ˈɔdiˌoː] *adj* **:** de sonido, de audio
audio[2] *n* **:** audio *m*
audiovisual [ˌɔdioˈvɪʒʊəl] *adj* **:** audiovisual
audit[1] [ˈɔdət] *vt* **1 :** auditar (finanzas) **2 :** asistir como oyente a (una clase o un curso)
audit[2] *n* **:** auditoría *f*
audition[1] [ɔˈdɪʃən] *vi* **:** hacer una audición
audition[2] *n* **:** audición *f*

auditor [ˈɔdətər] *n* **1 :** auditor *m,* -tora *f* (de finanzas) **2** STUDENT **:** oyente *mf*
auditorium [ˌɔdəˈtoriəm] *n, pl* **-riums** *or* **-ria** [-riə] **:** auditorio *m,* sala *f*
auditory [ˈɔdəˌtori] *adj* **:** auditivo
auger [ˈɔgər] *n* **:** taladro *m,* barrena *f*
augment [ɔgˈmɛnt] *vt* **:** aumentar, incrementar
augmentation [ˌɔgmənˈteɪʃən] *n* **:** aumento *m,* incremento *m*
augur[1] [ˈɔgər] *vt* **:** augurar, presagiar — *vi* **to augur well :** ser de buen agüero
augur[2] *n* **:** augur *m*
augury [ˈɔgjʊri, -gər-] *n, pl* **-ries :** augurio *m,* presagio *m,* agüero *m*
august [ɔˈgʌst] *adj* **:** augusto
August [ˈɔgəst] *n* **:** agosto *m*
auk [ˈɔk] *n* **:** alca *f*
aunt [ˈænt, ˈant] *n* **:** tía *f*
aura [ˈɔrə] *n* **:** aura *f*
aural [ˈɔrəl] *adj* **:** auditivo
auricle [ˈɔrɪkəl] *n* **:** aurícula *f*
aurora borealis [əˈrorəˌboriˈæləs] *n* **:** aurora *f* boreal
auspices [ˈɔspəsəz, -ˌsiːz] *npl* **:** auspicios *mpl*
auspicious [ɔˈspɪʃəs] *adj* **:** prometedor, propicio, de buen augurio
austere [ɔˈstɪr] *adj* **:** austero, severo, adusto — **austerely** *adv*
austerity [ɔˈstɛrəti] *n, pl* **-ties :** austeridad *f*
Australian [ɔˈstreɪljən] *n* **:** australiano *m,* -na *f* — **Australian** *adj*
Austrian [ˈɔstriən] *n* **:** austriaco *m,* -ca *f* — **Austrian** *adj*
authentic [əˈθɛntɪk, ɔ-] *adj* **:** auténtico, genuino — **authentically** [-tɪkli] *adv*
authenticate [əˈθɛntɪˌkeɪt, ɔ-] *vt* **-cated; -cating :** autenticar, autentificar
authenticity [ɔˌθɛnˈtɪsəti] *n* **:** autenticidad *f*
author [ˈɔθər] *n* **1** WRITER **:** escritor *m,* -tora *f;* autor *m,* -tora *f* **2** CREATOR **:** autor *m,* -tora *f;* creador *m,* -dora *f;* artífice *mf*
authoritarian [ɔˌθɔrəˈtɛriən, ə-] *adj* **:** autoritario
authoritative [əˈθɔrəˌteɪtɪv, ɔ-] *adj* **1** RELIABLE **:** fidedigno, autorizado **2** DICTATORIAL **:** autoritario, dictatorial, imperioso
authoritatively [əˈθɔrəˌteɪtɪvli, ɔ-] *adv* **1** RELIABLY **:** con autoridad **2** DICTATORIALLY **:** de manera autoritaria
authority [əˈθɔrəti, ɔ-] *n, pl* **-ties 1** EXPERT **:** autoridad *f;* experto *m,* -ta *f* **2** POWER **:** autoridad *f,* poder *m* **3** AUTHORIZATION **:** autorización *f,* licencia *f* **4 the authorities :** las autoridades *fpl* **5 on good authority :** de buena fuente
authorization [ˌɔθərəˈzeɪʃən] *n* **:** autorización *f*
authorize [ˈɔθəˌraɪz] *vt* **-rized; -rizing :** autorizar, facultar
authorship [ˈɔθərˌʃɪp] *n* **:** autoría *f*
auto [ˈɔto] → **automobile**
autobiographical [ˌɔtoˌbaɪəˈgræfɪkəl] *adj* **:** autobiográfico
autobiography [ˌɔtobaɪˈɑgrəfi] *n, pl* **-phies :** autobiografía *f*
autocracy [ɔˈtɑkrəsi] *n, pl* **-cies :** autocracia *f*
autocrat [ˈɔtəˌkræt] *n* **:** autócrata *mf*
autocratic [ˌɔtəˈkrætɪk] *adj* **:** autocrático — **autocratically** [-tɪkli] *adv*
autograph[1] [ˈɔtəˌgræf] *vt* **:** autografiar
autograph[2] *n* **:** autógrafo *m*
automate [ˈɔtəˌmeɪt] *vt* **-mated; -mating :** automatizar
automatic [ˌɔtəˈmætɪk] *adj* **:** automático — **automatically** [-tɪkli] *adv*
automation [ˌɔtəˈmeɪʃən] *n* **:** automatización *f*
automaton [ɔˈtɑməˌtɑn] *n, pl* **-atons** *or* **-ata** [-tə, -ˌtɑ] **:** autómata *m*
automobile [ˌɔtəmoˈbiːl, -ˈmoːˌbiːl] *n* **:** automóvil *m,* auto *m,* carro *m,* coche *m*
automotive [ˌɔtəˈmoːtɪv] *adj* **:** automotor
autonomous [ɔˈtɑnəməs] *adj* **:** autónomo — **autonomously** *adv*
autonomy [ɔˈtɑnəmi] *n, pl* **-mies :** autonomía *f*
autopsy [ˈɔˌtɑpsi, -təp-] *n, pl* **-sies :** autopsia *f*
autumn [ˈɔtəm] *n* **:** otoño *m*
autumnal [ɔˈtʌmnəl] *adj* **:** otoñal
auxiliary[1] [ɔgˈzɪljəri, -ˈzɪləri] *adj* **:** auxiliar
auxiliary[2] *n, pl* **-ries :** auxiliar *mf,* ayudante *mf*
avail[1] [əˈveɪl] *vt* **to avail oneself :** aprovecharse, valerse
avail[2] *n* **1 :** provecho *m,* utilidad *f* **2 to no avail :** en vano **3 to be of no avail :** no servir de nada, ser inútil
availability [əˌveɪləˈbɪləti] *n, pl* **-ties :** disponibilidad *f*
available [əˈveɪləbəl] *adj* **:** disponible
avalanche [ˈævəˌlæntʃ] *n* **:** avalancha *f,* alud *m*
avarice [ˈævərəs] *n* **:** avaricia *f,* codicia *f*
avaricious [ˌævəˈrɪʃəs] *adj* **:** avaricioso, codicioso
avenge [əˈvɛndʒ] *vt* **avenged; avenging :** vengar
avenger [əˈvɛndʒər] *n* **:** vengador *m,* -dora *f*
avenue [ˈævəˌnuː, -ˌnjuː] *n* **1 :** avenida *f* **2** MEANS **:** vía *f,* camino *m*
average[1] [ˈævrɪdʒ, ˈævə-] *vt* **-aged; -aging 1 :** hacer un promedio de <he averages 8 hours a day : hace un promedio de 8 horas diarias> **2 :** calcular el promedio de, promediar (en matemáticas)
average[2] *adj* **1** MEAN **:** medio <the average temperature : la temperatura media> **2** ORDINARY **:** común, ordinario <the average man : el hombre común>

average[3] *n* : promedio *m*

averse [ə'vərs] *adj* : reacio, opuesto

aversion [ə'vərʒən] *n* : aversión *f*

avert [ə'vərt] *vt* **1** : apartar, desviar <he averted his eyes from the scene : apartó los ojos de la escena> **2** AVOID, PREVENT : evitar, prevenir

aviary ['eɪvi,ɛri] *n, pl* **-aries** : pajarera *f*

aviation [,eɪvi'eɪʃən] *n* : aviación *f*

aviator ['eɪvi,eɪt̬ər] *n* : aviador *m,* -dora *f*

avid ['ævɪd] *adj* **1** GREEDY : ávido, codicioso **2** ENTHUSIASTIC : ávido, entusiasta, ferviente — **avidly** *adv*

avocado [,ævə'kɑdo, ,ɑvə-] *n, pl* **-dos** : aguacate *m,* palta *f*

avocation [,ævə'keɪʃən] *n* : pasatiempo *m,* afición *f*

avoid [ə'vɔɪd] *vt* **1** SHUN : evitar, eludir **2** FORGO : evitar, abstenerse de <I always avoided gossip : siempre evitaba los chismes> **3** EVADE : evitar <if I can avoid it : si puedo evitarlo>

avoidable [ə'vɔɪdəbəl] *adj* : evitable

avoidance [ə'vɔɪdənts] *n* : el evitar

avoirdupois [,ævərdə'pɔɪz] *n* : sistema *m* inglés de pesos y medidas

avow [ə'vaʊ] *vt* : reconocer, confesar

avowal [ə'vaʊəl] *n* : reconocimiento *m,* confesión *f*

await [ə'weɪt] *vt* : esperar

awake[1] [ə'weɪk] *v* **awoke** [ə'wo:k]; **awoken** [ə'wo:kən] *or* **awaked; awaking** : despertar

awake[2] *adj* : despierto

awaken [ə'weɪkən] → **awake**[1]

award[1] [ə'wɔrd] *vt* : otorgar, conceder, conferir

award[2] *n* **1** PRIZE : premio *m,* galardón *m* **2** MEDAL : condecoración *f*

aware [ə'wær] *adj* : consciente <to be aware of : darse cuenta de, estar consciente de>

awareness [ə'wærnəs] *n* : conciencia *f,* conocimiento *m*

awash [ə'wɔʃ] *adj* : inundado

away[1] [ə'weɪ] *adv* **1** : de aquí <go away! : ¡fuera de aquí!, ¡vete!> **2** : de distancia <10 miles away : 10 millas de distancia, queda a 10 millas> **3 far away** : lejos, a lo lejos **4 right away** : en seguida, ahora mismo **5 to be away** : estar ausente, estar de viaje **6 to give away** : regalar (una posesión), revelar (un secreto) **7 to go away** : irse, largarse **8 to put away** : guardar **9 to turn away** : volver la cara

away[2] *adj* **1** ABSENT : ausente <away for the week : ausente por la semana> **2 away game** : partido *m* que se juega fuera

awe[1] ['ɔ] *vt* **awed; awing** : abrumar, asombrar, impresionar

awe[2] *n* : asombro *m*

awesome ['ɔsəm] *adj* **1** IMPOSING : imponente, formidable **2** AMAZING : asombroso

awestruck ['ɔ,strʌk] *adj* : asombrado

awful ['ɔfəl] *adj* **1** AWESOME : asombroso **2** DREADFUL : horrible, terrible, atroz **3** ENORMOUS : enorme, tremendo <an awful lot of people : muchísima gente, la mar de gente>

awfully ['ɔfəli] *adv* **1** EXTREMELY : terriblemente, extremadamente **2** BADLY : muy mal, espantosamente

awhile [ə'*h*waɪl] *adv* : un rato, algún tiempo

awkward ['ɔkwərd] *adj* **1** CLUMSY : torpe, desmañado **2** EMBARRASSING : embarazoso, delicado — **awkwardly** *adv*

awkwardness ['ɔkwərdnəs] *n* **1** CLUMSINESS : torpeza *f* **2** INCONVENIENCE : incomodidad *f*

awl ['ɔl] *n* : punzón *m*

awning ['ɔnɪŋ] *n* : toldo *m*

awry [ə'raɪ] *adj* 1 ASKEW : torcido **2 to go awry** : salir mal, fracasar

ax *or* **axe** ['æks] *n* : hacha *m*

axiom ['æksiəm] *n* : axioma *m*

axiomatic [,æksiə'mæt̬ɪk] *adj* : axiomático

axis ['æksɪs] *n, pl* **axes** [-,si:z] : eje *m*

axle ['æksəl] *n* : eje *m*

aye[1] ['aɪ] *adv* : sí

aye[2] *n* : sí *m*

azalea [ə'zeɪljə] *n* : azalea *f*

azimuth ['æzəməθ] *n* : azimut *m,* acimut *m*

azure[1] ['æʒər] *adj* : azur, celeste

azure[2] *n* : azur *m*

B

b ['bi:] *n, pl* **b's** *or* **bs** ['bi:z] : segunda letra del alfabeto inglés

babble[1] ['bæbəl] *vi* **-bled; -bling 1** PRATTLE : balbucear **2** CHATTER : charlatanear, parlotear *fam* **3** MURMUR : murmurar

babble[2] *n* : balbuceo *m* (de bebé), parloteo *m* (de adultos), murmullo *m* (de voces, de un arroyo)

babe ['beɪb] → **baby**[3]

babel ['beɪbəl, 'bæ-] *n* : babel *f,* caos *m*

baboon [bæ'bu:n] *n* : babuino *m*

baby[1] ['beɪbi] *vt* **-bied; -bying** : mimar, consentir

baby[2] *adj* **1** : de niño <a baby carriage : un cochecito> <baby talk : habla infantil> **2** TINY : pequeño, minúsculo

baby[3] *n, pl* **-bies** : bebé *m;* niño *m,* -ña *f*

babyhood ['beɪbi,hʊd] *n* : niñez *f,* primera infancia *f*

babyish ['beɪbiɪʃ] *adj* : infantil, pueril

baby–sit [ˈbeɪbiˌsɪt] *vi* **-sat** [-ˌsæt]; **-sitting** : cuidar niños, hacer de canguro *Spain*
baby–sitter [ˈbeɪbiˌsɪt̬ər] *n* : niñero *m,* -ra *f;* canguro *mf Spain*
baccalaureate [ˌbækəˈlɔriət] *n* : licenciatura *f*
bachelor [ˈbætʃələr] *n* **1** : soltero *m* **2** : licenciado *m,* -da *f* <bachelor of arts degree : licenciatura en filosofía y letras>
bacillus [bəˈsɪləs] *n, pl* **-li** [-ˌlaɪ] : bacilo *m*
back[1] [ˈbæk] *vt* **1** *or* **to back up** SUPPORT : apoyar, respaldar **2** *or* **to back up** REVERSE : darle marcha atrás a (un vehículo) **3** : estar detrás de, formar el fondo de <trees back the garden : unos árboles están detrás del jardín> — *vi* **1** *or* **to back up** : retroceder **2 to back away** : echarse atrás **3 to back down** *or* **to back out** : volverse atrás, echarse para atrás
back[2] *adv* **1** : atrás, hacia atrás, detrás <to move back : moverse atrás> <back and forth : de acá para allá> **2** AGO : atrás, antes, ya <some years back : unos años atrás, ya unos años> <10 months back : hace diez meses> **3** : de vuelta, de regreso <we're back : estamos de vuelta> <she ran back : volvió corriendo> <to call back : llamar de nuevo>
back[3] *adj* **1** REAR : de atrás, posterior, trasero **2** OVERDUE : atrasado **3 back pay** : atrasos *mpl*
back[4] *n* **1** : espalda *f* (de un ser humano), lomo *m* (de un animal) **2** : respaldo *m* (de una silla), espalda *f* (de ropa) **3** REVERSE : reverso *m,* dorso *m,* revés *m* **4** REAR : fondo *m,* parte *f* de atrás **5** : defensa *mf* (en deportes)
backache [ˈbækˌeɪk] *n* : dolor *m* de espalda
backbite [ˈbækˌbaɪt] *v* **-bit** [-ˌbɪt]; **-bitten** [-ˌbɪtən]; **-biting** *vt* : calumniar, hablar mal de — *vi* : murmurar
backbiter [ˈbækˌbaɪt̬ər] *n* : calumniador *m,* -dora *f*
backbone [ˈbækˌboːn] *n* **1** : columna *f* vertebral **2** FIRMNESS : firmeza *f,* carácter *m*
backdrop [ˈbækˌdrɑp] *n* : telón *m* de fondo
backer [ˈbækər] *n* **1** SUPPORTER : partidario *m,* -ria *f* **2** SPONSOR : patrocinador *m,* -dora *f*
backfire[1] [ˈbækˌfaɪr] *vi* **-fired; -firing 1** : petardear (dícese de un automóvil) **2** FAIL : fallar, salir el tiro por la culata
backfire[2] *n* : petardeo *m,* explosión *f*
background [ˈbækˌgraʊnd] *n* **1** : fondo *m* (de un cuadro, etc.), antecedentes *mpl* (de una situación) **2** EXPERIENCE, TRAINING : experiencia *f* profesional, formación *f*
backhand[1] [ˈbækˌhænd] *adv* : de revés, con el revés
backhand[2] *n* : revés *m*
backhanded [ˈbækˌhændəd] *adj* **1** : dado con el revés, de revés **2** INDIRECT : indirecto, ambiguo
backing [ˈbækɪŋ] *n* **1** SUPPORT : apoyo *m,* respaldo *m* **2** REINFORCEMENT : refuerzo *m* **3** SUPPORTERS : partidarios *mpl,* -rias *fpl*
backlash [ˈbækˌlæʃ] *n* : reacción *f* violenta
backlog [ˈbækˌlɔg] *n* : atraso *m,* trabajo *m* acumulado
backpack[1] [ˈbækˌpæk] *vi* : viajar con mochila
backpack[2] *n* : mochila *f*
backrest [ˈbækˌrɛst] *n* : respaldo *m*
backslide [ˈbækˌslaɪd] *vi* **-slid** [-ˌslɪd]; **-slid** *or* **-slidden** [-ˌslɪdən]; **-sliding** : recaer, reincidir
backstage [ˌbækˈsteɪdʒ, ˈbækˌ-] *adv & adj* : entre bastidores
backtrack [ˈbækˌtræk] *vi* : dar marcha atrás, volverse atrás
backup [ˈbækˌʌp] *n* **1** SUPPORT : respaldo *m,* apoyo *m* **2** : copia *f* de seguridad (para computadoras)
backward[1] [ˈbækwərd] *or* **backwards** [-wərdz] *adv* **1** : hacia atrás **2** : de espaldas <he fell backwards : se cayó de espaldas> **3** : al revés <you're doing it backwards : lo estás haciendo al revés> **4 to bend over backwards** : hacer todo lo posible
backward[2] *adj* **1** : hacia atrás <a backward glance : una mirada hacia atrás> **2** RETARDED : retrasado **3** SHY : tímido **4** UNDERDEVELOPED : atrasado
backwardness [ˈbækwərdnəs] *n* : atraso *m* (dícese de una región), retraso *m* (dícese de una persona)
backwoods [ˌbækˈwʊdz] *npl* : monte *m,* región *f* alejada
bacon [ˈbeɪkən] *n* : tocino *m,* tocineta *f Col, Ven,* bacon *m Spain*
bacterial [bækˈtɪriəl] *adj* : bacteriano
bacteriologist [bækˌtɪriˈɑlədʒɪst] *n* : bacteriólogo *m,* -ga *f*
bacteriology [bækˌtɪriˈɑlədʒi] *n* : bacteriología *f*
bacterium [bækˈtɪriəm] *n, pl* **-ria** [-iə] : bacteria *f*
bad[1] [ˈbæd] *adv* → **badly**
bad[2] *adj* **1** : malo **2** ROTTEN : podrido **3** SERIOUS, SEVERE : grave **4** DEFECTIVE : defectuoso <a bad check : un cheque sin fondos> **5** HARMFUL : perjudicial **6** CORRUPT, EVIL : malo, corrompido **7** NAUGHTY : travieso **8 from bad to worse** : de mal en peor **9 too bad!** : ¡qué lástima!
bad[3] *n* : lo malo <the good and the bad : lo bueno y lo malo>
bade → **bid**
badge [ˈbædʒ] *n* : insignia *f,* botón *m,* chapa *f*
badger[1] [ˈbædʒər] *vt* : fastidiar, acosar, importunar
badger[2] *n* : tejón *m*

badly ['bædli] *adv* **1 :** mal **2** URGENTLY **:** mucho, con urgencia **3** SEVERELY **:** gravemente
badminton ['bæd,mɪntən, -,mɪt-] *n* **:** bádminton *m*
badness ['bædnəs] *n* **:** maldad *f*
baffle[1] ['bæfəl] *vi* **-fled; -fling 1** PERPLEX **:** desconcertar, confundir **2** FRUSTRATE **:** frustrar
baffle[2] *n* **:** deflector *m,* bafle *m* (acústico)
bafflement ['bæfəlmənt] *n* **:** desconcierto *m,* confusión *f*
bag[1] ['bæg] *v* **bagged; bagging** *vi* SAG **:** formar bolsas — *vt* **1 :** ensacar, poner en una bolsa **2 :** cobrar (en la caza), cazar
bag[2] *n* **1 :** bolsa *f,* saco *m* **2** HANDBAG **:** cartera *f,* bolso *m,* bolsa *f Mex* **3** SUITCASE **:** maleta *f,* valija *f*
bagatelle [,bægə'tɛl] *n* **:** bagatela *f*
bagel ['beɪgəl] *n* **:** rosquilla *f* de pan
baggage ['bægɪdʒ] *n* **:** equipaje *m*
baggy ['bægi] *adj* **-gier; -est :** holgado, ancho
bagpipe ['bæg,paɪp] *n* **:** gaita *f*
bail[1] ['beɪl] *vt* **1 :** achicar (agua de un bote) **2 to bail out :** poner en libertad (de una cárcel) bajo fianza **3 to bail out** EXTRICATE **:** sacar de apuros
bail[2] *n* **:** fianza *f,* caución *f*
bailiff ['beɪləf] *n* **:** aguacil *mf*
bailiwick ['beɪli,wɪk] *n* **:** dominio *m*
bailout ['beɪl,aʊt] *n* **:** rescate *m* (financial)
bait[1] ['beɪt] *vt* **1 :** cebar (un anzuelo o cepo) **2** HARASS **:** acosar
bait[2] *n* **:** cebo *m,* carnada *f*
bake[1] ['beɪk] *vt* **baked; baking :** hornear, hacer al horno
bake[2] *n* **:** fiesta con platos hechos al horno
baker ['beɪkər] *n* **:** panadero *m,* -ra *f*
baker's dozen *n* **:** docena *f* de fraile
bakery ['beɪkəri] *n, pl* **-ries :** panadería *f*
bakeshop ['beɪk,ʃɑp] *n* **:** pastelería *f,* panadería *f*
baking powder *n* **:** levadura *f* en polvo
baking soda → **sodium bicarbonate**
balance[1] ['bæləntś] *v* **-anced; -ancing** *vt* **1 :** hacer el balance de (una cuenta) <to balance the books : cuadrar las cuentas> **2** EQUALIZE **:** balancear, equilibrar **3** HARMONIZE **:** armonizar — *vi* **:** balancearse
balance[2] *n* **1** SCALES **:** balanza *f,* báscula *f* **2** COUNTERBALANCE **:** contrapeso *m* **3** EQUILIBRIUM **:** equilibrio *m* **4** REMAINDER **:** balance *m,* resto *m*
balanced ['bæləntst] *adj* **:** equilibrado, balanceado
balcony ['bælkəni] *n, pl* **-nies 1 :** balcón *m,* terraza *f* (de un edificio) **2 :** galería *f* (de un teatro)
bald ['bɔld] *adj* **1 :** calvo, pelado, pelón **2** PLAIN **:** simple, puro <the bald truth : la pura verdad>
balding ['bɔldɪŋ] *adj* **:** quedándose calvo
baldly ['bɔldli] *adv* **:** sin reparos, sin rodeos, francamente
baldness ['bɔldnəs] *n* **:** calvicie *f*
bale[1] ['beɪl] *vt* **baled; baling :** empacar, hacer balas de
bale[2] *n* **:** bala *f,* fardo *m,* paca *f*
baleful ['beɪlfəl] *adj* **1** DEADLY **:** mortífero **2** SINISTER **:** siniestro, funesto, torvo <a baleful glance : una mirada torva>
balk[1] ['bɔk] *vt* **:** obstaculizar, impedir — *vi* **1 :** plantarse *fam* (dícese de un caballo, etc.) **2 to balk at :** resistarse a, mostrarse reacio a
balk[2] *n* **:** obstáculo *m*
Balkan ['bɔlkən] *adj* **:** balcánico
balky ['bɔki] *adj* **balkier; -est :** reacio, obstinado, terco
ball[1] ['bɔl] *vt* **:** apelotonar, ovillar
ball[2] *n* **1 :** pelota *f,* bola *f,* balón *m,* ovillo *m* (de lana) **2 :** juego *m* con pelota o bola **3** DANCE **:** baile *m,* baile *m* de etiqueta
ballad ['bæləd] *n* **:** romance *m,* balada *f*
balladeer [,bælə'dɪr] *n* **:** cantante *mf* de baladas
ballast[1] ['bæləst] *vt* **:** lastrear
ballast[2] *n* **:** lastre *m*
ball bearing *n* **:** cojinete *m* de bola
ballerina [,bælə'ri:nə] *n* **:** bailarina *f*
ballet [bæ'leɪ, 'bæ,leɪ] *n* **:** ballet *m*
ballistic [bə'lɪstɪk] *adj* **:** balístico
ballistics [bə'lɪstɪks] *ns & pl* **:** balística *f*
balloon[1] [bə'lu:n] *vi* **1 :** viajar en globo **2** SWELL **:** hincharse, inflarse
balloon[2] *n* **:** globo *m*
balloonist [bə'lu:nɪst] *n* **:** aeróstata *mf*
ballot[1] ['bælət] *vi* **:** votar
ballot[2] *n* **1 :** papeleta *f* (de voto) **2** BALLOTING **:** votación *f* **3** VOTE **:** voto *m*
ballpoint pen ['bɔl,pɔɪnt] *n* **:** bolígrafo *m*
ballroom ['bɔl,ru:m, -,rʊm] *n* **:** sala *f* de baile
ballyhoo ['bæli,hu:] *n* **:** propaganda *f,* publicidad *f,* bombo *m fam*
balm ['bɑm, 'bɑlm] *n* **:** bálsamo *m,* ungüento *m*
balmy ['bɑmi, 'bɑl-] *adj* **balmier; -est 1** MILD **:** templado, agradable **2** SOOTHING **:** balsámico **3** CRAZY **:** chiflado *fam,* chalado *fam*
baloney [bə'lo:ni] *n* NONSENSE **:** tonterías *fpl,* estupideces *fpl*
balsa ['bɔlsə] *n* **:** balsa *f*
balsam ['bɔlsəm] *n* **1 :** bálsamo *m* **2** *or* **balsam fir :** abeto *m* balsámico
baluster ['bæləstər] *n* **:** balaustre *m*
balustrade ['bælə,streɪd] *n* **:** balaustrada *f*
bamboo [bæm'bu:] *n* **:** bambú *m*
bamboozle [bæm'bu:zəl] *vt* **-zled; -zling :** engañar, embaucar
ban[1] ['bæn] *vt* **banned; banning :** prohibir, proscribir

ban[2] *n* : prohibición *f,* proscripción *f*
banal [bə'nɑl, bə'næl, 'beɪnəl] *adj* : banal, trivial
banality [bə'næləṭi] *n, pl* **-ties** : banalidad *f,* trivialidad *f*
banana [bə'nænə] *n* : banano *m,* plátano *m,* banana *f,* cambur *m Ven,* guineo *m Car*
band[1] ['bænd] *vt* **1** BIND : fajar, atar **2 to band together** : unirse, juntarse
band[2] *n* **1** STRIP : banda *f,* cinta *f* (de un sombrero, etc.) **2** STRIPE : franja *f* **3** : banda *f* (de radiofrecuencia) **4** RING : anillo *m* **5** GROUP : banda *f,* grupo *m,* conjunto *m* <jazz band : conjunto de jazz>
bandage[1] ['bændɪdʒ] *vt* **-daged; -daging** : vendar
bandage[2] *n* : vendaje *m,* venda *f*
bandanna *or* **bandana** [bæn'dænə] *n* : pañuelo *m* (de colores)
bandit ['bændət] *n* : bandido *m,* -da *f;* bandolero *m,* -ra *f*
banditry ['bændətri] *n* : bandolerismo *m,* bandidaje *m*
bandstand ['bænd,stænd] *n* : quiosco *m* de música
bandwagon ['bænd,wægən] *n* **1** : carroza *f* de músicos **2 to jump on the bandwagon** : subirse al carro, seguir la moda
bandy[1] ['bændi] *vt* **-died; -dying 1** EXCHANGE : intercambiar **2 to bandy about** : circular, propagar
bandy[2] *adj* : arqueado, torcido <bandy-legged : de piernas arqueadas>
bane ['beɪn] *n* **1** POISON : veneno *m* **2** RUIN : ruina *f,* pesadilla *f*
baneful ['beɪnfəl] *adj* : nefasto, funesto
bang[1] ['bæŋ] *vt* **1** STRIKE : golpear, darse <he banged his elbow against the door : se dio con el codo en la puerta> **2** SLAM : cerrar (la puerta) con un portazo — *vi* **1** SLAM : cerrarse de un golpe **2 to bang on** : aporrear, golpear <she was banging on the table : aporreaba la mesa>
bang[2] *adv* : directamente, exactamente
bang[3] *n* **1** BLOW : golpe *m,* porrazo *m,* trancazo *m* **2** EXPLOSION : explosión *f,* estallido *m* **3** SLAM : portazo *m* **4 bangs** *npl* : flequilla *f,* fleco *m*
Bangladeshi [,bɑŋglə'dɛʃi, ,bæŋ-, ,bʌŋ-, -'deɪ-] *n* : bangladesí *mf* — **Bangladeshi** *adj*
bangle ['bæŋgəl] *n* : brazalete *m,* pulsera *f*
banish ['bænɪʃ] *vt* **1** EXILE : desterrar, exiliar **2** EXPEL : expulsar
banishment ['bænɪʃmənt] *n* **1** EXILE : destierro *m,* exilio *m* **2** EXPULSION : expulsión *f*
banister ['bænəstər] *n* **1** BALUSTER : balaustre *m* **2** HANDRAIL : pasamanos *m,* barandilla *f,* barandal *m*
banjo ['bæn,dʒoː] *n, pl* **-jos** : banjo *m*
bank[1] ['bæŋk] *vt* **1** TILT : peraltar (una carretera), ladear (un avión) **2** HEAP : amontonar **3** : cubrir (un fuego) **4** : depositar (dinero en un banco) — *vi* **1** : ladearse (dícese de un avión) **2** : tener una cuenta (en un banco) **3 to bank on** : contar con
bank[2] *n* **1** MASS : montón *m,* montículo *m,* masa *f* **2** : orilla *f,* ribera *f* (de un río) **3** : peralte *m* (de una carretera) **4** : banco *m* <World Bank : Banco Mundial> <banco de sangre : blood bank>
bankbook ['bæŋk,bʊk] *n* : libreta *f* bancaria, libreta *f* de ahorros
banker ['bæŋkər] *n* : banquero *m,* -ra *f*
bankrupt[1] ['bæŋ,krʌpt] *vt* : hacer quebrar, llevar a la quiebra, arruinar
bankrupt[2] *adj* **1** : en bancarrota, en quiebra **2 ~ of** LACKING : carente de, falto de
bankrupt[3] *n* : fallido *m,* -da *f;* quebrado *m,* -da *f*
bankruptcy ['bæŋ,krʌptsi] *n, pl* **-cies** : ruina *f,* quiebra *f,* bancarrota *f*
banner[1] ['bænər] *adj* : excelente
banner[2] *n* : estandarte *m,* bandera *f*
banns ['bænz] *npl* : amonestaciones *fpl*
banquet[1] ['bæŋkwət] *vi* : celebrar un banquete
banquet[2] *n* : banquete *m*
banter[1] ['bæntər] *vi* : bromear, hacer bromas
banter[2] *n* : bromas *fpl*
baptism ['bæp,tɪzəm] *n* : bautismo *m*
baptismal [bæp'tɪzməl] *adj* : bautismal
baptize [bæp'taɪz, 'bæp,taɪz] *vt* **-tized; -tizing** : bautizar
bar[1] ['bɑr] *vt* **barred; barring 1** OBSTRUCT : obstruir, bloquear **2** EXCLUDE : excluir **3** PROHIBIT : prohibir **4** SECURE : atrancar, asegurar <bar the door! : ¡atranca la puerta!>
bar[2] *n* **1** : barra *f,* barrote *m* (de una ventana), tranca *f* (de una puerta) **2** BARRIER : barrera *f,* obstáculo *m* **3** LAW : abogacía *f* **4** STRIPE : franja *f* **5** COUNTER : mostrador *m,* barra *f* **6** TAVERN : bar *m,* taberna *f*
bar[3] *prep* **1** : excepto, con excepción de **2 bar none** : sin excepción
barb ['bɑrb] *n* **1** POINT : púa *f,* lengüeta *f* **2** GIBE : pulla *f*
barbarian[1] [bɑr'bæriən] *adj* **1** : bárbaro **2** CRUDE : tosco, bruto
barbarian[2] *n* : bárbaro *m,* -ra *f*
barbaric [bɑr'bærɪk] *adj* **1** PRIMITIVE : primitivo **2** CRUEL : brutal, cruel
barbarity [bɑr'bærəṭi] *n, pl* **-ties** : barbaridad *f*
barbarous ['bɑrbərəs] *adj* **1** UNCIVILIZED : bárbaro **2** MERCILESS : despiadado, cruel
barbarously ['bɑrbərəsli] *adv* : bárbaramente

barbecue[1] [ˈbɑrbɪˌkjuː] *vt* **-cued; -cuing** : asar a la parrilla

barbecue[2] *n* : barbacoa *f,* parrillada *f*

barber [ˈbɑrbər] *n* : barbero *m,* -ra *f*

barbiturate [bɑrˈbɪtʃərət] *n* : barbitúrico *m*

bard [ˈbɑrd] *n* : bardo *m*

bare[1] [ˈbær] *vt* **bared; baring** : desnudar

bare[2] *adj* **1** NAKED : desnudo **2** EXPOSED : descubierto, sin protección **3** EMPTY : desprovisto, vacío **4** MINIMUM : mero, mínimo <the bare necessities : las necesidades mínimas> **5** PLAIN : puro, sencillo

bareback [ˈbærˌbæk] *or* **barebacked** [-ˌbækt] *adv & adj* : a pelo

barefaced [ˈbærˌfeɪst] *adj* : descarado

barefoot [ˈbærˌfʊt] *or* **barefooted** [-ˌfʊt̬əd] *adv & adj* : descalzo

bareheaded [ˈbærˈhɛdəd] *adv & adj* : sin sombrero, con la cabeza descubierta

barely [ˈbærli] *adv* : apenas, por poco

bareness [ˈbærnəs] *n* : desnudez *f*

bargain[1] [ˈbɑrgən] *vi* HAGGLE : regatear, negociar — *vt* BARTER : trocar, cambiar

bargain[2] *n* **1** AGREEMENT : acuerdo *m,* convenio *m* <to strike a bargain : cerrar un trato> **2** : ganga *f* <bargain price : precio de ganga>

barge[1] [ˈbɑrdʒ] *vi* **barged; barging 1** : mover con torpeza **2 to barge in** : entrometerse, interrumpir

barge[2] *n* : barcaza *f,* gabarra *f*

bar graph *n* : gráfico *m* de barras

baritone [ˈbærəˌtoːn] *n* : barítono *m*

barium [ˈbæriəm] *n* : bario *m*

bark[1] [ˈbɑrk] *vi* : ladrar — *vt or* **to bark out** : gritar <to bark out an order : dar una orden a gritos>

bark[2] *n* **1** : ladrido *m* (de un perro) **2** : corteza *f* (de un árbol) **3** *or* **barque** : tipo de embarcación con velas de proa y popa

barley [ˈbɑrli] *n* : cebada *f*

barn [ˈbɑrn] *n* : granero *m* (para cosechas), establo *m* (para ganado)

barnacle [ˈbɑrnɪkəl] *n* : percebe *m*

barnyard [ˈbɑrnˌjɑrd] *n* : corral *m*

barometer [bəˈrɑmət̬ər] *n* : barómetro *m*

barometric [ˌbærəˈmɛtrɪk] *adj* : barométrico

baron [ˈbærən] *n* **1** : barón *m* **2** TYCOON : magnate *mf*

baroness [ˈbærənɪs, -nəs, -ˌnɛs] *n* : baronesa *f*

baronet [ˌbærəˈnɛt, ˈbærənət] *n* : baronet *m*

baronial [bəˈroːniəl] *adj* **1** : de barón **2** STATELY : señorial, majestuoso

baroque [bəˈroːk, -ˈrɑk] *adj* : barroco

barracks [ˈbærəks] *ns & pl* : cuartel *m*

barracuda [ˌbærəˈkuːdə] *n, pl* **-da** *or* **-das** : barracuda *f*

barrage [bəˈrɑʒ, -ˈrɑdʒ] *n* **1** : descarga *f* (de artillería) **2** DELUGE : aluvión *m* <a barrage of questions : un aluvión de preguntas>

barred [ˈbɑrd] *adj* : excluido, prohibido

barrel[1] [ˈbærəl] *v* **-reled** *or* **-relled; -reling** *or* **-relling** *vt* : embarrilar — *vi* : ir disparado

barrel[2] *n* **1** : barril *m,* tonel *m* **2** : cañón *m* (de un arma de fuego), cilindro *m* (de una cerradura)

barren [ˈbærən] *adj* **1** STERILE : estéril (dícese de las plantas o la mujer), árido (dícese del suelo) **2** DESERTED : yermo, desierto

barrette [bɑˈrɛt, bə-] *n* : pasador *m,* broche *m* para el cabello

barricade[1] [ˈbærəˌkeɪd, ˌbærəˈ-] *vt* **-caded; -cading** : cerrar con barricadas

barricade[2] *n* : barricada *f*

barrier [ˈbæriər] *n* **1** : barrera *f* **2** OBSTACLE : obstáculo *m,* impedimento *m*

barring [ˈbɑrɪŋ] *prep* : excepto, salvo, a excepción de

barrio [ˈbɑrio, ˈbær-] *n* : barrio *m*

barroom [ˈbɑrˌruːm, -ˌrʊm] *n* : bar *m*

barrow [ˈbærˌoː] → **wheelbarrow**

bartender [ˈbɑrˌtɛndər] *n* : camarero *m,* -ra *f;* barman *m*

barter[1] [ˈbɑrt̬ər] *vt* : cambiar, trocar

barter[2] *n* : trueque *m,* permuta *f*

basalt [bəˈsɔlt, ˈbeɪˌ-] *n* : basalto *m*

base[1] [ˈbeɪs] *vt* **based; basing** : basar, fundamentar, establecer

base[2] *adj* **baser; basest 1** : de baja ley (dícese de un metal) **2** CONTEMPTIBLE : vil, despreciable

base[3] *n, pl* **bases** : base *f*

baseball [ˈbeɪsˌbɔl] *n* : beisbol *m,* béisbol *m*

baseless [ˈbeɪsləs] *adj* : infundado

basely [ˈbeɪsli] *adv* : vilmente

basement [ˈbeɪsmənt] *n* : sótano *m*

baseness [ˈbeɪsnəs] *n* : vileza *f,* bajeza *f*

bash[1] [ˈbæʃ] *vt* : golpear violentamente

bash[2] *n* **1** BLOW : golpe *m,* porrazo *m,* madrazo *m Mex fam* **2** PARTY: fiesta *f,* juerga *f fam*

bashful [ˈbæʃfəl] *adj* : tímido, vergonzoso, penoso

bashfulness [ˈbæʃfəlnəs] *n* : timidez *f*

basic [ˈbeɪsɪk] *adj* **1** FUNDAMENTAL : básico, fundamental **2** RUDIMENTARY : básico, elemental **3** : básico (en química)

basically [ˈbeɪsɪkli] *adv* : fundamentalmente

basil [ˈbeɪzəl, ˈbæzəl] *n* : albahaca *f*

basilica [bəˈsɪlɪkə] *n* : basílica *f*

basin [ˈbeɪsən] *n* **1** WASHBOWL : palangana *f,* lavamanos *m,* lavabo *m* **2** : cuenca *f* (de un río)

basis [ˈbeɪsəs] *n, pl* **bases** [-ˌsiːz] **1** BASE : base *f,* pilar *m* **2** FOUNDATION : fundamento *m,* base *f* **3 on a weekly basis** : semanalmente

bask [ˈbæsk] *vi* **:** disfrutar, deleitarse <to bask in the sun : disfrutar del sol>

basket [ˈbæskət] *n* **:** cesta *f,* cesto *m,* canasta *f*

basketball [ˈbæskətˌbɔl] *n* **:** baloncesto *m,* basquetbol *m*

bas–relief [ˌbɑrɪˈliːf] *n* **:** bajorrelieve *m*

bass[1] [ˈbæs] *n, pl* **bass** *or* **basses** **:** róbalo *m* (pesca)

bass[2] [ˈbeɪs] *n* **:** bajo *m* (tono, voz, cantante)

bass drum *n* **:** bombo *m*

basset hound [ˈbæsətˌhaʊnd] *n* **:** basset *m*

bassinet [ˌbæsəˈnɛt] *n* **:** moisés *m,* cuna *f*

bassoon [bəˈsuːn, bæ-] *n* **:** fagot *m*

bass viol [ˈbeɪsˈvaɪəl, -ˌoːl] → **double bass**

bastard[1] [ˈbæstərd] *adj* **:** bastardo

bastard[2] *n* **:** bastardo *m,* -da *f*

bastardize [ˈbæstərˌdaɪz] *vt* **-ized; -izing** DEBASE **:** degradar, envilecer

baste [ˈbeɪst] *vt* **basted; basting** **1** STITCH **:** hilvanar **2 :** bañar (con su jugo durante la cocción)

bastion [ˈbæstʃən] *n* **:** bastión *m,* baluarte *m*

bat[1] [ˈbæt] *vt* **batted; batting** **1** HIT **:** batear **2 without batting an eye :** sin pestañear

bat[2] *n* **1 :** murciélago *m* (animal) **2 :** bate *m* <baseball bat : bate de beisbol>

batch [ˈbætʃ] *n* **:** hornada *f,* tanda *f,* grupo *m,* cantidad *f*

bate [ˈbeɪt] *vt* **bated; bating** **1 :** aminorar, reducir **2 with bated breath :** con ansiedad, aguantando la respiración

bath [ˈbæθ, ˈbaθ] *n, pl* **baths** [ˈbæðz, ˈbæθs, ˈbaðz, ˈbaθs] **1** BATHING **:** baño *m* <to take a bath : bañarse> **2 :** baño *m* (en fotografía, etc.) **3** BATHROOM **:** baño *m,* cuarto *m* de baño **4** SPA **:** balneario *m* **5** LOSS **:** pérdida *f*

bathe [ˈbeɪð] *v* **bathed; bathing** *vt* **1** WASH **:** bañar, lavar **2** SOAK **:** poner en remojo **3** FLOOD **:** inundar <to bathe with light : inundar de luz> — *vi* **:** bañarse, ducharse

bather [ˈbeɪðər] *n* **:** bañista *mf*

bathrobe [ˈbæθˌroːb] *n* **:** bata *f* (de baño)

bathroom [ˈbæθˌruːm, -ˌrʊm] *n* **:** baño *m,* cuarto *m* de baño

bathtub [ˈbæθˌtʌb] *n* **:** bañera *f,* tina *f* (de baño)

batiste [bəˈtiːst] *n* **:** batista *f*

baton [bəˈtɑn] *n* **:** batuta *f,* bastón *m*

battalion [bəˈtæljən] *n* **:** batallón *m*

batten [ˈbætən] *vt* **to batten down the hatches :** cerrar las escotillas

batter[1] [ˈbæt̬ər] *vt* **1** BEAT **:** aporrear, golpear **2** MISTREAT **:** maltratar

batter[2] *n* **1 :** masa *f* para rebozar **2** HITTER **:** bateador *m,* -dora *f*

battering ram *n* **:** ariete *m*

battery [ˈbæt̬əri] *n, pl* **-teries** **1 :** lesiones *fpl* <assault and battery : agresión con lesiones> **2** ARTILLERY **:** batería *f* **3 :** batería *f,* pila *f* (de electricidad) **4** SERIES **:** serie *f*

batting [ˈbæt̬ɪŋ] *n* **1** *or* **cotton batting :** algodón *m* en láminas **2 :** bateo *m* (en beisbol)

battle[1] [ˈbæt̬əl] *vi* **-tled; -tling :** luchar, pelear

battle[2] *n* **:** batalla *f,* lucha *f,* pelea *f*

battle–ax [ˈbæt̬əlˌæks] *n* **:** hacha *f* de guerra

battlefield [ˈbæt̬əlˌfiːld] *n* **:** campo *m* de batalla

battlements [ˈbæt̬əlmənts] *npl* **:** almenas *fpl*

battleship [ˈbæt̬əlˌʃɪp] *n* **:** acorazado *m*

batty [ˈbæt̬i] *adj* **-tier; -est :** chiflado *fam,* chalado *fam*

bauble [ˈbɔbəl] *n* **:** chuchería *f,* baratija *f*

bawdiness [ˈbɔdinəs] *n* **:** picardía *f*

bawdy [ˈbɔdi] *adj* **bawdier; -est :** subido de tono, verde, colorado *Mex*

bawl[1] [ˈbɔl] *vi* **:** llorar a gritos

bawl[2] *n* **:** grito *m,* alarido *m*

bawl out *vt* SCOLD **:** regañar

bay[1] [ˈbeɪ] *vi* HOWL **:** aullar

bay[2] *adj* **:** castaño, zaino (dícese de los caballos)

bay[3] *n* **1 :** bahía *f* <Bay of Campeche : Bahía de Campeche> **2** *or* **bay horse :** caballo *m* castaño **3** LAUREL **:** laurel *m* **4** HOWL **:** aullido *m* **5 :** saliente *m* <bay window : ventana en saliente> **6** COMPARTMENT **:** área *f,* compartimento *m* **7 at ~ :** acorralado

bayberry [ˈbeɪˌbɛri] *n, pl* **-ries :** arrayán *m* brabántico

bayonet[1] [ˌbeɪəˈnɛt, ˈbeɪəˌnɛt] *vt* **-neted; -neting :** herir (*o* matar) con bayoneta

bayonet[2] *n* **:** bayoneta *f*

bayou [ˈbaɪˌuː, -ˌoː] *n* **:** pantano *m*

bazaar [bəˈzɑr] *n* **1 :** bazar *m* **2** SALE **:** venta *f* benéfica

bazooka [bəˈzuːkə] *n* **:** bazuca *f*

BB [ˈbiːbi] *n* **:** balín *m*

be [ˈbiː] *v* **was** [ˈwəz, ˈwɑz], **were** [ˈwər]; **been** [ˈbɪn]; **being; am** [ˈæm], **is** [ˈɪz], **are** [ˈɑr] *vi* **1** (*expressing equality*) **:** ser <José is a doctor : José es doctor> <I'm Ana's sister : soy la hermana de Ana> **2** (*expressing quality*) **:** ser <the tree is tall : el árbol es alto> <you're silly! : ¡eres tonto!> **3** (*expressing origin or possession*) **:** ser <she's from Managua : es de Managua> <it's mine : es mío> **4** (*expressing location*) **:** estar <my mother is at home : mi madre está en casa> <the cups are on the table : las tazas están en la mesa> **5** (*expressing existence*) **:** ser, existir <to be or not to be : ser, o no ser> <I think, therefore I am : pienso, luego existo> **6** (*expressing a state of being*)

: estar, tener <how are you? : ¿cómo estás?> <I'm cold : tengo frío> <she's 10 years old : tiene 10 años> <they're both sick : están enfermos los dos> — *v impers* **1** (*indicating time*) : ser <it's eight o'clock : son las ocho> <it's Friday : hoy es viernes> **2** (*indicating a condition*) : hacer, estar <it's sunny : hace sol> <it's very dark outside : está bien oscuro afuera> — *v aux* **1** (*expressing progression*) : estar <what are you doing? —I'm working : ¿qué haces? —estoy trabajando> **2** (*expressing occurrence*) : ser <it was finished yesterday : fue acabado ayer, se acabó ayer> <it was cooked in the oven : se cocinó en el horno> **3** (*expressing possibility*) : poderse <can she be trusted? : ¿se puede confiar en ella?> **4** (*expressing obligation*) : deber <you are to stay here : debes quedarte aquí> <he was to come yesterday : se esperaba que viniese ayer>

beach[1] [ˈbiːtʃ] *vt* : hacer embarrancar, hacer varar, hacer encallar

beach[2] *n* : playa *f*

beachcomber [ˈbiːtʃˌkoːmər] *n* : raquero *m,* -ra *f*

beachhead [ˈbiːtʃˌhɛd] *n* : cabeza *f* de playa

beacon [ˈbiːkən] *n* : faro *m*

bead[1] [ˈbiːd] *vi* : formarse en gotas

bead[2] *n* **1** : cuenta *f* **2** DROP : gota *f* **3 beads** *npl* NECKLACE : collar *m*

beady [ˈbiːdi] *adj* **beadier; -est 1** : de forma de cuenta **2 beady eyes** : ojos *mpl* pequeños y brillantes

beagle [ˈbiːgəl] *n* : beagle *m*

beak [ˈbiːk] *n* : pico *m*

beaker [ˈbiːkər] *n* **1** CUP : taza *f* alta **2** : vaso *m* de precipitados (en un laboratorio)

beam[1] [ˈbiːm] *vi* **1** SHINE : brillar **2** SMILE : sonreír radiantemente — *vt* BROADCAST : transmitir, emitir

beam[2] *n* **1** : viga *f,* barra *f* **2** RAY : rayo *m,* haz *m* de luz **3** : haz *m* de radiofaro (para guiar pilotos, etc.)

bean [ˈbiːn] *n* **1** : habichuela *f,* frijol *m* **2 broad bean** : haba *f* **3 string bean** : judía *f*

bear[1] [ˈbær] *v* **bore** [ˈbor]; **borne** [ˈbɔrn]; **bearing** *vt* **1** CARRY : llevar, portar **2** : dar a luz a (un niño) **3** PRODUCE : dar (frutas, cosechas) **4** ENDURE, SUPPORT : soportar, resistir, aguantar — *vi* **1** TURN : doblar, dar la vuelta <bear right : doble a la derecha> **2 to bear up** : resistir

bear[2] *n, pl* **bears** *or* **bear** : oso *m,* osa *f*

bearable [ˈbærəbəl] *adj* : soportable

beard [ˈbɪrd] *n* **1** : barba *f* **2** : arista *f* (de plantas)

bearded [ˈbɪrdəd] *adj* : barbudo, de barba

bearer [ˈbærər] *n* : portador *m,* -dora *f*

bearing [ˈbærɪŋ] *n* **1** CONDUCT, MANNERS : comportamiento *m,* modales *mpl* **2** SUPPORT : soporte *f* **3** SIGNIFICANCE : relacíon *f,* importancia *f* <to have no bearing on : no tener nada que ver con> **4** : cojinete *m,* rodamiento *m* (de una máquina) **5** COURSE, DIRECTION : dirección *f,* rumbo *m* <to get one's bearings : orientarse>

beast [ˈbiːst] *n* **1** : bestia *f,* fiera *f* <beast of burden : animal de carga> **2** BRUTE : bruto *m,* -ta *f;* bestia *mf*

beastly [ˈbiːstli] *adj* : detestable, repugnante

beat[1] [ˈbiːt] *v* **beat; beaten** [ˈbiːtən] *or* **beat; beating** *vt* **1** STRIKE : golpear, pegar, darle una paliza (a alguien) **2** DEFEAT : vencer, derrotar **3** AVOID : anticiparse a, evitar <to beat the crowd : evitar el gentío> **4** MASH, WHIP : batir — *vi* THROB : palpitar, latir

beat[2] *adj* EXHAUSTED : derrengado, muy cansado <I'm beat! : ¡estoy molido!>

beat[3] *n* **1** : golpe *m,* redoble *m* (de un tambor), latido *m* (del corazón) **2** RHYTHM : ritmo *m,* tiempo *m*

beater [ˈbiːtər] *n* **1** : batidor *m,* -dora *f* **2** EGGBEATER : batidor *m*

beatific [ˌbiːəˈtɪfɪk] *adj* : beatífico

beatitude [biˈætəˌtuːd] *n* **1** : beatitud *f* **2 the Beatitudes** : las bienaventuranzas

beau [ˈboː] *n, pl* **beaux** *or* **beaus** : pretendiente *m,* galán *m*

beautification [ˌbjuːtəfəˈkeɪʃən] *n* : embellecimiento *m*

beautiful [ˈbjuːtɪfəl] *adj* : hermoso, bello, lindo, precioso

beautifully [ˈbjuːtɪfəli] *adv* **1** ATTRACTIVELY : hermosamente **2** EXCELLENTLY : maravillosamente, excelentemente

beauty [ˈbjuːti] *n, pl* **-ties** : belleza *f,* hermosura *f,* beldad *f*

beauty shop *or* **beauty salon** *n* : salón *m* de belleza

beaver [ˈbiːvər] *n* : castor *m*

because [bɪˈkʌz, -ˈkɔz] *conj* : porque

because of *prep* : por, a causa de, debido a

beck [ˈbɛk] *n* **to be at the beck and call of** : estar a la entera disposición de, estar sometido a la voluntad de

beckon [ˈbɛkən] *vi* **to beckon to someone** : hacerle señas a alguien

become [bɪˈkʌm] *v* **-came** [-ˈkeɪm]; **-come; -coming** *vi* : hacerse, volverse, ponerse <he became famous : se hizo famoso> <to become sad : ponerse triste> <to become accustomed to : acostumbrarse a> — *vt* **1** BEFIT : ser apropiado para **2** SUIT : favorecer, quedarle bien (a alguien) <that dress becomes you : ese vestido te favorece>

becoming [bɪˈkʌmɪŋ] *adj* **1** SUITABLE : apropiado **2** FLATTERING : favorecedor

bed[1] [ˈbɛd] *v* **bedded; bedding** *vt* : acostar — *vi* : acostarse

bed[2] *n* **1** : cama *f,* lecho *m* **2** : cauce *m* (de un río), fondo *m* (del mar) **3**

: arriate *m* (para plantas) **4** LAYER, STRATUM : estrato *m,* capa *f*

bedbug [ˈbɛd,bʌg] *n* : chinche *f*

bedclothes [ˈbɛd,klo:ðz, -,klo:z] *npl* : ropa *f* de cama, sábanas *fpl*

bedding [ˈbɛdɪŋ] *n* **1** → **bedclothes 2** : cama *f* (para animales)

bedeck [bɪˈdɛk] *vt* : adornar, engalanar

bedevil [bɪˈdɛvəl] *vt* **-iled** *or* **-illed; -iling** *or* **-illing** : acosar, plagar

bedlam [ˈbɛdləm] *n* : locura *f,* caos *m,* alboroto *m*

bedraggled [bɪˈdrægəld] *adj* : desaliñado, despeinado

bedridden [ˈbɛd,rɪdən] *adj* : postrado en cama

bedrock [ˈbɛd,rɑk] *n* : lecho *m* de roca

bedroom [ˈbɛd,ru:m, -,rʊm] *n* : dormitorio *m,* habitación *f,* pieza *f,* recámara *f Col, Mex, Pan*

bedspread [ˈbɛd,sprɛd] *n* : cubrecama *m,* colcha *f,* cobertor *m*

bee [ˈbi:] *n* **1** : abeja *f* (insecto) **2** GATHERING : círculo *m,* reunión *f*

beech [ˈbi:tʃ] *n, pl* **beeches** *or* **beech** : haya *f*

beechnut [ˈbi:tʃ,nʌt] *n* : hayuco *m*

beef[1] [ˈbi:f] *vt* **to beef up** : fortalecer, reforzar — *vi* COMPLAIN : quejarse

beef[2] *n, pl* **beefs** [ˈbi:fs] *or* **beeves** [ˈbi:vz] : carne *f* de vaca, carne *f* de res *CA, Mex*

beefsteak [ˈbi:f,steɪk] *n* : filete *m,* bistec *m*

beehive [ˈbi:,haɪv] *n* : colmena *f*

beekeeper [ˈbi:,ki:pər] *n* : apicultor *m,* -tora *f*

beeline [ˈbi:,laɪn] *n* **to make a beeline for** : ir derecho a, ir directo hacia

been → **be**

beep[1] [ˈbi:p] *v* : pitar

beep[2] *n* : pitido *m*

beeper [ˈbi:pər] *n* : busca *m,* buscapersonas *m*

beer [ˈbɪr] *n* : cerveza *f*

beeswax [ˈbi:z,wæks] *n* : cera *f* de abejas

beet [ˈbi:t] *n* : remolacha *f,* betabel *m Mex*

beetle [ˈbi:təl] *n* : escarabajo *m*

befall [bɪˈfɔl] *v* **-fell** [-ˈfɛl]; **-fallen** [-ˈfɔlən] *vt* : sucederle a, acontecerle a — *vi* : acontecer

befit [bɪˈfɪt] *vt* **-fitted; -fitting** : convenir a, ser apropiado para

before[1] [bɪˈfor] *adv* **1** : antes <before and after : antes y después> **2** : anterior <the month before : el mes anterior>

before[2] *conj* : antes que <he would die before surrendering : moriría antes que rendirse>

before[3] *prep* **1** : antes de <before eating : antes de comer> **2** : delante de, ante <I stood before the house : estaba parada delante de la casa> <before the judge : ante el juez>

beforehand [bɪˈfor,hænd] *adv* : antes, por adelantado, de antemano, con anticipación

befriend [bɪˈfrɛnd] *vt* : hacerse amigo de

befuddle [bɪˈfʌdəl] *vt* **-dled; -dling** : aturdir, ofuscar, confundir

beg [ˈbɛg] *v* **begged; begging** *vt* : pedir, mendigar, suplicar <I begged him to go : le supliqué que fuera> — *vi* : mendigar, pedir limosna

beget [bɪˈgɛt] *vt* **-got** [-ˈgɑt]; **-gotten** [-ˈgɑtən] *or* **-got; -getting** : engendrar

beggar [ˈbɛgər] *n* : mendigo *m,* -ga *f;* pordiosero *m,* -ra *f*

begin [bɪˈgɪn] *v* **-gan** [-ˈgæn]; **-gun** [-ˈgʌn]; **-ginning** *vt* : empezar, comenzar, iniciar — *vi* **1** START : empezar, comenzar, iniciarse **2** ORIGINATE : nacer, originarse **3 to begin with** : en primer lugar, para empezar

beginner [bɪˈgɪnər] *n* : principiante *mf*

beginning [bɪˈgɪnɪŋ] *n* : principio *m,* comienzo *m*

begone [biˈgɔn] *interj* : ¡fuera de aquí!

begonia [bɪˈgo:njə] *n* : begonia *f*

begrudge [bɪˈgrʌdʒ] *vt* **-grudged; -grudging 1** : dar de mala gana **2** ENVY : envidiar, resentir

beguile [bɪˈgaɪl] *vt* **-guiled; -guiling 1** DECEIVE : engañar **2** AMUSE : divertir, entretener

behalf [bɪˈhæf, -ˈhaf] *n* **1** : favor *m,* beneficio *m,* parte *f* **2 on behalf of** *or* **in behalf of** : de parte de, en nombre de

behave [bɪˈheɪv] *vi* **-haved; -having** : comportarse, portarse

behavior [bɪˈheɪvjər] *n* : comportamiento *m,* conducta *f*

behead [bɪˈhɛd] *vt* : decapitar

behest [bɪˈhɛst] *n* **1** : mandato *m,* orden *f* **2 at the behest of** : a instancia de

behind[1] [bɪˈhaɪnd] *adv* : atrás, detrás <to fall behind : quedarse atrás>

behind[2] *prep* **1** : atrás de, detrás de, tras <behind the house : detrás de la casa> <one behind another : uno tras otro> **2** : atrasado con, después de <behind schedule : atrasado con el trabajo> <I arrived behind the others : llegué después de los otros> **3** SUPPORTING : en apoyo de, detrás

behold [bɪˈho:ld] *vt* **-held; -holding** : contemplar

beholder [bɪˈho:ldər] *n* : observador *m,* -dora *f*

behoove [bɪˈhu:v] *vt* **-hooved; -hooving** : convenirle a, corresponderle a <it behooves us to help him : nos conviene ayudarlo>

beige[1] [ˈbeɪʒ] *adj* : beige

beige[2] *n* : beige *m*

being [ˈbi:ɪŋ] *n* **1** EXISTENCE : ser *m,* existencia *f* **2** CREATURE : ser *m,* ente *m*

belabor [bɪˈleɪbər] *vt* **to belabor the point** : extenderse sobre el tema

belated [bɪˈleɪt̬əd] *adj* : tardío, retrasado
belch[1] [ˈbɛltʃ] *vi* 1 BURP : eructar 2 EXPEL : expulsar, arrojar
belch[2] *n* : eructo *m*
beleaguer [bɪˈliːgər] *vt* 1 BESIEGE : asediar, sitiar 2 HARASS : fastidiar, molestar
belfry [ˈbɛlfri] *n, pl* **-fries** : campanario *m*
Belgian [ˈbɛldʒən] *n* : belga *mf* — **Belgian** *adj*
belie [bɪˈlaɪ] *vt* **-lied; -lying** 1 MISREPRESENT : falsear, ocultar 2 CONTRADICT : contradecir, desmentir
belief [bəˈliːf] *n* 1 TRUST : confianza *f* 2 CONVICTION : creencia *f*, convicción *f* 3 FAITH : fe *f*
believable [bəˈliːvəbəl] *adj* : verosímil, creíble
believe [bəˈliːv] *v* **-lieved; -lieving** : creer
believer [bəˈliːvər] *n* 1 : creyente *mf* 2 : partidario *m*, -ria *f*; entusiasta *mf* <she's a great believer in vitamins : ella es una gran partidaria de las vitaminas>
belittle [bɪˈlɪt̬əl] *vt* **-littled; -littling** 1 DISPARAGE : menospreciar, denigrar, rebajar 2 MINIMIZE : minimizar, quitar importancia a
Belizean [bəˈliːziən] *n* : beliceño *m*, -ña *f* — **Belizean** *adj*
bell[1] [ˈbɛl] *vt* : ponerle un cascabel a
bell[2] *n* : campana *f*, cencerro *m* (para una vaca o cabra), cascabel *m* (para un gato), timbre *m* (de teléfono, de la puerta)
belladonna [ˌbɛləˈdɑnə] *n* : belladona *f*
belle [ˈbɛl] *n* : belleza *f*, beldad *f*
bellhop [ˈbɛlˌhɑp] *n* : botones *m*
bellicose [ˈbɛlɪˌkoːs] *adj* : belicoso *m* — **bellicosity** [ˌbɛlɪˈkɑsət̬i] *n*
belligerence [bəˈlɪdʒərənts] *n* : agresividad *f*, beligerancia *f*
belligerent[1] [bəˈlɪdʒərənt] *adj* : agresivo, beligerante
belligerent[2] *n* : beligerante *mf*
bellow[1] [ˈbɛˌloː] *vi* : bramar, mugir — *vt* : gritar
bellow[2] *n* : bramido *m*, grito *m*
bellows [ˈbɛˌloːz] *ns & pl* : fuelle *m*
bellwether [ˈbɛlˌwɛðər] *n* : líder *mf*
belly[1] [ˈbɛli] *vi* **-lied; -lying** SWELL : hincharse, inflarse
belly[2] *n, pl* **-lies** : abdomen *m*, vientre *m*, barriga *f*, panza *f*
belong [bɪˈlɔŋ] *vi* 1 : pertenecer (a), ser propiedad (de) <it belongs to her : pertenece a ella, es suyo, es de ella> 2 : ser parte (de), ser miembro (de) <he belongs to the club : es miembro del club> 3 : deber estar, ir <your coat belongs in the closet : tu abrigo va en el ropero>
belongings [bɪˈlɔŋɪŋz] *npl* : pertenencias *fpl*, efectos *mpl* personales
beloved[1] [bɪˈlʌvəd, -ˈlʌvd] *adj* : querido, amado
beloved[2] *n* : amado *m*, -da *f*; enamorado *m*, -da *f*; amor *m*
below[1] [bɪˈloː] *adv* : abajo
below[2] *prep* 1 : abajo de, debajo de <below the window : debajo de la ventana> 2 : por debajo de, bajo <below average : por debajo del promedio> <5 degrees below zero : 5 grados bajo cero>
belt[1] [ˈbɛlt] *vt* 1 : ceñir con un cinturón, ponerle un cinturón a 2 THRASH : darle una paliza a, darle un trancazo a
belt[2] *n* 1 : cinturón *m*, cinto *m* (para el talle) 2 BAND, STRAP : cinta *f*, correa *f*, banda *f Mex* 3 AREA : frente *m*, zona *f*
bemoan [bɪˈmoːn] *vt* : lamentarse de
bemuse [bɪˈmjuːz] *vt* **-mused; -musing** 1 BEWILDER : confundir, desconcertar 2 ENGROSS : absorber
bench [ˈbɛntʃ] *n* 1 SEAT : banco *m*, escaño *m*, banca *f* 2 : estrado *m* (de un juez) 3 COURT : tribunal *m*
bend[1] [ˈbɛnd] *v* **bent** [ˈbɛnt]; **bending** *vt* : torcer, doblar, curvar, flexionar — *vi* 1 : torcerse, agacharse <to bend over : inclinarse> 2 TURN : torcer, hacer una curva
bend[2] *n* 1 TURN : vuelta *f*, recodo *m* 2 CURVE : curva *f*, ángulo *m*, codo *m*
beneath[1] [bɪˈniːθ] *adv* : bajo, abajo, debajo
beneath[2] *prep* : bajo de, abajo de, por debajo de
benediction [ˌbɛnəˈdɪkʃən] *n* : bendición *f*
benefactor [ˈbɛnəˌfæktər] *n* : benefactor *m*, -tora *f*
beneficence [bəˈnɛfəsənts] *n* : beneficencia *f*
beneficent [bəˈnɛfəsənt] *adj* : benéfico, caritativo
beneficial [ˌbɛnəˈfɪʃəl] *adj* : beneficioso, provechoso — **beneficially** *adv*
beneficiary [ˌbɛnəˈfɪʃiˌɛri, -ˈfɪʃəri] *n, pl* **-ries** : beneficiario *m*, -ria *f*
benefit[1] [ˈbɛnəfɪt] *vt* : beneficiar — *vi* : beneficiarse
benefit[2] *n* 1 ADVANTAGE : beneficio *m*, ventaja *f*, provecho *m* 2 AID : asistencia *f*, beneficio *m* 3 : función *f* benéfica (para recaudar fondos)
benevolence [bəˈnɛvələnts] *n* : bondad *f*, benevolencia *f*
benevolent [bəˈnɛvələnt] *adj* : benévolo, bondadoso — **benevolently** *adv*
Bengali [bɛnˈgɔli, bɛŋ-] *n* 1 : bengalí *mf* 2 : bengalí *m* (idioma) — **Bengali** *adj*
benign [bɪˈnaɪn] *adj* 1 GENTLE, KIND : benévolo, amable 2 FAVORABLE : propicio, favorable 3 MILD : benigno <a benign tumor : un tumor benigno>

Beninese [bə,nɪ'ni:z, -,ni:-, -'ni:s; ,bɛnɪ'-] *n* : beninés *m,* -nesa *f* — **Beninese** *adj*
bent ['bɛnt] *n* : aptitud *f,* inclinación *f*
benumb [bɪ'nʌm] *vt* : entumecer
benzene ['bɛn,zi:n] *n* : benceno *m*
bequeath [bɪ'kwi:θ, -'kwi:ð] *vt* : legar, dejar en testamento
bequest [bɪ'kwɛst] *n* : legado *m*
berate [bɪ'reɪt] *vt* **-rated; -rating** : reprender, regañar
bereaved[1] [bɪ'ri:vd] *adj* : que está de luto, afligido (por la muerte de alguien)
bereaved[2] *n* **the bereaved** : los deudos del difunto (o de la difunta)
bereavement [bɪ'ri:vmənt] *n* **1** SORROW : dolor *m,* pesar *m* **2** LOSS : pérdida *f*
bereft [bɪ'rɛft] *adj* : privado, desprovisto
beret [bə'reɪ] *n* : boina *f*
beriberi [,bɛri'bɛri] *n* : beriberi *m*
berm ['bərm] *n* : arcén *m*
berry ['bɛri] *n, pl* **-ries** : baya *f*
berserk [bər'sərk, -'zərk] *adj* **1** : enloquecido **2 to go beserk** : volverse loco
berth[1] ['bərθ] *vi* : atracar
berth[2] *n* **1** DOCK : atracadero *m* **2** ACCOMMODATION : litera *f,* camarote *m* **3** POSITION : trabajo *m,* puesto *m*
beryl ['bɛrəl] *n* : berilo *m*
beseech [bɪ'si:tʃ] *vt* **-sought** [-'sɔt] *or* **-seeched; -seeching** : suplicar, implorar, rogar
beset [bɪ'sɛt] *vt* **-set; -setting 1** HARASS : acosar **2** SURROUND : rodear
beside [bɪ'saɪd] *prep* : al lado de, junto a
besides[1] [bɪ'saɪdz] *adv* **1** ALSO : además, también, aparte **2** MOREOVER : además, por otra parte
besides[2] *prep* **1** : además de, aparte de <six others besides you : seis otros además de ti> **2** EXCEPT : excepto, fuera de, aparte de
besiege [bɪ'si:dʒ] *vt* **-sieged; -sieging** : asediar, sitiar, cercar
besmirch [bɪ'smərtʃ] *vt* : ensuciar, mancillar
best[1] ['bɛst] *vt* : superar, ganar a
best[2] *adv* (*superlative of* **well**) : mejor <as best I can : lo mejor que puedo>
best[3] *adj* (*superlative of* **good**) : mejor <my best friend : mi mejor amigo>
best[4] *n* **1 the best** : lo mejor, el mejor, la mejor, los mejores, las mejores **2 at ~** : a lo más **3 to do one's best** : hacer todo lo posible
bestial ['bɛstʃəl, 'bi:s-] *adj* **1** : bestial **2** BRUTISH : brutal, salvaje
best man *n* : padrino *m*
bestow [bɪ'sto:] *vt* : conferir, otorgar, conceder
bestowal [bɪ'sto:əl] *n* : concesión *f,* otorgamiento *m*
bet[1] ['bɛt] *v* **bet; betting** *vt* : apostar — *vi* **to bet on** : apostarle a
bet[2] *n* : apuesta *f*
betoken [bɪ'to:kən] *vt* : denotar, ser indicio de
betray [bɪ'treɪ] *vt* **1** : traicionar <to betray one's country : traicionar uno a su patria> **2** DIVULGE, REVEAL : delatar, revelar <to betray a secret : revelar un secreto>
betrayal [bɪ'treɪəl] *n* : traición *f,* delación *f,* revelación *f* <betrayal of trust : abuso de confianza>
betrothal [bɪ'tro:ðəl, -'trɔ-] *n* : esponsales *mpl,* compromiso *m*
betrothed [bɪ'tro:ðd, -'trɔθt] *n* FIANCÉ : prometido *m,* -da *f*
better[1] ['bɛt̬ər] *vt* **1** IMPROVE : mejorar **2** SURPASS : superar
better[2] *adv* (*comparative of* **well**) **1** : mejor **2** MORE : más <better than 50 miles : más de 50 millas>
better[3] *adj* (*comparative of* **good**) **1** : mejor <the weather is better today : hace mejor tiempo hoy> <I was sick, but now I'm better : estuve enfermo, pero ahora estoy mejor> **2** : mayor <the better part of a month : la mayor parte de un mes>
better[4] *n* **1** : el mejor, la mejor <the better of the two : el mejor de los dos> **2 to get the better of** : vencer a, quedar por encima de, superar
betterment ['bɛt̬ərmənt] *n* : mejoramiento *m,* mejora *f*
bettor *or* **better** ['bɛt̬ər] *n* : apostador *m,* -dora *f*
between[1] [bɪ'twi:n] *adv* **1** : en medio, por lo medio **2 in ~** : intermedio
between[2] *prep* : entre
bevel[1] ['bɛvəl] *v* **-eled** *or* **-elled; -eling** *or* **-elling** *vt* : biselar — *vi* INCLINE : inclinarse
bevel[2] *n* : bisel *m*
beverage ['bɛvrɪdʒ, 'bɛvə-] *n* : bebida *f*
bevy ['bɛvi] *n, pl* **bevies** : grupo *m* (de personas), bandada *f* (de pájaros)
bewail [bɪ'weɪl] *vt* : lamentarse de, llorar
beware [bɪ'wær] *vi* **to beware of** : tener cuidado con <beware of the dog! : ¡cuidado con el perro!> — *vt* : guardarse de, cuidarse de
bewilder [bɪ'wɪldər] *vt* : desconcertar, dejar perplejo
bewilderment [bɪ'wɪldərmənt] *n* : desconcierto *m,* perplejidad *f*
bewitch [bɪ'wɪtʃ] *vt* **1** : hechizar, embrujar **2** CHARM : cautivar, encantar
bewitchment [bɪ'wɪtʃmənt] *n* : hechizo *m*
beyond[1] [bi'jɑnd] *adv* **1** FARTHER, LATER : más allá, más lejos (en el espacio), más adelante (en el tiempo) **2** MORE : más <$50 and beyond : $50 o más>
beyond[2] *n* **the beyond** : el más allá, lo desconocido
beyond[3] *prep* **1** : más allá de <beyond the frontier : más allá de la frontera>

2 : fuera de <beyond one's reach : fuera de su alcance> **3** BESIDES : además de

biannual [ˌbaɪˈænjʊəl] *adj* : bianual — **biannually** *adv*

bias¹ [ˈbaɪəs] *vt* **-ased** *or* **-assed; -asing** *or* **-assing 1** : predisponer, sesgar, influir en, afectar **2 to be biased against** : tener prejuicio contra

bias² *n* **1** : sesgo *m,* bies *m* (en la costura) **2** PREJUDICE : prejuicio *m* **3** TENDENCY : inclinación *f,* tendencia *f*

biased [ˈbaɪəst] *adj* : tendencioso, parcial

bib [ˈbɪb] *n* **1** : peto *m* **2** : babero *m* (para niños)

Bible [ˈbaɪbəl] *n* : Biblia *f*

biblical [ˈbɪblɪkəl] *adj* : bíblico

bibliographer [ˌbɪbliˈɑgrəfər] *n* : bibliógrafo *m,* -fa *f*

bibliographic [ˌbɪbliəˈgræfɪk] *adj* : bibliográfico

bibliography [ˌbɪbliˈɑgrəfi] *n, pl* **-phies** : bibliografía *f*

bicameral [ˌbaɪˈkæmərəl] *adj* : bicameral

bicarbonate [ˌbaɪˈkɑrbənət, -ˌneɪt] *n* : bicarbonato *m*

bicentennial [ˌbaɪsɛnˈtɛniəl] *n* : bicentenario *m*

biceps [ˈbaɪˌsɛps] *ns & pl* : bíceps *m*

bicker¹ [ˈbɪkər] *vi* : pelear, discutir, reñir

bicker² *n* : pelea *f,* riña *f,* discusión *f*

bicuspid [baɪˈkʌspɪd] *n* : premolar *m,* diente *m* bicúspide

bicycle¹ [ˈbaɪsɪkəl, -ˌsɪ-] *vi* **-cled; -cling** : ir en bicicleta

bicycle² *n* : bicicleta *f*

bicycling [ˈbaɪsɪkəlɪŋ] *n* : ciclismo *m*

bicyclist [ˈbaɪsɪkəlɪst] *n* : ciclista *mf*

bid¹ [ˈbɪd] *vt* **bade** [ˈbæd, ˈbeɪd] *or* **bid; bidden** [ˈbɪdən] *or* **bid; bidding 1** ORDER : pedir, mandar **2** INVITE : invitar **3** SAY : dar, decir <to bid good evening : dar las buenas noches> <to bid farewell to : decir adiós a> **4** : ofrecer (en una subasta), declarar (en juegos de cartas)

bid² *n* **1** OFFER : oferta *f* (en una subasta), declaración *f* (en juegos de cartas) **2** INVITATION : invitación *f* **3** ATTEMPT : intento *m,* tentativa *f*

bidder [ˈbɪdər] *n* : postor *m,* -tora *f*

bide [ˈbaɪd] *v* **bode** [ˈboːd] *or* **bided; bided; biding** *vt* : esperar, aguardar <to bide one's time : esperar el momento oportuno> — *vi* DWELL : morar, vivir

biennial [baɪˈɛniəl] *adj* : bienal — **biennially** *adv*

bier [ˈbɪr] *n* **1** STAND : andas *fpl* **2** COFFIN : ataúd *m,* féretro *m*

bifocals [ˈbaɪˌfoːkəlz] *npl* : lentes *mpl* bifocales, bifocales *mpl*

big [ˈbɪg] *adj* **bigger; biggest 1** LARGE : grande **2** PREGNANT : embarazada **3** IMPORTANT, MAJOR : importante, grande <a big decision : una gran decisión> **4** POPULAR : popular, famoso, conocido

bigamist [ˈbɪgəmɪst] *n* : bígamo *m,* -ma *f*

bigamous [ˈbɪgəməs] *adj* : bígamo

bigamy [ˈbɪgəmi] *n* : bigamia *f*

Big Dipper → **dipper**

bighorn [ˈbɪgˌhɔrn] *n, pl* **-horn** *or* **-horns** *or* **bighorn sheep** : oveja *f* salvaje de las montañas

bight [ˈbaɪt] *n* : bahía *f,* ensenada *f,* golfo *m*

bigot [ˈbɪgət] *n* : intolerante *mf*

bigoted [ˈbɪgət̬əd] *adj* : intolerante, prejuiciado, fanático

bigotry [ˈbɪgətri] *n, pl* **-tries** : intolerancia *f,* fanaticismo *m*

big shot *n* : pez *m* gordo *fam,* mandamás *mf*

bigwig [ˈbɪgˌwɪg] → **big shot**

bike [ˈbaɪk] *n* **1** : bicicleta *f,* bici *f fam* **2** : motocicleta *f,* moto *f*

bikini [bəˈkiːni] *n* : bikini *m*

bilateral [baɪˈlæt̬ərəl] *adj* : bilateral — **bilaterally** *adv*

bile [ˈbaɪl] *n* **1** : bilis *f* **2** IRRITABILITY : mal genio *m*

bilingual [baɪˈlɪŋgwəl] *adj* : bilingüe

bilious [ˈbɪliəs] *adj* **1** : bilioso **2** IRRITABLE : bilioso, colérico

bilk [ˈbɪlk] *vt* : burlar, estafar, defraudar

bill¹ [ˈbɪl] *vt* : pasarle la cuenta a — *vi* : acariciar <to bill and coo : acariciarse>

bill² *n* **1** LAW : proyecto *m* de ley, ley *f* **2** INVOICE : cuenta *f,* factura *f* **3** POSTER : cartel *m* **4** PROGRAM : programa *m* (del teatro) **5** : billete *m* <a five-dollar bill : un billete de cinco dólares> **6** BEAK : pico *m*

billboard [ˈbɪlˌbɔrd] *n* : cartelera *f*

billet¹ [ˈbɪlət] *vt* : acuartelar, alojar

billet² *n* : alojamiento *m*

billfold [ˈbɪlˌfoːld] *n* : billetera *f,* cartera *f*

billiards [ˈbɪljərdz] *n* : billar *m*

billion [ˈbɪljən] *n, pl* **billions** *or* **billion** : mil millones *mpl*

billow¹ [ˈbɪlo] *vi* : hincharse, inflarse

billow² *n* **1** WAVE : ola *f* **2** CLOUD : nube *f* <a billow of smoke : un nube de humo>

billowy [ˈbɪlowi] *adj* : ondulante

billy goat [ˈbɪliˌgoːt] *n* : macho *m* cabrío

bin [ˈbɪn] *n* : cubo *m,* cajón *m*

binary [ˈbaɪnəri, -ˌnɛri] *adj* : binario *m*

bind [ˈbaɪnd] *vt* **bound** [ˈbaʊnd]; **binding 1** TIE : atar, amarrar **2** OBLIGATE : obligar **3** UNITE : aglutinar, ligar, unir **4** BANDAGE : vendar **5** : encuadernar (un libro)

binder [ˈbaɪndər] *n* **1** FOLDER : carpeta *f* **2** : encuadernador *m,* -dora *f* (de libros)

binding [ˈbaɪndɪŋ] *n* **1** : encuadernación *f* (de libros) **2** COVER : cubierta *f,* forro *m*

binge [ˈbɪndʒ] *n* : juerga *f,* parranda *f fam*
bingo [ˈbɪŋˌgoː] *n, pl* **-gos** : bingo *m*
binocular [baɪˈnɑkjələr, bə-] *adj* : binocular
binoculars [bəˈnɑkjələrz, baɪ-] *npl* : binoculares *mpl*
biochemical[1] [ˌbaɪoˈkɛmɪkəl] *adj* : bioquímico
biochemical[2] *n* : bioquímico *m*
biochemist [ˌbaɪoˈkɛmɪst] *n* : bioquímico *m,* -ca *f*
biochemistry [ˌbaɪoˈkɛməstri] *n* : bioquímica *f*
biodegradable [ˌbaɪodɪˈgreɪdəbəl] *adj* : biodegradable
biodegradation [ˌbaɪodɛgrəˈdeɪʃən] *n* : biodegradación *f*
biodegrade [ˌbaɪodɪˈgreɪd] *vi* **-graded; -grading** : biodegradarse
biographer [baɪˈɑgrəfər] *n* : biógrafo *m,* -fa *f*
biographical [ˌbaɪəˈgræfɪkəl] *adj* : biográfico
biography [baɪˈɑgrəfi, biː-] *n, pl* **-phies** : biografía *f*
biologic [ˌbaɪəˈlɑdʒɪk] *or* **biological** [-dʒɪkəl] *adj* : biológico
biologist [baɪˈɑlədʒɪst] *n* : biólogo *m,* -ga *f*
biology [baɪˈɑlədʒi] *n* : biología *f*
biophysical [ˌbaɪoˈfɪzɪkəl] *adj* : biofísico
biophysicist [ˌbaɪoˈfɪzəsɪst] *n* : biofísico *m,* -ca *f*
biophysics [ˌbaɪoˈfɪzɪks] *ns & pl* : biofísica *f*
biopsy [ˈbaɪˌɑpsi] *n, pl* **-sies** : biopsia *f*
biotechnology [ˌbaɪotɛkˈnɑlədʒi] *n* : biotecnología *f*
biotic [baɪˈɑtɪk] *adj* : biótico
bipartisan [baɪˈpɑrtəzən, -sən] *adj* : bipartidista, de dos partidas
biped [ˈbaɪˌpɛd] *n* : bípedo *m*
birch [ˈbərtʃ] *n* : abedul *m*
bird [ˈbərd] *n* : pájaro *m* (pequeño), ave *f* (grande)
birdbath [ˈbərdˌbæθ, -ˌbaθ] *n* : pila *f* para pájaros
bird dog *n* : perro *m,* -rra *f* de caza
bird of prey *n* : ave *f* rapaz, ave *f* de presa
birdseed [ˈbərdˌsiːd] *n* : alpiste *m*
bird's–eye [ˈbərdzˌaɪ] *adj* **1** : visto desde arriba <bird's-eye view : vista aérea> **2** CURSORY : rápido, somero
birth [ˈbərθ] *n* **1** : nacimiento *m,* parto *m* **2** ORIGIN : origen *m,* nacimiento *m*
birthday [ˈbərθˌdeɪ] *n* : cumpleaños *m,* aniversario *m*
birthmark [ˈbərθˌmɑrk] *n* : mancha *f* de nacimiento
birthplace [ˈbərθˌpleɪs] *n* : lugar *m* de nacimiento
birthrate [ˈbərθˌreɪt] *n* : índice *m* de natalidad
birthright [ˈbərθˌraɪt] *n* : derecho *m* de nacimiento
biscuit [ˈbɪskət] *n* : bizcocho *m*
bisect [ˈbaɪˌsɛkt, ˌbaɪˈ-] *vt* : bisecar
bisector [ˈbaɪˌsɛktər, ˌbaɪˈ-] *n* : bisectriz *f*
bishop [ˈbɪʃəp] *n* : obispo *m*
bismuth [ˈbɪzməθ] *n* : bismuto *m*
bison [ˈbaɪzən, -sən] *ns & pl* : bisonte *m*
bistro [ˈbiːstro, ˈbɪs-] *n, pl* **-tros** : bar *m,* restaurante *m* pequeño
bit [ˈbɪt] *n* **1** FRAGMENT, PIECE : pedazo *m,* trozo *m* <a bit of luck : un poco de suerte> **2** : freno *m,* bocado *m* (de una brida) **3** : broca *f* (de un taladro) **4** : bit *m* (de información)
bitch[1] [ˈbɪtʃ] *vi* COMPLAIN : quejarse, reclamar
bitch[2] *n* : perra *f*
bite[1] [ˈbaɪt] *v* **bit** [ˈbɪt]; **bitten** [ˈbɪtən]; **biting** *vt* **1** : morder **2** STING : picar **3** PUNCTURE : punzar, pinchar **4** GRIP : agarrar — *vi* **1** : morder <that dog bites : ese perro muerde> **2** STING : picar (dícese de un insecto), cortar (dícese del viento) **3** : picar <the fish are biting now : ya están picando los peces> **4** GRAB : agarrarse
bite[2] *n* **1** BITING : mordisco *m,* dentellada *f* **2** SNACK : bocado *m* <a bite to eat : algo de comer> **3** : picadura *f* (de un insecto), mordedura *f* (de un animal) **4** SHARPNESS : mordacidad *f,* penetración *f*
biting *adj* **1** PENETRATING : cortante, penetrante **2** CAUSTIC : mordaz, sarcástico
bitter [ˈbɪtər] *adj* **1** ACRID : amargo, acre **2** PENETRATING : cortante, penetrante <bitter cold : frío glacial> **3** HARSH : duro, amargo <to the bitter end : hasta el final> **4** INTENSE, RELENTLESS : intenso, extremo, implacable <bitter hatred : odio implacable>
bitterly [ˈbɪtərli] *adv* : amargamente
bittern [ˈbɪtərn] *n* : avetoro *m* común
bitterness [ˈbɪtərnəs] *n* : amargura *f*
bituminous coal [bəˈtuːmənəs, -ˈtjuː-] *n* : carbón *m* bituminoso
bivalve [ˈbaɪˌvælv] *n* : bivalvo *m* — **bivalve** *adj*
bivouac[1] [ˈbɪvəˌwæk, ˈbɪvˌwæk] *vi* **-ouacked; -ouacking** : acampar, vivaquear
bivouac[2] *n* : vivaque *m*
bizarre [bəˈzɑr] *adj* : extraño, singular, estrafalario, estrambótico — **bizarrely** *adv*
blab [ˈblæb] *vi* **blabbed; blabbing** : parlotear *fam,* cotorrear *fam*
black[1] [ˈblæk] *vt* : ennegrecer
black[2] *adj* **1** : negro (color, raza) **2** SOILED : sucio **3** DARK : oscuro, negro **4** WICKED : malvado, perverso, malo **5** GLOOMY : negro, sombrío, deprimente
black[3] *n* **1** : negro *m* (color) **2** : negro *m,* -gra *f* (persona)
black–and–blue [ˌblækənˈbluː] *adj* : amoratado

blackball ['blæk,bɔl] *vt* **1** OSTRACIZE : hacerle el vacío a, aislar **2** BOYCOTT : boicotear
blackberry ['blæk,bɛri] *n, pl* **-ries** : mora *f*
blackbird ['blæk,bərd] *n* : mirlo *m*
blackboard ['blæk,bɔrd] *n* : pizarra *f*, pizarrón *m*
blacken ['blækən] *vt* **1** BLACK : ennegrecer **2** DEFAME : deshonrar, difamar, manchar
blackhead ['blæk,hɛd] *n* : espinilla *f*, punto *m* negro
black hole *n* : agujero *m* negro
blackjack ['blæk,jæk] *n* **1** : cachiporra *f* (arma) **2** : veintiuna *f* (juego de cartas)
blacklist[1] ['blæk,lɪst] *vt* : poner en la lista negra
blacklist[2] *n* : lista *f* negra
blackmail[1] ['blæk,meɪl] *vt* : chantajear, hacer chantaje a
blackmail[2] *n* : chantaje *m*
blackmailer ['blæk,meɪlər] *n* : chantajista *mf*
blackout ['blæk,aʊt] *n* **1** : apagón *m* (de poder eléctrico) **2** FAINT : desmayo *m*, desvanecimiento *m*
black out *vt* : dejar sin luz — *vi* FAINT : perder el conocimiento, desmayarse
blacksmith ['blæk,smɪθ] *n* : herrero *m*
blacktop ['blæk,tɑp] *n* : asfalto *m*
bladder ['blædər] *n* : vejiga *f*
blade ['bleɪd] *n* : hoja *f* (de un cuchillo), cuchilla *f* (de un patín), pala *f* (de un remo o una hélice), brizna *f* (de hierba)
blamable ['bleɪməbəl] *adj* : culpable
blame[1] ['bleɪm] *vt* **blamed; blaming** : culpar, echar la culpa a
blame[2] *n* : culpa *f*
blameless ['bleɪmləs] *adj* : intachable, sin culpa, inocente — **blamelessly** *adv*
blameworthiness ['bleɪm,wərðinəs] *n* : culpa *f*, culpabilidad *f*
blameworthy ['bleɪm,wərði] *adj* : culpable, reprochable, censurable
blanch ['blæntʃ] *vt* WHITEN : blanquear — *vi* PALE : palidecer
bland ['blænd] *adj* : soso, insulso, desabrido <a bland smile : una sonrisa insulsa> <a bland diet : una dieta fácil de digerir>
blandishments ['blændɪʃmənts] *npl* : lisonjas *fpl*, halagos *mpl*
blandly ['blændli] *adv* : de manera insulsa
blandness ['blændnəs] *n* : lo insulso, lo desabrido
blank[1] ['blæŋk] *vt* OBLITERATE : borrar
blank[2] *adj* **1** DAZED : perplejo, desconcertado **2** EXPRESSIONLESS : sin expresión, inexpresivo **3** : en blanco (dícese de un papel), liso (dícese de una pared) **4** EMPTY : vacío, en blanco <a blank stare : una mirada vacía> <his mind went blank : se quedó en blanco>
blank[3] *n* **1** SPACE : espacio *m* en blanco **2** FORM : formulario *m* **3** CARTRIDGE : cartucho *m* de fogueo **4** *or* **blank key** : llave *f* ciega
blanket[1] [blæŋkət] *vt* : cubrir
blanket[2] *adj* : global
blanket[3] *n* : manta *f*, cobija *f*, frazada *f*
blankly ['blænkli] *adv* : sin comprender
blankness ['blænknəs] *n* **1** PERPLEXITY : desconcierto *m*, perplejidad *f* **2** EMPTINESS : vacío *m*, vacuidad *f*
blare[1] ['blær] *vi* **blared; blaring** : resonar
blare[2] *n* : estruendo *m*
blarney ['blɑrni] *n* : labia *f fam*
blasé [blɑ'zeɪ] *adj* : displicente, indiferente
blaspheme [blæs'fiːm, 'blæs,-] *vi* **-phemed; -pheming** : blasfemar
blasphemer [blæs'fiːmər, 'blæs,-] *n* : blasfemo *m*, -ma *f*
blasphemous ['blæsfəməs] *adj* : blasfemo
blasphemy ['blæsfəmi] *n, pl* **-mies** : blasfemia *f*
blast[1] ['blæst] *vt* **1** BLOW UP : volar, hacer volar **2** ATTACK : atacar, arremeter contra
blast[2] *n* **1** GUST : ráfaga *f* **2** EXPLOSION : explosión *f*
blast-off ['blæst,ɔf] *n* : despegue *m*
blast off *vi* : despegar
blatant ['bleɪtənt] *adj* : descarado — **blatantly** ['bleɪtəntli] *adv*
blaze[1] ['bleɪz] *v* **blazed; blazing** *vi* SHINE : arder, brillar, resplandecer — *vt* MARK : marcar, señalar <to blaze a trail : abrir un camino>
blaze[2] *n* **1** FIRE : fuego *m* **2** BRIGHTNESS : resplandor *m*, brillantez *f* **3** OUTBURST : arranque *m* <a blaze of anger : un arranque de cólera> **4** DISPLAY : alarde *m*, llamarada *f* <a blaze of color : un derroche de color>
blazer ['bleɪzər] *n* : chaqueta *f* deportiva, blazer *m*
bleach[1] ['bliːtʃ] *vt* : blanquear, decolorar
bleach[2] *n* : lejía *f*, blanqueador *m*
bleachers ['bliːtʃərz] *ns & pl* : gradas *fpl*, tribuna *f* descubierta
bleak ['bliːk] *adj* **1** DESOLATE : inhóspito, sombrío, desolado **2** DEPRESSING : deprimente, triste, sombrío
bleakly ['bliːkli] *adv* : sombríamente
bleakness ['bliːknəs] *n* : lo inhóspito, lo sombrío
blear ['blɪr] *adj* : empañado, nublado
bleary ['blɪri] *adj* **1** : adormilado, fatigado **2** **bleary–eyed** : con los ojos nublados
bleat[1] ['bliːt] *vi* : balar
bleat[2] *n* : balido *m*
bleed ['bliːd] *v* **bled** ['blɛd]; **bleeding** *vi* **1** : sangrar **2** GRIEVE : sufrir, afligirse **3** EXUDE : exudar (dícese de una planta), correrse (dícese de los colo-

res) — *vt* **1 :** sangrar (a una persona), purgar (frenos) **2 to bleed someone dry :** sacarle todo el dinero a alguien
blemish[1] ['blɛmɪʃ] *vt* **:** manchar, marcar
blemish[2] *n* **:** imperfección *f,* mancha *f,* marca *f*
blend[1] ['blɛnd] *vt* **1** MIX **:** mezclar **2** COMBINE **:** combinar, aunar
blend[2] *n* **:** mezcla *f,* combinación *f*
blender ['blɛndər] *n* **:** licuadora *f*
bless ['blɛs] *vt* **blessed** ['blɛst]; **blessing 1** CONSECRATE **:** bendecir, consagrar **2 :** bendecir <may God bless you! : ¡que Dios te bendiga!> **3 to bless with :** dotar de **4 to bless oneself :** santiguarse
blessed ['blɛsəd] *or* **blest** ['blɛst] *adj* **:** bienaventurado, bendito, dichoso
blessedly ['blɛsədli] *adv* **:** felizmente, alegremente, afortunadamente
blessing ['blɛsɪŋ] *n* **1 :** bendición *f* **2** APPROVAL **:** aprobación *f,* consentimiento *m*
blew → **blow**
blight[1] ['blaɪt] *vt* **:** arruinar, infestar
blight[2] *n* **1 :** añublo *m* **2** PLAGUE **:** peste *f,* plaga *f* **3** DECAY **:** deterioro *m,* ruina *f*
blimp ['blɪmp] *n* **:** dirigible *m*
blind[1] ['blaɪnd] *vt* **1 :** cegar, dejar ciego **2** DAZZLE **:** deslumbrar
blind[2] *adj* **1** SIGHTLESS **:** ciego **2** INSENSITIVE **:** ciego, insensible, sin razón **3** CLOSED **:** sin salida <blind alley : callejón sin salida>
blind[3] *n* **1 :** persiana *f* (para una ventana) **2** COVER **:** escondite *m,* escondrijo *m*
blindfold[1] ['blaɪnd,fo:ld] *vt* **:** vendar los ojos
blindfold[2] *n* **:** venda *f* (para los ojos)
blindly ['blaɪndli] *adv* **:** a ciegas, ciegamente
blindness ['blaɪndnəs] *n* **:** ceguera *f*
blink[1] ['blɪŋk] *vi* **1** WINK **:** pestañear, parpadear **2 :** brillar intermitentemente
blink[2] *n* **:** pestañeo *m,* parpadeo *m*
blinker ['blɪŋkər] *n* **:** intermitente *m,* direccional *f*
bliss ['blɪs] *n* **1** HAPPINESS **:** dicha *f,* felicidad *f* absoluta **2** PARADISE **:** paraíso *m*
blissful ['blɪsfəl] *adj* **:** dichoso, feliz — **blissfully** *adv*
blister[1] ['blɪstər] *vi* **:** ampollarse
blister[2] *n* **:** ampolla *f* (en la piel o una superficie), burbuja *f* (en una superficie)
blithe ['blaɪθ, 'blaɪð] *adj* **blither; blithest 1** CAREFREE **:** despreocupado **2** CHEERFUL **:** alegre, risueño — **blithely** *adv*
blitz[1] ['blɪts] *vt* **1** BOMBARD **:** bombardear **2 :** atacar con rapidez
blitz[2] *n* **1 :** bombardeo *m* aéreo **2** CAMPAIGN **:** ataque *m,* acometida *f*
blizzard ['blɪzərd] *n* **:** tormenta *f* de nieve, ventisca *f*
bloat ['blo:t] *vi* **:** hincharse, inflarse
blob ['blɑb] *n* **:** gota *f,* mancha *f,* borrón *m*
bloc ['blɑk] *n* **:** bloque *m*
block[1] ['blɑk] *vt* **1** OBSTRUCT **:** obstruir, bloquear **2** CLOG **:** atascar, atorar
block[2] *n* **1** PIECE **:** bloque *m* <building blocks : cubos de construcción> <auction block : plataforma de subastas> <starting block : taco de salida> **2** OBSTRUCTION **:** obstrucción *f,* bloqueo *m* **3 :** cuadra *f,* manzana *f* (de edificios) <to go around the block : dar la vuelta a la cuadra> **4** BUILDING **:** edificio *m* (de apartamentos, oficinas, etc.) **5** GROUP, SERIES **:** serie *f,* grupo *m* <a block of tickets : una serie de entradas> **6 block and tackle :** aparejo *m* de poleas
blockade[1] [blɑ'keɪd] *vt* **-aded; -ading :** bloquear
blockade[2] *n* **:** bloqueo *m*
blockage ['blɑkɪdʒ] *n* **:** bloqueo *m,* obstrucción *f*
blockhead ['blɑk,hɛd] *n* **:** bruto *m,* -ta *f;* estúpido *m,* -da *f*
blond[1] *or* **blonde** ['blɑnd] *adj* **:** rubio, güero *Mex,* claro (dícese de la madera)
blond[2] *or* **blonde** *n* **:** rubio *m,* -bia *f;* güero *m,* -ra *f Mex*
blood ['blʌd] *n* **1 :** sangre *f* **2** LIFEBLOOD **:** vida *f,* alma *f* **3** LINEAGE **:** linaje *m,* sangre *f*
blood bank *n* **:** banco *m* de sangre
bloodcurdling ['blʌd,kərdəlɪŋ] *adj* **:** espeluznante, aterrador
blooded ['blʌdəd] *adj* **:** de sangre <cold-blooded animal : animal de sangre fría>
bloodhound ['blʌd,haʊnd] *n* **:** sabueso *m*
bloodless ['blʌdləs] *adj* **1 :** incruento, sin derramamiento de sangre **2** LIFELESS **:** desanimado, insípido, sin vida
bloodmobile ['blʌdmo,bi:l] *n* **:** unidad *f* móvil para donantes de sangre
blood pressure *n* **:** tensión *f,* presión *f* (arterial)
bloodshed ['blʌd,ʃɛd] *n* **:** derramamiento *m* de sangre
bloodshot ['blʌd,ʃɑt] *adj* **:** inyectado de sangre
bloodstain ['blʌd,steɪn] *n* **:** mancha *f* de sangre
bloodstained ['blʌd,steɪnd] *adj* **:** manchado de sangre
bloodstream ['blʌd,stri:m] *n* **:** torrente *m* sanguíneo, corriente *f* sanguínea
bloodsucker ['blʌd,sʌkər] *n* **:** sanguijuela *f*
bloodthirsty ['blʌd,θərsti] *adj* **:** sanguinario
blood vessel *n* **:** vaso *m* sanguíneo
bloody ['blʌdi] *adj* **bloodier; -est :** ensangrentado, sangriento

bloom[1] [ˈbluːm] *vi* **1** FLOWER : florècer **2** MATURE : madurar

bloom[2] *n* **1** FLOWER : flor *f* <to be in bloom : estar en flor> **2** FLOWERING : floración *f* <in full bloom : en plena floración> **3** : rubor *m* (de la tez) <in the bloom of youth : en plena juventud, en la flor de la vida>

bloomers [ˈbluːmərz] *npl* : bombachos *mpl*

blooper [ˈbluːpər] *n* : metedura *f* de pata *fam*

blossom[1] [ˈblɑsəm] *vi* : florecer, dar flor

blossom[2] *n* : flor *f*

blot[1] [ˈblɑt] *vt* **blotted; blotting 1** SPOT : emborronar, borronear **2** DRY : secar

blot[2] *n* **1** STAIN : mancha *f,* borrón *m* **2** BLEMISH : mancha *f,* tacha *f*

blotch[1] [ˈblɑtʃ] *vt* : emborronar, borronear

blotch[2] *n* : mancha *f,* borrón *m*

blotchy [ˈblɑtʃi] *adj* **blotchier; -est** : lleno de manchas

blotter [ˈblɑtər] *n* : hoja *f* de papel secante, secante *m*

blouse [ˈblaʊs, ˈblaʊz] *n* : blusa *f*

blow[1] [ˈbloː] *v* **blew** [ˈbluː]; **blown** [ˈbloːn]; **blowing** *vi* **1** : soplar, volar <the wind is blowing hard : el viento está soplando con fuerza> <it blew out the door : voló por la puerta> <the window blew shut : se cerró la ventana> **2** SOUND : sonar <the whistle blew : sonó el silbato> **3 to blow out** : fundirse (dícese de un fusible eléctrico), reventarse (dícese de una llanta) — *vt* **1** : soplar, echar <to blow smoke : echar humo> **2** SOUND : tocar, sonar **3** SHAPE : soplar, dar forma a <to blow glass : soplar vidrio> **4** BUNGLE : echar a perder

blow[2] *n* **1** PUFF : soplo *m,* soplido *m* **2** GALE : vendaval *f* **3** HIT, STROKE : golpe *m* **4** CALAMITY : golpe *m,* desastre *m* **5 to come to blows** : llegar a las manos

blower [ˈbloːər] *n* FAN : ventilador *m*

blowout [ˈbloːˌaʊt] *n* : reventón *m*

blowtorch [ˈbloːˌtɔrtʃ] *n* : soplete *m*

blow up *vi* EXPLODE : estallar, hacer explosión — *vt* BLAST : volar, hacer volar

blubber[1] [ˈblʌbər] *vi* : lloriquear

blubber[2] *n* : esperma *f* de ballena

bludgeon [ˈblʌdʒən] *vt* : aporrear

blue[1] [ˈbluː] *adj* **bluer; bluest 1** : azul **2** MELANCHOLY : melancólico, triste

blue[2] *n* : azul *m*

blueberry [ˈbluːˌbɛri] *n, pl* **-ries** : arándano *m*

bluebird [ˈbluːˌbərd] *n* : azulejo *m*

blue cheese *n* : queso *m* azul

blueprint [ˈbluːˌprɪnt] *n* **1** : plano *m,* proyecto *m,* cianotipo *m* **2** PLAN : anteproyecto *m,* programa *m*

blues [ˈbluːz] *npl* **1** DEPRESSION : depresión *f,* melancolía *f* **2** : blues *m* <to sing the blues : cantar blues>

bluff[1] [ˈblʌf] *vi* : hacer un farol, blofear *Col, Mex*

bluff[2] *adj* **1** STEEP : escarpado **2** FRANK : campechano, franco, directo

bluff[3] *n* **1** : farol *m,* blof *m Col, Mex* **2** CLIFF : acantilado *m,* risco *m*

bluffer [ˈblʌfər] *n* : farolero *m,* -ra *f fam;* blofeador *m,* -dora *f Col, Mex*

bluing *or* **blueing** [ˈbluːɪŋ] *n* : añil *m,* azulete *m*

bluish [ˈbluːɪʃ] *adj* : azulado

blunder[1] [ˈblʌndər] *vi* **1** STUMBLE : tropezar, dar traspiés **2** ERR : cometer un error, tropezar, meter la pata *fam*

blunder[2] *n* : error *m,* fallo *m* garrafal, metedura *f* de pata *fam*

blunderbuss [ˈblʌndərˌbʌs] *n* : trabuco *m*

blunt[1] [ˈblʌnt] *vt* : despuntar (aguja o lápiz), desafilar (cuchillo o tijeras), suavizar (crítica)

blunt[2] *adj* **1** DULL : desafilado, despuntado **2** DIRECT : directo, franco, categórico

bluntly [ˈblʌntli] *adv* : sin rodeos, francamente, bruscamente

bluntness [ˈblʌntnəs] *n* **1** DULLNESS : falta *f* de filo, embotadura *f* **2** FRANKNESS : franqueza *f*

blur[1] [ˈblər] *vt* **blurred; blurring** : desdibujar, hacer borroso

blur[2] *n* **1** SMEAR : mancha *f,* borrón *m* **2** : aspecto *m* borroso <everything was just a blur : todo se volvió borroso>

blurb [ˈblərb] *n* : propaganda *f,* nota *f* publicitaria

blurt [ˈblərt] *vt* : espetar, decir impulsivamente

blush[1] [ˈblʌʃ] *vi* : ruborizarse, sonrojarse, hacerse colorado

blush[2] *n* : rubor *m,* sonrojo *m*

bluster[1] [ˈblʌstər] *vi* **1** BLOW : soplar con fuerza **2** BOAST : fanfarronear, echar bravatas

bluster[2] *n* : fanfarronada *f,* bravata *f*

blustery [ˈblʌstəri] *adj* : borrascoso, tempestuoso

boa [ˈboːə] *n* : boa *f*

boar [ˈbor] *n* : cerdo *m* macho, verraco *m*

board[1] [ˈbord] *vt* **1** : embarcarse en, subir a bordo de (una nave o un avión), subir a (un tren o carro) **2** LODGE : hospedar, dar hospedaje con comidas a **3 to board up** : cerrar con tablas

board[2] *n* **1** PLANK : tabla *f,* tablón *m* **2** : tablero *m* <chessboard : tablero de ajedrez> **3** MEALS : comida *f* <board and lodging : comida y alojamiento> **4** COMMITTEE, COUNCIL : junta *f,* consejo *m*

boarder [ˈbordər] *n* LODGER : huésped *m,* -peda *f*

boardinghouse [ˈbordɪŋˌhaʊs] *n* : casa *f* de huéspedes

boarding school *n* : internado *m*

boardwalk [ˈbɔrd,wɔk] *n* : paseo *m* marítimo entablado

boast[1] [ˈboːst] *vi* : alardear, presumir, jactarse

boast[2] *n* : jactancia *f,* alarde *m*

boaster [ˈboːstər] *n* : presumido *m,* -da *f;* fanfarrón *m,* -rrona *f fam*

boastful [ˈboːstfəl] *adj* : jactancioso, fanfarrón *fam*

boastfully [ˈboːstfəli] *adv* : de manera jactanciosa

boat[1] [ˈboːt] *vt* : transportar en barco, poner a bordo

boat[2] *n* : barco *m,* embarcación *f,* bote *m,* barca *f*

boatman [ˈboːtmən] *n, pl* **-men** [-mən, -,mɛn] : barquero *m*

boatswain [ˈboːsən] *n* : contramaestre *m*

bob[1] [ˈbɑb] *v* **bobbed; bobbing** *vi* **1** : balancearse, mecerse <to bob up and down : subir y bajar> **2** *or* **to bob up** APPEAR : presentarse, surgir — *vt* **1** : inclinar (la cabeza o el cuerpo) **2** CUT : cortar, recortar <she bobbed her hair : se cortó el pelo>

bob[2] *n* **1** : inclinación *f* (de la cabeza, del cuerpo), sacudida *f* **2** FLOAT : flotador *m,* corcho *m* (de pesca) **3** : pelo *m* corto

bobbin [ˈbɑbən] *n* : bobina *f,* carrete *m*

bobby pin [ˈbɑbi,pɪn] *n* : horquilla *f*

bobcat [ˈbɑb,kæt] *n* : lince *m* rojo

bobolink [ˈbɑbə,lɪŋk] *n* : tordo *m* arrocero

bobsled [ˈbɑb,slɛd] *n* : bobsleigh *m*

bobwhite [ˈbɑbˈ*h*waɪt] *n* : codorniz *m* (del Nuevo Mundo)

bode[1] [ˈboːd] *v* **boded; boding** *vt* : presagiar, augurar — *vi* **to bode well** : ser de buen agüero

bode[2] → **bide**

bodice [ˈbɑdəs] *n* : corpiño *m*

bodied [ˈbɑdid] *adj* : de cuerpo <lean-bodied : de cuerpo delgado> <able-bodied : no discapacitado>

bodiless [ˈbɑdiləs, ˈbɑdələs] *adj* : incorpóreo

bodily[1] [ˈbɑdəli] *adv* : en peso <to lift someone bodily : levantar a alguien en peso>

bodily[2] *adj* : corporal, del cuerpo <bodily harm : daños corporales>

body [ˈbɑdi] *n, pl* **bodies 1** : cuerpo *m,* organismo *m* **2** CORPSE : cadáver *m* **3** PERSON : persona *f,* ser *m* humano **4** : nave *f* (de una iglesia), carrocería (de un automóvil), fuselaje *m* (de un avión), casco *m* (de una nave) **5** COLLECTION, MASS : conjunto *m,* grupo *m,* masa *f* <in a body : todos juntos, en masa> **6** ORGANIZATION : organismo *m,* organización *f*

bodyguard [ˈbɑdi,gɑrd] *n* : guardaespaldas *mf*

bog[1] [ˈbɑg, ˈbɔg] *vt* **bogged; bogging** : empantanar, inundar <to get bogged down : empantanarse>

bog[2] *n* : lodazal *m,* ciénaga *f,* cenagal *m*

bogey [ˈbʊgi, ˈboː-] *n, pl* **-geys** : terror *m,* coco *m fam*

boggle [ˈbɑgəl] *vi* **-gled; -gling** : quedarse atónito, quedarse pasmado <the mind boggles! : ¡es increíble!>

boggy [ˈbɑgi, ˈbɔ-] *adj* **boggier; -est** : cenagoso

bogus [ˈboːgəs] *adj* : falso, fingido, falaz

bohemian [boːˈhiːmiən] *n* : bohemio *m,* -mia *f* — **bohemian** *adj*

boil[1] [ˈbɔɪl] *vi* **1** : hervir **2 to make one's blood boil** : hervirle la sangre a uno — *vt* **1** : hervir, hacer hervir <to boil water : hervir agua> **2** : cocer, hervir <to boil potatoes : cocer papas>

boil[2] *n* **1** BOILING : hervor *m* **2** : furúnculo *m,* divieso *m* (in medicine)

boiler [ˈbɔɪlər] *n* : caldera *f*

boisterous [ˈbɔɪstərəs] *adj* : bullicioso, escandaloso — **boisterously** *adv*

bold [ˈboːld] *adj* **1** COURAGEOUS : valiente **2** INSOLENT : insolente, descarado **3** DARING : atrevido, andaz — **boldly** *adv*

boldface [ˈboːld,feɪs] *n or* **boldface type** : negrita *f*

boldness [ˈboːldnəs] *n* **1** COURAGE : valor *m,* coraje *m* **2** INSOLENCE : atrevimiento *m,* insolencia *f,* descaro *m* **3** DARING : audacia *f*

bolero [bəˈlɛro] *n, pl* **-ros** : bolero *m*

Bolivian [bəˈlɪviən] *n* : boliviano *m,* -na *f* — **Bolivian** *adj*

boll [ˈboːl] *n* : cápsula *f* (del algodón)

boll weevil *n* : gorgojo *m* del algodón

bologna [bəˈloːni] *n* : salchicha *f* ahumada

bolster[1] [ˈboːlstər] *vt* **-stered; -stering** : reforzar, reafirmar <to bolster morale : levantar la moral>

bolster[2] *n* : cabezal *m,* almohadón *m*

bolt[1] [ˈboːlt] *vt* **1** atornillar, sujetar con pernos <bolted to the floor : sujetado con pernos al suelo> **2** : cerrar con pestillo, echar el cerrojo a <to bolt the door : echar el cerrojo a la puerta> **3 to bolt down** : engullir <she bolted down her dinner : engulló su comida> — *vi* : echar a correr, salir corriendo <he bolted from the room : salió corriendo de la sala>

bolt[2] *n* **1** LATCH : pestillo *m,* cerrojo *m* **2** : tornillo *m,* perno *m* <nuts and bolts : tuercas y tornillos> **3** : rollo *m* <a bolt of cloth : un rollo de tela> **4 lightning bolt** : relámpago *m,* rayo *m*

bomb[1] [ˈbɑm] *vt* : bombardear

bomb[2] *n* : bomba *f*

bombard [bɑmˈbɑrd, bəm-] *vt* : bombardear

bombardier [,bɑmbəˈdɪr] *n* : bombardero *m,* -ra *f*

bombardment [bɑmˈbɑrdmənt] *n* : bombardeo *m*

bombast [ˈbɑmˌbæst] *n* **:** grandilocuencia *f,* ampulosidad *f*
bombastic [bɑmˈbæstɪk] *adj* **:** grandilocuente, ampuloso, bombástico
bomber [ˈbɑmər] *n* **:** bombardero *m*
bombproof [ˈbɑmˌpruːf] *adj* **:** a prueba de bombas
bombshell [ˈbɑmˌʃɛl] *n* **:** bomba *f* <a political bombshell **:** una bomba política>
bona fide [ˈboːnəˌfaɪd, ˈbɑ-; ˌboːnəˈfaɪdi] *adj* **1 :** de buena fe <a bona fide offer **:** una oferta de buena fe> **2** GENUINE **:** genuino, auténtico
bonanza [bəˈnænzə] *n* **:** bonanza *f*
bonbon [ˈbɑnˌbɑn] *n* **:** bombón *m*
bond[1] [ˈbɑnd] *vt* **1** INSURE **:** dar fianza a, asegurar **2** STICK **:** adherir, pegar — *vi* **:** adherirse, pegarse
bond[2] *n* **1** LINK, TIE **:** vínculo *m,* lazo *m* **2** BAIL **:** fianza *f,* caución *f* **3 :** bono *m* <stocks and bonds **:** acciones y bonos> **4 bonds** *npl* FETTERS **:** cadenas *fpl*
bondage [ˈbɑndɪdʒ] *n* **:** esclavitud *f*
bondholder [ˈbɑndˌhoːldər] *n* **:** tenedor *m,* -dora *f* de bonos
bondsman [ˈbɑndzmən] *n, pl* **-men** [-mən, -ˌmɛn] **1** SLAVE **:** esclavo *m* **2** SURETY **:** fiador *m,* -dora *f*
bone[1] [ˈboːn] *vt* **boned; boning :** deshuesar
bone[2] *n* **:** hueso *m*
boneless [ˈboːnləs] *adj* **:** sin huesos, sin espinas
boner [ˈboːnər] *n* **:** metedura *f* de pata, metida *f* de pata
bonfire [ˈbɑnˌfaɪr] *n* **:** hoguera *f,* fogata *f,* fogón *m*
bonito [bəˈniːt̬o] *n, pl* **-tos** *or* **-to :** bonito *m*
bonnet [ˈbɑnət] *n* **:** sombrero *m* (de mujer), gorra *f* (de niño)
bonus [ˈboːnəs] *n* **1 :** prima *f,* bonificación *f* (pagado al empleado) **2** ADVANTAGE, BENEFIT **:** beneficio *m,* provecho *m*
bony [ˈboːni] *adj* **bonier; -est :** huesudo, osudo
boo[1] [ˈbuː] *vt* **:** abuchear
boo[2] *n, pl* **boos :** abucheo *m*
booby [ˈbuːbi] *n, pl* **-bies :** bobo *m,* -ba *f;* tonto *m,* -ta *f*
book[1] [ˈbʊk] *vt* **:** reservar <to book a flight **:** reservar un vuelo>
book[2] *n* **1 :** libro *m* **2 the Book :** la Biblia **3 by the book :** según las reglas
bookcase [ˈbʊkˌkeɪs] *n* **:** estantería *f,* librero *m Mex*
bookend [ˈbʊkˌɛnd] *n* **:** sujetalibros *m*
bookie [ˈbʊki] → **bookmaker**
bookish [ˈbʊkɪʃ] *adj* **:** libresco
bookkeeper [ˈbʊkˌkiːpər] *n* **:** tenedor *m,* -dora *f* de libros; contable *mf Spain*
bookkeeping [ˈbʊkˌkiːpɪŋ] *n* **:** contabilidad *f,* teneduría *f* de libros
booklet [ˈbʊklət] *n* **:** folleto *m*
bookmaker [ˈbʊkˌmeɪkər] *n* **:** corredor *m,* -dora *f* de apuestas
bookmark [ˈbʊkˌmɑrk] *n* **:** señalador *m* de libros, marcador *m* de libros
bookseller [ˈbʊkˌsɛlər] *n* **:** librero *m,* -ra *f*
bookshelf [ˈbʊkˌʃɛlf] *n, pl* **-shelves 1 :** estante *m* **2 bookshelves** *npl* **:** estantería *f*
bookstore [ˈbʊkˌstor] *n* **:** librería *f*
bookworm [ˈbʊkˌwərm] *n* **:** ratón *m* de biblioteca *fam*
boom[1] [ˈbuːm] *vi* **1** THUNDER **:** tronar, resonar **2** FLOURISH, PROSPER **:** estar en auge, prosperar
boom[2] *n* **1** BOOMING **:** bramido *m,* estruendo *m* **2** FLOURISHING **:** auge *m* <population boom **:** auge de población>
boomerang [ˈbuːməˌræŋ] *n* **:** bumerán *m*
boon[1] [ˈbuːn] *adj* **boon companion :** amigo *m,* -ga *f* del alma
boon[2] *n* **:** ayuda *f,* beneficio *m,* adelanto *m*
boondocks [ˈbuːnˌdɑks] *npl* **:** area *f* rural remota, región *f* alejada
boor [ˈbʊr] *n* **:** grosero *m,* -ra *f*
boorish [ˈbʊrɪʃ] *adj* **:** grosero
boost[1] [ˈbuːst] *vt* **1** LIFT **:** levantar, alzar **2** INCREASE **:** aumentar, incrementar **3** PROMOTE **:** promover, fomentar, hacer publicidad por
boost[2] *n* **1** THRUST **:** impulso *m,* empujón *m* **2** ENCOURAGEMENT **:** estímulo *m,* aliento *m* **3** INCREASE **:** aumento *m,* incremento *m*
booster [ˈbuːstər] *n* **1** SUPPORTER **:** partidario *m,* -ria *f* **2 booster rocket :** cohete *m* propulsor **3 booster shot :** vacuna *f* de refuerzo
boot[1] [ˈbuːt] *vt* KICK **:** dar una patada a, patear
boot[2] *n* **1 :** bota *f,* botín *m* **2** KICK **:** puntapié *m,* patada *f*
bootee *or* **bootie** [ˈbuːt̬i] *n* **:** botita *f,* botín *m*
booth [ˈbuːθ] *n, pl* **booths** [ˈbuːðz, ˈbuːθs] **:** cabina *f* (de teléfono, de votar), caseta *f* (de información), barraca *f* (a una feria)
bootlegger [ˈbuːtˌlɛgər] *n* **:** contrabandista *mf* del alcohol
booty [ˈbuːt̬i] *n, pl* **-ties :** botín *m*
booze [ˈbuːz] *n* **:** trago *m,* bebida *f* (alcohólica)
borax [ˈbɔrˌæks] *n* **:** bórax *m*
border[1] [ˈbɔrdər] *vt* **1** EDGE **:** ribetear, bordear **2** BOUND **:** limitar con, lindar con — *vi* VERGE **:** rayar, lindar <that borders on absurdity **:** eso raya en el absurdo>
border[2] *n* **1** EDGE **:** borde *m,* orilla *f* **2** TRIM **:** ribete *m* **3** FRONTIER **:** frontera *f*
bore[1] [ˈbor] *vt* **bored; boring 1** PIERCE **:** taladrar, perforar <to bore metals **:** taladrar metales> **2** OPEN **:** hacer, abrir <to bore a tunnel **:** abrir un túnel> **3** WEARY **:** aburrir

bore[2] → **bear**[1]
bore[3] *n* **1 :** pesado *m,* -da *f* (persona aburrida) **2** TEDIOUSNESS **:** pesadez *f,* lo aburrido **3** DIAMETER **:** calibre *m*
boredom [ˈbordəm] *n* **:** aburrimiento *m*
boring [ˈborɪŋ] *adj* **:** aburrido, pesado
born [ˈbɔrn] *adj* **1 :** nacido **2 :** nato <she's a born singer : es una cantante nata> <he's a born leader : nació para mandar>
borne → **bear**[1]
boron [ˈborˌɑn] *n* **:** boro *m*
borough [ˈbəro] *n* **:** distrito *m* municipal
borrow [ˈbɑro] *vt* **1 :** pedir prestado, tomar prestado **2** APPROPRIATE **:** apropiarse de, adoptar
Bosnian [ˈbɑzniən, ˈbɔz-] *n* **:** bosnio *m,* -nia *f* — **Bosnian** *adj*
bosom[1] [ˈbʊzəm, ˈbuː-] *adj* **:** íntimo
bosom[2] *n* **1** CHEST **:** pecho *m* **2** BREAST **:** pecho *m,* seno *m* **3** CLOSENESS **:** seno *m* <in the bosom of her family : en el seno de su familia>
bosomed [ˈbʊzəmd, ˈbuː-] *adj* **:** con busto <big-bosomed : con mucho busto>
boss[1] [ˈbɔs] *vt* **1** SUPERVISE **:** dirigir, supervisar **2 to boss around :** mandonear *fam,* mangonear *fam*
boss[2] *n* **:** jefe *m,* -fa *f;* patrón *m,* -trona *f*
bossy [ˈbɔsi] *adj* **bossier; -est :** mandón *fam,* autoritario, dominante
botanist [ˈbɑtənɪst] *n* **:** botánico *m,* -ca *f*
botany [ˈbɑtəni] *n* **:** botánica *f* — **botanical** [bəˈtænɪkəl] *adj*
botch[1] [ˈbɑtʃ] *vt* **:** hacer una chapuza de, estropear
botch[2] *n* **:** chapuza *f*
both[1] [ˈboːθ] *adj* **:** ambos, los dos, las dos <both books : ambos libros, los dos libros>
both[2] *conj* **:** tanto como <both Ana and her mother are tall : tanto Ana como su madre son altas>
both[3] *pron* **:** ambos *m,* -bas *f;* los dos, las dos
bother[1] [ˈbɑðər] *vt* **1** IRK **:** preocupar <nothing's bothering me : nada me preocupa> <what's bothering him? : ¿qué le pasa?> **2** PESTER **:** molestar, fastidiar — *vi* **to bother to :** molestarse en, tomar la molestia de
bother[2] *n* **1** TROUBLE **:** molestia *f,* problemas *mpl* **2** ANNOYANCE **:** molestia *f,* fastidio *m*
bothersome [ˈbɑðərsəm] *adj* **:** molesto, fastidioso
bottle[1] [ˈbɑtəl] *vt* **bottled; bottling :** embotellar, envasar
bottle[2] *n* **:** botella *f,* frasco *m*
bottleneck [ˈbɑtəlˌnɛk] *n* **1 :** cuello *m* de botello (en un camino) **2 :** embotellamiento *m,* atasco *m* (de tráfico) **3** OBSTACLE **:** obstáculo *m*
bottom[1] [ˈbɑtəm] *adj* **:** más bajo, inferior, de abajo
bottom[2] *n* **1 :** fondo *m* (de una caja, de una taza, del mar), pie *m* (de una escalera, una página, una montaña), asiento *m* (de una silla), parte *f* de abajo (de una pila) **2** CAUSE **:** origen *m,* causa *f* <to get to the bottom of : llegar al fondo de> **3** BUTTOCKS **:** trasero *m,* nalgas *fpl*
bottomless [ˈbɑtəmləs] *adj* **:** sin fondo, sin límites
botulism [ˈbɑtʃəˌlɪzəm] *n* **:** botulismo *m*
boudoir [bəˈdwɑr, bʊ-; ˈbuːˌ-, ˈbʊ-] *n* **:** tocador *m*
bough [ˈbaʊ] *n* **:** rama *f*
bought → **buy**[1]
bouillon [ˈbuːˌjɑn; ˈbʊlˌjɑn, -jən] *n* **:** caldo *m*
boulder [ˈboːldər] *n* **:** canto *m* rodado, roca *f* grande
boulevard [ˈbʊləˌvɑrd, ˈbuː-] *n* **:** bulevar *m,* boulevard *m*
bounce[1] [ˈbaʊnts] *v* **bounced; bouncing** *vt* **:** hacer rebotar — *vi* **:** rebotar
bounce[2] *n* **:** rebote *m*
bouncy [ˈbaʊntsi] *adj* **bouncier; -est 1** LIVELY **:** vivo, exuberante, animado **2** RESILIENT **:** elástico, flexible **3 :** que rebota (dícese de una pelota)
bound[1] [ˈbaʊnd] *vt* **:** delimitar, rodear — *vi* LEAP **:** saltar, dar brincos
bound[2] *adj* **1** OBLIGED **:** obligado **2 :** encuadernado, empastado <a book bound in leather : un libro encuadernado en cuero> **3** DETERMINED **:** decidido, empeñado **4 to be bound to :** ser seguro que, tener que, no caber duda que <it was bound to happen : tenía que suceder> **5 bound for :** con rumbo a <bound for Chicago : con rumbo a Chicago> <to be homeward bound : ir camino a casa>
bound[3] *n* **1** LIMIT **:** límite *m* **2** LEAP **:** salto *m,* brinco *m*
boundary [ˈbaʊndri, -dəri] *n, pl* **-aries :** límite *m,* línea *f* divisoria, linde *mf*
boundless [ˈbaʊndləs] *adj* **:** sin límites, infinito
bounteous [ˈbaʊntiəs] *adj* **1** GENEROUS **:** generoso **2** ABUNDANT **:** copioso, abundante — **bounteously** *adv*
bountiful [ˈbaʊntɪfəl] *adj* **1** GENEROUS, LIBERAL **:** munificente, pródigo, generoso **2** ABUNDANT **:** copioso, abundante
bounty [ˈbaʊnti] *n, pl* **-ties 1** GENEROSITY **:** generosidad *f,* munificiencia *f* **2** REWARD **:** recompensa *f*
bouquet [boːˈkeɪ, buː-] *n* **1 :** ramo *m,* ramillete *m* **2** FRAGRANCE **:** bouquet *m,* aroma *m*
bourbon [ˈbərbən, ˈbʊr-] *n* **:** bourbon *m,* whiskey *m* americano
bourgeois[1] [ˈbʊrʒˌwɑ, bʊrʒˈwɑ] *adj* **:** burgués
bourgeois[2] *n* **:** burgués *m,* -guesa *f*
bourgeoisie [ˌbʊrʒˌwɑˈzi] *n* **:** burguesía *f*

bout [ˈbaʊt] *n* **1** : encuentro *m,* combate *m* (en deportes) **2** ATTACK : ataque *m* (de una enfermedad) **3** PERIOD, SPELL : período *m* (de actividad)
boutique [buːˈtiːk] *n* : boutique *f*
bovine[1] [ˈboːˌvaɪn, -ˌviːn] *adj* : bovino, vacuno
bovine[2] *n* : bovino *m*
bow[1] [ˈbaʊ] *vi* **1** : hacer una reverencia, inclinarse **2** SUBMIT : ceder, resignarse, someterse — *vt* **1** LOWER : inclinar, bajar **2** BEND : doblar
bow[2] [ˈbaʊː] *n* **1** BOWING : reverencia *f,* inclinación *f* **2** : proa *f* (de un barco)
bow[3] [ˈboː] *vi* CURVE : arquearse, doblarse
bow[4] [ˈboː] *n* **1** ARCH, CURVE : arco *m,* curva *f* **2** : arco *m* (arma o vara para tocar varios instrumentos de música) **3** : lazo *m,* moño *m* <to tie a bow : hacer un moño>
bowels [ˈbaʊəls] *npl* **1** INTESTINES : intestinos *mpl* **2** : entrañas *fpl* <in the bowels of the earth : en las entrañas de la tierra>
bower [ˈbaʊər] *n* : enramada *f*
bowl[1] [ˈboːl] *vi* : jugar a los bolos
bowl[2] *n* : tazón *m,* cuenco *m*
bowler [ˈboːlər] *n* : jugador *m,* -dora *f* de bolos
bowling [ˈboːlɪŋ] *n* : bolos *mpl*
box[1] [ˈbɑks] *vt* **1** PACK : empaquetar, embalar, encajonar **2** SLAP : bofetear, cachetear — *vi* : boxear
box[2] *n* **1** CONTAINER : caja *f,* cajón *m* **2** COMPARTMENT : compartimento *m,* palco *m* (en el teatro) **3** SLAP : bofetada *f,* cachetada *f* **4** : boj *m* (planta)
boxcar [ˈbɑksˌkɑr] *n* : vagón *m* de carga, furgón *m*
boxer [ˈbɑksər] *n* : boxeador *m,* -dora *f*
boxing [ˈbɑksɪŋ] *n* : boxeo *m*
box office *n* : taquilla *f,* boletería *f*
boxwood [ˈbɑksˌwʊd] *n* : boj *m*
boy [ˈbɔɪ] *n* : niño *m,* chico *m*
boycott[1] [ˈbɔɪˌkɑt] *vt* : boicotear
boycott[2] *n* : boicot *m*
boyfriend [ˈbɔɪˌfrɛnd] *n* **1** FRIEND : amigo *m* **2** SWEETHEART : novio *m*
boyhood [ˈbɔɪˌhʊd] *n* : niñez *f*
boyish [ˈbɔɪɪʃ] *adj* : de niño, juvenil
bra [ˈbrɑ] → **brassiere**
brace[1] [ˈbreɪs] *v* **braced; bracing** *vt* **1** PROP UP, SUPPORT : apuntalar, apoyar, sostener **2** INVIGORATE : vigorizar **3** REINFORCE : reforzar — *vi* **to brace oneself** PREPARE : prepararse
brace[2] *n* **1** : berbiquí *m* <brace and bit : berbiquí y barrena> **2** CLAMP, REINFORCEMENT : abrazadera *f,* refuerzo *m* **3** : llave *f* (signo de puntuación) **4 braces** *npl* : aparatos *mpl* (de ortodoncia), frenos *mpl Mex*
bracelet [ˈbreɪslət] *n* : brazalete *m,* pulsera *f*
bracken [ˈbrækən] *n* : helecho *m*
bracket[1] [ˈbrækət] *vt* **1** SUPPORT : asegurar, apuntalar **2** : poner entre corchetes **3** CATEGORIZE, GROUP : catalogar, agrupar
bracket[2] *n* **1** SUPPORT : soporte *m* **2** : corchete *m* (marca de puntuación) **3** CATEGORY, CLASS : clase *f,* categoría *f*
brackish [ˈbrækɪʃ] *adj* : salobre
brad [ˈbræd] *n* : clavo *m* con cabeza pequeña, clavito *m*
brag[1] [ˈbræg] *vi* **bragged; bragging** : alardear, fanfarronear, jactarse
brag[2] *n* : alarde *m,* jactancia *f,* fanfarronada *f*
braggart [ˈbrægərt] *n* : fanfarrón *m,* -rrona *f fam;* jactancioso *m,* -sa *f*
braid[1] [ˈbreɪd] *vt* : trenzar
braid[2] *n* : trenza *f*
braille [ˈbreɪl] *n* : braille *m*
brain[1] [ˈbreɪn] *vt* : romper la crisma a, aplastar el cráneo a
brain[2] *n* **1** : cerebro *m* **2 brains** *npl* INTELLECT : inteligencia *f,* sesos *mpl*
brainless [ˈbreɪnləs] *adj* : estúpido, tonto
brainstorm [ˈbreɪnˌstɔrm] *n* : idea *f* brillante, idea *f* genial
brainy [ˈbreɪni] *adj* **brainier; -est** : inteligente, listo
braise [ˈbreɪz] *vt* **braised; braising** : cocer a fuego lento, estofar
brake[1] [ˈbreɪk] *v* **braked; braking** : frenar
brake[2] *n* : freno *m*
bramble [ˈbræmbəl] *n* : zarza *f,* zarzamora *f*
bran [ˈbræn] *n* : salvado *m*
branch[1] [ˈbræntʃ] *vi* **1** : echar ramas (dícese de una planta) **2** DIVERGE : ramificarse, separarse
branch[2] *n* **1** : rama *f* (de una planta) **2** EXTENSION : ramal *m* (de un camino, un ferrocarril, un río), rama *f* (de una familia o un campo de estudiar), sucursal *f* (de una empresa), agencia *f* (del gobierno)
brand[1] [ˈbrænd] *vt* **1** : marcar (ganado) **2** LABEL : tachar, tildar <they branded him as a liar : lo tacharon de mentiroso>
brand[2] *n* **1** : marca *f* (de ganado) **2** STIGMA : estigma *m* **3** MAKE : marca *f* <brand name : marca de fábrica>
brandish [ˈbrændɪʃ] *vt* : blandir
brand–new [ˈbrændˈnuː, -ˈnjuː] *adj* : nuevo, flamante
brandy [ˈbrændi] *n, pl* **-dies** : brandy *m*
brash [ˈbræʃ] *adj* **1** IMPULSIVE : impulsivo, impetuoso **2** BRAZEN : excesivamente desenvuelto, descarado
brass [ˈbræs] *n* **1** : latón *m* **2** GALL, NERVE : descaro *m,* cara *f fam* **3** OFFICERS : mandamases *mpl fam*
brassiere [brəˈzɪr, brɑ-] *n* : sostén *m,* brasier *m Col, Mex*
brassy [ˈbræsi] *adj* **brassier; -est** : dorado
brat [ˈbræt] *n* : mocoso *m,* -sa *f;* niño *m* mimado, niña *f* mimada

bravado [brə'vɑdo] *n, pl* **-does** *or* **-dos** : bravuconadas *fpl,* bravatas *fpl*
brave[1] ['breɪv] *vt* **braved; braving** : afrontar, hacer frente a
brave[2] *adj* **braver; bravest** : valiente, valeroso — **bravely** *adv*
brave[3] *n* : guerrero *m* indio
bravery ['breɪvəri] *n* : valor *m,* valentía *f*
bravo ['brɑˌvoː] *n, pl* **-vos** : bravo *m*
brawl[1] ['brɔl] *vi* : pelearse, pegarse
brawl[2] *n* : pelea *f,* reyerta *f*
brawn ['brɔn] *n* : fuerza *f* muscular
brawny ['brɔni] *adj* **brawnier; -est** : musculoso
bray[1] ['breɪ] *vi* : rebuznar
bray[2] *n* : rebuzno *m*
brazen ['breɪzən] *adj* **1** : de latón **2** BOLD : descarado, directo
brazenly ['breɪzənli] *adv* : descaradamente, insolentemente
brazenness ['breɪzənnəs] *n* : descaro *m,* atrevimiento *m*
brazier ['breɪʒər] *n* : brasero *m*
Brazilian [brə'zɪljən] *n* : brasileño *m,* -ña *f* — **Brazilian** *adj*
Brazil nut [brə'zɪlˌnʌt] *n* : nuez *f* de Brasil
breach[1] ['briːtʃ] *vt* **1** PENETRATE : abrir una brecha en, penetrar **2** VIOLATE : infringir, violar
breach[2] *n* **1** VIOLATION : infracción *f,* violación *f* <breach of trust : abuso de confianza> **2** GAP, OPENING : brecha *f*
bread[1] ['brɛd] *vt* : empanar
bread[2] *n* : pan *m*
breadth ['brɛtθ] *n* : ancho *m,* anchura *f*
breadwinner ['brɛdˌwɪnər] *n* : sostén *m* de la familia
break[1] ['breɪk] *v* **broke** ['broːk]; **broken** ['broːkən]; **breaking** *vt* **1** SMASH : romper, quebrar **2** VIOLATE : infringir, violar, romper **3** SURPASS : batir, superar **4** CRUSH, RUIN : arruinar, deshacer, destrozar <to break one's spirit : quebrantar su espíritu> **5** : dar, comunicar <to break the news : dar las noticias> **6** INTERRUPT : cortar, interrumpir — *vi* **1** : romperse, quebrarse <my calculator broke : se me rompió la calculadora> **2** DISPERSE : dispersarse, despejarse **3** : estallar (dícese de una tormenta), romper (dícese del día) **4** CHANGE : cambiar (dícese del tiempo o de la voz) **5** DECREASE : bajar <my fever broke : me bajó la fiebre> **6** : divulgarse, revelarse <the news broke : la noticia se divulgó> **7 to break into** : forzar, abrir **8 to break out of** : escaparse de **9 to break through** : penetrar
break[2] *n* **1** : ruptura *f,* rotura *f,* fractura *f* (de un hueso), claro *m* (entre las nubes), cambio *m* (del tiempo) **2** CHANCE : oportunidad *f* <a lucky break : un golpe de suerte> **3** REST : descanso *m* <to take a break : tomar(se) un descanso>
breakable ['breɪkəbəl] *adj* : quebradizo, frágil
breakage ['breɪkɪdʒ] *n* **1** BREAKING : rotura *f* **2** DAMAGE : destrozos *mpl,* daños *mpl*
breakdown ['breɪkˌdaʊn] *n* **1** : avería *f* (de máquinas), interrupción *f* (de comunicaciones), fracaso *m* (de negociaciones) **2** ANALYSIS : análisis *m,* desglose *m* **3** *or* **nervous breakdown** : crisis *f* nerviosa
break down *vi* **1** : estropearse, descomponerse <the machine broke down : la máquina se descompuso> **2** FAIL : fracasar **3** CRY : echarse a llorar — *vt* **1** DESTROY : derribar, echar abajo **2** OVERCOME : vencer (la resistencia), disipar (sospechas) **3** ANALYZE : analizar, descomponer
breaker ['breɪkər] *n* **1** WAVE : ola *f* grande **2** : interruptor *m* automático (de electricidad)
breakfast[1] ['brɛkfəst] *vi* : desayunar
breakfast[2] *n* : desayuno *m*
breakneck ['breɪkˌnɛk] *adj* **at breakneck speed** : a una velocidad vertiginosa
break out *vi* **1** : salirse <she broke out in spots : le salieron granos> **2** ERUPT : estallar (dícese de una guerra, la violencia, etc.) **3** ESCAPE : fugarse, escaparse
break up *vt* **1** DIVIDE : dividir **2** : disolver (una muchedumbre, una pelea, etc.) — *vi* **1** BREAK : romperse **2** SEPARATE : deshacerse, separarse <I broke up with him : terminé con él>
breast ['brɛst] *n* **1** : pecho *m,* seno *m* (de una mujer) **2** CHEST : pecho *m*
breastbone ['brɛstˌboːn] *n* : esternón *m*
breast–feed ['brɛstˌfiːd] *vt* **-fed** [-ˌfɛd]; **-feeding** : amamantar, darle de mamar (a un niño)
breath ['brɛθ] *n* **1** BREATHING : aliento *m* <to hold one's breath : aguantar la respiración>**2** BREEZE : soplo *m* <a breath of fresh air : un soplo de aire fresco>
breathe ['briːð] *v* **breathed; breathing** *vi* **1** : respirar **2** LIVE : vivir, respirar — *vt* **1** : respirar, aspirar <to breathe fresh air : respirar el aire fresco> **2** UTTER : decir <I won't breathe a word of this : no diré nada de esto>
breathless ['brɛθləs] *adj* : sin aliento, jadeante
breathlessly ['brɛθləsli] *adv* : entrecortadamente, jadeando
breathlessness ['brɛθləsnəs] *n* : dificultad *f* al respirar
breathtaking ['brɛθˌteɪkɪŋ] *adj* IMPRESSIVE : impresionante, imponente
breeches ['brɪtʃəz, 'briː-] *npl* : pantalones *mpl,* calzones *mpl,* bombachos *mpl*
breed[1] ['briːd] *v* **bred** ['brɛd]; **breeding** *vt* **1** : criar (animales) **2** ENGENDER

: engendrar, producir <familiarity breeds contempt : la confianza hace perder el respeto> **3** RAISE, REAR : criar, educar — *vi* REPRODUCE : reproducirse

breed[2] *n* **1** : variedad *f* (de plantas), raza *f* (de animales) **2** CLASS : clase *f*, tipo *m*

breeder ['bri:dər] *n* : criador *m*, -dora *f* (de animales); cultivador *m*, -dora *f* (de plantas)

breeze[1] ['bri:z] *vi* **breezed; breezing** : pasar con ligereza <to breeze in : entrar como si nada>

breeze[2] *n* : brisa *f*, soplo *m* (de aire)

breezy ['bri:zi] *adj* **breezier; -est 1** AIRY, WINDY : aireado, ventoso **2** LIVELY : animado, alegre **3** NONCHALANT : despreocupado

brethren → **brother**

brevity ['brɛvəti] *n, pl* **-ties** : brevedad *f*, concisión *f*

brew[1] ['bru:] *vt* **1** : fabricar, elaborar (cerveza) **2** FOMENT : tramar, maquinar, fomentar — *vi* **1** : fabricar cerveza **2** : amenazar <a storm is brewing : una tormenta amenaza>

brew[2] *n* **1** BEER : cerveza *f* **2** POTION : brebaje *m*

brewer ['bru:ər] *n* : cervecero *m*, -ra *f*

brewery ['bru:əri, 'brʊri] *n, pl* **-eries** : cervecería *f*

briar ['braɪər] → **brier**

bribe[1] ['braɪb] *vt* **bribed; bribing** : sobornar, cohechar, coimear *Arg, Chile, Peru*

bribe[2] *n* : soborno *m*, cohecho *m*, coima *f Arg, Chile, Peru*, mordida *f CA, Mex*

bribery ['braɪbəri] *n, pl* **-eries** : soborno *m*, cohecho *m*, coima *f*, mordida *f CA, Mex*

bric–a–brac ['brɪkə,bræk] *npl* : baratijas *fpl*, chucherías *fpl*

brick[1] ['brɪk] *vt* **to brick up** : tabicar, tapiar

brick[2] *n* : ladrillo *m*

bricklayer ['brɪk,leɪər] *n* : albañil *mf*

bricklaying ['brɪk,leɪɪŋ] *n* : albañilería *f*

bridal ['braɪdəl] *adj* : nupcial, de novia

bride ['braɪd] *n* : novia *f*

bridegroom ['braɪd,gru:m] *n* : novio *m*

bridesmaid ['braɪdz,meɪd] *n* : dama *f* de honor

bridge[1] ['brɪdʒ] *vt* **bridged; bridging 1** : tender un puente sobre **2 to bridge the gap** : salvar las diferencias

bridge[2] *n* **1** : puente *m* **2** : caballete *m* (de la nariz) **3** : puente *m* de mando (de un barco) **4** DENTURE : puente *m* (dental) **5** : bridge *m* (juego de naipes)

bridle[1] ['braɪdəl] *v* **-dled; -dling** *vt* **1** : embridar (un caballo) **2** RESTRAIN : refrenar, dominar, contener — *vi* **to bridle at** : molestarse por, picarse por

bridle[2] *n* : brida *f*

brief[1] ['bri:f] *vt* : dar órdenes a, instruir

brief[2] *adj* : breve, sucinto, conciso

brief[3] *n* : resumen *m*, sumario *m*

briefcase ['bri:f,keɪs] *n* : portafolio *m*, maletín *m*

briefly ['bri:fli] *adv* : brevemente, por poco tiempo <to speak briefly : discursar en pocas palabras>

brier ['braɪər] *n* **1** BRAMBLE : zarza *f*, rosal *m* silvestre **2** HEATH : brezo *m* veteado

brig ['brɪg] *n* **1** : bergantín *m* (barco) **2** : calabozo *m* (en un barco)

brigade [brɪ'geɪd] *n* : brigada *f*

brigadier general [,brɪgə'dɪr] *n* : general *m* de brigada

brigand ['brɪgənd] *n* : bandolero *m*, -ra *f*; forajido *m*, -da *f*

bright ['braɪt] *adj* **1** : brillante (dícese del sol, de los ojos), vivo (dícese de un color), claro, fuerte **2** CHEERFUL : alegre, animado <bright and early : muy temprano> **3** INTELLIGENT : listo, inteligente <a bright idea : una idea luminosa>

brighten ['braɪtən] *vt* **1** ILLUMINATE : iluminar **2** ENLIVEN : alegrar, animar — *vi* **1** : hacerse más brillante **2 to brighten up** : animarse, alegrarse, mejorar

brightly ['braɪtli] *adv* : vivamente, intensamente, alegremente

brightness ['braɪtnəs] *n* **1** LUMINOSITY : luminosidad *f*, brillantez *f*, resplandor *m*, brillo *m* **2** CHEERFULNESS : alegría *f*, ánimo *m*

brilliance ['brɪljənts] *n* **1** BRIGHTNESS : resplandor *m*, fulgor *m*, brillo *m*, brillantez *f* **2** INTELLIGENCE : inteligencia *f*, brillantez *f*

brilliancy ['brɪljəntsi] → **brilliance**

brilliant ['brɪljənt] *adj* : brillante

brilliantly ['brɪljəntli] *adv* : brillantemente, con brillantez

brim[1] ['brɪm] *vi* **brimmed; brimming 1** *or* **to brim over** : desbordarse, rebosar **2 to brim with tears** : llenarse de lágrimas

brim[2] *n* **1** : ala *f* (de un sombrero) **2** : borde *m* (de una taza o un vaso)

brimful ['brɪm'fʊl] *adj* : lleno hasta el borde, repleto, rebosante

brimless ['brɪmləs] *adj* : sin ala

brimstone ['brɪm,sto:n] *n* : azufre *m*

brindled ['brɪndəld] *adj* : manchado, pinto

brine ['braɪn] *n* **1** : salmuera *f*, escabeche *m* (para encurtir) **2** OCEAN : océano *m*, mar *m*

bring ['brɪŋ] *vt* **brought** ['brɔt]; **bringing 1** CARRY : traer <bring me some coffee : tráigame un café> **2** PRODUCE : traer, producir, conseguir <his efforts will bring him success : sus esfuerzos le conseguirán el éxito> **3** PERSUADE : convencer, persuadir **4** YIELD : rendir, alcanzar, venderse por <to bring a good price : alcanzar un

precio alto> **5 to bring to an end** : terminar (con) **6 to bring to light** : sacar a la luz
bring about *vt* : ocasionar, provocar, determinar
bring forth *vt* PRODUCE : producir
bring out *vt* : sacar, publicar (un libro, etc.)
bring to *vt* REVIVE : resucitar
bring up *vt* **1** REAR : criar **2** MENTION : sacar, mencionar
brininess [ˈbraɪninəs] *n* : salinidad *f*
brink [ˈbrɪŋk] *n* : borde *m*
briny [ˈbraɪni] *adj* **brinier; -est** : salobre
briquette *or* **briquet** [brɪˈkɛt] *n* : briqueta *f*
brisk [ˈbrɪsk] *adj* **1** LIVELY : rápido, enérgico, brioso **2** INVIGORATING : fresco, estimulante
brisket [ˈbrɪskət] *n* : falda *f*
briskly [ˈbrɪskli] *adv* : rápidamente, enérgicamente, con brío
briskness [ˈbrɪsknəs] *n* : brío *m*, rapidez *f*
bristle[1] [ˈbrɪsəl] *vi* **-tled; -tling 1** : erizarse, ponerse de punta **2** : enfurecerse, enojarse <she bristled at the suggestion : se enfureció ante tal sugerencia> **3** : estar plagado, estar repleto <a city bristling with tourists : una ciudad repleta de turistas>
bristle[2] *n* : cerda *f* (de un animal), pelo *m* (de una planta)
bristly [ˈbrɪsəli] *adj* **bristlier; -est** : erizado, cerdoso, hirsuto
British[1] [ˈbrɪtɪʃ] *adj* : británico
British[2] *n* **the British** *npl* : los británicos
brittle [ˈbrɪtəl] *adj* **-tler; -tlest** : frágil, quebradizo
brittleness [ˈbrɪtəlnəs] *n* : fragilidad *f*
broach [ˈbroːtʃ] *vt* BRING UP : mencionar, abordar, sacar
broad [ˈbrɔd] *adj* **1** WIDE : ancho **2** SPACIOUS : amplio, extenso **3** FULL : pleno <in broad daylight : en pleno día> **4** OBVIOUS : claro, evidente **5** TOLERANT : tolerante, liberal **6** GENERAL : general **7** ESSENTIAL : principal, esencial <the broad outline : los rasgos esenciales>
broadcast[1] [ˈbrɔdˌkæst] *vt* **-cast; -casting 1** SCATTER : esparcir, diseminar **2** CIRCULATE, SPREAD : divulgar, difundir, propagar **3** TRANSMIT : transmitir, emitir
broadcast[2] *n* **1** TRANSMISSION : transmisión *f*, emisión *f* **2** PROGRAM : programa *m*, emisión *f*
broadcaster [ˈbrɔdˌkæstər] *n* : presentador *m*, -dora *f*; locutor *m*, -tora *f*
broadcloth [ˈbrɔdˌklɔθ] *n* : paño *m* fino
broaden [ˈbrɔdən] *vt* : ampliar, ensanchar — *vi* : ampliarse, ensancharse
broadloom [ˈbrɔdˌluːm] *adj* : tejido en telar ancho
broadly [ˈbrɔdli] *adv* **1** GENERALLY : en general, aproximadamente **2** WIDELY : extensivamente
broad–minded [ˈbrɔdˈmaɪndəd] *adj* : tolerante, de amplias miras
broad–mindedness [brɔdˈmaɪndədnəs] *n* : tolerancia *f*
broadside [ˈbrɔdˌsaɪd] *n* **1** VOLLEY : andanada *f* **2** ATTACK : ataque *m*, invectiva *f*, andanada *f*
brocade [broˈkeɪd] *n* : brocado *m*
broccoli [ˈbrɑkəli] *n* : brócoli *m*, brécol *m*
brochure [broˈʃʊr] *n* : folleto *m*
brogue [ˈbroːg] *n* : acento *m* irlandés
broil[1] [ˈbrɔɪl] *vt* : asar a la parrilla
broil[2] *n* : asado *m*
broiler [ˈbrɔɪlər] *n* **1** GRILL : parrilla *f* **2** : pollo *m* para asar
broke[1] [ˈbroːk] → **break**[1]
broke[2] *adj* : pelado, arruinado <to go broke : arruinarse, quebrar>
broken [ˈbroːkən] *adj* **1** DAMAGED, SHATTERED : roto, quebrado, fracturado **2** IRREGULAR, UNEVEN : accidentado, irregular, recortado **3** VIOLATED : roto, quebrantado **4** INTERRUPTED : interrumpido, descontinuo **5** CRUSHED : abatido, quebrantado <a broken man : un hombre destrozado> **6** IMPERFECT : mal <to speak broken English : hablar el inglés con dificultad>
brokenhearted [ˌbroːkənˈhɑrtəd] *adj* : descorazonado, desconsolado
broker[1] [ˈbroːkər] *vt* : hacer corretaje de
broker[2] *n* **1** : agente *mf;* corredor *m*, -dora *f* **2** → **stockbroker**
brokerage [ˈbroːkərɪdʒ] *n* : corretage *m*, agencia *f* de corredores
bromine [ˈbroːˌmiːn] *n* : bromo *m*
bronchitis [brɑnˈkaɪt̬əs, brɑŋ-] *n* : bronquitis *f*
bronze[1] [ˈbrɑnz] *vt* **bronzed; bronzing** : broncear
bronze[2] *n* : bronce *m*
brooch [ˈbroːtʃ, ˈbruːtʃ] *n* : broche *m*, prendedor *m*
brood[1] [ˈbruːd] *vt* **1** INCUBATE : empollar, incubar **2** PONDER : sopesar, considerar — *vi* **1** INCUBATE : empollar **2** REFLECT : rumiar, reflexionar **3** WORRY : ponerse melancólico, inquietarse
brood[2] *adj* : de cría
brood[3] *n* : nidada *f* (de pájaros), camada *f* (de mamíferos)
brooder [ˈbruːdər] *n* **1** THINKER : pensador *m*, -dora *f* **2** INCUBATOR : incubadora *f*
brook[1] [ˈbrʊk] *vt* TOLERATE : tolerar, admitir
brook[2] *n* : arroyo *m*
broom [ˈbruːm, ˈbrʊm] *n* **1** : retama *f*, hiniesta *f* **2** : escoba *f* (para barrer)
broomstick [ˈbruːmˌstɪk, ˈbrʊm-] *n* : palo *m* de escoba
broth [ˈbrɔθ] *n, pl* **broths** [ˈbrɔθs, ˈbrɔðz] : caldo *m*

brothel ['brɑθəl, 'brɔ-] *n* : burdel *m*
brother ['brʌðər] *n, pl* **brothers** *also* **brethren** ['brɛðrən, -ðərn] **1** : hermano *m* **2** KINSMAN : pariente *m,* familiar *m*
brotherhood ['brʌðərˌhʊd] *n* **1** FELLOWSHIP : fraternidad *f* **2** ASSOCIATION : hermandad *f*
brother-in-law ['brʌðərɪnˌlɔ] *n, pl* **brothers-in-law**: cuñado *m*
brotherly ['brʌðərli] *adj* : fraternal
brought → **bring**
brow ['braʊ] *n* **1** EYEBROW : ceja *f* **2** FOREHEAD : frente *f* **3** : cima *f* <the brow of a hill : la cima de una colina>
browbeat ['braʊˌbiːt] *vt* **-beat; -beaten** [-ˌbiːtən] *or* **-beat; -beating** : intimidar
brown¹ ['braʊn] *vt* **1** : dorar (en cocinar) **2** TAN : broncear — *vi* **1** : dorarse (en cocinar) **2** TAN : broncearse
brown² *adj* : marrón, café, castaño (dícese del pelo), moreno (dícese de la piel)
brown³ *n* : marrón *m,* café *m*
brownish ['braʊnɪʃ] *adj* : pardo
browse ['braʊz] *vi* **browsed; browsing 1** GRAZE : pacer **2** LOOK : mirar, echar un vistazo
bruin ['bruːɪn] *n* BEAR : oso *m*
bruise¹ ['bruːz] *vt* **bruised; bruising 1** : contusionar, machucar, magullar (a una persona) **2** DAMAGE : magullar, dañar (frutas) **3** CRUSH : majar **4** HURT : herir (los sentimientos)
bruise² *n* : moretón *m,* cardenal *m,* magulladura *f* (dícese de frutas)
brunch ['brʌntʃ] *n* : combinación *f* de desayuno y almuerzo
brunet¹ *or* **brunette** [bruː'nɛt] *adj* : moreno
brunet² *or* **brunette** *n* : moreno *m,* -na *f*
brunt ['brʌnt] *n* **to bear the brunt of** : llevar el peso de, aguantar el mayor impacto de
brush¹ ['brʌʃ] *vt* **1** : cepillar <to brush one's teeth : cepillarse uno los dientes> **2** SWEEP : barrer, quitar con un cepillo **3** GRAZE : rozar **4 to brush off** DISREGARD : hacer caso omiso de, ignorar — *vi* **to brush up on** : repasar, refrescar, dar un repaso a
brush² *n* **1** *or* **brushwood** ['brʌʃˌwʊd] : broza *f* **2** SCRUB, UNDERBRUSH : maleza *f* **3** : cepillo *m,* pincel *m* (de artista), brocha *f* (de pintor) **4** TOUCH : roce *m* **5** SKIRMISH : escaramuza *f*
brush-off ['brʌʃˌɔf] *n* **to give the brush-off to** : dar calabazas a
brusque ['brʌsk] *adj* : brusco — **brusquely** *adv*
brussels sprout ['brʌsəlzˌspraʊt] *n* : col *f* de Bruselas
brutal ['bruːtəl] *adj* : brutal, cruel, salvaje — **brutally** *adv*
brutality [bruː'tæləti] *n, pl* **-ties** : brutalidad *f*
brutalize ['bruːtəlˌaɪz] *vt* **-ized; -izing** : brutalizar, maltratar
brute¹ ['bruːt] *adj* : bruto <brute force : fuerza bruta>
brute² *n* **1** BEAST : bestia *f,* animal *m* **2** : bruto *m,* -ta *f;* bestia *mf* (persona)
brutish ['bruːtɪʃ] *adj* **1** : de animal **2** CRUEL : brutal, salvaje **3** STUPID : bruto, estúpido
bubble¹ ['bʌbəl] *vi* **-bled; -bling** : burbujear <to bubble over with joy : rebosar de alegría>
bubble² *n* : burbuja *f*
bubbly ['bʌbəli] *adj* **bubblier; -est 1** BUBBLING : burbujeante **2** LIVELY : vivaz, lleno de vida
bubonic plague [buː'bɑnɪk, 'bjuː-] *n* : peste *f* bubónica
buccaneer [ˌbʌkə'nɪr] *n* : bucanero *m*
buck¹ ['bʌk] *vi* **1** : corcovear (dícese de un caballo o un burro) **2** JOLT : dar sacudidas **3 to buck against** : resistirse a, rebelarse contra **4 to buck up** : animarse, levantar el ánimo — *vt* OPPOSE : oponerse a, ir en contra de
buck² *n, pl* **buck** *or* **bucks 1** : animal *m* macho, ciervo *m* (macho) **2** DOLLAR : dólar *m* **3 to pass the buck** *fam* : pasar la pelota *fam*
bucket ['bʌkət] *n* : balde *m,* cubo *m,* cubeta *f Mex*
bucketful ['bʌkətˌfʊl] *n* : balde *m* lleno
buckle¹ ['bʌkəl] *v* **-led; -ling** *vt* **1** FASTEN : abrochar **2** BEND, TWIST : combar, torcer — *vi* **1** BEND, TWIST : combarse, torcerse, doblarse (dícese de las rodillas) **2 to buckle down** : ponerse a trabajar con esmero **3 to buckle up** : abrocharse
buckle² *n* **1** : hebilla *f* **2** TWISTING : torcedura *f*
buckshot ['bʌkˌʃɑt] *n* : perdigón *m*
buckskin ['bʌkˌskɪn] *n* : gamuza *f*
bucktooth ['bʌkˌtuːθ] *n* : diente *m* saliente, diente *m* salido
buckwheat ['bʌkˌhwiːt] *n* : trigo *m* rubión, alforfón *m*
bucolic [bjuː'kɑlɪk] *adj* : bucólico
bud¹ ['bʌd] *v* **budded; budding** *vt* GRAFT : injertar — *vi* : brotar, hacer brotes
bud² *n* : brote *m,* yema *f,* capullo *m* (de una flor)
Buddhism ['buːˌdɪzəm, 'bʊ-] *n* : Budismo *m*
Buddhist ['buːdɪst, 'bʊ-] *n* : budista *mf* — **Buddhist** *adj*
buddy ['bʌdi] *n, pl* **-dies** : amigo *m,* -ga *f;* compinche *mf fam;* cuate *m,* -ta *f Mex fam*
budge ['bʌdʒ] *vi* **budged; budging 1** MOVE : moverse, desplazarse **2** YIELD : ceder
budget¹ ['bʌdʒət] *vt* : presupuestar (gastos), asignar (dinero) — *vi* : presupuestar, planear el presupuesto
budget² *n* : presupuesto

budgetary [ˈbʌdʒəˌtɛri] *adj* : presupuestario

buff¹ [ˈbʌf] *vt* POLISH : pulir, sacar brillo a, lustrar

buff² *adj* : beige, amarillento

buff³ *n* **1** : beige *m,* amarillento *m* **2** ENTHUSIAST : aficionado *m,* -da *f;* entusiasta *mf*

buffalo [ˈbʌfəˌloː] *n, pl* **-lo** *or* **-loes 1** : búfalo *m* **2** BISON : bisonte *m*

buffer [ˈbʌfər] *n* **1** BARRIER : barrera *f* <buffer state : estado tapón> **2** SHOCK ABSORBER : amortiguador *m*

buffet¹ [ˈbʌfət] *vt* : golpear, zarandear, sacudir

buffet² *n* BLOW : golpe *m*

buffet³ [ˌbʌˈfeɪ, ˌbuː-] *n* **1** : bufete *m,* bufé *m* (comida) **2** SIDEBOARD : aparador *m*

buffoon [ˌbʌˈfuːn] *n* : bufón *m,* -fona *f;* payaso *m,* -sa *f*

buffoonery [ˌbʌˈfuːnəri] *n, pl* **-eries** : bufonada *f,* payasada *f*

bug¹ [ˈbʌg] *vt* **bugged; bugging 1** PESTER : fastidiar, molestar **2** : ocultar micrófonos en

bug² *n* **1** INSECT : bicho *m,* insecto *m* **2** DEFECT : defecto *m,* falla *f,* problema *m* **3** GERM : microbio *m,* virus *m* **4** MICROPHONE : micrófono *m*

bugaboo [ˈbʌgəˌbuː] → **bogey**

bugbear [ˈbʌgˌbær] *n* : pesadilla *f,* coco *m*

buggy [ˈbʌgi] *n, pl* **-gies** : calesa *f* (tirada por caballos), cochecito *m* (para niños)

bugle [ˈbjuːgəl] *n* : clarín *m,* corneta *f*

bugler [ˈbjuːgələr] *n* : corneta *mf*

build¹ [ˈbɪld] *v* **built** [ˈbɪlt]; **building** *vt* **1** CONSTRUCT : construir, edificar, ensamblar, levantar **2** DEVELOP : desarrollar, elaborar, forjar **3** INCREASE : incrementar, aumentar — *vi* **to build up** : aumentar, intensificar

build² *n* PHYSIQUE : físico *m,* complexión *f*

builder [ˈbɪldər] *n* : constructor *m,* -tora *f;* contratista *mf*

building [ˈbɪldɪŋ] *n* **1** EDIFICE : edificio *m* **2** CONSTRUCTION : construcción *f*

built-in [ˈbɪltˈɪn] *adj* **1** : empotrado <built-in cabinets : armarios empotrados> **2** INHERENT : incorporado, intrínseco

bulb [ˈbʌlb] *n* **1** : bulbo *m* (de una planta), cabeza *f* (de ajo), cubeta *f* (de un termómetro) **2** LIGHTBULB : bombilla *f,* foco *m,* bombillo *m CA, Col, Ven*

bulbous [ˈbʌlbəs] *adj* : bulboso

Bulgarian [bʌlˈgæriən, bʊl-] *n* **1** : búlgaro *m,* -ra *f* **2** : búlgaro *m* (idioma) — **Bulgarian**

bulge¹ [ˈbʌldʒ] *vi* **bulged; bulging** : abultar, sobresalir

bulge² *n* : bulto *m,* protuberancia *f*

bulk¹ [ˈbʌlk] *vt* : hinchar — *vi* EXPAND, SWELL : ampliarse, hincharse

bulk² *n* **1** SIZE, VOLUME : volumen *m,* tamaño *m* **2** FIBER : fibra *f* **3** MASS : mole *f* **4 the bulk of** : la mayor parte de **5 in ~** : en grandes cantidades

bulkhead [ˈbʌlkˌhɛd] *n* : mamparo *m*

bulky [ˈbʌlki] *adj* **bulkier; -est** : voluminoso, grande

bull¹ [ˈbʊl] *adj* : macho

bull² *n* **1** : toro *m,* macho *m* (de ciertas especies) **2** : bula *f* (papal) **3** DECREE : decreto *m,* edicto *m*

bulldog [ˈbʊlˌdɔg] *n* : buldog *m*

bulldoze [ˈbʊlˌdoːz] *vt* **-dozed; -dozing 1** LEVEL : nivelar (el terreno), derribar (un edificio) **2** FORCE : forzar <he bulldozed his way through : se abrió paso a codazos>

bulldozer [ˈbʊlˌdoːzər] *n* : bulldozer *m*

bullet [ˈbʊlət] *n* : bala *f*

bulletin [ˈbʊlətən, -lətən] *n* **1** NOTICE : comunicado *m,* anuncio *m,* boletín *m* **2** NEWSLETTER : boletín *m* (informativo)

bulletin board *n* : tablón *m* de anuncios

bulletproof [ˈbʊlətˌpruːf] *adj* : antibalas, a prueba de balas

bullfight [ˈbʊlˌfaɪt] *n* : corrida *f* (de toros)

bullfighter [ˈbʊlˌfaɪt̬ər] *n* : torero *m,* -ra *f;* matador *m*

bullfrog [ˈbʊlˌfrɔg] *n* : rana *f* toro

bullheaded [ˈbʊlˈhɛdəd] *adj* : testarudo

bullion [ˈbʊljən] *n* : oro *m* en lingotes, plata *f* en lingotes

bullock [ˈbʊlək] *n* **1** STEER : buey *m,* toro *m* castrado **2** : toro *m* joven, novillo *m*

bull's–eye [ˈbʊlzˌaɪ] *n, pl* **bull's–eyes** : diana *f,* blanco *m*

bully¹ [ˈbʊli] *vt* **-lied; -lying** : intimidar, amendrentar, mangonear

bully² *n, pl* **-lies** : matón *m;* bravucón *m,* -cona *f*

bulrush [ˈbʊlˌrʌʃ] *n* : especie *f* de junco

bulwark [ˈbʊlˌwərk, -ˌwɔrk; ˈbʌlˌwərk] *n* : baluarte *m,* bastión *f*

bum¹ [ˈbʌm] *v* **bummed; bumming** *vi* **to bum around** : vagabundear, vagar — *vt* : gorronear *fam,* sablear *fam*

bum² *adj* : inútil, malo <a bum rap : una acusación falsa>

bum³ *n* **1** LOAFER : vago *m,* -ga *f* **2** HOBO, TRAMP : vagabundo *m,* -da *f*

bumblebee [ˈbʌmbəlˌbiː] *n* : abejorro *m*

bump¹ [ˈbʌmp] *vt* : chocar contra, golpear contra, dar <to bump one's head : darse (un golpe) en la cabeza> — *vi* **to bump into** MEET : encontrarse con, tropezarse con

bump² *n* **1** BULGE : bulto *m,* protuberancia *f* **2** IMPACT : golpe *m,* choque *m* **3** JOLT : sacudida *f*

bumper¹ [ˈbʌmpər] *adj* : extraordinario, récord <a bumper crop : una cosecha abundante>

bumper[2] *n* : parachoques *mpl*
bumpkin [ˈbʌmpkən] *n* : palurdo *m,* -da *f*
bumpy [ˈbʌmpi] *adj* **bumpier; -est** : desigual, lleno de baches (dícese de un camino), agitado (dícese de un vuelo en avión)
bun [ˈbʌn] *n* : bollo *m*
bunch[1] [ˈbʌntʃ] *vt* : agrupar, amontonar — *vi* **to bunch up** : amontarse, agruparse, fruncirse (dícese de una tela)
bunch[2] *n* : grupo *m,* montón *m,* ramo *m* (de flores)
bundle[1] [ˈbʌndəl] *vt* **-dled; -dling** : liar, atar
bundle[2] *n* **1** : fardo *m,* atado *m,* bulto *m,* haz *m* (de palos) **2** PARCEL : paquete *m* **3** LOAD : montón *m* <a bundle of money : un montón de dinero>
bungalow [ˈbʌŋgəˌloː] *n* : tipo de casa de un solo piso
bungle[1] [ˈbʌŋgəl] *vt* **-gled; -gling** : echar a perder, malograr
bungle[2] *n* : chapuza *f,* desatino *m*
bungler [ˈbʌŋgələr] *n* : chapucero *m,* -ra *f;* inepto *m,* -ta *f*
bunion [ˈbʌnjən] *n* : juanete *m*
bunk[1] [ˈbʌŋk] *vi* : dormir (en una litera)
bunk[2] *n* **1** *or* **bunk bed** : litera *f* **2** NONSENSE : tonterías *fpl,* bobadas *fpl*
bunker [ˈbʌŋkər] *n* **1** : carbonera *f* (en un barco) **2** SHELTER : búnker *m*
bunny [ˈbʌni] *n, pl* **-nies** : conejo *m,* -ja *f*
buoy[1] [ˈbuːi, ˈbɔɪ] *vt* **to buoy up 1** : mantener a flote **2** CHEER, HEARTEN : animar, levantar el ánimo a
buoy[2] *n* : boya *f*
buoyancy [ˈbɔɪəntsi, ˈbuːjən-] *n* **1** : flotabilidad *f* **2** OPTIMISM : confianza *f,* optimismo *m*
buoyant [ˈbɔɪənt, ˈbuːjənt] *adj* : boyante, flotante
bur *or* **burr** [ˈbər] *n* : abrojo *m* (de una planta)
burden[1] [ˈbərdən] *vt* : cargar, oprimir
burden[2] *n* : carga *f,* peso *m*
burdensome [ˈbərdənsəm] *adj* : oneroso
burdock [ˈbərˌdɑk] *n* : bardana *f*
bureau [ˈbjʊro] *n* **1** CHEST OF DRAWERS : cómoda *f* **2** DEPARTMENT : departamento *m* (del gobierno) **3** AGENCY : agencia *f* <travel bureau : agencia de viajes>
bureaucracy [bjʊˈrɑkrəsi] *n, pl* **-cies** : burocracia *f*
bureaucrat [ˈbjʊrəˌkræt] *n* : burócrata *mf*
bureaucratic [ˌbjʊrəˈkræt̬ɪk] *adj* : burocrático
burgeon [ˈbərdʒən] *vi* : florecer, retoñar, crecer
burglar [ˈbərglər] *n* : ladrón *m,* -drona *f*
burglarize [ˈbərgləˌraɪz] *vt* **-ized; -izing** : robar
burglary [ˈbərgləri] *n, pl* **-glaries** : robo *m*
burgle [ˈbərgəl] *vt* **-gled; -gling** : robar
burgundy [ˈbərgəndi] *n, pl* **-dies** : borgoña *m,* vino *m* de Borgoña
burial [ˈbɛriəl] *n* : entierro *m,* sepelio *m*
burlap [ˈbərˌlæp] *n* : arpillera *f*
burlesque[1] [bərˈlɛsk] *vt* **-lesqued; -lesquing** : parodiar
burlesque[2] *n* **1** PARODY : parodia *f* **2** REVUE : revista *f* (musical)
burly [ˈbərli] *adj* **-lier; -liest** : fornido, corpulento, musculoso
burn[1] [ˈbərn] *v* **burned** [ˈbərnd, ˈbərnt] *or* **burnt** [ˈbərnt]; **burning** *vt* **1** : quemar, incendiar <to burn a building : incendiar un edificio> <I burned my hand : me quemé la mano> **2** CONSUME : usar, gastar, consumir — *vi* **1** : arder (dícese de un fuego o un edificio), quemarse (dícese de la comida, etc.) **2** : estar prendido, estar encendido <we left the lights burning : dejamos las luces encendidas> **3 to burn out** : consumirse, apagarse **4 to burn with** : arder de <he was burning with jealousy : ardía de celos>
burn[2] *n* : quemadura *f*
burner [ˈbərnər] *n* : quemador *m*
burnish [ˈbərnɪʃ] *vt* : bruñir
burp[1] [ˈbərp] *vi* : eructar — *vt* : hacer eructar
burp[2] *n* : eructo *m*
burr → **bur**
burro [ˈbəro, ˈbʊr-] *n, pl* **-os** : burro *m*
burrow[1] [ˈbəro] *vi* **1** : cavar, hacer una madriguera **2 to burrow into** : hurgar en — *vt* : cavar, excavar
burrow[2] *n* : madriguera *f,* conejera *f* (de un conejo)
bursar [ˈbərsər] *n* : administrador *m,* -dora *f*
bursitis [bərˈsaɪt̬əs] *n* : bursitis *f*
burst[1] [ˈbərst] *v* **burst** *or* **bursted; bursting** *vi* **1** : reventarse (dícese de una llanta o un globo), estallar (dícese de obuses o fuegos artificiales), romperse (dícese de un dique) **2 to burst in** : irrumpir en **3 to burst into** : empezar a, echar a <to burst into tears : echarse a llorar> — *vt* : reventar
burst[2] *n* **1** EXPLOSION : estallido *m,* explosión *f,* reventón *m* (de una llanta) **2** OUTBURST : arranque *m* (de actividad, de velocidad), arrebato *m* (de ira), salva *f* (de aplausos)
Burundian [bʊˈruːndiən, -ˈrʊn-] *n* : burundés *m,* -desa *f* — **Burundian** *adj*
bury [ˈbɛri] *vt* **buried; burying 1** INTER : enterrar, sepultar **2** HIDE : esconder, ocultar **3 to bury oneself in** : enfrascarse en
bus[1] [ˈbʌs] *v* **bused** *or* **bussed** [ˈbʌst]; **busing** *or* **bussing** [ˈbʌsɪŋ] *vt* : trans-

portar en autobús — *vi* : viajar en autobús

bus[2] *n* : autobús *m,* bus *m,* camión *m Mex,* colectivo *m Arg, Bol, Peru*

busboy [ˈbʌsˌbɔɪ] *n* : ayudante *mf* de camarero

bush [ˈbʊʃ] *n* **1** SHRUB : arbusto *m,* mata *f* **2** THICKET : maleza *f,* matorral *m*

bushel [ˈbʊʃəl] *n* : medida de áridos igual a 35.24 litros

bushing [ˈbʊʃɪŋ] *n* : cojinete *m*

bushy [ˈbʊʃi] *adj* **bushier; -est** : espeso, poblado <bushy eyebrows : cejas pobladas>

busily [ˈbɪzəli] *adv* : afanosamente, diligentemente

business [ˈbɪznəs, -nəz] *n* **1** OCCUPATION : ocupación *f,* oficio *m* **2** DUTY, MISSION : misión *f,* deber *m,* responsabilidad *f* **3** ESTABLISHMENT, FIRM : empresa *f,* firma *f,* negocio *m,* comercio *m* **4** COMMERCE : negocios *mpl,* comercio *m* **5** AFFAIR, MATTER : asunto *m,* cuestión *f,* cosa *f* <it's none of your business : no es asunto tuyo>

businessman [ˈbɪznəsˌmæn, -nəz-] *n, pl* **-men** [-mən, -ˌmɛn] : empresario *m,* hombre *m* de negocios

businesswoman [ˈbɪznəsˌwʊmən, -nəz-] *n, pl* **-women** [-ˌwɪmən] : empresaria *f,* mujer *f* de negocios

bust[1] [ˈbʌst] *vt* **1** BREAK, SMASH : romper, estropear, destrozar **2** TAME : domar, amansar (un caballo) — *vi* : romperse, estropearse

bust[2] *n* **1** : busto *m* (en la escultura) **2** BREASTS : pecho *m,* senos *mpl,* busto *m*

bustle[1] [ˈbʌsəl] *vi* **-tled; -tling to bustle about** : ir y venir, trajinar, ajetrearse

bustle[2] *n* **1** *or* **hustle and bustle** : bullicio *m,* ajetreo *m* **2** : polisón *m* (en la ropa femenina)

busy[1] [ˈbɪzi] *vt* **busied; busying to busy oneself with** : ocuparse con, ponerse a, entretenerse con

busy[2] *adj* **busier; -est 1** OCCUPIED : ocupado, atareado <he's busy working : está ocupado en su trabajo> <the telephone was busy : el teléfono estaba ocupado> **2** BUSTLING : concurrido, animado <a busy street : una calle concurrida, una calle con mucho tránsito>

busybody [ˈbɪziˌbɑdi] *n, pl* **-bodies** : entrometido *m,* -da *f;* metiche *mf fam;* metomentodo *mf*

but[1] [ˈbʌt] *conj* **1** THAT : que <there is no doubt but he is lazy : no cabe duda que sea perezoso> **2** WITHOUT : sin que **3** NEVERTHELESS : pero, no obstante, sin embargo <I called her but she didn't answer : la llamé pero no contestó> **4** YET : pero <he was poor but proud : era pobre pero orgulloso>

but[2] *prep* EXCEPT : excepto, menos <everyone but Carlos : todos menos Carlos> <the last but one : el penúltimo>

butcher[1] [ˈbʊtʃər] *vt* **1** SLAUGHTER : matar (animales) **2** KILL : matar, asesinar, masacrar **3** BOTCH : estropear, hacer una chapuza

butcher[2] *n* **1** : carnicero *m,* -ra *f* **2** KILLER : asesino *m,* -na *f* **3** BUNGLER : chapucero *m,* -ra *f*

butler [ˈbʌtlər] *n* : mayordomo *m*

butt[1] [ˈbʌt] *vt* **1** : embestir (con los cuernos), darle un cabezazo a **2** ABUT : colindar con, bordear — *vi* **to butt in 1** INTERRUPT : interrumpir **2** MEDDLE : entrometerse, meterse

butt[2] *n* **1** BUTTING : embestida *f* (de cuernos), cabezazo *m* **2** TARGET : blanco *m* <the butt of their jokes : el blanco de sus bromas> **3** BOTTOM, END : extremo *m,* culata *f* (de un rifle), colilla *f* (de un cigarillo)

butte [ˈbjuːt] *n* : colina *f* empinada y aislada

butter[1] [ˈbʌtər] *vt* **1** : untar con mantequilla **2 to butter up** : halagar

butter[2] *n* : mantequilla *f*

buttercup [ˈbʌtərˌkʌp] *n* : ranúnculo *m*

butterfat [ˈbʌtərˌfæt] *n* : grasa *f* de la leche

butterfly [ˈbʌtərˌflaɪ] *n, pl* **-flies** : mariposa *f*

buttermilk [ˈbʌtərˌmɪlk] *n* : suero *m* de la leche

butternut [ˈbʌtərˌnʌt] *n* : nogal *m* ceniciento (árbol)

butterscotch [ˈbʌtərˌskɑtʃ] *n* : caramelo *m* duro hecho con mantequilla

buttery [ˈbʌtəri] *adj* : mantecoso

buttocks [ˈbʌtəks, -ˌtɑks] *npl* : nalgas *fpl,* trasero *m*

button[1] [ˈbʌtən] *vt* : abrochar, abotonar — *vi* : abrocharse, abotonarse

button[2] *n* : botón *m*

buttonhole[1] [ˈbʌtənˌhoːl] *vt* **-holed; -holing** : acorralar

buttonhole[2] *n* : ojal *m*

buttress[1] [ˈbʌtrəs] *vt* : apoyar, reforzar

buttress[2] *n* **1** : contrafuerte *m* (en la arquitectura) **2** SUPPORT : apoyo *m,* sostén *m*

buxom [ˈbʌksəm] *adj* : con mucho busto, con mucho pecho

buy[1] [ˈbaɪ] *vt* **bought** [ˈbɔt]; **buying** : comprar

buy[2] *n* BARGAIN : compra *f,* ganga *f*

buyer [ˈbaɪər] *n* : comprador *m,* -dora *f*

buzz[1] [ˈbʌz] *vi* : zumbar (dícese de un insecto), sonar (dícese de un teléfono o un despertador)

buzz[2] *n* **1** : zumbido *m* (de insectos) **2** : murmullo *m,* rumor *m* (de voces)

buzzard [ˈbʌzərd] *n* VULTURE : buitre *m,* zopilote *m CA, Mex*

buzzer [ˈbʌzər] *n* : timbre *m,* chicharra *f*

buzzword [ˈbʌzˌwərd] *n* : palabra *f* de moda

by[1] [ˈbaɪ] *adv* **1** NEAR : cerca <he lives close by : vive muy cerca> **2 to stop**

by : pasar por casa, hacer una visita **3 to go by** : pasar <they rushed by : pasaron corriendo> **4 to put by** : reservar, poner a un lado **5 by and by** : poco después, dentro de poco **6 by and large** : en general

by[2] *prep* **1** NEAR : cerca de, al lado de, junto a **2** VIA : por <she left by the door : salió por la puerta> **3** PAST : por, por delante de <they walked by him : pasaron por delante de él> **4** DURING : de, durante <by night : de noche> **5** (*in expressions of time*) : para <we'll be there by ten : estaremos allí para las diez> <by then : para entonces> **6** (*indicating cause or agent*) : por, de, a <built by the Romans : construido por los romanos> <a book by Borges : un libro de Borges> <made by hand : hecho a mano>

by and by *adv* : dentro de poco

bygone[1] [ˈbaɪˌgɔn] *adj* : pasado

bygone[2] *n* **let bygones be bygones** : lo pasado, pasado está

bylaw *or* **byelaw** [ˈbaɪˌlɔ] *n* : norma *f*, reglamento *m*

by–line [ˈbaɪˌlaɪn] *n* : data *f*

bypass[1] [ˈbaɪˌpæs] *vt* : evitar

bypass[2] *n* : carretera *f* de circunvalación, desvío *m*

by–product [ˈbaɪˌprɑdəkt] *n* : subproducto *m*, producto *m* derivado

bystander [ˈbaɪˌstændər] *n* : espectador *m*, -dora *f*

byway [ˈbaɪˌweɪ] *n* : camino *m* (apartado), carretera *f* secundaria

byword [ˈbaɪˌwərd] *n* **1** PROVERB : proverbio *m*, refrán *m* **2 to be a byword for** : estar sinónimo de

C

c [ˈsiː] *n, pl* **c's** *or* **cs** : tercera letra del alfabeto inglés

cab [ˈkæb] *n* **1** TAXI : taxi *m* **2** : cabina *f* (de un camión o una locomotora) **3** CARRIAGE : coche *m* de caballos

cabal [kəˈbɑl, -ˈbæl] *n* **1** INTRIGUE, PLOT : conspiración *f*, complot *m*, intriga *f* **2** : grupo *m* de conspiradores

cabaret [ˌkæbəˈreɪ] *n* : cabaret *m*

cabbage [ˈkæbɪdʒ] *n* : col *f*, repollo *m*

cabbie *or* **cabby** [ˈkæbi] *n* : taxista *mf*

cabin [ˈkæbən] *n* **1** HUT : cabaña *f*, choza *f*, barraca *f* **2** STATEROOM : camarote *m* **3** : cabina *f* (de un automóvil o avión)

cabinet [ˈkæbnət] *n* **1** CUPBOARD : armario *m* **2** : gabinete *m*, consejo *m* de ministros **3 medicine cabinet** : botiquín *m*

cabinetmaker [ˈkæbnətˌmeɪkər] *n* : ebanista *mf*

cabinetmaking [ˈkæbnətˌmeɪkɪŋ] *n* : ebanistería *f*

cable[1] [ˈkeɪbəl] *vt* **-bled; -bling** : enviar un cable, telegrafiar

cable[2] *n* **1** : cable *m* (para colgar o sostener algo) **2** : cable *m* eléctrico **3** → **cablegram**

cablegram [ˈkeɪbəlˌgræm] *n* : telegrama *m*, cable *m*

caboose [kəˈbuːs] *n* : furgón *m* de cola, cabús *m Mex*

cabstand [ˈkæbˌstænd] *n* : parada *f* de taxis

cacao [kəˈkaʊ, -ˈkeɪo] *n, pl* **cacaos** : cacao *m*

cache[1] [ˈkæʃ] *vt* **cached; caching** : esconder, guardar en un escondrijo

cache[2] *n* **1** : escondite *m*, escondrijo *m* <cache of weapons : escondite de armas> **2** : cache *m* <cache memory : memoria cache>

cachet [kæˈʃeɪ] *n* : caché *m*, prestigio *m*

cackle[1] [ˈkækəl] *vi* **-led; -ling 1** CLUCK : cacarear **2** : reírse o carcajearse estridentemente <he was cackling with delight : estaba carcajeándose de gusto>

cackle[2] *n* **1** : cacareo *m* (de una polla) **2** LAUGH : risa *f* estridente

cacophony [kæˈkɑfəni, -ˈkɔ-] *n, pl* **-nies** : cacofonía *f*

cactus [ˈkæktəs] *n, pl* **cacti** [-ˌtaɪ] *or* **-tuses** : cacto *m*, cactus *m*

cadaver [kəˈdævər] *n* : cadáver *m*

cadaverous [kəˈdævərəs] *adj* : cadavérico

caddie[1] *or* **caddy** [ˈkædi] *vi* **caddied; caddying** : trabajar de caddie, hacer de caddie

caddie[2] *or* **caddy** *n, pl* **-dies** : caddie *mf*

caddy [ˈkædi] *n, pl* **-dies** : cajita *f* para té

cadence [ˈkeɪdənts] *n* : cadencia *f*, ritmo *m*

cadenced [ˈkeɪdəntst] *adj* : cadencioso, rítmico

cadet [kəˈdɛt] *n* : cadete *mf*

cadmium [ˈkædmiəm] *n* : cadmio *m*

cadre [ˈkæˌdreɪ, ˈkɑ-, -ˌdriː] *n* : cuadro *m* (de expertos)

café [kæˈfeɪ, kə-] *n* : café *m*, cafetería *f*

cafeteria [ˌkæfəˈtɪriə] *n* : cafetería *f*, restaurante *m* de autoservicio

caffeine [kæˈfiːn] *n* : cafeína *f*

cage[1] [ˈkeɪdʒ] *vt* **caged; caging** : enjaular

cage[2] *n* : jaula *f*

cagey [ˈkeɪdʒi] *adj* **-gier; -est 1** CAUTIOUS : cauteloso, reservado **2** SHREWD : astuto, vivo — **cagily** [-dʒəli] *adv*

caisson ['keɪ,sɑn, -sən] *n* **1 :** cajón *m* de municiones **2 :** cajón *m* hidráulico

cajole [kə'ʤo:l] *vt* **-joled; -joling :** engatusar

cajolery [kə'ʤo:ləri] *n* **:** engatusamiento *m*

cake[1] ['keɪk] *v* **caked; caking** *vt* **:** cubrir <caked with mud : cubierto de barro> — *vi* **:** endurecerse

cake[2] *n* **1 :** torta *f,* bizcocho *m,* pastel *m* **2 :** pastilla *f* (de jabón) **3 to take the cake :** llevarse la palma, ser el colmo

calabash ['kælə,bæʃ] *n* **:** calabaza *f*

calamine ['kælə,maɪn] *n* **:** calamina *f* <calamine lotion : loción de calamina>

calamitous [kə'læmət̬əs] *adj* **:** desastroso, catastrófico, calamitoso — **calamitously** *adv*

calamity [kə'læmət̬i] *n, pl* **-ties :** desastre *m,* desgracia *f,* calamidad *f*

calcium ['kælsiəm] *n* **:** calcio *m*

calcium carbonate ['kɑrbə,neɪt, -nət] *n* **:** carbonato *m* de calcio

calculable ['kælkjələbəl] *adj* **:** calculable, computable

calculate ['kælkjə,leɪt] *v* **-lated; -lating** *vt* **1** COMPUTE **:** calcular, computar **2** ESTIMATE **:** calcular, creer **3** INTEND **:** planear, tener la intención de <I calculated on spending $100 : planeaba gastar $100> — *vi* **:** calcular, hacer cálculos

calculated ['kælkjə,leɪt̬əd] *adj* **1** ESTIMATED **:** calculado **2** DELIBERATE **:** intencional, premeditado, deliberado

calculating ['kælkjə,leɪt̬ɪŋ] *adj* SHREWD **:** calculador, astuto

calculation [,kælkjə'leɪʃən] *n* **:** cálculo *m*

calculator ['kælkjə,leɪt̬ər] *n* **:** calculadora *f*

calculus ['kælkjələs] *n, pl* **-li** [-,laɪ] **1 :** cálculo *m* <differential calculus : cálculo diferencial> **2** TARTAR **:** sarro *m* (dental)

caldron ['kɔldrən] → **cauldron**

calendar ['kæləndər] *n* **1 :** calendario *m* **2** SCHEDULE **:** calendario *m,* programa *m,* agenda *f*

calf ['kæf, 'kaf] *n, pl* **calves** ['kævz, 'kavz] **1 :** becerro *m,* -rra *f;* ternero *m,* -ra *f* (de vacunos) **2 :** cría *f* (de otros mamíferos) **3 :** pantorrilla *f* (de la pierna)

calfskin ['kæf,skɪn] *n* **:** piel *f* de becerro

caliber *or* **calibre** ['kæləbər] *n* **1 :** calibre *m* <a .38 caliber gun : una pistola de calibre .38> **2** ABILITY **:** calibre *m,* valor *m,* capacidad *f*

calibrate ['kælə,breɪt] *vt* **-brated; -brating :** calibrar (armas), graduar (termómetros)

calibration [,kælə'breɪʃən] *n* **:** calibrado *m,* calibración *f*

calico ['kælɪ,ko:] *n, pl* **-coes** *or* **-cos 1 :** calicó *m,* percal *m* **2** *or* **calico cat :** gato *m* manchado

calipers ['kæləpərz] *npl* **:** calibrador *m*

caliph *or* **calif** ['keɪləf, 'kæ-] *n* **:** califa *m*

calisthenics [,kæləs'θɛnɪks] *ns & pl* **:** calistenia *f*

calk ['kɔk] → **caulk**

call[1] ['kɔl] *vi* **1** CRY, SHOUT **:** gritar, vociferar **2** VISIT **:** hacer (una) visita, visitar **3 to call for :** exigir, requerir, necesitar <it calls for patience : requiere mucha paciencia> — *vt* **1** SUMMON **:** llamar, convocar **2** TELEPHONE **:** llamar por teléfono, telefonear **3** NAME **:** llamar, apodar

call[2] *n* **1** SHOUT **:** grito *m,* llamada *f* **2 :** grito *m* (de un animal), reclamo *m* (de un pájaro) **3** SUMMONS **:** llamada *f* **4** DEMAND **:** llamado *m,* petición *f* **5** VISIT **:** visita *f* **6** DECISION **:** decisión *f* (en deportes) **7** *or* **telephone call :** llamada *f* (telefónica)

call down *vt* REPRIMAND **:** reprender, reñir

caller ['kɔlər] *n* **1** VISITOR **:** visita *f* **2 :** persona *f* que llama (por teléfono)

calling ['kɔlɪŋ] *n* **:** vocación *f,* profesión *f*

calliope [kə'laɪə,pi:, 'kæli,o:p] *n* **:** órgano *m* de vapor

call off *vt* CANCEL **:** cancelar, suspender

callous[1] ['kæləs] *vt* **:** encallecer

callous[2] *adj* **1** CALLUSED **:** calloso, encallecido **2** UNFEELING **:** insensible, desalmado, cruel

callously ['kæləsli] *adv* **:** cruelmente, insensiblemente

callousness ['kæləsnəs] *n* **:** insensibilidad *f,* crueldad *f*

callow ['kælo] *adj* **:** inexperto, inmaduro

callus ['kæləs] *n* **:** callo m

callused ['kæləst] *adj* **:** encallecido, calloso

calm[1] ['kɑm, 'kɑlm] *vt* **:** tranquilizar, calmar, sosegar — *vi* **:** tranquilizarse, calmarse <calm down! : ¡tranquilízate!>

calm[2] *adj* **1** TRANQUIL **:** calmo, tranquilo, sereno, ecuánime **2** STILL **:** en calma (dícese del mar), sin viento (dícese del aire)

calm[3] *n* **:** tranquilidad *f,* calma *f*

calmly ['kɑmli, 'kɑlm-] *adv* **:** con calma, tranquilamente

calmness ['kɑmnəs, 'kɑlm-] *n* **:** calma *f,* tranquilidad *f*

caloric [kə'lɔrɪk] *adj* **:** calórico (dícese de los alimentos), calorífico (dícese de la energía)

calorie ['kæləri] *n* **:** caloría *f*

calumniate [kə'lʌmni,eɪt] *vt* **-ated; -ating :** calumniar, difamar

calumny ['kæləmni] *n, pl* **-nies :** calumnia *f,* difamación *f*

calve ['kæv, 'kav] *vi* **calved; calving :** parir (dícese de los mamíferos)

calves → **calf**

calypso [kə'lɪp,so:] *n, pl* **-sos :** calipso *m*

calyx [ˈkeɪlɪks, ˈkæ-] *n, pl* **-lyxes** *or* **-lyces** [-ləˌsiːz] : cáliz *m*
cam [ˈkæm] *n* : leva *f*
camaraderie [ˌkɑmˈrɑdəri, ˌkæm-; ˌkɑməˈrɑ-] *n* : compañerismo *m,* camaradería *f*
Cambodian [kæmˈboːdiən] *n* : camboyano *m,* -na *f* — **Cambodian** *adj*
came → **come**
camel [ˈkæməl] *n* : camello *m*
camellia [kəˈmiːljə] *n* : camelia *f*
cameo [ˈkæmiˌoː] *n, pl* **-eos 1** : camafeo *m* **2** *or* **cameo performance** : actuación *f* especial
camera [ˈkæmrə, ˈkæmərə] *n* : cámara *f,* máquina *f* fotográfica
Cameroonian [ˌkæməˈruːniən] *n* : camerunés *m,* -nesa *f*
camouflage[1] [ˈkæməˌflɑʒ, -ˌflɑdʒ] *vt* **-flaged; -flaging** : camuflajear, camuflar
camouflage[2] *n* : camuflaje *m*
camp[1] [ˈkæmp] *vi* : acampar, ir de camping
camp[2] *n* **1** : campamento *m* **2** FACTION : campo *m,* bando *m* <in the same camp : del mismo bando> **3 to pitch camp** : acampar, poner el campamento **4 to break camp** : levantar el campamento
campaign[1] [kæmˈpeɪn] *vi* : hacer (una) campaña
campaign[2] *n* : campaña *f*
campanile [ˌkæmpəˈniːˌliː, -ˈniːl] *n, pl* **-niles** *or* **-nili** [-ˈniːˌliː] : campanario *m*
camper [ˈkæmpər] *n* **1** : campista *mf* (persona) **2** : cámper *m* (vehículo)
campground [ˈkæmpˌgraʊnd] *n* : campamento *m,* camping *m*
camphor [ˈkæmpfər] *n* : alcanfor *m*
campsite [ˈkæmpˌsaɪt] *n* : campamento *m,* camping *m*
campus [ˈkæmpəs] *n* : campus *m,* recinto *m* universitario
can[1] [ˈkæn] *v aux, past* **could** [ˈkʊd]; *present s & pl* **can 1** : poder <could you help me? : ¿podría ayudarme?> **2** : saber <she can't drive yet : todavía no sabe manejar> **3** MAY : poder, tener permiso para <can I sit down? : ¿puedo sentarme?> **4** : poder <it can't be! : ¡no puede ser!> <where can they be? : ¿dónde estarán?>
can[2] [ˈkæn] *vt* **canned; canning 1** : enlatar, envasar <to can tomatoes : enlatar tomates> **2** DISMISS, FIRE : despedir, echar
can[3] *n* : lata *f,* envase *m,* cubo *m* <a can of beer : una lata de cerveza> <garbage can : cubo de basura>
Canadian [kəˈneɪdiən] *n* : canadiense *mf* — **Canadian** *adj*
canal [kəˈnæl] *n* **1** : canal *m,* tubo *m* <alimentary canal : tubo digestivo> **2** : canal *m* <Panama Canal : Canal de Panamá>
canapé [ˈkænəpi, -ˌpeɪ] *n* : canapé *m*
canary [kəˈnɛri] *n, pl* **-naries** : canario *m*
cancel [ˈkæntsəl] *vt* **-celed** *or* **-celled; -celing** *or* **-celling** : cancelar
cancellation [ˌkæntsəˈleɪʃən] *n* : cancelación *f*
cancer [ˈkæntsər] *n* : cáncer *m*
Cancer *n* : Cáncer *mf*
cancerous [ˈkæntsərəs] *adj* : canceroso
candelabrum [ˌkændəˈlɑbrəm, -ˈlæ-] *or* **candelabra** [-brə] *n, pl* **-bra** *or* **-bras** : candelabro *m*
candid [ˈkændɪd] *adj* **1** FRANK : franco, sincero, abierto **2** : natural, espontáneo (en la fotografía)
candidacy [ˈkændədəsi] *n, pl* **-cies** : candidatura *f*
candidate [ˈkændəˌdeɪt, -dət] *n* : candidato *m,* -ta *f*
candidly [ˈkændɪdli] *adv* : con franqueza
candied [ˈkændid] *adj* : confitado
candle [ˈkændəl] *n* : vela *f,* candela *f,* cirio *m* (ceremonial)
candlestick [ˈkændəlˌstɪk] *n* : candelero *m*
candor [ˈkændər] *n* : franqueza *f*
candy [ˈkændi] *n, pl* **-dies** : dulce *m,* caramelo *m*
cane[1] [ˈkeɪn] *vt* **caned; caning 1** : tapizar (muebles) con mimbre **2** FLOG : azotar con una vara
cane[2] *n* **1** : bastón *m* (para andar), vara *f* (para castigar) **2** REED : caña *f,* mimbre *m* (para muebles)
canine[1] [ˈkeɪˌnaɪn] *adj* : canino
canine[2] *n* **1** DOG : canino *m;* perro *m,* -rra *f* **2** *or* **canine tooth** : colmillo *m,* diente *m* canino
canister [ˈkænəstər] *n* : lata *f,* bote *m*
canker [ˈkæŋkər] *n* : úlcera *f* bucal
cannery [ˈkænəri] *n, pl* **-ries** : fábrica *f* de conservas
cannibal [ˈkænəbəl] *n* : caníbal *mf;* antropófago *m,* -ga *f*
cannibalism [ˈkænəbəˌlɪzəm] *n* : canibalismo *m,* antropofagia *f*
cannily [ˈkænəbəˌlaɪz] *adv* : astutamente, sagazmente
cannon [ˈkænən] *n, pl* **-nons** *or* **-non** : cañón *m*
cannot (can not) [ˈkænˌɑt, kəˈnɑt] → **can**[1]
canny [ˈkæni] *adj* **-nier; -est** SHREWD : astuto, sagaz
canoe[1] [kəˈnuː] *vt* **-noed; -noeing** : ir en canoa
canoe[2] *n* : canoa *f,* piragua *f*
canon [ˈkænən] *n* **1** : canon *m* <canon law : derecho canónico> **2** WORKS : canon *m* <the canon of American literature : el canon de la literatura americana> **3** : canónigo *m* (de una catedral) **4** STANDARD : canon *m,* norma *f*
canonize [ˈkænəˌnaɪz] *vt* **-ized; -izing** : canonizar

canopy [ˈkænəpi] *n, pl* **-pies** : dosel *m*, toldo *m*

cant¹ [ˈkænt] *vt* TILT : ladear, inclinar — *vi* **1** SLANT : ladearse, inclinarse, escorar (dícese de un barco) **2** : hablar insinceramente

cant² *n* **1** SLANT : plano *m* inclinado **2** JARGON : jerga *f* **3** : palabras *fpl* insinceras

can't [ˈkænt, ˈkant] (*contraction of* **can not**) → **can¹**

cantaloupe [ˈkæntəlˌoːp] *n* : melón *m*, cantalupo *m*

cantankerous [kænˈtæŋkərəs] *adj* : irritable, irascible — **cantankerously** *adv*

cantankerousness [kænˈtæŋkərəsnəs] *n* : irritabilidad *f*, irascibilidad *f*

cantata [kənˈtɑtə] *n* : cantata *f*

canteen [kænˈtiːn] *n* **1** FLASK : cantimplora *f* **2** CAFETERIA : cantina *f*, comedor *m* **3** : club *m* para actividades sociales y recreativas

canter¹ [ˈkæntər] *vi* : ir a medio galope

canter² *n* : medio galope *m*

cantilever [ˈkæntəˌliːvər, -ˌlɛvər] *n* **1** : viga *f* voladiza **2 cantilever bridge** : puente *m* voladizo

canto [ˈkænˌtoː] *n, pl* **-tos** : canto *m*

cantor [ˈkæntər] *n* : solista *mf*

canvas [ˈkænvəs] *n* **1** : lona *f* **2** SAILS : velas *fpl* (de un barco) **3** : lienzo *m*, tela *f* (de pintar) **4** PAINTING : pintura *f*, óleo *m*, cuadro *m*

canvass¹ [ˈkænvəs] *vt* **1** SOLICIT : solicitar votos o pedidos de, hacer campaña entre **2** SOUND OUT : sondear (opiniones, etc.)

canvass² *n* SURVEY : sondeo *m*, encuesta *f*

canyon [ˈkænjən] *n* : cañón *m*

cap¹ [ˈkæp] *vt* **capped; capping 1** COVER : tapar (un recipiente), enfundar (un diente), cubrir (una montaña) **2** CLIMAX : coronar, ser el punto culminante de <to cap it all off : para colmo> **3** LIMIT : limitar, poner un tope a

cap² *n* **1** : gorra *f*, gorro *m*, cachucha *f* *Mex* <baseball cap : gorra de béisbol> **2** COVER, TOP : tapa *f*, tapón *m* (de botellas), corcholata *f* *Mex* **3** LIMIT : tope *m*, límite *m*

capability [ˌkeɪpəˈbɪləti] *n, pl* **-ties** : capacidad *f*, habilidad *f*, competencia *f*

capable [ˈkeɪpəbəl] *adj* : competente, capaz, hábil — **capably** [-bli] *adv*

capacious [kəˈpeɪʃəs] *adj* : amplio, espacioso, de gran capacidad *f*

capacity¹ [kəˈpæsəti] *adj* : completo, total <a capacity crowd : un lleno completo>

capacity² *n, pl* **-ties 1** ROOM, SPACE : capacidad *f*, cabida *f*, espacio *m* **2** CAPABILITY : habilidad *f*, competencia *f* **3** FUNCTION, ROLE : calidad *f*, función *f* <in his capacity as ambassador : en su calidad de embajador>

cape [ˈkeɪp] *n* **1** : capa *f* **2** : cabo *m* <Cape Horn : el Cabo de Hornos>

caper¹ [ˈkeɪpər] *vi* : dar saltos, correr y brincar

caper² *n* **1** : alcaparra *f* <olives and capers : aceitunas y alcaparras> **2** ANTIC, PRANK : broma *f*, travesura *f* **3** LEAP : brinco *m*, salto *m*

Cape Verdean [ˈkeɪpˈvərdiən] *n* : caboverdiano *m*, -na *f* — **Cape Verdean** *adj*

capful [ˈkæpˌfʊl] *n* : tapa *f*, tapita *f*

capillary¹ [ˈkæpəˌlɛri] *adj* : capilar

capillary² *n, pl* **-ries** : capilar *m*

capital¹ [ˈkæpəṭəl] *adj* **1** : capital <capital punishment : pena capital> **2** : mayúsculo (dícese de las letras) **3** : de capital <capital assets : activo fijo> <capital gain : ganancia de capital, plusvalía> **4** EXCELLENT : excelente, estupendo

capital² *n* **1** *or* **capital city** : capital *f*, sede *f* del gobierno **2** WEALTH : capital *m* **3** *or* **capital letter** : mayúscula *f* **4** : capitel *m* (de una columna)

capitalism [ˈkæpəṭəlˌɪzəm] *n* : capitalismo *m*

capitalist¹ [ˈkæpəṭəlˌɪst] *or* **capitalistic** [ˌkæpəṭəlˈɪstɪk] *adj* : capitalista

capitalist² *n* : capitalista *mf*

capitalization [ˌkæpəṭələˈzeɪʃən] *n* : capitalización *f*

capitalize [ˈkæpəṭəlˌaɪz] *v* **-ized; -izing** *vt* **1** FINANCE : capitalizar, financiar **2** : escribir con mayúscula — *vi* **to capitalize on** : sacar partido de, aprovechar

capitol [ˈkæpəṭəl] *n* : capitolio *m*

capitulate [kəˈpɪtʃəˌleɪt] *vi* **-lated; -lating** : capitular

capitulation [kəˌpɪtʃəˈleɪʃən] *n* : capitulación *f*

capon [ˈkeɪˌpɑn, -pən] *n* : capón *m*

caprice [kəˈpriːs] *n* : capricho *m*, antojo *m*

capricious [kəˈprɪʃəs, -ˈpriː-] *adj* : caprichoso — **capriciously** *adv*

Capricorn [ˈkæprɪˌkɔrn] *n* : Capricornio *mf*

capsize [ˈkæpˌsaɪz, kæpˈsaɪz] *v* **-sized; -sizing** *vi* : volcar, volcarse — *vt* : hacer volcar

capstan [ˈkæpstən, -ˌstæn] *n* : cabrestante *m*

capsule [ˈkæpsəl, -ˌsuːl] *n* **1** : cápsula *f* (en la farmacéutica y botánica) **2 space capsule** : cápsula *f* espacial

captain¹ [ˈkæptən] *vt* : capitanear

captain² *n* **1** : capitán *m*, -tana *f* **2** HEADWAITER : jefe *m*, -fa *f* de comedor **3 captain of industry** : magnate *mf*

caption¹ [ˈkæpʃən] *vt* : ponerle una leyenda a (una ilustración), titular (un artículo), subtitular (una película)

caption² *n* **1** HEADING : titular *m*, encabezamiento *m* **2** : leyenda *f* (al pie de una ilustración) **3** SUBTITLE : subtítulo *m*

captivate ['kæptə,veɪt] *vt* **-vated; -vating** CHARM : cautivar, hechizar, encantar

captivating ['kæptə,veɪt̬ɪŋ] *adj* : cautivador, hechicero, encantador

captive[1] ['kæptɪv] *adj* : cautivo

captive[2] *n* : cautivo *m,* -va *f*

captivity [kæp'tɪvət̬i] *n* : cautiverio *m*

captor ['kæptər] *n* : captor *m,* -tora *f*

capture[1] ['kæpʃər] *vt* **-tured; -turing 1** SEIZE : capturar, apresar **2** CATCH : captar <to capture one's interest : captar el interés de uno>

capture[2] *n* : captura *f,* apresamiento *m*

car ['kɑr] *n* **1** AUTOMOBILE : automóvil *m,* coche *m,* carro *m* **2** : vagón *m,* coche *m* (de un tren) **3** : cabina *f* (de un ascensor)

carafe [kə'ræf, -'rɑf] *n* : garrafa *f*

caramel ['kɑrməl; 'kærəməl, -,mɛl] *n* **1** : caramelo *m,* azúcar *f* quemada **2** *or* **caramel candy** : caramelo *m,* dulce *m* de leche

carat ['kærət] *n* : quilate *m*

caravan ['kærə,væn] *n* : caravana *f*

caraway ['kærə,weɪ] *n* : alcaravea *f*

carbine ['kɑr,baɪn, -,bi:n] *n* : carabina *f*

carbohydrate [,kɑrbo'haɪ,dreɪt, -drət] *n* : carbohidrato *m,* hidrato *m* de carbono

carbon ['kɑrbən] *n* **1** : carbono *m* **2** → **carbon paper 3** → **carbon copy**

carbonated ['kɑrbə,neɪt̬əd] *adj* : carbonatado (dícese del agua), gaseoso (dícese de las bebidas)

carbon copy *n* **1** : copia *f* al carbón **2** DUPLICATE : duplicado *m,* copia *f* exacta

carbon paper *n* : papel *m* carbón

carbuncle ['kɑr,bʌŋkəl] *n* : carbunco *m*

carburetor ['kɑrbə,reɪt̬ər, -bjə-] *n* : carburador *m*

carcass ['kɑrkəs] *n* : cuerpo *m* (de un animal muerto)

carcinogen [kɑr'sɪnədʒən, 'kɑrsənə,dʒɛn] *n* : carcinógeno *m,* cancerígeno *m*

carcinogenic [,kɑrsəno'dʒɛnɪk] *adj* : carcinogénico

card[1] ['kɑrd] *vt* : cardar (fibras)

card[2] *n* **1** : carta *f,* naipe *m* <to play cards : jugar a las cartas> <a deck of cards : una baraja> **2** : tarjeta *f* <birthday card : tarjeta de cumpleaños> <business card : tarjeta (de visita)> **3** : carda *f* (para cardar fibras)

cardboard ['kɑrd,bord] *n* : cartón *m,* cartulina *f*

cardiac ['kɑrdi,æk] *adj* : cardíaco, cardiaco

cardigan ['kɑrdɪgən] *n* : cárdigan *m,* chaqueta *f* de punto

cardinal[1] ['kɑrdənəl] *adj* FUNDAMENTAL : cardinal, fundamental

cardinal[2] *n* : cardenal *m*

cardinal number *n* : número *m* cardinal

cardinal point *n* : punto *m* cardinal

cardiologist [,kɑrdi'ɑlədʒɪst] *n* : cardiólogo *m,* -ga *f*

cardiology [,kɑrdi'ɑlədʒi] *n* : cardiología *f*

cardiovascular [,kɑrdio'væskjələr] *adj* : cardiovascular

care[1] ['kær] *v* **cared; caring** *vi* **1** : importarle a uno <they don't care : no les importa> **2** : preocuparse, inquietarse <she cares about the poor : se preocupa por los pobres> **3 to care for** TEND : cuidar (de), atender, encargarse de **4 to care for** CHERISH : querer, sentir cariño por **5 to care for** LIKE : gustarle (algo a uno) <I don't care for your attitude : tu actitud no me agrada> — *vt* WISH : desear, querer <if you care to go : si deseas ir>

care[2] *n* **1** ANXIETY : inquietud *f,* preocupación *f* **2** CAREFULNESS : cuidado *m,* atención *f* <handle with care : manejar con cuidado> **3** CHARGE : cargo *m,* cuidado *m* **4 to take care of** : cuidar (de), atender, encargarse de

careen [kə'ri:n] *vi* **1** SWAY : oscilar, balancearse **2** CAREER : ir a toda velocidad

career[1] [kə'rɪr] *vi* : ir a toda velocidad

career[2] *n* VOCATION : vocación *f,* profesión *f,* carrera *f*

carefree ['kær,fri:, ,kær'-] *adj* : despreocupado

careful ['kærfəl] *adj* **1** CAUTIOUS : cuidadoso, cauteloso **2** PAINSTAKING : cuidadoso, esmerado, meticuloso

carefully ['kærfəli] *adv* : con cuidado, cuidadosamente

carefulness ['kærfəlnəs] *n* **1** CAUTION : cuidado *m,* cautela *f* **2** METICULOUSNESS : esmero *m,* meticulosidad *f*

caregiver ['kær,gɪvər] *n* : persona *f* que cuida a niños o enfermos

careless ['kærləs] *adj* : descuidado, negligente — **carelessly** *adv*

carelessness ['kærləsnəs] *n* : descuido *m,* negligencia *f*

caress[1] [kə'rɛs] *vt* : acariciar

caress[2] *n* : caricia *f*

caret ['kærət] *n* : signo *m* de intercalación

caretaker ['kɛr,teɪkər] *n* : conserje *mf;* velador *m,* -dora *f*

cargo ['kɑr,go:] *n, pl* **-goes** *or* **-gos** : cargamento *m,* carga *f*

caribou ['kærə,bu:] *n, pl* **-bou** *or* **-bous** : caribú *m*

caricature[1] ['kærɪkə,tʃʊr] *vt* **-tured; -turing** : caricaturizar

caricature[2] *n* : caricatura *f*

caricaturist ['kærɪkə,tʃʊrɪst] *n* : caricaturista *mf*

caries ['kær,i:z] *n, pl* **caries** : caries *f*

carillon ['kærə,lɑn] *n* : carillón *m*

carmine ['kɑrmən, -,maɪn] *n* : carmín *m*

carnage ['kɑrnɪdʒ] *n* : matanza *f,* carnicería *f*

carnal [ˈkɑrnəl] *adj* **:** carnal
carnation [kɑrˈneɪʃən] *n* **:** clavel *m*
carnival [ˈkɑrnəvəl] *n* **:** carnaval *m,* feria *f*
carnivore [ˈkɑrnəˌvor] *n* **:** carnívoro *m*
carnivorous [kɑrˈnɪvərəs] *adj* **:** carnívoro
carol[1] [ˈkærəl] *vi* **-oled** *or* **-olled; -oling** *or* **-olling :** cantar villancicos
carol[2] *n* **:** villancico *m*
caroler *or* **caroller** [ˈkærələr] *n* **:** persona *f* que canta villancicos
carom[1] [ˈkærəm] *vi* **1** REBOUND **:** rebotar <the bullet caromed off the wall : la bala rebotó contra el muro> **2 :** hacer carambola (en billar)
carom[2] *n* **:** carambola *f*
carouse [kəˈraʊz] *vt* **-roused; -rousing :** irse de parranda, irse de juerga
carousel *or* **carrousel** [ˌkærəˈsɛl, ˈkærəˌ-] *n* **:** carrusel *m,* tiovivo *m*
carouser [kəˈraʊzər] *n* **:** juerguista *mf*
carp[1] [ˈkɑrp] *vi* **1** COMPLAIN **:** quejarse **2 to carp at :** criticar
carp[2] *n, pl* **carp** *or* **carps :** carpa *f*
carpel [ˈkɑrpəl] *n* **:** carpelo *m*
carpenter [ˈkɑrpəntər] *n* **:** carpintero *m,* -ra *f*
carpentry [ˈkɑrpəntri] *n* **:** carpintería *f*
carpet[1] [ˈkɑrpət] *vt* **:** alfombrar
carpet[2] *n* **:** alfombra *f*
carpeting [ˈkɑrpətɪŋ] *n* **:** alfombrado *m*
carport [ˈkɑrˌpɔrt] *n* **:** cochera *f,* garaje *m* abierto
carriage [ˈkærɪdʒ] *n* **1** TRANSPORT **:** transporte *m* **2** POSTURE **:** porte *m,* postura *f* **3 horse–drawn carriage :** carruaje *m,* coche *m* **4 baby carriage :** cochecito *m*
carrier [ˈkæriər] *n* **1 :** transportista *mf,* empresa *f* de transportes **2 :** portador *m,* -dora *f* (de una enfermedad) **3 aircraft carrier :** portaaviones *m*
carrier pigeon : paloma *f* mensajera
carrion [ˈkæriən] *n* **:** carroña *f*
carrot [ˈkærət] *n* **:** zanahoria *f*
carry [ˈkæri] *v* **-ried; -rying** *vt* **1** TRANSPORT **:** llevar, cargar, transportar (cargamento), conducir (electricidad), portar (un virus) <to carry a bag : cargar una bolsa> <to carry money : llevar dinero encima, traer dinero consigo> **2** BEAR **:** soportar, aguantar, resistir (peso) **3** STOCK **:** vender, tener en abasto **4** ENTAIL **:** llevar, implicar, acarrear **5** WIN **:** ganar (una elección o competición), aprobar (una moción) **6 to carry oneself :** portarse, comportarse <he carried himself honorably : se comportó dignamente> — *vi* **:** oírse, proyectarse <her voice carries well : su voz se puede oír desde lejos>
carryall [ˈkæriˌɔl] *n* **:** bolsa *f* de viaje
carry away *vt* **to get carried away :** exaltarse, entusiasmarse
carry on *vt* CONDUCT **:** realizar, ejercer, mantener <to carry on research : realizar investigaciones> <to carry on a correspondence : mantener una correspondencia> — *vi* **1 :** portarse de manera escandalosa o inapropiada <it's embarrassing how he carries on : su manera de comportarse da vergüenza> **2** CONTINUE **:** seguir, continuar
carry out *vt* **1** PERFORM **:** llevar a cabo, realizar **2** FULFILL **:** cumplir
cart[1] [ˈkɑrt] *vt* **:** acarrear, llevar
cart[2] *n* **:** carreta *f,* carro *m*
cartel [kɑrˈtɛl] *n* **:** cártel *m*
cartilage [ˈkɑrtəlɪdʒ] *n* **:** cartílago *m*
cartilaginous [ˌkɑrtəlˈædʒənəs] *adj* **:** cartilaginoso
cartographer [kɑrˈtɑgrəfər] *n* **:** cartógrafo *m,* -fa *f*
cartography [kɑrˈtɑgrəfi] *n* **:** cartografía *f*
carton [ˈkɑrtən] *n* **:** caja *f* de cartón
cartoon [kɑrˈtuːn] *n* **1 :** chiste *m* (gráfico), caricatura *f* <a political cartoon : un chiste político> **2** COMIC STRIP **:** tira *f* cómica, historieta *f* **3** *or* **animated cartoon :** dibujo *m* animado
cartoonist [kɑrˈtuːnɪst] *n* **:** caricaturista *mf,* dibujante *mf* (de chistes)
cartridge [ˈkɑrtrɪdʒ] *n* **:** cartucho *m*
carve [ˈkɑrv] *vt* **carved; carving 1 :** tallar (madera), esculpir (piedra), grabar <he carved his name in the bark : grabó su nombre en la corteza> **2** SLICE **:** cortar, trinchar (carne)
cascade[1] [kæsˈkeɪd] *vi* **-caded; -cading :** caer en cascada
cascade[2] *n* **:** cascada *f,* salto *m* de agua
case[1] [ˈkeɪs] *vt* **cased; casing 1** BOX, PACK **:** embalar, encajonar **2** INSPECT **:** observar, inspeccionar (antes de cometer un delito)
case[2] *n* **1 :** caso *m* <an unusual case : un caso insólito> <ablative case : caso ablativo> <a case of the flu : un caso de gripe> **2** BOX **:** caja *f* **3** CONTAINER **:** funda *f,* estuche *m* **4 in any case :** de todos modos, en cualquier caso **5 in case :** como precaución <just in case : por si acaso> **6 in case of :** en caso de
casement [ˈkeɪsmənt] *n* **:** ventana *f* con bisagras
cash[1] [ˈkæʃ] *vt* **:** convertir en efectivo, cobrar, cambiar (un cheque)
cash[2] *n* **:** efectivo *m,* dinero *m* en efectivo
cashew [ˈkæˌʃuː, kəˈʃuː] *n* **:** anacardo *m*
cashier[1] [kæˈʃɪr] *vt* **:** destituir, despedir
cashier[2] *n* **:** cajero *m,* -ra *f*
cashmere [ˈkæʒˌmɪr, ˈkæʃ-] *n* **:** cachemir *m*
casino [kəˈsiːˌnoː] *n, pl* **-nos :** casino *m*
cask [ˈkæsk] *n* **:** tonel *m,* barrica *f,* barril *m*
casket [ˈkæskət] *n* COFFIN **:** ataúd *m,* féretro *m*

casserole [ˈkæsəˌroːl] *n* **1** : cazuela *f* **2** : guiso *m,* guisado *m* <tuna casserole : guiso de atún>

cassette [kəˈsɛt, kæ-] *n* : cassette *mf*

cassock [ˈkæsək] *n* : sotana *f*

cast[1] [ˈkæst] *vt* **cast; casting 1** THROW : tirar, echar, arrojar <the die is cast : la suerte está echada> **2** : depositar (un voto) **3** : asignar (papeles en una obra de teatro) **4** MOLD : moldear, fundir, vaciar **5 to cast off** ABANDON : desamparar, abandonar

cast[2] *n* **1** THROW : lance *m,* lanzamiento *m* **2** APPEARANCE : aspecto *m,* forma *f* **3** : elenco *m,* reparto *m* (de una obra de teatro) **4 plaster cast** : molde *m* de yeso, escayola *f*

castanets [ˌkæstəˈnɛts] *npl* : castañuelas *fpl*

castaway[1] [ˈkæstəˌweɪ] *adj* : náufrago

castaway[2] *n* : náufrago *m,* -ga *f*

caste [ˈkæst] *n* : casta *f*

caster [ˈkæstər] *n* : ruedita *f* (de un mueble)

castigate [ˈkæstəˌgeɪt] *vt* **-gated; -gating** : castigar severamente, censurar, reprobar

cast iron *n* : hierro *m* fundido

castle [ˈkæsəl] *n* **1** : castillo *m* **2** : torre *f* (en ajedrez)

cast–off [ˈkæstˌɔf] *adj* : desechado

castoff [ˈkæstˌɔf] *n* : desecho *m*

castrate [ˈkæsˌtreɪt] *vt* **-trated; -trating** : castrar

castration [kæˈstreɪʃən] *n* : castración *f*

casual [ˈkæʒʊəl] *adj* **1** FORTUITOUS : casual, fortuito **2** INDIFFERENT : indiferente, despreocupado **3** INFORMAL : informal — **casually** [ˈkæʒʊəli, ˈkæʒəli] *adv*

casualness [ˈkæʒʊəlnəs] *n* **1** FORTUITOUSNESS : casualidad *f* **2** INDIFFERENCE : indiferencia *f,* despreocupación *f* **3** INFORMALITY : informalidad *f*

casualty [ˈkæʒʊəlti, ˈkæʒəl-] *n, pl* **-ties 1** ACCIDENT : accidente *m* serio, desastre *m* **2** VICTIM : víctima *f;* baja *f;* herido *m,* -da *f*

cat [ˈkæt] *n* : gato *m,* -ta *f*

cataclysm [ˈkæṭəˌklɪzəm] *n* : cataclismo *m*

cataclysmal [ˌkæṭəˈklɪzməl] *or* **cataclysmic** [ˌkæṭəˈklɪzmɪk] *adj* : catastrófico

catacombs [ˈkæṭəˌkoːmz] *npl* : catacumbas *fpl*

catalog[1] *or* **catalogue** [ˈkæṭəˌlɔg] *vt* **-loged** *or* **-logued; -loging** *or* **-loguing** : catalogar

catalog[2] *n* : catálogo *m*

catalpa [kəˈtælpə, -ˈtɔl-] *n* : catalpa *f*

catalyst [ˈkæṭələst] *n* : catalizador *m*

catalytic [ˌkæṭəlˈɪtɪk] *adj* : catalítico

catamaran [ˌkæṭəməˈræn, ˈkæṭəməˌræn] *n* : catamarán *m*

catapult[1] [ˈkæṭəˌpʌlt, -ˌpʊlt] *vt* : catapultar

catapult[2] *n* : catapulta *f*

cataract [ˈkæṭəˌrækt] *n* : catarata *f*

catarrh [kəˈtɑr] *n* : catarro *m*

catastrophe [kəˈtæstrəˌfiː] *n* : catástrofe *f*

catastrophic [ˌkæṭəˈstrɑfɪk] *adj* : catastrófico — **catastrophically** [-fɪkli] *adv*

catcall [ˈkætˌkɔl] *n* : rechifla *f,* abucheo *m*

catch[1] [ˈkætʃ, ˈkɛtʃ] *v* **caught** [ˈkɔt]; **catching** *vt* **1** CAPTURE, TRAP : capturar, agarrar, atrapar, coger **2** : agarrar, pillar *fam,* tomar de sorpresa <they caught him red-handed : lo pillaron con las manos en la masa> **3** GRASP : agarrar, captar **4** ENTANGLE : enganchar, enredar **5** : tomar (un tren, etc.) **6** : contagiarse de <to catch a cold : contagiarse de un resfriado, resfriarse> — *vi* **1** GRASP : agarrar **2** HOOK : engancharse **3** IGNITE : prender, agarrar

catch[2] *n* **1** CATCHING : captura *f,* atrapada *f,* parada *f* (de una pelota) **2** : redada *f* (de pescado), presa *f* (de caza) <he's a good catch : es un buen partido> **3** LATCH : pestillo *m,* pasador *m* **4** DIFFICULTY, TRICK : problema *m,* trampa *f,* truco *m*

catcher [ˈkætʃər, ˈkɛ-] *n* : catcher *mf;* receptor *m* , -tora *f* (en béisbol)

catching [ˈkætʃɪŋ, ˈkɛ-] *adj* : contagioso

catchup [ˈkætʃəp, ˈkɛ-] → **ketchup**

catchword [ˈkætʃˌwərd, ˈkɛtʃ-] *n* : eslogan *m,* lema *m*

catchy [ˈkætʃi, ˈkɛ-] *adj* **catchier; -est** : pegajoso <a catchy song : una canción pegajosa>

catechism [ˈkæṭəˌkɪzəm] *n* : catecismo *m*

categorical [ˌkæṭəˈgɔrɪkəl] *adj* : categórico, absoluto, rotundo — **categorically** [-kli] *adv*

categorize [ˈkæṭɪgəˌraɪz] *vt* **-rized; -rizing** : clasificar, catalogar

category [ˈkæṭəˌgori] *n, pl* **-ries** : categoría *f,* género *m,* clase *f*

cater [ˈkeɪṭər] *vi* **1** : proveer alimentos (para fiestas, bodas, etc.) **2 to cater to** : atender a <to cater to all tastes : atender a todos los gustos>

catercorner[1] [ˈkæṭiˌkɔrnər, ˈkæṭə-, ˈkɪṭi-] *or* **cater–cornered** [-ˌkɔrnərd] *adv* : diagonalmente, en diagonal

catercorner[2] *or* **cater–cornered** *adj* : diagonal

caterer [ˈkeɪṭərər] *n* : proveedor *m,* -dora *f* de comida

caterpillar [ˈkæṭərˌpɪlər] *n* : oruga *f*

catfish [ˈkætˌfɪʃ] *n* : bagre *m*

catgut [ˈkætˌgʌt] *n* : cuerda *f* de tripa

catharsis [kəˈθɑrsɪs] *n, pl* **catharses** [-ˌsiːz] : catarsis *f*

cathartic[1] [kəˈθɑrtɪk] *adj* : catártico

cathartic[2] *n* : purgante *m*

cathedral [kəˈθiːdrəl] *n* : catedral *f*

catheter [ˈkæθəṭər] *n* : catéter *m,* sonda *f*

cathode ['kæ,θoːd] *n* : cátodo *m*

catholic ['kæθəlɪk] *adj* **1** BROAD, UNIVERSAL : liberal, universal **2 Catholic** : católico

Catholic *n* : católico *m*, -ca *f*

Catholicism [kə'θɑlə,sɪzəm] *n* : catolicismo *m*

catkin ['kætkɪn] *n* : amento *m*, candelilla *f*

catlike ['kæt,laɪk] *adj* : gatuno, felino

catnap[1] ['kæt,næp] *vi* **-napped; -napping** : tomarse una siestecita

catnap[2] *n* : siesta *f* breve, siestecita *f*

catnip ['kæt,nɪp] *n* : nébeda *f*

catsup ['kɛtʃəp, 'kætsəp] → **ketchup**

cattail ['kæt,teɪl] *n* : espadaña *f*, anea *f*

cattiness ['kæṭinəs] *n* : malicia *f*

cattle ['kæṭəl] *npl* : ganado *m*, reses *mpl*

cattleman ['kæṭəlmən, -,mæn] *n, pl* **-men** [-mən, -,mɛn] : ganadero *m*

catty ['kæṭi] *adj* **-tier; -est** : malicioso, malintencionado

catwalk ['kæt,wɔk] *n* : pasarela *f*

Caucasian[1] [kɔ'keɪʒən] *adj* : caucásico

Caucasian[2] *n* : caucásico *m*, -ca *f*

caucus ['kɔkəs] *n* : junta *f* de políticos

caught → **catch**

cauldron ['kɔldrən] *n* : caldera *f*

cauliflower ['kɑlɪ,flaʊər, 'kɔ-] *n* : coliflor *f*

caulk[1] ['kɔk] *vt* : calafatear (un barco), enmasillar (una grieta)

caulk[2] *n* : masilla *f*

causal ['kɔzəl] *adj* : causal

cause[1] ['kɔz] *vt* **caused; causing** : causar, provocar, ocasionar

cause[2] *n* **1** ORIGIN : causa *f*, origen *m* **2** REASON : causa *f*, razón *f*, motivo *m* **3** LAWSUIT : litigio *m*, pleito *m* **4** MOVEMENT : causa *f*, movimiento *m*

causeless ['kɔzləs] *adj* : sin causa

causeway ['kɔz,weɪ] *n* : camino *m* elevado

caustic ['kɔstɪk] *adj* **1** CORROSIVE : cáustico, corrosivo **2** BITING : mordaz, sarcástico

cauterize ['kɔṭə,raɪz] *vt* **-ized; -izing** : cauterizar

caution[1] ['kɔʃən] *vt* : advertir

caution[2] *n* **1** WARNING : advertencia *f*, aviso *m* **2** CARE, PRUDENCE : precaución *f*, cuidado *m*, cautela *f*

cautionary ['kɔʃə,nɛri] *adv* : admonitorio <cautionary tale : cuento moral>

cautious ['kɔʃəs] *adj* : cauteloso, cuidadoso, precavido

cautiously ['kɔʃəsli] *adv* : cautelosamente, con precaución

cautiousness ['kɔʃəsnəs] *n* : cautela *f*, precaución *f*

cavalcade [,kævəl'keɪd, 'kævəl,-] *n* **1** : cabalgata *f* **2** SERIES : serie *f*

cavalier[1] [,kævə'lɪr] *adj* : altivo, desdeñoso — **cavalierly** *adv*

cavalier[2] *n* : caballero *m*

cavalry ['kævəlri] *n, pl* **-ries** : caballería *f*

cave[1] ['keɪv] *vi* **caved; caving** *or* **to cave in** : derrumbarse

cave[2] *n* : cueva *f*

cavern ['kævərn] *n* : caverna *f*

cavernous ['kævərnəs] *adj* : cavernoso — **cavernously** *adv*

caviar *or* **caviare** ['kævi,ɑr, 'kɑ-] *n* : caviar *m*

cavity ['kævəṭi] *n, pl* **-ties 1** HOLE : cavidad *f*, hueco *m* **2** CARIES : caries *f*

cavort [kə'vɔrt] *vi* : brincar, hacer cabriolas

caw[1] ['kɔ] *vi* : graznar

caw[2] *n* : graznido *m*

cayenne pepper [,kaɪ'ɛn, ,keɪ-] *n* : pimienta *f* cayena, pimentón *m*

CD [,siː'diː] *n* : CD *m*, disco *m* compacto

cease ['siːs] *v* **ceased; ceasing** *vt* : dejar de <they ceased bickering : dejaron de discutir> — *vi* : cesar, pasarse

ceaseless ['siːsləs] *adj* : incesante, continuo

cedar ['siːdər] *n* : cedro *m*

cede ['siːd] *vt* **ceded; ceding** : ceder, conceder

ceiling ['siːlɪŋ] *n* **1** : techo *m*, cielo *m* **2** LIMIT : límite *m*, tope *m*

celebrant ['sɛləbrənt] *n* : celebrante *mf*, oficiante *mf*

celebrate ['sɛlə,breɪt] *v* **-brated; -brating** *vt* **1** : celebrar, oficiar <to celebrate Mass : celebrar la misa> **2** : celebrar, festejar <we're celebrating our anniversary : estamos celebrando nuestro aniversario> **3** EXTOL : alabar, ensalzar, exaltar — *vi* : estar de fiesta, divertirse

celebrated ['sɛlə,breɪṭəd] *adj* : célebre, famoso, renombrado

celebration [,sɛlə'breɪʃən] *n* : celebración *f*, festejos *mpl*

celebrity [sə'lɛbrəṭi] *n, pl* **-ties 1** RENOWN : fama *f*, renombre *m*, celebridad *f* **2** PERSONALITY : celebridad *f*, personaje *m*

celery ['sɛləri] *n, pl* **-eries** : apio *m*

celestial [sə'lɛstʃəl, -'lɛstiəl] *adj* **1** : celeste **2** HEAVENLY : celestial, paradisiaco

celibacy ['sɛləbəsi] *n* : celibato *m*

celibate[1] ['sɛləbət] *adj* : célibe

celibate[2] *n* : célibe *mf*

cell ['sɛl] *n* **1** : célula *f* (de un organismo) **2** : celda *f* (en una cárcel, etc.) **3** : elemento *m* (de una pila)

cellar ['sɛlər] *n* **1** BASEMENT : sótano *m* **2** : bodega *f* (de vinos)

cellist ['tʃɛlɪst] *n* : violonchelista *mf*

cello ['tʃɛ,loː] *n, pl* **-los** : violonchelo *m*

cellophane ['sɛlə,feɪn] *n* : celofán *m*

cellular ['sɛljələr] *adj* : celular

cellulose ['sɛljə,loːs] *n* : celulosa *f*

Celsius ['sɛlsiəs] *adj* : centígrado <100 degrees Celsius : 100 grados centígrados>

Celt ['kɛlt, 'sɛlt] *n* : celta *mf*

Celtic[1] ['kɛltɪk, 'sɛl-] *adj* : celta

Celtic[2] *n* : celta *m* (idioma)

cement[1] [sɪ'mɛnt] *vi* : unir o cubrir algo con cemento, cementar

cement[2] *n* **1** : cemento *m* **2** GLUE : pegamento *m*

cemetery ['sɛmə,tɛri] *n, pl* **-teries** : cementerio *m,* panteón *m*

censer ['sɛntsər] *n* : incensario *m*

censor[1] ['sɛntsər] *vt* : censurar

censor[2] *n* : censor *m,* -sora *f*

censorious [sɛn'soriəs] *adj* : de censura, crítico

censorship ['sɛntsər,ʃɪp] *n* : censura *f*

censure[1] ['sɛntʃər] *vt* **-sured; -suring** : censurar, criticar, reprobar — **censurable** [-tʃərəbəl] *adj*

censure[2] *n* : censura *f,* reproche *f* oficial

census ['sɛntsəs] *n* : censo *m*

cent ['sɛnt] *n* : centavo *m*

centaur ['sɛn,tɔr] *n* : centauro *m*

centennial[1] [sɛn'tɛniəl] *adj* : del centenario

centennial[2] *n* : centenario *m*

center[1] ['sɛntər] *vt* **1** : centrar **2** CONCENTRATE : concentrar, fijar, enfocar — *vi* : centrarse, enfocarse

center[2] *n* **1** : centro *m* <center of gravity : centro de gravedad> **2** : centro *mf* (en futbol americano), pívot *mf* (en basquetbol)

centerpiece ['sɛntər,pi:s] *n* : centro *m* de mesa

centigrade ['sɛntə,greɪd, 'sɑn-] *adj* : centígrado

centigram ['sɛntə,græm, 'sɑn-] *n* : centigramo *m*

centimeter ['sɛntə,mi:t̬ər, 'sɑn-] *n* : centímetro *m*

centipede ['sɛntə,pi:d] *n* : ciempiés *m*

central ['sɛntrəl] *adj* **1** : céntrico, central <in a central location : en un lugar céntrico> **2** MAIN, PRINCIPAL : central, fundamental, principal

Central American[1] *adj* : centroamericano

Central American[2] *n* : centroamericano *m,* -na *f*

centralization [,sɛntrələ'zeɪʃən] *n* : centralización *f*

centralize ['sɛntrə,laɪz] *vt* **-ized; -izing** : centralizar

centrally ['sɛntrəli] *adv* **1 centrally heated** : con calefacción central **2 centrally located** : céntrico, en un lugar céntrico

centre ['sɛntər] → **center**

centrifugal force [sɛn'trɪfjəgəl, -'trɪfɪgəl] *n* : fuerza *f* centrífuga

century ['sɛntʃəri] *n, pl* **-ries** : siglo *m*

ceramic[1] [sə'ræmɪk] *adj* : de cerámica

ceramic[2] *n* **1** : objeto *m* de cerámica, cerámica *f* **2 ceramics** *npl* : cerámica *f*

cereal[1] ['sɪriəl] *adj* : cereal

cereal[2] *n* : cereal *m*

cerebellum [,sɛrə'bɛləm] *n, pl* **-bellums** *or* **-bella** [-'bɛlə] : cerebelo *m*

cerebral [sə'ri:brəl, 'sɛrə-] *adj* : cerebral

cerebral palsy *n* : parálisis *f* cerebral

cerebrum [sə'ri:brəm, 'sɛrə-] *n, pl* **-brums** *or* **-bra** [-brə] : cerebro *m*

ceremonial[1] [,sɛrə'mo:niəl] *adj* : ceremonial

ceremonial[2] *n* : ceremonial *m*

ceremonious [,sɛrə'mo:niəs] *adj* **1** FORMAL : ceremonioso, formal **2** CEREMONIAL : ceremonial

ceremony ['sɛrə,mo:ni] *n, pl* **-nies** : ceremonia *f*

cerise [sə'ri:s] *n* : rojo *m* cereza

certain[1] ['sərtən] *adj* **1** DEFINITE : cierto, determinado <a certain percentage : un porcentaje determinado> **2** TRUE : cierto, con certeza <I don't know for certain : no sé exactamente> **3** : cierto, alguno <it has a certain charm : tiene cierta gracia> **4** INEVITABLE : seguro, inevitable **5** ASSURED : seguro, asegurado <she's certain to do well : seguro que le irá bien>

certain[2] *pron* : ciertos *pl,* algunos *pl* <certain of my friends : algunos de mis amigos>

certainly ['sərtənli] *adv* **1** DEFINITELY : ciertamente, seguramente **2** OF COURSE : por supuesto

certainty ['sərtənti] *n, pl* **-ties** : certeza *f,* certidumbre *f,* seguridad *f*

certifiable [,sərt̬ə'faɪəbəl] *adj* : certificable

certificate [sər'tɪfɪkət] *n* : certificado *m,* acta *f* <birth certificate : acta de nacimiento>

certification [,sərt̬əfə'keɪʃən] *n* : certificación *f*

certify ['sərt̬ə,faɪ] *vt* **-fied; -fying 1** VERIFY : certificar, verificar, confirmar **2** ENDORSE : endosar, aprobar oficialmente

certitude ['sərt̬ə,tu:d, -,tju:d] *n* : certeza *f,* certidumbre *f*

cervical ['sərvɪkəl] *adj* **1** : cervical (dícese del cuello) **2** : del cuello del útero

cervix ['sərvɪks] *n, pl* **-vices** [-və-,si:z] *or* **-vixes 1** NECK : cerviz *f* **2** *or* **uterine cervix** : cuello *m* del útero

cesarean[1] [sɪ'zæriən] *adj* : cesáreo

cesarean[2] *n* : cesárea *f*

cesium ['si:ziəm] *n* : cesio *m*

cessation [sɛ'seɪʃən] *n* : cesación *f,* cese *m*

cesspool ['sɛs,pu:l] *n* : pozo *m* séptico

Chadian ['tʃædiən] *n* : chadiano *m,* -na *f* — **Chadian** *adj*

chafe ['tʃeɪf] *v* **chafed; chafing** *vi* : enojarse, irritarse — *vt* : rozar

chaff ['tʃæf] *n* **1** : barcia *f,* granzas *fpl* **2 to separate the wheat from the chaff** : separar el grano de la paja

chafing dish [ˈtʃeɪfɪŋˌdɪʃ] *n* : escalfador *m*

chagrin[1] [ʃəˈgrɪn] *vt* : desilusionar, avergonzar

chagrin[2] *n* : desilusión *f,* disgusto *m*

chain[1] [ˈtʃeɪn] *vt* : encadenar

chain[2] *n* **1** : cadena *f* <steel chain : cadena de acero> <restaurant chain : cadena de restaurantes> **2** SERIES : serie *f* <chain of events : serie de eventos> **3 chains** *npl* FETTERS : grillos *mpl*

chair[1] [ˈtʃɛr] *vt* : presidir, moderar

chair[2] *n* **1** : silla *f* **2** CHAIRMANSHIP : presidencia *f* **3** → **chairman, chairwoman**

chairman [ˈtʃɛrmən] *n, pl* **-men** [-mən, -ˌmɛn] : presidente *m*

chairmanship [ˈtʃɛrmənˌʃɪp] *n* : presidencia *f*

chairwoman [ˈtʃɛrˌwʊmən] *n, pl* **-women** [-ˌwɪmən] : presidenta *f*

chaise longue [ˈʃeɪzˈlɔŋ] *n, pl* **chaise longues** [-lɔŋ, -ˈlɔŋz] : chaise longue *f*

chalet [ʃæˈleɪ] *n* : chalet *m,* chalé *m*

chalice [ˈtʃælɪs] *n* : cáliz *m*

chalk[1] [ˈtʃɔk] *vt* : escribir con tiza

chalk[2] *n* **1** LIMESTONE : creta *f,* caliza *f* **2** : tiza *f,* gis *m Mex* (para escribir)

chalkboard [ˈtʃɔkˌbord] → **blackboard**

chalk up *vt* **1** ASCRIBE : atribuir, adscribir **2** SCORE : apuntarse, anotarse (una victoria, etc.)

chalky [ˈtʃɔki] *adj* **chalkier; -est** : calcáreo

challenge[1] [ˈtʃælɪndʒ] *vt* **-lenged; -lenging 1** DISPUTE : disputar, cuestionar, poner en duda **2** DARE : desafiar, retar **3** STIMULATE : estimular, incentivar

challenge[2] *n* : reto *m,* desafío *m*

challenger [ˈtʃælɪndʒər] *n* : retador *m,* -dora *f;* contendiente *mf*

chamber [ˈtʃeɪmbər] *n* **1** ROOM : cámara *f,* sala *f* <the senate chamber : la cámara del senado> **2** : recámara *f* (de un arma de fuego), cámara *f* (de combustión) **3** : cámara *f* <chamber of commerce : cámara de comercio> **4 chambers** *npl or* **judge's chambers** : despacho *m* del juez

chambermaid [ˈtʃeɪmbərˌmeɪd] *n* : camarera *f*

chamber music *n* : música *f* de cámara

chameleon [kəˈmiːljən, -liən] *n* : camaleón *m*

chamois [ˈʃæmi] *n, pl* **chamois** [-mi, -miz] : gamuza *f*

champ[1] [ˈtʃæmp, ˈtʃɑmp] *vi* **1** : masticar ruidosamente **2 to champ at the bit** : impacientarse, comerle a uno la impaciencia

champ[2] [ˈtʃæmp] *n* : campeón *m,* -peona *f*

champagne [ʃæmˈpeɪn] *n* : champaña *m,* champán *m*

champion[1] [ˈtʃæmpiən] *vt* : defender, luchar por (una causa)

champion[2] *n* **1** ADVOCATE, DEFENDER : paladín *m;* campeón *m,* -peona *f;* defensor *m,* -sora *f* **2** WINNER : campeón *m,* -peona *f* <world champion : campeón mundial>

championship [ˈtʃæmpiənˌʃɪp] *n* : campeonato *m*

chance[1] [ˈtʃænts] *v* **chanced; chancing** *vi* **1** HAPPEN : ocurrir por casualidad **2 to chance upon** : encontrar por casualidad — *vt* RISK : arriesgar

chance[2] *adj* : fortuito, casual <a chance encounter : un encuentro casual>

chance[3] *n* **1** FATE, LUCK : azar *m,* suerte *f,* fortuna *f* **2** OPPORTUNITY : oportunidad *f,* ocasión *f* **3** PROBABILITY : probabilidad *f,* posibilidad *f* **4** RISK : riesgo *m* **5** : boleto *m* (de una rifa o lotería) **6 by chance** : por casualidad

chancellor [ˈtʃæntsələr] *n* **1** : canciller *m* **2** : rector *m,* -tora *f* (de una universidad)

chancre [ˈʃæŋkər] *n* : chancro *m*

chancy [ˈtʃæntsi] *adj* **chancier; -est** : riesgoso, arriesgado

chandelier [ˌʃændəˈlɪr] *n* : araña *f* de luces

change[1] [ˈtʃeɪndʒ] *v* **changed; changing** *vt* **1** ALTER : cambiar, alterar, modificar **2** EXCHANGE : cambiar de, intercambiar <to change places : cambiar de sitio> — *vi* **1** VARY : cambiar, variar, transformarse <you haven't changed : no has cambiado> **2** *or* **to change clothes** : cambiarse (de ropa)

change[2] *n* **1** ALTERATION : cambio *m* **2** : cambio *m,* vuelto *m* <two dollars change : dos dólares de vuelto> **3** COINS : cambio *m,* monedas *fpl*

changeable [ˈtʃeɪndʒəbəl] *adj* : cambiante, variable

changeless [ˈtʃeɪndʒləs] *adj* : invariable, constante

changer [ˈtʃeɪndʒər] *n* **1** : cambiador *m* <record changer : cambiador de discos> **2** *or* **money changer** : cambista *mf* (de dinero)

channel[1] [ˈtʃænəl] *vt* **-neled** *or* **-nelled; -neling** *or* **-nelling** : encauzar, canalizar

channel[2] *n* **1** RIVERBED : cauce *m* **2** STRAIT : canal *m,* estrecho *m* <English Channel : Canal de la Mancha> **3** COURSE, MEANS : vía *f,* conducto *m* <the usual channels : las vías normales> **4** : canal *m* (de televisión)

chant[1] [ˈtʃænt] *v* : salmodiar, cantar

chant[2] *n* : **1** : salmodia *f* **2 Gregorian chant** : canto *m* gregoriano

Chanukah [ˈxɑnəkə, ˈhɑ-] → **Hanukkah**

chaos [ˈkeɪˌɑs] *n* : caos *m*

chaotic [keɪˈɑtɪk] *adj* : caótico — **chaotically** [-tɪkli] *adv*

chap[1] [ˈtʃæp] *vi* **chapped; chapping** : partirse, agrietarse

chap[2] *n* FELLOW : tipo *m,* hombre *m*

chapel [ˈtʃæpəl] *n* : capilla *f*

chaperon[1] *or* **chaperone** [ˈʃæpəˌroːn] *vt* **-oned; -oning** : ir de chaperón, acompañar

chaperon[2] *or* **chaperone** *n* : chaperón *m*, -rona *f;* acompañante *mf*

chaplain [ˈtʃæplɪn] *n* : capellán *m*

chapter [ˈtʃæptər] *n* **1** : capítulo *m* (de un libro) **2** BRANCH : sección *f,* división *f* (de una organización)

char [ˈtʃɑr] *vt* **charred; charring 1** BURN : carbonizar **2** SCORCH : chamuscar

character [ˈkærɪktər] *n* **1** LETTER, SYMBOL : carácter *m* <Chinese characters : caracteres chinos> **2** DISPOSITION : carácter *m,* personalidad *f* <of good character : de buena reputación> **3** : tipo *m,* personaje *m* peculiar <he's quite a character! : ¡él es algo serio!> **4** : personaje *m* (ficticio)

characteristic[1] [ˌkærɪktəˈrɪstɪk] *adj* : característico, típico — **characteristically** [-tɪkli] *adv*

characteristic[2] *n* : característica *f*

characterization [ˌkærɪktərəˈzeɪʃən] *n* : caracterización *f*

characterize [ˈkærɪktəˌraɪz] *vt* **-ized; -izing** : caracterizar

charades [ʃəˈreɪdz] *ns & pl* : charada *f*

charcoal [ˈtʃɑrˌkoːl] *n* : carbón *m*

chard [ˈtʃɑrd] → **Swiss chard**

charge[1] [ˈtʃɑrdʒ] *v* **charged; charging** *vt* **1** : cargar <to charge the batteries : cargar las pilas> **2** ENTRUST : encomendar, encargar **3** COMMAND : ordenar, mandar **4** ACCUSE : acusar <charged with robbery : acusado de robo> **5** : cargar a una cuenta, comprar a crédito — *vi* **1** : cargar (contra el enemigo) <charge! : ¡a la carga!> **2** : cobrar <they charge too much : cobran demasiado>

charge[2] *n* **1** : carga *f* (eléctrica) **2** BURDEN : carga *f,* peso *m* **3** RESPONSIBILITY : cargo *m,* responsabilidad *f* <to take charge of : hacerse cargo de> **4** ACCUSATION : cargo *m,* acusación *f* **5** COST : costo *m,* cargo *m,* precio *m* **6** ATTACK : carga *f,* ataque *m*

charge card → **credit card**

chargeable [ˈtʃɑrdʒəbəl] *adj* **1** : acusable, perseguible (dícese de un delito) **2 ~ to** : a cargo de (una cuenta)

charger [ˈtʃɑrdʒər] *n* : corcel *m,* caballo *m* (de guerra)

chariot [ˈtʃæriət] *n* : carro *m* (de guerra)

charisma [kəˈrɪzmə] *n* : carisma *m*

charismatic [ˌkærəzˈmætɪk] *adj* : carismático

charitable [ˈtʃærət̬əbəl] *adj* **1** GENEROUS : caritativo <a charitable organization : una organización benéfica> **2** KIND, UNDERSTANDING : generoso, benévolo, comprensivo — **charitably** [-bli] *adv*

charitableness [ˈtʃærət̬əbəlnəs] *n* : caridad *f*

charity [ˈtʃærət̬i] *n, pl* **-ties 1** GENEROSITY : caridad *f* **2** ALMS : caridad *f,* limosna *f* **3** : organización *f* benéfica, obra *f* de beneficencia

charlatan [ˈʃɑrlətən] *n* : charlatán *m,* -tana *f;* farsante *mf*

charley horse [ˈtʃɑrliˌhɔrs] *n* : calambre *m*

charm[1] [ˈtʃɑrm] *vt* : encantar, cautivar, fascinar

charm[2] *n* **1** AMULET : amuleto *m,* talismán *m* **2** ATTRACTION : encanto *m,* atractivo *m* <it has a certain charm : tiene cierto atractivo> **3** : dije *m,* colgante *m* <charm bracelet : pulsera de dijes>

charmer [ˈtʃɑrmər] *n* : persona *f* encantadora

charming [ˈtʃɑrmɪŋ] *adj* : encantador, fascinante

chart[1] [ˈtʃɑrt] *vt* **1** : trazar un mapa de, hacer un gráfico de **2** PLAN : trazar, planear <to chart a course : trazar un derrotero>

chart[2] *n* **1** MAP : carta *f,* mapa *m* **2** DIAGRAM : gráfico *m,* cuadro *m,* tabla *f*

charter[1] [ˈtʃɑrt̬ər] *vt* **1** : establecer los estatutos de (una organización) **2** RENT : alquilar, fletar

charter[2] *n* **1** STATUTES : estatutos *mpl* **2** CONSTITUTION : carta *f,* constitución *f*

chartreuse [ʃɑrˈtruːz, -ˈtruːs] *n* : color *m* verde-amarillo intenso

chary [ˈtʃæri] *adj* **charier; -est 1** WARY : cauteloso, precavido **2** SPARING : parco

chase[1] [ˈtʃeɪs] *vt* **chased; chasing 1** PURSUE : perseguir, ir a la caza de **2** DRIVE : ahuyentar, echar <he chased the dog from the garden : ahuyentó al perro del jardín> **3** : grabar (metales)

chase[2] *n* **1** PURSUIT : persecución *f,* caza *f* **2 the chase** HUNTING : caza *f*

chaser [ˈtʃeɪsər] *n* **1** PURSUER : perseguidor *m,* -dora *f* **2** : bebida *f* que se toma después de un trago de licor

chasm [ˈkæzəm] *n* : abismo *m,* sima *f*

chassis [ˈtʃæsi, ˈʃæsi] *n, pl* **chassis** [-siz] : chasis *m,* armazón *m*

chaste [ˈtʃeɪst] *adj* **chaster; -est 1** : casto **2** MODEST : modesto, puro **3** AUSTERE : austero, sobrio

chastely [ˈtʃeɪstli] *adv* : castamente

chasten [ˈtʃeɪsən] *vt* : castigar, sancionar

chasteness [ˈtʃeɪstnəs] *n* **1** MODESTY : modestia *f,* castidad *f* **2** AUSTERITY : sobriedad *f,* austeridad *f*

chastise [ˈtʃæsˌtaɪz, tʃæsˈ-] *vt* **-tised; -tising 1** REPRIMAND : reprender, corregir, reprobar **2** PUNISH : castigar

chastisement [ˈtʃæsˌtaɪzmənt, tʃæsˈtaɪz-, ˈtʃæstəz-] *n* : castigo *m,* corrección *f*

chastity [ˈtʃæstət̬i] *n* : castidad *f,* decencia *f,* modestia *f*

chat[1] [ˈtʃæt] *vi* **chatted; chatting** : charlar, platicar

chat[2] *n* : charla *f,* plática *f*

château [ʃæˈtoː] *n, pl* **-teaus** [-ˈtoː, -ˈtoːz] *or* **-teaux** [-ˈtoːz] : mansión *f* campestre

chattel [ˈtʃætəl] *n* : bienes *fpl* muebles, enseres *mpl*

chatter[1] [ˈtʃætər] *vi* **1** : castañetear (dícese de los dientes) **2** GAB : parlotear *fam,* cotorrear *fam*

chatter[2] *n* **1** CHATTERING : castañeteo *m* (de dientes) **2** GABBING : parloteo *m fam,* cotorreo *m fam,* cháchara *f fam*

chatterbox [ˈtʃætər,bɑks] *n* : parlanchín *m,* -china *f;* charlatán *m,* -tana *f;* hablador *m,* -dora *f*

chatty [ˈtʃæti] *adj* **chattier; chattiest** **1** TALKATIVE : parlanchín, charlatán **2** CONVERSATIONAL : familiar, conversador <a chatty letter : una carta llena de noticias>

chauffeur[1] [ˈʃoːfər, ʃoˈfər] *vi* : trabajar de chofer privado — *vt* : hacer de chofer para

chauffeur[2] *n* : chofer *m* privado

chauvinism [ˈʃoːvə,nɪzəm] *n* : chauvinismo *m,* patriotería *f*

chauvinist [ˈʃoːvənɪst] *n* : chauvinista *mf;* patriotero *m,* -ta *f*

chauvinistic [,ʃoːvəˈnɪstɪk] *adj* : chauvinista, patriotero

cheap[1] [ˈtʃiːp] *adv* : barato <to sell cheap : vender barato>

cheap[2] *adj* **1** INEXPENSIVE : barato, económico **2** SHODDY : barato, mal hecho **3** STINGY : tacaño, agarrado *fam,* codo *Mex*

cheapen [ˈtʃiːpən] *vt* : degradar, rebajar

cheaply [ˈtʃiːpli] *adv* : barato, a precio bajo

cheapness [ˈtʃiːpnəs] *n* **1** : baratura *f,* precio *m* bajo **2** STINGINESS : tacañería *f*

cheapskate [ˈtʃiːp,skeɪt] *n* : tacaño *m,* -ña *f;* codo *m,* -da *f Mex*

cheat[1] [ˈtʃiːt] *vt* : defraudar, estafar, engañar — *vi* : hacer trampa

cheat[2] *n* **1** CHEATING : engaño *m,* fraude *m,* trampa *f* **2** → **cheater**

cheater [ˈtʃiːtər] *n* : estafador *m,* -dora *f;* tramposo *m,* -sa *f*

check[1] [ˈtʃɛk] *vt* **1** HALT : frenar, parar, detener **2** RESTRAIN : refrenar, contener, reprimir **3** VERIFY : verificar, comprobar **4** INSPECT : revisar, chequear, inspeccionar **5** MARK : marcar, señalar **6** : chequear, facturar (maletas, equipaje) **7** CHECKER : marcar con cuadros **8 to check in** : registrarse en un hotel **9 to check out** : irse de un hotel

check[2] *n* **1** HALT : detención *f* súbita, parada *f* **2** RESTRAINT : control *m,* freno *m* **3** INSPECTION : inspección *f,* verificación *f,* chequeo *m* **4** : cheque *m* <to pay by check : pagar con cheque> **5** VOUCHER : resguardo *m,* comprobante *m* **6** BILL : cuenta *f* (en un restaurante) **7** SQUARE : cuadro *m* **8** MARK : marca *f* **9** : jaque *m* (en ajedrez)

checker[1] [ˈtʃɛkər] *vt* : marcar con cuadros

checker[2] *n* **1** : pieza *f* (en el juego de damas) **2** : verificador *m,* -dora *f;* revisador *m,* -dora *f*

checkerboard [ˈtʃɛkər,bord] *n* : tablero *m* de damas

checkers [ˈtʃɛkərz] *n* : damas *fpl*

checkmate[1] [ˈtʃɛk,meɪt] *vt* **-mated; -mating** **1** : dar jaque mate a (en ajedrez) **2** THWART : frustrar, arruinar

checkmate[2] *n* : jaque mate *m*

checkpoint [ˈtʃɛk,pɔɪnt] *n* : puesto *m* de control

checkup [ˈtʃɛk,ʌp] *n* : examen *m* médico, chequeo *m*

cheddar [ˈtʃɛdər] *n* : queso *m* Cheddar

cheek [ˈtʃiːk] *n* **1** : mejilla *f,* cachete *m* **2** IMPUDENCE : insolencia *f,* descaro *m*

cheeky [ˈtʃiːki] *adj* **cheekier; -est** : descarado, insolente, atrevido

cheep[1] [ˈtʃiːp] *vi* : piar

cheep[2] *n* : pío *m*

cheer[1] [ˈtʃɪr] *vt* **1** ENCOURAGE : alentar, animar **2** GLADDEN : alegrar, levantar el ánimo a **3** ACCLAIM : aclamar, vitorear, echar porras a

cheer[2] *n* **1** CHEERFULNESS : alegría *f,* buen humor *m,* jovialidad *f* **2** APPLAUSE : aclamación *f,* ovación *f,* aplausos *mpl* <three cheers for the chief! : ¡viva el jefe!> **3 cheers!** : ¡salud!

cheerful [ˈtʃɪrfəl] *adj* : alegre, de buen humor

cheerfully [ˈtʃɪrfəli] *adv* : alegremente, jovialmente

cheerfulness [ˈtʃɪrfəlnəs] *n* : buen humor *m,* alegría *f*

cheerily [ˈtʃɪrəli] *adv* : alegremente

cheeriness [ˈtʃɪrinəs] *n* : buen humor *m,* alegría *f*

cheerleader [ˈtʃɪr,liːdər] *n* : porrista *mf*

cheerless [ˈtʃɪrləs] *adj* BLEAK : triste, sombrío

cheerlessly [ˈtʃɪrləsli] *adv* : desanimadamente

cheery [ˈtʃɪri] *adj* **cheerier; -est** : alegre, de buen humor

cheese [ˈtʃiːz] *n* : queso *m*

cheesecloth [ˈtʃiːz,kloθ] *n* : estopilla *f*

cheesy [ˈtʃiːzi] *adj* **cheesier; -est** **1** : a queso **2** : que contiene queso **3** CHEAP : barato, de mala calidad

cheetah [ˈtʃiːtə] *n* : guepardo *m*

chef [ˈʃɛf] *n* : chef *m*

chemical[1] [ˈkɛmɪkəl] *adj* : químico — **chemically** [-mɪkli] *adv*

chemical[2] *n* : sustancia *f* química

chemise [ʃəˈmiːz] *n* **1** : camiseta *f,* prenda *f* interior de una pieza **2** : vestido *m* holgado

chemist [ˈkɛmɪst] *n* : químico *m,* -ca *f*

chemistry [ˈkɛmɪstri] *n, pl* **-tries** : química *f*

chemotherapy [,kiːmoˈθɛrəpi, ,kɛmo-] *n, pl* **-pies** : quimioterapia *f*

chenille [ʃə'niːl] *n* **:** felpilla *f*
cherish ['tʃɛrɪʃ] *vt* **1** VALUE **:** apreciar, valorar **2** HARBOR **:** abrigar, albergar
cherry ['tʃɛri] *n, pl* **-ries 1 :** cereza *f* (fruta) **2 :** cerezo *m* (árbol)
cherub ['tʃɛrəb] *n* **1** *pl* **-ubim** ['tʃɛrə,bɪm, 'tʃɛrjə-] ANGEL **:** ángel *m,* querubín *m* **2** *pl* **-ubs :** niño *m* regordete, niña *f* regordeta
cherubic [tʃə'ruːbɪk] *adj* **:** querúbico, angelical
chess ['tʃɛs] *n* **:** ajedrez *m*
chessboard ['tʃɛs,bord] *n* **:** tablero *m* de ajedrez
chessman ['tʃɛsmən, -,mæn] *n, pl* **-men** [-mən, -,mɛn] **:** pieza *f* de ajedrez
chest ['tʃɛst] *n* **1 :** cofre *m,* baúl *m* **2 :** pecho *m* <chest pains : dolores de pecho>
chestnut ['tʃɛst,nʌt] *n* **1 :** castaña *f* (fruto) **2 :** castaño *m* (árbol)
chest of drawers *n* **:** cómoda *f*
chevron ['ʃɛvrən] *n* **:** galón *m* (de un oficial militar)
chew[1] ['tʃuː] *vt* **:** masticar, mascar
chew[2] *n* **:** algo que se masca (como tabaco)
chewable ['tʃuːəbəl] *adj* **:** masticable
chewing gum *n* **:** goma *f* de mascar, chicle *m*
chewy ['tʃuːi] *adj* **chewier; -est 1 :** fibroso (dícese de las carnes o los vegetales) **2 :** pegajoso, chicloso (dícese de los los dulces)
chic[1] ['ʃiːk] *adj* **:** chic, elegante, de moda
chic[2] *n* **:** chic *m,* elegancia *f*
Chicano [tʃɪ'kɑno] *n* **:** chicano *m,* -na *f* **— Chicano** *adj*
chick ['tʃɪk] *n* **:** pollito *m,* -ta *f;* polluelo *m,* -la *f*
chicken ['tʃɪkən] *n* **1** FOWL **:** pollo *m* **2** COWARD **:** cobarde *mf*
chickenhearted ['tʃɪkən,hɑrt̬əd] *n* **:** miedoso, cobarde
chicken pox *n* **:** varicela *f*
chicle ['tʃɪkəl] *n* **:** chicle *m* (resina)
chicory ['tʃɪkəri] *n, pl* **-ries 1 :** endibia *f* (para ensaladas) **2 :** achicoria *f* (aditivo de café)
chide ['tʃaɪd] *vt* **chid** ['tʃɪd] *or* **chided; chid** *or* **chidden** ['tʃɪdən] *or* **chided; chiding** ['tʃaɪdɪŋ] **:** regañar, reprender
chief[1] ['tʃiːf] *adj* **:** principal, capital <chief negotiator : negociador en jefe> **— chiefly** *adv*
chief[2] *n* **:** jefe *m,* -fa *f*
chieftain ['tʃiːftən] *n* **:** jefe *m,* -fa *f* (de una tribu)
chiffon [ʃɪ'fɑn, 'ʃɪ,-] *n* **:** chifón *m*
chigger ['tʃɪgər] *n* **:** nigua *f*
chignon ['ʃiːn,jɑn, -,jɔn] *n* **:** moño *m,* chongo *m Mex*
chilblain ['tʃɪl,bleɪn] *n* **:** sabañón *m*
child ['tʃaɪld] *n, pl* **children** ['tʃɪldrən] **1** BABY, YOUNGSTER **:** niño *m,* -ña *f;* criatura *f* **2** OFFSPRING **:** hijo *m,* -ja *f;* progenie *f*
childbearing[1] ['tʃaɪlbɛrɪŋ] *adj* **:** relativo al parto <of childbearing age : en edad fértil>
childbearing[2] **→ childbirth**
childbirth ['tʃaɪld,bərθ] *n* **:** parto *m*
childhood ['tʃaɪld,hʊd] *n* **:** infancia *f,* niñez *f*
childish ['tʃaɪldɪʃ] *adj* **:** infantil, inmaduro **— childishly** *adv*
childishness ['tʃaɪldɪʃnəs] *n* **:** infantilismo *m,* inmadurez *f*
childless ['tʃaɪldləs] *adj* **:** sin hijos
childlike ['tʃaɪld,laɪk] *adj* **:** infantil, inocente <a childlike imagination : una imaginación infantil>
childproof ['tʃaɪld,pruːf] *adj* **:** a prueba de niños
Chilean ['tʃɪliən, tʃɪ'leɪən] **:** chileno *m,* -na *f* **— Chilean** *adj*
chili *or* **chile** *or* **chilli** ['tʃɪli] *n, pl* **chilies** *or* **chiles** *or* **chillies 1** *or* **chili pepper :** chile *m,* ají *m* **2 :** chile *m* con carne
chill[1] ['tʃɪl] *v* **:** enfriar
chill[2] *adj* **:** frío, gélido <a chill wind : un viento frío>
chill[3] *n* **1** CHILLINESS **:** fresco *m,* frío *m* **2** SHIVER **:** escalofrío *m* **3** DAMPER **:** enfriamiento *m,* frío *m* <to cast a chill over : enfriar>
chilliness ['tʃɪlinəs] *n* **:** frío *m,* fresco *m*
chilly ['tʃɪli] *adj* **chillier; -est :** frío <it's chilly tonight : hace frío esta noche>
chime[1] ['tʃaɪm] *v* **chimed; chiming** *vt* **:** hacer sonar (una campana) **—** *vi* **:** sonar una campana, dar campanadas
chime[2] *n* **1** BELLS **:** juego *m* de campanitas sintonizadas, carillón *m* **2** PEAL **:** tañido *m,* campanada *f*
chime in *vi* **:** meterse en una conversación
chimera *or* **chimaera** [kaɪ'mɪrə, kə-] *n* **:** quimera *f*
chimney ['tʃɪmni] *n, pl* **-neys :** chimenea *f*
chimney sweep *n* **:** deshollinador *m,* -dora *f*
chimp ['tʃɪmp, 'ʃɪmp] **→ chimpanzee**
chimpanzee [,tʃɪm,pæn'ziː, ,ʃɪm-; tʃɪm'pænzi, ʃɪm-] *n* **:** chimpancé *m*
chin ['tʃɪn] *n* **:** barbilla *f,* mentón *m,* barba *f*
china ['tʃaɪnə] *n* **1** PORCELAIN **:** porcelana *f,* loza *f* **2** CROCKERY, TABLEWARE **:** loza *f,* vajilla *f*
chinchilla [tʃɪn'tʃɪlə] *n* **:** chinchilla *f*
Chinese ['tʃaɪ'niːz, -'niːs] *n* **1 :** chino *m,* -na *f* **2 :** chino *m* (idioma) **— Chinese** *adj*
chink ['tʃɪŋk] *n* **:** grieta *f,* abertura *f*
chintz ['tʃɪnts] *n* **:** chintz *m,* chinz *m*
chip[1] ['tʃɪp] *v* **chipped; chipping** *vt* **:** desportillar, desconchar, astillar (madera) **—** *vi* **:** desportillarse, desconcharse, descascararse (dícese de la pintura, etc.)
chip[2] *n* **1 :** astilla *f* (de madera o vidrio), lasca *f* (de piedra) <he's a chip

off the old block : de tal palo, tal astilla> **2** : bocado *m* pequeño (en rodajas o rebanadas) <tortilla chips : totopos, tortillitas tostadas> **3** : ficha *f* (de póker, etc.) **4** NICK : desportilladura *f,* mella *f* **5** : chip *m* <memory chip : chip de memoria>

chip in *v* CONTRIBUTE : contribuir

chipmunk ['tʃɪp,mʌŋk] *n* : ardilla *f* listada

chipper ['tʃɪpər] *adj* : alegre y vivaz

chiropodist [kə'rɑpədɪst, ʃə-] *n* : podólogo *m,* -ga *f*

chiropody [kə'rɑpədi, ʃə-] *n* : podología *f*

chiropractic ['kaɪrə,præktɪk] *n* : quiropráctica *f*

chiropractor ['kaɪrə,præktər] *n* : quiropráctico *m,* -ca *f*

chirp[1] ['tʃərp] *vi* : gorjear (dícese de los pájaros), chirriar (dícese de los grillos)

chirp[2] *n* : gorjeo *m* (de un pájaro), chirrido *m* (de un grillo)

chisel[1] ['tʃɪzəl] *vt* **-eled** *or* **-elled; -eling** *or* **-elling 1** : cincelar, tallar, labrar **2** CHEAT : estafar, defraudar

chisel[2] *n* : cincel *m* (para piedras y metales), escoplo *m* (para madera), formón *m*

chiseler ['tʃɪzələr] *n* SWINDLER : estafador *m,* -dora *f;* fraude *mf*

chit ['tʃɪt] *n* : resguardo *m,* recibo *m*

chitchat ['tʃɪt,tʃæt] *n* : cotorreo *m,* charla *f*

chivalric [ʃə'vælrɪk] → **chivalrous**

chivalrous ['ʃɪvəlrəs] *adj* **1** KNIGHTLY : caballeresco, relativo a la caballería **2** GENTLEMANLY : caballeroso, honesto, cortés

chivalrousness ['ʃɪvəlrəsnəs] *n* : caballerosidad *f,* cortesía *f*

chivalry ['ʃɪvəlri] *n, pl* **-ries 1** KNIGHTHOOD : caballería *f* **2** CHIVALROUSNESS : caballerosidad *f,* nobleza *f,* cortesía *f*

chive ['tʃaɪv] *n* : cebollino *m*

chloride ['klor,aɪd] *n* : cloruro *m*

chlorinate ['klorə,neɪt] *vt* **-nated; -nating** : clorar

chlorination [,klorə'neɪʃən] *n* : cloración *f*

chlorine ['klor,i:n] *n* : cloro *m*

chloroform[1] ['klorə,fɔrm] *vt* : cloroformizar

chloroform[2] *n* : cloroformo *m*

chlorophyll ['klorə,fɪl] *n* : clorofila *f*

chock–full ['tʃɑk'fʊl, 'tʃʌk-] *adj* : colmado, repleto

chocolate ['tʃɑkələt, 'tʃɔk-] *n* **1** : chocolate *m* **2** BONBON : bombón *m* **3** : color *m* chocolate, marrón *m*

choice[1] ['tʃɔɪs] *adj* **choicer; -est** : selecto, escogido, de primera calidad

choice[2] *n* **1** CHOOSING : elección *f,* selección *f* **2** OPTION : elección *f,* opción *f* <I have no choice : no tengo alternativa> **3** PREFERENCE : preferencia *f,* elección *f* **4** VARIETY : surtido *m,* selección *f* <a wide choice : un gran surtido>

choir ['kwaɪr] *n* : coro *m*

choirboy ['kwaɪr,bɔɪ] *n* : niño *m* de coro

choke[1] ['tʃo:k] *v* **choked; choking** *vt* **1** ASPHYXIATE, STRANGLE : sofocar, asfixiar, ahogar, estrangular **2** BLOCK : tapar, obstruir — *vi* **1** SUFFOCATE : asfixiarse, sofocarse, ahogarse, atragantarse (con comida) **2** CLOG : taparse, obstruirse

choke[2] *n* **1** CHOKING : estrangulación *f* **2** : choke *m* (de un motor)

choker ['tʃo:kər] *n* : gargantilla *f*

cholera ['kɑlərə] *n* : cólera *m*

cholesterol [kə'lɛstə,rɔl] *n* : colesterol *m*

choose ['tʃu:z] *v* **chose** ['tʃo:z]; **chosen** ['tʃo:zən]; **choosing** *vt* **1** SELECT : escoger, elegir <choose only one : escoja sólo uno> **2** DECIDE : decidir <he chose to leave : decidió irse> **3** PREFER : preferir <which one do you choose? : ¿cuál prefiere?> — *vi* : escoger <much to choose from : mucho de donde escoger>

choosy *or* **choosey** ['tʃu:zi] *adj* **choosier; -est** : exigente, remilgado

chop[1] ['tʃɑp] *vt* **chopped; chopping 1** MINCE : picar, cortar, moler (carne) **2 to chop down** : cortar, talar (un árbol)

chop[2] *n* **1** CUT : hachazo *m* (con una hacha), tajo *m* (con una cuchilla) **2** BLOW : golpe *m* (penetrante) <karate chop : golpe de karate> **3** : chuleta *f* <pork chops : chuletas de cerdo>

chopper ['tʃɑpər] → **helicopter**

choppy ['tʃɑpi] *adj* **choppier; -est 1** : agitado, picado (dícese del mar) **2** DISCONNECTED : incoherente, inconexo

chops ['tʃɑps] *npl* **1** : quijada *f,* mandíbula *f,* boca *f* (de una persona) **2 to lick one's chops** : relamerse

chopsticks ['tʃɑp,stɪks] *npl* : palillos *mpl*

choral ['korəl] *adj* : coral

chorale [kə'ræl, -'rɑl] *n* **1** : coral *f* (composición musical vocal) **2** CHOIR, CHORUS : coral *f,* coro *m*

chord ['kɔrd] *n* **1** : acorde *m* (en música) **2** : cuerda *f* (en anatomía o geometría)

chore ['tʃor] *n* **1** TASK : tarea *f* rutinaria **2** BOTHER, NUISANCE : lata *f fam,* fastidio *m* **3 chores** *npl* WORK : quehaceres *mpl,* faenas *fpl*

choreograph ['koriə,græf] *vt* : coreografiar

choreographer [,kori'ɑgrəfər] *n* : coreógrafo *m,* -fa *f*

choreographic [,koriə'græfɪk] *adj* : coreográfico

choreography [,kori'ɑgrəfi] *n, pl* **-phies** : coreografía *f*

chorister ['korəstər] *n* : corista *mf*

chortle[1] ['tʃɔrtəl] *vi* **-tled; -tling** : reírse (con satisfacción o júbilo)

chortle[2] *n* : risa *f* (de satisfacción o júbilo)

chorus[1] [ˈkorəs] *vt* : corear

chorus[2] *n* **1** : coro *m* (grupo o composición musical) **2** REFRAIN : coro *m*, estribillo *m*

chose *pp* → **choose**

chosen [ˈtʃoːzən] *adj* : elegido, selecto

chow [ˈtʃaʊ] *n* **1** FOOD : comida *f* **2** : chow-chow *m* (perro)

chowder [ˈtʃaʊdər] *n* : sopa *f* de pescado

christen [ˈkrɪsən] *vt* **1** BAPTIZE : bautizar **2** NAME : bautizar con el nombre de

Christendom [ˈkrɪsəndəm] *n* : cristiandad *f*

christening [ˈkrɪsənɪŋ] *n* : bautismo *m*, bautizo *m*

Christian[1] [ˈkrɪstʃən] *adj* : cristiano

Christian[2] *n* : cristiano *m*, -na *f*

Christianity [ˌkrɪstʃiˈænəṭi, ˌkrɪsˈtʃæ-] *n* : cristianismo *m*

Christian name *n* : nombre *m* de pila

Christmas [ˈkrɪsməs] *n* : Navidad *f* <Christmas season : las Navidades>

chromatic [kroːˈmæṭɪk] *adj* : cromático <chromatic scale : escala cromática>

chrome [ˈkroːm] *n* : cromo *m* (metal)

chromium [ˈkroːmiəm] *n* : cromo *m* (elemento)

chromosome [ˈkroːməˌsoːm, -ˌzoːm] *n* : cromosoma *m*

chronic [ˈkrɑnɪk] *adj* : crónico — **chronically** [-nɪkli] *adv*

chronicle[1] [ˈkrɑnɪkəl] *vt* **-cled; -cling** : escribir (una crónica o historia)

chronicle[2] *n* : crónica *f*, historia *f*

chronicler [ˈkrɑnɪklər] *n* : historiador *m*, -dora *f*; cronista *mf*

chronological [ˌkrɑnəlˈɑdʒɪkəl] *adj* : cronológico — **chronologically** [-kli] *adv*

chronology [krəˈnɑlədʒi] *n, pl* **-gies** : cronología *f*

chronometer [krəˈnɑməṭər] *n* : cronómetro *m*

chrysalis [ˈkrɪsələs] *n, pl* **chrysalides** [krɪˈsæləˌdiːz] *or* **chrysalises** : crisálida *f*

chrysanthemum [krɪˈsæntθəməm] *n* : crisantemo *m*

chubbiness [ˈtʃʌbinəs] *n* : gordura *f*

chubby [ˈtʃʌbi] *adj* **-bier; -est** : gordito, regordete, rechoncho

chuck[1] [ˈtʃʌk] *vt* **1** TOSS : tirar, lanzar, aventar *Col, Mex* **2 to chuck under the chin** : hacer la mamola

chuck[2] *n* **1** PAT : mamola *f*, palmada *f* **2** TOSS : lanzamiento *m* **3** *or* **chuck steak** : corte *m* de carne de res

chuckle[1] [ˈtʃʌkəl] *vi* **-led; -ling** : reírse entre dientes

chuckle[2] *n* : risita *f*, risa *f* ahogada

chug[1] [ˈtʃʌg] *vi* **chugged; chugging** : resoplar, traquetear

chug[2] *n* : resoplido *m*, traqueteo *m*

chum[1] [ˈtʃʌm] *vi* **chummed; chumming** : ser camaradas, ser cuates *Mex fam*

chum[2] *n* : amigo *m*, -ga *f*; camarada *mf*; compinche *mf fam*

chummy [ˈtʃʌmi] *adj* **-mier; -est** : amistoso <they're very chummy : son muy amigos>

chump [ˈtʃʌmp] *n* : tonto *m*, -ta *f*; idiota *mf*

chunk [ˈtʃʌnk] *n* **1** PIECE : cacho *m*, pedazo *m*, trozo *m* **2** : cantidad *f* grande <a chunk of money : mucho dinero>

chunky [ˈtʃʌnki] *adj* **chunkier; -est 1** STOCKY : fornido, robusto **2** : que contiene pedazos

church [ˈtʃərtʃ] *n* **1** : iglesia *f* <to go to church : ir a la iglesia> **2** CHRISTIANS : iglesia *f*, conjunto *m* de fieles cristianos **3** DENOMINATION : confesión *f*, secta *f* **4** CONGREGATION : feligreses *mpl*, fieles *mpl*

churchgoer [ˈtʃərtʃˌgoːər] *n* : practicante *mf*

churchyard [ˈtʃərtʃˌjɑrd] *n* : cementerio *m* (junto a una iglesia)

churn[1] [ˈtʃərn] *vt* **1** : batir (crema), hacer (mantequilla) **2** : agitar con fuerza, revolver — *vi* : agitarse, arremolinarse

churn[2] *n* : mantequera *f*

chute [ˈʃuːt] *n* : conducto *m* inclinado, vertedero *m* (para basuras)

chutney [ˈtʃʌtni] *n, pl* **-neys** : chutney *m*

chutzpah [ˈhʊtspə, ˈxʊt-, -ˌspɑ] *n* : descaro *m*, frescura *f*, cara *f fam*

cicada [səˈkeɪdə, -ˈkɑ-] *n* : cigarra *f*, chicharra *f*

cider [ˈsaɪdər] *n* **1** : jugo *m* (de manzana, etc.) **2 hard cider** : sidra *f*

cigar [sɪˈgɑr] *n* : puro *m*, cigarro *m*

cigarette [ˌsɪgəˈrɛt, ˈsɪgəˌrɛt] *n* : cigarrillo *m*, cigarro *m*

cinch[1] [ˈsɪntʃ] *vt* **1** : cinchar (un caballo) **2** ASSURE : asegurar

cinch[2] *n* **1** : cincha *f* (para caballos) **2** : algo fácil o seguro <it's a cinch : es bien fácil, es pan comido>

cinchona [sɪŋˈkoːnə] *n* : quino *m*

cinder [ˈsɪndər] *n* **1** EMBER : brasa *f*, ascua *f* **2 cinders** *npl* ASHES : cenizas *fpl*

cinema [ˈsɪnəmə] *n* : cine *m*

cinematic [ˌsɪnəˈmæṭɪk] *adj* : cinematográfico

cinnamon [ˈsɪnəmən] *n* : canela *f*

cipher [ˈsaɪfər] *n* **1** ZERO : cero *m* **2** CODE : cifra *f*, clave *f*

circa [ˈsərkə] *prep* : alrededor de, hacia <circa 1800 : hacia el año 1800>

circle[1] [ˈsərkəl] *v* **-cled; -cling** *vt* **1** : encerrar en un círculo, poner un círculo alrededor de **2** : girar alrededor de, dar vueltas a <we circled the building twice : le dimos vueltas al edificio dos veces> — *vi* : dar vueltas

circle[2] *n* **1** : círculo *m* **2** CYCLE : ciclo *m* <to come full circle : volver al punto de partida> **3** GROUP : círculo *m,* grupo *m* (social)

circuit [ˈsərkət] *n* **1** BOUNDARY : circuito *m,* perímetro *m* (de una zona o un territorio) **2** TOUR : circuito *m,* recorrido *m,* tour *m* **3** : circuito *m* (eléctrico) <a short circuit : un cortocircuito>

circuitous [ˌsərˈkjuːət̬əs] *adj* : sinuoso, tortuoso

circuitry [ˈsərkətri] *n, pl* **-ries** : sistema *m* de circuitos

circular[1] [ˈsərkjələr] *adj* ROUND : circular, redondo

circular[2] *n* : circular *f*

circulate [ˈsərkjəˌleɪt] *v* **-lated; -lating** *vi* : circular — *vt* **1** : circular (noticias, etc.) **2** DISSEMINATE : hacer circular, divulgar

circulation [ˌsərkjəˈleɪʃən] *n* : circulación *f*

circulatory [ˈsərkjələˌtori] *adj* : circulatorio

circumcise [ˈsərkəmˌsaɪz] *vt* **-cised; -cising** : circuncidar

circumcision [ˌsərkəmˈsɪʒən, ˈsərkəmˌ-] *n* : circuncisión *f*

circumference [sərˈkʌmpfrənts] *n* : circunferencia *f*

circumflex [ˈsərkəmˌflɛks] *n* : acento *m* circunflejo

circumlocution [ˌsərkəmloˈkjuːʃən] *n* : circunlocución *f*

circumnavigate [ˌsərkəmˈnævəˌgeɪt] *vt* **-gated; -gating** : circunnavegar

circumscribe [ˈsərkəmˌskraɪb] *vt* **-scribed; -scribing 1** : circunscribir, trazar una figura alrededor de **2** LIMIT : circunscribir, limitar

circumspect [ˈsərkəmˌspɛkt] *adj* : circunspecto, prudente, cauto

circumspection [ˌsərkəmˈspɛkʃən] *n* : circunspección *f,* cautela *f*

circumstance [ˈsərkəmˌstænts] *n* **1** EVENT : circunstancia *f,* acontecimiento *m* **2 circumstances** *npl* SITUATION : circunstancias *fpl,* situación *f* <under the circumstances : dadas las circunstancias> <under no circumstances : de ninguna manera, bajo ningún concepto> **3 circumstances** *npl* : situación *f* económica

circumstantial [ˌsərkəmˈstæntʃəl] *adj* : circunstancial

circumvent [ˌsərkəmˈvɛnt] *vt* : evadir, burlar (una ley o regla), sortear (una responsabilidad o dificultad)

circumvention [ˌsərkəmˈvɛntʃən] *n* : evasión *f*

circus [ˈsərkəs] *n* : circo *m*

cirrhosis [səˈroːsɪs] *n* : cirrosis *f*

cirrus [ˈsɪrəs] *n, pl* **-ri** [ˈsɪrˌaɪ] : cirro *m*

cistern [ˈsɪstərn] *n* : cisterna *f,* aljibe *m*

citadel [ˈsɪt̬ədəl, -ˌdɛl] *n* FORTRESS : ciudadela *f,* fortaleza *f*

citation [saɪˈteɪʃən] *n* **1** SUMMONS : emplazamiento *m,* citación *f,* convocatoria *f* (judicial) **2** QUOTATION : cita *f* **3** COMMENDATION : elogio *m,* mención *f* (de honor)

cite [ˈsaɪt] *vt* **cited; citing 1** ARRAIGN, SUBPOENA : emplazar, citar, hacer comparecer (ante un tribunal) **2** QUOTE : citar **3** COMMEND : elogiar, honrar (oficialmente)

citizen [ˈsɪt̬əzən] *n* : ciudadano *m,* -na *f*

citizenry [ˈsɪt̬əzənri] *n, pl* **-ries** : ciudadanía *f,* conjunto *m* de ciudadanos

citizenship [ˈsɪt̬əzənˌʃɪp] *n* : ciudadanía *f* <Nicaraguan citizenship : ciudadanía nicaragüense>

citron [ˈsɪtrən] *n* : cidra *f*

citrus [ˈsɪtrəs] *n, pl* **-rus** *or* **-ruses** : cítrico *m*

city [ˈsɪt̬i] *n, pl* **cities** : ciudad *f*

civic [ˈsɪvɪk] *adj* : cívico

civics [ˈsɪvɪks] *ns & pl* : civismo *m*

civil [ˈsɪvəl] *adj* **1** : civil <civil law : derecho civil> **2** POLITE : civil, cortés

civilian [səˈvɪljən] *n* : civil *mf* <soldiers and civilians : soldados y civiles>

civility [səˈvɪlət̬i] *n, pl* **-ties** : cortesía *f,* educación *f*

civilization [ˌsɪvələˈzeɪʃən] *n* : civilización *f*

civilize [ˈsɪvəˌlaɪz] *vt* **-lized; -lizing** : civilizar — **civilized** *adj*

civil liberties *npl* : derechos *mpl* civiles

civilly [ˈsɪvəli] *adv* : cortésmente

civil rights *npl* : derechos *mpl* civiles

civil service *n* : administración *f* pública

civil war *n* : guerra *f* civil

clack[1] [ˈklæk] *vi* : tabletear

clack[2] *n* : tableteo *m*

clad [ˈklæd] *adj* **1** CLOTHED : vestido **2** COVERED : cubierto

claim[1] [ˈkleɪm] *vt* **1** DEMAND : reclamar, reivindicar <she claimed her rights : reclamó sus derechos> **2** MAINTAIN : afirmar, sostener <they claim it's theirs : sostienen que es suyo>

claim[2] *n* **1** DEMAND : demanda *f,* reclamación *f* **2** DECLARATION : declaración *f,* afirmación *f* **3 to stake a claim** : reclamar, reivindicar

claimant [ˈkleɪmənt] *n* : demandante *mf* (ante un juez), pretendiente *mf* (al trono, etc.)

clairvoyance [klærˈvɔɪənts] *n* : clarividencia *f*

clairvoyant[1] [klærˈvɔɪənt] *adj* : clarividente

clairvoyant[2] *n* : clarividente *mf*

clam [ˈklæm] *n* : almeja *f*

clamber [ˈklæmbər] *vi* : treparse o subirse torpemente

clammy [ˈklæmi] *adj* **-mier; -est** : húmedo y algo frío

clamor[1] [ˈklæmər] *vi* : gritar, clamar

clamor[2] *n* **:** clamor *m*
clamorous [ˈklæmərəs] *adj* **:** clamoroso, ruidoso, estrepitoso
clamp[1] [ˈklæmp] *vt* **:** sujetar con abrazaderas
clamp[2] *n* **:** abrazadera *f*
clan [ˈklæn] *n* **:** clan *m*
clandestine [klænˈdɛstɪn] *adj* **:** clandestino, secreto
clang[1] [ˈklæŋ] *vi* **:** hacer resonar (dícese de un objeto metálico)
clang[2] *n* **:** ruido *m* metálico fuerte
clangor [ˈklæŋər, -gər] *n* **:** estruendo *m* metálico
clank[1] [ˈklæŋk] *vi* **:** producir un ruido metálico seco
clank[2] *n* **:** ruido *m* metálico seco
clannish [ˈklænɪʃ] *adj* **:** exclusivista
clap[1] [ˈklæp] *v* **clapped; clapping** *vt* **1** SLAP, STRIKE **:** golpear ruidosamente, dar una palmada <to clap one’s hands : batir palmas, dar palmadas> **2** APPLAUD **:** aplaudir — *vi* APPLAUD **:** aplaudir
clap[2] *n* **1** SLAP **:** palmada *f,* golpecito *m* **2** NOISE **:** ruido *m* seco <a clap of thunder : un trueno>
clapboard [ˈklæbərd, ˈklæp,bord] *n* **:** tabla *f* de madera (para revestir muros)
clapper [ˈklæpər] *n* **:** badajo *m* (de una campana)
clarification [ˌklærəfəˈkeɪʃən] *n* **:** clarificación *f*
clarify [ˈklærə,faɪ] *vt* **-fied; -fying 1** EXPLAIN **:** aclarar **2 :** clarificar (un líquido)
clarinet [ˌklærəˈnɛt] *n* **:** clarinete *m*
clarinetist *or* **clarinettist** [ˌklærəˈnɛt̬ɪst] *n* **:** clarinetista *mf*
clarion [ˈklæriən] *adj* **:** claro y sonoro
clarity [ˈklærət̬i] *n* **:** claridad *f,* nitidez *f*
clash[1] [ˈklæʃ] *vi* **1 :** sonar, chocarse <the cymbals clashed : los platillos sonaron> **2 :** chocar, enfrentarse <the students clashed with the police : los estudiantes se enfrentaron con la policía> **3** CONFLICT **:** estar en conflicto, oponerse **4 :** desentonar (dícese de los colores), coincidir (dícese de los datos)
clash[2] *n* **1 :** ruido *m* (producido por un choque) **2** CONFLICT, CONFRONTATION **:** enfrentamiento *m,* conflicto *m,* choque *m* **3 :** desentono *m* (de colores), coincidencia *f* (de datos)
clasp[1] [ˈklæsp] *vt* **1** FASTEN **:** sujetar, abrochar **2** EMBRACE, GRASP **:** agarrar, sujetar, abrazar
clasp[2] *n* **1** FASTENING **:** broche *m,* cierre *m* **2** EMBRACE, SQUEEZE **:** apretón *m,* abrazo *m*
class[1] [ˈklæs] *vt* **:** clasificar, catalogar
class[2] *n* **1** KIND, TYPE **:** clase *f,* tipo *m,* especie *f* **2 :** clase *f,* rango *m* social <the working class : la clase obrera> **3** LESSON **:** clase *f,* curso *m* <English class : clase de inglés> **4 :** conjunto *m* de estudiantes, clase *f* <the class of ’97 : la promoción del 97>
classic[1] [ˈklæsɪk] *adj* **:** clásico
classic[2] *n* **:** clásico *m,* obra *f* clásica
classical [ˈklæsɪkəl] *adj* **:** clásico — **classically** [-kli] *adv*
classicism [ˈklæsə,sɪzəm] *n* **:** clasicismo *m*
classification [ˌklæsəfəˈkeɪʃən] *n* **:** clasificación *f*
classified [ˈklæsə,faɪd] *adj* **1 :** clasificado <classified ads : avisos clasificados> **2** RESTRICTED **:** confidencial, secreto <classified documents : documentos secretos>
classify [ˈklæsə,faɪ] *vt* **-fied; -fying :** clasificar, catalogar
classless [ˈklæsləs] *adj* **:** sin clases
classmate [ˈklæs,meɪt] *n* **:** compañero *m,* -ra *f* de clase
classroom [ˈklæs,ruːm] *n* **:** aula *f,* salón *m* de clase
clatter[1] [ˈklæt̬ər] *vi* **:** traquetear, hacer ruido
clatter[2] *n* **:** traqueteo *m,* ruido *m,* estrépito *m*
clause [ˈklɔz] *n* **:** cláusula *f*
claustrophobia [ˌklɔstrəˈfoːbiə] *n* **:** claustrofobia *f*
clavicle [ˈklævɪkəl] *n* **:** clavícula *f*
claw[1] [ˈklɔ] *v* **:** arañar
claw[2] *n* **:** garra *f,* uña *f* (de un gato), pinza *f* (de un crustáceo)
clay [ˈkleɪ] *n* **:** arcilla *f,* barro *m*
clayey [ˈkleɪi] *adj* **:** arcilloso
clean[1] [ˈkliːn] *vt* **:** limpiar, lavar, asear
clean[2] *adv* **:** limpio, limpiamente <to play clean : jugar limpio>
clean[3] *adj* **1 :** limpio **2** UNADULTERATED **:** puro **3** IRREPROACHABLE **:** intachable, sin mancha <to have a clean record : no tener antecedentes penales> **4** DECENT **:** decente **5** COMPLETE **:** completo, absoluto <a clean break with the past : un corte radical con el pasado>
cleaner [ˈkliːnər] *n* **1 :** limpiador *m,* -dora *f* **2 :** producto *m* de limpieza **3** DRY CLEANER **:** tintorería *f* (servicio)
cleanliness [ˈklɛnlinəs] *n* **:** limpieza *f,* aseo *m*
cleanly[1] [ˈkliːnli] *adv* **:** limpiamente, con limpieza
cleanly[2] [ˈklɛnli] *adj* **-lier; -est :** limpio, pulcro
cleanness [ˈkliːnnəs] *n* **:** limpieza *f*
cleanse [ˈklɛnz] *vt* **cleansed; cleansing :** limpiar, purificar
cleanser [ˈklɛnzər] *n* **:** limpiador *m,* purificador *m*
clear[1] [ˈklɪr] *vt* **1** CLARIFY **:** aclarar, clarificar (un líquido) **2 :** despejar (una superficie), desatascar (un tubo), desmontar (una selva) <to clear the table : levantar la mesa> <to clear one’s throat : carraspear, aclararse la voz> **3** EXONERATE **:** absolver, limpiar el nombre de **4** EARN **:** ganar, sacar (una ganancia de) **5 :** pasar sin tocar

<he cleared the hurdle : saltó por encima de la valla> **6 to clear up** RESOLVE : aclarar, resolver, esclarecer — *vi* **1** DISPERSE : irse, despejarse, disiparse **2** : ser compensado (dícese de un cheque) **3 to clear up** : despejar (dícese del tiempo), mejorarse (dícese de una enfermedad)

clear[2] *adv* : claro, claramente

clear[3] *adj* **1** BRIGHT : claro, lúcido **2** FAIR : claro, despejado **3** TRANSPARENT : transparente, translúcido **4** EVIDENT, UNMISTAKABLE : evidente, claro, obvio **5** CERTAIN : seguro **6** UNOBSTRUCTED : despejado, libre

clear[4] *n* **1 in the clear** : inocente, libre de toda sospecha **2 in the clear** SAFE : fuera de peligro

clearance [ˈklɪrən*t*s] *n* **1** CLEARING : despeje *m* **2** SPACE : espacio *m* (libre), margen *m* **3** AUTHORIZATION : autorización *f,* despacho *m* (de la aduana)

clearing [ˈklɪrɪŋ] *n* : claro *m* (de un bosque)

clearly [ˈklɪrli] *adv* **1** DISTINCTLY : claramente, directamente **2** OBVIOUSLY : obviamente, evidentemente

cleat [ˈkliːt] *n* **1** : taco *m* **2 cleats** *npl* : zapatos *mpl* deportivos (con tacos)

cleavage [ˈkliːvɪdʒ] *n* **1** CLEFT : hendidura *f,* raja *f* **2** : escote *m* (del busto)

cleave[1] [ˈkliːv] *vi* **cleaved** [ˈkliːvd] *or* **clove** [ˈkloːv]; **cleaving** ADHERE : adherirse, unirse

cleave[2] *vt* **cleaved; cleaving** SPLIT : hender, dividir, partir

cleaver [ˈkliːvər] *n* : cuchilla *f* de carnicero

clef [ˈklɛf] *n* : clave *f*

cleft [ˈklɛft] *n* : hendidura *f,* raja *f,* grieta *f*

clemency [ˈklɛmən*t*si] *n* : clemencia *f*

clement [ˈklɛmənt] *adj* **1** MERCIFUL : clemente, piadoso **2** MILD : clemente, apacible

clench [ˈklɛntʃ] *vt* **1** CLUTCH : agarrar **2** TIGHTEN : apretar (el puño, los dientes)

clergy [ˈklərdʒi] *n, pl* **-gies** : clero *m*

clergyman [ˈklərdʒimən] *n, pl* **-men** [-mən, -ˌmɛn] : clérigo *m*

cleric [ˈklɛrɪk] *n* : clérigo *m,* -ga *f*

clerical [ˈklɛrɪkəl] *adj* **1** : clerical <a clerical collar : un alzacuello> **2** : de oficina <clerical staff : personal de oficina>

clerk[1] [ˈklərk, *Brit* ˈklɑrk] *vi* : trabajar de oficinista, trabajar de dependiente

clerk[2] *n* **1** : funcionario *m,* -ria *f* (de una oficina gubernamental) **2** : oficinista *mf,* empleado *m,* -da *f* de oficina **3** SALESPERSON : dependiente *m,* -ta *f*

clever [ˈklɛvər] *adj* **1** SKILLFUL : ingenioso, hábil **2** SMART : listo, inteligente, astuto

cleverly [ˈklɛvərli] *adv* **1** SKILLFULLY : ingeniosamente, hábilmente **2** INTELLIGENTLY : inteligentemente

cleverness [ˈklɛvərnəs] *n* **1** SKILL : ingenio *m,* habilidad *f* **2** INTELLIGENCE : inteligencia *f*

clew [ˈkluː] → **clue**

cliché [kliˈʃeɪ] *n* : cliché *m,* tópico *m*

click[1] [ˈklɪk] *vt* : chasquear (la lengua, los dedos) — *vi* **1** : chasquear **2** SUCCEED : tener éxito **3** GET ALONG : congeniar, llevarse bien

click[2] *n* : chasquido *m*

client [ˈklaɪənt] *n* : cliente *m,* -ta *f*

clientele [ˌklaɪənˈtɛl, ˌkliː-] *n* : clientela *f*

cliff [ˈklɪf] *n* : acantilado *m,* precipicio *m,* risco *m*

climate [ˈklaɪmət] *n* : clima *m*

climax[1] [ˈklaɪˌmæks] *vi* : llegar al punto culminante, culminar — *vt* : ser el punto culminante de

climax[2] *n* : clímax *m,* punto *m* culminante

climb[1] [ˈklaɪm] *vt* : escalar, trepar a, subir a <to climb a mountain : escalar una montaña> — *vi* **1** RISE : subir, ascender <prices are climbing : los precios están subiendo> **2** subirse, treparse <to climb up a tree : treparse a un árbol>

climb[2] *n* : ascenso *m,* subida *f*

climber [ˈklaɪmər] *n* **1** : escalador *m,* -dora *f* <a mountain climber : un alpinista> **2** : trepadora *f* (planta)

clinch[1] [ˈklɪntʃ] *vt* **1** FASTEN, SECURE : remachar (un clavo), afianzar, abrochar **2** SETTLE : decidir, cerrar <to clinch the title : ganar el título>

clinch[2] *n* : abrazo *m,* clinch *m* (en el boxeo)

clincher [ˈklɪntʃər] *n* : argumento *m* decisivo

cling [ˈklɪŋ] *vi* **clung** [ˈklʌŋ]; **clinging** **1** STICK : adherirse, pegarse **2** : aferrarse, agarrarse <he clung to the railing : se aferró a la barandilla>

clinic [ˈklɪnɪk] *n* : clínica *f*

clinical [ˈklɪnɪkəl] *adj* : clínico — **clinically** [-kli] *adv*

clink[1] [ˈklɪŋk] *vi* : tintinear

clink[2] *n* : tintineo *m*

clip[1] [ˈklɪp] *vt* **clipped; clipping 1** CUT : cortar, recortar **2** HIT : golpear, dar un puñetazo a **3** FASTEN : sujetar (con un clip)

clip[2] *n* **1** → **clippers 2** BLOW : golpe *m,* puñetazo *m* **3** PACE : paso *m* rápido **4** FASTENER : clip *m* <a paper clip : un sujetapapeles>

clipper [ˈklɪpər] *n* **1** : clíper *m* (buque de vela) **2 clippers** *npl* : tijeras *fpl* <nail clippers : cortauñas>

clique [ˈkliːk, ˈklɪk] *n* : grupo *m* exclusivo, camarilla *f* (de políticos)

clitoris [ˈklɪtərəs, klɪˈtorəs] *n, pl* **clitorides** [-ˈtorəˌdiːz] : clítoris *m*

cloak[1] [ˈkloːk] *vt* : encubrir, envolver (en un manto de)

cloak[2] *n* : capa *f,* capote *m,* manto *m* <under the cloak of darkness : al amparo de la oscuridad>

clobber ['klɑbər] *vt* : dar una paliza a

clock[1] ['klɑk] *vt* : cronometrar

clock[2] *n* **1** : reloj *m* (de pared), cronómetro *m* (en deportes o competencias) **2 around the clock** : las veinticuatro horas

clockwise ['klɑk,waɪz] *adv & adj* : en la dirección de las manecillas del reloj

clockwork ['klɑk,wərk] *n* : mecanismo *m* de relojería

clod ['klɑd] *n* **1** : terrón *m* **2** OAF : zoquete *mf*

clog[1] ['klɑg] *v* **clogged; clogging** *vt* **1** HINDER : estorbar, impedir **2** BLOCK : atascar, tapar — *vi* : atascarse, taparse

clog[2] *n* **1** OBSTACLE : traba *f,* impedimento *m,* estorbo *m* **2** : zueco *m* (zapato)

cloister[1] ['klɔɪstər] *vt* : enclaustrar

cloister[2] *n* : claustro *m*

clone ['klo:n] *n* **1** : clon *m* (de un organismo) **2** COPY : copia *f,* reproducción *f*

close[1] ['klo:z] *v* **closed; closing** *vt* : cerrar — *vi* **1** : cerrarse, cerrar **2** TERMINATE : concluirse, terminar **3 to close in** APPROACH : acercarse, aproximarse

close[2] ['klo:s] *adv* : cerca, de cerca

close[3] *adj* **closer; closest 1** CONFINING : restrictivo, estrecho **2** SECRETIVE : reservado **3** STRICT : estricto, detallado **4** STUFFY : cargado, bochornoso (dícese del tiempo) **5** TIGHT : apretado, entallado, ceñido <it's a close fit : es muy apretado> **6** NEAR : cercano, próximo **7** INTIMATE : íntimo <close friends : amigos íntimos> **8** ACCURATE : fiel, exacto **9** : reñido <a close election : una elección muy reñida>

close[4] ['klo:z] *n* : fin *m,* final *m,* conclusión *f*

closely ['klo:sli] *adv* : cerca, de cerca

closeness ['klo:snəs] *n* **1** NEARNESS : cercanía *f,* proximidad *f* **2** INTIMACY : intimidad *f*

closet[1] ['klɑzət] *vt* **to be closeted with** : estar encerrado con

closet[2] *n* : armario *m,* guardarropa *f,* clóset *m*

closure ['klo:ʒər] *n* **1** CLOSING, END : cierre *m,* clausura *f,* fin *m* **2** FASTENER : cierre *m*

clot[1] ['klɑt] *v* **clotted; clotting** *vt* : coagular, cuajar — *vi* : cuajarse, coagularse

clot[2] *n* : coágulo *m*

cloth ['klɔθ] *n, pl* **cloths** ['klɔðz, 'klɔθs] **1** FABRIC : tela *f* **2** RAG : trapo *m* **3** TABLECLOTH : mantel *m*

clothe ['klo:ð] *vt* **clothed** *or* **clad** ['klæd]; **clothing** DRESS : vestir, arropar, ataviar

clothes ['klo:z, 'klo:ðz] *npl* **1** CLOTHING : ropa *f* **2** BEDCLOTHES : ropa *f* de cama

clothespin ['klo:z,pɪn] *n* : pinza *f* (para la ropa)

clothing ['klo:ðɪŋ] *n* : ropa *f,* indumentaria *f*

cloud[1] ['klaʊd] *vt* : nublar, oscurecer — *vi* **to cloud over** : nublarse

cloud[2] *n* : nube *f*

cloudburst ['klaʊd,bərst] *n* : chaparrón *m,* aguacero *m*

cloudless ['klaʊdləs] *adj* : despejado, claro

cloudy ['klaʊdi] *adj* **cloudier; -est** : nublado, nuboso

clout[1] ['klaʊt] *vt* : bofetear, dar un tortazo a

clout[2] *n* **1** BLOW : golpe *m,* tortazo *m fam* **2** INFLUENCE : influencia *f,* palanca *f fam*

clove[1] ['klo:v] *n* **1** : diente *m* (de ajo) **2** : clavo *m* (especia)

clove[2] → **cleave**

cloven hoof ['klo:vən] : pezuña *f* hendida

clover ['klo:vər] *n* : trébol *m*

cloverleaf ['klo:vər,li:f] *n, pl* **-leafs** *or* **-leaves** [-,li:vz] : intersección *f* en trébol

clown[1] ['klaʊn] *vi* : payasear, bromear <stop clowning around : déjate de payasadas>

clown[2] *n* : payaso *m,* -sa *f*

clownish ['klaʊnɪʃ] *adj* **1** : de payaso **2** BOORISH : grosero — **clownishly** *adv*

cloying ['klɔɪɪŋ] *adj* : empalagoso, meloso

club[1] ['klʌb] *vt* **clubbed; clubbing** : aporrear, dar garrotazos a

club[2] *n* **1** CUDGEL : garrote *m,* porra *f* **2** : palo *m* <golf club : palo de golf> **3** : trébol *m* (naipe) **4** ASSOCIATION : club *m*

clubfoot ['klʌb,fʊt] *n, pl* **-feet** : pie *m* deforme

clubhouse ['klʌb,haʊs] *n* : sede *f* de un club

cluck[1] ['klʌk] *vi* : cloquear, cacarear

cluck[2] *n* : cloqueo *m,* cacareo *m*

clue[1] ['klu:] *vt* **clued; clueing** *or* **cluing** *or* **to clue in** : dar una pista a, informar

clue[2] *n* : pista *f,* indicio *m*

clump[1] ['klʌmp] *vi* **1** : caminar con pisadas fuertes **2** LUMP : agruparse, aglutinarse — *vt* : amontonar

clump[2] *n* **1** : grupo *m* (de arbustos o árboles), terrón *m* (de tierra) **2** : pisada *f* fuerte

clumsily ['klʌmzəli] *adv* : torpemente, sin gracia

clumsiness ['klʌmzinəs] *n* : torpeza *f*

clumsy ['klʌmzi] *adj* **-sier; -est 1** AWKWARD : torpe, desmañado **2** TACTLESS : carente de tacto, poco delicado

clung → **cling**

cluster[1] ['klʌstər] *vt* : agrupar, juntar — *vi* : agruparse, apiñarse, arracimarse

cluster[2] *n* : grupo *m,* conjunto *m,* racimo *m* (de uvas)

clutch[1] ['klʌtʃ] *vt* : agarrar, asir — *vi* **to clutch at** : tratar de agarrar

clutch[2] *n* **1** GRASP, GRIP **:** agarre *m,* apretón *m* **2 :** embrague *m,* clutch *m* (de una máquina) **3 clutches** *npl* **:** garras *fpl* <he fell into their clutches : cayó en sus garras>
clutter[1] [ˈklʌtər] *vt* **:** atiborrar o atestar de cosas, llenar desordenadamente
clutter[2] *n* **:** desorden *m,* revoltijo *m*
coach[1] [ˈkoːtʃ] *vt* **:** entrenar (atletas, artistas), preparar (alumnos)
coach[2] *n* **1** CARRIAGE **:** coche *m,* carruaje *m,* carroza *f* **2 :** vagón *m* de pasajeros (de un tren) **3** BUS **:** autobús *m,* ómnibus *m* **4 :** pasaje *m* aéreo de segunda clase **5** TRAINER **:** entrenador *m,* -dora *f*
coagulate [koˈæɡjəˌleɪt] *v* **-lated; -lating** *vt* **:** coagular, cuajar — *vi* **:** coagularse, cuajarse
coal [ˈkoːl] *n* **1** EMBER **:** ascua *f,* brasa *f* **2 :** carbón *m* <a coal mine : una mina de carbón>
coalesce [ˌkoːəˈlɛs] *vi* **-alesced; -alescing :** unirse
coalition [ˌkoːəˈlɪʃən] *n* **:** coalición *f*
coarse [ˈkors] *adj* **coarser; -est 1 :** grueso (dícese de la arena o la sal), basto (dícese de las telas), áspero (dícese de la piel) **2** CRUDE, ROUGH **:** basto, tosco, ordinario **3** VULGAR **:** grosero — **coarsely** *adv*
coarsen [ˈkorsən] *vt* **:** hacer áspero o basto — *vi* **:** volverse áspero o basto
coarseness [ˈkorsnəs] *n* **:** aspereza *f,* tosquedad *f*
coast[1] [ˈkoːst] *vi* **:** deslizarse, rodar sin impulso
coast[2] *n* **:** costa *f,* litoral *m*
coastal [ˈkoːstəl] *adj* **:** costero
coaster [ˈkoːstər] *n* **:** posavasos *m*
coast guard *n* **:** guardia *f* costera, guardacostas *mpl*
coastline [ˈkoːstˌlaɪn] *n* **:** costa *f*
coat[1] [ˈkoːt] *vt* **:** cubrir, revestir, bañar (en un líquido)
coat[2] *n* **1 :** abrigo *m* <a sport coat : una chaqueta, un saco> **2 :** pelaje *m* (de animales) **3** LAYER **:** capa *f,* mano *f* (de pintura)
coating [ˈkoːtɪŋ] *n* **:** capa *f*
coat of arms *n* **:** escudo *m* de armas
coax [ˈkoːks] *vt* **:** engatusar, persuadir
cob [ˈkɑb] → **corncob**
cobalt [ˈkoːˌbɔlt] *n* **:** cobalto *m*
cobble [ˈkɑbəl] *vt* **cobbled; cobbling 1 :** fabricar o remendar (zapatos) **2 to cobble together :** improvisar, hacer apresuradamente
cobbler [ˈkɑblər] *n* **1** SHOEMAKER **:** zapatero *m,* -ra *f* **2 fruit cobbler :** tarta *f* de fruta
cobblestone [ˈkɑbəlˌstoːn] *n* **:** adoquín *m*
cobra [ˈkoːbrə] *n* **:** cobra *f*
cobweb [ˈkɑbˌwɛb] *n* **:** telaraña *f*
cocaine [koːˈkeɪn, ˈkoːˌkeɪn] *n* **:** cocaína *f*
cock[1] [ˈkɑk] *vt* **1 :** ladear <to cock one's head : ladear la cabeza> **2 :** montar, amartillar (un arma de fuego)
cock[2] *n* **1** ROOSTER **:** gallo *m* **2** FAUCET **:** grifo *m,* llave *f* **3 :** martillo *m* (de un arma de fuego)
cockatoo [ˈkɑkəˌtuː] *n, pl* **-toos :** cacatúa *f*
cockeyed [ˈkɑkˌaɪd] *adj* **1** ASKEW **:** ladeado, torcido, chueco **2** ABSURD **:** disparatado, absurdo
cockfight [ˈkɑkˌfaɪt] *n* **:** pelea *f* de gallos
cockiness [ˈkɑkinəs] *n* **:** arrogancia *f*
cockle [ˈkɑkəl] *n* **:** berberecho *m*
cockpit [ˈkɑkˌpɪt] *n* **:** cabina *f*
cockroach [ˈkɑkˌroːtʃ] *n* **:** cucaracha *f*
cocktail [ˈkɑkˌteɪl] *n* **1 :** coctel *m,* cóctel *m* **2** APPETIZER **:** aperitivo *m*
cocky [ˈkɑki] *adj* **cockier; -est :** creído, engreído
cocoa [ˈkoːˌkoː] *n* **1** CACAO **:** cacao *m* **2 :** cocoa *f,* chocolate *m* (bebida)
coconut [ˈkoːkəˌnʌt] *n* **:** coco *m*
cocoon [kəˈkuːn] *n* **:** capullo *m*
cod [ˈkɑd] *n, pl* **cod :** bacalao *m*
coddle [ˈkɑdəl] *vt* **-dled; -dling :** mimar, consentir
code [ˈkoːd] *n* **1 :** código *m* <civil code : código civil> **2 :** código *m,* clave *f* <secret code : clave secreta>
codeine [ˈkoːˌdiːn] *n* **:** codeína *f*
codger [ˈkɑdʒər] *n* **:** viejo *m,* vejete *m*
codify [ˈkɑdəˌfaɪ, ˈkoː-] *vt* **-fied; -fying :** codificar
coeducation [ˌkoːˌɛdʒəˈkeɪʃən] *n* **:** coeducación *f,* enseñanza *f* mixta
coeducational [ˌkoːˌɛdʒəˈkeɪʃənəl] *adj* **:** mixto
coefficient [ˌkoːəˈfɪʃənt] *n* **:** coeficiente *m*
coerce [koˈərs] *vt* **-erced; -ercing :** coaccionar, forzar, obligar
coercion [koˈərʒən, -ʃən] *n* **:** coacción *f*
coercive [koˈərsɪv] *adj* **:** coactivo
coexist [ˌkoːɪɡˈzɪst] *vi* **:** coexistir
coexistence [ˌkoːɪɡˈzɪstənts] *n* **:** coexistencia *f*
coffee [ˈkɔfi] *n* **:** café *m*
coffeepot [ˈkɔfiˌpɑt] *n* **:** cafetera *f*
coffer [ˈkɔfər] *n* **:** cofre *m*
coffin [ˈkɔfən] *n* **:** ataúd *m,* féretro *m*
cog [ˈkɑɡ] *n* **:** diente *m* (de una rueda dentada)
cogent [ˈkoːdʒənt] *adj* **:** convincente, persuasivo
cogitate [ˈkɑdʒəˌteɪt] *vi* **-tated; -tating :** reflexionar, meditar, discurrir
cogitation [ˌkɑdʒəˈteɪʃən] *n* **:** reflexión *f,* meditación *f*
cognac [ˈkoːnˌjæk] *n* **:** coñac *m*
cognate [ˈkɑɡˌneɪt] *adj* **:** relacionado, afín
cogwheel [ˈkɑɡˌhwiːl] *n* **:** rueda *f* dentada
cohabit [ˌkoːˈhæbət] *vi* **:** cohabitar
cohere [koˈhɪr] *vi* **-hered; -hering 1** ADHERE **:** adherirse, pegarse **2 :** ser coherente o congruente

coherence [ko'hɪrənts] *n* **:** coherencia *f*, congruencia *f*
coherent [ko'hɪrənt] *adj* **:** coherente, congruente — **coherently** *adv*
cohesion [ko'hiːʒən] *n* **:** cohesión *f*
cohort ['koːˌhɔrt] *n* **1 :** cohorte *f* (de soldados) **2** COMPANION **:** compañero *m*, -ra *f*; colega *mf*
coiffure [kwɑ'fjʊr] *n* **:** peinado *m*
coil[1] ['kɔɪl] *vt* **:** enrollar — *vi* **:** enrollarse, enroscarse
coil[2] *n* **:** rollo *m* (de cuerda, etc.), espiral *f* (de humo)
coin[1] ['kɔɪn] *vt* **1** MINT **:** acuñar (moneda) **2** INVENT **:** acuñar, crear, inventar <to coin a phrase : como se suele decir>
coin[2] *n* **:** moneda *f*
coincide [ˌkoːɪn'saɪd, 'koːɪnˌsaɪd] *vi* **-cided; -ciding :** coincidir
coincidence [ko'ɪntsədənts] *n* **:** coincidencia *f*, casualidad *f* <what a coincidence! : ¡qué casualidad!>
coincident [ko'ɪntsədənt] *adj* **:** coincidente, concurrente
coincidental [koˌɪntsə'dɛntəl] *adj* **:** casual, accidental, fortuito
coitus ['koːət̬əs] *n* **:** coito *m*
coke ['koːk] *n* **:** coque *m*
colander ['kɑləndər, 'kʌ-] *n* **:** colador *m*
cold[1] ['koːld] *adj* **:** frío <it's cold out : hace frío> <a cold reception : una fría recepción> <in cold blood : a sangre fría>
cold[2] *n* **1 :** frío *m* <to feel the cold : sentir frío> **2 :** resfriado *m*, catarro *m* <to catch a cold : resfriarse>
cold–blooded ['koːld'blʌdəd] *adj* **1** CRUEL **:** cruel, despiadado **2 :** de sangre fría (dícese de los reptiles, etc.)
coldly ['koːldli] *adv* **:** fríamente, con frialdad
coldness ['koːldnəs] *n* **:** frialdad *f* (de una persona o una actitud), frío *m* (de la temperatura)
coleslaw ['koːlˌslɔ] *n* **:** ensalada *f* de col
colic ['kɑlɪk] *n* **:** cólico *m*
coliseum [ˌkɑlə'siːəm] *n* **:** coliseo *m*, arena *f*
collaborate [kə'læbəˌreɪt] *vi* **-rated; -rating :** colaborar
collaboration [kəˌlæbə'reɪʃən] *n* **:** colaboración *f*
collaborator [kə'læbəˌreɪt̬ər] *n* **1** COLLEAGUE **:** colaborador *m*, -dora *f* **2** TRAITOR **:** colaboracionista *mf*
collapse[1] [kə'læps] *vi* **-lapsed; -lapsing 1 :** derrumbarse, desplomarse, hundirse <the building collapsed : el edificio se derrumbó> **2** FALL **:** desplomarse, caerse <he collapsed on the bed : se desplomó en la cama> <to collapse with laughter : morirse de risa> **3** FAIL **:** fracasar, quebrar, arruinarse **4** FOLD **:** plegarse
collapse[2] *n* **1** FALL **:** derrumbe *m*, desplome *m* **2** BREAKDOWN, FAILURE **:** fracaso *m*, colapso *m* (físico), quiebra *f* (económica)
collapsible [kə'læpsəbəl] *adj* **:** plegable
collar[1] ['kɑlər] *vt* **:** agarrar, atrapar
collar[2] *n* **:** cuello *m*
collarbone ['kɑlərˌboːn] *n* **:** clavícula *f*
collate [kə'leɪt; 'kɑˌleɪt, 'koː-] *vt* **-lated; -lating 1** COMPARE **:** cotejar, comparar **2 :** ordenar, recopilar (páginas)
collateral[1] [kə'læt̬ərəl] *adj* **:** colateral
collateral[2] *n* **:** garantía *f*, fianza *f*, prenda *f*
colleague ['kɑˌliːg] *n* **:** colega *mf*; compañero *m*, -ra *f*
collect[1] [kə'lɛkt] *vt* **1** GATHER **:** recopilar, reunir, recoger <she collected her thoughts : puso en orden sus ideas> **2 :** coleccionar, juntar <to collect stamps : coleccionar timbres> **3 :** cobrar (una deuda), recaudar (un impuesto) **4** DRAW **:** cobrar, percibir (un sueldo, etc.) — *vi* **1** ACCUMULATE **:** acumularse, juntarse **2** CONGREGATE **:** congregarse, reunirse
collect[2] *adv & adj* **:** por cobrar, a cobro revertido
collectible *or* **collectable** [kə'lɛktəbəl] *adj* **:** coleccionable
collection [kə'lɛkʃən] *n* **1** COLLECTING **:** colecta *f* (de contribuciones), cobro *m* (de deudas), recaudación *f* (de impuestos) **2** GROUP **:** colección *f* (de objetos), grupo *m* (de personas)
collective[1] [kə'lɛktɪv] *adj* **:** colectivo — **collectively** *adv*
collective[2] *n* **:** colectivo *m*
collector [kə'lɛktər] *n* **1 :** coleccionista *mf* (de objetos) **2 :** cobrador *m*, -dora *f* (de deudas)
college ['kɑlɪdʒ] *n* **1 :** universidad *f* **2 :** colegio *m* (de electores o profesionales)
collegiate [kə'liːdʒət] *adj* **:** universitario
collide [kə'laɪd] *vi* **-lided; -liding :** chocar, colisionar, estrellarse
collie ['kɑli] *n* **:** collie *mf*
collision [kə'lɪʒən] *n* **:** choque *m*, colisión *f*
colloquial [kə'loːkwiəl] *adj* **:** coloquial
colloquialism [kə'loːkwiəˌlɪzəm] *n* **:** expresión *f* coloquial
collusion [kə'luːʒən] *n* **:** colusión *f*
cologne [kə'loːn] *n* **:** colonia *f*
Colombian [kə'lʌmbiən] *n* **:** colombiano *m*, -na *f* — **Colombian** *adj*
colon[1] ['koːlən] *n, pl* **colons** *or* **cola** [-lə] **:** colon *m* (de los intestinos)
colon[2] *n, pl* **colons :** dos puntos *mpl* (signo ortográfico)
colonel ['kərnəl] *n* **:** coronel *m*
colonial[1] [kə'loːniəl] *adj* **:** colonial
colonial[2] *n* **:** colono *m*, -na *f*
colonist ['kɑlənɪst] *n* **:** colono *m*, -na *f*; colonizador *m*, -dora *f*

colonization [ˌkɑlənəˈzeɪʃən] *n* : colonización *f*
colonize [ˈkɑləˌnaɪz] *vt* **-nized; -nizing** **1** : establecer una colonia en **2** SETTLE : colonizar
colonnade [ˌkɑləˈneɪd] *n* : columnata *f*
colony [ˈkɑləni] *n, pl* **-nies** : colonia *f*
color[1] [ˈkʌlər] *vt* **1** : colorear, pintar **2** INFLUENCE : influir en, influenciar — *vi* BLUSH : sonrojarse, ruborizarse
color[2] *n* **1** : color *m* <primary colors : colores primarios> **2** INTEREST, VIVIDNESS : color *m,* colorido *m* <local color : color local>
color–blind [ˈkʌlərˌblaɪnd] *adj* : daltónico
color blindness *n* : daltonismo *m*
colored [ˈkʌlərd] *adj* **1** : de color (dícese de los objetos) **2** : de color, negro (dícese de las personas)
colorfast [ˈkʌlərˌfæst] *adj* : que no se destiñe
colorful [ˈkʌlərfəl] *adj* **1** : lleno de colorido, de colores vivos **2** PICTURESQUE, STRIKING : pintoresco, llamativo
colorless [ˈkʌlərləs] *adj* **1** : incoloro, sin color **2** DULL : soso, aburrido
colossal [kəˈlɑsəl] *adj* : colosal
colossus [kəˈlɑsəs] *n, pl* **-si** [-ˌsaɪ] : coloso *m*
colt [ˈkoːlt] *n* : potro *m*
column [ˈkɑləm] *n* : columna *f*
columnist [ˈkɑləmnɪst, -ləmɪst] *n* : columnista *mf*
coma [ˈkoːmə] *n* : coma *m,* estado *m* de coma
comatose [ˈkoːməˌtoːs, ˈkɑ-] *adj* : comatoso, en estado de coma
comb[1] [ˈkoːm] *vt* **1** : peinar (el pelo) **2** SEARCH : peinar, rastrear, registrar a fondo
comb[2] *n* **1** : peine *m* **2** : cresta *f* (de un gallo)
combat[1] [kəmˈbæt, ˈkɑmˌbæt] *vt* **-bated** *or* **-batted; -bating** *or* **-batting** : combatir, luchar contra
combat[2] [ˈkɑmˌbæt] *n* : combate *m,* lucha *f*
combatant [kəmˈbætənt] *n* : combatiente *mf*
combative [kəmˈbætɪv] *adj* : combativo
combination [ˌkɑmbəˈneɪʃən] *n* : combinación *f*
combine[1] [kəmˈbaɪn] *v* **-bined; -bining** *vt* : combinar, aunar — *vi* : combinarse, mezclarse
combine[2] [ˈkɑmˌbaɪn] *n* **1** ALLIANCE : alianza *f* comercial o política **2** HARVESTER : cosechadora *f*
combustible [kəmˈbʌstəbəl] *adj* : inflamable, combustible
combustion [kəmˈbʌstʃən] *n* : combustión *f*
come [ˈkʌm] *vi* **came** [ˈkeɪm]; **come; coming** **1** APPROACH : venir, aproximarse <here they come : acá vienen> **2** ARRIVE : venir, llegar, alcanzar <they came yesterday : vinieron ayer> **3** ORIGINATE : venir, provenir <this wine comes from France : este vino viene de Francia> **4** AMOUNT : llegar, ascender <the investment came to two million : la inversión llegó a dos millones> **5 to come clean** : confesar, desahogar la conciencia **6 to come into** ACQUIRE : adquirir <to come into a fortune : heredar una fortuna> **7 to come off** SUCCEED : tener éxito, ser un éxito **8 to come out** : salir, aparecer, publicarse **9 to come to** REVIVE : recobrar el conocimiento, volver en sí **10 to come to pass** HAPPEN : acontecer **11 to come to terms** : llegar a un acuerdo
comeback [ˈkʌmˌbæk] *n* **1** RETORT : réplica *f,* respuesta *f* **2** RETURN : retorno *m,* regreso *m* <the champion announced his comeback : el campeón anunció su regreso>
come back *vi* **1** RETORT : replicar, contestar **2** RETURN : volver <come back here! : ¡vuelve acá!> <that style's coming back : ese estilo está volviendo>
comedian [kəˈmiːdiən] *n* : cómico *m,* -ca *f;* humorista *mf*
comedienne [kəˌmiːdiˈɛn] *n* : cómica *f,* humorista *f*
comedy [ˈkɑmədi] *n, pl* **-dies** : comedia *f*
comely [ˈkʌmli] *adj* **-lier; -est** : bello, bonito
comet [ˈkɑmət] *n* : cometa *m*
comfort[1] [ˈkʌmpfərt] *vt* **1** CHEER : confortar, alentar **2** CONSOLE : consolar
comfort[2] *n* **1** CONSOLATION : consuelo *m* **2** WELL-BEING : confort *m,* bienestar *m* **3** CONVENIENCE : comodidad *f* <the comforts of home : las comodidades del hogar>
comfortable [ˈkʌmpfərtəbəl, ˈkʌmpftə-] *adj* : cómodo, confortable — **comfortably** [ˈkʌmpfərtəbli, ˈkʌmpftə-] *adv*
comforter [ˈkʌmpfərtər] *n* **1** : confortador *m,* -dora *f* **2** QUILT : edredón *m,* cobertor *m*
comic[1] [ˈkɑmɪk] *adj* : cómico, humorístico
comic[2] *n* **1** COMEDIAN : cómico *m,* -ca *f;* humorista *mf* **2** *or* **comic book** : historieta *f,* cómic *m*
comical [ˈkɑmɪkəl] *adj* : cómico, gracioso, chistoso
comic strip *n* : tira *f* cómica, historieta *f*
coming [ˈkʌmɪŋ] *adj* : siguiente, próximo, que viene
comma [ˈkɑmə] *n* : coma *f*
command[1] [kəˈmænd] *vt* **1** ORDER : ordenar, mandar **2** CONTROL, DIRECT : comandar, tener el mando de — *vi* **1** : dar órdenes **2** GOVERN : estar al mando *m,* gobernar

command[2] *n* **1** CONTROL, LEADERSHIP : mando *m,* control *m,* dirección *f* **2** ORDER : orden *f,* mandato *m* **3** MASTERY : maestría *f,* destreza *f,* dominio *m* **4** : tropa *f* asignada a un comandante

commandant ['kamən,dant, -,dænt] *n* : comandante *mf*

commandeer [,kamən'dɪr] *vt* : piratear, secuestrar (un vehículo, etc.)

commander [kə'mændər] *n* : comandante *mf*

commandment [kə'mændmənt] *n* : mandamiento *m,* orden *f* <the Ten Commandments : los diez mandamientos>

commemorate [kə'mɛmə,reɪt] *vt* **-rated; -rating** : conmemorar

commemoration [kə,mɛmə'reɪʃən] *n* : conmemoración *f*

commemorative [kə'mɛmrətɪv, -'mɛmə,reɪtɪv] *adj* : conmemorativo

commence [kə'mɛnts] *v* **-menced; -mencing** *vt* : iniciar, comenzar — *vi* : iniciarse, comenzar

commencement [kə'mɛntsmənt] *n* **1** BEGINNING : inicio *m,* comienzo *m* **2** : ceremonia *f* de graduación

commend [kə'mɛnd] *vt* **1** ENTRUST : encomendar **2** RECOMMEND : recomendar **3** PRAISE : elogiar, alabar

commendable [kə'mɛndəbəl] *adj* : loable, meritorio, encomiable

commendation [,kamən'deɪʃən, -,mɛn-] *n* : elogio *m,* encomio *m*

commensurate [kə'mɛntsərət, -'mɛntʃʊrət] *adj* : proporcionado <commensurate with : en proporción a>

comment[1] ['ka,mɛnt] *vi* **1** : hacer comentarios **2 to comment on** : comentar, hacer observaciones sobre

comment[2] *n* : comentario *m,* observación *f*

commentary ['kamən,tɛri] *n, pl* **-taries** : comentario *m,* crónica *f* (deportiva)

commentator ['kamən,teɪtər] *n* : comentarista *mf,* cronista *mf* (de deportes)

commerce ['kamərs] *n* : comercio *m*

commercial[1] [kə'mərʃəl] *adj* : comercial — **commercially** *adv*

commercial[2] *n* : comercial *m*

commercialize [kə'mərʃə,laɪz] *vt* **-ized; -izing** : comercializar

commiserate [kə'mɪzə,reɪt] *vi* **-ated; -ating** : compadecerse, consolarse

commiseration [kə,mɪzə'reɪʃən] *n* : conmiseración *f*

commission[1] [kə'mɪʃən] *vt* **1** : nombrar (un oficial) **2** : comisionar, encargar <to commission a painting : encargar una pintura>

commission[2] *n* **1** : nombramiento *m* (al grado de oficial) **2** COMMITTEE : comisión *f,* comité *m* **3** COMMITTING : comisión *f,* realización *f* (de un acto) **4** PERCENTAGE : comisión *f* <sales commissions : comisiones de venta>

commissioned officer *n* : oficial *mf*

commissioner [kə'mɪʃənər] *n* **1** : comisionado *m,* -da *f;* miembro *m* de una comisión **2** : comisario *m,* -ria *f* (de policía, etc.)

commit [kə'mɪt] *vt* **-mitted; -mitting** **1** ENTRUST : encomendar, confiar **2** CONFINE : internar (en un hospital), encarcelar (en una prisión) **3** PERPETRATE : cometer <to commit a crime : cometer un crimen> **4 to commit oneself** : comprometerse

commitment [kə'mɪtmənt] *n* **1** RESPONSIBILITY : compromiso *m,* responsabilidad *f* **2** DEDICATION : dedicación *f,* devoción *f* <commitment to the cause : devoción a la causa>

committee [kə'mɪti] *n* : comité *m*

commodious [kə'mo:diəs] *adj* SPACIOUS : amplio, espacioso

commodity [kə'madəti] *n, pl* **-ties** : artículo *m* de comercio, mercancía *f,* mercadería *f*

commodore ['kamə,dor] *n* : comodoro *m*

common[1] ['kamən] *adj* **1** PUBLIC : común, público <the common good : el bien común> **2** SHARED : común <a common interest : un interés común> **3** GENERAL : común, general <it's common knowledge : todo el mundo lo sabe> **4** ORDINARY : ordinario, común y corriente <the common man : el hombre medio, el hombre de la calle>

common[2] *n* **1** : tierra *f* comunal **2 in ~** : en común

common cold *n* : resfriado *m* común

common denominator *n* : denominador *m* común

commoner ['kamənər] *n* : plebeyo *m,* -ya *f*

commonly ['kamənli] *adv* **1** FREQUENTLY : comúnmente, frecuentemente **2** USUALLY : normalmente

common noun *n* : nombre *m* común

commonplace[1] ['kamən,pleɪs] *adj* : común, ordinario

commonplace[2] *n* : cliché *m,* tópico *m*

common sense *n* : sentido *m* común

commonwealth ['kamən,wɛlθ] *n* : entidad *f* política <the British Commonwealth : la Mancomunidad Británica>

commotion [kə'mo:ʃən] *n* **1** RUCKUS : alboroto *m,* jaleo *m,* escándalo *m* **2** STIR, UPSET : revuelo *m,* conmoción *f*

communal [kə'mju:nəl] *adj* : communal

commune[1] [kə'mju:n] *vi* **-muned; -muning** : estar en comunión *f*

commune[2] ['ka,mju:n, kə'mju:n] *n* : comuna *f*

communicable [kə'mju:nɪkəbəl] *adj* CONTAGIOUS : transmisible, contagioso

communicate [kə'mju:nə,keɪt] *v* **-cated; -cating** *vt* **1** CONVEY : comunicar, expresar, hacer saber **2** TRANSMIT : transmitir (una enfermedad), contagiar — *vi* : comunicarse, expresarse

communication [kə,mjuːnə'keɪʃən] *n* : comunicación *f*

communicative [kə'mjuːnɪ,keɪṯɪv, -kəṯɪv] *adj* : comunicativo

communion [kə'mjuːnjən] *n* **1** SHARING : comunión *f* **2 Communion** : comunión *f,* eucaristía *f*

communiqué [kə'mjuːnə,keɪ, -,mjuːnə'keɪ] *n* : comunicado *m*

communism *or* **Communism** ['kɑmjə,nɪzəm] *n* : comunismo *m*

communist[1] *or* **Communist** ['kɑmjə,nɪst] *adj* : comunista <the Communist Party : el Partido Comunista>

communist[2] *or* **Communist** *n* : comunista *mf*

communistic *or* **Communistic** [,kɑmjə'nɪstɪk] *adj* : comunista

community [kə'mjuːnəṯi] *n, pl* **-ties** : comunidad *f*

commute [kə'mjuːt] *v* **-muted; -muting** *vt* REDUCE : conmutar, reducir (una sentencia) — *vi* : viajar de la residencia al trabajo

commuter [kə'mjuːtər] *n* : persona *f* que viaja diariamente al trabajo

compact[1] [kəm'pækt, 'kɑm,pækt] *vt* : compactar, consolidar, comprimir

compact[2] [kəm'pækt, 'kɑm,pækt] *adj* **1** DENSE, SOLID : compacto, macizo, denso **2** CONCISE : breve, conciso

compact[3] ['kɑm,pækt] *n* **1** AGREEMENT : acuerdo *m,* pacto *m* **2** : polvera *f,* estuche *m* de maquillaje **3** *or* **compact car** : auto *m* compacto

compact disc ['kɑm,pækt'dɪsk] *n* : disco *m* compacto, compact disc *m*

compactly [kəm'pæktli, 'kɑm,pækt-] *adv* **1** DENSELY : densamente, macizamente **2** CONCISELY : concisamente, brevemente

companion [kəm'pænjən] *n* **1** COMRADE : compañero *m,* -ra *f;* acompañante *mf* **2** MATE : pareja *f* (de un zapato, etc.)

companionable [kəm'pænjənəbəl] *adj* : sociable, amigable

companionship [kəm'pænjən,ʃɪp] *n* : compañerismo *m,* camaradería *f*

company ['kʌmpəni] *n, pl* **-nies 1** FIRM : compañía *f,* empresa *f* **2** GROUP : compañía *f* (de actores o soldados) **3** GUESTS : visita *f* <we have company : tenemos visita>

comparable ['kɑmpərəbəl] *adj* : comparable, parecido

comparative[1] [kəm'pærəṯiv] *adj* RELATIVE : comparativo, relativo — **comparatively** *adv*

comparative[2] *n* : comparativo *m*

compare[1] [kəm'pær] *v* **-pared; -paring** *vt* : comparar — *vi* **to compare with** : poder comparar con, tener comparación con

compare[2] *n* : comparación *f* <beyond compare : sin igual, sin par>

comparison [kəm'pærəsən] *n* : comparación *f*

compartment [kəm'pɑrtmənt] *n* : compartimento *m,* compartimiento *m*

compass ['kʌmpəs, 'kɑm-] *n* **1** RANGE, SCOPE : alcance *m,* extensión *f,* límites *mpl* **2** : compás *m* (para trazar circunferencias) **3** : compás *m,* brújula *f* <the points of the compass : los puntos cardinales>

compassion [kəm'pæʃən] *n* : compasión *f,* piedad *f,* misericordia *f*

compassionate [kəm'pæʃənət] *adj* : compasivo

compatibility [kəm,pæṯə'bɪləṯi] *n* : compatibilidad *f*

compatible [kəm'pæṯəbəl] *adj* : compatible, afín

compatriot [kəm'peɪtriət, -'pæ-] *n* : compatriota *mf;* paisano *m,* -na *f*

compel [kəm'pɛl] *vt* **-pelled; -pelling** : obligar, compeler

compendium [kəm'pɛndiəm] *n, pl* **-diums** *or* **-dia** [-diə] : compendio *m*

compensate ['kɑmpən,seɪt] *v* **-sated; -sating** *vi* **to compensate for** : compensar — *vt* : indemnizar, compensar

compensation [,kɑmpən'seɪʃən] *n* : compensación *f,* indemnización *f*

compensatory [kəm'pɛntsə,tori] *adj* : compensatorio

compete [kəm'piːt] *vi* **-peted; -peting** : competir, contender, rivalizar

competence ['kɑmpətənts] *n* : competencia *f,* aptitud *f*

competency ['kɑmpətəntsi] → **competence**

competent ['kɑmpətənt] *adj* : competente, capaz

competition [,kɑmpə'tɪʃən] *n* : competencia *f,* concurso *m*

competitive [kəm'pɛṯəṯiv] *adj* : competitivo

competitor [kəm'pɛṯəṯər] *n* : competidor *m,* -dora *f*

compile [kəm'paɪl] *vt* **-piled; -piling** : compilar, recopilar

complacency [kəm'pleɪsəntsi] *n* : satisfacción *f* consigo mismo, suficiencia *f*

complacent [kəm'pleɪsənt] *adj* : satisfecho de sí mismo, suficiente

complain [kəm'pleɪn] *vi* **1** GRIPE : quejarse, regañar, rezongar **2** PROTEST : reclamar, protestar

complaint [kəm'pleɪnt] *n* **1** GRIPE : queja *f* **2** AILMENT : afección *f,* dolencia *f* **3** ACCUSATION : reclamo *m,* acusación *f*

complement[1] ['kɑmplə,mɛnt] *vt* : complementar

complement[2] ['kɑmpləmənt] *n* : complemento *m*

complementary [,kɑmplə'mɛntəri] *adj* : complementario

complete[1] [kəm'pliːt] *vt* **-pleted; -pleting 1** : completar, hacer entero <this piece completes the collection : esta pieza completa la colección> **2** FINISH : completar, acabar, terminar

<she completed her studies : completó sus estudios>
complete[2] *adj* **-pleter; -est 1** WHOLE : completo, entero, íntegro **2** FINISHED : terminado, acabado **3** TOTAL : completo, total, absoluto
completely [kəm'pli:tli] *adv* : completamente, totalmente
completion [kəm'pli:ʃən] *n* : finalización *f,* cumplimiento *m*
complex[1] [kɑm'plɛks, kəm-; 'kɑm,plɛks] *adj* : complejo, complicado
complex[2] ['kɑm,plɛks] *n* : complejo *m*
complexion [kəm'plɛkʃən] *n* : cutis *m,* tez *f* <of dark complexion : de tez morena>
complexity [kəm'plɛksət̬i, kɑm-] *n, pl* **-ties** : complejidad *f*
compliance [kəm'plaɪənts] *n* : conformidad *f* <in compliance with the law : conforme a la ley>
compliant [kəm'plaɪənt] *adj* : dócil, sumiso
complicate ['kɑmplə,keɪt] *vt* **-cated; -cating** : complicar
complicated ['kɑmplə,keɪt̬əd] *adj* : complicado
complication [,kɑmplə'keɪʃən] *n* : complicación *f*
complicity [kəm'plɪsət̬i] *n, pl* **-ties** : complicidad *f*
compliment[1] ['kɑmplə,mɛnt] *vt* : halagar, florear *Mex*
compliment[2] ['kɑmpləmənt] *n* **1** : halago *m,* cumplido *m* **2 compliments** *npl* : saludos *mpl* <give them my compliments : déles saludos de mi parte>
complimentary [,kɑmplə'mɛntəri] *adj* **1** FLATTERING : halagador, halagüeño **2** FREE : de cortesía, gratis
comply [kəm'plaɪ] *vi* **-plied; -plying** : cumplir, acceder, obedecer
component[1] [kəm'po:nənt, 'kɑm,po:-] *adj* : componente
component[2] *n* : componente *m,* elemento *m,* pieza *f*
compose [kəm'po:z] *vt* **-posed; -posing 1** : componer, crear <to compose a melody : componer una melodía > **2** CALM : calmar, serenar <to compose oneself : serenarse> **3** CONSTITUTE : constar, componer <to be composed of : constar de> **4** : componer (un texto a imprimirse)
composer [kəm'po:zər] *n* : compositor *m,* -tora *f*
composite[1] [kɑm'pɑzət, kəm-; 'kɑmpəzət] *adj* : compuesto (de varias partes)
composite[2] *n* : compuesto *m,* mezcla *f*
composition [,kɑmpə'zɪʃən] *n* **1** MAKEUP : composición *f* **2** ESSAY : ensayo *m,* trabajo *m*
compost ['kɑm,po:st] *n* : abono *m* vegetal
composure [kəm'po:ʒər] *n* : compostura *f,* serenidad *f*
compound[1] [kɑm'paʊnd, kəm-; 'kɑm,paʊnd] *vt* **1** COMBINE, COMPOSE : combinar, componer **2** AUGMENT : agravar, aumentar <to compound a problem : agravar un problema>
compound[2] ['kɑm,paʊnd; kɑm'paʊnd, kəm-] *adj* : compuesto <compound interest : interés compuesto>
compound[3] ['kɑm,paʊnd] *n* **1** MIXTURE : compuesto *m,* mezcla *f* **2** ENCLOSURE : recinto *m* (de residencias, etc.)
compound fracture *n* : fractura *f* complicada
comprehend [,kɑmprɪ'hɛnd] *vt* **1** UNDERSTAND : comprender, entender **2** INCLUDE : comprender, incluir, abarcar
comprehensible [,kɑmprɪ'hɛntsəbəl] *adj* : comprensible
comprehension [,kɑmprɪ'hɛntʃən] *n* : comprensión *f*
comprehensive [,kɑmprɪ'hɛntsɪv] *adj* **1** INCLUSIVE : inclusivo, exhaustivo **2** BROAD : extenso, amplio
compress[1] [kəm'prɛs] *vt* : comprimir
compress[2] ['kɑm,prɛs] *n* : compresa *f*
compression [kəm'prɛʃən] *n* : compresión *f*
comprise [kəm'praɪz] *vt* **-prised; -prising 1** INCLUDE : comprender, incluir **2** : componerse de, constar de <the installation comprises several buildings : la instalación está compuesta de varios edificios>
compromise[1] ['kɑmprə,maɪz] *v* **-mised; -mising** *vi* : transigir, avenirse — *vt* JEOPARDIZE : comprometer, poner en peligro
compromise[2] *n* : acuerdo *m* mutuo, compromiso *m*
comptroller [kən'tro:lər, 'kɑmp,tro:-] *n* : contralor *m,* -lora *f;* interventor *m,* -tora *f*
compulsion [kəm'pʌlʃən] *n* **1** COERCION : coacción *f* **2** URGE : compulsión *f,* impulso *m*
compulsive [kəm'pʌlsɪv] *adj* : compulsivo
compulsory [kəm'pʌlsəri] *adj* : obligatorio
compunction [kəm'pʌŋkʃən] *n* **1** QUALM : reparo *m,* escrúpulo *m* **2** REMORSE : remordimiento *m*
computation [,kɑmpjʊ'teɪʃən] *n* : cálculo *m,* cómputo *m*
compute [kəm'pju:t] *vt* **-puted; -puting** : computar, calcular
computer [kəm'pju:tər] *n* : computadora *f,* computador *m,* ordenador *m* *Spain*
computerize [kəm'pju:t̬ə,raɪz] *vt* **-ized; -izing** : computarizar, informatizar
comrade ['kɑm,ræd] *n* : camarada *mf;* compañero *m,* -ra *f*
con[1] ['kɑn] *vt* **conned; conning** SWINDLE : estafar, timar
con[2] *adv* : contra

con[3] *n* : contra *m* <the pros and cons : los pros y los contras>

concave [kɑn'keɪv, 'kɑn,keɪv] *adj* : cóncavo

conceal [kən'si:l] *vt* : esconder, ocultar, disimular

concealment [kən'si:lmənt] *n* : escondimiento *m,* ocultación *f*

concede [kən'si:d] *vt* **-ceded; -ceding** **1** ALLOW, GRANT : conceder **2** ADMIT : conceder, reconocer <to concede defeat : reconocer la derrota>

conceit [kən'si:t] *n* : engreimiento *m,* presunción *f*

conceited [kən'si:ṭəd] *adj* : presumido, engreído, presuntuoso

conceivable [kən'si:vəbəl] *adj* : concebible, imaginable

conceivably [kən'si:vəbli] *adv* : posiblemente, de manera concebible

conceive [kən'si:v] *v* **-ceived; -ceiving** *vi* : concebir, embarazarse — *vt* IMAGINE : concebir, imaginar

concentrate[1] ['kɑntsən,treɪt] *v* **-trated; -trating** *vt* : concentrar — *vi* : concentrarse

concentrate[2] *n* : concentrado *m*

concentration [,kɑntsən'treɪʃən] *n* : concentración *f*

concentric [kən'sɛntrɪk] *adj* : concéntrico

concept ['kɑn,sɛpt] *n* : concepto *m,* idea *f*

conception [kən'sɛpʃən] *n* **1** : concepción *f* (de un bebé) **2** IDEA : concepto *m,* idea *f*

concern[1] [kən'sərn] *vt* **1** : tratarse de, tener que ver con <the novel concerns a sailor : la novela se trata de un marinero> **2** INVOLVE : concernir, incumbir a, afectar <that does not concern me : eso no me incumbe>

concern[2] *n* **1** AFFAIR : asunto *m* **2** WORRY : inquietud *f,* preocupación *f* **3** BUSINESS : negocio *m*

concerned [kən'sərnd] *adj* **1** ANXIOUS : preocupado, ansioso **2** INTERESTED, INVOLVED : interesado, afectado

concerning [kən'sərnɪŋ] *prep* REGARDING : con respecto a, acerca de, sobre

concert ['kɑn,sərt] *n* **1** AGREEMENT : concierto *m,* acuerdo *m* **2** : concierto *m* (musical)

concerted [kən'sərṭəd] *adj* : concertado, coordinado <to make a concerted effort : coordinar los esfuerzos>

concertina [,kɑntsər'ti:nə] *n* : concertina *f*

concerto [kən'tʃɛrto:] *n, pl* **-ti** [-ti, -,ti:] *or* **-tos** : concierto *m* <violin concerto : concierto para violín>

concession [kən'sɛʃən] *n* : concesión *f*

conch ['kɑŋk, 'kɑntʃ] *n, pl* **conchs** ['kɑŋks] *or* **conches** ['kɑntʃəz] : caracol *m* (animal), caracola *f* (concha)

conciliatory [kən'sɪliə,tori] *adj* : conciliador, conciliatorio

concise [kən'saɪs] *adj* : conciso, breve — **concisely** *adv*

conclave ['kɑn,kleɪv] *n* : cónclave *m*

conclude [kən'klu:d] *v* **-cluded; -cluding** *vt* **1** END : concluir, finalizar <to conclude a meeting : concluir una reunión> **2** DECIDE : concluir, llegar a la conclusión de — *vi* END : concluir, terminar

conclusion [kən'klu:ʒən] *n* **1** INFERENCE : conclusión *f* **2** END : fin *m,* final *m*

conclusive [kən'klu:sɪv] *adj* : concluyente, decisivo — **conclusively** *adv*

concoct [kən'kɑkt, kɑn-] *vt* **1** PREPARE : preparar, confeccionar **2** DEVISE : inventar, tramar

concoction [kən'kɑkʃən] *n* : invención *f,* mejunje *m,* brebaje *m*

concord ['kɑn,kɔrd, 'kɑŋ-] *n* **1** HARMONY : concordia *f,* armonía *f* **2** AGREEMENT : acuerdo *m*

concordance [kən'kɔrdənts] *n* : concordancia *f*

concourse ['kɑn,kors] *n* : explanada *f,* salón *m* (para pasajeros)

concrete[1] [kɑn'kri:t, 'kɑn,kri:t] *adj* **1** REAL : concreto <concrete objects : objetos concretos> **2** SPECIFIC : determinado, específico **3** : de concreto, de hormigón <concrete walls : paredes de concreto>

concrete[2] ['kɑn,kri:t, kɑn'kri:t] *n* : concreto *m,* hormigón *m*

concur [kən'kər] *vi* **concurred; concurring** **1** COINCIDE : concurrir, coincidir **2** AGREE : concurrir, estar de acuerdo

concurrent [kən'kərənt] *adj* : concurrente, simultáneo

concussion [kən'kʌʃən] *n* : conmoción *f* cerebral

condemn [kən'dɛm] *vt* **1** CENSURE : condenar, reprobar, censurar **2** : declarar insalubre (alimentos), declarar ruinoso (un edificio) **3** SENTENCE : condenar <condemned to death : condenado a muerte>

condemnation [,kɑn,dɛm'neɪʃən] *n* : condena *f,* reprobación *f*

condensation [,kɑn,dɛn'seɪʃən, -dən-] *n* : condensación *f*

condense [kən'dɛnts] *v* **-densed; -densing** *vt* **1** ABRIDGE : condensar, resumir **2** : condensar (vapor, etc.) — *vi* : condensarse

condescend [,kɑndɪ'sɛnd] *vi* **1** DEIGN : condescender, dignarse **2 to condescend to someone** : tratar a alguien con condescendencia

condescension [,kɑndɪ'sɛntʃən] *n* : condescendencia *f*

condiment ['kɑndəmənt] *n* : condimento *m*

condition[1] [kən'dɪʃən] *vt* **1** DETERMINE : condicionar, determinar **2** : acondicionar (el pelo o el aire), poner en forma (el cuerpo)

condition² *n* **1** STIPULATION : condición *f,* estipulación *f* <on the condition that : a condición de que> **2** STATE : condición *f,* estado *m* <in poor condition : en malas condiciones> **3 conditions** *npl* : condiciones *fpl,* situación *f* <working conditions : condiciones del trabajo>

conditional [kən'dɪʃənəl] *adj* : condicional — **conditionally** *adv*

condolence [kən'do:ləntś] *n* **1** SYMPATHY : condolencia *f* **2 condolences** *npl* : pésame *m*

condominium [ˌkɑndə'mɪniəm] *n, pl* **-ums** : condominio *m*

condone [kən'do:n] *vt* **-doned; -doning** : aprobar, perdonar, tolerar

condor ['kɑndər, -ˌdɔr] *n* : cóndor *m*

conducive [kən'du:sɪv, -'dju:-] *adj* : propicio, favorable

conduct¹ [kən'dʌkt] *vt* **1** GUIDE : guiar, conducir <to conduct a tour : guiar una visita> **2** DIRECT : conducir, dirigir <to conduct an orchestra : dirigir una orquesta> **3** CARRY OUT : realizar, llevar a cabo <to conduct an investigation : llevar a cabo una investigación> **4** TRANSMIT : conducir, transmitir (calor, electricidad, etc.) **5 to conduct oneself** BEHAVE : conducirse, comportarse

conduct² ['kɑnˌdʌkt] *n* **1** MANAGEMENT : conducción *f,* dirección *f,* manejo *m* <the conduct of foreign affairs : la conducción de asuntos exteriores> **2** BEHAVIOR : conducta *f,* comportamiento *m*

conduction [kən'dʌkʃən] *n* : conducción *f*

conductivity [ˌkɑnˌdʌk'tɪvəṭi] *n, pl* **-ties** : conductividad *f*

conductor [kən'dʌktər] *n* **1** : conductor *m,* -tora *f;* revisor *m,* -sora *f* (en un tren); cobrador *m,* -dora *f* (en un bus); director *m,* -tora *f* (de una orquesta) **2** : conductor *m* (de electricidad, etc.)

conduit ['kɑnˌdu:ət, -ˌdju:-] *n* : conducto *m,* canal *m,* vía *f*

cone ['ko:n] *n* **1** : piña *f* (fruto de las coníferas) **2** : cono *m* (en geometría) **3 ice-cream cone** : cono *m,* barquillo *m,* cucurucho *m*

confection [kən'fɛkʃən] *n* : dulce *m*

confectioner [kən'fɛkʃənər] *n* : confitero *m,* -ra *f*

confederacy [kən'fɛdərəsi] *n, pl* **-cies** : confederación *f*

confederate¹ [kən'fɛdəˌreɪt] *v* **-ated; -ating** *vt* : unir, confederar — *vi* : confederarse, aliarse

confederate² [kən'fɛdərət] *adj* : confederado

confederate³ *n* : cómplice *mf;* aliado *m,* -da *f*

confederation [kənˌfɛdə'reɪʃən] *n* : confederación *f,* alianza *f*

confer [kən'fər] *v* **-ferred; -ferring** *vt* : conferir, otorgar — *vi* **to confer with** : consultar

conference ['kɑnfrəntś, -fərəntś] *n* : conferencia *f* <press conference : conferencia de prensa>

confess [kən'fɛs] *vt* : confesar — *vi* **1** : confesar <the prisoner confessed : el detenido confesó> **2** : confesarse (en religión)

confession [kən'fɛʃən] *n* : confesión *f*

confessional [kən'fɛʃənəl] *n* : confesionario *m*

confetti [kən'fɛṭi] *n* : confeti *m*

confidant ['kɑnfəˌdɑnt, -ˌdænt] *n* : confidente *mf*

confide [kən'faɪd] *v* **-fided; -fiding** : confiar

confidence ['kɑnfədəntś] *n* **1** TRUST : confianza *f* **2** SELF-ASSURANCE : confianza *f* en sí mismo, seguridad *f* en sí mismo **3** SECRET : confidencia *f,* secreto *m*

confident ['kɑnfədənt] *adj* **1** SURE : seguro **2** SELF-ASSURED : confiado, seguro de sí mismo

confidential [ˌkɑnfə'dɛntʃəl] *adj* : confidencial — **confidentially** [ˌkɑnfə'dɛntʃəli] *adv*

confidently ['kɑnfədəntli] *adv* : con seguridad, con confianza

configuration [kənˌfɪgjə'reɪʃən] *n* : configuración *f*

confine [kən'faɪn] *vt* **-fined; -fining 1** LIMIT : confinar, restringir, limitar **2** IMPRISON : recluir, encarcelar, encerrar

confinement [kən'faɪnmənt] *n* : confinamiento *m,* reclusión *f,* encierro *m*

confines ['kɑnˌfaɪnz] *npl* : límites *mpl,* confines *mpl*

confirm [kən'fərm] *vt* **1** RATIFY : ratificar **2** VERIFY : confirmar, verificar **3** : confirmar (en religión)

confirmation [ˌkɑnfər'meɪʃən] *n* : confirmación *f*

confiscate ['kɑnfəˌskeɪt] *vt* **-cated; -cating** : confiscar, incautar, decomisar

confiscation [ˌkɑnfə'skeɪʃən] *n* : confiscación *f,* incautación *f,* decomiso *m*

conflagration [ˌkɑnflə'greɪʃən] *n* : conflagración *f*

conflict¹ [kən'flɪkt] *vi* : estar en conflicto, oponerse

conflict² ['kɑnˌflɪkt] *n* : conflicto *m* <to be in conflict : estar en desacuerdo>

conform [kən'fɔrm] *vi* **1** ACCORD, COMPLY : ajustarse, adaptarse, conformarse <it conforms with our standards : se ajusta a nuestras normas> **2** CORRESPOND : corresponder, encajar <to conform to the truth : corresponder a la verdad>

conformity [kən'fɔrməṭi] *n, pl* **-ties** : conformidad *f*

confound [kən'faʊnd, kɑn-] *vt* : confundir, desconcertar

confront [kən'frʌnt] *vt* : afrontar, enfrentarse a, encarar

confrontation [ˌkɑnfrən'teɪʃən] *n* : enfrentamiento *m,* confrontación *f*

confuse [kən'fju:z] *vt* **-fused; -fusing 1** PUZZLE **:** confundir, enturbiar **2** COMPLICATE **:** confundir, enredar, complicar <to confuse the issue **:** complicar las cosas>

confusion [kən'fju:ʒən] *n* **1** PERPLEXITY **:** confusión *f* **2** MESS, TURMOIL **:** confusión *f,* embrollo *m,* lío *m fam*

congeal [kən'dʒi:l] *vi* **1** FREEZE **:** congelarse **2** COAGULATE, CURDLE **:** coagularse, cuajarse

congenial [kən'dʒi:niəl] *adj* **:** agradable, simpático

congenital [kən'dʒɛnətəl] *adj* **:** congénito

congest [kən'dʒɛst] *vt* **1 :** congestionar (en la medicina) **2** OVERCROWD **:** abarrotar, atestar, congestionar (el tráfico) — *vi* **:** congestionarse

congestion [kən'dʒɛstʃən] *n* **:** congestión *f*

conglomerate¹ [kən'glɑmərət] *adj* **:** conglomerado

conglomerate² [kən'glɑmərət] *n* **:** conglomerado *m*

conglomeration [kən,glɑmə'reɪʃən] *n* **:** conglomerado *m,* acumulación *f*

Congolese [,kɑŋgə'li:z, -'li:s] *n* **:** congoleño *m,* -ña *f* — **Congolese** *adj*

congratulate [kən'grædʒə,leɪt, -'grætʃə-] *vt* **-lated; -lating :** felicitar

congratulation [kən,grædʒə'leɪʃən, -,grætʃə-] *n* **:** felicitación *f* <congratulations! **:** ¡felicidades!, ¡enhorabuena!>

congregate ['kɑŋgrɪ,geɪt] *v* **-gated; -gating** *vt* **:** congregar, reunir — *vi* **:** congregarse, reunirse

congregation [,kɑŋgrɪ'geɪʃən] *n* **1** GATHERING **:** congregación *f,* fieles *mpl* (a un servicio religioso) **2** PARISHIONERS **:** feligreses *mpl*

congress ['kɑŋgrəs] *n* **:** congreso *m*

congressional [kən'grɛʃənəl, kɑn-] *adj* **:** del congreso

congressman ['kɑŋgrəsmən] *n, pl* **-men** [-mən, -,mɛn] **:** congresista *m,* diputado *m*

congresswoman ['kɑŋgrəs,wʊmən] *n, pl* **-women** [-,wɪmən] **:** congresista *f,* diputada *f*

congruence [kən'gru:ən*t*s, 'kɑŋgrʊən*t*s] *n* **:** congruencia *f*

congruent [kən'gru:ənt, 'kɑŋgrʊənt] *adj* **:** congruente

conic ['kɑnɪk] → **conical**

conical ['kɑnɪkəl] *adj* **:** cónico

conifer ['kɑnəfər, 'ko:-] *n* **:** conífera *f*

coniferous [ko:'nɪfərəs, kə-] *adj* **:** conífero

conjecture¹ [kən'dʒɛktʃər] *v* **-tured; -turing :** conjeturar

conjecture² *n* **:** conjetura *f,* presunción *f*

conjugal ['kɑndʒɪgəl, kən'dʒu:-] *adj* **:** conyugal

conjugate ['kɑndʒə,geɪt] *vt* **-gated; -gating :** conjugar

conjugation [,kɑndʒə'geɪʃən] *n* **:** conjugación *f*

conjunction [kən'dʒʌŋkʃən] *n* **:** conjunción *f* <in conjunction with **:** en combinación con>

conjure ['kɑndʒər, 'kʌn-] *v* **-jured; -juring** *vt* **1** ENTREAT **:** rogar, suplicar **2 to conjure up :** hacer aparecer (apariciones), evocar (memorias, etc.) — *vi* **:** practicar la magia

conjurer *or* **conjuror** ['kɑndʒərər, 'kʌn-] *n* **:** mago *m,* -ga *f;* prestidigitador *m,* -dora *f*

connect [kə'nɛkt] *vi* **:** conectar, enlazar, empalmar, comunicarse — *vt* **1** JOIN, LINK **:** conectar, unir, juntar, vincular **2** RELATE **:** relacionar, asociar (ideas)

connection [kə'nɛkʃən] *n* **:** conexión *f,* enlace *m* <professional connections **:** relaciones profesionales>

connective [kə'nɛktɪv] *adj* **:** conectivo, conjuntivo <connective tissue **:** tejido conjuntivo>

connector [kə'nɛktər] *n* **:** conector *m*

connivance [kə'naɪvən*t*s] *n* **:** connivencia *f,* complicidad *f*

connive [kə'naɪv] *vi* **-nived; -niving** CONSPIRE, PLOT **:** actuar en connivencia, confabularse, conspirar

connoisseur [,kɑnə'sər, -'sʊr] *n* **:** conocedor *m,* -dora *f;* entendido *m,* -da *f*

connotation [,kɑnə'teɪʃən] *n* **:** connotación *f*

connote [kə'no:t] *vt* **-noted; -noting :** connotar

conquer ['kɑŋkər] *vt* **:** conquistar, vencer

conqueror ['kɑŋkərər] *n* **:** conquistador *m,* -dora *f*

conquest ['kɑn,kwɛst, 'kɑŋ-] *n* **:** conquista *f*

conscience ['kɑntʃən*t*s] *n* **:** conciencia *f,* consciencia *f* <to have a clear conscience **:** tener la conciencia limpia>

conscientious [,kɑntʃi'ɛntʃəs] *adj* **:** concienzudo — **conscientiously** *adv*

conscious ['kɑntʃəs] *adj* **1** AWARE **:** consciente <to become conscious of **:** darse cuenta de> **2** ALERT, AWAKE **:** consciente **3** INTENTIONAL **:** intencional, deliberado

consciously ['kɑntʃəsli] *adv* INTENTIONALLY **:** intencionalmente, deliberadamente, a propósito

consciousness ['kɑntʃəsnəs] *n* **1** AWARENESS **:** conciencia *f,* consciencia *f* **2** conocimiento *m* <to lose consciousness **:** perder el conocimiento>

conscript¹ [kən'skrɪpt] *vt* **:** reclutar, alistar, enrolar

conscript² ['kɑn,skrɪpt] *n* **:** conscripto *m,* -ta *f;* recluta *mf*

consecrate ['kɑn*t*sə,kreɪt] *vt* **-crated; -crating :** consagrar

consecration [,kɑn*t*sə'kreɪʃən] *n* **:** consagración *f,* dedicación *f*

consecutive [kən'sɛkjət̬iv] *adj* : consecutivo, seguido <on five consecutive days : cinco días seguidos>
consecutively [kən'sɛkjət̬ivli] *adv* : consecutivamente
consensus [kən'sɛntsəs] *n* : consenso *m*
consent¹ [kən'sɛnt] *vi* **1** AGREE : acceder, ponerse de acuerdo **2 to consent to do something** : consentir en hacer algo
consent² *n* : consentimiento *m,* permiso *m* <by common consent : de común acuerdo>
consequence ['kɑntsəˌkwɛnts, -kwənts] *n* **1** RESULT : consecuencia *f,* secuela *f* **2** IMPORTANCE : importancia *f,* trascendencia *f*
consequent ['kɑntsəkwənt, -ˌkwɛnt] *adj* : consiguiente
consequential [ˌkɑntsə'kwɛntʃəl] *adj* **1** CONSEQUENT : consiguiente **2** IMPORTANT : importante, trascendente, trascendental
consequently ['kɑntsəkwəntli, -ˌkwɛnt-] *adv* : por consiguiente, por ende, por lo tanto
conservation [ˌkɑntsər'veɪʃən] *n* : conservación *f,* protección *f*
conservationist [ˌkɑntsər'veɪʃənɪst] *n* : conservacionista *mf*
conservatism [kən'sərvəˌtɪzəm] *n* : conservadurismo *m*
conservative¹ [kən'sərvət̬iv] *adj* **1** : conservador **2** CAUTIOUS : moderado, cauteloso <a conservative estimate : un cálculo moderado>
conservative² *n* : conservador *m,* -dora *f*
conservatory [kən'sərvəˌtori] *n, pl* **-ries** : conservatorio *m*
conserve¹ [kən'sərv] *vt* **-served; -serving** : conservar, preservar
conserve² ['kɑnˌsərv] *n* PRESERVES : confitura *f*
consider [kən'sɪdər] *vt* **1** CONTEMPLATE : considerar, pensar en <we'd considered attending : habíamos pensado en asistir> **2** : considerar, tener en cuenta <consider the consequences : considera las consecuencias> **3** JUDGE, REGARD : considerar, estimar
considerable [kən'sɪdərəbəl] *adj* : considerable — **considerably** [-bli] *adv*
considerate [kən'sɪdərət] *adj* : considerado, atento
consideration [kənˌsɪdə'reɪʃən] *n* : consideración *f* <to take into consideration : tener en cuenta>
considering [kən'sɪdərɪŋ] *prep* : teniendo en cuenta, visto
consign [kən'saɪn] *vt* **1** COMMIT, ENTRUST : confiar, encomendar **2** TRANSFER : consignar, transferir **3** SEND : consignar, enviar (mercancía)
consignment [kən'saɪnmənt] *n* **1** : envío *m,* remesa *f* **2 on ~** : en consignación
consist [kən'sɪst] *vi* **1** LIE : consistir <success consists in hard work : el éxito consiste en trabajar duro> **2** : constar, componerse <the set consists of 5 pieces : el juego se compone de 5 piezas>
consistency [kən'sɪstəntsi] *n, pl* **-cies 1** : consistencia *f* (de una mezcla o sustancia) **2** COHERENCE : coherencia *f* **3** UNIFORMITY : regularidad *f,* uniformidad *f*
consistent [kən'sɪstənt] *adj* **1** COMPATIBLE : compatible, coincidente <consistent with policy : coincidente con la política> **2** UNIFORM : uniforme, constante, regular — **consistently** [kən'sɪstəntli] *adv*
consolation [ˌkɑntsə'leɪʃən] *n* **1** : consuelo *m* **2 consolation prize** : premio *m* de consolación
console¹ [kən'soːl] *vt* **-soled; -soling** : consolar
console² ['kɑnˌsoːl] *n* : consola *f*
consolidate [kən'sɑləˌdeɪt] *vt* **-dated; -dating** : consolidar, unir
consolidation [kənˌsɑlə'deɪʃən] *n* : consolidación *f*
consommé [ˌkɑntsə'meɪ] *n* : consomé *m*
consonant ['kɑntsənənt] *n* : consonante *m*
consort¹ [kən'sɔrt] *vi* : asociarse, relacionarse, tener trato <to consort with criminals : tener trato con criminales>
consort² ['kɑnˌsɔrt] *n* : consorte *mf*
conspicuous [kən'spɪkjʊəs] *adj* **1** OBVIOUS : visible, evidente **2** STRIKING : llamativo
conspicuously [kən'spɪkjʊəsli] *adv* : de manera llamativa
conspiracy [kən'spɪrəsi] *n, pl* **-cies** : conspiración *f,* complot *m,* confabulación *f*
conspirator [kən'spɪrət̬ər] *n* : conspirador *m,* -dora *f*
conspire [kən'spaɪr] *vi* **-spired; -spiring** : conspirar, confabularse
constable ['kɑntstəbəl, 'kʌntstə-] *n* : agente *mf* de policía (en un pueblo)
constancy ['kɑntstəntsi] *n, pl* **-cies** : constancia *f*
constant¹ ['kɑntstənt] *adj* **1** FAITHFUL : leal, fiel **2** INVARIABLE : constante, invariable **3** CONTINUAL : constante, continuo
constant² *n* : constante *f*
constantly ['kɑntstəntli] *adv* : constantemente, continuamente
constellation [ˌkɑntstə'leɪʃən] *n* : constelación *f*
consternation [ˌkɑntstər'neɪʃən] *n* : consternación *f*
constipate ['kɑntstəˌpeɪt] *vt* **-pated; -pating** : estreñir
constipation ['kɑntstə'peɪʃən] *n* : estreñimiento *m,* constipación *f* (de vientre)

constituency [kən'stɪtʃʊəntsi] *n, pl* **-cies 1 :** distrito *m* electoral **2 :** residentes *mpl* de un distrito electoral

constituent[1] [kən'stɪtʃʊənt] *adj* **1** COMPONENT **:** constituyente, componente **2 :** constituyente, constitutivo <a constituent assembly **:** una asamblea constituyente>

constituent[2] *n* **1** COMPONENT **:** componente *m* **2** ELECTOR, VOTER **:** elector *m,* -tora *f;* votante *mf*

constitute ['kɑntstə,tu:t, -,tju:t] *vt* **-tuted; -tuting 1** ESTABLISH **:** constituir, establecer **2** COMPOSE, FORM **:** constituir, componer

constitution [,kɑntstə'tu:ʃən, -'tju:-] *n* **:** constitución *f*

constitutional [,kɑntstə'tu:ʃənəl, -'tju:-] *adj* **:** constitucional

constitutionality [,kɑntstə,tu:ʃə 'næləti, -,tju:-] *n* **:** constitucionalidad *f*

constrain [kən'streɪn] *vt* **1** COMPEL **:** constreñir, obligar **2** CONFINE **:** constreñir, limitar, restringir **3** RESTRAIN **:** contener, refrenar

constraint [kən'streɪnt] *n* **:** restricción *f,* limitación *f*

constrict [kən'strɪkt] *vt* **:** estrechar, apretar, comprimir

constriction [kən'strɪkʃən] *n* **:** estrechamiento *m,* compresión *f*

construct [kən'strʌkt] *vt* **:** construir

construction [kən'strʌkʃən] *n* **:** construcción *f*

constructive [kən'strʌktɪv] *adj* **:** constructivo

construe [kən'stru:] *vt* **-strued; -struing :** interpretar

consul ['kɑntsəl] *n* **:** cónsul *mf*

consular ['kɑntsələr] *adj* **:** consular

consulate ['kɑntsələt] *n* **:** consulado *m*

consult [kən'sʌlt] *vt* **:** consultar — *vi* **to consult with :** consultar con, solicitar la opinión de

consultant [kən'sʌltənt] *n* **:** consultor *m,* -tora *f;* asesor *m,* -sora *f*

consultation [,kɑntsəl'teɪʃən] *n* **:** consulta *f*

consumable [kən'su:məbəl] *adj* **:** consumible

consume [kən'su:m] *vt* **-sumed; -suming :** consumir, usar, gastar

consumer [kən'su:mər] *n* **:** consumidor *m,* -dora *f*

consummate[1] ['kɑntsə,meɪt] *vt* **-mated; -mating :** consumar

consummate[2] [kən'sʌmət, 'kɑntsəmət] *adj* **:** consumado, perfecto

consummation [,kɑntsə'meɪʃən] *n* **:** consumación *f*

consumption [kən'sʌmpʃən] *n* **1** USE **:** consumo *m,* uso *m* <consumption of electricity **:** consumo de electricidad> **2** TUBERCULOSIS **:** tisis *f,* consunción *f*

contact[1] ['kɑn,tækt, kən'-] *vt* **:** ponerse en contacto con, contactar (con)

contact[2] ['kɑn,tækt] *n* **1** TOUCHING **:** contacto *m,* tocamiento *m* <to come into contact with **:** entrar en contacto con> **2** TOUCH **:** contacto *m,* comunicación *f* <to lose contact with **:** perder contacto con> **3** CONNECTION **:** contacto *m* (en negocios) **4 → contact lens**

contact lens ['kɑn,tækt'lɛnz] *n* **:** lente *mf* de contacto, pupilente *m Mex*

contagion [kən'teɪdʒən] *n* **:** contagio *m*

contagious [kən'teɪdʒəs] *adj* **:** contagioso

contain [kən'teɪn] *vt* **1 :** contener **2 to contain oneself :** contenerse

container [kən'teɪnər] *n* **:** recipiente *m,* envase *m*

contaminate [kən'tæmə,neɪt] *vt* **-nated; -nating :** contaminar

contamination [kən,tæmə'neɪʃən] *n* **:** contaminación *f*

contemplate ['kɑntəm,pleɪt] *v* **-plated; -plating** *vt* **1** VIEW **:** contemplar **2** PONDER **:** contemplar, considerar **3** CONSIDER, PROPOSE **:** proponerse, proyectar, pensar en <to contemplate a trip **:** pensar en viajar> — *vi* MEDITATE **:** meditar

contemplation [,kɑntəm'pleɪʃən] *n* **:** contemplación *f*

contemplative [kən'tɛmplətiv, 'kɑntəm,pleɪtɪv] *adj* **:** contemplativo

contemporaneous [kən,tɛmpə'reɪniəs] **→ contemporary**[1]

contemporary[1] [kən'tɛmpə,rɛri] *adj* **:** contemporáneo

contemporary[2] *n, pl* **-raries :** contemporáneo *m,* -nea *f*

contempt [kən'tɛmpt] *n* **1** DISDAIN **:** desprecio *m,* desdén *m* <to hold in contempt **:** despreciar> **2 :** desacato *m* (ante un tribunal)

contemptible [kən'tɛmptəbəl] *adj* **:** despreciable, vil

contemptuous [kən'tɛmptʃʊəs] *adj* **:** despectivo, despreciativo, desdeñoso

contemptuously [kən'tɛmptʃʊəsli] *adv* **:** despectivamente, con desprecio

contend [kən'tɛnd] *vi* **1** STRUGGLE **:** luchar, lidiar, contender <to contend with a problem **:** lidiar con un problema> **2** COMPETE **:** competir <to contend for a position **:** competir por un puesto> — *vt* **1** ARGUE, MAINTAIN **:** argüir, sostener, afirmar <he contended that he was right **:** afirmó que tenía razón> **2** CONTEST **:** protestar contra (una decisión, etc.), disputar

contender [kən'tɛndər] *n* **:** contendiente *mf;* aspirante *mf;* competidor *m,* -dora *f*

content[1] [kən'tɛnt] *vt* SATISFY **:** contentar, satisfacer

content[2] *adj* **:** conforme, contento, satisfecho

content[3] *n* CONTENTMENT **:** contento *m,* satisfacción *f* <to one's heart's content **:** hasta quedar satisfecho, a más no poder>

content[4] [ˈkɑnˌtɛnt] *n* **1** MEANING : contenido *m*, significado *m* **2** PROPORTION : contenido *m*, proporción *f* <fat content : contenido de grasa> **3 contents** *npl* : contenido *m*, sumario *m* (de un libro) <table of contents : índice de materias>

contented [kənˈtɛntəd] *adj* : conforme, satisfecho <a contented smile : una sonrisa de satisfacción>

contentedly [kənˈtɛntədli] *adv* : con satisfacción

contention [kənˈtɛntʃən] *n* **1** DISPUTE : disputa *f*, discusión *f* **2** COMPETITION : competencia *f*, contienda *f* **3** OPINION : argumento *m*, opinión *f*

contentious [kənˈtɛntʃəs] *adj* : disputador, pugnaz, combativo

contentment [kənˈtɛntmənt] *n* : satisfacción *f*, contento *m*

contest[1] [kənˈtɛst] *vt* : disputar, cuestionar, impugnar <to contest a will : impugnar un testamento>

contest[2] [ˈkɑnˌtɛst] *n* **1** STRUGGLE : lucha *f*, contienda *f* **2** GAME : concurso *m*, competencia *f*

contestable [kənˈtɛstəbəl] *adj* : discutible, cuestionable

contestant [kənˈtɛstənt] *n* : concursante *mf*; competidor *m*, -dora *f*

context [ˈkɑnˌtɛkst] *n* : contexto *m*

contiguous [kənˈtɪgjʊəs] *adj* : contiguo

continence [ˈkɑntənənts] *n* : continencia *f*

continent[1] [ˈkɑntənənt] *adj* : continente

continent[2] *n* : continente *m* — **continental** [ˌkɑntənˈɛntəl] *adj*

contingency [kənˈtɪndʒəntsi] *n, pl* **-cies** : contingencia *f*, eventualidad *f*

contingent[1] [kənˈtɪndʒənt] *adj* **1** POSSIBLE : contingente, eventual **2** ACCIDENTAL : fortuito, accidental **3 to be contingent on** : depender de, estar sujeto a

contingent[2] *n* : contingente *m*

continual [kənˈtɪnjʊəl] *adj* : continuo, constante — **continually** [kənˈtɪnjʊəli, -ˈtɪnjəli] *adv*

continuance [kənˈtɪnjʊənts] *n* **1** CONTINUATION : continuación *f* **2** DURATION : duración *f* **3** : aplazamiento *m* (de un proceso)

continuation [kənˌtɪnjʊˈeɪʃən] *n* : continuación *f*, prolongación *f*

continue [kənˈtɪnjuː] *v* **-tinued; -tinuing** *vi* **1** CARRY ON : continuar, seguir, proseguir <please continue : continúe, por favor> **2** ENDURE, LAST : continuar, prolongarse, durar **3** RESUME : continuar, reanudarse — *vt* **1** : continuar, seguir <she continued writing : continuó escribiendo> **2** RESUME : continuar, reanudar **3** EXTEND, PROLONG : continuar, prolongar

continuity [ˌkɑntənˈuːəti, -ˈjuː-] *n, pl* **-ties** : continuidad *f*

continuous [kənˈtɪnjʊəs] *adj* : continuo — **continuously** *adv*

contort [kənˈtɔrt] *vt* : torcer, retorcer, contraer (el rostro) — *vi* : contraerse, demudarse

contortion [kənˈtɔrʃən] *n* : contorsión *f*

contour [ˈkɑnˌtʊr] *n* **1** OUTLINE : contorno *m* **2 contours** *npl* SHAPE : forma *f*, curvas *fpl* **3 contour map** : mapa *m* topográfico

contraband [ˈkɑntrəˌbænd] *n* : contrabando *m*

contraception [ˌkɑntrəˈsɛpʃən] *n* : anticoncepción *f*, contracepción *f*

contraceptive[1] [ˌkɑntrəˈsɛptɪv] *adj* : anticonceptivo, contraceptivo

contraceptive[2] *n* : anticonceptivo *m*, contraceptivo *m*

contract[1] [kənˈtrækt, 1 *usu* ˈkɑnˌtrækt] *vt* **1** : contratar (servicios profesionales) **2** : contraer (una enfermedad, una deuda) **3** TIGHTEN : contraer (un músculo) **4** SHORTEN : contraer (una palabra) — *vi* : contraerse, reducirse

contract[2] [ˈkɑnˌtrækt] *n* : contrato *m*

contraction [kənˈtrækʃən] *n* : contracción *f*

contractor [ˈkɑnˌtræktər, kənˈtræk-] *n* : contratista *mf*

contractual [kənˈtræktʃʊəl] *adj* : contractual — **contractually** *adv*

contradict [ˌkɑntrəˈdɪkt] *vt* : contradecir, desmentir

contradiction [ˌkɑntrəˈdɪkʃən] *n* : contradicción *f*

contradictory [ˌkɑntrəˈdɪktəri] *adj* : contradictorio

contralto [kənˈtrælˌtoː] *n, pl* **-tos** : contralto *m* (voz), contralto *mf* (vocalista)

contraption [kənˈtræpʃən] *n* DEVICE : aparato *m*, artefacto *m*

contrary[1] [ˈkɑnˌtrɛri, *2 often* kənˈtrɛri] *adj* **1** OPPOSITE : contrario, opuesto **2** BALKY, STUBBORN : terco, testarudo **3 contrary to** : al contrario de, en contra de <contrary to the facts : en contra de los hechos>

contrary[2] [ˈkɑnˌtrɛri] *n, pl* **-traries 1** OPPOSITE : lo contrario, lo opuesto **2 on the contrary** : al contrario, todo lo contrario

contrast[1] [kənˈtræst] *vi* DIFFER : contrastar, diferir — *vt* COMPARE : contrastar, comparar

contrast[2] [ˈkɑnˌtræst] *n* : contraste *m*

contravene [ˌkɑntrəˈviːn] *vt* **-vened; -vening** : contravenir, infringir

contribute [kənˈtrɪbjət] *v* **-uted; -uting** *vt* : contribuir, aportar (dinero, bienes, etc.) — *vi* : contribuir

contribution [ˌkɑntrəˈbjuːʃən] *n* : contribución *f*

contributor [kənˈtrɪbjətər] *n* : contribuidor *m*, -dora *f*; colaborador *m*, -dora *f* (en periodismo)

contrite [ˈkɑnˌtraɪt, kənˈtraɪt] *adj* REPENTANT : contrito, arrepentido
contrition [kənˈtrɪʃən] *n* : contrición *f,* arrepentimiento *m*
contrivance [kənˈtraɪvənts] *n* **1** DEVICE : aparato *m,* artefacto *m* **2** SCHEME : artimaña *f,* treta *f,* ardid *m*
contrive [kənˈtraɪv] *vt* **-trived; -triving 1** DEVISE : idear, ingeniar, maquinar **2** MANAGE : lograr, ingeniárselas para <she contrived a way out of the mess : se las ingenió para salir del enredo>
control[1] [kənˈtroːl] *vt* **-trolled; -trolling** : controlar, dominar
control[2] *n* **1** : control *m,* dominio *m,* mando *m* <to be under control : estar bajo control> **2** RESTRAINT : control *m,* limitación *f* <birth control : control natal> **3** : control *m,* dispositivo *m* de mando <remote control : control remoto>
controllable [kənˈtroːləbəl] *adj* : controlable
controller [kənˈtroːlər, ˈkɑnˌ-] *n* **1** → **comptroller 2** : controlador *m,* -dora *f* <air traffic controller : controlador aéreo>
controversial [ˌkɑntrəˈvərʃəl, -siəl] *adj* : controvertido <a controversial decision : una decisión controvertida>
controversy [ˈkɑntrəˌvərsi] *n, pl* **-sies** : controversia *f*
controvert [ˈkɑntrəˌvərt, ˌkɑntrəˈ-] *vt* : controvertir, contradecir
contusion [kənˈtuːʒən, -tjuː-] *n* BRUISE : contusión *f,* moretón *m*
conundrum [kəˈnʌndrəm] *n* RIDDLE : acertijo *m,* adivinanza *f*
convalesce [ˌkɑnvəˈlɛs] *vi* **-lesced; -lescing** : convalecer
convalescence [ˌkɑnvəˈlɛsənts] *n* : convalecencia *f*
convalescent[1] [ˌkɑnvəˈlɛsənt] *adj* : convaleciente
convalescent[2] *n* : convaleciente *mf*
convection [kənˈvɛkʃən] *n* : convección *f*
convene [kənˈviːn] *v* **-vened; -vening** *vt* : convocar — *vi* : reunirse
convenience [kənˈviːnjənts] *n* **1** : conveniencia *f* <at your convenience : cuando le resulte conveniente> **2** AMENITY : comodidad *f* <modern conveniences : comodidades modernas>
convenient [kənˈviːnjənt] *adj* : conveniente, cómodo — **conveniently** *adv*
convent [ˈkɑnvənt, -ˌvɛnt] *n* : convento *m*
convention [kənˈvɛntʃən] *n* **1** PACT : convención *f,* convenio *m,* pacto *m* <the Geneva Convention : la Convención de Ginebra> **2** MEETING : convención *f,* congreso *m* **3** CUSTOM : convención *f,* convencionalismo *m*
conventional [kənˈvɛntʃənəl] *adj* : convencional — **conventionally** *adv*
converge [kənˈvərdʒ] *vi* **-verged; -verging** : converger, convergir
conversant [kənˈvərsənt] *adj* **conversant with** : versado con, experto en
conversation [ˌkɑnvərˈseɪʃən] *n* : conversación *f*
conversational [ˌkɑnvərˈseɪʃənəl] *adj* : familiar <a conversational style : un estilo familiar>
converse[1] [kənˈvərs] *vi* **-versed; -versing** : conversar
converse[2] [kənˈvərs, ˈkɑnˌvɛrs] *adj* : contrario, opuesto, inverso
conversely [kənˈvərsli, ˈkɑnˌvɛrs-] *adv* : a la inversa
conversion [kənˈvərʒən] *n* **1** CHANGE : conversión *f,* transformación *f,* cambio *m* **2** : conversión *f* (a una religión)
convert[1] [kənˈvərt] *vt* **1** : convertir (a una religión o un partido) **2** CHANGE : convertir, cambiar — *vi* : convertirse
convert[2] [ˈkɑnˌvərt] *n* : converso *m,* -sa *f*
converter *or* **convertor** [kənˈvərtər] *n* : convertidor *m*
convertible[1] [kənˈvərtəbəl] *adj* : convertible
convertible[2] *n* : convertible *m,* descapotable *m*
convex [kɑnˈvɛks, ˈkɑnˌ-, kənˈ-] *adj* : convexo
convey [kənˈveɪ] *vt* **1** TRANSPORT : transportar, conducir **2** TRANSMIT : transmitir, comunicar, expresar (noticias, ideas, etc.)
conveyance [kənˈveɪənts] *n* **1** TRANSPORT : transporte *m,* transportación *f* **2** COMMUNICATION : transmisión *f,* comunicación *f* **3** TRANSFER : transferencia *f,* traspaso *m* (de una propiedad)
conveyor [kənˈveɪər] *n* : transportador *m,* -dora *f* <conveyor belt : cinta transportadora>
convict[1] [kənˈvɪkt] *vt* : declarar culpable
convict[2] [ˈkɑnˌvɪkt] *n* : preso *m,* -sa *f;* presidiario *m,* -ria *f;* recluso *m,* -sa *f*
conviction [kənˈvɪkʃən] *n* **1** : condena *f* (de un acusado) **2** BELIEF : convicción *f,* creencia *f*
convince [kənˈvɪnts] *vt* **-vinced; -vincing** : convencer
convincing [kənˈvɪntsɪŋ] *adj* : convincente, persuasivo
convincingly [kənˈvɪntsɪŋli] *adv* : de forma convincente
convivial [kənˈvɪvjəl, -ˈvɪviəl] *adj* : jovial, festivo, alegre
conviviality [kənˌvɪviˈæləti] *n, pl* **-ties** : jovialidad *f*
convoke [kənˈvoːk] *vt* **-voked; -voking** : convocar
convoluted [ˈkɑnvəˌluːtəd] *adj* : intrincado, complicado
convoy [ˈkɑnˌvɔɪ] *n* : convoy *m*
convulse [kənˈvʌls] *v* **-vulsed; -vulsing** *vt* : convulsionar <convulsed with laughter : muerto de risa> — *vi* : sufrir convulsiones

convulsion [kən'vʌlʃən] *n* : convulsión *f*

convulsive [kən'vʌlsɪv] *adj* : convulsivo — **convulsively** *adv*

coo[1] ['ku:] *vi* : arrullar

coo[2] *n* : arrullo *m* (de una paloma)

cook[1] ['kʊk] *vi* : cocinar — *vt* **1** : preparar (comida) **2 to cook up** CONCOCT : inventar, tramar

cook[2] *n* : cocinero *m*, -ra *f*

cookbook ['kʊk,bʊk] *n* : libro *m* de cocina

cookery ['kʊkəri] *n, pl* **-eries** : cocina *f*

cookie *or* **cooky** ['kʊki] *n, pl* **-ies** : galleta *f* (dulce)

cookout ['kʊk,aʊt] *n* : comida *f* al aire libre

cool[1] ['ku:l] *vt* : refrescar, enfriar — *vi* **1** : refrescarse, enfriarse <the pie is cooling : el pastel se está enfriando> **2** : calmarse, tranquilizarse <his anger cooled : su ira se calmó>

cool[2] *adj* **1** : fresco, frío <cool weather : tiempo fresco> **2** CALM : tranquilo, sereno **3** ALOOF : frío, distante

cool[3] *n* **1** : fresco *m* <the cool of the evening : el fresco de la tarde> **2** COMPOSURE : calma *f*, serenidad *f*

coolant ['ku:lənt] *n* : refrigerante *m*

cooler ['ku:lər] *n* : nevera *f* portátil

coolie ['ku:li] *n* : culi *m*

coolly ['ku:lli] *adv* **1** CALMLY : con calma, tranquilamente **2** COLDLY : fríamente, con frialdad

coolness ['ku:lnəs] *n* **1** : frescura *f*, frescor *m* <the coolness of the evening : el frescor de la noche> **2** CALMNESS : tranquilidad *f*, serenidad *f* **3** COLDNESS, INDIFFERENCE : frialdad *f*, indiferencia

coop[1] ['ku:p, 'kʊp] *vt or* **to coop up** : encerrar <cooped up in the house : encerrado en la casa>

coop[2] *n* : gallinero *m*

co–op ['ko:,ɑp] → **cooperative**[2]

cooperate [ko'ɑpə,reɪt] *vi* **-ated; -ating** : cooperar, colaborar

cooperation [ko,ɑpə'reɪʃən] *n* : cooperación *f*, colaboración *f*

cooperative[1] [ko'ɑpərətɪv, -'ɑpə,reɪtɪv] *adj* : cooperativo

cooperative[2] [ko'ɑpərətɪv] *n* : cooperativa *f*

co–opt [ko'ɑpt] *vt* **1** : nombrar como miembro, cooptar **2** APPROPRIATE : apropiarse de

coordinate[1] [ko'ɔrdən,eɪt] *v* **-nated; -nating** *vt* : coordinar — *vi* : coordinarse, combinar, acordar

coordinate[2] [ko'ɔrdənət] *adj* **1** COORDINATED : coordinado **2** EQUAL : igual, semejante

coordinate[3] [ko'ɔrdənət] *n* : coordenada *f*

coordination [ko,ɔrdən'eɪʃən] *n* : coordinación *f*

coordinator [ko'ɔrdən,eɪtər] *n* : coordinador *m*, -dora *f*

cop ['kɑp] → **police officer**

cope ['ko:p] *vi* **coped; coping 1** : arreglárselas **2 to cope with** : hacer frente a, poder con <I can't cope with all this! : ¡no puedo con todo esto!>

copier ['kɑpiər] *n* : copiadora *f*, fotocopiadora *f*

copilot ['ko:,paɪlət] *n* : copiloto *m*

copious ['ko:piəs] *adj* : copioso, abundante — **copiously** *adv*

copiousness ['ko:piəsnəs] *n* : abundancia *f*

copper ['kɑpər] *n* : cobre *m*

coppery ['kɑpəri] *adj* : cobrizo

copra ['ko:prə, 'kɑ-] *n* : copra *f*

copse ['kɑps] *n* THICKET : soto *m*, matorral *m*

copulate ['kɑpjə,leɪt] *vi* **-lated; -lating** : copular

copulation [,kɑpjə'leɪʃən] *n* : cópula *f*, relaciones *fpl* sexuales

copy[1] ['kɑpi] *vt* **copied; copying 1** DUPLICATE : hacer una copia de, duplicar, reproducir **2** IMITATE : copiar, imitar

copy[2] *n, pl* **copies 1** : copia *f*, duplicado *m* (de un documento), reproducción *f* (de una obra de arte) **2** : ejemplar *m* (de un libro), número *m* (de una revista) **3** TEXT : manuscrito *m*, texto *m*

copyright[1] ['kɑpi,raɪt] *vt* : registrar los derechos de

copyright[2] *n* : derechos *mpl* de autor

coral[1] ['kɔrəl] *adj* : de coral <a coral reef : un arrecife de coral>

coral[2] *n* : coral *m*

coral snake *n* : serpiente *f* de coral

cord ['kɔrd] *n* **1** ROPE, STRING : cuerda *f*, cordón *m*, cordel *m* **2** : cuerda *f*, cordón *m*, médula *f* (en la anatomía) <vocal cords : cuerdas vocales> **3** : cuerda *f* <a cord of firewood : una cuerda de leña> **4** *or* **electric cord** : cable *m* eléctrico

cordial[1] ['kɔrdʒəl] *adj* : cordial — **cordially** *adv*

cordial[2] *n* : cordial *m*

cordiality [,kɔrdʒi'æləti] *n* : cordialidad *f*

cordon[1] ['kɔrdən] *vt* **to cordon off** : acordonar

cordon[2] *n* : cordón *m*

corduroy ['kɔrdə,rɔɪ] *n* **1** : pana *f* **2 corduroys** *npl* : pantalones *mpl* de pana

core[1] ['kor] *vt* **cored; coring** : quitar el corazón a (una fruta)

core[2] *n* **1** : corazón *m*, centro *m* (de algunas frutas) **2** CENTER : núcleo *m*, centro *m* **3** ESSENCE : núcleo *m*, meollo *m* <to the core : hasta la médula>

cork[1] ['kɔrk] *vt* : ponerle un corcho a

cork[2] *n* : corcho *m*

corkscrew ['kɔrk,skru:] *n* : tirabuzón *m*, sacacorchos *m*

cormorant ['kɔrmərənt, -,rænt] *n* : cormorán *m*

corn[1] ['kɔrn] *vt* : conservar en salmuera <corned beef : carne en conserva>

corn[2] *n* **1** GRAIN : grano *m* **2** : maíz *m,* elote *m Mex* <corn tortillas : tortillas de maíz> **3** : callo *m* <corn plaster : emplasto para callos>

corncob [ˈkɔrn,kɑb] *n* : mazorca *f* (de maíz), choclo *m,* elote *m CA, Mex*

cornea [ˈkɔrniə] *n* : córnea *f*

corner[1] [ˈkɔrnər] *vt* **1** TRAP : acorralar, arrinconar **2** MONOPOLIZE : monopolizar, acaparar (un mercado) — *vi* : tomar una curva, doblar una esquina (en un automóvil)

corner[2] *n* **1** ANGLE : rincón *m,* esquina *f,* ángulo *m* <the corner of a room : el rincón de una sala> <all corners of the world : todos los rincones del mundo> <to cut corners : atajar, economizar esfuerzos> **2** INTERSECTION : esquina *f* **3** IMPASSE, PREDICAMENT : aprieto *m,* impasse *m* <to be backed into a corner : estar acorralado>

cornerstone [ˈkɔrnər,sto:n] *n* : piedra *f* angular

cornet [kɔrˈnɛt] *n* : corneta *f*

cornice [ˈkɔrnɪs] *n* : cornisa *f*

cornmeal [ˈkɔrn,mi:l] *n* : harina *f* de maíz

cornstalk [ˈkɔrn,stɔk] *n* : tallo *m* del maíz

cornstarch [ˈkɔrn,stɑrtʃ] *n* : maicena *f,* almidón *m* de maíz

cornucopia [,kɔrnəˈko:piə, -njə-] *n* : cornucopia *f*

corolla [kəˈrɑlə] *n* : corola *f*

corollary [ˈkɔrə,lɛri] *n, pl* **-laries** : corolario *m*

corona [kəˈro:nə] *n* : corona *f* (del sol)

coronary[1] [ˈkɔrə,nɛri] *adj* : coronario

coronary[2] *n, pl* **-naries 1** : trombosis *f* coronaria **2** HEART ATTACK : infarto *m,* ataque *m* al corazón

coronation [,kɔrəˈneɪʃən] *n* : coronación *f*

coroner [ˈkɔrənər] *n* : médico *m* forense

corporal[1] [ˈkɔrpərəl] *adj* : corporal <corporal punishment : castigos corporales>

corporal[2] *n* : cabo *m*

corporate [ˈkɔrpərət] *adj* : corporativo, empresarial

corporation [,kɔrpəˈreɪʃən] *n* : sociedad *f* anónima, corporación *f,* empresa *f*

corporeal [kɔrˈporiəl] *adj* **1** PHYSICAL : corpóreo **2** MATERIAL : material, tangible — **corporeally** *adv*

corps [ˈkor] *n, pl* **corps** [ˈkorz] : cuerpo *m* <medical corps : cuerpo médico> <diplomatic corps : cuerpo diplomático>

corpse [ˈkɔrps] *n* : cadáver *m*

corpulence [ˈkɔrpjələn*t*s] *n* : obesidad *f,* gordura *f*

corpulent [ˈkɔrpjələnt] *adj* : obeso, gordo

corpuscle [ˈkɔr,pʌsəl] *n* : corpúsculo *m,* glóbulo *m* (sanguíneo)

corral[1] [kəˈræl] *vt* **-ralled; -ralling** : acorralar, encorralar (ganado)

corral[2] *n* : corral *m*

correct[1] [kəˈrɛkt] *vt* **1** RECTIFY : corregir, rectificar **2** REPRIMAND : corregir, reprender

correct[2] *adj* **1** ACCURATE, RIGHT : correcto, exacto <to be correct : estar en lo cierto> **2** PROPER : correcto, apropiado

correction [kəˈrɛkʃən] *n* : corrección *f*

corrective [kəˈrɛktɪv] *adj* : correctivo

correctly [kəˈrɛktli] *adv* : correctamente

correlate [ˈkɔrə,leɪt] *vt* **-lated; -lating** : relacionar, poner en correlación

correlation [,kɔrəˈleɪʃən] *n* : correlación *f*

correspond [,kɔrəˈspɑnd] *vi* **1** MATCH : corresponder, concordar, coincidir **2** WRITE : corresponderse, escribirse

correspondence [,kɔrəˈspɑndən*t*s] *n* : correspondencia *f*

correspondent [,kɔrəˈspɑndənt] *n* : corresponsal *mf*

correspondingly [,kɔrəˈspɑndɪŋli] *adv* : en consecuencia, de la misma manera

corridor [ˈkɔrədər, -,dɔr] *n* : corredor *m,* pasillo *m*

corroborate [kəˈrɑbə,reɪt] *vt* **-rated; -rating** : corroborar

corroboration [kə,rɑbəˈreɪʃən] *n* : corroboración *f*

corrode [kəˈro:d] *v* **-roded; -roding** *vt* : corroer — *vi* : corroerse

corrosion [kəˈro:ʒən] *n* : corrosión *f*

corrosive [kəˈro:sɪv] *adj* : corrosivo

corrugate [ˈkɔrə,geɪt] *vt* **-gated; -gating** : ondular, acanalar, corrugar

corrugated [ˈkɔrə,geɪtəd] *adj* : ondulado, acanalado <corrugated cardboard : cartón ondulado>

corrupt[1] [kəˈrʌpt] *vt* **1** PERVERT : corromper, pervertir, degradar (información) **2** BRIBE : sobornar

corrupt[2] *adj* : corrupto, corrompido

corruptible [kəˈrʌptəbəl] *adj* : corruptible

corruption [kəˈrʌpʃən] *n* : corrupción *f*

corsage [kɔrˈsɑʒ, -ˈsɑdʒ] *n* : ramillete *m* que se lleva como adorno

corset [ˈkɔrsət] *n* : corsé *m*

cortex [ˈkɔr,tɛks] *n, pl* **-tices** [ˈkɔrtə,si:z] *or* **-texes** : corteza *f* <cerebral cortex : corteza cerebral>

cortisone [ˈkɔrtə,so:n, -zo:n] *n* : cortisona *f*

cosmetic[1] [kɑzˈmɛtɪk] *adj* : cosmético

cosmetic[2] *n* : cosmético *m*

cosmic [ˈkɑzmɪk] *adj* **1** : cósmico <cosmic ray : rayo cósmico> **2** VAST : grandioso, inmenso, vasto

cosmonaut [ˈkɑzmə,nɔt] *n* : cosmonauta *mf*

cosmopolitan[1] [,kɑzməˈpɑlətən] *adj* : cosmopolita

cosmopolitan[2] *n* : cosmopolita *mf*

cosmos [ˈkɑzməs, -ˌmoːs, -ˌmɑs] *n* : cosmos *m,* universo *m*

cost[1] [ˈkɔst] *v* **cost; costing** *vt* : costar <how much does it cost? : ¿cuánto cuesta?, ¿cuánto vale?> — *vi* : costar <these cost more : éstos cuestan más>

cost[2] *n* : costo *m,* precio *m,* coste *m* <cost of living : costo de vida> <victory at all costs : victoria a toda costa>

Costa Rican[1] [ˌkɔstəˈriːkən] *adj* : costarricense

Costa Rican[2] *n* : costarricense *mf*

costly [ˈkɔstli] *adj* : costoso, caro

costume [ˈkɑsˌtuːm, -ˌtjuːm] *n* **1** : traje *m* <national costume : traje típico> **2** : disfraz *m* <costume party : fiesta de disfraces> **3** OUTFIT : vestimenta *f,* traje *m,* conjunto *m*

cosy [ˈkoːzi] → **cozy**

cot [ˈkɑt] *n* : catre *m*

coterie [ˈkoːţəˌri, ˌkoːţəˈ-] *n* : tertulia *f,* círculo *m* (social)

cottage [ˈkɑţɪdʒ] *n* : casita *f* (de campo)

cottage cheese *n* : requesón *m*

cotton [ˈkɑtən] *n* : algodón *m*

cottonmouth [ˈkɑtənˌmaʊθ] → **moccasin**

cottonseed [ˈkɑtənˌsiːd] *n* : semilla *f* de algodón

cotton swab → **swab**

cottontail [ˈkɑtənˌteɪl] *n* : conejo *m* de cola blanca

couch[1] [ˈkaʊtʃ] *vt* : expresar, formular <couched in strong language : expresado en lenguaje enérgico>

couch[2] *n* SOFA : sofá *m*

cougar [ˈkuːgər] *n* : puma *m*

cough[1] [ˈkɔf] *vi* : toser

cough[2] *n* : tos *f*

could [ˈkʊd] → **can**

council [ˈkaʊntsəl] *n* **1** : concejo *m* <city council : concejo municipal, ayuntamiento> **2** MEETING : concejo *m,* junta *f* **3** BOARD : consejo *m* **4** : concilio *m* (eclesiástico)

councillor *or* **councilor** [ˈkaʊntsələr] *n* : concejal *m,* -jala *f*

councilman [ˈkaʊntsəlmən] *n, pl* **-men** [-mən, -ˌmɛn] : concejal *m*

councilwoman [ˈkaʊntsəlˌwʊmən] *n, pl* **-women** [-ˌwɪmən] : concejala *f*

counsel[1] [ˈkaʊntsəl] *v* **-seled** *or* **-selled; -seling** *or* **-selling** *vt* ADVISE : aconsejar, asesorar, recomendar — *vi* CONSULT : consultar

counsel[2] *n* **1** ADVICE : consejo *m,* recomendación *f* **2** CONSULTATION : consulta *f* **3** **counsel** *ns & pl* LAWYER : abogado *m,* -da *f*

counselor *or* **counsellor** [ˈkaʊntsələr] *n* : consejero *m,* -ra *f;* consultor *m,* -tora *f;* asesor *m,* -sora *f*

count[1] [ˈkaʊnt] *vt* : contar, enumerar — *vi* **1** : contar <to count out loud : contar en voz alta> **2** MATTER : contar, valer, importar <that's what counts : eso es lo que cuenta> **3** **to count on** : contar con

count[2] *n* **1** COMPUTATION : cómputo *m,* recuento *m,* cuenta *f* <to lose count : perder la cuenta> **2** CHARGE : cargo *m* <two counts of robbery : dos cargos de robo> **3** : conde *m* (noble)

countable [ˈkaʊntəbəl] *adj* : numerable

countdown [ˈkaʊntˌdaʊn] *n* : cuenta *f* atrás

countenance[1] [ˈkaʊntənənts] *vt* **-nanced; -nancing** : permitir, tolerar

countenance[2] *n* FACE : semblante *m,* rostro *m*

counter[1] [ˈkaʊntər] *vt* **1** → **counteract** **2** OPPOSE : oponerse a, resistir — *vi* RETALIATE : responder, contraatacar

counter[2] *adv* **counter to** : contrario a, en contra de

counter[3] *adj* : contrario, opuesto

counter[4] *n* **1** PIECE : ficha *f* (de un juego) **2** : mostrador *m* (de un negocio), ventanilla *f* (en un banco) **3** : contador *m* (aparato) **4** COUNTERBALANCE : fuerza *f* opuesta, contrapeso *m*

counteract [ˌkaʊntərˈækt] *vt* : contrarrestar

counterattack [ˈkaʊntərəˌtæk] *n* : contraataque *m*

counterbalance[1] [ˌkaʊntərˈbælənts] *vt* **-anced; -ancing** : contrapesar

counterbalance[2] [ˈkaʊntərˌbælənts] *n* : contrapeso *m*

counterclockwise [ˌkaʊntərˈklɑkˌwaɪz] *adv & adj* : en el sentido opuesto al de las manecillas del reloj

counterfeit[1] [ˈkaʊntərˌfɪt] *vt* **1** : falsificar (dinero) **2** PRETEND : fingir, aparentar

counterfeit[2] *adj* : falso, inauténtico

counterfeit[3] *n* : falsificación *f*

counterfeiter [ˈkaʊntərˌfɪţər] *n* : falsificador *m,* -dora *f*

countermand [ˈkaʊntərˌmænd, ˌkaʊntərˈ-] *vt* : contramandar

countermeasure [ˈkaʊntərˌmɛʒər] *n* : contramedida *f*

counterpart [ˈkaʊntərˌpɑrt] *n* : homólogo *m,* contraparte *f Mex*

counterpoint [ˈkaʊntərˌpɔɪnt] *n* : contrapunto *m*

counterproductive [ˌkaʊntərprəˈdʌktɪv] *adj* : contraproducente

counterrevolution [ˌkaʊntərˌrɛvəˈluːʃən] *n* : contrarrevolución *f*

counterrevolutionary[1] [ˌkaʊntərˌrɛvəˈluːʃənˌɛri] *adj* : contrarrevolucionario

counterrevolutionary[2] *n, pl* **-ries** : contrarrevolucionario *m,* -ria *f*

countersign [ˈkaʊntərˌsaɪn] *n* : contraseña *f*

countess [ˈkaʊntɪs] *n* : condesa *f*

countless [ˈkaʊntləs] *adj* : incontable, innumerable

country[1] [ˈkʌntri] *adj* : campestre, rural

country[2] *n, pl* **-tries** **1** NATION : país *m,* nación *f,* patria *f* <country of origin : país de origen> <love of one's country : amor a la patria> **2** : campo *m*

<they left the city for the country : se fueron de la ciudad al campo>
countryman [ˈkʌntrimən] *n, pl* **-men** [-mən, -ˌmɛn] : compatriota *mf;* paisano *m,* -na *f*
countryside [ˈkʌntriˌsaɪd] *n* : campo *m,* campiña *f*
county [ˈkaʊnti] *n, pl* **-ties** : condado *m*
coup [ˈkuː] *n, pl* **coups** [ˈkuːz] **1** : golpe *m* maestro **2** *or* **coup d'etat** : golpe *m* (de estado), cuartelazo *m*
coupe [ˈkuːp] *n* : cupé *m*
couple[1] [ˈkʌpəl] *vt* **-pled; -pling** : acoplar, enganchar, conectar
couple[2] *n* **1** PAIR : par *m* <a couple of hours : un par de horas, unas dos horas> **2** : pareja *f* <a young couple : una pareja joven>
coupling [ˈkʌplɪŋ] *n* : acoplamiento *m*
coupon [ˈkuːˌpɑn, ˈkjuː-] *n* : cupón *m*
courage [ˈkərɪdʒ] *n* : valor *m,* valentía *f,* coraje *m*
courageous [kəˈreɪdʒəs] *adj* : valiente, valeroso
courier [ˈkʊriər, ˈkəriər] *n* : mensajero *m,* -ra *f*
course[1] [ˈkors] *vi* **coursed; coursing** : correr (a toda velocidad)
course[2] *n* **1** PROGRESS : curso *m,* transcurso *m* <to run its course : seguir su curso> **2** DIRECTION : rumbo *m* (de un avión), derrota *f,* derrotero *m* (de un barco) **3** PATH, WAY : camino *m,* vía *f* <course of action : línea de conducta> **4** : plato *m* (de una cena) <the main course : el plato principal> **5** : curso *m* (académico) **6 of course** : desde luego, por supuesto <yes, of course! : ¡claro que sí!>
court[1] [ˈkort] *vt* WOO : cortejar, galantear
court[2] *n* **1** PALACE : palacio *m* **2** RETINUE : corte *f,* séquito *m* **3** COURTYARD : patio *m* **4** : cancha *f* (de tenis, baloncesto, etc.) **5** TRIBUNAL : corte *f,* tribunal *m* <the Supreme Court : la Corte Suprema>
courteous [ˈkərt̬iəs] *adj* : cortés, atento, educado — **courteously** *adv*
courtesan [ˈkort̬əzən, ˈkər-] *n* : cortesana *f*
courtesy [ˈkərt̬əsi] *n, pl* **-sies** : cortesía *f*
courthouse [ˈkortˌhaʊs] *n* : palacio *m* de justicia, juzgado *m*
courtier [ˈkortiər, ˈkortjər] *n* : cortesano *m,* -na *f*
courtly [ˈkortli] *adj* **-lier; -est** : distinguido, elegante, cortés
court–martial[1] [ˈkortˌmɑrʃəl] *vt* : someter a consejo de guerra
court–martial[2] *n, pl* **courts–martial** [ˈkortsˌmɑrʃəl] : consejo *m* de guerra
court order *n* : mandamiento *m* judicial
courtroom [ˈkortˌruːm] *n* : tribunal *m,* corte *f*
courtship [ˈkortˌʃɪp] *n* : cortejo *m,* noviazgo *m*
courtyard [ˈkortˌjɑrd] *n* : patio *m*
cousin [ˈkʌzən] *n* : primo *m,* -ma *f*
cove [ˈkoːv] *n* : ensenada *f,* cala *f*
covenant [ˈkʌvənənt] *n* : pacto *m,* contrato *m*
cover[1] [ˈkʌvər] *vt* **1** : cubrir, tapar <cover your head : tápate la cabeza> <covered with mud : cubierto de lodo> **2** HIDE, PROTECT : encubrir, proteger **3** TREAT : tratar **4** INSURE : asegurar, cubrir
cover[2] *n* **1** SHELTER : cubierta *f,* abrigo *m,* refugio *m* <to take cover : ponerse a cubierto> <under cover of darkness : al amparo de la oscuridad> **2** LID, TOP : cubierta *f,* tapa *f* **3** : cubierta *f* (de un libro), portada *f* (de una revista) **4 covers** *npl* BEDCLOTHES : ropa *f* de cama, cobijas *fpl,* mantas *fpl*
coverage [ˈkʌvərɪdʒ] *n* : cobertura *f*
coverlet [ˈkʌvərlət] *n* : cobertor *m*
covert[1] [ˈkoːˌvərt, ˈkʌvərt] *adj* : encubierto, secreto <covert operations : operaciones encubiertas>
covert[2] [ˈkʌvərt, ˈkoː-] *n* THICKET : espesura *f,* maleza *f*
cover–up [ˈkʌvərˌʌp] *n* : encubrimiento
covet [ˈkʌvət] *vt* : codiciar
covetous [ˈkʌvət̬əs] *adj* : codicioso
covey [ˈkʌvi] *n, pl* **-eys 1** : bandada *f* pequeña (de codornices, etc.) **2** GROUP : grupo *m*
cow[1] [ˈkaʊ] *vt* : intimidar, acobardar
cow[2] *n* : vaca *f,* hembra *f* (de ciertas especies)
coward [ˈkaʊərd] *n* : cobarde *mf*
cowardice [ˈkaʊərdɪs] *n* : cobardía *f*
cowardly [ˈkaʊərdli] *adj* : cobarde
cowboy [ˈkaʊˌbɔɪ] *n* : vaquero *m,* cowboy *m*
cower [ˈkaʊər] *vi* : encogerse (de miedo), acobardarse
cowgirl [ˈkaʊˌgərl] *n* : vaquera *f*
cowherd [ˈkaʊˌhərd] *n* : vaquero *m,* -ra *f*
cowhide [ˈkaʊˌhaɪd] *n* : cuero *m,* piel *f* de vaca
cowl [ˈkaʊl] *n* : capucha *f* (de un monje)
cowlick [ˈkaʊˌlɪk] *n* : remolino *m*
cowpuncher [ˈkaʊˌpʌntʃər] → **cowboy**
cowslip [ˈkaʊˌslɪp] *n* : prímula *f,* primavera *f*
coxswain [ˈkɑksən, -ˌsweɪn] *n* : timonel *m*
coy [ˈkɔɪ] *adj* **1** SHY : tímido, cohibido **2** COQUETTISH : coqueto
coyote [kaɪˈoːt̬i, ˈkaɪˌoːt] *n, pl* **coyotes** *or* **coyote** : coyote *m*
cozy [ˈkoːzi] *adj* **-zier; -est** : acogedor, cómodo
crab [ˈkræb] *n* : cangrejo *m,* jaiba *f*
crabby [ˈkræbi] *adj* **-bier; -est** : gruñón, malhumorado
crabgrass [ˈkræbˌgræs] *n* : garranchuelo *m*

crack[1] ['kræk] *vi* **1** : chasquear, restallar <the whip cracked : el látigo restalló> **2** SPLIT : rajarse, resquebrajarse, agrietarse **3** : quebrarse (dícese de la voz) — *vt* **1** : restallar, chasquear (un látigo, etc.) **2** SPLIT : rajar, agrietar, resquebrajar **3** BREAK : romper (un huevo), cascar (nueces), forzar (una caja fuerte) **4** SOLVE : resolver, descifrar (un código)

crack[2] *adj* FIRST-RATE : buenísimo, de primera

crack[3] *n* **1** : chasquido *m,* restallido *m,* estallido *m* (de un arma de fuego), crujido *m* (de huesos) <a crack of thunder : un trueno> **2** WISECRACK : chiste *m,* ocurrencia *f,* salida *f* **3** CREVICE : raja *f,* grieta *f,* fisura *f* **4** BLOW : golpe *m* **5** ATTEMPT : intento *m*

crackdown ['kræk,daʊn] *n* : medidas *fpl* enérgicas

crack down *vt* : tomar medidas enérgicas

cracker ['krækər] *n* : galleta *f* (de soda, etc.)

crackle[1] ['krækəl] *vi* **-led; -ling** : crepitar, chisporrotear

crackle[2] *n* : crujido *m,* chisporroteo *m*

crackpot ['kræk,pɑt] *n* : excéntrico *m,* -ca *f;* chiflado *m,* -da *f*

crack–up ['kræk,ʌp] *n* **1** CRASH : choque *m,* estrellamiento *m* **2** BREAKDOWN : crisis *f* nerviosa

crack up *vt* WRECK : estrellar (un vehículo) — *vi* : sufrir una crisis nerviosa

cradle[1] ['kreɪdəl] *vt* **-dled; -dling** : acunar, mecer (a un niño)

cradle[2] *n* : cuna *f*

craft ['kræft] *n* **1** TRADE : oficio *m* <the craft of carpentry : el oficio de carpintero> **2** CRAFTSMANSHIP, SKILL : arte *m,* artesanía *f,* destreza *f* **3** CRAFTINESS : astucia *f,* maña *f* **4** *pl usually* **craft** BOAT : barco *m,* embarcación *f* **5** *pl usually* **craft** AIRCRAFT : avión *m,* aeronave *f*

craftiness ['kræftinəs] *n* : astucia *f,* maña *f*

craftsman ['kræftsmən] *n, pl* **-men** [-mən, -,mɛn] : artesano *m,* -na *f*

craftsmanship ['kræftsmən,ʃɪp] *n* : artesanía *f,* destreza *f*

crafty ['kræfti] *adj* **craftier; -est** : astuto, taimado

crag ['kræg] *n* : peñasco *m*

craggy ['krægi] *adj* **-gier; -est** : peñascoso

cram ['kræm] *v* **crammed; cramming** *vt* **1** JAM : embutir, meter **2** STUFF : atiborrar, abarrotar <crammed with people : atiborrado de gente> — *vi* : estudiar a última hora, memorizar (para un examen)

cramp[1] ['kræmp] *vt* **1** : dar calambre en **2** RESTRICT : limitar, restringir, entorpecer <to cramp someone's style : cortarle el vuelo a alguien> — *vi or* **to cramp up** : acalambrarse

cramp[2] *n* **1** SPASM : calambre *m,* espasmo *m* (de los músculos) **2 cramps** *npl* : retorcijones *mpl* <stomach cramps : retorcijones de estómago>

cranberry ['kræn,bɛri] *n, pl* **-berries** : arándano *m* (rojo y agrio)

crane[1] ['kreɪn] *vi* **craned; craning** : estirar <to crane one's neck : estirar el cuello>

crane[2] *n* **1** : grulla *f* (ave) **2** : grúa *f* (máquina)

cranial ['kreɪniəl] *adj* : craneal, craneano

cranium ['kreɪniəm] *n, pl* **-niums** *or* **-nia** [-niə]: cráneo *m*

crank[1] ['kræŋk] *vt or* **to crank up** : arrancar (con una manivela)

crank[2] *n* **1** : manivela *f,* manubrio *m* **2** ECCENTRIC : excéntrico *m,* -ca *f*

cranky ['kræŋki] *adj* **crankier; -est** : irritable, malhumorado, enojadizo

cranny ['kræni] *n, pl* **-nies** : grieta *f* <every nook and cranny : todos los rincones>

crash[1] ['kræʃ] *vi* **1** SMASH : caerse con estrépito, estrellarse **2** COLLIDE : estrellarse, chocar **3** BOOM, RESOUND : retumbar, resonar — *vt* **1** SMASH : estrellar **2 to crash one's car** : tener un accidente

crash[2] *n* **1** DIN : estrépito *m* **2** COLLISION : choque *m,* colisión *f* <car crash : accidente automovilístico> **3** FAILURE : quiebra *f* (de un negocio), crac *m* (de la bolsa)

crass ['kræs] *adj* : grosero, de mal gusto

crate[1] ['kreɪt] *vt* **crated; crating** : empacar en un cajón

crate[2] *n* : cajón *m* (de madera)

crater ['kreɪtər] *n* : cráter *m*

cravat [krə'væt] *n* : corbata *f*

crave ['kreɪv] *vt* **craved; craving** : ansiar, apetecer, tener muchas ganas de

craven ['kreɪvən] *adj* : cobarde, pusilánime

craving ['kreɪvɪŋ] *n* : ansia *f,* antojo *m,* deseo *m*

crawfish ['krɔ,fɪʃ] → **crayfish**

crawl[1] ['krɔl] *vi* **1** CREEP : arrastrarse, gatear (dícese de un bebé) **2** TEEM : estar plagado

crawl[2] *n* : paso *m* lento

crayfish ['kreɪ,fɪʃ] *n* **1** : ástaco *m* (de agua dulce) **2** : langostino *m* (de mar)

crayon ['kreɪ,ɑn, -ən] *n* : crayón *m*

craze ['kreɪz] *n* : moda *f* pasajera, manía *f*

crazed ['kreɪzd] *adj* : enloquecido

crazily ['kreɪzəli] *adv* : locamente, erráticamente, insensatamente

craziness ['kreɪzinəs] *n* : locura *f,* demencia *f*

crazy ['kreɪzi] *adj* **-zier; -est** **1** INSANE : loco, demente <to go crazy : volverse loco> **2** ABSURD, FOOLISH : loco, insensato, absurdo **3 to be crazy about** : estar loco por

creak[1] [ˈkriːk] *vi* : chirriar, rechinar, crujir

creak[2] *n* : chirrido *m,* crujido *m*

creaky [ˈkriːki] *adj* **creakier; -est** : chirriante, que cruje

cream[1] [ˈkriːm] *vt* **1** BEAT, MIX : batir, mezclar (azúcar y mantequilla, etc.) **2** : preparar (alimentos) con crema

cream[2] *n* **1** : crema *f* (de leche) **2** LOTION : crema *f,* loción *f* **3** ELITE : crema *f,* elite *f* <the cream of the crop : la crema y nata, lo mejor>

creamery [ˈkriːməri] *n, pl* **-eries** : fábrica *f* de productos lácteos

creamy [ˈkriːmi] *adj* **creamier; -est** : cremoso

crease[1] [ˈkriːs] *vt* **creased; creasing 1** : plegar, poner una raya en (pantalones) **2** WRINKLE : arrugar

crease[2] *n* : pliegue *m,* doblez *m,* raya *f* (de pantalones)

create [kriˈeɪt] *vt* **-ated; -ating** : crear, hacer

creation [kriˈeɪʃən] *n* : creación *f*

creative [kriˈeɪtɪv] *adj* : creativo, original <creative people : personas creativas> <a creative work : un obra original>

creatively [kriˈeɪtɪvli] *adv* : creativamente, con originalidad

creativity [ˌkriːeɪˈtɪvəti] *n* : creatividad *f*

creator [kriˈeɪtər] *n* : creador *m,* -dora *f*

creature [ˈkriːtʃər] *n* : ser *m* viviente, criatura *f,* animal *m*

credence [ˈkriːdənts] *n* : crédito *m*

credentials [krɪˈdɛntʃəlz] *npl* : referencias *fpl* oficiales, cartas *fpl* credenciales

credibility [ˌkrɛdəˈbɪləti] *n* : credibilidad *f*

credible [ˈkrɛdəbəl] *adj* : creíble

credit[1] [ˈkrɛdɪt] *vt* **1** BELIEVE : creer, dar crédito a **2** : ingresar, abonar <to credit $100 to an account : ingresar $100 en (una) cuenta> **3** ATTRIBUTE : atribuir <they credit the invention to him : a él se le atribuye el invento>

credit[2] *n* **1** : saldo *m* positivo, saldo *m* a favor (de una cuenta) **2** : crédito *m* <to buy on credit : comprar a crédito> <credit card : tarjeta de crédito> **3** CREDENCE : crédito *m* <I gave credit to everything he said : di crédito a todo lo que dijo> **4** RECOGNITION : reconocimiento *m* **5** : orgullo *m,* honor *m* <she's a credit to the school : ella es el orgullo de la escuela>

creditable [ˈkrɛdɪtəbəl] *adj* : encomiable, loable — **creditably** [-bli] *adv*

credit card *n* : tarjeta de crédito

creditor [ˈkrɛdɪtər] *n* : acreedor *m,* -dora *f*

credulity [krɪˈduːləti, -ˈdjuː-] *n* : credulidad *f*

credulous [ˈkrɛdʒələs] *adj* : crédulo

creed [ˈkriːd] *n* : credo *m*

creek [ˈkriːk, ˈkrɪk] *n* : arroyo *m,* riachuelo *m*

creel [ˈkriːl] *n* : nasa *f,* cesta *f* (de pescador)

creep[1] [ˈkriːp] *vi* **crept** [ˈkrɛpt]; **creeping 1** CRAWL : arrastrarse, gatear **2** : moverse lentamente o sigilosamente <he crept out of the house : salió sigilosamente de la casa> **3** SPREAD : trepar (dícese de una planta)

creep[2] *n* **1** CRAWL : paso *m* lento **2 creeps** *npl* : escalofríos *mpl* <that gives me the creeps : eso me da escalofríos>

creeper [ˈkriːpər] *n* : planta *f* trepadora, trepadora *f*

cremate [ˈkriːˌmeɪt] *vt* **-mated; -mating** : cremar

cremation [krɪˈmeɪʃən] *n* : cremación *f*

creosote [ˈkriːəˌsoːt] *n* : creosota *f*

crepe *or* **crêpe** [ˈkreɪp] *n* **1** : crespón *m* (tela) **2** PANCAKE : crepe *mf,* crepa *f Mex*

crescendo [krɪˈʃɛnˌdoː] *n, pl* **-dos** *or* **-does** : crescendo *m*

crescent [ˈkrɛsənt] *n* : creciente *m*

crest [ˈkrɛst] *n* **1** : cresta *f,* penacho *m* (de un ave) **2** PEAK, TOP : cresta *f* (de una ola), cima *f* (de una colina) **3** : emblema *m* (sobre un escudo de armas)

crestfallen [ˈkrɛstˌfɔlən] *adj* : alicaído, abatido

cretin [ˈkriːtən] *n* : cretino *m,* -na *f*

crevasse [krɪˈvæs] *n* : grieta *f,* fisura *f*

crevice [ˈkrɛvɪs] *n* : grieta *f,* hendidura *f*

crew [ˈkruː] *n* **1** : tripulación *f* (de una nave) **2** TEAM : equipo *m* (de trabajadores o atletas)

crib [ˈkrɪb] *n* **1** MANGER : pesebre *m* **2** GRANARY : granero *m* **3** : cuna *f* (de un bebé)

crick [ˈkrɪk] *n* : calambre *m,* espasmo *m* muscular

cricket [ˈkrɪkət] *n* **1** : grillo *m* (insecto) **2** : críquet *m* (juego)

crime [ˈkraɪm] *n* **1** : crimen *m,* delito *m* <to commit a crime : cometer un delito> **2** : crimen *m,* delincuencia *f* <organized crime : crimen organizado>

criminal[1] [ˈkrɪmənəl] *adj* : criminal

criminal[2] *n* : criminal *mf,* delincuente *mf*

crimp [ˈkrɪmp] *vt* : ondular, rizar (el pelo), arrugar (una tela, etc.)

crimson [ˈkrɪmzən] *n* : carmesí *m*

cringe [ˈkrɪndʒ] *vi* **cringed; cringing** : encogerse

crinkle[1] [ˈkrɪŋkəl] *v* **-kled; -kling** *vt* : arrugar — *vi* : arrugarse

crinkle[2] *n* : arruga *f*

crinkly [ˈkrɪŋkəli] *adj* : arrugado

cripple[1] [ˈkrɪpəl] *vt* **-pled; -pling 1** DISABLE : lisiar, dejar inválido **2** INCAPACITATE : inutilizar, incapacitar

cripple[2] *n* : lisiado *m,* -da *f*

crisis ['kraɪsɪs] *n, pl* **crises** [-ˌsiːz] : crisis *f*
crisp[1] ['krɪsp] *vt* : tostar, hacer crujiente
crisp[2] *adj* **1** CRUNCHY : crujiente, crocante **2** FIRM, FRESH : firme, fresco <crisp lettuce : lechuga fresca> **3** LIVELY : vivaz, alegre <a crisp tempo : un ritmo alegre> **4** INVIGORATING : fresco, vigorizante <the crisp autumn air : el fresco aire otoñal> — **crisply** *adv*
crispy ['krɪspi] *adj* **crispier; -est** : crujiente <crispy potato chips : papitas crujientes>
crisscross ['krɪsˌkrɔs] *vt* : entrecruzar
criterion [kraɪ'tɪriən] *n, pl* **-ria** [-iə] : criterio *m*
critic ['krɪt̬ɪk] *n* **1** : crítico *m*, -ca *f* (de las artes) **2** FAULTFINDER : detractor *m*, -tora *f*; criticón *m*, -cona *f*
critical ['krɪtɪkəl] *adj* : crítico
critically ['krɪtɪkli] *adv* : críticamente <critically ill : gravemente enfermo>
criticism ['krɪtəˌsɪzəm] *n* : crítica *f*
criticize ['krɪtəˌsaɪz] *vt* **-cized; -cizing** **1** EVALUATE, JUDGE : criticar, analizar, evaluar **2** CENSURE : criticar, reprobar
critique [krɪ'tiːk] *n* : crítica *f*, evaluación *f*
croak[1] ['kroːk] *vi* : croar
croak[2] *n* : croar *m*, canto *m* (de la rana)
Croatian [kro'eɪʃən] *n* : croata *mf* — **Croatian** *adj*
crochet[1] [kroː'ʃeɪ] *v* : tejer al croché
crochet[2] *n* : croché *m*, crochet *m*
crock ['krɑk] *n* : vasija *f* de barro
crockery ['krɑkəri] *n* : vajilla *f* (de barro)
crocodile ['krɑkəˌdaɪl] *n* : cocodrilo *m*
crocus ['kroːkəs] *n, pl* **-cuses** : azafrán *m*
crone ['kroːn] *n* : vieja *f* arpía, vieja *f* bruja
crony ['kroːni] *n, pl* **-nies** : amigote *m fam*; compinche *mf fam*
crook[1] ['krʊk] *vt* : doblar (el brazo o el dedo)
crook[2] *n* **1** STAFF : cayado *m* (de pastor), báculo *m* (de obispo) **2** THIEF : ratero *m*, -ra *f*; ladrón *m*, -drona *f*
crooked ['krʊkəd] *adj* **1** BENT : chueco, torcido **2** DISHONEST : deshonesto
crookedness ['krʊkədnəs] *n* **1** : lo torcido, lo chueco **2** DISHONESTY : falta *f* de honradez
croon ['kruːn] *v* : cantar suavemente
crop[1] ['krɑp] *v* **cropped; cropping** *vt* TRIM : recortar, cortar — *vi* **to crop up** : aparecer, surgir <these problems keep cropping up : estos problemas no cesan de surgir>
crop[2] *n* **1** : buche *m* (de un ave o insecto) **2** WHIP : fusta *f* (de jinete) **3** HARVEST : cosecha *f*, cultivo *m*
croquet [ˌkroː'keɪ] *n* : croquet *m*
croquette [ˌkroː'kɛt] *n* : croqueta *f*
cross[1] ['krɔs] *vt* **1** : cruzar, atravesar <to cross the street : cruzar la calle> <several canals cross the city : varios canales atraviesan la ciudad> **2** CANCEL : tachar, cancelar <he crossed his name off the list : tachó su nombre de la planilla> **3** INTERBREED : cruzar (en genética)
cross[2] *adj* **1** : que atraviesa <cross ventilation : ventilación que atraviesa un cuarto> **2** CONTRARY : contrario, opuesto <cross purposes : objetivos opuestos> **3** ANGRY : enojado, de mal humor
cross[3] *n* **1** : cruz *f* <the sign of the cross : la señal de la cruz> **2** : cruza *f* (en biología)
crossbones ['krɔsˌboːnz] *npl* **1** : huesos *mpl* cruzados **2** → **skull**
crossbow ['krɔsˌboː] *n* : ballesta *f*
crossbreed ['krɔsˌbriːd] *vt* **-bred** [-ˌbred]; **-breeding** : cruzar
cross–examination [ˌkrɔsɪgˌzæmə'neɪʃən] *n* : repreguntas *fpl*, interrogatorio *m*
cross–examine [ˌkrɔsɪg'zæmən] *vt* **-ined; -ining** : repreguntar
cross–eyed ['krɔsˌaɪd] *adj* : bizco
crossing ['krɔsɪŋ] *n* **1** INTERSECTION : cruce *m*, paso *m* <pedestrian crossing : paso de peatones> **2** VOYAGE : travesía *f* (del mar)
crossly ['krɔsli] *adv* : con enojo, con enfado
cross–reference [ˌkrɔs'rɛfrənts, -'rɛfərənts] *n* : referencia *f*, remisión *f*
crossroads ['krɔsˌroːdz] *n* : cruce *m*, encrucijada *f*, crucero *m Mex*
cross section *n* **1** SECTION : corte *m* transversal **2** SAMPLE : muestra *f* representativa <a cross section of the population : una muestra representativa de la población>
crosswalk ['krɔsˌwɔk] *n* : cruce *m* peatonal, paso *m* de peatones
crossways ['krɔsˌweɪz] → **crosswise**
crosswise[1] ['krɔsˌwaɪz] *adv* : transversalmente, diagonalmente
crosswise[2] *adj* : transversal, diagonal
crossword puzzle ['krɔsˌwərd] *n* : crucigrama *m*
crotch ['krɑtʃ] *n* : entrepierna *f*
crotchety ['krɑtʃət̬i] *adj* CRANKY : malhumorado, irritable, enojadizo
crouch ['kraʊtʃ] *vi* : agacharse, ponerse de cuclillas
croup ['kruːp] *n* : crup *m*
crouton ['kruːˌtɑn] *n* : crutón *m*
crow[1] ['kroː] *vi* **1** : cacarear, cantar (como un cuervo) **2** BRAG : alardear, presumir
crow[2] *n* **1** : cuervo *m* (ave) **2** : cantar *m* (del gallo)
crowbar ['kroːˌbɑr] *n* : palanca *f*
crowd[1] ['kraʊd] *vi* : aglomerarse, amontonarse — *vt* : atestar, atiborrar, llenar
crowd[2] *n* : multitud *f*, muchedumbre *f*, gentío *m*
crown[1] ['kraʊn] *vt* : coronar
crown[2] *n* : corona *f*

crow's nest *n* : cofa *f*
crucial [ˈkruːʃəl] *adj* : crucial, decisivo
crucible [ˈkruːsəbəl] *n* : crisol *m*
crucifix [ˈkruːsəˌfɪks] *n* : crucifijo *m*
crucifixion [ˌkruːsəˈfɪkʃən] *n* : crucifixión *f*
crucify [ˈkruːsəˌfaɪ] *vt* **-fied; -fying** : crucificar
crude [ˈkruːd] *adj* **cruder; -est 1** RAW, UNREFINED : crudo, sin refinar <crude oil : petróleo crudo> **2** VULGAR : grosero, de mal gusto **3** ROUGH : tosco, burdo, rudo
crudely [ˈkruːdli] *adv* **1** VULGARLY : groseramente **2** ROUGHLY : burdamente, de manera rudimentaria
crudity [ˈkruːdət̬i] *n, pl* **-ties 1** VULGARITY : grosería *f* **2** COARSENESS, ROUGHNESS : tosquedad *f,* rudeza *f*
cruel [ˈkruːəl] *adj* **-eler** *or* **-eller; -elest** *or* **-ellest** : cruel
cruelly [ˈkruːəli] *adv* : cruelmente
cruelty [ˈkruːəlti] *n, pl* **-ties** : crueldad *f*
cruet [ˈkruːɪt] *n* : vinagrera *f,* aceitera *f*
cruise[1] [ˈkruːz] *vi* **cruised; cruising 1** : hacer un crucero **2** : navegar o conducir a una velocidad constante <cruising speed : velocidad de crucero>
cruise[2] *n* : crucero *m*
cruiser [ˈkruːzər] *n* **1** WARSHIP : crucero *m,* buque *m* de guerra **2** : patrulla *f* (de policía)
crumb [ˈkrʌm] *n* : miga *f,* migaja *f*
crumble [ˈkrʌmbəl] *v* **-bled; -bling** *vt* : desmigajar, desmenuzar — *vi* : desmigajarse, desmoronarse, desmenuzarse
crumbly [ˈkrʌmbli] *adj* : que se desmenuza fácilmente, friable
crumple [ˈkrʌmpəl] *v* **-pled; -pling** *vt* RUMPLE : arrugar — *vi* **1** WRINKLE : arrugarse **2** COLLAPSE : desplomarse
crunch[1] [ˈkrʌntʃ] *vt* **1** : ronzar (con los dientes) **2** : hacer crujir (con los pies, etc.) — *vi* : crujir
crunch[2] *n* : crujido *m*
crunchy [ˈkrʌntʃi] *adj* **crunchier; -est** : crujiente
crusade[1] [kruːˈseɪd] *vi* **-saded; -sading** : hacer una campaña (a favor de o contra algo)
crusade[2] *n* **1** : campaña *f* (de reforma, etc.) **2 Crusade** : cruzada *f*
crusader [kruːˈseɪdər] *n* **1** : cruzado *m* (en la Edad Media) **2** : campeón *m,* -peona *f* (de una causa)
crush[1] [ˈkrʌʃ] *vt* **1** SQUASH : aplastar, apachurrar **2** GRIND, PULVERIZE : triturar, machacar **3** SUPPRESS : aplastar, suprimir
crush[2] *n* **1** CROWD, MOB : gentío *m,* multitud *f,* aglomeración *f* **2** INFATUATION : enamoramiento *m*
crushing [ˈkrʌʃɪŋ] *adj* : aplastante, abrumador
crust [ˈkrʌst] *n* **1** : corteza *f,* costra *f* (de pan) **2** : tapa *f* de masa, pasta *f* (de un pastel) **3** LAYER : capa *f,* corteza *f* <the earth's crust : la corteza terrestre>
crustacean [ˌkrʌsˈteɪʃən] *n* : crustáceo *m*
crusty [ˈkrʌsti] *adj* **crustier; -est 1** : de corteza dura **2** CROSS, GRUMPY : enojado, malhumorado
crutch [ˈkrʌtʃ] *n* : muleta *f*
crux [ˈkrʌks, ˈkrʊks] *n, pl* **cruxes** : quid *m,* esencia *f,* meollo *m* <the crux of the problem : el quid del problema>
cry[1] [ˈkraɪ] *vi* **cried; crying 1** SHOUT : gritar <they cried for more : a gritos pidieron más> **2** WEEP : llorar
cry[2] *n, pl* **cries 1** SHOUT : grito *m* **2** WEEPING : llanto *m* **3** : chillido *m* (de un animal)
crybaby [ˈkraɪˌbeɪbi] *n, pl* **-bies** : llorón *m,* -rona *f*
crypt [ˈkrɪpt] *n* : cripta *f*
cryptic [ˈkrɪptɪk] *adj* : enigmático, críptico
crystal [ˈkrɪstəl] *n* : cristal *m*
crystalline [ˈkrɪstəlɪn] *adj* : cristalino
crystallize [ˈkrɪstəˌlaɪz] *v* **-lized; -lizing** *vt* : cristalizar, materializar <to crystallize one's thoughts : cristalizar uno sus pensamientos> — *vi* : cristalizarse
cub [ˈkʌb] *n* : cachorro *m*
Cuban [ˈkjuːbən] *n* : cubano *m,* -na *f* — **Cuban** *adj*
cubbyhole [ˈkʌbiˌhoːl] *n* : chiribitil *m*
cube[1] [ˈkjuːb] *vt* **cubed; cubing 1** : elevar (un número) al cubo **2** : cortar en cubos
cube[2] *n* **1** : cubo *m* **2 ice cube** : cubito *m* de hielo **3 sugar cube** : terrón *m* de azúcar
cubic [ˈkjuːbɪk] *adj* : cúbico
cubicle [ˈkjuːbɪkəl] *n* : cubículo *m*
cuckoo[1] [ˈkuːˌkuː, ˈkʊ-] *adj* : loco, chiflado
cuckoo[2] *n, pl* **-oos** : cuco *m,* cuclillo *m*
cucumber [ˈkjuːˌkʌmbər] *n* : pepino *m*
cud [ˈkʌd] *n* **to chew the cud** : rumiar
cuddle [ˈkʌdəl] *v* **-dled; -dling** *vi* : abrazarse tiernamente, acurrucarse — *vt* : abrazar
cudgel[1] [ˈkʌdʒəl] *vt* **-geled** *or* **-gelled; -geling** *or* **-gelling** : apalear, aporrear
cudgel[2] *n* : garrote *m,* porra *f*
cue[1] [ˈkjuː] *vt* **cued; cuing** *or* **cueing** : darle el pie a, darle la señal a
cue[2] *n* **1** SIGNAL : señal *f,* pie *m* (en teatro), entrada *f* (en música) **2** : taco *m* (de billar)
cuff[1] [ˈkʌf] *vt* : bofetear, cachetear
cuff[2] *n* **1** : puño *m* (de una camisa), vuelta *f* (de pantalones) **2** SLAP : bofetada *f,* cachetada *f* **3 cuffs** *npl* HANDCUFFS : esposas *fpl*
cuisine [kwɪˈziːn] *n* : cocina *f* <Mexican cuisine : la cocina mexicana>

culinary [ˈkʌləˌnɛri, ˈkjuːlə-] *adj* : culinario

cull [ˈkʌl] *vt* : seleccionar, entresacar

culminate [ˈkʌlməˌneɪt] *vi* **-nated; -nating** : culminar

culmination [ˌkʌlməˈneɪʃən] *n* : culminación *f,* punto *m* culminante

culpable [ˈkʌlpəbəl] *adj* : culpable

culprit [ˈkʌlprɪt] *n* : culpable *mf*

cult [ˈkʌlt] *n* : culto *m*

cultivate [ˈkʌltəˌveɪt] *vt* **-vated; -vating 1** TILL : cultivar, labrar **2** FOSTER : cultivar, fomentar **3** REFINE : cultivar, refinar <to cultivate the mind : cultivar la mente>

cultivation [ˌkʌltəˈveɪʃən] *n* **1** : cultivo *m* <under cultivation : en cultivo> **2** CULTURE, REFINEMENT : cultura *f,* refinamiento *m*

cultural [ˈkʌltʃərəl] *adj* : cultural — **culturally** *adv*

culture [ˈkʌltʃər] *n* **1** CULTIVATION : cultivo *m* **2** REFINEMENT : cultura *f,* educación *f,* refinamiento *m* **3** CIVILIZATION : cultura *f,* civilización *f* <the Incan culture : la cultura inca>

cultured [ˈkʌltʃərd] *adj* **1** EDUCATED, REFINED : culto, educado, refinado **2** : de cultivo, cultivado <cultured pearls : perlas de cultivo>

culvert [ˈkʌlvərt] *n* : alcantarilla *f*

cumbersome [ˈkʌmbərsəm] *adj* : torpe y pesado, difícil de manejar

cumulative [ˈkjuːmjələt̬iv, -ˌleɪt̬ɪv] *adj* : acumulativo

cumulus [ˈkjuːmjələs] *n, pl* **-li** [-ˌlaɪ, -ˌliː] : cúmulo *n*

cunning[1] [ˈkʌnɪŋ] *adj* **1** CRAFTY : astuto, taimado **2** CLEVER : ingenioso, hábil **3** CUTE : mono, gracioso, lindo

cunning[2] *n* **1** SKILL : habilidad *f* **2** CRAFTINESS : astucia *f,* maña *f*

cup[1] [ˈkʌp] *vt* **cupped; cupping** : ahuecar (las manos)

cup[2] *n* **1** : taza *f* <a cup of coffee : una taza de café> **2** CUPFUL : taza *f* **3** : media pinta *f* (unidad de medida) **4** GOBLET : copa *f* **5** TROPHY : copa *f,* trofeo *m*

cupboard [ˈkʌbərd] *n* : alacena *f,* armario *m*

cupcake [ˈkʌpˌkeɪk] *n* : pastelito *m*

cupful [ˈkʌpˌfʊl] *n* : taza *f*

cupola [ˈkjuːpələ, -ˌloː] *n* : cúpula *f*

cur [ˈkər] *n* : perro *m* callejero, perro *m* corriente *Mex*

curate [ˈkjʊrət] *n* : cura *m,* párroco *m*

curator [ˈkjʊrˌeɪt̬ər, kjʊˈreɪt̬ər] *n* : conservador *m,* -dora *f* (de un museo); director *m,* -tora *f* (de un zoológico)

curb[1] [ˈkərb] *vt* : refrenar, restringir, controlar

curb[2] *n* **1** RESTRAINT : freno *m,* control *m* **2** : borde *m* de la acera

curd [ˈkərd] *n* : cuajada *f*

curdle [ˈkərdəl] *v* **-dled; -dling** *vi* : cuajarse — *vt* : cuajar <to curdle one's blood : helarle la sangre a uno>

cure[1] [ˈkjʊr] *vt* **cured; curing 1** HEAL : curar, sanar **2** REMEDY : remediar **3** PROCESS : curar (alimentos, etc.)

cure[2] *n* **1** RECOVERY : curación *f,* recuperación *f* **2** REMEDY : cura *f,* remedio *m*

curfew [ˈkərˌfjuː] *n* : toque *m* de queda

curio [ˈkjʊriˌoː] *n, pl* **-rios** : curiosidad *f,* objeto *m* curioso

curiosity [ˌkjʊriˈɑsət̬i] *n, pl* **-ties** : curiosidad *f*

curious [ˈkjʊriəs] *adj* **1** INQUISITIVE : curioso **2** STRANGE : curioso, raro

curl[1] [ˈkərl] *vt* **1** : rizar, ondular (el pelo) **2** COIL : enrollar **3** TWIST : torcer <to curl one's lip : hacer una mueca> — *vi* **1** : rizarse, ondularse **2 to curl up** : acurrucarse (con un libro, etc.)

curl[2] *n* **1** RINGLET : rizo *m* **2** COIL : espiral *f,* rosca *f*

curler [ˈkərlər] *n* : rulo *m*

curlew [ˈkərˌluː, ˈkərlˌjuː] *n, pl* **-lews** *or* **-lew** : zarapito *m*

curly [ˈkərli] *adj* **curlier; -est** : rizado, crespo

currant [ˈkərənt] *n* **1** : grosella *f* (fruta) **2** RAISIN : pasa *f* de Corinto

currency [ˈkərəntsi] *n, pl* **-cies 1** PREVALENCE, USE : uso *m,* aceptación *f,* difusión *f* <to be in currency : estar en uso> **2** MONEY : moneda *f,* dinero *m*

current[1] [ˈkərənt] *adj* **1** PRESENT : actual <current events : actualidades> **2** PREVALENT : corriente, común — **currently** *adv*

current[2] *n* : corriente *f*

curriculum [kəˈrɪkjələm] *n, pl* **-la** [-lə] : currículum *m,* currículo *m,* programa *m* de estudio

curriculum vitae [ˈviːˌtaɪ, ˈvaɪt̬i] *n, pl* **curricula vitae** : currículum *m,* currículo *m*

curry[1] [ˈkəri] *vt* **-ried; -rying 1** GROOM : almohazar (un caballo) **2** : condimentar con curry **3 to curry favor** : congraciarse (con alguien)

curry[2] *n, pl* **-ries** : curry *m*

curse[1] [ˈkərs] *v* **cursed; cursing** *vt* **1** DAMN : maldecir **2** INSULT : injuriar, insultar, decir malas palabras a **3** AFFLICT : afligir — *vi* : maldecir, decir malas palabras

curse[2] *n* **1** : maldición *f* <to put a curse on someone : echarle una maldición a alguien> **2** AFFLICTION : maldición *f,* aflicción *f,* cruz *f*

cursor [ˈkərsər] *n* : cursor *m*

cursory [ˈkərsəri] *adj* : rápido, superficial, somero

curt [ˈkərt] *adj* : cortante, brusco, seco — **curtly** *adv*

curtail [kərˈteɪl] *vt* : acortar, limitar, restringir

curtailment [kərˈteɪlmənt] *n* : restricción *f,* limitación *f*

curtain [ˈkərtən] *n* : cortina *f* (de una ventana), telón *m* (en un teatro)

curtness [ˈkərtnəs] *n* : brusquedad *f,* sequedad *f*

curtsy[1] *or* **curtsey** [ˈkərtsi] *vt* **-sied** *or* **-seyed; -sying** *or* **-seying :** hacer una reverencia
curtsy[2] *or* **curtsey** *n, pl* **-sies** *or* **-seys :** reverencia *f*
curvature [ˈkərvəˌtʃʊr] *n* **:** curvatura *f*
curve[1] [ˈkərv] *v* **curved; curving** *vi* **:** torcerse, describir una curva — *vt* **:** encorvar
curve[2] *n* **:** curva *f*
cushion[1] [ˈkʊʃən] *vt* **1 :** poner cojines o almohadones a **2** SOFTEN **:** amortiguar, mitigar, suavizar <to cushion a blow : amortiguar un golpe>
cushion[2] *n* **1 :** cojín *m,* almohadón *m* **2** PROTECTION **:** colchón *m,* protección *f*
cusp [ˈkʌsp] *n* **:** cúspide *f* (de un diente), cuerno *m* (de la luna)
cuspid [ˈkʌspɪd] *n* **:** diente *m* canino, colmillo *m*
custard [ˈkʌstərd] *n* **:** natillas *fpl*
custodian [ˌkʌˈstoːdiən] *n* **:** custodio *m,* -dia *f;* guardián, -diana *f*
custody [ˈkʌstədi] *n, pl* **-dies :** custodia *f,* cuidado *m* <to be in custody : estar detenido>
custom[1] [ˈkʌstəm] *adj* **:** a la medida, a la orden
custom[2] *n* **1 :** costumbre *f,* tradición *f* **2 customs** *npl* **:** aduana *f*
customarily [ˌkʌstəˈmɛrəli] *adv* **:** habitualmente, normalmente, de costumbre
customary [ˈkʌstəˌmɛri] *adj* **1** TRADITIONAL **:** tradicional **2** USUAL **:** habitual, de costumbre
customer [ˈkʌstəmər] *n* **:** cliente *m,* -ta *f*
custom–made [ˈkʌstəmˈmeɪd] *adj* **:** hecho a la medida
cut[1] [ˈkʌt] *v* **cut; cutting** *vt* **1 :** cortar <to cut paper : cortar papel> **2 :** cortarse <to cut one's finger : cortarse uno el dedo> **3** TRIM **:** cortar, recortar <to have one's hair cut : cortarse el pelo> **4** INTERSECT **:** cruzar, atravesar **5** SHORTEN **:** acortar, abreviar **6** REDUCE **:** reducir, rebajar <to cut prices : rebajar los precios> **7 to cut one's teeth :** salirle los dientes a uno — *vi* **1 :** cortar, cortarse **2 to cut in :** entrometerse
cut[2] *n* **1 :** corte *m* <a cut of meat : un corte de carne> **2** SLASH **:** tajo *m,* corte *m,* cortadura *f* **3** REDUCTION **:** rebaja *f,* reducción *f* <a cut in the rates : una rebaja en las tarifas>
cute [ˈkjuːt] *adj* **cuter; -est :** mono *fam,* lindo
cuticle [ˈkjuːtɪkəl] *n* **:** cutícula *f*
cutlass [ˈkʌtləs] *n* **:** alfanje *m*
cutlery [ˈkʌtləri] *n* **:** cubiertos *mpl*
cutlet [ˈkʌtlət] *n* **:** chuleta *f*
cutter [ˈkʌtər] *n* **1 :** cortadora *f* (implemento) **2 :** cortador *m,* -dora *f* (persona) **3 :** cúter *m* (embarcación)
cutthroat [ˈkʌtˌθroːt] *adj* **:** despiadado, desalmado <cutthroat competition : competencia feroz>
cutting[1] [ˈkʌtɪŋ] *adj* **1 :** cortante <a cutting wind : un viento cortante> **2** CAUSTIC **:** mordaz
cutting[2] *n* **:** esqueje *m* (de una planta)
cuttlefish [ˈkʌtəlˌfɪʃ] *n, pl* **-fish** *or* **-fishes :** jibia *f,* sepia *f*
cyanide [ˈsaɪəˌnaɪd, -nɪd] *n* **:** cianuro *m*
cycle[1] [ˈsaɪkəl] *vi* **-cled; -cling :** andar en bicicleta, ir en bicicleta
cycle[2] *n* **1 :** ciclo *m* <life cycle : ciclo de vida, ciclo vital> **2** BICYCLE **:** bicicleta *f* **3** MOTORCYCLE **:** motocicleta *f*
cyclic [ˈsaɪklɪk, ˈsɪ-] *or* **cyclical** [-klɪkəl] *adj* **:** cíclico
cyclist [ˈsaɪklɪst] *n* **:** ciclista *mf*
cyclone [ˈsaɪˌkloːn] *n* **1 :** ciclón *m* **2** TORNADO **:** tornado *m*
cyclopedia *or* **cyclopaedia** [ˌsaɪkləˈpiːdiə] → **encyclopedia**
cylinder [ˈsɪləndər] *n* **:** cilindro *m*
cylindrical [səˈlɪndrɪkəl] *adj* **:** cilíndrico
cymbal [ˈsɪmbəl] *n* **:** platillo *m,* címbalo *m*
cynic [ˈsɪnɪk] *n* **:** cínico *m,* -ca *f*
cynical [ˈsɪnɪkəl] *adj* **:** cínico
cynicism [ˈsɪnəˌsɪzəm] *n* **:** cinismo *m*
cypress [ˈsaɪprəs] *n* **:** ciprés *m*
Cypriot [ˈsɪpriət, -ˌɑt] *n* **:** chipriota *mf* — **Cypriot** *adj*
cyst [ˈsɪst] *n* **:** quiste *m*
cytoplasm [ˈsaɪtoˌplæzəm] *n* **:** citoplasma *m*
czar [ˈzɑr, ˈsɑr] *n* **:** zar *m*
czarina [zɑˈriːnə, sɑ-] *n* **:** zarina *f*
Czech [ˈtʃɛk] *n* **1 :** checo *m,* -ca *f* **2 :** checo *m* (idioma) — **Czech** *adj*
Czechoslovak [ˌtʃɛkoˈsloːˌvɑk, -ˌvæk] *or* **Czechoslovakian** [-sloˈvɑkiən, -ˈvæ-] *n* **:** checoslovaco *m,* -ca *f* — **Czechoslovak** *or* **Czechoslovakian** *adj*

D

d [ˈdiː] *n, pl* **d's** *or* **ds** [ˈdiːz] **:** cuarta letra del alfabeto inglés
dab[1] [ˈdæb] *vt* **dabbed; dabbing :** darle toques ligeros a, aplicar suavemente
dab[2] *n* **1** BIT **:** toque *m,* pizca *f,* poco *m* <a dab of ointment : un toque de ungüento> **2** PAT **:** toque *m* ligero, golpecito *m*
dabble [ˈdæbəl] *v* **-bled; -bling** *vt* SPATTER **:** salpicar — *vi* **1** SPLASH **:** chapotear **2** TRIFLE **:** jugar, interesarse superficialmente

dabbler [ˈdæbələr] *n* **:** diletante *mf*
dachshund [ˈdɑksˌhʊnt, -ˌhʊnd; ˈdɑksənt, -sənd] *n* **:** perro *m* salchicha
dad [ˈdæd] *n* **:** papá *m fam*
daddy [ˈdædi] *n, pl* **-dies :** papi *m fam*
daffodil [ˈdæfəˌdɪl] *n* **:** narciso *m*
daft [ˈdæft] *adj* **:** tonto, bobo
dagger [ˈdægər] *n* **:** daga *f,* puñal *m*
dahlia [ˈdæljə, ˈdɑl-, ˈdeɪl-] *n* **:** dalia *f*
daily¹ [ˈdeɪli] *adv* **:** a diario, diariamente
daily² *adj* **:** diario, cotidiano
daily³ *n, pl* **-lies :** diario *m,* periódico *m*
daintily [ˈdeɪntəli] *adv* **:** delicadamente, con delicadeza
daintiness [ˈdeɪntinəs] *n* **:** delicadeza *f,* finura *f*
dainty¹ [ˈdeɪnti] *adj* **-tier; -est 1** DELICATE **:** delicado **2** FASTIDIOUS **:** remilgado, melindroso **3** DELICIOUS **:** exquisito, sabroso
dainty² *n, pl* **-ties** DELICACY **:** exquisitez *f,* manjar *m*
dairy [ˈdæri] *n, pl* **-ies 1** *or* **dairy store :** lechería *f* **2** *or* **dairy farm :** granja *f* lechera
dairymaid [ˈdæriˌmeɪd] *n* **:** lechera *f*
dairyman [ˈdærimən, -ˌmæn] *n, pl* **-men** [-mən, -ˌmɛn] **:** lechero *m*
dais [ˈdeɪəs] *n* **:** tarima *f,* estrado *m*
daisy [ˈdeɪzi] *n, pl* **-sies :** margarita *f*
dale [ˈdeɪl] *n* **:** valle *m*
dally [ˈdæli] *vi* **-lied; -lying 1** TRIFLE **:** juguetear **2** DAWDLE **:** entretenerse, perder tiempo
dalmatian [dælˈmeɪʃən, dɔl-] *n* **:** dálmata *m*
dam¹ [ˈdæm] *vt* **dammed; damming :** represar, embalsar
dam² *n* **1 :** represa *f,* dique *m* **2 :** madre *f* (de animales domésticos)
damage¹ [ˈdæmɪdʒ] *vt* **-aged; -aging :** dañar (un objeto o una máquina), perjudicar (la salud o una reputación)
damage² *n* **1 :** daño *m,* perjuicio *m* **2 damages** *npl* **:** daños y perjuicios *mpl*
damask [ˈdæməsk] *n* **:** damasco *m*
dame [ˈdeɪm] *n* LADY **:** dama *f,* señora *f*
damn¹ [ˈdæm] *vt* **1** CONDEMN **:** condenar **2** CURSE **:** maldecir
damn² *or* **damned** [ˈdæmd] *adj* **:** condenado *fam,* maldito *fam*
damn³ *n* **:** pito *m,* bledo *m,* comino *m* <it's not worth a damn : no vale un pito> <I don't give a damn : me importa un comino>
damnable [ˈdæmnəbəl] *adj* **:** condenable, detestable
damnation [dæmˈneɪʃən] *n* **:** condenación *f*
damned¹ [ˈdæmd] *adv* VERY **:** muy
damned² *adj* **1 → damnable 2** REMARKABLE **:** extraordinario
damp¹ [ˈdæmp] *vt* **→ dampen**
damp² *adj* **:** húmedo
damp³ *n* MOISTURE **:** humedad *f*
dampen [ˈdæmpən] *vt* **1** MOISTEN **:** humedecer **2** DISCOURAGE **:** desalentar, desanimar
damper [ˈdæmpər] *n* **1 :** regulador *m* de tiro (de una chimenea) **2 :** sordina *f* (de un piano) **3 to put a damper on :** desanimar, apagar (el entusiasmo), enfriar
dampness [ˈdæmpnəs] *n* **:** humedad *f*
damsel [ˈdæmzəl] *n* **:** damisela *f*
dance¹ [ˈdænts] *v* **danced; dancing :** bailar
dance² *n* **:** baile *m*
dancer [ˈdæntsər] *n* **:** bailarín *m,* -rina *f*
dandelion [ˈdændəlˌaɪən] *n* **:** diente *m* de león
dandruff [ˈdændrəf] *n* **:** caspa *f*
dandy¹ [ˈdændi] *adj* **-dier; -est :** excelente, magnífico, macanudo *fam*
dandy² *n, pl* **-dies 1** FOP **:** dandi *m* **2 :** algo *m* excelente <this new program is a dandy : este programa nuevo es algo excelente>
Dane [ˈdeɪn] *n* **:** danés *m,* -nesa *f*
Danish¹ [ˈdeɪnɪʃ] *adj* **:** danés
Danish² *n* **:** danés *m* (idioma)
danger [ˈdeɪndʒər] *n* **:** peligro *m*
dangerous [ˈdeɪndʒərəs] *adj* **:** peligroso
dangle [ˈdæŋgəl] *v* **-gled; -gling** *vi* HANG **:** colgar, pender — *vt* **1** SWING **:** hacer oscilar **2** PROFFER **:** ofrecer (como incentivo) **3 to keep someone dangling :** dejar a alguien en suspenso
dank [ˈdæŋk] *adj* **:** frío y húmedo
dapper [ˈdæpər] *adj* **:** pulcro, atildado
dappled [ˈdæpəld] *adj* **:** moteado <a dappled horse : un caballo rodado>
dare¹ [ˈdær] *v* **dared; daring** *vi* **:** osar, atreverse <how dare you! : ¡cómo te atreves!> — *vt* **1** CHALLENGE **:** desafiar, retar **2 to dare to do something :** atreverse a hacer algo, osar hacer algo
dare² *n* **:** desafío *m,* reto *m*
daredevil [ˈdærˌdɛvəl] *n* **:** persona *f* temeraria
daring¹ [ˈdærɪŋ] *adj* **:** osado, atrevido, audaz
daring² *n* **:** arrojo *m,* coraje *m,* audacia *f*
dark [ˈdɑrk] *adj* **1 :** oscuro (dícese del ambiente o de los colores), moreno (dícese del pelo o de la piel) **2** SOMBER **:** sombrío, triste
darken [ˈdɑrkən] *vt* **1** DIM **:** oscurecer **2** SADDEN **:** entristecer — *vi* **:** ensombrecerse, nublarse
darkly [ˈdɑrkli] *adv* **1** DIMLY **:** oscuramente **2** GLOOMILY **:** tristemente **3** MYSTERIOUSLY **:** misteriosamente, enigmáticamente
darkness [ˈdɑrknəs] *n* **:** oscuridad *f,* tinieblas *f*
darling¹ [ˈdɑrlɪŋ] *adj* **1** BELOVED **:** querido, amado **2** CHARMING **:** encantador, mono *fam*

darling[2] *n* **1** BELOVED : querido *m,* -da *f;* amado *m,* -da *f;* cariño *m,* -ña *f* **2** FAVORITE : preferido *m,* -da *f;* favorito *m,* -ta *f*

darn[1] [ˈdɑrn] *vt* : zurcir

darn[2] *n* **1** : zurcido *m* **2** → **damn**[3]

dart[1] [ˈdɑrt] *vt* THROW : lanzar, tirar — *vi* DASH : lanzarse, precipitarse

dart[2] *n* **1** : dardo *m* **2 darts** *npl* : juego *m* de dardos

dash[1] [ˈdæʃ] *vt* **1** SMASH : romper, estrellar **2** HURL : arrojar, lanzar **3** SPLASH : salpicar **4** FRUSTRATE : frustrar **5 to dash off** : hacer (algo) rápidamente — *vi* **1** SMASH : romperse, estrellarse **2** DART : lanzarse, irse apresuradamente

dash[2] *n* **1** BURST, SPLASH : arranque *m,* salpicadura *f* (de aguas) **2** : guión *m* largo (signo de puntuación) **3** DROP : gota *f,* pizca *f* **4** VERVE : brío *m* **5** RACE : carrera *f* <a 100-meter dash : una carrera de 100 metros> **6 to make a dash for it** : precipitarse (hacia), echarse a correr **7** → **dashboard**

dashboard [ˈdæʃˌbord] *n* : tablero *m* de instrumentos

dashing [ˈdæʃɪŋ] *adj* : gallardo, apuesto

data [ˈdeɪṭə, ˈdæ-, ˈdɑ-] *ns & pl* : datos *mpl,* información *f*

database [ˈdeɪṭəˌbeɪs, ˈdæ-, ˈdɑ-] *n* : base *f* de datos

date[1] [ˈdeɪt] *v* **dated; dating** *vt* **1** : fechar (una carta, etc.), datar (un objeto) <it was dated June 9 : estaba fechada el 9 de junio> **2** : salir con <she's dating my brother : sale con mi hermano> — *vi* : datar

date[2] *n* **1** : fecha *f* <to date : hasta la fecha> **2** EPOCH, PERIOD : época *f,* período *m* **3** APPOINTMENT : cita *f* **4** COMPANION : acompañante *mf* **5** : dátil *m* (fruta)

dated [ˈdeɪṭəd] *adj* OUT-OF-DATE : anticuado, pasado de moda

datum [ˈdeɪṭəm, ˈdæ-, ˈdɑ-] *n, pl* **-ta** [-ṭə] *or* **-tums** : dato *m*

daub[1] [ˈdɔb] *vt* : embadurnar

daub[2] *n* : mancha *f*

daughter [ˈdɔṭər] *n* : hija *f*

daughter–in–law [ˈdɔṭərɪnˌlɔ] *n, pl* **daughters–in–law** : nuera *f,* hija *f* política

daunt [ˈdɔnt] *vt* : amilanar, acobardar, intimidar

dauntless [ˈdɔntləs] *adj* : intrépido, impávido

davenport [ˈdævənˌport] *n* : sofá *m*

dawdle [ˈdɔdəl] *vi* **-dled; -dling 1** DALLY : demorarse, entretenerse, perder tiempo **2** LOITER : vagar, holgazanear, haraganear

dawn[1] [ˈdɔn] *vi* **1** : amanecer, alborear, despuntar <Saturday dawned clear and bright : el sábado amaneció claro y luminoso> **2 to dawn on** : hacerse obvio <it dawned on me that she was right : me di cuenta de que tenía razón>

dawn[2] *n* **1** DAYBREAK : amanecer *m,* alba *f* **2** BEGINNING : albor *m,* comienzo *m* <the dawn of history : los albores de la historia> **3 from dawn to dusk** : de sol a sol

day [ˈdeɪ] *n* **1** : día *m* **2** DATE : fecha *f* **3** TIME : día *m,* tiempo *m* <in olden days : antaño> **4** WORKDAY : jornada *f* laboral

daybreak [ˈdeɪˌbreɪk] *n* : alba *f,* amanecer *m*

day care *n* : servicio *m* de guardería infantil

daydream[1] [ˈdeɪˌdriːm] *vi* : soñar despierto, fantasear

daydream[2] *n* : ensueño *m,* ensoñación *f,* fantasía *f*

daylight [ˈdeɪˌlaɪt] *n* **1** : luz *f* del día <in broad daylight : a plena luz del día> **2** → **daybreak 3** → **daytime**

daylight saving time *n* : hora *f* de verano

daytime [ˈdeɪˌtaɪm] *n* : horas *fpl* diurnas, día *m*

daze[1] [ˈdeɪz] *vt* **dazed; dazing 1** STUN : aturdir **2** DAZZLE : deslumbrar, ofuscar

daze[2] *n* **1** : aturdimiento *m* **2 in a daze** : aturdido, atonado

dazzle[1] [ˈdæzəl] *vt* **-zled; -zling** : deslumbrar, ofuscar

dazzle[2] *n* : resplandor *m,* brillo *m*

DDT [ˌdiːˌdiːˈtiː] *n* : DDT *m*

deacon [ˈdiːkən] *n* : diácono *m*

dead[1] [ˈdɛd] *adv* **1** ABRUPTLY : repentinamente, súbitamente <to stop dead : parar en seco> **2** ABSOLUTELY : absolutamente <I'm dead certain : estoy absolutamente seguro> **3** DIRECTLY : justo <dead ahead : justo adelante>

dead[2] *adj* **1** LIFELESS : muerto **2** NUMB : entumecido **3** INDIFFERENT : indiferente, frío **4** INACTIVE : inactivo <a dead volcano : un volcán inactivo> **5** : desconectado (dícese del teléfono), descargado (dícese de una batería) **6** EXHAUSTED : agotado, derrengado, muerto **7** OBSOLETE : obsoleto, muerto <a dead language : una lengua muerta> **8** EXACT : exacto <in the dead center : justo en el blanco>

dead[3] *n* **1 the dead** : los muertos **2 in the dead of night** : a las altas horas de la noche **3 in the dead of winter** : en pleno invierno

deadbeat [ˈdɛdˌbiːt] *n* **1** LOAFER : vago *m,* -ga *f;* holgazán *m,* -zana *f* **2** FREELOADER : gorrón *m,* -rrona *f fam;* gorrero *m,* -ra *f fam*

deaden [ˈdɛdən] *vt* **1** : atenuar (un dolor), entorpecer (sensaciones) **2** DULL : deslustrar **3** DISPIRIT : desanimar **4** MUFFLE : amortiguar, reducir (sonidos)

dead–end [ˈdɛdˈɛnd] *adj* **1** : sin salida <dead-end street : calle sin salida> **2** : sin futuro <a dead-end job : un trabajo sin porvenir>

dead end *n* : callejón *m* sin salida

dead heat *n* **:** empate *m*
deadline [ˈdɛd,laɪn] *n* **:** fecha *f* límite, fecha *f* tope, plazo *m* (determinado)
deadlock[1] [ˈdɛd,lɑk] *vt* **:** estancar — *vi* **:** estancarse, llegar a punto muerto
deadlock[2] *n* **:** punto *m* muerto, impasse *m*
deadly[1] [ˈdɛdli] *adv* **:** extremadamente, sumamente <deadly serious : muy en serio>
deadly[2] *adj* **-lier; -est 1** LETHAL **:** mortal, letal, mortífero **2** ACCURATE **:** certero, preciso <a deadly aim : una puntería infalible> **3** CAPITAL **:** capital <the seven deadly sins : los siete pecados capitales> **4** DULL **:** funesto, aburrido **5** EXTREME **:** extremo, absoluto <a deadly calm : una calma absoluta>
deadpan[1] [ˈdɛd,pæn] *adv* **:** de manera inexpresiva, sin expresión
deadpan[2] *adj* **:** inexpresivo, impasible
deaf [ˈdɛf] *adj* **:** sordo
deafen [ˈdɛfən] *vt* **-ened; -ening :** ensordecer
deaf–mute [ˈdɛfˈmjuːt] *n* **:** sordomudo *m*, -da *f*
deafness [ˈdɛfnəs] *n* **:** sordera *f*
deal[1] [ˈdiːl] *v* **dealt; dealing** *vt* **1** APPORTION **:** repartir <to deal justice : repartir la justicia> **2** DISTRIBUTE **:** repartir, dar (naipes) **3** DELIVER **:** asestar, propinar <to deal a blow : asestar un golpe> — *vi* **1 :** dar, repartir (en juegos de naipes) **2 to deal in :** comerciar en, traficar con (drogas) **3 to deal with** CONCERN **:** tratar de, tener que ver con <the book deals with poverty : el libro trata de la pobreza> **4 to deal with** HANDLE **:** tratar (con), encargarse de **5 to deal with** TREAT **:** tratar <the judge dealt with him severely : el juez lo trató con severidad> **6 to deal with** ACCEPT **:** aceptar (una situación o desgracia)
deal[2] *n* **1 :** reparto *m* (de naipes) **2** AGREEMENT, TRANSACTION **:** trato *m*, acuerdo *m*, transacción *f* **3** TREATMENT **:** trato *m* <he got a raw deal : le hicieron una injusticia> **4** BARGAIN **:** ganga *f*, oferta *f* **5 a good deal** *or* **a great deal :** mucho, una gran cantidad
dealer [ˈdiːlər] *n* **:** comerciante *mf*, traficante *mf*
dealings [ˈdiːlɪŋz] *npl* **1 :** relaciones *fpl* (personales) **2** TRANSACTIONS **:** negocios *mpl*, transacciones *fpl*
dean [ˈdiːn] *n* **1 :** deán *m* (del clero) **2 :** decano *m*, -na *f* (de una facultad o profesión)
dear[1] [ˈdɪr] *adj* **1** ESTEEMED, LOVED **:** querido, estimado <a dear friend : un amigo querido> <Dear Sir : Estimado Señor> **2** COSTLY **:** caro, costoso
dear[2] *n* **:** querido *m*, -da *f*; amado *m*, -da *f*
dearly [ˈdɪrli] *adv* **1 :** mucho <I love them dearly : los quiero mucho> **2 :** caro <to pay dearly : pagar caro>
dearth [ˈdərθ] *n* **:** escasez *f*, carestía *f*
death [ˈdɛθ] *n* **1 :** muerte *f*, fallecimiento *m* <to be the death of : matar> **2** FATALITY **:** víctima *f* (mortal); muerto *m*, -ta *f* **3** END **:** fin *m* <the death of civilization : el fin de la civilización>
deathbed [ˈdɛθ,bɛd] *n* **:** lecho *m* de muerte
deathblow [ˈdɛθ,bloː] *n* **:** golpe *m* mortal
deathless [ˈdɛθləs] *adj* **:** eterno, inmortal
deathly [ˈdɛθli] *adj* **:** de muerte, sepulcral (dícese del silencio), cadavérico (dícese de la palidez)
debacle [dɪˈbɑkəl, -ˈbæ-] *n* **:** desastre *m*, debacle *m*, fiasco *m*
debar [diˈbɑr] *vt* **-barred; -barring :** excluir, prohibir
debase [diˈbeɪs] *vt* **-based; -basing :** degradar, envilecer
debasement [diˈbeɪsmənt] *n* **:** degradación *f*, envilecimiento *m*
debatable [diˈbeɪtəbəl] *adj* **:** discutible
debate[1] [diˈbeɪt] *vt* **-bated; -bating :** debatir, discutir
debate[2] *n* **:** debate *m*, discusión *f*
debauch [diˈbɔtʃ] *vt* **:** pervertir, corromper
debauchery [diˈbɔtʃəri] *n, pl* **-eries :** libertinaje *m*, disipación *f*, intemperancia *f*
debilitate [diˈbɪlə,teɪt] *vt* **-tated; -tating :** debilitar
debility [diˈbɪləṭi] *n, pl* **-ties :** debilidad *f*
debit[1] [ˈdɛbɪt] *vt* **:** adeudar, cargar, debitar
debit[2] *n* **:** débito *m*, cargo *m*, debe *m*
debonair [,dɛbəˈnær] *adj* **:** elegante y desenvuelto, apuesto
debris [dəˈbriː, deɪ-; ˈdeɪ,briː] *n, pl* **-bris** [-ˈbriːz, -,briːz] **1** RUBBLE, RUINS **:** escombros *mpl*, ruinas *fpl*, restos *mpl* **2** RUBBISH **:** basura *f*, deshechos *mpl*
debt [ˈdɛt] *n* **1 :** deuda *f* <to pay a debt : saldar una deuda> **2** INDEBTEDNESS **:** endeudamiento *m*
debtor [ˈdɛṭər] *n* **:** deudor *m*, -dora *f*
debunk [diˈbʌŋk] *vt* DISCREDIT **:** desacreditar, desprestigiar
debut[1] [deɪˈbjuː, ˈdeɪ,bjuː] *vi* **:** debutar
debut[2] *n* **1 :** debut *m* (de un actor), estreno *m* (de una obra) **2 :** debut *m*, presentación *f* (en sociedad)
debutante [ˈdɛbjʊ,tɑnt] *n* **:** debutante *f*
decade [ˈdɛ,keɪd, dɛˈkeɪd] *n* **:** década *f*
decadence [ˈdɛkədənts] *n* **:** decadencia *f*
decadent [ˈdɛkədənt] *adj* **:** decadente
decal [ˈdiː,kæl, diˈkæl] *n* **:** calcomanía *f*

decamp [di'kæmp] *vi* : irse, largarse *fam*
decant [di'kænt] *vt* : decantar
decanter [di'kæntər] *n* : licorera *f,* garrafa *f*
decapitate [di'kæpə,teɪt] *vt* **-tated; -tating** : decapitar
decay[1] [di'keɪ] *vi* **1** DECOMPOSE : descomponerse, pudrirse **2** DETERIORATE : deteriorarse **3** : cariarse (dícese de los dientes)
decay[2] *n* **1** DECOMPOSITION : descomposición *f* **2** DECLINE, DETERIORATION : decadencia *f,* deterioro *m* **3** : caries *f* (de los dientes)
decease[1] [di'siːs] *vi* **-ceased; -ceasing** : morir, fallecer
decease[2] *n* : fallecimiento *m,* defunción *f,* deceso *m*
deceit [di'siːt] *n* **1** DECEPTION : engaño *m* **2** DISHONESTY : deshonestidad *f*
deceitful [di'siːtfəl] *adj* : falso, embustero, engañoso, mentiroso
deceitfully [di'siːtfəli] *adv* : con engaño, con falsedad
deceitfulness [di'siːtfəlnəs] *n* : falsedad *f,* engaño *m*
deceive [di'siːv] *vt* **-ceived; -ceiving** : engañar, burlar
deceiver [di'siːvər] *n* : impostor *m,* -tora *f*
decelerate [di'sɛlə,reɪt] *vi* **-ated; -ating** : reducir la velocidad, desacelerar
December [di'sɛmbər] *n* : diciembre *m*
decency ['disəntsi] *n, pl* **-cies** : decencia *f,* decoro *m*
decent ['diːsənt] *adj* **1** CORRECT, PROPER : decente, decoroso, correcto **2** CLOTHED : vestido, presentable **3** MODEST : púdico, modesto **4** ADEQUATE : decente, adecuado <decent wages : paga adecuada>
decently ['diːsəntli] *adv* : decentemente
deception [di'sɛpʃən] *n* : engaño *m*
deceptive [di'sɛptɪv] *adj* : engañoso, falaz — **deceptively** *adv*
decibel ['dɛsəbəl, -,bɛl] *n* : decibelio *m*
decide [di'saɪd] *v* **-cided; -ciding** *vt* **1** CONCLUDE : decidir, llegar a la conclusión de <he decided what to do : decidió qué iba a hacer> **2** DETERMINE : decidir, determinar <one blow decided the fight : un solo golpe determinó la pelea> **3** CONVINCE : decidir <her pleas decided me to help : sus súplicas me decidieron a ayudarla> **4** RESOLVE : resolver — *vi* : decidirse
decided [di'saɪdəd] *adj* **1** UNQUESTIONABLE : indudable **2** RESOLUTE : decidido, resuelto — **decidedly** *adv*
deciduous [di'sɪdʒʊəs] *adj* : caduco, de hoja caduca
decimal[1] ['dɛsəməl] *adj* : decimal
decimal[2] *n* : número *m* decimal
decipher [di'saɪfər] *vt* : descifrar — **decipherable** [-əbəl] *adj*
decision [dɪ'sɪʒən] *n* : decisión *f,* determinación *f* <to make a decision : tomar una decisión>
decisive [dɪ'saɪsɪv] *adj* **1** DECIDING : decisivo <the decisive vote : el voto decisivo> **2** CONCLUSIVE : decisivo, concluyente, contundente <a decisive victory : una victoria contundente> **3** RESOLUTE : decidido, resuelto, firme
decisively [dɪ'saɪsɪvli] *adv* : con decisión, de manera decisiva
decisiveness [dɪ'saɪsɪvnəs] *n* **1** FORCEFULNESS : contundencia *f* **2** RESOLUTION : firmeza *f,* decisión *f,* determinación *f*
deck[1] ['dɛk] *vt* **1** FLOOR : tumbar, derribar <she decked him with one blow : lo tumbó de un solo golpe> **2 to deck out** : adornar, engalanar
deck[2] *n* **1** : cubierta *f* (de un barco) **2** *or* **deck of cards** : baraja *f* (de naipes)
declaim [di'kleɪm] *v* : declamar
declaration [,dɛklə'reɪʃən] *n* : declaración *f,* pronunciamiento *m* (oficial)
declare [di'klær] *vt* **-clared; -claring** : declarar, manifestar <to declare war : declarar la guerra> <they declared their support : manifestaron su apoyo>
decline[1] [di'klaɪn] *v* **-clined; -clining** *vi* **1** DESCEND : descender **2** DETERIORATE : deteriorarse, decaer <her health is declining : su salud se está deteriorando> **3** DECREASE : disminuir, decrecer, decaer **4** REFUSE : rehusar — *vt* **1** INFLECT : declinar **2** REFUSE, TURN DOWN : declinar, rehusar
decline[2] *n* **1** DETERIORATION : decadencia *f,* deterioro *m* **2** DECREASE : disminución *f,* descenso *m* **3** SLOPE : declive *m,* pendiente *f*
decode [di'koːd] *vt* **-coded; -coding** : descifrar (un mensaje), descodificar (una señal)
decompose [,diːkəm'poːz] *v* **-posed; -posing** *vt* **1** BREAK DOWN : descomponer **2** ROT : descomponer, pudrir — *vi* : descomponerse, pudrirse
decomposition [,diː,kɑmpə'zɪʃən] *n* : descomposición *f*
decongestant [,diːkən'dʒɛstənt] *n* : descongestionante *m*
decor *or* **décor** [deɪ'kɔr, 'deɪ,kɔr] *n* : decoración *f*
decorate ['dɛkə,reɪt] *vt* **-rated; -rating 1** ADORN : decorar, adornar **2** : condecorar <he was decorated for bravery : lo condecoraron por valor>
decoration [,dɛkə'reɪʃən] *n* **1** ADORNMENT : decoración *f,* adorno *m* **2** : condecoración *f* (de honor)
decorative ['dɛkərət̬ɪv, -,reɪ-] *adj* : decorativo, ornamental, de adorno
decorator ['dɛkə,reɪt̬ər] *n* : decorador *m,* -dora *f*
decorum [di'korəm] *n* : decoro *m*

decoy[1] ['diː,kɔɪ, di'-] *vt* : atraer (con señuelo)
decoy[2] *n* : señuelo *m,* reclamo *m,* cimbel *m*
decrease[1] [di'kriːs] *v* **-creased; -creasing** *vi* : decrecer, disminuir, bajar — *vt* : reducir, disminuir
decrease[2] ['diː,kriːs] *n* : disminución *f,* descenso *m,* bajada *f*
decree[1] [di'kriː] *vt* **-creed; -creeing** : decretar
decree[2] *n* : decreto *m*
decrepit [di'krɛpɪt] *adj* **1** FEEBLE : decrépito, débil **2** DILAPIDATED : deteriorado, ruinoso
decry [di'kraɪ] *vt* **-cried; -crying** : censurar, criticar
dedicate ['dɛdɪ,keɪt] *vt* **-cated; -cating 1** : dedicar <she dedicated the book to Carlos : le dedicó el libro a Carlos> **2** : consagrar, dedicar <to dedicate one's life : consagrar uno su vida>
dedication [,dɛdɪ'keɪʃən] *n* **1** DEVOTION : dedicación *f,* devoción *f* **2** : dedicatoria *f* (de un libro, una canción, etc.) **3** CONSECRATION : dedicación *f*
deduce [di'duːs, -'djuːs] *vt* **-duced; -ducing** : deducir, inferir
deduct [di'dʌkt] *vt* : deducir, descontar, restar
deductible [di'dʌktəbəl] *adj* : deducible
deduction [di'dʌkʃən] *n* : deducción *f*
deed[1] ['diːd] *vt* : ceder, transferir
deed[2] *n* **1** ACT : acto *m,* acción *f,* hecho *m* <a good deed : una buena acción> **2** FEAT : hazaña *f,* proeza *f* **3** TITLE : escritura *f,* título *m*
deem ['diːm] *vt* : considerar, juzgar
deep[1] ['diːp] *adv* : hondo, profundamente <to dig deep : cavar hondo>
deep[2] *adj* **1** : hondo, profundo <the deep end : la parte honda> <a deep wound : una herida profunda> **2** WIDE : ancho **3** INTENSE : profundo, intenso **4** DARK : intenso, subido <deep red : rojo subido> **5** LOW : profundo <a deep tone : un tono profundo> **6** ABSORBED : absorto <deep in thought : absorto en la meditación>
deep[3] *n* **1 the deep** : lo profundo, el piélago **2 the deep of night** : lo más profundo de la noche
deepen ['diːpən] *vt* **1** : ahondar, profundizar **2** INTENSIFY : intensificar — *vi* **1** : hacerse más profundo **2** INTENSIFY : intensificarse
deeply ['diːpli] *adv* : hondo, profundamente <I'm deeply sorry : lo siento sinceramente>
deep–seated ['diːp'siːtəd] *adj* : profundamente arraigado, enraizado
deer ['dɪr] *ns & pl* : ciervo *m,* venado *m*
deerskin ['dɪr,skɪn] *n* : piel *f* de venado
deface [di'feɪs] *vt* **-faced; -facing** MAR : desfigurar
defacement [di'feɪsmənt] *n* : desfiguración *f*
defamation [,dɛfə'meɪʃən] *n* : difamación *f*
defamatory [di'fæmə,tori] *adj* : difamatorio
defame [di'feɪm] *vt* **-famed; -faming** : difamar, calumniar
default[1] [di'fɔlt, 'diː,fɔlt] *vi* **1** : no cumplir (con una obligación), no pagar **2** : no presentarse (en un tribunal)
default[2] *n* **1** NEGLECT : omisión *f,* negligencia *f* **2** NONPAYMENT : impago *m,* falta *f* de pago **3 to win by default** : ganar por abandono
defaulter [di'fɔltər] *n* : moroso *m,* -sa *f;* rebelde *mf* (en un tribunal)
defeat[1] [di'fiːt] *vt* **1** FRUSTRATE : frustrar **2** BEAT : vencer, derrotar
defeat[2] *n* : derrota *f,* rechazo *m* (de legislación), fracaso *m* (de planes, etc.)
defecate ['dɛfɪ,keɪt] *vi* **-cated; -cating** : defecar
defect[1] [di'fɛkt] *vi* : desertar
defect[2] ['diː,fɛkt, di'fɛkt] *n* : defecto *m*
defection [di'fɛkʃən] *n* : deserción *f,* defección *f*
defective [di'fɛktɪv] *adj* **1** FAULTY : defectuoso **2** DEFICIENT : deficiente
defector [di'fɛktər] *n* : desertor *m,* -tora *f*
defend [di'fɛnd] *vt* : defender
defendant [di'fɛndənt] *n* : acusado *m,* -da *f;* demandado *m,* -da *f*
defender [di'fɛndər] *n* **1** ADVOCATE : defensor *m,* -sora *f* **2** : defensa *mf* (en deportes)
defense [di'fɛn*t*s, 'diː,fɛn*t*s] *n* : defensa *f*
defenseless [di'fɛn*t*sləs] *adj* : indefenso
defensive[1] [di'fɛn*t*sɪv] *adj* : defensivo
defensive[2] *n* **on the defensive** : a la defensiva
defer [di'fər] *v* **-ferred; -ferring** *vt* POSTPONE : diferir, aplazar, posponer — *vi* **to defer to** : deferir a
deference ['dɛfərən*t*s] *n* : deferencia *f*
deferential [,dɛfə'rɛntʃəl] *adj* : respetuoso
deferment [di'fərmənt] *n* : aplazamiento *m*
defiance [di'faɪən*t*s] *n* : desafío *m*
defiant [di'faɪənt] *adj* : desafiante, insolente
deficiency [di'fɪʃən*t*si] *n, pl* **-cies** : deficiencia *f,* carencia *f*
deficient [di'fɪʃənt] *adj* : deficiente, carente
deficit ['dɛfəsɪt] *n* : déficit *m*
defile [di'faɪl] *vt* **-filed; -filing 1** DIRTY : ensuciar, manchar **2** CORRUPT : corromper **3** DESECRATE, PROFANE : profanar **4** DISHONOR : deshonrar
defilement [di'faɪlmənt] *n* **1** DESECRATION : profanación *f* **2** CORRUPTION

: corrupción *f* **3** CONTAMINATION : contaminación *f*

define [di'faɪn] *vt* **-fined; -fining 1** BOUND : delimitar, demarcar **2** CLARIFY : aclarar, definir **3** : definir <to define a word : definir una palabra>

definite ['dɛfənɪt] *adj* **1** CERTAIN : definido, determinado **2** CLEAR : claro, explícito **3** UNQUESTIONABLE : seguro, incuestionable

definite article *n* : artículo *m* definido

definitely ['dɛfənɪtli] *adv* **1** DOUBTLESSLY : indudablemente, sin duda **2** DEFINITIVELY : definitivamente, seguramente

definition [ˌdɛfə'nɪʃən] *n* : definición *f*

definitive [di'fɪnət̬ɪv] *adj* **1** CONCLUSIVE : definitivo, decisivo **2** AUTHORITATIVE : de autoridad, autorizado

deflate [di'fleɪt] *v* **-flated; -flating** *vt* **1** : desinflar (una llanta, etc.) **2** REDUCE : rebajar <to deflate one's ego : bajarle los humos a uno> — *vi* : desinflarse

deflect [di'flɛkt] *vt* : desviar — *vi* : desviarse

defoliant [di'foːliənt] *n* : defoliante *m*

deform [di'fɔrm] *vt* : deformar

deformed [di'fɔrmd] *adj* : deforme

deformity [di'fɔrmət̬i] *n, pl* **-ties** : deformidad *f*

defraud [di'frɔd] *vt* : estafar, defraudar

defray [di'freɪ] *vt* : sufragar, costear

defrost [di'frɔst] *vt* : descongelar, deshelar — *vi* : descongelarse, deshelarse

deft ['dɛft] *adj* : hábil, diestro — **deftly** *adv*

defunct [di'fʌŋkt] *adj* **1** DECEASED : difunto, fallecido **2** EXTINCT : extinto, fenecido

defy [di'faɪ] *vt* **-fied; -fying 1** CHALLENGE : desafiar, retar **2** DISOBEY : desobedecer **3** RESIST : resistir, hacer imposible, hacer inútil

degenerate[1] [di'dʒɛnəˌreɪt] *vi* **-ated; -ating** : degenerar

degenerate[2] [di'dʒɛnərət] *adj* : degenerado

degeneration [diˌdʒɛnə'reɪʃən] *n* : degeneración *f*

degradation [ˌdɛgrə'deɪʃən] *n* : degradación *f*

degrade [di'greɪd] *vt* **-graded; -grading 1** : degradar, envilecer **2 to degrade oneself** : rebajarse

degree [di'griː] *n* **1** EXTENT : grado *m* <a third degree burn : una quemadura de tercer grado> **2** : título *m* (de enseñanza superior) **3** : grado *m* (de un círculo, de la temperatura) **4 by degrees** : gradualmente, poco a poco

dehydrate [di'haɪˌdreɪt] *v* **-drated; -drating** *vt* : deshidratar — *vi* : deshidratarse

dehydration [ˌdiːhaɪ'dreɪʃən] *n* : deshidratación *f*

deice [ˌdiː'aɪs] *vt* **-iced; -icing** : deshelar, descongelar

deify ['diːəˌfaɪ, 'deɪ-] *vt* **-fied; -fying** : deificar

deign ['deɪn] *vi* : dignarse, condescender

deity ['diːət̬i, 'deɪ-] *n, pl* **-ties 1 the Deity** : Dios *m* **2** GOD, GODDESS : deidad *f;* dios *m,* diosa *f*

dejected [di'dʒɛktəd] *adj* : abatido, desalentado, desanimado

dejection [di'dʒɛkʃən] *n* : abatimiento *m,* desaliento *m,* desánimo *m*

delay[1] [di'leɪ] *vt* **1** POSTPONE : posponer, postergar **2** HOLD UP : retrasar, demorar — *vi* : tardar, demorar

delay[2] *n* **1** LATENESS : tardanza *f* **2** HOLDUP : demora *f,* retraso *m*

delectable [di'lɛktəbəl] *adj* **1** DELICIOUS : delicioso, exquisito **2** DELIGHTFUL : encantador

delegate[1] ['dɛlɪˌgeɪt] *v* **-gated; -gating** : delegar

delegate[2] ['dɛlɪgət, -ˌgeɪt] *n* : delegado *m,* -da *f*

delegation [ˌdɛlɪ'geɪʃən] *n* : delegación *f*

delete [di'liːt] *vt* **-leted; -leting** : suprimir, tachar, eliminar

deletion [di'liːʃən] *n* : supresión *f,* tachadura *f,* eliminación *f*

deliberate[1] [dɪ'lɪbəˌreɪt] *v* **-ated; -ating** *vt* : deliberar sobre, reflexionar sobre, considerar — *vi* : deliberar

deliberate[2] [dɪ'lɪbərət] *adj* **1** CONSIDERED : reflexionado, premeditado **2** INTENTIONAL : deliberado, intencional **3** SLOW : lento, pausado

deliberately [dɪ'lɪbərətli] *adv* **1** INTENTIONALLY : adrede, a propósito **2** SLOWLY : pausadamente, lentamente

deliberation [dɪˌlɪbə'reɪʃən] *n* **1** CONSIDERATION : deliberación *f,* consideración *f* **2** SLOWNESS : lentitud *f*

delicacy ['dɛlɪkəsi] *n, pl* **-cies 1** : manjar *m,* exquisitez *f* <caviar is a real delicacy : el caviar es un verdadero manjar> **2** FINENESS : delicadeza *f* **3** FRAGILITY : fragilidad *f*

delicate ['dɛlɪkət] *adj* **1** SUBTLE : delicado <a delicate fragrance : una fragancia delicada> **2** DAINTY : delicado, primoroso, fino **3** FRAGILE : frágil **4** SENSITIVE : delicado <a delicate matter : un asunto delicado>

delicately ['dɛlɪkətli] *adv* : delicadamente, con delicadeza

delicatessen [ˌdɛlɪkə'tɛsən] *n* : charcutería *f,* fiambrería *f,* salchichonería *f Mex*

delicious [di'lɪʃəs] *adj* : delicioso, exquisito, rico — **deliciously** *adv*

delight[1] [dɪ'laɪt] *vt* : deleitar, encantar — *vi* **to delight in** : deleitarse con, complacerse en

delight[2] *n* **1** JOY : placer *m,* deleite *m,* gozo *m* **2** : encanto *m* <your garden is a delight : su jardín es un encanto>

delightful [dɪˈlaɪtfəl] *adj* **:** delicioso, encantador

delightfully [dɪˈlaɪtfəli] *adv* **:** de manera encantadora, de maravilla

delineate [diˈlɪni,eɪt] *vt* **-eated; -eating :** delinear, trazar, bosquejar

delinquency [diˈlɪŋkwən*t*si] *n, pl* **-cies :** delincuencia *f*

delinquent[1] [diˈlɪŋkwənt] *adj* **1 :** delincuente **2** OVERDUE **:** vencido y sin pagar, moroso

delinquent[2] *n* **:** delincuente *mf* <juvenile delinquent : delincuente juvenil>

delirious [diˈlɪriəs] *adj* **:** delirante <delirious with joy : loco de alegría>

delirium [diˈlɪriəm] *n* **:** delirio *m,* desvarío *m*

deliver [diˈlɪvər] *vt* **1** FREE **:** liberar, librar **2** DISTRIBUTE, HAND **:** entregar, repartir **3 :** asistir en el parto de (un niño) **4 :** pronunciar <to deliver a speech : pronunciar un discurso> **5** PROJECT **:** despachar, lanzar <he delivered a fast ball : lanzó un pelota rápida> **6** DEAL **:** propinar, asestar <to deliver a blow : asestar un golpe>

deliverance [diˈlɪvərən*t*s] *n* **:** liberación *f,* rescate *m,* salvación *f*

deliverer [diˈlɪvərər] *n* RESCUER **:** libertador *m,* -dora *f;* salvador *m,* -dora *f*

delivery [diˈlɪvəri] *n, pl* **-eries 1** LIBERATION **:** liberación *f* **2 :** entrega *f,* reparto *m* <cash on delivery : entrega contra reembolso> <home delivery : servicio a domicilio> **3** CHILDBIRTH **:** parto *m,* alumbramiento *m* **4** SPEECH **:** expresión *f* oral, modo *m* de hablar **5** THROW **:** lanzamiento *m*

dell [ˈdɛl] *n* **:** hondonada *f,* valle *m* pequeño

delta [ˈdɛltə] *n* **:** delta *m*

delude [diˈluːd] *vt* **-luded; -luding 1 :** engañar **2 to delude oneself :** engañarse

deluge[1] [ˈdɛl,juːdʒ, -,juːʒ] *vt* **-uged; -uging 1** FLOOD **:** inundar **2** OVERWHELM **:** abrumar <deluged with requests : abrumado de pedidos>

deluge[2] *n* **1** FLOOD **:** inundación *f* **2** DOWNPOUR **:** aguacero *m* **3** BARRAGE **:** aluvión *m*

delusion [diˈluːʒən] *n* **1 :** ilusión *f* (falsa) **2 delusions of grandeur :** delirios *mpl* de grandeza

deluxe [diˈlʌks, -ˈlʊks] *adj* **:** de lujo

delve [ˈdɛlv] *vi* **delved; delving 1** DIG **:** escarbar **2 to delve into** PROBE **:** cavar en, ahondar en

demand[1] [diˈmænd] *vt* **:** demandar, exigir, reclamar

demand[2] *n* **1** REQUEST **:** petición *f,* pedido *m,* demanda *f* <by popular demand : a petición del público> **2** CLAIM **:** reclamación *f,* exigencia *f* **3** MARKET **:** demanda *f* <supply and demand : la oferta y la demanda>

demarcation [,diː,mɑrˈkeɪʃən] *n* **:** demarcación *f,* deslinde *m*

demean [diˈmiːn] *vt* **:** degradar, rebajar

demeanor [diˈmiːnər] *n* **:** comportamiento *m,* conducta *f*

demented [diˈmɛntəd] *adj* **:** demente, loco

demerit [diˈmɛrət] *n* **:** demérito *m*

demigod [ˈdɛmi,gɑd, -,gɔd] *n* **:** semidiós *m*

demise [dɪˈmaɪz] *n* **1** DEATH **:** fallecimiento *m,* deceso *m* **2** END **:** hundimiento *m,* desaparición *f* (de una institución, etc.)

demitasse [ˈdɛmi,tæs, -,tɑs] *n* **:** taza *f* pequeña (de café)

demobilization [di,moːbələˈzeɪʃən] *n* **:** desmovilización *f*

demobilize [diˈmoːbə,laɪz] *vt* **-lized; -lizing :** desmovilizar

democracy [diˈmɑkrəsi] *n, pl* **-cies :** democracia *f*

democrat [ˈdɛmə,kræt] *n* **:** demócrata *mf*

democratic [,dɛməˈkræt̬ɪk] *adj* **:** democrático — **democratically** [-tɪkli] *adv*

demolish [diˈmɑlɪʃ] *vt* **1** RAZE **:** demoler, derribar, arrasar **2** DESTROY **:** destruir, destrozar

demolition [,dɛməˈlɪʃən, ,diː-] *n* **:** demolición *f,* derribo *m*

demon [ˈdiːmən] *n* **:** demonio *m,* diablo *m*

demonstrably [diˈmɑn*t*strəbli] *adv* **:** manifiestamente, claramente

demonstrate [ˈdɛmən,streɪt] *vt* **-strated; -strating 1** SHOW **:** demostrar **2** PROVE **:** probar, demostrar **3** EXPLAIN **:** explicar, ilustrar

demonstration [,dɛmənˈstreɪʃən] *n* **1** SHOW **:** muestra *f,* demostración *f* **2** RALLY **:** manifestación *f*

demonstrative [diˈmɑn*t*strət̬ɪv] *adj* **1** EFFUSIVE **:** efusivo, expresivo, demostrativo **2 :** demostrativo (en lingüística) <demonstrative pronoun : pronombre demostrativo>

demonstrator [ˈdɛmən,streɪt̬ər] *n* **1 :** demostrador *m,* -dora *f* (de productos) **2** PROTESTER **:** manifestante *mf*

demoralize [diˈmɔrə,laɪz] *vt* **-ized; -izing :** desmoralizar

demote [diˈmoːt] *vt* **-moted; -moting :** degradar, bajar de categoría

demotion [diˈmoːʃən] *n* **:** degradación *f,* descenso *m* de categoría

demur [diˈmər] *vi* **-murred; -murring 1** OBJECT **:** oponerse **2 to demur at :** ponerle objeciones a (algo)

demure [diˈmjʊr] *adj* **:** recatado, modesto — **demurely** *adv*

den [ˈdɛn] *n* **1** LAIR **:** cubil *m,* madriguera *f* **2** HIDEOUT **:** guarida *f* **3** STUDY **:** estudio *m,* gabinete *m*

denature [diˈneɪtʃər] *vt* **-tured; -turing :** desnaturalizar

denial [diˈnaɪəl] *n* **1** REFUSAL **:** rechazo *m,* denegación *f,* negativa *f* **2** REPUDIATION **:** negación *f* (de una creencia, etc.), rechazo *m*

denim [ˈdɛnəm] *n* **1** : tela *f* vaquera, mezclilla *f Chile, Mex* **2 denims** *npl* → **jeans**

denizen [ˈdɛnəzən] *n* : habitante *mf;* morador *m,* -dora *f*

denomination [dɪˌnɑməˈneɪʃən] *n* **1** FAITH : confesión *f,* fe *f* **2** VALUE : denominación *f,* valor *m* (de una moneda)

denominator [dɪˈnɑməˌneɪt̬ər] *n* : denominador *m*

denote [diˈnoːt] *vt* **-noted; -noting 1** INDICATE, MARK : indicar, denotar, señalar **2** MEAN : significar

denouement [ˌdeɪˌnuːˈmɑ] *n* : desenlace *m*

denounce [diˈnaʊnts] *vt* **-nounced; -nouncing 1** CENSURE : denunciar, censurar **2** ACCUSE : denunciar, acusar, delatar

dense [ˈdɛnts] *adj* **denser; -est 1** THICK : espeso, denso <dense vegetation : vegetación densa> <a dense fog : una niebla espesa> **2** STUPID : estúpido, burro *fam*

densely [ˈdɛntsli] *adv* **1** THICKLY : densamente **2** STUPIDLY : torpemente

denseness [ˈdɛntsnəs] *n* **1** → **density 2** STUPIDITY : estupidez *f*

density [ˈdɛntsət̬i] *n, pl* **-ties** : densidad *f*

dent¹ [ˈdɛnt] *vt* : abollar, mellar

dent² *n* : abolladura *f,* mella *f*

dental [ˈdɛntəl] *adj* : dental

dental floss *n* : hilo *m* dental

dentifrice [ˈdɛntəfrɪs] *n* : dentífrico *m,* pasta *f* de dientes

dentist [ˈdɛntɪst] *n* : dentista *mf*

dentistry [ˈdɛntɪstri] *n* : odontología *f*

dentures [ˈdɛntʃərz] *npl* : dentadura *f* postiza

denude [diˈnuːd, -ˈnjuːd] *vt* **-nuded; -nuding** STRIP : desnudar, despojar

denunciation [diˌnʌntsiˈeɪʃən] *n* : denuncia *f,* acusación *f*

deny [diˈnaɪ] *vt* **-nied; -nying 1** REFUTE : desmentir, negar **2** DISOWN, REPUDIATE : negar, renegar de **3** REFUSE : denegar **4 to deny oneself** : privarse, sacrificarse

deodorant [diˈoːdərənt] *n* : desodorante *m*

deodorize [diˈoːdəˌraɪz] *vt* **-ized; -izing** : desodorizar

depart [diˈpɑrt] *vt* : salirse de — *vi* **1** LEAVE : salir, partir, irse **2** DIE : morir

department [diˈpɑrtmənt] *n* **1** DIVISION : sección *f* (de una tienda, una organización, etc.), departamento *m* (de una empresa, una universidad, etc.), ministerio *m* (del gobierno) **2** PROVINCE, SPHERE : esfera *f,* campo *m,* competencia *f*

departmental [diˌpɑrtˈmɛntəl, ˌdiː-] *adj* : departamental

department store *n* : grandes almacenes *mpl*

departure [diˈpɑrtʃər] *n* **1** LEAVING : salida *f,* partida *f* **2** DEVIATION : desviación *f*

depend [diˈpɛnd] *vi* **1** RELY : contar (con), confiar (en) <depend on me! : ¡cuenta conmigo!> **2 to depend on** : depender de <success depends on hard work : el éxito depende de trabajar duro> **3 that depends** : según, eso depende

dependable [diˈpɛndəbəl] *adj* : responsable, digno de confianza, fiable

dependence [diˈpɛndənts] *n* : dependencia *f*

dependency [diˈpɛndəntsi] *n, pl* **-cies 1** → **dependence 2** : posesión *f* (de una unidad política)

dependent¹ [diˈpɛndənt] *adj* : dependiente

dependent² *n* : persona *f* a cargo de alguien

depict [diˈpɪkt] *vt* **1** PORTRAY : representar **2** DESCRIBE : describir

depiction [diˈpɪkʃən] *n* : representación *f,* descripción *f*

deplete [diˈpliːt] *vt* **-pleted; -pleting 1** EXHAUST : agotar **2** REDUCE : reducir

depletion [diˈpliːʃən] *n* **1** EXHAUSTION : agotamiento *m* **2** REDUCTION : reducción *f,* disminución *f*

deplorable [diˈplorəbəl] *adj* **1** CONTEMPTIBLE : deplorable, despreciable **2** LAMENTABLE : lamentable

deplore [diˈplor] *vt* **-plored; -ploring 1** REGRET : deplorar, lamentar **2** CONDEMN : condenar, deplorar

deploy [diˈplɔɪ] *vt* : desplegar

deployment [diˈplɔɪmənt] *n* : despliegue *m*

deport [diˈport] *vt* **1** EXPEL : deportar, expulsar (de un país) **2 to deport oneself** BEHAVE : comportarse

deportment [diˈportmənt] *n* : conducta *f,* comportamiento *f*

depose [diˈpoːz] *v* **-posed; -posing** *vt* : deponer

deposit¹ [diˈpɑzət] *vt* **-ited; -iting** : depositar

deposit² *n* **1** : depósito *m* (en el banco) **2** DOWN PAYMENT : entrega *f* inicial **3** : depósito *m,* yacimiento *m* (en geología)

depositor [diˈpɑzət̬ər] *n* : depositante *mf*

depository [diˈpɑzəˌtori] *n, pl* **-ries** : almacén *m,* depósito *m*

depot [*in sense 1 usu* ˈdɛˌpoː, *2 usu* ˈdiː-] *n* **1** STOREHOUSE : almacén *m,* depósito *m* **2** STATION, TERMINAL : terminal *mf,* estación *f* (de autobuses, ferrocarriles, etc.)

deprave [diˈpreɪv] *vt* **-praved; -praving** : depravar, pervertir

depraved [diˈpreɪvd] *adj* : depravado, degenerado

depravity [diˈprævət̬i] *n, pl* **-ties** : depravación *f*

depreciate [diˈpriːʃiˌeɪt] *v* **-ated; -ating** *vt* **1** DEVALUE : depreciar, devaluar 2 DISPARAGE : menospreciar, despreciar — *vi* : depreciarse, devaluarse

depreciation [di͵priːʃiˈeɪʃən] *n* : depreciación *f,* devaluación *f*

depress [diˈprɛs] *vt* **1** PRESS, PUSH : apretar, presionar, pulsar **2** REDUCE : reducir, hacer bajar (precios, ventas, etc.) **3** SADDEN : deprimir, abatir, entristecer **4** DEVALUE : depreciar

depressant[1] [diˈprɛsənt] *adj* : depresivo

depressant[2] *n* : depresivo *m*

depressed [diˈprɛst] *adj* **1** DEJECTED : deprimido, abatido **2** : deprimido, en crisis (dícese de la economía)

depressing [diˈprɛsɪŋ] *adj* : deprimente, triste

depression [diˈprɛʃən] *n* **1** DESPONDENCY : depresión *f,* abatimiento *m* **2** : depresión (en una superficie) **3** RECESSION : depresión *f* económica, crisis *f*

deprivation [͵dɛprəˈveɪʃən] *n* : privación *f*

deprive [diˈpraɪv] *vt* **-prived; -priving** : privar

depth [ˈdɛpθ] *n, pl* **depths** [ˈdɛpθs, ˈdɛps] : profundidad *f,* fondo *m* <to study in depth : estudiar a fondo> <in the depths of winter : en pleno invierno>

deputize [ˈdɛpjʊ͵taɪz] *vt* **-tized; -tizing** : nombrar como segundo

deputy [ˈdɛpjʊti] *n, pl* **-ties** : suplente *mf;* sustituto *m,* -ta *f*

derail [diˈreɪl] *v* : descarrilar

derailment [diˈreɪlmənt] *n* : descarrilamiento *m*

derange [diˈreɪndʒ] *vt* **-ranged; -ranging 1** DISARRANGE : desarreglar, desordenar **2** DISTURB, UPSET : trastornar, perturbar **3** MADDEN : enloquecer, volver loco

derangement [diˈreɪndʒmənt] *n* **1** DISTURBANCE, UPSET : trastorno *m* **2** INSANITY : locura *f,* perturbación *f* mental

derby [ˈdərbi] *n, pl* **-bies 1** : derby *m* <the Kentucky Derby : el Derby de Kentucky> **2** : sombrero *m* hongo

deregulate [diˈrɛgjʊ͵leɪt] *vt* **-lated; -lating** : desregular

deregulation [di͵rɛgjʊˈleɪʃən] *n* : desregularización *f*

derelict[1] [ˈdɛrə͵lɪkt] *adj* **1** ABANDONED : abandonado, en ruinas **2** REMISS : negligente, remiso

derelict[2] *n* **1** : propiedad *f* abandonada **2** VAGRANT : vagabundo *m,* -da *f*

deride [diˈraɪd] *vt* **-rided; -riding** : ridiculizar, burlarse de

derision [diˈrɪʒən] *n* : escarnio *m,* irrisión *f,* mofa *f*

derisive [diˈraɪsɪv] *adj* : burlón

derivative[1] [diˈrɪvət̬ɪv] *adj* **1** DERIVED : derivado **2** BANAL : carente de originalidad, banal

derivative[2] *n* : derivado *m*

derive [diˈraɪv] *v* **-rived; -riving** *vt* **1** OBTAIN : obtener, sacar **2** DEDUCE : deducir, inferir — *vi* : provenir, derivar, proceder

dermatologist [͵dərməˈtɑlədʒɪst] *n* : dermatólogo *m,* -ga *f*

dermatology [͵dərməˈtɑlədʒi] *n* : dermatología *f*

derogatory [diˈrɑgə͵tori] *adj* : despectivo, despreciativo

derrick [ˈdɛrɪk] *n* **1** CRANE : grúa *f* **2** : torre *f* de perforación (sobre un pozo de petróleo)

descend [diˈsɛnd] *vt* : descender, bajar — *vi* **1** : descender, bajar <he descended from the platform : descendió del estrado> **2** DERIVE : descender, provenir **3** STOOP : rebajarse <I descended to his level : me rebajé a su nivel> **4 to descend upon** : caer sobre, invadir

descendant[1] [diˈsɛndənt] *adj* : descendente

descendant[2] *n* : descendiente *mf*

descent [diˈsɛnt] *n* **1** : bajada *f,* descenso *m* <the descent from the mountain : el descenso de la montaña> **2** ANCESTRY : ascendencia *f,* linaje *f* **3** SLOPE : pendiente *f,* cuesta *f* **4** FALL : caída *f* **5** ATTACK : incursión *f,* ataque *m*

describe [diˈskraɪb] *vt* **-scribed; -scribing** : describir

description [diˈskrɪpʃən] *n* : descripción *f*

descriptive [diˈskrɪptɪv] *adj* : descriptivo <descriptive adjective : adjetivo calificativo>

desecrate [ˈdɛsɪ͵kreɪt] *vt* **-crated; -crating** : profanar

desecration [͵dɛsɪˈkreɪʃən] *n* : profanación *f*

desegregate [diˈsɛgrə͵geɪt] *vt* **-gated; -gating** : eliminar la segregación racial de

desegregation [di͵sɛgrəˈgeɪʃən] *n* : eliminación *f* de la segregación racial

desert[1] [diˈzərt] *vt* : abandonar (una persona o un lugar), desertar de (una causa, etc.) — *vi* : desertar

desert[2] [ˈdɛzərt] *adj* : desierto <a desert island : una isla desierta>

desert[3] *n* **1** [ˈdɛzərt] : desierto *m* (en geografía) **2** [diˈzərt] → **deserts**

deserter [diˈzərt̬ər] *n* : desertor *m,* -tora *f*

desertion [diˈzərʃən] *n* : abandono *m,* deserción *f* (militar)

deserts [diˈzərts] *npl* : merecido *m* <to get one's just deserts : llevarse uno su merecido>

deserve [diˈzərv] *vt* **-served; -serving** : merecer, ser digno de

desiccate [ˈdɛsɪ͵keɪt] *vt* **-cated; -cating** : desecar, deshidratar

design[1] [diˈzaɪn] *vt* **1** DEVISE : diseñar, concebir, idear **2** PLAN : proyectar **3** SKETCH : trazar, bosquejar

design² *n* **1** PLAN, SCHEME : plan *m,* proyecto *m* <by design : a propósito, intencionalmente> **2** SKETCH : diseño *m,* bosquejo *m* **3** PATTERN, STYLE : diseño *m,* estilo *m* **4 designs** *npl* INTENTIONS : propósitos *mpl,* designios *mpl*
designate [ˈdɛzɪgˌneɪt] *vt* **-nated; -nating 1** INDICATE, SPECIFY : indicar, especificar **2** APPOINT : nombrar, designar
designation [ˌdɛzɪgˈneɪʃən] *n* **1** NAMING : designación *f* **2** NAME : denominación *f,* nombre *m* **3** APPOINTMENT : designación *f,* nombramiento *m*
designer [diˈzaɪnər] *n* : diseñador *m,* -dora *f*
desirability [diˌzaɪrəˈbɪləti] *n, pl* **-ties 1** ADVISABILITY : conveniencia *f* **2** ATTRACTIVENESS : atractivo *m*
desirable [diˈzaɪrəbəl] *adj* **1** ADVISABLE : conveniente, aconsejable **2** ATTRACTIVE : deseable, atractivo
desire¹ [diˈzaɪr] *vt* **-sired; -siring 1** WANT : desear **2** REQUEST : rogar, solicitar
desire² *n* : deseo *m,* anhelo *m,* ansia *m*
desist [diˈsɪst, -ˈzɪst] *vi* **to desist from** : desistir de, abstenerse de
desk [ˈdɛsk] *n* : escritorio *m,* pupitre *m* (en la escuela)
desolate¹ [ˈdɛsəˌleɪt, -zə-] *vt* **-lated; -lating** : devastar, desolar
desolate² [ˈdɛsələt, -zə-] *adj* **1** BARREN : desolado, desierto, yermo **2** DISCONSOLATE : desconsolado, desolado
desolation [ˌdɛsəˈleɪʃən, -zə-] *n* : desolación *f*
despair¹ [diˈspær] *vi* : desesperar, perder las esperanzas
despair² *n* : desesperación *f,* desesperanza *f*
desperate [ˈdɛspərət] *adj* **1** HOPELESS : desesperado, sin esperanzas **2** RASH : desesperado, precipitado **3** SERIOUS, URGENT : grave, urgente, apremiante <a desperate need : una necesidad apremiante>
desperately [ˈdɛspərətli] *adv* : desesperadamente, urgentemente
desperation [ˌdɛspəˈreɪʃən] *n* : desesperación *f*
despicable [diˈspɪkəbəl, ˈdɛspɪ-] *adj* : vil, despreciable, infame
despise [diˈspaɪz] *vt* **-spised; -spising** : despreciar
despite [dəˈspaɪt] *prep* : a pesar de, aún con
despoil [diˈspɔɪl] *vt* : saquear
despondency [diˈspɑndən*t*si] *n* : desaliento *m,* desánimo *m,* depresión *f*
despondent [diˈspɑndənt] *adj* : desalentado, desanimado
despot [ˈdɛspət, -ˌpɑt] *n* : déspota *mf;* tirano *m,* -na *f*
despotic [dɛsˈpɑtɪk] *adj* : despótico
despotism [ˈdɛspəˌtɪzəm] *n* : despotismo *m*
dessert [diˈzərt] *n* : postre *m*
destination [ˌdɛstəˈneɪʃən] *n* : destino *m,* destinación *f*
destined [ˈdɛstənd] *adj* **1** FATED : predestinado **2** BOUND : destinado, con destino (a), con rumbo (a)
destiny [ˈdɛstəni] *n, pl* **-nies** : destino *m*
destitute [ˈdɛstəˌtuːt, -ˌtjuːt] *adj* **1** LACKING : carente, desprovisto **2** POOR : indigente, en miseria
destitution [ˌdɛstəˈtuːʃən, -ˈtjuː-] *n* : indigencia *f,* miseria *f*
destroy [diˈstrɔɪ] *vt* **1** KILL : matar **2** DEMOLISH : destruir, destrozar
destroyer [diˈstrɔɪər] *n* : destructor *m* (buque)
destructible [diˈstrʌktəbəl] *adj* : destructible
destruction [diˈstrʌkʃən] *n* : destrucción *f,* ruina *f*
destructive [diˈstrʌktɪv] *adj* : destructor, destructivo
desultory [ˈdɛsəlˌtori] *adj* **1** AIMLESS : sin rumbo, sin objeto **2** DISCONNECTED : inconexo
detach [diˈtætʃ] *vt* : separar, quitar, desprender
detached [diˈtætʃt] *adj* **1** SEPARATE : separado, suelto **2** ALOOF : distante, indiferente **3** IMPARTIAL : imparcial, objetivo
detachment [diˈtætʃmənt] *n* **1** SEPARATION : separación *f* **2** DETAIL : destacamento *m* (de tropas) **3** ALOOFNESS : reserva *f,* indiferencia *f* **4** IMPARTIALITY : imparcialidad *f*
detail¹ [diˈteɪl, ˈdiːˌteɪl] *vt* : detallar, exponer en detalle
detail² *n* **1** : detalle *m,* pormenor *m* **2** : destacamento *m* (de tropas)
detailed [diˈteɪld, ˈdiːˌteɪld] *adj* : detallado, minucioso
detain [diˈteɪn] *vt* **1** HOLD : detener **2** DELAY : entretener, demorar, retrasar
detect [diˈtɛkt] *vt* : detectar, descubrir
detection [diˈtɛkʃən] *n* : descubrimiento *m*
detective [diˈtɛktɪv] *n* : detective *mf* <private detective : detective privado>
detention [diˈtɛntʃən] *n* : detención *m*
deter [diˈtər] *vt* **-terred; -terring** : disuadir, impedir
detergent [diˈtərdʒənt] *n* : detergente *m*
deteriorate [diˈtɪriəˌreɪt] *vi* **-rated; -rating** : deteriorarse, empeorar
deterioration [diˌtɪriəˈreɪʃən] *n* : deterioro *m,* empeoramiento *m*
determination [dɪˌtərməˈneɪʃən] *n* **1** DECISION : determinación *f,* decisión *f* **2** RESOLUTION : resolución *f,* determinación *f* <with grim determination : con una firme resolución>
determine [diˈtərmən] *vt* **-mined; -mining 1** ESTABLISH : determinar, establecer **2** SETTLE : decidir **3** FIND OUT : averiguar **4** BRING ABOUT : determinar

determined [di'tərmənd] *adj* RESOLUTE : decidido, resuelto

deterrent [di'tərənt] *n* : medida *f* disuasiva

detest [di'tɛst] *vt* : detestar, odiar, aborrecer

detestable [di'tɛstəbəl] *adj* : detestable, odioso, aborrecible

dethrone [di'θroːn] *vt* **-throned; -throning** : destronar

detonate ['dɛtən,eɪt] *v* **-nated; -nating** *vt* : hacer detonar — *vi* : detonar, estallar

detonator ['dɛtən,eɪt̬ər] *n* : detonador *m*

detour[1] ['diː,tʊr, di'tʊr] *vi* : desviarse

detour[2] *n* : desvío *m*, rodeo *m*

detract [di'trækt] *vi* **to detract from** : restarle valor a, quitarle méritos a

detriment ['dɛtrəmənt] *n* : detrimento *m*, perjuicio *m*

detrimental [,dɛtrə'mɛntəl] *adj* : perjudicial — **detrimentally** *adv*

devaluation [di,væljʊ'eɪʃən] *n* : devaluación *f*

devalue [di'væl,juː] *vt* **-ued; -uing** : devaluar, depreciar

devastate ['dɛvə,steɪt] *vt* **-tated; -tating** : devastar, arrasar, asolar

devastation [,dɛvə'steɪʃən] *n* : devastación *f*, estragos *mpl*

develop [di'vɛləp] *vt* **1** FORM, MAKE : desarrollar, elaborar, formar **2** : revelar (en fotografía) **3** FOSTER : desarrollar, fomentar **4** EXPLOIT : explotar (recursos), urbanizar (un área) **5** ACQUIRE : adquirir <to develop an interest : adquirir un interés> **6** CONTRACT : contraer (una enfermedad) — *vi* **1** GROW : desarrollarse **2** ARISE : aparecer, surgir

developed [di'vɛləpt] *adj* : avanzado, desarrollado

development [di'vɛləpmənt] *n* **1** : desarrollo *m* <physical development : desarrollo físico> **2** : urbanización *f* (de un área), explotación *f* (de recursos), creación *f* (de inventos) **3** EVENT : acontecimiento *m*, suceso *m* <to await developments : esperar acontecimientos>

deviant ['diːviənt] *adj* : desviado, anormal

deviate ['diːvi,eɪt] *v* **-ated; -ating** *vi* : desviarse, apartarse — *vt* : desviar

deviation [,diːvi'eɪʃən] *n* : desviación *f*

device [di'vaɪs] *n* **1** MECHANISM : dispositivo *m*, aparato *m*, mecanismo *m* **2** EMBLEM : emblema *m*

devil[1] ['dɛvəl] *vt* **-iled** *or* **-illed; -iling** *or* **-illing 1** : sazonar con picante y especias **2** PESTER : molestar

devil[2] *n* **1** SATAN : el diablo, Satanás *m* **2** DEMON : diablo *m*, demonio *m* **3** FIEND : persona *f* diabólica; malvado *m*, -da *f*

devilish ['dɛvəlɪʃ] *adj* : diabólico

devilry ['dɛvəlri] *n, pl* **-ries** : diabluras *fpl*, travesuras *fpl*

devious ['diːviəs] *adj* **1** CRAFTY : taimado, artero **2** WINDING : tortuoso, sinuoso

devise [di'vaɪz] *vt* **-vised; -vising 1** INVENT : idear, concebir, inventar **2** PLOT : tramar

devoid [di'vɔɪd] *adj* **~ of** : carente de, desprovisto de

devote [di'voːt] *vt* **-voted; -voting 1** DEDICATE : consagrar, dedicar <to devote one's life : dedicar uno su vida> **2 to devote oneself** : dedicarse

devoted [di'voːt̬əd] *adj* **1** FAITHFUL : leal, fiel **2 to be devoted to someone** : tenerle mucho cariño a alguien

devotee [,dɛvə'tiː, -'teɪ] *n* : devoto *m*, -ta *f*

devotion [di'voːʃən] *n* **1** DEDICATION : dedicación *f*, devoción *f* **2 devotions** PRAYERS : oraciones *fpl*, devociones *fpl*

devour [di'vaʊər] *vt* : devorar

devout [di'vaʊt] *adj* **1** PIOUS : devoto, piadoso **2** EARNEST, SINCERE : sincero, ferviente — **devoutly** *adv*

devoutness [di'vaʊtnəs] *n* : devoción *f*, piedad *f*

dew ['duː, 'djuː] *n* : rocío *m*

dewlap ['du,læp, 'dju-] *n* : papada *f*

dew point *n* : punto *m* de condensación

dewy ['duːi, 'djuːi] *adj* **dewier; -est** : cubierto de rocío

dexterity [dɛk'stɛrət̬i] *n, pl* **-ties** : destreza *f*, habilidad *f*

dexterous ['dɛkstrəs] *adj* : diestro, hábil

dexterously ['dɛkstrəsli] *adv* : con destreza, con habilidad, hábilmente

dextrose ['dɛk,stroːs] *n* : dextrosa *f*

diabetes [,daɪə'biːtiz] *n* : diabetes *f*

diabetic[1] [,daɪə'bɛt̬ɪk] *adj* : diabético

diabetic[2] *n* : diabético *m*, -ca *f*

diabolic [,daɪə'bɑlɪk] *or* **diabolical** [-lɪkəl] *adj* : diabólico, satánico

diacritical mark [,daɪə'krɪt̬ɪkəl] *n* : signo *m* diacrítico

diadem ['daɪə,dɛm, -dəm] *n* : diadema *f*

diagnose ['daɪɪg,noːs, ,daɪɪg'noːs] *vt* **-nosed; -nosing** : diagnosticar

diagnosis [,daɪɪg'noːsɪs] *n, pl* **-noses** [-'noː,siːz] : diagnóstico *m*

diagnostic [,daɪɪg'nɑstɪk] *adj* : diagnóstico

diagonal[1] [daɪ'ægənəl] *adj* : diagonal, en diagonal

diagonal[2] *n* : diagonal *f*

diagonally [daɪ'ægənəli] *adv* : diagonalmente, en diagonal

diagram[1] ['daɪə,græm] *vt* **-gramed** *or* **-grammed; -graming** *or* **-gramming** : hacer un diagrama de

diagram[2] *n* : diagrama *m*, gráfico *m*, esquema *m*

dial[1] ['daɪl] *v* **dialed** *or* **dialled; dialing** *or* **dialling** : marcar, discar

dial[2] *n* : esfera *f* (de un reloj), dial *m* (de un radio), disco *m* (de un teléfono)

dialect [ˈdaɪəˌlɛkt] *n* : dialecto *m*

dialogue [ˈdaɪəˌlɔg] *n* : diálogo *m*

diameter [daɪˈæməṭər] *n* : diámetro *m*

diamond [ˈdaɪmənd, ˈdaɪə-] *n* **1** : diamante *m,* brillante *m* <a diamond necklace : un collar de brillantes> **2** : rombo *m,* forma *f* de rombo **3** : diamante *m* (en naipes) **4** INFIELD : cuadro *m,* diamante *m* (en béisbol)

diaper [ˈdaɪpər, ˈdaɪə-] *n* : pañal *m*

diaphragm [ˈdaɪəˌfræm] *n* : diafragma *m*

diarrhea [ˌdaɪəˈriːə] *n* : diarrea *f*

diary [ˈdaɪəri] *n, pl* **-ries:** diario *m*

diatribe [ˈdaɪəˌtraɪb] *n* : diatriba *f*

dice[1] [ˈdaɪs] *vt* **diced; dicing** : cortar en cubos

dice[2] *ns & pl* **1** → **die**[2] **2** : dados *mpl* (juego)

dicker [ˈdɪkər] *vt* : regatear

dictate[1] [ˈdɪkˌteɪt, dɪkˈteɪt] *v* **-tated; -tating** *vt* **1** : dictar <to dictate a letter : dictar una carta> **2** ORDER : mandar, ordenar — *vi* : dar órdenes

dictate[2] [ˈdɪkˌteɪt] *n* **1** : mandato *m,* orden *f* **2 dictates** *npl* : dictados *mpl* <the dictates of conscience : los dictados de la conciencia>

dictation [dɪkˈteɪʃən] *n* : dictado *m*

dictator [ˈdɪkˌteɪṭər] *n* : dictador *m,* -dora *f*

dictatorial [ˌdɪktəˈtoriəl] *adj* : dictatorial — **dictatorially** *adv*

dictatorship [dɪkˈteɪṭərˌʃɪp, ˈdɪkˌ-] *n* : dictadura *f*

diction [ˈdɪkʃən] *n* **1** : lenguaje *m,* estilo *m* **2** ENUNCIATION : dicción *f,* articulación *f*

dictionary [ˈdɪkʃəˌnɛri] *n, pl* **-naries** : diccionario *m*

did → **do**

didactic [daɪˈdæktɪk] *adj* : didáctico

die[1] [ˈdaɪ] *vi* **died** [ˈdaɪd]; **dying** [ˈdaɪɪŋ] **1** : morir **2** CEASE : morir, morirse <a dying civilization : una civilización moribunda> **3** STOP : apagarse, dejar de funcionar <the motor died : el motor se apagó> **4 to die down** SUBSIDE : amainar, disminuir **5 to die out** : extinguirse **6 to be dying for** *or* **to be dying to** : morirse por <I'm dying to leave : me muero por irme>

die[2] [ˈdaɪ] *n, pl* **dice** [ˈdaɪs] : dado *m*

die[3] *n, pl* **dies** [ˈdaɪz] **1** STAMP : troquel *m,* cuño *m* **2** MOLD : matriz *f,* molde *m*

diesel [ˈdiːzəl, -səl] *n* : diesel *m*

diet[1] [ˈdaɪət] *vi* : ponerse a régimen, hacer dieta

diet[2] *n* : régimen *m,* dieta *f*

dietary [ˈdaɪəˌtɛri] *adj* : alimenticio, dietético

dietitian *or* **dietician** [ˌdaɪəˈtɪʃən] *n* : dietista *mf*

differ [ˈdɪfər] *vi* **-ferred; -ferring 1** : diferir, diferenciarse **2** VARY : variar **3** DISAGREE : discrepar, diferir, no estar de acuerdo

difference [ˈdɪfrən*t*s, ˈdɪfərən*t*s] *n* : diferencia *f*

different [ˈdɪfrənt, ˈdɪfərənt] *adj* : distinto, diferente

differentiate [ˌdɪfəˈrɛnʧiˌeɪt] *v* **-ated; -ating** *vt* **1** : hacer diferente **2** DISTINGUISH : distinguir, diferenciar — *vi* : distinguir

differentiation [ˌdɪfəˌrɛnʧiˈeɪʃən] *n* : diferenciación *f*

differently [ˈdɪfrəntli, ˈdɪfərənt-] *adv* : de otra manera, de otro modo, distintamente

difficult [ˈdɪfɪˌkʌlt] *adj* : difícil

difficulty [ˈdɪfɪˌkʌlti] *n, pl* **-ties 1** : dificultad *f* **2** PROBLEM : problema *f,* dificultad *f*

diffidence [ˈdɪfədən*t*s] *n* **1** SHYNESS : retraimiento *m,* timidez *f,* apocamiento *m* **2** RETICENCE : reticencia *f*

diffident [ˈdɪfədənt] *adj* **1** SHY : tímido, apocado, inseguro **2** RESERVED : reservado

diffuse[1] [dɪˈfjuːz] *v* **-fused; -fusing** *vt* : difundir, esparcir — *vi* : difundirse, esparcirse

diffuse[2] [dɪˈfjuːs] *adj* **1** WORDY : prolijo, verboso **2** WIDESPREAD : difuso

diffusion [dɪˈjuːʒən] *n* : difusión *f*

dig[1] [ˈdɪg] *v* **dug** [ˈdʌg]; **digging** *vt* **1** : cavar, excavar <to dig a hole : cavar un hoyo> **2** EXTRACT : sacar <to dig up potatoes : sacar papas del suelo> **3** POKE, THRUST : clavar, hincar <he dug me in the ribs : me dio un codazo en las costillas> **4 to dig up** DISCOVER : descubrir, sacar a luz — *vi* : cavar, excavar

dig[2] *n* **1** POKE : codazo *m* **2** GIBE : pulla *f* **3** EXCAVATION : excavación *f*

digest[1] [daɪˈʤɛst, dɪ-] *vt* **1** ASSIMILATE : digerir, asimilar **2** : digerir (comida) **3** SUMMARIZE : compendiar, resumir

digest[2] [ˈdaɪˌʤɛst] *n* : compendio *m,* resumen *m*

digestible [daɪˈʤɛstəbəl, dɪ-] *adj* : digerible

digestion [daɪˈʤɛsʧən, dɪ-] *n* : digestión *f*

digestive [daɪˈʤɛstɪv, dɪ-] *adj* : digestivo <the digestive system : el sistema digestivo>

digit [ˈdɪʤət] *n* **1** NUMERAL : dígito *m,* número *m* **2** FINGER, TOE : dedo *m*

digital [ˈdɪʤəṭəl] *adj* : digital — **digitally** *adv*

dignified [ˈdɪgnəˌfaɪd] *adj* : digno, decoroso

dignify [ˈdɪgnəˌfaɪ] *vt* **-fied; -fying** : dignificar, honrar

dignitary [ˈdɪgnəˌtɛri] *n, pl* **-taries** : dignatario *m,* -ria *f*

dignity [ˈdɪgnəṭi] *n, pl* **-ties** : dignidad *f*

digress [daɪˈgrɛs, də-] *vi* : desviarse del tema, divagar

digression [daɪˈgrɛʃən, də-] *n* : digresión *f*

dike *or* **dyke** [ˈdaɪk] *n* : dique *m*

dilapidated [dəˈlæpəˌdeɪtəd] *adj* : ruinoso, desvencijado, destartalado

dilapidation [dəˌlæpəˈdeɪʃən] *n* : deterioro *m*, estado *m* ruinoso

dilate [daɪˈleɪt, ˈdaɪˌleɪt] *v* **-lated; -lating** *vt* : dilatar — *vi* : dilatarse

dilemma [dɪˈlɛmə] *n* : dilema *m*

dilettante [ˈdɪləˌtɑnt, -ˌtænt] *n, pl* **-tantes** [-ˌtɑnts, -ˌtænts] *or* **-tanti** [ˌdɪləˈtɑnti, -ˈtæn-] : diletante *mf*

diligence [ˈdɪlədʒənts] *n* : diligencia *f*, aplicación *f*

diligent [ˈdɪlədʒənt] *adj* : diligente <a diligent search : una búsqueda minuciosa> — **diligently** *adv*

dill [ˈdɪl] *n* : eneldo *m*

dillydally [ˈdɪliˌdæli] *vi* **-lied; lying** : demorarse, perder tiempo

dilute [daɪˈluːt, də-] *vt* **-luted; -luting** : diluir, aguar

dilution [daɪˈluːʃən, də-] *n* : dilución *f*

dim[1] [ˈdɪm] *v* **dimmed; dimming** *vt* : atenuar (la luz), nublar (la vista), borrar (la memoria), opacar (una superficie) — *vi* : oscurecerse, apagarse

dim[2] *adj* **dimmer; dimmest 1** FAINT : oscuro, tenue (dícese de la luz), nublado (dícese de la vista), borrado (dícese de la memoria) **2** DULL : deslustrado **3** STUPID : tonto, torpe

dime [ˈdaɪm] *n* : moneda *f* de diez centavos

dimension [dəˈmɛntʃən, daɪ-] *n* **1** : dimensión *f* **2 dimensions** *npl* EXTENT, SCOPE : dimensiones *fpl*, extensión *f*, medida *f*

diminish [dəˈmɪnɪʃ] *vt* LESSEN : disminuir, reducir, amainar — *vi* DWINDLE, WANE : menguar, reducirse

diminutive [dəˈmɪnjʊtɪv] *adj* : diminutivo, minúsculo

dimly [ˈdɪmli] *adv* : indistintamente, débilmente

dimmer [ˈdɪmər] *n* : potenciómetro *m*, conmutador *m* de luces (en automóviles)

dimness [ˈdɪmnəs] *n* : oscuridad *f*, debilidad *f* (de la vista), imprecisión *f* (de la memoria)

dimple [ˈdɪmpəl] *n* : hoyuelo *m*

din [ˈdɪn] *n* : estrépito *m*, estruendo *m*

dine [ˈdaɪn] *vi* **dined; dining** : cenar

diner [ˈdaɪnər] *n* **1** : comensal *mf* (persona) **2** : vagón *m* restaurante (en un tren) **3** : cafetería *f*, restaurante *m* barato

dinghy [ˈdɪŋi, ˈdɪŋgi, ˈdɪŋki] *n, pl* **-ghies** : bote *m*

dinginess [ˈdɪndʒinəs] *n* **1** DIRTINESS : suciedad *f* **2** SHABBINESS : lo gastado, lo deslucido

dingy [ˈdɪndʒi] *adj* **-gier; -est 1** DIRTY : sucio **2** SHABBY : gastado, deslucido

dinner [ˈdɪnər] *n* : cena *f*, comida *f*

dinosaur [ˈdaɪnəˌsɔr] *n* : dinosaurio *m*

dint [ˈdɪnt] *n* **by dint of** : a fuerza de

diocese [ˈdaɪəsəs, -ˌsiːz, -ˌsiːs] *n, pl* **-ceses** [ˈdaɪəsəsəz] : diócesis *f*

dip[1] [ˈdɪp] *v* **dipped; dipping** *vt* **1** DUNK, PLUNGE : sumergir, mojar, meter **2** LADLE : servir con cucharón **3** LOWER : bajar, arriar (una bandera) — *vi* **1** DESCEND, DROP : bajar en picada, descender **2** SLOPE : bajar, inclinarse

dip[2] *n* **1** SWIM : chapuzón *m* **2** DROP : descenso *m*, caída *f* **3** SLOPE : cuesta *f*, declive *m* **4** SAUCE : salsa *f*

diphtheria [dɪfˈθɪriə] *n* : difteria *f*

diphthong [ˈdɪfˌθɔŋ] *n* : diptongo *m*

diploma [dəˈploːmə] *n, pl* **-mas** : diploma *m*

diplomacy [dəˈploːməsi] *n* **1** : diplomacia *f* **2** TACT : tacto *m*, discreción *f*

diplomat [ˈdɪpləˌmæt] *n* **1** : diplomático *m*, -ca *f* (en relaciones internacionales) **2** : persona *f* diplomática

diplomatic [ˌdɪpləˈmætɪk] *adj* : diplomático <diplomatic immunity : inmunidad diplomática>

dipper [ˈdɪpər] *n* **1** LADLE : cucharón *m*, cazo *m* **2 Big Dipper** : Osa *f* Mayor **3 Little Dipper** : Osa *f* Menor

dire [ˈdaɪr] *adj* **direr; direst 1** HORRIBLE : espantoso, terrible, horrendo **2** EXTREME : extremo <dire poverty : pobreza extrema>

direct[1] [dəˈrɛkt, daɪ-] *vt* **1** ADDRESS : dirigir, mandar **2** AIM, POINT : dirigir **3** GUIDE : indicarle el camino (a alguien), orientar **4** MANAGE : dirigir <to direct a film : dirigir una película> **5** COMMAND : ordenar, mandar

direct[2] *adv* : directamente

direct[3] *adj* **1** STRAIGHT : directo **2** FRANK : franco

direct current *n* : corriente *f* continua

direction [dəˈrɛkʃən, daɪ-] *n* **1** SUPERVISION : dirección *f* **2** INSTRUCTION, ORDER : instrucción *f*, orden *f* **3** COURSE : dirección *f*, rumbo *m* <to change direction : cambiar de dirección> **4 to ask directions** : pedir indicaciones

directly [dəˈrɛktli, daɪ-] *adv* **1** STRAIGHT : directamente <directly north : directamente al norte> **2** FRANKLY : francamente **3** EXACTLY : exactamente, justo <directly opposite : justo enfrente> **4** IMMEDIATELY : en seguida, inmediatamente

directness [dəˈrɛktnəs, daɪ-] *n* : franqueza *f*

director [dəˈrɛktər, daɪ-] *n* **1** : director *m*, -tora *f* **2 board of directors** : junta *f* directiva, directorio *m*

directory [dəˈrɛktəri, daɪ-] *n, pl* **-ries** : guía *f*, directorio *m* <telephone directory : directorio telefónico>

dirge [ˈdərdʒ] *n* : canto *m* fúnebre

dirigible [ˈdɪrədʒəbəl, dəˈrɪdʒə-] *n* : dirigible *m*, zepelín *m*

dirt [ˈdərt] *n* **1** FILTH : suciedad *f*, mugre *f*, porquería *f* **2** SOIL : tierra *f*

dirtiness [ˈdərtinəs] *n* : suciedad *f*

dirty[1] [ˈdərti] *vt* **dirtied; dirtying** : ensuciar, manchar

dirty[2] *adj* **dirtier; -est 1** SOILED, STAINED : sucio, manchado **2** DISHONEST : sucio, deshonesto <a dirty player : un jugador tramposo> <a dirty trick : una mala pasada> **3** INDECENT : indecente, cochino <a dirty joke : un chiste verde>

disability [ˌdɪsəˈbɪləṭi] *n, pl* **-ties** : minusvalía *f,* discapacidad *f,* invalidez *f*

disable [dɪsˈeɪbəl] *vt* **-abled; -abling** : dejar inválido, inutilizar, incapacitar

disabled [dɪsˈeɪbəld] *adj* : minusválido, discapacitado

disabuse [ˌdɪsəˈbjuːz] *vt* **-bused; -busing** : desengañar, sacar del error

disadvantage [ˌdɪsədˈvæntɪdʒ] *n* : desventaja *f*

disadvantageous [ˌdɪsˌædˌvænˈteɪdʒəs] *adj* : desventajoso, desfavorable

disagree [ˌdɪsəˈgriː] *vi* **1** DIFFER : discrepar, no coincidir **2** DISSENT : disentir, discrepar, no estar de acuerdo

disagreeable [ˌdɪsəˈgriːəbəl] *adj* : desagradable

disagreement [ˌdɪsəˈgriːmənt] *n* **1** : desacuerdo *m* **2** DISCREPANCY : discrepancia *f* **3** ARGUMENT : discusión *f,* altercado *m,* disputa *f*

disappear [ˌdɪsəˈpɪr] *vi* : desaparecer, desvanecerse <to disappear from view : perderse de vista>

disappearance [ˌdɪsəˈpɪrənts] *n* : desaparición *f*

disappoint [ˌdɪsəˈpɔɪnt] *vt* : decepcionar, defraudar, fallar

disappointment [ˌdɪsəˈpɔɪntmənt] *n* : decepción *f,* desilusión *f,* chasco *m*

disapproval [ˌdɪsəˈpruːvəl] *n* : desaprobación *f*

disapprove [ˌdɪsəˈpruːv] *vi* **-proved; -proving** : desaprobar, estar en contra

disapprovingly [ˌdɪsəˈpruːvɪŋli] *adv* : con desaprobación

disarm [dɪsˈɑrm] *vt* : desarmar

disarmament [dɪsˈɑrməmənt] *n* : desarme *m* <nuclear disarmament : desarme nuclear>

disarrange [ˌdɪsəˈreɪndʒ] *vt* **-ranged; -ranging** : desarreglar, desordenar

disarray [ˌdɪsəˈreɪ] *n* : desorden *m,* confusión *f,* desorganización *f*

disaster [dɪˈzæstər] *n* : desastre *m,* catástrofe *f*

disastrous [dɪˈzæstrəs] *adj* : desastroso

disband [dɪsˈbænd] *vt* : disolver — *vi* : disolverse, dispersarse

disbar [dɪsˈbɑr] *vt* **-barred; -barring** : prohibir de ejercer la abogacía

disbelief [ˌdɪsbɪˈliːf] *n* : incredulidad *f*

disbelieve [ˌdɪsbɪˈliːv] *v* **-lieved; -lieving** : no creer, dudar

disburse [dɪsˈbərs] *vt* **-bursed; -bursing** : desembolsar

disbursement [dɪsˈbərsmənt] *n* : desembolso *m*

disc → **disk**

discard [dɪsˈkɑrd, ˈdɪsˌkɑrd] *vt* : desechar, deshacerse de, botar — *vi* : descartarse (en juegos de naipes)

discern [dɪˈsərn, -ˈzərn] *vt* : discernir, distinguir, percibir

discernible [dɪˈsərnəbəl, -ˈzər-] *adj* : perceptible, visible

discernment [dɪˈsərnmənt, -ˈzərn-] *n* : discernimiento *m,* criterio *m*

discharge[1] [dɪsˈtʃɑrdʒ, ˈdɪsˌ-] *v* **-charged; -charging 1** UNLOAD : descargar (carga), desembarcar (pasajeros) **2** SHOOT : descargar, disparar **3** FREE : liberar, poner en libertad **4** DISMISS : despedir **5** EMIT : despedir (humo, etc.), descargar (electricidad) **6** : cumplir con (una obligación), saldar (una deuda) — *vi* **1** : descargarse (dícese de una batería) **2** OOZE : supurar

discharge[2] [ˈdɪsˌtʃɑrdʒ, dɪsˈ-] *n* **1** EMISSION : descarga *f* (de electricidad), emisión *f* (de gases) **2** DISMISSAL : despido *m* (del empleo), baja *f* (del ejército) **3** SECRETION : secreción *f*

disciple [dɪˈsaɪpəl] *n* : discípulo *m,* -la *f*

discipline[1] [ˈdɪsəplən] *vt* **-plined; -plining 1** PUNISH : castigar, sancionar (a los empleados) **2** CONTROL : disciplinar **3 to discipline oneself** : disciplinarse

discipline[2] *n* **1** FIELD : disciplina *f,* campo *m* **2** TRAINING : disciplina *f* **3** PUNISHMENT : castigo *m* **4** SELF-CONTROL : dominio *m* de sí mismo

disc jockey *n* : disc jockey *mf*

disclaim [dɪsˈkleɪm] *vt* DENY : negar

disclose [dɪsˈkloːz] *vt* **-closed; -closing** : revelar, poner en evidencia

disclosure [dɪsˈkloːʒər] *n* : revelación *f*

discolor [dɪsˈkʌlər] *vt* **1** BLEACH : decolorar **2** FADE : desteñir **3** STAIN : manchar — *vi* : decolorarse, desteñirse

discoloration [dɪsˌkʌləˈreɪʃən] *n* **1** FADING : decoloración *f* **2** STAIN : mancha *f*

discomfort [dɪsˈkʌmfərt] *n* **1** PAIN : molestia *f,* malestar *m* **2** UNEASINESS : inquietud *f*

disconcert [ˌdɪskənˈsərt] *vt* : desconcertar

disconnect [ˌdɪskəˈnɛkt] *vt* : desconectar

disconnected [ˌdɪskəˈnɛktəd] *adj* : inconexo

disconsolate [dɪsˈkɑntsələt] *adj* : desconsolado

discontent [ˌdɪskənˈtɛnt] *n* : descontento *m*

discontented [ˌdɪskənˈtɛntəd] *adj* : descontento

discontinue [ˌdɪskənˈtɪnˌjuː] *vt* **-ued; -uing** : suspender, descontinuar

discord [ˈdɪsˌkɔrd] *n* **1** STRIFE : discordia *f,* discordancia *f* **2** : disonancia *f* (en música)

discordant [dɪsˈkɔrdənt] *adj* **:** discordante, discorde — **discordantly** *adv*

discount¹ [ˈdɪsˌkaʊnt, dɪsˈ-] *vt* **1** REDUCE **:** descontar, rebajar (precios) **2** DISREGARD **:** descartar, ignorar

discount² [ˈdɪsˌkaʊnt] *n* **:** descuento *m,* rebaja *f*

discourage [dɪsˈkərɪdʒ] *vt* **-aged; -aging 1** DISHEARTEN **:** desalentar, desanimar **2** DISSUADE **:** disuadir

discouragement [dɪsˈkərɪdʒmənt] *n* **:** desánimo *m,* desaliento *m*

discourse¹ [dɪsˈkors] *vi* **-coursed; -coursing :** disertar, conversar

discourse² [ˈdɪsˌkors] *n* **1** TALK **:** conversación *f* **2** SPEECH, TREATISE **:** discurso *m,* tratado *m*

discourteous [dɪsˈkərt̬iəs] *adj* **:** descortés — **discourteously** *adv*

discourtesy [dɪsˈkərt̬əsi] *n, pl* **-sies :** descortesía *f*

discover [dɪsˈkʌvər] *vt* **:** descubrir

discoverer [dɪsˈkʌvərər] *n* **:** descubridor *m,* -dora *f*

discovery [dɪsˈkʌvəri] *n, pl* **-ries :** descubrimiento *m*

discredit¹ [dɪsˈkrɛdət] *vt* **1** DISBELIEVE **:** no creer, dudar **2 :** desacreditar, desprestigiar, poner en duda <they discredited his research : desacreditaron sus investigaciones>

discredit² *n* **1** DISREPUTE **:** descrédito *m,* desprestigio *m* **2** DOUBT **:** duda *f*

discreet [dɪsˈkriːt] *adj* **:** discreto — **discreetly** *adv*

discrepancy [dɪsˈkrɛpəntsi] *n, pl* **-cies :** discrepancia *f*

discretion [dɪsˈkrɛʃən] *n* **1** CIRCUMSPECTION **:** discreción *f,* circunspección *f* **2** JUDGMENT **:** discernimiento *m,* criterio *m*

discriminate [dɪsˈkrɪməˌneɪt] *v* **-nated; -nating** *vt* DISTINGUISH **:** distinguir, discriminar, diferenciar — *vi* **:** discriminar <to discriminate against women : discriminar a las mujeres>

discrimination [dɪsˌkrɪməˈneɪʃən] *n* **1** PREJUDICE **:** discriminación *f* **2** DISCERNMENT **:** discernimiento *m*

discriminatory [dɪsˈkrɪmənəˌtori] *adj* **:** discriminatorio

discus [ˈdɪskəs] *n, pl* **-cuses** [-kəsəz] **:** disco *m*

discuss [dɪsˈkʌs] *vt* **:** hablar de, discutir, tratar (de)

discussion [dɪsˈkʌʃən] *n* **:** discusión *f,* debate *m,* conversación *f*

disdain¹ [dɪsˈdeɪn] *vt* **:** desdeñar, despreciar <they disdained to reply : no se dignaron a responder>

disdain² *n* **:** desdén *m*

disdainful [dɪsˈdeɪnfəl] *adj* **:** desdeñoso — **disdainfully** *adv*

disease [dɪˈziːz] *n* **:** enfermedad *f,* mal *m,* dolencia *f*

diseased [dɪˈziːzd] *adj* **:** enfermo

disembark [ˌdɪsɪmˈbɑrk] *v* **:** desembarcar

disembarkation [dɪsˌɛmˌbɑrˈkeɪʃən] *n* **:** desembarco *m,* desembarque *m*

disembodied [ˌdɪsɪmˈbɑdid] *adj* **:** incorpóreo

disenchant [ˌdɪsɪnˈtʃænt] *vt* **:** desilusionar, desencantar, desengañar

disenchantment [ˌdɪsɪnˈtʃæntmənt] *n* **:** desencanto *m,* desilusión *f*

disengage [ˌdɪsɪnˈgeɪdʒ] *vt* **-gaged; -gaging 1 :** soltar, desconectar (un mecanismo) **2 to disengage the clutch :** desembragar

disentangle [ˌdɪsɪnˈtæŋgəl] *vt* **-gled; -gling** UNTANGLE **:** desenredar, desenmarañar

disfavor [dɪsˈfeɪvər] *n* **:** desaprobación *f*

disfigure [dɪsˈfɪgjər] *vt* **-ured; -uring :** desfigurar (a una persona), afear (un edificio, un área)

disfigurement [dɪsˈfɪgjərmənt] *n* **:** desfiguración *f,* afeamiento *m*

disfranchise [dɪsˈfrænˌtʃaɪz] *vt* **-chised; -chising :** privar del derecho a votar

disgrace¹ [dɪˈskreɪs] *vt* **-graced; -gracing :** deshonrar

disgrace² *n* **1** DISHONOR **:** desgracia *f,* deshonra *f* **2** SHAME **:** vergüenza *f* <he's a disgrace to his family : es una vergüenza para su familia>

disgraceful [dɪˈskreɪsfəl] *adj* **:** vergonzoso, deshonroso, ignominioso

disgracefully [dɪˈskreɪsfəli] *adv* **:** vergonzosamente

disgruntle [dɪsˈgrʌntəl] *vt* **-tled; -tling :** enfadar, contrariar

disguise¹ [dɪˈskaɪz] *vt* **-guised; -guising 1 :** disfrazar, enmascarar (el aspecto) **2** CONCEAL **:** encubrir, disimular

disguise² *n* **:** disfraz *m*

disgust¹ [dɪˈskʌst] *vt* **:** darle asco (a alguien), asquear, repugnar <eso me da asco : that disgusts me>

disgust² *n* **:** asco *m,* repugnancia *f*

disgusting [dɪˈskʌstɪŋ] *adj* **:** asqueroso, repugnante — **disgustingly** *adv*

dish¹ [ˈdɪʃ] *vt* SERVE **:** servir

dish² *n* **1 :** plato *m* <the national dish : el plato nacional> **2** PLATE **:** plato *m* <to wash the dishes : lavar los platos> **3 serving dish :** fuente *f*

dishcloth [ˈdɪʃˌklɔθ] *n* **:** paño *m* de cocina (para secar), trapo *m* de fregar (para lavar)

dishearten [dɪsˈhɑrtən] *vt* **:** desanimar, desalentar

dishevel [dɪˈʃɛvəl] *vt* **-eled** *or* **-elled; -eling** *or* **-elling :** desarreglar, despeinar (el pelo)

disheveled *or* **dishevelled** [dɪˈʃɛvəld] *adj* **:** despeinado (dícese del pelo), desarreglado, desaliñado

dishonest [dɪˈsɑnəst] *adj* **:** deshonesto, fraudulento — **dishonestly** *adv*

dishonesty [dɪˈsɑnəsti] *n, pl* **-ties :** deshonestidad *f,* falta *f* de honradez

dishonor¹ [dɪˈsɑnər] *vt* **:** deshonrar

dishonor[2] *n* : deshonra *f*
dishonorable [dɪˈsɑnərəbəl] *adj* : deshonroso — **dishonorably** [-bli] *adv*
dishrag [ˈdɪʃˌræg] → **dishcloth**
dishwasher [ˈdɪʃˌwɔʃər] *n* : lavaplatos *m*, lavavajillas *m*
disillusion [ˌdɪsəˈluːʒən] *vt* : desilusionar, desencantar, desengañar
disillusionment [ˌdɪsəˈluːʒənmənt] *n* : desilusión *f*, desencanto *m*
disinclination [dɪsˌɪnkləˈneɪʃən, -ˌɪŋ-] *n* : aversión *f*
disinclined [ˌdɪsɪnˈklaɪnd] *adv* : poco dispuesto
disinfect [ˌdɪsɪnˈfɛkt] *vt* : desinfectar
disinfectant[1] [ˌdɪsɪnˈfɛktənt] *adj* : desinfectante
disinfectant[2] *n* : desinfectante *m*
disinherit [ˌdɪsɪnˈhɛrət] *vt* : desheredar
disintegrate [dɪsˈɪntəˌgreɪt] *v* **-grated; -grating** *vt* : desintegrar, deshacer — *vi* : desintegrarse, deshacerse
disintegration [dɪsˌɪntəˈgreɪʃən] *n* : desintegración *f*
disinterested [dɪsˈɪntərəstəd, -ˌrɛs-] *adj* **1** INDIFFERENT : indiferente **2** IMPARTIAL : imparcial, desinteresado
disinterestedness [dɪsˈɪntərəstədnəs, -ˌrɛs-] *n* : desinterés *m*
disjointed [dɪsˈdʒɔɪntəd] *adj* : inconexo, incoherente
disk *or* **disc** [ˈdɪsk] *n* : disco *m*
dislike[1] [dɪsˈlaɪk] *vt* **-liked; -liking** : tenerle aversión a (algo), tenerle antipatía (a alguien), no gustarle (algo a uno)
dislike[2] *n* : aversión *f*, antipatía *f*
dislocate [ˈdɪsloˌkeɪt, dɪsˈloː-] *vt* **-cated; -cating** : dislocar
dislocation [ˌdɪsloˈkeɪʃən] *n* : dislocación *f*
dislodge [dɪsˈlɑdʒ] *vt* **-lodged; -lodging** : sacar, desalojar, desplazar
disloyal [dɪsˈlɔɪəl] *adj* : desleal
disloyalty [dɪsˈlɔɪəlti] *n, pl* **-ties** : deslealtad *f*
dismal [ˈdɪzməl] *adj* **1** GLOOMY : sombrío, lúgubre, tétrico **2** DEPRESSING : deprimente, triste
dismantle [dɪsˈmæntəl] *vt* **-tled; -tling** : desmantelar, desmontar, desarmar
dismay[1] [dɪsˈmeɪ] *vt* : consternar
dismay[2] *n* : consternación *f*
dismember [dɪsˈmɛmbər] *vt* : desmembrar
dismiss [dɪsˈmɪs] *vt* **1** : dejar salir, darle permiso (a alguien) para retirarse **2** DISCHARGE : despedir, destituir **3** REJECT : descartar, desechar, rechazar
dismissal [dɪsˈmɪsəl] *n* **1** : permiso *m* para retirarse **2** DISCHARGE : despido *m* (de un empleado), destitución *f* (de un funcionario) **3** REJECTION : rechazo *m*
dismount [dɪsˈmaʊnt] *vi* : desmontar, bajarse, apearse
disobedience [ˌdɪsəˈbiːdiənts] *n* : desobediencia *f* — **disobedient** [-ənt] *adj*
disobey [ˌdɪsəˈbeɪ] *v* : desobedecer
disorder[1] [dɪsˈɔrdər] *vt* : desordenar, desarreglar
disorder[2] *n* **1** DISARRAY : desorden *m* **2** UNREST : disturbios *mpl*, desórdenes *mpl* **3** AILMENT : afección *f*, indisposición *f*, dolencia *f*
disorderly [dɪsˈɔrdərli] *adj* **1** UNTIDY : desordenado, desarreglado **2** UNRULY : indisciplinado, alborotado **3 disorderly conduct** : conducta *f* escandalosa
disorganization [dɪsˌɔrgənəˈzeɪʃən] *n* : desorganización *f*
disorganize [dɪsˈɔrgəˌnaɪz] *vt* **-nized; -nizing** : desorganizar
disown [dɪsˈoːn] *vt* : renegar de, repudiar
disparage [dɪsˈpærɪdʒ] *vt* **-aged; -aging** : menospreciar, denigrar
disparagement [dɪsˈpærɪdʒmənt] *n* : menosprecio *m*
disparate [ˈdɪspərət, dɪsˈpærət] *adj* : dispar, diferente
disparity [dɪsˈpærət̬i] *n, pl* **-ties** : disparidad *f*
dispassionate [dɪsˈpæʃənət] *adj* : desapasionado, imparcial — **dispassionately** *adv*
dispatch[1] [dɪsˈpætʃ] *vt* **1** SEND : despachar, enviar **2** KILL : despachar, matar **3** HANDLE : despachar
dispatch[2] *n* **1** SENDING : envío *m*, despacho *m* **2** MESSAGE : despacho *m*, reportaje *m* (de un periodista), parte *m* (en el ejército) **3** PROMPTNESS : prontitud *f*, rapidez *f*
dispel [dɪsˈpɛl] *vt* **-pelled; -pelling** : disipar, desvanecer
dispensation [ˌdɪspɛnˈseɪʃən] *n* EXEMPTION : exención *m*, dispensa *f*
dispense [dɪsˈpɛnts] *v* **-pensed; -pensing** *vt* **1** DISTRIBUTE : repartir, distribuir, dar **2** ADMINISTER, BESTOW : administrar (justicia), conceder (favores, etc.) **3** : preparar y despachar (medicamentos) — *vi* **to dispense with** : prescindir de
dispenser [dɪsˈpɛntsər] *n* : dispensador *m*, distibuidor *m* automático
dispersal [dɪsˈpərsəl] *n* : dispersión *f*
disperse [dɪsˈpərs] *v* **-persed; -persing** *vt* : dispersar, diseminar — *vi* : dispersarse
dispirit [dɪˈspɪrət] *vt* : desalentar, desanimar
displace [dɪsˈpleɪs] *vt* **-placed; -placing** **1** : desplazar (un líquido, etc.) **2** REPLACE : reemplazar
displacement [dɪsˈpleɪsmənt] *n* **1** : desplazamiento *m* (de personas) **2** REPLACEMENT : sustitución *f*, reemplazo *m*
display[1] [dɪsˈpleɪ] *vt* : exponer, exhibir, mostrar
display[2] *n* : muestra *f*, exposición *m*, alarde *m*

displease [dɪs'pli:z] *vt* **-pleased; -pleasing** : desagradar a, disgustar, contrariar

displeasure [dɪs'plɛʒər] *n* : desagrado *m*

disposable [dɪs'po:zəbəl] *adj* **1** : desechable <disposable diapers : pañales desechables> **2** AVAILABLE : disponible

disposal [dɪs'po:zəl] *n* **1** PLACEMENT : disposición *f*, colocación *f* **2** REMOVAL : eliminación *f* **3 to have at one's disposal** : disponer de, tener a su disposición

dispose [dɪs'po:z] *v* **-posed; -posing** *vt* **1** ARRANGE : disponer, colocar **2** INCLINE : predisponer — *vi* **1 to dispose of** DISCARD : desechar, deshacerse de **2 to dispose of** HANDLE : despachar

disposition [ˌdɪspə'zɪʃən] *n* **1** ARRANGEMENT : disposición *f* **2** TENDENCY : predisposición *f*, inclinación *f* **3** TEMPERAMENT : temperamento *m*, carácter *m*

disproportion [ˌdɪsprə'porʃən] *n* : desproporción *f*

disproportionate [ˌdɪsprə'porʃənət] *adj* : desproporcionado — **disproportionately** *adv*

disprove [dɪs'pru:v] *vt* **-proved; -proving** : rebatir, refutar

disputable [dɪs'pju:təbəl, 'dɪspjʊtəbəl] *adj* : disputable, discutible

dispute[1] [dɪs'pju:t] *v* **-puted; -puting** *vt* **1** QUESTION : discutir, cuestionar **2** OPPOSE : combatir, resistir — *vi* ARGUE, DEBATE : discutir

dispute[2] *n* **1** DEBATE : debate *m*, discusión *f* **2** QUARREL : disputa *f*, discusión *f*

disqualification [dɪsˌkwɑləfə'keɪʃən] *n* : descalificación *f*

disqualify [dɪs'kwɑləˌfaɪ] *vt* **-fied; -fying** : descalificar, inhabilitar

disquiet[1] *vt* [dɪs'kwaɪət] : inquietar

disquiet[2] *n* : ansiedad *f*, inquietud *f*

disregard[1] [ˌdɪsrɪ'gɑrd] *vt* : ignorar, no prestar atención a

disregard[2] *n* : indiferencia *f*

disrepair [ˌdɪsrɪ'pær] *n* : mal estado *m*

disreputable [dɪs'rɛpjʊtəbəl] *adj* : de mala fama (dícese de una persona o un lugar), vergonzoso (dícese de la conducta)

disreputably [dɪs'rɛpjʊtəbli] *adv* : vergonzosamente

disrepute [ˌdɪsrɪ'pju:t] *n* : descrédito *m*, mala fama *f*, deshonra *f*

disrespect [ˌdɪsrɪ'spɛkt] *n* : falta *f* de respeto

disrespectful [ˌdɪsrɪ'spɛktfəl] *adj* : irrespetuoso — **disrespectfully** *adv*

disrobe [dɪs'ro:b] *v* **-robed; -robing** *vt* : desvestir, desnudar — *vi* : desvestirse, desnudarse

disrupt [dɪs'rʌpt] *vt* : trastornar, perturbar

disruption [dɪs'rʌpʃən] *n* : trastorno *m*

disruptive [dɪs'rʌptɪv] *adj* : perjudicial, perturbador — **disruptively** *adv*

dissatisfaction [dɪsˌsætəs'fækʃən] *n* : descontento *m*, insatisfacción *f*

dissatisfied [dɪs'sætəsˌfaɪd] *adj* : descontento, insatisfecho

dissatisfy [dɪs'sætəsˌfaɪ] *vt* **-fied; -fying** : no contentar, no satisfacer

dissect [dɪ'sɛkt] *vt* : disecar

dissemble [dɪ'sɛmbəl] *v* **-bled; -bling** *vt* HIDE : ocultar, disimular — *vi* PRETEND : fingir, disimular

disseminate [dɪ'sɛməˌneɪt] *vt* **-nated; -nating** : diseminar, difundir, divulgar

dissemination [dɪˌsɛmə'neɪʃən] *n* : diseminación *f*, difusión *f*

dissension [dɪ'sɛntʃən] *n* : disensión *f*, desacuerdo *m*

dissent[1] [dɪ'sɛnt] *vi* : disentir

dissent[2] *n* : disentimiento *m*, disensión *f*

dissertation [ˌdɪsər'teɪʃən] *n* **1** DISCOURSE : disertación *f*, discurso *m* **2** THESIS : tesis *f*

disservice [dɪs'sərvɪs] *n* : perjuicio *m*

dissident[1] ['dɪsədənt] *adj* : disidente

dissident[2] *n* : disidente *mf*

dissimilar [dɪ'sɪmələr] *adj* : distinto, diferente, disímil

dissipate ['dɪsəˌpeɪt] *vt* **-pated; -pating 1** DISPERSE : disipar, dispersar **2** SQUANDER : malgastar, desperdiciar, derrochar, disipar

dissipation [ˌdɪsə'peɪʃən] *n* : disipación *f*, libertinaje *m*

dissolute ['dɪsəˌlu:t] *adj* : disoluto

dissolution [ˌdɪsə'lu:ʃən] *n* : disolución *f*

dissolve [dɪ'zɑlv] *v* **-solved; -solving** *vt* : disolver — *vi* : disolverse

dissonance ['dɪsənənts] *n* : disonancia *f*

dissuade [dɪ'sweɪd] *vt* **-suaded; -suading** : disuadir

distance ['dɪstənts] *n* **1** : distancia *f* <the distance between two points : la distancia entre dos puntos> <in the distance : a lo lejos> **2** RESERVE : actitud *f* distante, reserva *f* <to keep one's distance : guardar las distancias>

distant ['dɪstənt] *adj* **1** FAR : distante, lejano **2** REMOTE : distante, lejano, remoto **3** ALOOF : distante, frío

distantly ['dɪstəntli] *adv* **1** LOOSELY : aproximadamente, vagamente **2** COLDLY : fríamente, con frialdad

distaste [dɪs'teɪst] *n* : desagrado *m*, aversión *f*

distasteful [dɪs'teɪstfəl] *adj* : desagradable, de mal gusto

distemper [dɪs'tɛmpər] *n* : moquillo *m*

distend [dɪs'tɛnd] *vt* : dilatar, hinchar — *vi* : dilatarse, hincharse

distill [dɪ'stɪl] *vt* : destilar

distillation [ˌdɪstə'leɪʃən] *n* : destilación *f*

distiller [dɪˈstɪlər] *n* : destilador *m,* -dora *f*
distinct [dɪˈstɪŋkt] *adj* **1** DIFFERENT : distinto, diferente **2** CLEAR, UNMISTAKABLE : marcado, claro, evidente <a distinct possibility : una clara posibilidad>
distinction [dɪˈstɪŋkʃən] *n* **1** DIFFERENTIATION : distinción *f* **2** DIFFERENCE : diferencia *f* **3** EXCELLENCE : distinción *f,* excelencia *f* <a writer of distinction : un escritor destacado>
distinctive [dɪˈstɪŋktɪv] *adj* : distintivo, característico — **distinctively** *adv*
distinctiveness [dɪˈstɪŋktɪvnəs] *n* : peculiaridad *f*
distinctly [dɪˈstɪŋktli] *adv* : claramente, con claridad
distinguish [dɪsˈtɪŋgwɪʃ] *vt* **1** DIFFERENTIATE : distinguir, diferenciar **2** DISCERN : distinguir <he distinguished the sound of the piano : distinguió el sonido del piano> **3 to distinguish oneself** : señalarse, distinguirse — *vi* DISCRIMINATE : distinguir
distinguishable [dɪsˈtɪŋgwɪʃəbəl] *adj* : distinguible
distinguished [dɪsˈtɪŋgwɪʃt] *adj* : distinguido
distort [dɪˈstɔrt] *vt* **1** MISREPRESENT : distorsionar, tergiversar **2** DEFORM : distorsionar, deformar
distortion [dɪˈstɔrʃən] *n* : distorsión *f,* deformación *f,* tergiversación *f*
distract [dɪˈstrækt] *vt* : distraer, entretener
distracted [dɪˈstræktəd] *adj* : distraído
distraction [dɪˈstrækʃən] *n* **1** INTERRUPTION : distracción *f,* interrupción *f* **2** CONFUSION : confusión *f* **3** AMUSEMENT : diversión *f,* entretenimiento *m,* distracción *f*
distraught [dɪˈstrɔt] *adj* : afligido, turbado
distress¹ [dɪˈstrɛs] *vt* : afligir, darle pena (a alguien), hacer sufrir
distress² *n* **1** SORROW : dolor *m,* angustia *f,* aflicción *f* **2** PAIN : dolor *m* **3 in ~** : en peligro
distressful [dɪˈstrɛsfəl] *adj* : doloroso, penoso
distribute [dɪˈstrɪˌbjuːt, -bjʊt] *vt* **-uted; -uting** : distribuir, repartir
distribution [ˌdɪstrəˈbjuːʃən] *n* : distribución *f,* reparto *m*
distributive [dɪˈstrɪbjʊṯɪv] *adj* : distributivo
distributor [dɪˈstrɪbjʊṯər] *n* : distribuidor *m,* -dora *f*
district [ˈdɪsˌtrɪkt] *n* **1** REGION : región *f,* zona *f,* barrio *m* (de una ciudad) **2** : distrito *m* (zona política)
distrust¹ [dɪsˈtrʌst] *vt* : desconfiar de
distrust² *n* : desconfianza *f,* recelo *m*
distrustful [dɪsˈtrʌstfəl] *adj* : desconfiado, receloso, suspicaz
disturb [dɪˈstərb] *vt* **1** BOTHER : molestar, perturbar <sorry to disturb you : perdone la molestia> **2** DISARRANGE : desordenar **3** WORRY : inquietar, preocupar **4 to disturb the peace** : alterar el orden público
disturbance [dɪˈstərbənts] *n* **1** COMMOTION : alboroto *m,* disturbio *m* **2** INTERRUPTION : interrupción *f*
disuse [dɪsˈjuːs] *n* : desuso *m*
ditch¹ [ˈdɪtʃ] *vt* **1** : cavar zanjas en **2** DISCARD : deshacerse de, botar
ditch² *n* : zanja *f,* fosa *f,* cuneta *f* (en una carretera)
dither [ˈdɪðər] *n* **to be in a dither** : estar nervioso, ponerse como loco
ditto [ˈdɪṯoː] *n, pl* **-tos 1** : lo mismo, ídem *m* **2 ditto marks** : comillas *fpl*
ditty [ˈdɪṯi] *n, pl* **-ties** : canción *f* corta y simple
diurnal [daɪˈərnəl] *adj* **1** DAILY : diario, cotidiano **2** : diurno <a diurnal animal : un animal diurno>
divan [ˈdaɪˌvæn, dɪˈ-] *n* : diván *m*
dive¹ [ˈdaɪv] *vi* **dived** *or* **dove** [ˈdoːv]; **dived; diving 1** PLUNGE : tirarse al agua, zambullirse, dar un clavado **2** SUBMERGE : sumergirse **3** DROP : bajar en picada (dícese de un avión), caer en picada
dive² *n* **1** PLUNGE : zambullida *f,* clavado *m* (en el agua) **2** DESCENT : descenso *m* en picada **3** BAR, JOINT : antro *m*
diver [ˈdaɪvər] *n* : saltador *m,* -dora *f;* clavadista *mf*
diverge [dəˈvərdʒ, daɪ-] *vi* **-verged; -verging 1** SEPARATE : divergir, separarse **2** DIFFER : divergir, discrepar
divergence [dəˈvərdʒənts, daɪ-] *n* : divergencia *f* — **divergent** [-ənt] *adj*
diverse [daɪˈvərs, də-, ˈdaɪˌvərs] *adj* : diverso, variado
diversify [daɪˈvərsəˌfaɪ, də-] *vt* **-fied; -fying** : diversificar, variar
diversion [daɪˈvərʒən, də-] *n* **1** DEVIATION : desviación *f* **2** AMUSEMENT, DISTRACTION : diversión *f,* distracción *f,* entretenimiento *m*
diversity [daɪˈvərsəṯi, də-] *n, pl* **-ties** : diversidad *f*
divert [dəˈvərt, daɪ-] *vt* **1** DEVIATE : desviar **2** DISTRACT : distraer **3** AMUSE : divertir, entretener
divest [daɪˈvɛst, də-] *vt* **1** UNDRESS : desnudar, desvestir **2 to divest of** : despojar de
divide [dəˈvaɪd] *v* **-vided; -viding** *vt* **1** HALVE : dividir, partir por la mitad **2** SHARE : repartir, dividir **3** : dividir (números) — *vi* : dividirse, dividir (en matemáticas)
dividend [ˈdɪvəˌdɛnd, -dənd] *n* **1** : dividendo *m* (en finanzas) **2** BONUS : beneficio *m,* provecho *m* **3** : dividendo *m* (en matemáticas)
divider [dɪˈvaɪdər] *n* **1** : separador *m* (para ficheros, etc.) **2** *or* **room divider** : mampara *f,* biombo *m*

divine[1] [də'vaɪn] *adj* **-viner; -est 1** : divino **2** SUPERB : divino, espléndido — **divinely** *adv*
divine[2] *n* : clérigo *m,* eclesiástico *m*
divinity [də'vɪnət̬i] *n, pl* **-ties** : divinidad *f*
divisible [dɪ'vɪzəbəl] *adj* : divisible
division [dɪ'vɪʒən] *n* **1** DISTRIBUTION : división *f,* reparto *m* <division of labor : distribución del trabajo> **2** PART : división *f,* sección *f* **3** : división *f* (en matemáticas)
divisor [dɪ'vaɪzər] *n* : divisor *m*
divorce[1] [də'vors] *v* **-vorced; -vorcing** *vt* : divorciar — *vi* : divorciarse
divorce[2] *n* : divorcio *m*
divorcé [dɪˌvor'seɪ, -'si:; -'vorˌ-] *n* : divorciado *m*
divorcée [dɪˌvor'seɪ, -'si:; -'vorˌ-] *n* : divorciada *f*
divulge [də'vʌldʒ, daɪ-] *vt* **-vulged; -vulging** : revelar, divulgar
dizzily ['dɪzəli] *adv* : vertiginosamente
dizziness ['dɪzinəs] *n* : mareo *m,* vahído *m,* vértigo *m*
dizzy ['dɪzi] *adj* **dizzier; -est 1** : mareado <I feel dizzy : estoy mareado> **2** : vertiginoso <a dizzy speed : una velocidad vertiginosa>
DNA [ˌdi:ˌɛn'eɪ] *n* : AND *m*
do ['du:] *v* **did** ['dɪd]; **done** ['dʌn]; **doing; does** ['dʌz] *vt* **1** CARRY OUT, PERFORM : hacer, realizar, llevar a cabo <she did her best : hizo todo lo posible> **2** PREPARE : preparar, hacer <do your homework : haz tu tarea> **3** ARRANGE : arreglar, peinar (el pelo) **4 to do in** RUIN : estropear, arruinar **5 to do in** KILL : matar, liquidar *fam* — *vi* **1** : hacer <you did well : hiciste bien> **2** FARE : estar, ir, andar <how are you doing? : ¿cómo estás?, ¿cómo te va?> **3** FINISH : terminar <now I'm done : ya terminé> **4** SERVE : servir, ser suficiente, alcanzar <this will do for now : esto servirá por el momento> **5 to do away with** ABOLISH : abolir, suprimir **6 to do away with** KILL : eliminar, matar **7 to do by** TREAT : tratar <he does well by her : él la trata bien> — *v aux* **1** (*used in interrogative sentences and negative statements*) <do you know her? : ¿la conoces?> <I don't like that : a mí no me gusta eso> **2** (*used for emphasis*) <I do hope you'll come : espero que vengas> **3** (*used as a substitute verb to avoid repetition*) <do you speak English? yes, I do : ¿habla inglés? sí>
docile ['dɑsəl] *adj* : dócil, sumiso
dock[1] ['dɑk] *vt* **1** CUT : cortar **2** : descontar dinero de (un sueldo) — *vi* ANCHOR, LAND : fondear, atracar
dock[2] *n* **1** PIER : atracadero *m* **2** WHARF : muelle *m* **3** : banquillo *m* de los acusados (en un tribunal)
doctor[1] ['dɑktər] *vt* **1** TREAT : tratar, curar **2** ALTER : adulterar, alterar, falsificar (un documento)
doctor[2] *n* **1** : doctor *m,* -tora *f* <Doctor of Philosophy : doctor en filosofía> **2** PHYSICIAN : médico *m,* -ca *f;* doctor *m,* -tora *f*
doctrine ['dɑktrɪn] *n* : doctrina *f*
document[1] ['dɑkjʊˌmɛnt] *vt* : documentar
document[2] ['dɑkjʊmənt] *n* : documento *m*
documentary[1] [ˌdɑkjʊ'mɛntəri] *adj* : documental
documentary[2] *n, pl* **-ries** : documental *m*
documentation [ˌdɑkjʊmən'teɪʃən] *n* : documentación *f*
dodge[1] ['dɑdʒ] *v* **dodged; dodging** *vt* : esquivar, eludir, evadir (impuestos) — *vi* : echarse a un lado
dodge[2] *n* **1** RUSE : truco *m,* treta *f,* artimaña *f* **2** EVASION : regate *m,* evasión *f*
dodo ['do:ˌdo:] *n, pl* **-does** *or* **-dos** : dodo *m*
doe ['do:] *n, pl* **does** *or* **doe** : gama *f,* cierva *f*
doer ['du:ər] *n* : hacedor *m,* -dora *f*
does → **do**
doff ['dɑf, 'dɔf] *vt* : quitarse <to doff one's hat : quitarse el sombrero>
dog[1] ['dɔg, 'dɑg] *vt* **dogged; dogging** : seguir de cerca, perseguir, acosar <to dog someone's footsteps : seguir los pasos de alguien> <dogged by bad luck : perseguido por la mala suerte>
dog[2] *n* : perro *m,* -rra *f*
dogcatcher ['dɔgˌkætʃər] *n* : perrero *m,* -ra *f*
dog–eared ['dɔgˌɪrd] *adj* : con las esquinas dobladas
dogged ['dɔgəd] *adj* : tenaz, terco, obstinado
doggy ['dɔgi] *n, pl* **doggies** : perrito *m,* -ta *f*
doghouse ['dɔgˌhaʊs] *n* : casita *f* de perro
dogma ['dɔgmə] *n* : dogma *m*
dogmatic [dɔg'mæt̬ɪk] *adj* : dogmático
dogmatism ['dɔgməˌtɪzəm] *n* : dogmatismo *m*
dogwood ['dɔgˌwʊd] *n* : cornejo *m*
doily ['dɔɪli] *n, pl* **-lies** : pañito *m*
doings ['du:ɪŋz] *npl* : eventos *mpl,* actividades *fpl*
doldrums ['do:ldrəmz, 'dɑl-] *npl* **1** : zona *f* de las calmas ecuatoriales **2 to be in the doldrums** : estar abatido (dícese de una persona), estar estancado (dícese de una empresa)
dole ['do:l] *n* **1** ALMS : distribución *f* a los necesitados, limosna *f* **2** : subsidios *mpl* de desempleo
doleful ['do:lfəl] *adj* : triste, lúgubre
dolefully ['do:lfəli] *adv* : con pesar, de manera triste
dole out *vt* **doled out; doling out** : repartir
doll ['dɑl, 'dɔl] *n* : muñeco *m,* -ca *f*
dollar ['dɑlər] *n* : dólar *m*

dolly [ˈdɑli] *n, pl* **-lies 1** → **doll 2** : plataforma *f* rodante
dolphin [ˈdɑlfən, ˈdɔl-] *n* : delfín *m*
dolt [ˈdoːlt] *n* : imbécil *mf;* tonto *m,* -ta *f*
domain [doˈmeɪn, də-] *n* **1** TERRITORY : dominio *m,* territorio *m* **2** FIELD : campo *m,* esfera *f,* ámbito *m* <the domain of art : el ámbito de las artes>
dome [ˈdoːm] *n* : cúpula *f,* bóveda *f*
domestic[1] [dəˈmɛstɪk] *adj* **1** HOUSEHOLD : doméstico, casero **2** : nacional, interno <domestic policy : política interna> **3** TAME : domesticado
domestic[2] *n* : empleado *m* doméstico, empleada *f* doméstica
domestically [dəˈmɛstɪkli] *adv* : domésticamente
domesticate [dəˈmɛstɪˌkeɪt] *vt* **-cated; -cating** : domesticar
domicile [ˈdɑməˌsaɪl, ˈdoː-; ˈdɑməsɪl] *n* : domicilio *m*
dominance [ˈdɑmənənts] *n* : dominio *m,* dominación *f*
dominant [ˈdɑmənənt] *adj* : dominante
dominate [ˈdɑməˌneɪt] *v* **-nated; -nating** : dominar
domination [ˌdɑməˈneɪʃən] *n* : dominación *f*
domineer [ˌdɑməˈnɪr] *vt* : dominar sobre, avasallar, tiranizar
Dominican [dəˈmɪnɪkən] *n* : dominicano *m,* -na *f* — **Dominican** *adj*
dominion [dəˈmɪnjən] *n* **1** POWER : dominio *m* **2** DOMAIN, TERRITORY : dominio *m,* territorio *m*
domino [ˈdɑməˌnoː] *n, pl* **-noes** *or* **-nos 1** : dominó *m* **2 dominoes** *npl* : dominó *m* (juego)
don [ˈdɑn] *vt* **donned; donning** : ponerse
donate [ˈdoːˌneɪt, doːˈ-] *vt* **-nated; -nating** : donar, hacer un donativo de
donation [doːˈneɪʃən] *n* : donación *f,* donativo *m*
done[1] [ˈdʌn] → **do**
done[2] *adj* **1** FINISHED : terminado, acabado, concluido **2** COOKED : cocinado
donkey [ˈdɑŋki, ˈdʌŋ-] *n, pl* **-keys** : burro *m,* asno *m*
donor [ˈdoːnər] *n* : donante *mf;* donador *m,* -dora *f*
doodle[1] [ˈduːdəl] *v* **-dled; -dling** : garabatear
doodle[2] *n* : garabato *m*
doom[1] [ˈduːm] *vt* : condenar
doom[2] *n* **1** JUDGMENT : sentencia *f,* condena *f* **2** DEATH : muerte *f* **3** FATE : destino *m* **4** RUIN : perdición *f,* ruina *f*
door [ˈdor] *n* : puerta *f*
doorbell [ˈdorˌbɛl] *n* : timbre *m*
doorknob [ˈdorˌnɑb] *n* : pomo *m,* perilla *f*
doorman [ˈdormən] *n, pl* **-men** [-mən, -ˌmɛn] : portero *m*
doormat [ˈdorˌmæt] *n* : felpudo *m*
doorstep [ˈdorˌstɛp] *n* : umbral *m*
doorway [ˈdorˌweɪ] *n* : entrada *f,* portal *m*
dope[1] [ˈdoːp] *vt* **doped; doping** : drogar, narcotizar
dope[2] *n* **1** DRUG : droga *f,* estupefaciente *m,* narcótico *m* **2** IDIOT : idiota *mf;* tonto *m,* -ta *f* **3** INFORMATION : información *f*
dormant [ˈdɔrmənt] *adj* : inactivo, latente
dormer [ˈdɔrmər] *n* : buhardilla *f*
dormitory [ˈdɔrməˌtori] *n, pl* **-ries** : dormitorio *m,* residencia *f* de estudiantes
dormouse [ˈdɔrˌmaʊs] *n* : lirón *m*
dorsal [ˈdɔrsəl] *adj* : dorsal — **dorsally** *adv*
dory [ˈdori] *n, pl* **-ries** : bote *m* de fondo plano
dosage [ˈdoːsɪdʒ] *n* : dosis *f*
dose[1] [ˈdoːs] *vt* **dosed; dosing** : medicinar
dose[2] *n* : dosis *f*
dot[1] [ˈdɑt] *vt* **dotted; dotting 1** : poner el punto sobre (una letra) **2** SCATTER : esparcir, salpicar
dot[2] *n* : punto *m* <at six on the dot : a las seis en punto> <dots and dashes : puntos y rayas>
dote [ˈdoːt] *vi* **doted; doting** : chochear
double[1] [ˈdʌbəl] *v* **-bled; -bling** *vt* **1** : doblar, duplicar (una cantidad), redoblar (esfuerzos) **2** FOLD : doblar, plegar **3 to double one's fist** : apretar el puño — *vi* **1** : doblarse, duplicarse **2 to double over** : retorcerse
double[2] *adj* : doble — **doubly** *adv*
double[3] *n* : doble *mf*
double bass *n* : contrabajo *m*
double–cross [ˌdʌbəlˈkrɔs] *vt* : traicionar
double–crosser [ˌdʌbəlˈkrɔsər] *n* : traidor *m,* -dora *f*
double–jointed [ˌdʌbəlˈdʒɔintəd] *adj* : con articulaciones dobles
double–talk [ˈdʌbəlˌtɔk] *n* : ambigüedades *fpl,* lenguaje *m* con doble sentido
doubt[1] [ˈdaʊt] *vt* **1** QUESTION : dudar de, cuestionar **2** DISTRUST : desconfiar de **3** : dudar, creer poco probable <I doubt it very much : lo dudo mucho>
doubt[2] *n* **1** UNCERTAINTY : duda *f,* incertidumbre *f* **2** DISTRUST : desconfianza *f* **3** SKEPTICISM : duda *f,* escepticismo *m*
doubtful [ˈdaʊtfəl] *adj* **1** QUESTIONABLE : dudoso **2** UNCERTAIN : dudoso, incierto
doubtfully [ˈdaʊtfəli] *adv* : dudosamente, sin estar convencido
doubtless [ˈdaʊtləs] *or* **doubtlessly** *adv* : sin duda
douche[1] [ˈduːʃ] *vt* **douched; douching** : irrigar
douche[2] *n* : ducha *f,* irrigación *f*
dough [ˈdoː] *n* : masa *f*

doughnut ['doː,nʌt] *n* : rosquilla *f*, dona *f Mex*
doughty ['daʊ̬ti] *adj* **-tier; -est** : fuerte, valiente
dour ['daʊər, 'dʊr] *adj* **1** STERN : severo, adusto **2** SULLEN : hosco, taciturno — **dourly** *adv*
douse ['daʊs, 'daʊz] *vt* **doused; dousing 1** DRENCH : empapar, mojar **2** EXTINGUISH : extinguir, apagar
dove[1] ['doːv] → **dive**
dove[2] ['dʌv] *n* : paloma *f*
dovetail ['dʌv,teɪl] *vi* : encajar, enlazar
dowdy ['daʊdi] *adj* **dowdier; -est** : sin gracia, poco elegante
dowel ['daʊəl] *n* : clavija *f*
down[1] ['daʊn] *vt* **1** FELL : tumbar, derribar, abatir **2** DEFEAT : derrotar
down[2] *adv* **1** DOWNWARD : hacia abajo **2 to lie down :** acostarse, echarse **3 to put down (money) :** pagar un depósito (de dinero) **4 to sit down :** sentarse **5 to take down, to write down** : apuntar, anotar
down[3] *adj* **1** DESCENDING : de bajada <the down elevator : el ascensor de bajada> **2** REDUCED : reducido, rebajado <attendance is down : la concurrencia ha disminuido> **3** DOWNCAST : abatido, deprimido
down[4] *n* : plumón *m*
down[5] *prep* **1** : (hacia) abajo <down the mountain : montaña abajo> <I walked down the stairs : bajé por la escalera> **2** ALONG : por, a lo largo de <we ran down the beach : corrimos por la playa> **3** : a través de <down the years : a través de los años>
downcast ['daʊn,kæst] *adj* **1** SAD : triste, abatido **2 with downcast eyes** : con los ojos bajos, con los ojos mirando al suelo
downfall ['daʊn,fɔl] *n* : ruina *f*, perdición *f*
downgrade[1] ['daʊn,greɪd] *vt* **-graded; -grading** : bajar de categoría
downgrade[2] *n* : bajada *f*
downhearted ['daʊn,hɑrt̬əd] *adj* : desanimado, descorazonado
downhill ['daʊn'hɪl] *adv & adj* : cuesta abajo
down payment *n* : entrega *f* inicial
downpour ['daʊn,por] *n* : aguacero *m*, chaparrón *m*
downright[1] ['daʊn,raɪt] *adv* THOROUGHLY : absolutamente, completamente
downright[2] *adj* : patente, manifiesto, absoluto <a downright refusal : un rechazo categórico>
downstairs[1] ['daʊn'stærz] *adv* : abajo
downstairs[2] ['daʊn,stærz] *adj* : del piso de abajo
downstairs[3] ['daʊn'stærz, -,stærz] *n* : planta *f* baja
downstream ['daʊn'striːm] *adv* : río abajo
down–to–earth [,daʊntu'ərth] *adj* : práctico, realista
downtown[1] [,daʊn'taʊn] *adv* : hacia el centro, al centro, en el centro (de la ciudad)
downtown[2] *adj* : del centro (de la ciudad) <downtown Chicago : el centro de Chicago>
downtown[3] [,daʊn'taʊn, 'daʊn,taʊn] *n* : centro *m* (de la ciudad)
downtrodden ['daʊn,trɑdən] *adj* : oprimido
downward ['daʊnwərd] *or* **downwards** [-wərdz] *adv & adj* : hacia abajo
downwind ['daʊn'wɪnd] *adv & adj* : en la dirección del viento
downy ['daʊni] *adj* **downier; -est 1** : cubierto de plumón, plumoso **2** VELVETY : aterciopelado, velloso
dowry ['daʊri] *n, pl* **-ries** : dote *f*
doze[1] ['doːz] *vi* **dozed; dozing** : dormitar
doze[2] *n* : sueño *m* ligero, cabezada *f*
dozen ['dʌzən] *n, pl* **dozens** *or* **dozen** : docena *f*
drab ['dræb] *adj* **drabber; drabbest 1** BROWNISH : pardo **2** DULL, LACKLUSTER : monótono, gris, deslustrado
draft[1] ['dræft, 'draft] *vt* **1** CONSCRIPT : reclutar **2** COMPOSE, SKETCH : hacer el borrador de, redactar
draft[2] *adj* **1** : de barril <draft beer : cerveza de barril> **2** : de tiro <draft horses : caballos de tiro>
draft[3] *n* **1** HAULAGE : tiro *m* **2** DRINK, GULP : trago *m* **3** OUTLINE, SKETCH : bosquejo *m*, borrador *m*, versión *f* **4** : corriente *f* de aire, chiflón *m*, tiro *m* (de una chimenea) **5** CONSCRIPTION : conscripción *f* **6 bank draft :** giro *m* bancario, letra *f* de cambio
draftee [dræf'tiː] *n* : recluta *mf*
draftsman ['dræftsmən] *n, pl* **-men** [-mən, -,mɛn] : dibujante *mf*
drafty ['dræfti] *adj* **draftier; -est :** con corrientes de aire
drag[1] ['dræg] *v* **dragged; dragging** *vt* **1** HAUL : arrastrar, jalar **2** DREDGE : dragar — *vi* **1** TRAIL : arrastrarse **2** LAG : rezagarse **3** : hacerse pesado, hacerse largo <the day dragged on : el día se hizo largo>
drag[2] *n* **1** RESISTANCE : resistencia *f* (aerodinámica) **2** HINDRANCE : traba *f*, estorbo *m* **3** BORE : pesadez *f*, plomo *m fam*
dragnet ['dræg,nɛt] *n* **1** : red *f* barredera (en pesca) **2** : operativo *m* policial de captura
dragon ['drægən] *n* : dragón *m*
dragonfly ['drægən,flaɪ] *n, pl* **-flies** : libélula *f*
drain[1] ['dreɪn] *vt* **1** EMPTY : vaciar, drenar **2** EXHAUST : agotar, consumir — *vi* **1** : escurrir, escurrirse <the dishes are draining : los platos están escurriéndose> **2** EMPTY : desaguar **3 to drain away :** irse agotando

drain[2] *n* **1** : desagüe *m* **2** SEWER : alcantarilla *f* **3** GRATING : sumidero *m,* resumidero *m,* rejilla *f* **4** EXHAUSTION : agotamiento *m,* disminución *f* (de energía, etc.) <to be a drain on : agotar, consumir> **5 to throw down the drain** : tirar por la ventana

drainage ['dreɪnɪdʒ] *n* : desagüe *m,* drenaje *m*

drainpipe ['dreɪn,paɪp] *n* : tubo *m* de desagüe, caño *m*

drake ['dreɪk] *n* : pato *m* (macho)

drama ['drɑmə, 'dræ-] *n* **1** THEATER : drama *m,* teatro *m* **2** PLAY : obra *f* de teatro, drama *m*

dramatic [drə'mæt̬ɪk] *adj* : dramático — **dramatically** [-t̬ɪkli] *adv*

dramatist ['dræmət̬ɪst, 'drɑ-] *n* : dramaturgo *m,* -ga *f*

dramatization [,dræmət̬ə'zeɪʃən, ,drɑ-] *n* : dramatización *f*

dramatize ['dræmə,taɪz, 'drɑ-] *vt* **-tized; -tizing** : dramatizar

drank → **drink**

drape[1] ['dreɪp] *vt* **draped; draping 1** COVER : cubrir (con tela) **2** HANG : drapear, disponer los pliegues de

drape[2] *n* **1** HANG : caída *f* **2 drapes** *npl* : cortinas *fpl*

drapery ['dreɪpəri] *n, pl* **-eries 1** CLOTH : pañería *f,* tela *f* para cortinas **2 draperies** *npl* : cortinas *fpl*

drastic ['dræstɪk] *adj* **1** HARSH, SEVERE : drástico, severo **2** EXTREME : radical, excepcional — **drastically** [-tɪkli] *adv*

draught ['dræft, 'draft] → **draft**[3]

draughty ['drafti] → **drafty**

draw[1] ['drɔ] *v* **drew** ['dru:]; **drawn** ['drɔn]; **drawing** *vt* **1** PULL : tirar de, jalar, correr (cortinas) **2** ATTRACT : atraer **3** PROVOKE : provocar, suscitar **4** INHALE : aspirar <to draw breath : respirar> **5** EXTRACT : sacar, extraer **6** TAKE : sacar <to draw a number : sacar un número> **7** COLLECT : cobrar, percibir (un sueldo, etc.) **8** BEND : tensar (un arco) **9** TIE : empatar (en deportes) **10** SKETCH : dibujar, trazar **11** FORMULATE : sacar, formular, llegar a <to draw a conclusion : llegar a una conclusión> **12 to draw out** : hacer hablar (sobre algo), hacer salir de sí mismo **13 to draw up** DRAFT : redactar — *vi* **1** SKETCH : dibujar **2** TUG : tirar, jalar **3 to draw near** : acercarse **4 to draw to a close** : terminar, finalizar **5 to draw up** STOP : parar

draw[2] *n* **1** DRAWING, RAFFLE : sorteo *m* **2** TIE : empate *m* **3** ATTRACTION : atracción *f* **4** PUFF : chupada *f* (de un cigarrillo, etc.)

drawback ['drɔ,bæk] *n* : desventaja *f,* inconveniente *m*

drawbridge ['drɔ,brɪdʒ] *n* : puente *m* levadizo

drawer ['drɔr, 'drɔər] *n* **1** ILLUSTRATOR : dibujante *mf* **2** : gaveta *f,* cajón *m* (en un mueble) **3 drawers** *npl* UNDERPANTS : calzones *mpl*

drawing ['drɔɪŋ] *n* **1** LOTTERY : sorteo *m,* lotería *f* **2** SKETCH : dibujo *m,* bosquejo *m*

drawl[1] ['drɔl] *vi* : hablar arrastrando las palabras

drawl[2] *n* : habla *f* lenta y con vocales prolongadas

dread[1] ['drɛd] *vt* : tenerle pavor a, temer

dread[2] *adj* : pavoroso, aterrado

dread[3] *n* : pavor *m,* temor *m*

dreadful ['drɛdfəl] *adj* **1** DREAD : pavoroso **2** TERRIBLE : espantoso, atroz, terrible — **dreadfully** *adv*

dream[1] ['dri:m] *v* **dreamed** ['drɛmpt, 'dri:md] *or* **dreamt** ['drɛmpt]; **dreaming** *vi* **1** : soñar <to dream about : soñar con> **2** FANTASIZE : fantasear — *vt* **1** : soñar **2** IMAGINE : imaginarse **3 to dream up** : inventar, idear

dream[2] *n* **1** : sueño *m,* ensueño *m* **2 bad dream** NIGHTMARE : pesadilla *f*

dreamer ['dri:mər] *n* : soñador *m,* -dora *f*

dreamlike ['dri:m,laɪk] *adj* : de ensueño

dreamy ['dri:mi] *adj* **dreamier; -est 1** DISTRACTED : soñador, distraído **2** DREAMLIKE : de ensueño **3** MARVELOUS : maravilloso

drearily ['drɪrəli] *adv* : sombríamente

dreary ['drɪri] *adj* **-rier; -est** : deprimente, lóbrego, sombrío

dredge[1] ['drɛdʒ] *vt* **dredged; dredging 1** DIG : dragar **2** COAT : espolvorear, enharinar

dredge[2] *n* : draga *f*

dredger ['drɛdʒər] *n* : draga *f*

dregs ['drɛgz] *npl* **1** LEES : posos *mpl,* heces *fpl* (de un líquido) **2** : heces *fpl,* escoria *f* <the dregs of society : la escoria de la sociedad>

drench ['drɛntʃ] *vt* : empapar, mojar, calar

dress[1] ['drɛs] *vt* **1** CLOTHE : vestir **2** DECORATE : decorar, adornar **3** : preparar (pollo o pescado), aliñar (ensalada) **4** : curar, vendar (una herida) **5** FERTILIZE : abonar (la tierra) — *vi* **1** : vestirse **2 to dress up** : ataviarse, engalanarse, ponerse de etiqueta

dress[2] *n* **1** APPAREL : indumentaria *f,* ropa *f* **2** : vestido *m,* traje *m* (de mujer)

dresser ['drɛsər] *n* : cómoda *f* con espejo

dressing ['drɛsɪŋ] *n* **1** : vestirse *m* **2** : aderezo *m,* aliño *m* (de ensalada), relleno *m* (de pollo) **3** BANDAGE : vendaje *m,* gasa *f*

dressmaker ['drɛs,meɪkər] *n* : modista *mf*

dressmaking ['drɛs,meɪkɪŋ] *n* : costura *f*

dressy ['drɛsi] *adj* **dressier; -est** : de mucho vestir, elegante

drew → **draw**

dribble[1] ['drɪbəl] *vi* **-bled; -bling 1** DRIP : gotear **2** DROOL : babear **3** : driblar (en basquetbol)

dribble[2] *n* **1** TRICKLE : goteo *m,* hilo *m* **2** DROOL : baba *f* **3** : drible *m* (en basquetbol)

drier → **dry**[2], **dryer**

driest → **dry**[2]

drift[1] ['drɪft] *vi* **1** : dejarse llevar por la corriente, ir a la deriva (dícese de un bote), ir sin rumbo (dícese de una persona) **2** ACCUMULATE : amontonarse, acumularse, apilarse

drift[2] *n* **1** DRIFTING : deriva *f* **2** HEAP, MASS : montón *m* (de arena, etc.), ventisquero *m* (de nieve) **3** MEANING : sentido *m*

drifter ['drɪftər] *n* : vagabundo *m,* -da *f*

driftwood ['drɪft,wʊd] *n* : madera *f* flotante

drill[1] ['drɪl] *vt* **1** BORE : perforar, taladrar **2** INSTRUCT : instruir por repetición — *vi* **1** TRAIN : entrenarse **2 to drill for oil** : perforar en busca de petróleo

drill[2] *n* **1** : taladro *m,* barrena *f* **2** EXERCISE, PRACTICE : ejercicio *m,* instrucción *f*

drily → **dryly**

drink[1] ['drɪŋk] *v* **drank** ['dræŋk]; **drunk** ['drʌŋk] *or* **drank; drinking** *vt* **1** IMBIBE : beber, tomar **2 to drink up** ABSORB : absorber — *vi* **1** : beber **2** : beber alcohol, tomar

drink[2] *n* **1** : bebida *f* **2** : bebida *f* alcohólica

drinkable ['drɪŋkəbəl] *adj* : potable

drinker ['drɪŋkər] *n* : bebedor *m,* -dora *f*

drip[1] ['drɪp] *vi* **dripped; dripping** : gotear, chorrear

drip[2] *n* **1** DROP : gota *f* **2** DRIPPING : goteo *m*

drive[1] ['draɪv] *v* **drove** ['dro:v]; **driven** ['drɪvən]; **driving** *vt* **1** IMPEL : impeler, impulsar **2** OPERATE : guiar, conducir, manejar (un vehículo) **3** COMPEL : obligar, forzar **4** : clavar, hincar <to drive a stake : clavar una estaca> **5** *or* **to drive away** : ahuyentar, echar **6 to drive crazy** : volver loco — *vi* : manejar, conducir <do you know how to drive? : ¿sabes manejar?>

drive[2] *n* **1** RIDE : paseo *m* en coche **2** CAMPAIGN : campaña *f* <fund-raising drive : campaña para recaudar fondos> **3** DRIVEWAY : camino *m* de entrada, entrada *f* **4** TRANSMISSION : transmisión *f* <front-wheel drive : tracción delantera> **5** ENERGY : dinamismo *m,* energía *f* **6** INSTINCT, NEED : instinto *m,* necesidad *f* básica

drivel ['drɪvəl] *n* : tontería *f,* estupidez *f*

driver ['draɪvər] *n* : conductor *m,* -tora *f;* chofer *m*

driveway ['draɪv,weɪ] *n* : camino *m* de entrada, entrada *f* (para coches)

drizzle[1] ['drɪzəl] *vi* **-zled; -zling** : lloviznar, garuar

drizzle[2] *n* : llovizna *f,* garúa *f*

droll ['dro:l] *adj* : cómico, gracioso, chistoso — **drolly** *adv*

dromedary ['drɑmə,dɛri] *n, pl* **-daries** : dromedario *m*

drone[1] ['dro:n] *vi* **droned; droning 1** BUZZ : zumbar **2** MURMUR : hablar con monotonía, murmurar

drone[2] *n* **1** : zángano *m* (abeja) **2** FREELOADER : gorrón *m,* -rrona *f fam;* parásito *m,* -ta *f* **3** BUZZ, HUM : zumbido *m,* murmullo *m*

drool[1] ['dru:l] *vi* : babear

drool[2] *n* : baba *f*

droop[1] ['dru:p] *vi* **1** HANG : inclinarse (dícese de la cabeza), encorvarse (dícese de los escombros), marchitarse (dícese de las flores) **2** FLAG : decaer, flaquear <his spirits drooped : se desanimó>

droop[2] *n* : inclinación *f,* caída *f*

drop[1] ['drɑp] *v* **dropped; dropping** *vt* **1** : dejar caer, soltar <she dropped the glass : se le cayó el vaso> <to drop a hint : dejar caer una indirecta> **2** SEND : mandar <drop me a line : mándame unas líneas> **3** ABANDON : abandonar, dejar <to drop the subject : cambiar de tema> **4** LOWER : bajar <he dropped his voice : bajó la voz> **5** OMIT : omitir **6 to drop off** : dejar — *vi* **1** DRIP : gotear **2** FALL : caer(se) **3** DECREASE, DESCEND : bajar, descender <the wind dropped : amainó el viento> **4 to drop back** *or* **to drop behind** : rezagarse, quedarse atrás **5 to drop by** *or* **to drop in** : pasar

drop[2] *n* **1** : gota *f* (de líquido) **2** DECLINE : caída *f,* bajada *f,* descenso *m* **3** INCLINE : caída *f,* pendiente *f* <a 20-foot drop : una caída de 20 pies> **4** SWEET : pastilla *f,* dulce *m* **5 drops** *npl* : gotas *fpl* (de medicina)

droplet ['drɑplət] *n* : gotita *f*

dropper ['drɑpər] *n* : gotero *m,* cuentagotas *m*

dross ['drɑs, 'drɔs] *n* : escoria *f*

drought ['draʊt] *n* : sequía *f*

drove[1] → **drive**

drove[2] ['dro:v] *n* : multitud *f,* gentío *m,* manada *f* (de ganado) <in droves : en manada>

drown ['draʊn] *vt* **1** : ahogar **2** INUNDATE : anegar, inundar **3 to drown out** : ahogar — *vi* : ahogarse

drowse[1] ['draʊz] *vi* **drowsed; drowsing** DOZE : dormitar

drowse[2] *n* : sueño *m* ligero, cabezada *f*

drowsiness ['draʊzinəs] *n* : somnolencia *f,* adormecimiento *m*

drowsy ['draʊzi] *adj* **drowsier; -est** : somnoliento, soñoliento

drub [ˈdrʌb] *vt* **drubbed; drubbing 1** BEAT, THRASH : golpear, apalear **2** DEFEAT : derrotar por completo

drudge[1] [ˈdrʌdʒ] *vi* **drudged; drudging** : trabajar como esclavo, trabajar duro

drudge[2] *n* : esclavo *m,* -va *f* del trabajo

drudgery [ˈdrʌdʒəri] *n, pl* **-eries** : trabajo *m* pesado

drug[1] [ˈdrʌg] *vt* **drugged; drugging** : drogar, narcotizar

drug[2] *n* **1** MEDICATION : droga *f,* medicina *f,* medicamento *m* **2** NARCOTIC : narcótico *m,* estupefaciente *m,* droga *f*

druggist [ˈdrʌgɪst] *n* : farmacéutico *m,* -ca *f*

drugstore [ˈdrʌgˌstor] *n* : farmacia *f,* botica *f,* droguería *f*

drum[1] [ˈdrʌm] *v* **drummed; drumming** *vt* : meter a fuerza <he drummed it into my head : me lo metió en la cabeza a fuerza> — *vi* : tocar el tambor

drum[2] *n* **1** : tambor *m* **2** : bidón *m* <oil drum : bidón de petróleo>

drummer [ˈdrʌmər] *n* : baterista *mf*

drumstick [ˈdrʌmˌstɪk] *n* **1** : palillo *m* (de tambor), baqueta *f* **2** : muslo *m* de pollo

drunk[1] *pp* → **drink**

drunk[2] [ˈdrʌŋk] *adj* : borracho, embriagado, ebrio

drunk[3] *n* : borracho *m,* -cha *f*

drunkard [ˈdrʌŋkərd] *n* : borracho *m,* -cha *f*

drunken [ˈdrʌŋkən] *adj* : borracho, ebrio <drunken driver : conductor ebrio> <drunken brawl : pleito de borrachos>

drunkenly [ˈdrʌŋkənli] *adv* : como un borracho

drunkenness [ˈdrʌŋkənnəs] *n* : borrachera *f,* embriaguez *f,* ebriedad *f*

dry[1] [ˈdraɪ] *v* **dried; drying** *vt* : secar — *vi* : secarse

dry[2] *adj* **drier; driest 1** : seco **2** THIRSTY : sediento **3** : donde la venta de bebidas alcohólicas está prohibida <a dry county : un condado seco> **4** DULL : aburrido, árido **5** : seco (dícese del vino), brut (dícese de la champaña)

dry–clean [ˈdraɪˌkliːn] *v* : limpiar en seco

dry cleaner *n* : tintorería *f* (servicio)

dry cleaning *n* : limpieza *f* en seco

dryer [ˈdraɪər] *n* **1 hair dryer** : secador *m* **2 clothes dryer** : secadora *f*

dry goods *npl* : artículos *mpl* de confección

dry ice *n* : hielo *m* seco

dryly [ˈdraɪli] *adv* : secamente

dryness [ˈdraɪnəs] *n* : sequedad *f,* aridez *f*

dual [ˈduːəl, ˈdjuː-] *adj* : doble

dub [ˈdʌb] *vt* **dubbed; dubbing 1** CALL : apodar **2** : doblar (una película), mezclar (una grabación)

dubious [ˈduːbiəs, ˈdjuː-] *adj* **1** UNCERTAIN : dudoso, indeciso **2** QUESTIONABLE : sospechoso, dudoso, discutible

dubiously [ˈduːbiəsli, ˈdjuː-] *adv* **1** UNCERTAINLY : dudosamente, con desconfianza **2** SUSPICIOUSLY : de modo sospechoso, con recelo

duchess [ˈdʌtʃəs] *n* : duquesa *f*

duck[1] [ˈdʌk] *vt* **1** LOWER : agachar, bajar (la cabeza) **2** PLUNGE : zambullir **3** EVADE : eludir, evadir — *vi* **to duck down** : agacharse

duck[2] *n, pl* **duck** *or* **ducks** : pato *m,* -ta *f*

duckling [ˈdʌklɪŋ] *n* : patito *m,* -ta *f*

duct [ˈdʌkt] *n* : conducto *m*

ductile [ˈdʌktəl] *adj* : dúctil

dude [ˈduːd, ˈdjuːd] *n* **1** DANDY : dandi *m,* dandy *m* **2** GUY : tipo *m*

due[1] [ˈduː, ˈdjuː] *adv* : justo a, derecho hacia <due north : derecho hacia el norte>

due[2] *adj* **1** PAYABLE : pagadero, sin pagar **2** APPROPRIATE : debido, apropiado <after due consideration : con las debidas consideraciones> **3** EXPECTED : esperado <the train is due soon : esperamos el tren muy pronto, el tren debe llegar pronto> **4 due to** : debido a, por

due[3] *n* **1 to give someone his (her) due** : darle a alguien su merecido **2 dues** *npl* : cuota *f*

duel[1] [ˈduːəl, ˈdjuː-] *vi* : batirse en duelo

duel[2] *n* : duelo *m*

duet [duˈɛt, dju-] *n* : dúo *m*

due to *prep* : debido a

dug *pp* → **dig**

dugout [ˈdʌgˌaʊt] *n* **1** CANOE : piragua *f* **2** SHELTER : refugio *m* subterráneo

duke [ˈduːk, ˈdjuːk] *n* : duque *m*

dull[1] [ˈdʌl] *vt* **1** DIM : opacar, quitar el brillo a, deslustrar **2** BLUNT : embotar (un filo), entorpecer (los sentidos), aliviar (el dolor), amortiguar (sonidos)

dull[2] *adj* **1** STUPID : torpe, lerdo, lento **2** BLUNT : desafilado, despuntado **3** LACKLUSTER : sin brillo, deslustrado **4** BORING : aburrido, soso, pesado — **dully** *adv*

dullness [ˈdʌlnəs] *n* **1** STUPIDITY : estupidez *f* **2** : embotamiento *m* (de los sentidos) **3** MONOTONY : monotonía *f,* insipidez *f* **4** : falta *f* de brillo **5** BLUNTNESS : falta *f* de filo, embotadura *f*

duly [ˈduːli, ˈdjuː-] *adv* PROPERLY : debidamente, a su debido tiempo

dumb [ˈdʌm] *adj* **1** MUTE : mudo **2** STUPID : estúpido, tonto, bobo — **dumbly** *adv*

dumbbell [ˈdʌmˌbɛl] *n* **1** WEIGHT : pesa *f* **2** : estúpido *m,* -da *f*

dumbfound *or* **dumfound** [ˌdʌmˈfaʊnd] *vt* : dejar atónito, dejar sin habla

dummy [ˈdʌmi] *n, pl* **-mies 1** SHAM : imitación *f,* sustituto *m* **2** PUPPET

: muñeco *m* 3 MANNEQUIN : maniquí *m* 4 IDIOT : tonto *m,* -ta *f;* idiota *mf*
dump[1] ['dʌmp] *vt* : descargar, verter
dump[2] *n* 1 : vertedero *m,* tiradero *m Mex* 2 **down in the dumps** : triste, deprimido
dumpling ['dʌmplɪŋ] *n* : bola *f* de masa hervida
dumpy ['dʌmpi] *adj* **dumpier; -est** : rechoncho, regordete
dun[1] ['dʌn] *vt* **dunned; dunning** : apremiar (a un deudor)
dun[2] *adj* : pardo (color)
dunce ['dʌnts] *n* : estúpido *m,* -da *f;* burro *m,* -rra *f fam*
dune ['du:n, 'dju:n] *n* : duna *f*
dung ['dʌŋ] *n* 1 FECES : excrementos *mpl* 2 MANURE : estiércol *m*
dungaree [ˌdʌŋgə'ri:] *n* 1 DENIM : tela *f* vaquera, mezclilla *f Chile, Mex* 2 **dungarees** *npl* : pantalones *mpl* de trabajo hechos de tela vaquera
dungeon ['dʌndʒən] *n* : mazmorra *f,* calabozo *m*
dunk ['dʌŋk] *vt* : mojar, ensopar
duo ['du:o:, 'dju:-] *n, pl* **duos** : dúo *m,* par *m*
dupe[1] ['du:p, dju:p] *vt* **duped; duping** : engañar, embaucar
dupe[2] *n* : inocentón *m,* -tona *f;* simple *mf*
duplex[1] ['du:ˌplɛks, 'dju:-] *adj* : doble
duplex[2] *n* : casa *f* de dos viviendas, dúplex *m*
duplicate[1] ['du:plɪˌkeɪt, 'dju:-] *vt* **-cated; -cating** 1 COPY : duplicar, hacer copias de 2 REPEAT : repetir, reproducir
duplicate[2] ['du:plɪkət, 'dju:-] *adj* : duplicado <a duplicate invoice : una factura por duplicado>
duplicate[3] ['du:plɪkət, 'dju:-] *n* : duplicado *m,* copia *f*
duplication [ˌdu:plɪ'keɪʃən, ˌdju:-] *n* 1 DUPLICATING : duplicación *f,* repetición *f* (de esfuerzos) 2 DUPLICATE : copia *f,* duplicado *m*
duplicity [dʊ'plɪsəti, ˌdju:-] *n, pl* **-ties** : duplicidad *f*
durability [ˌdʊrə'bɪləti, ˌdjʊr-] *n* : durabilidad *f* (de un producto), permanencia *f*
durable ['dʊrəbəl, 'djʊr-] *adj* : duradero
duration [dʊ'reɪʃən, djʊ-] *n* : duración *f*
duress [dʊ'rɛs, djʊ-] *n* : coacción *f*
during ['dʊrɪŋ, 'djʊr-] *prep* : durante
dusk ['dʌsk] *n* : anochecer *m,* crepúsculo *m*
dusky ['dʌski] *adj* **duskier; -est** : oscuro (dícese de los colores)
dust[1] ['dʌst] *vt* 1 : quitar el polvo de 2 SPRINKLE : espolvorear
dust[2] *n* : polvo *m*
duster ['dʌstər] *n* 1 *or* **dust cloth** : trapo *m* de polvo 2 HOUSECOAT : guardapolvo *m* 3 **feather duster** : plumero *m*
dustpan ['dʌstˌpæn] *n* : recogedor *m*
dusty ['dʌsti] *adj* **dustier; -est** : cubierto de polvo, polvoriento
Dutch[1] ['dʌtʃ] *adj* : holandés
Dutch[2] *n* 1 : holandés *m* (idioma) 2 **the Dutch** *npl* : los holandeses
Dutch treat *n* : invitación *f* o pago *m* a escote
dutiful ['du:tɪfəl, 'dju:-] *adj* : motivado por sus deberes, responsable
duty ['du:ti, 'dju:-] *n, pl* **-ties** 1 OBLIGATION : deber *m,* obligación *f,* responsabilidad *f* 2 TAX : impuesto *m,* arancel *m*
dwarf[1] ['dwɔrf] *vt* 1 STUNT : arrestar el crecimiento de 2 : hacer parecer pequeño
dwarf[2] *n, pl* **dwarfs** ['dwɔrfs] *or* **dwarves** ['dwɔrvz] : enano *m,* -na *f*
dwell ['dwɛl] *vi* **dwelled** *or* **dwelt** ['dwɛlt]; **dwelling** 1 RESIDE : residir, morar, vivir 2 **to dwell on** : pensar demasiado en, insistir en
dweller ['dwɛlər] *n* : habitante *mf*
dwelling ['dwɛlɪŋ] *n* : morada *f,* vivienda *f,* residencia *f*
dwindle ['dwɪndəl] *vi* **-dled; -dling** : menguar, reducirse, disminuir
dye[1] ['daɪ] *vt* **dyed; dyeing** : teñir
dye[2] *n* : tintura *f,* tinte *m*
dying → **die**
dyke → **dike**
dynamic [daɪ'næmɪk] *adj* : dinámico
dynamite[1] ['daɪnəˌmaɪt] *vt* **-mited; -miting** : dinamitar
dynamite[2] *n* : dinamita *f*
dynamo ['daɪnəˌmo:] *n, pl* **-mos** : dínamo *m,* generador *m* de electricidad
dynasty ['daɪnəsti, -ˌnæs-] *n, pl* **-ties** : dinastía *f*
dysentery ['dɪsənˌtɛri] *n, pl* **-teries** : disentería *f*
dystrophy ['dɪstrəfi] *n, pl* **-phies** 1 : distrofia *f* 2 → **muscular dystrophy**

E

e ['i:] *n, pl* **e's** *or* **es** ['i:z] : quinta letra del alfabeto inglés
each[1] ['i:tʃ] *adv* : cada uno, por persona <they cost $10 each : costaron $10 cada uno>
each[2] *adj* : cada <each student : cada estudiante> <each and every one : todos sin excepción>
each[3] *pron* 1 : cada uno *m,* cada una *f* <each of us : cada uno de nosotros>

2 each other : el uno al otro, mutuamente <we are helping each other : nos ayudamos el uno al otro> <they love each other : se aman>

eager [ˈiːgər] *adj* **1** ENTHUSIASTIC **:** entusiasta, ávido, deseoso **2** ANXIOUS **:** ansioso, impaciente

eagerly [ˈiːgərli] *adv* **:** con entusiasmo, ansiosamente

eagerness [ˈiːgərnəs] *n* **:** entusiasmo *m,* deseo *m,* impaciencia *f*

eagle [ˈiːgəl] *n* **:** águila *f*

ear [ˈɪr] *n* **1 :** oído *m,* oreja *f* <inner ear : oído interno> <big ears : orejas grandes> **2 ear of corn :** mazorca *f,* choclo *m*

earache [ˈɪr,eɪk] *n* **:** dolor *m* de oído

eardrum [ˈɪr,drʌm] *n* **:** tímpano *m*

earl [ˈərl] *n* **:** conde *m*

earlobe [ˈɪr,loːb] *n* **:** lóbulo *m* de la oreja, perilla *f* de la oreja

early[1] [ˈərli] *adv* **earlier; -est :** temprano, pronto <he arrived early : llegó temprano> <as early as possible : lo más pronto posible, cuanto antes> <ten minutes early : diez minutos de adelanto>

early[2] *adj* **earlier; -est 1** (*referring to a beginning*) **:** primero <the early stages : las primeras etapas> <in early May : a principios de mayo> **2** (*referring to antiquity*) **:** primitivo, antiguo <early man : el hombre primitivo> <early painting : la pintura antigua> **3** (*referring to a designated time*) **:** temprano, antes de la hora, prematuro <he was early : llegó temprano> <early fruit : frutas tempraneras> <an early death : una muerte prematura>

earmark [ˈɪr,mɑrk] *vt* **:** destinar <earmarked funds : fondos destinados>

earn [ˈərn] *vt* **1 :** ganar <to earn money : ganar dinero> **2** DESERVE **:** ganarse, merecer

earnest[1] [ˈərnəst] *adj* **:** serio, sincero

earnest[2] *n* **in ~ :** en serio, de verdad <we began in earnest : empezamos de verdad>

earnestly [ˈərnəstli] *adv* **1** SERIOUSLY **:** con seriedad, en serio **2** FERVENTLY **:** de todo corazón

earnestness [ˈərnəstnəs] *n* **:** seriedad *f,* sinceridad *f*

earnings [ˈərnɪŋz] *npl* **:** ingresos *mpl,* ganancias *fpl,* utilidades *fpl*

earphone [ˈɪr,foːn] *n* **:** audífono *m*

earring [ˈɪr,rɪŋ] *n* **:** zarcillo *m,* arete *m,* aro *m Arg, Chile, Uru,* pendiente *m Spain*

earshot [ˈɪr,ʃɑt] *n* **:** alcance *m* del oído

earth [ˈərθ] *n* **1** LAND, SOIL **:** tierra *f,* suelo *m* **2 the Earth :** la Tierra

earthen [ˈərθən, -ðən] *adj* **:** de tierra, de barro

earthenware [ˈərθən,wær, -ðən-] *n* **:** loza *f,* vajillas *fpl* de barro

earthly [ˈərθli] *adj* **:** terrenal, mundano

earthquake [ˈərθ,kweɪk] *n* **:** terremoto *m,* temblor *m*

earthworm [ˈərθ,wərm] *n* **:** lombriz *f* (de tierra)

earthy [ˈərθi] *adj* **earthier; -est 1 :** terroso <earthy colors : colores terrosos> **2** DOWN-TO-EARTH **:** realista, práctico, llano **3** COARSE, CRUDE **:** basto, grosero, tosco <earthy jokes : chistes groseros>

earwax [ˈɪr,wæks] → **wax**[2]

earwig [ˈɪr,wɪg] *n* **:** tijereta *f*

ease[1] [ˈiːz] *v* **eased; easing** *vt* **1** ALLEVIATE **:** aliviar, calmar, hacer disminuir **2** LOOSEN, RELAX **:** aflojar (una cuerda), relajar (restricciones), descargar (tensiones) **3** FACILITATE **:** facilitar — *vi* **:** calmarse, relajarse

ease[2] *n* **1** CALM, RELIEF **:** tranquilidad *f,* comodidad *f,* desahogo *m* **2** FACILITY **:** facilidad *f* **3 at ~ :** relajado, cómodo <to put someone at ease : tranquilizar a alguien>

easel [ˈiːzəl] *n* **:** caballete *m*

easily [ˈiːzəli] *adv* **1 :** fácilmente, con facilidad **2** UNQUESTIONABLY **:** con mucho, de lejos

easiness [ˈiːzinəs] *n* **:** facilidad *f,* soltura *f*

east[1] [ˈiːst] *adv* **:** al este

east[2] *adj* **:** este, del este, oriental <east winds : vientos del este>

east[3] *n* **1 :** este *m* **2 the East :** el Oriente

Easter [ˈiːstər] *n* **:** Pascua *f* (de Resurrección)

easterly [ˈiːstərli] *adv & adj* **:** del este

eastern [ˈiːstərn] *adj* **1 :** Oriental, del Este <Eastern Europe : Europa del Este> **2 :** oriental, este

Easterner [ˈiːstərnər] *n* **:** habitante *mf* del este

eastward [ˈiːstwərd] *adv & adj* **:** hacia el este

easy [ˈiːzi] *adj* **easier; -est 1 :** fácil **2** LENIENT **:** indulgente

easygoing [,iːziˈgoːɪŋ] *adj* **:** acomodaticio, tolerante, poco exigente

eat [ˈiːt] *v* **ate** [ˈeɪt]; **eaten** [ˈiːtən]; **eating** *vt* **1 :** comer **2** CONSUME **:** consumir, gastar, devorar <expenses ate up profits : los gastos devoraron las ganancias> **3** CORRODE **:** corroer — *vi* **1 :** comer **2 to eat away at** *or* **to eat into :** comerse **3 to eat out :** comer fuera

eatable[1] [ˈiːtəbəl] *adj* **:** comestible, comible *fam*

eatable[2] *n* **1 :** algo para comer **2 eatables** *npl* **:** comestibles *mpl,* alimentos *mpl*

eater [ˈiːtər] *n* **:** comedor *m,* **-dora** *f*

eaves [ˈiːvz] *npl* **:** alero *m*

eavesdrop [ˈiːvz,drɑp] *vi* **-dropped; -dropping :** escuchar a escondidas

eavesdropper [ˈiːvz,drɑpər] *n* **:** persona *f* que escucha a escondidas

ebb[1] [ˈɛb] *vi* **1 :** bajar, menguar (dícese de la marea) **2** DECLINE **:** decaer, disminuir

ebb[2] *n* **1** : reflujo *m* (de una marea) **2** DECLINE : decadencia *f,* declive *m,* disminución *f*

ebony[1] [ˈɛbəni] *adj* **1** : de ébano **2** BLACK : de color ébano, negro

ebony[2] *n, pl* **-nies** : ébano *m*

ebullience [ɪˈbʊljən*t*s, -ˈbʌl-] *n* : efervescencia *f,* vivacidad *f*

ebullient [ɪˈbʊljənt, -ˈbʌl-] *adj* : efervescente, vivaz

eccentric[1] [ɪkˈsɛntrɪk] *adj* **1** : excéntrico <an eccentric wheel : una rueda excéntrica> **2** ODD, SINGULAR : excéntrico, extraño, raro — **eccentrically** [-trɪkli] *adv*

eccentric[2] *n* : ecéntrico *m,* -ca *f*

eccentricity [ˌɛkˌsɛnˈtrɪsət̬i] *n, pl* **-ties** : excentricidad *f*

ecclesiastic [ɪˌkli:ziˈæstɪk] *n* : eclesiástico *m,* clérigo *m*

ecclesiastical [ɪˌkli:ziˈæstɪkəl] *or* **ecclesiastic** *adj* : eclesiástico — **ecclesiastically** *adv*

echelon [ˈɛʃəˌlɑn] *n* **1** : escalón *m* (de tropas o aviones) **2** LEVEL : nivel *m,* esfera *f,* estrato *m*

echo[1] [ˈɛˌko:] *v* **echoed; echoing** *vi* : hacer eco, resonar — *vt* : repetir

echo[2] *n, pl* **echoes** : eco *m*

éclair [eɪˈklær, i-] *n* : pastel *m* relleno de crema

eclectic [ɛˈklɛktɪk, ɪ-] *adj* : ecléctico

eclipse[1] [ɪˈklɪps] *vt* **eclipsed; eclipsing** : eclipsar

eclipse[2] *n* : eclipse *m*

ecological *adj* [ˌi:kəˈlɑdʒɪkəl, ˌɛkə-] : ecológico — **ecologically** *adv*

ecologist [iˈkɑlədʒɪst, ɛ-] *n* : ecólogo *m,* -ga *f*

ecology [iˈkɑlədʒi, ɛ-] *n, pl* **-gies** : ecología *f*

economic [ˌi:kəˈnɑmɪk, ˌɛkə-] *adj* : económico

economical [ˌi:kəˈnɑmɪkəl, ˌɛkə-] *adj* : económico — **economically** *adv*

economics [ˌi:kəˈnɑmɪks, ˌɛkə-] *n* : economía *f*

economist [iˈkɑnəmɪst] *n* : economista *mf*

economize [iˈkɑnəˌmaɪz] *v* **-mized; -mizing** : economizar, ahorrar

economy [iˈkɑnəmi] *n, pl* **-mies** **1** : economía *f,* sistema *m* económico **2** THRIFT : economía *f,* ahorro *m*

ecosystem [ˈi:koˌsɪstəm] *n* : ecosistema *m*

ecru [ˈɛˌkru:, ˈeɪ-] *n* : color *m* crudo

ecstasy [ˈɛkstəsi] *n, pl* **-sies** : éxtasis *m*

ecstatic [ɛkˈstæt̬ɪk, ɪk-] *adj* : extático

ecstatically [ɛkˈstæt̬ɪkli, ɪk-] *adv* : con éxtasis, con gran entusiasmo

Ecuadoran [ˌɛkwəˈdorən] *or* **Ecuadorean** *or* **Ecuadorian** [-ˈdoriən] *n* : ecuatoriano *m,* -na *f* — **Ecuadorean** *or* **Ecuadorian** *adj*

ecumenical [ˌɛkjʊˈmɛnɪkəl] *adj* : ecuménico

eczema [ɪgˈzi:mə, ˈɛgzəmə, ˈɛksə-] *n* : eczema *m*

eddy[1] [ˈɛdi] *vi* **eddied; eddying** : arremolinarse, hacer remolinos

eddy[2] *n, pl* **-dies** : remolino *m*

edema [ɪˈdi:mə] *n* : edema *m*

Eden [ˈi:dən] *n* : Edén *m*

edge[1] [ˈɛdʒ] *v* **edged; edging** *vt* **1** BORDER : bordear, ribetear, orlar **2** SHARPEN : afilar, aguzar **3** *or* **to edge one's way** : avanzar poco a poco **4** **to edge out** : derrotar por muy poco — *vi* ADVANCE : ir avanzando (poco a poco)

edge[2] *n* **1** : filo *m* (de un cuchillo) **2** BORDER : borde *m,* orilla *f,* margen *m* **3** ADVANTAGE : ventaja *f*

edger [ˈɛdʒər] *n* : cortabordes *m*

edgewise [ˈɛdʒˌwaɪz] *adv* SIDEWAYS : de lado, de canto

edginess [ˈɛdʒinəs] *n* : tensión *f,* nerviosismo *m*

edgy [ˈɛdʒi] *adj* **edgier; -est** : tenso, nervioso

edible [ˈɛdəbəl] *adj* : comestible

edict [ˈi:ˌdɪkt] *n* : edicto *m,* mandato *m,* orden *f*

edification [ˌɛdəfəˈkeɪʃən] *n* : edificación *f,* instrucción *f*

edifice [ˈɛdəfɪs] *n* : edificio *m*

edify [ˈɛdəˌfaɪ] *vt* **-fied; -fying** : edificar

edit [ˈɛdɪt] *vt* **1** : editar, redactar, corregir **2** *or* **to edit out** DELETE : recortar, cortar

edition [ɪˈdɪʃən] *n* : edición *f*

editor [ˈɛdɪt̬ər] *n* : editor *m,* -tora *f;* redactor *m,* -tora *f*

editorial[1] [ˌɛdɪˈtoriəl] *adj* **1** : de redacción **2** : editorial <an editorial comment : un comentario editorial>

editorial[2] *n* : editorial *m*

editorship [ˈɛdətərˌʃɪp] *n* : dirección *f*

educable [ˈɛdʒəkəbəl] *adj* : educable

educate [ˈɛdʒəˌkeɪt] *vt* **-cated; -cating** **1** TEACH : educar, enseñar **2** INSTRUCT : formar, educar, instruir **3** INFORM : informar, concientizar

education [ˌɛdʒəˈkeɪʃən] *n* : educación *f*

educational [ˌɛdʒəˈkeɪʃənəl] *adj* **1** : docente, de enseñanza <an educational institution : una institución docente> **2** PEDAGOGICAL : pedagógico **3** INSTRUCTIONAL : educativo, instructivo

educator [ˈɛdʒəˌkeɪt̬ər] *n* : educador *m,* -dora *f*

eel [ˈi:l] *n* : anguila *f*

eerie [ˈɪri] *adj* **-rier; -est** : extraño, misterioso, fantasmagórico

eerily [ˈɪrəli] *adv* : de manera extraña y misteriosa

efface [ɪˈfeɪs, ɛ-] *vt* **-faced; -facing** : borrar

effect[1] [ɪˈfɛkt] *vt* **1** CARRY OUT : efectuar, llevar a cabo **2** ACHIEVE : lograr, realizar

effect[2] *n* **1** RESULT : efecto *m,* resultado *m,* consecuencia *f* <to no effect : sin resultado> **2** MEANING : sentido *m* <something to that effect : algo por el estilo> **3** INFLUENCE : efecto *m,* influencia *f* **4 effects** *npl* BELONGINGS **:** efectos *mpl,* pertenencias *fpl* **5 to go into effect :** entrar en vigor **6 in ~** REALLY **:** en realidad, efectivamente

effective [ɪˈfɛktɪv] *adj* **1** EFFECTUAL **:** efectivo, eficaz **2** OPERATIVE **:** vigente **— effectively** *adv*

effectiveness [ɪˈfɛktɪvnəs] *n* **:** eficacia *f,* efectividad *f*

effectual [ɪˈfɛktʃʊəl] *adj* **:** eficaz, efectivo **— effectually** *adv*

effeminate [əˈfɛmənət] *adj* **:** afeminado

effervesce [ˌɛfərˈvɛs] *vi* **-vesced; -vescing 1 :** estar en efervescencia, burbujear (dícese de líquidos) **2 :** estar eufórico, estar muy animado (dícese de las personas)

effervescence [ˌɛfərˈvɛsənts] *n* **1 :** efervescencia *f* **2** LIVELINESS **:** vivacidad *f*

effervescent [ˌɛfərˈvɛsənt] *adj* **1 :** efervescente **2** LIVELY, VIVACIOUS **:** vivaz, animado

effete [ɛˈfiːt, ɪ-] *adj* **1** WORN- OUT **:** desgastado, agotado **2** DECADENT **:** decadente **3** EFFEMINATE **:** afeminado

efficacious [ˌɛfəˈkeɪʃəs] *adj* **:** eficaz, efectivo

efficacy [ˈɛfɪkəsi] *n, pl* **-cies :** eficacia *f*

efficiency [ɪˈfɪʃəntsi] *n, pl* **-cies :** eficiencia *f*

efficient [ɪˈfɪʃənt] *adj* **:** eficiente **— efficiently** *adv*

effigy [ˈɛfədʒi] *n, pl* **-gies :** efigie *f*

effluent [ˈɛˌfluːənt, ɛˈfluː-] *n* **:** efluente *m* **— effluent** *adj*

effort [ˈɛfərt] *n* **1** EXERTION **:** esfuerzo *m* **2** ATTEMPT **:** tentativa *f,* intento *m* <it's not worth the effort : no vale la pena>

effortless [ˈɛfərtləs] *adj* **:** fácil, sin esfuerzo

effortlessly [ˈɛfərtləsli] *adv* **:** sin esfuerzo, fácilmente

effrontery [ɪˈfrʌntəri] *n, pl* **-teries :** insolencia *f,* desfachatez *f,* descaro *m*

effusion [ɪˈfjuːʒən, ɛ-] *n* **:** efusión *f*

effusive [ɪˈfjuːsɪv, ɛ-] *adj* **:** efusivo **— effusively** *adv*

egg¹ [ˈɛg] *vt* **to egg on :** incitar, azuzar, provocar

egg² *n* **1 :** huevo *m* **2** OVUM **:** óvulo *m*

eggbeater [ˈɛgˌbiːt̬ər] *n* **:** batidor *m* (de huevos)

eggnog [ˈɛgˌnɑg] *n* **:** ponche *m* de huevo, rompope *m CA, Mex*

eggplant [ˈɛgˌplænt] *n* **:** berenjena *f*

eggshell [ˈɛgˌʃɛl] *n* **:** cascarón *m*

ego [ˈiːˌgoː] *n, pl* **egos 1** SELF-ESTEEM **:** amor *m* propio **2** SELF **:** ego *m,* yo *m*

egocentric [ˌiːgoˈsɛntrɪk] *adj* **:** egocéntrico

egoism [ˈiːgoˌwɪzəm] *n* **:** egoísmo *m*

egoist [ˈiːgowɪst] *n* **:** egoísta *mf*

egoistic [ˌiːˌgoˈwɪstɪk] *adj* **:** egoísta

egotism [ˈiːgəˌtɪzəm] *n* **:** egotismo *m*

egotist [ˈiːgətɪst] *n* **:** egotista *mf*

egotistic [ˌiːgəˈtɪstɪk] *or* **egotistical** [-ˈtɪstɪkəl] *adj* **:** egotista **— egotistically** *adv*

egregious [ɪˈgriːdʒəs] *adj* **:** atroz, flagrante, mayúsculo **— egregiously** *adv*

egress [ˈiːˌgrɛs] *n* **:** salida *f*

egret [ˈiːgrət, -ˌgrɛt] *n* **:** garceta *f*

eiderdown [ˈaɪdərˌdaʊn] *n* **1 :** plumón *m* **2** COMFORTER **:** edredón *m*

eight¹ *adj* [ˈeɪt] **:** ocho

eight² *n* **:** ocho *m*

eight hundred¹ *adj* **:** ochocientos

eight hundred² *n* **:** ochocientos *m*

eighteen¹ [eitˈtiːn] *adj* **:** dieciocho

eighteen² *n* **:** dieciocho *m*

eighteenth¹ [eɪtˈtiːnθ] *adj* **:** decimoctavo

eighteenth² *n* **1 :** decimoctavo *m,* -va *f* (en una serie) **2 :** dieciochoavo *m,* dieciochoava parte *f*

eighth¹ [ˈeɪtθ] *adj* **:** octavo

eighth² *n* **1 :** octavo *m,* -va *f* (en una serie) **2 :** octavo *m,* octava parte *f*

eightieth¹ [ˈeɪt̬iəθ] *adj* **:** octagésimo

eightieth² *n* **1 :** octogésimo *m,* -ma *f* (en una serie) **2 :** ochentavo *m,* ochentava parte *f*

eighty¹ [ˈeɪt̬i] *adj* **:** ochenta

eighty² *n, pl* **eighties 1 :** ochenta *m* **2 the eighties :** los ochenta *mpl*

either¹ [ˈiːðər, ˈaɪ-] *adj* **1 :** cualquiera (de los dos) <we can watch either movie : podemos ver cualquiera de las dos películas> **2 :** ninguno de los dos <she wasn't in either room : no estaba en ninguna de las dos salas> **3** EACH **:** cada <on either side of the street : a cada lado de la calle>

either² *pron* **1 :** cualquiera *mf* (de los dos) <either is fine : cualquiera de los dos está bien> **2 :** ninguno *m,* -na *f* (de los dos) <I don't like either : no me gusta ninguno> **3 :** algún *m,* alguna *f* <is either of you interested? : ¿está alguno de ustedes (dos) interesado?>

either³ *conj* **1 :** o, u <either David or Daniel could go : puede ir (o) David o Daniel> **2 :** ni <we won't watch either this movie or the other : no veremos ni esta película ni la otra>

ejaculate [iˈdʒækjəˌleɪt] *v* **-lated; -lating** *vt* **1 :** eyacular **2** EXCLAIM **:** exclamar **—** *vi* **:** eyacular

ejaculation [iˌdʒækjəˈleɪʃən] *n* **1 :** eyaculación *f* (en fisiología) **2** EXCLAMATION **:** exclamación *f*

eject [iˈdʒɛkt] *vt* **:** expulsar, expeler

ejection [iˈdʒɛkʃən] *n* **:** expulsión *f*

eke [ˈiːk] *vt* **eked; eking** *or* **to eke out :** ganar a duras penas

elaborate¹ [iˈlæbəˌreɪt] *v* **-rated; -rating** *vt* **:** elaborar, idear, desarrollar **—** *vi* **to elaborate on :** ampliar, entrar en detalles

elaborate² [iˈlæbərət] *adj* **1** DETAILED **:** detallado, minucioso, elaborado **2** COMPLICATED **:** complicado, intrincado, elaborado **— elaborately** *adv*

elaboration [i,læbə'reɪʃən] *n* : elaboración *f*
elapse [i'læps] *vi* **elapsed; elapsing** : transcurrir, pasar
elastic[1] [i'læstɪk] *adj* : elástico
elastic[2] *n* **1** : elástico *m* **2** RUBBER BAND : goma *f*, gomita *f*, elástico *m*, liga *f*
elasticity [i,læs'tɪsəti, ,iː,læs-] *n, pl* **-ties** : elasticidad *f*
elate [i'leɪt] *vt* **elated; elating** : alborozar, regocijar
elation [i'leɪʃən] *n* : euforia *f*, júbilo *m*, alborozo *m*
elbow[1] ['ɛl,boː] *vt* : darle un codazo a
elbow[2] *n* : codo *m*
elder[1] ['ɛldər] *adj* : mayor
elder[2] *n* **1 to be someone's elder** : ser mayor que alguien **2** : anciano *m*, -na *f* (de un pueblo o una tribu) **3** : miembro *m* del consejo (en varias religiones)
elderberry ['ɛldər,bɛri] *n, pl* **-berries** : baya *f* de saúco (fruta), saúco *m* (árbol)
elderly ['ɛldərli] *adj* : mayor, de edad, anciano
eldest ['ɛldəst] *adj* : mayor, de más edad
elect[1] [i'lɛkt] *vt* : elegir
elect[2] *adj* : electo <the president-elect : el presidente electo>
elect[3] *npl* **the elect** : los elegidos *mpl*
election [i'lɛkʃən] *n* : elección *f*
elective[1] [i'lɛktɪv] *adj* **1** : electivo **2** OPTIONAL : facultativo, optativo
elective[2] *n* : asignatura *f* electiva
elector [i'lɛktər] *n* : elector *m*, -tora *f*
electoral [i'lɛktərəl] *adj* : electoral
electorate [i'lɛktərət] *n* : electorado *m*
electric [i'lɛktrɪk] *adj* **1** *or* **electrical** [-trɪkəl] : eléctrico **2** THRILLING : electrizante, emocionante
electrician [i,lɛk'trɪʃən] *n* : electricista *mf*
electricity [i,lɛk'trɪsəti] *n, pl* **-ties 1** : electricidad *f* **2** CURRENT : corriente *m* eléctrica
electrification [i,lɛktrəfə'keɪʃən] *n* : electrificación *f*
electrify [i'lɛktrə,faɪ] *vt* **-fied; -fying 1** : electrificar **2** THRILL : electrizar, emocionar
electrocardiogram [i,lɛktro'kɑrdiə,græm] *n* : electrocardiograma *m*
electrocardiograph [i,lɛktro'kɑrdiə,græf] *n* : electrocardiógrafo *m*
electrocute [i'lɛktrə,kjuːt] *vt* **-cuted; -cuting** : electrocutar
electrocution [i,lɛktrə'kjuːʃən] *n* : electrocución *f*
electrode [i'lɛk,troːd] *n* : electrodo *m*
electrolysis [i,lɛk'trɑləsɪs] *n* : electrólisis *f*
electrolyte [i'lɛktrə,laɪt] *n* : electrolito *m*
electromagnet [i,lɛktro'mægnət] *n* : electroimán *m*
electromagnetic [i,lɛktromæg'nɛtɪk] *adj* : electromagnético — **electromagnetically** [-tɪkli] *adv*
electromagnetism [i,lɛktro'mægnə,tɪzəm] *n* : electromagnetismo *m*
electron [i'lɛk,trɑn] *n* : electrón *m*
electronic [i,lɛk'trɑnɪk] *adj* : electrónico — **electronically** [-nɪkli] *adv*
electronic mail *n* : correo *m* electrónico
electronics [i,lɛk'trɑnɪks] *n* : electrónica *f*
electroplate [i'lɛktrə,pleɪt] *vt* **-plated; plating** : galvanizar mediante electrólisis
elegance ['ɛlɪgənts] *n* : elegancia *f*
elegant ['ɛlɪgənt] *adj* : elegante — **elegantly** *adv*
elegy ['ɛlədʒi] *n, pl* **-gies** : elegía *f*
element ['ɛləmənt] *n* **1** COMPONENT : elemento *m*, factor *m* **2** : elemento *m* (en la química) **3** MILIEU : elemento *m*, medio *m* <to be in one's element : estar en su elemento> **4 elements** *npl* RUDIMENTS : elementos *mpl*, rudimentos *mpl*, bases *fpl* **5 the elements** WEATHER : los elementos *mpl*
elemental [,ɛlə'mɛntəl] *adj* **1** BASIC : elemental, primario **2** : elemental (dícese de los elementos químicos)
elementary [,ɛlə'mɛntri] *adj* **1** SIMPLE : elemental, simple, fundamental **2** : de enseñanza primaria
elementary school *n* : escuela *f* primaria
elephant ['ɛləfənt] *n* : elefante *m*, -ta *f*
elevate ['ɛlə,veɪt] *vt* **-vated; -vating 1** RAISE : elevar, levantar, alzar **2** EXALT, PROMOTE : elevar, exaltar, ascender **3** ELATE : alborozar, regocijar
elevation [,ɛlə'veɪʃən] *n* **1** : elevación *f* **2** ALTITUDE : altura *f*, altitud *f* **3** PROMOTION : ascenso *m*
elevator ['ɛlə,veɪtər] *n* : ascensor *m*, elevador *m*
eleven[1] [ɪ'lɛvən] *adj* : once *m*
eleven[2] *n* : once *m*
eleventh[1] [ɪlɛvəntθ] *adj* : undécimo
eleventh[2] *n* **1** : undécimo *m*, -ma *f* (en una serie) **2** : onceavo *m*, onceava parte *f*
elf ['ɛlf] *n, pl* **elves** ['ɛlvz] : elfo *m*, geniecillo *m*, duende *m*
elfin ['ɛlfən] *adj* **1** : de elfo, menudo **2** ENCHANTING, MAGIC : mágico, encantador
elfish ['ɛlfɪʃ] *adj* **1** : de elfo **2** MISCHIEVOUS : travieso
elicit [ɪ'lɪsət] *vt* : provocar
eligibility [,ɛlədʒə'bɪləti] *n, pl* **-ties** : elegibilidad *f*
eligible ['ɛlədʒəbəl] *adj* **1** QUALIFIED : elegible **2** SUITABLE : idóneo
eliminate [ɪ'lɪmə,neɪt] *vt* **-nated; -nating** : eliminar
elimination [ɪ,lɪmə'neɪʃən] *n* : eliminación *f*
elite [eɪ'liːt, i-] *n* : elite *f*

elixir [iˈlɪksər] *n* **:** elixir *m*
elk [ˈɛlk] *n* **:** alce *m* (de Europa), uapití *m* (de América)
ellipse [ɪˈlɪps, ɛ-] *n* **:** elipse *f*
ellipsis [ɪˈlɪpsəs, ɛ-] *n, pl* **-lipses** [-ˌsiːz] **1 :** elipsis *f* **2 :** puntos *mpl* suspensivos (en la puntuación)
elliptical [ɪˈlɪptɪkəl, ɛ-] *or* **elliptic** [-tɪk] *adj* **:** elíptico
elm [ˈɛlm] *n* **:** olmo *m*
elocution [ˌɛləˈkjuːʃən] *n* **:** elocución *f*
elongate [iˈlɔŋˌgeɪt] *vt* **-gated; -gating :** alargar
elongation [ˌiːˌlɔŋˈgeɪʃən] *n* **:** alargamiento *m*
elope [iˈloːp] *vi* **eloped; eloping :** fugarse
elopement [iˈloːpmənt] *n* **:** fuga *f*
eloquence [ˈɛləkwənts] *n* **:** elocuencia *f*
eloquent [ˈɛləkwənt] *adj* **:** elocuente — **eloquently** *adv*
El Salvadoran [ˌɛlˌsælvəˈdorən] *n* **:** salvadoreño *m*, -ña *f* — **El Salvadoran** *adj*
else[1] [ˈɛls] *adv* **1** DIFFERENTLY **:** de otro modo, de otra manera <how else? : ¿de qué otro modo?> **2** ELSEWHERE **:** de otro sitio, de otro lugar <where else? : ¿en qué otro sitio?> **3 or else** OTHERWISE **:** si no, de lo contrario
else[2] *adj* **1** OTHER **:** otro <anyone else : cualquier otro> <everyone else : todos los demás> <nobody else : ningún otro, nadie más> <somebody else : otra persona> **2** MORE **:** más <nothing else : nada más> <what else? : ¿qué más?>
elsewhere [ˈɛlsˌhwɛr] *adv* **:** en otra parte, en otro sitio, en otro lugar
elucidate [iˈluːsəˌdeɪt] *vt* **-dated; -dating :** dilucidar, elucidar, esclarecer
elucidation [iˌluːsəˈdeɪʃən] *n* **:** elucidación *f*, esclarecimiento *m*
elude [iˈluːd] *vt* **eluded; eluding :** eludir, evadir
elusive [iˈluːsɪv] *adj* **1** EVASIVE **:** evasivo, esquivo **2** SLIPPERY **:** huidizo, escurridizo **3** FLEETING, INTANGIBLE **:** impalpable, fugaz
elusively [iˈluːsɪvli] *adv* **:** de manera esquiva
elves → **elf**
emaciate [iˈmeɪʃiˌeɪt] *vt* **-ated; -ating :** enflaquecer
emaciation [iˌmeɪsiˈeɪʃən, -ʃi-] *n* **:** enflaquecimiento *m*, escualidez *f*, delgadez *f* extrema
E–mail [ˈiːˌmeɪl] → **electronic mail**
emanate [ˈɛməˌneɪt] *v* **-nated; -nating** *vi* **:** emanar, provenir, proceder — *vt* **:** emanar
emanation [ˌɛməˈneɪʃən] *n* **:** emanación *f*
emancipate [iˈmæntsəˌpeɪt] *vt* **-pated; -pating :** emancipar
emancipation [iˌmæntsəˈpeɪʃən] *n* **:** emancipación *f*
emasculate [iˈmæskjəˌleɪt] *vt* **-lated; -lating 1** CASTRATE **:** castrar, emascular **2** WEAKEN **:** debilitar
embalm [ɪmˈbɑm, ɛm-, -ˈbɑlm] *vt* **:** embalsamar
embankment [ɪmˈbæŋkmənt, ɛm-] *n* **:** terraplén *m*, muro *m* de contención
embargo[1] [ɪmˈbɑrgo, ɛm-] *vt* **-goed; -going :** imponer un embargo sobre
embargo[2] *n, pl* **-goes :** embargo *m*
embark [ɪmˈbɑrk, ɛm-] *vt* **:** embarcar — *vi* **1 :** embarcarse **2 to embark on** START **:** emprender, embarcarse en
embarkation [ˌɛmˌbɑrˈkeɪʃən] *n* **:** embarque *m*, embarco *m*
embarrass [ɪmˈbærəs, ɛm-] *vt* **:** avergonzar, abochornar
embarrassing [ɪmˈbærəsɪŋ, ɛm-] *adj* **:** embarazoso, violento
embarrassment [ɪmˈbærəsmənt, ɛm-] *n* **:** vergüenza *f*, pena *f*
embassy [ˈɛmbəsi] *n, pl* **-sies :** embajada *f*
embed [ɪmˈbɛd, ɛm-] *vt* **-bedded; -bedding :** incrustar, empotrar, grabar (en la memoria)
embellish [ɪmˈbɛlɪʃ, ɛm-] *vt* **:** adornar, embellecer
embellishment [ɪmˈbɛlɪʃmənt, ɛm-] *n* **:** adorno *m*
ember [ˈɛmbər] *n* **:** ascua *f*, brasa *f*
embezzle [ɪmˈbɛzəl, ɛm-] *vt* **-zled; -zling :** desfalcar, malversar
embezzlement [ɪmˈbɛzəlmənt, ɛm-] *n* **:** desfalco *m*, malversación *f*
embezzler [ɪmˈbɛzələr, ɛm-] *n* **:** desfacador *m*, -dora *f*; malversador *m*, -dora *f*
embitter [ɪmˈbɪtər, ɛm-] *vt* **:** amargar
emblem [ˈɛmbləm] *n* **:** emblema *m*, símbolo *m*
emblematic [ˌɛmbləˈmætɪk] *adj* **:** emblemático, simbólico
embodiment [ɪmˈbɑdɪmənt, ɛm-] *n* **:** encarnación *f*, personificación *f*
embody [ɪmˈbɑdi, ɛm-] *vt* **-bodied; -bodying :** encarnar, personificar
emboss [ɪmˈbɑs, ɛm-, -ˈbɔs] *vt* **:** repujar, grabar en relieve
embrace[1] [ɪmˈbreɪs, ɛm-] *vt* **-braced; -bracing 1** HUG **:** abrazar **2** ADOPT, TAKE ON **:** adoptar, aceptar **3** INCLUDE **:** abarcar, incluir
embrace[2] *n* **:** abrazo *m*
embroider [ɪmˈbrɔɪdər, ɛm-] *vt* **:** bordar (una tela), adornar (una historia)
embroidery [ɪmˈbrɔɪdəri, ɛm-] *n, pl* **-deries :** bordado *m*
embroil [ɪmˈbrɔɪl, ɛm-] *vt* **:** embrollar, enredar
embryo [ˈɛmbriˌoː] *n, pl* **embryos :** embrión *m*
embryonic [ˌɛmbriˈɑnɪk] *adj* **:** embrionario
emend [iˈmɛnd] *vt* **:** enmendar, corregir

emendation [ˌiːˌmɛnˈdeɪʃən] *n* : enmienda *f*

emerald[1] [ˈɛmrəld, ˈɛmə-] *adj* : verde esmeralda

emerald[2] *n* : esmeralda *f*

emerge [iˈmərdʒ] *vi* **emerged; emerging** : emerger, salir, aparecer, surgir

emergence [iˈmərdʒən*t*s] *n* : aparición *f,* surgimiento *m*

emergency [iˈmərdʒən*t*si] *n, pl* **-cies** : emergencia *f*

emergent [iˈmərdʒənt] *adj* : emergente

emery [ˈɛməri] *n, pl* **-eries** : esmeril *m*

emetic[1] [iˈmɛt̬ɪk] *adj* : vomitivo, emético

emetic[2] *n* : vomitivo *m,* emético *m*

emigrant [ˈɛmɪgrənt] *n* : emigrante *mf*

emigrate [ˈɛməˌgreɪt] *vi* **-grated; -grating** : emigrar

emigration [ˌɛməˈgreɪʃən] *n* : emigración *f*

eminence [ˈɛmənən*t*s] *n* **1** PROMINENCE : eminencia *f,* prestigio *m,* renombre *m* **2** DIGNITARY : eminencia *f;* dignatario *m,* -ria *f* <Your Eminence : Su Eminencia>

eminent [ˈɛmənənt] *adj* : eminente, ilustre

eminently [ˈɛmənəntli] *adv* : sumamente

emissary [ˈɛməˌsɛri] *n, pl* **-saries** : emisario *m,* **-ria** *f*

emission [iˈmɪʃən] *n* : emisión *f*

emit [iˈmɪt] *vt* **emitted; emitting** : emitir, despedir, producir

emote [iˈmoːt] *vi* **emoted; emoting** : exteriorizar las emociones

emotion [iˈmoːʃən] *n* : emoción *f,* sentimiento *m*

emotional [iˈmoːʃənəl] *adj* **1** : emocional, afectivo <an emotional reaction : una reacción emocional> **2** MOVING : emocionante, emotivo, conmovedor

emotionally [iˈmoːʃənəli] *adv* : emocionalmente

emperor [ˈɛmpərər] *n* : emperador *m*

emphasis [ˈɛmfəsɪs] *n, pl* **-phases** [-ˌsiːz] : énfasis *m,* hincapié *m*

emphasize [ˈɛmfəˌsaɪz] *vt* **-sized; -sizing** : enfatizar, destacar, subrayar, hacer hincapié en

emphatic [ɪmˈfætɪk, ɛm-] *adj* : enfático, enérgico, categórico — **emphatically** [-ɪkli] *adv*

empire [ˈɛmˌpaɪr] *n* : imperio *m*

empirical [ɪmˈpɪrɪkəl, ɛm-] *adj* : empírico — **empirically** [-ɪkli] *adv*

employ[1] [ɪmˈplɔɪ, ɛm-] *vt* **1** USE : usar, utilizar **2** HIRE : contratar, emplear **3** OCCUPY : ocupar, dedicar, emplear

employ[2] [ɪmˈplɔɪ, ɛm-; ˈɪmˌ-, ˈɛmˌ-] *n* **1** : puesto *m,* cargo *m,* ocupación *f* **2 to be in the employ of** : estar al servicio de, trabajar para

employee [ɪmˌplɔɪˈiː, ɛm-, -ˈplɔɪˌiː] *n* : empleado *m,* **-da** *f*

employer [ɪmˈplɔɪər, ɛm-] *n* : patrón *m,* -trona *f;* empleador *m,* -dora *f*

employment [ɪmˈplɔɪmənt, ɛm-] *n* : trabajo *m,* empleo *m*

empower [ɪmˈpaʊər, ɛm-] *vt* : facultar, autorizar, conferirle poder a

empowerment [ɪmˈpaʊərmənt, ɛm-] *n* : autorización *f*

empress [ˈɛmprəs] *n* : emperatriz *f*

emptiness [ˈɛmptinəs] *n* : vacío *m,* vacuidad *f*

empty[1] [ˈɛmpti] *v* **-tied; -tying** *vt* : vaciar — *vi* : desaguar (dícese de un río)

empty[2] *adj* **emptier; -est 1** : vacío **2** VACANT : desocupado, libre **3** MEANINGLESS : vacío, hueco, vano

empty–handed [ˌɛmptiˈhændəd] *adj* : con las manos vacías

empty–headed [ˌɛmptiˈhɛdəd] *adj* : cabeza hueca, tonto

emu [ˈiːˌmjuː] *n* : emú *m*

emulate [ˈɛmjəˌleɪt] *vt* **-lated; -lating** : emular

emulation [ˌɛmjəˈleɪʃən] *n* : emulación *f*

emulsifier [ɪˈmʌlsəˌfaɪər] *n* : emulsionante *m*

emulsify [ɪˈmʌlsəˌfaɪ] *vt* **-fied; -fying** : emulsionar

emulsion [ɪˈmʌlʃən] *n* : emulsión *f*

enable [ɪˈneɪbəl, ɛ-] *vt* **-abled; -abling 1** EMPOWER : habilitar, autorizar, facultar **2** PERMIT : hacer posible, posibilitar, permitar

enact [ɪˈnækt, ɛ-] *vt* **1** : promulgar (un ley o decreto) **2** : representar (un papel en el teatro)

enactment [ɪˈnæktmənt, ɛ-] *n* : promulgación *f*

enamel[1] [ɪˈnæməl] *vt* **-eled** *or* **-elled; -eling** *or* **-elling** : esmaltar

enamel[2] *n* : esmalte *m*

enamor [ɪˈnæmər] *vt* **1** : enamorar **2 to be enamored of** : estar enamorado de (una persona), estar entusiasmado con (algo)

encamp [ɪnˈkæmp, ɛn-] *vi* : acampar

encampment [ɪnˈkæmpmənt, ɛn-] *n* : campamento *m*

encase [ɪnˈkeɪs, ɛn-] *vt* **-cased; -casing** : encerrar, revestir

encephalitis [ɪnˌsɛfəˈlaɪt̬əs, ɛn-] *n, pl* **-litides** [-ˈlɪt̬əˌdiːz] : encefalitis *f*

enchant [ɪnˈtʃænt, ɛn-] *vt* **1** BEWITCH : hechizar, encantar, embrujar **2** CHARM, FASCINATE : cautivar, fascinar, encantar

enchanting [ɪnˈtʃæntɪŋ, ɛn-] *adj* : encantador

enchanter [ɪnˈtʃæntər, ɛn-] *n* SORCERER : mago *m,* encantador *m*

enchantment [ɪnˈtʃæntmənt, ɛn-] *n* **1** SPELL : encanto *m,* hechizo *m* **2** CHARM : encanto *m*

enchantress [ɪnˈtʃæntrəs, ɛn-] *n* **1** SORCERESS : maga *f,* hechicera *f* **2** CHARMER : mujer *f* cautivadora

encircle [ɪnˈsərkəl, ɛn-] *vt* **-cled; -cling** : rodear, ceñir, cercar

enclose [ɪnˈkloːz, ɛn-] *vt* **-closed; -closing 1** SURROUND : encerrar, cercar, rodear 2 INCLUDE : incluir, adjuntar, acompañar <please find enclosed : le enviamos adjunto>

enclosure [ɪn'klo:ʒər, ɛn-] *n* **1** ENCLOSING : encierro *m* **2** : cercado *m* (de terreno), recinto *m* <an enclosure for the press : un recinto para la prensa> **3** ADJUNCT : anexo *m* (con una carta), documento *m* adjunto

encompass [ɪn'kʌmpəs, ɛn-, -'kɑm-] *vt* **1** SURROUND : circundar, rodear **2** INCLUDE : abarcar, comprender

encore ['ɑn,kor] *n* : bis *m,* repetición *f*

encounter[1] [ɪn'kaʊntər, ɛn-] *vt* **1** MEET : encontrar, encontrarse con, toparse con, tropezar con **2** FIGHT : combatir, luchar contra

encounter[2] *n* : encuentro *m*

encourage [ɪn'kərɪdʒ, ɛn-] *vt* **-aged; -aging 1** HEARTEN, INSPIRE : animar, alentar **2** FOSTER : fomentar, promover

encouragement [ɪn'kərɪdʒmənt, ɛn-] *n* : ánimo *m,* aliento *m*

encroach [ɪn'kro:tʃ, ɛn-] *vi* **to encroach on** : invadir, abusar (derechos), quitar (tiempo)

encroachment [ɪn'kro:tʃmənt, ɛn-] *n* : invasión *f,* usurpación *f*

encrust [ɪn'krʌst, ɛn-] *vt* **1** : recubrir con una costra **2** INLAY : incrustar <encrusted with gems : incrustado de gemas>

encumber [ɪn'kʌmbər, ɛn-] *vt* **1** BLOCK : obstruir, estorbar **2** BURDEN : cargar, gravar

encumbrance [ɪn'kʌmbrənts, ɛn-] *n* : estorbo *m,* carga *f,* gravamen *m*

encyclopedia [ɪn,saɪklə'pi:diə, ɛn-] *n* : enciclopedia *f*

encyclopedic [ɪn,saɪklə'pi:dɪk, ɛn-] *adj* : enciclopédico

end[1] ['ɛnd] *vt* **1** STOP : terminar, poner fin a **2** CONCLUDE : concluir, terminar — *vi* : terminar(se), acabar, concluir(se)

end[2] *n* **1** EXTREMITY : extremo *m,* final *m,* punta *f* **2** CONCLUSION : fin *m,* final *m* **3** AIM : fin *m*

endanger [ɪn'deɪndʒər, ɛn-] *vt* : poner en peligro

endear [ɪn'dɪr, ɛn-] *vt* **to endear oneself to** : ganarse la simpatía de, granjearse el cariño de

endearment [ɪn'dɪrmənt, ɛn-] *n* : expresión *f* de cariño

endeavor[1] [ɪn'dɛvər, ɛn-] *vt* : intentar, esforzarse por <he endeavored to improve his work : intentó por mejorar su trabajo>

endeavor[2] *n* : intento *m,* esfuerzo *m*

ending ['ɛndɪŋ] *n* **1** CONCLUSION : final *m,* desenlace *m* **2** SUFFIX : sufijo *m,* terminación *f*

endive ['ɛn,daɪv, ,ɑn'di:v] *n* : endibia *f,* endivia *f*

endless ['ɛndləs] *adj* **1** INTERMINABLE : interminable, inacabable, sin fin **2** INNUMERABLE : innumerable, incontable

endlessly ['ɛndləsli] *adv* : interminablemente, eternamente, sin parar

endocrine ['ɛndəkrən, -,kraɪn, -,kri:n] *adj* : endocrino

endorse [ɪn'dɔrs, ɛn-] *vt* **-dorsed; -dorsing 1** SIGN : endosar, firmar **2** APPROVE : aprobar, sancionar

endorsement [ɪn'dɔrsmənt, ɛn-] *n* **1** SIGNATURE : endoso *m,* firma *f* **2** APPROVAL : aprobación *f,* aval *m*

endow [ɪn'daʊ, ɛn-] *vt* : dotar

endowment [ɪn'daʊmənt, ɛn-] *n* **1** FUNDING : dotación *f* **2** DONATION : donación *f,* legado *m* **3** ATTRIBUTE, GIFT : atributo *m,* dotes *fpl*

endurable [ɪn'dʊrəbəl, ɛn-, -'djʊr-] *adj* : tolerable, soportable

endurance [ɪn'dʊrənts, ɛn-, -'djʊr-] *n* : resistencia *f,* aguante *m*

endure [ɪn'dʊr, ɛn-, -'djʊr] *v* **-dured; -during** *vt* **1** BEAR : resistir, soportar, aguantar **2** TOLERATE : tolerar, soportar — *vi* LAST : durar, perdurar

enema ['ɛnəmə] *n* : enema *m,* lavativa *f*

enemy ['ɛnəmi] *n, pl* **-mies** : enemigo *m,* -ga *f*

energetic [,ɛnər'dʒɛtɪk] *adj* : enérgico, vigoroso — **energetically** [-tɪkli] *adv*

energize ['ɛnər,dʒaɪz] *vt* **-gized; -gizing 1** ACTIVATE : activar **2** INVIGORATE : vigorizar

energy ['ɛnərdʒi] *n, pl* **-gies 1** VITALITY : energía *f,* vitalidad *f* **2** EFFORT : esfuerzo *m,* energías *fpl* **3** POWER : energía *f* <atomic energy : energía atómica>

enervate ['ɛnər,veɪt] *vt* **-vated; -vating** : enervar, debilitar

enervation [,ɛnər'veɪʃən] *n* : enervación *f,* debilidad *f*

enfold [ɪn'fo:ld, ɛn-] *vt* : envolver

enforce [ɪn'fors, ɛn-] *vt* **-forced; -forcing 1** : hacer respetar, hacer cumplir (una ley, etc.) **2** IMPOSE : imponer <to enforce obedience : imponer la obediencia>

enforcement [ɪn'forsmənt, ɛn-] *n* : imposición *f*

enfranchise [ɪn'fræn,tʃaɪz, ɛn-] *vt* **-chised; -chising** : conceder el voto a

enfranchisement [ɪn'fræn,tʃaɪzmənt, ɛn-] *n* : concesión *f* del voto

engage [ɪn'geɪdʒ, ɛn-] *v* **-gaged; -gaging** *vt* **1** ATTRACT : captar, atraer, llamar <to engage one's attention : captar la atención> **2** MESH : engranar <to engage the clutch : embragar> **3** COMMIT : comprometer <to get engaged : comprometerse> **4** HIRE : contratar **5** : entablar combate con (un enemigo) — *vi* **1** PARTICIPATE : participar **2 to engage in combat** : entrar en combate

engagement [ɪn'geɪdʒmənt, ɛn-] *n* **1** APPOINTMENT **:** cita *f,* hora *f* **2** BETROTHAL **:** compromiso *m*
engaging [ɪn'geɪdʒɪŋ, ɛn-] *adj* **:** atractivo, encantador, interesante
engender [ɪn'dʒɛndər, ɛn-] *vt* **-dered; -dering :** engendrar
engine ['ɛndʒən] *n* **1** MOTOR **:** motor *m* **2** LOCOMOTIVE **:** locomotora *f,* máquina *f*
engineer[1] [ˌɛndʒə'nɪr] *vt* **1 :** diseñar, construir (un sistema, un mecanismo, etc.) **2** CONTRIVE **:** maquinar, tramar, fraguar
engineer[2] *n* **1 :** ingeniero *m,* -ra *f* **2 :** maquinista *mf* (de locomotoras)
engineering [ˌɛndʒə'nɪrɪŋ] *n* **:** ingeniería *f*
English[1] ['ɪŋglɪʃ, 'ŋlɪʃ] *adj* **:** inglés
English[2] *n* **1 :** inglés *m* (idioma) **2 the English :** los ingleses
Englishman ['ɪŋglɪʃmən, 'ɪŋlɪʃ-] *n, pl* **-men** [-mən, -ˌmɛn] **:** inglés *m*
Englishwoman ['ɪŋglɪʃˌwʊmən, 'ɪŋlɪʃ-] *n, pl* **-women** [-ˌwɪmən] **:** inglesa *f*
engrave [ɪn'greɪv, ɛn-] *vt* **-graved; -graving :** grabar
engraver [ɪn'greɪvər, ɛn-] *n* **:** grabador *m,* -dora *f*
engraving [ɪn'greɪvɪŋ, ɛn-] *n* **:** grabado *m*
engross [ɪn'groːs, ɛn-] *vt* **:** absorber
engrossed [ɪn'groːst, ɛn-] *adj* **:** absorto
engulf [ɪn'gʌlf, ɛn-] *vt* **:** envolver, sepultar
enhance [ɪn'hænts, ɛn-] *vt* **-hanced; -hancing :** realzar, aumentar, mejorar
enhancement [ɪn'hæntsmənt, ɛn-] *n* **:** mejora *f,* realce *m,* aumento *m*
enigma [ɪ'nɪgmə] *n* **:** enigma *m*
enigmatic [ˌɛnɪg'mæṭɪk, ˌiːnɪg-] *adj* **:** enigmático — **enigmatically** [-ṭɪkli] *adv*
enjoin [ɪn'dʒɔɪn, ɛn-] *vt* **1** COMMAND **:** ordenar, imponer **2** FORBID **:** prohibir, vedar
enjoy [ɪn'dʒɔɪ, ɛn-] *vt* **1 :** disfrutar, gozar de <did you enjoy the book? : ¿te gustó el libro?> <to enjoy good health : gozar de buena salud> **2 to enjoy oneself :** divertirse, pasarlo bien
enjoyable [ɪn'dʒɔɪəbəl, ɛn-] *adj* **:** agradable, placentero, divertido
enjoyment [ɪn'dʒɔɪmənt, ɛn-] *n* **:** placer *m,* goce *m,* disfrute *m,* deleite *m*
enlarge [ɪn'lɑrdʒ, ɛn-] *v* **-larged; -larging** *vt* **:** extender, agrandar, ampliar — *vi* **1 :** ampliarse **2 to enlarge upon :** extenderse sobre, entrar en detalles sobre
enlargement [ɪn'lɑrdʒmənt, ɛn-] *n* **:** expansión *f,* ampliación *f* (dícese de fotografías)
enlarger [ɪn'lɑrdʒər, ɛn-] *n* **:** ampliadora *f*
enlighten [ɪn'laɪtən, ɛn-] *vt* **:** iluminar, aclarar
enlightenment [ɪn'laɪtənmənt, ɛn-] *n* **1 :** ilustración *f* <the Enlightenment : la Ilustración> **2** CLARIFICATION **:** aclaración *f*
enlist [ɪn'lɪst, ɛn-] *vt* **1** ENROLL **:** alistar, reclutar **2** SECURE **:** conseguir <to enlist the support of : conseguir el apoyo de> — *vi* **:** alistarse
enlisted man [ɪn'lɪstəd, ɛn-] *n* **:** soldado *m* raso
enlistment [ɪn'lɪstmənt, ɛn-] *n* **:** alistamiento *m,* reclutamiento *m*
enliven [ɪn'laɪvən, ɛn-] *vt* **:** animar, alegrar, darle vida a
enmity ['ɛnməṭi] *n, pl* **-ties :** enemistad *f,* animadversión *f*
ennoble [ɪ'noːbəl, ɛ-] *vt* **-bled; -bling :** ennoblecer
ennui [ˌɑn'wiː] *n* **:** hastío *m,* tedio *m,* fastidio *m,* aburrimiento *m*
enormity [ɪ'nɔrməṭi] *n, pl* **-ties 1** ATROCITY **:** atrocidad *f,* barbaridad *f* **2** IMMENSITY **:** enormidad *f,* inmensidad *f*
enormous [ɪ'nɔrməs] *adj* **:** enorme, inmenso, tremendo — **enormously** *adv*
enough[1] [ɪ'nʌf] *adv* **1 :** bastante, suficientemente **2 fair enough! :** ¡está bien!, ¡de acuerdo! **3 strangely enough :** por extraño que parezca **4 sure enough :** en efecto, sin duda alguna **5 well enough :** muy bien, bastante bien
enough[2] *adj* **:** bastante, suficiente <do we have enough chairs? : ¿tenemos suficientes sillas?>
enough[3] *pron* **:** (lo) suficiente, (lo) bastante <enough to eat : lo suficiente para comer> <it's not enough : no basta> <I've had enough! : ¡estoy harto!, ¡está bueno ya!>
enquire [ɪn'kwaɪr, ɛn-], **enquiry** ['ɪnˌkwaɪri, 'ɛn-, -kwəri; ɪn'kwaɪri, ɛn'-] → **inquire, inquiry**
enrage [ɪn'reɪdʒ, ɛn-] *vt* **-raged; -raging :** enfurecer, encolerizar
enraged [ɪn'reɪdʒd, ɛn-] *adj* **:** enfurecido, furioso
enrich [ɪn'rɪtʃ, ɛn-] *vt* **:** enriquecer
enrichment [ɪn'rɪtʃmənt, ɛn-] *n* **:** enriquecimiento *m*
enroll *or* **enrol** [ɪn'roːl, ɛn-] *v* **-rolled; -rolling** *vt* **:** matricular, inscribir — *vi* **:** matricularse, inscribirse
enrollment [ɪn'roːlmənt, ɛn-] *n* **:** matrícula *f,* inscripción *f*
en route [ɑ'ruːt, ɛn'raʊt] *adv* **:** de camino, por el camino
ensconce [ɪn'skɑnts, ɛn-] *vt* **-sconced; -sconcing :** acomodar, instalar, establecer cómodamente
ensemble [ɑn'sɑmbəl] *n* **:** conjunto *m*
enshrine [ɪn'ʃraɪn, ɛn-] *vt* **-shrined; -shrining :** conservar religiosamente, preservar
ensign ['ɛntsən, 'ɛnˌsaɪn] *n* **1** FLAG **:** enseña *f,* pabellón *m* **2 :** alférez *mf* (de fragata)

enslave [ɪn'sleɪv, ɛn-] *vt* **-slaved; -slaving :** esclavizar

enslavement [ɪn'sleɪvmənt, ɛn-] *n* **:** esclavización *f*

ensnare [ɪn'snær, ɛn-] *vt* **-snared; -snaring :** atrapar

ensue [ɪn'suː, ɛn-] *vi* **-sued; -suing :** seguir, resultar

ensure [ɪn'ʃʊr, ɛn-] *vt* **-sured; -suring :** asegurar, garantizar

entail [ɪn'teɪl, ɛn-] *vt* **:** implicar, suponer, conllevar

entangle [ɪn'tæŋgəl, ɛn-] *vt* **-gled; -gling :** enredar

entanglement [ɪn'tæŋgəlmənt, ɛn-] *n* **:** enredo *m*

enter ['ɛntər] *vt* **1 :** entrar en, entrar a **2** BEGIN **:** entrar en, comenzar, iniciar **3** RECORD **:** anotar, inscribir, dar entrada a **4** JOIN **:** entrar en, alistarse en, hacerse socio de — *vi* **1 :** entrar **2 to enter into :** entrar en, firmar (un acuerdo), entablar (negociaciones, etc.)

enterprise ['ɛntər,praɪz] *n* **1** UNDERTAKING **:** empresa *f* **2** BUSINESS **:** empresa *f*, firma *f* **3** INITIATIVE **:** iniciativa *f*, empuje *m*

enterprising ['ɛntər,praɪzɪŋ] *adj* **:** emprendedor

entertain [,ɛntər'teɪn] *vt* **1 :** recibir, agasajar <to entertain guests : tener invitados> **2** CONSIDER **:** considerar, contemplar **3** AMUSE **:** entretener, divertir

entertainer [,ɛntər'teɪnər] *n* **:** artista *mf*

entertainment [,ɛntər'teɪnmənt] *n* **:** entretenimiento *m*, diversión *f*

enthrall *or* **enthral** [ɪn'θrɔl, ɛn-] *vt* **-thralled; -thralling :** cautivar, embelesar

enthusiasm [ɪn'θuːzi,æzəm, ɛn-, -'θjuː-] *n* **:** entusiasmo *m*

enthusiast [ɪn'θuːzi,æst, ɛn-, -'θjuː-, -əst] *n* **:** entusiasta *mf;* aficionado *m*, -da *f*

enthusiastic [ɪn,θuːzi'æstɪk, ɛn-, -,θjuː-] *adj* **:** entusiasta, aficionado

enthusiastically [ɪn,θuːzi'æstɪkli, ɛn-, -,θjuː-] *adv* **:** con entusiasmo

entice [ɪn'taɪs, ɛn-] *vt* **-ticed; -ticing :** atraer, tentar

enticement [ɪn'taɪsmənt, ɛn-] *n* **:** tentación *f*, atracción *f*, señuelo *m*

entire [ɪn'taɪr, ɛn-] *adj* **:** entero, completo

entirely [ɪn'taɪrli, ɛn-] *adv* **:** completamente, totalmente

entirety [ɪn'taɪrti, ɛn-, -'taɪrəṭi] *n, pl* **-ties :** totalidad *f*

entitle [ɪn'taɪṭəl, ɛn-] *vt* **-tled; -tling 1** NAME **:** titular, intitular **2 :** dar derecho a <it entitles you to enter free : le da derecho a entrar gratis> **3 to be entitled to :** tener derecho a

entitlement [ɪn'taɪṭəlmənt, ɛn-] *n* RIGHT **:** derecho *m*

entity ['ɛntəṭi] *n, pl* **-ties :** entidad *f*, ente *m*

entomologist [,ɛntə'mɑlədʒɪst] *n* **:** entomólogo *m*, -ga *f*

entomology [,ɛntə'mɑlədʒi] *n* **:** entomología *f*

entourage [,ɑntʊ'rɑʒ] *n* **:** séquito *m*

entrails ['ɛn,treɪlz, -trəlz] *npl* **:** entrañas *fpl*, vísceras *fpl*

entrance¹ [ɪn'træn*t*s, ɛn-] *vt* **-tranced; -trancing :** encantar, embelesar, fascinar

entrance² ['ɛntrən*t*s] *n* **1** ENTERING **:** entrada *f* <to make an entrance : entrar en escena> **2** ENTRY **:** entrada *f*, puerta *f* **3** ADMISSION **:** entrada *f*, ingreso *m* <entrance examination : examen de ingreso>

entrant ['ɛntrənt] *n* **:** candidato *m*, -ta *f* (en un examen); participante *mf* (en un concurso)

entrap [ɪn'træp, ɛn-] *vt* **-trapped; -trapping :** atrapar, entrampar, hacer caer en una trampa

entrapment [ɪn'træpmənt, ɛn-] *n* **:** captura *f*

entreat [ɪn'triːt, ɛn-] *vt* **:** suplicar, rogar

entreaty [ɪn'triːṭi, ɛn-] *n, pl* **-treaties :** ruego *m*, súplica *f*

entrée *or* **entree** ['ɑn,treɪ, ,ɑn'-] *n* **:** plato *m* principal

entrench [ɪn'trɛntʃ, ɛn-] *vt* **1** FORTIFY **:** atrincherar (una posición militar) **2 :** consolidar, afianzar <firmly entrenched in his job : afianzado en su puesto>

entrepreneur [,ɑntrəprə'nər, -'njʊr] *n* **:** empresario *m*, -ria *f*

entrust [ɪn'trʌst, ɛn-] *vt* **:** confiar, encomendar

entry ['ɛntri] *n, pl* **-tries 1** ENTRANCE **:** entrada *f* **2** NOTATION **:** entrada *f*, anotación *f*

entwine [ɪn'twaɪn, ɛn-] *vt* **-twined; -twining :** entrelazar, entretejer, entrecruzar

enumerate [ɪ'nuːmə,reɪt, ɛ-, -'njuː-] *vt* **-ated; -ating 1** LIST **:** enumerar **2** COUNT **:** contar, enumerar

enumeration [ɪ,nuːmə'reɪʃən, ɛ-, -,njuː-] *n* **:** enumeración *f*, lista *f*

enunciate [i'nʌn*t*si,eɪt, ɛ-] *vt* **-ated; -ating 1** STATE **:** enunciar, decir **2** PRONOUNCE **:** articular, pronunciar

enunciation [i,nʌn*t*si'eɪʃən, ɛ-] *n* **1** STATEMENT **:** enunciación *f*, declaración *f* **2** ARTICULATION **:** articulación *f*, pronunciación *f*, dicción *f*

envelop [ɪn'vɛləp, ɛn-] *vt* **:** envolver, cubrir

envelope ['ɛnvə,loːp, 'ɑn-] *n* **:** sobre *m*

enviable ['ɛnviəbəl] *adj* **:** envidiable

envious ['ɛnviəs] *adj* **:** envidioso — **enviously** *adv*

environment [ɪn'vaɪrənmənt, ɛn-, -'vaɪərn-] *n* **:** medio *m* (ambiente), ambiente *m*, entorno *m*

environmental [ɪn,vaɪrən'mɛntəl, ɛn-, -,vaɪərn-] *adj* **:** ambiental

environmentalist [ɪnˌvaɪrənˈmɛntəlɪst, ɛn-, -ˌvaɪərn-] *n* : ecologista *mf*
environs [ɪnˈvaɪrənz, ɛn-, -ˈvaɪərnz] *npl* : alrededores *mpl*, entorno *m*, inmediaciones *fpl*
envisage [ɪnˈvɪzɪdʒ, ɛn-] *vt* **-aged; -aging 1** IMAGINE : imaginarse, concebir **2** FORESEE : prever
envision [ɪnˈvɪʒən, ɛn-] *vt* : imaginar
envoy [ˈɛnˌvɔɪ, ˈɑn-] *n* : enviado *m*, -da *f*
envy[1] [ˈɛnvi] *vt* **-vied; -vying** : envidiar
envy[2] *n, pl* **envies** : envidia *f*
enzyme [ˈɛnˌzaɪm] *n* : enzima *f*
eon [ˈiːən, iːˌɑn] → **aeon**
epaulet [ˌɛpəˈlɛt] *n* : charretera *f*
ephemeral [ɪˈfɛmərəl, -ˈfiː-] *adj* : efímero, fugaz
epic[1] [ˈɛpɪk] *adj* : épico
epic[2] *n* : poema *m* épico, epopeya *f*
epicure [ˈɛpɪˌkjʊr] *n* : epicúreo *m*, -rea *f*; gastrónomo *m*, -ma *f*
epicurean [ˌɛpɪkjʊˈriːən, -ˈkjʊriən] *adj* : epicúreo
epidemic[1] [ˌɛpəˈdɛmɪk] *adj* : epidémico
epidemic[2] *n* : epidemia *f*
epidermis [ˌɛpəˈdərməs] *n* : epidermis *f*
epigram [ˈɛpəˌgræm] *n* : epigrama *m*
epilepsy [ˈɛpəˌlɛpsi] *n, pl* **-sies** : epilepsia *f*
epileptic[1] [ˌɛpəˈlɛptɪk] *adj* : epiléptico
epileptic[2] *n* : epiléptico *m*, -ca *f*
episcopal [ɪˈpɪskəpəl] *adj* : episcopal
episode [ˈɛpəˌsoːd] *n* : episodio *m*
episodic [ˌɛpəˈsɑdɪk] *adj* : episódico
epistle [ɪˈpɪsəl] *n* : epístola *f*, carta *f*
epitaph [ˈɛpəˌtæf] *n* : epitafio *m*
epithet [ˈɛpəˌθɛt, -θət] *n* : epíteto *m*
epitome [ɪˈpɪt̬əmi] *n* **1** SUMMARY : epítome *m*, resumen *m* **2** EMBODIMENT : personificación *f*
epitomize [ɪˈpɪt̬əˌmaɪz] *vt* **-mized; -mizing 1** SUMMARIZE : resumir **2** EMBODY : ser la personificación de, personificar
epoch [ˈɛpək, ˈɛˌpɑk, ˈiːˌpɑk] *n* : época *f*, era *f*
equable [ˈɛkwəbəl, ˈiː-] *adj* **1** CALM, STEADY : ecuánime **2** UNIFORM : estable (dícese de la temperatura), constante (dícese del clima), uniforme
equably [ˈɛkwəbli, ˈiː-] *adv* : con ecuanimidad
equal[1] [ˈiːkwəl] *vt* **equaled** *or* **equalled; equaling** *or* **equalling 1** : ser igual a <two plus three equals five : dos más tres es igual a cinco> **2** MATCH : igualar
equal[2] *adj* **1** SAME : igual **2** ADEQUATE : adecuado, capaz
equal[3] *n* : igual *mf*
equality [ɪˈkwɑləṭi] *n, pl* **-ties** : igualdad *f*
equalize [ˈiːkwəˌlaɪz] *vt* **-ized; -izing** : igualar, equiparar
equally [ˈiːkwəli] *adv* : igualmente, por igual
equanimity [ˌiːkwəˈnɪməṭi, ˌɛ-] *n, pl* **-ties** : ecuanimidad *f*
equate [ɪˈkweɪt] *vt* **equated; equating** : equiparar, identificar
equation [ɪˈkweɪʒən] *n* : ecuación *f*
equator [ɪˈkweɪṭər] *n* : ecuador *m*
equatorial [ˌiːkwəˈtoriəl, ˌɛ-] *adj* : ecuatorial
equestrian[1] [ɪˈkwɛstriən, ɛ-] *adj* : ecuestre
equestrian[2] *n* : jinete *mf*, caballista *mf*
equilateral [ˌiːkwəˈlæṭərəl, ˌɛ-] *adj* : equilátero
equilibrium [ˌiːkwəˈlɪbriəm, ˌɛ-] *n, pl* **-riums** *or* **-ria** [-briə] : equilibrio *m*
equine [ˈiːˌkwaɪn, ˈɛ-] *adj* : equino, hípico
equinox [ˈiːkwəˌnɑks, ˈɛ-] *n* : equinoccio *m*
equip [ɪˈkwɪp] *vt* **equipped; equipping 1** FURNISH : equipar **2** PREPARE : preparar
equipment [ɪˈkwɪpmənt] *n* : equipo *m*
equitable [ˈɛkwəṭəbəl] *adj* : equitativo, justo, imparcial
equity [ˈɛkwəṭi] *n, pl* **-ties 1** FAIRNESS : equidad *f*, imparcialidad *f* **2** VALUE : valor *m* líquido
equivalence [ɪˈkwɪvələnts] *n* : equivalencia *f*
equivalent[1] [ɪˈkwɪvələnt] *adj* : equivalente
equivalent[2] *n* : equivalente *m*
equivocal [ɪˈkwɪvəkəl] *adj* **1** AMBIGUOUS : equívoco, ambiguo **2** QUESTIONABLE : incierto, dudoso, sospechoso
equivocate [ɪˈkwɪvəˌkeɪt] *vi* **-cated; -cating** : usar lenguaje equívoco, andarse con evasivas
equivocation [ɪˌkwɪvəˈkeɪʃən] *n* : evasiva *f*, subterfugio *m*
era [ˈɪrə, ˈɛrə, ˈiːrə] *n* : era *f*, época *f*
eradicate [ɪˈrædəˌkeɪt] *vt* **-cated; -cating** : erradicar
erase [ɪˈreɪs] *vt* **erased; erasing** : borrar
eraser [ɪˈreɪsər] *n* : goma *f* de borrar, borrador *m*
erasure [ɪˈreɪʃər] *n* : tachadura *f*
ere[1] [ˈɛr] *conj* : antes de que
ere[2] *prep* **1** : antes de **2 ere long** : dentro de poco
erect[1] [ɪˈrɛkt] *vt* **1** CONSTRUCT : erigir, construir **2** RAISE : levantar **3** ESTABLISH : establecer
erect[2] *adj* : erguido, derecho, erecto
erection [ɪˈrɛkʃən] *n* **1** : erección *f* (en fisiología) **2** BUILDING : construcción *f*
ermine [ˈərmən] *n* : armiño *m*
erode [ɪˈroːd] *vt* **eroded; eroding** : erosionar (el suelo), corroer (metales)
erosion [ɪˈroːʒən] *n* : erosión *f*, corrosión *f*
erotic [ɪˈrɑṭɪk] *adj* : erótico — **erotically** [-ṭɪkli] *adv*

eroticism [ɪˈrɑtəˌsɪzəm] *n* : erotismo *m*

err [ˈɛr, ˈər] *vi* : cometer un error, equivocarse, errar

errand [ˈɛrənd] *n* : mandado *m,* encargo *m,* recado *m Spain* <an errand of mercy : una misión de caridad>

errant [ˈɛrənt] *adj* **1** WANDERING : errante **2** ASTRAY : descarriado

erratic [ɪˈræt̬ɪk] *adj* **1** INCONSISTENT : errático, irregular, inconsistente **2** ECCENTRIC : excéntrico, raro

erratically [ɪˈræt̬ɪkli] *adv* : erráticamente, de manera irregular

erroneous [ɪˈroːniəs, ɛ-] *adj* : erróneo — **erroneously** *adv*

error [ˈɛrər] *n* : error *m,* equivocación *f* <to be in error : estar equivocado>

ersatz [ˈɛrˌsɑts, ˈərˌsæts] *adj* : artificial, sustituto

erstwhile [ˈərstˌhwaɪl] *adj* : antiguo

erudite [ˈɛrəˌdaɪt, ˈɛrjʊ-] *adj* : erudito, letrado

erudition [ˌɛrəˈdɪʃən, ˌɛrjʊ-] *n* : erudición *f*

erupt [ɪˈrʌpt] *vi* **1** : hacer erupción (dícese de un volcán o un sarpullido) **2** : estallar (dícese de la cólera o la violencia)

eruption [ɪˈrʌpʃən] *n* : erupción *f,* estallido *m*

eruptive [ɪˈrʌptɪv] *adj* : eruptivo

escalate [ˈɛskəˌleɪt] *v* **-lated; -lating** *vt* : intensificar (un conflicto), aumentar (precios) — *vi* : intensificarse, aumentarse

escalation [ˌɛskəˈleɪʃən] *n* : intensificación *f,* escalada *f,* aumento *m,* subida *f*

escalator [ˈɛskəˌleɪt̬ər] *n* : escalera *f* mecánica

escapade [ˈɛskəˌpeɪd] *n* : aventura *f*

escape[1] [ɪˈskeɪp, ɛ-] *v* **-caped; -caping** *vt* : escaparse de, librarse de, evitar — *vi* : escaparse, fugarse, huir

escape[2] *n* **1** FLIGHT : fuga *f,* huida *f,* escapada *f* **2** LEAKAGE : escape *m,* fuga *f* **3** : escapatoria *f,* evasión *f* <to have no escape : no tener escapatoria> <escape from reality : evasión de la realidad>

escapee [ɪˌskeɪˈpiː, ˌɛ-] *n* : fugitivo *m,* -va *f*

escarole [ˈɛskəˌroːl] *n* : escarola *f*

escarpment [ɪsˈkɑrpmənt, ɛs-] *n* : escarpa *f,* escarpadura *f*

eschew [ɛˈʃuː, ɪsˈtʃuː] *vt* : evitar, rehuir, abstenerse de

escort[1] [ɪˈskɔrt, ɛ-] *vt* **1** : escoltar <to escort a ship : escoltar un barco> **2** ACCOMPANY : acompañar

escort[2] [ˈɛsˌkɔrt] *n* **1** : escolta *f* <armed escort : escolta armada> **2** COMPANION : acompañante *mf;* compañero *m,* -ra *f*

escrow [ˈɛsˌkroː] *n* **in escrow** : en depósito, en custodia de un tercero

esophagus [ɪˈsɑfəgəs, iː-] *n, pl* **-gi** [-ˌgaɪ, -ˌdʒaɪ] : esófago *m*

esoteric [ˌɛsəˈtɛrɪk] *adj* : esotérico, hermético

especially [ɪˈspɛʃəli] *adv* : especialmente, particularmente

espionage [ˈɛspiəˌnɑʒ, -ˌnɑdʒ] *n* : espionaje *m*

espouse [ɪˈspaʊz, ɛ-] *vt* **espoused; espousing 1** MARRY : casarse con **2** ADOPT, ADVOCATE : apoyar, adherirse a, adoptar

espresso [ɛˈsprɛˌsoː] *n, pl* **-sos** : café *m* exprés

essay[1] [ɛˈseɪ, ˈɛˌseɪ] *vt* : intentar, tratar

essay[2] [ˈɛˌseɪ] *n* **1** COMPOSITION : ensayo *m,* trabajo *m* **2** ATTEMPT : intento *m*

essayist [ˈɛˌseɪɪst] *n* : ensayista *mf*

essence [ˈɛsənts] *n* **1** CORE : esencia *f,* núcleo *m,* meollo *m* <in essence : esencialmente> **2** EXTRACT : esencia *f,* extracto *m* **3** PERFUME : esencia *f,* perfume *m*

essential[1] [ɪˈsɛntʃəl] *adj* : esencial, imprescindible, fundamental — **essentially** *adv*

essential[2] *n* : elemento *m* esencial, lo imprescindible

establish [ɪˈstæblɪʃ, ɛ-] *vt* **1** FOUND : establecer, fundar **2** SET UP : establecer, instaurar, instituir **3** PROVE : demostrar, probar

establishment [ɪˈstæblɪʃmənt, ɛ-] *n* **1** ESTABLISHING : establecimiento *m,* fundación *f,* instauración *f* **2** BUSINESS : negocio *m,* establecimiento *m* **3 the Establishment** : la clase dirigente

estate [ɪˈsteɪt, ɛ-] *n* **1** POSSESSIONS : bienes *mpl,* propiedad *f,* patrimonio *m* **2** PROPERTY : hacienda *f,* finca *f,* propiedad *f*

esteem[1] [ɪˈstiːm, ɛ-] *vt* : estimar, apreciar

esteem[2] *n* : estima *f,* aprecio *m*

ester [ˈɛstər] *n* : éster *m*

esthetic [ɛsˈθɛt̬ɪk] → **aesthetic**

estimable [ˈɛstəməbəl] *adj* : estimable

estimate[1] [ˈɛstəˌmeɪt] *vt* **-mated; -mating** : calcular, estimar

estimate[2] [ˈɛstəmət] *n* **1** : cálculo *m* aproximado <to make an estimate : hacer un cálculo> **2** ASSESSMENT : valoración *f,* estimación *f*

estimation [ˌɛstəˈmeɪʃən] *n* **1** JUDGMENT : juicio *m,* opinión *f* <in my estimation : en mi opinión, según mis cálculos> **2** ESTEEM : estima *f,* aprecio *m*

estimator [ˈɛstəˌmeɪt̬ər] *n* : tasador *m,* -dora *f*

Estonian [ɛˈstoːniən] *n* : estonio *m,* -nia *f* — **Estonian** *adj*

estrange [ɪˈstreɪndʒ, ɛ-] *vt* **-tranged; -tranging** : enajenar, apartar, alejar

estrangement [ɪˈstreɪndʒmənt, ɛ-] *n* : alejamiento *m,* distanciamiento *m*

estrogen [ˈɛstrədʒən] *n* : estrógeno *m*

estrus [ˈɛstrəs] *n* : celo *m*

estuary [ˈɛstʃʊˌwɛri] *n, pl* **-aries** : estuario *m,* -ria *f*

et cetera [ɛt'sɛt̬ərə, -'sɛtrə] : etcétera
etch ['ɛtʃ] *v* : grabar al aguafuerte
etching ['ɛtʃɪŋ] *n* : aguafuerte *m,* grabado *m* al aguafuerte
eternal [ɪ'tərnəl, iː-] *adj* **1** EVERLASTING : eterno **2** INTERMINABLE : constante, incesante
eternally [ɪ'tərnəli, iː-] *adv* : eternamente, para siempre
eternity [ɪ'tərnət̬i, iː-] *n, pl* **-ties** : eternidad *f*
ethane ['ɛ,θeɪn] *n* : etano *m*
ethanol ['ɛθə,nɔl, -,noːl] *n* : etanol *m*
ether ['iːθər] *n* : éter *m*
ethereal [ɪ'θɪriəl, iː-] *adj* **1** CELESTIAL : etéreo, celeste **2** DELICATE : delicado
ethical ['ɛθɪkəl] *adj* : ético — **ethically** *adv*
ethics ['ɛθɪks] *ns & pl* **1** : ética *f* **2** MORALITY : ética *f,* moral *f,* moralidad *f*
Ethiopian [,iːθi'oːpiən] *n* : etíope *mf* — **Ethiopian** *adj*
ethnic ['ɛθnɪk] *adj* : étnico
ethnologist [ɛθ'nɑlədʒɪst] *n* : etnólogo *m,* -ga *f*
ethnology [ɛθ'nɑlədʒi] *n* : etnología *f*
etiquette ['ɛtɪkət, -,kɛt] *n* : etiqueta *f,* protocolo *m*
etymological [,ɛt̬əmə'lɑdʒɪkəl] *adj* : etimológico
etymology [,ɛt̬ə'mɑlədʒi] *n, pl* **-gies** : etimología *f*
eucalyptus [,juːkə'lɪptəs] *n, pl* **-ti** [-,taɪ] *or* **-tuses** [-təsəz] : eucalipto *m*
Eucharist ['juːkərɪst] *n* : Eucaristía *f*
eulogize ['juːlə,dʒaɪz] *vt* **-gized; -gizing** : elogiar, encomiar
eulogy ['juːlədʒi] *n, pl* **-gies** : elogio *m,* encomio *m,* panegírico *m*
eunuch ['juːnək] *n* : eunuco *m*
euphemism ['juːfə,mɪzəm] *n* : eufemismo *m*
euphemistic [,juːfə'mɪstɪk] *adj* : eufemístico
euphony ['juːfəni] *n, pl* **-nies** : eufonía *f*
euphoria [jʊ'foriə] *n* : euforia *f*
euphoric [jʊ'forɪk] *adj* : eufórico
euthanasia [,juːθə'neɪʒə, -ʒiə] *n* : eutanasia *f*
evacuate [ɪ'vækjʊ,eɪt] *v* **-ated; -ating** *vt* VACATE : evacuar, desalojar — *vi* WITHDRAW : retirarse
evacuation [ɪ,vækjʊ'eɪʃən] *n* : evacuación *f,* desalojo *m*
evade [ɪ'veɪd] *vt* **evaded; evading** : evadir, eludir, esquivar
evaluate [ɪ'væljʊ,eɪt] *vt* **-ated; -ating** : evaluar, valorar, tasar
evaluation [ɪ,væljʊ'eɪʃən] *n* : evaluación *f,* valoración *f,* tasación *f*
evangelical [,iː,væn'dʒɛlɪkəl, ,ɛvən-] *adj* : evangélico
evangelist [ɪ'vændʒəlɪst] *n* **1** : evangelista *m* **2** PREACHER : predicador *m,* -dora *f*
evaporate [ɪ'væpə,reɪt] *vi* **-rated; -rating 1** VAPORIZE : evaporarse **2** VANISH : evaporarse, desvanecerse, esfumarse
evaporation [ɪ,væpə'reɪʃən] *n* : evaporación *f*
evasion [ɪ'veɪʒən] *n* : evasión *f*
evasive [ɪ'veɪsɪv] *adj* : evasivo
evasiveness [ɪ'veɪsɪvnəs] *n* : carácter *m* evasivo
eve ['iːv] *n* **1** : víspera *f* <on the eve of the festivities : en vísperas de las festividades> **2** → **evening**
even[1] ['iːvən] *vt* **1** LEVEL : allanar, nivelar, emparejar **2** EQUALIZE : igualar, equilibrar — *vi* **to even out** : nivelarse, emparejarse
even[2] *adv* **1** : hasta, incluso <even a child can do it : hasta un niño puede hacerlo> <he looked content, even happy : se le veía satisfecho, incluso feliz> **2** (*in negative constructions*) : ni siquiera <he didn't even try : ni siquiera lo intentó> **3** (*in comparisons*) : aún, todavía <even better : aún mejor, todavía mejor> **4 even if** : aunque **5 even so** : aun así **6 even though** : aun cuando, a pesar de que
even[3] *adj* **1** SMOOTH : uniforme, liso, parejo **2** FLAT : plano, llano **3** EQUAL : igual, igualado <an even score : un marcador igualado> **4** REGULAR : regular, constante <an even pace : un ritmo constante> **5** EXACT : exacto, justo **6** : par <even number : número par> **7 to be even** : estar en paz, estar a mano **8 to get even** : desquitarse, vengarse
evening ['iːvnɪŋ] *n* : tarde *f,* noche *f* <in the evening : por la noche>
evenly ['iːvənli] *adv* **1** UNIFORMLY : de modo uniforme, de manera constante **2** FAIRLY : igualmente, equitativamente
evenness ['iːvənnəs] *n* : uniformidad *f,* igualdad *f,* regularidad *f*
event [ɪ'vɛnt] *n* **1** : acontecimiento *m,* suceso *m,* prueba *f* (en deportes) **2 in the event that** : en caso de que
eventful [ɪ'vɛntfəl] *adj* : lleno de incidentes, memorable
eventual [ɪ'vɛntʃʊəl] *adj* : final, consiguiente
eventuality [ɪ,vɛntʃʊ'ælət̬i] *n, pl* **-ties** : eventualidad *f*
eventually [ɪ'vɛntʃʊəli] *adv* : al fin, con el tiempo, algún día
ever ['ɛvər] *adv* **1** ALWAYS : siempre <as ever : como siempre> <ever since : desde entonces> **2** (*in questions*) : alguna vez, algún día <have you ever been to Mexico? : ¿has estado en México alguna vez?> **3** (*in negative constructions*) : nunca <doesn't he ever work? : ¿es que nunca trabaja?> <nobody ever helps me : nadie nunca me ayuda> **4** (*in comparisons*) : nunca <better than ever : mejor que nunca> **5** (*as intensifier*) <I'm ever so happy! : ¡estoy tan y tan feliz!> <he

looks ever so angry : parece estar muy enojado>

evergreen[1] ['ɛvər,gri:n] *adj* : de hoja perenne

evergreen[2] *n* : planta *f* de hoja perenne

everlasting [,ɛvər'læstɪŋ] *adj* : eterno, perpetuo, imperecedero

evermore [,ɛvər'mor] *adv* : eternamente

every ['ɛvri] *adj* **1** EACH : cada <every time : cada vez> <every other house : cada dos casas> **2** ALL : todo <every month : todos los meses> <every woman : toda mujer, todas las mujeres> **3** COMPLETE : pleno, entero <to have every confidence : tener plena confianza>

everybody ['ɛvri,bʌdi, -,bɑ-] *pron* : todos *mpl,* -das *fpl*; todo el mundo

everyday [,ɛvri'deɪ, 'ɛvri,-] *adj* : cotidiano, diario, corriente <everyday clothes : ropa de todos los días>

everyone ['ɛvri ,wʌn] → **everybody**

everything ['ɛvri,θɪŋ] *pron* : todo

everywhere ['ɛvri,*h*wɛr] *adv* : en todas partes, por todas partes, dondequiera <I looked everywhere : busqué en todas partes> <everywhere we go : dondequiera que vayamos>

evict [ɪ'vɪkt] *vt* : desalojar, desahuciar

eviction [ɪ'vɪkʃən] *n* : desalojo *m,* desahucio *m*

evidence ['ɛvədən*t*s] *n* **1** INDICATION : indicio *m,* señal *m* <to be in evidence : estar a la vista> **2** PROOF : evidencia *f,* prueba *f* **3** TESTIMONY : testimonio *m,* declaración *f* <to give evidence : declarar como testigo, prestar declaración>

evident ['ɛvidənt] *adj* : evidente, patente, manifiesto

evidently ['ɛvidəntli, ,ɛvi'dɛntli] *adv* **1** CLEARLY : claramente, obviamente **2** APPARENTLY : aparentemente, evidentemente, al parecer

evil[1] ['i:vəl, -vɪl] *adj* **eviler** *or* **eviller; evilest** *or* **evillest 1** WICKED : malvado, malo, maligno **2** HARMFUL : nocivo, dañino, pernicioso **3** UNPLEASANT : desagradable <an evil odor : un olor horrible>

evil[2] *n* **1** WICKEDNESS : mal *m,* maldad *f* **2** MISFORTUNE : desgracia *f,* mal *m*

evildoer [,i:vəl'du:ər, ,i:vɪl-] *n* : malvado *m,* -da *f*

evince [ɪ'vɪn*t*s] *vt* **evinced; evincing** : mostrar, manifestar, revelar

eviscerate [ɪ'vɪsə,reɪt] *vt* **-ated; -ating** : eviscerar, destripar (un pollo, etc.)

evocation [,i:vo'keɪʃən, ,ɛ-] *n* : evocación *f*

evocative [i'vɑkətɪv] *adj* : evocador

evoke [i'vo:k] *vt* **evoked; evoking** : evocar, provocar

evolution [,ɛvə'lu:ʃən, ,i:-] *n* : evolución *f,* desarrollo *m*

evolutionary [,ɛvə'lu:ʃə,nɛri, ,i:-] *adj* : evolutivo

evolve [i'vɑlv] *vi* **evolved; evolving** : evolucionar, desarrollarse

ewe ['ju:] *n* : oveja *f*

exact[1] [ɪg'zækt, ɛ-] *vt* : exigir, imponer, arrancar

exact[2] *adj* : exacto, preciso — **exactly** *adv*

exacting [ɪ'zæktɪŋ, ɛg-] *adj* : exigente, riguroso

exactitude [ɪg'zæktə,tu:d, ɛg-, -,tju:d] *n* : exactitud *f,* precisión *f*

exaggerate [ɪg'zædʒə,reɪt, ɛg-] *v* **-ated; -ating** : exagerar

exaggerated [ɪg'zædʒə,reɪtəd, ɛg-] *adj* : exagerado — **exaggeratedly** *adv*

exaggeration [ɪg,zædʒə'reɪʃən, ɛg-] *n* : exageración *f*

exalt [ɪg'zɔlt, ɛg-] *vt* : exaltar, ensalzar, glorificar

exaltation [,ɛg,zɔl'teɪʃən, ,ɛk,sɔl-] *n* : exaltación *f*

exam [ɪg'zæm, ɛg-] → **examination**

examination [ɪg,zæmə'neɪʃən, ɛg-] *n* **1** TEST : examen *m* **2** INSPECTION : inspección *f,* revisión *f* **3** INVESTIGATION : examen *m,* estudio *m*

examine [ɪg'zæmən, ɛg-] *vt* **-ined; -ining 1** TEST : examinar **2** INSPECT : inspeccionar, revisar **3** STUDY : examinar

example [ɪg'zæmpəl, ɛg-] *n* : ejemplo *m* <for example : por ejemplo> <to set an example : dar ejemplo>

exasperate [ɪg'zæspə,reɪt, ɛg-] *vt* **-ated; -ating** : exasperar, sacar de quicio

exasperation [ɪg,zæspə'reɪʃən, ɛg-] *n* : exasperación *f*

excavate ['ɛkskə,veɪt] *vt* **-vated; -vating** : excavar

excavation [,ɛkskə'veɪʃən] *n* : excavación *f*

exceed [ɪk'si:d, ɛk-] *vt* **1** SURPASS : exceder, rebasar, sobrepasar **2** : exceder de, sobrepasar <not exceeding two months : que no exceda de dos meses>

exceedingly [ɪk'si:dɪŋli, ɛk-] *adv* : extremadamente, sumamente

excel [ɪk'sɛl, ɛk-] *v* **-celled; -celling** *vi* : sobresalir, descollar, lucirse — *vt* : superar

excellence ['ɛksələn*t*s] *n* : excelencia *f*

excellency ['ɛksələn*t*si] *n, pl* **-cies** : excelencia *f* <His Excellency : Su Excelencia>

excellent ['ɛksələnt] *adj* : excelente, sobresaliente — **excellently** *adv*

except[1] [ɪk'sɛpt] *vt* : exceptuar, excluir

except[2] *conj* : pero, si no fuera por

except[3] *prep* : excepto, menos, salvo <everyone except Carlos : todos menos Carlos>

exception [ɪk'sɛpʃən] *n* **1** : excepción *f* **2 to take exception to** : ofenderse por, objetar a

exceptional [ɪk'sɛpʃənəl] *adj* : excepcional, extraordinario — **exceptionally** *adv*

excerpt[1] [ɛk'sərpt, ɛg'zərpt, 'ɛk,-, 'ɛg,-] *vt* : escoger, seleccionar

excerpt[2] ['ɛk,sərpt, 'ɛg,zərpt] *n* : pasaje *m,* selección *f*

excess[1] ['ɛk,sɛs, ɪk'sɛs] *adj* **1** : excesivo, de sobra **2 excess baggage** : exceso *m* de equipaje

excess[2] [ɪk'sɛs, 'ɛk,sɛs] *n* **1** SUPERFLUITY : exceso *m,* superfluidad *f* <an excess of energy : un exceso de energía> **2** SURPLUS : excedente *m,* sobrante *m* <in excess of : superior a>

excessive [ɪk'sɛsɪv, ɛk-] *adj* : excesivo, exagerado, desmesurado — **excessively** *adv*

exchange[1] [ɪks'tʃeɪndʒ, ɛks-; 'ɛks,tʃeɪndʒ] *vt* **-changed; -changing** : cambiar, intercambiar, canjear

exchange[2] *n* **1** : cambio *m,* intercambio *m,* canje *m* **2 stock exchange** : bolsa *f* (de valores)

exchangeable [ɪks'tʃeɪndʒəbəl, ɛks-] *adj* : canjeable

excise[1] [ɪk'saɪz, ɛk-] *vt* **-cised; -cising** : extirpar

excise[2] ['ɛk,saɪz] *n* **excise tax** : impuesto *m* interno, impuesto *m* sobre el consumo

excision [ɪk'sɪʒən, ɛk-] *n* : extirpación *f,* excisión *f*

excitability [ɪk,saɪtə'bɪləti, ɛk-] *n* : excitabilidad *f*

excitable [ɪk'saɪtəbəl, ɛk-] *adj* : excitable

excitation [,ɛk,saɪ'teɪʃən] *n* : excitación *f*

excite [ɪk'saɪt, ɛk-] *vt* **-cited; -citing 1** AROUSE, STIMULATE : excitar, mover, estimular **2** ANIMATE : entusiasmar, animar **3** EVOKE, PROVOKE : provocar, despertar, suscitar <to excite curiousity : despertar la curiosidad>

excited [ɪk'saɪtəd, ɛk-] *adj* **1** STIMULATED : excitado, estimulado **2** ENTHUSIASTIC : entusiasmado, emocionado

excitedly [ɪk'saɪtədli, ɛk-] *adv* : con excitación, con entusiasmo

excitement [ɪk'saɪtmənt, ɛk-] *n* **1** ENTHUSIASM : entusiasmo *m,* emoción *f* **2** AGITATION : agitación *f,* alboroto *m,* conmoción *f* **3** AROUSAL : excitación *f*

exclaim [ɪks'kleɪm, ɛk-] *v* : exclamar

exclamation [,ɛksklə'meɪʃən] *n* : exclamación *f*

exclamation point *n* : signo *m* de admiración

exclamatory [ɪks'klæmə,tori, ɛks-] *adj* : exclamativo

exclude [ɪks'klu:d, ɛks-] *vt* **-cluded; -cluding 1** BAR : excluir, descartar, no admitir **2** EXPEL : expeler, expulsar

exclusion [ɪks'klu:ʒən, ɛks-] *n* : exclusión *f*

exclusive[1] [ɪks'klu:sɪv, ɛks-] *adj* **1** SOLE : exclusivo, único **2** SELECT : exclusivo, selecto

exclusive[2] *n* : exclusiva *f*

exclusively [ɪks'klu:sɪvli, ɛks-] *adv* : exclusivamente, únicamente

exclusiveness [ɪks'klu:sɪvnəs, ɛks-] *n* : exclusividad *f*

excommunicate [,ɛkskə'mju:nə,keɪt] *vt* **-cated; -cating** : excomulgar

excommunication [,ɛkskə,mju:nə'keɪʃən] *n* : excomunión *f*

excrement ['ɛkskrəmənt] *n* : excremento *m*

excrete [ɪk'skri:t, ɛk-] *vt* **-creted; -creting** : excretar

excretion [ɪk'skri:ʃən, ɛk-] *n* : excreción *f*

excruciating [ɪk'skru:ʃi,eɪtɪŋ, ɛk-] *adj* : insoportable, atroz, terrible — **excruciatingly** *adv*

exculpate ['ɛkskəl,peɪt] *vt* **-pated; -pating** : exculpar

excursion [ɪk'skərʒən, ɛk-] *n* **1** OUTING : excursión *f,* paseo *m* **2** DIGRESSION : digresión *f*

excuse[1] [ɪk'skju:z, ɛk-] *vt* **-cused; -cusing 1** PARDON : disculpar, perdonar <excuse me : con permiso, perdóneme, perdón> **2** EXEMPT : eximir, disculpar **3** JUSTIFY : excusar, justificar

excuse[2] [ɪk'skju:s, ɛk-] *n* **1** JUSTIFICATION : excusa *f,* justificación *f* **2** PRETEXT : pretexto *m* **3 to make one's excuses to someone** : pedirle disculpas a alguien

execute ['ɛksɪ,kju:t] *vt* **-cuted; -cuting 1** CARRY OUT : ejecutar, llevar a cabo, desempeñar **2** ENFORCE : ejecutar, cumplir (un testamento, etc.) **3** KILL : ejecutar, ajusticiar

execution [,ɛksɪ'kju:ʃən] *n* **1** PERFORMANCE : ejecución *f,* desempeño *m* **2** IMPLEMENTATION : cumplimiento *m* **3** : ejecución *f* (por un delito)

executioner [,ɛksɪ'kju:ʃənər] *n* : verdugo *m*

executive[1] [ɪg'zɛkjətɪv, ɛg-] *adj* : ejecutivo

executive[2] *n* : ejecutivo *m,* **-va** *f*

executor [ɪg'zɛkjətər, ɛg-] *n* : albacea *m,* testamentario *m*

executrix [ɪg'zɛkjə,trɪks, ɛg-] *n, pl* **executrices** [-,zɛkjə'traɪ,si:z] *or* **executrixes** [-'zɛkjə,trɪksəz] : albacea *f,* testamentaria *f*

exemplary [ɪg'zɛmpləri, ɛg-] *adj* : ejemplar

exemplify [ɪg'zɛmplə,faɪ, ɛg-] *vt* **-fied; -fying** : ejemplificar, ilustrar, demostrar

exempt[1] [ɪg'zɛmpt, ɛg-] *vt* : eximir, dispensar, exonerar

exempt[2] *adj* : exento, eximido

exemption [ɪg'zɛmpʃən, ɛg-] *n* : exención *f*

exercise[1] ['ɛksər,saɪz] *v* **-cised; -cising** *vt* **1** : ejercitar (el cuerpo) **2** USE : ejercer, hacer uso de — *vi* : hacer ejercicio

exercise[2] *n* **1** : ejercicio *m* **2 exercises** *npl* WORKOUT : ejercicios *mpl* físicos **3 exercises** *npl* CEREMONY : ceremonia *f*

exert [ɪg'zərt, ɛg-] *vt* **1** : ejercer, emplear **2 to exert oneself** : esforzarse

exertion [ɪg'zərʃən, ɛg-] *n* **1** USE : ejercicio *m* (de autoridad, etc.), uso *m* (de fuerza, etc.) **2** EFFORT : esfuerzo *m,* empeño *m*
exhalation [ˌɛksə'leɪʃən, ˌɛkshə-] *n* : exhalación *f,* espiración *f*
exhale [ɛks'heɪl] *v* **-haled; -haling** *vt* **1** : exhalar, espirar **2** EMIT : exhalar, despedir, emitir — *vi* : espirar
exhaust¹ [ɪg'zɔst, ɛg-] *vt* **1** DEPLETE : agotar **2** TIRE : cansar, fatigar, agotar **3** EMPTY : vaciar
exhaust² *n* **1 exhaust fumes** : gases *mpl* de escape **2 exhaust pipe** : tubo *m* de escape **3 exhaust system** : sistema *m* de escape
exhausted [ɪg'zɔstəd, ɛg-] *adj* : agotado, derrengado
exhausting [ɪg'zɔstɪŋ, ɛg-] *adj* : extenuante, agotador
exhaustion [ɪg'zɔstʃən, ɛg-] *n* : agotamiento *m*
exhaustive [ɪg'zɔstɪv, ɛg-] *adj* : exhaustivo
exhibit¹ [ɪg'zɪbət, ɛg-] *vt* **1** DISPLAY : exhibir, exponer **2** PRODUCE, SHOW : mostrar, presentar
exhibit² *n* **1** OBJECT : objeto *m* expuesto **2** EXHIBITION : exposición *f,* exhibición *f* **3** EVIDENCE : prueba *f* instrumental
exhibition [ˌɛksə'bɪʃən] *n* **1** : exposición *f,* exhibición *f* **2 to make an exhibition of oneself** : dar el espectáculo, hacer el ridículo
exhilarate [ɪg'zɪləˌreɪt, ɛg-] *vt* **-rated; -rating** : alegrar, levantar el ánimo de
exhilaration [ɪgˌzɪlə'reɪʃən, ɛg-] *n* : alegría *f,* regocijo *m,* júbilo *m*
exhort [ɪg'zɔrt, ɛg-] *vt* : exhortar
exhortation [ˌɛkˌsɔr'teɪʃən, -sər-; ˌɛgˌzɔr-] *n* : exhortación *f*
exhumation [ˌɛksju'meɪʃən, -hju-; ˌɛgzu-, -zju-] *n* : exhumación *f*
exhume [ɪg'zuːm, -'zjuːm; ɪks'juːm, -'hjuːm] *vt* **-humed; -huming** : exhumar, desenterrar
exigencies ['ɛksɪdʒəntsiz, ɪg'zɪdʒənˌsiːz] *npl* : exigencias *fpl*
exile¹ ['ɛgˌzaɪl, 'ɛkˌsaɪl] *vt* **exiled; exiling** : exiliar, desterrar
exile² *n* **1** BANISHMENT : exilio *m,* destierro *m* **2** OUTCAST : exiliado *m,* **-da** *f;* desterrado *m,* **-da** *f*
exist [ɪg'zɪst, ɛg-] *vi* **1** BE : existir **2** LIVE : subsistir, vivir
existence [ɪg'zɪstənts, ɛg-] *n* : existencia *f*
existent [ɪg'zɪstənt, ɛg-] *adj* : existente
exit¹ ['ɛgzət, 'ɛksət] *vi* : salir, hacer mutis (en el teatro) — *vt* : salir de
exit² *n* **1** DEPARTURE : salida *f,* partida *f* **2** EGRESS : salida *f* <emergency exit : salida de emergencia>
exodus ['ɛksədəs] *n* : éxodo *m*
exonerate [ɪg'zɑnəˌreɪt, ɛg-] *vt* **-ated; -ating** : exonerar, disculpar, absolver
exoneration [ɪgˌzɑnə'reɪʃən, ɛg-] *n* : exoneración *f*
exorbitant [ɪg'zɔrbətənt, ɛg-] *adj* : exorbitante, excesivo
exorcise ['ɛkˌsɔrˌsaɪz, -sər-] *vt* **-cised; -cising** : exorcizar
exorcism ['ɛksərˌsɪzəm] *n* : exorcismo *m*
exotic¹ [ɪg'zɑtɪk, ɛg-] *adj* : exótico — **exotically** [-ɪkli] *adv*
exotic² *n* : planta *f* exótica
expand [ɪk'spænd, ɛk-] *vt* **1** ENLARGE : expandir, dilatar, aumentar, ampliar **2** EXTEND : extender — *vi* **1** ENLARGE : ampliarse, extenderse **2** : expandirse, dilatarse (dícese de los metales, gases, etc.)
expanse [ɪk'spænts, ɛk-] *n* : extensión *f*
expansion [ɪk'spæntʃən, ɛk-] *n* **1** ENLARGEMENT : expansión *f,* ampliación *f* **2** EXPANSE : extensión *f*
expansive [ɪk'spæntsɪv, ɛk-] *adj* **1** : expansivo **2** OUTGOING : expansivo, comunicativo **3** AMPLE : ancho, amplio — **expansively** *adv*
expansiveness [ɪk'spæntsɪvnəs, ɛk-] *n* : expansibilidad *f*
expatriate¹ [ɛks'peɪtriˌeɪt] *vt* **-ated; -ating** : expatriar
expatriate² [ɛks'peɪtriət, -ˌeɪt] *adj* : expatriado
expatriate³ [ɛks'peɪtriət, -ˌeɪt] *n* : expatriado *m,* **-da** *f*
expect [ɪk'spɛkt, ɛk-] *vt* **1** SUPPOSE : suponer, imaginarse **2** ANTICIPATE : esperar **3** COUNT ON, REQUIRE : contar con, esperar — *vi* **to be expecting** : estar embarazada
expectancy [ɪk'spɛktəntsi, ɛk-] *n, pl* **-cies** : expectativa *f,* esperanza *f*
expectant [ɪk'spɛktənt, ɛk-] *adj* **1** ANTICIPATING : expectante **2** EXPECTING : futuro <expectant mother : futura madre>
expectantly [ɪk'spɛktəntli, ɛk-] *adv* : con expectación
expectation [ˌɛkˌspɛk'teɪʃən] *n* **1** ANTICIPATION : expectación *f* **2** EXPECTANCY : expectativa *f*
expedient¹ [ɪk'spiːdiənt, ɛk-] *adj* : conveniente, oportuno
expedient² *n* : expediente *m,* recurso *m*
expedite ['ɛkspəˌdaɪt] *vt* **-dited; -diting 1** FACILITATE : facilitar, dar curso a **2** HASTEN : acelerar
expedition [ˌɛkspə'dɪʃən] *n* : expedición *f*
expeditious [ˌɛkspə'dɪʃəs] *adj* : pronto, rápido
expel [ɪk'spɛl, ɛk-] *vt* **-pelled; -pelling** : expulsar, expeler
expend [ɪk'spɛnd, ɛk-] *vt* **1** DISBURSE : gastar, desembolsar **2** CONSUME : consumir, agotar
expendable [ɪk'spɛndəbəl, ɛk-] *adj* : prescindible
expenditure [ɪk'spɛndɪtʃər, ɛk-, -ˌtʃʊr] *n* : gasto *m*
expense [ɪk'spɛnts, ɛk-] *n* **1** COST : gasto *m* **2 expenses** *npl* : gastos *mpl,*

expensas *fpl* **3 at the expense of :** a expensas de

expensive [ɪk'spɛn*t*sɪv, ɛk-] *adj* **:** costoso, caro — **expensively** *adv*

experience[1] [ɪk'spɪriən*t*s, ɛk-] *vt* **-enced; -encing :** experimentar (sentimientos), tener (dificultades), sufrir (una pérdida)

experience[2] *n* **:** experiencia *f*

experiment[1] [ɪk'spɛrəmənt, ɛk-, -'spɪr-] *vi* **:** experimentar, hacer experimentos

experiment[2] *n* **:** experimento *m*

experimental [ɪk,spɛrə'mɛntəl, ɛk-, -,spɪr-] *adj* **:** experimental — **experimentally** *adv*

experimentation [ɪk,spɛrəmən'teɪʃən, ɛk-, -,spɪr-] *n* **:** experimentación *f*

expert[1] ['ɛk,spərt, ɪk'spərt] *adj* **:** experto, de experto, pericial (dícese de un testigo) — **expertly** *adv*

expert[2] ['ɛk,spərt] *n* **:** experto *m*, -ta *f*; perito *m*, -ta *f*; especialista *mf*

expertise [,ɛkspər'tiːz] *n* **:** pericia *f*, competencia *f*

expiate ['ɛkspi,eɪt] *vt* **-ated; -ating :** expiar

expiation [,ɛkspi'eɪʃən] *n* **:** expiación *f*

expiration [,ɛkspə'reɪʃən] *n* **1** EXHALATION **:** exhalación *f*, espiración *f* **2** DEATH **:** muerte *f* **3** TERMINATION **:** vencimiento *m*, caducidad *f*

expire [ɪk'spaɪr, ɛk-] *vi* **-pired; -piring 1** EXHALE **:** espirar **2** DIE **:** expirar, morir **3** TERMINATE **:** caducar, vencer

explain [ɪk'spleɪn, ɛk-] *vt* **:** explicar

explanation [,ɛksplə'neɪʃən] *n* **:** explicación *f*

explanatory [ɪk'splænə,tori, ɛk-] *adj* **:** explicativo, aclaratorio

expletive ['ɛksplət̬ɪv] *n* **:** improperio *m*, palabrota *f fam*, grosería *f*

explicable [ɛk'splɪkəbəl, 'ɛksplɪ-] *adj* **:** explicable

explicit [ɪk'splɪsət, ɛk-] *adj* **:** explícito, claro, categórico, rotundo — **explicitly** *adv*

explicitness [ɪk'splɪsətnəs, ɛk-] *n* **:** claridad *f*, carácter *m* explícito

explode [ɪk'sploːd, ɛk-] *v* **-ploded; -ploding** *vt* **1** BURST **:** explosionar, hacer explotar **2** REFUTE **:** rebatir, refutar, desmentir — *vi* **1** BURST **:** explotar, estallar, reventar **2** SKYROCKET **:** dispararse

exploit[1] [ɪk'splɔɪt, ɛk-] *vt* **:** explotar, aprovecharse de

exploit[2] ['ɛk,splɔɪt] *n* **:** hazaña *f*, proeza *f*

exploitation [,ɛk,splɔɪ'teɪʃən] *n* **:** explotación *f*

exploration [,ɛksplə'reɪʃən] *n* **:** exploración *f*

exploratory [ɪk'splorə,tori, ɛk-] *adj* **:** exploratorio

explore [ɪk'splor, ɛk-] *vt* **-plored; -ploring :** explorar, investigar, examinar

explorer [ɪk'splorər, ɛk-] *n* **:** explorador *m*, -dora *f*

explosion [ɪk'sploːʒən, ɛk-] *n* **:** explosión *f*, estallido *m*

explosive[1] [ɪk'sploːsɪv, ɛk-] *adj* **:** explosivo, fulminante — **explosively** *adv*

explosive[2] *n* **:** explosivo *m*

exponent [ɪk'spoːnənt, 'ɛk,spoː-] *n* **1 :** exponente *m* **2** ADVOCATE **:** defensor *m*, -sora *f*; partidario *m*, -ria *f*

exponential [,ɛkspə'nɛntʃəl] *adj* **:** exponencial — **exponentially** *adv*

export[1] [ɛk'sport, 'ɛk,sport] *vt* **:** exportar

export[2] ['ɛk,sport] *n* **1 :** artículo *m* de exportación **2 → exportation**

exportation [,ɛk,spor'teɪʃən] *n* **:** exportación *f*

exporter [ɛk'sport̬ər, 'ɛk,spor-] *n* **:** exportador *m*, -dora *f*

expose [ɪk'spoːz, ɛk-] *vt* **-posed; -posing 1 :** exponer (al peligro, a los elementos, a una enfermedad) **2 :** exponer (una película a la luz) **3** DISCLOSE **:** descubrir, revelar, poner en evidencia **4** UNMASK **:** desenmascarar

exposé *or* **expose** [,ɛkspo'zeɪ] *n* **:** exposición *f* (de hechos), relevación *f* (de un escándalo)

exposed [ɪk'spoːzd, ɛk-] *adj* **:** descubierto, sin protección

exposition [,ɛkspə'zɪʃən] *n* **:** exposición *f*

exposure [ɪk'spoːʒər, ɛk-] *n* **1 :** exposición *f* **2** CONTACT **:** exposición *f*, experiencia *f*, contacto *m* **3** UNMASKING **:** desenmascaramiento *m* **4** ORIENTATION **:** orientación *f* <a room with a northern exposure : una sala orientada al norte>

expound [ɪk'spaʊnd, ɛk-] *vt* **:** exponer, explicar — *vi* **:** hacer comentarios detallados

express[1] [ɪk'sprɛs, ɛk-] *vt* **1** SAY **:** expresar, comunicar **2** SHOW **:** expresar, manifestar, externar *Mex* **3** SQUEEZE **:** exprimir <to express the juice from a lemon : exprimir el jugo de un limón>

express[2] *adv* **:** por correo exprés, por correo urgente

express[3] *adj* **1** EXPLICIT **:** expreso, manifiesto **2** SPECIFIC **:** específico <for that express purpose : con ese fin específico> **3** RAPID **:** expreso, rápido

express[4] *n* **1 :** correo *m* exprés, correo *m* urgente **2 :** expreso *m* (tren)

expression [ɪk'sprɛʃən, ɛk-] *n* **1** UTTERANCE **:** expresión *f* <freedom of expression : libertad de expresión> **2 :** expresión *f* (en la matemática) **3** PHRASE **:** frase *f*, expresión *f* **4** LOOK **:** expresión *f*, cara *f*, gesto *m* <with a sad expression : con un gesto de tristeza>

expressionless [ɪk'sprɛʃənləs, ɛk-] *adj* **:** inexpresivo

expressive [ɪk'sprɛsɪv, ɛk-] *adj* : expresivo

expressway [ɪk'sprɛs,weɪ, ɛk-] *n* : autopista *f*

expulsion [ɪk'spʌlʃən, ɛk-] *n* : expulsión *f*

expurgate ['ɛkspər,geɪt] *vt* **-gated; -gating** : expurgar

exquisite [ɛk'skwɪzət, 'ɛk,skwɪ-] *adj* **1** FINE : exquisito, delicado, primoroso **2** INTENSE : intenso, extremo

extant ['ɛkstənt, ɛk'stænt] *adj* : existente

extemporaneous [ɛk,stɛmpə'reɪniəs] *adj* : improvisado — **extemporaneously** *adv*

extend [ɪk'stɛnd, ɛk-] *vt* **1** STRETCH : extender, tender **2** PROLONG : prolongar, prorrogar **3** ENLARGE : agrandar, ampliar, aumentar **4** PROFFER : extender, dar, ofrecer — *vi* : extenderse

extended [ɪk'stɛndəd, ɛk-] *adj* LENGTHY : prolongado, largo

extension [ɪk'stɛntʃən, ɛk-] *n* **1** EXTENDING : extensión *f,* ampliación *f,* prórroga *f,* prolongación *f* **2** ANNEX : ampliación *f,* anexo *m* **3** : extensión *f* (de teléfono)

extensive [ɪk'stɛntsɪv, ɛk-] *adj* : extenso, vasto, amplio — **extensively** *adv*

extent [ɪk'stɛnt, ɛk-] *n* **1** SIZE : extensión *f,* magnitud *f* **2** DEGREE, SCOPE : alcance *m,* grado *m* <to a certain extent : hasta cierto punto>

extenuate [ɪk'stɛnjə,weɪt, ɛk-] *vt* **-ated; -ating** : atenuar, aminorar, mitigar <extenuating circumstances : circunstancias atenuantes>

extenuation [ɪk,stɛnjə'weɪʃən, ɛk-] *n* : atenuación *f,* aminoración *f*

exterior¹ [ɛk'stɪriər] *adj* : exterior

exterior² *n* : exterior *m*

exterminate [ɪk'stərmə,neɪt, ɛk-] *vt* **-nated; -nating** : exterminar

extermination [ɪk,stərmə'neɪʃən, ɛk-] *n* : exterminación *f,* exterminio *m*

exterminator [ɪk'stərmə,neɪtər, ɛk-] *n* : exterminador *m,* -dora *f*

external [ɪk'stərnəl, ɛk-] *adj* : externo, exterior — **externally** *adv*

extinct [ɪk'stɪŋkt, ɛk-] *adj* : extinto

extinction [ɪk'stɪŋkʃən, ɛk-] *n* : extinción *f*

extinguish [ɪk'stɪŋgwɪʃ, ɛk-] *vt* : extinguir, apagar

extinguisher [ɪk'stɪŋgwɪʃər, ɛk-] *n* : extinguidor *m,* extintor *m*

extirpate ['ɛkstər,peɪt] *vt* **-pated; -pating** : extirpar, exterminar

extol [ɪk'stoːl, ɛk-] *vt* **-tolled; -tolling** : exaltar, ensalzar, alabar

extort [ɪk'stɔrt, ɛk-] *vt* : extorsionar

extortion [ɪk'stɔrʃən, ɛk-] *n* : extorsión *f*

extra¹ ['ɛkstrə] *adv* : extra, más, extremadamente, super <extra special : super especial>

extra² *adj* **1** ADDITIONAL : adicional, suplementario, de más **2** SUPERIOR : superior

extra³ *n* : extra *m*

extract¹ [ɪk'strækt, ɛk-] *vt* : extraer, sacar

extract² ['ɛk,strækt] *n* **1** EXCERPT : pasaje *m,* selección *f,* trozo *m* **2** : extracto *m* <vanilla extract : extracto de vainilla>

extraction [ɪk'strækʃən, ɛk-] *n* : extracción *f*

extractor [ɪk'stræktər, ɛk-] *n* : extractor *m*

extracurricular [,ɛkstrəkə'rɪkjələr] *adj* : extracurricular

extradite ['ɛkstrə,daɪt] *vt* **-dited; -diting** : extraditar

extradition [,ɛkstrə'dɪʃən] *n* : extradición *f*

extramarital [,ɛkstrə'mærətəl] *adj* : extramatrimonial

extraneous [ɛk'streɪniəs] *adj* **1** OUTSIDE : extrínseco, externo **2** SUPERFLUOUS : superfluo, ajeno — **extraneously** *adv*

extraordinary [ɪk'strɔrdən,ɛri, ,ɛkstrə'ɔrd-] *adj* : extraordinario, excepcional — **extraordinarily** [ɪk,strɔrdən'ɛrəli, ,ɛkstrə,ɔrd-] *adv*

extrasensory [,ɛkstrə'sɛntsəri] *adj* : extrasensorial

extraterrestrial¹ [,ɛkstrətə'rɛstriəl] *adj* : extraterrestre

extraterrestrial² *n* : extraterrestre *mf*

extravagance [ɪk'strævɪgənts, ɛk-] *n* **1** EXCESS : exceso *m,* extravagancia *f* **2** WASTEFULNESS : derroche *m,* despilfarro *m* **3** LUXURY : lujo *m*

extravagant [ɪk'strævɪgənt, ɛk-] *adj* **1** EXCESSIVE : excesivo, extravagante **2** WASTEFUL : despilfarrador, derrochador, gastador **3** EXORBITANT : costoso, exorbitante

extravagantly [ɪk'strævɪgəntli, ɛk-] *adv* **1** LAVISHLY : a lo grande **2** EXCESSIVELY : exageradamente, desmesuradamente

extravaganza [ɪk,strævə'gænzə, ɛk-] *n* : gran espectáculo *m*

extreme¹ [ɪk'striːm, ɛk-] *adj* **1** UTMOST : extremo, sumo <of extreme importance : de suma importancia> **2** INTENSE : intenso, extremado <extreme cold : frío extremado> **3** EXCESSIVE : excesivo, extremo <extreme views : opiniones extremas> <extreme measures : medidas excepcionales, medidas drásticas> **4** OUTERMOST : extremo <the extreme north : el norte extremo>

extreme² *n* **1** : extremo *m* **2 in the extreme** : en extremo, en sumo grado

extremely [ɪk'striːmli, ɛk-] *adv* : sumamente, extremadamente, terriblemente

extremity [ɪk'strɛməti, ɛk-] *n, pl* **-ties** **1** EXTREME : extremo *m* **2 extremities** *npl* LIMBS : extremidades *fpl*

extricate ['ɛkstrə,keɪt] *vt* **-cated; -cating** : librar, sacar
extrinsic [ɪk'strɪnzɪk, -'strɪntsɪk] *adj* : extrínseco
extrovert ['ɛkstrə,vərt] *n* : extrovertido *m*, -da *f*
extroverted ['ɛkstrə,vərtəd] *adj* : extrovertido
extrude [ɪk'struːd, ɛk-] *vt* **-truded; -truding** : extrudir, expulsar
exuberance [ɪg'zuːbərənts, ɛg-] *n* **1** JOYOUSNESS : euforia *f*, exaltación *f* **2** VIGOR : exuberancia *f*, vigor *m*
exuberant [ɪg'zuːbərənt, ɛg-] *adj* **1** JOYOUS : eufórico **2** LUSH : exuberante — **exuberantly** *adv*
exude [ɪg'zuːd, ɛg-] *vt* **-uded; -uding** **1** OOZE : rezumar, exudar **2** EMANATE : emanar, irradiar
exult [ɪg'zʌlt, ɛg-] *vi* : exultar, regocijarse
exultant [ɪg'zʌltənt, ɛg-] *adj* : exultante, jubiloso — **exultantly** *adv*
exultation [,ɛksəl'teɪʃən, ,ɛgzəl-] *n* : exultación *f*, júbilo *m*, alborozo *m*
eye¹ ['aɪ] *vt* **eyed; eyeing** *or* **eying** : mirar, observar
eye² *n* **1** : ojo *m* **2** VISION : visión *f*, vista *f*, ojo *m* <a good eye for bargains : un buen ojo para las gangas> **3** GLANCE : mirada *f*, ojeada *f* **4** ATTENTION : atención *f* <to catch one's eye : llamar la atención> **5** POINT OF VIEW : punto *m* de vista <in the eyes of the law : según la ley> **6** : ojo *m* (de una aguja, una papa, una tormenta)
eyeball ['aɪ,bɔl] *n* : globo *m* ocular
eyebrow ['aɪ,braʊ] *n* : ceja *f*
eyedropper ['aɪ,drɑpər] *n* : cuentagotas *f*
eyeglasses ['aɪ,glæsəz] *npl* : anteojos *mpl*, lentes *mpl*, espejuelos *mpl*, gafas *fpl*
eyelash ['aɪ,læʃ] *n* : pestaña *f*
eyelet ['aɪlət] *n* : ojete *m*
eyelid ['aɪ,lɪd] *n* : párpado *m*
eye–opener ['aɪ,oːpənər] *n* : revelación *f*, sorpresa *f*
eye–opening ['aɪ,oːpənɪŋ] *adj* : revelador
eyepiece ['aɪ,piːs] *n* : ocular *m*
eyesight ['aɪ,saɪt] *n* : vista *f*, visión *f*
eyesore ['aɪ,sor] *n* : monstruosidad *f*, adefesio *m*
eyestrain ['aɪ,streɪn] *n* : fatiga *f* visual, vista *f* cansada
eyetooth ['aɪ,tuːθ] *n* : colmillo *m*
eyewitness ['aɪ'wɪtnəs] *n* : testigo *mf* ocular, testigo *mf* presencial
eyrie ['aɪri] → **aerie**

F

f ['ɛf] *n*, *pl* **f's** *or* **fs** ['ɛfs] : sexta letra del alfabeto inglés
fable ['feɪbəl] *n* : fábula *f*
fabled ['feɪbəld] *adj* : legendario, fabuloso
fabric ['fæbrɪk] *n* **1** MATERIAL : tela *f*, tejido *m* **2** STRUCTURE : estructura *f* <the fabric of society : la estructura de la sociedad>
fabricate ['fæbrɪ,keɪt] *vt* **-cated; -cating** **1** CONSTRUCT, MANUFACTURE : construir, fabricar **2** INVENT : inventar (excusas o mentiras)
fabrication [,fæbrɪ'keɪʃən] *n* **1** LIE : mentira *f*, invención *f* **2** MANUFACTURE : fabricación *f*
fabulous ['fæbjələs] *adj* **1** LEGENDARY : fabuloso, legendario **2** INCREDIBLE : increíble, fabuloso <fabulous wealth : riqueza fabulosa> **3** WONDERFUL : magnífico, estupendo, fabuloso — **fabulously** *adv*
facade [fə'sɑd] *n* : fachada *f*
face¹ ['feɪs] *v* **faced; facing** *vt* **1** LINE : recubrir (una superficie), forrar (ropa) **2** CONFRONT : enfrentarse a, afrontar, hacer frente a <to face the music : afrontar las consecuencias> <to face the facts : aceptar la realidad> **3** : estar de cara a, estar enfrente de <she's facing her brother : está de cara a su hermano> **4** OVERLOOK : dar a — *vi* : mirar (hacia), estar orientado (a)
face² *n* **1** : cara *f*, rostro *m* <he told me to my face : me lo dijo a la cara> **2** EXPRESSION : cara *f*, expresión *f* <to pull a long face : poner mala cara> **3** GRIMACE : mueca *f* <to make faces : hacer muecas> **4** APPEARANCE : fisonomía *f*, aspecto *m* <the face of society : la fisonomía de la sociedad> **5** EFFRONTERY : desfachatez *f* **6** PRESTIGE : prestigio *m* <to lose face : desprestigiarse> **7** FRONT, SIDE : cara *f* (de una moneda), esfera *f* (de un reloj), fachada *f* (de un edificio), pared *f* (de una montaña) **8** SURFACE : superficie *f*, faz *f* (de la tierra), cara *f* (de la luna) **9 in the face of** DESPITE : en medio de, en visto de, ante
facedown ['feɪs,daʊn] *adv* : boca abajo
faceless ['feɪsləs] *adj* ANONYMOUS : anónimo
face–lift ['feɪs,lɪft] *n* **1** : estiramiento *m* facial **2** RENOVATION : renovación *f*, remozamiento *m*
facet ['fæsət] *n* **1** : faceta *f* (de una piedra) **2** ASPECT : faceta *f*, aspecto *m*
facetious [fə'siːʃəs] *adj* : gracioso, burlón, bromista
facetiously [fə'siːʃəsli] *adv* : en tono de burla
facetiousness [fə'siːʃəsnəs] *n* : jocosidad *f*
face–to–face *adv & adj* : cara a cara
faceup ['feɪs'ʌp] *adv* : boca arriba

face value *n* **:** valor *m* nominal

facial[1] ['feɪʃəl] *adj* **:** de la cara, facial

facial[2] *n* **:** tratamiento *m* facial, limpieza *f* de cutis

facile ['fæsəl] *adj* SUPERFICIAL **:** superficial, simplista

facilitate [fə'sɪlə,teɪt] *vt* **-tated; -tating :** facilitar

facility [fə'sɪləti] *n, pl* **-ties 1** EASE **:** facilidad *f* **2** CENTER, COMPLEX **:** centro *m*, complejo *m* **3 facilities** *npl* AMENITIES **:** comodidades *fpl*, servicios *mpl*

facing ['feɪsɪŋ] *n* **1** LINING **:** entretela *f* (de una prenda) **2 :** revestimiento *m* (de un edificio)

facsimile [fæk'sɪməli] *n* **:** facsímile *m*, facsímil *m*

fact ['fækt] *n* **1 :** hecho *m* <as a matter of fact : de hecho> **2** INFORMATION **:** información *f*, datos *mpl* <facts and figures : datos y cifras> **3** REALITY **:** realidad *f* <in fact : en realidad>

faction ['fækʃən] *n* **:** facción *m*, bando *m*

factional ['fækʃənəl] *adj* **:** entre facciones

factious ['fækʃəs] *adj* **:** faccioso, contencioso

factitious [fæk'tɪʃəs] *adj* **:** artificial, facticio

factor ['fæktər] *n* **:** factor *m*

factory ['fæktəri] *n, pl* **-ries :** fábrica *f*

factual ['fæktʃʊəl] *adj* **:** basado en hechos, objetivo

factually ['fæktʃʊəli] *adv* **:** en cuanto a los hechos

faculty ['fækəlti] *n, pl* **-ties 1 :** facultad *f* <the faculty of sight : las facultades visuales, el sentido de la vista> **2** APTITUDE **:** aptitud *f*, facilidad *f* **3** TEACHERS **:** cuerpo *m* docente

fad ['fæd] *n* **:** moda *f* pasajera, manía *f*

fade ['feɪd] *v* **faded; fading** *vi* **1** WITHER **:** debilitarse (dícese de las personas), marchitarse (dícese de las flores y las plantas) **2** DISCOLOR **:** desteñirse, decolorarse **3** DIM **:** apagarse (dícese de la luz), perderse (dícese de los sonidos), fundirse (dícese de las imágenes) **4** VANISH **:** desvanecerse, decaer — *vt* DISCOLOR **:** desteñir

fag ['fæg] *vt* **fagged; fagging** EXHAUST **:** cansar, fatigar

fagot *or* **faggot** ['fægət] *n* **:** haz *m* de leña

Fahrenheit ['færən,haɪt] *adj* **:** Fahrenheit

fail[1] ['feɪl] *vi* **1** WEAKEN **:** fallar, deteriorarse **2** STOP **:** fallar, detenerse <his heart failed : le falló el corazón> **3 :** fracasar, fallar <her plan failed : su plan fracasó> <the crops failed : se perdió la cosecha> **4 :** quebrar <a business about to fail : una empresa a punto de quebrar> **5 to fail in :** faltar a, no cumplir con <to fail in one's duties : faltar a sus deberes> — *vt* **1** FLUNK **:** reprobar (un examen) **2 :** fallar <words fail me : las palabras me fallan, no encuentro palabras> **3** DISAPPOINT **:** fallar, decepcionar <don't fail me! : ¡no me falles!>

fail[2] *n* **:** fracaso *m*

failing ['feɪlɪŋ] *n* **:** defecto *m*

failure ['feɪljər] *n* **1 :** fracaso *m*, malogro *m* <crop failure : pérdida de la cosecha> <heart failure : insuficiencia cardíaca> <engine failure : falla mecánica> **2** BANKRUPTCY **:** bancarrota *f*, quiebra *f* **3 :** fracaso *m* (persona) <he was a failure as a manager : como gerente, fue un fracaso>

faint[1] ['feɪnt] *vi* **:** desmayarse

faint[2] *adj* **1** COWARDLY, TIMID **:** cobarde, tímido **2** DIZZY **:** mareado <faint with hunger : desfallecido de hambre> **3** SLIGHT **:** leve, ligero, vago <I haven't the faintest idea : no tengo la más mínima idea> **4** INDISTINCT **:** tenue, indistinto, apenas perceptible

faint[3] *n* **:** desmayo *m*

fainthearted ['feɪnt'hɑrṭəd] *adj* **:** cobarde, pusilánime

faintly ['feɪntli] *adv* **:** débilmente, ligeramente, levemente

faintness ['feɪntnəs] *n* **1** INDISTINCTNESS **:** lo débil, falta *f* de claridad **2** FAINTING **:** desmayo *m*, desfallecimiento *m*

fair[1] ['fær] *adj* **1** ATTRACTIVE, BEAUTIFUL **:** bello, hermoso, atractivo **2** (*relating to weather*) **:** bueno, despejado <fair weather : tiempo despejado> **3** JUST **:** justo, imparcial **4** ALLOWABLE **:** permisible **5** BLOND, LIGHT **:** rubio (dícese del pelo), blanco (dícese de la tez) **6** ADEQUATE **:** bastante, adecuado <fair to middling : mediano, regular> **7 fair game :** presa *f* fácil **8 to play fair :** jugar limpio

fair[2] *n* **:** feria *f*

fairground ['fær,graʊnd] *n* **:** parque *m* de diversiones

fairly ['færli] *adv* **1** IMPARTIALLY **:** imparcialmente, limpiamente, equitativamente **2** QUITE **:** bastante **3** MODERATELY **:** medianamente

fairness ['færnəs] *n* **1** IMPARTIALITY **:** imparcialidad *f*, justicia *f* **2** LIGHTNESS **:** blancura *f* (de la piel), lo rubio (del pelo)

fairy ['færi] *n, pl* **fairies 1 :** hada *f* **2 fairy tale :** cuento *m* de hadas

fairyland ['færi,lænd] *n* **1 :** país *m* de las hadas **2 :** lugar *m* encantador

faith ['feɪθ] *n, pl* **faiths** ['feɪθs, 'feɪðz] **1** BELIEF **:** fe *f* **2** ALLEGIANCE **:** lealtad *f* **3** CONFIDENCE, TRUST **:** confianza *f*, fe *f* **4** RELIGION **:** religión *f*

faithful ['feɪθfəl] *adj* **:** fiel — **faithfully** *adv*

faithfulness ['feɪθfəlnəs] *n* **:** fidelidad *f*

faithless ['feɪθləs] *adj* **1** DISLOYAL **:** desleal **2 :** infiel (en la religión) — **faithlessly** *adv*

faithlessness [ˈfeɪθləsnəs] *n* : deslealtad *f*

fake[1] [ˈfeɪk] *v* **faked; faking** *vt* **1** FALSIFY : falsificar, falsear **2** FEIGN : fingir — *vi* **1** PRETEND : fingir **2** : hacer un engaño, hacer una finta (en deportes)

fake[2] *adj* : falso, fingido, postizo

fake[3] *n* **1** IMITATION : imitación *f,* falsificación *f* **2** IMPOSTOR : impostor *m,* -tora *f;* charlatán *m,* -tana *f;* farsante *mf* **3** FEINT : engaño *m,* finta *f* (en deportes)

faker [ˈfeɪkər] *n* : impostor *m,* -tora *f;* charlatán *m,* -tana *f;* farsante *mf*

fakir [fəˈkɪr, ˈfeɪkər] *n* : faquir *m*

falcon [ˈfælkən, ˈfɔl-] *n* : halcón *m*

falconry [ˈfælkənri, ˈfɔl-] *n* : cetrería *f*

fall[1] [ˈfɔl] *vi* **fell** [ˈfɛl]; **fallen** [fɔlən]; **falling 1** : caer, caerse <to fall out of bed : caer de la cama> <to fall down : caerse> **2** HANG : caer **3** DESCEND : caer (dícese de la lluvia o de la noche), bajar (dícese de los precios), descender (dícese de la temperatura) **4** : caer (a un enemigo), rendirse <the city fell : la ciudad se rindió> **5** OCCUR : caer <Christmas falls on a Friday : la Navidad cae en viernes> **6 to fall asleep** : dormirse, quedarse dormido **7 to fall from grace** SIN : perder la gracia **8 to fall sick** : caer enfermo, enfermarse **9 to fall through** : fracasar, caer en la nada **10 to fall to** : tocar a, corresponder a <the task fell to him : le tocó hacerlo>

fall[2] *n* **1** TUMBLE : caída *f* <to break one's fall : frenar uno su caída> <a fall of three feet : una caída de tres pies> **2** FALLING : derrumbe *m* (de rocas), aguacero *m* (de lluvia), nevada *f* (de nieve), bajada *f* (de precios), disminución *f* (de cantidades) **3** AUTUMN : otoño *m* **4** DOWNFALL : caída *f,* ruina *f* **5 falls** *npl* WATERFALL : cascada *f,* catarata *f*

fallacious [fəˈleɪʃəs] *adj* : erróneo, engañoso, falaz

fallacy [ˈfæləsi] *n, pl* **-cies** : falacia *f*

fall back *vi* **1** RETREAT : retirarse, replegarse **2 to fall back on** : recurrir a

fall guy *n* SCAPEGOAT : chivo *m* expiatorio

fallible [ˈfæləbəl] *adj* : falible

fallout [ˈfɔlˌaʊt] *n* **1** : lluvia *f* radioactiva **2** CONSEQUENCES : secuelas *fpl,* consecuencias *fpl*

fallow[1] [ˈfælo] *vt* : barbechar

fallow[2] *adj* **to lie fallow** : estar en barbecho

fallow[3] *n* : barbecho *m*

false [ˈfɔls] *adj* **falser; falsest 1** UNTRUE : falso **2** ERRONEOUS : erróneo, equivocado **3** FAKE : falso, postizo **4** UNFAITHFUL : infiel **5** FRAUDULENT : fraudulento <under false pretenses : por fraude>

falsehood [ˈfɔlsˌhʊd] *n* : mentira *f,* falsedad *f*

falsely [ˈfɔlsli] *adv* : falsamente, con falsedad

falseness [ˈfɔlsnəs] *n* : falsedad *f*

falsetto [fɔlˈsɛt̬oː] *n, pl* **-tos** : falsete *m*

falsification [ˌfɔlsəfəˈkeɪʃən] *n* : falsificación *f,* falseamiento *m*

falsify [ˈfɔlsəˌfaɪ] *vt* **-fied; fying** : falsificar, falsear

falsity [ˈfɔlsət̬i] *n, pl* **-ties** : falsedad *f*

falter [ˈfɔltər] *vi* **-tered; -tering 1** TOTTER : tambalearse **2** STAMMER : titubear, tartamudear **3** WAVER : vacilar

faltering [ˈfɔltərɪŋ] *adj* : titubeante, vacilante

fame [ˈfeɪm] *n* : fama *f*

famed [ˈfeɪmd] *adj* : famoso, célebre, afamado

familial [fəˈmɪljəl, -liəl] *adj* : familiar

familiar[1] [fəˈmɪljər] *adj* **1** KNOWN : familiar, conocido <to be familiar with : estar familiarizado con> **2** INFORMAL : familiar, informal **3** INTIMATE : íntimo, de confianza **4** FORWARD : confianzudo, atrevido — **familiarly** *adv*

familiar[2] *n* : espíritu *m* guardián

familiarity [fəˌmɪliˈærət̬i, -ˌmɪlˈjær-] *n, pl* **-ties 1** KNOWLEDGE : conocimiento *m,* familiaridad *f* **2** INFORMALITY, INTIMACY : confianza *f,* familiaridad *f* **3** FORWARDNESS : exceso *m* de confianza, descaro *m*

familiarize [fəˈmɪljəˌraɪz] *vt* **-ized; -izing 1** : familiarizar **2 to familiarize oneself** : familiarizarse

family [ˈfæmli, ˈfæmə-] *n, pl* **-lies** : familia *f*

family tree *n* : árbol *m* genealógico

famine [ˈfæmən] *n* : hambre *f,* hambruna *f*

famish [ˈfæmɪʃ] *vi* **to be famished** : estar famélico, estar hambriento, morir de hambre *fam*

famous [ˈfeɪməs] *adj* : famoso

famously [ˈfeɪməsli] *adv* **to get on famously** : llevarse de maravilla

fan[1] [ˈfæn] *vt* **fanned; fanning 1** : abanicar (a una persona), avivar (un fuego) **2** STIMULATE : avivar, estimular

fan[2] *n* **1** : ventilador *m,* abanico *m* **2** ADMIRER, ENTHUSIAST : aficionado *m,* -da *f;* entusiasta *mf;* admirador *m,* -dora *f*

fanatic[1] [fəˈnæt̬ɪk] *or* **fanatical** [-t̬ɪkəl] *adj* : fanático

fanatic[2] *n* : fanático *m,* -ca *f*

fanaticism [fəˈnæt̬əˌsɪzəm] *n* : fanatismo *m*

fanciful [ˈfæntsɪfəl] *adj* **1** CAPRICIOUS : caprichoso, fantástico, extravagante **2** IMAGINATIVE : imaginativo — **fancifully** *adv*

fancy[1] [ˈfæntsi] *vt* **-cied; -cying 1** IMAGINE : imaginarse, figurarse <fancy that! : ¡figúrate!, ¡imagínate!> **2** CRAVE : apetecer, tener ganas de

fancy[2] *adj* **-cier; -est 1** ELABORATE : elaborado **2** LUXURIOUS : lujoso, elegante — **fancily** [ˈfæntsəli] *adv*

fancy[3] *n, pl* **-cies** **1** LIKING : gusto *m,* afición *f* **2** WHIM : antojo *m,* capricho *m* **3** IMAGINATION : fantasía *f,* imaginación *f*

fandango [fæn'dæŋgo] *n, pl* **-gos** : fandango *m*

fanfare ['fæn,fær] *n* : fanfarria *f*

fang ['fæŋ] *n* : colmillo *m* (de un animal), diente *m* (de una serpiente)

fanlight ['fæn,laɪt] *n* : tragaluz *m*

fantasia [fæn'teɪʒə, -ziə; ,fæntə'ziːə] *n* : fantasía *f*

fantasize ['fæntə,saɪz] *vi* **-sized; -sizing** : fantasear

fantastic [fæn'tæstɪk] *adj* **1** UNBELIEVABLE : fantástico, increíble, extraño **2** ENORMOUS : fabuloso, inmenso <fantastic sums : sumas fabulosas> **3** WONDERFUL : estupendo, fantástico, bárbaro *fam,* macanudo *fam* — **fantastically** [-tɪkli] *adv*

fantasy ['fæntəsi] *n, pl* **-sies** : fantasía *f*

far[1] ['fɑr] *adv* **farther** ['fɑrðər] *or* **further** ['fər-]; **farthest** *or* **furthest** [-ðəst] **1** : lejos <far from here : lejos de aquí> <to go far : llegar lejos> <as far as Chicago : hasta Chicago> <far away : a lo lejos> **2** MUCH : muy, mucho <far bigger : mucho más grande> <far superior : muy superior> <it's by far the best : es con mucho el mejor> **3** (*expressing degree or extent*) <the results are far off : salieron muy inexactos los resultados> <to go so far as : decir tanto como> <to go far enough : tener el alcance necesario> **4** (*expressing progress*) <the work is far advanced : el trabajo está muy avanzado> <to take (something) too far : llevar (algo) demasiado lejos> **5 far and wide** : por todas partes **6 far from it!** : ¡todo lo contrario! **7 so far** : hasta ahora, todavía

far[2] *adj* **farther** *or* **further; farthest** *or* **furthest** **1** REMOTE : lejano, remoto <the Far East : el Lejano Oriente, el Extremo Oriente> <a far country : un país lejano> **2** LONG : largo <a far journey : un viaje largo> **3** EXTREME : extremo <the far right : la extrema derecha> <at the far end of the room : en el otro extremo de la sala>

faraway ['fɑrə,weɪ] *adj* : remoto, lejano

farce ['fɑrs] *n* : farsa *f*

farcical ['fɑrsɪkəl] *adj* : absurdo, ridículo

fare[1] ['fær] *vi* **fared; faring** : ir, salir <how did you fare? : ¿cómo te fue?>

fare[2] *n* **1** : pasaje *m,* billete *m,* boleto *m* <half fare : medio pasaje> **2** FOOD : comida *f*

farewell[1] [fær'wɛl] *adj* : de despedida

farewell[2] *n* : despedida *f*

far–fetched ['fɑr'fɛtʃt] *adj* : improbable, exagerado

farina [fə'riːnə] *n* : harina *f*

farm[1] ['fɑrm] *vt* **1** : cultivar, labrar **2** : criar (animales) — *vi* : ser agricultor

farm[2] *n* : granja *f,* hacienda *f,* finca *f,* estancia *f*

farmer ['fɑrmər] *n* : agricultor *m,* granjero *m*

farmhand ['fɑrm,hænd] *n* : peón *m*

farmhouse ['fɑrm,haʊs] *n* : granja *f,* vivienda *f* del granjero, casa *f* de hacienda

farming ['fɑrmɪŋ] *n* : labranza *f,* cultivo *m,* crianza *f* (de animales)

farmland ['fɑrm,lænd] *n* : tierras *fpl* de labranza

farmyard ['fɑrm,jɑrd] *n* : corral *m*

far–off ['fɑr,ɔf, -'ɔf] *adj* : remoto, distante, lejano

far–reaching ['fɑr'riːtʃɪŋ] *adj* : de gran alcance

farsighted ['fɑr,saɪtəd] *adj* **1** : hipermétrope **2** JUDICIOUS : con visión de futuro, previsor, precavido

farsightedness ['fɑr,saɪtədnəs] *n* **1** : hipermetropía *f* **2** PRUDENCE : previsión *f*

farther[1] ['fɑrðər] *adv* **1** AHEAD : más lejos (en el espacio), más adelante (en el tiempo) **2** MORE : más

farther[2] *adj* : más lejano, más remoto

farthermost ['fɑrðər,moːst] *adj* : (el) más lejano

farthest[1] ['fɑrðəst] *adv* **1** : lo más lejos <I jumped farthest : salté lo más lejos> **2** : lo más avanzado <he progressed farthest : progresó al punto más avanzado> **3** : más <the farthest developed plan : el plan más desarrollado>

farthest[2] *adj* : más lejano

fascicle ['fæsɪkəl] *n* : fascículo *m*

fascinate ['fæsən,eɪt] *vt* **-nated; -nating** : fascinar, cautivar

fascination [,fæsən'eɪʃən] *n* : fascinación *f*

fascism ['fæʃ,ɪzəm] *n* : fascismo *m*

fascist[1] ['fæʃɪst] *adj* : fascista

fascist[2] *n* : fascista *mf*

fashion[1] ['fæʃən] *vt* : formar, moldear

fashion[2] *n* **1** MANNER : manera *f,* modo *m* **2** CUSTOM : costumbre *f* **3** STYLE : moda *f*

fashionable ['fæʃənəbəl] *adj* : de moda, chic

fashionably ['fæʃənəbli] *adv* : a la moda

fast[1] ['fæst] *vi* : ayunar

fast[2] *adv* **1** SECURELY : firmemente, seguramente <to hold fast : agarrarse bien> **2** RAPIDLY : rápidamente, rápido, de prisa **3** SOUNDLY : profundamente <fast asleep : profundamente dormido>

fast[3] *adj* **1** SECURE : firme, seguro <to make fast : amarrar (un barco)> **2** FAITHFUL : leal <fast friends : amigos leales> **3** RAPID : rápido, veloz **4** : adelantado <10 minutes fast : 10 minutos adelantado> **5** DEEP : profundo <a fast sleep : un sueño pro-

fundo> 6 COLORFAST : inalterable, que no destiñe 7 DISSOLUTE : extravagante, disipado, disoluto
fast[4] *n* : ayuno *m*
fasten [ˈfæsən] *vt* **1** ATTACH : sujetar, atar **2** FIX : fijar <to fasten one's eyes on : fijar los ojos en> **3** SECURE : abrochar (ropa o cinturones), atar (cordones), cerrar (una maleta) — *vi* : abrocharse, cerrar
fastener [ˈfæsənər] *n* : cierre *m*, sujetador *m*
fastening [ˈfæsənɪŋ] *n* : cierre *m*, sujetador *m*
fastidious [fæsˈtɪdiəs] *adj* : quisquilloso, exigente — **fastidiously** *adv*
fat[1] [ˈfæt] *adj* **fatter; fattest 1** OBESE : gordo, obeso **2** THICK : grueso
fat[2] *n* : grasa *f*
fatal [ˈfeɪtəl] *adj* **1** DEADLY : mortal **2** ILL-FATED : malhadado, fatal **3** MOMENTOUS : fatídico
fatalism [ˈfeɪtəlˌɪzəm] *n* : fatalismo *m*
fatalist [ˈfeɪtəlɪst] *n* : fatalista *mf*
fatalistic [ˌfeɪtəlˈɪstɪk] *adj* : fatalista
fatality [feɪˈtæləti, fə-] *n, pl* **-ties** : víctima *f* mortal
fatally [ˈfeɪtəli] *adv* : mortalmente
fate [ˈfeɪt] *n* **1** DESTINY : destino *m* **2** END, LOT : final *m*, suerte *f*
fated [ˈfeɪtəd] *adj* : predestinado
fateful [ˈfeɪtfəl] *adj* **1** MOMENTOUS : fatídico, aciago **2** PROPHETIC : profético — **fatefully** *adv*
father[1] [ˈfɑðər] *vt* : engendrar
father[2] *n* **1** : padre *m* <my father and my mother : mi padre y mi madre> <Father Smith : el padre Smith> **2 the Father** GOD : el Padre, Dios *m*
fatherhood [ˈfɑðərˌhʊd] *n* : paternidad *f*
father-in-law [ˈfɑðərɪnˌlɔ] *n, pl* **fathers-in-law** : suegro *m*
fatherland [ˈfɑðərˌlænd] *n* : patria *f*
fatherless [ˈfɑðərləs] *adj* : huérfano de padre, sin padre
fatherly [ˈfɑðərli] *adj* : paternal
fathom[1] [ˈfæðəm] *vt* UNDERSTAND : entender, comprender
fathom[2] *n* : braza *f*
fatigue[1] [fəˈtiːg] *vt* **-tigued; -tiguing** : fatigar, cansar
fatigue[2] *n* : fatiga *f*
fatness [ˈfætnəs] *n* : gordura *f* (de una persona o un animal), grosor *m* (de un objeto)
fatten [ˈfætən] *vt* : engordar, cebar
fatty [ˈfæti] *adj* **fattier; -est** : graso, grasoso, adiposo (dícese de los tejidos)
fatuous [ˈfætʃʊəs] *adj* : necio, fatuo — **fatuously** *adv*
faucet [ˈfɔsət] *n* : llave *f*, canilla *f Arg,Uru*, grifo *m*
fault[1] [ˈfɔlt] *vt* : encontrar defectos a
fault[2] *n* **1** SHORTCOMING : defecto *m*, falta *f* **2** DEFECT : falta *f*, defecto *m*, falla *f* **3** BLAME : culpa *f* **4** FRACTURE : falla *f* (geológica)
faultfinder [ˈfɔltˌfaɪndər] *n* : criticón *m*, -cona *f*
faultfinding [ˈfɔltˌfaɪndɪŋ] *n* : crítica *f*
faultless [ˈfɔltləs] *adj* : sin culpa, sin imperfecciones, impecable
faultlessly [ˈfɔltləsli] *adv* : impecablemente, perfectamente
faulty [ˈfɔlti] *adj* **faultier; -est** : defectuoso, imperfecto — **faultily** [ˈfɔltəli] *adv*
fauna [ˈfɔnə] *n* : fauna *f*
faux pas [ˌfoːˈpɑ] *n, pl* **faux pas** [*same or* -ˈpɑz] : metedura *f* de pata *fam*
favor[1] [ˈfeɪvər] *vt* **1** SUPPORT : estar a favor de, ser partidario de, apoyar **2** OBLIGE : hacerle un favor a **3** PREFER : preferir **4** RESEMBLE : parecerse a, salir a
favor[2] *n* : favor *m* <in favor of : a favor de> <an error in his favor : un error a su favor>
favorable [ˈfeɪvərəbəl] *adj* : favorable, propicio
favorably [ˈfeɪvərəbli] *adv* : favorablemente, bien
favorite[1] [ˈfeɪvərət] *adj* : favorito, preferido
favorite[2] *n* : favorito *m*, -ta *f*; preferido *m*, -da *f*
favoritism [ˈfeɪvərəˌtɪzəm] *n* : favoritismo *m*
fawn[1] [ˈfɔn] *vi* : adular, lisonjear
fawn[2] *n* : cervato *m*
fax [ˈfæks] *n* : facsímil *m*, facsímile *m*
faze [ˈfeɪz] *vt* **fazed; fazing** : desconcertar, perturbar
fear[1] [ˈfɪr] *vt* : temer, tener miedo de — *vi* : temer
fear[2] *n* : miedo *m*, temor *m* <for fear of : por temor a>
fearful [ˈfɪrfəl] *adj* **1** FRIGHTENING : espantoso, aterrador, horrible **2** FRIGHTENED : temeroso, miedoso
fearfully [ˈfɪrfəli] *adv* **1** EXTREMELY : extremadamente, terriblemente **2** TIMIDLY : con temor
fearless [ˈfɪrləs] *adj* : intrépido, impávido
fearlessly [ˈfɪrləsli] *adv* : sin temor
fearlessness [ˈfɪrləsnəs] *n* : intrepidez *f*, impavidez *f*
fearsome [ˈfɪrsəm] *adj* : aterrador
feasibility [ˌfiːzəˈbɪləti] *n* : viabilidad *f*, factibilidad *f*
feasible [ˈfiːzəbəl] *adj* : viable, factible, realizable
feast[1] [ˈfiːst] *vi* : banquetear — *vt* **1** : agasajar, festejar **2 to feast one's eyes on** : regalarse la vista con
feast[2] *n* **1** BANQUET : banquete *m*, festín *m* **2** FESTIVAL : fiesta *f*
feat [ˈfiːt] *n* : proeza *f*, hazaña *f*
feather[1] [ˈfɛðər] *vt* **1** : emplumar **2 to feather one's nest** : hacer su agosto
feather[2] *n* **1** : pluma *f* **2 a feather in one's cap** : un triunfo personal
feathered [ˈfɛðərd] *adj* : con plumas
feathery [ˈfɛðəri] *adj* **1** DOWNY : plumoso **2** LIGHT : liviano

feature[1] [ˈfiːtʃər] *v* **-tured; -turing** *vt* **1** IMAGINE : imaginarse **2** PRESENT : presentar — *vi* : figurar

feature[2] *n* **1** CHARACTERISTIC : característica *f*, rasgo *m* **2** : largometraje *m* (en el cine), artículo *m* (en un periódico), documental *m* (en la televisión) **3 features** *npl* : rasgos *mpl*, facciones *fpl* <delicate features : facciones delicadas>

February [ˈfɛbjʊˌɛri, ˈfɛbʊ-, ˈfɛbrʊ-] *n* : febrero *m*

fecal [ˈfiːkəl] *adj* : fecal

feces [ˈfiːˌsiːz] *npl* : heces *fpl*, excrementos *mpl*

feckless [ˈfɛkləs] *adj* : irresponsable

fecund [ˈfɛkənd, ˈfiː-] *adj* : fecundo

fecundity [fɪˈkʌndəti, fɛ-] *n* : fecundidad *f*

federal [ˈfɛdrəl, -dərəl] *adj* : federal

federalism [ˈfɛdrəˌlɪzəm, -dərə-] *n* : federalismo *m*

federalist[1] [ˈfɛdrəlɪst, -dərə-] *adj* : federalista

federalist[2] *n* : federalista *mf*

federate [ˈfɛdəˌreɪt] *vt* **-ated; -ating** : federar

federation [ˌfɛdəˈreɪʃən] *n* : federación *f*

fedora [fɪˈdorə] *n* : sombrero *m* flexible de fieltro

fed up *adj* : harto

fee [ˈfiː] *n* **1** : honorarios *mpl* (a un médico, un abogado, etc.) **2 entrance fee** : entrada *f*

feeble [ˈfiːbəl] *adj* **-bler; -blest 1** WEAK : débil, endeble **2** INEFFECTIVE : flojo, pobre, poco convincente

feebleminded [ˌfiːbəlˈmaɪndəd] *adj* **1** : débil mental **2** FOOLISH, STUPID : imbécil, tonto

feebleness [ˈfiːbəlnəs] *n* : debilidad *f*

feebly [ˈfiːbli] *adv* : débilmente

feed[1] [ˈfiːd] *v* **fed** [ˈfɛd]; **feeding** *vt* **1** : dar de comer a, nutrir, alimentar (a una persona) **2** : alimentar (un fuego o una máquina), proveer (información), introducir (datos) — *vi* : comer, alimentarse

feed[2] *n* **1** NOURISHMENT : alimento *m* **2** FODDER : pienso *m*

feel[1] [ˈfiːl] *v* **felt** [ˈfɛlt]; **feeling** *vi* **1** : sentirse, encontrarse <I feel tired : me siento cansada> <he feels hungry : tiene hambre> <she feels like a fool : se siente como una idiota> <to feel like doing something : tener ganas de hacer algo> **2** SEEM : parecer <it feels like spring : parece primavera> **3** THINK : parecerse, opinar, pensar <how does he feel about that? : ¿qué opina él de eso?> — *vt* **1** TOUCH : tocar, palpar **2** SENSE : sentir <to feel the cold : sentir el frío> **3** CONSIDER : sentir, creer, considerar <to feel (it) necessary : creer necesario>

feel[2] *n* **1** SENSATION, TOUCH : sensación *f*, tacto *m* **2** ATMOSPHERE : ambiente *m*, atmósfera *f* **3 to have a feel for** : tener un talento especial para

feeler [ˈfiːlər] *n* : antena *f*, tentáculo *m*

feeling [ˈfiːlɪŋ] *n* **1** SENSATION : sensación *f*, sensibilidad *f* **2** EMOTION : sentimiento *m* **3** OPINION : opinión *f* **4 feelings** *npl* SENSIBILITIES : sentimientos *mpl* <to hurt someone's feelings : herir los sentimientos de alguien>

feet → **foot**

feign [ˈfeɪn] *vt* : simular, aparentar, fingir

feint[1] [ˈfeɪnt] *vi* : fintar, fintear

feint[2] *n* : finta *f*

felicitate [fɪˈlɪsəˌteɪt] *vt* **-tated; -tating** : felicitar, congratular

felicitation [fɪˌlɪsəˈteɪʃən] *n* : felicitación *f*

felicitous [fɪˈlɪsət̬əs] *adj* : acertado, oportuno

feline[1] [ˈfiːˌlaɪn] *adj* : felino

feline[2] *n* : felino *m*, -na *f*

fell[1] [ˈfɛl] *vt* : talar (un árbol), derribar (a una persona)

fell[2] → **fall**

fellow [ˈfɛˌloː] *n* **1** COMPANION : compañero *m*, -ra *f*; camarada *mf* **2** ASSOCIATE : socio *m*, -cia *f* **3** MAN : tipo *m*, hombre *m*

fellowman [ˌfɛloˈmæn] *n, pl* **-men** : prójimo *m*, semejante *m*

fellowship [ˈfɛloˌʃɪp] *n* **1** COMPANIONSHIP : camaradería *f*, compañerismo *m* **2** ASSOCIATION : fraternidad *f* **3** GRANT : beca *f* (de investigación)

felon [ˈfɛlən] *n* : malhechor *m*, -chora *f*; criminal *mf*

felonious [fəˈloːniəs] *adj* : criminal

felony [ˈfɛləni] *n, pl* **-nies** : delito *m* grave

felt[1] [ˈfɛlt] *n* : fieltro *m*

felt[2] → **feel**

female[1] [ˈfiːˌmeɪl] *adj* : femenino

female[2] *n* **1** : hembra *f* (de animal) **2** WOMAN : mujer *f*

feminine [ˈfɛmənən] *adj* : femenino

femininity [ˌfɛməˈnɪnət̬i] *n* : feminidad *f*, femineidad *f*

feminism [ˈfɛməˌnɪzəm] *n* : feminismo *m*

feminist[1] [ˈfɛmənɪst] *adj* : feminista

feminist[2] *n* : feminista *mf*

femoral [ˈfɛmərəl] *adj* : femoral

femur [ˈfiːmər] *n, pl* **femurs** *or* **femora** [ˈfɛmərə] : fémur *m*

fence[1] [ˈfɛn*t*s] *v* **fenced; fencing** *vt* : vallar, cercar — *vi* : hacer esgrima

fence[2] *n* : cerca *f*, valla *f*, cerco *m*

fencer [ˈfɛn*t*sər] *n* : esgrimista *mf*; esgrimidor *m*, -dora *f*

fencing [ˈfɛn*t*sɪŋ] *n* **1** : esgrima *m* (deporte) **2** : materiales *mpl* para cercas **3** ENCLOSURE : cercado *m*

fend [ˈfɛnd] *vt* **to fend off** : rechazar (un enemigo), parar (un golpe), eludir (una pregunta) — *vi* **to fend for oneself** : arreglárselas sólo, valerse por sí mismo

fender [ˈfɛndər] *n* : guardabarros *mpl,* salpicadera *f Mex*
fennel [ˈfɛnəl] *n* : hinojo *m*
ferment1 [fərˈmɛnt] *v* : fermentar
ferment2 [ˈfər,mɛnt] *n* **1** : fermento *m* (en la química) **2** TURMOIL : agitación *f,* conmoción *f*
fermentation [ˌfərmənˈteɪʃən, -ˌmɛn-] *n* : fermentación *f*
fern [ˈfərn] *n* : helecho *m*
ferocious [fəˈroːʃəs] *adj* : feroz — **ferociously** *adv*
ferociousness [fəˈroːʃəsnəs] *n* : ferocidad *f*
ferocity [fəˈrɑsət̬i] *n* : ferocidad *f*
ferret1 [ˈfɛrət] *vi* SNOOP : hurgar, husmear — *vt* **to ferret out** : descubrir
ferret2 *n* : hurón *m*
ferric [ˈfɛrɪk] *or* **ferrous** [ˈfɛrəs] *adj* : férrico
Ferris wheel [ˈfɛrɪs] *n* : noria *f*
ferry1 [ˈfɛri] *vt* **-ried; -rying** : llevar, transportar
ferry2 *n, pl* **-ries** : transbordador *m,* ferry *m*
ferryboat [ˈfɛriˌboːt] *n* : transbordador *m,* ferry *m*
fertile [ˈfərt̬əl] *adj* : fértil, fecundo
fertility [fərˈtɪlət̬i] *n* : fertilidad *f*
fertilization [ˌfərt̬ələˈzeɪʃən] *n* : fertilización *f* (del suelo), fecundación (de un huevo)
fertilize [ˈfərt̬əlˌaɪz] *vt* **-ized; -izing 1** : fecundar (un huevo) **2** : fertilizar, abonar (el suelo)
fertilizer [ˈfərt̬əlˌaɪzər] *n* : fertilizante *m,* abono *m*
fervent [ˈfərvənt] *adj* : ferviente, fervoroso, ardiente — **fervently** *adv*
fervid [ˈfərvɪd] *adj* : ardiente, apasionado — **fervidly** *adv*
fervor [ˈfərvər] *n* : fervor *m,* ardor *m*
fester [ˈfɛstər] *vi* : enconarse, supurar
festival [ˈfɛstəvəl] *n* : fiesta *f,* festividad *f,* festival *m*
festive [ˈfɛstɪv] *adj* : festivo — **festively** *adv*
festivity [fɛsˈtɪvət̬i] *n, pl* **-ties** : festividad *f,* celebración *f*
festoon1 [fɛsˈtuːn] *vt* : adornar, engalanar
festoon2 *n* GARLAND : guirnalda *f*
fetal [ˈfiːt̬əl] *adj* : fetal
fetch [ˈfɛtʃ] *vt* **1** BRING : traer, recoger, ir a buscar **2** REALIZE : realizar, venderse por <the jewelry fetched $10,000 : las joyas se vendieron por $10,000>
fetching [ˈfɛtʃɪŋ] *adj* : atractivo, encantador
fête1 [ˈfeɪt, ˈfɛt] *vt* **fêted; fêting** : festejar, agasajar
fête2 *n* : fiesta *f*
fetid [ˈfɛt̬əd] *adj* : fétido
fetish [ˈfɛt̬ɪʃ] *n* : fetiche *m*
fetlock [ˈfɛtˌlɑk] *n* : espolón *m*
fetter [ˈfɛt̬ər] *vt* : encadenar, poner grillos a
fetters [ˈfɛt̬ərz] *npl* : grillos *mpl,* grilletes *mpl,* cadenas *fpl*
fettle [ˈfɛt̬əl] *n* **in fine fettle** : en buena forma, en plena forma
fetus [ˈfiːt̬əs] *n* : feto *m*
feud1 [ˈfjuːd] *vi* : pelear, contender
feud2 *n* : contienda *f,* enemistad *f* (heredada)
feudal [ˈfjuːdəl] *adj* : feudal
feudalism [ˈfjuːdəlˌɪzəm] *n* : feudalismo *m*
fever [ˈfiːvər] *n* : fiebre *f,* calentura *f*
feverish [ˈfiːvərɪʃ] *adj* **1** : afiebrado, con fiebre, febril **2** FRANTIC : febril, frenético
few1 [ˈfjuː] *adj* : pocos <with few exceptions : con pocas excepciones> <a few times : varias veces>
few2 *pron* **1** : pocos <few (of them) were ready : pocos estaban listos> **2 a few** : algunos, unos cuantos **3 few and far between** : contados
fewer [ˈfjuːər] *pron* : menos <the fewer the better : cuantos menos mejor>
fez [ˈfɛz] *n, pl* **fezzes** : fez *m*
fiancé [ˌfiːˌɑnˈseɪ, ˌfiːˈɑnˌseɪ] *n* : prometido *m,* novio *m*
fiancée [ˌfiːˌɑnˈseɪ, ˌfiːˈɑnˌseɪ] *n* : prometida *f,* novia *f*
fiasco [fiˈæsˌkoː] *n, pl* **-coes** : fiasco *m,* fracaso *m*
fiat [ˈfiːˌɑt, -ˌæt, -ət; ˈfaɪət, -ˌæt] *n* : decreto *m,* orden *m*
fib1 [ˈfɪb] *vi* **fibbed; fibbing** : decir mentirillas
fib2 *n* : mentirilla *f,* bola *f fam*
fibber [ˈfɪbər] *n* : mentirosillo *m,* -lla *f;* cuentista *mf fam*
fiber *or* **fibre** [ˈfaɪbər] *n* : fibra *f*
fiberboard [ˈfaɪbərˌbord] *n* : cartón *m* madera
fiberglass [ˈfaɪbərˌglæs] *n* : fibra *f* de vidrio
fibrillate [ˈfɪbrəˌleɪt, ˈfaɪ-] *vi* **-lated; -lating** : fibrilar
fibrillation [ˌfɪbrəˈleɪʃən, ˌfaɪ-] *n* : fibrilación *f*
fibrous [ˈfaɪbrəs] *adj* : fibroso
fibula [ˈfɪbjələ] *n, pl* **-lae** [-ˌliː, -ˌlaɪ] *or* **-las** : peroné *m*
fickle [ˈfɪkəl] *adj* : inconstante, voluble, veleidoso
fickleness [ˈfɪkəlnəs] *n* : volubilidad *f,* inconstancia *f,* veleidad *f*
fiction [ˈfɪkʃən] *n* : ficción *f*
fictional [ˈfɪkʃənəl] *adj* : ficticio
fictitious [fɪkˈtɪʃəs] *adj* **1** IMAGINARY : ficticio, imaginario **2** FALSE : falso, ficticio
fiddle1 [ˈfɪdəl] *vi* **-dled; -dling 1** : tocar el violín **2 to fiddle with** : juguetear con, toquetear
fiddle2 *n* : violín *m*
fiddler [ˈfɪdlər, ˈfɪdələr] *n* : violinista *mf*
fiddlesticks [ˈfɪdəlˌstɪks] *interj* : ¡tonterías!
fidelity [fəˈdɛlət̬i, faɪ-] *n, pl* **-ties** : fidelidad *f*

fidget[1] [ˈfɪdʒət] *vi* **1 :** moverse, estarse inquieto **2 to fidget with :** juguetear con

fidget[2] *n* **1 :** persona *f* inquieta **2 fidgets** *npl* RESTLESSNESS **:** inquietud *f*

fidgety [ˈfɪdʒəti] *adj* **:** inquieto

fiduciary[1] [fəˈduːʃiˌɛri, -ˈdjuː-, -ʃəri] *adj* **:** fiduciario

fiduciary[2] *n, pl* **-ries :** fiduciario *m,* -ria *f*

field[1] [ˈfiːld] *vt* **:** interceptar y devolver (una pelota), presentar (un candidato), sortear (una pregunta)

field[2] *adj* **:** de campaña, de campo <field hospital : hospital de campaña> <field goal : gol de campo> <field trip : viaje de estudio>

field[3] *n* **1 :** campo *m* (de cosechas, de batalla, de magnetismo) **2 :** campo *m,* cancha *f* (en deportes) **3 :** campo *m* (de trabajo), esfera *f* (de actividades)

fielder [ˈfiːldər] *n* **:** jugador *m,* -dora *f* de campo; fildeador *m,* -dora *f*

field glasses *n* **:** binoculares *mpl,* gemelos *mpl*

fiend [ˈfiːnd] *n* **1** DEMON **:** demonio *m* **2** EVILDOER **:** persona *f* maligna; malvado *m,* -da *f* **3** FANATIC **:** fanático *m,* -ca *f*

fiendish [ˈfiːndɪʃ] *adj* **:** diabólico — **fiendishly** *adv*

fierce [ˈfɪrs] *adj* **fiercer; -est 1** FEROCIOUS **:** fiero, feroz **2** HEATED **:** acalorado **3** INTENSE **:** intenso, violento, fuerte — **fiercely** *adv*

fierceness [ˈfɪrsnəs] *n* **1** FEROCITY **:** ferocidad *f,* fiereza *f* **2** INTENSITY **:** intensidad *f,* violencia *f*

fieriness [ˈfaɪərinəs] *n* **:** pasión *f,* ardor *m*

fiery [ˈfaɪəri] *adj* **fierier; -est 1** BURNING **:** ardiente, llameante **2** GLOWING **:** encendido **3** PASSIONATE **:** acalorado, ardiente, fogoso

fiesta [fiˈɛstə] *n* **:** fiesta *f*

fife [ˈfaɪf] *n* **:** pífano *m*

fifteen[1] [fɪfˈtiːn] *adj* **:** quince

fifteen[2] *n* **:** quince *m*

fifteenth[1] [fɪfˈtiːnθ] *adj* **:** decimoquinto

fifteenth[2] *n* **1 :** decimoquinto *m,* -ta *f* (en una serie) **2 :** quinceavo *m,* quinceava parte *f*

fifth[1] [ˈfɪfθ] *adj* **:** quinto

fifth[2] *n* **1 :** quinto *m,* -ta *f* (en una serie) **2 :** quinto *m,* quinta parte *f* **3 :** quinta *f* (en la música)

fiftieth[1] [ˈfɪftiəθ] *adj* **:** quincuagésimo

fiftieth[2] *n* **1 :** quincuagésimo *m,* -ma *f* (en una serie) **2 :** cincuentavo *m,* cincuentava parte *f*

fifty[1] [ˈfɪfti] *adj* **:** cincuenta

fifty[2] *n, pl* **-ties :** cincuenta *m*

fifty–fifty[1] [ˌfɪftiˈfɪfti] *adv* **:** a medias, mitad y mitad

fifty–fifty[2] *adj* **to have a fifty–fifty chance :** tener un cincuenta por ciento de posibilidades

fig [ˈfɪg] *n* **:** higo *m*

fight[1] [ˈfaɪt] *v* **fought** [ˈfɔt]; **fighting** *vi* **:** luchar, combatir, pelear — *vt* **:** luchar contra, combatir contra

fight[2] *n* **1** COMBAT **:** lucha *f,* pelea *f,* combate *m* **2** MATCH **:** pelea *f,* combate *m* (en boxeo) **3** QUARREL **:** disputa *f,* pelea *f,* pleito *m*

fighter [ˈfaɪtər] *n* **1** COMBATANT **:** luchador *m,* -dora *f;* combatiente *mf* **2** BOXER **:** boxeador *m,* -dora *f*

figment [ˈfɪgmənt] *n* **figment of the imagination :** producto *m* de la imaginación

figurative [ˈfɪgjərətɪv, -gə-] *adj* **:** figurado, metafórico

figuratively [ˈfɪgjərətɪvli, -gə-] *adv* **:** en sentido figurado, de manera metafórica

figure[1] [ˈfɪgjər, -gər] *v* **-ured; -uring** *vt* **1** CALCULATE **:** calcular **2** ESTIMATE **:** figurarse, calcular <he figured it was possible : se figuró que era posible> — *vi* **1** FEATURE, STAND OUT **:** figurar, destacar **2 that figures! :** ¡obvio!, ¡no me extraña nada!

figure[2] *n* **1** DIGIT **:** número *m,* cifra *f* **2** PRICE **:** precio *m,* cifra *f* **3** PERSONAGE **:** figura *f,* personaje *m* **4 :** figura *f,* tipo *m,* físico *m* <to have a good figure : tener buen tipo, tener un buen físico> **5** DESIGN, OUTLINE **:** figura *f* **6 figures** *npl* **:** aritmética *f*

figurehead [ˈfɪgjərˌhɛd, -gər-] *n* **:** testaferro *m,* líder *mf* sin poder

figure of speech *n* **:** figura *f* retórica, figura *f* de hablar

figure out *vt* **1** UNDERSTAND **:** entender **2** RESOLVE **:** resolver (un problema, etc.)

figurine [ˌfɪgjəˈriːn] *n* **:** estatuilla *f*

Fijian [ˈfiːdʒiən, fɪˈjiːən] *n* **:** fijiano *m,* -na *f* — **Fijian** *adj*

filament [ˈfɪləmənt] *n* **:** filamento *m*

filbert [ˈfɪlbərt] *n* **:** avellana *f*

filch [ˈfɪltʃ] *vt* **:** hurtar, birlar *fam*

file[1] [ˈfaɪl] *v* **filed; filing** *vt* **1** CLASSIFY **:** clasificar **2 :** archivar (documentos) **3** SUBMIT **:** presentar <to file charges : presentar cargos> **4** SMOOTH **:** limar — *vi* **:** desfilar, entrar (o salir) en fila

file[2] *n* **1 :** lima *f* <nail file : lima de uñas> **2** DOCUMENTS **:** archivo *m* **3** LINE **:** fila *f*

filial [ˈfɪliəl, ˈfɪljəl] *adj* **:** filial

filibuster[1] [ˈfɪləˌbʌstər] *vi* **:** practicar el obstruccionismo

filibuster[2] *n* **:** obstruccionismo *m*

filibusterer [ˈfɪləˌbʌstərər] *n* **:** obstruccionista *mf*

filigree [ˈfɪləˌgriː] *n* **:** filigrana *f*

Filipino [ˌfɪləˈpiːnoː] *n* **:** filipino *m,* -na *f* — **Filipino** *adj*

fill[1] [ˈfɪl] *vt* **1 :** llenar, ocupar <to fill a cup : llenar una taza> <to fill a room : ocupar una sala> **2** STUFF **:** rellenar **3** PLUG **:** tapar, rellenar, empastar (un diente) **4** SATISFY **:** cumplir con, satisfacer **5** *or* **to fill out :** llenar, rellenar <to fill out a form : rellenar un formulario>

fill[2] *n* **1** FILLING, STUFFING : relleno *m* **2 to eat one's fill :** comer lo suficiente **3 to have one's fill of :** estar harto de

filler [ˈfɪlər] *n* : relleno *m*

fillet[1] [ˈfɪlət, fɪˈleɪ, ˈfɪˌleɪ] *vt* : cortar en filetes

fillet[2] *n* : filete *m*

fill in *vt* INFORM : informar, poner al corriente — *vi* **to fill in for** : reemplazar a

filling [ˈfɪlɪŋ] *n* **1** : relleno *m* **2** : empaste *m* (de un diente)

filling station → service station

filly [ˈfɪli] *n, pl* **-lies** : potra *f,* potranca *f*

film[1] [ˈfɪlm] *vt* : filmar — *vi* : rodar

film[2] *n* **1** COATING : capa *f,* película *f* **2** : película *f* (fotográfica) **3** MOVIE : película *f,* filme *m*

filmy [ˈfɪlmi] *adj* **filmier; -est 1** GAUZY : diáfano, vaporoso **2** : cubierto de una película

filter[1] [ˈfɪltər] *vt* : filtrar

filter[2] *n* : filtro *m*

filth [ˈfɪlθ] *n* : mugre *f,* porquería *f,* roña *f*

filthiness [ˈfɪlθinəs] *n* : suciedad *f*

filthy [ˈfɪlθi] *adj* **filthier; -est 1** DIRTY : mugriento, sucio **2** OBSCENE : obsceno, indecente

filtration [fɪlˈtreɪʃən] *n* : filtración *f*

fin [ˈfɪn] *n* **1** : aleta *f* **2** : alerón *m* (de un automóvil o un avión)

finagle [fəˈneɪgəl] *vt* **-gled; -gling** : arreglárselas para conseguir

final[1] [ˈfaɪnəl] *adj* **1** DEFINITIVE : definitivo, final, inapelable **2** ULTIMATE : final **3** LAST : último, final

final[2] *n* **1** : final *f* (en deportes) **2 finals** *npl* : exámenes *mpl* finales

finale [fɪˈnæli, -ˈnɑ-] *n* : final *m* <grand finale : final triunfal>

finalist [ˈfaɪnəlɪst] *n* : finalista *mf*

finality [faɪˈnæləṭi, fə-] *n, pl* **-ties** : finalidad *f*

finalize [ˈfaɪnəlˌaɪz] *vt* **-ized; -izing** : finalizar

finally [ˈfaɪnəli] *adv* **1** LASTLY : por último, finalmente **2** EVENTUALLY : por fin, al final **3** DEFINITIVELY : definitivamente

finance[1] [fəˈnænts, ˈfaɪˌnænts] *vt* **-nanced; -nancing** : financiar

finance[2] *n* **1** : finanzas *fpl* **2 finances** *npl* RESOURCES : recursos *mpl* financieros

financial [fəˈnæntʃəl, faɪ-] *adj* : financiero, económico

financially [fəˈnæntʃəli, faɪ-] *adv* : económicamente

financier [ˌfɪnənˈsɪr, ˌfaɪˌnæn-] *n* : financiero *m,* -ra *f;* financista *mf*

finch [ˈfɪntʃ] *n* : pinzón *m*

find[1] [ˈfaɪnd] *vt* **found** [ˈfaʊnd]; **finding 1** LOCATE : encontrar, hallar <I can't find it : no lo encuentro> <to find one's way : encontrar el camino, orientarse> **2** DISCOVER, REALIZE : descubrir, darse cuenta de <he found it difficult : descubrió que era difícil> **3** DECLARE : declarar, hallar <they found him guilty : lo declararon culpable>

find[2] *n* : hallazgo *m*

finder [ˈfaɪndər] *n* : descubridor *m,* -dora *f*

finding [ˈfaɪndɪŋ] *n* **1** FIND : hallazgo *m* **2 findings** *npl* : conclusiones *fpl*

find out *vt* DISCOVER : descubrir, averiguar — *vi* LEARN : enterarse

fine[1] [ˈfaɪn] *vt* **fined; fining** : multar

fine[2] *adj* **finer; -est 1** PURE : puro (dícese del oro y de la plata) **2** THIN : fino, delgado **3** : fino <fine sand : arena fina> **4** SMALL : pequeño, minúsculo <fine print : letras minúsculas> **5** SUBTLE : sutil, delicado **6** EXCELLENT : excelente, magnífico, selecto **7** FAIR : bueno <it's a fine day : hace buen tiempo> **8** EXQUISITE : exquisito, delicado, fino **9 fine arts** : bellas artes *fpl*

fine[3] *n* : multa *f*

finely [ˈfaɪnli] *adv* **1** EXCELLENTLY : con arte **2** ELEGANTLY : elegantemente **3** PRECISELY : con precisión **4 to chop finely** : picar muy fino, picar en trozos pequeños

fineness [ˈfaɪnnəs] *n* **1** EXCELLENCE : excelencia *f* **2** ELEGANCE : elegancia *f,* refinamiento *m* **3** DELICACY : delicadeza *f,* lo fino **4** PRECISION : precisión *f* **5** SUBTLETY : sutileza *f* **6** PURITY : ley *f* (de oro y plata)

finery [ˈfaɪnəri] *n* : galas *fpl,* adornos *mpl*

finesse[1] [fəˈnɛs] *vt* **-nessed; -nessing** : ingeniar

finesse[2] *n* **1** REFINEMENT : refinamiento *m,* finura *f* **2** TACT : delicadeza *f,* tacto *m,* diplomacia *f* **3** CRAFTINESS : astucia *f*

finger[1] [ˈfɪŋgər] *vt* **1** HANDLE : tocar, toquetear **2** ACCUSE : acusar, delatar

finger[2] *n* : dedo *m*

fingerling [ˈfɪŋgərlɪŋ] *n* : pez *m* pequeño y joven

fingernail [ˈfɪŋgərˌneɪl] *n* : uña *f*

fingerprint[1] [ˈfɪŋgərˌprɪnt] *vt* : tomar las huellas digitales a

fingerprint[2] *n* : huella *f* digital

fingertip [ˈfɪŋgərˌtɪp] *n* : punta *f* del dedo, yema *f* del dedo

finicky [ˈfɪnɪki] *adj* : maniático, melindroso, mañoso

finish[1] [ˈfɪnɪʃ] *vt* **1** COMPLETE : acabar, terminar **2** : aplicar un acabado a (muebles, etc.)

finish[2] *n* **1** END : fin *m,* final *m* **2** REFINEMENT : refinamiento *m* **3** : acabado *m* <a glossy finish : un acabado brillante>

finite [ˈfaɪˌnaɪt] *adj* : finito

fink [ˈfɪŋk] *n* : mequetrefe *mf fam*

Finn [ˈfɪn] *n* : finlandés *m,* -desa *f*

Finnish[1] [ˈfɪnɪʃ] *adj* : finlandés

Finnish[2] *n* : finlandés *m* (idioma)

fiord [fiˈɔrd] → **fjord**

fir [ˈfər] *n* : abeto *m*
fire[1] [ˈfaɪr] *vt* **fired; firing 1** IGNITE, KINDLE : encender **2** ENLIVEN : animar, avivar **3** DISMISS : despedir **4** SHOOT : disparar **5** BAKE : cocer (cerámica)
fire[2] *n* **1** : fuego *m* **2** BURNING : incendio *m* <fire alarm : alarma contra incendios> <to be on fire : estar en llamas> **3** ENTHUSIASM : ardor *m,* entusiasmo *m* **4** SHOOTING : disparos *mpl,* fuego *m*
firearm [ˈfaɪrˌɑrm] *n* : arma *f* de fuego
fireball [ˈfaɪrˌbɔl] *n* **1** : bola *f* de fuego **2** METEOR : bólido *m*
firebreak [ˈfaɪrˌbreɪk] *n* : cortafuegos *m*
firebug [ˈfaɪrˌbʌg] *n* : pirómano *m,* -na *f;* incendiario *m,* -ria *f*
firecracker [ˈfaɪrˌkrækər] *n* : petardo *m*
fire escape *n* : escalera *f* de incendios
firefighter [ˈfaɪrˌfaɪt̬ər] *n* : bombero *m,* -ra *f*
firefly [ˈfaɪrˌflaɪ] *n, pl* **-flies** : luciérnaga *f*
fireman [ˈfaɪrmən] *n, pl* **-men** [-mən, -ˌmɛn] **1** FIREFIGHTER : bombero *m,* -ra *f* **2** STOKER : fogonero *m,* -ra *f*
fireplace [ˈfaɪrˌpleɪs] *n* : hogar *m,* chimenea *f*
fireproof[1] [ˈfaɪrˌpruːf] *vt* : hacer incombustible
fireproof[2] *adj* : incombustible, ignífugo
fireside[1] [ˈfaɪrˌsaɪd] *adj* : informal <fireside chat : charla informal>
fireside[2] *n* **1** HEARTH : chimenea *f,* hogar *m* **2** HOME : hogar *m,* casa *f*
firewood [ˈfaɪrˌwʊd] *n* : leña *f*
fireworks [ˈfaɪrˌwərks] *npl* : fuegos *mpl* artificiales, pirotecnia *f*
firm[1] [ˈfərm] *vi* : endurecer
firm[2] *adj* **1** VIGOROUS : fuerte, vigoroso **2** SOLID, UNYIELDING : firme, duro, sólido **3** UNCHANGING : firme, inalterable **4** RESOLUTE : firme, resuelto
firm[3] *n* : empresa *f,* firma *f,* compañía *f*
firmament [ˈfərməmənt] *n* : firmamento *m*
firmly [ˈfərmli] *adv* : firmemente
firmness [ˈfərmnəs] *n* : firmeza *f*
first[1] [ˈfərst] *adv* **1** : primero <finish your homework first : primero termina tu tarea> <first and foremost : ante todo> <first of all : en primer lugar> **2** : por primera vez <I saw it first in Boston : lo vi por primera vez en Boston>
first[2] *adj* **1** : primero <the first time : la primera vez> <at first sight : a primera vista> <in the first place : en primer lugar> <the first ten applicants : los diez primeros candidatos> **2** FOREMOST : principal, primero <first tenor : tenor principal>
first[3] *n* **1** : primero *m,* -ra *f* (en una serie) **2** : primero *m,* primera parte *f* **3** *or* **first gear** : primera *f* **4 at ~** : al principio
first aid *n* : primeros auxilios *mpl*
first–class[1] [ˈfərstˈklæs] *adv* : en primera <to travel first-class : viajar en primera>
first–class[2] *adj* : de primera
first class *n* : primera clase *f*
firsthand[1] [ˈfərstˈhænd] *adv* : directamente
firsthand[2] *adj* : de primera mano
first lieutenant *n* : teniente *mf;* teniente primero *m,* teniente primera *f*
firstly [ˈfərstli] *adv* : primeramente, principalmente, en primer lugar
first–rate[1] [ˈfərstˈreɪt] *adv* : muy bien
first–rate[2] *adj* : de primera, de primera clase
first sergeant *n* : sargento *mf*
firth [ˈfərθ] *n* : estuario *m*
fiscal [ˈfɪskəl] *adj* : fiscal — **fiscally** *adv*
fish[1] [ˈfɪʃ] *vi* **1** : pescar **2 to fish for** SEEK : buscar, rebuscar <to fish for compliments : andar a la caza de cumplidos> — *vt* : pescar
fish[2] *n, pl* **fish** *or* **fishes** : pez *m* (vivo), pescado *m* (para comer)
fisherman [ˈfɪʃərmən] *n, pl* **-men** [-mən, -ˌmɛn] : pescador *m,* -dora *f*
fishery [ˈfɪʃəri] *n, pl* **-eries 1** → **fishing 2** : zona *f* pesquera, pesquería *f*
fishhook [ˈfɪʃˌhʊk] *n* : anzuelo *m*
fishing [ˈfɪʃɪŋ] *n* : pesca *f,* industria *f* pesquera
fishing pole *n* : caña *f* de pescar
fish market *n* : pescadería *f*
fishy [ˈfɪʃi] *adj* **fishier; -est 1** : a pescado <a fishy taste : un sabor a pescado> **2** QUESTIONABLE : dudoso, sospechoso <there's something fishy going on : aquí hay gato encerrado>
fission [ˈfɪʃən, -ʒən] *n* : fisión *f*
fissure [ˈfɪʃər] *n* : fisura *f,* hendidura *f*
fist [ˈfɪst] *n* : puño *m*
fistful [ˈfɪstˌfʊl] *n* : puñado *m*
fisticuffs [ˈfɪstɪˌkʌfs] *npl* : lucha *f* a puñetazos
fit[1] [ˈfɪt] *v* **fitted; fitting** *vt* **1** MATCH : corresponder a, coincidir con <the punishment fits the crime : el castigo corresponde al crimen> **2** : quedar <the dress doesn't fit me : el vestido no me queda> **3** GO : caber, encajar en <her key fits the lock : su llave encaja en la cerradura> **4** INSERT, INSTALL : poner, colocar **5** ADAPT : adecuar, ajustar, adaptar **6** *or* **to fit out** EQUIP : equipar — *vi* **1** : quedar, entallar <these pants don't fit : estos pantalones no me quedan> **2** CONFORM : encajar, cuadrar **3 to fit in** : encajar, estar integrado
fit[2] *adj* **fitter; fittest 1** SUITABLE : adecuado, apropiado, conveniente **2** QUALIFIED : calificado, competente **3** HEALTHY : sano, en forma
fit[3] *n* **1** ATTACK : ataque *m,* acceso *m,* arranque *m* **2 to be a good fit** : quedar bien **3 to be a tight fit** : ser muy

entallado (de ropa), estar apretado (de espacios)
fitful ['fɪtfəl] *adj* : irregular, intermitente — **fitfully** *adv*
fitness ['fɪtnəs] *n* **1** HEALTH : salud *f,* buena forma *f* (física) **2** SUITABILITY : idoneidad *f*
fitting[1] ['fɪtɪŋ] *adj* : adecuado, apropiado
fitting[2] *n* : accesorio *m*
five[1] ['faɪv] *adj* : cinco
five[2] *n* : cinco *m*
five hundred[1] *adj* : quinientos
five hundred[2] *n* : quinientos *m*
fix[1] ['fɪks] *vt* **1** ATTACH, SECURE : sujetar, asegurar, fijar **2** ESTABLISH : fijar, concretar, establecer **3** REPAIR : arreglar, reparar **4** PREPARE : preparar <to fix dinner : preparar la cena> **5** : arreglar, amañar <to fix a race : arreglar una carrera> **6** RIVET : fijar (los ojos, la mirada, etc.)
fix[2] *n* **1** PREDICAMENT : aprieto *m,* apuro *m* **2** : posición *f* <to get a fix on : establecer la posición de>
fixate ['fɪk,seɪt] *vi* **-ated; -ating** : obsesionarse
fixation [fɪk'seɪʃən] *n* : fijación *f,* obsesión *f*
fixed ['fɪkst] *adj* **1** STATIONARY : estacionario, inmóvil **2** UNCHANGING : fijo, inalterable **3** INTENT : fijo <a fixed stare : una mirada fija> **4 to be comfortably fixed** : estar en posición acomodada
fixedly ['fɪksədli] *adv* : fijamente
fixedness ['fɪksədnəs, 'fikst-] *n* : rigidez *f*
fixture ['fɪkstʃər] *n* **1** : parte *f* integrante, elemento *m* fijo **2 fixtures** *npl* : instalaciones *fpl* (de una casa)
fizz[1] ['fɪz] *vi* : burbujear
fizz[2] *n* : efervescencia *f,* burbujeo *m*
fizzle[1] ['fɪzəl] *vi* **-zled; -zling 1** FIZZ : burbujear **2** FAIL : fracasar
fizzle[2] *n* : fracaso *m,* fiasco *m*
fjord [fi'ɔrd] *n* : fiordo *m*
flab ['flæb] *n* : gordura *f*
flabbergast ['flæbər,gæst] *vt* : asombrar, pasmar, dejar atónito
flabby ['flæbi] *adj* **-bier; -est** : blando, fofo, aguado *CA, Col, Mex*
flaccid ['flæksəd, 'flæsəd] *adj* : fláccido
flag[1] ['flæg] *vi* **flagged; flagging 1** : hacer señales con banderas **2** WEAKEN : flaquear, desfallecer
flag[2] *n* : bandera *f,* pabellón *m,* estandarte *m*
flagon ['flægən] *n* : jarra *f* grande
flagpole ['flæg,po:l] *n* : asta *f,* mástil *m*
flagrant ['fleɪgrənt] *adj* : flagrante — **flagrantly** *adv*
flagship ['flæg,ʃɪp] *n* : buque *m* insignia
flagstaff ['flæg,stæf] → **flagpole**
flagstone ['flæg,sto:n] *n* : losa *f,* piedra *f*
flail[1] ['fleɪl] *vt* **1** : trillar (grano) **2** : sacudir, agitar (los brazos)
flail[2] *n* : mayal *m*
flair ['flær] *n* : don *m,* facilidad *f*
flak ['flæk] *ns & pl* **flak 1** : fuego *m* antiaéreo **2** CRITICISM : críticas *fpl*
flake[1] ['fleɪk] *vi* **flaked; flaking** : desmenuzarse, pelarse (dícese de la piel)
flake[2] *n* : copo *m* (de nieve), escama *f* (de la piel), astilla *f* (de madera)
flamboyance [flæm'bɔɪənts] *n* : extravagancia *f,* rimbombancia *f*
flamboyant [flæm'bɔɪənt] *adj* : exuberante, extravagante, rimbombante
flame[1] ['fleɪm] *vi* **flamed; flaming 1** BLAZE : arder, llamear **2** GLOW : brillar, encenderse
flame[2] *n* BLAZE : llama *f* <to burst into flames : estallar en llamas> <to go up in flame : incendiarse>
flamethrower ['fleɪm,θro:ər] *n* : lanzallamas *m*
flamingo [flə'mɪŋgo] *n, pl* **-gos** : flamenco *m*
flammable ['flæməbəl] *adj* : inflamable, flamable
flange ['flændʒ] *n* : reborde *m,* pestaña *f*
flank[1] ['flæŋk] *vt* **1** : flanquear (para defender o atacar) **2** BORDER, LINE : bordear
flank[2] *n* : ijada *f* (de un animal), costado *m* (de una persona), falda *f* (de una colina), flanco *m* (de un cuerpo de soldados)
flannel ['flænəl] *n* : franela *f*
flap[1] ['flæp] *v* **flapped; flapping** *vi* **1** : aletear <the bird was flapping (its wings) : el pájaro aleteaba> **2** FLUTTER : ondear, agitarse — *vt* : batir, agitar
flap[2] *n* **1** FLAPPING : aleteo *m,* aletazo *m* (de alas) **2** : soplada *f* (de un sobre), hoja *f* (de una mesa), faldón *m* (de una chaqueta)
flapjack ['flæp,dʒæk] → **pancake**
flare[1] ['flær] *vi* **flared; flaring 1** FLAME, SHINE : llamear, brillar **2 to flare up** : estallar, explotar (de cólera)
flare[2] *n* **1** FLASH : destello *m* **2** SIGNAL : (luz *f* de) bengala *f* **3 solar flare** : erupción *f* solar
flash[1] ['flæʃ] *vi* **1** SHINE, SPARKLE : destellar, brillar, relampaguear **2** : pasar como un relámpago <an idea flashed through my mind : una idea me cruzó la mente como un relámpago> — *vt* : despedir, lanzar (una luz), transmitir (un mensaje)
flash[2] *adj* SUDDEN : repentino
flash[3] *n* **1** : destello *m* (de luz), fogonazo *m* (de una explosión) **2 flash of lightning** : relámpago *m* **3 in a flash** : de repente, de un abrir y cerrar los ojos
flashiness ['flæʃinəs] *n* : ostentación *f*
flashlight ['flæʃ,laɪt] *n* : linterna *f*
flashy ['flæʃi] *adj* **flashier; -est** : llamativo, ostentoso
flask ['flæsk] *n* : frasco *m*

flat[1] [ˈflæt] *vt* **flatted; flatting 1** FLATTEN : aplanar, achatar **2** : bajar de tono (en música)
flat[2] *adv* **1** EXACTLY : exactamente <in ten minutes flat : en diez minutos exactos> **2** : desafinado, demasiado bajo (en la música)
flat[3] *adj* **flatter; flattest 1** EVEN, LEVEL : plano, llano **2** SMOOTH : liso **3** DEFINITE : categórico, rotundo, explícito <a flat refusal : una negativa categórica> **4** DULL : aburrido, soso, monótono (dícese la voz) **5** DEFLATED : desinflado, pinchado, ponchado *Mex* **6** : bemol (en música) <to sing flat : cantar desafinado>
flat[4] *n* **1** PLAIN : llano *m,* terreno *m* llano **2** : bemol *m* (en la música) **3** APARTMENT : apartamento *m,* departamento *m* **4** *or* **flat tire** : pinchazo *m,* ponchadura *f Mex*
flatbed [ˈflæt,bɛd] *n* : camión *m* de plataforma
flatcar [ˈflæt,kɑr] *n* : vagón *m* abierto
flatfish [ˈflæt,fɪʃ] *n* : platija *f*
flat–footed [ˈflæt,fʊt̬əd, ,flætˈ-] *adj* : de pies planos
flatly [ˈflætli] *adv* DEFINITELY : categóricamente, rotundamente
flatness [ˈflætnəs] *n* **1** EVENNESS : lo llano, lisura *f,* uniformidad *f* **2** DULLNESS : monotonía *f*
flat–out [ˈflætˈaʊt] *adj* **1** : frenético, a toda máquina <a flat-out effort : un esfuerzo frenético> **2** CATEGORICAL : descarado, rotundo, categórico
flatten [ˈflætən] *vt* : aplanar, achatar
flatter [ˈflæt̬ər] *vt* **1** OVERPRAISE : adular **2** COMPLIMENT : halagar **3** : favorecer <the photo flatters you : la foto te favorece>
flatterer [ˈflæt̬ərər] *n* : adulador *m,* -dora *f*
flattering [ˈflæt̬ərɪŋ] *adj* **1** COMPLIMENTARY : halagador **2** BECOMING : favorecedor
flattery [ˈflæt̬əri] *n, pl* **-ries** : halagos *mpl*
flatulence [ˈflætʃələnts] *n* : flatulencia *f,* ventosidad *f*
flatulent [ˈflætʃələnt] *adj* : flatulento
flatware [ˈflæt,wær] *n* : cubertería *f,* cubiertos *mpl*
flaunt[1] [ˈflɔnt] *vt* : alardear, hacer alarde de
flaunt[2] *n* : alarde *m,* ostentación *f*
flavor[1] [ˈfleɪvər] *vt* : dar sabor a, sazonar
flavor[2] *n* **1** : gusto *m,* sabor *m* **2** FLAVORING : sazón *f,* condimento *m*
flavorful [ˈfleɪvərfəl] *adj* : sabroso
flavoring [ˈfleɪvərɪŋ] *n* : condimento *m,* sazón *f*
flavorless [ˈfleɪvərləs] *adj* : sin sabor
flaw [ˈflɔ] *n* : falla *f,* defecto *m,* imperfección *f*
flawless [ˈflɔləs] *adj* : impecable, perfecto — **flawlessly** *adv*
flax [ˈflæks] *n* : lino *m*
flaxen [ˈflæksən] *adj* : rubio, blondo (dícese del pelo)
flay [ˈfleɪ] *vt* **1** SKIN : desollar, despellejar **2** VILIFY : criticar con dureza, vilipendiar
flea [ˈfliː] *n* : pulga *f*
fleck[1] [ˈflɛk] *vt* : salpicar
fleck[2] *n* : mota *f,* pinta *f*
fledgling [ˈflɛdʒlɪŋ] *n* : polluelo *m,* pollito *m*
flee [ˈfliː] *v* **fled** [ˈflɛd]; **fleeing** *vi* : huir, escapar(se) — *vt* : huir de
fleece[1] [ˈfliːs] *vt* **fleeced; fleecing 1** SHEAR : esquilar, trasquilar **2** SWINDLE : estafar, defraudar
fleece[2] *n* : lana *f,* vellón *m*
fleet[1] [ˈfliːt] *vi* : moverse con rapidez
fleet[2] *adj* SWIFT : rápido, veloz
fleet[3] *n* : flota *f*
fleet admiral *n* : almirante *mf*
fleeting [ˈfliːtɪŋ] *adj* : fugaz, breve
flesh [ˈflɛʃ] *n* **1** : carne *f* (de seres humanos y animales) **2** : pulpa *f* (de frutas)
flesh out *vt* : desarrollar, darle cuerpo a
fleshy [ˈflɛʃi] *adj* **fleshier; -est** : gordo (dícese de las personas), carnoso (dícese de la fruta)
flew → **fly**
flex [ˈflɛks] *vt* : doblar, flexionar
flexibility [,flɛksəˈbɪlət̬i] *n, pl* **-ties** : flexibilidad *f,* elasticidad *f*
flexible [ˈflɛksəbəl] *adj* : flexible — **flexibly** [-bli] *adv*
flick[1] [ˈflɪk] *vt* : dar un capirotazo a (con el dedo) <to flick a switch : darle al interruptor> — *vi* **1** FLIT : revolotear **2 to flick through** : hojear (un libro)
flick[2] *n* : coletazo *m* (de una cola), capirotazo *m* (de un dedo)
flicker[1] [ˈflɪkər] *vi* **1** FLUTTER : revolotear, aletear **2** BLINK, TWINKLE : parpadear, titilar
flicker[2] *n* **1** : parpadeo *m,* titileo *m* **2** HINT, TRACE : indicio *m,* rastro *m* <a flicker of hope : un rayo de esperanza>
flier [ˈflaɪər] *n* **1** AVIATOR : aviador *m,* -dora *f* **2** CIRCULAR : folleto *m* publicitario, circular *f*
flight [ˈflaɪt] *n* **1** : vuelo *m* (de aves o aviones), trayectoria *f* (de proyectiles) **2** TRIP : vuelo *m* **3** FLOCK, SQUADRON : bandada *f* (de pájaros), escuadrilla *f* (de aviones) **4** ESCAPE : huida *f,* fuga *f* **5 flight of fancy** : ilusiones *fpl,* fantasía *f* **6 flight of stairs** : tramo *m*
flightless [ˈflaɪtləs] *adj* : no volador
flighty [ˈflaɪt̬i] *adj* **flightier; -est** : caprichoso, frívolo
flimsy [flɪmzi] *adj* **flimsier; -est 1** LIGHT, THIN : ligero, fino **2** WEAK : endeble, poco sólido **3** IMPLAUSIBLE : pobre, flojo, poco convincente <a flimsy excuse : una excusa floja>
flinch [ˈflɪntʃ] *vi* **1** WINCE : estremecerse **2** RECOIL : recular, retroceder

fling[1] [ˈflɪŋ] *vt* **flung** [ˈflʌŋ]; **flinging 1** THROW : lanzar, tirar, arrojar **2 to fling oneself** : lanzarse, tirarse, precipitarse

fling[2] *n* **1** THROW : lanzamiento *m* **2** ATTEMPT : intento *m* **3** AFFAIR : aventura *f* **4** BINGE : juerga *f*

flint [ˈflɪnt] *n* : pedernal *m*

flinty [ˈflɪnti] *adj* **flintier; -est 1** : de pedernal **2** STERN, UNYIELDING : severo, inflexible

flip[1] [ˈflɪp] *v* **flipped; flipping** *vt* **1** TOSS : tirar <to flip a coin : echar a cara o cruz> **2** OVERTURN : dar la vuelta a, voltear — *vi* **1** : moverse bruscamente **2 to flip through** : hojear (un libro)

flip[2] *adj* : insolente, descarado

flip[3] *n* **1** FLICK : capirotazo *m,* golpe *m* ligero **2** SOMERSAULT : voltereta *f*

flippancy [ˈflɪpəntsi] *n, pl* **-cies** : ligereza *f,* falta *f* de seriedad

flippant [ˈflɪpənt] *adj* : ligero, frívolo, poco serio

flipper [ˈflɪpər] *n* : aleta *f*

flirt[1] [ˈflərt] *vi* **1** : coquetear, flirtear **2** TRIFLE : jugar <to flirt with death : jugar con la muerte>

flirt[2] *n* : coqueto *m,* -ta *f*

flirtation [ˌflərˈteɪʃən] *n* : devaneo *m,* coqueteo *m*

flirtatious [ˌflərˈteɪʃəs] *adj* : insinuante, coqueto

flit [ˈflɪt] *vi* **flitted; flitting 1** : revolotear **2 to flit about** : ir y venir rápidamente

float[1] [ˈfloːt] *vi* **1** : flotar **2** WANDER : vagar, errar — *vt* **1** : poner a flote, hacer flotar (un barco) **2** LAUNCH : hacer flotar (una empresa) **3** ISSUE : emitir (acciones en la bolsa)

float[2] *n* **1** : flotador *m,* corcho *m* (para pescar) **2** BUOY : boya *f* **3** : carroza *f* (en un desfile)

flock[1] [ˈflɑk] *vi* **1** : moverse en rebaño **2** CONGREGATE : congregarse, reunirse

flock[2] *n* : rebaño *m* (de ovejas), bandada *f* (de pájaros)

floe [ˈfloː] *n* : témpano *m* de hielo

flog [ˈflɑg] *vt* **flogged; flogging** : azotar, fustigar

flood[1] [ˈflʌd] *vt* : inundar, anegar

flood[2] *n* **1** INUNDATION : inundación *f* **2** TORRENT : avalancha *f,* diluvio *m,* torrente *m* <a flood of tears : un mar de lágrimas>

floodlight [ˈflʌdˌlaɪt] *n* : foco *m*

floodwater [ˈflʌdˌwɔţər] *n* : crecida *f,* creciente *f*

floor[1] [ˈflor] *vt* **1** : solar, poner suelo a (una casa o una sala) **2** KNOCK DOWN : derribar, echar al suelo **3** NONPLUS : desconcertar, confundir, dejar perplejo

floor[2] *n* **1** : suelo *m,* piso *m* <dance floor : pista de baile> **2** STORY : piso *m,* planta *f* <ground floor : planta baja> <second floor : primer piso> **3** : mínimo *m* (de sueldos, precios, etc.)

floorboard [ˈflorˌbord] *n* : tabla *f* del suelo, suelo *m,* piso *m*

flop[1] [ˈflɑp] *vi* **flopped; flopping 1** FLAP : golpearse, agitarse **2** COLLAPSE : dejarse caer, desplomarse **3** FAIL : fracasar

flop[2] *n* **1** FAILURE : fracaso *m* **2 to take a flop** : caerse

floppy [ˈflɑpi] *adj* **-pier; -est 1** : blando, flexible **2 floppy disk** : diskette *m,* disquete *m*

flora [ˈflorə] *n* : flora *f*

floral [ˈflorəl] *adj* : floral, floreado

florid [ˈflorɪd] *adj* **1** FLOWERY : florido **2** REDDISH : rojizo

florist [ˈflorɪst] *n* : florista *mf*

floss[1] [ˈflɔs] *vi* : limpiarse los dientes con hilo dental

floss[2] *n* **1** : hilo *m* de seda (de brodar) **2** → **dental floss**

flotation [floˈteɪʃən] *n* : flotación *f*

flotilla [floˈtɪlə] *n* : flotilla *f*

flotsam [ˈflɑtsəm] *n* **1** : restos *mpl* flotantes (en el mar) **2 flotsam and jetsam** : desechos *mpl,* restos *mpl*

flounce[1] [ˈflaʊnts] *vi* **flounced; flouncing** : moverse haciendo aspavientos <she flounced into the room : entró en la sala haciendo aspavientos>

flounce[2] *n* **1** RUFFLE : volante *m* **2** FLOURISH : aspaviento *m*

flounder[1] [ˈflaʊndər] *vi* **1** STRUGGLE : forcejear **2** STUMBLE : no saber qué hacer o decir, perder el hilo (en un discurso)

flounder[2] *n, pl* **flounder** *or* **flounders** : platija *f*

flour[1] [ˈflaʊər] *vt* : enharinar

flour[2] *n* : harina *f*

flourish[1] [ˈflərɪʃ] *vi* THRIVE : florecer, prosperar, crecer (dícese de las plantas) — *vt* BRANDISH : blandir

flourish[2] *n* : floritura *f,* floreo *m*

flourishing [ˈflərɪʃɪŋ] *adj* : floreciente, próspero

flout [ˈflaʊt] *vt* : desacatar, burlarse de

flow[1] [ˈfloː] *vi* **1** COURSE : fluir, manar, correr **2** CIRCULATE : circular, correr <traffic is flowing smoothly : el tránsito está circulando con fluidez>

flow[2] *n* **1** FLOWING : flujo *m,* circulación *f* **2** STREAM : corriente *f,* chorro *m*

flower[1] [ˈflaʊər] *vi* : florecer, florear

flower[2] *n* : flor *f*

flowered [ˈflaʊərd] *adj* : florido, floreado

floweriness [ˈflaʊərinəs] *n* : floritura *f*

flowering[1] [ˈflaʊərɪŋ] *adj* : floreciente

flowering[2] *n* : floración *f,* florecimiento *m*

flowerpot [ˈflaʊərˌpɑt] *n* : maceta *f,* tiesto *m,* macetero *m*

flowery [ˈflaʊəri] *adj* **1** : florido **2** FLOWERED : floreado, de flores

flowing [ˈfloːɪŋ] *adj* : fluido, corriente

flown → **fly**

flu [ˈfluː] *n* : gripe *f,* gripa *f Col, Mex*

fluctuate [ˈflʌktʃʊˌeɪt] *vi* **-ated; -ating** : fluctuar
fluctuation [ˌflʌktʃʊˈeɪʃən] *n* : fluctuación *f*
flue [ˈfluː] *n* : tiro *m,* salida *f* de humos
fluency [ˈfluːən*t*si] *n* : fluidez *f,* soltura *f*
fluent [ˈfluːənt] *adj* : fluido
fluently [ˈfluːəntli] *adv* : con soltura, con fluidez
fluff[1] [ˈflʌf] *vt* **1** : mullir <to fluff up the pillows : mullir las almohadas> **2** BUNGLE : echar a perder, equivocarse
fluff[2] *n* **1** FUZZ : pelusa *f* **2** DOWN : plumón *m*
fluffy [ˈflʌfi] *adj* **fluffier; -est 1** DOWNY : lleno de pelusa, velloso **2** SPONGY : esponjoso
fluid[1] [ˈfluːɪd] *adj* : fluido
fluid[2] *n* : fluido *m,* líquido *m*
fluidity [fluˈɪdəti] *n* : fluidez *f*
fluid ounce *n* : onza *f* líquida (29.57 mililitros)
fluke [ˈfluːk] *n* : golpe *m* de suerte, chiripa *f,* casualidad *f*
flung → **fling**
flunk [ˈflʌŋk] *vt* FAIL : reprobar — *vi* : salir reprobando
fluorescence [ˌflʊrˈɛsən*t*s, ˌflɔr-] *n* : fluorescencia *f*
fluorescent [ˌflʊrˈɛsənt, ˌflɔr-] *adj* : fluorescente
fluoridate [ˈflɔrəˌdeɪt, ˈflʊr-] *vt* **-dated; -dating** : fluorizar
fluoridation [ˌflɔrəˈdeɪʃən, ˌflʊr-] *n* : fluorización *f,* fluoración *f*
fluoride [ˈflɔrˌaɪd, ˈflʊr-] *n* : fluoruro *m*
fluorine [ˈflʊrˌiːn] *n* : flúor *m*
fluorocarbon [ˌflɔroˈkɑrbən, ˌflʊr-] *n* : fluorocarbono *m*
flurry [ˈfləri] *n, pl* **-ries 1** GUST : ráfaga *f* **2** SNOWFALL : nevisca *f* **3** BUSTLE : frenesí *m,* bullicio *m* **4** BARRAGE : aluvión *m,* oleada *f* <a flurry of questions : un aluvión de preguntas>
flush[1] [ˈflʌʃ] *vt* **1** : limpiar con agua <to flush the toilet : jalar la cadena> **2** RAISE : hacer salir, levantar (en la caza) — *vi* BLUSH : ruborizarse, sonrojarse
flush[2] *adv* : al mismo nivel, a ras
flush[3] *adj* **1** *or* **flushed** [ˈflʌʃt] : colorado, rojo, encendido (dícese de la cara) **2** FILLED : lleno a rebosar **3** ABUNDANT : copioso, abundante **4** AFFLUENT : adinerado **5** ALIGNED, SMOOTH : alineado, liso **6 flush against** : pegado a, contra
flush[4] *n* **1** FLOW, JET : chorro *m,* flujo *m* rápido **2** SURGE : arrebato *m,* arranque *m* <a flush of anger : un arrebato de cólera> **3** BLUSH : rubor *m,* sonrojo *m* **4** GLOW : resplandor *m,* flor *f* <the flush of youth : la flor de la juventud> <in the flush of victory : en la euforia del triunfo>
fluster[1] [ˈflʌstər] *vt* : poner nervioso, aturdir
fluster[2] *n* : agitación *f,* confusión *f*
flute [ˈfluːt] *n* : flauta *f*
fluted [ˈfluːtəd] *adj* **1** GROOVED : estriado, acanalado **2** WAVY : ondulado
fluting [ˈfluːtɪŋ] *n* : estrías *fpl*
flutist [ˈfluːtɪst] *n* : flautista *mf*
flutter[1] [ˈflʌtər] *vi* **1** : revolotear (dícese de un pájaro), ondear (dícese de una bandera), palpitar con fuerza (dícese del corazón) **2 to flutter about** : ir y venir, revoltear — *vt* : sacudir, batir
flutter[2] *n* **1** FLUTTERING : revoloteo *m,* aleteo *m* **2** COMMOTION, STIR : revuelo *m,* agitación *f*
flux [ˈflʌks] *n* **1** : flujo *m* (en física y medicina) **2** CHANGE : cambio *m* <to be in a state of flux : estar cambiando continuamente>
fly[1] [ˈflaɪ] *v* **flew** [ˈfluː]; **flown** [ˈfloːn]; **flying** *vi* **1** : volar (dícese de los pájaros, etc.) **2** TRAVEL : volar (dícese de los aviones), ir en avión (dícese de los pasajeros) **3** FLOAT : flotar, ondear **4** FLEE : huir, escapar **5** RUSH : correr, irse volando **6** PASS : pasar (volando) <how time flies! : ¡cómo pasa el tiempo!> **7 to fly open** : abrir de golpe — *vt* : pilotar (un avión), hacer volar (una cometa)
fly[2] *n, pl* **flies 1** : mosca *f* <to drop like flies : caer como moscas> **2** : bragueta *f* (de pantalones, etc.)
flyer → **flier**
flying saucer → **UFO**
flypaper [ˈflaɪˌpeɪpər] *n* : papel *m* matamoscas
flyspeck [ˈflaɪˌspɛk] *n* **1** : excremento *m* de mosca **2** SPECK : motita *f,* puntito *m*
flyswatter [ˈflaɪˌswɑtər] *n* : matamoscas *m*
flywheel [ˈflaɪˌ*h*wiːl] *n* : volante *m*
foal[1] [ˈfoːl] *vi* : parir
foal[2] *n* : potro *m,* -tra *f*
foam[1] [ˈfoːm] *vi* : hacer espuma
foam[2] *n* : espuma *f*
foamy [ˈfoːmi] *adj* **foamier; -est** : espumoso
focal [ˈfoːkəl] *adj* **1** : focal, central **2 focal point** : foco *m,* punto *m* de referencia
fo'c'sle [ˈfoːksəl] → **forecastle**
focus[1] [ˈfoːkəs] *v* **-cused** *or* **-cussed; -cusing** *or* **-cussing** *vt* **1** : enfocar (un instrumento) **2** CONCENTRATE : concentrar, centrar — *vi* : enfocar, fijar la vista
focus[2] *n, pl* **-ci** [ˈfoːˌsaɪ, -ˌkaɪ] **1** : foco *m* <to be in focus : estar enfocado> **2** FOCUSING : enfoque *m* **3** CENTER : centro *m,* foco *m*
fodder [ˈfɑdər] *n* : pienso *m,* forraje *m*
foe [ˈfoː] *n* : enemigo *m,* -ga *f*
fog[1] [ˈfɔg, ˈfɑg] *v* **fogged; fogging** *vt* : empañar — *vi* **to fog up** : empañarse
fog[2] *n* : niebla *f,* neblina *f*
foggy [ˈfɔgi, ˈfɑ-] *adj* **foggier; -est** : nebuloso, brumoso

foghorn [ˈfɔg,hɔrn, ˈfɑg-] *n* **:** sirena *f* de niebla
fogy [ˈfoːgi] *n, pl* **-gies :** carca *mf fam,* persona *f* chapada a la antigua
foible [ˈfɔɪbəl] *n* **:** flaqueza *f,* debilidad *f*
foil[1] [ˈfɔɪl] *vt* **:** frustrar, hacer fracasar
foil[2] *n* **1 :** lámina *f* de metal, papel *m* de aluminio **2** CONTRAST **:** contraste *m,* complemento *m* **3** SWORD **:** florete *m* (en esgrima)
foist [ˈfɔɪst] *vt* **:** encajar, endilgar *fam,* colocar
fold[1] [ˈfoːld] *vt* **1** BEND **:** doblar, plegar **2** CLASP **:** cruzar (brazos), enlazar (manos), plegar (alas) **3** EMBRACE **:** estrechar, abrazar — *vi* **1** FAIL **:** fracasar **2 to fold up :** doblarse, plegarse
fold[2] *n* **1** SHEEPFOLD **:** redil *m* (para ovejas) **2** FLOCK **:** rebaño *m* <to return to the fold : volver al redil> **3** CREASE **:** pliegue *m,* doblez *m*
folder [ˈfoːldər] *n* **1** CIRCULAR **:** circular *f,* folleto *m* **2** BINDER **:** carpeta *f*
foliage [ˈfoːliɪdʒ, -lɪdʒ] *n* **:** follaje *m*
folio [ˈfoːli,oː] *n, pl* **-lios :** folio *m*
folk[1] [ˈfoːk] *adj* **:** popular, folklórico <folk customs : costumbres populares> <folk dance : danza folklórica>
folk[2] *n, pl* **folk** *or* **folks 1** PEOPLE **:** gente *f* **2 folks** *npl* **:** familia *f,* padres *mpl*
folklore [ˈfoːk,lor] *n* **:** folklore *m*
folklorist [ˈfoːk,lorɪst] *n* **:** folklorista *mf*
folksy [ˈfoːksi] *adj* **folksier; -est :** campechano
follicle [ˈfɑlɪkəl] *n* **:** folículo *m*
follow [ˈfɑlo] *vt* **1 :** seguir <follow the guide : siga al guía> <she followed the road : siguió el camino, continuó por el camino> **2** PURSUE **:** perseguir, seguir **3** OBEY **:** seguir, cumplir, observar **4** UNDERSTAND **:** entender — *vi* **1 :** seguir **2** UNDERSTAND **:** entender **3 it follows that... :** se deduce que...
follower [ˈfɑloər] *n* **:** seguidor *m,* -dora *f*
following[1] [ˈfɑloɪŋ] *adj* NEXT **:** siguiente
following[2] *n* FOLLOWERS **:** seguidores *mpl*
following[3] *prep* AFTER **:** después de
follow through *vi* **to follow through with :** continuar con, realizar
follow up *vt* **:** seguir (una sugerencia, etc.), investigar (una huella)
folly [ˈfɑli] *n, pl* **-lies :** locura *f,* desatino *m*
foment [foˈmɛnt] *vt* **:** fomentar
fond [ˈfɑnd] *adj* **1** LOVING **:** cariñoso, tierno **2** PARTIAL **:** aficionado **3** FERVENT **:** ferviente, fervoroso
fondle [ˈfɑndəl] *vt* **-dled; -dling :** acariciar
fondly [ˈfɑndli] *adv* **:** cariñosamente, afectuosamente
fondness [ˈfɑndnəs] *n* **1** LOVE **:** cariño *m* **2** LIKING **:** afición *f*
fondue [fɑnˈduː, -ˈdjuː] *n* **:** fondue *f*
font [ˈfɑnt] *n* **1** *or* **baptismal font :** pila *f* bautismal **2** FOUNTAIN **:** fuente *f*
food [ˈfuːd] *n* **:** comida *f,* alimento *m*
food chain *n* **:** cadena *f* alimenticia
foodstuffs [ˈfuːd,stʌfs] *npl* **:** comestibles *mpl*
fool[1] [ˈfuːl] *vi* **1** JOKE **:** bromear, hacer el tonto **2** TOY **:** jugar, juguetear <don't fool with the computer : no juegues con la computadora> **3 to fool around :** perder el tiempo <he fools around instead of working : pierde el tiempo en vez de trabajar> — *vt* DECEIVE **:** engañar, burlar
fool[2] *n* **1** IDIOT **:** idiota *mf;* tonto *m,* -ta *f;* bobo *m,* -ba *f* **2** JESTER **:** bufón *m,* -fona *f*
foolhardiness [ˈfuːl,hɑrdinəs] *n* **:** imprudencia *f*
foolhardy [ˈfuːl,hɑrdi] *adj* RASH **:** imprudente, temerario, precipitado
foolish [ˈfuːlɪʃ] *adj* **1** STUPID **:** insensato, estúpido **2** SILLY **:** idiota, tonto
foolishly [ˈfuːlɪʃli] *adv* **:** tontamente
foolishness [ˈfuːlɪʃnəs] *n* **:** insensatez *f,* estupidez *f,* tontería *f*
foolproof [ˈfuːl,pruːf] *adj* **:** infalible
foot [ˈfʊt] *n, pl* **feet** [ˈfiːt] **:** pie *m*
footage [ˈfʊtɪdʒ] *n* **:** medida *f* en pies, metraje *m* (en el cine)
football [ˈfʊt,bɔl] *n* **:** futbol *m* americano, fútbol *m* americano
footbridge [ˈfʊt,brɪdʒ] *n* **:** pasarela *f,* puente *m* peatonal
foothills [ˈfʊt,hɪlz] *npl* **:** estribaciones *fpl*
foothold [ˈfʊt,hoːld] *n* **1 :** punto *m* de apoyo **2 to gain a foothold :** afianzarse en una posición
footing [ˈfʊtɪŋ] *n* **1** BALANCE **:** equilibrio *m* **2** FOOTHOLD **:** punto *m* de apoyo **3** BASIS **:** base *f* <on an equal footing : en igualdad>
footlights [ˈfʊt,laɪts] *npl* **:** candilejas *fpl*
footlocker [ˈfʊt,lɑkər] *n* **:** baúl *m* pequeño, cofre *m*
footloose [ˈfʊt,luːs] *adj* **:** libre y sin compromiso
footman [ˈfʊtmən] *n, pl* **-men** [-mən, -,mɛn] **:** lacayo *m*
footnote [ˈfʊt,noːt] *n* **:** nota *f* al pie de la página
footpath [ˈfʊt,pæθ] *n* **:** sendero *m,* senda *f,* vereda *f*
footprint [ˈfʊt,prɪnt] *n* **:** huella *f*
footrace [ˈfʊt,reɪs] *n* **:** carrera *f* pedestre
footrest [ˈfʊt,rɛst] *n* **:** apoyapiés *m,* reposapiés *m*
footstep [ˈfʊt,stɛp] *n* **1** STEP **:** paso *m* **2** FOOTPRINT **:** huella *f*
footstool [ˈfʊt,stuːl] *n* **:** taburete *m,* escabel *m*
footwear [ˈfʊt,wær] *n* **:** calzado *m*
footwork [ˈfʊt,wərk] *n* **:** juego *m* de piernas, juego *m* de pies
fop [ˈfɑp] *n* **:** petimetre *m,* dandi *m*

for[1] [ˈfɔr] *conj* **:** puesto que, porque

for[2] *prep* **1** (*indicating purpose*) **:** para, de <clothes for children : ropa para niños> <it's time for dinner : es la hora de comer> **2** BECAUSE OF **:** por <for fear of : por miedo de> **3** (*indicating a recipient*) **:** para, por <a gift for you : un regalo para ti> **4** (*indicating support*) **:** por <he fought for his country : luchó por su patria> **5** (*indicating a goal*) **:** por, para <a cure for cancer : una cura para el cáncer> <for your own good : por tu propio bien> **6** (*indicating correspondence or exchange*) **:** por, para <I bought it for $5 : lo compré por $5> <a lot of trouble for nothing : mucha molestia para nada> **7** AS FOR **:** para, con respecto a **8** (*indicating duration*) **:** durante, por <he's going for two years : se va por dos años> <I spoke for ten minutes : hablé (durante) diez minutos> <she has known it for three months : lo sabe desde hace tres meses>

forage[1] [ˈfɔrɪdʒ] *v* **-aged; -aging** *vi* **:** hurgar (en busca de alimento) — *vt* **:** buscar (provisiones)

forage[2] *n* **:** forraje *m*

foray [ˈfɔrˌeɪ] *n* **:** incursión *f*

forbear[1] [fɔrˈbær] *vi* **-bore** [-ˈbor]; **-borne** [-ˈborn]; **-bearing 1** ABSTAIN **:** abstenerse **2 :** tener paciencia

forbear[2] → **forebear**

forbearance [fɔrˈbærənts] *n* **1** ABSTAINING **:** abstención *f* **2** PATIENCE **:** paciencia *f*

forbid [fərˈbɪd] *vt* **-bade** [-ˈbæd, -ˈbeɪd] *or* **-bad** [-ˈbæd]; **-bidden** [-ˈbɪdən]; **-bidding 1** PROHIBIT **:** prohibir **2** PREVENT **:** impedir

forbidding [fərˈbɪdɪŋ] *adj* **1** IMPOSING **:** imponente **2** DISAGREEABLE **:** desagradable, ingrato **3** GRIM **:** severo

force[1] [ˈfors] *vt* **forced; forcing 1** COMPEL **:** obligar, forzar **2 :** forzar <to force open the window : forzar la ventana> <to force a lock : forzar una cerradura> **3** IMPOSE **:** imponer, obligar

force[2] *n* **1 :** fuerza *f* **2 by force :** por la fuerza **3 in force :** en vigor, en vigencia

forced [ˈforst] *adj* **:** forzado, forzoso

forceful [ˈforsfəl] *adj* **:** fuerte, energético, contundente

forcefully [ˈforsfəli] *adv* **:** con energía, con fuerza

forcefulness [ˈforsfəlnəs] *n* **:** contundencia *f,* fuerza *f*

forceps [ˈfɔrsəps, -ˌsɛps] *ns & pl* **:** fórceps *m*

forcible [ˈforsəbəl] *adj* **1** FORCED **:** forzoso **2** CONVINCING **:** contundente, convincente — **forcibly** [-bli] *adv*

ford[1] [ˈford] *vt* **:** vadear

ford[2] *n* **:** vado *m*

fore[1] [ˈfor] *adv* **1** FORWARD **:** hacia adelante **2 fore and aft :** de popa a proa

fore[2] *adj* **1** FORWARD **:** delantero, de adelante **2** FORMER **:** anterior

fore[3] *n* **1 :** frente *m,* delantera *f* **2 to come to the fore :** empezar a destacar, saltar a primera plana

fore–and–aft [ˈforənˈæft, -ənd-] *adj* **:** longitudinal

forearm [ˈforˌɑrm] *n* **:** antebrazo *m*

forebear [ˈforˌbær] *n* **:** antepasado *m,* -da *f*

foreboding [forˈboːdɪŋ] *n* **:** premonición *f,* presentimiento *m*

forecast[1] [ˈforˌkæst] *vt* **-cast; -casting :** pronosticar, predecir

forecast[2] *n* **:** predicción *f,* pronóstico *m*

forecastle [ˈfoːksəl] *n* **:** castillo *m* de proa

foreclose [forˈkloːz] *vt* **-closed; -closing :** ejecutar (una hipoteca)

forefather [ˈforˌfɑðər] *n* **:** antepasado *m,* ancestro *m*

forefinger [ˈforˌfɪŋgər] *n* **:** índice *m,* dedo *m* índice

forefoot [ˈforˌfʊt] *n* **:** pata *f* delantera

forefront [ˈforˌfrʌnt] *n* **:** frente *m,* vanguardia *f* <in the forefront : a la vanguardia>

forego [forˈgoː] *vt* **-went; -gone; -going 1** PRECEDE **:** preceder **2** → **forgo**

foregoing [forˈgoːɪŋ] *adj* **:** precedente, anterior

foregone [forˈgɔn] *adj* **:** previsto <a foregone conclusion : un resultado inevitable>

foreground [ˈforˌgraʊnd] *n* **:** primer plano *m*

forehand[1] [ˈforˌhænd] *adj* **:** directo, derecho

forehand[2] *n* **:** golpe *m* del derecho

forehead [ˈfɔrəd, ˈforˌhɛd] *n* **:** frente *f*

foreign [ˈfɔrən] *adj* **1 :** extranjero, exterior <foreign countries : países extranjeros> <foreign trade : comercio exterior> **2** ALIEN **:** ajeno, extraño <foreign to their nature : ajeno a su carácter> <a foreign body : un cuerpo extraño>

foreigner [ˈfɔrənər] *n* **:** extranjero *m,* -ra *f*

foreknowledge [forˈnɑlɪdʒ] *n* **:** conocimiento *m* previo

foreleg [ˈforˌlɛg] *n* **:** pata *f* delantera

foreman [ˈformən] *n, pl* **-men** [-mən, -ˌmɛn] **:** capataz *mf* <foreman of the jury : presidente del jurado>

foremost[1] [ˈforˌmoːst] *adv* **:** en primer lugar

foremost[2] *adj* **:** más importante, principal, grande

forenoon [ˈforˌnuːn] *n* **:** mañana *m*

forensic [fəˈrɛntsɪk] *adj* **1** RHETORICAL **:** retórico, de argumentación **2 :** forense <forensic medicine : medicina forense>

foreordain [ˌforɔrˈdeɪn] *vt* **:** predestinar, predeterminar
forequarter [ˈforˌkwɔrt̬ər] *n* **:** cuarto *m* delantero
forerunner [ˈforˌrʌnər] *n* **:** precursor *m*, -sora *f*
foresee [forˈsiː] *vt* **-saw; -seen; -seeing :** prever
foreseeable [forˈsiːəbəl] *adj* **:** previsible <in the foreseeable future **:** en el futuro inmediato>
foreshadow [forˈʃædoː] *vt* **:** anunciar, prefigurar
foresight [ˈforˌsaɪt] *n* **:** previsión *f*
foresighted [ˈforˌsaɪt̬əd] *adj* **:** previsto
forest [ˈfɔrəst] *n* **:** bosque *m* (en zonas templadas), selva *f* (en zonas tropicales)
forestall [forˈstɔl] *vt* **1** PREVENT **:** prevenir, impedir **2** PREEMPT **:** adelantarse a
forested [ˈfɔrəstəd] *adj* **:** arbolado
forester [ˈfɔrəstər] *n* **:** silvicultor *m*, -tora *f*
forestland [ˈfɔrəstˌlænd] *n* **:** zona *f* boscosa
forest ranger → **ranger**
forestry [ˈfɔrəstri] *n* **:** silvicultura *f*, ingeniería *f* forestal
foreswear → **forswear**
foretaste[1] [ˈforˌteɪst] *vt* **-tasted; -tasting :** anticipar
foretaste[2] *n* **:** anticipo *m*
foretell [forˈtɛl] *vt* **-told; -telling :** predecir, pronosticar, profetizar
forethought [ˈforˌθɔt] *n* **:** previsión *f*, reflexión *f* previa
forever [fɔrˈɛvər] *adv* **1** PERPETUALLY **:** para siempre, eternamente **2** CONTINUALLY **:** siempre, constantemente
forevermore [fɔrˌɛvərˈmor] *adv* **:** por siempre jamás
forewarn [forˈwɔrn] *vt* **:** prevenir, advertir
foreword [ˈforwərd] *n* **:** prólogo *m*
forfeit[1] [ˈfɔrfət] *vt* **:** perder el derecho a
forfeit[2] *n* **1** FINE, PENALTY **:** multa *f* **2 :** prenda *f* (en un juego)
forge[1] [ˈfordʒ] *v* **forged; forging** *vt* **1 :** forjar (metal o un plan) **2** COUNTERFEIT **:** falsificar — *vi* **to forge ahead :** avanzar, seguir adelante
forge[2] *n* **:** forja *f*
forger [ˈfordʒər] *n* **:** falsificador *m*, -dora *f*
forgery [ˈfordʒəri] *n, pl* **-eries :** falsificación *f*
forget [fərˈgɛt] *v* **-got** [-ˈgɑt]; **-gotten** [-ˈgɑtən] *or* **-got; -getting** *vt* **:** olvidar — *vi* **to forget about :** olvidarse de, no acordarse de
forgetful [fərˈgɛtfəl] *adj* **:** olvidadizo
forget–me–not [fərˈgɛtmiˌnɑt] *n* **:** nomeolvides *mf*
forgettable [fərˈgɛt̬əbəl] *adj* **:** poco memorable
forgivable [fərˈgɪvəbəl] *adj* **:** perdonable
forgive [fərˈgɪv] *vt* **-gave** [-ˈgeɪv]; **-given** [-ˈgɪvən]; **-giving :** perdonar
forgiveness [fərˈgɪvnəs] *n* **:** perdón *m*
forgiving [fərˈgɪvɪŋ] *adj* **:** indulgente, comprensivo, clemente
forgo *or* **forego** [forˈgoː] *vt* **-went; -gone; -going :** privarse de, renunciar a
fork[1] [ˈfɔrk] *vi* **:** ramificarse, bifurcarse — *vt* **1 :** levantar (con un tenedor, una horca, etc.) **2 to fork over :** desembolsar
fork[2] *n* **1 :** tenedor *m* (utensilio de cocina) **2** PITCHFORK **:** horca *f*, horquilla *f* **3 :** bifurcación *f* (de un río o camino), horqueta *f* (de un árbol)
forked [ˈfɔrkt, ˈfɔrkəd] *adj* **:** bífido, ahorquillado
forklift [ˈfɔrkˌlɪft] *n* **:** carretilla *f* elevadora
forlorn [fɔrˈlɔrn] *adj* **1** DESOLATE **:** abandonado, desolado, desamparado **2** SAD **:** triste **3** DESPERATE **:** desesperado
forlornly [fɔrˈlɔrnli] *adv* **1** SADLY **:** con tristeza **2** HALFHEARTEDLY **:** sin ánimo
form[1] [ˈfɔrm] *vt* **1** FASHION, MAKE **:** formar **2** DEVELOP **:** moldear, desarrollar **3** CONSTITUTE **:** constituir, formar **4** ACQUIRE **:** adquirir (un hábito), formar (una idea) — *vi* **:** tomar forma, formarse
form[2] *n* **1** SHAPE **:** forma *f*, figura *f* **2** MANNER **:** manera *f*, forma *f* **3** DOCUMENT **:** formulario *m* **4 :** forma *f* <in good form **:** en buena forma> <true to form **:** en forma consecuente> **5** MOLD **:** molde *m* **6** KIND, VARIETY **:** clase *f*, tipo *m* **7 :** forma *f* (en gramática) <plural forms **:** formas plurales>
formal[1] [ˈfɔrməl] *adj* **1** CEREMONIOUS **:** formal, de etiqueta, ceremonioso **2** OFFICIAL **:** formal, oficial, de forma
formal[2] *n* **1** BALL **:** baile *m* formal, baile *m* de etiqueta **2** *or* **formal dress :** traje *m* de etiqueta
formaldehyde [fɔrˈmældəˌhaɪd] *n* **:** formaldehído *m*
formality [fɔrˈmæləti] *n, pl* **-ties :** formalidad *f*
formalize [ˈfɔrməˌlaɪz] *vt* **-ized; -izing :** formalizar
formally [ˈfɔrməli] *adv* **:** formalmente
format[1] [ˈfɔrˌmæt] *vt* **-matted; -matting :** formatear
format[2] *n* **:** formato *m*
formation [fɔrˈmeɪʃən] *n* **1** FORMING **:** formación *f* **2** SHAPE **:** forma *f* **3 in formation :** en formación
formative [ˈfɔrmət̬ɪv] *adj* **:** formativo
former [ˈfɔrmər] *adj* **1** PREVIOUS **:** antiguo, anterior <the former president **:** el antiguo presidente> **2 :** primero (de dos)
formerly [ˈfɔrmərli] *adv* **:** anteriormente, antes
formidable [ˈfɔrmədəbəl, fɔrˈmɪdə-] *adj* **:** formidable — **formidably** *adv*

formless [ˈfɔrmləs] *adj* : informe, amorfo
formula [ˈfɔrmjələ] *n, pl* **-las** *or* **-lae** [-ˌliː, -ˌlaɪ] **1** : fórmula *f* **2 baby formula** : preparado *m* para biberón
formulate [ˈfɔrmjəˌleɪt] *vt* **-lated; -lating** : formular, hacer
formulation [ˌfɔrmjəˈleɪʃən] *n* : formulación *f*
fornicate [ˈfɔrnəˌkeɪt] *vi* **-cated; -cating** : fornicar
fornication [ˌfɔrnəˈkeɪʃən] *n* : fornicación *f*
forsake [fərˈseɪk] *vt* **-sook** [-ˈsʊk]; **-saken** [-ˈseɪkən]; **-saking 1** ABANDON : abandonar, desamparar **2** RELINQUISH : renunciar a
forswear [fɔrˈswær] *v* **-swore; -sworn; -swearing** *vt* RENOUNCE : renunciar a — *vi* : perjurar
forsythia [fərˈsɪθiə] *n* : forsitia *f*
fort [ˈfort] *n* **1** STRONGHOLD : fuerte *m,* fortaleza *f,* fortín *m* **2** BASE : base *f* militar
forte [ˈfort, ˈforˌteɪ] *n* : fuerte *m*
forth [ˈforθ] *adv* **1** : adelante <from this day forth : de hoy en adelante> **2 and so forth** : etcétera
forthcoming [forθˈkʌmɪŋ, ˈforθˌ-] *adj* **1** COMING : próximo **2** DIRECT, OPEN : directo, franco, comunicativo
forthright [ˈforθˌraɪt] *adj* : directo, franco — **forthrightly** *adv*
forthrightness [ˈforθˌraɪtnəs] *n* : franqueza *f*
forthwith [forθˈwɪθ, -ˈwɪð] *adv* : inmediatamente, en el acto, enseguida
fortieth[1] [ˈfɔrtiəθ] *adj* : cuadragésimo
fortieth[2] *n* **1** : cuadragésimo *m,* -ma *f* (en una serie) **2** : cuarentavo *m,* cuarentava parte *f*
fortification [ˌfɔrtəfəˈkeɪʃən] *n* : fortificación *f*
fortify [ˈfɔrtəˌfaɪ] *vt* **-fied; -fying** : fortificar
fortitude [ˈfɔrtəˌtuːd, -ˌtjuːd] *n* : fortaleza *f,* valor *m*
fortnight [ˈfortˌnaɪt] *n* : quince días *mpl,* dos semanas *fpl*
fortnightly[1] [ˈfortˌnaɪtli] *adv* : cada quince días
fortnightly[2] *adj* : quincenal
fortress [ˈfɔrtrəs] *n* : fortaleza *f*
fortuitous [fɔrˈtuːətəs, -ˈtjuː-] *adj* : fortuito, accidental
fortunate [ˈfɔrtʃənət] *adj* : afortunado
fortunately [ˈfɔrtʃənətli] *adv* : afortunadamente, con suerte
fortune [ˈfɔrtʃən] *n* **1** : fortuna *f* <to seek one's fortune : buscar uno su fortuna> **2** LUCK : suerte *f,* fortuna *f* **3** DESTINY, FUTURE : destino *m,* buenaventura *f* **4** : dineral *m,* platal *m* <she spent a fortune : se gastó un dineral>
fortune-teller [ˈfɔrtʃənˌtɛlər] *n* : adivino *m,* -na *f*
fortune-telling [ˈfɔrtʃənˌtɛlɪŋ] *n* : adivinación *f*
forty[1] [ˈfɔrti] *adj* : cuarenta
forty[2] *n, pl* **forties** : cuarenta *m*
forum [ˈforəm] *n, pl* **-rums** : foro *m*
forward[1] [ˈfɔrwərd] *vt* **1** PROMOTE : promover, adelantar, fomentar **2** SEND : remitir, enviar
forward[2] *adv* **1** : adelante, hacia adelante <to go forward : irse adelante> **2 from this day forward** : de aquí en adelante
forward[3] *adj* **1** : hacia adelante, delantero **2** BRASH : atrevido, descarado
forward[4] *n* : delantero *m,* -ra *f* (en deportes)
forwarder [ˈfɔrwərdər] *n* : agencia *f* de transportes, agente *mf* expedidor
forwardness [ˈfɔrwərdnəs] *n* : atrevimiento *m,* descaro *m*
forwards [ˈfɔrwərdz] → **forward**[2]
fossil[1] [ˈfɑsəl] *adj* : fósil
fossil[2] *n* : fósil *m*
fossilize [ˈfɑsəˌlaɪz] *vt* **-ized; -izing** : fosilizar — *vi* : fosilizarse
foster[1] [ˈfɔstər] *vt* : promover, fomentar
foster[2] *adj* : adoptivo <foster child : niño adoptivo>
fought → **fight**
foul[1] [ˈfaʊl] *vi* : cometer faltas (en deportes) — *vt* **1** DIRTY, POLLUTE : contaminar, ensuciar **2** TANGLE : enredar
foul[2] *adv* **1** → **foully 2** : contra las reglas
foul[3] *adj* **1** REPULSIVE : asqueroso, repugnante **2** CLOGGED : atascado, obstruido **3** TANGLED : enredado **4** OBSCENE : obsceno **5** BAD : malo <foul weather : mal tiempo> **6** : antirreglamentario (en deportes)
foul[4] *n* : falta *f,* faul *m*
foully [ˈfaʊli] *adv* : asquerosamente
foulmouthed [ˈfaʊlˌmæʊːðd, -ˌmaʊθt] *adj* : malhablado
foulness [ˈfaʊlnəs] *n* **1** DIRTINESS : suciedad *f* **2** INCLEMENCY : inclemencia *f* **3** OBSCENITY : obscenidad *f,* grosería *f*
foul play *n* : actos *mpl* criminales
foul-up [ˈfaʊlˌʌp] *n* : lío *m,* confusión *f,* desastre *m*
foul up *vt* SPOIL : estropear, arruinar — *vi* BUNGLE : echar todo a perder
found[1] → **find**
found[2] [ˈfaʊnd] *vt* : fundar, establecer
foundation [faʊnˈdeɪʃən] *n* **1** FOUNDING : fundación *f* **2** BASIS : fundamento *m,* base *f* **3** INSTITUTION : fundación *f* **4** : cimientos *mpl* (de un edificio)
founder[1] [ˈfaʊndər] *vi* SINK : hundirse, irse a pique
founder[2] *n* : fundador *m,* -dora *f*
foundling [ˈfaʊndlɪŋ] *n* : expósito *m,* -ta *f*
foundry [ˈfaʊndri] *n, pl* **-dries** : fundición *f*
fount [ˈfaʊnt] *n* SOURCE : fuente *f,* origen *m*

fountain ['faʊntən] *n* **1** SPRING : fuente *f,* manantial *m* **2** SOURCE : fuente *f,* origen *m* **3** JET : chorro *m* (de agua), surtidor *m*
fountain pen *n* : pluma *f* fuente
four[1] ['for] *adj* : cuatro
four[2] *n* : cuatro *m*
fourfold ['for,fo:ld, -'fo:ld] *adj* : cuadruple
four hundred[1] *adj* : cuatrocientos
four hundred[2] *n* : cuatrocientos *m*
fourscore ['for'skor] *adj* EIGHTY : ochenta *m*
fourteen[1] [for'ti:n] *adj* : catorce
fourteen[2] *n* : catorce *m*
fourteenth[1] [for'ti:nθ] *adj* : decimocuarto
fourteenth[2] *n* **1** : decimocuarto *m,* -ta *f* (en una serie) **2** : catorceavo *m,* catorceava parte *f*
fourth[1] ['forθ] *adj* : cuarto
fourth[2] *n* **1** : cuarto *m,* -ta *f* (en una serie) **2** : cuarto *m,* cuarta parte *f*
fowl ['faʊl] *n, pl* **fowl** *or* **fowls** **1** BIRD : ave *f* **2** CHICKEN : pollo *m*
fox[1] ['fɑks] *vt* **1** TRICK : engañar **2** BAFFLE : confundir
fox[2] *n, pl* **foxes** : zorro *m,* -ra *f*
foxglove ['fɑks,glʌv] *n* : dedalera *f,* digital *f*
foxhole ['fɑks,ho:l] *n* : hoyo *m* para atrincherarse, trinchera *f* individual
foxy ['fɑksi] *adj* **foxier; -est** SHREWD : astuto
foyer ['fɔɪər, 'fɔɪ,jeɪ] *n* : vestíbulo *m*
fracas ['freɪkəs, 'fræ-] *n, pl* **-cases** [-kəsəz] : altercado *m,* pelea *f,* reyerta *f*
fraction ['frækʃən] *n* **1** : fracción *f,* quebrado *m* **2** PORTION : porción *f,* parte *f*
fractional ['frækʃənəl] *adj* **1** : fraccionario **2** TINY : minúsculo, mínimo, insignificante
fractious ['frækʃəs] *adj* **1** UNRULY : rebelde **2** IRRITABLE : malhumorado, irritable
fracture[1] ['fræktʃər] *vt* **-tured; -turing** : fracturar
fracture[2] *n* **1** : fractura *f* (de un hueso) **2** CRACK : fisura *f,* grieta *f,* falla *f* (geológica)
fragile ['frædʒəl, -,dʒaɪl] *adj* : frágil
fragility [frə'dʒɪləṭi] *n, pl* **-ties** : fragilidad *f*
fragment[1] ['fræg,mɛnt] *vt* : fragmentar — *vi* : fragmentarse, hacerse añicos
fragment[2] ['frægmənt] *n* : fragmento *m,* trozo *m,* pedazo *m*
fragmentary ['frægmən,tɛri] *adj* : fragmentario, incompleto
fragmentation [,frægmən'teɪʃən, -,mɛn-] *n* : fragmentación *f*
fragrance ['freɪgrənts] *n* : fragancia *f,* aroma *m*
fragrant ['freɪgrənt] *adj* : fragante, aromático — **fragrantly** *adv*
frail ['freɪl] *adj* : débil, delicado
frailty ['freɪlti] *n, pl* **-ties** : debilidad *f,* flaqueza *f*
frame[1] ['freɪm] *vt* **framed; framing** **1** FORMULATE : formular, elaborar **2** BORDER : enmarcar, encuadrar **3** INCRIMINATE : incriminar
frame[2] *n* **1** BODY : cuerpo *m* **2** : armazón *f* (de un edificio, un barco, o un avión), bastidor *m* (de un automóvil), cuadro *m* (de una bicicleta), marco *m* (de un cuadro, una ventana, una puerta, etc.) **3** **frames** *npl* : armazón *mf,* montura *f* (para anteojos) **4** **frame of mind** : estado *m* de ánimo
framework ['freɪm,wərk] *n* **1** SKELETON, STRUCTURE : armazón *f,* estructura *f* **2** BASIS : marco *m*
franc ['fræŋk] *n* : franco *m*
franchise ['fræn,tʃaɪz] *n* **1** LICENSE : licencia *f* exclusiva, concesión *f* (en comercio) **2** SUFFRAGE : sufragio *m*
franchisee [,fræn,tʃaɪ'zi:, -tʃə-] *n* : concesionario *m,* -ria *f*
frank[1] ['fræŋk] *vt* : franquear
frank[2] *adj* : franco, sincero, cándido — **frankly** *adv*
frank[3] *n* : franqueo *m* (de correo)
frankfurter ['fræŋkfərṭər, -,fər-] *or* **frankfurt** [-fərt] *n* : salchicha *f* (de Frankfurt, de Viena), perro *m* caliente
frankincense ['fræŋkən,sɛnts] *n* : incienso *m*
frankness ['fræŋknəs] *n* : franqueza *f,* sinceridad *f,* candidez *f*
frantic ['fræntɪk] *adj* : frenético, desesperado — **frantically** *adv*
fraternal [frə'tərnəl] *adj* : fraterno, fraternal
fraternity [frə'tərnəṭi] *n, pl* **-ties** : fraternidad *f*
fraternization [,fræṭərnə'zeɪʃən] *n* : fraternización *f,* confraternización *f*
fraternize ['fræṭər,naɪz] *vi* **-nized; -nizing** : fraternizar, confraternizar
fratricidal [,frætrə'saɪdəl] *adj* : fratricida
fratricide ['frætrə,saɪd] *n* : fratricidio *m*
fraud ['frɔd] *n* **1** DECEPTION, SWINDLE : fraude *m,* estafa *f,* engaño *m* **2** IMPOSTOR : impostor *m,* -tora *f;* farsante *mf*
fraudulent ['frɔdʒələnt] *adj* : fraudulento — **fraudulently** *adv*
fraught ['frɔt] *adj* **fraught with** : lleno de, cargado de
fray[1] ['freɪ] *vt* **1** WEAR : desgastar, deshilachar **2** IRRITATE : crispar, irritar (los nervios) — *vi* : desgastarse, deshilacharse
fray[2] *n* : pelea *f,* lucha *f,* refriega *f*
frazzle[1] ['fræzəl] *vt* **-zled; -zling** **1** FRAY : desgastar, deshilachar **2** EXHAUST : agotar, fatigar
frazzle[2] *n* EXHAUSTION : agotamiento *m*
freak ['fri:k] *n* **1** ODDITY : ejemplar *m* anormal, fenómeno *m,* rareza *f* **2** ENTHUSIAST : entusiasta *mf*

freakish [ˈfriːkɪʃ] *adj* : extraño, estrafalario, raro
freckle[1] [ˈfrɛkəl] *vi* **-led; -ling** : cubrirse de pecas
freckle[2] *n* : peca *f*
free[1] [ˈfriː] *vt* **freed; freeing 1** LIBERATE : libertar, liberar, poner en libertad **2** RELIEVE, RID : librar, eximir **3** RELEASE, UNTIE : desatar, soltar **4** UNCLOG : desatascar, destapar
free[2] *adv* **1** FREELY : libremente **2** GRATIS : gratuitamente, gratis
free[3] *adj* **freer; freest 1** : libre <free as a bird : libre como un pájaro> **2** EXEMPT : libre <tax-free : libre de impuestos> **3** GRATIS : gratuito, gratis **4** VOLUNTARY : espontáneo, voluntario, libre **5** UNOCCUPIED : desocupado, libre **6** LOOSE : suelto
freebooter [ˈfriːˌbuːtər] *n* : pirata *mf*
freeborn [ˈfriːˈbɔrn] *adj* : nacido libre
freedom [ˈfriːdəm] *n* : libertad *f*
free–for–all [ˈfriːfərˌɔl] *n* : pelea *f*, batalla *f* campal
freelance[1] [ˈfriːˌlænts] *vi* **-lanced; -lancing** : trabajar por cuenta propia
freelance[2] *adj* : por cuenta propia, independiente
freeload [ˈfriːˌloːd] *vi* : gorronear *fam*, gorrear *fam*
freeloader [ˈfriːˌloːdər] *n* : gorrón *m*, -rrona *f*; gorrero *m*, -ra *f*; vividor *m*, -dora *f*
freely [ˈfriːli] *adv* **1** FREE : libremente **2** GRATIS : gratis, gratuitamente
freestanding [ˈfriːˈstændɪŋ] *adj* : de pie, no empotrado, independiente
freeway [ˈfriːˌweɪ] *n* : autopista *f*
freewill [ˈfriːˌwɪl] *adj* : de propia voluntad
free will *n* : libre albedrío *m*, propia voluntad *f*
freeze[1] [ˈfriːz] *v* **froze** [ˈfroːz]; **frozen** [ˈfroːzən]; **freezing** *vi* **1** : congelarse, helarse <the water froze in the lake : el agua se congeló en el lago> <my blood froze : se me heló la sangre> <I'm freezing : me estoy helando> **2** STOP : quedarse inmóvil — *vt* : helar, congelar (líquidos), congelar (alimentos, precios, activos)
freeze[2] *n* **1** FROST : helada *f* **2** FREEZING : congelación *f*, congelamiento *m*
freeze–dried [ˈfriːzˈdraɪd] *adj* : liofilizado
freeze–dry [ˈfriːzˈdraɪ] *vt* **-dried; -drying** : liofilizar
freezer [ˈfriːzər] *n* : congelador *m*
freezing [ˈfriːzɪŋ] *adj* : helando <it's freezing! : ¡hace un frío espantoso!>
freezing point *n* : punto *m* de congelación
freight[1] [ˈfreɪt] *vt* : enviar como carga
freight[2] *n* **1** SHIPPING, TRANSPORT : transporte *m*, porte *m*, flete *m* **2** GOODS : mercancías *fpl*, carga *f*
freighter [ˈfreɪtər] *n* : carguero *m*, buque *m* de carga
French[1] [ˈfrɛntʃ] *adj* : francés
French[2] *n* **1** : francés *m* (idioma) **2 the French** *npl* : los franceses
Frenchman [ˈfrɛntʃmən] *n, pl* **-men** [-mən, -ˌmɛn] : francés *m*
Frenchwoman [ˈfrɛntʃˌwʊmən] *n, pl* **-women** [-ˌwɪmən] : francesa *f*
french fries [ˈfrɛntʃˌfraɪz] *npl* : papas *fpl* fritas
frenetic [frɪˈnɛtɪk] *adj* : frenético — **frenetically** [-tɪkli] *adv*
frenzied [ˈfrɛnzid] *adj* : frenético
frenzy [ˈfrɛnzi] *n, pl* **-zies** : frenesí *m*
frequency [ˈfriːkwəntsi] *n, pl* **-cies** : frecuencia *f*
frequent[1] [friˈkwɛnt, ˈfriːkwənt] *vt* : frecuentar
frequent[2] [ˈfriːkwənt] *adj* : frecuente — **frequently** *adv*
fresco [ˈfrɛsˌkoː] *n, pl* **-coes** : fresco *m*
fresh [ˈfrɛʃ] *adj* **1** : dulce <freshwater : agua dulce> **2** PURE : puro **3** : fresco <fresh fruits : frutas frescas> **4** CLEAN, NEW : limpio, nuevo <fresh clothes : ropa limpia> <fresh evidence : evidencia nueva> **5** REFRESHED : fresco, descansado **6** IMPERTINENT : descarado, impertinente
freshen [ˈfrɛʃən] *vt* : refrescar, arreglar — *vi* **to freshen up** : arreglarse, lavarse
freshet [ˈfrɛʃət] *n* : arroyo *m* desbordado
freshly [ˈfrɛʃli] *adv* : recientemente, recién
freshman [ˈfrɛʃmən] *n, pl* **-men** [-mən, -ˌmɛn] : estudiante *mf* de primer año universitario
freshness [ˈfrɛʃnəs] *n* : frescura *f*
freshwater [ˈfrɛʃˌwɔtər] *n* : agua *f* dulce
fret[1] [ˈfrɛt] *vi* **fretted; fretting** : preocuparse, inquietarse
fret[2] *n* **1** VEXATION : irritación *f*, molestia *f* **2** WORRY : preocupación *f* **3** : traste *m* (de un instrumento musical)
fretful [ˈfrɛtfəl] *adj* : fastidioso, quejoso, neurótico
fretfully [ˈfrɛtfəli] *adv* : ansiosamente, fastidiosamente, inquieto
fretfulness [ˈfrɛtfəlnəs] *n* : inquietud *f*, irritabilidad *f*
friable [ˈfraɪəbəl] *adj* : friable, pulverizable
friar [ˈfraɪər] *n* : fraile *m*
fricassee[1] [ˈfrɪkəˌsiː, ˌfrɪkəˈsiː] *vt* **-seed; -seeing** : cocinar al fricasé
fricassee[2] *n* : fricasé *m*
friction [ˈfrɪkʃən] *n* **1** RUBBING : fricción *f* **2** CONFLICT : fricción *f*, roce *m*
Friday [ˈfraɪˌdeɪ, -di] *n* : viernes *m*
fridge [ˈfrɪdʒ] → **refrigerator**
friend [ˈfrɛnd] *n* : amigo *m*, -ga *f*
friendless [ˈfrɛndləs] *adj* : sin amigos
friendliness [ˈfrɛndlinəs] *n* : simpatía *f*, amabilidad *f*
friendly [ˈfrɛndli] *adj* **-lier; -est 1** : simpático, amable, de amigo <a friendly child : un niño simpático> <friendly advice : consejo de amigo>

2 : agradable, acogedor <a friendly atmosphere : un ambiente agradable> 3 GOOD-NATURED : amigable, amistoso <friendly competition : competencia amistosa>

friendship [ˈfrɛnd,ʃɪp] *n* : amistad *f*

frieze [ˈfriːz] *n* : friso *m*

frigate [ˈfrɪgət] *n* : fragata *f*

fright [ˈfraɪt] *n* : miedo *m,* susto *m*

frighten [ˈfraitən] *vt* : asustar, espantar

frightened [ˈfraitənd] *adj* : asustado, temeroso

frightening [ˈfraitənɪŋ] *adj* : espantoso, aterrador

frightful [ˈfraɪtfəl] *adj* **1** → **frightening 2** TREMENDOUS : espantoso, tremendo

frightfully [ˈfraɪtfəli] *adv* : terriblemente, tremendamente

frigid [ˈfrɪdʒɪd] *adj* : glacial, extremadamente frío

frigidity [frɪˈdʒɪdəti] *n* **1** COLDNESS : frialdad *f* **2** : frigidez *f* (sexual)

frill [ˈfrɪl] *n* **1** RUFFLE : volante *m* **2** EMBELLISHMENT : floritura *f,* adorno *m*

frilly [ˈfrɪli] *adj* **frillier; -est 1** RUFFLY : con volantes **2** OVERDONE : recargado

fringe[1] [ˈfrɪndʒ] *vt* **fringed; fringing** : orlar, bordear

fringe[2] *n* **1** BORDER : fleco *m,* orla *f* **2** EDGE : periferia *f,* margen *m* **3 fringe benefits** : incentivos *mpl*, extras *mpl*

frisk [ˈfrɪsk] *vi* FROLIC : retozar, juguetear — *vt* SEARCH : cachear, registrar

friskiness [ˈfrɪskinəs] *n* : vivacidad *f*

frisky [ˈfrɪski] *adj* **friskier; -est** : retozón, juguetón

fritter[1] [ˈfrɪtər] *vt* : desperdiciar, malgastar <I frittered away the money : malgasté el dinero>

fritter[2] *n* : buñuelo *m*

frivolity [frɪˈvɑləṭi] *n, pl* **-ties** : frivolidad *f*

frivolous [ˈfrɪvələs] *adj* : frívolo, de poca importancia

frivolously [ˈfrɪvələsli] *adv* : frívolamente, a la ligera

frizz[1] [ˈfrɪz] *vi* : rizarse, encresparse, ponerse chino *Mex*

frizz[2] *n* : rizos *mpl* muy apretados

frizzy [ˈfrɪzi] *adj* **frizzier; -est** : rizado, crespo, chino *Mex*

fro [ˈfroː] *adv* **to and fro** : de aquí para allá, de un lado para otro

frock [ˈfrɑk] *n* DRESS : vestido *m*

frog [ˈfrɔg, ˈfrɑg] *n* **1** : rana *f* **2** FASTENER : alamar *m* 3 **to have a frog in one's throat** : tener carraspera

frogman [ˈfrɔg,mæn, ˈfrɑg-, -mən] *n, pl* **-men** [-mən, -,mɛn] : hombre *m* rana, submarinista *mf*

frolic[1] [ˈfrɑlɪk] *vi* **-icked; -icking** : retozar, juguetear

frolic[2] *n* FUN : diversión *f*

frolicsome [ˈfrɑlɪksəm] *adj* : juguetón

from [ˈfrʌm, ˈfrɑm] *prep* **1** (*indicating a starting point*) : desde, de, a partir de <from Cali to Bogota : de Cali a Bogotá> <where are you from? : ¿de dónde eres?> <from that time onward : desde entonces> <from tomorrow : a partir de mañana> **2** (*indicating a source or sender*) : de <a letter from my friend : una carta de mi amiga> <a quote from Shakespeare : una cita de Shakespeare> **3** (*indicating distance*) : de <10 feet from the entrance : a 10 pies de la entrada> **4** (*indicating a cause*) : de <red from crying : rojos de llorar> <he died from the cold : murió del frío> **5** OFF, OUT OF : de <she took it from the drawer : lo sacó del cajón> **6** (*with adverbs or adverbial phrases*) : de, desde <from above : desde arriba> <from among : de entre>

frond [ˈfrɑnd] *n* : fronda *f,* hoja *f*

front[1] [ˈfrʌnt] *vi* **1** FACE : dar, estar orientado <the house fronts north : la casa da al norte> **2** : servir de pantalla <he fronts for his boss : sirve de pantalla para su jefe>

front[2] *adj* : delantero, de adelante, primero <the front row : la primera fila>

front[3] *n* **1** : frente *m,* parte *f* de adelante, delantera *f* <the front of the class : el frente de la clase> <at the front of the train : en la parte delantera del tren> **2** AREA, ZONE : frente *m,* zona *f* <the Eastern front : el frente oriental> <on the educational front : en el frente de la enseñanza> **3** FACADE : fachada *f* (de un edificio o una persona> **4** : frente *m* (en meteorología)

frontage [ˈfrʌntɪdʒ] *n* : fachada *f,* frente *m*

frontal [ˈfrʌntəl] *adj* : frontal, de frente

frontier [,frʌnˈtɪr] *n* : frontera *f*

frontiersman [,frʌnˈtɪrzmən] *n, pl* **-men** [-mən, -,mɛn] : hombre *m* de la frontera

frontispiece [ˈfrʌntəs,piːs] *n* : frontispicio *m*

frost[1] [ˈfrɔst] *vt* **1** FREEZE : helar **2** ICE : escarchar (pasteles)

frost[2] *n* **1** : helada *f* (en meteorología) **2** : escarcha *f* <frost on the window : escarcha en la ventana>

frostbite [ˈfrɔst,baɪt] *n* : congelación *f*

frostbitten [ˈfrɔst,bɪtən] *adj* : congelado (dícese de una persona), quemado (dícese de una planta)

frosting [ˈfrɔstɪŋ] *n* ICING : glaseado *m,* betún *m Mex*

frosty [ˈfrɔsti] *adj* **frostier; -est 1** CHILLY : helado, frío **2** COOL, UNFRIENDLY : frío, glacial

froth [ˈfrɔθ] *n, pl* **froths** [ˈfrɔθs, ˈfrɔðz] : espuma *f*

frothy [ˈfrɔθi] *adj* **frothier; -est** : espumoso

frown[1] [ˈfraʊn] *vi* **1** : fruncir el ceño, fruncir el entrecejo **2 to frown at**

: mirar (algo) con ceño, mirar (a alguien) con ceño
frown[2] *n* : ceño *m* (fruncido)
frowsy *or* **frowzy** ['fraʊzi] *adj* **frowsier** *or* **frowzier; -est** : desaliñado, desaseado
froze → **freeze**
frozen → **freeze**
frugal ['fruːgəl] *adj* : frugal, ahorrativo, parco — **frugally** *adv*
frugality [fru'gæləṭi] *n* : frugalidad *f*
fruit[1] ['fruːt] *vi* : dar fruto
fruit[2] *n* **1** : fruta *f* (término genérico), fruto *m* (término particular) **2 fruits** *npl* REWARDS : frutos *mpl* <the fruits of his labor : los frutos de su trabajo>
fruitcake ['fruːt,keɪk] *n* : pastel *m* de frutas
fruitful ['fruːtfəl] *adj* : fructífero, provechoso
fruition [fru'ɪʃən] *n* **1** : cumplimiento *m*, realización *f* **2 to bring to fruition** : realizar
fruitless ['fruːtləs] *adj* : infructuoso, inútil — **fruitlessly** *adv*
fruity ['fruːṭi] *adj* **fruitier; -est** : (con sabor) a fruta
frumpy ['frʌmpi] *adj* **frumpier; -est** : anticuado y sin atractivo
frustrate ['frʌs,treɪt] *vt* **-trated; -trating** : frustrar
frustrating ['frʌs,treɪṭɪŋ] *adj* : frustrante — **frustratingly** *adv*
frustration [,frʌs'treɪʃən] *n* : frustración *f*
fry[1] ['fraɪ] *vt* **fried; frying** : freír
fry[2] *n, pl* **fries 1** : fritura *f*, plato *m* frito **2** : fiesta *f* en que se sirven frituras **3** *pl* **fry** : alevín *m* (pez)
fuddle ['fʌdəl] *vt* **-dled; -dling** : confundir, atontar
fuddy–duddy ['fʌdi,dʌdi] *n, pl* **-dies** : persona *f* chapada a la antigua, carca *mf*
fudge[1] ['fʌdʒ] *vt* **fudged; fudging 1** FALSIFY : amañar, falsificar **2** DODGE : esquivar
fudge[2] *n* : dulce *m* blando de chocolate y leche
fuel[1] ['fjuːəl] *vt* **-eled** *or* **-elled; -eling** *or* **-elling 1** : abastecer de combustible **2** STIMULATE : estimular
fuel[2] *n* : combustible *m*, carburante *m* (para motores)
fugitive[1] ['fjuːdʒəṭɪv] *adj* **1** RUNAWAY : fugitivo **2** FLEETING : efímero, pasajero, fugaz
fugitive[2] *n* : fugitivo *m*, -va *f*
fulcrum ['fʊlkrəm, 'fʌl-] *n, pl* **-crums** *or* **-cra** [-krə] : fulcro *m*
fulfill *or* **fulfil** [fʊl'fɪl] *vt* **-filled; -filling 1** PERFORM : cumplir con, realizar, llevar a cabo **2** SATISFY : satisfacer
fulfillment [fʊl'fɪlmənt] *n* **1** PERFORMANCE : cumplimiento *m*, ejecución *f* **2** SATISFACTION : satisfacción *f*, realización *f*
full[1] ['fʊl, 'fʌl] *adv* **1** VERY : muy <full well : muy bien, perfectamente> **2** ENTIRELY : completamente <she swung full around : giró completamente> **3** DIRECTLY : de lleno, directamente <he looked me full in the face : me miró directamente a la cara>
full[2] *adj* **1** FILLED : lleno **2** COMPLETE : completo, detallado **3** MAXIMUM : todo, pleno <at full speed : a toda velocidad> <in full bloom : en plena flor> **4** PLUMP : redondo, llenito *fam*, regordete *fam* <a full face : una cara redonda> <a full figure : un cuerpo llenito> **5** AMPLE : amplio <a full skirt : una falda amplia>
full[3] *n* **1 to pay in full** : pagar en su totalidad **2 to the full** : al máximo
full–fledged ['fʊl'flɛdʒd] *adj* : hecho y derecho
fullness ['fʊlnəs] *n* **1** ABUNDANCE : plenitud *f*, abundancia *f* **2** : amplitud *f* (de una falda)
fully ['fʊli] *adv* **1** COMPLETELY : completamente, totalmente **2** : al menos, por lo menos <fully half of them : al menos la mitad de ellos>
fulsome ['fʊlsəm] *adj* : excesivo, exagerado, efusivo
fumble[1] ['fʌmbəl] *v* **-bled; -bling** *vt* **1** : dejar caer, fumblear **2 to fumble one's way** : ir a tientas — *vi* **1** GROPE : hurgar, tantear **2 to fumble with** : manejar con torpeza
fumble[2] *n* : fumble *m* (en futbol americano)
fume[1] ['fjuːm] *vi* **fumed; fuming 1** SMOKE : echar humo, humear **2** : enfadarse, enojarse
fume[2] *n* : gas *m*, humo *m*, vapor *m*
fumigate ['fjuːmə,geɪt] *vt* **-gated; -gating** : fumigar
fumigation [,fjuːmə'geɪʃən] *n* : fumigación *m*
fun[1] ['fʌn] *adj* : divertido, entretenido
fun[2] *n* **1** AMUSEMENT : diversión *f*, entretenimiento *m* **2** ENJOYMENT : disfrute *m* **3 to have fun** : divertirse **4 to make fun of** : reírse de, burlarse de
function[1] ['fʌŋkʃən] *vi* : funcionar, desempeñarse, servir
function[2] *n* **1** PURPOSE : función *f* **2** GATHERING : reunión *f* social, recepción *f* **3** CEREMONY : ceremonia *f*, acto *m*
functional ['fʌŋkʃənəl] *adj* : funcional — **functionally** *adv*
functionary ['fʌŋkʃə,nɛri] *n, pl* **-aries** : funcionario *m*, -ria *f*
fund[1] ['fʌnd] *vt* : financiar
fund[2] *n* **1** SUPPLY : reserva *f*, cúmulo *m* **2** : fondo *m* <investment fund : fondo de inversiones> **3 funds** *npl* RESOURCES : fondos *mpl*
fundamental[1] [,fʌndə'mɛntəl] *adj* **1** BASIC : fundamental, básico **2** PRINCIPAL : esencial, principal **3** INNATE : innato, intrínseco
fundamental[2] *n* : fundamento *m*

fundamentally [ˌfʌndəˈmɛntəli] *adv* : fundamentalmente, básicamente
funding [ˈfʌndɪŋ] *n* : financiación *f*
funeral[1] [ˈfjuːnərəl] *adj* **1** : funeral, funerario, fúnebre <funeral procession : cortejo fúnebre> **2 funeral home** : funeraria *f*
funeral[2] *n* : funeral *m,* funerales *mpl*
funereal [fjuːˈnɪriəl] *adj* : fúnebre
fungal [ˈfʌŋgəl] *adj* : de hongos, micótico
fungicidal [ˌfʌndʒəˈsaɪdəl, ˌfʌŋgə-] *adj* : fungicida
fungicide [ˈfʌndʒəˌsaɪd, ˈfʌŋgə-] *n* : fungicida *m*
fungous [ˈfʌŋgəs] *adj* : fungoso
fungus [ˈfʌŋgəs] *n, pl* **fungi** [ˈfʌnˌdʒaɪ, ˈfʌŋˌgaɪ] : hongo *m*
funk [ˈfʌŋk] *n* **1** FEAR : miedo *m* **2** DEPRESSION : depresión *f*
funky [ˈfʌŋki] *adj* **funkier; -est** ODD, QUAINT : raro, extraño, original
funnel[1] [ˈfʌnəl] *vt* **-neled; -neling** CHANNEL : canalizar, encauzar
funnel[2] *n* **1** : embudo *m* **2** SMOKESTACK : chimenea *f* (de un barco o vapor)
funnies [ˈfʌniz] *npl* : tiras *fpl* cómicas
funny [ˈfʌni] *adj* **funnier; -est 1** AMUSING : divertido, cómico **2** STRANGE : extraño, raro
fur[1] [ˈfər] *adj* : de piel
fur[2] *n* **1** : pelaje *m,* piel *f* **2** : prenda *f* de piel
furbish [ˈfərbɪʃ] *vt* : pulir, limpiar
furious [ˈfjʊriəs] *adj* **1** ANGRY : furioso **2** FRANTIC : violento, frenético, vertiginoso (dícese de la velocidad)
furiously [ˈfjʊriəsli] *adv* **1** ANGRILY : furiosamente **2** FRANTICALLY : frenéticamente
furlong [ˈfərˌlɔŋ] *n* : estadio *m* (201.2 m)
furlough[1] [ˈfərˌloː] *vt* : dar permiso a, dar licencia a
furlough[2] *n* LEAVE : permiso *m,* licencia *f*
furnace [ˈfərnəs] *n* : horno *m*
furnish [ˈfərnɪʃ] *vt* **1** SUPPLY : proveer, suministrar **2** : amueblar <furnished apartment : departamento amueblado>
furnishings [ˈfərnɪʃɪŋz] *npl* **1** ACCESSORIES : accesorios *mpl* **2** FURNITURE : muebles *mpl,* mobiliario *m*
furniture [ˈfərnɪtʃər] *n* : muebles *mpl,* mobiliario *m*
furor [ˈfjʊrˌɔr, -ər] *n* **1** RAGE : furia *f,* rabia *f* **2** UPROAR : escándalo *m,* jaleo *m,* alboroto *m*
furrier [ˈfəriər] *n* : peletero *m,* -ra *f*
furrow[1] [ˈfəroː] *vt* **1** : surcar **2 to furrow one's brow** : fruncir el ceño
furrow[2] *n* **1** GROOVE : surco *m* **2** WRINKLE : arruga *f,* surco *m*
furry [ˈfəri] *adj* **furrier; -est** : peludo (dícese de un animal), peluche (dícese de un objeto)
further[1] [ˈfərðər] *vt* : promover, fomentar
further[2] *adv* **1** FARTHER : más lejos, más adelante **2** MOREOVER : además **3** MORE : más <I'll consider it further in the morning : lo consideraré más en la mañana>
further[3] *adj* **1** FARTHER : más lejano **2** ADDITIONAL : adicional, más
furtherance [ˈfərðərənts] *n* : promoción *f,* fomento *m,* adelantamiento *m*
furthermore [ˈfərðərˌmor] *adv* : además
furthermost [ˈfərðərˌmoːst] *adj* : más lejano, más distante
furthest [ˈfərðəst] → **farthest**[1], **farthest**[2]
furtive [ˈfərtɪv] *adj* : furtivo, sigiloso — **furtively** *adv*
furtiveness [ˈfərtɪvnəs] *n* STEALTH : sigilo *m*
fury [ˈfjʊri] *n, pl* **-ries 1** RAGE : furia *f,* ira *f* **2** VIOLENCE : furia *f,* furor *m*
fuse[1] [ˈfjuːz] *or* **fuze** *vt* **fused** *or* **fuzed; fusing** *or* **fuzing** : equipar con un fusible
fuse[2] *v* **fused; fusing** *vt* **1** SMELT : fundir **2** MERGE : fusionar, fundir — *vi* : fundirse, fusionarse
fuse[3] *n* : fusible *m*
fuselage [ˈfjuːsəˌlɑʒ, -zə-] *n* : fuselage *m*
fusillade [ˈfjuːsəˌlɑd, -ˌleɪd, ˌfjuːsəˈ-, -zə-] *n* : descarga *f* de fusilería
fusion [ˈfjuːʒən] *n* : fusión *f*
fuss[1] [ˈfʌs] *vi* **1** WORRY : preocuparse **2 to fuss with** : juguetear con, toquetear **3 to fuss over** : mimar
fuss[2] *n* **1** COMMOTION : alboroto *m,* escándalo *m* **2** ATTENTION : atenciones *fpl* **3** COMPLAINT : quejas *fpl*
fussbudget [ˈfʌsˌbʌdʒət] *n* : quisquilloso *m,* -sa *f;* melindroso *m,* -sa *f*
fussiness [ˈfʌsinəs] *n* **1** IRRITABILITY : irritabilidad *f* **2** ORNATENESS : lo recargado **3** METICULOUSNESS : meticulosidad *f*
fussy [ˈfʌsi] *adj* **fussier; -est 1** IRRITABLE : irritable, nervioso **2** OVERELABORATE : recargado **3** METICULOUS : meticuloso **4** FASTIDIOUS : quisquilloso, exigente
futile [ˈfjuːtəl, ˈfjuːˌtaɪl] *adj* : inútil, vano
futility [fjuˈtɪləti] *n, pl* **-ties** : inutilidad *f*
future[1] [ˈfjuːtʃər] *adj* : futuro
future[2] *n* : futuro *m*
futuristic [ˌfjuːtʃəˈrɪstɪk] *adj* : futurista
fuze → **fuse**[1]
fuzz [ˈfʌz] *n* : pelusa *f*
fuzziness [ˈfʌzinəs] *n* **1** DOWNINESS : vellosidad *f* **2** INDISTINCTNESS : falta *f* de claridad
fuzzy [ˈfʌzi] *adj* **fuzzier; -est 1** FLUFFY, FURRY : con pelusa, peludo **2** INDISTINCT : indistinto, borroso

G

g [ˈdʒiː] *n, pl* **g's** *or* **gs** [ˈdʒiːz] : séptima letra del alfabeto inglés
gab[1] [ˈgæb] *vi* **gabbed; gabbing** : charlar, cotorrear *fam,* parlotear *fam*
gab[2] *n* CHATTER : cotorreo *m fam,* parloteo *m fam*
gabardine [ˈgæbərˌdiːn] *n* : gabardina *f*
gabby [ˈgæbi] *adj* **gabbier; -est** : hablador, parlanchín
gable [ˈgeɪbəl] *n* : hastial *m,* aguilón *m*
Gabonese [ˌgæbəˈniːz, -ˈniːs] *n* : gabonés *m,* -nesa *f* — **Gabonese** *adj*
gad [ˈgæd] *vi* **gadded; gadding** WANDER : deambular, vagar, callejear
gadfly [ˈgædˌflaɪ] *n, pl* **-flies 1** : tábano *m* (insecto) **2** FAULTFINDER : criticón *m,* -cona *f fam*
gadget [ˈgædʒət] *n* : artilugio *m,* aparato *m*
gadgetry [ˈgædʒətri] *n* : artilugios *mpl,* aparatos *mpl*
gaff [ˈgæf] *n* **1** : garfio *m* **2** → **gaffe**
gaffe [ˈgæf] *n* : metedura *f* de pata *fam*
gag[1] [ˈgæg] *v* **gagged; gagging** *vt* : amordazar <to tie up and gag : atar y amordazar> — *vi* **1** CHOKE : atragantarse **2** RETCH : hacer arcadas
gag[2] *n* **1** : mordaza *f* (para la boca) **2** JOKE : chiste *m*
gage → **gauge**
gaggle [ˈgægəl] *n* : bandada *f,* manada *f* (de gansos)
gaiety [ˈgeɪəti] *n, pl* **-eties 1** MERRYMAKING : juerga *f* **2** MERRIMENT : alegría *f,* regocijo *m*
gaily [ˈgeɪli] *adv* : alegremente
gain[1] [ˈgeɪn] *vt* **1** ACQUIRE, OBTAIN : ganar, obtener, adquirir, conseguir <to gain knowledge : adquirir conocimientos> <to gain a victory : obtener una victoria> **2** REACH : alcanzar, llegar a **3** INCREASE : ganar, aumentar <to gain weight : aumentar de peso> **4** : adelantarse, ganar <the watch gains two minutes a day : el reloj se adelanta dos minutos por día> — *vi* **1** PROFIT : beneficiarse **2** INCREASE : aumentar
gain[2] *n* **1** PROFIT : beneficio *m,* ganancia *f,* lucro *m,* provecho *m* **2** INCREASE : aumento *m*
gainful [ˈgeɪnfəl] *adj* : lucrativo, beneficioso, provechoso <gainful employment : trabajo remunerado>
gait [ˈgeɪt] *n* : paso *m,* andar *m,* manera *f* de caminar
gal [ˈgæl] *n* : muchacha *f*
gala[1] [ˈgeɪlə, ˈgæ-, ˈgɑ-] *adj* : de gala
gala[2] *n* : gala *f,* fiesta *f*
galactic [gəˈlæktɪk] *adj* : galáctico
galaxy [ˈgæləksi] *n, pl* **-axies** : galaxia *f*
gale [ˈgeɪl] *n* **1** WIND : vendaval *f,* viento *m* fuerte **2 gales of laughter** : carcajadas *fpl*
gall[1] [ˈgɔl] *vt* **1** CHAFE : rozar **2** IRRITATE, VEX : irritar, molestar
gall[2] *n* **1** BILE : bilis *f,* hiel *f* **2** INSOLENCE : audacidad *f,* insolencia *f,* descaro *m* **3** SORE : rozadura *f* (de un caballo) **4** : agalla *f* (de una planta)
gallant [ˈgælənt] *adj* **1** BRAVE : valiente, gallardo **2** CHIVALROUS, POLITE : galante, cortés
gallantry [ˈgæləntri] *n, pl* **-ries** : galantería *f,* caballerosidad *f*
gallbladder [ˈgɔlˌblædər] *n* : vesícula *f* biliar
galleon [ˈgæljən] *n* : galeón *m*
gallery [ˈgæləri] *n, pl* **-leries 1** BALCONY : galería *f* (para espectadores) **2** CORRIDOR : pasillo *m,* galería *f,* corredor *m* **3** : galería *f* (para exposiciones)
galley [ˈgæli] *n, pl* **-leys** : galera *f*
gallium [ˈgæliəm] *n* : galio *m*
gallivant [ˈgæləˌvænt] *vi* : callejear
gallon [ˈgælən] *n* : galón *m*
gallop[1] [ˈgæləp] *vi* : galopar
gallop[2] *n* : galope *m*
gallows [ˈgæˌloːz] *n, pl* **-lows** *or* **-lowses** [-ˌloːzəz] : horca *f*
gallstone [ˈgɔlˌstoːn] *n* : cálculo *m* biliar
galore [gəˈlor] *adj* : en abundancia <bargains galore : muchísimas gangas>
galoshes [gəˈlɑʃəz] *n* : galochas *fpl,* chanclos *mpl*
galvanize [ˈgælvənˌaɪz] *vt* **-nized; -nizing 1** STIMULATE : estimular, excitar, impulsar **2** : galvanizar (metales)
Gambian [ˈgæmbiən] *n* : gambiano *m,* -na *f* — **Gambian** *adj*
gambit [ˈgæmbɪt] *n* **1** : gambito *m* (en ajedrez) **2** STRATAGEM : estratagema *f,* táctica *f*
gamble[1] [ˈgæmbəl] *v* **-bled; -bling** *vi* : jugar, arriesgarse — *vt* **1** BET, WAGER : apostar, jugarse **2** RISK : arriesgar
gamble[2] *n* **1** BET : apuesta *f* **2** RISK : riesga *f*
gambler [ˈgæmbələr] *n* : jugador *m,* -dora *f*
gambol [ˈgæmbəl] *vi* **-boled** *or* **-bolled; -boling** *or* **-bolling** FROLIC : retozar, juguetear
game[1] [ˈgeɪm] *adj* **1** READY : listo, dispuesto <we're game for anything : estamos listos para lo que sea> **2** LAME : cojo
game[2] *n* **1** AMUSEMENT : juego *m,* diversión *f* **2** CONTEST : juego *m,* partido *m,* concurso *m* **3** : caza *f* <big game : caza mayor>
gamecock [ˈgeɪmˌkɑk] *n* : gallo *m* de pelea
gamekeeper [ˈgeɪmˌkiːpər] *n* : guardabosque *mf*
gamely [ˈgeɪmli] *adv* : animosamente

gamma ray [ˈgæmə] *n* : rayo *m* gamma

gamut [ˈgæmət] *n* : gama *f,* espectro *m* <to run the gamut : pasar por toda la gama>

gamy *or* **gamey** [ˈgeɪmi] *adj* **gamier; -est** : con sabor de animal de caza, fuerte

gander [ˈgændər] *n* **1** : ganso *m* (animal) **2** GLANCE : mirada *f,* vistazo *m,* ojeada *f*

gang[1] [ˈgæŋ] *vi* **to gang up** : agruparse, unirse

gang[2] *n* : banda *f,* pandilla *f*

gangling [ˈgæŋglɪŋ] *adj* LANKY : larguirucho *fam*

ganglion [ˈgæŋgliən] *n, pl* **-glia** [-gliə] : ganglio *m*

gangplank [ˈgæŋˌplæŋk] *n* : pasarela *f*

gangrene [ˈgæŋˌgriːn, ˈgæn-; gæŋˈ-, gænˈ-] *n* : gangrena *f*

gangrenous [ˈgæŋgrənəs] *adj* : gangrenoso

gangster [ˈgæŋstər] *n* : gángster *mf*

gangway [ˈgæŋˌweɪ] *n* **1** : pasarela *f* **2 gangway!** : ¡abran paso!

gap [ˈgæp] *n* **1** BREACH, OPENING : espacio *m,* brecha *f,* abertura *f* **2** GORGE : desfiladero *m,* barranco *m* **3** : laguna *f* <a gap in my education : una laguna en mi educación> **4** INTERVAL : pausa *f,* intervalo *m* **5** DISPARITY : brecha *f,* disparidad *f*

gape[1] [ˈgeɪp] *vi* **gaped; gaping 1** OPEN : abrirse, estar abierto **2** STARE : mirar fijamente con la boca abierta, mirar boquiabierto

gape[2] *n* **1** OPENING : abertura *f,* brecha *f* **2** STARE : mirada *f* boquiabierta

garage[1] [gəˈrɑʒ, -ˈrɑdʒ] *vt* **-raged; -raging** : dejar en un garaje

garage[2] *n* : garaje *m,* cochera *f*

garb[1] [ˈgɑrb] *vt* : vestir, ataviar

garb[2] *n* : vestimenta *f,* atuendo *f*

garbage [ˈgɑrbɪdʒ] *n* : basura *f,* desechos *mpl*

garbageman [ˈgɑrbɪdʒmən] *n, pl* **-men** [-mən, -ˌmɛn] : basurero *m*

garble [ˈgɑrbəl] *vt* **-bled; -bling** : tergiversar, distorsionar

garbled [ˈgɑrbəld] *adj* : incoherente, incomprensible

garden[1] [ˈgɑrdən] *vi* : trabajar en el jardín

garden[2] *n* : jardín *m*

gardener [ˈgɑrdənər] *n* : jardinero *m,* -ra *f*

gardenia [gɑrˈdiːnjə] *n* : gardenia *f*

gargantuan [gɑrˈgæntʃʊən] *adj* : gigantesco, colosal

gargle[1] [ˈgɑrgəl] *vi* **-gled; -gling** : hacer gárgaras, gargarizar

gargle[2] *n* : gárgara *f*

gargoyle [ˈgɑrˌgɔɪl] *n* : gárgola *f*

garish [ˈgærɪʃ] *adj* GAUDY : llamativo, chillón, charro — **garishly** *adv*

garland[1] [ˈgɑrlənd] *vt* : adornar con guirnaldas

garland[2] *n* : guirnalda *f*

garlic [ˈgɑrlɪk] *n* : ajo *m*

garment [ˈgɑrmənt] *n* : prenda *f*

garner [ˈgɑrnər] *vt* : recoger, cosechar

garnet [ˈgɑrnət] *n* : granate *m*

garnish[1] [ˈgɑrnɪʃ] *vt* : aderezar, guarnecer

garnish[2] *n* : aderezo *m,* guarnición *f*

garret [ˈgærət] *n* : buhardilla *f,* desván *m*

garrison[1] [ˈgærəsən] *vt* **1** QUARTER : acuartelar (tropas) **2** OCCUPY : guarnecer, ocupar (con tropas)

garrison[2] *n* **1** : guarnición *f* (ciudad) **2** FORT : fortaleza *f,* poste *m* militar

garrulous [ˈgærələs] *adj* : charlatán, parlanchín, garlero *Col fam*

garter [ˈgɑrtər] *n* : liga *f*

gas[1] [ˈgæs] *v* **gassed; gassing** *vt* : gasear — *vi* **to gas up** : llenar el tanque con gasolina

gas[2] *n, pl* **gases** [ˈgæsəz] **1** : gas *m* <tear gas : gas lacrimógeno> **2** GASOLINE : gasolina *f*

gaseous [ˈgæʃəs, ˈgæsiəs] *adj* : gaseoso

gash[1] [ˈgæʃ] *vt* : hacer un tajo en, cortar

gash[2] *n* : cuchillada *f,* tajo *m*

gasket [ˈgæskət] *n* : junta *f*

gas mask *n* : máscara *f* antigás

gasoline [ˈgæsəˌliːn, ˌgæsəˈ-] *n* : gasolina *f,* nafta *f*

gasp[1] [ˈgæsp] *vi* **1** : boquear <to gasp with surprise : gritar de asombro> **2** PANT : jadear, respirar con dificultad

gasp[2] *n* **1** : boqueada *f* <a gasp of surprise : un grito sofocado> **2** PANTING : jadeo *m*

gas station → **service station**

gastric [ˈgæstrɪk] *adj* : gástrico <gastric juice : jugo gástrico>

gastronomic [ˌgæstrəˈnɑmɪk] *adj* : gastronómico

gastronomy [gæsˈtrɑnəmi] *n* : gastronomía *f*

gate [ˈgeɪt] *n* : portón *m,* verja *f,* puerta *f*

gatekeeper [ˈgeɪtˌkiːpər] *n* : guarda *mf;* guardián *m,* -diana *f*

gateway [ˈgeɪtˌweɪ] *n* : puerta *f* (de acceso), entrada *f*

gather [ˈgæðər] *vt* **1** ASSEMBLE : juntar, recoger, reunir **2** HARVEST : recoger, cosechar **3** : fruncir (una tela) **4** INFER : deducir, suponer

gathering [ˈgæðərɪŋ] *n* : reunión *f*

gauche [ˈgoːʃ] *adj* : torpe, falto de tacto

gaudy [ˈgɔdi] *adj* **gaudier; -est** : chillón, llamativo

gauge[1] [ˈgeɪdʒ] *vt* **gauged; gauging 1** MEASURE : medir **2** ESTIMATE, JUDGE : estimar, evaluar, juzgar

gauge[2] *n* **1** : indicador *m* <pressure gauge : indicador de presión> **2** CALIBER : calibre *m* **3** INDICATION : indicio *m,* muestra *f*

gaunt ['gɔnt] *adj* : demacrado, enjuto, descarnado
gauntlet ['gɔntlət] *n* : guante *m* <to run the gauntlet of : exponerse a>
gauze ['gɔz] *n* : gasa *f*
gauzy ['gɔzi] *adj* **gauzier; -est** : diáfano, vaporoso
gave → **give**
gavel ['gævəl] *n* : martillo *m* (de un juez, un subastador, etc.)
gawk ['gɔk] *vi* GAPE : mirar boquiabierto
gawky ['gɔki] *adj* **gawkier; -est** : desmañado, torpe, desgarbado
gay ['geɪ] *adj* **1** MERRY : alegre **2** BRIGHT, COLORFUL : vistoso, vivo **3** HOMOSEXUAL : homosexual
gaze¹ ['geɪz] *vi* **gazed; gazing** : mirar (fijamente)
gaze² *n* : mirada *f* (fija)
gazelle [gə'zɛl] *n* : gacela *f*
gazette [gə'zɛt] *n* : gaceta *f*
gazetteer [ˌgæzə'tɪr] *n* : diccionario *m* geográfico
gear¹ ['gɪr] *vt* ADAPT, ORIENT : adaptar, ajustar, orientar <a book geared to children : un libro adaptado a los niños> — *vi* **to gear up** : prepararse
gear² *n* **1** CLOTHING : ropa *f* **2** BELONGINGS : efectos *mpl* personales **3** EQUIPMENT, TOOLS : equipo *m,* aparejo *m,* herramientas *fpl* <fishing gear : aparejo de pescar> <landing gear : tren de aterrizaje> **4** COGWHEEL : rueda *f* dentada **5** : marcha *f,* velocidad *f* (de un vehículo) <to put in gear : poner en marcha> <to change gear(s) : cambiar de velocidad>
gearshift ['gɪrˌʃɪft] *n* : palanca *f* de cambio, palanca *f* de velocidad
geese → **goose**
Geiger counter ['gaɪgərˌkaʊntər] *n* : contador *m* Geiger
gelatin ['dʒɛlətən] *n* : gelatina *f*
gem ['dʒɛm] *n* : joya *f,* gema *f,* alhaja *f*
Gemini ['dʒɛməˌnaɪ] *n* : Géminis *mf*
gemstone ['dʒɛmˌstoːn] *n* : piedra *f* (semipreciosa o preciosa), gema *f*
gender ['dʒɛndər] *n* **1** SEX : sexo *m* **2** : género *m* (en la gramática)
gene ['dʒiːn] *n* : gen *m,* gene *m*
genealogical [ˌdʒiːniə'lɑdʒɪkəl] *adj* : genealógico
genealogy [ˌdʒiːni'ɑlədʒi, ˌdʒɛ-, -'æ-] *n, pl* **-gies** : genealogía *f*
genera → **genus**
general¹ ['dʒɛnrəl, 'dʒɛnə-] *adj* : general <in general : en general, por lo general>
general² *n* : general *mf*
generality [ˌdʒɛnə'ræləṭi] *n, pl* **-ties** : generalidad *f*
generalization [ˌdʒɛnrələ'zeɪʃən, ˌdʒɛnərə-] *n* : generalización *f*
generalize ['dʒɛnrəˌlaɪz, 'dʒɛnərə-] *v* **-ized; -izing** : generalizar
generally ['dʒɛnrəli, 'dʒɛnərə-] *adv* : generalmente, por lo general, en general
generate ['dʒɛnəˌreɪt] *vt* **-ated; -ating** : generar, producir
generation [ˌdʒɛnə'reɪʃən] *n* : generación *f*
generator ['dʒɛnəˌreɪṭər] *n* : generador *m*
generic [dʒə'nɛrɪk] *adj* : genérico
generosity [ˌdʒɛnə'rɑsəṭi] *n, pl* **-ties** : generosidad *f*
generous ['dʒɛnərəs] *adj* **1** OPENHANDED : generoso, dadivoso, desprendido **2** ABUNDANT, AMPLE : abundante, amplio, generoso — **generously** *adv*
genetic [dʒə'nɛṭɪk] *adj* : genético — **genetically** [-ṭɪkli] *adv*
geneticist [dʒə'nɛṭəsɪst] *n* : genetista *mf*
genetics [dʒə'nɛṭɪks] *n* : genética *f*
genial ['dʒiːniəl] *adj* GRACIOUS : simpático, cordial, afable — **genially** *adv*
geniality [ˌdʒiːni'æləṭi] *n* : simpatía *f,* afabilidad *f*
genie ['dʒiːni] *n* : genio *m*
genital ['dʒɛnəṭəl] *adj* : genital
genitals ['dʒɛnəṭəlz] *npl* : genitales *mpl*
genius ['dʒiːnjəs] *n* : genio *m*
genocide ['dʒɛnəˌsaɪd] *n* : genocidio *m*
genre ['ʒɑnrə, 'ʒɑr] *n* : género *m*
genteel [dʒɛn'tiːl] *adj* : cortés, fino, refinado
gentile¹ ['dʒɛnˌtaɪl] *adj* : gentil
gentile² *n* : gentil *mf*
gentility [dʒɛn'tɪləṭi] *n, pl* **-ties** **1** : nobleza *f* (de nacimiento) **2** POLITENESS, REFINEMENT : cortesía *f,* refinamiento *m*
gentle ['dʒɛntəl] *adj* **-tler; -tlest** **1** NOBLE : bien nacido, noble **2** DOCILE : dócil, manso **3** KINDLY : bondadoso, amable **4** MILD : suave, apacible <a gentle breeze : una brisa suave> **5** SOFT : suave (dícese de un sonido), ligero (dícese del tacto) **6** MODERATE : moderado, gradual <a gentle slope : una cuesta gradual>
gentleman ['dʒɛntəlmən] *n, pl* **-men** [-mən, -ˌmɛn] : caballero *m,* señor *m*
gentlemanly ['dʒɛntəlmənli] *adj* : caballeroso
gentleness ['dʒɛntəlnəs] *n* : delicadeza *f,* suavidad *f,* ternura *f*
gentlewoman ['dʒɛntəlˌwʊmən] *n, pl* **-women** [-ˌwɪmən] : dama *f,* señora *f*
gently ['dʒɛntli] *adv* **1** CAREFULLY, SOFTLY : con cuidado, suavemente, ligeramente **2** KINDLY : amablemente, con delicadeza
gentry ['dʒɛntri] *n, pl* **-tries** : aristocracia *f*
genuflect ['dʒɛnjʊˌflɛkt] *vi* : doblar la rodilla, hacer una genuflexión
genuflection [ˌdʒɛnjʊ'flɛkʃən] *n* : genuflexión *f*

genuine ['dʒɛnjʊwən] *adj* **1** AUTHENTIC, REAL : genuino, verdadero, auténtico **2** SINCERE : sincero — **genuinely** *adv*

genus ['dʒiːnəs] *n, pl* **genera** ['dʒɛnərə] : género *m*

geographer [dʒi'ɑgrəfər] *n* : geógrafo *m,* -fa *f*

geographical [ˌdʒiːə'græfɪkəl] *or* **geographic** [-fɪk] *adj* : geográfico — **geographically** [-fɪkli] *adv*

geography [dʒi'ɑgrəfi] *n, pl* **-phies** : geografía *f*

geologic [ˌdʒiːə'lɑdʒɪk] *or* **geological** [-dʒɪkəl] *adj* : geológico — **geologically** [-dʒɪkli] *adv*

geologist [dʒi'ɑlədʒɪst] *n* : geólogo *m,* -ga *f*

geology [dʒi'ɑlədʒi] *n* : geología *f*

geometric [ˌdʒiːə'mɛtrɪk] *or* **geometrical** [-trɪkəl] *adj* : geométrico

geometry [dʒi'ɑmətri] *n, pl* **-tries** : geometría *f*

geranium [dʒə'reɪniəm] *n* : geranio *m*

gerbil ['dʒərbəl] *n* : jerbo *m,* gerbo *m*

geriatric [ˌdʒɛri'ætrɪk] *adj* : geriátrico

geriatrics [ˌdʒɛri'ætrɪks] *n* : geriatría *f*

germ ['dʒərm] *n* **1** MICROORGANISM : microbio *m,* germen *m* **2** BEGINNING : germen *m,* principio *m* <the germ of a plan : el germen de un plan>

German ['dʒərmən] *n* **1** : alemán *m,* -mana *f* **2** : alemán *m* (idioma) — **German** *adj*

germane [dʒər'meɪn] *adj* : relevante, pertinente

germanium [dʒər'meɪniəm] *n* : germanio *m*

germ cell *n* : célula *f* germen

germicide ['dʒərməˌsaɪd] *n* : germicida *m*

germinate ['dʒərməˌneɪt] *v* **-nated; -nating** *vi* : germinar — *vt* : hacer germinar

germination [ˌdʒərmə'neɪʃən] *n* : germinación *f*

gerund ['dʒɛrənd] *n* : gerundio *m*

gestation [dʒɛ'steɪʃən] *n* : gestación *f*

gesture[1] ['dʒɛstʃər] *vi* **-tured; -turing** : gesticular, hacer gestos

gesture[2] *n* **1** : gesto *m,* ademán *m* **2** SIGN, TOKEN : gesto *m,* señal *f* <a gesture of friendship : una señal de amistad>

get ['gɛt] *v* **got** ['gɑt]; **got** *or* **gotten** ['gɑtən]; **getting** *vt* **1** OBTAIN : conseguir, obtener, adquirir **2** RECEIVE : recibir <to get a letter : recibir una carta> **3** EARN : ganar <he gets $10 an hour : gana $10 por hora> **4** FETCH : traer <get me my book : tráigame el libro> **5** CATCH : tomar (un tren, etc.), agarrar (una pelota, una persona, etc.) **6** CONTRACT : contagiarse de, contraer <she got the measles : le dio el sarampión> **7** PREPARE : preparar (una comida) **8** PERSUADE : persuadir, mandar a hacer <I got him to agree : logré convencerlo> **9** (*to cause to be*) <to get one's hair cut : cortarse el pelo> **10** UNDERSTAND : entender <now I get it! : ¡ya entiendo!> **11 to have got** : tener <I've got a headache : tengo un dolor de cabeza> **12 to have got to** : tener que <you've got to come : tienes que venir> — *vi* **1** BECOME : ponerse, volverse, hacerse <to get angry : ponerse furioso, enojarse> **2** GO, MOVE : ir, avanzar <he didn't get far : no avanzó mucho> **3** ARRIVE : llegar <to get home : llegar a casa> **4 to get to be** : llegar a ser <she got to be the director : llegó a ser directora> **5 to get ahead** : adelantarse, progresar **6 to get along** : llevarse bien (con alguien), congeniar **7 to get by** MANAGE : arreglárselas **8 to get over** OVERCOME : superar, consolarse de **9 to get together** MEET : reunirse **10 to get up** : levantarse

getaway ['gɛtəˌweɪ] *n* ESCAPE : fuga *f,* huida *f,* escapada *f*

geyser ['gaɪzər] *n* : géiser *m*

Ghanaian ['gɑniən, 'gæ-] *n* : ghanés *m,* -nesa *f* — **Ghanaian** *adj*

ghastly ['gæstli] *adj* **-lier; -est 1** HORRIBLE : horrible, espantoso **2** PALE : pálido, cadavérico

gherkin ['gərkən] *n* : pepinillo *m*

ghetto ['gɛtoː] *n, pl* **-tos** *or* **-toes** : gueto *m*

ghost ['goːst] *n* **1** : fantasma *f,* espectro *m* **2 the Holy Ghost** : el Espíritu Santo

ghostly ['goːstli] *adv* : fantasmal

ghoul ['guːl] *n* **1** : demonio *m* necrófago **2** : persona *f* de gustos macabros

GI [ˌdʒiː'aɪ] *n, pl* **GI's** *or* **GIs** : soldado *m* estadounidense

giant[1] ['dʒaɪənt] *adj* : gigante, gigantesco, enorme

giant[2] *n* : gigante *m,* -ta *f*

gibberish ['dʒɪbərɪʃ] *n* : galimatías *m,* jerigonza *f*

gibbon ['gɪbən] *n* : gibón *m*

gibe[1] ['dʒaɪb] *vi* **gibed; gibing** : mofarse, burlarse

gibe[2] *n* : pulla *f,* burla *f,* mofa *f*

giblets ['dʒɪbləts] *npl* : menudos *mpl,* menudencias *fpl*

giddiness ['gɪdinəs] *n* **1** DIZZINESS : vértigo *m,* mareo *m* **2** SILLINESS : frivolidad *f,* estupidez *f*

giddy ['gɪdi] *adj* **-dier; -est 1** DIZZY : mareado, vertiginoso **2** FRIVOLOUS, SILLY : frívolo, tonto

gift ['gɪft] *n* **1** TALENT : don *m,* talento *m,* dotes *fpl* **2** PRESENT : regalo *m,* obsequio *m*

gifted ['gɪftəd] *adj* TALENTED : talentoso

gigantic [dʒaɪ'gæntɪk] *adj* : gigantesco, enorme, colosal

giggle[1] ['gɪgəl] *vi* **-gled; -gling** : reírse tontamente

giggle[2] *n* : risita *f,* risa *f* tonta

gild ['gɪld] *vt* **gilded** *or* **gilt** ['gɪlt]; **gilding** : dorar

gill ['gɪl] *n* : agalla *f,* branquia *f*

gilt[1] ['gɪlt] *adj* **:** dorado
gilt[2] *n* **:** dorado *m*
gimlet ['gɪmlət] *n* **1 :** barrena *f* (herramiento) **2 :** bebida *f* de vodka o ginebra y limón
gimmick ['gɪmɪk] *n* **1** GADGET **:** artilugio *m* **2** CATCH **:** engaño *m,* trampa *f* **3** SCHEME, TRICK **:** ardid *m,* truco *m*
gin[1] ['dʒɪn] *vt* **ginned; ginning :** desmotar (algodón)
gin[2] *n* **1 :** desmotadora *f* (de algodón) **2 :** ginebra *f* (bebida alcohólica)
ginger ['dʒɪndʒər] *n* **:** jengibre *m*
ginger ale *n* **:** ginger ale *m,* gaseosa *f* de jengibre
gingerbread ['dʒɪndʒərˌbrɛd] *n* **:** pan *m* de jengibre
gingerly ['dʒɪndʒərli] *adv* **:** con cuidado, cautelosamente
gingham ['gɪŋəm] *n* **:** guinga *f*
ginseng ['dʒɪnˌsɪŋ, -ˌsɛŋ] *n* **:** ginseng *m*
giraffe [dʒə'ræf] *n* **:** jirafa *f*
gird ['gərd] *vt* **girded** *or* **girt** ['gərt]; **girding 1** BIND **:** ceñir, atar **2** ENCIRCLE **:** rodear **3 to gird oneself :** prepararse
girder ['gərdər] *n* **:** viga *f*
girdle[1] ['gərdəl] *vt* **-dled; -dling 1** GIRD **:** ceñir, atar **2** SURROUND **:** rodear, circundar
girdle[2] *n* **:** faja *f*
girl ['gərl] *n* **1 :** niña *f,* muchacha *f,* chica *f* **2** SWEETHEART **:** novia *f* **3** DAUGHTER **:** hija *f*
girlfriend ['gərlˌfrɛnd] *n* **:** novia *f,* amiga *f*
girlhood ['gərlˌhʊd] *n* **:** niñez *f,* juventud *f* (de una muchacha)
girlish ['gərlɪʃ] *adj* **:** de niña
girth ['gərθ] *n* **1 :** circunferencia *f* (de un árbol, etc.), cintura *f* (de una persona) **2** CINCH **:** cincha *f* (para caballos, etc.)
gist ['dʒɪst] *n* **:** quid *m,* meollo *m*
give[1] ['gɪv] *v* **gave** ['geɪv]; **given** ['gɪvən]; **giving** *vt* **1** HAND, PRESENT **:** dar, regalar, obsequiar <give it to me : dámelo> <they gave him a gold watch : le regalaron un reloj de oro> **2** PAY **:** dar, pagar <I'll give you $10 for this one : te daré $10 por éste> **3** UTTER **:** dar, pronunciar <to give a shout : dar un grito> <to give a speech : pronunciar un discurso> <to give a verdict : dictar sentencia> **4** PROVIDE **:** dar <to give one's word : dar uno su palabra> <to give a party : dar una fiesta> **5** CAUSE **:** dar, causar, ocasionar <to give trouble : causar problemas> <to give someone to understand : darle a entender a alguien> **6** GRANT **:** dar, otorgar <to give permission : dar permiso> — *vi* **1 :** hacer regalos **2** YIELD **:** ceder, romperse <it gave under the weight of the crowd : cedió bajo el peso de la muchedumbre> **3 to give in** *or* **to give up** SURRENDER **:** rendirse, entregarse **4 to give out :** agotarse, acabarse <the supplies gave out : las provisiones se agotaron>
give[2] *n* FLEXIBILITY **:** flexibilidad *f,* elasticidad *f*
giveaway ['gɪvəˌweɪ] *n* **1 :** revelación *f* involuntaria **2** GIFT **:** regalo *m,* obsequio *m*
given ['gɪvən] *adj* **1** INCLINED **:** dado, inclinado <he's given to quarreling : es muy dado a discutir> **2** SPECIFIC **:** dado, determinado <at a given time : en un momento dado>
given name *n* **:** nombre *m* de pila
give up *vt* **:** dejar, renunciar a, abandonar <to give up smoking : dejar de fumar>
gizzard ['gɪzərd] *n* **:** molleja *f*
glacial ['gleɪʃəl] *adj* **:** glacial — **glacially** *adv*
glacier ['gleɪʃər] *n* **:** glaciar *m*
glad ['glæd] *adj* **gladder; gladdest 1** PLEASED **:** alegre, contento <she was glad I came : se alegró de que haya venido> <glad to meet you! : ¡mucho gusto!> **2** HAPPY, PLEASING **:** feliz, agradable <glad tidings : buenas nuevas> **3** WILLING **:** dispuesto, gustoso <I'll be glad to do it : lo haré con mucho gusto>
gladden ['glædən] *vt* **:** alegrar
glade ['gleɪd] *n* **:** claro *m*
gladiator ['glædiˌeɪţər] *n* **:** gladiador *m*
gladiolus [ˌglædi'oːləs] *n, pl* **-li** [-li, -ˌlaɪ] **:** gladiolo *m,* gladíolo *m*
gladly ['glædli] *adv* **:** con mucho gusto
gladness ['glædnəs] *n* **:** alegría *f,* gozo *m*
glamor *or* **glamour** ['glæmər] *n* **:** atractivo *m,* hechizo *m,* encanto *m*
glamorous ['glæmərəs] *adj* **:** atractivo, encantador
glance[1] ['glænts] *vi* **glanced; glancing 1** RICOCHET **:** rebotar <it glanced off the wall : rebotó en la pared> **2 to glance at :** mirar, echar un vistazo a **3 to glance away :** apartar los ojos
glance[2] *n* **:** mirada *f,* vistazo *m,* ojeada *f*
gland ['glænd] *n* **:** glándula *f*
glandular ['glændʒʊlər] *adj* **:** glandular
glare[1] ['glær] *vi* **glared; glaring 1** SHINE **:** brillar, relumbrar **2** STARE **:** mirar con ira, lanzar una mirada feroz
glare[2] *n* **1** BRIGHTNESS **:** resplandor *m,* luz *f* deslumbrante **2 :** mirada *f* feroz
glaring ['glærɪŋ] *adj* **1** BRIGHT **:** deslumbrante, brillante **2** FLAGRANT, OBVIOUS **:** flagrante, manifiesto <a glaring error : un error que salta a la vista>
glass ['glæs] *n* **1 :** vidrio *m,* cristal *m* <stained glass : vidrio de color> **2 :** vaso *m* <a glass of milk : un vaso de leche> **3 glasses** *npl* SPECTACLES **:** gafas *fpl,* anteojos *mpl,* lentes *mpl,* espejuelos *mpl*

glassblowing [ˈglæs,bloːɪŋ] *n* : soplado *m* del vidrio

glassful [ˈglæs,fʊl] *n* : vaso *m*, copa *f*

glassware [ˈglæs,wær] *n* : cristalería *f*

glassy [ˈglæsi] *adj* **glassier; -est 1** VITREOUS : vítreo **2** : vidrioso <glassy eyes : ojos vidriosos>

glaze[1] [ˈgleɪz] *vt* **glazed; glazing 1** : ponerle vidrios a (una ventana, etc.) **2** : vidriar (cerámica) **3** : glasear (papel, verduras, etc.)

glaze[2] *n* : vidriado *m*, glaseado *m*, barniz *m*

glazier [ˈgleɪʒər] *n* : vidriero *m*, -ra *f*

gleam[1] [ˈgliːm] *vi* : brillar, destellar, relucir

gleam[2] *n* **1** LIGHT : luz *f* (oscura) **2** GLINT : destello *m* **3** GLIMMER : rayo *m*, vislumbre *f* <a gleam of hope : un rayo de esperanza>

glean [ˈgliːn] *vt* : recoger, espigar

glee [ˈgliː] *n* : alegría *f*, júbilo *m*, regocijo *m*

gleeful [ˈgliːfəl] *adj* : lleno de alegría

glen [ˈglɛn] *n* : cañada *f*

glib [ˈglɪb] *adj* **glibber; glibbest 1** : simplista <a glib reply : una respuesta simplista> **2** : con mucha labia (dícese de una persona)

glibly [ˈglɪbli] *adv* : con mucha labia

glide[1] [ˈglaɪd] *vi* **glided; gliding** : deslizarse (en una superficie), planear (en el aire)

glide[2] *n* : planeo *m*

glider [ˈglaɪdər] *n* **1** : planeador *m* (aeronave) **2** : mecedor *m* (tipo de columpio)

glimmer[1] [ˈglɪmər] *vi* : brillar con luz trémula

glimmer[2] *n* **1** : luz *f* trémula, luz *f* tenue **2** GLEAM : rayo *m*, vislumbre *f* <a glimmer of understanding : un rayo de entendimiento>

glimpse[1] [ˈglɪmps] *vt* **glimpsed; glimpsing** : vislumbrar, entrever

glimpse[2] *n* : mirada *f* breve <to catch a glimpse of : alcanzar a ver, vislumbrar>

glint[1] [ˈglɪnt] *vi* GLEAM, SPARKLE : destellar, fulgurar

glint[2] *n* **1** SPARKLE : destello *m*, centelleo *m* **2 to have a glint in one's eye** : chispearle los ojos a uno

glisten[1] [ˈglɪsən] *vi* : brillar, centellear

glisten[2] *n* : brillo *m*, centelleo *m*

glitter[1] [ˈglɪt̬ər] *vi* **1** SPARKLE : destellar, relucir, brillar **2** FLASH : relampaguear <his eyes glittered in anger : le relampagueaban los ojos de ira>

glitter[2] *n* **1** BRIGHTNESS : brillo *m* **2** : purpurina *f* (para decoración)

gloat [ˈgloːt] *vi* **to gloat over** : regodearse en

glob [ˈglɑb] *n* : plasta *f*, masa *f*, grumo *m*

global [ˈgloːbəl] *adj* **1** SPHERICAL : esférico **2** WORLDWIDE : global, mundial — **globally** *adv*

globe [ˈgloːb] *n* **1** SPHERE : esfera *f*, globo *m* **2** EARTH : globo *m*, Tierra *f* **3** : globo *m* terráqueo (modelo de la Tierra)

globe–trotter [ˈgloːb,trɑt̬ər] *n* : trotamundos *mf*

globular [ˈglɑbjʊlər] *adj* : globular

globule [ˈglɑ,bjuːl] *n* : glóbulo *m*

gloom [ˈgluːm] *n* **1** DARKNESS : penumbra *f*, oscuridad *f* **2** MELANCHOLY : melancolía *f*, tristeza *f*

gloomily [ˈgluːməli] *adv* : tristemente

gloomy [ˈgluːmi] *adj* **gloomier; -est 1** DARK : oscuro, tenebroso <gloomy weather : tiempo gris> **2** MELANCHOLY : melancólico **3** PESSIMISTIC : pesimista **4** DEPRESSING : deprimente, lúgubre

glorification [,glorəfəˈkeɪʃən] *n* : glorificación *f*

glorify [ˈglorə,faɪ] *vt* **-fied; -fying** : glorificar

glorious [ˈgloriəs] *adj* **1** ILLUSTRIOUS : glorioso, ilustre **2** MAGNIFICENT : magnífico, espléndido, maravilloso — **gloriously** *adv*

glory[1] [ˈglori] *vi* **-ried; -rying** EXULT : exultar, regocijarse

glory[2] *n, pl* **-ries 1** RENOWN : gloria *f*, fama *f*, honor *m* **2** PRAISE : gloria *f* <glory to God : gloria a Dios> **3** MAGNIFICENCE : magnificencia *f*, esplendor *m*, gloria *f* **4 to be in one's glory** : estar uno en su gloria

gloss[1] [ˈglɔs, ˈglɑs] *vt* **1** EXPLAIN : glosar, explicar **2** POLISH : lustrar, pulir **3 to gloss over** : quitarle importancia a, minimizar

gloss[2] *n* **1** SHINE : lustre *m*, brillo *m* **2** EXPLANATION : glosa *f*, explicación *f* breve **3** → **glossary**

glossary [ˈglɔsəri, ˈglɑ-] *n, pl* **-ries** : glosario *m*

glossy [ˈglɔsi, ˈglɑ-] *adj* **glossier; -est** : brillante, lustroso, satinado (dícese del papel)

glove [ˈglʌv] *n* : guante *m*

glow[1] [ˈgloː] *vi* **1** SHINE : brillar, resplandecer **2** BRIM : rebosar <to glow with health : rebosar de salud>

glow[2] *n* **1** BRIGHTNESS : resplandor *m*, brillo *m*, luminosidad *f* **2** FEELING : sensación *f* (de bienestar), oleada *f* (de sentimiento) **3** INCANDESCENCE : incandescencia *f*

glower [ˈglaʊər] *vi* : fruncir el ceño

glowworm [ˈgloː,wərm] *n* : luciérnaga *f*

glucose [ˈgluː,koːs] *n* : glucosa *f*

glue[1] [ˈgluː] *vt* **glued; gluing** *or* **glueing** : pegar, encolar

glue[2] *n* : pegamento *m*, cola *f*

gluey [ˈgluːi] *adj* **gluier; -est** : pegajoso

glum [ˈglʌm] *adj* **glummer; glummest 1** SULLEN : hosco, sombrío **2** DREARY, GLOOMY : sombrío, triste, melancólico

glut[1] [ˈglʌt] *vt* **glutted; glutting 1** SATIATE : saciar, hartar **2** : inundar (el mercado)

glut[2] *n* : exceso *m,* superabundancia *f*

glutinous [ˈgluːtənəs] *adj* STICKY : pegajoso, glutinoso

glutton [ˈglʌtən] *n* : glotón *m,* -tona *f*

gluttonous [ˈglʌtənəs] *adj* : glotón

gluttony [ˈglʌtəni] *n, pl* **-tonies** : glotonería *f,* gula *f*

gnarled [ˈnɑrld] *adj* **1** KNOTTY : nudoso **2** TWISTED : retorcido

gnash [ˈnæʃ] *vt* : hacer rechinar (los dientes)

gnat [ˈnæt] *n* : jején *m*

gnaw [ˈnɔ] *vt* : roer

gnome [ˈnoːm] *n* : gnomo *m*

gnu [ˈnuː, ˈnjuː] *n, pl* **gnu** *or* **gnus** : ñu *m*

go[1] [ˈgoː] *v* **went** [ˈwɛnt]; **gone** [ˈgɔn, ˈgɑn]; **going; goes** [ˈgoːz] *vi* **1** PROCEED : ir <to go slow : ir despacio> <to go shopping : ir de compras> **2** LEAVE : irse, marcharse, salir <let's go! : ¡vámonos!> <the train went on time : el tren salió a tiempo> **3** DISAPPEAR : desaparecer, pasarse, irse <her fear is gone : se le ha pasado el miedo> <my pen is gone! : ¡mi pluma desapareció!> **4** EXTEND : ir, extenderse, llegar <this road goes to the river : este camino se extiende hasta el río> <to go from top to bottom : ir de arriba abajo> **5** FUNCTION : funcionar, marchar <the car won't go : el coche no funciona> <to get something going : poner algo en marcha> **6** SELL : venderse <it goes for $15 : se vende por $15> **7** PROGRESS : ir, andar, seguir <my exam went well : me fue bien en el examen> <how did the meeting go? : ¿qué tal la reunión?> **8** BECOME : volverse, quedarse <he's going crazy : está volviéndose loco> <the tire went flat : la llanta se desinfló> **9** FIT : caber <it will go through the door : cabe por la puerta> **10 anything goes!** : ¡todo vale! **11 to go** : faltar <only 10 days to go : faltan sólo 10 días> **12 to go back on** : faltar uno a (su promesa) **13 to go bad** SPOIL : estropearse, echarse a perder **14 to go for** : interesarse uno en, gustarle a uno (algo, alguien) <I don't go for that : eso no me interesa> **15 to go off** EXPLODE : estallar **16 to go with** MATCH : armonizar con, hacer juego con — *v aux* **to be going to** : ir a <I'm going to write a letter : voy a escribir una carta> <it's not going to last : no va a durar>

go[2] *n, pl* **goes 1** ATTEMPT : intento *m* <to have a go at : intentar, probar> **2** SUCCESS : éxito *m* **3** ENERGY : energía *f,* empuje *m* <to be on the go : no parar, no descansar>

goad[1] [ˈgoːd] *vt* : aguijonear (un animal), incitar (a una persona)

goad[2] *n* : aguijón *m*

goal [ˈgoːl] *n* **1** : gol *m* (en deportes) <to score a goal : anotar un gol> **2** *or* **goalposts** : portería *f* **3** AIM, OBJECTIVE : meta *m,* objetivo *m*

goalie [ˈgoːli] → **goalkeeper**

goalkeeper [ˈgoːlˌkiːpər] *n* : portero *m,* -ra *f;* guardameta *mf;* arquero *m,* -ra *f*

goaltender [ˈgoːlˌtɛndər] → **goalkeeper**

goat [ˈgoːt] *n* **1** : cabra *f* (hembra) **2 billy goat** : macho *m* cabrío, chivo *m*

goatee [goːˈtiː] *n* : barbita *f* de chivo, piocha *f Mex*

goatskin [ˈgoːtˌskɪn] *n* : piel *f* de cabra

gob [ˈgɑb] *n* : masa *f,* grumo *m*

gobble [ˈgɑbəl] *v* **-bled; -bling** *vt* **to gobble up** : tragar, engullir — *vi* : hacer ruidos de pavo

gobbledygook [ˈgɑbəldiˌgʊk, -ˌguːk] *n* GIBBERISH : jerigonza *f*

go–between [ˈgoːbɪˌtwiːn] *n* : intermediario *m,* -ria *f;* mediador *m,* -dora *f*

goblet [ˈgɑblət] *n* : copa *f*

goblin [ˈgɑblən] *n* : duende *m,* trasgo *m*

god [ˈgɑd, ˈgɔd] *n* **1** : dios *m* **2 God** : Dios *m*

godchild [ˈgɑdˌtʃaɪld, ˈgɔd-] *n, pl* **-children** : ahijado *m,* -da *f*

goddess [ˈgɑdəs, ˈgɔ-] *n* : diosa *f*

godfather [ˈgɑdˌfɑðər, ˈgɔd-] *n* : padrino *m*

godless [ˈgɑdləs, ˈgɔd-] *adj* : ateo

godlike [ˈgɑdˌlaɪk, ˈgɔd-] *adj* : divino

godly [ˈgɑdli, ˈgɔd-] *adj* **-lier; -est 1** DIVINE : divino **2** DEVOUT, PIOUS : piadoso, devoto, beato

godmother [ˈgɑdˌmʌðər, ˈgɔd-] *n* : madrina *f*

godparents [ˈgɑdˌpærənts, ˈgɔd-] *npl* : padrinos *mpl*

godsend [ˈgɑdˌsɛnd, ˈgɔd-] *n* : bendición *f,* regalo *m* divino

goes → **go**

go–getter [ˈgoːˌgɛtər] *n* : persona *f* ambiciosa, buscavidas *mf fam*

goggle [ˈgɑgəl] *vi* **-gled; -gling** : mirar con ojos desorbitados

goggles [ˈgɑgəlz] *npl* : gafas *fpl* (protectoras), anteojos *mpl*

goings–on [ˌgoːɪŋzˈɑn, -ˈɔn] *npl* : sucesos *mpl,* ocurrencias *fpl*

goiter [ˈgɔɪtər] *n* : bocio *m*

gold [ˈgoːld] *n* : oro *m*

golden [ˈgoːldən] *adj* **1** : (hecho) de oro **2** : dorado, de color oro <golden hair : pelo rubio> **3** FLOURISHING, PROSPEROUS : dorado, próspero <golden years : años dorados> **4** FAVORABLE : favorable, excelente <a golden opportunity : una excelente oportunidad>

goldenrod [ˈgoːldənˌrɑd] *n* : vara *f* de oro

golden rule *n* : regla *f* de oro

goldfinch [ˈgoːldˌfɪntʃ] *n* : jilguero *m*

goldfish [ˈgoːldˌfɪʃ] *n* : pez *m* de colores

goldsmith [ˈgoːldˌsmɪθ] *n* : orífice *mf,* orfebre *mf*

golf[1] [ˈgɑlf, ˈgɔlf] *vi* : jugar (al) golf

golf[2] *n* : golf *m*

golfer [ˈgɑlfər, ˈgɔl-] *n* : golfista *mf*

gondola [ˈgɑndələ, gɑnˈdoːlə] *n* : góndola *f*

gone [ˈgɔn] *adj* **1** DEAD : muerto **2** PAST : pasado, ido **3** LOST : perdido, desaparecido **4 to be far gone :** estar muy avanzado **5 to be gone on :** estar loco por

goner [ˈgɔnər] *n* **to be a goner :** estar en las últimas

gong [ˈgɔŋ, ˈgɑŋ] *n* : gong *m*

gonorrhea [ˌgɑnəˈriːə] *n* : gonorrea *f*

good[1] [ˈgʊd] *adv* **1** (*used as an intensifier*) : bien <a good strong rope : una cuerda bien fuerte> **2** WELL : bien

good[2] *adj* **better** [ˈbɛt̬ər]; **best** [ˈbɛst] **1** PLEASANT : bueno, agradable <good news : buenas noticias> <to have a good time : divertirse> **2** BENEFICIAL : bueno, beneficioso <good for a cold : beneficioso para los resfriados> <it's good for you : es bueno para uno> **3** FULL : completo, entero <a good hour : una hora entera> **4** CONSIDERABLE : bueno, bastante <a good many people : muchísima gente, un buen número de gente> **5** ATTRACTIVE, DESIRABLE : bueno, bien <a good salary : un buen sueldo> <to look good : quedar bien> **6** KIND, VIRTUOUS : bueno, amable <she's a good person : es buena gente> <that's good of you! : ¡qué amable!> <good deeds : buenas obras> **7** SKILLED : bueno, hábil <to be good at : tener facilidad para> **8** SOUND : bueno, sensato <good advice : buenos consejos> **9** (*in greetings*) : bueno <good morning : buenos días> <good afternoon (evening) : buenas tardes> <good night : buenas noches>

good[3] *n* **1** RIGHT : bien *m* <to do good : hacer el bien> **2** GOODNESS : bondad *f* **3** BENEFIT : bien *m,* provecho *m* <it's for your own good : es por tu propio bien> **4 goods** *npl* PROPERTY : efectos *mpl* personales, posesiones *fpl* **5 goods** *npl* WARES : mercancía *f,* mercadería *f,* artículos *mpl* **6 for ~ :** para siempre

good-bye *or* **good-by** [gʊdˈbaɪ] *n* : adiós *m*

good-for-nothing [ˈgʊdfərˌnʌθɪŋ] *n* : inútil *mf;* haragán *m,* -gana *f;* holgazán *m,* -zana *f*

Good Friday *n* : Viernes *m* Santo

good-hearted [ˈgʊdˈhɑrt̬əd] *adj* : bondadoso, benévolo, de buen corazón

good-looking [ˈgʊdˈlʊkɪŋ] *adj* : bello, bonito, guapo

goodly [ˈgʊdli] *adj* **-lier; -est :** considerable, importante <a goodly number : un número considerable>

good-natured [ˈgʊdˈneɪtʃərd] *adj* : amigable, amistoso, bonachón *fam*

goodness [ˈgʊdnəs] *n* **1** : bondad *f* **2 thank goodness! :** ¡gracias a Dios!, ¡menos mal!

good-tempered [ˈgʊdˈtɛmpərd] *adj* : de buen genio

goodwill [ˌgʊdˈwɪl] *n* **1** BENEVOLENCE : benevolencia *f,* buena voluntad *f* **2** : buen nombre *m* (de comercios), renombre *m* comercial

goody [ˈgʊdi] *n, pl* **goodies :** cosa *f* rica para comer, golosina *f*

gooey [ˈguːi] *adj* **gooier; gooiest :** pegajoso

goof[1] [ˈguːf] *vi* **1 to goof off :** holgazanear **2 to goof around :** hacer tonterías **3 to goof up** BLUNDER : cometer un error

goof[2] *n* **1** : bobo *m,* -ba *f;* tonto *m,* -ta *f* **2** BLUNDER : error *m,* planchazo *m fam*

goofy [ˈguːfi] *adj* **goofier; -est** SILLY : tonto, bobo

goose [ˈguːs] *n, pl* **geese** [ˈgiːs] : ganso *m,* -sa *f;* ánsar *m;* oca *f*

gooseberry [ˈguːsˌbɛriː, ˈguːz-] *n, pl* **-berries :** grosella *f* espinosa

goose bumps *npl* : carne *f* de gallina

gooseflesh [ˈguːsˌflɛʃ] → **goose bumps**

goose pimples → **goose bumps**

gopher [ˈgoːfər] *n* : taltuza *f*

gore[1] [ˈgor] *vt* **gored; goring :** cornear

gore[2] *n* BLOOD : sangre *f*

gorge[1] [ˈgɔrdʒ] *vt* **gorged; gorging 1** SATIATE : saciar, hartar **2 to gorge oneself :** hartarse, atiborrarse, atracarse *fam*

gorge[2] *n* RAVINE : desfiladero *m*

gorgeous [ˈgɔrdʒəs] *adj* : hermoso, espléndido, magnífico

gorilla [gəˈrɪlə] *n* : gorila *m*

gory [ˈgori] *adj* **gorier; -est** BLOODY : sangriento

gosling [ˈgɑzlɪŋ, ˈgɔz-] *n* : ansarino *m*

gospel [ˈgɑspəl] *n* **1** *or* **Gospel :** evangelio *m* <the four Gospels : los cuatro evangelios> **2 the gospel truth :** el evangelio, la pura verdad

gossamer [ˈgɑsəmər, ˈgɑzə-] *adj* : tenue, sutil <gossamer wings : alas tenues>

gossip[1] [ˈgɑsɪp] *vi* : chismear, contar chismes

gossip[2] *n* **1** : chismoso *m,* -sa *f* (persona) **2** RUMOR : chisme *m,* rumor *m*

gossipy [ˈgɑsɪpi] *adj* : chismoso

got → **get**

Gothic [ˈgɑθɪk] *adj* : gótico

gotten → **get**

gouge[1] [ˈgaʊdʒ] *vt* **gouged; gouging 1** : excavar, escoplear (con una gubia) **2** SWINDLE : estafar, extorsionar

gouge[2] *n* **1** CHISEL : gubia *f,* formón *m* **2** GROOVE : ranura *f,* hoyo *m* (hecho por un formón)

goulash ['gu:ˌlɑʃ, -ˌlæʃ] *n* : estofado *m,* guiso *m* al estilo húngaro

gourd ['gord, 'gʊrd] *n* : calabaza *f*

gourmand ['gʊrˌmɑnd] *n* **1** GLUTTON : glotón *m,* -tona *f* **2** → **gourmet**

gourmet ['gʊrˌmeɪ, gʊr'meɪ] *n* : gourmet *mf;* gastrónomo *m,* -ma *f*

gout ['gaʊt] *n* : gota *f*

govern ['gʌvərn] *vt* **1** RULE : gobernar **2** CONTROL, DETERMINE : determinar, controlar, guiar **3** RESTRAIN : dominar (las emociones, etc.) — *vi* : gobernar

governess ['gʌvərnəs] *n* : institutriz *f*

government ['gʌvərmənt] *n* : gobierno *m*

governmental [ˌgʌvər'mɛntəl] *adj* : gubernamental, gubernativo

governor ['gʌvənər, 'gʌvərnər] *n* **1** : gobernador *m,* -dora *f* (de un estado, etc.) **2** : regulador *m* (de una máquina)

governorship ['gʌvənərˌʃɪp, 'gʌvərnər-] *n* : cargo *m* de gobernador

gown ['gaʊn] *n* **1** : vestido *m* <evening gown : traje de fiesta> **2** : toga *f* (de magistrados, clérigos, etc.)

grab[1] ['græb] *v* **grabbed; grabbing** *vt* SNATCH : agarrar, arrebatar — *vi* : agarrarse

grab[2] *n* **1 to make a grab for** : tratar de agarrar **2 up for grabs** : disponible, libre

grace[1] ['greɪs] *vt* **graced; gracing 1** HONOR : honrar **2** ADORN : adornar, embellecer

grace[2] *n* **1** : gracia *f* <by the grace of God : por la gracia de Dios> **2** BLESSING : bendición *f* (de la mesa) **3** RESPITE : plazo *m,* gracia *f* <a five days' grace (period) : un plazo de cinco días> **4** GRACIOUSNESS : gentileza *f,* cortesía *f* **5** ELEGANCE : elegancia *f,* gracia *f* **6 to be in the good graces of** : estar en buenas relaciones con **7 with good grace** : de buena gana

graceful ['greɪsfəl] *adj* : lleno de gracia, garboso, grácil

gracefully ['greɪsfəli] *adv* : con gracia, con garbo

gracefulness ['greɪsfəlnəs] *n* : gracilidad *f,* apostura *f,* gallardía *f*

graceless ['greɪsləs] *adj* **1** DISCOURTEOUS : descortés **2** CLUMSY, INELEGANT : torpe, desgarbado, poco elegante

gracious ['greɪʃəs] *adj* : cortés, gentil, cordial

graciously ['greɪʃəsli] *adv* : gentilmente

graciousness ['greɪʃəsnəs] *n* : gentileza *f*

gradation [greɪ'deɪʃən, grə-] *n* : gradación *f*

grade[1] ['greɪd] *vt* **graded; grading 1** SORT : clasificar **2** LEVEL : nivelar **3** : calificar (exámenes, alumnos)

grade[2] *n* **1** QUALITY : categoría *f,* calidad *f* **2** RANK : grado *m,* rango *m* (militar) **3** YEAR : grado *m,* curso *m,* año *m* <sixth grade : el sexto grado> **4** MARK : nota *f,* calificación *f* (en educación) **5** SLOPE : cuesta *f,* pendiente *f,* gradiente *f*

grade school → **elementary school**

gradual ['grædʒʊəl] *adj* : gradual, paulatino

gradually ['grædʒʊəli, 'grædʒəli] *adv* : gradualmente, poco a poco

graduate[1] ['grædʒʊˌeɪt] *v* **-ated; -ating** *vi* : graduarse, licenciarse — *vt* : graduar <a graduated thermometer : un termómetro graduado>

graduate[2] ['grædʒʊət] *adj* : de postgrado <graduate course : curso de postgrado>

graduate[3] *n* **1** : licenciado *m,* -da *f;* graduado *m,* -da *f* (de la universidad) **2** : bachiller *mf* (de la escuela secundaria)

graduate student *n* : postgraduado *m,* -da *f*

graduation [ˌgrædʒʊ'eɪʃən] *n* : graduación *f*

graffiti [grə'fi:ti, græ-] *npl* : pintadas *fpl,* graffiti *mpl*

graft[1] ['græft] *vt* : injertar

graft[2] *n* **1** : injerto *m* <skin graft : injerto cutáneo> **2** CORRUPTION : soborno *m* (político), ganancia *f* ilegal

grain ['greɪn] *n* **1** : grano *m* <a grain of corn : un grano de maíz> <like a grain of sand : como grano de arena> **2** CEREALS : cereales *mpl* **3** : veta *f,* vena *f,* grano *m* (de madera) **4** SPECK, TRACE : pizca *f,* ápice *m* <a grain of truth : una pizca de verdad> **5** : grano *m* (unidad de peso)

gram ['græm] *n* : gramo *m*

grammar ['græmər] *n* : gramática *f*

grammar school → **elementary school**

grammatical [grə'mæt̬ɪkəl] *adj* : gramatical — **grammatically** [-kli] *adv*

granary ['greɪnəri, 'græ-] *n, pl* **-ries** : granero *m*

grand ['grænd] *adj* **1** FOREMOST : grande **2** IMPRESSIVE : impresionante, magnífico <a grand view : una vista magnífica> **3** LAVISH : grandioso, suntuoso, lujoso <to live in a grand manner : vivir a lo grande> **4** FABULOUS : fabuloso, magnífico <to have a grand time : pasarlo estupendamente, pasarlo en grande> **5 grand total** : total *m,* suma *f* total

grandchild ['grændˌtʃaɪld] *n, pl* **-children** : nieto *m,* -ta *f*

granddaughter ['grændˌdɔt̬ər] *n* : nieta *f*

grandeur ['grændʒər] *n* : grandiosidad *f,* esplendor *m*

grandfather ['grændˌfɑðər] *n* : abuelo *m*

grandiose ['grændiˌo:s, ˌgrændi'-] *adj* **1** IMPOSING : imponente, grandioso **2** POMPOUS : pomposo, presuntuoso

grandmother [ˈgrænd,mʌðər] *n* : abuela *f*
grandparents [ˈgrænd,pærənts] *npl* : abuelos *mpl*
grandson [ˈgrænd,sʌn] *n* : nieto *m*
grandstand [ˈgrænd,stænd] *n* : tribuna *f*
granite [ˈgrænɪt] *n* : granito *m*
grant[1] [ˈgrænt] *vt* **1** ALLOW : conceder <to grant a request : conceder una petición> **2** BESTOW : conceder, dar, otorgar <to grant a favor : otorgar un favor> **3** ADMIT : reconocer, admitir <I'll grant that he's clever : reconozco que es listo> **4 to take for granted** : dar (algo) por sentado
grant[2] *n* **1** GRANTING : concesión *f*, otorgamiento *m* **2** SCHOLARSHIP : beca *f* **3** SUBSIDY : subvención *f*
granular [ˈgrænjʊlər] *adj* : granular
granulated [ˈgrænjʊ,leɪt̬əd] *adj* : granulado
grape [ˈgreɪp] *n* : uva *f*
grapefruit [ˈgreɪp,fruːt] *n* : toronja *f*, pomelo *m*
grapevine [ˈgreɪp,vaɪn] *n* **1** : vid *f*, parra *f* **2 through the grapevine** : por vías secretas <I heard it through the grapevine : me lo contaron>
graph [ˈgræf] *n* : gráfica *f*, gráfico *m*
graphic [ˈgræfɪk] *adj* **1** VIVID : vívido, gráfico **2 graphic arts** : artes gráficas
graphically [ˈgræfɪkli] *adv* : gráficamente
graphite [ˈgræ,faɪt] *n* : grafito *m*
grapnel [ˈgræpnəl] *n* : rezón *m*
grapple [ˈgræpəl] *vi* **-pled; -pling 1** GRIP : agarrar (con un garfio) **2** STRUGGLE : forcejear, luchar (con un problema, etc.)
grasp[1] [ˈgræsp] *vt* **1** GRIP, SEIZE : agarrar, asir **2** COMPREHEND : entender, comprender — *vi* **to grasp at** : aprovechar
grasp[2] *n* **1** GRIP : agarre *m* **2** CONTROL : control *m*, garras *fpl* **3** REACH : alcance *m* <within your grasp : a su alcance> **4** UNDERSTANDING : comprensión *f*, entendimiento *m*
grass [ˈgræs] *n* **1** : hierba *f* (planta) **2** PASTURE : pasto *m*, zacate *m CA, Mex* **3** LAWN : césped *m*, pasto *m*
grasshopper [ˈgræs,hɑpər] *n* : saltamontes *m*
grassland [ˈgræs,lænd] *n* : pradera *f*
grassy [ˈgræsi] *adj* **grassier; -est** : cubierto de hierba
grate[1] [ˈgreɪt] *v* **grated; -ing** *vt* **1** : rallar (en cocina) **2** SCRAPE : rascar **3 to grate one's teeth** : hacer rechinar los dientes — *vi* **1** RASP, SQUEAK : chirriar **2** IRRITATE : irritar <to grate on one's nerves : crisparle los nervios a uno>
grate[2] *n* **1** : parrilla *f* (para cocinar) **2** GRATING : reja *f*, rejilla *f*, verja *f* (en una ventana)
grateful [ˈgreɪtfəl] *adj* : agradecido
gratefully [ˈgreɪtfəli] *adv* : con agradecimiento
gratefulness [ˈgreɪtfəlnəs] *n* : gratitud *f*, agradecimiento *m*
grater [ˈgreɪt̬ər] *n* : rallador *m*
gratification [,græt̬əfəˈkeɪʃən] *n* : gratificación *f*
gratify [ˈgræt̬ə,faɪ] *vt* **-fied; -fying 1** PLEASE : complacer **2** SATISFY : satisfacer, gratificar
grating [ˈgreɪt̬ɪŋ] *n* : reja *f*, rejilla *f*
gratis[1] [ˈgræt̬əs, ˈgreɪ-] *adv* : gratis, gratuitamente
gratis[2] *adj* : gratis, gratuito
gratitude [ˈgræt̬ə,tuːd, -,tjuːd] *n* : gratitud *f*, agradecimiento *m*
gratuitous [grəˈtuːət̬əs] *adj* : gratuito
gratuity [grəˈtuːət̬i] *n, pl* **-ities** TIP : propina *f*
grave[1] [ˈgreɪv] *adj* **graver; -est 1** IMPORTANT : grave, de mucha gravedad **2** SERIOUS, SOLEMN : grave, serio
grave[2] *n* : tumba *f*, sepultura *f*
gravel [ˈgrævəl] *n* : grava *f*, gravilla *f*
gravelly [ˈgrævəli] *adj* **1** : de grava **2** HARSH : áspero (dícese de la voz)
gravely [ˈgreɪvli] *adv* : gravemente
gravestone [ˈgreɪv,stoːn] *n* : lápida *f*
graveyard [ˈgreɪv,jɑrd] *n* CEMETERY : cementerio *m*, panteón *m*, camposanto *m*
gravitate [ˈgrævə,teɪt] *vi* **-tated; -tating** : gravitar
gravitation [,grævəˈteɪʃən] *n* : gravitación *f*
gravitational [,grævəˈteɪʃənəl] *adj* : gravitacional
gravity [ˈgrævət̬i] *n, pl* **-ties 1** SERIOUSNESS : gravedad *f*, seriedad *f* **2** : gravedad *f* <the law of gravity : la ley de la gravedad>
gravy [ˈgreɪvi] *n, pl* **-vies** : salsa *f* (preparada con el jugo de la carne asada)
gray[1] [ˈgreɪ] *vt* : hacer gris — *vi* : encanecer, ponerse gris
gray[2] *adj* **1** : gris (dícese del color) **2** : cano, canoso <gray hair : pelo canoso> <to go gray : volverse cano> **3** DISMAL, GLOOMY : gris, triste
gray[3] *n* : gris *m*
grayish [ˈgreɪɪʃ] *adj* : grisáceo
graze [ˈgreɪz] *v* **grazed; grazing** *vi* : pastar, pacer — *vt* **1** : pastorear (ganado) **2** BRUSH : rozar **3** SCRATCH : raspar
grease[1] [ˈgriːs, ˈgriːz] *vt* **greased; greasing** : engrasar, lubricar
grease[2] [ˈgriːs] *n* : grasa *f*
greasy [ˈgriːsi, -zi] *adj* **greasier; -est 1** : grasiento **2** OILY : graso, grasoso
great [ˈgreɪt] *adj* **1** LARGE : grande <a great mountain : una montaña grande> <a great crowd : una gran muchedumbre> **2** INTENSE : intenso, fuerte, grande <great pain : gran dolor> **3** EMINENT : grande, eminente, distinguido <a great poet : un gran poeta> **4** EXCELLENT, TERRIFIC : excelente, estupendo, fabuloso <to have a

great time : pasarlo en grande> **5 a great while :** mucho tiempo

great-aunt [ˌgreɪtˈænt, -ˈant] *n* **:** tía *f* abuela

greater [ˈgreɪt̬ər] (*comparative of* **great**) **:** mayor

greatest [ˈgreɪt̬əst] (*superlative of* **great**) **:** el mayor, la mayor

great–grandchild [ˌgreɪtˈgrændˌtʃaɪld] *n, pl* **-children** [-ˌtʃɪldrən] **:** bisnieto *m*, -ta *f*

great–grandfather [ˌgreɪtˈgrændˌfɑðər] *n* **:** bisabuelo *m*

great–grandmother [ˌgreɪtˈgrændˌmʌðər] *n* **:** bisabuela *f*

greatly [ˈgreɪtli] *adv* **1** MUCH **:** mucho, sumamente <to be greatly improved : haber mejorado mucho> **2** VERY **:** muy <greatly superior : muy superior>

greatness [ˈgreɪtnəs] *n* **:** grandeza *f*

great–uncle [ˌgreɪtˈʌŋkəl] *n* **:** tío *m* abuelo

grebe [ˈgriːb] *n* **:** somorgujo *m*

greed [ˈgriːd] *n* **1** AVARICE **:** avaricia *f*, codicia *f* **2** GLUTTONY **:** glotonería *f*, gula *f*

greedily [ˈgriːdəli] *adv* **:** con avaricia, con gula

greediness [ˈgriːdinəs] → **greed**

greedy [ˈgriːdi] *adj* **greedier; -est 1** AVARICIOUS **:** codicioso, avaricioso **2** GLUTTONOUS **:** glotón

Greek [ˈgriːk] *n* **1 :** griego *m*, -ga *f* **2 :** griego *m* (idioma) — **Greek** *adj*

green¹ [ˈgriːn] *adj* **1 :** verde (dícese del color) **2** UNRIPE **:** verde, inmaduro **3** INEXPERIENCED **:** verde, novato

green² *n* **1 :** verde *m* **2 greens** *npl* VEGETABLES **:** verduras *fpl*

greenery [ˈgriːnəri] *n, pl* **-eries :** plantas *fpl* verdes, vegetación *f*

greenhorn [ˈgriːnˌhɔrn] *n* **:** novato *m*, -ta *f*

greenhouse [ˈgriːnˌhaʊs] *n* **:** invernadero *m*

greenhouse effect : efecto *m* invernadero

greenish [ˈgriːnɪʃ] *adj* **:** verdoso

Greenlander [ˈgriːnləndər, -ˌlæn-] *n* **:** groenlandés *m*, -desa *f*

greenness [ˈgriːnnəs] *n* **1 :** verdor *m* **2** INEXPERIENCE **:** inexperiencia *f*

green thumb *n* **to have a green thumb :** tener buena mano para las plantas

greet [ˈgriːt] *vt* **1 :** saludar <to greet a friend : saludar a un amigo> **2 :** acoger, recibir <they greeted him with boos : lo recibieron con abucheos>

greeting [ˈgriːt̬ɪŋ] *n* **1 :** saludo *m* **2 greetings** *npl* REGARDS **:** saludos *mpl*, recuerdos *mpl*

gregarious [grɪˈgæriəs] *adj* **:** gregario (dícese de los animales), sociable (dícese de las personas) — **gregariously** *adv*

gregariousness [grɪˈgæriəsnəs] *n* **:** sociabilidad *f*

gremlin [ˈgrɛmlən] *n* **:** duende *m*

grenade [grəˈneɪd] *n* **:** granada *f*

Grenadian [grəˈneɪdiən] *n* **:** granadino *m*, -na *f* — **Grenadian** *adj*

grew → **grow**

grey → **gray**

greyhound [ˈgreɪˌhaʊnd] *n* **:** galgo *m*

grid [ˈgrɪd] *n* **1** GRATING **:** rejilla *f* **2** NETWORK **:** red *f* (de electricidad, etc.) **3 :** cuadriculado *m* (de un mapa)

griddle [ˈgrɪdəl] *n* **:** plancha *f*

griddle cake → **pancake**

gridiron [ˈgrɪdˌaɪərn] *n* **1** GRILL **:** parrilla *f* **2 :** campo *m* de futbol americano

grief [ˈgriːf] *n* **1** SORROW **:** dolor *m*, pena *f* **2** ANNOYANCE, TROUBLE **:** problemas *mpl*, molestia *f*

grievance [ˈgriːvənts] *n* COMPLAINT **:** queja *f*

grieve [ˈgriːv] *v* **grieved; grieving** *vt* DISTRESS **:** afligir, entristecer, apenar — *vi* **1 :** sufrir, afligirse **2 to grieve for** *or* **to grieve over :** llorar, lamentar

grievous [ˈgriːvəs] *adj* **1** OPPRESSIVE **:** gravoso, opresivo, severo **2** GRAVE, SERIOUS **:** grave, severo, doloroso

grievously [ˈgriːvəsli] *adv* **:** gravemente, de gravedad

grill¹ [ˈgrɪl] *vt* **1 :** asar (a la parrilla) **2** INTERROGATE **:** interrogar

grill² *n* **1 :** parrilla *f* (para cocinar) **2 :** parrillada *f* (comida) **3** RESTAURANT **:** grill *m*

grille *or* **grill** [ˈgrɪl] *n* **:** reja *f*, enrejado *m*

grim [ˈgrɪm] *adj* **grimmer; grimmest 1** CRUEL **:** cruel, feroz **2** STERN **:** adusto, severo <a grim expression : un gesto severo> **3** GLOOMY **:** sombrío, deprimente **4** SINISTER **:** macabro, siniestro **5** UNYIELDING **:** inflexible, persistente <with grim determination : con una voluntad de hierro>

grimace¹ [ˈgrɪməs, grɪˈmeɪs] *vi* **-maced; -macing :** hacer muecas

grimace² *n* **:** mueca *f*

grime [ˈgraɪm] *n* **:** mugre *f*, suciedad *f*

grimly [ˈgrɪmli] *adv* **1** STERNLY **:** severamente **2** RESOLUTELY **:** inexorablemente

grimy [ˈgraɪmi] *adj* **grimier; -est :** mugriento, sucio

grin¹ [ˈgrɪn] *vi* **grinned; grinning :** sonreír abiertamente

grin² *n* **:** sonrisa *f* abierta

grind¹ [ˈgraɪnd] *v* **ground** [ˈgraʊnd]; **grinding** *vt* **1** CRUSH **:** moler, machacar, triturar **2** SHARPEN **:** afilar **3** POLISH **:** pulir, esmerilar (lentes, espejos) **4 to grind one's teeth :** rechinarle los dientes a uno **5 to grind down** OPPRESS **:** oprimir, agobiar — *vi* **1 :** funcionar con dificultad, rechinar <to grind to a halt : pararse

poco a poco, llegar a un punto muerto> 2 STUDY : estudiar mucho
grind[2] *n* : trabajo *m* pesado <the daily grind : la rutina diaria>
grinder ['graɪndər] *n* : molinillo *m* <coffee grinder : molinillo de café>
grindstone ['graɪnd,sto:n] *n* : piedra *m* de afilar
grip[1] ['grɪp] *vt* **gripped; gripping 1** GRASP : agarrar, asir **2** HOLD, INTEREST : captar el interés de
grip[2] *n* **1** GRASP : agarre *m,* asidero *m* <to have a firm grip on something : agarrarse bien de algo> **2** CONTROL, HOLD : control *m,* dominio *m* <to lose one's grip on : perder el control de> <inflation tightened its grip on the economy : la inflación se afianzó en su dominio de la economía> **3** UNDERSTANDING : comprensión *f,* entendimiento *m* <to come to grips with : llegar a entender> **4** HANDLE : asidero *m,* empuñadura *f* (de un arma)
gripe[1] ['graɪp] *v* **griped; griping** *vt* IRRITATE, VEX : irritar, fastidiar, molestar — *vi* COMPLAIN : quejarse, rezongar
gripe[2] *n* : queja *f*
grippe ['grɪp] *n* : influenza *f,* gripe *f,* gripa *f Col, Mex*
grisly ['grɪzli] *adj* **-lier; -est** : horripilante, horroroso, truculento
grist ['grɪst] *n* : molienda *f* <it's all grist for the mill : todo ayuda, todo es provechoso>
gristle ['grɪsəl] *n* : cartílago *m*
gristly ['grɪsli] *adj* **-tlier; -est** : cartilaginoso
grit[1] ['grɪt] *vt* **gritted; gritting** : hacer rechinar (los dientes, etc.)
grit[2] *n* **1** SAND : arena *f* **2** GRAVEL : grava *f* **3** COURAGE : valor *m,* coraje *m* **4 grits** *npl* : sémola *f* de maíz
gritty ['grɪti] *adj* **-tier; -est 1** : arenoso <a gritty surface : una superficie arenosa> **2** PLUCKY : valiente
grizzled ['grɪzəld] *adj* : entrecano
grizzly bear ['grɪzli] *n* : oso *m* pardo
groan[1] ['gro:n] *vi* **1** MOAN : gemir, quejarse **2** CREAK : crujir
groan[2] *n* **1** MOAN : gemido *m,* quejido *m* **2** CREAK : crujido *m*
grocer ['gro:sər] *n* : tendero *m,* -ra *f*
grocery ['gro:səri, -ʃəri] *n, pl* **-ceries 1** *or* **grocery store** : tienda *f* de comestibles, tienda *f* de abarrotes **2 groceries** *npl* : comestibles *mpl,* abarrotes *mpl*
groggy ['grɑgi] *adj* **-gier; -est** : atontado, grogui, tambaleante
groin ['grɔɪn] *n* : ingle *f*
grommet ['grɑmət, 'grʌ-] *n* : arandela *f*
groom[1] ['gru:m, 'grʊm] *vt* **1** : cepillar, almohazar (un animal) **2** : arreglar, cuidar <well-groomed : bien arreglado> **3** PREPARE : preparar
groom[2] *n* **1** : mozo *m,* -za *f* de cuadra **2** BRIDEGROOM : novio *m*
groove[1] ['gru:v] *vt* **grooved; grooving** : acanalar, hacer ranuras en, surcar
groove[2] *n* **1** FURROW, SLOT : ranura *f,* surco *m* **2** RUT : rutina *f*
grope ['gro:p] *v* **groped; groping** *vi* : andar a tientas, tantear <he groped for the switch : buscó el interruptor a tientas> — *vt* **to grope one's way** : avanzar a tientas
gross[1] ['gro:s] *vt* : tener entrada bruta de, recaudar en bruto
gross[2] *adj* **1** FLAGRANT : flagrante, grave <a gross error : un error flagrante> <a gross injustice : una injusticia grave> **2** FAT : muy gordo, obeso **3** : bruto <gross national product : producto nacional bruto> **4** COARSE, VULGAR : grosero, basto
gross[3] *n* **1** *pl* **gross** : gruesa *f* (12 docenas) **2** *or* **gross income** : ingresos *mpl* brutos
grossly ['gro:sli] *adv* **1** EXTREMELY : extremadamente <grossly unfair : totalmente injusto> **2** CRUDELY : groseramente
grotesque [gro:'tɛsk] *adj* : grotesco
grotesquely [gro:'tɛskli] *adv* : de forma grotesca
grotto ['grɑto:] *n, pl* **-toes** : gruta *f*
grouch[1] ['graʊtʃ] *vi* : refunfuñar, rezongar
grouch[2] *n* **1** COMPLAINT : queja *f* **2** GRUMBLER : gruñón *m,* -ñona *f;* cascarrabias *mf fam*
grouchy ['graʊtʃi] *adj* **grouchier; -est** : malhumorado, gruñon
ground[1] ['graʊnd] *vt* **1** BASE : fundar, basar **2** INSTRUCT : enseñar los conocimientos básicos a <to be well grounded in : ser muy entendido en> **3** : conectar a tierra (un aparato eléctrico) **4** : varar, hacer encallar (un barco) **5** : restringir (un avión o un piloto) a la tierra
ground[2] *n* **1** EARTH, SOIL : suelo *m,* tierra *f* <to dig (in) the ground : cavar la tierra> <to fall to the ground : caerse al suelo> **2** LAND, TERRAIN : terreno *m* <hilly ground : terreno alto> <to lose ground : perder terreno> **3** BASIS, REASON : razón *f,* motivo *m* <grounds for complaint : motivos de queja> **4** BACKGROUND : fondo *m* **5** FIELD : campo *m,* plaza *f* <parade ground : plaza de armas> **6** : tierra *f* (para electricidad) **7 grounds** *npl* PREMISES : recinto *m,* terreno *m* **8 grounds** *npl* DREGS : posos *mpl* (de café)
ground[3] → **grind**
groundhog ['graʊnd,hɔg] *n* : marmota *f* (de América)
groundless ['graʊndləs] *adj* : infundado
groundwork ['graʊnd,wərk] *n* **1** FOUNDATION : fundamento *m,* base *f* **2** PREPARATION : trabajo *m* preparatorio
group[1] ['gru:p] *vt* : agrupar
group[2] *n* : grupo *m,* agrupación *f,* conjunto *m,* compañía *f*

grouper ['gruːpər] *n* : mero *m*

grouse¹ ['graʊs] *vi* **groused; grousing** : quejarse, rezongar, refunfuñar

grouse² *n, pl* **grouse** *or* **grouses** : urogallo *m* (ave)

grout ['graʊt] *n* : lechada *f*

grove ['groːv] *n* : bosquecillo *m,* arboleda *f,* soto *m*

grovel ['grɑvəl, 'grʌ-] *vi* **-eled** *or* **-elled; -eling** *or* **-elling 1** CRAWL : arrastrarse **2** : humillarse, postrarse <to grovel before someone : postrarse ante alguien>

grow ['groː] *v* **grew** ['gruː]; **grown** ['groːn]; **growing** *vi* **1** : crecer <palm trees grow on the islands : las palmas crecen en las islas> <my hair grows very fast : mi pelo crece muy rápido> **2** DEVELOP, MATURE : desarrollarse, madurar **3** INCREASE : crecer, aumentar **4** BECOME : hacerse, volverse, ponerse <she was growing angry : se estaba poniendo furiosa> <to grow dark : oscurecerse> **5 to grow up** : hacerse mayor <grow up! : ¡no seas niño!> — *vt* **1** CULTIVATE, RAISE : cultivar **2** : dejar crecer <to grow one's hair : dejarse crecer el pelo>

grower ['groːər] *n* : cultivador *m,* -dora *f*

growl¹ ['graʊl] *vi* : gruñir (dícese de un animal), refunfuñar (dícese de una persona)

growl² *n* : gruñido *m*

grown–up¹ ['groːn,əp] *adj* : adulto, mayor

grown–up² *n* : adulto *m,* -ta *f;* persona *f* mayor

growth ['groːθ] *n* **1** : crecimiento *m* <to stunt one's growth : detener el crecimiento> **2** INCREASE : aumento *m,* crecimiento *m,* expansión *f* **3** DEVELOPMENT : desarrollo *m* <economic growth : desarrollo económico> <a five days' growth of beard : una barba de cinco días> **4** LUMP, TUMOR : bulto *m,* tumor *m*

grub¹ ['grʌb] *vi* **grubbed; grubbing 1** DIG : escarbar **2** RUMMAGE : hurgar, buscar **3** DRUDGE : trabajar duro

grub² *n* **1** : larva *f* <beetle grub : larva del escarabajo> **2** DRUDGE : esclavo *m,* -va *f* del trabajo **3** FOOD : comida *f*

grubby ['grʌbi] *adj* **grubbier; -est** : mugriento, sucio

grudge¹ ['grʌdʒ] *vt* **grudged; grudging** : resentir, envidiar

grudge² *n* : rencor *m,* resentimiento *m* <to hold a grudge : guardar rencor>

grueling *or* **gruelling** ['gruːlɪŋ, 'gruːə-] *adj* : extenuante, agotador, duro

gruesome ['gruːsəm] *adj* : horripilante, truculento, horroroso

gruff ['grʌf] *adj* **1** BRUSQUE : brusco <a gruff reply : una respuesta brusca> **2** HOARSE : ronco — **gruffly** *adv*

grumble¹ ['grʌmbəl] *vi* **-bled; -bling 1** COMPLAIN : refunfuñar, rezongar, quejarse **2** RUMBLE : hacer un ruido sordo, retumbar (dícese del trueno)

grumble² *n* **1** COMPLAINT : queja *f* **2** RUMBLE : ruido *m* sordo, estruendo *m*

grumbler ['grʌmbələr] *n* : gruñón *m,* -ñona *f*

grumpy ['grʌmpi] *adj* **grumpier; -est** : malhumorado, gruñón

grunt¹ ['grʌnt] *vi* : gruñir

grunt² *n* : gruñido *m*

guacamole [,gwɑkə'moːli] *n* : guacamole *m,* guacamol *m*

guarantee¹ [,gærən'tiː] *vt* **-teed; -teeing 1** PROMISE : asegurar, prometer **2** : poner bajo garantía, garantizar (un producto o servicio)

guarantee² *n* **1** PROMISE : garantía *f,* promesa *f* <lifetime guarantee : garantía de por vida> **2** → **guarantor**

guarantor [,gærən'tɔr] *n* : garante *mf;* fiador *m,* -dora *f*

guaranty [,gærən'tiː] → **guarantee**

guard¹ ['gɑrd] *vt* **1** DEFEND, PROTECT : defender, proteger **2** : guardar, vigilar, custodiar <to guard the frontier : vigilar la frontera> <she guarded my secret well : guardó bien mi secreto> — *vi* **to guard against** : protegerse contra, evitar

guard² *n* **1** WATCHMAN : guarda *mf* <security guard : guarda de seguridad> **2** VIGILANCE : guardia *f,* vigilancia *f* <to be on guard : estar en guardia> <to let one's guard down : bajar la guardia> **3** SAFEGUARD : salvaguardia *f,* dispositivo *m* de seguridad (en una máquina) **4** PRECAUTION : precaución *f,* protección *f*

guardhouse ['gɑrd,haʊs] *n* : cuartel *m* de la guardia

guardian ['gɑrdiən] *n* **1** PROTECTOR : guardián *m,* -diana *f;* custodio *m,* -dia *f* **2** : tutor *m,* -tora *f* (de un niño)

guardianship ['gɑrdiən,ʃɪp] *n* : custodia *f,* tutela *f*

Guatemalan [,gwɑtə'mɑlən] *n* : guatemalteco *m,* -ca *f* — **Guatemalan** *adj*

guava ['gwɑvə] *n* : guayaba *f*

gubernatorial [,guːbənə'toriːəl, ,gjuː-] *adj* : del gobernador

guerrilla *or* **guerilla** [gə'rɪlə] *n* : guerrillero *m,* -ra *f*

guess¹ ['gɛs] *vt* **1** CONJECTURE : adivinar, conjeturar <guess what happened! : ¡adivina lo que pasó!> **2** SUPPOSE : pensar, creer, suponer <I guess so : supongo que sí> **3** : adivinar correctamente, acertar <to guess the answer : acertar la respuesta> — *vi* : adivinar

guess² *n* : conjetura *f,* suposición *f*

guesswork ['gɛs,wərk] *n* : suposiciones *fpl,* conjeturas *fpl*

guest ['gɛst] *n* : huésped *mf;* invitado *m,* -da *f*

guffaw¹ [gə'fɔ] *vi* : reírse a carcajadas, carcajearse *fam*

guffaw[2] [gə'fɔ, 'gʌ,fɔ] *n* **:** carcajada *f,* risotada *f*

guidance ['gaɪdənts] *n* **:** orientación *f,* consejos *mpl*

guide[1] ['gaɪd] *vt* **guided; guiding 1** DIRECT, LEAD **:** guiar, dirigir, conducir **2** ADVISE, COUNSEL **:** aconsejar, orientar

guide[2] *n* **:** guía *f*

guidebook ['gaɪd,bʊk] *n* **:** guía *f* (para viajeros)

guideline ['gaɪd,laɪn] *n* **:** pauta *f,* directriz *f*

guild ['gɪld] *n* **:** gremio *m,* sindicato *m,* asociación *f*

guile ['gaɪl] *n* **:** astucia *f,* engaño *m*

guileless ['gaɪlləs] *adj* **:** inocente, cándido, sin malicia

guillotine[1] ['gɪlə,tiːn, 'giːjə,-] *vt* **-tined; -tining :** guillotinar

guillotine[2] *n* **:** guillotina *f*

guilt ['gɪlt] *n* **:** culpa *f,* culpabilidad *f*

guilty ['gɪlti] *adj* **guiltier; -est :** culpable

guinea fowl ['gɪni] *n* **:** gallina *f* de Guinea

guinea pig *n* **:** conejillo *m* de Indias, cobaya *f*

guise ['gaɪz] *n* **:** apariencia *f,* aspecto *m,* forma *f*

guitar [gə'tɑr, gɪ-] *n* **:** guitarra *f*

gulch ['gʌltʃ] *n* **:** barranco *m,* quebrada *f*

gulf ['gʌlf] *n* **1 :** golfo *m* <the Gulf of Mexico : el Golfo de México> **2** GAP **:** brecha *f* <the gulf between generations : la brecha entre las generaciones> **3** CHASM **:** abismo *m*

gull ['gʌl] *n* **:** gaviota *f*

gullet ['gʌlət] *n* **:** garganta *f*

gullible ['gʌlɪbəl] *adj* **:** crédulo

gully ['gʌli] *n, pl* **-lies :** barranco *m,* hondonada *f*

gulp[1] ['gʌlp] *vt* **1 :** engullir, tragar <he gulped down the whiskey : engulló el whisky> **2** SUPPRESS **:** suprimir, reprimir, tragar <to gulp down a sob : reprimir un sollozo> — *vi* **:** tragar saliva, tener un nudo en la garganta

gulp[2] *n* **:** trago *m*

gum ['gʌm] *n* **1** CHEWING GUM **:** goma *f* de mascar, chicle *m* **2 gums** *npl* **:** encías *fpl*

gumbo ['gʌm,boː] *n* **:** sopa *f* de quingombó

gumdrop ['gʌm,drɑp] *n* **:** pastilla *f* de goma

gummy ['gʌmi] *adj* **gummier; -est :** gomoso

gumption ['gʌmpʃən] *n* **:** iniciativa *f,* agallas *fpl fam*

gun[1] ['gʌn] *vt* **gunned; gunning 1** *or* **to gun down :** matar a tiros, asesinar **2 :** acelerar (rápidamente) <to gun the engine : acelerar el motor>

gun[2] *n* **1** CANNON **:** cañón *m* **2** FIREARM **:** arma *f* de fuego **3** SPRAY GUN **:** pistola *f* **4 to jump the gun :** adelantarse, salir antes de tiempo

gunboat ['gʌn,boːt] *n* **:** cañonero *m*

gunfight ['gʌn,faɪt] *n* **:** tiroteo *m,* balacera *f*

gunfire ['gʌn,faɪr] *n* **:** disparos *mpl*

gunman ['gʌnmən] *n, pl* **-men** [-mən, -,mɛn] **:** pistolero *m,* gatillero *m Mex*

gunner ['gʌnər] *n* **:** artillero *m,* -ra *f*

gunnysack ['gʌni,sæk] *n* **:** saco *m* de yute

gunpowder ['gʌn,paʊdər] *n* **:** pólvora *f*

gunshot ['gʌn,ʃɑt] *n* **:** disparo *m,* tiro *m,* balazo *m*

gunwale ['gʌnəl] *n* **:** borda *f*

guppy ['gʌpi] *n, pl* **-pies :** lebistes *m*

gurgle[1] ['gərgəl] *vi* **-gled; -gling 1 :** borbotar, gorgotear (dícese de un líquido) **2 :** gorjear (dícese de un niño)

gurgle[2] *n* **1 :** borboteo *m,* gorgoteo *m* (de un líquido) **2 :** gorjeo *m* (de un niño)

gush ['gʌʃ] *vi* **1** SPOUT **:** surgir, salir a chorros, chorrear **2 :** hablar con entusiasmo efusivo <she gushed with praise : se deshizo en elogios>

gust ['gʌst] *n* **:** ráfaga *f,* racha *f*

gusto ['gʌs,toː] *n, pl* **gustoes :** entusiasmo *m* <with gusto : con deleite, con ganas>

gusty ['gʌsti] *adj* **gustier; -est :** racheado

gut[1] ['gʌt] *vt* **gutted; gutting 1** EVISCERATE **:** destripar (un pollo, etc.), limpiar (un pescado) **2 :** destruir el interior de (un edificio)

gut[2] *n* **1** INTESTINE **:** intestino *m* **2 guts** *npl* INNARDS **:** tripas *fpl fam,* entrañas *fpl* **3 guts** *npl* COURAGE **:** valentía *f,* agallas *fpl*

gutter ['gʌtər] *n* **1 :** canal *mf,* canaleta *f* (de un techo) **2 :** cuneta *f,* arroyo *m* (de una calle)

guttural ['gʌtərəl] *adj* **:** gutural

guy ['gaɪ] *n* **1** *or* **guyline :** cuerda *f* tensora, cable *m* **2** FELLOW **:** tipo *m,* hombre *m*

guzzle ['gʌzəl] *vt* **-zled; -zling :** chupar, tragarse

gym ['dʒɪm] → **gymnasium**

gymnasium [dʒɪm'neɪziəm, -ʒəm] *n, pl* **-siums** *or* **-sia** [-ziːə, -ʒə] **:** gimnasio *m*

gymnast ['dʒɪmnəst, -,næst] *n* **:** gimnasta *mf*

gymnastic [dʒɪm'næstɪk] *adj* **:** gimnástico

gymnastics [dʒɪm'næstɪks] *ns & pl* **:** gimnasia *f*

gynecologist [,gaɪnə'kɑlədʒɪst, ,dʒɪnə-] *n* **:** ginecólogo *m,* -ga *f*

gynecology [,gaɪnə'kɑlədʒi, ,dʒɪnə-] *n* **:** ginecología *f*

gyp[1] ['dʒɪp] *vt* **gypped; gypping :** estafar, timar

gyp[2] *n* **1** SWINDLER **:** estafador *m,* -dora *f* **2** FRAUD, SWINDLE **:** estafa *f,* timo *m fam*

gypsum ['dʒɪpsəm] *n* **:** yeso *m*

Gypsy [ˈdʒɪpsi] *n, pl* **-sies** : gitano *m,* -na *f*

gyrate [ˈdʒaɪˌreɪt] *vi* **-rated; -rating** : girar, rotar

gyration [dʒaɪˈreɪʃən] *n* : giro *m,* rotación *f*

gyroscope [ˈdʒaɪrəˌskoːp] *n* : giroscopio *m,* giróscopo *m*

H

h [ˈeɪtʃ] *n, pl* **h's** *or* **hs** [ˈeɪtʃəz] : octava letra del alfabeto inglés

haberdashery [ˈhæbərˌdæʃəri] *n, pl* **-eries** : tienda *f* de ropa para caballeros

habit [ˈhæbɪt] *n* **1** CUSTOM : hábito *m,* costumbre *f* **2** : hábito *m* (de un monje o una religiosa) **3** ADDICTION : dependencia *f,* adicción *f*

habitable [ˈhæbɪtəbəl] *adj* : habitable

habitat [ˈhæbɪˌtæt] *n* : hábitat *m*

habitation [ˌhæbɪˈteɪʃən] *n* **1** OCCUPANCY : habitación *f* **2** RESIDENCE : residencia *f,* morada *f*

habit–forming [ˈhæbɪtˌfɔrmɪŋ] *adj* : que crea dependencia

habitual [həˈbɪtʃʊəl] *adj* **1** CUSTOMARY : habitual, acostumbrado **2** INVETERATE : incorregible, empedernido — **habitually** *adv*

habituate [həˈbɪtʃʊˌeɪt] *vt* **-ated; -ating** : habituar, acostumbrar

hack[1] [ˈhæk] *vt* : cortar, tajar <to hack one's way : abrirse paso> — *vi* **1** : hacer tajos **2** COUGH : toser

hack[2] *n* **1** CHOP : hachazo *m,* tajo *m* **2** HORSE : caballo *m* de alquiler **3** WRITER : escritor *m,* -tora *f* a sueldo; escritorzuelo *m,* -la *f* **4** COUGH : tos *f* seca

hackles [ˈhækəlz] *npl* **1** : pluma *f* erizada (de un ave), pelo *m* erizado (de un perro, etc.) **2 to get one's hackles up** : ponerse furioso

hackney [ˈhækni] *n, pl* **-neys** : caballo *m* de silla, caballo *m* de tiro

hackneyed [ˈhæknid] *adj* TRITE : trillado, gastado

hacksaw [ˈhækˌsɔ] *n* : sierra *f* para metales

had → **have**

haddock [ˈhædək] *ns & pl* : eglefino *m*

hadn't [ˈhædənt] (*contraction of* **had not**) → **have**

haft [ˈhæft] *n* : mango *m,* empuñadura *f*

hag [ˈhæg] *n* **1** WITCH : bruja *f,* hechicera *f* **2** CRONE : vieja *f* fea

haggard [ˈhægərd] *adj* : demacrado, macilento — **haggardly** *adv*

haggle [ˈhægəl] *vi* **-gled; -gling** : regatear

ha–ha [ˌhɑˈhɑ, ˈhɑˈhɑ] *interj* : ¡ja, ja!

hail[1] [ˈheɪl] *vt* **1** GREET : saludar **2** SUMMON : llamar <to hail a taxi : llamar un taxi> — *vi* : granizar (en meteorología)

hail[2] *n* **1** : granizo *m* **2** BARRAGE : alud *m,* lluvia *f*

hail[3] *interj* : ¡salve!

hailstone [ˈheɪlˌstoːn] *n* : granizo *m,* piedra *f* de granizo

hailstorm [ˈheɪlˌstɔrm] *n* : granizada *f*

hair [ˈhær] *n* **1** : pelo *m,* cabello *m* <to get one's hair cut : cortarse el pelo> **2** : vello *m* (en las piernas, etc.)

hairbreadth [ˈhærˌbrɛdθ] *or* **hairsbreadth** [ˈhærz-] *n* **by a hairbreadth** : por un pelo

hairbrush [ˈhærˌbrʌʃ] *n* : cepillo *m* (del pelo)

haircut [ˈhærˌkʌt] *n* : corte *m* de pelo

hairdo [ˈhærˌduː] *n, pl* **-dos** : peinado *m*

hairdresser [ˈhærˌdrɛsər] *n* : peluquero *m,* -ra *f*

hairiness [ˈhærinəs] *n* : vellosidad *f*

hairless [ˈhærləs] *adj* : sin pelo, calvo, pelón

hairline [ˈhærˌlaɪn] *n* **1** : línea *f* delgada **2** : nacimiento *m* del pelo <to have a receding hairline : tener entradas>

hairpin [ˈhærˌpɪn] *n* : horquilla *f*

hair–raising [ˈhærˌreɪzɪŋ] *adj* : espeluznante

hairy [ˈhæri] *adj* **hairier; -est** : peludo, velludo

Haitian [ˈheɪʃən, ˈheɪtiən] *n* : haitiano *m,* -na *f* — **Haitian** *adj*

hake [ˈheɪk] *n* : merluza *f*

hale[1] [ˈheɪl] *vt* **haled; haling** : arrastrar, halar <to hale to court : arrastrar al tribunal>

hale[2] *adj* : saludable, robusto

half[1] [ˈhæf, ˈhaf] *adv* : medio, a medias <half cooked : medio cocido>

half[2] *adj* : medio, a medias <a half hour : una media hora> <a half truth : una verdad a medias>

half[3] *n, pl* **halves** [ˈhævz, ˈhavz] **1** : mitad *f* <half of my friends : la mitad de mis amigos> <in half : por la mitad> **2** : tiempo *m* (en deportes)

half brother *n* : medio hermano *m,* hermanastro *m*

halfhearted [ˈhæfˈhɑrtəd] *adj* : sin ánimo, poco entusiasta

halfheartedly [ˈhæfˈhɑrtədli] *adv* : con poco entusiasmo, sin ánimo

half–life [ˈhæfˌlaɪf] *n, pl* **half–lives** : media vida *f*

half sister *n* : media hermana *f,* hermanastra *f*

halfway[1] [ˈhæfˈweɪ] *adv* : a medio camino, a mitad de camino

halfway[2] *adj* : medio, intermedio <a halfway point : un punto intermedio>

half–wit [ˈhæfˌwɪt] *n* : tonto *m,* -ta *f;* imbécil *mf*

half–witted ['hæf,wɪṭəd] *adj* : estúpido

halibut ['hælɪbət] *ns & pl* : halibut *m*

hall ['hɔl] *n* **1** BUILDING : residencia *f* estudiantil, facultad *f* (de una universidad) **2** VESTIBULE : entrada *f,* vestíbulo *m,* zaguán *m* **3** CORRIDOR : corredor *m,* pasillo *m* **4** AUDITORIUM : sala *f,* salón *m* <concert hall : sala de conciertos> **5 city hall** : ayuntamiento *m*

hallelujah [,hælə'lu:jə, ,hɑ-] *interj* : ¡aleluya!

hallmark ['hɔl,mɑrk] *n* : sello *m* (distintivo)

hallow ['hæ,lo:] *vt* : santificar, consagrar

hallowed ['hæ,lo:d, 'hæ,lo:əd, 'hɑ,lo:d] *adj* : sagrado

Halloween [,hælə'wi:n, ,hɑ-] *n* : víspera *f* de Todos los Santos

hallucinate [hæ'lu:sən,eɪt] *vi* **-nated; -nating** : alucinar

hallucination [hə,lu:sən'eɪʃən] *n* : alucinación *f*

hallucinatory [hə'lu:sənə,tori] *adj* : alucinante

hallucinogen [hə'lu:sənədʒən] *n* : alucinógeno *m*

hallucinogenic [hə,lu:sənə'dʒɛnɪk] *adj* : alucinógeno

hallway ['hɔl,weɪ] *n* **1** ENTRANCE : entrada *f* **2** CORRIDOR : corredor *m,* pasillo *m*

halo ['heɪ,lo:] *n, pl* **-los** *or* **-loes** : aureola *f,* halo *m*

halt[1] ['hɔlt] *vi* : detenerse, pararse — *vt* **1** STOP : detener, parar (a una persona) **2** INTERRUPT : interrumpir (una actividad)

halt[2] *n* **1** : alto *m,* parada *f* **2 to come to a halt** : pararse, detenerse

halter ['hɔltər] *n* **1** : cabestro *m,* ronzal *m* (para un animal) **2** : blusa *f* sin espalda

halting ['hɔltɪŋ] *adj* HESITANT : vacilante, titubeante — **haltingly** *adv*

halve ['hæv, 'hav] *vt* **halved; halving** **1** DIVIDE : partir por la mitad **2** REDUCE : reducir a la mitad

halves → **half**

ham ['hæm] *n* **1** : jamón *m* **2** *or* **ham actor** : comicastro *m,* -tra *f* **3** *or* **ham radio operator** : radioaficionado *m,* -da *f* **4 hams** *npl* HAUNCHES : ancas *fpl*

hamburger ['hæm,bərgər] *or* **hamburg** [-,bərg] *n* **1** : carne *f* molida **2** : hamburguesa *f* (emparedado)

hamlet ['hæmlət] *n* VILLAGE : aldea *f,* poblado *m*

hammer[1] ['hæmər] *vt* **1** STRIKE : clavar, golpear **2** NAIL : clavar, martillar **3 to hammer out** NEGOTIATE : elaborar, negociar, llegar a — *vi* : martillar, golpear

hammer[2] *n* **1** : martillo *m* **2** : percusor *m,* percutor *m* (de un arma de fuego)

hammock ['hæmək] *n* : hamaca *f*

hamper[1] ['hæmpər] *vt* : obstaculizar, dificultar

hamper[2] *n* : cesto *m,* canasta *f*

hamster ['hæmpstər] *n* : hámster *m*

hamstring ['hæm,strɪŋ] *vt* **-strung** [-,strʌŋ]; **-stringing** **1** : cortarle el tendón del corvejón a (un animal) **2** INCAPACITATE : incapacitar, inutilizar

hand[1] ['hænd] *vt* : pasar, dar, entregar

hand[2] *n* **1** : mano *f* <made by hand : hecho a mano> **2** POINTER : manecilla *f,* aguja *f* (de un reloj o instrumento) **3** SIDE : lado *m* <on the other hand : por otro lado> **4** HANDWRITING : letra *f,* escritura *f* **5** APPLAUSE : aplauso *m* **6** : mano *f,* cartas *fpl* (en juegos de naipes) **7** WORKER : obrero *m,* -ra *f;* trabajador *m,* -dora *f* **8 to ask for someone's hand (in marriage)** : pedir la mano de alguien **9 to lend a hand** : echar una mano

handbag ['hænd,bæg] *n* : cartera *f,* bolso *m,* bolsa *f Mex*

handball ['hænd,bɔl] *n* : frontón *m*

handbill ['hænd,bɪl] *n* : folleto *m,* volante *m*

handbook ['hænd,bʊk] *n* : manual *m*

handcuff ['hænd,kʌf] *vt* : esposar, ponerle esposas (a alguien)

handcuffs ['hænd,kʌfs] *npl* : esposas *fpl*

handful ['hænd,fʊl] *n* : puñado *m*

handgun ['hænd,gʌn] *n* : pistola *f,* revólver *m*

handicap[1] ['hændi,kæp] *vt* **-capped; -capping** **1** : asignar un handicap a (en deportes) **2** HAMPER : obstaculizar, poner en desventaja

handicap[2] *n* **1** DISABILITY : minusvalía *f,* discapacidad *f* **2** DISADVANTAGE : desventaja *f,* handicap *m* (en deportes)

handicapped ['hændi,kæpt] *adj* DISABLED : minusválido, discapacitado

handicraft ['hændi,kræft] *n* : artesanía *f*

handily ['hændəli] *adv* EASILY : fácilmente, con facilidad

handiwork ['hændi,wərk] *n* **1** WORK : trabajo *m* **2** CRAFTS : artesanías *fpl*

handkerchief ['hæŋkərtʃəf, -,tʃi:f] *n, pl* **-chiefs** : pañuelo *m*

handle[1] ['hændəl] *v* **-dled; -dling** *vt* **1** TOUCH : tocar **2** MANAGE : tratar, manejar, despachar **3** SELL : comerciar con, vender — *vi* : responder, conducirse (dícese de un vehículo)

handle[2] *n* : asa *m,* asidero *m,* mango *m* (de un cuchillo, etc.), pomo *m* (de una puerta), tirador *m* (de un cajón)

handlebars ['hændəl,bɑrz] *npl* : manubrio *m,* manillar *m*

handler ['hændələr] *n* : cuidador *m,* -dora *f*

handmade ['hænd,meɪd] *adj* : hecho a mano

hand–me–downs ['hændmi,daʊnz] *npl* : ropa *f* usada

handout [ˈhænd,aʊt] *n* **1** AID **:** dádiva *f,* limosna *f* **2** LEAFLET **:** folleto *m*
handpick [ˈhændˈpɪk] *vt* **:** seleccionar con cuidado
handrail [ˈhænd,reɪl] *n* **:** pasamanos *m,* barandilla *f,* barandal *m*
handsaw [ˈhænd,sɔ] *n* **:** serrucho *m*
hands down *adv* **1** EASILY **:** con facilidad **2** UNQUESTIONABLY **:** con mucho, de lejos
handshake [ˈhænd,ʃeɪk] *n* **:** apretón *m* de manos
handsome [ˈhæn*t*səm] *adj* **-somer; -est 1** ATTRACTIVE **:** apuesto, guapo, atractivo **2** GENEROUS **:** generoso **3** SIZABLE **:** considerable
handsomely [ˈhæn*t*səmli] *adv* **1** ELEGANTLY **:** elegantemente **2** GENEROUSLY **:** con generosidad
handspring [ˈhænd,sprɪŋ] *n* **:** voltereta *f*
handstand [ˈhænd,stænd] *n* **to do a handstand :** pararse de manos
hand–to–hand [ˈhæn*d*təˈhænd] *adj* **:** cuerpo a cuerpo
handwriting [ˈhænd,raɪt̬ɪŋ] *n* **:** letra *f,* escritura *f*
handwritten [ˈhænd,rɪtən] *adj* **:** escrito a mano
handy [ˈhændi] *adj* **handier; -est 1** NEARBY **:** a mano, cercano **2** USEFUL **:** útil, práctico **3** DEXTEROUS **:** hábil
hang[1] [ˈhæŋ] *v* **hung** [ˈhʌŋ]; **hanging** *vt* **1** SUSPEND **:** colgar, tender, suspender **2** (*past tense often* **hanged**) EXECUTE **:** colgar, ahorcar **3 to hang one's head :** bajar la cabeza — *vi* **1** FALL **:** caer (dícese de las telas y la ropa) **2** DANGLE **:** colgar **3** HOVER **:** flotar, sostenerse en el aire **4 :** ser ahorcado **5** DROOP **:** inclinarse **6 to hang up :** colgar <he hung up on me : me colgó>
hang[2] *n* **1** DRAPE **:** caída *f* **2 to get the hang of something :** colgarle el truco a algo, lograr entender algo
hangar [ˈhæŋər, ˈhæŋgər] *n* **:** hangar *m*
hanger [ˈhæŋər] *n* **:** percha *f,* gancho *m* (para ropa)
hangman [ˈhæŋmən] *n, pl* **-men** [-mən, -,mɛn] **:** verdugo *m*
hangnail [ˈhæŋ,neɪl] *n* **:** padrastro *m*
hangout [ˈhæŋ,aʊt] *n* **:** lugar *m* popular, sitio *m* muy frecuentado
hangover [ˈhæŋ,oːvər] *n* **:** resaca *f*
hank [ˈhæŋk] *n* **:** madeja *f*
hanker [ˈhæŋkər] *vi* **to hanker for :** ansiar, anhelar, tener ganas de
hankering [ˈhæŋkərɪŋ] *n* **:** ansia *f,* anhelo *m*
hansom [ˈhæn*t*səm] *n* **:** coche *m* de caballos
Hanukkah [ˈxɑnəkə, ˈhɑ-] *n* **:** Januká, Hanukkah
haphazard [hæpˈhæzərd] *adj* **:** casual, fortuito, al azar — **haphazardly** *adv*
hapless [ˈhæpləs] *adj* UNFORTUNATE **:** desafortunado, desventurado — **haplessly**
happen [ˈhæpən] *vi* **1** OCCUR **:** pasar, ocurrir, suceder, tener lugar **2** BEFALL **:** pasar, acontecer <what happened to her? : ¿qué le ha pasado?> **3** CHANCE **:** resultar, ocurrir por casualidad <it happened that I wasn't home : resulta que estaba fuera de casa> <he happens to be right : da la casualidad de que tiene razón>
happening [ˈhæpənɪŋ] *n* **:** suceso *m,* acontecimiento *m*
happiness [ˈhæpinəs] *n* **:** felicidad *f,* dicha *f*
happy [ˈhæpi] *adj* **-pier; -est 1** JOYFUL **:** feliz, contento, alegre **2** FORTUNATE **:** afortunado, feliz — **happily** [-pəli] *adv*
happy–go–lucky [ˈhæpigoːˈlʌki] *adj* **:** despreocupado
harangue[1] [həˈræŋ] *vt* **-rangued; -ranguing :** arengar
harangue[2] *n* **:** arenga *f*
harass [həˈræs, ˈhærəs] *vt* **1** BESIEGE, HOUND **:** acosar, asediar, hostigar **2** ANNOY **:** molestar
harassment [həˈræsmənt, ˈhærəsmənt] *n* **:** acoso *m,* hostigamiento *m* <sexual harrassment : acoso sexual>
harbinger [ˈhɑrbɪndʒər] *n* **1** HERALD **:** heraldo *m,* precursor *m* **2** OMEN **:** presagio *m*
harbor[1] [ˈhɑrbər] *vt* **1** SHELTER **:** dar refugio a, albergar **2** CHERISH, KEEP **:** abrigar, guardar, albergar <to harbor doubts : guardar dudas>
harbor[2] *n* **1** REFUGE **:** refugio *m* **2** PORT **:** puerto *m*
hard[1] [ˈhɑrd] *adv* **1** FORCEFULLY **:** fuerte, con fuerza <the wind blew hard : el viento sopló fuerte> **2** STRENUOUSLY **:** duro, mucho <to work hard : trabajar duro> **3 to take something hard :** tomarse algo muy mal, estar muy afectado por algo
hard[2] *adj* **1** FIRM, SOLID **:** duro, firme, sólido **2** DIFFICULT **:** difícil, arduo **3** SEVERE **:** severo, duro <a hard winter : un invierno severo> **4** UNFEELING **:** insensible, duro **5** DILIGENT **:** diligente <to be a hard worker : ser muy trabajador> **6 hard liquor :** bebidas *fpl* fuertes **7 hard water :** agua *f* dura
harden [ˈhɑrdən] *vt* **:** endurecer
hardheaded [,hɑrdˈhɛdəd] *adj* **1** STUBBORN **:** testarudo, terco **2** REALISTIC **:** realista, práctico — **hardheadedly** *adv*
hard–hearted [,hɑrdˈhɑrt̬əd] *adj* **:** despiadado, insensible — **hard–heartedly** *adv*
hard–heartedness [,hɑrdˈhɑrt̬ədnəs] *n* **:** dureza *f* de corazón
hardly [ˈhɑrdli] *adv* **1** SCARCELY **:** apenas, casi <I hardly knew her : apenas la conocía> <hardly ever : casi nunca> **2** NOT **:** difícilmente,

poco, no <they can hardly blame me! : ¡difícilmente pueden echarme la culpa!> <it's hardly likely : es poco probable>

hardness ['hɑrdnəs] *n* **1** FIRMNESS : dureza *f* **2** DIFFICULTY : dificultad *f* **3** SEVERITY : severidad *f*

hardship ['hɑrd,ʃɪp] *n* : dificultad *f,* privación *f*

hardware ['hɑrd,wær] *n* **1** TOOLS : ferretería *f* **2** : hardware *m* (de una computadora)

hardwood ['hɑrd,wʊd] *n* : madera *f* dura, madera *f* noble

hardy ['hɑrdi] *adj* **-dier; -est** : fuerte, robusto, resistente (dícese de las plantas) — **hardily** [-dəli] *adv*

hare ['hær] *n, pl* **hare** *or* **hares** : liebre *f*

harebrained ['hær,breɪnd] *adj* : estúpido, absurdo, disparatado

harelip ['hær,lɪp] *n* : labio *m* leporino

harem ['hærəm] *n* : harén *m*

hark ['hɑrk] *vi* **1** (*used only in the imperative*) LISTEN : escuchar **2 hark back** RETURN : volver **3 hark back** RECALL : recordar

harlequin ['hɑrlɪkən, -kwən] *n* : arlequín *m*

harm[1] ['hɑrm] *vt* : hacerle daño a, perjudicar

harm[2] *n* : daño *m,* perjuicio *m*

harmful ['hɑrmfəl] *adj* : dañino, perjudicial — **harmfully** *adv*

harmless ['hɑrmləs] *adj* : inofensivo, inocuo — **harmlessly** *adv*

harmlessness ['hɑrmləsnəs] *n* : inocuidad *f*

harmonic [hɑr'mɑnɪk] *adj* : armónico — **harmonically** [-nɪkli] *adv*

harmonica [hɑr'mɑnɪkə] *n* : armónica *f*

harmonious [hɑr'mo:niəs] *adj* : armonioso — **harmoniously** *adv*

harmonize ['hɑrmə,naɪz] *v* **-nized; -nizing** : armonizar

harmony ['hɑrməni] *n, pl* **-nies** : armonía *f*

harness[1] ['hɑrnəs] *vt* **1** : enjaezar (un animal) **2** UTILIZE : utilizar, aprovechar

harness[2] *n* : arreos *mpl,* guarniciones *fpl,* arnés *m*

harp[1] ['hɑrp] *vi* **to harp on** : insistir sobre, machacar sobre

harp[2] *n* : arpa *m*

harpist ['hɑrpɪst] *n* : arpista *mf*

harpoon[1] [hɑr'pu:n] *vt* : arponear

harpoon[2] *n* : arpón *m*

harpsichord ['hɑrpsɪ,kɔrd] *n* : clavicémbalo *m*

harrow[1] ['hær,o:] *vt* **1** CULTIVATE : gradar, labrar (la tierra) **2** TORMENT : atormentar

harrow[2] *n* : grada *f,* rastra *f*

harry ['hæri] *vt* **-ried; -rying** HARASS : acosar, hostigar

harsh ['hɑrʃ] *adj* **1** ROUGH : áspero **2** SEVERE : duro, severo **3** : discordante (dícese de los sonidos) — **harshly** *adv*

harshness ['hɑrʃnəs] *n* **1** ROUGHNESS : aspereza *f* **2** SEVERITY : dureza *f,* severidad *f*

harvest[1] ['hɑrvəst] *v* : cosechar

harvest[2] *n* **1** HARVESTING : siega *f,* recolección *f* **2** CROP : cosecha *f*

harvester ['hɑrvəstər] *n* : segador *m,* -dora *f;* cosechadora *f* (máquina)

has → **have**

hash[1] ['hæʃ] *vt* **1** MINCE : picar **2 to hash over** DISCUSS : discutir, repasar

hash[2] *n* **1** : picadillo *m* (comida) **2** JUMBLE : revoltijo *m,* fárrago *m*

hasn't ['hæzənt] (*contraction of* **has not**) → **has**

hasp ['hæsp] *n* : picaporte *m,* pestillo *m*

hassle[1] ['hæsəl] *vt* **-sled; -sling** : fastidiar, molestar

hassle[2] *n* **1** ARGUMENT : discusión *f,* disputa *f,* bronca *f* **2** FIGHT : pelea *f,* riña *f* **3** BOTHER, TROUBLE : problemas *mpl,* lío *m*

hassock ['hæsək] *n* **1** CUSHION : almohadón *m,* cojín *m* **2** FOOTSTOOL : escabel *m*

haste ['heɪst] *n* **1** : prisa *f,* apuro *m* **2 to make haste** : darse prisa, apurarse

hasten ['heɪsən] *vt* : acelerar, precipitar — *vi* : apresurarse, apurarse

hasty ['heɪsti] *adj* **hastier; -est 1** HURRIED, QUICK : rápido, apresurado, apurado **2** RASH : precipitado — **hastily** [-təli] *adv*

hat ['hæt] *n* : sombrero *m*

hatch[1] ['hætʃ] *vt* **1** : incubar, empollar (huevos) **2** DEVISE : idear, tramar — *vi* : salir del cascarón

hatch[2] *n* : escotilla *f*

hatchery ['hætʃəri] *n, pl* **-ries** : criadero *m*

hatchet ['hætʃət] *n* : hacha *f*

hatchway ['hætʃ,weɪ] *n* : escotilla *f*

hate[1] ['heɪt] *vt* **hated; hating** : odiar, aborrecer, detestar

hate[2] *n* : odio *m*

hateful ['heɪtfəl] *adj* : odioso, aborrecible, detestable — **hatefully** *adv*

hatred ['heɪtrəd] *n* : odio *m*

hatter ['hætər] *n* : sombrerero *m,* -ra *f*

haughtiness ['hɔtinəs] *n* : altanería *f,* altivez *f*

haughty ['hɔti] *adj* **-tier; -est** : altanero, altivo — **haughtily** [-təli] *adv*

haul[1] ['hɔl] *vt* **1** DRAG, PULL : arrastrar, jalar **2** TRANSPORT : transportar

haul[2] *n* **1** PULL : tirón *m,* jalón *m* **2** CATCH : redada *f* **3** JOURNEY : viaje *m,* trayecto *m* <it's a long haul : es un trayecto largo>

haulage ['hɔlɪdʒ] *n* : transporte *m,* tiro *m*

hauler ['hɔlər] *n* : transportista *mf*

haunch [ˈhɔntʃ] *n* **1** HIP : cadera *f* **2 haunches** *npl* HINDQUARTERS : ancas *fpl*, cuartos *mpl* traseros

haunt[1] [ˈhɔnt] *vt* **1** : aparecer en (dícese de un fantasma) **2** FREQUENT : frecuentar, rondar **3** PREOCCUPY : perseguir, obsesionar

haunt[2] *n* : guarida *f* (de animales o ladrones), lugar *m* predilecto

haunting [ˈhɔntɪŋ] *adj* : obsesionante, evocador — **hauntingly** *adv*

have [ˈhæv, *in sense 3 as an auxiliary verb usu* ˈhæf] *v* **had** [ˈhæd]; **having; has** [ˈhæz, *in sense 3 as an auxiliary verb usu* ˈhæs] *vt* **1** POSSESS : tener <do you have change? : ¿tienes cambio?> **2** EXPERIENCE, UNDERGO : tener, experimentar, sufrir <I have a toothache : tengo un dolor de muelas> **3** INCLUDE : tener, incluir <April has 30 days : abril tiene 30 días> **4** CONSUME : comer, tomar **5** RECEIVE : tener, recibir <he had my permission : tenía mi permiso> **6** ALLOW : permitir, dejar <I won't have it! : ¡no lo permitiré!> **7** HOLD : hacer <to have a party : dar una fiesta> <to have a meeting : convocar una reunión> **8** HOLD : tener <he had me in his power : me tenía en su poder> **9** BEAR : tener (niños) **10** (*indicating causation*) <she had a dress made : mandó hacer un vestido> <to have one's hair cut : cortarse el pelo> — *v aux* **1** : haber <she has been very busy : ha estado muy ocupada> <I've lived here three years : hace tres años que vivo aquí> **2** (*used in tags*) <you've finished, haven't you? : ha terminado, ¿no?> **3 to have to** : deber, tener que <we have to leave : tenemos que salir>

haven [ˈheɪvən] *n* : refugio *m*

havoc [ˈhævək] *n* **1** DESTRUCTION : estragos *mpl*, destrucción *f* **2** CHAOS, DISORDER : desorden *m*, caos *m*

Hawaiian[1] [həˈwaɪən] *adj* : hawaiano

Hawaiian[2] *n* : hawaiano *m*, -na *f*

hawk[1] [ˈhɔk] *vt* : pregonar, vender (mercancías) en la calle

hawk[2] *n* : halcón *m*

hawker [ˈhɔkər] *n* : vendedor *m*, -dora *f* ambulante

hawthorn [ˈhɔˌθɔrn] *n* : espino *m*

hay [ˈheɪ] *n* : heno *m*

hay fever *n* : fiebre *f* del heno

hayloft [ˈheɪˌlɔft] *n* : pajar *m*

hayseed [ˈheɪˌsiːd] *n* : palurdo *m*, -da *f*

haystack [ˈheɪˌstæk] *n* : almiar *m*

haywire [ˈheɪˌwaɪr] *adj* : descompuesto, desbaratado <to go haywire : estropearse>

hazard[1] [ˈhæzərd] *vt* : arriesgar, aventurar

hazard[2] *n* **1** DANGER : peligro *m*, riesgo *m* **2** CHANCE : azar *m*

hazardous [ˈhæzərdəs] *adj* : arriesgado, peligroso

haze[1] [ˈheɪz] *vt* **hazed; hazing** : abrumar, acosar

haze[2] *n* : bruma *f*, neblina *f*

hazel [ˈheɪzəl] *n* **1** : avellano *m* (árbol) **2** : color *m* avellana

hazelnut [ˈheɪzəlˌnʌt] *n* : avellana *f*

haziness [ˈheɪzinəs] *n* **1** MISTINESS : nebulosidad *f* **2** VAGUENESS : vaguedad *f*

hazy [ˈheɪzi] *adj* **hazier; -est 1** MISTY : brumoso, neblinoso, nebuloso **2** VAGUE : vago, confuso

he [ˈhiː] *pron* : él

head[1] [ˈhɛd] *vt* **1** LEAD : encabezar **2** DIRECT : dirigir — *vi* : dirigirse

head[2] *adj* MAIN : principal <the head office : la oficina central, la sede>

head[3] *n* **1** : cabeza *f* <from head to foot : de pies a cabeza> **2** MIND : mente *f*, cabeza *f* **3** TIP, TOP : cabeza *f* (de un clavo, un martillo, etc.), cabecera *f* (de una mesa o un río), punta *f* (de una flecha), flor *m* (de un repollo, etc.), encabezamiento *m* (de una carta, etc.), espuma *f* (de cerveza) **4** DIRECTOR, LEADER : director *m*, -tora *f*; jefe *m*, -fa *f*; cabeza *f* (de una familia) **5** : cara *f* (de una moneda) <heads or tails : cara o cruz> **6** : cabeza *f* <500 head of cattle : 500 cabezas de ganado> <$10 a head : $10 por cabeza> **7 to come to a head** : llegar a un punto crítico

headache [ˈhɛdˌeɪk] *n* : dolor *m* de cabeza, jaqueca *f*

headband [ˈhɛdˌbænd] *n* : cinta *f* del pelo

headdress [ˈhɛdˌdrɛs] *n* : tocado *m*

headfirst [ˈhɛdˈfərst] *adv* : de cabeza

headgear [ˈhɛdˌgɪr] *n* : gorro *m*, casco *m*, sombrero *m*

heading [ˈhɛdɪŋ] *n* **1** DIRECTION : dirección *f* **2** TITLE : encabezamiento *m*, título *m* **3** : membrete *m* (de una carta)

headland [ˈhɛdlənd, -ˌlænd] *n* : cabo *m*

headlight [ˈhɛdˌlaɪt] *n* : faro *m*, foco *m*, farol *m Mex*

headline [ˈhɛdˌlaɪn] *n* : titular *m*

headlong[1] [ˈhɛdˈlɔŋ] *adv* **1** HEADFIRST : de cabeza **2** HASTILY : precipitadamente

headlong[2] [ˈhɛdˌlɔŋ] *adj* : precipitado

headmaster [ˈhɛdˌmæstər] *n* : director *m*

headmistress [ˈhɛdˌmɪstrəs, -ˈmɪs-] *n* : directora *f*

head–on [ˈhɛdˈɑn, -ˈɔn] *adv & adj* : de frente

headphones [ˈhɛdˌfoːnz] *npl* : audífonos *mpl*, cascos *mpl*

headquarters [ˈhɛdˌkwɔrtərz] *ns & pl* **1** SEAT : oficina *f* central, sede *f* **2** : cuartel *m* general (de los militares)

headrest [ˈhɛdˌrɛst] *n* : apoyacabezas *m*

headship [ˈhɛdˌʃɪp] *n* : dirección *f*

head start *n* : ventaja *f*

headstone [ˈhɛdˌstoːn] *n* : lápida *f*

headstrong ['hɛd'strɔŋ] *adj* : testarudo, obstinado, empecinado

headwaiter ['hɛd'weɪt̬ər] *n* : jefe *m*, -fa *f* de comedor

headwaters ['hɛd,wɔt̬ərz, -,wɑ-] *npl* : cabecera *f*

headway ['hɛd,weɪ] *n* : progreso *m* <to make headway against : avanzar contra>

heady ['hɛdi] *adj* **headier; -est** **1** INTOXICATING : embriagador, excitante **2** SHREWD : astuto, sagaz

heal ['hi:l] *vt* : curar, sanar — *vi* **1** : sanar, curarse **2** **to heal up** : cicatrizarse

healer ['hi:lər] *n* : curador *m*, -dora *f*

health ['hɛlθ] *n* : salud *f*

healthful ['hɛlθfəl] *adj* : saludable, salubre — **healthfully** *adv*

healthy ['hɛlθi] *adj* **healthier; -est** : sano, bien — **healthily** [-θəli] *adv*

heap¹ ['hi:p] *vt* **1** PILE : amontonar, apilar **2** SHOWER : colmar

heap² *n* : montón *m*, pila *f*

hear ['hɪr] *v* **heard** ['hərd]; **hearing** *vt* **1** : oír <do you hear me? : ¿me oyes?> **2** HEED : oír, prestar atención a **3** LEARN : oír, enterarse de — *vi* **1** : oír <to hear about : oír hablar de> **2** **to hear from** : tener noticias de

hearing ['hɪrɪŋ] *n* **1** : oído *m* <hard of hearing : duro de oído> **2** : vista *f* (en un tribunal) **3** ATTENTION : consideración *f*, oportunidad *f* de expresarse **4** EARSHOT : alcance *m* del oído

hearing aid *n* : audífono *m*

hearken ['hɑrkən] *vt* : escuchar

hearsay ['hɪr,seɪ] *n* : rumores *mpl*

hearse ['hərs] *n* : coche *m* fúnebre

heart ['hɑrt] *n* **1** : corazón *m* **2** CENTER, CORE : corazón *m*, centro *m* <the heart of the matter : el meollo del asunto> **3** FEELINGS : corazón *m*, sentimientos *mpl* <a broken heart : un corazón destrozado> <to have a good heart : tener buen corazón> <to take something to heart : tomarse algo a pecho> **4** COURAGE : valor *m*, corazón *m* <to take heart : animarse, cobrar ánimos> **5** **hearts** *npl* : corazones *mpl* (en juegos de naipes) **6** **by heart** : de memoria

heartache ['hɑrt̬,eɪk] *n* : pena *f*, angustia *f*

heart attack *n* : infarto *m*, ataque *m* al corazón

heartbeat ['hɑrt,bi:t] *n* : latido *m* (del corazón)

heartbreak ['hɑrt,breɪk] *n* : congoja *f*, angustia *f*

heartbreaking ['hɑrt,breɪkɪŋ] *adj* : desgarrador, que parte el corazón

heartbroken ['hɑrt,bro:kən] *adj* : desconsolado, destrozado

heartburn ['hɑrt,bərn] *n* : acidez *f* estomacal

hearten ['hɑrtən] *vt* : alentar, animar

hearth ['hɑrθ] *n* : hogar *m*, chimenea *f*

heartily ['hɑrt̬əli] *adv* **1** ENTHUSIASTICALLY : de buena gana, con entusiasmo **2** TOTALLY : totalmente, completamente

heartless ['hɑrtləs] *adj* : desalmado, despiadado, cruel

heartsick ['hɑrt,sɪk] *adj* : abatido, desconsolado

heartstrings ['hɑrt,strɪŋz] *npl* : fibras *fpl* del corazón

heartwarming ['hɑrt,wɔrmɪŋ] *adj* : conmovedor, emocionante

hearty ['hɑrt̬i] *adj* **heartier; -est** **1** CORDIAL, WARM : cordial, caluroso **2** STRONG : fuerte <to have a hearty appetite : ser de buen comer> **3** SUBSTANTIAL : abundante, sustancioso <a hearty breakfast : un desayuno abundante>

heat¹ ['hi:t] *vt* : calentar

heat² *n* **1** WARMTH : calor *m* **2** HEATING : calefacción *f* **3** EXCITEMENT : calor *m*, entusiasmo *m* <in the heat of the moment : en el calor del momento> **4** ESTRUS : celo *m*

heated ['hi:t̬əd] *adj* **1** WARMED : calentado **2** IMPASSIONED : acalorado, apasionado

heater ['hi:t̬ər] *n* : calentador *m*, estufa *f*, calefactor *m*

heath ['hi:θ] *n* **1** MOOR : brezal *m*, páramo *m* **2** HEATHER : brezo *m*

heathen¹ ['hi:ðən] *adj* : pagano

heathen² *n, pl* **-thens** *or* **-then** : pagano *m*, -na *f*; infiel *mf*

heather ['hɛðər] *n* : brezo *m*

heave¹ ['hi:v] *v* **heaved** *or* **hove** ['ho:v]; **heaving** *vt* **1** LIFT, RAISE : levantar con esfuerzo **2** HURL : lanzar, tirar **3** **to heave a sigh** : echar un suspiro, suspirar — *vi* **1** : subir y bajar, palpitar (dícese del pecho) **2** **to heave up** RISE : levantarse

heave² *n* **1** EFFORT : gran esfuerzo *m* (para levantar algo) **2** THROW : lanzamiento *m*

heaven ['hɛvən] *n* **1** : cielo *m* <for heaven's sake : por Dios> **2** **heavens** *npl* SKY : cielo *m* <the heavens opened up : empezó a llover a cántaros>

heavenly ['hɛvənli] *adj* **1** : celestial, celeste **2** DELIGHTFUL : divino, encantador

heavily ['hɛvəli] *adv* **1** : pesadamente, con mucho peso **2** LABORIOUSLY : trabajosamente, penosamente **3** : mucho

heaviness ['hɛvinəs] *n* : peso *m*, pesadez *f*

heavy ['hɛvi] *adj* **heavier; -est** **1** WEIGHTY : pesado **2** DENSE, THICK : denso, espeso, grueso **3** BURDENSOME : oneroso, gravoso **4** PROFOUND : profundo **5** SLUGGISH : lento, tardo **6** STOUT : corpulento **7** SEVERE : severo, duro, fuerte

heavy–duty ['hɛvi'du:t̬i, -'dju:-] *adj* : muy resistente, fuerte

heavyweight ['hɛvi,weɪt] *n* : peso *m* pesado (en deportes)

Hebrew[1] [ˈhiːˌbruː] *adj* : hebreo

Hebrew[2] *n* **1** : hebreo *m,* -brea *f* **2** : hebreo *m* (idioma)

heckle [ˈhɛkəl] *vt* **-led; -ling** : interrumpir (a un orador)

hectic [ˈhɛktɪk] *adj* : agitado, ajetreado — **hectically** [-tɪkli] *adv*

he'd [ˈhiːd] (*contraction of* **he had** *or* **he would**) → **have, would**

hedge[1] [ˈhɛdʒ] *v* **hedged; hedging** *vt* **1** : cercar con un seto **2 to hedge one's bet** : cubrirse — *vi* **1** : dar rodeos, contestar con evasivas **2 to hedge against** : cubrirse contra, protegerse contra

hedge[2] *n* **1** : seto *m* vivo **2** SAFEGUARD : salvaguardia *f,* protección *f*

hedgehog [ˈhɛdʒˌhɔg, -hɑg] *n* : erizo *m*

heed[1] [ˈhiːd] *vt* : prestar atención a, hacer caso de

heed[2] *n* : atención *f*

heedless [ˈhiːdləs] *adj* : descuidado, despreocupado, inconsciente <to be heedless of : hacer caso omiso de> — **heedlessly** *adv*

heel[1] [ˈhiːl] *vi* : inclinarse

heel[2] *n* : talón *m* (del pie), tacón *m* (de calzado)

heft [ˈhɛft] *vt* : sopesar

hefty [ˈhɛfti] *adj* **heftier; -est** : robusto, fornido, pesado

heifer [ˈhɛfər] *n* : novilla *f*

height [ˈhaɪt] *n* **1** PEAK : cumbre *f,* cima *f,* punto *m* alto <at the height of her career : en la cumbre de su carrera> <the height of stupidity : el colmo de la estupidez> **2** TALLNESS : estatura *f* (de una persona), altura *f* (de un objeto) **3** ALTITUDE : altura *f*

heighten [ˈhaɪtən] *vt* **1** : hacer más alto **2** INTENSIFY : aumentar, intensificar — *vi* : aumentarse, intensificarse

heinous [ˈheɪnəs] *adj* : atroz, abominable, nefando

heir [ˈær] *n* : heredero *m,* -ra *f*

heiress [ˈærəs] *n* : heredera *f*

heirloom [ˈærˌluːm] *n* : reliquia *f* de familia

held → **hold**

helicopter [ˈhɛləˌkɑptər] *n* : helicóptero *m*

helium [ˈhiːliəm] *n* : helio *m*

hell [ˈhɛl] *n* : infierno *m*

he'll [ˈhiːl, ˈhɪl] (*contraction of* **he shall** *or* **he will**) → **shall, will**

hellish [ˈhɛlɪʃ] *adj* : horroroso, infernal

hello [həˈloː, hɛ-] *interj* : ¡hola!

helm [ˈhɛlm] *n* **1** : timón *m* **2 to take the helm** : tomar el mando

helmet [ˈhɛlmət] *n* : casco *m*

help[1] [ˈhɛlp] *vt* **1** AID, ASSIST : ayudar, auxiliar, socorrer, asistir **2** ALLEVIATE : aliviar **3** SERVE : servir <help yourself! : ¡sírvete!> **4** AVOID : evitar <it can't be helped : no lo podemos evitar, no hay más remedio> <I couldn't help smiling : no pude menos que sonreír>

help[2] *n* **1** ASSISTANCE : ayuda *f* <help! : ¡socorro!, ¡auxilio!> **2** STAFF : personal *m* (en una oficina), servicio *m* doméstico

helper [ˈhɛlpər] *n* : ayudante *mf*

helpful [ˈhɛlpfəl] *adj* **1** OBLIGING : servicial, amable, atento **2** USEFUL : útil, práctico — **helpfully** *adv*

helpfulness [ˈhɛlpfəlnəs] *n* **1** KINDNESS : bondad *f,* amabilidad *f* **2** USEFULNESS : utilidad *f*

helping [ˈhɛlpɪŋ] *n* : porción *f*

helpless [ˈhɛlpləs] *adj* **1** POWERLESS : incapaz, impotente **2** DEFENSELESS : indefenso

helplessly [ˈhɛlpləsli] *adv* : en vano, inútilmente

helplessness [ˈhɛlpləsnəs] *n* POWERLESSNESS : incapacidad *f,* impotencia *f*

helter–skelter [ˌhɛltərˈskɛltər] *adv* : atropelladamente, precipitadamente

hem[1] [ˈhɛm] *vt* **hemmed; hemming 1** : dobladillar **2 to hem in** : encerrar

hem[2] *n* : dobladillo *m,* bastilla *f*

hemisphere [ˈhɛməˌsfɪr] *n* : hemisferio *m*

hemispheric [ˌhɛməˈsfɪrɪk, -ˈsfɛr-] *or* **hemispherical** [-ɪkəl] *adj* : hemisférico

hemlock [ˈhɛmˌlɑk] *n* : cicuta *f*

hemoglobin [ˈhiːməˌgloːbən] *n* : hemoglobina *f*

hemophilia [ˌhiːməˈfɪliə] *n* : hemofilia *f*

hemorrhage[1] [ˈhɛmərɪdʒ] *vi* **-rhaged; -rhaging** : sufrir una hemorragia

hemorrhage[2] *n* : hemorragia *f*

hemorrhoids [ˈhɛməˌrɔɪdz, ˈhɛmˌrɔɪdz] *npl* : hemorroides *fpl,* almorranas *fpl*

hemp [ˈhɛmp] *n* : cáñamo *m*

hen [ˈhɛn] *n* : gallina *f*

hence [ˈhɛnts] *adv* **1** : de aquí, de ahí <10 years hence : de aquí a 10 años> <a dog bit me, hence my dislike of animals : un perro me mordió, de ahí mi aversión a los animales> **2** THEREFORE : por lo tanto, por consiguiente

henceforth [ˈhɛntsˌforθ, ˌhɛntsˈ-] *adv* : de ahora en adelante

henchman [ˈhɛntʃmən] *n, pl* **-men** [-mən, -ˌmɛn] : secuaz *mf,* esbirro *m*

henpeck [ˈhɛnˌpɛk] *vt* : dominar (al marido)

hepatitis [ˌhɛpəˈtaɪtəs] *n, pl* **-titides** [-ˈtɪtəˌdiːz] : hepatitis *f*

her[1] [ˈhər] *adj* : su, sus, de ella <her house : su casa, la casa de ella>

her[2] [ˈhər, ər] *pron* **1** (*used as direct object*) : la <I saw her yesterday : la vi ayer> **2** (*used as indirect object*) : le, se <he gave her the book : le dio el libro> <he sent it to her : se lo mandó> **3** (*used as object of a preposition*) : ella <we did it for her : lo hicimos por ella> <taller than her : más alto que ella>

herald[1] ['hɛrəld] *vt* ANNOUNCE **:** anunciar, proclamar

herald[2] *n* **1** MESSENGER **:** heraldo *m* **2** HARBINGER **:** precursor *m*

heraldic [hɛ'rældɪk, hə-] *adj* **:** heráldico

heraldry ['hɛrəldri] *n, pl* **-ries :** heráldica *f*

herb ['ərb, 'hərb] *n* **:** hierba *f*

herbal ['ərbəl, 'hər-] *adj* **:** herbario

herbicide ['ərbə,saɪd, 'hər-] *n* **:** herbicida *m*

herbivore ['ərbə,vor, 'hər-] *n* **:** herbívoro *m*

herbivorous [,ər'bɪvərəs, ,hər-] *adj* **:** herbívoro

herculean [,hərkjə'liːən, ,hər'kjuːliən] *adj* **:** hercúleo, sobrehumano

herd[1] ['hərd] *vt* **:** reunir en manada, conducir en manada — *vi* **:** ir en manada (dícese de los animales), apiñarse (dícese de la gente)

herd[2] *n* **:** manada *f*

herder ['hərdər] → **herdsman**

herdsman ['hərdzmən] *n, pl* **-men** [-mən, -,mɛn] **:** vaquero *m* (de ganado), pastor *m* (de ovejas)

here ['hɪr] *adv* **1 :** aquí, acá <come here! **:** ¡ven acá!> <right here **:** aquí mismo> **2** NOW **:** en este momento, ahora, ya <here he comes **:** ya viene> <here it's three o'clock (already) **:** ahora son las tres> **3 :** en este punto <here we agree **:** estamos de acuerdo en este punto> **4 here you are! :** ¡toma!

hereabouts ['hɪrə,baʊts] *or* **hereabout** [-,baʊt] *adv* **:** por aquí (cerca)

hereafter[1] [hɪr'æftər] *adv* **1 :** de aquí en adelante, a continuación **2 :** en el futuro

hereafter[2] *n* **the hereafter :** el más allá

hereby [hɪr'baɪ] *adv* **:** por este medio

hereditary [hə'rɛdə,tɛri] *adj* **:** hereditario

heredity [hə'rɛdəti] *n* **:** herencia *f*

herein [hɪr'ɪn] *adv* **:** aquí

hereof [hɪr'ʌv] *adv* **:** de aquí

hereon [hɪr'ɑn, -'ɔn] *adv* **:** sobre esto

heresy ['hɛrəsi] *n, pl* **-sies :** herejía *f*

heretic ['hɛrə,tɪk] *n* **:** hereje *mf*

heretical [hə'rɛtɪkəl] *adj* **:** herético

hereto [hɪr'tuː] *adv* **:** a esto

heretofore ['hɪrtə,for] *adv* HITHERTO **:** hasta ahora

hereunder [hɪr'ʌndər] *adv* **:** a continuación, abajo

hereupon [hɪrə'pɑn, -'pɔn] *adv* **:** con esto, en ese momento

herewith [hɪr'wɪθ] *adv* **:** adjunto

heritage ['hɛrətɪdʒ] *n* **:** patrimonio *m* (nacional)

hermaphrodite [hər'mæfrə,daɪt] *n* **:** hermafrodita *mf*

hermetic [hər'mɛtɪk] *adj* **:** hermético — **hermetically** [-tɪkli] *adv*

hermit ['hərmət] *n* **:** ermitaño *m*, -ña *f*; eremita *mf*

hernia ['hərniə] *n, pl* **-nias** *or* **-niae** [-ni,iː, -ni,aɪ] **:** hernia *f*

hero ['hiː,roː, 'hɪr,oː] *n, pl* **-roes 1 :** héroe *m* **2** PROTAGONIST **:** protagonista *mf*

heroic [hɪ'roːɪk] *adj* **:** heroico — **heroically** [-ɪkli] *adv*

heroics [hɪ'roːɪks] *npl* **:** actos *mpl* heroicos

heroin ['hɛroən] *n* **:** heroína *f*

heroine ['hɛroən] *n* **1 :** heroína *f* **2** PROTAGONIST **:** protagonista *f*

heroism ['hɛro,ɪzəm] *n* **:** heroísmo *m*

heron ['hɛrən] *n* **:** garza *f*

herpes ['hər,piːz] *n* **:** herpes *m*

herpetology [,hərpə'tɑlədʒi] *n* **:** herpetología *f*

herring ['hɛrɪŋ] *n, pl* **-ring** *or* **-rings :** arenque *m*

hers ['hərz] *pron* **:** suyo, -ya; suyos, -yas; de ella <these shoes are hers **:** estos zapatos son suyos> <hers are bigger **:** los de ella son más grandes>

herself [hər'sɛlf] *pron* **1** (*used reflexively*) **:** se <she dressed herself **:** se vistió> **2** (*used emphatically*) **:** ella misma <she fixed it herself **:** lo arregló ella misma, lo arregló por sí sola>

hertz ['hərts, 'hɛrts] *ns & pl* **:** hercio *m*

he's ['hiːz] (*contraction of* **he is** *or* **he has**) → **be, have**

hesitancy ['hɛzətəntsi] *n, pl* **-cies :** vacilación *f*, titubeo *m*, indecisión *f*

hesitant ['hɛzətənt] *adj* **:** titubeante, vacilante — **hesitantly** *adv*

hesitate ['hɛzə,teɪt] *vi* **-tated; -tating :** vacilar, titubear

hesitation [,hɛzə'teɪʃən] *n* **:** vacilación *f*, indecisión *f*, titubeo *m*

heterogeneous [,hɛtərə'dʒiːniəs, -njəs] *adj* **:** heterogéneo

heterosexual[1] [,hɛtəro'sɛkʃʊəl] *adj* **:** heterosexual

heterosexual[2] *n* **:** heterosexual *mf*

heterosexuality [,hɛtəro,sɛkʃʊ'æləti] *n* **:** heterosexualidad *f*

hew ['hjuː] *v* **hewed; hewed** *or* **hewn** ['hjuːn]; **hewing** *vt* **1** CUT **:** cortar, talar (árboles) **2** SHAPE **:** labrar, tallar — *vi* CONFORM **:** conformarse, ceñirse

hex[1] ['hɛks] *vt* **:** hacerle un maleficio (a alguien)

hex[2] *n* **:** maleficio *m*

hexagon ['hɛksə,gɑn] *n* **:** hexágono *m*

hexagonal [hɛk'sægənəl] *adj* **:** hexagonal

hey ['heɪ] *interj* **:** ¡eh!, ¡oye!

heyday ['heɪ,deɪ] *n* **:** auge *m*, apogeo *m*

hi ['haɪ] *interj* **:** ¡hola!

hiatus [haɪ'eɪtəs] *n* **1 :** hiato *m* **2** PAUSE **:** pausa *f*

hibernate ['haɪbər,neɪt] *vi* **-nated; -nating :** hibernar, invernar

hibernation [,haɪbər'neɪʃən] *n* **:** hibernación *f*

hiccup[1] ['hɪkəp] *vi* **-cuped; -cuping :** hipar, tener hipo

hiccup[2] *n* **:** hipo *m* <to have the hiccups : tener hipo>

hick [ˈhɪk] *n* BUMPKIN **:** palurdo *m,* -da *f*

hickory [ˈhɪkəri] *n, pl* **-ries :** nogal *m* americano

hidden [ˈhɪdən] *adj* **:** oculto

hide[1] [ˈhaɪd] *v* **hid** [ˈhɪd]; **hidden** [ˈhɪdən] *or* **hid; hiding** *vt* **1** CONCEAL **:** esconder **2** ocultar <to hide one's motives : ocultar uno sus motivos> **3** SCREEN **:** tapar, no dejar ver — *vi* **:** esconderse

hide[2] *n* **:** piel *f,* cuero *m* <to save one's hide : salvar el pellejo>

hide–and–seek [ˈhaɪdənd'siːk] *n* **to play hide–and–seek :** jugar a las escondidas

hidebound [ˈhaɪdˌbaʊnd] *adj* **:** rígido, conservador

hideous [ˈhɪdiəs] *adj* **:** horrible, horroroso, espantoso — **hideously** *adv*

hideout [ˈhaɪdˌaʊt] *n* **:** guarida *f,* escondrijo *m*

hierarchical [ˌhaɪəˈrɑrkɪkəl] *adj* **:** jerárquico

hierarchy [ˈhaɪəˌrɑrki] *n, pl* **-chies :** jerarquía *f*

hieroglyphic [ˌhaɪərəˈglɪfɪk] *n* **:** jeroglífico *m*

hi–fi [ˈhaɪˈfaɪ] *n* **1** → **high fidelity 2 :** equipo *m* de alta fidelidad

high[1] [ˈhaɪ] *adv* **:** alto

high[2] *adj* **1** TALL **:** alto <a high wall : una pared alta> **2** ELEVATED **:** alto, elevado <high prices : precios elevados> <high blood pressure : presión alta> **3** GREAT, IMPORTANT **:** grande, importante, alto <a high number : un número grande> <high society : alta sociedad> <high hopes : grandes esperanzas> **4 :** alto (en música) **5** INTOXICATED **:** borracho, drogado

high[3] *n* **1 :** récord *m,* punto *m* máximo <to reach an all-time high : batir el récord> **2 :** zona *f* de alta presión (en meteorología) **3** *or* **high gear :** directa *f* **4 on high :** en las alturas

highbrow [ˈhaɪˌbraʊ] *n* **:** intelectual *mf*

higher [ˈhaɪər] *adj* **:** superior

high fidelity *n* **:** alta fidelidad *f*

high–flown [ˈhaɪˈfloːn] *adj* **:** altisonante

high–handed [ˈhaɪˈhændəd] *adj* **:** arbitrario

highlands [ˈhaɪləndz] *npl* **:** tierras *fpl* altas, altiplano *m*

highlight[1] [ˈhaɪˌlaɪt] *vt* **1** EMPHASIZE **:** destacar, poner en relieve, subrayar **2 :** ser el punto culminante de

highlight[2] *n* **:** punto *m* culminante

highly [ˈhaɪli] *adv* **1** VERY **:** muy, sumamente **2** FAVORABLY **:** muy bien <to speak highly of : hablar muy bien de> <to think highly of : tener en mucho a>

highness [ˈhaɪnəs] *n* **1** HEIGHT **:** altura *f* **2 Highness :** Alteza *f* <Your Royal Highness : Su Alteza Real>

high–rise [ˈhaɪˌraɪz] *adj* **:** alto, de muchas plantas

high school *n* **:** escuela *f* superior, escuela *f* secundaria

high seas *npl* **:** alta mar *f*

high–spirited [ˈhaɪˈspɪrət̬əd] *adj* **:** vivaz, muy animado, brioso

high–strung [ˌhaɪˈstrʌŋ] *adj* **:** nervioso, excitable

highway [ˈhaɪˌweɪ] *n* **:** carretera *f*

highwayman [ˈhaɪˌweɪmən] *n, pl* **-men** [-mən, -ˌmɛn] **:** salteador *m* (de caminos), bandido *m*

hijack[1] [ˈhaɪˌdʒæk] *vt* **:** secuestrar

hijack[2] *n* **:** secuestro *m*

hijacker [ˈhaɪˌdʒækər] *n* **:** secuestrador *m,* -dora *f*

hike[1] [ˈhaɪk] *v* **hiked; hiking** *vi* **:** hacer una caminata — *vt* RAISE **:** subir

hike[2] *n* **1 :** caminata *f,* excursión *f* **2** INCREASE **:** subida *f* (de precios)

hiker [ˈhaɪkər] *n* **:** excursionista *mf*

hilarious [hɪˈlæriəs, haɪˈ-] *adj* **:** muy divertido, hilarante

hilarity [hɪˈlærət̬i, haɪ-] *n* **:** hilaridad *f*

hill [ˈhɪl] *n* **1 :** colina *f,* cerro *m* **2** SLOPE **:** cuesta *f,* pendiente *f*

hillbilly [ˈhɪlˌbɪli] *n, pl* **-lies :** palurdo *m,* -da *f* (de las montañas)

hillock [ˈhɪlək] *n* **:** loma *f,* altozano *m,* otero *m*

hillside [ˈhɪlˌsaɪd] *n* **:** ladera *f,* cuesta *f*

hilltop [ˈhɪlˌtɑp] *n* **:** cima *f,* cumbre *f*

hilly [ˈhɪli] *adj* **hillier; -est :** montañoso, accidentado

hilt [ˈhɪlt] *n* **:** puño *m,* empuñadura *f*

him [ˈhɪm, əm] *pron* **1** (*used as direct object*) **:** lo <I found him : lo encontré> **2** (*used as indirect object*) **:** le, se <we gave him a present : le dimos un regalo> <I sent it to him : se lo mandé> **3** (*used as object of a preposition*) **:** él <she was thinking of him : pensaba en él> <younger than him : más joven que él>

himself [hɪmˈsɛlf] *pron* **1** (*used reflexively*) **:** se <he washed himself : se lavó> **2** (*used emphatically*) **:** él mismo <he did it himself : lo hizo él mismo, lo hizo por sí solo>

hind[1] [ˈhaɪnd] *adj* **:** trasero, posterior <hind legs : patas traseras>

hind[2] *n* **:** cierva *f*

hinder [ˈhɪndər] *vt* **:** dificultar, impedir, estorbar

hindquarters [ˈhaɪndˌkwɔrt̬ərz] *npl* **:** cuartos *mpl* traseros

hindrance [ˈhɪndrənts] *n* **:** estorbo *m,* obstáculo *m,* impedimento *m*

hindsight [ˈhaɪndˌsaɪt] *n* **:** retrospectiva *f* <with the benefit of hindsight : en retrospectiva, con la perspectiva que da la experiencia>

Hindu[1] [ˈhɪnˌduː] *adj* **:** hindú

Hindu[2] *n* **:** hindú *mf*

Hinduism [ˈhɪnduːˌɪzəm] *n* **:** hinduismo *m*

hinge[1] [ˈhɪndʒ] *v* **hinged; hinging** *vt* : unir con bisagras — *vi* **to hinge on** : depender de
hinge[2] *n* : bisagra *f,* gozne *m*
hint[1] [ˈhɪnt] *vt* : insinuar, dar a entender — *vi* : soltar indirectas
hint[2] *n* **1** INSINUATION : insinuación *f,* indirecta *f* **2** TIP : consejo *m,* sugerencia *f* **3** TRACE : pizca *f,* indicio *m*
hinterland [ˈhɪntərˌlænd, -lənd] *n* : interior *m* (de un país)
hip [ˈhɪp] *n* : cadera *f*
hippopotamus [ˌhɪpəˈpɑt̬əməs] *n, pl* **-muses** *or* **-mi** [-ˌmaɪ] : hipopótamo *m*
hippo [ˈhɪpoː] *n, pl* **hippos** → **hippopotamus**
hire[1] [ˈhaɪr] *vt* **hired; hiring 1** EMPLOY : contratar, emplear **2** RENT : alquilar, arrendar
hire[2] *n* **1** RENT : alquiler *m* <for hire : se alquila> **2** WAGES : paga *f,* sueldo *m* **3** EMPLOYEE : empleado *m,* -da *f*
his[1] [ˈhɪz, ɪz] *adj* : su, sus, de él <his hat : su sombrero, el sombrero de él>
his[2] *pron* : suyo, -ya; suyos, suyas; de él <the decision is his : la decisión es suya> <it's his, not hers : es de él, no de ella>
Hispanic[1] [hɪˈspænɪk] *adj* : hispano, hispánico
Hispanic[2] *n* : hispano *m,* -na *f;* hispánico *m,* -ca *f*
hiss[1] [ˈhɪs] *vi* : sisear, silbar — *vt* : decir entre dientes
hiss[2] *n* : siseo *m,* silbido *m*
historian [hɪˈstɔriən] *n* : historiador *m,* -dora *f*
historic [hɪˈstɔrɪk] *or* **historical** [-ɪkəl] *adj* : histórico — **historically** [-ɪkli] *adv*
history [ˈhɪstəri] *n, pl* **-ries 1** : historia *f* **2** RECORD : historial *m*
histrionics [ˌhɪstriˈɑnɪks] *ns & pl* : histrionismo *m*
hit[1] [ˈhɪt] *v* **hit; hitting** *vt* **1** STRIKE : golpear, pegar, batear (una pelota) <he hit the dog : le pegó al perro> **2** : chocar contra, dar con, dar en (el blanco) <the car hit a tree : el coche chocó contra un árbol> **3** AFFECT : afectar <the news hit us hard : la noticia nos afectó mucho> **4** ENCOUNTER : tropezar con, toparse con <to hit a snag : tropezar con un obstáculo> **5** REACH : llegar a, alcanzar <the price hit $10 a pound : el precio alcanzó los $10 dólares por libra> <to hit town : llegar a la ciudad> <to hit the headlines : ser noticia> **6 to hit on** *or* **to hit upon** : dar con — *vi* : golpear
hit[2] *n* **1** BLOW : golpe *m* **2** : impacto *m* (de un arma) **3** SUCCESS : éxito *m*
hitch[1] [ˈhɪtʃ] *vt* **1** : mover con sacudidas **2** ATTACH : enganchar, atar, amarrar **3** → **hitchhike 4 to hitch up** : subirse (los pantalones, etc.)
hitch[2] *n* **1** JERK : tirón *m,* jalón *m* **2** OBSTACLE : obstáculo *m,* impedimento *m,* tropiezo *m*
hitchhike [ˈhɪtʃˌhaɪk] *vi* **-hiked; -hiking** : hacer autostop, ir de aventón *Col, Mex fam*
hitchhiker [ˈhɪtʃˌhaɪkər] *n* : autostopista *mf*
hither [ˈhɪðər] *adv* : acá, por aquí
hitherto [ˈhɪðərˌtuː, ˌhɪðərˈ-] *adv* : hasta ahora
hitter [ˈhɪt̬ər] *n* BATTER : bateador *m,* -dora *f*
HIV [ˌeɪtʃˌaɪˈviː] *n* : VIH *m,* virus *m* del sida
hive [ˈhaɪv] *n* **1** : colmena *f* **2** SWARM : enjambre *m* **3** : lugar *m* muy activo <a hive of activity : un hervidero de actividad>
hives [ˈhaɪvz] *ns & pl* : urticaria *f*
hoard[1] [ˈhord] *vt* : acumular, atesorar
hoard[2] *n* : tesoro *m,* reserva *f,* provisión *f*
hoarfrost [ˈhorˌfrɔst] *n* : escarcha *f*
hoarse [ˈhors] *adj* **hoarser; -est** : ronco — **hoarsely** *adv*
hoarseness [ˈhorsnəs] *n* : ronquera *f*
hoary [ˈhori] *adj* **hoarier; -est 1** : cano, canoso **2** OLD : vetusto, antiguo
hoax[1] [ˈhoːks] *vt* : engañar, embaucar, bromar
hoax[2] *n* : engaño *m,* broma *f*
hobble[1] [ˈhɑbəl] *v* **-bled; -bling** *vi* LIMP : cojear, renguear — *vt* : manear (un animal)
hobble[2] *n* **1** LIMP : cojera *f,* rengo *m* **2** : maniota *f* (para un animal)
hobby [ˈhɑbi] *n, pl* **-bies** : pasatiempo *m,* afición *f*
hobgoblin [ˈhɑbˌgɑblən] *n* : duende *m*
hobnail [ˈhɑbˌneɪl] *n* : tachuela *f*
hobnob [ˈhɑbˌnɑb] *vi* **-nobbed; -nobbing** : codearse
hobo [ˈhoːˌboː] *n, pl* **-boes** : vagabundo *m,* -da *f*
hock[1] [ˈhɑk] *vt* PAWN : empeñar
hock[2] *n* **in hock** : empeñado
hockey [ˈhɑki] *n* : hockey *m*
hod [ˈhɑd] *n* : capacho *m* (de albañil)
hodgepodge [ˈhɑdʒˌpɑdʒ] *n* : mezcolanza *f*
hoe[1] [ˈhoː] *vt* **hoed; hoeing** : azadonar
hoe[2] *n* : azada *f,* azadón *m*
hog[1] [ˈhɔg, ˈhɑg] *vt* **hogged; hogging** : acaparar, monopolizar
hog[2] *n* **1** PIG : cerdo *m,* -da *f* **2** GLUTTON : glotón *m,* -tona *f*
hogshead [ˈhɔgzˌhɛd, ˈhɑgz-] *n* : tonel *m*
hoist[1] [ˈhɔɪst] *vt* : levantar, alzar, izar (una bandera, una vela)
hoist[2] *n* : grúa *f*
hold[1] [ˈhoːld] *v* **held** [ˈhɛld]; **holding** *vt* **1** POSSESS : tener <to hold office : ocupar un puesto> **2** RESTRAIN : detener, controlar <to hold one's temper : controlar su mal genio> **3** CLASP, GRASP : agarrar, coger <to hold hands : agarrarse de la mano> **4** : sujetar,

mantener fijo <hold this nail for me : sujétame este clavo> **5** CONTAIN : contener, dar cabida a **6** SUPPORT : aguantar, sostener **7** REGARD : considerar, tener <he held me responsible : me consideró responsable> **8** CONDUCT : celebrar (una reunión), realizar (un evento), mantener (una conversación) — *vi* **1** : aguantar, resistir <the rope will hold : la cuerda resistirá> **2** : ser válido, valer <my offer still holds : mi oferta todavía es válida> **3 to hold forth** : perorar, arengar **4 to hold to** : mantenerse firme en **5 to hold with** : estar de acuerdo con

hold[2] *n* **1** GRIP : agarre *m,* llave *f* (en deportes) **2** CONTROL : control *m,* dominio *m* <to get hold of oneself : controlarse> **3** DELAY : demora *f* <to put on hold : suspender temporalmente> **4** : bodega *f* (en un barco o un avión) **5 to get hold of** : conseguir, localizar

holder [ˈhoːldər] *n* : poseedor *m,* -dora *f;* titular *mf*

holdings [ˈhoːldɪŋz] *npl* : propiedades *fpl*

hold out *vi* **1** LAST : aguantar, durar **2** RESIST : resistir

holdup [ˈhoːldˌʌp] *n* **1** ROBBERY : atraco *m* **2** DELAY : retraso *m,* demora *f*

hold up *vt* **1** ROB : robarle (a alguien), atracar, asaltar **2** DELAY : retrasar

hole [ˈhoːl] *n* : agujero *m,* hoyo *m*

holiday [ˈhɑləˌdeɪ] *n* **1** : día *m* feriado, fiesta *f* **2** VACATION : vacaciones *fpl*

holiness [ˈhoːlinəs] *n* **1** : santidad *f* **2 His Holiness** : Su Santidad

holistic [hoːˈlɪstɪk] *adj* : holístico

holler[1] [ˈhɑlər] *vi* : gritar, chillar

holler[2] *n* : grito *m,* chillido *m*

hollow[1] [ˈhɑˌloː] *vt or* **to hollow out** : ahuecar

hollow[2] *adj* **-lower; -est 1** : hueco, hundido (dícese de las mejillas, etc.), cavernoso (dícese de un sonido) **2** EMPTY, FALSE : vacío, falso

hollow[3] *n* **1** CAVITY : hueco *m,* depresión *f,* cavidad *f* **2** VALLEY : hondonada *f,* valle *m*

hollowness [ˈhɑˌloːnəs] *n* **1** HOLLOW : hueco *m,* cavidad *f* **2** FALSENESS : falsedad *f* **3** EMPTINESS : vacuidad *f*

holly [ˈhɑli] *n, pl* **-lies** : acebo *m*

hollyhock [ˈhɑliˌhɑk] *n* : malvarrosa *f*

holocaust [ˈhɑləˌkɔst, ˈhoː-, ˈhɔ-] *n* : holocausto *m*

holster [ˈhoːlstər] *n* : pistolera *f*

holy [ˈhoːli] *adj* **-lier; -est** : santo, sagrado

Holy Ghost → **Holy Spirit**

Holy Spirit *n* **the Holy Spirit** : el Espíritu Santo

homage [ˈɑmɪdʒ, ˈhɑ-] *n* : homenaje *m*

home [ˈhoːm] *n* **1** : casa *f,* hogar *m,* domicilio *m* <to feel at home : sentirse en casa> **2** INSTITUTION : residencia *f,* asilo *m*

homecoming [ˈhoːmˌkʌmɪŋ] *n* : regreso *m* (a casa)

homegrown [ˈhoːmˈgroːn] *adj* **1** : de cosecha propia **2** LOCAL : local

homeland [ˈhoːmˌlænd] *n* : patria *f,* tierra *f* natal, terruño *m*

homeless [ˈhoːmləs] *adj* : sin hogar, sin techo

homely [ˈhoːmli] *adj* **-lier; -est 1** DOMESTIC : casero, hogareño **2** UGLY : feo, poco atractivo

homemade [ˈhoːmˈmeɪd] *adj* : casero, hecho en casa

homemaker [ˈhoːmˌmeɪkər] *n* : ama *f* de casa, persona *f* que se ocupa de la casa

home plate *n* : base *f* del bateador

home run *n* : jonrón *m*

homesick [ˈhoːmˌsɪk] *adj* : nostálgico <to be homesick : echar de menos a la familia>

homesickness [ˈhoːmˌsɪknəs] *n* : nostalgia *f,* morriña *f*

homespun [ˈhoːmˌspʌn] *adj* : simple, sencillo

homestead [ˈhoːmˌstɛd] *n* : estancia *f,* hacienda *f*

homeward[1] [ˈhoːmwərd] *or* **homewards** [-wərdz] *adv* : de vuelta a casa, hacia casa

homeward[2] *adj* : de vuelta, de regreso

homework [ˈhoːmˌwərk] *n* : tarea *f,* deberes *mpl Spain,* asignación *f PRi*

homey [ˈhoːmi] *adj* **homier; -est** : hogareño

homicidal [ˌhɑməˈsaɪdəl, ˌhoː-] *adj* : homicida

homicide [ˈhɑməˌsaɪd, ˈhoː-] *n* : homicidio *m*

hominy [ˈhɑməni] *n* : maíz *m* descascarillado

homogeneous [ˌhoːməˈdʒiːniəs, -njəs] *adj* : homogéneo — **homogeneously** *adv*

homogenize [hoːˈmɑdʒəˌnaɪz, hə-] *vt* **-nized; -nizing** : homogeneizar

homograph [ˈhɑməˌgræf, ˈhoː-] *n* : homógrafo *m*

homonym [ˈhɑməˌnɪm, ˈhoː-] *n* : homónimo *m*

homophone [ˈhɑməˌfoːn, ˈhoː-] *n* : homófono *m*

homosexual[1] [ˌhoːməˈsɛkʃʊəl] *adj* : homosexual

homosexual[2] *n* : homosexual *mf*

homosexuality [ˌhoːməˌsɛkʃʊˈæləti] *n* : homosexualidad *f*

Honduran [hɑnˈdʊrən, -ˈdjʊr-] *n* : hondureño *m,* -ña *f* — **Honduran** *adj*

hone [ˈhoːn] *vt* **honed; honing** : afilar

honest [ˈɑnəst] *adj* : honesto, honrado — **honestly** *adv*

honesty [ˈɑnəsti] *n, pl* **-ties** : honestidad *f,* honradez *f*

honey [ˈhʌni] *n, pl* **-eys** : miel *f*

honeybee [ˈhʌniˌbiː] *n* : abeja *f*

honeycomb [ˈhʌniˌkoːm] *n* : panal *m*

honeymoon[1] ['hʌni,mu:n] *vi* : pasar la luna de miel
honeymoon[2] *n* : luna *f* de miel
honeysuckle ['hʌni,sʌkəl] *n* : madreselva *f*
honk[1] ['haŋk, 'hɔŋk] *vi* **1** : graznar (dícese del ganso) **2** : tocar la bocina (dícese de un vehículo), pitar
honk[2] *n* : graznido *m* (del ganso), bocinazo *m* (de un vehículo)
honor[1] ['anər] *vt* **1** RESPECT : honrar **2** : cumplir con <to honor one's word : cumplir con su palabra> **3** : aceptar (un cheque, etc.)
honor[2] *n* **1** : honor *m* <in honor of : en honor de> **2 honors** *npl* AWARDS : honores *mpl*, condecoraciones *fpl* **3 Your Honor** : Su Señoría
honorable ['anərəbəl] *adj* : honorable, honroso — **honorably** [-bli] *adv*
honorary ['anə,rɛri] *adj* : honorario
hood ['hʊd] *n* **1** : capucha *f* **2** : capó *m*, bonete *m Car* (de un automóvil)
hooded ['hʊdəd] *adj* : encapuchado
hoodlum ['hʊdləm, 'hu:d-] *n* THUG : maleante *mf*, matón *m*
hoodwink ['hʊd,wɪŋk] *vt* : engañar
hoof ['hʊf, 'hu:f] *n, pl* **hooves** ['hʊvz, 'hu:vz] *or* **hoofs** : pezuña *f*, casco *m*
hoofed ['hʊft, 'hu:ft] *adj* : ungulado
hook[1] ['hʊk] *vt* : enganchar — *vi* : abrocharse, engancharse
hook[2] *n* : gancho *m*, percha *f*
hookworm ['hʊk,wərm] *n* : anquilostoma *m*
hooligan ['hu:lɪgən] *n* : gamberro *m*, -rra *f*
hoop ['hu:p] *n* : aro *m*
hooray [hʊ'reɪ] → **hurrah**
hoot[1] ['hu:t] *vi* **1** SHOUT : gritar <to hoot with laughter : morirse de risa, reírse a carcajadas> **2** : ulular (dícese de un búho), tocar la bocina (dícese de un vehículo), silbar (dícese de un tren o un barco)
hoot[2] *n* **1** : ululato *m* (de un búho), silbido *m* (de un tren), bocinazo *m* (de un vehículo) **2** GUFFAW : carcajada *f*, risotada *f* **3 I don't give a hoot** : me vale un comino, me importa un pito
hop[1] ['hap] *vi* **hopped; hopping** : brincar, saltar
hop[2] *n* **1** LEAP : salto *m*, brinco *m* **2** FLIGHT : vuelo *m* corto **3** : lúpulo *m* (planta)
hope[1] ['ho:p] *v* **hoped; hoping** *vi* : esperar — *vt* : esperar que <we hope she comes : esperamos que venga> <I hope not : espero que no>
hope[2] *n* : esperanza *f*
hopeful ['ho:pfəl] *adj* : esperanzado — **hopefully** *adv*
hopeless ['ho:pləs] *adj* **1** DESPAIRING : desesperado **2** IMPOSSIBLE : imposible <a hopeless case : un caso perdido>
hopelessly ['ho:pləsli] *adv* **1** : sin esperanzas, desesperadamente **2** COMPLETELY : totalmente, completamente **3** IMPOSSIBLY : imposiblemente
hopelessness ['ho:pləsnəs] *n* : desesperanza *f*
hopper ['hapər] *n* : tolva *f*
hopscotch ['hap,skatʃ] *n* : tejo *m*
horde ['hord] *n* : horda *f*, multitud *f*
horizon [hə'raɪzən] *n* : horizonte *m*
horizontal [,hɔrə'zantəl] *adj* : horizontal — **horizontally** *adv*
hormone ['hɔr,mo:n] *n* : hormona *f* — **hormonal** [hɔr'mo:nəl] *adj*
horn ['hɔrn] *n* **1** : cuerno *m* (de un toro, una vaca, etc.) **2** : cuerno *m*, trompa *f* (instrumento musical) **3** : bocina *f*, claxon *m* (de un vehículo)
horned ['hɔrnd, 'hɔrnəd] *adj* : cornudo, astado, con cuernos
hornet ['hɔrnət] *n* : avispón *m*
horn of plenty → **cornucopia**
horny ['hɔrni] *adj* **hornier; -est** CALLOUS : calloso
horoscope ['hɔrə,sko:p] *n* : horóscopo *m*
horrendous [hɔ'rɛndəs] *adj* : horrendo, horroroso, atroz
horrible ['hɔrəbəl] *adj* : horrible, espantoso, horroroso — **horribly** [-bli] *adv*
horrid ['hɔrɪd] *adj* : horroroso, horrible — **horridly** *adv*
horrify ['hɔrə,faɪ] *vt* **-fied; -fying** : horrorizar
horrifying ['hɔrə,faɪɪŋ] *adj* : horripilante, horroroso
horror ['hɔrər] *n* : horror *m*
hors d'oeuvre [ɔr'dərv] *n, pl* **hors d'oeuvres** [-'dərvz] : entremés *m*
horse ['hɔrs] *n* : caballo *m*
horseback ['hɔrs,bæk] *n* **on** ~ : a caballo
horse chestnut *n* : castaña *f* de Indias
horsefly ['hɔrs,flaɪ] *n, pl* **-flies** : tábano *m*
horsehair ['hɔrs,hær] *n* : crin *f*
horseman ['hɔrsmən] *n, pl* **-men** [-mən, -,mɛn] : jinete *m*, caballista *m*
horsemanship ['hɔrsmən,ʃɪp] *n* : equitación *f*
horseplay ['hɔrs,pleɪ] *n* : payasadas *fpl*
horsepower ['hɔrs,paʊər] *n* : caballo *m* de fuerza
horseradish ['hɔrs,rædɪʃ] *n* : rábano *m* picante
horseshoe ['hɔrs,ʃu:] *n* : herradura *f*
horsewhip ['hɔrs,*h*wɪp] *vt* **-whipped; -whipping** : azotar, darle fuetazos (a alguien)
horsewoman ['hɔrs,wʊmən] *n, pl* **-women** [-,wɪmən] : amazona *f*, jinete *f*, caballista *f*
horsey *or* **horsy** ['hɔrsi] *adj* **horsier; -est** : relacionado a los caballos, caballar
horticultural [,hɔrṭə'kʌltʃərəl] *adj* : hortícola
horticulture ['hɔrṭə,kʌltʃər] *n* : horticultura *f*

hose[1] [ˈhoːz] *vt* **hosed; hosing :** regar o lavar con manguera

hose[2] *n* **1** *pl* **hose** SOCKS **:** calcetines *mpl,* medias *fpl* **2** *pl* **hose** STOCKINGS **:** medias *fpl* **3** *pl* **hoses :** manguera *f,* manga *f*

hosiery [ˈhoːʒəri, ˈhoːzə-] *n* **:** calcetería *f,* medias *fpl*

hospice [ˈhɑspəs] *n* **:** hospicio *m*

hospitable [hɑˈspɪt̬əbəl, ˈhɑs͵pɪ-] *adj* **:** hospitalario — **hospitably** [-bli] *adv*

hospital [ˈhɑs͵pɪt̬əl] *n* **:** hospital *m*

hospitality [͵hɑspəˈtæləti] *n, pl* **-ties :** hospitalidad *f*

hospitalization [͵hɑs͵pɪt̬ələˈzeɪʃən] *n* **:** hospitalización *f*

hospitalize [ˈhɑs͵pɪt̬əl͵aɪz] *vt* **-ized; -izing :** hospitalizar

host[1] [ˈhoːst] *vt* **:** presentar (un programa de televisión, etc.)

host[2] *n* **1 :** anfitrión *m,* -triona *f* (en la casa, a un evento); presentador *m,* -dora *f* (de un programa de televisión, etc.) **2** *or* **host organism :** huésped *m* **3** TROOPS **:** huestes *fpl* **4** MULTITUDE **:** multitud *f* <for a host of reasons : por muchas razones> **5** EUCHARIST **:** hostia *f,* Eucaristía *f*

hostage [ˈhɑstɪdʒ] *n* **:** rehén *m*

hostel [ˈhɑstəl] *n* **:** albergue *m* juvenil

hostess [ˈhoːstɪs] *n* **:** anfitriona *f* (en la casa), presentadora *f* (de un programa)

hostile [ˈhɑstəl, -͵taɪl] *adj* **:** hostil — **hostilely** *adv*

hostility [hɑsˈtɪləti] *n, pl* **-ties :** hostilidad *f*

hot [ˈhɑt] *adj* **hotter; hottest 1 :** caliente, cálido, caluroso <hot water : agua caliente> <a hot climate : un clima cálido> <a hot day : un día caluroso> **2** ARDENT, FIERY **:** ardiente, acalorado <to have a hot temper : tener mal genio> **3** SPICY **:** picante **4** FRESH **:** reciente, nuevo <hot news : noticias de última hora> **5** EAGER **:** ávido **6** STOLEN **:** robado

hot air *n* **:** palabrería *f*

hotbed [ˈhɑt͵bɛd] *n* **1 :** semillero *m* (de plantas) **2 :** hervidero *m,* semillero *m* (de crimen, etc.)

hot dog *n* **:** perro *m* caliente

hotel [hoːˈtɛl] *n* **:** hotel *m*

hothead [ˈhɑt͵hɛd] *n* **:** exaltado *m,* -da *f*

hotheaded [ˈhɑtˈhɛdəd] *adj* **:** exaltado

hothouse [ˈhɑt͵haʊs] *n* **:** invernadero *m*

hot plate *n* **:** placa *f* (de cocina)

hot rod *n* **:** coche *m* con motor modificado

hot water *n* **to get into hot water :** meterse en un lío

hound[1] [ˈhaʊnd] *vt* **:** acosar, perseguir

hound[2] *n* **:** perro *m* (de caza)

hour [ˈaʊər] *n* **:** hora *f*

hourglass [ˈaʊər͵glæs] *n* **:** reloj *m* de arena

hourly [ˈaʊərli] *adv & adj* **:** cada hora, por hora

house[1] [ˈhaʊz] *vt* **housed; housing :** albergar, alojar, hospedar

house[2] [ˈhaʊs] *n, pl* **houses** [ˈhaʊzəz, -səz] **1** HOME **:** casa *f* **2 :** cámara *f* (del gobierno) **3** BUSINESS **:** casa *f,* empresa *f*

houseboat [ˈhaʊs͵boːt] *n* **:** casa *f* flotante

housebroken [ˈhaʊs͵broːkən] *adj* **:** enseñado

housefly [ˈhaʊs͵flaɪ] *n, pl* **-flies :** mosca *f* común

household[1] [ˈhaʊs͵hoːld] *adj* **1** DOMESTIC **:** doméstico, de la casa **2** FAMILIAR **:** conocido por todos

household[2] *n* **:** casa *f,* familia *f*

householder [ˈhaʊs͵hoːldər] *n* **:** dueño *m,* -ña *f* de casa

housekeeper [ˈhaʊs͵kiːpər] *n* **:** ama *f* de llaves

housekeeping [ˈhaʊs͵kiːpɪŋ] *n* **:** gobierno *m* de la casa, quehaceres *mpl* domésticos

housemaid [ˈhaʊs͵meɪd] *n* **:** criada *f,* mucama *f,* muchacha *f,* sirvienta *f*

housewarming [ˈhaʊs͵wɔrmɪŋ] *n* **:** fiesta *f* de estreno de una casa

housewife [ˈhaʊs͵waɪf] *n, pl* **-wives :** ama *f* de casa

housework [ˈhaʊs͵wərk] *n* **:** faenas *fpl* domésticas, quehaceres *mpl* domésticos

housing [ˈhaʊzɪŋ] *n* **1** HOUSES **:** vivienda *f* **2** COVERING **:** caja *f* protectora

hove → **heave**

hovel [ˈhʌvəl, ˈhɑ-] *n* **:** casucha *f,* tugurio *m*

hover [ˈhʌvər, ˈhɑ-] *vi* **1 :** cernerse, sostenerse en el aire **2 to hover about :** rondar

how [ˈhaʊ] *adv* **1 :** cómo <how are you? : ¿cómo estas?> <I don't know how to fix it : no se cómo arreglarlo> **2 :** qué <how beautiful! : ¡qué bonito!> **3 :** cuánto <how old are you? : ¿cuántos años tienes?> **4 how about...? :** ¿qué te parece...?

however[1] [haʊˈɛvər] *adv* **1 :** por mucho que, por más que <however hot it is : por mucho calor que haga> **2** NEVERTHELESS **:** sin embargo, no obstante

however[2] *conj* **:** comoquiera que, de cualquier manera que

howl[1] [ˈhaʊl] *vi* **:** aullar

howl[2] *n* **:** aullido *m,* alarido *m*

hub [ˈhʌb] *n* **1** CENTER **:** centro *m* **2 :** cubo *m* (de una rueda)

hubbub [ˈhʌ͵bʌb] *n* **:** algarabía *f,* alboroto *m,* jaleo *m*

hubcap [ˈhʌb͵kæp] *n* **:** tapacubos *m*

huckster [ˈhʌkstər] *n* **:** buhonero *m,* -ra *f;* vendedor *m,* -dora *f* ambulante

huddle[1] [ˈhʌdəl] *vi* **-dled; -dling 1 :** apiñarse, amontonarse **2 to huddle together :** acurrucarse

huddle[2] *n* : grupo *m* (cerrado) <to go into a huddle : conferenciar en secreto>

hue [ˈhjuː] *n* : color *m,* tono *m*

huff [ˈhʌf] *n* : enojo *m,* enfado *m* <to be in a huff : estar enojado>

huffy [ˈhʌfi] *adj* **huffier; -est** : enojado, enfadado

hug[1] [ˈhʌg] *vt* **hugged; hugging 1** EMBRACE : abrazar **2** : ir pegado a <the road hugs the river : el camino está pegado al río>

hug[2] *n* : abrazo *m*

huge [ˈhjuːdʒ] *adj* **huger; hugest** : inmenso, enorme — **hugely** *adv*

hulk [ˈhʌlk] *n* **1** : persona *f* fornida **2** : casco *m* (barco), armatoste *m* (edificio, etc.)

hulking [ˈhʌlkɪŋ] *adj* : grandote *fam,* pesado

hull[1] [ˈhʌl] *vt* : pelar

hull[2] *n* **1** HUSK : cáscara *f* **2** : casco *m* (de un barco, un avión, etc.)

hullabaloo [ˈhʌləbəˌluː] *n, pl* **-loos** : alboroto *m,* jaleo *m*

hum[1] [ˈhʌm] *v* **hummed; humming** *vi* **1** BUZZ : zumbar **2** : estar muy activo, moverse <to hum with activity : bullir de actividad> — *vt* : tararear (una melodía)

hum[2] *n* : zumbido *m,* murmullo *m*

human[1] [ˈhjuːmən, ˈjuː-] *adj* : humano — **humanly** *adv*

human[2] *n* : ser *m* humano

humane [hjuːˈmeɪn, ˌjuː-] *adj* : humano, humanitario — **humanely** *adv*

humanism [ˈhjuːməˌnɪzəm, ˈjuː-] *n* : humanismo *m*

humanist [ˈhjuːmənɪst, ˈjuː-] *n* : humanista *mf*

humanitarian[1] [hjuːˌmænəˈtɛriən, juː-] *adj* : humanitario

humanitarian[2] *n* : humanitario *m,* -ria *f*

humanity [hjuːˈmænət̬i, juː-] *n, pl* **-ties** : humanidad *f*

humankind [ˈhjuːmənˈkaɪnd, ˈjuː-] *n* : género *m* humano

humble[1] [ˈhʌmbəl] *vt* **-bled; -bling 1** : humillar **2 to humble oneself** : humillarse

humble[2] *adj* **-bler; -blest** : humilde, modesto — **humbly** [ˈhʌmbli] *adv*

humbug [ˈhʌmˌbʌg] *n* **1** FRAUD : charlatán *m,* -tana *f;* farsante *mf* **2** NONSENSE : patrañas *fpl,* tonterías *fpl*

humdrum [ˈhʌmˌdrʌm] *adj* : monótono, rutinario

humid [ˈhjuːməd, ˈjuː-] *adj* : húmedo

humidifier [hjuːˈmɪdəˌfaɪər, juː-] *n* : humidificador *m*

humidify [hjuːˈmɪdəˌfaɪ, juː-] *vt* **-fied; -fying** : humidificar

humidity [hjuːˈmɪdət̬i, juː-] *n, pl* **-ties** : humedad *f*

humiliate [hjuːˈmɪliˌeɪt, juː-] *vt* **-ated; -ating** : humillar

humiliating [hjuːˈmɪliˌeɪt̬ɪŋ, juː-] *adj* : humillante

humiliation [hjuːˌmɪliˈeɪʃən, juː-] *n* : humillación *f*

humility [hjuːˈmɪlət̬i, juː-] *n* : humildad *f*

hummingbird [ˈhʌmɪŋˌbərd] *n* : colibrí *m,* picaflor *m*

hummock [ˈhʌmək] *n* : montículo *m*

humor[1] [ˈhjuːmər, ˈjuː-] *vt* : seguir el humor a, complacer

humor[2] *n* : humor *m*

humorist [ˈhjuːmərɪst, ˈjuː-] *n* : humorista *mf*

humorless [ˈhjuːmərləs, ˈjuː-] *adj* : sin sentido del humor <a humorless smile : una sonrisa forzada>

humorous [ˈhjuːmərəs, ˈjuː-] *adj* : humorístico, cómico — **humorously** *adv*

hump [ˈhʌmp] *n* : joroba *f,* giba *f*

humpback [ˈhʌmpˌbæk] *n* **1** HUMP : joroba *f,* giba *f* **2** HUNCHBACK : jorobado *m,* -da *f;* giboso *m,* -sa *f*

humpbacked [ˈhʌmpˌbækt] *adj* : jorobado, giboso

humus [ˈhjuːməs, ˈjuː-] *n* : humus *m*

hunch[1] [ˈhʌntʃ] *vt* : encorvar — *vi or* **to hunch up** : encorvarse

hunch[2] *n* PREMONITION : presentimiento *m*

hunchback [ˈhʌntʃˌbæk] *n* **1** HUMP : joroba *f,* giba *f* **2** HUMPBACK : jorobado *m,* -da *f;* giboso *m,* -sa *f*

hunchbacked [ˈhʌntʃˌbækt] *adj* : jorobado, giboso

hundred[1] [ˈhʌndrəd] *adj* : cien, ciento

hundred[2] *n, pl* **-dreds** *or* **-dred** : ciento *m*

hundredth[1] [ˈhʌndrədθ] *adj* : centésimo

hundredth[2] *n* **1** : centésimo *m,* -ma *f* (en una serie) **2** : centésimo *m,* centésima parte *f*

hung → **hang**

Hungarian [hʌŋˈgæriən] *n* **1** : húngaro *m,* -ra *f* **2** : húngaro *m* (idioma) — **Hungarian** *adj*

hunger[1] [ˈhʌŋgər] *vi* **1** : tener hambre **2 to hunger for** : ansiar, anhelar

hunger[2] *n* : hambre *m*

hungrily [ˈhʌŋgrəli] *adv* : ávidamente

hungry [ˈhʌŋgri] *adj* **-grier; -est 1** : hambriento **2 to be hungry** : tener hambre

hunk [ˈhʌŋk] *n* : trozo *m,* pedazo *m*

hunt[1] [ˈhʌnt] *vt* **1** PURSUE : cazar **2 to hunt for** : buscar

hunt[2] *n* **1** PURSUIT : caza *f,* cacería *f* **2** SEARCH : búsqueda *f,* busca *f*

hunter [ˈhʌntər] *n* : cazador *m,* -dora *f*

hunting [ˈhʌntɪŋ] *n* : caza *f* <to go hunting : ir de caza>

hurdle[1] [ˈhərdəl] *vt* **-dled; -dling** : saltar, salvar (un obstáculo)

hurdle[2] *n* : valla *f* (en deportes), obstáculo *m*

hurl [ˈhərl] *vt* : arrojar, tirar, lanzar

hurrah [hʊˈrɑ, -ˈrɔ] *interj* : ¡hurra!

hurricane [ˈhərəˌkeɪn] *n* : huracán *m*

hurried [ˈhərid] *adj* : apresurado, precipitado
hurriedly [ˈhərədli] *adv* : apresuradamente, de prisa
hurry[1] [ˈhəri] *v* **-ried; -rying** *vi* : apurarse, darse prisa, apresurarse — *vt* : apurar, darle prisa (a alguien)
hurry[2] *n* : prisa *f,* apuro *f*
hurt[1] [ˈhərt] *v* **hurt; hurting** *vt* **1** INJURE : hacer daño a, herir, lastimar <to hurt oneself : hacerse daño> **2** DISTRESS, OFFEND : hacer sufrir, ofender, herir — *vi* : doler <my foot hurts : me duele el pie>
hurt[2] *n* **1** INJURY : herida *f* **2** DISTRESS, PAIN : dolor *m,* pena *f*
hurtful [ˈhərtfəl] *adj* : hiriente, doloroso
hurtle [ˈhərtəl] *vi* **-tled; -tling** : lanzarse, precipitarse
husband[1] [ˈhʌzbənd] *vt* : economizar, bien administrar
husband[2] *n* : esposo *m,* marido *m*
husbandry [ˈhʌzbəndri] *n* **1** MANAGEMENT, THRIFT : economía *f,* buena administración *f* **2** AGRICULTURE : agricultura *f* <animal husbandry : cría de animales>
hush[1] [ˈhʌʃ] *vt* **1** SILENCE : hacer callar, acallar **2** CALM : calmar, apaciguar
hush[2] *n* : silencio *m*
hush–hush [ˈhʌʃˌhʌʃ, ˌhʌʃˈhʌʃ] *adj* : muy secreto, confidencial
husk[1] [ˈhʌsk] *vt* : descascarar
husk[2] *n* : cáscara *f*
huskily [ˈhʌskəli] *adv* : con voz ronca
husky[1] [ˈhʌski] *adj* **-kier; -est 1** HOARSE : ronco **2** BURLY : fornido
husky[2] *n, pl* **-kies** : perro *m,* -rra *f* esquimal
hustle[1] [ˈhəsəl] *v* **-tled; -tling** *vt* : darle prisa (a alguien), apurar <they hustled me in : me hicieron entrar a empujones> — *vi* : apurarse, ajetrearse
hustle[2] *n* BUSTLE : ajetreo *m*
hut [ˈhʌt] *n* : cabaña *f,* choza *f,* barraca *f*
hutch [ˈhʌtʃ] *n* **1** CUPBOARD : alacena *f* **2 rabbit hutch** : conejera *f*
hyacinth [ˈhaɪəˌsɪnθ] *n* : jacinto *m*
hybrid[1] [ˈhaɪbrɪd] *adj* : híbrido
hybrid[2] *n* : híbrido *m*
hydrant [ˈhaɪdrənt] *n* : boca *f* de riego, hidrante *m CA, Col* <fire hydrant : boca de incendios>
hydraulic [haɪˈdrɔlɪk] *adj* : hidráulico — **hydraulically** *adv*
hydrocarbon [ˌhaɪdroˈkɑrbən] *n* : hidrocarburo *m*
hydrochloric acid [ˌhaɪdroˈklorɪk] *n* : ácido *m* clorohídrico
hydroelectric [ˌhaɪdroɪˈlɛktrɪk] *adj* : hidroeléctrico
hydrogen [ˈhaɪdrədʒən] *n* : hidrógeno *m*
hydrogen bomb *n* : bomba *f* de hidrógeno
hydrogen peroxide *n* : agua *f* oxigenada, peróxido *m* de hidrógeno
hydrophobia [ˌhaɪdrəˈfoːbiə] *n* : hidrofobia *f,* rabia *f*
hydroplane [ˈhaɪdrəˌpleɪn] *n* : hidroplano *m*
hyena [haɪˈiːnə] *n* : hiena *f*
hygiene [ˈhaɪˌdʒiːn] *n* : higiene *f*
hygienic [haɪˈdʒɛnɪk, -ˈdʒiː-; ˌhaɪdʒiˈɛnɪk] *adj* : higiénico — **hygienically** [-nɪkli] *adv*
hygienist [haɪˈdʒiːnɪst, -ˈdʒɛ-; ˈhaɪˌdʒiː-] *n* : higienista *mf*
hygrometer [haɪˈgrɑmətər] *n* : higrómetro *m*
hymn [ˈhɪm] *n* : himno *m*
hymnal [ˈhɪmnəl] *n* : himnario *m*
hype [ˈhaɪp] *n* : bombo *m* publicitario
hyperactive [ˌhaɪpərˈæktɪv] *adj* : hiperactivo
hyperbole [haɪˈpərbəli] *n* : hipérbole *f*
hypercritical [ˌhaɪpərˈkrɪtəkəl] *adj* : hipercrítico
hypersensitivity [ˌhaɪpərˌsɛntsəˈtɪvəti] *n* : hipersensibilidad *f*
hypertension [ˈhaɪpərˌtɛntʃən] *n* : hipertensión *f*
hyphen [ˈhaɪfən] *n* : guión *m*
hyphenate [ˈhaɪfənˌeɪt] *vt* **-ated; -ating** : escribir con guión
hypnosis [hɪpˈnoːsɪs] *n, pl* **-noses** [-ˌsiːz] : hipnosis *f*
hypnotic [hɪpˈnɑtɪk] *adj* : hipnótico, hipnotizador
hypnotism [ˈhɪpnəˌtɪzəm] *n* : hipnotismo *m*
hypnotize [ˈhɪpnəˌtaɪz] *vt* **-tized; -tizing** : hipnotizar
hypochondria [ˌhaɪpəˈkɑndriə] *n* : hipocondría *f*
hypochondriac [ˌhaɪpəˈkɑndriˌæk] *n* : hipocondríaco *m,* -ca *f*
hypocrisy [hɪpˈɑkrəsi] *n, pl* **-sies** : hipocresía *f*
hypocrite [ˈhɪpəˌkrɪt] *n* : hipócrita *mf*
hypocritical [ˌhɪpəˈkrɪtɪkəl] *adj* : hipócrita
hypodermic[1] [ˌhaɪpəˈdərmɪk] *adj* : hipodérmico
hypodermic[2] *n* : aguja *f* hipodérmica
hypotenuse [haɪˈpɑtənˌuːs, -ˌuːz, -ˌjuːs, -ˌjuːz] *n* : hipotenusa *f*
hypothesis [haɪˈpɑθəsɪs] *n, pl* **-eses** [-ˌsiːz] : hipótesis *f*
hypothetical [ˌhaɪpəˈθɛtɪkəl] *adj* : hipotético — **hypothetically** [-tɪkli] *adv*
hysteria [hɪsˈtɛriə, -tɪr-] *n* : histeria *f,* histerismo *m*
hysterical [hɪsˈtɛrɪkəl] *adj* : histérico — **hysterically** [-ɪkli] *adv*
hysterics [hɪsˈtɛrɪks] *n* : histeria *f,* histerismo *m*

I

i ['aɪ] *n, pl* **i's** *or* **is** ['aɪz] : novena letra del alfabeto inglés
I ['aɪ] *pron* : yo
ibis ['aɪbəs] *n, pl* **ibis** *or* **ibises** : ibis *f*
ice[1] ['aɪs] *v* **iced; icing** *vt* **1** FREEZE : congelar, helar **2** CHILL : enfriar **3 to ice a cake** : escarchar un pastel — *vi* : helarse, congelarse
ice[2] *n* **1** : hielo *m* **2** SHERBET : sorbete *m,* nieve *f Cuba, Mex, PRi*
iceberg ['aɪs,bərg] *n* : iceberg *m*
icebox ['aɪs,bɑks] → **refrigerator**
icebreaker ['aɪs,breɪkər] *n* : rompehielos *m*
ice cap *n* : casquete *m* glaciar
ice–cold ['aɪs'ko:ld] *adj* : helado
ice cream *n* : helado *m,* mantecado *m PRi*
Icelander ['aɪs,lændər, -lən-] *n* : islandés *m,* -desa *f*
Icelandic[1] [aɪs'lændɪk] *adj* : islandés
Icelandic[2] *n* : islandés *m* (idioma)
ice–skate ['aɪs,skeɪt] *vi* **-skated; -skating** : patinar
ice skater *n* : patinador *m,* -dora *f*
ichthyology [,ɪkθi'ɑlədʒi] *n* : ictiología *f*
icicle ['aɪ,sɪkəl] *n* : carámbano *m*
icily ['aɪsəli] *adv* : fríamente, con frialdad <he stared at me icily : me fijó la mirada con mucha frialdad>
icing ['aɪsɪŋ] *n* : glaseado *m,* betún *m Mex*
icon ['aɪ,kɑn, -kən] *n* : icono *m*
iconoclasm [aɪ'kɑnə,klæzəm] *n* : iconoclasia *f*
iconoclast [aɪ'kɑnə,klæst] *n* : iconoclasta *mf*
icy ['aɪsi] *adj* **icier; -est 1** : cubierto de hielo <an icy road : una carretera cubierta de hielo> **2** FREEZING : helado, gélido, glacial **3** ALOOF : frío, distante
id ['ɪd] *n* : id *m*
I'd ['aɪd] (*contraction of* **I should** *or* **I would**) → **should, would**
idea [aɪ'di:ə] *n* : idea *f*
ideal[1] [aɪ'di:əl] *adj* : ideal
ideal[2] *n* : ideal *m*
idealism [aɪ'di:ə,lɪzəm] *n* : idealismo *m*
idealist [aɪ'di:əlɪst] *n* : idealista *mf*
idealistic [aɪ,di:ə'lɪstɪk] *adj* : idealista
idealistically [aɪ,di:ə'lɪstɪkli] *adv* : con idealismo
idealization [aɪ,di:ələ'zeɪʃən] *n* : idealización *f*
idealize [aɪ'di:ə,laɪz] *vt* **-ized; -izing** : idealizar
ideally [aɪ'di:əli] *adv* : perfectamente
identical [aɪ'dɛntɪkəl] *adj* : idéntico — **identically** [-tɪkli] *adv*
identifiable [aɪ,dɛntə'faɪəbəl] *adj* : identificable
identification [aɪ,dɛntəfə'keɪʃən] *n* **1** : identificación *f* **2 identification card** : carnet *m,* cédula *f* de identidad, identificación *f*
identify [aɪ'dɛntə,faɪ] *v* **-fied; -fying** *vt* : identificar — *vi* **to identify with** : identificarse con
identity [aɪ'dɛntəṭi] *n, pl* **-ties** : identidad *f*
ideological [,aɪdiə'lɑdʒɪkəl, ,ɪ-] *adj* : ideológico — **ideologically** [-dʒɪkli] *adv*
ideology [,aɪdi'ɑlədʒi, ,ɪ-] *n, pl* **-gies** : ideología *f*
idiocy ['ɪdiəsi] *n, pl* **-cies 1** : idiotez *f* **2** NONSENSE : estupidez *f,* tontería *f*
idiom ['ɪdiəm] *n* **1** LANGUAGE : lenguaje *m* **2** EXPRESSION : modismo *m,* expresión *f* idiomática
idiomatic [,ɪdiə'mæṭɪk] *adj* : idiomático
idiosyncrasy [,ɪdio'sɪŋkrəsi] *n, pl* **-sies** : idiosincrasia *f*
idiosyncratic [,ɪdiosɪn'kræṭɪk] *adj* : idiosincrásico — **idiosyncratically** [-ṭɪkli] *adv*
idiot ['ɪdiət] *n* **1** : idiota *mf* (en medicina) **2** FOOL : idiota *mf;* tonto *m,* -ta *f;* imbécil *mf fam*
idiotic [,ɪdi'ɑtɪk] *adj* : estúpido, idiota
idiotically [,ɪdi'ɑṭɪkli] *adv* : estúpidamente
idle[1] ['aɪdəl] *v* **idled; idling** *vi* **1** LOAF : holgazanear, flojear, haraganear **2** : andar al ralentí (dícese de un automóvil), marchar en vacío (dícese de una máquina) — *vt* : dejar sin trabajo
idle[2] *adj* **idler; idlest 1** VAIN : frívolo, vano, infundado <idle curiosity : pura curiosidad> **2** INACTIVE : inactivo, parado, desocupado **3** LAZY : holgazán, haragán, perezoso
idleness ['aɪdəlnəs] *n* **1** INACTIVITY : inactividad *f,* ociosidad *f* **2** LAZINESS : holgazanería *f,* flojera *f,* pereza *f*
idler ['aɪdələr] *n* : haragán *m,* -gana *f;* holgazán *m,* -zana *f*
idly ['aɪdəli] *adv* : ociosamente
idol ['aɪdəl] *n* : ídolo *m*
idolater *or* **idolator** [aɪ'dɑləṭər] *n* : idólatra *mf*
idolatrous [aɪ'dɑlətrəs] *adj* : idólatra
idolatry [aɪ'dɑlətri] *n, pl* **-tries** : idolatría *f*
idolize ['aɪdəlaɪz] *vt* **-ized; -izing** : idolatrar
idyll ['aɪdəl] *n* : idilio *m*
idyllic [aɪ'dɪlɪk] *adj* : idílico
if ['ɪf] *conj* **1** : si <I would do it if I could : lo haría si pudiera> <if so : si es así> <as if : como si> <if I were you : yo que tú> **2** WHETHER : si <I don't know if they're ready : no sé si están listos> **3** THOUGH : aunque, si bien <it's pretty, if somewhat old-fashioned : es lindo aunque algo anticuado>
igloo ['ɪ,glu:] *n, pl* **-loos** : iglú *m*

ignite [ɪg'naɪt] *v* **-nited; -niting** *vt* : prenderle fuego a, encender — *vi* : prender, encenderse

ignition [ɪg'nɪʃən] *n* **1** IGNITING : ignición *f*, encendido *m* **2** *or* **ignition switch** : encendido *m*, arranque *m* <to turn on the ignition : arrancar el motor>

ignoble [ɪg'noːbəl] *adj* : innoble — **ignobly** *adv*

ignominious [ˌɪgnə'mɪniəs] *adj* : ignominioso, deshonroso — **ignominiously** *adv*

ignominy ['ɪgnəˌmɪni] *n, pl* **-nies** : ignominia *f*

ignoramus [ˌɪgnə'reɪməs] *n* : ignorante *mf;* bestia *mf;* bruto *m*, -ta *f*

ignorance ['ɪgnərənts] *n* : ignorancia *f*

ignorant ['ɪgnərənt] *adj* **1** : ignorante **2 to be ignorant of** : no ser consciente de, desconocer, ignorar

ignorantly ['ɪgnərəntli] *adv* : ignorantemente, con ignorancia

ignore [ɪg'nor] *vt* **-nored; -noring** : ignorar, hacer caso omiso de, no hacer caso de

iguana [ɪ'gwɑnə] *n* : iguana *f*, garrobo *f CA*

ilk ['ɪlk] *n* : tipo *m*, clase *f*, índole *f*

ill[1] ['ɪl] *adv* **worse** ['wərs]; **worst** ['wərst] : mal <to speak ill of : hablar mal de> <he can ill afford to fail : mal puede permitirse el lujo de fracasar>

ill[2] *adj* **worse; worst 1** SICK : enfermo **2** BAD : malo <ill luck : mala suerte>

ill[3] *n* **1** EVIL : mal *m* **2** MISFORTUNE : mal *m*, desgracia *f* **3** AILMENT : enfermedad *f*

I'll ['aɪl] (*contraction of* **I shall** *or* **I will**) → **shall, will**

illegal [ɪl'liːgəl] *adj* : ilegal — **illegally** *adv*

illegality [ɪli'gæləti] *n* : ilegalidad *f*

illegibility [ɪlˌlɛdʒə'bɪləti] *n, pl* **-ties** : ilegibilidad *f*

illegible [ɪl'lɛdʒəbəl] *adj* : ilegible — **illegibly** [-bli] *adv*

illegitimacy [ˌɪlɪ'dʒɪtəməsi] *n* : ilegitimidad *f*

illegitimate [ˌɪlɪ'dʒɪtəmət] *adj* **1** BASTARD : ilegítimo, bastardo **2** UNLAWFUL : ilegítimo, ilegal — **illegitimately** *adv*

ill–fated ['ɪl'feɪtəd] *adj* : malhadado, infortunado, desventurado

illicit [ɪl'lɪsət] *adj* : ilícito — **illicitly** *adv*

illiteracy [ɪl'lɪtərəsi] *n, pl* **-cies** : analfabetismo *m*

illiterate[1] [ɪl'lɪtərət] *adj* : analfabeto

illiterate[2] *n* : analfabeto *m*, -ta *f*

ill–mannered [ˌɪl'manərd] *adj* : descortés, maleducado

ill–natured [ˌɪl'neɪtʃərd] *adj* : desagradable, de mal genio

ill–naturedly [ˌɪl'neɪtʃərdli] *adv* : desagradablemente

illness ['ɪlnəs] *n* : enfermedad *f*

illogical [ɪl'lɑdʒɪkəl] *adj* : ilógico — **illogically** [-kli] *adv*

ill–tempered [ˌɪl'tempərd] → **ill–natured**

ill–treat [ˌɪl'triːt] *vt* : maltratar

ill–treatment [ˌɪl'triːtmənt] *n* : maltrato *m*

illuminate [ɪ'luːməˌneɪt] *vt* **-nated; -nating 1** : iluminar, alumbrar **2** ELUCIDATE : esclarecer, elucidar

illumination [ɪˌluːmə'neɪʃən] *n* **1** LIGHTING : iluminación *f*, luz *f* **2** ELUCIDATION : esclarecimiento *m*, elucidación *f*

ill–use ['ɪl'juːz] → **ill–treat**

illusion [ɪ'luːʒən] *n* : ilusión *f*

illusory [ɪ'luːsəri, -zəri] *adj* : engañoso, ilusorio

illustrate ['ɪləsˌtreɪt] *v* **-trated; -trating** : ilustrar

illustration [ˌɪlə'streɪʃən] *n* **1** PICTURE : ilustración *f* **2** EXAMPLE : ejemplo *m*, ilustración *f*

illustrative [ɪ'lʌstrətɪv, 'ɪləˌstreɪtɪv] *adj* : ilustrativo — **illustratively** *adv*

illustrator ['ɪləˌstreɪtər] *n* : ilustrador *m*, -dora *f;* dibujante *mf*

illustrious [ɪ'lʌstriəs] *adj* : ilustre, eminente, glorioso

illustriousness [ɪ'lʌstriəsnəs] *n* : eminencia *f*, prestigio *m*

ill will *n* : animosidad *f*, malquerencia *f*, mala voluntad *f*

I'm ['aɪm] (*contraction of* **I am**) → **be**

image[1] ['ɪmɪdʒ] *vt* **-aged; -aging** : imaginar, crear una imagen de

image[2] *n* : imagen *f*

imagery ['ɪmɪdʒri] *n, pl* **-eries 1** IMAGES : imágenes *fpl* **2** : imaginería *f* (en el arte)

imaginable [ɪ'mædʒənəbəl] *adj* : imaginable — **imaginably** [-bli] *adv*

imaginary [ɪ'mædʒəˌnɛri] *adj* : imaginario

imagination [ɪˌmædʒə'neɪʃən] *n* : imaginación *f*

imaginative [ɪ'mædʒənətɪv, -əˌneɪtɪv] *adj* : imaginativo — **imaginatively** *adv*

imagine [ɪ'mædʒən] *vt* **-ined; -ining** : imaginar(se)

imbalance [ɪm'bælənts] *n* : desajuste *m*, desbalance *m*, desequilibrio *m*

imbecile[1] ['ɪmbəsəl, -ˌsɪl] *or* **imbecilic** [ˌɪmbə'sɪlɪk] *adj* : imbécil, estúpido

imbecile[2] *n* **1** : imbécil *mf* (en medicina) **2** FOOL : idiota *mf;* imbécil *mf fam;* estúpido *m*, -da *f*

imbecility [ˌɪmbə'sɪləti] *n, pl* **-ties** : imbecilidad *f*

imbibe [ɪm'baɪb] *v* **-bibed; -bibing** *vt* **1** DRINK : beber **2** ABSORB : absorber, embeber — *vi* : beber

imbue [ɪm'bjuː] *vt* **-bued; -buing** : imbuir

imitate ['ɪməˌteɪt] *vt* **-tated; -tating** : imitar, remedar

imitation[1] [ˌɪməˈteɪʃən] *adj* **:** de imitación, artificial
imitation[2] *n* **:** imitación *f*
imitative [ˈɪməˌteɪt̬ɪv] *adj* **:** imitativo, imitador, poco original
imitator [ˈɪməˌteɪt̬ər] *n* **:** imitador *m*, -dora *f*
immaculate [ɪˈmækjələt] *adj* **1** PURE **:** inmaculado, puro **2** FLAWLESS **:** impecable, intachable — **immaculately** *adv*
immaterial [ˌɪməˈtɪriəl] *adj* **1** INCORPOREAL **:** incorpóreo **2** UNIMPORTANT **:** irrelevante, sin importancia
immature [ˌɪməˈtʃʊr, -ˈtjʊr, -ˈtʊr] *adj* **:** inmaduro, verde (dícese de la fruta)
immaturity [ˌɪməˈtʃʊrət̬i, -ˈtjʊr-, -ˈtʊr-] *n, pl* **-ties :** inmadurez *f*, falta *f* de madurez
immeasurable [ɪˈmɛʒərəbəl] *adj* **:** inconmensurable, incalculable — **immeasurably** [-bli] *adv*
immediate [ɪˈmiːdiət] *adj* **1** INSTANT **:** inmediato, instantáneo <immediate relief : alivio instantáneo> **2** DIRECT **:** inmediato, directo <the immediate cause of death : la causa directa de la muerte> **3** URGENT **:** urgente, apremiante **4** CLOSE **:** cercano, próximo, inmediato <her immediate family : sus familiares más cercanos> <in the immediate vicinity : en los alrededores, en las inmediaciones>
immediately [ɪˈmiːdiətli] *adv* **:** inmediatamente, enseguida
immemorial [ˌɪməˈmoriəl] *adj* **:** inmemorial
immense [ɪˈmɛnts] *adj* **:** inmenso, enorme — **immensely** *adv*
immensity [ɪˈmɛntsət̬i] *n, pl* **-ties :** inmensidad *f*
immerse [ɪˈmərs] *vt* **-mersed; -mersing 1** SUBMERGE **:** sumergir **2 to immerse oneself in :** enfrascarse en
immersion [ɪˈmərʒən] *n* **1 :** inmersión *f* (en un líquido) **2 :** enfrascamiento *m* (en una actividad)
immigrant [ˈɪmɪgrənt] *n* **:** inmigrante *mf*
immigrate [ˈɪməˌgreɪt] *vi* **-grated; -grating :** inmigrar
immigration [ˌɪməˈgreɪʃən] *n* **:** inmigración *f*
imminence [ˈɪmənənts] *n* **:** inminencia *f*
imminent [ˈɪmənənt] *adj* **:** inminente — **imminently** *adv*
immobile [ɪmˈoːbəl] *adj* **1** FIXED, IMMOVABLE **:** inmovible, fijo **2** MOTIONLESS **:** inmóvil
immobility [ˌɪmoˈbɪlət̬i] *n, pl* **-ties :** inmovilidad *f*
immobilize [ɪˈmoːbəˌlaɪz] *vt* **-lized; -lizing :** inmovilizar, paralizar
immoderate [ɪˈmɑdərət] *adj* **:** inmoderado, desmesurado, desmedido, excesivo — **immoderately** *adv*
immodest [ɪˈmɑdəst] *adj* **1** INDECENT **:** inmodesto, indecente, impúdico **2** CONCEITED **:** inmodesto, presuntuoso, engreído — **immodestly** *adv*
immodesty [ɪˈmɑdəsti] *n* **:** inmodestia *f*
immoral [ɪˈmɔrəl] *adj* **:** inmoral
immorality [ˌɪmɔˈrælət̬i, ˌɪmə-] *n, pl* **-ties :** inmoralidad *f*
immorally [ɪˈmɔrəli] *adv* **:** de manera inmoral
immortal[1] [ɪˈmɔrtəl] *adj* **:** inmortal
immortal[2] *n* **:** inmortal *mf*
immortality [ˌɪˌmɔrˈtælət̬i] *n* **:** inmortalidad *f*
immortalize [ɪˈmɔrtəlˌaɪz] *vt* **-ized; -izing :** inmortalizar
immovable [ɪˈmuːvəbəl] *adj* **1** FIXED **:** fijo, inmovible **2** UNYIELDING **:** inflexible
immune [ɪˈmjuːn] *adj* **1 :** inmune <immune to smallpox : inmune a la viruela> **2** EXEMPT **:** exento, inmune
immune system *n* **:** sistema *m* inmunológico
immunity [ɪˈmjuːnət̬i] *n, pl* **-ties 1 :** inmunidad *f* **2** EXEMPTION **:** exención *f*
immunization [ˌɪmjʊnəˈzeɪʃən] *n* **:** inmunización *f*
immunize [ˈɪmjʊˌnaɪz] *vt* **-nized; -nizing :** inmunizar
immunology [ˌɪmjʊˈnɑləʤi] *n* **:** inmunología *f*
immutable [ɪˈmjuːt̬əbəl] *adj* **:** inmutable
imp [ˈɪmp] *n* RASCAL **:** diablillo *m;* pillo *m*, -lla *f*
impact[1] [ɪmˈpækt] *vt* **1** STRIKE **:** chocar con, impactar **2** AFFECT **:** afectar, impactar, impresionar — *vi* **1** STRIKE **:** hacer impacto, golpear **2 to impact on :** tener un impacto sobre
impact[2] [ˈɪmˌpækt] *n* **1** COLLISION **:** impacto *m*, choque *m*, colisión *f* **2** EFFECT **:** efecto *m*, impacto *m*, consecuencias *fpl*
impacted [ɪmˈpæktəd] *adj* **:** impactado, incrustado (dícese de los dientes)
impair [ɪmˈpær] *vt* **:** perjudicar, dañar, afectar
impairment [ɪmˈpærmənt] *n* **:** perjuicio *m*, daño *m*
impala [ɪmˈpɑlə, -ˈpæ-] *n, pl* **impalas** *or* **impala :** impala *m*
impale [ɪmˈpeɪl] *vt* **-paled; -paling :** empalar
impanel [ɪmˈpænəl] *vt* **-eled** *or* **-elled; -eling** *or* **-elling :** elegir (un jurado)
impart [ɪmˈpɑrt] *vt* **1** CONVEY **:** impartir, dar, conferir **2** DISCLOSE **:** revelar, divulgar
impartial [ɪmˈpɑrʃəl] *adj* **:** imparcial — **impartially** *adv*
impartiality [ɪmˌpɑrʃiˈælət̬i] *n, pl* **-ties :** imparcialidad *f*
impassable [ɪmˈpæsəbəl] *adj* **:** infranqueable, intransitable — **impassably** [-bli] *adv*

impasse [ˈɪm,pæs] *n* **1** DEADLOCK **:** impasse *m,* punto *m* muerto **2** DEAD END **:** callejón *m* sin salida
impassioned [ɪmˈpæʃənd] *adj* **:** apasionado, vehemente
impassive [ɪmˈpæsɪv] *adj* **:** impasible, indiferente
impassively [ɪmˈpæsɪvli] *adv* **:** impasiblemente, sin emoción
impatience [ɪmˈpeɪʃənts] *n* **:** impaciencia *f*
impatient [ɪmˈpeɪʃənt] *adj* **:** impaciente — **impatiently** *adv*
impeach [ɪmˈpiːtʃ] *vt* **:** destituir (a un funcionario) de su cargo
impeachment [ɪmˈpiːtʃmənt] *n* **1** ACCUSATION **:** acusación *f* **2** DISMISSAL **:** destitución *f*
impeccable [ɪmˈpɛkəbəl] *adj* **:** impecable — **impeccably** [-bli] *adv*
impecunious [,ɪmpɪˈkjuːniəs] *adj* **:** falto de dinero
impede [ɪmˈpiːd] *vt* **-peded; -peding :** impedir, dificultar, obstaculizar
impediment [ɪmˈpɛdəmənt] *n* **1** HINDRANCE **:** impedimento *m,* obstáculo *m* **2 speech impediment :** defecto *m* del habla
impel [ɪmˈpɛl] *vt* **-pelled; -pelling :** impeler
impend [ɪmˈpɛnd] *vi* **:** ser inminente
impenetrable [ɪmˈpɛnətrəbəl] *adj* **1 :** impenetrable <an impenetrable forest : una selva impenetrable> **2** INSCRUTABLE **:** incomprensible, inescrutable, impenetrable — **impenetrably** [-bli] *adv*
impenitent [ɪmˈpɛnətənt] *adj* **:** impenitente
imperative[1] [ɪmˈpɛrətɪv] *adj* **1** AUTHORITATIVE **:** imperativo, imperioso **2** NECESSARY **:** imprescindible — **imperatively** *adv*
imperative[2] *n* **:** imperativo *m*
imperceptible [,ɪmpərˈsɛptəbəl] *adj* **:** imperceptible — **imperceptibly** [-bli] *adv*
imperfect [ɪmˈpərfɪkt] *adj* **:** imperfecto, defectuoso — **imperfectly** *adv*
imperfection [ɪm,pərˈfɛkʃən] *n* **:** imperfección *f,* defecto *m*
imperial [ɪmˈpɪriəl] *adj* **1 :** imperial **2** SOVEREIGN **:** soberano **3** IMPERIOUS **:** imperioso, señorial
imperialism [ɪmˈpɪriə,lɪzəm] *n* **:** imperialismo *m*
imperialist[1] [ɪmˈpɪriəlɪst] *adj* **:** imperialista
imperialist[2] *n* **:** imperialista *mf*
imperialistic [ɪm,pɪriːəˈlɪstɪk] *adj* **:** imperialista
imperil [ɪmˈpɛrəl] *vt* **-iled** *or* **-illed; -iling** *or* **-illing :** poner en peligro
imperious [ɪmˈpɪriəs] *adj* **:** imperioso — **imperiously** *adv*
imperishable [ɪmˈpɛrɪʃəbəl] *adj* **:** imperecedero
impermanent [ɪmˈpərmənənt] *adj* **:** pasajero, inestable, efímero — **impermanently** *adv*
impermeable [ɪmˈpərmiəbəl] *adj* **:** impermeable
impersonal [ɪmˈpərsənəl] *adj* **:** impersonal — **impersonally** *adv*
impersonate [ɪmˈpərsən,eɪt] *vt* **-ated; -ating :** hacerse pasar por, imitar
impersonation [ɪm,pərsənˈeɪʃən] *n* **:** imitación *f*
impersonator [ɪmˈpərsən,eɪt̬ər] *n* **:** imitador *m,* -dora *f*
impertinence [ɪmˈpərtənənts] *n* **:** impertinencia *f*
impertinent [ɪmˈpərtənənt] *adj* **1** IRRELEVANT **:** impertinente, irrelevante **2** INSOLENT **:** impertinente, insolente
impertinently [ɪmˈpərtənəntli] *adv* **:** con impertinencia, impertinentemente
imperturbable [,ɪmpərˈtərbəbəl] *adj* **:** imperturbable
impervious [ɪmˈpərviəs] *adj* **1** IMPENETRABLE **:** impermeable **2** INSENSITIVE **:** insensible <impervious to criticism : insensible a la crítica>
impetuosity [ɪm,pɛtʃʊˈɑsət̬i] *n, pl* **-ties :** impetuosidad *f*
impetuous [ɪmˈpɛtʃʊəs] *adj* **:** impetuoso, impulsivo
impetuously [ɪmˈpɛtʃʊəsli] *adv* **:** de manera impulsiva, impetuosamente
impetus [ˈɪmpət̬əs] *n* **:** ímpetu *m,* impulso *m*
impiety [ɪmˈpaɪət̬i] *n, pl* **-ties :** impiedad *f*
impinge [ɪmˈpɪndʒ] *vi* **-pinged; -pinging 1 to impinge on** AFFECT **:** afectar a, incidir en **2 to impinge on** VIOLATE **:** violar, vulnerar
impious [ˈɪmpiəs, ɪmˈpaɪəs] *adj* **:** impío, irreverente
impish [ˈɪmpɪʃ] *adj* MISCHIEVOUS **:** pícaro, travieso
impishly [ˈɪmpɪʃli] *adv* **:** con picardía
implacable [ɪmˈplækəbəl] *adj* **:** implacable — **implacably** [-bli] *adv*
implant[1] [ɪmˈplænt] *vt* **1** INCULCATE, INSTILL **:** inculcar, implantar **2** INSERT **:** implantar, insertar
implant[2] [ˈɪm,plænt] *n* **:** implante *m* (de pelo), injerto *m* (de piel)
implantation [,ɪm,plænˈteɪʃən] *n* **:** implantación *f*
implausibility [ɪm,plɔzəˈbɪlət̬i] *n, pl* **-ties :** inverosimilitud *f*
implausible [ɪmˈplɔzəbəl] *adj* **:** inverosímil, poco convincente
implement[1] [ˈɪmplə,mɛnt] *vt* **:** poner en práctica, implementar
implement[2] [ˈɪmpləmənt] *n* **:** utensilio *m,* instrumento *m,* implemento *m*
implementation [,ɪmpləmənˈteɪʃən] *n* **:** implementación *f,* ejecución *f,* cumplimiento *m*
implicate [ˈɪmplə,keɪt] *vt* **-cated; -cating :** implicar, involucrar

implication [ˌɪmpləˈkeɪʃən] *n* **1** CONSEQUENCE : implicación *f,* consecuencia *f* **2** INFERENCE : insinuación *f,* inferencia *f*
implicit [ɪmˈplɪsət] *adj* **1** IMPLIED : implícito, tácito **2** ABSOLUTE : absoluto, completo <implicit faith : fe ciega> — **implicitly** *adv*
implied [ɪmˈplaɪd] *adj* : implícito, tácito
implode [ɪmˈploːd] *vi* **-ploded; -ploding** : implosionar
implore [ɪmˈplor] *vt* **-plored; -ploring** : implorar, suplicar
imply [ɪmˈplaɪ] *vt* **-plied; -plying 1** SUGGEST : insinuar, dar a entender **2** INVOLVE : implicar, suponer <rights imply obligations : los derechos implican unas obligaciones>
impolite [ˌɪmpəˈlaɪt] *adj* : descortés, maleducado
impoliteness [ˌɪmpəˈlaɪtnəs] *n* : descortesía *f,* falta *f* de educación
impolitic [ɪmˈpɑləˌtɪk] *adj* : imprudente, poco político
imponderable¹ [ɪmˈpɑndərəbəl] *adj* : imponderable
imponderable² *n* : imponderable *m*
import¹ [ɪmˈport] *vt* **1** SIGNIFY : significar **2** : importar <to import foreign cars : importar autos extranjeros>
import² [ˈɪmˌport] *n* **1** SIGNIFICANCE : importancia *f,* significación *f* **2** → **importation**
importance [ɪmˈportənts] *n* : importancia *f*
important [ɪmˈpɔrtənt] *adj* : importante
importantly [ɪmˈpɔrtəntli] *adv* **1** : con importancia **2 more importantly** : lo que es más importante
importation [ˌɪmˌpɔrˈteɪʃən] *n* : importación *f*
importer [ɪmˈporṭər] *n* : importador *m,* -dora *f*
importunate [ɪmˈpɔrtʃənət] *adj* : importuno, insistente
importune [ˌɪmpərˈtuːn, -ˈtjuːn; ɪmˈpɔrtʃən] *vt* **-tuned; -tuning** : importunar, implorar
impose [ɪmˈpoːz] *v* **-posed; -posing** *vt* : imponer <to impose a tax : imponer un impuesto> — *vi* **to impose on** : abusar de, molestar <to impose on her kindness : abusar de su bondad>
imposing [ɪmˈpoːzɪŋ] *adj* : imponente, impresionante
imposition [ˌɪmpəˈzɪʃən] *n* : imposición *f*
impossibility [ɪmˌpɑsəˈbɪləṭi] *n, pl* **-ties** : imposibilidad *f*
impossible [ɪmˈpɑsəbəl] *adj* **1** : imposible <an impossible task : una tarea imposible> <to make life impossible for : hacerle la vida imposible a> **2** UNACCEPTABLE : inaceptable
impossibly [ɪmˈpɑsəbli] *adv* : imposiblemente, increíblemente
impostor *or* **imposter** [ɪmˈpɑstər] *n* : impostor *m,* -tora *f*
imposture [ɪmˈpɑstʃər] *n* : impostura *f*
impotence [ˈɪmpətənts] *n* : impotencia *f*
impotency [ˈɪmpətəntsi] → **impotence**
impotent [ˈɪmpətənt] *adj* : impotente
impound [ɪmˈpaʊnd] *vt* : incautar, embargar, confiscar
impoverish [ɪmˈpɑvərɪʃ] *vt* : empobrecer
impoverishment [ɪmˈpɑvərɪʃmənt] *n* : empobrecimiento *m*
impracticable [ɪmˈpræktɪkəbəl] *adj* : impracticable
impractical [ɪmˈpræktɪkəl] *adj* : poco práctico
imprecise [ˌɪmprɪˈsaɪs] *adj* : impreciso
imprecisely [ˌɪmprɪˈsaɪsli] *adv* : con imprecisión
impreciseness [ˌɪmprɪˈsaɪsnəs] → **imprecision**
imprecision [ˌɪmprɪˈsɪʒən] *n* : imprecisión *f,* falta de precisión *f*
impregnable [ɪmˈprɛgnəbəl] *adj* : inexpugnable, impenetrable, inconquistable
impregnate [ɪmˈprɛgˌneɪt] *vt* **-nated; -nating 1** FERTILIZE : fecundar **2** PERMEATE, SATURATE : impregnar, empapar, saturar
impresario [ˌɪmprəˈsɑriˌo, -ˈsær-] *n, pl* **-rios** : empresario *m,* -ria *f*
impress [ɪmˈprɛs] *vt* **1** IMPRINT : imprimir, estampar **2** : impresionar, causar impresión a <I was not impressed : no me hizo buena impresión> **3 to impress (something) on someone** : recalcarle (algo) a alguien — *vi* : impresionar, hacer una impresión
impression [ɪmˈprɛʃən] *n* **1** IMPRINT : marca *f,* huella *f,* molde *m* (de los dientes) **2** EFFECT : impresión *f,* efecto *m,* impacto *m* **3** PRINTING : impresión *f* **4** NOTION : impresión *f,* noción *f*
impressionable [ɪmˈprɛʃənəbəl] *adj* : impresionable
impressive [ɪmˈprɛsɪv] *adj* : impresionante — **impressively** *adv*
impressiveness [ɪmˈprɛsɪvnəs] *n* : calidad de ser impresionante
imprint¹ [ɪmˈprɪnt, ˈɪmˌ-] *vt* : imprimir, estampar
imprint² [ˈɪmˌprɪnt] *n* : marca *f,* huella *f*
imprison [ɪmˈprɪzən] *vt* **1** JAIL : encarcelar, aprisionar **2** CONFINE : recluir, encerrar
imprisonment [ɪmˈprɪzənmənt] *n* : encarcelamiento *m*
improbability [ɪmˌprɑbəˈbɪləṭi] *n, pl* **-ties** : improbabilidad *f,* inverosimilitud *f*
improbable [ɪmˈprɑbəbəl] *adj* : improbable, inverosímil

impromptu[1] [ɪm'prɑmp,tu:, -,tju:] *adv* : sin preparación, espontáneamente

impromptu[2] *adj* : espontáneo, improvisado

impromptu[3] *n* : improvisación *f*

improper [ɪm'prɑpər] *adj* **1** INCORRECT : incorrecto, impropio **2** INDECOROUS : indecoroso

improperly [ɪm'prɑpərli] *adv* : incorrectamente, indebidamente

impropriety [,ɪmprə'praɪəṭi] *n, pl* **-eties 1** INDECOROUSNESS : indecoro *m,* falta *f* de decoro **2** ERROR : impropiedad *f,* incorrección *f*

improve [ɪm'pru:v] *v* **-proved; -proving** : mejorar

improvement [ɪm'pru:vmənt] *n* : mejoramiento *m,* mejora *f*

improvidence [ɪm'prɑvədənts] *n* : imprevisión *f*

improvident [ɪm'prɑvədənt] *adj* : sin previsión, imprevisor

improvisation [ɪm,prɑvə'zeɪʃən, ,ɪmprəvə-] *n* : improvisación *f*

improvise ['ɪmprə,vaɪz] *v* **-vised; -vising** : improvisar

imprudence [ɪm'pru:dənts] *n* : imprudencia *f,* indiscreción *f*

imprudent [ɪm'pru:dənt] *adj* : imprudente, indiscreto

impudence ['ɪmpjədənts] *n* : insolencia *f,* descaro *m*

impudent ['ɪmpjədənt] *adj* : insolente, descarado — **impudently** *adv*

impugn [ɪm'pju:n] *vt* : impugnar

impulse ['ɪm,pʌls] *n* **1** : impulso *m* **2 on impulse** : sin reflexionar

impulsive [ɪm'pʌlsɪv] *adj* : impulsivo — **impulsively** *adv*

impulsiveness [ɪm'pʌlsɪvnəs] *n* : impulsividad *f*

impunity [ɪm'pju:nəṭi] *n* **1** : impunidad *f* **2 with impunity** : impunemente

impure [ɪm'pjʊr] *adj* **1** : impuro <impure thoughts : pensamientos impuros> **2** CONTAMINATED : con impurezas, impuro

impurity [ɪm'pjʊrəṭi] *n, pl* **-ties** : impureza *f*

impute [ɪm'pju:t] *vt* **-puted; -puting** ATTRIBUTE : imputar, atribuir

in[1] ['ɪn] *adv* **1** INSIDE : dentro, adentro <let's go in : vamos adentro> **2** HARVESTED : recogido <the crops are in : las cosechas ya están recogidas> **3 to be in** : estar <is Linda in? : ¿está Linda?> **4 to be in** : estar en poder <the Democrats are in : los demócratas están en el poder> **5 to be in for** : ser objeto de, estar a punto de <they're in for a treat : los van a agasajar> <he's in for a surprise : se va a llevar una sorpresa> **6 to be in on** : participar en, tomar parte en

in[2] *adj* **1** INSIDE : interior <the in part : la parte interior> **2** FASHIONABLE : de moda

in[3] *prep* **1** (*indicating location or position*) <in the lake : en el lago> <a pain in the leg : un dolor en la pierna> <in the sun : al sol> <in the rain : bajo la lluvia> <the best restaurant in Buenos Aires : el mejor restaurante de Buenos Aires> **2** INTO : en, a <he broke it in pieces : lo rompió en pedazos> <she went in the house : se metió a la casa> **3** DURING : por, durante <in the afternoon : por la tarde> **4** WITHIN : dentro de <I'll be back in a week : vuelvo dentro de una semana> **5** (*indicating manner*) : en, con, de <in Spanish : en español> <written in pencil : escrito con lápiz> <in this way : de esta manera> **6** (*indicating states or circumstances*) <to be in luck : tener suerte> <to be in love : estar enamorado> <to be in a hurry : tener prisa> **7** (*indicating purpose*) : en <in reply : en respuesta, como réplica>

inability [,ɪnə'bɪləṭi] *n, pl* **-ties** : incapacidad *f*

inaccessibility [,ɪnɪk,sɛsə'bɪləṭi] *n, pl* **-ties** : inaccesibilidad *f*

inaccessible [,ɪnɪk'sɛsəbəl] *adj* : inaccesible

inaccuracy [ɪn'ækjərəsi] *n, pl* **-cies 1** : inexactitud *f* **2** MISTAKE : error *m*

inaccurate [ɪn'ækjərət] *n* : inexacto, erróneo, incorrecto

inaccurately [ɪn'ækjərətli] *adv* : incorrectamente, con inexactitud

inaction [ɪn'ækʃən] *n* : inactividad *f,* inacción *f*

inactive [ɪn'æktɪv] *n* : inactivo

inactivity [,ɪn,æk'tɪvəṭi] *n, pl* **-ties** : inactividad *f,* ociosidad *f*

inadequacy [ɪn'ædɪkwəsi] *n, pl* **-cies 1** INSUFFICIENCY : insuficiencia *f* **2** INCOMPETENCE : ineptitud *f,* incompetencia *f*

inadequate [ɪn'ædɪkwət] *adj* **1** INSUFFICIENT : insuficiente, inadecuado **2** INCOMPETENT : inepto, incompetente

inadmissible [,ɪnæd'mɪsəbəl] *adj* : inadmisible

inadvertent [,ɪnəd'vərtənt] *adj* : inadvertido, involuntario — **inadvertently** *adv*

inadvisable [,ɪnæd'vaɪzəbəl] *adj* : desaconsejable

inalienable [ɪn'eɪljənəbəl, -'eɪliənə-] *adj* : inalienable

inane [ɪ'neɪn] *adj* **inaner; -est** : estúpido, idiota, necio

inanimate [ɪn'ænəmət] *adj* : inanimado, exánime

inanity [ɪ'nænəṭi] *n, pl* **-ties 1** STUPIDITY : estupidez *f* **2** NONSENSE : idiotez *f,* disparate *m*

inapplicable [ɪn'æplɪkəbəl, ,ɪnə'plɪkəbəl] *adj* IRRELEVANT : inaplicable, irrelevante

inappreciable [,ɪnə'pri:ʃəbəl] *adj* : inapreciable, imperceptible

inappropriate [,ɪnə'pro:priət] *adj* : inapropiado, inadecuado, impropio

inappropriateness [ˌɪnəˈproːpriətnəs] *n* : lo inapropiado, impropiedad *f*

inapt [ɪnˈæpt] *adj* **1** UNSUITABLE : inadecuado, inapropiado **2** INEPT : inepto

inarticulate [ˌɪnɑrˈtɪkjələt] *adj* : inarticulado, incapaz de expresarse

inarticulately [ˌɪnɑrˈtɪkjələtli] *adv* : inarticuladamente

inasmuch as [ˌɪnæzˈmʌtʃæz] *conj* : ya que, dado que, puesto que

inattention [ˌɪnəˈtɛntʃən] *n* : falta *f* de atención, distracción *f*

inattentive [ˌɪnəˈtɛntɪv] *adj* : distraído, despistado

inattentively [ˌɪnəˈtɛntɪvli] *adv* : distraídamente, sin prestar atención

inaudible [ɪnˈɔdəbəl] *adj* : inaudible

inaudibly [ɪnˈɔdəbli] *adv* : de forma inaudible

inaugural[1] [ɪˈnɔgjərəl, -gərəl] *adj* : inaugural, de investidura

inaugural[2] *n* **1** *or* **inaugural address** : discurso *m* de investidura **2** INAUGURATION : investidura *f* (de una persona)

inaugurate [ɪˈnɔgjəˌreɪt, -gə-] *vt* **-rated; -rating 1** BEGIN : inaugurar **2** INDUCT : investir <to inaugurate the president : investir al presidente>

inauguration [ɪˌnɔgjəˈreɪʃən, -gə-] *n* **1** : inauguración *f* (de un edificio, un sistema, etc.) **2** : investidura *f* (de una persona)

inauspicious [ˌɪnɔˈspɪʃəs] *adj* : desfavorable, poco propicio

inborn [ˈɪnˌbɔrn] *adj* **1** CONGENITAL, INNATE : innato, congénito **2** HEREDITARY : hereditario

inbred [ˈɪnˌbrɛd] *adj* **1** : engendrado por endogamia **2** INNATE : innato

inbreed [ˈɪnˌbriːd] *vt* **-bred; -breeding** : engendrar por endogamia

inbreeding [ˈɪnˌbriːdɪŋ] *n* : endogamia *f*

incalculable [ɪnˈkælkjələbəl] *adj* : incalculable — **incalculably** [-bli] *adv*

incandescence [ˌɪnkənˈdɛsənts] *n* : incandescencia *f*

incandescent [ˌɪnkənˈdɛsənt] *adj* **1** : incandescente **2** BRILLIANT : brillante

incantation [ˌɪnˌkænˈteɪʃən] *n* : conjuro *m*, ensalmo *m*

incapable [ɪnˈkeɪpəbəl] *adj* : incapaz

incapacitate [ˌɪnkəˈpæsəˌteɪt] *vt* **-tated; -tating** : incapacitar

incapacity [ˌɪnkəˈpæsəti] *n, pl* **-ties** : incapacidad *f*

incarcerate [ɪnˈkɑrsəˌreɪt] *vt* **-ated; -ating** : encarcelar

incarceration [ɪnˌkɑrsəˈreɪʃən] *n* : encarcelamiento *m*, encarcelación *f*

incarnate[1] [ɪnˈkɑrˌneɪt] *vt* **-nated; -nating** : encarnar

incarnate[2] [ɪnˈkɑrnət, -ˌneɪt] *adj* : encarnado

incarnation [ˌɪnˌkɑrˈneɪʃən] *n* : encarnación *f*

incendiary[1] [ɪnˈsɛndiˌɛri] *adj* : incendiario

incendiary[2] *n, pl* **-aries** : incendiario *m*, -ria *f*; pirómano *m*, -na *f*

incense[1] [ɪnˈsɛnts] *vt* **-censed; -censing** : indignar, enfadar, enfurecer

incense[2] [ˈɪnˌsɛnts] *n* : incienso *m*

incentive [ɪnˈsɛntɪv] *n* : incentivo *m*, aliciente *m*, motivación *f*, acicate *m*

inception [ɪnˈsɛpʃən] *n* : comienzo *m*, principio *m*

incessant [ɪnˈsɛsənt] *adj* : incesante, continuo — **incessantly** *adv*

incest [ˈɪnˌsɛst] *n* : incesto *m*

incestuous [ɪnˈsɛstʃʊəs] *adj* : incestuoso

inch[1] [ˈɪntʃ] *v* : avanzar poco a poco

inch[2] *n* **1** : pulgada *f* **2 every inch** : absoluto, seguro <every inch a winner : un seguro ganador> **3 within an inch of** : a punto de

incidence [ˈɪntsədənts] *n* **1** FREQUENCY : frecuencia *f*, índice *m* <a high incidence of crime : un alto índice de crímenes> **2 angle of incidence** : ángulo *m* de incidencia

incident[1] [ˈɪntsədənt] *adj* : incidente

incident[2] *n* : incidente *m*, incidencia *f*, episodio *m* (en una obra de ficción)

incidental[1] [ˌɪntsəˈdɛntəl] *adj* **1** SECONDARY : incidental, secundario **2** ACCIDENTAL : casual, fortuito

incidental[2] *n* **1** : algo incidental **2 incidentals** *npl* : imprevistos *mpl*

incidentally [ˌɪntsəˈdɛntəli, -ˈdɛntli] *adv* **1** BY CHANCE : incidentalmente, casualmente **2** BY THE WAY : a propósito, por cierto

incinerate [ɪnˈsɪnəˌreɪt] *vt* **-ated; -ating** : incinerar

incinerator [ɪnˈsɪnəˌreɪtər] *n* : incinerador *m*

incipient [ɪnˈsɪpiənt] *adj* : incipiente, naciente

incise [ɪnˈsaɪz] *vt* **-cised; -cising 1** ENGRAVE : grabar, cincelar, inscribir **2** : hacer una incisión en

incision [ɪnˈsɪʒən] *n* : incisión *f*

incisive [ɪnˈsaɪsɪv] *adj* : incisivo, penetrante

incisively [ɪnˈsaɪsɪvli] *adv* : con agudeza

incisor [ɪnˈsaɪzər] *n* : incisivo *m*

incite [ɪnˈsaɪt] *vt* **-cited; -citing** : incitar, instigar

incitement [ɪnˈsaɪtmənt] *n* : incitación *f*

inclemency [ɪnˈklɛməntsi] *n, pl* **-cies** : inclemencia *f*

inclement [ɪnˈklɛmənt] *adj* : inclemente, tormentuoso

inclination [ˌɪnkləˈneɪʃən] *n* **1** PROPENSITY : inclinación *f*, tendencia *f* **2** DESIRE : deseo *m*, ganas *fpl* **3** BOW : inclinación *f*

incline[1] [ɪnˈklaɪn] *v* **-clined; -clining** *vi* **1** SLOPE : inclinarse **2** TEND : inclinarse, tender <he is inclined to be late : tiende a llegar tarde> — *vt* **1** LOWER : inclinar, bajar <to incline one's head

: bajar la cabeza> 2 SLANT : inclinar 3 PREDISPOSE : predisponer

incline² [ˈɪnˌklaɪn] *n* : inclinación *f*, pendiente *f*

inclined [ɪnˈklaɪnd] *adj* **1** SLOPING : inclinado **2** PRONE : prono, dispuesto, dado

inclose, inclosure → **enclose, enclosure**

include [ɪnˈkluːd] *vt* **-cluded; -cluding** : incluir, comprender

inclusion [ɪnˈkluːʒən] *n* : inclusión *f*

inclusive [ɪnˈkluːsɪv] *adj* : inclusivo

incognito [ˌɪnˌkɑɡˈniːto, ɪnˈkɑɡnəˌtoː] *adv & adj* : de incógnito

incoherence [ˌɪnkoˈhɪrənts, -ˈhɛr-] *n* : incoherencia *f*

incoherent [ˌɪnkoˈhɪrənt, -ˈhɛr-] *adj* : incoherente — **incoherently** *adv*

incombustible [ˌɪnkəmˈbʌstəbəl] *adj* : incombustible

income [ˈɪnˌkʌm] *n* : ingresos *mpl*, entradas *fpl*

income tax *n* : impuesto *m* sobre la renta

incoming [ˈɪnˌkʌmɪŋ] *adj* **1** ARRIVING : que se recibe (dícese del correo), que llega (dícese de las personas), ascendente (dícese de la marea) **2** NEW : nuevo, entrante <the incoming president : el nuevo presidente> <the incoming year : el año entrante>

incommunicado [ˌɪnkəˌmjuːnəˈkɑdo] *adj* : incomunicado

incomparable [ɪnˈkɑmpərəbəl] *adj* : incomparable, sin igual

incompatible [ˌɪnkəmˈpætəbəl] *adj* : incompatible

incompetence [ɪnˈkɑmpətənts] *n* : incompetencia *f*, impericia *f*, ineptitud *f*

incompetent [ɪnˈkɑmpətənt] *adj* : incompetente, inepto, incapaz

incomplete [ˌɪnkəmˈpliːt] *adj* : incompleto — **incompletely** *adv*

incomprehensible [ˌɪnˌkɑmpriˈhɛntsəbəl] *adj* : incomprensible

inconceivable [ˌɪnkənˈsiːvəbəl] *adj* **1** INCOMPREHENSIBLE : incomprensible **2** UNBELIEVABLE : inconcebible, increíble

inconceivably [ˌɪnkənˈsiːvəbli] *adv* : inconcebiblemente, increíblemente

inconclusive [ˌɪnkənˈkluːsɪv] *adj* : inconcluyente, no decisivo

incongruity [ˌɪnkənˈɡruːəti, -ˌkɑn-] *n, pl* **-ties** : incongruencia *f*

incongruous [ɪnˈkɑŋɡrʊəs] *adj* : incongruente, inapropiado, fuera de lugar

incongruously [ɪnˈkɑŋɡrʊəsli] *adv* : de manera incongruente, inapropiadamente

inconsequential [ˌɪnˌkɑnsəˈkwɛntʃəl] *adj* : intrascendente, de poco importancia

inconsiderable [ˌɪnkənˈsɪdərəbəl] *adj* : insignificante

inconsiderate [ˌɪnkənˈsɪdərət] *adj* : desconsiderado, sin consideración — **inconsiderately** *adv*

inconsistency [ˌɪnkənˈsɪstəntsi] *n, pl* **-cies** : inconsecuencia *f*, inconsistencia *f*

inconsistent [ˌɪnkənˈsɪstənt] *adj* : inconsecuente, inconsistente

inconsolable [ˌɪnkənˈsoːləbəl] *adj* : inconsolable — **inconsolably** [-bli] *adv*

inconspicuous [ˌɪnkənˈspɪkjʊəs] *adj* : discreto, no conspicuo, que no llama la atención

inconspicuously [ˌɪnkənˈspɪkjʊəsli] *adv* : discretamente, sin llamar la atención

incontestable [ˌɪnkənˈtɛstəbəl] *adj* : incontestable, indiscutible — **incontestably** [-bli] *adv*

incontinence [ɪnˈkɑntənənts] *n* : incontinencia *f*

incontinent [ɪnˈkɑntənənt] *adj* : incontinente

inconvenience¹ [ˌɪnkənˈviːnjənts] **-nienced; -niencing** *vt* : importunar, incomodar, molestar

inconvenience² *n* : incomodidad *f*, molestia *f*

inconvenient [ˌɪnkənˈviːnjənt] *adj* : inconveniente, importuno, incómodo — **inconveniently** *adv*

incorporate [ɪnˈkɔrpəˌreɪt] *vt* **-rated; -rating 1** INCLUDE : incorporar, incluir **2** : incorporar, constituir en sociedad (dícese de un negocio)

incorporation [ɪnˌkɔrpəˈreɪʃən] *n* : incorporación *f*

incorporeal [ˌɪnˌkɔrˈporiəl] *adj* : incorpóreo

incorrect [ˌɪnkəˈrɛkt] *adj* **1** INACCURATE : incorrecto **2** WRONG : equivocado, erróneo **3** IMPROPER : impropio — **incorrectly** *adv*

incorrigible [ɪnˈkɔrədʒəbəl] *adj* : incorregible

incorruptible [ˌɪnkəˈrʌptəbəl] *adj* : incorruptible

increase¹ [ɪnˈkriːs, ˈɪnˌkriːs] *v* **-creased; -creasing** *vi* GROW : aumentar, crecer, subir (dícese de los precios) — *vt* AUGMENT : aumentar, acrecentar

increase² [ˈɪnˌkriːs, ɪnˈkriːs] *n* : aumento *m*, incremento *m*, subida *f* (de precios)

increasing [ɪnˈkriːsɪŋ, ˈɪnˌkriːsɪŋ] *adj* : creciente

increasingly [ɪnˈkriːsɪŋli] *adv* : cada vez más

incredible [ɪnˈkrɛdəbəl] *adj* : increíble — **incredibly** [-bli] *adv*

incredulity [ˌɪnkrɪˈduːləti, -ˈdjuː-] *n* : incredulidad *f*

incredulous [ɪnˈkrɛdʒələs] *adj* : incrédulo, escéptico

incredulously [ɪnˈkrɛdʒələsli] *adv* : con incredulidad

increment [ˈɪŋkrəmənt, ˈɪn-] *n* : incremento *m*, aumento *m*

incremental [ˌɪŋkrəˈmɛntəl, ˌɪn-] *adj* : de incremento

incriminate [ɪnˈkrɪmə,neɪt] *vt* **-nated; -nating** : incriminar

incrimination [ɪn,krɪməˈneɪʃən] *n* : incriminación *f*

incriminatory [ɪnˈkrɪmənə,tori] *adj* : incriminatorio

incubate [ˈɪŋkjʊ,beɪt, ˈɪn-] *v* **-bated; -bating** *vt* : incubar, empollar — *vi* : incubar(se), empollar

incubation [,ɪŋkjʊˈbeɪʃən, ,ɪn-] *n* : incubación *f*

incubator [ˈɪŋkjʊ,beɪtər, ˈɪn-] *n* : incubadora *f*

inculcate [ɪnˈkʌl,keɪt, ˈɪn,kʌl-] *vt* **-cated; -cating** : inculcar

incumbency [ɪnˈkʌmbəntsi] *n, pl* **-cies** **1** OBLIGATION : incumbencia *f* **2** : mandato *m* (en la política)

incumbent[1] [ɪnˈkʌmbənt] *adj* : obligatorio

incumbent[2] *n* : titular *mf*

incur [ɪnˈkər] *vt* **incurred; incurring** : provocar (al enojo), incurrir en (gastos, obligaciones)

incurable [ɪnˈkjʊrəbəl] *adj* : incurable, sin remedio

incursion [ɪnˈkərʒən] *n* : incursión *f*

indebted [ɪnˈdɛtəd] *adj* **1** : endeudado **2 to be indebted to** : estar en deuda con, estarle agracido a

indebtedness [ɪnˈdɛtədnəs] *n* : endeudamiento *m*

indecency [ɪnˈdiːsəntsi] *n, pl* **-cies** : indecencia *f*

indecent [ɪnˈdiːsənt] *adj* : indecente — **indecently** *adv*

indecipherable [,ɪndɪˈsaɪfərəbəl] *adj* : indescifrable

indecision [,ɪndɪˈsɪʒən] *n* : indecisión *f*, irresolución *f*

indecisive [,ɪndɪˈsaɪsɪv] *adj* **1** INCONCLUSIVE : indeciso, que no es decisivo **2** IRRESOLUTE : indeciso, irresoluto, vacilante **3** INDEFINITE : indefinido — **indecisively** *adv*

indecorous [ɪnˈdɛkərəs, ,ɪndɪˈkorəs] *adj* : indecoroso — **indecorously** *adv*

indecorousness [ɪnˈdɛkərəsnəs, ,ɪndɪˈkorəs-] *n* : indecoro *m*

indeed [ɪnˈdiːd] *adv* **1** TRULY : verdaderamente, de veras **2** (*used as intensifier*) <thank you very much indeed : muchísimas gracias> **3** OF COURSE : claro, por supuesto

indefatigable [,ɪndɪˈfætɪgəbəl] *adj* : incansable, infatigable — **indefatigably** [-bli] *adv*

indefensible [,ɪndɪˈfɛntsəbəl] *adj* **1** VULNERABLE : indefendible, vulnerable **2** INEXCUSABLE : inexcusable

indefinable [,ɪndɪˈfaɪnəbəl] *adj* : indefinible

indefinite [ɪnˈdɛfənət] *adj* **1** : indefinido, indeterminado <indefinite pronouns : pronombres indefinidos> **2** VAGUE : vago, impreciso

indefinitely [ɪnˈdɛfənətli] *adv* : indefinidamente, por un tiempo indefinido

indelible [ɪnˈdɛləbəl] *adj* : indeleble, imborrable — **indelibly** [-bli] *adv*

indelicacy [ɪnˈdɛləkəsi] *n* : falta *f* de delicadeza

indelicate [ɪnˈdɛlɪkət] *adj* **1** IMPROPER : indelicado, indecoroso **2** TACTLESS : indiscreto, falto de tacto

indemnify [ɪnˈdɛmnə,faɪ] *vt* **-fied; -fying** **1** INSURE : asegurar **2** COMPENSATE : indemnizar, compensar

indemnity [ɪnˈdɛmnəti] *n, pl* **-ties** **1** INSURANCE : indemnidad *f* **2** COMPENSATION : indemnización *f*

indent [ɪnˈdɛnt] *vt* : sangrar (un párrafo)

indentation [,ɪn,dɛnˈteɪʃən] *n* **1** NOTCH : muesca *f*, mella *f* **2** INDENTING : sangría *f* (de un párrafo)

indenture[1] [ɪnˈdɛntʃər] *vt* **-tured; -turing** : ligar por contrato

indenture[2] *n* : contrato de aprendizaje

independence [,ɪndəˈpɛndənts] *n* : independencia *f*

Independence Day *n* : día *m* de la Independencia (4 de julio en los EE.UU.)

independent[1] [,ɪndəˈpɛndənt] *adj* : independiente — **independently** *adv*

independent[2] *n* : independiente *mf*

indescribable [,ɪndɪˈskraɪbəbəl] *adj* : indescriptible, incalificable — **indescribably** [-bli] *adv*

indestructibility [,ɪndɪ,strʌktəˈbɪləti] *n* : indestructibilidad *f*

indestructible [,ɪndɪˈstrʌktəbəl] *adj* : indestructible

indeterminate [,ɪndɪˈtərmənət] *adj* **1** VAGUE : vago, impreciso, indeterminado **2** INDEFINITE : indeterminado, indefinido

index[1] [ˈɪn,dɛks] *vt* **1** : ponerle un índice a (un libro o una revista) **2** : incluir en un índice <all proper names are indexed : todos los nombres propios están incluidos en el índice> **3** INDICATE : indicar, señalar **4** REGULATE : indexar, indiciar <to index prices : indiciar los precios>

index[2] *n, pl* **-dexes** *or* **-dices** [ˈɪndə,siːz] **1** : índice *m* (de un libro, de precios) **2** INDICATION : indicio *m*, índice *m*, señal *f* <an index of her character : una señal de su carácter>

index finger *n* FOREFINGER : dedo *m* índice

Indian [ˈɪndiən] *n* **1** : indio *m*, -dia *f* **2** → **American Indian** — **Indian** *adj*

indicate [ˈɪndə,keɪt] *vt* **-cated; -cating** **1** POINT OUT : indicar, señalar **2** SHOW, SUGGEST : ser indicio de, ser señal de **3** EXPRESS : expresar, señalar **4** REGISTER : marcar, poner (una medida, etc.)

indication [,ɪndəˈkeɪʃən] *n* : indicio *m*, señal *f*

indicative [ɪnˈdɪkətɪv] *adj* : indicativo

indicator [ˈɪndəˌkeɪt̬ər] *n* : indicador *m*
indict [ɪnˈdaɪt] *vt* : acusar, procesar (por un crímen)
indictment [ɪnˈdaɪtmənt] *n* : acusación *f*
indifference [ɪnˈdɪfrənts, -ˈdɪfə-] *n* : indiferencia *f*
indifferent [ɪnˈdɪfrənt, -ˈdɪfə-] *adj* **1** UNCONCERNED : indiferente **2** MEDIOCRE : mediocre
indifferently [ɪnˈdɪfrəntli, -ˈdɪfə-] *adv* **1** : con indiferencia, indiferentemente **2** so-so : de modo regular, más o menos
indigence [ˈɪndɪdʒənts] *n* : indigencia *f*
indigenous [ɪnˈdɪdʒənəs] *adj* : indígena, nativo
indigent [ˈɪndɪdʒənt] *adj* : indigente, pobre
indigestible [ˌɪndaɪˈdʒɛstəbəl, -dɪ-] *adj* : difícil de digerir
indigestion [ˌɪndaɪˈdʒɛstʃən, -dɪ-] *n* : indigestión *f*, empacho *m*
indignant [ɪnˈdɪgnənt] *adj* : indignado
indignantly [ɪnˈdɪgnəntli] *adv* : con indignación
indignation [ˌɪndɪgˈneɪʃən] *n* : indignación *f*
indignity [ɪnˈdɪgnət̬i] *n, pl* **-ties** : indignidad *f*
indigo [ˈɪndɪˌgoː] *n, pl* **-gos** *or* **-goes** : añil *m*, índigo *m*
indirect [ˌɪndəˈrɛkt, -daɪ-] *adj* : indirecto — **indirectly** *adv*
indiscernible [ˌɪndɪˈsərnəbəl, -ˈzər-] *adj* : imperceptible
indiscreet [ˌɪndɪˈskriːt] *adj* : indiscreto, imprudente — **indiscreetly** *adv*
indiscretion [ˌɪndɪˈskrɛʃən] *n* : indiscreción *f*, imprudencia *f*
indiscriminate [ˌɪndɪˈskrɪmənət] *adj* : indiscriminado
indiscriminately [ˌɪndɪˈskrɪmənətli] *adv* : sin discriminación, sin discernimiento
indispensable [ˌɪndɪˈspɛntsəbəl] *adj* : indispensable, necesario, imprescindible — **indispensably** [-bli] *adv*
indisposed [ˌɪndɪˈspoːzd] *adj* **1** ILL : indispuesto, enfermo **2** AVERSE, DISINCLINED : opuesto, reacio <to be indisposed toward working : no tener ganas de trabajar>
indisputable [ˌɪndɪˈspjuːt̬əbəl, ɪnˈdɪspjʊt̬ə-] *adj* : indiscutible, incuestionable, incontestable — **indisputably** [-bli] *adv*
indistinct [ˌɪndɪˈstɪŋkt] *adj* : indistinto — **indistinctly** *adv*
indistinctness [ˌɪndɪˈstɪŋktnəs] *n* : falta *f* de claridad
individual[1] [ˌɪndəˈvɪdʒʊəl] *adj* **1** PERSONAL : individual, personal <individual traits : características personales> **2** SEPARATE : individual, separado **3** PARTICULAR : particular, propio
individual[2] *n* : individuo *m*
individualist [ˌɪndəˈvɪdʒʊəlɪst] *n* : individualista *mf*
individuality [ˌɪndəˌvɪdʒʊˈælət̬i] *n, pl* **-ties** : individualidad *f*
individually [ˌɪndəˈvɪdʒʊəli, -dʒəli] *adv* : individualmente
indivisible [ˌɪndɪˈvɪzəbəl] *adj* : indivisible
indoctrinate [ɪnˈdɑktrəˌneɪt] *vt* **-nated; -nating 1** TEACH : enseñar, instruir **2** PROPAGANDIZE : adoctrinar
indoctrination [ɪnˌdɑktrəˈneɪʃən] *n* : adoctrinamiento *m*
indolence [ˈɪndələnts] *n* : indolencia *f*
indolent [ˈɪndələnt] *adj* : indolente
indomitable [ɪnˈdɑmət̬əbəl] *adj* : invencible, indomable, indómito — **indomitably** [-bli] *adv*
Indonesian [ˌɪndoˈniːʒən, -ʃən] *n* : indonesio *m*, -sia *f* — **Indonesian** *adj*
indoor [ˈɪnˈdor] *adj* : interior (dícese de las plantas), para estar en casa (dícese de la ropa), cubierto (dícese de las piscinas, etc.), bajo techo (dícese de los deportes)
indoors [ˈɪnˈdorz] *adv* : adentro, dentro
indubitable [ɪnˈduːbət̬əbəl, -ˈdjuː-] *adj* : indudable, incuestionable, indiscutible
indubitably [ɪnˈduːbət̬əbli, -ˈdjuː-] *adv* : indudablemente
induce [ɪnˈduːs, -ˈdjuːs] *vt* **-duced; -ducing 1** PERSUADE : persuadir, inducir **2** CAUSE : inducir, provocar <to induce labor : provocar un parto>
inducement [ɪnˈduːsmənt, -ˈdjuːs-] *n* **1** INCENTIVE : incentivo *m*, aliciente *m* **2** : inducción *f*, provocación *f* (de un parto)
induct [ɪnˈdʌkt] *vt* **1** INSTALL : instalar, investir **2** ADMIT : admitir (como miembro) **3** CONSCRIPT : reclutar (al servicio militar)
inductee [ˌɪnˌdʌkˈtiː] *n* : recluta *mf*, conscripto *m*, -ta *f*
induction [ɪnˈdʌkʃən] *n* **1** INTRODUCTION : iniciación *f*, introducción *f* **2** : inducción *f* (en la lógica o la electricidad)
inductive [ɪnˈdʌktɪv] *adj* : inductivo
indulge [ɪnˈdʌldʒ] *v* **-dulged; -dulging** *vt* **1** GRATIFY : gratificar, satisfacer **2** SPOIL : consentir, mimar — *vi* **to indulge in** : permitirse
indulgence [ɪnˈdʌldʒənts] *n* **1** SATISFYING : satisfacción *f*, gratificación *f* **2** HUMORING : complacencia *f*, indulgencia *f* **3** SPOILING : consentimiento *m* **4** : indulgencia *f* (en la religión)
indulgent [ɪŋˈdʌldʒənt] *adj* : indulgente, consentido — **indulgently** *adv*
industrial [ɪnˈdʌstriəl] *adj* : industrial — **industrially** *adv*
industrialist [ɪnˈdʌstriəlɪst] *n* : industrial *mf*

industrialization [ɪn,dʌstriələ'zeɪʃən] *n* **:** industrialización *f*
industrialize [ɪn'dʌstriə,laɪz] *vt* **-ized; -izing :** industrializar
industrious [ɪn'dʌstriəs] *adj* **:** diligente, industrioso, trabajador
industriously [ɪn'dʌstriəsli] *adv* **:** con diligencia, con aplicación
industriousness [ɪn'dʌstriəsnəs] *n* **:** diligencia *f,* aplicación *f*
industry ['ɪndəstri] *n, pl* **-tries 1** DILIGENCE **:** diligencia *f,* aplicación *f* **2 :** industria *f* <the steel industry : la industria siderúrgica>
inebriated [ɪ'ni:bri,eɪtəd] *adj* **:** ebrio, embriagado
inebriation [ɪ,ni:bri'eɪʃən] *n* **:** ebriedad *f,* embriaguez *f*
ineffable [ɪn'ɛfəbəl] *adj* **:** inefable — **ineffably** [-bli] *adv*
ineffective [,ɪnɪ'fɛktɪv] *adj* **1** INEFFECTUAL **:** ineficaz, inútil **2** INCAPABLE **:** incompetente, ineficiente, incapaz
ineffectively [,ɪnɪ'fɛktɪvli] *adv* **:** ineficazmente, infructuosamente
ineffectual [,ɪnɪ'fɛktʃʊəl] *adj* **:** inútil, ineficaz — **ineffectually** *adv*
inefficiency [,ɪnɪ'fɪʃəntsi] *n, pl* **-cies :** ineficiencia *f,* ineficacia *f*
inefficient [,ɪnɪ'fɪʃənt] *adj* **1 :** ineficiente, ineficaz **2** INCAPABLE, INCOMPETENT **:** incompetente, incapaz — **inefficiently** *adv*
inelegance [ɪn'ɛləgənts] *n* **:** inelegancia *f*
inelegant [ɪn'ɛləgənt] *adj* **:** inelegante, poco elegante
ineligibility [ɪn,ɛlədʒə'bɪləti] *n* **:** inelegibilidad *f*
ineligible [ɪn'ɛlədʒəbəl] *adj* **:** inelegible
inept [ɪ'nɛpt] *adj* **:** inepto <inept at : incapaz para>
ineptitude [ɪ'nɛptə,tu:d, -,tju:d] *n* **:** ineptitud *f,* incompetencia *f,* incapacidad *f*
inequality [,ɪnɪ'kwɑləti] *n, pl* **-ties :** desigualdad *f*
inert [ɪ'nərt] *adj* **1** INACTIVE **:** inerte, inactivo **2** SLUGGISH **:** lento
inertia [ɪ'nərʃə] *n* **:** inercia *f*
inescapable [,ɪnɪ'skeɪpəbəl] *adj* **:** inevitable, ineludible — **inescapably** [-bli] *adv*
inessential [,ɪnɪ'sɛntʃəl] *adj* **:** que no es esencial, innecesario
inestimable [ɪn'ɛstəməbəl] *adj* **:** inestimable, inapreciable
inevitability [ɪn,ɛvətə'bɪləti] *n, pl* **-ties :** inevitabilidad *f*
inevitable [ɪn'ɛvətəbəl] *adj* **:** inevitable — **inevitably** [-bli] *adv*
inexact [,ɪnɪg'zækt] *adj* **:** inexacto
inexactly [,ɪnɪg'zæktli] *adv* **:** sin exactitud
inexcusable [,ɪnɪk'skju:zəbəl] *adj* **:** inexcusable, imperdonable — **inexcusably** [-bli] *adv*
inexhaustible [,ɪnɪg'zɔstəbəl] *adj* **1** INDEFATIGABLE **:** infatigable, incansable **2** ENDLESS **:** inagotable — **inexhaustibly** [-bli] *adv*
inexorable [ɪn'ɛksərəbəl] *adj* **:** inexorable — **inexorably** [-bli] *adv*
inexpensive [,ɪnɪk'spɛntsɪv] *adj* **:** barato, económico
inexperience [,ɪnɪk'spɪriənts] *n* **:** inexperiencia *f*
inexperienced [,ɪnɪk'spɪriəntst] *adj* **:** inexperto, novato
inexplicable [,ɪnɪk'splɪkəbəl] *adj* **:** inexplicable — **inexplicably** [-bli] *adv*
inexpressible [,ɪnɪk'sprɛsəbəl] *adj* **:** inexpresable, inefable
inextricable [,ɪnɪk'strɪkəbəl, ɪ'nɛk-,strɪ-] *adj* **:** inextricable — **inextricably** [-bli] *adv*
infallibility [ɪn,fælə'bɪləti] *n* **:** infalibilidad *f*
infallible [ɪn'fæləbəl] *adj* **:** infalible — **infallibly** [-bli] *adv*
infamous ['ɪnfəməs] *adj* **:** infame — **infamously** *adv*
infamy ['ɪnfəmi] *n, pl* **-mies :** infamia *f*
infancy ['ɪnfəntsi] *n, pl* **-cies :** infancia *f*
infant ['ɪnfənt] *n* **:** bebé *m;* niño *m,* -ña *f*
infantile ['ɪnfən,taɪl, -təl, -,ti:l] *adj* **:** infantil, pueril
infantile paralysis → **poliomyelitis**
infantry ['ɪnfəntri] *n, pl* **-tries :** infantería *f*
infatuated [ɪn'fætʃʊ,eɪtəd] *adj* **to be infatuated with :** estar encaprichado con
infatuation [ɪn,fætʃʊ'eɪʃən] *n* **:** encaprichamiento *m,* enamoramiento *m*
infect [ɪn'fɛkt] *vt* **:** infectar, contagiar
infection [ɪn'fɛkʃən] *n* **:** infección *f,* contagio *m*
infectious [ɪn'fɛkʃəs] *adj* **:** infeccioso, contagioso
infer [ɪn'fər] *vt* **inferred; inferring 1** DEDUCE **:** deducir, inferir **2** SURMISE **:** concluir, suponer, tener entendido **3** IMPLY **:** sugerir, insinuar
inference ['ɪnfərənts] *n* **:** deducción *f,* inferencia *f,* conclusión *f*
inferior¹ [ɪn'fɪriər] *adj* **:** inferior, malo
inferior² *n* **:** inferior *mf*
inferiority [ɪn,fɪri'ɔrəti] *n, pl* **-ties :** inferioridad *f* <inferiority complex : complejo de inferioridad>
infernal [ɪn'fərnəl] *adj* **1 :** infernal <infernal fires : fuegos infernales> **2** DIABOLICAL **:** infernal, diabólico **3** DAMNABLE **:** maldito, condenado
inferno [ɪn'fər,no:] *n, pl* **-nos :** infierno *m*
infertile [ɪn'fərtəl, -,taɪl] *adj* **:** estéril, infecundo
infertility [,ɪnfər'tɪləti] *n* **:** esterilidad *f,* infecundidad *f*
infest [ɪn'fɛst] *vt* **:** infestar, plagar
infidel ['ɪnfədəl, -,dɛl] *n* **:** infiel *mf*

infidelity [ˌɪnfəˈdɛləṭi, -faɪ-] *n, pl* **-ties** **1** UNFAITHFULNESS **:** infidelidad *f* **2** DISLOYALTY **:** deslealtad *f*
infield [ˈɪnˌfiːld] *n* **:** cuadro *m,* diamante *m*
infiltrate [ɪnˈfɪlˌtreɪt, ˈɪnfɪl-] *v* **-trated; -trating** *vt* **:** infiltrar — *vi* **:** infiltrarse
infiltration [ˌɪnfɪlˈtreɪʃən] *n* **:** infiltración *f*
infinite [ˈɪnfənət] *adj* **1** LIMITLESS **:** infinito, sin límites **2** VAST **:** infinito, vasto, extenso
infinitely [ˈɪnfənətli] *adv* **:** infinitamente
infinitesimal [ˌɪnˌfɪnəˈtɛsəməl] *adj* **:** infinitésimo, infinitesimal — **infinitesimally** *adv*
infinitive [ɪnˈfɪnəṭɪv] *n* **:** infinitivo *m*
infinitude [ɪnˈfɪnəˌtuːd, -tjuːd] *n* **:** infinitud *f*
infinity [ɪnˈfɪnəṭi] *n, pl* **-ties** **1 :** infinito *m* (en matemáticas, etc.) **2 :** infinidad *f* <an infinity of stars **:** una infinidad de estrellas>
infirm [ɪnˈfərm] *adj* **1** FEEBLE **:** enfermizo, endeble **2** INSECURE **:** inseguro
infirmary [ɪnˈfərməri] *n, pl* **-ries :** enfermería *f,* hospital *m*
infirmity [ɪnˈfərməṭi] *n, pl* **-ties** **1** FRAILTY **:** debilidad *f,* endeblez *f* **2** AILMENT **:** enfermedad *f,* dolencia *f* <the infirmities of age **:** los achaques de la vejez>
inflame [ɪnˈfleɪm] *v* **-flamed; -flaming** *vt* **1** KINDLE **:** inflamar, encender **2 :** inflamar (una herida) **3** STIR UP **:** encender, provocar, inflamar — *vi* **:** inflamarse
inflammable [ɪnˈflæməbəl] *adj* **1** FLAMMABLE **:** inflamable **2** IRASCIBLE **:** irascible, explosivo
inflammation [ˌɪnfləˈmeɪʃən] *n* **:** inflamación *f*
inflammatory [ɪnˈflæməˌtori] *adj* **:** inflamatorio, incendiario
inflatable [ɪnˈfleɪṭəbəl] *adj* **:** inflable
inflate [ɪnˈfleɪt] *vt* **-flated; -flating** **:** inflar, hinchar
inflation [ɪnˈfleɪʃən] *n* **:** inflación *f*
inflationary [ɪnˈfleɪʃəˌnɛri] *adj* **:** inflacionario, inflacionista
inflect [ɪnˈflɛkt] *vt* **1** CONJUGATE, DECLINE **:** conjugar, declinar **2** MODULATE **:** modular (la voz)
inflection [ɪnˈflɛkʃən] *n* **:** inflexión *f*
inflexibility [ɪnˌflɛksəˈbɪləṭi] *n, pl* **-ties** **:** inflexibilidad *f*
inflexible [ɪnˈflɛksɪbəl] *adj* **:** inflexible
inflict [ɪnˈflɪkt] *vt* **1 :** infligir, causar, imponer **2 to inflict oneself on :** imponer uno su presencia (a alguien)
infliction [ɪnˈflɪkʃən] *n* **:** imposición *f*
influence¹ [ˈɪnˌfluːənts, ɪnˈfluːənts] *vt* **-enced; -encing :** influenciar, influir en
influence² *n* **1 :** influencia *f,* influjo *m* <to exert influence over **:** ejercer influencia sobre> <the influence of gravity **:** el influjo de la gravidad> **2 under the influence :** bajo la influencia del alcohol, embriagado
influential [ˌɪnfluˈɛntʃəl] *adj* **:** influyente
influenza [ˌɪnfluˈɛnzə] *n* **:** gripe *f,* influenza *f,* gripa *f Col, Mex*
influx [ˈɪnˌflʌks] *n* **:** afluencia *f* (de gente), entrada *f* (de mercancías), llegada *f* (de ideas)
inform [ɪnˈfɔrm] *vt* **:** informar, notificar, avisar — *vi* **to inform on :** delatar, denunciar
informal [ɪnˈfɔrməl] *adj* **1** UNCEREMONIOUS **:** sin ceremonia, sin etiqueta **2** CASUAL **:** informal, familiar (dícese del lenguaje) **3** UNOFFICIAL **:** extraoficial
informality [ˌɪnfɔrˈmæləṭi, -fər-] *n, pl* **-ties :** informalidad *f,* familiaridad *f,* falta *f* de ceremonia
informally [ɪnˈfɔrməli] *adv* **:** sin ceremonias, de manera informal, informalmente
informant [ɪnˈfɔrmənt] *n* **:** informante *mf;* informador *m,* -dora *f*
information [ˌɪnfərˈmeɪʃən] *n* **:** información *f*
informative [ɪnˈfɔrməṭɪv] *adj* **:** informativo, instructivo
informer [ɪnˈfɔrmər] *n* **:** informante *mf;* informador *m,* -dora *f*
infraction [ɪnˈfrækʃən] *n* **:** infracción *f,* violación *f,* transgresión *f*
infrared [ˌɪnfrəˈrɛd] *adj* **:** infrarrojo
infrastructure [ˈɪnfrəˌstrʌktʃər] *n* **:** infraestructura *f*
infrequent [ɪnˈfriːkwənt] *adj* **:** infrequente, raro
infrequently [ɪnˈfriːkwəntli] *adv* **:** raramente, con poca frecuencia
infringe [ɪnˈfrɪndʒ] *v* **-fringed; -fringing** *vt* **:** infringir, violar — *vi* **to infringe on :** abusar de, violar
infringement [ɪnˈfrɪndʒmənt] *n* **1** VIOLATION **:** violación *f* (de la ley), incumplimiento *m* (de un contrato) **2** ENCROACHMENT **:** usurpación *f* (de derechos, etc.)
infuriate [ɪnˈfjʊriˌeɪt] *vt* **-ated; -ating** **:** enfurecer, poner furioso
infuriating [ɪnˈfjʊriˌeɪṭɪŋ] *adj* **:** indignante, exasperante
infuse [ɪnˈfjuːz] *vt* **-fused; -fusing** **1** INSTILL **:** infundir **2** STEEP **:** hacer una infusión de
infusion [ɪnˈfjuːʒən] *n* **:** infusión *f*
ingenious [ɪnˈdʒiːnjəs] *adj* **:** ingenioso — **ingeniously** *adv*
ingenue *or* **ingénue** [ˈɑndʒəˌnuː, ˈæn-; ˈæʒə-, ˈɑ-] *n* **:** ingenua *f*
ingenuity [ˌɪndʒəˈnuːəṭi, -ˈnjuː-] *n, pl* **-ities :** ingenio
ingenuous [ɪnˈdʒɛnjʊəs] *adj* **1** FRANK **:** cándido, franco **2** NAIVE **:** ingenuo — **ingenuously** *adv*
ingenuousness [ɪnˈdʒɛnjʊəsnəs] *n* **1** FRANKNESS **:** candidez *f,* candor *m* **2** NAÏVETÉ **:** ingenuidad *f*

ingest [ɪnˈdʒɛst] *vt* : ingerir
inglorious [ɪnˈgloriəs] *adj* : deshonroso, ignominioso
ingot [ˈɪŋgət] *n* : lingote *m*
ingrained [ɪnˈgreɪnd] *adj* : arraigado
ingrate [ˈɪnˌgreɪt] *n* : ingrato *m,* -ta *f*
ingratiate [ɪnˈgreɪʃiˌeɪt] *vt* **-ated; -ating** : conseguir la benevolencia de <to ingratiate oneself with someone : congraciarse con alguien>
ingratiating [ɪnˈgreɪʃiˌeɪt̬ɪŋ] *adj* : halagador, zalamero, obsequioso
ingratitude [ɪnˈgræt̬əˌtuːd, -ˌtjuːd] *n* : ingratitud *f*
ingredient [ɪnˈgriːdiənt] *n* : ingrediente *m,* componente *m*
ingrown [ˈɪnˌgroːn] *adj* **1** : crecido hacia adentro **2 ingrown toenail** : uña *f* encarnada
inhabit [ɪnˈhæbət] *vt* : vivir en, habitar, ocupar
inhabitable [ɪnˈhæbət̬əbəl] *adj* : habitable
inhabitant [ɪnˈhæbət̬ənt] *n* : habitante *mf*
inhalant [ɪnˈheɪlənt] *n* : inhalante *m*
inhalation [ˌɪnhəˈleɪʃən, ˌɪnə-] *n* : inhalación *f*
inhale [ɪnˈheɪl] *v* **-haled; -haling** *vt* : inhalar, aspirar — *vi* : inspirar
inhaler [ɪnˈheɪlər] *n* : inhalador *m*
inhere [ɪnˈhɪr] *vi* **-hered; -hering** : ser inherente
inherent [ɪnˈhɪrənt, -ˈhɛr-] *adj* : inherente, intrínseco — **inherently** *adv*
inherit [ɪnˈhɛrət] *vt* : heredar
inheritance [ɪnˈhɛrət̬ən*t*s] *n* : herencia *f*
inheritor [ɪnˈhɛrət̬ər] *n* : heredero *m,* -da *f*
inhibit [ɪnˈhɪbət] *vt* IMPEDE : inhibir, impedir
inhibition [ˌɪnhəˈbɪʃən, ˌɪnə-] *n* : inhibición *f,* cohibición *f*
inhuman [ɪnˈhjuːmən, -ˈjuː-] *adj* : inhumano, cruel — **inhumanly** *adv*
inhumane [ˌɪnhjuˈmeɪn, -ju-] *adj* INHUMAN : inhumano, cruel
inhumanity [ˌɪnhjuˈmænət̬i, -ju-] *n, pl* **-ties** : inhumanidad *f,* crueldad *f*
inimical [ɪˈnɪmɪkəl] *adj* **1** UNFAVORABLE : adverso, desfavorable **2** HOSTILE : hostil — **inimically** *adv*
inimitable [ɪˈnɪmət̬əbəl] *adj* : inimitable
iniquitous [ɪˈnɪkwət̬əs] *adj* : inicuo, malvado
iniquity [ɪˈnɪkwət̬i] *n, pl* **-ties** : iniquidad *f*
initial[1] [ɪˈnɪʃəl] *vt* **-tialed** *or* **-tialled; -tialing** *or* **-tialling** : poner las iniciales a, firmar con las iniciales
initial[2] *adj* : inicial, primero — **initially** *adv*
initial[3] *n* : inicial *f*
initiate[1] [ɪˈnɪʃiˌeɪt] *vt* **-ated; -ating 1** BEGIN : comenzar, iniciar **2** INDUCT : instruir **3** INTRODUCE : introducir, instruir
initiate[2] [ɪˈnɪʃiət] *n* : iniciado *m,* -da *f*
initiation [ɪˌnɪʃiˈeɪʃən] *n* : iniciación *f*
initiative [ɪˈnɪʃət̬ɪv] *n* : iniciativa *f*
initiatory [ɪˈnɪʃiəˌtori] *adj* **1** INTRODUCTORY : introductorio **2** : de iniciación <initiatory rites : ritos de iniciación>
inject [ɪnˈdʒɛkt] *vt* : inyectar
injection [ɪnˈdʒɛkʃən] *n* : inyección *f*
injudicious [ˌɪndʒʊˈdɪʃəs] *adj* : imprudente, indiscreto, poco juicioso
injunction [ɪnˈdʒʌŋkʃən] *n* **1** ORDER : orden *f,* mandato *m* **2** COURT ORDER : mandamiento *m* judicial
injure [ˈɪndʒər] *vt* **-jured; -juring 1** WOUND : herir, lesionar **2** HURT : lastimar, dañar, herir **3 to injure oneself** : hacerse daño
injurious [ɪnˈdʒʊriəs] *adj* : perjudicial <injurious to one's health : perjudicial a la salud>
injury [ˈɪndʒəri] *n, pl* **-ries 1** WRONG : mal *m,* injusticia *f* **2** DAMAGE, HARM : herida *f,* daño *m,* perjuicio *m*
injustice [ɪnˈdʒʌstəs] *n* : injusticia *f*
ink[1] [ˈɪŋk] *vt* : entintar
ink[2] *n* : tinta *f*
inkling [ˈɪŋklɪŋ] *n* : presentimiento *m,* indicio *m,* sospecho *m*
inkwell [ˈɪŋkˌwɛl] *n* : tintero *m*
inky [ˈɪŋki] *adj* **1** : manchado de tinta **2** BLACK : negro, impenetrable <inky darkness : negra oscuridad>
inland[1] [ˈɪnˌlænd, -lənd] *adv* : hacia el interior, tierra adentro
inland[2] *adj* : interior
inland[3] *n* : interior *m*
in–law [ˈɪnˌlɔ] *n* **1** : pariente *m* político **2 in–laws** *npl* : suegros *mpl*
inlay[1] [ɪnˈleɪ, ˈɪnˌleɪ] *vt* **-laid** [-ˈleɪd, -ˌleɪd]; **-laying** : incrustar, taracear
inlay[2] [ˈɪnˌleɪ] *n* **1** : incrustación *f* **2** : empaste *m* (de un diente)
inlet [ˈɪnˌlɛt, -lət] *n* : cala *f,* ensenada *f*
inmate [ˈɪnˌmeɪt] *n* : paciente *mf* (en un hospital); preso *m,* -sa *f* (en una prisión); interno *m,* -na *f* (en un asilo)
in memoriam [ˌɪnməˈmoriəm] *prep* : en memoria de
inmost [ˈɪnˌmoːst] → **innermost**
inn [ˈɪn] *n* **1** : posada *f,* hostería *f,* fonda *f* **2** TAVERN : taberna *f*
innards [ˈɪnərdz] *npl* : entrañas *fpl,* tripas *fpl fam*
innate [ɪˈneɪt] *adj* **1** INBORN : innato **2** INHERENT : inherente
inner [ˈɪnər] *adj* : interior, interno
innermost [ˈɪnərˌmoːst] *adj* : más íntimo, más profundo
innersole [ˈɪnərˈsoːl] → **insole**
inning [ˈɪnɪŋ] *n* : entrada *f*
innkeeper [ˈɪnˌkiːpər] *n* : posadero *m,* -ra *f*
innocence [ˈɪnəsən*t*s] *n* : inocencia *f*
innocent[1] [ˈɪnəsənt] *adj* : inocente — **innocently** *adv*
innocent[2] *n* : inocente *mf*

innocuous [ɪ'nɑkjəwəs] *adj* **1** HARMLESS : inocuo **2** INOFFENSIVE : inofensivo

innovate ['ɪnə,veɪt] *vi* **-vated; -vating** : innovar

innovation [,ɪnə'veɪʃən] *n* : innovación *f*, novedad *f*

innovative ['ɪnə,veɪt̬ɪv] *adj* : innovador

innovator ['ɪnə,veɪt̬ər] *n* : innovador *m*, -dora *f*

innuendo [,ɪnjʊ'ɛndo] *n, pl* **-dos** *or* **-does** : insinuación *f*, indirecta *f*

innumerable [ɪ'nuːmərəbəl, -'njuː-] *adj* : innumerable

inoculate [ɪ'nɑkjə,leɪt] *vt* **-lated; -lating** : inocular

inoculation [ɪ,nɑkjə'leɪʃən] *n* : inoculación *f*

inoffensive [,ɪnə'fɛntsɪv] *adj* : inofensivo

inoperable [ɪn'ɑpərəbəl] *adj* : inoperable

inoperative [ɪn'ɑpərət̬ɪv, -,reɪ-] *adj* : inoperante

inopportune [ɪn,ɑpər'tuːn, -'tjuːn] *adj* : inoportuno — **inopportunely** *adv*

inordinate [ɪn'ɔrdənət] *adj* : excesivo, inmoderado, desmesurado — **inordinately** *adv*

inorganic [,ɪn,ɔr'gænɪk] *adj* : inorgánico

inpatient ['ɪn,peɪʃənt] *n* : paciente *mf* hospitalizado

input[1] ['ɪn,pʊt] *vt* **inputted** *or* **input; inputting** : entrar (datos, información)

input[2] *n* **1** CONTRIBUTION : aportación *f*, contribución *f* **2** ENTRY : entrada *f* (de datos) **3** ADVICE, OPINION : consejos *mpl*, opinión *f*

inquest ['ɪn,kwɛst] *n* INQUIRY, INVESTIGATION : investigación *f*, averiguación *f*, pesquisa *f* (judicial)

inquire [ɪn'kwaɪr] *v* **-quired; -quiring** *vt* : preguntar, informarse de, inquirir <he inquired how to get in : preguntó como entrar> — *vi* **1** ASK : preguntar, informarse <to inquire about : informarse sobre> <to inquire after (someone) : preguntar por (alguien)> **2 to inquire into** INVESTIGATE : investigar, inquirir sobre

inquirer [ɪn'kwaɪrər] *n* : inquiridor *m*, -dora *f*; investigador *m*, -dora *f*

inquiringly [ɪn'kwaɪrɪŋli] *adv* : inquisitivamente

inquiry ['ɪn,kwaɪri, ɪn'kwaɪri; 'ɪnkwəri, 'ɪŋ-] *n, pl* **-ries 1** QUESTION : pregunta *f* <to make inquiries about : pedir información sobre> **2** INVESTIGATION : investigación *f*, inquisición *f*, pesquisa *f*

inquisition [,ɪnkwə'zɪʃən, ,ɪŋ-] *n* **1** : inquisición *f*, interrogatorio *m*, investigación *f* **2 the Inquisition** : la Inquisición *f*

inquisitive [ɪn'kwɪzət̬ɪv] *adj* : inquisidor, inquisitivo, curioso — **inquisitively** *adv*

inquisitiveness [ɪn'kwɪzət̬ɪvnəs] *n* : curiosidad *f*

inquisitor [ɪn'kwɪzət̬ər] *n* : inquisidor *m*, -dora *f*; interrogador *m*, -dora *f*

inroad ['ɪn,roːd] *n* **1** ENCROACHMENT, INVASION : invasión *f*, incursión *f* **2 to make inroads into** : ocupar parte de (un tiempo), agotar parte de (ahorros, recursos), invadir (un territorio)

insane [ɪn'seɪn] *adj* **1** MAD : loco, demente <to go insane : volverse loco> **2** ABSURD : absurdo, insensato <an insane scheme : un proyecto insensato>

insanely [ɪn'seɪnli] *adv* : como un loco <insanely suspicious : loco de recelo>

insanity [ɪn'sænət̬i] *n, pl* **-ties 1** MADNESS : locura *f* **2** FOLLY : locura *f*, insensatez *f*

insatiable [ɪn'seɪʃəbəl] *adj* : insaciable — **insatiably** [-bli] *adv*

inscribe [ɪn'skraɪb] *vt* **-scribed; -scribing 1** ENGRAVE : inscribir, grabar **2** ENROLL : inscribir **3** DEDICATE : dedicar (un libro)

inscription [ɪn'skrɪpʃən] *n* : inscripción *f* (en un monumento), dedicación *f* (en un libro), leyenda *f* (de una ilustración, etc.)

inscrutable [ɪn'skruːt̬əbəl] *adj* : inescrutable, misterioso — **inscrutably** [-bli] *adv*

inseam ['ɪn,siːm] *n* : entrepierna *f*

insect ['ɪn,sɛkt] *n* : insecto *m*

insecticidal [ɪn,sɛktə'saɪdəl] *adj* : insecticida

insecticide [ɪn'sɛktə,saɪd] *n* : insecticida *m*

insecure [,ɪnsɪ'kjʊr] *adj* : inseguro, poco seguro — **insecurely** *adv*

insecurely [,ɪnsɪ'kjʊrli] *adv* : inseguramente

insecurity [,ɪnsɪ'kjʊrət̬i] *n, pl* **-ties** : inseguridad *f*

inseminate [ɪn'sɛmə,neɪt] *vt* **-nated; -nating** : inseminar

insemination [ɪn,sɛmə'neɪʃən] *n* : inseminación *f*

insensibility [ɪn,sɛntsə'bɪlət̬i] *n, pl* **-ties** : insensibilidad *f*

insensible [ɪn'sɛntsəbəl] *adj* **1** UNCONSCIOUS : inconsciente, sin conocimiento **2** NUMB : insensible, entumecido **3** UNAWARE : inconsciente

insensitive [ɪn'sɛntsət̬ɪv] *adj* : insensible

insensitivity [ɪn,sɛntsə'tɪvət̬i] *n, pl* **-ties** : insensibilidad *f*

inseparable [ɪn'sɛpərəbəl] *adj* : inseparable

insert[1] [ɪn'sərt] *vt* **1** : insertar, introducir, poner, meter <insert your key in the lock : mete tu llave en la cerradura> **2** INTERPOLATE : interpolar, intercalar

insert² [ˈɪn,sərt] *n* **:** inserción *f,* hoja *f* insertada (en una revista, etc.)
insertion [ɪnˈsərʃən] *n* **:** inserción *f*
inset [ˈɪn,sɛt] *n* **:** página *f* intercalada (en un libro), entredós *m* (de encaje en la ropa)
inshore¹ [ˈɪnˈʃor] *adv* **:** hacia la costa
inshore² *adj* **:** cercano a la costa, costero <inshore fishing : pesca costera>
inside¹ [ɪnˈsaɪd, ˈɪn,saɪd] *adv* **:** adentro, dentro <to run inside : correr para adentro> <inside and out : por dentro y por fuera>
inside² *adj* **1 :** interior, de adentro, de dentro <the inside lane : el carril interior> **2 :** confidencial <inside information : información confidencial>
inside³ *n* **1 :** interior *m,* parte *f* de adentro **2 insides** *npl* BELLY, GUTS **:** tripas *fpl fam* **3 inside out :** al revés
inside⁴ *prep* **1** INTO **:** al interior de **2** WITHIN **:** dentro de **3** (*referring to time*) **:** en menos de <inside an hour : en menos de una hora>
inside of *prep* INSIDE **:** dentro de
insider [ɪnˈsaɪdər] *n* **:** persona *f* enterada
insidious [ɪnˈsɪdiəs] *adj* **:** insidioso — **insidiously** *adv*
insidiousness [ɪnˈsɪdiəsnəs] *n* **:** insidia *f*
insight [ˈɪn,saɪt] *n* **:** perspicacia *f,* penetración *f*
insightful [ɪnˈsaɪtfəl] *adj* **:** perspicaz
insignia [ɪnˈsɪgniə] *or* **insigne** [-,niː] *n, pl* **-nia** *or* **-nias :** insignia *f,* enseña *f*
insignificance [,ɪnsɪgˈnɪfɪkənts] *n* **:** insignificancia *f*
insignificant [,ɪnsɪgˈnɪfɪkənt] *adj* **:** insignificante
insincere [,ɪnsɪnˈsɪr] *adj* **:** insincero, poco sincero
insincerely [,ɪnsɪnˈsɪrli] *adv* **:** con poca sinceridad
insincerity [,ɪnsɪnˈsɛrəṯi, -ˈsɪr-] *n, pl* **-ties :** insinceridad *f*
insinuate [ɪnˈsɪnjʊ,eɪt] *vt* **-ated; -ating :** insinuar
insinuation [ɪn,sɪnjʊˈeɪʃən] *n* **:** insinuación *f*
insipid [ɪnˈsɪpəd] *adj* **:** insípido
insist [ɪnˈsɪst] *v* **:** insistir
insistence [ɪnˈsɪstənts] *n* **:** insistencia *f*
insistent [ɪnˈsɪstənt] *adj* **:** insistente — **insistently** *adv*
insofar as [,ɪnsoˈfɑræz] *conj* **:** en la medida en que, en tanto que, en cuanto a
insole [ˈɪn,soːl] *n* **:** plantilla *f*
insolence [ˈɪntsələnts] *n* **:** insolencia *f*
insolent [ˈɪntsələnt] *adj* **:** insolente
insolubility [ɪn,sɑljʊˈbɪləṯi] *n* **:** insolubilidad *f*
insoluble [ɪnˈsɑljʊbəl] *adj* **:** insoluble
insolvency [ɪnˈsɑlvəntsi] *n, pl* **-cies :** insolvencia *f*
insolvent [ɪnˈsɑlvənt] *adj* **:** insolvente
insomnia [ɪnˈsɑmniə] *n* **:** insomnio *m*
insomuch as [,ɪnsoˈmʌtʃæz] → **inasmuch as**
insomuch that *conj* SO **:** así que, de manera que
inspect [ɪnˈspɛkt] *vt* **:** inspeccionar, examinar, revisar
inspection [ɪnˈspɛkʃən] *n* **:** inspección *f,* examen *m,* revisión *f,* revista *f* (de tropas)
inspector [ɪnˈspɛktər] *n* **:** inspector *m,* -tora *f*
inspiration [,ɪntspəˈreɪʃən] *n* **:** inspiración *f*
inspirational [,ɪntspəˈreɪʃənəl] *adj* **:** inspirador
inspire [ɪnˈspaɪr] *v* **-spired; -spiring** *vt* **1** INHALE **:** inhalar, aspirar **2** STIMULATE **:** estimular, animar, inspirar **3** INSTILL **:** inspirar, infundir — *vi* **:** inspirar
instability [,ɪntstəˈbɪləṯi] *n, pl* **-ties :** inestabilidad *f*
install [ɪnˈstɔl] *vt* **-stalled; -stalling 1 :** instalar <to install the new president : instalar el presidente nuevo> <to install a fan : montar un abanico> **2 to install oneself :** instalarse
installation [,ɪntstəˈleɪʃən] *n* **:** instalación *f*
installment [ɪnˈstɔlmənt] *n* **1 :** plazo *m,* cuota *f* <to pay in four installments : pagar a cuatro plazos> **2 :** entrega *f* (de una publicación o telenovela) **3** INSTALLATION **:** instalación *f*
instance [ˈɪntstənts] *n* **1** INSTIGATION **:** instancia *f* **2** EXAMPLE **:** ejemplo *m* <for instance : por ejemplo> **3** OCCASION **:** instancia *f,* caso *m,* ocasión *f* <he prefers, in this instance, to remain anonymous : en este caso prefiere quedarse anónimo>
instant¹ [ˈɪntstənt] *adj* **1** IMMEDIATE **:** inmediato, instantáneo <an instant reply : una respuesta inmediata> **2 :** instantáneo <instant coffee : café instantáneo>
instant² *n* **:** momento *m,* instante *m*
instantaneous [,ɪntstənˈteɪniəs] *adj* **:** instantáneo
instantaneously [,ɪntstənˈteɪniəsli] *adv* **:** instantáneamente, al instante
instantly [ˈɪntstəntli] *adv* **:** al instante, instantáneamente
instead [ɪnˈstɛd] *adv* **1 :** en cambio, en lugar de eso, en su lugar <Dad was going, but Mom went instead : papá iba a ir, pero mamá fue en su lugar> **2** RATHER **:** al contrario
instead of *prep* **:** en vez de, en lugar de
instep [ˈɪn,stɛp] *n* **:** empeine *m*
instigate [ˈɪntstə,geɪt] *vt* **-gated; -gating** INCITE, PROVOKE **:** instigar, incitar, provocar, fomentar
instigation [,ɪntstəˈgeɪʃən] *n* **:** instancia *f,* incitación *f*
instigator [ˈɪntstə,geɪtər] *n* **:** instigador *m,* -dora *f;* incitador *m,* -dora *f*

instill [ɪn'stɪl] *vt* **-stilled; -stilling :** inculcar, infundir

instinct ['ɪn,stɪŋkt] *n* **1** TALENT **:** instinto *m,* don *m* <an instinct for the right word : un don para escoger la palabra apropiada> **2 :** instinto *m* <maternal instincts : instintos maternales>

instinctive [ɪn'stɪŋktɪv] *adj* **:** instintivo

instinctively [ɪn'stɪŋktɪvli] *adv* **:** instintivamente, por instinto

instinctual [ɪn'stɪŋktʃʊəl] *adj* **:** instintivo

institute[1] ['ɪn*t*stə,tu:t, -,tju:t] *vt* **-tuted; -tuting 1** ESTABLISH**:** establecer, instituir, fundar **2** INITIATE **:** iniciar, empezar, entablar

institute[2] *n* **:** instituto *m*

institution [,ɪn*t*stə'tu:ʃən, -'tju:-] *n* **1** ESTABLISHING **:** institución *f,* establecimiento *m* **2** CUSTOM **:** institución *f,* tradición *f* <the institution of marriage : la institución del matrimonio> **3** ORGANIZATION **:** institución *f,* organismo *m* **4** ASYLUM **:** asilo *m*

institutional [,ɪn*t*stə'tu:ʃənəl, -'tju:-] *adj* **:** institucional

institutionalize [,ɪn*t*stə'tu:ʃənə,laɪz, -'tju:-] *vt* **-ized; -izing 1 :** institucionalizar <institutionalized values : valores institucionalizados> **2 :** internar <institutionalized orphans : huérfanos internados>

instruct [ɪn'strʌkt] *vt* **1** TEACH, TRAIN **:** instruir, adiestrar, enseñar **2** COMMAND **:** mandar, ordenar, dar instrucciones a

instruction [ɪn'strʌkʃən] *n* **1** TEACHING **:** instrucción *f,* enseñanza *f* **2** COMMAND **:** orden *f,* instrucción *f* **3 instructions** *npl* DIRECTIONS **:** instrucciones *fpl,* modo *m* de empleo

instructional [ɪn'strʌkʃənəl] *adj* **:** instructivo, educativo

instructive [ɪn'strʌktɪv] *adj* **:** instructivo

instructor [ɪn'strʌktər] *n* **:** instructor *m,* -tora *f*

instrument ['ɪn*t*strəmənt] *n* **:** instrumento *m*

instrumental [,ɪn*t*strə'mɛntəl] *adj* **:** instrumental

instrumentalist [,ɪn*t*strə'mɛntəlɪst] *n* **:** instrumentista *mf*

insubordinate [,ɪnsə'bɔrdənət] *adj* **:** insubordinado

insubordination [,ɪnsə,bɔrdən'eɪʃən] *n* **:** insubordinación *f*

insubstantial [,ɪnsəb'stæntʃəl] *adj* **:** insustancial, poco nutritivo (dícese de una comida), poco sólido (dícese de una estructura o un argumento)

insufferable [ɪn'sʌfərəbəl] *adj* UNBEARABLE **:** insufrible, intolerable, inaguantable, insoportable — **insufferably** [-bli] *adv*

insufficiency [,ɪnsə'fɪʃən*t*si] *n, pl* **-cies :** insuficiencia *f*

insufficient [,ɪnsə'fɪʃənt] *adj* **:** insuficiente — **insufficiently** *adv*

insular ['ɪn*t*sʊlər, -sjʊ-] *adj* **1 :** isleño (dícese de la gente), insular (dícese del clima) <insular residents : residentes de la isla> **2** NARROW-MINDED **:** de miras estrechas

insularity [,ɪn*t*sʊ'lærət̬i, -sjʊ-] *n* **:** insularidad *f*

insulate ['ɪn*t*sə,leɪt] *vt* **-lated; -lating :** aislar

insulation [,ɪn*t*sə'leɪʃən] *n* **:** aislamiento *m*

insulator ['ɪn*t*sə,leɪt̬ər] *n* **:** aislante *m,* aislador *m*

insulin ['ɪn*t*sələn] *n* **:** insulina *f*

insult[1] [ɪn'sʌlt] *vt* **:** insultar, ofender, injuriar

insult[2] ['ɪn,sʌlt] *n* **:** insulto *m,* injuria *f,* agravio *m*

insulting [ɪn'sʌltɪŋ] *adj* **:** ofensivo, injurioso, insultante

insultingly [ɪn'sʌltɪŋli] *adv* **:** ofensivamente, de manera insultante

insuperable [ɪn'su:pərəbəl] *adj* **:** insuperable — **insuperably** [-bli] *adv*

insurable [ɪn'ʃʊrəbəl] *adj* **:** asegurable

insurance [ɪn'ʃʊrən*t*s, 'ɪn,ʃʊr-] *n* **:** seguro *m* <life insurance : seguro de vida> <insurance company : compañía de seguros>

insure [ɪn'ʃʊr] *vt* **-sured; -suring 1** UNDERWRITE **:** asegurar **2** ENSURE **:** asegurar, garantizar

insured [ɪn'ʃʊrd] *n* **:** asegurado *m,* -da *f*

insurer [ɪn'ʃʊrər] *n* **:** asegurador *m,* -dora *f*

insurgent[1] [ɪn'sərdʒənt] *adj* **:** insurgente

insurgent[2] *n* **:** insurgente *mf*

insurmountable [,ɪnsər'maʊntəbəl] *adj* **:** insuperable, insalvable — **insurmountably** [-bli] *adv*

insurrection [,ɪnsə'rɛkʃən] *n* **:** insurrección *f,* levantamiento *m,* alzamiento *m*

intact [ɪn'tækt] *adj* **:** intacto

intake ['ɪn,teɪk] *n* **1** OPENING **:** entrada *f,* toma *f* <fuel intake : toma de combustible> **2 :** entrada *f* (de agua o aire), consumo *m* (de sustancias nutritivas) **3 intake of breath :** inhalación *f*

intangible [ɪn'tændʒəbəl] *adj* **:** intangible, impalpable — **intangibly** [-bli] *adv*

integer ['ɪntɪdʒər] *n* **:** entero *m*

integral ['ɪntɪgrəl] *adj* **:** integral, esencial

integrate ['ɪntə,greɪt] *v* **-grated; -grating** *vt* **1** UNITE **:** integrar, unir **2** DESEGREGATE **:** eliminar la segregación de — *vi* **:** integrarse

integration [,ɪntə'greɪʃən] *n* **:** integración *f*

integrity [ɪn'tɛgrət̬i] *n* **:** integridad *f*

intellect ['ɪntəl,ɛkt] *n* **:** intelecto *m,* inteligencia *f,* capacidad *f* intelectual

intellectual[1] [ˌɪntəˈlɛktʃʊəl] *adj* : intelectual — **intellectually** *adv*
intellectual[2] *n* : intelectual *mf*
intellectualism [ˌɪntəˈlɛktʃʊəˌlɪzəm] *n* : intelectualismo *m*
intelligence [ɪnˈtɛlədʒən*t*s] *n* **1** : inteligencia *f* **2** INFORMATION, NEWS : inteligencia *f,* información *f,* noticias *fpl*
intelligent [ɪnˈtɛlədʒənt] *adj* : inteligente — **intelligently** *adv*
intelligibility [ɪnˌtɛlədʒəˈbɪləṭi] *n* : inteligibilidad *f*
intelligible [ɪnˈtɛlədʒəbəl] *adj* : inteligible, comprensible — **intelligibly** [-bli] *adv*
intemperance [ɪnˈtɛmpərən*t*s] *n* : inmoderación *f,* intemperancia *f*
intemperate [ɪnˈtɛmpərət] *adj* : excesivo, inmoderado, desmedido
intend [ɪnˈtɛnd] *vt* **1** MEAN : querer decir <that's not what I intended : eso no es lo que quería decir> **2** PLAN : tener planeado, proyectar, proponerse <I intend to finish by Thursday : me propongo acabar para el jueves>
intended [ɪnˈtɛndəd] *adj* **1** PLANNED : previsto, proyectado **2** INTENTIONAL : intencional, deliberado
intense [ɪnˈtɛn*t*s] *adj* **1** EXTREME : intenso, extremo <intense pain : dolor intenso> **2** : profundo, intenso <to my intense relief : para mi alivio profundo> <intense enthusiasm : entusiasmo ardiente>
intensely [ɪnˈtɛn*t*sli] *adv* : sumamente, profundamente, intensamente
intensification [ɪnˌtɛn*t*səfəˈkeɪʃən] *n* : intensificación *f*
intensify [ɪnˈtɛn*t*səˌfaɪ] *v* **-fied; -fying** *vt* **1** STRENGTHEN : intensificar, redoblar <to intensify one's efforts : redoblar uno sus esfuerzos> **2** SHARPEN : intensificar, agudizar (dolor, ansiedad) — *vi* : intensificarse, hacerse más intenso
intensity [ɪnˈtɛn*t*səṭi] *n, pl* **-ties** : intensidad *f*
intensive [ɪnˈtɛn*t*sɪv] *adj* : intensivo — **intensively** *adv*
intent[1] [ɪnˈtɛnt] *adj* **1** FIXED : concentrado, fijo <an intent stare : una mirada fija> **2 intent on** *or* **intent upon** : resuelto a, atento a
intent[2] *n* **1** PURPOSE : intención *f,* propósito *m* **2 for all intents and purposes** : a todos los efectos, prácticamente
intention [ɪnˈtɛntʃən] *n* : intención *f,* propósito *m*
intentional [ɪnˈtɛntʃənəl] *adj* : intencional, deliberado
intentionally [ɪnˈtɛntʃənəli] *adv* : a propósito, adrede
intently [ɪnˈtɛntli] *adv* : atentamente, fijamente
inter [ɪnˈtər] *vt* **-terred; -terring** : enterrar, inhumar
interact [ˌɪntərˈækt] *vi* : interactuar, actuar recíprocamente, relacionarse
interaction [ˌɪntərˈækʃən] *n* : interacción *f,* interrelación *f*
interactive [ˌɪntərˈæktɪv] *adj* : interactivo
interbreed [ˌɪntərˈbriːd] *v* **-bred** [-ˈbrɛd]; **-breeding** *vt* : cruzar — *vi* : cruzarse
intercalate [ɪnˈtərkəˌleɪt] *vt* **-lated; -lating** : intercalar
intercede [ˌɪntərˈsiːd] *vi* **-ceded; -ceding** : interceder
intercept [ˌɪntərˈsɛpt] *vt* : interceptar
interception [ˌɪntərˈsɛpʃən] *n* : intercepción *f*
intercession [ˌɪntərˈsɛʃən] *n* : intercesión *f*
interchange[1] [ˌɪntərˈtʃeɪndʒ] *vt* **-changed; -changing** : intercambiar
interchange[2] [ˈɪntərˌtʃeɪndʒ] *n* **1** EXCHANGE : intercambio *m,* cambio *m* **2** JUNCTION : empalme *m,* enlace *m* de carreteras
interchangeable [ˌɪntərˈtʃeɪndʒəəl] *adj* : intercambiable
intercity [ˈɪntərˈsɪṭi] *adj* : interurbano
intercollegiate [ˌɪntərkəˈliːdʒət, -dʒiət] *adj* : interuniversitario
intercontinental [ˌɪntərˌkɑntənˈɛntəl] *adj* : intercontinental
intercourse [ˈɪntərˌkors] *n* **1** RELATIONS : relaciones *fpl,* trato *m* **2** COPULATION : acto *m* sexual, relaciones *fpl* sexuales, coito *m*
interdenominational [ˌɪntərdɪˌnɑməˈneɪʃənəl] *adj* : interconfesional
interdepartmental [ˌɪntərdɪˌpɑrtˈmɛntəl, -ˌdiː-] *adj* : interdepartamental
interdependence [ˌɪntərdɪˈpɛndən*t*s] *n* : interdependencia *f*
interdependent [ˌɪntərdɪˈpɛndənt] *adj* : interdependiente
interdict [ˌɪntərˈdɪkt] *vt* **1** PROHIBIT : prohibir **2** : cortar (las líneas de comunicación o provisión del enemigo)
interest[1] [ˈɪntrəst, -təˌrɛst] *vt* : interesar
interest[2] *n* **1** SHARE, STAKE : interés *m,* participación *f* **2** BENEFIT : provecho *m,* beneficio *m,* interés *m* <in the public interest : en el interés público> **3** CHARGE : interés *m,* cargo *m* <compound interest : interés compuesto> **4** CURIOSITY : interés *m,* curiosidad *f* **5** COLOR : color *m,* interés *m* <places of local interest : lugares de color local> **6** HOBBY : afición *f*
interesting [ˈɪntrəstɪŋ, -təˌrɛstɪŋ] *adj* : interesante — **interestingly** *adv*
interface [ˈɪntərˌfeɪs] *n* **1** : punto *m* de contacto <oil-water interface : punto de contacto entre el agua y el aceite> **2** : interfase *f,* interfaz *f* (de una computadora)
interfere [ˌɪntərˈfɪr] *vi* **-fered; -fering** **1** INTERPOSE : interponerse, hacer in-

terferencia <to interfere with a play : obstruir una jugada> **2** MEDDLE : entrometerse, interferir, intervenir **3 to interfere with** DISRUPT : afectar (una actividad), interferir (la radiotransmisión) **4 to interfere with** TOUCH : tocar <someone interfered with my papers : alguien tocó mis papeles>

interference [ˌɪntərˈfɪrənts] *n* : interferencia *f,* intromisión *f*

intergalactic [ˌɪntərgəˈlæktɪk] *adj* : intergaláctico

intergovernmental [ˌɪntərˌgʌvərˈmɛntəl, -vərn-] *adj* : intergubernamental

interim[1] [ˈɪntərəm] *adj* : interino, provisional

interim[2] *n* **1** : interín *m,* intervalo *m* **2 in the interim** : en el interín, mientras tanto

interior[1] [ɪnˈtɪriər] *adj* : interior

interior[2] *n* : interior *m*

interject [ˌɪntərˈdʒɛkt] *vt* : interponer, agregar

interjection [ˌɪntərˈdʒɛkʃən] *n* **1** : interjección *f* (en lingüística) **2** EXCLAMATION : exclamación *f* **3** INTERPOSITION, INTERRUPTION : interposición *f,* interrupción *f*

interlace [ˌɪntərˈleɪs] *vt* **-laced; -lacing 1** INTERWEAVE : entrelazar **2** INTERSPERSE : intercalar

interlock [ˌɪntərˈlɑk] *vt* **1** UNITE : trabar, unir **2** ENGAGE, MESH : engranar — *vi* : entrelazarse, trabarse

interloper [ˌɪntərˈloːpər] *n* **1** INTRUDER : intruso *m,* -sa *f* **2** MEDDLER : entrometido *m,* -da *f*

interlude [ˈɪntərˌluːd] *n* **1** INTERVAL : intervalo *m,* intermedio *m* (en el teatro) **2** : interludio *m* (en música)

intermarriage [ˌɪntərˈmærɪdʒ] *n* **1** : matrimonio *m* mixto (entre miembros de distintas razas o religiones) **2** : matrimonio *m* entre miembros del mismo grupo

intermarry [ˌɪntərˈmæri] *vi* **-married; -marrying 1** : casarse (con miembros de otros grupos) **2** : casarse entre sí (con miembros del mismo grupo)

intermediary[1] [ˌɪntərˈmiːdiˌɛri] *adj* : intermediario

intermediary[2] *n, pl* **-aries** : intermediario *m,* -ria *f*

intermediate[1] [ˌɪntərˈmiːdiət] *adj* : intermedio

intermediate[2] *n* GO-BETWEEN : intermediario *m,* -ria *f;* mediador *m,* -dora *f*

interment [ɪnˈtərmənt] *n* : entierro *m*

interminable [ɪnˈtərmənəbəl] *adj* : interminable, constante — **interminably** [-bli] *adv*

intermingle [ˌɪntərˈmɪŋgəl] *vt* **-mingled; -mingling** : entremezclar, mezclar — *vi* : entremezclarse

intermission [ˌɪntərˈmɪʃən] *n* : intermisión *f,* intervalo *m,* intermedio *m*

intermittent [ˌɪntərˈmɪtənt] *adj* : intermitente — **intermittently** *adv*

intermix [ˌɪntərˈmɪks] *vt* : entremezclar

intern[1] [ˈɪnˌtərn, ɪnˈtərn] *vt* : confinar (durante la guerra) — *vi* : servir de interno, hacer las prácticas

intern[2] [ˈɪnˌtərn] *n* : interno *m,* -na *f*

internal [ɪnˈtərnəl] *adj* : interno, interior <internal bleeding : hemorragia interna> <internal affairs : asuntos interiores, asuntos domésticos> — **internally** *adv*

international [ˌɪntərˈnæʃənəl] *adj* : internacional — **internationally** *adv*

internationalize [ˌɪntərˈnæʃənəˌlaɪz] *vt* **-ized; -izing** : internacionalizar

internee [ˌɪnˌtərˈniː] *n* : interno *m,* -na *f*

internist [ˈɪnˌtərnɪst] *n* : internista *mf*

interpersonal [ˌɪntərˈpərsənəl] *adj* : interpersonal

interplay [ˈɪntərˌpleɪ] *n* : interacción *f,* juego *m*

interpolate [ɪnˈtərpəˌleɪt] *vt* **-lated; -lating** : interpolar

interpose [ˌɪntərˈpoːz] *v* **-posed; -posing** *vt* : interponer, interrumpir con — *vi* : interponerse

interposition [ˌɪntərpəˈzɪʃən] *n* : interposición *f*

interpret [ɪnˈtərprət] *vt* : interpretar

interpretation [ɪnˌtərprəˈteɪʃən] *n* : interpretación *f*

interpretative [ɪnˈtərprəˌteɪt̬ɪv] *adj* : interpretativo

interpreter [ɪnˈtərprət̬ər] *n* : intérprete *mf*

interpretive [ɪnˈtərprət̬ɪv] *adj* : interpretativo

interracial [ˌɪntərˈreɪʃəl] *adj* : interracial

interrelate [ˌɪntərɪˈleɪt] *vi* **-related; -relating** : interelacionar

interrelationship [ˌɪntərɪˈleɪʃənˌʃɪp] *n* : interrelación *f*

interrogate [ɪnˈtɛrəˌgeɪt] *vt* **-gated; -gating** : interrogar, someter a un interrogatorio

interrogation [ɪnˌtɛrəˈgeɪʃən] *n* : interrogación *f*

interrogative[1] [ˌɪntəˈrɑgət̬ɪv] *adj* : interrogativo

interrogative[2] *n* : interrogativo *m*

interrogator [ɪnˈtɛrəˌgeɪt̬ər] *n* : interrogador *m,* -dora *f*

interrogatory [ˌɪntəˈrɑgəˌtori] → **interrogative[1]**

interrupt [ˌɪntəˈrʌpt] *v* : interrumpir

interruption [ˌɪntəˈrʌpʃən] *n* : interrupción *f*

intersect [ˌɪntərˈsɛkt] *vt* : cruzar, cortar — *vi* : cruzarse (dícese de los caminos), intersectarse (dícese de las líneas o figuras), cortarse

intersection [ˌɪntərˈsɛkʃən] *n* : intersección *f,* cruce *m*

intersperse [ˌɪntərˈspərs] *vt* **-spersed; -spersing** : intercalar, entremezclar

interstate [ˌɪntərˈsteɪt] *adj* : interestatal

interstellar [ˌɪntərˈstɛlər] *adj* : interestelar

interstice [ɪnˈtərstəs] *n, pl* **-stices** [-stəˌsiːz, -stəsəz] : intersticio *m*

intertwine [ˌɪntərˈtwaɪn] *vi* **-twined; -twining** : entrelazarse

interval [ˈɪntərvəl] *n* : intervalo *m*

intervene [ˌɪntərˈviːn] *vi* **-vened; -vening 1** ELAPSE : transcurrir, pasar <the intervening years : los años intermediarios> **2** INTERCEDE : intervenir, interceder, mediar

intervention [ˌɪntərˈvɛntʃən] *n* : intervención *f*

interview¹ [ˈɪntərˌvjuː] *vt* : entrevistar — *vi* : hacer entrevistas

interview² *n* : entrevista *f*

interviewer [ˈɪntərˌvjuːər] *n* : entrevistador *m,* -dora *f*

interweave [ˌɪntərˈwiːv] *v* **-wove** [-ˈwoːv]; **-woven** [-ˈwoːvən]; **-weaving** *vt* : entretejer, entrelazar — *vi* INTERTWINE : entrelazarse, entretejerse

interwoven [ˌɪntərˈwoːvən] *adj* : entretejido

intestate [ɪnˈtɛsˌteɪt, -tət] *adj* : intestado

intestinal [ɪnˈtɛstənəl] *adj* : intestinal

intestine [ɪnˈtɛstən] *n* **1** : intestino *m* **2 small intestine** : intestino *m* delgado **3 large intestine** : intestino *m* grueso

intimacy [ˈɪntəməsi] *n, pl* **-cies 1** CLOSENESS : intimidad *f* **2** FAMILIARITY : familiaridad *f*

intimate¹ [ˈɪntəˌmeɪt] *vt* **-mated; -mating** : insinuar, dar a entender

intimate² [ˈɪntəmət] *adj* **1** CLOSE : íntimo, de confianza <intimate friends : amigos íntimos> **2** PRIVATE : íntimo, privado <intimate clubs : clubes íntimos> **3** INNERMOST, SECRET : íntimo, secreto <intimate fantasies : fantasías secretas>

intimate³ *n* : amigo *m* íntimo, amiga *f* íntima

intimidate [ɪnˈtɪməˌdeɪt] *vt* **-dated; -dating** : intimidar

intimidation [ɪnˌtɪməˈdeɪʃən] *n* : intimidación *f*

into [ˈɪnˌtuː] *prep* **1** (*indicating motion*) : en, a, contra, dentro de <she got into bed : se metió en la cama> <to get into a plane : subir a un avión> <he crashed into the wall : chocó contra la pared> <looking into the sun : mirando al sol> **2** (*indicating state or condition*) : a, en <to burst into tears : echarse a llorar> <the water turned into ice : el agua se convirtió en hielo> <to translate into English : traducir al inglés> **3** (*indicating time*) <far into the night : hasta bien entrada la noche> <he's well into his eighties : tiene los ochenta bien cumplidos> **4** (*in mathematics*) <3 into 12 is 4 : 12 dividido por 3 es 4>

intolerable [ɪnˈtɑlərəbəl] *adj* : intolerable — **intolerably** [-bli] *adv*

intolerance [ɪnˈtɑlərənts] *n* : intolerancia *f*

intolerant [ɪnˈtɑlərənt] *adj* : intolerante

intonation [ˌɪntoˈneɪʃən] *n* : intonación *f*

intone [ɪnˈtoːn] *vt* **-toned; -toning** : entonar

intoxicant [ɪnˈtɑksɪkənt] *n* : bebida *f* alcohólica

intoxicate [ɪnˈtɑksəˌkeɪt] *vt* **-cated; -cating** : emborrachar, embriagar

intoxicated [ɪnˈtɑksəˌkeɪt̬əd] *adj* : borracho, embriagado

intoxicating [ɪnˈtɑksəˌkeɪt̬ɪŋ] *adj* : embriagador

intoxication [ɪnˌtɑksəˈkeɪʃən] *n* : embriaguez *f*

intractable [ɪnˈtræktəbəl] *adj* : obstinado, intratable

intramural [ˌɪntrəˈmjʊrəl] *adj* : interno, dentro de la universidad

intransigence [ɪnˈtræntsədʒənts, -ˈtrænzə-] *n* : intransigencia *f*

intransigent [ɪnˈtræntsədʒənt, -ˈtrænzə-] *adj* : intransigente

intravenous [ˌɪntrəˈviːnəs] *adj* : intravenoso — **intravenously** *adv*

intrepid [ɪnˈtrɛpəd] *adj* : intrépido

intricacy [ˈɪntrɪkəsi] *n, pl* **-cies** : complejidad *f,* lo intrincado

intricate [ˈɪntrɪkət] *adj* : intrincado, complicado — **intricately** *adv*

intrigue¹ [ɪnˈtriːg] *v* **-trigued; -triguing** : intrigar

intrigue² [ˈɪnˌtriːg, ɪnˈtriːg] *n* : intriga *f*

intriguing [ɪnˈtriːgɪŋli] *adj* : intrigante, fascinante

intrinsic [ɪnˈtrɪnzɪk, -ˈtrɪntsɪk] *adj* : intrínseco, esencial — **intrinsically** [-zɪkli, -sɪ-] *adv*

introduce [ˌɪntrəˈduːs, -ˈdjuːs] *vt* **-duced; -ducing 1** : presentar <let me introduce my father : permítame presentar a mi padre> **2** : introducir (algo nuevo), lanzar (un producto), presentar (una ley), proponer (una idea o un tema)

introduction [ˌɪntrəˈdʌkʃən] *n* : introducción *f,* presentación *f*

introductory [ˌɪntrəˈdʌktəri] *adj* : introductorio, preliminar, de introducción

introspection [ˌɪntrəˈspɛkʃən] *n* : introspección *f*

introspective [ˌɪntrəˈspɛktɪv] *adj* : introspectivo — **introspectively** *adv*

introvert [ˈɪntrəˌvərt] *n* : introvertido *m,* -da *f*

introverted [ˈɪntrəˌvərt̬əd] *adj* : introvertido

intrude [ɪnˈtruːd] *v* **-truded; -truding** *vi* **1** INTERFERE : inmiscuirse, entrometerse **2** DISTURB, INTERRUPT : molestar, estorbar, interrumpir — *vt* : introducir por fuerza

intruder [ɪnˈtruːdər] *n* **:** intruso *m,* -sa *f*

intrusion [ɪnˈtruːʒən] *n* **:** intrusión *f*

intrusive [ɪnˈtruːsɪv] *adj* **:** intruso

intuit [ɪnˈtuːɪt, -ˈtjuː-] *vt* **:** intuir

intuition [ˌɪntʊˈɪʃən, -tjʊ-] *n* **:** intuición *f*

intuitive [ɪnˈtuːətɪv, -ˈtjuː-] *adj* **:** intuitivo — **intuitively** *adv*

inundate [ˈɪnənˌdeɪt] *vt* **-dated; -dating :** inundar

inundation [ˌɪnənˈdeɪʃən] *n* **:** inundación *f*

inure [ɪˈnʊr, -ˈnjʊr] *vt* **-ured; -uring :** acostumbrar, habituar

invade [ɪnˈveɪd] *vt* **-vaded; -vading :** invadir

invader [ɪnˈveɪdər] *n* **:** invasor *m,* -sora *f*

invalid[1] [ɪnˈvæləd] *adj* **:** inválido, nulo

invalid[2] [ˈɪnvələd] *adj* **:** inválido, discapacitado

invalid[3] [ˈɪnvələd] *n* **:** inválido *m,* -da *f*

invalidate [ɪnˈvæləˌdeɪt] *vt* **-dated; -dating :** invalidar

invalidity [ˌɪnvəˈlɪdəti] *n, pl* **-ties :** invalidez *f,* falta de validez *f*

invaluable [ɪnˈvæljəbəl, -ˈvæljʊə-] *adj* **:** invalorable, inestimable, inapreciable

invariable [ɪnˈværiəbəl] *adj* **:** invariable, constante — **invariably** [-bli] *adv*

invasion [ɪnˈveɪʒən] *n* **:** invasión *f*

invasive [ɪnˈveɪsɪv] *adj* **:** invasivo

invective [ɪnˈvɛktɪv] *n* **:** invectiva *f,* improperio *m,* vituperio *m*

inveigh [ɪnˈveɪ] *vi* **to inveigh against :** arremeter contra, lanzar invectivas contra

inveigle [ɪnˈveɪgəl, -ˈviː-] *vt* **-gled; -gling :** engatusar, embaucar, persuadir con engaños

invent [ɪnˈvɛnt] *vt* **:** inventar

invention [ɪnˈvɛntʃən] *n* **:** invención *f,* invento *m*

inventive [ɪnˈvɛntɪv] *adj* **:** inventivo

inventiveness [ɪnˈvɛntɪvnəs] *n* **:** ingenio *m,* inventiva *f*

inventor [ɪnˈvɛntər] *n* **:** inventor *m,* -tora *f*

inventory[1] [ˈɪnvənˌtɔri] *vt* **-ried; -rying :** inventariar

inventory[2] *n, pl* **-ries 1** LIST **:** inventario *m* **2** STOCK **:** existencias *fpl*

inverse[1] [ɪnˈvərs, ˈɪnˌvərs] *adj* **:** inverso — **inversely** *adv*

inverse[2] *n* **:** inverso *m*

inversion [ɪnˈvərʒən] *n* **:** inversión *f*

invert [ɪnˈvərt] *vt* **:** invertir

invertebrate[1] [ɪnˈvərtəbrət, -ˌbreɪt] *adj* **:** invertebrado

invertebrate[2] *n* **:** invertebrado *m*

invest [ɪnˈvɛst] *vt* **1** AUTHORIZE **:** investir, autorizar **2** CONFER **:** conferir **3 :** invertir, dedicar <he invested his savings in stocks : invirtió sus ahorros en acciones> <to invest one's time : dedicar uno su tiempo>

investigate [ɪnˈvɛstəˌgeɪt] *v* **-gated; -gating :** investigar

investigation [ɪnˌvɛstəˈgeɪʃən] *n* **:** investigación *f,* estudio *m*

investigative [ɪnˈvɛstəˌgeɪtɪv] *adj* **:** investigador

investigator [ɪnˈvɛstəˌgeɪtər] *n* **:** investigador *m,* -dora *f*

investiture [ɪnˈvɛstəˌtʃʊr, -tʃər] *n* **:** investidura *f*

investment [ɪnˈvɛstmənt] *n* **:** inversión *f*

investor [ɪnˈvɛstər] *n* **:** inversor *m,* -sora *f;* inversionista *mf*

inveterate [ɪnˈvɛtərət] *adj* **1** DEEP-SEATED **:** inveterado, enraizado **2** HABITUAL **:** empedernido, incorregible

invidious [ɪnˈvɪdiəs] *adj* **1** OBNOXIOUS **:** repugnante, odioso **2** UNJUST **:** injusto — **invidiously** *adv*

invigorate [ɪnˈvɪgəˌreɪt] *vt* **-rated; -rating :** vigorizar, animar

invigorating [ɪnˈvɪgəˌreɪtɪŋ] *adj* **:** vigorizante, estimulante

invigoration [ɪnˌvɪgəˈreɪʃən] *n* **:** animación *f*

invincibility [ɪnˌvɪntsəˈbɪləti] *n* **:** invencibilidad *f*

invincible [ɪnˈvɪntsəbəl] *adj* **:** invencible — **invincibly** [-bli] *adv*

inviolable [ɪnˈvaɪələbəl] *adj* **:** inviolable

inviolate [ɪnˈvaɪələt] *adj* **:** inviolado, puro

invisibility [ɪnˌvɪzəˈbɪləti] *n* **:** invisibilidad *f*

invisible [ɪnˈvɪzəbəl] *adj* **:** invisible — **invisibly** [-bli] *adv*

invitation [ˌɪnvəˈteɪʃən] *n* **:** invitación *f*

invite [ɪnˈvaɪt] *vt* **-vited; -viting 1** ATTRACT **:** atraer, tentar <a book that invites interest : un libro que atrae el interés> **2** PROVOKE **:** provocar, buscar <to invite trouble : buscarse problemas> **3** ASK **:** invitar <we invited them for dinner : los invitamos a cenar> **4** SOLICIT **:** solicitar, buscar (preguntas, comentarios, etc.)

inviting [ɪnˈvaɪtɪŋ] *adj* **:** atractivo, atrayente

invocation [ˌɪnvəˈkeɪʃən] *n* **:** invocación *f*

invoice[1] [ˈɪnˌvɔɪs] *vt* **-voiced; -voicing :** facturar

invoice[2] *n* **:** factura *f*

invoke [ɪnˈvoːk] *vt* **-voked; -voking 1 :** invocar, apelar a <she invoked our aid : apeló a nuestra ayuda> **2** CITE **:** invocar, citar <to invoke a precedent : invocar un precedente> **3** CONJURE UP **:** hacer aparecer, invocar

involuntary [ɪnˈvɑlənˌtɛri] *adj* **:** involuntario — **involuntarily** [ɪnˌvɑlənˈtɛrəli] *adv*

involve [ɪn'vɑlv] *vt* **-volved; -volving** **1** ENGAGE : ocupar <workers involved in construction : trabajadores ocupados con la construcción> **2** IMPLICATE : involucrar, enredar, implicar <to be involved in a crime : estar involucrado en un crimen> **3** CONCERN : concernir, afectar **4** CONNECT : conectar, relacionar **5** ENTAIL, INCLUDE : suponer, incluir, consistir en <what does the job involve? : ¿en qué consiste el trabajo?> **6 to be involved with someone** : tener una relación (amorosa) con alguien

involved [ɪn'vɑlvd] *adj* **1** COMPLEX, INTRICATE : complicado, complejo, enrevesado **2** CONCERNED : interesado, afectado

involvement [ɪn'vɑlvmənt] *n* **1** PARTICIPATION : participación *f,* complicidad *f* **2** RELATIONSHIP : relación *f*

invulnerable [ɪn'vʌlnərəbəl] *adj* : invulnerable

inward[1] ['ɪnwərd] *or* **inwards** [-wərdz] *adv* : hacia adentro, hacia el interior

inward[2] *adj* INSIDE : interior, interno

inwardly ['ɪnwərdli] *adv* **1** MENTALLY, SPIRITUALLY : por dentro **2** INTERNALLY : internamente, interiormente **3** PRIVATELY : para sus adentros, para sí

iodide ['aɪə,daɪd] *n* : yoduro *m*

iodine ['aɪə,daɪn, -dən] *n* : yodo *m,* tintura *f* de yodo

iodize ['aɪə,daɪz] *vt* **-dized; -dizing** : yodar

ion ['aɪən, 'aɪ,ɑn] *n* : ion *m*

ionic [aɪ'ɑnɪk] *adj* : iónico

ionize ['aɪə,naɪz] *v* **ionized; ionizing** : ionizar

ionosphere [aɪ'ɑnə,sfɪr] *n* : ionosfera *f*

iota [aɪ'oːt̬ə] *n* : pizca *f,* ápice *m*

IOU [,aɪ,o'juː] *n* : pagaré *m,* vale *m*

Iranian [ɪ'reɪniən, -'ræ-, -'rɑ-; aɪ'-] *n* : iraní *mf* — **Iranian** *adj*

Iraqi [ɪ'rakiː] *n* : iraquí *mf* — **Iraqi** *adj*

irascibility [ɪ,ræsə'bɪlət̬i] *n* : irascibilidad *f*

irascible [ɪ'ræsəbəl] *adj* : irascible

irate [aɪ'reɪt] *adj* : furioso, airado, iracundo — **irately** *adv*

ire ['aɪr] *n* : ira *f,* cólera *f*

iridescence [,ɪrə'dɛsənts] *n* : iridiscencia *f*

iridescent [,ɪrə'dɛsənt] *adj* : iridiscente

iris ['aɪrəs] *n, pl* **irises** *or* **irides** ['aɪrə,diːz, 'ɪr-] **1** : iris *m* (del ojo) **2** : lirio *m* (planta)

Irish[1] ['aɪrɪʃ] *adj* : irlandés

Irish[2] **1** : irlandés *m* (idioma) **2 the Irish** *npl* : los irlandeses

Irishman ['aɪrɪʃmən] *n* : irlandés *m*

Irishwoman ['aɪrɪʃ,wʊmən] *n* : irlandesa *f*

irk ['ərk] *vt* : fastidiar, irritar, preocupar

irksome ['ərksəm] *adj* : irritante, fastidioso — **irksomely** *adv*

iron[1] ['aɪərn] *v* : planchar

iron[2] *n* **1** : hierro *m,* fierro *m* <a will of iron : una voluntad de hierro, una voluntad férrea> **2** : plancha *f* (para planchar la ropa)

ironclad ['aɪərn'klæd] *adj* **1** : acorazado, blindado **2** STRICT : riguroso, estricto

ironic [aɪ'rɑnɪk] *or* **ironical** [-nɪkəl] *adj* : irónico — **ironically** [-kli] *adv*

ironing ['aɪərnɪŋ] *n* **1** PRESSING : planchada *f* **2** : ropa *f* para planchar

ironing board *n* : tabla *f* (de planchar)

ironwork ['aɪərn,wərk] *n* **1** : obra *f* de hierro **2 ironworks** *npl* : fundición *f*

ironworker ['aɪərn,wərkər] *n* : fundidor *m,* -dora *f*

irony ['aɪrəni] *n, pl* **-nies** : ironía *f*

irradiate [ɪ'reɪdi,eɪt] *vt* **-ated; -ating** : irradiar, radiar

irradiation [ɪ,reɪdi'eɪʃən] *n* : irradiación *f,* radiación *f*

irrational [ɪ'ræʃənəl] *adj* : irracional — **irrationally** *adv*

irrationality [ɪ,ræʃə'nælət̬i] *n, pl* **-ties** : irracionalidad *f*

irreconcilable [ɪ,rɛkən'saɪləbəl] *adj* : irreconciliable

irrecoverable [,ɪrɪ'kʌvərəbəl] *adj* : irrecuperable — **irrecoverably** [-bli] *adv*

irredeemable [,ɪrɪ'diːməbəl] *adj* **1** : irredimible (dícese de un bono) **2** HOPELESS : irremediable, irreparable

irreducible [,ɪrɪ'duːsəbəl, -'djuː-] *adj* : irreducible — **irreducibly** [-bli] *adv*

irrefutable [,ɪrɪ'fjuːt̬əbəl, ɪr'rɛfjə-] *adj* : irrefutable

irregular[1] [ɪ'rɛgjələr] *adj* : irregular — **irregularly** *adv*

irregular[2] *n* **1** : soldado *m* irregular **2 irregulars** *npl* : artículos *mpl* defectuosos

irregularity [ɪ,rɛgjə'lærət̬i] *n, pl* **-ties** : irregularidad *f*

irrelevance [ɪ'rɛləvənts] *n* : irrelevancia *f*

irrelevant [ɪ'rɛləvənt] *adj* : irrelevante

irreligious [,ɪrɪ'lɪdʒəs] *adj* : irreligioso

irreparable [ɪ'rɛpərəbəl] *adj* : irreparable

irreplaceable [,ɪrɪ'pleɪsəbəl] *adj* : irreemplazable, insustituible

irrepressible [,ɪrɪ'prɛsəbəl] *adj* : incontenible, incontrolable

irreproachable [ɪrɪ'proːtʃəbəl] *adj* : irreprochable, intachable

irresistible [,ɪrɪ'zɪstəbəl] *adj* : irresistible — **irresistibly** [-bli] *adv*

irresolute [ɪ'rɛzə,luːt] *adj* : irresoluto, indeciso

irresolutely [ɪ'rɛzə,luːtli, -,rɛzə'luːt-] *adv* : de manera indecisa

irresolution [ɪ,rɛzə'luːʃən] *n* : irresolución *f*

irrespective of [ˌɪrɪˈspɛktɪvəv] *prep* : sin tomar en consideración, sin tener en cuenta
irresponsibility [ˌɪrɪˌspɑntsəˈbɪləṭi] *n, pl* **-ties** : irresponsabilidad *f,* falta *f* de responsabilidad
irresponsible [ˌɪrɪˈspɑntsəbəl] *adj* : irresponsable — **irresponsibly** [-bli] *adv*
irretrievable [ˌɪrɪˈtriːvəbəl] *adj* IRRECOVERABLE : irrecuperable
irreverence [ɪˈrɛvərənts] *n* : irreverencia *f,* falta *f* de respeto
irreverent [ɪˈrɛvərənt] *adj* : irreverente, irrespetuoso
irreversible [ˌɪrɪˈvərsəbəl] *adj* : irreversible
irrevocable [ɪˈrɛvəkəbəl] *adj* : irrevocable — **irrevocably** [-bli] *adv*
irrigate [ˈɪrəˌgeɪt] *vt* **-gated; -gating** : irrigar, regar
irrigation [ˌɪrəˈgeɪʃən] *n* : irrigación *f,* riego *m*
irritability [ˌɪrəṭəˈbɪləṭi] *n, pl* **-ties** : irritabilidad *f*
irritable [ˈɪrəṭəbəl] *adj* : irritable, colérico
irritably [ˈɪrəṭəbli] *adv* : con irritación
irritant¹ [ˈɪrəṭənt] *adj* : irritante
irritant² *n* : agente *m* irritante
irritate [ˈɪrəˌteɪt] *vt* **-tated; -tating 1** ANNOY : irritar, molestar **2** : irritar (en medicina)
irritating [ˈɪrəˌteɪṭɪŋ] *adj* : irritante
irritatingly [ˈɪrəˌteɪṭɪŋli] *adv* : de modo irritante, fastidiosamente
irritation [ˌɪrəˈteɪʃən] *n* : irritación *f*
is → **be**
Islam [ɪsˈlɑm, ɪz-, -ˈlæm; ˈɪsˌlɑm, ˈɪz-, -ˌlæm] *n* : el Islam
Islamic [ɪsˈlɑmɪk, ɪz-, -ˈlæ-] *adj* : islámico
island [ˈaɪlənd] *n* : isla *f*
islander [ˈaɪləndər] *n* : isleño *m,* -ña *f*
isle [ˈaɪl] *n* : isla *f,* islote *m*
islet [ˈaɪlət] *n* : islote *m*
isolate [ˈaɪsəˌleɪt] *vt* **-lated; -lating** : aislar
isolated [ˈaɪsəˌleɪṭəd] *adj* : aislado, solo
isolation [ˌaɪsəˈleɪʃən] *n* : aislamiento *m*
isometric [ˌaɪsəˈmɛtrɪk] *adj* : isométrico
isometrics [ˌaɪsəˈmɛtrɪks] *ns & pl* : isometría *f*
isosceles [aɪˈsɑsəˌliːz] *adj* : isósceles
isotope [ˈaɪsəˌtoːp] *n* : isótopo *m*
Israeli [ɪzˈreɪli] *n* : israelí *mf* — **Israeli** *adj*
issue¹ [ˈɪˌʃuː] *v* **-sued; -suing** *vi* **1** EMERGE : emerger, salir, fluir **2** DESCEND : descender (dícese de los padres o antepasados específicos) **3** EMANATE, RESULT : emanar, surgir, resultar — *vt* **1** EMIT : emitir **2** DISTRIBUTE : emitir, distribuir <to issue a new stamp : emitir un sello nuevo> **3** PUBLISH : publicar
issue² *n* **1** EMERGENCE, FLOW : emergencia *f,* flujo *m* **2** PROGENY : descendencia *f,* progenie *f* **3** OUTCOME, RESULT : desenlace *m,* resultado *m,* consecuencia *f* **4** MATTER, QUESTION : asunto *m,* cuestión *f* **5** PUBLICATION : publicación *f,* distribución *f,* emisión *f* **6** : número *m* (de un periódico o una revista)
isthmus [ˈɪsməs] *n* : istmo *m*
it [ˈɪt] *pron* **1** (*as subject; generally omitted*) : él, ella, ello <it's a big building : es un edificio grande> <who was it? : ¿quién era?> **2** (*as indirect object*) : le <I'll give it some water : voy a darle agua> **3** (*as direct object*) : lo, la <give it to me : dámelo> **4** (*as object of a preposition; generally omitted*) : él, ella, ello <behind it : detrás, detrás de él> **5** (*in impersonal constructions*) <it's raining : está lloviendo> <it's 8 o'clock : son las ocho> **6** (*as the implied subject or object of a verb*) <it is necessary to study : es necesario estudiar> <to give it all one's got : dar lo mejor de sí>
Italian [ɪˈtæliən, aɪ-] *n* **1** : italiano *m,* -na *f* **2** : italiano *m* (idioma) — **Italian** *adj*
italic¹ [ɪˈtælɪk, aɪ-] *adj* : en cursiva, en bastardilla
italic² *n* : cursiva *f,* bastardilla *f*
italicize [ɪˈtæləˌsaɪz, aɪ-] *vt* **-cized; -cizing** : poner en cursiva
itch¹ [ˈɪtʃ] *vi* **1** : picar <her arm itched : le pica el brazo> **2** : morirse <they were itching to go outside : se morían por salir> — *vt* : dar picazón, hacer picar
itch² *n* **1** ITCHING : picazón *f,* picor *m,* comezón *f* **2** RASH : sarpullido *m,* erupción *f* **3** DESIRE : ansia *f,* deseo *m*
itchy [ˈɪtʃi] *adj* **itchier; -est** : que pica, que da comezón
it'd [ˈɪṭəd] (*contraction of* **it had** *or* **it would**) → **have, would**
item [ˈaɪṭəm] *n* **1** OBJECT : artículo *m,* pieza *f* <item of clothing : prenda de vestir> **2** : punto *m* (en una agenda), número *m* (en el teatro), ítem *m* (en un documento) **3 news item** : noticia *f*
itemize [ˈaɪṭəˌmaɪz] *vt* **-ized; -izing** : detallar, enumerar, listar
itinerant [aɪˈtɪnərənt] *adj* : itinerante, ambulante
itinerary [aɪˈtɪnəˌrɛri] *n, pl* **-aries** : itinerario *m*
it'll [ˈɪṭəl] (*contraction of* **it shall** *or* **it will**) → **shall, will**
its [ˈɪts] *adj* : su, sus <its kennel : su perrera> <a city and its inhabitants : una ciudad y sus habitantes>
it's [ˈɪts] (*contraction of* **it is** *or* **it has**) → **be, have**
itself [ɪtˈsɛlf] *pron* **1** (*used reflexively*) : se <the cat gave itself a bath : el gato se bañó> **2** (*used for emphasis*) : (él) mismo, (ella) misma, sí (mismo), solo <he is courtesy itself : es la misma cortesía> <in and of itself : por sí

mismo> <it opened by itself : se abrió solo>

I've ['aɪv] (*contraction of* **I have**) → **have**

ivory ['aɪvəri] *n, pl* **-ries 1 :** marfil *m* **2 :** color *m* de marfil

ivy ['aɪvi] *n, pl* **ivies 1 :** hiedra *f,* yedra *f* **2** → **poison ivy**

J

j ['dʒeɪ] *n, pl* **j's** *or* **js** ['dʒeɪz] **:** décima letra del alfabeto inglés

jab[1] ['dʒæb] *v* **jabbed; jabbing** *vt* **1** PUNCTURE **:** clavar, pinchar **2** POKE **:** dar, golpear (con la punta de algo) <he jabbed me in the ribs : me dio un codazo en las costillas> — *vi* **to jab at :** dar, golpear

jab[2] *n* **1** PRICK **:** pinchazo *m* **2** POKE **:** golpe *m* abrupto

jabber[1] ['dʒæbər] *v* **:** farfullar

jabber[2] *n* **:** galimatías *m,* farfulla *f*

jack[1] ['dʒæk] *vt* **to jack up 1 :** levantar (con un gato) **2** INCREASE **:** subir, aumentar

jack[2] *n* **1 :** gato *m,* cric *m* <hydraulic jack : gato hidráulico> **2** FLAG **:** pabellón *m* **3** SOCKET **:** enchufe *m* hembra **4 :** jota *f,* valet *m* <jack of hearts : jota de corazones> **5 jacks** *npl* **:** cantillos *mpl*

jackal ['dʒækəl] *n* **:** chacal *m*

jackass ['dʒæk,æs] *n* **:** asno *m,* burro *m*

jacket ['dʒækət] *n* **1 :** chaqueta *f* **2** COVER **:** sobrecubierta *f* (de un libro), carátula *f* (de un disco)

jackhammer ['dʒæk,hæmər] *n* **:** martillo *m* neumático

jack–in–the–box ['dʒækɪnðə,bɑks] *n* **:** caja *f* de sorpresa

jackknife[1] ['dʒæk,naɪf] *vi* **-knifed; -knifing :** doblarse como una navaja, plegarse

jackknife[2] *n* **:** navaja *f*

jack–of–all–trades *n* **:** persona *f* que sabe un poco de todo, persona *f* de muchos oficios

jack–o'–lantern ['dʒækə,læntərn] *n* **:** linterna *f* hecha de una calabaza

jackpot ['dʒæk,pɑt] *n* **1 :** primer premio *m,* gordo *m* **2 to hit the jackpot :** sacarse la lotería, sacarse el gordo

jackrabbit ['dʒæk,ræbət] *n* **:** liebre *f* grande de Norteamérica

jade ['dʒeɪd] *n* **:** jade *m*

jaded ['dʒeɪdəd] *adj* **1** TIRED **:** agotado **2** BORED **:** hastiado

jagged ['dʒægəd] *adj* **:** dentado, mellado

jaguar ['dʒæg,wɑr, 'dʒægjʊ,wɑr] *n* **:** jaguar *m*

jai alai ['haɪ,laɪ] *n* **:** jai alai *m,* pelota *f* vasca

jail[1] ['dʒeɪl] *vt* **:** encarcelar

jail[2] *n* **:** cárcel *f*

jailbreak ['dʒeɪl,breɪk] *n* **:** fuga *f,* huida *f* (de la cárcel)

jailer *or* **jailor** ['dʒeɪlər] *n* **:** carcelero *m,* -ra *f*

jalapeño [,hɑlə'peɪnjo, ,hæ-, -'piːno] *n* **:** jalapeño *m*

jalopy [dʒə'lɑpi] *n, pl* **-lopies :** cacharro *m fam,* carro *m* destartalado

jalousie ['dʒæləsi] *n* **:** celosía *f*

jam[1] ['dʒæm] *v* **jammed; jamming** *vt* **1** CRAM **:** apiñar, embutir **2** BLOCK **:** atascar, atorar **3 to jam on the brakes :** frenar en seco — *vi* STICK **:** atascarse, atrancarse

jam[2] *n* **1** *or* **traffic jam :** atasco *m,* embotellamiento *m* (de tráfico) **2** PREDICAMENT **:** lío *m,* aprieto *m,* apuro *m* **3 :** mermelada *f* <strawberry jam : mermelada de fresa>

jamb ['dʒæm] *n* **:** jamba *f*

jamboree [,dʒæmbə'riː] *n* **:** fiesta *f* grande

jangle[1] ['dʒæŋgəl] *v* **-gled; -gling** *vi* **:** hacer un ruido metálico — *vt* **1 :** hacer sonar **2 to jangle one's nerves :** irritar, crispar

jangle[2] *n* **:** ruido *m* metálico

janitor ['dʒænət̬ər] *n* **:** portero *m,* -ra *f;* conserje *mf*

January ['dʒænjʊ,ɛri] *n* **:** enero *m*

Japanese [,dʒæpə'niːz, -'niːs] *n* **1 :** japonés *m,* -nesa *f* **2 :** japonés *m* (idioma) — **Japanese** *adj*

jar[1] ['dʒɑr] *v* **jarred; jarring** *vi* **1** GRATE **:** chirriar **2** CLASH **:** desentonar **3** SHAKE **:** sacudirse **4 to jar on :** crispar, enervar — *vt* JOLT **:** sacudir

jar[2] *n* **1** GRATING **:** chirrido *m* **2** JOLT **:** vibración *f,* sacudida *f* **3 :** tarro *m,* bote *m,* pote *m* <a jar of honey : un tarro de miel>

jargon ['dʒɑrgən] *n* **:** jerga *f*

jasmine ['dʒæzmən] *n* **:** jazmín *m*

jasper ['dʒæspər] *n* **:** jaspe *m*

jaundice ['dʒɔndɪs] *n* **:** ictericia *f*

jaundiced ['dʒɔndɪst] *adj* **1 :** ictérico **2** EMBITTERED, RESENTFUL **:** amargado, resentido, negativo <with a jaundiced eye : con una actitud de cinismo>

jaunt ['dʒɔnt] *n* **:** excursión *f,* paseo *m*

jauntily ['dʒɔnt̬əli] *adv* **:** animadamente

jauntiness ['dʒɔntinəs] *n* **:** animación *f,* vivacidad *f*

jaunty ['dʒɔnti] *adj* **-tier; -est 1** SPRIGHTLY **:** animado, alegre **2** RAKISH **:** desenvuelto, desenfadado

javelin ['dʒævələn] *n* **:** jabalina *f*

jaw[1] ['dʒɔ] *vi* GAB **:** cotorrear *fam,* parlotear *fam*

jaw[2] *n* **1 :** mandíbula *f,* quijada *f* **2 :** mordaza *f* (de una herramienta) **3 the jaws of death :** las garras *f* de la muerte

jawbone [ˈdʒɔˌboːn] *n* : mandíbula *f*
jay [ˈdʒeɪ] *n* : arrendajo *m*, chara *f Mex*, azulejo *m Mex*
jaybird [ˈdʒeɪˌbərd] → **jay**
jaywalk [ˈdʒeɪˌwɔk] *vi* : cruzar la calle sin prudencia
jaywalker [ˈdʒeɪˌwɔkər] *n* : peatón *m* imprudente
jazz[1] [ˈdʒæz] *vt* **to jazz up** : animar, alegrar
jazz[2] *n* : jazz *m*
jazzy [ˈdʒæzi] *adj* **jazzier; -est 1** : con ritmo de jazz **2** FLASHY, SHOWY : llamativo, ostentoso
jealous [ˈdʒɛləs] *adj* : celoso, envidioso — **jealously** *adv*
jealousy [ˈdʒɛləsi] *n* : celos *mpl*, envidia *f*
jeans [ˈdʒiːnz] *npl* : jeans *mpl*, vaqueros *mpl*
jeep [ˈdʒiːp] *n* : jeep *m*
jeer[1] [ˈdʒɪr] *vi* **1** BOO : abuchear **2** SCOFF : mofarse, burlarse — *vt* RIDICULE : mofarse de, burlarse de
jeer[2] *n* **1** : abucheo *m* **2** TAUNT : mofa *f*, burla *f*
Jehovah [dʒɪˈhoːvə] *n* : Jehová *m*
jell [ˈdʒɛl] *vi* **1** SET : gelificarse, cuajar **2** FORM : cuajar, formarse (una idea, etc.)
jelly[1] [ˈdʒɛli] *v* **jellied; jellying** *vi* **1** JELL : gelificarse, cuajar **2** : hacer jalea — *vt* : gelificar
jelly[2] *n, pl* **-lies 1** : jalea *f* **2** GELATIN : gelatina *f*
jellyfish [ˈdʒɛliˌfɪʃ] *n* : medusa *f*
jeopardize [ˈdʒɛpərˌdaɪz] *vt* **-dized; -dizing** : arriesgar, poner en peligro
jeopardy [ˈdʒɛpərdi] *n* : peligro *m*, riesgo *m*
jerk[1] [ˈdʒərk] *vt* **1** JOLT : sacudir **2** TUG, YANK : darle un tirón a — *vi* JOLT : dar sacudidas <the train jerked along : el tren iba moviéndose a sacudidas>
jerk[2] *n* **1** TUG : tirón *m*, jalón *m* **2** JOLT : sacudida *f* brusca **3** FOOL : estúpido *m*, -da *f*; idiota *mf*
jerkin [ˈdʒərkən] *n* : chaqueta *f* sin mangas, chaleco *m*
jerky [ˈdʒərki] *adj* **jerkier; -est 1** : espasmódico (dícese de los movimientos) **2** CHOPPY : inconexo (dícese de la prosa) — **jerkily** [-kəli] *adv*
jerry–built [ˈdʒɛriˌbɪlt] *adj* : mal construido, chapucero
jersey [ˈdʒərzi] *n, pl* **-seys** : jersey *m*
jest[1] [ˈdʒɛst] *vi* : bromear
jest[2] *n* : broma *f*, chiste *m*
jester [ˈdʒɛstər] *n* : bufón *m*, -fona *f*
Jesus [ˈdʒiːzəs, -zəz] *n* : Jesús *m*
jet[1] [ˈdʒɛt] *v* **jetted; jetting** *vt* SPOUT : arrojar a chorros — *vi* **1** GUSH : salir a chorros, chorrear **2** FLY : viajar en avión, volar
jet[2] *n* **1** STREAM : chorro *m* **2** *or* **jet airplane** : avión *m* a reacción, reactor *m* **3** : azabache *m* (mineral) **4 jet engine** : reactor *m*, motor *m* a reacción **5 jet lag** : desajuste *m* de horario (debido a un vuelo largo)
jet–propelled *adj* : a reacción
jetsam [ˈdʒɛtsəm] *n* **flotsam and jetsam** : restos *mpl*, desechos *mpl*
jettison [ˈdʒɛtəsən] *vt* **1** : echar al mar **2** DISCARD : desechar, deshacerse de
jetty [ˈdʒɛti] *n, pl* **-ties 1** PIER, WHARF : desembarcadero *m*, muelle *m* **2** BREAKWATER : malecón *m*, rompeolas *m*
Jew [ˈdʒuː] *n* : judío *m*, -día *f*
jewel [ˈdʒuːəl] *n* **1** : joya *f*, alhaja *f* **2** GEM : piedra *f* preciosa, gema *f* **3** : rubí *m* (de un reloj) **4** TREASURE : joya *f*, tesoro *m*
jeweler *or* **jeweller** [ˈdʒuːələr] *n* : joyero *m*, -ra *f*
jewelry [ˈdʒuːəlri] *n* : joyas *fpl*, alhajas *fpl*
Jewish [ˈdʒuːɪʃ] *adj* : judío
jib [ˈdʒɪb] *n* : foque *m* (de un barco)
jibe [ˈdʒaɪb] *vi* **jibed; jibing** AGREE : concordar
jiffy [ˈdʒɪfi] *n, pl* **-fies** : santiamén *m*, segundo *m*, momento *m*
jig[1] [ˈdʒɪg] *vi* **jigged; jigging** : bailar la giga
jig[2] *n* **1** : giga *f* **2 the jig is up** : se acabó la fiesta
jigger [ˈdʒɪgər] *n* : medida de 1 a 2 onzas (para licores)
jiggle[1] [ˈdʒɪgəl] *v* **-gled; -gling** *vt* : agitar o sacudir ligeramente — *vi* : agitarse, vibrar
jiggle[2] *n* : sacudida *f*, vibración *f*
jigsaw [ˈdʒɪgˌsɔ] *n* **1** : sierra *f* de vaivén **2 jigsaw puzzle** : rompecabezas *m*
jilt [ˈdʒɪlt] *vt* : dejar plantado, dar calabazas a
jimmy[1] [ˈdʒɪmi] *vt* **-mied; -mying** : forzar con una palanqueta
jimmy[2] *n, pl* **-mies** : palanqueta *f*
jingle[1] [ˈdʒɪŋgəl] *v* **-gled; -gling** *vi* : tintinear — *vt* : hacer sonar
jingle[2] *n* **1** TINKLE : tintineo *m*, retintín *m* **2** : canción *f* rimada
jingoism [ˈdʒɪŋgoˌɪzəm] *n* : jingoísmo *m*, patriotería *f*
jingoistic [ˌdʒɪŋgoˈɪstɪk] *or* **jingoist** [ˈdʒɪŋgoɪst] *adj* : jingoísta, patriotero
jinx[1] [ˈdʒɪŋks] *vt* : traer mala suerte a, salar *CoRi, Mex*
jinx[2] *n* **1** : cenizo *m*, -za *f* **2 to put a jinx on** : echarle el mal de ojo a
jitters [ˈdʒɪtərz] *npl* : nervios *mpl* <he got the jitters : se puso nervioso>
jittery [ˈdʒɪtəri] *adj* : nervioso
job [ˈdʒɑb] *n* **1** : trabajo *m* <he did odd jobs for her : le hizo algunos trabajos> **2** CHORE, TASK : tarea *f*, quehacer *m* **3** EMPLOYMENT : trabajo *m*, empleo *m*, puesto *m*
jobber [ˈdʒɑbər] *n* MIDDLEMAN : intermediario *m*, -ria *f*
jockey[1] [ˈdʒɑki] *v* **-eyed; -eying** *vt* **1** MANIPULATE : manipular **2** MANEUVER

: maniobrar — *vi* **to jockey for position** : maniobrar para conseguir algo

jockey[2] *n, pl* **-eys** : jockey *mf*

jocose [dʒo'ko:s] *adj* : jocoso

jocular ['dʒɑkjʊlər] *adj* : jocoso — **jocularly** *adv*

jocularity [ˌdʒɑkjʊ'lærət̬i] *n* : jocosidad *f*

jodhpurs ['dʒɑdpərz] *npl* : pantalones *mpl* de montar

jog[1] ['dʒɑg] *v* **jogged; jogging** *vt* **1** NUDGE : dar, empujar, codear **2 to jog one's memory** : refrescar la memoria — *vi* **1** RUN : correr despacio, trotar, hacer footing (como ejercicio) **2** TRUDGE : andar a trote corto

jog[2] *n* **1** PUSH, SHAKE : empujoncito *m*, sacudida *f* leve **2** TROT : trote *m* corto, footing *m* (en deportes) **3** TWIST : recodo *m*, vuelta *f*, curva *f*

jogger ['dʒɑgər] *n* : persona *f* que hace footing

join ['dʒɔɪn] *vt* **1** CONNECT, LINK : unir, juntar <to join in marriage : unir en matrimonio> **2** ADJOIN : lindar con, colindar con **3** MEET : reunirse con, encontrarse con <we joined them for lunch : nos reunimos con ellos para almorzar> **4** : hacerse socio de (una organización), afiliarse a (un partido), entrar en (una empresa) — *vi* **1** UNITE : unirse **2** MERGE : empalmar (dícese de las carreteras), confluir (dícese de los ríos) **3 to join up** : hacerse socio, enrolarse

joiner ['dʒɔɪnər] *n* **1** CARPENTER : carpintero *m*, -ra *f* **2** : persona *f* que se une a varios grupos

joint[1] ['dʒɔɪnt] *adj* : conjunto, colectivo, mutuo <a joint effort : un esfuerzo conjunto> — **jointly** *adv*

joint[2] *n* **1** : articulación *f*, coyuntura *f* <out of joint : dislocado> **2** ROAST : asado *m* **3** JUNCTURE : juntura *f*, unión *f* **4** DIVE : antro *m*, tasca *f*

joist ['dʒɔɪst] *n* : viga *f*

joke[1] ['dʒo:k] *vi* **joked; joking** : bromear

joke[2] *n* **1** STORY : chiste *m* **2** PRANK : broma *f*

joker ['dʒo:kər] *n* **1** PRANKSTER : bromista *mf* **2** : comodín *m* (en los naipes)

jokingly ['dʒo:kɪŋli] *adv* : en broma

jollity ['dʒɑlət̬i] *n, pl* **-ties** MERRIMENT : alegría *f*, regocijo *m*

jolly ['dʒɑli] *adj* **-lier; -est** : alegre, jovial

jolt[1] ['dʒo:lt] *vi* JERK : dar tumbos, dar sacudidas — *vt* : sacudir

jolt[2] *n* **1** JERK : sacudida *f* brusca **2** SHOCK : golpe *m* (emocional)

jonquil ['dʒɑnkwɪl] *n* : junquillo *m*

Jordanian [dʒɔr'deɪniən] *n* : jordano *m*, -na *f* — **Jordanian** *adj*

josh ['dʒɑʃ] *vt* TEASE : tomarle el pelo (a alguien) — *vi* JOKE : bromear

jostle ['dʒɑsəl] *v* **-tled; -tling** *vi* **1** SHOVE : empujar, dar empellones **2** CONTEND : competir — *vt* **1** SHOVE : empujar **2 to jostle one's way** : abrirse paso a empellones

jot[1] ['dʒɑt] *vt* **jotted; jotting** : anotar, apuntar <jot it down : apúntalo>

jot[2] *n* BIT : ápice *m*, jota *f*, pizca *f*

jounce[1] ['dʒæʊnts] *v* **jounced; jouncing** *vt* JOLT : sacudir — *vi* : dar tumbos, dar sacudidas

jounce[2] *n* JOLT : sacudida *f*, tumbo *m*

journal ['dʒərnəl] *n* **1** DIARY : diario *m* **2** PERIODICAL : revista *f*, publicación *f* periódica **3** NEWSPAPER : periódico *m*, diario *m*

journalism ['dʒərnəlˌɪzəm] *n* : periodismo *m*

journalist ['dʒərnəlɪst] *n* : periodista *mf*

journalistic [ˌdʒərnəl'ɪstɪk] *adj* : periodístico

journey[1] ['dʒərni] *vi* **-neyed; -neying** : viajar

journey[2] *n, pl* **-neys** : viaje *m*

journeyman ['dʒərnimən] *n, pl* **-men** [-mən, -ˌmɛn] : oficial *m*

joust[1] ['dʒæʊst] *vi* : justar

joust[2] *n* : justa *f*

jovial ['dʒo:viəl] *adj* : jovial — **jovially** *adv*

joviality [ˌdʒo:vi'ælət̬i] *n* : jovialidad *f*

jowl ['dʒæʊl] *n* **1** JAW : mandíbula *f* **2** CHEEK : mejilla *f*, cachete *m*

joy ['dʒɔɪ] *n* **1** HAPPINESS : gozo *m*, alegría *f*, felicidad *f* **2** DELIGHT : placer *m*, deleite *m* <the child is a real joy : el niño es un verdadero placer>

joyful ['dʒɔɪfəl] *adj* : gozoso, alegre, feliz — **joyfully** *adv*

joyless ['dʒɔɪləs] *adj* : sin alegría, triste

joyous ['dʒɔɪəs] *adj* : alegre, feliz, eufórico — **joyously** *adv*

joyousness ['dʒɔɪəsnəs] *n* : alegría *f*, felicidad *f*, euforia *f*

joyride ['dʒɔɪˌraɪd] *n* : paseo *m* temerario e irresponsable (en coche)

jubilant ['dʒu:bələnt] *adj* : jubiloso, alborozado — **jubilantly** *adv*

jubilation [ˌdʒu:bə'leɪʃən] *n* : júbilo *m*

jubilee ['dʒu:bəˌli:] *n* **1** : quincuagésimo aniversario *m* **2** CELEBRATION : celebración *f*, festejos *mpl*

Judaic [dʒʊ'deɪɪk] *adj* : judaico

Judaism ['dʒu:dəˌɪzəm, 'dʒu:di-, 'dʒu:ˌdeɪ-] *n* : judaísmo *m*

judge[1] ['dʒʌdʒ] *vt* **judged; judging 1** ASSESS : evaluar, juzgar **2** DEEM : juzgar, considerar **3** TRY : juzgar (ante el tribuno) **4 judging by** : a juzgar por

judge[2] *n* **1** : juez *mf*, jueza *f* **2 to be a good judge of** : saber juzgar a, entender mucho de

judgment *or* **judgement** ['dʒʌdʒmənt] *n* **1** RULING : fallo *m*, sentencia *f* **2** OPINION : opinión *f* **3** DISCERNMENT : juicio *m*, discernimiento *m*

judgmental [ˌdʒʌdʒ'mɛntəl] *adj* : crítico — **judgmentally** *adv*

judicature [ˈdʒuːdɪkəˌtʃʊr] *n* **:** judicatura *f*

judicial [dʒʊˈdɪʃəl] *adj* **:** judicial — **judicially** *adv*

judiciary[1] [dʒʊˈdɪʃiˌɛri, -ˈdɪʃəri] *adj* **:** judicial

judiciary[2] *n* **1** JUDICATURE **:** judicatura *f* **2 :** poder *m* judicial

judicious [dʒʊˈdɪʃəs] *adj* SOUND, WISE **:** juicioso, sensato — **judiciously** *adv*

judo [ˈdʒuːˌdoː] *n* **:** judo *m*

jug [ˈdʒʌg] *n* **1 :** jarra *f,* jarro *m,* cántaro *m* **2** JAIL **:** cárcel *f,* chirona *f fam*

juggernaut [ˈdʒʌgərˌnɔt] *n* **:** gigante *m,* fuerza *f* irresistible <a political juggernaut : un gigante político>

juggle [ˈdʒʌgəl] *v* **-gled; -gling** *vt* **1 :** hacer juegos malabares con **2** MANIPULATE **:** manipular, jugar con — *vi* **:** hacer juegos malabares

juggler [ˈdʒʌgələr] *n* **:** malabarista *mf*

jugular [ˈdʒʌgjʊlər] *adj* **:** yugular <jugular vein : vena yugular>

juice [ˈdʒuːs] *n* **1 :** jugo *m* (de carne, de frutas) *m,* zumo *m* (de frutas) **2** ELECTRICITY **:** electricidad *f,* luz *f*

juicer [ˈdʒuːsər] *n* **:** exprimidor *m*

juiciness [ˈdʒuːsinəs] *n* **:** jugosidad *f*

juicy [ˈdʒuːsi] *adj* **juicier; -est 1** SUCCULENT **:** jugoso, suculento **2** PROFITABLE **:** jugoso, lucrativo **3** RACY **:** picante

jukebox [ˈdʒuːkˌbɑks] *n* **:** rocola *f,* máquina *f* de discos

julep [ˈdʒuːləp] *n* **:** bebida *f* hecha con whisky americano y menta

July [dʒʊˈlaɪ] *n* **:** julio *m*

jumble[1] [ˈdʒʌmbəl] *vt* **-bled; -bling :** mezclar, revolver

jumble[2] *n* **:** revoltijo *m,* fárrago *m,* embrollo *m*

jumbo[1] [ˈdʒʌmˌboː] *adj* **:** gigante, enorme, de tamaño extra grande

jumbo[2] *n, pl* **-bos :** coloso *m,* cosa *f* de tamaño extra grande

jump[1] [ˈdʒʌmp] *vi* **1** LEAP **:** saltar, brincar **2** START **:** levantarse de un salto, sobresaltarse **3** MOVE, SHIFT **:** moverse, pasar <to jump from job to job : pasar de un empleo a otro> **4** INCREASE, RISE **:** dar un salto, aumentarse de golpe, subir bruscamente **5** BUSTLE **:** animarse, ajetrearse **6 to jump to conclusions :** sacar conclusiones precipitadas — *vt* **1 :** saltar <to jump a fence : saltar una valla> **2** SKIP **:** saltarse **3** ATTACK **:** atacar, asaltar **4 to jump the gun :** precipitarse

jump[2] *n* **1** LEAP **:** salto *m* **2** START **:** sobresalto *m,* respingo *m* **3** INCREASE **:** subida *f* brusca, aumento *m* **4** ADVANTAGE **:** ventaja *f* <we got the jump on them : les llevamos la ventaja>

jumper [ˈdʒʌmpər] *n* **1 :** saltador *m,* -dora *f* (en deportes) **2 :** jumper *m,* vestido *m* sin mangas

jumpy [ˈdʒʌmpi] *adj* **jumpier; -est :** asustadizo, nervioso

junction [ˈdʒʌŋkʃən] *n* **1** JOINING **:** unión *f* **2 :** cruce *m* (de calles), empalme *m* (de un ferrocarril), confluencia *f* (de ríos)

juncture [ˈdʒʌŋktʃər] *n* **1** UNION **:** juntura *f,* unión *f* **2** MOMENT, POINT **:** coyuntura *f* <at this juncture : en esta coyuntura, en este momento>

June [ˈdʒuːn] *n* **:** junio *m*

jungle [ˈdʒʌŋgəl] *n* **:** jungla *f,* selva *f*

junior[1] [ˈdʒuːnjər] *adj* **1** YOUNGER **:** más joven <John Smith, Junior : John Smith, hijo> **2** SUBORDINATE **:** subordinado, subalterno

junior[2] *n* **1 :** persona *f* de menor edad <she's my junior : es menor que yo> **2** SUBORDINATE **:** subalterno *m,* **-na** *f;* subordinado *m,* -da *f* **3 :** estudiante *mf* de penúltimo año

juniper [ˈdʒuːnəpər] *n* **:** enebro *m*

junk[1] [ˈdʒʌŋk] *vt* **:** echar a la basura

junk[2] *n* **1** RUBBISH **:** desechos *mpl,* desperdicios *mpl* **2** STUFF **:** trastos *mpl fam,* cachivaches *mpl fam* **3 piece of junk :** cacharro *m,* porquería *f*

junket [ˈdʒʌŋkət] *n* **:** viaje *m* (pagado con dinero público)

junta [ˈhʊntə, ˈdʒʌn-, ˈhʌn-] *n* **:** junta *f* militar

Jupiter [ˈdʒuːpətər] *n* **:** Júpiter *m*

jurisdiction [ˌdʒʊrəsˈdɪkʃən] *n* **:** jurisdicción *f*

jurisprudence [ˌdʒʊrəsˈpruːdənts] *n* **:** jurisprudencia *f*

jurist [ˈdʒʊrɪst] *n* **:** jurista *mf;* magistrado *m,* -da *f*

juror [ˈdʒʊrər] *n* **:** jurado *m,* -da *f*

jury [ˈdʒʊri] *n, pl* **-ries :** jurado *m*

just[1] [ˈdʒʌst] *adv* **1** EXACTLY **:** justo, precisamente, exactamente **2** POSSIBLY **:** posiblemente <it just might work : tal vez resulte> **3** BARELY **:** justo, apenas <just in time : justo a tiempo> **4** ONLY **:** sólo, solamente, nada más <just us : sólo nosotros> **5** QUITE **:** muy, simplemente <it's just horrible! : ¡qué horrible!> **6 to have just (done something) :** acabar de (hacer algo) <he just called : acaba de llamar>

just[2] *adj* **:** justo — **justly** *adv*

justice [ˈdʒʌstɪs] *n* **1 :** justicia *f* **2** JUDGE **:** juez *mf,* jueza *f*

justification [ˌdʒʌstəfəˈkeɪʃən] *n* **:** justificación *f*

justify [ˈdʒʌstəˌfaɪ] *vt* **-fied; -fying :** justificar — **justifiable** [ˌdʒʌstəˈfaɪəbəl] *adj*

jut [ˈdʒʌt] *vi* **jutted; jutting :** sobresalir

jute [ˈdʒuːt] *n* **:** yute *m*

juvenile[1] [ˈdʒuːvəˌnaɪl, -vənəl] *adj* **1 :** juvenil <juvenile delinquent : delincuente juvenil> <juvenile court : tribunal de menores> **2** CHILDISH **:** infantil

juvenile[2] *n* **:** menor *mf*

juxtapose [ˈdʒʌkstəˌpoːz] *vt* **-posed; -posing :** yuxtaponer

juxtaposition [ˌdʒʌkstəpəˈzɪʃən] *n* **:** yuxtaposición *f*

K

k [ˈkeɪ] *n, pl* **k's** *or* **ks** [ˈkeɪz] : undécima letra del alfabeto inglés

kaiser [ˈkaɪzər] *n* : káiser *m*

kale [ˈkeɪl] *n* : col *f* rizada

kaleidoscope [kəˈlaɪdəˌskoːp] *n* : calidoscopio *m*

kangaroo [ˌkæŋgəˈruː] *n, pl* **-roos** : canguro *m*

kaolin [ˈkeɪələn] *n* : caolín *m*

karat [ˈkærət] *n* : quilate *m*

karate [kəˈrɑt̬i] *n* : karate *m*

katydid [ˈkeɪt̬iˌdɪd] *n* : saltamontes *m*

kayak [ˈkaɪˌæk] *n* : kayac *m,* kayak *m*

keel[1] [ˈkiːl] *vi* **to keel over** : volcar (dícese de un barco), desplomarse (dícese de una persona)

keel[2] *n* : quilla *f*

keen [ˈkiːn] *adj* **1** SHARP : afilado, filoso <a keen blade : una hoja afilada> **2** PENETRATING : cortante, penetrante <a keen wind : un viento cortante> **3** ENTHUSIASTIC : entusiasta **4** ACUTE : agudo, fino <keen hearing : oído fino> <keen intelligence : inteligencia aguda>

keenly [ˈkiːnli] *adv* **1** ENTHUSIASTICALLY : con entusiasmo **2** INTENSELY : vivamente, profundamente <keenly aware of : muy consciente de>

keenness [ˈkiːnnəs] *n* **1** SHARPNESS : lo afilado, lo filoso **2** ENTHUSIASM : entusiasmo *m* **3** ACUTENESS : agudeza *f*

keep[1] [ˈkiːp] *v* **kept** [ˈkɛpt]; **keeping** *vt* **1** : cumplir (la palabra a uno), acudir a (una cita) **2** OBSERVE : observar (una fiesta) **3** GUARD : guardar, cuidar **4** CONTINUE : mantener <to keep silence : mantener silencio> **5** SUPPORT : mantener (una familia) **6** RAISE : criar (animales) **7** : llevar, escribir (un diario, etc.) **8** RETAIN : guardar, conservar, quedarse con **9** STORE : guardar **10** DETAIN : hacer quedar, detener **11** PRESERVE : guardar <to keep a secret : guardar un secreto> — *vi* **1** : conservarse (dícese de los alimentos) **2** CONTINUE : seguir, no dejar <he keeps on pestering us : no deja de molestarnos> **3 to keep from** : abstenerse de <I couldn't keep from laughing : no podía contener la risa>

keep[2] *n* **1** TOWER : torreón *m* (de un castillo), torre *f* del homenaje **2** SUSTENANCE : manutención *f,* sustento *m* **3 for keeps** : para siempre

keeper [ˈkiːpər] *n* **1** : guarda *mf* (en un zoológico); conservador *m,* -dora *f* (en un museo) **2** GAMEKEEPER : guardabosque *mf*

keeping [ˈkiːpɪŋ] *n* **1** CONFORMITY : conformidad *f,* acuerdo *m* <in keeping with : de acuerdo con> **2** CARE : cuidado *m* <in the keeping of : al cuidado de>

keepsake [ˈkiːpˌseɪk] *n* : recuerdo *m*

keep up *vt* CONTINUE, MAINTAIN : mantener, seguir con — *vi* **1** : mantenerse al corriente <he kept up with the news : se mantenía al tanto de las noticias> **2** CONTINUE : continuar **3 to keep up with someone** : mantener contacto con alguien

keg [ˈkɛg] *n* : barril *m*

kelp [ˈkɛlp] *n* : alga *f* marina

ken [ˈkɛn] *n* **1** SIGHT : vista *f,* alcance *m* de la vista **2** UNDERSTANDING : comprensión *f,* alcance *m* del conocimiento <it's beyond his ken : no lo puede entender>

kennel [ˈkɛnəl] *n* : caseta *f* para perros, perrera *f*

Kenyan [ˈkɛnjən, ˈkiːn-] *n* : keniano *m,* -na *f* — **Kenyan** *adj*

kept → **keep**

kerchief [ˈkərtʃəf, -ˌtʃiːf] *n* : pañuelo *m*

kernel [ˈkərnəl] *n* **1** : almendra *f* (de semillas y nueces) **2** : grano *m* (de cereales) **3** CORE : meollo *m* <a kernel of truth : un fondo de verdad>

kerosene *or* **kerosine** [ˈkɛrəˌsiːn, ˌkɛrəˈ-] *n* : queroseno *m,* kerosén *m,* kerosene *m*

ketchup [ˈkɛtʃəp, ˈkæ-] *n* : salsa *f* catsup

kettle [ˈkɛt̬əl] *n* **1** : hervidor *m,* pava *f Arg, Bol, Chile* **2** → **teakettle**

kettledrum [ˈkɛt̬əlˌdrʌm] *n* : timbal *m*

key[1] [ˈkiː] *vt* **1** ATTUNE : adaptar, adecuar **2 to key up** : poner nervioso, inquietar

key[2] *adj* : clave, fundamental

key[3] *n* **1** : llave *f* **2** SOLUTION : clave *f,* soluciones *fpl* **3** : tecla *f* (de un piano o una máquina) **4** : tono *m,* tonalidad *f* (en la música) **5** ISLET, REEF : cayo *m,* islote *m*

keyboard [ˈkiːˌbord] *n* : teclado *m*

keyhole [ˈkiːˌhoːl] *n* : bocallave *f,* ojo *m* (de una cerradura)

keynote[1] [ˈkiːˌnoːt] *vt* **-noted; -noting 1** : establecer la tónica de (en música) **2** : pronunciar el discurso principal de

keynote[2] *n* **1** : tónica *f* (en música) **2** : idea *f* fundamental

keystone [ˈkiːˌstoːn] *n* : clave *f,* dovela *f*

khaki [ˈkæki, ˈkɑ-] *n* : caqui *m*

khan [ˈkɑn, ˈkæn] *n* : kan *m*

kibbutz [kəˈbʊts, -ˈbuːts] *n, pl* **-butzim** [-ˌbʊtˈsiːm, -ˌbuːt-] : kibutz *m*

kibitz [ˈkɪbɪts] *vi* : dar consejos molestos

kibitzer [ˈkɪbɪtsər, kɪˈbɪt-] *n* : persona *f* que da consejos molestos

kick[1] [ˈkɪk] *vi* **1** : dar patadas (dícese de una persona), cocear (dícese de un animal) **2** PROTEST : patalear, protestar **3** RECOIL : dar un culatazo (dícese de un arma de fuego) — *vt* : patear, darle una patada (a alguien)

kick[2] *n* **1** : patada *f,* puntapié *m,* coz *f* (de un animal) **2** RECOIL : culatazo *m* (de un arma de fuego) **3** : fuerza *f* <a drink with a kick : una bebida fuerte>

kicker [ˈkɪkər] *n* : pateador *m,* -dora *f* (en deportes)

kickoff [ˈkɪkˌɔf] *n* : saque *m* (inicial)

kick off *vi* **1** : hacer el saque inicial (en deportes) **2** BEGIN : empezar — *vt* : empezar

kid[1] [ˈkɪd] *v* **kidded; kidding** *vt* **1** FOOL : engañar **2** TEASE : tomarle el pelo (a alguien) — *vi* JOKE : bromear <I'm only kidding : lo digo en broma>

kid[2] *n* **1** : chivo *m,* -va *f;* cabrito *m,* -ta *f* **2** CHILD : chico *m,* -ca *f;* niño *m,* -ña *f*

kidder [ˈkɪdər] *n* : bromista *mf*

kiddingly [ˈkɪdɪŋli] *adv* : en broma

kidnap [ˈkɪdˌnæp] *vt* **-napped** *or* **-naped** [-ˌnæpt]; **-napping** *or* **-naping** [-ˌnæpɪŋ] : secuestrar, raptar

kidnapper *or* **kidnaper** [ˈkɪdˌnæpər] *n* : secuestrador *m,* -dora *f;* raptor *m,* -tora *f*

kidney [ˈkɪdni] *n, pl* **-neys** : riñón *m*

kidney bean *n* : frijol *m*

kill[1] [ˈkɪl] *vt* **1** : matar **2** END : acabar con, poner fin a **3 to kill time** : matar el tiempo

kill[2] *n* **1** KILLING : matanza *f* **2** PREY : presa *f*

killer [ˈkɪlər] *n* : asesino *m,* -na *f*

kiln [ˈkɪl, ˈkɪln] *n* : horno *m*

kilo [ˈkiːˌloː] *n, pl* **-los** : kilo *m*

kilocycle [ˈkɪləˌsaɪkəl] *n* : kilociclo *m*

kilogram [ˈkɪləˌgræm, ˈkiː-] *n* : kilogramo *m*

kilohertz [ˈkɪləˌhərts] *n* : kilohertzio *m*

kilometer [kɪˈlɑmət̬ər, ˈkɪləˌmiː-] *n* : kilómetro *m*

kilowatt [ˈkɪləˌwɑt] *n* : kilovatio *m*

kilt [ˈkɪlt] *n* : falda *f* escocesa

kilter [ˈkɪltər] *n* **1** ORDER : buen estado *m* **2 out of kilter** : descompuesto, estropeado

kimono [kəˈmoːno, -nə] *n, pl* **-nos** : kimono *m,* quimono *m*

kin [ˈkɪn] *n* : familiares *mpl*, parientes *mpl*

kind[1] [ˈkaɪnd] *adj* : amable, bondadoso, benévolo

kind[2] *n* **1** ESSENCE : esencia *f* <a difference in degree, not in kind : una diferencia cuantitativa y no cualitativa> **2** CATEGORY : especie *f,* género *m* **3** TYPE : clase *f,* tipo *m,* índole *f*

kindergarten [ˈkɪndərˌgɑrtən, -dən] *n* : kinder *m,* kindergarten *m,* jardín *m* de infantes, jardín *m* de niños *Mex*

kindhearted [ˌkaɪndˈhɑrt̬əd] *adj* : bondadoso, de buen corazón

kindle [ˈkɪndəl] *v* **-dled; -dling** *vt* **1** IGNITE : encender **2** AROUSE : despertar, suscitar — *vi* : encenderse

kindliness [ˈkaɪndlinəs] *n* : bondad *f*

kindling [ˈkɪndlɪŋ, ˈkɪndlən] *n* : astillas *fpl*, leña *f*

kindly[1] [ˈkaɪndli] *adv* **1** AMIABLY : amablemente, bondadosamente **2** COURTEOUSLY : cortésmente, con cortesía <we kindly ask you not smoke : les rogamos que no fumen> **3** PLEASE : por favor **4 to take kindly to** : aceptar de buena gana

kindly[2] *adj* **-lier; -est** : bondadoso, amable

kindness [ˈkaɪndnəs] *n* : bondad *f*

kind of *adv* SOMEWHAT : un tanto, algo

kindred[1] [ˈkɪndrəd] *adj* SIMILAR : similar, afín <kindred spirits : almas gemelas>

kindred[2] *n* **1** FAMILY : familia *f,* parentela *f* **2** → **kin**

kinfolk [ˈkɪnˌfoːk] *or* **kinfolks** [-ˌfoːks] *npl* → **kin**

king [ˈkɪŋ] *n* : rey *m*

kingdom [ˈkɪŋdəm] *n* : reino *m*

kingfisher [ˈkɪŋˌfɪʃər] *n* : martín *m* pescador

kingly [ˈkɪŋli] *adj* **-lier; -est** : regio, real

king–size [ˈkɪŋˌsaɪz] *or* **king–sized** [-ˌsaɪzd] *adj* : de tamaño muy grande, extra largo (dícese de cigarillos)

kink [ˈkɪŋk] *n* **1** : rizo *m* (en el pelo), vuelta *f* (en una cuerda) **2** CRAMP : calambre *m* <to have a kink in the neck : tener tortícolis>

kinky [ˈkɪŋki] *adj* **-kier; -est** : rizado (dícese del pelo), enroscado (dícese de una cuerda)

kinship [ˈkɪnˌʃɪp] *n* : parentesco *m*

kinsman [ˈkɪnzmən] *n, pl* **-men** [-mən, -ˌmɛn] : familiar *m,* pariente *m*

kinswoman [ˈkɪnzˌwʊmən] *n, pl* **-women** [-ˌwɪmən] : familiar *f,* pariente *f*

kipper [ˈkɪpər] *n* : arenque *m* ahumado

kiss[1] [ˈkɪs] *vt* : besar — *vi* : besarse

kiss[2] *n* : beso *m*

kit [ˈkɪt] *n* **1** SET : juego *m,* kit *m* **2** CASE : estuche *m,* caja *f* **3 first–aid kit** : botiquín *m* **4 tool kit** : caja *f* de herramientas **5 travel kit** : neceser *m*

kitchen [ˈkɪtʃən] *n* : cocina *f*

kite [ˈkaɪt] *n* **1** : milano *m* (ave) **2** : cometa *f,* papalote *m Mex* <to fly a kite : hacer volar una cometa>

kith [ˈkɪθ] *n* : amigos *mpl* <kith and kin : amigos y parientes>

kitten [ˈkɪtən] *n* : gatito *m,* -ta *f*

kitty [ˈkɪt̬i] *n, pl* **-ties 1** FUND, POOL : bote *m,* fondo *m* común **2** CAT : gato *m,* gatito *m*

kitty–corner [ˈkɪt̬iˌkɔrnər] *or* **kitty–cornered** [-nərd] → **catercorner**

kiwi [ˈkiːˌwiː] *n* : kiwi *m*

kleptomania [ˌklɛptəˈmeɪniə] *n* : cleptomanía *f*

kleptomaniac [ˌklɛptəˈmeɪniˌæk] *n* : cleptómano *m,* -na *f*

knack [ˈnæk] *n* : maña *f,* facilidad *f*

knapsack [ˈnæpˌsæk] *n* : mochila *f,* morral *m*

knave [ˈneɪv] *n* **:** bellaco *m,* pícaro *m*
knead [ˈniːd] *vt* **1 :** amasar, sobar **2** MASSAGE **:** masajear
knee [ˈniː] *n* **:** rodilla *f*
kneecap [ˈniːˌkæp] *n* **:** rótula *f*
kneel [ˈniːl] *vi* **knelt** [ˈnɛlt] *or* **kneeled** [ˈniːld]; **kneeling :** arrodillarse, ponerse de rodillas
knell [ˈnɛl] *n* **:** doble *m,* toque *m* <death knell : toque de difuntos>
knew → **know**
knickers [ˈnɪkərz] *npl* **:** pantalones *mpl* bombachos de media pierna
knickknack [ˈnɪkˌnæk] *n* **:** chuchería *f,* baratija *f*
knife[1] [ˈnaɪf] *vt* **knifed** [ˈnaɪft]; **knifing :** acuchillar, apuñalar
knife[2] *n, pl* **knives** [ˈnaɪvz] **:** cuchillo *m*
knight[1] [ˈnaɪt] *vt* **:** conceder el título de *Sir* a
knight[2] *n* **1 :** caballero *m* <knight errant : caballero andante> **2 :** caballo *m* (en ajedrez) **3 :** uno que tiene el título de *Sir*
knighthood [ˈnaɪtˌhʊd] *n* **1 :** caballería *f* **2 :** título *m* de *Sir*
knightly [ˈnaɪtli] *adj* **:** caballeresco
knit[1] [ˈnɪt] *v* **knit** *or* **knitted** [ˈnɪt̬əd]; **knitting** *vt* **1** UNITE **:** unir, enlazar **2 :** tejer <to knit a sweater : tejer un suéter> **3 to knit one's brows :** fruncir el ceño — *vi* **1 :** tejer **2 :** soldarse (dícese de los huesos)
knit[2] *n* **:** prenda *f* tejida
knitter [ˈnɪt̬ər] *n* **:** tejedor *m,* -dora *f*
knob [ˈnɑb] *n* **1** LUMP **:** bulto *m,* protuberancia *f* **2** HANDLE **:** perilla *f,* tirador *m,* botón *m*
knobbed [ˈnɑbd] *adj* **1** KNOTTY **:** nudoso **2 :** que tiene perilla o botón
knobby [ˈnɑbi] *adj* **knobbier; -est 1** KNOTTY **:** nudoso **2 knobby knees :** rodillas *fpl* huesudas
knock[1] [ˈnɑk] *vt* **1** HIT, RAP **:** golpear, golpetear **2 :** hacer chocar <they knocked heads : se dieron en la cabeza> **3** CRITICIZE **:** criticar — *vi* **1** RAP **:** dar un golpe, llamar (a la puerta) **2** COLLIDE **:** darse, chocar
knock[2] *n* **:** golpe *m,* llamada *f* (a la puerta), golpeteo *m* (de un motor)
knock down *vt* **:** derribar, echar al suelo
knocker [ˈnɑkər] *n* **:** aldaba *f,* llamador *m*
knock–kneed [ˈnɑkˈniːd] *adj* **:** patizambo
knock out *vt* **:** dejar sin sentido, poner fuera de combate (en el boxeo)
knoll [ˈnoːl] *n* **:** loma *f,* otero *m,* montículo *m*
knot[1] [ˈnɑt] *v* **knotted; knotting** *vt* **:** anudar — *vi* **:** anudarse
knot[2] *n* **1 :** nudo *m* (en cordel o madera), nódulo *m* (en los músculos) **2** CLUSTER **:** grupo *m* **3 :** nudo *m* (unidad de velocidad)
knotty [ˈnɑt̬i] *adj* **-tier; -est 1** GNARLED **:** nudoso **2** COMPLEX **:** espinoso, enredado, complejo
know [ˈnoː] *v* **knew** [ˈnuː, ˈnjuː]; **known** [ˈnoːn]; **knowing** *vt* **1 :** saber <he knows the answer : sabe la respuesta> **2 :** conocer (a una persona, un lugar) <do you know Julia? : ¿conoces a Julia?> **3** RECOGNIZE **:** reconocer **4** DISCERN, DISTINGUISH **:** distinguir, discernir **5 to know how to :** saber <I don't know how to dance : no sé bailar> — *vi* **:** saber
knowable [ˈnoːəbəl] *adj* **:** conocible
knowing [ˈnoːɪŋ] *adj* **1** KNOWLEDGEABLE **:** informado <a knowing look : una mirada de complicidad> **2** ASTUTE **:** astuto **3** DELIBERATE **:** deliberado, intencional
knowingly [ˈnoːɪŋli] *adv* **1 :** con complicidad <she smiled knowingly : sonrió con una mirada de complicidad> **2** DELIBERATELY **:** a sabiendas, adrede, a propósito
know–it–all [ˈnoːɪt̬ˌɔl] *n* **:** sabelotodo *mf fam*
knowledge [ˈnɑlɪdʒ] *n* **1** AWARENESS **:** conocimiento *m* **2** LEARNING **:** conocimientos *mpl,* saber *m*
knowledgeable [ˈnɑlɪdʒəbəl] *adj* **:** informado, entendido, enterado
known [ˈnoːn] *adj* **:** conocido, familiar
knuckle [ˈnʌkəl] *n* **:** nudillo *m*
koala [koˈwɑlə] *n* **:** koala *m*
kohlrabi [ˌkoːlˈrɑbi, -ˈræ-] *n, pl* **-bies :** colinabo *m*
Koran [kəˈrɑn, -ˈræn] *n* **the Koran :** el Corán
Korean [kəˈriːən] *n* **:** coreano *m,* -na *f* — **Korean** *adj*
kosher [ˈkoːʃər] *adj* **:** aprobado por la ley judía
kowtow [ˌkaʊˈtaʊ, ˈkaʊˌtaʊ] *vi* **to kowtow to :** humillarse ante, doblegarse ante
krypton [ˈkrɪpˌtɑn] *n* **:** criptón *m*
kudos [ˈkjuːˌdɑs, ˈkuː-, -ˌdoːz] *n* **:** fama *f,* renombre *m*
kumquat [ˈkʌmˌkwɑt] *n* **:** naranjita *f* china
Kuwaiti [kʊˈweɪt̬i] *n* **:** kuwaití *mf* — **Kuwaiti** *adj*

L

l [ˈɛl] *n, pl* **l's** *or* **ls** [ˈɛlz] **:** duodécima letra del alfabeto inglés
lab [ˈlæb] → **laboratory**
label[1] [ˈleɪbəl] *vt* **-beled** *or* **-belled; -beling** *or* **-belling 1 :** etiquetar, poner etiqueta a **2** BRAND, CATEGORIZE

: calificar, tildar, tachar <they labeled him as a fraud : lo calificaron de farsante>

label[2] *n* **1** : etiqueta *f,* rótulo *m* **2** DESCRIPTION : calificación *f,* descripción *f* **3** BRAND : marca *f*

labial [ˈleɪbiəl] *adj* : labial

labor[1] [ˈleɪbər] *vi* **1** WORK : trabajar **2** STRUGGLE : avanzar penosamente (dícese de una persona), funcionar con dificultad (dícese de un motor) **3 to labor under a delusion** : hacerse ilusiones, tener una falsa impresión — *vt* BELABOR : insistir en, extenderse sobre

labor[2] *n* **1** EFFORT, WORK : trabajo *m,* esfuerzos *mpl* **2** : parto *m* <to be in labor : estar de parto> **3** TASK : tarea *f,* labor *m* **4** WORKERS : mano *f* de obra

laboratory [ˈlæbrəˌtori, ləˈbɔrə-] *n, pl* **-ries** : laboratorio *m*

Labor Day *n* : Día *m* del Trabajo

laborer [ˈleɪbərər] *n* : peón *m;* trabajador *m,* -dora *f*

laborious [ləˈboriəs] *adj* : laborioso, difícil

laboriously [ləˈboriəsli] *adv* : laboriosamente, trabajosamente

labor union → **union**

labyrinth [ˈlæbəˌrɪnθ] *n* : laberinto *m*

lace[1] [ˈleɪs] *vt* **laced; lacing 1** TIE : acordonar, atar los cordones de **2** : adornar de encaje <I laced the dress in white : adorné el vestido de encaje blanco> **3** SPIKE : echar licor a

lace[2] *n* **1** : encaje *m* **2** SHOELACE : cordón *m* (de zapatos), agujeta *f Mex*

lacerate [ˈlæsəˌreɪt] *vt* **-ated; -ating** : lacerar

laceration [ˌlæsəˈreɪʃən] *n* : laceración *f*

lack[1] [ˈlæk] *vt* : carecer de, no tener <she lacks patience : carece de paciencia> — *vi* : faltar <they lack for nothing : no les falta nada>

lack[2] *n* : falta *f,* carencia *f*

lackadaisical [ˌlækəˈdeɪzɪkəl] *adj* : apático, indiferente, lánguido — **lackadaisically** [-kli] *adv*

lackey [ˈlæki] *n, pl* **-eys 1** FOOTMAN : lacayo *m* **2** TOADY : adulador *m,* -dora *f*

lackluster [ˈlækˌlʌstər] *adj* **1** DULL : sin brillo, apagado, deslustrado **2** MEDIOCRE : deslucido, mediocre

laconic [ləˈkɑnɪk] *adj* : lacónico — **laconically** [-nɪkli] *adv*

lacquer[1] [ˈlækər] *vt* : laquear, pintar con laca

lacquer[2] *n* : laca *f*

lacrosse [ləˈkrɔs] *n* : lacrosse *f*

lactic acid [ˈlæktɪk] *n* : ácido *m* láctico

lacuna [ləˈkuːnə, -ˈkjuː-] *n, pl* **-nae** [-ˌniː, -ˌnaɪ] *or* **-nas** : laguna *f*

lacy [ˈleɪsi] *adj* **lacier; -est** : de encaje, como de encaje

lad [ˈlæd] *n* : muchacho *m,* niño *m*

ladder [ˈlædər] *n* : escalera *f*

laden [ˈleɪdən] *adj* : cargado

ladle[1] [ˈleɪdəl] *vt* **-dled; -dling** : servir con cucharón

ladle[2] *n* : cucharón *m,* cazo *m*

lady [ˈleɪdi] *n, pl* **-dies 1** : señora *f,* dama *f* **2** WOMAN : mujer *f*

ladybird [ˈleɪdiˌbərd] → **ladybug**

ladybug [ˈleɪdiˌbʌg] *n* : mariquita *f*

lag[1] [ˈlæg] *vi* **lagged; lagging** : quedarse atrás, retrasarse, rezagarse

lag[2] *n* **1** DELAY : retraso *m,* demora *f* **2** INTERVAL : lapso *m,* intervalo *m*

lager [ˈlɑgər] *n* : cerveza *f* rubia

laggard[1] [ˈlægərd] *adj* : retardado, retrasado

laggard[2] *n* : rezagado *m,* -da *f*

lagoon [ləˈguːn] *n* : laguna *f*

laid *pp* → **lay**

lain *pp* → **lie**

lair [ˈlær] *n* : guarida *f,* madriguera *f*

laissez–faire [ˌlɛˌseɪˈfær, ˌleɪˌzeɪ-] *n* : liberalismo *m* económico

laity [ˈleɪəṭi] *n* **the laity** : los laicos, el laicado

lake [ˈleɪk] *n* : lago *m*

lama [ˈlɑmə] *n* : lama *m*

lamb [ˈlæm] *n* **1** : cordero *m,* borrego *m* (animal) **2** : carne *f* de cordero

lambaste [læmˈbeɪst] *or* **lambast** [-ˈbæst] *vt* **-basted; -basting 1** BEAT, THRASH : golpear, azotar, darle una paliza (a alguien) **2** CENSURE : arremeter contre, censurar

lame[1] [ˈleɪm] *vt* **lamed; laming** : lisiar, hacer cojo

lame[2] *adj* **lamer; lamest 1** : cojo, renco, rengo **2** WEAK : pobre, débil, poco convincente <a lame excuse : una excusa débil>

lamé [lɑˈmeɪ, læ-] *n* : lamé *m*

lame duck *n* : persona *f* sin poder <a lame-duck President : un presidente saliente>

lamely [ˈleɪmli] *adv* : sin convicción

lameness [ˈleɪmnəs] *n* **1** : cojera *f,* renquera *f* **2** : falta *f* de convicción, debilidad *f,* pobreza *f* <the lameness of her response : la pobreza de su respuesta>

lament[1] [ləˈmɛnt] *vt* **1** MOURN : llorar, llorar por **2** DEPLORE : lamentar, deplorar — *vi* : llorar

lament[2] *n* : lamento *m*

lamentable [ˈlæməntəbəl, ləˈmɛntə-] *adj* : lamentable, deplorable — **lamentably** [-bli] *adv*

lamentation [ˌlæmənˈteɪʃən] *n* : lamentación *f,* lamento *m*

laminate[1] [ˈlæməˌneɪt] *vt* **-nated; -nating** : laminar

laminate[2] [ˈlæmənət] *n* : laminado *m*

laminated [ˈlæməˌneɪṭəd] *adj* : laminado

lamp [ˈlæmp] *n* : lámpara *f*

lampoon[1] [læmˈpuːn] *vt* : satirizar

lampoon[2] *n* : sátira *f*

lamprey [ˈlæmpri] *n, pl* **-preys** : lamprea *f*

lance[1] [ˈlænts] *vt* **lanced; lancing** : abrir con lanceta, sajar

lance[2] *n* : lanza *f*
lance corporal *n* : cabo *m* interino, soldado *m* de primera clase
lancet [ˈlæntsət] *n* : lanceta *f*
land[1] [ˈlænd] *vt* **1** : desembarcar (pasajeros de un barco), hacer aterrizar (un avión) **2** CATCH : pescar, sacar (un pez) del agua **3** GAIN, SECURE : conseguir, ganar <to land a job : conseguir empleo> **4** DELIVER : dar, asestar <he landed a punch : asestó un puñetazo> — *vi* **1** : aterrizar, tomar tierra, atracar <the plane just landed : el avión acaba de aterrizar> <the ship landed an hour ago : el barco atracó hace una hora>**2** ALIGHT : posarse, aterrizar <to land on one's feet : caer de pie>
land[2] *n* **1** GROUND : tierra *f* <dry land : tierra firme> **2** TERRAIN : terreno *m* **3** NATION : país *m,* nación *f* **4** DOMAIN : mundo *m,* dominio *m* <the land of dreams : el mundo de los sueños>
landfill [ˈlænd,fɪl] *n* : vertadero *m* (de basuras)
landing [ˈlændɪŋ] *n* **1** : aterrizaje *m* (de aviones), desembarco *m* (de barcos) **2** : descansillo *m* (de una escalera)
landing field *n* : campo *m* de aterrizaje
landing strip → **airstrip**
landlady [ˈlænd,leɪdi] *n, pl* **-dies** : casera *f,* dueña *f,* arrendadora *f*
landless [ˈlændləs] *adj* : sin tierra
landlocked [ˈlænd,lɑkt] *adj* : sin salida al mar
landlord [ˈlænd,lɔrd] *n* : dueño *m,* casero *m,* arrendador *m*
landlubber [ˈlænd,lʌbər] *n* : marinero *m* de agua dulce
landmark [ˈlænd,mɑrk] *n* **1** : señal *f* (geográfica), punto *m* de referencia **2** MILESTONE : hito *m* <a landmark in our history : un hito en nuestra historia> **3** MONUMENT : monumento *m* histórico
landowner [ˈlænd,oːnər] *n* : hacendado *m,* -da *f;* terrateniente *mf*
landscape[1] [ˈlænd,skeɪp] *vt* **-scaped; -scaping** : ajardinar
landscape[2] *n* : paisaje *m*
landslide [ˈlænd,slaɪd] *n* **1** : desprendimiento *m* de tierras, derrumbe *m* **2 landslide victory** : victoria *f* arrolladora
landward [ˈlændwərd] *adv* : en dirección de la tierra, hacia tierra
lane [ˈleɪn] *n* **1** PATH, WAY : camino *m,* sendero *m* **2** : carril *m* (de una carretera)
language [ˈlæŋgwɪdʒ] *n* **1** : idioma *m,* lengua *f* <the English language : el idioma inglés> **2** : lenguaje *m* <body language : lenguaje corporal>
languid [ˈlæŋgwɪd] *adj* : lánguido — **languidly** *adv*
languish [ˈlæŋgwɪʃ] *vi* **1** WEAKEN : languidecer, debilitarse **2** PINE : consumirse, suspirar (por) <to languish for love : suspirar por el amor> <he languished in prison : estuvo pudriéndose en la cárcel>
languor [ˈlæŋgər] *n* : languidez *f*
languorous [ˈlæŋgərəs] *adj* : lánguido — **languorously** *adv*
lank [ˈlæŋk] *adj* **1** THIN : delgado, larguirucho *fam* **2** LIMP : lacio
lanky [ˈlæŋki] *adj* **lankier; -est** : delgado, larguirucho *fam*
lanolin [ˈlænəlɪn] *n* : lanolina *f*
lantern [ˈlæntərn] *n* : linterna *f,* farol *m*
Laotian [leɪˈoːʃən, ˈlaʊʃən] *n* : laosiano *m,* -na *f* — **Laotian** *adj*
lap[1] [ˈlæp] *v* **lapped; lapping** *vt* **1** FOLD : plegar, doblar **2** WRAP : envolver **3** : lamer, besar <waves were lapping the shore : las olas lamían la orilla> **4 to lap up** : beber a lengüetadas (como un gato) — *vi* OVERLAP : traslaparse
lap[2] *n* **1** : falda *f,* regazo *m* (del cuerpo) **2** OVERLAP : traslapo *m* **3** : vuelta *f* (en deportes) **4** STAGE : etapa *f* (de un viaje)
lapdog [ˈlæp,dɔg] *n* : perro *m* faldero
lapel [ləˈpɛl] *n* : solapa *f*
Lapp [ˈlæp] *n* : lapón *m,* -pona *f* — **Lapp** *adj*
lapse[1] [ˈlæps] *vi* **lapsed; lapsing 1** FALL, SLIP : caer <to lapse into bad habits : caer en malos hábitos> <to lapse into unconsciousness : perder el conocimiento> <to lapse into silence : quedarse callado> **2** FADE : decaer, desvanecerse <her dedication lapsed : su dedicación se desvaneció> **3** CEASE : cancelarse, perderse **4** ELAPSE : transcurrir, pasar **5** EXPIRE : caducar
lapse[2] *n* **1** SLIP : lapsus *m,* deliz *m,* falla *f* <a lapse of memory : una falla de memoria> **2** INTERVAL : lapso *m,* intervalo *m,* período *m* **3** EXPIRATION : caducidad *f*
laptop [ˈlæp,tɑp] *adj* : portátil, laptop
larboard [ˈlɑrbərd] *n* : babor *m*
larcenous [ˈlɑrsənəs] *adj* : de robo
larceny [ˈlɑrsəni] *n, pl* **-nies** : robo *m,* hurto *m*
larch [ˈlɑrtʃ] *n* : alerce *f*
lard [ˈlɑrd] *n* : manteca *f* de cerdo
larder [ˈlɑrdər] *n* : despensa *f,* alacena *f*
large [ˈlɑrdʒ] *adj* **larger; largest 1** BIG : grande **2** COMPREHENSIVE : amplio, extenso **3 by and large** : por lo general
largely [ˈlɑrdʒli] *adv* : en gran parte, en su mayoría
largeness [ˈlɑrdʒnəs] *n* : lo grande
largesse *or* **largess** [lɑrˈʒɛs, -ˈdʒɛs] *n* : generosidad *f,* largueza *f*
lariat [ˈlæriət] *n* : lazo *m*
lark [ˈlɑrk] *n* **1** FUN : diversión *f* <what a lark! : ¡qué divertido!> **2** : alondra *f* (pájaro)
larva [ˈlɑrvə] *n, pl* **-vae** [-,viː, -,vaɪ] : larva *f* — **larval** [-vəl] *adj*
laryngitis [,lærənˈdʒaɪtəs] *n* : laringitis *f*

larynx [ˈlærɪŋks] *n, pl* **-rynges** [ləˈrɪn,dʒiːz] *or* **-ynxes** [ˈlærɪŋksəz] : laringe *f*
lasagna [ləˈzɑnjə] *n* : lasaña *f*
lascivious [ləˈsɪviəs] *adj* : lascivo
lasciviousness [ləˈsɪviəsnəs] *n* : lascivia *f,* lujuria *f*
laser [ˈleɪzər] *n* : láser *m*
lash[1] [ˈlæʃ] *vt* **1** WHIP : azotar **2** BIND : atar, amarrar
lash[2] *n* **1** WHIP : látigo *m* **2** STROKE : latigazo *m* **3** EYELASH : pestaña *f*
lass [ˈlæs] *or* **lassie** [ˈlæsi] *n* : muchacha *f,* chica *f*
lassitude [ˈlæsə,tuːd, -,tjuːd] *n* : lasitud *f*
lasso[1] [ˈlæ,soː, læˈsuː] *vt* : lazar
lasso[2] *n, pl* **-sos** *or* **-soes** : lazo *m,* reata *f Mex*
last[1] [ˈlæst] *vi* **1** CONTINUE : durar <how long will it last? : ¿cuánto durará?> **2** ENDURE : aguantar, durar **3** SURVIVE : durar, sobrevivir **4** SUFFICE : durar, bastar — *vt* **1** : durar <it will last a lifetime : durará toda la vida> **2 to last out** : aguantar
last[2] *adv* **1** : en último lugar, al último <we came in last : llegamos en último lugar> **2** : por última vez, la última vez <I saw him last in Bogota : lo vi por última vez en Bogotá> **3** FINALLY : por último, en conclusión
last[3] *adj* **1** FINAL : último, final **2** PREVIOUS : pasado <last year : el año pasado>
last[4] *n* **1** : el último, la última, lo último <at last : por fin, al fin, finalmente> **2** : horma *f* (de zapatero)
lasting [ˈlæstɪŋ] *adj* : perdurable, duradero, estable
lastly [ˈlæstli] *adv* : por último, finalmente
latch[1] [ˈlætʃ] *vt* : cerrar con picaporte
latch[2] *n* : picaporte *m,* pestillo *m,* pasador *m*
late[1] [ˈleɪt] *adv* **later; latest 1** : tarde <to arrive late : llegar tarde> <to sleep late : dormir hasta tarde> **2** : a última hora, a finales <late in the month : a finales del mes> **3** RECENTLY : recién, últimamente <as late as last year : todavía en el año pasado>
late[2] *adj* **later; latest 1** TARDY : tardío, de retraso <to be late : llegar tarde> **2** : avanzado <because of the late hour : a causa de la hora avanzada> **3** DECEASED : difunto, fallecido **4** RECENT : reciente, último <our late quarrel : nuestra última pelea>
latecomer [ˈleɪt,kʌmər] *n* : rezagado *m,* -da *f*
lately [ˈleɪtli] *adv* : recientemente, últimamente
lateness [ˈleɪtnəs] *n* **1** DELAY : retraso *m,* atraso *m,* tardanza *f* **2** : lo avanzado (de la hora)
latent [ˈleɪtənt] *adj* : latente — **latently** *adv*
lateral [ˈlæt̬ərəl] *adj* : lateral — **laterally** *adv*
latex [ˈleɪ,tɛks] *n, pl* **-tices** [ˈleɪt̬ə,siːz, ˈlæt̬ə-] *or* **-texes** : látex *m*
lath [ˈlæθ, ˈlæð] *n, pl* **laths** *or* **lath** : listón *m*
lathe [ˈleɪð] *n* : torno *m*
lather[1] [ˈlæðər] *vt* : enjabonar — *vi* : espumar, hacer espuma
lather[2] *n* **1** : espuma *f* (de jabón) **2** : sudor *m* (de caballo) **3 to get into a lather** : ponerse histérico
Latin[1] *adj* : latino
Latin[2] *n* **1** : latín *m* (idioma) **2** → **Latin American**
Latin–American [ˈlætənəˈmɛrikən] *adj* : latinoamericano
Latin American *n* : latinoamericano *m,* -na *f*
latitude [ˈlæt̬ə,tuːd, -,tjuːd] *n* : latitud *f*
latrine [ləˈtriːn] *n* : letrina *f*
latter[1] [ˈlæt̬ər] *adj* **1** SECOND : segundo **2** LAST : último
latter[2] *pron* **the latter** : éste, ésta, éstos *pl,* éstas *pl*
lattice [ˈlæt̬əs] *n* : enrejado *m,* celosía *f*
Latvian [ˈlætviən] *n* : letón *m,* -tona *f* — **Latvian** *adj*
laud[1] [ˈlɔd] *vt* : alabar, loar
laud[2] *n* : alabanza *f,* loa *f*
laudable [ˈlɔdəbəl] *adj* : loable — **laudably** [-bli] *adv*
laugh[1] [ˈlæf] *vi* : reír, reírse
laugh[2] *n* **1** LAUGHTER : risa *f* **2** JOKE : chiste *m,* broma *f* <he did it for a laugh : lo hizo en broma, lo hizo para divertirse>
laughable [ˈlæfəbəl] *adj* : risible, de risa
laughingstock [ˈlæfɪŋ,stɑk] *n* : hazmerreír *m*
laughter [ˈlæftər] *n* : risa *f,* risas *fpl*
launch[1] [ˈlɔntʃ] *vt* **1** HURL : lanzar **2** : botar (un barco) **3** START : iniciar, empezar
launch[2] *n* **1** : lancha *f* (bote) **2** LAUNCHING : lanzamiento *m*
launder [ˈlɔndər] *vt* **1** : lavar y planchar (ropa) **2** : blanquear, lavar (dinero)
launderer [ˈlɔndərər] *n* : lavandero *m,* -ra *f*
laundress [ˈlɔndrəs] *n* : lavandera *f*
laundry [ˈlɔndri] *n, pl* **laundries 1** : ropa *f* sucia, ropa *f* para lavar <to do the laundry : lavar la ropa> **2** : lavandería *f* (servicio de lavar)
laureate [ˈlɔriət] *n* : laureado *m,* -da *f* <poet laureate : poeta laureado>
laurel [ˈlɔrəl] *n* **1** : laurel *m* (planta) **2 laurels** *npl* : laureles *mpl* <to rest on one's laurels : dormirse uno en sus laureles>
lava [ˈlɑvə, ˈlæ-] *n* : lava *f*
lavatory [ˈlævə,tori] *n, pl* **-ries** : baño *m,* cuarto *m* de baño

lavender ['lævəndər] *n* : lavanda *f,* espliego *m*
lavish[1] ['lævɪʃ] *vt* : prodigar (a), colmar (de)
lavish[2] *adj* **1** EXTRAVAGANT : pródigo, generoso, derrochador **2** ABUNDANT : abundante **3** LUXURIOUS : lujoso, espléndido
lavishly ['lævɪʃli] *adv* : con generosidad, espléndidamente <to live lavishly : vivir a lo grande>
lavishness ['lævɪʃnəs] *n* : generosidad *f,* esplendidez *f*
law ['lɔ] *n* **1** : ley *f* <to break the law : violar la ley> **2** : derecho *m* <criminal law : derecho criminal> **3** : abogacía *f* <to practice law : ejercer la abogacía>
law–abiding ['lɔə,baɪdɪŋ] *adj* : observante de la ley
lawbreaker ['lɔ,breɪkər] *n* : infractor *m,* -tora *f* de la ley
lawful ['lɔfəl] *adj* : legal, legítimo, lícito — **lawfully** *adv*
lawgiver ['lɔ,gɪvər] *n* : legislador *m,* -dora *f*
lawless ['lɔləs] *adj* : anárquico, ingobernable — **lawlessly** *adv*
lawlessness ['lɔləsnəs] *n* : anarquía *f,* desorden *m*
lawmaker ['lɔ,meɪkər] *n* : legislador *m,* -dora *f*
lawman ['lɔmən] *n, pl* **-men** [-mən, -,mɛn] : agente *m* del orden
lawn ['lɔn] *n* : césped *m,* pasto *m*
lawn mower *n* : cortadora *f* de césped
lawsuit ['lɔ,su:t] *n* : pleito *m,* litigio *m,* demanda *f*
lawyer ['lɔɪər, 'lɔjər] *n* : abogado *m,* -da *f*
lax ['læks] *adj* : laxo, relajado — **laxly** *adv*
laxative ['læksətɪv] *n* : laxante *m*
laxity ['læksəti] *n* : relajación *f,* descuido *m,* falta *f* de rigor
lay[1] ['leɪ] *vt* **laid** ['leɪd]; **laying 1** PLACE, PUT : poner, colocar <she laid it on the table : lo puso en la mesa> <to lay eggs : poner huevos> **2** : hacer <to lay a bet : hacer una apuesta> **3** IMPOSE : imponer <to lay a tax : imponer un impuesto> <to lay the blame on : echarle la culpa a> **4 to lay out** PRESENT : presentar, exponer <he laid out his plan : presentó su proyecto> **5 to lay out** DESIGN : diseñar (el trazado de)
lay[2] *pp* → **lie**
lay[3] *adj* SECULAR : laico, lego
lay[4] *n* **1** : disposición *f,* configuración *f* <the lay of the land : la configuración del terreno> **2** BALLAD : romance *m,* balada *f*
layer ['leɪər] *n* **1** : capa *f* (de pintura, etc.), estrato *m* (de roca) **2** : gallina *f* ponedora
layman ['leɪmən] *n, pl* **-men** [-mən, -,mɛn] : laico *m,* lego *m*
layoff ['leɪ,ɔf] *n* : despido *m*
lay off *vt* : despedir
layout ['leɪ,aʊt] *n* : disposición *f,* distribución *f* (de una casa, etc.), trazado *m* (de una ciudad)
lay up *vt* **1** STORE : guardar, almacenar **2 to be laid up** : estar enfermo, tener que guardar cama
laywoman ['leɪ,wʊmən] *n, pl* **-women** [-,wɪmən] : laica *f,* lega *f*
laziness ['leɪzinəs] *n* : pereza *f,* flojera *f*
lazy ['leɪzi] *adj* **-zier; -est** : perezoso, holgazán — **lazily** ['leɪzəli] *adv*
leach ['li:tʃ] *vt* : filtrar
lead[1] ['li:d] *vt* **led** ['lɛd]; **leading 1** GUIDE : conducir, llevar, guiar **2** DIRECT : dirigir **3** HEAD : encabezar, ir al frente de **4 to lead to** : resultar en, llevar a <it only leads to trouble : sólo resulta en problemas>
lead[2] *n* : delantera *f,* primer lugar *m* <to take the lead : tomar la delantera>
lead[3] ['lɛd] *n* **1** : plomo *m* (metal) **2** : mina *f* (de lápiz) **3 lead poisoning** : saturnismo *m*
leaden ['lɛdən] *adj* **1** : plomizo <a leaden sky : un ciel plomizo> **2** HEAVY : pesado
leader ['li:dər] *n* : jefe *m,* -fa *f;* líder *mf;* dirigente *mf;* gobernante *mf*
leadership ['li:dər,ʃɪp] *n* : mando *m,* dirección *f*
leaf[1] ['li:f] *vi* **1** : echar hojas (dícese de un árbol) **2 to leaf through** : hojear (un libro)
leaf[2] *n, pl* **leaves** ['li:vz] **1** : hoja *f* (de plantas o libros) **2 to turn over a new leaf** : hacer borrón y cuenta nueva
leafless ['li:fləs] *adj* : sin hojas, pelado
leaflet ['li:flət] *n* : folleto *m*
leafy ['li:fi] *adj* **leafier; -est** : frondoso
league[1] ['li:g] *v* **leagued; leaguing** *vt* : aliar, unir — *vi* : aliarse, unirse
league[2] *n* **1** : legua *f* (medida de distancia) **2** ASSOCIATION : alianza *f,* sociedad *f,* liga *f*
leak[1] ['li:k] *vt* **1** : perder, dejar escapar (un líquido o un gas) **2** : filtrar (información) — *vi* **1** : gotear, escaparse, fugarse (dícese de un líquido o un gas) **2** : hacer agua (dícese de un bote) **3** : filtrarse, divulgarse (dícese de información)
leak[2] *n* **1** HOLE : agujero *m* (en recipientes), gotera *f* (en un tejado) **2** ESCAPE : fuga *f,* escape *m* **3** : filtración *f* (de información)
leakage ['li:kɪdʒ] *n* : escape *m,* fuga *f*
leaky ['li:ki] *adj* **leakier; -est** : agujereado (dícese de un recipiente), que hace agua (dícese de un bote), con goteras (dícese de un tejado)
lean[1] ['li:n] *vi* **1** BEND : inclinarse, ladearse **2** RECLINE : reclinarse **3** RELY : apoyarse (en), depender (de) **4** INCLINE, TEND : inclinarse, tender — *vt* : apoyar

lean[2] *adj* 1 THIN : delgado, flaco 2 : sin grasa, magro (dícese de la carne)
leanness [ˈliːnnəs] *n* : delgadez *f*
lean–to [ˈliːnˌtuː] *n* : cobertizo *m*
leap[1] [ˈliːp] *vi* **leapt** *or* **leaped** [ˈliːpt, ˈlɛpt]; **leaping** : saltar, brincar
leap[2] *n* : salto *m,* brinco *m*
leap year *n* : año *m* bisiesto
learn [ˈlərn] *vt* 1 : aprender <to learn to sing : aprender a cantar> 2 MEMORIZE : aprender de memoria 3 DISCOVER : saber, enterarse de — *vi* 1 : aprender <to learn from experience : aprender por experiencia> 2 FIND OUT : enterarse, saber
learned [ˈlərnəd] *adj* : erudito
learner [ˈlərnər] *n* : principiante *mf,* estudiante *mf*
learning [ˈlərnɪŋ] *n* : erudición *f,* saber *m*
lease[1] [ˈliːs] *vt* **leased; leasing** : arrendar
lease[2] *n* : contrato *m* de arrendamiento
leash[1] [ˈliːʃ] *vt* : atraillar (un animal)
leash[2] *n* : traílla *f*
least[1] [ˈliːst] *adv* : menos <when least expected : cuando menos se espera>
least[2] *adj* (*superlative of* **little**) : menor, más mínimo
least[3] *n* 1 : lo menos <at least : por lo menos> 2 **to say the least** : por no decir más
leather [ˈlɛðər] *n* : cuero *m*
leathery [ˈlɛðəri] *adj* : curtido (dícese de la piel), correoso (dícese de la carne)
leave[1] [ˈliːv] *v* **left** [ˈlɛft]; **leaving** *vt* 1 BEQUEATH : dejar, legar 2 DEPART : dejar, salir(se) de 3 ABANDON : abandonar, dejar 4 FORGET : dejar, olvidarse de <I left the books at the library : dejé los libros en la biblioteca> 5 **to be left** : quedar <it's all I have left : es todo lo que me queda> 6 **to be left over** : sobrar 7 **to leave out** : omitir, excluir — *vi* : irse, salir, partir, marcharse <she left yesterday morning : se fue ayer por la mañana>
leave[2] *n* 1 PERMISSION : permiso *m* <by your leave : con su permiso> 2 *or* **leave of absence** : permiso *m,* licencia *f* <maternity leave : licencia por maternidad> 3 **to take one's leave** : despedirse
leaven [ˈlɛvən] *n* : levadura *f*
leaves → **leaf**[2]
leaving [ˈliːvɪŋ] *n* 1 : salida *f,* partida *f* 2 **leavings** *npl* : restos *mpl,* sobras *fpl*
Lebanese [ˌlɛbəˈniːz, -ˈniːs] *n* : libanés *m,* -nesa *f* — **Lebanese** *adj*
lecherous [ˈlɛtʃərəs] *adj* : lascivo, libidinoso — **lecherously** *adv*
lechery [ˈlɛtʃəri] *n* : lascivia *f,* lujuria *f*
lecture[1] [ˈlɛktʃər] *v* **-tured; -turing** *vi* : dar clase, dictar clase, dar una conferencia — *vt* SCOLD : sermonear, echar una reprimenda a, regañar
lecture[2] *n* 1 : conferencia *f* 2 REPRIMAND : reprimenda *f*
led *pp* → **lead**[1]
ledge [ˈlɛdʒ] *n* : repisa *f* (de una pared), antepecho *m* (de una ventana), saliente *m* (de una montaña)
ledger [ˈlɛdʒər] *n* : libro *m* mayor, libro *m* de contabilidad
lee[1] [ˈliː] *adj* : de sotavento
lee[2] *n* : sotavento *m*
leech [ˈliːtʃ] *n* : sanguijuela *f*
leek [ˈliːk] *n* : puerro *m*
leer[1] [ˈlɪr] *vi* : mirar con lascivia
leer[2] *n* : mirada *f* lasciva
leery [ˈlɪri] *adj* : receloso
lees [ˈliːz] *npl* : posos *mpl,* heces *fpl*
leeward[1] [ˈliːwərd, ˈluːərd] *adj* : de sotavento
leeward[2] *n* : sotavento *m*
leeway [ˈliːˌweɪ] *n* : libertad *f,* margen *m*
left[1] [ˈlɛft] *adv* : hacia la izquierda
left[2] *pp* → **leave**
left[3] *adj* : izquierdo
left[4] *n* : izquierda *f* <on the left : a la izquierda>
left–hand [ˈlɛftˈhand] *adj* 1 : de la izquierda 2 → **left–handed**
left–handed [ˈlɛftˈhandəd] *adj* 1 : zurdo (dícese de una persona) 2 : con doble sentido <a left-handed compliment : un cumplido a medias>
leftovers [ˈlɛftˌoːvərz] *npl* : restos *mpl,* sobras *fpl*
left wing *n* **the left wing** : la izquierda
left–winger [ˈlɛftˈwɪŋər] *n* : izquierdista *mf*
leg [ˈlɛg] *n* 1 : pierna *f* (de una persona, de carne, de ropa), pata *f* (de un animal, de muebles) 2 STAGE : etapa *f* (de un viaje), vuelta *f* (de una carrera)
legacy [ˈlɛgəsi] *n, pl* **-cies** : legado *m,* herencia *f*
legal [ˈliːgəl] *adj* 1 : legal, jurídico <legal advisor : asesor jurídico> <the legal profession : la abogacía> 2 LAWFUL : legítimo, legal
legalistic [ˌliːgəˈlɪstɪk] *adj* : legalista
legality [lɪˈgæləṭi] *n, pl* **-ties** : legalidad *f*
legalize [ˈliːgəˌlaɪz] *vt* **-ized; -izing** : legalizar
legally [ˈliːgəli] *adv* : legalmente
legate [ˈlɛgət] *n* : legado *m*
legation [lɪˈgeɪʃən] *n* : legación *f*
legend [ˈlɛdʒənd] *n* 1 STORY : leyenda *f* 2 INSCRIPTION : leyenda *f,* inscripción *f* 3 : signos *mpl* convencionales (en un mapa)
legendary [ˈlɛdʒənˌdɛri] *adj* : lengendario
legerdemain [ˌlɛdʒərdəˈmeɪn] → **sleight of hand**
leggings [ˈlɛgɪŋz, ˈlɛgənz] *npl* : mallas *fpl*
legibility [ˌlɛdʒəˈbɪləṭi] *n* : legibilidad *f*
legible [ˈlɛdʒəbəl] *adj* : legible

legibly [ˈlɛdʒəbli] *adv* **:** de manera legible
legion [ˈliːdʒən] *n* **:** legión *f*
legionnaire [ˌliːdʒəˈnær] *n* **:** legionario *m,* -ria *f*
legislate [ˈlɛdʒəsˌleɪt] *vi* **-lated; -lating :** legislar
legislation [ˌlɛdʒəsˈleɪʃən] *n* **:** legislación *f*
legislative [ˈlɛdʒəsˌleɪt̬ɪv] *adj* **:** legislativo, legislador
legislator [ˈlɛdʒəsˌleɪt̬ər] *n* **:** legislador *m,* -dora *f*
legislature [ˈlɛdʒəsˌleɪtʃər] *n* **:** asamblea *f* legislativa
legitimacy [lɪˈdʒɪt̬əməsi] *n* **:** legitimidad *f*
legitimate [lɪˈdʒɪt̬əmət] *adj* **1** VALID **:** legítimo, válido, justificado **2** LAWFUL **:** legítimo, legal
legitimately [lɪˈdʒɪt̬əmətli] *adv* **:** legítimamente
legitimize [lɪˈdʒɪt̬əˌmaɪz] *vt* **-mized; -mizing :** legitimar, hacer legítimo
legume [ˈlɛˌgjuːm, lɪˈgjuːm] *n* **:** legumbre *f*
leisure [ˈliːʒər, ˈlɛ-] *n* **1 :** ocio *m,* tiempo *m* libre <a life of leisure : una vida de ocio> **2 to take one's leisure :** reposar **3 at your leisure :** cuando te venga bien, cuando tengas tiempo
leisurely [ˈliːʒərli, ˈlɛ-] *adj & adv* **:** lento, sin prisas
lemming [ˈlɛmɪŋ] *n* **:** lemming *m*
lemon [ˈlɛmən] *n* **:** limón *m*
lemonade [ˌlɛməˈneɪd] *n* **:** limonada *f*
lemony [ˈlɛməni] *adj* **:** a limón
lend [ˈlɛnd] *vt* **lent** [ˈlɛnt]; **lending 1 :** prestar <to lend money : prestar dinero> **2** GIVE **:** dar <it lends force to his criticism : da fuerza a su crítica> **3 to lend oneself to :** prestarse a
length [ˈlɛŋkθ] *n* **1 :** longitud *f,* largo *m* <10 feet in length : 10 pies de largo> **2** DURATION **:** duración *f* **3 :** trozo *m* (de madera), corte *m* (de tela) **4 to go to any lengths :** hacer todo lo posible **5 at ~ :** extensamente <to speak at length : hablar largo y tendido>
lengthen [ˈlɛŋkθən] *vt* **1 :** alargar <can they lengthen the dress? : ¿se puede alargar el vestido?> **2** EXTEND, PROLONG **:** prolongar, extender — *vi* **:** alargarse, crecer <the days are lengthening : los días están creciendo>
lengthways [ˈlɛŋkθˌweɪz] → **lengthwise**
lengthwise [ˈlɛŋkθˌwaɪz] *adv* **:** a lo largo, longitudinalmente
lengthy [ˈlɛŋkθi] *adj* **lengthier; -est 1** OVERLONG **:** largo y pesado **2** EXTENDED **:** prolongado, largo
leniency [ˈliːniəntsi] *n, pl* **-cies :** lenidad *f,* indulgencia *f*
lenient [ˈliːniənt] *adj* **:** indulgente, poco severo
leniently [ˈliːniəntli] *adv* **:** con lenidad, con indulgencia
lens [ˈlɛnz] *n* **1 :** cristalino *m* (del ojo) **2 :** lente *mf* (de un instrumento o una cámara) **3** → **contact lens**
lent → **lend**
Lent [ˈlɛnt] *n* **:** Cuaresma *f*
lentil [ˈlɛntəl] *n* **:** lenteja *f*
Leo [ˈliːoː] *n* **:** Leo *mf*
leopard [ˈlɛpərd] *n* **:** leopardo *m*
leotard [ˈliːəˌtɑrd] *n* **:** leotardo *m,* malla *f*
leper [ˈlɛpər] *n* **:** leproso *m,* -sa *f*
leprechaun [ˈlɛprəˌkɑn] *n* **:** duende *m* (irlandés)
leprosy [ˈlɛprəsi] *n* **:** lepra *f* — **leprous** [ˈlɛprəs] *adj*
lesbian[1] [ˈlɛzbiən] *adj* **:** lesbiano
lesbian[2] *n* **:** lesbiana *f*
lesbianism [ˈlɛzbiəˌnɪzəm] *n* **:** lesbianismo *m*
lesion [ˈliːʒən] *n* **:** lesión *f*
less[1] [ˈlɛs] *adv* (*comparative of* **little**[1]) **:** menos <the less you know, the better : cuanto menos sepas, mejor> <less and less : cada vez menos>
less[2] *adj* (*comparative of* **little**[2]) **:** menos <less than three : menos de tres> <less money : menos dinero> <nothing less than perfection : nada menos que la perfección>
less[3] *pron* **:** menos <I'm earning less : estoy ganando menos>
less[4] *prep* **:** menos <one month less two days : un mes menos dos días>
lessee [lɛˈsiː] *n* **:** arrendatario *m,* -ria *f*
lessen [ˈlɛsən] *vt* **:** disminuir, reducir — *vi* **:** disminuir, reducirse
lesser [ˈlɛsər] *adj* **:** menor <to a lesser degree : en menor grado>
lesson [ˈlɛsən] *n* **1** CLASS **:** clase *f,* curso *m* **2 :** lección *f* <the lessons of history : las lecciones de la historia>
lessor [ˈlɛˌsɔr, lɛˈsɔr] *n* **:** arrendador *m,* -dora *f*
lest [ˈlɛst] *conj* **:** para (que) no <lest we forget : para que no olvidemos>
let [ˈlɛt] *vt* **let; letting 1** ALLOW **:** dejar, permitir <let me see it : déjame verlo> **2** MAKE **:** hacer <let me know : házmelo saber, avísame> <let them wait : que esperen, haz que esperen> **3** RENT **:** alquilar **4** (*used in the first person plural imperative*) <let's go! : ¡vamos!, ¡vámonos!> <let us pray : oremos> **5 to let down** DISAPPOINT **:** fallar **6 to let off** FORGIVE **:** perdonar **7 to let out** REVEAL **:** revelar **8 to let up** ABATE **:** amainar, disminuir <the pace never lets up : el ritmo nunca disminuye>
letdown *n* **:** chasco *m,* decepción *f*
lethal [ˈliːθəl] *adj* **:** letal — **lethally** *adv*
lethargic [lɪˈθɑrdʒɪk] *adj* **:** letárgico
lethargy [ˈlɛθərdʒi] *n* **:** letargo *m*
let on *vi* **1** ADMIT **:** reconocer <don't let on! : ¡no digas nada!> **2** PRETEND **:** fingir
let's [ˈlɛts] (*contraction of* **let us**) → **let**

letter[1] [ˈlɛt̬ər] *vt* : marcar con letras, inscribir letras en

letter[2] *n* **1** : letra *f* (del alfabeto) **2** : carta *f* <a letter to my mother : una carta a mi madre> **3 letters** *npl* ARTS : letras *fpl* **4 to the letter** : al pie de la letra

lettering [ˈlɛt̬ərɪŋ] *n* : letra *f*

lettuce [ˈlɛt̬əs] *n* : lechuga *f*

leukemia [luːˈkiːmiə] *n* : leucemia *f*

levee [ˈlɛvi] *n* : dique *m*

level[1] [ˈlɛvəl] *vt* **-eled** *or* **-elled; -eling** *or* **-elling 1** FLATTEN : nivelar, aplanar **2** AIM : apuntar (una pistola), dirigir (una acusación) **3** RAZE : rasar, arrasar

level [2] *adj* **1** EVEN : llano, plano, parejo **2** CALM : tranquilo <to keep a level head : no perder la cabeza>

level [3] *n* : nivel *m*

leveler [ˈlɛvələr] *n* : nivelador *m*, -dora *f*

levelheaded [ˈlɛvəlˈhɛdəd] *adj* : sensato, equilibrado

levelly [ˈlɛvəli] *adv* CALMLY : con ecuanimidad *f*, con calma

levelness [ˈlɛvəlnəs] *n* : uniformidad *f*

lever [ˈlɛvər, ˈliː-] *n* : palanca *f*

leverage [ˈlɛvərɪdʒ, ˈliː-] *n* **1** : apalancamiento *m* (en física) **2** INFLUENCE : influencia *f*, palanca *f fam*

leviathan [lɪˈvaɪəθən] *n* : leviatán *m*, gigante *m*

levity [ˈlɛvət̬i] *n* : ligereza *f*, frivolidad *f*

levy[1] [ˈlɛvi] *vt* **levied; levying 1** IMPOSE : imponer, exigir, gravar (un impuesto) **2** COLLECT : recaudar (un impuesto)

levy[2] *n, pl* **levies** : impuesto *m*, gravamen *m*

lewd [ˈluːd] *adj* : lascivo — **lewdly** *adv*

lewdness [ˈluːdnəs] *n* : lascivia *f*

lexicographer [ˌlɛksəˈkɑgrəfər] *n* : lexicógrafo *m*, -fa *f*

lexicographical [ˌlɛksəkoˈgræfɪkəl] *or* **lexicographic** [-ˈgræfɪk] *adj* : lexicográfico

lexicography [ˌlɛksəˈkɑgrəfi] *n* : lexicografía *f*

lexicon [ˈlɛksɪˌkɑn] *n, pl* **-ica** [-kə] *or* **-icons** : léxico *m*, lexicón *m*

liability [ˌlaɪəˈbɪlət̬i] *n, pl* **-ties 1** RESPONSIBILITY : responsabilidad *f* **2** SUSCEPTIBILITY : propensión *f* **3** DRAWBACK : desventaja *f* **4 liabilities** *npl* DEBTS : deudas *fpl*, pasivo *m*

liable [ˈlaɪəbəl] *adj* **1** RESPONSIBLE : responsable **2** SUSCEPTIBLE : propenso **3** PROBABLE : probable <it's liable to happen : es probable que suceda>

liaison [ˈliːəˌzɑn, liˈeɪ-] *n* **1** CONNECTION : enlace *m*, relación *f* **2** AFFAIR : amorío *m*, aventura *f*

liar [ˈlaɪər] *n* : mentiroso *m*, -sa *f*; embustero *m*, -ra *f*

libel[1] [ˈlaɪbəl] *vt* **-beled** *or* **-belled; -beling** *or* **-belling** : difamar, calumniar

libel[2] *n* : difamación *f*, calumnia *f*

libeler [ˈlaɪbələr] *n* : difamador *m*, -dora *f*; calumniador *m*, -dora *f*; libelista *mf*

libelous *or* **libellous** [ˈlaɪbələs] *adj* : difamatorio, calumnioso, injurioso

liberal[1] [ˈlɪbrəl, ˈlɪbərəl] *adj* **1** TOLERANT : liberal, tolerante **2** GENEROUS : generoso **3** ABUNDANT : abundante **4 liberal arts** : humanidades *fpl*, artes *fpl* liberales

liberal[2] *n* : liberal *mf*

liberalism [ˈlɪbrəˌlɪzəm, ˈlɪbərə-] *n* : liberalismo *m*

liberality [ˌlɪbəˈræləṭi] *n, pl* **-ties** : liberalidad *f*, generosidad *f*

liberalize [ˈlɪbrəˌlaɪz, ˈlɪbərə-] *vt* **-ized; -izing** : liberalizar

liberally [ˈlɪbrəli, ˈlɪbərə-] *adv* **1** GENEROUSLY : generosamente **2** ABUNDANTLY : abundantemente **3** FREELY : libremente

liberate [ˈlɪbəˌreɪt] *vt* **-ated; -ating** : liberar, libertar

liberation [ˌlɪbəˈreɪʃən] *n* : liberación *f*

liberator [ˈlɪbəˌreɪt̬ər] *n* : libertador *m*, -dora *f*

Liberian [laɪˈbɪriən] *n* : liberiano *m*, -na *f* — **Liberian** *adj*

libertine [ˈlɪbərˌtiːn] *n* : libertino *m*, -na *f*

liberty [ˈlɪbərt̬i] *n, pl* **-ties 1** : libertad *f* **2 to take the liberty of** : tomarse la libertad de **3 to take liberties with** : tomarse confianzas con, tomarse libertades con

libido [ləˈbiːdoː, -ˈbaɪ-] *n, pl* **-dos** : libido *f* — **libidinous** [ləˈbɪdənəs] *adj*

Libra [ˈliːbrə] *n* : Libra *mf*

librarian [laɪˈbrɛriən] *n* : bibliotecario *m*, -ria *f*

library [ˈlaɪˌbrɛri] *n, pl* **-braries** : biblioteca *f*

librettist [lɪˈbrɛt̬ɪst] *n* : libretista *mf*

libretto [lɪˈbrɛt̬o] *n, pl* **-tos** *or* **-ti** [-tiː] : libreto *m*

Libyan [ˈlɪbiən] *n* : libio *m*, -bia *f* — **Libyan** *adj*

lice → **louse**

license[1] [ˈlaɪsənts] *vt* **licensed; licensing** : licenciar, autorizar, dar permiso a

license[2] *or* **licence** *n* **1** PERMISSION : licencia *f*, permiso *m* **2** PERMIT : licencia *f*, carnet *m Spain* <driver's license : licencia de conducir> **3** FREEDOM : libertad *f* **4** LICENTIOUSNESS : libertinaje *m*

licentious [laɪˈsɛntʃəs] *adj* : licencioso, disoluto — **licentiously** *adv*

licentiousness [laɪˈsɛntʃəsnəs] *n* : libertinaje *m*

lichen [ˈlaɪkən] *n* : liquen *m*

licit [ˈlɪsət] *adj* : lícito

lick[1] [ˈlɪk] *vt* **1** : lamer **2** BEAT : darle una paliza (a alguien)

lick[2] *n* **:** lamida *f,* lengüetada *f* <a lick of paint : una mano de pintura> **2** BIT **:** pizca *f,* ápice *m* **3 a lick and a promise :** una lavada a la carrera

licorice [ˈlɪkərɪʃ, -rəs] *n* **:** regaliz *m,* dulce *m* de regaliz

lid [ˈlɪd] *n* **1** COVER **:** tapa *f* **2** EYELID **:** párpado *m*

lie[1] [ˈlaɪ] *vi* **lay** [ˈleɪ]; **lain** [ˈleɪn]; **lying** [ˈlaɪɪŋ] **1 :** acostarse, echarse <I lay down : me acosté> **2 :** estar, estar situado, encontrarse <the book lay on the table : el libro estaba en la mesa> <the city lies to the south : la ciudad se encuentra al sur> **3** CONSIST **:** consistir **4 to lie in :** residir en <the power lies in the people : el poder reside en el pueblo>

lie[2] *vi* **lied; lying** [ˈlaɪɪŋ] **:** mentir

lie[3] *n* **1** UNTRUTH **:** mentira *f* <to tell lies : decir mentiras> **2** POSITION **:** posición *f*

liege [ˈliːdʒ] *n* **:** señor *m* feudal

lien [ˈliːn, ˈliːən] *n* **:** derecho *m* de retención

lieutenant [luːˈtɛnənt] *n* **:** teniente *mf*

lieutenant colonel *n* **:** teniente *mf* coronel

lieutenant commander *n* **:** capitán *m,* -tana *f* de corbeta

lieutenant general *n* **:** teniente *mf* general

life [ˈlaɪf] *n, pl* **lives** [ˈlaɪvz] **1 :** vida *f* <plant life : la vida vegetal> **2** EXISTENCE **:** vida *f,* existencia *f* **3** BIOGRAPHY **:** biografía *f,* vida *f* **4** DURATION **:** duración *f,* vida *f* **5** LIVELINESS **:** vivacidad *f,* animación *f*

lifeblood [ˈlaɪfˌblʌd] *n* **:** parte *f* vital, sustento *m*

lifeboat [ˈlaɪfˌboːt] *n* **:** bote *m* salvavidas

lifeguard [ˈlaɪfˌgɑrd] *n* **:** socorrista *mf,* salvavidas *mf*

lifeless [ˈlaɪfləs] *adj* **:** sin vida, muerto

lifelike [ˈlaɪfˌlaɪk] *adj* **:** que parece vivo, natural, verosímil

lifelong [ˈlaɪfˈlɔŋ] *adj* **:** de toda la vida <a lifelong friend : un amigo de toda la vida>

life preserver *n* **:** salvavidas *m*

lifesaver [ˈlaɪfˌseɪvər] *n* **1 :** salvación *f* **2** → **lifeguard**

lifesaving [ˈlaɪfˌseɪvɪŋ] *n* **:** socorrismo *m*

lifestyle [ˈlaɪfˌstaɪl] *n* **:** estilo *m* de vida

lifetime [ˈlaɪfˌtaɪm] *n* **:** vida *f,* curso *m* de la vida

lift[1] [ˈlɪft] *vt* **1** RAISE **:** levantar, alzar, subir **2** END **:** levantar <to lift a ban : levantar una prohibición> — *vi* **1** RISE **:** levantarse, alzarse **2** CLEAR UP **:** despejar <the fog lifted : se disipó la niebla>

lift[2] *n* **1** LIFTING **:** levantamiento *m,* alzamiento *m* **2** BOOST **:** impulso *m,* estímulo *m* **3 to give someone a lift :** llevar en coche a alguien

liftoff [ˈlɪftˌɔf] *n* **:** despegue *m*

ligament [ˈlɪgəmənt] *n* **:** ligamento *m*

ligature [ˈlɪgəˌtʃʊr, -tʃər] *n* **:** ligadura *f*

light[1] [ˈlaɪt] *v* **lit** [ˈlɪt] *or* **lighted; lighting** *vt* **1** ILLUMINATE **:** iluminar, alumbrar **2** IGNITE **:** encender, prenderle fuego a — *vi* **:** encenderse, prender

light[2] *vi* **lighted** *or* **lit** [ˈlɪt]; **lighting 1** LAND, SETTLE **:** posarse **2** DISMOUNT **:** bajarse, apearse

light[3] [ˈlaɪt] *adv* **1** LIGHTLY **:** suavemente, ligeramente **2 to travel light :** viajar con poco equipaje

light[4] *adj* **1** LIGHTWEIGHT **:** ligero, liviano, poco pesado **2** EASY **:** fácil, ligero, liviano <light reading : lectura fácil> <light work : trabajo liviano> **3** GENTLE, MILD **:** fino, suave, leve <a light breeze : una brisa suave> <a light rain : una lluvia fina> **4** FRIVOLOUS **:** de poca importancia, superficial **5** BRIGHT **:** bien iluminado, claro **6** PALE **:** claro (dícese de los colores), rubio (dícese del pelo)

light[5] *n* **1** ILLUMINATION **:** luz *f* **2** DAYLIGHT **:** luz *f* del día **3** DAWN **:** amanecer *m,* madrugada *f* **4** LAMP **:** lámpara *f* <to turn on off the light : apagar la luz> **5** ASPECT **:** aspecto *m* <in a new light : con otros ojos> <in the light of : en vista de, a la luz de> **6** MATCH **:** fósforo *m,* cerillo *m* **7 to bring to light :** sacar a (la) luz

lightbulb [ˈlaɪtˌbʌlb] *n* **:** bombilla *f,* foco *m,* bombillo *m CA, Col, Ven*

lighten [ˈlaɪtən] *vt* **1** ILLUMINATE **:** iluminar, dar más luz a **2 :** aclararse (el pelo) **3 :** aligerar (una carga, etc.) **4** RELIEVE **:** aliviar **5** GLADDEN **:** alegrar <it lightened his heart : alegró su corazón>

lighter [ˈlaɪtər] *n* **:** encendedor *m*

lighthearted [ˈlaɪtˈhɑrtəd] *adj* **:** alegre, despreocupado, desenfadado — **lightheartedly** *adv*

lightheartedness [ˈlaɪtˈhɑrtədnəs] *n* **:** desenfado *m,* alegría *f*

lighthouse [ˈlaɪtˌhaʊs] *n* **:** faro *m*

lighting [ˈlaɪtɪŋ] *n* **:** iluminación *f*

lightly [ˈlaɪtli] *adv* **1** GENTLY **:** suavemente **2** SLIGHTLY **:** ligeramente **3** FRIVOLOUSLY **:** a la ligera **4 to let off lightly :** tratar con indulgencia

lightness [ˈlaɪtnəs] *n* **1** BRIGHTNESS **:** luminosidad *f,* claridad *f* **2** GENTLENESS **:** ligereza *f,* suavidad *f,* delicadeza *f* **3 :** ligereza *f,* liviandad *f* (de peso)

lightning [ˈlaɪtnɪŋ] *n* **:** relámpago *m,* rayo *m*

lightning bug → **firefly**

lightproof [ˈlaɪtˌpruːf] *adj* **:** impenetrable por la luz, opaco

lightweight [ˈlaɪtˈweɪt] *adj* **:** ligero, liviano, de poco peso

light–year [ˈlaɪtˌjɪr] *n* **:** año *m* luz

lignite [ˈlɪgˌnaɪt] *n* **:** lignito *m*

likable *or* **likeable** [ˈlaɪkəbəl] *adj* **:** simpático, agradable

like[1] ['laɪk] *v* **liked; liking** *vt* **1 :** agradar, gustarle (algo a uno) <he likes rice : le gusta el arroz> <she doesn't like flowers : a ella no le gustan las flores> <I like you : me caes bien> **2** WANT : querer, desear <I'd like a hamburger : quiero una hamburguesa> <he would like more help : le gustaría tener más ayuda> — *vi* : querer <do as you like : haz lo que quieras>

like[2] *adj* : parecido, semejante, similar

like[3] *n* **1** PREFERENCE : preferencia *f,* gusto *m* **2 the like :** cosa *f* parecida, cosas *fpl* por el estilo <I've never seen the like : nunca he visto cosa parecida>

like[4] *conj* **1** AS IF : como si <they looked at me like I was crazy : se me quedaron mirando como si estuviera loca> **2** AS : como, igual que <she doesn't love you like I do : ella no te quiere como yo>

like[5] *prep* **1 :** como, parecido a <she acts like my mother : se comporta como mi madre> <he looks like me : se parece a mí> **2 :** propio de, típico de <that's just like her : eso es muy típico de ella> **3 :** como <animals like cows : animales como vacas> **4 like this, like that :** así <do it like that : hazlo así>

likelihood ['laɪkli,hʊd] *n* : probabilidad *f* <in all likelihood : con toda probabilidad>

likely[1] ['laɪkli] *adv* : probablemente <most likely he's sick : lo más probable es que esté enfermo> <they're likely to come : es probable que vengan>

likely[2] *adj* **-lier; -est 1** PROBABLE : probable <to be likely to : ser muy probable que> **2** SUITABLE : apropiado, adecuado **3** BELIEVABLE : verosímil, creíble **4** PROMISING : prometedor

liken ['laɪkən] *vt* : comparar

likeness ['laɪknəs] *n* **1** SIMILARITY : semejanza *f,* parecido *m* **2** PORTRAIT : retrato *m*

likewise ['laɪk,waɪz] *adv* **1** SIMILARLY : de la misma manera, asimismo **2** ALSO : también, además, asimismo

liking ['laɪkɪŋ] *n* **1** FONDNESS : afición *f* (por una cosa), simpatía *f* (por una persona) **2** TASTE : gusto *m* <is it to your liking? : ¿te gusta?>

lilac ['laɪlək, -,læk, -,lɑk] *n* : lila *f*

lilt ['lɪlt] *n* : cadencia *f,* ritmo *m* alegre

lily ['lɪli] *n, pl* **lilies 1 :** lirio *m,* azucena *f* **2 lily of the valley :** lirio *m* de los valles, muguete *m*

lima bean ['laɪmə] *n* : frijol *m* de media luna

limb ['lɪm] *n* **1** APPENDAGE : miembro *m,* extremidad *f* **2** BRANCH : rama *f*

limber[1] ['lɪmbər] *vi or* **to limber up** : calentarse, prepararse

limber[2] *adj* : ágil (dícese de las personas), flexible (dícese de los objetos)

limbo ['lɪm,boː] *n, pl* **-bos 1 :** limbo *m* (en la religión) **2** OBLIVION : olvido *m* <the project is in limbo : el proyecto ha caído en el olvido>

lime ['laɪm] *n* **1 :** cal *f* (óxido) **2 :** lima *f* (fruta), limón *m* verde *Mex*

limelight ['laɪm,laɪt] *n* **to be in the limelight :** ser el centro de atención, estar en el candelero

limerick ['lɪmərɪk] *n* : poema *m* jocoso de cinco versos

limestone ['laɪm,stoːn] *n* : piedra *f* caliza, caliza *f*

limit[1] ['lɪmət] *vt* : limitar, restringir

limit[2] *n* **1** MAXIMUM : límite *m,* máximo *m* <speed limit : límite de velocidad> **2 limits** *npl* : límites *mpl,* confines *mpl* <city limits : límites de la ciudad> **3 that's the limit! :** ¡eso es el colmo!

limitation [,lɪmə'teɪʃən] *n* : limitación *f,* restricción *f*

limited ['lɪmət̬əd] *adj* : limitado, restringido

limitless ['lɪmətləs] *adj* : ilimitado, sin límites

limousine ['lɪmə,ziːn, ,lɪmə'-] *n* : limusina *f*

limp[1] ['lɪmp] *vi* : cojear

limp[2] *adj* **1** FLACCID : fláccido **2** LANK : lacio (dícese del pelo) **3** WEAK : débil <to feel limp : sentirse desfallecer, sentirse sin fuerzas>

limp[3] *n* : cojera *f*

limpid ['lɪmpəd] *adj* : límpido, claro

limply ['lɪmpli] *adv* : sin fuerzas

limpness ['lɪmpnəs] *n* : flaccidez *f,* debilidad *f*

linden ['lɪndən] *n* : tilo *m*

line[1] ['laɪn] *v* **lined; lining** *vt* **1 :** forrar, cubrir <to line a dress : forrar un vestido> <to line the walls : cubrir las paredes> **2** MARK : rayar, trazar líneas en **3** BORDER : bordear **4** ALIGN : alinear — *vi* **to line up :** ponerse in fila, hacer cola

line[2] *n* **1** CORD, ROPE : cuerda *f* **2** WIRE : cable *m* <power line : cable eléctrico> **3 :** línea *f* (de teléfono) **4** ROW : fila *f,* hilera *f* **5** NOTE : nota *f,* líneas *fpl* <drop me a line : mándame unas líneas> **6** COURSE : línea *f* <line of inquiry : línea de investigación> **7** AGREEMENT : conformidad *f* <to be in line with : ser conforme a> <to fall into line : estar de acuerdo> **8** OCCUPATION : ocupación *f,* rama *f,* especialidad *f* **9** LIMIT : línea *f,* límite *m* <dividing line : línea divisoria> <to draw the line : fijar límites> **10** SERVICE : línea *f* <bus line : línea de autobuses> **11** MARK : línea *f,* arruga *f* (de la cara)

lineage ['lɪniɪdʒ] *n* : linaje *m,* abolengo *m*

lineal ['lɪniəl] *adj* : en línea directa

lineaments ['lɪniəmənts] *npl* : facciones *fpl* (de la cara), rasgos *mpl*

linear ['lɪniər] *adj* : lineal

linen ['lɪnən] *n* **:** lino *m*
liner ['laɪnər] *n* **1** LINING **:** forro *m* **2** SHIP **:** buque *m,* transatlántico *m*
lineup ['laɪn,əp] *n* **1 :** fila *f* de sospechosos **2 :** formación *f* (en deportes) **3** ALIGNMENT **:** alineación *f*
linger ['lɪŋgər] *vi* **1** TARRY **:** quedarse, entretenerse, rezagarse **2** PERSIST **:** persistir, sobrevivir
lingerie [,lɑndʒə'reɪ, ,læʒə'riː] *n* **:** ropa *f* íntima femenina, lencería *f*
lingo ['lɪŋgo] *n, pl* **-goes 1** LANGUAGE **:** idioma *m* **2** JARGON **:** jerga *f*
linguist ['lɪŋgwɪst] *n* **:** lingüista *mf*
linguistic [lɪŋ'gwɪstɪk] *adj* **:** lingüístico
linguistics [lɪŋ'gwɪstɪks] *n* **:** lingüística *f*
liniment ['lɪnəmənt] *n* **:** linimento *m*
lining ['laɪnɪŋ] *n* **:** forro *m*
link[1] ['lɪŋk] *vt* **:** unir, enlazar, conectar — *vi* **to link up :** unirse, conectar
link[2] *n* **1 :** eslabón *m* (de una cadena) **2** BOND **:** conexión *f,* lazo *m,* vínculo *m*
linkage ['lɪŋkɪdʒ] *n* **:** conexión *f,* unión *f,* enlace *m*
linoleum [lə'noːliəm] *n* **:** linóleo *m*
linseed oil ['lɪn,siːd] *n* **:** aceite *m* de linaza
lint ['lɪnt] *n* **:** pelusa *f*
lintel ['lɪntəl] *n* **:** dintel *m*
lion ['laɪən] *n* **:** león *m*
lioness ['laɪənɪs] *n* **:** leona *f*
lionize ['laɪə,naɪz] *vt* **-ized; -izing :** tratar a una persona como muy importante
lip ['lɪp] *n* **1 :** labio *m* **2** EDGE, RIM **:** pico *m* (de una jarra), borde *m* (de una taza)
lipreading ['lɪp,riːdɪŋ] *n* **:** lectura *f* de los labios
lipstick ['lɪp,stɪk] *n* **:** lápiz *m* de labios, barra *f* de labios
liquefy ['lɪkwə,faɪ] *v* **-fied; -fying** *vt* **:** licuar — *vi* **:** licuarse
liqueur [lɪ'kʊr, -'kər, -'kjʊr] *n* **:** licor *m*
liquid[1] ['lɪkwəd] *adj* **:** líquido
liquid[2] *n* **:** líquido *m*
liquidate ['lɪkwə,deɪt] *vt* **-dated; -dating :** liquidar
liquidation [,lɪkwə'deɪʃən] *n* **:** liquidación *f*
liquidity [lɪk'wɪdəti] *n* **:** liquidez *f*
liquor ['lɪkər] *n* **:** alcohol *m,* bebidas *fpl* alcohólicas, licor *m*
lisp[1] ['lɪsp] *vi* **:** cecear
lisp[2] *n* **:** ceceo *m*
lissome ['lɪsəm] *adj* **1** FLEXIBLE **:** flexible **2** LITHE **:** ágil y grácil
list[1] ['lɪst] *vt* **1** ENUMERATE **:** hacer una lista de, enumerar **2** INCLUDE **:** poner en una lista, incluir — *vi* **:** escorar (dícese de un barco)
list[2] *n* **1** ENUMERATION **:** lista *f* **2** SLANT **:** escora *f,* inclinación *f*
listen ['lɪsən] *vi* **1 :** escuchar, oír **2 to listen to** HEED **:** prestar atención a, hacer caso de, escuchar **3 to listen to reason :** atender a razones
listener ['lɪsənər] *n* **:** oyente *mf,* persona *f* que sabe escuchar
listless ['lɪstləs] *adj* **:** lánguido, apático — **listlessly** *adv*
listlessness ['lɪstləsnəs] *n* **:** apatía *f,* languidez *f,* desgana *f*
lit ['lɪt] *pp* → **light**
litany ['lɪtəni] *n, pl* **-nies :** letanía *f*
liter ['liːtər] *n* **:** litro *m*
literacy ['lɪtərəsi] *n* **:** alfabetismo *m*
literal ['lɪtərəl] *adj* **:** literal — **literally** *adv*
literary ['lɪtə,rɛri] *adj* **:** literario
literate ['lɪtərət] *adj* **:** alfabetizado
literature ['lɪtərə,tʃʊr, -tʃər] *n* **:** literatura *f*
lithe ['laɪð, 'laɪθ] *adj* **:** ágil y grácil
lithesome ['laɪðsəm, 'laɪθ-] → **lissome**
lithograph ['lɪθə,græf] *n* **:** litografía *f*
lithographer [lɪ'θɑgrəfər, 'lɪθə,græfər] *n* **:** litógrafo *m,* -fa *f*
lithography [lɪ'θɑgrəfi] *n* **:** litografía *f*
litigant ['lɪtɪgənt] *n* **:** litigante *mf*
litigate ['lɪtə,geɪt] *vi* **-gated; -gating :** litigar
litigation [,lɪtə'geɪʃən] *n* **:** litigio *m*
litmus paper ['lɪtməs] *n* **:** papel *m* de tornasol
litter[1] ['lɪtər] *vt* **:** tirar basura en, ensuciar — *vi* **:** tirar basura
litter[2] *n* **1 :** camada *f,* cría *f* <a litter of kittens : una cría de gatitos> **2** STRETCHER **:** camilla *f* **3** RUBBISH **:** basura *f* **4 :** arena *f* higiénica (para gatos)
little[1] ['lɪtəl] *adv* **less** ['lɛs]; **least** ['liːst] **1 :** poco <she sings very little : canta muy poco> **2 little did I know that... :** no tenía la menor idea de que ... **3 as little as possible :** lo menos posible
little[2] *adj* **littler** *or* **less** ['lɛs] *or* **lesser** ['lɛsər]; **littlest** *or* **least** ['liːst] **1** SMALL **:** pequeño **2 :** poco <they speak little Spanish : hablan poco español> <little by little : poco a poco> **3** TRIVIAL **:** sin importancia, trivial
little[3] *n* **1 :** poco *m* <little has changed : poco ha cambiado> **2 a little :** un poco, algo <it's a little surprising : es algo sorprendente>
Little Dipper → **dipper**
liturgical [lə'tərdʒɪkəl] *adj* **:** litúrgico — **liturgically** [-kli] *adv*
liturgy ['lɪtərdʒi] *n, pl* **-gies :** liturgia *f*
livable ['lɪvəbəl] *adj* **:** habitable
live[1] ['lɪv] *vi* **lived; living 1** EXIST **:** vivir <as long as I live : mientras viva> <to live from day to day : vivir al día> **2 :** llevar una vida, vivir <he lived simply : llevó una vida sencilla> **3** SUBSIST **:** mantenerse, vivir **4** RESIDE **:** vivir, residir
live[2] ['laɪv] *adj* **1** LIVING **:** vivo **2** BURNING **:** encendido <a live coal : una brasa> **3 :** con corriente <live wires

: cables con corriente> **4** : cargado, sin estallar <a live bomb : una bomba sin estallar> **5** CURRENT : de actualidad <a live issue : un asunto de actualidad> **6** : en vivo, en directo <a live interview : una entrevista en vivo>

livelihood [ˈlaɪvli,hʊd] *n* : sustento *m,* vida *f,* medio *m* de vida

liveliness [ˈlaɪvlinəs] *n* : animación *f,* vivacidad *f*

livelong [ˈlɪvˈlɔŋ] *adj* : entero, completo

lively [ˈlaɪvli] *adj* **-lier; -est** : animado, vivaz, vivo, enérgico

liven [ˈlaɪvən] *vt* : animar — *vi* : animarse

liver [ˈlɪvər] *n* : hígado *m*

livery [ˈlɪvəri] *n, pl* **-eries** : librea *f*

lives → **life**

livestock [ˈlaɪv,stɑk] *n* : ganado *m*

live wire *n* : persona *f* vivaz y muy activa

livid [ˈlɪvəd] *adj* **1** BLACK-AND-BLUE : amoratado **2** PALE : lívido **3** ENRAGED : furioso

living[1] [ˈlɪvɪŋ] *adj* : vivo

living[2] *n* **to make a living** : ganarse la vida

living room *n* : living *m,* sala *f* de estar

lizard [ˈlɪzərd] *n* : lagarto *m*

llama [ˈlɑmə, ˈjɑ-] *n* : llama *f*

load[1] [ˈloːd] *vt* : cargar, embarcar

load[2] *n* **1** CARGO : carga *f* **2** WEIGHT : peso *m* **3** BURDEN : carga *f,* peso *m* **4** **loads** *npl* : montón *m,* pila *f,* cantidad *f* <loads of work : un montón de trabajo>

loaf[1] [ˈloːf] *vi* : holgazanear, flojear, haraganear

loaf[2] *n, pl* **loaves** [ˈloːvz] **1** : pan *m,* pan *m* de molde, barra *f* de pan **2 meat loaf** : pan *m* de carne

loafer [ˈloːfər] *n* : holgazán *m,* -zana *f;* haragán *m,* -gana *f;* vago *m,* -ga *f*

loam [ˈloːm] *n* : marga *f,* suelo *m*

loan[1] [ˈloːn] *vt* : prestar

loan[2] *n* : préstamo *m,* empréstito *m* (del banco)

loath [ˈloːθ, ˈloːð] *adj* : poco dispuesto <I am loath to say it : me resisto a decirlo>

loathe [ˈloːð] *vt* **loathed; loathing** : odiar, aborrecer

loathing [ˈloːðɪŋ] *n* : aversión *f,* odio *m,* aborrecimiento *m*

loathsome [ˈloːθsəm, ˈloːð-] *adj* : odioso, repugnante

lob[1] [ˈlɑb] *vt* **lobbed; lobbing** : hacerle un globo (a otro jugador)

lob[2] *n* : globo *m* (en deportes)

lobby[1] [ˈlɑbi] *v* **-bied; -bying** *vt* : presionar, ejercer presión sobre — *vi* **to lobby for** : presionar para (lograr algo)

lobby[2] *n, pl* **-bies 1** FOYER : vestíbulo *m* **2** LOBBYISTS : grupo *m* de presión, lobby *m*

lobbyist [ˈlɑbiɪst] *n* : miembro *m* de un lobby

lobe [ˈloːb] *n* : lóbulo *m*

lobed [ˈloːbd] *adj* : lobulado

lobotomy [ləˈbɑţəmi, lo-] *n, pl* **-mies** : lobotomía *f*

lobster [ˈlɑbstər] *n* : langosta *f*

local[1] [ˈloːkəl] *adj* : local

local[2] *n* **1** : anestesia *f* local **2 the locals** : los vecinos del lugar, los habitantes

locale [loˈkæl] *n* : lugar *m,* escenario *m*

locality [loˈkæləţi] *n, pl* **-ties** : localidad *f*

localize [ˈloːkə,laɪz] *vt* **-ized; -izing** : localizar

locally [ˈloːkəli] *adv* : en la localidad, en la zona

locate [ˈloː,keɪt, loˈkeɪt] *v* **-cated; -cating** *vt* **1** POSITION : situar, ubicar **2** FIND : localizar, ubicar — *vi* SETTLE : establecerse

location [loˈkeɪʃən] *n* **1** POSITION : posición *f,* emplazamiento *m,* ubicación *f* **2** PLACE : lugar *m,* sitio *m*

lock[1] [ˈlɑk] *vt* **1** FASTEN : cerrar **2** CONFINE : encerrar <they locked me in the room : me encerraron en la sala> **3** IMMOBILIZE : bloquear (una rueda) — *vi* **1** : cerrarse (dícese de una puerta) **2** : trabarse, bloquearse (dícese de una rueda)

lock[2] *n* **1** : mechón *m* (de pelo) **2** FASTENER : cerradura *f,* cerrojo *m,* chapa *f* **3** : esclusa *f* (de un canal)

locker [ˈlɑkər] *n* : armario *m,* cajón *m* con llave, lócker *m*

locket [ˈlɑkət] *n* : medallón *m,* guardapelo *m,* relicario *m*

lockjaw [ˈlɑk,dʒɔ] *n* : tétano *m*

lockout [ˈlɑk,aʊt] *n* : cierre *m* patronal, lockout *m*

locksmith [ˈlɑk,smɪθ] *n* : cerrajero *m,* -ra *f*

lockup [ˈlɑk,ʌp] *n* JAIL : cárcel *f*

locomotion [,loːkəˈmoːʃən] *n* : locomoción *f*

locomotive[1] [,loːkəˈmoːţɪv] *adj* : locomotor

locomotive[2] *n* : locomotora *f*

locust [ˈloːkəst] *n* **1** : langosta *f,* chapulín *m CA, Mex* **2** CICADA : cigarra *f,* chicharra *f* **3** : acacia *f* blanca (árbol)

locution [loˈkjuːʃən] *n* : locución *f*

lode [ˈloːd] *n* : veta *f,* vena *f,* filón *m*

lodestar [ˈloːd,stɑr] *n* : estrella *f* polar

lodestone [ˈloːd,stoːn] *n* : piedra *f* imán

lodge[1] [ˈlɑdʒ] *v* **lodged; lodging** *vt* **1** HOUSE : hospedar, alojar **2** FILE : presentar <to lodge a complaint : presentar una demanda> — *vi* **1** : posarse, meterse <the bullet lodged in the door : la bala se incrustó en la puerta> **2** STAY : hospedarse, alojarse

lodge[2] *n* **1** : pabellón *m,* casa *f* de campo <hunting lodge : refugio de caza> **2** : madriguera *f* (de un castor) **3** : logia *f* <Masonic lodge : logia masónica>

lodger [ˈlɑdʒər] *n* **:** inquilino *m,* -na *f;* huésped *m,* -peda *f*

lodging [ˈlɑdʒɪŋ] *n* **1 :** alojamiento *m* **2 lodgings** *npl* ROOMS **:** habitaciones *fpl*

loft [ˈlɔft] *n* **1** ATTIC **:** desván *m,* ático *m,* buhardilla *f* **2 :** loft *m* (en un depósito comercial) **3** HAYLOFT **:** pajar *m* **4 :** galería *f* <choir loft : galería del coro>

loftily [ˈlɔftəli] *adv* **:** altaneramente, con altivez

loftiness [ˈlɔftinəs] *n* **1** NOBILITY **:** nobleza *f* **2** ARROGANCE **:** altanería *f,* arrogancia *f* **3** HEIGHT **:** altura *f,* elevación *f*

lofty [ˈlɔfti] *adj* **loftier; -est 1** NOBLE **:** noble, elevado **2** HAUGHTY **:** altivo, arrogante, altanero **3** HIGH **:** majestuoso, elevado

log[1] [ˈlɔg, ˈlɑg] *vi* **logged; logging 1 :** talar (árboles) **2** RECORD **:** registrar, anotar **3 to log on :** entrar (al sistema) **4 to log off :** salir (del sistema)

log[2] *n* **1 :** tronco *m,* leño *m* **2** RECORD **:** diario *m*

logarithm [ˈlɔgəˌrɪðəm, ˈlɑ-] *n* **:** logaritmo *m*

logger [ˈlɔgər, ˈlɑ-] *n* **:** leñador *m,* -dora *f*

loggerhead [ˈlɔgərˌhɛd, ˈlɑ-] *n* **1 :** tortuga *f* boba **2 to be at loggerheads :** estar en pugna, estar en desacuerdo

logic [ˈlɑdʒɪk] *n* **:** lógica *f* **— logical** [ˈlɑdʒɪkəl] *adj* **— logically** [-kli] *adv*

logistic [ləˈdʒɪstɪk, lo-] *adj* **:** logístico

logistics [ləˈdʒɪstɪks, lo-] *ns & pl* **:** logística *f*

logo [ˈloːˌgoː] *n, pl* **logos** [-ˌgoːz] **:** logotipo *m*

loin [ˈlɔɪn] *n* **1 :** lomo *m* <pork loin : lomo de cerdo> **2 loins** *npl* **:** lomos *mpl* <to gird one's loins : prepararse para la lucha>

loiter [ˈlɔɪt̬ər] *vi* **:** vagar, perder el tiempo

loll [ˈlɑl] *vi* **1** SLOUCH **:** repantigarse **2** IDLE **:** holgazanear, hacer el vago

lollipop *or* **lollypop** [ˈlɑliˌpɑp] *n* **:** dulce *m* en palito, chupete *m Chile, Peru,* paleta *f CA, Mex*

lone [ˈloːn] *adj* **1** SOLITARY **:** solitario **2** ONLY **:** único

loneliness [ˈloːnlinəs] *n* **:** soledad *f*

lonely [ˈloːnli] *adj* **-lier; -est 1** SOLITARY **:** solitario, aislado **2** LONESOME **:** solo <to feel lonely : sentirse muy solo>

loner [ˈloːnər] *n* **:** solitario *m,* -ria *f;* recluso *m,* -sa *f*

lonesome [ˈloːnsəm] *adj* **:** solo, solitario

long[1] [ˈlɔŋ] *vi* **1 to long for :** añorar, desear, anhelar **2 to long to :** anhelar, estar deseando <they longed to see her : estaban deseando verla, tenían muchas ganas de verla>

long[2] *adv* **1 :** mucho, mucho tiempo <it didn't take long : no llevó mucho tiempo> <will it last long? : ¿va a durar mucho?> **2 all day long :** todo el día **3 as long as** *or* **so long as :** mientras, con tal que **4 long before :** mucho antes **5 so long! :** ¡hasta luego!, ¡adiós!

long[3] *adj* **longer** [ˈlɔŋgər]; **longest** [ˈlɔŋgəst] **1** (*indicating length*) **:** largo <the dress is too long : el vestido es demasiado largo> <a long way from : bastante lejos de> <in the long run : a la larga> **2** (*indicating time*) **:** largo, prolongado <a long illness : una enfermedad prolongada> <a long walk : un paseo largo> <at long last : por fin> **3 to be long on :** estar cargado de

long[4] *n* **1 before long :** dentro de poco **2 the long and the short :** lo esencial, lo fundamental

longevity [lɑnˈdʒɛvət̬i] *n* **:** longevidad *f*

longhand [ˈlɔŋˌhænd] *n* **:** escritura *f* a mano, escritura *f* cursiva

longhorn [ˈlɔŋˌhɔrn] *n* **:** longhorn *mf*

longing [lɔŋɪŋ] *n* **:** vivo deseo *m,* ansia *f,* anhelo *m*

longingly [lɔŋɪŋlli] *adv* **:** ansiosamente, con ansia

longitude [ˈlɑndʒəˌtuːd, -ˌtjuːd] *n* **:** longitud *f*

longitudinal [ˌlɑndʒəˈtuːdənəl, -ˈtjuː-] *adj* **:** longitudinal **— longitudinally** *adv*

longshoreman [ˈlɔŋˈʃormən] *n, pl* **-men** [-mən, -ˌmɛn] **:** estibador *m,* -dora *f*

long–suffering [ˈlɔŋˈsʌfərɪŋ] *adj* **:** paciente, sufrido

look[1] [ˈlʊk] *vi* **1** GLANCE **:** mirar <to look out the window : mirar por la ventana> **2** INVESTIGATE **:** buscar, mirar <look in the closet : busca en el closet> <look before you leap : mira lo que haces> **3** SEEM **:** parecer <he looks happy : parece estar contento> <I look like my mother : me parezco a mi madre> **4 to look after :** cuidar, cuidar de **5 to look for** EXPECT **:** esperar **6 to look for** SEEK **:** buscar **—** *vt* **:** mirar

look[2] *n* **1** GLANCE **:** mirada *f* **2** EXPRESSION **:** cara *f* <a look of disapproval : una cara de desaprobación> **3** ASPECT **:** aspecto *m,* apariencia *f,* aire *m*

lookout [ˈlʊkˌaʊt] *n* **1 :** centinela *mf,* vigía *mf* **2 to be on the lookout for :** estar al acecho de, andar a la caza de

loom[1] [ˈluːm] *vi* **1 :** aparecer, surgir <the city loomed up in the distance : la ciudad surgió en la distancia> **2** IMPEND **:** amenazar, ser inminente **3 to loom large :** cobrar mucha importancia

loom[2] *n* **:** telar *m*

loon [ˈluːn] *n* **:** somorgujo *m,* somormujo *m*

loony *or* **looney** [ˈluːni] *adj* **-nier; -est :** loco, chiflado *fam*

loop[1] [ˈluːp] *vt* **1 :** hacer lazadas con **2 to loop around :** pasar alrededor de — *vi* **1 :** rizar el rizo (dícese de un avión) **2 :** serpentear (dícese de una carretera)

loop[2] *n* **1 :** lazada *f* (en hilo o cuerda) **2** BEND **:** curva *f* **3** CIRCUIT **:** circuito *m* cerrado **4 :** rizo *m* (en la aviación) <to loop the loop : rizar el rizo>

loophole [ˈluːpˌhoːl] *n* **:** escapatoria *f,* pretexto *m*

loose[1] [ˈluːs] *vt* **loosed; loosing 1** RELEASE **:** poner en libertad, soltar **2** UNTIE **:** deshacer, desatar **3** DISCHARGE, UNLEASH **:** descargar, desatar

loose[2] → **loosely**

loose[3] *adj* **looser; -est 1** INSECURE **:** flojo, suelto, poco seguro <a loose tooth : un diente flojo> **2** ROOMY **:** suelto, holgado <loose clothing : ropa holgada> **3** OPEN **:** suelto, abierto <loose soil : suelo suelto> <a loose weave : una tejida abierta> **4** FREE **:** suelto <to break loose : soltarse> **5** SLACK **:** flojo, flexible **6** APPROXIMATE **:** libre, aproximado <a loose translation : una traducción aproximada>

loosely [ˈluːsli] *adv* **1 :** sin apretar **2** ROUGHLY **:** aproximadamente, más o menos

loosen [ˈluːsən] *vt* **:** aflojar

loose–leaf [ˈluːsˈliːf] *adj* **:** de hojas sueltas

looseness [ˈluːsnəs] *n* **1 :** aflojamiento *m,* holgura *f* (de ropa) **2** IMPRECISION **:** imprecisión *f*

loot[1] [ˈluːt] *vt* **:** saquear, robar

loot[2] *n* **:** botín *m*

looter [ˈluːt̬ər] *n* **:** saqueador *m,* -dora *f*

lop [ˈlɑp] *vt* **lopped; lopping :** cortar, podar

lope[1] [ˈloːp] *vi* **loped; loping :** correr a paso largo

lope[2] *n* **:** paso *m* largo

lopsided [ˈlɑpˌsaɪdəd] *adj* **1** CROOKED **:** torcido, chueco, ladeado **2** ASYMETRICAL **:** asimétrico

loquacious [loˈkweɪʃəs] *adj* **:** locuaz

lord [ˈlɔrd] *n* **1 :** señor *m,* noble *m* **2 :** lord *m* (en la Gran Bretaña) **3 the Lord :** el Señor **4 good Lord! :** ¡Dios mío!

lordly [ˈlɔrdli] *adj* **-lier; -est** HAUGHTY **:** arrogante, altanero

lordship [ˈlɔrdˌʃɪp] *n* **:** señoría *f*

Lord's Supper *n* **:** Eucaristía *f*

lore [ˈlor] *n* **:** saber *m* popular, tradición *f*

lose [ˈluːz] *v* **lost** [ˈlɔst]; **losing** [ˈluːzɪŋ] *vt* **1 :** perder <I lost my umbrella : perdí mi paraguas> <to lose blood : perder sangre> <to lose one's voice : quedarse afónico> <to have nothing to lose : no tener nada que perder> <to lose no time : no perder tiempo> <to lose weight : perder peso, adelgazar> <to lose one's temper : perder los estribos, enojarse, enfadarse> <to lose sight of : perder de vista> **2 :** costar, hacer perder <the errors lost him his job : los errores le costaron su empleo> **3 :** atrasar <my watch loses 5 minutes a day : mi reloj atrasa 5 minutos por día> **4 to lose oneself :** perderse, ensimismarse — *vi* **1 :** perder <we lost to the other team : perdimos contra el otro equipo> **2 :** atrasarse <the clock loses time : el reloj se atrasa>

loser [ˈluːzər] *n* **:** perdedor *m,* -dora *f*

loss [ˈlɔs] *n* **1** LOSING **:** pérdida *f* <loss of memory : pérdida de memoria> <to sell at a loss : vender con pérdida> <to be at a loss to : no saber como> **2** DEFEAT **:** derrota *f,* juego *m* perdido **3 losses** *npl* DEATHS **:** muertos *mpl*

lost [ˈlɔst] *adj* **1 :** perdido <a lost cause : una causa perdida> <lost in thought : absorto> **2 to get lost :** perderse **3 to make up for lost time :** recuperar el tiempo perdido

lot [ˈlɑt] *n* **1** DRAWING **:** sorteo *m* <by lot : por sorteo> **2** SHARE **:** parte *f,* porción *f* **3** FATE **:** suerte *f* **4** LAND, PLOT **:** terreno *m,* solar *m,* lote *m,* parcela *f* **5 a lot of** *or* **lots of :** mucho, un montón de, bastante <lots of books : un montón de libros, muchos libros> <a lot of people : mucha gente>

loth [ˈloːθ, ˈloːð] → **loath**

lotion [ˈloːʃən] *n* **:** loción *f*

lottery [ˈlɑtəri] *n, pl* **-teries :** lotería *f*

lotus [ˈloːt̬əs] *n* **:** loto *m*

loud[1] [ˈlaʊd] *adv* **:** alto, fuerte <out loud : en voz alta>

loud[2] *adj* **1 :** alto, fuerte <a loud voice : una voz alta> **2** NOISY **:** ruidoso <a loud party : una fiesta ruidosa> **3** FLASHY **:** llamativo, chillón

loudly [ˈlaʊdli] *adv* **:** alto, fuerte, en voz alta

loudness [ˈlaʊdnəs] *n* **:** volumen *m,* fuerza *f* (del ruido)

loudspeaker [ˈlaʊdˌspiːkər] *n* **:** altavoz *m,* altoparlante *m*

lounge[1] [ˈlaʊndʒ] *vi* **lounged; lounging :** holgazanear, gandulear

lounge[2] *n* **:** salón *m,* sala *f* de estar

louse [ˈlaʊs] *n, pl* **lice** [ˈlaɪs] **:** piojo *m*

lousy [ˈlaʊzi] *adj* **lousier; -est 1 :** piojoso, lleno de piojos **2** BAD **:** pésimo, muy malo

lout [ˈlaʊt] *n* **:** bruto *m,* patán *m*

louver *or* **louvre** [ˈluːvər] *n* **:** persiana *f,* listón *m* de persiana

lovable [ˈlʌvəbəl] *adj* **:** adorable, amoroso, encantador

love[1] [ˈlʌv] *v* **loved; loving** *vt* **1 :** querer, amar <I love you : te quiero> **2** ENJOY **:** encantarle a alguien, ser (muy) aficionado a, gustarle mucho a uno (algo) <she loves flowers : le encantan las flores> <he loves golf : es muy aficionado al golf> <I'd love

to go with you : me gustaría mucho acompañarte> — *vi* : querer, amar

love[2] *n* **1** : amor *m,* cariño *m* <to be in love with : estar enamorado de> <to fall in love with : enamorarse de> **2** ENTHUSIASM, INTEREST : amor *m,* afición *m,* gusto *m* <love of music : afición a la música> **3** BELOVED : amor *m;* amado *m,* -da *f;* enamorado *m,* -da *f*

loveless [ˈlʌvləs] *adj* : sin amor

loveliness [ˈlʌvlinəs] *n* : belleza *f,* hermosura *f*

lovelorn [ˈlʌvˌlɔrn] *adj* : herido de amor, perdidamente enamorado

lovely [ˈlʌvli] *adj* **-lier; -est** : hermoso, bello, lindo, precioso

lover [ˈlʌvər] *n* : amante *mf* (de personas); aficionado *m,* -da *f* (a alguna actividad)

loving [ˈlʌvɪŋ] *adj* : amoroso, cariñoso

lovingly [ˈlʌvɪŋli] *adv* : cariñosamente

low[1] [ˈloː] *vi* : mugir

low[2] *adv* : bajo, profundo <to aim low : apuntar bajo> <to lie low : mantenerse escondido> <to turn the lights down low : bajar las luces>

low[3] *adj* **lower** [ˈloːər]; **-est 1** : bajo <a low building : un edificio bajo> <a low bow : una profunda reverencia> **2** SOFT : bajo, suave <in a low voice : en voz baja> **3** SHALLOW : bajo, poco profundo **4** HUMBLE : humilde, modesto **5** DEPRESSED : deprimido, bajo de moral **6** INFERIOR : bajo, inferior **7** UNFAVORABLE : mal <to have a low opinion of him : tener un mal concepto de él> **8 to be low on** : tener poco de, estar escaso de

low[4] *n* **1** : punto *m* bajo <to reach an all-time low : estar más bajo que nunca> **2** *or* **low gear** : primera velocidad *f* **3** : mugido *m* (de una vaca)

lowbrow [ˈloːˌbraʊ] *n* : persona *f* inculta

lower[1] [ˈloːər] *vt* **1** DROP : bajar <to lower one's voice : bajar la voz> **2** : arriar, bajar <to lower the flag : arriar la bandera> **3** REDUCE : reducir, bajar **4 to lower oneself** : rebajarse

lower[2] [ˈloːər] *adj* : inferior, más bajo, de abajo

lowland [ˈloːlənd, -ˌlænd] *n* : tierras *fpl* bajas

lowly [ˈloːli] *adj* **-lier; -est** : humilde, modesto

loyal [ˈlɔɪəl] *adj* : leal, fiel — **loyally** *adv*

loyalist [ˈlɔɪəlɪst] *n* : partidario *m,* -ria *f* del régimen

loyalty [ˈlɔɪəlti] *n, pl* **-ties** : lealtad *f,* fidelidad *f*

lozenge [ˈlɑzəndʒ] *n* : pastilla *f*

LSD [ˌɛlˌɛsˈdiː] *n* : LSD *m*

lubricant [ˈluːbrɪkənt] *n* : lubricante *m*

lubricate [ˈluːbrɪˌkeɪt] *vt* **-cated; -cating** : lubricar — **lubrication** [ˌluːbrɪˈkeɪʃən] *n*

lucid [ˈluːsəd] *adj* : lúcido, claro — **lucidly** *adv*

lucidity [luːˈsɪdəṭi] *n* : lucidez *f*

luck [ˈlʌk] *n* **1** : suerte *f* **2 to have bad luck** : tener mala suerte **3 good luck!** : ¡(buena) suerte!

luckily [ˈlʌkəli] *adv* : afortunadamente, por suerte

luckless [ˈlʌkləs] *adj* : desafortunado

lucky [ˈlʌki] *adj* **luckier; -est 1** : afortunado, que tiene suerte <a lucky woman : una mujer afortunada> **2** FORTUITOUS : fortuito, de suerte **3** OPPORTUNE : oportuno **4** : de (la) suerte <lucky number : número de la suerte>

lucrative [ˈluːkrəṭɪv] *adj* : lucrativo, provechoso — **lucratively** *adv*

ludicrous [ˈluːdəkrəs] *adj* : ridículo, absurdo — **ludicrously** *adv*

ludicrousness [ˈluːdəkrəsnəs] *n* : ridiculez *f,* absurdo *m*

lug [ˈlʌg] *vt* **lugged; lugging** : arrastrar, transportar con dificultad

luggage [ˈlʌgɪdʒ] *n* : equipaje *m*

lugubrious [lʊˈguːbriəs] *adj* : lúgubre — **lugubriously** *adv*

lukewarm [ˈluːkˈwɔrm] *adj* **1** TEPID : tibio **2** HALFHEARTED : poco entusiasta

lull[1] [ˈlʌl] *vt* **1** CALM, SOOTHE : calmar, sosegar **2 to lull to sleep** : arrullar, adormecer

lull[2] *n* : calma *f,* pausa *f*

lullaby [ˈlʌləˌbaɪ] *n, pl* **-bies** : canción *f* de cuna, arrullo *m,* nana *f*

lumbago [ˌlʌmˈbeɪgo] *n* : lumbago *m*

lumber[1] [ˈlʌmbər] *vt* : aserrar (madera) — *vi* : moverse pesadamente

lumber[2] *n* : madera *f*

lumberjack [ˈlʌmbərˌdʒæk] *n* : leñador *m,* -dora *f*

lumberyard [ˈlʌmbərˌjɑrd] *n* : almacén *m* de maderas

luminary [ˈluːməˌnɛri] *n, pl* **-naries** : lumbrera *f,* luminaria *f*

luminescence [ˌluːməˈnɛsənts] *n* : luminiscencia *f* — **luminescent** [-ˈnɛsənt] *adj*

luminosity [ˌluːməˈnɑsəṭi] *n, pl* **-ties** : luminosidad *f*

luminous [ˈluːmənəs] *adj* : luminoso — **luminously** *adv*

lump[1] [ˈlʌmp] *vt or* **to lump together** : juntar, agrupar, amontonar — *vi* CLUMP : agruparse, aglutinarse

lump[2] *n* **1** GLOB : grumo *m* **2** PIECE : pedazo *m,* trozo *m,* terrón *m* <a lump of coal : un trozo de carbón> <a lump of sugar : un terrón de azúcar> **3** SWELLING : bulto *m,* hinchazón *f,* protuberancia *f* **4 to have a lump in one's throat** : tener un nudo en la garganta

lumpy [ˈlʌmpi] *adj* **lumpier; -est 1** : lleno de grumos (dícese de una salsa) **2** UNEVEN : desigual, disparejo

lunacy [ˈluːnəsi] *n, pl* **-cies** : locura *f*

lunar [ˈluːnər] *adj* : lunar

lunatic[1] [ˈluːnəˌtɪk] *adj* : lunático, loco

lunatic[2] *n* : loco *m,* -ca *f*
lunch[1] [ˈlʌntʃ] *vi* : almorzar, comer
lunch[2] *n* : almuerzo *m,* comida *f,* lonche *m*
luncheon [ˈlʌntʃən] *n* **1** : comida *f,* almuerzo *m* **2 luncheon meat** : fiambres *fpl*
lung [ˈlʌŋ] *n* : pulmón *m*
lunge[1] [ˈlʌndʒ] *vi* **lunged; lunging 1** THRUST : atacar (en la esgrima) **2 to lunge forward** : arremeter, lanzarse
lunge[2] *n* **1** : arremetida *f,* embestida *f* **2** : estocada *f* (en la esgrima)
lurch[1] [ˈlərtʃ] *vi* **1** PITCH : cabecear, dar bandazos, dar sacudidas **2** STAGGER : tambalearse
lurch[2] *n* **1** : sacudida *f,* bandazo *m* (de un vehículo) **2** : tambaleo *m* (de una persona)
lure[1] [ˈlʊr] *vt* **lured; luring** : atraer
lure[2] *n* **1** ATTRACTION : atractivo *m* **2** ENTICEMENT : señuelo *m,* aliciente *m* **3** BAIT : cebo *m* artificial (en la pesca)
lurid [ˈlʊrəd] *adj* **1** GRUESOME : espeluznante, horripilante **2** SENSATIONAL : sensacionalista, chocante **3** GAUDY : chillón
lurk [ˈlərk] *vi* : estar al acecho
luscious [ˈlʌʃəs] *adj* **1** DELICIOUS : delicioso, exquisito **2** SEDUCTIVE : seductor, cautivador
lush [ˈlʌʃ] *adj* **1** LUXURIANT : exuberante, lozano **2** LUXURIOUS : suntuoso, lujoso
lust[1] [ˈlʌst] *vi* **to lust after** : desear (a una persona), codiciar (riquezas, etc.)
lust[2] *n* **1** LASCIVIOUSNESS : lujuria *f,* lascivia *f* **2** CRAVING : deseo *m,* ansia *f,* anhelo *m*
luster *or* **lustre** [ˈlʌstər] *n* **1** GLOSS, SHEEN : lustre *m,* brillo *m* **2** SPLENDOR : lustre *m,* esplendor *m*
lusterless [ˈlʌstərləs] *adj* : deslustrado, sin brillo
lustful [ˈlʌstfəl] *adj* : lujurioso, lascivo, lleno de deseo
lustrous [ˈlʌstrəs] *adj* : brillante, brilloso, lustroso
lusty [ˈlʌsti] *adj* **lustier; -est** : fuerte, robusto, vigoroso — **lustily** [ˈlʌstəli] *adv*
lute [ˈluːt] *n* : laúd *m*
luxuriant [ˌlʌgˈʒʊriənt, ˌlʌkˈʃʊr-] *adj* **1** : exuberante, lozano (dícese de las plantas) **2** : abundante y hermoso (dícese del pelo) — **luxuriantly** *adv*
luxuriate [ˌlʌgˈʒʊriˌeɪt, ˌlʌkˈʃʊr-] *vi* **-ated; -ating 1** : disfrutar **2 to luxuriate in** : deleitarse con
luxurious [ˌlʌgˈʒʊriəs, ˌlʌkˈʃʊr-] *adj* : lujoso, suntuoso — **luxuriously** *adv*
luxury [ˈlʌkʃəri, ˈlʌgʒə-] *n, pl* **-ries** : lujo *m*
lye [ˈlaɪ] *n* : lejía *f*
lying → **lie**[1], **lie**[2]
lymph [ˈlɪmpf] *n* : linfa *f*
lymphatic [lɪmˈfætɪk] *adj* : linfático
lynch [ˈlɪntʃ] *vt* : linchar
lynx [ˈlɪŋks] *n, pl* **lynx** *or* **lynxes** : lince *m*
lyre [ˈlaɪr] *n* : lira *f*
lyric[1] [ˈlɪrɪk] *adj* : lírico
lyric[2] *n* **1** : poema *m* lírico **2 lyrics** *npl* : letra *f* (de una canción)
lyrical [ˈlɪrɪkəl] *adj* : lírico, elocuente

M

m [ˈɛm] *n, pl* **m's** *or* **ms** [ˈɛmz] : decimotercera letra del alfabeto inglés
ma'am [ˈmæm] → **madam**
macabre [məˈkɑb, -ˈkɑbər, -ˈkɑbrə] *adj* : macabro
macadam [məˈkædəm] *n* : macadán *m*
macaroni [ˌmækəˈroːni] *n* : macarrones *mpl*
macaroon [ˌmækəˈruːn] *n* : macarrón *m,* mostachón *m*
macaw [məˈkɔ] *n* : guacamayo *m*
mace [ˈmeɪs] *n* **1** : maza *f* (arma o símbolo) **2** : macis *f* (especia)
machete [məˈʃɛti] *n* : machete *m*
machination [ˌmækəˈneɪʃən, ˌmæʃə-] *n* : maquinación *f,* intriga *f*
machine[1] [məˈʃiːn] *vt* **-chined; -chining** : trabajar a máquina
machine[2] *n* **1** : máquina *f* <machine shop : taller de máquinas> <machine language : lenguaje de la máquina> **2** : aparato *m,* maquinaria *f* (en política)
machine gun *n* : ametralladora *f*
machinery [məˈʃiːnəri] *n, pl* **-eries 1** : maquinaria *f* **2** WORKS : mecanismo *m*
machinist [məˈʃiːnɪst] *n* : maquinista *mf*
mackerel [ˈmækərəl] *n, pl* **-el** *or* **-els** : caballa *f*
mackinaw [ˈmækəˌnɔ] *n* : chaqueta *f* escocesa de lana
mad [ˈmæd] *adj* **madder; maddest 1** INSANE : loco, demente **2** RABID : rabioso **3** FOOLISH : tonto, insensato **4** ANGRY : enojado, furioso **5** CRAZY : loco <I'm mad about you : estoy loco por ti>
Madagascan [ˌmædəˈgæskən] *n* : malgache *mf* — **Madagascan** *adj*
madam [ˈmædəm] *n, pl* **mesdames** [meɪˈdɑm, -ˈdæm] : señora *f*
madcap[1] [ˈmædˌkæp] *adj* ZANY : alocado, disparatado
madcap[2] *n* : alocado *m,* -da *f*
madden [ˈmædən] *vt* : enloquecer, enfurecer
maddeningly [ˈmædənɪŋli] *adv* : irritantemente <maddeningly vague : tan vago que te exaspera>

made → **make**[1]
madhouse ['mæd,haʊs] *n* : manicomio *m* <the office was a madhouse : la oficina parecía una casa de locos>
madly ['mædli] *adv* : como un loco, locamente
madman ['mæd,mæn, -mən] *n, pl* **-men** [-mən, -,mɛn] : loco *m,* demente *m*
madness ['mædnəs] *n* : locura *f,* demencia *f*
madwoman ['mæd,wʊmən] *n, pl* **-women** [-,wɪmən] : loca *f,* demente *f*
maelstrom ['meɪlstrəm] *n* : remolino *m,* vorágine *f*
maestro ['maɪ,stroː] *n, pl* **-stros** *or* **-stri** [-,striː] : maestro *m*
Mafia ['mɑfiə] *n* : Mafia *f*
magazine ['mægə,ziːn] *n* **1** STOREHOUSE : almacén *m,* polvorín *m* (de explosivos) **2** PERIODICAL : revista *f* **3** : cargador *m* (de un arma de fuego)
magenta [mə'dʒɛntə] *n* : magenta *f,* color *m* magenta
maggot ['mægət] *n* : gusano *m*
magic[1] ['mædʒɪk] *or* **magical** ['mædʒɪkəl] *adj* : mágico
magic[2] *n* : magia *f*
magically ['mædʒɪkli] *adv* : mágicamente <they magically appeared : aparecieron como por arte de magia>
magician [mə'dʒɪʃən] *n* **1** SORCERER : mago *m,* -ga *f* **2** CONJURER : prestidigitador *m,* -dora *f;* mago *m,* -ga *f*
magistrate ['mædʒə,streɪt] *n* : magistrado *m,* -da *f*
magma ['mægmə] *n* : magma *m*
magnanimity [,mægnə'nɪməṭi] *n, pl* **-ties** : magnanimidad *f*
magnanimous [mæg'nænəməs] *adj* : magnánimo, generoso — **magnanimously** *adv*
magnate ['mæg,neɪt, -nət] *n* : magnate *mf*
magnesium [mæg'niːziəm, -ʒəm] *n* : magnesio *m*
magnet ['mægnət] *n* : imán *m*
magnetic [mæg'nɛṭɪk] *adj* : magnético — **magnetically** [-ṭɪkli] *adv*
magnetic field *n* : campo *m* magnético
magnetism ['mægnə,tɪzəm] *n* : magnetismo *m*
magnetize ['mægnə,taɪz] *vt* **-tized; -tizing 1** : magnetizar, imantar **2** ATTRACT : magnetizar, atraer
magnification [,mægnəfə'keɪʃən] *n* : aumento *m,* ampliación *f*
magnificence [mæg'nɪfəsənts] *n* : magnificencia *f*
magnificent [mæg'nɪfəsənt] *adj* : magnífico — **magnificently** *adv*
magnify ['mægnə,faɪ] *vt* **-fied; -fying 1** ENLARGE : ampliar **2** EXAGGERATE : magnificar, exagerar
magnifying glass *n* : lupa *f*
magnitude ['mægnə,tuːd, -,tjuːd] *n* **1** GREATNESS : magnitud *f,* grandeza *f* **2** QUANTITY : cantidad *f* **3** IMPORTANCE : magnitud *f,* envergadura *f*
magnolia [mæg'noːljə] *n* : magnolia *f* (flor), magnolio *m* (árbol)
magpie ['mæg,paɪ] *n* : urraca *f*
mahogany [mə'hɑgəni] *n, pl* **-nies** : caoba *f*
maid ['meɪd] *n* **1** MAIDEN : doncella *f* **2** *or* **maidservant** ['meɪd,sərvənt] : sirvienta *f,* muchacha *f,* mucama *f,* criada *f*
maiden[1] ['meɪdən] *adj* **1** UNMARRIED : soltera **2** FIRST : primero <maiden voyage : primera travesía>
maiden[2] *n* : doncella *f*
maidenhood ['meɪdən,hʊd] *n* : doncellez *f*
maiden name *n* : nombre *m* de soltera
mail[1] ['meɪl] *vt* : enviar por correo, echar al correo
mail[2] *n* **1** : correo *m* <airmail : correo aéreo> **2** : malla *f* <coat of mail : cota de malla>
mailbox ['meɪl,bɑks] *n* : buzón *m*
mailman ['meɪl,mæn, -mən] *n, pl* **-men** [-mən, -,mɛn] : cartero *m*
maim ['meɪm] *vt* : mutilar, desfigurar, lisiar
main[1] ['meɪn] *adj* : principal, central <the main office : la oficina central>
main[2] *n* **1** HIGH SEAS : alta mar *f* **2** : tubería *f* principal (de agua o gas), cable *m* principal (de un circuito) **3** **with might and main** : con todas sus fuerzas
mainframe ['meɪn,freɪm] *n* : mainframe *m,* computadora *f* central
mainland ['meɪn,lænd, -lənd] *n* : continente *m*
mainly ['meɪnli] *adv* **1** PRINCIPALLY : principalmente, en primer lugar **2** MOSTLY : principalmente, en la mayor parte
mainstay ['meɪn,steɪ] *n* : pilar *m,* sostén *m* principal
mainstream[1] ['meɪn,striːm] *adj* : dominante, corriente, convencional
mainstream[2] *n* : corriente *f* principal
maintain [meɪn'teɪn] *vt* **1** SERVICE : dar mantenimiento a (una máquina) **2** PRESERVE : mantener, conservar <to maintain silence : guardar silencio> **3** SUPPORT : mantener, sostener **4** ASSERT : mantener, sostener, afirmar
maintenance ['meɪntənənts] *n* : mantenimiento *m*
maize ['meɪz] *n* : maíz *m*
majestic [mə'dʒɛstɪk] *adj* : majestuoso — **majestically** [-tɪkli] *adv*
majesty ['mædʒəsti] *n, pl* **-ties 1** : majestad *f* <Your Majesty : su Majestad> **2** SPLENDOR : majestuosidad *f,* esplendor *m*
major[1] ['meɪdʒər] *vi* **-jored; -joring** : especializarse

major[2] *adj* **1** GREATER **:** mayor **2** NOTEWORTHY **:** mayor, notable **3** SERIOUS **:** grave **4 :** mayor (en la música)

major[3] *n* **1 :** mayor *mf,* comandante *mf* (en las fuerzas armadas) **2 :** especialidad *f* (universitaria)

Majorcan [mɑ'dʒɔrkən, mə-, -'jɔr-] *n* **:** mallorquín *m,* -quina *f* — **Majorcan** *adj*

major general *n* **:** general *mf* de división

majority [mə'dʒɔrəṭi] *n, pl* **-ties 1** ADULTHOOD **:** mayoría *f* de edad **2 :** mayoría *f,* mayor parte *f* <the vast majority : la inmensa mayoría>

make[1] ['meɪk] *v* **made** ['meɪd]; **making** *vt* **1** CREATE **:** hacer <to make noise : hacer ruido> **2** FASHION, MANUFACTURE **:** hacer, fabricar <she made a dress : hizo un vestido> **3** DEVISE, FORM **:** desarrollar, elaborar, formar **4** CONSTITUTE **:** hacer, constituir <made of stone : hecho de piedra> **5** PREPARE **:** hacer, preparar **6** RENDER **:** hacer, poner <it makes him nervous : lo pone nervioso> <to make someone happy : hacer feliz a alguien> <it made me sad : me dio pena> **7** PERFORM **:** hacer <to make a gesture : hacer un gesto> **8** COMPEL **:** hacer, forzar, obligar **9** EARN **:** ganar <to make a living : ganarse la vida> — *vi* **1** HEAD **:** ir, dirigirse <we made for home : nos fuimos a casa> **2 to make do :** arreglárselas **3 to make good** REPAY **:** pagar **4 to make good** SUCCEED **:** tener éxito

make[2] *n* BRAND **:** marca *f*

make–believe[1] [,meɪkbə'li:v] *adj* **:** imaginario

make–believe[2] *n* **:** fantasía *f,* invención *f* <a world of make-believe : un mundo de ensueño>

make out *vt* **1** WRITE **:** hacer (un cheque) **2** DISCERN **:** distinguir, divisar **3** UNDERSTAND **:** comprender, entender — *vi* **:** arreglárselas <how did you make out? : ¿qué tal te fue?>

maker ['meɪkər] *n* **:** fabricante *mf*

makeshift ['meɪk,ʃɪft] *adj* **:** provisional, improvisado

makeup ['meɪk,ʌp] *n* **1** COMPOSITION **:** composición *f* **2** CHARACTER **:** carácter *m,* temperamento *m* **3** COSMETICS **:** maquillaje *m*

make up *vt* **1** INVENT **:** inventar **2 :** recuperar <she made up the time : recuperó las horas perdidas> — *vi* RECONCILE **:** hacer las paces, reconciliarse

maladjusted [,mælə'dʒʌstəd] *adj* **:** inadaptado

malady ['mælədi] *n, pl* **-dies :** dolencia *f,* enfermedad *f,* mal *m*

malaise [mə'leɪz, mæ-] *n* **:** malestar *m*

malapropism ['mælə,prɑ,pɪzəm] *n* **:** uso *m* incorrecto y cómico de una palabra

malaria [mə'lɛriə] *n* **:** malaria *f,* paludismo *m*

malarkey [mə'lɑrki] *n* **:** tonterías *fpl,* estupideces *fpl*

Malawian [mə'lɑwiən] *n* **:** malauiano *m,* -na *f* — **Malawian** *adj*

Malay [mə'leɪ, 'meɪ,leɪ] *n* **1** *or* **Malayan** [mə'leɪən, meɪ-; 'meɪ,leɪən] **:** malayo *m,* -ya *f* **2 :** malayo *m* (idioma) — **Malay** *or* **Malayan** *adj*

male[1] ['meɪl] *adj* **1 :** macho **2** MASCULINE **:** masculino

male[2] *n* **:** macho *m* (de animales o plantas), varón *m* (de personas)

malefactor ['mælə,fæktər] *n* **:** malhechor *m,* -chora *f*

maleness ['meɪlnəs] *n* **:** masculinidad *f*

malevolence [mə'lɛvələnts] *n* **:** malevolencia *f*

malevolent [mə'lɛvələnt] *adj* **:** malévolo

malformation [,mælfɔr'meɪʃən] *n* **:** malformación *f*

malformed [mæl'fɔrmd] *adj* **:** mal formado, deforme

malfunction[1] [mæl'fʌŋkʃən] *vi* **:** funcionar mal

malfunction[2] *n* **:** mal funcionamiento *m*

malice ['mælɪs] *n* **1 :** malicia *f,* malevolencia *f* **2 with malice aforethought :** con premeditación

malicious [mə'lɪʃəs] *adj* **:** malicioso, malévolo — **maliciously** *adv*

malign[1] [mə'laɪn] *vt* **:** calumniar, difamar

malign[2] *adj* **:** maligno

malignancy [mə'lɪgnəntsi] *n, pl* **-cies :** malignidad *f*

malignant [mə'lɪgnənt] *adj* **:** maligno

malinger [mə'lɪŋgər] *vi* **:** fingirse enfermo

malingerer [mə'lɪŋgərər] *n* **:** uno que se finge enfermo

mall ['mɔl] *n* **1** PROMENADE **:** alameda *f,* paseo *m* (arbolado) **2 :** centro *m* comercial <shopping mall : galería comercial>

mallard ['mælərd] *n, pl* **-lard** *or* **-lards :** pato *m* real, ánade *mf* real

malleable ['mæliəbəl] *adj* **:** maleable

mallet ['mælət] *n* **:** mazo *m*

malnourished [mæl'nərɪʃt] *adj* **:** desnutrido, malnutrido

malnutrition [,mælnʊ'trɪʃən, -njʊ-] *n* **:** desnutrición *f,* malnutrición *f*

malodorous [mæl'o:dərəs] *adj* **:** maloliente

malpractice [,mæl'præktəs] *n* **:** mala práctica *f,* negligencia *f*

malt ['mɔlt] *n* **:** malta *f*

maltreat [mæl'tri:t] *vt* **:** maltratar

mama *or* **mamma** ['mɑmə] *n* **:** mamá *f*

mammal ['mæməl] *n* **:** mamífero *m*

mammalian [mə'meɪliən, mæ-] *adj* **:** mamífero

mammary ['mæməri] *adj* **1 :** mamario **2 mammary gland :** glándula mamaria

mammogram [ˈmæmə͵græm] *n* : mamografía *f*
mammoth[1] [ˈmæməθ] *adj* : colosal, gigantesco
mammoth[2] *n* : mamut *m*
man[1] [ˈmæn] *vt* **manned; manning** : tripular (un barco o avión), encargarse de (un servicio)
man[2] *n, pl* **men** [ˈmɛn] **1** PERSON : hombre *m,* persona *f* **2** MALE : hombre *m* **3** MANKIND : humanidad *f*
manacles [ˈmænɪkəlz] *npl* HANDCUFFS : esposas *fpl*
manage [ˈmænɪdʒ] *v* **-aged; -aging** *vt* **1** HANDLE : controlar, manejar **2** DIRECT : administrar, dirigir **3** CONTRIVE : lograr, ingeniárselas para — *vi* COPE : arreglárselas
manageable [ˈmænɪdʒəbəl] *adj* : manejable
management [ˈmænɪdʒmənt] *n* **1** DIRECTION : administración *f,* gestión *f,* dirección *f* **2** HANDLING : manejo *m* **3** MANAGERS : dirección *f,* gerencia *f*
manager [ˈmænɪdʒər] *n* : director *m,* -tora *f;* gerente *mf;* administrador *m,* -dora *f*
managerial [͵mænəˈdʒɪriəl] *adj* : directivo, gerencial
mandarin [ˈmændərən] *n* **1** : mandarín *m* **2** *or* **mandarin orange** : mandarina *f*
mandate [ˈmæn͵deɪt] *n* : mandato *m*
mandatory [ˈmændə͵tori] *adj* : obligatorio
mandible [ˈmændəbəl] *n* : mandíbula *f*
mandolin [͵mændəˈlɪn, ˈmændələn] *n* : mandolina *f*
mane [ˈmeɪn] *n* : crin *f* (de un caballo), melena *f* (de un león o una persona)
maneuver[1] [məˈnuːvər, -ˈnjuː-] *vt* **1** PLACE, POSITION : maniobrar, posicionar, colocar **2** MANIPULATE : manipular, maniobrar — *vi* : maniobrar
maneuver[2] *n* : maniobra *f*
manfully [ˈmænfəli] *adj* : valientemente
manganese [ˈmæŋgə͵niːz, -͵niːs] *n* : manganeso *m*
mange [ˈmeɪndʒ] *n* : sarna *f*
manger [ˈmeɪndʒər] *n* : pesebre *m*
mangle [ˈmæŋgəl] *vt* **-gled; -gling** **1** CRUSH, DESTROY : aplastar, despedazar, destrozar **2** MUTILATE : mutilar <to mangle a text : mutilar un texto>
mango [ˈmæŋ͵goː] *n, pl* **-goes** : mango *m*
mangrove [ˈmæn͵groːv, ˈmæŋ-] *n* : mangle *m*
mangy [ˈmeɪndʒi] *adj* **mangier; -est** **1** : sarnoso **2** SHABBY : gastoso
manhandle [ˈmæn͵hændəl] *vi* **-dled; -dling** : maltratar, tratar con poco cuidado
manhole [ˈmæn͵hoːl] *n* : boca *f* de alcantarilla
manhood [ˈmæn͵hʊd] *n* **1** : madurez *f* (de un hombre) **2** COURAGE, MANLINESS : hombría *f,* valor *m* **3** MEN : hombres *mpl*
manhunt [ˈmæn͵hʌnt] *n* : búsqueda *f* (de un criminal)
mania [ˈmeɪniə, -njə] *n* : manía *f*
maniac [ˈmeɪni͵æk] *n* : maníaco *m,* -ca *f;* maniático *m,* -ca *f*
maniacal [məˈnaɪəkəl] *adj* : maníaco, maniaco
manicure[1] [ˈmænə͵kjʊr] *vt* **-cured; -curing** **1** : hacer la manicura a **2** TRIM : recortar
manicure[2] *n* : manicura *f*
manicurist [ˈmænə͵kjʊrɪst] *n* : manicuro *m,* -ra *f*
manifest[1] [ˈmænə͵fɛst] *vt* : manifestar
manifest[2] *adj* : manifiesto, patente — **manifestly** *adv*
manifestation [͵mænəfəˈsteɪʃən] *n* : manifestación *f*
manifesto [͵mænəˈfɛs͵toː] *n, pl* **-tos** *or* **-toes** : manifiesto *m*
manifold[1] [ˈmænə͵foːld] *adj* : diverso, variado
manifold[2] *n* : colector *m* (de escape)
manipulate [məˈnɪpjə͵leɪt] *vt* **-lated; -lating** : manipular
manipulation [mə͵nɪpjəˈleɪʃən] *n* : manipulación *f*
manipulative [məˈnɪpjə͵leɪt̬ɪv, -lət̬ɪv] *adj* : manipulador
mankind [ˈmænˈkaɪnd, ͵kaɪnd] *n* : género *m* humano, humanidad *f*
manliness [ˈmænlinəs] *n* : hombría *f,* masculinidad *f*
manly [ˈmænli] *adj* **-lier; -est** : varonil, viril
man–made [ˈmænˈmeɪd] *adj* : artificial <man-made fabrics : telas sintéticas>
manna [ˈmænə] *n* : maná *m*
mannequin [ˈmænɪkən] *n* **1** DUMMY : maniquí *m* **2** MODEL : modelo *mf*
manner [ˈmænər] *n* **1** KIND, SORT : tipo *m,* clase *f* **2** WAY : manera *f,* modo *m* **3** STYLE : estilo *m* (artístico) **4** **manners** *npl* CUSTOMS : costumbres *fpl* <Victorian manners : costumbres victorianas> **5** **manners** *npl* ETIQUETTE : modales *mpl*, educación *f,* etiqueta *f* <good manners : buenos modales>
mannered [ˈmænərd] *adj* **1** AFFECTED, ARTIFICIAL : amanerado, afectado **2** **well–mannered** : educado, cortés **3** → **ill–mannered**
mannerism [ˈmænə͵rɪzəm] *n* : peculiaridad *f,* gesto *m* particular
mannerly [ˈmænərli] *adj* : cortés, bien educado
mannish [ˈmænɪʃ] *adj* : masculino, hombruno
man–of–war [͵mænəˈwɔr, -əvˈwɔr] *n, pl* **men–of–war** [͵mɛn-] WARSHIP : buque *m* de guerra
manor [ˈmænər] *n* **1** : casa *f* solariega, casa *f* señorial **2** ESTATE : señorío *m*

manpower ['mæn,paʊər] *n* : personal *m,* mano *f* de obra
mansion ['mæntʃən] *n* : mansión *f*
manslaughter ['mæn,slɔt̬ər] *n* : homicidio *m* sin premeditación
mantel ['mæntəl] *n* : repisa *f* de chimenea
mantelpiece ['mæntəl,piːs] → **mantel**
mantis ['mæntəs] *n, pl* **-tises** *or* **-tes** ['mæn,tiːz] : mantis *f* religiosa
mantle ['mæntəl] *n* : manto *m*
manual[1] ['mænjʊəl] *adj* : manual — **manually** *adv*
manual[2] *n* : manual *m*
manufacture[1] [,mænjə'fæktʃər] *vt* **-tured; -turing** : fabricar, manufacturar, confeccionar (ropa), elaborar (comestibles)
manufacture[2] *n* : manufactura *f,* fabricación *f,* confección *f* (de ropa), elaboración *f* (de comestibles)
manufacturer [,mænjə'fæktʃərər] *n* : fabricante *m;* manufacturero *m,* -ra *f*
manure [mə'nʊr, -'njʊr] *n* : estiércol *m*
manuscript ['mænjə,skrɪpt] *n* : manuscrito *m*
many[1] ['mɛni] *adj* **more** ['mor]; **most** ['moːst] : muchos
many[2] *pron* : muchos *pl,* -chas *pl*
map[1] ['mæp] *vt* **mapped; mapping** 1 : trazar el mapa de 2 PLAN : planear, proyectar <to map out a program : planear un programa>
map[2] *n* : mapa *m*
maple ['meɪpəl] *n* : arce *m*
mar ['mɑr] *vt* **marred; marring** 1 SPOIL : estropear, echar a perder 2 DEFACE : desfigurar
maraschino [,mærə'skiːnoː, -'ʃiː-] *n, pl* **-nos** : cereza *f* al marrasquino
marathon ['mærə,θɑn] *n* 1 RACE : maratón *m* 2 CONTEST : competencia *f* de resistencia
maraud [mə'rɔd] *vi* : merodear
marauder [mə'rɔdər] *n* : merodeador *m,* -dora *f*
marble ['mɑrbəl] *n* 1 : mármol *m* 2 : canica *f* <to play marbles : jugar a las canicas>
march[1] ['mɑrtʃ] *vi* 1 : marchar, desfilar <they marched past the grandstand : desfilaron ante la tribuna> 2 : caminar con resolución <she marched right up to him : se le acercó sin vacilación>
march[2] *n* 1 MARCHING : marcha *f* 2 PASSAGE : paso *m* (del tiempo) 3 PROGRESS : avance *m,* progreso *m* 4 : marcha *f* (en música)
March ['mɑrtʃ] *n* : marzo *m*
marchioness ['mɑrʃənɪs] *n* : marquesa *f*
Mardi Gras ['mɑrdi,grɑ] *n* : martes *m* de Carnaval
mare ['mær] *n* : yegua *f*
margarine ['mɑrdʒərən] *n* : margarina *f*
margin ['mɑrdʒən] *n* : margen *m*
marginal ['mɑrdʒənəl] *adj* 1 : marginal 2 MINIMAL : mínimo — **marginally** *adv*
marigold ['mærə,goːld] *n* : maravilla *f,* caléndula *f*
marijuana [,mærə'*h*wɑnə] *n* : marihuana *f*
marina [mə'riːnə] *n* : puerto *m* deportivo
marinate ['mærə,neɪt] *vt* **-nated; -nating** : marinar
marine[1] [mə'riːn] *adj* 1 : marino <marine life : vida marina> 2 NAUTICAL : náutico, marítimo 3 : de la infantería de marina
marine[2] *n* : soldado *m* de marina
mariner ['mærɪnər] *n* : marinero *m,* marino *m*
marionette [,mæriə'nɛt] *n* : marioneta *f,* títere *m*
marital ['mærət̬əl] *adj* 1 : matrimonial 2 **marital status** : estado *m* civil
maritime ['mærə,taɪm] *adj* : marítimo
marjoram ['mɑrdʒərəm] *n* : mejorana *f*
mark[1] ['mɑrk] *vt* 1 : marcar 2 CHARACTERIZE : caracterizar 3 SIGNAL : señalar 4 NOTICE : prestar atención a, hacer caso de 5 **to mark off** : demarcar, delimitar
mark[2] *n* 1 TARGET : blanco *m* 2 : marca *f,* señal *f* <put a mark where you left off : pon una señal donde terminaste> 3 INDICATION : señal *f,* indicio *m* 4 GRADE : nota *f* 5 IMPRINT : huella *f,* marca *f* 6 BLEMISH : marca *f,* imperfección *f*
marked ['mɑrkt] *adj* : marcado, notable — **markedly** ['mɑrkədli] *adv*
marker ['mɑrkər] *n* : marcador *m*
market[1] ['mɑrkət] *vt* : poner en venta, comercializar
market[2] *n* 1 MARKETPLACE : mercado *m* <the open market : el mercado libre> 2 DEMAND : demanda *f,* mercado *m* 3 STORE : tienda *f* 4 → **stock market**
marketable ['mɑrkət̬əbəl] *adj* : vendible
marketplace ['mɑrkət,pleɪs] *n* : mercado *m*
marksman ['mɑrksmən] *n, pl* **-men** [-mən, -,mɛn] : tirador *m*
marksmanship ['mɑrksmən,ʃɪp] *n* : puntería *f*
marlin ['mɑrlɪn] *n* : marlín *m*
marmalade ['mɑrmə,leɪd] *n* : mermelada *f*
marmoset ['mɑrmə,sɛt] *n* : tití *m*
marmot ['mɑrmət] *n* : marmota *f*
maroon[1] [mə'ruːn] *vt* : abandonar, aislar
maroon[2] *n* : rojo *m* oscuro, granate *m*
marquee [mɑr'kiː] *n* : marquesina *f*
marquess ['mɑrkwɪs] *or* **marquis** ['mɑrkwɪs, mɑr'kiː] *n, pl* **-quesses** *or* **-quises** [-'kiːz, -'kiːzəz] *or* **-quis** [-'kiː, -'kiːz] : marqués *m*
marquise [mɑr'kiːz] → **marchioness**

marriage ['mærɪdʒ] *n* **1** : matrimonio *m* **2** WEDDING : casamiento *m,* boda *f*

marriageable ['mærɪdʒəbəl] *adj* **of marriageable age** : de edad de casarse

married ['mærid] *adj* **1** : casado **2 to get married** : casarse

marrow ['mæroː] *n* : médula *f,* tuétano *m*

marry ['mæri] *vt* **-ried; -rying 1** : casar <the priest married them : el cura los casó> **2** : casarse con <she married John : se casó con John>

Mars ['mɑrz] *n* : Marte *m*

marsh ['mɑrʃ] *n* **1** : pantano *m* **2 salt marsh** : marisma *f*

marshal[1] ['mɑrʃəl] *vt* **-shaled** *or* **-shalled; -shaling** *or* **-shalling 1** : poner en orden, reunir **2** USHER : conducir

marshal[2] *n* **1** : maestro *m* de ceremonias **2** : mariscal *m* (en el ejército); jefe *m,* -fa *f* (de la policía, de los bomberos, etc.)

marshmallow ['mɑrʃˌmɛloː, -ˌmæloː] *n* : malvavisco *m*

marshy ['mɑrʃi] *adj* **marshier; -est** : pantanoso

marsupial [mɑr'suːpiəl] *n* : marsupial *m*

mart ['mɑrt] *n* MARKET : mercado *m*

marten ['mɑrtən] *n, pl* **-ten** *or* **-tens** : marta *f*

martial ['mɑrʃəl] *adj* : marcial

martin ['mɑrtən] *n* **1** SWALLOW : golondrina *f* **2** SWIFT : vencejo *m*

martyr[1] ['mɑrt̬ər] *vt* : martirizar

martyr[2] *n* : mártir *mf*

martyrdom ['mɑrt̬ərdəm] *n* : martirio *m*

marvel[1] ['mɑrvəl] *vi* **-veled** *or* **-velled; -veling** *or* **-velling** : maravillarse

marvel[2] *n* : maravilla *f*

marvelous ['mɑrvələs] *or* **marvellous** *adj* : maravilloso — **marvelously** *adv*

Marxism ['mɑrkˌsɪzəm] *n* : marxismo *m*

Marxist[1] ['mɑrksɪst] *adj* : marxista

Marxist[2] *n* : marxista *mf*

mascara [mæs'kærə] *n* : rímel *m,* rimel *m*

mascot ['mæsˌkɑt, -kət] *n* : mascota *f*

masculine ['mæskjələn] *adj* : masculino

masculinity [ˌmæskjə'lɪnət̬i] *n* : masculinidad *f*

mash[1] ['mæʃ] *vt* **1** : hacer puré de (papas, etc.) **2** CRUSH : aplastar, majar

mash[2] *n* **1** FEED : afrecho *m* **2** : malta *f* (para hacer bebidas alcohólicas) **3** PASTE, PULP : papilla *f,* pasta *f*

mask[1] ['mæsk] *vt* **1** CONCEAL, DISGUISE : enmascarar, ocultar **2** COVER : cubrir, tapar

mask[2] *n* : máscara *f,* careta *f,* mascarilla *f* (de un cirujano o dentista)

masochism ['mæsəˌkɪzəm, 'mæzə-] *n* : masoquismo *m*

masochist ['mæsəˌkɪst, 'mæzə-] *n* : masoquista *mf*

masochistic [ˌmæsə'kɪstɪk, ˌmæzə-] *adj* : masoquista

mason ['meɪsən] *n* **1** BRICKLAYER : albañil *mf* **2** *or* **stonemason** ['stoːnˌ-] : mampostero *m,* cantero *m*

masonry ['meɪsənri] *n, pl* **-ries 1** BRICKLAYING : albañería *f* **2** *or* **stonemasonry** ['stoːnˌ-] : mampostería *f*

masquerade[1] [ˌmæskə'reɪd] *vi* **-aded; -ading 1** : disfrazarse (de), hacerse pasar (por) **2** : asistir a una mascarada

masquerade[2] *n* **1** : mascarada *f,* baile *m* de disfraces **2** FACADE : farsa *f,* fachada *f*

mass[1] ['mæs] *vi* : concentrarse, juntarse en masa — *vt* : concentrar

mass[2] *n* **1** : masa *f* <atomic mass : masa atómica> **2** BULK : mole *f,* volumen *m* **3** MULTITUDE : cantidad *f,* montón *m* (de cosas), multitud *f* (de gente) **4 the masses** : las masas, el pueblo, el populacho

Mass ['mæs] *n* : misa *f*

massacre[1] ['mæsɪkər] *vt* **-cred; -cring** : masacrar

massacre[2] *n* : masacre *f*

massage[1] [mə'sɑʒ, -'sɑdʒ] *vt* **-saged; -saging** : masajear

massage[2] *n* : masaje *m*

masseur [mæ'sər] *n* : masajista *m*

masseuse [mæ'søz, -'suːz] *n* : masajista *f*

massive ['mæsɪv] *adj* **1** BULKY : voluminoso, macizo **2** HUGE : masivo, enorme — **massively** *adv*

mast ['mæst] *n* : mástil *m,* palo *m*

master[1] ['mæstər] *vt* **1** SUBDUE : dominar **2** : llegar a dominar <she mastered French : llegó a dominar el francés>

master[2] *n* **1** TEACHER : maestro *m,* profesor *m* **2** EXPERT : experto *m,* -ta *f;* maestro *m,* -tra *f* **3** : amo *m* (de animales o esclavos), señor *m* (de la casa) **4 master's degree** : maestría *f*

masterful ['mæstərfəl] *adj* **1** IMPERIOUS : autoritario, imperioso, dominante **2** SKILLFUL : magistral — **masterfully** *adv*

masterly ['mæstərli] *adj* : magistral

masterpiece ['mæstərˌpiːs] *n* : obra *f* maestra

masterwork ['mæstərˌwərk] → **masterpiece**

mastery ['mæstəri] *n* **1** DOMINION : dominio *m,* autoridad *f* **2** SUPERIORITY : superioridad *f* **3** EXPERTISE : maestría *f*

masticate ['mæstəˌkeɪt] *v* **-cated; -cating** : masticar

mastiff ['mæstɪf] *n* : mastín *m*

mastodon ['mæstəˌdɑn] *n* : mastodonte *m*

masturbate ['mæstərˌbeɪt] *v* **-bated; bating** *vi* : masturbarse — *vt* : masturbar

masturbation [ˌmæstər'beɪʃən] *n* : masturbación *f*

mat[1] [ˈmæt] *v* **matted; matting** *vt* TANGLE : enmarañar — *vi* : enmarañarse

mat[2] *n* **1** : estera *f* **2** TANGLE : maraña *f* **3** PAD : colchoneta *f* (de gimnasia) **4** *or* **matt** *or* **matte** [ˈmæt] FRAME : marco *m* (de cartón)

mat[3] → **matte**

matador [ˈmæt̬əˌdɔr] *n* : matador *m*

match[1] [ˈmætʃ] *vt* **1** PIT : enfrentar, oponer **2** EQUAL, FIT : igualar, corresponder a, coincidir con **3** : combinar con, hacer juego con <her shoes match her dress : sus zapatos hacen juego con su vestido> — *vi* **1** CORRESPOND : concordar, coincidir **2** : hacer juego <with a tie to match : con una corbata que hace juego>

match[2] *n* **1** EQUAL : igual *mf* <he's no match for her : no puede competir con ella> **2** FIGHT, GAME : partido *m,* combate *m* (en boxeo) **3** MARRIAGE : matrimonio *m,* casamiento *m* **4** : fósforo *m,* cerilla *f,* cerillo *m* (*in various countries*) <he lit a match : encendió un fósforo> **5 to be a good match** : hacer buena pareja (dícese de las personas), hacer juego (dícese de la ropa)

matchless [ˈmætʃləs] *adj* : sin igual, sin par

matchmaker [ˈmætʃˌmeɪkər] *n* : casamentero *m,* -ra *f*

mate[1] [ˈmeɪt] *v* **mated; mating** *vi* **1** FIT : encajar **2** PAIR : emparejarse **3** (*relating to animals*) : aparearse, copular — *vt* : aparear, acoplar (animales)

mate[2] *n* **1** COMPANION : compañero *m,* -ra *f;* camarada *mf* **2** : macho *m,* hembra *f* (de animales) **3** : oficial *mf* (de un barco) <first mate : primer oficial> **4** : compañero *m,* -ra *f;* pareja *f* (de un zapato, etc.)

material[1] [məˈtɪriəl] *adj* **1** PHYSICAL : material, físico <the material world : el mundo material> <material needs : necesidades materiales> **2** IMPORTANT : importante, esencial **3 material evidence** : prueba *f* sustancial

material[2] *n* **1** : material *m* **2** CLOTH : tejido *m,* tela *f*

materialism [məˈtɪriəˌlɪzəm] *n* : materialismo *m*

materialist [məˈtɪriəlɪst] *n* : materialista *mf*

materialistic [məˌtɪriəˈlɪstɪk] *adj* : materialista

materialize [məˈtɪriəˌlaɪz] *v* **-ized; -izing** *vt* : materializar, hacer aparecer — *vi* : materializarse, aparecer

maternal [məˈtərnəl] *adj* MOTHERLY : maternal — **maternally** *adv*

maternity[1] [məˈtərnət̬i] *adj* : de maternidad <maternity clothes : ropa de futura mamá> <maternity leave : licencia por maternidad>

maternity[2] *n, pl* **-ties** : maternidad *f*

math [ˈmæθ] → **mathematics**

mathematical [ˌmæθəˈmæt̬ɪkəl] *adj* : matemático — **mathematically** *adv*

mathematician [ˌmæθəməˈtɪʃən] *n* : matemático *m,* -ca *f*

mathematics [ˌmæθəˈmæt̬ɪks] *ns & pl* : matemáticas *fpl,* matemática *f*

matinee *or* **matinée** [ˌmætənˈeɪ] *n* : matiné *f*

matriarch [ˈmeɪtriˌɑrk] *n* : matriarca *f*

matriarchy [ˈmeɪtriˌɑrki] *n, pl* **-chies** : matriarcado *m*

matriculate [məˈtrɪkjəˌleɪt] *v* **-lated; -lating** *vt* : matricular — *vi* : matricularse

matriculation [məˌtrɪkjəˈleɪʃən] *n* : matrícula *f,* matriculación *f*

matrimony [ˈmætrəˌmoːni] *n* : matrimonio *m* — **matrimonial** [ˌmætrəˈmoːniəl] *adj*

matrix [ˈmeɪtrɪks] *n, pl* **-trices** [ˈmeɪtrəˌsiːz, ˈmæ-] *or* **-trixes** [ˈmeɪtrɪksəz] : matriz *f*

matron [ˈmeɪtrən] *n* : matrona *f*

matronly [ˈmeɪtrənli] *adj* : de matrona, matronal

matte [ˈmæt] *adj* : mate, de acabado mate

matter[1] [ˈmæt̬ər] *vi* : importar <it doesn't matter : no importa>

matter[2] *n* **1** QUESTION : asunto *m,* cuestión *f* <a matter of taste : una cuestión de gusto> **2** SUBSTANCE : materia *f,* sustancia *f* **3 matters** *npl* CIRCUMSTANCES : situación *f,* cosas *fpl* <to make matters worse : para colmo de males> **4 to be the matter** : pasar <what's the matter? : ¿qué pasa?> **5 as a matter of fact** : en efecto, en realidad **6 for that matter** : de hecho **7 no matter how much** : por mucho que

matter–of–fact [ˈmæt̬ərəvˈfækt] *adj* : práctico, realista

mattress [ˈmætrəs] *n* : colchón *m*

mature[1] [məˈtʊr, -ˈtjʊr, -ˈtʃʊr] *vi* **-tured; -turing 1** : madurar **2** : vencer <when does the loan mature? : ¿cuándo vence el préstamo?>

mature[2] *adj* **-turer; -est 1** : maduro **2** DUE : vencido

maturity [məˈtʊrət̬i, -ˈtjʊr-, -ˈtʃʊr-] *n* : madurez *f*

maudlin [ˈmɔdlɪn] *adj* : sensiblero

maul[1] [ˈmɔl] *vt* **1** BEAT : golpear, pegar **2** MANGLE : mutilar **3** MANHANDLE : maltratar

maul[2] *n* MALLET : mazo *m*

Mauritanian [ˌmɔrəˈteɪniən] *n* : mauritano *m,* -na *f* — **Mauritanian** *adj*

mausoleum [ˌmɔsəˈliːəm, ˌmɔzə-] *n, pl* **-leums** *or* **-lea** [-ˈliːə] : mausoleo *m*

mauve [ˈmoːv, ˈmɔv] *n* : malva *m*

maven *or* **mavin** [ˈmeɪvən] *n* EXPERT : experto *m,* -ta *f*

maverick [ˈmævrɪk, ˈmævə-] *n* **1** : ternero *m* sin marcar **2** NONCONFORMIST : inconformista *mf,* disidente *mf*

mawkish [ˈmɔkɪʃ] *adj* : sensiblero

maxim [ˈmæksəm] *n* : máxima *f*

maximize [ˈmæksəˌmaɪz] *vt* **-mized; -mizing** : maximizar, llevar al máximo

maximum[1] [ˈmæksəməm] *adj* : máximo

maximum[2] *n, pl* **-ma** [ˈmæksəmə] *or* **-mums** : máximo *m*

may [ˈmeɪ] *v aux, past* **might** [ˈmaɪt]; *present s & pl* **may 1** (*expressing permission*) : poder <you may go : puedes ir> **2** (*expressing possibility or probability*) : poder <you may be right : puede que tengas razón> <it may happen occasionally : puede pasar de vez en cuando> **3** (*expressing desires, intentions, or contingencies*) <may the best man win : que gane el mejor> <I laugh that I may not weep : me río para no llorar> <come what may : pase lo que pase>

May [ˈmeɪ] *n* : mayo *m*

maybe [ˈmeɪbi] *adv* PERHAPS : quizás, tal vez

mayfly [ˈmeɪˌflaɪ] *n, pl* **-flies** : efímera *f*

mayhem [ˈmeɪˌhɛm, ˈmeɪəm] *n* **1** MUTILATION : mutilación *f* **2** DEVASTATION : estragos *mpl*

mayonnaise [ˈmeɪəˌneɪz] *n* : mayonesa *f*

mayor [ˈmeɪər, ˈmɛr] *n* : alcalde *m*, -desa *f*

mayoral [ˈmeɪərəl, ˈmɛrəl] *adj* : de alcalde

maze [ˈmeɪz] *n* : laberinto *m*

me [ˈmiː] *pron* **1** : me <she called me : me llamó> <give it to me : dámelo> **2** (*after a preposition*) : mí <for me : para mí> <with me : conmigo> **3** (*after conjunctions and verbs*) : yo <it's me : soy yo> <as big as me : tan grande como yo> **4** (*emphatic use*) : yo <me, too! : ¡yo también!> <who, me? : ¿quién, yo?>

meadow [ˈmɛdoː] *n* : prado *m*, pradera *f*

meadowland [ˈmɛdoˌlænd] *n* : pradera *f*

meadowlark [ˈmɛdoˌlɑrk] *n* : pájaro *m* cantor con el pecho amarillo

meager *or* **meagre** [ˈmiːgər] *adj* **1** THIN : magro, flaco **2** POOR, SCANTY : exiguo, escaso, pobre

meagerly [ˈmiːgərli] *adv* : pobremente

meagerness [ˈmiːgərnəs] *n* : escasez *f*, pobreza *f*

meal [ˈmiːl] *n* **1** : comida *f* <a hearty meal : una comida sustanciosa> **2** : harina *f* (de maíz, etc.)

mealtime [ˈmiːlˌtaɪm] *n* : hora *f* de comer

mean[1] [ˈmiːn] *vt* **meant** [ˈmɛnt]; **meaning 1** INTEND : querer, pensar, tener la intención de <I didn't mean to do it : lo hice sin querer> <what do you mean to do? : ¿qué piensas hacer?> **2** SIGNIFY : querer decir, significar <what does that mean? : ¿qué quiere decir eso?> **3** : importar <health means everything : lo que más importa es la salud>

mean[2] *adj* **1** HUMBLE : humilde **2** NEGLIGIBLE : despreciable <it's no mean feat : no es poca cosa> **3** STINGY : mezquino, tacaño **4** CRUEL : malo, cruel <to be mean to someone : tratar mal a alguien> **5** AVERAGE, MEDIAN : medio

mean[3] *n* **1** MIDPOINT : término *m* medio **2** AVERAGE : promedio *m*, media *f* aritmética **3 means** *npl* WAY : medio *m*, manera *f*, vía *f* **4 means** *npl* RESOURCES : medios *mpl*, recursos *mpl* **5 by all means** : por supuesto, cómo no **6 by means of** : por medio de **7 by no means** : de ninguna manera, de ningún modo

meander [miˈændər] *vi* **-dered; -dering 1** WIND : serpentear **2** WANDER : vagar, andar sin rumbo fijo

meaning [ˈmiːnɪŋ] *n* **1** : significado *m*, sentido *m* <double meaning : doble sentido> **2** INTENT : intención *f*, propósito *m*

meaningful [ˈmiːnɪŋfəl] *adj* : significativo — **meaningfully** *adv*

meaningless [ˈmiːnɪŋləs] *adj* : sin sentido

meanness [ˈmiːnnəs] *n* **1** CRUELTY : crueldad *f*, mezquindad *f* **2** STINGINESS : tacañería *f*

meantime[1] [ˈmiːnˌtaɪm] *adv* → **meanwhile**[1]

meantime[2] *n* **1** : interín *m* **2 in the meantime** : entretanto, mientras tanto

meanwhile[1] [ˈmiːnˌhwaɪl] *adv* : entretanto, mientras tanto

meanwhile[2] *n* → **meantime**[2]

measles [ˈmiːzəlz] *ns & pl* : sarampión *m*

measly [ˈmiːzli] *adj* **-slier; -est** : miserable, mezquino

measurable [ˈmɛʒərəbəl, ˈmeɪ-] *adj* : mensurable — **measurably** [-bli] *adv*

measure[1] [ˈmɛʒər, ˈmeɪ-] *v* **-sured; -suring** : medir <he measured the table : midió la mesa> <it measures 15 feet tall : mide 15 pies de altura>

measure[2] *n* **1** AMOUNT : medida *f*, cantidad *f* <in large measure : en gran medida> <a full measure : una cantidad exacta> <a measure of proficiency : una cierta competencia> <for good measure : de ñapa, por añadidura> **2** DIMENSIONS, SIZE : medida *f*, tamaño *m* **3** RULER : regla *f* <tape measure : cinta métrica> **4** MEASUREMENT : medida *f* <cubic measure : medida de capacidad> **5** MEASURING : medición *f* **6 measures** *npl* : medidas *fpl* <security measures : medidas de seguridad>

measureless [ˈmɛʒərləs, ˈmeɪ-] *adj* : inmensurable

measurement [ˈmɛʒərmənt, ˈmeɪ-] *n* **1** MEASURING : medición *f* **2** DIMENSION : medida *f*

measure up *vi* **to measure up to** : estar a la altura de

meat [ˈmiːt] *n* **1** FOOD : comida *f* **2** : carne *f* <meat and fish : carne y pescado> **3** SUBSTANCE : sustancia *f,* esencia *f* <the meat of the story : la sustancia del cuento>

meatball [ˈmiːtˌbɔl] *n* : albóndiga *f*

meaty [ˈmiːṱi] *adj* **meatier; -est** : con mucha carne, carnoso

mechanic [mɪˈkænɪk] *n* : mecánico *m,* -ca *f*

mechanical [mɪˈkænɪkəl] *adj* : mecánico — **mechanically** *adv*

mechanics [mɪˈkænɪks] *ns & pl* **1** : mecánica *f* <fluid mechanics : la mecánica de fluidos> **2** MECHANISMS : mecanismos *mpl,* aspectos *mpl* prácticos

mechanism [ˈmɛkəˌnɪzəm] *n* : mecanismo *m*

mechanization [ˌmɛkənəˈzeɪʃən] *n* : mecanización *f*

mechanize [ˈmɛkəˌnaɪz] *vt* **-nized; -nizing** : mecanizar

medal [ˈmɛdəl] *n* : medalla *f,* condecoración *f*

medalist [ˈmɛdəlɪst] *or* **medallist** *n* : medallista *mf*

medallion [məˈdæljən] *n* : medallón *m*

meddle [ˈmɛdəl] *vi* **-dled; -dling** : meterse, entrometerse

meddler [ˈmɛdələr] *n* : entrometido *m,* -da *f*

meddlesome [ˈmɛdəlsəm] *adj* : entrometido

media [ˈmiːdiə] *npl* : medios *mpl* de comunicación

median[1] [ˈmiːdiən] *adj* : medio

median[2] *n* : valor *m* medio

mediate [ˈmiːdiˌeɪt] *vi* **-ated; -ating** : mediar

mediation [ˌmiːdiˈeɪʃən] *n* : mediación *f*

mediator [ˈmiːdiˌeɪṱər] *n* : mediador *m,* -dora *f*

medical [ˈmɛdɪkəl] *adj* : médico

medicate [ˈmɛdəˌkeɪt] *vt* **-cated; -cating** : medicar <medicated powder : polvos medicinales>

medication [ˌmɛdəˈkeɪʃən] *n* **1** TREATMENT : tratamiento *m,* medicación *f* **2** MEDICINE : medicamento *m* <to be on medication : estar medicado>

medicinal [məˈdɪsənəl] *adj* : medicinal

medicine [ˈmɛdəsən] *n* **1** MEDICATION : medicina *f,* medicamento *m* **2** : medicina *f* <he's studying medicine : estudia medicina>

medicine man *n* : hechicero *m*

medieval *or* **mediaeval** [mɪˈdiːvəl, ˌmiː-, ˌmɛ-, -diˈiːvəl] *adj* : medieval

mediocre [ˌmiːdiˈoːkər] *adj* : mediocre

mediocrity [ˌmiːdiˈɑkrəṱi] *n, pl* **-ties** : mediocridad *f*

meditate [ˈmɛdəˌteɪt] *vi* **-tated; -tating** : meditar

meditation [ˌmɛdəˈteɪʃən] *n* : meditación *f*

meditative [ˈmɛdəˌteɪṱɪv] *adj* : meditabundo

medium[1] [ˈmiːdiəm] *adj* : mediano <of medium height : de estatura mediana, de estatura regular>

medium[2] *n, pl* **-diums** *or* **-dia** [ˈmiːdiə] **1** MEAN : punto *m* medio, término *m* medio <happy medium : justo medio> **2** MEANS : medio *m* **3** SUBSTANCE : medio *m,* sustancia *f* <a viscous medium : un medio viscoso> **4** : medio *m* de comunicación **5** : medio *m* (artístico)

medley [ˈmɛdli] *n, pl* **-leys** : popurrí *m* (de canciones)

meek [ˈmiːk] *adj* **1** LONG-SUFFERING : paciente, sufrido **2** SUBMISSIVE : sumiso, dócil, manso

meekly [ˈmiːkli] *adv* : dócilmente

meekness [ˈmiːknəs] *n* : mansedumbre *f,* docilidad *f*

meet[1] [ˈmiːt] *v* **met** [ˈmɛt]; **meeting** *vt* **1** ENCOUNTER : encontrarse con **2** JOIN : unirse con **3** CONFRONT : enfrentarse a **4** SATISFY : satisfacer, cumplir con <to meet costs : pagar los gastos> **5** : conocer <I met his sister : conocí a su hermana> — *vi* ASSEMBLE : reunirse, congregarse

meet[2] *n* : encuentro *m*

meeting [ˈmiːṱɪŋ] *n* **1** : reunión *f* <to open the meeting : abrir la sesión> **2** ENCOUNTER : encuentro *m* **3** : entrevista *f* (formal)

meetinghouse [ˈmiːṱɪŋˌhaʊs] *n* : iglesia *f* (de ciertas confesiones protestantes)

megabyte [ˈmɛgəˌbaɪt] *n* : megabyte *m*

megahertz [ˈmɛgəˌhərts, -ˌhɛrts] *n* : megahercio *m*

megaphone [ˈmɛgəˌfoːn] *n* : megáfono *m*

melancholy[1] [ˈmɛlənˌkɑli] *adj* : melancólico, triste, sombrío

melancholy[2] *n, pl* **-cholies** : melancolía *f*

melanoma [ˌmɛləˈnoːmə] *n, pl* **-mas** : melanoma *m*

melee [ˈmeɪˌleɪ, meɪˈleɪ] *n* BRAWL : reyerta *f,* riña *f,* pelea *f*

meliorate [ˈmiːljəˌreɪt, ˈmiːliə-] → **ameliorate**

mellow[1] [ˈmɛloː] *vt* : suavizar, endulzar — *vi* : suavizarse, endulzarse

mellow[2] *adj* **1** RIPE : maduro **2** MILD : apacible <a mellow character : un carácter apacible> <mellow wines : vinos añejos> **3** : suave, dulce <mellow colors : colores suaves> <mellow tones : tonos dulces>

mellowness [ˈmɛlonəs] *n* : suavidad *f,* dulzura *f*

melodic [məˈlɑdɪk] *adj* : melódico — **melodically** [-dɪkli] *adv*

melodious [məˈloːdiəs] *adj* : melodioso — **melodiously** *adv*

melodiousness [mə'lo:diəsnəs] *n* : calidad *f* de melódico

melodrama ['mɛlə,drɑmə, -,dræ-] *n* : melodrama *m*

melodramatic [,mɛlədrə'mæt̬ɪk] *adj* : melodramático — **melodramatically** [-tɪkli] *adv*

melody ['mɛlədi] *n, pl* **-dies** : melodía *f*, tonada *f*

melon ['mɛlən] *n* : melón *m*

melt ['mɛlt] *vt* **1** : derretir, disolver **2** SOFTEN : ablandar <it melted his heart : ablandó su corazón> — *vi* **1** : derretirse, disolverse **2** SOFTEN : ablandarse **3** DISAPPEAR : desvanecerse, esfumarse <the clouds melted away : las nubes se desvanecieron>

melting point *n* : punto *m* de fusión

member ['mɛmbər] *n* **1** LIMB : miembro *m* **2** : miembro *m* (de un grupo); socio *m*, -cia *f* (de un club) **3** PART : miembro *m*, parte *f*

membership ['mɛmbər,ʃɪp] *n* **1** : membresía *f* <application for membership : solicitud de entrada> **2** MEMBERS : membresía *f*, miembros *mpl*, socios *mpl*

membrane ['mɛm,breɪn] *n* : membrana *f* — **membranous** ['mɛmbrənəs] *adj*

memento [mɪ'mɛn,to:] *n, pl* **-tos** *or* **-toes** : recuerdo *m*

memo ['mɛmo:] *n, pl* **memos** : memorándum *m*

memoirs ['mɛm,wɑrz] *npl* : memorias *fpl*, autobiografía *f*

memorabilia [,mɛmərə'biliə, -'bɪljə] *npl* **1** : objetos *mpl* de interés histórico **2** MEMENTOS : recuerdos *mpl*

memorable ['mɛmərəbəl] *adj* : memorable, notable — **memorably** [-bli] *adv*

memorandum [,mɛmə'rændəm] *n, pl* **-dums** *or* **-da** [-də] : memorándum *m*

memorial[1] [mə'moriəl] *adj* : conmemorativo

memorial[2] *n* : monumento *m* conmemorativo

Memorial Day *n* : el último lunes de mayo (observado en Estados Unidos como día feriado para conmemorar a los caídos en guerra)

memorialize [mə'moriə,laɪz] *vt* **-ized; -izing** COMMEMORATE : conmemorar

memorization [,mɛmərə'zeɪʃən] *n* : memorización *f*

memorize ['mɛmə,raɪz] *vt* **-rized; -rizing** : memorizar, aprender de memoria

memory ['mɛmri, 'mɛmə-] *n, pl* **-ries** **1** : memoria *f* <he has a good memory : tiene buena memoria> **2** RECOLLECTION : recuerdo *m* **3** COMMEMORATION : memoria *f*, conmemoración *f*

men → **man**[2]

menace[1] ['mɛnəs] *vt* **-aced; -acing** **1** THREATEN : amenazar **2** ENDANGER : poner en peligro

menace[2] *n* : amenaza *f*

menacing ['mɛnəsɪŋli] *adj* : amenazador, amenazante

menagerie [mə'nædʒəri, -'næʒəri] *n* : colección *f* de animales salvajes

mend[1] ['mɛnd] *vt* **1** CORRECT : enmendar, corregir <to mend one's ways : enmendarse> **2** REPAIR : remendar, arreglar, reparar — *vi* HEAL : curarse

mend[2] *n* : remiendo *m*

mendicant ['mɛndɪkənt] *n* BEGGAR : mendigo *m*, -ga *f*

menhaden [mɛn'heɪdən, mən-] *ns & pl* : pez *m* de la misma familia que los arenques

menial[1] ['mi:niəl] *adj* : servil, bajo

menial[2] *n* : sirviente *m*, -ta *f*

meningitis [,mɛnən'dʒaɪt̬əs] *n, pl* **-gitides** [-'dʒɪt̬ə,di:z] : meningitis *f*

menopause ['mɛnə,pɔz] *n* : menopausia *f*

menorah [mə'norə] *n* : candelabro *m* (usado en los oficios religiosos judíos)

menstrual ['mɛntstrʊəl] *adj* : menstrual

menstruate ['mɛntstrʊ,eɪt] *vi* **-ated; -ating** : menstruar

menstruation [,mɛntstrʊ'eɪʃən] *n* : menstruación *f*

mental ['mɛntəl] *adj* : mental <mental hospital : hospital psiquiátrico> — **mentally** *adv*

mentality [mɛn'tæləṭi] *n, pl* **-ties** : mentalidad *f*

menthol ['mɛn,θɔl, -,θo:l] *n* : mentol *m*

mentholated [,mɛntθə,leɪt̬əd] *adj* : mentolado

mention[1] ['mɛntʃən] *vt* : mencionar, mentar, referirse a <don't mention it! : ¡de nada!, ¡no hay de qué!>

mention[2] *n* : mención *f*

mentor ['mɛn,tɔr, 'mɛntər] *n* : mentor *m*

menu ['mɛn,ju:] *n* **1** : menú *m*, carta *f* (en un restaurante) **2** : menú *m* (de computadoras)

meow[1] [mi:'aʊ] *vi* : maullar

meow[2] *n* : maullido *m*, miau *m*

mercantile ['mərkən,ti:l, -,taɪl] *adj* : mercantil

mercenary[1] ['mərsən,ɛri] *adj* : mercenario

mercenary[2] *n, pl* **-naries** : mercenario *m*, -ria *f*

merchandise ['mərtʃən,daɪz, -,daɪs] *n* : mercancía *f*, mercadería *f*

merchandiser ['mərtʃən,daɪzər] *n* : comerciante *mf;* vendedor *m*, -dora *f*

merchant ['mərtʃənt] *n* : comerciante *mf*

merchant marine *n* : marina *f* mercante

merciful ['mərsɪfəl] *adj* : misericordioso, clemente

mercifully ['mərsɪfli] *adv* **1** : con misericordia, con compasión **2** FORTUNATELY : afortunadamente

merciless [ˈmərsɪləs] *adj* **:** despiadado — **mercilessly** *adv*
mercurial [ˌmərˈkjʊriəl] *adj* TEMPERAMENTAL **:** temperamental, volátil
mercury [ˈmərkjəri] *n, pl* **-ries :** mercurio *m*
Mercury *n* **:** Mercurio *m*
mercy [ˈmərsi] *n, pl* **-cies 1** CLEMENCY **:** misericordia *f,* clemencia *f* **2** BLESSING **:** bendición *f*
mere [ˈmɪr] *adj, superlative* **merest :** mero, simple
merely [ˈmɪrli] *adv* **:** solamente, simplemente
merge [ˈmərdʒ] *v* **merged; merging** *vi* **:** unirse, fusionarse (dícese de las compañías), confluir (dícese de los ríos, las calles, etc.) — *vt* **:** unir, fusionar, combinar
merger [ˈmərdʒər] *n* **:** unión *f,* fusión *f*
meridian [məˈrɪdiən] *n* **:** meridiano *m*
meringue [məˈræŋ] *n* **:** merengue *m*
merino [məˈriːno] *n, pl* **-nos 1 :** merino *m,* -na *f* **2** *or* **merino wool :** lana *f* merino
merit[1] [ˈmɛrət] *vt* **:** merecer, ser digno de
merit[2] *n* **:** mérito *m,* valor *m*
meritorious [ˌmɛrəˈtoriəs] *adj* **:** meritorio
mermaid [ˈmərˌmeɪd] *n* **:** sirena *f*
merriment [ˈmɛrɪmənt] *n* **:** alegría *f,* júbilo *m,* regocijo *m*
merry [ˈmɛri] *adj* **-rier; -est :** alegre — **merrily** [ˈmɛrəli] *adv*
merry–go–round [ˈmɛrigoˌraʊnd] *n* **:** carrusel *m,* tiovivo *m*
merrymaker [ˈmɛriˌmeɪkər] *n* **:** juerguista *mf*
merrymaking [ˈmɛriˌmeɪkɪŋ] *n* **:** juerga *f*
mesa [ˈmeɪsə] *n* **:** mesa *f*
mesdames → madam, Mrs.
mesh[1] [ˈmɛʃ] *vi* **1** ENGAGE **:** engranar (dícese de las piezas mecánicas) **2** TANGLE **:** enredarse **3** COORDINATE **:** coordinarse, combinar
mesh[2] *n* **1 :** malla *f* <wire mesh : malla metálica> **2** NETWORK **:** red *f* **3** MESHING **:** engranaje *m* <in mesh : engranado>
mesmerize [ˈmɛzməˌraɪz] *vt* **-ized; -izing 1** HYPNOTIZE **:** hipnotizar **2** FASCINATE **:** cautivar, embelesar, fascinar
mess[1] [ˈmɛs] *vt* **1** SOIL **:** ensuciar **2 to mess up** DISARRANGE **:** desordenar, desarreglar **3 to mess up** BUNGLE **:** echar a perder — *vi* **1** PUTTER **:** entretenerse **2** INTERFERE **:** meterse, entrometerse <don't mess with me : no te metas conmigo>
mess[2] *n* **1 :** rancho *m* (para soldados, etc.) **2** DISORDER **:** desorden *m* <your room is a mess : tienes el cuarto hecho un desastre> **3** CONFUSION, TURMOIL **:** confusión *f,* embrollo *m,* lío *m fam*
message [ˈmɛsɪdʒ] *n* **:** mensaje *m,* recado *m*
messenger [ˈmɛsəndʒər] *n* **:** mensajero *m,* -ra *f*
Messiah [məˈsaɪə] *n* **:** Mesías *m*
Messrs. → Mr.
messy [ˈmɛsi] *adj* **messier; -est** UNTIDY **:** desordenado, sucio
met → meet
metabolic [ˌmɛt̬əˈbɑlɪk] *adj* **:** metabólico
metabolism [məˈtæbəˌlɪzəm] *n* **:** metabolismo *m*
metabolize [məˈtæbəˌlaɪz] *vt* **-lized; -lizing :** metabolizar
metal [ˈmɛt̬əl] *n* **:** metal *m*
metallic [məˈtælɪk] *adj* **:** metálico
metallurgical [ˌmɛt̬əlˈərdʒɪkəl] *adj* **:** metalúrgico
metallurgy [ˈmɛt̬əlˌərdʒi] *n* **:** metalurgia *f*
metalwork [ˈmɛt̬əlˌwərk] *n* **:** objeto *m* de metal
metalworking [ˈmɛt̬əlˌwərkɪŋ] *n* **:** metalistería *f*
metamorphosis [ˌmɛt̬əˈmɔrfəsɪs] *n, pl* **-phoses** [-ˌsiːz] **:** metamorfosis *f*
metaphor [ˈmɛt̬əˌfɔr, -fər] *n* **:** metáfora *f*
metaphoric [ˌmɛt̬əˈfɔrɪk] *or* **metaphorical** [-ɪkəl] *adj* **:** metafórico
metaphysical [ˌmɛt̬əˈfɪzəkəl] *adj* **:** metafísico
metaphysics [ˌmɛt̬əˈfɪzɪks] *n* **:** metafísica *f*
mete [ˈmiːt] *vt* **meted; meting** ALLOT **:** repartir, distribuir <to mete out punishment : imponer castigos>
meteor [ˈmiːt̬iər, -tiːˌɔr] *n* **:** meteoro *m*
meteoric [ˌmiːt̬iˈɔrɪk] *adj* **:** meteórico
meteorite [ˈmiːt̬iəˌraɪt] *n* **:** meteorito *m*
meteorologic [ˌmiːt̬iˌɔrəˈlɑdʒɪk] *or* **meteorological** [-ˈlɑdʒɪkəl] *adj* **:** meteorológico
meteorologist [ˌmiːt̬iəˈrɑlədʒɪst] *n* **:** meteorólogo *m,* -ga *f*
meteorology [ˌmiːt̬iəˈrɑlədʒi] *n* **:** meteorología *f*
meter [ˈmiːt̬ər] *n* **1 :** metro *m* <it measures 2 meters : mide 2 metros> **2 :** contador *m,* medidor *m* (de electricidad, etc.) <parking meter : parquímetro> **3 :** metro *m* (en literatura o música)
methane [ˈmɛˌθeɪn] *n* **:** metano *m*
method [ˈmɛθəd] *n* **:** método *m*
methodical [məˈθɑdɪkəl] *adj* **:** metódico — **methodically** *adv*
meticulous [məˈtɪkjələs] *adj* **:** meticuloso — **meticulously** *adv*
meticulousness [məˈtɪkjələsnəs] *n* **:** meticulosidad *f*
metric [ˈmɛtrɪk] *or* **metrical** [-trɪkəl] *adj* **:** métrico
metric system *n* **:** sistema *m* métrico
metronome [ˈmɛtrəˌnoːm] *n* **:** metrónomo *m*
metropolis [məˈtrɑpələs] *n* **:** metrópoli *f,* metrópolis *f*
metropolitan [ˌmɛtrəˈpɑlətən] *adj* **:** metropolitano

mettle [ˈmɛt̬əl] *n* **:** temple *m,* valor *m* <on one's mettle **:** dispuesto a mostrar su valía>

Mexican [ˈmɛksɪkən] *n* **:** mexicano *m,* -na *f* — **Mexican** *adj*

mezzanine [ˈmɛzəˌniːn, ˌmɛzəˈniːn] *n* **1 :** entrepiso *m,* entresuelo *m* **2 :** primer piso *m* (de un teatro)

miasma [maɪˈæzmə] *n* **:** miasma *m*

mica [ˈmaɪkə] *n* **:** mica *f*

mice → **mouse**

micro [ˈmaɪkro] *adj* **:** muy pequeño, microscópico

microbe [ˈmaɪˌkroːb] *n* **:** microbio *m*

microbiology [ˌmaɪkrobaɪˈɑlədʒi] *n* **:** microbiología *f*

microcomputer [ˈmaɪkrokəmˌpjuːt̬ər] *n* **:** microcomputadora *f*

microcosm [ˈmaɪkroˌkɑzəm] *n* **:** microcosmo *m*

microfilm [ˈmaɪkroˌfɪlm] *n* **:** microfilm *m*

micrometer [maɪˈkrɑmət̬ər] *n* **:** micrómetro *m*

micron [ˈmaɪˌkrɑn] *n* **:** micrón *m*

microorganism [ˌmaɪkroˈɔrgəˌnɪzəm] *n* **:** microorganismo *m,* microbio *m*

microphone [ˈmaɪkrəˌfoːn] *n* **:** micrófono *m*

microprocessor [ˈmaɪkroˌprɑˌsɛsər] *n* **:** microprocesador *m*

microscope [ˈmaɪkrəˌskoːp] *n* **:** microscopio *m*

microscopic [ˌmaɪkrəˈskɑpɪk] *adj* **:** microscópico

microscopy [maɪˈkrɑskəpi] *n* **:** microscopía *f*

microwave [ˈmaɪkrəˌweɪv] *n* **1 :** microonda *f* **2** *or* **microwave oven :** microondas *m*

mid [ˈmɪd] *adj* **:** medio <mid morning **:** a media mañana> <in mid-August **:** a mediados de agosto> <in mid ocean **:** en alta mar>

midair [ˈmɪdˈær] *n* **in ~ :** en el aire <to catch in midair **:** agarrar al vuelo>

midday [ˈmɪdˈdeɪ] *n* NOON **:** mediodía *m*

middle[1] [ˈmɪdəl] *adj* **1** CENTRAL **:** medio, del medio, de en medio **2** INTERMEDIATE **:** intermedio, mediano <middle age **:** la mediana edad>

middle[2] *n* **1** CENTER **:** medio *m,* centro *m* <fold it down the middle **:** dóblalo por la mitad> **2 in the middle of :** en medio de (un espacio), a mitad de (una actividad) <in the middle of the month **:** a mediados del mes>

Middle Ages *npl* **:** Edad *f* Media

middle class *n* **:** clase *f* media

middleman [ˈmɪdəlˌmæn] *n, pl* **-men** [-mən, -ˌmɛn] **:** intermediario *m,* -ria *f*

middling [ˈmɪdlɪŋ, -lən] *adj* **1** MEDIUM, MIDDLE **:** mediano **2** MEDIOCRE **:** mediocre, regular

midge [ˈmɪdʒ] *n* **:** mosca *f* pequeña

midget [ˈmɪdʒət] *n* **1 :** enano *m,* -na *f* (persona) **2 :** cosa *f* diminuta

midland [ˈmɪdlənd, -ˌlænd] *n* **:** región *f* central (de un país)

midnight [ˈmɪdˌnaɪt] *n* **:** medianoche *f*

midpoint [ˈmɪdˌpɔɪnt] *n* **:** punto *m* medio, término *m* medio

midriff [ˈmɪdˌrɪf] *n* **:** diafragma *m*

midshipman [ˈmɪdˌʃɪpmən, ˌmɪdˈʃɪp-] *n, pl* **-men** [-mən, -ˌmɛn] **:** guardiamarina *m*

midst[1] [ˈmɪdst] *n* **:** medio *m* <in our midst **:** entre nosotros> <in the midst of **:** en medio de>

midst[2] *prep* **:** entre

midstream [ˈmɪdˈstriːm, -ˌstriːm] *n* **:** medio *m* de la corriente <in the midstream of his career **:** en medio de su carrera>

midsummer [ˈmɪdˈsʌmər, -ˌsʌ-] *n* **:** pleno verano *m*

midtown [ˈmɪdˌtaʊn] *n* **:** centro *m* (de una ciudad)

midway [ˈmɪdˌweɪ] *adv* HALFWAY **:** a mitad de camino

midweek [ˈmɪdˌwiːk] *n* **:** medio *m* de la semana <in midweek **:** a media semana>

midwife [ˈmɪdˌwaɪf] *n, pl* **-wives** [-ˌwaɪvz] **:** partera *f,* comadrona *f*

midwinter [ˈmɪdˈwɪntər, -ˌwɪn-] *n* **:** pleno invierno *m*

midyear [ˈmɪdˌjɪr] *n* **:** medio *m* del año <at midyear **:** a mediados del año>

mien [ˈmiːn] *n* **:** aspecto *m,* porte *m,* semblante *m*

miff [ˈmɪf] *vt* **:** ofender

might[1] [ˈmaɪt] (*used to express permission or possibility or as a polite alternative to* **may**) → **may** <it might be true **:** podría ser verdad> <might I speak with Sarah? **:** ¿se puede hablar con Sarah?>

might[2] *n* **:** fuerza *f,* poder *m*

mightily [ˈmaɪt̬əli] *adv* **:** con mucha fuerza, poderosamente

mighty[1] [ˈmaɪt̬i] *adv* VERY **:** muy <mighty good **:** muy bueno, buenísimo>

mighty[2] *adj* **mightier; -est 1** POWERFUL **:** poderoso, potente **2** GREAT **:** grande, imponente

migraine [ˈmaɪˌgreɪn] *n* **:** jaqueca *f,* migraña *f*

migrant [ˈmaɪgrənt] *n* **:** trabajador *m,* -dora *f* ambulante

migrate [ˈmaɪˌgreɪt] *vi* **-grated; -grating :** emigrar

migration [maɪˈgreɪʃən] *n* **:** migración *f*

migratory [ˈmaɪgrəˌtori] *adj* **:** migratorio

mild [ˈmaɪld] *adj* **1** GENTLE **:** apacible, suave <a mild disposition **:** un temperamento suave> **2** LIGHT **:** leve, ligero <a mild punishment **:** un castigo leve, un castigo poco severo> **3** TEMPERATE **:** templado (dícese del clima) — **mildly** *adv*

mildew[1] [ˈmɪlˌduː, -ˌdjuː] *vi* : enmohecerse
mildew[2] *n* : moho *m*
mildness [ˈmaɪldnəs] *n* : apacibilidad *f*, suavidad *f*
mile [ˈmaɪl] *n* : milla *f*
mileage [ˈmaɪlɪdʒ] *n* **1** ALLOWANCE : viáticos *mpl* (pagados por milla recorrida) **2** : distancia *f* recorrida (en millas), kilometraje *m*
milestone [ˈmaɪlˌstoːn] *n* LANDMARK : hito *m*, jalón *m* <a milestone in his life : un hito en su vida>
milieu [miːlˈjuː, -ˈjø] *n, pl* **-lieus** *or* **-lieux** [-ˈjuːz, -ˈjø] SURROUNDINGS : entorno *m*, medio *m*, ambiente *m*
militant[1] [ˈmɪlətənt] *adj* : militante, combativo
militant[2] *n* : militante *mf*
militarism [ˈmɪlətəˌrɪzəm] *n* : militarismo *m*
militaristic [ˌmɪlətəˈrɪstɪk] *adj* : militarista
military[1] [ˈmɪləˌtɛri] *adj* : militar
military[2] *n* **the military** : las fuerzas armadas
militia [məˈlɪʃə] *n* : milicia *f*
milk[1] [ˈmɪlk] *vt* **1** : ordeñar (una vaca, etc.) **2** EXPLOIT : explotar
milk[2] *n* : leche *f*
milkman [ˈmɪlkˌmæn, -mən] *n, pl* **-men** [-mən, -ˌmɛn] : lechero *m*
milk shake *n* : batido *m*, licuado *m*
milkweed [ˈmɪlkˌwiːd] *n* : algodoncillo *m*
milky [ˈmɪlki] *adj* **milkier; -est** : lechoso
Milky Way *n* : Vía *f* Láctea
mill[1] [ˈmɪl] *vt* : moler (granos), fresar (metales), acordonar (monedas) — *vi* **to mill about** : arremolinarse
mill[2] *n* **1** : molino *m* (para moler granos) **2** FACTORY : fábrica *f* <textile mill : fábrica textil> **3** GRINDER : molinillo *m*
millennium [məˈlɛniəm] *n, pl* **-nia** [-niə] *or* **-niums** : milenio *m*
miller [ˈmɪlər] *n* : molinero *m*, -ra *f*
millet [ˈmɪlət] *n* : mijo *m*
milligram [ˈmɪləˌgræm] *n* : miligramo *m*
milliliter [ˈmɪləˌliːtər] *n* : mililitro *m*
millimeter [ˈmɪləˌmiːtər] *n* : milímetro *m*
milliner [ˈmɪlənər] *n* : sombrerero *m*, -ra *f* (de señoras)
millinery [ˈmɪləˌnɛri] *n* : sombreros *mpl* de señora
million[1] [ˈmɪljən] *adj* **a million** : un millón de
million[2] *n, pl* **millions** *or* **million** : millón *m*
millionaire [ˌmɪljəˈnær, ˈmɪljəˌnær] *n* : millonario *m*, -ria *f*
millionth[1] [ˈmɪljənθ] *adj* : millonésimo
millionth[2] *n* : millonésimo *m*
millipede [ˈmɪləˌpiːd] *n* : milpiés *m*
millstone [ˈmɪlˌstoːn] *n* : rueda *f* de molino, muela *f*
mime[1] [ˈmaɪm] *v* **mimed; miming** *vt* MIMIC : imitar, remedar — *vi* PANTOMIME : hacer la mímica
mime[2] *n* **1** : mimo *mf* **2** PANTOMIME : pantomima *f*
mimeograph [ˈmɪmiəˌgræf] *n* : mimeógrafo *m*
mimic[1] [ˈmɪmɪk] *vt* **-icked; -icking** : imitar, remedar
mimic[2] *n* : imitador *m*, -dora *f*
mimicry [ˈmɪmɪkri] *n, pl* **-ries** : mímica *f*, imitación *f*
minaret [ˌmɪnəˈrɛt] *n* : alminar *m*, minarete *m*
mince [ˈmɪnts] *v* **minced; mincing** *vt* **1** CHOP : picar, moler (carne) **2 not to mince one's words** : no tener uno pelos en la lengua — *vi* : caminar de manera afectada
mincemeat [ˈmɪntsˌmiːt] *n* : mezcla *f* de fruta picada, sebo, y especias
mind[1] [ˈmaɪnd] *vt* **1** TEND : cuidar, atender <mind the children : cuida a los niños> **2** OBEY : obedecer **3** : preocuparse por, sentirse molestado por <I don't mind his jokes : sus bromas no me molestan> **4** : tener cuidado con <mind the ladder! : ¡cuidado con la escalera!> — *vi* **1** OBEY : obedecer **2** CARE : importarle a uno <I don't mind : no me importa, me es igual>
mind[2] *n* **1** MEMORY : memoria *f*, recuerdo *m* <keep it in mind : téngalo en cuenta> **2** : mente *f* <the mind and the body : la mente y el cuerpo> **3** INTENTION : intención *f*, propósito *m* <to have a mind to do something : tener intención de hacer algo> **4** : razón *f* <he's out of his mind : está loco> **5** OPINION : opinión *f* <to change one's mind : cambiar de opinión> **6** INTELLECT : capacidad *f* intelectual
minded [ˈmaɪndəd] *adj* **1** (*used in combination*) <narrow-minded : de mentalidad cerrada> <health-minded : preocupado por la salud> **2** INCLINED : inclinado
mindful [ˈmaɪndfəl] *adj* AWARE : consciente — **mindfully** *adv*
mindless [ˈmaɪndləs] *adj* **1** SENSELESS : estúpido, sin sentido <mindless violence : violencia sin sentido> **2** HEEDLESS : inconsciente
mindlessly [ˈmaɪndləsli] *adv* **1** SENSELESSLY : sin sentido **2** HEEDLESSLY : inconscientemente
mine[1] [ˈmaɪn] *vt* **mined; mining 1** : extraer (oro, etc.) **2** : minar (con artefactos explosivos)
mine[2] *n* : mina *f* <gold mine : mina de oro>
mine[3] *pron* : mío, mía <that one's mine : ése es el mío> <some friends of mine : unos amigos míos>
minefield [ˈmaɪnˌfiːld] *n* : campo *m* de minas
miner [ˈmaɪnər] *n* : minero *m*, -ra *f*

mineral ['mɪnərəl] *n* : mineral *m* — **mineral** *adj*

mineralogy [ˌmɪnə'rɑlədʒi, -'ræ-] *n* : mineralogía *f*

mingle ['mɪŋgəl] *v* **-gled; -gling** *vt* MIX : mezclar — *vi* **1** MIX : mezclarse **2** CIRCULATE : circular

miniature[1] ['mɪniəˌtʃʊr, 'mɪnɪˌtʃʊr, -tʃər] *adj* : en miniatura, diminuto

miniature[2] *n* : miniatura *f*

minibus ['mɪniˌbʌs] *n* : microbús *m*, pesera *f Mex*

minicomputer ['mɪnikəmˌpjuːt̬ər] *n* : minicomputadora *f*

minimal ['mɪnəməl] *adj* : mínimo

minimally ['mɪnəməli] *adv* : en grado mínimo

minimize ['mɪnəˌmaɪz] *vt* **-mized; -mizing** : minimizar

minimum[1] ['mɪnəməm] *adj* : mínimo

minimum[2] *n, pl* **-ma** ['mɪnəmə] *or* **-mums** : mínimo *m*

miniskirt ['mɪniˌskərt] *n* : minifalda *f*

minister[1] ['mɪnəstər] *vi* **to minister to** : cuidar (de), atender a

minister[2] *n* **1** : pastor *m*, -tora *f* (de una iglesia) **2** : ministro *m*, -tra *f* (en política)

ministerial [ˌmɪnə'stɪriəl] *adj* : ministerial

ministry ['mɪnəstri] *n, pl* **-tries 1** : ministerio *m* (en política) **2** : sacerdocio *m* (en el catolicismo), clerecía *f* (en el protestantismo)

minivan ['mɪniˌvæn] *n* : minivan *f*

mink ['mɪŋk] *n, pl* **mink** *or* **minks** : visón *m*

minnow ['mɪnoː] *n, pl* **-nows** : pececillo *m* de agua dulce

minor[1] ['maɪnər] *adj* : menor

minor[2] *n* **1** : menor *mf* (de edad) **2** : asignatura *f* secundaria (de estudios)

minority [mə'nɔrət̬i, maɪ-] *n, pl* **-ties** : minoría *f*

minstrel ['mɪn*t*strəl] *n* : juglar *m*, trovador *m* (en el medioevo)

mint[1] ['mɪnt] *vt* : acuñar

mint[2] *adj* : sin usar <in mint condition : como nuevo>

mint[3] *n* **1** : menta *f* <mint tea : té de menta> **2** : pastilla *f* de menta **3** : casa *f* de la moneda <the U.S. Mint : la casa de la moneda de los EE.UU.> **4** FORTUNE : dineral *m*, fortuna *f*

minuet [ˌmɪnjʊ'ɛt] *n* : minué *m*

minus[1] ['maɪnəs] *n* **1** : cantidad *f* negativa **2 minus sign** : signo *m* de menos

minus[2] *prep* **1** : menos <four minus two : cuatro menos dos> **2** WITHOUT : sin <minus his hat : sin su sombrero>

minuscule *or* **miniscule** ['mɪnəsˌkjuːl, mɪ'nʌs-] *adj* : minúsculo

minute[1] [maɪ'nuːt, mɪ-, -'njuːt] *adj* **-nuter; -est 1** TINY : diminuto, minúsculo **2** DETAILED : minucioso

minute[2] ['mɪnət] *n* **1** : minuto *m* <ten minutes late : diez minutos de retraso> **2** MOMENT : momento *m* **3 minutes** *npl* : actas *fpl* (de una reunión)

minutely [maɪ'nuːtli, mɪ-, -'njuːt-] *adv* : minuciosamente

miracle ['mɪrɪkəl] *n* : milagro *m*

miraculous [mə'rækjələs] *adj* : milagroso — **miraculously** *adv*

mirage [mɪ'rɑʒ, *chiefly Brit* 'mɪrˌɑʒ] *n* : espejismo *m*

mire[1] ['maɪr] *vi* **mired; miring** : atascarse

mire[2] *n* : lodo *m*, barro *m*, fango *m*

mirror[1] ['mɪrər] *vt* : reflejar

mirror[2] *n* : espejo *m*

mirth ['mərθ] *n* : alegría *f*, regocijo *m*

mirthful ['mərθfəl] *adj* : alegre, regocijado

misanthrope ['mɪsənˌθroːp] *n* : misántropo *m*, -pa *f*

misanthropic [ˌmɪsən'θrɑpɪk] *adj* : misantrópico

misanthropy [mɪ'sænθrəpi] *n* : misantropía *f*

misapprehend [ˌmɪsˌæprə'hɛnd] *vt* : entender mal

misapprehension [ˌmɪsˌæprə'hɛntʃən] *n* : malentendido *m*

misappropriate [ˌmɪsə'proːpriˌeɪt] *vt* **-ated; -ating** : malversar

misbegotten [ˌmɪsbi'gɑtən] *adj* **1** ILLEGITIMATE : ilegítimo **2** : mal concebido <misbegotten laws : leyes mal concebidas>

misbehave [ˌmɪsbi'heɪv] *vi* **-haved; -having** : portarse mal

misbehavior [ˌmɪsbi'heɪvjər] *n* : mala conducta *f*

miscalculate [mɪs'kælkjəˌleɪt] *v* **-lated; -lating** : calcular mal

miscalculation [mɪsˌkælkjə'leɪʃən] *n* : error *m* de cálculo, mal cálculo *m*

miscarriage [ˌmɪs'kærɪdʒ, 'mɪsˌkærɪdʒ] *n* **1** : aborto *m* **2** FAILURE : fracaso *m*, malogro *m* <a miscarriage of justice : una injusticia, un error judicial>

miscarry [ˌmɪs'kæri, 'mɪsˌkæri] *vi* **-ried; -rying 1** ABORT : abortar **2** FAIL : malograrse, fracasar

miscellaneous [ˌmɪsə'leɪniəs] *adj* : misceláneo

miscellany ['mɪsəˌleɪni] *n, pl* **-nies** : miscelánea *f*

mischance [mɪs'tʃæn*t*s] *n* : desgracia *f*, infortunio *m*, mala suerte *f*

mischief ['mɪstʃəf] *n* : diabluras *fpl*, travesuras *fpl*

mischievous ['mɪstʃəvəs] *adj* : travieso, pícaro

mischievously ['mɪstʃəvəsli] *adv* : de manera traviesa

misconception [ˌmɪskən'sɛpʃən] *n* : concepto *m* erróneo, idea *f* falsa

misconduct [mɪs'kɑndəkt] *n* : mala conducta *f*

misconstrue [ˌmɪskən'struː] *vt* **-strued; -struing** : malinterpretar

misdeed [mɪs'diːd] *n* : fechoría *f*

misdemeanor [ˌmɪsdɪˈmiːnər] *n* : delito *m* menor

miser [ˈmaɪzər] *n* : avaro *m,* -ra *f;* tacaño *m,* -ña *f*

miserable [ˈmɪzərəbəl] *adj* **1** UNHAPPY : triste, desdichado **2** WRETCHED : miserable, desgraciado <a miserable hut : una choza miserable> **3** UNPLEASANT : desagradable, malo <miserable weather : tiempo malísimo> **4** CONTEMPTIBLE : despreciable, mísero <for a miserable $10 : por unos míseros diez dólares>

miserably [ˈmɪzərəbli] *adv* **1** SADLY : tristemente **2** WRETCHEDLY : miserablemente, lamentablemente **3** UNFORTUNATELY : desgraciadamente

miserly [ˈmaɪzərli] *adj* : avaro, tacaño

misery [ˈmɪzəri] *n, pl* **-eries** : miseria *f,* sufrimiento *m*

misfire [mɪsˈfaɪr] *vi* **-fired; -firing** : fallar

misfit [ˈmɪsˌfɪt] *n* : inadaptado *m,* -da *f*

misfortune [mɪsˈfɔrtʃən] *n* : desgracia *f,* desventura *f,* infortunio *m*

misgiving [mɪsˈgɪvɪŋ] *n* : duda *f,* recelo *m*

misguided [mɪsˈgaɪdəd] *adj* : desacertado, equivocado, mal informado

mishap [ˈmɪsˌhæp] *n* : contratiempo *m,* percance *m,* accidente *m*

misinform [ˌmɪsɪnˈfɔrm] *vt* : informar mal

misinterpret [ˌmɪsɪnˈtərprət] *vt* : malinterpretar

misinterpretation [ˌmɪsɪnˌtərprəˈteɪʃən] *n* : mala interpretación *f,* malentendido *m*

misjudge [mɪsˈdʒʌdʒ] *vt* **-judged; -judging** : juzgar mal

mislay [mɪsˈleɪ] *vt* **-laid** [-leɪd]; **-laying** : extraviar, perder

mislead [mɪsˈliːd] *vt* **-led** [-ˈlɛd]; **-leading** : engañar

misleading [mɪsˈliːdɪŋ] *adj* : engañoso

mismanage [mɪsˈmænɪdʒ] *vt* **-aged; -aging** : administrar mal

mismanagement [mɪsˈmænɪdʒmənt] *n* : mala administración *f*

misnomer [mɪsˈnoːmər] *n* : nombre *m* inapropiado

misogynist [mɪˈsɑdʒənɪst] *n* : misógino *m*

misplace [mɪsˈpleɪs] *vt* **-placed; -placing** : extraviar, perder

misprint [ˈmɪsˌprɪnt, mɪsˈ-] *n* : errata *f,* error *m* de imprenta

mispronounce [ˌmɪsprəˈnaʊnts] *vt* **-nounced; -nouncing** : pronunciar mal

mispronunciation [ˌmɪsprəˌnʌntsiˈeɪʃən] *n* : pronunciación *f* incorrecta

misquote [mɪsˈkwoːt] *vt* **-quoted; -quoting** : citar incorrectamente

misread [mɪsˈriːd] *vt* **-read; -reading** **1** : leer mal <she misread the sentence : leyó mal la frase> **2** MISUNDERSTAND : malinterpretar <they misread his intention : malinterpretaron su intención>

misrepresent [ˌmɪsˌrɛprɪˈzɛnt] *vt* : distorsionar, falsear, tergiversar

misrule[1] [mɪsˈruːl] *vt* **-ruled; -ruling** : gobernar mal

misrule[2] *n* : mal gobierno *m*

miss[1] [ˈmɪs] *vt* **1** : errar, faltar <to miss the target : no dar en el blanco> **2** : no encontrar, perder <they missed each other : no se encontraron> <I missed the plane : perdí el avión> **3** : echar de menos, extrañar <we miss him a lot : lo echamos mucho de menos> **4** OVERLOOK : pasar por alto, perder (una oportunidad, etc.) **5** AVOID : evitar <they just missed hitting the tree : por muy poco chocan contra el árbol> **6** OMIT : saltarse <he missed breakfast : se saltó el desayuno>

miss[2] *n* **1** : fallo *m* (de un tiro, etc.) **2** FAILURE : fracaso *m* **3** : señorita *f* <Miss Jones : la señorita Jones> <excuse me, miss : perdone, señorita>

missal [ˈmɪsəl] *n* : misal *m*

misshapen [mɪˈʃeɪpən] *adj* : deforme

missile [ˈmɪsəl] *n* **1** : misil *m* <guided missile : misil guiado> **2** PROJECTILE : proyectil *m*

missing [ˈmɪsɪŋ] *adj* **1** ABSENT : ausente <who's missing? : ¿quién falta?> **2** LOST : perdido, desaparecido <missing persons : los desaparecidos>

mission [ˈmɪʃən] *n* **1** : misión *f* (mandada por una iglesia) **2** DELEGATION : misión *f,* delegación *f,* embajada *f* **3** TASK : misión *f*

missionary[1] [ˈmɪʃəˌnɛri] *adj* : misionero

missionary[2] *n, pl* **-aries** : misionero *m,* -ra *f*

missive [ˈmɪsɪv] *n* : misiva *f*

misspell [mɪsˈspɛl] *vt* : escribir mal

misspelling [mɪsˈspɛlɪŋ] *n* : falta *f* de ortografía

misstep [ˈmɪsˌstɛp] *n* : traspié *m,* tropezón *m*

mist [ˈmɪst] *n* **1** HAZE : neblina *f,* niebla *f* **2** SPRAY : rocío *m*

mistake[1] [mɪˈsteɪk] *vt* **-took** [-ˈstʊk]; **-taken** [-ˈsteɪkən]; **-taking** **1** MISINTERPRET : malinterpretar **2** CONFUSE : confundir <he mistook her for Clara : la confundió con Clara>

mistake[2] *n* **1** MISUNDERSTANDING : malentendido *m,* confusión *f* **2** ERROR : error *m* <I made a mistake : me equivoqué, cometí un error>

mistaken [mɪˈsteɪkən] *adj* WRONG : equivocado — **mistakenly** *adv*

mister [ˈmɪstər] *n* : señor *m* <watch out, mister : cuidado, señor>

mistiness [ˈmɪstinəs] *n* : nebulosidad *f*

mistletoe [ˈmɪsəlˌtoː] *n* : muérdago *m*

mistreat [mɪsˈtriːt] *vt* : maltratar

mistreatment [mɪsˈtriːtmənt] *n* : maltrato *m,* abuso *m*

mistress [ˈmɪstrəs] *n* **1** : dueña *f,* señora *f* (de una casa) **2** LOVER : amante *f*

mistrust[1] [mɪsˈtrʌst] *vt* : desconfiar de

mistrust[2] *n* : desconfianza *f*

mistrustful [mɪsˈtrʌstfəl] *adj* : desconfiado

misty [ˈmɪsti] *adj* **mistier; -est** **1** : neblinoso, nebuloso **2** TEARFUL : lloroso

misunderstand [ˌmɪsˌʌndərˈstænd] *vt* **-stood** [-ˈstʊd]; **-standing** **1** : entender mal **2** MISINTERPRET : malinterpretar <don't misunderstand me : no me malinterpretes>

misunderstanding [ˌmɪsˌʌndərˈstændɪŋ] *n* **1** MISINTERPRETATION : malentendido *m* **2** DISAGREEMENT, QUARREL : disputa *f,* discusión *f*

misuse[1] [mɪsˈjuːz] *vt* **-used; -using** **1** : emplear mal **2** ABUSE, MISTREAT : abusar de, maltratar

misuse[2] [mɪsˈjuːs] *n* **1** : mal empleo *m,* mal uso *m* **2** WASTE : derroche *m,* despilfarro *m* **3** ABUSE : abuso *m*

mite [ˈmaɪt] *n* **1** : ácaro *m* **2** BIT : poco *m* <a mite tired : un poquito cansado>

miter *or* **mitre** [ˈmaɪt̬ər] *n* **1** : mitra *f* (de un obispo) **2** *or* **miter joint** : inglete *m*

mitigate [ˈmɪt̬əˌgeɪt] *vt* **-gated; -gating** : mitigar, aliviar

mitigation [ˌmɪt̬əˈgeɪʃən] *n* : mitigación *f,* alivio *m*

mitosis [maɪˈtoːsɪs] *n, pl* **-toses** [-ˌsiːz] : mitosis *f*

mitt [ˈmɪt] *n* : manopla *f,* guante *m* (de béisbol)

mitten [ˈmɪtən] *n* : manopla *f,* mitón *m*

mix[1] [ˈmɪks] *vt* **1** COMBINE : mezclar **2** STIR : remover, revolver **3 to mix up** CONFUSE : confundir — *vi* : mezclarse

mix[2] *n* : mezcla *f*

mixer [ˈmɪksər] *n* **1** : batidora *f* (de la cocina) **2 cement mixer** : hormigonera *f*

mixture [ˈmɪkstʃər] *n* : mezcla *f*

mix–up [ˈmɪksˌʌp] *n* CONFUSION : confusión *f,* lío *m fam*

mnemonic [nɪˈmɑnɪk] *adj* : mnemónico

moan[1] [ˈmoːn] *vi* : gemir

moan[2] *n* : gemido *m*

moat [ˈmoːt] *n* : foso *m*

mob[1] [ˈmɑb] *vt* **mobbed; mobbing** **1** ATTACK : atacar en masa **2** HOUND : acosar, rodear

mob[2] *n* **1** THRONG : multitud *f,* turba *f,* muchedumbre *f* **2** GANG : pandilla *f*

mobile[1] [ˈmoːbəl, -ˌbiːl, -ˌbaɪl] *adj* : móvil <mobile home : caravana, casa rodante>

mobile[2] [ˈmoˌbiːl] *n* : móvil *m*

mobility [moˈbɪlət̬i] *n* : movilidad *f*

mobilize [ˈmoːbəˌlaɪz] *vt* **-lized; -lizing** : movilizar

moccasin [ˈmɑkəsən] *n* **1** : mocasín *m* **2** *or* **water moccasin** : serpiente *f* venenosa de Norteamérica

mocha [ˈmoːkə] *n* **1** : mezcla *f* de café y chocolate **2** : color *m* chocolate

mock[1] [ˈmɑk, ˈmɔk] *vt* **1** RIDICULE : burlarse de, mofarse de **2** MIMIC : imitar, remedar (de manera burlona)

mock[2] *adj* **1** SIMULATED : simulado **2** PHONY : falso

mockery [ˈmɑkəri, ˈmɔ-] *n, pl* **-eries** **1** JEER, TAUNT : burla *f,* mofa *f* <to make a mockery of : burlarse de> **2** FAKE : imitación *f* (burlona)

mockingbird [ˈmɑkɪŋˌbərd, ˈmɔ-] *n* : sinsonte *m*

mode [ˈmoːd] *n* **1** FORM : modo *m,* forma *f* **2** MANNER : modo *m,* manera *f,* estilo *m* **3** FASHION : moda *f*

model[1] [ˈmɑdəl] *v* **-eled** *or* **-elled; -eling** *or* **-elling** *vt* SHAPE : modelar — *vi* : trabajar de modelo

model[2] *adj* **1** EXEMPLARY : modelo, ejemplar <a model student : un estudiante modelo> **2** MINIATURE : en miniatura

model[3] *n* **1** PATTERN : modelo *m* **2** MINIATURE : modelo *m,* miniatura *f* **3** EXAMPLE : modelo *m,* ejemplo *m* **4** MANNEQUIN : modelo *mf* **5** DESIGN : modelo *m* <the '97 model : el modelo '97>

modem [ˈmoːdəm, -ˌdɛm] *n* : módem *m*

moderate[1] [ˈmɑdəˌreɪt] *v* **-ated; -ating** *vt* : moderar, temperar — *vi* **1** CALM : moderarse, calmarse **2** : fungir como moderador (en un debate, etc.)

moderate[2] [ˈmɑdərət] *adj* : moderado

moderate[3] [ˈmɑdərət] *n* : moderado *m,* -da *f*

moderately [ˈmɑdərətli] *adv* **1** : con moderación **2** FAIRLY : medianamente

moderation [ˌmɑdəˈreɪʃən] *n* : moderación *f*

moderator [ˈmɑdəˌreɪt̬ər] *n* : moderador *m,* -dora *f*

modern [ˈmɑdərn] *adj* : moderno

modernity [məˈdərnət̬i] *n* : modernidad *f*

modernization [ˌmɑdərnəˈzeɪʃən] *n* : modernización *f*

modernize [ˈmɑdərˌnaɪz] *v* **-ized; -izing** *vt* : modernizar — *vi* : modernizarse

modest [ˈmɑdəst] *adj* **1** HUMBLE : modesto **2** DEMURE : recatado, pudoroso **3** MODERATE : modesto, moderado — **modestly** *adv*

modesty [ˈmɑdəsti] *n* : modestia *f*

modicum [ˈmɑdɪkəm] *n* : mínimo *m,* pizca *f*

modification [ˌmɑdəfəˈkeɪʃən] *n* : modificación *f*

modifier [ˈmɑdəˌfaɪər] *n* : modificante *m,* modificador *m*

modify [ˈmɑdəˌfaɪ] *vt* **-fied; -fying** : modificar, calificar (en gramática)

modish [ˈmoːdɪʃ] *adj* STYLISH : a la moda, de moda

modular [ˈmɑdʒələr] *adj* : modular

modulate [ˈmɑdʒəˌleɪt] *vt* **-lated; -lating** : modular

modulation [ˌmɑdʒəˈleɪʃən] *n* : modulación *f*

module [ˈmɑˌdʒuːl] *n* : módulo *m*

mogul [ˈmoːgəl] *n* : magnate *mf;* potentado *m,* -da *f*

mohair [ˈmoːˌhær] *n* : mohair *m*

moist [ˈmɔɪst] *adj* : húmedo

moisten [ˈmɔɪsən] *vt* : humedecer

moistness [ˈmɔɪstnəs] *n* : humedad *f*

moisture [ˈmɔɪstʃər] *n* : humedad *f*

moisturize [ˈmɔɪstʃəˌraɪz] *vt* **-ized; -izing** : humedecer (el aire), humectar (la piel)

moisturizer [ˈmɔɪtʃəˌraɪzər] *n* : crema *f* hidratante, crema *f* humectante

molar [ˈmoːlər] *n* : muela *f,* molar *m*

molasses [məˈlæsəz] *n* : melaza *f*

mold¹ [ˈmoːld] *vt* : moldear, formar (carácter, etc.) — *vi* : enmohecerse <the bread will mold : el pan se enmohecerá>

mold² *n* **1** *or* **leaf mold** : mantillo *m* **2** FORM : molde *m* <to break the mold : romper el molde> **3** FUNGUS : moho *m*

molder [ˈmoːldər] *vi* CRUMBLE : desmoronarse

molding [ˈmoːldɪŋ] *n* : moldura *f* (en arquitectura)

moldy [ˈmoːldi] *adj* **moldier; -est** : mohoso

mole [ˈmoːl] *n* **1** : lunar *m* (en la piel) **2** : topo *m* (animal)

molecule [ˈmɑlɪˌkjuːl] *n* : molécula *f* — **molecular** [məˈlɛkjələr] *adj*

molehill [ˈmoːlˌhɪl] *n* : topera *f*

molest [məˈlɛst] *vt* **1** ANNOY, DISTURB : molestar **2** : abusar (sexualmente)

mollify [ˈmɑləˌfaɪ] *vt* **-fied; -fying** : apaciguar, aplacar

mollusk *or* **mollusc** [ˈmɑləsk] *n* : molusco *m*

mollycoddle [ˈmɑliˌkɑdəl] *vt* **-dled; -dling** PAMPER : consentir, mimar

molt [ˈmoːlt] *vi* : mudar, hacer la muda

molten [ˈmoːltən] *adj* : fundido

mom [ˈmɑm, ˈmʌm] *n* : mamá *f*

moment [ˈmoːmənt] *n* **1** INSTANT : momento *m* <one moment, please : un momento, por favor> **2** TIME : momento *m* <at the moment : de momento, actualmente> <from that moment : desde entonces> **3** IMPORTANCE : importancia *f* <of great moment : de gran importancia>

momentarily [ˌmoːmənˈtɛrəli] *adv* **1** : momentáneamente **2** SOON : dentro de poco, pronto

momentary [ˈmoːmənˌtɛri] *adj* : momentáneo

momentous [moˈmɛntəs] *adj* : de suma importancia, fatídico

momentum [moˈmɛntəm] *n, pl* **-ta** [-tə] *or* **-tums 1** : momento *m* (en física) **2** IMPETUS : ímpetu *m,* impulso *m*

monarch [ˈmɑˌnɑrk, -nərk] *n* : monarca *mf*

monarchism [ˈmɑˌnɑrˌkɪzəm, -nər-] *n* : monarquismo *m*

monarchist [ˈmɑˌnɑrkɪst, -nər-] *n* : monárquico *m,* -ca *f*

monarchy [ˈmɑˌnɑrki, -nər-] *n, pl* **-chies** : monarquía *f*

monastery [ˈmɑnəˌstɛri] *n, pl* **-teries** : monasterio *m*

monastic [məˈnæstɪk] *adj* : monástico — **monastically** [-tɪkli] *adv*

Monday [ˈmʌnˌdeɪ, -di] *n* : lunes *m*

monetary [ˈmɑnəˌtɛri, ˈmʌnə-] *adj* : monetario

money [ˈmʌni] *n, pl* **-eys** *or* **-ies** [ˈmʌniz] : dinero *m,* plata *f*

moneyed [ˈmʌnid] *adj* : adinerado

moneylender [ˈmʌniˌlɛndər] *n* : prestamista *mf*

money order *n* : giro *m* postal

Mongolian [mɑnˈgoːliən, mɑŋ-] *n* : mongol *m,* -gola *f* — **Mongolian** *adj*

mongoose [ˈmɑnˌguːs, ˈmɑŋ-] *n, pl* **-gooses** : mangosta *f*

mongrel [ˈmɑŋgrəl, ˈmʌŋ-] *n* **1** : perro *m* mestizo, perro *m* corriente *Mex* **2** HYBRID : híbrido *m*

monitor¹ [ˈmɑnət̬ər] *vt* : controlar, monitorear

monitor² *n* **1** : ayudante *mf* (en una escuela) **2** : monitor *m* (de una computadora, etc.)

monk [ˈmʌŋk] *n* : monje *m*

monkey¹ [ˈmʌŋki] *vi* **-keyed; -keying 1 to monkey around** : hacer payasadas, payasear **2 to monkey with** : juguetear con

monkey² *n, pl* **-keys** : mono *m,* -na *f*

monkeyshines [ˈmʌŋkiˌʃaɪnz] *npl* PRANKS : picardías *fpl,* travesuras *fpl*

monkey wrench *n* : llave *f* inglesa

monkshood [ˈmʌŋksˌhʊd] *n* : acónito *m*

monocle [ˈmɑnɪkəl] *n* : monóculo *m*

monogamous [məˈnɑgəməs] *adj* : monógamo

monogamy [məˈnɑgəmi] *n* : monogamia *f*

monogram¹ [ˈmɑnəˌgræm] *vt* **-grammed; -gramming** : marcar con monograma <monogrammed towels : toallas con monograma>

monogram² *n* : monograma *m*

monograph [ˈmɑnəˌgræf] *n* : monografía *f*

monolingual [ˌmɑnəˈlɪŋgwəl] *adj* : monolingüe

monolith [ˈmɑnəˌlɪθ] *n* : monolito *m*

monolithic [ˌmɑnəˈlɪθɪk] *adj* : monolítico

monologue [ˈmɑnəˌlɔg] *n* : monólogo *m*

monoplane [ˈmɑnəˌpleɪn] *n* : monoplano *m*

monopolize [məˈnɑpəˌlaɪz] *vt* **-lized; -lizing** : monopolizar

monopoly [məˈnɑpəli] *n, pl* **-lies** : monopolio *m*

monosyllabic [ˌmɑnosəˈlæbɪk] *adj* : monosilábico

monosyllable [ˈmɑno͵sɪləbəl] *n* : monosílabo *m*
monotheism [ˈmɑnoθiː͵ɪzəm] *n* : monoteísmo *m*
monotheistic [͵mɑnoθiːˈɪstɪk] *adj* : monoteísta
monotone [ˈmɑnə͵toːn] *n* : voz *f* monótona
monotonous [məˈnɑtənəs] *adj* : monótono — **monotonously** *adv*
monotony [məˈnɑtəni] *n* : monotonía *f*, uniformidad *f*
monoxide [məˈnɑk͵saɪd] *n* : monóxido *m*
monsoon [mɑnˈsuːn] *n* : monzón *m*
monster [ˈmɑntstər] *n* : monstruo *m*
monstrosity [mɑnˈstrɑsəṭi] *n, pl* **-ties** : monstruosidad *f*
monstrous [ˈmɑntstrəs] *adj* : monstruoso — **monstrously** *adv*
montage [mɑnˈtɑʒ] *n* : montaje *m*
month [ˈmʌnθ] *n* : mes *m*
monthly[1] [ˈmʌnθli] *adv* : mensualmente
monthly[2] *adj* : mensual
monthly[3] *n, pl* **-lies** : publicación *f* mensual
monument [ˈmɑnjəmənt] *n* : monumento *m*
monumental [͵mɑnjəˈmɛntəl] *adj* : monumental — **monumentally** *adv*
moo[1] [ˈmuː] *vi* : mugir
moo[2] *n* : mugido *m*
mood [ˈmuːd] *n* : humor *m* <to be in a good mood : estar de buen humor> <to be in the mood for : tener ganas de> <to be in no mood for : no estar para>
moodiness [ˈmuːdinəs] *n* **1** SADNESS : melancolía *f*, tristeza *f* **2** : cambios *mpl* de humor, carácter *m* temperamental
moody [ˈmuːdi] *adj* **moodier; -est 1** GLOOMY : melancólico, deprimido **2** TEMPERAMENTAL : temperamental, de humor variable
moon [ˈmuːn] *n* : luna *f*
moonbeam [ˈmuːn͵biːm] *n* : rayo *m* de luna
moonlight[1] [ˈmuːn͵laɪt] *vi* : estar pluriempleado
moonlight[2] *n* : claro *m* de luna, luz *f* de la luna
moonlit [ˈmuːn͵lɪt] *adj* : iluminado por la luna <a moonlit night : una noche de luna>
moonshine [ˈmuːn͵ʃaɪn] *n* **1** MOONLIGHT : luz *f* de la luna **2** NONSENSE : disparates *mpl*, tonterías *fpl* **3** : whiskey *m* destilado ilegalmente
moor[1] [ˈmʊr, ˈmɔr] *vt* : amarrar
moor[2] *n* : brezal *m*, páramo *m*
mooring [ˈmʊrɪŋ, ˈmɔr-] *n* DOCK : atracadero *m*
moose [ˈmuːs] *ns & pl* : alce *m* (norteamericano)
moot [ˈmuːt] *adj* DEBATABLE : discutible
mop[1] [ˈmɑp] *vt* **mopped; mopping** : trapear
mop[2] *n* : trapeador *m*
mope [ˈmoːp] *vi* **moped; moping** : andar deprimido, quedar abatido
moped [ˈmoː͵pɛd] *n* : ciclomotor *m*
moral[1] [ˈmɔrəl] *adj* : moral <moral judgment : juicio moral> <moral support : apoyo moral> — **morally** *adv*
moral[2] *n* **1** : moraleja *f* (de un cuento, etc.) **2 morals** *npl* : moral *f*, moralidad *f*
morale [məˈræl] *n* : moral *f*
morality [məˈræləṭi] *n, pl* **-ties** : moralidad *f*
morass [məˈræs] *n* **1** SWAMP : ciénaga *f*, pantano *m* **2** CONFUSION, MESS : lío *m fam*, embrollo *m*
moratorium [͵mɔrəˈtoriəm] *n, pl* **-riums** *or* **-ria** [-iə] : moratoria *f*
moray [ˈmɔr͵eɪ, məˈreɪ] *n* : morena *f*
morbid [ˈmɔrbɪd] *adj* **1** : mórbido, morboso (en medicina) **2** GRUESOME : morboso, horripilante
morbidity [mɔrˈbɪdəṭi] *n* : morbosidad *f*
more[1] [ˈmor] *adv* : más <what more can I say? : ¿qué más puedo decir?> <more important : más importante> <once more : una vez más>
more[2] *adj* : más <nothing more than that : nada más que eso> <more work : más trabajo>
more[3] *n* : más *m* <the more you eat, the more you want : cuanto más comes, tanto más quieres>
more[4] *pron* : más <more were found : se encontraron más>
moreover [morˈoːvər] *adv* : además
mores [ˈmɔr͵eɪz, -iːz] *npl* CUSTOMS : costumbres *fpl*, tradiciones *fpl*
morgue [ˈmɔrg] *n* : morgue *f*
moribund [ˈmɔrə͵bʌnd] *adj* : moribundo
morn [ˈmɔrn] → **morning**
morning [ˈmɔrnɪŋ] *n* : mañana *f* <good morning! : ¡buenos días!>
Moroccan [məˈrɑkən] *n* : marroquí *mf* — **Moroccan** *adj*
moron [ˈmor͵ɑn] *n* **1** : retrasado *m*, -da *f* mental **2** DUNCE : estúpido *m*, -da *f*; tonto *m*, -ta *f*
morose [məˈroːs] *adj* : hosco, sombrío — **morosely** *adv*
moroseness [məˈroːsnəs] *n* : malhumor *m*
morphine [ˈmɔr͵fiːn] *n* : morfina *f*
morrow [ˈmɑroː] *n* : día *m* siguiente
Morse code [ˈmɔrs] *n* : código *m* morse
morsel [ˈmɔrsəl] *n* **1** BITE : bocado *m* **2** FRAGMENT : pedazo *m*
mortal[1] [ˈmɔrṭəl] *adj* : mortal <mortal blow : golpe mortal> <mortal fear : miedo mortal> — **mortally** *adv*
mortal[2] *n* : mortal *mf*
mortality [mɔrˈtæləṭi] *n* : mortalidad *f*
mortar [ˈmɔrṭər] *n* **1** : mortero *m*, molcajete *m Mex* <mortar and pestle

: mortero y maja> **2** : mortero *m* <mortar shell : granada de mortero> **3** CEMENT : mortero *m,* argamasa *f*

mortgage[1] ['mɔrgɪdʒ] *vt* **-gaged; -gaging** : hipotecar

mortgage[2] *n* : hipoteca *f*

mortification [ˌmɔrtəfə'keɪʃən] *n* **1** : mortificación *f* **2** HUMILIATION : humillación *f,* vergüenza *f*

mortify ['mɔrtəˌfaɪ] *vt* **-fied; -fying 1** : mortificar (en religión) **2** HUMILIATE : humillar, avergonzar

mortuary ['mɔrtʃəˌwɛri] *n, pl* **-aries** FUNERAL HOME : funeraria *f*

mosaic [mo'zeɪɪk] *n* : mosaico *m*

Moslem ['mɑzləm] → **Muslim**

mosque ['mɑsk] *n* : mezquita *f*

mosquito [mə'skiːto] *n, pl* **-toes** : mosquito *m,* zancudo *m*

moss ['mɔs] *n* : musgo *m*

mossy ['mɔsi] *adj* **-ier; -est** : musgoso

most[1] ['moːst] *adv* : más <the most interesting book : el libro más interesante>

most[2] *adj* **1** : la mayoría de, la mayor parte de <most people : la mayoría de la gente> **2** GREATEST : más (dícese de los números), mayor (dícese de las cantidades) <the most ability : la mayor capacidad>

most[3] *n* : más *m,* máximo *m* <the most I can do : lo más que puedo hacer> <three weeks at the most : tres semanas como máximo>

most[4] *pron* : la mayoría, la mayor parte <most will go : la mayoría irá>

mostly ['moːstli] *adv* MAINLY : en su mayor parte, principalmente

mote ['moːt] *n* SPECK : mota *f*

motel [mo'tɛl] *n* : motel *m*

moth ['mɔθ] *n* : palomilla *f,* polilla *f*

mother[1] ['mʌðər] *vt* **1** BEAR : dar a luz a **2** PROTECT : cuidar de, proteger

mother[2] *n* : madre *f*

motherhood ['mʌðərˌhʊd] *n* : maternidad *f*

mother-in-law ['mʌðərɪnˌlɔ] *n, pl* **mothers-in-law** : suegra *f*

motherland ['mʌðərˌlænd] *n* : patria *f*

motherly ['mʌðərli] *adj* : maternal

mother-of-pearl [ˌmʌðərəv'pərl] *n* : nácar *m,* madreperla *f*

motif [mo'tiːf] *n* : motivo *m*

motion[1] ['moːʃən] *vt* : hacerle señas (a alguien) <she motioned us to come in : nos hizo señas para que entráramos>

motion[2] *n* **1** MOVEMENT : movimiento *m* <to set in motion : poner en marcha> **2** PROPOSAL : moción *f* <to second a motion : apoyar una moción>

motionless ['moːʃənləs] *adj* : inmóvil, quieto

motion picture *n* MOVIE : película *f*

motivate ['moːtəˌveɪt] *vt* **-vated; -vating** : motivar, mover, inducir

motivation [ˌmoːtə'veɪʃən] *n* : motivación *f*

motive[1] ['moːtɪv] *adj* : motor <motive power : fuerza motriz>

motive[2] *n* : motivo *m,* móvil *m*

motley ['mɑtli] *adj* : abigarrado, variopinto

motor[1] ['moːtər] *vi* : viajar en coche

motor[2] *n* : motor *m*

motorbike ['moːtərˌbaɪk] *n* : motocicleta *f* (pequeña), moto *f*

motorboat ['moːtərˌboːt] *n* : bote *m* a motor, lancha *f* motora

motorcar ['moːtərˌkɑr] *n* : automóvil *m*

motorcycle ['moːtərˌsaɪkəl] *n* : motocicleta *f*

motorcyclist ['moːtərˌsaɪkəlɪst] *n* : motociclista *mf*

motorist ['moːtərɪst] *n* : automovilista *mf,* motorista *mf*

mottle ['mɑtəl] *vt* **-tled; -tling** : manchar, motear <mottled skin : piel manchada> <a mottled surface : una superficie moteada>

motto ['mɑtoː] *n, pl* **-toes** : lema *m*

mould ['moːld] → **mold**

mound ['maʊnd] *n* **1** PILE : montón *m* **2** KNOLL : montículo *m* **3 burial mound** : túmulo *m*

mount[1] ['maʊnt] *vt* **1** : montar a (un caballo), montar en (una bicicleta), subir a **2** : montar (artillería, etc.) — *vi* INCREASE : aumentar

mount[2] *n* **1** SUPPORT : soporte *m* **2** HORSE : caballería *f,* montura *f* **3** MOUNTAIN : monte *m,* montaña *f*

mountain ['maʊntən] *n* : montaña *f*

mountaineer [ˌmaʊntən'ɪr] *n* : alpinista *mf;* montañero *m,* -ra *f*

mountainous ['maʊntənəs] *adj* : montañoso

mountaintop ['maʊntənˌtɑp] *n* : cima *f,* cumbre *f*

mourn ['morn] *vt* : llorar (por), lamentar <to mourn the death of : llorar la muerte de> — *vi* : llorar, estar de luto

mourner ['mornər] *n* : doliente *mf*

mournful ['mornfəl] *adj* **1** SORROWFUL : lloroso, plañidero, triste **2** GLOOMY : deprimente, entristecedor — **mournfully** *adv*

mourning ['mornɪŋ] *n* : duelo *m,* luto *m*

mouse ['maʊs] *n, pl* **mice** ['maɪs] **1** : ratón *m,* -tona *f* **2** : ratón *m* (de una computadora)

mousetrap ['maʊsˌtræp] *n* : ratonera *f*

moustache ['mʌˌstæʃ, mə'stæʃ] → **mustache**

mouth[1] ['maʊð] *vt* **1** : decir con poca sinceridad, repetir sin comprensión **2** : articular en silencio <she mouthed the words : formó las palabras con los labios>

mouth[2] ['maʊθ] *n* : boca *f* (de una persona o un animal), entrada *f* (de un túnel), desembocadura *f* (de un río)

mouthful ['maʊθˌfʊl] *n* : bocado *m* (de comida), bocanada *f* (de líquido o humo)

mouthpiece [ˈmaʊθˌpiːs] *n* : boquilla *f* (de un instrumento musical)

movable [ˈmuːvəbəl] *or* **moveable** *adj* : movible, móvil

move[1] [ˈmuːv] *v* **moved; moving** *vi* **1** GO : ir **2** RELOCATE : mudarse, trasladarse **3** STIR : moverse <¡no te muevas! : don't move!> **4** ACT : actuar — *vt* **1** : mover <move it over there : ponlo allí> <he kept moving his feet : no dejaba de mover los pies> **2** INDUCE, PERSUADE : inducir, persuadir, mover **3** TOUCH : conmover <it moved him to tears : lo hizo llorar> **4** PROPOSE : proponer

move[2] *n* **1** MOVEMENT : movimiento *m* **2** RELOCATION : mudanza *f* (de casa), traslado *m* **3** STEP : paso *m* <a good move : un paso acertado>

movement [ˈmuːvmənt] *n* : movimiento *m*

mover [ˈmuːvər] *n* : persona *f* que hace mudanzas

movie [ˈmuːvi] *n* **1** : película *f* **2 movies** *npl* : cine *m*

moving [ˈmuːvɪŋ] *adj* **1** : en movimiento <a moving target : un blanco móvil> **2** TOUCHING : conmovedor, emocionante

mow[1] [ˈmoː] *vt* **mowed; mowed** *or* **mown** [ˈmoːn]; **mowing** : cortar (la hierba)

mow[2] [ˈmaʊ] *n* : pajar *m*

mower [ˈmoːər] → **lawn mower**

Mr. [ˈmɪstər] *n, pl* **Messrs.** [ˈmɛsərz] : señor *m*

Mrs. [ˈmɪsəz, -səs, *esp South* ˈmɪzəz, -zəs] *n, pl* **Mesdames** [meɪˈdɑm, -ˈdæm] : señora *f*

Ms. [ˈmɪz] *n* : señora *f,* señorita *f*

much[1] [ˈmʌtʃ] *adv* **more** [ˈmor]; **most** [ˈmoːst] : mucho <I'm much happier : estoy mucho más contenta> <she talks as much as I do : habla tanto como yo>

much[2] *adj* **more; most** : mucho <it has much validity : tiene mucha validez> <too much time : demasiado tiempo>

much[3] *pron* : mucho, -cha <I don't need much : no necesito mucho>

mucilage [ˈmjuːsəlɪdʒ] *n* : mucílago *m*

muck [ˈmʌk] *n* **1** MANURE : estiércol *m* **2** DIRT, FILTH : mugre *f,* suciedad *f* **3** MIRE, MUD : barro *m,* fango *m,* lodo *m*

mucous [ˈmjuːkəs] *adj* : mucoso <mucous membrane : membrana mucosa>

mucus [ˈmjuːkəs] *n* : mucosidad *f*

mud [ˈmʌd] *n* : barro *m,* fango *m,* lodo *m*

muddle[1] [ˈmʌdəl] *v* **-dled; -dling** *vt* **1** CONFUSE : confundir **2** BUNGLE : echar a perder, malograr — *vi* : andar confundido <to muddle through : arreglárselas>

muddle[2] *n* : confusión *f,* embrollo *m,* lío *m*

muddleheaded [ˌmʌdəlˈhɛdəd, ˈmʌdəlˌ-] *adj* CONFUSED : confuso, despistado

muddy[1] [ˈmʌdi] *vt* **-died; -dying** : llenar de barro

muddy[2] *adj* **-dier; -est** : barroso, fangoso, lodoso, enlodado <you're all muddy : estás cubierto de barro>

muff[1] [ˈmʌf] *vt* BUNGLE : echar a perder, fallar (un tiro, etc.)

muff[2] *n* : manguito *m*

muffin [ˈmʌfən] *n* : magdalena *f,* mantecada *f Mex*

muffle [ˈmʌfəl] *vt* **-fled; -fling 1** ENVELOP : cubrir, tapar **2** DEADEN : amortiguar (un sonido)

muffler [ˈmʌflər] *n* **1** SCARF : bufanda *f* **2** : silenciador *m,* mofle *m CA, Mex* (de un automóvil)

mug[1] [ˈmʌg] *v* **mugged; mugging** *vi* : posar (con afectación), hacer muecas <mugging for the camera : haciendo muecas para la cámara> — *vt* ASSAULT : asaltar, atracar

mug[2] *n* CUP : tazón *m*

mugger [ˈmʌgər] *n* : atracador *m,* -dora *f*

mugginess [ˈmʌginəs] *n* : bochorno *m*

muggy [ˈmʌgi] *adj* **-gier; -est** : bochornoso

mulatto [mʊˈlɑto, -ˈlæ-] *n, pl* **-toes** *or* **-tos** : mulato *m,* -ta *f*

mulberry [ˈmʌlˌbɛri] *n, pl* **-ries** : morera *f* (árbol), mora *f* (fruta)

mulch[1] [ˈmʌltʃ] *vt* : cubrir con pajote

mulch[2] *n* : pajote *m*

mule [ˈmjuːl] *n* **1** : mula *f* **2** : obstinado *m,* -da *f;* terco *m,* -ca *f*

mulish [ˈmjuːlɪʃ] *adj* : obstinado, terco

mull [ˈmʌl] *vt* **to mull over** : reflexionar sobre

mullet [ˈmʌlət] *n, pl* **-let** *or* **-lets** : mújol *m,* múgil *m*

multicolored [ˌmʌltiˈkʌlərd, ˌmʌltaɪ-] *adj* : multicolor, abigarrado

multifaceted [ˌmʌltiˈfæsət̬əd, ˌmʌltaɪ-] *adj* : multifacético

multifamily [ˌmʌltiˈfæmli, ˌmʌltaɪ-] *adj* : multifamiliar

multifarious [ˌmʌltəˈfæriəs] *adj* DIVERSE : diverso, variado

multilateral [ˌmʌltiˈlæt̬ərəl, ˌmʌltaɪ-] *adj* : multilateral

multimedia [ˌmʌltiˈmiːdiə, ˌmʌltaɪ-] *adj* : multimedia

multimillionaire [ˌmʌltiˌmɪljəˈnær, ˌmʌltaɪ-, -ˈmɪljəˌnær] *adj* : multimillonario

multinational [ˌmʌltiˈnæʃənəl, ˌmʌltaɪ-] *adj* : multinacional

multiple[1] [ˈmʌltəpəl] *adj* : múltiple

multiple[2] *n* : múltiplo *m*

multiple sclerosis [skləˈroːsɪs] *n* : esclerosis *f* múltiple

multiplication [ˌmʌltəpləˈkeɪʃən] *n* : multiplicación *f*

multiplicity [ˌmʌltəˈplɪsət̬i] *n, pl* **-ties** : multiplicidad *f*

multiplier [ˈmʌltəˌplaɪər] *n* : multiplicador *m* (en matemáticas)

multiply [ˈmʌltəˌplaɪ] *v* **-plied; -plying** *vt* : multiplicar — *vi* : multiplicarse
multipurpose [ˌmʌltiˈpərpəs, ˌmʌlˌtaɪ-] *adj* : multiuso
multitude [ˈmʌltəˌtuːd, -ˌtjuːd] *n* **1** CROWD : multitud *f,* muchedumbre *f* **2** HOST : multitud *f,* gran cantidad *f* <a multitude of ideas : numerosas ideas>
multivitamin [ˌmʌltiˈvaɪtəmən, ˌmʌltaɪ-] *adj* : multivitamínico
mum¹ [ˈmʌm] *adj* SILENT : callado
mum² *n* → **chrysanthemum**
mumble¹ [ˈmʌmbəl] *v* **-bled; -bling** *vt* : mascullar, musitar — *vi* : mascullar, hablar entre dientes, murmurar
mumble² *n* **to speak in a mumble** : hablar entre dientes
mummy [ˈmʌmi] *n, pl* **-mies** : momia *f*
mumps [ˈmʌmps] *ns & pl* : paperas *fpl*
munch [ˈmʌntʃ] *v* : mascar, masticar
mundane [ˌmʌnˈdeɪn, ˈmʌnˌ-] *adj* **1** EARTHLY, WORLDLY : mundano, terrenal **2** COMMONPLACE : rutinario, ordinario
municipal [mjʊˈnɪsəpəl] *adj* : municipal
municipality [mjʊˌnɪsəˈpæləti] *n, pl* **-ties** : municipio *m*
munitions [mjʊˈnɪʃənz] *npl* : municiones *fpl*
mural¹ [ˈmjʊrəl] *adj* : mural
mural² [ˈmjʊrəlɪst] *n* : mural *m*
murder¹ [ˈmərdər] *vt* : asesinar, matar — *vi* : matar
murder² *n* : asesinato *m,* homicidio *m*
murderer [ˈmərdərər] *n* : asesino *m,* -na *f;* homicida *mf*
murderess [ˈmərdərɪs, -dəˌrɛs, -dərəs] *n* : asesina *f,* homicida *f*
murderous [ˈmərdərəs] *adj* : asesino, homicida
murk [ˈmərk] *n* DARKNESS : oscuridad *f,* tinieblas *fpl*
murkiness [ˈmərkinəs] *n* : oscuridad *f,* tenebrosidad *f*
murky [ˈmərki] *adj* **-kier; -est** : oscuro, tenebroso
murmur¹ [ˈmərmər] *vi* **1** DRONE : mumurar **2** GRUMBLE : refunfuñar, regañar, rezongar — *vt* MUMBLE : murmurar
murmur² *n* **1** COMPLAINT : queja *f* **2** DRONE : murmullo *m,* rumor *m*
muscle¹ [ˈmʌsəl] *vi* **-cled; -cling** : meterse <to muscle in on : meterse por la fuerza en, entrometerse en>
muscle² *n* **1** : músculo *m* **2** STRENGTH : fuerza *f*
muscular [ˈmʌskjələr] *adj* **1** : muscular <muscular tissue : tejido muscular> **2** BRAWNY : musculoso
muscular dystrophy *n* : distrofia *f* muscular
musculature [ˈmʌskjələˌtʃʊr, -tʃər] *n* : musculatura *f*
muse¹ [ˈmjuːz] *vi* **mused; musing** PONER, REFLECT : cavilar, meditar, reflexionar
muse² *n* : musa *f*
museum [mjʊˈziːəm] *n* : museo *m*
mush [ˈmʌʃ] *n* **1** : gachas *fpl* (de maíz) **2** SENTIMENTALITY : sensiblería *f*
mushroom¹ [ˈmʌʃˌruːm, -ˌrʊm] *vi* GROW, MULTIPLY : crecer rápidamente, multiplicarse
mushroom² *n* : hongo *m,* champiñón *m,* seta *f*
mushy [ˈmʌʃi] *adj* **mushier; -est 1** SOFT : blando **2** MAWKISH : sensiblero
music [ˈmjuːzɪk] *n* : música *f*
musical¹ [ˈmjuːzɪkəl] *adj* : musical, de música — **musically** *adv*
musical² *n* : comedia *f* musical
music box *n* : cajita *f* de música
musician [mjʊˈzɪʃən] *n* : músico *m,* -ca *f*
musk [ˈmʌsk] *n* : almizcle *m*
musket [ˈmʌskət] *n* : mosquete *m*
musketeer [ˌmʌskəˈtɪr] *n* : mosquetero *m*
muskrat [ˈmʌskˌræt] *n, pl* **-rat** *or* **-rats** : rata *f* almizclera
Muslim¹ [ˈmʌzləm, ˈmʊs-, ˈmʊz-] *adj* : musulmán
Muslim² *n* : musulmán *m,* -mana *f*
muslin [ˈmʌzlən] *n* : muselina *f*
muss¹ [ˈmʌs] *vt* : desordenar, despeinar (el pelo)
muss² *n* : desorden *m*
mussel [ˈmʌsəl] *n* : mejillón *m*
must¹ [ˈmʌst] *v aux* **1** (*expressing obligation or necessity*) : deber, tener que <you must stop : debes parar> <we must obey : tenemos que obedecer> **2** (*expressing probability*) : deber (de), haber de <you must be tired : debes de estar cansado> <it must be late : ha de ser tarde>
must² *n* : necesidad *f* <exercise is a must : el ejercicio es imprescindible>
mustache [ˈmʌˌstæʃ, mʌˈstæʃ] *n* : bigote *m,* bigotes *mpl*
mustang [ˈmʌˌstæŋ] *n* : mustang *m*
mustard [ˈmʌstərd] *n* : mostaza *f*
muster¹ [ˈmʌstər] *vt* **1** ASSEMBLE : reunir **2 to muster up** : armarse de, cobrar (valor, fuerzas, etc.)
muster² *n* **1** INSPECTION : revista *f* (de tropas) <it didn't pass muster : no resistió un examen minucioso> **2** COLLECTION : colección *f*
mustiness [ˈmʌstinəs] *n* : lo mohoso
musty [ˈmʌsti] *adj* **mustier; -est** : mohoso, que huele a moho, que huele a encerrado
mutant¹ [ˈmjuːtənt] *adj* : mutante
mutant² *n* : mutante *m*
mutate [ˈmjuːˌteɪt] *vi* **-tated; -tating 1** : mutar (genéticamente) **2** CHANGE : transformarse
mutation [mjuːˈteɪʃən] *n* : mutación *f* (genética)

mute[1] [ˈmjuːt] *vt* **muted; muting** MUFFLE : amortiguar, ponerle sordina a (un instrumento musical)
mute[2] *adj* **muter; mutest** : mudo — **mutely** *adv*
mute[3] *n* **1** : mudo *m,* -da *f* (persona) **2** : sordina *f* (para un instrumento musical)
mutilate [ˈmjuːtəˌleɪt] *vt* **-lated; -lating** : mutilar
mutilation [ˌmjuːtəˈleɪʃən] *n* : mutilación *f*
mutineer [ˌmjuːtənˈɪr] *n* : amotinado *m,* -da *f*
mutinous [ˈmjuːtənəs] *adj* : amotinado
mutiny[1] [ˈmjuːtəni] *vi* **-nied; -nying** : amotinarse
mutiny[2] *n, pl* **-nies** : amotinamiento *m,* motín *m*
mutt [ˈmʌt] *n* MONGREL : perro *m* mestizo, perro *m* corriente *Mex*
mutter [ˈmʌtər] *vi* **1** MUMBLE : mascullar, hablar entre dientes, murmurar **2** GRUMBLE : refunfuñar, regañar, rezongar
mutton [ˈmʌtən] *n* : carne *f* de carnero
mutual [ˈmjuːtʃʊəl] *adj* **1** : mutuo <mutual respect : respeto mutuo> **2** COMMON : común <a mutual friend : un amigo común>
mutually [ˈmjuːtʃʊəli, -tʃəli] *adv* **1** : mutuamente <mutually beneficial : mutuamente beneficioso> **2** JOINTLY : conjuntamente
muzzle[1] [ˈmʌzəl] *vt* **-zled; -zling** : ponerle un bozal a (un animal), amordazar
muzzle[2] *n* **1** SNOUT : hocico *m* **2** : bozal *m* (para un perro, etc.) **3** : boca *f* (de un arma de fuego)
my[1] [ˈmaɪ] *adj* : mi <my parents : mis padres>
my[2] *interj* : ¡caramba!, ¡Dios mío!
myopia [maɪˈoːpiə] *n* : miopía *f*
myopic [maɪˈoːpɪk, -ˈɑ-] *adj* : miope
myriad[1] [ˈmɪriəd] *adj* INNUMERABLE : innumerable
myriad[2] *n* : miríada *f*
myrrh [ˈmər] *n* : mirra *f*
myrtle [ˈmərtəl] *n* : mirto *m,* arrayán *m*
myself [maɪˈsɛlf] *pron* **1** (*used reflexively*) : me <I washed myself : me lavé> **2** (*used for emphasis*) : yo mismo, yo misma <I did it myself : lo hice yo mismo>
mysterious [mɪˈstɪriəs] *adj* : misterioso — **mysteriously** *adv*
mysteriousness [mɪˈstɪriəsnəs] *n* : lo misterioso
mystery [ˈmɪstəri] *n, pl* **-teries** : misterio *m*
mystic[1] [ˈmɪstɪk] *adj* : místico
mystic[2] *n* : místico *m,* -ca *f*
mystical [ˈmɪstɪkəl] *adj* : místico — **mystically** *adv*
mysticism [ˈmɪstəˌsɪzəm] *n* : misticismo *m*
mystify [ˈmɪstəˌfaɪ] *vt* **-fied; -fying** : dejar perplejo, confundir
mystique [mɪˈstiːk] *n* : aura *f* de misterio
myth [ˈmɪθ] *n* : mito *m*
mythical [ˈmɪθɪkəl] *adj* : mítico
mythological [ˌmɪθəˈlɑdʒɪkəl] *adj* : mitológico
mythology [mɪˈθɑlədʒi] *n, pl* **-gies** : mitología *f*

N

n [ˈɛn] *n, pl* **n's** *or* **ns** [ˈɛnz] : decimocuarta letra del alfabeto inglés
nab [ˈnæb] *vt* **nabbed; nabbing** : prender, pillar *fam,* pescar *fam*
nadir [ˈneɪdər, ˈneɪˌdɪr] *n* : nadir *m,* punto *m* más bajo
nag[1] [ˈnæg] *v* **nagged; nagging** *vi* **1** COMPLAIN : quejarse, rezongar **2 to nag at** HASSLE : molestar, darle (la) lata (a alguien) — *vt* **1** PESTER : molestar, fastidiar **2** SCOLD : regañar, estarle encima a *fam*
nag[2] *n* **1** GRUMBLER : gruñón *m,* -ñona *f* **2** HORSE : jamelgo *m*
naiad [ˈneɪəd, ˈnaɪ-, -ˌæd] *n, pl* **-iads** *or* **-iades** [-əˌdiːz] : náyade *f*
nail[1] [ˈneɪl] *vt* : clavar, sujetar con clavos
nail[2] *n* **1** FINGERNAIL : uña *f* <nail file : lima (de uñas)> <nail polish : laca de uñas> **2** : clavo *m* <to hit the nail on the head : dar en el clavo>
naive *or* **naïve** [nɑˈiːv] *adj* **-iver; -est 1** INGENUOUS : ingenuo, cándido **2** GULLIBLE : crédulo
naively [nɑˈiːvli] *adv* : ingenuamente
naïveté [ˌnɑˌiːvəˈteɪ, nɑˈiːvəˌ-] *n* : ingenuidad *f*
naked [ˈneɪkəd] *adj* **1** UNCLOTHED : desnudo **2** UNCOVERED : desenvainado (dícese de una espada), pelado (dícese de los árboles), expuesto al aire (dícese de una llama) **3** OBVIOUS, PLAIN : manifiesto, puro, desnudo <the naked truth : la pura verdad> **4 to the naked eye** : a simple vista
nakedly [ˈneɪkədli] *adv* : manifiestamente
nakedness [ˈneɪkədnəs] *n* : desnudez *f*
name[1] [ˈneɪm] *vt* **named; naming 1** CALL : llamar, bautizar, ponerle nombre a **2** MENTION : mentar, mencionar, dar el nombre de <they have named a suspect : han dado el nombre de un

sospechoso> 3 APPOINT : nombrar 4 **to name a price** : fijar un precio

name[2] *adj* 1 KNOWN : de nombre <name brand : marca conocida> 2 PROMINENT : de renombre, de prestigio

name[3] *n* 1 : nombre *m* <what is your name : ¿cómo se llama?> 2 SURNAME : apellido *m* 3 EPITHET : epíteto *m* <to call somebody names : llamar a alguien de todo> 4 REPUTATION : fama *f*, reputación *f* <to make a name for oneself : darse a conocer, hacerse famoso>

nameless [ˈneɪmləs] *adj* 1 ANONYMOUS : anónimo 2 INDESCRIBABLE : indecible, indescriptible

namelessly [ˈneɪmləsli] *adv* : anónimamente

namely [ˈneɪmli] *adv* : a saber

namesake [ˈneɪm,seɪk] *n* : tocayo *m*, -ya *f;* homónimo *m*, -ma *f*

Namibian [nəˈmɪbiən] *n* : namibio *m*, -bia *f* — **Namibian** *adj*

nap[1] [ˈnæp] *vi* **napped; napping** 1 : dormir, dormir la siesta 2 **to be caught napping** : estar desprevenido

nap[2] *n* 1 SLEEP : siesta *f* <to take a nap : echarse una siesta> 2 FUZZ, PILE : pelo *m*, pelusa *f* (de telas)

nape [ˈneɪp, ˈnæp] *n* : nuca *f*, cerviz *f*, cogote *m*

naphtha [ˈnæfθə] *n* : nafta *f*

napkin [ˈnæpkən] *n* : servilleta *f*

narcissism [ˈnɑrsə,sɪzəm] *n* : narcisismo *m*

narcissist [ˈnɑrsəsɪst] *n* : narcisista *mf*

narcissistic [,nɑrsəˈsɪstɪk] *adj* : narcisista

narcissus [nɑrˈsɪsəs] *n, pl* **-cissus** *or* **-cissuses** *or* **-cissi** [-ˈsɪ,saɪ, -,siː] : narciso *m*

narcotic[1] [nɑrˈkɑtɪk] *adj* : narcótico

narcotic[2] *n* : narcótico *m*, estupefaciente *m*

narrate [ˈnær,eɪt] *vt* **-rated; -rating** : narrar, relatar

narration [næˈreɪʃən] *n* : narración *f*

narrative[1] [ˈnærət̬ɪv] *adj* : narrativo

narrative[2] *n* : narración *f*, narrativa *f*, relato *m*

narrator [ˈnær,eɪt̬ər] *n* : narrador *m*, -dora *f*

narrow[1] [ˈnær,oː] *vi* : estrecharse, angostarse <the river narrowed : el río se estrechó> — *vt* 1 : estrechar, angostar 2 LIMIT : restringir, limitar <to narrow the search : limitar la búsqueda>

narrow[2] *adj* 1 : estrecho, angosto 2 LIMITED : estricto, limitado <in the narrowest sense of the word : en el sentido más estricto de la palabra> 3 **to have a narrow escape** : escapar por un pelo

narrowly [ˈnæroli] *adv* 1 BARELY : por poco 2 CLOSELY : de cerca

narrow-minded [,næroˈmaɪndəd] *adj* : de miras estrechas

narrowness [ˈnæronəs] *n* : estrechez *f*

narrows [ˈnæroːz] *npl* STRAIT : estrecho *m*

narwhal [ˈnɑr,*h*wɑl, ˈnɑrwəl] *n* : narval *m*

nasal [ˈneɪzəl] *adj* : nasal, gangoso <a nasal voice : una voz gangosa>

nasally [ˈneɪzəli] *adv* 1 : por la nariz 2 : con voz gangosa

nastily [ˈnæstəli] *adv* : con maldad, cruelmente

nastiness [ˈnæstinəs] *n* : porquería *f*

nasturtium [nəˈstərʃəm, næ-] *n* : capuchina *f*

nasty [ˈnæsti] *adj* **-tier; -est** 1 FILTHY : sucio, mugriento 2 OBSCENE : obsceno 3 MEAN, SPITEFUL : malo, malicioso 4 UNPLEASANT : desagradable, feo 5 REPUGNANT : asqueroso, repugnante <a nasty smell : un olor asqueroso>

natal [ˈneɪt̬əl] *adj* : natal

nation [ˈneɪʃən] *n* : nación *f*

national[1] [ˈnæʃənəl] *adj* : nacional

national[2] *n* : ciudadano *m*, -na *f;* nacional *mf*

nationalism [ˈnæʃənə,lɪzəm] *n* : nacionalismo *m*

nationalist[1] [ˈnæʃənəlɪst] *adj* : nacionalista

nationalist[2] *n* : nacionalista *mf*

nationalistic [,næʃənəˈlɪstɪk] *adj* : nacionalista

nationality [,næʃəˈnælət̬i] *n, pl* **-ties** : nacionalidad *f*

nationalization [,næʃənələˈzeɪʃən] *n* : nacionalización *f*

nationalize [ˈnæʃənə,laɪz] *vt* **-ized; -izing** : nacionalizar

nationally [ˈnæʃənəli] *adv* : a escala nacional, a nivel nacional

nationwide [ˈneɪʃənˈwaɪd] *adj* : en toda la nación, por todo el país

native[1] [ˈneɪt̬ɪv] *adj* 1 INNATE : innato 2 : natal <her native city : su ciudad natal> 3 INDIGENOUS : indígeno, autóctono

native[2] *n* 1 ABORIGINE : nativo *m*, -va *f;* indígena *mf* 2 : natural *m* <he's a native of Mexico : es natural de México>

Native American → **American Indian**

nativity [nəˈtɪvət̬i, neɪ-] *n, pl* **-ties** 1 BIRTH : navidad *f* 2 **the Nativity** : la Natividad, la Navidad

natty [ˈnæt̬i] *adj* **-tier; -est** : elegante, garboso

natural[1] [ˈnætʃərəl] *adj* 1 : natural, de la naturaleza <natural woodlands : bosques naturales> <natural childbirth : parto natural> 2 INNATE : innato, natural 3 UNAFFECTED : natural, sin afectación 4 LIFELIKE : natural, vivo

natural[2] *n* **to be a natural** : tener un talento innato (para algo)

natural gas *n* : gas *m* natural

natural history *n* : historia *f* natural

naturalist [ˈnætʃərəlɪst] *n* : naturalista *mf*
naturalization [ˌnætʃərələˈzeɪʃən] *n* : naturalización *f*
naturalize [ˈnætʃərəˌlaɪz] *vt* **-ized; -izing** : naturalizar
naturally [ˈnætʃərəli] *adv* **1** INHERENTLY : naturalmente, intrínsecamente **2** UNAFFECTEDLY : de manera natural **3** OF COURSE : por supuesto, naturalmente
naturalness [ˈnætʃərəlnəs] *n* : naturalidad *f*
natural science *n* : ciencias *fpl* naturales
nature [ˈneɪtʃər] *n* **1** : naturaleza *f* <the laws of nature : las leyes de la naturaleza> **2** KIND, SORT : índole *f,* clase *f* <things of this nature : cosas de esta índole> **3** DISPOSITION : carácter *m,* natural *m,* naturaleza *f* <it is his nature to be friendly : es de natural simpático> <human nature : la naturaleza humana>
naught [ˈnɔt] *n* **1** : nada *f* <to come to naught : reducirse a nada, fracasar> **2** ZERO : cero *m*
naughtily [ˈnɔt̬əli] *adv* : traviesamente, con malicia
naughtiness [ˈnɔt̬inəs] *n* : mala conducta *f,* travesuras *fpl*, malicia *f*
naughty [ˈnɔt̬i] *adj* **-tier; -est 1** MISCHIEVOUS : travieso, pícaro **2** RISQUÉ : picante, subido de tono
nausea [ˈnɔziə, ˈnɔʃə] *n* **1** SICKNESS : náuseas *fpl* **2** DISGUST : asco *m*
nauseate [ˈnɔziˌeɪt, -ʒi-, -si-, -ʃi-] *vt* **-ated; -ating 1** SICKEN : darle náuseas (a alguien) **2** DISGUST : asquear, darle asco (a alguien)
nauseating *adj* : nauseabundo, repugnante
nauseatingly [ˈnɔziˌeɪt̬ɪŋli, -ʒi-, -si-, -ʃi-] *adv* : hasta el punto de dar asco <nauseatingly sweet : tan dulce que da asco>
nauseous [ˈnɔʃəs, -ziəs] *adj* **1** SICK : mareado, con náuseas **2** SICKENING : nauseabundo
nautical [ˈnɔt̬ɪkəl] *adj* : náutico
nautilus [ˈnɔt̬ələs] *n, pl* **-luses** *or* **-li** [-ˌlaɪ, -ˌliː] : nautilo *m*
naval [ˈneɪvəl] *adj* : naval
nave [ˈneɪv] *n* : nave *f*
navel [ˈneɪvəl] *n* : ombligo *m*
navigability [ˌnævɪgəˈbɪlət̬i] *n* : navegabilidad *f*
navigable [ˈnævɪgəbəl] *adj* : navegable
navigate [ˈnævəˌgeɪt] *v* **-gated; -gating** *vi* : navegar — *vt* **1** STEER : gobernar (un barco), pilotar (un avión) **2** : navegar por (un río, etc.)
navigation [ˌnævəˈgeɪʃən] *n* : navegación *f*
navigator [ˈnævəˌgeɪt̬ər] *n* : navegante *mf*
navy [ˈneɪvi] *n, pl* **-vies 1** FLEET : flota *f* **2** : marina *f* de guerra, armada *f* <the United States Navy : la armada de los Estados Unidos> **3** *or* **navy blue** : azul *m* marino
nay[1] [ˈneɪ] *adv* : no
nay[2] *n* : no *m,* voto *m* en contra
Nazi [ˈnɑtsi, ˈnæt-] *n* : nazi *mf*
Nazism [ˈnɑtˌsɪzəm, ˈnæt-] *or* **Naziism** [ˈnɑtsiˌɪzəm, ˈnæt-] *n* : nazismo *m*
Neanderthal man [niˈændərˌθɔl, -ˌtɔl] *n* : hombre *m* de Neanderthal
near[1] [ˈnɪr] *vt* **1** : acercarse a <the ship is nearing port : el barco se está acercando al puerto> **2** : estar a punto de <she is nearing graduation : está a punto de graduarse>
near[2] *adv* **1** CLOSE : cerca <my family lives quite near : mi familia vive muy cerca> **2** NEARLY : casi <I came near to finishing : casi terminé>
near[3] *adj* **1** CLOSE : cercano, próximo **2** SIMILAR : parecido, semejante
near[4] *prep* : cerca de
nearby[1] [nɪrˈbaɪ, ˈnɪrˌbaɪ] *adv* : cerca
nearby[2] *adj* : cercano
nearly [ˈnɪrli] *adv* **1** ALMOST : casi <nearly asleep : casi dormido> **2 not nearly** : ni con mucho, ni mucho menos <it was not nearly so bad as I had expected : no fue ni con mucho tan malo como esperaba>
nearness [ˈnɪrnəs] *n* : proximidad *f*
nearsighted [ˈnɪrˌsaɪt̬əd] *adj* : miope, corto de vista
nearsightedly [ˈnɪrˌsaɪt̬ədli] *adv* : con miopía
nearsightedness [ˈnɪrˌsaɪt̬ədnəs] *n* : miopía *f*
neat [ˈniːt] *adj* **1** CLEAN, ORDERLY : ordenado, pulcro, limpio **2** UNDILUTED : solo, sin diluir **3** SIMPLE, TASTEFUL : sencillo y de buen gusto **4** CLEVER : hábil, ingenioso <a neat trick : un truco ingenioso>
neatly [ˈniːtli] *adv* **1** TIDILY : ordenadamente **2** CLEVERLY : ingeniosamente
neatness [ˈniːtnəs] *n* : pulcritud *f,* limpieza *f,* orden *m*
nebula [ˈnɛbjʊlə] *n, pl* **-lae** [-ˌliː, -ˌlaɪ] : nebulosa *f*
nebulous [ˈnɛbjʊləs] *adj* : nebuloso, vago
necessarily [ˌnɛsəˈsɛrəli] *adv* : necesariamente, forzosamente
necessary[1] [ˈnɛsəˌsɛri] *adj* **1** INEVITABLE : inevitable **2** COMPULSORY : necesario, obligatorio **3** ESSENTIAL : imprescindible, preciso, necesario
necessary[2] *n, pl* **-saries** : lo esencial, lo necesario
necessitate [nɪˈsɛsəˌteɪt] *vt* **-tated; -tating** : necesitar, requerir
necessity [nɪˈsɛsət̬i] *n, pl* **-ties 1** NEED : necesidad *f* **2** REQUIREMENT : requisito *m* indispensable **3** POVERTY : indigencia *f,* necesidad *f* **4** INEVITABILITY : inevitabilidad *f*
neck[1] [ˈnɛk] *vi* : besuquearse

neck[2] *n* **1 :** cuello *m* (de una persona), pescuezo *m* (de un animal) **2** COLLAR **:** cuello *m* **3 :** cuello *m* (de una botella), mástil *m* (de una guitarra)
neckerchief [ˈnɛkərtʃəf, -ˌtʃiːf] *n, pl* **-chiefs** [-tʃəfs, -ˌtʃiːfs] **:** pañuelo *m* (para el cuello), mascada *f Mex*
necklace [ˈnɛkləs] *n* **:** collar *m*
neckline [ˈnɛkˌlaɪn] *n* **:** escote *m*
necktie [ˈnɛkˌtaɪ] *n* **:** corbata *f*
nectar [ˈnɛktər] *n* **:** néctar *m*
nectarine [ˌnɛktəˈriːn] *n* **:** nectarina *f*
née *or* **nee** [ˈneɪ] *adj* **:** de soltera <Mrs. Smith, née Whitman : la señora Smith, de soltera Whitman>
need[1] [ˈniːd] *vt* **1 :** necesitar <I need your help : necesito su ayuda> <I need money : me falta dinero> **2** REQUIRE **:** requerir, exigir <that job needs patience : ese trabajo exige paciencia> **3 to need to :** tener que <he needs to study : tiene que estudiar> <they need to be scolded : hay que reprenderlos> — *v aux* **1** MUST **:** tener que, deber <need you shout? : ¿tienes que gritar?> **2 to be needed :** hacer falta <you needn't worry : no hace falta que te preocupes, no hay por qué preocuparse>
need[2] *n* **1** NECESSITY **:** necesidad *f* <in case of need : en caso de necesidad> **2** LACK **:** falta *f* <the need for better training : la falta de mejor capacitación> <to be in need : necesitar> **3** POVERTY **:** necesidad *f,* indigencia *f* **4 needs** *npl* **:** requisitos *mpl*, carencias *fpl*
needful [ˈniːdfəl] *adj* **:** necesario
needle[1] [ˈniːdəl] *vt* **-dled; -dling :** pinchar
needle[2] *n* **1 :** aguja *f* <to thread a needle : enhebrar una aguja> <knitting needle : aguja de tejer> **2** POINTER **:** aguja *f,* indicador *m*
needlepoint [ˈniːdəlˌpɔint] *n* **1** LACE **:** encaje *m* de mano **2** EMBROIDERY **:** bordado *m* en cañamazo
needless [ˈniːdləs] *adj* **:** innecesario
needlessly [ˈniːdləsli] *adv* **:** sin ninguna necesidad, innecesariamente
needlework [ˈniːdəlˌwərk] *n* **:** bordado *m*
needn't [ˈniːdənt] (*contraction of* **need not**) → **need**
needy[1] [ˈniːdi] **needier; -est** *adj* **:** necesitado
needy[2] *n* **the needy :** los necesitados *mpl*
nefarious [nɪˈfæriəs] *adj* **:** nefario, nefando, infame
negate [nɪˈgeɪt] *vt* **-gated; -gating 1** DENY **:** negar **2** NULLIFY **:** invalidar, anular
negation [nɪˈgeɪʃən] *n* **:** negación *f*
negative[1] [ˈnɛgət̬ɪv] *adj* **:** negativo
negative[2] *n* **1 :** negación *f* (en lingüística) **2 :** negativa *f* <to answer in the negative : contestar con una negativa> **3 :** término *m* negativo (en matemáticas) **4 :** negativo *m,* imagen *f* en negativo (en fotografía)
negatively [ˈnɛgət̬ɪvli] *adv* **:** negativamente
neglect[1] [nɪˈglɛkt] *vt* **1 :** desatender, descuidar <to neglect one's health : descuidar la salud> **2 :** no cumplir con, faltar a <to neglect one's obligations : faltar uno a sus obligaciones> <he neglected to tell me : omitió decírmelo>
neglect[2] *n* **1 :** negligencia *f,* descuido *m,* incumplimiento *m* <through neglect : por negligencia> <neglect of duty : incumplimiento del deber> **2 in a state of neglect :** abandonado, descuidado
neglectful [nɪˈglɛktfəl] *adj* **:** descuidado *m*
negligee [ˌnɛgləˈʒeɪ] *n* **:** negligé *m*
negligence [ˈnɛglɪdʒənts] *n* **:** descuido *m,* negligencia *f*
negligent [ˈnɛglɪdʒənt] *adj* **:** negligente, descuidado — **negligently** *adv*
negligible [ˈnɛglɪdʒəbəl] *adj* **:** insignificante, despreciable
negotiable [nɪˈgoːʃəbəl, -ʃiə-] *adj* **:** negociable
negotiate [nɪˈgoːʃiˌeɪt] *v* **-ated; -ating** *vi* **:** negociar — *vt* **1 :** negociar, gestionar <to negotiate a treaty : negociar un trato> **2 :** salvar, franquear <they negotiated the obstacles : salvaron los obstáculos> <to negotiate a turn : tomar una curva>
negotiation [nɪˌgoːʃiˈeɪʃən, -siˈeɪ-] *n* **:** negociación *f*
negotiator [nɪˈgoːʃiˌeɪt̬ər, -siˌeɪ-] *n* **:** negociador *m,* -dora *f*
Negro [ˈniːˌgroː] *n, pl* **-groes :** negro *m,* -gra *f*
neigh[1] [ˈneɪ] *vi* **:** relinchar
neigh[2] *n* **:** relincho *m*
neighbor[1] [ˈneɪbər] *vt* **:** ser vecino de, estar junto a <her house neighbors mine : su casa está junto a la mía> — *vi* **:** estar cercano, lindar, colindar <her land neighbors on mine : sus tierras lindan con las mías>
neighbor[2] *n* **1 :** vecino *m,* -na *f* **2 love thy neighbor :** ama a tu prójimo
neighborhood [ˈneɪbərˌhʊd] *n* **1 :** barrio *m,* vecindad *f,* vecindario *m* **2 in the neighborhood of :** alrededor de, cerca de
neighborly [ˈneɪbərli] *adv* **:** amable, de buena vecindad
neither[1] [ˈniːðər, ˈnaɪ-] *adj* **:** ninguno (de los dos)
neither[2] *conj* **1 :** ni <neither asleep nor awake : ni dormido ni despierto> **2** NOR **:** ni (tampoco) <I'm not asleep — neither am I : no estoy dormido — ni yo tampoco>
neither[3] *pron* **:** ninguno
nemesis [ˈnɛməsɪs] *n, pl* **-eses** [-ˌsiːz] **1** RIVAL **:** rival *mf* **2** RETRIBUTION **:** justo castigo *m*

neologism [ni'ɑlə,dʒɪzəm] *n* **:** neologismo *m*
neon[1] ['ni:,ɑn] *adj* **:** de neón <neon sign : letrero de neón>
neon[2] *n* **:** neón *m*
Nepali [nə'pɔli, -'pɑ-, -'pæ-] *n* **:** nepalés *m,* -lesa *f* — **Nepali** *adj*
neophyte ['ni:ə,faɪt] *n* **:** neófito *m,* -ta *f*
nephew ['nɛ,fju:, *chiefly British* 'nɛ,vju:] *n* **:** sobrino *m*
nepotism ['nɛpə,tɪzəm] *n* **:** nepotismo *m*
Neptune ['nɛp,tu:n, -,tju:n] *n* **:** Neptuno *m*
nerd ['nərd] *n* **:** ganso *m,* -sa *f*
nerve ['nərv] *n* **1 :** nervio *m* **2** COURAGE **:** coraje *m,* valor *m,* fuerza *f* de la voluntad <to lose one's nerve : perder el valor> **3** AUDACITY, GALL **:** atrevimiento *m,* descaro *m* <of all the nerve! : ¡qué descaro!> **4 nerves** *npl* **:** nervios *mpl* <a fit of nerves : un ataque de nervios>
nervous ['nərvəs] *adj* **1 :** nervioso <the nervous system : el sistema nervioso> **2** EXCITABLE **:** nervioso, excitable <to get nervous : excitarse, ponerse nervioso> **3** FEARFUL **:** miedoso, temeroso
nervously ['nərvəsli] *adv* **:** nerviosamente
nervousness ['nərvəsnəs] *n* **:** nerviosismo *m,* nerviosidad *f,* ansiedad *f*
nervy ['nərvi] *adj* **nervier; -est 1** COURAGEOUS **:** valiente **2** IMPUDENT **:** atrevido, descarado, fresco *fam* **3** NERVOUS **:** nervioso
nest[1] ['nɛst] *vi* **:** anidar
nest[2] *n* **1 :** nido *m* (de un ave), avispero *m* (de una avispa), madriguera *f* (de un animal) **2** REFUGE **:** nido *m,* refugio *m* **3** SET **:** juego *m* <a nest of tables : un juego de mesitas>
nestle ['nɛsəl] *vi* **-tled; -tling :** acurrucarse, arrimarse cómodamente
net[1] ['nɛt] *vt* **netted; netting 1** CATCH **:** pescar, atrapar con una red **2** CLEAR **:** ganar neto <they netted $5000 : ganaron $5000 netos> **3** YIELD **:** producir neto
net[2] *adj* **:** neto <net weight : peso neto> <net gain : ganancia neta>
net[3] *n* **:** red *f,* malla *f*
nether ['nɛðər] *adj* **1 :** inferior, más bajo **2 the nether regions :** el infierno
nettle[1] ['nɛtəl] *vt* **-tled; -tling :** irritar, provocar, molestar
nettle[2] *n* **:** ortiga *f*
network ['nɛt,wərk] *n* **1** SYSTEM **:** red *f* **2** CHAIN **:** cadena *f* <a network of supermarkets : una cadena de supermercados>
neural ['nʊrəl, 'njʊr-] *adj* **:** neural
neuralgia [nʊ'rældʒə, njʊ-] *n* **:** neuralgia *f*
neuritis [nʊ'raɪtəs, njʊ-] *n, pl* **-ritides** [-'rɪtə,di:z] *or* **-ritises :** neuritis *f*
neurological [,nʊrə'lɑdʒɪkəl, ,njʊr-] *or* **neurologic** [,nʊrə'lɑdʒɪk, ,njʊr-] *adj* **:** neurológico
neurologist [nʊ'rɑlədʒɪst, njʊ-] *n* **:** neurólogo *m,* -ga *f*
neurology [nʊ'rɑlədʒi, njʊ-] *n* **:** neurología *f*
neurosis [nʊ'ro:sɪs, njʊ-] *n, pl* **-roses** [-,si:z] **:** neurosis *f*
neurotic[1] [nʊ'rɑtɪk, njʊ-] *adj* **:** neurótico
neurotic[2] *n* **:** neurótico *m,* -ca *f*
neuter[1] ['nu:tər, 'nju:-] *vt* **:** castrar
neuter[2] *adj* **:** neutro
neutral[1] ['nu:trəl, 'nju:-] *adj* **1** IMPARTIAL **:** neutral, imparcial <to remain neutral : permanecer neutral> **2 :** neutro <a neutral color : un color neutro> **3 :** neutro (en la química o la electricidad)
neutral[2] *n* **:** punto *m* muerto (de un automóvil)
neutrality [nu:'trælət̬i:, nju:-] *n* **:** neutralidad *f*
neutralization [,nu:trələ'zeɪʃən, ,nju:-] *n* **:** neutralización *f*
neutralize ['nu:trə,laɪz, 'nju:-] *vt* **-ized; -izing :** neutralizar
neutron ['nu:,trɑn, 'nju:-] *n* **:** neutrón *m*
never ['nɛvər] *adv* **1 :** nunca, jamás <he never studies : nunca estudia> **2 never again :** nunca más, nunca jamás **3 never mind :** no importa
nevermore [,nɛvər'mor] *adv* **:** nunca más
nevertheless [,nɛvərðə'lɛs] *adv* **:** sin embargo, no obstante
new ['nu:, 'nju:] *adj* **1 :** nuevo <a new dress : un vestido nuevo> **2** RECENT **:** nuevo, reciente <what's new? : ¿qué hay de nuevo?> <a new arrival : un recién llegado> **3** DIFFERENT **:** nuevo, distinto <this problem is new : este problema es distinto> <new ideas : ideas nuevas> **4 like new :** como nuevo
newborn ['nu:,bɔrn, 'nju:-] *adj* **:** recién nacido
newcomer ['nu:,kʌmər, 'nju:-] *n* **:** recién llegado *m,* recién llegada *f*
newfangled ['nu:'fæŋgəld, 'nju:-] *adj* **:** novedoso
newfound ['nu:'faʊnd, 'nju:-] *adj* **:** recién descubierto
newly ['nu:li, 'nju:-] *adv* **:** recién, recientemente
newlywed ['nu:li,wɛd, 'nju:-] *n* **:** recién casado *m,* -da *f*
new moon *n* **:** luna *f* nueva
newness ['nu:nəs, 'nju:-] *n* **:** novedad *f*
news ['nu:z, 'nju:z] *n* **:** noticias *fpl*
newscast ['nu:z,kæst, 'nju:z-] *n* **:** noticiero *m,* informativo *m*
newscaster ['nu:z,kæstər, 'nju:z-] *n* **:** presentador *m,* -dora *f;* locutor *m,* -tora *f*

newsletter [ˈnuːzˌlɛt̬ər, ˈnjuːz-] *n* : boletín *m* informativo
newsman [ˈnuːzmən, ˈnjuːz-, -ˌmæn] *n, pl* **-men** [-mən, -ˌmɛn] : periodista *m,* reportero *m*
newspaper [ˈnuːzˌpeɪpər, ˈnjuːz-] *n* : periódico *m,* diario *m*
newspaperman [ˈnuːzˌpeɪpərˌmæn, ˈnjuːz-] *n, pl* **-men** [-mən, -ˌmɛn] **1** REPORTER : periodista *m,* reportero *m* **2** : dueño *m* de un periódico
newsprint [ˈnuːzˌprɪnt, ˈnjuːz-] *n* : papel *m* de prensa
newsstand [ˈnuːzˌstænd, ˈnjuːz-] *n* : quiosco *m,* puesto *m* de periódicos
newswoman [ˈnuːzˌwʊmən, ˈnjuːz-] *n, pl* **-women** [-ˌwɪmən] : periodista *f,* reportera *f*
newsworthy [ˈnuːzˌwərði, ˈnjuːz-] *adj* : de interés periodístico
newsy [ˈnuːziː, ˈnjuː-] *adj* **newsier; -est** : lleno de noticias
newt [ˈnuːt, ˈnjuːt] *n* : tritón *m*
New Year *n* : Año *m* Nuevo
New Year's Day *n* : día *m* del Año Nuevo
New Yorker [nuːˈjɔrkər, njuː-] *n* : neoyorquino *m,* -na *f*
New Zealander [nuːˈziːləndər, njuː-] *n* : neozelandés *m,* -desa *f*
next[1] [ˈnɛkst] *adv* **1** AFTERWARD : después, luego <what will you do next? : ¿qué harás después?> **2** NOW : después, ahora, entonces <next I will sing a song : ahora voy a cantar una canción> **3** : la próxima vez <when next we meet : la próxima vez que nos encontremos>
next[2] *adj* **1** ADJACENT : contiguo, de al lado **2** COMING : que viene, próximo <next Friday : el viernes que viene> **3** FOLLOWING : siguiente <the next year : el año siguiente>
next-door [ˈnɛkstˈdor] *adj* : de al lado
next to[1] *adv* ALMOST : casi, prácticamente <next to impossible : casi imposible>
next to[2] *prep* : junto a, al lado de
nib [ˈnɪb] *n* : plumilla *f*
nibble[1] [ˈnɪbəl] *v* **-bled; -bling** *vt* : pellizcar, mordisquear, picar — *vi* : picar
nibble[2] *n* : mordisco *m*
Nicaraguan [ˌnɪkəˈrɑgwən] *n* : nicaragüense *mf* — **Nicaraguan** *adj*
nice [ˈnaɪs] *adj* **nicer; nicest 1** REFINED : pulido, refinado **2** SUBTLE : fino, sutil **3** PLEASING : agradable, bueno, lindo <nice weather : buen tiempo> **4** RESPECTABLE : bueno, decente **5 nice and** : bien, muy <nice and hot : bien caliente> <nice and slow : despacito>
nicely [ˈnaɪsli] *adv* **1** KINDLY : amablemente **2** POLITELY : con buenos modales **3** ATTRACTIVELY : de buen gusto
niceness [ˈnaɪsnəs] *n* : simpatía *f,* amabilidad *f*
nicety [ˈnaɪsət̬i] *n, pl* **-ties 1** DETAIL, SUBTLETY : sutileza *f,* detalle *m* **2 niceties** *npl* : lujos *mpl,* detalles *mpl*
niche [ˈnɪtʃ] *n* **1** RECESS : nicho *m,* hornacina *f* **2** : nicho *m,* hueco *m* <to make a niche for oneself : hacerse un hueco, encontrarse una buena posición>
nick[1] [ˈnɪk] *vt* : cortar, hacer una muesca en
nick[2] *n* **1** CUT : corte *m,* muesca *f* **2 in the nick of time** : en el momento crítico, justo a tiempo
nickel [ˈnɪkəl] *n* **1** : níquel *m* **2** : moneda *f* de cinco centavos
nickname[1] [ˈnɪkˌneɪm] *vt* **-named; -naming** : apodar
nickname[2] *n* : apodo *m,* mote *m,* sobrenombre *m*
nicotine [ˈnɪkəˌtiːn] *n* : nicotina *f*
niece [ˈniːs] *n* : sobrina *f*
Nigerian [naɪˈdʒɪriən] *n* : nigeriano *m,* -na *f* — **Nigerian** *adj*
niggardly [ˈnɪgərdli] *adj* : mezquino, tacaño
niggling [ˈnɪgəlɪŋ] *adj* **1** PETTY : insignificante **2** PERSISTENT : constante, persistente <a niggling doubt : una duda constante>
nigh[1] [ˈnaɪ] *adv* **1** NEARLY : casi **2 to draw nigh** : acercarse, avecinarse
nigh[2] *adj* : cercano, próximo
night[1] [ˈnaɪt] *adj* : nocturno, de la noche <the night sky : el cielo nocturno> <night shift : turno de la noche>
night[2] *n* **1** EVENING : noche *f* <at night : de noche> <last night : anoche> <tomorrow night : mañana por la noche> **2** DARKNESS : noche *f,* oscuridad *f* <night fell : cayó la noche>
nightclothes [ˈnaɪtˌkloːðz, -ˌkloːz] *npl* : ropa *f* de dormir
nightclub [ˈnaɪtˌklʌb] *n* : cabaret *m,* club *m* nocturno
night crawler [ˈnaɪtˌkrɔlər] *n* EARTHWORM : lombriz *f* (de tierra)
nightfall [ˈnaɪtˌfɔl] *n* : anochecer *m*
nightgown [ˈnaɪtˌgaʊn] *n* : camisón *m* (de noche)
nightingale [ˈnaɪtənˌgeɪl, ˈnaɪt̬ɪŋ-] *n* : ruiseñor *m*
nightly[1] [ˈnaɪtli] *adv* : cada noche, todas las noches
nightly[2] *adj* : de todas las noches
nightmare [ˈnaɪtˌmær] *n* : pesadilla *f*
nightmarish [ˈnaɪtˌmærɪʃ] *adj* : de pesadilla
night owl *n* : noctámbulo *m,* -la *f*
nightshade [ˈnaɪtˌʃeɪd] *n* : hierba *f* mora
nightshirt [ˈnaɪtˌʃərt] *n* : camisa *f* de dormir
nightstick [ˈnaɪtˌstɪk] *n* : porra *f*
nighttime [ˈnaɪtˌtaɪm] *n* : noche *f*
nil [ˈnɪl] *n* : nada *f,* cero *m*
nimble [ˈnɪmbəl] *adj* **-bler; -blest 1** AGILE : ágil **2** CLEVER : hábil, ingenioso
nimbleness [ˈnɪmbəlnəs] *n* : agilidad *f*

nimbly ['nɪmbli] *adv* : con agilidad, ágilmente

nincompoop ['nɪnkəm,pu:p, 'nɪŋ-] *n* FOOL : tonto *m,* -ta *f;* bobo *m,* -ba *f*

nine[1] ['naɪn] *adj* **1** : nueve **2 nine times out of ten** : casi siempre

nine[2] *n* : nueve *m*

nine hundred[1] *adj* : novecientos

nine hundred[2] *n* : novecientos *m*

ninepins ['naɪn,pɪnz] *n* : bolos *mpl*

nineteen[1] [naɪn'ti:n] *adj* : diecinueve

nineteen[2] *n* : diecinueve *m*

nineteenth[1] [naɪn'ti:nθ] *adj* : decimonoveno, decimonono <the nineteenth century : el siglo diecinueve>

nineteenth[2] *n* : decimonoveno *m,* -na *f;* decimonono *m,* -na *f* (en una serie) **2** : diecinueveavo *m,* diecinueveava parte *f*

ninetieth[1] ['naɪntiəθ] *adj* : nonagésimo

ninetieth[2] *n* **1** : nonagésimo *m,* -ma *f* (en una serie) **2** : noventavo *m,* noventava parte *f*

ninety[1] ['naɪnti] *adj* : noventa

ninety[2] *n, pl* **-ties** : noventa *m*

ninth[1] ['naɪnθ] *adj* : noveno

ninth[2] *n* **1** : noveno *m,* -na *f* (en una serie) **2** : noveno *m,* novena parte *f*

ninny ['nɪni] *n, pl* **ninnies** FOOL : tonto *m,* -ta *f;* bobo *m,* -ba *f*

nip[1] ['nɪp] *vt* **nipped; nipping 1** PINCH : pellizcar **2** BITE : morder, mordisquear **3 to nip in the bud** : cortar de raíz

nip[2] *n* **1** TANG : sabor *m* fuerte **2** PINCH : pellizco *m* **3** NIBBLE : mordisco *m* **4** SWALLOW : trago *m,* traguito *m* **5 there's a nip in the air** : hace fresco

nipple ['nɪpəl] *n* : pezón *m* (de una mujer), tetilla *f* (de un hombre)

nippy ['nɪpi] *adj* **-pier; -est 1** SHARP : fuerte, picante **2** CHILLY : frío <it's nippy today : hoy hace frío>

nit ['nɪt] *n* : liendre *f*

nitrate ['naɪ,treɪt] *n* : nitrato *m*

nitric acid ['naɪtrɪk] *n* : ácido *m* nítrico

nitrite ['naɪ,traɪt] *n* : nitrito *m*

nitrogen ['naɪtrədʒən] *n* : nitrógen *m*

nitroglycerin *or* **nitroglycerine** [,naɪtro'glɪsərən] *n* : nitroglicerina *f*

nitwit ['nɪt,wɪt] *n* : zonzo *m,* -za *f;* bobo *m,* -ba *f*

no[1] ['no:] *adv* : no <are you leaving?—no : ¿te vas?—no> <no less than : no menos de> <to say no : decir que no> <like it or no : quieras o no quieras>

no[2] *adj* **1** : ninguno <it's no trouble : no es ningún problema> <she has no money : no tiene dinero> **2** (*indicating a small amount*) <we'll be there in no time : llegamos dentro de poco, no tardamos nada> **3** (*expressing a negation*) <he's no liar : no es mentiroso>

no[3] *n, pl* **noes** *or* **nos** ['no:z] **1** DENIAL : no *m* <I won't take no for an answer : no aceptaré un no por respuesta> **2** : vota *f* en contra <the noes have it : se ha rechazado la moción>

nobility [no'bɪləti] *n* : nobleza *f*

noble[1] ['no:bəl] *adj* **-bler; -blest 1** ILLUSTRIOUS : noble, glorioso **2** ARISTOCRATIC : noble **3** STATELY : majestuoso, magnífico **4** LOFTY : noble, elevado <noble sentiments : sentimientos elevados>

noble[2] *n* : noble *mf,* aristócrata *mf*

nobleman ['no:bəlmən] *n, pl* **-men** [-mən, -,mɛn] : noble *m,* aristócrata *m*

nobleness ['no:bəlnəs] *n* : nobleza *f*

noblewoman ['no:bəl,wʊmən] *n, pl* **-women** [-,wɪmən] : noble *f,* aristócrata *f*

nobly ['no:bli] *adv* : noblemente

nobody[1] ['no:bədi, -,bɑdi] *n, pl* **-bodies** : don nadie *m* <he's a mere nobody : es un don nadie>

nobody[2] *pron* : nadie

nocturnal [nɑk'tərnəl] *adj* : nocturno

nocturne ['nɑk,tərn] *n* : nocturno *m*

nod[1] ['nɑd] *v* **nodded; nodding** *vi* **1** : saludar con la cabeza, asentir con la cabeza **2 to nod off** : dormirse, quedarse dormido — *vt* : inclinar (la cabeza) <to nod one's head in agreement : asentir con la cabeza>

nod[2] *n* : saludo *m* con la cabeza, señal *m* con la cabeza, señal *m* de asentimiento

node ['no:d] *n* : nudo *m* (de una planta)

nodule ['nɑ,dʒu:l] *n* : nódulo *m*

noel [no'ɛl] *n* **1** CAROL : villancico *m* de Navidad **2 Noel** CHRISTMAS : Navidad *f*

noes → **no**[3]

noise[1] ['nɔɪz] *vt* **noised; noising** : rumorear, publicar

noise[2] *n* : ruido *m*

noiseless ['nɔɪzləs] *adj* : silencioso, sin ruido

noiselessly ['nɔɪzləsli] *adv* : silenciosamente

noisemaker ['nɔɪz,meɪkər] *n* : matraca *f*

noisiness ['nɔɪzinəs] *n* : ruido *m*

noisome ['nɔɪsəm] *adj* : maloliente, fétido

noisy ['nɔɪzi] *adj* **noisier; -est** : ruidoso — **noisily** ['nɔɪzəli] *adv*

nomad[1] ['no:,mæd] → **nomadic**

nomad[2] *n* : nómada *mf*

nomadic [no'mædɪk] *adj* : nómada

nomenclature ['no:mən,kleɪtʃər] *n* : nomenclatura *f*

nominal ['nɑmənəl] *adj* **1** : nominal <the nominal head of his party : el jefe nominal de su partido> **2** TRIFLING : insignificante

nominally ['nɑmənəli] *adv* : sólo de nombre, nominalmente

nominate ['nɑmə,neɪt] *vt* **-nated; -nating 1** PROPOSE : proponer (como candidato), nominar **2** APPOINT : nombrar

nomination [ˌnɑməˈneɪʃən] *n* **1** PROPOSAL : propuesta *f,* postulación *f* **2** APPOINTMENT : nombramiento *m*

nominative¹ [ˈnɑmənət̬ɪv] *adj* : nominativo

nominative² *n or* **nominative case** : nominativo *m*

nominee [ˌnɑməˈniː] *n* : candidato *m,* -ta *f*

nonaddictive [ˌnɑnəˈdɪktɪv] *adj* : que no crea dependencia

nonalcoholic [ˌnɑnˌælkəˈhɔlɪk] *adj* : sin alcohol, no alcohólico

nonaligned [ˌnɑnəˈlaɪnd] *adj* : no alineado

nonbeliever [ˌnɑnbəˈliːvər] *n* : no creyente *mf*

nonbreakable [ˌnɑnˈbreɪkəbəl] *adj* : irrompible

nonce [ˈnɑn*t*s] *n* **for the nonce** : por el momento

nonchalance [ˌnɑnʃəˈlɑn*t*s] *n* : indiferencia *f,* despreocupación *f*

nonchalant [ˌnɑnʃəˈlɑnt] *adj* : indiferente, despreocupado, impasible

nonchalantly [ˌnɑnʃəˈlɑntli] *adv* : con aire despreocupado, con indiferencia

noncombatant [ˌnɑnkəmˈbætənt, -ˈkɑmbə-] *adj* : no combatiente *mf*

noncommissioned officer [ˌnɑnkəˈmɪʃənd] *n* : suboficial *mf*

noncommittal [ˌnɑnkəˈmɪt̬əl] *adj* : evasivo, que no se compromete

nonconductor [ˌnɑnkənˈdʌktər] *n* : aislante *m*

nonconformist [ˌnɑnkənˈfɔrmɪst] *n* : inconformista *mf,* inconforme *mf*

nonconformity [ˌnɑnkənˈfɔrmət̬i] *n* : inconformidad *f,* no conformidad *f*

noncontagious [ˌnɑnkənˈteɪdʒəs] *adj* : no contagioso

nondenominational [ˌnɑndɪˌnɑməˈneɪʃənəl] *adj* : no sectario

nondescript [ˌnɑndɪˈskrɪpt] *adj* : anodino, soso

nondiscriminatory [ˌnɑndɪˈskrɪmənəˌtori] *adj* : no discriminatorio

nondrinker [ˌnɑnˈdrɪŋkər] *n* : abstemio *m,* -mia *f*

none¹ [ˈnʌn] *adv* : de ninguna manera, de ningún modo, nada <he was none too happy : no se sintió nada contento> <I'm none the worse for it : no estoy peor por ello> <none too soon : a buena hora>

none² *pron* : ninguno, ninguna

nonentity [ˌnɑnˈɛntət̬i] *n, pl* **-ties** : persona *f* insignificante, nulidad *f*

nonessential [ˌnɑnɪˈsɛntʃəl] *adj* : secundario, no esencial

nonessentials [ˌnɑnɪˈsɛntʃəlz] *npl* : cosas *fpl* secundarias, cosas *fpl* accesorias

nonetheless [ˌnʌnðəˈlɛs] *adv* : sin embargo, no obstante

nonexistence [ˌnɑnɪgˈzɪstən*t*s] *n* : inexistencia *f*

nonexistent [ˌnɑnɪgˈzɪstənt] *adj* : inexistente

nonfat [ˌnɑnˈfæt] *adj* : sin grasa

nonfattening [ˌnɑnˈfætənɪŋ] *adj* : que no engorda

nonfiction [ˌnɑnˈfɪkʃən] *n* : no ficción *f*

nonflammable [ˌnɑnˈflæməbəl] *adj* : no inflamable

nonintervention [ˌnɑnˌɪntərˈvɛntʃən] *n* : no intervención *f*

nonmalignant [ˌnɑnməˈlɪgnənt] *adj* : no maligno, benigno

nonnegotiable [ˌnɑnnɪˈgoːʃəbəl, -ʃiə-] *adj* : no negociable

nonpareil¹ [ˌnɑnpəˈrɛl] *adj* : sin parangón, sin par

nonpareil² *n* : persona *f* sin igual, cosa *f* sin par

nonpartisan [ˌnɑnˈpɑrt̬əzən, -sən] *adj* : imparcial

nonpaying [ˌnɑnˈpeɪɪŋ] *adj* : que no paga

nonpayment [ˌnɑnˈpeɪmənt] *n* : impago *m,* falta *f* de pago

nonperson [ˌnɑnˈpərsən] *n* : persona *f* sin derechos

nonplus [ˌnɑnˈplʌs] *vt* **-plussed; -plussing** : confundir, desconcertar, dejar perplejo

nonprescription [ˌnɑnprɪˈskrɪpʃən] *adj* : disponible sin receta del médico

nonproductive [ˌnɑnprəˈdʌktɪv] *adj* : improductivo

nonprofit [ˌnɑnˈprɑfət] *adj* : sin fines lucrativos

nonproliferation [ˌnɑnprəˌlɪfəˈreɪʃən] *adj* : no proliferación

nonresident [ˌnɑnˈrɛzədənt, -ˌdɛnt] *n* : no residente *mf*

nonscheduled [ˌnɑnˈskɛˌdʒuːld] *adj* : no programado, no regular

nonsectarian [ˌnɑnˌsɛkˈtæriən] *adj* : no sectario

nonsense [ˈnɑnˌsɛn*t*s, ˈnɑn*t*sən*t*s] *n* : tonterías *fpl,* disparates *mpl*

nonsensical [nɑnˈsɛn*t*sɪkəl] *adj* ABSURD : absurdo, disparatado — **nonsensically** [-kli] *adv*

nonsmoker [ˌnɑnˈsmoːkər] *n* : no fumador *m,* -dora *f;* persona *f* que no fuma

nonstandard [ˌnɑnˈstændərd] *adj* : no regular, no estándar

nonstick [ˌnɑnˈstɪk] *adj* : antiadherente

nonstop¹ [ˌnɑnˈstɑp] *adv* : sin parar <he talked nonstop : habló sin parar>

nonstop² *adj* : directo, sin escalas <nonstop flight : vuelo directo>

nonsupport [ˌnɑnsəˈpɔrt] *n* : falta *f* de manutención

nontaxable [ˌnɑnˈtæksəbəl] *adj* : exento de impuestos

nontoxic [ˌnɑnˈtɑksɪk] *adj* : no tóxico

nonviolence [ˌnɑnˈvaɪlən*t*s, -ˈvaɪə-] *n* : no violencia *f*

nonviolent [ˌnɑnˈvaɪlənt, -ˈvaɪə-] *adj* : pacífico, no violento

noodle [ˈnuːdəl] *n* : fideo *m,* tallarín *m*

nook [ˈnʊk] *n* **:** rincón *m,* recoveco *m,* escondrijo *m* <in every nook and cranny : en todos los rincones>
noon [ˈnuːn] *n* **:** mediodía *m*
noonday [ˈnuːnˌdeɪ] *n* **:** mediodía *m* <the noonday sun : el sol de mediodía>
no one *pron* NOBODY **:** nadie
noontime [ˈnuːnˌtaɪm] *n* **:** mediodía *m*
noose [ˈnuːs] *n* **1** LASSO **:** lazo *m* **2 hangman's noose:** dogal *m,* soga *f*
nor [ˈnɔr] *conj* **:** ni <neither good nor bad : ni bueno ni malo> <nor I! : ¡ni yo tampoco!>
Nordic [ˈnɔrdɪk] *adj* **:** nórdico
norm [ˈnɔrm] *n* **1** STANDARD **:** norma *f,* modelo *m* **2** CUSTOM, RULE **:** regla *f* general, lo normal
normal [ˈnɔrməl] *adj* **:** normal — **normally** *adv*
normalcy [ˈnɔrməlsi] *n* **:** normalidad *f*
normality [nɔrˈmæləṭi] *n* **:** normalidad *f*
normalize [ˈnɔrməˌlaɪz] *vt* **:** normalizar
Norse [ˈnɔrs] *adj* **:** nórdico
north[1] [ˈnɔrθ] *adv* **:** al norte
north[2] *adj* **:** norte, del norte <the north coast : la costa del norte>
north[3] *n* **1 :** norte *m* **2 the North :** el Norte *m*
northbound [ˈnɔrθˌbaʊnd] *adv* **:** con rumbo al norte
North American *n* **:** norteamericano *m,* -na *f* — **North American** *adj*
northeast[1] [nɔrθˈiːst] *adv* **:** hacia el nordeste
northeast[2] *adj* **:** nordeste, del nordeste
northeast[3] *n* **:** nordeste *m,* noreste *m*
northeasterly[1] [nɔrθˈiːstərli] *adv* **:** hacia el nordeste
northeasterly[2] *adj* **:** nordeste, del nordeste
northeastern [nɔrθˈiːstərn] *adj* **:** nordeste, del nordeste
northerly[1] [ˈnɔrðərli] *adv* **:** hacia el norte
northerly[2] *adj* **:** del norte <a northerly wind : un viento del norte>
northern [ˈnɔrðərn] *adj* **:** norte, norteño, septentrional
Northerner [ˈnɔrðərnər] *n* **:** norteño *m,* -ña *f*
northern lights → aurora borealis
North Pole : Polo *m* Norte
North Star *n* **:** estrella *f* polar
northward [ˈnɔrθwərd] *adv & adj* **:** hacia el norte
northwest[1] [nɔrθˈwɛst] *adv* **:** hacia el noroeste
northwest[2] *adj* **:** del noroeste
northwest[3] *n* **:** noroeste *m*
northwesterly[1] [nɔrθˈwɛstərli] *adv* **:** hacia el noroeste
northwesterly[2] *adj* **:** del noroeste
northwestern [nɔrθˈwɛstərn] *adj* **:** noroeste, del noroeste
Norwegian [nɔrˈwiːdʒən] *n* **1 :** noruego *m,* -ga *f* **2 :** noruego *m* (idioma) — **Norwegian** *adj*
nose[1] [ˈnoːz] *v* **nosed; nosing** *vt* **1** SMELL **:** olfatear **2 :** empujar con el hocico <the dog nosed open the bag : el perro abrió el saco con el hocico> **3** EDGE, MOVE **:** mover poco a poco — *vi* **1** PRY **:** entrometerse, meter las narices **2** EDGE **:** avanzar poco a poco
nose[2] *n* **1 :** nariz *f* (de una persona), hocico *m* (de un animal) <to blow one's nose : sonarse las narices> **2** SMELL **:** olfato *m,* sentido *m* del olfato **3** FRONT **:** parte *f* delantera, nariz *f* (de un avión), proa *f* (de un barco) **4 to follow one's nose :** dejarse guiar por el instinto
nosebleed [ˈnoːzˌbliːd] *n* **:** hemorragia *f* nasal
nosedive [ˈnoːzˌdaɪv] *n* **1 :** descenso *m* en picada (de un avión) **2 :** caída *f* súbita (de precios, etc.)
nose–dive [ˈnoːzˌdaɪv] *vi* **:** descender en picada, caer en picada
nostalgia [nɑˈstældʒə, nə-] *n* **:** nostalgia *f*
nostalgic [nɑˈstældʒɪk, nə-] *adj* **:** nostálgico
nostril [ˈnɑstrəl] *n* **:** ventana *f* de la nariz
nostrum [ˈnɑstrəm] *n* **:** panacea *f*
nosy *or* **nosey** [ˈnoːzi] *adj* **nosier; -est :** entrometido
not [ˈnɑt] *adv* **1** (*used to form a negative*) **:** no <she is not tired : no está cansada> <not to say something would be wrong : no decir nada sería injusto> **2** (*used to replace a negative clause*) **:** no <are we going or not? : ¿vamos a ir o no?> <of course not! : ¡claro que no!>
notable[1] [ˈnoːṭəbəl] *adj* **1** NOTEWORTHY **:** notable, de notar **2** DISTINGUISHED, PROMINENT **:** distinguido, destacado
notable[2] *n* **:** persona *f* importante, personaje *m*
notably [ˈnoːṭəbli] *adv* **:** notablemente, particularmente
notarize [ˈnoːṭəˌraɪz] *vt* **-rized; -rizing :** autenticar, autorizar
notary public [ˈnoːṭəri] *n, pl* **-ries public** *or* **-ry publics :** notario *m,* -ria *f;* escribano *m,* -na *f*
notation [noˈteɪʃən] *n* **1** NOTE **:** anotación *f,* nota *f* **2 :** notación *f* <musical notation : notación musical>
notch[1] [ˈnɑtʃ] *vt* **:** hacer una muesca en, cortar
notch[2] *n* **:** muesca *f,* corte *m*
note[1] [ˈnoːt] *vt* **noted; noting 1** NOTICE **:** notar, observar, tomar nota de **2** RECORD **:** anotar, apuntar
note[2] *n* **1 :** nota *f* (musical) **2** COMMENT **:** nota *f,* comentario *m* **3** LETTER **:** nota *f,* cartita *f* **4** PROMINENCE **:** prestigio *m* <a musician of note : un músico destacado> **5** ATTENTION **:** atención *f* <to take note of : prestar atención a>

notebook [ˈnoːtˌbʊk] *n* : libreta *f,* cuaderno *m*

noted [ˈnoːt̬əd] *adj* EMINENT : renombrado, eminente, celebrado

noteworthy [ˈnoːtˌwərði] *adj* : notable, de notar, de interés

nothing[1] [ˈnʌθɪŋ] *adv* **1** : de ninguna manera <nothing daunted, we carried on : sin amilanarnos, seguimos adelante> **2 nothing like** : no...en nada <he's nothing like his brother : no se parece en nada a su hermano>

nothing[2] *n* **1** NOTHINGNESS : nada *f* **2** ZERO : cero *m* **3** : persona *f* de poca importancia, cero *m* **4** TRIFLE : nimiedad *f*

nothing[3] *pron* : nada <there's nothing better : no hay nada mejor> <nothing else : nada más> <nothing but : solamente> <they mean nothing to me : ellos me son indiferentes>

nothingness [ˈnʌθɪŋnəs] *n* **1** VOID : vacío *m,* nada *f* **2** NONEXISTENCE : inexistencia *f* **3** TRIFLE : nimiedad *f*

notice[1] [ˈnoːt̬ɪs] *vt* **-ticed; -ticing** : notar, observar, advertir, darse cuenta de

notice[2] *n* **1** NOTIFICATION : aviso *m,* notificación *f* **2** ATTENTION : atención *f* <to take notice of : prestar atención a>

noticeable [ˈnoːt̬ɪsəbəl] *adj* : evidente, perceptible — **noticeably** [-bli] *adv*

notification [ˌnoːt̬əfəˈkeɪʃən] *n* : notificación *f,* aviso *m*

notify [ˈnoːt̬əˌfaɪ] *vt* **-fied; -fying** : notificar, avisar

notion [ˈnoːʃən] *n* **1** IDEA : idea *f,* noción *f* **2** WHIM : capricho *m,* antojo *m* **3 notions** *npl* : artículos *mpl* de mercería

notoriety [ˌnoːt̬əˈraɪət̬i] *n* : mala fama *f,* notoriedad *f*

notorious [noˈtoːriəs] *adj* : de mala fama, célebre, bien conocido

notwithstanding[1] [ˌnɑtwɪθˈstændɪŋ, -wɪð-] *adv* NEVERTHELESS : no obstante, sin embargo

notwithstanding[2] *conj* : a pesar de que

notwithstanding[3] *prep* : a pesar de, no obstante

nougat [ˈnuːgət] *n* : turrón *m*

nought [ˈnɔt, ˈnɑt] → **naught**

noun [ˈnaʊn] *n* : nombre *m,* sustantivo *m*

nourish [ˈnərɪʃ] *vt* **1** FEED : alimentar, nutrir, sustentar **2** FOSTER : fomentar, alentar

nourishing [ˈnərɪʃɪŋ] *adj* : alimenticio, nutritivo

nourishment [ˈnərɪʃmənt] *n* : nutrición *f,* alimento *m,* sustento *m*

novel[1] [ˈnɑvəl] *adj* : original, novedoso

novel[2] *n* : novela *f*

novelist [ˈnɑvəlɪst] *n* : novelista *mf*

novelty [ˈnɑvəlt̬i] *n, pl* **-ties 1** : novedad *f* **2 novelties** *npl* TRINKETS : baratijas *fpl,* chucherías *fpl*

November [noˈvɛmbər] *n* : noviembre *m*

novice [ˈnɑvɪs] *n* : novato *m,* -ta *f;* principiante *mf;* novicio *m,* -cia *f*

now[1] [ˈnaʊ] *adv* **1** PRESENTLY : ahora, ya, actualmente <from now on : de ahora en adelante> <long before now : ya hace tiempo> <now and then : de vez en cuando> **2** IMMEDIATELY : ahora (mismo), inmediatamente <do it right now! : ¡hazlo ahora mismo!> **3** THEN : ya, entonces <now they were ready : ya estaban listos> **4** (*used to introduce a statement, a question, a command, or a transition*) <now hear this! : ¡presten atención!> <now what do you think of that? : ¿qué piensas de eso?>

now[2] *n* (*indicating the present time*) <until now : hasta ahora> <by now : ya> <ten years from now : dentro de 10 años>

now[3] *conj* **now that** : ahora que, ya que

nowadays [ˈnaʊəˌdeɪz] *adv* : hoy en día, actualmente, en la actualidad

nowhere[1] [ˈnoːˌ*h*wɛr] *adv* **1** : en ninguna parte, a ningún lado <nowhere to be found : en ninguna parte, por ningún lado> <you're going nowhere : no estás yendo a ningún lado, no estás yendo a ninguna parte> **2 nowhere near** : ni con mucho, nada cerca <it's nowhere near here : no está nada cerca de aquí>

nowhere[2] *n* **1** : ninguna parte *f* **2 out of nowhere** : de la nada

noxious [ˈnɑkʃəs] *adj* : nocivo, dañino, tóxico

nozzle [ˈnɑzəl] *n* : boca *f*

nuance [ˈnuːˌɑnts, ˈnjuː-] *n* : matiz *m*

nub [ˈnʌb] *n* **1** KNOB, LUMP : protuberancia *f,* nudo *m* **2** GIST : quid *m,* meollo *m*

nuclear [ˈnuːkliər, ˈnjuː-] *adj* : nuclear

nucleus [ˈnuːkliəs, ˈnjuː-] *n, pl* **-clei** [-kliˌaɪ] : núcleo *m*

nude[1] [ˈnuːd, ˈnjuːd] *adj* **nuder; nudest** : desnudo

nude[2] *n* : desnudo *m*

nudge[1] [ˈnʌdʒ] *vt* **nudged; nudging** : darle con el codo (a alguien)

nudge[2] *n* : toque *m* que se da con el codo

nudism [ˈnuːˌdɪzəm, ˈnjuː-] *n* : nudismo *m*

nudist [ˈnuːdɪst, ˈnjuː-] *n* : nudista *mf*

nudity [ˈnuːdət̬i, ˈnjuː-] *n* : desnudez *f*

nugget [ˈnʌgət] *n* : pepita *f*

nuisance [ˈnuːsənts, ˈnjuː-] *n* **1** BOTHER : fastidio *m,* molestia *f,* lata *f* **2** PEST : peste *f;* pesado *m,* -da *f fam*

null [ˈnʌl] *adj* : nulo <null and void : nulo y sin efecto>

nullify [ˈnʌləˌfaɪ] *vt* **-fied; -fying** : invalidar, anular

numb[1] [ˈnʌm] *vt* : entumecer, adormecer

numb[2] *adj* : entumecido, dormido <numb with fear : paralizado de miedo>
number[1] ['nʌmbər] *vt* **1** COUNT, INCLUDE : contar, incluir **2** : numerar <number the pages : numera las páginas> **3** TOTAL : ascender a, sumar
number[2] *n* **1** : número *m* <in round numbers : en números redondos> <telephone number : número de teléfono> **2 a number of** : varios, unos pocos, unos cuantos
numberless ['nʌmbərləs] *adj* : innumerable, sin número
numbness ['nʌmnəs] *n* : entumecimiento *m*
numeral ['nu:mərəl, 'nju:-] *n* : número *m* <Roman numeral : número romano>
numerator ['nu:mə,reɪṭər, 'nju:-] *n* : numerador *m*
numeric [nʊ'mɛrɪk, njʊ-] *adj* : numérico
numerical [nʊ'mɛrɪkəl, njʊ-] *adj* : numérico — **numerically** [-kli] *adv*
numerous ['nu:mərəs, 'nju:-] *adj* : numeroso
numismatics [,nu:məz'mæṭɪks, ,nju:-] *n* : numismática *f*
numskull ['nʌm,skʌl] *n* : tonto *m*, -ta *f*; mentecato *m*, -ta *f*; zoquete *m fam*
nun ['nʌn] *n* : monja *f*
nuptial ['nʌpʃəl] *adj* : nupcial
nuptials ['nʌpʃəlz] *npl* WEDDING : nupcias *fpl*, boda *f*
nurse[1] ['nərs] *vt* **nursed; nursing 1** SUCKLE : amamantar **2** : cuidar (de), atender <to nurse the sick : cuidar a los enfermos> <to nurse a cold : curarse de un resfriado>
nurse[2] *n* **1** : enfermero *m*, -ra *f* **2** → **nursemaid**
nursemaid ['nərs,meɪd] *n* : niñera *f*
nursery ['nərsəri] *n*, *pl* **-eries 1** *or* **day nursery** : guardería *f* **2** : vivero *m* (de plantas)
nursing home *n* : hogar *m* de ancianos, clínica *f* de reposo
nurture[1] ['nərtʃər] *vt* **-tured; -turing 1** FEED, NOURISH : nutrir, alimentar **2** EDUCATE : criar, educar **3** FOSTER : alimentar, fomentar
nurture[2] *n* **1** UPBRINGING : crianza *f*, educación *f* **2** FOOD : alimento *m*
nut ['nʌt] *n* **1** : nuez *f* **2** : tuerca *f* <nuts and bolts : tuercas y tornillos> **3** LUNATIC : loco *m*, -ca *f*; chiflado *m*, -da *f fam* **4** ENTHUSIAST : fanático *m*, -ca *f*; entusiasta *mf*
nutcracker ['nʌt,krækər] *n* : cascanueces *m*
nuthatch ['nʌt,hætʃ] *n* : trepador *m*
nutmeg ['nʌt,mɛg] *n* : nuez *f* moscada
nutrient ['nu:triənt, 'nju:-] *n* : nutriente *m*, alimento *m* nutritivo
nutriment ['nu:trəmənt, 'nju:-] *n* : nutrimento *m*
nutrition [nʊ'trɪʃən, njʊ-] *n* : nutrición *f*
nutritional [nʊ'trɪʃənəl, njʊ-] *adj* : alimenticio
nutritious [nʊ'trɪʃəs, njʊ-] *adj* : nutritivo, alimenticio
nuts ['nʌts] *adj* **1** FANATICAL : fanático **2** CRAZY : loco, chiflado *fam*
nutshell ['nʌt,ʃɛl] *n* **1** : cáscara *f* de nuez **2 in a nutshell** : en pocas palabras
nutty ['nʌṭi] *adj* **-tier; -tiest** : loco, chiflado *fam*
nuzzle ['nʌzəl] *v* **-zled; -zling** *vi* NESTLE : acurrucarse, arrimarse — *vt* : acariciar con el hocico
nylon ['naɪ,lɑn] *n* **1** : nilón *m* **2 nylons** *npl* : medias *fpl* de nilón
nymph ['nɪmpf] *n* : ninfa *f*

O

o ['o:] *n*, *pl* **o's** *or* **os** ['o:z] **1** : decimoquinta letra del alfabeto inglés **2** ZERO : cero *m*
O ['o:] → **oh**
oaf ['o:f] *n* : zoquete *m*; bruto *m*, -ta *f*
oafish ['o:fɪʃ] *adj* : torpe, lerdo
oak ['o:k] *n*, *pl* **oaks** *or* **oak** : roble *m*
oaken ['o:kən] *adj* : de roble
oar ['or] *n* : remo *m*
oarlock ['or,lɑk] *n* : tolete *m*, escálamo *m*
oasis [o'eɪsɪs] *n*, *pl* **oases** [-,si:z] : oasis *m*
oat ['o:t] *n* : avena *f*
oath ['o:θ] *n*, *pl* **oaths** ['o:ðz, 'o:θs] **1** : juramento *m* <to take an oath : prestar juramento> **2** SWEARWORD : mala palabra *f*, palabrota *f*
oatmeal ['o:t,mi:l] *n* : avena *f* <instant oatmeal : avena instantánea>
obdurate ['ɑbdʊrət, -djʊ-] *adj* : inflexible, firme, obstinado
obedience [o'bi:diənts] *n* : obediencia *f*
obedient [o'bi:diənt] *adj* : obediente — **obediently** *adv*
obelisk ['ɑbə,lɪsk] *n* : obelisco *m*
obese [o'bi:s] *adj* : obeso
obesity [o'bi:səṭi] *n* : obesidad *f*
obey [o'beɪ] *v* **obeyed; obeying** : obedecer <to obey the law : cumplir la ley>
obfuscate ['ɑbfə,skeɪt] *vt* **-cated; -cating** : ofuscar, confundir
obituary [ə'bɪtʃʊ,ɛri] *n*, *pl* **-aries** : obituario *m*, necrología *f*
object[1] [əb'dʒɛkt] *vt* : objetar — *vi* : oponerse, poner reparos, hacer objeciones
object[2] ['ɑbdʒɪkt] *n* **1** : objeto *m* **2** OBJECTIVE, PURPOSE : objetivo *m*, pro-

pósito *m* **3** : complemento *m* (en gramática)

objection [əb'dʒɛkʃən] *n* : objeción *f*

objectionable [əb'dʒɛkʃənəbəl] *adj* : ofensivo, indeseable — **objectionably** [-bli] *adv*

objective[1] [əb'dʒɛktɪv] *adj* **1** IMPARTIAL : objetivo, imparcial **2** : de complemento, directo (en gramática)

objective[2] *n* **1** : objetivo *m* **2** *or* **objective case** : acusativo *m*

objectively [əb'dʒɛktɪvli] *adv* : objetivamente

objectivity [ˌɑbˌdʒɛk'tɪvət̬i] *n, pl* **-ties** : objetividad *f*

obligate ['ɑbləˌgeɪt] *vt* **-gated; -gating** : obligar

obligation [ˌɑblə'geɪʃən] *n* : obligación *f*

obligatory [ə'blɪgəˌtori] *adj* : obligatorio

oblige [ə'blaɪdʒ] *vt* **obliged; obliging** **1** COMPEL : obligar **2** : hacerle un favor (a alguien), complacer <to oblige a friend : hacerle un favor a un amigo> **3 to be much obliged** : estar muy agradecido

obliging [ə'blaɪdʒɪŋ] *adj* : servicial, complaciente — **obligingly** *adv*

oblique [o'bliːk] *adj* **1** SLANTING : oblicuo **2** INDIRECT : indirecto — **obliquely** *adv*

obliterate [ə'blɪt̬əˌreɪt] *vt* **-ated; -ating** **1** ERASE : obliterar, borrar **2** DESTROY : destruir, eliminar

obliteration [əˌblɪt̬ə'reɪʃən] *n* : obliteración *f*

oblivion [ə'blɪviən] *n* : olvido *m*

oblivious [ə'blɪviəs] *adj* : inconsciente — **obliviously** *adv*

oblong[1] ['ɑˌblɔŋ] *adj* : oblongo

oblong[2] *n* : figura *f* oblonga, rectángulo *m*

obnoxious [ɑb'nɑkʃəs, əb-] *adj* : repugnante, odioso — **obnoxiously** *adv*

oboe ['oːˌboː] *n* : oboe *m*

oboist ['oˌboɪst] *n* : oboe *mf*

obscene [ɑb'siːn, əb-] *adj* : obsceno, indecente — **obscenely** *adv*

obscenity [ɑb'sɛnət̬i, əb-] *n, pl* **-ties** : obscenidad *f*

obscure[1] [ɑb'skjʊr, əb-] *vt* **-scured; -scuring** **1** CLOUD, DIM : oscurecer, nublar **2** HIDE : ocultar

obscure[2] *adj* **1** DIM : oscuro **2** REMOTE, SECLUDED : recóndito **3** VAGUE : oscuro, confuso, vago **4** UNKNOWN : desconocido <an obscure poet : un poeta desconocido> — **obscurely** *adv*

obscurity [ɑb'skjʊrət̬i, əb-] *n, pl* **-ties** : oscuridad *f*

obsequious [əb'siːkwiəs] *adj* : servil, excesivamente atento

observable [əb'zərvəbəl] *adj* : observable, perceptible

observance [əb'zərvənts] *n* **1** FULFILLMENT : observancia *f*, cumplimiento *m* **2** PRACTICE : práctica *f*

observant [əb'zərvənt] *adj* : observador

observation [ˌɑbsər'veɪʃən, -zər-] *n* : observación *f*

observatory [əb'zərvəˌtori] *n, pl* **-ries** : observatorio *m*

observe [əb'zərv] *v* **-served; -serving** *vt* **1** OBEY : observar, obedecer **2** CELEBRATE : celebrar, guardar (una práctica religiosa) **3** WATCH : observar, mirar **4** REMARK : observar, comentar — *vi* LOOK : mirar

obsess [əb'sɛs] *vt* : obsesionar

obsession [ɑb'sɛʃən, əb-] *n* : obsesión *f*

obsessive [ɑb'sɛsɪv, əb-] *adj* : obsesivo — **obsessively** *adv*

obsolescence [ˌɑbsə'lɛsənts] *n* : obsolescencia *f*

obsolescent [ˌɑbsə'lɛsənt] *adj* : obsolescente <to become obsolescent : caer en desuso>

obsolete [ˌɑbsə'liːt, 'ɑbsəˌ-] *adj* : obsoleto, anticuado

obstacle ['ɑbstɪkəl] *n* : obstáculo *m*, impedimento *m*

obstetric [əb'stɛtrɪk] *or* **obstetrical** [-trɪkəl] *adj* : obstétrico

obstetrician [ˌɑbstə'trɪʃən] *n* : obstetra *mf;* tocólogo *m*, -ga *f*

obstetrics [əb'stɛtrɪks] *ns & pl* : obstetricia *f*, tocología *f*

obstinacy ['ɑbstənəsi] *n, pl* **-cies** : obstinación *f*, terquedad *f*

obstinate ['ɑbstənət] *adj* : obstinado, terco — **obstinately** *adv*

obstreperous [əb'strɛpərəs] *adj* **1** CLAMOROUS : ruidoso, clamoroso **2** UNRULY : rebelde, indisciplinado

obstruct [əb'strʌkt] *vt* : obstruir, bloquear

obstruction [əb'strʌkʃən] *n* : obstrucción *f*, bloqueo *m*

obstructive [əb'strəktɪv] *adj* : obstructor

obtain [əb'teɪn] *vt* : obtener, conseguir — *vi* PREVAIL : imperar, prevalecer

obtainable [əb'teɪnəbəl] *adj* : obtenible, asequible

obtrude [əb'truːd] *v* **-truded; -truding** *vt* **1** EXTRUDE : expulsar **2** IMPOSE : imponer — *vi* INTRUDE : inmiscuirse, entrometerse

obtrusive [əb'truːsɪv] *adj* **1** IMPERTINENT, MEDDLESOME : impertinente, entrometido **2** PROTRUDING : prominente

obtuse [ɑb'tuːs, əb-, -'tjuːs] *adj* : obtuso, torpe

obtuse angle *n* : ángulo obtuso

obviate ['ɑbviˌeɪt] *vt* **-ated; -ating** : obviar, evitar

obvious ['ɑbviəs] *adj* : obvio, evidente, manifiesto

obviously ['ɑbviəsli] *adv* **1** CLEARLY : obviamente, evidentemente **2** OF COURSE : claro, por supuesto

occasion[1] [ə'keɪʒən] *vt* : ocasionar, causar

occasion[2] *n* **1** OPPORTUNITY **:** oportunidad *f,* ocasión *f* **2** CAUSE **:** motivo *m,* razón *f* **3** INSTANCE **:** ocasión *f* **4** EVENT **:** ocasión *f,* acontecimiento *m* **5 on ~ :** de vez en cuando, ocasionalmente

occasional [ə'keɪʒənəl] *adj* **:** ocasional

occasionally [ə'keɪʒənəli] *adv* **:** de vez en cuando, ocasionalmente

occidental [ˌɑksə'dɛntəl] *adj* **:** oeste, del oeste, occidental

occult[1] [ə'kʌlt, 'ɑˌkʌlt] *adj* **1** HIDDEN, SECRET **:** oculto, secreto **2** ARCANE **:** arcano, esotérico

occult[2] *n* **the occult :** las ciencias ocultas

occupancy ['ɑkjəpəntsi] *n, pl* **-cies :** ocupación *f,* habitación *f*

occupant ['ɑkjəpənt] *n* **:** ocupante *mf*

occupation [ˌɑkjə'peɪʃən] *n* **:** ocupación *f,* profesión *f,* oficio *m*

occupational [ˌɑkjə'peɪʃənəl] *adj* **:** ocupacional

occupy ['ɑkjəˌpaɪ] *vt* **-pied; -pying :** ocupar

occur [ə'kər] *vi* **occurred; occurring 1** EXIST **:** encontrarse, existir **2** HAPPEN **:** ocurrir, acontecer, suceder, tener lugar **3 :** ocurrirse <it occurred to him that. . . : se le ocurrió que. . .>

occurrence [ə'kərənts] *n* **:** acontecimiento *m,* suceso *m,* ocurrencia *f*

ocean ['oːʃən] *n* **:** océano *m*

oceanic [ˌoːʃi'ænɪk] *adj* **:** oceánico

oceanography [ˌoːʃə'nɑgrəfi] *n* **:** oceanografía *f*

ocelot ['ɑsəˌlɑt, 'oː-] *n* **:** ocelote *m*

ocher *or* **ochre** ['oːkər] *n* **:** ocre *m*

o'clock [ə'klɑk] *adv* (*used in telling time*) <it's ten o'clock : son las diez> <at six o'clock : a las seis>

octagon ['ɑktəˌgɑn] *n* **:** octágono *m*

octagonal [ɑk'tægənəl] *adj* **:** octagonal

octave ['ɑktɪv] *n* **:** octava *f*

October [ɑk'toːbər] *n* **:** octubre *m*

octopus ['ɑktəˌpʊs, -pəs] *n, pl* **-puses** *or* **-pi** [-ˌpaɪ] **:** pulpo *m*

ocular ['ɑkjələr] *adj* **:** ocular

oculist ['ɑkjəlɪst] *n* **1** OPHTHALMOLOGIST **:** oftalmólogo *m,* -ga *f;* oculista *mf* **2** OPTOMETRIST **:** optometrista *mf*

odd ['ɑd] *adj* **1 :** sin pareja, suelto <an odd sock : un calcetín sin pareja> **2** UNEVEN **:** impar <odd numbers : números impares> **3 :** y pico, y tantos <forty odd years ago : hace cuarenta y pico años> **4 :** alguno, uno que otro <odd jobs : algunos trabajos> **5** STRANGE **:** extraño, raro

oddball ['ɑdˌbɔl] *n* **:** excéntrico *m,* -ca *f;* persona *f* rara

oddity ['ɑdəṭi] *n, pl* **-ties :** rareza *f,* cosa *f* rara

oddly ['ɑdli] *adv* **:** de manera extraña

oddness ['ɑdnəs] *n* **:** rareza *f,* excentricidad *f*

odds ['ɑdz] *npl* **1** CHANCES **:** probabilidades *fpl* **2 :** puntos *mpl* de ventaja (de una apuesta) **3 to be at odds :** estar en desacuerdo

odds and ends *npl* **:** costillas *fpl,* cosas *fpl* sueltas, cachivaches *mpl*

ode ['oːd] *n* **:** oda *f*

odious ['oːdiəs] *adj* **:** odioso **— odiously** *adv*

odor ['oːdər] *n* **:** olor *m*

odorless ['oːdərləs] *adj* **:** inodoro, sin olor

odorous ['oːdərəs] *adj* **:** oloroso

odyssey ['ɑdəsi] *n, pl* **-seys :** odisea *f*

o'er ['or] → **over**

of ['ʌv, 'ɑv] *prep* **1** FROM **:** de <a man of the city : un hombre de la ciudad> **2** (*indicating character or background*) **:** de <a woman of great ability : una mujer de gran capacidad> **3** (*indicating cause*) **:** de <he died of the flu : murió de la gripe> **4** BY **:** de <the works of Shakespeare : las obras de Shakespeare> **5** (*indicating contents, material or quantity*) **:** de <a house of wood : una casa de madera> <a glass of water : un vaso de agua> **6** (*indicating belonging or connection*) **:** de <the front of the house : el frente de la casa> **7** ABOUT **:** sobre, de <tales of the West : los cuentos del Oeste> **8** (*indicating a particular example*) **:** de <the city of Caracas : la ciudad de Caracas> **9** FOR **:** por, a <love of country : amor por la patria> **10** (*indicating time or date*) <five minutes of ten : las diez menos cinco> <the eighth of April : el ocho de abril>

off[1] ['ɔf] *adv* **1** (*indicating change of position or state*) <to march off : marcharse> <he dozed off : se puso a dormir> **2** (*indicating distance in space or time*) <some miles off : a varias millas> <the holiday is three weeks off : faltan tres semanas para la fiesta> **3** (*indicating removal*) <the knob came off : se le cayó el pomo> **4** (*indicating termination*) <shut the television off : apaga la televisión> **5** (*indicating suspension of work*) <to take a day off : tomarse un día de descanso> **6 off and on :** de vez en cuando

off[2] *adj* **1** FARTHER **:** más remoto, distante <the off side of the building : el lado distante del edificio> **2** STARTED **:** empezado <to be off on a spree : irse de juerga> **3** OUT **:** apagado <the light is off : la luz está apagada> **4** CANCELED **:** cancelado, suspendido **5** INCORRECT **:** erróneo, incorrecto **6** REMOTE **:** remoto, lejano <an off chance : una posibilidad remota> **7** FREE **:** libre <I'm off today : hoy estoy libre> **8 to be well off :** vivir con desahogo, tener bastante dinero

off[3] *prep* **1** (*indicating physical separation*) **:** de <she took it off the table : lo tomó de la mesa> <a shop off the main street : una tienda al lado de la calle principal> **2 :** a la costa de, a expensas de <he lives off his sister : vive a expensas de su hermana> **3** (*indicating the suspension of an activity*) <to be off duty : estar libre> <he's off liquor : ha dejado el alcohol> **4** BELOW **:** por debajo de <he's off his game : está por debajo de su juego normal>

offal [ˈɔfəl] *n* **1** RUBBISH, WASTE **:** desechos *mpl,* desperdicios *mpl* **2** VISCERA **:** vísceras *fpl,* asaduras *fpl*

offend [əˈfɛnd] *vt* **1** VIOLATE **:** violar, atentar contra **2** HURT **:** ofender <to be easily offended : ser muy susceptible>

offender [əˈfɛndər] *n* **:** delincuente *mf;* infractor *m,* -tora *f*

offense *or* **offence** [əˈfɛnts, ˈɔˌfɛnts] *n* **1** INSULT **:** ofensa *f,* injuria *f,* agravio *m* <to take offense : ofenderse> **2** ASSAULT **:** ataque *m* **3 :** ofensiva *f* (en deportes) **4** CRIME, INFRACTION **:** infracción *f,* delito *m*

offensive¹ [əˈfɛntsɪv, ˈɔˌfɛnt-] *adj* **:** ofensivo — **offensively** *adv*

offensive² *n* **:** ofensiva *f*

offer¹ [ˈɔfər] *vt* **1 :** ofrecer <they offered him the job : le ofrecieron el puesto> **2** PROPOSE **:** proponer, sugerir **3** SHOW **:** ofrecer, mostrar <to offer resistance : ofrecer resistencia>

offer² *n* **:** oferta *f,* ofrecimiento *m,* propuesta *f*

offering [ˈɔfərɪŋ] *n* **:** ofrenda *f*

offhand¹ [ˈɔfˈhænd] *adv* **:** sin preparación, sin pensarlo

offhand² *adj* **1** IMPROMPTU **:** improvisado **2** ABRUPT **:** brusco

office [ˈɔfəs] *n* **1 :** cargo *m* <to run for office : presentarse como candidato> **2 :** oficina *f,* despacho *m,* gabinete *m* (en la casa) <office hours : horas de oficina>

officeholder [ˈɔfəsˌhoːldər] *n* **:** titular *mf*

officer [ˈɔfəsər] *n* **1** *or* **police officer :** policía *mf,* agente *mf* de policía **2** OFFICIAL **:** oficial *mf;* funcionario *m,* -ria *f;* director *m,* -tora *f* (en una empresa) **3** COMMISSIONED OFFICER **:** oficial *mf*

official¹ [əˈfɪʃəl] *adj* **:** oficial — **officially** *adv*

official² *n* **:** funcionario *m,* -ria *f;* oficial *mf*

officiate [əˈfɪʃiˌeɪt] *v* **-ated; -ating** *vi* **1 :** arbitrar (en deportes) **2 to officiate at :** oficiar, celebrar — *vt* **:** arbitrar

officious [əˈfɪʃəs] *adj* **:** oficioso

offing [ˈɔfɪŋ] *n* **in the offing :** en perspectiva

offset [ˈɔfˌsɛt] *vt* **-set; -setting :** compensar

offshoot [ˈɔfˌʃuːt] *n* **1** OUTGROWTH **:** producto *m,* resultado *m* **2** BRANCH, SHOOT **:** retoño *m,* rama *f,* vástago *m* (de una planta)

offshore¹ [ˈɔfˈʃor] *adv* **:** a una distancia de la costa

offshore² *adj* **1 :** de (la) tierra <an offshore wind : un viento que sopla de tierra> **2 :** (de) costa afuera, cercano a la costa <an offshore island : una isla costera>

offspring [ˈɔfˌsprɪŋ] *ns & pl* **1** YOUNG **:** crías *fpl* (de los animales) **2** PROGENY **:** prole *f,* progenie *f*

off-the-road [ˈɔfðəˈroːd] *adj* **:** extraoficial

often [ˈɔfən, ˈɔftən] *adv* **:** muchas veces, a menudo, seguido

oftentimes [ˈɔfənˌtaɪmz, ˈɔftən-] *or* **ofttimes** [ˈɔftˌtaɪms] → **often**

ogle [ˈoːgəl] *vt* **ogled; ogling :** comerse con los ojos, quedarse mirando a

ogre [ˈoːgər] *n* **:** ogro *m*

oh [ˈoː] *interj* **:** ¡oh!, ¡ah!, ¡ay! <oh, of course : ah, por supuesto> <oh no! : ¡ay no!> <oh really? : ¿de veras?>

ohm [ˈoːm] *n* **:** ohm *m,* ohmio *m*

oil¹ [ˈɔɪl] *vt* **:** lubricar, engrasar, aceitar

oil² *n* **1 :** aceite *m* **2** PETROLEUM **:** petróleo *m* **3** *or* **oil painting :** óleo *m,* pintura *f* al óleo **4** *or* **oil paint(s) :** óleo *m*

oilcloth [ˈɔɪlˌklɔθ] *n* **:** hule *m*

oiliness [ˈɔɪlinəs] *n* **:** lo aceitoso

oilskin [ˈɔɪlˌskɪn] *n* **1 :** hule *m* **2 oilskins** *npl* **:** impermeable *m*

oily [ˈɔɪli] *adj* **oilier; -est :** aceitoso, grasiento, grasoso <oily fingers : dedos grasientos>

ointment [ˈɔɪntmənt] *n* **:** ungüento *m,* pomada *f*

OK¹ [ˌoːˈkeɪ] *vt* **OK'd** *or* **okayed** [ˌoːˈkeɪd]; **OK'ing** *or* **okaying** APPROVE, AUTHORIZE **:** dar el visto bueno a, autorizar, aprobar

OK² *or* **okay** [ˌoːˈkeɪ] *adv* **1** WELL **:** bien **2** YES **:** sí, por supuesto

OK³ *adj* **:** bien <he's OK : está bien> <it's OK with me : estoy de acuerdo>

OK⁴ *n* **:** autorización *f,* visto *m* bueno

okra [ˈoːkrə, *South also* -kri] *n* **:** quingombó *m*

old¹ [ˈoːld] *adj* **1** ANCIENT **:** antiguo <old civilizations : civilizaciones antiguas> **2** FAMILIAR **:** viejo <old friends : viejos amigos> <the same old story : el mismo cuento> **3** (*indicating a certain age*) <he's ten years old : tiene diez años (de edad)> **4** AGED **:** viejo, anciano <an old woman : una anciana> **5** FORMER **:** antiguo <her old neighborhood : su antiguo barrio> **6** WORN-OUT **:** viejo, gastado

old² *n* **1 the old :** los viejos, los ancianos **2 in the days of old :** antaño, en los tiempos antiguos

olden [ˈoːldən] *adj* **:** de antaño, de antigüedad

old–fashioned [ˈoːldˈfæʃənd] *adj* **:** anticuado, pasado de moda

old maid *n* **1** SPINSTER **:** soltera *f* **2** FUSSBUDGET **:** maniático *m,* -ca *f;* melindroso *m,* -sa *f*

old–time [ˈoːldˈtaɪm] *adj* **:** antiguo

old–timer [ˈoːldˈtaɪmər] *n* **1** VETERAN : veterano *m*, -na *f* **2** *or* **oldster** : anciano *m*, -na *f*
old–world [ˈoːldˈwərld] *adj* : pintoresco (de antaño)
oleander [ˈoːliˌændər] *n* : adelfa *f*
oleomargarine [ˌoːlioˈmɑrdʒərən] → **margarine**
olfactory [ɑlˈfæktəri,ol-] *adj* : olfativo
oligarchy [ˈɑləˌgɑrki, ˈoːlə-] *n, pl* **-chies** : oligarquía *f*
olive [ˈɑlɪv, -ləv] *n* **1** : aceituna *f*, oliva *f* (fruta) **2** : olivo *m* (árbol) **3** *or* **olive green** : color *m* aceituna, verde *m* oliva
Olympic Games [oˈlɪmpɪk] *npl* : Juegos *mpl* Olímpicos
Omani [oˈmɑni, -ˈmæ-] *n* : omaní *mf* — **Omani** *adj*
ombudsman [ˈɑmˌbʊdzmən, ɑmˈbʊdz-] *n, pl* **-men** [-mən, -ˌmɛn] : ombudsman *m*
omelet *or* **omelette** [ˈɑmlət, ˈɑmə-] *n* : omelette *mf*, tortilla *f* de huevo
omen [ˈoːmən] *n* : presagio *m*, augurio *m*, agüero *m*
ominous [ˈɑmənəs] *adj* : ominoso, agorero, de mal agüero
ominously [ˈɑmənəsli] *adv* : de manera amenazadora
omission [oˈmɪʃən] *n* : omisión *f*
omit [oˈmɪt] *vt* **omitted; omitting 1** LEAVE OUT : omitir, excluir **2** NEGLECT : omitir <they omitted to tell us : omitieron decírnoslo>
omnipotence [ɑmˈnɪpətənts] *n* : omnipotencia *f* — **omnipotent** [ɑmˈnɪpətənt] *adj*
omnipresent [ˌɑmnɪˈprɛzənt] *adj* : omnipresente
omniscient [ɑmˈnɪʃənt] *adj* : omnisciente
omnivorous [ɑmˈnɪvərəs] *adj* **1** : omnívoro **2** AVID : ávido, voraz
on[1] [ˈɑn, ˈɔn] *adv* **1** (*indicating contact with a surface*) <put the top on : pon la tapa> <he has a hat on : lleva un sombrero puesto> **2** (*indicating forward movement*) <from that moment on : a partir de ese momento> <farther on : más adelante> **3** (*indicating operation or an operating position*) <turn the light on : prende la luz>
on[2] *adj* **1** (*being in operation*) <the radio is on : el radio está prendido> **2** (*taking place*) <the game is on : el juego ha comenzado> **3 to be on to** : estar enterado de
on[3] *prep* **1** (*indicating position*) : en, sobre, encima de <on the table : en (sobre, encima de) la mesa> <shadows on the wall : sombras en la pared> <on horseback : a caballo> **2** AT, TO : a <on the right : a la derecha> **3** ABOARD, IN : en, a <on the plane : en el avión> <he got on the train : subió al tren> **4** (*indicating time*) <she worked on Saturdays : trabajaba los sábados> <every hour on the hour : a la hora en punto> **5** (*indicating means or agency*) : por <he cut himself on a tin can : se cortó con una lata> <to talk on the telephone : hablar por teléfono> **6** (*indicating a state or process*) : en <on fire : en llamas> <on the increase : en aumento> **7** (*indicating connection or membership*) : en <on a committee : en una comisión> **8** (*indicating an activity*) <on vacation : de vacaciones> <on a diet : a dieta> **9** ABOUT, CONCERNING : sobre <a book on insects : un libro sobre insectos> <reflect on that : reflexiona sobre eso>
once[1] [ˈwʌnts] *adv* **1** : una vez <once a month : una vez al mes> <once and for all : de una vez por todas> **2** EVER : alguna vez **3** FORMERLY : antes, anteriormente
once[2] *adj* FORMER : antiguo
once[3] *n* **1** : una vez **2 at ~** SIMULTANEOUSLY : al mismo tiempo, simultáneamente **3 at ~** IMMEDIATELY : inmediatamente, en seguida
once[4] *conj* : una vez que, tan pronto como
once–over [ˌwʌntsˈoːvər, ˈwʌntsˌ-] *n* **to give someone the once–over** : echarle un vistazo a alguien
oncoming [ˈɑnˌkʌmɪŋ, ˈɔn-] *adj* : que viene
one[1] [ˈwʌn] *adj* **1** (*being a single unit*) : un, una <he only wants one apple : sólo quiere una manzana> **2** (*being a particular one*) : un, una <he arrived early one morning : llegó temprano una mañana> **3** (*being the same*) : mismo, misma <they're all members of one team : todos son miembros del mismo equipo> <one and the same thing : la misma cosa> **4** SOME : alguno, alguna; un, una <I'll see you again one day : algún día te veré otra vez> <at one time or another : en una u otra ocasión>
one[2] *n* **1** : uno *m* (número) **2** (*indicating the first of a set or series*) <from day one : desde el primer momento> **3** (*indicating a single person or thing*) <the one (girl) on the right : la de la derecha> <he has the one but needs the other : tiene uno pero necesita el otro>
one[3] *pron* **1** : uno, una <one of his friends : una de sus amigas> <one never knows : uno nunca sabe, nunca se sabe> <to cut one's finger : cortarse el dedo> **2 one and all** : todos, todo el mundo **3 one another** : el uno al otro, se <they loved one another : se amaban> **4 that one** : aquél, aquella **5 which one?** : ¿cuál?
onerous [ˈɑnərəs, ˈoːnə-] *adj* : oneroso, gravoso
oneself [ˌwʌnˈsɛlf] *pron* **1** (*used reflexively or for emphasis*) : se, sí mismo, uno mismo <to control oneself : controlarse> <to talk to oneself

: hablarse a sí mismo> <to do it one-self : hacérselo uno mismo> **2 by ~** : solo

one–sided [ˈwʌnˈsaɪdəd] *adj* **1** : de un solo lado **2** LOPSIDED : asimétrico **3** BIASED : parcial, tendencioso **4** UNILATERAL : unilateral

onetime [ˈwʌnˈtaɪm] *adj* FORMER : antiguo

one–way [ˈwʌnˈweɪ] *adj* **1** : de sentido único, de una sola dirección <a one-way street : una calle de sentido único> **2** : de ida, sencillo <a one-way ticket : un boleto de ida>

ongoing [ˈɑnˌgoːɪŋ] *adj* **1** CONTINUING : en curso, corriente **2** DEVELOPING : en desarrollo

onion [ˈʌnjən] *n* : cebolla *f*

only[1] [ˈoːnli] *adv* **1** MERELY : sólo, solamente, nomás <for only two dollars : por tan sólo dos dólares> <only once : sólo una vez, no más de una vez> <I only did it to help : lo hice por ayudar nomás> **2** SOLELY : únicamente, sólo, solamente <only he knows it : solamente él lo sabe> **3** (*indicating a result*) <it will only cause him problems : no hará más que crearle problemas> **4 if only** : ojalá, por lo menos <if only it were true! : ¡ojalá sea cierto!> <if he could only dance : si por lo menos pudiera bailar>

only[2] *adj* : único <an only child : un hijo único> <the only chance : la única oportunidad>

only[3] *conj* BUT : pero <I would go, only I'm sick : iría, pero estoy enfermo>

onset [ˈɑnˌsɛt] *n* : comienzo *m*, llegada *f*

onslaught [ˈɑnˌslɔt, ˈɔn-] *n* : arremetida *f*, embestida *f*, embate *m*

onto [ˈɑnˌtuː, ˈɔn-] *prep* : sobre

onus [ˈoːnəs] *n* : responsabilidad *f*, carga *f*

onward[1] [ˈɑnwərd, ˈɔn-] *or* **onwards** *adv* FORWARD : adelante, hacia adelante

onward[2] *adj* : hacia adelante

onyx [ˈɑnɪks] *n* : ónix *m*

ooze[1] [ˈuːz] *v* **oozed; oozing** *vi* : rezumar — *vt* **1** : rezumar **2** EXUDE : irradiar, rebosar <to ooze confidence : irradiar confianza>

ooze[2] *n* SLIME : cieno *m*, limo *m*

opal [ˈoːpəl] *n* : ópalo *m*

opaque [oˈpeɪk] *adj* **1** : opaco **2** UNCLEAR : poco claro

open[1] [ˈoːpən] *vt* **1** : abrir <open the door : abre la puerta> **2** UNCOVER : destapar **3** UNFOLD : desplegar, abrir **4** CLEAR : abrir (un camino, etc.) **5** INAUGURATE : abrir (una tienda), inaugurar (una exposición, etc.) **6** INITIATE : initiar, entablar, abrir <to open the meeting : abrir la sesión> <to open a discussion : entablar un debate> — *vi* **1** : abrirse **2** BEGIN : empezar, comenzar

open[2] *adj* **1** : abierto <an open window : una ventana abierta> **2** FRANK : abierto, franco, directo **3** UNCOVERED : descubierto, abierto **4** EXTENDED : extendido, abierto <with open arms : con los brazos abiertos> **5** UNRESTRICTED : libre, abierto **6** UNDECIDED : pendiente, por decidir, sin resolver <an open question : una cuestión pendiente> **7** AVAILABLE : vacante, libre <the job is open : el puesto está vacante>

open[3] *n* **in the open 1** OUTDOORS : al aire libre **2** KNOWN : conocido, sacado a la luz

open-air [ˈoːpənˈær] *adj* OUTDOOR : al aire libre

open-and-shut [ˈoːpənəndˈʃʌt] *adj* : claro, evidente <an open-and-shut case : un caso muy claro>

opener [ˈoːpənər] *n* : destapador *m*, abrelatas *m*, abridor *m*

openhanded [ˌoːpənˈhændəd] *adj* : generoso, liberal

openhearted [ˌoːpənˈhɑrt̬əd] *adj* **1** FRANK : franco, sincero **2** : generoso, de gran corazón

opening [ˈoːpənɪŋ] *n* **1** BEGINNING : comienzo *m*, principio *m*, apertura *f* **2** APERTURE : abertura *f*, brecha *f*, claro *m* (en el bosque) **3** OPPORTUNITY : oportunidad *f*

openly [ˈoːpənli] *adv* **1** FRANKLY : abiertamente, francamente **2** PUBLICLY : públicamente, declaradamente

openness [ˈoːpənnəs] *n* : franqueza *f*

opera [ˈɑprə, ˈɑpərə] *n* **1** : ópera *f* **2** → **opus**

opera glasses *npl* : gemelos *mpl* de teatro

operate [ˈɑpəˌreɪt] *v* **-ated; -ating** *vi* **1** ACT, FUNCTION : operar, funcionar, actuar **2 to operate on (someone)** : operar a (alguien) — *vt* **1** WORK : operar, manejar, hacer funcionar (una máquina) **2** MANAGE : manejar, administrar (un negocio)

operatic [ˌɑpəˈrætɪk] *adj* : operístico

operation [ˌɑpəˈreɪʃən] *n* **1** FUNCTIONING : funcionamiento *m* **2** USE : uso *m*, manejo *m* (de máquinas) **3** SURGERY : operación *f*, intervención *f* quirúrgica

operational [ˌɑpəˈreɪʃənəl] *adj* : operacional, de operación

operative [ˈɑpərət̬ɪv, -ˌreɪ-] *adj* **1** OPERATING : vigente, en vigor **2** WORKING : operativo **3** SURGICAL : quirúrgico

operator [ˈɑpəˌreɪt̬ər] *n* : operador *m*, -dora *f*

operetta [ˌɑpəˈrɛt̬ə] *n* : opereta *f*

ophthalmologist [ˌɑfˌθælˈmɑlədʒɪst, -θəˈmɑ-] *n* : oftalmólogo *m*, -ga *f*

ophthalmology [ˌɑfˌθælˈmɑlədʒi, -θəˈmɑ-] *n* : oftalmología *f*

opiate [ˈoːpiət, -piˌeɪt] *n* : opiato *m*

opinion [əˈpɪnjən] *n* : opinión *f*

opinionated [əˈpɪnjəˌneɪt̬əd] *adj* : testarudo, dogmático

opium [ˈoːpiəm] *n* : opio *m*

opossum [əˈpɑsəm] *n* : zarigüeya *f,* oposum *m*

opponent [əˈpoːnənt] *n* : oponente *mf;* opositor *m,* -tora *f;* contrincante *mf* (en deportes)

opportune [ˌɑpərˈtuːn, -ˈtjuːn] *adj* : oportuno — **opportunely** *adv*

opportunist [ˌɑpərˈtuːnɪst, -ˈtjuː-] *n* : oportunista *mf*

opportunity [ˌɑpərˈtuːnəti, -ˈtjuː-] *n, pl* **-ties** : oportunidad *f,* ocasión *f,* chance *m,* posibilidades *fpl*

oppose [əˈpoːz] *vt* **-posed; -posing 1** : ir en contra de, oponerse a <good opposes evil : el bien se opone al mal> **2** COMBAT : luchar contra, combatir, resistir

opposite[1] [ˈɑpəzət] *adv* : enfrente

opposite[2] *adj* **1** FACING : de enfrente <the opposite side : el lado de enfrente> **2** CONTRARY : opuesto, contrario <in opposite directions : en direcciones contrarias> <the opposite sex : el sexo opuesto, el otro sexo>

opposite[3] *n* : lo contrario, lo opuesto

opposite[4] *prep* : enfrente de, frente a

opposition [ˌɑpəˈzɪʃən] *n* **1** : oposición *f,* resistencia *f* **2 in opposition to** AGAINST : en contra de

oppress [əˈprɛs] *vt* **1** PERSECUTE : oprimir, perseguir **2** BURDEN : oprimir, agobiar

oppression [əˈprɛʃən] *n* : opresión *f*

oppressive [əˈprɛsɪv] *adj* **1** HARSH : opresivo, severo **2** STIFLING : agobiante, sofocante <oppressive heat : calor sofocante>

oppressor [əˈprɛsər] *n* : opresor *m,* -sora *f*

opprobrium [əˈproːbriəm] *n* : oprobio *m*

opt [ˈɑpt] *vi* : optar

optic [ˈɑptɪk] *or* **optical** [-tɪkəl] *adj* : óptico

optician [ɑpˈtɪʃən] *n* : óptico *m,* -ca *f*

optics [ˈɑptɪks] *npl* : óptica *f*

optimal [ˈɑptəməl] *adj* : óptimo

optimism [ˈɑptəˌmɪzəm] *n* : optimismo *m*

optimist [ˈɑptəmɪst] *n* : optimista *mf*

optimistic [ˌɑptəˈmɪstɪk] *adj* : optimista

optimistically [ˌɑptəˈmɪstɪkli] *adv* : con optimismo, positivamente

optimum[1] [ˈɑptəməm] *adj* → **optimal**

optimum[2] *n, pl* **-ma** [ˈɑptəmə] : lo óptimo, lo ideal

option [ˈɑpʃən] *n* : opción *f* <she has no option : no tiene más remedio>

optional [ˈɑpʃənəl] *adj* : facultativo, optativo

optometrist [ɑpˈtɑmətrɪst] *n* : optometrista *mf*

optometry [ɑpˈtɑmətri] *n* : optometría *f*

opulence [ˈɑpjələn*t*s] *n* : opulencia *f*

opulent [ˈɑpjələnt] *adj* : opulento

opus [ˈoːpəs] *n, pl* **opera** [ˈoːpərə, ˈɑpə-] : opus *m,* obra *f* (de música)

or [ˈɔr] *conj* **1** (*indicating an alternative*) : o (u *before words beginning with* o *or* ho) <coffee or tea : café o té> <one day or another : un día u otro> **2** (*following a negative*) : ni <he didn't have his keys or his wallet : no llevaba ni sus llaves ni su billetera>

oracle [ˈɔrəkəl] *n* : oráculo *m*

oral [ˈorəl] *adj* : oral — **orally** *adv*

orange [ˈɔrɪndʒ] *n* **1** : naranja *f,* china *f PRi* (fruto) **2** : naranja *m* (color), color *m* de china *PRi*

orangeade [ˌɔrɪndʒˈeɪd] *n* : naranjada *f*

orangutan [əˈræŋəˌtæŋ, -ˈræŋgə-, -ˌtæn] *n* : orangután *m*

oration [əˈreɪʃən] *n* : oración *f,* discurso *m*

orator [ˈɔrət̬ər] *n* : orador *m,* -dora *f*

oratorio [ˌɔrəˈtoriˌoː] *n, pl* **-rios** : oratorio *m*

oratory [ˈɔrəˌtori] *n, pl* **-ries** : oratoria *f*

orb [ˈɔrb] *n* : orbe *m*

orbit[1] [ˈɔrbət] *vt* **1** CIRCLE : girar alrededor de **2** : poner en órbita (un satélite, etc.) — *vi* : orbitar

orbit[2] *n* : órbita *f*

orbital [ˈɔrbətəl] *adj* : orbital

orchard [ˈɔrtʃərd] *n* : huerto *m*

orchestra [ˈɔrkəstrə] *n* : orquesta *f*

orchestral [ɔrˈkɛstrəl] *adj* : orquestal

orchestrate [ˈɔrkəˌstreɪt] *vt* **-trated; -trating 1** : orquestar, instrumentar (en música) **2** ORGANIZE : arreglar, organizar

orchestration [ˌɔrkəˈstreɪʃən] *n* : orquestación *f*

orchid [ˈɔrkɪd] *n* : orquídea *f*

ordain [ɔrˈdeɪn] *vt* **1** : ordenar (en religión) **2** DECREE : decretar, ordenar

ordeal [ɔrˈdiːl, ˈɔrˌdiːl] *n* : prueba *f* dura, experiencia *f* terrible

order[1] [ˈɔrdər] *vt* **1** ORGANIZE : arreglar, ordenar, poner en orden **2** COMMAND : ordenar, mandar **3** REQUEST : pedir, encargar <to order a meal : pedir algo de comer> — *vi* : hacer un pedido

order[2] *n* **1** : orden *f* <a religious order : una orden religiosa> **2** COMMAND : orden *f,* mandato *m* <to give an order : dar una orden> **3** REQUEST : orden *f,* pedido *m* <purchase order : orden de compra> **4** ARRANGEMENT : orden *m* <in chronological order : por orden cronológico> **5** DISCIPLINE : orden *m* <law and order : el orden público> **6 in order to** : para **7 out of order** : descompuesto, averiado **8 orders** *npl or* **holy orders** : órdenes *fpl* sagradas

orderliness [ˈɔrdərlinəs] *n* : orden *m*

orderly[1] [ˈɔrdərli] *adj* **1** METHODICAL : ordenado, metódico **2** PEACEFUL : pacífico, disciplinado

orderly[2] *n, pl* **-lies 1** : ordenanza *m* (en el ejército) **2** : camillero *m* (en un hospital)

ordinal [ˈɔrdənəl] *n or* **ordinal number** : ordinal *m,* número *m* ordinal
ordinance [ˈɔrdənən*t*s] *n* : ordenanza *f,* reglamento *m*
ordinarily [ˌɔrdənˈɛrəli] *adv* : ordinariamente, por lo general
ordinary [ˈɔrdənˌɛri] *adj* **1** NORMAL, USUAL : normal, usual **2** AVERAGE : común y corriente, normal **3** MEDIOCRE : mediocre, ordinario
ordination [ˌɔrdənˈeɪʃən] *n* : ordenación *f*
ordnance [ˈɔrdnən*t*s] *n* : artillería *f*
ore [ˈor] *n* : mineral *m* (metalífero), mena *f*
oregano [əˈrɛgəˌnoː] *n* : orégano *m*
organ [ˈɔrgən] *n* **1** : órgano *m* (instrumento) **2** : órgano *m* (del cuerpo) **3** PERIODICAL : publicación *f* periódica, órgano *m*
organic [ɔrˈgænɪk] *adj* : orgánico — **organically** *adv*
organism [ˈɔrgəˌnɪzəm] *n* : organismo *m*
organist [ˈɔrgənɪst] *n* : organista *mf*
organization [ˌɔrgənəˈzeɪʃən] *n* **1** ORGANIZING : organización *f* **2** BODY : organización *f,* organismo *m*
organizational [ˌɔrgənəˈzeɪʃənəl] *adj* : organizativo
organize [ˈɔrgəˌnaɪz] *vt* **-nized; -nizing** : organizar, arreglar, poner en orden
organizer [ˈɔrgəˌnaɪzər] *n* : organizador *m,* -dora *f*
orgasm [ˈɔrˌgæzəm] *n* : orgasmo *m*
orgy [ˈɔrdʒi] *n, pl* **-gies** : orgía *f*
orient [ˈoriˌɛnt] *vt* : orientar
Orient *n* **the Orient** : el Oriente
oriental [ˌoriˈɛntəl] *adj* : del Oriente, oriental
Oriental *n* : oriental *mf*
orientation [ˌoriənˈteɪʃən] *n* : orientación *f*
orifice [ˈɔrəfəs] *n* : orificio *m*
origin [ˈɔrədʒən] *n* **1** ANCESTRY : origen *m,* ascendencia *f* **2** SOURCE : origen *m,* raíz *f,* fuente *f*
original[1] [əˈrɪdʒənəl] *adj* : original
original[2] *n* : original *m*
originality [əˌrɪdʒəˈnæləti] *n* : originalidad *f*
originally [əˈrɪdʒənəli] *adv* **1** AT FIRST : al principio, originariamente **2** CREATIVELY : originalmente, con originalidad
originate [əˈrɪdʒəˌneɪt] *v* **-nated; -nating** *vt* : originar, iniciar, crear — *vi* **1** BEGIN : originarse, empezar **2** COME : provenir, proceder, derivarse
originator [əˈrɪdʒəˌneɪtər] *n* : creador *m,* -dora *f;* inventor *m,* -tora *f*
oriole [ˈoriˌoːl, -iəl] *n* : oropéndola *f*
ornament[1] [ˈɔrnəmənt] *vt* : adornar, decorar, ornamentar
ornament[2] *n* : ornamento *m,* adorno *m,* decoración *f*
ornamental [ˌɔrnəˈmɛntəl] *adj* : ornamental, de adorno, decorativo
ornamentation [ˌɔrnəmənˈteɪʃən, -mɛn-] *n* : ornamentación *f*
ornate [ɔrˈneɪt] *adj* : elaborado, recargado
ornery [ˈɔrnəri, ˈɑrnəri] *adj* **ornerier; -est** : de mal genio, malhumorado
ornithologist [ˌɔrnəˈθɑlədʒɪst] *n* : ornitólogo *m,* -ga *f*
ornithology [ˌɔrnəˈθɑlədʒi] *n, pl* **-gies** : ornitología *f*
orphan[1] [ˈɔrfən] *vt* : dejar huérfano
orphan[2] *n* : huérfano *m,* -na *f*
orphanage [ˈɔrfənɪdʒ] *n* : orfelinato *m,* orfanato *m*
orthodontics [ˌɔrθəˈdɑntɪks] *n* : ortodoncia *f*
orthodontist [ˌɔrθəˈdɑntɪst] *n* : ortodoncista *mf*
orthodox [ˈɔrθəˌdɑks] *adj* : ortodoxo
orthodoxy [ˈɔrθəˌdɑksi] *n, pl* **-doxies** : ortodoxia *f*
orthographic [ˌɔrθəˈgræfɪk] *adj* : ortográfico
orthography [ɔrˈθɑgrəfi] *n, pl* **-phies** SPELLING : ortografía *f*
orthopedic [ˌɔrθəˈpiːdɪk] *adj* : ortopédico
orthopedics [ˌɔrθəˈpiːdɪks] *ns & pl* : ortopedia *f*
orthopedist [ˌɔrθəˈpiːdɪst] *n* : ortopedista *mf*
oscillate [ˈɑsəˌleɪt] *vi* **-lated; -lating** : oscilar
oscillation [ˌɑsəˈleɪʃən] *n* : oscilación *f*
osmosis [ɑzˈmoːsɪs, ɑs-] *n* : ósmosis *f,* osmosis *f*
ostensible [ɑˈstɛn*t*səbəl] *adj* APPARENT : aparente, ostensible — **ostensibly** [-bli] *adv*
ostentation [ˌɑstənˈteɪʃən] *n* : ostentación *f,* boato *m*
ostentatious [ˌɑstənˈteɪʃəs] *adj* : ostentoso — **ostentatiously** *adv*
osteopath [ˈɑstiəˌpæθ] *n* : osteópata *f*
osteopathy [ˌɑstiˈɑpəθi] *n* : osteopatía *f*
osteoporosis [ˌɑstiopəˈroːsɪs] *n, pl* **-roses** [-ˌsiːz] : osteoporosis *f*
ostracism [ˈɑstrəˌsɪzəm] *n* : ostracismo *m*
ostracize [ˈɑstrəˌsaɪz] *vt* **-cized; -cizing** : condenar al ostracismo, marginar, aislar
ostrich [ˈɑstrɪtʃ, ˈɔs-] *n* : avestruz *m*
other[1] [ˈʌðər] *adv* **other than** : aparte de, fuera de
other[2] *adj* : otro <the other boys : los otros muchachos> <smarter than other people : más inteligente que los demás> <on the other hand : por otra parte, por otro lado> <every other day : cada dos días>
other[3] *pron* : otro, otra <one in front of the other : uno tras otro> <myself and three others : yo y tres otros, yo y tres más> <somewhere or other : en alguna parte>

otherwise[1] [ˈʌðərˌwaɪz] *adv* **1** DIFFERENTLY **:** de otro modo, de manera distinta <he could not act otherwise : no pudo actuar de manera distinta> **2** **:** eso aparte, por lo demás <I'm dizzy, but otherwise I'm fine : estoy mareado pero, por lo demás, estoy bien> **3** OR ELSE **:** de lo contario, si no <do what I tell you, otherwise you'll be sorry : haz lo que te digo, de lo contario, te arrepentirás>

otherwise[2] *adj* **:** diferente, distinto <the facts are otherwise : la realidad es diferente>

otter [ˈɑt̬ər] *n* **:** nutria *f*

ought [ˈɔt] *v aux* **:** deber <you ought to take care of yourself : deberías cuidarte>

oughtn't [ˈɔtənt] (*contraction of* **ought not**) → **ought**

ounce [ˈaʊnts] *n* **:** onza *f*

our [ˈɑr, ˈaʊr] *adj* **:** nuestro

ours [ˈaʊrz, ˈɑrz] *pron* **:** nuestro, nuestra <a cousin of ours : un primo nuestro>

ourselves [ɑrˈsɛlvz, aʊr-] *pron* **1** (*used reflexively*) **:** nos, nosotros <we amused ourselves : nos divertimos> <we were always thinking of ourselves : siempre pensábamos en nosotros> **2** (*used for emphasis*) **:** nosotros mismos, nosotras mismas <we did it ourselves : lo hicimos nosotros mismos>

oust [ˈaʊst] *vt* **:** desbancar, expulsar

ouster [ˈaʊstər] *n* **:** expulsión *f* (de un país, etc.), destitución *f* (de un puesto)

out[1] [ˈaʊt] *vi* **:** revelarse, hacerse conocido

out[2] *adv* **1** (*indicating direction or movement*) **:** para afuera <she opened the door and looked out : abrió la puerta y miró para afuera> **2** (*indicating a location away from home or work*) **:** fuera, afuera <to eat out : comer afuera> **3** (*indicating loss of control or possession*) <they let the secret out : sacaron el secreto a la luz> **4** (*indicating completion or discontinuance*) <his money ran out : se le acabó el dinero> <to turn out the light : apagar la luz> **5** OUTSIDE **:** fuera, afuera <out in the garden : afuera en el jardín> **6** ALOUD **:** en voz alta, en alto <to cry out : gritar>

out[3] *adj* **1** EXTERNAL **:** externo, exterior **2** OUTLYING **:** alejado, distante <the out islands : las islas distantes> **3** ABSENT **:** ausente **4** UNFASHIONABLE **:** fuera de moda **5** EXTINGUISHED **:** apagado

out[4] *prep* **1** (*used to indicate an outward movement*) **:** por <I looked out the window : miré por la ventana> <she ran out the door : corrió por la puerta> **2** → **out of**

out–and–out [ˈaʊtənˈaʊt] *adj* UTTER **:** redomado, absoluto

outboard motor [ˈaʊtˌbord] *n* **:** motor *m* fuera de borde

outbound [ˈaʊtˌbaʊnd] *adj* **:** que sale, de salida

outbreak [ˈaʊtˌbreɪk] *n* **:** brote *m* (de una enfermedad), comienzo *m* (de guerra), ola *f* (de violencia), erupción *f* (de granos)

outbuilding [ˈaʊtˌbɪldɪŋ] *n* **:** edificio *m* anexo

outburst [ˈaʊtˌbərst] *n* **:** arranque *m,* arrebato *m*

outcast [ˈaʊtˌkæst] *n* **:** marginado *m,* -da *f;* paria *mf*

outcome [ˈaʊtˌkʌm] *n* **:** resultado *m,* desenlace *m,* consecuencia *f*

outcrop [ˈaʊtˌkrɑp] *n* **:** afloramiento *m*

outcry [ˈaʊtˌkraɪ] *n, pl* **-cries :** clamor *m,* protesta *f*

outdated [ˌaʊtˈdeɪt̬əd] *adj* **:** anticuado, fuera de moda

outdistance [ˌaʊtˈdɪstənts] *vt* **-tanced; -tancing :** aventajar, dejar atrás

outdo [ˌaʊtˈduː] *vt* **-did** [-ˈdɪd]; **-done** [-ˈdʌn]; **-doing**; **-does** [-ˈdʌz] **:** superar

outdoor [ˈaʊtˈdor] *adj* **:** al aire libre <outdoor sports : deportes al aire libre> <outdoor clothing : ropa de calle>

outdoors[1] [ˈaʊtˈdorz] *adv* **:** afuera, al aire libre

outdoors[2] *n* **:** aire *m* libre

outer [ˈaʊt̬ər] *adj* **1 :** exterior, externo **2 outer space :** espacio *m* exterior

outermost [ˈaʊt̬ərˌmoːst] *adj* **:** más remoto, más exterior, extremo

outfield [ˈaʊtˌfiːld] *n* **the outfield :** los jardines

outfielder [ˈaʊtˌfiːldər] *n* **:** jardinero *m,* -ra *f*

outfit[1] [ˈaʊtˌfɪt] *vt* **-fitted; -fitting** EQUIP **:** equipar

outfit[2] *n* **1** EQUIPMENT **:** equipo *m* **2** COSTUME, ENSEMBLE **:** traje *m,* conjunto *m* **3** GROUP **:** conjunto *m*

outgo [ˈaʊtˌgoː] *n, pl* **outgoes :** gasto *m*

outgoing [ˈaʊtˌgoːɪŋ] *adj* **1** OUTBOUND **:** que sale **2** DEPARTING **:** saliente <an outgoing president : un presidente saliente> **3** EXTROVERTED **:** extrovertido, expansivo

outgrow [ˌaʊtˈgroː] *vt* **-grew** [-ˈgruː]; **-grown** [-ˈgroːn]; **-growing 1 :** crecer más que <that tree outgrew all the others : ese árbol creció más que todos los otros> **2 to outgrow one's clothes :** quedarle pequeña la ropa a uno

outgrowth [ˈaʊtˌgroːθ] *n* **1** OFFSHOOT **:** brote *m,* vástago *m* (de una planta) **2** CONSEQUENCE **:** consecuencia *f,* producto *m,* resultado *m*

outing [ˈaʊt̬ɪŋ] *n* **:** excursión *f*

outlandish [aʊtˈlændɪʃ] *adj* **:** descabellado, muy extraño

outlast [ˌaʊtˈlæst] *vt* **:** durar más que

outlaw[1] [ˈaʊtˌlɔ] *vt* **:** hacerse ilegal, declarar fuera de la ley, prohibir

outlaw[2] *n* : bandido *m,* -da *f;* bandolero *m,* -ra *f;* forajido *m,* -da *f*

outlay ['aʊt,leɪ] *n* : gasto *m,* desembolso *m*

outlet ['aʊt,lɛt, -lət] *n* **1** EXIT : salida *f,* escape *m* <electrical outlet : toma de corriente> **2** RELIEF : desahogo *m* **3** MARKET : mercado *m,* salida *f*

outline[1] ['aʊt,laɪn] *vt* **-lined; -lining 1** SKETCH : diseñar, esbozar, bosquejar **2** DEFINE, EXPLAIN : perfilar, delinear, explicar <she outlined our responsibilities : delineó nuestras responsabilidades>

outline[2] *n* **1** PROFILE : perfil *m,* silueta *f,* contorno *m* **2** SKETCH : bosquejo *m,* boceto *m* **3** SUMMARY : esquema *m,* resumen *m,* sinopsis *m* <an outline of world history : un esquema de la historia mundial>

outlive [,aʊt'lɪv] *vt* **-lived; -living** : sobrevivir a

outlook ['aʊt,lʊk] *n* **1** VIEW : vista *f,* panorama *f* **2** POINT OF VIEW : punto *m* de vista **3** PROSPECTS : perspectivas *fpl*

outlying ['aʊt,laɪɪŋ] *adj* : alejado, distante, remoto <the outlying areas : las afueras>

outmoded [,aʊt'mo:dəd] *adj* : pasado de moda, anticuado

outnumber [,aʊt'nʌmbər] *vt* : superar en número a, ser más numeroso de

out of *prep* **1** (*indicating direction or movement from within*) : de, por <we ran out of the house : salimos corriendo de la casa> <to look out of the window : mirar por la ventana> **2** (*being beyond the limits of*) <out of control : fuera de control> <to be out of sight : desaparecer de vista> **3** OF : de <one out of four : uno de cada cuatro> **4** (*indicating absence or loss*) : sin <out of money : sin dinero> <we're out of matches : nos hemos quedado sin fósforos> **5** BECAUSE OF : por <out of curiosity : por curiosidad> **6** FROM : de <made out of plastic : hecho de plástico>

out–of–date [,aʊtəv'deɪt] *adj* : anticuado, obsoleto, pasado de moda

out-of-door [,aʊtəv'dor] *or* **out-of-doors** [-'dorz] *adj* → **outdoor**

out-of-doors *n* → **outdoors**

outpatient ['aʊt,peɪʃənt] *n* : paciente *m* externo, paciente *f* externa

outpost ['aʊt,po:st] *n* : puesto *m* avanzado

output[1] ['aʊt,pʊt] *vt* **-putted** *or* **-put; -putting** : producir

output[2] *n* : producción *f* (de una fábrica), rendimiento *m* (de una máquina), productividad *f* (de una persona)

outrage[1] ['aʊt,reɪdʒ] *vt* **-raged; -raging 1** INSULT : ultrajar, injuriar **2** INFURIATE : indignar, enfurecer

outrage[2] *n* **1** ATROCITY : atropello *m,* atrocidad *f,* atentado *m* **2** SCANDAL : escándalo *m* **3** ANGER : ira *f,* furia *f*

outrageous [,aʊt'reɪdʒəs] *adj* **1** SCANDALOUS : escandaloso, ofensivo, atroz **2** UNCONVENTIONAL : poco convencional, extravagante **3** EXORBITANT : exorbitante, excesivo (dícese de los precios, etc.)

outright[1] [,aʊt'raɪt] *adv* **1** COMPLETELY : por completo, totalmente <to sell outright : vender por completo> <he refused it outright : lo rechazó rotundamente> **2** DIRECTLY : directamente, sin reserva **3** INSTANTLY : al instante, en el acto

outright[2] ['aʊt,raɪt] *adj* **1** COMPLETE : completo, absoluto, categórico <an outright lie : una mentira absoluta> **2** : sin reservas <an outright gift : un regalo sin reservas>

outset ['aʊt,sɛt] *n* : comienzo *m,* principio *m*

outshine [,aʊt'ʃaɪn] *vt* **-shone** [-'ʃo:n, -'ʃɒn] *or* **-shined; -shining** : eclipsar

outside[1] [,aʊt'saɪd, 'aʊt,-] *adv* : fuera, afuera

outside[2] *adj* **1** : exterior, externo <the outside edge : el borde exterior> <outside influences : influencias externas> **2** REMOTE : remoto <an outside chance : una posibilidad remota>

outside[3] *n* **1** EXTERIOR : parte *f* de afuera, exterior *m* **2** MOST : máximo *m* <three weeks at the outside : tres semanas como máximo> **3 from the outside** : desde afuera, desde fuera

outside[4] *prep* : fuera de, afuera de <outside my window : fuera de mi ventana> <outside regular hours : fuera del horario normal> <outside the law : afuera de la ley>

outside of *prep* **1** → **outside**[4] **2** → **besides**[2]

outsider [,aʊt'saɪdər] *n* : forastero *m,* -ra *f*

outskirts ['aʊt,skərts] *npl* : afueras *fpl,* alrededores *mpl*

outsmart [,aʊt'smɑrt] → **outwit**

outspoken [,aʊt'spo:kən] *adj* : franco, directo

outstanding [,aʊt'stændɪŋ] *adj* **1** UNPAID : pendiente **2** NOTABLE : destacado, notable, excepcional, sobresaliente

outstandingly [,aʊt'stændɪŋli] *adv* : excepcionalmente

outstrip [,aʊt'strɪp] *vt* **-stripped** *or* **-stript** [-'strɪpt]; **-stripping 1** : aventajar, dejar atrás <he outstripped the other runners : aventajó a los otros corredores> **2** SURPASS : aventajar, sobrepasar

outward[1] ['aʊtwərd] *or* **outwards** [-wərdz] *adv* : hacia afuera, hacia el exterior

outward[2] *adj* **1** : hacia afuera <an outward flow : un flujo hacia afuera> **2** : externo, external <outward beauty : belleza externa>

outwardly [ˈaʊtwərdli] *adv* **1** EXTERNALLY : externalmente **2** APPARENTLY : aparentemente <outwardly friendly : aparentemente simpático>

outwit [ˌaʊtˈwɪt] *vt* **-witted; -witting** : ser más listo que

ova → **ovum**

oval[1] [ˈoːvəl] *adj* : ovalado, oval

oval[2] *n* : óvalo *m*

ovary [ˈoːvəri] *n, pl* **-ries** : ovario *m*

ovation [oˈveɪʃən] *n* : ovación *f*

oven [ˈʌvən] *n* : horno *m*

over[1] [ˈoːvər] *adv* **1** (*indicating movement across*) <he flew over to London : voló a Londres> <come on over! : ¡ven acá!> **2** (*indicating an additional amount*) <the show ran 10 minutes over : el espectáculo terminó 10 minutos de tarde> **3** ABOVE, OVERHEAD : por encima **4** AGAIN : otra vez, de nuevo <over and over : una y otra vez> <to start over : volver a empezar> **5 all over** EVERYWHERE : por todas partes **6 to fall over** : caerse **7 to turn over** : poner boca abajo, voltear

over[2] *adj* **1** HIGHER, UPPER : superior **2** REMAINING : sobrante, que sobra **3** ENDED : terminado, acabado <the work is over : el trabajo está terminado>

over[3] *prep* **1** ABOVE : encima de, arriba de, sobre <over the fireplace : encima de la chimenea> <the hawk flew over the hills : el halcón voló sobre los cerros> **2** : más de <over $50 : más de $50> **3** ALONG : por, sobre <to glide over the ice : deslizarse sobre el hielo> **4** (*indicating motion through a place or thing*) <they showed me over the house : me mostraron la casa> **5** ACROSS : por encima de, sobre <he jumped over the ditch : saltó por encima de la zanja> **6** UPON : sobre <a cape over my shoulders : una capa sobre los hombros> **7** ON : por <to speak over the telephone : hablar por teléfono> **8** DURING : en, durante <over the past 25 years : durante los últimos 25 años> **9** BECAUSE OF : por <they fought over the money : se pelearon por el dinero>

overabundance [ˌoːvərəˈbʌndənts] *n* : superabundancia *f*

overabundant [ˌoːvərəˈbʌndənt] *adj* : superabundante

overactive [ˌoːvərˈæktɪv] *adj* : hiperactivo

overall [ˌoːvərˈɔl] *adj* : total, global, de conjunto

overalls [ˈoːvərˌɔlz] *npl* : overol *m*

overawe [ˌoːvərˈɔ] *vt* **-awed; -awing** : intimidar, impresionar

overbearing [ˌoːvərˈbærɪŋ] *adj* : dominante, imperioso, prepotente

overboard [ˈoːvərˌbord] *adv* : por la borda, al agua

overburden [ˌoːvərˈbərdən] *vt* : sobrecargar, agobiar

overcast [ˈoːvərˌkæst] *adj* CLOUDY : nublado

overcharge [ˌoːvərˈtʃɑrdʒ] *vt* **-charged; -charging** : cobrarle de más (a alguien)

overcoat [ˈoːvərˌkoːt] *n* : abrigo *m*

overcome [ˌoːvərˈkʌm] *v* **-came** [-ˈkeɪm]; **-come; -coming** *vt* **1** CONQUER : vencer, derrotar, superar **2** OVERWHELM : abrumar, agobiar — *vi* : vencer

overconfidence [ˌoːvərˈkɑnfədənts] *n* : exceso *m* de confianza

overconfident [ˌoːvərˈkɑnfədənt] *adj* : demasiado confiado

overcook [ˌoːvərˈkʊk] *vt* : recocer, cocer demasiado

overcrowded [ˌoːvərˈkraʊdəd] *adj* **1** PACKED : abarrotado, atestado de gente **2** OVERPOPULATED : superpoblado

overdo [ˌoːvərˈduː] *vt* **-did** [-ˈdɪd]; **-done** [-ˈdʌn]; **-doing; -does** [-ˈdʌz] **1** : hacer demasiado **2** EXAGGERATE : exagerar **3** OVERCOOK : recocer

overdose [ˈoːvərˌdoːs] *n* : sobredosis *f*

overdraft [ˈoːvərˌdræft] *n* : sobregiro *m,* descubierto *m*

overdraw [ˌoːvərˈdrɔ] *vt* **-drew** [-ˈdruː]; **-drawn** [-ˈdrɔn]; **-drawing 1** : sobregirar <my account is overdrawn : tengo la cuenta en descubierto> **2** EXAGGERATE : exagerar

overdue [ˌoːvərˈduː] *adj* **1** UNPAID : vencido y sin pagar **2** TARDY : de retraso, tardío

overeat [ˌoːvərˈiːt] *vi* **-ate** [-ˈeɪt]; **-eaten** [-ˈiːtən]; **-eating** : comer demasiado

overelaborate [ˌoːvərɪˈlæbərət] *adj* : recargado

overestimate [ˌoːvərˈɛstəˌmeɪt] *vt* **-mated; -mating** : sobreestimar

overexcited [ˌoːvərɪkˈsaɪṭəd] *adj* : sobreexcitado

overexpose [ˌoːvərɪkˈspoːz] *vt* **-posed; -posing** : sobreexponer

overfeed [ˌoːvərˈfiːd] *vt* **-fed** [-ˈfɛd]; **-feeding** : sobrealimentar

overflow[1] [ˌoːvərˈfloː] *vt* **1** : desbordar **2** INUNDATE : inundar — *vi* : desbordarse, rebosar

overflow[2] [ˈoːvərˌfloː] *n* **1** : derrame *m,* desbordamiento *m* (de un río) **2** SURPLUS : exceso *m,* excedente *m*

overfly [ˌoːvərˈflaɪ] *vt* **-flew** [-ˈfluː]; **-flown** [-ˈfloːn]; **-flying** : sobrevolar

overgrown [ˌoːvərˈgroːn] *adj* **1** : cubierto <overgrown with weeds : cubierto de malas hierbas> **2** : demasiado grande

overhand[1] [ˈoːvərˌhænd] *adv* : por encima de la cabeza

overhand[2] *adj* : por lo alto (tirada)

overhang[1] [ˌoːvərˈhæŋ] *v* **-hung** [-ˈhʌŋ]; **-hanging** *vt* **1** : sobresalir por encima de **2** THREATEN : amenazar — *vi* : sobresalir

overhang[2] [ˈoːvərˌhæŋ] *n* : saliente *mf*

overhaul [ˌoːvərˈhɔl] *vt* **1** : revisar <to overhaul an engine : revisar un motor> **2** OVERTAKE : adelantar
overhead[1] [ˌoːvərˈhɛd] *adv* : por encima, arriba, por lo alto
overhead[2] [ˈoːvərˌhɛd] *adj* : de arriba
overhead[3] [ˈoːvərˌhɛd] *n* : gastos *mpl* generales
overhear [ˌoːvərˈhɪr] *vt* **-heard; -hearing** : oír por casualidad
overheat [ˌoːvərˈhiːt] *vt* : recalentar, sobrecalentar, calentar demasiado
overjoyed [ˌoːvərˈdʒɔɪd] *adj* : rebosante de alegría
overkill [ˈoːvərˌkɪl] *n* : exceso *m,* excedente *m*
overland[1] [ˈoːvərˌlænd, -lənd] *adv* : por tierra
overland[2] *adj* : terrestre, por tierra
overlap[1] [ˌoːvərˈlæp] *v* **-lapped; -lapping** *vt* : traslapar — *vi* : traslaparse, solaparse
overlap[2] [ˈoːvərˌlæp] *n* : traslapo *m*
overlay[1] [ˌoːvərˈleɪ] *vt* **-laid** [-ˈleɪd]; **-laying** : recubrir, revestir
overlay[2] [ˈoːvərˌleɪ] *n* : revestimiento *m*
overload [ˌoːvərˈloːd] *vt* : sobrecargar
overlong [ˌoːvərˈlɔŋ] *adj* : excesivamente largo, largo y pesado
overlook [ˌoːvərˈlʊk] *vt* **1** INSPECT : inspeccionar, revisar **2** : tener vista a, dar a <a house overlooking the valley : una casa que tiene vista al valle> **3** MISS : pasar por alto **4** EXCUSE : dejar pasar, disculpar
overly [ˈoːvərli] *adv* : demasiado
overnight[1] [ˌoːvərˈnaɪt] *adv* **1** : por la noche, durante la noche **2** : de la noche a la mañana <we can't do it overnight : no podemos hacerlo de la noche a la mañana>
overnight[2] [ˈoːvərˈnaɪt] *adj* **1** : de noche <an overnight stay : una estancia de una noche> <an overnight bag : una bolsa de viaje> **2** SUDDEN : repentino
overpass [ˈoːvərˌpæs] *n* : paso *m* elevado, paso *m* a desnivel *Mex*
overpopulated [ˌoːvərˈpɑpjəˌleɪt̬əd] *adj* : sobrepoblado
overpower [ˌoːvərˈpaʊər] *vt* **1** CONQUER, SUBDUE : vencer, superar **2** OVERWHELM : abrumar, agobiar <overpowered by the heat : sofocado por el calor>
overpraise [ˌoːvərˈpreɪz] *vt* **-praised; -praising** : adular
overrate [ˌoːvərˈreɪt] *vt* **-rated; -rating** : sobrevalorar, sobrevaluar
override [ˌoːvərˈraɪd] *vt* **-rode** [-ˈroːd]; **-ridden** [-ˈrɪdən]; **-riding 1** : predominar sobre, contar más que <hunger overrode our manners : el hambre predominó sobre los modales> **2** ANNUL : anular, invalidar <to override a veto : anular un veto>
overrule [ˌoːvərˈruːl] *vt* **-ruled; -ruling** : anular (una decisión), desautorizar (una persona), denegar (un pedido)
overrun [ˌoːvərˈrʌn] *v* **-ran** [-ˈræn]; **-running** *vt* **1** INVADE : invadir **2** INFEST : infestar, plagar **3** EXCEED : exceder, rebasar — *vi* : rebasar el tiempo previsto
overseas[1] [ˌoːvərˈsiːz] *adv* : en el extranjero <to travel overseas : viajar al extranjero>
overseas[2] [ˈoːvərˌsiːz] *adj* : extranjero, exterior
oversee [ˌoːvərˈsiː] *vt* **-saw** [-ˈsɔ]; **-seen** [-ˈsiːn]; **-seeing** SUPERVISE : supervisar
overseer [ˈoːvərˌsiːər] *n* : supervisor *m,* -sora *f;* capataz *mf*
overshadow [ˌoːvərˈʃæˌdoː] *vt* **1** DARKEN : oscurecer, ensombrecer **2** ECLIPSE, OUTSHINE : eclipsar
overshoe [ˈoːvərˌʃuː] *n* : chanclo *m*
overshoot [ˌoːvərˈʃuːt] *vt* **-shot** [-ˈʃɑt]; **-shooting** : pasarse de <to overshoot the mark : pasarse de la raya>
oversight [ˈoːvərˌsaɪt] *n* : descuido *m,* inadvertencia *f*
oversleep [ˌoːvərˈsliːp] *vi* **-slept** [-ˈslɛpt]; **-sleeping** : no despertarse a tiempo, quedarse dormido
overspread [ˌoːvərˈsprɛd] *vt* **-spread; -spreading** : extenderse sobre
overstaffed [ˌoːvərˈstæft] *adj* : con exceso de personal
overstate [ˌoːvərˈsteɪt] *vt* **-stated; -stating** EXAGGERATE : exagerar
overstatement [ˌoːvərˈsteɪtmənt] *n* : exageración *f*
overstep [ˌoːvərˈstɛp] *vt* **-stepped; -stepping** EXCEED : sobrepasar, traspasar, exceder
overt [oˈvərt, ˈoːˌvərt] *adj* : evidente, manifiesto, patente
overtake [ˌoːvərˈteɪk] *vt* **-took** [-ˈtʊk]; **-taken** [-ˈteɪkən]; **-taking** : pasar, adelantar, rebasar *Mex*
overthrow[1] [ˌoːvərˈθroː] *vt* **-threw** [-ˈθruː]; **-thrown** [-ˈθroːn]; **-throwing 1** OVERTURN : dar la vuelta a, volcar **2** DEFEAT, TOPPLE : derrocar, derribar, deponer
overthrow[2] [ˈoːvərˌθroː] *n* : derrocamiento *m,* caída *f*
overtime [ˈoːvərˌtaɪm] *n* **1** : horas *fpl* extras (de trabajo) **2** : prórroga *f* (en deportes)
overtly [oˈvərtli, ˈoːˌvərt-] *adv* OPENLY : abiertamente
overtone [ˈoːvərˌtoːn] *n* **1** : armónico *m* (en música) **2** HINT, SUGGESTION : tinte *m,* insinuación *f*
overture [ˈoːvərˌtʃʊr, -tʃər] *n* **1** PROPOSAL : propuesta *f* **2** : obertura *f* (en música)
overturn [ˌoːvərˈtərn] *vt* **1** UPSET : dar la vuelta a, volcar **2** NULLIFY : anular, invalidar — *vi* TURN OVER : volcar, dar un vuelco

overuse [ˌoːvərˈjuːz] *vt* **-used; -using** : abusar de

overview [ˈoːvərˌvjuː] *n* : resumen *m,* visión *f* general

overweening [ˌoːvərˈwiːnɪŋ] *adj* **1** ARROGANT : arrogante, soberbio **2** IMMODERATE : desmesurado

overweight [ˌoːvərˈweɪt] *adj* : demasiado gordo, demasiado pesado

overwhelm [ˌoːvərˈ*h*wɛlm] *vt* **1** CRUSH, DEFEAT : aplastar, arrollar **2** SUBMERGE : inundar, sumergir **3** OVERPOWER : abrumar, agobiar <overwhelmed by remorse : abrumado de remordimiento>

overwhelming [ˌoːvərˈ*h*wɛlmɪŋ] *adj* **1** CRUSHING : abrumador, apabullante **2** SWEEPING : arrollador, aplastante <an overwhelming majority : una mayoría aplastante>

overwork [ˌoːvərˈwərk] *vt* **1** : hacer trabajar demasiado **2** OVERUSE : abusar de — *vi* : trabajar demasiado

overwrought [ˌoːvərˈrɔt] *adj* : alterado, sobreexcitado

ovoid [ˈoːˌvɔɪd] *or* **ovoidal** [oˈvɔɪdəl] *adj* : ovoide

ovulate [ˈɑvjəˌleɪt, ˈoː-] *vi* **-lated; -lating** : ovular

ovulation [ˌɑvjəˈleɪʃən, ˌoː-] *n* : ovulación *f*

ovum [ˈoːvəm] *n, pl* **ova** [-və] : óvulo *m*

owe [ˈoː] *vt* **owed; owing** : deber <you owe me $10 : me debes $10> <he owes his wealth to his father : le debe su riqueza a su padre>

owing to *prep* : debido a

owl [ˈaʊl] *n* : búho *m,* lechuza *f,* tecolote *m Mex*

own[1] *v* [ˈoːn] *vt* **1** POSSESS : poseer, tener, ser dueño de **2** ADMIT : reconocer, admitir — *vi* **to own up** : reconocer (algo), admitir (algo)

own[2] *adj* : propio, personal, particular <his own car : su propio coche>

own[3] *pron* **my** (**your, his/her, our, their**) **own** : el mío, la mía; el tuyo, la tuya; el suyo, la suya; el nuestro, la nuestra <to each his own : cada uno a lo suyo> <money of my own : mi propio dinero> <to be on one's own : estar solo>

owner [ˈoːnər] *n* : dueño *m,* -ña *f;* propietario *m,* -ria *f*

ownership [ˈoːnərˌʃɪp] *n* : propiedad *f*

ox [ˈɑks] *n, pl* **oxen** [ˈɑksən] : buey *m*

oxidation [ˌɑksəˈdeɪʃən] *n* : oxidación *f*

oxide [ˈɑkˌsaɪd] *n* : óxido *m*

oxidize [ˈɑksəˌdaɪz] *vt* **-dized; -dizing** : oxidar

oxygen [ˈɑksɪdʒən] *n* : oxígeno *m*

oyster [ˈɔɪstər] *n* : ostra *f,* ostión *m Mex*

ozone [ˈoːˌzoːn] *n* : ozono *m*

P

p [ˈpiː] *n, pl* **p's** *or* **ps** [ˈpiːz] : decimosexta letra del alfabeto inglés

pace[1] [ˈpeɪs] *v* **paced; pacing** *vi* : caminar, ir y venir — *vt* **1** : caminar por <she paced the floor : caminaba de un lado a otro del cuarto> **2 to pace a runner** : marcarle el ritmo a un corredor

pace[2] *n* **1** STEP : paso *m* **2** RATE : paso *m,* ritmo *m* <to set the pace : marcar el paso, marcar la pauta>

pacemaker [ˈpeɪsˌmeɪkər] *n* : marcapasos *m*

pacific [pəˈsɪfɪk] *adj* : pacífico

pacifier [ˈpæsəˌfaɪər] *n* : chupete *m,* chupón *m,* mamila *f Mex*

pacifism [ˈpæsəˌfɪzəm] *n* : pacifismo *m*

pacifist [ˈpæsəfɪst] *n* : pacifista *mf*

pacify [ˈpæsəˌfaɪ] *vt* **-fied; -fying 1** SOOTHE : apaciguar, pacificar **2** : pacificar (un país, una región, etc.)

pack[1] [ˈpæk] *vt* **1** PACKAGE : empaquetar, embalar, envasar **2** : empacar, meter (en una maleta) <to pack one's bag : hacer la maleta> **3** FILL : llenar, abarrotar <a packed theater : un teatro abarrotado> **4 to pack off** SEND : mandar — *vi* : empacar, hacer las maletas

pack[2] *n* **1** BUNDLE : bulto *m,* fardo *m* **2** BACKPACK : mochila *f* **3** PACKAGE : paquete *m,* cajetilla *f* (de cigarillos, etc.) **4** : manada *f* (de lobos, etc.), jauría *f* (de perros) <a pack of thieves : una pandilla de ladrones>

package[1] [ˈpækɪdʒ] *vt* **-aged; -aging** : empaquetar, embalar

package[2] *n* : paquete *m,* bulto *m*

packer [ˈpækər] *n* : empacador *m,* -dora *f*

packet [ˈpækət] *n* : paquete *m*

pact [ˈpækt] *n* : pacto *m,* acuerdo *m*

pad[1] [ˈpæd] *vt* **padded; padding 1** FILL, STUFF : rellenar, acolchar (una silla, una pared) **2** : meter paja en, rellenar <to pad a speech : rellenar un discurso>

pad[2] *n* **1** CUSHION : almohadilla *f* <a shoulder pad : una hombrera> **2** TABLET : bloc *m* (de papel) **3** *or* **lily pad** : hoja *f* grande (de un nenúfar) **4 ink pad** : tampón *m* **5 launching pad** : plataforma *f* (de lanzamiento)

padding [ˈpædɪŋ] *n* **1** FILLING : relleno *m* **2** : paja *f* (en un discurso, etc.)

paddle[1] [ˈpædəl] *v* **-dled; -dling** *vt* **1** : hacer avanzar (una canoa) con canalete **2** HIT : azotar, darle nalgadas a (con una pala o paleta) — *vi* **1** : remar (en una canoa) **2** SPLASH : chapotear, mojarse los pies

paddle[2] *n* **1 :** canalete *m,* zagual *m* (de una canoa, etc.) **2 :** pala *f,* paleta *f* (en deportes)
paddock ['pædək] *n* **1** PASTURE **:** potrero *m* **2 :** paddock *m,* cercado *m* (en un hipódromo)
paddy ['pædi] *n, pl* **-dies :** arrozal *m*
padlock[1] ['pæd,lɑk] *vt* **:** cerrar con candado
padlock[2] *n* **:** candado *m*
pagan[1] ['peɪgən] *adj* **:** pagano
pagan[2] *n* **:** pagano *m,* -na *f*
paganism ['peɪgən,ɪzəm] *n* **:** paganismo *m*
page[1] ['peɪdʒ] *vt* **paged; paging :** llamar por altavoz
page[2] *n* **1** BELLHOP **:** botones *m* **2 :** página *f* (de un libro, etc.)
pageant ['pædʒənt] *n* **1** SPECTACLE **:** espectáculo *m* **2** PROCESSION **:** desfile *m*
pageantry ['pædʒəntri] *n* **:** pompa *f,* fausto *m*
pagoda [pə'goːdə] *n* **:** pagoda *f*
paid → **pay**
pail ['peɪl] *n* **:** balde *m,* cubo *m,* cubeta *f Mex*
pailful ['peɪl,fʊl] *n* **:** balde *m,* cubo *m,* cubeta *f Mex*
pain[1] ['peɪn] *vt* **:** doler
pain[2] *n* **1** PENALTY **:** pena *f* <under pain of death : so pena de muerte> **2** SUFFERING **:** dolor *m,* malestar *m,* pena *f* (mental) **3 pains** *npl* EFFORT **:** esmero *m,* esfuerzo *m* <to take pains : esmerarse>
painful ['peɪnfəl] *adj* **:** doloroso — **painfully** *adv*
painkiller ['peɪn,kɪlər] *n* **:** analgésico *m*
painless ['peɪnləs] *adj* **:** indoloro, sin dolor
painlessly ['peɪnləsli] *adv* **:** sin dolor
painstaking ['peɪn,steɪkɪŋ] *adj* **:** esmerado, cuidadoso, meticuloso — **painstakingly** *adv*
paint[1] ['peɪnt] *v* **:** pintar
paint[2] *n* **:** pintura *f*
paintbrush ['peɪnt,brʌʃ] *n* **:** pincel *m* (de un artista), brocha *f* (para pintar casas, etc.)
painter ['peɪntər] *n* **:** pintor *m,* -tora *f*
painting ['peɪntɪŋ] *n* **:** pintura *f*
pair[1] ['pær] *vt* **:** emparejar, poner en parejas — *vi* **:** emparejarse
pair[2] *n* **:** par *m* (de objetos), pareja *f* (de personas o animales) <a pair of scissors : unas tijeras>
pajamas [pə'dʒɑməz, -'dʒæ-] *npl* **:** pijama *m,* piyama *mf*
Pakistani [,pækɪ'stæni, ,pɑkɪ'stɑni] *n* **:** paquistaní *mf* — **Pakistani** *adj*
pal ['pæl] *n* **:** amigo *m,* -ga *f;* compinche *mf fam;* chamo *m,* -ma *f Ven fam;* cuate *m,* -ta *f Mex*
palace ['pæləs] *n* **:** palacio *m*
palatable ['pælətəbəl] *adj* **:** sabroso
palate ['pælət] *n* **1 :** paladar *m* (de la boca) **2** TASTE **:** paladar *m,* gusto *m*
palatial [pə'leɪʃəl] *adj* **:** suntuoso, espléndido
palaver [pə'lævər, -'lɑ-] *n* **:** palabrería *f*
pale[1] ['peɪl] *v* **paled; paling** *vi* **:** palidecer — *vt* **:** hacer pálido
pale[2] *adj* **paler; palest 1 :** pálido <to turn pale : palidecer, ponerse pálido> **2 :** claro (dícese de los colores)
paleness ['peɪlnəs] *n* **:** palidez *f*
Palestinian [,pælə'stɪniən] *n* **:** palestino *m,* -na *f* — **Palestinian** *adj*
palette ['pælət] *n* **:** paleta *f* (para mezclar pigmentos)
palisade [,pælə'seɪd] *n* **1** FENCE **:** empalizada *f,* estacada *f* **2** CLIFFS **:** acantilado *m*
pall[1] ['pɔl] *vi* **:** perder su sabor, dejar de gustar
pall[2] *n* **1 :** paño *m* mortuario (sobre un ataúd) **2** COVER **:** cortina *f* (de humo, etc.) **3 to cast a pall over :** ensombrecer
pallbearer ['pɔl,bɛrər] *n* **:** portador *m,* -dora *f* del féretro
pallet ['pælət] *n* **1** BED **:** camastro *m* **2** PLATFORM **:** plataforma *f* de carga
palliative ['pæli,eɪtɪv, 'pæljətɪv] *adj* **:** paliativo
pallid ['pæləd] *adj* **:** pálido
pallor ['pælər] *n* **:** palidez *f*
palm[1] ['pɑm, 'pɑlm] *vt* **1** CONCEAL **:** escamotear (un naipe, etc.) **2 to palm off :** encajar, endilgar *fam* <he palmed it off on me : me lo endilgó>
palm[2] *n* **1** *or* **palm tree :** palmera *f* **2 :** palma *f* (de la mano)
Palm Sunday *n* **:** Domingo *m* de Ramos
palomino [,pælə'miː,noː] *n, pl* **-nos :** caballo *m* de color dorado
palpable ['pælpəbəl] *adj* **:** palpable — **palpably** [-bli] *adv*
palpitate ['pælpə,teɪt] *vi* **-tated; -tating :** palpitar
palpitation [,pælpə'teɪʃən] *n* **:** palpitación *f*
palsy ['pɔlzi] *n, pl* **-sies 1 :** parálisis *f* **2** → **cerebral palsy**
paltry ['pɔltri] *adj* **-trier; -est :** mísero, mezquino, insignificante <a paltry excuse : una mala excusa>
pampas ['pæmpəz, 'pɑmpəs] *npl* **:** pampa *f*
pamper ['pæmpər] *vt* **:** mimar, consentir, chiquear *Mex*
pamphlet ['pæmpflət] *n* **:** panfleto *m,* folleto *m*
pan[1] ['pæn] *vt* **panned; panning** CRITICIZE **:** poner por los suelos — *vi* **to pan for gold :** cribar el oro con batea, lavar oro
pan[2] *n* **1 :** cacerola *f,* cazuela *f* **2 frying pan :** sartén *mf,* freidera *f Mex*
panacea [,pænə'siːə] *n* **:** panacea *f*
Panamanian [,pænə'meɪniən] *n* **:** panameño *m,* -ña *f* — **Panamanian** *adj*
pancake ['pæn,keɪk] *n* **:** panqueque *m*

pancreas ['pæŋkriəs, 'pæn-] *n* : páncreas *m*
panda ['pændə] *n* : panda *mf*
pandemonium [ˌpændə'moːniəm] *n* : pandemonio *m,* pandemónium *m*
pander ['pændər] *vi* **to pander to** : satisfacer, complacer (a alguien) <to pander to popular taste : satisfacer el gusto popular>
pane ['peɪn] *n* : cristal *m,* vidrio *m*
panel[1] ['pænəl] *vt* **-eled** *or* **-elled; -eling** *or* **-elling** : adornar con paneles
panel[2] *n* **1** : lista *f* de nombres (de un jurado, etc.) **2** GROUP : panel *m,* grupo *m* <discussion panel : panel de discusión> **3** : panel *m* (de una pared, etc.) **4 instrument panel** : tablero *m* de instrumentos
paneling ['pænəlɪŋ] *n* : paneles *mpl*
pang ['pæŋ] *n* : puntada *f,* punzada *f*
panic[1] ['pænɪk] *v* **-icked; -icking** *vt* : llenar de pánico — *vi* : ser presa de pánico
panic[2] *n* : pánico *m*
panicky ['pænɪki] *adj* : presa de pánico
panorama [ˌpænə'ræmə, -'rɑ-] *n* : panorama *m*
panoramic [ˌpænə'ræmɪk, -'rɑ-] *adj* : panorámico
pansy ['pænzi] *n, pl* **-sies** : pensamiento *m*
pant[1] ['pænt] *vi* : jadear, resoplar
pant[2] *n* : jadeo *m,* resoplo *m*
pantaloons [ˌpæntə'luːnz] → **pants**
panther ['pænθər] *n* : pantera *f*
panties ['pæntiz] *npl* : calzones *mpl,* pantaletas *fpl*
pantomime[1] ['pæntəˌmaɪm] *v* **-mimed; -miming** *vt* : representar mediante la pantomima — *vi* : hacer la mímica
pantomime[2] *n* : pantomima *f*
pantry ['pæntri] *n, pl* **-tries** : despensa *f*
pants ['pænts] *npl* **1** TROUSERS : pantalón *m,* pantalones *mpl* **2** → **panties**
pap ['pæp] *n* : papilla *f* (para bebés, etc.)
papal ['peɪpəl] *adj* : papal
papaya [pə'paɪə] *n* : papaya *f* (fruta)
paper[1] ['peɪpər] *vt* WALLPAPER : empapelar
paper[2] *adj* : de papel
paper[3] *n* **1** : papel *m* <a piece of paper : un papel> **2** DOCUMENT : papel *m,* documento *m* **3** NEWSPAPER : periódico *m,* diario *m*
paperback ['peɪpərˌbæk] *n* : libro *m* en rústica
paper clip *n* : clip *m,* sujetapapeles *m*
paperweight ['peɪpərˌweɪt] *n* : pisapapeles *m*
papery ['peɪpəri] *adj* : parecido al papel
papier–mâché [ˌpeɪpərmə'ʃeɪ, ˌpæˌpjeɪmæ'ʃeɪ] *n* : papel *m* maché
papoose [pæ'puːs, pə-] *n* : niño *m,* -ña *f* de los indios norteamericanos
paprika [pə'priːkə, pæ-] *n* : pimentón *m,* paprika *f*
papyrus [pə'paɪrəs] *n, pl* **-ruses** *or* **-ri** [-ri, -ˌraɪ] : papiro *m*
par ['pɑr] *n* **1** VALUE : valor *m* (nominal), par *f* <below par : debajo de la par> **2** EQUALITY : igualdad *f* <to be on a par with : estar al mismo nivel que> **3** : par *m* (en golf)
parable ['pærəbəl] *n* : parábola *f*
parachute[1] ['pærəˌʃuːt] *vi* **-chuted; -chuting** : lanzarse en paracaídas
parachute[2] *n* : paracaídas *m*
parachutist ['pærəˌʃuːtɪst] *n* : paracaidista *mf*
parade[1] [pə'reɪd] *vi* **-raded; -rading 1** MARCH : desfilar **2** SHOW OFF : pavonearse, lucirse
parade[2] *n* **1** PROCESSION : desfile *m* **2** DISPLAY : alarde *m*
paradigm ['pærəˌdaɪm] *n* : paradigma *m*
paradise ['pærəˌdaɪs, -ˌdaɪz] *n* : paraíso *m*
paradox ['pærəˌdɑks] *n* : paradoja *f*
paradoxical [ˌpærə'dɑksɪkəl] *adj* : paradójico — **paradoxically** *adv*
paraffin ['pærəfən] *n* : parafina *f*
paragraph[1] ['pærəˌgræf] *vt* : dividir en párrafos
paragraph[2] *n* : párrafo *m,* acápite *m*
Paraguayan [ˌpærə'gwaɪən, -'gweɪ-] *n* : paraguayo *m,* -ya *f* — **Paraguayan** *adj*
parakeet ['pærəˌkiːt] *n* : periquito *m*
parallel[1] ['pærəˌlɛl, -ləl] *vt* **1** MATCH, RESEMBLE : ser paralelo a, ser análogo a, corresponder con **2** : extenderse en línea paralela con <the road parallels the river : el camino se extiende a lo largo del río>
parallel[2] *adj* : paralelo
parallel[3] *n* **1** : línea *f* paralela, superficie *f* paralela **2** : paralelo *m* (en geografía) **3** SIMILARITY : paralelismo *m,* semejanza *f*
parallelogram [ˌpærə'lɛləˌgræm] *n* : paralelogramo *m*
paralysis [pə'ræləsɪs] *n, pl* **-yses** [-ˌsiːz] : parálisis *f*
paralyze ['pærəˌlaɪz] *vt* **-lyzed; -lyzing** : paralizar
parameter [pə'ræmətər] *n* : parámetro *m*
paramount ['pærəˌmaʊnt] *adj* : supremo <of paramount importance : de suma importancia>
paranoia [ˌpærə'nɔɪə] *n* : paranoia *f*
paranoid ['pærəˌnɔɪd] *adj* : paranoico
parapet ['pærəpət, -ˌpɛt] *n* : parapeto *m*
paraphernalia [ˌpærəfə'neɪljə, -fər-] *ns & pl* : parafernalia *f*
paraphrase[1] ['pærəˌfreɪz] *vt* **-phrased; -phrasing** : parafrasear
paraphrase[2] *n* : paráfrasis *f*
paraplegic[1] [ˌpærə'pliːdʒɪk] *adj* : parapléjico
paraplegic[2] *n* : parapléjico *m,* -ca *f*

parasite ['pærə,saɪt] *n* : parásito *m*
parasitic [,pærə'sɪtɪk] *adj* : parasitario
parasol ['pærə,sɔl] *n* : sombrilla *f*, quitasol *m*, parasol *m*
paratrooper ['pærə,truːpər] *n* : paracaidista *mf* (militar)
parboil ['pɑr,bɔɪl] *vt* : sancochar, cocer a medias
parcel¹ ['pɑrsəl] *vt* **-celed** *or* **-celled; -celing** *or* **-celling** *or* **to parcel out** : repartir, parcelar (tierras)
parcel² *n* **1** LOT : parcela *f*, lote *m* **2** PACKAGE : paquete *m*, bulto *m*
parch ['pɑrtʃ] *vt* : resecar
parchment ['pɑrtʃmənt] *n* : pergamino *m*
pardon¹ ['pɑrdən] *vt* **1** FORGIVE : perdonar, disculpar <pardon me! : ¡perdone!, ¡disculpe la molestia!> **2** REPRIEVE : indultar (a un delincuente)
pardon² *n* **1** FORGIVENESS : perdón *m* **2** REPRIEVE : indulto *m*
pardonable ['pɑrdənəbəl] *adj* : perdonable, disculpable
pare ['pær] *vt* **pared; paring 1** PEEL : pelar **2** TRIM : recortar **3** REDUCE : reducir <he pared it (down) to 50 pages : lo redujo a 50 páginas>
parent ['pærənt] *n* **1** : madre *f*, padre *m* **2 parents** *npl* : padres *mpl*
parentage ['pærəntɪdʒ] *n* : linaje *m*, abolengo *m*, origen *m*
parental [pə'rɛntəl] *adj* : de los padres
parenthesis [pə'rɛnθəsɪs] *n*, *pl* **-theses** [-,siːz] : paréntesis *m*
parenthetic [,pærən'θɛtɪk] *or* **parenthetical** [-tɪkəl] *adj* : parentético — **parenthetically** [-tɪkli] *adv*
parenthood ['pærənt,hʊd] *n* : paternidad *f*
parfait [pɑr'feɪ] *n* : postre *m* elaborado con frutas y helado
pariah [pə'raɪə] *n* : paria *mf*
parish ['pærɪʃ] *n* : parroquia *f*
parishioner [pə'rɪʃənər] *n* : feligrés *m*, -gresa *f*
parity ['pærəti] *n*, *pl* **-ties** : paridad *f*
park¹ ['pɑrk] *vt* : estacionar, parquear, aparcar *Spain* — *vi* : estacionarse, parquearse, aparcar *Spain*
park² *n* : parque *m*
parka ['pɑrkə] *n* : parka *f*
parkway ['pɑrk,weɪ] *n* : carretera *f* ajardinada, bulevar *m*
parley¹ ['pɑrli] *vi* : parlamentar, negociar
parley² *n*, *pl* **-leys** : negociación *f*, parlamento *m*
parliament ['pɑrləmənt, 'pɑrljə-] *n* : parlamento *m*
parliamentary [,pɑrlə'mɛntəri, ,pɑrljə-] *adj* : parlamentario
parlor ['pɑrlər] *n* **1** : sala *f*, salón *m* (en una casa) **2** : salón *m* <beauty parlor : salón de belleza> **3 funeral parlor** : funeraria *f*
parochial [pə'roːkiəl] *adj* **1** : parroquial **2** PROVINCIAL : pueblerino, de miras estrechas
parody¹ ['pærədi] *vt* **-died; -dying** : parodiar
parody² *n*, *pl* **-dies** : parodia *f*
parole [pə'roːl] *n* : libertad *f* condicional
paroxysm ['pærək,sɪzəm, pə'rɑk-] *n* : paroxismo *m*
parquet ['pɑr,keɪ, pɑr'keɪ] *n* : parquet *m*, parqué *m*
parrakeet → **parakeet**
parrot ['pærət] *n* : loro *m*, papagayo *m*
parry¹ ['pæri] *v* **-ried; -rying** *vi* : parar un golpe — *vt* EVADE : esquivar (una pregunta, etc.)
parry² *n*, *pl* **-ries** : parada *f*
parsimonious [,pɑrsə'moːniəs] *adj* : tacaño, mezquino
parsley ['pɑrsli] *n* : perejil *m*
parsnip ['pɑrsnɪp] *n* : chirivía *f*
parson ['pɑrsən] *n* : pastor *m*, -tora *f*; clérigo *m*
parsonage ['pɑrsənɪdʒ] *n* : rectoría *f*, casa *f* del párroco
part¹ ['pɑrt] *vi* **1** SEPARATE : separarse, despedirse <we should part as friends : debemos separarnos amistosamente> **2** OPEN : abrirse <the curtains parted : las cortinas se abrieron> **3 to part with** : dehacerse de — *vt* **1** SEPARATE : separar **2 to part one's hair** : hacerse la raya, peinarse con raya
part² *n* **1** SECTION, SEGMENT : parte *f*, sección *f* **2** PIECE : pieza *f* (de una máquina, etc.) **3** ROLE : papel *m* **4** : raya *f* (del pelo)
partake [pɑr'teɪk, pər-] *vi* **-took** [-'tʊk]; **-taken** [-'teɪkən]; **-taking 1 to partake of** CONSUME : comer, beber, tomar **2 to partake in** : participar en (una actividad, etc.)
partial ['pɑrʃəl] *adj* **1** BIASED : parcial, tendencioso **2** INCOMPLETE : parcial, incompleto **3 to be partial to** : ser aficionado a
partiality [,pɑrʃi'æləti] *n*, *pl* **-ties** : parcialidad *f*
partially ['pɑrʃəli] *adv* : parcialmente
participant [pər'tɪsəpənt, pɑr-] *n* : participante *mf*
participate [pər'tɪsə,peɪt, pɑr-] *vi* **-pated; -pating** : participar
participation [pər,tɪsə'peɪʃən, pɑr-] *n* : participación *f*
participle ['pɑrtə,sɪpəl] *n* : participio *m*
particle ['pɑrtɪkəl] *n* : partícula *f*
particular¹ [pɑr'tɪkjələr] *adj* **1** SPECIFIC : particular, en particular <this particular person : esta persona en particular> **2** SPECIAL : particular, especial <with particular emphasis : con un énfasis especial> **3** FUSSY : exigente, maniático <to be very particular : ser muy especial> <I'm not particular : me da igual>
particular² *n* **1** DETAIL : detalle *m*, sentido *m* **2 in particular** : en particular, en especial

particularly [pɑr'tɪkjələrli] *adv* **1** ESPECIALLY : particularmente, especialmente **2** SPECIFICALLY : específicamente, en especial

partisan ['pɑrtəzən, -sən] *n* **1** ADHERENT : partidario *m,* -ria *f* **2** GUERRILLA : partisano *m,* -na *f;* guerrillero *m,* -ra *f*

partition[1] [pər'tɪʃən, pɑr-] *vt* : dividir <to partition off (a room) : dividir con un tabique>

partition[2] *n* **1** DISTRIBUTION : partición *f,* división *f,* reparto *m* **2** DIVIDER : tabique *m,* mampara *f,* biombo *m*

partly ['pɑrtli] *adv* : en parte, parcialmente

partner ['pɑrtnər] *n* **1** COMPANION : compañero *m,* -ra *f* **2** : pareja *f* (en un juego, etc.) <dancing partner : pareja de baile> **3** SPOUSE : cónyuge *mf* **4** *or* **business partner** : socio *m,* -cia *f;* asociado *m,* -da *f*

partnership ['pɑrtnər,ʃɪp] *n* **1** ASSOCIATION : asociación *f,* compañerismo *m* **2** : sociedad *f* (de negociantes) <to form a partnership : asociarse>

part of speech : categoría *f* gramatical

partridge ['pɑrtrɪdʒ] *n, pl* **-tridge** *or* **-tridges** : perdiz *f*

party ['pɑrti] *n, pl* **-ties** **1** : partido *m* (político) **2** PARTICIPANT : parte *f,* participante *mf* **3** GROUP : grupo *m* (de personas) **4** GATHERING : fiesta *f* <to throw a party : dar una fiesta>

parvenu ['pɑrvə,nu:, -,nju:] *n* : advenedizo *m,* -za *f*

pass[1] ['pæs] *vi* **1** : pasar, cruzarse <a car passed by : pasó un coche> <we passed in the hallway : nos cruzamos en el pasillo> **2** CEASE : pasarse <the pain passed : se pasó el dolor> **3** ELAPSE : pasar, transcurrir **4** PROCEED : pasar <let me pass : déjame pasar> **5** HAPPEN : pasar, ocurrir **6** : pasar, aprobar (en un examen) **7** RULE : fallar <the jury passed on the case : el jurado falló en el caso> **8** *or* **to pass down** : pasar <the throne passed to his son : el trono pasó a su hijo> **9** **to let pass** OVERLOOK : pasar por alto **10** **to pass as** : pasar por **11** **to pass away** *or* **to pass on** DIE : fallecer, morir — *vt* **1** : pasar por <they passed the house : pasaron por la casa> **2** OVERTAKE : pasar, adelantar **3** SPEND : pasar (tiempo) **4** HAND : pasar <pass me the salt : pásame la sal> **5** : aprobar (un examen, una ley)

pass[2] *n* **1** CROSSING, GAP : paso *m,* desfiladero *m,* puerto *m* <mountain pass : puerto de montaña> **2** PERMIT : pase *m,* permiso *m* **3** : pase *m* (en deportes) **4** SITUATION : situación *f* (difícil) <things have come to a pretty pass! : ¡hasta dónde hemos llegado!>

passable ['pæsəbəl] *adj* **1** ADEQUATE : adecuado, pasable **2** : transitable (dícese de un camino, etc.)

passably ['pæsəbli] *adv* : pasablemente

passage ['pæsɪdʒ] *n* **1** PASSING : paso *m* <the passage of time : el paso del tiempo> **2** PASSAGEWAY : pasillo *m* (dentro de un edificio), pasaje *m* (entre edificios) **3** VOYAGE : travesía *f* (por el mar), viaje *m* <to grant safe passage : dar un salvoconducto> **4** SECTION : pasaje *m* (en música o literatura)

passageway ['pæsɪdʒ,weɪ] *n* : pasillo *m,* pasadizo *m,* corredor *m*

passbook ['pæs,bʊk] *n* BANKBOOK : libreta *f* de ahorros

passé [pæ'seɪ] *adj* : pasado de moda

passenger ['pæsəndʒər] *n* : pasajero *m,* -ra *f*

passerby [,pæsər'baɪ, 'pæsər,-] *n, pl* **passersby** : transeúnte *mf*

passing ['pæsɪŋ] *n* DEATH : fallecimiento *m*

passion ['pæʃən] *n* : pasión *f,* ardor *m*

passionate ['pæʃənət] *adj* **1** IRASCIBLE : irascible, iracundo **2** ARDENT : apasionado, ardiente, ferviente, fogoso

passionately ['pæʃənətli] *adv* : apasionadamente, fervientemente, con pasión

passive[1] ['pæsɪv] *adj* : pasivo — **passively** *adv*

passive[2] *n* : voz *f* pasiva (en gramática)

Passover ['pæs,o:vər] *n* : Pascua *f* (en el judaísmo)

passport ['pæs,port] *n* : pasaporte *m*

password ['pæs,wərd] *n* : contraseña *f*

past[1] ['pæst] *adv* : por delante <he drove past : pasamos en coche>

past[2] *adj* **1** AGO : hace <10 years past : hace 10 años> **2** LAST : último <the past few months : los últimos meses> **3** BYGONE : pasado <in past times : en tiempos pasados> **4** : pasado (en gramática)

past[3] *n* : pasado *m*

past[4] *prep* **1** BY : por, por delante de <he ran past the house : pasó por la casa corriendo> **2** BEYOND : más allá de <just past the corner : un poco más allá de la esquina> <we went past the exit : pasamos la salida> **3** AFTER : despúes de <past noon : después del mediodía> <half past two : las dos y media>

pasta ['pɑstə, 'pæs-] *n* : pasta *f*

paste[1] ['peɪst] *vt* **pasted; pasting** : pegar (con engrudo)

paste[2] *n* **1** : pasta *f* <tomato paste : pasta de tomate> **2** : engrudo *m* (para pegar)

pasteboard ['peɪst,bord] *n* : cartón *m,* cartulina *f*

pastel [pæ'stɛl] *n* : pastel *m* — **pastel** *adj*

pasteurization [,pæstʃərə'zeɪʃən, ,pæstjə-] *n* : pasteurización *f*

pasteurize ['pæstʃə,raɪz, 'pæstjə-] *vt* **-ized; -izing** : pasteurizar

pastime ['pæs,taɪm] *n* : pasatiempo *m*

pastor ['pæstər] *n* : pastor *m,* -tora *f*

pastoral [ˈpæstərəl] *adj* : pastoral
past participle *n* : participio *m* pasado
pastry [ˈpeɪstri] *n, pl* **-ries 1** DOUGH : pasta *f,* masa *f* **2 pastries** *npl* : pasteles *mpl*
pasture[1] [ˈpæstʃər] *v* **-tured; -turing** *vi* GRAZE : pacer, pastar — *vt* : apacentar, pastar
pasture[2] *n* : pastizal *m,* potrero *m,* pasto *m*
pasty [ˈpeɪsti] *adj* **pastier; -est 1** : pastoso (en consistencia) **2** PALLID : pálido
pat[1] [ˈpæt] *vt* **patted; patting** : dar palmaditas a, tocar
pat[2] *adv* : de memoria <to have down pat : saberse de memoria>
pat[3] *adj* **1** APT : apto, apropiado **2** GLIB : fácil **3** UNYIELDING : firme <to stand pat : mantenerse firme>
pat[4] *n* **1** TAP : golpecito *m,* palmadita *f* <a pat on the back : una palmadita en la espalda> **2** CARESS : caricia *f* **3** : porción *f* <a pat of butter : una porción de mantequilla>
patch[1] [ˈpætʃ] *vt* **1** MEND, REPAIR : remender, parchar, ponerle un parche a **2 to patch together** IMPROVISE : confeccionar, improvisar **3 to patch up** : arreglar <they patched things up : hicieron las paces>
patch[2] *n* **1** : parche *m,* remiendo *m* (para la ropa) <eye patch : parche para el ojo> **2** PIECE : mancha *f,* trozo *m* <a patch of sky : un trozo de cielo> **3** PLOT : parcela *f,* terreno *m* <cabbage patch : parcela de repollos>
patchwork [ˈpætʃˌwərk] *n* : labor *f* de retazos
patchy [ˈpætʃi] *adj* **patchier; -est 1** IRREGULAR : irregular, desigual **2** INCOMPLETE : parcial, incompleto
patent[1] [ˈpætənt] *vt* : patentar
patent[2] *adj* [ˈpætənt, ˈpeɪt-] **1** OBVIOUS : patente, evidente **2** [ˈpæt-] PATENTED : patentado
patent[3] [ˈpætənt] *n* : patente *f*
patently [ˈpætəntli] *adv* : patentemente, evidentemente
paternal [pəˈtərnəl] *adj* **1** FATHERLY : paternal **2** : paterno <paternal grandfather : abuelo paterno>
paternity [pəˈtərnəṭi] *n* : paternidad *f*
path [ˈpæθ, ˈpaθ] *n* **1** TRACK, TRAIL : camino *m,* sendero *m,* senda *f* **2** COURSE, ROUTE : recorrido *m,* trayecto *m,* trayectoria *f*
pathetic [pəˈθɛṭɪk] *adj* : patético — **pathetically** [-ṭɪkli] *adv*
pathological [ˌpæθəˈlɑdʒɪkəl] *adj* : patológico
pathologist [pəˈθɑlədʒɪst] *n* : patólogo *m,* -ga *f*
pathology [pəˈθɑlədʒi] *n, pl* **-gies** : patología *f*
pathos [ˈpeɪˌθɑs, ˈpæ-, -ˌθɔs] *n* : patetismo *m*
pathway [ˈpæθˌweɪ] *n* : camino *m,* sendero *m,* senda *f,* vereda *f*
patience [ˈpeɪʃənts] *n* : paciencia *f*
patient[1] [ˈpeɪʃənt] *adj* : paciente — **patiently** *adv*
patient[2] *n* : paciente *mf*
patio [ˈpæṭiˌoː] *n, pl* **-tios** : patio *m*
patriarch [ˈpeɪtriˌɑrk] *n* : patriarca *m*
patrimony [ˈpætrəˌmoːni] *n, pl* **-nies** : patrimonio *m*
patriot [ˈpeɪtriət] *n* : patriota *mf*
patriotic [ˌpeɪtriˈɑṭɪk] *adj* : patriótico — **patriotically** *adv*
patriotism [ˈpeɪtriəˌtɪzəm] *n* : patriotismo *m*
patrol[1] [pəˈtroːl] *v* **-trolled; -trolling** : patrullar
patrol[2] *n* : patrulla *f*
patrolman [pəˈtroːlmən] *n, pl* **-men** [-mən, -ˌmɛn] : policía *mf,* guardia *mf*
patron [ˈpeɪtrən] *n* **1** SPONSOR : patrocinador *m,* -dora *f* **2** CUSTOMER : cliente *m,* -ta *f* **3** *or* **patron saint** : patrono *m,* -na *f*
patronage [ˈpeɪtrənɪdʒ, ˈpæ-] *n* **1** SPONSORSHIP : patrocinio *m* **2** CLIENTELE : clientela *f* **3** : influencia *f* (política)
patronize [ˈpeɪtrəˌnaɪz, ˈpæ-] *vt* **-ized; -izing 1** SPONSOR : patrocinar **2** : ser cliente de (un negocio) **3** : tratar con condescendencia
patter[1] [ˈpæṭər] *vi* **1** TAP : golpetear, tamborilear (dícese de la lluvia) **2 to patter about** : corretear (con pasos ligeros)
patter[2] *n* **1** TAPPING : golpeteo *m,* tamborileo *m* (de la lluvia), correteo *m* (de pies) **2** CHATTER : palabrería *f,* parloteo *m fam*
pattern[1] [ˈpæṭərn] *vt* **1** BASE : basar (en un modelo) **2 to pattern after** : hacer imitación de
pattern[2] *n* **1** MODEL : modelo *m,* patrón *m* (de costura) **2** DESIGN : diseño *m,* dibujo *m,* estampado *m* (de tela) **3** NORM, STANDARD : pauta *f,* norma *f,* patrón *m*
patty [ˈpæṭi] *n, pl* **-ties** : porción *f* de carne picada (u otro alimento) en forma de ruedita <a hamburger patty : una hamburguesa>
paucity [ˈpɔsəṭi] *n* : escasez *f*
paunch [ˈpɔntʃ] *n* : panza *f,* barriga *f*
pauper [ˈpɔpər] *n* : pobre *mf,* indigente *mf*
pause[1] [ˈpɔz] *vi* **paused; pausing** : hacer una pausa, pararse (brevemente)
pause[2] *n* : pausa *f*
pave [ˈpeɪv] *vt* **paved; paving** : pavimentar <to pave with stones : empedrar>
pavement [ˈpeɪvmənt] *n* : pavimento *m,* empedrado *m*
pavilion [pəˈvɪljən] *n* : pabellón *m*
paving [ˈpeɪvɪŋ] → **pavement**
paw[1] [ˈpɔ] *vt* : tocar, manosear, sobar
paw[2] *n* : pata *f,* garra *f,* zarpa *f*
pawn[1] [ˈpɔn] *vt* : empeñar, prendar

pawn[2] *n* **1** PLEDGE, SECURITY : prenda *f* **2** PAWNING : empeño *m* **3** : peón *m* (en ajedrez)

pawnbroker [ˈpɔnˌbroːkər] *n* : prestamista *mf*

pawnshop [ˈpɔnˌʃɑp] *n* : casa *f* de empeños, monte *m* de piedad

pay[1] [ˈpeɪ] *v* **paid** [ˈpeɪd]; **paying** *vt* **1** : pagar (una cuenta, a un empleado, etc.) **2 to pay attention** : poner atención, prestar atención, hacer caso **3 to pay back** : pagar, devolver <she paid them back : les devolvió el dinero> <I'll pay you back for what you did! : ¡me las pagarás!> **4 to pay off** SETTLE : saldar, cancelar (una deuda, etc.) **5 to pay one's respects** : presentar uno sus respetos **6 to pay a visit** : hacer una visita — *vi* : valer la pena <crime doesn't pay : no hay crimen sin castigo>

pay[2] *n* : paga *f*

payable [ˈpeɪəbəl] *adj* DUE : pagadero

paycheck [ˈpeɪˌtʃɛk] *n* : sueldo *m*, cheque *m* del sueldo

payee [peɪˈiː] *n* : beneficiario *m*, -ria *f* (de un cheque, etc.)

payment [ˈpeɪmənt] *n* **1** : pago *m* **2** INSTALLMENT : plazo *m*, cuota *f* **3** REWARD : recompensa *f*

payroll [ˈpeɪˌroːl] *n* : nómina *f*

PC [ˌpiːˈsiː] *n, pl* **PCs** *or* **PC's** : PC *mf*, computadora *f* personal

pea [ˈpiː] *n* : chícharo *m*, guisante *m*, arveja *f*

peace [ˈpiːs] *n* **1** : paz *f* <peace treaty : tratado de paz> <peace and tranquillity : paz y tranquilidad> **2** ORDER : orden *m* (público)

peaceable [ˈpiːsəbəl] *adj* : pacífico — **peaceably** [-bli] *adv*

peaceful [ˈpiːsfəl] *adj* **1** PEACEABLE : pacífico **2** CALM, QUIET : tranquilo, sosegado — **peacefully** *adv*

peacemaker [ˈpiːsˌmeɪkər] *n* : conciliador *m*, -dora *f*; mediador *m*, -dora *f*

peach [ˈpiːtʃ] *n* : durazno *m*, melocotón *m*

peacock [ˈpiːˌkɑk] *n* : pavo *m* real

peak[1] [ˈpiːk] *vi* : alcanzar su nivel máximo

peak[2] *adj* : máximo

peak[3] *n* **1** POINT : punta *f* **2** CREST, SUMMIT : cima *f*, cumbre *f* **3** APEX : cúspide *f*, apogeo *m*, nivel *m* máximo

peaked [ˈpiːkəd] *adj* SICKLY : pálido

peal[1] [ˈpiːl] *vi* : repicar

peal[2] *n* : repique *m*, tañido *m* (de campanada) <peals of laughter : carcajadas>

peanut [ˈpiːˌnʌt] *n* : maní *m*, cacahuate *m Mex*, cacahuete *m Spain*

pear [ˈpær] *n* : pera *f*

pearl [ˈpərl] *n* : perla *f*

pearly [ˈpərli] *adj* **pearlier; -est** : nacarado

peasant [ˈpɛzənt] *n* : campesino *m*, -na *f*

peat [ˈpiːt] *n* : turba *f*

pebble [ˈpɛbəl] *n* : piedrita *f*, piedrecita *f*, guijarro *m*

pecan [pɪˈkɑn, -ˈkæn, ˈpiːˌkæn] *n* : pacana *f*, nuez *f Mex*

peccadillo [ˌpɛkəˈdɪlo] *n, pl* **-loes** *or* **-los** : pecadillo *m*

peccary [ˈpɛkəri] *n, pl* **-ries** : pécari *m*, pecarí *m*

peck[1] [ˈpɛk] *vt* : picar, picotear

peck[2] *n* **1** : medida *f* de áridos equivalente a 8.810 litros **2** : picotazo *m* (de un pájaro) <a peck on the cheek : un besito en la mejilla>

pectoral [ˈpɛktərəl] *adj* : pectoral

peculiar [pɪˈkjuːljər] *adj* **1** DISTINCTIVE : propio, peculiar, característico <peculiar to this area : propio de esta zona> **2** STRANGE : extraño, raro — **peculiarly** *adv*

peculiarity [pɪˌkjuːlˈjærəti, -ˌkjuːliˈær-] *n, pl* **-ties 1** DISTINCTIVENESS : peculiaridad *f* **2** ODDITY, QUIRK : rareza *f*, idiosincrasia *f*, excentricidad *f*

pecuniary [pɪˈkjuːniˌɛri] *adj* : pecuniario

pedagogical [ˌpɛdəˈgɑdʒɪkəl, -ˈgoː-] *adj* : pedagógico

pedagogy [ˈpɛdəˌgoːdʒi, -ˌgɑ-] *n* : pedagogía *f*

pedal[1] [ˈpɛdəl] *v* **-aled** *or* **-alled; -aling** *or* **-alling** *vi* : pedalear — *vt* : darle a los pedales de

pedal[2] *n* : pedal *m*

pedant [ˈpɛdənt] *n* : pedante *mf*

pedantic [pɪˈdæntɪk] *adj* : pedante

pedantry [ˈpɛdəntri] *n, pl* **-ries** : pedantería *f*

peddle [ˈpɛdəl] *vt* **-dled; -dling** : vender (en las calles)

peddler [ˈpɛdlər] *n* : vendedor *m*, -dora *f* ambulante; mercachifle *m*

pedestal [ˈpɛdəstəl] *n* : pedestal *m*

pedestrian[1] [pəˈdɛstriən] *adj* **1** COMMONPLACE : pedestre, ordinario **2** : de peatón <pedestrian crossing : paso de peatones>

pedestrian[2] *n* : peatón *m*, -tona *f*

pediatric [ˌpiːdiˈætrɪk] *adj* : pediátrico

pediatrician [ˌpiːdiəˈtrɪʃən] *n* : pediatra *mf*

pediatrics [ˌpiːdiˈætrɪks] *ns & pl* : pediatría *f*

pedigree [ˈpɛdəˌgriː] *n* **1** FAMILY TREE : árbol *m* genealógico **2** LINEAGE : pedigrí *m* (de un animal), linaje *m* (de una persona)

peek[1] [ˈpiːk] *vi* **1** PEEP : espiar, mirar furtivamente **2** GLANCE : echar un vistazo

peek[2] *n* **1** : miradita *f* (furtiva) **2** GLANCE : vistazo *m*, ojeada *f*

peel[1] [ˈpiːl] *vt* **1** : pelar (fruta, etc.) **2** *or* **to peel away** : quitar — *vi* : pelarse (dícese de la piel), desconcharse (dícese de la pintura)

peel[2] *n* : cáscara *f*

peep[1] ['piːp] *vi* **1** PEEK **:** espiar, mirar furtivamente **2** CHEEP **:** piar **3 to peep out** SHOW **:** asomarse

peep[2] *n* **1** CHEEP **:** pío *m* (de un pajarito) **2** GLANCE **:** vistazo *m,* ojeada *f*

peer[1] ['pɪr] *vi* **:** mirar detenidamente, mirar con atención

peer[2] *n* **1** EQUAL **:** par *m,* igual *mf* **2** NOBLE **:** noble *mf*

peerage ['pɪrɪdʒ] *n* **:** nobleza *f*

peerless ['pɪrləs] *adj* **:** sin par, incomparable

peeve[1] ['piːv] *vt* **peeved; peeving :** fastidiar, irritar, molestar

peeve[2] *n* **:** queja *f*

peevish ['piːvɪʃ] *adj* **:** quejoso, fastidioso — **peevishly** *adv*

peevishness ['piːvɪʃnəs] *n* **:** irritabilidad *f*

peg[1] ['pɛg] *vt* **pegged; pegging 1** PLUG **:** tapar (con una clavija) **2** FASTEN, FIX **:** sujetar (con estaquillas) **3 to peg out** MARK **:** marcar (con estaquillas)

peg[2] *n* **:** estaquilla *f* (para clavar), clavija *f* (para tapar)

pejorative [pɪ'dʒɔrət̬ɪv] *adj* **:** peyorativo — **pejoratively** *adv*

pelican ['pɛlɪkən] *n* **:** pelícano *m*

pellagra [pə'lægrə, -'leɪ-] *n* **:** pelagra *f*

pellet ['pɛlət] *n* **1** BALL **:** bolita *f* <food pellet : bolita de comida> **2** SHOT **:** perdigón *m*

pell–mell ['pɛl'mɛl] *adv* **:** desordenadamente, atropelladamente

pelt[1] ['pɛlt] *vt* **1** THROW **:** lanzar, tirar (algo a alguien) **2 to pelt with stones :** apedrear — *vi* BEAT **:** golpear con fuerza <the rain was pelting down : llovía a cántaros>

pelt[2] *n* **:** piel *f,* pellejo *m*

pelvic ['pɛlvɪk] *adj* **:** pélvico

pelvis ['pɛlvɪs] *n, pl* **-vises** *or* **-ves** ['pɛl,viːz] **:** pelvis *f*

pen[1] ['pɛn] *vt* **penned; penning 1** *or* **pen in :** encerrar (animales) **2** WRITE **:** escribir

pen[2] *n* **1** CORRAL **:** corral *m,* redil *m* (para ovejas) **2 :** pluma *f* <fountain pen : pluma fuente> <ballpoint pen : bolígrafo>

penal ['piːnəl] *adj* **:** penal

penalize ['piːnəl,aɪz, 'pɛn-] *vt* **-ized; -izing :** penalizar, sancionar, penar

penalty ['pɛnəlti] *n, pl* **-ties 1** PUNISHMENT **:** pena *f,* castigo *m* **2** DISADVANTAGE **:** desventaja *f,* castigo *m,* penalty *m* (en deportes) **3** FINE **:** multa *f*

penance ['pɛnənts] *n* **:** penitencia *f*

pence → **penny**

penchant ['pɛntʃənt] *n* **:** inclinación *f,* afición *f*

pencil[1] ['pɛntsəl] *vt* **-ciled** *or* **-cilled; -ciling** *or* **-cilling :** escribir con lápiz, dibujar con lápiz

pencil[2] *n* **:** lápiz *m*

pendant ['pɛndənt] *n* **:** colgante *m*

pending[1] ['pɛndɪŋ] *adj* **:** pendiente

pending[2] *prep* **1** DURING **:** durante **2** AWAITING **:** en espera de

pendulum ['pɛndʒələm, -djʊləm] *n* **:** péndulo *m*

penetrate ['pɛnə,treɪt] *vt* **-trated; -trating :** penetrar

penetrating ['pɛnə,treɪt̬ɪŋ] *adj* **:** penetrante, cortante

penetration [,pɛnə'treɪʃən] *n* **:** penetración *f*

penguin ['pɛŋgwɪn, 'pɛn-] *n* **:** pingüino *m*

penicillin [,pɛnə'sɪlən] *n* **:** penicilina *f*

peninsula [pə'nɪntsələ, -'nɪntʃʊlə] *n* **:** península *f*

penis ['piːnəs] *n, pl* **-nes** [-,niːz] *or* **-nises :** pene *m*

penitence ['pɛnət̬ənts] *n* **:** arrepentimiento *m,* penitencia *f*

penitent[1] ['pɛnət̬ənt] *adj* **:** arrepentido, penitente

penitent[2] *n* **:** penitente *mf*

penitentiary [,pɛnə'tɛntʃəri] *n, pl* **-ries :** penitenciaría *f,* prisión *m,* presidio *m*

penmanship ['pɛnmən,ʃɪp] *n* **:** escritura *f,* caligrafía *f*

pen name *n* **:** seudónimo *m*

pennant ['pɛnənt] *n* **:** gallardete *m* (de un barco), banderín *m*

penniless ['pɛniləs] *adj* **:** sin un centavo

penny ['pɛni] *n, pl* **-nies** *or* **pence** ['pɛnts] **1 :** penique *m* (del Reino Unido) **2** *pl* **-nies** CENT **:** centavo *m* (de los Estados Unidos)

pension[1] ['pɛntʃən] *vt or* **to pension off :** jubilar

pension[2] *n* **:** pensión *m,* jubilación *f*

pensive ['pɛntsɪv] *adj* **:** pensativo, meditabundo — **pensively** *adv*

pent ['pɛnt] *adj* **:** encerrado <pent-up feelings : emociones reprimidas>

pentagon ['pɛntə,gɑn] *n* **:** pentágono *m*

pentagonal [pɛn'tægənəl] *adj* **:** pentagonal

penthouse ['pɛnt,haʊs] *n* **:** ático *m,* penthouse *m*

penury ['pɛnjəri] *n* **:** penuria *f,* miseria *f*

peon ['piː,ɑn, -ən] *n, pl* **-ons** *or* **-ones** [peɪ'oːniːz] **:** peón *m*

peony ['piːəni] *n, pl* **-nies :** peonía *f*

people[1] ['piːpəl] *vt* **-pled; -pling :** poblar

people[2] *ns & pl* **1 people** *npl* **:** gente *f,* personas *fpl* <people like him : él le cae bien a la gente> <many people : mucha gente, muchas personas> **2** *pl* **peoples :** pueblo *m* <the Cuban people : el pueblo cubano>

pep[1] ['pɛp] *vt* **pepped; pepping** *or* **to pep up :** animar

pep[2] *n* **:** energía *f,* vigor *m*

pepper[1] ['pɛpər] *vt* **1 :** añadir pimienta a **2** RIDDLE **:** acribillar (a balazos) **3** SPRINKLE **:** salpicar <peppered with quotations : salpicado de citas>

pepper[2] *n* **1 :** pimienta *f* (condimento) **2 :** pimiento *m,* pimentón *m* (fruta) **3** → **chili**

peppermint [ˈpɛpərˌmɪnt] *n* **:** menta *f*

peppery [ˈpɛpəri] *adj* **:** picante

peppy [ˈpɛpi] *adj* **peppier; -est :** lleno de energía, vivaz

peptic [ˈpɛptɪk] *adj* **peptic ulcer :** úlcera *f* estomacal

per [ˈpər] *prep* **1 :** por <miles per hour : millas por hora> **2** ACCORDING TO **:** según <per his specifications : según sus especificaciones>

per annum [pərˈænəm] *adv* **:** al año, por año

percale [ˌpərˈkeɪl, ˈpər-ˌ; ˌpərˈkæl] *n* **:** percal *m*

per capita [pərˈkæpɪṭə] *adv & adj* **:** per cápita

perceive [pərˈsiːv] *vt* **-ceived; -ceiving 1** REALIZE **:** percatarse de, concientizarse de, darse cuenta de **2** NOTE **:** percibir, notar

percent[1] [pərˈsɛnt] *adv* **:** por ciento

percent[2] *n, pl* **-cent** *or* **-cents 1 :** por ciento <10 percent of the population : el 10 por ciento de la población> **2** → **percentage**

percentage [pərˈsɛntɪdʒ] *n* **:** porcentaje *m*

perceptible [pərˈsɛptəbəl] *adj* **:** perceptible — **perceptibly** [-bli] *adv*

perception [pərˈsɛpʃən] *n* **1 :** percepción *f* <color perception : la percepción de los colores> **2** INSIGHT **:** perspicacia *f* **3** IDEA **:** idea *f,* imagen *f*

perceptive [pərˈsɛptɪv] *adj* **:** perspicaz

perceptively [pərˈsɛptɪvli] *adv* **:** con perspicacia

perch[1] [ˈpərtʃ] *vi* **1** ROOST **:** posarse **2** SIT **:** sentarse (en un sitio elevado) — *vt* PLACE **:** posar, colocar

perch[2] *n* **1** ROOST **:** percha *f* (para los pájaros) **2** *pl* **perch** *or* **perches :** perca *f* (pez)

percolate [ˈpərkəˌleɪt] *vi* **-lated; -lating :** colarse, filtrarse <percolated coffee : café filtrado>

percolator [ˈpərkəˌleɪṭər] *n* **:** cafetera *f* de filtro

percussion [pərˈkʌʃən] *n* **1** STRIKING **:** percusión *f* **2** *or* **percussion instruments :** instrumentos *mpl* de percusión

peremptory [pəˈrɛmptəri] *adj* **:** perentorio

perennial[1] [pəˈrɛniəl] *adj* **1 :** perenne, vivaz <perennial flowers : flores perennes> **2** RECURRENT **:** perenne, continuo <a perennial problem : un problema eterno>

perennial[2] *n* **:** planta *f* perenne, planta *f* vivaz

perfect[1] [pərˈfɛkt] *vt* **:** perfeccionar

perfect[2] [ˈpərfɪkt] *adj* **:** perfecto — **perfectly** *adv*

perfection [pərˈfɛkʃən] *n* **:** perfección *f*

perfectionist [pərˈfɛkʃənɪst] *n* **:** perfeccionista *mf*

perfidious [pərˈfɪdiəs] *adj* **:** pérfido

perforate [ˈpərfəˌreɪt] *vt* **-rated; -rating :** perforar

perforation [ˌpərfəˈreɪʃən] *n* **:** perforación *f*

perform [pərˈfɔrm] *vt* **1** CARRY OUT **:** realizar, hacer, desempeñar **2** PRESENT **:** representar, dar (una obra teatral, etc.) — *vi* **:** actuar (en una obra teatral), cantar (en una ópera, etc.), tocar (en un concierto, etc.), bailar (en un ballet, etc.)

performance [pərˈfɔrmənts] *n* **1** EXECUTION **:** ejecución *f,* realización *f,* desempeño *m,* rendimiento *m* **2** INTERPRETATION **:** interpretación *f* <his performance of Hamlet : su interpretación de Hamlet> **3** PRESENTATION **:** representación *f* (de una obra teatral), función *f*

performer [pərˈfɔrmər] *n* **:** artista *mf;* actor *m,* -triz *f;* intérprete *mf* (de música)

perfume[1] [pərˈfjuːm, ˈpərˌ-] *vt* **-fumed; -fuming :** perfumar

perfume[2] [ˈpərˌfjuːm, pərˈ-] *n* **:** perfume *m*

perfunctory [pərˈfʌŋktəri] *adj* **:** mecánico, superficial, somero

perhaps [pərˈhæps] *adv* **:** tal vez, quizá, quizás

peril [ˈpɛrəl] *n* **:** peligro *m*

perilous [ˈpɛrələs] *adj* **:** peligroso — **perilously** *adv*

perimeter [pəˈrɪmətər] *n* **:** perímetro *m*

period [ˈpɪriəd] *n* **1 :** punto *m* (en puntuación) **2 :** período *m* <a two-hour period : un período de dos horas> **3** STAGE **:** época *f* (histórica), fase *f,* etapa *f*

periodic [ˌpɪriˈɑdɪk] *or* **periodical** [-dɪkəl] *adj* **:** periódico — **periodically** [-dɪkli] *adv*

periodical [ˌpɪriˈɑdɪkəl] *n* **:** publicación *f* periódica, revista *f*

peripheral [pəˈrɪfərəl] *adj* **:** periférico

periphery [pəˈrɪfəri] *n, pl* **-eries :** periferia *f*

periscope [ˈpɛrəˌskoːp] *n* **:** periscopio *m*

perish [ˈpɛrɪʃ] *vi* DIE **:** perecer, morirse

perishable[1] [ˈpɛrɪʃəbəl] *adj* **:** perecedero

perishable[2] *n* **:** producto *m* perecedero

perjure [ˈpərdʒər] *vt* **-jured; -juring** (*used in law*) **to perjure oneself :** perjurar, perjurarse

perjury [ˈpərdʒəri] *n* **:** perjurio *m*

perk[1] [ˈpərk] *vt* **1 :** levantar (las orejas, etc.) **2** *or* **to perk up** FRESHEN **:** arreglar — *vi* **to perk up :** animarse, reanimarse

perk[2] *n* **:** extra *m*

perky [ˈpərki] *adj* **perkier; -est :** animado, alegre, lleno de vida

permanence [ˈpərmənənts] *n* **:** permanencia *f*

permanent[1] [ˈpərmənənt] *adj* : permanente — **permanently** *adv*

permanent[2] *n* : permanente *f*

permeable [ˈpərmiəbəl] *adj* : permeable

permeate [ˈpərmi,eɪt] *v* **-ated; -ating** *vt* **1** PENETRATE : penetrar, impregnar **2** PERVADE : penetrar, difundirse por — *vi* : penetrar

permissible [pərˈmɪsəbəl] *adj* : permisible, lícito

permission [pərˈmɪʃən] *n* : permiso *m*

permissive [pərˈmɪsɪv] *adj* : permisivo

permit[1] [pərˈmɪt] *vt* **-mitted; -mitting** : permitir, dejar <weather permitting : si el tiempo lo permite>

permit[2] [ˈpər,mɪt, pərˈ-] *n* : permiso *m,* licencia *f*

pernicious [pərˈnɪʃəs] *adj* : pernicioso

peroxide [pəˈrɑk,saɪd] *n* **1** : peróxido *m* **2** → **hydrogen peroxide**

perpendicular[1] [,pərpənˈdɪkjələr] *adj* **1** VERTICAL : vertical **2** : perpendicular <perpendicular lines : líneas perpendiculares> — **perpendicularly** *adv*

perpendicular[2] *n* : perpendicular *f*

perpetrate [ˈpərpə,treɪt] *vt* **-trated; -trating** : perpetrar, cometer (un delito)

perpetrator [ˈpərpə,treɪtər] *n* : autor *m,* -tora *f* (de un delito)

perpetual [pərˈpɛtʃʊəl] *adj* **1** EVERLASTING : perpetuo, eterno **2** CONTINUAL : perpetuo, continuo, constante

perpetually [pərˈpɛtʃʊəli, -tʃəli] *adv* : para siempre, eternamente

perpetuate [pərˈpɛtʃʊ,eɪt] *vt* **-ated; -ating** : perpetuar

perpetuity [,pərpəˈtuːəti, -ˈtjuː-] *n, pl* **-ties** : perpetuidad *f*

perplex [pərˈplɛks] *vt* : dejar perplejo, confundir

perplexed [pərˈplɛkst] *adj* : perplejo

perplexity [pərˈplɛksəti] *n, pl* **-ties** : perplejidad *f,* confusión *f*

persecute [ˈpərsɪ,kjuːt] *vt* **-cuted; -cuting** : perseguir

persecution [,pərsɪˈkjuːʃən] *n* : persecución *f*

perseverance [,pərsəˈvɪrənts] *n* : perseverancia *f*

persevere [,pərsəˈvɪr] *vi* **-vered; -vering** : perseverar

Persian [ˈpərʒən] *n* **1** : persa *mf* **2** : persa *m* (idioma) — **Persian** *adj*

persist [pərˈsɪst] *vi* : persistir

persistence [pərˈsɪstənts] *n* **1** CONTINUATION : persistencia *f* **2** TENACITY : perseverancia *f,* tenacidad *f*

persistent [pərˈsɪstənt] *adj* : persistente — **persistently** *adv*

person [ˈpərsən] *n* **1** HUMAN, INDIVIDUAL : persona *f,* individuo *m,* ser *m* humano **2** : persona *f* (en gramática) **3 in person** : en persona

personable [ˈpərsənəbəl] *adj* : agradable

personage [ˈpərsənɪdʒ] *n* : personaje *m*

personal [ˈpərsənəl] *adj* **1** OWN, PRIVATE : personal, particular, privado <for personal reasons : por razones personales> **2** : en persona <to make a personal appearance : presentarse en persona, hacerse acto de presencia> **3** : íntimo, personal <personal hygiene : higiene personal> **4** INDISCREET, PRYING : indiscreto, personal

personality [,pərsənˈæləti] *n, pl* **-ties** **1** DISPOSITION : personalidad *f,* temperamento *m* **2** CELEBRITY : personalidad *f,* personaje *m,* celebridad *f*

personalize [ˈpərsənə,laɪz] *vt* **-ized; -izing** : personalizar

personally [ˈpərsənəli] *adv* **1** : personalmente, en persona <I'll do it personally : lo haré personalmente> **2** : como persona <personally she's very amiable : como persona es muy amable> **3** : personalmente <personally, I don't believe it : yo, personalmente, no me lo creo>

personification [pər,sɑnəfəˈkeɪʃən] *n* : personificación *f*

personify [pərˈsɑnə,faɪ] *vt* **-fied; -fying** : personificar

personnel [,pərsənˈɛl] *n* : personal *m*

perspective [pərˈspɛktɪv] *n* : perspectiva *f*

perspicacious [,pərspəˈkeɪʃəs] *adj* : perspicaz

perspiration [,pərspəˈreɪʃən] *n* : transpiración *f,* sudor *m*

perspire [pərˈspaɪr] *vi* **-spired; -spiring** : transpirar, sudar

persuade [pərˈsweɪd] *vt* **-suaded; -suading** : persuadir, convencer

persuasion [pərˈsweɪʒən] *n* : persuasión *f*

persuasive [pərˈsweɪsɪv, -zɪv] *adj* : persuasivo — **persuasively** *adv*

persuasiveness [pərˈsweɪsɪvnəs, -zɪv-] *n* : persuasión *f*

pert [ˈpərt] *adj* **1** SAUCY : descarado, impertinente **2** JAUNTY : alegre, animado <a pert little hat : un sombrero coqueto>

pertain [pərˈteɪn] *vi* **1** BELONG : pertenecer (a) **2** RELATE : estar relacionado (con)

pertinence [ˈpərtənənts] *n* : pertinencia *f*

pertinent [ˈpərtənənt] *adj* : pertinente

perturb [pərˈtərb] *vt* : perturbar

perusal [pəˈruːzəl] *n* : lectura *f* cuidadosa

peruse [pəˈruːz] *vt* **-rused; -rusing** **1** READ : leer con cuidado **2** SCAN : recorrer con la vista <he perused the newspaper : echó un vistazo al periódico>

Peruvian [pəˈruːviən] *n* : peruano *m,* -na *f* — **Peruvian** *adj*

pervade [pərˈveɪd] *vt* **-vaded; -vading** : penetrar, difundirse por

pervasive [pərˈveɪsɪv, -zɪv] *adj* : penetrante

perverse [pər'vərs] *adj* **1** CORRUPT : perverso, corrompido **2** STUBBORN : obstinado, porfiado, terco (sin razón) — **perversely** *adv*

perversion [pər'vərʒən] *n* : perversión *f*

perversity [pər'vərsəṭi] *n, pl* **-ties 1** CORRUPTION : corrupción *f* **2** STUBBORNNESS : obstinación *f,* terquedad *f*

pervert[1] [pər'vərt] *vt* **1** DISTORT : pervertir, distorsionar **2** CORRUPT : pervertir, corromper

pervert[2] ['pər,vərt] *n* : pervertido *m,* -da *f*

peso ['peɪ,soː] *n, pl* **-sos** : peso *m*

pessimism ['pɛsə,mɪzəm] *n* : pesimismo *m*

pessimist ['pɛsəmɪst] *n* : pesimista *mf*

pessimistic [,pɛsə'mɪstɪk] *adj* : pesimista

pest ['pɛst] *n* **1** NUISANCE : peste *f;* latoso *m,* -sa *f fam* <to be a pest : dar (la) lata> **2** : insecto *m* nocivo, animal *m* nocivo <the squirrels were pests : las ardillas eran una plaga>

pester ['pɛstər] *vt* **-tered; -tering** : molestar, fastidiar

pesticide ['pɛstə,saɪd] *n* : pesticida *m*

pestilence ['pɛstələn*t*s] *n* : pestilencia *f,* peste *f*

pestle ['pɛsəl, 'pɛstəl] *n* : mano *f* de mortero, mazo *m,* maja *f*

pet[1] ['pɛt] *vt* **petted; petting** : acariciar

pet[2] *n* **1** : animal *m* doméstico **2** FAVORITE : favorito *m,* -ta *f*

petal ['pɛṭəl] *n* : pétalo *m*

petite [pə'tiːt] *adj* : pequeña, menuda, chiquita

petition[1] [pə'tɪʃən] *vt* : peticionar

petition[2] *n* : petición *f*

petitioner [pə'tɪʃənər] *n* : peticionario *m,* -ria *f*

petrify ['pɛtrə,faɪ] *vt* **-fied; -fying** : petrificar

petroleum [pə'troːliəm] *n* : petróleo *m*

petticoat ['pɛṭi,koːt] *n* : enagua *f,* fondo *m Mex*

pettiness ['pɛṭinəs] *n* **1** INSIGNIFICANCE : insignificancia *f* **2** MEANNESS : mezquindad *f*

petty ['pɛṭi] *adj* **-tier; -est 1** MINOR : menor <petty cash : dinero para gastos menores> **2** INSIGNIFICANT : insignificante, trivial, nimio **3** MEAN : mezquino

petty officer *n* : suboficial *mf*

petulance ['pɛtʃələn*t*s] *n* : irritabilidad *f,* mal genio *m*

petulant ['pɛtʃələnt] *adj* : irritable, de mal genio

petunia [pɪ'tuːnjə, -'tjuː-] *n* : petunia *f*

pew ['pjuː] *n* : banco *m* (de iglesia)

pewter ['pjuːtər] *n* : peltre *m*

pH [,piː'eɪtʃ] *n* : pH *m*

phallic ['fælɪk] *adj* : fálico

phallus ['fæləs] *n, pl* **-li** ['fæ,laɪ] *or* **-luses** : falo *m*

phantasy ['fæntəsi] → **fantasy**

phantom ['fæntəm] *n* : fantasma *m*

pharaoh ['fɛr,oː, 'feɪ,roː] *n* : faraón *m*

pharmaceutical [,fɑrmə'suːṭɪkəl] *adj* : farmacéutico

pharmacist ['fɑrməsɪst] *n* : farmacéutico *m,* -ca *f*

pharmacology [,fɑrmə'kɑlədʒi] *n* : farmacología *f*

pharmacy ['fɑrməsi] *n, pl* **-cies** : farmacia *f*

pharynx ['færɪŋks] *n, pl* **pharynges** [fə'rɪn,dʒiːz] : faringe *f*

phase[1] ['feɪz] *vt* **phased; phasing 1** SYNCHRONIZE : sincronizar, poner en fase **2** STAGGER : escalonar **3 to phase in** : introducir progresivamente **4 to phase out** : retirar progresivamente, dejar de producir

phase[2] *n* **1** : fase *f* (de la luna, etc.) **2** STAGE : fase *f,* etapa *f*

pheasant ['fɛzənt] *n, pl* **-ant** *or* **-ants** : faisán *m*

phenomenal [fɪ'nɑmənəl] *adj* : extraordinario, excepcional

phenomenon [fɪ'nɑmə,nɑn, -nən] *n, pl* **-na** [-nə] *or* **-nons 1** : fenómeno *m* **2** *pl* **-nons** PRODIGY : fenómeno *m,* prodigio *m*

philanthropic [,fɪlən'θrɑpɪk] *adj* : filantrópico

philanthropist [fə'læn*t*θrəpɪst] *n* : filántropo *m,* -pa *f*

philanthropy [fə'læn*t*θrəpi] *n, pl* **-pies** : filantropía *f*

philately [fə'læṭəli] *n* : filatelia *f*

philodendron [,fɪlə'dɛndrən] *n, pl* **-drons** *or* **-dra** [-drə] : arácea *f*

philosopher [fə'lɑsəfər] *n* : filósofo *m,* -fa *f*

philosophic [,fɪlə'sɑfɪk] *or* **philosophical** [-fɪkəl] *adj* : filosófico — **philosophically** [-kli] *adv*

philosophize [fə'lɑsə,faɪz] *vi* **-phized; -phizing** : filosofar

philosophy [fə'lɑsəfi] *n, pl* **-phies** : filosofía *f*

phlebitis [flɪ'baɪṭəs] *n* : flebitis *f*

phlegm ['flɛm] *n* : flema *f*

phlox ['flɑks] *n, pl* **phlox** *or* **phloxes** : polemonio *m*

phobia ['foːbiə] *n* : fobia *f*

phoenix ['fiːnɪks] *n* : fénix *m*

phone[1] ['foːn] *v* → **telephone**[1]

phone[2] *n* → **telephone**[2]

phoneme ['foː,niːm] *n* : fonema *m*

phonetic [fə'nɛṭɪk] *adj* : fonético

phonetics [fə'nɛṭɪks] *n* : fonética *f*

phonics ['fɑnɪks] *n* : método *m* fonético de aprender a leer

phonograph ['foːnə,græf] *n* : fonógrafo *m,* tocadiscos *m*

phony[1] *or* **phoney** ['foːni] *adj* **-nier; -est** : falso

phony[2] *or* **phoney** *n, pl* **-nies** : farsante *mf;* charlatán *m,* -tana *f*

phosphate ['fɑs,feɪt] *n* : fosfato *m*

phosphorescence [,fɑsfə'rɛsən*t*s] *n* : fosforescencia *f*

phosphorescent [ˌfɑsfəˈrɛsənt] *adj* : fosforescente — **phosphorescently** *adv*
phosphorus [ˈfɑsfərəs] *n* : fósforo *m*
photo [ˈfoːˌtoː] *n, pl* **-tos** : foto *f*
photocopier [ˈfoːt̬oˌkɑpiər] *n* : fotocopiadora *f*
photocopy[1] [ˈfoːt̬oˌkɑpi] *vt* **-copied; -copying** : fotocopiar
photocopy[2] *n, pl* **-copies** : fotocopia *f*
photoelectric [ˌfoːt̬oɪˈlɛktrɪk] *adj* : fotoeléctrico
photogenic [ˌfoːt̬əˈdʒɛnɪk] *adj* : fotogénico
photograph[1] [ˈfoːt̬əˌgræf] *vt* : fotografiar
photograph[2] *n* : fotografía *f*, foto *f* <to take a photograph of : tomarle una fotografía a, tomar una fotografía de>
photographer [fəˈtɑgrəfər] *n* : fotógrafo *m*, -fa *f*
photographic [ˌfoːt̬əˈgræfɪk] *adj* : fotográfico — **photographically** [-fɪkli] *adv*
photography [fəˈtɑgrəfi] *n* : fotografía *f*
photosynthesis [ˌfoːt̬oˈsɪnθəsɪs] *n* : fotosíntesis *f*
photosynthetic [ˌfoːt̬osɪnˈθɛt̬ɪk] *adj* : fotosintético, de fotosíntesis
phrase[1] [ˈfreɪz] *vt* **phrased; phrasing** : expresar
phrase[2] *n* : frase *f*, locución *f* <to coin a phrase : para decirlo así>
phylum [ˈfaɪləm] *n, pl* **-la** [-lə] : phylum *m*
physical[1] [ˈfɪzɪkəl] *adj* **1** : físico <physical laws : leyes físicas> **2** MATERIAL : material, físico **3** BODILY : físico, corpóreo — **physically** [-kli] *adv*
physical[2] *n* CHECKUP : chequeo *m*, reconocimiento *m* médico
physician [fəˈzɪʃən] *n* : médico *m*, -ca *f*
physicist [ˈfɪzəsɪst] *n* : físico *m*, -ca *f*
physics [ˈfɪzɪks] *ns & pl* : física *f*
physiognomy [ˌfɪziˈɑgnəmi] *n, pl* **-mies** : fisonomía *f*
physiological [ˈfɪziəˈlɑdʒɪkəl] *or* **physiologic** [-dʒɪk] *adj* : fisiológico
physiologist [ˌfɪziˈɑlədʒɪst] *n* : fisiólogo *m*, -ga *f*
physiology [ˌfɪziˈɑlədʒi] *n* : fisiología *f*
physique [fəˈziːk] *n* : físico *m*
pi [ˈpaɪ] *n, pl* **pis** [ˈpaɪz] : pi *f*
pianist [piˈænɪst, ˈpiːənɪst] *n* : pianista *mf*
piano [piˈænoː] *n, pl* **-anos** : piano *m*
piazza [piˈæzə, -ˈɑtsə] *n, pl* **-zas** *or* **-ze** [-ˈɑtˌseɪ] : plaza *f*
picayune [ˌpɪkiˈjuːn] *adj* : trivial, nimio, insignificante
piccolo [ˈpɪkəˌloː] *n, pl* **-los** : flautín *m*
pick[1] [ˈpɪk] *vt* **1** : picar, labrar (con un pico) <he picked the hard soil : picó la tierra dura> **2** : quitar, sacar (poco a poco) <to pick meat off the bones : quitar pedazos de carne de los huesos> **3** : recoger, arrancar (frutas, flores, etc.) **4** SELECT : escoger, elegir **5** PROVOKE : provocar <to pick a quarrel : buscar pleito, buscar pelea> **6 to pick a lock** : forzar una cerradura **7 to pick someone's pocket** : robarle algo del bolsillo de alguien <someone picked my pocket! : ¡me robaron la cartera del bolsillo!> — *vi* **1** NIBBLE : picar, picotear **2 to pick and choose** : ser exigente **3 to pick at** : tocar, rascarse (una herida, etc.) **4 to pick on** TEASE : mofarse de, atormentar
pick[2] *n* **1** CHOICE : selección *f* **2** BEST : lo mejor <the pick of the crop : la crema y nata> **3** → **pickax**
pickax [ˈpɪkˌæks] *n* : pico *m*, zapapico *m*, piqueta *f*
pickerel [ˈpɪkərəl] *n, pl* **-el** *or* **-els** : lucio *m* pequeño
picket[1] [ˈpɪkət] *v* : piquetear
picket[2] *n* **1** STAKE : estaca *f* **2** STRIKER : huelguista *mf*, integrante *mf* de un piquete
pickle[1] [ˈpɪkəl] *vt* **-led; -ling** : encurtir, escabechar
pickle[2] *n* **1** BRINE : escabeche *m* **2** GHERKIN : pepinillo *m* (encurtido) **3** JAM, TROUBLE : lío *m*, apuro *m*
pickpocket [ˈpɪkˌpɑkət] *n* : carterista *mf*
pickup [ˈpɪkˌəp] *n* **1** IMPROVEMENT : mejora *f* **2** *or* **pickup truck** : camioneta *f*
pick up *vt* **1** LIFT : levantar **2** TIDY : arreglar, ordenar — *vi* IMPROVE : mejorar
picnic[1] [ˈpɪkˌnɪk] *vi* **-nicked; -nicking** : ir de picnic
picnic[2] *n* : picnic *m*
pictorial [pɪkˈtoriəl] *adj* : pictórico
picture[1] [ˈpɪktʃər] *vt* **-tured; -turing 1** DEPICT : representar **2** IMAGINE : imaginarse <can you picture it? : ¿te lo puedes imaginar?>
picture[2] *n* **1** : cuadro *m* (pintado o dibujado), ilustración *f*, fotografía *f* **2** DESCRIPTION : descripción *f* **3** IMAGE : imagen *f* <he's the picture of his father : es la viva imagen de su padre> **4** MOVIE : película *f*
picturesque [ˌpɪktʃəˈrɛsk] *adj* : pintoresco
pie [ˈpaɪ] *n* : pastel *m* (con fruta o carne), empanada *f* (con carne)
piebald [ˈpaɪˌbɔld] *adj* : picazo, pío
piece[1] [ˈpiːs] *vt* **pieced; piecing 1** PATCH : parchar, arreglar **2 to piece together** : construir pieza por pieza
piece[2] *n* **1** FRAGMENT : trozo *m*, pedazo *m* **2** COMPONENT : pieza *f* <a three-piece suit : un traje de tres piezas> **3** UNIT : pieza *f* <a piece of fruit : una (pieza de) fruta> **4** WORK : obra *f*, pieza *f* (de música, etc.) **5** (*in board games*) : ficha *f*, pieza *f*, figura *f* (en ajedrez)

piecemeal[1] ['piːsˌmiːl] *adv* : poco a poco, por partes

piecemeal[2] *adj* : hecho poco a poco, poco sistemático

pied ['paɪd] *adj* : pío

pier ['pɪr] *n* **1** : pila *f* (de un puente) **2** WHARF : muelle *m,* atracadero *m,* embarcadero *m* **3** PILLAR : pilar *m*

pierce ['pɪrs] *vt* **pierced; piercing 1** PENETRATE : atravesar, traspasar, penetrar (en) <the bullet pierced his leg : la bala le atravesó la pierna> <to pierce one's heart : traspasarle el corazón a uno> **2** PERFORATE : perforar, agujerear (las orejas, etc.) **3 to pierce the silence** : desgarrar el silencio

piety ['paɪəti] *n, pl* **-eties** : piedad *f*

pig ['pɪg] *n* **1** HOG, SWINE : cerdo *m,* -da *f;* puerco *m,* -ca *f* **2** SLOB : persona *f* desaliñada; cerdo *m,* -da *f* **3** GLUTTON : glotón *m,* -tona *f* **4** *or* **pig iron** : lingote *m* de hierro

pigeon ['pɪdʒən] *n* : paloma *f*

pigeonhole ['pɪdʒənˌhoːl] *n* : casilla *f*

pigeon–toed ['pɪdʒənˌtoːd] *adj* : patituerto

piggish ['pɪgɪʃ] *adj* **1** GREEDY : glotón **2** DIRTY : cochino, sucio

piggyback ['pɪgiˌbæk] *adv & adj* : a cuestas

pigheaded ['pɪgˌhɛdəd] *adj* : terco, obstinado

piglet ['pɪglət] *n* : cochinillo *m;* lechón *m,* -chona *f*

pigment ['pɪgmənt] *n* : pigmento *m*

pigmentation [ˌpɪgmən'teɪʃən] *n* : pigmentación *f*

pigmy → **pygmy**

pigpen ['pɪgˌpɛn] *n* : chiquero *m,* pocilga *f*

pigsty ['pɪgˌstaɪ] → **pigpen**

pigtail ['pɪgˌteɪl] *n* : coleta *f,* trenza *f*

pike ['paɪk] *n, pl* **pike** *or* **pikes 1** : lucio *m* (pez) **2** LANCE : pica *f* **3** → **turnpike**

pile[1] ['paɪl] *v* **piled; piling** *vt* : amontonar, apilar — *vi* **to pile up** : amontonarse, acumularse

pile[2] *n* **1** STAKE : pilote *m* **2** HEAP : montón *m,* pila *f* **3** NAP : pelo *m* (de telas)

piles ['paɪlz] *npl* HEMORRHOIDS : hemorroides *fpl,* almorranas *fpl*

pilfer ['pɪlfər] *vt* : robar (cosas pequeñas), ratear

pilgrim ['pɪlgrəm] *n* : peregrino *m,* -na *f*

pilgrimage ['pɪlgrəmɪdʒ] *n* : peregrinación *f*

pill ['pɪl] *n* : pastilla *f,* píldora *f*

pillage[1] ['pɪlɪdʒ] *vt* **-laged; -laging** : saquear

pillage[2] *n* : saqueo *m*

pillar ['pɪlər] *n* : pilar *m,* columna *f*

pillory ['pɪləri] *n, pl* **-ries** : picota *f*

pillow ['pɪˌloː] *n* : almohada *f*

pillowcase ['pɪˌloːˌkeɪs] *n* : funda *f*

pilot[1] ['paɪlət] *vt* : pilotar, pilotear

pilot[2] *n* : piloto *mf*

pilot light *n* : piloto *m*

pimento [pə'mɛnˌtoː] → **pimiento**

pimiento [pə'mɛnˌtoː, -'mjɛn-] *n, pl* **-tos** : pimiento *m* morrón

pimp ['pɪmp] *n* : proxeneta *m*

pimple ['pɪmpəl] *n* : grano *m*

pimply ['pɪmpəli] *adj* **-plier; -est** : cubierto de granos

pin[1] ['pɪn] *vt* **pinned; pinning 1** FASTEN : prender, sujetar (con alfileres) **2** HOLD, IMMOBILIZE : inmovilizar, sujetar **3 to pin one's hopes on** : poner sus esperanzas en

pin[2] *n* **1** : alfiler *m* <safety pin : alfiler de gancho> <a bobby pin : una horquilla> **2** BROOCH : alfiler *m,* broche *m,* prendedor *m* **3** *or* **bowling pin** : bolo *m*

pinafore ['pɪnəˌfor] *n* : delantal *m*

pincer ['pɪntsər] *n* **1** CLAW : pinza *f* (de una langosta, etc.) **2 pincers** *npl* : pinzas *fpl,* tenazas *fpl,* tenaza *f*

pinch[1] ['pɪntʃ] *vt* **1** : pellizcar <she pinched my cheek : me pellizcó el cachete> **2** STEAL : robar — *vi* : apretar <my shoes pinch : me aprietan los zapatos>

pinch[2] *n* **1** EMERGENCY : emergencia *f* <in a pinch : en caso necesario> **2** PAIN : dolor *m,* tormento *m* **3** SQUEEZE : pellizco *m* (con los dedos) **4** BIT : pizca *f,* pellizco *m* <a pinch of cinnamon : una pizca de canela>

pinch hitter *n* **1** SUBSTITUTE : sustituto *m,* -ta *f* **2** : bateador *m* emergente (en beisbol)

pincushion ['pɪnˌkʊʃən] *n* : acerico *m,* alfiletero *m*

pine[1] ['paɪn] *vi* **pined; pining 1 to pine away** : languidecer, consumirse **2 to pine for** : añorar, suspirar por

pine[2] *n* **1** : pino *m* (árbol) **2** : madera *f* de pino

pineapple ['paɪnˌæpəl] *n* : piña *f,* ananá *m,* ananás *m*

pinion[1] ['pɪnjən] *vt* : sujetar los brazos de, inmovilizar

pinion[2] *n* : piñón *m*

pink[1] ['pɪŋk] *adj* : rosa, rosado

pink[2] *n* **1** : clavelito *m* (flor) **2** : rosa *m,* rosado *m* (color) **3 to be in the pink** : estar en plena forma, rebosar de salud

pinkeye ['pɪŋkˌaɪ] *n* : conjuntivitis *f* aguda

pinkish ['pɪŋkɪʃ] *adj* : rosáceo

pinnacle ['pɪnɪkəl] *n* **1** : pináculo *m* (de un edificio) **2** PEAK : cima *f,* cumbre *f* (de una montaña) **3** ACME : pináculo *m,* cúspide *f,* apogeo *m*

pinpoint ['pɪnˌpɔɪnt] *vt* : precisar, localizar con precisión

pint ['paɪnt] *n* : pinta *f*

pinto ['pɪnˌtoː] *n, pl* **pintos** : caballo *m* pinto

pinworm ['pɪnˌwərm] *n* : oxiuro *m*

pioneer[1] [ˌpaɪə'nɪr] *vt* : promover, iniciar, introducir

pioneer[2] *n* : pionero *m,* -ra *f*

pious [ˈpaɪəs] *adj* **1** DEVOUT : piadoso, devoto **2** SANCTIMONIOUS : beato
piously [ˈpaɪəsli] *adv* **1** DEVOUTLY : piadosamente **2** SANCTIMONIOUSLY : santurronamente
pipe[1] [ˈpaɪp] *v* **piped; piping** *vi* : hablar en voz chillona — *vt* **1** PLAY : tocar (el caramillo o la flauta) **2** : conducir por tuberías <to pipe water : transportar el agua por tubería>
pipe[2] *n* **1** : caramillo *m* (instrumento musical) **2** BAGPIPE : gaita *f* **3** : tubo *m*, caño *m* <gas pipes : tubería de gas> **4** : pipa *f* (para fumar)
pipeline [ˈpaɪpˌlaɪn] *n* **1** : conducto *m*, oleoducto *m* (para petróleo), gasoducto *m* (para gas) **2** CONDUIT : vía *f* (de información, etc.)
piper [ˈpaɪpər] *n* : músico *m*, -ca *f* que toca el caramillo o la gaita
piping [ˈpaɪpɪŋ] *n* **1** : música *f* del caramillo o de la gaita **2** TRIM : cordoncillo *m*, ribete *m* con cordón
piquant [ˈpiːkənt, ˈpɪkwənt] *adj* **1** SPICY : picante **2** INTRIGUING : intrigante, estimulante
pique[1] [ˈpiːk] *vt* **piqued; piquing 1** IRRITATE : picar, irritar **2** AROUSE : despertar (la curiosidad, etc.)
pique[2] *n* : pique *m*, resentimiento *m*
piracy [ˈpaɪrəsi] *n*, *pl* **-cies** : piratería *f*
piranha [pəˈrɑnə, -ˈrɑnjə, -ˈrænjə] *n* : piraña *f*
pirate [ˈpaɪrət] *n* : pirata *mf*
pirouette [ˌpɪrəˈwɛt] *n* : pirueta *f*
pis → **pi**
Pisces [ˈpaɪˌsiːz, ˈpɪ-; ˈpɪsˌkeɪs] *n* : Piscis *mf*
pistachio [pəˈstæʃiˌoː, -ˈstɑ-] *n*, *pl* **-chios** : pistacho *m*
pistil [ˈpɪstəl] *n* : pistilo *m*
pistol [ˈpɪstəl] *n* : pistola *f*
piston [ˈpɪstən] *n* : pistón *m*, émbolo *m*
pit[1] [ˈpɪt] *v* **pitted; pitting** *vt* **1** : marcar de hoyos, picar (una superficie) **2** : deshuesar (una fruta) **3 to pit against** : enfrentar a, oponer a — *vi* : quedar marcado
pit[2] *n* **1** HOLE : fosa *f*, hoyo *m* <a bottomless pit : un pozo sin fondo> **2** MINE : mina *f* **3** : foso *m* <orchestra pit : foso orquestal> **4** POCKMARK : marca *f* (en la cara), cicatriz *f* de viruela **5** STONE : hueso *m*, pepa *f* (de una fruta) **6 pit of the stomach** : boca *f* del estómago
pitch[1] [ˈpɪtʃ] *vt* **1** SET UP : montar, armar (una tienda) **2** THROW : lanzar, arrojar **3** ADJUST, SET : dar el tono de (un discurso, un instrumento musical) — *vi* **1** *or* **pitch forward** FALL : caerse **2** LURCH : cabecear (dícese de un barco o un avión), dar bandazos
pitch[2] *n* **1** LURCHING : cabezada *f*, cabeceo *m* (de un barco o un avión) **2** SLOPE : (grado de) inclinación *f*, pendiente *f* **3** : tono *m* (en música) <perfect pitch : oído absoluto> **4** THROW : lanzamiento *m* **5** DEGREE : grado *m*, nivel *m*, punto *m* <the excitement reached a high pitch : la excitación llegó a un punto culminante> **6** *or* **sales pitch** : presentación *f* (de un vendedor) **7** TAR : pez *f*, brea *f*
pitcher [ˈpɪtʃər] *n* **1** JUG : jarra *f*, jarro *m*, cántaro *m*, pichel *m* **2** : lanzador *m*, -dora *f* (en béisbol, etc.)
pitchfork [ˈpɪtʃˌfɔrk] *n* : horquilla *f*, horca *f*
piteous [ˈpɪtiəs] *adj* : lastimoso, lastimero — **piteously** *adv*
pitfall [ˈpɪtˌfɔl] *n* : peligro *m* (poco obvio), dificultad *f*
pith [ˈpɪθ] *n* **1** : médula *f* (de una planta) **2** CORE : meollo *m*, entraña *f*
pithy [ˈpɪθi] *adj* **pithier; -est** : conciso y sustancioso <pithy comments : comentarios sucintos>
pitiable [ˈpɪtiəbəl] → **pitiful**
pitiful [ˈpɪtɪfəl] *adj* **1** LAMENTABLE : lastimero, lastimoso, lamentable **2** CONTEMPTIBLE : despreciable, lamentable — **pitifully** [-fli] *adv*
pitiless [ˈpɪtɪləs] *adj* : despiadado — **pitilessly** *adv*
pittance [ˈpɪtənts] *n* : miseria *f*
pituitary [pəˈtuːəˌtɛri, -ˈtjuː-] *adj* : pituitario
pity[1] [ˈpɪti] *vt* **pitied; pitying** : compadecer, compadecerse de
pity[2] *n*, *pl* **pities 1** COMPASSION : compasión *f*, piedad *f* **2** SHAME : lástima *f*, pena *f* <what a pity! : ¡qué lástima!>
pivot[1] [ˈpɪvət] *vi* **1** : girar sobre un eje **2 to pivot on** : girar sobre, depender de
pivot[2] *n* : pivote *m*
pivotal [ˈpɪvətəl] *adj* : fundamental, central
pixie *or* **pixy** [ˈpɪksi] *n*, *pl* **pixies** : elfo *m*, hada *f*
pizza [ˈpiːtsə] *n* : pizza *f*
pizzazz *or* **pizazz** [pəˈzæz] *n* **1** GLAMOR : encanto *m* **2** VITALITY : animación *f*, vitalidad *f*
placard [ˈplækərd, -ˌkɑrd] *n* POSTER : cartel *m*, póster *m*, afiche *m*
placate [ˈpleɪˌkeɪt, ˈplæ-] *vt* **-cated; -cating** : aplacar, apaciguar
place[1] [ˈpleɪs] *vt* **placed; placing 1** PUT, SET : poner, colocar **2** SITUATE : situar, ubicar, emplazar <to be well placed : estar bien situado> <to place in a job : colocar en un trabajo> **3** IDENTIFY, RECALL : identificar, ubicar, recordar <I can't place him : no lo ubico> **4 to place an order** : hacer un pedido
place[2] *n* **1** SPACE : sitio *m*, lugar *m* <there's no place to sit : no hay sitio para sentarse> **2** LOCATION, SPOT : lugar *m*, sitio *m*, parte *f* <place of work : lugar de trabajo> <our summer place : nuestra casa de verano> <all over the place : por todas partes> **3** RANK : lugar *m*, puesto *m* <he took first place : ganó el primer lugar> **4**

POSITION : lugar *m* <everything in its place : todo en su debido lugar> <to feel out of place : sentirse fuera de lugar> **5** SEAT : asiento *m,* cubierto *m* (a la mesa) **6** JOB : puesto *m* **7** ROLE : papel *m,* lugar *m* <to change places : cambiarse los papeles> **8 to take place :** tener lugar **9 to take the place of :** sustituir a

placebo [plə'siːˌboː] *n, pl* **-bos :** placebo *m*

placement ['pleɪsmənt] *n* **:** colocación *f*

placenta [plə'sɛntə] *n, pl* **-tas** *or* **-tae** [-ti, -ˌtaɪ] **:** placenta *f*

placid ['plæsəd] *adj* **:** plácido, tranquilo — **placidly** *adv*

plagiarism ['pleɪdʒəˌrɪzəm] *n* **:** plagio *m*

plagiarist ['pleɪdʒərɪst] *n* **:** plagiario *m,* -ria *f*

plagiarize ['pleɪdʒəˌraɪz] *vt* **-rized; -rizing :** plagiar

plague[1] ['pleɪg] *vt* **plagued; plaguing 1** AFFLICT **:** plagar, afligir **2** HARASS **:** acosar, atormentar

plague[2] *n* **1 :** plaga *f* (de insectos, etc.) **2 :** peste *f* (en medicina)

plaid[1] ['plæd] *adj* **:** escocés, de cuadros <a plaid skirt : una falda escocesa>

plaid[2] *n* TARTAN **:** tela *f* escocesa, tartán *m*

plain[1] ['pleɪn] *adj* **1** SIMPLE, UNADORNED **:** liso, sencillo, sin adornos **2** CLEAR **:** claro <in plain language : en palabras claras> **3** FRANK **:** franco, puro <the plain truth : la pura verdad> **4** HOMELY **:** ordinario, poco atractivo **5 in plain sight :** a la vista de todos

plain[2] *n* **:** llanura *f,* llano *m,* planicie *f*

plainly ['pleɪnli] *adv* **1** CLEARLY **:** claramente **2** FRANKLY **:** francamente, con franqueza **3** SIMPLY **:** sencillamente

plaintiff ['pleɪntɪf] *n* **:** demandante *mf*

plaintive ['pleɪntɪv] *adj* MOURNFUL **:** lastimero, plañidero

plait[1] ['pleɪt, 'plæt] *vt* **1** PLEAT **:** plisar **2** BRAID **:** trenzar

plait[2] *n* **1** PLEAT **:** pliegue *m* **2** BRAID **:** trenza *f*

plan[1] ['plæn] *v* **planned; planning** *vt* **1 :** planear, proyectar, planificar <to plan a trip : planear un viaje> <to plan a city : planificar una ciudad> **2** INTEND **:** tener planeado, proyectar — *vi* **:** hacer planes

plan[2] *n* **1** DIAGRAM **:** plano *m,* esquema *m* **2** SCHEME **:** plan *m,* proyecto *m,* programa *m* <to draw up a plan : elaborar un proyecto>

plane[1] ['pleɪn] *vt* **planed; planing :** cepillar (madera)

plane[2] *adj* **:** plano

plane[3] *n* **1 :** plano *m* (en matemáticas, etc.) **2** LEVEL **:** nivel *m* **3 :** cepillo *m* (de carpintero) **4 → airplane**

planet ['plænət] *n* **:** planeta *f*

planetarium [ˌplænə'tɛriəm] *n, pl* **-iums** *or* **-ia** [-iə] **:** planetario *m*

planetary ['plænəˌtɛri] *adj* **:** planetario

plank ['plæŋk] *n* **1** BOARD **:** tablón *m,* tabla *f* **2 :** artículo *m,* punto *m* (de una plataforma política)

plankton ['plæŋktən] *n* **:** plancton *m*

plant[1] ['plænt] *vt* **1 :** plantar (flores, árboles), sembrar (semillas) **2** PLACE **:** plantar, colocar <to plant an idea : inculcar una idea>

plant[2] *n* **1 :** planta *f* <leafy plants : plantas frondosas> **2** FACTORY **:** planta *f,* fábrica *f* <hydroelectric plant : planta hidroeléctrica> **3** MACHINERY **:** maquinaria *f,* equipo *m*

plantain ['plæntən] *n* **1 :** llantén *m* (mala hierba) **2 :** plátano *m,* plátano *m* macho *Mex* (fruta)

plantation [plæn'teɪʃən] *n* **:** plantación *f,* hacienda *f* <a coffee plantation : un cafetal>

planter ['plæntər] *n* **1 :** hacendado *m,* -da *f* (de una hacienda) **2** FLOWERPOT **:** tiesto *m,* maceta *f*

plaque ['plæk] *n* **1** TABLET **:** placa *f* **2 :** placa *f* (dental)

plasma ['plæzmə] *n* **:** plasma *m*

plaster[1] ['plæstər] *vt* **1 :** enyesar, revocar (con yeso) **2** COVER **:** cubrir, llenar <a wall plastered with notices : una pared cubierta de avisos>

plaster[2] *n* **1 :** yeso *m,* revoque *m* (para paredes, etc.) **2 :** escayola *f,* yeso *m* (en medicina) **3 plaster of Paris** ['pærɪs] **:** yeso *m* mate

plaster cast *n* **:** vaciado *m* de yeso

plasterer ['plæstərər] *n* **:** revocador *m,* -dora *f*

plastic[1] ['plæstɪk] *adj* **1 :** de plástico **2** PLIABLE **:** plástico, flexible **3 plastic surgery :** cirugía *f* plástica

plastic[2] *n* **:** plástico *m*

plate[1] ['pleɪt] *vt* **plated; plating :** chapar (en metal)

plate[2] *n* **1** PLAQUE, SHEET **:** placa *f* <a steel plate : una placa de acero> **2** UTENSILS **:** vajilla *f* (de metal) <silver plate : vajilla de plata> **3** DISH **:** plato *m* **4** DENTURES **:** dentadura *f* postiza **5** ILLUSTRATION **:** lámina *f* (en un libro) **6 license plate :** matrícula *f,* placa *f* de matrícula

plateau [plæ'toː] *n, pl* **-teaus** *or* **-teaux** [-'toːz] **:** meseta *f*

platform ['plætˌfɔrm] *n* **1** STAGE **:** plataforma *f,* estrado *m,* tribuna *f* **2 :** andén *m* (de una estación de ferrocarril) **3 political platform :** plataforma *f* política, programa *m* electoral

plating ['pleɪt̬ɪŋ] *n* **1 :** enchapado *m* **2 silver plating :** plateado *m*

platinum ['plætənəm] *n* **:** platino *m*

platitude ['plæt̬əˌtuːd, -ˌtjuːd] *n* **:** lugar *m* común, perogrullada *f*

platoon [plə'tuːn] *n* **:** sección *f* (en el ejército)

platter ['plæt̬ər] *n* **:** fuente *f*

platypus ['plætɪpəs, -ˌpʊs] *n, pl* **platypuses** *or* **platypi** [-ˌpaɪ, -ˌpiː] : ornitorrinco *m*

plausibility [ˌplɔzə'bɪləti] *n, pl* **-ties** : credibilidad *f,* verosimilitud *f*

plausible ['plɔzəbəl] *adj* : creíble, convincente, verosímil — **plausibly** [-bli] *adv*

play[1] ['pleɪ] *vi* **1** : jugar <to play with a doll : jugar con una muñeca> <to play with an idea : darle vueltas a una idea> **2** FIDDLE, TOY : jugar, juguetear <don't play with your food : no juegues con la comida> **3** : tocar <to play in a band : tocar en un grupo> **4** : actuar (en una obra de teatro) — *vt* **1** : jugar (un deporte, etc.), jugar a (un juego), jugar contra (un contrincante) **2** : tocar (música o un instrumento) **3** PERFORM : interpretar, hacer el papel de (un carácter), representar (una obra de teatro) <she plays the lead : hace el papel principal>

play[2] *n* **1** GAME, RECREATION : juego *m* <children at play : niños jugando> <a play on words : un juego de palabras> **2** ACTION : juego *m* <the ball is in play : la pelota está en juego> <to bring into play : poner en juego> **3** DRAMA : obra *f* de teatro, pieza *f* (de teatro) **4** MOVEMENT : juego *m* (de la luz, una brisa, etc.) **5** SLACK : juego *m* <there's not enough play in the wheel : la rueda no da lo suficiente>

playacting ['pleɪˌæktɪŋ] *n* : actuación *f,* teatro *m*

player ['pleɪər] *n* **1** : jugador *m,* -dora *f* (en un juego) **2** ACTOR : actor *m,* actriz *f* **3** MUSICIAN : músico *m,* -ca *f*

playful ['pleɪfəl] *adj* **1** FROLICSOME : juguetón **2** JOCULAR : jocoso — **playfully** *adv*

playfulness ['pleɪfəlnəs] *n* : lo juguetón, jocosidad *f,* alegría *f*

playground ['pleɪˌgraʊnd] *n* : patio *m* de recreo, jardín *m* para jugar

playhouse ['pleɪˌhaʊs] *n* **1** THEATER : teatro *m* **2** : casita *f* de juguete

playing card *n* : naipe *m,* carta *f*

playmate ['pleɪˌmeɪt] *n* : compañero *m,* -ra *f* de juego

play–off ['pleɪˌɔf] *n* : desempate *m*

playpen ['pleɪˌpɛn] *n* : corral *m* (para niños)

plaything ['pleɪˌθɪŋ] *n* : juguete *m*

playwright ['pleɪˌraɪt] *n* : dramaturgo *m,* -ga *f*

plaza ['plæzə, 'plɑ-] *n* **1** SQUARE : plaza *f* **2 shopping plaza** MALL : centro *m* comercial

plea ['pliː] *n* **1** : acto *m* de declararse <he entered a plea of guilty : se declaró culpable> **2** APPEAL : ruego *m,* súplica *f*

plead ['pliːd] *v* **pleaded** *or* **pled** ['plɛd]; **pleading** *vi* **1** : declararse (culpable o inocente) **2 to plead for** : suplicar, implorar — *vt* **1** : alegar, pretextar <he pleaded illness : pretextó la enfermedad> **2 to plead a case** : defender un caso

pleasant ['plɛzənt] *adj* : agradable, grato, bueno — **pleasantly** *adv*

pleasantness ['plɛzəntnəs] *n* : lo agradable, amenidad *f*

pleasantries ['plɛzəntriz] *npl* : cumplidos *mpl*, cortesías *fpl* <to exchange pleasantries : intercambiar cumplidos>

please[1] ['pliːz] *v* **pleased; pleasing** *vt* **1** GRATIFY : complacer <please yourself! : ¡cómo quieras!> **2** SATISFY : contentar, satisfacer — *vi* **1** SATISFY : complacer, agradar <anxious to please : deseoso de complacer> **2** LIKE : querer <do as you please : haz lo que quieras, haz lo que te parezca>

please[2] *adv* : por favor

pleased ['pliːzd] *adj* : contento, satisfecho, alegre

pleasing ['pliːzɪŋ] *adj* : agradable — **pleasingly** *adv*

pleasurable ['plɛʒərəbəl] *adj* PLEASANT : agradable

pleasure ['plɛʒər] *n* **1** WISH : deseo *m,* voluntad *f* <at your pleasure : cuando guste> **2** ENJOYMENT : placer *m,* disfrute *m,* goce *m* <with pleasure : con mucho gusto> **3** : placer *m,* gusto *m* <it's a pleasure to be here : me da gusto estar aquí> <the pleasures of reading : los placeres de leer>

pleat[1] ['pliːt] *vt* : plisar

pleat[2] *n* : pliegue *m*

plebeian [plɪ'biən] *adj* : ordinario, plebeyo

pledge[1] ['plɛdʒ] *vt* **pledged; pledging** **1** PAWN : empeñar, prendar **2** PROMISE : prometer, jurar

pledge[2] *n* **1** SECURITY : garantía *f,* prenda *f* **2** PROMISE : promesa *f*

plenteous ['plɛntiəs] *adj* : copioso, abundante

plentiful ['plɛntɪfəl] *adj* : abundante — **plentifully** [-fli] *adv*

plenty ['plɛnti] *n* : abundancia *f* <plenty of time : tiempo de sobra> <plenty of visitors : muchos visitantes>

plethora ['plɛθərə] *n* : plétora *f*

pleurisy ['plʊrəsi] *n* : pleuresía *f*

pliable ['plaɪəbəl] *adj* : flexible, maleable

pliant ['plaɪənt] → **pliable**

pliers ['plaɪərz] *npl* : alicates *mpl*, pinzas *fpl*

plight ['plaɪt] *n* : situación *f* difícil, apuro *m*

plod ['plɑd] *vi* **plodded; plodding** **1** TRUDGE : caminar pesadamente y lentamente **2** DRUDGE : trabajar laboriosamente

plot[1] ['plɑt] *v* **plotted; plotting** *vt* **1** DEVISE : tramar **2 to plot out** : trazar, determinar (una posición, etc.) — *vi* CONSPIRE : conspirar

plot[2] *n* **1** LOT : terreno *m,* parcela *f,* lote *m* **2** STORY : argumento *m* (en el teatro), trama *f* (en un libro, etc.) **3** CONSPIRACY, INTRIGUE **:** complot *m,* intriga *f*

plotter ['plɑt̬ər] *n* **:** conspirador *m,* -dora *f;* intrigante *mf*

plow[1] *or* **plough** ['plaʊ] *vt* **1 :** arar (la tierra) **2 to plow the seas :** surcar los mares

plow[2] *or* **plough** *n* **1 :** arado *m* **2** → **snowplow**

plowshare ['plaʊ,ʃɛr] *n* **:** reja *f* del arado

ploy ['plɔɪ] *n* **:** estratagema *f,* maniobra *f*

pluck[1] ['plʌk] *vt* **1** PICK **:** arrancar **2 :** desplumar (un pollo, etc.) — *vi* **to pluck at :** tirar de

pluck[2] *n* **1** TUG **:** tirón *m* **2** COURAGE, SPIRIT **:** valor *m,* ánimo *m*

plucky ['plʌki] *adj* **pluckier; -est :** valiente, animoso

plug[1] ['plʌg] *vt* **plugged; plugging 1** BLOCK **:** tapar **2** PROMOTE **:** hacerle publicidad a, promocionar **3 to plug in :** enchufar

plug[2] *n* **1** STOPPER **:** tapón *m* **2 :** enchufe *m* (eléctrico) **3** ADVERTISEMENT **:** publicidad *f,* propaganda *f*

plum ['plʌm] *n* **1 :** ciruela *f* (fruta) **2 :** color *m* ciruela **3** PRIZE **:** premio *m,* algo muy atractivo

plumage ['plu:mɪdʒ] *n* **:** plumaje *m*

plumb[1] ['plʌm] *vt* **1 :** aplomar <to plumb a wall : aplomar una pared> **2** SOUND **:** sondear, sondar

plumb[2] *adv* **1** VERTICALLY **:** a plomo, verticalmente **2** EXACTLY **:** justo, exactamente **3** COMPLETELY **:** completamente, absolutamente <plumb crazy : loco de remate>

plumb[3] *adj* **:** a plomo

plumb[4] *n or* **plumb line :** plomada *f*

plumber ['plʌmər] *n* **:** plomero *m,* -ra *f;* fontanero *m,* -ra *f*

plumbing ['plʌmɪŋ] *n* **1 :** plomería *f,* fontanería *f* (trabajo del plomero) **2** PIPES **:** cañería *f,* tubería *f*

plume ['plu:m] *n* **1** FEATHER **:** pluma *f* **2** TUFT **:** penacho *m* (en un sombrero, etc.)

plumed ['plu:md] *adj* **:** con plumas <white-plumed birds : aves de plumaje blanco>

plummet ['plʌmət] *vi* **:** caer en picada, desplomarse

plump[1] ['plʌmp] *vi or* **to plump down :** dejarse caer (pesadamente)

plump[2] *adv* **1** STRAIGHT **:** a plomo **2** DIRECTLY **:** directamente, sin rodeos <he ran plump into the door : dio de cara con la puerta>

plump[3] *adj* **:** llenito *fam,* regordete *fam,* rechoncho *fam*

plumpness ['plʌmpnəs] *n* **:** gordura *f*

plunder[1] ['plʌndər] *vi* **:** saquear, robar

plunder[2] *n* **:** botín *m*

plunderer ['plʌndərər] *n* **:** saqueador *m,* -dora *f*

plunge[1] ['plʌndʒ] *v* **plunged; plunging** *vt* **1** IMMERSE **:** sumergir **2** THRUST **:** hundir, clavar — *vi* **1** DIVE **:** zambullirse (en el agua) **2 :** meterse precipitadamente o violentamente <they plunged into war : se enfrascaron en una guerra> <he plunged into depression : cayó en la depresión> **3** DESCEND **:** descender en picada <the road plunges dizzily : la calle desciende vertiginosamente>

plunge[2] *n* **1** DIVE **:** zambullida *f* **2** DROP **:** descenso *m* abrupto <the plunge in prices : el desplome de los precios>

plural[1] ['plʊrəl] *adj* **:** plural

plural[2] *n* **:** plural *m*

plurality [plʊ'ræləţi] *n, pl* **-ties :** pluralidad *f*

pluralize ['plʊrə,laɪz] *vt* **-ized; -izing :** pluralizar

plus[1] ['plʌs] *adj* **1** POSITIVE **:** positivo <a plus factor : un factor positivo> **2** (*indicating a quantity in addition*) <a grade of C plus : una calificación entre C y B> <a salary of $30,000 plus : un sueldo de más de $30,000>

plus[2] *n* **1** *or* **plus sign :** más *m,* signo *m* de más **2** ADVANTAGE **:** ventaja *f*

plus[3] *prep* **:** más (en matemáticas)

plus[4] *conj* AND **:** y

plush[1] ['plʌʃ] *adj* **1 :** afelpado **2** LUXURIOUS **:** lujoso

plush[2] *n* **:** felpa *f,* peluche *m*

plushy ['plʌʃi] *adj* **plushier; -est :** lujoso

Pluto ['plu:ţo:] *n* **:** Plutón *m*

plutocracy [plu:'tɑkrəsi] *n, pl* **-cies :** plutocracia *f*

plutonium [plu:'to:niəm] *n* **:** plutonio *m*

ply[1] ['plaɪ] *v* **plied; plying** *vt* **1** USE, WIELD **:** manejar <to ply an ax : manejar un hacha> **2** PRACTICE **:** ejercer <to ply a trade : ejercer un oficio> **3 to ply with questions :** acosar con preguntas

ply[2] *n, pl* **plies 1** LAYER **:** chapa *f* (de madera), capa *f* (de papel) **2** STRAND **:** cabo *m* (de hilo, etc.)

plywood ['plaɪ,wʊd] *n* **:** contrachapado *m*

pneumatic [nʊ'mæţɪk, njʊ-] *adj* **:** neumático

pneumonia [nʊ'mo:njə, njʊ-] *n* **:** pulmonía *f,* neumonía *f*

poach ['po:tʃ] *vt* **1 :** cocer a fuego lento <to poach an egg : escalfar un huevo> **2 to poach game :** cazar ilegalmente — *vi* **:** cazar ilegalmente

poacher ['po:tʃər] *n* **:** cazador *m* furtivo, cazadora *f* furtiva

pock ['pɑk] *n* **1** PUSTULE **:** pústula *f* **2** → **pockmark**

pocket[1] ['pɑkət] *vt* **1 :** meterse en el bolsillo <he pocketed the pen : se metió la pluma en el bolsillo> **2** STEAL **:** embolsarse

pocket[2] *n* **1 :** bolsillo *m,* bolsa *f Mex* <a coat pocket : el bolsillo de un abrigo>

<air pockets : bolsas de aire> **2** CENTER : foco *m,* centro *m* <a pocket of resistance : un foco de resistencia>

pocketbook ['pɑkət,bʊk] *n* **1** PURSE : cartera *f,* bolso *m,* bolsa *f Mex* **2** MEANS : recursos *mpl*

pocketknife ['pɑkət,naɪf] *n, pl* **-knives** : navaja *f*

pocket-size ['pɑkət'saɪz] *adj* : de bolsillo

pockmark ['pɑk,mɑrk] *n* : cicatriz *f* de viruela, viruela *f*

pod ['pɑd] *n* : vaina *f* <pea pod : vaina de guisantes>

podiatrist [pə'daɪətrɪst, po-] *n* : podólogo *m,* -ga *f*

podiatry [pə'daɪətri, po-] *n* : podología *f,* podiatría *f*

podium ['po:diəm] *n, pl* **-diums** *or* **-dia** [-diə] : podio *m,* estrado *m,* tarima *f*

poem ['po:əm] *n* : poema *m,* poesía *f*

poet ['po:ət] *n* : poeta *mf*

poetic [po'ɛt̬ɪk] *or* **poetical** [-t̬ɪkəl] *adj* : poético

poetry ['po:ətri] *n* : poesía *f*

pogrom ['po:grəm, pə'grɑm, 'pɑgrəm] *n* : pogrom *m*

poignancy ['pɔɪnjəntsi] *n, pl* **-cies** : lo conmovedor

poignant ['pɔɪnjənt] *adj* **1** PAINFUL : penoso, doloroso <poignant grief : profundo dolor> **2** TOUCHING : conmovedor, emocionante

poinsettia [pɔɪn'sɛt̬iə, -'sɛt̬ə] *n* : flor *f* de Nochebuena

point[1] ['pɔɪnt] *vt* **1** SHARPEN : afilar (la punta de) **2** INDICATE : señalar, indicar <to point the way : señalar el camino> **3** AIM : apuntar **4 to point out** : señalar, indicar — *vi* **1 to point at** : señalar (con el dedo) **2 to point to** INDICATE : señalar, indicar

point[2] *n* **1** ITEM : punto *m* <the main points : los puntos principales> **2** QUALITY : cualidad *f* <her good points : sus buenas cualidades> <it's not his strong point : no es su (punto) fuerte> **3** (*indicating a chief idea or meaning*) <it's beside the point : no viene al caso> <to get to the point : ir al grano> <to stick to the point : no salirse del tema> **4** PURPOSE : fin *m,* propósito *m* <there's no point to it : no vale la pena, no sirve para nada> **5** PLACE : punto *m,* lugar *m* <points of interest : puntos interesantes> **6** : punto *m* (en una escala) <boiling point : punto de ebullición> **7** MOMENT : momento *m,* coyuntura *f* <at this point : en este momento> **8** TIP : punta *f* **9** HEADLAND : punta *f,* cabo *m* **10** PERIOD : punto *m* (marca de puntuación) **11** UNIT : punto *m* <he scored 15 points : ganó 15 puntos> <shares fell 10 points : las acciones bajaron 10 enteros> **12 compass points** : puntos *mpl* cardinales **13 decimal point** : punto *m* decimal, coma *f*

point–blank[1] ['pɔɪnt'blæŋk] *adv* **1** : a quemarropa <to shoot point-blank : disparar a quemarropa> **2** BLUNTLY, DIRECTLY : a bocajarro, sin rodeos, francamente

point–blank[2] *adj* **1** : a quemarropa <point-blank shots : disparos a quemarropa> **2** BLUNT, DIRECT : directo, franco

pointedly ['pɔɪntədli] *adv* : intencionadamente, directamente

pointer ['pɔɪntər] *n* **1** STICK : puntero *m* (para maestros, etc.) **2** INDICATOR, NEEDLE : indicador *m,* aguja *f* **3** : perro *m* de muestra **4** HINT, TIP : consejo *m*

pointless ['pɔɪntləs] *adj* : inútil, ocioso, vano <it's pointless to continue : no tiene sentido continuar>

point of view *n* : perspectiva *f,* punto *m* de vista

poise[1] ['pɔɪz] *vt* **poised; poising** BALANCE : equilibrar, balancear

poise[2] *n* : aplomo *m,* compostura *f*

poison[1] ['pɔɪzən] *vt* **1** : envenenar, intoxicar **2** CORRUPT : corromper

poison[2] *n* : veneno *m*

poison ivy *n* : hiedra *f* venenosa

poisonous ['pɔɪzənəs] *adj* : venenoso, tóxico, ponzoñoso

poke[1] ['po:k] *v* **poked; poking** *vt* **1** JAB : golpear (con la punta de algo), dar <he poked me with his finger : me dio con el dedo> **2** THRUST : introducir, asomar <I poked my head out the window : asomé la cabeza por la ventana> — *vi* **1 to poke around** RUMMAGE : hurgar **2 to poke along** DAWDLE : demorarse, entretenerse

poke[2] *n* : golpe *m* abrupto (con la punta de algo)

poker ['po:kər] *n* **1** : atizador *m* (para el fuego) **2** : póker *m,* poker *m* (juego de naipes)

polar ['po:lər] *adj* : polar

polar bear *n* : oso *m* blanco

Polaris [po'lærɪs, -'lɑr-] → **North Star**

polarize ['po:lə,raɪz] *vt* **-ized; -izing** : polarizar

pole ['po:l] *n* **1** : palo *m,* poste *m,* vara *f* <telephone pole : poste de teléfonos> **2** : polo *m* <the South Pole : el Polo Sur> **3** : polo *m* (eléctrico o magnético)

Pole ['po:l] *n* : polaco *m,* -ca *f*

polecat ['po:l,kæt] *n, pl* **polecats** *or* **polecat** **1** : turón *m* (de Europa) **2** SKUNK : mofeta *f,* zorrillo *m*

polemical [pə'lɛmɪkəl] *adj* : polémico

polemics [pə'lɛmɪks] *ns & pl* : polémica *f*

polestar ['po:l,stɑr] → **North Star**

police[1] [pə'li:s] *vt* **-liced; -licing** : mantener el orden en <to police the streets : patrullar las calles>

police[2] *ns & pl* **1** : policía *f* (organización) **2** POLICE OFFICERS : policías *mfpl*

policeman [pə'li:smən] *n, pl* **-men** [-mən, -,mɛn] : policía *m*

police officer *n* **:** policía *mf,* agente *mf* de policía

policewoman [pə'liːs,wʊmən] *n, pl* **-women** [-,wɪmən] **:** policía *f,* mujer *f* policía

policy ['pɑləsi] *n, pl* **-cies 1 :** política *f* <foreign policy : política exterior> **2** *or* **insurance policy :** póliza *f* de seguros, seguro *m*

polio¹ ['poːli,oː] *adj* **:** de polio <polio vaccine : vacuna contra la polio>

polio² *n* → **poliomyelitis**

poliomyelitis [,poːli,oː,maɪə'laɪt̬əs] *n* **:** poliomielitis *f,* polio *f*

polish¹ ['pɑlɪʃ] *vt* **1 :** pulir, lustrar, sacar brillo a <to polish one's nails : pintarse las uñas> **2** REFINE **:** pulir, perfeccionar

polish² *n* **1** LUSTER **:** brillo *m,* lustre *m* **2** REFINEMENT **:** refinamiento *m* **3 :** betún *m* (para zapatos), cera *f* (para suelos y muebles), esmalte *m* (para las uñas)

Polish¹ ['poːlɪʃ] *adj* **:** polaco

Polish² *n* **:** polaco *m* (idioma)

polite [pə'laɪt] *adj* **-liter; -est :** cortés, correcto, educado

politely [pə'laɪtli] *adv* **:** cortésmente, correctamente, con buenos modales

politeness [pə'laɪtnəs] *n* **:** cortesía *f*

politic ['pɑlə,tɪk] *adj* **:** diplomático, prudente

political [pə'lɪtɪkəl] *adj* **:** político — **politically** [-tɪkli] *adv*

politician [,pɑlə'tɪʃən] *n* **:** político *m,* -ca *f*

politics ['pɑlə,tɪks] *ns & pl* **:** política *f*

polka ['poːlkə, 'poːkə] *n* **:** polka *f*

polka dot ['poːkə,dɑt] *n* **:** lunar *m* (en un diseño)

poll¹ ['poːl] *vt* **1 :** obtener (votos) <she polled over 1000 votes : obtuvo más de 1000 votos> **2** CANVASS **:** encuestar, sondear — *vi* **:** obtener votos

poll² *n* **1** SURVEY **:** encuesta *f,* sondeo *m* **2 polls** *npl* **:** urnas *fpl* <to go to the polls : acudir a las urnas, ir a votar>

pollen ['pɑlən] *n* **:** polen *m*

pollinate ['pɑlə,neɪt] *vt* **-nated; -nating :** polinizar

pollination [,pɑlə'neɪʃən] *n* **:** polinización *f*

pollster ['poːlstər] *n* **:** encuestador *m,* -dora *f*

pollutant [pə'luːtənt] *n* **:** contaminante *m*

pollute [pə'luːt] *vt* **-luted; -luting :** contaminar

pollution [pə'luːʃən] *n* **:** contaminación *f*

pollywog *or* **polliwog** ['pɑli,wɔg] *n* TADPOLE **:** renacuajo *m*

polo ['poː,loː] *n* **:** polo *m*

poltergeist ['poːltər,gaɪst] *n* **:** poltergeist *m,* fantasma *m* travieso

polyester ['pɑli,ɛstər, ,pɑli'-] *n* **:** poliéster *m*

polygamous [pə'lɪgəməs] *adj* **:** polígamo

polygamy [pə'lɪgəmi] *n* **:** poligamia *f*

polygon ['pɑli,gɑn] *n* **:** polígono *m*

polymer ['pɑləmər] *n* **:** polímero *m*

polyunsaturated [,pɑli,ʌn'sætʃə,reɪt̬əd] *adj* **:** poliinsaturado

pomegranate ['pɑmə,grænət, 'pɑm,grænət] *n* **:** granada *f* (fruta)

pommel¹ ['pʌməl] *vt* → **pummel**

pommel² ['pʌməl, 'pɑ-] *n* **1 :** pomo *m* (de una espada) **2 :** perilla *f* (de una silla de montar)

pomp ['pɑmp] *n* **1** SPLENDOR **:** pompa *f,* esplendor *m* **2** OSTENTATION **:** boato *m,* ostentación *f*

pom-pom ['pɑm,pɑm] *n* **:** borla *f,* pompón *m*

pomposity [pɑm'pɑsət̬i] *n, pl* **-ties :** pomposidad *f*

pompous ['pɑmpəs] *adj* **:** pomposo — **pompously** *adv*

poncho ['pɑn,tʃoː] *n, pl* **-chos :** poncho *m*

pond ['pɑnd] *n* **:** charca *f* (natural), estanque *m* (artificial)

ponder ['pɑndər] *vt* **:** reflexionar, considerar — *vi* **to ponder over :** reflexionar sobre, sopesar

ponderous ['pɑndərəs] *adj* **:** pesado

pontiff ['pɑntɪf] *n* POPE **:** pontífice *m*

pontificate [pɑn'tɪfə,keɪt] *vi* **-cated; -cating :** pontificar

pontoon [pɑn'tuːn] *n* **:** pontón *m*

pony ['poːni] *n, pl* **-nies :** poni *m,* poney *m,* jaca *f*

ponytail ['poːni,teɪl] *n* **:** cola *f* de caballo, coleta *f*

poodle ['puːdəl] *n* **:** caniche *m*

pool¹ ['puːl] *vt* **:** mancomunar, hacer un fondo común de

pool² *n* **1 :** charca *f* <a swimming pool : una piscina> **2** PUDDLE **:** charco *m* **3** RESERVE, SUPPLY **:** fondo *m* común (de recursos), reserva *f* **4 :** billar *m* (juego)

poor ['pʊr, 'por] *adj* **1 :** pobre <poor people : los pobres> **2** SCANTY **:** pobre, escaso <poor attendance : baja asistencia> **3** UNFORTUNATE **:** pobre <poor thing! : ¡pobrecito!> **4** BAD **:** malo <to be in poor health : estar mal de salud>

poorly ['pʊrli, 'por-] *adv* **:** mal

pop¹ ['pɑp] *v* **popped; popping** *vi* **1** BURST **:** reventarse, estallar **2 :** ir, venir, o aparecer abruptamente <he popped into the house : se metió en la casa> <a menu pops up : aparece un menú> **3 to pop out** PROTRUDE **:** salirse, saltarse <my eyes popped out of my head : se me saltaban los ojos> — *vt* **1** BURST **:** reventar **2 :** hacer o meter abruptamente <he popped it into his mouth : se lo metió en la boca>

pop² *adj* **:** popular <pop music : música popular>

pop³ *n* **1 :** estallido *m* pequeño (de un globo, etc.) **2** SODA **:** refresco *m,* gaseosa *f*

popcorn [ˈpɑpˌkɔrn] *n* : palomitas *fpl* (de maíz)

pope [ˈpoːp] *n* : papa *m* <Pope John : el Papa Juan>

poplar [ˈpɑplər] *n* : álamo *m*

poplin [ˈpɑplɪn] *n* : popelín *m*, popelina *f*

poppy [ˈpɑpi] *n, pl* **-pies** : amapola *f*

populace [ˈpɑpjələs] *n* **1** MASSES : pueblo *m* **2** POPULATION : población *f*

popular [ˈpɑpjələr] *adj* **1** : popular <the popular vote : el voto popular> **2** COMMON : generalizado, común <popular beliefs : creencias generalizadas> **3** : popular, de gran popularidad <a popular singer : un cantante popular>

popularity [ˌpɑpjəˈlærət̬i] *n* : popularidad *f*

popularize [ˈpɑpjələˌraɪz] *vt* **-ized; -izing** : popularizar

popularly [ˈpɑpjələrli] *adv* : popularmente, vulgarmente

populate [ˈpɑpjəˌleɪt] *vt* **-lated; -lating** : poblar

population [ˌpɑpjəˈleɪʃən] *n* : población *f*

populous [ˈpɑpjələs] *adj* : populoso

porcelain [ˈporsələn] *n* : porcelana *f*

porch [ˈportʃ] *n* : porche *m*

porcupine [ˈpɔrkjəˌpaɪn] *n* : puerco *m* espín

pore[1] [ˈpor] *vi* **pored; poring 1** GAZE : mirar (con atención) **2 to pore over** : leer detenidamente, estudiar

pore[2] *n* : poro *m*

pork [ˈpork] *n* : carne *f* de cerdo, carne *f* de puerco

pornographic [ˌpɔrnəˈgræfɪk] *adj* : pornográfico

pornography [pɔrˈnɑgrəfi] *n* : pornografía *f*

porous [ˈporəs] *adj* : poroso

porpoise [ˈpɔrpəs] *n* **1** : marsopa *f* **2** DOLPHIN : delfín *m*

porridge [ˈpɔrɪdʒ] *n* : sopa *f* espesa de harina, gachas *fpl*

port[1] [ˈport] *adj* : de babor <on the port side : a babor>

port[2] *n* **1** HARBOR : puerto *m* **2** ORIFICE : orificio *m* (de una válvula, etc.) **3** : puerto *m* (de una computadora) **4** PORTHOLE : portilla *f* **5** *or* **port side** : babor *m* (de un barco) **6** : oporto *m* (vino)

portable [ˈport̬əbəl] *adj* : portátil

portal [ˈport̬əl] *n* : portal *m*

portend [pɔrˈtɛnd] *vt* : presagiar, augurar

portent [ˈpɔrˌtɛnt] *n* : presagio *m*, augurio *m*

portentous [pɔrˈtɛntəs] *adj* : profético, que presagia

porter [ˈportər] *n* : maletero *m*, mozo *m* (de estación)

portfolio [portˈfoːliˌo] *n, pl* **-lios 1** FOLDER : cartera *f* (para llevar papeles), carpeta *f* **2** : cartera *f* (diplomática) **3 investment portfolio** : cartera de inversiones

porthole [ˈportˌhoːl] *n* : portilla *f* (de un barco), ventanilla *f* (de un avión)

portico [ˈport̬ɪˌko] *n, pl* **-coes** *or* **-cos** : pórtico *m*

portion[1] [ˈporʃən] *vt* DISTRIBUTE : repartir

portion[2] *n* PART, SHARE : porción *f*, parte *f*

portly [ˈportli] *adj* **-lier; -est** : corpulento

portrait [ˈportrət, -ˌtreɪt] *n* : retrato *m*

portray [porˈtreɪ] *vt* **1** DEPICT : representar, retratar **2** DESCRIBE : describir **3** PLAY : interpretar (un personaje)

portrayal [porˈtreɪəl] *n* **1** REPRESENTATION : representación *f* **2** PORTRAIT : retrato *m*

Portuguese [ˌportʃəˈgiːz, -ˈgiːs] *n* **1** : portugués *m*, -guesa *f* (persona) **2** : portugués *m* (idioma) — **Portuguese** *adj*

pose[1] [ˈpoːz] *v* **posed; posing** *vt* PRESENT : plantear (una pregunta, etc.), representar (una amenaza) — *vi* **1** : posar (para una foto, etc.) **2 to pose as** : hacerse pasar por

pose[2] *n* **1** : pose *f* <to strike a pose : asumir una pose> **2** PRETENSE : pose *f*, afectación *f*

posh [ˈpɑʃ] *adj* : elegante, de lujo

position[1] [pəˈzɪʃən] *vt* : colocar, situar, ubicar

position[2] *n* **1** APPROACH, STANCE : posición *f*, postura *f*, planteamiento *m* **2** LOCATION : posición *f*, ubicación *f* **3** STATUS : posición *f* (en una jerarquía) **4** JOB : puesto *m*

positive [ˈpɑzət̬ɪv] *adj* **1** DEFINITE : incuestionable, inequívoco <positive evidence : pruebas irrefutables> **2** CONFIDENT : seguro **3** : positivo (en gramática, matemáticas, y física) **4** AFFIRMATIVE : positivo, afirmativo <a positive response : una respuesta positiva>

positively [ˈpɑzət̬ɪvli] *adv* **1** FAVORABLY : favorablemente **2** OPTIMISTICALLY : positivamente **3** DEFINITELY : definitivamente, en forma concluyente **4** (*used for emphasis*) : realmente, verdaderamente <it's positively awful! : ¡es verdaderamente malo!>

possess [pəˈzɛs] *vt* **1** HAVE, OWN : poseer, tener **2** SEIZE : apoderarse de <he was possessed by fear : el miedo se apoderó de él>

possession [pəˈzɛʃən] *n* **1** POSSESSING : posesión *f* **2** : posesión *f* (por un demonio, etc.) **3 possessions** *npl* PROPERTY : bienes *mpl*, propiedad *f*

possessive[1] [pəˈzɛsɪv] *adj* **1** : posesivo (en gramática) **2** JEALOUS : posesivo, celoso

possessive[2] *n or* **possessive case** : posesivo *m*

possessor [pəˈzɛsər] *n* **:** poseedor *m,* -dora *f*

possibility [ˌpɑsəˈbɪləṯi] *n, pl* **-ties** **:** posibilidad *f*

possible [ˈpɑsəbəl] *adj* **:** posible

possibly [ˈpɑsəbli] *adv* **1** CONCEIVABLY **:** posiblemente <it can't possibly be true! : ¡no puede ser!> **2** PERHAPS **:** quizás, posiblemente

possum [ˈpɑsəm] → **opossum**

post[1] [ˈpoːst] *vt* **1** MAIL **:** echar al correo, mandar por correo **2** ANNOUNCE **:** anunciar <they've posted the grades : han anunciado las notas> **3** AFFIX **:** fijar, poner (noticias, etc.) **4** STATION **:** apostar **5 to keep (someone) posted :** tener al corriente (a alguien)

post[2] *n* **1** POLE **:** poste *m,* palo *m* **2** STATION **:** puesto *m* **3** CAMP **:** puesto *m* (militar) **4** JOB, POSITION **:** puesto *m,* empleo *m,* cargo *m*

postage [ˈpoːstɪdʒ] *n* **:** franqueo *m*

postal [ˈpoːstəl] *adj* **:** postal

postcard [ˈpoːstˌkɑrd] *n* **:** postal *f,* tarjeta *f* postal

poster [ˈpoːstər] *n* **:** póster *m,* cartel *m,* afiche *m*

posterior[1] [pɑˈstɪriər, po-] *adj* **:** posterior

posterior[2] *n* BUTTOCKS **:** trasero *m,* nalgas *fpl,* asentaderas *fpl*

posterity [pɑˈstɛrəṯi] *n* **:** posteridad *f*

postgraduate[1] [ˌpoːstˈgrædʒʊət] *adj* **:** de postgrado

postgraduate[2] *n* **:** postgraduado *m,* -da *f*

posthaste [ˈpoːstˈheɪst] *adv* **:** a toda prisa

posthumous [ˈpɑstʃəməs] *adj* **:** póstumo — **posthumously** *adv*

postman [ˈpoːstmən, -ˌmæn] → **mailman**

postmark[1] [ˈpoːstˌmɑrk] *vt* **:** matasellar

postmark[2] *n* **:** matasellos *m*

postmaster [ˈpoːstˌmæstər] *n* **:** administrador *m,* -dora *f* de correos

postmortem [ˌpoːstˈmɔrṯəm] *n* **:** autopsia *f*

postnatal [ˌpoːstˈneɪṯəl] *adj* **:** postnatal <postnatal depression : depresión posparto>

post office *n* **:** correo *m,* oficina *f* de correos

postoperative [ˌpoːstˈɑpərəṯɪv, -ˌreɪ-] *adj* **:** posoperatorio

postpaid [ˌpoːstˈpeɪd] *adv* **:** con franqueo pagado

postpone [ˌpoːstˈpoːn] *vt* **-poned; -poning :** postergar, aplazar, posponer

postponement [ˌpoːstˈpoːnmənt] *n* **:** postergación *f,* aplazamiento *m*

postscript [ˈpoːstˌskrɪpt] *n* **:** postdata *f,* posdata *f*

postulate [ˈpɑstʃəˌleɪt] *vt* **-lated; -lating :** postular

posture[1] [ˈpɑstʃər] *vi* **-tured; -turing :** posar, asumir una pose

posture[2] *n* **:** postura *f*

postwar [ˌpoːstˈwɔr] *adj* **:** de (la) posguerra

posy [ˈpoːzi] *n, pl* **-sies 1** FLOWER **:** flor *f* **2** BOUQUET **:** ramo *m,* ramillete *m*

pot[1] [ˈpɑt] *vt* **potted; potting :** plantar (en una maceta)

pot[2] *n* **1 :** olla *f* (de cocina) **2 pots and pans :** cacharros *mpl*

potable [ˈpoːṯəbəl] *adj* **:** potable

potash [ˈpɑtˌæʃ] *n* **:** potasa *f*

potassium [pəˈtæsiəm] *n* **:** potasio *m*

potato [pəˈteɪṯo] *n, pl* **-toes :** papa *f,* patata *f Spain*

potato chips *npl* **:** papas *fpl* fritas (de bolsa)

potbellied [ˈpɑtˌbɛlid] *adj* **:** panzón, barrigón *fam*

potbelly [ˈpɑtˌbɛli] *n* **:** panza *f,* barriga *f*

potency [ˈpoːtəntsi] *n, pl* **-cies 1** POWER **:** fuerza *f,* potencia *f* **2** EFFECTIVENESS **:** eficacia *f*

potent [ˈpoːtənt] *adj* **1** POWERFUL **:** potente, poderoso **2** EFFECTIVE **:** eficaz <a potent medicine : una medicina bien fuerte>

potential[1] [pəˈtɛntʃəl] *adj* **:** potencial, posible

potential[2] *n* **1 :** potencial *m* <growth potential : potencial de crecimiento> <a child with potential : un niño que promete> **2 :** potencial *m* (eléctrico) — **potentially** *adv*

potful [ˈpɑtˌfʊl] *n* **:** contenido *m* de una olla <a potful of water : una olla de agua>

pothole [ˈpɑtˌhoːl] *n* **:** bache *m*

potion [ˈpoːʃən] *n* **:** brebaje *m,* poción *f*

potluck [ˈpɑtˌlʌk] *n* **to take potluck :** tomar lo que haya

potpourri [ˌpoːpʊˈriː] *n* **:** popurrí *m*

potshot [ˈpɑtˌʃɑt] *n* **1 :** tiro *m* al azar <to take potshots at : disparar al azar a> **2** CRITICISM **:** crítica *f* (hecha al azar)

potter [ˈpɑṯər] *n* **:** alfarero *m,* -ra *f*

pottery [ˈpɑṯəri] *n, pl* **-teries :** cerámica *f*

pouch [ˈpaʊtʃ] *n* **1** BAG **:** bolsa *f* pequeña **2 :** bolsa *f* (de un animal)

poultice [ˈpoːltəs] *n* **:** emplasto *m,* cataplasma *f*

poultry [ˈpoːltri] *n* **:** aves *fpl* de corral

pounce [ˈpaʊnts] *vi* **pounced; pouncing :** abalanzarse

pound[1] [ˈpaʊnd] *vt* **1** CRUSH **:** machacar, machucar, majar **2** BEAT **:** golpear, machacar <she pounded the lessons into them : les machacaba las lecciones> <he pounded home his point : les hizo entender su razonamiento> — *vi* **1** BEAT **:** palpitar (dícese del corazón) **2** RESOUND **:** retumbar, resonar **3 :** andar con paso pesado <we pounded through the mud : caminamos pesadamente por el barro>

pound[2] *n* **1 :** libra *f* (unidad de peso) **2 :** libra *f* (unidad monetaria) **3 dog pound :** perrera *f*

pour [ˈpor] *vt* **1 :** echar, verter, servir (bebidas) <pour it into a pot : viértalo en una olla> **2 :** proveer con abundancia <they poured money into it : le invirtieron mucho dinero> **3 to pour out :** dar salida a <he poured out his feelings to her : se desahogó con ella> — *vi* **1** FLOW **:** manar, fluir, salir <blood was pouring from the wound : la sangre le salía de la herida> **2 it's pouring (outside) :** está lloviendo a cántaros

pout[1] [ˈpaʊt] *vi* **:** hacer pucheros

pout[2] *n* **:** puchero *m*

poverty [ˈpɑvərt̬i] *n* **:** pobreza *f,* indigencia *f*

powder[1] [ˈpaʊdər] *vt* **1 :** empolvar <to powder one's face : empolvarse la cara> **2** PULVERIZE **:** pulverizar

powder[2] *n* **:** polvo *m,* polvos *mpl*

powdery [ˈpaʊdəri] *adj* **:** polvoriento, como polvo

power[1] [ˈpaʊər] *vt* **:** impulsar, propulsar

power[2] *n* **1** AUTHORITY **:** poder *m,* autoridad *f* <executive powers : poderes ejecutivos> **2** ABILITY **:** capacidad *f,* poder *m* **3 :** potencia *f* (política) <foreign powers : potencias extranjeras> **4** STRENGTH **:** fuerza *f* **5 :** potencia *f* (en física y matemáticas)

powerful [ˈpaʊərfəl] *adj* **:** poderoso, potente — **powerfully** *adv*

powerhouse [ˈpaʊərˌhaʊs] *n* **:** persona *f* dinámica

powerless [ˈpaʊərləs] *adj* **:** impotente

power plant *n* **:** central *f* eléctrica

powwow [ˈpaʊˌwaʊ] *n* **:** conferencia *f*

pox [ˈpɑks] *n, pl* **pox** *or* **poxes 1** CHICKEN POX **:** varicela *f* **2** SYPHILIS **:** sífilis *f*

practicable [ˈpræktɪkəbəl] *adj* **:** practicable, viable, factible

practical [ˈpræktɪkəl] *adj* **:** práctico

practicality [ˌpræktɪˈkæləti] *n, pl* **-ties :** factibilidad *f,* viabilidad *f*

practical joke *n* **:** broma *f* (pesada)

practically [ˈpræktɪkli] *adv* **1 :** de manera práctica **2** ALMOST **:** casi, prácticamente

practice[1] *or* **practise** [ˈpræktəs] *vt* **-ticed** *or* **-tised; -ticing** *or* **-tising 1 :** practicar <he practiced his German on us : practicó el alemán con nosotros> <to practice politeness : practicar la cortesía> **2 :** ejercer <to practice medicine : ejercer la medicina>

practice[2] *n* **1** USE **:** práctica *f* <to put into practice : poner en práctica> **2** CUSTOM **:** costumbre *f* <it's a common practice here : por aquí se acostumbra hacerlo> **3** TRAINING **:** práctica *f* **4 :** ejercicio *m* (de una profesión)

practitioner [prækˈtɪʃənər] *n* **1 :** profesional *mf* **2 general practitioner :** médico *m,* -ca *f*

pragmatic [prægˈmæt̬ɪk] *adj* **:** pragmático — **pragmatically** *adv*

pragmatism [ˈprægməˌtɪzəm] *n* **:** pragmatismo

prairie [ˈprɛri] *n* **:** pradera *f,* llanura *f*

praise[1] [ˈpreɪz] *vt* **praised; praising :** elogiar, alabar <to praise God : alabar a Dios>

praise[2] *n* **:** elogio *m,* alabanza *f*

praiseworthy [ˈpreɪzˌwərði] *adj* **:** digno de alabanza, loable

prance[1] [ˈprænts] *vi* **pranced; prancing 1 :** hacer cabriolas, cabriolar <a prancing horse : un caballo haciendo cabriolas> **2** SWAGGER **:** pavonearse

prance[2] *n* **:** cabriola *f*

prank [ˈpræŋk] *n* **:** broma *f,* travesura *f*

prankster [ˈpræŋkstər] *n* **:** bromista *mf*

prattle[1] [ˈprætəl] *vt* **-tled; -tling :** parlotear *fam,* cotorrear *fam,* balbucear (como un niño)

prattle[2] *n* **:** parloteo *m fam,* cotorreo *m fam,* cháchara *f fam*

prawn [ˈprɔn] *n* **:** langostino *m,* camarón *m,* gamba *f*

pray [ˈpreɪ] *vt* ENTREAT **:** rogar, suplicar — *vi* **:** rezar

prayer [ˈprɛr] *n* **1 :** plegaria *f,* oración *f* <to say one's prayers : orar, rezar> <the Lord's Prayer : el Padrenuestro> **2** PRAYING **:** rezo *m,* oración *f* <to kneel in prayer : arrodillarse para rezar>

praying mantis → **mantis**

preach [ˈpriːtʃ] *vi* **:** predicar — *vt* ADVOCATE **:** abogar por <to preach cooperation : promover la cooperación>

preacher [ˈpriːtʃər] *n* **1 :** predicador *m,* -dora *f* **2** MINISTER **:** pastor *m,* -tora *f*

preamble [ˈpriːˌæmbəl] *n* **:** preámbulo *m*

prearrange [ˌpriːəˈreɪndʒ] *vt* **-ranged; -ranging :** arreglar de antemano

precarious [priˈkæriəs] *adj* **:** precario — **precariously** *adv*

precariousness [priˈkæriəsnəs] *n* **:** precariedad *f*

precaution [priˈkɔʃən] *n* **:** precaución *f*

precautionary [priˈkɔʃəˌnɛri] *adj* **:** preventivo, cautelar, precautorio

precede [priˈsiːd] *v* **-ceded; -ceding :** preceder a

precedence [ˈprɛsədənts, prɪˈsiːdənts] *n* **:** precedencia *f*

precedent [ˈprɛsədənt] *n* **:** precedente *m*

precept [ˈpriːˌsɛpt] *n* **:** precepto *m*

precinct [ˈpriːˌsɪŋkt] *n* **1** DISTRICT **:** distrito *m* (policial, electoral, etc.) **2 precincts** *npl* PREMISES **:** recinto *m,* predio *m,* límites *mpl* (de una ciudad)

precious [ˈprɛʃəs] *adj* **1 :** precioso <precious gems : piedras preciosas> **2** DEAR **:** querido **3** AFFECTED **:** afectado

precipice [ˈprɛsəpəs] *n* **:** precipicio *m*

precipitate [priˈsɪpəˌteɪt] *v* **-tated; -tating** *vt* **1** HASTEN, PROVOKE **:** precipitar, provocar **2** HURL **:** arrojar **3**

: precipitar (en química) — *vi* : precipitarse (en química), condensarse (en meteorología)
precipitation [priˌsɪpəˈteɪʃən] *n* **1** HASTE : precipitación *f,* prisa *f* **2** : precipitaciones *fpl* (en meteorología)
precipitous [priˈsɪpət̬əs] *adj* **1** HASTY, RASH : precipitado **2** STEEP : escarpado, empinado <a precipitous drop : una caída vertiginosa>
précis [preɪˈsiː] *n, pl* **précis** [-ˈsiːz] : resumen *m*
precise [priˈsaɪs] *adj* **1** DEFINITE : preciso, explícito **2** EXACT : exacto, preciso <precise calculations : cálculos precisos> — **precisely** *adv*
preciseness [priˈsaɪsnəs] *n* : precisión *f,* exactitud *f*
precision [priˈsɪʒən] *n* : precisión *f*
preclude [priˈkluːd] *vt* **-cluded; -cluding** : evitar, impedir, excluir (una posibilidad, etc.)
precocious [priˈkoːʃəs] *adj* : precoz — **precociously** *adv*
precocity [priˈkɑsət̬i] *n* : precocidad *f*
preconceive [ˌpriːkənˈsiːv] *vt* **-ceived; -ceiving** : preconcebir
preconception [ˌpriːkənˈsɛpʃən] *n* : idea *f* preconcebida
precondition [ˌpriːkənˈdɪʃən] *n* : precondición *f,* condición *f* previa
precook [ˌpriːˈkʊk] *vt* : precocinar
precursor [priˈkərsər] *n* : precursor *m,* -sora *f*
predator [ˈprɛdət̬ər] *n* : depredador *m,* -dora *f*
predatory [ˈprɛdəˌtori] *adj* : depredador
predecessor [ˈprɛdəˌsɛsər, ˈpriː-] *n* : antecesor *m,* -sora *f;* predecesor *m,* -sora *f*
predestination [priˌdɛstəˈneɪʃən] *n* : predestinación *f*
predestine [priˈdɛstən] *vt* **-tined; -tining** : predestinar
predetermine [ˌpriːdɪˈtərmən] *vt* **-mined; -mining** : predeterminar
predicament [priˈdɪkəmənt] *n* : apuro *m,* aprieto *m*
predicate[1] [ˈprɛdəˌkeɪt] *vt* **-cated; -cating 1** AFFIRM : afirmar, aseverar **2 to be predicated on** : estar basado en
predicate[2] [ˈprɛdɪkət] *n* : predicado *m*
predict [priˈdɪkt] *vt* : pronosticar, predecir
predictable [priˈdɪktəbəl] *adj* : previsible — **predictably** [-bli] *adv*
prediction [priˈdɪkʃən] *n* : pronóstico *m,* predicción *f*
predilection [ˌprɛdəlˈɛkʃən, ˌpriː-] *n* : predilección *f*
predispose [ˌpriːdɪˈspoːz] *vt* **-posed; -posing** : predisponer
predominance [priˈdɑmənənts] *n* : predominio *m*
predominant [priˈdɑmənənt] *adj* : predominante — **predominantly** *adv*
predominate [priˈdɑməˌneɪt] *vi* **-nated; -nating 1** : predominar (en cantidad) **2** PREVAIL : prevalecer
preeminence [priˈɛmənənts] *n* : preeminencia *f*
preeminent [priˈɛmənənt] *adj* : preeminente
preeminently [priˈɛmənəntli] *adv* : especialmente
preempt [priˈɛmpt] *vt* **1** APPROPRIATE : apoderarse de, apropriarse de **2** : reemplazar (un programa de televisión, etc.) **3** FORESTALL : adelantarse a (un ataque, etc.)
preen [ˈpriːn] *vt* : arreglarse (el pelo, las plumas, etc.)
prefabricated [ˌpriːˈfæbrəˌkeɪt̬əd] *adj* : prefabricado
preface [ˈprɛfəs] *n* : prefacio *m,* prólogo *m*
prefatory [ˈprɛfəˌtori] *adj* : preliminar
prefer [priˈfər] *vt* **-ferred; -ferring 1** : preferir <I prefer coffee : prefiero café> **2 to prefer charges against** : presentar cargos contra
preferable [ˈprɛfərəbəl] *adj* : preferible
preferably [ˈprɛfərəbli] *adv* : preferentemente, de preferencia
preference [ˈprɛfrənts, ˈprɛfər-] *n* : preferencia *f,* gusto *m*
preferential [ˌprɛfəˈrɛntʃəl] *adj* : preferencial, preferente
prefigure [priˈfɪgjər] *vt* **-ured; -uring** FORESHADOW : prefigurar, anunciar
prefix [ˈpriːˌfɪks] *n* : prefijo *m*
pregnancy [ˈprɛgnəntsi] *n, pl* **-cies** : embarazo *m,* preñez *f*
pregnant [ˈprɛgnənt] *adj* **1** : embarazada (dícese de una mujer), preñada (dícese de un animal) **2** MEANINGFUL : significativo
preheat [ˌpriːˈhiːt] *vt* : precalentar
prehensile [priˈhɛntsəl, -ˈhɛnˌsaɪl] *adj* : prensil
prehistoric [ˌpriːhɪsˈtɔrɪk] *or* **prehistorical** [-ɪkəl] *adj* : prehistórico
prejudge [ˌpriːˈdʒʌdʒ] *vt* **-judged; -judging** : prejuzgar
prejudice[1] [ˈprɛdʒədəs] *vt* **-diced; -dicing 1** DAMAGE : perjudicar **2** BIAS : predisponer, influir en
prejudice[2] *n* **1** DAMAGE : perjuicio *m* (en derecho) **2** BIAS : prejuicio *m*
prelate [ˈprɛlət] *n* : prelado *m*
preliminary[1] [priˈlɪməˌnɛri] *adj* : preliminar
preliminary[2] *n, pl* **-naries 1** : preámbulo *m,* preludio *m* **2 preliminaries** *npl* : preliminares *mpl*
prelude [ˈprɛˌluːd, ˈprɛlˌjuːd; ˈpreɪˌluːd, ˈpriː-] *n* : preludio *m*
premarital [ˌpriːˈmærət̬əl] *adj* : prematrimonial
premature [ˌpriːməˈtʊr, -ˈtjʊr, -ˈtʃʊr] *adj* : prematuro — **prematurely** *adv*
premeditate [priˈmɛdəˌteɪt] *vt* **-tated; -tating** : premeditar

premeditation [pri,mɛdə'teɪʃən] *n* : premeditación *f*

premenstrual [pri'mɛntstrʊəl] *adj* : premenstrual

premier[1] [pri'mɪr, -'mjɪr; 'priːmiər] *adj* : principal

premier[2] *n* PRIME MINISTER : primer ministro *m,* primera ministra *f*

premiere[1] [prɪ'mjɛr, -'mɪr] *vt* **-miered; -miering** : estrenar

premiere[2] *n* : estreno *m*

premise ['prɛmɪs] *n* **1** : premisa *f* <the premise of his arguments : la premisa de sus argumentos> **2 premises** *npl* : recinto *m,* local *m*

premium ['priːmiəm] *n* **1** BONUS : prima *f* **2** SURCHARGE : recargo *m* <to sell at a premium : vender (algo) muy caro> **3 insurance premium** : prima *f* (de seguros) **4 to set a premium on** : darle un gran valor (a algo)

premonition [,priːmə'nɪʃən, ,prɛmə-] *n* : presentimiento *m,* premonición *f*

prenatal [,priː'neɪṭəl] *adj* : prenatal

preoccupation [pri,ɑkjə'peɪʃən] *n* : preocupación *f*

preoccupied [pri'ɑkjə,paɪd] *adj* : abstraído, ensimismado, preocupado

preoccupy [pri'ɑkjə,paɪ] *vt* **-pied; -pying** : preocupar

preparation [,prɛpə'reɪʃən] *n* **1** PREPARING : preparación *f* **2** MIXTURE : preparado *m* <a preparation for burns : un preparado para quemaduras> **3 preparations** *npl* ARRANGEMENTS : preparativos *mpl*

preparatory [pri'pærə,tori] *adj* : preparatorio

prepare [pri'pær] *v* **-pared; -paring** *vt* : preparar — *vi* : prepararse

prepay [,priː'peɪ] *vt* **-paid; -paying** : pagar por adelantado

preponderance [pri'pɑndərənts] *n* : preponderancia *f*

preponderant [pri'pɑndərənt] *adj* : preponderante — **preponderantly** *adv*

preposition [,prɛpə'zɪʃən] *n* : preposición *f*

prepositional [,prɛpə'zɪʃənəl] *adj* : preposicional

prepossessing [,priːpə'zɛsɪŋ] *adj* : atractivo, agradable

preposterous [pri'pɑstərəs] *adj* : absurdo, ridículo

prerequisite[1] [pri'rɛkwəzət] *adj* : necesario, esencial

prerequisite[2] *n* : condición *f* necesario, requisito *m* previo

prerogative [pri'rɑgəṭɪv] *n* : prerrogativa *f*

presage ['prɛsɪdʒ, pri'seɪdʒ] *vt* **-saged; -saging** : presagiar

preschool ['priː,skuːl] *adj* : preescolar <preschool students : estudiantes de preescolar>

prescribe [pri'skraɪb] *vt* **-scribed; -scribing 1** ORDAIN : prescribir, ordenar **2** : recetar (medicinas, etc.)

prescription [pri'skrɪpʃən] *n* : receta *f*

presence ['prɛzənts] *n* : presencia *f*

present[1] [pri'zɛnt] *vt* **1** INTRODUCE : presentar <to present oneself : presentarse> **2** : presentar (una obra de teatro, etc.) **3** GIVE : entregar (un regalo, etc.), regalar, obsequiar **4** SHOW : presentar, ofrecer <it presents a lovely view : ofrece una vista muy linda>

present[2] ['prɛzənt] *adj* **1** : actual <present conditions : condiciones actuales> **2** : presente <all the students were present : todos los estudiantes estaban presentes>

present[3] ['prɛzənt] *n* **1** GIFT : regalo *m,* obsequio *m* **2** : presente *m* <at present : en este momento> **3** *or* **present tense** : presente *m*

presentation [,priː,zɛn'teɪʃən, ,prɛzən-] *n* : presentación *f* <presentation ceremony : ceremonia de entrega>

presentiment [pri'zɛntəmənt] *n* : presentimiento *m,* premonición *f*

presently ['prɛzəntli] *adv* **1** SOON : pronto, dentro de poco **2** NOW : actualmente, ahora

present participle *n* : participio *m* presente, participio *m* activo

preservation [,prɛzər'veɪʃən] *n* : conservación *f,* preservación *f*

preservative [pri'zərvəṭɪv] *n* : conservante *m*

preserve[1] [pri'zərv] *vt* **-served; -serving 1** PROTECT : proteger, preservar **2** : conservar (los alimentos, etc.) **3** MAINTAIN : conservar, mantener

preserve[2] *n* **1** *or* **preserves** *npl* : conserva *f* <peach preserves : duraznos en conserva> **2** : coto *m* <game preserve : coto de caza>

preside [pri'zaɪd] *vi* **-sided; -siding 1 to preside over** : presidir <he presided over the meeting : presidió la reunión> **2 to preside over** : supervisar <she presides over the department : dirige el departamento>

presidency ['prɛzədəntsi] *n, pl* **-cies** : presidencia *f*

president ['prɛzədənt] *n* : presidente *m,* -ta *f*

presidential [,prɛzə'dɛntʃəl] *adj* : presidencial

press[1] ['prɛs] *vt* **1** PUSH : apretar **2** SQUEEZE : apretar, prensar (frutas, flores, etc.) **3** IRON : planchar (ropa) **4** URGE : instar, apremiar <he pressed me to come : insistió en que viniera> — *vi* **1** PUSH : apretar <press hard : aprieta con fuerza> **2** CROWD : apiñarse **3** : abrirse paso <I pressed through the crowd : me abrí paso entre el gentío> **4** URGE : presionar

press[2] *n* **1** CROWD : multitud *f* **2** : imprenta *f,* prensa *f* <to go to press : entrar en prensa> **3** URGENCY : urgencia *f,* prisa *f* **4** PRINTER, PUBLISHER : imprenta *f,* editorial *f* **5 the press** : la prensa <freedom of the press : libertad de prensa>

pressing [ˈprɛsɪŋ] *adj* URGENT : urgente

pressure[1] [ˈprɛʃər] *vt* **-sured; -suring** : presionar, apremiar

pressure[2] *n* **1** : presión *f* <to be under pressure : estar bajo presión> **2** → **blood pressure**

pressurize [ˈprɛʃəˌraɪz] *vt* **-ized; -izing** : presurizar

prestige [prɛˈstiːʒ, -ˈstiːdʒ] *n* : prestigio *m*

prestigious [prɛˈstɪdʒəs] *adj* : prestigioso

presto [ˈprɛsˌtoː] *adv* : de pronto

presumably [priˈzuːməbli] *adv* : es de suponer, supuestamente <presumably, he's guilty : supone que es culpable>

presume [priˈzuːm] *vt* **-sumed; -suming 1** ASSUME, SUPPOSE : suponer, asumir, presumir **2 to presume to** : atreverse a, osar

presumption [priˈzʌmpʃən] *n* **1** AUDACITY : atrevimiento *m,* osadía *f* **2** ASSUMPTION : presunción *f,* suposición *f*

presumptuous [priˈzʌmptʃʊəs] *adj* : descarado, atrevido

presuppose [ˌpriːsəˈpoːz] *vt* **-posed; -posing** : presuponer

pretend [priˈtɛnd] *vt* **1** CLAIM : pretender **2** FEIGN : fingir, simular — *vi* : fingir

pretense *or* **pretence** [ˈpriːˌtɛnts, priˈtɛnts] *n* **1** CLAIM : afirmación *f* (falsa), pretensión *f* **2** FEIGNING : fingimiento *m,* simulación *f* <to make a pretense of doing something : fingir hacer algo> <a pretense of order : una apariencia de orden> **3** PRETEXT : pretexto *m* <under false pretenses : con pretextos falsos, de manera fraudulenta>

pretension [priˈtɛntʃən] *n* **1** CLAIM : pretensión *f,* afirmación *f* **2** ASPIRATION : aspiración *f,* ambición *f* **3** PRETENTIOUSNESS : pretensiones *fpl*, presunción *f*

pretentious [priˈtɛntʃəs] *adj* : pretencioso

pretentiousness [priˈtɛntʃəsnəs] *n* : presunción *f,* pretenciones *fpl*

pretext [ˈpriːˌtɛkst] *n* : pretexto *m,* excusa *f*

prettily [ˈprɪtəli] *adv* : atractivamente

prettiness [ˈprɪtinəs] *n* : lindeza *f*

pretty[1] [ˈprɪti] *adv* : bastante, bien <it's pretty obvious : está bien claro> <it's pretty much the same : es más o menos igual>

pretty[2] *adj* **-tier; -est** : bonito, lindo, guapo <a pretty girl : una muchacha guapa> <what a pretty dress! : ¡qué vestido más lindo!>

pretzel [ˈprɛtsəl] *n* : galleta *f* salada (en forma de nudo)

prevail [priˈveɪl] *vi* **1** TRIUMPH : prevalecer **2** PREDOMINATE : predominar **3 to prevail upon** : persuadir, convencer <I prevailed upon her to sing : la convencí para que cantara>

prevalence [ˈprɛvələnts] *n* : preponderancia *f,* predominio *m*

prevalent [ˈprɛvələnt] *adj* **1** COMMON : común y corriente, general **2** WIDESPREAD : extendido

prevaricate [priˈværəˌkeɪt] *vi* **-cated; -cating** LIE : mentir

prevarication [priˌværəˈkeɪʃən] *n* : mentira *f*

prevent [priˈvɛnt] *vt* **1** AVOID : prevenir, evitar <steps to prevent war : medidas para evitar la guerra> **2** HINDER : impedir

preventable [priˈvɛntəbəl] *adj* : evitable

preventative [priˈvɛntət̬ɪv] → **preventive**

prevention [priˈvɛntʃən] *n* : prevención *f*

preventive [priˈvɛntɪv] *adj* : preventivo

preview [ˈpriːˌvju] *n* : preestreno *m*

previous [ˈpriːviəs] *adj* : previo, anterior <previous knowledge : conocimientos previos> <the previous day : el día anterior> <in the previous year : en el año pasado>

previously [ˈpriːviəsli] *adv* : antes

prewar [ˌpriːˈwɔr] *adj* : de antes de la guerra

prey [ˈpreɪ] *n, pl* **preys** : presa *f*

prey on *vt* **1** : cazar, alimentarse de <it preys on fish : se alimenta de peces> **2 to prey on one's mind** : hacer presa en alguien, atormentar a alguien

price[1] [ˈpraɪs] *vt* **priced; pricing** : poner un precio a

price[2] *n* : precio *m* <peace at any price : la paz a toda costa>

priceless [ˈpraɪsləs] *adj* : inestimable, inapreciable

prick[1] [ˈprɪk] *vt* **1** : pinchar **2 to prick up one's ears** : levantar las orejas — *vi* : pinchar

prick[2] *n* **1** STAB : pinchazo *m* <a prick of conscience : un remordimiento> **2** → **pricker**

pricker [ˈprɪkər] *n* THORN : espina *f*

prickle[1] [ˈprɪkəl] *vi* **-led; -ling** : sentir un cosquilleo, tener un hormigueo

prickle[2] *n* **1** : espina *f* (de una planta) **2** TINGLE : cosquilleo *m,* hormigueo *m*

prickly [ˈprɪkəli] *adj* **1** THORNY : espinoso **2** : que pica <a prickly sensation : un hormigueo>

prickly pear *n* : tuna *f*

pride[1] [ˈpraɪd] *vt* **prided; priding** : estar orgulloso de <to pride oneself on : preciarse de, enorgullecerse de>

pride[2] *n* : orgullo *m*

priest [ˈpriːst] *n* : sacerdote *m,* cura *m*

priestess [ˈpriːstɪs] *n* : sacerdotisa *f*

priesthood [ˈpriːstˌhʊd] *n* : sacerdocio *m*

priestly [ˈpriːstli] *adj* : sacerdotal

prig [ˈprɪg] *n* : mojigato *m,* -ta *f;* gazmoño *m,* -ña *f*

prim ['prɪm] *adj* **primmer; primmest** 1 PRISSY : remilgado 2 PRUDISH : mojigato, gazmoño

primarily [praɪ'mɛrəli] *adv* : principalmente, fundamentalmente

primary[1] ['praɪ,mɛri, 'praɪməri] *adj* 1 FIRST : primario 2 PRINCIPAL : principal 3 BASIC : fundamental

primary[2] *n, pl* **-ries** : elección *f* primaria

primary color *n* : color *m* primario

primary school → **elementary school**

primate *n* 1 ['praɪ,meɪt, -mət] : primado *m* (obispo) 2 [-,meɪt] : primate *m* (animal)

prime[1] ['praɪm] *vt* **primed; priming** 1 : cebar <to prime a pump : cebar una bomba> 2 PREPARE : preparar (una superficie para pintar) 3 COACH : preparar (a un testigo, etc.)

prime[2] *adj* 1 CHIEF, MAIN : principal, primero 2 EXCELLENT : de primera (categoría), excelente

prime[3] *n* **the prime of one's life** : la flor de la vida

prime minister *n* : primer ministro *m*, primera ministra *f*

primer[1] ['prɪmər] *n* 1 READER : cartilla *f* 2 MANUAL : manual *m*

primer[2] ['praɪmər] *n* 1 : cebo *m* (para explosivos) 2 : base *f* (de pintura)

primeval [praɪ'miːvəl] *adj* : primitivo, primigenio

primitive ['prɪmət̬ɪv] *adj* : primitivo

primly ['prɪmli] *adv* : mojigatamente

primness ['prɪmnəs] *n* : mojigatería *f*, gazmoñería *f*

primordial [praɪ'mɔrdiəl] *adj* : primordial, fundamental

primp ['prɪmp] *vi* : arreglarse, acicalarse

primrose ['prɪm,roːz] *n* : primavera *f*, prímula *f*

prince ['prɪnts] *n* : príncipe *m*

princely ['prɪntsli] *adj* : principesco

princess ['prɪntsəs, 'prɪn,sɛs] *n* : princesa *f*

principal[1] ['prɪntsəpəl] *adj* : principal — **principally** *adv*

principal[2] *n* 1 PROTAGONIST : protagonista *mf* 2 : director *m*, -tora *f* (de una escuela) 3 CAPITAL : principal *m*, capital *m* (en finanzas)

principality [,prɪntsə'pæləţi] *n, pl* **-ties** : principado *m*

principle ['prɪntsəpəl] *n* : principio *m*

print[1] ['prɪnt] *vt* : imprimir (libros, etc.) — *vi* : escribir con letra de molde

print[2] *n* 1 IMPRESSION : marca *f*, huella *f*, impresión *f* 2 : texto *m* impreso <to be out of print : estar agotado> 3 LETTERING : letra *f* 4 ENGRAVING : grabado *m* 5 : copia *f* (en fotografía) 6 : estampado *m* (de tela)

printer ['prɪntər] *n* 1 : impresor *m*, -sora *f* (persona) 2 : impresora *f* (máquina)

printing ['prɪntɪŋ] *n* 1 : impresión *f* (acto) <the third printing : la tercera tirada> 2 : imprenta *f* (profesión) 3 LETTERING : letras *fpl* de molde

printing press *n* : prensa *f*

print out *vt* : imprimir (de una computadora)

printout ['prɪnt,aʊt] *n* : copia *f* impresa (de una computadora)

prior ['praɪər] *adj* 1 : previo 2 **prior to** : antes de

priority [praɪ'ɔrəţi] *n, pl* **-ties** : prioridad *f*

priory ['praɪəri] *n, pl* **-ries** : priorato *m*

prism ['prɪzəm] *n* : prisma *m*

prison ['prɪzən] *n* : prisión *f*, cárcel *f*

prisoner ['prɪzənər] *n* : preso *m*, -sa *f*; recluso *m*, -sa *f* <prisoner of war : prisionero de guerra>

prissy ['prɪsi] *adj* **-sier; -est** : remilgado, melindroso

pristine ['prɪs,tiːn, prɪs'-] *adj* : puro, prístino

privacy ['praɪvəsi] *n, pl* **-cies** : privacidad *f*

private[1] ['praɪvət] *adj* 1 PERSONAL : privado, particular <private property : propiedad privada> 2 INDEPENDENT : privado, independiente <private studies : estudios privados> 3 SECRET : secreto 4 SECLUDED : aislado, privado — **privately** *adv*

private[2] *n* : soldado *m* raso

privateer [,praɪvə'tɪr] *n* : corsario *m*

privation [praɪ'veɪʃən] *n* : privación *f*

privilege ['prɪvlɪdʒ, 'prɪvə-] *n* : privilegio *m*

privileged ['prɪvlɪdʒd, 'prɪvə-] *adj* : privilegiado

privy[1] ['prɪvi] *adj* **to be privy to** : estar enterado de

privy[2] *n, pl* **privies** : excusado *m*, retrete *m* (exterior)

prize[1] ['praɪz] *vt* **prized; prizing** : valorar, apreciar

prize[2] *adj* 1 : premiado <a prize stallion : un semental premiado> 2 OUTSTANDING : de primera, excepcional

prize[3] *n* 1 AWARD : premio *m* <third prize : el tercer premio> 2 : joya *f*, tesoro *m* <he's a real prize : es un tesoro>

prizefighter ['praɪz,faɪţər] *n* : boxeador *m*, -dora *f* profesional

prizewinning ['praɪz,wɪnɪŋ] *adj* : premiado

pro[1] ['proː] *adv* : a favor

pro[2] *adj* → **professional**[1]

pro[3] *n* 1 : pro *m* <the pros and cons : los pros y los contras> 2 → **professional**[2]

probability [,prɑbə'bɪləţi] *n, pl* **-ties** : probabilidad *f*

probable ['prɑbəbəl] *adj* : probable — **probably** [-bli] *adv*

probate[1] ['proː,beɪt] *vt* **-bated; -bating** : autenticar (un testamento)

probate[2] *n* : autenticación *f* (de un testamento)

probation [proˈbeɪʃən] *n* **1 :** período *m* de prueba (para un empleado, etc.) **2 :** libertad *f* condicional (para un preso)
probationary [proˈbeɪʃəˌnɛri] *adj* **:** de prueba
probe[1] [ˈproːb] *vt* **probed; probing 1 :** sondar (en medicina y tecnología) **2** INVESTIGATE **:** investigar, sondear
probe[2] *n* **1 :** sonda *f* (en medicina, etc.) <space probe **:** sonda espacial> **2** INVESTIGATION **:** investigación *f,* sondeo *m*
probity [ˈproːbəti] *n* **:** probidad *f*
problem[1] [ˈprɑbləm] *adj* **:** difícil
problem[2] *n* **:** problema *m*
problematic [ˌprɑbləˈmætɪk] *or* **problematical** [-tɪkəl] *adj* **:** problemático
proboscis [prəˈbɑsɪs] *n, pl* **-cises** *also* **-cides** [-səˌdiːz] **:** probóscide *f*
procedural [prəˈsiːdʒərəl] *adj* **:** de procedimiento
procedure [prəˈsiːdʒər] *n* **:** procedimiento *m* <administrative procedures **:** trámites administrativos>
proceed [proˈsiːd] *vi* **1 :** proceder <to proceed to do something **:** proceder a hacer algo> **2** CONTINUE **:** continuar, proseguir, seguir <he proceeded to the next phase **:** pasó a la segunda fase> **3** ADVANCE **:** avanzar <as the conference proceeded **:** mientras seguía avanzando la conferencia> <the road proceeds south **:** la calle sigue hacia el sur>
proceeding [proˈsiːdɪŋ] *n* **1** PROCEDURE **:** procedimiento *m* **2 proceedings** *npl* EVENTS **:** acontecimientos *mpl* **3 proceedings** *npl* MINUTES **:** actas *fpl* (de una reunión, etc.)
proceeds [ˈproːˌsiːdz] *npl* **:** ganancias *fpl*
process[1] [ˈprɑˌsɛs, ˈproː-] *vt* **:** procesar, tratar
process[2] *n, pl* **-cesses** [ˈprɑˌsɛsəz, ˈproː-, -səsəz, -səˌsiːz] **1 :** proceso *m* <the process of elimination **:** el proceso de eliminación> **2** METHOD **:** proceso *m,* método *m* <manufacturing processes **:** procesos industriales> **3 :** acción *f* judicial <due process of law **:** el debido proceso (de la ley)> **4** SUMMONS **:** citación *f* **5** PROJECTION **:** protuberancia *f* (anatómica) **6 in the process of :** en vías de <in the process of repair **:** en reparaciones>
procession [prəˈsɛʃən] *n* **:** procesión *f,* desfile *m* <a funeral procession **:** un cortejo fúnebre>
processional [prəˈsɛʃənəl] *n* **:** himno *m* para una procesión
processor [ˈprɑˌsɛsər, ˈproː-, -səsər] *n* **1 :** procesador *m* (de una computadora) **2 food processor :** procesador *m* de alimentos
proclaim [proˈkleɪm] *vt* **:** proclamar
proclamation [ˌprɑkləˈmeɪʃən] *n* **:** proclamación *f*
proclivity [proˈklɪvəṭi] *n, pl* **-ties :** proclividad *f*
procrastinate [prəˈkræstəˌneɪt] *vi* **-nated; -nating :** demorar, aplazar las responsabilidades
procrastination [prəˌkræstəˈneɪʃən] *n* **:** aplazamiento *m,* demora *f,* dilación *f*
procreate [ˈproːkriˌeɪt] *vi* **-ated; -ating :** procrear
procreation [ˌproːkriˈeɪʃən] *n* **:** procreación *f*
proctor[1] [ˈprɑktər] *vt* **:** supervisar (un examen)
proctor[2] *n* **:** supervisor *m,* -sora *f* (de un examen)
procure [prəˈkjʊr] *vt* **-cured; -curing 1** OBTAIN **:** procurar, obtener **2** BRING ABOUT **:** provocar, lograr, conseguir
procurement [prəˈkjʊrmənt] *n* **:** obtención *f*
prod[1] [ˈprɑd] *vt* **prodded; prodding 1** JAB, POKE **:** pinchar, golpear (con la punta de algo) **2** GOAD **:** incitar, estimular
prod[2] *n* **1** JAB, POKE **:** golpe *m* (con la punta de algo), pinchazo *m* **2** STIMULUS **:** estímulo *m* **3 cattle prod :** picana *f,* aguijón *m*
prodigal[1] [ˈprɑdɪgəl] *adj* SPENDTHRIFT **:** pródigo, despilfarrador, derrochador
prodigal[2] *n* **:** pródigo *m,* -ga *f;* derrochador *m,* -dora *f*
prodigious [prəˈdɪdʒəs] *adj* **1** MARVELOUS **:** prodigioso, maravilloso **2** HUGE **:** enorme, vasto <prodigious sums **:** muchísimo dinero> **— prodigiously** *adv*
prodigy [ˈprɑdədʒi] *n, pl* **-gies :** prodigio *m* <child prodigy **:** niño prodigio>
produce[1] [prəˈduːs, -ˈdjuːs] *vt* **-duced; -ducing 1** EXHIBIT **:** presentar, mostrar **2** YIELD **:** producir **3** CAUSE **:** producir, causar **4** CREATE **:** producir <to produce a poem **:** escribir un poema> **5 :** poner en escena (una obra de teatro), producir (una película)
produce[2] [ˈprɑˌduːs, ˈproː-, -ˌdjuːs] *n* **:** productos *mpl* agrícolas
producer [prəˈduːsər, -ˈdjuː-] *n* **:** productor *m,* -tora *f*
product [ˈprɑˌdʌkt] *n* **:** producto *m*
production [prəˈdʌkʃən] *n* **:** producción *f*
productive [prəˈdʌktɪv] *adj* **:** productivo
productivity [ˌproːˌdʌkˈtɪvəṭi, ˌprɑ-] *n* **:** productividad *f*
profane[1] [proˈfeɪn] *vt* **-faned; -faning :** profanar
profane[2] *adj* **1** SECULAR **:** profano **2** IRREVERENT **:** irreverente, impío
profanity [proˈfænəṭi] *n, pl* **-ties 1** IRREVERENCE **:** irreverencia *f,* impiedad *f* **2 :** blasfemias *fpl,* obscenidades *fpl* <don't use profanity **:** no digas blasfemias>
profess [prəˈfɛs] *vt* **1** DECLARE **:** declarar, manifestar **2** CLAIM **:** pretender **3 :** profesar (una religión, etc.)

professedly [prəˈfɛsədli] *adv* **1** OPENLY : declaradamente **2** ALLEGEDLY : supuestamente
profession [prəˈfɛʃən] *n* : profesión *f*
professional[1] [prəˈfɛʃənəl] *adj* : profesional — **professionally** *adv*
professional[2] *n* : profesional *mf*
professionalism [prəˈfɛʃənəˌlizəm] *n* : profesionalismo *m*
professor [prəˈfɛsər] *n* : profesor *m* (universitario), profesora *f* (universitaria); catedrático *m*, -ca *f*
proffer [ˈprɑfər] *vt* **-fered; -fering** : ofrecer, dar
proficiency [prəˈfɪʃəntsi] *n* : competencia *f*, capacidad *f*
proficient [prəˈfɪʃənt] *adj* : competente, experto — **proficiently** *adv*
profile [ˈproːˌfaɪl] *n* : perfil *m* <a portrait in profile : un retrato de perfil> <to keep a low profile : no llamar la atención, hacerse pasar desapercibido>
profit[1] [ˈprɑfət] *vi* : sacar provecho (de), beneficiarse (de)
profit[2] *n* **1** ADVANTAGE : provecho *m*, partido *m*, beneficio *m* **2** GAIN : beneficio *m*, utilidad *f*, ganancia *f* <to make a profit : sacar beneficios>
profitable [ˈprɑfət̬əbəl] *adj* : rentable, lucrativo — **profitably** [-bli] *adv*
profitless [ˈprɑfətləs] *adj* : infructuoso, inútil
profligate [ˈprɑflɪgət, -ˌgeɪt] *adj* **1** DISSOLUTE : disoluto, licencioso **2** SPENDTHRIFT : despilfarrador, derrochador, pródigo
profound [prəˈfaʊnd] *adj* : profundo
profoundly [prəˈfaʊndli] *adv* : profundamente, en profundidad
profundity [prəˈfʌndət̬i] *n, pl* **-ties** : profundidad *f*
profuse [prəˈfjuːs] *adj* **1** COPIOUS : profuso, copioso **2** LAVISH : pródigo — **profusely** *adv*
profusion [prəˈfjuːʒən] *n* : abundancia *f*, profusión *f*
progeny [ˈprɑdʒəni] *n, pl* **-nies** : progenie *f*
progesterone [proˈdʒɛstəˌroːn] *n* : progesterona *f*
prognosis [prɑgˈnoːsɪs] *n, pl* **-noses** [-ˌsiːz] : pronóstico *m* (médico)
program[1] [ˈproːˌgræm, -grəm] *vt* **-grammed** *or* **-gramed; -gramming** *or* **-graming** : programar
program[2] *n* : programa *m*
programmer [ˈproːˌgræmər] *n* : programador *m*, -dora *f*
programming [ˈproːˌgræmɪŋ] *n* : programación *f*
progress[1] [prəˈgrɛs] *vi* **1** PROCEED : progresar, adelantar **2** IMPROVE : mejorar
progress[2] [ˈprɑgrəs, -ˌgrɛs] *n* **1** ADVANCE : progreso *m*, adelanto *m*, avance *m* <to make progress : hacer progresos> **2** BETTERMENT : mejora *f*, mejoramiento *m*
progression [prəˈgrɛʃən] *n* **1** ADVANCE : avance *m* **2** SEQUENCE : desarrollo *m* (de eventos)
progressive [prəˈgrɛsɪv] *adj* **1** : progresista <a progressive society : una sociedad progresista> **2** : progresivo <a progressive disease : una enfermedad progresiva> **3** *or* **Progressive** : progresista (en política) **4** : progresivo (en gramática)
progressively [prəˈgrɛsɪvli] *adv* : progresivamente, poco a poco
prohibit [proˈhɪbət] *vt* : prohibir
prohibition [ˌproːəˈbɪʃən, ˌproːhə-] *n* : prohibición *f*
prohibitive [proˈhɪbət̬ɪv] *adj* : prohibitivo
project[1] [prəˈdʒɛkt] *vt* **1** PLAN : proyectar, planear **2** : proyectar (imágenes, misiles, etc.) — *vi* PROTRUDE : sobresalir, salir
project[2] [ˈprɑˌdʒɛkt, -dʒɪkt] *n* : proyecto *m*, trabajo *m* (de un estudiante) <research project : proyecto de investigación>
projectile [prəˈdʒɛktəl, -ˌtaɪl] *n* : proyectil *m*
projection [prəˈdʒɛkʃən] *n* **1** PLAN : plan *m*, proyección *f* **2** : proyección *f* (de imágenes, misiles, etc.) **3** PROTRUSION : saliente *m*
projector [prəˈdʒɛktər] *n* : proyector *m*
proletarian[1] [ˌproːləˈtɛriən] *adj* : proletario
proletarian[2] *n* : proletario *m*, -ria *f*
proletariat [ˌproːləˈtɛriət] *n* : proletariado *m*
proliferate [prəˈlɪfəˌreɪt] *vi* **-ated; -ating** : proliferar
proliferation [prəˌlɪfəˈreɪʃən] *n* : proliferación *f*
prolific [prəˈlɪfɪk] *adj* : prolífico
prologue [ˈproːˌlɔg] *n* : prólogo *m*
prolong [prəˈlɔŋ] *vt* : prolongar
prolongation [ˌproːˌlɔŋˈgeɪʃən] *n* : prolongación *f*
prom [ˈprɑm] *n* : baile *m* formal (de un colegio)
promenade[1] [ˌprɑməˈneɪd, -ˈnɑd] *vi* **-naded; -nading** : pasear, pasearse, dar un paseo
promenade[2] *n* : paseo *m*
prominence [ˈprɑmənənts] *n* **1** PROJECTION : prominencia *f* **2** EMINENCE : eminencia *f*, prestigio *m*
prominent [ˈprɑmənənt] *adj* **1** OUTSTANDING : prominente, destacado **2** PROJECTING : prominente, saliente
prominently [ˈprɑmənəntli] *adv* : destacadamente, prominentemente
promiscuity [ˌprɑmɪsˈkjuːət̬i] *n, pl* **-ties** : promiscuidad *f*
promiscuous [prəˈmɪskjʊəs] *adj* : promiscuo — **promiscuously** *adv*
promise[1] [ˈprɑməs] *v* **-ised; -ising** : prometer

promise[2] *n* **1** : promesa *f* <he kept his promise : cumplió su promesa> **2 to show promise** : prometer

promising [ˈprɑməsɪŋ] *adj* : prometedor

promissory [ˈprɑməˌsori] *adj* : que promete <a promissory note : un pagaré>

promontory [ˈprɑmənˌtori] *n, pl* **-ries** : promontorio *m*

promote [prəˈmoːt] *vt* **-moted; -moting 1** : ascender (a un alumno o un empleado) **2** ADVERTISE : promocionar, hacerle publicidad a **3** FURTHER : promover, fomentar

promoter [prəˈmoːtər] *n* : promotor *m,* -tora *f;* empresario *m,* -ria *f* (en deportes)

promotion [prəˈmoːʃən] *n* **1** : ascenso *m* (de un alumno o un empleado) **2** FURTHERING : promoción *f,* fomento *m* **3** ADVERTISING : publicidad *f,* propaganda *f*

promotional [prəˈmoːʃənəl] *adj* : promocional

prompt[1] [ˈprɑmpt] *vt* **1** INDUCE : provocar (una cosa), inducir (a una persona) <curiosity prompted me to ask you : la curiosidad me indujo a preguntarle> **2** : apuntar (a un actor, etc.)

prompt[2] *adj* : pronto, rápido <prompt payment : pago puntual>

prompter [ˈprɑmptər] *n* : apuntador *m,* -dora *f* (en teatro)

promptly [ˈprɑmptli] *adv* : inmediatamente, rápidamente

promptness [ˈprɑmptnəs] *n* : prontitud *f,* rapidez *f*

prone [ˈproːn] *adj* **1** LIABLE : propenso, proclive <accident-prone : propenso a los accidentes> **2** : boca abajo, decúbito prono <in a prone position : en decúbito prono>

prong [ˈprɔŋ] *n* : punta *f,* diente *m*

pronoun [ˈproːˌnaʊn] *n* : pronombre *m*

pronounce [prəˈnaʊnts] *vt* **-nounced; -nouncing 1** : pronunciar <how do you pronounce your name? : ¿cómo se pronuncia su nombre?> **2** DECLARE : declarar **3 to pronounce sentence** : dictar sentencia, pronunciar un fallo

pronounced [prəˈnaʊntst] *adj* MARKED : pronunciado, marcado

pronouncement [prəˈnaʊntsmənt] *n* : declaración *f*

pronunciation [prəˌnʌntsiˈeɪʃən] *n* : pronunciación *f*

proof[1] [ˈpruːf] *adj* : a prueba <proof against tampering : a prueba de manipulación>

proof[2] *n* : prueba *f*

proofread [ˈpruːfˌriːd] *v* **-read; -reading** *vt* : corregir — *vi* : corregir pruebas

proofreader [ˈpruːfˌriːdər] *n* : corrector *m,* -tora *f* (de pruebas)

prop[1] [ˈprɑp] *vt* **propped; propping 1 to prop against** : apoyar contra **2 to prop up** SUPPORT : apoyar, apuntalar, sostener **3 to prop up** SUSTAIN : alentar (a alguien), darle ánimo (a alguien)

prop[2] *n* **1** SUPPORT : puntal *m,* apoyo *m,* soporte *m* **2** : accesorio *m* (en teatro)

propaganda [ˌprɑpəˈgændə, ˌproː-] *n* : propaganda *f*

propagandize [ˌprɑpəˈgænˌdaɪz, ˌproː-] *v* **-dized; -dizing** *vt* : someter a propaganda — *vi* : hacer propaganda

propagate [ˈprɑpəˌgeɪt] *v* **-gated; -gating** *vi* : propagarse — *vt* : propagar

propagation [ˌprɑpəˈgeɪʃən] *n* : propagación *f*

propane [ˈproːˌpeɪn] *n* : propano *m*

propel [prəˈpɛl] *vt* **-pelled; -pelling** : impulsar, propulsar, impeler

propellant *or* **propellent** [prəˈpɛlənt] *n* : propulsor *m*

propeller [prəˈpɛlər] *n* : hélice *f*

propensity [prəˈpɛntsəti] *n, pl* **-ties** : propensión *f,* tendencia *f,* inclinación *f*

proper [ˈprɑpər] *adj* **1** RIGHT, SUITABLE : apropiado, adecuado **2** : propio, mismo <the city proper : la propia ciudad> **3** CORRECT : correcto **4** GENTEEL : fino, refinado, cortés **5** OWN, SPECIAL : propio <proper name : nombre propio> — **properly** *adv*

property [ˈprɑpərti] *n, pl* **-ties 1** CHARACTERISTIC : característica *f,* propiedad *f* **2** POSSESSIONS : propiedad *f* **3** BUILDING : inmueble *m* **4** LAND, LOT : terreno *m,* lote *m,* parcela *f* **5** PROP : accesorio *m* (en teatro)

prophecy [ˈprɑfəsi] *n, pl* **-cies** : profecía *f,* vaticinio *m*

prophesy [ˈprɑfəˌsaɪ] *v* **-sied; -sying** *vt* **1** FORETELL : profetizar (como profeta) **2** PREDICT : profetizar, predecir, vaticinar — *vi* : hacer profecías

prophet [ˈprɑfət] *n* : profeta *m,* profetisa *f*

prophetic [prəˈfɛtɪk] *or* **prophetical** [-tɪkəl] *adj* : profético — **prophetically** [-tɪkli] *adv*

propitiate [proˈpɪʃiˌeɪt] *vt* **-ated; -ating** : propiciar

propitious [prəˈpɪʃəs] *adj* : propicio

proponent [prəˈpoːnənt] *n* : defensor *m,* -sora *f;* partidario *m,* -ria *f*

proportion[1] [prəˈporʃən] *vt* : proporcionar <well-proportioned : de buenas proporciones>

proportion[2] *n* **1** RATIO : proporción *f* **2** SYMMETRY : proporción *f,* simetría *f* <out of proportion : desproporcionado> **3** SHARE : parte *f* **4 proportions** *npl* SIZE : dimensiones *fpl*

proportional [prəˈporʃənəl] *adj* : proporcional — **proportionally** *adv*

proportionate [prəˈporʃənət] *adj* : proporcional — **proportionately** *adv*

proposal [prəˈpoːzəl] *n* **1** PROPOSITION : propuesta *f,* proposición *f* <marriage

proposal : propuesta de matrimonio> **2** PLAN : proyecto *m,* propuesta *f*

propose [prə'po:z] *v* **-posed; -posing** *vi* : proponer matrimonio — *vt* **1** INTEND : pensar, proponerse **2** SUGGEST : proponer

proposition [ˌprɑpə'zɪʃən] *n* **1** PROPOSAL : proposición *f,* propuesta *f* **2** STATEMENT : proposición *f*

propound [prə'paʊnd] *vt* : proponer, exponer

proprietary [prə'praɪəˌtɛri] *adj* : propietario, patentado

proprietor [prə'praɪət̬ər] *n* : propietario *m,* -ria *f*

propriety [prə'praɪət̬i] *n, pl* **-eties 1** DECORUM : decencia *f,* decoro *m* **2 proprieties** *npl* CONVENTIONS : convenciones *fpl,* cánones *mpl* sociales

propulsion [prə'pʌlʃən] *n* : propulsión *f*

prosaic [pro'zeɪɪk] *adj* : prosaico

proscribe [pro'skraɪb] *vt* **-scribed; -scribing** : proscribir

prose ['pro:z] *n* : prosa *f*

prosecute ['prɑsɪˌkju:t] *vt* **-cuted; -cuting 1** CARRY OUT : llevar a cabo **2** : procesar, enjuiciar <prosecuted for fraud : procesado por fraude>

prosecution [ˌprɑsɪ'kju:ʃən] *n* **1** : procesamiento *m* <the prosecution of forgers : el procesamiento de falsificadores> **2** PROSECUTORS : acusación *f* <witness for the prosecution : testigo de cargo>

prosecutor ['prɑsɪˌkju:t̬ər] *n* : acusador *m,* -dora *f;* fiscal *mf*

prospect¹ ['prɑˌspɛkt] *vi* : prospectar (el terreno) <to prospect for gold : buscar oro>

prospect² *n* **1** VISTA : vista *f,* panorama *m* **2** POSSIBILITY : posibilidad *f* **3** OUTLOOK : perspectiva *f* **4** : posible cliente *m,* -ta *f* <a salesman looking for prospects : un vendedor buscando nuevos clientes>

prospective [prə'spɛktɪv, 'prɑˌspɛk-] *adj* **1** EXPECTANT : futuro <prospective mother : futura madre> **2** POTENTIAL : potencial, posible <prospective employee : posible empleado>

prospector ['prɑˌspɛktər, prɑ'spɛk-] *n* : prospector *m,* -tora *f;* explorador *m,* -dora *f*

prospectus [prə'spɛktəs] *n* : prospecto *m*

prosper ['prɑspər] *vi* : prosperar

prosperity [prɑ'spɛrət̬i] *n* : prosperidad *f*

prosperous ['prɑspərəs] *adj* : próspero

prostate ['prɑˌsteɪt] *n* : próstata *f*

prosthesis [prɑs'θi:sɪs, 'prɑsθə-] *n, pl* **-theses** [-ˌsi:z] : prótesis *f*

prostitute¹ ['prɑstəˌtu:t, -ˌtju:t] *vt* **-tuted; -tuting 1** : prostituir **2 to prostitute oneself** : prostituirse

prostitute² *n* : prostituto *m,* -ta *f*

prostitution [ˌprɑstə'tu:ʃən, -'tju:-] *n* : prostitución *f*

prostrate¹ ['prɑˌstreɪt] *vt* **-trated; -trating 1** : postrar **2 to prostrate oneself** : postrarse

prostrate² *adj* : postrado

prostration [prɑ'streɪʃən] *n* : postración *f*

protagonist [pro'tægənɪst] *n* : protagonista *mf*

protect [prə'tɛkt] *vt* : proteger

protection [prə'tɛkʃən] *n* : protección *f*

protective [prə'tɛktɪv] *adj* : protector

protector [prə'tɛktər] *n* **1** : protector *m,* -tora *f* (persona) **2** GUARD : protector *m* (aparato)

protectorate [prə'tɛktərət] *n* : protectorado *m*

protégé ['pro:t̬əˌʒeɪ] *n* : protegido *m,* -da *f*

protein ['pro:ˌti:n] *n* : proteína *f*

protest¹ [pro'tɛst] *vt* **1** ASSERT : afirmar, declarar **2** : protestar <they protested the decision : protestaron (por) la decisión> — *vi* **to protest against** : protestar contra

protest² ['pro:ˌtɛst] *n* **1** DEMONSTRATION : manifestación *f* (de protesta) <a public protest : una manifestación pública> **2** COMPLAINT : queja *f,* protesta *f*

Protestant ['prɑt̬əstənt] *n* : protestante *mf*

Protestantism ['prɑt̬əstənˌtɪzəm] *n* : protestantismo *m*

protocol ['pro:t̬əˌkɔl] *n* : protocolo *m*

proton ['proˌtɑn] *n* : protón *m*

protoplasm ['pro:t̬əˌplæzəm] *n* : protoplasma *m*

prototype ['pro:t̬əˌtaɪp] *n* : prototipo *m*

protozoan [ˌpro:t̬ə'zo:ən] *n* : protozoario *m,* protozoo *m*

protract [pro'trækt] *vt* : prolongar

protractor [pro'træktər] *n* : transportador *m* (instrumento)

protrude [pro'tru:d] *vi* **-truded; -truding** : salir, sobresalir

protrusion [pro'tru:ʒən] *n* : protuberancia *f,* saliente *m*

protuberance [pro'tu:bərənts, -'tju:-] *n* : protuberancia *f*

proud ['praʊd] *adj* **1** HAUGHTY : altanero, orgulloso, arrogante **2** : orgulloso <she was proud of her work : estaba orgullosa de su trabajo> <too proud to beg : demasiado orgulloso para rogar> **3** GLORIOUS : glorioso — **proudly** *adv*

prove ['pru:v] *v* **proved; proved** *or* **proven** ['pru:vən]; **proving** *vt* **1** TEST : probar **2** DEMONSTRATE : probar, demostrar — *vi* : resultar <it proved effective : resultó efectivo>

Provençal [ˌpro:vɑn'sɑl, ˌprɑvən-] *n* **1** : provenzal *mf* **2** : provenzal *m* (idioma) — **Provençal** *adj*

proverb [ˈprɑˌvərb] *n* : proverbio *m*, refrán *m*

proverbial [prəˈvərbiəl] *adj* : proverbial

provide [prəˈvaɪd] *v* **-vided; -viding** *vt* **1** STIPULATE : estipular **2 to provide with** : proveer de, proporcionar — *vi* **1** : proveer <the Lord will provide : el Señor proveerá> **2 to provide for** SUPPORT : mantener **3 to provide for** ANTICIPATE : hacer previsiones para, prever

provided [prəˈvaɪdəd] *or* **provided that** *conj* : con tal (de) que, siempre que

providence [ˈprɑvədənts] *n* **1** PRUDENCE : previsión *f*, prudencia *f* **2** *or* **Providence** : providencia *f* <divine providence : la Divina Providencia> **3 Providence** GOD : Providencia *f*

provident [ˈprɑvədənt] *adj* **1** PRUDENT : previsor, prudente **2** FRUGAL : frugal, ahorrativo

providential [ˌprɑvəˈdɛntʃəl] *adj* : providencial

providing that → **provided**

province [ˈprɑvɪnts] *n* **1** : provincia *f* (de un país) <to live in the provinces : vivir en las provincias> **2** FIELD, SPHERE : campo *m*, competencia *f* <it's not in my province : no es de mi competencia>

provincial [prəˈvɪntʃəl] *adj* **1** : provincial <provincial government : gobierno provincial> **2** : provinciano, pueblerino <a provincial mentality : una mentalidad provinciana>

provision¹ [prəˈvɪʒən] *vt* : aprovisionar, abastecer

provision² *n* **1** PROVIDING : provisión *f*, suministro *m* **2** STIPULATION : condición *f*, salvedad *f*, estipulación *f* **3 provisions** *npl* : despensa *f*, víveres *mpl*, provisiones *fpl*

provisional [prəˈvɪʒənəl] *adj* : provisional, provisorio — **provisionally** *adv*

proviso [prəˈvaɪˌzoː] *n, pl* **-sos** *or* **-soes** : condición *f*, salvedad *f*, estipulación *f*

provocation [ˌprɑvəˈkeɪʃən] *n* : provocación *f*

provocative [prəˈvɑkət̬ɪv] *adj* : provocador, provocativo <a provocative article : un artículo que hace pensar>

provoke [prəˈvoːk] *vt* **-voked; -voking** : provocar

prow [ˈprаʊ] *n* : proa *f*

prowess [ˈpraʊəs] *n* **1** VALOR : valor *m*, valentía *f* **2** SKILL : habilidad *f*, destreza *f*

prowl [ˈpraʊl] *vi* : merodear, rondar — *vt* : rondar por

prowler [ˈpraʊlər] *n* : merodeador *m*, -dora *f*

proximity [prɑkˈsɪmət̬i] *n* : proximidad *f*

proxy [ˈprɑksi] *n, pl* **proxies 1** : poder *m* (de actuar en nombre de alguien) <by proxy : por poder> **2** AGENT : apoderado *m*, -da *f*; representante *mf*

prude [ˈpruːd] *n* : mojigato *m*, -ta *f*; gazmoño *m*, -ña *f*

prudence [ˈpruːdənts] *n* **1** SHREWDNESS : prudencia *f*, sagacidad *f* **2** CAUTION : prudencia *f*, cautela *f* **3** THRIFTINESS : frugalidad *f*

prudent [ˈpruːdənt] *adj* **1** SHREWD : prudente, sagaz **2** CAUTIOUS, FARSIGHTED : prudente, previsor, precavido **3** THRIFTY : frugal, ahorrativo — **prudently** *adv*

prudery [ˈpruːdəri] *n, pl* **-eries** : mojigatería *f*, gazmoñería *f*

prudish [ˈpruːdɪʃ] *adj* : mojigato, gazmoño

prune¹ [ˈpruːn] *vt* **pruned; pruning** : podar (arbustos, etc.), acortar (un texto), recortar (gastos, etc.)

prune² *n* : ciruela *f* pasa

prurient [ˈprʊriənt] *adj* : lascivo

pry [ˈpraɪ] *v* **pried; prying** *vi* : curiosear, huronear <to pry into other people's business : meterse uno en lo que no le importa> — *vt or* **to pry open** : abrir (con una palanca), apalancar

psalm [ˈsɑm, ˈsɑlm] *n* : salmo *m*

pseudonym [ˈsuːdəˌnɪm] *n* : seudónimo *m*

psoriasis [səˈraɪəsɪs] *n* : soriasis *f*, psoriasis *f*

psyche [ˈsaɪki] *n* : psique *f*, psiquis *f*

psychiatric [ˌsaɪkiˈætrɪk] *adj* : psiquiátrico, siquiátrico

psychiatrist [səˈkaɪətrɪst, saɪ-] *n* : psiquiatra *mf*, siquiatra *mf*

psychiatry [səˈkaɪətri, saɪ-] *n* : psiquiatría *f*, siquiatría *f*

psychic¹ [ˈsaɪkɪk] *adj* **1** : psíquico, síquico (en psicología) **2** CLAIRVOYANT : clarividente

psychic² *n* : vidente *mf*, clarividente *mf*

psychoanalysis [ˌsaɪkoəˈnæləsɪs] *n, pl* **-yses** : psicoanálisis *m*, sicoanálisis *m*

psychoanalyst [ˌsaɪkoˈænəlɪst] *n* : psicoanalista *mf*, sicoanalista *mf*

psychoanalytic [ˌsaɪkoˌænəlˈɪt̬ɪk] *adj* : psicoanalítico, sicoanalítico

psychoanalyze [ˌsaɪkoˈænəlˌaɪz] *vt* **-lyzed; -lyzing** : psicoanalizar, sicoanalizar

psychological [ˌsaɪkəˈlɑdʒɪkəl] *adj* : psicológico, sicológico — **psychologically** *adv*

psychologist [saɪˈkɑlədʒɪst] *n* : psicólogo *m*, -ga *f*; sicólogo *m*, -ga *f*

psychology [saɪˈkɑlədʒi] *n, pl* **-gies** : psicología *f*, sicología *f*

psychopath [ˈsaɪkəˌpæθ] *n* : psicópata *mf*, sicópata *mf*

psychopathic [ˌsaɪkəˈpæθɪk] *adj* : psicopático, sicopático

psychosis [saɪˈkoːsɪs] *n, pl* **-choses** [-ˈkoːˌsiːz] : psicosis *f*, sicosis *f*

psychosomatic [ˌsaɪkəsəˈmæt̬ɪk] *adj* : psicosomático, sicosomático

psychotherapist [ˌsaɪkoˈθɛrəpɪst] *n* : psicoterapeuta *mf*, sicoterapeuta *mf*

psychotherapy [ˌsaɪkoˈθɛrəpi] *n, pl* **-pies** : psicoterapia *f,* sicoterapia *f*

psychotic[1] [saɪˈkɑt̬ɪk] *adj* : psicótico, sicótico

psychotic[2] *n* : psicótico *m,* -ca *f;* sicótico *m,* -ca *f*

puberty [ˈpjuːbərt̬i] *n* : pubertad *f*

pubic [ˈpjuːbɪk] *adj* : pubiano, púbico

public[1] [ˈpʌblɪk] *adj* : público — **publicly** *adv*

public[2] *n* : público *m*

publication [ˌpʌbləˈkeɪʃən] *n* : publicación *f*

publicist [ˈpʌbləsɪst] *n* : publicista *mf*

publicity [pəˈblɪsət̬i] *n* : publicidad *f*

publicize [ˈpʌbləˌsaɪz] *vt* **-cized; -cizing** : publicitar

public school *n* : escuela *f* pública

publish [ˈpʌblɪʃ] *vt* : publicar

publisher [ˈpʌblɪʃər] *n* : casa *f* editorial (compañía); editor *m,* -tora *f* (persona)

pucker[1] [ˈpʌkər] *vt* : fruncir, arrugar — *vi* : arrugarse

pucker[2] *n* : arruga *f,* frunce *m,* fruncido *m*

pudding [ˈpʊdɪŋ] *n* : budín *m,* pudín *m*

puddle [ˈpʌdəl] *n* : charco *m*

pudgy [ˈpʌdʒi] *adj* **pudgier; -est** : regordete *fam,* rechoncho *fam,* gordinflón *fam*

puerile [ˈpjʊrəl] *adj* : pueril

Puerto Rican[1] [ˌpwɛrt̬əˈriːkən, ˌport̬ə-] *adj* : puertorriqueño

Puerto Rican[2] *n* : puertorriqueño *m,* -ña *f*

puff[1] [ˈpʌf] *vi* **1** BLOW : soplar **2** PANT : resoplar, jadear **3 to puff up** SWELL : hincharse — *vt* **1** BLOW : soplar <to puff smoke : echar humo> **2** INFLATE : inflar, hinchar <to puff out one's cheeks : inflar las mejillas>

puff[2] *n* **1** GUST : soplo *m,* ráfaga *f,* bocanada *f* (de humo) **2** DRAW : chupada *f* (a un cigarrillo) **3** SWELLING : hinchazón *f* **4 cream puff** : pastelito *m* de crema **5 powder puff** : borla *f*

puffy [ˈpʌfi] *adj* **puffier; -est 1** SWOLLEN : hinchado, inflado **2** SPONGY : esponjoso, suave

pug [ˈpʌg] *n* **1** : doguillo *m* (perro) **2** *or* **pug nose** : nariz *f* achatada

pugnacious [ˌpʌgˈneɪʃəs] *adj* : pugnaz, agresivo

puke [ˈpjuːk] *vi* **puked; puking** : vomitar, devolver

pull[1] [ˈpʊl, ˈpʌl] *vt* **1** DRAW, TUG : tirar de, jalar **2** EXTRACT : sacar, extraer <to pull teeth : sacar muelas> <to pull a gun on : amenazar a (alguien) con pistola> **3** TEAR : desgarrarse (un músculo, etc.) **4 to pull down** : bajar, echar abajo, derribar (un edificio) **5 to pull in** ATTRACT : atraer (una muchedumbre, etc.) <to pull in votes : conseguir votos> **6 to pull off** REMOVE : sacar, quitar **7 to pull oneself together** : calmarse, tranquilizarse **8 to pull up** RAISE : levantar, subir — *vi* **1** DRAW, TUG : tirar, jalar **2** (*indicating movement in a specific direction*) <they pulled in front of us : se nos metieron delante> <to pull to a stop : pararse> **3 to pull through** RECOVER : recobrarse, reponerse **4 to pull together** COOPERATE : trabajar juntos, cooperar

pull[2] *n* **1** TUG : tirón *m,* jalón *m* <he gave it a pull : le dio un tirón> **2** ATTRACTION : atracción *f,* fuerza *f* <the pull of gravity : la fuerza de la gravedad> **3** INFLUENCE : influencia *f* **4** HANDLE : tirador *m* (de un cajón, etc.) **5 bell pull** : cuerda *f*

pullet [ˈpʊlət] *n* : polla *f,* gallina *f* (joven)

pulley [ˈpʊli] *n, pl* **-leys** : polea *f*

pullover [ˈpʊlˌoːvər] *n* : suéter *m*

pulmonary [ˈpʊlməˌnɛri, ˈpʌl-] *adj* : pulmonar

pulp [ˈpʌlp] *n* **1** : pulpa *f* (de una fruta, etc.) **2** MASH : papilla *f,* pasta *f* <wood pulp : pasta de papel, pulpa de papel> <to beat to a pulp : hacer papilla (a alguien)> **3** : pulpa *f* (de los dientes)

pulpit [ˈpʊlˌpɪt] *n* : púlpito *m*

pulsate [ˈpʌlˌseɪt] *vi* **-sated; -sating 1** BEAT : latir, palpitar **2** VIBRATE : vibrar

pulsation [ˌpʌlˈseɪʃən] *n* : pulsación *f*

pulse [ˈpʌls] *n* : pulso *m*

pulverize [ˈpʌlvəˌraɪz] *vt* **-ized; -izing** : pulverizar

puma [ˈpuːmə, ˈpjuː-] *n* : puma *m;* león *m,* leona *f* (in various countries)

pumice [ˈpʌməs] *n* : piedra *f* pómez

pummel [ˈpʌməl] *vt* **-meled; -meling** : aporrear, apalear

pump[1] [ˈpʌmp] *vt* **1** : bombear <to pump water : bombear agua> <to pump (up) a tire : inflar una llanta> **2** : mover (una manivela, un pedal, etc.) de arriba abajo <to pump someone's hand : darle un fuerte apretón de manos (a alguien)> **3 to pump out** : sacar, vaciar (con una bomba)

pump[2] *n* **1** : bomba *f* <water pump : bomba de agua> **2** SHOE : zapato *m* de tacón

pumpernickel [ˈpʌmpərˌnɪkəl] *n* : pan *m* negro de centeno

pumpkin [ˈpʌmpkɪn, ˈpʌŋkən] *n* : calabaza *f,* zapallo *m Arg, Chile, Peru, Uru*

pun[1] [ˈpʌn] *vi* **punned; punning** : hacer juegos de palabras

pun[2] *n* : juego *m* de palabras, albur *m Mex*

punch[1] [ˈpʌntʃ] *vt* **1** HIT : darle un puñetazo (a alguien), golpear <she punched him in the nose : le dio un puñetazo en la nariz> **2** PERFORATE : perforar (papel, etc.), picar (un boleto)

punch[2] *n* **1** : perforadora *f* <paper punch : perforadora de papel> **2** BLOW : golpe *m,* puñetazo *m* **3** : ponche *m* <fruit punch : ponche de frutas>

punctilious [pəŋk'tɪliəs] *adj* **:** puntilloso

punctual ['pʌŋktʃʊəl] *adj* **:** puntual

punctuality [ˌpʌŋktʃʊ'æləṭi] *n* **:** puntualidad *f*

punctually ['pʌŋktʃʊəli] *adv* **:** puntualmente, a tiempo

punctuate ['pʌŋktʃʊˌeɪt] *vt* **-ated; -ating :** puntuar

punctuation [ˌpʌŋktʃʊ'eɪʃən] *n* **:** puntuación *f*

puncture[1] ['pʌŋktʃər] *vt* **-tured; -turing :** pinchar, punzar, perforar, ponchar *Mex*

puncture[2] *n* **:** pinchazo *m,* ponchadura *f Mex*

pundit ['pʌndɪt] *n* **:** experto *m,* -ta *f*

pungency ['pʌndʒən*t*si] *n* **:** acritud *f,* acrimonia *f*

pungent ['pʌndʒənt] *adj* **:** acre

punish ['pʌnɪʃ] *vt* **:** castigar

punishable ['pʌnɪʃəbəl] *adj* **:** punible

punishment ['pʌnɪʃmənt] *n* **:** castigo *m*

punitive ['pju:nəṭɪv] *adj* **:** punitivo

punt[1] ['pʌnt] *vt* **:** impulsar (un barco) con una pértiga — *vi* **:** despejar (en deportes)

punt[2] *n* **1 :** batea *f* (barco) **2 :** patada *f* de despeje (en deportes)

puny ['pju:ni] *adj* **-nier; -est :** enclenque, endeble

pup ['pʌp] *n* **:** cachorro *m,* -rra *f* (de un perro); cría *f* (de otros animales)

pupa ['pju:pə] *n, pl* **-pae** [-pi, -ˌpaɪ] *or* **-pas :** crisálida *f,* pupa *f*

pupil ['pju:pəl] *n* **1 :** alumno *m,* -na *f* (de colegio) **2 :** pupila *f* (del ojo)

puppet ['pʌpət] *n* **:** títere *m,* marioneta *f*

puppy ['pʌpi] *n, pl* **-pies :** cachorro *m,* -rra *f*

purchase[1] ['pərtʃəs] *vt* **-chased; -chasing :** comprar

purchase[2] *n* **1** PURCHASING **:** compra *f,* adquisición *f* **2 :** compra *f* <last-minute purchases : compras de última hora> **3** GRIP **:** agarre *m,* asidero *m* <she got a firm purchase on the wheel : se agarró bien del volante>

purchase order *n* **:** orden *f* de compra

pure ['pjʊr] *adj* **purer; purest :** puro

puree[1] [pjʊ'reɪ, -'ri:] *vt* **-reed; -reeing :** hacer un puré con

puree[2] *n* **:** puré *m*

purely ['pjʊrli] *adv* **1** WHOLLY **:** puramente, completamente <purely by chance : por pura casualidad> **2** SIMPLY **:** sencillamente, meramente

purgative ['pərgəṭɪv] *n* **:** purgante *m*

purgatory ['pərgəˌtori] *n, pl* **-ries :** purgatorio *m*

purge[1] ['pərdʒ] *vt* **purged; purging :** purgar

purge[2] *n* **:** purga *f*

purification [ˌpjʊrəfə'keɪʃən] *n* **:** purificación *f*

purify ['pjʊrəˌfaɪ] *vt* **-fied; -fying :** purificar

puritan ['pjʊrətən] *n* **:** puritano *m,* -na *f*

puritanical [ˌpju:rə'tænɪkəl] *adj* **:** puritano

purity ['pjʊrəṭi] *n* **:** pureza *f*

purl[1] ['pərl] *v* **:** tejer al revés, tejer del revés

purl[2] *n* **:** punto *m* del revés

purloin [pər'lɔɪn, 'pərˌlɔɪn] *vt* **:** hurtar, robar

purple ['pərpəl] *n* **:** morado *m,* color *m* púrpura

purport [pər'port] *vt* **:** pretender <to purport to be : pretender ser>

purpose ['pərpəs] *n* **1** INTENTION **:** propósito *m,* intención *f* <on purpose : a propósito, adrede> **2** FUNCTION **:** función *f* **3** RESOLUTION **:** resolución *f,* determinación *f*

purposeful ['pərpəsfəl] *adj* **:** determinado, decidido, resuelto

purposefully ['pərpəsfəli] *adv* **:** decididamente, resueltamente

purposely ['pərpəsli] *adv* **:** intencionadamente, a propósito, adrede

purr[1] ['pər] *vi* **:** ronronear

purr[2] *n* **:** ronroneo *m*

purse[1] ['pərs] *vt* **pursed; pursing :** fruncir <to purse one's lips : fruncir la boca>

purse[2] *n* **1** HANDBAG **:** cartera *f,* bolso *m,* bolsa *f Mex* <a change purse : un monedero> **2** FUNDS **:** fondos *mpl* **3** PRIZE **:** premio *m*

pursue [pər'su:] *vt* **-sued; -suing 1** CHASE **:** perseguir **2** SEEK **:** buscar, tratar de encontrar <to pursue pleasure : buscar el placer> **3** FOLLOW **:** seguir <the road pursues a northerly course : el camino sigue hacia el norte> **4 :** dedicarse a <to pursue a hobby : dedicarse a un pasatiempo>

pursuer [pər'su:ər] *n* **:** perseguidor *m,* -dora *f*

pursuit [pər'su:t] *n* **1** CHASE **:** persecución *f* **2** SEARCH **:** búsqueda *f,* busca *f* **3** ACTIVITY **:** actividad *f,* pasatiempo *m*

purveyor [pər'veɪər] *n* **:** proveedor *m,* -dora *f*

pus ['pʌs] *n* **:** pus *m*

push[1] ['pʊʃ] *vt* **1** SHOVE **:** empujar **2** PRESS **:** apretar, pulsar <push that button : aprieta ese botón> **3** PRESSURE, URGE **:** presionar **4 to push around** BULLY **:** intimidar, mangonear — *vi* **1** SHOVE **:** empujar **2** INSIST **:** insistir, presionar **3 to push off** LEAVE **:** marcharse, irse, largarse *fam* **4 to push on** PROCEED **:** seguir

push[2] *n* **1** SHOVE **:** empujón *m* **2** DRIVE **:** empuje *m,* energía *f,* dinamismo *m* **3** EFFORT **:** esfuerzo *m*

push-button ['pʊʃ'bʌtən] *adj* **:** de botones

pushcart ['pʊʃˌkart] *n* **:** carretilla *f* de mano

pushy ['pʊʃi] *adj* **pushier; -est :** mandón, prepotente

pussy [ˈpʊsi] *n, pl* **pussies :** gatito *m,* -ta *f;* minino *m,* -na *f*

pussy willow *n* **:** sauce *m* blanco

pustule [ˈpʌsˌtʃuːl] *n* **:** pústula *f*

put [ˈpʊt] *v* **put; putting** *vt* **1** PLACE **:** poner, colocar <put it on the table **:** ponlo en la mesa> **2** INSERT **:** meter **3** (*indicating causation of a state or feeling*) **:** poner <it put her in a good mood **:** la puso de buen humor> <to put into effect **:** poner en práctica> **4** IMPOSE **:** imponer <they put a tax on it **:** lo gravaron con un impuesto> **5** SUBJECT **:** someter, poner <to put to the test **:** poner a prueba> <to put to death **:** ejecutar> **6** EXPRESS **:** expresar, decir <he put it simply **:** lo dijo sencillamente> **7** APPLY **:** aplicar <to put one's mind to something **:** proponerse hacer algo> 8 SET **:** poner <I put him to work **:** lo puse a trabajar> **9** ATTACH **:** dar <to put a high value on **:** dar gran valor a> **10** PRESENT **:** presentar, exponer <to put a question to someone **:** hacer una pregunta a alguien> — *vi* **1 to put to sea :** hacerse a la mar **2 to put up with :** aguantar, soportar

put away *vt* **1** KEEP **:** guardar **2** *or* **to put aside :** dejar a un lado

put by *vt* SAVE **:** ahorrar

put down *vt* **1** SUPPRESS **:** aplastar, suprimir **2** ATTRIBUTE **:** atribuir <she put it down to luck **:** lo atribuyó a la suerte>

put in *vi* **:** presentarse <I've put in for the position **:** me presenté para el puesto> — *vt* DEVOTE **:** dedicar (unas horas, etc.)

put off *vt* DEFER **:** aplazar, posponer

put on *vt* **1** ASSUME **:** afectar, adoptar **2** PRODUCE **:** presentar (una obra de teatro, etc.) **3** WEAR **:** ponerse

put out *vt* INCONVENIENCE **:** importunar, incomodar

putrefy [ˈpjuːtrəˌfaɪ] *v* **-fied; -fying** *vt* **:** pudrir — *vi* **:** pudrirse

putrid [ˈpjuːtrɪd] *adj* **:** putrefacto, pútrido

putter [ˈpʌt̬ər] *vi or* **to putter around :** entretenerse

putty[1] [ˈpʌt̬i] *vt* **-tied; -tying :** poner masilla en

putty[2] *n, pl* **-ties :** masilla *f*

put up *vt* **1** LODGE **:** alojar **2** CONTRIBUTE **:** contribuir, pagar

puzzle[1] [ˈpʌzəl] *vt* **-zled; -zling 1** CONFUSE **:** confundir, dejar perplejo **2 to puzzle out :** dar vueltas a, tratar de resolver

puzzle[2] *n* **1 :** rompecabezas *m* <a crossword puzzle **:** un crucigrama> **2** MYSTERY **:** misterio *m,* enigma *m*

puzzlement [ˈpʌzəlmənt] *n* **:** desconcierto *m,* perplejidad *f*

pygmy[1] [ˈpɪgmi] *adj* **:** enano, pigmeo

pygmy[2] *n, pl* **-mies 1** DWARF **:** enano *m,* -na *f* **2 Pygmy :** pigmeo *m,* -mea *f*

pylon [ˈpaɪˌlɑn, -lən] *n* **1 :** torre *f* de conducta eléctrica **2 :** pilón *m* (de un puente)

pyramid [ˈpɪrəˌmɪd] *n* **:** pirámide *f*

pyre [ˈpaɪr] *n* **:** pira *f*

pyromania [ˌpaɪroˈmeɪniə] *n* **:** piromanía *f*

pyromaniac [ˌpaɪroˈmeɪniˌæk] *n* **:** pirómano *m,* -na *f*

pyrotechnics [ˌpaɪrəˈtɛknɪks] *npl* **1** FIREWORKS **:** fuegos *mpl* artificiales **2** DISPLAY, SHOW **:** espectáculo *m,* muestra *f* de virtuosismo <computer pyrotechnics **:** efectos especiales hechos por computadora>

python [ˈpaɪˌθɑn, -θən] *n* **:** pitón *f,* serpiente *f* pitón

Q

q [ˈkjuː] *n, pl* **q's** *or* **qs** [ˈkjuːz] **:** decimoséptima letra del alfabeto inglés

quack[1] [ˈkwæk] *vi* **:** graznar

quack[2] *n* **1 :** graznido *m* (de pato) **2** CHARLATAN **:** curandero *m,* -ra *f;* matasanos *m fam*

quadrangle [ˈkwɑˌdræŋgəl] *n* **1** COURTYARD **:** patio *m* interior **2** → **quadrilateral**

quadrant [ˈkwɑdrənt] *n* **:** cuadrante *m*

quadrilateral [ˌkwɑdrəˈlæt̬ərəl] *n* **:** cuadrilátero *m*

quadruped [ˈkwɑdrəˌpɛd] *n* **:** cuadrúpedo *m*

quadruple [kwɑˈdruːpəl, -ˈdrʌ-; ˈkwɑdrə-] *v* **-pled; -pling** *vt* **:** cuadruplicar — *vi* **:** cuadruplicarse

quadruplet [kwɑˈdruːplət, -ˈdrʌ-; ˈkwɑdrə-] *-n* **:** cuatrillizo *m,* -za *f*

quagmire [ˈkwægˌmaɪr, ˈkwɑg-] *n* **:** cenagal *m,* lodazal *m*

quail[1] [ˈkweɪl] *vi* **:** encogerse, acobardarse

quail[2] *n, pl* **quail** *or* **quails :** codorniz *f*

quaint [ˈkweɪnt] *adj* **1** ODD **:** extraño, curioso **2** PICTURESQUE **:** pintoresco — **quaintly** *adv*

quaintness [ˈkweɪntnəs] *n* **:** rareza *f,* lo curioso

quake[1] [ˈkweɪk] *vi* **quaked; quaking :** temblar

quake[2] *n* **:** temblor *m,* terremoto *m*

qualification [ˌkwɑləfəˈkeɪʃən] *n* **1** LIMITATION, RESERVATION **:** reserva *f,* limitación *f* <without qualification **:** sin reservas> **2** REQUIREMENT **:** requisito *m* **3 qualifications** *npl* ABILITY **:** aptitud *f,* capacidad *f*

qualified [ˈkwɑləˌfaɪd] *adj* **:** competente, capacitado

qualify [ˈkwɑləˌfaɪ] *v* **-fied; -fying** *vt* **1 :** matizar <to qualify a statement

: matizar una declaración> **2** MODIFY : calificar (en gramática) **3** : habilitar <the certificate qualified her to teach : el certificado la habilitó para enseñar> — *vi* **1** : obtener el título, recibirse <to qualify as an engineer : recibirse de ingeniero> **2** : clasificarse (en deportes)

quality [ˈkwɑləṭi] *n, pl* **-ties 1** NATURE : carácter *m* **2** ATTRIBUTE : cualidad *f* **3** GRADE : calidad *f* <of good quality : de buena calidad>

qualm [ˈkwɑm, ˈkwɑlm, ˈkwɔm] *n* **1** MISGIVING : duda *f*, aprensión *f* **2** RESERVATION, SCRUPLE : escrúpulo *m*, reparo *m*

quandary [ˈkwɑndri] *n, pl* **-ries** : dilema *m*

quantity [ˈkwɑntəṭi] *n, pl* **-ties** : cantidad *f*

quantum theory [ˈkwɑntəm] *n* : teoría *f* cuántica

quarantine[1] [ˈkwɔrən,tiːn] *vt* **-tined; -tining** : poner en cuarentena

quarantine[2] *n* : cuarentena *f*

quarrel[1] [ˈkwɔrəl] *vi* **-reled** *or* **-relled; -reling** *or* **-relling** : pelearse, reñir, discutir

quarrel[2] *n* : pelea *f*, riña *f*, disputa *f*

quarrelsome [ˈkwɔrəlsəm] *adj* : pendenciero, discutidor

quarry[1] [ˈkwɔri] *vt* **quarried; quarrying 1** EXTRACT : extraer, sacar <to quarry marble : extraer mármol> **2** EXCAVATE : excavar <to quarry a hill : excavar un cerro>

quarry[2] *n, pl* **quarries 1** PREY : presa *f* **2** *or* **stone quarry** : cantera *f*

quart [ˈkwɔrt] *n* : cuarto *m* de galón

quarter[1] [ˈkwɔrṭər] *vt* **1** : dividir en cuatro partes **2** LODGE : alojar, acuartelar (tropas)

quarter[2] *n* **1** : cuarto *m*, cuarta parte *f* <a foot and a quarter : un pie y cuarto> <a quarter after three : las tres y cuarto> **2** : moneda *f* de 25 centavos, cuarto *m* de dólar **3** DISTRICT : barrio *m* <business quarter : barrio comercial> **4** PLACE : parte *f* <from all quarters : de todas partes> <at close quarters : de muy cerca> **5** MERCY : clemencia *f*, cuartel *m* <to give no quarter : no dar cuartel> **6 quarters** *npl* LODGING : alojamiento *m*, cuartel *m* (militar)

quarterly[1] [ˈkwɔrṭərli] *adv* : cada tres meses, trimestralmente

quarterly[2] *adj* : trimestral

quarterly[3] *n, pl* **-lies** : publicación *f* trimestral

quartermaster [ˈkwɔrṭər,mæstər] *n* : intendente *mf*

quartet [kwɔrˈtɛt] *n* : cuarteto *m*

quartz [ˈkwɔrts] *n* : cuarzo *m*

quash [ˈkwɑʃ, ˈkwɔʃ] *vt* **1** ANNUL : anular **2** QUELL : sofocar, aplastar

quaver[1] [ˈkweɪvər] *vi* **1** SHAKE : temblar <her voice was quavering : su voz temblaba> **2** TRILL : trinar

quaver[2] *n* : temblor *m* (de la voz)

quay [ˈkiː, ˈkeɪ, ˈkweɪ] *n* : muelle *m*

queasiness [ˈkwiːzinəs] *n* : mareo *m*, náusea *f*

queasy [ˈkwiːzi] *adj* **-sier; -est** : mareado

queen [ˈkwiːn] *n* : reina *f*

queenly [ˈkwiːnli] *adj* **-lier; -est** : de reina, regio

queer [ˈkwɪr] *adj* : extraño, raro, curioso — **queerly** *adv*

quell [ˈkwɛl] *vt* : aplastar, sofocar

quench [ˈkwɛntʃ] *vt* **1** EXTINGUISH : apagar, sofocar **2** SATISFY : saciar, satisfacer (la sed)

querulous [ˈkwɛrələs, ˈkwɛrjələs, ˈkwɪr-] *adj* : quejumbroso, quejoso — **querulously** *adv*

query[1] [ˈkwɪri, ˈkwɛr-] *vt* **-ried; -rying 1** ASK : preguntar, interrogar <we queried the professor : preguntamos al profesor> **2** QUESTION : cuestionar, poner en duda <to query a matter : cuestionar un asunto>

query[2] *n, pl* **-ries 1** QUESTION : pregunta *f* **2** DOUBT : duda *f*

quest[1] [ˈkwɛst] *v* : buscar

quest[2] *n* : búsqueda *f*

question[1] [ˈkwɛstʃən] *vt* **1** ASK : preguntar **2** DOUBT : poner en duda, cuestionar **3** INTERROGATE : interrogar — *vi* INQUIRE : inquirir, preguntar

question[2] *n* **1** QUERY : pregunta *f* **2** ISSUE : asunto *m*, problema *f*, cuestión *f* **3** POSSIBILITY : posibilidad *f* <it's out of the question : es indiscutible> **4** DOUBT : duda *f* <to call into question : poner en duda>

questionable [ˈkwɛstʃənəbəl] *adj* : dudoso, discutible, cuestionable <questionable results : resultados discutibles> <questionable motives : motivos sospechosos>

questioner [ˈkwɛstʃənər] *n* : interrogador *m*, -dora *f*

question mark *n* : signo *m* de interrogación

questionnaire [,kwɛstʃəˈnær] *n* : cuestionario *m*

queue[1] [ˈkjuː] *vi* **queued; queuing** *or* **queueing** : hacer cola

queue[2] *n* **1** PIGTAIL : coleta *f*, trenza *f* **2** LINE : cola *f*, fila *f*

quibble[1] [ˈkwɪbəl] *vi* **-bled; -bling** : quejarse por nimiedades, andar con sutilezas

quibble[2] *n* : objeción *f* de poca monta, queja *f* insignificante

quick[1] [ˈkwɪk] *adv* : rápidamente

quick[2] *adj* **1** RAPID : rápido **2** ALERT, CLEVER : listo, vivo, agudo **3 a quick temper** : un genio vivo

quick[3] *n* **1** FLESH : carne *f* viva **2 to cut someone to the quick** : herir a alguien en lo más vivo

quicken [ˈkwɪkən] *vt* **1** REVIVE : resucitar **2** AROUSE : estimular, despertar **3** HASTEN : acelerar <she quickened her pace : aceleró el paso>

quickly [ˈkwɪkli] *adv* : rápidamente, rápido, de prisa
quickness [ˈkwɪknəs] *n* : rapidez *f*
quicksand [ˈkwɪkˌsænd] *n* : arena *f* movediza
quicksilver [ˈkwɪkˌsɪlvər] *n* : mercurio *m,* azogue *m*
quick–tempered [ˈkwɪkˈtɛmpərd] *adj* : irascible, de genio vivo
quick–witted [ˈkwɪkˈwɪt̬əd] *adj* : agudo
quiet[1] *v* [ˈkwaɪət] *vt* **1** SILENCE : hacer callar, acallar **2** CALM : calmar, tranquilizar — *vi* **to quiet down** : calmarse, tranquilizarse
quiet[2] *adv* : silenciosamente <a quiet-running engine : un motor silencioso>
quiet[3] *adj* **1** CALM : tranquilo, calmoso **2** MILD : sosegado, suave <a quiet disposition : un temperamento sosegado> **3** SILENT : silencioso **4** UNOBTRUSIVE : discreto **5** SECLUDED : aislado <a quiet nook : un rincón aislado> — **quietly** *adv*
quiet[4] *n* **1** CALM : calma *f,* tranquilidad *f* **2** SILENCE : silencio *m*
quietness [ˈkwaɪətnəs] *n* : suavidad *f,* tranquilidad *f,* quietud *f*
quietude [ˈkwaɪəˌtuːd, -ˌtjuːd] *n* : quietud *f,* reposo *m*
quill [ˈkwɪl] *n* **1** SPINE : púa *f* (de un puerco espín) **2** : pluma *f* (para escribir)
quilt[1] [ˈkwɪlt] *vt* : acolchar
quilt[2] *n* : colcha *f,* edredón *m*
quince [ˈkwɪn*t*s] *n* : membrillo *m*
quinine [ˈkwaɪˌnaɪn] *n* : quinina *f*
quintessence [kwɪnˈtɛsən*t*s] *n* : quintaesencia *f*
quintet [kwɪnˈtɛt] *n* : quinteto *m*
quintuple [kwɪnˈtuːpəl, -ˈtjuː-, -ˈtʌ-; ˈkwɪntə-] *adj* : quíntuplo
quintuplet [kwɪnˈtʌplət, -ˈtuː-, -ˈtjuː-; ˈkwɪntə-] *n* : quintillizo *m,* -za *f*
quip[1] [ˈkwɪp] *vi* **quipped; quipping** : bromear
quip[2] *n* : ocurrencia *f,* salida *f*
quirk [ˈkwərk] *n* : peculiaridad *f,* rareza *f* <a quirk of fate : un capricho del destino>
quirky [ˈkwərki] *adj* **-kier; -est** : peculiar, raro
quit [ˈkwɪt] *v* **quit; quitting** *vt* : dejar, abandonar <to quit smoking : dejar de fumar> — *vi* **1** STOP : parar **2** RESIGN : dimitir, renunciar
quite [ˈkwaɪt] *adv* **1** COMPLETELY : completamente, totalmente **2** RATHER : bastante <quite near : bastante cerca>
quits [ˈkwɪts] *adj* **to call it quits** : quedar en paz
quitter [ˈkwɪt̬ər] *n* : derrotista *mf*
quiver[1] [ˈkwɪvər] *vi* : temblar, estremecerse, vibrar
quiver[2] *n* **1** : carcaj *m,* aljaba *f* (para flechas) **2** TREMBLING : temblor *m,* estremecimiento *m*
quixotic [kwɪkˈsɑt̬ɪk] *adj* : quijotesco
quiz[1] [ˈkwɪz] *vt* **quizzed; quizzing** : interrogar, hacer una prueba a (en el colegio)
quiz[2] *n, pl* **quizzes** : examen *m* corto, prueba *f*
quizzical [ˈkwɪzɪkəl] *adj* **1** TEASING : burlón **2** CURIOUS : curioso, interrogativo
quorum [ˈkworəm] *n* : quórum *m*
quota [ˈkwoːt̬ə] *n* : cuota *f,* cupo *m*
quotable [ˈkwoːt̬əbəl] *adj* : citable
quotation [kwoˈteɪʃən] *n* **1** CITATION : cita *f* **2** ESTIMATE : presupuesto *m,* estimación *f* **3** PRICE : cotización *f*
quotation marks *npl* : comillas *fpl*
quote[1] [ˈkwoːt] *vt* **quoted; quoting 1** CITE : citar **2** VALUE : cotizar (en finanzas)
quote[2] *n* **1** → **quotation 2 quotes** *npl* → **quotation marks**
quotient [ˈkwoːʃənt] *n* : cociente *m*

R

r [ˈɑr] *n, pl* **r's** *or* **rs** [ˈɑrz] : decimoctava letra del alfabeto inglés
rabbi [ˈræˌbaɪ] *n* : rabino *m,* -na *f*
rabbit [ˈræbət] *n, pl* **-bit** *or* **-bits** : conejo *m,* -ja *f*
rabble [ˈræbəl] *n* **1** MASSES : populacho *m* **2** RIFFRAFF : chusma *f,* gentuza *f*
rabid [ˈræbɪd] *adj* **1** : rabioso, afectado con la rabia **2** FURIOUS : furioso **3** FANATIC : fanático
rabies [ˈreɪbiːz] *ns & pl* : rabia *f*
raccoon [ræˈkuːn] *n, pl* **-coon** *or* **-coons** : mapache *m*
race[1] [ˈreɪs] *vi* **raced; racing 1** : correr, competir (en una carrera) **2** RUSH : ir a toda prisa, ir corriendo
race[2] *n* **1** CURRENT : corriente *f* (de agua) **2** : carrera *f* <dog race : carrera de perros> <the presidential race : la carrera presidential> **3** : raza *f* <the black race : la raza negra> <the human race : el género humano>
racecourse [ˈreɪsˌkors] *n* : pista *f* (de carreras)
racehorse [ˈreɪsˌhors] *n* : caballo *m* de carreras
racer [ˈreɪsər] *n* : corredor *m,* -dora *f*
racetrack [ˈreɪsˌtræk] *n* : pista *f* (de carreras)
racial [ˈreɪʃəl] *adj* : racial — **racially** *adv*
racism [ˈreɪˌsɪzəm] *n* : racismo *m*
racist [ˈreɪsɪst] *n* : racista *mf*

rack[1] ['ræk] *vt* **1 :** atormentar <racked with pain : atormentado por el dolor> **2 to rack one's brains :** devanarse los sesos

rack[2] *n* **1** SHELF, STAND : estante *m* <a luggage rack : un portaequipajes> <a coatrack : un perchero, una percha> **2** : potro *m* (instrumento de la tortura)

racket ['rækət] *n* **1 :** raqueta *f* (en deportes) **2** DIN **:** estruendo *m,* bulla *f,* jaleo *m fam* **3** SWINDLE **:** estafa *f,* timo *m fam*

racketeer [ˌrækə'tɪr] *n* **:** estafador *m,* -dora *f*

raconteur [ˌræˌkɑn'tər] *n* **:** anecdotista *mf*

racy ['reɪsi] *adj* **racier; -est :** subido de tono, picante

radar ['reɪˌdɑr] *n* **:** radar *m*

radial ['reɪdiəl] *adj* **:** radial

radiance ['reɪdiənts] *n* **:** resplandor *m*

radiant ['reɪdiənt] *adj* **:** radiante — **radiantly** *adv*

radiate ['reɪdiˌeɪt] *v* **-ated; -ating** *vt* **:** irradiar, emitir <to radiate heat : irradiar el calor> <to radiate happiness : rebosar de alegría> — *vi* **1 :** irradiar **2** SPREAD **:** salir, extenderse <to radiate (out) from the center : salir del centro>

radiation [ˌreɪdi'eɪʃən] *n* **:** radiación *f*

radiator ['reɪdiˌeɪtər] *n* **:** radiador *m*

radical[1] ['rædɪkəl] *adj* **:** radical — **radically** [-kli] *adv*

radical[2] *n* **:** radical *mf*

radii → **radius**

radio[1] ['reɪdiˌoː] *v* **:** llamar por radio, transmitir por radio

radio[2] *n, pl* **-dios :** radio *m* (aparato), radio *f* (emisora, radiodifusión)

radioactive ['reɪdio'æktɪv] *adj* **:** radiactivo, radioactivo

radioactivity [ˌreɪdioˌæk'tɪvət̬i] *n, pl* **-ties :** radiactividad *f,* radioactividad *f*

radiologist [ˌreɪdi'ɑlədʒɪst] *n* **:** radiólogo *m,* -ga *f*

radiology [ˌreɪdi'ɑlədʒi] *n* **:** radiología *f*

radish ['rædɪʃ] *n* **:** rábano *m*

radium ['reɪdiəm] *n* **:** radio *m*

radius ['reɪdiəs] *n, pl* **radii** [-diˌaɪ] **:** radio *m*

radon ['reɪˌdɑn] *n* **:** radón *m*

raffle[1] ['ræfəl] *vt* **-fled; -fling :** rifar, sortear

raffle[2] *n* **:** rifa *f,* sorteo *m*

raft ['ræft] *n* **1 :** balsa *f* <rubber rafts : balsas de goma> **2** LOT, SLEW **:** montón *m* <a raft of documents : un montón de documentos>

rafter ['ræftər] *n* **:** par *m,* viga *f*

rag ['ræg] *n* **1** CLOTH **:** trapo *m* **2 rags** *npl* TATTERS **:** harapos *mpl,* andrapos *mpl*

ragamuffin ['rægəˌmʌfən] *n* **:** pilluelo *m,* -la *f*

rage[1] ['reɪdʒ] *vi* **raged; raging 1 :** estar furioso, rabiar <to fly into a rage : enfurecerse> **2 :** bramar, hacer estragos <the wind was raging : el viento bramaba> <flu raged through the school : la gripe hizo estragos por el colegio>

rage[2] *n* **1** ANGER **:** furia *f,* ira *f,* cólera *f* **2** FAD **:** moda *f,* furor *m*

ragged ['rægəd] *adj* **1** UNEVEN **:** irregular, desigual **2** TORN **:** hecho jirones **3** TATTERED **:** andrajoso, harapiento

ragout [ræ'guː] *n* **:** ragú *m,* estofado *m*

ragtime ['rægˌtaɪm] *n* **:** ragtime *m*

ragweed ['rægˌwiːd] *n* **:** ambrosía *f*

raid[1] ['reɪd] *vt* **1 :** invadir, hacer una incursión en <raided by enemy troops : invadido por tropas enemigas> **2 :** asaltar, atracar <the gang raided the warehouse : la pandilla asaltó el almacén> **3 :** allanar, hacer una redada en <police raided the house : la policía allanó la vivienda>

raid[2] *n* **1 :** invasión *f* (militar) **2 :** asalto *m* (por delincuentes) **3 :** redada *f,* allanamiento *m* (por la policía)

raider ['reɪdər] *n* **1** ATTACKER **:** asaltante *mf;* invasor *m,* -sora *f* **2 corporate raider :** tiburón *m*

rail[1] ['reɪl] *vi* **1 to rail against** REVILE **:** denostar contra **2 to rail at** SCOLD **:** regañar, reprender

rail[2] *n* **1** BAR **:** barra *f,* barrera *f* **2** HANDRAIL **:** pasamanos *m,* barandilla *f* **3** TRACK **:** riel *m* (para ferrocarriles) **4** RAILROAD **:** ferrocarril *m*

railing ['reɪlɪŋ] *n* **1 :** baranda *f* (de un balcón, etc.) **2** RAILS **:** verja *f*

raillery ['reɪləri] *n, pl* **-leries :** bromas *fpl*

railroad ['reɪlˌroːd] *n* **:** ferrocarril *m*

railway ['reɪlˌweɪ] → **railroad**

raiment ['reɪmənt] *n* **:** vestiduras *fpl*

rain[1] ['reɪn] *vi* **1 :** llover <it's raining : está lloviendo> **2 to rain down** SHOWER **:** llover <insults rained down on him : le llovieron los insultos>

rain[2] *n* **:** lluvia *f*

rainbow ['reɪnˌboː] *n* **:** arco *m* iris

raincoat ['reɪnˌkoːt] *n* **:** impermeable *m*

raindrop ['reɪnˌdrɑp] *n* **:** gota *f* de lluvia

rainfall ['reɪnˌfɔl] *n* **:** lluvia *f,* precipitación *f*

rainstorm ['reɪnˌstɔrm] *n* **:** temporal *m* (de lluvia)

rainwater ['reɪnˌwɔt̬ər] *n* **:** agua *f* de lluvia

rainy ['reɪni] *adj* **rainier; -est :** lluvioso

raise[1] ['reɪz] *vt* **raised; raising 1** LIFT **:** levantar, subir, alzar <to raise one's spirits : levantarle el ánimo a alguien> **2** ERECT **:** levantar, erigir **3** COLLECT **:** recaudar <to raise money : recaudar dinero> **4** REAR **:** criar <to raise one's children : criar uno a sus niños> **5** GROW **:** cultivar **6** INCREASE **:** aumentar, subir **7** PROMOTE **:** ascender **8** PROVOKE **:** provocar <it raised

a laugh : provocó una risa> **9** BRING UP : sacar (temas, objeciones, etc.)

raise[2] *n* : aumento *m*

raisin ['reɪzən] *n* : pasa *f*

raja *or* **rajah** ['rɑdʒə, -ˌdʒɑ, -ˌʒɑ] *n* : rajá *m*

rake[1] ['reɪk] *v* **raked; raking** *vt* **1** : rastrillar <to rake leaves : rastrillar las hojas> **2** SWEEP : barrer <raked with gunfire : barrido con metralla> — *vi* **to rake through** : revolver, hurgar en

rake[2] *n* **1** : rastrillo *m* **2** LIBERTINE : libertino *m*, -na *f;* calavera *m*

rakish ['reɪkɪʃ] *adj* **1** JAUNTY : desenvuelto, desenfadado **2** DISSOLUTE : libertino, disoluto

rally[1] ['ræli] *v* **-lied; -lying** *vi* **1** MEET, UNITE : reunirse, congregarse **2** RECOVER : recuperarse — *vt* **1** ASSEMBLE : reunir (tropas, etc.) **2** RECOVER : recobrar (la fuerza, el ánimo, etc.)

rally[2] *n, pl* **-lies** : reunión *f,* mitin *m,* manifestación *f*

ram[1] ['ræm] *v* **rammed; ramming** *vt* **1** DRIVE : hincar, clavar <he rammed it into the ground : lo hincó en la tierra> **2** SMASH : estrellar, embestir — *vi* COLLIDE : chocar (contra), estrellarse

ram[2] *n* **1** : carnero *m* (animal) **2 battering ram** : ariete *m*

RAM ['ræm] *n* : RAM *f*

ramble[1] ['ræmbəl] *vi* **-bled; -bling 1** WANDER : pasear, deambular **2 to ramble on** : divagar, perder el hilo **3** SPREAD : trepar (dícese de una planta)

ramble[2] *n* : paseo *m,* excursión *f*

rambler ['ræmblər] *n* **1** WALKER : excursionista *mf* **2** ROSE : rosa *f* trepadora

rambunctious [ræm'bʌŋkʃəs] *adj* UNRULY : alborotado

ramification [ˌræməfə'keɪʃən] *n* : ramificación *f*

ramify ['ræməˌfaɪ] *vi* **-fied; -fying** : ramificarse

ramp ['ræmp] *n* : rampa *f*

rampage[1] ['ræmˌpeɪdʒ, ræm'peɪdʒ] *vi* **-paged; -paging** : andar arrasando todo, correr destrozando

rampage[2] ['ræmˌpeɪdʒ] *n* : alboroto *m,* frenesí *m* (de violencia)

rampant ['ræmpənt] *adj* : desenfrenado

rampart ['ræmˌpɑrt] *n* : terraplén *m,* muralla *f*

ramrod ['ræmˌrɑd] *n* : baqueta *f*

ramshackle ['ræmˌʃækəl] *adj* : destartalado

ran → **run**

ranch ['ræntʃ] *n* **1** : hacienda *f,* rancho *m,* finca *f* ganadera **2** FARM : granja *f* <fruit ranch : granja de frutas>

rancher ['ræntʃər] *n* : estanciero *m,* -ra *f;* ranchero *m,* -ra *f*

rancid ['ræntsɪd] *adj* : rancio

rancor ['ræŋkər] *n* : rencor *m*

random ['rændəm] *adj* **1** : fortuito, aleatorio **2 at ~** : al azar — **randomly** *adv*

rang → **ring**

range[1] ['reɪndʒ] *v* **ranged; ranging** *vt* ARRANGE : alinear, ordenar, arreglar — *vi* **1** ROAM : deambular <to range through the town : deambular por el pueblo> **2** EXTEND : extenderse <the results range widely : los resultados se extienden mucho> **3** VARY : variar <discounts range from 20% to 40% : los descuentos varían entre 20% y 40%>

range[2] *n* **1** ROW : fila *f,* hilera *f* <a mountain range : una cordillera> **2** GRASSLAND : pradera *f,* pampa *f* **3** STOVE : cocina *f* **4** VARIETY : variedad *f,* gama *f* **5** SPHERE : ámbito *m,* esfera *f,* campo *m* **6** REACH : registro *m* (de la voz), alcance *m* (de un arma de fuego) **7 shooting range** : campo *m* de tiro

ranger ['reɪndʒər] *n or* **forest ranger** : guardabosque *mf*

rangy ['reɪndʒi] *adj* **rangier; -est** : alto y delgado

rank[1] ['ræŋk] *vt* **1** RANGE : alinear, ordenar, poner en fila **2** CLASSIFY : clasificar — *vi* **1 to rank above** : ser superior a **2 to rank among** : encontrarse entre, figurar entre

rank[2] *adj* **1** LUXURIANT : lozano, exuberante (dícese de una planta) **2** SMELLY : fétido, maloliente **3** OUTRIGHT : completo, absoluto <a rank injustice : una injusticia manifiesta>

rank[3] *n* **1** LINE, ROW : fila *f* <to close ranks : cerrar filas> **2** GRADE, POSITION : grado *m,* rango *m* (militar) <to pull rank : abusar de su autoridad> **3** CLASS : categoría *f,* clase *f* **4 ranks** *npl* : soldados *mpl* rasos

rank and file *n* **1** RANKS : soldados *mpl* rasos **2** : bases *fpl* (de un partido, etc.)

rankle ['ræŋkəl] *v* **-kled; -kling** *vi* : doler — *vt* : irritar, herir

ransack ['rænˌsæk] *vt* : revolver, desvalijar, registrar de arriba abajo

ransom[1] ['ræntsəm] *vt* : rescatar, pagar un rescate por

ransom[2] *n* : rescate *m*

rant ['rænt] *vi or* **to rant and rave** : despotricar, desvariar

rap[1] ['ræp] *v* **rapped; rapping** *vt* **1** KNOCK : golpetear, dar un golpe en **2** CRITICIZE : criticar — *vi* **1** CHAT : charlar, cotorrear *fam* **2** KNOCK : dar un golpe

rap[2] *n* **1** BLOW, KNOCK : golpe *m,* golpecito *m* **2** CHAT : charla *f* **3** *or* **rap music** : rap *m* **4 to take the rap** : pagar el pato *fam*

rapacious [rə'peɪʃəs] *adj* **1** GREEDY : avaricioso, codicioso **2** PREDATORY : rapaz, de rapiña **3** RAVENOUS : voraz

rape[1] ['reɪp] *vt* **raped; raping** : violar

rape[2] *n* **1** : colza *f* (planta) **2** : violación *f* (de una persona)

rapid [ˈræpɪd] *adj* : rápido — **rapidly** *adv*

rapidity [rəˈpɪdət̬i] *n* : rapidez *f*

rapids [ˈræpɪdz] *npl* : rápidos *mpl*

rapier [ˈreɪpiər] *n* : estoque *m*

rapist [ˈreɪpɪst] *n* : violador *m*, -dora *f*

rapport [ræˈpor] *n* : relación *f* armoniosa, entendimiento *m*

rapt [ˈræpt] *adj* : absorto, embelesado

rapture [ˈræptʃər] *n* : éxtasis *m*

rapturous [ˈræptʃərəs] *adj* : extasiado, embelesado

rare [ˈrær] *adj* **rarer; rarest 1** RAREFIED : enrarecido **2** FINE : excelente, excepcional <a rare talent : un talento excepcional> **3** UNCOMMON : raro, poco común **4** : poco cocido (dícese de la carne)

rarefy [ˈrærə͵faɪ] *vt* **-fied; -fying** : rarificar, enrarecer

rarely [ˈrærli] *adv* SELDOM : pocas veces, rara vez

raring [ˈrærən, -ɪŋ] *adj* : lleno de entusiasmo, con muchas ganas

rarity [ˈrærət̬i] *n, pl* **-ties** : rareza *f*

rascal [ˈræskəl] *n* : pillo *m*, -lla *f*; pícaro *m*, -ra *f*

rash[1] [ˈræʃ] *adj* : imprudente, precipitado — **rashly** *adv*

rash[2] *n* : sarpullido *m*, erupción *f*

rashness [ˈræʃnəs] *n* : precipitación *f*, impetuosidad *f*

rasp[1] [ˈræsp] *vt* **1** SCRAPE : raspar, escofinar **2 to rasp out** : decir en voz áspera

rasp[2] *n* : escofina *f*

raspberry [ˈræz͵bɛri] *n, pl* **-ries** : frambuesa *f*

rat [ˈræt] *n* : rata *f*

ratchet [ˈrætʃət] *n* : trinquete *m*

rate[1] [ˈreɪt] *vt* **rated; rating 1** CONSIDER, REGARD : considerar, estimar **2** DESERVE : merecer

rate[2] *n* **1** PACE, SPEED : velocidad *f*, ritmo *m* <at this rate : a este paso> **2** : índice *m*, tasa *f* <birth rate : índice de natalidad> <interest rate : tasa de interés> **3** CHARGE, PRICE : precio *m*, tarifa *f*

rather [ˈræðər, ˈrʌ-, ˈrɑ-] *adv* **1** (*indicating preference*) <she would rather stay in the house : preferiría quedarse en casa> <I'd rather not : mejor que no> **2** (*indicating preciseness*) <my father, or rather my stepfather : mi padre, o mejor dicho mi padrastro> **3** INSTEAD : sino que, más que, al contrario <I'm not pleased; rather I'm disappointed : no estoy satisfecho, sino desilusionado> **4** SOMEWHAT : algo, un tanto <rather strange : un poco extraño> **5** QUITE : bastante <rather difficult : bastante difícil>

ratification [͵ræt̬əfəˈkeɪʃən] *n* : ratificación *f*

ratify [ˈræt̬ə͵faɪ] *vt* **-fied; -fying** : ratificar

rating [ˈreɪt̬ɪŋ] *n* **1** STANDING : clasificación *f*, posición *f* **2 ratings** *npl* : índice *m* de audiencia

ratio [ˈreɪʃio] *n, pl* **-tios** : proporción *f*, relación *f*

ration[1] [ˈræʃən, ˈreɪʃən] *vt* : racionar

ration[2] *n* **1** : ración *f* **2 rations** *npl* PROVISIONS : víveres *mpl*

rational [ˈræʃənəl] *adj* : racional, razonable, lógico — **rationally** *adv*

rationale [͵ræʃəˈnæl] *n* **1** EXPLANATION : explicación *f* **2** BASIS : base *f*, razones *fpl*

rationalization [͵ræʃənələˈzeɪʃən] *n* : racionalización *f*

rationalize [ˈræʃənə͵laɪz] *vt* **-ized; -izing** : racionalizar

rattle[1] [ˈræt̬əl] *v* **-tled; -tling** *vi* **1** CLATTER : traquetear, hacer ruido **2 to rattle on** CHATTER : parlotear *fam* — *vt* **1** : hacer sonar, agitar <the wind rattled the door : el viento sacudió la puerta> **2** DISCONCERT, WORRY : desconcertar, poner nervioso **3 to rattle off** : despachar, recitar, decir de corrido

rattle[2] *n* **1** CLATTER : traqueteo *m*, ruido *m* **2** *or* **baby's rattle** : sonajero *m* **3** : cascabel *m* (de una culebra)

rattler [ˈræt̬ələr] → **rattlesnake**

rattlesnake [ˈræt̬əl͵sneɪk] *n* : serpiente *f* de cascabel

ratty [ˈræt̬i] *adj* **rattier; -est** : raído, andrajoso

raucous [ˈrɔkəs] *adj* **1** HOARSE : ronco **2** BOISTEROUS : escandaloso, bullicioso — **raucously** *adv*

ravage[1] [ˈrævɪdʒ] *vt* **-aged; -aging** : devastar, arrasar, hacer estragos

ravage[2] *n* : destrozo *m*, destrucción *f* <the ravages of war : los estragos de la guerra>

rave [ˈreɪv] *vi* **raved; raving 1** : delirar, desvariar <to rave like a maniac : desvariar como un loco> **2 to rave about** : hablar con entusiasmo sobre, entusiasmarse por

ravel [ˈrævəl] *v* **-eled** *or* **-elled; -eling** *or* **-elling** *vt* UNRAVEL : desenredar, desenmarañar — *vi* FRAY : deshilacharse

raven [ˈreɪvən] *n* : cuervo *m*

ravenous [ˈrævənəs] *adj* : hambriento, voraz — **ravenously** *adv*

ravine [rəˈviːn] *n* : barranco *m*, quebrada *f*

ravish [ˈrævɪʃ] *vt* **1** PLUNDER : saquear **2** ENCHANT : embelesar, cautivar, encantar

raw [ˈrɔ] *adj* **rawer; rawest 1** UNCOOKED : crudo **2** UNTREATED : sin tratar, sin refinar, puro <raw data : datos en bruto> <raw materials : materias primas> **3** INEXPERIENCED : novato, inexperto **4** OPEN : abierto, en carne viva <a raw sore : una llaga abierta> **5** : frío y húmedo <a raw day : un día crudo> **6** UNFAIR : injusto <a raw deal : un trato injusto, una injusticia>

rawhide [ˈrɔˌhaɪd] *n* : cuero *m* sin curtir

ray [ˈreɪ] *n* **1** : rayo *m* (de la luz, etc.) <a ray of hope : un resquicio de esperanza> **2** : raya *f* (pez)

rayon [ˈreɪˌɑn] *n* : rayón *m*

raze [ˈreɪz] *vt* **razed; razing** : arrasar, demoler

razor [ˈreɪzər] *n* **1 straight razor** : navaja *f* (de afeitar) **2 safety razor** : maquinilla *f* de afeitar, rastrillo *m Mex*

reach[1] [ˈriːtʃ] *vt* **1** EXTEND : extender, alargar <to reach out one's hand : extender la mano> **2** : alcanzar <I couldn't reach the apple : no pude alcanzar la manzana> **3** : llegar a, llegar hasta <the shadow reached the wall : la sombra llegó hasta la pared> **4** CONTACT : contactar, ponerse en contacto con — *vi* **1** *or* **to reach out** : extender la mano **2** STRETCH : extenderse **3 to reach for** : tratar de agarrar

reach[2] *n* : alcance *m*, extensión *f*

react [riˈækt] *vi* : reaccionar

reaction [riˈækʃən] *n* : reacción *f*

reactionary[1] [riˈækʃəˌnɛri] *adj* : reaccionario

reactionary[2] *n, pl* **-ries** : reaccionario *m*, -ria *f*

reactor [riˈæktər] *n* : reactor *m* <nuclear reactor : reactor nuclear>

read[1] [ˈriːd] *v* **read** [ˈrɛd]; **reading** *vt* **1** : leer <to read a story : leer un cuento> **2** INTERPRET : interpretar <it can be read two ways : se puede interpretar de dos maneras> **3** : decir, poner <the sign read "No smoking" : el letrero decía "No Fumar"> **4** : marcar <the thermometer reads 70° : el termómetro marca 70°> — *vi* **1** : leer <he can read : sabe leer> **2** SAY : decir <the list reads as follows : la lista dice lo siguiente>

read[2] *n* **to be a good read** : ser una lectura amena

readable [ˈriːdəbəl] *adj* : legible — **readably** [-bli] *adv*

reader [ˈriːdər] *n* : lector *m*, -tora *f*

readily [ˈrɛdəli] *adv* **1** WILLINGLY : de buena gana, con gusto **2** EASILY : fácilmente, con facilidad

readiness [ˈrɛdinəs] *n* **1** WILLINGNESS : buena disposición *f* **2 to be in readiness** : estar preparado

reading [ˈriːdɪŋ] *n* : lectura *f*

readjust [ˌriːəˈdʒʌst] *vt* : reajustar — *vi* : volverse a adaptar

readjustment [ˌriːəˈdʒʌstmənt] *n* : reajuste *m*

ready[1] [ˈrɛdi] *vt* **readied; readying** : preparar

ready[2] *adj* **readier; -est 1** PREPARED : listo, preparado **2** WILLING : dispuesto **3** : a punto de <ready to cry : a punto de llorar> **4** AVAILABLE : disponible <ready cash : efectivo> **5** QUICK : vivo, agudo <a ready wit : un ingenio agudo>

ready–made [ˈrɛdiˈmeɪd] *adj* : preparado, confeccionado

reaffirm [ˌriːəˈfərm] *vt* : reafirmar

real[1] [ˈriːl] *adv* VERY : muy <we had a real good time : lo pasamos muy bien>

real[2] *adj* **1** : inmobilario <real property : bien inmueble, bien raíz> **2** GENUINE : auténtico, genuino **3** ACTUAL, TRUE : real, verdadero <a real friend : un verdadero amigo> **4 for real** SERIOUSLY : de veras, de verdad

real estate *n* : propiedad *f* inmobiliaria, bienes *mpl* raíces

realign [ˌriːəˈlaɪn] *vt* : realinear

realignment [ˌriːəˈlaɪnmənt] *n* : realineamiento *m*

realism [ˈriːəˌlɪzəm] *n* : realismo *m*

realist [ˈriːəlɪst] *n* : realista *mf*

realistic [ˌriːəˈlɪstɪk] *adj* : realista

realistically [ˌriːəˈlɪstɪkli] *adv* : de manera realista

reality [riˈæləti] *n, pl* **-ties** : realidad *f*

realization [ˌriːələˈzeɪʃən] *n* : realización *f*

realize [ˈriːəˌlaɪz] *vt* **-ized; -izing 1** ACCOMPLISH : realizar, llevar a cabo **2** GAIN : obtener, realizar, sacar <to realize a profit : realizar beneficios> **3** UNDERSTAND : darse cuenta de, saber

really [ˈrɪli, ˈriː-] *adv* **1** ACTUALLY : de verdad, en realidad **2** TRULY : verdaderamente, realmente **3** FRANKLY : francamente, en serio

realm [ˈrɛlm] *n* **1** KINGDOM : reino *m* **2** SPHERE : esfera *f*, campo *m*

ream[1] [ˈriːm] *vt* : escariar

ream[2] *n* **1** : resma *f* (de papel) **2 reams** *npl* LOADS : montones *mpl*

reap [ˈriːp] *v* : cosechar

reaper [ˈriːpər] *n* **1** : cosechador *m*, -dora *f* (persona) **2** : cosechadora *f* (máquina)

reappear [ˌriːəˈpɪr] *vi* : reaparecer

reappearance [ˌriːəˈpɪrənts] *n* : reaparición *f*

rear[1] [ˈrɪr] *vt* **1** LIFT, RAISE : levantar **2** BREED, BRING UP : criar — *vi or* **to rear up** : encabritarse

rear[2] *adj* : trasero, posterior, de atrás

rear[3] *n* **1** BACK : parte *f* de atrás <to bring up the rear : cerrar la marcha> **2** *or* **rear end** : trasero *m*

rear admiral *n* : contraalmirante *mf*

rearrange [ˌriːəˈreɪndʒ] *vt* **-ranged; -ranging** : colocar de otra manera, volver a arreglar, reorganizar

reason[1] [ˈriːzən] *vt* THINK : pensar — *vi* : razonar <I can't reason with her : no puedo razonar con ella>

reason[2] *n* **1** CAUSE, GROUND : razón *f*, motivo *m* <the reason for his trip : el motivo de su viaje> <for this reason : por esta razón, por lo cual> <the reason why : la razón por la cual, el porqué> **2** SENSE : razón *f* <to lose

one's reason : perder los sesos> <to listen to reason : avenirse a razones>

reasonable [ˈriːzənəbəl] *adj* **1** SENSIBLE : razonable **2** INEXPENSIVE : barato, económico

reasonably [ˈriːzənəbli] *adv* **1** SENSIBLY : razonablemente **2** FAIRLY : bastante

reasoning [ˈriːzənɪŋ] *n* : razonamiento *m,* raciocinio *m,* argumentos *mpl*

reassess [ˌriːəˈsɛs] *vt* : revaluar, reconsiderar

reassurance [ˌriːəˈʃʊrənts] *n* : consuelo *m,* palabras *fpl* alentadoras

reassure [ˌriːəˈʃʊr] *vt* **-sured; -suring** : tranquilizar

reawaken [ˌriːəˈweɪkən] *vt* : volver a despertar, reavivar

rebate [ˈriːˌbeɪt] *n* : reembolso *m,* devolución *f*

rebel[1] [rɪˈbɛl] *vi* **-belled; -belling** : rebelarse, sublevarse

rebel[2] [ˈrɛbəl] *adj* : rebelde

rebel[3] [ˈrɛbəl] *n* : rebelde *mf*

rebellion [rɪˈbɛljən] *n* : rebelión *f*

rebellious [rɪˈbɛljəs] *adj* : rebelde

rebelliousness [rɪˈbɛljəsnəs] *n* : rebeldía *f*

rebirth [ˌriːˈbərθ] *n* : renacimiento *m*

rebound[1] [ˈriːˌbaʊnd, ˌriːˈbaʊnd] *vi* : rebotar

rebound[2] [ˈriːˌbaʊnd] *n* : rebote *m*

rebuff[1] [riˈbʌf] *vt* : desairar, rechazar

rebuff[2] *n* : desaire *m,* rechazo *m*

rebuild [ˌriːˈbɪld] *vt* **-built** [-ˈbɪlt]; **-building** : reconstruir

rebuke[1] [riˈbjuːk] *vt* **-buked; -buking** : reprender, regañar

rebuke[2] *n* : reprimenda *f,* reproche *m*

rebut [riˈbʌt] *vt* **-butted; -butting** : rebatir, refutar

rebuttal [riˈbʌtəl] *n* : refutación *f*

recalcitrant [riˈkælsətrənt] *adj* : recalcitrante

recall[1] [riˈkɔl] *vt* **1** : llamar, retirar <recalled to active duty : llamado al servicio activo> **2** REMEMBER : recordar, acordarse de **3** REVOKE : revocar

recall[2] [riˈkɔl, ˈriːˌkɔl] *n* **1** : retirada *f* (de personas o mercancías) **2** MEMORY : memoria *f* <to have total recall : poder recordar todo>

recant [riˈkænt] *vt* : retractarse de — *vi* : retractarse, renegar

recapitulate [ˌriːkəˈpɪtʃəˌleɪt] *v* **-lated; -lating** : resumir, recapitular

recapture [ˌriːˈkæptʃər] *vt* **-tured; -turing 1** REGAIN : volver a tomar, reconquistar **2** RELIVE : revivir (la juventud, etc.)

recede [riˈsiːd] *vi* **-ceded; -ceding 1** WITHDRAW : retirarse, retroceder **2** FADE : desvanecerse, alejarse **3** SLANT : inclinarse **4 to have a receding hairline** : tener entradas

receipt [riˈsiːt] *n* **1** : recibo *m* **2 receipts** *npl* : ingresos *mpl,* entradas *fpl*

receivable [riˈsiːvəbəl] *adj* **accounts receivable** : cuentas por cobrar

receive [riˈsiːv] *vt* **-ceived; -ceiving 1** GET : recibir <to receive a letter : recibir una carta> <to receive a blow : recibir un golpe> **2** WELCOME : acoger, recibir <to receive guests : tener invitados> **3** : recibir, captar (señales de radio)

receiver [riˈsiːvər] *n* **1** : receptor *m,* -tora *f* (en futbol americano) **2** : receptor *m* (de radio o televisión) **3 telephone receiver** : auricular *m*

recent [ˈriːsənt] *adj* : reciente — **recently** *adv*

receptacle [riˈsɛptɪkəl] *n* : receptáculo *m,* recipiente *m*

reception [riˈsɛpʃən] *n* : recepción *f*

receptionist [riˈsɛpʃənɪst] *n* : recepcionista *mf*

receptive [riˈsɛptɪv] *adj* : receptivo

receptivity [ˌriːˌsɛpˈtɪvəṭi] *n* : receptividad *f*

recess[1] [ˈriːˌsɛs, rɪˈsɛs] *vt* **1** : poner en un hueco <recessed lighting : iluminación empotrada> **2** ADJOURN : suspender, levantar

recess[2] *n* **1** ALCOVE : hueco *m,* nicho *m* **2** BREAK : receso *m,* descanso *m,* recreo *m* (en el colegio)

recession [riˈsɛʃən] *n* : recesión *f,* depresión *f* económica

recessive [riˈsɛsɪv] *adj* : recesivo

recharge [ˌriːˈtʃɑrdʒ] *vt* **-charged; -charging** : recargar

rechargeable [ˌriːˈtʃɑrdʒəbəl] *adj* : recargable

recipe [ˈrɛsəˌpiː] *n* : receta *f*

recipient [riˈsɪpiənt] *n* : recipiente *mf*

reciprocal [riˈsɪprəkəl] *adj* : recíproco

reciprocate [riˈsɪprəˌkeɪt] *vi* **-cated; -cating** : reciprocar

reciprocity [ˌrɛsəˈprɑsəṭi] *n, pl* **-ties** : reciprocidad *f*

recital [riˈsaɪṭəl] *n* **1** PERFORMANCE : recital *m* **2** ENUMERATION : relato *m,* enumeración *f*

recitation [ˌrɛsəˈteɪʃən] *n* : recitación *f*

recite [riˈsaɪt] *vt* **-cited; -citing 1** : recitar (un poema, etc.) **2** RECOUNT : narrar, relatar, enumerar

reckless [ˈrɛkləs] *adj* : imprudente, temerario — **recklessly** *adv*

recklessness [ˈrɛkləsnəs] *n* : imprudencia *f,* temeridad *f*

reckon [ˈrɛkən] *vt* **1** CALCULATE : calcular, contar **2** CONSIDER : considerar

reckoning [ˈrɛkənɪŋ] *n* **1** CALCULATION : cálculo *m* **2** SETTLEMENT : ajuste *m* de cuentas <day of reckoning : día del juicio final>

reclaim [riˈkleɪm] *vt* **1** : ganar, sanear <to reclaim marshy land : sanear las tierras pantanosas> **2** RECOVER : recobrar, reciclar <to reclaim old tires : reciclar llantas desechadas> **3** REGAIN : reclamar, recuperar <to reclaim one's rights : reclamar uno sus derechos>

recline [ri'klaɪn] *vi* **-clined; -clining 1** LEAN : reclinarse **2** REPOSE : recostarse

recluse ['rɛ,klu:s, ri'klu:s] *n* : solitario *m*, -ria *f*

recognition [,rɛkɪg'nɪʃən] *n* : reconocimiento *m*

recognizable ['rɛkəg,naɪzəbəl] *adj* : reconocible

recognize ['rɛkɪg,naɪz] *vt* **-nized; -nizing** : reconocer

recoil¹ [ri'kɔɪl] *vi* : retroceder, dar un culatazo

recoil² ['ri:,kɔɪl, ri'-] *n* : retroceso *m*, culatazo *m*

recollect [,rɛkə'lɛkt] *v* : recordar

recollection [,rɛkə'lɛkʃən] *n* : recuerdo *m*

recommend [,rɛkə'mɛnd] *vt* **1** : recomendar <she recommended the medicine : recomendó la medicina> **2** ADVISE, COUNSEL : aconsejar, recomendar

recommendation [,rɛkəmən'deɪʃən] *n* : recomendación *f*

recompense¹ ['rɛkəm,pɛnts] *vt* **-pensed; -pensing** : indemnizar, recompensar

recompense² *n* : indemnización *f*, compensación *f*

reconcile ['rɛkən,saɪl] *v* **-ciled; -ciling** *vt* **1** : reconciliar (personas), conciliar (ideas, etc.) **2 to reconcile oneself to** : resignarse a — *vi* MAKE UP : reconciliarse, hacer las paces

reconciliation [,rɛkən,sɪli'eɪʃən] *n* : reconciliación *f* (con personas), conciliación *f* (con ideas, etc.)

recondite ['rɛkən,daɪt, ri'kɑn-] *adj* : recóndito, abstruso

recondition [,ri:kən'dɪʃən] *vt* : reacondicionar

reconnaissance [ri'kɑnəzənts, -sənts] *n* : reconocimiento *m*

reconnoiter *or* **reconnoitre** [,ri:kə'nɔɪtər, ,rɛkə-] *v* **-tered** *or* **-tred; -tering** *or* **-tring** *vt* : reconocer — *vi* : hacer un reconocimiento

reconsider [,ri:kən'sɪdər] *vt* : reconsiderar, repensar

reconsideration [,ri:kən,sɪdə'reɪʃən] *n* : reconsideración *f*

reconstruct [,ri:kən'strʌkt] *vt* : reconstruir

record¹ [ri'kɔrd] *vt* **1** WRITE DOWN : anotar, apuntar **2** REGISTER : registrar, hacer constar **3** INDICATE : marcar (una temperatura, etc.) **4** TAPE : grabar

record² ['rɛkərd] *n* **1** DOCUMENT : registro *m*, documento *m* oficial **2** HISTORY : historial *m* <a good academic record : un buen historial académico> <criminal record : antecedentes penales> **3** : récord *m* <the world record : el récord mundial> **4** : disco *m* (de música, etc.) <to make a record : grabar un disco>

recorder [ri'kɔrdər] *n* **1** : flauta *f* dulce (instrumento de viento) **2 tape recorder** : grabadora *f*

recount¹ [ri'kaʊnt] *vt* **1** NARRATE : narrar, relatar **2** : volver a contar (votos, etc.)

recount² ['ri:,kaʊnt, ,ri'-] *n* : recuento *m*

recoup [ri'ku:p] *vt* : recuperar, recobrar

recourse ['ri:,kors, ri'-] *n* : recurso *m* <to have recourse to : recurrir a>

recover [ri'kʌvər] *vt* REGAIN : recobrar — *vi* RECUPERATE : recuperarse

recovery [ri'kʌvəri] *n, pl* **-eries** : recuperación *f*

re–create [,ri:kri'eɪt] *vt* **-ated; -ating** : recrear

recreation [,rɛkri'eɪʃən] *n* : recreo *m*, esparcimiento *m*, diversión *f*

recreational [,rɛkri'eɪʃənəl] *adj* : recreativo, de recreo

recrimination [ri,krɪmə'neɪʃən] *n* : recriminación *f*

recruit¹ [ri'kru:t] *vt* : reclutar

recruit² *n* : recluta *mf*

recruitment [ri'kru:tmənt] *n* : reclutamiento *m*, alistamiento *m*

rectal ['rɛktəl] *adj* : rectal

rectangle ['rɛk,tæŋgəl] *n* : rectángulo *m*

rectangular [rɛk'tæŋgjələr] *adj* : rectangular

rectify ['rɛktə,faɪ] *vt* **-fied; -fying** : rectificar

rectitude ['rɛktə,tu:d, -,tju:d] *n* : rectitud *f*

rector ['rɛktər] *n* : rector *m*, -tora *f*

rectory ['rɛktəri] *n, pl* **-ries** : rectoría *f*

rectum ['rɛktəm] *n, pl* **-tums** *or* **-ta** [-tə] : recto *m*

recuperate [ri'ku:pə,reɪt, -'kju:-] *v* **-ated; -ating** *vt* : recuperar — *vi* : recuperarse, restablecerse

recuperation [ri,ku:pə'reɪʃən, -,kju:-] *n* : recuperación *f*

recur [ri'kər] *vi* **-curred; -curring** : volver a ocurrir, volver a producirse, repetirse

recurrence [ri'kərənts] *n* : repetición *f*, reaparición *f*

recurrent [ri'kərənt] *adj* : recurrente, que se repite

recycle [ri'saɪkəl] *vt* **-cled; -cling** : reciclar

red¹ ['rɛd] *adj* **1** : rojo, colorado <to be red in the face : ponerse colorado> <to have red hair : ser pelirrojo> **2** COMMUNIST : rojo, comunista

red² *n* **1** : rojo *m*, colorado *m* **2 Red** COMMUNIST : comunista *mf*

red blood cell *n* : glóbulo *m* rojo

red–blooded ['rɛd'blʌdəd] *adj* : vigoroso

redcap ['rɛd,kæp] → **porter**

redden ['rɛdən] *vt* : enrojecer — *vi* BLUSH : enrojecerse, ruborizarse

reddish ['rɛdɪʃ] *adj* : rojizo

redecorate [,ri:'dɛkə,reɪt] *vt* **-rated; -rating** : renovar, pintar de nuevo

redeem [ri'di:m] *vt* **1** RESCUE, SAVE : rescatar, salvar **2** : desempeñar <she redeemed it from the pawnshop : lo desempeñó de la casa de empeños> **3** : redimir (en religión) **4** : canjear, vender <to redeem coupons : canjear cupones>

redeemer [ri'di:mər] *n* : redentor *m*, -tora *f*

redemption [ri'dɛmpʃən] *n* : redención *f*

redesign [ˌri:di'zaɪn] *vt* : rediseñar

red–handed ['rɛd'hændəd] *adj* : con las manos en la masa

redhead ['rɛdˌhɛd] *n* : pelirrojo *m*, -ja *f*

red–hot ['rɛd'hɑt] *adj* **1** : candente **2** ARDENT : ardiente, fervoroso

rediscover [ˌri:di'skʌvər] *vt* : redescubrir

redistribute [ˌri:di'strɪˌbju:t] *vt* **-uted; -uting** : redistribuir

red–letter ['rɛd'lɛt̬ər] *adj* **red–letter day** : día *m* memorable

redness ['rɛdnəs] *n* : rojez *f*

redo [ˌri:'du:] *vt* **-did** [-dɪd]; **-done** [-'dʌn]; **-doing 1** : hacer de nuevo **2** → **redecorate**

redolence ['rɛdələnts] *n* : fragancia *f*

redolent ['rɛdələnt] *adj* **1** FRAGRANT : fragante, oloroso **2** SUGGESTIVE : evocador

redouble [ri'dʌbəl] *vt* **-bled; -bling** : redoblar, intensificar (esfuerzos, etc.)

redoubtable [rɛ'daʊt̬əbəl] *adj* : temible

redress [ri'drɛs] *vt* : reparar, remediar, enmendar

red snapper *n* : pargo *m*, huachinango *m Mex*

red tape *n* : papeleo *m*

reduce [ri'du:s, -'dju:s] *v* **-duced; -ducing** *vt* **1** LESSEN : reducir, disminuir, rebajar (precios) **2** DEMOTE : bajar de categoría, degradar **3 to be reduced to :** verse rebajado a, verse forzado a **4 to reduce someone to tears :** hacer llorar a alguien — *vi* SLIM : adelgazar

reduction [ri'dʌkʃən] *n* : reducción *f*, rebaja *f*

redundant [ri'dʌndənt] *adj* : superfluo, redundante

redwood ['rɛdˌwʊd] *n* : secoya *f*

reed ['ri:d] *n* **1** : caña *f*, carrizo *m*, junco *m* **2** : lengüeta *f* (para instrumentos de viento)

reef ['ri:f] *n* : arrecife *m*, escollo *m*

reek[1] ['ri:k] *vi* : apestar

reek[2] *n* : hedor *m*

reel ['ri:l] *vt* **1 to reel in :** enrollar, sacar (un pez) del agua **2 to reel off** : recitar de un tirón — *vi* **1** SPIN, WHIRL : girar, dar vueltas **2** STAGGER : tambalearse

reel[2] *n* **1** : carrete *m* (de pescar etc.), rollo *m* (de fotos) **2** : baile *m* escocés **3** STAGGER : tambaleo *m*

reelect [ˌri:ɪ'lɛkt] *vt* : reelegir

reenact [ˌri:ɪ'nækt] *vt* : representar de nuevo, reconstruir

reenter [ˌri:'ɛntər] *vt* : volver a entrar

reestablish [ˌri:ɪ'stæblɪʃ] *vt* : restablecer

reevaluate [ˌri:ɪ'væljʊˌeɪt] *vt* **-ated; -ating** : revaluar

reevaluation [ˌri:ɪˌvæljʊ'eɪʃən] *n* : revaluación *f*

reexamine [ˌri:ɪg'zæmən, -ɛg-] *vt* **-ined; -ining** : volver a examinar, reexaminar

refer [ri'fər] *v* **-ferred; -ferring** *vt* DIRECT, SEND : remitir, enviar <to refer a patient to a specialist : enviar a un paciente a un especialista> — *vi* **to refer to** MENTION : referirse a, aludir a

referee[1] [ˌrɛfə'ri:] *v* **-eed; -eeing** : arbitrar

referee[2] *n* : árbitro *m*, -tra *f*; réferi *mf*

reference ['rɛfrənts, 'rɛfə-] *n* **1** ALLUSION : referencia *f*, alusión *f* <to make reference to : hacer referencia a> **2** CONSULTATION : consulta *f* <for future reference : para futuras consultas> **3** *or* **reference book** : libro *m* de consulta **4** TESTIMONIAL : informe *m*, referencia *f*, recomendación *f*

referendum [ˌrɛfə'rɛndəm] *n, pl* **-da** [-də] *or* **-dums** : referéndum *m*

refill[1] [ˌri:'fɪl] *vt* : rellenar

refill[2] ['ri:ˌfɪl] *n* : recambio *m*

refinance [ˌri:'faɪˌnænts] *vt* **-nanced; -nancing** : refinanciar

refine [ri'faɪn] *vt* **-fined; -fining 1** : refinar (azúcar, petróleo, etc.) **2** PERFECT : perfeccionar, pulir

refined [ri'faɪnd] *adj* **1** : refinado (dícese del azúcar, etc.) **2** CULTURED : culto, educado, refinado

refinement [ri'faɪnmənt] *n* : refinamiento *m*, fineza *f*, finura *f*

refinery [ri'faɪnəri] *n, pl* **-eries** : refinería *f*

reflect [ri'flɛkt] *vt* **1** : reflejar <to reflect light : reflejar la luz> <happiness is reflected in her face : la felicidad se refleja en su cara> **2 to reflect that** : pensar que, considerar que — *vi* **1 to reflect on** : reflexionar sobre **2 to reflect badly on** : desacreditar, perjudicar

reflection [ri'flɛkʃən] *n* **1** : reflexión *f*, reflejo *m* (de la luz, de imágenes, etc.) **2** THOUGHT : reflexión *f*, meditación *f*

reflective [ri'flɛktɪv] *adj* **1** THOUGHTFUL : reflexivo, pensativo **2** : reflectante (en física)

reflector [ri'flɛktər] *n* : reflector *m*

reflex ['ri:ˌflɛks] *n* : reflejo *m*

reflexive [ri'flɛksɪv] *adj* : reflexivo <a reflexive verb : un verbo reflexivo>

reform[1] [ri'fɔrm] *vt* : reformar — *vi* : reformarse

reform[2] *n* : reforma *f*

reformation [ˌrɛfər'meɪʃən] *n* : reforma *f* <the Reformation : la Reforma>

reformatory [ri'fɔrmə,tori] *n, pl* **-ries** : reformatorio *m*

reformer [ri'fɔrmər] *n* : reformador *m*, -dora *f*

refract [ri'frækt] *vt* : refractar — *vi* : refractarse

refraction [ri'frækʃən] *n* : refracción *f*

refractory [ri'fræktəri] *adj* OBSTINATE : refractario, obstinado

refrain[1] [ri'freɪn] *vi* **to refrain from** : abstenerse de

refrain[2] *n* : estribillo *m* (en música)

refresh [ri'frɛʃ] *vt* : refrescar <to refresh one's memory : refrescarle la memoria a uno>

refreshment [ri'frɛʃmənt] *n* **1** : refresco *m* **2 refreshments** *npl* : refrigerio *m*

refrigerate [ri'frɪdʒə,reɪt] *vt* **-ated; -ating** : refrigerar

refrigeration [ri,frɪdʒə'reɪʃən] *n* : refrigeración *f*

refrigerator [ri'frɪdʒə,reɪt̬ər] *n* : refrigerador *mf*, nevera *f*

refuel [riː'fjuːəl] *v* **-eled** *or* **-elled; -eling** *or* **-elling** *vi* : repostar — *vt* : llenar de combustible

refuge ['rɛ,fjuːdʒ] *n* : refugio *m*

refugee [,rɛfjʊ'dʒiː] *n* : refugiado *m*, -da *f*

refund[1] [ri'fʌnd, 'riː,fʌnd] *vt* : reembolsar, devolver

refund[2] ['riː,fʌnd] *n* : reembolso *m*, devolución *f*

refundable [ri'fʌndəbəl] *adj* : reembolsable

refurbish [ri'fərbɪʃ] *vt* : renovar, restaurar

refusal [ri'fjuːzəl] *n* : negativa *f*, rechazo *m*, denegación *f* (de una petición)

refuse[1] [ri'fjuːz] *vt* **-fused; -fusing 1** REJECT : rechazar, rehusar **2** DENY : negar, rehusar, denegar <to refuse permission : negar el permiso> **3 to refuse to** : negarse a

refuse[2] ['rɛ,fjuːs, -,fjuːz] *n* : basura *f*, desechos *mpl*, desperdicios *m*

refutation [,rɛfjʊ'teɪʃən] *n* : refutación *f*

refute [ri'fjuːt] *vt* **-futed; -futing 1** DENY : desmentir, negar **2** DISPROVE : refutar, rebatir

regain [riː'geɪn] *vt* **1** RECOVER : recuperar, recobrar **2** REACH : alcanzar <to regain the shore : llegar a la tierra>

regal ['riːgəl] *adj* : real, regio

regale [ri'geɪl] *vt* **-galed; -galing 1** ENTERTAIN : agasajar, entretener **2** AMUSE, DELIGHT : deleitar, divertir

regalia [ri'geɪljə] *npl* : ropaje *m*, vestiduras *fpl*, adornos *mpl*

regard[1] [ri'gɑrd] *vt* **1** OBSERVE : observar, mirar **2** HEED : tener en cuenta, hacer caso de **3** CONSIDER : considerar **4** RESPECT : respetar <highly regarded : muy estimado> **5 as regards** : en cuanto a, en lo que se refiere a

regard[2] *n* **1** CONSIDERATION : consideración *f* **2** ESTEEM : respeto *m*, estima *f* **3** PARTICULAR : aspecto *m*, sentido *m* <in this regard : en este sentido> **4 regards** *npl* : saludos *mpl*, recuerdos *mpl* **5 with regard to** : con relación a, con respecto a

regarding [ri'gɑrdɪŋ] *prep* : con respecto a, en cuanto a

regardless [ri'gɑrdləs] *adv* : a pesar de todo

regardless of *prep* : a pesar de, sin tener en cuenta <regardless of our mistakes : a pesar de nuestros errores> <regardless of age : sin tener en cuenta la edad>

regenerate [ri'dʒɛnə,reɪt] *v* **-ated; -ating** *vt* : regenerar — *vi* : regenerarse

regeneration [ri,dʒɛnə'reɪʃən] *n* : regeneración *f*

regent ['riːdʒənt] *n* **1** RULER : regente *mf* **2** : miembro *m* de la junta directiva (de una universidad, etc.)

regime [reɪ'ʒiːm, rɪ-] *n* : régimen *m*

regimen ['rɛdʒəmən] *n* : régimen *m*

regiment[1] ['rɛdʒə,mɛnt] *vt* : reglamentar

regiment[2] ['rɛdʒəmənt] *n* : regimiento *m*

region ['riːdʒən] *n* **1** : región *f* **2 in the region of** : alrededor de

regional ['riːdʒənəl] *adj* : regional — **regionally** *adv*

register[1] ['rɛdʒəstər] *vt* **1** RECORD : registrar, inscribir **2** INDICATE : marcar (temperatura, medidas, etc.) **3** REVEAL : manifestar, acusar <to register surprise : acusar sorpresa> **4** : certificar (correo) — *vi* ENROLL : inscribirse, matricularse

register[2] *n* : registro *m*

registrar ['rɛdʒə,strɑr] *n* : registrador *m*, -dora *f* oficial

registration [,rɛdʒə'streɪʃən] *n* **1** REGISTERING : inscripción *f*, matriculación *f*, registro *m* **2** *or* **registration number** : matrícula *f*, número *m* de matrícula

registry ['rɛdʒəstri] *n, pl* **-tries** : registro *m*

regress [ri'grɛs] *vi* : retroceder

regression [ri'grɛʃən] *n* : retroceso *m*, regresión *f*

regressive [ri'grɛsɪv] *adj* : regresivo

regret[1] [ri'grɛt] *vt* **-gretted; -gretting** : arrepentirse de, lamentar <he regrets nothing : no se arrepiente de nada> <I regret to tell you : lamento decirle>

regret[2] *n* **1** REMORSE : arrepentimiento *m*, remordimientos *mpl* **2** SADNESS : pesar *m*, dolor *m* **3 regrets** *npl* : excusas *fpl* <to send one's regrets : excusarse>

regretful [ri'grɛtfəl] *adj* : arrepentido, pesaroso

regretfully [ri'grɛtfəli] *adv* : con pesar

regrettable [ri'grɛt̬əbəl] *adj* : lamentable — **regrettably** [-bli] *adv*

regular[1] [ˈrɛgjələr] *adj* **1** NORMAL : regular, normal, usual **2** STEADY : uniforme, regular <a regular pace : un paso regular> **3** CUSTOMARY, HABITUAL : habitual, de costumbre

regular[2] *n* : cliente *mf* habitual

regularity [ˌrɛgjəˈlærət̬i] *n, pl* **-ties** : regularidad *f*

regularly [ˈrɛgjələrli] *adv* : regularmente, con regularidad

regulate [ˈrɛgjəˌleɪt] *vt* **-lated; -lating** : regular

regulation [ˌrɛgjəˈleɪʃən] *n* **1** REGULATING : regulación *f* **2** RULE : regla *f,* reglamento *m,* norma *f* <safety regulations : reglas de seguridad>

regurgitate [riˈgərdʒəˌteɪt] *v* **-tated; -tating** : regurgitar, vomitar

rehabilitate [ˌriːhəˈbɪləˌteɪt, ˌriːə-] *vt* **-tated; -tating** : rehabilitar

rehabilitation [ˌriːhəˌbɪləˈteɪʃən, ˌriːə-] *n* : rehabilitación *f*

rehearsal [riˈhərsəl] *n* : ensayo *m*

rehearse [riˈhərs] *v* **-hearsed; -hearsing** : ensayar

reheat [ˌriːˈhiːt] *vt* : recalentar

reign[1] [ˈreɪn] *vi* **1** RULE : reinar **2** PREVAIL : reinar, predominar

reign[2] *n* : reinado *m*

reimburse [ˌriːəmˈbərs] *vt* **-bursed; -bursing** : reembolsar

reimbursement [ˌriːəmˈbərsmənt] *n* : reembolso *m*

rein[1] [ˈreɪn] *vt* : refrenar (un caballo)

rein[2] *n* **1** : rienda *f* <to give free rein to : dar rienda suelta a> **2** CHECK : control *m* <to keep a tight rein on : llevar un estricto control de>

reincarnation [ˌriːɪnˌkɑrˈneɪʃən] *n* : reencarnación *f*

reindeer [ˈreɪnˌdɪr] *n* : reno *m*

reinforce [ˌriːənˈfors] *vt* **-forced; -forcing** : reforzar

reinforcement [ˌriːənˈforsmənt] *n* : refuerzo *m*

reinstate [ˌriːənˈsteɪt] *vt* **-stated; -stating 1** : reintegrar, restituir (una persona) **2** RESTORE : restablecer (un servicio, etc.)

reinstatement [ˌriːənˈsteɪtmənt] *n* : reintegración *f,* restitución *f,* restablecimiento *m*

reiterate [riˈɪt̬əˌreɪt] *vt* **-ated; -ating** : reiterar, repetir

reiteration [riˌɪt̬əˈreɪʃən] *n* : reiteración *f,* repetición *f*

reject[1] [riˈdʒɛkt] *vt* : rechazar

reject[2] [ˈriːˌdʒɛkt] *n* : desecho *m* (cosa), persona *f* rechazada

rejection [riˈdʒɛkʃən] *n* : rechazo *m*

rejoice [riˈdʒɔɪs] *vi* **-joiced; -joicing** : alegrarse, regocijarse

rejoin *vt* [ˌriːˈdʒɔɪn] **1** : reincorporarse a, reintegrarse a <he rejoined the firm : se reincorporó a la firma> **2** [riˈ-] REPLY, RETORT : replicar

rejoinder [riˈdʒɔɪndər] *n* : réplica *f*

rejuvenate [riˈdʒuːvəˌneɪt] *vt* **-nated; -nating** : rejuvenecer

rejuvenation [riˌdʒuːvəˈneɪʃən] *n* : rejuvenecimiento *m*

rekindle [ˌriːˈkɪndəl] *vt* **-dled; -dling** : reavivar

relapse[1] [riˈlæps] *vi* **-lapsed; -lapsing** : recaer, volver a caer

relapse[2] [ˈriːˌlæps, riˈlæps] *n* : recaída *f*

relate [riˈleɪt] *v* **-lated; -lating** *vt* **1** TELL : relatar, contar **2** ASSOCIATE : relacionar, asociar <to relate crime to poverty : relacionar la delincuencia a la pobreza> — *vi* **1** CONNECT : conectar, estar relacionado (con) **2** INTERACT : relacionarse (con), llevarse bien (con) **3 to relate to** UNDERSTAND : identificarse con, simpatizar con

related [riˈleɪt̬əd] *adj* : emparentado <to be related to : ser pariente de>

relation [riˈleɪʃən] *n* **1** NARRATION : relato *m,* narración *f* **2** RELATIVE : pariente *mf,* familiar *mf* **3** RELATIONSHIP : relación *f* <in relation to : en relación con, con relación a> **4 relations** *npl* : relaciones *fpl* <public relations : relaciones públicas>

relationship [riˈleɪʃənˌʃɪp] *n* **1** CONNECTION : relación *f* **2** KINSHIP : parentesco *m*

relative[1] [ˈrɛlət̬ɪv] *adj* : relativo — **relatively** *adv*

relative[2] *n* : pariente *mf,* familiar *mf*

relativity [ˌrɛləˈtɪvət̬i] *n, pl* **-ties** : relatividad *f*

relax [riˈlæks] *vt* : relajar, aflojar — *vi* : relajarse

relaxation [ˌriːˌlækˈseɪʃən] *n* **1** RELAXING : relajación *f,* aflojamiento *m* **2** DIVERSION : esparcimiento *m,* distracción *f*

relay[1] [ˈriːˌleɪ, riˈleɪ] *vt* **-layed; -laying** : transmitir

relay[2] [ˈriːˌleɪ] *n* **1** : relevo *m* **2** *or* **relay race** : carrera de relevos

release[1] [riˈliːs] *vt* **-leased; -leasing 1** FREE : liberar, poner en libertad **2** LOOSEN : soltar, aflojar <to release the brake : soltar el freno> **3** RELINQUISH : renunciar a, ceder **4** ISSUE : publicar (un libro), estrenar (una película), sacar (un disco)

release[2] *n* **1** LIBERATION : liberación *f,* puesta *f* en libertad **2** RELINQUISHMENT : cesión *f* (de propiedad, etc.) **3** ISSUE : estreno *m* (de una película), puesta *f* en venta (de un disco), publicación *f* (de un libro) **4** ESCAPE : escape *m,* fuga *f* (de un gas)

relegate [ˈrɛləˌgeɪt] *vt* **-gated; -gating** : relegar

relent [riˈlɛnt] *vi* : ablandarse, ceder

relentless [riˈlɛntləs] *adj* : implacable, sin tregua

relentlessly [riˈlɛntləsli] *adv* : implacablemente

relevance [ˈrɛləvənts] *n* : pertinencia *f,* relación *f*

relevant [ˈrɛləvənt] *adj* : pertinente — **relevantly** *adv*

reliability [ri,laɪə'bɪləti] *n, pl* **-ties 1** : fiabilidad *f,* seguridad *f* (de una cosa) **2** : formalidad *f,* seriedad *f* (de una persona)

reliable [ri'laɪəbəl] *adj* : confiable, fiable, fidedigno, seguro

reliably [ri'laɪəbli] *adv* : sin fallar <to be reliably informed : saber (algo) de fuentes fidedignas>

reliance [ri'laɪənts] *n* **1** DEPENDENCE : dependencia *f* **2** CONFIDENCE : confianza *f*

reliant [ri'laɪənt] *adj* : confiable, dependente

relic ['rɛlɪk] *n* **1** : reliquia *f* **2** VESTIGE : vestigio *m*

relief [ri'li:f] *n* **1** : alivio *m,* desahogo *m* <relief from pain : alivio del dolor> **2** AID, WELFARE : ayuda *f* (benéfica), asistencia *f* social **3** : relieve *m* (en la escultura) <relief map : mapa en relieve> **4** REPLACEMENT : relevo *m*

relieve [ri'li:v] *vt* **-lieved; -lieving 1** ALLEVIATE : aliviar, mitigar <to feel relieved : sentirse aliviado> **2** FREE : liberar, eximir <to relieve someone of responsibility for : eximir a alguien de la responsabilidad de> **3** REPLACE : relevar (a un centinela, etc.) **4** BREAK : romper <to relieve the monotony : romper la monotonía>

religion [ri'lɪdʒən] *n* : religión *f*

religious [ri'lɪdʒəs] *adj* : religioso — **religiously** *adv*

relinquish [ri'lɪŋkwɪʃ, -'lɪn-] *vt* **1** GIVE UP : renunciar a, abandonar **2** RELEASE : soltar

relish¹ ['rɛlɪʃ] *vt* : saborear (comida), disfrutar con (una idea, una perspectiva, etc.)

relish² *n* **1** ENJOYMENT : gusto *m,* deleite *m* **2** : salsa *f* (condimento)

relive [,ri:'lɪv] *vt* **-lived; -living** : revivir

relocate [,ri:'lo:,keɪt, ,ri:lo'keɪt] *v* **-cated; -cating** *vt* : reubicar, trasladar — *vi* : trasladarse

relocation [,ri:lo'keɪʃən] *n* : reubicación *f,* traslado *m*

reluctance [ri'lʌktənts] *n* : renuencia *f,* reticencia *f,* desgana *f*

reluctant [ri'lʌktənt] *adj* : renuente, reacio, reticente

reluctantly [ri'lʌktəntli] *adv* : a regañadientes

rely [ri'laɪ] *vi* **-lied; -lying 1** DEPEND : depender (de), contar (con) **2** TRUST : confiar (en)

remain [ri'meɪn] *vi* **1** : quedar <very little remains : queda muy poco> <the remaining 10 minutes : los 10 minutos que quedan> **2** STAY : quedarse, permanecer **3** CONTINUE : continuar, seguir <to remain the same : continuar siendo igual> **4 to remain to** : quedar por <to remain to be done : quedar por hacer> <it remains to be seen : está por ver>

remainder [ri'meɪndər] *n* : resto *m,* remanente *m*

remains [ri'meɪnz] *npl* : restos *mpl* <mortal remains : restos mortales>

remark¹ [ri'mɑrk] *vt* **1** NOTICE : observar **2** SAY : comentar, observar — *vi* **to remark on** : hacer observaciones sobre

remark² *n* : comentario *m,* observación *f*

remarkable [ri'mɑrkəbəl] *adj* : extraordinario, notable — **remarkably** [-bli] *adv*

rematch ['ri:,mætʃ] *n* : revancha *f*

remedial [ri'mi:diəl] *adj* : correctivo <remedial classes : clases para alumnos atrasados>

remedy¹ ['rɛmədi] *vt* **-died; -dying** : remediar

remedy² *n, pl* **-dies** : remedio *m,* medicamento *m*

remember [ri'mɛmbər] *vt* **1** RECOLLECT : acordarse de, recordar **2** : no olvidar <remember my words : no olvides mis palabras> <to remember to : acordarse de> **3** : dar saludos, dar recuerdos <remember me to her : dale saludos de mi parte> **4** COMMEMORATE : recordar, conmemorar

remembrance [ri'mɛmbrənts] *n* **1** RECOLLECTION : recuerdo *m* <in remembrance of : en conmemoración de> **2** MEMENTO : recuerdo *m*

remind [ri'maɪnd] *vt* : recordar <remind me to do it : recuérdame que lo haga> <she reminds me of Clara : me recuerda de Clara>

reminder [ri'maɪndər] *n* : recuerdo *m*

reminisce [,rɛmə'nɪs] *vi* **-nisced; -niscing** : rememorar los viejos tiempos

reminiscence [,rɛmə'nɪsənts] *n* : recuerdo *m,* reminiscencia *f*

reminiscent [,rɛmə'nɪsənt] *adj* **1** NOSTALGIC : reminiscente, nostálgico **2** SUGGESTIVE : evocador, que recuerda — **reminiscently** *adv*

remiss [ri'mɪs] *adj* : negligente, descuidado, remiso

remission [ri'mɪʃən] *n* : remisión *f*

remit [ri'mɪt] *vt* **-mitted; -mitting 1** PARDON : perdonar **2** SEND : remitir, enviar (dinero)

remittance [ri'mɪtənts] *n* : remesa *f*

remnant ['rɛmnənt] *n* : restos *mpl,* vestigio *m*

remodel [ri'mɑdəl] *vt* **-eled** *or* **-elled; -eling** *or* **-elling** : remodelar, reformar

remonstrate [ri'mɑn,streɪt] *vi* **-strated; -strating** : protestar <to remonstrate with someone : quejarse a alguien>

remorse [ri'mɔrs] *n* : remordimiento *m*

remorseful [ri'mɔrsfəl] *adj* : arrepentido, lleno de remordimiento

remorseless [ri'mɔrsləs] *adj* **1** PITILESS : despiadado **2** RELENTLESS : implacable

remote [ri'moːt] *adj* **-moter; -est 1** FAR-OFF : lejano, remoto <remote countries : países remotos> <in the remote past : en el pasado lejano> **2** SECLUDED : recóndito **3** : a distancia, remoto <remote control : control remoto> **4** SLIGHT : remoto **5** ALOOF : distante

remotely [ri'moːtli] *adv* **1** SLIGHTLY : remotamente **2** DISTANTLY : en un lugar remoto, muy lejos

remoteness [ri'moːtnəs] *n* : lejanía *f*

removable [ri'muːvəbəl] *adj* : movible, separable

removal [ri'muːvəl] *n* : separación *f,* extracción *f,* supresión *f* (en algo escrito), eliminación *f* (de problemas, etc.)

remove [ri'muːv] *vt* **-moved; -moving 1** : quitar, quitarse <remove the lid : quite la tapa> <to remove one's hat : quitarse el sombrero> **2** EXTRACT : sacar, extraer <to remove the contents of : sacar el contenido de> **3** ELIMINATE : eliminar, disipar

remunerate [ri'mjuːnəˌreɪt] *vt* **-ated; -ating** : remunerar

remuneration [riˌmjuːnə'reɪʃən] *n* : remuneración *f*

remunerative [ri'mjuːnərət̬ɪv, -ˌreɪ-] *adj* : remunerativo

renaissance [ˌrɛnə'sɑnts, -'zɑnts; 'rɛnəˌ-] *n* : renacimiento *m* <the Renaissance : el Renacimiento>

renal ['riːnəl] *adj* : renal

rename [ˌriː'neɪm] *vt* **-named; -naming** : ponerle un nombre nuevo a

rend ['rɛnd] *vt* **rent** ['rɛnt]; **rending** : desgarrar

render ['rɛndər] *vt* **1** : derretir <to render lard : derretir la manteca> **2** GIVE : prestar, dar <to render aid : prestar ayuda> **3** MAKE : hacer, volver, dejar <it rendered him helpless : lo dejó incapacitado> **4** TRANSLATE : traducir, verter <to render into English : traducir al inglés>

rendezvous ['rɑndɪˌvuː, -deɪ-] *ns & pl* : encuentro *m,* cita *f*

rendition [rɛn'dɪʃən] *n* : interpretación *f*

renegade ['rɛnɪˌgeɪd] *n* : renegado *m,* -da *f*

renege [ri'nɪg, -'nɛg] *vi* **-neged; -neging** : no cumplir con (una promesa, etc.)

renew [ri'nuː, -'njuː] *vt* **1** REVIVE : renovar, reavivar <to renew the sentiments of youth : renovar los sentimientos de la juventud> **2** RESUME : reanudar **3** EXTEND : renovar <to renew a subscription : renovar una suscripción>

renewable [ri'nuːəbəl, -'njuː-] *adj* : renovable

renewal [ri'nuːəl, -'njuː-] *n* : renovación *f*

renounce [ri'naʊnts] *vt* **-nounced; -nouncing** : renunciar a

renovate ['rɛnəˌveɪt] *vt* **-vated; -vating** : restaurar, renovar

renovation [ˌrɛnə'veɪʃən] *n* : restauración *f,* renovación *f*

renown [ri'naʊn] *n* : renombre *m,* fama *f,* celebridad *f*

renowned [ri'naʊnd] *adj* : renombrado, célebre, famoso

rent¹ ['rɛnt] *vt* : rentar, alquilar

rent² *n* **1** : renta *f,* alquiler *m* <for rent : se alquila> **2** RIP : rasgadura *f*

rental¹ ['rɛntəl] *adj* RENT : de alquiler

rental² *n* : alquiler *m*

renter ['rɛntər] *n* : arrendatario *m,* -ria *f*

renunciation [riˌnʌntsi'eɪʃən] *n* : renuncia *f*

reopen [ˌriː'oːpən] *vt* : volver a abrir

reorganization [ˌriːˌɔrgənə'zeɪʃən] *n* : reorganización *f*

reorganize [ˌriː'ɔrgənˌaɪz] *vt* **-nized; -nizing** : reorganizar

repair¹ [ri'pær] *vt* : reparar, arreglar, refaccionar

repair² *n* **1** : reparación *f,* arreglo *m* **2** CONDITION : estado *m* <in bad repair : en mal estado>

reparation [ˌrɛpə'reɪʃən] *n* **1** AMENDS : reparación *f* **2 reparations** *npl* COMPENSATION : indemnización *f*

repartee [ˌrɛpər'tiː, -ˌpɑr-, -'teɪ] *n* : intercambio *m* de réplicas ingeniosas

repast [ri'pæst, 'riːˌpæst] *n* : comida *f*

repatriate [ri'peɪtriˌeɪt] *vt* **-ated; -ating** : repatriar

repay [ri'peɪ] *vt* **-paid; -paying** : pagar, devolver, reembolsar

repeal¹ [ri'piːl] *vt* : abrogar, revocar

repeal² *n* : abrogación *f,* revocación *f*

repeat¹ [ri'piːt] *vt* : repetir

repeat² *n* : repetición *f*

repeatedly [ri'piːt̬ədli] *adv* : repetidamente, repetidas veces

repel [ri'pɛl] *vt* **-pelled; -pelling 1** REPULSE : repeler (un enemigo, etc.) **2** RESIST : repeler **3** REJECT : rechazar, repeler **4** DISGUST : repugnar, darle asco (a alguien)

repellent *or* **repellant** [ri'pɛlənt] *n* : repelente *m*

repent [ri'pɛnt] *vi* : arrepentirse

repentance [ri'pɛntənts] *n* : arrepentimiento *m*

repentant [ri'pɛntənt] *adj* : arrepentido

repercussion [ˌriːpər'kʌʃən, ˌrɛpər-] *n* : repercusión *f*

repertoire ['rɛpərˌtwɑr] *n* : repertorio *m*

repertory ['rɛpərˌtori] *n, pl* **-ries** : repertorio *m*

repetition [ˌrɛpə'tɪʃən] *n* : repetición *f*

repetitious [ˌrɛpə'tɪʃəs] *adj* : repetitivo, reiterativo — **repetitiously** *adv*

repetitive [ri'pɛt̬ət̬ɪv] *adj* : repetitivo, reiterativo
replace [ri'pleɪs] *vt* **-placed; -placing 1** : volver a poner <replace it in the drawer : vuelve a ponerlo en el cajón> **2** SUBSTITUTE : reemplazar, sustituir **3** : reponer <to replace the worn carpet : reponer la alfombra raída>
replaceable [ri'pleɪsəbəl] *adj* : reemplazable
replacement [ri'pleɪsmənt] *n* **1** SUBSTITUTION : reemplazo *m,* sustitución *f* **2** SUBSTITUTE : sustituto *m,* -ta *f;* suplente *mf* (persona) **3 replacement part** : repuesto *m,* pieza *f* de recambio
replenish [ri'plɛnɪʃ] *vt* : rellenar, llenar de nuevo
replenishment [ri'plɛnɪʃmənt] *n* : reabastecimiento *m*
replete [ri'pliːt] *adj* : repleto, lleno
replica ['rɛplɪkə] *n* : réplica *f,* reproducción *f*
reply[1] [ri'plaɪ] *vi* **-plied; -plying** : contestar, responder
reply[2] *n, pl* **-plies** : respuesta *f,* contestación *f*
report[1] [ri'port] *vt* **1** ANNOUNCE : relatar, anunciar **2** : dar parte de, informar de, reportar <he reported an accident : dio parte de un accidente> <to report a crime : denunciar un delito> **3** : informar acerca de (en un periódico, la televisión, etc.) — *vi* **1** : hacer un informe, informar **2 to report for duty** : presentarse, reportarse
report[2] *n* **1** RUMOR : rumor *m* **2** REPUTATION : reputación *f* <people of evil report : personas de mala fama> **3** ACCOUNT : informe *m,* reportaje *m* (en un periódico, etc.) **4** BANG : estallido *m* (de un arma de fuego)
report card *n* : boletín *m* de calificaciones, boletín *m* de notas
reportedly [ri'portədli] *adv* : según se dice, según se informa
reporter [ri'port̬ər] *n* : periodista *mf;* reportero *m,* -ra *f*
repose[1] [ri'poːz] *vi* **-posed; -posing** : reposar, descansar
repose[2] *n* **1** : reposo *m,* descanso *m* **2** CALM : calma *f,* tranquilidad *f*
repository [ri'pɑzə,tori] *n, pl* **-ries** : depósito *m*
repossess [,riːpə'zɛs] *vt* : recuperar, recobrar la posesión de
reprehensible [,rɛpri'hɛntsəbəl] *adj* : reprensible — **reprehensibly** *adv*
represent [,rɛprɪ'zɛnt] *vt* **1** SYMBOLIZE : representar <the flag represents our country : la bandera representa a nuestro país> **2** : representar, ser un representante de <an attorney who represents his client : un abogado que representa su cliente> **3** PORTRAY : presentar <he represents himself as a friend : se presenta como amigo>
representation [,rɛprɪ,zɛn'teɪʃən, -zən-] *n* : representación *f*
representative[1] [,rɛprɪ'zɛntət̬ɪv] *adj* : representativo
representative[2] *n* **1** : representante *mf* **2** : diputado *m,* -da *f* (en la política)
repress [ri'prɛs] *vt* : reprimir
repression [ri'prɛʃən] *n* : represión *f*
repressive [ri'prɛsɪv] *adj* : represivo
reprieve[1] [ri'priːv] *vt* **-prieved; -prieving** : indultar
reprieve[2] *n* : indulto *m*
reprimand[1] ['rɛprə,mænd] *vt* : reprender
reprimand[2] *n* : reprimenda *f*
reprint[1] [ri'prɪnt] *vt* : reimprimir
reprint[2] ['riː,prɪnt, ri'prɪnt] *n* : reedición *f*
reprisal [ri'praɪzəl] *n* : represalia *f*
reproach[1] [ri'proːtʃ] *vt* : reprochar
reproach[2] *n* **1** DISGRACE : deshonra *f* **2** REBUKE : reproche *m,* recriminación *f*
reproachful [ri'proːtʃfəl] *adj* : de reproche
reproduce [,riːprə'duːs, -'djuːs] *v* **-duced; -ducing** *vt* : reproducir — *vi* BREED : reproducirse
reproduction [,riːprə'dʌkʃən] *n* : reproducción *f*
reproductive [,riːprə'dʌktɪv] *adj* : reproductor
reproof [ri'pruːf] *n* : reprobación *f,* reprimenda *f,* reproche *m*
reprove [ri'pruːv] *vt* **-proved; -proving** : reprender, censurar
reptile ['rɛp,taɪl] *n* : reptil *m*
republic [ri'pʌblɪk] *n* : república *f*
republican[1] [ri'pʌblɪkən] *adj* : republicano
republican[2] *n* : republicano *m,* -na *f*
repudiate [ri'pjuːdi,eɪt] *vt* **-ated; -ating 1** REJECT : rechazar **2** DISOWN : repudiar, renegar de
repudiation [ri,pjuːdi'eɪʃən] *n* : rechazo *m,* repudio *m*
repugnance [ri'pʌgnənts] *n* : repugnancia *f*
repugnant [ri'pʌgnənt] *adj* : repugnante, asqueroso
repulse[1] [ri'pʌls] *vt* **-pulsed; -pulsing 1** REPEL : repeler **2** REBUFF : desairar, rechazar
repulse[2] *n* : rechazo *m*
repulsive [ri'pʌlsɪv] *adj* : repulsivo, repugnante, asqueroso — **repulsively** *adv*
reputable ['rɛpjət̬əbəl] *adj* : acreditado, de buena reputación
reputation [,rɛpjə'teɪʃən] *n* : reputación *f,* fama *f*
repute [ri'pjuːt] *n* : reputación *f,* fama *f*
reputed [ri'pjuːt̬əd] *adj* : reputado, supuesto <she's reputed to be the best : tiene fama de ser la mejor>
reputedly [ri'pjuːt̬ədli] *adv* : supuestamente, según se dice
request[1] [ri'kwɛst] *vt* : pedir, solicitar, rogar <to request assistance : solicitar asistencia, pedir ayuda> <I requested him to do it : le pedí que lo hiciera>

request² *n* : petición *f*, solicitud *f*, pedido *m*

requiem ['rɛkwiəm, 'reɪ-] *n* : réquiem *m*

require [ri'kwaɪr] *vt* **-quired; -quiring** **1** CALL FOR, DEMAND : requerir, exigir <if required : si se requiere> <to require that something be done : exigir que algo se haga> **2** NEED : necesitar, requerir

requirement [ri'kwaɪrmənt] *n* **1** NECESSITY : necesidad *f* **2** DEMAND : requisito *m*, demanda *f*

requisite¹ ['rɛkwəzɪt] *adj* : esencial, necesario

requisite² *n* : requisito *m*, necesidad *f*

requisition¹ [ˌrɛkwə'zɪʃən] *vt* : requisar

requisition² *n* : requisición *f*, requisa *f*

reread [ˌriː'riːd] *vt* **-read; -reading** : releer

reroute [ˌriː'ruːt, -'raʊt] *vt* **-routed; -routing** : desviar

resale ['riːˌseɪl, ˌriː'seɪl] *n* : reventa *f* <resale price : precio de venta>

rescind [ri'sɪnd] *vt* **1** CANCEL : rescindir, cancelar **2** REPEAL : abrogar, revocar

rescue¹ ['rɛsˌkjuː] *vt* **-cued; -cuing** : rescatar, salvar

rescue² *n* : rescate *m*

rescuer ['rɛskjuər] *n* : salvador *m*, -dora *f*

research¹ [ri'sərtʃ, 'riːˌsərtʃ] *v* : investigar

research² *n* : investigación *f*

researcher [ri'sərtʃər, 'riːˌ-] *n* : investigador *m*, -dora *f*

resemblance [ri'zɛmblənts] *n* : semejanza *f*, parecido *m*

resemble [ri'zɛmbəl] *vt* **-sembled; -sembling** : parecerse a, asemejarse a

resent [ri'zɛnt] *vt* : resentirse de, ofenderse por

resentful [ri'zɛntfəl] *adj* : resentido, rencoroso — **resentfully** *adv*

resentment [ri'zɛntmənt] *n* : resentimiento *m*

reservation [ˌrɛzər'veɪʃən] *n* **1** : reservación *f*, reserva *f* <to make a reservation : hacer una reservación> **2** DOUBT, MISGIVING : reserva *f*, duda *f* <without reservations : sin reservas> **3** : reserva *f* (de indios americanos)

reserve¹ [ri'zərv] *vt* **-served; -serving** : reservar

reserve² *n* **1** STOCK : reserva *f* <to keep in reserve : guardar en reserva> **2** RESTRAINT : reserva *f*, moderación *f* **3** **reserves** *npl* : reservas *fpl* (militares)

reserved [ri'zərvd] *adj* : reservado

reservoir ['rɛzərˌvwɑr, -ˌvwɔr, -ˌvɔr] *n* : embalse *m*

reset [ˌriː'sɛt] *vt* **-set; -setting** : reajustar, poner en hora (un reloj), reinicializar (una computadora)

reside [ri'zaɪd] *vi* **-sided; -siding** **1** DWELL : residir **2** LIE : radicar, residir

<the power resides in the presidency : el poder radica en la presidencia>

residence ['rɛzədənts] *n* : residencia *f*

resident¹ ['rɛzədənt] *adj* : residente

resident² *n* : residente *mf*

residential [ˌrɛzə'dɛntʃəl] *adj* : residencial

residual [ri'zɪdʒʊəl] *adj* : residual

residue ['rɛzəˌduː, -ˌdjuː] *n* : residuo *m*, resto *m*

resign [ri'zaɪn] *vt* **1** QUIT : dimitir, renunciar **2 to resign oneself** : aguantarse, resignarse

resignation [ˌrɛzɪg'neɪʃən] *n* : resignación *f*

resignedly [ri'zaɪnədli] *adv* : con resignación

resilience [ri'zɪljənts] *n* **1** : capacidad *f* de recuperación, adaptabilidad *f* **2** ELASTICITY : elasticidad *f*

resiliency [ri'zɪljəntsi] → **resilience**

resilient [ri'zɪljənt] *adj* **1** STRONG : resistente, fuerte **2** ELASTIC : elástico

resin ['rɛzən] *n* : resina *f*

resist [ri'zɪst] *vt* **1** WITHSTAND : resistir <to resist heat : resistir el calor> **2** OPPOSE : oponerse a

resistance [ri'zɪstənts] *n* : resistencia *f*

resistant [ri'zɪstənt] *adj* : resistente

resolute ['rɛzəˌluːt] *adj* : firme, resuelto, decidido

resolutely ['rɛzəˌluːtli, ˌrɛzə'-] *adv* : resueltamente, firmemente

resolution [ˌrɛzə'luːʃən] *n* **1** SOLUTION : solución *f* **2** RESOLVE : resolución *f*, determinación *f* **3** DECISION : propósito *m*, decisión *f* <New Year's resolutions : propósitos para el Año Nuevo> **4** MOTION, PROPOSAL : moción *f*, resolución *f* (legislativa)

resolve¹ [ri'zɑlv] *vt* **-solved; -solving** **1** SOLVE : resolver, solucionar **2** DECIDE : resolver <she resolved to get more sleep : resolvió dormir más>

resolve² *n* : resolución *f*, determinación *f*

resonance ['rɛzənənts] *n* : resonancia *f*

resonant ['rɛzənənt] *adj* : resonante, retumbante

resort¹ [ri'zɔrt] *vi* **to resort to** : recurrir <to resort to force : recurrir a la fuerza>

resort² *n* **1** RECOURSE : recurso *m* <as a last resort : como último recurso> **2** HANGOUT : lugar *m* popular, lugar *m* muy frecuentado **3** : lugar *m* de vacaciones <tourist resort : centro turístico>

resound [ri'zaʊnd] *vi* : retumbar, resonar

resounding [ri'zaʊndɪŋ] *adj* **1** RESONANT : retumbante, resonante **2** ABSOLUTE, CATEGORICAL : rotundo, tremendo <a resounding success : un éxito rotundo>

resource ['riːˌsors, ri'sors] *n* **1** RESOURCEFULNESS : ingenio *m*, recursos *mpl* **2 resources** *npl* : recursos *mpl*

<natural resources : recursos naturales> 3 **resources** *npl* MEANS : recursos *mpl*, medios *mpl*, fondos *mpl*

resourceful [ri'sorsfəl, -'zors-] *adj* : ingenioso

resourcefulness [ri'sorsfəlnəs, -'zors-] *n* : ingenio *m*, recursos *mpl*, inventiva *f*

respect[1] [ri'spɛkt] *vt* : respetar, estimar

respect[2] *n* **1** REFERENCE : relación *f*, respeto *m* <with respect to : en lo que respecta a> **2** ESTEEM : respeto *m*, estima *f* **3** DETAIL, PARTICULAR : detalle *m*, sentido *m*, respeto *m* <in some respects : en algunos sentidos> **4 respects** *npl* : respetos *mpl* <to pay one's respects : presentar uno sus respetos>

respectability [ri,spɛktə'bɪləti] *n* : respetabilidad *f*

respectable [ri'spɛktəbəl] *adj* **1** PROPER : respetable, decente **2** CONSIDERABLE : considerable, respetable <a respectable amount : una cantidad respetable> — **respectably** [-bli] *adv*

respectful [ri'spɛktfəl] *adj* : respetuoso — **respectfully** *adv*

respectfulness [ri'spɛktfəlnəs] *n* : respetuosidad *f*

respective [ri'spɛktɪv] *adj* : respectivo <their respective homes : sus casas respectivas> — **respectively** *adv*

respiration [,rɛspə'reɪʃən] *n* : respiración *f*

respirator ['rɛspə,reɪtər] *n* : respirador *m*

respiratory ['rɛspərə,tori, rɪ'spaɪrə-] *adj* : respiratorio

respite ['rɛspɪt, rɪ'spaɪt] *n* : respiro *m*, tregua *f*

resplendent [ri'splɛndənt] *adj* : resplandeciente — **resplendently** *adv*

respond [ri'spɑnd] *vi* **1** ANSWER : contestar, responder **2** REACT : responder, reaccionar <to respond to treatment : responder al tratamiento>

response [ri'spɑnts] *n* : respuesta *f*

responsibility [ri,spɑntsə'bɪləti] *n, pl* **-ties** : responsabilidad *f*

responsible [ri'spɑntsəbəl] *adj* : responsable — **responsibly** [-bli] *adv*

responsive [ri'spɑntsɪv] *adj* **1** ANSWERING : que responde **2** SENSITIVE : sensible, receptivo

responsiveness [ri'spɑntsɪvnəs] *n* : receptividad *f*, sensibilidad *f*

rest[1] ['rɛst] *vi* **1** REPOSE : reposar, descansar **2** RELAX : quedarse tranquilo **3** STOP : pararse, detenerse **4** DEPEND : basarse (en), descansar (sobre), depender (de) <the decision rests with her : la decisión pesa sobre ella> **5 to rest on** : apoyarse en, descansar sobre <to rest on one's arm : apoyarse en el brazo> — *vt* **1** RELAX : descansar **2** SUPPORT : apoyar **3 to rest one's eyes on** : fijar la mirada en

rest[2] *n* **1** RELAXATION, REPOSE : reposo *m*, descanso *m* **2** SUPPORT : soporte *m*, apoyo *m* **3** : silencio *m* (en música) **4** REMAINDER : resto *m* **5 to come to rest** : pararse

restatement [,riː'steɪtmənt] *n* : repetición *f*

restaurant ['rɛstə,rɑnt, -rənt] *n* : restaurante *m*

restful ['rɛstfəl] *adj* **1** RELAXING : relajante **2** PEACEFUL : tranquilo, sosegado

restitution [,rɛstə'tuːʃən, -'tjuː-] *n* : restitución *f*

restive ['rɛstɪv] *adj* : inquieto, nervioso

restless ['rɛstləs] *adj* **1** FIDGETY : inquieto, agitado **2** IMPATIENT : impaciente **3** SLEEPLESS : desvelado <a restless night : una noche en blanco>

restlessly ['rɛstləsli] *adv* : nerviosamente

restlessness ['rɛstləsnəs] *n* : inquietud *f*, agitación *f*

restoration [,rɛstə'reɪʃən] *n* : restauración *f*, restablecimiento *m*

restore [ri'stor] *vt* **-stored; -storing 1** RETURN : volver **2** REESTABLISH : restablecer **3** REPAIR : restaurar

restrain [ri'streɪn] *vt* **1** : refrenar, contener **2 to restrain oneself** : contenerse

restrained [ri'streɪnd] *adj* : comedido, templado, contenido

restraint [ri'streɪnt] *n* **1** RESTRICTION : restricción *f*, limitación *f*, control *m* **2** CONFINEMENT : encierro *m* **3** RESERVE : reserva *f*, control *m* de sí mismo

restrict [ri'strɪkt] *vt* : restringir, limitar, constreñir

restricted [ri'strɪktəd] *adj* **1** LIMITED : limitado, restringido **2** CLASSIFIED : secreto, confidencial

restriction [ri'strɪkʃən] *n* : restricción *f*

restrictive [ri'strɪktɪv] *adj* : restrictivo — **restrictively** *adv*

restructure [ri'strʌktʃər] *vt* **-tured; -turing** : reestructurar

result[1] [ri'zʌlt] *vi* : resultar <to result in : resultar en, tener por resultado>

result[2] *n* : resultado *m*, consecuencia *f* <as a result of : como consecuencia de>

resultant [ri'zʌltənt] *adj* : resultante

resume [ri'zuːm] *v* **-sumed; -suming** *vt* : reanudar — *vi* : reanudarse

résumé *or* **resume** *or* **resumé** ['rɛzə,meɪ, ,rɛzə'-] *n* **1** SUMMARY : resumen *m* **2** CURRICULUM VITAE : currículum *m*, currículo *m*

resumption [ri'zʌmpʃən] *n* : reanudación *f*

resurface [,riː'sərfəs] *v* **-faced; -facing** *vt* : pavimentar (una carretera) de nuevo — *vi* : volver a salir en la superficie

resurgence [ri'sərdʒənts] *n* : resurgimiento *m*

resurrect [ˌrɛzəˈrɛkt] *vt* **:** resucitar, desempolvar

resurrection [ˌrɛzəˈrɛkʃən] *n* **:** resurrección *f*

resuscitate [riˈsʌsəˌteɪt] *vt* **-tated; -tating :** resucitar, revivir

retail[1] [ˈriːˌteɪl] *vt* **:** vender al por menor, vender al detalle

retail[2] *adv* **:** al por menor, al detalle

retail[3] *adj* **:** detallista, minorista

retail[4] *n* **:** venta *f* al detalle, venta *f* al por menor

retailer [ˈriːˌteɪlər] *n* **:** detallista *mf,* minorista *mf*

retain [riˈteɪn] *vt* **:** retener, conservar, guardar

retainer [riˈteɪnər] *n* **1** SERVANT **:** criado *m,* -da *f* **2** ADVANCE **:** anticipo *m*

retaliate [riˈtæliˌeɪt] *vi* **-ated; -ating :** responder, contraatacar, tomar represalias

retaliation [riˌtæliˈeɪʃən] *n* **:** represalia *f,* retaliación *f*

retard [riˈtɑrd] *vt* **:** retardar, retrasar

retarded [riˈtɑrdəd] *adj* **:** retrasado

retch [ˈrɛtʃ] *vi* **:** hacer arcadas

retention [riˈtɛntʃən] *n* **:** retención *f*

retentive [riˈtɛntɪv] *adj* **:** retentivo

reticence [ˈrɛtəsən*t*s] *n* **:** reticencia *f*

reticent [ˈrɛtəsənt] *adj* **:** reticente

retina [ˈrɛtənə] *n, pl* **-nas** *or* **-nae** [-əni, -ənˌaɪ] **:** retina *f*

retinue [ˈrɛtənˌuː, -ˌjuː] *n* **:** séquito *m,* comitiva *f,* cortejo *m*

retire [riˈtaɪr] *vi* **-tired; -tiring 1** RETREAT, WITHDRAW **:** retirarse, retraerse **2 :** retirarse, jubilarse (de su trabajo) **3 :** acostarse, irse a dormir

retiree [riˌtaɪˈriː] *n* **:** jubilado *m,* -da *f*

retirement [riˈtaɪrmənt] *n* **:** jubilación *f*

retiring [riˈtaɪrɪŋ] *adj* SHY **:** retraído

retort[1] [riˈtɔrt] *vt* **:** replicar

retort[2] *n* **:** réplica *f*

retrace [ˌriːˈtreɪs] *vt* **-traced; -tracing :** volver sobre, desandar <to retrace one's steps **:** volver uno sobre sus pasos>

retract [riˈtrækt] *vt* **1** TAKE BACK, WITHDRAW **:** retirar, retractarse de **2 :** retraer (las garras) **—** *vi* **:** retractarse

retractable [riˈtræktəbəl] *adj* **:** retractable

retrain [ˌriːˈtreɪn] *vt* **:** reciclar, reconvertir

retreat[1] [riˈtriːt] *vi* **:** retirarse

retreat[2] *n* **1** WITHDRAWAL **:** retirada *f,* repliegue *m,* retiro *m* <to beat a retreat **:** batirse en retirada> **2** REFUGE **:** retiro *m,* refugio *m*

retrench [riˈtrɛntʃ] *vt* **:** reducir (gastos) **—** *vi* **:** economizar

retribution [ˌrɛtrəˈbjuːʃən] *n* PUNISHMENT **:** castigo *m,* pena *f* merecida

retrieval [riˈtriːvəl] *n* **:** recuperación *f* <beyond retrieval **:** irrecuperable> <data retrieval **:** recuperación de datos>

retrieve [riˈtriːv] *vt* **-trieved; -trieving 1 :** cobrar <to retrieve game **:** cobrar la caza> **2** RECOVER **:** recuperar

retriever [riˈtriːvər] *n* **:** perro *m* cobrador

retroactive [ˌrɛtroˈæktɪv] *adj* **:** retroactivo **— retroactively** *adv*

retrograde [ˈrɛtrəˌgreɪd] *adj* **:** retrógrado

retrospect [ˈrɛtrəˌspɛkt] *n* **in retrospect :** mirando hacia atrás, retrospectivamente

retrospective [ˌrɛtrəˈspɛktɪv] *adj* **:** retrospectivo

return[1] [riˈtərn] *vi* **1 :** volver, regresar <to return home **:** regresar a casa> **2** REAPPEAR **:** reaparecer, resurgir **3** ANSWER **:** responder **—** *vt* **1** REPLACE, RESTORE **:** devolver, volver (a poner), restituir <to return something to its place **:** volver a poner algo en su lugar> **2** YIELD **:** producir, redituar, rendir **3** REPAY **:** pagar, devolver <to return a compliment **:** devolver un cumplido>

return[2] *adj* **:** de vuelta

return[3] *n* **1** RETURNING **:** regreso *m,* vuelta *f,* retorno *m* **2** *or* **tax return :** declaración *f* de impuestos **3** YIELD **:** rédito *m,* rendimiento *m,* ganancia *f* **4 returns** *npl* DATA, RESULTS **:** resultados *mpl*, datos *mpl*

reunion [riˈjuːnjən] *n* **:** reunión *f,* reencuentro *m*

reunite [ˌriːjʊˈnaɪt] *v* **-nited; -niting** *vt* **:** (volver a) reunir **—** *vi* **:** (volver a) reunirse

reusable [riˈjuːzəbəl] *adj* **:** reutilizable

reuse [riˈjuːz] *vt* **-used; -using :** reutilizar, usar de nuevo

revamp [ˌriˈvæmp] *vt* **:** renovar

reveal [riˈviːl] *vt* **1** DIVULGE **:** revelar, divulgar <to reveal a secret **:** revelar un secreto> **2** SHOW **:** manifestar, mostrar, dejar ver

reveille [ˈrɛvəli] *n* **:** toque *m* de diana

revel[1] [ˈrɛvəl] *vi* **-eled** *or* **-elled; -eling** *or* **-elling 1** CAROUSE **:** ir de juerga **2 to revel in :** deleitarse en

revel[2] *n* **:** juerga *f,* parranda *f fam*

revelation [ˌrɛvəˈleɪʃən] *n* **:** revelación *f*

reveler *or* **reveller** [ˈrɛvələr] *n* **:** juerguista *mf*

revelry [ˈrɛvəlri] *n, pl* **–ries :** juerga *f,* parranda *f fam,* jarana *f fam*

revenge[1] [riˈvɛndʒ] *vt* **-venged; -venging :** vengar <to revenge oneself on **:** vengarse de>

revenge[2] *n* **:** venganza *f*

revenue [ˈrɛvəˌnuː, -ˌnjuː] *n* **:** ingresos *mpl*, rentas *fpl*

reverberate [riˈvərbəˌreɪt] *vi* **-ated; -ating :** reverberar

reverberation [riˌvərbəˈreɪʃən] *n* **:** reverberación *f*

revere [riˈvɪr] *vt* **-vered; -vering :** reverenciar, venerar

reverence ['rɛvərənts] *n* : reverencia *f,* veneración *f*

reverend ['rɛvərənd] *adj* : reverendo <the Reverend John Chapin : el reverendo John Chapin>

reverent ['rɛvərənt] *adj* : reverente — **reverently** *adv*

reverie ['rɛvəri] *n, pl* **-eries** : ensueño *m*

reversal ['rɛvərsəl] *n* **1** INVERSION : inversión *f* (del orden normal) **2** CHANGE : cambio *m* total **3** SETBACK : revés *m,* contratiempo *m*

reverse[1] [ri'vərs] *v* **-versed; -versing** *vt* **1** INVERT : invertir **2** CHANGE : cambiar totalmente **3** ANNUL : anular, revocar — *vi* : dar marcha atrás

reverse[2] *adj* **1** : inverso <in reverse order : en orden inverso> <the reverse side : el reverso> **2** OPPOSITE : contrario, opuesto

reverse[3] *n* **1** OPPOSITE : lo contrario, lo opuesto **2** SETBACK : revés *m,* contratiempo *m* **3** BACK : reverso *m,* dorso *m,* revés *m* **4** *or* **reverse gear** : marcha *f* atrás, reversa *f Col, Mex*

reversible [ri'vərsəbəl] *adj* : reversible

reversion [ri'vərʒən] *n* : reversión *f,* vuelta *f*

revert [ri'vərt] *vi* : revertir

review[1] [ri'vjuː] *vt* **1** REEXAMINE : volver a examinar, repasar (una lección) **2** CRITICIZE : reseñar, hacer una crítica de **3** EXAMINE : examinar, analizar <to review one's life : examinar su vida> **4 to review the troops** : pasar revista a las tropas

review[2] *n* **1** INSPECTION : revista *f* (de tropas) **2** ANALYSIS, OVERVIEW : resumen *m,* análisis *m* <a review of current affairs : un análisis de las actualidades> **3** CRITICISM : reseña *f,* crítica *f* (de un libro, etc.) **4** : repaso *m* (para un examen) **5** REVUE : revista *f* (musical)

reviewer [ri'vjuːər] *n* : crítico *m,* -ca *f*

revile [ri'vaɪl] *vt* **-viled; -viling** : injuriar, denostar

revise [ri'vaɪz] *vt* **-vised; -vising** : revisar, corregir, refundir <to revise a dictionary : corregir un diccionario>

revision [ri'vɪʒən] *n* : revisión *f*

revival [ri'vaɪvəl] *n* **1** : renacimiento *m* (de ideas, etc.), restablecimiento *m* (de costumbres, etc.), reactivación *f* (de la economía) **2** : reanimación *f,* resucitación *f* (en medicina) **3** *or* **revival meeting** : asamblea *f* evangelista

revive [ri'vaɪv] *v* **-vived; -viving** *vt* **1** REAWAKEN : reavivar, reanimar, reactivar (la economía), resucitar (a un paciente) **2** REESTABLISH : restablecer — *vi* **1** : renacer, reanimarse, reactivarse **2** COME TO : recobrar el sentido, volver en sí

revoke [ri'voːk] *vt* **-voked; -voking** : revocar

revolt[1] [ri'voːlt] *vi* **1** REBEL : rebelarse, sublevarse **2 to revolt at** : sentir repugnancia por — *vt* DISGUST : darle asco (a alguien), repugnar

revolt[2] *n* REBELLION : rebelión *f,* revuelta *f,* sublevación *f*

revolting [ri'voːltɪŋ] *adj* : asqueroso, repugnante

revolution [ˌrɛvə'luːʃən] *n* : revolución *f*

revolutionary[1] [ˌrɛvə'luːʃənˌɛri] *adj* : revolucionario

revolutionary[2] *n, pl* **-aries** : revolucionario *m,* -ria *f*

revolutionize [ˌrɛvə'luːʃənˌaɪz] *vt* **-ized; -izing** : cambiar radicalmente, revolucionar

revolve [ri'vɑlv] *v* **-volved; -volving** *vt* ROTATE : hacer girar — *vi* **1** ROTATE : girar <to revolve around : girar alrededor de> **2 to revolve in one's mind** : darle vueltas en la cabeza a alguien

revolver [ri'vɑlvər] *n* : revólver *m*

revue [ri'vjuː] *n* : revista *f* (musical)

revulsion [ri'vʌlʃən] *n* : repugnancia *f*

reward[1] [ri'wɔrd] *vt* : recompensar, premiar

reward[2] *n* : recompensa *f*

rewrite [ˌriː'raɪt] *vt* **-wrote; -written; -writing** : escribir de nuevo, volver a escribir

rhapsody ['ræpsədi] *n, pl* **-dies 1** : elogio *m* excesivo <to go into rhapsodies over : extasiarse por> **2** : rapsodia *f* (en música)

rhetoric ['rɛtərɪk] *n* : retórica *f*

rhetorical [rɪ'tɔrɪkəl] *adj* : retórico

rheumatic [rʊ'mætɪk] *adj* : reumático

rheumatism ['ruːməˌtɪzəm, 'rʊ-] *n* : reumatismo *m*

rhinestone ['raɪnˌstoːn] *n* : diamante *m* de imitación

rhino ['raɪˌnoː] *n, pl* **rhino** *or* **rhinos** → **rhinoceros**

rhinoceros [raɪ'nɑsərəs] *n, pl* **-eroses** *or* **-eros** *or* **-eri** [-ˌraɪ] : rinoceronte *m*

rhododendron [ˌroːdə'dɛndrən] *n* : rododendro *m*

rhombus ['rɑmbəs] *n, pl* **-buses** *or* **-bi** [-ˌbaɪ, -bi] : rombo *m*

rhubarb ['ruːˌbɑrb] *n* : ruibarbo *m*

rhyme[1] ['raɪm] *vi* **rhymed; rhyming** : rimar

rhyme[2] *n* **1** : rima *f* **2** VERSE : verso *m* (en rima)

rhythm ['rɪðəm] *n* : ritmo *m*

rhythmic ['rɪðmɪk] *or* **rhythmical** [-mɪkəl] *adj* : rítmico — **rhythmically** [-mɪkli] *adv*

rib[1] ['rɪb] *vt* **ribbed; ribbing 1** : hacer en canalé <a ribbed sweater : un suéter en canalé> **2** TEASE : tomarle el pelo (a alguien)

rib[2] *n* **1** : costilla *f* (de una persona o un animal) **2** : nervio *m* (de una bóveda o una hoja), varilla *f* (de un paraguas), canalé *m* (de una prenda tejida)

ribald [ˈrɪbəld] *adj* **:** escabroso, procaz

ribbon [ˈrɪbən] *n* **1 :** cinta *f* **2 to tear to ribbons :** hacer jirones

rice [ˈraɪs] *n* **:** arroz *m*

rich [ˈrɪtʃ] *adj* **1** WEALTHY **:** rico **2** SUMPTUOUS **:** suntuoso, lujoso **3 :** pesado <rich foods : comida pesada> **4** ABUNDANT **:** abundante **5 :** vivo, intenso <rich colors : colores vivos> **6** FERTILE **:** fértil, rico

riches [ˈrɪtʃəz] *npl* **:** riquezas *fpl*

richly [ˈrɪtʃli] *adv* **1** SUMPTUOUSLY **:** suntuosamente, ricamente **2** ABUNDANTLY **:** abundantemente **3 richly deserved :** bien merecido

richness [ˈrɪtʃnəs] *n* **:** riqueza *f*

rickets [ˈrɪkəts] *n* **:** raquitismo *m*

rickety [ˈrɪkəṭi] *adj* **:** desvencijado, destartalado

ricksha *or* **rickshaw** [ˈrɪkˌʃɔ] *n* **:** cochecillo *m* tirado por un hombre

ricochet[1] [ˈrɪkəˌʃeɪ] *vi* **-cheted** [-ˌʃeɪd] *or* **-chetted** [-ˌʃɛṭəd]; **-cheting** [-ˌʃeɪɪŋ] *or* **-chetting** [-ˌʃɛṭɪŋ] **:** rebotar

ricochet[2] *n* **:** rebote *m*

rid [ˈrɪd] *vt* **rid; ridding 1** FREE **:** librar <to rid the city of thieves : librar la ciudad de ladrones> **2 to rid oneself of :** desembarazarse de

riddance [ˈrɪdənts] *n* **:** libramiento *m* <good riddance! : ¡adiós y buen viaje!, ¡vete con viento fresco!>

riddle[1] [ˈrɪdəl] *vt* **-dled; -dling :** acribillar <riddled with bullets : acribillado a balazos> <riddled with errors : lleno de errores>

riddle[2] *n* **:** acertijo *m,* adivinanza *f*

ride[1] [ˈraɪd] *v* **rode** [ˈroːd]; **ridden** [ˈrɪdən]; **riding** *vt* **1 :** montar, ir, andar <to ride a horse : montar a caballo> <to ride a bicycle : montar en bicicleta, andar en bicicleta> <to ride the bus : ir en autobús> **2** TRAVERSE **:** recorrer <he rode 5 miles : recorrió 5 millas> **3** TEASE **:** burlarse de, ridiculizar **4** CARRY **:** llevar **5** WEATHER **:** capear <they rode out the storm : capearon el temporal> **6 to ride the waves :** surcar los mares — *vi* **1 :** montar a caballo, cabalgar **2** TRAVEL **:** ir, viajar (en coche, en bicicleta, etc.) **3** RUN **:** andar, marchar <the car rides well : el coche anda bien> **4 to ride at anchor :** estar fondeado **5 to let things ride :** dejar pasar las cosas

ride[2] *n* **1 :** paseo *m,* vuelta *f* (en coche, en bicicleta, a caballo) <to go for a ride : dar una vuelta> <to give someone a ride : llevar en coche a alguien> **2 :** aparato *m* (en un parque de diversiones)

rider [ˈraɪdər] *n* **1 :** jinete *mf* <the rider fell off his horse : el jinete se cayó de su caballo> **2** CYCLIST **:** ciclista *mf* **3** MOTORCYCLIST **:** motociclista *mf* **4** CLAUSE **:** cláusula *f* añadida

ridge [ˈrɪdʒ] *n* **1** CHAIN **:** cadena *f* (de montañas o cerros) **2 :** caballete *m* (de un techo), cresta *f* (de una ola o una montaña), cordoncillo *m* (de telas)

ridicule[1] [ˈrɪdəˌkjuːl] *vt* **-culed; -culing :** burlarse de, mofarse de, ridiculizar

ridicule[2] *n* **:** burlas *fpl*

ridiculous [rəˈdɪkjələs] *adj* **:** ridículo, absurdo

ridiculously [rəˈdɪkjələsli] *adv* **:** de forma ridícula

rife [ˈraɪf] *adj* **:** abundante, común <to be rife with : estar plagado de>

riffraff [ˈrɪfˌræf] *n* **:** chusma *f,* gentuza *f*

rifle[1] [ˈraɪfəl] *v* **-fled; -fling** *vt* RANSACK **:** desvalijar, saquear — *vi* **: to rifle through :** revolver

rifle[2] *n* **:** rifle *m,* fusil *m*

rift [ˈrɪft] *n* **1** FISSURE **:** grieta *f,* fisura *f* **2** BREAK **:** ruptura *f* (entre personas), división *f* (dentro de un grupo)

rig[1] [ˈrɪg] *vt* **rigged; rigging 1 :** aparejar (un barco) **2** EQUIP **:** equipar **3** FIX **:** amañar (una elección, etc.) **4 to rig up** CONSTRUCT **:** construir, erigir **5 to rig oneself out as :** vestirse de

rig[2] *n* **1 :** aparejo *m* (de un barco) **2** *or* **oil rig :** torre *f* de perforación, plataforma *f* petrolífera

rigging [ˈrɪgɪŋ, -gən] *n* **:** jarcia *f,* aparejo *m*

right[1] [ˈraɪt] *vt* **1** FIX, RESTORE **:** reparar <to right the economy : reparar la economía> **2** STRAIGHTEN **:** enderezar

right[2] *adv* **1 :** bien <to live right : vivir bien> **2** PRECISELY **:** precisamente, justo <right in the middle : justo en medio> **3** DIRECTLY, STRAIGHT **:** derecho, directamente <he went right home : fue derecho a casa> **4** IMMEDIATELY **:** inmediatamente <right after lunch : inmediatamente después del almuerzo> **5** COMPLETELY **:** completamente <he felt right at home : se sintió completamente cómodo> **6 :** a la derecha <to look left and right : mirar a la izquierda y a la derecha>

right[3] *adj* **1** UPRIGHT **:** bueno, honrado <right conduct : conducta honrada> **2** CORRECT **:** correcto <the right answer : la respuesta correcta> **3** APPROPRIATE **:** apropiado, adecuado, debido <the right man for the job : el hombre perfecto para el trabajo> **4** STRAIGHT **:** recto <a right line : una línea recta> **5 :** derecho <the right hand : la mano derecha> **6** SOUND **:** bien <he's not in his right mind : no está bien de la cabeza>

right[4] *n* **1** GOOD **:** bien *m* <to do right : hacer el bien> **2 :** derecha *f* <on the right : a la derecha> **3** *or* **right hand :** mano *f* derecha **4** ENTITLEMENT **:** derecho *m* <the right to vote : el derecho a votar> <women's rights : los derechos de la mujer> **5 the Right :** la derecha (en la política)

right angle *n* : ángulo *m* recto
right–angled [ˈraɪtˈæŋgəld] *or* **right–angle** [-gəl] *adj* **1** : en ángulo recto **2 right–angled triangle** : triángulo *m* rectángulo
righteous [ˈraɪtʃəs] *adj* : recto, honrado — **righteously** *adv*
righteousness [ˈraɪtʃəsnəs] *n* : rectitud *f*, honradez *f*
rightful [ˈraɪtfəl] *adj* **1** JUST : justo **2** LAWFUL : legítimo — **rightfully** *adv*
right–hand [ˈraɪtˈhænd] *adj* **1** : situado a la derecha **2** RIGHT-HANDED : para la mano derecha, con la mano derecha **3 right–hand man** : brazo *m* derecho
right–handed [ˈraɪtˈhændəd] *adj* **1** : diestro <a right-handed pitcher : un lanzador diestro> **2** : para la mano derecha, con la mano derecha **3** CLOCKWISE : en la dirección de las manecillas del reloj
rightly [ˈraɪtli] *adv* **1** JUSTLY : justamente, con razón **2** PROPERLY : debidamente, apropiadamente **3** CORRECTLY : correctamente
right–of–way [ˈraɪtəˈweɪ, -əv-] *n, pl* **rights–of–way 1** : preferencia (del tráfico) **2** ACCESS : derecho *m* de paso
rightward [ˈraɪtwərd] *adj* : a la derecha, hacia la derecha
right–wing [ˈraɪtˈwɪŋ] *adj* : derechista
right wing *n* **the right wing** : la derecha
right–winger [ˈraɪtˈwɪŋər] *n* : derechista *mf*
rigid [ˈrɪdʒɪd] *adj* : rígido — **rigidly** *adv*
rigidity [rɪˈdʒɪdət̬i] *n, pl* **-ties** : rigidez *f*
rigmarole [ˈrɪgməˌroːl, ˈrɪgə-] *n* **1** NONSENSE : galimatías *m*, disparates *mpl* **2** PROCEDURES : trámites *mpl*
rigor [ˈrɪgər] *n* : rigor *m*
rigor mortis [ˌrɪgərˈmɔrt̬əs] *n* : rigidez *f* cadavérica
rigorous [ˈrɪgərəs] *adj* : rigoroso — **rigorously** *adv*
rile [ˈraɪl] *vt* **riled; riling** : irritar
rill [ˈrɪl] *n* : riachuelo *m*
rim [ˈrɪm] *n* **1** EDGE : borde *m* **2** : llanta *f*, rin *m Col, Mex* (de una rueda) **3** FRAME : montura *f* (de anteojos)
rime [ˈraɪm] *n* : escarcha *f*
rind [ˈraɪnd] *n* : corteza *f*
ring[1] [ˈrɪŋ] *v* **rang** [ˈræŋ]; **rung** [ˈrʌŋ]; **ringing** *vi* **1** : sonar <the doorbell rang : el timbre sonó> <to ring for : llamar> **2** RESOUND : resonar **3** SEEM : parecer <to ring true : parecer cierto> — *vt* **1** : tocar, hacer sonar (un timbre, una alarma, etc.) **2** SURROUND : cercar, rodear
ring[2] *n* **1** : anillo *m*, sortija *f* <wedding ring : anillo de matrimonio> **2** BAND : aro *m*, anillo *m* <piston ring : aro de émbolo> **3** CIRCLE : círculo *m* **4** ARENA : arena *f*, ruedo *m* <a boxing ring : un cuadrilátero, un ring> **5** GANG : banda *f* (de ladrones, etc.) **6** SOUND : timbre *m*, sonido *m* **7** CALL : llamada *f* (por teléfono)
ringer [ˈrɪŋər] *n* **to be a dead ringer for** : ser un vivo retrato de
ringleader [ˈrɪŋˌliːdər] *n* : cabecilla *mf*
ringlet [ˈrɪŋlət] *n* : sortija *f*, rizo *m*
ringworm [ˈrɪŋˌwərm] *n* : tiña *f*
rink [ˈrɪŋk] *n* : pista *f* <skating rink : pista de patinaje>
rinse[1] [ˈrɪnts] *vt* **rinsed; rinsing** : enjuagar <to rinse out one's mouth : enjuagarse la boca>
rinse[2] *n* : enjuague *m*
riot[1] [ˈraɪət] *vi* : amotinarse
riot[2] *n* : motín *m*, tumulto *m*, alboroto *m*
rioter [ˈraɪət̬ər] *n* : alborotador *m*, -dora *f*
riotous [ˈraɪət̬əs] *adj* **1** UNRULY, WILD : desenfrenado, alborotado **2** ABUNDANT : abundante
rip[1] [ˈrɪp] *v* **ripped; ripping** *vt* : rasgar, arrancar, desgarrar — *vi* : rasgarse, desgarrarse
rip[2] *n* : rasgón *m*, desgarrón *m*
ripe [ˈraɪp] *adj* **riper; ripest 1** MATURE : maduro <ripe fruit : fruta madura> **2** READY : listo, preparado
ripen [ˈraɪpən] *v* : madurar
ripeness [ˈraɪpnəs] *n* : madurez *f*
rip–off [ˈrɪpˌɔf] *n* **1** THEFT : robo *m* **2** SWINDLE : estafa *f*, timo *m fam*
ripple[1] [ˈrɪpəl] *v* **-pled; -pling** *vi* : rizarse, ondear, ondular — *vt* : rizar
ripple[2] *n* : onda *f*, ondulación *f*
rise[1] [ˈraɪz] *vi* **rose** [ˈroːz]; **risen** [ˈrɪzən]; **rising 1** GET UP : levantarse <to rise to one's feet : ponerse de pie> **2** : elevarse, alzarse <the mountains rose to the west : las montañas se elevaron al oeste> **3** : salir (dícese del sol y de la luna) **4** : subir (dícese de las aguas, del humo, etc.) <the river rose : las aguas subieron de nivel> **5** INCREASE : aumentar, subir **6** ORIGINATE : nacer, proceder **7 to rise in rank** : ascender **8 to rise up** REBEL : sublevarse, rebelarse
rise[2] *n* **1** ASCENT : ascensión *f*, subida *f* **2** ORIGIN : origen *m* **3** ELEVATION : elevación *f* **4** INCREASE : subida *f*, aumento *m*, alzamiento *m* **5** SLOPE : pendiente *f*, cuesta *f*
riser [ˈraɪzər] *n* **1** : contrahuella *f* (de una escalera) **2 early riser** : madrugador *m*, -dora *f* **3 late riser** : dormilón *m*, -lona *f*
risk[1] [ˈrɪsk] *vt* : arriesgar
risk[2] *n* : riesgo *m*, peligro *m* <at risk : en peligro> <at your own risk : por su cuenta y riesgo>
risky [ˈrɪski] *adj* **riskier; -est** : arriesgado, peligroso, riesgoso
risqué [rɪˈskeɪ] *adj* : escabroso, picante, subido de tono
rite [ˈraɪt] *n* : rito *m*

ritual[1] ['rɪtʃʊəl] *adj* : ritual — **ritually** *adv*
ritual[2] *n* : ritual *m*
rival[1] ['raɪvəl] *vt* **-valed** *or* **-valled; -valing** *or* **-valling** : rivalizar con, competir con
rival[2] *adj* : competidor, rival
rival[3] *n* : rival *mf;* competidor *m,* -dora *f*
rivalry ['raɪvəlri] *n, pl* **-ries** : rivalidad *f,* competencia *f*
river ['rɪvər] *n* : río *m*
riverbank ['rɪvər,bæŋk] *n* : ribera *f,* orilla *f*
riverbed ['rɪvər,bɛd] *n* : cauce *m,* lecho *m*
riverside ['rɪvər,saɪd] *n* : ribera *f,* orilla *f*
rivet[1] ['rɪvət] *vt* **1** : remachar **2** FIX : fijar (los ojos, etc.) **3** FASCINATE : fascinar, cautivar
rivet[2] *n* : remache *m*
rivulet ['rɪvjələt] *n* : arroyo *m,* riachuelo *m* <rivulets of sweat : gotas de sudor>
roach ['ro:tʃ] → **cockroach**
road ['ro:d] *n* **1** : carretera *f,* calle *f,* camino *m* **2** PATH : camino *m,* sendero *m,* vía *f* <on the road to a solution : en vías de una solución>
roadblock ['ro:d,blɑk] *n* : control *m*
roadrunner ['ro:d,rʌnər] *n* : correcaminos *m*
roadside ['ro:d,saɪd] *n* : borde *m* de la carretera
roadway ['ro:d,weɪ] *n* : carretera *f,* calzada *f*
roam ['ro:m] *vi* : vagar, deambular, errar — *vt* : vagar por
roan[1] ['ro:n] *adj* : ruano
roan[2] *n* : caballo *m* ruano
roar[1] ['ror] *vi* : rugir, bramar <to roar with laughter : reírse a carcajadas> — *vt* : decir a gritos
roar[2] *n* **1** : rugido *m,* bramido *m* (de un animal) **2** DIN : clamor *m* (de gente), fragor *m* (del trueno), estruendo *m* (del tráfico, etc.)
roast[1] ['ro:st] *vt* : asar (carne, papas), tostar (café, nueces) — *vi* : asarse
roast[2] *adj* **1** : asado <roast chicken : pollo asado> **2 roast beef** : rosbif *m*
roast[3] *n* : asado *m*
rob ['rɑb] *v* **robbed; robbing** *vt* **1** STEAL : robar **2** DEPRIVE : privar, quitar — *vi* : robar
robber ['rɑbər] *n* : ladrón *m,* -drona *f*
robbery ['rɑbəri] *n, pl* **-beries** : robo *m*
robe[1] ['ro:b] *vt* **robed; robing** : vestirse
robe[2] *n* **1** : toga *f* (de magistrados, etc.), sotana *f* (de eclesiásticos) <robe of office : traje de ceremonias> **2** BATHROBE : bata *f*
robin ['rɑbən] *n* : petirrojo *m*
robot ['ro:,bɑt, -bət] *n* : robot *m*
robust [ro'bʌst, 'ro:,bʌst] *adj* : robusto, fuerte — **robustly** *adv*
rock[1] ['rɑk] *vt* **1** : acunar (a un niño), mecer (una cuna) **2** SHAKE : sacudir — *vi* SWAY : mecerse, balancearse
rock[2] *adj* : de rock
rock[3] *n* **1** ROCKING : balanceo *m* **2** *or* **rock music** : rock *m,* música *f* rock **3** : roca *f* (substancia) **4** STONE : piedra *f*
rock and roll *n* : rock and roll *m*
rocker ['rɑkər] *n* **1** : balancín *m* **2** *or* **rocking chair** : mecedora *f,* balancín *m* **3 to be off one's rocker** : estar chiflado, estar loco
rocket[1] ['rɑkət] *vi* : dispararse, subir rápidamente
rocket[2] *n* : cohete *m*
rocking horse *n* : caballito *m* (de balancín)
rock salt *n* : sal *f* gema
rocky ['rɑki] *adj* **rockier; -est 1** : rocoso, pedregoso **2** UNSTEADY : inestable
rod ['rɑd] *n* **1** BAR : barra *f,* varilla *f,* vara *f* (de madera) <a fishing rod : una caña (de pescar)> **2** : medida *f* de longitud equivalente a 5.03 metros (5 yardas)
rode → **ride**[1]
rodent ['ro:dənt] *n* : roedor *m*
rodeo ['ro:di,o:, ro'deɪ,o:] *n, pl* **-deos** : rodeo *m*
roe ['ro:] *n* : hueva *f*
roe deer *n* : corzo *m*
rogue ['ro:g] *n* SCOUNDREL : pícaro *m,* -ra *f;* pillo *m,* -lla *f*
roguish ['ro:gɪʃ] *adj* : pícaro, travieso
role ['ro:l] *n* : papel *m,* función *f,* rol *m*
roll[1] ['ro:l] *vt* **1** : hacer rodar <to roll the ball : hacer rodar la pelota> <to roll one's eyes : poner los ojos en blanco> **2** : liar (un cigarillo) **3** *or* **to roll up** : enrollar <to roll (oneself) up into a ball : hacerse una bola> **4** FLATTEN : estirar (masa), laminar (metales), pasar el rodillo por (el césped) **5 to roll up one's sleeves** : arremangarse — *vi* **1** : rodar <the ball kept on rolling : la pelota siguió rodando> **2** SWAY : balancearse <the ship rolled in the waves : el barco se balanceó en las olas> **3** REVERBERATE, SOUND : tronar (dícese del trueno), redoblar (dícese de un tambor) **4 to roll along** PROCEED : ponerse en marcha **5 to roll around** : revolcarse **6 to roll by** : pasar **7 to roll over** : dar una vuelta
roll[2] *n* **1** LIST : lista *f* <to call the roll : pasar lista> <to have on the roll : tener inscrito> **2** *or* **bread roll** : panecito *m,* bolillo *m Mex* **3** : rollo *m* (de papel, de tela, etc.) <a roll of film : un carrete> <a roll of bills : un fajo> **4** : redoble *m* (de tambores), retumbo *m* (del trueno, etc.) **5** ROLLING, SWAYING : balanceo *m*
roller ['ro:lər] *n* **1** : rodillo *m* **2** CURLER : rulo *m*
roller coaster ['ro:lər,ko:stər] *n* : montaña *f* rusa

roller–skate ['ro:lər,skeɪt] *vi* **-skated; -skating** : patinar (sobre ruedas)
roller skate *n* : patín *m* (de ruedas)
rollicking ['rɑlɪkɪŋ] *adj* : animado, alegre
rolling pin *n* : rodillo *m*
Roman[1] ['ro:mən] *adj* : romano
Roman[2] *n* : romano *m,* -na *f*
Roman Catholic *n* : católico *m,* -ca *f* — **Roman Catholic** *adj*
Roman Catholicism *n* : catolicismo *m*
romance[1] [ro'mænts, 'ro:,mænts] *vi* **-manced; -mancing** FANTASIZE : fantasear
romance[2] *n* **1** : romance *m,* novela *f* de caballerías **2** : novela *f* de amor, novela *f* romántica **3** AFFAIR : romance *m,* amorío *m*
Romanian [rʊ'meɪniən, ro-] *n* **1** : rumano *m,* -na *f* **2** : rumano *m* (idioma) — **Romanian** *adj*
Roman numeral *n* : número *m* romano
romantic [ro'mæntɪk] *adj* : romántico — **romantically** [-tɪkli] *adv*
romp[1] ['rɑmp] *vi* FROLIC : retozar, jugetear
romp[2] *n* : retozo *m*
roof[1] ['ru:f, 'rʊf] *vt* : techar
roof[2] *n, pl* **roofs** ['ru:fs, 'rʊfs; 'ru:vz, 'rʊvz] **1** : techo *m,* tejado *m,* techado *m* **2 roof of the mouth** : paladar *m*
roofing ['ru:fɪŋ, 'rʊfɪŋ] *n* : techumbre *f*
rooftop ['ru:f,tɑp, 'rʊf-] *n* ROOF : tejado *m*
rook[1] ['rʊk] *vt* CHEAT : defraudar, estafar, timar
rook[2] *n* **1** : grajo *m* (ave) **2** : torre *f* (en ajedrez)
rookie ['rʊki] *n* : novato *m,* -ta *f*
room[1] ['ru:m, 'rʊm] *vi* LODGE : alojarse, hospedarse
room[2] *n* **1** SPACE : espacio *m,* sitio *m,* lugar *m* <to make room for : hacer lugar para> **2** : cuarto *m,* habitación *f* (en una casa), sala *f* (para reuniones, etc.) **3** BEDROOM : dormitorio *m,* habitación *f,* pieza *f* **4** (*indicating possibility or opportunity*) <room for improvement : posibilidad de mejorar> <there's no room for error : no hay lugar para errores>
roomer ['ru:mər, 'rʊmər] *n* : inquilino *m,* -na *f*
rooming house *n* : pensión *f*
roommate ['ru:m,meɪt, 'rʊm-] *n* : compañero *m,* -ra *f* de cuarto
roomy ['ru:mi, 'rʊmi] *adj* **roomier; -est 1** SPACIOUS : espacioso, amplio **2** LOOSE : suelto, holgado <a roomy blouse : una blusa holgada>
roost[1] ['ru:st] *vi* : posarse, dormir (en una percha)
roost[2] *n* : percha *f*
rooster ['ru:stər, 'rʊs-] *n* : gallo *m*
root[1] ['ru:t, 'rʊt] *vi* **1** : arraigar <the plant rooted easily : la planta arraigó con facilidad> <deeply rooted traditions : tradiciones profundamente arraigadas> **2** : hozar (dícese de los cerdos) <to root around in : hurgar en> **3 to root for** : apoyar a, alentar — *vt* **to root out** *or* **to root up** : desarraigar (plantas), extirpar (problemas, etc.)
root[2] *n* **1** : raíz *f* (de una planta) **2** ORIGIN : origen *m,* raíz *f* **3** CORE : centro *m,* núcleo *m* <to get to the root of the matter : ir al centro del asunto>
rootless ['ru:tləs, 'rʊt-] *adj* : desarraigado
rope[1] ['ro:p] *vt* **roped; roping 1** TIE : amarrar, atar **2** LASSO : lazar **3 to rope off** : acordonar
rope[2] *n* : soga *f,* cuerda *f*
rosary ['ro:zəri] *n, pl* **-ries** : rosario *m*
rose[1] → **rise[1]**
rose[2] ['ro:z] *adj* : rosa, color de rosa
rose[3] *n* **1** : rosal *m* (planta), rosa *f* (flor) **2** : rosa *m* (color)
rosebush ['ro:z,bʊʃ] *n* : rosal *m*
rosemary ['ro:z,mɛri] *n, pl* **-maries** : romero *m*
rosette [ro'zɛt] *n* : escarapela *f* (hecho de cintas), roseta *f* (en arquitectura)
Rosh Hashanah [,rɑʃhɑ'ʃɑnə, ,ro:ʃ-] *n* : el Año Nuevo judío
rosin ['rɑzən] *n* : colofonia *f*
roster ['rɑstər] *n* : lista *f*
rostrum ['rɑstrəm] *n, pl* **-trums** *or* **-tra** [-trə] : tribuna *f,* estrado *m*
rosy ['ro:zi] *adj* **rosier; -est 1** : sonrosado, de color rosa **2** PROMISING : prometedor, halagüeno
rot[1] ['rɑt] *v* **rotted; rotting** *vi* : pudrirse, descomponerse — *vt* : pudrir, descomponer
rot[2] *n* : putrefacción *f,* descomposición *f,* podredumbre *f*
rotary[1] ['ro:ţəri] *adj* : rotativo, rotatorio
rotary[2] *n, pl* **-ries 1** : máquina *f* rotativa **2** TRAFFIC CIRCLE : rotonda *f,* glorieta *f*
rotate ['ro:,teɪt] *v* **-tated; -tating** *vi* REVOLVE : girar, rotar — *vt* **1** TURN : hacer girar, darle vueltas a **2** ALTERNATE : alternar
rotation [ro'teɪʃən] *n* : rotación *f*
rote ['ro:t] *n* **to learn by rote** : aprender de memoria
rotor ['ro:ţər] *n* : rotor *m*
rotten ['rɑţən] *adj* **1** PUTRID : podrido, putrefacto **2** CORRUPT : corrompido **3** BAD : malo <a rotten day : un día malísimo>
rottenness ['rɑtənnəs] *n* : podredumbre *f*
rotund [ro'tʌnd] *adj* **1** ROUNDED : redondeado **2** PLUMP : regordete *fam,* llenito *fam*
rouge ['ru:ʒ, 'ru:dʒ] *n* : colorete *m*
rough[1] ['rʌf] *vt* **1** ROUGHEN : poner áspero **2 to rough out** SKETCH : esbozar, bosquejar **3 to rough up** BEAT : darle una paliza (a alguien) **4 to rough it** : vivir sin comodidades

rough[2] *adj* **1** COARSE **:** áspero, basto **2** UNEVEN **:** desigual, escabroso, accidentado (dícese del terreno) **3 :** agitado (dícese del mar), tempestuoso (dícese del tiempo), violento (dícese del viento) **4** VIOLENT **:** violento, brutal <a rough neighborhood : un barrio peligroso> **5** DIFFICULT **:** duro, difícil **6** CRUDE **:** rudo, tosco, burdo <a rough cottage : una casita tosca> <a rough draft : un borrador> <a rough sketch : un bosquejo> **7** APPROXIMATE **:** aproximado <a rough idea : una idea aproximada>
rough[3] *n* **1 the rough :** el rough (en golf) **2 in the rough :** en borrador
roughage [ˈrʌfɪdʒ] *n* **:** fibra *f*
roughen [ˈrʌfən] *vt* **:** poner áspero — *vi* **:** ponerse áspero
roughly [ˈrʌfli] *adv* **1 :** bruscamente <to treat roughly : maltratar> **2** CRUDELY **:** burdamente **3** APPROXIMATELY **:** aproximadamente, más o menos
roughneck [ˈrʌfˌnɛk] *n* **:** matón *m*
roughness [ˈrʌfnəs] *n* **:** rudeza *f,* aspereza *f*
roulette [ruːˈlɛt] *n* **:** ruleta *f*
round[1] [ˈraʊnd] *vt* **1 :** redondear <she rounded the edges : redondeó los bordes> **2** TURN **:** doblar <to round the corner : dar la vuelta a la esquina> **3 to round off :** redondear (un número) **4 to round off** *or* **to round out** COMPLETE **:** rematar, terminar **5 to round up** GATHER **:** reunir
round[2] *adv* → **around**[1]
round[3] *adj* **1 :** redondo <a round table : una mesa redonda> <in round numbers : en números redondos> <round shoulders : espaldas cargadas> **2 round trip :** viaje *m* de ida y vuelta
round[4] *n* **1** CIRCLE **:** círculo *m* **2** SERIES **:** serie *f,* sucesión *f* <a round of talks : una ronda de negociaciones> <the daily round : la rutina cotidiana> **3 :** asalto *m* (en boxeo), recorrido *m* (en golf), vuelta *f* (en varios juegos) **4 :** salva *f* (de aplausos) **5 round of drinks :** ronda *f* **6 round of ammunition :** disparo *m,* cartucho *m* **7 rounds** *npl* **:** recorridos *mpl* (de un cartero), rondas *fpl* (de un vigilante), visitas *fpl* (de un médico) <to make the rounds : hacer visitas>
round[5] *prep* → **around**[2]
roundabout [ˈraʊndəˌbaʊt] *adj* **:** indirecto <to speak in a roundabout way : hablar con rodeos>
roundly [ˈraʊndli] *adv* **1** THOROUGHLY **:** completamente **2** BLUNTLY **:** francamente, rotundamente **3** VIGOROUSLY **:** con vigor
roundness [ˈraʊndnəs] *n* **:** redondez *f*
roundup [ˈraʊndˌʌp] *n* **1 :** rodeo *m* (de animales), redada *f* (de delincuentes, etc.) **2** SUMMARY **:** resumen *m*
round up *vt* **1 :** rodear (ganado), reunir (personas) **2** SUMMARIZE **:** hacer un resumen de
roundworm [ˈraʊndˌwərm] *n* **:** lombriz *f* intestinal
rouse [ˈraʊz] *vt* **roused; rousing 1** AWAKE **:** despertar **2** EXCITE **:** excitar <it roused him to fury : lo enfureció>
rout[1] [ˈraʊt] *vt* **1** DEFEAT **:** derrotar, aplastar **2 to rout out :** hacer salir
rout[2] *n* **1** DISPERSAL **:** desbandada *f,* dispersión *f* **2** DEFEAT **:** derrota *f* aplastante
route[1] [ˈruːt, ˈraʊt] *vt* **routed; routing :** dirigir, enviar, encaminar
route[2] *n* **:** camino *m,* ruta *f,* recorrido *m*
routine[1] [ruːˈtiːn] *adj* **:** rutinario — **routinely** *adv*
routine[2] *n* **:** rutina *f*
rove [ˈroːv] *v* **roved; roving** *vi* **:** vagar, errar — *vt* **:** errar por
rover [ˈroːvər] *n* **:** vagabundo *m,* -da *f*
row[1] [ˈroː] *vt* **1 :** avanzar a remo <to row a boat : remar> **2 :** llevar a remo <he rowed me to shore : me llevó hasta la orilla> — *vi* **:** remar
row[2] [ˈraʊ] *n* **1 :** paseo *m* en barca <to go for a row : salir a remar> **2** LINE, RANK **:** fila *f,* hilera *f* **3** SERIES **:** serie *f* <three days in a row : tres días seguidos> **4** RACKET **:** estruendo *m,* bulla *f* **5** QUARREL **:** pelea *f,* riña *f*
rowboat [ˈroːˌboːt] *n* **:** bote *m* de remos
rowdiness [ˈraʊdinəs] *n* **:** bulla *f*
rowdy[1] [ˈraʊdi] *adj* **-dier; -est :** escandaloso, alborotador
rowdy[2] *n, pl* **-dies :** alborotador *m,* -dora *f*
royal[1] [ˈrɔɪəl] *adj* **:** real — **royally** *adv*
royal[2] *n* **:** persona de linaje real, miembro de la familia real
royalty [ˈrɔɪəlti] *n, pl* **-ties 1 :** realeza *f* (posición) **2 :** miembros *mpl* de la familia real **3 royalties** *npl* **:** derechos *mpl* de autor
rub[1] [ˈrʌb] *v* **rubbed; rubbing** *vt* **1 :** frotar, restregar <to rub one's hands together : frotarse las manos> **2** MASSAGE **:** friccionar, masajear **3** CHAFE **:** rozar **4** POLISH **:** frotar, pulir **5** SCRUB **:** fregar **6 to rub elbows with :** codarse con **7 to rub someone the wrong way :** sacar de quicio a alguien, caerle mal a alguien — *vi* **to rub against :** rozar
rub[2] *n* **1** RUBBING **:** frotamiento *m,* fricción *f* **2** DIFFICULTY **:** problema *m*
rubber [ˈrʌbər] *n* **1 :** goma *f,* caucho *m,* hule *m Mex* **2 rubbers** *npl* OVERSHOES **:** chanclos *mpl*
rubber band *n* **:** goma *f* (elástica), gomita *f*
rubber–stamp [ˈrʌbərˈstæmp] *vt* **1** APPROVE **:** aprobar, autorizar **2** STAMP **:** sellar
rubber stamp *n* **:** sello *m* (de goma)
rubbery [ˈrʌbəri] *adj* **:** gomoso

rubbish [ˈrʌbɪʃ] *n* : basura *f,* desechos *mpl,* desperdicios *mpl*

rubble [ˈrʌbəl] *n* : escombros *mpl,* ripio *m*

ruble [ˈruːbəl] *n* : rublo *m*

ruby [ˈruːbi] *n, pl* **-bies 1** : rubí *m* (gema) **2** : color *m* de rubí

rudder [ˈrʌdər] *n* : timón *m*

ruddy [ˈrʌdi] *adj* **-dier; -est** : rubicundo (dícese de la cara, etc.), rojizo (dícese del cielo)

rude [ˈruːd] *adj* **ruder; rudest 1** CRUDE : tosco, rústico **2** IMPOLITE : grosero, descortés, maleducado **3** ABRUPT : brusco <a rude awakening : una sorpresa desagradable>

rudely [ˈruːdli] *adv* : groseramente

rudeness [ˈruːdnəs] *n* **1** IMPOLITENESS : grosería *f,* descortesía *f,* falta *f* de educación **2** ROUGHNESS : tosquedad *f* **3** SUDDENNESS : brusquedad *f*

rudiment [ˈruːdəmənt] *n* : rudimento *m,* noción *f* básica <the rudiments of Spanish : los rudimentos del español>

rudimentary [ˌruːdəˈmɛntəri] *adj* : rudimentario, básico

rue [ˈruː] *vt* **rued; ruing** : lamentar, arrepentirse de

rueful [ˈruːfəl] *adj* **1** PITIFUL : lastimoso **2** REGRETFUL : arrepentido, pesaroso

ruffian [ˈrʌfiən] *n* : matón *m*

ruffle[1] [ˈrʌfəl] *vt* **-fled; -fling 1** AGITATE : agitar, rizar (agua) **2** RUMPLE : arrugar (ropa), despeinar (pelo) **3** ERECT : erizar (plumas) **4** VEX : alterar, irritar, perturbar **5** : fruncir volantes en (tela)

ruffle[2] *n* FLOUNCE : volante *m*

ruffly [ˈrʌfəli] *adj* : con volantes

rug [ˈrʌg] *n* : alfombra *f,* tapete *m*

rugged [ˈrʌgəd] *adj* **1** ROUGH, UNEVEN : accidentado, escabroso <rugged mountains : montañas accidentadas> **2** HARSH : duro, severo **3** ROBUST, STURDY : robusto, fuerte

ruin[1] [ˈruːən] *vt* **1** DESTROY : destruir, arruinar **2** BANKRUPT : arruinar, hacer quebrar

ruin[2] *n* **1** : ruina *f* <to fall into ruin : caer en ruinas> **2** : ruina *f,* perdición *f* <to be the ruin of : ser la perdición de> **3 ruins** *npl* : ruinas *fpl,* restos *mpl* <the ruins of the ancient temple : las ruinas del templo antiguo>

ruinous [ˈruːənəs] *adj* : ruinoso

rule[1] [ˈruːl] *v* **ruled; ruling** *vt* **1** CONTROL, GOVERN : gobernar (un país), controlar (las emociones) **2** DECIDE : decidir, fallar <the judge ruled that... : el juez falló que...> **3** DRAW : trazar con una regla — *vi* **1** GOVERN : gobernar, reinar **2** PREVAIL : prevalecer, imperar **3 to rule against** : fallar en contra de

rule[2] *n* **1** REGULATION : regla *f,* norma *f* **2** CUSTOM, HABIT : regla *f* general <as a rule : por lo general> **3** GOVERNMENT : gobierno *m,* dominio *m* **4** RULER : regla *f* (para medir)

ruler [ˈruːlər] *n* **1** LEADER, SOVEREIGN : gobernante *mf;* soberano *m,* -na *f* **2** : regla *f* (para medir)

ruling [ˈruːlɪŋ] *n* : resolución *f,* fallo *m*

rum [ˈrʌm] *n* : ron *m*

Rumanian [rʊˈmeɪniən] → **Romanian**

rumble[1] [ˈrʌmbəl] *vi* **-bled; -bling** : retumbar, hacer ruidos (dícese del estómago)

rumble[2] *n* : estruendo *m,* ruido *m* sordo, retumbo *m*

ruminant[1] [ˈruːmənənt] *adj* : rumiante

ruminant[2] *n* : rumiante *m*

ruminate [ˈruːməˌneɪt] *vi* **-nated; -nating 1** : rumiar (en zoología) **2** REFLECT : reflexionar, rumiar

rummage [ˈrʌmɪdʒ] *v* **-maged; -maging** *vi* : hurgar — *vt* RANSACK : revolver <they rummaged the attic : revolvieron el ático>

rummy [ˈrʌmi] *n* : rummy *m* (juego de naipes)

rumor[1] [ˈruːmər] *vt* : rumorear <it is rumored that. . . : se rumorea que. . . , se dice que. . .>

rumor[2] *n* : rumor *m*

rump [ˈrʌmp] *n* **1** : ancas *fpl,* grupa *f* (de un animal) **2** : cadera *f* <rump steak : filete de cadera>

rumple [ˈrʌmpəl] *vt* **-pled; -pling** : arrugar (ropa, etc.), despeinar (pelo)

rumpus [ˈrʌmpəs] *n* : lío *m,* jaleo *m fam*

run[1] [ˈrʌn] *v* **ran** [ˈræn]; **run; running** *vi* **1** : correr <she ran to catch the bus : corrió para alcanzar el autobús> <run and fetch the doctor : corre a buscar al médico> **2** : circular, correr <the train runs between Detroit and Chicago : el tren circula entre Detroit y Chicago> <to run on time : ser puntual> **3** FUNCTION : funcionar, ir <the engine runs on gasoline : el motor funciona con gasolina> <to run smoothly : ir bien> **4** FLOW : correr, ir **5** LAST : durar <the movie runs for two hours : la película dura dos horas> <the contract runs for three years : el contrato es válido por tres años> **6** : desteñir, despintar (dícese de los colores) **7** EXTEND : correr, extenderse **8 to run for office** : postularse, presentarse — *vt* **1** : correr <to run 10 miles : correr 10 millas> <to run errands : hacer los mandados> <to run out of town : hacer salir del pueblo> **2** PASS : pasar **3** DRIVE : llevar en coche **4** OPERATE : hacer funcionar (un motor, etc.) **5** : echar <to run water : echar agua> **6** MANAGE : dirigir, llevar (un negocio, etc.) **7** EXTEND : tender (un cable, etc.) **8 to run a risk** : correr un riesgo

run[2] *n* **1** : carrera *f* <at a run : a la carrera, corriendo> <to go for a run : ir a correr> **2** TRIP : vuelta *f,* paseo *m* (en coche), viaje *m* (en avión) **3** SERIES : serie *f* <a run of disappointments : una serie de desilusiones> <in

the long run : a la larga> <in the short run : a corto plazo> 4 DEMAND : gran demanda *f* <a run on the banks : una corrida bancaria> **5** (*used for theatrical productions and films*) <to have a long run : mantenerse mucho tiempo en la cartelera> **6** TYPE : tipo *m* <the average run of students : el tipo más común de estudiante> **7** : carrera *f* (en béisbol) **8** : carrera *f* (en una media) **9 to have the run of** : tener libre acceso de (una casa, etc.) **10 ski run** : pista *f* (de esquí)

runaway[1] [ˈrʌnəˌweɪ] *adj* **1** FUGITIVE : fugitivo **2** UNCONTROLLABLE : incontrolable, fuera de control <runaway inflation : inflación desenfrenada> <a runaway success : un éxito aplastante>

runaway[2] *n* : fugitivo *m*, -va *f*

rundown [ˈrʌnˌdaʊn] *n* SUMMARY : resumen *m*

run–down [ˈrʌnˈdaʊn] *adj* **1** DILAPIDATED : ruinoso, destartalado **2** SICKLY, TIRED : cansado, débil

rung[1] → **ring**[1]

rung[2] [ˈrʌŋ] *n* : peldaño *m*, escalón *m*

run–in [ˈrʌnˌɪn] *n* : disputa *f*, altercado *m*

runner [ˈrʌnər] *n* **1** RACER : corredor *m*, -dora *f* **2** MESSENGER : mensajero *m*, -ra *f* **3** TRACK : riel *m* (de un cajón, etc.) **4** : patín *m* (de un trineo), cuchilla *f* (de un patín) **5** : estolón *m* (planta)

runner–up [ˌrʌnərˈʌp] *n, pl* **runners–up** : subcampeón *m*, -peona *f*

running [ˈrʌnɪŋ] *adj* **1** FLOWING : corriente <running water : agua corriente> **2** CONTINUOUS : continuo <a running battle : una lucha continua> **3** CONSECUTIVE : seguido <six days running : por seis días seguidos>

run over *vt* : atropellar — *vi* OVERFLOW : rebosar

runt [ˈrʌnt] *n* : animal *m* pequeño <the runt of the litter : el más pequeño de la camada>

runway [ˈrʌnˌweɪ] *n* : pista *f* de aterrizaje

rupee [ruːˈpiː, ˈruːˌ-] *n* : rupia *f*

rupture[1] [ˈrʌptʃər] *v* **-tured; -turing** *vt* **1** BREAK, BURST : romper, reventar **2** : causar una hernia en — *vi* : reventarse

rupture[2] *n* **1** BREAK : ruptura *f* **2** HERNIA : hernia *f*

rural [ˈrʊrəl] *adj* : rural, campestre

ruse [ˈruːs, ˈruːz] *n* : treta *f*, ardid *m*, estratagema *f*

rush[1] [ˈrʌʃ] *vi* : correr, ir de prisa <to rush around : correr de un lado a otro> <to rush off : irse corriendo> — *vt* **1** HURRY : apresurar, apurar **2** ATTACK : abalanzarse sobre, asaltar

rush[2] *adj* : urgente

rush[3] *n* **1** HASTE : prisa *f*, apuro *m* **2** SURGE : ráfaga *f* (de aire), torrente *m* (de aguas), avalancha *f* (de gente) **3** DEMAND : demanda *f* <a rush on sugar : una gran demanda para el azúcar> **4** : carga *f* (en futbol americano) **5** : junco *m* (planta)

russet [ˈrʌsət] *n* : color *m* rojizo

Russian [ˈrʌʃən] *n* **1** : ruso *m*, -sa *f* **2** : ruso *m* (idioma) — **Russian** *adj*

rust[1] [ˈrʌst] *vi* : oxidarse — *vt* : oxidar

rust[2] *n* **1** : herrumbre *f*, orín *m*, óxido *m* (en los metales) **2** : roya *f* (en las plantas)

rustic[1] [ˈrʌstɪk] *adj* : rústico, campestre — **rustically** [-tɪkli] *adv*

rustic[2] *n* : rústico *m*, -ca *f*; campesino *m*, -na *f*

rustle[1] [ˈrʌsəl] *v* **-tled; -tling** *vt* **1** : hacer susurrar, hacer crujir <to rustle a newspaper : hacer crujir un periódico> **2** STEAL : robar (ganado) — *vi* : susurrar, crujir

rustle[2] *n* : murmullo *m*, susurro *m*, crujido *m*

rustler [ˈrʌsələr] *n* : ladrón *m*, -drona *f* de ganado

rusty [ˈrʌsti] *adj* **rustier; -est** : oxidado, herrumbroso

rut [ˈrʌt] *n* **1** GROOVE, TRACK : rodada *f*, surco *m* **2 to be in a rut** : ser esclavo de la rutina

ruthless [ˈruːθləs] *adj* : despiadado, cruel — **ruthlessly** *adv*

ruthlessness [ˈruːθləsnəs] *n* : crueldad *f*, falta *f* de piedad

Rwandan [rʊˈɑndən] *n* : ruandés *m*, -desa *f* — **Rwandan** *adj*

rye [ˈraɪ] *n* **1** : centeno *m* **2** *or* **rye whiskey** : whisky *m* de centeno

S

s [ˈɛs] *n, pl* **s's** *or* **ss** [ˈɛsəz] : decimonovena letra del alfabeto inglés

Sabbath [ˈsæbəθ] *n* **1** : sábado *m* (en el judaísmo) **2** : domingo *m* (en el cristianismo)

saber [ˈseɪbər] *n* : sable *m*

sable [ˈseɪbəl] *n* **1** BLACK : negro *m* **2** : marta *f* cebellina (animal)

sabotage[1] [ˈsæbəˌtɑʒ] *vt* **-taged; -taging** : sabotear

sabotage[2] *n* : sabotaje *m*

sac [ˈsæk] *n* : saco *m* (anatómico)

saccharin [ˈsækərən] *n* : sacarina *f*

saccharine *adj* [ˈsækərən, -ˌriːn, -ˌraɪn] : meloso, empalagoso

sachet [sæˈʃeɪ] *n* : bolsita *f* (perfumada)

sack[1] [ˈsæk] *vt* **1** FIRE : echar (del trabajo), despedir **2** PLUNDER : saquear

sack[2] *n* BAG : saco *m*

sacrament [ˈsækrəmənt] *n* : sacramento *m*

sacramental [ˌsækrəˈmɛntəl] *adj* : sacramental

sacred [ˈseɪkrəd] *adj* **1** RELIGIOUS : sagrado, sacro <sacred texts : textos sagrados> **2** HOLY : sagrado **3 sacred to** : consagrado a

sacrifice[1] [ˈsækrəˌfaɪs] *vt* **-ficed; -ficing 1** : sacrificar **2 to sacrifice oneself** : sacrificarse

sacrifice[2] *n* : sacrificio *m*

sacrilege [ˈsækrəlɪdʒ] *n* : sacrilegio *m*

sacrilegious [ˌsækrəˈlɪdʒəs, -ˈliː-] *adj* : sacrílego

sacrosanct [ˈsækroˌsæŋkt] *adj* : sacrosanto

sad [ˈsæd] *adj* **sadder; saddest** : triste — **sadly** *adv*

sadden [ˈsædən] *vt* : entristecer

saddle[1] [ˈsædəl] *vt* **-dled; -dling** : ensillar

saddle[2] *n* : silla *f* (de montar)

sadism [ˈseɪˌdɪzəm, ˈsæ-] *n* : sadismo *m*

sadist [ˈseɪdɪst, ˈsæ-] *n* : sádico *m*, -ca *f*

sadistic [səˈdɪstɪk] *adj* : sádico — **sadistically** [-tɪkli] *adv*

sadness [ˈsædnəs] *n* : tristeza *f*

safari [səˈfɑri, -ˈfær-] *n* : safari *m*

safe[1] [ˈseɪf] *adj* **safer; safest 1** UNHARMED : ileso <safe and sound : sano y salvo> **2** SECURE : seguro **3 to be on the safe side** : para mayor seguridad **4 to play it safe** : ir a la segura

safe[2] *n* : caja *f* fuerte

safeguard[1] [ˈseɪfˌgɑrd] *vt* : salvaguardar, proteger

safeguard[2] *n* : salvaguarda *f*, protección *f*

safekeeping [ˈseɪfˈkiːpɪŋ] *n* : custodia *f*, protección *f* <to put into safekeeping : poner en buen recaudo>

safely [ˈseɪfli] *adv* **1** UNHARMED : sin incidentes, sin novedades <they landed safely : aterrizaron sin novedades> **2** SECURELY : con toda seguridad, sin peligro

safety [ˈseɪfti] *n, pl* **-ties** : seguridad *f*

safety belt *n* : cinturón *m* de seguridad

safety pin *n* : alfiler *m* de gancho, alfiler *m* de seguridad, imperdible *m Spain*

saffron [ˈsæfrən] *n* : azafrán *m*

sag[1] [ˈsæg] *vi* **sagged; sagging 1** DROOP, SINK : combarse, hundirse, inclinarse **2** : colgar, caer <his jowls sagged : le colgaban las mejillas> **3** FLAG : flaquear, decaer <his spirits sagged : se le flaqueó el ánimo>

sag[2] *n* : combadura *f*

saga [ˈsɑgə, ˈsæ-] *n* : saga *f*

sagacious [səˈgeɪʃəs] *adj* : sagaz

sage[1] [ˈseɪdʒ] *adj* **sager; -est** : sabio — **sagely** *adv*

sage[2] *n* **1** : sabio *m*, -bia *f* **2** : salvia *f* (planta)

sagebrush [ˈseɪdʒˌbrʌʃ] *n* : artemisa *f*

Sagittarius [ˌsædʒəˈtɛriəs] *n* : Sagitario *mf*

said → **say**

sail[1] [ˈseɪl] *vi* **1** : navegar (en un barco) **2** : ir fácilmente <we sailed right in : entramos sin ningún problema> — *vt* **1** : gobernar (un barco) **2 to sail the seas** : cruzar los mares

sail[2] *n* **1** : vela *f* (de un barco) **2** : viaje *m* en velero <to go for a sail : salir a navegar>

sailboat [ˈseɪlˌboːt] *n* : velero *m*, barco *m* de vela

sailfish [ˈseɪlˌfɪʃ] *n* : pez *m* vela

sailor [ˈseɪlər] *n* : marinero *m*

saint [ˈseɪnt, *before a name* ˌseɪnt *or* sənt] *n* : santo *m*, -ta *f* <Saint Francis : San Francisco> <Saint Rose : Santa Rosa>

saintliness [ˈseɪntlinəs] *n* : santidad *f*

saintly [ˈseɪntli] *adj* **saintlier; -est** : santo

sake [ˈseɪk] *n* **1** BENEFIT : bien *m* <for the children's sake : por el bien de los niños> **2** (*indicating an end or a purpose*) <art for art's sake : el arte por el arte> <let's say, for argument's sake, that he's wrong : pongamos que está equivocado> **3 for goodness' sake!** : ¡por (el amor de) Dios!

salable *or* **saleable** [ˈseɪləbəl] *adj* : vendible

salacious [səˈleɪʃəs] *adj* : salaz — **salaciously** *adv*

salad [ˈsæləd] *n* : ensalada *f*

salamander [ˈsæləˌmændər] *n* : salamandra *f*

salami [səˈlɑmi] *n* : salami *m*

salary [ˈsæləri] *n, pl* **-ries** : sueldo *m*

sale [ˈseɪl] *n* **1** SELLING : venta *f* **2** : liquidación *f*, rebajas *fpl* <on sale : de rebaja> **3 sales** *npl* : ventas *fpl* <to work in sales : trabajar en ventas>

salesman [ˈseɪlzmən] *n, pl* **-men** [-mən, -ˌmɛn] **1** : vendedor *m*, dependiente *m* (en una tienda) **2 traveling salesman** : viajante *m*, representante *m*

salesperson [ˈseɪlzˌpərsən] *n* : vendedor *m*, -dora *f*; dependiente *m*, -ta *f* (en una tienda)

saleswoman [ˈseɪlzˌwʊmən] *n, pl* **-women** [-ˌwɪmən] **1** : vendedora *f*, dependienta *f* (en una tienda) **2 traveling saleswoman** : viajante *f*, representante *f*

salient [ˈseɪljənt] *adj* : saliente, sobresaliente

saline [ˈseɪˌliːn, -ˌlaɪn] *adj* : salino

saliva [səˈlaɪvə] *n* : saliva *f*

salivary [ˈsæləˌvɛri] *adj* : salival <salivary gland : glándula salival>

salivate [ˈsæləˌveɪt] *vi* **-vated; -vating** : salivar

sallow [ˈsæloː] *adj* : amarillento, cetrino

sally[1] [ˈsæli] *vi* **-lied; -lying** SET OUT : salir, hacer una salida

sally[2] *n, pl* **-lies 1** : salida *f* (militar), misión *f* **2** QUIP : salida *f*, ocurrencia *f*

salmon ['sæmən] *ns & pl* **1** : salmón *m* (pez) **2** : color *m* salmón
salon [sə'lɑn, 'sæ,lɑn, sæ'lɔ̃] *n* : salón *m* <beauty salon : salón de belleza>
saloon [sə'lu:n] *n* **1** HALL : salón *m* (en un barco) **2** BARROOM : bar *m*
salsa ['sɔlsə, 'sɑl-] *n* : salsa *f* mexicana, salsa *f* picante
salt[1] ['sɔlt] *vt* : salar, echarle sal a
salt[2] *adj* : salado
salt[3] *n* : sal *f*
saltwater ['sɔlt,wɔtər, -,wɑ-] *adj* : de agua salada
salty ['sɔlti] *adj* **saltier; -est** : salado
salubrious [sə'lu:briəs] *adj* : salubre
salutary ['sæljə,tɛri] *adj* : saludable, salubre
salutation [,sæljə'teɪʃən] *n* : saludo *m,* salutación *f*
salute[1] [sə'lu:t] *v* **-luted; -luting** *vt* **1** : saludar (con gestos o ceremonias) **2** ACCLAIM : reconocer, aclamar — *vi* : hacer un saludo
salute[2] *n* **1** : saludo *m* (gesto), salva *f* (de cañonazos) **2** TRIBUTE : reconocimiento *m,* homenaje *m*
salvage[1] ['sælvɪdʒ] *vt* **-vaged; -vaging** : salvar, rescatar
salvage[2] *n* **1** SALVAGING : salvamento *m,* rescate *m* **2** : objetos *mpl* salvados
salvation [sæl'veɪʃən] *n* : salvación *f*
salve[1] ['sæv, 'sav] *vt* **salved; salving** : calmar, apaciguar <to salve one's conscience : aliviarse la conciencia>
salve[2] *n* : ungüento *m*
salvo ['sæl,vo:] *n, pl* **-vos** *or* **-voes** : salva *f*
same[1] ['seɪm] *adj* : mismo, igual <the results are the same : los resultados son iguales> <he said the same thing as you : dijo lo mismo que tú>
same[2] *pron* : mismo <it's all the same to me : me da lo mismo> <the same to you! : ¡igualmente!>
sameness ['seɪmnəs] *n* **1** SIMILARITY : identidad *f,* semejanza *f* **2** MONOTONY : monotonía *f*
sample[1] ['sæmpəl] *vt* **-pled; -pling** : probar
sample[2] *n* : muestra *f,* prueba *f*
sampler ['sæmplər] *n* : dechado *m* (en bordado)
sanatorium [,sænə'toriəm] *n, pl* **-riums** *or* **-ria** [-iə] : sanatorio *m*
sanctify ['sæŋktə,faɪ] *vt* **-fied; -fying** : santificar
sanctimonious [,sæŋktə'mo:niəs] *adj* : beato, santurrón
sanction[1] ['sæŋkʃən] *vt* : sancionar, aprobar
sanction[2] *n* **1** AUTHORIZATION : sanción *f,* autorización *f* **2 sanctions** *npl* : sanciones *fpl* <to impose sanctions on : imponer sanciones a>
sanctity ['sæŋktəti] *n, pl* **-ties** : santidad *f*
sanctuary ['sæŋktʃʊ,ɛri] *n, pl* **-aries 1** : presbiterio *m* (en una iglesia) **2** REFUGE : refugio *m,* asilo *m*
sand[1] ['sænd] *vt* : lijar (madera)
sand[2] *n* : arena *f*
sandal ['sændəl] *n* : sandalia *f*
sandbank ['sænd,bæŋk] *n* : banco *m* de arena
sandpaper *n* : papel *m* de lija
sandpiper ['sænd,paɪpər] *n* : andarríos *m*
sandstone ['sænd,sto:n] *n* : arenisca *f*
sandstorm ['sænd,stɔrm] *n* : tormenta *f* de arena
sandwich[1] ['sænd,wɪtʃ] *vt* : intercalar, encajonar, meter (entre dos cosas)
sandwich[2] *n* : sandwich *m,* emparedado *m,* bocadillo *m Spain*
sandy ['sændi] *adj* **sandier; -est** : arenoso
sane ['seɪn] *adj* **saner; sanest 1** : cuerdo **2** SENSIBLE : sensato, razonable
sang → **sing**
sanguine ['sæŋgwən] *adj* **1** RUDDY : sanguíneo, rubicundo **2** HOPEFUL : optimista
sanitarium [,sænə'tɛriəm] *n, pl* **-iums** *or* **-ia** [-iə] → **sanatorium**
sanitary ['sænətɛri] *adj* **1** : sanitario <sanitary measures : medidas sanitarias> **2** HYGIENIC : higiénico **3 sanitary napkin** : compresa *f,* paño *m* higiénico
sanitation [,sænə'teɪʃən] *n* : sanidad *f*
sanity ['sænəti] *n* : cordura *f,* razón *f* <to lose one's sanity : perder el juicio>
sank → **sink**
Santa Claus ['sæntə,klɔz] *n* : Papá Noel, San Nicolás
sap[1] ['sæp] *vt* **sapped; sapping 1** UNDERMINE : socavar **2** WEAKEN : minar, debilitar
sap[2] *n* **1** : savia *f* (de una planta) **2** SUCKER : inocentón *m,* -tona *f*
sapling ['sæplɪŋ] *n* : árbol *m* joven
sapphire ['sæ,faɪr] *n* : zafiro *m*
sarcasm ['sɑr,kæzəm] *n* : sarcasmo *m*
sarcastic [sɑr'kæstɪk] *adj* : sarcástico — **sarcastically** [-tɪkli] *adv*
sarcophagus [sɑr'kɑfəgəs] *n, pl* **-gi** [-,gaɪ, -,dʒaɪ] : sarcófago *m*
sardine [sɑr'di:n] *n* : sardina *f*
sardonic [sɑr'dɑnɪk] *adj* : sardónico — **sardonically** [-nɪkli] *adv*
sarsaparilla [,sæspə'rɪlə, ,sɑrs-] *n* : zarzaparrilla *f*
sash ['sæʃ] *n* **1** : faja *f* (de un vestido), fajín *m* (de un uniforme) **2** *pl* **sash** : marco *m* (de una ventana)
sassafras ['sæsə,fræs] *n* : sasafrás *m*
sassy ['sæsi] *adj* **sassier; -est** → **saucy**
sat → **sit**
Satan ['seɪtən] *n* : Satanás *m,* Satán *m*
satanic [sə'tænɪk, seɪ-] *adj* : satánico — **satanically** [-nɪkli] *adv*
satchel ['sætʃəl] *n* : cartera *f,* saco *m*
sate ['seɪt] *vt* **sated; sating** : saciar

satellite [ˈsæt̬əˌlaɪt] *n* : satélite *m* <spy satellite : satélite espía>
satiate [ˈseɪʃiˌeɪt] *vt* **-ated; -ating** : saciar, hartar
satin [ˈsætən] *n* : raso *m,* satín *m,* satén *m*
satire [ˈsæˌtaɪr] *n* : sátira *f*
satiric [səˈtɪrɪk] *or* **satirical** [-ɪkəl] *adj* : satírico
satirize [ˈsæt̬əˌraɪz] *vt* **-rized; -rizing** : satirizar
satisfaction [ˌsæt̬əsˈfækʃən] *n* : satisfacción *f*
satisfactory [ˌsæt̬əsˈfæktəri] *adj* : satisfactorio, bueno — **satisfactorily** [-rəli] *adv*
satisfy [ˈsæt̬əsˌfaɪ] *v* **-fied; -fying** *vt* **1** PLEASE : satisfacer, contentar **2** CONVINCE : convencer **3** FULFILL : satisfacer, cumplir con, llenar **4** SETTLE : pagar, saldar (una cuenta) — *vi* SUFFICE : bastar
saturate [ˈsætʃəˌreɪt] *vt* **-rated; -rating 1** SOAK : empapar **2** FILL : saturar
saturation [ˌsætʃəˈreɪʃən] *n* : saturación *f*
Saturday [ˈsæt̬ərˌdeɪ, -di] *n* : sábado *m*
Saturn [ˈsæt̬ərn] *n* : Saturno *m*
satyr [ˈseɪt̬ər, ˈsæ-] *n* : sátiro *m*
sauce [ˈsɔs] *n* : salsa *f*
saucepan [ˈsɔsˌpæn] *n* : cacerola *f,* cazo *m,* cazuela *f*
saucer [ˈsɔsər] *n* : platillo *m*
sauciness [ˈsɔsinəs] *n* : descaro *m,* frescura *f*
saucy [ˈsɔsi] *adj* **saucier; -est** IMPUDENT : descarado, fresco *fam* — **saucily** *adv*
sauna [ˈsɔnə, ˈsaʊnə] *n* : sauna *mf*
saunter [ˈsɔntər, ˈsɑn-] *vi* : pasear, parsearse
sausage [ˈsɔsɪdʒ] *n* : salchicha *f,* embutido *m*
sauté [sɔˈteɪ, soː-] *vt* **-téed** *or* **-téd; -téing** : saltear, sofreír
savage[1] [ˈsævɪdʒ] *adj* : salvaje, feroz — **savagely** *adv*
savage[2] *n* : salvaje *mf*
savagery [ˈsævɪdʒri, -dʒəri] *n, pl* **-ries 1** FEROCITY : ferocidad *f* **2** WILDNESS : salvajismo *m*
save[1] [ˈseɪv] *vt* **saved; saving 1** RESCUE : salvar, rescatar **2** PRESERVE : preservar, conservar **3** KEEP : guardar, ahorrar (dinero), almacenar (alimentos)
save[2] *prep* EXCEPT : salvo, excepto, a menos
savior [ˈseɪvjər] *n* **1** : salvador *m,* -dora *f* **2 the Savior** : el Salvador *m*
savor[1] [ˈseɪvər] *vt* : saborear
savor[2] *n* : sabor *m*
savory [ˈseɪvəri] *adj* : sabroso
saw[1] → **see**
saw[2] [ˈsɔ] *vt* **sawed; sawed** *or* **sawn** [ˈsɔn]; **sawing** : serrar, cortar (con sierra)
saw[3] *n* : sierra *f*
sawdust [ˈsɔˌdʌst] *n* : aserrín *m,* serrín *m*
sawhorse [ˈsɔˌhɔrs] *n* : caballete *m,* burro *m* (en carpintería)
sawmill [ˈsɔˌmɪl] *n* : aserradero *m*
saxophone [ˈsæksəˌfoːn] *n* : saxofón *m*
say[1] [ˈseɪ] *v* **said** [ˈsɛd]; **saying; says** [ˈsɛz] *vt* **1** EXPRESS, UTTER : decir, expresar <to say no : decir que no> <that goes without saying : ni que decir tiene> <no sooner said than done : dicho y hecho> <to say again : repetir> <to say one's prayers : rezar> **2** INDICATE : marcar, poner <my watch says three o'clock : mi reloj marca las tres> <what does the sign say? : ¿qué pone el letrero?> **3** ALLEGE : decir <it's said that she's pretty : se dice que es bonita> — *vi* : decir
say[2] *n, pl* **says** [ˈseɪz] : voz *f,* opinión *f* <to have no say : no tener ni voz ni voto> <to have one's say : dar uno su opinión>
saying [ˈseɪɪŋ] *n* : dicho *m,* refrán *m*
scab [ˈskæb] *n* **1** : costra *f,* postilla *f* (en una herida) **2** STRIKEBREAKER : rompehuelgas *mf,* esquirol *mf*
scabbard [ˈskæbərd] *n* : vaina *f* (de una espada), funda *f* (de un puñal, etc.)
scabby [ˈskæbi] *adj* **scabbier; -est** : lleno de costras
scaffold [ˈskæfəld, -ˌfoːld] *n* **1** *or* **scaffolding** : andamio *m* (para obreros, etc.) **2** : patíbulo *m,* cadalso *m* (para ejecuciones)
scald [ˈskɔld] *vt* **1** BURN : escaldar **2** HEAT : calentar (hasta el punto de ebullición)
scale[1] [ˈskeɪl] *v* **scaled; scaling** *vt* **1** : escamar (un pescado) **2** CLIMB : escalar (un muro, etc.) **3 to scale down** : reducir — *vi* WEIGH : pesar <he scaled in at 200 pounds : pesó 200 libras>
scale[2] *n* **1** *or* **scales** : balanza *f,* báscula *f* (para pesar) **2** : escama *f* (de un pez, etc.) **3** EXTENT : escala *f,* proporción *f* <wage scale : escala salarial> **4** : escala *f* (en música, en cartografía, etc.) <to draw to scale : dibujar a escala>
scallion [ˈskæljən] *n* : cebollino *m,* cebolleta *f*
scallop [ˈskɑləp, ˈskæ-] *n* **1** : vieira *f* (molusco) **2** : festón *m* (decoración)
scalp[1] [ˈskælp] *vt* : arrancar la cabellera a
scalp[2] *n* : cuero *m* cabelludo
scalpel [ˈskælpəl] *n* : bisturí *m,* escalpelo *m*
scaly [ˈskeɪli] *adj* **scalier; -est** : escamoso
scam [ˈskæm] *n* : estafa *f,* timo *m fam,* chanchullo *m fam*
scamp [ˈskæmp] *n* : bribón *m,* -bona *f;* granuja *mf;* travieso *m,* -sa *f*
scamper [ˈskæmpər] *vi* : corretear

scan[1] [ˈskæn] *vt* **scanned; scanning 1** : escandir (versos) **2** SCRUTINIZE : escudriñar, escrutar <to scan the horizon : escudriñar el horizonte> **3** PERUSE : echarle un vistazo a (un periódico, etc.) **4** EXPLORE : explorar (con radar), hacer un escáner de (en ecografía) **5** : escanear (una imagen)

scan[2] *n* **1** : ecografía *f*, examen *m* ultrasónico (en medicina) **2** : imagen *f* escaneada (en una computadora)

scandal [ˈskændəl] *n* **1** DISGRACE, OUTRAGE : escándalo *m* **2** GOSSIP : habladurías *fpl*, chismes *mpl*

scandalize [ˈskændəl,aɪz] *vt* **-ized; -izing** : escandalizar

scandalous [ˈskændələs] *adj* : de escándalo

Scandinavian[1] [,skændəˈneɪviən] *adj* : escandinavo

Scandinavian[2] *n* : escandinavo *m*, -va *f*

scanner [ˈskænər] *n* : escáner *m*, scanner *m*

scant [ˈskænt] *adj* : escaso

scanty [ˈskænti] *adj* **scantier; -est** : exiguo, escaso <a scanty meal : una comida insuficiente> — **scantily** [-təli] *adv*

scapegoat [ˈskeɪp,goːt] *n* : chivo *m* expiatorio, cabeza *f* de turco

scapula [ˈskæpjələ] *n, pl* **-lae** [-,liː, -,laɪ] *or* **-las** → **shoulder blade**

scar[1] [ˈskɑr] *v* **scarred; scarring** *vt* : dejar una cicatriz en — *vi* : cicatrizar

scar[2] *n* : cicatriz *f*, marca *f*

scarab [ˈskærəb] *n* : escarabajo *m*

scarce [ˈskɛrs] *adj* **scarcer; -est** : escaso

scarcely [ˈskɛrsli] *adv* **1** BARELY : apenas **2** : ni mucho menos, ni nada que se le parezca <he's scarcely an expert : ciertamente no es experto>

scarcity [ˈskɛrsəṭi] *n, pl* **-ties** : escasez *f*

scare[1] [ˈskɛr] *vt* **scared; scaring** : asustar, espantar

scare[2] *n* **1** FRIGHT : susto *m*, sobresalto *m* **2** ALARM : pánico *m*

scarecrow [ˈskɛr,kroː] *n* : espantapájaros *m*, espantajo *m*

scarf [ˈskɑrf] *n, pl* **scarves** [ˈskɑrvz] *or* **scarfs 1** MUFFLER : bufanda *f* **2** KERCHIEF : pañuelo *m*

scarlet [ˈskɑrlət] *n* : escarlata *f* — **scarlet** *adj*

scarlet fever *n* : escarlatina *f*

scary [ˈskɛri] *adj* **scarier; -est** : espantoso, pavoroso

scathing [ˈskeɪðɪŋ] *adj* : mordaz, cáustico

scatter [ˈskæṭər] *vt* : esparcir, desparramar — *vi* DISPERSE : dispersarse

scavenge [ˈskævəndʒ] *v* **-venged; -venging** *vt* : rescatar (de la basura), pepenar *CA, Mex* — *vi* : rebuscar, hurgar en la basura <to scavenge for food : andar buscando comida>

scavenger [ˈskævəndʒər] *n* **1** : persona *f* que rebusca en las basuras; pepenador *m*, -dora *f CA, Mex* **2** : carroñero *m*, -ra *f* (animal)

scenario [səˈnæri,oː, -ˈnɑr-] *n, pl* **-ios 1** PLOT : argumento *m* (en teatro), guión *m* (en cine) **2** SITUATION : situación *f* hipotética <in the worst-case scenario : en el peor de los casos>

scene [ˈsiːn] *n* **1** : escena *f* (en una obra de teatro) **2** SCENERY : decorado *m* (en el teatro) **3** VIEW : escena *f* **4** LOCALE : escenario *m* **5** COMMOTION, FUSS : escándalo *m*, escena *f* <to make a scene : armar un escándalo>

scenery [ˈsiːnəri] *n, pl* **-eries 1** : decorado *m* (en el teatro) **2** LANDSCAPE : paisaje *m*

scenic [ˈsiːnɪk] *adj* : pintoresco

scent[1] [ˈsɛnt] *vt* **1** SMELL : oler, olfatear **2** PERFUME : perfumar **3** SENSE : sentir, percibir

scent[2] *n* **1** ODOR : olor *m*, aroma *m* **2** : olfato *m* <a dog with a keen scent : un perro con un buen olfato> **3** PERFUME : perfume *m*

scented [ˈsɛntəd] *adj* : perfumado

scepter [ˈsɛptər] *n* : cetro *m*

sceptic [ˈskɛptɪk] → **skeptic**

schedule[1] [ˈskɛ,dʒuːl, -dʒəl, *esp Brit* ˈʃɛd,juːl] *vt* **-uled; -uling** : planear, programar

schedule[2] *n* **1** PLAN : programa *m*, plan *m* <on schedule : según lo previsto> <behind schedule : atrasado, con retraso> **2** TIMETABLE : horario *m*

scheme[1] [ˈskiːm] *vi* **schemed; scheming** : intrigar, conspirar

scheme[2] *n* **1** PLAN : plan *m*, proyecto *m* **2** PLOT, TRICK : intriga *f*, ardid *m* **3** FRAMEWORK : esquema *f* <a color scheme : una combinación de colores>

schemer [ˈskiːmər] *n* : intrigante *mf*

schism [ˈsɪzəm, ˈskɪ-] *n* : cisma *m*

schizophrenia [,skɪtsəˈfriːniə, ,skɪzə-, -ˈfrɛ-] *n* : esquizofrenia *f*

schizophrenic [,skɪtsəˈfrɛnɪk, ,skɪzə-] *n* : esquizofrénico *m*, -ca *f* — **schizophrenic** *adj*

scholar [ˈskɑlər] *n* **1** STUDENT : escolar *mf*; alumno *m*, -na *f* **2** EXPERT : especialista *mf*

scholarly [ˈskɑlərli] *adj* : erudito

scholarship [ˈskɑlər,ʃɪp] *n* **1** LEARNING : erudición *f* **2** GRANT : beca *f*

scholastic [skəˈlæstɪk] *adj* : académico

school[1] [ˈskuːl] *vt* : instruir, enseñar

school[2] *n* **1** : escuela *f*, colegio *m* (institución) **2** : estudiantes *mfpl* y profesores *mpl* (de una escuela) **3** : escuela *f* (en pintura, etc.) <the Flemish school : la escuela flamenca> **4** **school of fish** : banco *m*, cardumen *m*

schoolboy [ˈskuːl,bɔɪ] *n* : escolar *m*, colegial *m*

schoolgirl [ˈskuːl,gərl] *n* : escolar *f*, colegiala *f*

schoolhouse ['skuːlˌhaʊs] *n* : escuela *f*
schoolmate ['skuːlˌmeɪt] *n* : compañero *m,* -ra *f* de escuela
schoolroom ['skuːlˌruːm, -ˌrʊm] → **classroom**
schoolteacher ['skuːlˌtiːtʃər] *n* : maestro *m,* -tra *f;* profesor *m,* -sora *f*
schooner ['skuːnər] *n* : goleta *f*
science ['saɪən*t*s] *n* : ciencia *f*
scientific [ˌsaɪən'tɪfɪk] *adj* : científico — **scientifically** [-fɪkli] *adv*
scientist ['saɪəntɪst] *n* : científico *m,* -ca *f*
scintillating ['sɪntəˌleɪṱɪŋ] *adj* : chispeante, brillante
scissors ['sɪzərz] *npl* : tijeras *fpl*
scoff ['skɑf] *vi* **to scoff at** : burlarse de, mofarse de
scold ['skoːld] *vt* : regañar, reprender, reñir
scoop[1] ['skuːp] *vt* **1** : sacar (con pala o cucharón) **2 to scoop out** HOLLOW : vaciar, ahuecar
scoop[2] *n* : pala *f* (para harina, etc.), cucharón *m* (para helado, etc.)
scoot ['skuːt] *vi* : ir rápidamente <she scooted around the corner : volvió la esquina a toda prisa>
scooter ['skuːṱər] *n* : patineta *f,* monopatín *m,* patinete *m*
scope ['skoːp] *n* **1** RANGE : alcance *m,* ámbito *m,* extensión *f* **2** OPPORTUNITY : posibilidades *fpl,* libertad *f*
scorch ['skɔrtʃ] *vt* : chamuscar, quemar
score[1] ['skor] *v* **scored; scoring** *vt* **1** RECORD : anotar **2** MARK, SCRATCH : marcar, rayar **3** : marcar, meter (en deportes) **4** GAIN : ganar, apuntarse **5** GRADE : calificar (exámenes, etc.) **6** : instrumentar, orquestar (música) — *vi* **1** : marcar (en deportes) **2** : obtener una puntuación (en un examen)
score[2] *n, pl* **scores 1** *or pl* **score** TWENTY : veintena *f* **2** LINE, SCRATCH : línea *f,* marca *f* **3** : resultado *m* (en deportes) <what's the score? : ¿cómo va el marcador?> **4** GRADE, POINTS : calificación *f* (en un examen), puntuación *f* (en un concurso) **5** ACCOUNT : cuenta *f* <to settle a score : ajustar una cuenta> <on that score : a ese respecto> **6** : partitura *f* (musical)
scorn[1] ['skɔrn] *vt* : despreciar, menospreciar, desdeñar
scorn[2] *n* : desprecio *m,* menosprecio *m,* desdén *m*
scornful ['skɔrnfəl] *adj* : desdeñoso, despreciativo — **scornfully** *adv*
Scorpio ['skɔrpiˌoː] *n* : Escorpio *mf,* Escorpión *mf*
scorpion ['skɔrpiən] *n* : alacrán *m,* escorpión *m*
Scot ['skɑt] *n* : escocés *m,* -cesa *f*
Scotch[1] ['skɑtʃ] *adj* → **Scottish**[1]
Scotch[2] *npl* **the Scotch** : los escoceses
scot–free ['skɑt'friː] *adj* **to get off scot–free** : salir impune, quedar sin castigo
Scots ['skɑts] *n* : escocés *m* (idioma)
Scottish[1] ['skɑṱɪʃ] *adj* : escocés
Scottish[2] *n* → **Scots**
scoundrel ['skaʊndrəl] *n* : sinvergüenza *mf;* bellaco *m,* -ca *f*
scour ['skaʊər] *vt* **1** EXAMINE, SEARCH : registrar (un área), revisar (documentos, etc.) **2** SCRUB : fregar, restregar
scourge[1] ['skərdʒ] *vt* **scourged; scourging** : azotar
scourge[2] *n* : azote *m*
scout[1] ['skaʊt] *vi* **1** RECONNOITER : reconocer **2 to scout around for** : explorar en busca de
scout[2] *n* **1** : explorador *m,* -dora *f* **2** *or* **talent scout** : cazatalentos *mf*
scow ['skaʊ] *n* : barcaza *f,* gabarra *f*
scowl[1] ['skaʊl] *vi* : fruncir el ceño
scowl[2] *n* : ceño *m* fruncido
scram ['skræm] *vi* **scrammed; scramming** : largarse
scramble[1] ['skræmbəl] *v* **-bled; -bling** *vi* **1** : trepar, gatear (con torpeza) <he scrambled over the fence : se trepó a la cerca con dificultad> **2** STRUGGLE : pelearse (por) <they scrambled for seats : se pelearon por los asientos> — *vt* **1** JUMBLE : mezclar **2 to scramble eggs** : hacer huevos revueltos
scramble[2] *n* : rebatiña *f,* pelea *f*
scrap[1] ['skræp] *v* **scrapped; scrapping** *vt* DISCARD : desechar — *vi* FIGHT : pelearse
scrap[2] *n* **1** FRAGMENT : pedazo *m,* trozo *m* **2** FIGHT : pelea *f* **3** *or* **scrap metal** : chatarra *f* **4 scraps** *npl* LEFTOVERS : restos *mpl,* sobras *fpl*
scrapbook ['skræpˌbʊk] *n* : álbum *m* de recortes
scrape[1] ['skreɪp] *v* **scraped; scraping** *vt* **1** GRAZE, SCRATCH : rozar, rascar <to scrape one's knee : rasparse la rodilla> **2** CLEAN : raspar <to scrape carrots : raspar zanahorias> **3 to scrape off** : raspar (pintura, etc.) **4 to scrape up** *or* **to scrape together** : juntar, reunir poco a poco — *vi* **1** RUB : rozar **2 to scrape by** : arreglárselas, ir tirando
scrape[2] *n* **1** SCRAPING : raspadura *f* **2** SCRATCH : rasguño *m* **3** PREDICAMENT : apuro *m,* aprieto *m*
scratch[1] ['skrætʃ] *vt* **1** : arañar, rasguñar <to scratch an itch : rascarse> **2** MARK : rayar, marcar **3 to scratch out** : tachar
scratch[2] *n* **1** : rasguño *m,* arañazo *m* (en la piel), rayón *m* (en un mueble, etc.) **2** : sonido *m* rasposo <I heard a scratch at the door : oí como que raspaban a la puerta>
scratchy ['skrætʃi] *adj* **scratchier; -est** : áspero, que pica <a scratchy sweater : un suéter que pica>
scrawl[1] ['skrɔl] *v* : garabatear
scrawl[2] *n* : garabato *m*

scrawny [ˈskrɔni] *adj* **scrawnier; -est** : flaco, escuálido

scream[1] [ˈskriːm] *vi* : chillar, gritar

scream[2] *n* : chillido *m,* grito *m*

screech[1] [ˈskriːtʃ] *vi* : chillar (dícese de las personas o de los animales), chirriar (dícese de los frenos, etc.)

screech[2] *n* 1 : chillido *m,* grito *m* (de una persona o un animal) **2** : chirrido *m* (de frenos, etc.)

screen[1] [ˈskriːn] *vt* **1** SHIELD : proteger **2** CONCEAL : tapar, ocultar **3** EXAMINE : someter a una revisión, hacerle un chequeo (a un paciente) **4** SIEVE : cribar

screen[2] *n* **1** PARTITION : biombo *m,* pantalla *f* **2** SIEVE : criba *f* **3** : pantalla *f* (de un televisor, una computadora, etc.) **4** MOVIES : cine *m* **5** *or* **window screen** : ventana *f* de tela metálica

screw[1] [ˈskruː] *vt* : atornillar — *vi* **to screw in** : atornillarse

screw[2] *n* **1** : tornillo *m* (para fijar algo) **2** TWIST : vuelta *f* **3** PROPELLER : hélice *f*

screwdriver [ˈskruːˌdraɪvər] *n* : destornillador *m,* desarmador *m Mex*

scribble[1] [ˈskrɪbəl] *v* **-bled; -bling** : garabatear

scribble[2] *n* : garabato *m*

scribe [ˈskraɪb] *n* : escriba *m*

scrimp [ˈskrɪmp] *vi* **1 to scrimp on** : escatimar **2 to scrimp and save** : hacer economías

script [ˈskrɪpt] *n* **1** HANDWRITING : letra *f,* escritura *f* **2** : guión *m* (de una película, etc.)

scriptural [ˈskrɪptʃərəl] *adj* : bíblico

scripture [ˈskrɪptʃər] *n* **1** : escritos *mpl* sagrados (de una religión) **2 the Scriptures** *npl* : las Sagradas Escrituras

scroll [ˈskroːl] *n* **1** : rollo *m* (de pergamino, etc.) **2** : voluta *f* (adorno en arquitectura)

scrotum [ˈskroːtəm] *n, pl* **scrota** [-tə] *or* **scrotums** : escroto *m*

scrounge [ˈskraʊndʒ] *v* **scrounged; scrounging** *vt* **1** BUM : gorrear *fam,* sablear *fam* (dinero) **2 to scrounge around for** : buscar, andar a la busca de — *vi* **to scrounge off someone** : vivir a costa de alguien

scrub[1] [ˈskrʌb] *vt* **scrubbed; scrubbing** : restregar, fregar

scrub[2] *n* **1** THICKET, UNDERBRUSH : maleza *f,* matorral *m,* matorrales *mpl* **2** SCRUBBING : fregado *m,* restregadura *f*

scrubby [ˈskrʌbi] *adj* **-bier; -est 1** STUNTED : achaparrado **2** : cubierto de maleza

scruff [ˈskrʌf] *n* **by the scruff of the neck** : por el cogote, por el pescuezo

scrumptious [ˈskrʌmpʃəs] *adj* : delicioso, muy rico

scruple [ˈskruːpəl] *n* : escrúpulo *m*

scrupulous [ˈskruːpjələs] *adj* : escrupuloso — **scrupulously** *adv*

scrutinize [ˈskruːtənˌaɪz] *vt* **-nized; -nizing** : escrutar, escudriñar

scrutiny [ˈskruːtəni] *n, pl* **-nies** : escrutinio *m,* inspección *f*

scuff [ˈskʌf] *vt* : rayar, raspar <to scuff one's feet : arrastrar los pies>

scuffle[1] [ˈskʌfəl] *vi* **-fled; -fling 1** TUSSLE : pelearse **2** SHUFFLE : caminar arrastrando los pies

scuffle[2] *n* **1** TUSSLE : refriega *f,* pelea *f* **2** SHUFFLE : arrastre *m* de los pies

scull[1] [ˈskʌl] *vi* : remar (con espadilla)

scull[2] *n* OAR : espadilla *f*

sculpt [ˈskʌlpt] *v* : esculpir

sculptor [ˈskʌlptər] *n* : escultor *m,* -tora *f*

sculpture[1] [ˈskʌlptʃər] *vt* **-tured; -turing** : esculpir

sculpture[2] *n* : escultura *f*

scum [ˈskʌm] *n* **1** FROTH : espuma *f,* nata *f* **2** : verdín *m* (encima de un líquido)

scurrilous [ˈskərələs] *adj* : difamatorio, calumnioso, injurioso

scurry [ˈskəri] *vi* **-ried; -rying** : corretear

scurvy [ˈskərvi] *n* : escorbuto *m*

scuttle[1] [ˈskʌtəl] *v* **-tled; -tling** *vt* : hundir (un barco) — *vi* SCAMPER : corretear

scuttle[2] *n* : cubo *m* (para carbón)

scythe [ˈsaɪð] *n* : guadaña *f*

sea[1] [ˈsiː] *adj* : del mar

sea[2] *n* **1** : mar *mf* <the Black Sea : el Mar Negro> <on the high seas : en alta mar> <heavy seas : mar gruesa, mar agitada> **2** MASS : mar *m,* multitud *f* <a sea of faces : un mar de rostros>

seabird [ˈsiːˌbərd] *n* : ave *f* marina

seacoast [ˈsiːˌkoːst] *n* : costa *f,* litoral *m*

seafarer [ˈsiːˌfærər] *n* : marinero *m*

seafaring[1] [ˈsiːˌfærɪŋ] *adj* : marinero

seafaring[2] *n* : navegación *f*

seafood [ˈsiːˌfuːd] *n* : mariscos *mpl*

seagull [ˈsiːˌgʌl] *n* : gaviota *f*

sea horse [ˈsiːˌhɔrs] *n* : hipocampo *m,* caballito *m* de mar

seal[1] [ˈsiːl] *vt* **1** CLOSE : sellar, cerrar <to seal a letter : cerrar una carta> <to seal an agreement : sellar un acuerdo> **2 to seal up** : tapar, rellenar (una grieta, etc.)

seal[2] *n* **1** : foca *f* (animal) **2** : sello *m* <seal of approval : sello de aprobación> **3** CLOSURE : cierre *m,* precinto *m*

sea level *n* : nivel *m* del mar

sea lion *n* : león *m* marino

sealskin [ˈsiːlˌskɪn] *n* : piel *f* de foca

seam[1] [ˈsiːm] *vt* **1** STITCH : unir con costuras **2** MARK : marcar

seam[2] *n* **1** STITCHING : costura *f* **2** LODE, VEIN : veta *f,* filón *m*

seaman [ˈsiːmən] *n, pl* **-men** [-mən, -ˌmɛn] **1** SAILOR : marinero *m* **2** : marino *m* (en la armada)

seamless [ˈsiːmləs] *adj* **1** : sin costuras, de una pieza **2** : perfecto <a seamless transition : una transición fluida>

seamstress [ˈsiːmpstrəs] *n* : costurera *f*

seamy [ˈsiːmi] *adj* **seamier; -est** : sórdido

séance [ˈseɪˌɑnts] *n* : sesión *f* de espiritismo

seaplane [ˈsiːˌpleɪn] *n* : hidroavión *m*

seaport [ˈsiːˌport] *n* : puerto *m* marítimo

sear [ˈsɪr] *vt* **1** PARCH, WITHER : secar, resecar **2** SCORCH : chamuscar, quemar

search[1] [ˈsərtʃ] *vt* : registrar (un edificio, un área), cachear (a una persona), buscar en — *vi* **to search for** : buscar

search[2] *n* : búsqueda *f*, registro *m* (de un edificio, etc.), cacheo *m* (de una persona)

searchlight [ˈsərtʃˌlaɪt] *n* : reflector *m*

seashell [ˈsiːˌʃɛl] *n* : concha *f* (marina)

seashore [ˈsiːˌʃor] *n* : orilla *f* del mar

seasick [ˈsiːˌsɪk] *adj* : mareado <to get seasick : marearse>

seasickness [ˈsiːˌsɪknəs] *n* : mareo *m*

seaside → **seacoast**

season[1] [ˈsiːzən] *vt* **1** FLAVOR, SPICE : sazonar, condimentar **2** CURE : curar, secar <seasoned wood : madera seca> <a seasoned veteran : un veterano avezado>

season[2] *n* **1** : estación *f* (del año) **2** : temporada *f* (en deportes, etc.) <baseball season : temporada de beisbol>

seasonable [ˈsiːzənəbəl] *adj* **1** : propio de la estación (dícese del tiempo, de las temperaturas, etc.) **2** TIMELY : oportuno

seasonal [ˈsiːzənəl] *adj* : estacional — **seasonally** *adv*

seasoning [ˈsiːzənɪŋ] *n* : condimento *m*, sazón *f*

seat[1] [ˈsiːt] *vt* **1** SIT : sentar <please be seated : siéntense, por favor> **2** HOLD : tener cabida para <the stadium seats 40,000 : el estadio tiene 40,000 asientos>

seat[2] *n* **1** : asiento *m*, plaza *f* (en un vehículo) <take a seat : tome asiento> **2** BOTTOM : fondillos *mpl* (de la ropa), trasero *m* (del cuerpo) **3** : sede *f* (de un gobierno, etc.)

seat belt *n* : cinturón *m* de seguridad

sea urchin *n* : erizo *m* de mar

seawall [ˈsiːˌwɑl] *n* : rompeolas *m*, dique *m* marítimo

seawater [ˈsiːˌwɔt̬ər, -ˌwɑ-] *n* : agua *f* de mar

seaweed [ˈsiːˌwiːd] *n* : alga *f* marina

seaworthy [ˈsiːˌwərði] *adj* : en condiciones de navegar

secede [sɪˈsiːd] *vi* **-ceded; -ceding** : separarse (de una nación, etc.)

seclude [sɪˈkluːd] *vt* **-cluded; -cluding** : aislar

seclusion [sɪˈkluːʒən] *n* : aislamiento *m*

second[1] [ˈsɛkənd] *vt* : secundar, apoyar (una moción)

second[2] *or* **secondly** [ˈsɛkəndli] *adv* : en segundo lugar

second[3] *adj* : segundo

second[4] *n* **1** : segundo *m*, -da *f* (en una serie) **2** : segundo *m*, segunda parte *f* **3** : segundo *m*, ayudante *m* (en deportes) **4** MOMENT : segundo *m*, momento *m*

secondary [ˈsɛkənˌdɛri] *adj* : secundario

secondhand [ˈsɛkəndˈhænd] *adj* : de segunda mano

second lieutenant *n* : alférez *mf*, subteniente *mf*

second-rate [ˈsɛkəndˈreɪt] *adj* : mediocre, de segunda categoría

secrecy [ˈsiːkrəsi] *n, pl* **-cies** : secreto *m*

secret[1] [ˈsiːkrət] *adj* : secreto — **secretly** *adv*

secret[2] *n* : secreto *m*

secretarial [ˌsɛkrəˈtɛriəl] *adj* : de secretario, de oficina

secretariat [ˌsɛkrəˈtɛriət] *n* : secretaría *f*, secretariado *m*

secretary [ˈsɛkrəˌtɛri] *n, pl* **-taries 1** : secretario *m*, -ria *f* (en una oficina, etc.) **2** : ministro *m*, -tra *f*; secretario *m*, -ria *f* <Secretary of State : Secretario de Estado>

secrete [sɪˈkriːt] *vt* **-creted; -creting 1** : secretar, segregar (en fisiología) **2** HIDE : ocultar

secretion [sɪˈkriːʃən] *n* : secreción *f*

secretive [ˈsiːkrət̬ɪv, sɪˈkriːt̬ɪv] *adj* : reservado, callado, secreto

sect [ˈsɛkt] *n* : secta *f*

sectarian [sɛkˈtɛriən] *adj* : sectario

section [ˈsɛkʃən] *n* : sección *f*, parte *f* (de un mueble, etc.), sector *m* (de la población), barrio *m* (de una ciudad)

sectional [ˈsɛkʃənəl] *adj* **1** : en sección, en corte <a sectional diagram : un gráfico en corte> **2** FACTIONAL : de grupo, entre facciones **3** : modular <sectional furniture : muebles modulares>

sector [ˈsɛktər] *n* : sector *m*

secular [ˈsɛkjələr] *adj* **1** : secular, laico <secular life : la vida secular> **2** : seglar (dícese de los sacerdotes, etc.)

secure[1] [sɪˈkjʊr] *vt* **-cured; -curing 1** FASTEN : asegurar (una puerta, etc.), sujetar **2** GET : conseguir

secure[2] *adj* **-curer; -est** : seguro — **securely** *adv*

security [sɪˈkjʊrət̬i] *n, pl* **-ties 1** SAFETY : seguridad *f* **2** GUARANTEE : garantía *f* **3 securities** *npl* : valores *mpl*

sedan [sɪˈdæn] *n* **1** *or* **sedan chair** : silla *f* de manos **2** : sedán *m* (automóvil)

sedate[1] [sɪˈdeɪt] *vt* **-dated; -dating** : sedar

sedate[2] *adj* : sosegado — **sedately** *adv*

sedation [sɪˈdeɪʃən] *n* : sedación *f*

sedative[1] [ˈsɛdət̬ɪv] *adj* : sedante

sedative[2] *n* : sedante *m*, calmante *m*

sedentary [ˈsɛdənˌtɛri] *adj* : sedentario

sedge [ˈsɛdʒ] *n* : juncia *f*

sediment [ˈsɛdəmənt] *n* : sedimento *m* (geológico), poso *m* (en un líquido)

sedimentary [ˌsɛdəˈmɛntəri] *adj* : sedimentario

sedition [sɪˈdɪʃən] *n* : sedición *f*

seditious [sɪˈdɪʃəs] *adj* : sedicioso

seduce [sɪˈduːs, -ˈdjuːs] *vt* **-duced; -ducing** : seducir

seduction [sɪˈdʌkʃən] *n* : seducción *f*

seductive [sɪˈdʌktɪv] *adj* : seductor, seductivo

see[1] [ˈsiː] *v* **saw** [ˈsɔ]; **seen** [ˈsiːn]; **seeing** *vt* **1** : ver <I saw a dog : vi un perro> <see you later! : ¡hasta luego!> **2** EXPERIENCE : ver, conocer **3** UNDERSTAND : ver, entender **4** ENSURE : asegurarse <see that it's correct : asegúrese de que sea correcto> **5** ACCOMPANY : acompañar **6 to see off** : despedir, despedirse de — *vi* **1** : ver <seeing is believing : ver para creer> **2** UNDERSTAND : entender, ver <now I see! : ¡ya entiendo!> **3** CONSIDER : ver <let's see : vamos a ver> **4 to see to** : ocuparse de

see[2] *n* : sede *f* <the Holy See : la Santa Sede>

seed[1] [ˈsiːd] *vt* **1** SOW : sembrar **2** : despepitar, quitarle las semillas a

seed[2] *n, pl* **seed** *or* **seeds 1** : semilla *f,* pepita *f* (de una fruta) **2** SOURCE : germen *m,* semilla *f*

seedless [ˈsiːdləs] *adj* : sin semillas

seedling [ˈsiːdlɪŋ] *n* : plantón *m*

seedpod [ˈsiːdˌpɑd] → **pod**

seedy [ˈsiːdi] *adj* **seedier; -est 1** : lleno de semillas **2** SHABBY : raído (dícese de la ropa) **3** RUN-DOWN : ruinoso (dícese de los edificios, etc.), sórdido

seek [ˈsiːk] *v* **sought** [ˈsɔt]; **seeking** *vt* **1** : buscar <to seek an answer : buscar una solución> **2** REQUEST : solicitar, pedir **3 to seek to** : tratar de, intentar de — *vi* SEARCH : buscar

seem [ˈsiːm] *vi* : parecer

seeming [ˈsiːmɪŋ] *adj* : aparente, ostensible

seemingly [ˈsiːmɪŋli] *adv* : aparentemente, según parece

seemly [ˈsiːmli] *adj* **seemlier; -est** : apropiado, decoroso

seep [ˈsiːp] *vi* : filtrarse

seer [ˈsiːər] *n* : vidente *mf,* clarividente *mf*

seesaw[1] [ˈsiːˌsɔ] *vi* **1** : jugar en un subibaja **2** VACILLATE : vacilar, oscilar

seesaw[2] *n* : balancín *m,* subibaja *m*

seethe [ˈsiːð] *vi* **seethed; seething 1** : bullir, hervir **2 to seethe with anger** : rabiar, estar furioso

segment [ˈsɛgmənt] *n* : segmento *m*

segmented [ˈsɛgˌmɛntəd, sɛgˈmɛn-] *adj* : segmentado

segregate [ˈsɛgrɪˌgeɪt] *vt* **-gated; -gating** : segregar

segregation [ˌsɛgrɪˈgeɪʃən] *n* : segregación *f*

seismic [ˈsaɪzmɪk, ˈsaɪs-] *adj* : sísmico

seize [ˈsiːz] *v* **seized; seizing** *vt* **1** CAPTURE : capturar, tomar, apoderarse de **2** ARREST : detener **3** CLUTCH, GRAB : agarrar, coger, aprovechar (una oportunidad) **4 to be seized with** : estar sobrecogido por — *vi or* **to seize up** : agarrotarse

seizure [ˈsiːʒər] *n* **1** CAPTURE : toma *f,* captura *f* **2** ARREST : detención *f* **3** : ataque *m* <an epileptic seizure : un ataque epiléptico>

seldom [ˈsɛldəm] *adv* : pocas veces, rara vez, casi nunca

select[1] [səˈlɛkt] *vt* : escoger, elegir, seleccionar (a un candidato, etc.)

select[2] *adj* : selecto

selection [səˈlɛkʃən] *n* : selección *f,* elección *f*

selective [səˈlɛktɪv] *adj* : selectivo

selenium [səˈliːniəm] *n* : selenio *m*

self [ˈsɛlf] *n, pl* **selves** [ˈsɛlvz] **1** : ser *m,* persona *f* <the self : el yo> <with his whole self : con todo su ser> <her own self : su propia persona> **2** SIDE : lado (de la personalidad) <his better self : su lado bueno>

self-addressed [ˌsɛlfəˈdrɛst] *adj* : con la dirección del remitente <include a self-addressed envelope : incluya un sobre con su nombre y dirección>

self-appointed [ˌsɛlfəˈpɔɪntəd] *adj* : autoproclamado, autonombrado

self-assurance [ˌsɛlfəˈʃʊrənts] *n* : seguridad *f* en sí mismo

self-assured [ˌsɛlfəˈʃʊrd] *adj* : seguro de sí mismo

self-centered [ˌsɛlfˈsɛntərd] *adj* : egocéntrico

self-confidence [ˌsɛlfˈkɑnfədənts] *n* : confianza *f* en sí mismo

self-confident [ˌsɛlfˈkɑnfədənt] *adj* : seguro de sí mismo

self-conscious [ˌsɛlfˈkɑntʃəs] *adj* : cohibido, tímido

self-consciously [ˌsɛlfˈkɑntʃəsli] *adv* : de manera cohibida

self-consciousness [ˌsɛlfˈkɑntʃəsnəs] *n* : vergüenza *f,* timidez *f*

self-contained [ˌsɛlfkənˈteɪnd] *adj* **1** INDEPENDENT : independiente **2** RESERVED : reservado

self-control [ˌsɛlfkənˈtroːl] *n* : autocontrol *m,* control *m* de sí mismo

self-defense [ˌsɛlfdɪˈfɛnts] *n* : defensa *f* propia, defensa *f* personal <to act in self-defense : actuar en defensa propia> <self-defense class : clase de defensa personal>

self-denial [ˌsɛlfdɪˈnaɪəl] *n* : abnegación *f*

self-destructive [ˌsɛlfdɪˈstrʌktɪv] *adj* : autodestructivo

self-determination [ˌsɛlfdɪˌtərməˈneɪʃən] *n* : autodeterminación *f*

self-discipline [ˌsɛlfˈdɪsəplən] *n* : autodisciplina *f*

self–employed [ˌsɛlfɪm'plɔɪd] *adj* : que trabaja por cuenta propia, autónomo
self–esteem [ˌsɛlfɪ'stiːm] *n* : autoestima *f,* amor *m* propio
self–evident [ˌsɛlf'ɛvədənt] *adj* : evidente, manifiesto
self–explanatory [ˌsɛlfɪk'splænəˌtori] *adj* : fácil de entender, evidente
self–expression [ˌsɛlfɪk'sprɛʃən] *n* : expresión *f* personal
self–government [ˌsɛlf'gʌvərmənt, -vərn-] *n* : autogobierno *m*
self–help [ˌsɛlf'hɛlp] *n* : autoayuda *f*
self–important [ˌsɛlfɪm'pɔrtənt] *adj* **1** VAIN : vanidoso, presumido **2** ARROGANT : arrogante
self–indulgent [ˌsɛlfɪn'dʌldʒənt] *adj* : que se permite excesos
self–inflicted [ˌsɛlfɪn'flɪktəd] *adj* : autoinfligido
self–interest [ˌsɛlf'ɪntrəst, -təˌrɛst] *n* : interés *m* personal
selfish ['sɛlfɪʃ] *adj* : egoísta
selfishly ['sɛlfɪʃli] *adv* : de manera egoísta
selfishness ['sɛlfɪʃnəs] *n* : egoísmo *m*
selfless ['sɛlfləs] *adj* UNSELFISH : desinteresado
self–made [ˌsɛlf'meɪd] *adj* : próspero gracias a sus propios esfuerzos
self–pity [ˌsɛlf'pɪṯi] *n, pl* **-ties** : autocompasión *f*
self–portrait [ˌsɛlf'pɔrtrət] *n* : autorretrato *m*
self–propelled [ˌsɛlfpro'pɛld] *adj* : autopropulsado
self–reliance [ˌsɛlfri'laɪən*t*s] *n* : independencia *f,* autosuficiencia *f*
self–respect [ˌsɛlfri'spɛkt] *n* : autoestima *f,* amor *m* propio
self–restraint [ˌsɛlfri'streɪnt] *n* : autocontrol *m,* moderación *f*
self–righteous [ˌsɛlf'raɪtʃəs] *adj* : santurrón, moralista
self–sacrifice [ˌsɛlf'sækrəˌfaɪs] *n* : abnegación *f*
selfsame ['sɛlfˌseɪm] *adj* : mismo
self–service [ˌsɛlf'sərvɪs] *adj* **1** : de autoservicio **2 self-service restaurant** : autoservicio *m*
self–sufficiency [ˌsɛlfsə'fɪʃən*t*si] *n* : autosuficiencia *f*
self–sufficient [ˌsɛlfsə'fɪʃənt] *adj* : autosuficiente
self–taught [ˌsɛlf'tɔt] *adj* : autodidacto
sell ['sɛl] *v* **sold** ['soːld]; **selling** *vt* : vender — *vi* : venderse
seller ['sɛlər] *n* : vendedor *m,* -dora *f*
selves → **self**
semantics [sɪ'mæntɪks] *ns & pl* : semántica *f*
semaphore ['sɛməˌfor] *n* : semáforo *m*
semblance ['sɛmblən*t*s] *n* : apariencia *f*
semen ['siːmən] *n* : semen *m*
semester [sə'mɛstər] *n* : semestre *m*
semicolon ['sɛmiˌkoːlən, 'sɛˌmaɪ-] *n* : punto y coma *m*
semiconductor ['sɛmikənˌdʌktər, 'sɛˌmaɪ-] *n* : semiconductor *m*
semifinal ['sɛmiˌfaɪnəl, 'sɛˌmaɪ-] *n* : semifinal *f*
seminar ['sɛməˌnɑr] *n* : seminario *m*
seminary ['sɛməˌnɛri] *n, pl* **-naries** : seminario *m*
senate ['sɛnət] *n* : senado *m*
senator ['sɛnəṯər] *n* : senador *m,* -dora *f*
send ['sɛnd] *vt* **sent** ['sɛnt]; **sending 1** : mandar, enviar <to send a letter : mandar una carta> <to send word : avisar, mandar decir> **2** PROPEL : mandar, lanzar <he sent it into left field : lo mandó al jardín izquierdo> <to send up dust : alzar polvo> **3 to send into a rage** : poner furioso
sender ['sɛndər] *n* : remitente *mf* (de una carta, etc.)
Senegalese [ˌsɛnəgə'liːz, -'liːs] *n* : senegalés *m,* -lesa *f* — **Senegalese** *adj*
senile ['siːˌnaɪl] *adj* : senil
senility [sɪ'nɪləṯi] *n* : senilidad *f*
senior¹ ['siːnjər] *adj* **1** ELDER : mayor <John Doe, Senior : John Doe, padre> **2** : superior (en rango), más antiguo (en años de servicio) <a senior official : un alto oficial>
senior² *n* **1** : superior *m* (en rango) **2 to be someone's senior** : ser mayor que alguien <she's two years my senior : me lleva dos años>
seniority [ˌsiː'njɔrəṯi] *n* : antigüedad *f* (en años de servicio)
sensation [sɛn'seɪʃən] *n* : sensación *f*
sensational [sɛn'seɪʃənəl] *adj* : que causa sensación <sensational stories : historias sensacionalistas>
sense¹ ['sɛn*t*s] *vt* **sensed; sensing** : sentir <he sensed danger : se dio cuenta del peligro>
sense² *n* **1** MEANING : sentido *m,* significado *m* **2** : sentido *m* <the sense of smell : el sentido del olfato> **3 to make sense** : tener sentido
senseless ['sɛn*t*sləs] *adj* **1** MEANINGLESS : sin sentido, sin razón **2** UNCONSCIOUS : inconsciente
senselessly ['sɛn*t*sləsli] *adv* : sin sentido
sensibility [ˌsɛn*t*sə'bɪləṯi] *n, pl* **-ties** : sensibilidad *f*
sensible ['sɛn*t*səbəl] *adj* **1** PERCEPTIBLE : sensible, perceptible **2** AWARE : consciente **3** REASONABLE : sensato <a sensible man : un hombre sensato> <sensible shoes : zapatos prácticos> — **sensibly** [-bli] *adv*
sensibleness ['sɛn*t*səbəlnəs] *n* : sensatez *f,* solidez *f*
sensitive ['sɛn*t*səṯɪv] *adj* **1** : sensible, delicado <sensitive skin : piel sensible> **2** IMPRESSIONABLE : sensible, impresionable **3** TOUCHY : susceptible

sensitiveness [ˈsɛntsət̬ɪvnəs] → **sensitivity**
sensitivity [ˌsɛntsəˈtɪvət̬i] *n, pl* **-ties** : sensibilidad *f*
sensor [ˈsɛnˌsɔr, ˈsɛntsər] *n* : sensor *m*
sensory [ˈsɛntsəri] *adj* : sensorial
sensual [ˈsɛntʃʊəl] *adj* : sensual — **sensually** *adv*
sensuous [ˈsɛntʃʊəs] *adj* : sensual
sent → **send**
sentence[1] [ˈsɛntənts, -ənz] *vt* **-tenced; -tencing** : sentenciar
sentence[2] *n* **1** JUDGMENT : sentencia *f* **2** : oración *f,* frase *f* (en gramática)
sentiment [ˈsɛntəmənt] *n* **1** BELIEF : opinión *f* **2** FEELING : sentimiento *m* **3** → **sentimentality**
sentimental [ˌsɛntəˈmɛntəl] *adj* : sentimental
sentimentality [ˌsɛntəˌmɛnˈtæləţi] *n, pl* **-ties** : sentimentalismo *m,* sensiblería *f*
sentinel [ˈsɛntənəl] *n* : centinela *mf,* guardia *mf*
sentry [ˈsɛntri] *n, pl* **-tries** : centinela *mf*
sepal [ˈsiːpəl, ˈsɛ-] *n* : sépalo *m*
separable [ˈsɛpərəbəl] *adj* : separable
separate[1] [ˈsɛpəˌreɪt] *v* **-rated; -rating** *vt* **1** DETACH, SEVER : separar **2** DISTINGUISH : diferenciar, distinguir — *vi* PART : separarse
separate[2] [ˈsɛprət, ˈsɛpə-] *adj* **1** INDIVIDUAL : separado, aparte <a separate state : un estado separado> <in a separate envelope : en un sobre aparte> **2** DISTINCT : distinto
separately [ˈsɛprətli, ˈsɛpə-] *adv* : por separado, separadamente, aparte
separation [ˌsɛpəˈreɪʃən] *n* : separación *f*
sepia [ˈsiːpiə] *n* : color *m* sepia
September [sɛpˈtɛmbər] *n* : septiembre *m,* setiembre *m*
sepulchre [ˈsɛpəlkər] *n* : sepulcro *m*
sequel [ˈsiːkwəl] *n* **1** CONSEQUENCE : secuela *f,* consecuencia *f* **2** : continuación *f* (de una película, etc.)
sequence [ˈsiːkwənts] *n* **1** SERIES : serie *f,* sucesión *f,* secuencia *f* (matemática o musical) **2** ORDER : orden *m*
sequester [sɪˈkwɛstər] *vt* : aislar
sequin [ˈsiːkwən] *n* : lentejuela *f*
sequoia [sɪˈkwɔɪə] *n* : secoya *f,* secuoya *f*
sera → **serum**
Serb [ˈsərb] *or* **Serbian** [ˈsərbiən] *n* : serbio *m,* -bia *f* — **Serb** *or* **Serbian** *adj*
Serbo–Croatian [ˌsərbokroˈeɪʃən] *n* : serbocroata *m* (idioma) — **Serbo–Croatian** *adj*
serenade[1] [ˌsɛrəˈneɪd] *vt* **-naded; -nading** : darle una serenata (a alguien)
serenade[2] *n* : serenata *f*
serene [səˈriːn] *adj* : sereno — **serenely** *adv*
serenity [səˈrɛnəţi] *n* : serenidad *f*
serf [ˈsərf] *n* : siervo *m,* -va *f*
serge [ˈsərdʒ] *n* : sarga *f*
sergeant [ˈsɑrdʒənt] *n* : sargento *mf*
serial[1] [ˈsɪriəl] *adj* : seriado
serial[2] *n* : serie *f,* serial *m* (de radio o televisión), publicación *f* por entregas
serially [ˈsɪriəli] *adv* : en serie
series [ˈsɪrˌiːz] *n, pl* **series** : serie *f,* sucesión *f*
serious [ˈsɪriəs] *adj* **1** SOBER : serio **2** DEDICATED, EARNEST : serio, dedicado <to be serious about something : tomar algo en serio> **3** GRAVE : serio, grave <serious problems : problemas graves>
seriously [ˈsɪriəsli] *adv* **1** EARNESTLY : seriamente, con seriedad, en serio **2** SEVERELY : gravemente
seriousness [ˈsɪriəsnəs] *n* : seriedad *f,* gravedad *f*
sermon [ˈsərmən] *n* : sermón *m*
serpent [ˈsərpənt] *n* : serpiente *f*
serrated [səˈreɪţəd, ˈsɛrˌeɪţəd] *adj* : dentado, serrado
serum [ˈsɪrəm] *n, pl* **serums** *or* **sera** [ˈsɪrə] : suero *m*
servant [ˈsərvənt] *n* : criado *m,* -da *f;* sirviente *m,* -ta *f*
serve [ˈsərv] *v* **served; serving** *vi* **1** : servir <to serve in the navy : servir en la armada> <to serve on a jury : ser miembro de un jurado> **2** DO, FUNCTION : servir <to serve as : servir de, servir como> **3** : sacar (en deportes) — *vt* **1** : servir <to serve God : servir a Dios> **2** HELP : servir <it serves no purpose : no sirve para nada> **3** : servir (comida o bebida) <dinner is served : la cena está servida> **4** SUPPLY : abastecer **5** CARRY OUT : cumplir, hacer <to serve time : servir una pena> **6 to serve a summons** : entregar una citación
server [ˈsərvər] *n* **1** : camarero *m,* -ra *f;* mesero *m,* -ra *f* (en un restaurante) **2** *or* **serving dish** : fuente *f* (para servir comida)
service[1] [ˈsərvəs] *vt* **-viced; -vicing 1** MAINTAIN : darle mantenimiento a (una máquina), revisar **2** REPAIR : arreglar, reparar
service[2] *n* **1** HELP, USE : servicio *m* <to do someone a service : hacerle un servicio a alguien> <at your service : a sus órdenes> <to be out of service : no funcionar> **2** CEREMONY : oficio *m* (religioso) **3** DEPARTMENT, SYSTEM : servicio *m* <social services : servicios sociales> <train service : servicio de trenes> **4** SET : juego *m,* servicio *m* <tea service : juego de té> **5** MAINTENANCE : mantenimiento *m,* revisión *f,* servicio *m* **6** : saque *m* (en deportes) **7 armed services** : fuerzas *fpl* armadas
serviceable [ˈsərvəsəbəl] *adj* **1** USEFUL : útil **2** DURABLE : duradero
serviceman [ˈsərvəsˌmæn, -mən] *n, pl* **-men** [-mən, -ˌmɛn] : militar *m*

service station *n* : estación *f* de servicio

servicewoman [ˈsərvəsˌwʊmən] *n, pl* **-women** [-ˌwɪmən] : militar *f*

servile [ˈsərvəl, -ˌvaɪl] *adj* : servil

serving [ˈsərvɪŋ] *n* HELPING : porción *f,* ración *f*

servitude [ˈsərvəˌtuːd, -ˌtjuːd] *n* : servidumbre *f*

sesame [ˈsɛsəmi] *n* : ajonjolí *m,* sésamo *m*

session [ˈsɛʃən] *n* : sesión *f*

set[1] [ˈsɛt] *v* **set; setting** *vt* **1** SEAT : sentar **2** *or* **to set down** PLACE : poner, colocar **3** ARRANGE : fijar, establecer <to set the date : poner la fecha> <he set the agenda : estableció la agenda> **4** ADJUST : poner (un reloj, etc.) **5** (*indicating the causing of a certain condition*) <to set fire to : prenderle fuego a> <she set it free : lo soltó> **6** MAKE, START : poner, hacer <I set them working : los puse a trabajar> — *vi* **1** SOLIDIFY : fraguar (dícese del cemento, etc.), cuajar (dícese de la gelatina, etc.) **2** : ponerse (dícese del sol o de la luna)

set[2] *adj* **1** ESTABLISHED, FIXED : fijo, establecido **2** RIGID : inflexible <to be set in one's ways : tener costumbres muy arraigadas> **3** READY : listo, preparado

set[3] *n* **1** COLLECTION : juego *m* <a set of dishes : un juego de platos, una vajilla> <a tool set : una caja de herramientas> **2** *or* **stage set** : decorado *m* (en el teatro), plató *m* (en el cine) **3** APPARATUS : aparato *m* <a television set : un televisor> **4** : conjunto *m* (en matemáticas)

setback [ˈsɛtˌbæk] *n* : revés *m,* contratiempo *m*

set in *vi* BEGIN : comenzar, empezar

set off *vt* **1** PROVOKE : provocar **2** EXPLODE : hacer estallar (una bomba, etc.) — *vi or* **to set forth** : salir

set out *vi* : salir (de viaje) — *vt* INTEND : proponerse

settee [sɛˈtiː] *n* : sofá *m*

setter [ˈsɛt̬ər] *n* : setter *mf* <Irish setter : setter irlandés>

setting [ˈsɛt̬ɪŋ] *n* **1** : posición *f,* ajuste *m* (de un control) **2** : engaste *m,* montura *f* (de una gema) **3** SCENE : escenario *m* (de una novela, etc.) **4** SURROUNDINGS : ambiente *m,* entorno *m,* marco *m*

settle [ˈsɛt̬əl] *v* **settled; settling** *vi* **1** ALIGHT, LAND : posarse (dícese de las aves), depositarse (dícese del polvo) **2** SINK : asentarse (dícese de los edificios) <he settled into the chair : se arrellanó en la silla> **3** : instalarse (en una casa), establecerse (en una ciudad o región) **4 to settle down** : calmarse, tranquilizarse <settle down! : ¡tranquilízate!, ¡cálmate!> **5 to settle down** : sentar cabeza, hacerse sensato <to marry and settle down : casarse y sentar cabeza> — *vt* **1** ARRANGE, DECIDE : fijar, decidir, acordar (planes, etc.) **2** RESOLVE : resolver, solucionar <to settle an argument : resolver una discusión> **3** PAY : pagar <to settle an account : saldar una cuenta> **4** CALM : calmar (los nervios), asentar (el estómago) **5** COLONIZE : colonizar **6 to settle oneself** : acomodarse, hacerse cómodo

settlement [ˈsɛt̬əlmənt] *n* **1** PAYMENT : pago *m,* liquidación *f* **2** COLONY : asentamiento *m* **3** RESOLUTION : acuerdo *m*

settler [ˈsɛt̬ələr] *n* : poblador *m,* -dora *f;* colono *m,* -na *f*

set up *vt* **1** ASSEMBLE : montar, armar **2** ERECT : levantar, erigir **3** ESTABLISH : establecer, fundar, montar (un negocio) **4** CAUSE : armar <they set up a clamor : armaron un alboroto>

seven[1] [ˈsɛvən] *adj* : siete

seven[2] *n* : siete *m*

seven hundred[1] *adj* : setecientos

seven hundred[2] *n* : setecientos *m*

seventeen[1] [ˌsɛvənˈtiːn] *adj* : diecisiete

seventeen[2] *n* : diecisiete *m*

seventeenth[1] [ˌsɛvənˈtiːnθ] *adj* : decimoséptimo

seventeenth[2] *n* **1** : decimoséptimo *m,* -ma *f* (en una serie) **2** : diecisieteavo *m,* diecisieteava parte *f*

seventh[1] [ˈsɛvənθ] *adj* : séptimo

seventh[2] *n* **1** : séptimo *m,* -ma *f* (en una serie) **2** : séptimo *m,* séptima parte *f*

seventieth[1] [ˈsɛvəntiəθ] *adj* : septuagésimo

seventieth[2] *n* **1** : septuagésimo *m,* -ma *f* (en una serie) **2** : setentavo *m,* setentava parte *f,* septuagésima parte *f*

seventy[1] [ˈsɛvənti] *adj* : setenta

seventy[2] *n, pl* **-ties** : setenta *m*

sever [ˈsɛvər] *vt* **-ered; -ering** : cortar, romper

several[1] [ˈsɛvrəl, ˈsɛvə-] *adj* **1** DISTINCT : distinto **2** SOME : varios <several weeks : varias semanas>

several[2] *pron* : varios, varias

severance [ˈsɛvrənts, sɛvə-] *n* **1** : ruptura *f* (de relaciones, etc.) **2 severance pay** : indemnización *f* (por despido)

severe [səˈvɪr] *adj* **severer; -est 1** STRICT : severo **2** AUSTERE : sobrio, austero **3** SERIOUS : grave <a severe wound : una herida grave> <severe aches : dolores fuertes> **4** DIFFICULT : duro, difícil — **severely** *adv*

severity [səˈvɛrət̬i] *n* **1** HARSHNESS : severidad *f* **2** AUSTERITY : sobriedad *f,* austeridad *f* **3** SERIOUSNESS : gravedad *f* (de una herida, etc.)

sew [ˈsoː] *v* **sewed; sewn** [ˈsoːn] *or* **sewed; sewing** : coser

sewage [ˈsuːɪdʒ] *n* : aguas *fpl* negras, aguas *fpl* residuales

sewer[1] [ˈsoːər] *n* : uno que cose

sewer[2] [ˈsuːər] *n* : alcantarilla *f,* cloaca *f*

sewing [ˈsoːɪŋ] *n* : costura *f*
sex [ˈsɛks] *n* **1** : sexo *m* <the opposite sex : el sexo opuesto> **2** COPULATION : relaciones *fpl* sexuales
sexism [ˈsɛkˌsɪzəm] *n* : sexismo *m*
sexist[1] [ˈsɛksɪst] *adj* : sexista
sexist[2] *n* : sexista *mf*
sextant [ˈsɛkstənt] *n* : sextante *m*
sextet [sɛkˈstɛt] *n* : sexteto *m*
sexton [ˈsɛkstən] *n* : sacristán *m*
sexual [ˈsɛkʃʊəl] *adj* : sexual — **sexually** *adv*
sexuality [ˌsɛkʃʊˈæləṱi] *n* : sexualidad *f*
sexy [ˈsɛksi] *adj* **sexier; -est** : sexy
shabbily [ˈʃæbəli] *adv* **1** : pobremente <shabbily dressed : pobremente vestido> **2** UNFAIRLY : mal, injustamente
shabbiness [ˈʃæbinəs] *n* **1** : lo gastado (de ropa, etc.) **2** : lo mal vestido (de personas) **3** UNFAIRNESS : injusticia *f*
shabby [ˈʃæbi] *adj* **shabbier; -est 1** : gastado (dícese de la ropa, etc.) **2** : mal vestido (dícese de las personas) **3** UNFAIR : malo, injusto <shabby treatment : mal trato>
shack [ˈʃæk] *n* : choza *f,* rancho *m*
shackle[1] [ˈʃækəl] *vt* **-led; -ling** : ponerle grilletes (a alguien)
shackle[2] *n* : grillete *m*
shad [ˈʃæd] *n* : sábalo *m*
shade[1] [ˈʃeɪd] *v* **shaded; shading** *vt* **1** SHELTER : proteger (del sol o de la luz) **2** *or* **to shade in** : matizar los colores de — *vi* : convertirse gradualmente <his irritation shaded into rage : su irritación iba convirtiéndose en furia>
shade[2] *n* **1** : sombra *f* <to give shade : dar sombra> **2** : tono *m* (de un color) **3** NUANCE : matiz *m* **4** : pantalla *f* (de una lámpara), persiana *f* (de una ventana)
shadow[1] [ˈʃædoː] *vt* **1** DARKEN : ensombrecer **2** TRAIL : seguir de cerca, seguirle la pista (a alguien)
shadow[2] *n* **1** : sombra *f* **2** DARKNESS : oscuridad *f* **3** TRACE : sombra *f,* atisbo *m,* indicio *m* <without a shadow of a doubt : sin sombra de duda, sin lugar a dudas> **4 to cast a shadow over** : ensombrecer
shadowy [ˈʃædowi] *adj* **1** INDISTINCT : vago, indistinto **2** DARK : oscuro
shady [ˈʃeɪdi] *adj* **shadier; -est 1** : sombreado (dícese de un lugar), que da sombra (dícese de un árbol) **2** DISREPUTABLE : sospechoso (dícese de una persona), turbio (dícese de un negocio, etc.)
shaft [ˈʃæft] *n* **1** : asta *f* (de una lanza), astil *m* (de una flecha), mango *m* (de una herramienta) **2** *or* **mine shaft** : pozo *m*
shaggy [ˈʃægi] *adj* **shaggier; -est 1** HAIRY : peludo <a shaggy dog : un perro peludo> **2** UNKEMPT : enmarañado, despeinado (dícese del pelo, de las barbas, etc.)
shake[1] [ˈʃeɪk] *v* **shook** [ˈʃʊk]; **shaken** [ˈʃeɪkən]; **shaking** *vt* **1** : sacudir, agitar, hacer temblar <he shook his head : negó con la cabeza> **2** WEAKEN : debilitar, hacer flaquear <it shook her faith : debilitó su confianza> **3** UPSET : afectar, alterar **4 to shake hands with someone** : darle la mano a alguien, estrecharle la mano a alguien — *vi* : temblar, sacudirse
shake[2] *n* : sacudida *f,* apretón *m* (de manos)
shaker [ˈʃeɪkər] *n* **1 salt shaker** : salero *m* **2 pepper shaker** : pimentero *m* **3 cocktail shaker** : coctelera *f*
shake–up [ˈʃeɪkˌʌp] *n* : reorganización *f*
shakily [ˈʃeɪkəli] *adv* : temblorosamente
shaky [ˈʃeɪki] *adj* **shakier; -est 1** SHAKING : tembloroso **2** UNSTABLE : poco firme, inestable **3** PRECARIOUS : precario, incierto **4** QUESTIONABLE : dudoso, cuestionable <shaky arguments : argumentos discutibles>
shale [ˈʃeɪl] *n* : esquisto *m*
shall [ˈʃæl] *v aux, past* **should** [ˈʃʊd]; *present s & pl* **shall 1** (*used to express a command*) <you shall do as I say : harás lo que te digo> **2** (*used to express futurity*) <we shall see : ya veremos> <when shall we expect you? : ¿cuándo te podemos esperar?> **3** (*used to express determination*) <you shall have the money : tendrás el dinero> **4** (*used to express a condition*) <if he should die : si muriera> <if they should call, tell me : si llaman, dímelo> **5** (*used to express obligation*) <he should have said it : debería haberlo dicho> **6** (*used to express probability*) <they should arrive soon : deben (de) llegar pronto> <why should he lie? : ¿porqué ha de mentir?>
shallow [ˈʃæloː] *adj* **1** : poco profundo (dícese del agua, etc.) **2** SUPERFICIAL : superficial
shallows [ˈʃæloːz] *npl* : bajío *m,* bajos *mpl*
sham[1] [ˈʃæm] *v* **shammed; shamming** : fingir
sham[2] *adj* : falso, fingido
sham[3] *n* **1** FAKE, PRETENSE : farsa *f,* simulación *f,* imitación *f* **2** FAKER : impostor *m,* -tora *f;* farsante *mf*
shamble [ˈʃæmbəl] *vi* **-bled; -bling** : caminar arrastrando los pies
shambles [ˈʃæmbəlz] *ns & pl* : caos *m,* desorden *m,* confusión *f*
shame[1] [ˈʃeɪm] *vt* **shamed; shaming 1** : avergonzar <he was shamed by their words : sus palabras le dieron vergüenza> **2** DISGRACE : deshonrar
shame[2] *n* **1** : vergüenza *f* <to have no shame : no tener vergüenza> **2** DISGRACE : vergüenza *f,* deshonra *f* **3** PITY : lástima *f,* pena *f* <what a shame! : ¡qué pena!>

shamefaced [ˈʃeɪmˌfeɪst] *adj* : avergonzado

shameful [ˈʃeɪmfəl] *adj* : vergonzoso — **shamefully** *adv*

shameless [ˈʃeɪmləs] *adj* : descarado, desvergonzado — **shamelessly** *adv*

shampoo[1] [ʃæmˈpuː] *vt* : lavar (el pelo)

shampoo[2] *n, pl* **-poos** : champú *m*

shamrock [ˈʃæmˌrɑk] *n* : trébol *m*

shank [ˈʃæŋk] *n* : parte *f* baja de la pierna

shan't [ˈʃænt] (*contraction of* **shall not**) → **shall**

shanty [ˈʃænti] *n, pl* **-ties** : choza *f*, rancho *m*

shape[1] [ˈʃeɪp] *v* **shaped; shaping** *vt* **1** : dar forma a, modelar (arcilla, etc.), tallar (madera, piedra), formar (carácter) <to be shaped like : tener forma de> **2** DETERMINE : decidir, determinar — *vi or* **to shape up** : tomar forma

shape[2] *n* **1** : forma *f*, figura *f* <in the shape of a circle : en forma de círculo> **2** CONDITION : estado *m*, condiciones *fpl*, forma *f* (física) <to get in shape : ponerse en forma>

shapeless [ˈʃeɪpləs] *adj* : informe

shapely [ˈʃeɪpli] *adj* **shapelier; -est** : curvilíneo, bien proporcionado

shard [ˈʃɑrd] *n* : fragmento *m*, casco *m* (de cerámica, etc.)

share[1] [ˈʃɛr] *v* **shared; sharing** *vt* **1** APPORTION : dividir, repartir **2** : compartir <they share a room : comparten una habitación> — *vi* : compartir

share[2] *n* **1** PORTION : parte *f*, porción *f* <one's fair share : lo que le corresponde a uno> **2** : acción *f* (en una compañía) <to hold shares : tener acciones>

sharecropper [ˈʃɛrˌkrɑpər] *n* : aparcero *m*, -ra *f*

shareholder [ˈʃɛrˌhoːldər] *n* : accionista *mf*

shark [ˈʃɑrk] *n* : tiburón *m*

sharp[1] [ˈʃɑrp] *adv* : en punto <at two o'clock sharp : a las dos en punto>

sharp[2] *adj* **1** : afilado, filoso <a sharp knife : un cuchillo afilado> **2** PENETRATING : cortante, fuerte **3** CLEVER : agudo, listo, perspicaz **4** ACUTE : agudo <sharp eyesight : vista aguda> **5** HARSH, SEVERE : duro, severo, agudo <a sharp rebuke : una reprimenda mordaz> **6** STRONG : fuerte <sharp cheese : queso fuerte> **7** ABRUPT : brusco, repentino **8** DISTINCT : nítido, definido <a sharp image : una imagen bien definida> **9** ANGULAR : anguloso (dícese de la cara) **10** : sostenido (en música)

sharp[3] *n* : sostenido *m* (en música)

sharpen [ˈʃɑrpən] *vt* : afilar, aguzar <to sharpen a pencil : sacarle punta a un lápiz> <to sharpen one's wits : aguzar el ingenio>

sharpener [ˈʃɑrpənər] *n* : afilador *m* (para cuchillos, etc.), sacapuntas *m* (para lápices)

sharply [ˈʃɑrpli] *adv* **1** ABRUPTLY : bruscamente **2** DISTINCTLY : claramente, marcadamente

sharpness [ˈʃɑrpnəs] *n* **1** : lo afilado (de un cuchillo, etc.) **2** ACUTENESS : agudeza *f* (de los sentidos o de la mente) **3** INTENSITY : intensidad *f*, agudeza *f* (de dolores, etc.) **4** HARSHNESS : dureza *f*, severidad *f* **5** ABRUPTNESS : brusquedad *f* **6** CLARITY : nitidez *f*

sharpshooter [ˈʃɑrpˌʃuːtər] *n* : tirador *m*, -dora *f* de primera

shatter [ˈʃætər] *vt* **1** : hacer añicos <to shatter the silence : romper el silencio> **2 to be shattered by** : quedar destrozado por — *vi* : hacerse añicos, romperse en pedazos

shave[1] [ˈʃeɪv] *v* **shaved; shaved** *or* **shaven** [ˈʃeɪvən]; **shaving** *vt* **1** : afeitar, rasurar <she shaved her legs : se rasuró las piernas> <they shaved (off) his beard : le afeitaron la barba> **2** SLICE : cortar (en pedazos finos) — *vi* : afeitarse, rasurarse

shave[2] *n* : afeitada *f*, rasurada *f*

shaver [ˈʃeɪvər] *n* : afeitadora *f*, máquina *f* de afeitar, rasuradora *f*

shawl [ˈʃɔl] *n* : chal *m*, mantón *m*, rebozo *m*

she [ˈʃiː] *pron* : ella

sheaf [ˈʃiːf] *n, pl* **sheaves** [ˈʃiːvz] : gavilla *f* (de cereales), haz *m* (de flechas), fajo *m* (de papeles)

shear [ˈʃɪr] *vt* **sheared; sheared** *or* **shorn** [ˈʃorn]; **shearing 1** : esquilar, trasquilar <to shear sheep : trasquilar ovejas> **2** CUT : cortar (el pelo, etc.)

shears [ˈʃɪrz] *npl* : tijeras *fpl* (grandes)

sheath [ˈʃiːθ] *n, pl* **sheaths** [ˈʃiːðz, ˈʃiːθs] : funda *f*, vaina *f*

sheathe [ˈʃiːð] *vt* **sheathed; sheathing** : envainar, enfundar

shed[1] [ˈʃɛd] *vt* **shed; shedding 1** : derramar (sangre o lágrimas) **2** EMIT : emitir (luz) <to shed light on : aclarar> **3** DISCARD : mudar (la piel, etc.) <to shed one's clothes : quitarse uno la ropa>

shed[2] *n* : cobertizo *m*

she'd [ˈʃiːd] (*contraction of* **she had** *or* **she would**) → **have, would**

sheen [ˈʃiːn] *n* : brillo *m*, lustre *m*

sheep [ˈʃiːp] *ns & pl* : oveja *f*

sheepfold [ˈʃiːpˌfoːld] *n* : redil *m*

sheepish [ˈʃiːpɪʃ] *adj* : avergonzado

sheepskin [ˈʃiːpˌskɪn] *n* : piel *f* de oveja, piel *f* de borrego

sheer[1] [ˈʃɪr] *adv* **1** COMPLETELY : completamente, totalmente **2** VERTICALLY : verticalmente

sheer[2] *adj* **1** TRANSPARENT : vaporoso, transparente **2** ABSOLUTE, UTTER : puro <by sheer luck : por pura suerte> **3** STEEP : escarpado, vertical

sheet [ˈʃiːt] *n* **1** *or* **bedsheet** [ˈbɛdˌʃiːt] : sábana *f* **2** : hoja *f* (de papel) **3**

: capa *f* (de hielo, etc.) **4 :** lámina *f,* placa *f* (de vidrio, metal, etc.), plancha *f* (de metal, madera, etc.) <baking sheet : placa de horno>

sheikh *or* **sheik** [ˈʃiːk, ˈʃeɪk] *n* **:** jeque *m*

shelf [ˈʃɛlf] *n, pl* **shelves** [ˈʃɛlvz] **1 :** estante *m,* anaquel *m* (en una pared) **2 :** banco *m,* arrecife *m* (en geología) <continental shelf : plataforma continental>

shell[1] [ˈʃɛl] *vt* **1 :** desvainar (chícharos), pelar (nueces, etc.) **2** BOMBARD **:** bombardear

shell[2] *n* **1** SEASHELL **:** concha *f* **2 :** cáscara *f* (de huevos, nueces, etc.), vaina *f* (de chícharos, etc.), caparazón *m* (de crustáceos, tortugas, etc.) **3 :** cartucho *m,* casquillo *m* <a .45 caliber shell : un cartucho calibre .45> **4** *or* **racing shell :** bote *m* (para hacer regatas de remos)

she'll [ˈʃiːl, ˈʃɪl] (*contraction of* **she shall** *or* **she will**) → **shall, will**

shellac[1] [ʃəˈlæk] *vt* **-lacked; -lacking 1 :** laquear (madera, etc.) **2** DEFEAT **:** darle una paliza (a alguien), derrotar

shellac[2] *n* **:** laca *f*

shellfish [ˈʃɛlˌfɪʃ] *n* **:** marisco *m*

shelter[1] [ˈʃɛltər] *vt* **1** PROTECT **:** proteger, abrigar **2** HARBOR **:** dar refugio a, albergar

shelter[2] *n* **:** refugio *m,* abrigo *m* <to take shelter : refugiarse>

shelve [ˈʃɛlv] *vt* **shelved; shelving 1 :** poner en estantes **2** DEFER **:** dar carpetazo a

shenanigans [ʃəˈnænɪgənz] *npl* **1** TRICKERY **:** artimañas *fpl* **2** MISCHIEF **:** travesuras *fpl*

shepherd[1] [ˈʃɛpərd] *vt* **1 :** cuidar (ovejas, etc.) **2** GUIDE **:** conducir, guiar

shepherd[2] *n* **:** pastor *m*

shepherdess [ˈʃɛpərdəs] *n* **:** pastora *f*

sherbet [ˈʃərbət] *or* **sherbert** [-bərt] *n* **:** sorbete *m,* nieve *f Cuba, Mex, PRi*

sheriff [ˈʃɛrɪf] *n* **:** sheriff *mf*

sherry [ˈʃɛri] *n, pl* **-ries :** jerez *m*

she's [ˈʃiːz] (*contraction of* **she is** *or* **she has**) → **be, have**

shield[1] [ˈʃiːld] *vt* **1** PROTECT **:** proteger **2** CONCEAL **:** ocultar <to shield one's eyes : taparse los ojos>

shield[2] *n* **1 :** escudo *m* (armadura) **2** PROTECTION **:** protección *f,* blindaje *m* (de un cable)

shier, shiest → **shy**

shift[1] [ˈʃɪft] *vt* **1** CHANGE **:** cambiar <to shift gears : cambiar de velocidad> **2** MOVE **:** mover **3** TRANSFER **:** transferir <to shift the blame : echarle la culpa (a otro)> — *vi* **1** CHANGE **:** cambiar **2** MOVE **:** moverse **3 to shift for oneself :** arreglárselas solo

shift[2] *n* **1** CHANGE, TRANSFER **:** cambio *m* <a shift in priorities : un cambio de prioridades> **2 :** turno *m* <night shift : turno de noche> **3** DRESS **:** vestido *m* (suelto) **4** → **gearshift**

shiftless [ˈʃɪftləs] *adj* **:** perezoso, vago, holgazán

shifty [ˈʃɪfti] *adj* **shiftier; -est :** taimado, artero <a shifty look : una mirada huidiza>

shilling [ˈʃɪlɪŋ] *n* **:** chelín *m*

shimmer [ˈʃɪmər] *vi* GLIMMER **:** brillar con luz trémula

shin[1] [ˈʃɪn] *vi* **shinned; shinning :** trepar, subir <she shinned up the pole : subió al poste>

shin[2] *n* **:** espinilla *f,* canilla *f*

shine[1] [ˈʃaɪn] *v* **shone** [ˈʃoːn, *esp Brit and Canadian* ˈʃɒn] *or* **shined; shining** *vi* **1 :** brillar, relucir <the stars were shining : las estrellas brillaban> **2** EXCEL **:** brillar, lucirse — *vt* **1 :** alumbrar <he shined the flashlight at it : lo alumbró con la linterna> **2** POLISH **:** sacarle brillo a, lustrar

shine[2] *n* **:** brillo *m,* lustre *m*

shingle[1] [ˈʃɪŋgəl] *vt* **-gled; -gling :** techar

shingle[2] *n* **:** tablilla *f* (para techar)

shingles [ˈʃɪŋgəlz] *npl* **:** herpes *m*

shinny [ˈʃɪni] *vi* **-nied; -nying** → **shin[1]**

shiny [ˈʃaɪni] *adj* **shinier; -est :** brillante

ship[1] [ˈʃɪp] *vt* **shipped; shipping 1** LOAD **:** embarcar (en un barco) **2** SEND **:** transportar (en barco), enviar <to ship by air : enviar por avión>

ship[2] *n* **1 :** barco *m,* buque *m* **2** → **spaceship**

shipboard [ˈʃɪpˌbord] *n* **on ~ :** a bordo

shipbuilder [ˈʃɪpˌbɪldər] *n* **:** constructor *m,* -tora *f* naval

shipment [ˈʃɪpmənt] *n* **1** SHIPPING **:** transporte *m,* embarque *m* **2 :** envío *m,* remesa *f* <a shipment of medicine : un envío de medicina>

shipping [ˈʃɪpɪŋ] *n* **1** SHIPS **:** barcos *mpl,* embarcaciones *fpl* **2** TRANSPORTATION **:** transporte *m* (de mercancías)

shipshape [ˈʃɪpˈʃeɪp] *adj* **:** ordenado

shipwreck[1] [ˈʃɪpˌrɛk] *vt* **to be shipwrecked :** naufragar

shipwreck[2] *n* **:** naufragio *m*

shipyard [ˈʃɪpˌjɑrd] *n* **:** astillero *m*

shirk [ˈʃərk] *vt* **:** eludir, rehuir <to shirk one's responsibilities : esquivar uno sus responsabilidades>

shirt [ˈʃərt] *n* **:** camisa *f*

shiver[1] [ˈʃɪvər] *vi* **1 :** tiritar (de frío) **2** TREMBLE **:** estremecerse, temblar

shiver[2] *n* **:** escalofrío *m,* estremecimiento *m*

shoal [ˈʃoːl] *n* **:** banco *m,* bajío *m*

shock[1] [ˈʃɑk] *vt* **1** UPSET **:** conmover, conmocionar **2** STARTLE **:** asustar, sobresaltar **3** SCANDALIZE **:** escandalizar **4 :** darle una descarga eléctrica a

shock[2] *n* **1** COLLISION, JOLT **:** choque *m,* sacudida *f* **2** UPSET **:** conmoción *f,* golpe *m* emocional **3 :** shock *m* (en medicina) **4** *or* **electric shock :** descarga *f* eléctrica **5** SHEAVES **:** gavillas *fpl* **6 shock of hair :** mata *f* de pelo

shock absorber *n* : amortiguador *m*
shoddy [ˈʃɑdi] *adj* **shoddier; -est** : de mala calidad <a shoddy piece of work : un trabajo chapucero>
shoe[1] [ˈʃuː] *vt* **shod** [ˈʃɑd]; **shoeing** : herrar (un caballo)
shoe[2] *n* **1** : zapato *m* <the shoe industry : la industria del calzado> **2** HORSESHOE : herradura *f* **3 brake shoe** : zapata *f*
shoelace [ˈʃuːˌleɪs] *n* : cordón *m* (de zapatos)
shoemaker [ˈʃuːˌmeɪkər] *n* : zapatero *m*, -ra *f*
shone → **shine**
shook → **shake**
shoot[1] [ˈʃuːt] *v* **shot** [ˈʃɑt]; **shooting** *vt* **1** : disparar, tirar <to shoot a bullet : tirar una bala> **2** : pegarle un tiro a, darle un balazo a <he shot her : le pegó un tiro> <they shot and killed him : lo mataron a balazos> **3** THROW : lanzar (una pelota, etc.), echar (una mirada) **4** PHOTOGRAPH : fotografiar **5** FILM : filmar — *vi* **1** : disparar (con un arma de fuego) **2** DART : ir rápidamente <it shot past : pasó como una bala>
shoot[2] *n* : brote *m*, retoño *m*, vástago *m*
shooting star *n* : estrella *f* fugaz
shop[1] [ˈʃɑp] *vi* **shopped; shopping** : hacer compras <to go shopping : ir de compras>
shop[2] *n* **1** WORKSHOP : taller *m* **2** STORE : tienda *f*
shopkeeper [ˈʃɑpˌkiːpər] *n* : tendero *m*, -ra *f*
shoplift [ˈʃɑpˌlɪft] *vi* : hurtar mercancía (de una tienda) — *vt* : hurtar (de una tienda)
shoplifter [ˈʃɑpˌlɪftər] *n* : ladrón *m*, -drona *f* (que roba en una tienda)
shopper [ˈʃɑpər] *n* : comprador *m*, -dora *f*
shore[1] [ˈʃor] *vt* **shored; shoring** : apuntalar <they shored up the wall : apuntalaron la pared>
shore[2] *n* **1** : orilla *f* (del mar, etc.) **2** PROP : puntal *m*
shoreline [ˈʃorˌlaɪn] *n* : orilla *f*
shorn → **shear**
short[1] [ˈʃɔrt] *adv* **1** ABRUPTLY : repentinamente, súbitamente <the car stopped short : el carro se paró en seco> **2 to fall short** : no alcanzar, quedarse corto
short[2] *adj* **1** : corto (de medida), bajo (de estatura) **2** BRIEF : corto <short and sweet : corto y bueno> <a short time ago : hace poco> **3** CURT : brusco, cortante, seco **4** : corto (de tiempo, de dinero) <I'm one dollar short : me falta un dólar>
short[3] *n* **1 shorts** *npl* : shorts *mpl*, pantalones *mpl* cortos **2** → **short circuit**
shortage [ˈʃɔrtɪdʒ] *n* : falta *f*, escasez *f*, carencia *f*
shortcake [ˈʃɔrtˌkeɪk] *n* : tarta *f* de fruta
shortchange [ˈʃɔrtˈtʃeɪndʒ] *vt* **-changed; -changing** : darle mal el cambio (a alguien)
short circuit *n* : cortocircuito *m*, corto *m* (eléctrico)
shortcoming [ˈʃɔrtˌkʌmɪŋ] *n* : defecto *m*
shortcut [ˈʃɔrtˌkʌt] *n* **1** : atajo *m* <to take a shortcut : cortar camino> **2** : alternativa *f* fácil, método *m* rápido
shorten [ˈʃɔrtən] *vt* : acortar — *vi* : acortarse
shorthand [ˈʃɔrtˌhænd] *n* : taquigrafía *f*
short–lived [ˈʃɔrtˈlɪvd, -ˈlaɪvd] *adj* : efímero
shortly [ˈʃɔrtli] *adv* **1** BRIEFLY : brevemente <to put it shortly : para decirlo en pocas palabras> **2** SOON : dentro de poco
shortness [ˈʃɔrtnəs] *n* **1** : lo corto <shortness of stature : estatura baja> **2** BREVITY : brevedad *f* **3** CURTNESS : brusquedad *f* **4** SHORTAGE : falta *f*, escasez *f*, carencia *f*
shortsighted [ˈʃɔrtˌsaɪt̬əd] → **nearsighted**
shot [ˈʃɑt] *n* **1** : disparo *m*, tiro *m* <to fire a shot : disparar> **2** PELLETS : perdigones *mpl* **3** : tiro *m* (en deportes) **4** ATTEMPT : intento *m*, tentativa *f* <to have a shot at : hacer un intento por> **5** RANGE : alcance *m* <a long shot : una posibilidad remota> **6** PHOTOGRAPH : foto *f* **7** INJECTION : inyección *f* **8** : trago *m* (de licor)
shotgun [ˈʃɑtˌgʌn] *n* : escopeta *f*
should → **shall**
shoulder[1] [ˈʃoːldər] *vt* **1** JOSTLE : empujar (con el hombro) **2** : ponerse al hombro (una mochila, etc.) **3** : cargar con (la responsabilidad, etc.)
shoulder[2] *n* **1** : hombro *m* <to shrug one's shoulders : encogerse los hombros> **2** : arcén *m* (de una carretera)
shoulder blade *n* : omóplato *m*, omoplato *m*, escápula *f*
shouldn't [ˈʃʊdənt] (*contraction of* **should not**) → **should**
shout[1] [ˈʃaʊt] *v* : gritar, vocear
shout[2] *n* : grito *m*
shove[1] [ˈʃʌv] *v* **shoved; shoving** : empujar bruscamente
shove[2] *n* : empujón *m*, empellón *m*
shovel[1] [ˈʃʌvəl] *vt* **-veled** *or* **-velled; -veling** *or* **-velling 1** : mover con (una) pala <they shoveled the dirt out : sacaron la tierra con palas> **2** DIG : cavar (con una pala)
shovel[2] *n* : pala *f*
show[1] [ˈʃoː] *v* **showed; shown** [ˈʃoːn] *or* **showed; showing** *vt* **1** DISPLAY : mostrar, enseñar **2** REVEAL : demostrar, manifestar, revelar <he showed himself to be a coward : se reveló como cobarde> **3** TEACH : enseñar **4** PROVE : demostrar, probar **5** CON-

DUCT, DIRECT : llevar, acompañar <to show someone the way : indicarle el camino a alguien> **6** : proyectar (una película), dar (un programa de televisión) — *vi* **1** : notarse, verse <the stain doesn't show : la mancha no se ve> **2** APPEAR : aparecer, dejarse ver

show² *n* **1** : demostración *f* <a show of force : una demostración de fuerza> **2** EXHIBITION : exposición *f,* exhibición *f* <flower show : exposición de flores> <to be on show : estar expuesto> **3** : espectáculo *m* (teatral), programa *m* (de televisión, etc.) <to go to a show : ir al teatro>

showcase [ˈʃoːˌkeɪs] *n* : vitrina *f*

showdown [ˈʃoːˌdaʊn] *n* : confrontación *f* (decisiva)

shower¹ [ˈʃaʊər] *vt* **1** SPRAY : regar, mojar **2** HEAP : colmar <they showered him with gifts : lo colmaron de regalos, le llovieron los regalos> — *vi* **1** BATHE : ducharse, darse una ducha **2** RAIN : llover

shower² *n* **1** : chaparrón *m,* chubasco *m* <a chance of showers : una posibilidad de chaparrones> **2** : ducha *f* <to take a shower : ducharse> **3** PARTY : fiesta *f* <a bridal shower : una despedida de soltera>

show off *vt* : hacer alarde de, ostentar — *vi* : lucirse

show up *vi* APPEAR : aparecer — *vt* EXPOSE : revelar

showy [ˈʃoːi] *adj* **showier; -est** : llamativo, ostentoso — **showily** *adv*

shrank → **shrink**

shrapnel [ˈʃræpnəl] *ns & pl* : metralla *f*

shred¹ [ˈʃrɛd] *vt* **shredded; shredding** : hacer trizas, desmenuzar (con las manos), triturar (con una máquina) <to shred vegetables : cortar verduras en tiras>

shred² *n* **1** STRIP : tira *f,* jirón *m* (de tela) **2** BIT : pizca *f* <not a shred of evidence : ni la mínima prueba>

shrew [ˈʃruː] *n* **1** : musaraña *f* (animal) **2** : mujer *f* regañona, arpía *f*

shrewd [ˈʃruːd] *adj* : astuto, inteligente, sagaz — **shrewdly** *adv*

shrewdness [ˈʃruːdnəs] *n* : astucia *f*

shriek¹ [ˈʃriːk] *vi* : chillar, gritar

shriek² *n* : chillido *m,* alarido *m,* grito *m*

shrill [ˈʃrɪl] *adj* : agudo, estridente

shrilly [ˈʃrɪli] *adv* : agudamente

shrimp [ˈʃrɪmp] *n* : camarón *m,* langostino *m*

shrine [ˈʃraɪn] *n* **1** TOMB : sepulcro *m* (de un santo) **2** SANCTUARY : lugar *m* sagrado, santuario *m*

shrink [ˈʃrɪŋk] *vi* **shrank** [ˈʃræŋk]; **shrunk** [ˈʃrʌŋk] *or* **shrunken** [ˈʃrʌŋkən]; **shrinking 1** RECOIL : retroceder <he shrank back : se echó para atrás> **2** : encogerse (dícese de la ropa)

shrinkage [ˈʃrɪŋkɪdʒ] *n* : encogimiento *m* (de ropa, etc.), contracción *f,* reducción *f*

shrivel [ˈʃrɪvəl] *vi* **-veled** *or* **-velled; -veling** *or* **-velling** : arrugarse, marchitarse

shroud¹ [ˈʃraʊd] *vt* : envolver

shroud² *n* **1** : sudario *m,* mortaja *f* **2** VEIL : velo *m* <wrapped in a shroud of mystery : envuelto en un aura de misterio>

shrub [ˈʃrʌb] *n* : arbusto *m,* mata *f*

shrubbery [ˈʃrʌbəri] *n, pl* **-beries** : arbustos *mpl,* matas *fpl*

shrug [ˈʃrʌg] *vi* **shrugged; shrugging** : encogerse de hombros

shrunk → **shrink**

shuck¹ [ˈʃʌk] *vt* : pelar (mazorcas, etc.), abrir (almejas, etc.)

shuck² *n* **1** HUSK : cascarilla *f,* cáscara *f* (de una nuez, etc.), hojas *fpl* (de una mazorca) **2** SHELL : concha *f* (de una almeja, etc.)

shudder¹ [ˈʃʌdər] *vi* : estremecerse

shudder² *n* : estremecimiento *m,* escalofrío *m*

shuffle¹ [ˈʃʌfəl] *v* **-fled; -fling** *vt* MIX : mezclar, revolver, barajar (naipes) — *vi* : caminar arrastrando los pies

shuffle² *n* **1** : acto *m* de revolver <each player gets a shuffle : a cada jugador le toca barajar> **2** JUMBLE : revoltijo *m* **3** : arrastramiento *m* de los pies

shun [ˈʃʌn] *vi* **shunned; shunning** : evitar, esquivar, eludir

shunt [ˈʃʌnt] *vt* : desviar, cambiar de vía (un tren)

shut [ˈʃʌt] *v* **shut; shutting** *vt* **1** CLOSE : cerrar <shut the lid : tápalo> **2 to shut out** EXCLUDE : excluir, dejar fuera a (personas), no dejar que entre (luz, ruido, etc.) **3 to shut up** CONFINE : encerrar — *vi* : cerrarse <the factory shut down : la fábrica cerró sus puertas>

shut–in [ˈʃʌtˌɪn] *n* : inválido *m,* -da *f* (que no puede salir de casa)

shutter [ˈʃʌtər] *n* **1** : contraventana *f,* postigo *m* (de una ventana o puerta) **2** : obturador *m* (de una cámara)

shuttle¹ [ˈʃʌtəl] *v* **-tled; -tling** *vt* : transportar <she shuttled him back and forth : lo llevaba de acá para allá> — *vi* : ir y venir

shuttle² *n* **1** : lanzadera *f* (para tejer) **2** : vehículo *m* que hace recorridos cortos **3** → **space shuttle**

shuttlecock [ˈʃʌtəlˌkɑk] *n* : volante *m*

shut up *vi* : callarse <shut up! : ¡cállate (la boca)!>

shy¹ [ˈʃaɪ] *vi* **shied; shying** : retroceder, asustarse

shy² *adj* **shier** *or* **shyer** [ˈʃaɪər]; **shiest** *or* **shyest** [ˈʃaɪəst] **1** TIMID : tímido **2** WARY : cauteloso <he's not shy about asking : no vacila en preguntar> **3** SHORT : corto (de dinero, etc.) <I'm two dollars shy : me faltan dos dólares>

shyly [ˈʃaɪli] *adv* : tímidamente
shyness [ˈʃaɪnəs] *n* : timidez *f*
sibling [ˈsɪblɪŋ] *n* : hermano *m,* hermana *f*
Sicilian [səˈsɪljən] *n* : siciliano *m,* -na *f* — **Sicilian** *adj*
sick [ˈsɪk] *adj* **1** : enfermo **2** NAUSEOUS : mareado, con náuseas <to get sick : vomitar> **3** : para uso de enfermos <sick day : día de permiso (por enfermedad)>
sickbed [ˈsɪkˌbɛd] *n* : lecho *m* de enfermo
sicken [ˈsɪkən] *vt* **1** : poner enfermo **2** REVOLT : darle asco (a alguien) — *vi* : enfermar(se), caer enfermo
sickening [ˈsɪkənɪŋ] *adj* : asqueroso, repugnante, nauseabundo
sickle [ˈsɪkəl] *n* : hoz *f*
sickly [ˈsɪkli] *adj* **sicklier; -est 1** : enfermizo **2** → **sickening**
sickness [ˈsɪknəs] *n* **1** : enfermedad *f* **2** NAUSEA : náuseas *fpl*
side [ˈsaɪd] *n* **1** : lado *m,* costado *m* (de una persona), ijada *f* (de un animal) **2** : lado *m,* cara *f* (de una moneda, etc.) **3** : lado *m,* parte *f* <he's on my side : está de mi parte> <to take sides : tomar partido>
sideboard [ˈsaɪdˌbord] *n* : aparador *m*
sideburns [ˈsaɪdˌbərnz] *npl* : patillas *fpl*
sided [ˈsaɪdəd] *adj* : que tiene lados <one-sided : de un lado>
side effect *n* : efecto *m* secundario
sideline [ˈsaɪdˌlaɪn] *n* **1** : línea *f* de banda (en deportes) **2** : actividad *f* suplementaria (en negocios) **3 to be on the sidelines** : estar al margen
sidelong [ˈsaɪdˌlɔŋ] *adj* : de reojo, de soslayo
sideshow [ˈsaɪdˌʃoː] *n* : espectáculo *m* secundario, atracción *f* secundaria
sidestep [ˈsaɪdˌstɛp] *v* **-stepped; -stepping** *vi* : dar un paso hacia un lado — *vt* AVOID : esquivar, eludir
sidetrack [ˈsaɪdˌtræk] *vt* : desviar (una conversación, etc.), distraer (a una persona)
sidewalk [ˈsaɪdˌwɔk] *n* : acera *f,* vereda *f,* andén *m CA, Col,* banqueta *f Mex*
sideways¹ [ˈsaɪdˌweɪz] *adv* **1** : hacia un lado <it leaned sideways : se inclinaba hacia un lado> **2** : de lado, de costado <lie sideways : acuéstese de costado>
sideways² *adj* : hacia un lado <a sideways glance : una mirada de reojo>
siding [ˈsaɪdɪŋ] *n* **1** : apartadero *m* (para trenes) **2** : revestimiento *m* exterior (de un edificio)
sidle [ˈsaɪdəl] *vi* **-dled; -dling** : moverse furtivamente
siege [ˈsiːdʒ, ˈsiːʒ] *n* : sitio *m* <to be under siege : estar sitiado>
siesta [siːˈɛstə] *n* : siesta *f*
sieve [ˈsɪv] *n* : tamiz *m,* cedazo *m,* criba *f* (en minerología)
sift [ˈsɪft] *vt* **1** : tamizar, cerner <sift the flour : tamice la harina> **2** *or* **sift through** : examinar cuidadosamente, pasar por el tamiz
sifter [ˈsɪftər] *n* : tamiz *m,* cedazo *m*
sigh¹ [ˈsaɪ] *vi* : suspirar
sigh² *n* : suspiro *m*
sight¹ [ˈsaɪt] *vt* : ver (a una persona), divisar (la tierra, un barco)
sight² *n* **1** : vista *f* (facultad) <out of sight : fuera de vista> **2** : algo visto <it's a familiar sight : se ve con frecuencia> <she's a sight for sore eyes : da gusto verla> **3** : lugar *m* de interés (para turistas, etc.) **4** : mira *f* (de un rifle, etc.) **5** GLIMPSE : mirada *f* breve <I caught sight of her : la divisé, alcancé a verla>
sightless [ˈsaɪtləs] *adj* : invidente, ciego
sightseer [ˈsaɪtˌsiːər] *n* : turista *mf*
sign¹ [ˈsaɪn] *vt* **1** : firmar <to sign a check : firmar un cheque> **2** *or* **to sign on** HIRE : contratar (a un empleado), fichar (a un jugador) — *vi* **1** : hacer una seña <she signed for him to stop : le hizo una seña para que se parara> **2** : comunicarse por señas
sign² *n* **1** SYMBOL : símbolo *m,* signo *m* <minus sign : signo de menos> **2** GESTURE : seña *f,* señal *f,* gesto *m* **3** : letrero *m,* cartel *m* <neon sign : letrero de neón> **4** TRACE : señal *f,* indicio *m*
signal¹ [ˈsɪgnəl] *vt* **-naled** *or* **-nalled; -naling** *or* **-nalling 1** : hacerle señas (a alguien) <she signaled me to leave : me hizo señas para que saliera> **2** INDICATE : señalar, indicar — *vi* : hacer señas, comunicar por señas
signal² *adj* NOTABLE : señalado, notable
signal³ *n* : señal *f*
signature [ˈsɪgnəˌtʃʊr] *n* : firma *f*
signet [ˈsɪgnət] *n* : sello *m*
significance [sɪgˈnɪfɪkən*t*s] *n* **1** MEANING : significado *m* **2** IMPORTANCE : importancia *f*
significant [sɪgˈnɪfɪkənt] *adj* **1** IMPORTANT : importante **2** MEANINGFUL : significativo — **significantly** *adv*
signify [ˈsɪgnəˌfaɪ] *vt* **-fied; -fying 1** : indicar <he signified his desire for more : haciendo señas indicó que quería más> **2** MEAN : significar
sign language *n* : lenguaje *m* por señas
signpost [ˈsaɪnˌpoːst] *n* : poste *m* indicador
silence¹ [ˈsaɪlən*t*s] *vt* **-lenced; -lencing** : silenciar, acallar
silence² *n* : silencio *m*
silent [ˈsaɪlənt] *adj* **1** : callado <to remain silent : quedarse callado, guardar silencio> **2** QUIET, STILL : silencioso **3** MUTE : mudo <a silent letter : una letra muda>
silently [ˈsaɪləntli] *adv* : silenciosamente, calladamente
silhouette¹ [ˌsɪləˈwɛt] *vt* **-etted; -etting** : destacar la silueta de <it was

silhouetted against the sky : se perfilaba contra el cielo>
silhouette[2] *n* : silueta *f*
silica [ˈsɪlɪkə] *n* : sílice *f*
silicon [ˈsɪlɪkən, -ˌkɑn] *n* : silicio *m*
silk [ˈsɪlk] *n* : seda *f*
silken [ˈsɪlkən] *adj* **1** : de seda <a silken veil : un velo de seda> **2** SILKY : sedoso <silken hair : cabellos sedosos>
silkworm [ˈsɪlkˌwərm] *n* : gusano *m* de seda
silky [ˈsɪlki] *adj* **silkier; -est** : sedoso
sill [ˈsɪl] *n* : alféizar *m* (de una ventana), umbral *m* (de una puerta)
silliness [ˈsɪlinəs] *n* : tontería *f*, estupidez *f*
silly [ˈsɪli] *adj* **sillier; -est** : tonto, estúpido, ridículo
silo [ˈsaɪˌloː] *n, pl* **silos** : silo *m*
silt [ˈsɪlt] *n* : cieno *m*
silver[1] [ˈsɪlvər] *adj* **1** : de plata <a silver spoon : una cuchara de plata> **2** → **silvery**
silver[2] *n* **1** : plata *f* **2** COINS : monedas *fpl* **3** → **silverware 4** : color *m* plata
silverware [ˈsɪlvərˌwær] *n* **1** : artículos *mpl* de plata, platería *f* **2** FLATWARE : cubertería *f*
silvery [ˈsɪlvəri] *adj* : plateado
similar [ˈsɪmələr] *adj* : similar, parecido, semejante
similarity [ˌsɪməˈlærəṭi] *n, pl* **-ties** : semejanza *f*, parecido *m*
similarly [ˈsɪmələrli] *adv* : de manera similar
simile [ˈsɪməˌliː] *n* : símil *m*
simmer [ˈsɪmər] *v* : hervir a fuego lento
simper[1] [ˈsɪmpər] *vi* : sonreír como un tonto
simper[2] *n* : sonrisa *f* tonta
simple [ˈsɪmpəl] *adj* **simpler; -plest 1** INNOCENT : inocente **2** PLAIN : sencillo, simple **3** EASY : simple, sencillo, fácil **4** STRAIGHTFORWARD : puro, simple <the simple truth : la pura verdad> **5** NAIVE : ingenuo, simple
simpleton [ˈsɪmpəltən] *n* : bobo *m*, -ba *f*; tonto *m*, -ta *f*
simplicity [sɪmˈplɪsəṭi] *n* : simplicidad *f*, sencillez *f*
simplification [ˌsɪmpləfəˈkeɪʃən] *n* : simplificación *f*
simplify [ˈsɪmpləˌfaɪ] *vt* **-fied; -fying** : simplificar
simply [ˈsɪmpli] *adv* **1** PLAINLY : sencillamente **2** SOLELY : simplemente, sólo **3** REALLY : absolutamente
simulate [ˈsɪmjəˌleɪt] *vt* **-lated; -lating** : simular
simultaneous [ˌsaɪməlˈteɪniəs] *adj* : simultáneo — **simultaneously** *adv*
sin[1] [ˈsɪn] *vi* **sinned; sinning** : pecar
sin[2] *n* : pecado *m*
since[1] [ˈsɪnts] *adv* **1** : desde entonces <they've been friends ever since : desde entonces han sido amigos> <she's since become mayor : más tarde se hizo alcalde> **2** AGO : hace <he's long since dead : murió hace mucho>
since[2] *conj* **1** : desde que <since he was born : desde que nació> **2** INASMUCH AS : ya que, puesto que, dado que
since[3] *prep* : desde
sincere [sɪnˈsɪr] *adj* **-cerer; -est** : sincero — **sincerely** *adv*
sincerity [sɪnˈsɛrəṭi] *n* : sinceridad *f*
sinew [ˈsɪnˌjuː, ˈsɪˌnuː] *n* **1** TENDON : tendón *m*, nervio *m* (en la carne) **2** POWER : fuerza *f*
sinewy [ˈsɪnjʊi, ˈsɪnʊi] *adj* **1** STRINGY : fibroso **2** STRONG, WIRY : fuerte, nervudo
sinful [ˈsɪnfəl] *adj* : pecador (dícese de las personas), pecaminoso
sing [ˈsɪŋ] *v* **sang** [ˈsæŋ] *or* **sung** [ˈsʌŋ]; **sung; singing** : cantar
singe [ˈsɪndʒ] *vt* **singed; singeing** : chamuscar, quemar
singer [ˈsɪŋər] *n* : cantante *mf*
single[1] [ˈsɪŋgəl] *vt* **-gled; -gling** *or* **to single out 1** SELECT : escoger **2** DISTINGUISH : señalar
single[2] *adj* **1** UNMARRIED : soltero **2** SOLE : solo <a single survivor : un solo sobreviviente> <every single one : cada uno, todos>
single[3] *n* **1** : soltero *m*, -ra *f* <for married couples and singles : para los matrimonios y los solteros> **2** *or* **single room** : habitación *f* individual **3** DOLLAR : billete *m* de un dólar
single–handed [ˈsɪŋgəlˈhændəd] *adj* : sin ayuda, solo
singly [ˈsɪŋgli] *adv* : individualmente, uno por uno
singular[1] [ˈsɪŋgjələr] *adj* **1** : singular (en gramática) **2** OUTSTANDING : singular, sobresaliente **3** STRANGE : singular, extraño
singular[2] *n* : singular *m*
singularly [ˈsɪŋgjələrli] *adv* : singularmente
sinister [ˈsɪnəstər] *adj* : siniestro
sink[1] [ˈsɪŋk] *v* **sank** [ˈsæŋk] *or* **sunk** [ˈsʌŋk]; **sunk; sinking** *vi* **1** : hundirse (dícese de un barco) **2** DROP, FALL : descender, caer <to sink into a chair : dejarse caer en una silla> <her heart sank : se le cayó el alma a los pies> **3** DECREASE : bajar — *vt* **1** : hundir (un barco, etc.) **2** EXCAVATE : excavar (un pozo para minar), perforar (un pozo de agua) **3** PLUNGE, STICK : clavar, hincar **4** INVEST : invertir (fondos)
sink[2] *n* **1 kitchen sink** : fregadero *m*, lavaplatos *m Chile, Col, Mex* **2 bathroom sink** : lavabo *m*, lavamanos *m*
sinner [ˈsɪnər] *n* : pecador *m*, -dora *f*
sinuous [ˈsɪnjʊəs] *adj* : sinuoso — **sinuously** *adv*
sinus [ˈsaɪnəs] *n* : seno *m*
sip[1] [ˈsɪp] *v* **sipped; sipping** *vt* : sorber — *vi* : beber a sorbos
sip[2] *n* : sorbo *m*
siphon[1] [ˈsaɪfən] *vt* : sacar con sifón

siphon[2] *n* : sifón *m*

sir ['sər] *n* **1** (*in titles*) : sir *m* **2** (*as a form of address*) : señor *m* <Dear Sir : Muy señor mío> <yes sir! : ¡sí, señor!>

sire[1] ['saɪr] *vt* **sired; siring** : engendrar, ser el padre de

sire[2] *n* : padre *m*

siren ['saɪrən] *n* : sirena *f*

sirloin ['sər,lɔɪn] *n* : solomillo *m*

sirup → **syrup**

sisal ['saɪsəl, -zəl] *n* : sisal *m*

sissy ['sɪsi] *n, pl* **-sies** : mariquita *f fam*

sister ['sɪstər] *n* : hermana *f*

sisterhood ['sɪstər,hʊd] *n* **1** : condición *f* de ser hermana **2** : sociedad *f* de mujeres

sister-in-law ['sɪstərɪn,lɔ] *n, pl* **sisters-in-law** : cuñada *f*

sisterly ['sɪstərli] *adj* : de hermana

sit ['sɪt] *v* **sat** ['sæt]; **sitting** *vi* **1** : sentarse, estar sentado <he sat down : se sentó> **2** ROOST : posarse **3** : sesionar <the legislature is sitting : la legislatura está en sesión> **4** POSE : posar (para un retrato) **5** LIE, REST : estar (ubicado) <the house sits on a hill : la casa está en una colina> — *vt* SEAT : sentar, colocar <I sat him on the sofa : lo senté en el sofá>

site ['saɪt] *n* 1 PLACE : sitio *m,* lugar *m* **2** LOCATION : emplazamiento *m,* ubicación *f*

sitting room → **living room**

sitter ['sɪt̬ər] → **baby-sitter**

situated ['sɪtʃʊ,eɪt̬əd] *adj* LOCATED : ubicado, situado

situation [,sɪtʃʊ'eɪʃən] *n* **1** LOCATION : situación *f,* ubicación *f,* emplazamiento *m* **2** CIRCUMSTANCES : situación *f* **3** JOB : empleo *m*

six[1] ['sɪks] *adj* : seis

six[2] *n* : seis *m*

six-gun ['sɪks,gʌn] *n* : revólver *m* (con seis cámaras)

six hundred[1] *adj* : seiscientos

six hundred[2] *n* : seiscientos *m*

six-shooter ['sɪks,ʃuːt̬ər] → **six-gun**

sixteen[1] [sɪks'tiːn] *adj* : dieciséis

sixteen[2] *n* : dieciséis *m*

sixteenth[1] [sɪks'tiːnθ] *adj* : decimosexto

sixteenth[2] *n* **1** : decimosexto *m,* -ta *f* (en una serie) **2** : dieciseisavo *m,* dieciseisava parte *f*

sixth[1] ['sɪksθ, 'sɪkst] *adj* : sexto

sixth[2] *n* **1** : sexto *m,* -ta *f* (en una serie) **2** : sexto *m,* sexta parte *f*

sixtieth[1] ['sɪkstiəθ] *adj* : sexagésimo

sixtieth[2] *n* **1** : sexagésimo *m,* -ma *f* (en una serie) **2** : sesentavo *m,* sesentava parte *f*

sixty[1] ['sɪksti] *adj* : sesenta

sixty[2] *n, pl* **-ties** : sesenta *m*

sizable *or* **sizeable** ['saɪzəbəl] *adj* : considerable

size[1] ['saɪz] *vt* **sized; sizing 1** : clasificar según el tamaño **2 to size up** : evaluar, apreciar

size[2] *n* **1** DIMENSIONS : tamaño *m,* talla *f* (de ropa), número *m* (de zapatos) **2** MAGNITUDE : magnitud *f*

sizzle ['sɪzəl] *vi* **-zled; -zling** : chisporrotear

skate[1] ['skeɪt] *vi* **skated; skating** : patinar

skate[2] *n* **1** : patín *m* <roller skate : patín de ruedas> **2** : raya *f* (pez)

skateboard ['skeɪt,bord] *n* : monopatín *m*

skater ['skeɪt̬ər] *n* : patinador *m,* -dora *f*

skein ['skeɪn] *n* : madeja *f*

skeletal ['skɛlət̬əl] *adj* **1** : óseo (en anatomía) **2** EMACIATED : esquelético

skeleton ['skɛlətən] *n* **1** : esqueleto *m* (anatómico) **2** FRAMEWORK : armazón *mf*

skeptic ['skɛptɪk] *n* : escéptico *m,* -ca *f*

skeptical ['skɛptɪkəl] *adj* : escéptico

skepticism ['skɛptə,sɪzəm] *n* : escepticismo *m*

sketch[1] ['skɛtʃ] *vt* : bosquejar — *vi* : hacer bosquejos

sketch[2] *n* **1** DRAWING, OUTLINE : esbozo *m,* bosquejo *m* **2** ESSAY : ensayo *m*

sketchy ['skɛtʃi] *adj* **sketchier; -est** : incompleto, poco detallado

skewer[1] ['skjuːər] *vt* : ensartar (carne, etc.)

skewer[2] *n* : brocheta *f,* broqueta *f*

ski[1] ['skiː] *vi* **skied; skiing** : esquiar

ski[2] *n, pl* **skis** : esquí *m*

skid[1] ['skɪd] *vi* **skidded; skidding** : derrapar, patinar

skid[2] *n* : derrape *m,* patinazo *m*

skier ['skiːər] *n* : esquiador *m,* -dora *f*

skiff ['skɪf] *n* : esquife *m*

skill ['skɪl] *n* **1** DEXTERITY : habilidad *f,* destreza *f* **2** CAPABILITY : capacidad *f,* arte *m,* técnica *f* <organizational skills : la capacidad para organizar>

skilled ['skɪld] *adj* : hábil, experto

skillet ['skɪlət] *n* : sartén *mf*

skillful ['skɪlfəl] *adj* : hábil, diestro

skillfully ['skɪlfəli] *adv* : con habilidad, con destreza

skim[1] ['skɪm] *vt* **skimmed; skimming 1** *or* **to skim off** : espumar, descremar (leche) **2** : echarle un vistazo a (un libro, etc.), pasar rozando (un superficie)

skim[2] *adj* : descremado <skim milk : leche descremada>

skimp ['skɪmp] *vi* **to skimp on** : escatimar

skimpy ['skɪmpi] *adj* **skimpier; -est** : exiguo, escaso, raquítico

skin[1] ['skɪn] *vt* **skinned; skinning** : despellejar, desollar

skin[2] *n* **1** : piel *f,* cutis *m* (de la cara) <dark skin : piel morena> **2** RIND : piel *f*

skin diving *n* : buceo *m,* submarinismo *m*

skinflint ['skɪn,flɪnt] *n* : tacaño *m,* -ña *f*

skinned [ˈskɪnd] *adj* : de piel <tough-skinned : de piel dura>

skinny [ˈskɪni] *adj* **skinnier; -est** : flaco

skip¹ [ˈskɪp] *v* **skipped; skipping** *vi* : ir dando brincos — *vt* : saltarse

skip² *n* : brinco *m,* salto *m*

skipper [ˈskɪpər] *n* : capitán *m,* -tana *f*

skirmish¹ [ˈskərmɪʃ] *vi* : escaramuzar

skirmish² *n* : escaramuza *f,* refriega *f*

skirt¹ [ˈskərt] *vt* **1** BORDER : bordear **2** EVADE : evadir, esquivar

skirt² *n* : falda *f,* pollera *f*

skit [ˈskɪt] *n* : sketch *m* (teatral)

skittish [ˈskɪt̬ɪʃ] *adj* : asustadizo, nervioso

skulk [ˈskʌlk] *vi* : merodear

skull [ˈskʌl] *n* **1** : cráneo *m,* calavera *f* **2 skull and crossbones** : calavera *f* (bandera pirata)

skunk [ˈskʌŋk] *n* : zorrillo *m,* mofeta *f*

sky [ˈskaɪ] *n, pl* **skies** : cielo *m*

skylark [ˈskaɪˌlɑrk] *n* : alondra *f*

skylight [ˈskaɪˌlaɪt] *n* : claraboya *f,* tragaluz *m*

skyline [ˈskaɪˌlaɪn] *n* : horizonte *m*

skyrocket [ˈskaɪˌrɑkət] *vi* : dispararse

skyscraper [ˈskaɪˌskreɪpər] *n* : rascacielos *m*

slab [ˈslæb] *n* : losa *f* (de piedra), tabla *f* (de madera), pedazo *m* grueso (de pan, etc.)

slack¹ [ˈslæk] *adj* **1** CARELESS : descuidado, negligente **2** LOOSE : flojo **3** SLOW : de poco movimiento

slack² *n* **1** : parte *f* floja <to take up the slack : tensar (una cuerda, etc.)> **2 slacks** *npl* : pantalones *mpl*

slacken [ˈslækən] *vt* : aflojar — *vi* : aflojarse

slag [ˈslæg] *n* : escoria *f*

slain → **slay**

slake [ˈsleɪk] *vt* **slaked; slaking** : saciar (la sed), satisfacer (la curiosidad)

slam¹ [ˈslæm] *v* **slammed; slamming** *vt* **1** : cerrar de golpe <he slammed the door : dio un portazo> **2** : tirar o dejar caer de golpe <he slammed down the book : dejó caer el libro de un golpe> — *vi* **1** : cerrarse de golpe **2 to slam into** : chocar contra

slam² *n* : golpe *m,* portazo *m* (de una puerta)

slander¹ [ˈslændər] *vt* : calumniar, difamar

slander² *n* : calumnia *f,* difamación *f*

slanderous [ˈslændərəs] *adj* : difamatorio, calumnioso

slang [ˈslæŋ] *n* : argot *m,* jerga *f*

slant¹ [ˈslænt] *vi* : inclinarse, ladearse — *vt* **1** SLOPE : inclinar **2** ANGLE : sesgar, orientar, dirigir <a story slanted towards youth : un artículo dirigido a los jóvenes>

slant² *n* **1** INCLINE : inclinación *f* **2** PERSPECTIVE : perspectiva *f,* enfoque *m*

slap¹ [ˈslæp] *vt* **slapped; slapping** : bofetear, cachetear, dar una palmada (en la espalda, etc.)

slap² *n* : bofetada *f,* cachetada *f,* palmada *f*

slash¹ [ˈslæʃ] *vt* **1** GASH : cortar, hacer un tajo en **2** REDUCE : reducir, rebajar (precios)

slash² *n* : tajo *m,* corte *m*

slat [ˈslæt] *n* : tablilla *f,* listón *m*

slate [ˈsleɪt] *n* **1** : pizarra *f* <a slate roof : un techo de pizarra> **2** : lista *f* de candidatos (políticos)

slaughter¹ [ˈslɔt̬ər] *vt* **1** BUTCHER : matar (animales) **2** MASSACRE : masacrar (personas)

slaughter² *n* **1** : matanza *f* (de animales) **2** MASSACRE : masacre *f,* carnicería *f*

slaughterhouse [ˈslɔt̬ərˌhaʊs] *n* : matadero *m*

Slav [ˈslɑv, ˈslæv] *n* : eslavo *m,* -va *f*

slave¹ [ˈsleɪv] *vi* **slaved; slaving** : trabajar como un burro

slave² *n* : esclavo *m,* -va *f*

slaver [ˈslævər, ˈsleɪ-] *vi* : babear

slavery [ˈsleɪvəri] *n* : esclavitud *f*

Slavic [ˈslɑvɪk, ˈslæ-] *adj* : eslavo

slavish [ˈsleɪvɪʃ] *adj* **1** SERVILE : servil **2** IMITATIVE : poco original

slay [ˈsleɪ] *vt* **slew** [ˈsluː]; **slain** [ˈsleɪn]; **slaying** : asesinar, matar

slayer [ˈsleɪər] *n* : asesino *m,* -na *f*

sleazy [ˈsliːzi] *adj* **sleazier; -est 1** SHODDY : chapucero, de mala calidad **2** DILAPIDATED : ruinoso **3** DISREPUTABLE : de mala fama

sled¹ [ˈslɛd] *v* **sledded; sledding** *vi* : ir en trineo — *vt* : transportar en trineo

sled² *n* : trineo *m*

sledge [ˈslɛdʒ] *n* **1** : trineo *m* (grande) **2** → **sledgehammer**

sledgehammer [ˈslɛdʒˌhæmər] *n* : almádena *f,* combo *m Chile, Peru*

sleek¹ [ˈsliːk] *vt* SLICK : alisar

sleek² *adj* : liso y brillante

sleep¹ [ˈsliːp] *vi* **slept** [ˈslɛpt]; **sleeping** : dormir

sleep² *n* **1** : sueño *m* **2 to go to sleep** : dormirse

sleeper [ˈsliːpər] *n* **1** : durmiente *mf* <to be a light sleeper : tener el sueño ligero> **2** *or* **sleeping car** : coche *m* cama, coche *m* dormitorio

sleepily [ˈsliːpəli] *adv* : de manera somnolienta

sleepiness [ˈsliːpinəs] *n* : somnolencia *f*

sleepless [ˈsliːpləs] *adj* : sin dormir, desvelado <to have a sleepless night : pasar la noche en blanco>

sleepwalker [ˈsliːpˌwɔkər] *n* : sonámbulo *m,* -la *f*

sleepy [ˈsliːpi] *adj* **sleepier; -est 1** DROWSY : somnoliento, soñoliento <to be sleepy : tener sueño> **2** LETHARGIC : aletargado, letárgico

sleet¹ [ˈsliːt] *vi* **to be sleeting** : caer aguanieve

sleet[2] *n* : aguanieve *f*

sleeve [ˈsliːv] *n* : manga *f* (de una camisa, etc.)

sleeveless [ˈsliːvləs] *adj* : sin mangas

sleigh[1] [ˈsleɪ] *vi* : ir en trineo

sleigh[2] *n* : trineo *m* (tirado por caballos)

sleight of hand [ˌslaɪtəvˈhænd] : prestidigitación *f,* juegos *mpl* de manos

slender [ˈslɛndər] *adj* **1** SLIM : esbelto, delgado **2** SCANTY : exiguo, escaso <a slender hope : una esperanza lejana>

sleuth [ˈsluːθ] *n* : detective *mf;* sabueso *m,* -sa *f*

slew → **slay**

slice[1] [ˈslaɪs] *vt* **sliced; slicing** : cortar

slice[2] *n* : rebanada *f,* tajada *f,* lonja *f* (de carne, etc.), rodaja *f* (de una verdura, fruta, etc.), trozo *m* (de pastel, etc.)

slick[1] [ˈslɪk] *vt* : alisar

slick[2] *adj* **1** SLIPPERY : resbaladizo, resbaloso **2** CRAFTY : astuto, taimado

slicker [ˈslɪkər] *n* : impermeable *m*

slide[1] [ˈslaɪd] *v* **slid** [ˈslɪd]; **sliding** [ˈslaɪdɪŋ] *vi* **1** SLIP : resbalar **2** GLIDE : deslizarse **3** DECLINE : bajar <to let things slide : dejar pasar las cosas> — *vt* : correr, deslizar

slide[2] *n* **1** SLIDING : deslizamiento *m* **2** SLIP : resbalón *m* **3** : tobogán *m* (para niños) **4** : TRANSPARENCY : diapositiva *f* (fotográfica) **5** DECLINE : descenso *m*

slier, sliest → **sly**

slight[1] [ˈslaɪt] *vt* : desairar, despreciar

slight[2] *adj* **1** SLENDER : esbelto, delgado **2** FLIMSY : endeble **3** TRIFLING : leve, insignificante <a slight pain : un leve dolor> **4** SMALL : pequeño, ligero <not in the slightest : en absoluto>

slight[3] *n* SNUB : desaire *m*

slightly [ˈslaɪtli] *adv* : ligeramente, un poco

slim[1] [ˈslɪm] *v* **slimmed; slimming** : adelgazar

slim[2] *adj* **slimmer; slimmest 1** SLENDER : esbelto, delgado **2** SCANTY : exiguo, escaso

slime [ˈslaɪm] *n* **1** : baba *f* (secretado por un animal) **2** MUD, SILT : fango *m,* cieno *m*

slimy [ˈslaɪmi] *adj* **slimier; -est** : viscoso

sling[1] [ˈslɪŋ] *vt* **slung** [ˈslʌŋ]; **slinging 1** THROW : lanzar, tirar **2** HANG : colgar

sling[2] *n* **1** : honda *f* (arma) **2** : cabestrillo *m* <my arm is in a sling : llevo el brazo en cabestrillo>

slingshot [ˈslɪŋˌʃɑt] *n* : tiragomas *m,* resortera *f Mex*

slink [ˈslɪŋk] *vi* **slunk** [ˈslʌŋk]; **slinking** : caminar furtivamente

slip[1] [ˈslɪp] *v* **slipped; slipping** *vi* **1** STEAL : ir sigilosamente <to slip away : escabullirse> <to slip out the door : escaparse por la puerta> **2** SLIDE : resbalarse, deslizarse **3** LAPSE : caer <to slip into error : equivocarse> **4 to let slip** : dejar escapar **5 to slip into** PUT ON : ponerse — *vt* **1** PUT : meter, poner **2** PASS : pasar <she slipped me a note : me pasó una nota> **3 to slip one's mind** : olvidársele a uno

slip[2] *n* **1** PIER : atracadero *m* **2** MISHAP : percance *m,* contratiempo *m* **3** MISTAKE : error *m,* desliz *m* <a slip of the tongue : un lapsus> **4** PETTICOAT : enagua *f* **5** : injerto *m,* esqueje *m* (de una planta) **6 slip of paper** : papelito *m*

slipper [ˈslɪpər] *n* : zapatilla *f,* pantufla *f*

slipperiness [ˈslɪpərinəs] *n* **1** : lo resbaloso, lo resbaladizo **2** TRICKINESS : astucia *f*

slippery [ˈslɪpəri] *adj* **slipperier; -est 1** : resbaloso, resbaladizo <a slippery road : un camino resbaloso> **2** TRICKY : artero, astuto, taimado **3** ELUSIVE : huidizo, escurridizo

slipshod [ˈslɪpˌʃɑd] *adj* : descuidado, chapucero

slip up *vi* : equivocarse

slit[1] [ˈslɪt] *vt* **slit; slitting** : cortar, abrir por lo largo

slit[2] *n* **1** OPENING : abertura *f,* rendija *f* **2** CUT : corte *m,* raja *f,* tajo *m*

slither [ˈslɪðər] *vi* : deslizarse

sliver [ˈslɪvər] *n* : astilla *f*

slob [ˈslɑb] *n* : persona *f* desaliñada <what a slob! : ¡qué cerdo!>

slobber[1] [ˈslɑbər] *vi* : babear

slobber[2] *n* : baba *f*

slogan [ˈsloːgən] *n* : lema *m,* eslogan *m*

sloop [ˈsluːp] *n* : balandra *f*

slop[1] [ˈslɑp] *v* **slopped; slopping** *vt* : derramar — *vi* : derramarse

slop[2] *n* : bazofia *f*

slope[1] [ˈsloːp] *vi* **sloped; sloping** : inclinarse <the road slopes upward : el camino sube (en pendiente)>

slope[2] *n* : inclinación *f,* pendiente *f,* declive *m*

sloppy [ˈslɑpi] *adj* **sloppier; -est 1** MUDDY, SLUSHY : lodoso, fangoso **2** UNTIDY : descuidado (en el trabajo, etc.), desaliñado (de aspecto)

slot [ˈslɑt] *n* : ranura *f*

sloth [ˈslɔθ, ˈsloːθ] *n* **1** LAZINESS : pereza *f* **2** : perezoso *m* (animal)

slouch[1] [ˈslaʊtʃ] *vi* : andar con los hombros caídos, repantigarse (en un sillón)

slouch[2] *n* **1** SLUMPING : mala postura *f* **2** BUNGLER, IDLER : haragán *m,* -gana *f;* inepto *m,* -ta *f* <to be no slouch : no quedarse atrás>

slough[1] [ˈslʌf] *vt* : mudar de (piel)

slough[2] [ˈsluː, ˈslaʊ] *n* SWAMP : ciénaga *f*

Slovak [ˈsloːˌvɑk, -ˌvæk] *or* **Slovakian** [sloːˈvɑkiən, -ˈvæ-] *n* : eslovaco *m,* -ca *f* — **Slovak** *or* **Slovakian** *adj*

Slovene [ˈsloːˌviːn] *or* **Slovenian** [sloːˈviːniən] *n* : esloveno *m,* -na *f* — **Slovene** *or* **Slovenian** *adj*

slovenly ['slɑvənli, 'slʌv-] *adj* : descuidado (en el trabajo, etc.), desaliñado (de aspecto)

slow[1] [slo:] *vt* : retrasar, reducir la marcha de — *vi* : ir más despacio

slow[2] *adv* : despacio, lentamente

slow[3] *adj* **1** : lento <a slow process : un proceso lento> **2** : atrasado <my watch is slow : mi reloj está atrasado, mi reloj se atrasa> **3** SLUGGISH : lento, poco activo **4** STUPID : lento, torpe, corto de alcances

slowly [slo:li] *adv* : lentamente, despacio

slowness [slo:nəs] *n* : lentitud *f*, torpeza *f*

sludge ['slʌdʒ] *n* : aguas *fpl* negras, aguas *fpl* residuales

slug[1] ['slʌg] *vt* **slugged; slugging** : pegarle un porrazo (a alguien)

slug[2] *n* **1** : babosa *f* (molusco) **2** BULLET : bala *f* **3** TOKEN : ficha *f* **4** BLOW : porrazo *m*, puñetazo *m*

sluggish ['slʌgɪʃ] *adj* : aletargado, lento

sluice[1] ['slu:s] *vt* **sluiced; sluicing** : lavar en agua corriente

sluice[2] *n* : canal *m*

slum ['slʌm] *n* : barriada *f*, barrio *m* bajo

slumber[1] ['slʌmbər] *vi* : dormir

slumber[2] *n* : sueño *m*

slump[1] ['slʌmp] *vi* **1** DECLINE, DROP : disminuir, bajar **2** SLOUCH : encorvarse, dejarse caer (en una silla, etc.)

slump[2] *n* : bajón *m*, declive *m* (económico)

slung → **sling**

slunk → **slink**

slur[1] ['slər] *vt* **slurred; slurring** : ligar (notas musicales), tragarse (las palabras)

slur[2] *n* **1** : ligado *m* (en música), mala pronunciación *f* (de las palabras) **2** ASPERSION : calumnia *f*, difamación *f*

slurp[1] ['slərp] *vi* : beber o comer haciendo ruido — *vt* : sorber ruidosamente

slurp[2] *n* : sorbo *m* (ruidoso)

slush ['slʌʃ] *n* : nieve *f* medio derretida

slut ['slʌt] *n* PROSTITUTE : ramera *f*, fulana *f*

sly ['slaɪ] *adj* **slier** ['slaɪər]; **sliest** ['slaɪəst] **1** CUNNING : astuto, taimado **2** UNDERHANDED : soplado — **slyly** *adv*

slyness ['slaɪnəs] *n* : astucia *f*

smack[1] ['smæk] *vi* **to smack of** : oler a, saber a — *vt* **1** KISS : besar, plantarle un beso (a alguien) **2** SLAP : pegarle una bofetada (a alguien) **3 to smack one's lips** : relamerse

smack[2] *adv* : justo, exactamente <smack in the face : en plena cara>

smack[3] *n* **1** TASTE, TRACE : sabor *m*, indicio *m* **2** : chasquido *m* (de los labios) **3** SLAP : bofetada *f* **4** KISS : beso *m*

small ['smɔl] *adj* **1** : pequeño, chico <a small house : una casa pequeña> <small change : monedas de poco valor> **2** TRIVIAL : pequeño, insignificante

smallness ['smɔlnəs] *n* : pequeñez *f*

smallpox ['smɔl,pɑks] *n* : viruela *f*

smart[1] ['smɑrt] *vi* **1** STING : escocer, picar, arder **2** HURT : dolerse, resentirse <to smart under a rejection : dolerse ante un rechazo>

smart[2] *adj* **1** BRIGHT : listo, vivo, inteligente **2** STYLISH : elegante — **smartly** *adv*

smart[3] *n* : escozor *m*, dolor *m*

smartness ['smɑrtnəs] *n* **1** INTELLIGENCE : inteligencia *f* **2** ELEGANCE : elegancia *f*

smash[1] ['smæʃ] *vt* **1** BREAK : romper, quebrar, hacer pedazos **2** WRECK : destrozar, arruinar **3** CRASH : estrellar, chocar — *vi* **1** SHATTER : hacerse pedazos, hacerse añicos **2** COLLIDE, CRASH : estrellarse, chocar

smash[2] *n* **1** BLOW : golpe *m* **2** COLLISION : choque *m* **3** BANG, CRASH : estrépito *m*

smattering ['smætərɪŋ] *n* **1** : nociones *fpl* <she has a smattering of programming : tiene nociones de programación> **2** : un poco, unos cuantos <a smattering of spectators : unos cuantos espectadores>

smear[1] ['smɪr] *vt* **1** DAUB : embadurnar, untar (mantequilla, etc.) **2** SMUDGE : emborronar **3** SLANDER : calumniar, difamar

smear[2] *n* **1** SMUDGE : mancha *f* **2** SLANDER : calumnia *f*

smell[1] ['smɛl] *v* **smelled** *or* **smelt** ['smɛlt]; **smelling** *vt* : oler, olfatear <to smell danger : olfatear el peligro> — *vi* : oler <to smell good : oler bien>

smell[2] *n* **1** : olfato *m*, sentido *m* del olfato **2** ODOR : olor *m*

smelly ['smɛli] *adj* **smellier; -est** : maloliente

smelt[1] ['smɛlt] *vt* : fundir

smelt[2] *n, pl* **smelts** *or* **smelt** : eperlano *m* (pez)

smile[1] ['smaɪl] *vi* **smiled; smiling** : sonreír

smile[2] *n* : sonrisa *f*

smirk[1] ['smərk] *vi* : sonreír con suficiencia

smirk[2] *n* : sonrisa *f* satisfecha

smite ['smaɪt] *vt* **smote** ['smo:t]; **smitten** ['smɪtən] *or* **smote; smiting 1** STRIKE : golpear **2** AFFLICT : afligir

smith ['smɪθ] *n* : herrero *m*, -ra *f*

smithy ['smɪθi] *n, pl* **smithies** : herrería *f*

smock ['smɑk] *n* : bata *f*, blusón *m*

smog ['smɑg, 'smɔg] *n* : smog *m*

smoke[1] ['smo:k] *v* **smoked; smoking** *vi* **1** : echar humo, humear <a smoking chimney : una chimenea que echa humo> **2** : fumar <I don't smoke : no fumo> — *vt* : ahumar (carne, etc.)

smoke[2] *n* : humo *m*

smoke detector [dɪˈtɛktər] *n* : detector *m* de humo
smoker [ˈsmoːkər] *n* : fumador *m*, -dora *f*
smokestack [ˈsmoːkˌstæk] *n* : chimenea *f*
smoky [ˈsmoːki] *adj* **smokier; -est 1** SMOKING : humeante **2** : a humo <a smoky flavor : un sabor a humo> **3** : lleno de humo <a smoky room : un cuarto lleno de humo>
smolder [ˈsmoːldər] *vi* **1** : arder sin llama **2** : arder (en el corazón) <his anger smoldered : su rabia ardía>
smooth[1] [ˈsmuːð] *vt* : alisar
smooth[2] *adj* **1** : liso (dícese de una superficie) <smooth skin : piel lisa> **2** : suave (dícese de un movimiento) <a smooth landing : un aterrizaje suave> **3** : sin grumos <a smooth sauce : una salsa sin grumos> **4** : fluido <smooth writing : escritura fluida>
smoothly [ˈsmuːðli] *adv* **1** GENTLY, SOFTLY : suavemente **2** EASILY : con facilidad, sin problemas
smoothness [ˈsmuːðnəs] *n* : suavidad *f*
smother [ˈsmʌðər] *vt* **1** SUFFOCATE : ahogar, sofocar **2** COVER : cubrir **3** SUPPRESS : contener — *vi* : asfixiarse
smudge[1] [ˈsmʌdʒ] *v* **smudged; smudging** *vt* : emborronar — *vi* : correrse
smudge[2] *n* : mancha *f*, borrón *m*
smug [ˈsmʌg] *adj* **smugger; smuggest** : suficiente, pagado de sí mismo
smuggle [ˈsmʌgəl] *vt* **-gled; -gling** : contrabandear, pasar de contrabando
smuggler [ˈsmʌgələr] *n* : contrabandista *mf*
smugly [ˈsmʌgli] *adv* : con suficiencia
smut [ˈsmʌt] *n* **1** SOOT : tizne *m*, hollín *m* **2** FUNGUS : tizón *m* **3** OBSCENITY : obscenidad *f*, inmundicia *f*
smutty [ˈsmʌti] *adj* **smuttier; -est 1** SOOTY : tiznado **2** OBSCENE : obsceno, indecente
snack [ˈsnæk] *n* : refrigerio *m*, bocado *m*, tentempié *m fam* <an afternoon snack : una merienda>
snag[1] [ˈsnæg] *v* **snagged; snagging** *vt* : enganchar — *vi* : engancharse
snag[2] *n* : problema *m*, inconveniente *m*
snail [ˈsneɪl] *n* : caracol *m*
snake [ˈsneɪk] *n* : culebra *f*, serpiente *f*
snakebite [ˈsneɪkˌbaɪt] *n* : mordedura *f* de serpiente
snap[1] [ˈsnæp] *v* **snapped; snapping** *vi* **1** : intentar morder (dícese de un perro, etc.), picar (dícese de un pez) **2** : hablar con severidad <he snapped at me! : ¡me gritó!> **3** BREAK : romperse, quebrarse (haciendo un chasquido) — *vt* **1** BREAK : partir (en dos), quebrar **2** : hacer (algo) de un golpe <to snap open : abrir de golpe> **3** RETORT : decir bruscamente **4** CLICK : chasquear <to snap one's fingers : chasquear los dedos>
snap[2] *n* **1** CLICK, CRACK : chasquido *m* **2** FASTENER : broche *m* **3** CINCH : cosa *f* fácil <it's a snap : es facilísimo>
snapdragon [ˈsnæpˌdrægən] *n* : dragón *m* (flor)
snapper [ˈsnæpər] → **red snapper**
snappy [ˈsnæpi] *adj* **snappier; -est 1** FAST : rápido <make it snappy! : ¡date prisa!> **2** LIVELY : vivaz **3** CHILLY : frío **4** STYLISH : elegante
snapshot [ˈsnæpˌʃɑt] *n* : instantánea *f*
snare[1] [ˈsnær] *vt* **snared; snaring** : atrapar
snare[2] *n* : trampa *f*, red *f*
snare drum *n* : tambor *m* con bordón
snarl[1] [ˈsnɑrl] *vi* **1** TANGLE : enmarañar, enredar **2** GROWL : gruñir
snarl[2] *n* **1** TANGLE : enredo *m*, maraña *f* **2** GROWL : gruñido *m*
snatch[1] [ˈsnætʃ] *vt* : arrebatar
snatch[2] *n* : fragmento *m*
sneak[1] [ˈsniːk] *vi* : ir a hurtadillas — *vt* : hacer furtivamente <to sneak a look : mirar con disimulo> <he sneaked a smoke : fumó un cigarrillo a escondidas>
sneak[2] *n* : soplón *m*, -plona *f*
sneakers [ˈsniːkərz] *npl* : tenis *mpl*, zapatillas *fpl*
sneaky [ˈsniːki] *adj* **sneakier; -est** : solapado
sneer[1] [ˈsnɪr] *vi* : sonreír con desprecio
sneer[2] *n* : sonrisa *f* de desprecio
sneeze[1] [ˈsniːz] *vi* **sneezed; sneezing** : estornudar
sneeze[2] *n* : estornudo *m*
snicker[1] [ˈsnɪkər] *vi* : reírse disimuladamente
snicker[2] *n* : risita *f*
snide [ˈsnaɪd] *adj* : sarcástico
sniff[1] [ˈsnɪf] *vi* **1** SMELL : oler, husmear (dícese de los animales) **2 to sniff at** : despreciar, desdeñar — *vt* **1** SMELL : oler **2 to sniff out** : olerse, husmear
sniff[2] *n* **1** SNIFFING : aspiración *f* por la nariz **2** SMELL : olor *m*
sniffle [ˈsnɪfəl] *vi* **-fled; -fling** : respirar con la nariz congestionada
sniffles [ˈsnɪfəlz] *npl* : resfriado *m*
snip[1] [ˈsnɪp] *vt* **snipped; snipping** : cortar (con tijeras)
snip[2] *n* : tijeretada *f*, recorte *m*
snipe[1] [ˈsnaɪp] *vi* **sniped; sniping** : disparar
snipe[2] *n, pl* **snipes** *or* **snipe** : agachadiza *f*
sniper [ˈsnaɪpər] *n* : francotirador *m*, -dora *f*
snivel [ˈsnɪvəl] *vi* **-veled** *or* **-velled; -veling** *or* **-velling 1** → **snuffle 2** WHINE : lloriquear
snob [ˈsnɑb] *n* : esnob *mf*, snob *mf*
snobbery [ˈsnɑbəri] *n, pl* **-beries** : esnobismo *m*
snobbish [ˈsnɑbɪʃ] *adj* : esnob, snob
snobbishness [ˈsnɑbɪʃnəs] *n* : esnobismo *m*
snoop[1] [ˈsnuːp] *vi* : husmear, curiosear
snoop[2] *n* : fisgón *m*, -gona *f*

snooze[1] [ˈsnuːz] *vi* **snoozed; snoozing** : dormitar

snooze[2] *n* : siestecita *f,* siestita *f*

snore[1] [ˈsnor] *vi* **snored; snoring** : roncar

snore[2] *n* : ronquido *m*

snort[1] [ˈsnɔrt] *vi* : bufar, resoplar

snort[2] *n* : bufido *m,* resoplo *m*

snout [ˈsnaʊt] *n* : hocico *m,* morro *m*

snow[1] [ˈsnoː] *vi* **1** : nevar <I'm snowed in : estoy aislado por la nieve> **2 to be snowed under** : estar inundado

snow[2] *n* : nieve *f*

snowball [ˈsnoːˌbɔl] *n* : bola *f* de nieve

snowdrift [ˈsnoːˌdrɪft] *n* : ventisquero *m*

snowfall [ˈsnoːˌfɔl] *n* : nevada *f*

snowplow [ˈsnoːˌplaʊ] *n* : quitanieves *m*

snowshoe [ˈsnoːˌʃuː] *n* : raqueta *f* (para nieve)

snowstorm [ˈsnoːˌstɔrm] *n* : tormenta *f* de nieve, ventisca *f*

snowy [ˈsnoːi] *adj* **snowier; -est** : nevoso <a snowy road : un camino nevado>

snub[1] [ˈsnʌb] *vi* **snubbed; snubbing** : desairar

snub[2] *n* : desaire *m*

snub–nosed [ˈsnʌbˌnoːzd] *adj* : de nariz respingada

snuff[1] [ˈsnʌf] *vt* **1** : apagar (una vela) **2** : sorber (algo) por la nariz

snuff[2] *n* : rapé *m*

snuffle [ˈsnʌfəl] *vi* **-fled; -fling** : respirar con la nariz congestionada

snug [ˈsnʌg] *adj* **snugger; snuggest 1** COMFORTABLE : cómodo **2** TIGHT : ajustado, ceñido <snug pants : pantalones ajustados>

snuggle [ˈsnʌgəl] *vi* **-gled; -gling** : acurrucarse <to snuggle up to someone : arrimársele a alguien>

snugly [ˈsnʌgli] *adv* **1** COMFORTABLY : cómodamente **2** : de manera ajustada <the shirt fits snugly : la camisa queda ajustada>

so[1] [ˈsoː] *adv* **1** (*referring to something indicated or suggested*) <do you think so? : ¿tú crees?> <so it would seem : eso parece> <I told her so : se lo dije> <he's ready, or so he says : según dice, está listo> <it so happened that. . . : resultó que. . .> <do it like so : hazlo así> <so be it : así sea> **2** ALSO : también <so do I : yo también> **3** THUS : así, de esta manera **4** : tan <he'd never been so happy : nunca había estado tan contento> **5** CONSEQUENTLY : por lo tanto

so[2] *conj* **1** THEREFORE : así que **2** *or* **so that** : para que, así que, de manera que **3 so what?** : ¿y qué?

soak[1] [ˈsoːk] *vi* : estar en remojo — *vt* **1** : poner en remojo **2 to soak up** ABSORB : absorber

soak[2] *n* : remojo *m*

soap[1] [ˈsoːp] *vt* : enjabonar

soap[2] *n* : jabón *m*

soapsuds [ˈsoːpˌsʌdz] → **suds**

soapy [ˈsoːpi] **soapier; -est** *adj* : jabonoso <a soapy taste : un gusto a jabón> <a soapy texture : una textura de jabón>

soar [ˈsor] *vi* **1** FLY : volar **2** RISE : remontar el vuelo (dícese de las aves) <her hopes soared : su esperanza renació> <prices are soaring : los precios están subiendo vertiginosamente>

sob[1] [ˈsɑb] *vi* **sobbed; sobbing** : sollozar

sob[2] *n* : sollozo *m*

sober [ˈsoːbər] *adj* **1** : sobrio <he's not sober enough to drive : está demasiado borracho para manejar> **2** SERIOUS : serio

soberly [ˈsoːbərli] *adv* **1** : sobriamente **2** SERIOUSLY : seriamente

sobriety [səˈbraɪəṭi, so-] *n* **1** : sobriedad *f* <sobriety test : prueba de alcoholemia> **2** SERIOUSNESS : seriedad *f*

so–called [ˈsoːˈkɔld] *adj* : supuesto, presunto <the so-called experts : los expertos, así llamados>

soccer [ˈsɑkər] *n* : futbol *m,* fútbol *m*

sociable [ˈsoːʃəbəl] *adj* : sociable

social[1] [ˈsoːʃəl] *adj* : social — **socially** *adv*

social[2] *n* : reunión *f* social

socialism [ˈsoːʃəˌlɪzəm] *n* : socialismo *m*

socialist[1] [ˈsoːʃəlɪst] *adj* : socialista

socialist[2] *n* : socialista *mf*

socialize [ˈsoːʃəˌlaɪz] *v* **-ized; -izing** *vt* **1** NATIONALIZE : nacionalizar **2** : socializar (en psicología) — *vi* : alternar, circular <to socialize with friends : alternar con amigos>

social work *n* : asistencia *f* social

society [səˈsaɪəṭi] *n, pl* **-eties 1** COMPANIONSHIP : compañía *f* **2** : sociedad *f* <a democratic society : una sociedad democrática> <high society : alta sociedad> **3** ASSOCIATION : sociedad *f,* asociación *f*

sociology [ˌsoːsiˈɑlədʒi] *n* : sociología *f*

sociological [ˌsoːsiəˈlɑdʒɪkəl] *adj* : sociológico

sociologist [ˌsoːsiˈɑlədʒɪst] *n* : sociólogo *m,* -ga *f*

sock[1] [ˈsɑk] *vt* : pegar, golpear, darle un puñetazo a

sock[2] *n* **1** *pl* **socks** *or* **sox** [ˈsɑks] : calcetín *m,* media *f* <shoes and socks : zapatos y calcetines> **2** *pl* **socks** [ˈsɑks] PUNCH : puñetazo *m*

socket [ˈsɑkət] *n* **1** *or* **electric socket** : enchufe *m,* toma *f* de corriente **2** : glena *f* (de una articulación) <shoulder socket : glena del hombro> **3 eye socket** : órbita *f,* cuenca *f*

sod[1] [ˈsɑd] *vt* **sodded; sodding** : cubrir de césped

sod[2] *n* TURF : césped *m,* tepe *m*

soda [ˈsoːdə] *n* **1** *or* **soda water :** soda *f* **2** *or* **soda pop :** gaseosa *f,* refresco *m* **3** *or* **ice–cream soda :** refresco *m* con helado
sodden [ˈsɑdən] *adj* SOGGY **:** empapado
sodium [ˈsoːdiəm] *n* **:** sodio *m*
sodium bicarbonate *n* **:** bicarbonato *m* de soda
sodium chloride → **salt**
sofa [ˈsoːfə] *n* **:** sofá *m*
soft [ˈsɔft] *adj* **1 :** blando <a soft pillow : una almohada blanda> **2** SMOOTH **:** suave (dícese de las texturas, de los sonidos, etc.) **3** NONALCOHOLIC **:** no alcohólico <a soft drink : un refresco>
softball [ˈsɔftˌbɔl] *n* **:** softbol *m*
soften [ˈsɔfən] *vt* **:** ablandar (algo sólido), suavizar (la piel, un golpe, etc.), amortiguar (un impacto) — *vi* **:** ablandarse, suavizarse
softly [ˈsɔftli] *adv* **:** suavemente <she spoke softly : habló en voz baja>
softness [ˈsɔftnəs] *n* **1 :** blandura *f,* lo blando (de una almohada, de la mantequilla, etc.) **2** SMOOTHNESS **:** suavidad *f*
software [ˈsɔftˌwær] *n* **:** software *m*
soggy [ˈsɑgi] *adj* **soggier; -est :** empapado
soil[1] [ˈsɔɪl] *vt* **:** ensuciar — *vi* **:** ensuciarse
soil[2] *n* **1** DIRTINESS **:** suciedad *f* **2** DIRT, EARTH **:** suelo *m,* tierra *f* **3** COUNTRY **:** patria *f* <her native soil : su tierra natal>
sojourn[1] [ˈsoːˌdʒərn, soːˈdʒərn] *vi* **:** pasar una temporada
sojourn[2] *n* **:** estadía *f,* estancia *f,* permanencia *f*
solace [ˈsɑləs] *n* **:** consuelo *m*
solar [ˈsoːlər] *adj* **:** solar <the solar system : el sistema solar>
sold → **sell**
solder[1] [ˈsɑdər, ˈsɔ-] *vt* **:** soldar
solder[2] *n* **:** soldadura *f*
soldier[1] [ˈsoːldʒər] *vi* **:** servir como soldado
soldier[2] *n* **:** soldado *mf*
sole[1] [ˈsoːl] *adj* **:** único
sole[2] *n* **1 :** suela *f* (de un zapato) **2 :** lenguado *m* (pez)
solely [ˈsoːli] *adv* **:** únicamente, sólo
solemn [ˈsɑləm] *adj* **:** solemne, serio — **solemnly** *adv*
solemnity [səˈlɛmnət̬i] *n, pl* **-ties :** solemnidad *f*
solicit [səˈlɪsət] *vt* **:** solicitar
solicitous [səˈlɪsət̬əs] *adj* **:** solícito
solicitude [səˈlɪsəˌtuːd, -ˌtjuːd] *n* **:** solicitud *f*
solid[1] [ˈsɑləd] *adj* **1 :** macizo <a solid rubber ball : una bola maciza de caucho> **2** CUBIC **:** tridimensional **3** COMPACT **:** compacto, denso **4** STURDY **:** sólido **5** CONTINUOUS **:** seguido, continuo <two solid hours : dos horas seguidas> <a solid line : una línea continua> **6** UNANIMOUS **:** unánime **7** DEPENDABLE **:** serio, fiable **8** PURE **:** macizo, puro <solid gold : oro macizo>
solid[2] *n* **:** sólido *m*
solidarity [ˌsɑləˈdærət̬i] *n* **:** solidaridad *f*
solidify [səˈlɪdəˌfaɪ] *v* **-fied; -fying** *vt* **:** solidificar — *vi* **:** solidificarse
solidity [səˈlɪdət̬i] *n, pl* **-ties :** solidez *f*
solidly [ˈsɑlədli] *adv* **1 :** sólidamente **2** UNANIMOUSLY **:** unánimemente
soliloquy [səˈlɪləkwi] *n, pl* **-quies :** soliloquio *m*
solitaire [ˈsɑləˌtɛr] *n* **:** solitario *m*
solitary [ˈsɑləˌtɛri] *adj* **1** ALONE **:** solitario **2** SECLUDED **:** apartado, retirado **3** SINGLE **:** solo
solitude [ˈsɑləˌtuːd, -ˌtjuːd] *n* **:** soledad *f*
solo[1] [ˈsoːˌloː] *vi* **:** volar en solitario (dícese de un piloto)
solo[2] *adv & adj* **:** en solitario, a solas
solo[3] *n, pl* **solos :** solo *m*
soloist [ˈsoːloɪst] *n* **:** solista *mf*
solstice [ˈsɑlstɪs] *n* **:** solsticio *m*
soluble [ˈsɑljəbəl] *adj* **:** soluble
solution [səˈluːʃən] *n* **:** solución *f*
solve [ˈsɑlv] *vt* **solved; solving :** resolver, solucionar
solvency [ˈsɑlvəntsi] *n* **:** solvencia *f*
solvent [ˈsɑlvənt] *n* **:** solvente *m*
Somali [soˈmɑli, sə-] *n* **:** somalí *mf* — **Somali** *adj*
somber [ˈsɑmbər] *adj* **1** DARK **:** sombrío, oscuro <somber colors : colores oscuros> **2** GRAVE **:** sombrío, serio **3** MELANCHOLY **:** sombrío, lúgubre
sombrero [səmˈbrɛrˌoː] *n, pl* **-ros :** sombrero *m* (mexicano)
some[1] [ˈsʌm] *adj* **1 :** un, algún <some lady stopped me : una mujer me detuvo> <some distant galaxy : alguna galaxia lejana> **2 :** algo de, un poco de <he drank some water : tomó (un poco de) agua> **3 :** unos <do you want some apples? : ¿quieres unas manzanas?> <some years ago : hace varios años>
some[2] *pron* **1 :** algunos <some went, others stayed : algunos se fueron, otros se quedaron> **2 :** un poco, algo <there's some left : queda un poco> <I have gum; do you want some? : tengo chicle, ¿quieres?>
somebody [ˈsʌmbədi, -ˌbɑdi] *pron* **:** alguien
someday [ˈsʌmˌdeɪ] *adv* **:** algún día
somehow [ˈsʌmˌhaʊ] *adv* **1 :** de alguna manera, de algún modo <I'll do it somehow : lo haré de alguna manera> **2 :** por alguna rázon <somehow I don't trust her : por alguna razón no me fío de ella>
someone [ˈsʌmˌwʌn] *pron* **:** alguien
somersault[1] [ˈsʌmərˌsɔlt] *vi* **:** dar volteretas, dar un salto mortal
somersault[2] *n* **:** voltereta *f,* salto *m* mortal

something ['sʌmθɪŋ] *pron* : algo <I want something else : quiero otra cosa> <she's writing a novel or something : está escribiendo una novela o no sé qué>
sometime ['sʌm,taɪm] *adv* : algún día, en algún momento <sometime next month : durante el mes que viene>
sometimes ['sʌm,taɪmz] *adv* : a veces, algunas veces, de vez en cuando
somewhat ['sʌm,hwʌt, -,hwɑt] *adv* : algo, un tanto
somewhere ['sʌm,*h*wɛr] *adv* **1** : en alguna parte, a algún lugar **2 somewhere else** : en otro sitio
son ['sʌn] *n* : hijo *m*
sonar ['so:,nɑr] *n* : sonar *m*
sonata [sə'nɑt̬ə] *n* : sonata *f*
song ['sɔŋ] *n* : canción *f,* canto *m* (de un pájaro)
songbird ['sɔŋ,bərd] *n* : pájaro *m* cantor
sonic ['sɑnɪk] *adj* **1** : sónico **2 sonic boom** : estampido *m* sónico
son–in–law ['sʌnɪn,lɔ] *n, pl* **sons–in–law** : yerno *m,* hijo *m* político
sonnet ['sɑnət] *n* : soneto *m*
sonorous ['sɑnərəs, sə'norəs] *adj* : sonoro
soon ['su:n] *adv* **1** : pronto, dentro de poco <he'll arrive soon : llegará pronto> **2** QUICKLY : pronto <as soon as possible : lo más pronto posible> <the sooner the better : cuanto antes mejor>
soot ['sʊt, 'su:t, 'sʌt] *n* : hollín *m,* tizne *m*
soothe ['su:ð] *vt* **soothed; soothing 1** CALM : calmar, tranquilizar **2** RELIEVE : aliviar
soothsayer ['su:θ,seɪər] *n* : adivino *m,* -na *f*
sooty ['sʊt̬i, 'su:-, 'sʌ-] *adj* **sootier; -est** : cubierto de hollín, tiznado
sop[1] ['sɑp] *vt* **sopped; sopping 1** DIP : mojar **2** SOAK : empapar **3 to sop up** : rebañar, absorber
sop[2] *n* **1** CONCESSION : concesión *f* **2** BRIBE : soborno *m*
sophisticated [sə'fɪstə,keɪt̬əd] *adj* **1** COMPLEX : complejo **2** WORLDLY-WISE : sofisticado
sophistication [sə,fɪstə'keɪʃən] *n* **1** COMPLEXITY : complejidad *f* **2** URBANITY : sofisticación *f*
sophomore ['sɑf,mor, 'sɑfə,mor] *n* : estudiante *mf* de segundo año
soporific [,sɑpə'rɪfɪk, ,so:-] *adj* : soporífero
soprano [sə'præ,no:] *n, pl* **-nos** : soprano *mf*
sorcerer ['sɔrsərər] *n* : hechicero *m,* brujo *m,* mago *m*
sorceress ['sɔrsərəs] *n* : hechicera *f,* bruja *f,* maga *f*
sorcery ['sɔrsəri] *n* : hechicería *f,* brujería *f*
sordid ['sɔrdɪd] *adj* : sórdido
sore[1] ['sor] *adj* **sorer; sorest 1** PAINFUL : dolorido, doloroso <I have a sore throat : me duele la garganta> **2** ACUTE, SEVERE : extremo, grande <in sore straits : en grandes apuros> **3** ANGRY : enojado, enfadado
sore[2] *n* : llaga *f*
sorely ['sorli] *adv* : muchísimo <it was sorely needed : se necesitaba urgentemente> <she was sorely missed : la echaban mucho de menos>
soreness ['sornəs] *n* : dolor *m*
sorghum ['sɔrgəm] *n* : sorgo *m*
sorority [sə'rɔrət̬i] *n, pl* **-ties** : hermandad *f* (de estudiantes femeninas)
sorrel ['sɔrəl] *n* **1** : alazán *m* (color o animal) **2** : acedera *f* (hierba)
sorrow ['sɑr,o:] *n* : pesar *m,* dolor *m,* pena *f*
sorrowful ['sɑrofəl] *adj* : triste, afligido, apenado
sorrowfully ['sɑrofəli] *adv* : con tristeza
sorry ['sɑri] *adj* **sorrier; -est 1** PITIFUL : lastimero, lastimoso **2 to be sorry** : sentir, lamentar <I'm sorry : lo siento> **3 to feel sorry for** : compadecer <I feel sorry for him : me da pena>
sort[1] ['sɔrt] *vt* : clasificar
sort[2] *n* **1** KIND : tipo *m,* clase *f* <a sort of writer : una especie de escritor> **2** NATURE : índole *f* **3 out of sorts** : de mal humor
sortie ['sɔrt̬i, sɔr'ti:] *n* : salida *f*
SOS [,ɛs,o:'ɛs] *n* : SOS *m*
so–so ['so:'so:] *adj & adv* : así así, de modo regular
soufflé [su:'fleɪ] *n* : suflé *m*
sought → **seek**
soul ['so:l] *n* **1** SPIRIT : alma *f* **2** ESSENCE : esencia *f* **3** PERSON : persona *f,* alma *f*
soulful ['so:lfəl] *adj* : conmovedor, lleno de emoción
sound[1] ['saʊnd] *vt* **1** : sondar (en navegación) **2** *or* **to sound out** PROBE : sondear **3** : hacer sonar, tocar (una trompeta, etc.) — *vi* **1** : sonar <the alarm sounded : la alarma sonó> **2** SEEM : parecer
sound[2] *adj* **1** HEALTHY : sano <safe and sound : sano y salvo> <of sound mind and body : en pleno uso de sus facultades> **2** FIRM, SOLID : sólido **3** SENSIBLE : lógico, sensato **4** DEEP : profundo <a sound sleep : un sueño profundo>
sound[3] *n* **1** : sonido *m* <the speed of sound : la velocidad del sonido> **2** NOISE : sonido *m,* ruido *m* <I heard a sound : oí un sonido> **3** CHANNEL : brazo *m* de mar, canal *m* (ancho)
soundless ['saʊndləs] *adj* : sordo
soundlessly ['saʊndləsli] *adv* : silenciosamente
soundly ['saʊndli] *adv* **1** SOLIDLY : sólidamente **2** SENSIBLY : lógicamente, sensatamente **3** DEEPLY : profunda-

mente <sleeping soundly : durmiendo profundamente>
soundness ['saʊndnəs] *n* **1** SOLIDITY : solidez *f* **2** SENSIBLENESS : sensatez *f,* solidez *f*
soundproof ['saʊnd,pru:f] *adj* : insonorizado
sound wave *n* : onda *f* sonora
soup ['su:p] *n* : sopa *f*
sour[1] ['saʊər] *vi* : agriarse, cortarse (dícese de la leche) — *vt* : agriar, cortar (leche)
sour[2] *adj* **1** ACID : agrio, ácido (dícese de la fruta, etc.), cortado (dícese de la leche) **2** DISAGREEABLE : desagradable, agrio
source ['sors] *n* : fuente *f,* origen *m,* nacimiento *m* (de un río)
sourness ['saʊərnəs] *n* : acidez *f*
south[1] ['saʊθ] *adv* : al sur, hacia el sur <the window looks south : la ventana mira al sur> <she continued south : continuó hacia el sur>
south[2] *adj* : sur, del sur <the south entrance : la entrada sur> <South America : Sudamérica, América del Sur>
south[3] *n* : sur *m*
South African *n* : sudafricano *m,* -na *f* — **South African** *adj*
South American[1] *adj* : sudamericano, suramericano
South American[2] *n* : sudamericano *m,* -na *f;* suramericano *m,* -na *f*
southbound ['saʊθ,baʊnd] *adj* : con rumbo al sur
southeast[1] [saʊ'θi:st] *adj* : sureste, sudeste, del sureste
southeast[2] *n* : sureste *m,* sudeste *m*
southeasterly [saʊ'θi:stərli] *adv & adj* **1** : del sureste (dícese del viento) **2** : hacia el sureste
southeastern [saʊ'θi:stərn] → **southeast**[1]
southerly ['sʌðərli] *adv & adj* : del sur
southern ['sʌðərn] *adj* : sur, sureño, meridional, austral <a southern city : una ciudad del sur del país, una ciudad meridional> <the southern side : el lado sur>
Southerner ['sʌðərnər] *n* : sureño *m,* -ña *f*
South Pole : Polo *m* Sur
southward ['saʊθwərd] *or* **southwards** [-wərdz] *adv & adj* : hacia el sur
southwest[1] [saʊθ'wɛst, *as a nautical term often* saʊ'wɛst] *adj* : suroeste, sudoeste, del suroeste
southwest[2] *n* : suroeste *m,* sudoeste *m*
southwesterly [saʊθ'wɛstərli] *adv & adj* **1** : del suroeste (dícese del viento) **2** : hacia el suroeste
southwestern [saʊθ'wɛstərn] → **southwest**[1]
souvenir [,su:və'nɪr, 'su:və,-] *n* : recuerdo *m,* souvenir *m*
sovereign[1] ['sɑvərən] *adj* : soberano
sovereign[2] *n* **1** : soberano *m,* -na *f* (monarca) **2** : soberano *m* (moneda)
sovereignty ['sɑvərənti] *n, pl* **-ties** : soberanía *f*
Soviet ['so:vi,ɛt, 'sɑ-, -viət] *adj* : soviético
sow[1] ['so:] *vt* **sowed; sown** ['so:n] *or* **sowed; sowing 1** PLANT : sembrar **2** SCATTER : esparcir
sow[2] ['saʊ] *n* : cerda *f*
sox → **sock**
soybean ['sɔɪ,bi:n] *n* : soya *f,* soja *f*
spa ['spɑ] *n* : balneario *m*
space[1] ['speɪs] *vt* **spaced; spacing** : espaciar
space[2] *n* **1** PERIOD : espacio *m,* lapso *m,* período *m* **2** ROOM : espacio *m,* sitio *m,* lugar *m* <is there space for me? : ¿hay sitio para mí?> **3** : espacio *m* <blank space : espacio en blanco> **4** : espacio *m* (en física) **5** PLACE : plaza *f,* sitio *m* <to reserve space : reservar plazas> <parking space : sitio para estacionarse>
spacecraft ['speɪs,kræft] *n* : nave *f* espacial
spaceflight ['speɪs,flaɪt] *n* : vuelo *m* espacial
spaceman ['speɪsmən, -,mæn] *n, pl* **-men** [-mən, -,mɛn] : astronauta *m,* cosmonauta *m*
spaceship ['speɪs,ʃɪp] *n* : nave *f* espacial
space shuttle *n* : transbordador *m* espacial
space suit *n* : traje *m* espacial
spacious ['speɪʃəs] *adj* : espacioso, amplio
spade[1] ['speɪd] *v* **spaded; spading** *vt* : palear — *vi* : usar una pala
spade[2] *n* **1** SHOVEL : pala *f* **2** : pica *f* (naipe)
spaghetti [spə'gɛti] *n* : espagueti *m,* espaguetis *mpl,* spaghetti *mpl*
span[1] ['spæn] *vt* **spanned; spanning** : abarcar (un período de tiempo), extenderse sobre (un espacio)
span[2] *n* **1** : lapso *m,* espacio *m* (de tiempo) <life span : duración de la vida> **2** : luz *f* (entre dos soportes)
spangle ['spæŋgəl] *n* : lentejuela *f*
Spaniard ['spænjərd] *n* : español *m,* -ñola *f*
spaniel ['spænjəl] *n* : spaniel *m*
Spanish[1] ['spænɪʃ] *adj* : español
Spanish[2] *n* **1** : español *m* (idioma) **2** **the Spanish** *npl* : los españoles
spank ['spæŋk] *vt* : darle nalgadas (a alguien)
spar[1] ['spɑr] *vi* **sparred; sparring** : entrenarse (en boxeo)
spar[2] *n* : palo *m,* verga *f* (de un barco)
spare[1] ['spær] *vt* **spared; sparing 1** : perdonar <to spare someone's life : perdonarle la vida a alguien> **2** SAVE : ahorrar, evitar <I'll spare you the trouble : le evitaré la molestia> **3** : prescindir de <I can't spare her : no puedo prescindir de ella> <can you

spare a dollar? : ¿me das un dólar?> 4 STINT : escatimar <they spared no expense : no repararon en gastos> 5 **to spare** : de sobra
spare² *adj* **1** : de repuesto, de recambio <spare tire : llanta de repuesto> **2** EXCESS : de más, de sobra <spare time : tiempo libre> **3** LEAN : delgado
spare³ *n or* **spare part** : repuesto *m,* recambio *m*
sparing ['spærɪŋ] *adj* : parco, económico — **sparingly** *adv*
spark¹ ['spɑrk] *vi* : chispear, echar chispas — *vt* PROVOKE : despertar, provocar <to spark interest : despertar interés>
spark² *n* **1** : chispa *f* <to throw off sparks : echar chispas> **2** GLIMMER, TRACE : destello *m,* pizca *f*
sparkle¹ ['spɑrkəl] *vi* **-kled; -kling 1** FLASH, SHINE : destellar, centellear, brillar **2** : estar muy animado (dícese de una conversación, etc.)
sparkle² *n* : destello *m,* centelleo *m*
sparkler ['spɑrklər] *n* : luz *f* de bengala
spark plug *n* : bujía *f*
sparrow ['spæroː] *n* : gorrión *m*
sparse ['spɑrs] *adj* **sparser; -est** : escaso — **sparsely** *adv*
spasm ['spæzəm] *n* **1** : espasmo *m* (muscular) **2** BURST, FIT : arrebato *m*
spasmodic [spæz'mɑdɪk] *adj* **1** : espasmódico **2** SPORADIC : irregular, esporádico — **spasmodically** [-dɪkli] *adv*
spastic ['spæstɪk] *adj* : espástico
spat¹ → **spit¹**
spat² ['spæt] *n* : discusión *f,* disputa *f,* pelea *f*
spatial ['speɪʃəl] *adj* : espacial
spatter¹ ['spæt̬ər] *v* : salpicar
spatter² *n* : salpicadura *f*
spatula ['spætʃələ] *n* : espátula *f,* paleta *f* (para servir)
spawn¹ ['spɔn] *vi* : desovar, frezar — *vt* GENERATE : generar, producir
spawn² *n* : hueva *f,* freza *f*
spay ['speɪ] *vt* : esterilizar (una perra, etc.)
speak ['spiːk] *v* **spoke** ['spoːk]; **spoken** ['spoːkən]; **speaking** *vi* **1** TALK : hablar <to speak to someone : hablar con alguien> <who's speaking? : ¿de parte de quien?> <so to speak : por así decirlo> **2 to speak out** : hablar claramente **3 to speak out against** : denunciar **4 to speak up** : hablar en voz alta **5 to speak up for** : defender — *vt* **1** SAY : decir <she spoke her mind : habló con franqueza> **2** : hablar (un idioma)
speaker ['spiːkər] *n* **1** : hablante *mf* <a native speaker : un hablante nativo> **2** : orador *m,* -dora *f* <the keynote speaker : el orador principal> **3** LOUDSPEAKER : altavoz *m,* altoparlante *m*
spear¹ ['spɪr] *vt* : atravesar con una lanza
spear² *n* : lanza *f*
spearhead¹ ['spɪr,hɛd] *vt* : encabezar
spearhead² *n* : punta *f* de lanza
spearmint ['spɪrmɪnt] *n* : menta *f* verde
special ['spɛʃəl] *adj* : especial <nothing special : nada en especial, nada en particular> — **specially** *adv*
specialist ['spɛʃəlɪst] *n* : especialista *mf*
specialization [,spɛʃələ'zeɪʃən] *n* : especialización *f*
specialize ['spɛʃə,laɪz] *vi* **-ized; -izing** : especializarse
specialty ['spɛʃəlt̬i] *n, pl* **-ties** : especialidad *f*
species ['spiː,ʃiːz, -,siːz] *ns & pl* : especie *f*
specific [spɪ'sɪfɪk] *adj* : específico, determinado — **specifically** [-fɪkli] *adv*
specification [,spɛsəfə'keɪʃən] *n* : especificación *f*
specify ['spɛsə,faɪ] *vt* **-fied; -fying** : especificar
specimen ['spɛsəmən] *n* **1** SAMPLE : espécimen *m,* muestra *f* **2** EXAMPLE : espécimen *m,* ejemplar *m*
speck ['spɛk] *n* **1** SPOT : manchita *f* **2** BIT, TRACE : mota *f,* pizca *f,* ápice *m*
speckled ['spɛkəld] *adj* : moteado
spectacle ['spɛktɪkəl] *n* **1** : espectáculo *m* **2 spectacles** *npl* GLASSES : lentes *fpl,* gafas *fpl,* anteojos *mpl,* espejuelos *mpl*
spectacular [spɛk'tækjələr] *adj* : espectacular
spectator ['spɛk,teɪt̬ər] *n* : espectador *m,* -dora *f*
specter *or* **spectre** ['spɛktər] *n* : espectro *m,* fantasma *m*
spectrum ['spɛktrəm] *n, pl* **spectra** [-trə] *or* **spectrums 1** : espectro *m* (de colores, etc.) **2** RANGE : gama *f,* abanico *m*
speculate ['spɛkjə,leɪt] *vi* **-lated; -lating 1** : especular (en finanza) **2** WONDER : preguntarse, hacer conjeturas
speculation [,spɛkjə'leɪʃən] *n* : especulación *f*
speculative ['spɛkjə,leɪt̬ɪv] *adj* : especulativo
speculator ['spɛkjə,leɪt̬ər] *n* : especulador *m,* -dora *f*
speech ['spiːtʃ] *n* **1** : habla *f,* modo *m* de hablar, expresión *f* **2** ADDRESS : discurso *m*
speechless ['spiːtʃləs] *adj* : enmudecido, estupefacto
speed¹ ['spiːd] *v* **sped** ['spɛd] *or* **speeded; speeding** *vi* **1** : ir a toda velocidad, correr a toda prisa <he sped off : se fue a toda velocidad> **2** : conducir a exceso de velocidad <a ticket for speeding : una multa por exceso de velocidad> — *vt* **to speed up** : acelerar
speed² *n* **1** SWIFTNESS : rapidez *f* **2** VELOCITY : velocidad *f*

speedboat [ˈspiːdˌboːt] *n* : lancha *f* motora
speed bump *n* : badén *m*
speed limit *n* : velocidad *f* máxima, límite *m* de velocidad
speedometer [spɪˈdɑmət̬ər] *n* : velocímetro *m*
speedup [ˈspiːdˌʌp] *n* : aceleracion *f*
speedy [ˈspiːdi] *adj* **speedier, -est** : rápido — **speedily** [-dəli] *adv*
spell[1] [ˈspɛl] *vt* **1** : escribir, deletrear (verbalmente) <how do you spell it? : ¿cómo se escribe?, ¿cómo se deletrea?> **2** MEAN : significar <that could spell trouble : eso puede significar problemas> **3** RELIEVE : relevar
spell[2] *n* **1** TURN : turno *m* **2** PERIOD, TIME : período *m* (de tiempo) **3** ENCHANTMENT : encanto *m,* hechizo *m,* maleficio *m*
spellbound [ˈspɛlˌbaʊnd] *adj* : embelesado
speller [ˈspɛlər] *n* : persona *f* que escribe <she's a good speller : tiene buena ortografía>
spelling [ˈspɛlɪŋ] *n* : ortografía *f*
spend [ˈspɛnd] *vt* **spent** [ˈspɛnt]; **spending** **1** : gastar (dinero, etc.) **2** PASS : pasar (el tiempo) <to spend time on : dedicar tiempo a>
spendthrift [ˈspɛndˌθrɪft] *n* : derrochador *m,* -dora *f;* despilfarrador *m,* -dora *f*
sperm [ˈspərm] *n, pl* **sperm** *or* **sperms** : esperma *mf*
spew [ˈspjuː] *vi* : salir a chorros — *vt* : vomitar, arrojar (lava, etc.)
sphere [ˈsfɪr] *n* : esfera *f*
spherical [ˈsfɪrɪkəl, ˈsfɛr-] *adj* : esférico
spice[1] [ˈspaɪs] *vt* **spiced; spicing** **1** SEASON : condimentar, sazonar **2** *or* **to spice up** : salpimentar, hacer más interesante
spice[2] *n* **1** : especia *f* **2** FLAVOR, INTEREST : sabor *m* <the spice of life : la sal de la vida>
spick–and–span [ˈspɪkənd*ˈ*spæn] *adj* : limpio y ordenado
spicy [ˈspaɪsi] *adj* **spicier; -est** **1** SPICED : condimentado, sazonado **2** HOT : picante **3** RACY : picante
spider [ˈspaɪdər] *n* : araña *f*
spigot [ˈspɪgət, -kət] *n* : llave *f,* grifo *m,* canilla *Arg, Uru*
spike[1] [ˈspaɪk] *vt* **spiked; spiking** **1** FASTEN : clavar (con clavos grandes) **2** PIERCE : atravesar **3** : añadir alcohol a <he spiked her drink with rum : le puso ron a la bebida>
spike[2] *n* : clavo *m* grande
spill[1] [ˈspɪl] *vt* **1** SHED : derramar, verter <to spill blood : derrame sangre> **2** DIVULGE : revelar, divulgar — *vi* : derramarse
spill[2] *n* **1** SPILLING : derrame *m,* vertido *m* <oil spill : derrame de petróleo> **2** FALL : caída *f*
spin[1] [ˈspɪn] *v* **spun** [ˈspʌn]; **spinning** *vi* **1** : hilar **2** TURN : girar **3** REEL : dar vueltas <my head is spinning : la cabeza me está dando vueltas> — *vt* **1** : hilar (hilo, etc.) **2** : tejer <to spin a web : tejer una telaraña> **3** TWIRL : hacer girar
spin[2] *n* : vuelta *f,* giro *m* <to go for a spin : dar una vuelta (en coche)>
spinach [ˈspɪnɪtʃ] *n* : espinacas *fpl,* espinaca *f*
spinal column [ˈspaɪnəl] *n* BACKBONE : columna *f* vertebral
spinal cord *n* : médula *f* espinal
spindle [ˈspɪndəl] *n* **1** : huso *m* (para hilar) **2** : eje *m* (de un mecanismo)
spindly [ˈspɪndli] *adj* : larguirucho *fam,* largo y débil (dícese de una planta)
spine [ˈspaɪn] *n* **1** BACKBONE : columna *f* vertebral, espina *f* dorsal **2** QUILL : púa *f* (de un animal) **3** THORN : espina *f* **4** : lomo *m* (de un libro)
spineless [ˈspaɪnləs] *adj* **1** : sin púas, sin espinas **2** INVERTEBRATE : invertebrado **3** WEAK : débil (de carácter)
spinet [ˈspɪnət] *n* : espineta *f*
spinster [ˈspɪn*t*stər] *n* : soltera *f*
spiny [ˈspaɪni] *adj* **spinier; -est** : con púas (dícese de los animales), espinoso (dícese de las plantas)
spiral[1] [ˈspaɪrəl] *vi* **-raled** *or* **-ralled; -raling** *or* **-ralling** : ir en espiral
spiral[2] *adj* : espiral, en espiral <a spiral staircase : una escalera de caracol>
spiral[3] *n* : espiral *f*
spire [ˈspaɪr] *n* : aguja *f*
spirit[1] [ˈspɪrət] *vt* **to spirit away** : hacer desaparecer
spirit[2] *n* **1** : espíritu *m* <body and spirit : cuerpo y espíritu> **2** GHOST : espíritu *m,* fantasma *m* **3** MOOD : espíritu *m,* humor *m* <in the spirit of friendship : en el espíritu de amistad> <to be in good spirits : estar de buen humor> **4** ENTHUSIASM, VIVACITY : espíritu *m,* ánimo *m,* brío *m* **5 spirits** *npl* : licores *mpl*
spirited [ˈspɪrət̬əd] *adj* : animado, energético
spiritless [ˈspɪrətləs] *adj* : desanimado
spiritual[1] [ˈspɪrɪtʃʊəl, -tʃəl] *adj* : espiritual — **spiritually** *adv*
spiritual[2] *n* : espiritual *m* (canción)
spiritualism [ˈspɪrɪtʃʊəˌlɪzəm, -tʃə-] *n* : espiritismo *m*
spirituality [ˌspɪrɪtʃʊˈælət̬i] *n, pl* **-ties** : espiritualidad *f*
spit[1] [ˈspɪt] *v* **spit** *or* **spat** [ˈspæt]; **spitting** : escupir
spit[2] *n* **1** SALIVA : saliva *f* **2** ROTISSERIE : asador *m* **3** POINT : lengua *f* (de tierra)
spite[1] [ˈspaɪt] *vt* **spited; spiting** : fastidiar, molestar
spite[2] *n* **1** : despecho *m,* rencor *m* **2 in spite of** : a pesar de (que), pese a (que)

spiteful ['spaɪtfəl] *adj* **:** malicioso, rencoroso

spitting image *n* **to be the spitting image of :** ser el vivo retrato de

spittle ['spɪt̬əl] *n* **:** saliva *f*

splash[1] ['splæʃ] *vt* **:** salpicar — *vi* **1 :** salpicar **2 to splash around :** chapotear

splash[2] *n* **1** SPLASHING **:** salpicadura *f* **2** SQUIRT **:** chorrito *m* **3** SPOT **:** mancha *f*

splatter ['splæt̬ər] → **spatter**

splay ['spleɪ] *vt* **:** extender (hacia afuera) <to splay one's fingers : abrir los dedos> — *vi* **:** extenderse (hacia afuera)

spleen ['spliːn] *n* **1 :** bazo *m* (órgano) **2** ANGER, SPITE **:** ira *f,* rencor *m*

splendid ['splɛndəd] *adj* **:** espléndido — **splendidly** *adv*

splendor ['splɛndər] *n* **:** esplendor *m*

splice[1] ['splaɪs] *vt* **spliced; splicing :** empalmar, unir

splice[2] *n* **:** empalme *m,* unión *f*

splint ['splɪnt] *n* **:** tablilla *f*

splinter[1] ['splɪntər] *vt* **:** astillar — *vi* **:** astillarse

splinter[2] *n* **:** astilla *f*

split[1] ['splɪt] *v* **split; splitting** *vt* **1** CLEAVE **:** partir, hender <to split wood : partir madera> **2** BURST **:** romper, rajar <to split open : abrir> **3** DIVIDE, SHARE **:** dividir, repartir — *vi* **1 :** partirse (dícese de la madera, etc.) **2** BURST, CRACK **:** romperse, rajarse **3** *or* **to split up :** dividirse

split[2] *n* **1** CRACK **:** rajadura *f* **2** TEAR **:** rotura *f* **3** DIVISION **:** división *f,* escisión *f*

splurge[1] ['splərdʒ] *v* **splurged; splurging** *vt* **:** derrochar — *vi* **:** derrochar dinero

splurge[2] *n* **:** derroche *m*

spoil[1] ['spɔɪl] *v* **spoiled** *or* **spoilt** ['spɔɪlt]; **spoiling** *vt* **1** PILLAGE **:** saquear **2** RUIN **:** estropear, arruinar **3** PAMPER **:** consentir, mimar — *vi* **:** estropearse, echarse a perder

spoil[2] *n* PLUNDER **:** botín *m*

spoke[1] → **speak**

spoke[2] ['spoːk] *n* **:** rayo *m* (de una rueda)

spoken → **speak**

spokesman ['spoːksmən] *n, pl* **-men** [-mən, -ˌmɛn] **:** portavoz *mf;* vocero *m,* -ra *f*

spokeswoman ['spoːksˌwʊmən] *n, pl* **-women** [-ˌwɪmən] **:** portavoz *f,* vocera *f*

sponge[1] ['spʌndʒ] *vt* **sponged; sponging :** limpiar con una esponja

sponge[2] *n* **:** esponja *f*

spongy ['spʌndʒi] *adj* **spongier; -est :** esponjoso

sponsor[1] ['spɑntsər] *vt* **:** patrocinar, auspiciar, apadrinar (a una persona)

sponsor[2] *n* **:** patrocinador *m,* -dora *f;* padrino *m,* madrina *f*

sponsorship ['spɑntsərˌʃɪp] *n* **:** patrocinio *m,* apadrinamiento *m*

spontaneity [ˌspɑntə'niːət̬i, -'neɪ-] *n* **:** espontaneidad *f*

spontaneous [spɑn'teɪniəs] *adj* **:** espontáneo — **spontaneously** *adv*

spoof ['spuːf] *n* **:** burla *f,* parodia *f*

spook[1] ['spuːk] *vt* **:** asustar

spook[2] *n* **:** fantasma *m,* espíritu *m,* espectro *m*

spooky ['spuːki] *adj* **spookier; -est :** que da miedo, espeluzante

spool ['spuːl] *n* **:** carrete *m*

spoon[1] ['spuːn] *vt* **:** comer, servir, o echar con cuchara

spoon[2] *n* **:** cuchara *f*

spoonful ['spuːnˌfʊl] *n* **:** cucharada *f* <by the spoonful : a cucharadas>

spoor ['spʊr, 'spor] *n* **:** rastro *m,* pista *f*

sporadic [spə'rædɪk] *adj* **:** esporádico — **sporadically** [-dɪkli] *adv*

spore ['spor] *n* **:** espora *f*

sport[1] ['sport] *vi* FROLIC **:** retozar, juguetear — *vt* SHOW OFF **:** lucir, ostentar

sport[2] *n* **1 :** deporte *m* <outdoor sports : deportes al aire libre> **2** JEST **:** broma *f* **3 to be a good sport :** tener espíritu deportivo

sportsman ['sportsmən] *n, pl* **-men** [-mən, -ˌmɛn] **:** deportista *m*

sportsmanship ['sportsmənˌʃɪp] *n* **:** espíritu *m* deportivo, deportividad *f Spain*

sportswoman ['sportsˌwʊmən] *n, pl* **-women** [-ˌwɪmən] **:** deportista *f*

sporty ['sport̬i] *adj* **sportier; -est :** deportivo

spot[1] ['spɑt] *v* **spotted; spotting** *vt* **1** STAIN **:** manchar **2** RECOGNIZE, SEE **:** ver, reconocer <to spot an error : descubrir un error> — *vi* **:** mancharse

spot[2] *adj* **:** hecho al azar <a spot check : un vistazo, un control aleatorio>

spot[3] *n* **1** STAIN **:** mancha *f* **2** DOT **:** punto *m* **3** PIMPLE **:** grano *m* <to break out in spots : salirle granos a alguien> **4** PREDICAMENT **:** apuro *m,* aprieto *m,* lío *m* <in a tight spot : en apuros> **5** PLACE **:** lugar *m,* sitio *m* <to be on the spot : estar en el lugar>

spotless ['spɑtləs] *adj* **:** impecable, inmaculado — **spotlessly** *adv*

spotlight[1] ['spɑtˌlaɪt] *vt* **-lighted** *or* **-lit** [-ˌlɪt]; **-lighting 1** LIGHT **:** iluminar (con un reflector) **2** HIGHLIGHT **:** destacar, poner en relieve

spotlight[2] *n* **1 :** reflector *m,* foco *m* **2 to be in the spotlight :** ser el centro de atención

spotty ['spɑti] *adj* **spottier; -est :** irregular, desigual

spouse ['spaʊs] *n* **:** cónyuge *mf*

spout[1] ['spaʊt] *vt* **1 :** lanzar chorros de **2** DECLAIM **:** declamar — *vi* **:** salir a chorros

spout[2] *n* **1 :** pico *m* (de una jarra, etc.) **2** STREAM **:** chorro *m*

sprain[1] ['spreɪn] *vt* **:** sufrir un esguince en

sprain[2] *n* : esguince *m,* torcedura *f*
sprawl[1] ['sprɔl] *vi* **1** LIE : tumbarse, echarse, despatarrarse **2** EXTEND : extenderse
sprawl[2] *n* **1** : postura *f* despatarrada **2** SPREAD : extensión *f,* expansión *f*
spray[1] ['spreɪ] *vt* : rociar (una superficie), pulverizar (un líquido)
spray[2] *n* **1** BOUQUET : ramillete *m* **2** MIST : rocío *m* **3** ATOMIZER : atomizador *m,* pulverizador *m*
spray gun *n* : pistola *f*
spread[1] ['sprɛd] *v* **spread; spreading** *vt* **1** *or* **to spread out** : desplegar, extender **2** SCATTER, STREW : esparcir **3** SMEAR : untar (mantequilla, etc.) **4** DISSEMINATE : difundir, sembrar, propagar — *vi* **1** : difundirse, correr, propagarse **2** EXTEND : extenderse
spread[2] *n* **1** EXTENSION : extensión *f,* difusión *f* (de noticias, etc.), propagación *f* (de enfermedades, etc.) **2** : colcha *f* (para una cama), mantel *m* (para una mesa) **3** PASTE : pasta *f* <cheese spread : pasta de queso>
spreadsheet ['sprɛd,ʃiːt] *n* : hoja *f* de cálculo
spree ['spri] *n* **1** : acción *f* desenfrenada <to go on a shopping spree : comprar como loco> **2** BINGE : parranda *f,* juerga *f* <on a spree : de parranda, de juerga>
sprig ['sprɪg] *n* : ramita *f,* ramito *m*
sprightly ['spraɪtli] *adj* **sprightlier; -est** : vivo, animado <with a sprightly step : con paso ligero>
spring[1] ['sprɪŋ] *v* **sprang** ['spræŋ] *or* **sprung** ['sprʌŋ]; **sprung; springing** *vi* **1** LEAP : saltar **2** : mover rápidamente <the lid sprang shut : la tapa se cerró de un golpe> <he sprang to his feet : se paró de un salto> **3 to spring up** : brotar (dícese de las plantas), surgir **4 to spring from** : surgir de — *vt* **1** RELEASE : soltar (de repente) <to spring the news on someone : sorprender a alguien con las noticias> <to spring a trap : hacer saltar una trampa> **2** ACTIVATE : accionar (un mecanismo) **3 to spring a leak** : hacer agua
spring[2] *n* **1** SOURCE : fuente *f,* origen *m* **2** : manantial *m,* fuente *f* <hot spring : fuente termal> **3** : primavera *f* <spring and summer : la primavera y el verano> **4** : resorte *m,* muelle *m* (de metal, etc.) **5** LEAP : salto *m,* brinco *m* **6** RESILIENCE : elasticidad *f*
springboard ['sprɪŋ,bord] *n* : trampolín *m*
springtime ['sprɪŋ,taɪm] *n* : primavera *f*
springy ['sprɪŋi] *adj* **springier; -est 1** RESILIENT : elástico **2** LIVELY : enérgico
sprinkle[1] ['sprɪŋkəl] *vt* **-kled; -kling** : rociar (con agua), espolvorear (con azúcar, etc.), salpicar
sprinkle[2] *n* : llovizna *f*
sprinkler ['sprɪŋkələr] *n* : rociador *m,* aspersor *m*
sprint[1] ['sprɪnt] *vi* : echar la carrera, esprintar (en deportes)
sprint[2] *n* : esprint *m* (en deportes)
sprite ['spraɪt] *n* : hada *f,* elfo *m*
sprocket ['sprɑkət] *n* : diente *m* (de una rueda dentada)
sprout[1] ['spraʊt] *vi* : brotar
sprout[2] *n* : brote *m,* retoño *m,* vástago *m*
spruce[1] ['spruːs] *v* **spruced; sprucing** *vt* : arreglar — *vi or* **to spruce up** : arreglarse, acicalarse
spruce[2] *adj* **sprucer; sprucest** : pulcro, arreglado
spruce[3] *n* : picea *f* (árbol)
spry ['spraɪ] *adj* **sprier** *or* **spryer** ['spraɪər]; **spriest** *or* **spryest** ['spraɪəst] : ágil, activo
spun → **spin**
spunk ['spʌŋk] *n* : valor *m,* coraje *m,* agallas *fpl fam*
spunky ['spʌŋki] *adj* **spunkier; -est** : animoso, corajudo
spur[1] ['spər] *vt* **spurred; spurring** *or* **to spur on** : espolear (un caballo), motivar (a una persona, etc.)
spur[2] *n* **1** : espuela *f,* acicate *m* **2** STIMULUS : acicate *m* **3** : espolón *m* (de aves gallináceas)
spurious ['spjʊriəs] *adj* : espurio
spurn ['spərn] *vt* : desdeñar, rechazar
spurt[1] ['spərt] *vt* SQUIRT : lanzar un chorro de — *vi* SPOUT : salir a chorros
spurt[2] *n* **1** : actividad *f* repentina <a spurt of energy : una explosión de energía> <to do in spurts : hacer por rachas> **2** JET : chorro *m* (de agua, etc.)
sputter[1] ['spʌtər] *vi* **1** JABBER : farfullar **2** : chisporrotear (dícese de la grasa, etc.), petardear (dícese de un motor)
sputter[2] *n* **1** JABBER : farfulla *f* **2** : chisporroteo *m* (de grasa, etc.), petardeo *m* (de un motor)
spy[1] ['spaɪ] *v* **spied; spying** *vt* SEE : ver, divisar — *vi* : espiar <to spy on someone : espiar a alguien>
spy[2] *n* : espía *mf*
squab ['skwɑb] *n, pl* **squabs** *or* **squab** : pichón *m*
squabble[1] ['skwɑbəl] *vi* **-bled; -bling** : reñir, pelearse, discutir
squabble[2] *n* : riña *f,* pelea *f,* discusión *f*
squad ['skwɑd] *n* : pelotón *m* (militar), brigada *f* (de policías), cuadrilla *f* (de obreros, etc.)
squadron ['skwɑdrən] *n* : escuadrón *m* (de militares), escuadrilla *f* (de aviones), escuadra *f* (de naves)
squalid ['skwɑlɪd] *adj* : miserable
squall ['skwɔl] *n* **1** : aguacero *m* tormentoso, chubasco *m* tormentoso **2 snow squall** : tormenta *f* de nieve
squalor ['skwɑlər] *n* : miseria *f*
squander ['skwɑndər] *vt* : derrochar (dinero, etc.), desaprovechar (una

oportunidad, etc.), desperdiciar (talentos, energías, etc.)

square[1] ['skwær] *vt* **squared; squaring 1 :** cuadrar **2 :** elevar al cuadrado (en matemáticas) **3** CONFORM **:** conciliar (con), ajustar (con) **4** SETTLE **:** saldar (una cuenta) <I squared it with him : lo arreglé con él>

square[2] *adj* **squarer; -est 1 :** cuadrado <a square house : una casa cuadrada> **2** RIGHT-ANGLED **:** a escuadra, en ángulo recto **3 :** cuadrado (en matemáticas) <a square mile : una milla cuadrada> **4** HONEST **:** justo <a square deal : un buen acuerdo> <fair and square : en buena lid>

square[3] *n* **1 :** escuadra *f* (instrumento) **2 :** cuadrado *m,* cuadro *m* <to fold into squares : plegar en cuadrados> **3 :** plaza *f* (de una ciudad) **4 :** cuadrado *m* (en matemáticas)

squarely ['skwærli] *adv* **1** EXACTLY **:** exactamente, directamente, justo **2** HONESTLY **:** honradamente, justamente

square root *n* **:** raíz *f* cuadrada

squash[1] ['skwɑʃ, 'skwɔʃ] *vt* **1** CRUSH **:** aplastar **2** SUPPRESS **:** acallar (protestas), sofocar (una rebelión)

squash[2] *n* **1** *pl* **squashes** *or* **squash :** calabaza *f* (vegetal) **2** *or* **squash racquets :** squash *m* (deporte)

squat[1] ['skwɑt] *vi* **squatted; squatting 1** CROUCH **:** agacharse, ponerse en cuclillas **2 :** ocupar un lugar sin derecho

squat[2] *adj* **squatter; squattest :** bajo y ancho, rechoncho *fam* (dícese de una persona)

squat[3] *n* **1 :** posición *f* en cuclillas **2 :** ocupación *f* ilegal (de un lugar)

squaw ['skwɔ] *n* **:** india *f* (norteamericana)

squawk[1] ['skwɔk] *vi* **:** graznar (dícese de las aves), chillar

squawk[2] *n* **:** graznido *m* (de un ave), chillido *m*

squeak[1] ['skwiːk] *vi* **:** chillar (dícese de un animal), chirriar (dícese de un objeto)

squeak[2] *n* **:** chillido *m,* chirrido *m*

squeaky ['skwiːki] *adj* **squeakier; -est :** chirriante <a squeaky voice : una voz chillona>

squeal[1] ['skwiːl] *vi* **1 :** chillar (dícese de las personas o los animales), chirriar (dícese de los frenos, etc.) **2** PROTEST **:** quejarse

squeal[2] *n* **1 :** chillido *m* (de una persona o un animal) **2** SCREECH **:** chirrido *m* (de frenos, etc.)

squeamish ['skwiːmɪʃ] *adj* **:** impresionable, sensible <he's squeamish about cockroaches : las cucarachas le dan asco>

squeeze[1] ['skwiːz] *vt* **squeezed; squeezing 1** PRESS **:** apretar, exprimir (naranjas, etc.) **2** EXTRACT **:** extraer (jugo, etc.)

squeeze[2] *n* **:** apretón *m*

squelch ['skwɛltʃ] *vt* **:** aplastar (una rebelión, etc.)

squid ['skwɪd] *n, pl* **squid** *or* **squids :** calamar *m*

squint[1] ['skwɪnt] *vi* **:** mirar con los ojos entornados

squint[2] *adj* *or* **squint-eyed** ['skwɪnt,aɪd] **:** bizco

squint[3] *n* **:** ojos *mpl* bizcos, bizquera *f*

squire ['skwaɪr] *n* **:** hacendado *m,* -da *f;* terrateniente *mf*

squirm ['skwərm] *vi* **:** retorcerse

squirrel ['skwərəl] *n* **:** ardilla *f*

squirt[1] ['skwərt] *vt* **:** lanzar un chorro de — *vi* SPURT **:** salir a chorros

squirt[2] *n* **:** chorrito *m*

stab[1] [stæb] *vt* **stabbed; stabbing 1** KNIFE **:** acuchillar, apuñalar **2** STICK **:** clavar (con una aguja, etc.), golpear (con el dedo, etc.)

stab[2] *n* **1 :** puñalada *f,* cuchillada *f* **2** JAB **:** pinchazo *m* (con una aguja, etc.), golpe *m* (con un dedo, etc.) **3 to take a stab at :** intentar

stability [stə'bɪləti] *n, pl* **-ties :** estabilidad *f*

stabilize ['steɪbə,laɪz] *v* **-lized; -lizing** *vt* **:** estabilizar — *vi* **:** estabilizarse

stable[1] ['steɪbəl] *vt* **-bled; -bling :** poner (ganado) en un establo, poner (caballos) en una caballeriza

stable[2] *adj* **-bler; -blest 1** FIXED, STEADY **:** fijo, sólido, estable **2** LASTING **:** estable, perdurable <a stable government : un gobierno estable> **3 :** estacionario (en medicina), equilibrado (en psicología)

stable[3] *n* **:** establo *m* (para ganado), caballeriza *f* o cuadra *f* (para caballos)

staccato [stə'kɑtoː] *adj* **:** staccato

stack[1] ['stæk] *vt* **1** PILE **:** amontonar, apilar **2** COVER **:** cubrir, llenar <he stacked the table with books : cubrió la mesa de libros>

stack[2] *n* **1** PILE **:** montón *m,* pila *f* **2** SMOKESTACK **:** chimenea *f*

stadium ['steɪdiəm] *n, pl* **-dia** [-diə] *or* **-diums :** estadio *m*

staff[1] ['stæf] *vt* **:** proveer de personal

staff[2] *n, pl* **staffs** ['stæfs, stævz] *or* **staves** ['stævz, 'steɪvz] **1 :** bastón *m* (de mando), báculo *m* (de obispo) **2** *pl* **staffs** PERSONNEL **:** personal *m* **3** *pl* **staffs :** pentagrama *m* (en música)

stag[1] ['stæg] *adv* **:** solo, sin pareja <to go stag : ir solo>

stag[2] *adj* **:** sólo para hombres

stag[3] *n, pl* **stags** *or* **stag :** ciervo *m,* venado *m*

stage[1] ['steɪdʒ] *vt* **staged; staging :** poner en escena (una obra de teatro)

stage[2] *n* **1** PLATFORM **:** estrado *m,* tablado *m,* escenario *m* (de un teatro) **2** PHASE, STEP **:** fase *f,* etapa *f* <stage of development : fase de desarrollo> <in stages : por etapas> **3 the stage :** el teatro *m*

stagecoach ['steɪdʒ,koːtʃ] *n* **:** diligencia *f*

stagger[1] [ˈstægər] *vi* TOTTER : tambalearse — *vt* **1** ALTERNATE : alternar, escalonar (turnos de trabajo) **2** : hacer tambalear <to be staggered by : quedarse estupefacto por>
stagger[2] *n* : tambaleo *m*
staggering [ˈstægərɪŋli] *adj* : asombroso
stagnant [ˈstægnənt] *adj* : estancado
stagnate [ˈstæg,neɪt] *vi* **-nated; -nating** : estancarse
staid [ˈsteɪd] *adj* : serio, sobrio
stain[1] [ˈsteɪn] *vt* **1** DISCOLOR : manchar **2** DYE : teñir (madera, etc.) **3** SULLY : manchar, empañar
stain[2] *n* **1** SPOT : mancha *f* **2** DYE : tinte *m,* tintura *f* **3** BLEMISH : mancha *f,* mácula *f*
stainless [ˈsteɪnləs] *adj* : sin mancha <stainless steel : acero inoxidable>
stair [ˈstær] *n* **1** STEP : escalón *m,* peldaño *m* **2 stairs** *npl* : escalera *f,* escaleras *fpl*
staircase [ˈstær,keɪs] *n* : escalera *f,* escaleras *fpl*
stairway [ˈstær,weɪ] *n* : escalera *f,* escaleras *fpl*
stake[1] [ˈsteɪk] *vt* **staked; staking 1** : estacar, marcar con estacas (una propiedad) **2** BET : jugarse, apostar **3 to stake a claim to** : reclamar, reivindicar
stake[2] *n* **1** POST : estaca *f* **2** BET : apuesta *f* <to be at stake : estar en juego> **3** INTEREST, SHARE : interés *m,* participación *f*
stalactite [stəˈlæk,taɪt] *n* : estalactita *f*
stalagmite [stəˈlæg,maɪt] *n* : estalagmita *f*
stale [ˈsteɪl] *adj* **staler; stalest** : viejo <stale bread : pan duro> <stale news : viejas noticias>
stalemate [ˈsteɪl,meɪt] *n* : punto *m* muerto, impasse *m*
stalk[1] [ˈstɔk] *vt* : acechar — *vi* : caminar rígidamente (por orgullo, ira, etc.)
stalk[2] *n* : tallo *m* (de una planta)
stall[1] [ˈstɔl] *vt* **1** : parar (un motor) **2** DELAY : entretener (a una persona), demorar — *vi* **1** : pararse (dícese de un motor) **2** DELAY : demorar, andar con rodeos
stall[2] *n* **1** : compartimiento *m* (de un establo) **2** : puesto *m* (en un mercado, etc.)
stallion [ˈstæljən] *n* : caballo *m* semental
stalwart [ˈstɔlwərt] *adj* **1** STRONG : fuerte <a stalwart supporter : un firme partidario> **2** BRAVE : valiente, valeroso
stamen [ˈsteɪmən] *n* : estambre *m*
stamina [ˈstæmənə] *n* : resistencia *f*
stammer[1] [ˈstæmər] *vi* : tartamudear, titubear
stammer[2] *n* : tartamudeo *m,* titubeo *m*
stamp[1] [ˈstæmp] *vt* **1** : pisotear (con los pies) <to stamp one's feet : patear, dar una patada> **2** IMPRESS, IMPRINT : sellar (una factura, etc.), acuñar (monedas) **3** : franquear, ponerle estampillas a (correo)
stamp[2] *n* **1** : sello *m* (para documentos, etc.) **2** DIE : cuño *m* (para monedas) **3** *or* **postage stamp** : sello *m,* estampilla *f,* timbre *m CA, Mex*
stampede[1] [stæmˈpiːd] *vi* **-peded; -peding** : salir en estampida
stampede[2] *n* : estampida *f*
stance [ˈstænts] *n* : postura *f*
stanch [ˈstɔntʃ, ˈstɑntʃ] *vt* : detener, estancar (un líquido)
stand[1] [ˈstænd] *v* **stood** [ˈstʊd]; **standing** *vi* **1** : estar de pie, estar parado <I was standing on the corner : estaba parada en la esquina> **2** *or* **to stand up** : levantarse, pararse, ponerse de pie **3** *(indicating a specified position or location)* <they stand third in the country : ocupan el tercer lugar en el país> <the machines are standing idle : las máquinas están paradas> **4** *(referring to an opinion)* <how does he stand on the matter ? : ¿cuál es su postura respecto al asunto?> **5** BE : estar <the house stands on a hill : la casa está en una colina> **6** CONTINUE : seguir <the order still stands : el mandato sigue vigente> — *vt* **1** PLACE, SET : poner, colocar <he stood them in a row : los colocó en hilera> **2** TOLERATE : aguantar, soportar <he can't stand her : no la puede tragar> **3 to stand firm** : mantenerse firme **4 to stand guard** : hacer la guardia
stand[2] *n* **1** RESISTANCE : resistencia *f* <to make a stand against : resistir a> **2** BOOTH, STALL : stand *m,* puesto *m,* kiosko *m* (para vender periódicos, etc.) **3** BASE : pie *m,* base *f* **4** : grupo *m* (de árboles, etc.) **5** POSITION : posición *f,* postura *f* **6 stands** *npl* GRANDSTAND : tribuna *f*
standard[1] [ˈstændərd] *adj* **1** ESTABLISHED : estándar, oficial <standard measures : medidas oficiales> <standard English : el inglés estándar> **2** NORMAL : normal, estándar, común **3** CLASSIC : estándar, clásico <a standard work : una obra clásica>
standard[2] *n* **1** BANNER : estandarte *m* **2** CRITERION : criterio *m* **3** RULE : estándar *m,* norma *f,* regla *f* **4** LEVEL : nivel *m* <standard of living : nivel de vida> **5** SUPPORT : poste *m,* soporte *m*
standardize [ˈstændər,daɪz] *vt* **-ized; -izing** : estandarizar
standard time *n* : hora *f* oficial
stand by *vt* : atenerse a, cumplir con (una promesa, etc.) — *vi* **1** : mantenerse aparte <to stand by and do nothing : mirar sin hacer nada> **2** : estar preparado, estar listo (para un anuncio, un ataque, etc.)
stand for *vt* **1** REPRESENT : significar **2** PERMIT, TOLERATE : permitir, tolerar
standing [ˈstændɪŋ] *n* **1** POSITION, RANK : posición *f* **2** DURATION : duración *f*

stand out *vi* **1** : destacar(se) <she stands out from the rest : se destaca entre los otros> **2 to stand out against** RESIST : oponerse a

standpoint [ˈstændˌpɔint] *n* : punto *m* de vista

standstill [ˈstændˌstɪl] *n* **1** STOP : detención *f,* paro *m* <to come to a standstill : pararse> **2** DEADLOCK : punto *m* muerto, impasse *m*

stand up *vt* : dejar plantado <he stood me up again : otra vez me dejó plantado> — *vi* **1** ENDURE : durar, resistir **2 to stand up for** : defender **3 to stand up to** : hacerle frente (a alguien)

stank → **stink**

stanza [ˈstænzə] *n* : estrofa *f*

staple[1] [ˈsteɪpəl] *vt* **-pled; -pling** : engrapar, grapar

staple[2] *adj* : principal, básico <a staple food : un alimento básico>

staple[3] *n* **1** : producto *m* principal **2** : grapa *f* (para engrapar papeles)

stapler [ˈsteɪplər] *n* : engrapadora *f,* grapadora *f*

star[1] [ˈstɑr] *v* **starred; starring** *vt* **1** : marcar con una estrella o un asterisco **2** FEATURE : ser protagonizado por — *vi* : tener el papel principal <to star in : protagonizar>

star[2] *n* : estrella *f*

starboard [ˈstɑrbərd] *n* : estribor *m*

starch[1] [ˈstɑrtʃ] *vt* : almidonar

starch[2] *n* : almidón *m,* fécula *f* (comida)

starchy [ˈstɑrtʃi] *adj* **starchier; -est** : lleno de almidón <a starchy diet : una dieta feculenta>

stardom [ˈstɑrdəm] *n* : estrellato *m*

stare[1] [ˈstær] *vi* **stared; staring** : mirar fijamente

stare[2] *n* : mirada *f* fija

starfish [ˈstɑrˌfɪʃ] *n* : estrella *f* de mar

stark[1] [ˈstɑrk] *adv* : completamente <stark raving mad : loco de remate> <stark naked : completamente desnudo>

stark[2] *adj* **1** ABSOLUTE : absoluto **2** BARREN, DESOLATE : desolado, desierto **3** BARE : desnudo **4** HARSH : severo, duro

starlight [ˈstɑrˌlaɪt] *n* : luz *f* de las estrellas

starling [ˈstɑrlɪŋ] *n* : estornino *m*

starry [ˈstɑri] *adj* **starrier; -est** : estrellado

start[1] [ˈstɑrt] *vi* **1** JUMP : levantarse de un salto, sobresaltarse, dar un respingo **2** BEGIN : empezar, comenzar **3** SET OUT : salir (de viaje, etc.) **4** : arrancar (dícese de un motor) — *vt* **1** BEGIN : empezar, comenzar, iniciar **2** CAUSE : provocar, causar **3** ESTABLISH : fundar, montar, establecer <to start a business : montar un negocio> **4** : arrancar, poner en marcha, encender <to start the car : arrancar el motor>

start[2] *n* **1** JUMP : sobresalto *m,* respingo *m* **2** BEGINNING : principio *m,* comienzo *m* <to get an early start : salir temprano>

starter [ˈstɑrt̬ər] *n* **1** ENTRANT : participante *mf* (en deportes) **2** APPETIZER : entremés *m,* aperitivo *m* **3** : motor *m* de arranque (de un vehículo)

startle [ˈstɑrt̬əl] *vt* **-tled; -tling** : asustar, sobresaltar

starvation [stɑrˈveɪʃən] *n* : inanición *f,* hambre *f*

starve [ˈstɑrv] *v* **starved; starving** *vi* : morirse de hambre — *vt* : privar de comida

stash [ˈstæʃ] *vt* : esconder, guardar (en un lugar secreto)

state[1] [ˈsteɪt] *vt* **stated; stating 1** REPORT : puntualizar, exponer (los hechos, etc.) <state your name : diga su nombre> **2** ESTABLISH, FIX : establecer, fijar

state[2] *n* **1** CONDITION : estado *m,* condición *f* <a liquid state : un estado líquido> <state of mind : estado de ánimo> <in a bad state : en malas condiciones> **2** NATION : estado *m,* nación *f* **3** : estado *m* (dentro de un país) <the States : los Estados Unidos>

stateliness [ˈsteɪtlinəs] *n* : majestuosidad *f*

stately [ˈsteɪtli] *adj* **statelier; -est** : majestuoso

statement [ˈsteɪtmənt] *n* **1** DECLARATION : declaración *f,* afirmación *f* **2** *or* **bank statement** : estado *m* de cuenta

stateroom [ˈsteɪtˌruːm, -ˌrʊm] *n* : camarote *m*

statesman [ˈsteɪtsmən] *n, pl* **-men** [-mən, -ˌmɛn] : estadista *mf*

static[1] [ˈstæt̬ɪk] *adj* : estático

static[2] *n* : estática *f,* interferencia *f*

station[1] [ˈsteɪʃən] *vt* : apostar, estacionar

station[2] *n* **1** : estación *f* (de trenes, etc.) **2** RANK, STANDING : condición *f* (social) **3** : canal *m* (de televisión), estación *f* o emisora *f* (de radio) **4 police station** : comisaría *f* **5 fire station** : estación *f* de bomberos, cuartel *m* de bomberos

stationary [ˈsteɪʃəˌnɛri] *adj* **1** IMMOBILE : estacionario, inmovible **2** UNCHANGING : inmutable, inalterable

stationery [ˈsteɪʃəˌnɛri] *n* : papel *m* y sobres *mpl* (para correspondencia)

station wagon *n* : camioneta *f* guayín, camioneta *f* ranchera

statistic [stəˈtɪstɪk] *n* : estadística *f* <according to statistics : según las estadísticas>

statistical [stəˈtɪstɪkəl] *adj* : estadístico

statue [ˈstæˌtʃuː] *n* : estatua *f*

statuesque [ˌstætʃʊˈɛsk] *adj* : escultural

statuette [ˌstætʃʊˈɛt] *n* : estatuilla *f*

stature [ˈstætʃər] *n* **1** HEIGHT : estatura *f,* talla *f* **2** PRESTIGE : talla *f,* prestigio *m*

status [ˈsteɪtəs, ˈstæ-] *n* : condición *f*, situación *f*, estatus *m* (social) <marital status : estado civil>

statute [ˈstæˌtʃuːt] *n* : ley *f*, estatuto *m*

staunch [ˈstɔntʃ] *adj* : acérrimo, incondicional, leal <a staunch supporter : un partidario incondicional> — **staunchly** *adv*

stave[1] [ˈsteɪv] *vt* **staved** *or* **stove** [ˈstoːv]; **staving 1 to stave in** : romper **2 to stave off** : evitar (un ataque), prevenir (un problema)

stave[2] *n* : duela *f* (de un barril)

staves → **staff**

stay[1] [ˈsteɪ] *vi* **1** REMAIN : quedarse, permanecer <to stay in : quedarse en casa> <he stayed in the city : permaneció en la ciudad> **2** CONTINUE : seguir, quedarse <it stayed cloudy : siguió nublado> <to stay awake : mantenerse despierto> **3** LODGE : hospedarse, alojarse (en un hotel, etc.) — *vt* **1** HALT : detener, suspender (una ejecución, etc.) **2 to stay the course** : aguantar hasta el final

stay[2] *n* **1** SOJOURN : estadía *f*, estancia *f*, permanencia *f* **2** SUSPENSION : suspensión *f* (de una sentencia) **3** SUPPORT : soporte *m*

stead [ˈstɛd] *n* **1** : lugar *m* <she went in his stead : fue en su lugar> **2 to stand (someone) in good stead** : ser muy útil a, servir de mucho a

steadfast [ˈstɛdˌfæst] *adj* : firme, resuelto <a steadfast friend : un fiel amigo> <a steadfast refusal : una negativa categórica>

steadily [ˈstɛdəli] *adv* **1** CONSTANTLY : continuamente, sin parar **2** FIRMLY : con firmeza **3** FIXEDLY : fijamente

steady[1] [ˈstɛdi] *v* **steadied; steadying** *vt* : sujetar <she steadied herself : recobró el equilibrio> — *vi* : estabilizarse

steady[2] *adj* **steadier; -est 1** FIRM, SURE : seguro, firme <to have a steady hand : tener buen pulso> **2** FIXED, REGULAR : fijo <a steady income : ingresos fijos> **3** CALM : tranquilo, ecuánime <she has steady nerves : es imperturbable> **4** DEPENDABLE : responsable, fiable **5** CONSTANT : constante

steak [ˈsteɪk] *n* : bistec *m*, filete *m*, churrasco *m*, bife *m Arg, Chile, Uru*

steal [ˈstiːl] *v* **stole** [ˈstoːl]; **stolen** [ˈstoːlən]; **stealing** *vt* : robar, hurtar — *vi* **1** : robar, hurtar **2** : ir sigilosamente <to steal away : escabullirse>

stealth [ˈstɛlθ] *n* : sigilo *m*

stealthily [ˈstɛlθəli] *adv* : furtivamente

stealthy [ˈstɛlθi] *adj* **stealthier; -est** : furtivo, sigiloso

steam[1] [ˈstiːm] *vi* : echar vapor <to steam away : moverse echando vapor> — *vt* **1** : cocer al vapor (en cocina) **2 to steam open** : abrir con vapor

steam[2] *n* **1** : vapor *m* **2 to let off steam** : desahogarse

steamboat [ˈstiːmˌboːt] → **steamship**

steam engine *n* : motor *m* de vapor

steamroller [ˈstiːmˌroːlər] *n* : apisonadora *f*

steamship [ˈstiːmˌʃɪp] *n* : vapor *m*, barco *m* de vapor

steamy [ˈstiːmi] *adj* **steamier; -est 1** : lleno de vapor **2** EROTIC : erótico <a steamy romance : un tórrido romance>

steed [ˈstiːd] *n* : corcel *m*

steel[1] [ˈstiːl] *vt* **to steel oneself** : armarse de valor

steel[2] *adj* : de acero

steel[3] *n* : acero *m*

steely [ˈstiːli] *adj* **steelier; -est** : como acero <a steely gaze : una mirada fría> <steely determination : determinación férrea>

steep[1] [ˈstiːp] *vt* : remojar, dejar (té, etc.) en infusión

steep[2] *adj* **1** : empinado, escarpado <a steep cliff : un precipicio escarpado> **2** CONSIDERABLE : considerable, marcado **3** EXCESSIVE : excesivo <steep prices : precios muy altos>

steeple [ˈstiːpəl] *n* : aguja *f*, campanario *m*

steeplechase [ˈstiːpəlˌtʃeɪs] *n* : carrera *f* de obstáculos

steeply [ˈstiːpli] *adv* : abruptamente

steer[1] [ˈstɪr] *vt* **1** : conducir (un coche), gobernar (un barco) **2** GUIDE : dirigir, guiar

steer[2] *n* : buey *m*

steering wheel *n* : volante *m*

stein [ˈstaɪn] *n* : jarra *f* (para cerveza)

stellar [ˈstɛlər] *adj* : estelar

stem[1] [ˈstɛm] *v* **stemmed; stemming** *vt* : detener, contener, parar <to stem the tide : detener el curso> — *vi* **to stem from** : provenir de, ser el resultado de

stem[2] *n* : tallo *m* (de una planta)

stench [ˈstɛntʃ] *n* : hedor *m*, mal olor *m*

stencil[1] [ˈstɛn*t*səl] *vt* **-ciled** *or* **-cilled; -ciling** *or* **-cilling** : marcar utilizando una plantilla

stencil[2] *n* : plantilla *f* (para marcar)

stenographer [stəˈnɑgrəfər] *n* : taquígrafo *m*, -fa *f*

stenographic [ˌstɛnəˈgræfɪk] *adj* : taquigráfico

stenography [stəˈnɑgrəfi] *n* : taquigrafía *f*

step[1] [ˈstɛp] *vi* **stepped; stepping 1** : dar un paso <step this way, please : pase por aquí, por favor> <he stepped outside : salió> **2 to step on** : pisar

step[2] *n* **1** : paso *m* <step by step : paso por paso> **2** STAIR : escalón *m*, peldaño *m* **3** RUNG : escalón *m*, travesaño *m* **4** MEASURE, MOVE : medida *f*, paso *m* <to take steps : tomar medidas> **5** STRIDE : paso *m* <with a quick step : con paso rápido>

stepbrother ['stɛp,brʌðər] *n* : hermanastro *m*
stepdaughter ['stɛp,dɔt̬ər] *n* : hijastra *f*
stepfather ['stɛp,fɑðər, -,fa-] *n* : padrastro *m*
stepladder ['stɛp,lædər] *n* : escalera *f* de tijera
stepmother ['stɛp,mʌðər] *n* : madrastra *f*
steppe ['stɛp] *n* : estepa *f*
stepping–stone ['stɛpɪŋ,stoːn] *n* : pasadera *f* (en un río, etc.), trampolín *m* (al éxito)
stepsister ['stɛp,sɪstər] *n* : hermanastra *f*
stepson ['stɛp,sʌn] *n* : hijastro *m*
step up *vt* INCREASE : aumentar
stereo[1] ['stɛri,oː, 'stɪr-] *adj* : estéreo
stereo[2] *n, pl* **stereos** : estéreo *m*
stereophonic [,stɛrio'fɑnɪk, ,stɪr-] *adj* : estereofónico
stereotype[1] ['stɛrio,taɪp, 'stɪr-] *vt* **-typed; -typing** : estereotipar
stereotype[2] *n* : estereotipo *m*
sterile ['stɛrəl] *adj* : estéril
sterility [stə'rɪlət̬i] *n* : esterilidad *f*
sterilization [,stɛrələ'zeɪʃən] *n* : esterilización *f*
sterilize ['stɛrə,laɪz] *vt* **-ized; -izing** : esterilizar
sterling ['stərlɪŋ] *adj* **1** : de ley <sterling silver : plata de ley> **2** EXCELLENT : excelente
stern[1] ['stərn] *adj* : severo, adusto — **sternly** *adv*
stern[2] *n* : popa *f*
sternness ['stərnnəs] *n* : severidad *f*
sternum ['stərnəm] *n, pl* **sternums** *or* **sterna** [-nə] : esternón *m*
stethoscope ['stɛθə,skoːp] *n* : estetoscopio *m*
stevedore ['stiːvə,dor] *n* : estibador *m*, -dora *f*
stew[1] ['stuː, 'stjuː] *vt* : estofar, guisar — *vi* **1** : cocer (dícese de la carne, etc.) **2** FRET : preocuparse
stew[2] *n* **1** : estofado *m*, guiso *m* **2 to be in a stew** : estar agitado
steward ['stuːərd, 'stjuː-] *n* **1** MANAGER : administrador *m* **2** : auxiliar *m* de vuelo (en un avión), camarero *m* (en un barco)
stewardess ['stuːərdəs, 'stjuː-] *n* **1** MANAGER : administradora *f* **2** : camarera *f* (en un barco) **3** : auxiliar *f* de vuelo, azafata *f*, aeromoza *f* (en un avión)
stick[1] ['stɪk] *v* **stuck** ['stʌk]; **sticking** *vt* **1** STAB : clavar **2** ATTACH : pegar **3** PUT : poner **4 to stick out** : sacar (la lengua, etc.), extender (la mano) — *vi* **1** ADHERE : pegarse, adherirse **2** JAM : atascarse **3 to stick around** : quedarse **4 to stick out** PROJECT : sobresalir (de una superficie), asomar (por detrás o debajo de algo) **5 to stick to** : no abandonar <stick to your guns : manténgase firme> **6 to stick up** : estar parado (dícese del pelo, etc.), sobresalir (de una superficie) **7 to stick with** : serle fiel a (una persona), seguir con (una cosa) <I'll stick with what I know : prefiero lo conocido>
stick[2] *n* **1** BRANCH, TWIG : ramita *f* **2** : palo *m*, vara *f* <a walking stick : un bastón>
sticker ['stɪkər] *n* : etiqueta *f* adhesiva
stickler ['stɪklər] *n* : persona *f* exigente <to be a stickler for : insistir mucho en>
sticky ['stɪki] *adj* **stickier; -est 1** ADHESIVE : pegajoso, adhesivo **2** MUGGY : bochornoso **3** DIFFICULT : difícil
stiff ['stɪf] *adj* **1** RIGID : rígido, tieso <a stiff dough : una masa firme> **2** : agarrotado, entumecido <stiff muscles : músculos entumecidos> **3** STILTED : acartonado, poco natural **4** STRONG : fuerte (dícese del viento, etc.) **5** DIFFICULT, SEVERE : severo, difícil, duro
stiffen ['stɪfən] *vt* **1** STRENGTHEN : fortalecer, reforzar (tela, etc.) **2** : hacer más duro (un castigo, etc.) — *vi* **1** HARDEN : endurecerse **2** : entumecerse (dícese de los músculos)
stiffly ['stɪfli] *adv* **1** RIGIDLY : rígidamente **2** COLDLY : con frialdad
stiffness ['stɪfnəs] *n* **1** RIGIDITY : rigidez *f* **2** COLDNESS : frialdad *f* **3** SEVERITY : severidad *f*
stifle ['staɪfəl] *vt* **-fled; -fling** SMOTHER, SUPPRESS : sofocar, reprimir, contener <to stifle a yawn : reprimir un bostezo>
stigma ['stɪgmə] *n, pl* **stigmata** [stɪg'mɑt̬ə, 'stɪgmət̬ə] *or* **stigmas** : estigma *m*
stigmatize ['stɪgmə,taɪz] *vt* **-tized; -tizing** : estigmatizar
stile ['staɪl] *n* : escalones *mpl* para cruzar un cerco
stiletto [stə'lɛ,t̬oː] *n, pl* **-tos** *or* **-toes** : estilete *m*
still[1] ['stɪl] *vt* CALM : pacificar, apaciguar — *vi* : pacificarse, apaciguarse
still[2] *adv* **1** QUIETLY : quieto <sit still! : ¡quédate quieto!> **2** : de todos modos, aún, todavía <she still lives there : aún vive allí> <it's still the same : sigue siendo lo mismo> **3** IN ANY CASE : de todos modos, aún así <he still has doubts : aún así le quedan dudas> <I still prefer that you stay : de todos modos prefiero que te quedes>
still[3] *adj* **1** MOTIONLESS : quieto, inmóvil **2** SILENT : callado
still[4] *n* **1** SILENCE : quietud *f*, calma *f* **2** : alambique *m* (para destilar alcohol)
stillborn ['stɪl,bɔrn] *adj* : nacido muerto
stillness ['stɪlnəs] *n* : calma *f*, silencio *m*
stilt ['stɪlt] *n* : zanco *m*
stilted ['stɪltəd] *adj* : afectado, poco natural

stimulant [ˈstɪmjələnt] *n* : estimulante *m* — **stimulant** *adj*

stimulate [ˈstɪmjəˌleɪt] *vt* **-lated; -lating** : estimular

stimulation [ˌstɪmjəˈleɪʃən] *n* **1** STIMULATING : estimulación *f* **2** STIMULUS : estímulo *m*

stimulus [ˈstɪmjələs] *n, pl* **-li** [-ˌlaɪ] **1** : estímulo *m* **2** INCENTIVE : acicate *m*

sting[1] [ˈstɪŋ] *v* **stung** [ˈstʌŋ]; **stinging** *vt* **1** : picar <a bee stung him : le picó una abeja> **2** HURT : hacer escocer (físicamente), herir (emocionalmente) — *vi* **1** : picar (dícese de las abejas, etc.) **2** SMART : escocer, arder

sting[2] *n* : picadura *f* (herida), escozor *m* (sensación)

stinger [ˈstɪŋər] *n* : aguijón *m* (de una abeja, etc.)

stinginess [ˈstɪndʒinəs] *n* : tacañería *f*

stingy [ˈstɪndʒi] *adj* **stingier; -est 1** MISERLY : tacaño, avaro **2** PALTRY : mezquino, mísero

stink[1] [ˈstɪŋk] *vi* **stank** [ˈstæŋk] *or* **stunk** [ˈstʌŋk]; **stunk; stinking** : apestar, oler mal

stink[2] *n* : hedor *m,* mal olor *m,* peste *f*

stint[1] [ˈstɪnt] *vt* : escatimar <to stint oneself of : privarse de> — *vi* **to stint on** : escatimar

stint[2] *n* : período *m*

stipend [ˈstaɪˌpɛnd, -pənd] *n* : estipendio *m*

stipulate [ˈstɪpjəˌleɪt] *vt* **-lated; -lating** : estipular

stipulation [ˌstɪpjəˈleɪʃən] *n* : estipulación *f*

stir[1] [ˈstər] *v* **stirred; stirring** *vt* **1** AGITATE : mover, agitar **2** MIX : revolver, remover **3** INCITE : incitar, impulsar, motivar **4** *or* **to stir up** AROUSE : despertar (memorias, etc.), provocar (ira, etc.) — *vi* : moverse, agitarse

stir[2] *n* **1** MOTION : movimiento *m* **2** COMMOTION : revuelo *m*

stirrup [ˈstərəp, ˈstɪr-] *n* : estribo *m*

stitch[1] [ˈstɪtʃ] *vt* : coser, bordar (para decorar) — *vi* : coser

stitch[2] *n* **1** : puntada *f* **2** TWINGE : punzada *f,* puntada *f*

stock[1] [ˈstɑk] *vt* : surtir, abastecer, vender — *vi* **to stock up** : abastecerse

stock[2] *n* **1** SUPPLY : reserva *f,* existencias *fpl* (en comercio) <to be out of stock : estar agotadas las existencias> **2** SECURITIES : acciones *fpl,* valores *mpl* **3** LIVESTOCK : ganado *m* **4** ANCESTRY : linaje *m,* estirpe *f* **5** BROTH : caldo *m* **6 to take stock** : evaluar

stockade [stɑˈkeɪd] *n* : estacada *f*

stockbroker [ˈstɑkˌbroːkər] *n* : corredor *m,* -dora *f* de bolsa

stockholder [ˈstɑkˌhoːldər] *n* : accionista *mf*

stocking [ˈstɑkɪŋ] *n* : media *f* <a pair of stockings : unas medias>

stock market *n* : bolsa *f*

stockpile[1] [ˈstɑkˌpaɪl] *vt* **-piled; -piling** : acumular, almacenar

stockpile[2] *n* : reservas *fpl*

stocky [ˈstɑki] *adj* **stockier; -est** : robusto, fornido

stockyard [ˈstɑkˌjɑrd] *n* : corral *m*

stodgy [ˈstɑdʒi] *adj* **stodgier; -est 1** DULL : aburrido, pesado **2** OLD-FASHIONED : anticuado

stoic[1] [ˈstoːɪk] *or* **stoical** [-ɪkəl] *adj* : estoico — **stoically** [-ɪkli] *adv*

stoic[2] *n* : estoico *m,* -ca *f*

stoicism [ˈstoːəˌsɪzəm] *n* : estoicismo *m*

stoke [ˈstoːk] *vt* **stoked; stoking** : atizar (un fuego), echarle carbón a (un horno)

stole[1] → **steal**

stole[2] [ˈstoːl] *n* : estola *f*

stolen → **steal**

stolid [ˈstɑlɪd] *adj* : impasible, imperturbable — **stolidly** *adv*

stomach[1] [ˈstʌmɪk] *vt* : aguantar, soportar

stomach[2] *n* **1** : estómago *m* **2** BELLY : vientre *m,* barriga *f,* panza *f* **3** DESIRE : ganas *fpl* <he had no stomach for a fight : no quería pelea>

stomachache [ˈstʌmɪkˌeɪk] *n* : dolor *m* de estómago

stomp [ˈstɑmp, ˈstɔmp] *vt* : pisotear — *vi* : pisar fuerte

stone[1] [ˈstoːn] *vt* **stoned; stoning** : apedrear, lapidar

stone[2] *n* **1** : piedra *f* **2** PIT : hueso *m,* pepa *f* (de una fruta)

Stone Age *n* : Edad *f* de Piedra

stony [ˈstoːni] *adj* **stonier; -est 1** ROCKY : pedregoso **2** UNFEELING : insensible, frío <a stony stare : una mirada glacial>

stood → **stand**

stool [ˈstuːl] *n* **1** SEAT : taburete *m,* banco *m* **2** FOOTSTOOL : escabel *m* **3** FECES : deposición *f* de heces

stoop[1] [ˈstuːp] *vi* **1** CROUCH : agacharse **2 to stoop to** : rebajarse a

stoop[2] *n* **1** : espaldas *fpl* encorvadas <to have a stoop : ser encorvado> **2** : entrada *f* (de una casa)

stop[1] [ˈstɑp] *v* **stopped; stopping** *vt* **1** PLUG : tapar **2** PREVENT : impedir, evitar <she stopped me from leaving : me impidió que saliera> **3** HALT : parar, detener **4** CEASE : dejar de <he stopped talking : dejó de hablar> — *vi* **1** HALT : detenerse, parar **2** CEASE : cesar, terminar <the rain won't stop : no deja de llover> **3** STAY : quedarse <she stopped with friends : se quedó en casa de unos amigos> **4 to stop by** : visitar

stop[2] *n* **1** STOPPER : tapón *m* **2** HALT : parada *f,* alto *m* <to come to a stop : pararse, detenerse> <to put a stop to : poner fin a> **3** : parada *f* <bus stop : parada de autobús>

stopgap [ˈstɑpˌgæp] *n* : arreglo *m* provisorio

stoplight [ˈstɑpˌlaɪt] *n* : semáforo *m*

stoppage ['stɑpɪdʒ] *n* : acto *m* de parar <a work stoppage : un paro>

stopper ['stɑpər] *n* : tapón *m*

storage ['storɪdʒ] *n* : almacenamiento *m,* almacenaje *m*

storage battery *n* : acumulador *m*

store[1] ['stor] *vt* **stored; storing** : guardar, almacenar

store[2] *n* **1** RESERVE, SUPPLY : reserva *f* **2** SHOP : tienda *f* <grocery store : tienda de comestibles>

storehouse ['stor,haʊs] *n* : almacén *m,* depósito *m*

storekeeper ['stor,kiːpər] *n* : tendero *m,* -ra *f*

storeroom ['stor,ruːm, -,rʊm] *n* : almacén *m,* depósito *m*

stork ['stɔrk] *n* : cigüeña *f*

storm[1] ['stɔrm] *vi* **1** : llover o nevar tormentosamente **2** RAGE : ponerse furioso, vociferar **3 to storm out** : salir echando pestes — *vt* ATTACK : asaltar

storm[2] *n* **1** : tormenta *f,* tempestad *f* **2** UPROAR : alboroto *m,* revuelo *m,* escándalo *m* <a storm of abuse : un torrente de abusos>

stormy ['stɔrmi] *adj* **stormier; -est** : tormentoso

story ['stori] *n, pl* **stories 1** NARRATIVE : cuento *m,* relato *m* **2** ACCOUNT : historia *f,* relato *m* **3** : piso *m,* planta *f* (de un edificio) <first story : planta baja>

stout ['staʊt] *adj* **1** FIRM, RESOLUTE : firme, resuelto **2** STURDY : fuerte, robusto, sólido **3** FAT : corpulento, gordo

stove[1] ['stoːv] *n* : cocina *f* (para cocinar), estufa *f* (para calentar)

stove[2] → **stave**[1]

stow ['stoː] *vt* **1** STORE : poner, meter, guardar **2** LOAD : cargar — *vi* **to stow away** : viajar de polizón

stowaway ['stoːə,weɪ] *n* : polizón *m*

straddle ['strædəl] *vt* **-dled; -dling** : sentarse a horcajadas sobre

straggle ['strægəl] *vi* **-gled; -gling** : rezagarse, quedarse atrás

straggler ['strægələr] *n* : rezagado *m,* -da *f*

straight[1] ['streɪt] *adv* **1** : derecho, directamente <go straight, then turn right : sigue derecho, luego gira a la derecha> **2** HONESTLY : honestamente <to go straight : enmendarse> **3** CLEARLY : con claridad **4** FRANKLY : francamente, con franqueza

straight[2] *adj* **1** : recto (dícese de las líneas, etc.), derecho (dícese de algo vertical), lacio (dícese del pelo) **2** HONEST, JUST : honesto, justo **3** NEAT, ORDERLY : arreglado, ordenado

straighten ['streɪtən] *vt* **1** : enderezar, poner derecho **2 to straighten up** : arreglar, ordenar <he straightened up the house : arregló la casa>

straightforward [streɪt'fɔrwərd] *adj* **1** FRANK : franco, sincero **2** CLEAR, PRECISE : puro, simple, claro

straightway ['streɪt'weɪ, -,weɪ] *adv* : inmediatamente

strain[1] ['streɪn] *vt* **1** EXERT : forzar (la vista, la voz) <to strain oneself : hacer un gran esfuerzo> **2** FILTER : colar, filtrar **3** INJURE : lastimarse, hacerse daño en <to strain a muscle : sufrir un esguince>

strain[2] *n* **1** LINEAGE : linaje *m,* abolengo *m* **2** STREAK, TRACE : veta *f* **3** VARIETY : tipo *m,* variedad *f* **4** STRESS : tensión *f,* presión *f* **5** SPRAIN : esguince *m,* torcedura *f* (del tobillo, etc.) **6 strains** *npl* TUNE : melodía *f,* acordes *mpl,* compases *fpl*

strainer ['streɪnər] *n* : colador *m*

strait ['streɪt] *n* **1** : estrecho *m* **2 straits** *npl* DISTRESS : aprietos *mpl,* apuros *mpl* <in dire straits : en serios aprietos>

straitened ['streɪtənd] *adj* **in straitened circumstances** : en apuros económicos

strand[1] ['strænd] *vt* **1** : varar **2 to be left stranded** : quedar(se) varado, quedar colgado <they left me stranded : me dejaron abandonado>

strand[2] *n* **1** : hebra *f* (de hilo, etc.) <a strand of hair : un pelo> **2** BEACH : playa *f*

strange ['streɪndʒ] *adj* **stranger; -est 1** QUEER, UNUSUAL : extraño, raro **2** UNFAMILIAR : desconocido, nuevo

strangely ['streɪndʒli] *adv* ODDLY : de manera extraña <to behave strangely : portarse de una manera rara> <strangely, he didn't call : curiosamente, no llamó>

strangeness ['streɪndʒnəs] *n* **1** ODDNESS : rareza *f* **2** UNFAMILIARITY : lo desconocido

stranger ['streɪndʒər] *n* : desconocido *m,* -da *f;* extraño *m,* -ña *f*

strangle ['stræŋgəl] *vt* **-gled; -gling** : estrangular

strangler ['stræŋglər] *n* : estrangulador *m,* -dora *f*

strap[1] ['stræp] *vt* **strapped; strapping 1** FASTEN : sujetar con una correa **2** FLOG : azotar (con una correa)

strap[2] *n* **1** : correa *f* **2 shoulder strap** : tirante *m*

strapless ['stræpləs] *n* : sin tirantes

strapping ['stræpɪŋ] *adj* : robusto, fornido

stratagem ['strætədʒəm, -,dʒɛm] *n* : estratagema *f,* artimaña *f*

strategic [strə'tiːdʒɪk] *adj* : estratégico

strategy ['strætədʒi] *n, pl* **-gies** : estrategia *f*

stratified ['strætə,faɪd] *adj* : estratificado

stratosphere ['strætə,sfɪr] *n* : estratosfera *f*

stratum ['streɪtəm, 'stræ-] *n, pl* **strata** [-tə] : estrato *m,* capa *f*

straw *n* **1** : paja *f* <the last straw : el colmo> **2** *or* **drinking straw** : pajita *f,* popote *m Mex*

strawberry ['strɔˌbɛri] *n, pl* **-ries** : fresa *f*
stray[1] ['streɪ] *vi* **1** WANDER : alejarse, extraviarse <the cattle strayed away : el ganado se descarrió> **2** DIGRESS : desviarse, divagar
stray[2] *adj* : perdido, callejero (dícese de un perro o un gato), descarriado (dícese del ganado)
stray[3] *n* : animal *m* perdido, animal *m* callejero
streak[1] ['stri:k] *vt* : hacer rayas en <blue streaked with grey : azul veteado con gris> — *vi* : ir como una flecha
streak[2] *n* **1** : raya *f,* veta *f* (en mármol, queso, etc.), mechón *m* (en el pelo) **2** : rayo *m* (de luz) **3** TRACE : veta *f* **4** : racha *f* <a streak of luck : una racha de suerte>
stream[1] ['stri:m] *vi* : correr, salir a chorros <tears streamed from his eyes : las lágrimas brotaban de sus ojos> — *vt* : derramar, dejar correr <to stream blood : derramar sangre>
stream[2] *n* **1** BROOK : arroyo *m,* riachuelo *m* **2** RIVER : río *m* **3** FLOW : corriente *f,* chorro *m*
streamer ['stri:mər] *n* **1** PENNANT : banderín *m* **2** RIBBON : serpentina *f* (de papel), cinta *f* (de tela)
streamlined ['stri:mˌlaɪnd] *adj* **1** : aerodinámico (dícese de los automóviles, etc.) **2** EFFICIENT : eficiente, racionalizado
street ['stri:t] *n* : calle *f*
streetcar ['stri:tˌkɑr] *n* : tranvía *m*
strength ['strɛŋ*k*θ] *n* **1** POWER : fuerza *f* **2** SOLIDITY, TOUGHNESS : solidez *f,* resistencia *f,* dureza *f* **3** INTENSITY : intensidad *f* (de emociones, etc.), lo fuerte (de un sabor, etc.) **4** : punto *m* fuerte <strengths and weaknesses : virtudes y defectos> **5** NUMBER : número *m,* complemento *m* <in full strength : en gran número>
strengthen ['strɛŋ*k*θən] *vt* **1** : fortalecer (los músculos, el espíritu, etc.) **2** REINFORCE : reforzar **3** INTENSIFY : intensificar, redoblar (esfuerzos, etc.) — *vi* **1** : fortalecerse, hacerse más fuerte **2** INTENSIFY : intensificarse
strenuous ['strɛnjʊəs] *adj* **1** VIGOROUS : vigoroso, enérgico **2** ARDUOUS : duro, riguroso
strenuously ['strɛnjʊəsli] *adv* : vigorosamente, duro
stress[1] ['strɛs] *vt* **1** : someter a tensión (física) **2** EMPHASIZE : enfatizar, recalcar **3** **to stress out** : estresar
stress[2] *n* **1** : tensión *f* (en un material) **2** EMPHASIS : énfasis *m,* acento *m* (en lingüística) **3** TENSION : tensión *f* (nerviosa), estrés *m*
stressful ['strɛsfəl] *adj* : estresante
stretch[1] ['strɛtʃ] *vt* **1** EXTEND : estirar, extender, desplegar (alas) **2** **to stretch the truth** : forzar la verdad, exagerar — *vi* : estirarse
stretch[2] *n* **1** STRETCHING : extensión *f,* estiramiento *m* (de músculos) **2** ELASTICITY : elasticidad *f* **3** EXPANSE : tramo *m,* trecho *m* <the home stretch : la recta final> **4** PERIOD : período *m* (de tiempo)
stretcher ['strɛtʃər] *n* : camilla *f*
strew ['stru:] *vt* **strewed; strewed** *or* **strewn** ['stru:n]; **strewing** **1** SCATTER : esparcir (semillas, etc.), desparramar (papeles, etc.) **2** **to strew with** : cubrir de
stricken ['strɪkən] *adj* **stricken with** : aquejado de (una enfermedad), afligido por (tristeza, etc.)
strict ['strɪkt] *adj* : estricto — **strictly** *adv*
strictness ['strɪktnəs] *n* : severidad *f,* lo estricto
stricture ['strɪktʃər] *n* : crítica *f,* censura *f*
stride[1] ['straɪd] *vi* **strode** ['stro:d]; **stridden** ['strɪdən]; **striding** : ir dando trancos, ir dando zancadas
stride[2] *n* : tranco *m,* zancada *f*
strident ['straɪdənt] *adj* : estridente
strife ['straɪf] *n* : conflictos *mpl,* disensión *f*
strike[1] ['straɪk] *v* **struck** ['strʌk]; **struck; striking** *vt* **1** HIT : golpear (a una persona) <to strike a blow : pegar un golpe> **2** DELETE : suprimir, tachar **3** COIN, MINT : acuñar (monedas) **4** : dar (la hora) **5** AFFLICT : sobrevenir <he was stricken with a fever : le sobrevino una fiebre> **6** IMPRESS : impresionar, parecer <her voice struck me : su voz me impresionó> <it struck him as funny : le pareció chistoso> **7** : encender (un fósforo) **8** FIND : descubrir (oro, petróleo) **9** ADOPT : adoptar (una pose, etc.) — *vi* **1** HIT : golpear <to strike against : chocar contra> **2** ATTACK : atacar **3** : declararse en huelga
strike[2] *n* **1** BLOW : golpe *m* **2** : huelga *f,* paro *m* <to be on strike : estar en huelga> **3** ATTACK : ataque *m*
strikebreaker ['straɪkˌbreɪkər] *n* : rompehuelgas *mf,* esquirol *mf*
strike out *vi* **1** HEAD : salir (para) **2** : ser ponchado (en béisbol) <the batter struck out : poncharon al bateador>
striker ['straɪkər] *n* : huelgista *mf*
strike up *vt* START : entablar, empezar
striking ['straɪkɪŋ] *adj* : notable, sorprendente, llamativo <a striking beauty : una belleza imponente> — **strikingly** *adv*
string[1] ['strɪŋ] *vt* **strung** ['strʌŋ]; **stringing** **1** THREAD : ensartar <to string beads : ensartar cuentas> **2** HANG : colgar (con un cordel)
string[2] *n* **1** : cordel *m,* cuerda *f* **2** SERIES : serie *f,* sarta *f* (de insultos, etc.) **3** **strings** *npl* : cuerdas *fpl* (en música)
string bean *n* : judía *f,* ejote *m Mex*
stringent ['strɪndʒənt] *adj* : estricto, severo

stringy [ˈstrɪŋi] *adj* **stringier; -est** : fibroso
strip[1] [ˈstrɪp] *v* **stripped; stripping** *vt* : quitar (ropa, pintura, etc.), desnudar, despojar — *vi* UNDRESS : desnudarse
strip[2] *n* : tira *f* <a strip of land : una faja>
stripe[1] [ˈstraɪp] *vt* **striped** [ˈstraɪpt]; **striping** : marcar con rayas o listas
stripe[2] *n* **1** : raya *f,* lista *f* **2** BAND : franja *f*
striped [ˈstraɪpt, ˈstraɪpəd] *adj* : a rayas, de rayas, rayado, listado
strive [ˈstraɪv] *vi* **strove** [ˈstroːv]; **striven** [ˈstrɪvən] *or* **strived; striving 1 to strive for** : luchar por lograr **2 to strive to** : esforzarse por
strode → **stride**
stroke[1] [ˈstroːk] *vt* **stroked; stroking** : acariciar
stroke[2] *n* : golpe *m* <a stroke of luck : un golpe de suerte>
stroll[1] [ˈstroːl] *vi* : pasear, pasearse, dar un paseo
stroll[2] *n* : paseo *m*
stroller [ˈstroːlər] *n* : cochecito *m* (para niños)
strong [ˈstrɔŋ] *adj* **1** : fuerte **2** HEALTHY : sano **3** ZEALOUS : ferviente
stronghold [ˈstrɔŋˌhoːld] *n* : fortaleza *f,* fuerte *m,* bastión *m* <a cultural stronghold : un baluarte de la cultura>
strongly [ˈstrɔŋli] *adv* **1** POWERFULLY : fuerte, con fuerza **2** STURDILY : fuertemente, sólidamente **3** INTENSELY : intensamente, profundamente **4** WHOLEHEARTEDLY : totalmente
struck → **strike**[1]
structural [ˈstrʌktʃərəl] *adj* : estructural
structure[1] [ˈstrʌktʃər] *vt* **-tured; -turing** : estructurar
structure[2] *n* **1** BUILDING : construcción *f* **2** ARRANGEMENT, FRAMEWORK : estructura *f*
struggle[1] [ˈstrʌgəl] *vi* **-gled; -gling 1** CONTEND : forcejear (físicamente), luchar, contender **2** : hacer con dificultad <she struggled forward : avanzó con dificultad>
struggle[2] *n* : lucha *f,* pelea *f* (física)
strum [ˈstrʌm] *vt* **strummed; strumming** : rasguear
strung → **string**[1]
strut[1] [ˈstrʌt] *vi* **strutted; strutting** : pavonearse
strut[2] *n* **1** : pavoneo *m* <he walked with a strut : se pavoneaba> **2** : puntal *m* (en construcción, etc.)
strychnine [ˈstrɪkˌnaɪn, -nən, -ˌniːn] *n* : estricnina *f*
stub[1] [ˈstʌb] *vt* **stubbed; stubbing 1 to stub one's toe** : darse en el dedo (del pie) **2 to stub out** : apagarse
stub[2] *n* : colilla *f* (de un cigarrillo), cabo *m* (de un lápiz, etc.), talón *m* (de un cheque)
stubble [ˈstʌbəl] *n* **1** : rastrojo *m* (de plantas) **2** BEARD : barba *f*
stubborn [ˈstʌbərn] *adj* **1** OBSTINATE : terco, obstinado, empecinado **2** PERSISTENT : pertinaz, persistente — **stubbornly** *adv*
stubbornness [ˈstʌbərnnəs] *n* **1** OBSTINACY : terquedad *f,* obstinación *f* **2** PERSISTENCE : persistencia *f*
stubby [ˈstʌbi] *adj* **stubbier; -est** : corto y grueso <stubby fingers : dedos regordetes>
stucco [ˈstʌkoː] *n, pl* **stuccos** *or* **stuccoes** : estuco *m*
stuck → **stick**[1]
stuck–up [ˈstʌkˈʌp] *adj* : engreído, creído *fam*
stud[1] [ˈstʌd] *vt* **studded; studding** : tachonar, salpicar
stud[2] *n* **1** *or* **stud horse** : semental *m* **2** : montante *m* (en construcción) **3** HOBNAIL : tachuela *f,* tachón *m*
student [ˈstuːdənt, ˈstjuː-] *n* : estudiante *mf;* alumno *m,* -na *f* (de un colegio)
studied [ˈstʌdid] *adj* : intencionado, premeditado
studio [ˈstuːdiˌoː, ˈstjuː-] *n, pl* **studios** : estudio *m*
studious [ˈstuːdiəs, ˈstjuː-] *adj* : estudioso — **studiously** *adv*
study[1] [ˈstʌdi] *v* **studied; studying 1** : estudiar **2** EXAMINE : examinar, estudiar
study[2] *n, pl* **studies 1** STUDYING : estudio *m* **2** OFFICE : estudio *m,* gabinete *m* (en una casa) **3** RESEARCH : investigación *f,* estudio *m*
stuff[1] [ˈstʌf] *vt* : rellenar, llenar, atiborrar
stuff[2] *n* **1** POSSESSIONS : cosas *fpl* **2** ESSENCE : esencia *f* **3** SUBSTANCE : cosa *f,* cosas *fpl* <some sticky stuff : una cosa pegajosa> <she knows her stuff : es experta>
stuffing [ˈstʌfɪŋ] *n* : relleno *m*
stuffy [ˈstʌfi] *adj* **stuffier; -est 1** CLOSE : viciado, cargado <a stuffy room : una sala mal ventilada> <stuffy weather : tiempo bochornoso> **2** : tapado (dícese de la nariz) **3** STODGY : pesado, aburrido
stumble[1] [ˈstʌmbəl] *vi* **-bled; -bling 1** TRIP : tropezar, dar un traspié **2** FLOUNDER : quedarse sin saber qué hacer o decir **3 to stumble across** *or* **to stumble upon** : dar con, tropezar con
stumble[2] *n* : tropezón *m,* traspié *m*
stump[1] [ˈstʌmp] *vt* : dejar perplejo <to be stumped : no tener respuesta>
stump[2] *n* **1** : muñón *m* (de un brazo o una pierna) **2** *or* **tree stump** : cepa *f,* tocón *m* **3** STUB : cabo *m*
stun [ˈstʌn] *vt* **stunned; stunning 1** : aturdir (con un golpe) **2** ASTONISH, SHOCK : dejar estupefacto, dejar atónito, aturdir
stung → **sting**[1]
stunk → **stink**[1]

stunning ['stʌnɪŋ] *adj* **1** ASTONISHING : asombroso, pasmoso, increíble **2** STRIKING : imponente, impresionante (dícese de la belleza)

stunt[1] ['stʌnt] *vt* : atrofiar

stunt[2] *n* : proeza *f* (acrobática)

stupefy ['stuːpəˌfaɪ, 'stjuː-] *vt* **-fied; -fying 1** : aturdir, atontar (con drogas, etc.) **2** AMAZE : dejar estupefacto, dejar atónito

stupendous [stʊ'pɛndəs, stjʊ-] *adj* **1** MARVELOUS : estupendo, maravilloso **2** TREMENDOUS : tremendo — **stupendously** *adv*

stupid ['stuːpəd, 'stjuː-] *adj* **1** IDIOTIC, SILLY : tonto, bobo, estúpido **2** DULL, OBTUSE : lento, torpe, lerdo

stupidity [stʊ'pɪdət̬i, stjʊ-] *n* : tontería *f,* estupidez *f*

stupidly ['stuːpədli, 'stjuː-] *adv* **1** IDIOTICALLY : estúpidamente, tontamente **2** DENSELY : torpemente

stupor ['stuːpər, 'stjuː-] *n* : estupor *m*

sturdily ['stərdəli] *adv* : sólidamente

sturdiness ['stərdinəs] *n* : solidez *f* (de muebles, etc.), robustez *f* (de una persona)

sturdy ['stərdi] *adj* **sturdier; -est** : fuerte, robusto, sólido

sturgeon ['stərdʒən] *n* : esturión *m*

stutter[1] ['stʌt̬ər] *vi* : tartamudear

stutter[2] *n* STAMMER : tartamudeo *m*

sty ['staɪ] *n* **1** *pl* **sties** PIGPEN : chiquero *m,* polcilga *f* **2** *pl* **sties** *or* **styes** : orzuelo *m* (en el ojo)

style[1] ['staɪl] *vt* **styled; styling 1** NAME : llamar **2** : peinar (pelo), diseñar (vestidos, etc.) <carefully styled prose : prosa escrita con gran esmero>

style[2] *n* **1** : estilo *m* <that's just his style : él es así> <to live in style : vivir a lo grande> **2** FASHION : moda *f*

stylish ['staɪlɪʃ] *adj* : de moda, elegante, chic

stylishly ['staɪlɪʃli] *adv* : con estilo

stylishness ['staɪlɪʃnəs] *n* : estilo *m*

stylize ['staɪˌlaɪz, 'staɪə-] *vt* : estilizar

stylus ['staɪləs] *n, pl* **styli** ['staɪˌlaɪ] **1** PEN : estilo *m* **2** NEEDLE : aguja *f* (de un tocadiscos)

stymie ['staɪmi] *vt* **-mied; -mieing** : obstaculizar

suave ['swɑv] *adj* : fino, urbano

sub[1] ['sʌb] *vi* **subbed; subbing** → **substitute**[1]

sub[2] *n* **1** → **substitute**[2] **2** → **submarine**

subcommittee ['sʌbkəˌmɪt̬i] *n* : subcomité *m*

subconscious[1] [səb'kɑntʃəs] *adj* : subconsciente — **subconsciously** *adv*

subconscious[2] *n* : subconsciente *m*

subcontract [ˌsʌb'kɑnˌtrækt] *vt* : subcontratar

subdivide [ˌsʌbdə'vaɪd, 'sʌbdəˌvaɪd] *vt* **-vided; -viding** : subdividir

subdivision ['sʌbdəˌvɪʒən] *n* : subdivisión *f*

subdue [səb'duː, -'djuː] *vt* **-dued; -duing 1** OVERCOME : sojuzgar (a un enemigo), vencer, superar **2** CONTROL : dominar **3** SOFTEN : suavizar, atenuar (luz, etc.), moderar (lenguaje)

subhead ['sʌbˌhɛd] *or* **subheading** [-ˌhɛdɪŋ] *n* : subtítulo *m*

subject[1] [səb'dʒɛkt] *vt* **1** CONTROL, DOMINATE : controlar, dominar **2** : someter <they subjected him to pressure : lo sometieron a presiones>

subject[2] ['sʌbdʒɪkt] *adj* **1** : subyugado, sometido <a subject nation : una nación subyugada> **2** PRONE : sujeto, propenso <subject to colds : sujeto a resfriarse> **3 subject to** : sujeto a <subject to congressional approval : sujeto a la aprobación del congreso>

subject[3] ['sʌbdʒɪkt] *n* **1** : súbdito *m,* -ta *f* (de un gobierno) **2** TOPIC : tema *m* **3** : sujeto *m* (en gramática)

subjection [səb'dʒɛkʃən] *n* : sometimiento *m*

subjective [səb'dʒɛktɪv] *adj* : subjetivo — **subjectively** *adv*

subjectivity [ˌsʌbˌdʒɛk'tɪvət̬i] *n* : subjetividad *f*

subjugate ['sʌbdʒɪˌgeɪt] *vt* **-gated; -gating** : subyugar, someter, sojuzgar

subjunctive [səb'dʒʌŋktɪv] *n* : subjuntivo *m* — **subjunctive** *adj*

sublet ['sʌbˌlɛt] *vt* **-let; -letting** : subarrendar

sublime [sə'blaɪm] *adj* : sublime

sublimely [sə'blaɪmli] *adv* **1** : de manera sublime **2** UTTERLY : absolutamente, completamente

submarine[1] ['sʌbməˌriːn, ˌsʌbmə'-] *adj* : submarino

submarine[2] *n* : submarino *m*

submerge [səb'mərdʒ] *v* **-merged; -merging** *vt* : sumergir — *vi* : sumergirse

submission [səb'mɪʃən] *n* **1** YIELDING : sumisión *f* **2** PRESENTATION : presentación *f*

submissive [səb'mɪsɪv] *adj* : sumiso, dócil

submit [səb'mɪt] *v* **-mitted; -mitting** *vi* YIELD : rendirse <to submit to : someterse a> — *vt* PRESENT : presentar

subnormal [ˌsʌb'nɔrməl] *adj* : por debajo de lo normal

subordinate[1] [sə'bɔrdənˌeɪt] *vt* **-nated; -nating** : subordinar

subordinate[2] [sə'bɔrdənət] *adj* : subordinado <a subordinate clause : una oración subordinada>

subordinate[3] *n* : subordinado *m,* -da *f;* subalterno *m,* -na *f*

subordination [səˌbɔrdən'eɪʃən] *n* : subordinación *f*

subpoena[1] [sə'piːnə] *vt* **-naed; -naing** : citar

subpoena[2] *n* : citación *f,* citatorio *m*

subscribe [səb'skraɪb] *vi* **-scribed; -scribing 1** : suscribirse (a una revista, etc.) **2 to subscribe to** : suscribir (una opinión, etc.), estar de acuerdo con

subscriber [səb'skraɪbər] *n* **:** suscriptor *m,* -tora *f* (de una revista, etc.); abonado *m,* -da *f* (de un servicio)

subscription [səb'skrɪpʃən] *n* **:** suscripción *f*

subsequent ['sʌbsɪkwənt, -sə,kwɛnt] *adj* **:** subsiguiente <subsequent to : posterior a>

subsequently ['sʌb,kwɛntli, -kwənt-] *adv* **:** posteriormente

subservient [səb'sərviənt] *adj* **:** servil

subside [səb'saɪd] *vi* **-sided; -siding 1** SINK **:** hundirse, descender **2** ABATE **:** calmarse (dícese de las emociones), amainar (dícese del viento, etc.)

subsidiary[1] [səb'sɪdi,ɛri] *adj* **:** secundario

subsidiary[2] *n, pl* **-ries :** filial *f,* subsidiaria *f*

subsidize ['sʌbsə,daɪz] *vt* **-dized; -dizing :** subvencionar, subsidiar

subsidy ['sʌbsədi] *n, pl* **-dies :** subvención *f,* subsidio *m*

subsist [səb'sɪst] *vi* **:** subsistir, mantenerse, vivir

subsistence [səb'sɪstən*t*s] *n* **:** subsistencia *f*

substance ['sʌbstən*t*s] *n* **1** ESSENCE **:** sustancia *f,* esencia *f* **2 :** sustancia *f* <a toxic substance : una sustancia tóxica> **3** WEALTH **:** riqueza *f* <a woman of substance : una mujer acaudalada>

substandard [,sʌb'stændərd] *adj* **:** inferior, deficiente

substantial [səb'stænt∫əl] *adj* **1** ABUNDANT **:** sustancioso <a substantial meal : una comida sustanciosa> **2** CONSIDERABLE **:** considerable, apreciable **3** SOLID, STURDY **:** sólido

substantially [səb'stænt∫əli] *adv* **:** considerablemente

substantiate [səb'stænt∫i,eɪt] *vt* **-ated; -ating :** confirmar, probar, justificar

substitute[1] ['sʌbstə,tu:t, -,tju:t] *v* **-tuted; -tuting** *vt* **:** sustituir — *vi* **to substitute for :** sustituir

substitute[2] *n* **1 :** sustituto *m,* -ta *f;* suplente *mf* (persona) **2 :** sucedáneo *m* <sugar substitute : sucedáneo de azúcar>

substitute teacher *n* **:** profesor *m,* -sora *f* suplente

substitution [,sʌbstə'tu:ʃən, -'tju:-] *n* **:** sustitución *f*

subterfuge ['sʌbtər,fju:dʒ] *n* **:** subterfugio *m*

subterranean [,sʌbtə'reɪniən] *adj* **:** subterráneo

subtitle ['sʌb,taɪtəl] *n* **:** subtítulo *m*

subtle ['sʌtəl] *adj* **-tler; -tlest 1** DELICATE, ELUSIVE **:** sutil, delicado **2** CLEVER **:** sutil, ingenioso

subtlety ['sʌtəlti] *n, pl* **-ties :** sutileza *f*

subtly ['sʌtəli] *adv* **:** sutilmente

subtotal ['sʌb,to:təl] *n* **:** subtotal *m*

subtract [səb'trækt] *vt* **:** restar, sustraer

subtraction [səb'trækʃən] *n* **:** resta *f,* sustracción *f*

suburb ['sʌ,bərb] *n* **:** municipio *m* periférico, suburbio *m*

suburban [sə'bərbən] *adj* **:** de las afueras (de una ciudad), suburbano

subversion [səb'vərʒən] *n* **:** subversión *f*

subversive [səb'vərsɪv] *adj* **:** subversivo

subway ['sʌb,weɪ] *n* **:** metro *m,* subterráneo *m Arg, Uru*

succeed [sək'si:d] *vt* FOLLOW **:** suceder a — *vi* **:** tener éxito (dícese de las personas), dar resultado (dícese de los planes, etc.) <she succeeded in finishing : logró terminar>

success [sək'sɛs] *n* **:** éxito *m*

successful [sək'sɛsfəl] *adj* **:** exitoso, logrado — **successfully** *adv*

succession [sək'sɛʃən] *n* **:** sucesión *f* <in succesion : sucesivamente>

successive [sək'sɛsɪv] *adj* **:** sucesivo, consecutivo — **successively** *adv*

successor [sək'sɛsər] *n* **:** sucesor *m,* -sora *f*

succinct [sək'sɪŋkt, sə'sɪŋkt] *adj* **:** sucinto — **succinctly** *adv*

succor[1] ['sʌkər] *vt* **:** socorrer

succor[2] *n* **:** socorro *m*

succotash ['sʌkə,tæʃ] *n* **:** guiso *m* de maíz y frijoles

succulent[1] ['sʌkjələnt] *adj* **:** suculento, jugoso

succulent[2] *n* **:** suculenta *f* (planta)

succumb [sə'kʌm] *vi* **:** sucumbir

such[1] ['sʌtʃ] *adv* **1** SO **:** tan <such tall buildings : edificios tan grandes> **2** VERY **:** muy <he's not in such good shape : anda un poco mal> **3 such that :** de tal manera que

such[2] *adj* **:** tal <there's no such thing : no existe tal cosa> <in such cases : en tales casos> <animals such as cows and sheep : animales como vacas y ovejas>

such[3] *pron* **1 :** tal <such was the result : tal fue el resultado> <he's a child, and acts as such : es un niño, y se porta como tal> **2 :** algo o alguien semejante <books, papers and such : libros, papeles y cosas por el estilo>

suck ['sʌk] *vi* **1 :** chupar (por la boca), aspirar (dícese de las máquinas) **2** SUCKLE **:** mamar — *vt* **:** sorber (bebidas), chupar (dulces, etc.)

sucker ['sʌkər] *n* **1 :** ventosa *f* (de un insecto, etc.) **2 :** chupón *m* (de una planta) **3 → lollipop 4** FOOL **:** tonto *m,* -ta *f;* idiota *mf*

suckle ['sʌkəl] *v* **-led; -ling** *vt* **:** amamantar — *vi* **:** mamar

suckling ['sʌklɪŋ] *n* **:** lactante *mf*

sucrose ['su:,kro:s, -,kro:z] *n* **:** sacarosa *f*

suction ['sʌkʃən] *n* **:** succión *f*

Sudanese [ˌsuːdənˈiːz, -ˈiːs] *n* : sudanés *m*, -nesa *f* — **Sudanese** *adj*
sudden [ˈsʌdən] *adj* **1** : repentino, súbito <all of a sudden : de pronto, de repente> **2** UNEXPECTED : inesperado, improvisto **3** ABRUPT, HASTY : precipitado, brusco
suddenly [ˈsʌdənli] *adv* **1** : de repente, de pronto **2** ABRUPTLY : bruscamente
suddenness [ˈsʌdənnəs] *n* **1** : lo repentino **2** ABRUPTNESS : brusquedad *f* **3** HASTINESS : lo precipitado
suds [ˈsʌdz] *npl* : espuma *f* (de jabón)
sue [ˈsuː] *v* **sued; suing** *vt* : demandar — *vi* **to sue for** : demandar por (daños, etc.)
suede [ˈsweɪd] *n* : ante *m*, gamuza *f*
suet [ˈsuːət] *n* : sebo *m*
suffer [ˈsʌfər] *vi* : sufrir — *vt* **1** : sufrir, padecer (dolores, etc.) **2** PERMIT : permitir, dejar
sufferer [ˈsʌfərər] *n* : persona que padece (una enfermedad, etc.)
suffering [ˈsʌfərɪŋ] *n* : sufrimiento *m*
suffice [səˈfaɪs] *vi* **-ficed; -ficing** : ser suficiente, bastar
sufficient [səˈfɪʃənt] *adj* : suficiente
sufficiently [səˈfɪʃəntli] *adv* : (lo) suficientemente, bastante
suffix [ˈsʌˌfɪks] *n* : sufijo *m*
suffocate [ˈsʌfəˌkeɪt] *v* **-cated; -cating** *vt* : asfixiar, ahogar — *vi* : asfixiarse, ahogarse
suffocation [ˌsʌfəˈkeɪʃən] *n* : asfixia *f*, ahogo *m*
suffrage [ˈsʌfrɪdʒ] *n* : sufragio *m*, derecho *m* al voto
suffuse [səˈfjuːz] *vt* **-fused; -fusing** : impregnar (de olores, etc.), bañar (de luz), teñir (de colores), llenar (de emociones)
sugar[1] [ˈʃʊgər] *vt* : azucarar
sugar[2] *n* : azúcar *mf*
sugarcane [ˈʃʊgərˌkeɪn] *n* : caña *f* de azúcar
sugary [ˈʃʊgəri] *adj* **1** : azucarado <sugary desserts : postres azucarados> **2** SACCHARINE : empalagoso
suggest [səgˈdʒɛst, sə-] *vt* **1** PROPOSE : sugerir **2** IMPLY : indicar, dar a entender
suggestible [səgˈdʒɛstəbəl, sə-] *adj* : influenciable
suggestion [səgˈdʒɛstʃən, sə-] *n* **1** PROPOSAL : sugerencia *f* **2** INDICATION : indicio *m* **3** INSINUATION : insinuación *f*
suggestive [səgˈdʒɛstɪv, sə-] *adj* : insinuante — **suggestively** *adv*
suicidal [ˌsuːəˈsaɪdəl] *adj* : suicida
suicide [ˈsuːəˌsaɪd] *n* **1** : suicidio *m* (acto) **2** : suicida *mf* (persona)
suit[1] [ˈsuːt] *vt* **1** ADAPT : adaptar **2** BEFIT : convenir a, ser apropiado a **3** BECOME : favorecer, quedarle bien (a alguien) <the dress suits you : el vestido te queda bien> **4** PLEASE : agradecer, satisfacer, convenirle bien (a alguien) <does Friday suit you? : ¿le conviene el viernes?> <suit yourself! : ¡como quieras!>
suit[2] *n* **1** LAWSUIT : pleito *m*, litigio *m* **2** : traje *m* (ropa) **3** : palo *m* (de naipes)
suitability [ˌsuːtəˈbɪləṭi] *n* : idoneidad *f*, lo apropiado
suitable [ˈsuːṭəbəl] *adj* : apropiado, idóneo — **suitably** [-bli] *adv*
suitcase [ˈsuːtˌkeɪs] *n* : maleta *f*, valija *f*, petaca *f Mex*
suite [ˈswiːt, *for 2 also* ˈsuːt] *n* **1** : suite *f* (de habitaciones) **2** SET : juego *m* (de muebles)
suitor [ˈsuːtər] *n* : pretendiente *m*
sulfur [ˈsʌlfər] *n* : azufre *m*
sulfuric acid [ˌsʌlˈfjʊrɪk] *adj* : ácido *m* sulfúrico
sulfurous [ˌsʌlˈfjʊrəs, ˈsʌlfərəs, ˈsʌlfjə-] *adj* : sulfuroso
sulk[1] [ˈsʌlk] *vi* : estar de mal humor, enfurruñarse *fam*
sulk[2] *n* : mal humor *m*
sulky [ˈsʌlki] *adj* **sulkier; -est** : malhumorado, taimado *Chile*
sullen [ˈsʌlən] *adj* **1** MOROSE : hosco, taciturno **2** DREARY : sombrío, deprimente
sullenly [ˈsʌlənli] *adv* **1** MOROSELY : hoscamente **2** GLOOMILY : sombríamente
sully [ˈsʌli] *vt* **sullied; sullying** : manchar, empañar
sultan [ˈsʌltən] *n* : sultán *m*
sultry [ˈsʌltri] *adj* **sultrier; -est 1** : bochornoso <sultry weather : tiempo sofocante, tiempo bochornoso> **2** SENSUAL : sensual, seductor
sum[1] [ˈsʌm] *vt* **summed; summing 1** : sumar (números) **2** → **sum up**
sum[2] *n* **1** AMOUNT : suma *f*, cantidad *f* **2** TOTAL : suma *f*, total *f* **3** : suma *f*, adición *f* (en matemáticas)
sumac [ˈʃuːˌmæk, ˈsuː-] *n* : zumaque *m*
summarize [ˈsʌməˌraɪz] *v* **-rized; -rizing** : resumir, compendiar
summary[1] [ˈsʌməri] *adj* **1** CONCISE : breve, conciso **2** IMMEDIATE : inmediato <a summary dismissal : un despido inmediato>
summary[2] *n, pl* **-ries** : resumen *m*, compendio *m*
summer [ˈsʌmər] *n* : verano *m*
summery [ˈsʌməri] *adj* : veraniego
summit [ˈsʌmət] *n* **1** : cumbre *f*, cima *f* (de una montaña) **2** *or* **summit conference** : cumbre *f*
summon [ˈsʌmən] *vt* **1** CALL : convocar (una reunión, etc.), llamar (a una persona) **2** : citar (en derecho) **3 to summon up** : armarse de (valor, etc.) <to summon up one's strength : reunir fuerzas>
summons [ˈsʌmənz] *n, pl* **summonses 1** SUBPOENA : citación *f*, citatorio *m Mex* **2** CALL : llamada *f*, llamamiento *m*
sumptuous [ˈsʌmptʃʊəs] *adj* : suntuoso

sum up *vt* **1** SUMMARIZE : resumir **2** EVALUATE : evaluar — *vi* : recapitular

sun[1] [ˈsʌn] *vt* **sunned; sunning 1** : poner al sol **2 to sun oneself** : asolearse, tomar el sol

sun[2] *n* **1** : sol *m* **2** SUNSHINE : luz *f* del sol

sunbeam [ˈsʌnˌbiːm] *n* : rayo *m* de sol

sunblock [ˈsʌnˌblɑk] *n* : filtro *m* solar

sunburn[1] [ˈsʌnˌbərn] *vi* **-burned** [-ˌbərnd] *or* **-burnt** [-ˌbərnt]; **-burning** : quemarse por el sol

sunburn[2] [ˈsʌnˌbərn] *n* : quemadura *f* de sol

sundae [ˈsʌndi] *n* : sundae *m*

Sunday [ˈsʌnˌdeɪ, -di] *n* : domingo *m*

sundial [ˈsʌnˌdaɪl] *n* : reloj *m* de sol

sundown [ˈsʌnˌdaʊn] → **sunset**

sundries [ˈsʌndriz] *npl* : artículos *mpl* diversos

sundry [ˈsʌndri] *adj* : varios, diversos

sunflower [ˈsʌnˌflaʊər] *n* : girasol *m*, mirasol *m*

sung → **sing**

sunglasses [ˈsʌnˌglæsəz] *npl* : gafas *fpl* de sol, lentes *mpl* de sol

sunk → **sink**[1]

sunken [ˈsʌŋkən] *adj* : hundido

sunlight [ˈsʌnˌlaɪt] *n* : sol *m*, luz *f* del sol

sunny [ˈsʌni] *adj* **sunnier; -est** : soleado

sunrise [ˈsʌnˌraɪz] *n* : salida *f* del sol

sunset [ˈsʌnˌsɛt] *n* : puesta *f* del sol

sunshine [ˈsʌnˌʃaɪn] *n* : sol *m*, luz *f* del sol

sunspot [ˈsʌnˌspɑt] *n* : mancha *f* solar

sunstroke [ˈsʌnˌstroːk] *n* : insolación *f*

suntan [ˈsʌnˌtæn] *n* : bronceado *m*

sup [ˈsʌp] *vi* **supped; supping** : cenar

super [ˈsuːpər] *adj* : súper <super! : ¡fantástico!>

superabundance [ˌsuːpərəˈbʌndən*t*s] *n* : superabundancia *f*

superb [sʊˈpərb] *adj* : magnífico, espléndido — **superbly** *adv*

supercilious [ˌsuːpərˈsɪliəs] *adj* : altivo, altanero, desdeñoso

supercomputer [ˈsuːpərkəmˌpjuːt̬ər] *n* : supercomputadora *f*

superficial [ˌsuːpərˈfɪʃəl] *adj* : superficial — **superficially** *adv*

superfluous [sʊˈpərfluəs] *adj* : superfluo

superhighway [ˈsuːpərˌhaɪˌweɪ, ˌsuːpərˈ-] *n* : autopista *f*

superhuman [ˌsuːpərˈ*h*juːmən] *adj* **1** SUPERNATURAL : sobrenatural **2** HERCULEAN : sobrehumano

superimpose [ˌsuːpərɪmˈpoːz] *vt* **-posed; -posing** : superponer, sobreponer

superintend [ˌsuːpərɪnˈtɛnd] *vt* : supervisar

superintendent [ˌsuːpərɪnˈtɛndənt] *n* : portero *m*, -ra *f* (de un edificio); director *m*, -tora *f* (de una escuela, etc.); superintendente *mf* (de policía)

superior[1] [sʊˈpɪriər] *adj* **1** BETTER : superior **2** HAUGHTY : altivo, altanero

superior[2] *n* : superior *m*

superiority [sʊˌpɪriˈɔrət̬i] *n, pl* **-ties** : superioridad *f*

superlative[1] [sʊˈpərlət̬ɪv] *adj* **1** : superlativo (en gramática) **2** SUPREME : supremo **3** EXCELLENT : excelente, excepcional

superlative[2] *n* : superlativo *m*

supermarket [ˈsuːpərˌmɑrkət] *n* : supermercado *m*

supernatural [ˌsuːpərˈnætʃərəl] *adj* : sobrenatural

supernaturally [ˌsuːpərˈnætʃərəli] *adv* : de manera sobrenatural

superpower [ˈsuːpərˌpaʊər] *n* : superpotencia *f*

supersede [ˌsuːpərˈsiːd] *vt* **-seded; -seding** : suplantar, reemplazar, sustituir

supersonic [ˌsuːpərˈsɑnɪk] *adj* : supersónico

superstition [ˌsuːpərˈstɪʃən] *n* : superstición *f*

superstitious [ˌsuːpərˈstɪʃəs] *adj* : supersticioso

superstructure [ˈsuːpərˌstrʌktʃər] *n* : superestructura *f*

supervise [ˈsuːpərˌvaɪz] *vt* **-vised; -vising** : supervisar, dirigir

supervision [ˌsuːpərˈvɪʒən] *n* : supervisión *f*, dirección *f*

supervisor [ˈsuːpərˌvaɪzər] *n* : supervisor *m*, -sora *f*

supervisory [ˌsuːpərˈvaɪzəri] *adj* : de supervisor

supine [sʊˈpaɪn] *adj* **1** : en decúbito supino, en decúbito dorsal **2** ABJECT, INDIFFERENT : indiferente, apático

supper [ˈsʌpər] *n* : cena *f*, comida *f*

supplant [səˈplænt] *vt* : suplantar

supple [ˈsʌpəl] *adj* **-pler; -plest** : flexible

supplement[1] [ˈsʌpləˌmɛnt] *vt* : complementar, completar

supplement[2] [ˈsʌpləmənt] *n* **1** : complemento *m* <dietary supplement : complemento alimenticio> **2** : suplemento *m* (de un libro o periódico)

supplementary [ˌsʌpləˈmɛntəri] *adj* : suplementario

supplicate [ˈsʌpləˌkeɪt] *v* **-cated; -cating** *vi* : rezar — *vt* : suplicar

supplier [səˈplaɪər] *n* : proveedor *m*, -dora *f*; abastecedor *m*, -dora *f*

supply[1] [səˈplaɪ] *vt* **-plied; -plying** : suministrar, proveer de, proporcionar

supply[2] *n, pl* **-plies 1** PROVISION : provisión *f*, suministro *m* <supply and demand : la oferta y la demanda> **2** STOCK : reserva *f*, existencias *fpl* (de un negocio) **3 supplies** *npl* PROVISIONS : provisiones *fpl*, víveres *mpl*, despensa *f*

support[1] [səˈport] *vt* **1** BACK : apoyar, respaldar **2** MAINTAIN : mantener, sostener, sustentar 3 PROP UP : sostener, apoyar, apuntalar, soportar

support[2] *n* **1** : apoyo *m* (moral), ayuda *f* (económica) **2** PROP : soporte *m*, apoyo *m*

supporter [sə'portər] *n* : partidario *m*, -ria *f*

suppose [sə'po:z] *vt* **-posed; -posing 1** ASSUME : suponer, imaginarse **2** BELIEVE : suponer, creer **3 to be supposed to** : tener que, deber

supposition [ˌsʌpə'zɪʃən] *n* : suposición *f*

suppository [sə'pɑzəˌtori] *n, pl* **-ries** : supositorio *m*

suppress [sə'prɛs] *vt* **1** SUBDUE : sofocar, suprimir, reprimir (una rebelión, etc.) **2** : suprimir, ocultar (información) **3** REPRESS : reprimir, contener <to suppress a yawn : reprimir un bostezo>

suppression [sə'prɛʃən] *n* **1** SUBDUING : represión *f* **2** : supresión *f* (de información) **3** REPRESSION : represión *f*, inhibición *f*

supremacy [sʊ'prɛməsi] *n, pl* **-cies** : supremacía *f*

supreme [sʊ'pri:m] *adj* : supremo

Supreme Being *n* : Ser *m* Supremo

supremely [sʊ'pri:mli] *adv* : totalmente, sumamente

surcharge ['sərˌtʃɑrdʒ] *n* : recargo *m*

sure[1] ['ʃʊr] *adv* **1** ALL RIGHT : por supuesto, claro **2** (*used as an intensifier*) <it sure is hot! : ¡hace tanto calor!> <she sure is pretty! : ¡qué linda es!>

sure[2] *adj* **surer; -est** : seguro <to be sure about something : estar seguro de algo> <a sure sign : una clara señal> <for sure : seguro, con seguridad>

surely ['ʃʊrli] *adv* **1** CERTAINLY : seguramente **2** (*used as an intensifier*) <you surely don't mean that! : ¡no me digas que estás hablando en serio!>

sureness ['ʃʊrnəs] *n* : certeza *f*, seguridad *f*

surety ['ʃʊrəti] *n, pl* **-ties** : fianza *f*, garantía *f*

surf ['sərf] *n* **1** WAVES : oleaje *m* **2** FOAM : espuma *f*

surface[1] ['sərfəs] *v* **-faced; -facing** *vi* : salir a la superficie — *vt* : revestir (una carretera)

surface[2] *n* **1** : superficie *f* **2 on the surface** : en apariencia

surfboard ['sərfˌbord] *n* : tabla *f* de surf, tabla *f* de surfing

surfeit ['sərfət] *n* : exceso *m*

surfing ['sərfɪŋ] *n* : surf *m*, surfing *m*

surge[1] ['sərdʒ] *vi* **surged; surging 1** : hincharse (dícese del mar), levantarse (dícese de las olas) **2** SWARM : salir en tropel (dícese de la gente, etc.)

surge[2] *n* **1** : oleaje *m* (del mar), oleada *f* (de gente) **2** FLUSH : arranque *m*, arrebato *m* (de ira, etc.) **3** INCREASE : aumento *m* (súbito)

surgeon ['sərdʒən] *n* : cirujano *m*, -na *f*

surgery ['sərdʒəri] *n, pl* **-geries** : cirugía *f*

surgical ['sərdʒɪkəl] *adj* : quirúrgico — **surgically** [-kli] *adv*

surly ['sərli] *adj* **surlier; -est** : hosco, arisco

surmise[1] [sər'maɪz] *vt* **-mised; -mising** : conjeturar, suponer, concluir

surmise[2] *n* : conjetura *f*

surmount [sər'maʊnt] *vt* **1** OVERCOME : superar, vencer, salvar **2** CLIMB : escalar **3** CAP, TOP : coronar

surname ['sərˌneɪm] *n* : apellido *m*

surpass [sər'pæs] *vt* : superar, exceder, rebasar, sobrepasar

surplus ['sərˌplʌs] *n* : excedente *m*, sobrante *m*, superávit *m* (de dinero)

surprise[1] [sə'praɪz, sər-] *vt* **-prised; -prising** : sorprender

surprise[2] *n* : sorpresa *f* <to take by surprise : sorprender>

surprising [sə'praɪzɪŋ, sər-] *adj* : sorprendente — **surprisingly** *adv*

surrender[1] [sə'rɛndər] *vt* **1** : entregar, rendir **2 to surrender oneself** : entregarse — *vi* : rendirse

surrender[2] *n* : rendición *m* (de una ciudad, etc.), entrega *f* (de posesiones)

surreptitious [ˌsərəp'tɪʃəs] *adj* : subrepticio — **surreptitiously** *adv*

surrogate ['sərəgət, -ˌgeɪt] *n* : sustituto *m*

surround [sə'raʊnd] *vt* : rodear

surroundings [sə'raʊndɪŋz] *npl* : ambiente *m*, entorno *m*

surveillance [sər'veɪlənts, -'veɪljənts, -'veɪənts] *n* : vigilancia *f*

survey[1] [sər'veɪ] *vt* **-veyed; -veying 1** : medir (un terreno) **2** EXAMINE : inspeccionar, examinar, revisar **3** POLL : hacer una encuesta de, sondear

survey[2] ['sərˌveɪ] *n, pl* **-veys 1** INSPECTION : inspección *f*, revisión *f* **2** : medición *f* (de un terreno) **3** POLL : encuesta *f*, sondeo *m*

surveyor [sər'veɪər] *n* : agrimensor *m*, -sora *f*

survival [sər'vaɪvəl] *n* : supervivencia *f*, sobrevivencia *f*

survive [sər'vaɪv] *v* **-vived; -viving** *vi* : sobrevivir — *vt* OUTLIVE : sobrevivir a

survivor [sər'vaɪvər] *n* : superviviente *mf*, sobreviviente *mf*

susceptibility [səˌsɛptə'bɪləti] *n, pl* **-ties** : vulnerabilidad *f*, propensión *f* (a enfermedades, etc.)

susceptible [sə'sɛptəbəl] *adj* **1** VULNERABLE : vulnerable, sensible <susceptible to flattery : sensible a halagos> **2** PRONE : propenso <susceptible to colds : propenso a resfriarse>

suspect[1] [sə'spɛkt] *vt* **1** DISTRUST : dudar de **2** : sospechar (algo), sospechar de (una persona) **3** IMAGINE, THINK : imaginarse, creer

suspect² ['sʌsˌpɛkt, sə'spɛkt] *adj* : sospechoso, dudoso, cuestionable
suspect³ ['sʌsˌpɛkt] *n* : sospechoso *m*, -sa *f*
suspend [sə'spɛnd] *vt* : suspender
suspenders [sə'spɛndərz] *npl* : tirantes *mpl*
suspense [sə'spɛn*t*s] *n* : incertidumbre *f*, suspenso *m* (en una película, etc.)
suspenseful [sə'spɛn*t*sfəl] *adj* : de suspenso
suspension [sə'spɛntʃən] *n* : suspensión *f*
suspicion [sə'spɪʃən] *n* **1** : sospecha *f* **2** TRACE : pizca *f*, atisbo *m*
suspicious [sə'spɪʃəs] *adj* **1** QUESTIONABLE : sospechoso, dudoso **2** DISTRUSTFUL : suspicaz, desconfiado
suspiciously [sə'spɪʃəsli] *adv* : de modo sospechoso, con recelo
sustain [sə'steɪn] *vt* **1** NOURISH : sustentar **2** PROLONG : sostener **3** SUFFER : sufrir **4** SUPPORT, UPHOLD : apoyar, respaldar, sostentar
sustenance ['sʌstənən*t*s] *n* **1** NOURISHMENT : sustento *m* **2** SUPPORT : sostén *m*
svelte ['sfɛlt] *adj* : esbelto
swab¹ ['swɑb] *vt* **swabbed; swabbing** **1** CLEAN : lavar, limpiar **2** : aplicar a (con hisopo)
swab² *n or* **cotton swab** : hisopo *m* (para aplicar medicinas, etc.)
swaddle ['swɑdəl] *vt* **-dled; -dling** ['swɑdəlɪŋ] : envolver (en pañales)
swagger¹ ['swægər] *vi* : pavonearse
swagger² *n* : pavoneo *m*
swallow¹ ['swɑloː] *vt* **1** : tragar (comida, etc.) **2** ENGULF : tragarse, envolver **3** REPRESS : tragarse (insultos, etc.) — *vi* : tragar
swallow² *n* **1** : golondrina *f* (pájaro) **2** GULP : trago *m*
swam → **swim¹**
swamp¹ ['swɑmp] *vt* : inundar
swamp² *n* : pantano *m*, ciénaga *f*
swampy ['swɑmpi] *adj* **swampier; -est** : pantanoso, cenagoso
swan ['swɑn] *n* : cisne *f*
swap¹ ['swɑp] *vt* **swapped; swapping** : cambiar, intercambiar <to swap places : cambiarse de sitio>
swap² *n* : cambio *m*, intercambio *m*
swarm¹ ['swɔrm] *vi* : enjambrar
swarm² *n* : enjambre *m*
swarthy ['swɔrði, -θi] *adj* **swarthier; -est** : moreno
swashbuckling ['swɑʃˌbʌklɪŋ] *adj* : de aventurero
swat¹ ['swɑt] *vt* **swatted; swatting** : aplastar (un insecto), darle una palmada (a alguien)
swat² *n* : palmada *f* (con la mano), golpe *m* (con un objeto)
swatch ['swɑtʃ] *n* : muestra *f*
swath ['swɑθ, 'swɔθ] *or* **swathe** ['swɑð, 'swɔð, 'sweɪð] *n* : franja *f* (de grano segado)
swathe ['swɑð, 'swɔð, 'sweɪð] *vt* **swathed; swathing** : envolver
swatter ['swɑtər] → **flyswatter**
sway¹ ['sweɪ] *vi* : balancearse, mecerse — *vt* INFLUENCE : influir en, convencer
sway² *n* **1** SWINGING : balanceo *m* **2** INFLUENCE : influjo *m*
swear ['swær] *v* **swore** ['swor]; **sworn** ['sworn]; **swearing** *vi* **1** VOW : jurar **2** CURSE : decir palabrotas — *vt* : jurar
swearword ['swærˌwərd] *n* : mala palabra *f*, palabrota *f*
sweat¹ ['swɛt] *vi* **sweat** *or* **sweated; sweating** **1** PERSPIRE : sudar, transpirar **2** OOZE : rezumar **3 to sweat over** : sudar la gota gorda por
sweat² *n* : sudor *m*, transpiración *f*
sweater ['swɛtər] *n* : suéter *m*
sweatshirt ['swɛtˌʃərt] *n* : sudadera *f*
sweaty ['swɛti] *adj* **sweatier; -est** : sudoroso, sudado, transpirado
Swede ['swiːd] *n* : sueco *m*, -ca *f*
Swedish¹ ['swiːdɪʃ] *adj* : sueco
Swedish² *n* **1** : sueco *m* (idioma) **2 the Swedish** *npl* : los suecos
sweep¹ ['swiːp] *v* **swept** ['swɛpt]; **sweeping** *vt* **1** : barrer (el suelo, etc.), limpiar (suciedad, etc.) <he swept the books aside : apartó los libros de un manotazo> **2** *or* **to sweep through** : extenderse por (dícese del fuego, etc.), azotar (dícese de una tormenta) — *vi* **1** : barrer, limpiar **2** : extenderse (en una curva), describir una curva <the sun swept across the sky : el sol describía una curva en el cielo>
sweep² *n* **1** : barrido *m*, barrida *f* (con una escoba) **2** : movimiento *m* circular **3** SCOPE : alcance *m*
sweeper ['swiːpər] *n* : barrendero *m*, -ra *f*
sweeping ['swiːpɪŋ] *adj* **1** WIDE : amplio (dícese de un movimiento) **2** EXTENSIVE : extenso, radical **3** INDISCRIMINATE : indiscriminado, demasiado general **4** OVERWHELMING : arrollador, aplastante
sweepstakes ['swiːpˌsteɪks] *ns & pl* **1** : carrera *f* (en que el ganador se lleva el premio entero) **2** LOTTERY : lotería *f*
sweet¹ ['swiːt] *adj* **1** : dulce <sweet desserts : postres dulces> **2** FRESH : fresco **3** : sin sal (dícese de la mantequilla, etc.) **4** PLEASANT : dulce, agradable **5** DEAR : querido
sweet² *n* : dulce *m*
sweeten ['swiːtən] *vt* : endulzar
sweetener ['swiːtənər] *n* : endulzante *m*
sweetheart ['swiːtˌhɑrt] *n* : novio *m*, -via *f* <thanks, sweetheart : gracias, cariño>
sweetly ['swiːtli] *adv* : dulcemente
sweetness ['swiːtnəs] *n* : dulzura *f*
sweet potato *n* : batata *f*, boniato *m*
swell¹ ['swɛl] *vi* **swelled; swelled** *or* **swollen** ['swoːlən, 'swʌl-]; **swelling** **1** *or* **to swell up** : hincharse <her

ankle swelled : se le hinchó el tobillo> **2** *or* **to swell out** : inflarse, hincharse (dícese de las velas, etc.) **3** INCREASE : aumentar, crecer
swell[2] *n* **1** : oleaje *m* (del mar) **2** → **swelling**
swelling [ˈswɛlɪŋ] *n* : hinchazón *f*
swelter [ˈswɛltər] *vi* : sofocarse de calor
swept → **sweep**[1]
swerve[1] [ˈswərv] *vi* **swerved; swerving** : virar bruscamente
swerve[2] *n* : viraje *m* brusco
swift[1] [ˈswɪft] *adj* **1** FAST : rápido, veloz **2** SUDDEN : repentino, súbito — **swiftly** *adv*
swift[2] *n* : vencejo *m* (pájaro)
swiftness [ˈswɪftnəs] *n* : rapidez *f,* velocidad *f*
swig[1] [ˈswɪg] *vi* **swigged; swigging** : tomar a tragos, beber a tragos
swig[2] *n* : trago *m*
swill[1] [ˈswɪl] *vt* : chupar, beber a tragos grandes
swill[2] *n* **1** SLOP : bazofia *f* **2** GARBAGE : basura *f*
swim[1] [ˈswɪm] *vi* **swam** [ˈswæm]; **swum** [ˈswʌm]; **swimming 1** : nadar **2** FLOAT : flotar **3** REEL : dar vueltas <his head was swimming : la cabeza le daba vueltas>
swim[2] *n* : baño *m,* chapuzón *m* <to go for a swim : ir a nadar>
swimmer [ˈswɪmər] *n* : nadador *m,* -dora *f*
swindle[1] [ˈswɪndəl] *vt* **-dled; -dling** : estafar, timar
swindle[2] *n* : estafa *f,* timo *m fam*
swindler [ˈswɪndələr] *n* : estafador *m,* -dora *f;* timador *m,* -dora *f*
swine [ˈswaɪn] *ns & pl* : cerdo *m,* -da *f*
swing[1] [ˈswɪŋ] *v* **swung** [ˈswʌŋ]; **swinging** *vt* **1** : describir una curva con <he swung the ax at the tree : le dio al arbol con el hacha> **2** : balancear (los brazos, etc.), hacer oscilar **3** SUSPEND : colgar — *vi* **1** SWAY : balancearse (dícese de los brazos, etc.), oscilar (dícese de un objeto), columpiarse, mecerse (en un columpio) **2** SWIVEL : girar (en un pivote) <the door swung shut : la puerta se cerró> **3** CHANGE : virar, cambiar (dícese de las opiniones, etc.)
swing[2] *n* **1** SWINGING : vaivén *m,* balanceo *m* **2** CHANGE, SHIFT : viraje *m,* movimiento *m* **3** : columpio *m* (para niños) **4 to take a swing at someone** : intentar pegarle a alguien
swipe[1] [ˈswaɪp] *vt* **swiped; swiping 1** STRIKE : dar, pegar (con un movimiento amplio) **2** WIPE : limpiar **3** STEAL : birlar *fam,* robar
swipe[2] *n* BLOW : golpe *m*
swirl[1] [ˈswərl] *vi* : arremolinarse
swirl[2] *n* **1** EDDY : remolino *m* **2** SPIRAL : espiral *f*
swish[1] [ˈswɪʃ] *vt* : mover (produciendo un sonido) <she swished her skirt : movía la falda> — *vi* : moverse (produciendo un sonido) <the cars swished by : se oían pasar los coches>
swish[2] *n* : silbido *m* (de un látigo, etc.), susurro *m* (de agua), crujido *m* (de ropa, etc.)
Swiss [ˈswɪs] *n* : suizo *m,* -za *f* — **Swiss** *adj*
swiss chard *n* : acelga *f*
switch[1] [ˈswɪtʃ] *vt* **1** LASH, WHIP : azotar **2** CHANGE : cambiar de **3** EXCHANGE : intercambiar **4 to switch on** : encender, prender **5 to switch off** : apagar — *vi* **1** : moverse de un lado al otro **2** CHANGE : cambiar **3** SWAP : intercambiarse
switch[2] *n* **1** WHIP : vara *f* **2** CHANGE, SHIFT : cambio *m* **3** : interruptor *m,* llave *f* (de la luz, etc.)
switchboard [ˈswɪtʃˌbord] *n* : conmutador *m,* centralita *f*
swivel[1] [ˈswɪvəl] *vi* **-veled** *or* **-velled; -veling** *or* **-velling** : girar (sobre un pivote)
swivel[2] *n* : base *f* giratoria
swollen → **swell**[1]
swoon[1] [ˈswuːn] *vi* : desvanecerse, desmayarse
swoon[2] *n* : desvanecimiento *m,* desmayo *m*
swoop[1] [ˈswuːp] *vi* : abatirse (dícese de las aves), descender en picada (dícese de un avión)
swoop[2] *n* : descenso *m* en picada
sword [ˈsɔrd] *n* : espada *f*
swordfish [ˈsɔrdˌfɪʃ] *n* : pez *m* espada
swore, sworn → **swear**
swum → **swim**[1]
swung → **swing**[1]
sycamore [ˈsɪkəˌmor] *n* : sicomoro *m*
sycophant [ˈsɪkəfənt, -ˌfænt] *n* : adulador *m,* -dora *f*
syllabic [səˈlæbɪk] *adj* : silábico
syllable [ˈsɪləbəl] *n* : sílaba *f*
syllabus [ˈsɪləbəs] *n, pl* **-bi** [-ˌbaɪ] *or* **-buses** : programa *m* (de estudios)
symbol [ˈsɪmbəl] *n* : símbolo *m*
symbolic [sɪmˈbɑlɪk] *adj* : simbólico — **symbolically** [-kli] *adv*
symbolism [ˈsɪmbəˌlɪzəm] *n* : simbolismo *m*
symbolize [ˈsɪmbəˌlaɪz] *vt* **-ized; -izing** : simbolizar
symmetrical [səˈmɛtrɪəl] *or* **symmetric** [-trɪk] *adj* : simétrico — **symmetrically** [-trɪkli] *adv*
symmetry [ˈsɪmətri] *n, pl* **-tries** : simetría *f*
sympathetic [ˌsɪmpəˈθɛt̬ɪk] *adj* **1** PLEASING : agradable **2** RECEPTIVE : receptivo, favorable **3** COMPASSIONATE, UNDERSTANDING : comprensivo, compasivo
sympathetically [ˌsɪmpəˈθɛtɪkli] *adv* : con compasión, con comprensión

sympathize [ˈsɪmpəˌθaɪz] *vi* **-thized; -thizing :** compadecer <I sympathize with you : te compadezco>
sympathy [ˈsɪmpəθi] *n, pl* **-thies 1** COMPASSION **:** compasión *f* **2** UNDERSTANDING **:** comprensión *f* **3** AGREEMENT **:** solidaridad *f* <in sympathy with : de acuerdo con> **4** CONDOLENCES **:** pésame *m,* condolencias *fpl*
symphonic [sɪmˈfɑnɪk] *adj* **:** sinfónico
symphony [ˈsɪmpfəni] *n, pl* **-nies :** sinfonía *f*
symposium [sɪmˈpoːziəm] *n, pl* **-sia** [-ziə] *or* **-siums :** simposio *m*
symptom [ˈsɪmptəm] *n* **:** síntoma *m*
symptomatic [ˌsɪmptəˈmæṭɪk] *adj* **:** sintomático
synagogue [ˈsɪnəˌgɑg, -ˌgɔg] *n* **:** sinagoga *f*
synchronize [ˈsɪŋkrəˌnaɪz, ˈsɪn-] *v* **-nized; -nizing** *vi* **:** estar sincronizado — *vt* **:** sincronizar
syncopate [ˈsɪŋkəˌpeɪt, ˈsɪn-] *vt* **-pated; -pating :** sincopar
syncopation [ˌsɪŋkəˈpeɪʃən, ˌsɪn-] *n* **:** síncopa *f*
syndicate[1] [ˈsɪndəˌkeɪt] *vi* **-cated; -cating :** formar una asociación
syndicate[2] [ˈsɪndɪkət] *n* **:** asociación *f,* agrupación *f*
syndrome [ˈsɪnˌdroːm] *n* **:** síndrome *m*
synonym [ˈsɪnəˌnɪm] *n* **:** sinónimo *m*
synonymous [səˈnɑnəməs] *adj* **:** sinónimo
synopsis [səˈnɑpsɪs] *n, pl* **-opses** [-ˌsiːz] **:** sinopsis *f*
syntax [ˈsɪnˌtæks] *n* **:** sintaxis *f*
synthesis [ˈsɪnθəsɪs] *n, pl* **-theses** [-ˌsiːz] **:** síntesis *f*
synthesize [ˈsɪnθəˌsaɪz] *vt* **-sized; -sizing :** sintetizar
synthetic[1] [sɪnˈθɛṭɪk] *adj* **:** sintético, artificial — **synthetically** [-ṭɪkli] *adv*
synthetic[2] *n* **:** producto *m* sintético
syphilis [ˈsɪfələs] *n* **:** sífilis *f*
Syrian [ˈsɪriən] *n* **:** sirio *m,* -ria *f* — **Syrian** *adj*
syringe [səˈrɪndʒ, ˈsɪrɪndʒ] *n* **:** jeringa *f,* jeringuilla *f*
syrup [ˈsərəp, ˈsɪrəp] *n* **:** jarabe *m,* almíbar *m* (de azúcar y agua)
system [ˈsɪstəm] *n* **1** METHOD **:** sistema *m,* método *m* **2** APPARATUS **:** sistema *m,* instalación *f,* aparato *m* <electrical system : instalación eléctrica> <digestive system : aparato digestivo> **3** BODY **:** organismo *m,* cuerpo *m* <diseases that affect the whole system : enfermedades que afectan el organismo entero> **4** NETWORK **:** red *f*
systematic [ˌsɪstəˈmæṭɪk] *adj* **:** sistemático — **systematically** [-ṭɪkli] *adv*
systematize [ˈsɪstəməˌtaɪz] *vt* **-tized; -tizing :** sistematizar
systemic [sɪsˈtɛmɪk] *adj* **:** sistémico

T

t [ˈtiː] *n, pl* **t's** *or* **ts** [ˈtiːz] **:** vigésima letra del alfabeto inglés
tab [ˈtæb] *n* **1** FLAP, TAG **:** lengüeta *f* (de un sobre, una caja, etc.), etiqueta *f* (de ropa) **2 → tabulator 3** BILL, CHECK **:** cuenta *f* **4 to keep tabs on :** tener bajo vigilancia
tabby [ˈtæbi] *n, pl* **-bies 1** *or* **tabby cat :** gato *m* atigrado **2 :** gata *f*
tabernacle [ˈtæbərˌnækəl] *n* **:** tabernáculo *m*
table [ˈteɪbəl] *n* **1 :** mesa *f* <a table for two : una mesa para dos> **2** LIST **:** tabla *f* <multiplication table : tabla de multiplicar> **3 table of contents :** índice *m* de materias
tableau [tæˈbloː, ˈtæˌ-] *n, pl* **-leaux** [-ˈbloːz, -ˌbloːz] **:** retablo *m,* cuadro *m* vivo (en teatro)
tablecloth [ˈteɪbəlˌklɔθ] *n* **:** mantel *m*
tablespoon [ˈteɪbəlˌspuːn] *n* **1 :** cuchara *f* (de mesa) **2 → tablespoonful**
tablespoonful [ˈteɪbəlˌspuːnˌfʊl] *n* **:** cucharada *f*
tablet [ˈtæblət] *n* **1** PLAQUE **:** placa *f* **2** PAD **:** bloc *m* (de papel) **3** PILL **:** tableta *f,* pastilla *f,* píldora *f* <an aspirin tablet : una tableta de aspirina>
table tennis *n* **:** tenis *m* de mesa
tableware [ˈteɪbəlˌwær] *n* **:** vajillas *fpl,* cubiertos *mpl* (de mesa)
tabloid [ˈtæˌblɔɪd] *n* **:** tabloide *m*
taboo[1] [təˈbuː, tæ-] *adj* **:** tabú
taboo[2] *n* **:** tabú *m*
tabular [ˈtæbjələr] *adj* **:** tabular
tabulate [ˈtæbjəˌleɪt] *vt* **-lated; -lating :** tabular
tabulator [ˈtæbjəˌleɪṭər] *n* **:** tabulador *m*
tacit [ˈtæsɪt] *adj* **:** tácito, implícito — **tacitly** *adv*
taciturn [ˈtæsɪˌtərn] *adj* **:** taciturno
tack[1] [ˈtæk] *vt* **1 :** sujetar con tachuelas **2 to tack on** ADD **:** añadir, agregar
tack[2] *n* **1 :** tachuela *f* **2** COURSE **:** rumbo *m* <to change tack : cambiar de rumbo>
tackle[1] [ˈtækəl] *vt* **-led; -ling 1 :** taclear (en futbol americano) **2** CONFRONT **:** abordar, enfrentar, emprender (un problema, un trabajo, etc.)
tackle[2] *n* **1** EQUIPMENT, GEAR **:** equipo *m,* aparejo *m* **2 :** aparejo *m* (de un buque) **3 :** tacleada *f* (en futbol americano)
tacky [ˈtæki] *adj* **tackier; -est 1** STICKY **:** pegajoso **2** CHEAP, GAUDY **:** de mal gusto, naco *Mex*
tact [ˈtækt] *n* **:** tacto *m,* delicadeza *f,* discreción *f*

tactful [ˈtæktfəl] *adj* : discreto, diplomático, de mucho tacto

tactfully [ˈtæktfəli] *adv* : discretamente, con mucho tacto

tactic [ˈtæktɪk] *n* : táctica *f*

tactical [ˈtæktɪkəl] *adj* : táctico, estratégico

tactics [ˈtæktɪks] *ns & pl* : táctica *f*, estrategia *f*

tactile [ˈtæktəl, -ˌtaɪl] *adj* : táctil

tactless [ˈtæktləs] *adj* : indiscreto, poco delicado

tactlessly [ˈtæktləsli] *adv* : rudamente, sin tacto

tadpole [ˈtædˌpoːl] *n* : renacuajo *m*

taffeta [ˈtæfətə] *n* : tafetán *m*, tafeta *f Arg, Mex, Uru*

taffy [ˈtæfi] *n, pl* **-fies** : caramelo *m* de melaza, chicloso *m Mex*

tag[1] [ˈtæg] *v* **tagged; tagging** *vt* **1** LABEL : etiquetar **2** TAIL : seguir de cerca **3** TOUCH : tocar (en varios juegos) — *vi* **to tag along** : pegarse, acompañar

tag[2] *n* **1** LABEL : etiqueta *f* **2** SAYING : dicho *m*, refrán *m*

tail[1] [ˈteɪl] *vt* FOLLOW : seguir de cerca, pegarse

tail[2] *n* **1** : cola *f*, rabo *m* (de un animal) **2** : cola *f*, parte *f* posterior <a comet's tail : la cola de un cometa> **3 tails** *npl* : cruz *f* (de una moneda) <heads or tails : cara o cruz>

tailed [ˈteɪld] *adj* : que tiene cola

tailgate[1] [ˈteɪlˌgeɪt] *vi* **-gated; -gating** : seguir a un vehículo demasiado de cerca

tailgate[2] *n* : puerta *f* trasera (de un vehículo)

taillight [ˈteɪlˌlaɪt] *n* : luz *f* trasera (de un vehículo), calavera *f Mex*

tailor[1] [ˈteɪlər] *vt* **1** : confeccionar o alterar (ropa) **2** ADAPT : adaptar, ajustar

tailor[2] *n* : sastre *m*, -tra *f*

tailpipe [ˈteɪlˌpaɪp] *n* : tubo *m* de escape

tailspin [ˈteɪlˌspɪn] *n* : barrena *f*

taint[1] [ˈteɪnt] *vt* : contaminar, corromper

taint[2] *n* : corrupción *f*, impureza *f*

take[1] [ˈteɪk] *v* **took** [ˈtʊk]; **taken** [ˈteɪkən]; **taking** *vt* **1** CAPTURE : capturar, apresar **2** GRASP : tomar, agarrar <to take the bull by the horns : tomar al toro por los cuernos> **3** CATCH : tomar, agarrar <taken by surprise : tomado por sorpresa> **4** CAPTIVATE : encantar, fascinar **5** INGEST : tomar, ingerir <take two pills : tome dos píldoras> **6** REMOVE : sacar, extraer <take an orange : saca una naranja> **7** : tomar, coger (un tren, un autobús, etc.) **8** NEED, REQUIRE : tomar, requirir <these things take time : estas cosas toman tiempo> **9** BRING, CARRY : llevar, sacar, cargar <take them with you : llévalos contigo> <take the trash out : saca la basura> **10** BEAR, ENDURE : soportar, aguantar (dolores, etc.) **11** ACCEPT : aceptar (un cheque, etc.), seguir (consejos), asumir (la responsabilidad) **12** SUPPOSE : suponer <I take it that... : supongo que...> **13** (*indicating an action or an undertaking*) <to take a walk : dar un paseo> <to take a class : tomar una clase> **14 to take place** HAPPEN : tener lugar, suceder, ocurrir — *vi* : agarrar (dícese de un tinte), prender (dícese de una vacuna)

take[2] *n* **1** PROCEEDS : recaudación *f*, ingresos *mpl*, ganancias *fpl* **2** : toma *f* (de un rodaje o una grabación)

take back *vt* : retirar (palabras, etc.)

take in *vt* **1** : tomarle a, achicar (un vestido, etc.) **2** INCLUDE : incluir, abarcar **3** ATTEND : ir a <to take in a movie : ir al cine> **4** GRASP, UNDERSTAND : captar, entender **5** DECEIVE : engañar

takeoff [ˈteɪkˌɔf] *n* **1** PARODY : parodia *f* **2** : despegue *m* (de un avión o cohete)

take off *vt* REMOVE : quitar <take off your hat : quítate el sombrero> — *vi* **1** : despegar (dícese de un avión o un cohete) **2** LEAVE : irse, partir

take on *vt* **1** TACKLE : abordar, emprender (problemas, etc.) **2** ACCEPT : aceptar, encargarse de, asumir (una responsabilidad) **3** CONTRACT : contratar (trabajadores) **4** ASSUME : adoptar, asumir, adquirir <the neighborhood took on a dingy look : el barrio asumió una apariencia deprimente>

takeover [ˈteɪkˌoːvər] *n* : toma *f* (de poder o de control), adquisición *f* (de una empresa por otra)

take over *vt* : tomar el poder de, tomar las riendas de — *vi* : asumir el mando

taker [ˈteɪkər] *n* : persona *f* interesada <available to all takers : disponible a cuantos estén interesados>

take up *vt* **1** LIFT : levantar **2** SHORTEN : acortar (una falda, etc.) **3** BEGIN : empezar, dedicarse a (un pasatiempo, etc.) **4** OCCUPY : ocupar, llevar (tiempo, espacio) **5** PURSUE : volver a (una cuestión, un asunto) **6** CONTINUE : seguir con

talc [ˈtælk] *n* : talco *m*

talcum powder [ˈtælkəm] *n* : talco *m*, polvos *mpl* de talco

tale [ˈteɪl] *n* **1** ANECDOTE, STORY : cuento *m*, relato *m*, anécdota *f* **2** FALSEHOOD : cuento *m*, mentira *f*

talent [ˈtælənt] *n* : talento *m*, don *m*

talented [ˈtæləntəd] *adj* : talentoso

talisman [ˈtælɪsmən, -lɪz-] *n, pl* **-mans** : talismán *m*

talk[1] [ˈtɔk] *vi* **1** : hablar <he talks for hours : se pasa horas hablando> **2** CHAT : charlar, platicar — *vt* **1** SPEAK : hablar <to talk French : hablar francés> <to talk business : hablar de negocios> **2** PERSUADE : influenciar, convencer <she talked me out of it : me convenció que no lo hiciera> **3**

to talk over DISCUSS : hablar de, discutir

talk[2] *n* **1** CONVERSATION : charla *f,* plática *f,* conversación *f* **2** GOSSIP, RUMOR : chisme *m,* rumores *mpl*

talkative [ˈtɔkətɪv] *adj* : locuaz, parlanchín, charlatán

talker [ˈtɔkər] *n* : conversador *m,* -dora *f;* hablador *m,* -dora *f*

tall [ˈtɔl] *adj* : alto <how tall is he? : ¿cuánto mide?>

tallness [ˈtɔlnəs] *n* HEIGHT : estatura *f* (de una persona), altura *f* (de un objeto)

tallow [ˈtæloː] *n* : sebo *m*

tally[1] [ˈtæli] *v* **-lied; -lying** *vt* RECKON : contar, hacer una cuenta de — *vi* MATCH : concordar, corresponder, cuadrar

tally[2] *n, pl* **-lies** : cuenta *f* <to keep a tally : llevar la cuenta>

talon [ˈtælən] *n* : garra *f* (de un ave de rapiña)

tambourine [ˌtæmbəˈriːn] *n* : pandero *m,* pandereta *f*

tame[1] [ˈteɪm] *vt* **tamed; taming** : domar, amansar, domesticar

tame[2] *adj* **tamer; -est** **1** DOMESTICATED : domesticado, manso **2** DOCILE : manso, dócil **3** DULL : aburrido, soso

tamely [ˈteɪmli] *adv* : mansamente, dócilmente

tamer [ˈteɪmər] *n* : domador *m,* -dora *f*

tamp [ˈtæmp] *vt* : apisonar

tamper [ˈtæmpər] *vi* **to tamper with** : adulterar (una sustancia), forzar (un sello, una cerradura), falsear (documentos), manipular (una máquina)

tampon [ˈtæmˌpɑn] *n* : tampón *m*

tan[1] [ˈtæn] *v* **tanned; tanning** *vt* **1** : curtir (pieles) **2** : broncear — *vi* : broncearse

tan[2] *n* **1** SUNTAN : bronceado *m* <to get a tan : broncearse> **2** : color *m* canela, color *m* café con leche

tandem[1] [ˈtændəm] *adv or* **in tandem** : en tándem

tandem[2] *n* : tándem *m* (bicicleta)

tang [ˈtæŋ] *n* : sabor *m* fuerte

tangent [ˈtændʒənt] *n* : tangente *f* <to go off on a tangent : irse por la tangente>

tangerine [ˈtændʒəˌriːn, ˌtændʒəˈ-] *n* : mandarina *f*

tangible [ˈtændʒəbəl] *adj* : tangible, palpable — **tangibly** [-bli] *adv*

tangle[1] [ˈtæŋgəl] *v* **-gled; -gling** *vt* : enredar, enmarañar — *vi* : enredarse

tangle[2] *n* : enredo *m,* maraña *f*

tango[1] [ˈtæŋˌgoː] *vi* : bailar el tango

tango[2] *n, pl* **-gos** : tango *m*

tangy [ˈtæŋi] *adj* **tangier; -est** : que tiene un sabor fuerte

tank [ˈtæŋk] *n* : tanque *m,* depósito *m* <fuel tank : depósito de combustibles>

tankard [ˈtæŋkərd] *n* : jarra *f*

tanker [ˈtæŋkər] *n* : buque *m* cisterna, camión *m* cisterna, avión *m* cisterna <an oil tanker : un petrolero>

tanner [ˈtænər] *n* : curtidor *m,* -dora *f*

tannery [ˈtænəri] *n, pl* **-neries** : curtiduría *f,* tenería *f*

tannin [ˈtænən] *n* : tanino *m*

tantalize [ˈtæntəˌlaɪz] *vt* **-lized; -lizing** : tentar, atormentar (con algo inasequible)

tantalizing [ˈtæntəˌlaɪzɪŋ] *adj* : tentador, seductor

tantamount [ˈtæntəˌmaʊnt] *adj* : equivalente

tantrum [ˈtæntrəm] *n* : rabieta *f,* berrinche *m* <to throw a tantrum : hacer un berrinche>

tap[1] [ˈtæp] *vt* **tapped; tapping** **1** : ponerle una espita a, sacar líquido de (un barril, un tanque, etc.) **2** : intervenir (una línea telefónica) **3** PAT, TOUCH : tocar, golpear ligeramente <he tapped me on the shoulder : me tocó en el hombro>

tap[2] *n* **1** FAUCET : llave *f,* grifo *m* <beer on tap : cerveza de barril> **2** : extracción *f* (de líquido) <a spinal tap : una punción lumbar> **3** PAT, TOUCH : golpecito *m,* toque *m*

tape[1] [ˈteɪp] *vt* **taped; taping** **1** : sujetar o mendar con cinta adhesiva **2** RECORD : grabar

tape[2] *n* **1** : cinta *f* (adhesiva, magnética, etc.) **2** → **tape measure**

tape measure *n* : cinta *f* métrica

taper[1] [ˈteɪpər] *vi* **1** : estrecharse gradualmente <its tail tapers towards the tip : su cola va estrechándose hacia la punta> **2** *or* **to taper off** : disminuir gradualmente

taper[2] *n* **1** CANDLE : vela *f* larga y delgada **2** TAPERING : estrechamiento *m* gradual

tapestry [ˈtæpəstri] *n, pl* **-tries** : tapiz *m*

tapeworm [ˈteɪpˌwərm] *n* : solitaria *f,* tenia *f*

tapioca [ˌtæpiˈoːkə] *n* : tapioca *f*

tar[1] [ˈtɑr] *vt* **tarred; tarring** : alquitranar

tar[2] *n* : alquitrán *m,* brea *f,* chapopote *m Mex*

tarantula [təˈræntʃələ, -ˈræntələ] *n* : tarántula *f*

tardiness [ˈtɑrdinəs] *n* : tardanza *f,* retraso *m*

tardy [ˈtɑrdi] *adj* **-dier; -est** LATE : tardío, de retraso

target[1] [ˈtɑrgət] *vt* : fijar como objetivo, dirigir, destinar

target[2] *n* **1** : blanco *m* <target practice : tiro al blanco> **2** GOAL, OBJECTIVE : meta *f,* objetivo *m*

tariff [ˈtærɪf] *n* DUTY : tarifa *f,* arancel *m*

tarnish[1] [ˈtɑrnɪʃ] *vt* **1** DULL : deslustrar **2** SULLY : empañar, manchar (una reputación, etc.) — *vi* : deslustrarse

tarnish[2] *n* : deslustre *m*

tarpaulin [tɑr'pɔlən, 'tɑrpə-] *n* **:** lona *f* (impermeable)
tarry[1] ['tæri] *vi* **-ried; -rying :** demorarse, entretenerse
tarry[2] ['tɑri] *adj* **1 :** parecido al alquitrán **2 :** cubierto de alquitrán
tart[1] ['tɑrt] *adj* **1** SOUR **:** ácido, agrio **2** CAUSTIC **:** mordaz, acrimonioso — **tartly** *adv*
tart[2] *n* **:** tartaleta *f*
tartan ['tɑrtən] *n* **:** tartán *m*
tartar ['tɑrtər] *n* **1 :** tártaro *m* <tartar sauce : salsa tártara> **2 :** sarro *m* (dental)
tartness ['tɑrtnəs] *n* **1** SOURNESS **:** acidez *f* **2** ACRIMONY, SHARPNESS **:** mordacidad *f,* acrimonia *f,* acritud *f*
task ['tæsk] *n* **:** tarea *f,* trabajo *m*
taskmaster ['tæsk,mæstər] *n* **to be a hard taskmaster :** ser exigente, ser muy estricto
tassel ['tæsəl] *n* **:** borla *f*
taste[1] ['teɪst] *v* **tasted; tasting** *vt* **:** probar (alimentos), degustar, catar (vinos) <taste this soup : prueba esta sopa> — *vi* **:** saber <this tastes good : esto sabe bueno>
taste[2] *n* **1** SAMPLE **:** prueba *f,* bocado *m* (de comida), trago *m* (de bebidas) **2** FLAVOR **:** gusto *m,* sabor *m* **3 :** gusto *m* <she has good taste : tiene buen gusto> <in bad taste : de mal gusto>
taste bud *n* **:** papila *f* gustativa
tasteful ['teɪstfəl] *adj* **:** de buen gusto
tastefully ['teɪstfəli] *adv* **:** con buen gusto
tasteless ['teɪstləs] *adj* **1** FLAVORLESS **:** sin sabor, soso, insípido **2 :** de mal gusto <a tasteless joke : un chiste de mal gusto>
taster ['teɪstər] *n* **:** degustador *m,* -dora *f;* catador *m,* -dora *f* (de vinos)
tastiness ['teɪstinəs] *n* **:** lo sabroso
tasty ['teɪsti] *adj* **tastier; -est :** sabroso, gustoso
tatter ['tæt̬ər] *n* **1** SHRED **:** tira *f,* jirón *m* (de tela) **2 tatters** *npl* **:** andrajos *mpl,* harapos *mpl* <to be in tatters : estar por los suelos>
tattered ['tæt̬ərd] *adj* **:** andrajoso, en jirones
tattle ['tæt̬əl] *vi* **-tled; -tling 1** CHATTER **:** parlotear *fam,* cotorrear *fam* **2 to tattle on someone :** acusar a alguien
tattletale ['tæt̬əl,teɪl] *n* **:** soplón *m,* -plona *f fam*
tattoo[1] [tæ'tu:] *vt* **:** tatuar
tattoo[2] *n* **:** tatuaje *m* <to get a tattoo : tatuarse>
taught → **teach**
taunt[1] ['tɔnt] *vt* MOCK **:** mofarse de, burlarse de
taunt[2] *n* **:** mofa *f,* burla *f*
Taurus ['tɔrəs] *n* **:** Tauro *mf*
taut ['tɔt] *adj* **:** tirante, tenso — **tautly** *adv*
tautness ['tɔtnəs] *n* **:** tirantez *f,* tensión *f*
tavern ['tævərn] *n* **:** taberna *f*
tawdry ['tɔdri] *adj* **-drier; -est :** chabacano, vulgar
tawny ['tɔni] *adj* **-nier; -est :** leonado
tax[1] ['tæks] *vt* **1 :** gravar, cobrar un impuesto sobre **2** CHARGE **:** acusar <they taxed him with neglect : fue acusado de incumplimiento> **3 to tax someone's strength :** ponerle a prueba las fuerzas (a alguien)
tax[2] *n* **1 :** impuesto *m,* tributo *m* **2** BURDEN **:** carga *f*
taxable ['tæksəbəl] *adj* **:** sujeto a un impuesto
taxation [tæk'seɪʃən] *n* **:** impuestos *mpl*
tax–exempt ['tæksɪg'zɛmpt, -ɛg-] *adj* **:** libre de impuestos
taxi[1] ['tæksi] *vi* **taxied; taxiing** *or* **taxying; taxis** *or* **taxies 1 :** ir en taxi **2 :** rodar sobre la pista de aterrizaje (dícese de un avión)
taxi[2] *n, pl* **taxis :** taxi *m,* libre *m Mex*
taxicab ['tæksi,kæb] → **taxi**[2]
taxidermist ['tæksə,dərmɪst] *n* **:** taxidermista *mf*
taxidermy ['tæksə,dərmi] *n* **:** taxidermia *f*
taxpayer ['tæks,peɪər] *n* **:** contribuyente *mf,* causante *mf Mex*
TB [,ti:'bi:] → **tuberculosis**
tea ['ti:] *n* **1 :** té *m* (planta y bebida) **2 :** merienda *f,* té *m* (comida)
teach ['ti:tʃ] *v* **taught** ['tɔt]; **teaching** *vt* **:** enseñar, dar clases de <she teaches math : da clases de matemáticas> <she taught me everything I know : me enseñó todo lo que sé> — *vi* **:** enseñar, dar clases
teacher ['ti:tʃər] *n* **:** maestro *m,* -tra *f* (de enseñanza primaria); profesor *m,* -sora *f* (de enseñanza secundaria)
teaching ['ti:tʃɪŋ] *n* **:** enseñanza *f*
teacup ['ti:,kʌp] *n* **:** taza *f* para té
teak ['ti:k] *n* **:** teca *f*
teakettle ['ti:,kɛtəl] *n* **:** tetera *f*
teal ['ti:l] *n, pl* **teal** *or* **teals :** cerceta *f* (pato)
team[1] ['ti:m] *vi or* **to team up 1 :** formar un equipo (en deportes) **2** COLLABORATE **:** asociarse, juntarse, unirse
team[2] *adj* **:** de equipo
team[3] *n* **1 :** tiro *m* (de caballos), yunta *f* (de bueyes o mulas) **2 :** equipo *m* (en deportes, etc.)
teammate ['ti:m,meɪt] *n* **:** compañero *m,* -ra *f* de equipo
teamster ['ti:mstər] *n* **:** camionero *m,* -ra *f*
teamwork ['ti:m,wərk] *n* **:** trabajo *m* en equipo, cooperación *f*
teapot ['ti:,pɑt] *n* **:** tetera *f*
tear[1] ['tær] *v* **tore** ['tor]; **torn** ['torn]; **tearing** *vt* **1** RIP **:** desgarrar, romper, rasgar (tela) <to tear to pieces : hacer pedazos> **2** *or* **to tear apart** DIVIDE **:** dividir **3** REMOVE **:** arrancar <torn from his family : arrancado de su familia> **4 to tear down :** derribar — *vi* **1** RIP **:** desgarrarse, romperse **2** RUSH

: ir a gran velocidad <she went tearing down the street : se fue como rayo por la calle>

tear[2] *n* : desgarradura *f,* rotura *f,* desgarro *m* (muscular)

tear[3] [ˈtɪr] *n* : lágrima *f*

teardrop [ˈtɪrˌdrɑp] → **tear**[3]

tearful [ˈtɪrfəl] *adj* : lloroso, triste — **tearfully** *adv*

tease[1] [ˈtiːz] *vt* **teased; teasing 1** MOCK : burlarse de, mofarse de **2** ANNOY : irritar, fastidiar

tease[2] *n* **1** TEASING : burla *f,* mofa *f* **2** : bromista *mf;* guasón *m,* -sona *f*

teaspoon [ˈtiːˌspuːn] *n* **1** : cucharita *f* **2** → **teaspoonful**

teaspoonful [ˈtiːˌspuːnˌfʊl] *n, pl* **-spoonfuls** [-ˌfʊlz] *or* **-spoonsful** [-ˌspuːnzˌfʊl] : cucharadita *f*

teat [ˈtiːt] *n* : tetilla *f*

technical [ˈtɛknɪkəl] *adj* : técnico — **technically** [-kli] *adv*

technicality [ˌtɛknəˈkæləṱi] *n, pl* **-ties** : detalle *m* técnico

technician [tɛkˈnɪʃən] *n* : técnico *m,* -ca *f*

technique [tɛkˈniːk] *n* : técnica *f*

technological [ˌtɛknəˈlɑdʒɪkəl] *adj* : tecnológico

technology [tɛkˈnɑlədʒi] *n, pl* **-gies** : tecnología *f*

teddy bear [ˈtɛdi] *n* : oso *m* de peluche

tedious [ˈtiːdiəs] *adj* : aburrido, pesado, monótono — **tediously** *adv*

tediousness [ˈtiːdiəsnəs] *n* : lo aburrido, lo pesado

tedium [ˈtiːdiəm] *n* : tedio *m,* pesadez *f*

tee [ˈtiː] *n* : tee *mf*

teem [ˈtiːm] *vi* **to teem with** : estar repleto de, estar lleno de

teenage [ˈtiːnˌeɪdʒ] *or* **teenaged** [-eɪdʒd] *adj* : adolescente, de adolescencia

teenager [ˈtiːnˌeɪdʒər] *n* : adolescente *mf*

teens [ˈtiːnz] *npl* : adolescencia *f*

teepee → **tepee**

teeter[1] [ˈtiːṱər] *vi* : balancearse, tambalearse

teeter[2] *n or* **teeter–totter** [ˈtiːṱərˌtɑṱər] → **seesaw**

teeth → **tooth**

teethe [ˈtiːð] *vi* **teethed; teething** : formársele a uno los dientes <the baby's teething : le están saliendo los dientes al niño>

telecast[1] [ˈtɛləˌkæst] *vt* **-cast; -casting** : televisar, transmitir por televisión

telecast[2] *n* : transmisión *f* por televisión

telecommunication [ˈtɛləkəˌmjuːnəˈkeɪʃən] *n* : telecomunicación *f*

telegram [ˈtɛləˌgræm] *n* : telegrama *m*

telegraph[1] [ˈtɛləˌgræf] *v* : telegrafiar

telegraph[2] *n* : telégrafo *m*

telepathic [ˌtɛləˈpæθɪk] *adj* : telepático — **telepathically** [-θɪkli] *adv*

telepathy [təˈlɛpəθi] *n* : telepatía *f*

telephone[1] [ˈtɛləˌfoːn] *v* **-phoned; -phoning** *vt* : llamar por teléfono a, telefonear — *vi* : telefonear

telephone[2] *n* : teléfono *m*

telescope[1] [ˈtɛləˌskoːp] *vi* **-scoped; -scoping** : plegarse (como un telescopio)

telescope[2] *n* : telescopio *m*

telescopic [ˌtɛləˈskɑpɪk] *adj* : telescópico

televise [ˈtɛləˌvaɪz] *vt* **-vised; -vising** : televisar

television [ˈtɛləˌvɪʒən] *n* : televisión *f*

tell [ˈtɛl] *v* **told** [ˈtoːld]; **telling** *vt* **1** COUNT : contar, enumerar <all told : en total> **2** INSTRUCT : decir <he told me how to fix it : me dijo cómo arreglarlo> <they told her to wait : le dijeron que esperara> **3** RELATE : contar, relatar, narrar <to tell a story : contar una historia> **4** DIVULGE, REVEAL : revelar, divulgar <he told me everything about her : me contó todo acerca de ella> **5** DISCERN : discernir, notar <I can't tell the difference : no noto la diferencia> — *vi* **1** SAY : decir <I won't tell : no voy a decírselo a nadie> **2** KNOW : saber <you never can tell : nunca se sabe> **3** SHOW : notarse, hacerse sentir <the strain is beginning to tell : la tensión se empieza a notar>

teller [ˈtɛlər] *n* **1** NARRATOR : narrador *m,* -dora *f* **2** *or* **bank teller** : cajero *m,* -ra *f*

temerity [təˈmɛrəṱi] *n, pl* **-ties** : temeridad *f*

temp [ˈtɛmp] *n* : empleado *m,* -da *f* temporal

temper[1] [ˈtɛmpər] *vt* **1** MODERATE : moderar, temperar **2** ANNEAL : templar (acero, etc.)

temper[2] *n* **1** DISPOSITION : carácter *m,* genio *m* **2** HARDNESS : temple *m,* dureza *f* (de un metal) **3** COMPOSURE : calma *f,* serenidad *f* <to lose one's temper : perder los estribos> **4** RAGE : furia *f* <to fly into a temper : ponerse furioso>

temperament [ˈtɛmpərmənt, -prə-, -pərə-] *n* : temperamento *m*

temperamental [ˌtɛmpərˈmɛntəl, -prə-, -pərə-] *adj* : temperamental

temperance [ˈtɛmprənts] *n* : templanza *f,* temperancia *f*

temperate [ˈtɛmpərət] *adj* : templado (dícese del clima, etc.), moderado

temperature [ˈtɛmpərˌtʃʊr, -prə-, -pərə-, -tʃər] *n* **1** : temperatura *f* **2** FEVER : calentura *f,* fiebre *f*

tempest [ˈtɛmpəst] *n* : tempestad *f*

tempestuous [tɛmˈpɛstʃʊəs] *adj* : tempestuoso

temple [ˈtɛmpəl] *n* **1** : templo *m* (en religión) **2** : sien *f* (en anatomía)

tempo [ˈtɛmˌpoː] *n, pl* **-pi** [-ˌpiː] *or* **-pos** : ritmo *m,* tempo *m* (en música)

temporal [ˈtɛmpərəl] *adj* : temporal

temporarily [ˌtɛmpəˈrɛrəli] *adv* : temporalmente, provisionalmente

temporary [ˈtɛmpəˌrɛri] *adj* : temporal, provisional, provisorio
tempt [ˈtɛmpt] *vt* : tentar
temptation [tɛmpˈteɪʃən] *n* : tentación *f*
tempter [ˈtɛmptər] *n* : tentador *m*
temptress [ˈtɛmptrəs] *n* : tentadora *f*
ten[1] [ˈtɛn] *adj* : diez
ten[2] *n* **1** : diez *m* (número) **2** : decena *f* <tens of thousands : decenas de millares>
tenable [ˈtɛnəbəl] *adj* : sostenible, defendible
tenacious [təˈneɪʃəs] *adj* : tenaz
tenacity [təˈnæsət̬i] *n* : tenacidad *f*
tenancy [ˈtɛnəntsi] *n, pl* **-cies** : tenencia *f,* inquilinato *m* (de un inmueble)
tenant [ˈtɛnənt] *n* : inquilino *m,* -na *f;* arrendatario *m,* -ria *f*
tend [ˈtɛnd] *vt* : atender, cuidar (de), ocuparse de — *vi* : tender <it tends to benefit the consumer : tiende a beneficiar al consumidor>
tendency [ˈtɛndəntsi] *n, pl* **-cies** : tendencia *f,* proclividad *f,* inclinación *f*
tender[1] [ˈtɛndər] *vt* : entregar, presentar <I tendered my resignation : presenté mi renuncia>
tender[2] *adj* **1** : tierno, blando <tender steak : bistec tierno> **2** AFFECTIONATE, LOVING : tierno, cariñoso, afectuoso **3** DELICATE : tierno, sensible, delicado
tender[3] *n* **1** OFFER : propuesta *f,* oferta *f* (en negocios) **2 legal tender** : moneda *f* de curso legal
tenderize [ˈtɛndəˌraɪz] *vt* **-ized; -izing** : ablandar (carnes)
tenderloin [ˈtɛndərˌlɔɪn] *n* : lomo *f* (de res o de puerco)
tenderly [ˈtɛndərli] *adv* : tiernamente, con ternura
tenderness [ˈtɛndərnəs] *n* : ternura *f*
tendon [ˈtɛndən] *n* : tendón *m*
tendril [ˈtɛndrɪl] *n* : zarcillo *m*
tenement [ˈtɛnəmənt] *n* : casa *f* de vecindad
tenet [ˈtɛnət] *n* : principio *m*
tennis [ˈtɛnəs] *n* : tenis *m*
tenor [ˈtɛnər] *n* **1** PURPORT : tenor *m,* significado *m* **2** : tenor *m* (en música)
tenpins [ˈtɛnˌpɪnz] *npl* : bolos *mpl,* boliche *m*
tense[1] [ˈtɛnts] *v* **tensed; tensing** *vt* : tensar — *vi* : tensarse, ponerse tenso
tense[2] *adj* **tenser; tensest 1** TAUT : tenso, tirante **2** NERVOUS : tenso, nervioso
tense[3] *n* : tiempo *m* (de un verbo)
tensely [ˈtɛntsli] *adv* : tensamente
tenseness [ˈtɛntsnəs] → **tension**
tension [ˈtɛntʃən] *n* **1** TAUTNESS : tensión *f,* tirantez *f* **2** STRESS : tensión *f,* nerviosismo *m,* estrés *m*
tent [ˈtɛnt] *n* : tienda *f* de campaña
tentacle [ˈtɛntɪkəl] *n* : tentáculo *m*
tentative [ˈtɛntət̬ɪv] *adj* **1** HESITANT : indeciso, vacilante **2** PROVISIONAL : sujeto a cambios, provisional
tentatively [ˈtɛntət̬ɪvli] *adv* : provisionalmente
tenth[1] [ˈtɛnθ] *adj* : décimo
tenth[2] *n* **1** : décimo *m,* -ma *f* (en una serie) **2** : décimo *m,* décima parte *f*
tenuous [ˈtɛnjʊəs] *adj* : tenue, débil <tenuous reasons : razones poco convincentes>
tenuously [ˈtɛnjʊəsli] *adv* : tenuemente, ligeramente
tenure [ˈtɛnjər] *n* : tenencia *f* (de un cargo o una propiedad), titularidad *f* (de un puesto académico)
tepee [ˈtiːˌpiː] *n* : tipi *m*
tepid [ˈtɛpɪd] *adj* : tibio
term[1] [ˈtərm] *vt* : calificar de, llamar, nombrar
term[2] *n* **1** PERIOD : término *m,* plazo *m,* período *m* **2** : término *m* (en matemáticas) **3** WORD : término *m,* vocablo *m* <legal terms : términos legales> **4 terms** *npl* CONDITIONS : términos *mpl,* condiciones *fpl* **5 terms** *npl* RELATIONS : relaciones *fpl* <to be on good terms with : tener buenas relaciones con> **6 in terms of** : con respecto a, en cuanto a
terminal[1] [ˈtərmənəl] *adj* : terminal
terminal[2] *n* **1** : terminal *m,* polo *m* (en electricidad) **2** : terminal *m* (de una computadora) **3** STATION : terminal *f,* estación *f* (de transporte público)
terminate [ˈtərməˌneɪt] *v* **-nated; -nating** *vi* : terminar(se), concluirse — *vt* : terminar, poner fin a
termination [ˌtərməˈneɪʃən] *n* : cese *m,* terminación *f*
terminology [ˌtərməˈnɑlədʒi] *n, pl* **-gies** : terminología *f*
terminus [ˈtərmənəs] *n, pl* **-ni** [-ˌnaɪ] *or* **-nuses 1** END : término *m,* fin *m* **2** : terminal *f* (de transporte público)
termite [ˈtərˌmaɪt] *n* : termita *f*
tern [ˈtərn] *n* : golondrina *f* de mar
terrace[1] [ˈtɛrəs] *vt* **-raced; -racing** : formar en terrazas, disponer en bancales
terrace[2] *n* **1** PATIO : terraza *f,* patio *m* **2** : terraplén *m,* terraza *f,* bancal *m* (en agricultura)
terra–cotta [ˌtɛrəˈkɑt̬ə] *n* : terracota *f*
terrain [təˈreɪn] *n* : terreno *m*
terrapin [ˈtɛrəpɪn] *n* : galápago *m* norteamericano
terrarium [təˈræriəm] *n, pl* **-ia** [-iə] *or* **-iums** : terrario *m*
terrestrial [təˈrɛstriəl] *adj* : terrestre
terrible [ˈtɛrəbəl] *adj* : atroz, horrible, terrible
terribly [ˈtɛrəbli] *adv* **1** BADLY : muy mal **2** EXTREMELY : terriblemente, extremadamente
terrier [ˈtɛriər] *n* : terrier *mf*
terrific [təˈrɪfɪk] *adj* **1** FRIGHTFUL : aterrador **2** EXTRAORDINARY : extraordinario, excepcional **3** EXCELLENT : excelente, estupendo
terrify [ˈtɛrəˌfaɪ] *vt* **-fied; -fying** : aterrorizar, aterrar, espantar

terrifying [ˈtɛrəˌfaɪɪŋ] *adj* **:** espantoso, aterrador
territory [ˈtɛrəˌtori] *n, pl* **-ries :** territorio *m* — **territorial** [ˌtɛrəˈtoriəl] *adj*
terror [ˈtɛrər] *n* **:** terror *m*
terrorism [ˈtɛrərˌɪzəm] *n* **:** terrorismo *m*
terrorist¹ [ˈtɛrərɪst] *adj* **:** terrorista
terrorist² *n* **:** terrorista *mf*
terrorize [ˈtɛrərˌaɪz] *vt* **-ized; -izing :** aterrorizar
terry [ˈtɛri] *n, pl* **-ries** *or* **terry cloth :** (tela de) toalla *f*
terse [ˈtərs] *adj* **terser; tersest :** lacónico, conciso, seco — **tersely** *adv*
tertiary [ˈtərʃiˌɛri] *adj* **:** terciario
test¹ [ˈtɛst] *vt* **:** examinar, evaluar — *vi* **:** hacer pruebas
test² *n* **:** prueba *f,* examen *m,* test *m* <to put to the test **:** poner a prueba>
testament [ˈtɛstəmənt] *n* **1** WILL **:** testamento *m* **2 :** Testamento *m* (en la Biblia) <the Old Testament **:** el Antiguo Testamento>
testicle [ˈtɛstɪkəl] *n* **:** testículo *m*
testify [ˈtɛstəˌfaɪ] *v* **-fied; -fying** *vi* **:** testificar, atestar, testimoniar — *vt* **:** testificar
testimonial [ˌtɛstəˈmoːniəl] *n* **1** REFERENCE **:** recomendación *f* **2** TRIBUTE **:** homenaje *m,* tributo *m*
testimony [ˈtɛstəˌmoːni] *n, pl* **-nies :** testimonio *m,* declaración *f*
test tube *n* **:** probeta *f,* tubo *m* de ensayo
testy [ˈtɛsti] *adj* **-tier; -est :** irritable
tetanus [ˈtɛtənəs] *n* **:** tétano *m,* tétanos *m*
tête-à-tête [ˌtɛtəˈtɛt, ˌteɪtəˈteɪt] *n* **:** conversación *f* en privado
tether¹ [ˈtɛðər] *vt* **:** atar (con una cuerda), amarrar
tether² *n* **:** atadura *f,* cadena *f,* correa *f*
text [ˈtɛkst] *n* **1 :** texto *m* **2** TOPIC **:** tema *m* **3 → textbook**
textbook [ˈtɛkstˌbʊk] *n* **:** libro *m* de texto
textile [ˈtɛkˌstaɪl, ˈtɛkstəl] *n* **:** textil *m,* tela *f* <the textile industry **:** la industria textil>
textual [ˈtɛkstʃʊəl] *adj* **:** textual
texture [ˈtɛkstʃər] *n* **:** textura *f*
than¹ [ˈðæn] *conj* **:** que, de <it's worth more than that **:** vale más que eso> <more than you think **:** más de lo que piensas>
than² *prep* **:** que, de <you're better than he is **:** eres mejor que él> <more than once **:** más de una vez>
thank [ˈθæŋk] *vt* **:** agradecer, darle (las) gracias (a alguien) <thank you! **:** ¡gracias!> <I thanked her for the present **:** le di las gracias por el regalo> <I thank you for your help **:** le agradezco su ayuda>
thankful [ˈθæŋkfəl] *adj* **:** agradecido
thankfully [ˈθæŋkfəli] *adv* **1** GRATEFULLY **:** con agradecimiento **2** FORTUNATELY **:** afortunadamente, por suerte <thankfully, it's over **:** se acabó, gracias a Dios>
thankfulness [ˈθæŋkfəlnəs] *n* **:** agradecimiento *m,* gratitud *f*
thankless [ˈθæŋkləs] *adj* **:** ingrato <a thankless task **:** un trabajo ingrato>
thanks [ˈθæŋks] *npl* **1 :** agradecimiento *m* **2 thanks! :** ¡gracias!
Thanksgiving [θæŋksˈgɪvɪŋ, ˈθæŋksˌ-] *n* **:** el día de Acción de Gracias (fiesta estadounidense)
that¹ [ˈðæt] *adv* (*in negative constructions*) **:** tan <it's not that expensive **:** no es tan caro> <not that much **:** no tanto>
that² *adj, pl* **those :** ese, esa, aquel, aquella <do you see those children? **:** ¿ves a aquellos niños?>
that³ *conj & pron* **:** que <he said that he was afraid **:** dijo que tenía miedo> <the book that he wrote **:** el libro que escribió>
that⁴ *pron, pl* **those** [ˈðoːz] **1 :** ése, ésa, eso <that's my father **:** ése es mi padre> <those are the ones he likes **:** ésos son los que le gustan> <what's that? **:** ¿qué es eso?> **2** (*referring to more distant objects or time*) **:** aquél, aquélla, aquello <those are maples and these are elms **:** aquéllos son arces y éstos son olmos> <that came to an end **:** aquello se acabó>
thatch¹ [ˈθætʃ] *vt* **:** cubrir o techar con paja
thatch² *n* **:** paja *f* (usada para techos)
thaw¹ [ˈθɔ] *vt* **:** descongelar — *vi* **:** derretirse (dícese de la nieve), descongelarse (dícese de los alimentos)
thaw² *n* **:** deshielo *m*
the¹ [ðə, *before vowel sounds usu* ðiː] *adv* **1** (*used to indicate comparison*) <the sooner the better **:** cuanto más pronto, mejor> <she likes this one the best **:** éste es el que más le gusta> **2** (*used as a conjunction*) **:** cuanto <the more I learn, the less I understand **:** cuanto más aprendo, menos entiendo>
the² *art* **:** el, la, los, las <the gloves **:** los guantes> <the suitcase **:** la maleta> <forty cookies to the box **:** cuarenta galletas por caja>
theater *or* **theatre** [ˈθiːətər] *n* **1 :** teatro *m* (edificio) **2** DRAMA **:** teatro *m,* drama *m*
theatrical [θiˈætrɪkəl] *adj* **:** teatral, dramático
thee [ˈðiː] *pron* **:** te, ti
theft [ˈθɛft] *n* **:** robo *m,* hurto *m*
their [ˈðɛr] *adj* **:** su <their friends **:** sus amigos>
theirs [ˈðɛrz] *pron* **:** (el) suyo, (la) suya, (los) suyos, (las) suyas <they came for theirs **:** vinieron por el suyo> <theirs is bigger **:** la suya es más grande, la de ellos es más grande> <a brother of theirs **:** un hermano suyo, un hermano de ellos>

them [ˈðɛm] *pron* **1** (*as a direct object*) **:** los (*Spain sometimes* les), las <I know them **:** los conozco> **2** (*as indirect object*) **:** les, se <I sent them a letter **:** les mandé una carta> <give it to them **:** dáselo (a ellos)> **3** (*as object of a preposition*) **:** ellos, ellas <go with them **:** ve con ellos> **4** (*for emphasis*) **:** ellos, ellas <I wasn't expecting them **:** no los esperaba a ellos>

theme [ˈθiːm] *n* **1** SUBJECT, TOPIC **:** tema *m* **2** COMPOSITION **:** composición *f,* trabajo *m* (escrito) **3 :** tema *m* (en música)

themselves [ðəmˈsɛlvz, ðɛm-] *pron* **1** (*as a reflexive*) **:** se, sí <they enjoyed themselves **:** se divirtieron> <they divided it among themselves **:** lo repartieron entre sí, se lo repartieron> **2** (*for emphasis*) **:** ellos mismos, ellas mismas <they built it themselves **:** ellas mismas lo construyeron>

then[1] [ˈðɛn] *adv* **1 :** entonces, en ese tiempo <I was sixteen then **:** tenía entonces dieciséis años> <since then **:** desde entonces> **2** NEXT **:** después, luego <we'll go to Toronto, then to Winnipeg **:** iremos a Toronto, y luego a Winnipeg> **3** BESIDES **:** además, aparte <then there's the tax **:** y aparte está el impuesto> **4 :** entonces, en ese caso <if you like music, then you should attend **:** si te gusta la música, entonces deberías asistir>

then[2] *adj* **:** entonces <the then governor of Georgia **:** el entonces gobernador de Georgia>

thence [ˈðɛnts, ˈθɛnts] *adv* **:** de ahí, de ahí en adelante

theologian [ˌθiːəˈloːdʒən] *n* **:** teólogo *m,* -ga *f*

theological [ˌθiːəˈlɑdʒɪkəl] *adj* **:** teológico

theology [θiˈɑlədʒi] *n, pl* **-gies :** teología *f*

theorem [ˈθiːərəm, ˈθɪrəm] *n* **:** teorema *m*

theoretical [ˌθiːəˈrɛtɪkəl] *adj* **:** teórico — **theoretically** *adv*

theorize [ˈθiːəˌraɪz] *vi* **-rized; -rizing :** teorizar

theory [ˈθiːəri, ˈθɪri] *n, pl* **-ries :** teoría *f*

therapeutic [ˌθɛrəˈpjuːtɪk] *adj* **:** terapéutico — **therapeutically** *adv*

therapist [ˈθɛrəpɪst] *n* **:** terapeuta *mf*

therapy [ˈθɛrəpi] *n, pl* **-pies :** terapia *f*

there[1] [ˈðær] *adv* **1 :** ahí, allí, allá <stand over there **:** párate ahí> <over there **:** por allí, por allá> <who's there? **:** ¿quién es?> **2 :** ahí, en esto, en eso <there is where we disagree **:** en eso es donde no estamos de acuerdo>

there[2] *pron* **1** (*introducing a sentence or clause*) <there comes a time to decide **:** llega un momento en que tiene uno que decidir> **2 there is, there are :** hay <there are many children here **:** aquí hay muchos niños> <there's a good hotel downtown **:** hay un buen hotel en el centro>

thereabouts [ðærəˈbaʊts, ˈðærəˌ-] *or* **thereabout** [-ˈbaʊt, -ˌbaʊt] *adv* **or thereabouts :** por ahí, más o menos <at five o'clock or thereabouts **:** por ahí de las cinco>

thereafter [ðærˈæftər] *adv* **:** después <shortly thereafter **:** poco después>

thereby [ðærˈbaɪ, ˈðærˌbaɪ] *adv* **:** de tal modo, de ese manera, así

therefore [ˈðærˌfor] *adv* **:** por lo tanto, por consiguiente

therein [ðærˈɪn] *adv* **1 :** allí adentro, ahí adentro <the contents therein **:** lo que allí se contiene> **2 :** allí, en ese aspecto <therein lies the problem **:** allí está el problema>

thereof [ðærˈʌv, -ˈɑv] *adv* **:** de eso, de esto

thereupon [ˈðærəˌpɑn, -ˌpɔn; ˌðærəˈpɑn, -ˈpɔn] *adv* **:** acto seguido, inmediatamente (después)

therewith [ðærˈwɪð, -ˈwɪθ] *adv* **:** con eso, con ello

thermal [ˈθərməl] *adj* **1 :** térmico (en física) **2** HOT **:** termal

thermodynamics [ˌθərmodaɪˈnæmɪks] *ns & pl* **:** termodinámica *f*

thermometer [θərˈmɑmət̬ər] *n* **:** termómetro *m*

thermos [ˈθərməs] *n* **:** termo *m*

thermostat [ˈθərməˌstæt] *n* **:** termostato *m*

thesaurus [θɪˈsɔrəs] *n, pl* **-sauri** [-ˈsɔrˌaɪ] *or* **-sauruses** [-ˈsɔrəsəz] **:** diccionario *m* de sinónimos

these → **this**

thesis [ˈθiːsɪs] *n, pl* **theses** [ˈθiːˌsiːz] **:** tesis *f*

they [ˈðeɪ] *pron* **:** ellos, ellas <they are here **:** están aquí> <they don't know **:** ellos no saben>

they'd [ˈðeɪd] (*contraction of* **they had** *or* **they would**) → **have, would**

they'll [ˈðeɪl, ˈðɛl] (*contraction of* **they shall** *or* **they will**) → **shall, will**

they're [ˈðɛr] (*contraction of* **they are**) → **be**

they've [ˈðeɪv] (*contraction of* **they have**) → **have**

thiamine [ˈθaɪəmɪn, -ˌmiːn] *n* **:** tiamina *f*

thick[1] [ˈθɪk] *adj* **1 :** grueso <a thick plank **:** una tabla gruesa> **2 :** espeso, denso <thick syrup **:** jarabe espeso> — **thickly** *adv*

thick[2] *n* **1 in the thick of :** en medio de <in the thick of the battle **:** en lo más reñido de la batalla> **2 through thick and thin :** a las duras y a las maduras

thicken [ˈθɪkən] *vt* **:** espesar (un líquido) — *vi* **:** espesarse

thickener [ˈθɪkənər] *n* **:** espesante *m*

thicket [ˈθɪkət] *n* **:** matorral *m,* maleza *f,* espesura *f*

thickness [ˈθɪknəs] *n* **:** grosor *m,* grueso *m,* espesor *m*

thickset [ˈθɪkˈsɛt] *adj* STOCKY **:** robusto, fornido

thick–skinned [ˈθɪkˈskɪnd] *adj* **:** poco sensible, que no se ofende fácilmente

thief [ˈθiːf] *n, pl* **thieves** [ˈθiːvz] **:** ladrón *m,* -drona *f*

thieve [ˈθiːv] *v* **thieved; thieving :** hurtar, robar

thievery [ˈθiːvəri] *n* **:** hurto *m,* robo *m,* latrocinio *m*

thigh [ˈθaɪ] *n* **:** muslo *m*

thighbone [ˈθaɪˌboːn] *n* **:** fémur *m*

thimble [ˈθɪmbəl] *n* **:** dedal *m*

thin[1] [ˈθɪn] *v* **thinned; thinning** *vt* **:** hacer menos denso, diluir, aguar (un líquido), enrarecer (un gas) — *vi* **:** diluirse, aguarse (dícese de un líquido), enrarecerse (dícese de un gas)

thin[2] *adj* **thinner; -est 1** LEAN, SLIM **:** delgado, esbelto, flaco **2** SPARSE **:** ralo, escaso <a thin beard **:** una barba rala> **3** WATERY **:** claro, aguado, diluido **4** FINE **:** delgado, fino <thin slices **:** rebanadas finas>

thing [ˈθɪŋ] *n* **1** AFFAIR, MATTER **:** cosa *f,* asunto *m* <don't talk about those things **:** no hables de esas cosas> <how are things? **:** ¿cómo van las cosas?> **2** ACT, EVENT **:** cosa *f,* suceso *m,* evento *m* <the flood was a terrible thing **:** la inundación fue una cosa terrible> **3** OBJECT **:** cosa *f,* objeto *m* <don't forget your things **:** no olvides tus cosas>

think [ˈθɪŋk] *v* **thought** [ˈθɔt]; **thinking** *vt* **1 :** pensar <I thought to return early **:** pensaba regresar temprano> **2** BELIEVE **:** pensar, creer, opinar **3** PONDER **:** pensar, reflexionar **4** CONCEIVE **:** ocurrirse, concebir <we've thought up a plan **:** se nos ha ocurrido un plan> — *vi* **1** REASON **:** pensar, razonar **2** CONSIDER **:** pensar, considerar <think of your family first **:** primero piensa en tu familia>

thinker [ˈθɪŋkər] *n* **:** pensador *m,* -dora *f*

thinly [ˈθɪnli] *adv* **1** LIGHTLY **:** ligeramente **2** SPARSELY **:** escasamente <thinly populated **:** poco populado> **3** BARELY **:** apenas

thinness [ˈθɪnnəs] *n* **:** delgadez *f*

thin–skinned [ˈθɪnˈskɪnd] *adj* **:** susceptible, muy sensible

third[1] [ˈθərd] *or* **thirdly** [-li] *adv* **:** en tercer lugar <she came in third **:** llegó en tercer lugar>

third[2] *adj* **:** tercero <the third day **:** el tercer día>

third[3] *n* **1 :** tercero *m,* -ra *f* (en una serie) **2 :** tercero *m,* tercera parte *f*

third world *n* **the Third World :** el Tercer Mundo *m*

thirst[1] [ˈθərst] *vi* **1 :** tener sed **2 to thirst for** DESIRE **:** tener sed de, estar sediento de

thirst[2] *n* **:** sed *f*

thirsty [ˈθərsti] *adj* **thirstier; -est :** sediento, que tiene sed <I'm thirsty **:** tengo sed>

thirteen[1] [ˌθərˈtiːn] *adj* **:** trece

thirteen[2] *n* **:** trece *m*

thirteenth[1] [ˌθərˈtiːnθ] *adj* **:** décimo tercero

thirteenth[2] *n* **1 :** decimotercero *m,* -ra *f* (en una serie) **2 :** treceavo *m,* treceava parte *f*

thirtieth[1] [ˈθərtiəθ] *adj* **:** trigésimo

thirtieth[2] *n* **1 :** trigésimo *m,* -ma *f* (en una serie) **2 :** treintavo *m,* treintava parte *f*

thirty[1] [ˈθərti] *adj* **:** treinta

thirty[2] *n, pl* **thirties :** treinta *m*

this[1] [ˈðɪs] *adv* **:** así, a tal punto <this big **:** así de grande>

this[2] *adj, pl* **these** [ˈðiːz] **:** este <these things **:** estas cosas> <read this book **:** lee este libro>

this[3] *pron, pl* **these :** esto <what's this? **:** ¿qué es esto?> <this wasn't here yesterday **:** esto no estaba aquí ayer>

thistle [ˈθɪsəl] *n* **:** cardo *m*

thong [ˈθɔŋ] *n* **1** STRAP **:** correa *f,* tira *f* **2** *or* **thong sandal :** chancla *f,* chancleta *f*

thorax [ˈθorˌæks] *n, pl* **-raxes** *or* **-races** [ˈθorəˌsiːz] **:** tórax *m*

thorn [ˈθɔrn] *n* **:** espina *f*

thorny [ˈθɔrni] *adj* **thornier; -est :** espinoso

thorough [ˈθəroː] *adj* **1** CONSCIENTIOUS **:** concienzudo, meticuloso **2** COMPLETE **:** absoluto, completo — **thoroughly** *adv*

thoroughbred [ˈθəroˌbrɛd] *adj* **:** de pura sangre (dícese de un caballo)

Thoroughbred *n or* **Thoroughbred horse :** pura sangre *mf*

thoroughfare [ˈθəroˌfær] *n* **:** vía *f* pública, carretera *f*

thoroughness [ˈθəronəs] *n* **:** esmero *m,* meticulosidad *f*

those → **that**

thou [ˈðaʊ] *pron* **:** tú

though[1] [ˈðoː] *adv* **1** HOWEVER, NEVERTHELESS **:** sin embargo, no obstante **2 as ~ :** como si <as though nothing had happened **:** como si nada hubiera pasado>

though[2] *conj* **:** aunque, a pesar de <though it was raining, we went out **:** salimos a pesar de la lluvia>

thought[1] → **think**

thought[2] [ˈθɔt] *n* **1** THINKING **:** pensamiento *m,* ideas *fpl* <Western thought **:** el pensamiento occidental> **2** COGITATION **:** pensamiento *m,* reflexión *f,* raciocinio *m* **3** IDEA **:** idea *f,* ocurrencia *f* <it was just a thought **:** fue sólo una idea>

thoughtful [ˈθɔtfəl] *adj* **1** PENSIVE **:** pensativo, meditabundo **2** CONSIDERATE **:** considerado, atento, cortés — **thoughtfully** *adv*

thoughtfulness [ˈθɔtfəlnəs] *n* **:** consideración *f,* atención *f,* cortesía *f*

thoughtless [ˈθɔtləs] *adj* **1** CARELESS : descuidado, negligente **2** INCONSIDERATE : desconsiderado — **thoughtlessly** *adv*

thousand[1] [ˈθaʊzənd] *adj* : mil

thousand[2] *n, pl* **-sands** *or* **-sand** : mil *m*

thousandth[1] [ˈθaʊzəntθ] *adj* : milésimo

thousandth[2] *n* **1** : milésimo *m,* -ma *f* (en una serie) **2** : milésimo *m,* milésima parte *f*

thrash [ˈθræʃ] *vt* **1** → **thresh 2** BEAT : golpear, azotar, darle una paliza (a alguien) **3** FLAIL : sacudir, agitar bruscamente

thread[1] [ˈθrɛd] *vt* **1** : enhilar, enhebrar (una aguja) **2** STRING : ensartar (cuentas en un hilo) **3 to thread one's way** : abrirse paso

thread[2] *n* **1** : hilo *m,* hebra *f* <needle and thread : aguja e hilo> <the thread of an argument : el hilo de un debate> **2** : rosca *f,* filete *m* (de un tornillo)

threadbare [ˈθrɛdˈbær] *adj* **1** SHABBY, WORN : raído, gastado **2** TRITE : trillado, tópico, manido

threat [ˈθrɛt] *n* : amenaza *f*

threaten [ˈθrɛtən] *v* : amenazar

threatening [ˈθrɛtənɪŋ] *adj* : amenazador — **threateningly** *adv*

three[1] [ˈθriː] *adj* : tres

three[2] *n* : tres *m*

threefold [ˈθriːˌfoːld] *adj* TRIPLE : triple

three hundred[1] *adj* : trescientos

three hundred[2] *n* : trescientos *m*

threescore [ˈθriːˈskor] *adj* SIXTY : sesenta

thresh [ˈθrɛʃ] *vt* : trillar (grano)

thresher [ˈθrɛʃər] *n* : trilladora *f*

threshold [ˈθrɛʃˌhoːld, -ˌoːld] *n* : umbral *m*

threw → **throw**[1]

thrice [ˈθraɪs] *adv* : tres veces

thrift [ˈθrɪft] *n* : economía *f,* frugalidad *f*

thriftless [ˈθrɪftləs] *adj* : despilfarrador, manirroto

thrifty [ˈθrɪfti] *adj* **thriftier; -est** : económico, frugal — **thriftily** [ˈθrɪftəli] *adv*

thrill[1] [ˈθrɪl] *vt* : emocionar — *vi* **to thrill to** : dejarse conmover por, estremecerse con

thrill[2] *n* : emoción *f*

thriller [ˈθrɪlər] *n* **1** : evento *m* emocionante **2** : obra *f* de suspenso

thrilling [ˈθrɪlɪŋ] *adj* : emocionante, excitante

thrive [ˈθraɪv] *vi* **throve** [ˈθroːv] *or* **thrived; thriven** [ˈθrɪvən] **1** FLOURISH : florecer, crecer abundantemente **2** PROSPER : prosperar

throat [ˈθroːt] *n* : garganta *f*

throaty [ˈθroːti] *adj* **throatier; -est** : ronco (dícese de la voz)

throb[1] [ˈθrɑb] *vi* **throbbed; throbbing** : palpitar, latir (dícese del corazón), vibrar (dícese de un motor, etc.)

throb[2] *n* : palpitación *f,* latido *m,* vibración *f*

throe [ˈθroː] *n* **1** PAIN, SPASM : espasmo *m,* dolor *m* <the throes of childbirth : los dolores de parto> **2 throes** *npl* : lucha *f* larga y ardua <in the throes of : en el medio de>

throne [ˈθroːn] *n* : trono *m*

throng[1] [ˈθrɔŋ] *vt* CROWD : atestar, atiborrar, llenar — *vi* : aglomerarse, amontonarse

throng[2] *n* : muchedumbre *f,* gentío *m,* multitud *f*

throttle[1] [ˈθrɑtəl] *vt* **-tled; -tling 1** STRANGLE : estrangular, ahogar **2 to throttle down** : desacelerar (un motor)

throttle[2] *n* **1** : válvula *f* reguladora **2 at full throttle** : a toda máquina

through[1] [ˈθruː] *adv* **1** : a través, de un lado a otro <let them through : déjenlos pasar> **2** : de principio a fin <she read the book through : leyó el libro de principio a fin> **3** COMPLETELY : completamente <soaked through : completamente empapado>

through[2] *adj* **1** DIRECT : directo <a through train : un tren directo> **2** FINISHED : terminado, acabado <we're through : hemos terminado>

through[3] *prep* **1** : a través de, por <through the door : por la puerta> <a road through the woods : un camino que atraviesa el bosque> **2** BETWEEN : entre <a path through the trees : un sendero entre los árboles> **3** BECAUSE OF : a causa de, como consecuencia de **4** (*in expressions of time*) <through the night : durante la noche> <to go through an experience : pasar por una experiencia> **5** : a, hasta <from Monday through Friday : de lunes a viernes>

throughout[1] [θruːˈaʊt] *adv* **1** EVERYWHERE : por todas partes **2** THROUGH : desde el principio hasta el fin de (algo)

throughout[2] *prep* **1** : en todas partes de, a través de <throughout the United States : en todo Estados Unidos> **2** : de principio a fin de, durante <throughout the winter : durante todo el invierno>

throve → **thrive**

throw[1] [ˈθroː] *vt* **threw** [ˈθruː]; **thrown** [ˈθroːn]; **throwing 1** TOSS : tirar, lanzar, echar, arrojar, aventar *Col, Mex* <to throw a ball : tirar una pelota> **2** UNSEAT : desmontar (a un jinete) **3** CAST : proyectar <it threw a long shadow : proyectó una sombra larga> **4 to throw a party** : dar una fiesta **5 to throw into confusion** : desconcertar **6 to throw out** DISCARD : botar, tirar (en la basura)

throw[2] *n* TOSS : tiro *m,* tirada *f,* lanzamiento *m,* lance *m* (de dados)
thrower [ˈθro:ər] *n* : lanzador *m,* -dora *f*
throw up *v* VOMIT : vomitar, devolver
thrush [ˈθrʌʃ] *n* : tordo *m,* zorzal *m*
thrust[1] [ˈθrʌst] *vt* **thrust; thrusting 1** SHOVE : empujar bruscamente **2** PLUNGE, STAB : apuñalar, clavar <he thrust a dagger into her heart : la apuñaló en el corazón> **3 to thrust one's way** : abrirse paso **4 to thrust upon** : imponer a
thrust[2] *n* **1** PUSH, SHOVE : empujón *m,* empellón *m* **2** LUNGE : estocada *f* (en esgrima) **3** IMPETUS : ímpetu *m,* impulso *m,* propulsión *f* (de un motor)
thud[1] [ˈθʌd] *vi* **thudded; thudding** : producir un ruido sordo
thud[2] *n* : ruido *m* sordo (que produce un objeto al caer)
thug [ˈθʌg] *n* : matón *m*
thumb[1] [ˈθʌm] *vt* : hojear (con el pulgar)
thumb[2] *n* : pulgar *m,* dedo *m* pulgar
thumbnail [ˈθʌm,neɪl] *n* : uña *f* del pulgar
thumbtack [ˈθʌm,tæk] *n* : tachuela *f,* chinche *f*
thump[1] [ˈθʌmp] *vt* POUND : golpear, aporrear — *vi* : latir con vehemencia (dícese del corazón)
thump[2] *n* THUD : ruido *m* sordo
thunder[1] [ˈθʌndər] *vi* **1** : tronar <it rained and thundered all night : llovió y tronó durante la noche> **2** BOOM : retumbar, bramar, resonar — *vt* ROAR, SHOUT : decir a gritos, vociferar
thunder[2] *n* : truenos *mpl*
thunderbolt [ˈθʌndər,bo:lt] *n* : rayo *m*
thunderclap [ˈθʌndər,klæp] *n* : trueno *m*
thunderous [ˈθʌndərəs] *adj* : atronador, ensordecedor, estruendoso
thundershower [ˈθʌndər,ʃaʊər] *n* : lluvia *f* con truenos y relámpagos
thunderstorm [ˈθʌndər,stɔrm] *n* : tormenta *f* con truenos y relámpagos
thunderstruck [ˈθʌndər,strʌk] *adj* : atónito
Thursday [ˈθərz,deɪ, -di] *n* : jueves *m*
thus [ˈðʌs] *adv* **1** : así, de esta manera **2** SO : hasta (cierto punto) <the weather's been nice thus far : hasta ahora ha hecho buen tiempo> **3** HENCE : por consiguiente, por lo tanto
thwart [ˈθwɔrt] *vt* : frustrar
thy [ˈðaɪ] *adj* : tu
thyme [ˈtaɪm, ˈθaɪm] *n* : tomillo *m*
thyroid [ˈθaɪ,rɔɪd] *n or* **thyroid gland** : tiroides *mf,* glándula *f* tiroidea
thyself [ðaɪˈsɛlf] *pron* : ti, ti mismo
tiara [tiˈærə, -ˈɑr-] *n* : diadema *f*
tibia [ˈtɪbiə] *n, pl* **-iae** [-bi,i:] : tibia *f*
tic [ˈtɪk] *n* : tic *m*
tick[1] [ˈtɪk] *vi* **1** : hacer tictac **2** OPERATE, RUN : operar, andar (dícese de un mecanismo) <what makes him tick? : ¿qué es lo que lo mueve?> — *vt or* **to tick off** CHECK : marcar
tick[2] *n* **1** : tictac *m* (de un reloj) **2** CHECK : marca *f* **3** : garrapata *f* (insecto)
ticket[1] [ˈtɪkət] *vt* LABEL : etiquetar
ticket[2] *n* **1** : boleto *m,* entrada *f* (de un espectáculo), pasaje *m* (de avión, tren, etc.) **2** SLATE : lista *f* de candidatos
tickle[1] [ˈtɪkəl] *v* **-led; -ling** *vt* **1** AMUSE : divertir, hacerle gracia (a alguien) **2** : hacerle cosquillas (a alguien) <don't tickle me! : ¡no me hagas cosquillas!> — *vi* : picar
tickle[2] *n* : cosquilla *f*
ticklish [ˈtɪkəlɪʃ] *adj* **1** : cosquilloso (dícese de una persona) **2** DELICATE, TRICKY : delicado, peliagudo
tidal [ˈtaɪdəl] *adj* : de marea, relativo a la marea
tidal wave *n* : maremoto *m*
tidbit [ˈtɪd,bɪt] *n* **1** BITE, SNACK : bocado *m,* golosina *f* **2** : dato *m* o noticia *f* interesante <useful tidbits of information : informaciones útiles>
tide[1] [ˈtaɪd] *vt* **tided; tiding** *or* **to tide over** : proveer lo necesario para aguantar una dificultad <this money will tide you over until you find work : este dinero te mantendrá hasta que encuentres empleo>
tide[2] *n* **1** : marea *f* **2** CURRENT : corriente *f* (de eventos, opiniones, etc.)
tidily [ˈtaɪdəli] *adv* : ordenadamente
tidiness [ˈtaɪdinəs] *n* : aseo *m,* limpieza *f,* orden *m*
tidings [ˈtaɪdɪŋz] *npl* : nuevas *fpl*
tidy[1] [ˈtaɪdi] *vt* **-died; -dying** : asear, limpiar, poner en orden
tidy[2] *adj* **-dier; -est 1** CLEAN, NEAT : limpio, aseado, en orden **2** SUBSTANTIAL : grande, considerable <a tidy sum : una suma considerable>
tie[1] [ˈtaɪ] *v* **tied; tying** *or* **tieing** *vt* **1** : atar, amarrar <to tie a knot : atar un nudo> <to tie one's shoelaces : atarse los cordones> **2** BIND, UNITE : ligar, atar **3** : empatar <they tied the score : empataron el marcador> — *vi* : empatar <the two teams were tied : los dos equipos empataron>
tie[2] *n* **1** : ligadura *f,* cuerda *f,* cordón *m* (para atar algo) **2** BOND, LINK : atadura *f,* ligadura *f,* vínculo *m,* lazo *m* <family ties : lazos familiares> **3** *or* **railroad tie** : traviesa *f* **4** DRAW : empate *m* (en deportes) **5** NECKTIE : corbata *f*
tier [ˈtɪr] *n* : hilera *f,* escalón *m*
tiff [ˈtɪf] *n* : disgusto *m,* disputa *f*
tiger [ˈtaɪgər] *n* : tigre *m*
tight[1] [ˈtaɪt] *adv* TIGHTLY : bien, fuerte <shut it tight : ciérralo bien>
tight[2] *adj* **1** : bien cerrado, hermético <a tight seal : un cierre hermético> **2** STRICT : estricto, severo **3** TAUT : tirante, tenso **4** SNUG : apretado, ajustado, ceñido <a tight dress : un vestido ceñido> **5** DIFFICULT : difícil <to be in a tight spot : estar en un aprieto> **6** STINGY : apretado, avaro, agarrado

fam **7** CLOSE : reñido <a tight game : un juego reñido> **8** SCARCE : escaso <money is tight : escasea el dinero>

tighten ['taɪtən] *vt* : tensar (una cuerda, etc.), apretar (un nudo, un tornillo, etc.), apretarse (el cinturón), reforzar (las reglas)

tightly ['taɪtli] *adv* : bien, fuerte

tightness ['taɪtnəs] *n* : lo apretado, lo tenso, tensión *f*

tightrope ['taɪt,ro:p] *n* : cuerda *f* floja

tights ['taɪts] *npl* : leotardo *m,* malla *f*

tightwad ['taɪt,wɑd] *n* : avaro *m,* -ra *f;* tacaño *m,* -ña *f*

tigress ['taɪgrəs] *n* : tigresa *f*

tile[1] ['taɪl] *vt* **tiled; tiling** : embaldosar (un piso), revestir de azulejos (una pared), tejar (un techo)

tile[2] *n* **1** *or* **floor tile** : losa *f,* baldosa *f,* mosaico *m Mex* (de un piso) **2** : azulejo *m* (de una pared) **3** : teja *f* (de un techo)

till[1] ['tɪl] *vt* : cultivar, labrar

till[2] *n* : caja *f,* caja *f* registradora

till[3] *prep & conj* → **until**

tiller ['tɪlər] *n* **1** : cultivador *m,* -dora *f* (de la tierra) **2** : caña *f* del timón (de un barco)

tilt[1] ['tɪlt] *vt* : ladear, inclinar — *vi* : ladearse, inclinarse

tilt[2] *n* **1** SLANT : inclinación *f* **2 at full tilt** : a toda velocidad

timber ['tɪmbər] *n* **1** : madera *f* (para construcción) **2** BEAM : viga *f*

timberland ['tɪmbər,lænd] *n* : bosque *m* maderero

timbre ['tæmbər, 'tɪm-] *n* : timbre *m*

time[1] ['taɪm] *vt* **timed; timing 1** SCHEDULE : fijar la hora de, calcular el momento oportuno para **2** CLOCK : cronometrar, medir el tiempo de (una competencia, etc.)

time[2] *n* **1** : tiempo *m* <the passing of time : el paso del tiempo> <she doesn't have time : no tiene tiempo> **2** MOMENT : tiempo *m,* momento *m* <this is not the time to bring it up : no es el momento de sacar el tema> **3** : vez *f* <she called you three times : te llamó tres veces> <three times greater : tres veces mayor> **4** AGE : tiempo *m,* era *f* <in your grandparents' time : en el tiempo de tus abuelos> **5** TEMPO : tiempo *m,* ritmo *m* (en música) **6** : hora *f* <what time is it? : ¿qué hora es?> <at the usual time : a la hora acostumbrada> <to keep time : ir a la hora> <to lose time : atrasar> **7** EXPERIENCE : rato *m,* experiencia *f* <we had a nice time together : pasamos juntos un rato agradable> <to have a rough time : pasarlo mal> <have a good time! : ¡que se diviertan!> **8 at times** SOMETIMES : a veces **9 for the time being** : por el momento, de momento **10 from time to time** OCCASIONALLY : de vez en cuando **11 in time** PUNCTUALLY : a tiempo **12 in time** EVENTUALLY : con el tiempo **13 time after time** : una y otra vez

timekeeper ['taɪm,ki:pər] *n* : cronometrador *m,* -dora *f*

timeless ['taɪmləs] *adj* : eterno

timely ['taɪmli] *adj* **-lier; -est** : oportuno

timepiece ['taɪm,pi:s] *n* : reloj *m*

timer ['taɪmər] *n* : temporizador *m,* cronómetro *m*

times ['taɪmz] *prep* : por <3 times 4 is 12 : 3 por 4 son 12>

timetable ['taɪm,teɪbəl] *n* : horario *m*

timid ['tɪmɪd] *adj* : tímido — **timidly** *adv*

timidity [tə'mɪdəti] *n* : timidez *f*

timorous ['tɪmərəs] *adj* : timorato, miedoso

timpani ['tɪmpəni] *npl* : timbales *mpl*

tin ['tɪn] *n* **1** : estaño *m,* hojalata *f* (metal) **2** CAN : lata *f,* bote *m,* envase *m*

tincture ['tɪŋktʃər] *n* : tintura *f*

tinder ['tɪndər] *n* : yesca *f*

tine ['taɪn] *n* : diente *m* (de un tenedor, etc.)

tinfoil ['tɪn,fɔɪl] *n* : papel *m* (de) aluminio

tinge[1] ['tɪndʒ] *vt* **tinged; tingeing** *or* **tinging** ['tɪndʒɪŋ] TINT : matizar, teñir ligeramente

tinge[2] *n* **1** TINT : matiz *m,* tinte *m* sutil **2** TOUCH : dejo *m,* sensación *f* ligera

tingle[1] ['tɪŋgəl] *vi* **-gled; -gling** : sentir (un) hormigueo, sentir (un) cosquilleo

tingle[2] *n* : hormigueo *m,* cosquilleo *m*

tinker ['tɪŋkər] *vi* **to tinker with** : arreglar con pequeños ajustes, toquetear (con intento de arreglar)

tinkle[1] ['tɪŋkəl] *vi* **-kled; -kling** : tintinear

tinkle[2] *n* : tintineo *m*

tinsel ['tɪntsəl] *n* : oropel *m*

tint[1] ['tɪnt] *vt* : teñir, colorar

tint[2] *n* : tinte *m*

tiny ['taɪni] *adj* **-nier; -est** : diminuto, minúsculo

tip[1] ['tɪp] *v* **tipped; tipping** *vt* **1** *or* **to tip over** : volcar, voltear, hacer caer **2** TILT : ladear, inclinar <to tip one's hat : saludar con el sombrero> **3** TAP : tocar, golpear ligeramente **4** : darle una propina (a un mesero, etc.) <I tipped him $5 : le di $5 de propina> **5** : adornar o cubrir la punta de <wings tipped in red : alas que tienen las puntas rojas> **6 to tip off** : dar información a — *vi* TILT : ladearse, inclinarse

tip[2] *n* **1** END, POINT : punta *f,* extremo *m* <on the tip of one's tongue : en la punta de la lengua> **2** GRATUITY : propina *f* **3** ADVICE, INFORMATION : consejo *m,* información *f* (confidencial)

tip–off ['tɪp,ɔf] *n* **1** SIGN : indicación *f,* señal *f* **2** TIP : información *f* (confidencial)

tipple [ˈtɪpəl] *vi* **-pled; -pling** : tomarse unas copas
tipsy [ˈtɪpsi] *adj* **-sier; -est** : achispado
tiptoe[1] [ˈtɪp,toː] *vi* **-toed; -toeing** : caminar de puntillas
tiptoe[2] *adv* : de puntillas
tiptoe[3] *n* : punta *f* del pie
tip–top[1] [ˈtɪpˈtɑp, -,tɑp] *adj* EXCELLENT : excelente
tip–top[2] *n* SUMMIT : cumbre *f,* cima *f*
tirade [ˈtaɪ,reɪd] *n* : diatriba *f*
tire[1] [ˈtaɪr] *v* **tired; tiring** *vt* : cansar, agotar, fatigar — *vi* : cansarse
tire[2] *n* : llanta *f,* neumático *m,* goma *f*
tired [ˈtaɪrd] *adj* : cansado, agotado, fatigado <to get tired : cansarse>
tireless [ˈtaɪrləs] *adj* : incansable, infatigable — **tirelessly** *adv*
tiresome [ˈtaɪrsəm] *adj* : fastidioso, pesado, tedioso — **tiresomely** *adv*
tissue [ˈtɪ,ʃuː] *n* **1** : pañuelo *m* de papel **2** : tejido *m* <lung tissue : tejido pulmonar>
titanic [taɪˈtænɪk, tə-] *adj* GIGANTIC : titánico, gigantesco
titanium [taɪˈteɪniəm, tə-] *n* : titanio *m*
titillate [ˈtɪtəl,eɪt] *vt* **-lated; -lating** : excitar, estimular placenteramente
title[1] [ˈtaɪṱəl] *vt* **-tled; -tling** : titular, intitular
title[2] *n* : título *m*
titter[1] [ˈtɪṱər] *vi* GIGGLE : reírse tontamente
titter[2] *n* : risita *f,* risa *f* tonta
tizzy [ˈtɪzi] *n, pl* **tizzies** : estado *m* agitado o nervioso <I'm all in a tizzy : estoy todo alterado>
TNT [,tiː,ɛnˈtiː] *n* : TNT *m*
to[1] [ˈtuː] *adv* **1** : a un estado consciente <to come to : volver en sí> **2 to and fro** : de aquí para allá, de un lado para otro
to[2] *prep* **1** (*indicating a place*) : a <to go to the doctor : ir al médico> <I'm going to John's : voy a la casa de John> **2** TOWARD : a, hacia <two miles to the south : dos millas hacia el sur> **3** ON : en, sobre <apply salve to the wound : póngale ungüento a la herida> **4** UP TO : hasta, a <to a degree : hasta cierto grado> <from head to toe : de pies a cabeza> **5** (*in expressions of time*) <it's quarter to seven : son las siete menos cuarto> **6** UNTIL : a, hasta <from May to December : de mayo a diciembre> **7** (*indicating belonging or possession*) : de, a <the key to the lock : la llave del candado> **8** (*indicating response*) : a <dancing to the rhythm : bailando al compás> **9** (*indicating comparison or proportion*) : a <it's similar to mine : es parecido al mío> <they won 4 to 2 : ganaron 4 a 2> **10** (*indicating agreement or conformity*) : a, de acuerdo con <made to order : hecho a la orden> <to my knowledge : a mi saber> **11** (*indicating inclusion*) : en cada, por <twenty to the box : veinte por caja> **12** (*used to form the infinitive*) <to understand : entender> <to go away : irse>
toad [ˈtoːd] *n* : sapo *m*
toadstool [ˈtoːd,stuːl] *n* : hongo *m* (no comestible)
toady [ˈtoːdi] *n, pl* **toadies** : adulador *m,* -dora *f*
toast[1] [ˈtoːst] *vt* **1** : tostar (pan) **2** : brindar por <to toast the victors : brindar por los vencedores> **3** WARM : calentar <to toast oneself : calentarse>
toast[2] *n* **1** : pan *m* tostado, tostadas *fpl* **2** : brindis *m* <to propose a toast : proponer un brindis>
toaster [ˈtoːstər] *n* : tostador *m*
tobacco [təˈbækoː] *n, pl* **-cos** : tabaco *m*
toboggan[1] [təˈbɑgən] *vi* : deslizarse en tobogán
toboggan[2] *n* : tobogán *m*
today[1] [təˈdeɪ] *adv* **1** : hoy <she arrives today : hoy llega> **2** NOWADAYS : hoy en día
today[2] *n* : hoy *m* <today is a holiday : hoy es día de fiesta>
toddle [ˈtɑdəl] *vi* **-dled; -dling** : hacer pininos, hacer pinitos
toddler [ˈtɑdələr] *n* : niño *m* pequeño, niña *f* pequeña (que comienza a caminar)
to–do [təˈduː] *n, pl* **to–dos** [-ˈduːz] FUSS : lío *m,* alboroto *m*
toe [ˈtoː] *n* : dedo *m* del pie
toenail [ˈtoː,neɪl] *n* : uña *f* del pie
toffee *or* **toffy** [ˈtɔfi, ˈtɑ-] *n, pl* **toffees** *or* **toffies** : caramelo *m* elaborado con azúcar y mantequilla
toga [ˈtoːgə] *n* : toga *f*
together [təˈgɛðər] *adv* **1** : juntamente, juntos (el uno con el otro) <Susan and Sarah work together : Susan y Sarah trabajan juntas> **2 ~ with** : junto con
togetherness [təˈgɛðərnəs] *n* : unión *f,* compañerismo *m*
togs [ˈtɑgz, ˈtɔgz] *npl* : ropa *f*
toil[1] [ˈtɔɪl] *vi* : trabajar arduamente
toil[2] *n* : trabajo *m* arduo
toilet [ˈtɔɪlət] *n* **1** : arreglo *m* personal **2** BATHROOM : (cuarto de) baño *m,* servicios *mpl* (públicos), sanitario *m Col, Mex, Ven* **3** : inodoro *m* <to flush the toilet : jalar la cadena>
toilet paper *n* : papel *m* higiénico
toiletries [ˈtɔɪlətriz] *npl* : artículos *mpl* de tocador
token [ˈtoːkən] *n* **1** PROOF, SIGN : prueba *f,* muestra *f,* señal *m* **2** SYMBOL : símbolo *m* **3** SOUVENIR : recuerdo *m* **4** : ficha *f* (para transporte público, etc.)
told → **tell**
tolerable [ˈtɑlərəbəl] *adj* : tolerable — **tolerably** [-bli] *adv*
tolerance [ˈtɑlərənts] *n* : tolerancia *f*
tolerant [ˈtɑlərənt] *adj* : tolerante — **tolerantly** *adv*

tolerate ['tɑlə,reɪt] *vt* **-ated; -ating 1** ACCEPT : tolerar, aceptar **2** BEAR, ENDURE : tolerar, aguantar, soportar

toleration [,tɑlə'reɪʃən] *n* : tolerancia *f*

toll[1] ['to:l] *vt* : tañer, sonar (una campana) — *vi* : sonar, doblar (dícese de las campanas)

toll[2] *n* **1** : peaje *m* (de una carretera, un puente, etc.) **2** CASUALTIES : pérdida *f,* número *m* de víctimas **3** TOLLING : tañido *m* (de campanas)

tollbooth ['to:l,bu:θ] *n* : caseta *f* de peaje

tollgate ['to:l,geɪt] *n* : barrera *f* de peaje

tomahawk ['tɑmə,hɔk] *n* : hacha *f* de guerra (de los indígenas norteamericanos)

tomato [tə'meɪt̬o, -'mɑ-] *n, pl* **-toes** : tomate *m*

tomb ['tu:m] *n* : sepulcro *m,* tumba *f*

tomboy ['tɑm,bɔɪ] *n* : marimacho *mf;* niña *f* que se porta como muchacho

tombstone ['tu:m,sto:n] *n* : lápida *f*

tomcat ['tɑm,kæt] *n* : gato *m* (macho)

tome ['to:m] *n* : tomo *m*

tomorrow[1] [tə'mɑro] *adv* : mañana

tomorrow[2] *n* : mañana *m*

tom–tom ['tɑm,tɑm] *n* : tam-tam *m*

ton ['tən] *n* : tonelada *f*

tone[1] ['to:n] *vt* **toned; toning 1** *or* **to tone down** : atenuar, suavizar, moderar **2** *or* **to tone up** STRENGTHEN : tonificar, vigorizar

tone[2] *n* : tono *m* <in a friendly tone : en tono amistoso> <a greyish tone : un tono grisáceo>

tongs ['tɑŋz, 'tɔŋz] *npl* : tenazas *fpl*

tongue ['tʌŋ] *n* **1** : lengua *f* **2** LANGUAGE : lengua *f,* idioma *m*

tongue–tied ['tʌŋ,taɪd] *adj* **to get tongue–tied** : trabársele la lengua a uno

tonic[1] ['tɑnɪk] *adj* : tónico

tonic[2] *n* **1** : tónico *m* **2** *or* **tonic water** : tónica *f*

tonight[1] [tə'naɪt] *adv* : esta noche

tonight[2] *n* : esta noche *f*

tonsil ['tɑn*t*səl] *n* : amígdala *f,* angina *f Mex*

tonsillitis [,tɑn*t*sə'laɪt̬əs] *n* : amigdalitis *f,* anginas *fpl Mex*

too ['tu:] *adv* **1** ALSO : también **2** EXCESSIVELY : demasiado <it's too hot in here : aquí hace demasiado calor>

took → **take**[1]

tool[1] ['tu:l] *vt* **1** : fabricar, confeccionar (con herramientas) **2** EQUIP : instalar maquinaria en (una fábrica)

tool[2] *n* : herramienta *f*

toolbox ['tu:l,bɑks] *n* : caja *f* de herramientas

toot[1] ['tu:t] *vt* : sonar (un claxon o un pito)

toot[2] *n* : pitido *m,* bocinazo *m* (de un claxon)

tooth ['tu:θ] *n, pl* **teeth** ['ti:θ] : diente *m*

toothache ['tu:θ,eɪk] *n* : dolor *m* de muelas

toothbrush ['tu:θ,brʌʃ] *n* : cepillo *m* de dientes

toothless ['tu:θləs] *adj* : desdentado

toothpaste ['tu:θ,peɪst] *n* : pasta *f* de dientes, crema *f* dental, dentífrico *m*

toothpick ['tu:θ,pɪk] *n* : palillo *m* (de dientes), mondadientes *m*

top[1] ['tɑp] *vt* **topped; topping 1** COVER : cubrir, coronar **2** SURPASS : sobrepasar, superar **3** CLEAR : pasar por encima de

top[2] *adj* : superior <the top shelf : la repisa superior> <one of the top lawyers : uno de los mejores abogados>

top[3] *n* **1** : parte *f* superior, cumbre *f,* cima *f* (de un monte, etc.) <to climb to the top : subir a la cumbre> **2** COVER : tapa *f,* cubierta *f* **3** : trompo *m* (juguete) **4 on top of** : encima de

topaz ['to:,pæz] *n* : topacio *m*

topcoat ['tɑp,ko:t] *n* : sobretodo *m,* abrigo *m*

topic ['tɑpɪk] *n* : tema *f,* tópico *m*

topical ['tɑpɪkəl] *adj* : de interés actual

topmost ['tɑp,mo:st] *adj* : más alto

top–notch ['tɑp'nɑtʃ] *adj* : de lo mejor, de primera categoría

topographic [,tɑpə'græfɪk,] *or* **topographical** [-fɪkəl] *adj* : topográfico

topography [tə'pɑgrəfi] *n, pl* **-phies** : topografía *f*

topple ['tɑpəl] *v* **-pled; -pling** *vi* : caerse, venirse abajo — *vt* : volcar, derrocar (un gobierno, etc.)

topsoil ['tɑp,sɔɪl] *n* : capa *f* superior del suelo

topsy–turvy [,tɑpsi'tərvi] *adv & adj* : patas arriba, al revés

torch ['tɔrtʃ] *n* : antorcha *f*

tore → **tear**[1]

torment[1] [tɔr'mɛnt, 'tɔr,-] *vt* : atormentar, torturar, martirizar

torment[2] ['tɔr,mɛnt] *n* : tormento *m,* suplicio *m,* martirio *m*

tormentor [tɔr'mɛntər] *n* : atormentador *m,* -dora *f*

torn → **tear**[1]

tornado [tɔr'neɪdo] *n, pl* **-does** *or* **-dos** : tornado *m*

torpedo[1] [tɔr'pi:do] *vt* : torpedear

torpedo[2] *n, pl* **-does** : torpedo *m*

torpid ['tɔrpɪd] *adj* **1** SLUGGISH : aletargado **2** APATHETIC : apático

torpor ['tɔrpər] *n* : letargo *m,* apatía *f*

torrent ['tɔrənt] *n* : torrente *m*

torrential [tɔ'rɛntʃəl, tə-] *adj* : torrencial

torrid ['tɔrɪd] *adj* : tórrido

torso ['tɔr,so:] *n, pl* **-sos** *or* **-si** [-,si:] : torso *m*

tortilla [tɔr'ti:jə] *n* : tortilla *f*

tortoise ['tɔrt̬əs] *n* : tortuga *f* (terrestre)

tortoiseshell ['tɔrt̬əs,ʃɛl] *n* : carey *m,* concha *f*

tortuous ['tɔrtʃʊəs] *adj* : tortuoso

torture[1] [ˈtɔrtʃər] *vt* **-tured; -turing** : torturar, atormentar

torture[2] *n* : tortura *f,* tormento *m* <it was sheer torture! : ¡fue un verdadero suplicio!>

torturer [ˈtɔrtʃərər] *n* : torturador *m,* -dora *f*

toss[1] [ˈtɔs, ˈtɑs] *vt* **1** AGITATE, SHAKE : sacudir, agitar, mezclar (una ensalada) **2** THROW : tirar, echar, lanzar — *vi* : sacudirse, moverse agitadamente <to toss and turn : dar vueltas>

toss[2] *n* THROW : lanzamiento *m,* tiro *m,* tirada *f,* lance *m* (de dados, etc.)

toss–up [ˈtɔs,ʌp] *n* : posibilidad *f* igual <it's a toss-up : quizá sí, quizá no>

tot [ˈtɑt] *n* : pequeño *m,* -ña *f*

total[1] [ˈto:tǝl] *vt* **-taled** *or* **-talled; -taling** *or* **-talling 1** *or* **to total up** ADD : sumar, totalizar **2** AMOUNT TO : ascender a, llegar a

total[2] *adj* : total, completo, absoluto — **totally** *adv*

total[3] *n* : total *m*

totalitarian [to:,tæləˈtɛriən] *adj* : totalitario

totalitarianism [to:,tæləˈtɛriə,nɪzəm] *n* : totalitarismo *m*

totality [to:ˈtælǝti] *n, pl* **-ties** : totalidad *f*

tote [ˈto:t] *vt* **toted; toting** : cargar, llevar

totem [ˈto:təm] *n* : tótem *m*

totter [ˈtɑtər] *vi* : tambalearse

touch[1] [ˈtʌtʃ] *vt* **1** FEEL, HANDLE : tocar, tentar **2** AFFECT, MOVE : conmover, afectar, tocar <his gesture touched our hearts : su gesto nos tocó el corazón> — *vi* : tocarse

touch[2] *n* **1** : tacto *m* (sentido) **2** DETAIL : toque *m,* detalle *m* <a touch of color : un toque de color> **3** BIT : pizca *f,* gota *f,* poco *m* **4** ABILITY : habilidad *f* <to lose one's touch : perder la habilidad> **5** CONTACT : contacto *m,* comunicación *f* <to keep in touch : mantenerse en contacto>

touchdown [ˈtʌtʃ,daʊn] *n* : touchdown *m* (en futbol americano)

touch up *vt* : retocar

touchy [ˈtʌtʃi] *adj* **touchier; -est 1** : sensible, susceptible (dícese de una persona) **2** : delicado <a touchy subject : un tema delicado>

tough[1] [ˈtʌf] *adj* **1** STRONG : fuerte, resistente (dícese de materiales) **2** LEATHERY : correoso <a tough steak : un bistec duro> **3** HARDY : fuerte, robusto (dícese de una persona) **4** STRICT : severo, exigente **5** DIFFICULT : difícil **6** STUBBORN : terco, obstinado

tough[2] *n* : matón *m,* persona *f* ruda y brusca

toughen [ˈtʌfən] *vt* : fortalecer, endurecer — *vi* : endurecerse, hacerse más fuerte

toughness [ˈtʌfnəs] *n* : dureza *f*

toupee [tu:ˈpeɪ] *n* : peluquín *m,* bisoñé *m*

tour[1] [ˈtʊr] *vi* : tomar una excursión, viajar — *vt* : recorrer, hacer una gira por

tour[2] *n* **1** : gira *f,* tour *m,* excursión *f* **2 tour of duty** : período *m* de servicio

tourist [ˈtʊrɪst, ˈtər-] *n* : turista *mf*

tournament [ˈtərnəmənt, ˈtʊr-] *n* : torneo *m*

tourniquet [ˈtərnɪkət, ˈtʊr-] *n* : torniquete *m*

tousle [ˈtaʊzəl] *vt* **-sled; -sling** : desarreglar, despeinar (el cabello)

tout [ˈtaʊt] *vt* : promocionar, elogiar (con exageración)

tow[1] [ˈto:] *vt* : remolcar

tow[2] *n* : remolque *m*

toward [ˈtord, təˈwɔrd] *or* **towards** [ˈtordz, təˈwɔrdz] *prep* **1** (*indicating direction*) : hacia, rumbo a <heading toward town : dirigiéndose rumbo al pueblo> <efforts towards peace : esfuerzos hacia la paz> **2** (*indicating time*) : alrededor de <toward midnight : alrededor de la medianoche> **3** REGARDING : hacia, con respecto a <his attitude toward life : su actitud hacia la vida> **4** FOR : para, como pago parcial de (una compra o deuda)

towel [ˈtaʊəl] *n* : toalla *f*

tower[1] [ˈtaʊər] *vi* **to tower over** : descollar sobre, elevarse sobre, dominar

tower[2] *n* : torre *f*

towering [ˈtaʊərɪŋ] *adj* : altísimo, imponente

town [ˈtaʊn] *n* : pueblo *m,* ciudad *f* (pequeña)

township [ˈtaʊn,ʃɪp] *n* : municipio *m*

tow truck [ˈto:,trʌk] *n* : grúa *f*

toxic [ˈtɑksɪk] *adj* : tóxico

toxicity [tɑkˈsɪsəti] *n, pl* **-ties** : toxicidad *f*

toxin [ˈtɑksɪn] *n* : toxina *f*

toy[1] [ˈtɔɪ] *vi* : juguetear, jugar

toy[2] *adj* : de juguete <a toy rifle : un rifle de juguete>

toy[3] *n* : juguete *m*

trace[1] [ˈtreɪs] *vt* **traced; tracing 1** : calcar (un dibujo, etc.) **2** OUTLINE : delinear, trazar (planes, etc.) **3** TRACK : describir (un curso, una historia) **4** FIND : localizar, ubicar

trace[2] *n* **1** SIGN, TRACK : huella *f,* rastro *m,* indicio *m,* vestigio *m* <he disappeared without a trace : desapareció sin dejar rastro> **2** BIT, HINT : pizca *f,* ápice *m,* dejo *m*

trachea [ˈtreɪkiə] *n, pl* **-cheae** [-ki,i:] : tráquea *f*

tracing paper *n* : papel *m* de calcar

track[1] [ˈtræk] *vt* **1** TRAIL : seguir la pista de, rastrear **2** : dejar huellas de <he tracked mud all over : dejó huellas de lodo por todas partes>

track[2] *n* **1** : rastro *m,* huella *f* (de animales), pista *f* (de personas) **2** PATH : pista *f,* sendero *m,* camino *m* **3** *or* **railroad track** : vía *f* (férrea) **4** → **racetrack 5** : oruga *f* (de un tanque,

etc.) **6** : pista *f* (deporte) **7 to keep track of** : llevar la cuenta de
track–and–field [ˈtrækəndˈfiːld] *adj* : de pista y campo
tract [ˈtrækt] *n* **1** AREA : terreno *m*, extensión *f*, área *f* **2** : tracto *m* <digestive tract : tracto digestivo> **3** PAMPHLET : panfleto *m*, folleto *m*
traction [ˈtrækʃən] *n* : tracción *f*
tractor [ˈtræktər] *n* **1** : tractor *m* (vehículo agrícola) **2** TRUCK : camión *m* (con remolque)
trade¹ [ˈtreɪd] *v* **traded; trading** *vi* : comerciar, negociar — *vt* EXCHANGE : intercambiar, canjear
trade² *n* **1** OCCUPATION : oficio *m*, profesión *f*, ocupación *f* <a carpenter by trade : carpintero de oficio> **2** COMMERCE : comercio *m*, industria *f* <free trade : libre comercio> <the book trade : la industria del libro> **3** EXCHANGE : intercambio *m*, canje *m*
trade–in [ˈtreɪdˌɪn] *n* : artículo *m* que se canjea por otro
trademark [ˈtreɪdˌmɑrk] *n* **1** : marca *f* registrada **2** CHARACTERISTIC : sello *m* característico (de un grupo, una persona, etc.)
trader [ˈtreɪdər] *n* : negociante *mf*, tratante *mf*, comerciante *mf*
tradesman [ˈtreɪdzmən] *n, pl* **-men** [-mən, -ˌmɛn] **1** CRAFTSMAN : artesano *m*, -na *f* **2** SHOPKEEPER : tendero *m*, -ra *f*; comerciante *mf*
trade wind *n* : viento *m* alisio
tradition [trəˈdɪʃən] *n* : tradición *f*
traditional [trəˈdɪʃənəl] *adj* : tradicional — **traditionally** *adv*
traffic¹ [ˈtræfɪk] *vi* **trafficked; trafficking** : traficar (en)
traffic² *n* **1** COMMERCE : tráfico *m*, comercio *m* <the drug traffic : el narcotráfico> **2** : tráfico *m*, tránsito *m*, circulación *f* (de vehículos, etc.)
traffic circle *n* : rotonda *f*, glorieta *f*
trafficker [ˈtræfɪkər] *n* : traficante *mf*
traffic light *n* : semáforo *m*, luz *f* (de tránsito)
tragedy [ˈtrædʒədi] *n, pl* **-dies** : tragedia *f*
tragic [ˈtrædʒɪk] *adj* : trágico — **tragically** *adv*
trail¹ [ˈtreɪl] *vi* **1** DRAG : arrastrarse **2** LAG : quedarse atrás, retrasarse **3 to trail away** *or* **to trail off** : disminuir, menguar, desvanecerse — *vt* **1** DRAG : arrastrar **2** PURSUE : perseguir, seguir la pista de
trail² *n* **1** TRACK : rastro *m*, huella *f*, pista *f* <a trail of blood : un rastro de sangre> **2** : cola *f*, estela *f* (de un meteoro) **3** PATH : sendero *m*, camino *m*, vereda *f*
trailer [ˈtreɪlər] *n* **1** : remolque *m*, tráiler *m* (de un camión) **2** : caravana *f* (vivienda ambulante)
train¹ [ˈtreɪn] *vt* **1** : entrenar (atletas), capacitar (empleados), adiestrar, amaestrar (animales) **2** POINT : apuntar (un arma, etc.) — *vi* : entrenar(se) (físicamente), prepararse (profesionalmente) <she's training at the gym : se está entrenando en el gimnasio>
train² *n* **1** : cola *f* (de un vestido) **2** RETINUE : cortejo *m*, séquito *m* **3** SERIES : serie *f* (de eventos) **4** : tren *m* <passenger train : tren de pasajeros>
trainee [treɪˈniː] *n* : aprendiz *m*, -diza *f*
trainer [ˈtreɪnər] *n* : entrenador *m*, -dora *f*
traipse [ˈtreɪps] *vi* **traipsed; traipsing** : andar de un lado para otro, vagar
trait [ˈtreɪt] *n* : rasgo *m*, característica *f*
traitor [ˈtreɪtər] *n* : traidor *m*, -dora *f*
traitorous [ˈtreɪtərəs] *adj* : traidor
trajectory [trəˈdʒɛktəri] *n, pl* **-ries** : trayectoria *f*
tramp¹ [ˈtræmp] *vi* : caminar (a paso pesado) — *vt* : deambular por, vagar por <to tramp the streets : vagar por las calles>
tramp² *n* **1** VAGRANT : vagabundo *m*, -da *f* **2** HIKE : caminata *f*
trample [ˈtræmpəl] *vt* **-pled; -pling** : pisotear, hollar
trampoline [ˌtræmpəˈliːn, ˈtræmpəˌ-] *n* : trampolín *m*, cama *f* elástica
trance [ˈtrænts] *n* : trance *m*
tranquil [ˈtræŋkwəl] *adj* : calmo, tranquilo, sereno — **tranquilly** *adv*
tranquilize [ˈtræŋkwəˌlaɪz] *vt* **-ized; -izing** : tranquilizar
tranquilizer [ˈtræŋkwəˌlaɪzər] *n* : tranquilizante *m*
tranquillity *or* **tranquility** [træŋˈkwɪləti] *n* : sosiego *m*, tranquilidad *f*
transact [trænˈzækt] *vt* : negociar, gestionar, hacer (negocios)
transaction [trænˈzækʃən] *n* **1** : transacción *f*, negocio *m*, operación *f* **2 transactions** *npl* RECORDS : actas *fpl*
transatlantic [ˌtræntsətˈlæntɪk, ˌtrænz-] *adj* : transatlántico
transcend [trænˈsɛnd] *vt* : trascender, sobrepasar
transcribe [trænˈskraɪb] *vt* **-scribed; -scribing** : transcribir
transcript [ˈtrænˌskrɪpt] *n* : copia *f* oficial
transcription [trænˈskrɪpʃən] *n* : transcripción *f*
transfer¹ [træntsˈfər, ˈtræntsˌfər] *v* **-ferred; -ferring** *vt* **1** : trasladar (a una persona), transferir (fondos) **2** : transferir, traspasar, ceder (propiedad) **3** PRINT : imprimir (un diseño) — *vi* **1** MOVE : trasladarse, cambiarse **2** CHANGE : transbordar, cambiar (de un transporte a otro) <she transferred at E Street : hizo un transborde a la calle E>
transfer² [ˈtræntsˌfər] *n* **1** TRANSFERRING : transferencia *f* (de fondos, de

propiedad, etc.), traslado *m* (de una persona) **2** DECAL **:** calcomanía *f* **3** **:** boleto *m* (para cambiar de un avión, etc., a otro)

transferable [trænts'fərəbəl] *adj* **:** transferible

transference [trænts'fərənts] *n* **:** transferencia *f*

transfigure [trænts'fɪgjər] *vt* **-ured; -uring :** transfigurar, transformar

transfix [trænts'fɪks] *vt* **1** PIERCE **:** traspasar, atravesar **2** IMMOBILIZE **:** paralizar

transform [trænts'fɔrm] *vt* **:** transformar

transformation [ˌtræntsfər'meɪʃən] *n* **:** transformación *f*

transformer [trænts'fɔrmər] *n* **:** transformador *m*

transfusion [trænts'fju:ʒən] *n* **:** transfusión *f*

transgress [trænts'grɛs, trænz-] *vt* **:** transgredir, infringir

transgression [trænts'grɛʃən, trænz-] *n* **:** transgresión *f*

transient1 ['træntʃənt, 'trænsiənt] *adj* **:** pasajero, transitorio — **transiently** *adv*

transient2 *n* **:** transeúnte *mf*

transistor [træn'zɪstər, -'sɪs-] *n* **:** transistor *m*

transit ['træntsɪt, 'trænzɪt] *n* **1** PASSAGE **:** pasaje *m*, tránsito *m* <in transit : en tránsito> **2** TRANSPORTATION **:** transporte *m* (público) **3 :** teodolito *m* (instrumento topográfico)

transition [træn'sɪʃən, -'zɪʃ-] *n* **:** transición *f*

transitional [træn'sɪʃənəl, -'zɪʃ-] *adj* **:** de transición

transitive ['træntsət̬ɪv, 'trænzə-] *adj* **:** transitivo

transitory ['træntsəˌtori, 'trænzə-] *adj* **:** transitorio

translate [trænts'leɪt, trænz-; 'trænts,-, 'træns,-] *vt* **-lated; -lating :** traducir

translation [trænts'leɪʃən, trænz-] *n* **:** traducción *f*

translator [trænts'leɪt̬ər, trænz-; 'trænts,-, 'træns,-] *n* **:** traductor *m*, -tora *f*

translucent [trænts'lu:sənt, trænz-] *adj* **:** translúcido

transmission [trænts'mɪʃən, trænz-] *n* **:** transmisión *f*

transmit [trænts'mɪt, trænz-] *vt* **-mitted; -mitting :** transmitir

transmitter [trænts'mɪt̬ər, trænz-; 'trænts,-, 'træns,-] *n* **:** transmisor *m*, emisor *m*

transom ['træntsəm] *n* **:** montante *m* (de una puerta), travesaño *m* (de una ventana)

transparency [trænts'pærəntsi] *n, pl* **-cies :** transparencia *f*

transparent [trænts'pærənt] *adj* **1** **:** transparente, traslúcido <a transparent fabric : una tela transparente> **2** OBVIOUS **:** transparente, obvio, claro — **transparently** *adv*

transpiration [ˌtræntspə'reɪʃən] *n* **:** transpiración *f*

transpire [trænts'paɪr] *vi* **-spired; -spiring 1 :** transpirar (en biología y botanía) **2** TURN OUT **:** resultar **3** HAPPEN **:** suceder, ocurrir, tener lugar

transplant1 [trænts'plænt] *vt* **:** trasplantar

transplant2 ['trænts,plænt] *n* **:** trasplante *m*

transport1 [trænts'port, 'trænts,-] *vt* **1** CARRY **:** transportar, acarrear **2** ENRAPTURE **:** transportar, extasiar

transport2 ['trænts,port] *n* **1** TRANSPORTATION **:** transporte *m*, transportación *f* **2** RAPTURE **:** éxtasis *m* **3** *or* **transport ship :** buque *m* de transporte (de personal militar)

transportation [ˌtræntspər'teɪʃən] *n* **:** transporte *m*, transportación *f*

transpose [trænts'po:z] *vt* **-posed; -posing :** trasponer, trasladar, transportar (una composición musical)

transverse [trænts'vərs, trænz-] *adj* **:** transversal, transverso, oblicuo — **transversely** *adv*

trap1 ['træp] *vt* **trapped; trapping :** atrapar, apresar (en una trampa)

trap2 *n* **:** trampa *f* <to set a trap : tender una trampa>

trapdoor ['træp'dor] *n* **:** trampilla *f*, escotillón *m*

trapeze [træ'pi:z] *n* **:** trapecio *m*

trapezoid ['træpəˌzɔɪd] *n* **:** trapezoide *m*, trapecio *m*

trapper ['træpər] *n* **:** trampero *m*, -ra *f*; cazador *m*, -dora *f* (que usa trampas)

trappings ['træpɪŋz] *npl* **1 :** arreos *mpl*, jaeces *mpl* (de un caballo) **2** ADORNMENTS **:** adornos *mpl*, pompa *f*

trash ['træʃ] *n* **:** basura *f*

trauma ['trɔmə, 'traʊ-] *n* **:** trauma *m*

traumatic [trə'mæt̬ɪk, trɔ-, traʊ-] *adj* **:** traumático

travel1 ['trævəl] *vi* **-eled** *or* **-elled; -eling** *or* **-elling 1** JOURNEY **:** viajar **2** GO, MOVE **:** desplazarse, moverse, ir <the waves travel at uniform speed : las ondas se desplazan a una velocidad uniforme>

travel2 *n* **:** viajes *mpl*

traveler *or* **traveller** ['trævələr] *n* **:** viajero *m*, -ra *f*

traverse [trə'vərs, træ'vərs, 'trævərs] *vt* **-versed; -versing** CROSS **:** atravesar, extenderse a través de, cruzar

travesty ['trævəsti] *n, pl* **-ties :** parodia *f*

trawl1 ['trɔl] *vi* **:** pescar con red de arrastre, rastrear

trawl2 *n or* **trawl net :** red *f* de arrastre

trawler ['trɔlər] *n* **:** barco *m* de pesca (utilizado para rastrear)

tray ['treɪ] *n* **:** bandeja *f*, charola *f Bol, Mex, Peru*

treacherous [ˈtrɛtʃərəs] *adj* **1** TRAITOROUS : traicionero, traidor **2** DANGEROUS : peligroso
treacherously [ˈtrɛtʃərəsli] *adv* : a traición
treachery [ˈtrɛtʃəri] *n, pl* **-eries** : traición *f*
tread[1] [ˈtrɛd] *v* **trod** [ˈtrɑd]; **trodden** [ˈtrɑdən] *or* **trod; treading** *vt* TRAMPLE : pisotear, hollar — *vi* **1** WALK : caminar, andar **2 to tread on** : pisar
tread[2] *n* **1** STEP : paso *m,* andar *m* **2** : banda *f* de rodadura (de un neumático, etc.) **3** : escalón *m* (de una escalera)
treadle [ˈtrɛdəl] *n* : pedal *m* (de una máquina)
treadmill [ˈtrɛdˌmɪl] *n* **1** : rueda *f* de andar **2** ROUTINE : rutina *f*
treason [ˈtriːzən] *n* : traición *f* (a la patria, etc.)
treasure[1] [ˈtrɛʒər, ˈtreɪ-] *vt* **-sured; -suring** : apreciar, valorar
treasure[2] *n* : tesoro *m*
treasurer [ˈtrɛʒərər, ˈtreɪ-] *n* : tesorero *m,* -ra *f*
treasury [ˈtrɛʒəri, ˈtreɪ-] *n, pl* **-suries** : tesorería *f,* tesoro *m*
treat[1] [ˈtriːt] *vt* **1** DEAL WITH : tratar (un asunto) <the article treats of poverty : el artículo trata de la pobreza> **2** HANDLE : tratar (a una persona), manejar (un objeto) <to treat something as a joke : tomar(se) algo a broma> **3** INVITE : invitar, convidar <he treated me to a meal : me invitó a comer> **4** : tratar, atender (en medicina) **5** PROCESS : tratar <to treat sewage : tratar las aguas negras>
treat[2] *n* : gusto *m,* placer *m* <it was a treat to see you : fue un placer verte> <it's my treat : yo invito>
treatise [ˈtriːt̬ɪs] *n* : tratado *m,* estudio *m*
treatment [ˈtriːtmənt] *n* : trato *m,* tratamiento *m* (médico)
treaty [ˈtriːt̬i] *n, pl* **-ties** : tratado *m,* convenio *m*
treble[1] [ˈtrɛbəl] *vt* **-bled; -bling** : triplicar
treble[2] *adj* **1** → **triple 2** : de tiple, soprano (en música) **3 treble clef** : clave *f* de sol
treble[3] *n* : tiple *m,* parte *f* soprana
tree [ˈtriː] *n* : árbol *m*
treeless [ˈtriːləs] *adj* : carente de árboles
trek[1] [ˈtrɛk] *vi* **trekked; trekking** : hacer un viaje largo y difícil
trek[2] *n* : viaje *m* largo y difícil
trellis [ˈtrɛlɪs] *n* : enrejado *m,* espaldera *f,* celosía *f*
tremble [ˈtrɛmbəl] *vi* **-bled; -bling** : temblar
tremendous [trɪˈmɛndəs] *adj* : tremendo — **tremendously** *adv*
tremor [ˈtrɛmər] *n* : temblor *m*
tremulous [ˈtrɛmjələs] *adj* : trémulo, tembloroso
trench [ˈtrɛntʃ] *n* **1** DITCH : zanja *f* **2** : trinchera *f* (militar)
trenchant [ˈtrɛntʃənt] *adj* : cortante, mordaz
trend[1] [ˈtrɛnd] *vi* : tender, inclinarse
trend[2] *n* **1** TENDENCY : tendencia *f* **2** FASHION : moda *f*
trendy [ˈtrɛndi] *adj* **trendier; -est** : de moda
trepidation [ˌtrɛpəˈdeɪʃən] *n* : inquietud *f,* ansiedad *f*
trespass[1] [ˈtrɛspəs, -ˌpæs] *vi* **1** SIN : pecar, transgredir **2** : entrar ilegalmente (en propiedad ajena)
trespass[2] *n* **1** SIN : pecado *m,* transgresión *f* <forgive us our trespasses : perdónanos nuestras deudas> **2** : entrada *f* ilegal (en propiedad ajena)
tress [ˈtrɛs] *n* : mechón *m*
trestle [ˈtrɛsəl] *n* **1** : caballete *m* (armazón) **2** *or* **trestle bridge** : puente *m* de caballete
triad [ˈtraɪˌæd] *n* : tríada *f*
trial[1] [ˈtraɪəl] *adj* : de prueba <trial period : período de prueba>
trial[2] *n* **1** : juicio *m,* proceso *m* <to stand trial : ser sometido a juicio> **2** AFFLICTION : aflicción *f,* tribulación *f* **3** TEST : prueba *f,* ensayo *m*
triangle [ˈtraɪˌæŋgəl] *n* : triángulo *m*
triangular [traɪˈæŋgjələr] *adj* : triangular
tribal [ˈtraɪbəl] *adj* : tribal
tribe [ˈtraɪb] *n* : tribu *f*
tribesman [ˈtraɪbzmən] *n, pl* **-men** [-mən, -ˌmɛn] : miembro *m* de una tribu
tribulation [ˌtrɪbjəˈleɪʃən] *n* : tribulación *f*
tribunal [traɪˈbjuːnəl, trɪ-] *n* : tribunal *m,* corte *f*
tributary [ˈtrɪbjəˌtɛri] *n, pl* **-taries** : afluente *m*
tribute [ˈtrɪbˌjuːt] *n* : tributo *m*
trick[1] [ˈtrɪk] *vt* : engañar, embaucar
trick[2] *n* **1** RUSE : trampa *f,* treta *f,* artimaña *f* **2** PRANK : broma *f* <we played a trick on her : le gastamos una broma> **3** : truco *m* <magic tricks : trucos de magia> <the trick is to wait five minutes : el truco está en esperar cinco minutos> **4** MANNERISM : peculiaridad *f,* manía *f* **5** : baza *f* (en juegos de naipes)
trickery [ˈtrɪkəri] *n* : engaños *mpl,* trampas *fpl*
trickle[1] [ˈtrɪkəl] *vi* **-led; -ling** : gotear, chorrear
trickle[2] *n* : goteo *m,* hilo *m*
trickster [ˈtrɪkstər] *n* : estafador *m,* -dora *f;* embaucador *m,* -dora *f*
tricky [ˈtrɪki] *adj* **trickier; -est 1** SLY : astuto, taimado **2** DIFFICULT : delicado, peliagudo, difícil
tricycle [ˈtraɪsəkəl, -ˌsɪkəl] *n* : triciclo *m*
trident [ˈtraɪdənt] *n* : tridente *m*
triennial [ˈtraɪˈɛniəl] *adj* : trienal
trifle[1] [ˈtraɪfəl] *vi* **-fled; -fling** : jugar, juguetear

trifle[2] *n* : nimiedad *f,* insignificancia *f*
trifling ['traɪflɪŋ] *adj* : trivial, insignificante
trigger[1] ['trɪgər] *vt* : causar, provocar
trigger[2] *n* : gatillo *m*
trigonometry [ˌtrɪgə'nɑmətri] *n* : trigonometría *f*
trill[1] ['trɪl] *vi* QUAVER : trinar, gorjear — *vt* : vibrar <to trill the *r* : vibrar la *r*>
trill[2] *n* **1** QUAVER : trino *m,* gorjeo *m* **2** : vibración *f* (en fonología)
trillion ['trɪljən] *n* : billón *m*
trilogy ['trɪlədʒi] *n, pl* **-gies** : trilogía *f*
trim[1] ['trɪm] *vt* **trimmed; trimming 1** DECORATE : adornar, decorar **2** CUT : recortar **3** REDUCE : recortar, reducir <to trim the excess : recortar el exceso>
trim[2] *adj* **trimmer; trimmest 1** SLIM : esbelto **2** NEAT : limpio y arreglado, bien cuidado
trim[3] *n* **1** CONDITION : condición *f,* estado *m* <to keep in trim : mantenerse en buena forma> **2** CUT : recorte *m* **3** TRIMMING : adornos *mpl*
trimming ['trɪmɪŋ] *n* : adornos *mpl,* accesorios *mpl*
Trinity ['trɪnət̬i] *n* : Trinidad *f*
trinket ['trɪŋkət] *n* : chuchería *f,* baratija *f*
trio ['triːˌoː] *n, pl* **trios** : trío *m*
trip[1] ['trɪp] *v* **tripped; tripping** *vi* **1** : caminar (a paso ligero) **2** STUMBLE : tropezar **3 to trip up** ERR : equivocarse, cometer un error — *vt* **1** : hacerle una zancadilla (a alguien) <you tripped me on purpose! : ¡me hiciste la zancadilla a propósito!> **2** ACTIVATE : activar (un mecanismo) **3 to trip up** : hacer equivocar (a alguien)
trip[2] *n* **1** JOURNEY : viaje *m* <to take a trip : hacer un viaje> **2** STUMBLE : tropiezo *m,* traspié *m*
tripartite [traɪ'pɑrˌtaɪt] *adj* : tripartito
tripe ['traɪp] *n* **1** : mondongo *m,* callos *mpl,* pancita *f Mex* **2** TRASH : porquería *f*
triple[1] ['trɪpəl] *vt* **-pled; -pling** : triplicar
triple[2] *adj* : triple
triple[3] *n* : triple *m*
triplet ['trɪplət] *n* **1** : terceto *m* (en poesía, música, etc.) **2** : trillizo *m,* -za *f* (persona)
triplicate ['trɪplɪkət] *n* : triplicado *m*
tripod ['traɪˌpɑd] *n* : trípode *m*
trite ['traɪt] *adj* **triter; tritest** : trillado, tópico, manido
triumph[1] ['traɪəmpf] *vi* : triunfar
triumph[2] *n* : triunfo *m*
triumphal [traɪ'ʌmpfəl] *adj* : triunfal
triumphant [traɪ'ʌmpfənt] *adj* : triunfante, triunfal — **triumphantly** *adv*
trivia ['trɪviə] *ns & pl* : trivialidades *fpl,* nimiedades *fpl*
trivial ['trɪviəl] *adj* : trivial, intrascendente, insignificante
triviality [ˌtrɪvi'ælət̬i] *n, pl* **-ties** : trivialidad *f*
trod, trodden → **tread**[1]
troll ['troːl] *n* : duende *m* o gigante *m* de cuentos folklóricos
trolley ['trɑli] *n, pl* **-leys** : tranvía *m*
trombone [trɑm'boːn] *n* : trombón *m*
trombonist [trɑm'boːnɪst] *n* : trombón *m*
troop[1] ['truːp] *vi* : desfilar, ir en tropel
troop[2] *n* **1** : escuadrón *m* (de caballería) **2** GROUP : grupo *m,* banda *f* (de personas) **3 troops** *npl* SOLDIERS : tropas *fpl,* soldados *mpl*
trooper ['truːpər] *n* **1** : soldado *m* (de caballería) **2** : policía *m* montado **3** : policía *m* (estatal)
trophy ['troːfi] *n, pl* **-phies** : trofeo *m*
tropic[1] ['trɑpɪk] *or* **tropical** [-pɪkəl] *adj* : tropical
tropic[2] *n* **1** : trópico *m* <tropic of Cancer : trópico de Cáncer> **2 the tropics** : el trópico
trot[1] ['trɑt] *vi* **trotted; trotting** : trotar
trot[2] *n* : trote *m*
trouble[1] ['trʌbəl] *v* **-bled; -bling** *vt* **1** DISTURB, WORRY : molestar, perturbar, inquietar **2** AFFLICT : afligir, afectar — *vi* : molestarse, hacer un esfuerzo <they didn't trouble to come : no se molestaron en venir>
trouble[2] *n* **1** PROBLEMS : problemas *mpl,* dificultades *fpl* <to be in trouble : estar en un aprieto> <heart trouble : problemas de corazón> **2** EFFORT : molestia *f,* esfuerzo *m* <to take the trouble : tomarse la molestia> <it's not worth the trouble : no vale la pena>
troublemaker ['trʌbəlˌmeɪkər] *n* : agitador *m,* -dora *f;* alborotador *m,* -dora *f*
troublesome ['trʌbəlsəm] *adj* : problemático, dificultoso — **troublesomely** *adv*
trough ['trɔf] *n, pl* **troughs** ['trɔfs, 'trɔvz] **1** : comedero *m,* bebedero *m* (de animales) **2** CHANNEL, HOLLOW : depresión *f* (en el suelo), seno *m* (de olas)
trounce ['traʊnts] *vt* **trounced; trouncing 1** THRASH : apalear, darle una paliza (a alguien) **2** DEFEAT : derrotar contundentemente
troupe ['truːp] *n* : troupe *f*
trousers ['traʊzərz] *npl* : pantalón *m,* pantalones *mpl*
trout ['traʊt] *n, pl* **trout** : trucha *f*
trowel ['traʊəl] *n* **1** : llana *f,* paleta *f* (de albañil) **2** : desplantador *m* (de jardinero)
truant ['truːənt] *n* : alumno *m,* -na *f* que falta a clase sin permiso
truce ['truːs] *n* : tregua *f,* armisticio *m*
truck[1] ['trʌk] *vt* : transportar en camión
truck[2] *n* **1** : camión *m* (vehículo automóvil), carro *m* (manual) **2** DEAL-

INGS : tratos *mpl* <to have no truck with : no tener nada que ver con>

trucker [ˈtrʌkər] *n* : camionero *m,* -ra *f*

truculent [ˈtrʌkjələnt] *adj* : agresivo, beligerante

trudge [ˈtrʌdʒ] *vi* **trudged; trudging** : caminar a paso pesado

true[1] [ˈtruː] *vt* **trued; trueing** : aplomar (algo vertical), nivelar (algo horizontal), centrar (una rueda)

true[2] *adv* **1** TRUTHFULLY : lealmente, sinceramente **2** ACCURATELY : exactamente, certeramente

true[3] *adj* **truer; truest 1** LOYAL : fiel, leal **2** : cierto, verdadero, verídico <it's true : es cierto, es la verdad> <a true story : una historia verídica> **3** GENUINE : auténtico, genuino — **truly** *adv*

true–blue [ˈtruːˈbluː] *adj* LOYAL : leal, fiel

truffle [ˈtrʌfəl] *n* : trufa *f*

truism [ˈtruːˌɪzəm] *n* : perogrullada *f,* verdad *f* obvia

trump[1] [ˈtrʌmp] *vt* : matar (en juegos de naipes)

trump[2] *n* : triunfo *m* (en juegos de naipes)

trumped–up [ˈtrʌmptˈʌp] *adj* : inventado, fabricado <trumped-up charges : falsas acusaciones>

trumpet[1] [ˈtrʌmpət] *vi* **1** : sonar una trompeta **2** : berrear, bramar (dícese de un animal) — *vt* : proclamar a los cuatro vientos

trumpet[2] *n* : trompeta *f*

trumpeter [ˈtrʌmpətər] *n* : trompetista *mf*

truncate [ˈtrʌŋˌkeɪt, ˈtrʌn-] *vt* **-cated; -cating** : truncar

trundle [ˈtrʌndəl] *v* **-dled; -dling** *vi* : rodar lentamente — *vt* : hacer rodar, empujar lentamente

trunk [ˈtrʌŋk] *n* **1** : tronco *m* (de un árbol o del cuerpo) **2** : trompa *f* (de un elefante) **3** CHEST : baúl *m* **4** : maletero *m,* cajuela *f Mex* (de un auto) **5 trunks** *npl* : traje *m* de baño (de caballero)

truss[1] [ˈtrʌs] *vt* : atar (con fuerza)

truss[2] *n* **1** FRAMEWORK : armazón *m* (de una estructura) **2** : braguero *m* (en medicina)

trust[1] [ˈtrʌst] *vi* : confiar, esperar <to trust in God : confiar en Dios> — *vt* **1** ENTRUST : confiar, encomendar **2** : confiar en, tenerle confianza a <I trust you : te tengo confianza>

trust[2] *n* **1** CONFIDENCE : confianza *f* **2** HOPE : esperanza *f,* fe *f* **3** CREDIT : crédito *m* <to sell on trust : fiar> **4** : fideicomiso *m* <to hold in trust : guardar en fideicomiso> **5** : trust *m* (consorcio empresarial) **6** CUSTODY : responsabilidad *f,* custodia *f*

trustee [ˌtrʌsˈtiː] *n* : fideicomisario *m,* -ria *f;* fiduciario *m,* -ria *f*

trustful [ˈtrʌstfəl] *adj* : confiado — **trustfully** *adv*

trustworthiness [ˈtrəstˌwərðinəs] *n* : integridad *f,* honradez *f*

trustworthy [ˈtrəstˌwərði] *adj* : digno de confianza, confiable

trusty [ˈtrəsti] *adj* **trustier; -est** : fiel, confiable

truth [ˈtruːθ] *n, pl* **truths** [ˈtruːðz, ˈtruːθs] : verdad *f*

truthful [ˈtruːθfəl] *adj* : sincero, veraz — **truthfully** *adv*

truthfulness [ˈtruːθfəlnəs] *n* : sinceridad *f,* veracidad *f*

try[1] [ˈtraɪ] *v* **tried; trying** *vt* **1** : enjuiciar, juzgar, procesar <he was tried for murder : fue procesado por homicidio> **2** : probar <did you try the salad? : ¿probaste la ensalada?> **3** TEST : tentar, poner a prueba <to try one's patience : tentarle la paciencia a uno> **4** ATTEMPT : tratar (de), intentar **5** *or* **to try on** : probarse (ropa) — *vi* : tratar, intentar

try[2] *n, pl* **tries** : intento *m,* tentativa *f*

tryout [ˈtraɪˌaʊt] *n* : prueba *f*

tsar [ˈzɑr, ˈtsɑr, ˈsɑr] → **czar**

T–shirt [ˈtiːˌʃərt] *n* : camiseta *f*

tub [ˈtʌb] *n* **1** CASK : cuba *f,* barril *m,* tonel *m* **2** CONTAINER : envase *m* (de plástico, etc.) <a tub of margarine : un envase de margarina> **3** BATHTUB : tina *f* (de baño), bañera *f*

tuba [ˈtuːbə, ˈtjuː-] *n* : tuba *f*

tube [ˈtuːb, ˈtjuːb] *n* **1** PIPE : tubo *m* **2** : tubo *m* (de dentífrico, etc.) **3** *or* **inner tube** : cámara *f* **4** : tubo *m* (de un aparato electrónico) **5** : trompa *f* (en anatomía)

tubeless [ˈtuːbləs, ˈtjuːb-] *adj* : sin cámara (dícese de una llanta)

tuber [ˈtuːbər, ˈtjuː-] *n* : tubérculo *m*

tubercular [tʊˈbərkjələr, tjʊ-] → **tuberculous**

tuberculosis [tʊˌbərkjəˈloːsɪs, tjʊ-] *n, pl* **-loses** [-ˌsiːz] : tuberculosis *f*

tuberculous [tʊˈbərkjələs, tjʊ-] *adj* : tuberculoso

tuberous [ˈtuːbərəs, ˈtjuː-] *adj* : tuberoso

tubing [ˈtuːbɪŋ, ˈtjuː-] *n* : tubería *f*

tubular [ˈtuːbjələr, ˈtjuː-] *adj* : tubular

tuck[1] [ˈtʌk] *vt* **1** PLACE, PUT : meter, colocar <tuck in your shirt : métete la camisa> **2** : guardar, esconder <to tuck away one's money : guardar uno bien su dinero> **3** COVER : arropar (a un niño en la cama)

tuck[2] *n* : pliegue *m,* alforza *f*

Tuesday [ˈtuːzˌdeɪ, ˈtjuːz-, -di] *n* : martes *m*

tuft [ˈtʌft] *n* : penacho *m* (de plumas), copete *m* (de pelo)

tug[1] [ˈtʌg] *v* **tugged; tugging** *vi* : tirar, jalar, dar un tirón — *vt* : jalar, arrastrar, remolcar (con un barco)

tug[2] *n* **1** : tirón *m,* jalón *m* **2** → **tugboat**

tugboat [ˈtʌgˌboːt] *n* : remolcador *m*

tug–of–war [ˌtʌgəˈwɔr] *n, pl* **tugs–of–war** : tira y afloja *m*

tulip [ˈtuːlɪp, ˈtjuː-] *n* : tulipán *m*

tumble[1] ['tʌmbəl] *v* **-bled; -bling** *vi* **1** : dar volteretas (en acrobacia) **2** FALL : caerse, venirse abajo — *vt* **1** TOPPLE : volcar **2** TOSS : hacer girar

tumble[2] *n* : voltereta *f,* caída *f*

tumbler ['tʌmblər] *n* **1** ACROBAT : acróbata *mf,* saltimbanqui *mf* **2** GLASS : vaso *m* (de mesa) **3** : clavija *f* (de una cerradura)

tummy ['tʌmi] *n, pl* **-mies** BELLY : panza *f,* vientre *m*

tumor ['tuːmər 'tjuː-] *n* : tumor *m*

tumult ['tuːˌmʌlt 'tjuː-] *n* : tumulto *m,* alboroto *m*

tumultuous [tʊ'mʌltʃʊəs, tjuː-] *adj* : tumultuoso

tuna ['tuːnə 'tjuː-] *n, pl* **-na** *or* **-nas** : atún *m*

tundra ['tʌndrə] *n* : tundra *f*

tune[1] ['tuːn, 'tjuːn] *v* **tuned; tuning** *vt* **1** ADJUST : ajustar, hacer más preciso, afinar (un motor) **2** : afinar (un instrumento musical) **3** : sintonizar (un radio o televisor) — *vi* **to tune in** : sintonizar (con una emisora)

tune[2] *n* **1** MELODY : tonada *f,* canción *f,* melodía *f* **2 in tune** : afinado (dícese de un instrumento o de la voz), sintonizado, en sintonía

tuneful ['tuːnfəl, 'tjuːn-] *adj* : armonioso, melódico

tuner ['tuːnər, 'tjuː-] *n* : afinador *m,* -dora *f* (de instrumentos); sintonizador *m* (de un radio o un televisior)

tungsten ['tʌŋkstən] *n* : tungsteno *m*

tunic ['tuːnɪk, 'tjuː-] *n* : túnica *f*

tuning fork *n* : diapasón *m*

Tunisian [tuː'niːʒən, tjuː'nɪziən] *n* : tunecino *m,* -na *f* — **Tunisian** *adj*

tunnel[1] ['tʌnəl] *vi* **-neled** *or* **-nelled; -neling** *or* **-nelling** : hacer un túnel

tunnel[2] *n* : túnel *m*

turban ['tərbən] *n* : turbante *m*

turbid ['tərbɪd] *adj* : turbio

turbine ['tərbən, -ˌbaɪn] *n* : turbina *f*

turboprop ['tərboːˌprɑp] *n* : turbopropulsor *m* (motor), avión *m* turbopropulsado

turbulence ['tərbjələnts] *n* : turbulencia *f*

turbulent ['tərbjələnt] *adj* : turbulento — **turbulently** *adv*

tureen [tə'riːn, tjʊ-] *n* : sopera *f*

turf ['tərf] *n* SOD : tepe *m*

turgid ['tərdʒɪd] *adj* **1** SWOLLEN : turgente **2** : ampuloso, hinchado <turgid style : estilo ampuloso>

turkey ['tərki] *n, pl* **-keys** : pavo *m*

turmoil ['tərˌmɔɪl] *n* : agitación *f,* desorden *m,* confusión *f*

turn[1] ['tərn] *vt* **1** : girar, voltear, volver <to turn one's head : voltear la cabeza> <she turned her chair toward the fire : giró su asiento hacia la hoguera> **2** ROTATE : darle vuelta a, hacer girar <turn the handle : dale vuelta a la manivela> **3** SPRAIN, WRENCH : dislocar, torcer **4** UPSET : revolver (el estómago) **5** TRANSFORM : convertir <to turn water into wine : convertir el agua en vino> **6** SHAPE : tornear (en carpintería) — *vi* **1** ROTATE : girar, dar vueltas **2** : girar, doblar, dar una vuelta <turn left : doble a la izquierda> <to turn around : dar la media vuelta> **3** BECOME : hacerse, volverse, ponerse **4** SOUR : agriarse, cortarse (dícese de la leche) **5 to turn to** : recurrir a <they have no one to turn to : no tienen quien les ayude>

turn[2] *n* **1** : vuelta *f,* giro *m* <a sudden turn : una vuelta repentina> **2** CHANGE : cambio *m* **3** CURVE : curva *f* (en un camino) **4** : turno *m* <they're awaiting their turn : están esperando su turno> <whose turn is it? : ¿a quién le toca?>

turncoat ['tərnˌkoːt] *n* : traidor *m,* -dora *f*

turn down *vt* **1** REFUSE : rehusar, rechazar <they turned down our invitation : rehusaron nuestra invitación> **2** LOWER : bajar (el volumen)

turn in *vt* : entregar <to turn in one's work : entregar uno su trabajo> <they turned in the suspect : entregaron al sospechoso> — *vi* : acostarse, irse a la cama

turnip ['tərnəp] *n* : nabo *m*

turn off *vt* : apagar (la luz, la radio, etc.)

turn on *vt* : prender (la luz, etc.), encender (un motor, etc.)

turnout ['tərnˌaʊt] *n* : concurrencia *f*

turn out *vt* **1** EVICT, EXPEL : expulsar, echar, desalojar **2** PRODUCE : producir **3** → **turn off** — *vi* **1** : concurrir, presentarse <many turned out to vote : muchos concurrieron a votar> **2** PROVE, RESULT : resultar

turnover ['tərnˌoːvər] *n* **1** : tarta *f* (rellena de fruta) **2** : volumen *m* (de ventas) **3** : rotación *f* (de personal) <a high turnover : un alto nivel de rotación>

turn over *vt* **1** TRANSFER : entregar, transferir (un cargo o una responsabilidad) **2** : voltear, darle la vuelta a <turn the cassette over : voltea el cassette>

turnpike ['tərnˌpaɪk] *n* : carretera *f* de peaje

turnstile ['tərnˌstaɪl] *n* : torniquete *m* (de acceso)

turntable ['tərnˌteɪbəl] *n* : tornamesa *mf*

turn up *vi* **1** APPEAR : aparecer, presentarse **2** HAPPEN : ocurrir, suceder (inesperadamente) — *vt* : subir (el volumen)

turpentine ['tərpənˌtaɪn] *n* : aguarrás *m,* trementina *f*

turquoise ['tərˌkɔɪz, -ˌkwɔɪz] *n* : turquesa *f*

turret ['tərət] *n* **1** TOWER : torre *f* pequeña **2** : torreta *f* (de un tanque, un avión, etc.)

turtle ['tərtəl] *n* : tortuga *f* (marina)

turtledove [ˈtərtəlˌdʌv] *n* : tórtola *f*
turtleneck [ˈtərtəlˌnɛk] *n* : cuello *m* de tortuga, cuello *m* alto
tusk [ˈtʌsk] *n* : colmillo *m*
tussle[1] [ˈtʌsəl] *vi* **-sled; -sling** SCUFFLE : pelearse, reñir
tussle[2] *n* : riña *f,* pelea *f*
tutor[1] [ˈtuːtər, ˈtjuː-] *vt* : darle clases particulares (a alguien)
tutor[2] *n* : tutor *m,* -tora *f;* maestro *m,* -tra *f* (particular)
tuxedo [ˌtəkˈsiːˌdoː] *n, pl* **-dos** *or* **-does** : esmoquin *m,* smoking *m*
TV [ˌtiːˈviː, ˈtiːˌviː] → **television**
twain [ˈtweɪn] *n* : dos *m*
twang[1] [ˈtwæŋ] *vt* : pulsar la cuerda de (una guitarra) — *vi* : hablar en tono nasal
twang[2] *n* **1** : tañido *m* (de una cuerda de guitarra) **2** : tono *m* nasal (de voz)
tweak[1] [ˈtwiːk] *vt* : pellizcar
tweak[2] *n* : pellizco *m*
tweed [ˈtwiːd] *n* : tweed *m*
tweet[1] [ˈtwiːt] *vi* : piar
tweet[2] *n* : gorjeo *m,* pío *m*
tweezers [ˈtwiːzərz] *npl* : pinzas *fpl*
twelfth[1] [ˈtwɛlfθ] *adj* : duodécimo
twelfth[2] *n* **1** : duodécimo *m,* -ma *f* (en una serie) **2** : doceavo *m,* doceava parte *f*
twelve[1] [ˈtwɛlv] *adj* : doce
twelve[2] *n* : doce *m*
twentieth[1] [ˈtwʌntiəθ, ˈtwɛn-] *adj* : vigésimo
twentieth[2] *n* **1** : vigésimo *m,* -ma *f* (en una serie) **2** : veinteavo *m,* veinteava parte *f*
twenty[1] [ˈtwʌnti, ˈtwɛn-] *adj* : veinte
twenty[2] *n, pl* **-ties** : veinte *m*
twice [ˈtwaɪs] *adv* : dos veces <twice a day : dos veces al día> <it costs twice as much : cuesta el doble>
twig [ˈtwɪg] *n* : ramita *f*
twilight [ˈtwaɪˌlaɪt] *n* : crepúsculo *m*
twill [ˈtwɪl] *n* : sarga *f,* tela *f* cruzada
twin[1] [ˈtwɪn] *adj* : gemelo, mellizo
twin[2] *n* : gemelo *m,* -la *f;* mellizo *m,* -za *f*
twine[1] [ˈtwaɪn] *v* **twined; twining** *vt* : entrelazar, entrecruzar — *vi* : enroscarse (alrededor de algo)
twine[2] *n* : cordel *m,* cuerda *f,* mecate *m* *CA, Mex, Ven*
twinge[1] [ˈtwɪndʒ] *vi* **twinged; twinging** *or* **twingeing** : sentir punzadas
twinge[2] *n* : punzada *f,* dolor *m* agudo
twinkle[1] [ˈtwɪŋkəl] *vi* **-kled; -kling 1** : centellear, titilar (dícese de las estrellas o de la luz) **2** : chispear, brillar (dícese de los ojos)
twinkle[2] *n* : centelleo *m* (de las estrellas), brillo *m* (de los ojos)
twirl[1] [ˈtwərl] *vt* : girar, darle vueltas a — *vi* : girar, dar vueltas (rápidamente)
twirl[2] *n* : giro *m,* vuelta *f*
twist[1] [ˈtwɪst] *vt* : torcer, retorcer <he twisted my arm : me torció el brazo> — *vi* : retorcerse, enroscarse, serpentear (dícese de un río, un camino, etc.)
twist[2] *n* **1** BEND : vuelta *f,* recodo *m* (en el camino, el río, etc.) **2** TURN : giro *m* <give it a twist : hazlo girar> **3** SPIRAL : espiral *f* <a twist of lemon : una rodajita de limón> **4** : giro *m* inesperado (de eventos, etc.)
twister [ˈtwɪstər] **1** → **tornado 2** → **waterspout**
twitch[1] [ˈtwɪtʃ] *vi* : moverse nerviosamente, contraerse espasmódicamente (dícese de un músculo)
twitch[2] *n* : espasmo *m,* sacudida *f* <a nervous twitch : un tic nervioso>
twitter[1] [ˈtwɪtər] *vi* CHIRP : gorjear, cantar (dícese de los pájaros)
twitter[2] *n* : gorjeo *m*
two[1] [ˈtuː] *adj* : dos
two[2] *n, pl* **twos** : dos *m*
twofold[1] [ˈtuːˈfoːld] *adv* : al doble
twofold[2] [ˈtuːˌfoːld] *adj* : doble
two hundred[1] *adj* : doscientos
two hundred[2] *n* : doscientos *m*
twosome [ˈtuːsəm] *n* COUPLE : pareja *f*
tycoon [taɪˈkuːn] *n* : magnate *mf*
tying → **tie**[1]
type[1] [ˈtaɪp] *v* **typed; typing** *vt* **1** TYPEWRITE : escribir a máquina, pasar (un texto) a máquina **2** CATEGORIZE : categorizar, identificar — *vi* : escribir a máquina
type[2] *n* **1** KIND : tipo *m,* clase *f,* categoría *f* **2** *or* **printing type** : tipo *m*
typewrite [ˈtaɪpˌraɪt] *v* **-wrote; -written** : escribir a máquina
typewriter [ˈtaɪpˌraɪtər] *n* : máquina *f* de escribir
typhoid[1] [ˈtaɪˌfɔɪd, taɪˈ-] *adj* : relativo al tifus o a la tifoidea
typhoid[2] *n or* **typhoid fever** : tifoidea *f*
typhoon [taɪˈfuːn] *n* : tifón *m*
typhus [ˈtaɪfəs] *n* : tifus *m,* tifo *m*
typical [ˈtɪpɪkəl] *adj* : típico, característico — **typically** *adv*
typify [ˈtɪpəˌfaɪ] *vt* **-fied; -fying** : ser típico o representativo de (un grupo, una clase, etc.)
typist [ˈtaɪpɪst] *n* : mecanógrafo *m,* -fa *f*
typographic [ˌtaɪpəˈgræfɪk] *or* **typographical** [-fɪkəl] *adj* : tipográfico — **typographically** [-fɪkli] *adv*
typography [taɪˈpɑgrəfi] *n* : tipografía *f*
tyrannical [təˈrænɪkəl, taɪ-] *adj* : tiránico — **tyrannically** [-nɪkli] *adv*
tyrannize [ˈtɪrəˌnaɪz] *vt* **-nized; -nizing** : tiranizar
tyranny [ˈtɪrəni] *n, pl* **-nies** : tiranía *f*
tyrant [ˈtaɪrənt] *n* : tirano *m,* -na *f*
tzar [ˈzɑr, ˈtsɑr, ˈsɑr] → **czar**

U

u [ˈjuː] *n, pl* **u's** *or* **us** [ˈjuːz] : vigésima primera letra del alfabeto inglés
ubiquitous [juːˈbɪkwət̬əs] *adj* : ubicuo, omnipresente
udder [ˈʌdər] *n* : ubre *f*
UFO [ˌjuːˌɛfˈoː, ˈjuːˌfoː] *n, pl* **UFO's** *or* **UFOs** (*unidentified flying object*) : ovni *m,* OVNI *m*
Ugandan [juːˈgændən, -ˈgɑn-; uːˈgɑn-] *n* : ugandés *m,* -desa *f* — **Ugandan** *adj*
ugliness [ˈʌglinəs] *n* : fealdad *f*
ugly [ˈʌgli] *adj* **uglier; -est** **1** UNATTRACTIVE : feo **2** DISAGREEABLE : desagradable, feo <ugly weather : tiempo feo> <to have an ugly temper : tener mal genio>
Ukrainian [juːˈkreɪniən, -ˈkraɪ-] *n* : ucraniano *m,* -na *f* — **Ukrainian** *adj*
ukulele [ˌjuːkəˈleɪli] *n* : ukelele *m*
ulcer [ˈʌlsər] *n* : úlcera *f* (interna), llaga *f* (externa)
ulcerate [ˈʌlsəˌreɪt] *vi* **-ated; -ating** : ulcerarse
ulceration [ˌʌlsəˈreɪʃən] *n* **1** : ulceración *f* **2** ULCER : úlcera *f,* llaga *f*
ulcerous [ˈʌlsərəs] *adj* : ulceroso
ulna [ˈʌlnə] *n* : cúbito *m*
ulterior [ˌʌlˈtɪriər] *adj* : oculto <ulterior motive : motivo oculto, segunda intención>
ultimate [ˈʌltəmət] *adj* **1** FINAL : último, final **2** SUPREME : supremo, máximo **3** FUNDAMENTAL : fundamental, esencial
ultimately [ˈʌltəmətli] *adv* **1** FINALLY : por último, finalmente **2** EVENTUALLY : a la larga, con el tiempo
ultimatum [ˌʌltəˈmeɪt̬əm, -ˈmɑ-] *n, pl* **-tums** *or* **-ta** [-t̬ə] : ultimátum *m*
ultraviolet [ˌʌltrəˈvaɪələt] *adj* : ultravioleta
umbilical cord [ˌʌmˈbɪlɪkəl] *adj* : cordón umbilical
umbrage [ˈʌmbrɪdʒ] *n* **to take umbrage at** : ofenderse por
umbrella [ˌʌmˈbrɛlə] *n* **1** : paraguas *m* **2 beach umbrella** : sombrilla *f*
umpire[1] [ˈʌmˌpaɪr] *v* **-pired; -piring** : arbitrar
umpire[2] *n* : árbitro *m,* -tra *f*
umpteenth [ˌʌmpˈtiːnθ] *adj* : enésimo
unable [ˌʌnˈeɪbəl] *adj* : incapaz <to be unable to : no poder>
unabridged [ˌʌnəˈbrɪdʒd] *adj* : íntegro
unacceptable [ˌʌnɪkˈsɛptəbəl] *adj* : inaceptable
unaccompanied [ˌʌnəˈkʌmpənid] *adj* : solo, sin acompañamiento (en música)
unaccountable [ˌʌnəˈkaʊntəbəl] *adj* : inexplicable, incomprensible — **unaccountably** [-bli] *adv*
unaccustomed [ˌʌnəˈkʌstəmd] *adj* **1** UNUSUAL : desacostumbrado, inusual **2** UNUSED : inhabituado <unaccustomed to noise : inhabituado al ruido>
unacquainted [ˌʌnəˈkweɪnt̬əd] *adj* **to be unacquainted with** : desconocer, ignorar
unadorned [ˌʌnəˈdɔrnd] *adj* : sin adornos, puro y simple
unadulterated [ˌʌnəˈdʌltəˌreɪt̬əd] *adj* **1** PURE : puro <unadulterated food : comida pura> **2** ABSOLUTE : completo, absoluto
unaffected [ˌʌnəˈfɛktəd] *adj* **1** : no afectado, indiferente **2** NATURAL : sin afectación, natural
unaffectedly [ˌʌnəˈfɛktədli] *adv* : de manera natural
unafraid [ˌʌnəˈfreɪd] *adj* : sin miedo
unaided [ˌʌnˈeɪdəd] *adj* : sin ayuda, solo
unambiguous [ˌʌnæmˈbɪgjʊəs] *adj* : inequívoco
unanimity [ˌjuːnəˈnɪmət̬i] *n* : unanimidad *f*
unanimous [jʊˈnænəməs] *adj* : unánime — **unanimously** *adv*
unannounced [ˌʌnəˈnaʊnst] *adj* : sin dar aviso
unanswered [ˌʌnˈæntsərd] *adj* : sin contestar
unappealing [ˌʌnəˈpiːlɪŋ] *adj* : desagradable
unappetizing [ˌʌnˈæpəˌtaɪzɪŋ] *adj* : poco apetitoso, poco apetecible
unarmed [ˌʌnˈɑrmd] *adj* : sin armas, desarmado
unassisted [ˌʌnəˈsɪstəd] *adj* : sin ayuda
unassuming [ˌʌnəˈsuːmɪŋ] *adj* : modesto, sin pretensiones
unattached [ˌʌnəˈtætʃt] *adj* **1** LOOSE : suelto **2** INDEPENDENT : independiente **3** : solo (ni casado ni prometido)
unattractive [ˌʌnəˈtræktɪv] *adj* : poco atractivo
unauthorized [ˌʌnˈɔθəˌraɪzd] *adj* : sin autorización, no autorizado
unavailable [ˌʌnəˈveɪləbəl] *adj* : no disponible
unavoidable [ˌʌnəˈvɔɪdəbəl] *adj* : inevitable, ineludible
unaware[1] [ˌʌnəˈwær] *adv* → **unawares**
unaware[2] *adj* : inconsciente
unawares [ˌʌnəˈwærz] *adv* **1** : por sorpresa <to catch someone unawares : agarrar a alguien desprevenido> **2** UNINTENTIONALLY : inconscientemente, inadvertidamente
unbalanced [ˌʌnˈbælən*t*st] *adj* : desequilibrado
unbearable [ˌʌnˈbærəbəl] *adj* : insoportable, inaguantable — **unbearably** [-bli] *adv*
unbecoming [ˌʌnbɪˈkʌmɪŋ] *adj* **1** UNSEEMLY : impropio, indecoroso **2** UNFLATTERING : poco favorecedor

unbelievable [ˌʌnbəˈliːvəbəl] *adj* : increíble — **unbelievably** [-bli] *adv*
unbend [ˌʌnˈbɛnd] *vi* **-bent** [-ˈbɛnt]; **-bending** RELAX : relajarse
unbending [ˌʌnˈbɛndɪŋ] *adj* : inflexible
unbiased [ˌʌnˈbaɪəst] *adj* : imparcial, objetivo
unbind [ˌʌnˈbaɪnd] *vt* **-bound** [-ˈbaʊnd]; **-binding 1** UNFASTEN, UNTIE : desatar, desamarrar **2** RELEASE : liberar
unbolt [ˌʌnˈboːlt] *vt* : abrir el cerrojo de, descorrer el pestillo de
unborn [ˌʌnˈbɔrn] *adj* : aún no nacido, que va a nacer
unbosom [ˌʌnˈbʊzəm, -ˈbuː-] *vt* : revelar, divulgar
unbreakable [ˌʌnˈbreɪkəbəl] *adj* : irrompible
unbridled [ˌʌnˈbraɪdəld] *adj* : desenfrenado
unbroken [ˌʌnˈbroːkən] *adj* **1** INTACT : intacto, sano **2** CONTINUOUS : continuo, ininterrumpido
unbuckle [ˌʌnˈbʌkəl] *vt* **-led; -ling** : desabrochar
unburden [ˌʌnˈbərdən] *vt* **1** UNLOAD : descargar **2 to unburden oneself** : desahogarse
unbutton [ˌʌnˈbʌtən] *vt* : desabrochar, desabotonar
uncalled–for [ˌʌnˈkɔldˌfɔr] *adj* : inapropiado, innecesario
uncanny [ənˈkæni] *adj* **-nier; -est 1** STRANGE : extraño **2** EXTRAORDINARY : raro, extraordinario — **uncannily** [-ˈkænəli] *adv*
unceasing [ˌʌnˈsiːsɪŋ] *adj* : incesante, continuo — **unceasingly** *adv*
unceremonious [ˌʌnˌsɛrəˈmoːniəs] *adj* **1** INFORMAL : sin ceremonia, sin pompa **2** ABRUPT : abrupto, brusco — **unceremoniously** *adv*
uncertain [ˌʌnˈsərtən] *adj* **1** INDEFINITE : indeterminado **2** UNSURE : incierto, dudoso **3** CHANGEABLE : inestable, variable <uncertain weather : tiempo inestable> **4** HESITANT : indeciso **5** VAGUE : poco claro
uncertainly [ˌʌnˈsərtənli] *adv* : dudosamente, con desconfianza
uncertainty [ˌʌnˈərtənti] *n, pl* **-ties** : duda *f,* incertidumbre *f*
unchangeable [ˌʌnˈtʃeɪndʒəbəl] *adj* : inalterable, inmutable
unchanged [ˌʌnˈtʃeɪndʒd] *adj* : sin cambiar
unchanging [ˌʌnˈtʃeɪdʒɪŋ] *adj* : inalterable, inmutable, firme
uncharacteristic [ˌʌnˌkærɪktəˈrɪstɪk] *adj* : inusual, desacostumbrado
uncharged [ˌʌnˈtʃɑrdʒd] *adj* : sin carga (eléctrica)
uncivilized [ˌʌnˈsɪvəˌlaɪzd] *adj* **1** BARBAROUS : incivilizado, bárbaro **2** WILD : salvaje
uncle [ˈʌŋkəl] *n* : tío *m*
unclean [ˌʌnˈkliːn] *adj* **1** IMPURE : impuro **2** DIRTY : sucio
unclear [ˌʌnˈklɪr] *adj* : confuso, borroso, poco claro
Uncle Sam [ˈsæm] *n* : el Tío Sam
unclog [ˌʌnˈklɑg] *vt* **-clogged; -clogging** : desatascar, destapar
unclothed [ˌʌnˈkloːðd] *adj* : desnudo
uncomfortable [ˌʌnˈkʌmpfərṭəbəl] *adj* **1** : incómodo (dícese de una silla, etc.) **2** UNEASY : inquieto, incómodo
uncommitted [ˌʌnkəˈmɪṭəd] *adj* : sin compromisos
uncommon [ˌʌnˈkɑmən] *adj* **1** UNUSUAL : raro, poco común **2** REMARKABLE : excepcional, extraordinario
uncommonly [ˌʌnˈkɑmənli] *adv* : extraordinariamente
uncompromising [ˌʌnˈkɑmprəˌmaɪzɪŋ] *adj* : inflexible, intransigente
unconcerned [ˌʌnkənˈsərnd] *adj* : indiferente — **unconcernedly** [-ˈsərnədli] *adv*
unconditional [ˌʌnkənˈdɪʃənəl] *adj* : incondicional — **unconditionally** *adv*
unconscious[1] [ˌʌnˈkɑntʃəs] *adj* : inconsciente — **unconsciously** *adv*
unconscious[2] *n* : inconsciente *m*
unconsciousness [ˌʌnˈkɑntʃəsnəs] *n* : inconsciencia *f*
unconstitutional [ˌʌnˌkɑntstəˈtuːʃənəl, -ˈtjuː-] *adj* : inconstitucional
uncontrollable [ˌʌnkənˈtroːləbəl] *adj* : incontrolable, incontenible — **uncontrollably** [-bli] *adv*
uncontrolled [ˌʌnkənˈtroːld] *adj* : incontrolado
unconventional [ˌʌnkənˈvɛntʃənəl] *adj* : poco convencional
unconvincing [ˌʌnkənˈvɪntsɪŋ] *adj* : poco convincente
uncouth [ˌʌnˈkuːθ] *adj* CRUDE, ROUGH : grosero, rudo
uncover [ˌʌnˈkʌvər] *vt* **1** : destapar (un objeto), dejar al descubierto **2** EXPOSE, REVEAL : descubrir, revelar, exponer
uncultivated [ˌʌnˈkʌltəˌveɪṭəd] *adj* : inculto
uncurl [ˌʌnˈkərl] *vt* UNROLL : desenrollar — *vi* : desenrollarse, desrizarse (dícese del pelo)
uncut [ˌʌnˈkʌt] *adj* **1** : sin cortar <uncut grass : hierba sin cortar> **2** : sin tallar, en bruto <an uncut diamond : un diamante en bruto> **3** UNABRIDGED : completo, íntegro
undaunted [ˌʌnˈdɔntəd] *adj* : impávido
undecided [ˌʌndiˈsaɪdəd] *adj* **1** IRRESOLUTE : indeciso, irresoluto **2** UNRESOLVED : pendiente, no resuelto
undefeated [ˌʌndiˈfiːṭəd] *adj* : invicto
undeniable [ˌʌndiˈnaɪəbəl] *adj* : innegable — **undeniably** [-bli] *adv*
under[1] [ˈʌndər] *adv* **1** LESS : menos <$10 or under : $10 o menos> **2** UNDERWATER : debajo del agua **3** : bajo los efectos de la anestesia

under[2] *adj* **1** LOWER : (más) bajo, inferior **2** SUBORDINATE : inferior **3** : insuficiente <an under dose of medicine : una dosis insuficiente de medicina>

under[3] *prep* **1** BELOW, BENEATH : debajo de, abajo de <under the table : abajo de la mesa> <we walked under the arch : pasamos por debajo del arco> <under the sun : bajo el sol> **2** : menos de <in under 20 minutes : en menos de 20 minutos> **3** (*indicating rank or authority*) : bajo <under the command of : bajo las órdenes de> **4** SUBJECT TO : bajo <under suspicion : bajo sospecha> <under the circumstances : dadas las circunstancias> **5** ACCORDING TO : según, de acuerdo con, conforme a <under the present laws : según las leyes actuales>

underage [ˌʌndərˈeɪdʒ] *adj* : menor de edad

underbrush [ˈʌndərˌbrəʃ] *n* : maleza *f*

underclothes [ˈʌndərˌkloːz, -ˌkloːðz] → **underwear**

underclothing [ˈʌndərˌkloːðɪŋ] → **underwear**

undercover [ˌʌndərˈkʌvər] *adj* : secreto, clandestino

undercurrent [ˈʌndərˌkərənt] *n* **1** : corriente *f* submarina **2** UNDERTONE : corriente *f* oculta, trasfondo *m*

undercut [ˌʌndərˈkʌt] *vt* **-cut; -cutting** : vender más barato que

underdeveloped [ˌʌndərdɪˈvɛləpt] *adj* : subdesarrollado, atrasado

underdog [ˈʌndərˌdɔg] *n* : persona *f* que tiene menos posibilidades

underdone [ˌʌndərˈdʌn] *adj* RARE : poco cocido

underestimate [ˌʌndərˈɛstəˌmeɪt] *vt* **-mated; -mating** : subestimar, menospreciar

underexposed [ˌʌndərɪkˈspoːzd] *adj* : subexpuesto (en fotografía)

underfoot [ˌʌndərˈfʊt] *adv* **1** : bajo los pies <to trample underfoot : pisotear> **2 to be underfoot** : estorbar <they're always underfoot : están siempre estorbando>

undergarment [ˈʌndərˌgɑrmənt] *n* : prenda *f* íntima

undergo [ˌʌndərˈgoː] *vt* **-went** [-ˈwɛnt;]; **-gone** [-ˈgɔn]; **-going** : sufrir, experimentar <to undergo an operation : someterse a una intervención quirúrgica>

undergraduate [ˌʌndərˈgrædʒʊət] *n* : estudiante *m* universitario, estudiante *f* universitaria

underground[1] [ˌʌndərˈgraʊnd] *adv* **1** : bajo tierra **2** SECRETLY : clandestinamente, en secreto <to go underground : pasar a la clandestinidad>

underground[2] [ˈʌndərˌgraʊnd] *adj* **1** SUBTERRANEAN : subterráneo **2** SECRET : secreto, clandestino

underground[3] [ˈʌndərˌgraʊnd] *n* : movimiento *m* o grupo *m* clandestino

undergrowth [ˈʌndərˈgroːθ] *n* : maleza *f*, broza *f*

underhand[1] [ˈʌndərˌhænd] *adv* **1** SECRETLY : de manera clandestina **2** *or* **underhanded** : sin levantar el brazo por encima del hombro (en deportes)

underhand[2] *adj* **1** SLY : solapado **2** : por debajo del hombro (en deportes)

underhanded [ˌʌndərˈhændəd] *adj* **1** SLY : solapado **2** SHADY : turbio, poco limpio

underline [ˈʌndərˌlaɪn] *vt* **-lined; -lining 1** : subrayar **2** EMPHASIZE : subrayar, acentuar, hacer hincapié en

underlying [ˌʌndərˈlaɪɪŋ] *adj* **1** : subyacente <the underlying rock : la roca subyacente> **2** FUNDAMENTAL : fundamental, esencial

undermine [ˌʌndərˈmaɪn] *vt* **-mined; -mining 1** : socavar (una estructura, etc.) **2** SAP, WEAKEN : minar, debilitar

underneath[1] [ˌʌndərˈniːθ] *adv* : debajo, abajo <the part underneath : la parte de abajo>

underneath[2] *prep* : debajo de, abajo de

undernourished [ˌʌndərˈnərɪʃt] *adj* : desnutrido

underpants [ˈʌndərˌpænts] *npl* : calzoncillos *mpl*, calzones *mpl*

underpass [ˈʌndərˌpæs] *n* : paso *m* a desnivel

underprivileged [ˌʌndərˈprɪvlɪdʒd] *adj* : desfavorecido

underrate [ˌʌndərˈreɪt] *vt* **-rated; -rating** : subestimar, menospreciar

underscore [ˈʌndərˌskor] *vt* **-scored; -scoring** → **underline**

undersea[1] [ˌʌndərˈsiː] *or* **underseas** [-ˈsiːz] *adv* : bajo la superficie del mar

undersea[2] *adj* : submarino

undersecretary [ˌʌndərˈsɛkrəˌtɛri] *n, pl* **-ries** : subsecretario *m*, -ria *f*

undersell [ˌʌndərˈsɛl] *vt* **-sold; -selling** : vender más barato que

undershirt [ˈʌndərˌʃərt] *n* : camiseta *f*

undershorts [ˈʌndərˌʃɔrts] *npl* : calzoncillos *mpl*

underside [ˈʌndərˌsaɪd, ˌʌndərˈsaɪd] *n* : parte *f* de abajo

undersized [ˌʌndərˈsaɪzd] *adj* : más pequeño de lo normal

understand [ˌʌndərˈstænd] *v* **-stood** [-ˈstʊd;]; **-standing** *vt* **1** COMPREHEND : comprender, entender <I don't understand it : no lo entiendo> <that's understood : eso se comprende> <to make oneself understood : hacerse entender> **2** BELIEVE : entender <to give someone to understand : dar a alguien a entender> **3** INFER : tener entendido <I understand that she's leaving : tengo entendido que se va> — *vi* : comprender, entender

understandable [ˌʌndərˈstændəbəl] *adj* : comprensible

understanding[1] [ˌʌndərˈstændɪŋ] *adj* : comprensivo, compasivo

understanding[2] *n* **1** GRASP : comprensión *f*, entendimiento *m* **2** SYMPATHY : comprensión *f* (mutua) **3** INTERPRETATION : interpretación *f* <it's my understanding that... : tengo la impresión de que..., tengo entendido que...> **4** AGREEMENT : acuerdo *m*, arreglo *m*

understate [ˌʌndərˈsteɪt] *vt* **-stated; -stating** : minimizar, subestimar

understatement [ˌʌndərˈsteɪtmənt] *n* : atenuación *f* <that's an understatement : decir sólo eso es quedarse corto>

understudy [ˈʌndərˌstʌdi] *n, pl* **-dies** : sobresaliente *mf*, suplente *mf* (en el teatro)

undertake [ˌʌndərˈteɪk] *vt* **-took** [-ˈtʊk]; **-taken** [-ˈteɪkən]; **-taking 1** : emprender (una tarea), asumir (una responsabilidad) **2** PROMISE : comprometerse (a hacer algo)

undertaker [ˈʌndərˌteɪkər] *n* : director *m*, -tora *f* de funeraria

undertaking [ˈʌndərˌteɪkɪŋ, ˌʌndərˈ-] *n* **1** ENTERPRISE, TASK : empresa *f*, tarea *f* **2** PLEDGE : promesa *f*, garantía *f*

undertone [ˈʌndərˌtoːn] *n* **1** : voz *f* baja <to speak in an undertone : hablar en voz baja> **2** HINT, UNDERCURRENT : trasfondo *m*, matiz *m*

undertow [ˈʌndərˌtoː] *n* : resaca *f*

undervalue [ˌʌndərˈvælˌjuː] *vt* **-ued; -uing** : menospreciar, subestimar

underwater[1] [ˌʌndərˈwɔt̬ər, -ˈwɑ-] *adv* : debajo (del agua)

underwater[2] *adj* : submarino

under way [ˌʌndərˈweɪ] *adv* : en marcha, en camino <to get under way : ponerse en marcha>

underwear [ˈʌndərˌwær] *n* : ropa *f* interior, ropa *f* íntima

underworld [ˈʌndərˌwərld] *n* **1** HELL : infierno *m* **2 the underworld** CRIMINALS : la hampa, los bajos fondos

underwrite [ˈʌndərˌraɪt, ˌʌndərˈ-] *vt* **-wrote** [-ˌroːt, -ˈroːt]; **-written** [-ˌrɪtən, -ˈrɪtən]; **-writing 1** INSURE : asegurar **2** FINANCE : financiar **3** BACK, ENDORSE : suscribir, respaldar

underwriter [ˈʌndərˌraɪt̬ər, ˌʌndərˈ-] *n* INSURER : asegurador *m*, -dora *f*

undeserving [ˌʌndiˈzərvɪŋ] *adj* : indigno

undesirable[1] [ˌʌndiˈzaɪrəbəl] *adj* : indeseable

undesirable[2] *n* : indeseable *mf*

undeveloped [ˌʌndiˈvɛləpt] *adj* : sin desarrollar, sin revelar (dícese de una película)

undies [ˈʌndiːz] → **underwear**

undignified [ˌʌnˈdɪgnəfaɪd] *adj* : indecoroso

undiluted [ˌʌndaɪˈluːt̬əd, -də-] *adj* : sin diluir, concentrado

undiscovered [ˌʌndɪˈskʌvərd] *adj* : no descubierto

undisputed [ˌʌndɪˈspjuːt̬əd] *adj* : indiscutible

undisturbed [ˌʌndɪˈstərbd] *adj* : tranquilo (dícese de una persona), sin tocar (dícese de un objeto)

undivided [ˌʌndɪˈvaɪdəd] *adj* : íntegro, completo

undo [ˌʌnˈduː] *vt* **-did** [-ˈdɪd]; **-done** [-ˈdʌn]; **-doing 1** UNFASTEN : desabrochar, desatar, abrir **2** ANNUL : anular **3** REVERSE : deshacer, reparar (daños, etc.) **4** RUIN : arruinar, destruir

undoing [ˌʌnˈduːɪŋ] *n* : ruina *f*, perdición *f*

undoubted [ˌʌnˈdaʊt̬əd] *adj* : cierto, indudable — **undoubtedly** *adv*

undress [ˌʌnˈdrɛs] *vt* : desvestir, desabrigar, desnudar — *vi* : desvestirse, desnudarse

undrinkable [ˌʌnˈdrɪŋkəbəl] *adj* : no potable

undue [ˌʌnˈduː, -ˈdjuː] *adj* : excesivo, indebido — **unduly** *adv*

undulate [ˈʌndʒəˌleɪt] *vi* **-lated; -lating** : ondular

undulation [ˌʌndʒəˈleɪʃən] *n* : ondulación *f*

undying [ˌʌnˈdaɪɪŋ] *adj* : perpetuo, imperecedero

unearth [ˌʌnˈərθ] *vt* **1** EXHUME : desenterrar, exhumar **2** DISCOVER : descubrir

unearthly [ˌʌnˈərθli] *adj* **-lier; -est** : sobrenatural, de otro mundo

uneasily [ˌʌnˈiːzəli] *adv* : inquietamente, con inquietud

uneasiness [ˌʌnˈiːzinəs] *n* : inquietud *f*

uneasy [ˌʌnˈiːzi] *adj* **-easier; -est 1** AWKWARD : incómodo **2** WORRIED : preocupado, inquieto **3** RESTLESS : inquieto, agitado

uneducated [ˌʌnˈɛdʒəˌkeɪt̬əd] *adj* : inculto, sin educación

unemployed [ˌʌnɪmˈplɔɪd] *adj* : desempleado

unemployment [ˌʌnɪmˈplɔɪmənt] *n* : desempleo *m*

unending [ˌʌnˈɛndɪŋ] *adj* : sin fin, interminable

unendurable [ˌʌnɪnˈdʊrəbəl, -ɛn-, -ˈdjʊr-] *adj* : insoportable, intolerable

unequal [ˌʌnˈiːkwəl] *adj* **1** : desigual **2** INADEQUATE : incapaz, incompetente <to be unequal to a task : no estar a la altura de una tarea>

unequaled *or* **unequalled** [ˌʌnˈiːkwəld] *adj* : sin igual

unequivocal [ˌʌnɪˈkwɪvəkəl] *adj* : inequívoco, claro — **unequivocally** *adv*

unerring [ˌʌnˈɛrɪŋ, -ˈər-] *adj* : infalible

unethical [ˌʌnˈɛθɪkəl] *adj* : poco ético

uneven [ˌʌnˈiːvən] *adj* **1** ODD : impar (dícese de un número) **2** : desigual, desnivelado (dícese de una superficie) <uneven terrain : terreno accidentado> **3** IRREGULAR : irregular, poco uniforme **4** UNEQUAL : desigual

unevenly [ˌʌnˈiːvənli] *adv* : desigualmente, irregularmente

uneventful [ˌʌnɪˈvɛntfəl] *adj* : sin incidentes, tranquilo

unexpected [ˌʌnɪkˈspɛktəd] *adj* : imprevisto, inesperado — **unexpectedly** *adv*

unfailing [ˌʌnˈfeɪlɪŋ] *adj* **1** CONSTANT : constante **2** INEXHAUSTIBLE : inagotable **3** SURE : a toda prueba, indefectible

unfair [ˌʌnˈfær] *adj* : injusto — **unfairly** *adv*

unfairness [ˌʌnˈfærnəs] *n* : injusticia *f*

unfaithful [ˌʌnˈfeɪθfəl] *adj* : desleal, infiel — **unfaithfully** *adv*

unfaithfulness [ˌʌnˈfeɪθfəlnəs] *n* : infidelidad *f,* deslealtad *f*

unfamiliar [ˌʌnfəˈmɪljər] *adj* **1** STRANGE : desconocido, extraño <an unfamiliar place : un lugar nuevo> **2 to be unfamiliar with** : no estar familiarizado con, desconocer

unfamiliarity [ˌʌnfəˌmɪliˈærət̬i] *n* : falta *f* de familiaridad

unfashionable [ˌʌnˈfæʃənəbəl] *adj* : fuera de moda

unfasten [ˌʌnˈfæsən] *vt* : desabrochar, desatar (una cuerda, etc.), abrir (una puerta)

unfavorable [ˌʌnˈfeɪvərəbəl] *adj* : desfavorable, mal — **unfavorably** [-bli] *adv*

unfeeling [ˌʌnˈfiːlɪŋ] *adj* : insensible — **unfeelingly** *adv*

unfinished [ˌʌnˈfɪnɪʃd] *adj* : inacabado, incompleto

unfit [ˌʌnˈfɪt] *adj* **1** UNSUITABLE : inadecuado, impropio **2** UNSUITED : no apto, incapaz **3** : incapacitado (físicamente) <to be unfit : no estar en forma>

unflappable [ˌʌnˈflæpəbəl] *adj* : imperturbable

unflattering [ˌʌnˈflæt̬ərɪŋ] *adj* : poco favorecedor

unfold [ˌʌnˈfoːld] *vt* **1** EXPAND : desplegar, desdoblar, extender <to unfold a map : desplegar un mapa> **2** DISCLOSE, REVEAL : revelar, exponer (un plan, etc.) — *vi* **1** DEVELOP : desarrollarse, desenvolverse <the story unfolded : el cuento se desarrollaba> **2** EXPAND : extenderse, desplegarse

unforeseeable [ˌʌnforˈsiːəbəl] *adj* : imprevisible

unforeseen [ˌʌnforˈsiːn] *adj* : imprevisto

unforgettable [ˌʌnfərˈgɛt̬əbəl] *adj* : inolvidable, memorable — **unforgettably** [-bli] *adv*

unforgivable [ˌʌnfərˈgɪvəbəl] *adj* : imperdonable

unfortunate[1] [ˌʌnˈfɔrtʃənət] *adj* **1** UNLUCKY : desgraciado, infortunado, desafortunado <how unfortunate! : ¡qué mala suerte!> **2** INAPPROPRIATE : inoportuno <an unfortunate comment : un comentario poco feliz>

unfortunate[2] *n* : desgraciado *m,* -da *f*

unfortunately [ˌʌnˈfɔrtʃənətli] *adv* : desafortunadamente

unfounded [ˌʌnˈfaʊndəd] *adj* : infundado

unfreeze [ˌʌnˈfriːz] *v* **-froze** [-ˈfroːz]; **-frozen** [-ˈfroːzən]; **-freezing** *vt* : descongelar — *vi* : descongelarse

unfriendliness [ˌʌnˈfrɛndlinəs] *n* : hostilidad *f,* antipatía *f*

unfriendly [ˌʌnˈfrɛndli] *adj* **-lier; -est** : poco amistoso, hostil

unfurl [ˌʌnˈfərl] *vt* : desplegar, desdoblar — *vi* : desplegarse

unfurnished [ˌʌnˈfərnɪʃt] *adj* : desamueblado

ungainly [ˌʌnˈgeɪnli] *adj* : desgarbado

ungodly [ˌʌnˈgɔdli, -ˈgɑd-] *adj* **1** IMPIOUS : impío **2** OUTRAGEOUS : atroz, terrible <at an ungodly hour : a una hora intempestiva>

ungrateful [ˌʌnˈgreɪtfəl] *adj* : desagradecido, ingrato — **ungratefully** *adv*

ungratefulness [ˌʌnˈgreɪtfəlnəs] *n* : ingratitud *f*

unhappily [ˌʌnˈhæpəli] *adv* **1** SADLY : tristemente **2** UNFORTUNATELY : desafortunadamente, lamentablemente

unhappiness [ˌʌnˈhæpinəs] *n* : infelicidad *f,* tristeza *f,* desdicha *f*

unhappy [ˌʌnˈhæpi] *adj* **-pier; -est 1** UNFORTUNATE : desafortunado, desventurado **2** MISERABLE, SAD : infeliz, triste, desdichado **3** INOPPORTUNE : inoportuno, poco feliz

unharmed [ˌʌnˈhɑrmd] *adj* : salvo, ileso

unhealthy [ˌʌnˈhɛlθi] *adj* **-thier; -est 1** UNWHOLESOME : insalubre, malsano, nocivo a la salud <an unhealthy climate : un clima insalubre> **2** SICKLY : de mala salud, enfermizo

unheard–of [ˌʌnˈhərdəv] *adj* : sin precedente, inaudito, insólito

unhinge [ˌʌnˈhɪndʒ] *vt* **-hinged; -hinging 1** : desquiciar (una puerta, etc.) **2** DISRUPT, UNSETTLE : trastornar, perturbar

unholy [ˌʌnˈhoːli] *adj* **-lier; -est 1** : profano, impío **2** UNGODLY : atroz, terrible

unhook [ˌʌnˈhʊk] *vt* **1** : desenganchar, descolgar (de algo) **2** UNDO : desabrochar

unhurt [ˌʌnˈhərt] *adj* : ileso

unicorn [ˈjuːnəˌkɔrn] *n* : unicornio *m*

unidentified [ˌʌnaɪˈdɛntəˌfaɪd] *adj* : no identificado <unidentified flying object : objeto volador no identificado>

unification [ˌjuːnəfəˈkeɪʃən] *n* : unificación *f*

uniform[1] [ˈjuːnəˌfɔrm] *adj* : uniforme, homogéneo, constante

uniform[2] *n* : uniforme *m*

uniformity [ˌjuːnəˈfɔrmət̬i] *n, pl* **-ties** : uniformidad *f*

unify [ˈjuːnəˌfaɪ] *vt* **-fied; -fying** : unificar, unir

unilateral [ˌjuːnəˈlæt̬ərəl] *adj* : unilateral — **unilaterally** *adv*

unimaginable [ˌʌnɪˈmædʒənəbəl] *adj* : inimaginable, inconcebible

unimportant [ˌʌnɪmˈpɔrtənt] *adj* : intrascendente, insignificante, sin importancia

uninhabited [ˌʌnɪnˈhæbət̬əd] *adj* : deshabitado, desierto, despoblado

uninhibited [ˌʌnɪnˈhɪbət̬əd] *adj* : desenfadado, desinhibido, sin reservas

uninjured [ˌʌnˈindʒərd] *adj* : ileso

unintelligent [ˌʌnɪnˈtɛlədʒənt] *adj* : poco inteligente

unintelligible [ˌʌnɪnˈtɛlədʒəbəl] *adj* : ininteligible, incomprensible

unintentional [ˌʌnɪnˈtɛntʃənəl] *adj* : no deliberado, involuntario

unintentionally [ˌʌnɪnˈtɛntʃənəli] *adv* : involuntariamente, sin querer

uninterested [ˌʌnˈɪntəˌrɛstəd, -trəstəd] *adj* : indiferente

uninteresting [ˌʌnˈɪntəˌrɛstɪŋ, -trəstɪŋ] *adj* : poco interesante, sin interés

uninterrupted [ˌʌnˌɪntəˈrʌptəd] *adj* : ininterrumpido, continuo

union [ˈjuːnjən] *n* **1** : unión *f* **2** *or* **labor union** : sindicato *m,* gremio *m*

unionize [ˈjuːnjəˌnaɪz] *v* **-ized; -izing** *vt* : sindicalizar, sindicar — *vi* : sindicalizarse

unique [jʊˈniːk] *adj* **1** SOLE : único, solo **2** UNUSUAL : extraordinario

uniquely [jʊˈniːkli] *adv* **1** EXCLUSIVELY : exclusivamente **2** EXCEPTIONALLY : excepcionalmente

unison [ˈjuːnəsən, -zən] *n* **1** : unísono *m* (en música) **2** CONCORD : acuerdo *m,* armonía *f,* concordia *f* **3 in ~** SIMULTANEOUSLY : simultáneamente, al unísono

unit [ˈjuːnɪt] *n* **1** : unidad *f* **2** : módulo *m* (de un mobiliario)

unite [jʊˈnaɪt] *v* **united; uniting** *vt* : unir, juntar, combinar — *vi* : unirse, juntarse

unity [ˈjuːnət̬i] *n, pl* **-ties 1** UNION : unidad *f,* unión *f* **2** HARMONY : armonía *f,* acuerdo *m*

universal [ˌjuːnəˈvərsəl] *adj* **1** GENERAL : general, universal <a universal rule : una regla universal> **2** WORLDWIDE : universal, mundial — **universally** *adv*

universe [ˈjuːnəˌvərs] *n* : universo *m*

university [ˌjuːnəˈvərsət̬i] *n, pl* **-ties** : universidad *f*

unjust [ˌʌnˈdʒʌst] *adj* : injusto — **unjustly** *adv*

unjustifiable [ˌʌnˌdʒʌstəˈfaɪəbəl] *adj* : injustificable

unjustified [ˌʌnˈdʒʌstəˌfaɪd] *adj* : injustificado

unkempt [ˌʌnˈkɛmpt] *adj* : descuidado, desaliñado, despeinado (dícese del pelo)

unkind [ˌʌnˈkaɪnd] *adj* : poco amable, cruel — **unkindly** *adv*

unkindness [ˌʌnˈkaɪndnəs] *n* : crueldad *f,* falta *f* de amabilidad

unknowing [ˌʌnˈnoːɪŋ] *adj* : inconsciente, ignorante — **unknowingly** *adv*

unknown [ˌʌnˈnoːn] *adj* : desconocido

unlawful [ˌʌnˈlɔfəl] *adj* : ilícito, ilegal — **unlawfully** *adv*

unleash [ˌʌnˈliːʃ] *vt* : soltar, desatar

unless [ənˈlɛs] *conj* : a menos que, salvo que, a no ser que

unlike¹ [ˌʌnˈlaɪk] *adj* **1** DIFFERENT : diferente, distinto **2** UNEQUAL : desigual

unlike² *prep* **1** : diferente de, distinto de <unlike the others : distinto a los demás> **2** : a diferencia de <unlike her sister, she is shy : a diferencia de su hermana, es tímida>

unlikelihood [ˌʌnˈlaɪkliˌhʊd] *n* : improbabilidad *f*

unlikely [ˌʌnˈlaɪkli] *adj* **-lier; -est 1** IMPROBABLE : improbable, poco probable **2** UNPROMISING : poco prometedor

unlimited [ˌʌnˈlɪmət̬əd] *adj* : ilimitado

unload [ˌʌnˈloːd] *vt* **1** REMOVE : descargar, desembarcar (mercancías o pasajeros) **2** : descargar (un avión, un camión, etc.) **3** DUMP : deshacerse de — *vi* : descargar (dícese de un avión, un camión, etc.)

unlock [ˌʌnˈlɑk] *vt* **1** : abrir (con llave) **2** DISCLOSE, REVEAL : revelar

unluckily [ˌʌnˈlʌkəli] *adv* : desgraciadamente

unlucky [ˌʌnˈlʌki] *adj* **-luckier; -est 1** : de mala suerte, desgraciado, desafortunado <an unlucky year : un año de mala suerte> **2** INAUSPICIOUS : desfavorable, poco propicio **3** REGRETTABLE : lamentable

unmanageable [ˌʌnˈmænɪdʒəbəl] *adj* : difícil de controlar, poco manejable, ingobernable

unmarried [ˌʌnˈmærid] *adj* : soltero

unmask [ˌʌnˈmæsk] *vt* EXPOSE : desenmascarar

unmerciful [ˌʌnˈmərsɪfəl] *adj* MERCILESS : despiadado — **unmercifully** *adv*

unmistakable [ˌʌnmɪˈsteɪkəbəl] *adj* : evidente, inconfundible, obvio — **unmistakably** [-bli] *adv*

unmoved [ˌʌnˈmuːvd] *adj* : impasible <to be unmoved by : permanecer impasible ante>

unnatural [ˌʌnˈnætʃərəl] *adj* **1** ABNORMAL, UNUSUAL : anormal, poco natural, poco normal **2** AFFECTED : afectado, forzado <an unnatural smile : una sonrisa forzada> **3** PERVERSE : perverso, antinatural

unnecessary [ˌʌnˈnɛsəˌsɛri] *adj* : innecesario — **unnecessarily** [-ˌnɛsəˈsɛrəli] *adv*

unnerve [ˌʌnˈnərv] *vt* **-nerved; -nerving :** turbar, desconcertar, poner nervioso

unnoticed [ˌʌnˈnoːt̬əst] *adj* **:** inadvertido <to go unnoticed **:** pasar inadvertido>

unobstructed [ˌʌnəbˈstrʌktəd] *adj* **:** libre, despejado

unobtainable [ˌʌnəbˈteɪnəbəl] *adj* **:** inasequible

unobtrusive [ˌʌnəbˈstruːsɪv] *adj* **:** discreto

unoccupied [ˌʌnˈɑkjəˌpaɪd] *adj* **1** IDLE **:** desempleado, desocupado **2** EMPTY **:** desocupado, libre, deshabitado

unofficial [ˌʌnəˈfɪʃəl] *adj* **:** extraoficial, oficioso, no oficial

unorganized [ˌʌnˈɔrgəˌnaɪzd] *adj* **:** desorganizado

unorthodox [ˌʌnˈɔrθəˌdɑks] *adj* **:** poco ortodoxo, poco convencional

unpack [ˌʌnˈpæk] *vt* **:** desempacar — *vi* **:** desempacar, deshacer las maletas

unpaid [ˌʌnˈpeɪd] *adj* **:** no remunerado, no retribuido <an unpaid bill **:** una cuenta pendiente>

unparalleled [ˌʌnˈpærəˌlɛld] *adj* **:** sin igual

unpatriotic [ˌʌnˌpeɪtriˈɑt̬ɪk] *adj* **:** antipatriótico

unpleasant [ˌʌnˈplɛzənt] *adj* **:** desagradable — **unpleasantly** *adv*

unplug [ˌʌnˈplʌg] *vt* **-plugged; -plugging 1** UNCLOG **:** destapar, desatascar **2** DISCONNECT **:** desconectar, desenchufar

unpopular [ˌʌnˈpɑpjələr] *adj* **:** impopular, poco popular

unpopularity [ˌʌnˌpɑpjəˈlærət̬i] *n* **:** impopularidad *f*

unprecedented [ˌʌnˈprɛsəˌdɛntəd] *adj* **:** sin precedentes, inaudito, nuevo

unpredictable [ˌʌnpriˈdɪktəbəl] *adj* **:** impredecible

unprejudiced [ˌʌnˈprɛdʒədəst] *adj* **:** imparcial, objetivo

unprepared [ˌʌnpriˈpærd] *adj* **:** no preparado <an unprepared speech **:** un discurso improvisado>

unpretentious [ˌʌnpriˈtɛntʃəs] *adj* **:** modesto, sin pretensiones

unprincipled [ˌʌnˈprɪn*t*səpəld] *adj* **:** sin principios, carente de escrúpulos

unproductive [ˌʌnprəˈdʌktɪv] *adj* **:** improductivo

unprofitable [ˌʌnˈprɑfət̬əbəl] *adj* **:** no rentable, poco provechoso

unpromising [ˌʌnˈprɑməsɪŋ] *adj* **:** poco prometedor

unprotected [ˌʌnprəˈtɛktəd] *adj* **:** sin protección, desprotegido

unprovoked [ˌʌnprəˈvoːkt] *adj* **:** no provocado

unpunished [ˌʌnˈpʌnɪʃt] *adj* **:** impune <to go unpunished **:** escapar sin castigo>

unqualified [ˌʌnˈkwɑləˌfaɪd] *adj* **1 :** no calificado, sin título **2** COMPLETE **:** completo, absoluto <an unqualified denial **:** una negación incondicional>

unquestionable [ˌʌnˈkwɛstʃənəbəl] *adj* **:** incuestionable, indudable, indiscutible — **unquestionably** [-bli] *adv*

unquestioning [ˌʌnˈkwɛstʃənɪŋ] *adj* **:** incondicional, absoluto, ciego

unravel [ˌʌnˈrævəl] *v* **-eled** *or* **-elled; -eling** *or* **-elling** *vt* **1** DISENTANGLE **:** desenmarañar, desenredar **2** SOLVE **:** aclarar, desenmarañar, desentrañar — *vi* **:** deshacerse

unreal [ˌʌnˈriːl] *adj* **:** irreal

unrealistic [ˌʌnˌriːəˈlɪstɪk] *adj* **:** poco realista

unreasonable [ˌʌnˈriːzənəbəl] *adj* **1** IRRATIONAL **:** poco razonable, irrazonable, irracional **2** EXCESSIVE **:** excesivo <unreasonable prices **:** precios excesivos>

unreasonably [ˌʌnˈriːzənəbli] *adv* **1** IRRATIONALLY **:** irracionalmente, de manera irrazonable **2** EXCESSIVELY **:** excesivamente

unrefined [ˌʌnriˈfaɪnd] *adj* **1 :** no refinado, sin refinar (dícese del azúcar, de la harina, etc.) **2 :** poco refinado, inculto (dícese de una persona)

unrelated [ˌʌnriˈleɪt̬əd] *adj* **:** no relacionado, inconexo

unrelenting [ˌʌnriˈlɛntɪŋ] *adj* **1** STERN **:** severo, inexorable **2** CONSTANT, RELENTLESS **:** constante, implacable

unreliable [ˌʌnriˈlaɪəbəl] *adj* **:** que no es de fiar, de poca confianza, inestable (dícese del tiempo)

unrepentant [ˌʌnriˈpɛntənt] *adj* **:** impenitente

unresolved [ˌʌnriˈzɑlvd] *adj* **:** pendiente, no resuelto

unrest [ˌʌnˈrɛst] *n* **:** inquietud *f,* malestar *m* <political unrest **:** disturbios políticos>

unrestrained [ˌʌnriˈstreɪnd] *adj* **:** desenfrenado, incontrolado

unrestricted [ˌʌnriˈstrɪktəd] *adj* **:** sin restricción <unrestricted access **:** libre acceso>

unrewarding [ˌʌnriˈwɔrdɪŋ] *adj* THANKLESS **:** ingrato

unripe [ˌʌnˈraɪp] *adj* **:** inmaduro, verde

unrivaled *or* **unrivalled** [ˌʌnˈraɪvəld] *adj* **:** incomparable

unroll [ˌʌnˈroːl] *vt* **:** desenrollar — *vi* **:** desenrollarse

unruffled [ˌʌnˈrʌfəld] *adj* **1** SERENE **:** sereno, tranquilo **2** SMOOTH **:** tranquilo, liso <unruffled waters **:** aguas tranquilas>

unruliness [ˌʌnˈruːlinəs] *n* **:** indisciplina *f*

unruly [ˌʌnˈruːli] *adj* **:** indisciplinado, díscolo, rebelde

unsafe [ˌʌnˈseɪf] *adj* **:** inseguro

unsaid [ˌʌnˈsɛd] *adj* **:** sin decir <to leave unsaid **:** quedar por decir>

unsanitary [ˌʌnˈsænəˌtɛri] *adj* **:** antihigiénico

unsatisfactory [ˌʌnˌsæt̬əsˈfæktəri] *adj* : insatisfactorio

unsatisfied [ˌʌnˈsæt̬əsˌfaɪd] *adj* : insatisfecho

unscathed [ˌʌnˈskeɪðd] *adj* UNHARMED : ileso

unscheduled [ˌʌnˈskɛˌdʒuːld] *adj* : no programado, imprevisto

unscientific [ˌʌnˌsaɪənˈtɪfɪk] *adj* : poco científico

unscrupulous [ˌʌnˈskruːpjələs] *adj* : inescrupuloso, sin escrúpulos — **unscrupulously** *adv*

unseal [ˌʌnˈsiːl] *vt* : abrir, quitarle el sello a

unseasonable [ˌʌnˈsiːzənəbəl] *adj* **1** : extemporáneo <unseasonable rain : lluvia extemporánea> **2** UNTIMELY : extemporáneo, inoportuno

unseemly [ˌʌnˈsiːmli] *adj* **-lier; -est 1** INDECOROUS : indecoroso **2** INAPPROPRIATE : impropio, inapropiado

unseen [ˌʌnˈsiːn] *adj* **1** UNNOTICED : inadvertido **2** INVISIBLE : oculto, invisible

unselfish [ˌʌnˈsɛlfɪʃ] *adj* : generoso, desinteresado — **unselfishly** *adv*

unselfishness [ˌʌnˈsɛlfɪʃnəs] *n* : generosidad *f,* desinterés *m*

unsettle [ˌʌnˈsɛt̬əl] *vt* **-tled; -tling** DISTURB : trastornar, alterar, perturbar

unsettled [ˌʌnˈsɛt̬əld] *adj* **1** CHANGEABLE : inestable, variable <unsettled weather : tiempo inestable> **2** DISTURBED : agitado, inquieto <unsettled waters : aguas agitadas> **3** UNDECIDED : pendiente (dícese de un asunto), indeciso (dícese de una persona) **4** UNPAID : sin saldar, pendiente **5** UNINHABITED : despoblado, no colonizado

unshaped [ˌʌnˈʃeɪpt] *adj* : sin forma, informe

unsightly [ˌʌnˈsaɪtli] *adj* UGLY : feo, de aspecto malo

unskilled [ˌʌnˈskɪld] *adj* : no calificado

unskillful [ˌʌnˈskɪlfəl] *adj* : inexperto, poco hábil

unsnap [ˌʌnˈsnæp] *vt* **-snapped; -snapping** : desabrochar

unsociable *adj* : poco sociable

unsolved [ˌʌnˈsɔlvd] *adj* : no resuelto, sin resolver

unsophisticated [ˌʌnsəˈfɪstəˌkeɪt̬əd] *adj* **1** NAIVE, UNWORLDLY : ingenuo, de poco mundo **2** SIMPLE : simple, poco sofisticado, rudimentario

unsound [ˌʌnˈsaʊnd] *adj* **1** UNHEALTHY : enfermizo, de mala salud **2** : poco sólido, defectuoso (dícese de una estructura, etc.) **3** INVALID : inválido, erróneo **4 of unsound mind** : mentalmente incapacitado

unspeakable [ˌʌnˈspiːkəbəl] *adj* **1** INDESCRIBABLE : indecible, inexpresable, incalificable **2** HEINOUS : atroz, nefando, abominable — **unspeakably** [-bli] *adv*

unspecified [ˌʌnˈspɛsəˌfaɪd] *adj* : indeterminado, sin especificar

unspoiled [ˌʌnˈspɔɪld] *adj* **1** : conservado, sin estropear (dícese de un lugar) **2** : que no está mimado (dícese de un niño)

unstable [ˌʌnˈsteɪbəl] *adj* **1** CHANGEABLE : variable, inestable, cambiable <an unstable pulse : un pulso irregular> **2** UNSTEADY : inestable, poco sólido (dícese de una estructura)

unsteadily [ˌʌnˈstɛdəli] *adv* : de modo inestable

unsteadiness [ˌʌnˈstɛdinəs] *n* : inestabilidad *f,* inseguridad *f*

unsteady [ˌʌnˈstɛdi] *adj* **1** UNSTABLE : inestable, variable **2** SHAKY : tembloroso

unstoppable [ˌʌnˈstɑpəbəl] *adj* : irrefrenable, incontenible

unsubstantiated [ˌʌnsəbˈstæntʃiˌeɪt̬əd] *adj* : no corroborado, no demostrado

unsuccessful [ˌʌnsəkˈsɛsfəl] *adj* : fracasado, infructuoso

unsuitable [ˌʌnˈsuːt̬əbəl] *adj* : inadecuado, impropio, inapropiado <an unsuitable time : una hora inconveniente>

unsuited [ˌʌnˈsuːt̬əd] *adj* : inadecuado, inepto

unsung [ˌʌnˈsʌŋ] *adj* : olvidado

unsure [ˌʌnˈʃʊr] *adj* : incierto, dudoso

unsurpassed [ˌʌnsərˈpæst] *adj* : sin par, sin igual

unsuspecting [ˌʌnsəˈspɛktɪŋ] *adj* : desprevenido, desapercibido, confiado

unsympathetic [ˌʌnˌsɪmpəˈθɛt̬ɪk] *adj* : poco comprensivo, indiferente

untangle [ˌʌnˈteɪŋgəl] *vt* **-gled; -gling** : desenmarañar, desenredar

unthinkable [ˌʌnˈθɪŋkəbəl] *adj* : inconcebible, impensable

unthinking [ˌʌnˈθɪŋkɪŋ] *adj* : irreflexivo, inconsciente — **unthinkingly** *adv*

untidy [ˌʌnˈtaɪdi] *adj* **1** SLOVENLY : desaliñado **2** DISORDERLY : desordenado, desarreglado

untie [ˌʌnˈtaɪ] *vt* **-tied; -tying** *or* **-tieing** : desatar, deshacer

until¹ [ˌʌnˈtɪl] *prep* : hasta <until now : hasta ahora>

until² *conj* : hasta que <until they left : hasta que salieron> <don't answer until you're sure : no contestes hasta que (no) estés seguro>

untimely [ˌʌnˈtaɪmli] *adj* **1** PREMATURE : prematuro <an untimely death : una muerte prematura> **2** INOPPORTUNE : inoportuno, intempestivo

untold [ˌʌnˈtoːld] *adj* **1** : nunca dicho <the untold secret : el secreto sin contar> **2** INCALCULABLE : incalculable, indecible

untouched [ˌʌnˈtʌtʃt] *adj* **1** INTACT : intacto, sin tocar, sin probar (dícese de la comida) **2** UNAFFECTED : insensible, indiferente

untoward [ˌʌnˈtɔrd, -ˈtoːərd, -təˈwɔrd] *adj* **1** : indecoroso, impropio (dícese del comportamiento) **2** ADVERSE, UNFORTUNATE : desafortunado, adverso <untoward effects : efectos perjudiciales> **3** UNSEEMLY : indecoroso

untrained [ˌʌnˈtreɪnd] *adj* : inexperto, no capacitado

untreated [ˌʌnˈtriːtəd] *adj* : no tratado (dícese de una enfermedad, etc.), sin tratar (dícese de un material)

untroubled [ˌʌnˈtrʌbəld] *adj* : tranquilo <to be untroubled by : no estar afectado por>

untrue [ˌʌnˈtruː] *adj* **1** UNFAITHFUL : infiel **2** FALSE : falso

untrustworthy [ˌʌnˈtrʌstˌwərði] *adj* : de poca confianza (dícese de una persona), no fidedigno (dícese de la información)

untruth [ˌʌnˈtruːθ, ˈʌnˌ-] *n* : mentira *f*, falsedad *f*

untruthful [ˌʌnˈtruːθfəl] *adj* : mentiroso, falso

unusable [ˌʌnˈjuːzəbəl] *adj* : inútil, inservible

unused [ˌʌnˈjuːzd, *in sense 1 usually* -ˈjuːst] *adj* **1** UNACCUSTOMED : inhabituado **2** NEW : nuevo **3** IDLE : no utilizado (dícese de la tierra) **4** REMAINING : restante <the unused portion : la porción restante>

unusual [ˌʌnˈjuːʒʊəl] *adj* : inusual, poco común, raro

unusually [ˌʌnˈjuːʒʊəli, -ˈjuːʒəli] *adv* : excepcionalmente, extraordinariamente, fuera de lo común

unwanted [ˌʌnˈwɑntəd] *adj* : superfluo, de sobre

unwarranted [ˌʌnˈwɔrəntəd] *adj* : injustificado

unwary [ˌʌnˈwæri] *adj* : incauto

unwavering [ˌʌnˈweɪvərɪŋ] *adj* : firme, inquebrantable <an unwavering gaze : una mirada fija>

unwelcome [ˌʌnˈwɛlkəm] *adj* : importuno, molesto

unwell [ˌʌnˈwɛl] *adj* : enfermo, mal

unwholesome [ˌʌnˈhoːlsəm] *adj* **1** UNHEALTHY : malsano, insalubre **2** PERNICIOUS : pernicioso **3** LOATHSOME : repugnante, muy desagradable

unwieldy [ˌʌnˈwiːldi] *adj* CUMBERSOME : difícil de manejar, torpe y pesado

unwilling [ˌʌnˈwɪlɪŋ] *adj* : poco dispuesto <to be unwilling to : no estar dispuesto a>

unwillingly [ˌʌnˈwɪlɪŋli] *adv* : a regañadientes, de mala gana

unwind [ˌʌnˈwaɪnd] *v* **-wound** [-ˈwaʊnd]; **-winding** *vt* **1** UNROLL : desenrollar **2** RELAX : relajar — *vi* : desenrollarse

unwise [ˌʌnˈwaɪz] *adj* : imprudente, desacertado, poco aconsejable

unwisely [ˌʌnˈwaɪzli] *adv* : imprudentemente

unwitting [ˌʌnˈwɪtɪŋ] *adj* **1** UNAWARE : inconsciente **2** INADVERTENT : involuntario, inadvertido <an unwitting mistake : un error inadvertido> — **unwittingly** *adv*

unworthiness [ˌʌnˈwərðinəs] *n* : falta *f* de valía

unworthy [ˌʌnˈwərði] *adj* **1** UNDESERVING : indigno <to be unworthy of : no ser digno de> **2** UNMERITED : inmerecido

unwrap [ˌʌnˈræp] *vt* **-wrapped; -wrapping** : desenvolver, deshacer

unwritten [ˌʌnˈrɪtən] *adj* : no escrito

unyielding [ˌʌnˈjiːldɪŋ] *adj* : firme, inflexible, rígido

unzip [ˌʌnˈzɪp] *vt* **-zipped; -zipping** : abrir el cierre de

up[1] [ˈʌp] *v* **upped** [ˈʌpt]; **upping; ups** *vt* INCREASE : aumentar, subir <they upped the prices : aumentaron los precios> — *vi* **to up and** : agarrar y *fam* <she up and left : agarró y se fue>

up[2] *adv* **1** ABOVE : arriba, en lo alto <up in the mountains : arriba en las montañas> **2** UPWARDS : hacia arriba <push it up : empújalo hacia arriba> <the sun came up : el sol salió> <prices went up : los precios subieron> **3** (*indicating an upright position or waking state*) <to sit up : ponerse derecho> <they got up late : se levantaron tarde> <I stayed up all night : pasé toda la noche sin dormir> **4** (*indicating volume or intensity*) <to speak up : hablar más fuerte> **5** (*indicating a northerly direction*) <the climate up north : el clima del norte> <I'm going up to Canada : voy para Canadá> **6** (*indicating the appearance or existence of something*) <the book turned up : el libro apareció> **7** (*indicating consideration*) <she brought the matter up : mencionó el asunto> **8** COMPLETELY : completamente <eat it up : cómetelo todo> **9** : en pedazos <he tore it up : lo rompió en pedazos> **10** (*indicating a stopping*) <the car pulled up to the curb : el carro paró al borde de la acera> **11** (*indicating an even score*) <the game was 10 up : empataron a 10>

up[3] *adj* **1** (*risen above the horizon*) <the sun is up : ha salido el sol> **2** (*being above a normal or former level*) <prices are up : los precios han aumentado> <the river is up : las aguas están altas> **3** : despierto, levantado <up all night : despierto toda la noche> **4** BUILT : construido <the house is up : la casa está construida> **5** OPEN : abierto <the windows are up : las ventanas están abiertas> **6** (*moving or going upward*) <the up staircase : la escalera para subir> **7** ABREAST : enterado, al día, al corriente <to be up on the news : estar al corriente de las noticias> **8** PREPARED : preparado <we were up for the test

: estuvimos preparados para el examen> **9** FINISHED : terminado, acabado <time is up : se ha terminado el tiempo permitido> **10 to be up** : pasar <what's up? : ¿qué pasa?>

up[4] *prep* **1** (*to, toward, or at a higher point of*) <he went up the stairs : subió la escalera> **2** (*to or toward the source of*) <to go up the river : ir río arriba> **3** ALONG : a lo largo, por <up the coast : a lo largo de la costa> <just up the way : un poco más adelante> <up and down the city : por toda la ciudad>

upbraid [ˌʌpˈbreɪd] *vt* : reprender, regañar

upbringing [ˈʌpˌbrɪŋɪŋ] *n* : crianza *f,* educación *f*

upcoming [ˌʌpˈkʌmɪŋ] *adj* : próximo

update[1] [ˌʌpˈdeɪt] *vt* **-dated; -dating** : poner al día, poner al corriente, actualizar

update[2] [ˈʌpˌdeɪt] *n* : actualización *f,* puesta *f* al día

upend [ˌʌpˈɛnd] *vt* **1** : poner vertical **2** OVERTURN : volcar

upgrade[1] [ˈʌpˌgreɪd, ˌʌpˈ-] *vt* **-graded; -grading** : elevar la categoría de (un puesto, etc.), implementar mejoras a (una facilidad, etc.)

upgrade[2] [ˈʌpˌgreɪd] *n* **1** SLOPE : cuesta *f,* pendiente *f* **2** RISE : aumento *m* de categoría (de un puesto), ascenso *m* (de un empleado)

upheaval [ˌʌpˈhiːvəl] *n* **1** : levantamiento *m* (en geología) **2** DISTURBANCE, UPSET : trastorno *m,* agitación *f,* conmoción *f*

uphill[1] [ˌʌpˈhɪl] *adv* : cuesta arriba

uphill[2] [ˈʌpˌhɪl] *adj* **1** ASCENDING : en subida **2** DIFFICULT : difícil, arduo

uphold [ˌʌpˈhoːld] *vt* **-held; -holding** **1** SUPPORT : sostener, apoyar, mantener **2** RAISE : levantar **3** CONFIRM : confirmar (una decisión judicial)

upholster [ˌʌpˈhoːlstər] *vt* : tapizar

upholsterer [ˌʌpˈhoːlstərər] *n* : tapicero *m,* -ra *f*

upholstery [ˌʌpˈhoːlstəri] *n, pl* **-steries** : tapicería *f*

upkeep [ˈʌpˌkiːp] *n* : mantenimiento *m*

upland [ˈʌplənd, -ˌlænd] *n* : altiplanicie *f,* altiplano *m*

uplift[1] [ˌʌpˈlɪft] *vt* **1** RAISE : elevar, levantar **2** ELEVATE : elevar, animar (el espíritu, la mente, etc.)

uplift[2] [ˈʌpˌlɪft] *n* : elevación *f*

upon [əˈpɔn, əˈpɑn] *prep* : en, sobre <upon the desk : sobre el escritorio> <upon leaving : al salir> <questions upon questions : pregunta tras pregunta>

upper[1] [ˈʌpər] *adj* **1** HIGHER : superior <the upper classes : las clases altas> **2** : alto (en geografía) <the upper Mississippi : el alto Mississippi>

upper[2] *n* : parte *f* superior (del calzado, etc.)

uppercase [ˌʌpərˈkeɪs] *adj* : mayúsculo

upper hand *n* : ventaja *f,* dominio *m*

uppermost [ˈʌpərˌmoːst] *adj* : más alto <it was uppermost in his mind : era lo que más le preocupaba>

upright[1] [ˈʌpˌraɪt] *adj* **1** VERTICAL : vertical **2** ERECT : erguido, derecho <to sit upright : sentarse derecho>**3** JUST : recto, honesto, justo

upright[2] *n* : montante *m,* poste *m,* soporte *m*

uprising [ˈʌpˌraɪzɪŋ] *n* : insurrección *f,* revuelta *f,* alzamiento *m*

uproar [ˈʌpˌror] *n* COMMOTION : alboroto *m,* jaleo *m,* escándalo *m*

uproarious [ˌʌpˈroriəs] *adj* **1** CLAMOROUS : estrepitoso, clamoroso **2** HILARIOUS : muy divertido, hilarante — **uproariously** *adv*

uproot [ˌʌpˈruːt, -ˈrʊt] *vt* : desarraigar

upset[1] [ˌʌpˈsɛt] *vt* **-set; -setting** **1** OVERTURN : volcar **2** SPILL : derramar **3** DISTURB : perturbar, disgustar, inquietar, alterar **4** SICKEN : sentar mal a <it upsets my stomach : me sienta mal al estómago> **5** DISRUPT : trastornar, desbaratar (planes, etc.) **6** DEFEAT : derrotar (en deportes)

upset[2] *adj* **1** DISPLEASED, DISTRESSED : disgustado, alterado **2 to have an upset stomach** : estar mal del estómago, estar descompuesto (de estómago)

upset[3] [ˈʌpˌsɛt] *n* **1** OVERTURNING : vuelco *m* **2** DISRUPTION : trastorno *m* (de planes, etc.) **3** DEFEAT : derrota *f* (en deportes)

upshot [ˈʌpˌʃɑt] *n* : resultado *m* final

upside–down [ˌʌpˌsaɪdˈdaʊn] *adj* : al revés

upside down [ˌʌpˌsaɪdˈdaʊn] *adv* **1** : al revés **2** : en confusión, en desorden

upstairs[1] [ˌʌpˈstærz] *adv* : arriba, en el piso superior

upstairs[2] [ˈʌpˌstærz, ˌʌpˈ-] *adj* : de arriba

upstairs[3] [ˈʌpˌstærz, ˌʌpˈ-] *ns & pl* : piso *m* de arriba, planta *f* de arriba

upstanding [ˌʌpˈstændɪŋ, ˈʌpˌ-] *adj* HONEST, UPRIGHT : honesto, íntegro, recto

upstart [ˈʌpˌstɑrt] *n* : advenedizo *m,* -za *f*

upswing [ˈʌpˌswɪŋ] *n* : alza *f,* mejora *f* notable <to be on the upswing : estar mejorándose>

uptight [ˌʌpˈtaɪt] *adj* : tenso, nervioso

up to *prep* **1** : hasta <up to a year : hasta un año> <in mud up to my ankles : en barro hasta los tobillos> **2 to be up to** : estar a la altura de <I'm not up to going : no estoy en condiciones de ir> **3 to be up to** : depender de <it's up to the director : depende del director>

up–to–date [ˌʌptəˈdeɪt] *adj* **1** CURRENT : corriente, al día <to keep up-to-date

: mantenerse al corriente> 2 MODERN : moderno

uptown [ˈʌpˈtaʊn] *adv* : hacia la parte alta de la ciudad, hacia el distrito residencial

upturn [ˈʌpˌtərn] *n* : mejora *f,* auge *m* (económico)

upward[1] [ˈʌpwərd] *or* **upwards** [-wərdz] *adv* : hacia arriba

upward[2] *adj* : ascendente, hacia arriba

upwind [ˌʌpˈwɪnd] *adv & adj* : contra el viento

uranium [jʊˈreɪniəm] *n* : uranio *m*

Uranus [jʊˈreɪnəs, ˈjʊrənəs] *n* : Urano *m*

urban [ˈərbən] *adj* : urbano

urbane [ˌərˈbeɪn] *adj* : urbano, cortés

urchin [ˈərtʃən] *n* **1** SCAMP : granuja *mf;* pillo *m,* -lla *f* **2 sea urchin** : erizo *m* de mar

urethra [jʊˈriːθrə] *n, pl* **-thras** *or* **-thrae** [-ˌθriː] : uretra *f*

urge[1] [ˈərdʒ] *vt* **urged; urging 1** PRESS : instar, apremiar, insistir <we urged him to come : insistimos en que viniera> **2** ADVOCATE : recomendar, abogar por **3 to urge on** : animar, alentar

urge[2] *n* : impulso *m,* ganas *fpl,* compulsión *f*

urgency [ˈərdʒəntsi] *n, pl* **-cies** : urgencia *f*

urgent [ˈərdʒənt] *adj* **1** PRESSING : urgente, apremiante **2** INSISTENT : insistente **3 to be urgent** : urgir

urgently [ˈərdʒəntli] *adv* : urgentemente

urinal [ˈjʊrənəl, *esp Brit* jʊˈraɪnəl] *n* : orinal *m* (recipiente), urinario *m* (lugar)

urinary [ˈjʊrəˌnɛri] *adj* : urinario

urinate [ˈjʊrəˌneɪt] *vi* **-nated; -nating** : orinar

urination [ˌjʊrəˈneɪʃən] *n* : orinación *f*

urine [ˈjʊrən] *n* : orina *f*

urn [ˈərn] *n* **1** VASE : urna *f* **2** : recipiente *m* (para servir café, etc.)

Uruguayan [ˌʊrəˈgwaɪən, ˌjʊr-, -ˈgweɪ-] *n* : uruguayo *m,* -ya *f* — **Uruguayan** *adj*

us [ˈʌs] *pron* **1** (*as direct object*) : nos <they were visiting us : nos visitaban> **2** (*as indirect object*) : nos <he gave us a present : nos dio un regalo> **3** (*as object of preposition*) : nosotros, nosotras <stay with us : quédese con nosotros> <both of us : nosotros dos> **4** (*for emphasis*) : nosotros <it's us! : ¡somos nosotros!>

usable [ˈjuːzəbəl] *adj* : utilizable

usage [ˈjuːsɪdʒ, -zɪdʒ] *n* **1** HABIT : costumbre *f,* hábito *m* **2** USE : uso *m*

use[1] [ˈjuːz] *v* **used** [ˈjuːzd, *in phrase "used to" usually* ˈjuːstuː]; **using** *vt* **1** EMPLOY : emplear, usar **2** CONSUME : consumir, tomar (drogas, etc.) **3** UTILIZE : usar, utilizar <to use tact : usar tacto> <he used his friends to get ahead : usó a sus amigos para mejorar su posición> **4** TREAT : tratar <they used the horse cruelly : maltrataron al caballo> **5 to use up** : agotar, consumir, gastar — *vi* (*used in the past with* **to** *to indicate a former fact or state*) : soler, acostumbrar <winters used to be colder : los inviernos solían ser más fríos, los inviernos eran más fríos> <she used to dance : acostumbraba bailar>

use[2] [ˈjuːs] *n* **1** APPLICATION, EMPLOYMENT : uso *m,* empleo *m,* utilización *f* <out of use : en desuso> <ready for use : listo para usar> <to be in use : usarse, estar funcionando> <to make use of : servirse de, aprovechar> **2** USEFULNESS : utilidad *f* <to be of no use : no servir (para nada)> <it's no use! : ¡es inútil!> **3 to have the use of** : poder usar, tener acceso a **4 to have no use for** : no necesitar <she has no use for poetry : a ella no le gusta la poesía>

used [ˈjuːzd] *adj* **1** SECONDHAND : usado, de segunda mano <used cars : coches usados> **2 used to** ACCUSTOMED : acostumbrado <used to the heat : acostumbrado al calor>

useful [ˈjuːsfəl] *adj* : útil, práctico — **usefully** *adv*

usefulness [ˈjuːsfəlnəs] *n* : utilidad *f*

useless [ˈjuːsləs] *adj* : inútil — **uselessly** *adv*

uselessness [ˈjuːsləsnəs] *n* : inutilidad *f*

user [ˈjuːzər] *n* : usuario *m,* -ria *f*

usher[1] [ˈʌʃər] *vt* **1** ESCORT : acompañar, conducir **2 to usher in** : hacer pasar (a alguien) <to usher in a new era : anunciar una nueva época>

usher[2] *n* : acomodador *m,* -dora *f*

usherette [ˌʌʃəˈrɛt] *n* : acomodadora *f*

usual [ˈjuːʒʊəl] *adj* **1** NORMAL : usual, normal **2** CUSTOMARY : acostumbrado, habitual, de costumbre **3** ORDINARY : ordinario, típico

usually [ˈjuːʒʊəli, ˈjuːʒəli] *adv* : usualmente, normalmente

usurp [jʊˈsərp, -ˈzərp] *vt* : usurpar

usurper [jʊˈsərpər, -ˈzər-] *n* : usurpador *m,* -dora *f*

utensil [jʊˈtɛntsəl] *n* **1** : utensilio *m* (de cocina) **2** IMPLEMENT : implemento *m,* útil *m* (de labranza, etc.)

uterus [ˈjuːtərəs] *n, pl* **uteri** [-ˌraɪ] : útero *m,* matriz *f*

utilitarian [juːˌtɪləˈtɛriən] *adj* : utilitario

utility [juːˈtɪləti] *n, pl* **-ties 1** USEFULNESS : utilidad *f* **2 public utility** : empresa *f* de servicio público

utilization [ˌjuːtələˈzeɪʃən] *n* : utilización *f*

utilize [ˈjuːtəlˌaɪz] *vt* **-lized; -lizing** : utilizar, hacer uso de

utmost[1] [ˈʌtˌmoːst] *adj* **1** FARTHEST : extremo, más lejano **2** GREATEST : sumo, mayor <of the utmost importance : de suma importancia>

utmost[2] *n* : lo más posible <to the utmost : al máximo>

utopia [jʊˈto:piə] *n* : utopía *f*

utopian [jʊˈto:piən] *adj* : utópico

utter[1] [ˈʌt̬ər] *vt* : decir, articular, pronunciar (palabras)

utter[2] *adj* : absoluto — **utterly** *adv*

utterance [ˈʌt̬ərənts] *n* : declaración *f*, articulación *f*

V

v [ˈvi:] *n, pl* **v's** *or* **vs** [ˈvi:z] : vigésima segunda letra del alfabeto inglés

vacancy [ˈveɪkəntsi] *n, pl* **-cies 1** EMPTINESS : vacío *m*, vacuidad *f* **2** : vacante *f*, puesto *m* vacante <to fill a vacancy : ocupar un puesto> **3** : habitación *f* libre (en un hotel) <no vacancies : completo>

vacant [ˈveɪkənt] *adj* **1** EMPTY : libre, desocupado (dícese de los edificios, etc.) **2** : vacante (dícese de los puestos) **3** BLANK : vacío, ausente <a vacant stare : una mirada ausente>

vacate [ˈveɪˌkeɪt] *vt* **-cated; -cating** : desalojar, desocupar

vacation[1] [veɪˈkeɪʃən, və-] *vi* : pasar las vacaciones, vacacionar *Mex*

vacation[2] *n* : vacaciones *fpl* <to be on vacation : estar de vacaciones>

vacationer [veɪˈkeɪʃənər, və-] *n* : turista *mf*, veraneante *mf*, vacacionista *mf CA, Mex*

vaccinate [ˈvæksəˌneɪt] *vt* **-nated; -nating** : vacunar

vaccination [ˌvæksəˈneɪʃən] *n* : vacunación *f*

vaccine [vækˈsi:n, ˈvækˌ-] *n* : vacuna *f*

vacillate [ˈvæsəˌleɪt] *vi* **-lated; -lating 1** HESITATE : vacilar **2** SWAY : oscilar

vacillation [ˌvæsəˈleɪʃən] *n* : indecisión *f*, vacilación *f*

vacuous [ˈvækjʊəs] *adj* **1** EMPTY : vacío **2** INANE : vacuo, necio, estúpido

vacuum[1] [ˈvæˌkju:m, -kjəm] *vt* : limpiar con aspiradora, pasar la aspiradora por

vacuum[2] *n, pl* **vacuums** *or* **vacua** [ˈvækjʊə] : vacío *m*

vacuum cleaner *n* : aspiradora *f*

vagabond[1] [ˈvægəˌbɑnd] *adj* : vagabundo

vagabond[2] *n* : vagabundo *m*, -da *f*

vagary [ˈveɪgəri, vəˈgɛri] *n, pl* **-ries** : capricho *m*

vagina [vəˈdʒaɪnə] *n, pl* **-nae** [-ˌni:, -ˌnaɪ] *or* **-nas** : vagina *f*

vagrancy [ˈveɪgrəntsi] *n* : vagancia *f*

vagrant[1] [ˈveɪgrənt] *adj* : vagabundo

vagrant[2] *n* : vagabundo *m*, -da *f*

vague [ˈveɪg] *adj* **vaguer; -est 1** IMPRECISE : vago, impreciso <a vague feeling : una sensación indefinida> <I haven't the vaguest idea : no tengo la más remota idea> **2** UNCLEAR : borroso, poco claro <a vague outline : un perfil indistinto> **3** ABSENTMINDED : distraído

vaguely [ˈveɪgli] *adv* : vagamente, de manera imprecisa

vagueness [ˈveɪgnəs] *n* : vaguedad *f*, imprecisión *f*

vain [ˈveɪn] *adj* **1** WORTHLESS : vano **2** FUTILE : vano, inútil <in vain : en vano> **3** CONCEITED : vanidoso, presumido

vainly [ˈveɪnli] *adv* : en vano, vanamente, inútilmente

valance [ˈvæləntś, ˈveɪ-] *n* **1** FLOUNCE : volante *m* (de una cama, etc.) **2** : galería *f* de cortina (sobre una ventana)

vale [ˈveɪl] *n* : valle *m*

valedictorian [ˌvæləˌdɪkˈtoriən] *n* : estudiante *mf* que pronuncia el discurso de despedida en ceremonia de graduación

valedictory [ˌvæləˈdɪktəri] *adj* : de despedida

valentine [ˈvælənˌtaɪn] *n* : tarjeta *f* que se manda el Día de los Enamorados (el 14 de febrero)

Valentine's Day *n* : Día *m* de los Enamorados

valet [ˈvæˌleɪ, væˈleɪ, ˈvælət] *n* : ayuda *m* de cámara

valiant [ˈvæljənt] *adj* : valiente, valeroso

valiantly [ˈvæljəntli] *adv* : con valor, valientemente

valid [ˈvæləd] *adj* : válido

validate [ˈvæləˌdeɪt] *vt* **-dated; -dating** : validar, dar validez a

validity [vəˈlɪdət̬i, væ-] *n* : validez *f*

valise [vəˈli:s] *n* : maleta *f* (de mano)

valley [ˈvæli] *n, pl* **-leys** : valle *m*

valor [ˈvælər] *n* : valor *m*, valentía *f*

valorous [ˈvælərəs] *adj* : valeroso, valiente

valuable[1] [ˈvæljʊəbəl, ˈvæljəbəl] *adj* **1** EXPENSIVE : valioso, de valor **2** WORTHWHILE : valioso, apreciable

valuable[2] *n* : objeto *m* de valor

valuation [ˌvæljʊˈeɪʃən] *n* **1** APPRAISAL : valoración *f*, tasación *f* **2** VALUE : valuación *f*

value[1] [ˈvælˌju:] *vt* **-ued; -uing 1** APPRAISE : valorar, avaluar, tasar **2** APPRECIATE : valorar, apreciar

value[2] *n* **1** : valor *m* <of little value : de poco valor> <to be a good value : estar bien de precio, tener buen precio> <at face value : en su sentido literal>

2 values *npl* **:** valores *mpl* (morales), principios *mpl*
valueless ['væljuːləs] *adj* **:** sin valor
valve ['vælv] *n* **:** válvula *f*
vampire ['væmˌpaɪr] *n* **1 :** vampiro *m* **2** *or* **vampire bat :** vampiro *m*
van[1] ['væn] → **vanguard**
van[2] *n* **:** furgoneta *f,* camioneta *f*
vanadium [və'neɪdiəm] *n* **:** vanadio *m*
vandal ['vændəl] *n* **:** vándalo *m*
vandalism ['vændəlˌɪzəm] *n* **:** vandalismo *m*
vandalize ['vændəlˌaɪz] *vt* **:** destrozar, destruir, estropear
vane ['veɪn] *n or* **weather vane :** veleta *f*
vanguard ['vænˌgɑrd] *n* **:** vanguardia *f*
vanilla [və'nɪlə, -'nɛ-] *n* **:** vainilla *f*
vanish ['vænɪʃ] *vi* **:** desaparecer, disiparse, desvanecerse
vanity ['vænət̬i] *n, pl* **-ties 1 :** vanidad *f* **2** *or* **vanity table :** tocador *m*
vanquish ['væŋkwɪʃ, 'væn-] *vt* **:** vencer, conquistar
vantage point ['væntɪdʒ] *n* **:** posición *f* ventajosa
vapid ['væpəd, 'veɪ-] *adj* **:** insípido, insulso
vapor ['veɪpər] *n* **:** vapor *m*
vaporize ['veɪpəˌraɪz] *v* **-rized; -rizing** *vt* **:** vaporizar — *vi* **:** vaporizarse, evaporarse
vaporizer ['veɪpəˌraɪzər] *n* **:** vaporizador *m*
variability [ˌvɛriə'bɪlət̬i] *n, pl* **-ties :** variabilidad *f*
variable[1] ['vɛriəbəl] *adj* **:** variable <variable cloudiness **:** nubosidad variable>
variable[2] *n* **:** variable *f,* factor *m*
variance ['vɛriənts] *n* **1** DISCREPANCY **:** varianza *f,* discrepancia *f* **2** DISAGREEMENT **:** desacuerdo *m* <at variance with **:** en desacuerdo con>
variant[1] ['vɛriənt] *adj* **:** variante, divergente
variant[2] *n* **:** variante *f*
variation [ˌvɛri'eɪʃən] *n* **:** variación *f,* diferencias *fpl*
varicose ['værəˌkoːs] *adj* **:** varicoso
varicose veins *npl* **:** varices *fpl*, várices *fpl*
varied ['vɛrid] *adj* **:** variado, dispar, diferente
variegated ['vɛriəˌgeɪt̬ɛd] *adj* **:** abigarrado, multicolor
variety [və'raɪət̬i] *n, pl* **-ties 1** DIVERSITY **:** diversidad *f,* variedad *f* **2** ASSORTMENT **:** surtido *m* <for a variety of reasons **:** por diversas razones> **3** SORT **:** clase *f* **4** BREED **:** variedad *f* (de plantas)
various ['vɛriəs] *adj* **:** varios, diversos
varnish[1] ['vɑrnɪʃ] *vt* **:** barnizar
varnish[2] *n* **:** barniz *f*
varsity ['vɑrsət̬i] *n, pl* **-ties :** equipo *m* universitario
vary ['vɛri] *v* **varied; varying** *vt* **:** variar, diversificar — *vi* **1** CHANGE **:** variar, cambiar **2** DEVIATE **:** desviarse
vascular ['væskjələr] *adj* **:** vascular
vase ['veɪs, 'veɪz, 'vɑz] *n* **:** jarrón *m,* florero *m*
vassal ['væsəl] *n* **:** vasallo *m,* -lla *f*
vast ['væst] *adj* **:** inmenso, enorme, vasto
vastly ['væstli] *adv* **:** enormemente
vastness ['væstnəs] *n* **:** vastedad *f,* inmensidad *f*
vat ['væt] *n* **:** cuba *f,* tina *f*
vaudeville ['vɔdvəl, -ˌvɪl; 'vɔdəˌvɪl] *n* **:** vodevil *m*
vault[1] ['vɔlt] *vi* LEAP **:** saltar
vault[2] *n* **1** JUMP **:** salto *m* <pole vault **:** salto de pértiga, salto con garrocha> **2** DOME **:** bóveda *f* **3 :** bodega *f* (para vino), bóveda *f* de seguridad (de un banco) **4** CRYPT **:** cripta *f*
vaulted ['vɔltəd] *adj* **:** abovedado
vaunted ['vɔntəd] *adj* **:** cacareado, alardeado <a much vaunted wine **:** un vino muy alardeado>
VCR [ˌviːˌsiː'ɑr] *n* **:** video *m,* videocasetera *f*
veal ['viːl] *n* **:** ternera *f,* carne *f* de ternera
veer ['vɪr] *vi* **:** virar (dícese de un barco), girar (dícese de un coche), torcer (dícese de un camino)
vegetable[1] ['vɛdʒtəbəl, 'vɛdʒət̬ə-] *adj* **:** vegetal
vegetable[2] *n* **1 :** vegetal *m* <the vegetable kingdom **:** el reino vegetal> **2 :** verdura *f,* hortaliza *f* (para comer)
vegetarian [ˌvɛdʒə'tɛriən] *n* **:** vegetariano *mf*
vegetarianism [ˌvɛdʒə'tɛriəˌnɪzəm] *n* **:** vegetarianismo *m*
vegetate ['vɛdʒəˌteɪt] *vi* **-tated; -tating :** vegetar
vegetation [ˌvɛdʒə'teɪʃən] *n* **:** vegetación *f*
vehemence ['viːəmənts] *n* **:** intensidad *f,* vehemencia *f*
vehement ['viːəmənt] *adj* **:** intenso, vehemente
vehemently ['viːəməntli] *adv* **:** vehementemente, con vehemencia
vehicle ['viːəkəl, 'viːˌhɪkəl] *n* **1** *or* **motor vehicle :** vehículo *m* **2** MEDIUM **:** vehículo *m,* medio *m*
vehicular [vi'hɪkjələr, və-] *adj* **:** vehicular <vehicular homicide **:** muerte por atropello>
veil[1] ['veɪl] *vt* **1** CONCEAL **:** velar, disimular **2 :** cubrir con un velo <to veil one's face **:** cubrirse con un velo>
veil[2] *n* **:** velo *m* <bridal veil **:** velo de novia>
vein ['veɪn] *n* **1 :** vena *f* (en anatomía, botánica, etc.) **2** LODE **:** veta *f,* vena *f,* filón *m* **3** STYLE **:** vena *f* <in a humorous vein **:** en vena humorística>
veined ['veɪnd] *adj* **:** veteado (dícese del queso, de los minerales, etc.)

velocity [və'lɑsəṭi] *n, pl* **-ties :** velocidad *f*
velour [və'lʊr] *or* **velours** [-'lʊrz] *n* **:** velour *m*
velvet[1] ['vɛlvət] *adj* **1 :** de terciopelo **2** → **velvety**
velvet[2] *n* **:** terciopelo *m*
velvety ['vɛlvəṭi] *adj* **:** aterciopelado
venal ['vi:nəl] *adj* **:** venal, sobornable
vend ['vɛnd] *vt* **:** vender
vendetta [vɛn'dɛṭə] *n* **:** vendetta *f*
vendor ['vɛndər] *n* **:** vendedor *m,* -dora *f;* puestero *m,* -ra *f*
veneer[1] [və'nɪr] *vt* **:** enchapar, chapar
veneer[2] *n* **1 :** enchapado *m,* chapa *f* **2** APPEARANCE **:** apariencia *f,* barniz *m* <a veneer of culture **:** un barniz de cultura>
venerable ['vɛnərəbəl] *adj* **:** venerable
venerate ['vɛnə,reɪt] *vt* **-ated; -ating :** venerar
veneration [,vɛnə'reɪʃən] *n* **:** veneración *f*
venereal disease [və'nɪriəl] *n* **:** enfermedad *f* venérea
venetian blind [və'ni:ʃən] *n* **:** persiana *f* veneciana
Venezuelan [,vɛnə'zweɪlən, -zʊ'eɪ-] *n* **:** venezolano *m,* -na *f* — **Venezuelan** *adj*
vengeance ['vɛndʒənts] *n* **:** venganza *f* <to take vengeance on **:** vengarse de>
vengeful ['vɛndʒfəl] *adj* **:** vengativo
venial ['vi:niəl] *adj* **:** venial <a venial sin **:** un pecado venial>
venison ['vɛnəsən, -zən] *n* **:** venado *m,* carne *f* de venado
venom ['vɛnəm] *n* **1 :** veneno *m* **2** MALICE **:** veneno *m,* malevolencia *f*
venomous ['vɛnəməs] *adj* **:** venenoso
vent[1] ['vɛnt] *vt* **:** desahogar, dar salida a <to vent one's feelings **:** desahogarse>
vent[2] *n* **1** OPENING **:** abertura *f* (de escape), orificio *m* **2** *or* **air vent :** respiradero *m,* rejilla *f* de ventilación **3** OUTLET **:** desahogo *m* <to give vent to one's anger **:** desahogar la ira>
ventilate ['vɛntəl,eɪt] *vt* **-lated; -lating :** ventilar
ventilation [,vɛntəl'eɪʃən] *n* **:** ventilación *f*
ventilator ['vɛntəl,eɪṭər] *n* **:** ventilador *m*
ventricle ['vɛntrɪkəl] *n* **:** ventrículo *m*
ventriloquism [vɛn'trɪlə,kwɪzəm] *n* **:** ventriloquia *f*
ventriloquist [vɛn'trɪlə,kwɪst] *n* **:** ventrílocuo *m,* -cua *f*
venture[1] ['vɛntʃər] *v* **-tured; -turing** *vt* **1** RISK **:** arriesgar **2** OFFER **:** aventurar <to venture an opinion **:** aventurar una opinión> — *vi* **:** arriesgarse, atreverse, aventurarse
venture[2] *n* **1** UNDERTAKING **:** empresa *f* **2** GAMBLE, RISK **:** aventura *f,* riesgo *m*
venturesome ['vɛntʃərsəm] *adj* **1** ADVENTUROUS **:** audaz, atrevido **2** RISKY **:** arriesgado
venue ['vɛn,ju:] *n* **1** PLACE **:** lugar *m* **2 :** jurisdicción *f* (en derecho)
Venus ['vi:nəs] *n* **:** Venus *m*
veracity [və'ræsəṭi] *n, pl* **-ties :** veracidad *f*
veranda *or* **verandah** [və'rændə] *n* **:** terraza *f,* veranda *f*
verb ['vərb] *n* **:** verbo *m*
verbal ['vərbəl] *adj* **:** verbal
verbalize ['vərbə,laɪz] *vt* **-ized; -izing :** expresar con palabras, verbalizar
verbally ['vərbəli] *adv* **:** verbalmente, de palabra
verbatim[1] [vər'beɪṭəm] *adv* **:** palabra por palabra, textualmente
verbatim[2] *adj* **:** literal, textual
verbose [vər'bo:s] *adj* **:** verboso, prolijo
verdant ['vərdənt] *adj* **:** verde, verdeante
verdict ['vərdɪkt] *n* **1 :** veredicto *m* (de un jurado) **2** JUDGMENT, OPINION **:** juicio *m,* opinión *f*
verge[1] ['vərdʒ] *vi* **verged; verging :** estar al borde, rayar <it verges on madness **:** raya en la locura>
verge[2] *n* **1** EDGE **:** borde *m* **2 to be on the verge of :** estar a pique de, estar al borde de, estar a punto de
verification [,vɛrəfə'keɪʃən] *n* **:** verificación *f*
verify ['vɛrə,faɪ] *vt* **-fied; -fying :** verificar, comprobar, confirmar
veritable ['vɛrəṭəbəl] *adj* **:** verdadero — **veritably** *adv*
vermicelli [,vərmə'tʃɛli, -'sɛli] *n* **:** fideos *mpl* finos
vermin ['vərmən] *ns & pl* **:** alimañas *fpl,* bichos *mpl,* sabandijas *fpl*
vermouth [vər'mu:th] *n* **:** vermut *m*
vernacular[1] [vər'nækjələr] *adj* **:** vernáculo
vernacular[2] *n* **:** lengua *f* vernácula
versatile ['vərsəṭəl] *adj* **:** versátil
versatility [,vərsə'tɪləṭi] *n* **:** versatilidad *f*
verse ['vərs] *n* **1** LINE, STANZA **:** verso *m,* estrofa *f* **2** POETRY **:** poesía *f* **3 :** versículo *m* (en la Biblia)
versed ['vərst] *adj* **:** versado <to be well versed in **:** ser muy versado en>
version ['vərʒən] *n* **:** versión *f*
versus ['vərsəs] *prep* **:** versus
vertebra ['vərṭəbrə] *n, pl* **-brae** [-,breɪ, -,bri:] *or* **-bras :** vértebra *f*
vertebrate[1] ['vərṭəbrət, -,breɪt] *adj* **:** vertebrado
vertebrate[2] *n* **:** vertebrado *m*
vertex ['vər,tɛks] *n, pl* **vertices** ['vərṭə,si:z] **1 :** vértice *m* (en matemáticas y anatomía) **2** SUMMIT, TOP **:** ápice *m,* cumbre *f,* cima *f*
vertical[1] ['vərṭɪkəl] *adj* **:** vertical — **verticalmente** *adv*
vertical[2] *n* **:** vertical *f*
vertigo ['vərṭɪ,go:] *n, pl* **-goes** *or* **-gos :** vértigo *m*
verve ['vərv] *n* **:** brío *m*

very[1] [ˈvɛri] *adv* **1** EXTREMELY **:** muy, sumamente <very few : muy pocos> <I am very sorry : lo siento mucho> **2** (*used for emphasis*) <at the very least : por lo menos, como mínimo> <the same dress : el mismo vestido>
very[2] *adj* **verier; -est 1** EXACT, PRECISE **:** mismo, exacto <at that very moment : en ese mismo momento> <it's the very thing : es justo lo que hacía falta> **2** BARE, MERE **:** solo, mero <the very thought of it : sólo pensarlo> **3** EXTREME **:** extremo, de todo <at the very top : arriba de todo>
vespers [ˈvɛspərz] *npl* **:** vísperas *fpl*
vessel [ˈvɛsəl] *n* **1** CONTAINER **:** vasija *f,* recipiente *m* **2** BOAT, CRAFT **:** nave *f,* barco *m,* buque *m* **3 :** vaso *m* <blood vessel : vaso sanguíneo>
vest[1] [ˈvɛst] *vt* **1** CONFER **:** conferir <to vest authority in : conferirle la autoridad a> **2** CLOTHE **:** vestir
vest[2] *n* **1 :** chaleco *m* **2** UNDERSHIRT **:** camiseta *f*
vestibule [ˈvɛstəˌbjuːl] *n* **:** vestíbulo *m*
vestige [ˈvɛstɪdʒ] *n* **:** vestigio *m,* rastro *m*
vestment [ˈvɛstmənt] *n* **:** vestidura *f*
vestry [ˈvɛstri] *n, pl* **-tries :** sacristía *f*
vet [ˈvɛt] *n* **1** → **veterinarian 2** → **veteran**[2]
veteran[1] [ˈvɛt̬ərən, ˈvɛtrən] *adj* **:** veterano
veteran[2] *n* **:** veterano *m,* -na *f*
Veterans Day *n* **:** día *m* del Armisticio (celebrado el 11 de noviembre en los Estados Unidos)
veterinarian [ˌvɛt̬ərəˈnɛriən, ˌvɛt̬əˈnɛr-] *n* **:** veterinario *m,* -ria *f*
veterinary [ˈvɛt̬ərəˌnɛri] *adj* **:** veterinario
veto[1] [ˈviːt̬o] *vt* **1** FORBID **:** prohibir **2 :** vetar <to veto a bill : vetar un proyecto de ley>
veto[2] *n, pl* **-toes 1 :** veto *m* <the power of veto : el derecho de veto> **2** BAN **:** veto *m,* prohibición *f*
vex [ˈvɛks] *vt* **:** contrariar, molestar, irritar
vexation [vɛkˈseɪʃən] *n* **:** contrariedad *f,* irritación *f*
via [ˈvaɪə, ˈviːə] *prep* **:** por, vía
viability [ˌvaɪəˈbɪlət̬i] *n* **:** viabilidad *f*
viable [ˈvaɪəbəl] *adj* **:** viable
viaduct [ˈvaɪəˌdʌkt] *n* **:** viaducto *m*
vial [ˈvaɪəl] *n* **:** frasco *m*
vibrant [ˈvaɪbrənt] *adj* **1** LIVELY **:** vibrante, animado, dinámico **2** BRIGHT **:** fuerte, vivo (dícese de los colores)
vibrate [ˈvaɪˌbreɪt] *vi* **-brated; -brating 1** OSCILLATE **:** vibrar, oscilar **2** THRILL **:** bullir <to vibrate with excitement : bullir de emoción>
vibration [vaɪˈbreɪʃən] *n* **:** vibración *f*
vicar [ˈvɪkər] *n* **:** vicario *m,* -ria *f*
vicarious [vaɪˈkæriːəs, vɪ-] *adj* **:** indirecto — **vicariously** *adv*
vice [ˈvaɪs] *n* **:** vicio *m*
vice admiral *n* **:** vicealmirante *mf*
vice president *n* **:** vicepresidente *m,* -ta *f*
viceroy [ˈvaɪsˌrɔɪ] *n* **:** virrey *m,* -rreina *f*
vice versa [ˌvaɪsɪˈvərsə, ˌvaɪsˈvər-] *adv* **:** viceversa
vicinity [vəˈsɪnət̬i] *n, pl* **-ties 1** NEIGHBORHOOD **:** vecindad *f,* inmediaciones *fpl* **2** NEARNESS **:** proximidad *f*
vicious [ˈvɪʃəs] *adj* **1** DEPRAVED **:** depravado, malo **2** SAVAGE **:** malo, fiero, salvaje <a vicious dog : un perro feroz> **3** MALICIOUS **:** malicioso
viciously [ˈvɪʃəsli] *adv* **:** con saña, brutalmente
viciousness [ˈvɪʃəsnəs] *n* **:** brutalidad *f,* ferocidad *f* (de un animal), malevolencia *f* (de un comentario, etc.)
vicissitudes [vəˈsɪsəˌtuːdz, vaɪ-, -ˌtjuːdz] *npl* **:** vicisitudes *fpl*
victim [ˈvɪktəm] *n* **:** víctima *f*
victimize [ˈvɪktəˌmaɪz] *vt* **-mized; -mizing :** tomar como víctima, perseguir, victimizar *Arg, Mex*
victor [ˈvɪktər] *n* **:** vencedor *m,* -dora *f*
Victorian [vɪkˈtoːriən] *adj* **:** victoriano
victorious [vɪkˈtoːriəs] *adj* **:** victorioso — **victoriously** *adv*
victory [ˈvɪktəri] *n, pl* **-ries :** victoria *f,* triunfo *m*
victuals [ˈvɪt̬əlz] *npl* **:** víveres *mpl,* provisiones *fpl*
video[1] [ˈvɪdiˌoː] *adj* **:** de video <video recording : grabación de video>
video[2] *n* **1 :** video *m* (medio o grabación) **2** → **videotape**[2]
videocassette [ˌvɪdiokəˈsɛt] *n* **:** videocasete *m,* videocassette *m*
videocassette recorder → **VCR**
videotape[1] [ˈvɪdioˌteɪp] *vt* **-taped; -taping :** grabar en video, videograbar
videotape[2] *n* **:** videocinta *f*
vie [ˈvaɪ] *vi* **vied; vying** [ˈvaɪɪŋ] **:** competir, rivalizar
Vietnamese [viˌɛtnəˈmiːz, -ˈmiːs] *n* **:** vietnamita *mf* — **Vietnamese** *adj*
view[1] [ˈvjuː] *vt* **1** OBSERVE **:** mirar, ver, observar **2** CONSIDER **:** considerar, contemplar
view[2] *n* **1** SIGHT **:** vista *f* <to come into view : aparecer> **2** ATTITUDE, OPINION **:** opinión *f,* parecer *m,* actitud *f* <in my view : en mi opinión> **3** SCENE **:** vista *f,* panorama *f* **4** INTENTION **:** idea *f,* vista *f* <with a view to : con vistas a, con la idea de> **5 in view of :** dado que, en vista de (que)
viewer [ˈvjuːər] *n or* **television viewer :** telespectador *m,* -dora *f;* televidente *mf*
viewpoint [ˈvjuːˌpɔɪnt] *n* **:** punto *m* de vista
vigil [ˈvɪdʒəl] *n* **1 :** vigilia *f,* vela *f* **2 to keep vigil :** velar
vigilance [ˈvɪdʒələnts] *n* **:** vigilancia *f*
vigilant [ˈvɪdʒələnt] *adj* **:** vigilante

vigilante [ˌvɪdʒəˈlænˌtiː] *n* **:** integrante *mf* de un comité de vigilancia (que actúa como policía)
vigilantly [ˈvɪdʒələntli] *adv* **:** con vigilancia
vigor [ˈvɪgər] *n* **:** vigor *m,* energía *f,* fuerza *f*
vigorous [ˈvɪgərəs] *adj* **:** vigoroso, enérgico — **vigorously** *adv*
Viking [ˈvaɪkɪŋ] *n* **:** vikingo *m,* -ga *f*
vile [ˈvaɪl] *adj* **viler; vilest 1** WICKED **:** vil, infame **2** REVOLTING **:** asqueroso, repugnante **3** TERRIBLE **:** horrible, atroz <vile weather : tiempo horrible> <to be in a vile mood : estar de un humor de perros>
vilify [ˈvɪləˌfaɪ] *vt* **-fied; -fying :** vilipendiar, denigrar, difamar
villa [ˈvɪlə] *n* **:** casa *f* de campo, quinta *f*
village [ˈvɪlɪdʒ] *n* **:** pueblo *m* (grande), aldea *f* (pequeña)
villager [ˈvɪlɪdʒər] *n* **:** vecino *m,* -na *f* (de un pueblo); aldeano *m,* -na *f* (de una aldea)
villain [ˈvɪlən] *n* **:** villano *m,* -na *f;* malo *m,* -la *f* (en ficción, películas, etc.)
villainess [ˈvɪlənɪs, -nəs] *n* **:** villana *f*
villainous [ˈvɪlənəs] *adj* **:** infame, malvado
villainy [ˈvɪləni] *n, pl* **-lainies :** vileza *f,* maldad *f*
vim [ˈvɪm] *n* **:** brío *m,* vigor *m,* energía *f*
vindicate [ˈvɪndəˌkeɪt] *vt* **-cated; -cating 1** EXONERATE **:** vindicar, disculpar **2** JUSTIFY **:** justificar
vindication [ˌvɪndəˈkeɪʃən] *n* **:** vindicación *f,* justificación *f*
vindictive [vɪnˈdɪktɪv] *adj* **:** vengativo
vine [ˈvaɪn] *n* **1** GRAPEVINE **:** vid *f,* parra *f* **2 :** planta *f* trepadora, enredadera *f*
vinegar [ˈvɪnɪgər] *n* **:** vinagre *m*
vinegary [ˈvɪnɪgəri] *adj* **:** avinagrado
vineyard [ˈvɪnjərd] *n* **:** viña *f,* viñedo *m*
vintage[1] [ˈvɪntɪdʒ] *adj* **1 :** añejo (dícese de un vino) **2** CLASSIC **:** clásico, de época
vintage[2] *n* **1 :** cosecha *f* <the 1947 vintage : la cosecha de 1947> **2** ERA **:** época *f,* era *f* <slang of recent vintage : argot de la época reciente>
vinyl [ˈvaɪnəl] *n* **:** vinilo
viola [viːˈoːlə] *n* **:** viola *f*
violate [ˈvaɪəˌleɪt] *vt* **-lated; -lating 1** BREAK **:** infringir, violar, quebrantar <to violate the rules : violar las reglas> **2** RAPE **:** violar **3** DESECRATE **:** profanar
violation [ˌvaɪəˈleɪʃən] *n* **1 :** violación *f,* infracción *f* (de una ley) **2** DESECRATION **:** profanación *f*
violence [ˈvaɪlənts, ˈvaɪə-] *n* **:** violencia *f*
violent [ˈvaɪlənt, ˈvaɪə-] *adj* **:** violento
violently [ˈvaɪləntli, ˈvaɪə-] *adv* **:** violentamente, con violencia
violet [ˈvaɪlət, ˈvaɪə-] *n* **:** violeta *f*
violin [ˌvaɪəˈlɪn] *n* **:** violín *m*
violinist [ˌvaɪəˈlɪnɪst] *n* **:** violinista *mf*
violoncello [ˌvaɪələnˈtʃɛloː, ˌviː-] → **cello**
VIP [ˌviːˌaɪˈpiː] *n, pl* **VIPs** [-ˈpiːz] **:** VIP *mf,* persona *f* de categoría
viper [ˈvaɪpər] *n* **:** víbora *f*
viral [ˈvaɪrəl] *adj* **:** viral, vírico <viral pneumonia : pulmonía viral>
virgin[1] [ˈvərdʒən] *adj* **1** CHASTE **:** virginal <the virgin birth : el alumbramiento virginal> **2 :** virgen, intacto <a virgin forest : una selva virgen> <virgin wool : lana virgen>
virgin[2] *n* **:** virgen *mf*
virginity [vərˈdʒɪnəti] *n* **:** virginidad *f*
Virgo [ˈvərˌgoː, ˈvɪr-] *n* **:** Virgo *mf*
virile [ˈvɪrəl, -ˌaɪl] *adj* **:** viril, varonil
virility [vəˈrɪləti] *n* **:** virilidad *f*
virtual [ˈvərtʃʊəl] *adj* **:** virtual <a virtual dictator : un virtual dictador> <virtual reality : realidad virtual>
virtually [ˈvərtʃʊəli, ˈvərtʃəli] *adv* **:** en realidad, de hecho, casi
virtue [ˈvərˌtʃuː] *n* **1 :** virtud *f* **2 by virtue of :** en virtud de, debido a
virtuosity [ˌvərtʃʊˈɑsəti] *n, pl* **-ties :** virtuosismo *m*
virtuoso [ˌvərtʃʊˈoːsoː, -zoː] *n, pl* **-sos** *or* **-si** [-ˌsiː, -ˌziː] **:** virtuoso *m,* -sa *f*
virtuous [ˈvərtʃʊəs] *adj* **:** virtuoso, bueno — **virtuously** *adv*
virulence [ˈvɪrələnts, ˈvɪrjə-] *n* **:** virulencia *f*
virulent [ˈvɪrələnt, ˈvɪrjə-] *adj* **:** virulento
virus [ˈvaɪrəs] *n* **:** virus *m*
visa [ˈviːzə, -sə] *n* **:** visa *f*
vis–à–vis [ˌviːzəˈviː, -sə-] *prep* **:** con relación a, con respecto a
viscera [ˈvɪsərə] *npl* **:** vísceras *fpl*
visceral [ˈvɪsərəl] *adj* **:** visceral
viscosity [vɪsˈkɑsəti] *n, pl* **-ties :** viscosidad *f*
viscount [ˈvaɪˌkæʊnt] *n* **:** vizconde *m*
viscountess [ˈvaɪˌkæʊntɪs] *n* **:** vizcondesa *f*
viscous [ˈvɪskəs] *adj* **:** viscoso
vise [ˈvaɪs] *n* **:** torno *m* de banco, tornillo *m* de banco
visibility [ˌvɪzəˈbɪləti] *n, pl* **-ties :** visibilidad *f*
visible [ˈvɪzəbəl] *adj* **1 :** visible <the visible stars : las estrellas visibles> **2** OBVIOUS **:** evidente, patente
visibly [ˈvɪzəbli] *adv* **:** visiblemente
vision [ˈvɪʒən] *n* **1** EYESIGHT **:** vista *f,* visión *f* **2** APPARITION **:** visión *f,* aparición *f* **3** FORESIGHT **:** visión *f* (del futuro), previsión *f* **4** IMAGE **:** imagen *f* <she had visions of a disaster : se imaginaba un desastre>
visionary[1] [ˈvɪʒəˌnɛri] *adj* **1** FARSIGHTED **:** visionario, con visión de futuro **2** UTOPIAN **:** utópico, poco realista
visionary[2] *n, pl* **-ries :** visionario *m,* -ria *f*

visit[1] [ˈvɪzət] *vt* **1 :** visitar, ir a ver **2** AFFLICT **:** azotar, afligir <visited by troubles : afligido con problemas> — *vi* **:** hacer (una) visita

visit[2] *n* **:** visita *f*

visitor [ˈvɪzətər] *n* **:** visitante *mf* (a una ciudad, etc.), visita *f* (a una casa)

visor [ˈvaɪzər] *n* **:** visera *f*

vista [ˈvɪstə] *n* **:** vista *f*

visual [ˈvɪʒʊəl] *adj* **:** visual <the visual arts : las artes visuales> — **visually** *adv*

visualize [ˈvɪʒʊəˌlaɪz] *vt* **-ized; -izing :** visualizar, imaginarse, hacerse una idea de

vital [ˈvaɪtəl] *adj* **1 :** vital <vital organs : órganos vitales> **2** CRUCIAL **:** esencial, crucial, decisivo <of vital importance : de suma importancia> **3** LIVELY **:** enérgico, lleno de vida, vital

vitality [vaɪˈtæləṯi] *n, pl* **-ties :** vitalidad *f,* energía *f*

vitally [ˈvaɪtəli] *adv* **:** sumamente

vital statistics *npl* **:** estadísticas *fpl* demográficas

vitamin [ˈvaɪtəmən] *n* **:** vitamina *f* <vitamin deficiency : carencia vitamínica>

vitreous [ˈvɪtriəs] *adj* **:** vítreo

vitriolic [ˌvɪtriˈɑlɪk] *adj* **:** mordaz, virulento

vituperation [vaɪˌtuːpəˈreɪʃən, -ˌtjuː-] *n* **:** vituperio *m*

vivacious [vəˈveɪʃəs, vaɪ-] *adj* **:** vivaz, animado, lleno de vida

vivaciously [vəˈveɪʃəsli, vaɪ-] *adv* **:** con vivacidad, animadamente

vivacity [vəˈvæsəṯi, vaɪ-] *n* **:** vivacidad *f*

vivid [ˈvɪvəd] *adj* **1** LIVELY **:** lleno de vitalidad **2** BRILLIANT **:** vivo, intenso <vivid colors : colores vivos> **3** INTENSE, SHARP **:** vívido, gráfico <a vivid dream : un sueño vívido>

vividly [ˈvɪvədli] *adv* **1** BRIGHTLY **:** con colores vivos **2** SHARPLY **:** vívidamente

vividness [ˈvɪvədnəs] *n* **1** BRIGHTNESS **:** intensidad *f,* viveza *f* **2** SHARPNESS **:** lo gráfico, nitidez *f*

vivisection [ˌvɪvəˈsɛkʃən, ˈvɪvəˌ-] *n* **:** vivisección *f*

vixen [ˈvɪksən] *n* **:** zorra *f,* raposa *f*

vocabulary [voːˈkæbjəˌlɛri] *n, pl* **-laries 1 :** vocabulario *m* **2** LEXICON **:** léxico *m*

vocal [ˈvoːkəl] *adj* **1 :** vocal **2** LOUD, OUTSPOKEN **:** ruidoso, muy franco

vocal cords *npl* **:** cuerdas *fpl* vocales

vocalist [ˈvoːkəlɪst] *n* **:** cantante *mf,* vocalista *mf*

vocalize [ˈvoːkəlˌaɪz] *vt* **-ized; -izing :** vocalizar

vocation [voˈkeɪʃən] *n* **:** vocación *f* <to have a vocation for : tener vocación de>

vocational [voˈkeɪʃənəl] *adj* **:** profesional <vocational guidance : orientación profesional>

vociferous [voˈsɪfərəs] *adj* **:** ruidoso, vociferante

vodka [ˈvɑdkə] *n* **:** vodka *m*

vogue [ˈvoːg] *n* **:** moda *f,* boga *f* <to be in vogue : estar de moda, estar en boga>

voice[1] [ˈvɔɪs] *vt* **voiced; voicing :** expresar

voice[2] *n* **1 :** voz *f* <in a low voice : en voz baja> <to lose one's voice : quedarse sin voz> <the voice of the people : la voz del pueblo> **2 to make one's voice heard :** hacerse oír

voice box → **larynx**

voiced [ˈvɔɪst] *adj* **:** sonoro

void[1] [ˈvɔɪd] *vt* **:** anular, invalidar <to void a contract : anular un contrato>

void[2] *adj* **1** EMPTY **:** vacío, desprovisto <void of content : desprovisto de contenido> **2** INVALID **:** inválido, nulo

void[3] *n* **:** vacío *m*

volatile [ˈvɑləṯəl] *adj* **:** volátil, inestable

volatility [ˌvɑləˈtɪləṯi] *n* **:** volatilidad *f,* inestabilidad *f*

volcanic [vɑlˈkænɪk] *adj* **:** volcánico

volcano [vɑlˈkeɪˌnoː] *n, pl* **-noes** *or* **-nos :** volcán *m*

vole [ˈvoːl] *n* **:** campañol *m*

volition [voˈlɪʃən] *n* **:** volición *f,* voluntad *f* <of one's own volition : por voluntad propia>

volley [ˈvɑli] *n, pl* **-leys 1 :** descarga *f* (de tiros) **2 :** torrente *m,* lluvia *f* (de insultos, etc.) **3 :** salva *f* (de aplausos) **4 :** volea *f* (en deportes)

volleyball [ˈvɑliˌbɔl] *n* **:** voleibol *m*

volt [ˈvoːlt] *n* **:** voltio *m*

voltage [ˈvoːltɪdʒ] *n* **:** voltaje *m*

volubility [ˌvɑljəˈbɪləṯi] *n* **:** locuacidad *f*

voluble [ˈvɑljəbəl] *adj* **:** locuaz

volume [ˈvɑljəm, -ˌjuːm] *n* **1** BOOK **:** volumen *m,* tomo *m* **2** SPACE **:** capacidad *f,* volumen *m* (en física) **3** AMOUNT **:** cantidad *f,* volumen *m* **4** LOUDNESS **:** volumen *m*

voluminous [vəˈluːmənəs] *adj* **:** voluminoso

voluntary [ˈvɑlənˌtɛri] *adj* **:** voluntario — **voluntarily** [ˌvɑlənˈtɛrəli] *adv*

volunteer[1] [ˌvɑlənˈtɪr] *vt* **:** ofrecer, dar <to volunteer one's assistance : ofrecer la ayuda> — *vi* **:** ofrecerse, alistarse como voluntario

volunteer[2] *n* **:** voluntario *m,* -ria *f*

voluptuous [vəˈlʌptʃʊəs] *adj* **:** voluptuoso

vomit[1] [ˈvɑmət] *v* **:** vomitar

vomit[2] *n* **:** vómito *m*

voodoo [ˈvuːˌduː] *n, pl* **voodoos :** vudú *m*

voracious [vɔˈreɪʃəs, və-] *adj* **:** voraz

voraciously [vɔˈreɪʃəsli, və-] *adv* **:** vorazmente, con voracidad

vortex [ˈvɔrˌtɛks] *n, pl* **vortices** [ˈvɔrtəˌsiːz] **:** vórtice *m*

vote[1] ['vo:t] *vi* **voted; voting** : votar <to vote Democratic : votar por los demócratas>

vote[2] *n* **1** : voto *m* **2** SUFFRAGE : sufragio *m,* derecho *m* al voto

voter ['vo:t̬ər] *n* : votante *mf*

voting ['vo:t̬ɪŋ] *n* : votación *f*

vouch ['væʊtʃ] *vi* **to vouch for** : garantizar (algo), responder de (algo), responder por (alguien)

voucher ['væʊtʃər] *n* **1** RECEIPT : comprobante *m* **2** : vale *m* <travel voucher : vale de viajar>

vow[1] [væʊ] *vt* : jurar, prometer, hacer voto de

vow[2] *n* : promesa *f,* voto *m* (en la religión) <a vow of poverty : un voto de pobreza>

vowel ['væʊəl] *n* : vocal *m*

voyage[1] ['vɔɪɪdʒ] *vi* **-aged; -aging** : viajar

voyage[2] *n* : viaje *m*

voyager ['vɔɪɪdʒər] *n* : viajero *m,* -ra *f*

vulcanize ['vʌlkə,naɪz] *vt* **-nized; -nizing** : vulcanizar

vulgar ['vʌlgər] *adj* **1** COMMON, PLEBIAN : ordinario, populachero, del vulgo **2** COARSE, CRUDE : grosero, de mal gusto, majadero *Mex* **3** INDECENT : indecente, colorado (dícese de un chiste, etc.)

vulgarity [,vʌl'gærət̬i] *n, pl* **-ties** : grosería *f,* vulgaridad *f*

vulgarly ['vʌlgərli] *adv* : vulgarmente, groseramente

vulnerability [,vʌlnərə'bɪlət̬i] *n, pl* **-ties** : vulnerabilidad *f*

vulnerable ['vʌlnərəbəl] *adj* : vulnerable

vulture ['vʌltʃər] *n* : buitre *m,* zopilote *m CA, Mex*

vying → **vie**

W

w ['dʌbəl,ju:] *n, pl* **w's** *or* **ws** [-,ju:z] : vigésima tercera letra del alfabeto inglés

wad[1] ['wɑd] *vt* **wadded; wadding 1** : hacer un taco con, formar en una masa **2** STUFF : rellenar

wad[2] *n* : taco *m* (de papel), bola *f* (de algodón, etc.), fajo *m* (de billetes)

waddle[1] ['wɑdəl] *vi* **-dled; -dling** : andar como un pato

waddle[2] *n* : andar *m* de pato

wade ['weɪd] *v* **waded; wading** *vi* **1** : caminar por el agua **2 to wade through** : leer (algo) con dificultad — *vt or* **to wade across** : vadear

wading bird *n* : zancuda *f,* ave *f* zancuda

wafer ['weɪfər] *n* : barquillo *m,* galleta *f* de barquillo

waffle ['wɑfəl] *n* **1** : wafle *m* **2 waffle iron** : waflera *f*

waft ['wɑft, 'wæft] *vt* : llevar por el aire — *vi* : flotar

wag[1] ['wæg] *v* **wagged; wagging** *vt* : menear — *vi* : menearse, moverse

wag[2] *n* **1** : meneo *m* (de la cola) **2** JOKER, WIT : bromista *mf*

wage[1] ['weɪdʒ] *vt* **waged; waging** : hacer, librar <to wage war : hacer la guerra>

wage[2] *n or* **wages** *npl* : sueldo *m,* salario *m* <minimum wage : salario mínimo>

wager[1] ['weɪdʒər] *v* : apostar

wager[2] *n* : apuesta *f*

waggish ['wægɪʃ] *adj* : burlón, bromista (dícese de una persona), chistoso (dícese de un comentario)

waggle ['wægəl] *vt* **-gled; -gling** : menear, mover (de un lado a otro)

wagon ['wægən] *n* **1** : carro *m* (tirado por caballos) **2** CART : carrito *m* **3** → **station wagon**

waif ['weɪf] *n* : niño *m* abandonado, animal *m* sin hogar

wail[1] ['weɪl] *vi* : gemir, lamentarse

wail[2] *n* : gemido *m,* lamento *m*

wainscot ['weɪnskət, -,skɑt, -,sko:t] *or* **wainscoting** [-skət̬ɪŋ, -,skɑ-, -,sko:-] *n* : boiserie *f,* revestimiento *m* de paneles de madera

waist ['weɪst] *n* : cintura *f* (del cuerpo humano), talle *m* (de ropa)

waistline ['weɪst,laɪn] → **waist**

wait[1] ['weɪt] *vi* : esperar <to wait for something : esperar algo> <wait and see! : ¡espera y verás!> <I can't wait : me muero de ganas> — *vt* **1** AWAIT : esperar **2** DELAY : retrasar <don't wait lunch : no retrase el almuerzo> **3** SERVE : servir, atender <to wait tables : servir (a la mesa)>

wait[2] *n* **1** : espera *f* **2 to lie in wait** : estar al acecho

waiter ['weɪt̬ər] *n* : mesero *m,* camarero *m,* mozo *m Arg, Chile, Col, Peru*

waiting room *n* : sala *f* de espera

waitress ['weɪtrəs] *n* : mesera *f,* camarera *f,* moza *f Arg, Chile, Col, Peru*

waive ['weɪv] *vt* **waived; waiving** : renunciar a <to waive one's rights : renunciar a sus derechos> <to waive the rules : no aplicar las reglas>

waiver ['weɪvər] *n* : renuncia *f*

wake[1] ['weɪk] *v* **woke** ['wo:k]; **woken** ['wo:kən] *or* **waked; waking** *vi or* **to wake up** : despertar(se) <he woke at noon : se despertó al mediodía> <wake up! : ¡despiértate!> — *vt* : despertar

wake[2] *n* **1** VIGIL : velatorio *m,* velorio *m* (de un difunto) **2** TRAIL : estela *f* (de un barco, un huracán, etc.) **3** AFTERMATH : consecuencias *fpl* <in the wake of : tras, como consecuencia de>

wakeful [ˈweɪkfəl] *adj* **1** SLEEPLESS **:** desvelado **2** VIGILANT **:** alerta, vigilante

waken [ˈweɪkən] → **awake**

walk[1] [ˈwɔk] *vi* **1 :** caminar, andar, pasear <you're walking too fast : estás caminando demasiado rápido> <to walk around the city : pasearse por la ciudad> **2 :** ir andando, ir a pie <we had to walk home : tuvimos que ir a casa a pie> **3 :** darle base por bolas (a un bateador) — *vt* **1 :** recorrer, caminar <she walked two miles : caminó dos millas> **2** ACCOMPANY **:** acompañar **3 :** sacar a pasear (a un perro)

walk[2] *n* **1 :** paseo *m,* caminata *f* <to go for a walk : ir a caminar, dar un paseo> **2** PATH **:** camino *m* **3** GAIT **:** andar *m* **4 :** marcha *f* (en beisbol) **5 walk of life :** esfera *f,* condición *f*

walker [ˈwɔkər] *n* **1 :** paseante *mf;* andador *m,* -dora *f* **2** HIKER **:** excursionista *mf* **3** *or* **baby walker :** andador *m*

walking stick *n* **:** bastón *m*

walkout [ˈwɔkˌaʊt] *n* STRIKE **:** huelga *f*

walk out *vi* **1** STRIKE **:** declararse en huelga **2** LEAVE **:** salir, irse **3 to walk out on :** abandonar, dejar

wall[1] [ˈwɔl] *vt* **1 to wall in :** cercar con una pared o un muro, tapiar, amurallar **2 to wall off :** separar con una pared o un muro **3 to wall up :** tapiar, condenar (una ventana, etc.)

wall[2] *n* **1 :** muro *m* (exterior) <the walls of the city : las murallas de la ciudad> **2 :** pared *f* (interior) **3** BARRIER **:** barrera *f* <a wall of mountains : una barrera de montañas> **4 :** pared *f* (en anatomía)

wallaby [ˈwɑləbi] *n, pl* **-bies :** ualabí *m*

walled [ˈwɔld] *adj* **:** amurallado

wallet [ˈwɑlət] *n* **:** billetera *f,* cartera *f*

wallflower [ˈwɔlˌflaʊər] *n* **1 :** alhelí *m* (flor) **2 to be a wallflower :** comer pavo

wallop[1] [ˈwɑləp] *vt* **1** TROUNCE **:** darle una paliza (a alguien) **2** SOCK **:** pegar fuerte

wallop[2] *n* **:** golpe *m* fuerte, golpazo *m*

wallow[1] [ˈwɑˌloː] *vi* **1 :** revolcarse <to wallow in the mud : revolcarse en el lodo> **2** DELIGHT **:** deleitarse <to wallow in luxury : nadar en lujos>

wallow[2] *n* **:** revolcadero *m* (para animales)

wallpaper[1] [ˈwɔlˌpeɪpər] *vt* **:** empapelar

wallpaper[2] *n* **:** papel *m* pintado

walnut [ˈwɔlˌnʌt] *n* **1 :** nuez *f* (fruta) **2 :** nogal *m* (árbol y madera)

walrus [ˈwɔlrəs, ˈwɑl-] *n, pl* **-rus** *or* **-ruses :** morsa *f*

waltz[1] [ˈwɔlts] *vi* **1 :** valsar, bailar el vals **2** BREEZE **:** pasar con ligereza <to waltz in : entrar tan campante>

waltz[2] *n* **:** vals *m*

wan [ˈwɑn] *adj* **wanner; -est 1** PALLID **:** pálido **2** DIM **:** tenue <wan light : luz tenue> **3** LANGUID **:** lánguido <a wan smile : una sonrisa lánguida> — **wanly** *adv*

wand [ˈwɑnd] *n* **:** varita *f* (mágica)

wander [ˈwɑndər] *vi* **1** RAMBLE **:** deambular, vagar, vagabundear **2** STRAY **:** alejarse, desviarse, divagar <she let her mind wander : dejó vagar la imaginación> — *vt* **:** recorrer <to wander the streets : vagar por las calles>

wanderer [ˈwɑndərər] *n* **:** vagabundo *m,* -da *f;* viajero *m,* -ra *f*

wanderlust [ˈwɑndərˌlʌst] *n* **:** pasión *f* por viajar

wane[1] [ˈweɪn] *vi* **waned; waning 1 :** menguar (dícese de la luna) **2** DECLINE **:** disminuir, decaer, menguar

wane[2] *n* **on the wane :** decayendo, en decadencia

wangle [ˈwæŋgəl] *vt* **-gled; -gling** FINAGLE **:** arreglárselas para conseguir

want[1] [ˈwɑnt, ˈwɔnt] *vt* **1** LACK **:** faltar **2** REQUIRE **:** requerir, necesitar **3** DESIRE **:** querer, desear

want[2] *n* **1** LACK **:** falta *f* **2** DESTITUTION **:** indigencia *f,* miseria *f* **3** DESIRE, NEED **:** deseo *m,* necesidad *f*

wanting [ˈwɑntɪŋ, ˈwɔn-] *adj* **1** ABSENT **:** ausente **2** DEFICIENT **:** deficiente <he's wanting in common sense : le falta sentido común>

wanton [ˈwɑntən, ˈwɔn-] *adj* **1** LEWD, LUSTFUL **:** lascivo, lujurioso, licencioso **2** INHUMANE, MERCILESS **:** despiadado <wanton cruelty : crueldad despiadada>

wapiti [ˈwɑpəti] *n, pl* **-ti** *or* **-tis :** uapití *m*

war[1] [ˈwɔr] *vi* **warred; warring :** combatir, batallar, hacer la guerra

war[2] *n* **:** guerra *f* <to go to war : entrar en guerra>

warble[1] [ˈwɔrbəl] *vi* **-bled; -bling :** gorjear, trinar

warble[2] *n* **:** trino *m,* gorjeo *m*

warbler [ˈwɔrblər] *n* **:** pájaro *m* gorjeador, curruca *f*

ward[1] [ˈwɔrd] *vt* **to ward off :** desviar, protegerse contra

ward[2] *n* **1 :** sala *f* (de un hospital, etc.) <maternity ward : sala de maternidad> **2 :** distrito *m* electoral o administrativo (de una ciudad) **3 :** pupilo *m,* -la *f* (de un tutor, etc.)

warden [ˈwɔrdən] *n* **1** KEEPER **:** guarda *mf;* guardián *m,* -diana *f* <game warden : guardabosque> **2** *or* **prison warden :** alcaide *m*

wardrobe [ˈwɔrdˌroːb] *n* **1** CLOSET **:** armario *m* **2** CLOTHES **:** vestuario *m,* guardarropa *f*

ware [ˈwær] *n* **1** POTTERY **:** cerámica *f* **2 wares** *npl* GOODS **:** mercancía *f,* mercadería *f*

warehouse [ˈwærˌhaʊs] *n* **:** depósito *m,* almacén *m,* bodega *f* *Chile, Col, Mex*

warfare [ˈwɔrˌfær] *n* **1** WAR : guerra *f* **2** STRUGGLE : lucha *f* <the warfare against drugs : la lucha contra las drogas>

warhead [ˈwɔrˌhɛd] *n* : ojiva *f,* cabeza *f* (de un misil)

warily [ˈwærəli] *adv* : cautelosamente, con cautela

wariness [ˈwærinəs] *n* : cautela *f*

warlike [ˈwærˌlaɪk] *adj* : belicoso, guerrero

warm1 [ˈwɔrm] *vt* **1** HEAT : calentar, recalentar **2 to warm one's heart** : reconfortar a uno, alegrar el corazón **3 to warm up** : calentar (los músculos, un automóvil, etc.) — *vi* **1** : calentarse **2 to warm to** : tomarle simpatía (a alguien), entusiasmarse con (algo)

warm2 *adj* **1** LUKEWARM : tibio, templado **2** : caliente, cálido, caluroso <a warm wind : un viento cálido> <a warm day : un día caluroso, un día de calor> <warm hands : manos calientes> **3** : caliente, que abriga <warm clothes : ropa de abrigo> <I feel warm : tengo calor> **4** CARING, CORDIAL : cariñoso, cordial **5** : cálido (dícese de colores) **6** FRESH : fresco, reciente <a warm trail : un rastro reciente> **7** (*used for riddles*) : caliente

warm–blooded [ˈwɔrmˈblʌdəd] *adj* : de sangre caliente

warmhearted [ˈwɔrmˈhɑrt̬əd] *adj* : cariñoso

warmly [ˈwɔrmli] *adv* **1** AFFECTIONATELY : calurosamente, afectuosamente **2 to dress warmly** : abrigarse

warmonger [ˈwɔrˌmɑŋgər, -ˌmʌŋ-] *n* : belicista *mf*

warmth [ˈwɔrmpθ] *n* **1** : calor *m* **2** AFFECTION : cariño *m,* afecto *m* **3** ENTHUSIASM : ardor *m,* entusiasmo *m*

warm–up [ˈwɔrmˌʌp] *n* : calentamiento *m*

warn [ˈwɔrn] *vt* **1** CAUTION : advertir, alertar **2** INFORM : avisar, informar

warning [ˈwɔrnɪŋ] *n* **1** ADVICE : advertencia *f,* aviso *m* **2** ALERT : alerta *f,* alarma *f*

warp1 [ˈwɔrp] *vt* **1** : alabear, combar **2** PERVERT : pervertir, deformar — *vi* : pandearse, alabearse, combarse

warp2 *n* **1** : urdimbre *f* <the warp and the weft : la urdimbre y la trama> **2** : alabeo *m* (en la madera, etc.)

warrant1 [ˈwɔrənt] *vt* **1** ASSURE : asegurar, garantizar **2** GUARANTEE : garantizar **3** JUSTIFY, MERIT : justificar, merecer

warrant2 *n* **1** AUTHORIZATION : autorización *f,* permiso *m* <an arrest warrant : una orden de detención> **2** JUSTIFICATION : justificación *f*

warranty [ˈwɔrənti, ˌwɔrənˈtiː] *n, pl* **-ties** : garantía *f*

warren [ˈwɔrən] *n* : madriguera *f* (de conejos)

warrior [ˈwɔriər] *n* : guerrero *m,* -ra *f*

warship [ˈwɔrˌʃɪp] *n* : buque *m* de guerra

wart [ˈwɔrt] *n* : verruga *f*

wartime [ˈwɔrˌtaɪm] *n* : tiempo *m* de guerra

wary [ˈwæri] *adj* **warier; -est** : cauteloso, receloso <to be wary of : desconfiar de>

was → **be**

wash1 [ˈwɔʃ, ˈwɑʃ] *vt* **1** CLEAN : lavar(se), limpiar, fregar <to wash the dishes : lavar los platos> <to wash one's hands : lavarse las manos> **2** DRENCH : mojar **3** LAP : bañar <waves were washing the shore : las olas bañaban la orilla> **4** CARRY, DRAG : arrastrar **5 to wash away** : llevarse (un puente, etc.) — *vi* **1** : lavarse (dícese de una persona o la ropa) <the dress washes well : el vestido se lava bien> **2 to wash against** *or* **to wash over** : bañar

wash2 *n* **1** : lavado *m* <to give something a wash : lavar algo> **2** LAUNDRY : artículos *mpl* para lavar, ropa *f* sucia **3** : estela *f* (de un barco)

washable [ˈwɔʃəbəl, ˈwɑ-] *adj* : lavable

washboard [ˈwɔʃˌbord, ˈwɑʃ-] *n* : tabla *f* de lavar

washbowl [ˈwɔʃˌboːl, ˈwɑʃ-] *n* : lavabo *m,* lavamanos *m*

washcloth [ˈwɔʃˌklɔθ, ˈwɑʃ-] *n* : toallita *f* (para lavarse)

washed–out [ˈwɔʃtˈaʊt, ˈwɑʃt-] *adj* **1** : desvaído (dícese de colores) **2** EXHAUSTED : agotado, desanimado

washed–up [ˈwɔʃtˈʌp, ˈwɑʃt-] *adj* : acabado (dícese de una persona), fracasado (dícese de un negocio, etc.)

washer [ˈwɔʃər, ˈwɑ-] *n* **1** → **washing machine 2** : arandela *f* (de una llave, etc.)

washing [ˈwɔʃɪŋ, ˈwɑ-] *n* WASH : ropa *f* para lavar

washing machine *n* : máquina *f* de lavar, lavadora *f*

washout [ˈwɔʃˌaʊt, ˈwɑʃ-] *n* **1** : erosión *f* (de la tierra) **2** FAILURE : fracaso *m* <she's a washout : es un desastre>

washroom [ˈwɔʃˌruːm, ˈwɑʃ-, -ˌrʊm] *n* : servicios *mpl* (públicos), baño *m,* sanitario *m Col, Mex, Ven*

wasn't [ˈwʌzənt] (*contraction of* **was not**) → **be**

wasp [ˈwɑsp] *n* : avispa *f*

waspish [ˈwɑspɪʃ] *adj* **1** IRRITABLE : irritable, irascible **2** CAUSTIC : cáustico, mordaz

waste1 [ˈweɪst] *v* **wasted; wasting** *vt* **1** DEVASTATE : arrasar, arruinar, devastar **2** SQUANDER : desperdiciar, despilfarrar, malgastar <to waste time : perder tiempo> — *vi or* **to waste away** : consumirse, chuparse

waste2 *adj* **1** BARREN : yermo, baldío **2** DISCARDED : de desecho **3** EXCESS : sobrante

waste[3] *n* **1** → **wasteland 2** MISUSE : derroche *m,* desperdicio *m,* despilfarro *m* <a waste of time : una pérdida de tiempo> **3** RUBBISH : basura *f,* desechos *mpl,* desperdicios *mpl* **4** EXCREMENT : excremento *m*

wastebasket [ˈweɪstˌbæskət] *n* : cesto *m* (de basura), papelera *f,* zafacón *m Car*

wasteful [ˈweɪstfəl] *adj* : despilfarrador, derrochador, pródigo

wastefulness [ˈweɪstfəlnəs] *n* : derroche *m,* despilfarro *m*

wasteland [ˈweɪstˌlænd, -lənd] *n* : baldío *m,* yermo *m,* desierto *m*

watch[1] [ˈwɑtʃ] *vi* **1** *or* **to keep watch** : velar **2** OBSERVE : mirar, ver, observar **3 to watch for** AWAIT : esperar, quedar a la espera de **4 to watch out** : tener cuidado <watch out! : ¡ten cuidado!, ¡ojo!> — *vt* **1** OBSERVE : mirar, observar **2** *or* **to watch over** : vigilar, cuidar **3** : tener cuidado de <watch what you do : ten cuidado con lo que haces>

watch[2] *n* **1** : guardia *f* <to be on watch : estar de guardia> **2** SURVEILLANCE : vigilancia *f* **3** LOOKOUT : guardia *mf,* centinela *f,* vigía *mf* **4** TIMEPIECE : reloj *m*

watchdog [ˈwɑtʃˌdɔg] *n* : perro *m* guardián

watcher [ˈwɑtʃər] *n* : observador *m,* -dora *f*

watchful [ˈwɑtʃfəl] *adj* : alerta, vigilante, atento

watchfulness [ˈwɑtʃfəlnəs] *n* : vigilancia *f*

watchman [ˈwɑtʃmən] *n, pl* **-men** [-mən, -ˌmɛn] : vigilante *m,* guarda *m*

watchword [ˈwɑtʃˌwərd] *n* **1** PASSWORD : contraseña *f* **2** SLOGAN : lema *m,* eslogan *m*

water[1] [ˈwɔt̬ər, ˈwɑ-] *vt* **1** : regar (el jardín, etc.) **2 to water down** DILUTE : diluir, aguar — *vi* : lagrimar (dícese de los ojos), hacérsele agua la boca a uno <my mouth is watering : se me hace agua la boca>

water[2] *n* : agua *f*

water buffalo *n* : búfalo *m* de agua

watercolor [ˈwɔt̬ərˌkʌlər, ˈwɑ-] *n* : acuarela *f*

watercourse [ˈwɔt̬ərˌkors, ˈwɑ-] *n* : curso *m* de agua

watercress [ˈwɔt̬ərˌkrɛs, ˈwɑ-] *n* : berro *m*

waterfall [ˈwɔt̬ərˌfɔl, ˈwɑ-] *n* : cascada *f,* salto *m* de agua, catarata *f*

waterfowl [ˈwɔt̬ərˌfaʊl, ˈwɑ-] *n* : ave *f* acuática

waterfront [ˈwɔt̬ərˌfrʌnt, ˈwɑ-] *n* **1** : tierra *f* que bordea un río, un lago, o un mar **2** WHARF : muelle *m*

water lily *n* : nenúfar *m*

waterlogged [ˈwɔt̬ərˌlɔgd, ˈwɑt̬ərˌlɑgd] *adj* : lleno de agua, empapado, inundado (dícese del suelo)

watermark [ˈwɔt̬ərˌmɑrk, ˈwɑ-] *n* **1** : marca *f* del nivel de agua **2** : filigrana *f* (en el papel)

watermelon [ˈwɔt̬ərˌmɛlən, ˈwɑ-] *n* : sandía *f*

water moccasin → **moccasin**

waterpower [ˈwɔt̬ərˌpaʊər, ˈwɑ-] *n* : energía *f* hidráulica

waterproof[1] [ˈwɔt̬ərˌpruːf, ˈwɑ-] *vt* : hacer impermeable, impermeabilizar

waterproof[2] *adj* : impermeable, a prueba de agua

watershed [ˈwɔt̬ərˌʃɛd, ˈwɑ-] *n* **1** : línea *f* divisoria de aguas **2** BASIN : cuenca *f* (de un río)

waterskiing [ˈwɔt̬ərˌskiːɪŋ, ˈwɑ-] *n* : esquí *m* acuático

waterspout [ˈwɔt̬ərˌspaʊt, ˈwɑ-] *n* WHIRLWIND : tromba *f* marina

watertight [ˈwɔt̬ərˌtaɪt, ˈwɑ-] *adj* **1** : hermético **2** IRREFUTABLE : irrebatible, irrefutable <a watertight contract : un contrato sin lagunas>

waterway [ˈwɔt̬ərˌweɪ, ˈwɑ-] *n* : vía *f* navegable

waterworks [ˈwɔt̬ərˌwərks, ˈwɑ-] *npl* : central *f* de abastecimiento de agua

watery [ˈwɔt̬əri, ˈwɑ-] *adj* **1** : acuoso, como agua **2** : aguado, diluido <watery soup : sopa aguada> **3** : lloroso <watery eyes : ojos llorosos> **4** WASHED-OUT : desvaído (dícese de colores)

watt [ˈwɑt] *n* : vatio *m*

wattage [ˈwɑt̬ɪdʒ] *n* : vataje *m*

wattle [ˈwɑt̬əl] *n* : carúncula *f* (de un ave, etc.)

wave[1] [ˈweɪv] *v* **waved; waving** *vi* **1** : saludar con la mano, hacer señas con la mano <she waved at him : lo saludó con la mano> **2** FLUTTER, SHAKE : ondear, agitarse **3** UNDULATE : ondular — *vt* **1** SHAKE : agitar **2** BRANDISH : blandir **3** CURL : ondular, marcar (el pelo) **4** SIGNAL : hacerle señas a (con la mano) <he waved farewell : se despidió con la mano>

wave[2] *n* **1** : ola *f* (de agua) **2** CURL : onda *f* (en el pelo) **3** : onda *f* (en física) **4** SURGE : oleada *f* <a wave of enthusiasm : una oleada de entusiasmo> **5** GESTURE : señal *f* con la mano, saludo *m* con la mano

wavelength [ˈweɪvˌlɛŋkθ] *n* : longitud *f* de onda

waver [ˈweɪvər] *vi* **1** VACILLATE : vacilar, fluctuar **2** FLICKER : parpadear, titilar, oscilar **3** FALTER : flaquear, tambalearse

wavy [ˈweɪvi] *adj* **wavier; -est** : ondulado

wax[1] [ˈwæks] *vi* **1** : crecer (dícese de la luna) **2** BECOME : volverse, ponerse <to wax indignant : indignarse> — *vt* : encerar

wax[2] *n* **1** BEESWAX : cera *f* de abejas **2** : cera *f* <floor wax : cera para el piso>

3 *or* **earwax** [ˈɪr,wæks] : cerilla *f,* cerumen *m*

waxen [ˈwæksən] *adj* : de cera

waxy [ˈwæksi] *adj* **waxier; -est** : ceroso

way [ˈweɪ] *n* **1** PATH, ROAD : camino *m,* vía *f* **2** ROUTE : camino *m,* ruta *f* <to go the wrong way : equivocarse de camino> <I'm on my way : estoy de camino> **3** : línea *f* de conducta, camino *m* <he chose the easy way : optó por el camino fácil> **4** MANNER, MEANS : manera *f,* modo *m,* forma *f* <in the same way : del mismo modo, igualmente> <there are no two ways about it : no cabe la menor duda> **5** (*indicating a wish*) <have it your way : como tú quieras> <to get one's own way : salirse uno con la suya> **6** STATE : estado *m* <things are in a bad way : las cosas marchan mal> **7** RESPECT : aspecto *m,* sentido *m* **8** CUSTOM : costumbre *f* <to mend one's ways : dejar las malas costumbres> **9** PASSAGE : camino *m* <to get in the way : meterse en el camino> **10** DISTANCE : distancia *f* <to come a long way : hacer grandes progresos> **11** DIRECTION : dirección *f* <come this way : venga por aquí> <which way did he go? : ¿por dónde fue?> **12 by the way** : a propósito, por cierto **13 by way of** VIA : vía, pasando por **14 out of the way** REMOTE : remoto, recóndito **15 → under way**

wayfarer [ˈweɪ,færər] *n* : caminante *mf*

waylay [ˈweɪ,leɪ] *vt* **-laid** [-,leɪd]; **-laying** ACCOST : abordar

wayside [ˈweɪ,saɪd] *n* : borde *m* del camino

wayward [ˈweɪwərd] *adj* **1** UNRULY : díscolo, rebelde **2** UNTOWARD : adverso

we [ˈwiː] *pron* : nosotros, nosotras

weak [ˈwiːk] *adj* **1** FEEBLE : débil, endeble **2** : flojo, pobre <a weak excuse : una excusa poco convincente> **3** DILUTED : aguado, diluido <weak tea : té poco cargado> **4** FAINT : tenue (dícese de los colores, las luces, los sonidos, etc.)

weaken [ˈwiːkən] *vt* : debilitar — *vi* : debilitarse, flaquear

weakling [ˈwiːklɪŋ] *n* : alfeñique *m fam;* debilucho *m,* -cha *f*

weakly[1] [ˈwiːkli] *adv* : débilmente

weakly[2] *adj* **weaklier; -est** : débil, enclenque

weakness [ˈwiːknəs] *n* **1** FEEBLENESS : debilidad *f* **2** FAULT, FLAW : flaqueza *f,* punto *m* débil

wealth [ˈwɛlθ] *n* **1** RICHES : riqueza *f* **2** PROFUSION : abundancia *f,* profusión *f*

wealthy [ˈwɛlθi] *adj* **wealthier; -est** : rico, acaudalado, adinerado

wean [ˈwiːn] *vt* **1** : destetar (a los niños o las crías) **2 to wean someone away from** : quitarle a alguien la costumbre de

weapon [ˈwɛpən] *n* : arma *f*

weaponless [ˈwɛpənləs] *adj* : desarmado

wear[1] [ˈwær] *v* **wore** [ˈwor]; **worn** [ˈworn]; **wearing** *vt* **1** : llevar (ropa, un reloj, etc.), calzar (zapatos) <to wear a happy smile : sonreír alegremente> **2** *or* **to wear away** : desgastar, erosionar (rocas, etc.) **3 to wear out** : gastar <he wore out his shoes : gastó sus zapatos> **4 to wear out** EXHAUST : agotar, fatigar <to wear oneself out : agotarse> — *vi* **1** LAST : durar **2 to wear off** DIMINISH : disminuir **3 to wear out** : gastarse

wear[2] *n* **1** USE : uso *m* <for everyday wear : para todos los días>**2** CLOTHING : ropa *f* <children's wear : ropa de niños> **3** DETERIORATION : desgaste *m* <to be the worse for wear : estar deteriorado>

wearable [ˈwærəbəl] *adj* : que puede ponerse (dícese de una prenda)

wear and tear *n* : desgaste *m*

weariness [ˈwɪrinəs] *n* : fatiga *f,* cansancio *m*

wearisome [ˈwɪrisəm] *adj* : aburrido, pesado, cansado

weary[1] [ˈwɪri] *v* **-ried; -rying** *vt* **1** TIRE : cansar, fatigar **2** BORE : hastiar, aburrir — *vi* : cansarse

weary[2] *adj* **-rier; -est 1** TIRED : cansado **2** FED UP : harto **3** BORED : aburrido

weasel [ˈwiːzəl] *n* : comadreja *f*

weather[1] [ˈwɛðər] *vt* **1** WEAR : erosionar, desgastar **2** ENDURE : aguantar, sobrellevar, capear <to weather the storm : capear el temporal>

weather[2] *n* : tiempo *m*

weather–beaten [ˈwɛðər,biːtən] *adj* : curtido

weatherman [ˈwɛðər,mæn] *n, pl* **-men** [-mən, -,mɛn] METEOROLOGIST : meteorólogo *m,* -ga *f*

weatherproof [ˈwɛðər,pruːf] *adj* : que resiste a la intemperie, impermeable

weather vane → vane

weave[1] [ˈwiːv] *v* **wove** [ˈwoːv] *or* **weaved; woven** [ˈwoːvən] *or* **weaved; weaving** *vt* **1** : tejer (tela) **2** INTERLACE : entretejer, entrelazar **3 to weave one's way through** : abrirse camino por — *vi* **1** : tejer **2** WIND : serpentear, zigzaguear

weave[2] *n* : tejido *m,* trama *f*

weaver [ˈwiːvər] *n* : tejedor *m,* -dora *f*

web[1] [ˈwɛb] *vt* **webbed; webbing** : cubrir o proveer con una red

web[2] *n* **1** COBWEB, SPIDERWEB : telaraña *f,* tela *f* de araña **2** ENTANGLEMENT, SNARE : red *f,* enredo *m* <a web of intrigue : una red de intriga> **3** : membrana *f* interdigital (de aves) **4** NETWORK : red *f* <a web of highways : una red de carreteras>

webbed [ˈwɛbd] *adj* : palmeado <webbed feet : patas palmeadas>
wed [ˈwɛd] *vt* **wedded; wedding 1** MARRY : casarse con **2** UNITE : ligar, unir
we'd [ˈwiːd] (*contraction of* **we had, we should,** *or* **we would**) → **have, should, would**
wedding [ˈwɛdɪŋ] *n* : boda *f,* casamiento *m*
wedge[1] [ˈwɛdʒ] *vt* **wedged; wedging 1** : apretar (con una cuña) <to wedge open : mantener abierto con una cuña> **2** CRAM : meter, embutir
wedge[2] *n* **1** : cuña *f* **2** PIECE : porción *f,* trozo *m*
wedlock [ˈwɛd,lɑk] → **marriage**
Wednesday [ˈwɛnz,deɪ, -di] *n* : miércoles *m*
wee [ˈwiː] *adj* : pequeño, minúsculo <in the wee hours : a las altas horas>
weed[1] [ˈwiːd] *vt* **1** : desherbar, desyerbar **2 to weed out** : eliminar, quitar
weed[2] *n* : mala hierba *f*
weedy [ˈwiːdi] *adj* **weedier; -est 1** : cubierto de malas hierbas **2** LANKY, SKINNY : flaco, larguirucho *fam*
week [ˈwiːk] *n* : semana *f*
weekday [ˈwiːk,deɪ] *n* : día *m* laborable
weekend [ˈwiːk,ɛnd] *n* : fin *m* de semana
weekly[1] [ˈwiːkli] *adv* : semanalmente
weekly[2] *adj* : semanal
weekly[3] *n, pl* **-lies** : semanario *m*
weep [ˈwiːp] *v* **wept** [ˈwɛpt]; **weeping** : llorar
weeping willow *n* : sauce *m* llorón
weepy [ˈwiːpi] *adj* **weepier; -est** : lloroso, triste
weevil [ˈwiːvəl] *n* : gorgojo *m*
weft [ˈwɛft] *n* : trama *f*
weigh [ˈweɪ] *vt* **1** : pesar **2** CONSIDER : considerar, sopesar **3 to weigh anchor** : levar anclas **4 to weigh down** : sobrecargar (con una carga), abrumar (con preocupaciones, etc.) — *vi* **1** : pesar <it weighs 10 pounds : pesa 10 libras> **2** COUNT : tener importancia, contar **3 to weigh on one's mind** : preocuparle a uno
weight[1] [ˈweɪt] *vt* **1** : poner peso en, sujetar con un peso **2** BURDEN : cargar, oprimir
weight[2] *n* **1** HEAVINESS : peso *m* <to lose weight : bajar de peso, adelgazar> **2** : peso *m* <weights and measures : pesos y medidas> **3** : pesa *f* <to lift weights : levantar pesas> **4** BURDEN : peso *m,* carga *f* <to take a weight off one's mind : quitarle un peso de encima a uno> **5** IMPORTANCE : peso *m* **6** INFLUENCE : influencia *f,* autoridad *f* <to throw one's weight around : hacer sentir su influencia>
weighty [ˈweɪti] *adj* **weightier; -est 1** HEAVY : pesado **2** IMPORTANT : importante, de peso
weird [ˈwɪrd] *adj* **1** MYSTERIOUS : misterioso **2** STRANGE : extraño, raro — **weirdly** *adv*
welcome[1] [ˈwɛlkəm] *vt* **-comed; -coming** : darle la bienvenida a, recibir
welcome[2] *adj* : bienvenido <to make someone welcome : acoger bien a alguien> <you're welcome! : ¡de nada!, ¡no hay de qué!>
welcome[3] *n* : bienvenida *f,* recibimiento *m,* acojida *f*
weld[1] [ˈwɛld] *v* : soldar
weld[2] *n* : soldadura *f*
welder [ˈwɛldər] *n* : soldador *m,* -dora *f*
welfare [ˈwɛl,fær] *n* **1** WELL-BEING : bienestar *m* **2** : asistencia *f* social
well[1] [ˈwɛl] *vi or* **to well up** : brotar, manar
well[2] *adv* **better** [ˈbɛt̬ər]; **best** [ˈbɛst] **1** RIGHTLY : bien, correctamente **2** SATISFACTORILY : bien <to turn out well : resultar bien, salir bien> **3** COMPLETELY : completamente <well-hidden : completamente escondido> **4** INTIMATELY : bien <I knew him well : lo conocía bien> **5** CONSIDERABLY, FAR : muy, bastante <well ahead : muy adelante> <well before the deadline : bastante antes de la fecha> **6 as well** ALSO : también **7** → **as well**
well[3] *adj* **1** SATISFACTORY : bien <all is well : todo está bien> **2** DESIRABLE : conveniente <it would be well if you left : sería conveniente que te fueras> **3** HEALTHY : bien, sano
well[4] *n* **1** : pozo *m* (de agua, petróleo, gas, etc.), aljibe *m* (de agua) **2** SOURCE : fuente *f* <a well of information : una fuente de información> **3** *or* **stairwell** : caja *f,* hueco *m* (de la escalera)
well[5] *interj* **1** (*used to introduce a remark*) : bueno **2** (*used to express surprise*) : ¡vaya!
we'll [ˈwiːl, wɪl] (*contraction of* **we shall** *or* **we will**) → **shall, will**
well–balanced [ˈwɛlˈbælənst] *adj* : equilibrado
well–being [ˈwɛlˈbiːɪŋ] *n* : bienestar *m*
well–bred [ˈwɛlˈbrɛd] *adj* : fino, bien educado
well–done [ˈwɛlˈdʌn] *adj* **1** : bien hecho <well-done! : ¡bravo!> **2** : bien cocido
well–known [ˈwɛlˈnoːn] *adj* : famoso, bien conocido
well–meaning [ˈwɛlˈmiːnɪŋ] *adj* : bienintencionado, que tiene buenas intenciones
well–nigh [ˈwɛlˈnaɪ] *adv* : casi <well-nigh impossible : casi imposible>
well–off [ˈwɛlˈɔf] → **well–to–do**
well–rounded [ˈwɛlˈraʊndəd] *adj* : completo, equilibrado
well–to–do [,wɛltəˈduː] *adj* : próspero, adinerado, rico

welt ['wɛlt] *n* **1 :** vira *f* (de un zapato) **2** WHEAL **:** verdugón *m*

welter ['wɛltər] *n* **:** fárrago *m,* revoltijo *m* <a welter of data : un fárrago de datos>

wend ['wɛnd] *vi* **to wend one's way :** ponerse en camino, encaminar sus pasos

went → **go**

wept → **weep**

were → **be**

we're ['wɪr, 'wər, 'wiːər] (*contraction of* **we are**) → **be**

werewolf ['wɪrˌwʊlf, 'wɛr-, 'wər-, -ˌwʌlf] *n, pl* **-wolves** [-ˌwʊlvz, -ˌwʌlvz] **:** hombre *m* lobo

west[1] ['wɛst] *adv* **:** al oeste

west[2] *adj* **:** oeste, del oeste, occidental <west winds : vientos del oeste>

west[3] *n* **1 :** oeste *m* **2 the West :** el Oeste, el Occidente

westerly ['wɛstərli] *adv & adj* **:** del oeste

western ['wɛstərn] *adj* **1 :** Occidental, del Oeste **2 :** occidental, oeste

Westerner ['wɛstərnər] *n* **:** habitante *mf* del oeste

West Indian *n* **:** antillano *m,* -na *f* — **West Indian** *adj*

westward ['wɛstwərd] *adv & adj* **:** hacia el oeste

wet[1] ['wɛt] *vt* **wet** *or* **wetted; wetting :** mojar, humedecer

wet[2] *adj* **wetter; wettest 1 :** mojado, húmedo <wet clothes : ropa mojada> **2** RAINY **:** lluvioso **3 wet paint :** pintura *f* fresca

wet[3] *n* **1** MOISTURE **:** humedad *f* **2** RAIN **:** lluvia *f*

we've ['wiːv] (*contraction of* **we have**) → **have**

whack[1] ['hwæk] *vt* **:** golpear (fuertemente), aporrear

whack[2] *n* **1 :** golpe *m* fuerte, porrazo *m* **2** ATTEMPT **:** intento *m,* tentativa *f*

whale[1] ['hweɪl] *vi* **whaled; whaling :** cazar ballenas

whale[2] *n, pl* **whales** *or* **whale :** ballena *f*

whaleboat ['hweɪlˌboːt] *n* **:** ballenero *m*

whalebone ['hweɪlˌboːn] *n* **:** barba *f* de ballena

whaler ['hweɪlər] *n* **1 :** ballenero *m,* -ra *f* **2** → **whaleboat**

wharf ['hwɔrf] *n, pl* **wharves** ['hwɔrvz] **:** muelle *m,* embarcadero *m*

what[1] ['hwɑt, 'hwʌt] *adv* **1** HOW **:** cómo, cúanto <what he suffered! : ¡cómo sufría!> **2 what with :** entre <what with one thing and another : entre una cosa y otra>

what[2] *adj* **1** (*used in questions*) **:** qué <what more do you want? : ¿qué más quieres?> <what color is it? : ¿de qué color es?> **2** (*used in exclamations*) **:** qué <what an idea! : ¡qué idea!> **3** ANY, WHATEVER **:** cualquier <give what help you can : da cualquier contribución que puedas>

what[3] *pron* **1** (*used in direct questions*) **:** qué <what happened? : ¿qué pasó?> <what does it cost? : ¿cuánto cuesta?> **2** (*used in indirect statements*) **:** lo que, que <I don't know what to do : no sé que hacer> <do what I tell you : haz lo que te digo> **3 what for** WHY **:** porqué **4 what if :** y si <what if he knows? : ¿y si lo sabe?>

whatever[1] [hwɑt'ɛvər, ˌhwʌt-] *adj* **1** ANY **:** cualquier, cualquier...que <whatever way you prefer : de cualquier manera que prefiera, como prefiera> **2** (*in negative constructions*) <there's no chance whatever : no hay ninguna posibilidad> <nothing whatever : nada en absoluto>

whatever[2] *pron* **1** ANYTHING **:** (todo) lo que <I'll do whatever I want : haré lo que quiera> **2** (*no matter what*) <whatever it may be : sea lo que sea> **3** WHAT **:** qué <whatever do you mean? : ¿qué quieres decir?>

whatsoever[1] [ˌhwɑtso'ɛvər, ˌhwʌt-] *adj* → **whatever**[1]

whatsoever[2] *pron* → **whatever**[2]

wheal ['hwiːl] *n* **:** verdugón *m*

wheat ['hwiːt] *n* **:** trigo *m*

wheaten ['hwiːtən] *adj* **:** de trigo

wheedle ['hwiːdəl] *vt* **-dled; -dling** CAJOLE **:** engatusar <to wheedle something out of someone : sonsacarle algo a alguien>

wheel[1] ['hwiːl] *vt* **:** empujar (una bicicleta, etc.), mover (algo sobre ruedas) — *vi* **1** ROTATE **:** girar, rotar **2 to wheel around** TURN **:** darse la vuelta

wheel[2] *n* **1 :** rueda *f* **2** *or* **steering wheel :** volante *m* (de automóviles, etc.), timón *m* (de barcos o aviones) **3 wheels** *npl* **:** maquinaria *f,* fuerza *f* impulsora <the wheels of government : la maquinaria del gobierno>

wheelbarrow ['hwiːlˌbærˌoː] *n* **:** carretilla *f*

wheelchair ['hwiːlˌtʃær] *n* **:** silla *f* de ruedas

wheeze[1] ['hwiːz] *vi* **wheezed; wheezing :** resollar, respirar con dificultad

wheeze[2] *n* **:** resuello *m*

whelk ['hwɛlk] *n* **:** buccino *m*

whelp[1] ['hwɛlp] *vi* **:** parir

whelp[2] *n* **:** cachorro *m,* -rra *f*

when[1] ['hwɛn] *adv* **:** cuándo <when will you return? : ¿cuándo volverás?> <he asked me when I would be home : me preguntó cuándo estaría en casa>

when[2] *conj* **1** (*referring to a particular time*) **:** cuando, en que <when you are ready : cuando estés listo> <the days when I clean the house : los días en que limpio la casa> **2** IF **:** cuando, si <how can I go when I have no money? : ¿cómo voy a ir si no tengo dinero?> **3** ALTHOUGH **:** cuando <you said it was big when actually it's

small : dijiste que era grande cuando en realidad es pequeño>

when[3] *pron* : cuándo <since when are you the boss? : ¿desde cuándo eres el jefe?>

whence [ˈ*h*wɛnts] *adv* : de donde

whenever[1] [*h*wɛnˈɛvər] *adv* **1 :** cuando sea <tomorrow or whenever : mañana o cuando sea> **2** (*in questions*) : cuándo

whenever[2] *conj* **1 :** siempre que, cada vez que <whenever I go, I'm disappointed : siempre que voy, quedo desilusionado> **2** WHEN : cuando <whenever you like : cuando quieras>

where[1] [ˈ*h*wɛr] *adv* : dónde, adónde <where is he? : ¿dónde está?> <where did they go? : ¿adónde fueron?>

where[2] *conj* : donde, adonde <she knows where the house is : sabe donde está la casa> <she goes where she likes : va adonde quiera>

where[3] *pron* : donde <Chicago is where I live : Chicago es donde vivo>

whereabouts[1] [ˈ*h*wɛrəˌbaʊts] *adv* : dónde, por dónde <whereabouts is the house? : ¿dónde está la casa?>

whereabouts[2] *ns & pl* : paradero *m*

whereas [*h*wɛrˈæz] *conj* **1 :** considerando que (usado en documentos legales) **2 :** mientras que <I like the white one whereas she prefers the black : me gusta el blanco mientras que ella prefiere el negro>

whereby [*h*wɛrˈbaɪ] *adv* : por lo cual

wherefore [ˈ*h*wɛrˌfor] *adv* : por qué

wherein [*h*wɛrˈɪn] *adv* : en el cual, en el que

whereof [*h*wɛrˈʌv, -ɑv] *conj* : de lo cual

whereupon [ˈ*h*wɛrəˌpɑn, -ˌpɔn] *conj* : con lo cual, después de lo cual

wherever[1] [*h*wɛrˈɛvər] *adv* **1** WHERE : dónde, adónde **2 :** en cualquier parte <or wherever : o donde sea>

wherever[2] *conj* : dondequiera que, donde sea <wherever you go : dondequiera que vayas>

wherewithal [ˈ*h*wɛrwɪˌðɔl, -ˌθɔl] *n* : medios *mpl*, recursos *mpl*

whet [ˈ*h*wɛt] *vt* **whetted; whetting 1** SHARPEN : afilar **2** STIMULATE : estimular <to whet the appetite : estimular el apetito>

whether [ˈ*h*wɛðər] *conj* **1 :** si <I don't know whether it is finished : no sé si está acabado> <we doubt whether he'll show up : dudamos que aparezca> **2** (*used in comparisons*) <whether I like it or not : tanto si quiero como si no> <whether he comes or he doesn't : venga o no>

whetstone [ˈ*h*wɛtˌstoːn] *n* : piedra *f* de afilar

whey [ˈ*h*weɪ] *n* : suero *m* (de la leche)

which[1] [ˈ*h*wɪtʃ] *adj* : qué, cuál <which tie do you prefer? : ¿cuál corbata prefieres?> <which ones? : ¿cuáles?> <tell me which house is yours : dime qué casa es la tuya>

which[2] *pron* **1 :** cuál <which is the right answer? : ¿cuál es la respuesta correcta?> **2 :** que, el (la) cual <the cup which broke : la taza que se quebró> <the house, which is made of brick : la casa, la cual es de ladrillo>

whichever[1] [*h*wɪtʃˈɛvər] *adj* : el (la) que, cualquiera que <whichever book you like : cualquier libro que te guste>

whichever[2] *pron* : el (la) que, cualquiera que <take whichever you want : toma el que quieras> <whichever I choose : cualquiera que elija>

whiff[1] [ˈ*h*wɪf] *v* PUFF : soplar

whiff[2] *n* **1** PUFF : soplo *m,* ráfaga *f* **2** SNIFF : olor *m* **3** HINT : dejo *m,* pizca *f*

while[1] [ˈ*h*waɪl] *vt* **whiled; whiling** : pasar <to while away the time : matar el tiempo>

while[2] *n* **1** TIME : rato *m,* tiempo *m* <after a while : después de un rato> <in a while : dentro de poco> **2 to be worth one's while :** valer la pena

while[3] *conj* **1 :** mientras <whistle while you work : silba mientras trabajas> **2** WHEREAS : mientras que **3** ALTHOUGH : aunque <while it's very good, it's not perfect : aunque es muy bueno, no es perfecto>

whim [ˈ*h*wɪm] *n* : capricho *m,* antojo *m*

whimper[1] [ˈ*h*wɪmpər] *vi* : lloriquear, gimotear

whimper[2] *n* : quejido *m*

whimsical [ˈ*h*wɪmzɪkəl] *adj* **1** CAPRICIOUS : caprichoso, fantasioso **2** ERRATIC : errático — **whimsically** *adv*

whine[1] [ˈ*h*waɪn] *vi* **whined; whining 1** : lloriquear, gimotear, gemir **2** COMPLAIN : quejarse

whine[2] *n* : quejido *m,* gemido *m*

whinny[1] [ˈ*h*wɪni] *vi* **-nied; -nying** : relinchar

whinny[2] *n, pl* **-nies** : relincho *m*

whip[1] [ˈ*h*wɪp] *v* **whipped; whipping** *vt* **1** SNATCH : sacar (rápidamente), arrebatar <she whipped the cloth off the table : arrebató el mantel de la mesa> **2** LASH : azotar **3** DEFEAT : vencer, derrotar **4** INCITE : incitar, despertar <to whip up enthusiasm : despertar el entusiasmo> **5** BEAT : batir (huevos, crema, etc.) — *vi* FLAP : agitarse

whip[2] *n* **1 :** látigo *m,* azote *m,* fusta *f* (de jinete) **2 :** miembro *m* de un cuerpo legislativo encargado de disciplina

whiplash [ˈ*h*wɪpˌlæʃ] *n or* **whiplash injury** : traumatismo *m* cervical

whippet [ˈ*h*wɪpət] *n* : galgo *m* pequeño, galgo *m* inglés

whippoorwill [ˈ*h*wɪpərˌwɪl] *n* : chotacabras *mf*

whir[1] [ˈ*h*wər] *vi* **whirred; whirring** : zumbar

whir[2] *n* : zumbido *m*

whirl[1] ['hwərl] *vi* **1** SPIN : dar vueltas, girar <my head is whirling : la cabeza me está dando vueltas> **2 to whirl about** : arremolinarse, moverse rápidamente

whirl[2] *n* **1** SPIN : giro *m,* vuelta *f,* remolino *m* (dícese del polvo, etc.) **2** BUSTLE : bullicio *m,* torbellino *m* (de actividad, etc.) **3 to give it a whirl** : intentar hacer, probar

whirlpool ['hwərl,pu:l] *n* : vorágine *f,* remolino *m*

whirlwind ['hwərl,wɪnd] *n* : remolino *m,* torbellino *m,* tromba *f*

whisk[1] ['hwɪsk] *vt* **1** : llevar <she whisked the children off to bed : llevó a los niños a la cama> **2** : batir <to whisk eggs : batir huevos> **3 to whisk away** *or* **to whisk off** : sacudir

whisk[2] *n* **1** WHISKING : sacudida *f* (movimiento) **2** : batidor *m* (para batir huevos, etc.)

whisk broom *n* : escobilla *f*

whisker ['hwɪskər] *n* **1** : pelo *m* (de la barba o el bigote) **2 whiskers** *npl* : bigotes *mpl* (de animales)

whiskey *or* **whisky** ['hwɪski] *n, pl* **-keys** *or* **-kies** : whisky *m*

whisper[1] ['hwɪspər] *vi* : cuchichear, susurrar — *vt* : decir en voz baja, susurrar

whisper[2] *n* **1** WHISPERING : susurro *m,* cuchicheo *m* **2** RUMOR : rumor *m* **3** TRACE : dejo *m,* pizca *f*

whistle[1] ['hwɪsəl] *v* **-tled; -tling** *vi* : silbar, chiflar, pitar (dícese de un tren, etc.) — *vt* : silbar <to whistle a tune : silbar una melodía>

whistle[2] *n* **1** WHISTLING : chiflido *m,* silbido *m* **2** : silbato *m,* pito *m* (instrumento)

whit ['hwɪt] *n* BIT : ápice *m,* pizca *f*

white[1] ['hwaɪt] *adj* **whiter; -est** : blanco

white[2] *n* **1** : blanco *m* (color) **2** : clara *f* (de huevos) **3** *or* **white person** : blanco *m,* -ca *f*

white blood cell *n* : glóbulo *m* blanco

whitecaps ['hwaɪt,kæps] *npl* : cabrillas *fpl*

white–collar ['hwaɪt'kɑlər] *adj* **1** : de oficina **2 white–collar worker** : oficinista *mf*

whitefish ['hwaɪt,fɪʃ] *n* : pescado *m* blanco

whiten ['hwaɪtən] *vt* : blanquear — *vi* : ponerse blanco

whiteness ['hwaɪtnəs] *n* : blancura *f*

white–tailed deer ['hwaɪt'teɪld] *n* : ciervo *f* de Virginia

whitewash[1] ['hwaɪt,wɔʃ] *vt* **1** : enjalbegar, blanquear <to whitewash a fence : enjalbegar una valla> **2** CONCEAL : encubrir (un escándalo, etc.)

whitewash[2] *n* **1** : jalbegue *m,* lechada *f* **2** COVER-UP : encubrimiento *m*

whither ['hwɪðər] *adv* : adónde

whiting ['hwaɪt̬ɪŋ] *n* : merluza *f,* pescadilla *f* (pez)

whitish ['hwaɪt̬ɪʃ] *adj* : blancuzco

whittle ['hwɪt̬əl] *vt* **-tled; -tling 1** : tallar (madera) **2 to whittle down** : reducir, recortar <to whittle down expenses : reducir los gastos>

whiz[1] *or* **whizz** ['hwɪz] *vi* **whizzed; whizzing 1** BUZZ : zumbar **2 to whiz by** : pasar muy rápido, pasar volando

whiz[2] *or* **whizz** *n, pl* **whizzes 1** BUZZ : zumbido *m* **2 to be a whiz** : ser un prodigio, ser muy hábil

who ['hu:] *pron* **1** (*used in direct and indirect questions*) : quién <who is that? : ¿quién es ése?> <who did it? : ¿quién lo hizo?> <we know who they are : sabemos quiénes son> **2** (*used in relative clauses*) : que, quien <the lady who lives there : la señora que vive allí> <for those who wait : para los que esperan, para quienes esperan>

whodunit [hu:'dʌnɪt] *n* : novela *f* policíaca

whoever [hu:'ɛvər] *pron* **1** : quienquiera que, quien <whoever did it : quienquiera que lo hizo> <give it to whoever you want : dalo a quien quieras> **2** (*used in questions*) : quién <whoever could that be? : ¿quién podría ser?>

whole[1] ['ho:l] *adj* **1** UNHURT : ileso **2** INTACT : intacto, sano **3** ENTIRE : entero, íntegro <the whole island : toda la isla> <whole milk : leche entera> **4 a whole lot** : muchísimo

whole[2] *n* **1** : todo *m* **2 as a whole** : en conjunto **3 on the whole** : en general

wholehearted ['ho:l'hɑrt̬əd] *adj* : sin reservas, incondicional

whole number *n* : entero *m*

wholesale[1] ['ho:l,seɪl] *v* **-saled; -saling** *vt* : vender al por mayor — *vi* : venderse al por mayor

wholesale[2] *adv* : al por mayor

wholesale[3] *adj* **1** : al por mayor <wholesale grocer : tendero al por mayor> **2** TOTAL : total, absoluto <wholesale slaughter : matanza sistemática>

wholesale[4] *n* : mayoreo *m*

wholesaler ['ho:l,seɪlər] *n* : mayorista *mf*

wholesome ['ho:lsəm] *adj* **1** : sano <wholesome advice : consejo sano> **2** HEALTHY : sano, saludable

whole wheat *adj* : de trigo integral

wholly ['ho:li] *adv* **1** COMPLETELY : completamente **2** SOLELY : exclusivamente, únicamente

whom ['hu:m] *pron* **1** (*used in direct questions*) : a quién <whom did you choose? : ¿a quién elegiste?> **2** (*used in indirect questions*) : de quién, con quién, en quién <I don't know whom to consult : no sé con quién consultar> **3** (*used in relative clauses*) : que, a quien <the lawyer whom I recommended to you : el abogado que te recomendé>

whomever [huːm'ɛvər] *pron* : a quienquiera que, a quien
whoop[1] ['*h*wuːp, '*h*wʊp] *vi* : gritar, chillar
whoop[2] *n* : grito *m*
whooping cough *n* : tos *f* ferina
whopper ['*h*wɑpər] *n* **1** : cosa *f* enorme **2** LIE : mentira *f* colosal
whopping ['*h*wɑpɪŋ] *adj* : enorme
whore ['hor] *n* : puta *f*, ramera *f*
whorl ['*h*wɔrl, '*h*wərl] *n* : espiral *f*, espira *f* (de una concha), línea *f* (de una huella digital)
whose[1] ['huːz] *adj* **1** (*used in questions*) : de quién <whose truck is that? : ¿de quién es ese camión?> **2** (*used in relative clauses*) : cuyo <the person whose work is finished : la persona cuyo trabajo está terminado>
whose[2] *pron* : de quién <tell me whose it was : dime de quién era>
why[1] ['*h*waɪ] *adv* : por qué <why did you do it? : ¿por qué lo hizo?>
why[2] *n, pl* **whys** REASON : porqué *m*, razón *f*
why[3] *conj* : por qué <I know why he left : yo sé por qué salió> <there's no reason why it should exist : no hay razón para que exista>
why[4] *interj* (*used to express surprise*) : ¡vaya!, ¡mira!
wick ['wɪk] *n* : mecha *f*
wicked ['wɪkəd] *adj* **1** EVIL : malo, malvado **2** MISCHIEVOUS : travieso, pícaro <a wicked grin : una sonrisa traviesa> **3** TERRIBLE : terrible, horrible <a wicked storm : una tormenta horrible>
wickedly ['wɪkədli] *adv* : con maldad
wickedness ['wɪkədnəs] *n* : maldad *f*
wicker[1] ['wɪkər] *adj* : de mimbre
wicker[2] *n* **1** : mimbre *m* **2** → **wickerwork**
wickerwork ['wɪkər,wərk] *n* : artículos *mpl* de mimbre
wicket ['wɪkət] *n* **1** WINDOW : ventanilla *f* **2** *or* **wicket gate** : postigo *m* **3** : aro *m* (en croquet), palos *mpl* (en críquet)
wide[1] ['waɪd] *adv* **wider; widest 1** WIDELY : por todas partes <to travel far and wide : viajar por todas partes> **2** COMPLETELY : completamente, totalmente <wide open : abierto de par en par> **3 wide apart** : muy separados
wide[2] *adj* **wider; widest 1** VAST : vasto, extensivo <a wide area : una área extensiva> **2** : ancho <three meters wide : tres metros de ancho> **3** BROAD : ancho, amplio **4** *or* **wide–open** : muy abierto **5 wide of the mark** : desviado, lejos del blanco
wide–awake ['waɪdə'weɪk] *adj* : (completamente) despierto
wide–eyed ['waɪd'aɪd] *adj* **1** : con los ojos muy abiertos **2** NAIVE : inocente, ingenuo
widely ['waɪdli] *adv* : extensivamente, por todas partes
widen ['waɪdən] *vt* : ampliar, ensanchar — *vi* : ampliarse, ensancharse
widespread ['waɪd'sprɛd] *adj* : extendido, extenso, difuso
widow[1] ['wɪ,doː] *vt* : dejar viuda <to be widowed : enviudar>
widow[2] *n* : viuda *f*
widower ['wɪdowər] *n* : viudo *m*
width ['wɪdθ] *n* : ancho *m*, anchura *f*
wield ['wiːld] *vt* **1** USE : usar, manejar <to wield a broom : usar una escoba> **2** EXERCISE : ejercer <to wield influence : influir>
wiener ['wiːnər] → **frankfurter**
wife ['waɪf] *n, pl* **wives** ['waɪvz] : esposa *f*, mujer *f*
wifely ['waɪfli] *adj* : de esposa, conyugal
wig ['wɪg] *n* : peluca *f*
wiggle[1] ['wɪgəl] *v* **-gled; -gling** *vt* : menear, contonear <to wiggle one's hips : contonearse> — *vi* : menearse
wiggle[2] *n* : meneo *m*, contoneo *m*
wiggly ['wɪgəli] *adj* **-glier; -est 1** : que se menea **2** WAVY : ondulado
wigwag ['wɪg,wæg] *vi* **-wagged; -wagging** : comunicar por señales
wigwam ['wɪg,wɑm] *n* : wigwam *m*
wild[1] ['waɪld] *adv* **1** → **wildly 2 to run wild** : descontrolarse
wild[2] *adj* **1** : salvaje, silvestre, cimarrón <wild horses : caballos salvajes> <wild rice : arroz silvestre> **2** DESOLATE : yermo, agreste **3** UNRULY : desenfrenado **4** CRAZY : loco, fantástico <wild ideas : ideas locas> **5** BARBAROUS : salvaje, bárbaro **6** ERRATIC : errático <a wild throw : un tiro errático>
wild[3] *n* → **wilderness**
wildcat ['waɪld,kæt] *n* **1** : gato *m* montés **2** BOBCAT : lince *m* rojo
wilderness ['wɪldərnəs] *n* : yermo *m*, desierto *m*
wildfire ['waɪld,faɪr] *n* **1** : fuego *m* descontrolado **2 to spread like wildfire** : propagarse como un reguero de pólvora
wildflower ['waɪld,flaʊər] *n* : flor *f* silvestre
wildfowl ['waɪld,faʊl] *n* : ave *f* de caza
wildlife ['waɪld,laɪf] *n* : fauna *f*
wildly ['waɪldli] *adv* **1** FRANTICALLY : frenéticamente, como un loco **2** EXTREMELY : extremadamente <wildly happy : loco de felicidad>
wile[1] ['waɪl] *vt* **wiled; wiling** LURE : atraer
wile[2] *n* : ardid *m*, artimaña *f*
will[1] ['wɪl] *v past* **would** ['wʊd]; *pres sing & pl* **will** *vi* WISH : querer <do what you will : haz lo que quieras> — *v aux* **1** (*expressing willingness*) <no one would take the job : nadie aceptaría el trabajo> <I won't do it : no lo haré> **2** (*expressing habitual action*) <he will get angry over nothing : se pone furioso por cualquier cosa> **3** (*forming the future tense*)

<tomorrow we will go shopping : mañana iremos de compras> **4** (*expressing capacity*) <the couch will hold three people : en el sofá cabrán tres personas> **5** (*expressing determination*) <I will go despite them : iré a pesar de ellos> **6** (*expressing probability*) <that will be the mailman : eso ha de ser el cartero> **7** (*expressing inevitability*) <accidents will happen : los accidentes ocurrirán> **8** (*expressing a command*) <you will do as I say : harás lo que digo>

will[2] *vt* **1** ORDAIN **:** disponer, decretar <if God wills it : si Dios lo dispone, si Dios quiere> **2 :** lograr a fuerza de voluntad <they were willing him to succeed : estaban deseando que tuviera éxito> **3** BEQUEATH **:** legar

will[3] *n* **1** DESIRE **:** deseo *m,* voluntad *f* **2** VOLITION **:** voluntad *f* <free will : libre albedrío> **3** WILLPOWER **:** voluntad *f,* fuerza *f* de voluntad <a will of iron : una voluntad férrea> **4 :** testamento *m* <to make a will : hacer testamento>

willful *or* **wilful** ['wɪlfəl] *adj* **1** OBSTINATE **:** obstinado, terco **2** INTENTIONAL **:** intencionado, deliberado — **willfully** *adv*

willing ['wɪlɪŋ] *adj* **1** INCLINED, READY **:** listo, dispuesto **2** OBLIGING **:** servicial, complaciente

willingly ['wɪlɪŋli] *adv* **:** con gusto

willingness ['wɪlɪŋnəs] *n* **:** buena voluntad *f*

willow ['wɪ,loː] *n* **:** sauce *m*

willowy ['wɪlowi] *adj* **:** esbelto

willpower ['wɪl,paʊər] *n* **:** voluntad *f,* fuerza *f* de voluntad

wilt ['wɪlt] *vi* **1 :** marchitarse (dícese de las flores) **2** LANGUISH **:** debilitarse, languidecer

wily ['waɪli] *adj* **wilier; -est :** artero, astuto

win[1] ['wɪn] *v* **won** ['wʌn]; **winning** *vi* **:** ganar — *vt* **1 :** ganar, conseguir **2 to win over :** ganarse a **3 to win someone's heart :** conquistar a alguien

win[2] *n* **:** triunfo *m,* victoria *f*

wince[1] ['wɪnts] *vi* **winced; wincing :** estremecerse, hacer una mueca de dolor

wince[2] *n* **:** mueca *f* de dolor

winch ['wɪntʃ] *n* **:** torno *m*

wind[1] ['wɪnd] *vt* **:** dejar sin aliento <to be winded : quedarse sin aliento>

wind[2] ['waɪnd] *v* **wound** ['waʊnd]; **winding** *vi* MEANDER **:** serpentear — *vt* **1** COIL, ROLL **:** envolver, enrollar **2** TURN **:** hacer girar <to wind a clock : darle cuerda a un reloj>

wind[3] ['wɪnd] *n* **1 :** viento *m* <against the wind : contra el viento> **2** BREATH **:** aliento *m* **3** FLATULENCE **:** flatulencia *f,* ventosidad *f* **4 to get wind of :** enterarse de

wind[4] ['waɪnd] *n* **1** TURN **:** vuelta *f* **2** BEND **:** recodo *m,* curva *f*

windbreak ['wɪnd,breɪk] *n* **:** barrera *f* contra el viento, abrigadero *m*

windfall ['wɪnd,fɔl] *n* **1 :** fruta *f* caída **2 :** beneficio *m* imprevisto

wind instrument *n* **:** instrumento *m* de viento

windlass ['wɪndləs] *n* **:** cabrestante *m*

windmill ['wɪnd,mɪl] *n* **:** molino *m* de viento

window ['wɪn,doː] *n* **1 :** ventana *f* (de un edificio o una computadora), ventanilla *f* (de un vehículo o avión), vitrina *f* (de una tienda) **2 → windowpane**

windowpane ['wɪn,doː,peɪn] *n* **:** vidrio *m*

window–shop ['wɪndo,ʃɑp] *vi* **-shopped; -shopping :** mirar las vitrinas

windpipe ['wɪnd,paɪp] *n* **:** tráquea *f*

windshield ['wɪnd,ʃiːld] *n* **1 :** parabrisas *m* **2 windshield wiper :** limpiaparabrisas *m*

windup ['waɪnd,ʌp] *n* **:** conclusión *f*

wind up *vt* END **:** terminar, concluir — *vi* **:** terminar, acabar

windward[1] ['wɪndwərd] *adj* **:** de barlovento

windward[2] *n* **:** barlovento *m*

windy ['wɪndi] *adj* **windier; -est 1 :** ventoso <it's windy : hace viento> **2** VERBOSE **:** verboso, prolijo

wine[1] ['waɪn] *v* **wined; wining** *vi* **:** beber vino — *vt* **to wine and dine :** agasajar

wine[2] *n* **:** vino *m*

wing[1] ['wɪŋ] *vi* FLY **:** volar

wing[2] *n* **1 :** ala *f* (de un ave, un avión, o un edificio) **2** FACTION **:** ala *f* <the right wing of the party : el ala derecha del partido> **3 wings** *npl* **:** bastidores *mpl* (de un teatro) **4 on the wing :** al vuelo, volando **5 under one's wing :** bajo el cargo de uno

winged ['wɪŋd, 'wɪŋəd] *adj* **:** alado

wink[1] ['wɪŋk] *vi* **1 :** guiñar el ojo **2** BLINK **:** pestañear, parpadear **3** FLICKER **:** parpadear, titilar

wink[2] *n* **1 :** guiño *m* (del ojo) **2** NAP **:** siesta *f* <not to sleep a wink : no pegar el ojo>

winner ['wɪnər] *n* **:** ganador *m,* -dora *f*

winning ['wɪnɪŋ] *adj* **1** VICTORIOUS **:** ganador **2** CHARMING **:** encantador

winnings ['wɪnɪŋz] *npl* **:** ganancias *fpl*

winnow ['wɪ,noː] *vt* **:** aventar (el grano, etc.)

winsome ['wɪnsəm] *adj* CHARMING **:** encantador

winter[1] ['wɪntər] *adj* **:** invernal, de invierno

winter[2] *n* **:** invierno *m*

wintergreen ['wɪntər,griːn] *n* **:** gaulteria *f*

wintertime ['wɪntər,taɪm] *n* **:** invierno *m*

wintry ['wɪntri] *adj* **wintrier; -est 1** WINTER **:** invernal, de invierno **2** COLD

: frío <she gave us a wintry greeting : nos saludó fríamente>

wipe[1] ['waɪp] *vt* **wiped; wiping 1** : limpiar, pasarle un trapo a <to wipe one's feet : limpiarse los pies> **2 to wipe away** : enjugar (lágrimas), borrar (una memoria) **3 to wipe out** ANNIHILATE : aniquilar, destruir

wipe[2] *n* : pasada *f* (con un trapo, etc.)

wire[1] ['waɪr] *vt* **-wired; wiring 1** : instalar el cableado en (una casa, etc.) **2** BIND : atar con alambre **3** TELEGRAPH : telegrafiar, mandarle un telegrama (a alguien)

wire[2] *n* **1** : alambre *m* <barbed wire : alambre de púas> **2** : cable *m* (eléctrico o telefónico) **3** CABLEGRAM, TELEGRAM : telegrama *m,* cable *m*

wireless ['waɪrləs] *adj* : inalámbrico

wiretapping ['waɪrˌtæpɪŋ] *n* : intervención *f* electrónica

wiring ['waɪrɪŋ] *n* : cableado *m*

wiry ['waɪri] *adj* **wirier; -est 1** : hirsuto, tieso (dícese del pelo) **2** : esbelto y musculoso (dícese del cuerpo)

wisdom ['wɪzdəm] *n* **1** KNOWLEDGE : sabiduría *f* **2** JUDGMENT, SENSE : sensatez *f*

wisdom tooth *n* : muela *f* de juicio

wise[1] ['waɪz] *adj* **wiser; wisest 1** LEARNED : sabio **2** SENSIBLE : sabio, sensato, prudente **3** KNOWLEDGEABLE : entendido, enterado <they're wise to his tricks : conocen muy bien sus mañas>

wise[2] *n* : manera *f,* modo *m* <in no wise : de ninguna manera>

wisecrack ['waɪzˌkræk] *n* : broma *f,* chiste *m*

wisely ['waɪzli] *adv* : sabiamente, sensatamente

wish[1] ['wɪʃ] *vt* **1** WANT : desear, querer **2 to wish (something) for** : desear <they wished me well : me desearon lo mejor> — *vi* **1** : pedir (como deseo) **2** : querer <as you wish : como quieras>

wish[2] *n* **1** : deseo *m* <to grant a wish : conceder un deseo> **2 wishes** *npl* : saludos *mpl,* recuerdos *mpl* <to send best wishes : mandar muchos recuerdos>

wishbone ['wɪʃˌboːn] *n* : espoleta *f*

wishful ['wɪʃfəl] *adj* **1** HOPEFUL : deseoso, lleno de esperanza **2 wishful thinking** : ilusiones *fpl*

wishy–washy ['wɪʃiˌwɔʃi, -ˌwɑʃi] *adj* : insípido, soso

wisp ['wɪsp] *n* **1** BUNCH : manojo *m* (de paja) **2** STRAND : mechón *m* (de pelo) **3** : voluta *f* (de humo)

wispy ['wɪspi] *adj* **wispier; -est** : tenue, ralo (dícese del pelo)

wisteria [wɪs'tɪriə] *n* : glicinia *f*

wistful ['wɪstfəl] *adj* : añorante, anhelante, melancólico — **wistfully** *adv*

wistfulness ['wɪstfəlnəs] *n* : añoranza *f,* melancolía *f*

wit ['wɪt] *n* **1** INTELLIGENCE : inteligencia *f* **2** CLEVERNESS : ingenio *m,* gracia *f,* agudeza *f* **3** HUMOR : humorismo *m* **4** JOKER : chistoso *m,* -sa *f* **5 wits** *npl* : razón *f,* buen juicio *m* <scared out of one's wits : muerto de miedo> <to be at one's wits' end : estar desesperado>

witch ['wɪtʃ] *n* : bruja *f*

witchcraft ['wɪtʃˌkræft] *n* : brujería *f,* hechicería *f*

witch doctor *n* : hechicero *m,* -ra *f*

witchery ['wɪtʃəri] *n, pl* **-eries 1** → **witchcraft 2** CHARM : encanto *m*

witch–hunt ['wɪtʃˌhʌnt] *n* : caza *f* de brujas

with ['wɪð, 'wɪθ] *prep* **1** : con <I'm going with you : voy contigo> <coffee with milk : café con leche> **2** AGAINST : con <to argue with someone : discutir con alguien> **3** (*used in descriptions*) : con, de <the girl with red hair : la muchacha de pelo rojo> **4** (*indicating manner, means, or cause*) : con <to cut with a knife : cortar con un cuchillo> <fix it with tape : arréglalo con cinta> <with luck : con suerte> **5** DESPITE : a pesar de, aún con <with all his work, the business failed : a pesar de su trabajo, el negocio fracasó> **6** REGARDING : con respecto a, con <the trouble with your plan : el problema con su plan> **7** ACCORDING TO : según <it varies with the season : varía según la estación> **8** (*indicating support or understanding*) : con <I'm with you all the way : estoy contigo hasta el fin>

withdraw [wɪð'drɔ, wɪθ-] *v* **-drew** [-'druː]; **-drawn** [-'drɔn]; **-drawing** *vt* **1** REMOVE : retirar, apartar, sacar (dinero) **2** RETRACT : retractarse de — *vi* : retirarse, recluirse (de la sociedad)

withdrawal [wɪð'drɔəl, wɪθ-] *n* **1** : retirada *f,* retiro *m* (de fondos, etc.), retraimiento *m* (social) **2** RETRACTION : retractación *f* **3 withdrawal symptoms** : síndrome *m* de abstinencia

withdrawn [wɪð'drɔn, wɪθ-] *adj* : retraído, reservado, introvertido

wither ['wɪðər] *vt* : marchitar, agostar — *vi* **1** WILT : marchitarse **2** WEAKEN : decaer, debilitarse

withhold [wɪθ'hoːld, wɪð-] *vt* **-held** [-'hɛld]; **-holding** : retener (fondos), aplazar (una decisión), negar (permiso, etc.)

within[1] [wɪð'ɪn, wɪθ-] *adv* : dentro

within[2] *prep* **1** : dentro de <within the limits : dentro de los límites> **2** (*in expressions of distance*) : a menos de <within 10 miles of the ocean : a menos de 10 millas del mar> **3** (*in expressions of time*) : dentro de <within an hour : dentro de una hora> <within a month of her birthday : a poco menos de un mes de su cumpleaños>

without[1] [wɪð'aʊt, wɪθ-] *adv* **1** OUTSIDE : fuera **2 to do without** : pasar sin algo

without[2] *prep* **1** OUTSIDE : fuera de **2** : sin <without fear : sin temor> <he left without his briefcase : se fue sin su portafolios>

withstand [wɪθ'stænd, wɪð-] *vt* **-stood** [-'stʊd]; **-standing 1** BEAR : aguantar, soportar **2** RESIST : resistir, resistirse a

witless ['wɪtləs] *adj* : estúpido, tonto

witness[1] ['wɪtnəs] *vt* **1** SEE : presenciar, ver, ser testigo de **2** : atestiguar (una firma, etc.) — *vi* TESTIFY : atestiguar, testimoniar

witness[2] *n* **1** TESTIMONY : testimonio *m* <to bear witness : atestiguar, testimoniar> **2** : testigo *mf* <witness for the prosecution : testigo de cargo>

witticism ['wɪtə,sɪzəm] *n* : agudeza *f*, ocurrencia *f*

witty ['wɪti] *adj* **-tier; -est** : ingenioso, ocurrente, gracioso

wives → **wife**

wizard ['wɪzərd] *n* **1** SORCERER : mago *m*, brujo *m*, hechicero *m* **2** : genio *m* <a math wizard : un genio en matemáticas>

wizened ['wɪzənd, 'wiː-] *adj* : arrugado, marchito

wobble[1] ['wɑbəl] *vi* **-bled; -bling** : bambolearse, tambalearse, temblar (dícese de la voz)

wobble[2] *n* : tambaleo *m*, bamboleo *m*

wobbly ['wɑbəli] *adj* : bamboleante, tambaleante, inestable

woe ['woː] *n* **1** GRIEF, MISFORTUNE : desgracia *f*, infortunio *m*, aflicción *f* **2 woes** *npl* TROUBLES : penas *fpl*, males *mpl*

woeful ['woːfəl] *adj* **1** SORROWFUL : afligido, apenado, triste **2** UNFORTUNATE : desgraciado, infortunado **3** DEPLORABLE : lamentable

woke, woken → **wake**[1]

wolf[1] ['wʊlf] *vt or* **to wolf down** : engullir

wolf[2] *n, pl* **wolves** ['wʊlvz] : lobo *m*, -ba *f*

wolfram ['wʊlfrəm] → **tungsten**

wolverine [,wʊlvə'riːn] *n* : glotón *m* (animal)

woman ['wʊmən] *n, pl* **women** ['wɪmən] : mujer *f*

womanhood ['wʊmən,hʊd] *n* **1** : condición *f* de mujer **2** WOMEN : mujeres *fpl*

womanly ['wʊmənli] *adj* : femenino

womb ['wuːm] *n* : útero *m*, matriz *f*

won → **win**

wonder[1] ['wʌndər] *vi* **1** SPECULATE : preguntarse, pensar <to wonder about : preguntarse por> **2** MARVEL : asombrarse, maravillarse — *vt* : preguntarse <I wonder if they're coming : me pregunto si vendrán>

wonder[2] *n* **1** MARVEL : maravilla *f*, milagro *m* <to work wonders : hacer maravillas> **2** AMAZEMENT : asombro *m*

wonderful ['wʌndərfəl] *adj* : maravilloso, estupendo

wonderfully ['wʌndərfəli] *adv* : maravillosamente, de maravilla

wonderland ['wʌndər,lænd, -lənd] *n* : país *m* de las maravillas

wonderment ['wʌndərmənt] *n* : asombro *m*

wondrous ['wʌndrəs] → **wonderful**

wont[1] ['wɔnt, 'woːnt, 'wɑnt] *adj* : acostumbrado, habituado

wont[2] *n* : hábito *m*, costumbre *f*

won't ['woːnt] (*contraction of* **will not**) → **will**[1]

woo ['wuː] *vt* **1** COURT : cortejar **2** : buscar el apoyo de (clientes, votantes, etc.)

wood[1] ['wʊd] *adj* : de madera

wood[2] *n* **1** *or* **woods** *npl* FOREST : bosque *m* **2** : madera *f* (materia) **3** FIREWOOD : leña *f*

woodchuck ['wʊd,tʃʌk] *n* : marmota *f* de América

woodcut ['wʊd,kʌt] *n* **1** : plancha *f* de madera (para imprimir imágenes) **2** : grabado *m* en madera

woodcutter ['wʊd,kʌtər] *n* : leñador *m*, -dora *f*

wooded ['wʊdəd] *adj* : arbolado, boscoso

wooden ['wʊdən] *adj* **1** : de madera <a wooden cross : una cruz de madera> **2** STIFF : rígido, inexpresivo (dícese del estilo, de la cara, etc.)

woodland ['wʊdlənd, -,lænd] *n* : bosque *m*

woodpecker ['wʊd,pɛkər] *n* : pájaro *m* carpintero

woodshed ['wʊd,ʃɛd] *n* : leñera *f*

woodsman ['wʊdzmən] → **woodcutter**

woodwind ['wʊd,wɪnd] *n* : instrumento *m* de viento de madera

woodworking ['wʊd,wərkɪŋ] *n* : carpintería *f*

woody ['wʊdi] *adj* **woodier; -est 1** → **wooded 2** : leñoso <woody plants : plantas leñosas> **3** : leñoso (dícese de la textura), a madera (dícese del aroma, etc.)

woof ['wʊf] → **weft**

wool ['wʊl] *n* : lana *f*

woolen[1] *or* **woollen** ['wʊlən] *adj* : de lana

woolen[2] *or* **woollen** *n* **1** : lana *f* (tela) **2 woolens** *npl* : prendas *fpl* de lana

woolly ['wʊli] *adj* **-lier; -est 1** : lanudo **2** CONFUSED : confuso, vago

woozy ['wuːzi] *adj* **-zier; -est** : mareado

word[1] ['wərd] *vt* : expresar, formular, redactar

word[2] *n* **1** : palabra *f*, vocablo *m*, voz *f* <word for word : palabra por palabra> <in one's own words : en sus

propias palabras> <words fail me : me quedo sin habla> **2** REMARK : palabra *f* <by word of mouth : de palabra> <to have a word with : hablar (dos palabras) con> **3** COMMAND : orden *f* <to give the word : dar la orden> <just say the word : no tienes que decirlo> **4** MESSAGE, NEWS : noticias *fpl* <is there any word from her? : ¿hay noticias de ella?> <to send word : mandar un recado> **5** PROMISE : palabra *f* <to keep one's word : cumplir uno su palabra> **6 words** *npl* QUARREL : palabra *f*, riña *f* <to have words with : tener unas palabras con, reñir con> **7 words** *npl* TEXT : letra *f* (de una canción, etc.)

wordiness ['wərdinəs] *n* : verbosidad *f*

wording ['wərdɪŋ] *n* : redacción *f*, lenguaje *m* (de un documento)

word processing *n* : procesamiento *m* de textos

word processor *n* : procesador *m* de textos

wordy ['wərdi] *adj* **wordier; -est** : verboso, prolijo

wore → **wear[1]**

work[1] ['wərk] *v* **worked** ['wərkt] *or* **wrought** ['rɔt]; **working** *vt* **1** OPERATE : trabajar, operar <to work a machine : operar una máquina> **2** : lograr, conseguir (algo) con esfuerzo <to work one's way up : lograr subir por sus propios esfuerzos> **3** EFFECT : efectuar, llevar a cabo, obrar (milagros) **4** MAKE, SHAPE : elaborar, fabricar, formar <a beautifully wrought vase : un florero bellamente elaborado> **5 to work up** : estimular, excitar <don't get worked up : no te agites> — *vi* **1** LABOR : trabajar <to work full-time : trabajar a tiempo completo> **2** FUNCTION : funcionar, servir

work[2] *adj* : laboral

work[3] *n* **1** LABOR : trabajo *m*, labor *f* **2** EMPLOYMENT : trabajo *m*, empleo *m* **3** TASK : tarea *f*, faena *f* **4** DEED : obra *f*, labor *f* <works of charity : obras de caridad> **5** : obra *f* (de arte o literatura) **6** → **workmanship 7 works** *npl* FACTORY : fábrica *f* **8 works** *npl* MECHANISM : mecanismo *m*

workable ['wərkəbəl] *adj* **1** : explotable (dícese de una mina, etc.) **2** FEASIBLE : factible, realizable

workaday ['wərkəˌdeɪ] *adj* : ordinario, banal

workbench ['wərkˌbɛntʃ] *n* : mesa *f* de trabajo

workday ['wərkˌdeɪ] *n* **1** : jornada *f* laboral **2** WEEKDAY : día *m* hábil, día *m* laborable

worker ['wərkər] *n* : trabajador *m*, -dora *f*; obrero *m*, -ra *f*

working ['wərkɪŋ] *adj* **1** : que trabaja <working mothers : madres que trabajan> <the working class : la clase obrera> **2** : de trabajo <working hours : horas de trabajo> **3** FUNCTIONING : que funciona, operativo **4** SUFFICIENT : suficiente <a working majority : una mayoría suficiente> <working knowledge : conocimientos básicos>

workingman ['wərkɪŋˌmæn] *n, pl* **-men** [-mən, -ˌmɛn] : obrero *m*

workman ['wərkmən] *n, pl* **-men** [-mən, -ˌmɛn] **1** → **workingman 2** ARTISAN : artesano *m*

workmanlike ['wərkmənˌlaɪk] *adj* : bien hecho, competente

workmanship ['wərkmənˌʃɪp] *n* **1** WORK : ejecución *f*, trabajo *m* **2** CRAFTSMANSHIP : artesanía *f*, destreza *f*

workout ['wərkˌaʊt] *n* : ejercicios *mpl* físicos, entrenamiento *m*

work out *vt* **1** DEVELOP, PLAN : idear, planear, desarrollar **2** RESOLVE : solucionar, resolver <to work out the answer : calcular la solución> — *vi* **1** TURN OUT : resultar **2** SUCCEED : lograr, dar resultado, salir bien **3** EXERCISE : hacer ejercicio

workroom ['wərkˌru:m, -ˌrʊm] *n* : taller *m*

workshop ['wərkˌʃɑp] *n* : taller *m* <ceramics workshop : taller de cerámica>

world[1] ['wərld] *adj* : mundial, del mundo <world championship : campeonato mundial>

world[2] *n* : mundo *m* <around the world : alrededor del mundo> <a world of possibilities : un mundo de posibilidades> <to think the world of someone : tener a alguien en alta estima> <to be worlds apart : no tener nada que ver (uno con otro)>

worldly ['wərldli] *adj* **1** : mundano <wordly goods : bienes materiales> **2** SOPHISTICATED : sofisticado, de mundo

worldwide[1] ['wərld'waɪd] *adv* : mundialmente, en todo el mundo

worldwide[2] *adj* : global, mundial

worm[1] ['wərm] *vi* **1** CRAWL : arrastrarse, deslizarse (como gusano) <to worm one's way into someone's confidence : ganarse la confianza de alguien> **2 to worm something out of someone** : sonsacarle algo a alguien — *vt* : desparasitar (un animal)

worm[2] *n* **1** : gusano *m*, lombriz *f* **2 worms** *npl* : lombrices *fpl* (parásitos)

wormy ['wərmi] *adj* **wormier; -est** : infestado de gusanos

worn → **wear[1]**

worn–out ['worn'aʊt] *adj* **1** USED : gastado, desgastado **2** TIRED : agotado

worried ['wərid] *adj* : inquieto, preocupado

worrier ['wəriər] *n* : persona *f* que se preocupa mucho

worrisome ['wərisəm] *adj* **1** DISTURBING : preocupante, inquietante **2** : que se preocupa mucho (dícese de una persona)

worry[1] ['wəri] *v* **-ried; -rying** *vt* : preocupar, inquietar — *vi* : preocuparse, inquietarse, angustiarse

worry[2] *n, pl* **-ries :** preocupación *f,* inquietud *f,* angustia *f*
worse[1] [ˈwərs] *adv* (*comparative of* **bad** *or of* **ill**) **:** peor <to feel worse : sentirse peor>
worse[2] *adj* (*comparative of* **bad** *or of* **ill**) **:** peor <from bad to worse : de mal en peor> <to get worse : empeorar>
worse[3] *n* **:** estado *m* peor <to take a turn for the worse : ponerse peor> <so much the worse : tanto peor>
worsen [ˈwərsən] *vt* **:** empeorar — *vi* **:** empeorar(se)
worship[1] [ˈwərʃəp] *v* **-shiped** *or* **-shipped; -shiping** *or* **-shipping** *vt* **:** adorar, venerar <to worship God : adorar a Dios> — *vi* **:** practicar una religión
worship[2] *n* **:** adoración *f,* culto *m*
worshiper *or* **worshipper** [ˈwərʃəpər] *n* **:** devoto *m,* -ta *f;* adorador *m,* -dora *f*
worst[1] [ˈwərst] *vt* DEFEAT **:** derrotar
worst[2] *adv* (*superlative of* **ill** *or of* **bad** *or* **badly**) **:** peor <the worst dressed of all : el peor vestido de todos>
worst[3] *adj* (*superlative of* **bad** *or of* **ill**) **:** peor <the worst movie : la peor película>
worst[4] *n* **the worst :** lo peor, el (la) peor <the worst is over : ya ha pasado lo peor>
worsted [ˈwʊstəd, ˈwərstəd] *n* **:** estambre *m*
worth[1] [ˈwərθ] *n* **1 :** valor *m* (monetario) <ten dollars' worth of gas : diez dólares de gasolina> **2** MERIT **:** valor *m,* mérito *m,* valía *f* <an employee of great worth : un empleado de gran valía>
worth[2] *prep* **to be worth :** valer <her holdings are worth a fortune : sus propiedades valen una fortuna> <it's not worth it : no vale la pena>
worthiness [ˈwərðinəs] *n* **:** mérito *m*
worthless [ˈwərθləs] *adj* **1 :** sin valor <worthless trinkets : chucherías sin valor> **2** USELESS **:** inútil
worthwhile [wərθˈ*h*waɪl] *adj* **:** que vale la pena
worthy [ˈwərði] *adj* **-thier; -est 1 :** digno <worthy of promotion : digno de un ascenso> **2** COMMENDABLE **:** meritorio, encomiable
would [ˈwʊd] *past of* **will 1** (*expressing preference*) <I would rather go alone than with her : preferiría ir sola que con ella> **2** (*expressing intent*) <those who would ban certain books : aquellos que prohibirían ciertos libros> **3** (*expressing habitual action*) <he would often take his kids to the park : solía llevar a sus hijos al parque> **4** (*expressing contingency*) <I would go if I had the money : iría yo si tuviera el dinero> **5** (*expressing probability*) <she would have won if she hadn't tripped : habría ganado si no hubiera tropezado> **6** (*expressing a request*) <would you kindly help me with this? : ¿tendría la bondad de ayudarme con esto?>
would–be [ˈwʊdˈbiː] *adj* **:** potencial <a would-be celebrity : un aspirante a celebridad>
wouldn't [ˈwʊdˈənt] (*contraction of* **would not**) → **would**
wound[1] [ˈwuːnd] *vt* **:** herir
wound[2] *n* **:** herida *f*
wound[3] [ˈwaʊnd] → **wind**[2]
wove, woven → **weave**[1]
wrangle[1] [ˈræŋgəl] *vi* **-gled; -gling :** discutir, reñir <to wrangle over : discutir por>
wrangle[2] *n* **:** riña *f,* disputa *f*
wrap[1] [ˈræp] *v* **wrapped; wrapping** *vt* **1** COVER **:** envolver, cubrir <to wrap a package : envolver un paquete> <wrapped in mystery : envuelto en misterio> **2** ENCIRCLE **:** rodear, ceñir <to wrap one's arms around someone : estrechar a alguien> **3 to wrap up** FINISH **:** darle fin a (algo) — *vi* **1** COIL **:** envolverse, enroscarse **2 to wrap up** DRESS **:** abrigarse <wrap up warmly : abrígate bien>
wrap[2] *n* **1** WRAPPER **:** envoltura *f* **2 :** prenda *f* que envuelve (como un chal, una bata, etc.)
wrapper [ˈræpər] *n* **:** envoltura *f,* envoltorio *m*
wrapping [ˈræpɪŋ] *n* **:** envoltura *f,* envoltorio *m*
wrath [ˈræθ] *n* **:** ira *f,* cólera *f*
wrathful [ˈræθfəl] *adj* **:** iracundo
wreak [ˈriːk] *vt* **:** infligir, causar <to wreak havoc : crear caos, causar estragos>
wreath [ˈriːθ] *n, pl* **wreaths** [ˈriːðz, ˈriːθs] **:** corona *f* (de flores, etc.)
wreathe [ˈriːð] *vt* **wreathed; wreathing 1** ADORN **:** coronar (de flores, etc.) **2** ENVELOP **:** envolver <wreathed in mist : envuelto en niebla>
wreck[1] [ˈrɛk] *vt* **:** destruir, arruinar, estrellar (un automóvil), naufragar (un barco)
wreck[2] *n* **1** WRECKAGE **:** restos *mpl* (de un buque naufragado, un avión siniestrado, etc.) **2** RUIN **:** ruina *f,* desastre *m* <this place is a wreck! : ¡este lugar está hecho un desastre!> <to be a nervous wreck : tener los nervios destrozados>
wreckage [ˈrɛkɪdʒ] *n* **:** restos *mpl* (de un buque naufragado, un avión siniestrado, etc.), ruinas *fpl* (de un edificio)
wrecker [ˈrɛkər] *n* **1** TOW TRUCK **:** grúa *f* **2 :** desguazador *m* (de autos, barcos, etc.), demoledor *m* (de edificios)
wren [ˈrɛn] *n* **:** chochín *m*
wrench[1] [ˈrɛntʃ] *vt* **1** PULL **:** arrancar (de un tirón) **2** SPRAIN, TWIST **:** torcerse (un tobillo, un músculo, etc.)
wrench[2] *n* **1** TUG **:** tirón *m,* jalón *m* **2** SPRAIN **:** torcedura *f* **3** *or* **monkey wrench :** llave *f* inglesa

wrest ['rɛst] *vt* **:** arrancar
wrestle[1] ['rɛsəl] *v* **-tled; -tling** *vi* **1 :** luchar, practicar la lucha (en deportes) **2** STRUGGLE **:** luchar <to wrestle with a dilemma : lidiar con un dilema> — *vt* **:** luchar contra
wrestle[2] *n* STRUGGLE **:** lucha *f*
wrestler ['rɛsələr] *n* **:** luchador *m*, -dora *f*
wrestling ['rɛsəlɪŋ] *n* **:** lucha *f*
wretch ['rɛtʃ] *n* **:** infeliz *mf;* desgraciado *m*, -da *f*
wretched ['rɛtʃəd] *adj* **1** MISERABLE, UNHAPPY **:** desdichado, afligido <I feel wretched : me siento muy mal> **2** UNFORTUNATE **:** miserable, desgraciado, lastimoso <wretched weather : tiempo espantoso> **3** INFERIOR **:** inferior, malo
wretchedly ['rɛtʃədli] *adv* **:** miserablemente, lamentablemente
wriggle ['rɪgəl] *vi* **-gled; -gling :** retorcerse, menearse
wring ['rɪŋ] *vt* **wrung** ['rʌŋ]; **wringing 1** *or* **to wring out :** escurrir, exprimir (el lavado) **2** EXTRACT **:** arrancar, sacar (por la fuerza) **3** TWIST **:** torcer, retorcer **4 to wring someone's heart :** partirle el corazón a alguien
wringer ['rɪŋər] *n* **:** escurridor *m*
wrinkle[1] ['rɪŋkəl] *v* **-kled; -kling** *vt* **:** arrugar — *vi* **:** arrugarse
wrinkle[2] *n* **:** arruga *f*
wrinkly ['rɪŋkəli] *adj* **wrinklier; -est :** arrugado
wrist ['rɪst] *n* **1 :** muñeca *f* (en anatomía) **2** *or* **wristband** ['rɪst,bænd] CUFF **:** puño *m*
writ ['rɪt] *n* **:** orden *f* (judicial)
write ['raɪt] *v* **wrote** ['ro:t]; **written** ['rɪtən]; **writing :** escribir
write down *vt* **:** apuntar, anotar
write off *vt* CANCEL **:** cancelar
writer ['raɪt̬ər] *n* **:** escritor *m*, -tora *f*
writhe ['raɪð] *vi* **writhed; writhing :** retorcerse
writing ['raɪt̬ɪŋ] *n* **:** escritura *f*
wrong[1] ['rɔŋ] *vt* **wronged; wronging :** ofender, ser injusto con
wrong[2] *adv* **:** mal, incorrectamente
wrong[3] *adj* **wronger** ['rɔŋər]; **wrongest** ['rɔŋəst] **1** EVIL, SINFUL **:** malo, injusto, inmoral **2** IMPROPER, UNSUITABLE **:** inadecuado, inapropiado, malo **3** INCORRECT **:** incorrecto, erróneo, malo <a wrong answer : una mala respuesta> **4 to be wrong :** equivocarse, estar equivocado
wrong[4] *n* **1** INJUSTICE **:** injusticia *f*, mal *m* **2** OFFENSE **:** ofensa *f*, agravio *m* (en derecho) **3 to be in the wrong :** haber hecho mal, estar equivocado
wrongdoer ['rɔŋ,du:ər] *n* **:** malhechor *m*, -chora *f*
wrongdoing ['rɔŋ,du:ɪŋ] *n* **:** fechoría *f*, maldad *f*
wrongful ['rɔŋfəl] *adj* **1** UNJUST **:** injusto **2** UNLAWFUL **:** ilegal
wrongly ['rɔŋli] *adv* **1 :** injustamente **2** INCORRECTLY **:** erróneamente, incorrectamente
wrote → **write**
wrought ['rɔt] *adj* **1** SHAPED **:** formado, forjado <wrought iron : hierro forjado> **2** *or* **wrought up :** agitado, excitado
wrung → **wring**
wry ['raɪ] *adj* **wrier** ['raɪər]; **wriest** ['raɪəst] **1** TWISTED **:** torcido <a wry neck : un cuello torcido> **2 :** irónico, sardónico (dícese del humor)

X

x[1] *n, pl* **x's** *or* **xs** ['ɛksəz] **1 :** vigésima cuarta letra del alfabeto inglés **2 :** incógnita *f* (en matemáticas)
x[2] ['ɛks] *vt* **x–ed** ['ɛkst]; **x–ing** *or* **x'ing** ['ɛksiŋ] DELETE **:** tachar
xenon ['zi:,nɑn, 'zɛ-] *n* **:** xenón *m*
xenophobia [,zɛnə'fo:biə, ,zi:-] *n* **:** xenofobia *f*
Xmas ['krɪsməs] *n* **:** Navidad *f*
x–ray ['ɛks,reɪ] *vt* **:** radiografiar
X ray ['ɛks,reɪ] *n* **1 :** rayo *m* X **2** *or* **X–ray photograph :** radiografía *f*
xylophone ['zaɪlə,fo:n] *n* **:** xilófono *m*

Y

y ['waɪ] *n, pl* **y's** *or* **ys** ['waɪz] **:** vigésima quinta letra del alfabeto inglés
yacht[1] ['jɑt] *vi* **:** navegar (a vela), ir en yate <to go yachting : irse a navegar>
yacht[2] *n* **:** yate *m*
yak ['jæk] *n* **:** yac *m*
yam ['jæm] *n* **1 :** ñame *m* **2** SWEET POTATO **:** batata *f*, boniato *m*
yank[1] ['jæŋk] *vt* **:** tirar de, jalar, darle un tirón a
yank[2] *n* **:** tirón *m*
Yankee ['jæŋki] *n* **:** yanqui *mf*
yap[1] ['jæp] *vi* **yapped; yapping 1** BARK, YELP **:** ladrar, gañir **2** CHATTER **:** cotorrear *fam*, parlotear *fam*
yap[2] *n* **:** ladrido *m*, gañido *m*

yard ['jɑrd] *n* **1** : yarda *f* (medida) **2** SPAR : verga *f* (de un barco) **3** COURTYARD : patio *m* **4** : jardín *m* (de una casa) **5** : depósito *m* (de mercancías, etc.)

yardage ['jɑrdɪdʒ] *n* : medida *f* en yardas

yardarm ['jɑrd,ɑrm] *n* : penol *m*

yardstick ['jɑrd,stɪk] *n* **1** : vara *f* **2** CRITERION : criterio *m,* norma *f*

yarn ['jɑrn] *n* **1** : hilado *m* **2** TALE : historia *f,* cuento *m* <to spin a yarn : inventar una historia>

yawl ['jɔl] *n* : yola *f*

yawn[1] ['jɔn] *vi* **1** : bostezar **2** OPEN : abrirse

yawn[2] *n* : bostezo *m*

ye ['jiː] *pron* : vosotros, vosotras

yea[1] ['jeɪ] *adv* YES : sí

yea[2] *n* : voto *m* a favor

year ['jɪr] *n* **1** : año *m* <last year : el año pasado> <he's ten years old : tiene diez años> **2** : curso *m,* año *m* (escolar) **3 years** *npl* AGES : siglos *mpl,* años *mpl* <I haven't seen them in years : hace siglos que no los veo>

yearbook ['jɪr,bʊk] *n* : anuario *m*

yearling ['jɪrlɪŋ, 'jərlən] *n* : animal *m* menor de dos año

yearly[1] ['jɪrli] *adv* : cada año, anualmente

yearly[2] *adj* : anual

yearn ['jərn] *vi* : anhelar, ansiar

yearning ['jərnɪŋ] *n* : anhelo *m*

yeast ['jiːst] *n* : levadura *f*

yell[1] ['jɛl] *vi* : gritar, chillar — *vt* : gritar

yell[2] *n* : grito *m,* alarido *m* <to let out a yell : dar un grito>

yellow[1] ['jɛlo] *vi* : ponerse amarillo, volverse amarillo

yellow[2] *adj* **1** : amarillo **2** COWARDLY : cobarde

yellow[3] *n* : amarillo *m*

yellow fever *n* : fiebre *f* amarilla

yellowish ['jɛloɪʃ] *adj* : amarillento

yellow jacket *n* : avispa *f* (con rayas amarillas)

yelp[1] ['jɛlp] *vi* : dar un gañido (dícese de un animal), dar un grito (dícese de una persona)

yelp[2] *n* : gañido *m* (de un animal), grito *m* (de una persona)

yen ['jɛn] *n* **1** DESIRE : deseo *m,* ganas *fpl* **2** : yen *m* (moneda japonesa)

yeoman ['joːmən] *n, pl* **-men** [-mən, -mɛn] : suboficial *mf* de marina

yes[1] ['jɛs] *adv* : sí <to say yes : decir que sí>

yes[2] *n* : sí *m*

yesterday[1] ['jɛstər,deɪ, -di] *adv* : ayer

yesterday[2] *n* **1** : ayer *m* **2 the day before yesterday** : anteayer

yet[1] ['jɛt] *adv* **1** BESIDES, EVEN : aún <yet more problems : más problemas aún> <yet again : otra vez> **2** SO FAR : aún, todavía <not yet : todavía no> <as yet : hasta ahora, todavía> **3** : ya <has he come yet? : ¿ya ha venido?> **4** EVENTUALLY : todavía, algún día **5** NEVERTHELESS : sin embargo

yet[2] *conj* : pero

yew ['juː] *n* : tejo *m*

yield[1] ['jiːld] *vt* **1** SURRENDER : ceder <to yield the right of way : ceder el paso> **2** PRODUCE : producir, dar, rendir (en finanzas) — *vi* **1** GIVE : ceder <to yield under pressure : ceder por la presión> **2** GIVE IN, SURRENDER : ceder, rendirse, entregarse

yield[2] *n* : rendimiento *m,* rédito *m* (en finanzas)

yodel[1] ['joːdəl] *vi* **-deled** *or* **-delled; -deling** *or* **-delling** : cantar al estilo tirolés

yodel[2] *n* : canción *f* al estilo tirolés

yoga ['joːgə] *n* : yoga *m*

yogurt ['joːgərt] *n* : yogur *m,* yogurt *m*

yoke[1] ['joːk] *vt* **yoked; yoking** : uncir (animales)

yoke[2] *n* **1** : yugo *m* (para uncir animales) <the yoke of oppression : el yugo de la opresión> **2** TEAM : yunta *f* (de bueyes) **3** : canesú *m* (de ropa)

yokel ['joːkəl] *n* : palurdo *m,* -da *f*

yolk ['joːk] *n* : yema *f* (de un huevo)

Yom Kippur [,joːmkɪ'pʊr, ,jɑm-, -'kɪpər] *n* : el Día *m* del Perdón, Yom Kippur

yon ['jɑn] → **yonder**

yonder[1] ['jɑndər] *adv* : allá <over yonder : allá lejos>

yonder[2] *adj* : aquel <yonder hill : aquella colina>

yore ['joːr] *n* **in days of yore** : antaño

you ['juː] *pron* **1** (*used as subject — familiar*) : tú; vos (*in some Latin American countries*); ustedes *pl;* vosotros, vosotras *pl Spain* **2** (*used as subject — formal*) : usted, ustedes *pl* **3** (*used as indirect object — familiar*) : te, les *pl* (se *before lo, la, los, las*), os *pl Spain* <he told it to you : te lo contó> <I gave them to (all of, both of) you : se los di> **4** (*used as indirect object — formal*) : lo (*Spain sometimes* le), la; los (*Spain sometimes* les), las *pl* **5** (*used after a preposition — familiar*) : ti; vos (*in some Latin American countries*); ustedes *pl;* vosotros, vosotras *pl Spain* **6** (*used after a preposition — formal*) : usted, ustedes *pl* **7** (*used as an impersonal subject*) <you never know : nunca se sabe> <you have to be aware : hay que ser consciente> <you mustn't do that : eso no se hace> **8 with you** (*familiar*) : contigo; con ustedes *pl;* con vosotros, con vosotras *pl Spain* **9 with you** (*formal*) : con usted, con ustedes *pl*

you'd ['juːd, 'jʊd] (*contraction of* **you had** *or* **you would**) → **have, would**

you'll ['juːl, 'jʊl] (*contraction of* **you shall** *or* **you will**) → **shall, will**

young[1] ['jʌŋ] *adj* **younger** ['jʌŋgər]; **youngest** [-gəst] **1** : joven, pequeño, menor <young people : los jóvenes>

<my younger brother : mi hermano menor> <she is the youngest : es la más pequeña> **2** FRESH, NEW : tierno (dícese de las verduras), joven (dícese del vino) **3** YOUTHFUL : joven, juvenil

young² *npl* : jóvenes *mfpl* (de los humanos), crías *fpl* (de los animales)

youngster [ˈjʌŋkstər] *n* **1** YOUTH : joven *mf* **2** CHILD : chico *m,* -ca *f;* niño *m,* -ña *f*

your [ˈjʊr, ˈjoːr, jər] *adj* **1** (*familiar singular*) : tu <your cat : tu gato> <your books : tus libros> <wash your hands : lávate las manos> **2** (*familiar plural*) su, vuestro *Spain* <your car : su coche, el coche de ustedes> **3** (*formal*) : su <your houses : sus casas> **4** (*impersonal*) : el, la, los, las <on your left : a la izquierda>

you're [ˈjʊr, ˈjoːr, ˈjər, ˈjuːər] (*contraction of* **you are**) → **be**

yours [ˈjʊrz, ˈjoːrz] *pron* **1** (*belonging to one person — familiar*) : (el) tuyo, (la) tuya, (los) tuyos, (las) tuyas <those are mine; yours are there : ésas son mías; las tuyas están allí> <is this one yours? : ¿éste es tuyo?> **2** (*belonging to more than one person — familiar*) : (el) suyo, (la) suya, (los) suyos, (las) suyas; (el) vuestro, (la) vuestra, (los) vuestros, (las) vuestras *Spain* <our house and yours : nuestra casa y la suya> **3** (*formal*) : (el) suyo, (la) suya, (los) suyos, (las) suyas

yourself [jərˈsɛlf] *pron, pl* **yourselves** [-ˈsɛlvz] **1** (*used reflexively — familiar*) : te, se *pl,* os *pl Spain* <wash yourself : lávate> <you dressed yourselves : se vistieron, os vestisteis> **2** (*used reflexively — formal*) : se <did you hurt yourself? : ¿se hizo daño?> <you've gotten yourselves dirty : se ensuciaron> **3** (*used for emphasis*) : tú mismo, tú misma; usted mismo, usted misma; ustedes mismos, ustedes mismas *pl;* vosotros mismos, vosotras mismas *pl Spain* <you did it yourselves? : ¿lo hicieron ustedes mismos?, ¿lo hicieron por sí solos?>

youth [ˈjuːθ] *n, pl* **youths** [ˈjuːðz, ˈjuːθs] **1** : juventud *f* <in her youth : en su juventud> **2** BOY : joven *m* **3** : jóvenes *mfpl,* juventud *f* <the youth of our city : los jóvenes de nuestra ciudad>

youthful [ˈjuːθfəl] *adj* **1** : de juventud **2** YOUNG : joven **3** JUVENILE : juvenil

youthfulness [ˈjuːθfəlnəs] *n* : juventud *f*

you've [ˈjuːv] (*contraction of* **you have**) → **have**

yowl¹ [ˈjæʊl] *vi* : aullar

yowl² *n* : aullido *m*

yo–yo [ˈjoːˌjoː] *n, pl* **-yos** : yoyo *m,* yoyó *m*

yucca [ˈjʌkə] *n* : yuca *f*

Yugoslavian [ˌjuːgoˈslɑviən] *n* : yugoslavo *m,* -va *f* — **Yugoslavian** *adj*

yule [ˈjuːl] *n* CHRISTMAS : Navidad *f*

yuletide [ˈjuːlˌtaɪd] *n* : Navidades *fpl*

Z

z [ˈziː] *n, pl* **z's** *or* **zs** : vigésima sexta letra del alfabeto inglés

Zambian [ˈzæmbiən] *n* : zambiano *m,* -na *f* — **Zambian** *adj*

zany¹ [ˈzeɪni] *adj* **-nier; -est** : alocado, disparatado

zany² *n, pl* **-nies** : bufón *m,* -fona *f*

zeal [ˈziːl] *n* : fervor *m,* celo *m,* entusiasmo *m*

zealot [ˈzɛlət] *n* : fanático *m,* -ca *f*

zealous [ˈzɛləs] *adj* : celoso — **zealously** *adv*

zebra [ˈziːbrə] *n* : cebra *f*

zenith [ˈziːnəθ] *n* **1** : cenit *m* (en astronomía) **2** PEAK : apogeo *m,* cenit *m* <at the zenith of his career : en el apogeo de su carrera>

zephyr [ˈzɛfər] *n* : céfiro *m*

zeppelin [ˈzɛplən, -pəlɪn] *n* : zepelín *m*

zero¹ [ˈziːro, ˈzɪro] *vi* **to zero in on** : apuntar hacia, centrarse en (un problema, etc.)

zero² *adj* : cero, nulo <zero degrees : cero grados> <zero opportunities : oportunidades nulas>

zero³ *n, pl* **-ros** : cero *m* <below zero : bajo cero>

zest [ˈzɛst] *n* **1** GUSTO : entusiasmo *m,* brío *m* **2** FLAVOR : sabor *m,* sazón *f*

zestful [ˈzɛstfəl] *adj* : brioso

zigzag¹ [ˈzɪgˌzæg] *vi* **-zagged; -zagging** : zigzaguear

zigzag² *adv & adj* : en zigzag

zigzag³ *n* : zigzag *m*

Zimbabwean [zɪmˈbɑbwiən, -bweɪ-] *n* : zimbabuense *mf* — **Zimbabwean** *adj*

zinc [ˈzɪŋk] *n* : cinc *m,* zinc *m*

zing [ˈzɪŋ] *n* **1** HISS, HUM : zumbido *m,* silbido *m* **2** ENERGY : brío *m*

zinnia [ˈzɪniə, ˈziː-, -njə] *n* : zinnia *f*

Zionism [ˈzaɪəˌnɪzəm] *n* : sionismo *m*

Zionist [ˈzaɪənɪst] *n* : sionista *mf*

zip¹ [ˈzɪp] *v* **zipped; zipping** *vt or* **to zip up** : cerrar el cierre de — *vi* **1** SPEED : pasarse volando <the day zipped by : el día se pasó volando> **2** HISS, HUM : silbar, zumbar

zip² *n* **1** ZING : zumbido *m,* silbido *m* **2** ENERGY : brío *m*

zip code *n* : código *m* postal

zipper [ˈzɪpər] *n* : cierre *m,* cremallera *f,* zíper *m CA, Mex*

zippy [ˈzɪpi] *adj* **-pier; -est** : brioso

zircon ['zər,kɑn] *n* **:** circón *m,* zircón *m*
zirconium [,zər'ko:niəm] *n* **:** circonio *m*
zither ['zɪðər, -θər] *n* **:** cítara *f*
zodiac ['zo:di,æk] *n* **:** zodíaco *m*
zombie ['zɑmbi] *n* **:** zombi *mf,* zombie *mf*
zone[1] ['zo:n] *vt* **zoned; zoning 1 :** dividir en zonas **2** DESIGNATE **:** declarar <to zone for business **:** declarar como zona comercial>
zone[2] *n* **:** zona *f*
zoo ['zu:] *n, pl* **zoos :** zoológico *m,* zoo *m*
zoological [,zo:ə'lɑdʒɪkəl, ,zu:ə-] *adj* **:** zoológico
zoologist [zo'ɑlədʒɪst, zu:-] *n* **:** zoólogo *m,* -ga *f*
zoology [zo'ɑlədʒi, zu:-] *n* **:** zoología *f*
zoom[1] ['zu:m] *vi* **1 :** zumbar, ir volando <to zoom past **:** pasar volando> **2** CLIMB **:** elevarse <the plane zoomed up **:** el avión se elevó>
zoom[2] *n* **1 :** zumbido *m* <the zoom of an engine **:** el zumbido de un motor> **2 :** subida *f* vertical (de un avión, etc.) **3** *or* **zoom lens :** zoom *m*
zucchini [zʊ'ki:ni] *n, pl* **-ni** *or* **-nis :** calabacín *m,* calabacita *f Mex*
zygote ['zaɪ,go:t] *n* **:** zigoto *m,* cigoto *m*

Common Spanish Abbreviations
Abreviaturas comunes en español

SPANISH ABBREVIATION AND EXPANSION		ENGLISH EQUIVALENT	
abr.	abril	**Apr.**	April
A.C., a.C.	antes de Cristo	**BC**	before Christ
a. de J.C.	antes de Jesucristo	**BC**	before Christ
admon., admón.	administración	—	administration
a/f	a favor	—	in favor
ago.	agosto	**Aug.**	August
Apdo.	apartado (de correos)	—	P.O. box
aprox.	aproximadamente	**approx.**	approximately
Aptdo.	apartado (de correos)	—	P.O. box
Arq.	arquitecto	**arch.**	architect
A.T.	Antiguo Testamento	**O. T.**	Old Testament
atte.	atentamente	—	sincerely
atto., atta.	atento, atenta	—	kind, courteous
av., avda.	avenida	**ave.**	avenue
a/v.	a vista	—	on receipt
BID	Banco Interamericano de Desarrollo	**IDB**	Interamerican Development Bank
B^{0}	banco	—	bank
BM	Banco Mundial		World Bank
c/, C/	calle	**st.**	street
C	centígrado, Celsius	**C**	centigrade, Celsius
C.	compañía	**Co.**	company
CA	corriente alterna	**AC**	alternating current
cap.	capítulo	**ch., chap.**	chapter
c/c	cuenta corriente	—	current account, checking account
c.c.	centímetros cúbicos	**cu. cm**	cubic centimeters
CC	corriente continua	**DC**	direct current
c/d	con descuento	—	with discount
Cd.	ciudad	—	city
CE	Comunidad Europea	**EC**	European Community
CEE	Comunidad Económica Europea	**EEC**	European Economic Community
cf.	confróntese	**cf.**	compare
cg.	centígramo	**cg**	centigram
CGT	Confederación General de Trabajadores *or* del Trabajo	—	confederation of workers, workers' union
CI	coeficiente intelectual *or* de inteligencia	**IQ**	intelligence quotient
Cía.	compañía	**Co.**	company
cm.	centímetro	**cm**	centimeter

SPANISH ABBREVIATION AND EXPANSION		ENGLISH EQUIVALENT	
Cnel.	coronel	**Col.**	colonel
col.	columna	**col.**	column
Col. *Mex*	Colonia	—	—
Com.	comandante	**Cmdr.**	commander
comp.	compárese	**comp.**	compare
Cor.	coronel	**Col.**	colonel
C.P.	código postal	—	zip code
CSF, c.s.f.	coste, seguro y flete	**c.i.f.**	cost, insurance, and freight
cta.	cuenta	**ac., acct.**	account
cte.	corriente	**cur.**	current
c/u	cada uno, cada una	**ea.**	each
CV	caballo de vapor	**hp**	horsepower
D.	Don	—	—
Da., D.ª	Doña	—	—
d.C.	después de Cristo	**AD**	anno Domini (in the year of our Lord)
dcha.	derecha	—	right
d. de J.C.	después de Jesucristo	**AD**	anno Domini (in the year of our Lord)
dep.	departamento	**dept.**	department
DF, D.F.	Distrito Federal	—	Federal District
dic.	diciembre	**Dec.**	December
dir.	director, directora	**dir.**	director
dir.	dirección	—	address
Dña.	Doña	—	—
do.	domingo	**Sun.**	Sunday
dpto.	departamento	**dept.**	department
Dr.	doctor	**Dr.**	doctor
Dra.	doctora	**Dr.**	doctor
dto.	descuento	—	discount
E, E.	Este, este	**E**	East, east
Ed.	editorial	—	publishing house
Ed., ed.	edición	**ed.**	edition
edif.	edificio	**bldg.**	building
edo.	estado	**st.**	state
EEUU, EE.UU.	Estados Unidos	**US, U.S.**	United States
ej.	por ejemplo	**e.g.**	for example
E.M.	esclerosis multiple	**MS**	multiple sclerosis
ene.	enero	**Jan.**	January
etc.	etcétera	**etc.**	et cetera
ext.	extensión	**ext.**	extension
F	Fahrenheit	**F**	Fahrenheit
f.a.b.	franco a bordo	**f.o.b.**	free on board
FC	ferrocarril	**RR**	railroad
feb.	febrero	**Feb.**	February
FF AA, FF.AA.	Fuerzas Armadas	—	armed forces
FMI	Fondo Monetario Internacional	**IMF**	International Monetary Fund
g.	gramo	**g., gm, gr.**	gram
G.P.	giro postal	**M.O.**	money order
gr.	gramo	**g., gm, gr.**	gram

SPANISH ABBREVIATION AND EXPANSION		ENGLISH EQUIVALENT	
Gral.	general	**Gen.**	general
h.	hora	**hr.**	hour
Hnos.	hermanos	**Bros.**	brothers
I + D, I & D, I y D	investigación y desarrollo	**R & D**	research and development
i.e.	esto es, es decir	**i.e.**	that is
incl.	inclusive	**incl.**	inclusive, inclusively
Ing.	ingeniero, ingeniera	**eng.**	engineer
IPC	indice de precios al consumo	**CPI**	consumer price index
IVA	impuesto al valor agregado	**VAT**	value-added tax
izq.	izquierda	**l.**	left
juev.	jueves	**Thurs.**	Thursday
jul.	julio	**Jul.**	July
jun.	junio	**Jun.**	June
kg.	kilogramo	**kg**	kilogram
km.	kilómetro	**km**	kilometer
km/h	kilómetros por hora	**kph**	kilometers per hour
kv, kV	kilovatio	**kw, kW**	kilowatt
l.	litro	**l, lit.**	liter
Lic.	licenciado, licenciada	—	*usually indicates a college graduate*
Ltda.	limitada	**Ltd.**	limited
lun.	lunes	**Mon.**	Monday
m	masculino	**m**	masculine
m	metro	**m**	meter
m	minuto	**m**	minute
mar.	marzo	**Mar.**	March
mart.	martes	**Tues.**	Tuesday
mg.	miligramo	**mg**	milligram
miérc.	miércoles	**Wednes.**	Wednesday
min	minuto	**min.**	minute
mm.	milímetro	**mm**	millimeter
M-N, m/n	moneda nacional	—	national currency
Mons.	monseñor	**Msgr.**	monsignor
Mtro.	maestro	—	teacher
Mtra.	maestra	—	teacher
N, N.	Norte, norte	**N, no.**	North, north
n/	nuestro	—	our
n.º	número	**no.**	number
N. de (la) R.	nota de (la) redacción	—	editor's note
NE	nordeste	**NE**	northeast
NN.UU.	Naciones Unidas	**UN**	United Nations
NO	noroeste	**NW**	northwest
nov.	noviembre	**Nov.**	November
N.T.	Nuevo Testamento	**N.T.**	New Testament
ntra., ntro.	nuestra, nuestro	—	our
NU	Naciones Unidas	**UN**	United Nations
núm.	número	**num.**	number
O, O.	Oeste, oeste	**W**	West, west
oct.	octubre	**Oct.**	October
OEA, O.E.A.	Organización de Estados Americanos	**OAS**	Organization of American States

SPANISH ABBREVIATION AND EXPANSION		ENGLISH EQUIVALENT	
OMS	Organización Mundial de la Salud	**WHO**	World Health Organization
ONG	organización no gubernamental	**NGO**	non-governmental organization
ONU	Organización de las Naciones Unidas	**UN**	United Nations
OTAN	Organización del Tratado del Atlántico Norte	**NATO**	North Atlantic Treaty Organization
p.	página	**p.**	page
P, P.	padre (*in religion*)	**Fr.**	father
pág.	página	**pg.**	page
pat.	patente	**pat.**	patent
PCL	pantalla de cristal líquido	**LCD**	liquid crystal display
P.D.	postdata	**P.S.**	postscript
p. ej.	por ejemplo	**e.g.**	for example
PNB	Producto Nacional Bruto	**GNP**	gross national product
P^0	paseo	**Ave.**	avenue
p.p.	porte pagado	**ppd.**	postpaid
PP, p.p.	por poder, por poderes	**p.p.**	by proxy
prom.	promedio	**av., avg.**	average
ptas., pts.	pesetas	—	—
q.e.p.d.	que en paz descanse	**R.I.P.**	may he/she rest in peace
R, R/	remite	—	sender
RAE	Real Academia Española	—	—
ref., ref.^{a}	referencia	**ref.**	reference
rep.	república	**rep.**	republic
r.p.m.	revoluciones por minuto	**rpm.**	revolutions per minute
rte.	remite, remitente	—	sender
s.	siglo	**c., cent.**	century
s/	su, sus	—	his, her, your, their
S, S.	Sur, sur	**S, so.**	South, south
S.	san, santo	**St.**	saint
S.A.	sociedad anónima	**Inc.**	incorporated (company)
sáb.	sábado	**Sat.**	Saturday
s/c	su cuenta	—	your account
SE	sudeste, sureste	**SE**	southeast
seg.	segundo, segundos	**sec.**	second, seconds
sep., sept.	septiembre	**Sept.**	September
s.e.u.o.	salvo error u omisión	—	errors and omissions excepted
Sgto.	sargento	**Sgt.**	sergeant
S.L.	sociedad limitada	**Ltd.**	limited (corporation)
S.M.	Su Majestad	**HM**	His Majesty, Her Majesty
s/n	sin número	—	no (street) number
s.n.m.	sobre el nivel de mar	**a.s.l.**	above sea level
SO	sudoeste/suroeste	**SW**	southwest

SPANISH ABBREVIATION AND EXPANSION		ENGLISH EQUIVALENT	
S.R.C.	se ruega contestación	**R.S.V.P.**	please reply
ss.	siguientes	—	the following ones
SS, S.S.	Su Santidad	**H.H.**	His Holiness
Sta.	santa	**St.**	saint
Sto.	santo	**St.**	saint
t, t.	tonelada	**t., tn.**	ton
TAE	tasa anual efectiva	**APR**	annual percentage rate
tb.	también	—	also
tel., Tel.	teléfono	**tel.**	telephone
Tm.	tonelada métrica	**MT**	metric ton
Tn.	tonelada	**t., tn.**	ton
trad.	traducido	**tr., trans., transl.**	translated
UE	Unión Europea	**EU**	European Union
Univ.	universidad	**Univ., U.**	university
UPC	unidad procesadora central	**CPU**	central processing unit
Urb.	urbanización	—	residential area
v	versus	**v., vs.**	versus
v	verso	**v., ver., vs.**	verse
v.	véase	**vid.**	see
Vda.	viuda	—	widow
v.g., v.gr.	verbigracia	**e.g.**	for example
vier., viern.	viernes	**Fri.**	Friday
V.M.	Vuestra Majestad	—	Your Majesty
$V^{0}B^{0}$, $V.^{0}B.^{0}$	visto bueno	—	OK, approved
vol, vol.	volumen	**vol.**	volume
vra., vro.	vuestra, vuestro	—	your

Common English Abbreviations
Abreviaturas comunes en inglés

ENGLISH ABBREVIATION AND EXPANSION		SPANISH EQUIVALENT	
AAA	American Automobile Association	—	—
AD	anno Domini (in the year of our Lord)	**d.C., d. de J.C.**	después de Cristo, después de Jesucristo
AK	Alaska	—	Alaska
AL, Ala.	Alabama	—	Alabama
Alas.	Alaska	—	Alaska
a.m., AM	ante meridiem (before noon)	**a.m.**	ante meridiem (de la mañana)
Am., Amer.	America, American	—	América, americano
amt.	amount	—	cantidad
anon.	anonymous	—	anónimo
ans.	answer	—	respuesta
Apr.	April	**abr.**	abril
AR	Arkansas	—	Arkansas
Ariz.	Arizona	—	Arizona
Ark.	Arkansas	—	Arkansas
asst.	assistant	**ayte.**	ayudante
atty.	attorney	—	abogado, -da
Aug.	August	**ago.**	agosto
ave.	avenue	**av., avda.**	avenida
AZ	Arizona	—	Arizona
BA	Bachelor of Arts	**Lic.**	Licenciado, -da en Filosofía y Letras
BA	Bachelor of Arts (degree)	—	Licenciatura en Filosofía y Letras
BC	before Christ	**a.C., A.C., a. de J.C.**	antes de Cristo, antes de Jesucristo
BCE	before the Christian Era, before the Common Era	—	antes de la era cristiana, antes de la era común
bet.	between	—	entre
bldg.	building	**edif.**	edificio
blvd.	boulevard	**blvar., br.**	bulevar
Br., Brit.	Britain, British	—	Gran Bretaña, británico
Bro(s).	brother(s)	**Hno(s),**	hermano(s)
BS	Bachelor of Science	**Lic.**	Licenciado, -da en Ciencias
BS	Bachelor of Science (degree)	—	Licenciatura en Ciencias
c	carat	—	quilate
c	cent	—	centavo

ENGLISH ABBREVIATION AND EXPANSION		SPANISH EQUIVALENT	
c	centimeter	**cm.**	centímetro
c	century	**s.**	siglo
c	cup	—	taza
C	Celsius, centigrade	**C**	Celsius, centígrado
CA, Cal., Calif.	California	—	California
Can., Canad.	Canada, Canadian	—	Canadá, canadiense
cap.	capital	—	capital
cap.	capital	—	mayúscula
Capt.	captain	—	capitán
cent.	century	**s.**	siglo
CEO	chief executive officer	—	presidente, -ta (de una corporación)
ch., chap.	chapter	**cap.**	capítulo
CIA	Central Intelligence Agency	—	—
cm	centimeter	**cm.**	centímetro
Co.	company	**C., Cía.**	compañía
co.	county	—	condado
CO	Colorado	—	Colorado
c/o	care of	**a/c**	a cargo de
COD	cash on delivery, collect on delivery	—	(pago) contra reembolso
col.	column	**col.**	columna
Col., Colo.	Colorado	—	Colorado
Conn.	Connecticut	—	Connecticut
corp.	corporation	—	corporación
CPR	cardiopulmonary resuscitation	**RCP**	reanimación cardiopulmonar, resucitación cardiopulmonar
ct.	cent	—	centavo
CT	Connecticut	—	Connecticut
D.A.	district attorney	—	fiscal (del distrito)
DC	District of Columbia	—	—
DDS	Doctor of Dental Surgery	—	doctor de cirugía dental
DE	Delaware	—	Delaware
Dec.	December	**dic.**	diciembre
Del.	Delaware	—	Delaware
DJ	disc jockey		disc-jockey
dept.	department	**dep., dpto.**	departamento
DMD	Doctor of Dental Medicine	—	doctor de medicina dental
doz.	dozen	—	docena
Dr.	doctor	**Dr., Dra.**	doctor, doctora
DST	daylight saving time	—	—
DVM	Doctor of Veterinary Medicine	—	doctor de medicina veterinaria
E	East, east	**E, E.**	Este, este
ea.	each	**c/u**	cada uno, cada una
e.g.	for example	**v.g., v.gr.**	verbigracia

ENGLISH ABBREVIATION AND EXPANSION		SPANISH EQUIVALENT	
EMT	emergency medical technician	—	técnico, -ca en urgencias médicas
Eng.	England, English	—	Inglaterra, inglés
esp.	especially	—	especialmente
EST	eastern standard time	—	—
etc.	et cetera	**etc.**	etcétera
f	false	—	falso
f	female	**f**	femenino
F	Fahrenheit	**F**	Fahrenheit
FBI	Federal Bureau of Investigation	—	—
Feb.	February	**feb.**	febrero
fem.	feminine	—	femenino
FL, Fla.	Florida	—	Florida
Fri.	Friday	**vier., viern.**	viernes
ft.	feet, foot	—	pie(s)
g	gram	**g., gr.**	gramo
Ga., GA	Georgia	—	Georgia
gal.	gallon	—	galón
Gen.	general	**Gral.**	general
gm	gram	**g., gr.**	gramo
gov.	governor	—	gobernador, -dora
govt.	government	—	gobierno
gr.	gram	**g., gr.**	gramo
HI	Hawaii	—	Hawai, Hawaii
hr.	hour	**h.**	hora
HS	high school	—	colegio secundario
ht.	height	—	altura
Ia., IA	Iowa	—	Iowa
ID	Idaho	—	Idaho
i.e.	id est (that is)	**i.e.**	id est (esto es, es decir)
IL, Ill	Illinois	—	Illinois
in.	inch	—	pulgada
IN	Indiana	—	Indiana
Inc.	incorporated (company)	**S.A.**	sociedad anónima
Ind.	Indian, Indiana	—	Indiana
Jan.	January	**ene.**	enero
Jul.	July	**jul.**	julio
Jun.	June	**jun.**	junio
Jr., Jun.	Junior	**Jr.**	Júnior
Kan., Kans.	Kansas	—	Kansas
kg	kilogram	**kg.**	kilogramo
km	kilometer	**km.**	kilómetro
KS	Kansas	—	Kansas
Ky., KY	Kentucky	—	Kentucky
l	liter	**l.**	litro
l.	left	**izq.**	izquierda
L	large	**G**	(talla) grande
La, LA	Louisiana	—	Luisiana, Louisiana
lb.	pound	—	libra

ENGLISH ABBREVIATION AND EXPANSION		SPANISH EQUIVALENT	
Ltd.	limited (corporation)	**S.L.**	sociedad limitada
m	male	**m**	masculino
m	meter	**m**	metro
m	mile	—	milla
M	medium	**M**	(talla) mediana
MA	Massachusetts	—	Massachusetts
Maj.	major	—	mayor
Mar.	March	**mar.**	marzo
masc.	masculine	—	masculino
Mass.	Massachusetts	—	Massachusetts
Md., MD	Maryland	—	Maryland
M.D.	Doctor of Medicine	—	doctor de medicina
Me., ME	Maine	—	Maine
Mex.	Mexican, Mexico	**Méx.**	mexicano, México
mg	milligram	**mg.**	miligramo
mi.	mile	—	milla
MI, Mich.	Michigan	—	Michigan
min.	minute	**min**	minuto
Minn.	Minnesota	—	Minnesota
Miss.	Mississippi	—	Mississippi, Misisipí
ml	mililiter	**ml.**	mililitro
mm	millimeter	**mm.**	milímetro
MN	Minnesota	—	Minnesota
mo.	month	—	mes
Mo., MO	Missouri	—	Missouri
Mon.	Monday	**lun.**	lunes
Mont.	Montana	—	Montana
mpg	miles per gallon	—	millas pør galón
mph	miles per hour	—	millas por hora
MS	Mississippi	—	Mississippi, Misisipí
mt.	mount, mountain	—	monte, montaña
MT	Montana	—	Montana
mtn.	mountain	—	montaña
N	North, north	**N**	Norte, norte
NASA	National Aeronautics and Space Administration	—	—
NC	North Carolina	—	Carolina del Norte, North Carolina
ND, N. Dak.	North Dakota	—	Dakota del Norte, North Dakota
NE	northeast	**NE**	nordeste
NE, Neb., Nebr.	Nebraska	—	Nebraska
Nev.	Nevada	—	Nevada
NH	New Hampshire	—	New Hampshire
NJ	New Jersey	—	Nueva Jersey, New Jersey
NM., N. Mex.	New Mexico	—	Nuevo México, New Mexico
no.	north	**N**	norte
no.	number	**n.º**	número
Nov.	November	**nov.**	noviembre
N.T.	New Testament	**N.T.**	Nuevo Testamento

ENGLISH ABBREVIATION AND EXPANSION		SPANISH EQUIVALENT	
NV	Nevada	—	Nevada
NW	northwest	**NO**	noroeste
NY	New York	**NY**	Nueva York, New York
O	Ohio	—	Ohio
Oct.	October	**oct.**	octubre
OH	Ohio	—	Ohio
OK, Okla.	Oklahoma	—	Oklahoma
OR, Ore., Oreg.	Oregon	—	Oregon
O.T.	Old Testament	**A.T.**	Antiguo Testamento
oz.	ounce, ounces	—	onza, onzas
p.	page	**p.**	página
Pa., PA	Pennsylvania	—	Pennsylvania, Pensilvania
pat.	patent	**pat.**	patente
PD	police department	—	departamento de policía
PE	physical education	—	educación física
Penn., Penna.	Pennsylvania	—	Pennsylvania, Pensilvania
pg.	page	**pág.**	página
PhD	Doctor of Philosophy	—	doctor, -tora (en filosofía)
pkg.	package	—	paquete
p.m., PM	post meridiem (afternoon)	**p.m.**	post meridiem (de la tarde)
P.O.	post office	—	oficina de correos, correo
pp.	pages	**págs.**	páginas
PR	Puerto Rico	**PR**	Puerto Rico
pres.	present	—	presente
pres.	president		presidente, -ta
prof.	professor	—	profesor, -sora
P.S.	postscript	**P.D.**	postdata
P.S.	public school	—	escuela pública
pt.	pint	—	pinta
pt.	point	**pto.**	punto
PTA	Parent-Teacher Association	—	—
PTO	Parent-Teacher Organization	—	—
q, qt.	quart	—	cuarto de galón
r.	right	**dcha.**	derecha
rd.	road	**c/, C/**	calle
RDA	recommended daily allowance	—	consumo diario recomendado
recd.	received	—	recibido
Rev.	reverend	**Rdo.**	reverendo
RI	Rhode Island	—	Rhode Island
rpm	revolutions per minute	**r.p.m.**	revoluciones por minuto
RR	railroad	**FC**	ferrocarril

ENGLISH ABBREVIATION AND EXPANSION		SPANISH EQUIVALENT	
R.S.V.P	please reply (répondez s'il vous plaît)	**S.R.C.**	se ruega contestación
rt.	right	**dcha.**	derecha
rte.	route	—	ruta
S	small	**P**	(talla) pequeña
S	South, south	**S**	Sur, sur
S.A.	South America	—	Sudamérica, América del Sur
Sat.	Saturday	**sáb.**	sábado
SC	South Carolina	—	Carolina del Sur, South Carolina
SD, S. Dak.	South Dakota	—	Dakota del Sur, South Dakota
SE	southeast	**SE**	sudeste, sureste
Sept.	September	**sep., sept.**	septiembre
so.	south	**S**	sur
sq.	square		cuadrado
Sr.	Senior	**Sr.**	Sénior
Sr.	sister (*in religion*)	—	sor
st.	state	—	estado
st.	street	**c/, C/**	calle
St.	saint	**S., Sto., Sta.**	santo, santa
Sun.	Sunday	**dom.**	domingo
SW	southwest	**SO**	sudoeste, suroeste
t.	teaspoon	—	cucharadita
T, tb., tbsp.	tablespoon	—	cucharada (grande)
Tenn.	Tennessee	—	Tennessee
Tex.	Texas	—	Texas
Thu., Thur., Thurs.	Thursday	**juev.**	jueves
TM	trademark	—	marca (de un producto)
TN	Tennessee	—	Tennessee
tsp.	teaspoon	—	cucharadita
Tue., Tues.	Tuesday	**mart.**	martes
TX	Texas	—	Texas
UN	United Nations	**NU, NN.UU.**	Naciones Unidas
US	United States	**EEUU, EE.UU.**	Estados Unidos
USA	United States of America	**EEUU, EE.UU.**	Estados Unidos de América
usu.	usually	—	usualmente
UT	Utah	—	Utah
v.	versus	**v**	versus
Va., VA	Virginia	—	Virginia
vol.	volume	**vol.**	volumen
VP	vice president	—	vicepresidente, -ta
vs.	versus	**v**	versus
Vt., VT	Vermont	—	Vermont

ENGLISH ABBREVIATION AND EXPANSION		SPANISH EQUIVALENT	
W	West, west	**O**	Oeste, oeste
WA, Wash.	Washington (state)	—	Washington
Wed.	Wednesday	**miérc.**	miércoles
WI, Wis., Wisc.	Wisconsin	—	Wisconsin
wt.	weight	—	peso
WV, W. Va.	West Virginia	—	Virginia del Oeste, West Virginia
WY, Wyo.	Wyoming	—	Wyoming
yd.	yard	—	yarda
yr.	year	—	año

Metric System : Conversions
Sistema métrico : conversiones

Length

unit	number of meters	approximate U.S. equivalents	
millimeter	0.001	0.039	inch
centimeter	0.01	0.39	inch
meter	1	39.37	inches
kilometer	1,000	0.62	mile

Longitud

unidad	número de metros	equivalentes aproximados de los EE.UU.	
milímetro	0.001	0.039	pulgada
centímetro	0.01	0.39	pulgada
metro	1	39.37	pulgadas
kilómetro	1,000	0.62	milla

Area

unit	number of square meters	approximate U.S. equivalents	
square centimeter	0.0001	0.155	square inch
square meter	1	10.764	square feet
hectare	10,000	2.47	acres
square kilometer	1,000,000	0.3861	square mile

Superficie

unidad	número de metros cuadrados	equivalentes aproximados de los EE.UU.	
centímetro cuadrado	0.0001	0.155	pulgada cuadrada
metro cuadrado	1	10.764	pies cuadrados
hectárea	10,000	2.47	acres
kilómetro cuadrado	1,000,000	0.3861	milla cuadrada

Volume

unit	number of cubic meters	approximate U.S. equivalents	
cubic centimeter	0.000001	0.061	cubic inch
cubic meter	1	1.307	cubic yards

Volumen

unidad	número de metros cúbicos	equivalentes aproximados de los EE.UU	
centímetro cúbico	0.000001	0.061	pulgada cúbica
metro cúbico	1	1.307	yardas cúbicas

Capacity

unit	number of liters	approximate U.S. equivalents		
		CUBIC	DRY	LIQUID
liter	1	61.02 cubic inches	0.908 quart	1.057 quarts

Capacidad

unidad	número de litros	equivalentes aproximados de los EE.UU.		
		CÚBICO	SECO	LIQUIDO
litro	1	61.02 pulgadas cúbicas	0.908 cuarto	1.057 cuartos

Mass and Weight

unit	number of grams	approximate U.S. equivalents	
milligram	0.001	0.015	grain
centigram	0.01	0.154	grain
gram	1	0.035	ounce
kilogram	1,000	2.2046	pounds
metric ton	1,000,000	1.102	short tons

Masa y peso

unidad	número de gramos	equivalentes aproximados de los EE.UU.	
miligramo	0.001	0.015	grano
centigramo	0.01	0.154	grano
gramo	1	0.035	onza
kilogramo	1.000	2.2046	libras
tonelada métrica	1,000,000	1.102	toneladas cortas